# Dispelling the Myths
# of Abortion History

# Dispelling the Myths of Abortion History

**Joseph W. Dellapenna**

PROFESSOR OF LAW
VILLANOVA UNIVERSITY SCHOOL OF LAW

CAROLINA ACADEMIC PRESS
Durham, North Carolina

Library of Congress Cataloging-in-Publication Data

Dellapenna, Joseph W.
   Dispelling the myths of abortion history / by Joseph W. Dellapenna.
      p. cm.
ISBN 0-89089-509-0 (alk. paper)
1. Abortion--Law and legislation--United States--History. 2. Abortion--Law and legislation--Great Britain--History. 3. Abortion--Social aspects. I. Title.

KF3771.D45 2005
342.7308'4--dc22                                        2005015243

Carolina Academic Press
700 Kent Street
Durham, North Carolina 27701
Telephone (919) 489-7486
Fax (919) 493-5668
www.cap-press.com

Printed in the United States of America

# Contents

# A Personal Aside

*Coming to terms with the presence of the traditions from which we are derived is, or should be, a fundamental part of growing up.*

—Jaroslav Pelikan[1]

I have been working on this book—as such—for about 15 years, but if one looks back to when I first began to examine the history of abortion, one could say that I have been at it for more than 30 years. The earliest fruit of that effort was a law review article published some 26 years ago.[2] How I, a white man who has fathered at least five children, became so concerned about the conflicting stories we tell about abortion and so concerned about discovering the forces that have shaped those stories down through the centuries as to undertake this effort demands an explanation. Indeed, some will even consider me physiologically disqualified from thinking or writing seriously about abortion (except were I to agree with "politically correct" women). I have little to say to anyone who believes that except that I do not agree.

My race and gender, of course, might be relevant in evaluating my stories. Abortion, however, raises questions that are too important to be the exclusive domain of any particular group. Furthermore, I have had several close encounters with abortion in my life, including professional and personal relationships with women who have had abortions. Finally, while most of my children were planned, as a father of three daughters I am highly conscious of the special risks they face from unwanted pregnancy.

Some readers might assume that I am a Catholic given my family name and that I have taught at a Catholic university for 29 years. Law professor David Garrow, for example, assumed that I am a Catholic even while conceding that my work has been "among the more significant hostile critiques" of the Supreme Court's constitutionalization of abortion rights.[3] I need not address whether this too would disqualify me for I am not a Catholic. I am and have been for most of my life, by choice, a Unitarian. (Today, one might describe me as a lapsed Unitarian, for I find even that church too restrictive.) Nor am I an absolutist on abortion, as Garrow also appears to suppose. I wrote more than twenty years ago in support of a policy of unlimited choice early in pregnancy and of a carefully tailored—albeit highly restrictive—indications policy thereafter.[4] I still adhere to that view.

---

1. Jaroslav Pelikan, The Vindication of Tradition 12 (1984).

2. Joseph Dellapenna, *The History of Abortion: Technology, Morality, and Law,* 40 U. Pitt. L. Rev. 359, 422–27 (1979).

3. David Garrow, Liberty and Sexuality: The Right of Privacy and the Making of Roe v. Wade 609, 913–14 n.16 (2nd ed. 1998).

4. Joseph Dellapenna, *Nor Piety Nor Wit: The Supreme Court on Abortion,* 6 Colum. H. Rts. L. Rev. 379, 406–9 (1974). *See also* Michael Lockwood, *When Does Life Begin?,* in Moral Dilemmas in Modern Medicine 9 (Michael Lockwood ed. 1985).

My view, based on the emergence of fetal brain activity,[5] would legalize choice only up to eight weeks of gestation—but that would take in about half of the abortions currently performed and the percentage would rise if women were concerned to beat the deadline.[6] If women did not accelerate their abortions appreciably, the law I proposed would mean approximately 500–600,000 fewer abortions annually. Such a law would have a greater impact on younger women (under 20 years of age) than on older women because younger women account for the majority of abortions performed after 8 weeks of gestation. While only 10.2 percent of all abortions occur after the first trimester, the rate rises to 16 percent for teenagers 15 to 19 years of age, and to 22.5 percent for teenagers under 15. The rate for women over 20 is only 8.7 percent.[7] One side effect of pressuring for abortions to occur earlier in the gestation process would be a marked increase in the safety of abortions for the mother.[8] I do not argue the merits of that or any other position in this book, except to note that my position places me among those whom philosopher Ann Davis has identified as "moderates" on abortion, neither "Pro-Life" nor "Pro-Choice."[9] None of this, however, answers the question of how I came to research the topic of abortion.

---

5. *See also* BARUCH BRODY, ABORTION AND THE SANCTITY OF HUMAN LIFE 83 (1975); R. Alta Charo, *Biological Determinism in Legal Decision Making: The Parent Trap*, 3 TEX. J. WOMEN & LAW 265, 278 (1994); Joel Cornwell, *The Concept of Brain Life: Shifting the Abortion Standard without Imposing Religious Values*, 25 DUQ. L. REV. 471 (1987); Michael Flower, *Coming into Being: The Prenatal Development of Humans* in ABORTION, MEDICINE, AND THE LAW 437, 442–45 (J. Douglas Butler & David Walbert eds., 3rd ed. 1986); Michael Flower, *Neuromaturation and the Moral Status of Human Fetal Life*, in ABORTION RIGHTS AND FETAL PERSONHOOD 71, 79 (Edd Doerr & James Prescott eds. 1989); Gary Gertler, Note, *Brain Birth: A Proposal for Defining When a Fetus Is Entitled to Human Life Status*, 59 S. CAL. L. REV. 1061 (1986); John Goldenring, *The Brain-Life Theory: Towards a Considered Biological Definition of Humanness*, 11 J. MED. ETHICS 198 (1985); Donald Hope, *The Hand as an Emblem of Human Identity: A Solution to the Abortion Controversy Based on Science and Reason*, 32 U. TOL. L. REV. 205, 216–18 (2001); D. Gareth Jones, *Brain Birth and Personal Identity*, 15 J. MED. ETHICS 173 (1989); J. Korein, *Ontogenesis of the Fetal Nervous System: The Onset of Brain Life*, 22 TRANSPLANTATION PROC. 982 (1990); Julian Savluescu, *Why Human Research Cannot Be Locked in a Cell*, SYDNEY (Austral.) MORNING HERALD, Aug. 27, 2001, at 10; Katherine Sheehan, *The Hand that Rocks the Cradle*, 32 U. TOL. L. REV. 229, 238–39 (2001); Peter Steinfels, *Scholar Proposes "Brain Birth" Law*, N.Y. TIMES, Nov. 8, 1990, at A28; Timothy Vinceguerra, *Notes of a Footsoldier*, 62 ALB. L. REV. 1167, 1180–81 (1999).

6. Centers for Disease Control, *Abortion Surveillance: Prelminiary Data—United States, 1992*, 43 MWWR MORBIDITY & MORTALITY WKLY. REP. 933 (1994); Kenneth Kochanek, *Induced Terminations of Pregnancy: Reporting States, 1987*, 38 MONTHLY VITAL STATISTICS REP. 1, 5–6 (1990); Lynn Wardle, *The Quandary of Pro-Life Free Speech: A Lesson from the Abolitionists*, 62 ALB. L. REV. 853, 943, 962 (1999). Note that RU-486—the "abortion pill"—has been approved for use only up to the end of seven weeks gestation because its efficacy falls off sharply thereafter. *See* Beverly Winikoff *et al.*, *Acceptability and Feasibility of Early Pregnancy Termination by Mifepristone-Misoprostol: Results of a Large Multicenter Trial in the United States*, 7 ARCHIVES FAM. MED. 360, 361–62 (1998). To the extent that RU-486 gains acceptance, it will tend to push more abortions into this early period. Mandee Silverman, Note, *RU-486: A Dramatic New Choice or Forum for Continued Abortion Controversy*, 57 NYU ANN. SURV. AM. L. 247, 262–63 (2000); Aaron Zitner, *Abortion Pill's Effects in U.S. Hard to Predict*, L.A. TIMES, Sept. 30, 2000, at A1.

7. Kochanek, *supra* note 6, at 6; Allen Rosenfield, *The Difficult Issue of Second-Trimester Abortion*, 267 JAMA 324, 324 (1994).

8. Rosenfield, *supra* note 7, at 324. The mortality rates per 100,000 abortions by week of gestation are:

| | |
|---|---|
| up to 10 weeks | 0.3 |
| weeks 11 & 12 | 0.6 |
| weeks 13–15 | 1.8 |
| weeks 16–20 | 3.7 |
| 21st week & beyond | 12.7 |

9. Nancy (Ann) Davis, *The Abortion Debate: The Search for Common Ground, Part I*, 103 ETHICS 516, 518–21 (1993). Philosophy professor Davis identifies several recent scholarly works as expressing "moderate" positions, while indicating that these works support widely differing specific positions: L.W. SUMMER, ABORTION AND MORAL THEORY (1981); Roger Wertheimer, *Understanding the Abortion Argument*, 1 PHIL. & PUB. AFF. 67 (1971); Jane English, *Abortion and the Concept of a Person*, 5 CAN. J. PHIL. 233 (1975).

When I began this project, shortly after *Roe v. Wade*[10] was decided in 1973, most law professors—especially male law professors—did not write about the decision with less than enthusiasm for the outcome of the decision for much the same reasons that made the legal academy ignore motherhood generally: "too soft, not important, no funding, few colleagues, and who cares."[11] Unitarians were even more likely to support abortion rights—if they bothered much about the question at all. This was true even though the founding president of Americans United for Life was a Unitarian minister—George Huntson Williams, Hollis Professor of Divinity at Harvard Divinity School.[12] Yet I felt something was seriously amiss in the thinking on both sides of the abortion controversy that was coming to divide the nation. I concluded that I actually had something to contribute that might help clarify the issues even if my contribution could not resolve the dispute.

To understand why I felt I had something to contribute, one might examine my rather convoluted career path between graduating from law school in 1968 and the decision of *Roe v. Wade* less than five years later, in early 1973. My first position as a lawyer was a short stint as an attorney-advisor at NASA (during which I worked, among other things, on Apollo XI). I then found employment as a research attorney at the Program for Policy Studies in Science and Technology at the George Washington University, a "think tank" working on technology assessment issues. I spent the better part of a year with the Program for Policy Studies, leaving in 1970 when I was hired at Willamette University as the first person to teach environmental law there.[13] Armed with an advance law degree in international law (earned while working at NASA and at the think tank), I set about to combine these several concerns and experiences by studying the technological aspects of world population policy, beginning about two years before *Roe* was decided.[14]

Given my interests, I was struck by the technological claims underlying the abortion history in the majority opinion in *Roe* and its companion case of *Doe v. Bolton*.[15] Justice Harry Blackmun, the author of the majority opinion in *Roe*, derived these claims from the work of law professor Cyril Means.[16] Upon reading Means' work, I found those claims seriously deficient even based on the evidence Means himself presented. During a year I spent at Columbia University earning another advanced law degree, I researched and wrote a preliminary review of Means' history.[17] This is the work that David Garrow found to be among the more significant hostile critiques of *Roe*. The rest, as they say, is history.

I seek to elucidate the history of abortion in English and American law. The focus is very much on law as the existence of the legal tradition relating to abortion is at least highly significant to any claim that our Constitution protects a right a right to choose to abort. No doubt, there are those who will doubt the relevance of history to our understanding of the Constitution. Indeed, some will object to recourse to history as unjustly elevating certain texts and certain readings of the chosen texts over other texts and variant readings of the chosen texts. At the ex-

---

10. 410 U.S. 113 (1973).

11. Carol Sanger, *M Is for the Many Things*, 1 REV. L. & WOMEN'S STUD. 15, 21 (1992).

12. JOHN NOONAN, JR., A PRIVATE CHOICE: ABORTION IN AMERICA IN THE SEVENTIES 62 (1979).

13. Later, I would be the first person to teach a course on Environmental Law in the Republic of China (as a Fulbright Professor at National Chengchi University—1978) and the first to teach such a course in the People's Republic of China (as a Fulbright Professor at Jilin University—1987).

14. *See* Joseph Dellapenna & Philip Schuster II, *Meeting the Challenge of Population Change: Institutional Reform to Assess Population Trends*, 7 WILLAMETTE L. REV. 232 (1972).

15. 410 U.S. 179 (1973).

16. Cyril Means, jr., *The Law of New York Concerning Abortion and the Status of the Foetus, 1664–1968: A Case of Cessation of Constitutionality*, 14 N.Y.L.F. 411 (1968); Cyril Means, jr., *The Phoenix of Abortional Freedom: Is a Penumbral Right or Ninth-Amendment Right About to Arise from the Nineteenth-Century Legislative Ashes of a Fourteenth-Century Common-Law Liberty?*, 17 N.Y.L.F. 335 (1971).

17. Dellapenna, *supra* note 4.

treme, such critics will conclude that reliance on historical legal materials will result in stodgy, rule-bound decision making that stifles creative reasoning.

Those who think along these lines should read *Roe v. Wade* again. They will find that Justice Blackmun structured the argument in the majority opinion as an argument about the history of abortion laws. Yet Blackmun himself, facing searing critiques of the history he presented, silently abandoned his reliance on history.[18] No doubt, like Blackmun, the staunchest defenders of abortion rights will not abandon their faith in abortion simply because history does not support their claims. Yet even they recognize the importance—whether merely as a rhetorical tool or otherwise—of history. Why else would they put so much effort into recasting history into a form that supports their position?

This is an argumentative book. In this book, I set about to set the record straight regarding the history of abortion. In order to do so, I critique the received histories presented by those who currently dominate the debate over the rights and wrongs of abortion. I am more critical of the "pro-choice" historians—their distortions of the history are far greater, and they are, after all, the current orthodoxy. Yet the anti-abortion historians also come in for a share of the criticism.[19]

Despite my focus on the Anglo-American law of abortion, I frequently examine general legal practices and the social and medical practices relative to abortion contemporary with the particular legal practices directed to abortion. I also examine related social activities occurring at about the same time. Only by placing the strictly legal materials in social, political, and technological contexts can one properly understand what happened in the past and how the law specific to abortion changed through time.

I do not say very much about events in Europe generally. In part this is because of my concern to elucidate the meaning of our Constitution, and in part this is necessary to make the project manageable given the depth of analysis I attempt in this book. In particular, I write very little about the practices of ancient Greeks and Romans or of the Teutons who replaced the Roman Empire. Although I do occasionally refer to certain aspects of the history of these practices, they did not directly influence later English practice or the resulting American practices. I do provide somewhat greater attention to the practices elsewhere in Europe (particularly western Europe) contemporary with English practices as these practices did influence events in England and later in America. Still, the focus remains throughout on English and American law.

I argue in this book that Anglo-American law has always treated abortion as a serious crime, generally even including early in pregnancy, presenting evidence of prosecutions and even executions, occurring as long as 800 years ago in England, and less serious punishments in colonial America. The reasons provided for these prosecutions and penalties consistently focused on protecting the life of the unborn child. This unbroken tradition tends to refute the claims that unborn children have not been treated as persons in our law or as persons under the Constitution of the United States.

The tradition of treating abortion as a crime was unbroken through nearly 800 years of English and American history until the "reform" movement of the later twentieth century. During much of that time, abortion was not punished as severely as the homicide of an adult human being. More than a few observers have argued from this that the prohibition of abortion was not truly based on a belief that the abortus was a "person." Perhaps, the argument goes, the law was meant to vindicate the mother's interest in continuing her pregnancy (many early cases involved involuntary abortions) or to protect the mother's health, rather than to protect the life of the child.

---

18. *See* Planned Parenthood of Southeastern Pennsylvania v. Casey, 505 U.S. 833, 922–43 (1992) (Blackmun, J., partially concurring, and saying not one word in defense of his historical arguments in *Roe*).

19. This point is developed more fully in Chapter 1, at notes 49–140.

Ronald Dworkin, one of the leading legal philosophers of the second half of the twentieth century made just such an argument in his book on the problems of abortion and euthanasia. He argued that the existence in times past of laws that punished some or even most abortions less severely than "true" homicide demonstrates that abortion was not considered the equivalent of the killing of a person.[20] He also argued that if abortion were truly considered homicide, the killing of an innocent infant could not be justified even in order to save the mother's life.[21] These appear to be compelling arguments, but Dworkin himself demonstrated that these arguments are hardly dispositive.

Dworkin described at some length the emotional reality of loss that occurs to someone close to the deceased.[22] As Dworkin put it, our sense of loss grows the later from birth the death occurs (and grows similarly even during pregnancy as birth approaches) until reaching a plateau sometime in adolescence or early adulthood. The sense of loss remains roughly on this level plateau until late in life when the sense of loss declines to the point where, in at least some instances, one feels more relief than loss when death finally comes. This appears to me to be a credible account that reflects our sense of investment (both of material resources and of hopes) in a growing child and of our growing sense of loss as age takes its toll prior to death.

Consider now the legal response to a professional murderer who guns down an adult of, say 30 years of age, in order to achieve some criminal goal. Compare that to the legal response to an elderly person who kills her diseased and despairing spouse at his request. Both have traditionally been treated as murder, but upon conviction the professional murderer will likely receive the maximum sentence, perhaps the death penalty itself, while the elderly widow is likely to receive the minimum sentence, perhaps even probation. A similar comparison arises if the killer is a mother who kills a newborn infant, where the event might even be excused as representing "post-partum psychosis"—murder, but excused by a mental disease or defect.

While some, including Dworkin, would now argue that the killing of the spouse in the circumstances described ought not to be classed as homicide, traditionally all three crimes were so classified. And not even Dworkin would argue that either the elderly spouse (sentient enough to request death) or the infant are not persons just because many of us are willing to countenance their deaths. The same points apply as well to the unborn infant if we examine how the historical actors explained themselves to themselves. They consistently spoke of punishing abortion, at whatever level punishment might take, as a means of protecting the life of an unborn child, a statement that sounds suspiciously like the protection of a "person."[23]

This book opens with an extended discussion (in two chapters) of the social practices that framed abortion laws down through the centuries. This discussion explores how abortions were done, and how else people undertook to prevent or dispose of unwanted pregnancies before the nineteenth century. The book then turns to the evolution of abortion laws from the earliest days of the common law in twelfth century England and America to the opening of the twenty-first century. The final two chapters explore certain deeper questions about how we do and understand history, and how the doing and the understanding of history—the stories we tell ourselves about our past—might be relevant to the current abortion controversy.

The history of abortion demonstrates that societies around the world had to respond to the moral challenges posed by the newfound ability to abort women with minimal risk to the physical well being of the woman undergoing the abortion. In the nineteenth century, nearly all per-

---

20. RONALD DWORKIN, LIFE'S DOMINION: AN ARGUMENT ABOUT ABORTION, EUTHENASIA, AND INDIVIDUAL FREEDOM 44, 111–12 (1993).

21. *Id.* at 94–95, 114.

22. *Id.* at 84–89, 169–70.

23. *See* Chapters 3 & 4.

sons in society—led by feminists, physicians, and religious leaders—dealt with the moral challenge by treating the problem as a legal challenge, with legislatures around the world enacting statutes to repress or prohibit abortion.[24] Changing medical technologies that made the practice less dangerous for the mother and more difficult to detect undermined the prohibition of abortion. In the later years of the twentieth century, as the medical profession perfected the techniques for doing abortions and as many men and women found that their personal goals were best served by reducing or even eliminating the role of children in their lives, many came to prefer to manage abortion as a medical problem rather than a legal problem. Legislatures in many nations consequently remolded their abortion statutes to facilitate the choices of women (and often of their men) to abort pregnancies.[25]

In the United States, supporters of abortion rights grew impatient with the slow, difficult, and uncertain legislative process; they turned, initially successfully, to the courts to establish a constitutional right to choose whether to abort.[26] Unlike the legislative solutions embraced in other countries, however, the American solution generated enormous controversy and even violence, leading the Supreme Court to disavow judicial management of the moral questions posed by abortion[27]—and of other medical technologies that upended some of our most cherished moral traditions regarding the value of life.[28] The problem thus was mostly returned to the legislative branches where perhaps it should have been all along.[29] Yet ultimately the majority on the Court could not keep their hands off the abortion controversy, leaving society confused about the possible direction abortion laws would or could take in the near future.[30]

I do not contend that anyone will ever recover the "complete truth" about any past event. But we can distinguish between the truth and the untruth of certain facts about the past even while we quarrel about the significance of these truths. History is more than a process of projecting our wishes onto the past. As for its relevance, recall again that the main opinion in *Roe v. Wade* itself was structured as an argument about history.

This book, unlike so many others dealing with abortion these days, was not supported by foundations or by time off from teaching. I never applied for such funding, and indeed turned down more than one invitation to apply for such funding, in order to avoid any taint that my work reflected the prejudices of my funding sources. I did receive several grants from the Law Alumni Fund of Villanova University for work during summers on this project. Right or wrong, the work and its conclusions are entirely my responsibility.

As a result of my determination to finish this work without significant outside funding, the time and attention for its writing came at the expense of my family. I begin by acknowledging their contribution, primarily their ability to tolerate my obsessive attention to the minutiae of abortion history. Thanks are particularly due them given the small likelihood that the publication of the results would provide recompense to the family either in material terms or in terms of widespread good will or likely influence on public policy, yet without their support this work could not have been completed.

---

24. *See* Chapters 5–8.

25. *See* Chapters 13, 15.

26. *See* Chapter 14.

27. *See* Chapters 16, 17.

28. See the text *supra* at notes 88–159.

29. On the range of legislative responses to abortion, see Eva Rubin, Abortion, Politics, and the Courts 126–49 (rev. ed. 1987). On possible applications of the "undue burden" test to abortion regulations, see Richard Wilkins, Richard Sherlock, & Stephen Clark, *Mediating the Polar Extremes: A Guide to Post-*Webster *Abortion Policy*, in Abortion and the States: Political Change and Future Regulation 139, 157–64 (Jane Wishner ed. 1993).

30. *See* Chapter 19.

Neither this book nor those briefs could ever have been written without the help of the many people who have kindly shared their research with me or otherwise assisted me in this work. So many have done so that thanking them all is impossible. In particular, the many research assistants that I have employed at two different law schools (the University of Cincinnati and Villanova) are just too many to list or to single out for special praise. I must also thank the staff of the Historical Medical Library of the College of Physicians of Pennsylvania, the repository in which my research assistants found many of the more obscure sources.

Apart from my research assistants, three people deserve special mention for their assistance in this project. The first is Philip Rafferty, of the California Bar, who shared his own extensive research unstintingly and frequently critiqued my work. Virtually every case, and many other sources cited in this article appear in full in the appendixes to his book.[31] That he and I differ in our interpretation of some of these sources does not detract from the importance of his work in uncovering and collecting these original sources, some of which were unknown before he found them and most of which were scattered in obscure historical studies or even more obscure collections of almost randomly assembled cases. Mr. Rafferty or I can provide copies of the originals of these sources, which until recent times are all recorded in either medieval Latin script or Law French.

Special mention is also due to John Keown, then Professor of Law and Medicine at the University of Leicester and now at Georgetown University. The research he shared with me included several early cases and, most especially, the legislative history of *Lord Ellenborough's Act* and other nineteenth-century English sources. He has published his own major work on the history of English abortion statutes.[32]

Finally, John Baker, Professor of Legal History at Cambridge University and at New York University, was also a great help, both directly and through his aid to Mr. Rafferty's research. Dr. Baker provided original translations from medieval Latin or Law French for all of the numerous records of medieval English legal proceedings, all of which he verified from the original public records. He has written the leading text on English legal history that is used in universities throughout the Commonwealth.[33]

A good deal of the material I have used in this paper was actually uncovered by historians and others seeking to establish or to refute a constitutional right to abortion, including Means, Keown, and Rafferty. One might also mention historian James Mohr, whose book on the history of abortion in nineteenth century America[34] opens a window onto the many relevant sources even though I find his analysis of the materials nearly always wrong. My own original research was mostly, but not entirely, related to the medical history that plays such a prominent part in this book. All interpretations of all data that I rely on in this book, regardless of how the data came to my attention, are, of course, my own and any errors in reporting or interpreting the data are my sole responsibility.

Earlier (and much shorter) versions of this history were presented at meetings of the Section of Legal History at the Association of American Law Schools Annual Meeting in San Francisco and at the Second International Conference on Argumentation held at the University of Amsterdam, both in 1990. I also take this opportunity to thank Frederick Dyer, Kathleen Farrell, Clarke Forsythe, Mary Ann Glendon, Kent Greenawalt, Paul Linton, Christopher Tietze, and William

---

31. PHILIP RAFFERTY, ROE V. WADE: THE BIRTH OF A CONSTITUTIONAL RIGHT (University Microfilm International Dissertation Information Service, Ann Arbor, MI 1993).

32. JOHN KEOWN, ABORTION, DOCTORS AND THE LAW (1988).

33. J.H. BAKER, AN INTRODUCTION TO ENGLISH LEGAL HISTORY (3rd ed. 1990).

34. JAMES MOHR, ABORTION IN AMERICA: THE ORIGINS AND EVOLUTION OF NATIONAL POLICY, 1800–1900 (1978).

Valente, all of whom reviewed and commented on drafts of parts of this work during various stages of my work.

Finally, one should note that I have cut off the research as of January 1, 2004. The year 2004 had many interesting and complex events that carry forward the story set forth in these pages, but they did not, as it turned out, result in any fundamental change of direction from what appeared to be in store at the end of 2003. While I finished the manuscript somewhat later than I expected when I chose this cut-off date, I thought it better to stick to it than to attempt to undertake to write yet more to cover the year 2004.

# Dispelling the Myths
# of Abortion History

# Chapter 1

# Only Women Bleed[1]

*Continuity with the past is only a necessity, not a duty.*
    —Oliver Wendell Holmes[2]

Women have a rather more difficult time giving birth than most mammals, more difficult than most other primates.[3] Because of the size of human brains, infant human heads barely fit through a pelvis that must remain narrow to allow walking upright on only two feet.[4] The infant must twist and turn like a contortionist to find a pathway through the birth canal, and must be born with a brain that is not fully grown and with a skull that has not yet fused, allowing the skull to be compressed and stretched during birth. The result is a long period of infantile dependence while the infant's brain finishes growing and maturing. In terms of cerebral development, human infants essentially remain fetuses for about nine months after birth.[5] And human babies normally are born facing away from the mother, so the mother cannot assist the baby out of the birth canal without bending the baby's spine back, risking fatal injury to the infant. Nor can the mother clear mucus from the baby's mouth, or unwind the umbilical cord should it have wrapped around the baby's neck, both essential steps to enable the infant to breathe. As result of these problems, women giving birth unassisted probably experienced some of the highest rates of fetal and maternal death during birth of any mammal.

Most mammals, including other primates, give birth alone and in seclusion. Women, with the ability to foresee and to discuss what they faced, chose otherwise. They sought others to help

---

1. Alice Cooper, *Only Women Bleed* (1977).

2. Oliver Wendell Holmes, *Law in Science and Science in Law,* in Collected Legal papers of Oliver Wendell Holmes 210, 211 (1920).

3. *See generally* Wenda Trevathan, Human Birth: An Evolutionary Perspective (1987). *See also* Sarah Blaffer Hrdy, Mother Nature: A History of Mothers, Infants, and Natural Selection 165 fig. 7.8 (1999).

4. Hrdy, *supra* note 3, at 165, 478–79; Karen Rosenberg & Wenda Trevathan, *Bipedalism and Human Birth: The Obstetrical Dilemma Revised,* 4 Evolutionary Anthropology 161, 166 (1996); Peter Rodman & Henry McHenry, *Bioenergetics and the Origins of Hominid Bipedalism,* 52 Am. J. Physical Anthropology 103 (1980).

Human babies are also born, on average, with four times as much subcutaneous body fat as other primates. Hrdy, *supra,* at 475–84; M.C. Elphick & W.W. Wilkinson, *The Effects of Starvation and Surgical Injury on the Plasma Levels of Glucose, Free Fatty Acids, and Neutral Lipidss in Newborn Babies Suffering from Various Congenital Anomalies,* 15 Pediatric Research 313 (1981); David Haig, *Genetic Conflicts of Human Pregnancy,* 68 Q. Rev. Biology 495, 500–03 (1993); Paul Harvey, R.D. Martin, & T.H. Clutton-Brock, *Life Histories in Comparative Perspectives,* in Primate Societies 181 (Barbara Smuts ed. 1987); E.M. Widdowson, *The Chemical Composition of Newly Born Mammals,* 166 Nature 769 (1950). According to one theory, the extra fat is "critical for the development of fast-growing, lipid guzzling human brains." Hrdy, *supra,* at 478. The brain accounts for more than 50% of the total basal metabolic rate of a human infant. Leslie Aiello & Peter Wheeler, *The Expensive Tissue Hypothesis,* 36 Current Anthropology 199 (1995); Toni Ziegler *et al., Body Composition of the Reference Fetus,* 40 Growth 329 (1976).

5. Trevathan, *supra* note 3, at 143–45. *See also* Hrdy, *supra* note 3, at 479–80.

them and their infants through the birth process, creating a cultural solution to a biological problem. While we have no direct evidence of when or where this practice began, it probably began shortly after the advent of upright walking by humans, perhaps as early as 5,000,000 years ago and almost certainly by the time modern humans emerged somewhat over 100,000 years ago. The need to cooperate in birthing, rather than the needs of hunting and gathering, might have been the source of language, and hence of culture.

Assisted delivery was universal by the time written records began, and continues to be universal today. Two anthropologists, Wenda Trevathan and Karen Rosenberg, surveyed 298 cultures and found only 24 in which a significant minority of women—nearly always experienced mothers—sometimes gave birth alone.[6] For most women around the world until well into the twentieth century, these helpers were other, more experienced women.[7] As some women demonstrated superior skill and learning in birthing, they began to assist at many, even most, births in their communities. Thus was born the profession of midwives, from the Old English *mit wif*, meaning someone who was "with the wife."[8]

Midwives developed into a group of persons sharing a specialized knowledge particularly useful to their society. Although no one can document it, midwifery would appear to be truly the oldest profession. Midwives, however, remained largely self-taught or (at best) learned as apprentices assisting more experienced midwives.[9] Indeed, the experience of giving birth was considered the most important part of a midwife's training.[10] Predictably, there were no standard procedures, disagreement reaching such basic questions as to whether the midwife should "encourage" birth by vigorous manipulations or pressures on the mother's abdomen or should largely allow nature to take its course.[11]

---

6. Rosenberg & Trevathan, *supra* note 4, at 163–64.

7. *See, e.g.*, Thomas Darlington, *The Present State of the Midwife*, 63 Am. J. Obstet. & Gynaecology 870 (1911). *See also* Nanette Davis, From Crime to Choice 89 (1985); Raymond DeVries, Making Midwives Legal: Childbirth, Medicine, and the Law 23–26 (2nd ed. 1996); Jean Donnison, Midwives and Medical Men: A History of the Struggle for the Control of Childbirth 22, 85 (2nd ed. 1988); Mireille Laget, *Naissances: l'accouchemnet avant l'age de la clinique* 138 (1982); Judy Barrett Litoff, American Midwives: 1860 to the Present 27, 136 (1978); Richard Meckel, Save the Babies: American Public Health Reform and the Prevention of Infant Mortality 174 (1990); Kerry Petersen, Abortion Regimes 40 (1993); Debra Susie, In the Way of Our Grandmothers: A Cultural View of Twentieth-Century Midwifery in Florida (1988); Dorothy & Richard Wertz, Lying In: A History of Childbirth in America 55–59 (1977); Bruce Bellingham & Mary Pugh Mathis, *Race, Citizenship, and the Bio-Politics of the Maternalist Welfare State: "Traditional" Midwifery in the American South under the Sheppard-Towner Act, 1921–1929*, 1 Soc. Pol. 157 (1994).

8. Donnison, *supra* note 7, at 11. Italian uses a term with a similar derivation: *comare* (with the mother). *Id.*

9. *See, e.g.*, Pierre Dionis, Traité général des accouchements, qui instruit ce tout ce qu'il faut faire pour être habile accoucheur 414–15 (1711); Elizabeth Nihell, A Treatise on the Art of Midwifery 217–18 (1760); Sarah Stone, A Complete Practice of Midwifery xv–xvii (1737); Laurel Thatcher Ulrich, The Midwife's Tale: The Life of Martha Ballard Based on Her Diary, 1785–1812, at 11–12 (1991) ("Ulrich, The Midwife's Tale"); Percival Willughby, Observations in Midwifery: As also the Countrey Midwifes Opusculum and Vade Mecum 2, 72 (Henry Blenkinsop ed. 1863; original pub. ca. 1663). *See also* Alice Clark, Working Life of Women in the Seventeenth Century 269–73 (1968); Donnison, *supra* note 7, at 20–22, 31, 36–40, 50–52, 55, 60–67, 70, 77–78, 82–85, 96, 105, 111, 117–20; Joan Donegan, Women and Men Midwives: Medicine, Morality, and Misogyny in Early America 12, 42–43 (1978); Laurel Thatcher Ulrich, Goodwives: Image and Reality in the Lives of Women in Northern New England, 1650–1750, at 134 (1983) ("Ulrich, Goodwives"); Mary Roth Walsh, Doctors Wanted: No Women Need Apply 5–6 (1977).

10. Stone, *supra* note 9, at xiv; Ulrich, The Midwife's Tale, *supra* note 9, at 12. *See also* Donnison, *supra* note 7, at 14, 28; Walsh, *supra* note 9, at 5–6.

11. David Hunt, Parents and Children in History: The Psychology of Family Life in Early Modern France 86 (1970). These debates continue today as disputes over whether midwives should be qualified

Sanitation was barely considered. As historian David Hunt noted, "[i]t was hoped that she [the midwife] would cut her nails, wash, and remove the rings from her hands before beginning."[12] Hunt does not say who was hoping, but one suspects that the hope that hands were washed was not felt in the same manner as the hope that nails would be clipped and rings removed. No wonder eighteenth-century midwife Martha Ballard's first loss of a woman while tending her labor, in 1787 after nearly a decade of midwifing, occurred when Ballard was also busy treating an epidemic of scarlet fever.[13] And a midwife could do little if she encountered major difficulties. Usually a midwife had no instruments other than her own hands, and only alcohol or crude folk concoctions for easing pain.[14] Cesarean sections were rarely attempted unless the mother was already dead, for such surgery was nearly always fatal.[15]

These patterns were still real enough in the opening years of the twentieth century to lend plausibility to the charge that midwives were the major cause of maternal deaths in childbirth.[16] Not so long before, delivery by a physician was clearly more dangerous than delivery by a midwife.[17] Furthermore, midwives continually experimented with herbs and with various other

---

to use modern technology (such as fetal heart monitors) or should rely on nature taking its course. *See* DE-VRIES, *supra* note 7, at 28–29; Paula Laurillard-Lampe, *Giving Birth in Holland in a Time of Changes,* 9 Assoc. RADICAL MIDWIVES NEWSL. 10 (1981); Jen Thomas, *Extracts from a Review of the Fifth International Congress of Psychosomatic Obstetrics and Gynecology,* 4 Assoc. RADICAL MIDWIVES NEWSL. 14 (1979); W.G. van Arkel, A.J. Ament, & N. Bell, *The Politics of Home Delivery in the Netherlands,* 7 BIRTH & FAM. J. 101 (1980).

12. HUNT, *supra* note 11, at 86. For a contemporary observation about the "notorious harshness" of midwives, see *Female Physicians,* 54 BOS. MED. & SURGICAL J. 169, 171–72 (1856). *See also* DONNISON, *supra* note 7, at 25, 28–29, 106–08.

13. ULRICH, THE MIDWIFE'S TALE, *supra* note 9, at 42–45, 192–93. *See generally* DONNISON, *supra* note 7, at 62–63.

14. *See, e.g.,* LOUISE BOURGEOIS, RECUIL DES SECRETS DE LOUYSE BOURGEOIS 115–30 (1635); DIONIS, *supra* note 9, at 206; JACQUES GUILLEMEAU, CHILDBIRTH, OR THE HAPPY DELIVERY OF WOMEN... 115 (1635); 2 AMBROISE PARÉ, *OUEVRES COMPLÈTES* 704–06 (1840). *See generally* HUNT, *supra* note 11, at 87–88; ULRICH, GOODWIVES, *supra* note 9, at 134–38, 184, 190.

15. J.L. BADELOQUE, TWO MEMOIRES ON THE CAESARIAN OPERATION (John Hull trans. 1801); 1 LOUISE BOURGEOIS, *OBSERVATIONS DIVERSES SUR LA STÉRILITÉ, PERTE DE FRUIT FEOCONDITÉ, ACCOUCHEMENS ET MALADIES DES FEMMES ET ENFANTS NOUVEAUX NAIZ* 189 (1626); GUILLEMEAU, *supra* note 14, at 185–88; FRANÇOIS MAURICEAU, *TRAITÉ DES MALADES DES FEMMES GROSSES...* 348 (1675). The first successful Cesarean section in which the mother and child both lived appears to have been performed by an Irish midwife in 1738. *See* DONNISON, *supra* note 7, at 59 [citing to SAMUEL MERRIMAN, DIFFICULT PARTURITION 163 (1820)].

16. *See, e.g.,* Eliza Root, *The Status of Obstetrics in General Practice,* TRANS. FIRST PAN-AM. MED. CONG., pt. I, at 901 (1895); Ralph Waldo Lobenstine, *The Influence of the Midwife upon Infant and Maternal Morbidity and Mortality,* 63 AM. J. OBSTET. & DISEASES OF WOMEN & CHILDREN 878 (1911). *See generally* DONNISON, *supra* note 7, at 137; LESLIE REAGAN, WHEN ABORTION WAS A CRIME: WOMEN, MEDICINE, AND LAW IN THE UNITED STATES, 1867–1973, at 90–93 (1997); Constance Backhouse, *Involuntary Motherhood: Abortion, Birth Control and the Law in Nineteenth Century Canada,* 3 WINDSOR Y.B. OF ACCESS TO JUSTICE 61, 63 (1983); Charles King, *The New York Maternal Mortality Study: A Conflict of Professionalization,* 65 BULL. MED. HIST. 476 (1991).

17. Considerable evidence suggests that birthing with the help of a midwife even now is safer than birthing with the help of a physician; in evaluating such claims, however, one must keep in mind that in settings where both sorts of birthing are common, physicians get all the complicated births, midwives sending to a doctor any birth posing serious problems. *See* SUZANNE ARMS, IMMACULATE DECEPTION: A NEW LOOK AT WOMEN AND CHILDBIRTH 53–54 (1977); DONNISON, *supra* note 7, at 192–93; LITOFF, *supra* note 7, at 83, 147; BARBARA KATZ ROTHMAN, IN LABOR: WOMEN AND POWER IN THE BIRTHPLACE 42 (1982); LYNN SILVER & SIDNEY WOLFE, UNNECESSARY CESAREAN SECTIONS: HOW TO CURE A NATIONAL EPIDEMIC (1989); MARJORIE TEW, SAFER CHILDBIRTH? 289 (1990); WERTZ & WERTZ, *supra* note 17, at 161; Robbie Davis-Floyd, *The Role of Obstetrical Rituals in the Resolution of Cultural Anomaly,* 31 SOC. SCI. MED. 175 (1990); A. Mark Durand, *The Safety of Home Birth: The Farm Study,* 82 AM. J. PUB. HEALTH 450 (1992); Ken Nagaya *et al., Causes of Maternal Mortality in Japan,* 283 JAMA 2661 (2000); Francis Notzon, *International Differences in the Use of Obstetric Interventions,* 263 JAMA 3286 (1990); Roger Rosenblatt, *The Perinatal Paradox: Doing More and Accomplishing Less,* 1989 HEALTH AFF. 158; Marjorie Tew, *Do Obstetric Intranatal Interventions Make Birth Safer?,* 93 BRIT. J.

techniques for easing the pain and reducing the risk of childbirth. From these simple beginnings, midwives gave birth to the profession of medicine generally. As late as the nineteenth century in many parts of England and the United States, midwives and "wise women" practiced an informal medicine, primarily but not entirely as herbalists.[18]

Of course, not all women were happy to be pregnant or willing to give birth. Because midwives had a long and intimate association with gestation and birth, at some point (also probably very early) women who did not want to bear a child began to turn to midwives for help in disposing of unwanted children. Even assuming that many or most midwives did not do abortions or infanticide, the association of midwives with abortion and infanticide was common enough that eventually an unsavory reputation became attached to midwives.[19] Indeed, nurse Elizabeth Crowell could write in 1907 that "some go so far as to as to say that the two terms 'midwife' and 'abortionist' are synonymous."[20]

It is no wonder then that even the earliest regulations enacted for midwives included requirements that midwives demonstrate themselves to be "of good character" and prohibited them from certifying the cause of death of someone under their care (mother or child).[21] Ecclesiastical regulations requiring midwives to have licenses from the church expressly forbade abortion and infanticide, as well as price gouging, favoritism, concealing births and deaths, and misreporting

---

OBSTET. & GYNAECOLOGY 659 (1986); Marsden Wagner, *Infant Mortality in Europe: Implications for the United States, Statement to the National Commission to Prevent Infant Mortality,* 9 J. PUB. HEALTH 473, 481 (1988).

18. *See generally* JEANNE ACHTERBERG, WOMAN AS HEALER (1990); MARY CHAMBERLAIN, OLD WIVES' TAILS: THEIR HISTORY, REMEDIES, AND SPELLS (1991); CARL DEGLER, AT ODDS: WOMEN AND THE FAMILY IN AMERICA FROM THE REVOLUTION TO THE PRESENT 56–57 (1980); Donegan, *supra* note 9; DONNISON, *supra* note 7, at 12–13, 17–19, 21; BARBARA EHRENREICH & DEIDRE ENGLISH, WITCHES, MIDWIVES, & NURSES: A HISTORY OF WOMEN HEALERS 44–48 (1973); LINDA GORDON, WOMAN'S BODY, WOMAN'S RIGHT: A SOCIAL HISTORY OF BIRTH CONTROL IN AMERICA 172 (1976); KATE CAMPBELL HURD-MEAD, A HISTORY OF WOMEN IN MEDICINE FROM THE EARLIEST TIMES TO THE BEGINNING OF THE NINETEENTH CENTURY (1938); PAUL STARR, THE SOCIAL TRANSFORMATION OF AMERICAN MEDICINE: THE RISE OF A SOVEREIGN PROFESSION AND THE MAKING OF A VAST INDUSTRY 32–37, 49–50, 54–59, 124 (1982); REAY TANNAHILL, SEX IN HISTORY 62 (1980); ULRICH, THE MIDWIFE'S TALE, *supra* note 9, at 254–61, 339–40; WALSH, *supra* note 9, at 1–10.

19. *See, e.g.,* GEORGE ELLINGTON, THE WOMEN OF NEW YORK, OR THE UNDERWORLD OF A GREAT CITY 399–400 (1869); 2 NED WARD, THE LONDON SPY COMPLEAT, IN EIGHTEEN PARTS 396–99 (1704–06); VICE COMMISSION OF CHICAGO, THE SOCIAL EVIL IN CHICAGO: A CASE STUDY OF EXISTING CONDITIONS WITH RECOMMENDATIONS BY THE VICE COMMISSION OF CHICAGO 225–27 (1911); Charles Bacon, *The Midwife Question in America,* 29 JAMA 1091 (1897); F. Elisabeth Crowell, *The Midwives of New York,* 17 CHARITIES & THE COMMONS 667 (1907); Caroline Hedger, *Investigation of 363 Midwives in Chicago,* 3 TRANS. AM. ASSOC. FOR STUDY OF INFANT MORTALITY 264 (1912); Rudolph Holmes et al., *The Midwives of Chicago,* 50 JAMA 1346 (1908); James Lincoln Huntington, *The Midwives of Massachusetts,* 167 BOS. MED. & SURGICAL J. 547 (1912); Mary Sherwood, *The Midwives of Baltimore,* 52 JAMA 2009 (1909); Horatio Robinson Storer, *Contributions to Obstetric Jurisprudence—Criminal Abortion V: Its Perpetrators,* 3 N. AM. MEDICO-CHIRURGICAL REV. 465, 465–66 (1859). *See generally* DEVRIES, *supra* note 7, at 22; DONNISION, *supra* note 7, at 45–46, 86–87, 113–14, 118–19, 129, 135–36, 168–69; T.R. FORBES, THE MIDWIFE AND THE WITCH (1966); KRISTIN LUKER, ABORTION AND THE POLITICS OF MOTHERHOOD 41–45 (1984); ANGUS MCLAREN, BIRTH CONTROL IN NINETEENTH-CENTURY ENGLAND 241 (1978); JAMES MOHR, ABORTION IN AMERICA: THE ORIGINS AND EVOLUTION OF NATIONAL POLICY, 1800–1900, at 11, 161 (1978); REGINA MORANTZ-SANCHEZ, SYMPATHY AND SCIENCE: WOMEN PHYSICIANS IN AMERICAN MEDICINE 188–89 (1985); PETERSEN, *supra* note 7, at 13, 40–41; REAGAN, *supra* note 16, at 52–53, 70–76, 90–112 (1997); RICKIE SOLINGER, THE ABORTIONIST: A WOMAN AGAINST THE LAW 202–04 (paperback ed. 1996); Dennis Horan & Thomas Marzen, *Abortion and Midwifery: A Footnote in Legal History,* in NEW PERSPECTIVES ON HUMAN ABORTION 199 (Dennis Horan & David Mall eds. 1981); Ann Oakley, *Wise Women and Medicine Man: Changes in the Management of Childbirth,* in THE RIGHTS AND WRONGS OF WOMEN 17, 23–30 (Juliet Mitchell & Ann Oakley eds. 1976). *But see* MARGARET STEPHEN, THE DOMESTIC MIDWIFE 105 (1795) (denying charges that midwives are disposed towards "intemperance, or even obscenity" as motivated by those who seek to discredit the profession).

20. Crowell, *supra* note 19, at 673.

21. DONNISON, *supra* note 7, at 4–7; MOHR, *supra* note 19, at 86–90; PETERSEN, *supra* note 7, at 13, 41.

paternity.[22] At times in Medieval Europe, the sons of midwives were barred from apprenticing to the trade guilds because of their mothers' profession.[23] Only later—beginning as early as the sixteenth century in France and even later in England—did licensing authorities (by then secularized) begin to insist on competency in the midwifery arts in addition to promises not to kill or give false reports.[24] It did not help the image of midwives that many of them, whether from ignorance or from a choice to defy the regulations, remained unlicensed.[25] By the nineteenth century, the moral reputation of midwives had become so suspect that they were often characterized by novelists as "drunken incompetent slattern[s]."[26] That such an unsavory reputation arose in large measure from association with abortion and infanticide belies the claim of abortion rights activists that abortion was socially accepted until the late nineteenth century.

Under the circumstances, one can understand why abortions were often depicted as something done by women to women, although that was always too simple a picture of the social and physical reality of abortion. Some nineteenth-century anti-abortion crusaders even saw abortion as a women's conspiracy against men.[27] More recently, feminists and other abortion rights promoters have painted the same picture as a basis for claiming that abortion has always been the secret knowledge of women that never was, and is not now, any business of men.[28] An inconsistent claim is that the demographic transition that began in the United States in the

---

22. DeVries, *supra* note 7, at 31–32; Donnison, *supra* note 7, at 14–15, 19; James Hitchock, *A Sixteenth Century Midwife's License*, 41 Bull. Hist. Med. 75 (1967). *See also* Forbes, *supra* note 19, at 143–49.

23. Forbes, *supra* note 19, at 113.

24. J.H. Aveling, English Midwives: Their History and Prospects 14 (1872); Clark, *supra* note 9, at 276–79; DeVries, *supra* note 7, at 33–36; Donnison, *supra* note 7, at 20, 25–32; Wertz & Wertz, *supra* note 7, at 31–33; Richard Petrelli, *The Regulation of French Midwives during the Ancient Regime*, 26 J. Hist. Med. 276 (1971).

25. *See, e.g.*, Alexander Boorde, The Breviary of Helthe fol. xvii (1547). *See generally* Donnison, *supra* note 7, at 20, 32; R.S. Roberts, *The Personnel and Practice of Medicine in Tudor and Stuart Times*, 6 Med. Hist. 363, 363–64 (1962).

26. Dianne Martin, *The Midwife's Tale: Old Wisdom and a New Challenge to the Control of Reproduction*, 3 Colum. J. Gender & L. 417, 433 (1992). *See also* Donnison, *supra* note 7, at 45, 54, 70, 103, 113, 115; Nancy Schrom Dye, *History of Childbirth in America*, 6 Signs 97, 102 (1980); Robert Erickson, *"The Books of Generation": Some Observations on the Style of the British Midwife Books, 1671–1761*, in Sexuality in Eighteenth-Century Britain 75, 85 (Paul-Gabriel Boucé ed. 1982).

27. *See, e.g.*, Edwin Hale, The Great Crime of the Nineteenth Century, Why Is It Committed? Who Are the Criminals? How Shall They Be Detected? How Shall They Be Punished? 17 (1867); Horatio Robinson Storer & Franklin Fiske Heard, Criminal Abortion: Its Nature, Its Evidence and Its Law 97–103 (1868); John Todd, Serpent in a Dove's Nest 4 (1867). *See generally* Walsh, *supra* note 9, at 72 n.86, 106–77; Reva Siegel, *Abortion as a Sex Equality Right: Its Basis in Feminist Theory* ("Siegel, *Sex Equality*"), in Mothers in Law: Feminist Theory and the Legal Regulation of Motherhood 43, 49–51 (Martha Albertson Fineman & Isabel Karpin eds. 1995); Reva Siegel, *Reasoning from the Body: A Historical Perspective on Abortion Regulation and Questions of Equal Protection*, 44 Stan. L. Rev. 261, 300–01 (1992) ("Siegel, *Reasoning from the Body*").

28. Kingsley Davis & Judith Blake, *Social Structure and Fertility: An Analytical Framework*, 4 Econ. Dev. & Cultural Change 230 (1956), as quoted in Mohr, *supra* note 19, at 103 (abortion alone "is a woman's method [of limiting fertility] and can be practiced without the man's knowledge"). *See also* Gordon, *supra* note 18, at 26–32, 36, 39, 47; Rosalind Pollack Petchesky, Abortion and Women's Choice: The State, Sexuality, and Reproductive Freedom 179 (rev. ed. 1990); Petersen, *supra* note 7, at 2, 10–13, 18, 23; Reagan, *supra* note 16, at 25–31, 34–35; Women's Medicine: A Cross-Cultural Study of Indigenous Fertility Regulation (Lucille Newman ed. 1985); Susan Klepp, *Lost, Hidden, Obstructed, and Repressed*, in Early American Technology: Making and Doing Things from the Colonial Era to 1850, at 68, 71–73, 82 (Judith McGaw ed. 1994). *See generally* Georges Devereux, A Study of Abortion in Primitive Societies 136–37 (1955); DeVries, *supra* note 7, at 21–23; Angus McLaren, Reproductive Rituals 111 (1984); John Riddle, Contraception and Abortion from the Ancient World to the Renaissance 16, 58–59, 81, 91–92, 109–10, 116–17, 155–56 (1992); Abraham Rongy, Abortion: Legal or Illegal? 35–36 (1933).

early years of the nineteenth century is evidence of a "domestic feminism" whereby women began to take control of their bodies by persuading their husbands to limit the size of the family.[29] Others argued that women had undertaken to prevent children without the knowledge or cooperation of their husbands.[30] It has even become fashionable in some circles to decry the medicalization of birth as a male conspiracy to subordinate women's bodies (and hence their lives) to the control of men (physicians rather than husbands).[31] In these circles, the demand

---

29. Daniel Scott Smith, *Family Limitation, Sexual Conduct, and Domestic Feminism in Victorian America*, 1 FEMINIST STUD. 40 (1973).

30. *See, e.g.,* 1 BONNIE ANDERSON & JUDITH ZINSSER, A HISTORY OF THEIR OWN: WOMEN IN EUROPE FROM PREHISTORY TO THE PRESENT 136–37 (1988); BARBARA BROOKES, ABORTION IN ENGLAND 1900–1967, at 52 (1988); DEGLER, *supra* note 18, at 227–28; GORDON, *supra* note 18, at 28–30, 47; BEVERLY WILDUNG HARRISON, OUR RIGHT TO CHOOSE: TOWARD A NEW ETHIC OF ABORTION 162, 165–66 (1983); MOHR, *supra* note 19, at 82–85, 103, 106–07; PETCHESKY, *supra* note 28, at 29–33, 51–53, 71–73; PATRICK SHEERAN, WOMEN, SOCIETY, THE STATE, AND ABORTION: A STRUCTURALIST ANALYSIS 51 (1987); CARROLL SMITH-ROSENBERG, DISORDERLY CONDUCT: VISIONS OF GENDER IN VICTORIAN AMERICA 226 (1985).

31. ARMS, *supra* note 17, at 54–61, 109, 178–81, 202, 268, 304–05; G.J. BARKER-BENFIELD, THE HORRORS OF THE HALF-KNOWN LIFE: MALE ATTITUDES TOWARD WOMEN AND SEXUALITY IN NINETEENTH CENTURY AMERICA 61 (1976); CHARLOTTE BORST, CATCHING BABIES: THE PROFESSIONALIZATION OF BIRTH, 1870–1920 (1995); JANET FARRELL BRODIE, CONTRACEPTION AND ABORTION IN NINETEENTH-CENTURY AMERICA 287 (1994); GENA COREA, THE HIDDEN MALPRACTICE: HOW AMERICAN MEDICINE MISTREATS WOMEN (updated ed. 1985); DeVRIES, *supra* note 7, at 23–27, 39–46, 51, 112; DONNISON, *supra* note 7, at 11, 28–29, 38–39, 191–95, 198–206; BARBARA EHRENREICH & DIERDRE ENGLISH, FOR HER OWN GOOD: 150 YEARS OF THE EXPERTS' ADVICE TO WOMEN (1982); BARBARA EHRENREICH & DIERDRE ENGLISH, COMPLAINTS AND DISORDERS: THE SEXUAL POLITICS OF SICKNESS (1973); GORDON, *supra* note 18, at 19–25; HARRISON, *supra* note 30, at 36; ROBBIE PFEUFER KAHN, BEARING MEANING: THE LANGUAGE OF BIRTH (1995); CATHARINE MacKINNON, TOWARD A FEMINIST THEORY OF THE STATE 192 (1989); SUSAN McCUTCHEON-ROSEGG, NATURAL CHILDBIRTH THE BRADLEY WAY 130–31, 189, 211–12, 222–24 (1984); McLAREN, *supra* note 19, at 231–32; WENDY MITCHINSON, THE NATURE OF THEIR BODIES: WOMAN AND THEIR DOCTORS IN VICTORIAN CANADA (1991); REGINA MORANTZ-SANCHEZ, CONDUCT UNBECOMING A WOMAN: MEDICINE ON TRIAL IN BROOKLYN 114–26 (1999); ANN OAKLEY, THE CAPTURED WOMB: A HISTORY OF THE MEDICAL CARE OF PREGNANT WOMEN (1984); PETCHESKY, *supra* note 27, at 49–55; KATHRYN ALLEN RABUZZI, MOTHER WITH CHILD: TRANSFORMATION THROUGH CHILDBIRTH (1994); KERREEN REIGER, THE DISENCHANTMENT OF THE HOME 94 (1985); CYNTHIA EAGLE RUSSETT, SEXUAL SCIENCE: THE VICTORIAN CONSTRUCTION OF WOMANHOOD (1989); BEVERLY SAVAGE & DIANA SIMKIN, PREPARATION FOR BIRTH 194–97 (1987); SUSAN SHERWIN, NO LONGER PATIENT 193–96 (1992); ELAINE SHOWALTER, THE FEMALE MALADY (1985); SOLINGER, *supra* note 19, at 204–18; SARAH STAGE, FEMALE COMPLAINTS: LYDIA PINKHAM AND THE BUSINESS OF WOMEN'S MEDICINE (1979); STARR, *supra* note 18, at 81, 117, 123–26; ALEXANDER DUNDAS TODD, INTIMATE ADVERSARIES: CULTURAL CONFLICT BETWEEN DOCTORS AND WOMEN PATIENTS (1989); PATRICIA VERTINSKY, THE ETERNALLY WOUNDED WOMAN: WOMEN, DOCTORS, AND EXERCISE IN THE LATE NINETEENTH CENTURY (1994); WERTZ & WERTZ, *supra* note 7, at 257–63; Lynda Birke *et al., Technology in the Lying-in Room*, in ALICE THROUGH THE MICROSCOPE: THE POWER OF SCIENCE OVER WOMEN'S LIVES 165, 177–79 (Linda Birke *et al.* eds. 1980); Erin Daly, *Reconsidering Abortion Law: Liberty, Equality, and the New Rhetoric of* Planned Parenthood v. Casey, 45 AM. U. L. REV. 77, 85–86, 108–09, 116 (1995); Frances Kobrin, *The American Midwife Controversy: A Crisis of Professionalization,* 40 BULL. HIST. MED. 350 (1966); Janna Merrick & Robert Blank, *The Politics of Pregnancy: Policy Dilemmas in the Maternal-Fetal Relationship,* 13 WOMEN & POL. 1 (1993); Regina Markell Morantz & Sue Zschoche, *Professionalism, Feminism, and Gender Roles: A Comparative Study of Nineteenth-Century Medical Therapeutics,* 67 J. AM. HIST. 568 (1980); Regina Morantz-Sanchez, *Physicians,* in WOMEN, HEALTH & MEDICINE IN AMERICA (Rima Apple ed. 1990); Charles Rosenberg & Carroll Smith-Rosenberg, *The Female Animal: Medical and Biological Views of Women and Her Role in Nineteenth-Century America,* 4 J. INTERDISCIPLINARY HIST. 25 (1973); Robyn Rowland, *Technology and Motherhood: Reproductive Choice Reconsidered,* 12 SIGNS 512 (1987); Siegel, *Reasoning from the Body, supra* note 27, at 287–88, 314–15; Siegel, *Sex Equality, supra* note 27, at 48–49; Brenda Waugh, *Repro-Woman: A View of the Labyrinth (from the Lithotomy Position),* 3 YALE J.L. & FEMINISM 5 (1991); Laura Woliver, *Reproductive Technologies, Surrogacy Arrangements, and the Politics of Motherhood,* in MOTHERS IN LAW, *supra* note 27, at 346, 352–53. *See also* Irving Zola, *Medicine as an Instrument of Social Control,* 20 SOC. RES. 487 (1972).

arises that women "seize" back control through "demedicalizing" the practice of gynecology and obstetrics.[32]

The supposition that women routinely, yet secretly, controlled birth patterns independently of their husbands actually belies the evidence. In the remarkably detailed diary of midwife Martha Ballard for the period from 1785 to 1812, when many historians now insist that midwives were commonly performing abortions, there is no mention of even a single abortion.[33] We cannot assume that Ballard simply did not report such activities; her diary includes accounts of incest, illegitimacy, child abuse, and other unsavory activities. If Ballard did abortions so routinely that they did not strike her as significant, it would still be extraordinary that, in such a detailed record of the events of her life, she would not mention it even once. Either Ballard considered abortions even viler than the activities she recorded or she neither did nor knew of any.

# Assumptions Instead of Evidence

*Those who can't remember the past are condemned to trust historians.*
—Carlin Romano[34]

Historians have found direct evidence of "women's networks" for providing abortions only from the late nineteenth century.[35] British historian Angus McLaren simply asserted that abortion was always women's secret, but he immediately followed that claim with a brief description of several cases in which a man instructed women in the necessary "art" or in which a man coerced a woman into undergoing an abortion.[36] Similarly, historian James Mohr sought to support the same idea by pointing out that in one Indiana abortion trial several affiants notarized

---

32. An early and classic statement is BOSTON WOMEN'S HEALTH COLLECTIVE, OUR BODIES, OUR SELVES (1971). This book has been reissued in at least six editions. *See also* ARMS, *supra* note 17; R. CAMPBELL & A. MACFARLANE, WHERE TO BE BORN: THE DEBATE AND THE EVIDENCE (1987); ANN CARTWRIGHT, THE DIGNITY OF LABOUR? A STUDY OF CHILDBIRTH AND INDUCTION (1979); REBECCA CHALKER & CAROL DOWNER, A WOMAN'S BOOK OF CHOICES: ABORTION, MENSTRUAL EXTRACTION, RU 486, at 9 (1993); DONNISON, *supra* note 7, at 195–98, 206–09; MARGO EDWARDS & MARY WALDORF, RECLAIMING BIRTH: HISTORY AND HEROINES OF AMERICAN CHILDBIRTH REFORM (1984); FEDERATION OF WOMEN'S HEALTH CTRS., HOW TO STAY OUT OF THE GYNECOLOGIST'S OFFICE (Carol Downer, Rebecca Chalker, & Lorraine Rothman eds. 1981); MYRA MARX FERREE & BETH HESS, CONTROVERSY AND COALITION: THE NEW FEMINIST MOVEMENT ACROSS THREE DECADES OF CHANGE 107–08 (rev. ed. 1994); INA MAY GASKIN, SPIRITUAL MIDWIFERY (1977); SALLY INCH, BIRTHRIGHTS: A PARENT'S GUIDE TO MODERN CHILDBIRTH (1982); JUDY BARRETT LITOFF, THE AMERICAN MIDWIFE DEBATE 13–14 (1986); EMILY MARTIN, THE WOMAN IN THE BODY: A CULTURAL ANALYSIS OF REPRODUCTION (1987); MICHEL ODENT, BIRTH REBORN: WHAT BIRTH CAN AND SHOULD BE (1984); REAGAN, *supra* note 16, at 224–26; ADRIEN RICH, OF WOMEN BORN: MOTHERHOOD AS EXPERIENCE AND INSTITUTION (1976); SUE ROSSER, WOMEN'S HEALTH — MISSING FROM U.S. MEDICINE (1994); ROTHMAN, *supra* note 17; SHERYL BURT RUZEK, THE WOMEN'S HEALTH MOVEMENT: FEMINIST ALTERNATIVES TO MEDICAL CONTROL (1978); Marie Ashe, *Zig-Zag Stitching and the Seamless Web: Thoughts on "Reproduction" and the Law,* 13 NOVA L. REV. 355 (1989); Diane Curtis, *Doctored Rights: Menstrual Extraction, Self-Help Gynecological Care, and the Law,* 20 REV. L. & SOC. CHANGE 427 (1994); D. & N.J. Wikler, *Turkey-Baster Babies: The Demedicalization of Artificial Insemination,* 69 MILBANK Q. 5 (1991).

33. ULRICH, THE MIDWIFE'S TALE, *supra* note 8.

34. Carlin Romano, *How a Heretical School of History Found Its Place,* PHILA. INQUIRER, July 29, 1991, at 3-I.

35. *See* EUROPEAN WOMEN: A DOCUMENTARY HISTORY, 1789–1945, at 207–09 (Eleanor Riemer & John Fouts eds. 1980); MCLAREN, *supra* note 19, at 226–28; PETCHESKY, *supra* note 28, at 51–55.

36. MCLAREN, *supra* note 19, at 89–93, 111–12, 231–32, 240–42.

their depositions with marks rather than signatures.[37] Nevertheless, the defendant in the case was a male doctor and not the illiterate member of a "women's underground." Or consider historian John Riddle's recent study of the technology of abortion. Riddle repeatedly claimed that abortion was part of a "women's subculture" unknown to men, yet he cites book after book written by men reciting techniques for procuring abortions dating back to the Roman Empire.[38] Riddle's one direct report of what he considered a women's subculture involved a man giving a woman a potion as part of a seduction.[39] Historian Leslie Reagan, who introduces her study of abortion with page after page of anecdotes describing women's role in helping each other obtain abortions in the early years of the twentieth century,[40] does at least acknowledge that "[w]omen also counted on men."[41] Additionally, numerous legal records dating back centuries record men as pressuring women into abortions they did not want, and even as physically forcing abortions on unwilling women.[42]

Rather than abortion being a "women's secret," men seem to have been involved in decisions regarding abortion, and the doing of abortions, for as long as we have recorded history. Accounts that seek to portray abortion as a "women's secret" also neglect or deny the coercive aspects of male involvement in abortion—or that even purely female networks could be and often were coercive, whether from fear of possible male intervention or otherwise.[43] Nor do those who decry the medicalization of birth seem to consider the health effects of that achievement or the probable effects of a genuine return of control to mothers through a truly natural birth.[44]

Fifty years ago, abortion was not a topic for polite conversation. Abortion was a crime and there were no significant advocates for the changing the law. Only in a few Communist and socialist countries and in Japan was abortion legal and commonly available.[45] Yet the law did change. Abortion went, in a mere fifteen years (1958–1973), from a practice shrouded in shame and guilt to a fundamental right protected by the Constitution in the United States and by legislative reform in many other countries. This remarkable change provoked great controversy in

---

37. MOHR, *supra* note 19, at 106–07.

38. RIDDLE, *supra* note 28, at 16, 58–59, 81, 91–92, 109–10, 116–17, 155–56.

39. *Id.* at 144–45.

40. REAGAN, *supra* note 16, at 25–31.

41. *Id.* at 31. *See id.* at 31–36.

42. *See, e.g.,* Rex v. Hallowell, 9 SUPER. CT. RECORDS Nos. 113, 173, 175 (Wyndham Cnty., Conn., Super. Ct. Files, box 172) (1745–47), described in Cornelia Hughes Dayton, *Taking the Trade: Abortion and Gender Relations in an Eighteenth-Century New England Village,* 48 WM. & MARY Q. 19 (1991); Commonwealth v. Mitchell, 10 MD. ARCHIVES 171–86 (1652; published 1891); Rex v. Powell (1635), *in Cnty. Ct. Records of Accomack-Northampton, Virginia, 1632–1640,* 7 AM. LEGAL RECORDS 43 (Susie Ames ed. 1954); Rex v. Anonymous (1670), 1 MATTHEW HALE, HISTORY OF PLEAS OF THE CROWN 429–30 (1736); Rex v. Wodlake, K.B. 9/513/m23 (1530); Rex v. de Bourton, Y.B. Mich. 1 Edw. 3, f. 23, pl. 28 (K.B. 1327); Agnes's Appeal (1200), SELECT PLEAS OF THE CROWN (1 SELDEN SOC'Y) 39 (no. 82) (F.W. Maitland ed. 1887). *See also* RIDDLE, *supra* note 28, at 32–36; Anne Burnet, *Abortion as the Exciting Cause of Insanity,* 9 WOMEN'S MED. J. 400, 401 (1899).

43. *See generally* MARY ODEM, DELINQUENT DAUGHTERS: PROTECTING AND POLICING ADOLESCENT FEMALE SEXUALITY IN THE UNITED STATES, 1885–1920 (1995); REAGAN, *supra* note 16, at 32–34; Carole Joffe, *Comments on MacKinnon,* 18 RADICAL AM. 68 (Mar.–June 1984); Catharine MacKinnon, *The Male Ideology of Privacy: A Feminist Perspective on the Right to Abortion,* 17 RADICAL AM. 23 (July–Aug. 1983); Rosalind Pollack Petchesky, *Abortion as "Violence against Women": A Feminist Critique,* 18 RADICAL AM. 64 (Mar.–June 1984).

44. Franklin Miller, *Book Rev.* (of SHERWIN, *supra* note 31), 91 APA NEWSLETTERS 88, 89 (Fall 1992).

45. *See generally* DANIEL CALLAHAN, ABORTION: LAW, CHOICE, AND MORALITY 185–223, 253–57 (1970); SAMUEL COLEMAN, FAMILY PLANNING IN JAPAN 19–20 (1983); PAUL GEBHARD *et al.,* PREGNANCY, BIRTH AND ABORTION 221–32 (1958); GERMAIN GRISEZ, ABORTION: THE MYTHS, THE REALITIES, AND THE ARGUMENTS 194–206, 253–56 (1970).

the United States[46] and abroad.[47] As a result, we are engaged in an intense struggle over the stories we tell ourselves about abortion.[48]

The story of abortion as told in recent years in American legal and political discourse has been described by some as "propagating a philosophy of extreme individualism, if not selfishness, that negates the conception of the family, although this comes about in a haphazard and unplanned fashion."[49] Others, however, tell the story differently, seeing women gaining control of their reproductive capacity to become whole individuals, with family and governmental insti-

---

46. *See generally* DALLAS BLANCHARD, THE ANTI-ABORTION MOVEMENT AND THE RISE OF THE RELIGIOUS RIGHT: FROM POLITE TO FIERY PROTEST (1994); ETHAN BRONNER, BATTLE FOR JUSTICE: HOW THE BORK NOMINATION SHOOK AMERICA (1988); ELIZABETH ADELL COOK, TED JELEN, & CLYDE WILCOX, BETWEEN TWO ABSOLUTES: PUBLIC OPINION AND THE POLITICS OF ABORTION (1992); DONALD CRITCHLOW, INTENDED CONSEQUENCES: BIRTH CONTROL, ABORTION, AND THE FEDERAL GOVERNMENT IN MODERN AMERICA 200–24 (1999); MARIAN FAUX, CRUSADERS: VOICES FROM THE ABORTION FRONT (1990); FEDERAL ABORTION POLITICS: A DOCUMENTARY HISTORY (Neil Devins & Wendy Watson eds. 1995); BARBARA HINKINSON CRAIG & DAVID O'BRIEN, ABORTION AND AMERICAN POLITICS (1993); KENNETH KARST, LAW'S PROMISE, LAW'S EXPRESSION: VISIONS OF POWER IN THE POLITICS OF RACE, GENDER, AND RELIGION 31–66 (1993); LUKER, *supra* note 19; STEPHEN MARKMAN, JUDICIAL SELECTION: MERIT, IDEOLOGY AND POLITICS—THE REAGAN YEARS (1990); PATRICK MCGUIGAN & DAWN WEYRICH, NINTH JUSTICE: THE BATTLE FOR BORK (1990); MICHELLE MCKEEGAN, ABORTION POLITICS: MUTINY IN THE RANKS OF THE RIGHT (1992); MICHAEL PERTSCHUK & WENDY SCHAETZEL, THE PEOPLE RISING: THE CAMPAIGN AGAINST THE BORK NOMINATION (1989); PETCHESKY, *supra* note 28, at 241–76; EVA RUBIN, ABORTION, POLITICS, AND THE COURTS (rev. ed. 1987); ROBERT SPITZLER, THE RIGHT TO LIFE MOVEMENT AND THIRD PARTY POLITICS (1987); SUZANNE STAGGENBORG, THE PRO-CHOICE MOVEMENT: ORGANIZATION AND ACTIVISM IN THE ABORTION CONFLICT (1991); UNDERSTANDING THE NEW POLITICS OF ABORTION (Michael Goggin ed. 1993); MATTHEW WETSTEIN, ABORTION RATES IN THE UNITED STATES: THE INFLUENCE OF OPINION AND POLICY (1996); CATHERINE WHITNEY, WHOSE LIFE? A BALANCED, COMPREHENSIVE VIEW OF ABORTION FROM ITS HISTORICAL CONTEXT TO THE CURRENT DEBATE (1991); BARBARA YARNOLD, ABORTION POLITICS IN THE FEDERAL COURTS: RIGHT VERSUS RIGHT (1995); Merrill McLaughlin, *America's New Civil War,* U.S. NEWS & WORLD REP., Oct. 3, 1988, at 23; Fawn Vrazo, *Conservative Ascendancy Propels Abortion to the Crossroads,* PHILA. INQUIRER, Nov. 13, 1994, at A15. Note that these sources often make no pretense of neutrality, generally evidencing a strong bias against those who oppose abortion rights. In this regard, Catherine Whitney's book, subtitled *A Balanced, Comprehensive View,* is typical in being neither balanced nor comprehensive.

47. *See, e.g.,* F.L. MORTON, PRO-CHOICE VS. PRO-LIFE AND THE COURTS IN CANADA (1993); Sabine Berghahn, *Gender in the Legal Discourse in Post-Unification Germany: Old and New Lines of Conflict,* 2 SOC. POL.: INT'L STUD. IN GENDER, STATE & SOC'Y 37, 43–45 (1995); David Cole, *"Going to England": Irish Abortion Law and the European Community,* 17 HASTINGS INT'L & COMP. L. REV. 113 (1993); *Despite Pope's Protest, Polish Deputies Vote to Ease Abortion Law,* N.Y. TIMES, Oct. 25, 1996, at A4; Deborah Goldberg, *Developments in German Abortion Law: A U.S. Perspective,* 5 UCLA WOMEN'S L.J. 531 (1995); Ewa Maleck-Lewy, *Between Self-Determination and State Supervision: Women and the Abortion Law in Post-Unification Germany,* 2 SOC. POL.: INT'L STUD. IN GENDER, STATE & SOC'Y 62 (1995); Susan Walther, *Thou Shalt Not (But Thou Mayest): Abortion after the German Constitutional Court's 1993 Landmark Decision,* 36 GERMAN Y.B. IN'TL L. 385 (1993); Eleanora Zielinska, *Recent Trends in Abortion Legislation in Eastern Europe, with Particular Reference to Poland,* 4 CRIM. L.F. 47 (Regina Gorzkowska trans. 1993).

48. CELESTE MICHELLE CONDIT, DECODING ABORTION RHETORIC: COMMUNICATING SOCIAL CHANGE (1990); FAYE GINSBURG, CONTESTED LIVES: THE ABORTION DEBATE IN AN AMERICAN COMMUNITY (1989); CHRISTOPHER LASCH, THE TRUE AND ONLY HEAVEN: PROGRESS AND ITS CRITICS 487–96 (1991); Peggy Cooper Davis, *Neglected Stories and the Lawfulness of* Roe v. Wade, 28 HARV. C.R.-C.L. L. REV. 299 (1993); Sally Sheldon, *"Who Is the Mother to Make the Judgment?": The Constructions of Woman in English Abortion Law,* 1 FEMINIST LEG. STUD. 3 (1993); Joan Williams, *Gender Wars: Selfless Women in the Republic of Choice,* 66 NYU L. REV. 1559 (1991). *See generally* RONALD DWORKIN, LAW'S EMPIRE 228–50, 313 (1986); ROBIN WEST, NARRATIVE, AUTHORITY, AND LAW (1993); JAMES BOYD WHITE, JUSTICE AS TRANSLATION 89–112, 257–69 (1990).

49. Walter Otto Weyrauch, *Book Review,* 37 AM J. COMP. L. 832, 833 (1989) (reviewing MARY ANN GLENDON, HERMENEUTICS, ABORTION AND DIVORCE: A REVIEW OF ABORTION AND DIVORCE IN WESTERN LAW (1989)]. *See also* GLENDON, *supra,* at 112–42.

tutions as oppressors.[50] For example, news reports tell of a community in Nebraska, strongly opposed to abortion, that banded together to seize and hold an unmarried pregnant teenager to prevent her from aborting. As presented in the *New York Times*, the story is one of the family of the putative father, conspiring with a doctor, the local sheriff's office and police, the County Attorney, and a local Juvenile Court judge to deprive the girl (and her family) of their freedom, both to choose abortion and in a broader sense, by kidnapping the girl and by court order.[51] One could as easily cast the "conspirators" as heroes intervening to save the life of an unborn child of 23 weeks gestation—now an infant girl described in the article as a "darling little baby" being raised by the parents of the unnamed teenage girl.

Pennsylvania provides a somewhat similar story, but with intervention on the side of "choice" rather than "life." There, Rosa Marie Hartford was convicted of interfering with the custody of a 13-year old girl by taking the girl to New York for an abortion without the knowledge or consent of the girl's mother—who did not even know that the girl was pregnant.[52] Hartford, apparently seeking (in vain as it turned out) to avoid a statutory rape conviction for her 19-year old son, faced a jail sentence of up to seven years after her conviction. Many persons (including, apparently, the seven men and five women on the jury) see Hartford's actions as a selfish exploitation of a vulnerable child and a high-handed disregard of the right of a parent to determine the medical procedures and cultural values that should play a role in her daughter's life. Others, led by attorney Kathryn Kolbert of the Center for Reproductive Law and Policy who defended Hartford, see Hartford as a heroine who facilitated a young woman's lawful choice in the face of an uncaring and hostile world.

The struggle over the stories we tell ourselves about abortion inevitably has become in part a struggle to control the history of abortion. The history of Anglo-American abortion laws is central to the abortion controversy, serving to connect today's stories to the story of the Constitution and establishing a contemporary social context for appraising the ongoing value debates embodied in the story of abortion. Until 1968, the history of abortion in English and American law was considered unproblematic. Sir James Fitzjames Stephen, historian of the English criminal law, wrote in 1883 that he could "pass over many sections punishing particular acts of violence to the person, and in particular the whole series of offenses relating to the abduction of women, rape, and other such crimes. Their history possesses no special interest and does not illustrate either our political or our social history."[53]

At the time, Stephen was embroiled in a harsh debate with John Stuart Mill in which Stephen supported the propriety of the legal enforcement morality.[54] Under the circumstances, one would have expected Stephen to explore a topic like abortion if he had found any reason to ques-

---

50. Weyrauch, *supra* note 49, at 836. *See also* Planned Parenthood of S.E. Pa. v. Casey, 505 U.S. 833, 852–57 (1992) (Kennedy, O'Connor, & Souter, JJ., joint plurality op.); Robin West, *Jurisprudence and Gender*, 55 U. Chi. L. Rev. 1 (1988); Williams, *supra* note 48, at 1572–94.

51. Tamar Lewin, *Nebraska Abortion Case: The Issue is Interference*, N.Y. Times, Sept. 25, 1995, at A8.

52. Marie McCullough, *Abortion Case Taps Some of Parents' Deepest Fears*, Phila. Inquirer, Oct. 27, 1996, at A1; Marie McCullough, *For Young Teen's Mother, a Hollow Victory in Court*, Phila. Inquirer, Nov. 3,1996, at E2; David Stout, *Woman Who Took Girl for Abortion Is Guilty in Custody Case*, N.Y. Times, Oct. 31, 1996, at A15. *See also* Susan Dundon, *The Verdict Is in, but There's No Simple Answer When It Comes to Abortion*, Phila. Inquirer, Nov. 3, 1996, at E7.

53. 3 James Fitzjames Stephen, History of the Criminal Law of England 117–18 (1883).

54. *Compare* John Stuart Mill, On Liberty (1859), *with* James Fitzjames Stephen, Liberty, Equality and Fraternity (1873). The debate is reviewed in Stefan Petrow, *The Legal Enforcement of Morality in Late-Victorian England*, 11 U. Tasmania L. Rev. 60 (1992). *See generally* James Colalaco, James Fitzjames Stephen and the Crisis of Victorian Thought (1983).

tion its historic status as a crime. Stephen barely mentioned abortion, however, merely indicating his conclusion that under pre-Norman law (*i.e.*, before 1066), abortion was a crime exclusively within the ecclesiastical jurisdiction.[55] Such neglect of abortion is characteristic of historical writing until quite recently. We generally find abortion presented merely as an adjunct to discussions of what clearly were taken as significant social problems rather than as a topic of importance in its own right.[56] Sir William Holdsworth hardly mentioned abortion in his 23-volume history of English law.[57]

Stephen's attitude towards such crimes went unchallenged for another three-quarters of a century. Modern feminists seem inclined to see in such silences contempt for women that rendered women's concerns beneath the notice of serious students of the law.[58] Others might assume that the earlier silence rather as indicating either that such laws were largely uncontroversial in our history or were relatively unchanging through time or both. Yet the lack of attention by mainline historians both left the relevant historical materials largely undeveloped and left abortion history open to unfettered exploitation by all sides once women's concerns came to the fore and the legal status of abortion became controversial. Many historians now subscribe to a new orthodoxy regarding the history of abortion derived from the writings of Cyril Means, jr., and James Mohr, as well as Justice Harry Blackmun's majority opinion in *Roe v. Wade.*[59]

The late Cyril Means, jr., was a law professor at New York Law School when he became the first to undertake to revise our notions of abortion history. Means propounded two hitherto unsuspected historical "facts": First, that abortion was not criminal in England or America before the nineteenth century;[60] and second, that abortion was criminalized during the nineteenth century solely to protect the life or health of mothers, and not to protect the lives or health of unborn children.[61] Regardless of how many times these claims are repeated, however, they are not facts; they are myths. Means concluded from his myths that abortion was "a common law liberty" in 1791 (when the Ninth Amendment was adopted),[62] and that whatever restrictions on

---

55. 1 STEPHEN, *supra* note 53, at 54. One might add his mention that under Roman law abortion was an "extraordinary crime," but not homicide. *Id.* at 25. *See also* 2 STEPHEN, *supra*, at 411 (the ecclesiastical jurisdiction over marriage and incontinence covers all crimes arising out of the relationship between the sexes, including abortion).

56. ROGER ROSENBLATT, LIFE ITSELF: ABORTION IN THE AMERICAN MIND 58 (1992).

57. Holdsworth was content simply to report the adoption of Lord Ellenborough's Act, the first statutory prohibition of abortion. 11 W.S. HOLDSWORTH, A HISTORY OF ENGLISH LAW 537 (23 vols., 7th ed. 1956).

58. *See, e.g.,* Catharine MacKinnon, *Reflections on Sex Equality under Law,* 100 YALE L.J. 1281, 1281–82 (1991).

59. Roe v. Wade, 410 U.S. 113 (1973); MOHR, *supra* note 19; Cyril Means, jr., *The Law of New York Concerning Abortion and the Status of the Foetus, 1664–1968: A Case of Cessation of Constitutionality,* 14 N.Y.L.F. 411 (1968) ("Means I"); Cyril Means, jr., *The Phoenix of Abortional Freedom: Is a Penumbral Right or Ninth-Amendment Right About to Arise from the Nineteenth-Century Legislative Ashes of a Fourteenth-Century Common-Law Liberty?,* 17 N.Y.L.F. 335 (1971) ("Means II").

60. Means II, *supra* note 59, at 336–76.

61. *Id.* at 382–92. *See also* Means I, *supra* note 59, at 511–15. Means did not bother to explain why a modern legislature would need to re-enact a statute that already serves its purposes simply because its purposes have changed. *See* Richard Epstein, *Substantive Due Process by Any Other Name: The Abortion Cases,* 1973 SUP. CT. REV. 159, 168 n.34 ("There is no reason to require a legislature to protect or rehabilitate an old statute with a new preamble.").

62. Means II, *supra* note 59, at 336, 351–54, 374–75, 409–10 n.175. *See also* Roe v. Wade, 410 U.S. 113, 140 (1973); Beecham v. Leahy, 287 A.2d 836, 839 (Vt. 1972); *Amicus Brief of 250 American Historians in support of Appellants in* Planned Parenthood of Southeastern Pennsylvania v. Casey, [505 U.S. 833 (1992)], at 5–6 ("*Casey Historians' Brief*"); *Amicus Brief of 281 American Historians supporting Appellees in* Webster v. Reproductive Health Services [492 U.S. 490 (1989)] ("*Webster Historians' Brief*"), reprinted at 11 WOMEN'S RTS. L. RPTR. 163, 170 (1989), and in 8 DOCUMENTARY HISTORY OF THE LEGAL ASPECTS OF ABORTION IN THE

that "liberty" were enacted between 1791 and 1868 (when the Fourteenth Amendment was adopted) did not displace that "liberty" because the statutes, like the "liberty," were designed to protect women, not to subordinate women's interests to the interests of others.[63]

Unfortunately, Professor Means' history of abortion was neither objective nor accurate.[64] When Means wrote his first article, he was General Counsel for the National Association for the Repeal of Abortion Laws (NARAL—later the National Abortion Rights Action League, then the National Abortion and Reproductive Rights Action League, and now NARAL-Pro Choice America), and was still devoted to the "movement" when he wrote his second article.[65] Means' research was funded by the Association for the Study of Abortion (ASA), another branch of the abortion reform movement.[66] He revealed neither the funding nor his advocacy position in his published "scholarship"— "scholarship" that was relied on by the Court and accepted by much of the public as redefining the history of abortion.[67]

Means presented his radical revision of the history of abortion—a history that had been unquestioned for centuries—to the Supreme Court in an *amicus* brief to *Roe v. Wade*. Sarah Weddington, the attorney who argued for "Jane Roe" in the case, has stated that the Justices had copies of Means' articles on the bench with them during the oral arguments.[68] The effort was successful. Justice Harry Blackmun devoted fully half of the majority opinion in *Roe* to the history of abortion, using that history to inform his interpretation of the values involved in the case and ultimately whether the statutory prohibition of abortion was constitutional.[69] Blackmun re-

---

UNITED STATES: WEBSTER V. REPRODUCTIVE HEALTH SERVICES 107 (Roy Mersky & Gary Hartman eds. 1990) ("DOCUMENTARY HISTORY") (specific pagination will be given only to the version in the *Women's Rts. L. Rptr.*); GORDON, *supra* note 18, at 52–53, 57; MOHR, *supra* note 19, at 20–21, 128–29, 134–36, 144–45, 201, 208–11, 226, 229, 235–36; REAGAN, *supra* note 16, at 10; Laura Flanders, *Abortion: The Usable Past*, THE NATION, Aug. 7, 1989, at 175; Morton Kondracke, *The Abortion Wars*, NEW REP., Aug. 28, 1989, 17, at 19, col. 2; Siegel, *Reasoning from the Body, supra* note 27; Rickie Solinger, *"A Complete Disaster": Abortion and the Politics of Hospital Abortion Committees, 1950–1970*, 19 FEMINIST STUD. 241, 243 (1993). Few leaders in the abortion rights movement have conceded that even if the law did not prohibit early abortions, it did not create a legal right to an abortion. *See, e.g.*, LUKER, *supra* note 19, at 92; Mark Graber, *The Clintonification of American Law: Abortion, Welfare, and Liberal Constitutional Theory*, 58 OHIO ST. L.J. 731, 765–66 (1997).

63. Means II, *supra* note 59, at 376–410.

64. J. KEOWN, ABORTION, DOCTORS AND THE LAW 3–11 (1988); PHILIP RAFFERTY, *ROE V. WADE:* THE BIRTH OF A CONSTITUTIONAL RIGHT (University Microfilm International Dissertation Information Service, Ann Arbor, MI 1993); Joseph Dellapenna, *The History of Abortion: Technology, Morality, and Law*, 40 U. PITT. L. REV. 359 (1979). *See also* GLANVILLE WILLIAMS, THE SANCTITY OF LIFE AND THE CRIMINAL LAW 191 (1957).

65. FAUX, *supra* note 46, at 73, 81, 216–19, 222–23, 234, 237, 240, 289–92. Faux's book was written with the full cooperation of those who argued on behalf of Roe in *Roe v. Wade*, which is not surprising given, as one admiring reviewer aptly put it, that her book exhibits a clear bias "in favor of the pro-choice decision in *Roe v. Wade*." Francine Adkins Tone, *Book Review*, 19 LINCOLN L. REV. 67, 69 (1990).

66. FAUX, *supra* note 46, at 216–19.

67. This is a prime example of the advocacy scholarship denounced by Mary Ann Glendon and Ronald Collins. *See* MARY ANN GLENDON, A NATION UNDER LAWYERS: HOW THE CRISIS IN THE LEGAL PROFESSION IS TRANSFORMING AMERICAN SOCIETY 208 (1994); Ronald Collins, *A Letter on Scholarly Ethics*, 45 J. LEGAL EDUC. 139 (1995). Skeptics of advocacy scholarship occasionally deride those who denounce such scholarship for not naming names. *See, e.g.*, Sanford Levinson, *Book Review* (of Glendon, *supra*), 45 J. LEGAL EDUC. 143, 146 (1995); Michael Sean Quinn, *"Scholarly Ethics": A Response*, 46 J. LEGAL EDUC. 110 (1996). Cyril Means more than satisfies their demand.

68. Sarah Weddington, *Introduction*, in ABORTION IN THE SEVENTIES: PROCEEDINGS OF THE WESTERN REGIONAL CONFERENCE ON ABORTION, DENVER, COLORADO FEBRUARY 27–29, 1976, at 187, 189 (Dr. Warren Hern & Bonnie Andrikopoulos eds. 1977).

69. 410 U.S. at 136–52, 158 n. 54.

lied heavily and uncritically on Means' history, citing Means (and no other historian) no less than seven times.[70] Like Means, Blackmun's conclusions were wrong on all points.[71]

The purported history in the *Roe* majority opinion came under sustained criticism that succeeded in refuting many of the purported details of that history without coming to grips with what was perhaps the central historical point of the Means/Blackmun myths. Neither Means nor most of his critics uncovered any evidence of systematic or sustained efforts to seek out and suppress abortion before the nineteenth century.[72] Still, the challenges to the Means/Blackmun myths were strong enough to prompt a response by historian James Mohr. Without seriously questioning Means' work, Mohr presented an alternative explanation of the enactment of the nineteenth century abortion statutes by creating two further, somewhat overlapping, historical theses in his book *Abortion in America:* that abortion was a generally accepted and common practice in American society at the opening of the nineteenth century;[73] and that the nineteenth-century statutes were actually a device by men for oppressing women, particularly useful for the "organized" (largely male) medical profession to suppress competition from disorganized (largely female) "irregular" practitioners.[74] Mohr's book has become so central to disputes over the history of abortion that *amicus* briefs on both sides of later abortion cases have relied on Mohr's work to advance their own claims about the significance of that history.[75] These theses are also myths.

The myths propounded by Means and Mohr have become the new orthodox history of abortion on which the claim of a constitutionally protected liberty to abort is based. The very political convenience of this new orthodoxy ought to suggest a need for cautious examination of its truth. It would be well if those who insist that somehow the founders intended to make access to abortion a right protected by the Constitution but neglected to mention that supposed right in the document were to keep in mind the admonition of law professor Jefferson Powell:

> If your history uniformly confirms your predilections, it is probably bad history.... If the founders, as you understand them, always agree with you, it is logically possible that you are in incredible harmony with them. It is considerably more likely that your reconstruction of their views is being systematically warped by your personal opinions on constitutional construction.[76]

---

70. *Id.* at 136–39. *See also* Wolfgang Saxon, *Obituary: Cyril C. Means, 73, A Specialist in Laws Regarding Abortion,* N.Y. Times, Oct. 6, 1992, at A15. Edward Steegman noted the imbalance in Justice Blackmun's review of history without observing its source; instead, he suggested that the imbalance was a direct result of Blackmun's exaggerated distaste for "religious intolerance" to which the Justice would apparently attribute all historical prohibition of abortion. Edward Steegman, Note, *Of History and Due Process,* 63 Ind. L.J. 369, 390–94, 396–97 (1987).

71. *See generally* Keown, *supra* note 64, at 3–25; Rafferty, *supra* note 64; Dellapenna, *supra* note 64. *See also* Eugene Quay, *Justifiable Abortion — Medical and Legal Foundations (Pt. II),* 49 Geo. L.J. 395 (1961).

72. *See, e.g.,* Keown, *supra* note 64, at 3–11; Robert Byrn, *An American Tragedy: The Supreme Court on Abortion,* 41 Fordham L. Rev. 807 (1973); Robert Destro, *Abortion and the Constitution: The Need for a Life-Protective Amendment,* 63 Cal. L. Rev. 1250 (1975); John Noonan, jr., *An Almost Absolute Value in History,* in The Morality of Abortion: Legal and Historical Perspectives 1, 3–7 (John Noonan, jr., ed. 1970); Quay, *supra* note 71; James Witherspoon, *Reexamining* Roe: *Nineteenth-Century Abortion Statutes and the Fourteenth Amendment,* 17 St. Mary's L.J. 29 (1985).

73. Mohr, *supra* note 19, at 6–19.

74. *Id.* at 32–37, 147–82.

75. *Casey Historians' Brief, supra* note 62; *Webster Historians' Brief, supra* note 62; *Amicus Brief of the United States supporting Appellants in* Webster v. Reproductive Health Services, reprinted in 5 Documentary History, *supra* note 62, at 25.

76. H. Jefferson Powell, *Rules for Originalists,* 73 Va. L. Rev. 659, 667 (1987). *Cf.* Russell Korobkin, *A Multi-Disciplinary Approach to Legal Scholarship: Economics, Behavioral Economics, and Evolutionary Psychol-*

Yet with the Supreme Court's imprimatur still apparently secure on *Roe's* version of abortion history, that history continues to be regarded as true without question in ever widening circles.[77] The new orthodoxy has been recently reiterated by such well-known scholars as Ronald Dworkin in such respected, general circulation periodicals as the *New York Review of Books*,[78] as well as in leading newspapers and magazines,[79] in books by lawyers and others,[80] in scholarly ar-

---

*ogy*, 41 JURIMETRICS J. 319, 350–51 (2001) (arguing that scholars should always be skeptical if their research conforms to their preconceived notions).

77. For relatively recent references to *Roe* as the definitive account of abortion history, see CRAIG & O'BRIEN, *supra* note 46, at 342; PETCHESKY, *supra* note 28, at 98 n.37; RUBIN, *supra* note 46, at 11, 73–75; Lisa Allegrucci & Paul Kunz, Note, *The Future of* Roe v. Wade *in the Supreme Court: Devolution of the Right of Abortion and Resurgence of State Control*, 7 ST. L.U. J. LEGAL COMMENTARY 295, 295–96 n.1 (1991); Curtis, *supra* note 32, at 435 n.41; Bonnie Hertberg, Note, *Resolving the Abortion Debate: Compromise Legislation, an Analysis of the Abortion Policies of the United States, France, and Germany*, 16 SUFF. TRANSNAT'L L. REV. 513, 514–16 (1993); Nadine Taub & Elizabeth Schneider, *Women's Subordination and the Role of Law*, in FEMINIST LEGAL THEORY: FOUNDATIONS 9, 11 (D. Kelly Weisberger ed. 1993); Mark Woltz, Note, *A Bold Reaffirmation?* Planned Parenthood v. Casey *Opens the Door to Enact New Laws to Discourage Abortion*, 71 N. CAR. L. REV. 1787, 1787 (1993).

78. Ronald Dworkin, *The Great Abortion Case*, N.Y. REV. BOOKS, June 29, 1989, at 49, 50 n.10. *See also* Flanders, *supra* note 62; Katie Monagle, *How We Got Here*, Ms., May–June 1995, at 54; Tim Stafford, *The Abortion Wars*, CHRISTIANITY TODAY, Oct. 6, 1989, at 16. Dworkin himself has pronounced history generally irrelevant to legal argument. *See* RONALD DWORKIN, LIFE'S DOMINION: AN ARGUMENT ABOUT ABORTION, EUTHENASIA, AND INDIVIDUAL FREEDOM 13–14 (1993) ("DWORKIN, LIFE'S DOMINION").

79. *See, e.g.,* Katha Pollitt, *Abortion in American History* (book rev.), ATLANTIC MONTHLY, May 1998, at 111; Andrew Rosenthal, *Strong Foe of* Roe v. Wade *Gets Platform Post*, N.Y. TIMES, Jan. 23, 1992, at A1.

80. THE ABORTION CONTROVERSY: A DOCUMENTARY HISTORY 10–26 (Eva Rubin ed. 1994); NINIA BAEHR, ABORTION WITHOUT APOLOGY: A RADICAL HISTORY FOR THE 1990s, at 1–2 (1990); MARY BECKER, CYNTHIA GRANT BOWMAN, & MORRISON TORREY, FEMINIST JURISPRUDENCE: TAKING WOMEN SERIOUSLY 368 (1994); BLANCHARD, *supra* note 46, at 12–18; ROBERT BLANK & JANNA MERRICK, HUMAN REPRODUCTION, EMERGING TECHNOLOGIES, AND CONFLICTING RIGHTS 33–36 (1995); JUDITH BOSS, THE BIRTH LOTTERY: PRENATAL DIAGNOSIS AND SELECTIVE ABORTION 109–10 (1993); BRODIE, *supra* note 31, at 33, 143–44, 253–55, 258, 266–72; BROOKES, *supra* note 30, at 22–26, 54–56; JAMES MACGREGOR BURNS & STEWART BURNS, A PEOPLE'S CHARTER: THE PURSUIT OF RIGHTS IN AMERICA 351 (1991); ELLEN CHESLER, WOMEN OF VALOR: MARGARET SANGER AND THE BIRTH CONTROL MOVEMENT 38, 60–64 (1992); ANNE COLLINS, THE BIG EVASION: ABORTION, THE ISSUE THAT WON'T GO AWAY 207–15 (1985); CONDIT, *supra* note 48, at 22, 100–02; CRAIG & O'BRIEN, *supra* note 46, at 9–10, 39–41, 213–21; CRITCHLOW, *supra* note 46, at 269 n.63; DAVIS, *supra* note 7, at 11, 41–44, 210–13, 217; DEGLER, *supra* note 18, at 227–48; JOHN D'EMILIO & ESTELLE FREEDMAN, INTIMATE MATTERS: A HISTORY OF SEXUALITY IN AMERICA 145–47 (1988); DWORKIN, LIFE'S DOMINION, *supra* note 78, at 45, 112; LEE EPSTEIN & JOSEPH KOBYLKA, THE SUPREME COURT AND LEGAL CHANGE: ABORTION AND THE DEATH PENALTY 139–40 (1992); FAUX, *supra* note 46, at 53, 55–56; MARIAN FAUX, *ROE V. WADE: THE UNTOLD STORY OF THE LANDMARK SUPREME COURT DECISION THAT MADE ABORTION LEGAL* 51–57, 90, 222, 290–91, 297–98 (1988); COLIN FRANCOME, ABORTION FREEDOM: A WORLDWIDE MOVEMENT 30–31, 122–27 (1984); DAVID GARROW, LIBERTY AND SEXUALITY: THE RIGHT OF PRIVACY AND THE MAKING OF *ROE V. WADE* 271–72 (2nd ed. 1998); JOYCE GELB & MARIAN LIEF PALLEY, WOMEN AND PUBLIC POLICIES 129–31 (1982); GINSBURG, *supra* note 8, at 14–15, 23–33; GORDON, *supra* note 18, at 415–16; MICHAEL GROSSBERG, GOVERNING THE HEARTH: LAW AND THE FAMILY IN NINETEENTH-CENTURY AMERICA 11, 155–56, 159–87, 193–95 (1985); ROBERT HARDAWAY, POPULATION, LAW, AND THE ENVIRONMENT 115–17 (1994); JANET HADLEY, ABORTION: BETWEEN FREEDOM AND NECESSITY 33–36 (1996); HARRISON, *supra* note 28, at 149–51, 165–67; BETSY HARTMANN, REPRODUCTIVE RIGHTS AND WRONGS 259 (1995); KERRY JACOBY, SOULS, BODIES, SPIRITS: THE DRIVE TO ABOLISH ABORTION SINCE 1973, at 2 (1998); DONALD JUDGES, HARD CHOICES, LOST VOICES 83–84, 90–106 (1993); EDWARD LAZARUS, CLOSED CHAMBERS: THE FIRST EYEWITNESS ACCOUNT OF THE EPIC STRUGGLES INSIDE THE SUPREME COURT 343, 370 (1998); JETHRO LIEBERMAN, THE EVOLVING CONSTITUTION 23 (1992); LUKER, *supra* note 18, at 11–39; CHERYL MEYER, THE WANDERING UTERUS: POLITICS AND THE REPRODUCTIVE RIGHTS OF WOMEN 133–34 (1997); BARBARA MILBAUER & BERT OBRENTZ, THE LAW GIVETH: LEGAL ASPECTS OF THE ABORTION CONTROVERSY 14, 110–42 (1983); MAUREEN MULDOON, THE ABORTION DEBATE IN THE UNITED STATES AND CANADA: A SOURCE BOOK 159–60 (1991); KAREN O'CONNOR, NO NEUTRAL GROUND? ABORTION POLITICS IN AN AGE OF ABSOLUTES 19–22 (1997); PETCHESKEY, *supra* note 28, at 76–84, 248–49; PETERSEN, *supra* note 7, at 1–3, 17–18, 34–36, 65; REAGAN, *supra* note 16, at 8–14; DEBORAH RHODE, JUSTICE AND GENDER 202–05 (1989); JAMES RISEN & JUDY THOMAS, WRATH OF ANGELS: THE

ticles,[81] and in an occasional judicial decision.[82] Few of these authors have undertaken original research on, or have even shown any awareness of evidence that might contradict, the history of abortion that they so confidently espouse.[83] As a result, even strongly anti-abortion authors

---

AMERICAN ABORTION WAR 6–10 (1998); HYMAN RODMAN, BETTY SARVIS, & JOY BONAR, THE ABORTION QUESTION 3 (1987); ROSENBLATT, *supra* note 56, at 68–71, 82–88, 97–98; JACQUES ROSSIAUD, MEDIEVAL PROSTITUTION 125 (1988); RUBIN, *supra* note 46, at 11–17, 64, 73–75; SHULAMITH SHAHAR, THE FOURTH ESTATE: A HISTORY OF WOMEN IN THE MIDDLE AGES 124 (1983); SHEERAN *supra* note 30, at 49–58, 73–75; SMITH-ROSENBERG, *supra* note 30, at 23–24, 217–44; SOLINGER, *supra* note 19, at 10–12; DOROTHY MCBRIDE STETSON, WOMEN'S RIGHTS IN THE U.S.A.: POLICY DEBATES AND GENDER ROLES 80–81 (1991); RAYMOND TATALOVICH & BYRON DAYNES, THE POLITICS OF ABORTION: A STUDY OF COMMUNITY CONFLICT IN PUBLIC POLICY MAKING 16–23 (1981); LAURENCE TRIBE, ABORTION: THE CLASH OF ABSOLUTES 30–34 (1990) ("TRIBE, CLASH OF ABSOLUTES"); LAURENCE TRIBE, AMERICAN CONSTITUTIONAL LAW 1355–56 (2nd ed. 1988); JEFFREY WEEKS, SEX, POLITICS AND SOCIETY 27–76 (1981); WHITNEY, *supra* note 46, at 44–46; MAJORIE WORTMAN, WOMEN IN AMERICAN LAW: FROM COLONIAL TIMES TO THE NEW DEAL 163–65 (1985);

81. *See, e.g.,* Backhouse, *supra* note 16; Thomas Blumenthal, *Judicial Activism—The Politicization of the Right of Privacy,* 11 ST. L.U. PUB. L. REV. 329, 350–51 (1992); Samuel Buell, Note, *Criminal Abortion Revisited,* 66 NYU L. REV. 1774, 1780–94 (1991); Jane Maslow Cohen, *A Jurisprudence of Doubt: Deliberative Autonomy and Abortion,* 3 COLUM. J. GENDER & LAW. 175, 204–17 (1992); Rhonda Copelon, *Losing the Negative Right of Privacy: Building Sexual and Reproductive Freedom,* 18 NYU REV. L. & SOC. CHANGE 15, 27 (1990); Barbara Cox, *Refocusing Abortion Jurisprudence to Include the Woman: A Response to Bopp and Coleson and* Webster v. Reproductive Health Services, 1990 UTAH L. REV. 543, 558–63; Curtis, *supra* note 32, at 442–44; Daly, *supra* note 31, at 99; Walter Dellinger & Gene Sperling, *Abortion and the Supreme Court: The Retreat from* Roe v. Wade, 138 U. PA. L. REV. 83, 109–11 (1989); Susan Estrich & Kathleen Sullivan, *Abortion Politics: Writing for an Audience of One,* 138 U. PA. L. REV. 119, 152–54 (1989); Kathryn Ann Farr, *Shaping Policy through Litigation: Abortion Law in the United States,* 39 CRIME & DELINQUENCY 167, 169–70 (1993); Margaret Farrell, *Revisiting* Roe v. Wade: *Substance and Due Process in the Abortion Debate,* 68 IND. L.J. 269, 316 (1993); Thomas Grey, *Eros, Civilization, and the Burger Court,* 43 L. & CONTEMP. PROB. 83, 90 (Summer 1980); Julia Hanigsberg, *Book Rev.,* 37 MCGILL L.J. 928, 929–30 (1992) (purportedly describing Canadian history, but citing to Mohr and several American sources and to only one Canadian source); Amy Johnson, *Abortion, Personhood, and Privacy in Texas,* 68 TEX. L. REV. 1521, 1522–24 (1990); Sylvia Law, *Abortion and Compromise—Inevitable and Impossible,* 1992 U. ILL. L. REV. 921, 934 n.76; Deborah Mathieu, *Crime and Punishment: Abortion as Murder?,* 24 J. SOC. PHILOS. 1, 18–20 (1993); Jon Merz, Catherine Jackson, & Jacob Klerman, *A Review of Abortion Policy: Legality, Medicaid Funding, and Parental Involvement, 1967–1994,* 17 WOMEN'S RTS. L. RPTR. 1, 4 (1995); Mary Odem, *Fallen Women and Thieving Ladies: Historical Approaches to Women and Crime in the United States,* 17 LAW & SOC. INQUIRY 351, 352 (1992); James O'Hair, *A Brief History of Abortion in the United States,* 262 JAMA 1875 (1989); Frances Olsen, *Unraveling Compromise,* 103 HARV. L. REV. 105, 118 n.65 (1989); Elizabeth Reilly, *The Rhetoric of Disrespect: Uncovering the Faulty Premises Infecting Reproductive Rights,* 5 J. GENDER & L. 147, 149–52 (1996); Deborah Rhode, *Adolescent Pregnancy and Public Policy,* 108 POLI. SCI. Q. 635, 641–44 (1994); Frank Scaturro, *Abortion and the Supreme Court:* Roe, Casey, *the Myth of* Stare Decisis, *and the Court as a Political Insitution,* 3 HOLY CROSS J.L. & PUB. POL'Y 133, 136–43 (1998); Stephen Schnably, *Beyond* Griswold: *Foucauldian and Republican Approaches to Privacy,* 23 CONN. L. REV. 861, 866 n.25, 907 (1991); Elsa Shartsis, Casey *and Abortion Rights in Michigan,* 10 COOLEY L. REV. 313, 314–17 (1993); Siegel, *Reasoning from the Body, supra* note 27; Cass Sunstein, *Neutrality in Constitutional Law (with Special Reference to Pornography, Abortion, and Surrogacy),* 92 COLUM. L. REV. 1, 36–37 n.134 (1992); Jeremy Telman, *Abortion and Women's Legal Personhood in Germany: A Contribution to the Feminist Theory of the State,* 24 REV. L. & SOC. CHANGE 91, 95 n.16 (1998); Sara Walsh, *Liquid Lives and Liquid Laws,* 7 INT'L LEG. PERSPECTIVES 187, 213–20 (1995); Sarah Weddington, *The Donohue Lecture Series:* Roe v. Wade: *Past and Future,* 24 SUFF. U. L. REV. 601, 607–08 (1990); Williams, *supra* note 48, at 1573, 1575–76.

82. Stam v. State, 267 S.E.2d 335, 340 (N.C. 1980).

83. For three of the few attempts at a balanced account of the competing versions of abortion history, see JACOBY, *supra* note 80, at 2, 59–64; David Margolick, *At the Bar: Battle over Abortion Rights Rescues Some Forgotten Women from Centuries of Anonymity,* N.Y. TIMES, April 24, 1992, at B7; Jim Stone, *Abortion as Murder? A Response,* 26 J. SOC. PHILOS. 129, 134–36 (1995). Law professor Donald Judges does recount the history as provided by both sides, but he utterly fails to see the significance of the stories he retells, largely because he assumes that abortion was a common practice throughout history. JUDGES, *supra* note 80, at 90–110. Law professor Jane Maslow Cohen does acknowledge my own work in criticizing the claims of Blackmun, Means, and

like George Will have reiterated the new orthodoxy,[84] presumably because this spurious history has become so thoroughly embedded in the popular culture that it has taken on the aura of unquestionable truth. We have yet to learn that simply because the Supreme Court has the power to bind us to their law does not empower the Justices to bind us to their history.[85]

Those who approach history from an anti-abortion perspective also distort what actually happened in the past. They also assume that abortion was a common practice in the past, and, relying on the considerable evidence that abortion was always considered a serious crime, they assert that it was frequently and vigorously prosecuted for several thousand years of European history.[86] Their story is closer to the reality of history than the new orthodoxy is. Abortion was considered a serious crime throughout most of European history. Where their story breaks down is in the assumption that abortion was a common practice before the nineteenth century, and that prosecution was therefore common. In fact, prosecutions were relatively rare; the question is why. These "pro-life" historians did not even seriously examine the evidence pertaining to their a most basic—and erroneous—assumption, that abortion was always a common practice.

Followers of the new orthodoxy propound a theory that women in the past controlled abortion and performed the procedure routinely, safely, and easily, tending to assume that the knowledge of how to do an abortion in times long past was similar to our own knowledge, without attempting to explore the relevant evidence that allegedly proves the claim.[87] The real question,

---

Mohr, but sees the two lines of work as mere expressions of different "interpretive spins" without seriously evaluating the evidence. Cohen, *supra* note 81, at 205–06 n.116. The quality of Professor Cohen's analysis is suggested by her explanation of why she speaks of the intent of legislatures when her deconstructive technique precludes any such imputation: "Although I am uncomfortable with any such ascription, *I have allowed my text to behave similarly.*" Cohen, *supra,* at 206 n.116 (emphasis added).

84. George Will, *Abortion Is a State Question,* WASH. POST, June 18, 1989, at C7, col. 1. *See also* R. Randall Rainey, Gerard Magill, & Kevin O'Rourke, *Introduction: Abortion,the Catholic Church, and Public Policy,* in ABORTION AND PUBLIC POLICY: AN INTERDISCIPLINARY INVESTIGATION WITHIN THE CATHOLIC TRADITION 1, 8–9 (R. Randall Rainey & Gerard Magill eds. 1996).

85. MARK DEWOLFE HOWE, THE GARDEN AND THE WILDERNESS: RELIGION AND GOVERNMENT IN AMERICAN CONSTITUTIONAL HISTORY 4–5 (1965).

86. *See, e.g.,* KEOWN, *supra* note 64, at 3–11; Byrn, *supra* note 72; Destro, *supra* note 72; Noonan, *supra* note 72; Quay, *supra* note 71; Witherspoon, *supra* note 72.

87. *See, e.g.,* 1 ANDERSON & ZINSSER, *supra* note 30, at 137–38; BRODIE, *supra* note 31, at 33, 41–44, 224–25; BROOKES, *supra* note 30, at 1, 24; CHALKER & DOWNER, *supra* note 30, at 9; CONDIT, *supra* note 48, at 77 n.29; D'EMILIO & FREEDMAN, *supra* note 80, at 63, 145–50; AUDREY ECCLES, OBSTETRICS AND GYNAECOLOGY IN TUDOR AND STUART ENGLAND 67 (1982); MARIE-THÉRÈSE FONTANILLE, *ABORTEMENT ET CONTRACEPTION DANS LA MÉDECINE GRÈCO-ROMAINE* (1977); GINSBURG, *supra* note 48, at 23–24, 30; GORDON, *supra* note 18, at 28–29, 35–39, 52–54; MICHAEL GORMAN, ABORTION AND THE EARLY CHURCH: CHRISTIAN, JEWISH & PAGAN ATTITUDES IN THE GRECO-ROMAN WORLD 14–15, 18–19, 25–28, 94 (1982); HADLEY, *supra* note 80, at 33–34; HARRISON, *supra* note 30, at 238–44; OLWEN HUFTON, THE POOR IN EIGHTEENTH CENTURY FRANCE 331 (1974); MARTIN INGRAM, CHURCH COURTS, SEX AND MARRIAGE IN ENGLAND, 1570–1640, at 159 (1987); RALPH JACKSON, DOCTORS AND DISEASES IN THE ROMAN EMPIRE 105–09 (1988); JUDGES, *supra* note 80, at 32, 83–84, 96–97, 101; McLAREN, *supra* note 19, at 34, 241; McLAREN, *supra* note 28, at 5–7, 107, 111–12, 114; J.S. MILNE, SURGICAL INSTRUMENTS IN GREEK & ROMAN TIMES 81–82 (1907); MOHR, *supra* note 19, at 11–14, 18, 25–40, 85–118, 128, 147–82; PETCHESKY, *supra* note 28, at 1–2, 28–30, 48–57, 70–71, 76–78; PETERSEN, *supra* note 7, at 1, 12; G.R. QUAIFE, WANTON WENCHES AND WAYWARD WIVES: PEASANTS AND ILLICIT SEX IN EARLY SEVENTEENTH CENTURY ENGLAND 118–20 (1979); RHODE, *supra* note 80, at 202; SHEERAN, *supra* note 30, at 49–51, 54, 58, 73, 75; EDWARD SHORTER, A HISTORY OF WOMEN'S BODIES 177–91 (Pelican Books ed. 1984); REAGAN, *supra* note 16, at 6–8; SMITH-ROSENBERG, *supra* note 30, at 217; VERA ST. ERLICH, FAMILY IN TRANSITION: A STUDY OF 300 YUGOSLAV VILLAGES 257, 295 (1966); TRIBE, CLASH OF ABSOLUTES, *supra* note 80, at 30–34; JEFFREY WEEKS, SEX, POLITICS AND SOCIETY 72 (1981); WHITNEY, *supra* note 46, at 39–44; *Casey Historians' Brief, supra* note 62, at 4–10; *Webster Historians' Brief, supra* note 62, at 170–77; Backhouse, *supra* note 16, at 63; Cohen, *supra* note 81, at 206–07; Curtis, *supra* note 32, at 435; Dayton, *supra* note 42, at 19–20, 23; Sheila Dickinson, *Abortion in Antiquity,* 6 ARETHUSA 159 (1973); James Hitchcock, *Respect for Life and the Health Care Professions: A Historical Study,* in HUMAN LIFE AND HEALTH

however, is not whether it was men or women who controlled abortion in the past, but whether anyone in times past could perform abortions successfully. For example, Janet Brodie would have us believe that the mere fact that people must have attempted to control their fertility demonstrates that contraception and abortion were real social practices in past times.[88] Yet Brodie herself acknowledged that the evidence strongly shows birth patterns reflecting copulation without contraceptive or abortive intervention and that such private communications regarding the matter of childbirth as have come down to us exhibit an air of "resigned inevitability" rather than control.[89] This is similar to Linda Gordon's insistence that knowledge of how to do safe and effective abortions was widespread even while she herself referred to numerous letters sent to birth control advocates in the early twentieth century that, directly or indirectly, indicated that numerous couples had not the foggiest notion of how to go about having an abortion.[90] Beverly Wildung Harrison expressly assumed that abortion was a common practice in earlier centuries through recourse to techniques similar to our own.[91] Yet elsewhere in the same book she twice wrote that "until recently any act of abortion *always endangered the life of the mother* every bit as much as it imperiled the prenatal life in her womb."[92] Or consider Connie Paige's assumption that abortions were always readily available even while conceding that the success rate would not have been any higher than for natural miscarriages.[93]

Because James Mohr's book, *Abortion in America*,[94] remains so highly influential, Mohr's assumptions deserve special attention. Some of his assumptions are rather obvious failures of logic, as when he assumed that falling birth rates prove that there were rising rates of abortion — as if that were the only possible explanation.[95] In a similar vein, he assumes that statements regarding the relieving "obstructed menses" must always have been understood by the persons making the statements as having meant an abortion rather than the relieving of some other medical condition.[96] Most convenient to Mohr's story of abortion in America is his assumption that any evidence contrary to his theses represents a subterfuge by the persons who produced the evidence rather than an honest description of that persons' (or group's) goals or motives.[97]

Some of Mohr's other assumptions are so contrary to the evidence that he himself contradicted his own assumption. Thus, he assumed that relatively safe and effective means were available for accomplishing abortions throughout history even while denying the safety and effectiveness of those same techniques elsewhere in his book.[98] So intent was Mohr on finding safe and

CARE ETHICS 37, 37–38, 46 (James Bopp, jr., ed. 1985); Klepp, *supra* note 28, at 90–93; Elizabeth Karlin, *"We Called It Kindness": Establishing a Feminist Abortion Practice,* in ABORTION WARS: A HALF CENTURY OF STRUGGLE, 1950–2000, at 273, 273 (Rickie Solinger ed. 1998); Loretta Ross, *African-American Women and Abortion,* in ABORTION WARS, *supra,* at 161, 164–65; Siegel, *Reasoning from the Body, supra* note 27, at 318 n.235; Étienne van de Walle, *Motivations and Technology and the Decline of French Fertility,* in FAMILY AND SEXUALITY IN FRENCH HISTORY 135, 144–45 (Robert Wheaton & Tamara Hareven eds. 1980); Ray Bowen Ward, *The Use of the Bible in the Abortion Debate,* 13 ST. L. U. PUB. L. REV. 391, 392–93 (1993).

88. BRODIE, *supra* note 31, at 39–41.

89. *Id.* at 41.

90. *Compare* GORDON, *supra* note 18, at 28–29, 35–39, 52–54, *with id.* at 367–68.

91. HARRISON, *supra* note 30, at 238–44.

92. *Id.* at 124, 167 (emphasis added). *Also compare* van de Walle, *supra* note 87, at 144–45, *with* John Knodel & Étienne van de Walle, *Lessons from the Past: Policy Implications of Historical Fertility Studies,* 5 POPULATION & DEV. STUD. 217, 219 (1979).

93. CONNIE PAIGE, THE RIGHT TO LIFERS: WHO THEY ARE; HOW THEY OPERATE; WHERE THEY GET THEIR MONEY 32–33 (1983).

94. MOHR, *supra* note 19.

95. *Id.* at 78–84.

96. *Id.* at 4, 6–7, 10.

97. *See, e.g., id.* at 32–37, 85–118, 128, 147–82.

98. *Compare id.* at 11–14, 18, 25–40, 85–118, 128, 147–82, *with Id.* at 53–58, 71–73.

effective means for aborting that he assumed that electric shock was used to induce abortion in 1800 even while recognizing that his sources indicated that no mechanism existed for generating a powerful enough shock before 1840.[99] But then he reported that cottonroot was widely used between 1840 and 1880 as a "mild and effective" abortifacient,[100] but never bothered to ask why the product thereafter disappeared from use if it were truly effective without danger and if abortion were as popular an activity as he alleged. Historian Janet Brodie, herself as anxious to find evidence of abortifacients in the past as Mohr, indicated, however, that cottonroot was a "dangerous poison."[101] Cottonroot, incidentally, was reportedly used by slaves to defy masters who reportedly wanted to kill their offspring rather than have them born into slavery.[102] The steady growth of the number of slaves after the end of legal importation,[103] however, suggests that if cottonroot were in use among slaves, its use could not have been all that common—or at least, all that successful.

Eventually, Mohr even admitted that "[t]he nineteenth century had no preparations capable of directly producing abortions, though contemporary physicians and the public believed otherwise."[104] He hid that admission even more effectively than some others, burying it in an endnote appended to his discussion of the advertising of abortifacients rather than to his discussion of the efficacy of those techniques. Because various potions were so widely reported as in use for abortions, Mohr concluded that many women must have taken them in the hope of an abortion. He immediately undercut his conclusion by noting that "these preparations helped to trigger a relatively small number of actual abortions" and that "they [the women taking the potions] did not know that the drugs were incapable of doing what their advertisers claimed."[105] He also noted that one formula for an abortifacient would produce a "sweet and sour cocktail" that "may or may not have induced an abortion, but must certainly have jolted the system of any woman who tried one."[106] Mohr assumed that, having tried to obtain an abortion by using an ineffective potion, "many of the women who failed to get results with medicines would turn next to surgical methods" notwithstanding the known dangers of such techniques.[107] All of this is hardly a ringing endorsement of his own claim that abortion "was, if not common, almost certainly not rare in the United States during the first decades of the nineteenth century."[108]

---

99. *Id.* at 9, 66–67. Mohr's source for assuming that electric shock was in use was JOSEPH BREVITT, THE FEMALE MEDICAL REPOSITORY 46–47 (1810). For the lateness of the invention of adequate means, Mohr cites FREDERICK HOLLICK, DISEASES OF WOMEN, THEIR CAUSES AND CURE FAMILIARLY EXPLAINED; WITH PRACTICAL HINTS FOR THEIR PREVENTION, AND FOR THE PRESERVATION OF FEMALE HEALTH; FOR EVERY FEMALE'S PRIVATE USE 155–58 (1849).

100. MOHR, *supra* note 19, at 59. *See also* BRODIE, *supra* note 31, at 44, 225–26, 236; D'EMILIO & FREEDMAN, *supra* note 80, at 65; REAGAN, *supra* note 16, at 9.

101. BRODIE, *supra* note 31, at 44. For similar admissions by Janet Hadley, who also never heard of an abortifacient she didn't believe in, see HADLEY, *supra* note 80, at 37–38.

102. BRODIE, *supra* note 31, at 44, 225–26, 236; D'EMILIO & FREEDMAN, *supra* note 80, at 65; MOHR, *supra* note 19, at 59; REAGAN, *supra* note 16, at 9.

103. *See* PAUL DAVID ET AL., RECKONING WITH SLAVERY: A CRITICAL STUDY IN THE QUANTITATIVE HISTORY OF AMERICAN NEGRO SLAVERY (1976); ROGER FOGEL & STANLEY ENGERMAN, TIME ON THE CROSS: THE ECONOMICS OF AMERICAN SLAVERY (1974).

104. MOHR, *supra* note 19, at 276 n.15.

105. *Id.* at 67. *See also id.* at 44–45; PETCHESKY, *supra* note 28, at 77–78; THE ROMANCE OF PHILANTHROPY 158–59 (W.A. Coote ed. 1916); BRITISH MED. ASS'N, MORE SECRET REMEDIES: WHAT THEY COST AND WHAT THEY CONTAIN 184–206 (1912) ("SECRET REMEDIES"). Angus Mclaren listed no less than five articles in the well-known English medical journal *The Lancet* in 1898 and 1899 that listed such false advertisements. MCLAREN, *supra* note 28, at 251 n.11.

106. MOHR, *supra* note 19, at 14.

107. *Id.* at 53.

108. *Id.* at 16. *See also id.* at 155, 171–72.

Mohr's remarkable trust in dubious sources is best shown by his strong reliance on what was apparently the only mid-nineteenth-century source he found that actually claimed that there was then available an abortion technique that was "perfectly safe...and would 'impart no pain.'"[109] The claim is found in a book written under an assumed name (Dr. A.M. Mauriceau—the actual name of a famous eighteenth-century French obstetrician) by Charles Lohman, the husband of Madame Restell—the most notorious professional abortionist in the United States at the time.[110] Not only did Lohman use a pseudonym, but (as Mohr well knew) Lohman also falsely claimed in the book to be a "Professor of Diseases of Women" who had conducted many famous operations reported in the *Bulletin of the Academy of Medicine*.[111] Lohman assumed the name in order to claim that the author was both European trained and famous in Paris for his skill.[112] Readers were instructed that the pills "Dr. Mauriceau" recommended could be obtained by mail from yet another fictitious character invented by Lohman—M.M. Desomeaux—for $5 (then the cost of a month's rent for a New York City apartment).[113] The entire work appears to be a fraud designed to promote the sale of ineffective or dangerous abortifacients rather than a reliable source on the qualities of the techniques described in the book.[114] Mohr never discussed this possibility although elsewhere in the book he quoted from a pharmacist contemporary of Lohman who described the fraudulent nature of such claims within his profession.[115]

Mohr's reasoning is remarkable in other respects as well. He asserted that the quickening distinction sometimes applied in the common law demonstrates that people did not believe that killing a living fetus at any time was wrong even while acknowledging that women at the

---

109. *Id.*, at 65, quoting A.M. Mauriceau [Charles Lohman], The Married Woman's Private Medical Companion, Embracing the Treatment of Menstruation, or Monthly Turns, During Their Stoppage, Irregularity, or Entire Suppression. Pregnancy, and How It May Be Determined; with the Treatment of Its Various Diseases. Discovery to Prevent Pregnancy; Its Great and Important Necessity Where Malformation or Inability Exists to Give Birth. To Prevent Miscarriage or Abortion. When Proper and Necessary To Effect Miscarriage When Attended with Entire Safety 169 (1847).

110. On the career of Madame Restell, whose real name was Ann Lohman, see Brodie, *supra* note 31, at 229–31; Gordon, *supra* note 18, at 54–58; Grossberg, *supra* note 80, at 167; Allen Keller, Scandalous Lady: The Life and Times of Madame Restell, New York's Most Famous Abortionist (1981); Milbauer & Obrentz, *supra* note 80, at 138–42; Mohr, *supra* note 19, at 48–53, 88–89, 94, 96, 125–28, 182, 199. On the career of Restell's husband, see Mohr, *supra*, at 62–65.

Janet Brodie has identified the pseudo-Mauriceau as Joseph Trow, Ann Lohman's brother, rather than as Restelle's husband. Brodie, *supra*, at 66, 231. Apparently Trow held the copyright at one point; who really was the author does not affect the point in the text. Brodie is as unconcerned about the fraudulent nature of the publication as Mohr was. *Id.* at 71–72.

111. Mauriceau, *supra* note 109, at 181. *See also* Mohr, *supra* note 19, at 63.

112. Mauriceau, *supra* note 109, at 15–16.

113. *Id.* at 169.

114. *See also* Secret Remedies, *supra* note 105, at 184–85. The pills and nostrums collected in this report were sold for from 30 to as much as 500 times their cost. *Id.* at 192–206. The British Medical Society found that some pills then advertised for relieving "obstructed menses" had no active ingredient at all. *Id.* at 200–03. *See also* Brookes, *supra* note 30, at 29, 117–18; Mary Kenny, Abortion: The Whole Story 186–87 (1986).

115. Mohr, *supra* note 19, at 60. For Mohr's entire discussion of the Mauriceau book, see Mohr, *supra*, at 62–65. Historian Carl Degler also relied on Lohman's work to suggest that there was widespread public support for contraception and abortion. Degler revealed even less of Lohman's background that Mohr, mentioning only that "Mauriceau" was married to "New York's most notorious woman abortionist." Degler, *supra* note 18, at 199–201, 203, 216–17, 219–220, 243. Linda Gordon described Lohman as the prime example of "dishonest, avaricious, and ignoble men" whose quackery endangered women's lives. Gordon, *supra* note 18, at 165–66. Gordon did not mention Lohman's connection to Madame Restell, whom Gordon described as a martyr for women's rights without considering whether Restell's practices might also have involved quackery. Gordon, *supra*, at 54–58.

time considered the pre-quickening fetus to be "inert non-beings."[116] He attributed a supposed rise in abortion rates at least in major part to the emergence of nineteenth century feminism, although he also cites the evidence of the strong feminist opposition to abortion.[117] In sum, Mohr's book simply does not withstand careful reading even without additional research into his claims.

British historian Angus McLaren achieved similar prominence regarding the history of abortion in England in a pair of books: *Birth Control in Nineteenth-Century England* (1978) and *Reproductive Rituals* (1984).[118] We have already noted the contradiction in his assumption that women had secret knowledge regarding abortion that no man knew.[119] McLaren's ultimate argument for concluding that there were safe and effective abortifacients in times past is that to think otherwise is a sexist refusal to believe that women could have taken such "an active part in determining family size."[120] Even McLaren could not rest on that argument, so in his second book he argued that because women so desperately wanted to control their own fertility the magical rituals and procedures they followed must necessarily have worked.[121] Yet he also concluded that the search for herbal abortifacients was evidence of the desire of women to procure abortions rather than as evidence that their desire was realized.[122] In the end, he could only claim that adequate techniques existed simply because people so desperately wanted to abort:

> [F]irst,...concerns for health and family well-being could have led many to contemplate abortion; second...there existed a wide range of techniques that were *believed* to be effective in precipitating miscarriages; and third...the concept of "quickening" permitted women to consider the action as legitimate. For these reasons we have to conclude that abortion played a far more important role in the regulation of fertility than has usually been believed.[123]

McLaren backed this remarkable conclusion with a short list of reputed abortifacients without examining their safety or their efficacy.[124] His faith in the efficacy of folk medicine for accomplishing abortions is all the more remarkable given that he himself had studied the late nineteenth-century London frauds in the abortion industry.[125] McLaren's reasoning leads ineluctably to the conclusion that the ancients must have possessed the "elixir of life" that would confer immortality, for they surely sought it, apparently believed it existed, and some at least thought it was a legitimate pursuit. We also would be reduced to believing that alchemists could indeed transmute base metals into gold simply because their desire to do so was so intense.[126]

Finally, consider the first book in the English language to investigate the history of techniques for doing abortions. Historian John Riddle published *Contraception and Abortion from*

---

116. *Compare* MOHR, *supra* note 19, at 4–10, *with id.* at 6, 73–77.

117. *Id.* at 102–14.

118. MCLAREN, *supra* note 19; MCLAREN, *supra* note 28.

119. See the text *supra* at note 36.

120. MCLAREN, *supra* note 28, at 231.

121. *Id.* at 5–8, 98–99.

122. *Id.* at 98 (the statement is quoted below at note 124).

123. *Id.* at 111 (emphasis added). Rosalind Petchesky quoted E.A. Wrigley for a similar argument. PETCHESKY, *supra* note 28, at 29 [quoting E.A. WRIGLEY, POPULATION AND HISTORY 125 (1969)]. *See also* REAGAN, *supra* note 16, at 12–13; Angus McLaren, *Abortion in France: Women and the Regulation of Family Size, 1800–1914*, 10 FRENCH HIST. STUD. 461, 462 (1978).

124. MCLAREN, *supra* note 28, at 106–07.

125. Angus McLaren, *Abortion in England, 1890–1914*, 20 VICTORIAN STUDIES 379, 400 (1977).

126. *See, e.g.,* JACQUES SADOUL, ALCHEMISTS AND GOLD (Olga Sieveking trans. 1972)

*the Ancient World to the Renaissance* in 1992.[127] Riddle undertook to demonstrate that doctors and midwives during Roman and Medieval times knew and used many safe and effective means to procure abortion, even while conceding that some dangers were known and counseled against in ancient times. To achieve his purpose, Riddle felt it necessary not only to discover what techniques were reported for the doing of abortions in these ancient times, but also to discover whether these means really worked and how safe they were. To answer the latter question, Riddle employed a pharmacologist (Dr. J. Worth Estes of the Boston University School of Medicine) to provide information regarding the tests of the efficacy of ancient abortifacients. Riddle concluded that the ancient abortifacients were safe and effective, even though Dr. Estes strongly and publicly disagreed with these conclusions.[128] Several other reputable historians (Vivian Nutton of the University of London and Josiah Russell of the University of New Mexico) also disputed Riddle's conclusions when interviewed by a reporter for the *New York Times*.[129]

Riddle's book is riddled with admissions that contradict his conclusions. He admitted that many of his reconstructions of ancient abortifacient recipes were based on uncertain identifications of herbal ingredients and went on to admonish that no one should try to use them because "possibility for error is too great and the risk might be considerable."[130] Riddle also noted that these drugs had, at best, highly varied success rates and that success rates approaching 100 percent "in natural-product drugs [are] seldom the case."[131] Indeed, Riddle even admitted that "[s]ome of the plants...had marginal value, if any."[132] He also admitted that given the lack of precise recipes he can only rely on "reasonable case probability" for concluding that the recipes worked.[133] Riddle even admitted that for many (if not for all) of the claimed abortifacients, "there is an unresolvable ambiguity as to whether the words describe an action or a desired effect."[134]

So intent was Riddle on "proving" that Roman and medieval practitioners could successfully (and safely) induce abortion that he was reduced to accepting the validity of claims for "amulets and incantations," although he did not seek to catalogue or analyze such claims.[135] Yet Riddle never considered, giving the intermixing of the pharmacological remedies with magical rituals or devices, why we should assume that the ingestives are any more reliable than the magicals. Riddle's willingness to believe in the magical powers of ancient amulets and potions rivals the occasional "historian" who claims that alchemists really could transform base metals into gold.[136]

Even if one accepts a rather generous reading of the evidence, Riddle himself reports that only a little over half (56 percent by the most favorable study) of the drugs he lists have shown any effects that could be claimed to be either abortifacient or contraceptive under modern conditions of refining and concentrating.[137] Riddle found the relationship to be even less impressive when run the other way—less than 30 percent of the plants modern pharmacists have identified as having abortifacient or contraceptive properties are found in the an-

127. RIDDLE, *supra* note 28, at 7, 9–10.

128. *See* Gina Kolata, *In Ancient Times, Flowers and Fennel for Family Planning,* N.Y. TIMES, Mar. 8, 1994, at C1, C10.

129. *Id.*

130. RIDDLE, *supra* note 28, at viii–ix. *See also* GORDON, *supra* note 18, at 30.

131. RIDDLE, *supra* note 28, at 38.

132. *Id.* at 84.

133. *Id.* at 52.

134. *Id.* at 50.

135. *Id.* at viii, 96, 137.

136. *See, e.g.,* SADOUL, *supra* note 126.

137. RIDDLE, *supra* note 28, at 52–53.

cient texts.[138] Is this, as Riddle asserts, an overlap that is "too great to attribute to chance"[139]—especially given the vast number of substances for which the ancients claimed abortifacient or contraceptive effect? Riddle, like McLaren, is reduced to arguing that because certain potions were used for centuries in the hope of obtaining an abortion, they must have worked. How else could their use have persisted for so long?[140] At this point, he might have asked, but did not, how innumerable other discredited medical practices persisted for centuries, ranging from the purely ritualistic to such physical procedures as the ingestion of poisons and bleeding, when such procedures undoubtedly helped to bring about many more deaths than cures.

The reader should not be surprised that in this book I am more critical of the "pro-choice" historians than of the "pro-life" historians—their distortions of the history are far greater, and they are, after all, the current orthodoxy. I begin in this Chapter by examining the point that most historians simply assume away, the most basic point of all: How common were abortions in prior centuries? We approach this question first by considering a small but significant problem—the persistent belief over many centuries that a woman's menstruation could be obstructed for reasons other than pregnancy and that medications or procedures would alleviate the problem.

# "Obstructed Menses"

*Ignorance, especially the ignorance of educated men, can be a more powerful force than knowledge.*
—Michael Howard[141]

What are now regarded as purported abortifacients were often recommended over the centuries as remedies for "obstructed menses" rather than as the means to accomplish an abortion as such.[142] Such remedies were called "emmenagogues." This expression tells us something about how people in times past thought about abortion and how they thought about the functioning of the human body generally. How modern historians treat the expression will tell us something about how they "decode" the past.

Several historians have assumed that the phrase "obstructed menses" always was a conscious euphemism for abortion—that is, a midwife or physician who claimed to be treating a woman for obstructed menses must have realized that in fact she was only attempting to induce an abortion.[143] These historians offer no evidence for their assumption, and several even report a euphemism ("taking the cold") for obstructed menses.[144] It is therefore worth examining whether the ancient sources really did mean "obstructed menses" when using the term, or whether the authors of those sources understood that obstructed menses nearly always signaled

---

138. *Id.*

139. *Id.* at 52.

140. *Id.* at 144–45.

141. HOWARD, *supra* note 2, at 16.

142. MOHR, *supra* note 19, at 6–7, 278 n.37; SMITH-ROSENBERG, *supra* note 30, at 219; ULRICH, THE MIDWIFE'S TALE, *supra* note 9, at 56; Klepp, *supra* note 28, at 76–81.

143. *See* BRODIE, *supra* note 31, at 146, 287–88; McLAREN, *supra* note 19, at 35, 246; McLAREN, *supra* note 28, at 9–10, 14–15; MARVIN OLASKY, ABORTION RIGHTS: A SOCIAL HISTORY OF ABORTION IN AMERICA 95–96 (1992); REAGAN, *supra* note 17, at 8–10; RIDDLE, *supra* note 29, at 23, 27, 29, 83, 85, 89–90, 102–05, 114–17, 119–20, 122–126, 131–32, 134, 136–38, 142, 148, 150, 152–54, 158–61; Klepp, *supra* note 28, at 80.

144. MOHR, *supra* note 19, at 7; Klepp, *supra* note 28, at 78–79.

a pregnancy. How we resolve this question goes a long way towards resolving whether there was widespread social acceptance of abortion if only you would call it something else, or whether there was mere toleration of a crude medical procedure that might incidentally induce an abortion although no such outcome was desired. Understanding that just might help us understand the import of the legal and other materials addressing abortion from earlier times to be examined in later chapters.

The first point to note is that until the twentieth century there was no certain test for pregnancy before the baby could be felt to move in the womb ("quicken")—as even those who assume that the expression "curing obstructed menses" was a euphemism for abortion admit.[145] There were no sonograms, no checking blood samples for tell-tale hormones, no x-rays, no dead rabbits, in short no clinical test for verifying a probable pregnancy until Cecil Vogue devised the rabbit test in 1926.[146] While tests for detecting HCG (human chorionic gonadotropin) in a woman's blood to confirm pregnancy ("the rabbit test") became standard in the 1930s, the tests continued to yield a significant number of false results until refined in the 1960s.[147]

One need not rely only on the lack of modern medical tests to decide that many women in the past would remain uncertain whether they were pregnant for weeks or even months. There is plenty of direct evidence of this fact in the historical record. Numerous legal proceedings spread across centuries turned crucially on the fact of pregnancy, yet that fact was found to be utterly indeterminate.[148] Early writers on the law focused their discussion of abortion on the evidentiary impossibility of determining whether a woman was pregnant and of determining whether the fetus was still alive when an abortionist began.[149] In 1855, we find physicians still complaining that they cannot determine whether a woman had been pregnant or had aborted after the event.[150]

These difficulties were not just because men (jurists, lawyers, and physicians) were more ignorant in these matters than the women undergoing the pregnancy. Even experienced "matrons" were as unsure as the men. The diary of Mary Poor provides an example. Poor, the wife of a founder of Standard and Poor's, bore seven children and had at least two miscarriages during a period of 22 years. She frequently fretted for months even near the end of her childbearing years over whether a missed period signaled another pregnancy or some other problem.[151]

---

145. MOHR, *supra* note 19, at 72–73, 230–33; TANNAHILL, *supra* note 18, at 65–66; Klepp, *supra* note 28, at 77–78.

146. THOMAS EDEN & EARDLEY HOLLAND, A MANUAL OF MIDWIFERY 77–78 (7th ed. 1931). *See also* JUDITH WALZER LEAVITT, BROUGHT TO BED: CHILDBEARING IN AMERICA 1750–1950, at 268 (1986).

147. CARL PAUERSTEIN *et al.*, CLINICAL OBSTETRICS 110–14 (1987); PATRICIA MILLER, THE WORST OF TIMES 19 (1993).

148. *See, e.g.,* People v. Murphy, 101 N.Y. 126 (1886); Lohman v. People, 1 N.Y. 379 (1848); Regina v. Sims, 75 ENG. REP. 1075 (K.B. 1601).

149. *See, e.g.,* EDWARD COKE, THIRD INSTITUTE 50–51 (1644); 1 MATTHEW HALE, HISTORY OF PLEAS OF THE CROWN 433 (1736); MATTHEW HALE, PLEAS OF THE CROWN: OR, A METHODICAL SUMMARY OF THE PRINCIPAL MATTERS RELATING TO THAT SUBJECT 53 (1678); JAMES PARKER, CONDUCTOR GENERALIS: OR, THE OFFICE, DUTY, AND AUTHORITY OF JUSTICES OF THE PEACE 216–17 (1764).

150. FRANCIS WHARTON & MORETON STILLÉ, TREATISE ON MEDICAL JURISPRUDENCE 277 (1855). *See also* 1 WILLIAM BARTON, OUTLINES OF LECTURES ON *MATERIA MEDICA* AND BOTANY, DELIVERED IN JEFFERSON MEDICAL COLLEGE, PHILADELPHIA 104 (1827–28); SAMUEL JENNINGS, THE MARRIED LADIES COMPANION; OR, POOR MAN'S FRIEND 54, 75 (2nd ed. 1808; reprinted 1972); HORATIO ROBINSON STORER, ON CRIMINAL ABORTION IN AMERICA 44, 46 (1860). *See generally* MARY BETH NORTON, LIBERTY'S DAUGHTERS: THE REVOLUTIONARY EXPERIENCE OF AMERICAN WOMEN, 1750–1800, at 80 (1980); Klepp, *supra* note 78, at 77–78.

151. BRODIE, *supra* note 31, at 21–25. *See generally* DEGLER, *supra* note 18, at 235; GORDON, *supra* note 18, at 57; GROSSBERG, *supra* note 80, at 183; LILIAN WYLES, A WOMAN OF SCOTLAND YARD 227 (1952); Byrn, *supra* note 72, at 817–19; Shelley Gavigan, *The Criminal Sanction as It Relates to Human Reproduction: The Genesis of the Statutory Prohibition of Abortion,* 5 J. LEGAL HIST. 20, 20 (1984); Witherspoon, *supra* note 72, at 31–32, 56–57.

Against this background, it is no wonder that the notion that the flow of menstrual blood might be "blocked" without pregnancy, posing serious health risks for women, has a long history in both folk medicine and the medical profession.[152] Historian Linda Gordon apparently still believes that there are emmenagogues that are not abortifacients.[153] People who believed that menstrual blockages were common also appear to have believed that the resulting health problems could be alleviated by "unblocking" the menses. Whether this was generally a euphemism or often a genuine belief we perhaps will never know for certain, although if a euphemism it was both remarkably long-lived and consistently employed. The euphemism even turns up in medieval Japanese in the form of *gekkei yaku* (literally, "menstrual medicine") and such expressions are still common in some parts of the world.[154]

When doctors complained that some women have fooled some doctors into inducing abortions by feigning obstructed menses, the complaining doctors at least appear to have believed sincerely that other women did actually suffer from menses obstructed from causes other than pregnancy. Consider this passage from a manual for midwives from the seventeenth century:

> Above all things, you must beware (for any treasure in the world) of adhering to one vice, such as they are guilty of who give Remedies to cause Abortion; for those that do ill, and those that seek a damnable remedy, are wicked in a high degree. But it is a higher degree of wickedness for those that are no way ingaged in the business [of midwifery], for lucre's sake to kill both the body and the soul of an infant. This I do not speak that thou shouldest refuse to give a Remedy upon just occasions: but to take heed how you be cheated by subtle persons, who shall tell you fine stories of the diseases of their Wives or Daughters, which they may say are very honest, hoping to get them from you some Receipts to effect their wicked designs.[155]

Belief in the sincerity of at least some of those physicians is enhanced when we occasionally find one who, while reporting the use of mild "emmenagogues," declined to describe "stronger remedies" for fear that they might be used to induce abortions.[156] Even anti-abortion crusader Dr. Horatio Robinson Storer believed that there were medical treatments appropriate to restoring a woman's menses,[157] and no one has ever accused him of secretly approving abortions. In-

---

152. *See, e.g.,* Medieval Woman's Guide to Health: The First English Gynecological Handbook (Beryl Rowland ed. 1981). *See generally* Shorter, *supra* note 87, at 180–81; John Benton, *Trotula, Women's Problems, and the Professionalization of Medicine in the Middle Ages,* 59 Bull. Hist. Med. 59 (1985); Patricia Crawford, *Attitudes to Menstruation in Seventeenth-Century England,* 91 Past & Present 47 (1981).

153. Gordon, *supra* note 18, at 30, 40, 54.

154. Susan Hanley & Kozo Yamamura, Economic and Demographic Change in Preindustrial Japan 1600–1868, at 233–34 (1977). *See also* Eugene Brody, Sex, Contraception, and Motherhood in Jamaica 45 (1981). *See generally* McLaren, *supra* note 28, at 102–05, 110–11. Historian Janet Brodie used the expression as recently as 1994 in writing about the banning of the advertisement of certain abortifacients by the Federal Trade Commission. *See* Brodie, *supra* note 31, at 226.

155. John Pechey, The Compleat Midwife's Practice Enlarged 346 (1694). *See also* Brevitt, *supra* note 99, at 47.

156. Hollick, *supra* note 99, at 149–53; George Gregory, Medical Morals, Illustrated with Plates and Extracts from Medical Works: Designed to Show the Pernicious Social and Moral Influence of the Present System of Medical Practice, and the Importance of Establishing Female Medical Colleges, and Educating Female Physicians for Their Own Sex 13–16 (1853). *See also* Alexander Berg, Der Krankheitskomplex der Kolik — und Gebärmutterlieden in Volksmedizin 50–53 (1935); G. Lammert, Volskmedizin und medizinischer Aberglaube in Bayern 252 (1869); Carl Seyfarth, Aberglaube und Zauberei in der Volksmedezin Sachsens 89 (1913); Ilza Verth, Hysteria: The History of a Disease ch. 2 (1965). *See generally* Mary Lefkowitz & Maureen Fant, Women's Lives in Greece and Rome: A Source Book in Translation 81–87 (1982); G.E.R. Lloyd, Science, Folklore and Ideology: Studies in the Life Sciences in Ancient Greece 84 (1983); Shorter, *supra* note 87, at 180, 286–87.

157. Horatio Robinson Storer, Why Not? A Book for Everywoman 26, 41, 48 (1866).

deed, some women considered the use of contraceptive devices to be against nature and a sin even while seeing the use of emmenagogues as natural and harmless.[158] This idea persisted to some extent among the poor of London at least as late as the 1950s.[159] In dismissing such evidence, James Mohr is reduced simply to stating that he does not believe it, even though he cites, warnings to decline to use stronger emmenagogues for fear of abortion from 1694, 1800, and 1875.[160]

True enough, by the end of the nineteenth century the occasional claims by physicians facing prosecution for criminal abortion that they had not thought the woman to be pregnant but had been treating her for "obstructed menses" had begun to appear as rank hypocrisies.[161] Perhaps the earliest assertion that such claims were fraudulent appears in a book by Dr. Charles Meigs published in 1842.[162] Yet as late as 1871 an English court found itself unable to decide whether emmenagogic agents (pennyroyal, iron, and myrrh) were capable of producing abortions as well as restoring menses obstructed for some reason other than pregnancy.[163] Given the inability at the time even to determine whether the woman was pregnant, such persistent uncertainty is hardly a surprise. Even in the early twentieth century physicians could not entirely rule out the possibility that the menses actually were obstructed for reasons other than pregnancy.[164] Only gradually did physicians and others come to realize that "if a healthy woman's menstrual periods cease, the cause in 999 cases out of 1000 is pregnancy."[165] Yet we even encounter such claims by abortion advocates today who seek to absolve women who might be tempted to engage in "menstrual extraction" from any sense of moral guilt over possibly having committed an abortion.[166]

The utter rejection of such evidence by Mohr and others relies on the appearance of such claims as implausible to a modern audience. General gynecological knowledge, however, was remarkably primitive even as late as 1800. Some folkloric traditions in Europe as late as 1800 still embraced a belief that the uterus was a living and dangerous thing that could travel up inside a woman's body to choke her.[167] As late as 1878, the *British Medical Journal* could print correspondence over a period of six months debating whether the touch of a menstruating woman would turn a ham rancid.[168] Belief in an ambient uterus led many to believe that the uterus traveled

---

158. Claud Mullins, Marriage, Children and God 141 (1922); Marie Stopes, Mother England: A Contemporary History 183 (1929). *See also* Brookes, *supra* note 30, at 4, 6, 8; Robert Roberts, The Classic Slum: Salford Life in the First Quarter of the Century 100 (1971).

159. Madeline Kerr, The People of Ship Street 137, 174 (1958).

160. Mohr, *supra* note 19, at 11, 65–66, 68, 267–68 n.21, 141–42, 278 n.37.

161. *See* Regina v. Collins (Q.B. 1898), as summarized in Leonard Parry, Famous Medical Trials 40 (1927). *See also* Thomas Radford, Observations on the Caesarean Section, Craniotomy, and on Other Obstetric Operations 42 (2nd ed. 1880).

162. Charles Meigs, The Philadelphia Practice of Midwifery 133–34 (1842). *See also* Charles Meigs, Women: Their Diseases and Remedies 405 (1848).

163. Regina v. Wallace (Winchester Aut. Ass. 1871) [described in Riddle, *supra* note 28, at 158–59; and 2 Alfred Taylor, The Principles and Practice of Medical Jurisprudence 168–69 (Frederick Smith ed., 5th ed. 1905)].

164. Secret Remedies, *supra* note 105, at 185. *See also* Olasky, *supra* note 143, at 110–11; Riddle, *supra* note 28, at 27.

165. F.J. McCann, *Letter,* Brit. Med. J., Feb. 2, 1929, at 203

166. *See* Chalker & Downer, *supra* note 32; Hadley, *supra* note 80, at 124–27; Curtis, *supra* note 32, at 439–40; Laura Punnett, *Menstrual Extraction Politics,* 4 Quest 48 (No. 3, 1978).

167. *See, e.g.,* 1 J.B. Chomel, Abregé de l'histoire des plantes usuelles 149–50 (1739). *See also* Natalie Zemon Davis, Society and Culture in Early Modern France 124–25 (1975); Cheryl Meyer, The Wandering Uterus: Politics and the Reproductive Rights of Women 1–3 (1997); Sherwin Nuland, The Mysteries within: A Surgeon Reflects on Medical Myths 212–25, 228–30 (2000).

168. Fraser Harrison, The Dark Angel: Aspects of Victorian Sexuality 57 (1977); Tannahill, *supra* note 18, at 352.

down into the vagina to "embrace" the penis during intercourse and to receive the sperm directly into itself.[169] Such ideas, so bizarre to us today, might have been inspired by the recognition (at least as early as 1900 BCE) of the possibility of a prolapsed (dropped) uterus.[170]

Another long-standing belief was that a woman could not become pregnant if she did not herself experience orgasm—on a theory that she needed to ejaculate similarly to a man.[171] In later centuries, noted midwives and others wrote to advise pregnant mothers that the mere expression of their imagination could mark the child they would carry, and thus that while pregnant they must strictly control their thoughts and dwell only on the beautiful and joyful.[172] Some midwives apparently believed that a fetus was "stuck" to a woman's back or that stretching the cervix with their fingers during labor would hasten the birth when in fact it not only would not speed dilation but could cause severe injuries to the mother.[173]

While such ideas came under harsh attack during the eighteenth century,[174] they had not been entirely displaced by the nineteenth century.[175] Indeed, such ideas were still in circulation in some circles in the twentieth century.[176] Remember that debate in the *British Medical Journal* in 1878 over whether the touch of a menstruating woman could spoil a ham.[177] Some people apparently still believe today that intercourse with an immature girl will cure venereal disease.[178] And, of course, the modern word "hysteria," referring to what some still think of as a problem peculiar to women, is simply the Greek name for the uterus.[179]

Given such widespread beliefs, a sincere belief even by well-educated physicians and midwives in obstructed menses cannot be ruled out. John Riddle has conceded as much—but Riddle was intent on showing that the ancients could do the trick rather than on what they

---

169. *See, e.g.,* Henry Bracken The Midwife's Companion 10 (1737); James McMath, The Expert Midwife 3 (1694); Lazaerus Riverius *et al.,* The Practice of Physick 503 (1658); E. Sibly, The Medical Mirror, or Treatise on the Impregnation of the Human Female 17 (1794). *See generally* Eccles, *supra* note 87, at 29.

170. Nuland, *supra* note 167, at 228; Henry Sigerist, On the History of Medicine 332–34 (Felix Marti-Ibañez ed. 1960); Tannahill, *supra* note 18, at 64–65.

171. *See, e.g.,* Antonio Guainerius, *Tractatus de Matricibus* f. Z4 verso (Pavia 1481); Guilielmus de Saliceto, *Summa Conservationis et Curationis* f. 13vb. (Venice 1489). *See generally* Nuland, *supra* note 167, at 237.

172. Aristotle's Masterpiece 89–90 (1749); Marguerite de la Marche, *Instruction familière et tres utile pour les accouchemens* 29 (1710); Daniel Turner, De Morbis Cutaneis 155–90 (1723).

173. *See, e.g.,* Bracken, *supra* note 169, at 123–24; William Harvey, Anatomical Exercitation Concerning the Generation of Living Creatures 509 (1653); Willoughby, *supra* note 9A, at 6.

174. Isaac Bellet, *Lettres sur le pouvoir de l'imagination des femmes enceintes* (1745); James Augustus Blondel, The Strength of the Imagination in Pregnant Women Examin'd (1727).

175. Louis-Nicole Bablot, *Dissertation sur le pouvoir de l'imagination des femmes enceintes* (1788). *See also* J. Marion Sims, Clinical Notes on Uterine Surgery, with Special Reference to the Management of the Sterile Condition 369 (1871); George Napheys, The Physical Life of Women: Advice to the Maiden, Wife, and Mother 104–05 (1873); Alice Bunker Stockham, Tokology 326 (1887). *See generally* Degler, *supra* note 18, at 257–58, 261; Paul-Gabriel Boucé, *Imagination, Pregnant Women, and Monsters, in Eighteenth-Century England and France,* in Sexual Underworlds of the Enlightenment 86 (G.S. Rousseau & Roy Porter eds. 1988); Roy Porter, *Lay Medical Knowledge in the Eighteenth Century: The Evidence of the Gentleman's Magazine,* 29 Med. Hist. 148 (1985).

176. Boucé, *supra* note 175, at 349, 99–100 n.8.

177. See the references collected *supra* at note 168.

178. Allan Brandt, No Magic Bullet: A Social History of Venereal Disease in the United States since 1880, at 20–21 (1985); Wayland Hand, Magical Medicine: The Folkloric Component of Medicine in the Folk Belief, Custom and Ritual of the Peoples of Europe and America 18–19, 309–10 (1980).

179. *See* Nuland, *supra* note 167, at 214–31; Cohen, *supra* note 87, at 198 nn.87–88

thought they were doing.[180] If we conclude that doctors and midwives until recently believed what we now consider nonsense, it wouldn't be the first time. Consider the "anatomical" reports of renaissance physicians.[181] Nor should we too hastily assume that women knew better—they seemed to have shared in what to us appear to be absurd folkloric traditions such as the magical powers of menstrual blood and of the placenta or in evil emanations from a pregnant uterus.[182] If these beliefs were sincere, then to assert that the acceptance of remedies for obstructed menses shows that people at that time considered early abortions unobjectionable, as Mohr does,[183] can only be an anachronistic projection of modern ideas into the past. And if the expressed concern over obstructed menses really was a euphemism for abortion, what does the felt need for such a euphemism really tell us about the social acceptability of that practice?

# A Typology of Abortion Techniques

*"The time has come," the Walrus said,*
*"To talk of many things:*
*Of shoes—and ships—and sealing wax—*
*Of cabbages—and Kings—*
*Of why the sea is boiling hot—*
*And whether pigs have wings."*

—Lewis Carroll[184]

Many of the same historians who refuse to credit the apparently widespread belief in "obstructed menses" seem to have no difficulty in believing that wondrous folk medicines were used in times past or in medically primitive cultures today to bring about abortions that were safe and relatively painless for the mother (at least as compared to the birth process).[185] Neither historical nor anthropological evidence supports a belief in such wondrous folk medicines. So persistent is the contrary belief, however, that the belief itself long ago became something of an anthropological curiosity. Bronislaw Malinowski noted the phenomenon more than sixty years ago in discussing Western interest in certain sexual practices in the Trobriand islands:

> …They [the Melanesians] never practice coitus interruptus, and still less have any notion about chemical or mechanical preventatives.

> But though I am quite certain on this point, I cannot speak with the same conviction about abortion, though probably it is not practiced to any large extent. I may say at once that the natives, when discussing these matters, feel neither fear nor constraint, so there can be no question of any difficulties in finding out the state of affairs because of reticence or concealment. My informants told me that a magic exists to bring about premature birth, but I was not able either to obtain instances in which it was performed, nor to find out the spells or rites made use of. Some of the herbs employed in

---

180. RIDDLE, *supra* note 28, at 27.

181. *See, e.g.*, Le Roy Crummer, *The "Anatomia Infantis" of Gabriel de Zerbi*, 18 AM. J. OBST. & GYN. 1 (1927) (a translation of Zerbi's anatomical studies first published in 1502).

182. SHORTER, *supra* note 87, at 287–92.

183. MOHR, *supra* note 19, at 6, 9–10.

184. LEWIS CARROLL, THROUGH THE LOOKING GLASS 78 (1977).

185. *See, e.g.*, WILLIAM GRAHAM SUMNER, FOLKWAYS 320–27 (1906).

this magic were mentioned to me, but I am certain that none of them possesses any physiological properties. Abortion by mechanical means[186] seems, in fine, the only effective method practiced to check the increase in population, and there is no doubt that it is used on a large scale.

...It is amusing to find that the average white resident or visitor to the Trobriands is deeply interested in this subject, and in this subject only, of all the ethnological problems opened to him for consideration. There is a belief prevalent among the white citizens of eastern New Guinea that the Trobrianders are in possession of some mysterious and powerful means of prevention or abortion.[187]

A well-known example of such beliefs being propagated by anthropologists is Herbert Aptheker's study, *Anjea: Infanticide, Abortion, and Contraception in Savage Society.*[188] Aptheker glowingly told us in some detail about a purported Eskimo abortion technique that involved using a whale-bone knife to puncture a uterus, as if this wouldn't be fatal to the mother as well.[189] He similarly credited reports of African potions that taken monthly for six months eventually produced an abortion, along with repeated bouts of "severe vomiting, acute abdominal pains, diarrhea, and exhaustion for two days."[190] On the basis of such stories, without examining what the effects of such attempts at abortion would have been, Aptheker felt justified in concluding not only that abortion was rife in "primitive" societies along with infanticide, but that the incidence of abortion and infanticide increased when effective contraceptives became available.[191]

Unquestionably abortions were attempted in all human societies and in all eras. Our task is to investigate what techniques actually were used and how, if at all, those techniques actually worked. We must do so without preconceptions about what we must find based upon faith in the ability of people to construct the reality they wish for, or the supposition that women, as powerful people, must always have been able to control their own fertility. In order to achieve our task, we must create a typology of abortifacients,[192] organized by method but appraised as to effectiveness and safety. Such a typology will enable us, in later chapters, to relate the techniques and changes in techniques to changing patterns of social attitudes towards abortion and to changing patterns of legal control. I take it as axiomatic that some people, perhaps most people, down through history have attempted to control their own fertility. Unless one can identify effective means, however, there is no basis for assuming that they either could or did in fact control their fertility. Unwanted children, after all, could be

---

186. While Malinowski did not specify what means he had in mind, George Deveraux indicated that, in such medically primitive societies, the only "mechanical means" used were the injury techniques discussed below. DEVEREUX, *supra* note 28, at 30–35, 171–358. *See also* JEROME BATES & EDWARD ZAWADSKI, CRIMINAL ABORTION 87–88 (1964); 87–88; McLAREN, *supra* note 28, at 100–08; FREDERICK TAUSSIG, ABORTION: SPONTANEOUS AND INDUCED 41–45, 355 (1936).

187. BRONISLAW MALINOWSKI, THE SEXUAL LIFE OF SAVAGES IN NORTH-WESTERN MELANESIA 168–69 (3rd ed. 1932).

188. HERBERT APTHEKER, ANJEA: INFANTICIDE, ABORTION, AND CONTRACEPTION IN SAVAGE SOCIETY (1931).

189. *Id.* at 142–43.

190. *Id.* at 143–44.

191. *Id.* at 150–51.

192. *See generally* SHORTER, *supra* note 87, at 177–191; Dellapenna, *supra* note 64, at 372–76; Georges Devereux, *A Typological Study of Abortion in 350 Primitive, Ancient, and Pre-Industrial Societies,* in THERAPEUTIC ABORTION at 97 (Harold Rosen ed. 1954) (this book was reissued in 1967 under the title ABORTION IN AMERICA).

disposed of through different means than abortion or contraception, as we shall see in the next chapter.

We can begin to construct our typology by examining the legal cases described by Cyril Means, jr., in his second article on the history of abortion that so influenced the Supreme Court in *Roe v. Wade*.[193] All of the cases he reported before 1670 apparently were coerced rather than voluntary. The cases involved crude physical batterings of the mother — often to her serious injury or death (injury techniques).[194] Interestingly, the only mention of abortion in the Old Testament also involves a physical battering of the mother.[195] Means reported a case, referred to by Sir Matthew Hale, of an abortion induced by a "noxious potion" in 1670 (ingestion techniques).[196] Means described only two cases involving abortions induced through the insertion of pointed objects into the uterus, either puncturing the amniotic sac or introducing infection to procure the abortion, both appearing after 1780 (insertion techniques).[197]

In all of the six cases that Means reported the mother either died or suffered severe, debilitating injuries. From this, one might infer, as Means did, that the law was directed at protecting the mother's life or health — but only if one assumes, as many historians have, that abortion was always readily available through relatively safe and effective means.[198] As I will describe below, however, the ingestion and insertion techniques, if effective, appear to have been nearly as deadly as the batterings or other injury techniques. Abortion has been attempted in every society.[199] Modern research strongly suggests that the assumption that such attempts were safe and effective is false.[200] Instead, we find a pattern of attempting abortion through largely ritualistic activities progressing to painful and dangerous activities, including eventually injury, ingestion, and intrusion techniques. This pattern was reported in the nineteenth century[201] and continued into the twentieth century.[202] We shall examine each technique in turn.

---

193. Means II, *supra* note 59. The *Roe* majority opinion cites Means' two articles seven times while citing no other legal historian. Roe v. Wade, 410 U.S. 113, 136–39 (1973).

194. Regina v. Sims, 75 Eng. Rep. 1075 (Q.B. 1601), reported in Means II, *supra* note 59, at 344; Rex v. Anonymous, ANTHONY FITZHERBERT, GRAUNDE ABRIDGEMENT tit. Corone, f. 268, pl. 263 (1st ed. 1516) [K.B. 1348?], reported in Means II, *supra* note 59, at 339, as "The Abortionist's Case"; Rex v. de Bourton, Y.B. Mich. 1 Edw. 3, f. 23, pl. 28 (K.B. 1327), reported in Means II, *supra*, at 337, as "The Twinslayer's Case."

195. *Exodus* 21:22–25.

196. Rex v. Anonymous (1670), 1 MATTHEW HALE, HISTORY OF PLEAS OF THE CROWN 429–30 (1736), reported in Means II, *supra* note 59, at 350.

197. Rex v. Tinckler (1781), 1 EDWARD HYDE EAST, A TREATISE ON THE PLEAS OF THE CROWN 354 (1803), reported in Means II, *supra* note 59, at 363; Rex v. Anonymous (1802), 3 JOSEPH CHITTY, CRIMINAL LAW 798–801 (1816), reported in Means II, *supra*, at 355.

198. See the references collected *supra* at note 87.

199. Devereux, *supra* note 192, at 106–17, 133–34. *See also* McLAREN, *supra* note 28, at 5–6.

200. *See generally* LESTER ADELSON, THE PATHOLOGY OF HOMICIDE 693–95 (1974); BATES & ZAWADSKI, *supra* note 186, at 14–23, 85–91; DEVEREUX, *supra* note 28, at 28, 40–42, 149–50, 171–358; HRDY, *supra* note 3, at 470; TAUSSIG, *supra* note 186, at 31–45, 352–57; TAYLOR'S PRINCIPLES AND PRACTICE OF MEDICAL JURISPRUDENCE 328–29 (A. Keith Mant ed., 13th ed. 1984); WILLIAMS OBSTETRICS 505–06 (F. Gary Cunningham, Paul MacDonald, & Norman Grant eds., 18th ed. 1989); Leopold & Rudiger Breitenecker, *Abortion in German-Speaking Countries of Europe,* in ABORTION AND THE LAW 206, 218–20 (David Smith ed. 1967); Russell Fisher, *Criminal Abortion,* in THERAPEUTIC ABORTION, *supra* note 192, at 3, 6–10. Consider also the inconsistencies in John Riddle's attempt to prove the contrary. See the text *supra* at notes 127–40.

201. *See* JOHN BECK, AN INAUGURAL DISSERTATION ON INFANTICIDE 25 (1817); STORER, *supra* note 150, at 30; Meredeth Reese, *Report on Infant Mortality in Large Cities,* 12 TRANS. A.M.A. 98 (1857); Montrose Pallen, *Foeticide,* 3 MED. ARCHIVES (St. L. n.s.) 201–02 (1869).

202. BROOKES, *supra* note 30, at 31–32; HADLEY, *supra* note 80, at 39–40; REAGAN, *supra* note 19, at 28, 31, 42–43, 72, 209.

# Injury Techniques

*If anyone strikes a pregnant woman or gives her a poison in order to make an abortion,*
*if the foetus is already formed, especially if it is quickened, he commits homicide.*

—Henry de Bracton[203]

The earliest techniques to appear in the common law legal records were external manipulations of the mother's body designed to prompt or force her to miscarry. Such techniques have ranged from wholly ritualistic and largely ineffective simple bodily maneuvers through strenuous physical exertions up to savage assaults. I term such techniques "injury techniques" because the forms that appear most likely to have been effective would have succeeded precisely because of severe injury to the mother.

There are reports of ritualistic manipulations of the mother's body that some claim to have been successful. These appear to have involved symbolic magic rather than techniques that were likely to succeed. Thus Georges Devereux reported a story of a witch among the Montagnards of Indo-China who could induce abortion by a "light touch."[204] This would appear to be similar to the belief, long held in England, France, and elsewhere, that a "royal touch"—a touch by the reigning monarch—would could certain ills.[205] We do not need to list the numerous reports of other forms of purely ritualistic abortions involving wholly verbal incantations or other forms of symbolic magic.[206] While history abounds with examples of psychosomatic healing, no one has been able to develop such techniques with even minimal consistency.[207] While some historians insist that purely ritualistic techniques might have worked through psychological effect,[208] the vast numbers of women who have prayed without success not to be pregnant or otherwise sought unsuccessfully through denial or other psychological devices to end a pregnancy suggests that such occasions must have been rare—unless perhaps coupled with some extraordinary exertion on the part of the mother.

The ancient Greek physician Hippocrates is reputed to have arranged one of the best known examples of a successful ritualistic abortion. He is said to have advised a young woman to jump in the air while striking her heels against her hips a magical seven times in order to abort.[209] This report may not be accurate. After all, in the traditional form of the Hippocratic Oath (*i.e.*, its

---

203. 2 Henry de Bracton, The Laws and Customs of England 341 (in Latin, 1256?) (Samuel Thorne ed. 1968).

204. Devereux, *supra* note 192, at 104–05.

205. *See generally* Mark Bloch, The Royal Touch (1973). Belief in the power of the "royal touch" buttressed the claims of kings to divine authority, although not enough to protect Charles I from execution in 1649. *See* C.V. Wedgwood, A Coffin for King Charles 10, 68 (1964).

206. Aptheker, *supra* note 188, at 119; Gordon, *supra* note 18, at 29–32; Norman Himes, Medical History of Contraception 6, 9, 20, 174–77 (1936); McLaren, *supra* note 28, at 100–01; Enid Porter, Cambridgeshire Customs and Folklore 10–11 (1969); Keith Thomas, Religion and the Decline of Magic 177–211 (1971); Devereux, *supra* note 192, at 118, 124–25, 132–33; Helen Lemay, *Women and the Literature of Obstetrics and Gynecology,* in Medieval Women and the Sources of Medieval History 189, 194–99 (Joel Rosenthal ed. 1990).

207. *See* Vincent Buranelli, The Wizard from Vienna: Franz Mesmer and the Origins of Hypnotism (1976); Robert Darnton, Mesmerism and the End of the Enlightenment in France (1968); A. Brian Laver, *Miracles No Wonder! The Mesmeric Phenomenon and Organic Cures of Valentine Greatrokes,* 33 J. Hist. Med. 35 (1978); Nicholas Steneck, *Greatrakes the Stroker: The Interpretation of Historians,* 73 Isis 159 (1982).

208. Gordon, *supra* note 18, at 30; Riddle, *supra* note 28, at viii.

209. 7 Hippocrates, *Ouevres complètes d'Hippocrate: traduction nouvelle avec le texte grec en regard* 490 (Emile Littré ed. reprinted 1973); 11 Hippocrites, *supra,* at 55 (Robert Joly ed. 1970). *See also* Taussig, *supra* note 186, at 33; Devereux, *supra* note 192, at 123–24, 137.

form before it was amended after *Roe v. Wade*) doctors swore not to administer a pessary to induce an abortion.[210] Perhaps Hippocrates was unremittingly hostile to abortion, or perhaps he considered pessaries too dangerous for use but did not oppose other abortions, or perhaps he simply meant that abortion should be left to the experts—midwives.[211] In any event, the reading of Hippocrates (and medical ethics generally) as prohibiting all abortions dates back at least to Scribonius and the Stoics in the first century of the Common Era.[212] Finally if the report that Hyprocrites recommended abortion by jumping is accurate, any resulting abortion, if one resulted, was more likely to have been induced by the extraordinary exertion of the jumping than by the mere suggestibility of the mother.[213]

For some reported techniques, we simply do not know enough about the how the technique was used to decide whether it involved only ritual or something more. Thus Susan Hanley and Kozo Yamamura report the use of continuous pressure vibration to induce abortion.[214] If a gentle rubbing were enough, one would expect that the practice would, by now, be widely known and frequently used. What else might have gone along with the "pressure vibrations" we do not know as Hanley and Yamamura do not tell us anything about how intense the rubbings were to be, or what further steps were necessary before an abortion would be induced.

Rituals have also been combined with other steps that might possibly contribute to bringing on an abortion, although less likely to succeed than physical exertion. One fairly common practice was the wearing of tightly laced clothing.[215] Another common practice was for the woman to soak herself in a hot bath.[216] The idea of bathing to bring on an abortion can be traced at least as far back as the physician Soranus in the second century.[217] Bathing was not common through much of history, and the idea that a hot bath ("as hot as the woman can stand") would bring on an abortion seems simply to express the hope that the pregnancy or menstrual obstruction would simply wash away, a kind of sympathetic magic.[218] Modern folklore still sometimes ad-

---

210. ARTURO CASTIGLIONI, A HISTORY OF MEDICINE 148 (2nd ed. 1947); LUDWIG EDELSTEIN, THE HIPPOCRATIC OATH 3 (1943).

211. *See* SIGERIST, *supra* note 170, at 38; RIDDLE, *supra* note 28, at 7–10.

212. SCRIBONIUS LARGUS, *COMPOSITIONES PRAEF.* 5.20–23, at 2 (S. Sconocchia ed. 1983). *See also* ETHICS IN MEDICINE: HISTORICAL PERSPECTIVES AND CONTEMPORARY CONCERNS 5, 10 (Stanley Reiser et al. eds. 1977); Martin Arbagi, *Roe and the Hippocratic Oath,* in ABORTION AND THE CONSTITUTION: REVERSING *ROE v. WADE* THROUGH THE COURTS 159 (Dennis Horan, Edward Grant, & Paige Cunningham eds. 1987); Edmund & Alice Pellegrino, *Humanism and Ethics in Roman Medicine: Translation and Commentary on a Text of Scribonius Largus,* 7 LITERATURE & MED. 22 (1988).

213. That sufficiently strenuous exertion is thought to bring an abortion, see Devereux, *supra* note 192, at 116, 123. *See also* HANLEY & YAMAMURA, *supra* note 154, at 234; MOHR, *supra* note 19, at 7; REAGAN, *supra* note 16, at 42; Klepp, *supra* note 28, at 80–82.

214. HANLEY & YAMAMURA, *supra* note 154, at 233. *See also* HADLEY, *supra* note 80, at 37 (claiming that there are hundreds of thousands of such abortions annually in Thailand).

215. *See, e.g.,* JAMES RUEFF, THE EXPERT MIDWIFE 58, 60 (1637). *See also* GORMAN, *supra* note 87, at 16–17.

216. WILLIAM BUCHAN, DOMESTIC MEDICINE, OR A TREATISE ON THE PREVENTION AND CURE OF DISEASES BY REGIMEN AND SIMPLE MEDICINE 400 (1816 ed.); JENNINGS, *supra* note 150, at 43–47; H.S. POMEROY, THE ETHICS OF MARRIAGE 64 (1888). *See also* BRODIE, *supra* note 31, at 19, 119; DEGLER, *supra* note 18, at 236; D'EMILIO & FREEDMAN, *supra* note 80, at 63; GORDON, *supra* note 18, at 38; HADLEY, *supra* note 80, at 36; MOHR, *supra* note 19, at 6, 10; RIDDLE, *supra* note 28, at 32, 46–47, 97, 100–01; REAGAN, *supra* note 16, at 26, 42, 75; SOLINGER, *supra* note 19, at 208, 211; Devereux, *supra* note 192, at 121, 124–25, 132. Susan Klepp asserts that "bathing" was a euphemism for a vaginal douche, although she provides no documentation for her assertion. Klepp, *supra* note 28, at 81. Given her serious factual errors elsewhere in her study, one would want more substantial documentation before acception her inferences. *See, e.g.,* Klepp, *supra,* at 73–74, 76 (discussing at length a non-existent English abortion statute from 1623).

217. SORANUS, GYNECOLOGY ¶ 1.64, at 66 (Oswei Temkin trans. 1956).

218. ANTHONY HORDERN, LEGAL ABORTION: THE ENGLISH EXPERIENCE 2 (1971); Devereux, *supra* note 192, at 103.

vises hot baths.[219] Like other forms of sympathetic magic, the hot bath was often combined with other, potentially more effective measures. Thus, one letter written in 1847 describes the recipe used to bring on an "obstructed menses" in these words: "A hot bath, a tremendous walk, and a great dose have succeeded...."[220] Anthropologist Georges Devereux suggested that reports of abortions induced by ritual or other forms of suggestion, or by simple physical maneuvers, might actually reflect the results of widespread venereal disease or because of inadequate medical care after prior births, either of which could make women susceptible to abortion, often spontaneous.[221] One might also add general malnutrition and poor health that might also have induced some spontaneous abortions.[222]

In some cultures, women are told to drink boiling water rather than to bath in it.[223] Other cultures have used steam, hot ashes or coals, or warmed stones or similar objects, applied to the woman's abdomen, for much the same purposes.[224] By the time we reach the drinking of boiling water and or the laying of hot coals on the woman's abdomen, we are moving away from mere ritual and treading close to true injury techniques. If neither ritual nor exertion succeeded, a woman could indeed attempt self-injury, such as falls, starving, or bleeding herself, in an effort to induce an abortion.[225] If extreme enough, such efforts might work. Favored places for bleeding were from the thighs or the feet. Bleeding in order to bring about an abortion also can be traced back at least to Hippocrates in the fifth century BCE.[226] As with Hippocrates' purported jumping abortion, bloodletting, unless carried to an extreme threatening to the mother's life, would work only as a kind of sympathetic magic with the flowing blood serving to symbolize the desired return of the flow of menstrual blood.

Sympathetic magic might also be found in the practice of pulling a tooth in the hope of inducing an abortion.[227] This practice continued at least into the 1870s in the United

---

219. Brookes, *supra* note 30, at 31; Nancy Mitford, The Ladies of Aderley 169–71 (1938); Petchesky, *supra* note 28, at 51; Reagan, *supra* note 16, at 209; Ted Willis, Whatever Happened to Tom Mix? 8 (1970); Fisher, *supra* note 200, at 6; Denslow Lewis, *Facts Regarding Criminal Abortion*, 35 JAMA 944 (1900); Noonan, *supra* note 72, at 4–5.

220. From a letter of Henrietta Stanley to her husband in 1847, quoted in McLaren, *supra* note 28, at 97. *See also* Gordon, *supra* note 18, at 32; Himes, *supra* note 206, at 95; Mohr, *supra* note 19, at 7–8; Riddle, *supra* note 28, at 46–47.

221. Devereux, *supra* note 192, at 121, 132–33. *See also* Gordon, *supra* note 18, at 38; Herbert Gutman, The Black Family in Slavery and Freedom 81 (1976); Riddle, *supra* note 28, at 46–47, 97, 101.

222. Brookes, *supra* note 30, at 118; Harrison, *supra* note 30, at 175; Ingram, *supra* note 87, at 159; Riddle, *supra* note 28, at 122–23; Tannahill, *supra* note 18, at 30.

223. Devereux, *supra* note 192, at 122. *See also* Lewis, *supra* note 216, at 944 ("hot drinks").

224. Gordon, *supra* note 18, at 38; Hanley & Yamamura, *supra* note 154, at 234; Himes, *supra* note 206, at 138; Devereux, *supra* note 192, at 124–25.

225. Brevitt, *supra* note 99, at 117 (bleeding); Buchan, *supra* note 216, at 403–04 (same). *See generally* Brodie, *supra* note 31, at 22, 24, 33–34, 227; Degler, *supra* note 18, at 230; D'Emilio & Freedman, *supra* note 80, at 63; Devereux, *supra* note 28, at 123–24; Gordon, *supra* note 18, at 38–39; Hadley, *supra* note 80, at 36; McLaren, *supra* note 28, at 101; Ministry of Health & Home Office, Report of the Interdepartmental Committee on Abortion 43 (1939) ("Interdepartmental Committee"); Mohr, *supra* note 19, at 6–7, 9; Petchesky, *supra* note 28, at 51; Pomeroy, *supra* note 216, at 64; Quaife, *supra* note 87, at 118; Reagan, *supra* note 16, at 26; Riddle, *supra* note 28, at 47–48, 98; Ulrich, The Midwife's Tale, *supra* note 9, at 259; Devereux, *supra* note 192, at 101, 103, 123–26; Lewis, *supra* note 216, at 944.

226. Riddle, supra note 28, at 47. *See also* Soranus, *supra* note 217, ¶ 1.65, at 67–68.

227. *See, e.g.,* John Burns, Observations on Abortion: Containing an Account of the Manner in Which It Takes Place, the Causes Which Produce It, and the Method of Preventing or Treating It 45, 74 (1806); Thomas Ewell, Letter to Ladies, Detailing Important Information Concerning Themselves and Infants 48–54 (1817).

States.[228] Before analgesics, anesthetics, antiseptics, and antibiotics, the pain-induced shock and any resulting infection might have lead to an abortion, but more likely the procedure was meant to symbolize pulling a plug preventing the draining of the uterus. Or, the practice of pulling a tooth at a time when there was no means of stemming the flow of blood might simply have been meant as a cover should the abortion produce serious complications or the death of the mother.[229]

If the attacks on the mother's body suggested so far had not worked, a sufficiently desperate woman might have accepted even more violent attacks on her body.[230] Such techniques included pressing or squeezing the abdomen with hands or heavy objects; twisting the uterus through the abdominal wall; or striking the mother's belly with fists, stones, or other objects.[231] Often these procedures would be pursued until there was vaginal bleeding, by which time true (and serious) injury to the woman as well as to the fetus was likely.[232] Even the wearing of a constricting belt in the hopes of inducing an abortion has been pursued to the point of maternal death.[233]

The records of early English cases abound with reports of injury techniques. The earliest reports generally involve injury techniques of the crudest sort. A woman was beaten and "wounded" until she is delivered of twins "to the great despair of her life."[234] Few of these records go into detail, but one case records a beating with a pole and another a striking with a stone.[235] At an extreme, the assailant might have gone so far as to slash the woman's belly open in order to tear out the unwanted children. No legal record of such an extreme has been found, although it might lie hidden in proceedings based on axe murders of women.[236]

Even extreme attacks producing severe injuries might not succeed.[237] Yet despite the evident pain and danger of true injury techniques, injury techniques were more likely actually to achieve the desired result than less extreme techniques, including ingestion techniques and lesser injury techniques—as even those who insist that safe and effective abortion techniques were widely known and used in preliterate cultures sometimes concede.[238] Because of the greater certainty of

---

228. MOHR, *supra* note 19, at 7–8.

229. *Id.* at 8.

230. *See* BATES & ZAWADSKI, *supra* note 186, at 87–88; DEGLER, *supra* note 18, at 230; DEVEREUX, *supra* note 28, at 30–35; GORMAN, *supra* note 87, at 17; QUAIFE, *supra* note 87, at 120; TAUSSIG, *supra* note 186, at 41–45, 355; Devereux, *supra* note 192, at 104, 125–27. Physical batterings continue to be used to cause abortions today. *See* Elaine Hilberman *et al.*, *Sixty Battered Women*, 2 VICTIMOLOGY 460 (1978).

231. APTHEKER, *Supra* note 188, at 141; DEVEREUX, *supra* note 28, at 123–33; GORDON, *supra* note 18, at 38–39; HANLEY & YAMAMURA, *supra* note 154, at 234; QUAIFE, *supra* note 87, at 26, 118; Devereux, *supra* note 192, at 113, 115, 117–18, 122, 124–27, 138, 142.

232. HORDERN, *supra* note 218, at 2.

233. Devereux, *supra* note 192, at 126.

234. Rex v. Cokkes (1415), 7 CALENDAR OF INQUISITIONS MISC. (CH.) PRESERVED IN THE PUB. REC. OFF. 1399–1422, at 296 (no. 523) (1968). *See also, e.g.,* Rex v. de Bourton, Y.B. Mich. 1 Edw. 3, f. 23, pl. 28 (K.B. 1327); Juliana's Appeal (1256?), SOMERSET PLEAS (CIV. & CRIM.) FROM THE ROLLS OF THE ITINERANT JUSTICES 321 (no. 1243) (C. Chadwyck-Healey ed. 1897); Amice's Appeal, JUST 1/274, m.14d (1247). Most of these cases and those cited in the next several footnotes are quoted in full at appropriate points in other chapters of this book.

235. Rex v. Mercer (Oxford Eyre 1285), JUST 1/710, m.45 (striking with a stone); Agnes' Appeal (1200), 1 SELDEN SOC'Y 39 (no. 82, 1887) (beating with a pole).

236. *See, e.g.,* Marra's Appeal, JUST 1/82 (Cambridgeshire Eyre 1261).

237. *See, e.g.,* William Cummin, *Lectures on Forensic Medicine*, LONDON MED. GAZETTE, Feb. 4, 1837, at 679–80 (describing an attempted abortion in which the father sat on the mother, trampled on her, and lacerated her uterus with a scissors—all without inducing an abortion).

238. *See, e.g.,* GORDON, *supra* note 18, at 36.

"success" from such grisly techniques, anthropologists have found true injury techniques to be the most common among medically primitive cultures.[239] It hardly needs demonstration that true injury techniques were not popular with women, as even those who view abortion favorably have recognized. Medical historian Edward Shorter, no foe of legalized abortion, concluded that before 1880 only women who were truly desperate would risk abortion.[240] Historian Geoffrey Quaife, another friend of legalized abortion, described injury techniques in connection with his analysis of violence, and not with abortion.[241]

A woman simply was not likely to undergo an effective injury abortion voluntarily unless she was suicidal because of the pregnancy. Georges Devereux, in the most extensive anthropological survey of abortion in medically primitive cultures, concluded that suicide and abortion were alternative responses to unwanted pregnancies in such societies.[242] His conclusion is particularly telling as he also indicated that he believed abortion to be "an absolutely universal phenomenon,"[243] something I suppose he would have said about suicide as well if he had been asked. Still, he was far more skeptical of reports of abortion as a practice in his completed study (1955) than he was in his preliminary study (1954).[244] An extreme example of his earlier uncritical acceptance of all reports of abortion practices was his approval of a rather unlikely report that in one medically primitive culture all pregnancies were aborted unless the woman were between 34 and 37 years old.[245] Pro-abortion historians are fond of quoting Devereux's early conclusion that abortion is a universal phenomenon without, however, mentioning its link to suicide.[246] Nor do they bother to mention Devereux's observation that condemnation and punishment (actual or symbolic, ranging from cursing and social ridicule to death) for abortion are just as universal as were attempts to abort.[247]

Devereux is not the only observer to note the link to suicide. A British doctor concluded in 1815 that abortion was tantamount to suicide.[248] Nineteenth-century Swedish medical authorities routinely recorded failed abortions as "suicide."[249] That nearly all the English cases reporting such techniques read quite clearly as cases of assault by persons outside the family that were resisted by the woman and, sometimes, by her husband or other members of her family, or that the only mention of abortion in the Old Testament involved a similar event,[250] suggests that such abortions, when they did occur, were unlikely to have been voluntary as far as the woman goes. It is possible that the father of the child instigated the attack,[251] although the terse legal records of the early cases seldom even hint at this possibility.

---

239. DEVEREUX, *supra* note 28, at 30–35, 171–358. *See also* BATES & ZAWADSKI, *supra* note 186, at 87–88; MCLAREN, *supra* note 28, at 100–08; TAUSSIG, *supra* note 186, at 41–45, 355.

240. SHORTER, *supra* note 87, at 177.

241. QUAIFE, *supra* note 87, at 26, 118.

242. DEVEREUX, *supra* note 28, at 28, 149–50; Devereux, *supra* note 192, at 101, 119, 122.

243. Devereux, *supra* note 192, at 98.

244. *Compare* DEVEREUX, *supra* note 28, at 30–35, 171–358, *with* Devereux, *supra* note 192, at 106–17, 133–34.

245. Devereux, *supra* note 192, at 107, 120.

246. *See, e.g.,* PETCHESKY, *supra* note 28, at 1–2, 29.

247. Devereux, *supra* note 192, at 98, 139–52.

248. O.W. BARTLEY, A TREATISE ON FORENSIC MEDICINE 3 (1815).

249. Jonas Frykman, *Sexual Intercourse and Social Norms: A Study of Illegitimate Births in Sweden, 1831–1933,* 1975 ETHNOLOGIA SCANDINAVIA 135. *See also* Dellapenna, *supra* note 64, at 372–76, 393–95; Fisher, *supra* note 200, at 6–10.

250. *Exodus* 21:22–25.

251. QUAIFE, *supra* note 87, at 26.

# Ingestion Techniques

*[T]he vast range of references to herbal abortifacients is chiefly of interest because of the light it casts, not on the rate of successful induction of abortions, but on the reality of a widespread tradition of women seeking to limit births by herbal means.*

—Angus McLaren[252]

Throughout most of history, the ingestion of various pharmacological concoctions was the major alternative to injury techniques for abortions. Closely related to the taking of a drug were the practices of douching with what were believed to be abortifacient potions or the insertion of pessaries into the vagina. I group these pharmacological methods together under the label "ingestion techniques."

Ingestion techniques were nearly as painful and deadly as the worst injury techniques until well into the nineteenth century, and thus also were tantamount to suicide, particularly as ingestion techniques were generally less likely to induce an abortion than injury techniques, and thus could lead to the ingesting of excessive doses.[253] The conclusion that ingestive abortions were suicidal was seldom expressed over the centuries, perhaps because it was so obvious that few felt it necessary to mention. Nonetheless, we can trace occasional acknowledgments of this reality back nearly two millennia. St. Jerome, in the fourth century of the Common Era, described the use of potions to obtain an abortion as involving both the sin of abortion and the sin of suicide, while also being likely to involve the sin of adultery.[254] St. Basil of Caesarea (in Palestine) reached this same conclusion at nearly the same time:

> She who deliberately destroyed a fetus has to pay the penalty of murder. And there is no exact inquiry among us as to whether the fetus was formed or unformed. For here it is not only the child to be born that is vindicated, but also the woman herself who made an attempt against her own life, because usually the women die in such attempts.[255]

We find similar observations by writers in the eighteenth century,[256] and we find the conclusion confirmed in the twentieth century as well.[257] Even some modern commentators who have been reluctant to conclude that voluntary abortion was rare (and thus deny that abortion was linked to suicide) have still ended by conceding facts that tend to confirm the rarity they deny. Thus, historian Geoffrey Quaife conceded that mothers were rarely anxious to use ingestion techniques.[258] While feminist historians Linda Gordon and Rosalind Petchesky have assumed that most abortions were voluntary throughout history, even they acknowledged the dangers and pain of the early techniques.[259] With or without the father's aggressive participation, for cen-

---

252. McLaren, *supra* note 28, at 107.

253. Gebhard *et al.*, *supra* note 45, at 193–96; Gordon, *supra* note 18, at 36, 53.

254. St. Jerome, *Letter to Eustochium* ¶ 22.13 (quoted in Gorman, *supra* note 87, at 68).

255. St. Basil the Great, *Epistularum* § 188.2, in 2 Fathers of the Church 12–13 (2) (Agnes Clare Way trans. 1951–55).

256. Alexander Hamilton, A Treatise on the Management of Female Complaints 231 (1792); Martha Mears, The Pupil of Nature: or Candid Advice to the Fair Sex 92–93 (1797); Thomas Short, New Observations 74 (1750). *See generally* McLaren, *supra* note 28, at 92–94.

257. Devereux, *supra* note 28, at 149–50; Gordon, *supra* note 18, at 37, 53; Mohr, *supra* note 19, at 21–22, 55–58; Dellapenna, *supra* note 64, at 372–76, 393–95; Fisher, *supra* note 200, at 6–7.

258. Quaife, *supra* note 87, at 26, 118.

259. Gordon, *supra* note 18, at 39; Petchesky, *supra* note 28, at 49–55.

turies an abortion that was not a crime against the mother was rare. This reality underlies the long-held tradition that an aborting mother was seen as a victim rather than a criminal.[260]

Surveys of medical literature in early societies supports the conclusion that the potions ingested in attempts at an abortion were ineffective, highly dangerous, or both.[261] The rarity of induced abortions until recent times is confirmed by the little direct evidence as we have of abortion rates. Historian Peter Laslett, in searching church records in England (which do not distinguish between spontaneous and induced abortions), found that recorded abortions in the seventeenth century amounted to 6–7 percent of total births.[262] If we take seriously the claim by pro-abortion historians that no social opprobrium attached to abortion before the twentieth century, there is no reason to believe these records systematically excluded induced abortions. In the twentieth century, spontaneous abortions range from 7.5 to 11 percent with our more advanced medical technology.[263] The seventeenth century figures reveal few, if any, induced abortions.

Despite the overwhelming evidence that there were no consistently safe and effective ingestive techniques, the belief persists that women at many places around the world secretly used "magic potions" that enabled them to terminate unwanted pregnancies.[264] Those making this assumption apparently seldom pause to consider how this knowledge, of obvious practical importance, could have been lost not just once or twice, but everywhere it supposedly existed; they certainly do not attempt to explain this mystery. We have already seen how the efforts of historian John Riddle and others to prove the existence of such potions founder on inconsistencies and a lack of credible evidence.[265]

While we have no way of knowing every potion used in ancient and medieval times in efforts to induce abortions, we can in fact form a fairly clear overall picture of what was available and used openly or even secretly among women. For example, the now published diary of midwife Martha Ballard, who was active in Maine from 1785 to 1812, has entries recording her gathering of herbs and is entirely consistent with the patterns recorded in the herbal directories compiled by physicians and male pharmacists and in circulation at the time — even though there is no evidence that Martha Ballard ever consulted such a text or any text at all.[266] Ballard's compounds were simpler than some in the herbals and she exhibited no interest in "Indian" or "Negro" "cures." Nor does Ballard ever mention inducing an abortion during her nearly 40 years of midwifing.

Our sources disclose long lists of herbs that were reputed abortifacients. The list goes on and on until one suspects that someone somewhere has attributed abortifacient properties to virtually any ingestible substance and some uningestible substances as well. We begin our survey of

---

260. Wm. L. Clark, jr., Hand-Book of Criminal Law 182 (1894); Annotation, *Woman upon Whom Abortion Is Committed as Accomplice for Purposes of Rule Requiring Corroboration of Accomplice Testimony*, 34 A.L.R.3d 858 (1970); Thomas Harris, Note, *A Functional Study of Existing Abortion Laws*, 35 Colum. L. Rev. 87, 90–91 (1935). *See also* Brookes, *supra* note 30, at 40; Grossberg, *supra* note 80, at 211–12; Backhouse, *supra* note 16, at 83–84.

261. Bates & Zawadski, *supra* note 186, at 14–23, 85–91; Degler, *supra* note 18, at 230; Devereux, *supra* note 28, at 36–43, 249, 279; Gordon, *supra* note 18, at 36–37, 40; Himes, *supra* note 206, at 139–51; Hordern, *supra* note 218, at 3; Eve Levin, Sex and Society in the World of the Orthodox Slavs, 900–1700, at 175–78 (1989); Mohr, *supra* note 19, at 49–58, 71–73, 125; John Noonan, jr., Contraception 222–30 (1965); Shorter, *supra* note 87, at 179–88; Taussig, *supra* note 186, at 31–45, 352–57; Dellapenna, *supra* note 64, at 373–76; Carl Djerassi, *Book Review*, 329 N. Eng. J. Med. 143 (1993).

262. Peter Laslett, The World We Have Lost 123 (1966).

263. *Id.* at 266. *See also* Paige, *supra* note 93, at 33.

264. See the references collected *supra* at note 87.

265. See the text *supra* at notes 87–140.

266. Ulrich, The Midwife's Tale, *supra* note 9, at 49–53.

ingestion techniques with examples of utterly ineffective reputed "abortifacients." It doesn't matter whether we examine reputed abortifacients available in England or America during the period of this study (1200–present), or go back to the ancients or look outside the European cultural zone. For example, one source found enough reputed abortifacient drugs recommended by Greek physicians or found in Greek folk medicine to fill twelve pages—all ineffective.[267] We find that reputed abortifacients have included "acid food,"[268] anise,[269] cardamom,[270] seeds of wild carrot (Queen Anne's Lace),[271] celery or celery seed,[272] chamomile,[273] chicory,[274] cinnamon,[275] coriander,[276] cottonroot,[277] cumin,[278] raw eggs,[279] ginger,[280] goat dung or urine,[281] chopped animal hair,[282] hops,[283] horseradish,[284] extract of iris or lily root,[285] laurel,[286] lavender,[287] leeks,[288] licorice,[289] marjoram,[290] marigolds,[291] human milk,[292] mint,[293] mustard,[294] oranges in white

267. BATES & ZAWADSKI, *supra* note 186, at 16–27.

268. MICHAEL ETMULLERUS, DESCRIPTION OF ALL DISEASES INCIDENT TO MEN, WOMEN, AND CHILDREN 563 (3rd ed. 1712); TAUSSIG, *supra* note 186, at 33.

269. RIDDLE, *supra* note 28, at 80, 91, 124, 134; Norman Farnsworth *et al., Potential Value of Plants as Sources of New Antifertility Agents (Pt. I),* 64 J. PHARMACEUTICAL SCI. 535, 536 (1975) ("Farnsworth I").

270. RIDDLE, *supra* note 28, at 47–48, 56, 100, 130, 138.

271. SCRIBONIUS, *supra* note 212, ¶ 121, at 64. *See also* RIDDLE, *supra* note 28, at 58–59, 80, 83–84, 91, 102, 106, 119, 123, 152; Farnsworth I, *supra* note 269, at 554; M.M. Sharma *et al., Estrogenic and Pregnancy Interceptory Effects of Carrot Daucus Carota Seeds,* 14 INDIAN J. EXPERIMENTAL BIOL. 506 (1976).

272. RIDDLE, *supra* note 28, at 72–73, 76, 82, 91, 104, 119, 121, 126, 129; J.M. WATT & M.G. BREYER-BRANDWIJK, THE MEDICINAL AND POISONOUS PLANTS OF SOUTHERN AFRICA 117–18 (1982); R.C.D. Casey, *Alleged Anti-Fertility Plants of India,* 14 INDIAN J. MED. SCIENCES 590, 592 (1960); R.R. Chaudhury, *Plants with Possible Antifertility Activity,* 55 INDIAN COUNCIL FOR MED. RESEARCH: SPEC. REP. SER. 1, 4, 14 (1966); Farnsworth I, *supra* note 269, at 554; Klepp, *supra* note 28, at 86.

273. RIDDLE, *supra* note 28, at 83, 101, 114, 119, 123–24; Farnsworth I, *supra* note 269, at 559.

274. RIDDLE, *supra* note 28, at 83.

275. *Id.* at 84, 114, 127, 132, 138.

276. *Id.* at 79, 91.

277. BRODIE, *supra* note 31, at 44, 225–26, 236; D'EMILIO & FREEDMAN, *supra* note 80, at 65; MOHR, *supra* note 19, at 59.

278. RIDDLE, *supra* note 28, at 78, 80, 101–02, 124.

279. DEVEREUX, *supra* note 28, at 38, 249.

280. GEBHARD *et al., supra* note 45, at 195; GORDON, *supra* note 18, at 37; RIDDLE, *supra* note 28, at 85, 91; Klepp, *supra* note 28, at 84, 86.

281. DEVEREUX, *supra* note 28, at 38, 279; Lemay, *supra* note 206, at 194; Lucille Pinto, *The Folk Practice of Obstetrics and Gynecology in the Middle Ages,* 47 BULL. HIST. MED. 513, 523 (1973).

282. GORDON, *supra* note 18, at 36; Devereux, *supra* note 192, at 123, 129–31.

283. VIRGINIA SCULLY, A TREASURY OF AMERICAN INDIAN HERBS 120 (1971).

284. GEBHARD *et al., supra* note 45, at 195; GORDON, *supra* note 18, at 37.

285. McLAREN, *supra* note 28, at 101; RIDDLE, *supra* note 28, at 37, 42, 46, 56, 89–90, 92, 100–02, 104, 114, 119–20, 123, 131–32; Norman Farnsworth *et al., Potential Value of Plants as Sources of New Antifertility Agents (Pt. II),* 64 J. PHARMACEUTICAL SCI. 717, 718 (1975) ("Farnsworth II").

286. RIDDLE, *supra* note 28, at 47–48, 56, 98, 123, 161.

287. BRODIE, *supra* note 31, at 43; GEBHARD *et al., supra* note 45, at 195; GORDON, *supra* note 18, at 36, 37; HIMES, *supra* note 206, at 170–71; RIDDLE, *supra* note 28, at 84, 119; Klepp, *supra* note 28, at 91.

288. RIDDLE, *supra* note 28, at 78, 82, 89.

289. *Id.* at 42, 105.

290. BRODIE, *supra* note 31, at 43; GORDON, *supra* note 18, at 36; HIMES, *supra* note 206, at 170–71; RIDDLE, *supra* note 28, at 53, 114, 119, 124.

291. Brody, *supra* note 31, at 45; McLAREN, *supra* note 28, at 102, 104; ROGER THOMPSON, SEX IN MIDDLESEX: POPULAR MORES IN A MASSACHUSETTS COUNTY, 1649–1699, at 183 (1986).

292. Lemay, *supra* note 206, at 194–95; Pinto, *supra* note 281, at 516–17.

293. BRODIE, *supra* note 31, at 43–44; RIDDLE, *supra* note 28, at 79–80, 83–84, 123, 126, 130–31, 136, 138, 161; Farnsworth I, *supra* note 269, at 564; Klepp, *supra* note 28, at 91.

294. GEBHARD *et al., supra* note 45, at 195; GORDON, *supra* note 18, at 37; GORMAN, *supra* note 87, at 16.

wine,[295] parsley,[296] rabbit innards,[297] sage,[298] stallion meat,[299] "ungrateful strong smells,"[300] wine,[301] and chopped women's hair.[302] We have reports of women drinking water in which rusty nails had been soaked while rubbing their breasts with gunpowder.[303] Later reports describe women attempting abortion by drinking gunpowder dissolved in gin while performing certain rituals.[304]

As these last descriptions suggests, many ingestion techniques depended, just like the simpler injury techniques, on sympathetic magic rather than chemical action.[305] One perhaps reaches the limit of such claims in reading that the ingestion of garlic both prevents conception and induces abortions.[306] This was too much even for John Riddle. Despite his determination to accept nearly every claim about every reputed pharmacological abortifacients and contraceptives from times past, Riddle could not help pointing out that "[i]f garlic is a contraceptive or abortifacient, one might wonder why there is any population in the Mediterranean at all."[307]

Space does not allow a detailed examination of each of these reputed but utterly ineffective abortifacients. A few examples will have to suffice. Parsley is a particularly good example as it was long recommended to prevent as well as to induce abortions, and functioned as an aphrodisiac and as a contraceptive.[308] Such contradictory reports are actually fairly common in anthropological studies.[309] We have already noted such reports for garlic. Sage was similarly recommended to help conception and to prevent miscarriages.[310] Mint had a similarly varied reputation.[311] Eating a human placenta was believed both to induce and to prevent conception.[312]

The varied powers attributed to these herbs suggest that the herbs, now simple cooking staples unless an extract is heavily refined, had no relevant effect at all, except perhaps through the excessive suggestibility of a very few women. Yet at least one medieval physician described parsley not only as an extremely powerful emmenagogue (for unblocking "obstructed menses") but also as an extremely

295. McLaren, *supra* note 28, at 103.

296. Brodie, *supra* note 31, at 13 n.47, 170; 2 A. Goris & A. Liot, *Pharmacie Galénique* 1833 (1939); Gordon, *supra* note 18, at 36; Hadley, *supra* note 80, at 37; McLaren, *supra* note 28, at 104; Riddle, *supra* note 28, at 82, 84, 86, 91, 102, 119, 161, 208 n.64; Taussig, *supra* note 186, at 32; Klepp, *supra* note 28, at 86.

297. Pinto, *supra* note 281, at 520.

298. Brodie, *supra* note 31, at 42; 2 Compleat Herbal 94–95 (G. Swindells ed. 1787); Riddle, *supra* note 28, at 53, 83, 102, 115, 124, 138, 155, 208 n.64; Shorter, *supra* note 87, at 183.

299. Devereux, *supra* note 192, at 121–22.

300. Etmullerus, *supra* note 268, at 563. *See also* Riddle, *supra* note 28, at 45, 91, 128, 136, 181 n.15.

301. Etmullerus, *supra* note 268, at 563. *See also* Riddle, *supra* note 28, at 26, 34, 47, 54–55, 71, 77–78, 98, 101, 104–05, 115; Shorter, *supra* note 87, at 182. Wine generally appears as part of a formula in which the wine might actually have been meant merely as a vehicle of ingestion rather than as an abortifacient ingredient in itself. Dioscorides, in the first century, reported that wine made from grapes grown in the proximity of certain herbs would induce an abortion. Riddle, *supra*, at 54.

302. Riddle, *supra* note 28, at 98.

303. Aptheker, *supra* note 188, at 120. *See also* D'Emilio & Freedman, *supra* note 80, at 63; Gebhard *et al.*, *supra* note 45, at 195; Gordon, *supra* note 18, at 36–37; Himes, *supra* note 206, at 92, 162; Riddle, *supra* note 28, at 51.

304. Brookes, *supra* note 30, at 5, 117.

305. *See, e.g.,* Aptheker, *supra* note 188, at 140; Gordon, *supra* note 18, at 36; Lemay, *supra* note 206, at 194–95; Pinto, *supra* note 281, at 516–17, 523.

306. Riddle, *supra* note 28, at 77, 89, 98; Casey, *supra* note 272, at 595; Farnsworth I, *supra* note 269, at 561; Farnsworth II, *supra* note 285, at 735.

307. Riddle, *supra* note 28, at 37–38.

308. Noonan, *supra* note 261, at 208; Riddle, *supra* note 28, at 82; Taussig, *supra* note 186, at 32.

309. Devereux, *supra* note 192, at 130.

310. 1 Compleat Herbal, *supra* note 298, at 94–95.

311. Constantinus Africanus, *De gratibus* 359 (1536 ed.; original from ca. 1085). *See also* Riddle, *supra* note 28, at 119.

312. Levin, *supra* note 261, at 177–78; Riddle, *supra* note 28, at 154; Joseph Needham & Gwi-Djen Lu, *Sex Hormones in the Middle Ages*, 27 Endeavor 130 (1968).

dangerous one.[313] An extract of parsley, apiole, actually is capable of inducing paralysis of the nervous system.[314] Apiole, however, is not effective for abortions short of producing such a general nerve paralysis as to endanger the mother's life or health.[315] While historian Edward Shorter claims that apiole could be effective without such a general debilitative effect, even he admits that apiole was only discovered in 1715, and apparently was not put to use, as an abortifacient or otherwise, before the middle of the nineteenth century.[316] While apiole appears on lists of abortifacients in use in the twentieth century,[317] there is no evidence that it was employed in ancient or medieval times.

If the foregoing drugs were ingested and failed, a woman might go on to ingest drugs that, in dangerous quantities, could induce an abortion. The ancient physician Soranus directly delineated the pattern of ingesting progressively more dangerous substances in an attempt to secure an abortion.[318] We find reports of the following such potentially dangerous substances used as abortifacients before 1800: assarabacca,[319] camphor,[320] castor oil,[321] cloves,[322] croton oil,[323] ergot of rye,[324] ivy,[325] jalappa,[326] mandrake root,[327] myrrh,[328] myrtle,[329] nutmeg,[330]

313. Constantinus Africanus, *supra* note 311, at 386.

314. Taussig, *supra* note 186, at 353–54.

315. Himes, *supra* note 206, at 13 n.47, 170; Interdepartmental Committee, *supra* note 225, at 42.

316. Shorter, *supra* note 87, at 214–24.

317. Brodie, *supra* note 31, at 226; Brookes, *supra* note 30, at 4–5; Secret Remedies, *supra* note 105, at 195, 199, 205; Fisher, *supra* note 200, at 6.

318. Soranus, *supra* note 217, ¶¶1.63–1.65, at 65–68. *See also* Brodie, *supra* note 31, at 42–43, 226; Burns, *supra* note 227, at 79; Devereux, *supra* note 28, at 42–43; Kenny, *supra* note 114, at 185; Mohr, *supra* note 19, at 58; Noonan, *supra* note 261, at 211; Riddle, *supra* note 28, at 46–49, 97–103, 119–20; Breitenecker & Breitenecker, *supra* note 200, at 218–19; Fisher, *supra* note 200, at 6–7.

319. 1 Compleat Herbal, *supra* note 298, at 69–71; John Pechey, Compleat Herbal of Physical Plants 13 (1707).

320. Gutman, *supra* note 221, at 81; Reagan, *supra* note 16, at 137; You May Plow Here: The Narrative of Sara Brooks 176–77 (Thordis Simonson ed. 1986).

321. Bates & Zawadski, *supra* note 186, at 89; Brodie, *supra* note 31, at 44; Brookes, *supra* note 30, at 32; Gebhard *et al.*, *supra* note 45, at 195; Gordon, *supra* note 18, at 36; Hordern, *supra* note 218, at 3; Reagan, *supra* note 16; Riddle, *supra* note 28, at 102; Farnsworth II, *supra* note 285, at 737; Fisher, *supra* note 200, at 6.

322. Bates & Zawadski, *supra* note 186, at 89.

323. Fisher, *supra* note 200, at 6.

324. James Ashton, The Book of Nature; Containing Information for Young People Who Think of Getting Married, on the Philosophy of Procreation and Sexual Intercourse; Showing How to Prevent Conception and to Avoid Child-Bearing 61 (1860); Richard Carlile, Every Woman's Book 23–24 (1838); Robert Christison, A Treatise on Poisons 670–71 (1829); John Morgan, *An Essay on the Causes of Abortion among the Negro Population,* 19 Nashville J. Med. 117, 120 (1860). *See also* Bates & Zawadski, *supra* note 186, at 88; Brodie, *supra* note 31, at 142, 187, 225–26, 236, 294, 305 n.23; Brookes, *supra* note 30, at 119; Hordern, *supra* note 218, at 3; Interdepartmental Committee, *supra* note 225, at 42; McLaren, *supra* note 19, at 241; McLaren, *supra* note 28, at 104; Reagan, *supra* note 16, at 9, 209; Riddle, *supra* note 28, at 17, 163; Shorter, *supra* note 87, at 182–84; Solinger, *supra* note 19, at 208, 211; Taussig, *supra* note 186, at 353; Backhouse, *supra* note 16, at 85; Fisher, *supra* note 200, at 6; Klepp, *supra* note 28, at 87. Taussig suggests that ergot of rye is not effective even in large doses. Whatever its effect, ergot grows on other crops as well. Riddle, *supra,* at 55, 83.

325. Mohr , *supra* note 19, at 12; Riddle, *supra* note 28, at 35, 104, 133; J.M. Watt & M.G. Breyer-Brandwijk, The Medicinal and Poisonous Plants of Southern Africa 117–18 (1982). On the dangers of ingesting ivy, see Walter Lewis & Memory Elvin-Lewis, Medical Botany: Plants Affecting Man's Health 49 (1977).

326. Warren Dawson, A Leechbook or Collection of Medical Recipes of the Fifteenth Century 125 (1934); McLaren, *supra* note 28, at 106; Mohr, *supra* note 19, at 9; Secret Remedies, *supra* note 105, at 192–93, 196; Shorter, *supra* note 87, at 180.

327. Riddle, *supra* note 28, at 84, 86, 133; Farnsworth I, *supra* note 269, at 546, 553, 574–75.

328. Mohr, *supra* note 19, at 12; Riddle, *supra* note 28, at 29, 32, 47, 56–58, 81, 83–85, 89–90, 92, 98, 100–05, 119, 124, 127, 129–31, 161; Backhouse, *supra* note 16, at 85; Klepp, *supra* note 28, at 84.

329. Gorman, *supra* note 87, at 16; Riddle, *supra* note 28, at 29, 32, 47, 77–79, 161.

opium,[331] pennyroyal,[332] quinine,[333] rosemary,[334] rue,[335] saffron,[336] saltpeter,[337] sassafras,[338] savin (or other forms of juniper),[339] savory,[340] seaweed,[341] slippery elm,[342] squills,[343] tansy,[344]

330. BATES & ZAWADSKI, *supra* note 186, at 89; HORDERN, *supra* note 218, at 3; REAGAN, *supra* note 16, at 137; SCULLY, *supra* note 283, at 120; YOU MAY PLOW HERE, *supra* note 320, at 176–77.

331. RIDDLE, *supra* note 28, at 84, 89, 101, 105, 124.

332. CATHARINE BROOKS, THE COMPLEAT ENGLISH COOK 120–21 (1765); 2 COMPLEAT HERBAL, *supra* note 298, at 33; ELIZABETH SMITH, THE COMPLEAT HOUSEWIFE 237, 320, 324 (1725); JOHN WESLEY, PRIMITIVE PHYSICKE 90 (1776); HANNAH WOOLEY, THE ACCOMPLISHED LADY'S DELIGHT 152 (1677). *See also* BRODIE, *supra* note 31, at 42–44, 119; BROOKES, *supra* note 30, at 4; DAWSON, *supra* note 326, at 97; WALTER GREENWOOD, THERE WAS A TIME 62 (1967); GUTMAN, *supra* note 221, at 81; HADLEY, *supra* note 80, at 37; HORDERN, *supra* note 218, at 3; INTERDEPARTMENTAL COMMITTEE, *supra* note 225, at 42; MCLAREN, *supra* note 19, at 241; MCLAREN, *supra* note 28, at 103–04; REAGAN, *supra* note 16, at 9, 44; RIDDLE, *supra* note 28, at 53–54, 57, 59–61, 79, 83, 85, 89–91, 100–04, 115, 123–24, 130–31, 133, 136, 138, 152, 155, 161; ROBERT ROBERTS, THE CLASSIC SLUM: SALFORD LIFE IN THE FIRST QUARTER OF THE CENTURY 100 (1971); SECRET REMEDIES, *supra* note 105, at 192–93, 195–98, 204–05; SHORTER, *supra* note 87, at 182–83, 188; THOMPSON, *supra* note 291, at 183; WATT & BREYER-BRANDWIJK, *supra* note 325, at 523; WILLIS, *supra* note 219, at 8; Backhouse, *supra* note 16, at 85; Farnsworth I, *supra* note 269, at 564; Jennifer Fiore, *Pennyroyal Roulette,* NEW AGE J., May/June, 1995, at 88; Fisher, *supra* note 200, at 6; Klepp, *supra* note 28, at 83–85, 87.

333. BROOKES, *supra* note 30, at 4, 55, 117, 119; GORDON, *supra* note 18, at 36; HADLEY, *supra* note 80, at 37; HORDERN, *supra* note 218, at 3; LEWIS & ELVIN-LEWIS, *supra* note 325, at 645, at 324; MCLAREN, *supra* note 19, at 241, 247–48; MOHR, *supra* note 19, at 6; RIDDLE, *supra* note 28, at 153, 160; SECRET REMEDIES, *supra* note 105, at 194, 200–03; SOLINGER, *supra* note 19, at 208; Fisher, *supra* note 200, at 6.

334. BRODIE, *supra* note 31, at 43; GEBHARD *et al., supra* note 45, at 195; GORDON, *supra* note 18, at 37; SHORTER, supra note 87, at 183; Klepp, *supra* note 28, at 86–87.

335. BATES & ZAWADSKI, *supra* note 186, at 89; BRODIE, *supra* note 31, at 43–44, 119, 225; D'EMILIO & FREEDMAN, *supra* note 80, at 63; 2 GORIS & LIOT, *supra* note 296, at 1833; GUTMAN, *supra* note 221, at 81; HORDERN, *supra* note 218, at 3; MCLAREN, *supra* note 19, at 241; MCLAREN, *supra* note 28, at 103–04; QUAIFE, *supra* note 87, at 118; RIDDLE, *supra* note 28, at 28–29, 32, 47, 56, 79, 82–92, 98, 100–04, 108, 115, 119–20, 123, 126–27, 129–32, 136–38, 153–55, 161; SECRET REMEDIES, *supra* note 105, at 195, 203–05; SHORTER, *supra* note 87, at 184–85; Fisher, *supra* note 200, at 6; Klepp, *supra* note 28, at 83–84, 86–87; Morgan, *supra* note 324, at 118; John Scarborough, *Drugs and Medicines in the Roman World,* 38 EXPEDITION, No.2, at 38, 41 (1996). Rue has been used successfully to abort horses. Farnsworth I, *supra* note 269, at 561. It has also been used successfully on rats. Mirko Guerra & A.T.L. Andrade, *Contraceptive Effects of Native Plants in Rats,* 18 CONTRACEPTION 191 (1974).

336. BATES & ZAWADSKI, *supra* note 186, at 89; 2 GORIS & LIOT, *supra* note 296, at 1833; HORDERN, *supra* note 218, at 3; MCLAREN, *supra* note 28, at 103; RIDDLE, *supra* note 28, at 80, 85, 90, 104–05, 161; SHORTER, *supra* note 87, at 182.

337. RIDDLE, *supra* note 28, at 79–81.

338. BATES & ZAWADSKI, *supra* note 186, at 89.

339. 2 BARTON, *supra* note 150, at 196; 2 WILLIAM BARTON, COMPENDIUM FLORAE PHILADELPHICAE 200 (1818); BOORDE, *supra* note 27, fol. lxxxxiii; BREVITT, *supra* note 99, at 47; 2 COMPLEAT HERBAL, *supra* note 298, at 103; WILLIAM COLES, ADAM IN EDEN, OR NATURE'S PARADISE 593 (1657); JEHAN GOEURIOT, THE REGIMENT OF LIFE fol. lviii (Thomas Phayre ed. 1544); JOHN GREGORY, MEDICAL LECTURES 379 (1770); ROBERT LOVELL, A COMPLEAT HERBAL 385 (1665); *MALLEUS MALEFICARUM* 66 (Montague Summers ed. 1966; orig. date 1488); CHARLES MILLSPAUGH, AMERICAN MEDICINAL PLANTS pl. 166 (1887); 1 C.S. RAFINESQUE, MEDICAL FLORA; OR, MANUAL OF THE MEDICAL BOTANY OF THE UNITED STATES OF NORTH AMERICA 232 (1828–30). *See also* BRODIE, *supra* note 31, at 42–44, 119, 225–26; BROOKES, *supra* note 30, at 119; 2 GORIS & LIOT, *supra* note 296, at 1833; HORDERN, *supra* note 218, at 3; INTERDEPARTMENTAL COMMITTEE, *supra* note 225, at 41–42; MCLAREN, *supra* note 19, at 241; MCLAREN, *supra* note 28, at 92, 103–06; MOHR, *supra* note 19, at 8–9, 12–13, 71; MALCOLM POTTS, PETER DIGGORY, & JOHN PEEL, ABORTION 170–72 (1977); QUAIFE, *supra* note 87, at 118, 172; REAGAN, *supra* note 16, at 9; RIDDLE, *supra* note 28, at 36, 71, 79–80, 82, 85–86, 89–90, 102, 115, 119, 122, 124, 130–34, 136, 148, 151, 160–61, 163; SCULLY, *supra* note 283, at 120; SECRET REMEDIES, *supra* note 105, at 197; SHORTER, *supra* note 87, at 186–87; TAUSSIG, *supra* note 186, at 353; THOMPSON, *supra* note 291, at 25–26, 107, 182–83; Bakhouse, *supra* note 16, at 103; Fisher, *supra* note 200, at 6; Klepp, *supra* note 28, at 82–83, 86–87, 89. One could add numerous literary references to savin. MCLAREN, *supra,* at 105.

340. RIDDLE, *supra* note 28, at 115; SHORTER, *supra* note 87, at 182.

341. MCLAREN, *supra* note 19, at 241.

342. *Id.;* BRODIE, *supra* note 31, at 42; BROOKES, *supra* note 30, at 3–4, 22, 119; SOLINGER, *supra* note 19, at 208.

343. MCLAREN, *supra* note 19, at 241.

thyme,[345] turpentine,[346] and yarrow.[347]

As with the wholly ineffective ingestives, some of these were also reported to have contradictory or symbolic effects. Myrrh was reputed to aid conception as well as to be an abortifacient.[348] Pennyroyal was also reputedly good for expelling stomach worms. As historian Janet Brodie commented, the logic linking the expulsion of stomach worms to the expulsion of an unwanted foetus was "primitive but obvious."[349] Brodie also tells us that pennyroyal was reputed to have various gynecological uses among American Indians, so much so that it was often called "squaw mint." Pharmacologist Charles Millspaugh found, in 1887, that tansy tea was quite ineffective as an abortifacient while being rather deadly.[350] Dr. Frederick Taussig also considered it ineffective, although he thought it was "relatively harmless."[351] Tansy tea, like rue, apparently was more useful for expelling worms than for expelling a fetus.[352] On the other hand, more than one source recommended tansy for preventing miscarriage or to promote conception as well as for inducing abortion.[353] Rather than adding yet other similar substances to these lists,[354] one should consider how these substances operated, if they operated at all.

Generally the more dangerous substances did not operate on the uterus itself; they were effective, if at all, only by so debilitating the woman (often through attacks on her lower digestive track) that she could no longer sustain the pregnancy.[355] For example, while rue continues to be recommended in traditional (non-Western) medicine for human use as a contraceptive and an abortifacient,[356] the ancients recognized the dangers of rue for human use.[357] Despite Janet Brodie's apparent enthusiasm for many of these substances, she described pennyroyal, rue, savin, and tansy as "dangerous poisons."[358] Yarrow was also notably dangerous, although historian Vir-

---

344. BRODIE, *supra* note 31, at 43–44, 119, 146, 225; D'EMILIO & FREEDMAN, *supra* note 80, at 63; GEBHARD *et al.*, *supra* note 45, at 195; GORDON, *supra* note 18, at 36; GUTMAN, *supra* note 221, at 81; HORDERN, *supra* note 218, at 3; KENNY, *supra* note 114, at 185; McLAREN, *supra* note 28, at 104; REAGAN, *supra* note 19, at 9, 44; RIDDLE, *supra* note 28, at 116–17, 161, 163, 208 n.64; SECRET REMEDIES, *supra* note 105, at 204; SHORTER, *supra* note 87, at 185–86; SOLINGER, *supra* note 19, at 208; TAUSSIG, *supra* note 186, at 353; R. Frank Chander *et al.*, *Herbal Remedies of the Maritime Indians*, 1 J. ETHNOPHARMACOLOGY 62 (1979); Backhouse, *supra* note 16, at 85; George Conway & John Slocumb, *Plants Used as Abortifacients and Emmenagogues by Spanish New Mexicans*, 1 J. ETHNOPHARMACOLOGY 253 (1979); Morgan, *supra* note 324, at 117–18; J.C. Saha *et al.*, *Ecbolic Properties of Indian Medicinal Plants*, 49 IND. J. MED. RES. 130, at 141 (1961); Fisher, *supra* note 200, at 6.

345. BATES & ZAWADSKI, *supra* note 186, at 89; BRODIE, *supra* note 31, at 119; GORDON, *supra* note 18, at 36; HIMES, *supra* note 206, at 170; McLAREN, *supra* note 28, at 104; RIDDLE, *supra* note 28, at 53, 83, 90, 102, 104, 119, 132, 137, 152, 161; SHORTER, *supra* note 87, at 183.

346. GEBHARD *et al.*, *supra* note 45, at 195; GORDON, *supra* note 18, at 36; KENNY, *supra* note 114, at 185; REAGAN, *supra* note 16, at 138; YOU MAY PLOW HERE, *supra* note 320, at 177.

347. SCULLY, *supra* note 283, at 120.

348. GORMAN, *supra* note 87, at 16; RIDDLE, *supra* note 28, at 126.

349. BRODIE, *supra* note 31, at 44.

350. MILLSPAUGH, *supra* note 339, pl. 86.

351. TAUSSIG, *supra* note 186, at 353.

352. ULRICH, THE MIDWIFE'S TALE, *supra* note 9, at 56.

353. BRODIE, *supra* note 31, at 43.

354. *See* GUTMAN, *supra* note 221, at 81; McLAREN, *supra* note 28, at 104; RIDDLE, *supra* note 28, *passim*.

355. BROOKES, *supra* note 87, at 118; GORDON, *supra* note 18, at 37, 53; INTERDEPARTMENTAL COMMITTEE, *supra* note 225, at 42; McLAREN, *supra* note 28, at 107; PAIGE, *supra* note 93, at 33; STORER, *supra* note 157, at 43, 45; Michael Eshleman, *Diet during Pregnancy in the Sixteenth and Seventeenth Centuries*, 30 J. HIST. MED. & ALLIED SCIENCES 23 (1975); J.J. Mulheron, *Foeticide*, 10 PENINSULAR J. MED. 387, 389 (1874). *See also* APTHEKER, *supra* note 188, at 145.

356. RIDDLE, *supra* note 28, at 29, 154.

357. SORANUS, *supra* note 217, ¶ 1.63, at 65–66.

358. BRODIE, *supra* note 31, at 44.

ginia Scully noted that it was "not as dangerous as nutmeg."[359] Soranus, perhaps the leading gynecologist of the Roman Empire, summarized the matter early in the second century of the
Common Era: "the evil from these things [ingestive abortifacients] is too great, since they damage and upset the stomach, and besides cause congestion of the head and induce sympathetic reactions."[360] All too often, debilitation would progress so far that the mother could not sustain her
own life—as the ancients well knew. No wonder St. Basil reported in 374 CE, "usually the
woman dies in such attempts."[361]

One of the mysteries to be unraveled is why did so many sources report a substance of the
sort listed here as useful as an abortifacient despite frequent reports of the substance's dire effects
when successful. Edward Shorter has explained the apparent confusion about the effects of purported abortifacients as arising from the fact that many of the intermediately "effective" abortifacients were volatile oils, including pennyroyal, rosemary, rue, sage, savin, tansy, and thyme.[362]
Unlike fatty oils, volatile oils evaporate easily when heated; in fact, they evaporate so easily that
aromatic volatile oils form the basis of the perfume industry, evaporating from body heat
alone.[363] Pennyroyal itself is used in some perfumes in the United States.[364] This volatility makes
volatile oils extremely difficult to work with. The amount of oil in an herb or other plant could
vary dramatically depending on whether the growing season had been wet or dry, or depending
on the month in which it was harvested.[365] The amount of oil could also vary with soil conditions, with the part of the plant used to prepare the potion or to extract the oil, and with the
processing techniques.[366]

Given the enormous variability of the herbs used to produce the volatile oils, a midwife (or a
modern pharmacist) could never be certain precisely how potent an oil or tea brewed from one
of these plants really was. Exactly the same recipe could produce an utterly ineffective potion one
time and a deadly toxic concoction the next simply because of small variations in the factors already suggested, in the heat applied, the age of herbs being used, and so on.[367] In *Rex v. Skeete,*[368]
a seventeenth century English case, the court heard testimony of repeated use of several potions
without significant effect. More than one person intent on achieving an abortion must have
compensated for these uncertainties by increasing the strength of the potion, with predictable
results[369]—a phenomenon still observable where folk medicine continues to predominate.[370]

Savin oil appears to have been the most popular abortifacient through the centuries.[371] Its
story is typical of the rest. Savin oil is one of the volatile oils. It was easily obtained from juniper

359. SCULLY, *supra* note 283, at 120.

360. SORANUS, *supra* note 217, ¶1.63, at 65–66. *See also* AËTIUS OF AMIDA, THE GYNAECOLOGY AND OB-
STETRICS OF THE VITH CENTURY, A.D., at 26–27 (James Ricci trans. 1950); CLAUDIUS GALEN, *DE NATURAL-
IBUS FACULTATIBUS* ¶3.12 (Arthur John Brock trans. 1952); 1 JOSEPH PITTON DE TOURNEFORT, THE COMPLEAT
HERBAL; OR, THE BOTANICAL INSTITUTIONS OF MR. TOURNEFORT 149 (1719).

361. ST. BASIL THE GREAT, LETTER ¶188.2 (374 A.D.) [quoted in GORMAN, *supra* note 18, at 66–67]; ST.
JEROME, *supra* note 254.

362. SHORTER, *supra* note 87, at 183–88. *See also* RIDDLE, *supra* note 28, at 159; SECRET REMEDIES, *supra*
note 105, at 192.

363. SHORTER, *supra* note 87, at 183.

364. RIDDLE, *supra* note 28, at 54.

365. *See, e.g.,* 1 ERNEST GUENTHER, ESSENTIAL OILS 68–77 (1948).

366. G. Marczal *et al., Phenol-Ether Components of Diuretic Effect in Parsley,* 26 ACTA AGRONOMICA ACAD-
EMIAE SCIENTIARUM HUNGARICAE 7 (1977).

367. RIDDLE, *supra* note 28, at 156; SHORTER, *supra* note 87, at 187–88.

368. E.R.O. (Chelmsford) T/A 465/27, at 14–15, 22–23 (1638).

369. SHORTER, *supra* note 87, at 188.

370. Caroline Rendle Short, *Causes of Maternal Death among Africans in Kampala, Uganda,* 68 J. OBSTET-
RICS & GYN. OF BRIT. COMMW. 45 (1961).

371. MOHR, *supra* note 19, at 8–9; SHORTER, *supra* note 87, at 186–87.

berries growing wild in related species on both sides of the Atlantic.[372] Tea made from, or oil extracted from, savin or juniper berries has been reported back to antiquity as an abortifacient, and because of this reputation the planting of the bush was forbidden in several European states from about the end of the eighteenth century.[373] This belief persists today. Historians who note in passing that particular attempts to abort with savin simply failed nonetheless assume that the technique must have been generally reliable.[374] There is, however, surprisingly little evidence to support the notion that savin oil would induce an abortion although self-styled experts on abortion often seem unaware of this fact.[375]

Numerous researchers have studied savin carefully. Edward Shorter reported experiments suggesting that savin oil worked directly on the uterus and was satisfactorily effective,[376] yet even he admitted that "in the medical literature poisoning cases far outweigh those in which the mother suffered no grave side effects."[377] Dr. Frederick Taussig confirmed this with a report of a modern attempt to test savin's efficacy.[378] The drug was administered to 21 women according to a standard medieval recipe, producing 10 abortions. Nine of the 10 "successful" women died, as did four of the "unsuccessful" ones. Similarly, Dr. Louis Lewin, in a survey of the medical literature, found that women had aborted 21 of the 32 times in which savin was ingested, but 13 of the 32 women had died.[379] In the nineteenth century, Rudolf Lex concluded that "when abortion does happen, almost without exception it is tied to the death of the mother."[380] At the end of the seventeenth century, we find four criminal prosecutions for abortion or attempted abortion in the colony of Massachusetts in which the defendants reportedly used savin—and in the three of the four attempts, no abortion resulted.[381] Even Janet Brodie, intent on proving the availability of workable abortifacients and having praised savin as a well-known and well-used abortifacient, went on to describe oil of savin (a concentrated form) as "a dangerous poison."[382]

As medical research proceeded to test the effectiveness of volatile oils as abortifacients, physicians became steadily more skeptical of their claimed utility. For example, in 1865 Dr. Alfred Taylor described pennyroyal as an effective abortifacient, yet the 1905 edition of the same work (edited by Dr. Frederick Smith) concluded that "[i]t has neither emmenagogue nor ecbolic [abortifacient] properties."[383] In one recent episode involving pennyroyal, one of three women who used it in an attempt to abort died, one had to be hospitalized, and only one suffered no serious ill effects—but

---

372. The European variety is *Juniperus sabina;* the American variety is *Juniperus Virginiana. See* Millspaugh, *supra* note 339, pl. 66; Scully, *supra* note 283, at 120; Shorter, *supra* note 87, at 186.

373. Shorter, *supra* note 87, at 186–87.

374. *See, e.g.,* F.G. Emmison, Elizabethan Life: Disorder 41 (1970); Peter Laslett, Bastardy and Its Comparative History 76–77 (1980); Mohr, *supra* note 19, at 9, 71.

375. *See, e.g.,* Potts, Diggory, & Peel, *supra* note 339, at 172.

376. Shorter, *supra* note 87, at 186, *citing* Lucy Prochnow, *Experimentelle Beiträge zur Kenntnis der Wirkung der Volksabortiva,* 12 Archives internationales de pharmacodynamie 317 (1911); Jean Renaux, *À propos de propriétés abortives des essences de rue et de sabine,* 66 Archives internationales de pharmacodynamie 472 (1941).

377. Shorter, *supra* note 87, at 187.

378. Taussig, *supra* note 186, at 353. *See also* André Patoir *et al., Étude expérimentale compararitive de quelques abortifs,* 39 Gynécologie et obstétrique 201, 204–05 (1939).

379. Louis Lewin, Die Fruchtabtreibung durch Gifte und andere Mittel 333–35 (1922). For a graphic description of a savin death in the nineteenth century, see T.R. Forbes, *Early Forensic Medicine in England: The Angus Murder Trial,* 36 J. Hist. Med. 296 (1981). *See also* Gordon, *supra* note 18, at 37; Shorter, *supra* note 87, at 186–88.

380. Rudolf Lex, *Die Abtreibung des Leibesfrucht,* 4 Vierteljahrschrift für gerichtliche und öffentliche Medicin 239–40 (1866), as translated and quoted by Shorter, *supra* note 87, at 187.

381. Thompson, *supra* note 291, at 25–26, 78.

382. Brodie, *supra* note 31, at 42–44. *See also* Mohr, *supra* note 19, at 21–22.

383. *Compare* Alfred Taylor, The Principles and Practice of Medical Jurisprudence 786 (10th ed. 1865), *with* 2 Taylor, *supra* note 163, at 168.

none aborted.[384] Tansy tea was perhaps even more popular in the United States than savin oil despite its extreme toxicity.[385] Rue is also extremely toxic.[386] Only by drastically altering the method and form of administration—say, intra-amniotic injection of a standardized and highly refined extract—can such traditional substances be used with a modicum of safety and with a predictable rate of success, something no one before the late nineteenth century could do. John Riddle, who claims that savin and many other traditional ingestive substances were safe and effective as abortifacients, relies heavily on tests employing just such modern techniques.[387] As Riddle himself noted, "the exact details concerning preparation, amounts, and frequencies are crucial."[388] But then Riddle was not discouraged in describing something as an abortifacient even when modern laboratory tests failed to confirm any such effects.[389] Historian Marvin Olasky has more aptly described recourse to such potions as equivalent to playing Russian roulette with three bullets in the chamber.[390]

The "abortifacients" that were not volatile oils, like ergot, generally were alkaloids.[391] Ergot is a hard, black fungus that grows on various grains, most commonly rye. This made the drug easy to procure, and it was believed since ancient times to work on the uterus, being used to strengthen contractions during labor as well as an abortifacient.[392] Because of its reputed abortifacient properties, in 1778 a Hanoverian law prohibited midwives from using ergot.[393] As an alkaloid, ergot is "oxytocic." Such drugs can induce labor, but these effects seem limited to late in the pregnancy and in any event produce dangerous side effects when taken in quantities sufficient to induce labor significantly earlier than the natural term of the pregnancy.[394] Ironically, modern research indicates that oxytocins provide the hormonal basis of maternal bonding to gestating and newly born infants.[395]

It is hardly an answer to such facts to insist, as herbalist/educator Susan Weed claims, that "women [intuitively] know the difference between taking enough of something to 'poison' themselves and taking enough of something to kill themselves."[396] Yet in an approach all too typical of those searching for the elusive safe and effective abortifacient, Edward Shorter, who credits everything his sources say that is positive about ergot, reports its toxicity as merely a "reputation."[397] He does not indicate why its abortifacient effects should not also be considered merely a reputation. Shorter's attitude towards ergot contrasts sharply with his hesitancy regarding the abortifacient effects of rue.[398] Even here, however, Shorter fully credits reports that rue works directly on the uterus while dropping a report that rue is nearly always fatal to an unnumbered footnote.[399]

---

384. RIDDLE, *supra* note 28, at 54
385. SHORTER, *supra* note 87, at 186.
386. Patoir *et al., supra* note 378, at 201.
387. RIDDLE, *supra* note 28, at 36–38.
388. *Id.* at 45, 83.
389. *Id.* at 104.
390. OLASKY, *supra* note 143, at 29.
391. SHORTER, *supra* note 87, at 183–84.
392. *Id.* at 184.
393. *Id.* The Kings of England were, at this time, the Electors of Hanover.
394. *Id.* at 184. *See also* LOUIS GOODMAN & ALFRED GILMAN, THE PHARMACOLOGICAL BASIS OF THERAPEUTICS 874 (5th ed. 1975); JAMES WHITEHEAD, ON THE CAUSES AND TREATMENT OF ABORTION AND STERILITY 254 (1847); Morgan, *supra* note 324, at 120; O. Vago, *Toxische und kautische Komplikationen durch Begrauch sogenannter fruchtabtreibender,* 170 ZEITSCHRIFT FÜR GEBURTSHILFE UND GYNÄKOLOGIE 273 (1969); Dr. Weihe, *Use of Ergot in Inducing Abortion,* 18 LONDON MED. GAZ. 543 (1836).
395. Natalie Angier, *What Makes a Parent Put Up with It All? The Uxorious Vole Offers a Clue to the Role of Hormones,* N.Y. TIMES, Nov. 2, 1993, at C1, C14.
396. As quoted (including the interpolation) in Fiore, *supra* note 332, at 131.
397. SHORTER, *supra* note 87, at 184.
398. *Id.* at 185 n.*.
399. *Id. See also* MCLAREN, *supra* note 28, at 104.

Historian Jeffrey Weeks, another of those who presumed explicitly (and optimistically) that knowledge of safe and effective abortifacients was widespread over the centuries, also noted that lead poisoning was "epidemic" (at various times) because of the use of the abortifacients.[400] Angus McLaren goes even further. He attempted to prove his belief in the availability of safe and effective abortifacients by quoting from ballads and poems dating back to the early Middle Ages in which the abortion either failed or the woman died![401]

Eventually, if a woman failed to achieve an abortion after ingesting (perhaps repeatedly) one or more intermediately effective potions, a sufficiently desperate woman could ingest (or be made to ingest) a substance that is lethal even in small doses but which is reputed to be an abortifacient. Our records report such "abortifacients" as absinthe (wormwood),[402] aloes,[403] arsenic,[404] artemisia,[405] cantharides ("Spanish fly"),[406] foxglove,[407] hellebore,[408] lupine,[409] mistletoe,[410] nightshade,[411] "ratsbane" (rat poison),[412] seneca snakeroot,[413] snake venom,[414] oil of wintergreen,[415] and various metallic salts (including antimony, copper, iron, lead, mercury, phosphorus, and silver salts).[416] One might add to this list such thoroughly modern substances as

---

400. WEEKS, *supra* note 87, at 72.

401. MCLAREN, *supra* note 28, at 91–93.

402. 2 GORIS & LIOT, *supra* note 296, at 1833; RIDDLE, *supra* note 28, at 47–48, 56, 83, 89–90, 92, 98, 100, 102, 114, 119, 122, 126, 161, 208 n.64.

403. BREVITT, *supra* note 99, at 46; JENNINGS, *supra* note 150, at 78; Ely van de Warker, *The Detection of Criminal Abortion (Pt. III)*, 6 J. GYNECOLOGICAL SOC'Y OF BOSTON 350 (1871). *See also* BATES & ZAWADSKI, *supra* note 186, at 89; BRODIE, *supra* note 31, at 44, 225–26; D'EMILIO & FREEDMAN, *supra* note 80, at 63; HORDERN, *supra* note 218, at 3; MCLAREN, *supra* note 19, at 241; MCLAREN, *supra* note 28, at 103–04, 106; MOHR, *supra* note 19, at 7–10, 12; RIDDLE, *supra* note 28, at 86, 161; SECRET REMEDIES, *supra* note 105, at 192–93, 195–96, 198–200, 204–05; SHORTER, *supra* note 87, at 180; TAUSSIG, *supra* note 186, at 353; Fisher, *supra* note 200, at 6; Klepp, *supra* note 28, at 83–84.

404. SECRET REMEDIES, *supra* note 105, at 206; TAUSSIG, *supra* note 186, at 354.

405. 2 GORIS & LIOT, *supra* note 296, at 1833; RIDDLE, *supra* note 28, at 56, 83, 85–86, 89–90, 92, 98, 103, 114, 122–24, 126, 137, 161; Farnsworth I, *supra* note 269, at 549.

406. BREVITT, *supra* note 99, at 45. *See also* BATES & ZAWADSKI, *supra* note 186, at 89; MOHR, *supra* note 19, at 9; RIDDLE, *supra* note 28, at 71, 76–77; TAUSSIG, *supra* note 186, at 354; Backhouse, *supra* note 16, at 85.

407. BRODIE, *supra* note 31, at 44.

408. BOORDE, *supra* note 27, at lxxxxiii; BREVITT, *supra* note 99, at 46; BUCHAN, *supra* note 217, at 400; GOEURIOT, *supra* note 339, fol. lviii; JOHN WESLEY, PRIMITIVE PHYSICKE 90 (1776). *See also* BATES & ZAWADSKI, *supra* note 186, at 89; BRODIE, *supra* note 31, at 225–26; MCLAREN, *supra* note 28, at 103–04; MOHR, *supra* note 19, at 6, 8–9; RIDDLE, *supra* note 28, at 54–55, 81, 89, 101, 115, 117, 119; SCULLY, *supra* note 283, at 120; Backhouse, *supra* note 16, at 85; Casey, *supra* note 272, at 593; Klepp, *supra* note 28, at 84, 86. Apparently, hellebore could produce sterility for life.

409. RIDDLE, *supra* note 28, at 47, 56, 85, 92, 98, 129, 131. Lupine is a bean that is poisonous if not properly prepared.

410. BRODIE, *supra* note 31, at 44.

411. *Id.*

412. See, e.g., Regina v. Webb (Q.B. 1602), CALENDAR OF ASSIZE REC., SURREY INDICTMENTS, ELIZ. I, at 512 (no. 3146) (J. Cockburn ed. 1980). *See also* BROOKES, *supra* note 30, at 117.

413. JOHN BIDDLE, MATERIA MEDICA FOR THE USE OF STUDENTS 257 (4th ed. 1871). *See also* BRODIE, *supra* note 31, at 44; Klepp, *supra* note 28, at 85–87.

414. BATES & ZAWADSKI, *supra* note 186, at 90; TAUSSIG, *supra* note 186, at 355.

415. Fisher, *supra* note 200, at 6.

416. BATES & ZAWADSKI, *supra* note 186, at 15, 89–90; BROOKES, *supra* note 30, at 4–5, 117, 119; HANLEY & YAMAMURA, *supra* note 154, at 233; HORDERN, *supra* note 218, at 3; KENNY, *supra* note 114, at 185–86; MCLAREN, *supra* note 28, at 103; RIDDLE, *supra* note 28, at 74–77, 80–81, 102; MARY WALKER STANDLEE, THE GREAT PULSE: JAPANESE MIDWIFERY AND OBSTETRICS THROUGH THE AGES 155 (1959); TAUSSIG, *supra* note 186, at 31, 354–55; Devereux, *supra* note 192, at 130; Fisher, *supra* note 200, at 6–7; Klepp, *supra* note 28, at 84, 92.

benzene, formaldehyde, kerosene, Lysol, and an antiseptic sold under the brand name "Ultra-Jel."[417] In fact, the British Medical Association found in 1912 that nearly all advertised pills for "obstructed menses" also included iron salts although these salts seem not to have had "any active effect."[418] Still, belief in their efficacy persisted over centuries.[419]

As the list of inherently dangerous substances used as abortifacients suggests, many modern poisons were discovered through the search for a safe dosage of abortifacients.[420] Indeed, the Latin *medicamenta* can be translated as "drug," "medicine," or "remedy," but also as "poison," "cosmetic," or "dye."[421] This is not simply a characteristic of ancient medicine. The first (1899) *Merck's Manual of the Materia Medica*—described as "a ready-reference pocket book for the practicing physician"—recommended that men take arsenic orally as a cure for baldness, that people be made to inhale formaldehyde for the common cold, that doctors rub an iodine-turpentine mixture into the skin for tubercular meningitis, and that people take strychnine as a cure for diptheria.[422] People at the time knew the dangers; what they didn't know was that all of these recommendations are useless at best.

The dangers of "abortifacient potions" certainly were not a secret in centuries past. The dangers were so well known that in early English slang the term "poisoned" meant pregnant.[423] And at least in Connecticut, a slang term for trashy merchandise and bad medicines ("the trade") was apparently used to signify abortifacients.[424] Consider particularly those metallic salts. Copper and mercury might have been effective occasionally, producing an abortion by poisoning the mother's kidneys and intestines; mercury was frequently used as a treatment for many diseases, and undoubtedly killed often.[425] Lead poisoning causes death or blindness, while phosphorus might also some times cause an abortion, but it always produces jaundice (and occasionally death) as it poisons the mother's liver.[426]

The inefficacy or risk (or both) of the potions used in ingestion techniques—whether deadly only when taken in large dosages or deadly even in minuscule quantities—were well-known in the seventeenth century.[427] Pharmacologist John Pechey, writing in 1707, could note that a reputed abortifacient worked because it would "purge violently, upwards and downwards."[428] In 1782, another pharmacologist noted that "they weaken nature, nor shall ever advise them to be used, unless upon urgent necessity."[429] As the usages of eighteenth-century English slang suggests,[430] the dangers of ingestion techniques were well known to the public, and not just to erudite physicians. Even earlier, medieval ballads were full of tales of failed, and fatal, attempted

---

417. Fisher, *supra* note 200, at 6–7.

418. SECRET REMEDIES, *supra* note 105, at 192–206. *See also* McLAREN, *supra* note 28, at 106; MOHR, *supra* note 19, at 6, 12.

419. *See* P.S. Brown, *Female Pills and the Reputation of Iron as an Abortifacient*, 21 MEDICAL HIST. 291 (1977).

420. BATES & ZAWADSKI, *supra* note 186, at 88.

421. Scarborough, *supra* note 335, at 39.

422. Abigail Zuger, *Take Some Strychnine and Call Me in the Morning*, N.Y. TIMES, Apr. 20, 1999, at F1.

423. FRANCIS GROSE, A CLASSICAL DICTIONARY OF THE VULGAR TONGUE (1785); McLAREN, *supra* note 28, at 92–94, 102.

424. Dayton, *supra* note 42, at 24.

425. ERWIN ACKERKNECHT, THERAPEUTICS: FROM THE PRIMITIVES TO THE 20TH CENTURY 81 (1973); ULRICH, THE MIDWIFE'S TALE, *supra* note 9, at 56.

426. INTERDEPARTMENTAL COMMITTEE, *supra* note 225, at 42; McLAREN, *supra* note 19, at 241–42, 248; SHORTER, *supra* note 87, at 211–13.

427. QUAIFE, *supra* note 87, at 118, 120.

428. PECHEY, *supra* note 319, at 13.

429. 1 COMPLEAT HERBAL, *supra* note 298, at 69–71. *See also* INTERDEPARTMENTAL COMMITTEE, *supra* note 225, at 42, and the sources collected *supra* in note 200.

430. *See* GROSE, *supra* note 423.

abortions.[431] Finally, American courts in nineteenth century were well aware of the limited effectiveness of such "potions" unless taken in doses dangerous to the health or the life of the mother.[432] A New Jersey court went so far as to declare in 1881 that abortion "in almost every case endangers the life and health of the woman."[433] Well into the twentieth century, folk remedies intended to bring on an abortion remained dangerous.[434]

Despite the foregoing evidence, one cannot entirely rule out the possibility that a safe and effective drug escaped notice in the legal, medical, and popular literature of the day, unlikely as it may be. Such a belief is implicit in the widespread assumption that safe and effective means existed prior to the nineteenth century. Yet neither do the Arabic medical texts which were standard medical references of the later middle ages describe anything better,[435] nor do later works in English add anything significant.[436] Indeed, the same drugs appear as reputed abortifacients in folk cultures thousands of miles apart with little likelihood of contact among the practitioners of folk medicine before the recipes were first recorded.[437] These and other texts also describe abortifacient effects in language markedly different from their descriptions of other pharmacological effects. Such effects are always introduced with phrases such as "it is said" or warnings against using a medication on pregnant women for fear of inadvertently aborting her, but almost never as a recommendation of abortion as such.[438] Such phrases suggest either uncertainty about the efficacy of the potion or unwillingness to be thought to favor the practice.[439]

Given the general slow rate of inventiveness of pre-scientific societies, the lack of significant variation in reported abortion techniques over at least six centuries in England and America, and for longer periods globally, is hardly a surprise.[440] Indeed, reports persisted of the continuance of these older folk traditions well into the twentieth century in the more remote parts of Europe.[441] On the basis of such unproved folk beliefs, Edward Shorter was left

---

431. McLaren, *supra* note 28, at 91–93.

432. *See, e.g.,* Commonwealth v. W.M.W., 3 Pitts. Rep. 462 (1871); Moore v. State, 40 S.W. 287 (Tex Crim. 1897). *See also* Secret Remedies, *supra* note 105, at 185.

433. State v. Gedicke, 43 N.J.L. 86, 96 (1881).

434. Interdepartmental Committee, *supra* note 225, at 42.

435. Avicenna, *Libri Canonis Medicinae* (Gerard of Cremona trans. printed 1595; Gerard's translation dates from ca. 1150); Rhazes, *Liber ad Almansorem* ¶ 5.73, at 140 (Gerard of Cremona trans. printed 1497; Gerard's translation dates from ca. 1150). Avicenna is the Latin name for the Arab physician Ibn Sina; his book, written in the middle of the tenth century, became the standard medical text throughout Europe from the middle of the twelfth century to the middle of the seventeenth century. Himes, *supra* note 206, at 141; Riddle, *supra* note 28, at 128, 133, 145, 149; Tannahill, *supra* note 18, at 243 n*; A.D. Farr, *The Marquis de Sade and Induced Abortion,* 6 J. Med. Ethics 7, 7 (1980). *See generally* Nancy Siraisi, Avicenna in Renaissance Italy: The Canon and Medical Training in Italian Universities after 1500 (1987); Himes, *supra* note 206, at 139–51. On the influence of Arab texts on European medicine in the high Middle Ages, see Helen Rodnite Lemay, *Human Sexuality in Twelfth- through Fifteenth-Century Scientific Writings,* in Sexual Practices and the Medieval Church 187, 187–92 (Vern Bullough & James Brundage eds. 1982).

436. 1 Compleat Herbal, *supra* note 298, at 69–71, 94–95; Daniel Dafoe, A Treatise Concerning the Use and Abuse of the Marriage Bed 152–55 (1727); Etmullerus, *supra* note 268, at 563; Pechey, *supra* note 319, at 13. *See also* Levin, *supra* note 261, at 177.

437. Yun Cheung Kong, *Potential Anti-Fertility Plants from Chinese Medicine,* 4 Am. J. Chinese Med. 105 (1976); R. Moreno & B. Schvartzman, *268 plantas medicinales utilizadas para regular la fecundidad en algunos paises de Sudamérica,* 2 Reproducción 163 (1975); Saha *et al., supra* note 344, at 130. *See generally* Devereux, *supra* note 28; Shorter, *supra* note 87, at 183.

438. *See, e.g.,* Guilielmus de Saliceto, *Summa Conservationis et Curationis* f. 13vb. (Venice 1489); Brevitt, *supra* note 99, at 117. *See also* Riddle, *supra* note 28, at 120–22, 148, 154–57, 160.

439. *See also* McLaren, *supra* note 28, at 102–04, 123; Noonan, *supra* note 261, at 201–07, 217.

440. Devereux, *supra* note 28, at 28.

441. 1 Anderson & Zinsser, *supra* note 30, at 137; St. Erlich, *supra* note 87, at 257, 295. *See also* Gordon, *supra* note 18, at 35–36; Petchesky, *supra* note 28, at 49–55.

rather lamely to conclude that, as these substances were reputed to be abortifacients for centuries, they "must have some efficacy."[442] Shorter acknowledged, however, that the British Interdepartmental Committee on Abortion found as late as 1939 that although the oral administration of a drug was the most commonly attempted means for aborting, in fact the commonly-used drugs were "successful only to a very limited extent."[443] Pro-choice historian Connie Paige was reduced to concluding that abortifacient potions were effective at a rate of "7 to 14 percent," which, as even she conceded, correlated "with the normal rate of spontaneous miscarriage."[444] As historian Carl Djerassi noted, belief in the efficacy of ingestion techniques are naïve in the extreme.[445]

Closely related to the ingestion practices already described are the use of douches and pessaries. A douche is the washing of the vaginal canal.[446] Often the "solution" used to wash the canal was merely soapy water, although substances as strong as lye were sometimes used.[447] Other popular ingredients included boiling water, brandy, brine, vinegar, and wine.[448] By the twentieth century, we find women douching with detergents, orange juice, and even Coca Cola.[449]

As an abortifacient, douches seem mostly to have represented another form of sympathetic magic expressing the hope of cleansing the womb of the pregnancy. One-hundred-fifty years ago, Eugene Becklard advised that merely douching with cold water could bring on an abortion, yet he also advised that douching with cold water could prevent an abortion.[450] Only if the douching substance was actually injected into the womb was an abortion likely, and that was highly dangerous; if an abortion did result, it was likely to have been from the dangerous pharmacological substances contained in the douche as from the act of douching itself.[451] Douches were also used as contraceptives, to wash out the sperm from the vaginal canal.[452] Lacking an effective spermicide, however, douches can hardly have been effective in this role, and might (by increasing the fluid available to the sperm to swim in) actually have increased the risk of pregnancy.[453]

A pessary is a vaginal suppository laced with the same sort of abortifacient drugs as in oral ingestion techniques.[454] The reported "drugs" included, among others, iris root, sowbread root,

---

442. SHORTER, *supra* note 87, at 186.

443. INTERDEPARTMENTAL COMMITTEE, *supra* note 225, at 41. *See* SHORTER, *supra* note 87, at 209; TAUSSIG, *supra* note 186, at 386–87.

444. PAIGE, *supra* note 93, at 33.

445. Djerassi, *supra* note 261, at 143.

446. EWELL, *supra* note 227, at 74–76.

447. BRODIE, *supra* note 31, at 31, 69; HADLEY, *supra* note 80, at 36–37; HORDERN, *supra* note 218, at 3; PETCHESKY, *supra* note 28, at 51; REAGAN, *supra* note 16, at 208–09.

448. EWELL, *supra* note 227, at 74–76. *See also* MOHR, *supra* note 19, at 10–11; REAGAN, *supra* note 16, at 26, 75; MARTHA WARD, POOR WOMEN, POWERFUL MEN: AMERICA'S GREAT EXPERIMENT IN FAMILY PLANNING 14 (1986); Lewis, *supra* note 216, at 944; Ross, *supra* note 87, at 175.

449. WARD, *supra* note 448, at 14.

450. EUGENE BECKLARD, PHYSIOLOGICAL MYSTERIES AND REVELATIONS IN LOVE, COURTSHIP, AND MARRIAGE 35–45 (1845). Even Janet Brodie was compelled to admit that Becklard's book was "a jumbled mixture of superstition, ancient folklore, and plagiarized ideas." BRODIE, *supra* note 31, at 69. Brodie, by the way, mentioned one manufacturer of douching syringes that provided interchangeable nozzles so the syringe could also be used to water house plants. BRODIE, *supra*, at 70.

451. *See, e.g.,* J.C. Gleason, *A Medico-Legal Case of Abortion Followed by Conviction of the Accused Abortionist*, 101 BOS. MED. & SURGICAL J. 185 (1879). *See generally* BRODIE, *supra* note 31, at 69–70; MOHR, *supra* note 19, at 10–11.

452. BRODIE, *supra* note 31, at 58, 67–79; DEGLER, *supra* note 18, at 215–16; GORDON, *supra* note 18, at 42, 64–66; GUTMAN, *supra* note 221, at 81; JAMES REED, FROM PRIVATE VICE TO PUBLIC VIRTUE: THE BIRTH CONTROL MOVEMENT AND AMERICAN SOCIETY SINCE 1830, at 10 (1978).

453. DEGLER, *supra* note 18, at 227.

454. LEONARD SOWERBY, THE LADIES DISPENSATORY 158–61 (1651).

and unwashed wool.[455] John Riddle, of course, finds that "suppositories" (as he calls pessaries) must have worked safely and effectively as they were so widely reported.[456] Even Angus McLaren, who also was willing to credit almost any report of ancient abortifacients, eventually conceded that how pessaries might work "is not always clear."[457] Like douches, most pessaries seem not to have been effective as abortifacients[458]—at least if there were no intrusion into a woman's cervix, in which case the intrusion was the probable cause of the abortion regardless of any drug that might have been used.[459] Such an insertion would open a pathway for infection into the uterus.[460] The invention of a technique involving insertion of a pessary into the uterus as late as the seventeenth century made one Japanese abortionist famous, although he cautioned that if the pessary, upon insertion into the uterus, were to puncture the amniotic sac it could prove fatal.[461] The use of mercury as a principle ingredient in Japanese pessaries must have made them deadly even without penetration into the uterus.[462]

The few pessaries that might have been effective without penetration were, like other ingestible abortifacients, highly dangerous for the woman.[463] The general ineffectiveness of pessaries did not prevent doctors from swearing a Hippocratic Oath not to administer them, at least until the oath was amended after *Roe v. Wade*.[464] Even as contraceptives, however, pessaries had limited success.[465] After all, even in 1966 a study found that modern contraceptive sponges, laced with effective spermicides, could be expected to produce 28 to 35 pregnancies per 100 woman-years of use (i.e., if 100 women used these for one year, approximately 1/3 of them would be pregnant).[466]

# Intrusion Techniques

*The danger that an abortion always poses a mother, independent of this love for her children which nature always inspires, will make this a rare crime.*

— J.P. Brissot de Warville[467]

---

455. McLaren, *supra* note 28, at 101–02.

456. Riddle, *supra* note 28, at 25–26, 32, 69–72, 76–77, 80–82, 98–100, 120, 144–45, 148.

457. McLaren, *supra* note 28, at 102. This has not stopped McLaren in other articles from endorsing the efficacy of pessaries without bothering to explain how they were effective. *See, e.g.,* Angus McLaren, *Birth Control and Abortion in Canada, 1870–1920,* 59 Can. Hist. Rev. 319, 326 (1978).

458. McLaren, *supra* note 28, at 101–02; Devereux, *supra* note 28, at 37; Secret Remedies, *supra* note 105, at 202–03; Taussig, *supra* note 186, at 355–56; Devereux, *supra* note 192, at 129; Fisher, *supra* note 200, at 7.

459. Bates & Zawadski, *supra* note 186, at 21–22, 85–87; Devereux, *supra* note 28, at 36, 42–43, 129; Himes, *supra* note 206, at 179; Taussig, *supra* note 186, at 219–20; Fisher, *supra* note 200, at 8.

460. Potts, Diggory, & Peel, *supra* note 339, at 181.

461. Standlee, *supra* note 416, at 154.

462. Hanley & Yamamura, *supra* note 154, at 233; William LaFleur, Liquid Life: Abortion and Buddhism in Japan 113 (1992); Lynn Wardle, *"Crying Stones": A Comparison of Abortion in Japan and the United States,* 14 N.Y.L.S. J. Int'l & Comp. L. 183, 188 (1993).

463. Riddle, *supra* note 28, at 36–37, 66–69.

464. Castiglioni, *supra* note 211, at 148.

465. Charles Knowlton, The Fruits of Philosophy 59–60 (1832); Marie Kopp, Birth Control in Practice: An Analysis of 10,000 Case Histories 133 (1934). *See also* Brodie, *supra* note 31, at 212–24; Gordon, *supra* note 18, at 42–43, 67–68; Himes, *supra* note 206, at 100; Riddle, *supra* note 28, at 7, 25–26, 35–38; Keith Hopkins, *Contraception in the Roman Empire,* 8 Comp. Stud. in Soc'y & Hist. 135 (1965).

466. Brodie, *supra* note 31, at 215.

467. J.P. Brissot de Warville, *Les moyens d'adoucir la rigeur des lois penales en France* 108 (1793).

Singularly missing from European legal, medical, and popular literature before the eighteenth century is any mention of techniques involving the successful intrusion of an object or instrument through the cervix into the uterus to induce abortion (intrusion techniques).[468] Certain pro-abortion activists make great claims about the availability of intrusion techniques in ancient times.[469] They lump them together with techniques ranging from hot baths to physically injury, and are likely to have been as effective and as dangerous.[470] Dr. Alan Guttmacher, a leader in the early abortion legalization movement, did report descriptions of the necessary instruments for dilation and curettage from Greek times and alleged that such instruments were found in Pompeii, although his conclusion as to their use is be based more on surmise than on any actual record.[471] Even Guttmacher admitted that all evidence of such possibilities disappeared with the rise of Christianity, which he concedes could reflect a "retrogression in medicine during the Middle Ages" as much as a change mores. Norman Himes, an advocate of abortion reform from the 1930s, described an intrusion technique from medieval Persia—a thousand or more years after Pompeii.[472] There also appears to be some evidence of intrusive abortions in Japan back to the late seventeenth century.[473] Whether such techniques were any more refined, effective, and safe than early intrusive abortions in Europe and America is not clear.

The scant evidence hardly supports a firm conclusion that intrusion techniques were widely known or used. Furthermore, the ancients themselves tell us that they knew little or nothing about intrusion techniques. Soranus, the leading gynecologist of the Roman Empire with whom we are familiar, was active early in the second century the Common Era. He wrote extensively about what were believed to be ingestive abortifacients, making careful recommendations about their use.[474] Yet about intrusive abortions he wrote only that "one must, however, beware of things that are too powerful and of separating the embryo by means of something sharp-edged, for danger arises that some of the adjacent parts be wounded."[475] The Japanese writers, from more than a thousand years later and at a time when intrusive abortions were apparently well-known, continued to lament that abortion was considerably more dangerous than childbirth.[476] As a result, infanticide remained far more common than abortion in Japan well into the twentieth century.[477]

The underlying reason intrusive abortions were both rare and dangerous was the remarkably primitive knowledge of women's reproductive anatomy prevalent until quite recently. Anthropologist Georges Devereux reported that people in at least one culture attempted abortions through manipulation of the breasts because that is where the fetus was located early in pregnancy.[478] We

---

468. Bates & Zawadski, *supra* note 186, at 21–22, 85–87; Devereux, *supra* note 28, at 36, 42–43; Shorter, *supra* note 87, at 189; Taussig, *supra* note 186, at 43, 355; Breitenecker & Breitenecker, *supra* note 186, at 219–20.

469. *See, e.g.,* Gordon, *supra* note 18, at 37–38; Paige, *supra* note 93, at 33.

470. Grisez, *supra* note 87, at 149.

471. Alan Guttmacher, *The Shrinking Non-Psychiatric Indications for Therapeutic Abortion,* in Therapeutic Abortion, *supra* note 188, at 12, 13.

472. Himes, *supra* note 206, at 138

473. Standlee, *supra* note 416, at 111; Wardle, *supra* note 462, at 187–89; Hiromi Maruyama, *Abortion in Japan: A Feminist Critique,* 10 Wis. Women's L.J. 131, 132 (1995). The earliest book to describe this method was published in 1692. Hanley & Yamamura, *supra* note 154, at 233.

474. Soranus, *supra* note 217, ¶¶ 1.63–1.65, at 65–68.

475. *Id.* at ¶ 1.65, at 68. *See also* St. Augustine, *Enchiridion* ¶ 86; Celsus, *De Medicina* ¶ 7.29; Tertullian, *De Anima* ¶ 25 (T.R. Glove trans. 1966). *See generally* Gormon, *supra* note 87, at 17–18.

476. Standlee, *supra* note 416, at 101.

477. Maruyama, *supra* note 473, at 132. *See also* Hanley & Yamamura, *supra* note 154, at 233; George De Vos & Hiroshi Wagatsuma, *Status and Role Behavior in Changing Japan,* in Sex Roles in Changing Society 334, 350 (Georgene Seward & Robert Williamson eds. 1970); Wardle, *supra* note 462, at 187.

478. Devereux, *supra* note 192, at 126.

have already noted the folkloric traditions relating to the functioning of the uterus that could only have compounded the dangers of attempting an intrusive abortion.[479] With the continuing profound ignorance of the female reproductive anatomy, intrusive intervention can rarely have been safe for the mother, let alone accomplished with acceptable levels of pain. Indeed, Soranus and the Japanese indicated that intrusion abortions were inordinately painful and dangerous.[480]

Physicians, with their limited experience with vaginal procedures before taking over birthing from midwives during the nineteenth century, probably would have done even more poorly than "nonprofessional" abortionists.[481] We do have some evidence suggestive of this outcome in that the medicalization of birth did increase the rates of complications and of infant mortality in the nineteenth century.[482] Even in 1973, when a fair number of obstetricians/gynecologists began to perform abortions on a regular basis for the first time in their career, they discovered to their chagrin that complication rates were "uncomfortably high" until they gained considerable experience with the procedure.[483]

If a skilled abortionist could be found to undertake an intrusion procedure, the mother would find that the procedure had opened a "broad highway" for infection into her uterus.[484] Lacking any notion of sanitary precautions, adequate means to kill pain (with a resulting likelihood of shock), and knowledge of how to prevent or cure infections, the procedures, whether performed by a physician or a midwife, would likely have been as painful and as deadly as injury techniques.[485] Before 1880, physicians were rarely called upon to treat incomplete abortions or "septic abortions" (abortions requiring medical attention because of resulting infection), which is strong and direct evidence of the rarity of intrusion techniques before that time.[486] In the face of such evidence, Edward Shorter, who assumed that abortions were readily available throughout the Middle Ages, has conceded that instrumental abortions were not a realistic possibility before the nineteenth century.[487] Historian Linda Gordon, on the other had, insisted that intrusion techniques have an ancient lineage, but she was reduced to asking her readers to disregard part of the long description of an Eskimo intrusion technique which she quoted when the informant told us that the purpose was to puncture the uterus.[488]

---

479. See the text *supra* at notes 167–79.

480. See the text *supra* at notes 474–77. On the difficulties in intrusive abortions generally, see Harrison, *supra* note 30, at 167; Fisher, *supra* 200, at 8–10. On the prevalence of ingestive abortions and rarity of intrusive abortions, see Riddle, *supra* note 28, at 64.

481. Reagan, *supra* note 16, at 77–79; Calvin Schmid, Social Saga of Two Cities: An Ecological and Statistical Study of Social Trends in Minneapolis and St. Paul 410–11 (1937); Shorter, *supra* note 87, at 190, 207–08; Smith-Rosenberg, *supra* note 30, at 234; Taussig, *supra* note 186, at 225–26. For an account of the difficulties an experienced surgeon had in inducing a therapeutic abortion at the end of the third trimester of pregnancy in 1849, see Henry Oldham, *Clinical Lecture on the Induction of Abortion in a Case of Contracted Vagina from Cicaterization*, 9 (N.S.) London Med. Gaz. 45 (1849). For nineteenth-century statements to the effect that intrusive abortions were highly dangerous, see Storer, *supra* note 157, at 43, 45–47; H. Gibbons, sr., *On Foeticide*, 21 Pac. Med. & Surgical J. 97, 111 (1878). Horatio Storer reported one study that found that 22 of 34 intrusive abortions resulted in maternal death. Storer, *supra*, at 47.

482. Ulrich, The Midwife's Tale, *supra* note 9, at 171–72.

483. Warren Hern, Abortion Practice 104 (2nd ed. 1990).

484. Bates & Zawadski, *supra* note 186, at 85–87; Fisher, *supra* note 200, at 9.

485. Storer, *supra* note 157, at 44–48, 54, 58; Devereux, *supra* note 192, at 127–29; Means II, *supra* note 59, at 382–92. Recall here the hope that midwives would remove their rings before assisting at a birth, quoted *supra* at note 12. See Hunt, *supra* note 11, at 86.

486. Shorter, *supra* note 87, at 191–96.

487. *Id.* at 188–91. *See also* Devereux, *supra* note 28, at 28, 36–37; Jacques Guillemeau, The Nursing of Children 7, 85 (1612); Jane Sharp, The Midwives Book 38 (1671).

488. Gordon, *supra* note 18, at 37–38. *See also* Aptheker, *supra* note 188, at 142–43; Devereux, *supra* note 192, at 128.

The closest one finds to intrusion techniques in records from before 1700 are occasional mentions of the "douches" and "pessaries" already discussed in connection with ingestion techniques.[489] The earliest actual record of an intrusion abortion in Europe now known was reported in Diderot's *Encyclopedie* as having been performed in Nuremberg in 1714.[490] The author, noted French naturalist Philippe-Laurent de Joubert, considered the procedure to have been a true medical oddity.[491] The curette, which would become the tool of choice for intrusive abortions, apparently was invented in France in 1723,[492] although possibly it was kept as as trade secret for some years before then. These developments followed the first reported use of intrusion techniques in Japan by only 20 to 30 years.[493]

The historical record in England and America is equally devoid of any evidence of intrusive abortions before the early eighteenth century. Thus, Daniel Defoe, satirizing the "abuse of the marriage bed" in 1727, listed abortion techniques in use without any mention of intrusive techniques: "Drugs and Physicians whether Astringents, Diureticks, Emeticks, or of whatever kind, nay even to Purgations, Potions, Poisons, or any thing that Apothecaries can supply....Devil Spells, Filtres, Charms, Witchcraft,..."[494] The first record of a true intrusion abortion in England or America is from an informally published report of a prosecution in England in 1732.[495] The judge and the prosecutors appear shocked at the novelty of the procedure.

The lateness of these developments should not surprise us. Anthropologist Georges Devereux remarked on how uncharacteristic "true inventiveness" was regarding abortion among medically primitive peoples.[496] Various prevalent beliefs effectively barred experimentation with intrusion techniques. One belief in particular—that upon becoming pregnant a woman's cervix would close so tightly that not even the sharpest needle could penetrate to the uterus except with "much violence" seems to have persisted over many centuries.[497] Other beliefs that might have impeded research into intrusion techniques were the the long prevalent notion that abortifacient drugs were really "emmenagogues," means of bringing on a merely delayed menstruation, and the widespread belief that the uterus was a living being capable of moving about a woman's body and thus of "attacking" her if it were "attacked."[498]

The belief in the impenetrability of the cervix might reflect knowledge of the mucous plug that forms in the cervix during pregnancy and which requires considerable surgical skill to overcome without injury to the mother.[499] Furthermore, abortionists seeking to use intrusive devises had to operative blindly, by touch, inside a fairly inaccessible and vulnerable organ

---

489. See the text *supra* at notes 447–67.

490. Philippe-Laurent de Joubert, *Fausse couche*, in 6 Encyclopédie 452 (Denis Diderot ed. 1766).

491. *See* Shorter, supra note 87, at 191.

492. Potts, Diggory, & Peel, *supra* note 339, at 180.

493. Hanley & Yamamura, *supra* note 154, at 233; Standlee, *supra* note 416, at 111; Wardle, *supra* note 462, at 187–89.

494. Dafoe, *supra* note 436, at 152.

495. Rex v. Beare, 2 The Gentleman's Magazine 931 (Aug. 1732). The case is discussed in Chapter 5, at notes 27–32.

496. Devereux, *supra* note 192, at 121–23.

497. Bartholinus' Anatomy 72 (Nicholas Culpeper & Abdiah Cole trans. 1668); Nicholas Culpeper, A Directory for Midwives pt. I, at 26 (2nd ed. 1675); Helkish Crooke, Μικpoκoεμoτpαiα: A Description of the Body of Man 262 (2nd ed. 1631); Guillemeau, *supra* note 487, at 7, 85; Francis Mauriceau, The Accomplisht Midwife 23 (Hugh Chamberlin trans. 1672); Thomas Raynolde, The Birth of Mankynde, Otherwyse Named the Womans Book bk. 1, ch. 6, fol. 11, bk. 2, ch. 2, fol. 55, & bk. 4, ch. 4, fol. 124 (2nd ed. 1565); Sharp, *supra* note 487, at 38. *See also* Eccles, *supra* note 87, at 28.

498. See the text *supra* at notes 141–73.

499. *See, e.g.,* Potts, Diggory, & Peel, *supra* note 339, at 179; Taylor's Manual of Medical Jurisprudence 515 (Clark Bell ed., 11th Am. ed. 1892). *See also* James Scanlon, Albert the Great: Man and the Beast: "De Animalibus" (Books 22–26) 62 n.5.3 (47 Medieval & Renaissance Stud. 1987).

that the abortionist might never have examined anatomically.[500] Apparently that level of skill simply did not emerge for a long time, not until the beginning of the eighteenth century Europe according to Joubert and also according to the legal evidence from that time. Prosecutions for intrusive abortions were never challenged as not being crimes, but they remained notably more rare than for injurious or ingestive abortions until the nineteenth century.[501] By the nineteenth century, however, we find doctors lecturing on the possibility of surgical abortions.[502]

Once a corps of abortionists experienced in intrusion techniques was created, the procedure might well have been less dangerous and less painful for the mother than either injury or ingestion techniques. The development of intrusion techniques was the first recorded significant technological change affecting abortions, but remained highly dangerous.[503] At first, intrusive abortions were almost as dangerous as injurious or ingestive abortions. In addition to being performed without analgesics, antiseptics, anesthetics, or antibiotics, for many years lack of skill resulted in the frequent puncturing of the uterine wall—as was especially likely through the use of rigid probes, as appears to have been common for at least the first century or so of the procedure.[504] Another complication could arise if an inexperienced abortionist erroneously sought to evacuate the contents of the bladder rather than of the uterus.[505] Then, if an object were successfully inserted into the uterus, the object, as already noted, served as a highway for deadly infection, and the pain of the procedure induced life-threatening shock.[506] Intrusive abortions could be expected to kill one-third or more of the women undergoing them early in the 19th century.[507] The gradual refinement of the technique, which apparently took place among midwives and other "irregular" abortionists long before allopathic physicians developed suitable skills,[508] made the procedure steadily safer and more certain until intrusion techniques became the technique of choice.

Medical evidence for intrusive abortions remained sparse until the later nineteenth century.[509] As a contemporary observer noted, "[t]he danger that an abortion always poses a mother, independent of this love for her children which nature always inspires, will make this a rare crime...."[510] James Mohr, intent on proving the prevalence of intrusive abortions in the nineteenth century, could find only a single contemporary source—a statement by Heber Kimball—that claimed that physicians commonly performed such abortions.[511] Even Mohr, however, did not credit Kimball as a reliable source, although one must read carefully to realize this. Mohr

---

500. POTTS, DIGGORY, & PEEL, *supra* note 339, at 179.

501. *See* Chapter 5.

502. HARVEY GRAHAM, ETERNAL EVE: THE HISTORY OF GYNAECOLOGY AND OBSTETRICS 356–66 (1951).

503. M.K. HARD, WOMAN'S MEDICAL GUIDE: BEING A COMPLETE REVIEW OF THE PECULIARITIES OF THE FEMALE CONSTITUTION AND THE DERANGEMENTS TO WHICH IT IS SUBJECT, WITH A DESCRIPTION OF SIMPLE YET CERTAIN MEANS FOR THEIR CURE 3–4, 34, 38, 90 (1848). *See also* BATES & ZAWADSKI, *supra* note 186, at 85–87; KEOWN, *supra* note 64, at 35–38, 59–78; MOHR, *supra* note 19, at 25–30; SMITH-ROSENBERG, *supra* note 30, at 219–20; DAVID WALBERT & J. DOUGLAS BUTLER, ABORTION, SOCIETY AND THE LAW 327–28 (1973); Dellapenna, *supra* note 64, at 393–95, 406–07, 411–17; Zad Leavy & Jerome Kummer, *Criminal Abortion: Human Hardship and Unyielding Laws*, 35 S. CAL. L. REV. 123 (1962); Means I, *supra* note 59; Means II, *supra* note 59, at 382–401.

504. BATES & ZAWADSKI, *supra* note 186, at 87; D'EMILIO & FREEDMAN, *supra* note 80, at 63; INTERDEPARTMENTAL COMMITTEE, *supra* note 225, at 41; MILBAUER & OBRENTZ, *supra* note 80, at 128–29; TAUSSIG, *supra* note 186, at 231.

505. BATES & ZAWADSKI, *supra* note 186, at 87.

506. *Id.,* at 85–87.

507. Dellapenna, *supra* note 64, at 400, 412.

508. SHORTER, *supra* note 87, at 190, 207–08.

509. *Id.,* at 191–96.

510. BRISSOT DE WARVILLE, *supra* note 467, at 108.

511. MOHR, *supra* note 19, at 16.

buried in a remote endnote his reservations based on the fact that Kimball, a Mormon perse-cuted for polygamy, was intent on demonstrating the immorality of the traditional culture and could possibly have indulged in libel to accomplish his aim.[512] That Mohr nonetheless quotes Kimball in the text as the only direct authority on intrusive abortions by trained physicians sug-gests how sparse such evidence is.

Mohr's cavalier attitude towards evidence becomes even more obvious when one discovers that, notwithstanding Kimball's statement, Mohr noted that abortionists doubled as sellers of cadavers for "secret midnight lectures on secret surgical cliniques."[513] But then, Mohr had al-ready observed that some of the intrusion techniques that he reports in glowing terms would not have worked without the aid of an "emmenagogue"[514]—in other words, the ingestion of a drug that Mohr has already noted would itself be highly dangerous.[515] Yet the enduring search for a safe and effective intrusion technique is the best evidence we have of the ineffec-tiveness (or unsafety) of the injury and ingestion techniques that were more commonly re-ported in prior centuries. Given the rather grim reality, one can understand why Irish femi-nist Mary Kenny could write that before the nineteenth century, "[t]he traditional forms of abortion had been infanticide and abandonment."[516] But this thought leads us to the next chapter.

---

512. *Id.* at 268–69 n.31. Edward Shorter considered Mohr's confidence in the early availability of intrusion techniques to have been a result of "naïveté." SHORTER, *supra* note 87, at 191 n.*.

513. MOHR, *supra* note 19, at 125. The quotation is from 1 NATIONAL POLICE GAZETTE 220 (Feb. 28, 1846). *See also* 1 NATIONAL POLICE GAZETTE 284–85 (Apr. 25, 1846), 291–93 (May 2, 1846). Mohr tells us the bodies "went for about $20 apiece if you bagged them and delivered them yourself," but only $12 if the cus-tomer had to provide those services. MOHR, *supra*, at 291 n.22.

514. MOHR, *supra* note 19, at 61.

515. *Id.* at 21–22, 55–58.

516. KENNY, *supra* note 114, at 181. *See also* L.A. PARRY, CRIMINAL ABORTION 35–36 (1932); Gavigan, *supra* note 151, at 24; William Ian Miller, *Of Outlaws, Christians, Horsemeat, and Writing: Uniform Laws and Saga Iceland,* 89 MICH. L. REV. 2081, 2086 (1991).

# Chapter 2

# Dead Babies Can Take Care of Themselves[1]

*Even the most optimistic historian can agree that the past is not completely knowable; but then, neither is the present.*

—Donald Boyle, Jr.[2]

As we saw in chapter 1, abortion techniques were so crude before 1800 as virtually to amount to suicide—as anthropologist Georges Devereux noted.[3] Historian Edward Shorter concluded that before 1880 only the truly desperate would risk abortion.[4] Historian Geoffrey Quaife described injury techniques for inducing an abortion with his analysis of violence, and not with abortion generally.[5] Quaife also conceded that girls were rarely anxious to use ingestion techniques.[6] The evidence strongly suggests that, before the nineteenth century, abortion remained a sometime thing that seldom came before a court, with unequivocally elective or voluntary abortions being truly rare. Even purely theological condemnations of abortion remained few and undeveloped, often thrown in with more extended condemnations of contraception, infanticide, or sexual promiscuity rather than being dealt with as a serious social problem.[7]

I take it as axiomatic that as long as there have been humans there have been people who did not want to be burdened by a child, and would seek to do whatever it took to be rid of an unwanted infant. The question is what could they do to prevent pregnancies or to dispose of an unwanted pregnancy if one resulted and abortion was too dangerous to perform. The short answer regarding contraception—methods enabling one to have intercourse without risk of pregnancy—is that such methods as were available before the middle of the twentieth century were highly unreliable. The only truly reliable method for preventing pregnancy was sexual abstinence. As for getting rid of an unwanted pregnancy, Irish feminist Mary Kenny summarized

---

1. Alice Cooper, *Dead Babies* (1972).
2. Donald Boyle, jr., Note, *Philosophy, History, and Judging*, 30 Wm. & Mary L. Rev. 181, 183 (1988)
3. Georges Devereux, A Study of Abortion in Primitive Societies 28, 149–50 (1955). *See also* Linda Gordon, Woman's Body, Woman's Right: A Social History of Birth Control in America 39 (1976); Rosalind Pollack Petchesky, Abortion and Women's Choice: The State, Sexuality, and Reproductive Freedom 49–55 (rev. ed. 1990); Joseph Dellapenna, *The History of Abortion: Technology, Morality, and Law,* 40 U. Pitt. L. Rev. 359, 372–76, 393–95 (1979).
4. Edward Shorter, A History of Women's Bodies 177 (Pelican Books ed. 1984).
5. G.R. Quaife, Wanton Wenches and Wayward Wives: Peasants and Illicit Sex in Early Seventeenth Century England 26 (1979).
6. *Id.* at 118.
7. Beverly Wildung Harrison, Our Right to Choose: Toward a New Ethic of Abortion 127, 130–44 (1983); Donald Judges, Hard Choices, Lost Voices 87–90 (1993); John Noonan, jr., Contraception 162–99 (1965); John Riddle, Contraception and Abortion from the Ancient World to the Renaissance 108–14 (1992).

the matter succinctly: "The traditional forms of abortion had been infanticide and abandonment" before the nineteenth century.[8]

Remarkably, many today seem as ready to assume that safe and effective contraceptives were widely available in times past as they are to assume that safe and effective techniques for doing abortions were widely known in centuries past.[9] Both assumptions are simply unfounded. Historian John Riddle wrote an entire book to prove that the abortifacient and contraceptive recipes that have come down from the ancients were safe and effective, but he does include a cautionary note in his preface that readers should not attempt to use any of the recipes he provides.[10] Even more remarkably, we as a society have largely managed to put infanticide out of mind when regarding our own past; infanticide is something that happens in strange and alien lands. Even apparently sophisticated historians have assumed that Christian moral constraints were enough to inhibit infanticide and to make infanticide a rare event in the history of western societies.[11] The actual practices regarding contraception and infanticide in western societies were in fact very different from what many people suppose. And, as a result, sexual abstinence, even within marriage, was far more than many today would suspect. This chapter examines the actual practices regarding contraception, abstinence, and infanticide.

# Contraception

*Probably 80% of the present population of this country have been born through "being careful."*
—Helena Wright[12]

Apart from sexual abstinence, there are just two methods for preventing conception: the prevention of the production of ova or sperm or the prevention of the union of ovum and sperm

---

8. MARY KENNY, ABORTION: THE WHOLE STORY 181 (1986). *See also* GORDON, *supra* note 3, at 32; HARRISON, *supra* note 6, at 182–83; PETER HOFFER & N.E.H. HULL, MURDERING MOTHERS: INFANTICIDE IN ENGLAND AND NEW ENGLAND 1558–1803, at 154 (1981); BARBARA MILLER, THE ENDANGERED SEX: THE NEGLECT OF CHILDREN IN RURAL NORTH INDIA (1981); L.A. PARRY, CRIMINAL ABORTION 35–36 (1932); R. THOMPSON, UNFIT FOR MODEST EARS 160–61 (1979); Georges Devereux, *A Typological Study of Abortion in 350 Primitive, Ancient, and Pre-Industrial Societies,* in THERAPEUTIC ABORTION, at 97, 113–14, 119–21 (Harold Rosen ed. 1954) (this book was reissued in 1967 under the title ABORTION IN AMERICA); Leigh Minturn & Jerry Stashak, *Infanticide as a Terminal Abortion Procedure,* 17 BEHAVIOR SCI. RESEARCH 70 (1982). Some might see a link between this fact and the pervasiveness of infanticide among primates generally, despite the often very different motivations involved among the several species. *See* SARAH BLAFFER HRDY, MOTHER NATURE: A HISTORY OF MOTHERS, INFANTS, AND NATURAL SELECTION 31–36, 51–52, 178–84 (1999) ("HRDY, MOTHER NATURE"); SARAH BLAFFER HRDY, THE WOMAN THAT NEVER EVOLVED 108–09 (1981); INFANTICIDE BY MALES AND ITS IMPLICATIONS (C. van Schaik & C. Jansen eds. 1994); INFANTICIDE: COMPARATIVE AND EVOLUTIONARY PERSPECTIVES (G. Hausfater & S. Blaffer Hrdy eds. 1984); RICHARD BORSHAY LEE, THE !KUNG SAN: MEN, WOMEN AND WORK IN A FORAGING SOCIETY 317–20 (1979); Anne Pusey, Jennifer Williams, & Jane Goodall, *The Influence of Dominance Rank on the Reproductive Success of Female Chimpanzees,* 277 SCI. 828 (1997).

9. *See, e.g.,* JANET FARRELL BRODIE, CONTRACEPTION AND ABORTION IN NINETEENTH-CENTURY AMERICA 4 (1994); CARL DEGLER, AT ODDS: WOMEN AND THE FAMILY IN AMERICA FROM THE REVOLUTION TO THE PRESENT 210–26 (1980); JOHN D'EMILIO & ESTELLE FREEDMAN, INTIMATE MATTERS: A HISTORY OF SEXUALITY IN AMERICA 60–63 (1988); GORDON, *supra* note 3, at 39–46; JAMES REED, FROM PRIVATE VICE TO PUBLIC VIRTUE: THE BIRTH CONTROL MOVEMENT AND AMERICAN SOCIETY SINCE 1830, at 10–16 (1978); RIDDLE, *supra* note 7.

10. RIDDLE, *supra* note 7, at ix.

11. DEGLER, *supra* note 9, at 187–88.

12. As quoted in BARBARA BROOKES, ABORTION IN ENGLAND 1900–1967, at 113 (1988).

after intercourse. People seem to have realized these possibilities (without fully understanding the processes involved) very early in human society, and the resulting folklore provided even more suggested means for accomplishing contraception than the folklore provided for abortion. The several prescriptions can be roughly grouped into two types: mechanical and medicinal. Mechanical means included contraceptive barriers and castration. Medicinal means included recipes for substances that could be inserted into a vagina, spread over a penis, or eaten. Medicinal means were variously thought of as a spermicide, or as a means of preventing ovulation, or as a means of preventing implantation of a fertilized ovum.

As with the reputed abortifacients of ancient times, contraceptives—whether mechanical or medicinal—seem to have been either absurdly ineffective, highly dangerous, or both.[13] The earliest known medical manuscript, an Egyptian papyrus dated to around 1850 B.C.E., contains three fragmentary prescriptions for contraceptive pessaries (vaginal insertions), including such items as crocodile dung, honey, and (apparently) saltpeter.[14] Roman physician Claudius Galen simply refused to discuss either abortifacients and contraceptives on grounds of ineffectiveness and dangerousness.[15] In the high Middle Ages, Maimonides could advise thusly on contraception:

> Contraceptives before intercourse. The things that prevent conception are (1) from the man's side anointing [the penis] with juice of onion, wood tar, or gall bladder of chicken, and (2) from the woman's side inserting pessaries with juice of peppermint, or pennyroyal, or the seeds of leek after purity.[16]

Riddle sought to buttress the notion that such recipes might actually be effective by noting that changing patterns of fertility in the Roman Empire and the later Middle Ages did not correlate directly with the availability of food—suggesting that such changes merely reflected pre-

---

13. *See, e.g.,* Frederick Hollick, The Marriage Guide, or Natural History of Generation: A Private Instruction for Married Persons and Those about to Marry Both Male and Female 336–39 (1860). For a detailed review of the pattern of sexual behavior of one couple in the mid-nineteenth century, with repeated indicia of contraceptive failure, see Brodie, *supra* note 9, at 16. *See generally* 1 Bonnie Anderson & Judith Zinsser, A History of Their Own: Women in Europe from Prehistory to the Present 46 (1988); Philippe Ariès, *Histoire des populations françaises et de leurs attitudes devant la vie despuis le XVIII siècle* 494–531 (1948); Brodie, *supra,* at 50, 55; P.A. Brunt, Italian Manpower, 225 B.C.–A.D. 14, at 147 (1971); Degler, *supra* note 9, at 187, 227–28; D'Emilio & Freedman, *supra* note 9, at 5–6; Marie-Thérèse Fontanille, *Abortement et contraception dans la médecine gréco-romaine* 195 (1977); Antonia Fraser, The Weaker Vessel: Women's Lot in Seventeenth-Century England 66–68 (1984); Gordon, *supra* note 3, at 40; Danielle Gourevitch, *Le mal d'ètre femme: la femme et la médecine dans la Rome antique* 198–99 (1984); Norman Himes, Medical History of Contraception 83–92, 97, 100, 137–73, 182–84, 262–63 (1936); Peter Laslett, The World We Have Lost 116–18 (1966); Alan MacFarlane, Marriage and Love in England: Modes of Reproduction 240–41 (1986); Angus McLaren, Reproductive Rituals 57–87 (1984); Noonan, *supra* note 7, at 255–56; Petchesky, *supra* note 3, at 77; Shorter, *supra* note 4, at 77–79; Reay Tannahill, Sex in History 127–30 (1980); Keith Wrightson, English Society, 1580–1680, at 105 (1982); Keith Hopkins, *Contraception in the Roman Empire,* 8 Comp. Stud. in Soc'y & Hist. 135, 150 (1965); John Knodel & Étienne van de Walle, *Lessons from the Past: Policy Implications of Historical Fertility Studies,* 5 Population & Dev. Stud. 217 (1979); Michael La Sorte, *Nineteenth-Century Family Planning Practices,* 31 J. Psychohist. 163, 167–69 (1976); Robert Schnucker, *Elizabethan Birth Control and Puritan Attitudes,* 5 J. Interdisciplinary Hist. 655 (1975); Wilson Yates, *Birth Control Literature and the Medical Profession in Nineteenth Century America,* 31 J. Hist. Med. & Allied Sciences 42 (1976).

14. Riddle, *supra* note 7, at 66–69; Tannahill, *supra* note 13, at 71–73; Andrea Tone, Devices and Desires: A History of Contraceptives in America 13 (2001); Kirsti Dyer, *Curiosities of Contraception: A Historical Perspective,* 264 JAMA 2818, 2818 (1990).

15. 12 Claudius Galen, Opera Omnia 251–52 (Karl Gottlob Kühn ed. 1821–33; originally published 2d cent. CE).

16. B.F. Musallam, Sex and Society in Islam: Birth Control before the Nineteenth Century 66 (1983).

vailing tastes.[17] He did not consider, however, other material factors such as the availability of arable land for new families, the constraints of the Roman taxing system, and so on. Even in acknowledging the Black Death, Riddle insisted that this did not explain the population decline of the fourteenth century.[18] Historian Mary Matossian has noted that the variations in medieval populations correlate neatly with weather conditions that were conducive to the growth of ergot of rye which could have resulted in the inadvertent ingestion of a fertility suppressant in those dependent on rye bread.[19] The causes of changes in population growth rates in Roman and Medieval times remain far from clear; no one can claim on this basis alone that the people of those times must certainly have possessed the secrets of safe and effective contraception and abortion.

In any event, the existence of contraceptive recipes does not explain the continuing high incidence of infanticide and abandonment, as will be developed later in this chapter. Nor do such recipes explain why there should have been such a sharp decline in relevant knowledge after the fall of Rome, which one must suppose if one believes that the Greeks and Romans knew very well how to contracept.[20] John Riddle himself nearly conceded as much in his attempt to prove that the ancients knew how to abort and how to contracept for when he reached the Middle Ages in Europe, he was reduced to describing medical treatise after medical treatise which had "surprisingly little" or nothing to say about abortion, contraception, or emmenagogues. Riddle, however, consistently stated that while baffling, this should not be taken as either lack of knowledge or as censorship or condemnation.[21] He offered no reason for any of these suppositions. Riddle even admitted, in describing texts from this era, that "[a]s a physician it was normal for a writer virtually to avoid the subject [abortion and contraception],... or to be more circumspect, to avoid comment and merely to list the remedies."[22] Riddle also noted that when medical education moved into the universities, the study of medicine generally did not include information about birth control and abortion, so much so that he referred to the "broken trail of learning."[23] Riddle is reduced to arguing that there must have been available safe and effective contraceptive potions because prostitutes had fewer children although the prostitutes undoubtedly had intercourse more frequently than other women.[24]

Riddle's arguments ignore not only the possibility of infanticide, but also the likelihood that prostitutes were often sterile as a result of venereal disease—not to mention the prevalence of anal intercourse among ancient prostitutes, as evidenced by numerous vase paintings.[25] Nor should we overlook the likely, albeit unintended, effects of the pervasive lead poisoning experi-

---

17. Riddle, *supra* note 7, at 1–2. *But see* Tannahill, *supra* note 13, at 151 (arguing that population growth in medieval Europe did correspond to "a breakthrough in agriculture"). *See also* Reay Tannahill, Food in History 184–85, 190–94 (1973). Recent research suggests that a new and virulent strain of malaria swept through the Roman Empire in the fifth century, playing a major role both in the decline of population and in the fall of the Empire. John Noble Wilford, *DNA Shows Malaria Helped Topple Rome*, N.Y. Times, Feb. 20, 2001, at F1.

18. Riddle, *supra* note 7, at 2. *But see* Brunt, *supra* note 13; T.H. Hollingsworth, Historical Demography 375–88 (1969); William McNeill, Plagues and People (1977); J.C. Russell, British Medieval Population 92–117 (1948); Tannahill, *supra* note 13, at 130; S.J. Thrupp, *Plague Effects in Medieval Europe*, 18 Econ. Hist. Rev. 101 (1965).

19. Mary Kilbourne Matossian, Poisons of the Past: Molds, Epidemics, and History 67 (1989). *See also* Riddle, *supra* note 7, at 17.

20. W.V. Harris, *Old Wives' Tales*, N.Y. Rev. Books, Nov. 18, 1993, at 52, 53.

21. Riddle, *supra* note 7, at 106–07, 116–17, 120–26.

22. *Id.* at 136.

23. *Id.* at 137. *See also id.* at 145–49, 154–57, 160–63.

24. *Id.* at 143.

25. K.J. Dover, Greek Homosexuality 100–01 (1978); Tannahill, *supra* note 13, at 102–03, 128.

enced by the ancients generally from drinking from lead cups, eating off lead plates with lead utensils, bringing water to their homes or fountains in lead pipes, using lead powder for make-up, and so on.[26] The likely high levels of sterility from lead poisoning were compounded by the likely induction of male impotence from the alcoholism that pervaded Roman life, and the likely declines in sperm production from the long hours spent in the hot baths.[27]

Many of the contraceptive recipes we come across in old or ancient medical texts involved sympathetic magic rather than actual pharmacological effects.[28] For example, Dioscorides recommended eating the kidney of a mule. Because mules were sterile, the woman who ate its kidney would also become sterile, much as in many parts of the world the belief persists that eating animal testes will render men more virile.[29] Millennia later, Margaret Sanger recorded her fruitless effort, over a span of six months in 1913, to find contraceptive information in the Library of Congress, the New York Academy of Medicine, and the Boston Public Library.[30] As late as 1938, one researcher found that barely half of the white families in one rural Tennessee community knew of any method for limiting births.[31] Popular ignorance is hardly surprising given the social conventions against open discussion of the matter. Popular literature of the nineteenth century, even lurid novels of "fallen women," rarely even mention the topic and is never explicit about how one might go about limiting family size.[32]

When historian Janet Brodie wanted to claim that twentieth-century ignorance of contraception resulted from its criminalization in the late nineteenth century, Brodie was comparing the knowledge of working class women in the twentieth century with the knowledge of middle class women of the nineteenth century.[33] Even the evidence Brodie cites does not support her conclusion, however. Ignorance regarding contraception was more profound—and more pervasive—than Brodie seems able to imagine. Between 1892 and 1912, Clelia Duel Mosher, a physician at Stanford University, surveyed a group of 47 married women about their sexual practices.[34] The group overall relied most heavily douching (42 percent), followed by the rhythm method (24 percent), and then by *coitus interruptus* (20 percent). Pretty much the same list appeared in several other medical sources published at about the same time.[35] Often these and other techniques were used in combination, with the older women in the group (married between 1854 and 1882) relying most heavily on *coitus interruptus* and the younger women relying more on other techniques. These women generally experienced contraceptive failure, most dramatically in the case of a woman who experienced 12 pregnancies during 29 years of marriage. For those who would like to believe that such technical failures are peculiar to Western cultures, it is revealing to dis-

---

26. J.P.V.D. BALDSON, LIFE AND LEISURE IN ANCIENT ROME 195 (1969); TANNAHILL, *supra* note 13, at 131, 133–35.

27. TANNAHILL, *supra* note 13, at 131–35.

28. *See, e.g., id.* at 96, 98. *See also* TANNAHILL, *supra* note 13, at 128–29, 152–53; Dyer, *supra* note 14, at 2818.

29. RIDDLE, *supra* note 7, at 33–34. *See also id.* at 104–05, 132, 148, 150.

30. MARGARET SANGER, MY FIGHT FOR BIRTH CONTROL 57–61 (1931). *See also* LEE RAINWATER, AND THE POOR GET CHILDREN (1960).

31. FRANK DEWITT ALEXANDER, OWNERS AND TENANTS OF SMALL FARMS IN THE LIFE OF A SELECTED COMMUNITY: A CULTURAL ANALYSIS 16 (1938).

32. *See, e.g.,* LEO TOLSTOY, ANNA KARENINA 635 (New Am. Library ed.1980). *See generally* BRODIE, *supra* note 9, at 1–2.

33. BRODIE, *supra* note 9, at 281.

34. *See* JAMES MAHOOD & KRISTINE WENBURG, THE MOSHER SURVEY: SEXUAL ATTITUDES OF 45 VICTORIAN WOMEN (1980). *See also* BRODIE, *supra* note 9, at 57–59; DEGLER, *supra* note 9, at 262–66; D'EMILIO & FREEDMAN, *supra* note 9, at 175–78; TONE, *supra* note 14, at 73–75.

35. F. Wallace Abbott, *Limitation of Family,* 10 MASS. MED. J. 337 (1890); David Matteson, *Letter,* 59 MED. & SURGICAL RPTR. 759 (1888).

cover that Japanese writers of the pre-contact period also lamented that the performance of contraceptives always lagged "woefully" behind the sales talk of the sellers.[36]

Notice that douching seems to come into common use in the United States only in the later years of the nineteenth century. Douching probably was not widely used in colonial or federal times, if only because of lack or privacy for the married couple, with children, servants, and even visiting adults sleeping in the same room. The development of bedroom privacy in the more prosperous late-nineteenth century made douching a more practical possibility.[37] The women in Mosher's study used douches that were often nothing but water, although some women would add such things as alcohol, alum, borax, soap, or zinc to the water.[38] Other sources indicate that women added such substances as baking soda, carbolic acid, iodine, metallic salts, opium, prussic acid, salt, strychnine, tannin, turpentine, or vinegar to the douche.[39] As late as the 1950s, some women were douching with Coca-Cola in the hope that the carbonation bubbles would explode the heads of the sperm.[40]

While douching might have had some of the desired effect, it is in fact ineffective (with 20 to 40 pregnancies annually for each hundred woman douching for a year) and can be dangerous if inappropriate substances are used or if fluid or air is forced into the uterus.[41] The lasting popularity of the practice was linked to widespread belief in its hygienic benefits even if the woman did not seek contraceptive benefits, a fashion that perhaps explains the popularity of pure water douches.[42] Mosher's informants who douched experienced several accidental pregnancies each, perhaps because the popular pure water douches might actually have speeded the spermatozoa on their way rather than having impeded their journey.[43] One manufacturer made douching syringes with interchangeable nozzles so the syringe could also be used to water houseplants.[44]

The rhythm method was even less successful. Knowledge of the ovulation process was so undeveloped in the nineteenth century that even apparently knowledgeable physicians, analogizing the menstrual cycle to estrus in mammals, recommended the middle of the menstrual cycle as the "safe" period and advised the avoidance of intercourse just before and after a woman's

---

36. MARY WALKER STANDLEE, THE GREAT PULSE: JAPANESE MIDWIFERY AND OBSTETRICS THROUGH THE AGES 111 (1959).

37. BRODIE, *supra* note 9, at 77. *See generally Id.* at 58, 67–79; DEGLER, *supra* note 9, at 215–16; GORDON, *supra* note 3, at 42, 64–66; HERBERT GUTMAN, THE BLACK FAMILY IN SLAVERY AND FREEDOM 81 (1976); REED, *supra* note 9, at 10.

38. BRODIE, *supra* note 9, at 58, 66. One author explicitly recommended pure water douches as an abortifacient. EUGENE BECKLARD, PHYSIOLOGICAL MYSTERIES AND REVELATIONS IN LOVE, COURTSHIP, AND MARRIAGE 35–45 (1845). Even Brodie was compelled to admit that Becklard's book was "a jumbled mixture of superstition, ancient folklore, and plagiarized ideas." BRODIE, *supra*, at 69.

39. BRODIE, *supra* note 9, at 67–79, 130, 148–50; THOMAS EWELL, LETTER TO LADIES, DETAILING IMPORTANT INFORMATION CONCERNING THEM SELVES AND INFANTS 74–76 (1817); ANTHONY HORDERN, LEGAL ABORTION: THE ENGLISH EXPERIENCE 3 (1971); JAMES MOHR, ABORTION IN AMERICA: THE ORIGINS AND EVOLUTION OF NATIONAL POLICY, 1800–1900, at 10–11 (1978); PETCHESKY, *supra* note 3, at 51; TONE, *supra* note 14, at 151–52, 159–82.

40. BETH BAILEY, SEX IN THE HEARTLAND 76–77 (1999).

41. BRODIE, *supra* note 9, at 73–75; ROBERT KISTNER, GYNECOLOGY: PRINCIPLES AND PRACTICE 676 (2nd ed. 1971); BOSTON WOMEN'S HEALTH COLLECTIVE, OUR BODIES, OUR SELVES 223, 255, 518 (1971); MALCOLM POTTS, PETER DIGGORY, & JOHN PEEL, ABORTION 170–72 (1977); TONE, *supra* note 14, at 169–73.

42. BRODIE, *supra* note 9, at 78–79. *See generally* TONE, *supra* note 14, at 151–82.

43. DEGLER, *supra* note 9, at 227. *See also* CONSUMER REPORTS, A REPORT ON CONTRACEPTIVE MATERIALS 18–20, 29–30 (1945); RACHEL LYNN PALMER & SARAH GREENBERG, FACTS AND FRAUD IN WOMEN'S HYGIENE 99, 123–36 (1936); Royal Brown, *Changes of the Consistency of Contraceptive Preparations during Storage,* 7 HUM. FERTILITY 161 (Dec. 1942). *See generally* TONE, *supra* note 14, at 169–70.

44. BRODIE, *supra* note 9, at 70.

menses.[45] This tradition has been traced back to the ancient Greeks,[46] and is precisely the opposite of the correct approach. Couples can achieve significant success with the rhythm method—but only if they use it correctly and consistently.[47] While a few nineteenth-century authors did more or less accurately assess the safe period,[48] some, like the self-styled physician Frederick Hollick, demonstrated their lack of knowledge in later writings in which they got the matter wrong and gave the same backwards advice so common in the work of others.[49] Some got it right only because they recommended abstinence for nearly the entire cycle.[50]

The idea of a safe period depended on the discovery of the ovulation process making the menstrual cycle at least minimally comprehensible. As a result, the very existence of an infertile period during the menstrual cycle was hotly contested during the middle of the nineteenth century, when the new discoveries were being made.[51] Physicians did not identify the fertile period for women until the 1920s.[52] Even today some physicians disagree precisely when, in her men-

45. ANNIE BESANT, THE LAW OF POPULATION: IT CONSEQUENCES, AND ITS BEARING UPON HUMAN CONDUCT AND MORALS 33 (1878); P. HENRY CHEVASSE, PHYSICAL LIFE OF MAN AND WOMAN; OR ADVICE TO BOTH SEXES 23 (1871); JOHN COWAN, THE SCIENCE OF NEW LIFE 110–11 (1869); AUGUSTUS GARDNER, THE CAUSES AND CURATIVE TREATMENT OF STERILITY 18 (1856) ("GARDNER, STERILITY"); AUGUSTUS GARDNER, CONJUGAL SINS AGAINST THE LAWS OF LIFE AND HEALTH AND THEIR EFFECTS UPON THE FATHER, MOTHER, AND THE CHILD 182–83 (1876) ("GARDNER, CONJUGAL SINS"); WINFIELD SCOTT HALL, SEXUAL KNOWLEDGE 215 (1916); EZRA HEYWOOD, CUPID'S YOKE; OR, THE BINDING FORCES OF CONJUGAL LIFE 16, 19–20 (1887); B.G. JEFFERIS & J.L. NICHOLS, LIGHT ON DARK CORNERS: A COMPLETE SEXUAL SCIENCE AND GUIDE TO PURITY 248 (1897); H.W. LONG, SANE SEX LIFE 60, 66–67 (1919); GEORGE NAPHEYS, THE PHYSICAL LIFE OF WOMEN: ADVICE TO THE MAIDEN, WIFE, AND MOTHER 96–97 (1873); FÉLIX POUCHET, *THÉORIE POSITIVE DE LA FÉCUNDATION DES MAMMIFÈRES* 275–76 (1842); P.B. SAUER, MATERNITY: A BOOK FOR EVERY WIFE AND MOTHER 151 (1891); J. MARION SIMS, CLINICAL NOTES ON UTERINE SURGERY, WITH SPECIAL REFERENCE TO THE MANAGEMENT OF THE STERILE CONDITION 371 (1871); HORATIO ROBINSON STORER, WHY NOT? A BOOK FOR EVERYWOMAN preface (1866); RUSSELL TRALL, SEXUAL PHYSIOLOGY: A SCIENTIFIC AND POPULAR EXPOSITION OF THE FUNDAMENTAL PROBLEMS IN SOCIOLOGY 206–07 (1866); O.E. Herrick, *Specialties,* 4 MICH. MED. NEWS 41 (1881). *See generally* BRODIE, *supra* note 9, at 28–31, 79–86, 130; DEGLER, *supra* note 9, at 213–15; GORDON, *supra* note 3, at 63, 101, 159; JOHN & ROBIN HALLER, THE PHYSICIAN AND SEXUALITY IN VICTORIAN AMERICA 118–19 (1974); DAVID KENNEDY, BIRTH CONTROL IN AMERICA: THE CAREER OF MARGARET SANGER 210 (1970); STEPHEN KERN, ANATOMY AND DESTINY: A CULTURAL HISTORY OF THE HUMAN BODY 97–98, 155 (1975); MARGARET MARSH & WANDA RONNER, THE EMPTY CRADLE: INFERTILITY IN AMERICA FROM COLONIAL TIMES TO THE PRESENT 85 (1996); PETCHESKY, *supra* note 3, at 77; RIDDLE, *supra* note 7, at 5–7, 155; TONE, *supra* note 14, at 72–73, 81; Thomas Laqueur, *Orgasm, Generation, and the Politics of Reproductive Biology,* 14 REPRESENTATIONS 1, 25–31 (1986); Angus McLaren, *Birth Control and Abortion in Canada, 1870–1920,* 59 CAN. HIST. REV. 319, 324–25 (1978).

46. Lesley Dean-Jones, *Menstrual Bleeding According to the Hypocrites and Aristotle,* 119 TRANS. AM. PHILOLOGICAL SOC'Y 177 (1989).

47. John Barrett & John Marshall, *The Risk of Conception on Different Days of the Menstrual Cycle,* 23 POPULATION STUD. 455 (1969); P.A. Lachenbruch, *Frequency and Timing of Intercourse: Its Relation to the Probability of Conception,* 21 POPULATION STUD. 23 (1967).

48. *See* FREDERICK HOLLICK, DISEASES OF WOMEN, THEIR CAUSES AND CURE FAMILIARLY EXPLAINED; WITH PRACTICAL HINTS FOR THEIR PREVENTION, AND FOR THE PRESERVATION OF FEMALE HEALTH; FOR EVERY FEMALE'S PRIVATE USE 340 (1849).

49. *See* HOLLICK, *supra* note 13, at 204.

50. *See, e.g.,* ADAM RACIBORSKI, *DE LA PUBERTÉ ET DE L'ÂGE CRITIQUE CHEZ LA FEMME, AU POINT DE VUE PHYSIOLOGIQUE, HYGIÉNIQUE ET MÉDICALE ET DE LA PONTE PÉRIODIQUE CHEZ LA FEMME ET LES MAMMIFÈRES* 135 (1844) (recommending abstinence for 25 days of the 28–32 day cycle).

51. *See, e.g.,* P.C. DUNNE & A.F. DERBOIS, THE YOUNG MARRIED LADY'S PRIVATE MEDICAL GUIDE 207–09 (F. Harrison Doane trans. 4th ed. 1854); A. Reeves Jackson, *The Ovulation Theory of Menstruation: Will It Stand?,* TRANS. 28TH MEETING ILL. ST. MED. SOC'Y 143–44 (1876); Henry Oldham, *Clinical Lecture on the Induction of Abortion in a Case of Contracted Vagina from Cicaterization,* 9 (N.S.) LONDON MED. GAZ. 45 (1849). *See generally* BRODIE, *supra* note 9, at 80.

52. ERIC MATSNER & FREDERICK HOLDEN, THE TECHNIQUE OF CONTRACEPTION 37 (1938); John Rock & Marshall Bartlett, *Biopsy Studies of Human Endometrium,* 108 JAMA 2022 (1937); Irving Stein & Melvin

strual cycle, a woman is fertile.[53] One thus could not expect very much success in attempts to regulate birth patterns through the timing and frequency of intercourse.

One might think that withdrawal—*coitus interruptus*—would be the most obvious solution for those without effective mechanical or medicinal means of contraception.[54] Yet the technique turned up in a rather poor third place in the 1912 Mosher study, being reported by only 20 percent of the interviewees.[55] This is less than half of the number who relied on largely symbolic douches, and less than those who relied on a very poorly understood rhythm method. Attempting to determine the incidence of the practice in earlier times turns out to be rather more problematic than determining the extent of successful recourse to mechanical or medicinal devices.[56]

Withdrawal is the one form of contraception unequivocally mentioned in the Bible, where it is condemned as a serious sin.[57] (In the Biblical account, the actual sin was the refusal of Onan to impregnate his brother's widow so that his brother could have an heir, rather than the fact that Onan practiced withdrawal.[58]) Nor does the practice of withdrawal appear to have been common in Rome. Even John Riddle, usually ready to infer every sort of contraceptive and abortive practice from unclear and incomplete ancient records, noted that even though the pre-Christian Roman Empire had no religious strictures against the practice of *coitus interruptus*, there is virtually no evidence for the practice in pre-Christian Rome.[59] Riddle was intent on proving that women could control their fertility by their own actions; he therefore was willing to be skeptical of the practice because it depends on male cooperation.[60] Given the frankness of Roman authors' in describing a myriad of other sexual practices, such silence strongly suggests that they did not indulge in the practice.[61]

The term "Onanism" came into Christian usage as a condemnation of any "unnatural" waste of sperm. Christians usually applied the term "Onanism" to male masturbation rather than to its original signification of *coitus interruptus,* but the condemnation of either activity was general and harsh—and continued down to the opening of the twentieth century.[62] On the other hand,

---

Cohen, *An Evaluation of the Safe Period,* 110 JAMA 257 (1938). *See generally* GORDON, *supra* note 3, at 45; KENNEDY, *supra* note 45, at 210; MARSH & RONNER, *supra* note 45, at 85; TONE, *supra* note 14, at 72.

53. Lawrence Altman, *Study Challenges Beliefs on Conception Period,* N.Y. TIMES, Dec. 7, 1995, at A28 (reporting a finding that a woman is fertile only if she has intercourse within the five days before ovulation, not by having intercourse during a period of about 10 days centered on ovulation as most doctors believe).

54. TANNAHILL, *supra* note 13, at 73.

55. See the text *supra* at notes 34–35.

56. *See generally* BRODIE, *supra* note 9, at 27, 41, 49, 58–65, 130, 185–86; DEGLER, *supra* note 9, at 211–12; D'EMILIO & FREEDMAN, *supra* note 9, at 15, 18–20, 26, 30, 33, 68–69; GARDNER, CONJUGAL SINS, *supra* note 45, at 149; GORDON, *supra* note 3, at 161–62; HIMES, *supra* note 13, at 70–71; DAVID HUNT, PARENTS AND CHILDREN IN HISTORY: THE PSYCHOLOGY OF FAMILY LIFE IN EARLY MODERN FRANCE 82 (1970); NOONAN, *supra* note 7, at 10–11, 50, 95; RIDDLE, *supra* note 7, at 4–5; Susan Klepp, *Lost, Hidden, Obstructed, and Repressed,* in EARLY AMERICAN TECHNOLOGY: MAKING AND DOING THINGS FROM THE COLONIAL ERA TO 1850, at 68, 71 (Judith McGaw ed. 1994); R.H. MacDonald, *The Frightful Consequences of Onanism: Notes on the History of a Delusion,* 28 J. HIST. OF IDEAS 423 (1967).

57. *Genesis* 38:8–10.

58. *See also* LOUIS EPSTEIN, MARRIAGE LAWS IN THE BIBLE AND TALMUD 77–144 (1942); HIMES, *supra* note 13, at 59–78; TANNAHILL, *supra* note 13, at 74–75.

59. RIDDLE, *supra* note 7, at 4.

60. *Id.* at 143.

61. HOPKINS, *supra* note 13, at 124, 143–50.

62. *See, e.g.,* WILLIAM ALCOTT, THE PHYSIOLOGY OF MARRIAGE 190 (1866); GARDNER, STERILITY, *supra* note 45, at 90–102; 2 G. STANLEY HALL, ADOLESCENCE 438 (1904); HOLLICK, *supra* note 13, at 336; JOHN HARVEY KELLOGG, PLAIN FACTS FOR OLD AND YOUNG 255 (1881); ABBOTT KINNEY, THE CONQUEST OF DEATH 99 (1893); THOMAS LAQUEUR, SOLITARY SEX: A CULTURAL HISTORY OF MASTURBATION (2003); NAPHEYS, *supra* note 45, at 97–98; A PHYSICIAN (NATHANIAL FRANCIS COOKE), SATAN IN SOCIETY: A PLEA FOR SOCIAL PURITY. A DISCUSSION OF THE TRUE RIGHTS OF WOMAN, MARITAL AND SOCIAL 96 (1871); SAMUEL-AUGUSTE-

at least one medieval physician did recommend *coitus interruptus* as a contraceptive practice.[63] Despite this evidence, some historians have concluded that withdrawal was virtually unknown in medieval Europe because of the vehement Christian denunciations of the practice and the general lack of evidence for its practice.[64] Some modern historians have assumed that *coitus interruptus* was widespread despite the almost complete absence of direct evidence of the practice and the formal condemnation of the practice simply because they can imagine nothing else that might account for successful family limitation prior to the late nineteenth century.[65] We shall probably never know precisely how extensive the practice of withdrawal was in societies caught between the unequivocal condemnation of the practice and the practical need for it. A closer examination of the attitudes and realities of nineteenth century America perhaps will illuminate the longer-term pattern in Western societies.

Evidence of heterosexual anal intercourse is also sparse among western societies except as a charge against one's enemies.[66] Rather extensive evidence of such practices does turn up in some non-western societies.[67] This, of course, does not mean that rear entry did not happen in western societies, but it does suggest that it was not as common as modern sensibilities might assume. There is, in fact, no reason to think that it was any more common that *coitus interruptus*, and for many of the same reasons.

One can discount widespread recourse to *coitus interruptus* in the United States in colonial times or into the nineteenth century, at least among the middle and upper classes. Historian Martin Ingram reached much the same conclusion for England during the same period.[68] The moral strictures against the practice, the expressed dislike of men and women for the practice as found by researchers in the late nineteenth and early twentieth centuries, the fact that many people had to be taught the technique when open discussion of it became possible, and finally the limited achievements in birth spacing all are strongly suggestive that the practice either was not widespread or at least that it was not used successfully. We shall examine each of these reasons briefly in the ensuing paragraphs.

---

André Tissot, *L'Onanisme: Essai sur les maladies produites par la masturbation* (1758); William Goodell, *Clinical Lecture on Conjugal Onanism and Kindred Sin*, Phila. Med. Times, Feb. 1, 1872, at 161; Horatio Robinson Storer, *A Medico-Legal Study of Rape*, 2 N.Y. Med. J. 100 (1865). *See generally* Haller & Haller, *supra* note 45, at 207–08; Kern, *supra* note 42, at 119–22, 132–33, 155–57; Noonan, *supra* note 7, at 160; Tannahill, *supra* note 13, at 152, 342–44; René Spitz, *Authority and Masturbation*, 21 Psychoanalytic Q. 490 (1952). At least one man was executed in the colonies for "teaching masturbation." Cornelia Hughes Dayton, Women before the Bar: Gender, Law, and Society in Connecticut, 1639–1789, at 164 n.11 (1995).

63. Guilielmus de Saliceto, *Summa Conservationis et Curationis* f. 13vb. (Venice 1489).

64. Orest & Patricia Ranum, *Introduction,* in Popular Attitudes toward Birth Control in Pre-Industrial France and England 1, 6 (Orest & Patricia Ranum eds. 1972).

65. *See, e.g.,* Ariès, *supra* note 13, at 496–97, 516; James Brundage, Law, Sex, and Christian Society in Medieval Europe 358 (1987); Degler, *supra* note 9, at 196–98, 210–13; D'Emilio & Freedman, *supra* note 9, at 59, 175; Jean-Louis Flandrin, Families in Former Times: Kinship, Household and Sexuality 216–25 (Richard Southern trans. 1979); Gordon, *supra* note 3, at 13, 41, 85; Himes, *supra* note 13, at 190; Kern, *supra* note 13, at 155; Petchesky, *supra* note 3, at 29, 35, 42–45; Tannahill, *supra* note 13, at 285, 408; E.A. Wrigley, Population and History 188 (1969); P.A. Biller, *Birth-Control in the West in the Thirteenth and Early Fourteenth Centuries,* 94 Past & Present 3, 19 (1982); Pierre Goubert, *Historical Demography and the Reinterpretation of Early Modern French History: A Research Review,* 1 J. Interdisciplinary Hist. 44 (1970).

66. Tannahill, *supra* note 13, at 285–86.

67. *Id.* at 296–99, 320–22. *See also* Francisco Guerra, The Pre-Columbian Mind: A Study into the Aberrant Nature of Sexual Drives, Drugs Affecting Behavior, and the Attitude towards Life and Death, with a Survey of Psychotherapy, in Pre-Columbian America 256–58 (1971).

68. Martin Ingram, Church Courts, Sex and Marriage in England, 1570–1640, at 158–59 (1987).

One suspects that the strong moral strictures against "Onanism" must have had some effect, although how much we cannot say. We know of one criminal prosecution in Massachusetts in 1710 in which a woman testified against her husband for the crime of "Onan's abominable sin," a practice which she scorned.[69] Whether this was typical, we cannot know. We do not even know whether the woman was referring to masturbation or withdrawal. What we can know is that the condemnation of masturbation became remarkably extravagant in the nineteenth century. For example, Dr. Nathaniel Francis Cooke, writing under the pseudonym "A Physician," described the case of a youth of seventeen in these terms:

> He delivered himself to masturbation which he repeated three times a day.…In less than one year he began to experience great weakness after each act.…The spasm which formerly occurred only at the consumption of the act and ceased at the same time, had become habitual, and often seized him…in so violent a fashion that during the whole time of the paroxysm, which sometimes lasted 15 hours…he experienced in the back of the neck such violent pains that he commonly raised not cries merely, but howls.…I visited him; I found less a living being than a corpse groaning upon the straw; emaciated, pale, filthy, exhaling an infectious Oder; almost incapable of any movement…a constant slime flowed from his mouth…a being far below a brute; a spectacle of which it is impossible to conceive the horror; one would with difficulty recognize that he formerly belonged to the human species.[70]

Another doctor described those who masturbated as exhibiting a "masturbatic insanity" that induced in its victims a strong resemblance to Mr. Hyde of someone who would otherwise act as a mild-mannered Dr. Jeckyll.[71] Yet another doctor defended such exaggerated accounts in the following terms:

> One would fain be spared the sickening task of dealing with this disgusting subject; but as he who would exterminate the wild beasts that ravage his fields must not fear to enter their dark and noisome dens, and drag them out of their lair; so he who would rid humanity of a pest must not shrink from dragging it from its hiding places, to perish in the light of day. If men deified him who delivered Lerna from its hydra, and canonized him who rid Ireland of its serpents, what should they do for one who could extirpate this monster vice?[72]

The same author went on to describe masturbation as "a pestilence which walketh in darkness, because, while it saps and weakens all the higher qualities of the mind, it so strengthens low cunning and deceit that the victim goes on in his habit unsuspected.…"[73] Nor was this attitude uniquely American or Anglo-American. We find similarly extravagant condemnations of "Onanism" both in France and in Germany.[74]

Female masturbation was, if anything, subject to more condemnation than male masturbation.[75] Even bicycling by girls or women became controversial because of its supposed masturba-

---

69. Brodie, *supra* note 9, at 41.

70. A Physician, *supra* note 62, at 96–98.

71. E.C. Spitzka, *Cases of Masturbation (Masturbatic Insanity)*, 34 J. Mental Sci. 52, 52–53 (1888).

72. S.G. Howe, On the Causes of Idiocy 29 (1858).

73. *Id.* at 30.

74. Pierre Garnier, *Onanisme seul et à deux sous toutes ses formes et leur conséquences* (1894); Hermann Rohleder, *Die Masturbation* (1899). *See generally* Théodore Tarczylo, *Sexe et liberté au siècle des lumières* 108–14, 151 (1983).

75. Kern, *supra* note 45, at 100–01, 157–60.

tory effect.[76] Some doctors went so far as to perform surgical clitoridectomies to "cure" "excessive" masturbation.[77] One could hardly imagine doctors (mostly men) performing surgical castration for the same reasons. To gynecologist Robert Dickinson goes the honor of being the first physician to defend the physiological utility of female masturbation; he wrote on the subject only at the end of the nineteenth century.[78]

The evidence regarding condemnation of *coitus interruptus* is not as clear as the condemnation of masturbation. This in itself might suggest that the practice was not perceived as common, or perhaps that the practice was so common that it was not really condemned at all. We can discount the latter possibility when we find a religious zealot (John Humphrey Noyes) so opposed to *coitus interruptus* that he re-invented a form of *coitus reservatus* in which intercourse was to occur without male ejaculation.[79] Noyes' Oneida Community apparently practiced *coitus reservatus* with considerable success, reporting only 31 accidental pregnancies in 21 years in a group of around 200 people; on the other hand, the practice of *coitus reservatus* was denounced by others as health threatening.[80] Some nineteenth century feminists and free-love advocates attempted to popularize this method beyond a narrow religious sect.[81] Even these zealots did not advocate anal or oral intercourse, although we cannot rule out recourse to such practices by persons seeking to avoid pregnancy.[82]

The evidence of attitude is thus at least suggestive regarding the infrequency of the practice. That evidence is reinforced when one finds evidence that many people, including the women in Dr. Mosher's study, disliked their experience with withdrawal in part because of their belief that it was bad for one or the other spouse's health.[83] Even such a strong supporter of birth control in general as Margaret Sanger was strongly critical of *coitus interruptus* on the grounds of its supposed "evil effect upon the woman's nervous condition."[84] Only occasional observers argued that

---

76. *See* Robert Dickinson, *Bicycling for Women from the Standpoint of the Gynecologist,* 31 Am. J. Obstetrics 24 (1895).

77. Kern, *supra* note 45, at 101–02.

78. Dickinson, *supra* note 78; Robert Dickinson, *Hypertrophies of the Labia Minora and Their Significance,* 1 Am. Gynecology 223 (1902).

79. *See* John Humphrey Noyes, Male Continence (1872). Although Noyes seems to have thought this was his own unique discovery, legal historian (now judge) John Noonan has traced the practice of *coitus reservatus* back to the Middle Ages. Noonan, *supra* note 7, at 296, 336–38, 447. Historian Reay Tannahill finds references to the practice in ancient Chinese and Hindu writings. Tannahill, *supra* note 13, at 171, 226–28, 413–14. *See also* Dyer, *supra* note 14, at 2818.

80. James Jackson, American Womanhood: Its Peculiarities and Necessities 47–48 (1870).

81. *See* Heywood, *supra* note 45, at 14–15; Alice Duncan Stockham, Karezza: The Ethics of Marriage 53, 82–83 (1898). *See generally* Brodie, *supra* note 9, at 65–67, 282; Gordon, *supra* note 3, at 62–63, 84–89, 101; Kern, *supra* note 45, at 155–56.

82. *See* Ariès, *supra* note 13, at 467; Danielle Jacquart & Claude Thomasset, Sexualité et savoir médical au moyen âge 241 (1985); Riddle, *supra* note 7, at 5.

83. *See, e.g.,* George Beard, Sexual Neurasthenia: Its Hygiene, Causes, Symptoms and Treatment 127 (1884); A.M. Mauriceau [Charles Lohman], The Married Woman's Private Medical Companion, Embracing the Treatment of Menstruation, or Monthly Turns, During Their Stoppage, Irregularity, or Entire Suppression. Pregnancy, and How It May Be Determined; with the Treatment of Its Various Diseases. Discovery to Prevent Pregnancy; Its Great and Important Necessity Where Malformation or Inability Exists to Give Birth. To Prevent Miscarriage or Abortion. When Proper and Necessary To Effect Miscarriage When Attended with Entire Safety 143 (1847); Napheys, *supra* note 45, at 97–99; L. Bolton Bangs, *Some of the Effects of Withdrawal,* 9 Trans. N.Y. Acad. Med. 119 (2d ser. 1893); Sigmund Freud, *Pre-Psychoanalytic Publications and Drafts,* 1 The Standard Edition of the Complete Works of Sigmund Freud 181–83 (1966); Goodell, *supra* note 62. *See generally* Brodie, *supra* note 9, at 58, 61–63; MacDonald, *supra* note 57.

84. Kennedy, *supra* note 45, at 130. *See also* Gordon, *supra* note 3, at 369.

the practice was too widespread to believe that it generally caused ill-effects—and even they argued that its frequent practice was in distant lands.[85] Only in the middle of the nineteenth century do we find open endorsement of the practice.[86]

Many men had an additional reason for disliking the practice: loss of sexual pleasure. Social reformer, Robert Dale Owen, the earliest known public advocate of *coitus interruptus* in England or America, rebuked such men, although again we cannot determine whether he had any success.[87] Withdrawal must also have reduced the woman's pleasure as well, although we have no actual record of such sentiments. Janet Brodie emphasized the displeasure women must have felt, both in physical terms and in terms of being wholly dependent on the man's decision to withdraw in order to eliminate the risk of pregnancy.[88] Despite the all too obvious level of male control, some historians have nonetheless argued that a supposed rising incidence of *coitus interruptus* in the nineteenth century indicated growing control by women over the frequency, timing, and style of sexual intercourse.[89] Such assertions perhaps indicate more about the personal experience of the historian rather than any actual information about historical practices.

The final reasons for doubting common recourse to withdrawal are the need to teach people the practice and the limited evidence of successful birth spacing. Remarkable as it may seem for such a self-evident birth control technique, there is indeed considerable evidence that the practice had to be taught to a good many people.[90] More centrally, although withdrawal can be quite an effective technique of birth control if used carefully and persistently,[91] the limited achievements in birth spacing in earlier times suggest at least that *coitus interruptus* was not used successfully, even if the practice was common, and perhaps that the practice simply was not common. To be successful, a couple would have to practice withdrawal correctly, one might almost say religiously. Helena Wright, an English woman testifying before a Parliamentary committee in 1938, felt free to comment that "probably 80 percent of the present population of this country have been born through 'being careful.'"[92] This could, once again, demonstrate a profound ignorance of the correct procedure rather than failure to attempt withdrawal. Janet Brodie concluded that many persons must have practiced partial withdrawal rather than true *coitus interruptus,* that is, ejaculation inside the opening of the vagina rather than full withdrawal, because success was so limited.[93] Even those who insist most strongly that coitus interruptus was a common practice in earlier times concede that the practice, in its various forms, was in fact "notoriously

---

85. Besant, *supra* note 45, at 33.

86. James Ashton, The Book of Nature; Containing Information for Young People Who Think of Getting Married, on the Philosophy of Procreation and Sexual Intercourse; Showing How to Prevent Conception and to Avoid Child-Bearing 42 (1860); L.F.E. Bergeret, The Preventive Obstacle, or Conjugal Onanism (P. DeMarmon trans., 3rd ed. 1870); Robert Dale Owen, Moral Physiology 65 (10th ed. Gilbert Vale ed. 1858).

87. Owen, *supra* note 86, at 65. *See also* Mauriceau, *supra* note 83, at 143. *See generally* Brodie, *supra* note 9, at 63–65.

88. Brodie, *supra* note 9, at 65.

89. *See, e.g.,* Daniel Scott Smith, *Family Limitation, Sexual Conduct, and Domestic Feminism in Victorian America,* 1 Feminist Stud. 40, 130–32 (1973).

90. *See, e.g.,* Owen, *supra* note 86, at 76. *See also* Brodie, *supra* note 9, at 60; Degler, *supra* note 9, at 211; M.K. Hopkins, *Contraception in the Roman Empire,* 8 Comp. Stud. in Soc'y & Hist. 124 (1965).

91. Kistner, *supra* note 41, at 676.

92. Quoted in Brookes, *supra* note 12, at 113. People were expressing similar concerns back in the eighteenth century. Klepp, *supra* note 56, at 72. *See generally* Brodie, *supra* note 9, at 63–65.

93. Brodie, *supra* note 9, at 61.

unreliable" because of difficulties in male self-control, as indeed was recognized by the nineteenth century advocates of the practice.[94]

Finally, there were attempts to create artificial barriers to be worn on a penis or inside a vagina. Early condoms, supposedly named after a Dr. Condom who was physician at the court of Charles II of England, were made out of a sheep's bladder or intestines, fish membranes, or the like; similar devices can be found back as early as ancient Egypt.[95] Such devices were both uncomfortable and unreliable, subject to considerable leakage. A woman writing in 1671 described condoms as "armor against enjoyment and a spider web against danger."[96] At the present writing, there is no known record of any form of condom being used in the American colonies,[97] although they certainly became available in the early years of the Republic.

Some historians have argued that vulcanized rubber condoms became widely and cheaply available as early as 1850, relying in part on the great many euphemisms (more than for any other contraceptive device) that appeared then or in the ensuing several decades to describe the device.[98] The notorious Anthony Comstock provided some indication that condoms were beginning to be in wide use in the 1870s, boasting that within six months of the enactment of the "Comstock Law" and his appointment as special agent to the U.S. Post Office to enforce the act that he had personally seized 60,000 "rubber articles." [99] Even the advent of more effective condoms hardly alters the analysis, particularly as there is good evidence that early in the twentieth century abstinence and withdrawal (and even simple douches) remained more common than condoms as means for preventing pregnancy,[100] which is hardly surprising when one finds that as late as 1924 physician and birth control advocate Dr. Robert Dickinson found a 50 percent failure rate among condoms issued at three birth control clinics in London and New York.[101] Thus we find one woman lawyer (Ada Bittenbender) advising other women lawyers in 1889 to occupy separate beds, and even separate bedrooms, from their husbands if they truly want to avoid or

---

94. *See* ASHTON, *supra* note 86, at 42; MAURICEAU, *supra* note 83, at 143; OWEN, *supra* note 86, at 65. *See generally* PETCHESKY, *supra* note 3, at 50.

95. BRODIE, *supra* note 9, at 205–11; ERIC CHEVALLIER, THE CONDOM: THREE THOUSAND YEARS OF SAFER SEX (1995); B.F. FINCH & HUGH GREEN, CONTRACEPTION THROUGH THE AGES 50–57; HIMES, *supra* note 13, at 100, 186–202; NOONAN, *supra* note 13, at 347–48; JEANNETTE PARISOT, JOHNNY COME LATELY: A SHORT HISTORY OF THE CONDOM (1985); RIDDLE, *supra* note 7, at 5; WILLIAM ROBERTSON, AN ILLUSTRATED HISTORY OF CONTRACEPTION 112–13 (1990); TANNAHILL, *supra* note 13, at 129–30, 336, 411 n*; TONE, *supra* note 14, at 14, 51–53.

96. *See* BRODIE, *supra* note 9, at 208. *See also* GARDNER, *supra* note 45, at 109; HIMES, *supra* note 13, at 190; PARISOT, *supra* note 95, at 13; TONE, *supra* note 14, at 67–69.

97. BRODIE, *supra* note 9, at 205. *See also* Klepp, *supra* note 56, at 71.

98. *Id.* at 190–92, 206–11; DEGLER, *supra* note 9, at 217; REED, *supra* note 9, at 15; RIDDLE, *supra* note 7, at 5; TANNAHILL, *supra* note 13, at 411; TONE, *supra* note 14, at 14–15, 54, 69; McLaren, *supra* note 45, at 326–27. On Charles Goodyear's discovery and development of the vulcanization process around 1840, see HOWARD & RALPH WOLF, RUBBER: A STORY OF GLORY AND GREED 15–29 (1936); H.J. Stern, *History,* in RUBBER TECHNOLOGY AND MANUFACTURE 1 (C.M. Blow & C. Hepburn eds. 1982).

99. Quoted in EDWARD DE GRAZIA, GIRLS LEAN BACK EVERYWHERE: THE LAW OF OBSCENITY AND THE ASSAULT ON GENIUS 4 (1992) (Comstock also reported seizing 31,500 boxes of pills and powders, although he described these as "mostly 'aphrodisiacs.'"). *See also* T.J.B. Buckingham, *The Trade in Questionable Rubber Goods,* INDIA RUBBER WORLD, Mar. 15, 1892, at 164. *See generally* TONE, *supra* note 14, at 54–55, 69–70; BRUCE WOYCKE, BIRTH CONTROL IN GERMANY 4, 36 (1988).

100. BROOKES, *supra* note 12, at 6; DEGLER, *supra* note 9, at 212–13, 222–23. *See generally* TONE, *supra* note 14; McLaren, *supra* note 45, at 326–27.

101. Robert Dickinson, *Contraception: A Medical Review of the Situation,* 8 AM. J. OBSTET. & GYNECOLOGY 584, 585–87 (1924). Another test, in 1934 and 1935, found a 59 percent failure rate. PALMER & GREENBERG, *supra* note 43, at 272. *See also* TONE, *supra* note 14, at 70–71.

limit pregnancies.[102] Because of careless manufacturing, rubber condoms often were more uncomfortable and more unreliable even than skin condoms.[103] Even today, condoms have a failure rate of about 15 percent.[104] No wonder Linda Gordon conceded that condoms were not in general use before World War I.[105]

Doctor Wilhelm Mensinga is usually identified as the inventor of the first successful contraceptive diaphragm in 1842.[106] Mensinga termed his invention an "occlusive pessary"—although in fact it was quite different from a true pessary. Somewhat similar devices were patented in the United States as early as the 1835, although there is no evidence that these were marketed widely.[107] Improvements were made steadily throughout the century. It is perhaps more than a coincidence that in the 1880s respectable women first began to wear attractive nightgowns in place of the "markedly unappealing" nightgowns that had formerly been the custom.[108]

Remarkably, quite a few physicians recommended certain "intrauterine pessaries" as a means of promoting rather than preventing conception, although today we would recognized these as "IUD's or as simple sponges intended to absorb sperm."[109] Linda Gordon has conceded that cervical diaphragms were not much in use in the United States before World War I.[110] She speculated that psychological concerns regarding sexuality probably deterred many women, particular middle and upper class women who could afford diaphragms in the nineteenth century, from using the devices. Janet Brodie was extremely skeptical of any such pruderies or anxieties inhibiting women from using diaphragms or pessaries.[111] Brodie would have us believe that effective diaphragms were in widespread use by 1840.[112]

---

102. Virginia Drachman, Sisters in Law: Women Lawyers in Modern American History 116 (1998).

103. Brodie, *supra* note 9, at 210.

104. Elise Jones & Jacqueline Darroch Forrest, *Contraceptive Failure Rates Based on the 1988 NSFG*, 24 Fam. Planning Perspectives 12 (Jan./Feb. 1992); David Lee Warner & Roberta Hatcher, & James Trussell, *Condom Slippage and Breakage Rates*, 24 Fam. Planning Perspectives 20 (Jan./Feb. 1992). John Kenyon Mason indicates that condoms are 98% successful, "given intelligent use." J.K. Mason, Medico-Legal Aspects of Reproduction and Parenthood 43 (2nd ed. 1998).

105. Gordon, *supra* note 3, at 63–64.

106. Himes, *supra* note 13, at 319; Reed, *supra* note 9, at 97–99; Robertson, *supra* note 95, at 114; Tannahill, *supra* note 13, at 411–12; Tone, *supra* note 14, at 56, 121, 126; Bullough, *supra* note 99, at 105.

107. Brodie, *supra* note 9, at 217–19. *See also* Reed, *supra* note 9, at 115; Tone, *supra* note 14, at 56–58; Bullough, *supra* note 99, at 114.

108. C. Willett & Phillis Cunningham, The History of Underclothes 16 (1951); Tannahill, *supra* note 13, at 411.

109. *See, e.g.,* William Goodell, Lessons in Gynecology 126 (1879); C.D. Meigs, Women: Their Diseases and Remedies 204–05 (1848). *See also* Brodie, *supra* note 9, at 221–23; Shirley Green, The Curious History of Contraception 114 (1971); Tannahill, *supra* note 13, at 410; Tone, *supra* note 14, at 59–61. Manufacturers of under-the-counter contraceptives also made and distributed a wide-variety of true pessaries. *See* Brodie, *supra*, at 72–73; Gordon, *supra* note 3, at 68; Tone, *supra*, at 61–66.

110. *Id.* at 179. *See also* Brodie, *supra* note 9, at 216–24; Himes, *supra* note 13, at 288, 319–21; Kern, *supra* note 45, at 155; Tannahill, *supra* note 13, at 412. Even today, IUDs—the most popular contraceptive worldwide—are seldom used in the United States. *See* Patricia Cohen, *The IUD: Birth-Control Device that the U.S. Market Won't Bear*, Wash. Post, Aug. 6, 1996, at A1; Sheldon Segal, *Contraceptive Update*, 23 NYU Rev. L. & Soc. Change 457, 459–60 (1997). The cause appears to be serious medical complications that led to widespread litigation over a popular form of IUD known as the Dalkon Shield. *See* Sylvia Law, *Tort Liability and the Availability of Contraceptive Drugs and Devices in the United States*, 23 NYU Rev. L. & Soc. Change 339, 362–68, 383–85 (1997).

111. Brodie, *supra* note 9, at 219–21, 224.

112. *Id.* at 188. *See also* Tone, *supra* note 14, at 59–61.

In any event, these devices were not entirely reliable. Even today, diaphragms and similar barrier contraceptives have failure rates of about 18 percent.[113] Furthermore, as Linda Gordon commented, diaphragms are "rich folks' contraceptive."[114] In addition to a careful fitting and knowledge of correct use, a diaphragm required running water and privacy; its use was sufficiently annoying that it was often "left in the drawer." No wonder that even Janet Brodie has stated that so much conflicting advice was being marketed in the nineteenth century that the dominant reaction of the intended audience was more likely to have been confusion than useful education.[115] Regardless of which historian is correct, diaphragms do not appear to have been widely used in (or before) the nineteenth century.

As late as 1931, one doctor wrote that there were no safe and effective methods for contraception, although this might have reflected a more stringent standard of effectiveness than others relied on.[116] The first large-scale clinical study of contraceptive use in the United States found that, for this New York clinic in 1924, contraceptive douches were used by 60 percent of the clients, condoms by 42 percent, male withdrawal (*coitus interruptus*) by 40 percent, nursing a child by 30 percent, male holding back (*coitus reservatus*) by 30 percent, a suppository by 12 percent, a "cervical cap" (an early form of vaginal diaphragm) by 10 percent, a contraceptive sponge by 4 percent, an IUD by 2 percent, and various powders and tablets by yet others.[117] Only 4 percent relied on complete abstinence. This sounds like a rather complete and potentially effective repertoire of techniques. Yet the very fact that the percentages add up to more than 200 percent indicates that people did not feel that these techniques were highly reliable.

The people of the time tried to assure control of their fertility by using two or more contraceptive techniques at a time.[118] This must have made for messy and unpleasant love-making, to say the least. How successful it was is another matter. Enid Charles, in study undertaken in England during the Depression, estimated the failure rate of condoms at 21 percent, diaphragms at 23 percent, douching at 73 percent, and quinine pessaries as virtually useless.[119] All in all, the ev-

---

113. *A Contraceptive Is Denied Approval*, N.Y. TIMES, Oct. 22, 1996, at C3 (reporting denial of approval to a new form of contraceptive shield because of ineffectiveness; Lisa Cox of the National Women's Health Network was quoted as demanding approval because of women's desperate need). Law professor Ruth Colker reports a 5% failure rate for the diaphragm when properly used, compared to 3% for condoms and less than 1% for the pill, but that given incorrect usage patterns the failure rate for diaphragms actually is about 18% (compared to 12% for condoms and about 3% for the pill). RUTH COLKER, ABORTION & DIALOGUE — PRO-CHOICE, PRO-LIFE, AND AMERICAN LAW 68 (1992). Colker's source is ROBERT HATCHER *et al.*, CONTRACEPTIVE TECHNOLOGY: 1988–89, at 151 (1988).

114. GORDON, *supra* note 3, at 308–11. *See also* BROOKES, *supra* note 12, at 135; TONE, *supra* note 14, at 152–55; Earl Lomon Koos, *Class Differences in the Employment of Contraceptive Measures*, 12 HUMAN FERTILITY 99 (Dec. 1947).

115. BRODIE, *supra* note 9, at 189–90.

116. A.J. Rongy, *Abortion and Birth Control: A Critical Study*, 37 AM. MED. 400, 404 (1931). *See also* MORRIS FISHBEIN, MEDICAL FOLLIES 142 (1925); PALMER & GREENBERG, *supra* note 43, at 271; *Editorial*, 94 JAMA 2806 (1930).

117. DOROTHY BOCKER, BIRTH CONTROL METHODS 4–7 (1924). On the prevalence of *coitus interruptus*, see also Dickinson, *supra*, at 602.

118. TONER, *supra* note 14, at 77–78, 82–83. *See also* GORDON, *supra* note 3, at 70 ("[T]he best available methods were not so good as they are today.")

119. ENID CHARLES, THE PRACTICE OF BIRTH CONTROL: AN ANALYSIS OF THE BIRTH CONTROL EXPERIENCES OF NINE HUNDRED WOMEN 43 (1932). Similar studies near the same period in time found that condoms failed at rates of 50–60 percent. PALMER & GREENBERG, *supra* note 43, at 272; Dickinson, *supra* note 101, at 585–87. *See also* TONE, *supra* note 14, at 70–72. Some studies found that douching failure rates were above 90 percent. BOCKER, *supra* note 117, at 5. *See also* TONE, *supra*, at 76–77; Dickinson, *supra*, at 586. Some observes considered diaphragms pretty much useless. TONE, *supra*, at 126 (noting one report of 100 percent failure for diaphragms). Kirsti Dyer reports that quinine pessaries were used in Japan during "ancient times."

idence suggests that there were no safe and effective contraceptive practices, devices, or medi-cines throughout most of human history other than sexual abstinence — except lactation.

Only after 1880 did mechanical and chemical means of birth control become available in America and England to any large extent, and even then only over considerable public opposi-tion.[120] The first public birth control clinic was established in the Netherlands in 1882.[121] As late as 1950, the only available form of artificial contraception wholly within the control of the woman was the vaginal diaphragm, a form that remained difficult to use correctly and thus prone to failure, particularly among the poorly educated.[122] To explain the pattern of a woman's ending of birthing well before menopause, and perhaps the spacing of births as well, we must turn to lactation and sexual abstinence.

# Lactation

*Nature has so wisely ordered things that did women suckle their children, they would preserve their own health, and there would be such an interval between the birth of each child, that we should seldom see a houseful of babes.*

— Mary Wollstonecraft[123]

Apart from sexual abstinence, the most likely means to assure birth spacing during most of the time humans have been on the planet has been prolonged lactation. Modern research has confirmed that prolonged lactation does indeed prevent the resumption of menstruation, partic-ularly for undernourished women, albeit somewhat unpredictably.[124] Undernourishment was the

---

Dyer, *supra* note 14, at 2818. She does not mention that quinine was introduced from Peru only sometime after Columbus. *See generally* Tone, *supra*, at 68–77; Bullough, *supra* note 101, at 104–06.

120. Brodie, *supra* note 9, at 205–24; Kern, *supra* note 45, at 155; Petchesky, *supra* note 3, at 34–35; Carroll Smith-Rosenberg, Disorderly Conduct: Visions of Gender in Victorian America 224 (1985); Vivien Walsh, *Contraception: The Growth of a Technology,* in Alice through the Microscope: The Power of Science over Women's Lives 108, 182–83 (Lynda Birke et al. eds. 1980). *See generally* Gordon, *supra* note 3, at 159–390.; Tone, *supra* note 14; Steven Polgar, *Population History and Population Policies from an Anthropological Perspective,* 13 Current Anthropology 203 (1972); Étienne van de Walle, *Motivations and Technology and the Decline of French Fertility,* in Family and Sexuality in French History 135 (Robert Wheaton & Tamara Hareven eds. 1980). On the public opposition, see Brodie, *supra,* at 87–288; David Garrow, Liberty and Sexuality: The Right of Privacy and the Making of *Roe v. Wade* 1–269 (2nd ed. 1998); Tone, *supra* note 14, at 3–200

121. Gordon, *supra* note 3, at 172.

122. *Id.* at 308–11; Palmer & Greenberg, *supra* note 43, at 272; Raymond Pearl, Biology of Population Growth 167 (1925); Tone, *supra* note 14, at 74–75; Dickinson, *supra* note 101, at 586.

123. Mary Wollstonecraft, Vindication of the Rights of Woman 315 (reprint ed. 1978; original pub. 1792).

124. Child Spacing in Tropical Africa (H.J. Page & R. Lesthaeghe eds. 1981); Carl Djerassi, The Politics of Contraception 10–13 (1979); Harrison, *supra* note 7, at 175–76; Hrdy, Mother Nature, *supra* note 8, at 104–05, 193–96, 364–65, 409–10, 449–50; Moni Nag, Factors Affecting Human Fertil-ity in Non-Industrial Societies: A Cross-Cultural Study 79 (1962); James Wood, The Dynamics of Human Reproduction 368–70 (1994); Eric Charnov & David Berrigan, *Why Do Female Primates Have Such Long Lifespans and So Few Babies? Or Life in the Slow Lane,* 1 Evolutionary Anthropology 191 (1993); Peter Ellison, *Breastfeeding, Fertility, and Maternal Condition,* in Breastfeeding: Biocultural Perspectives 305 (Patricia Stuart-Macadam & Katherine Dettwyler eds. 1995); Rose Frisch, *Fatness, Puberty, and Fertility,* 89 Nat. Hist. 16 (1980); B. Galdikas & J. Wood, *Birth Spacing in Humans and Apes,* 83 Am. J. Physical An-thropology 185 (1990); Robert May, *Human Reproduction Reconsidered,* 272 Nature 491 (1978); Melvin Konner & Carol Worthman, *Nursing Frequency, Gonadal Function, and Birth Spacing among !Kung Hunter-Gatherers,* 207 Science 788 (1980); Robert Potter *et al., Applications of Field Studies to Research on the Physiol-*

lot of most women (and men) before the nineteenth century. Prolonged lactation was particularly common in the United States as resort to wet nurses remained expensive and therefore rare in the American colonies and on into the nineteenth century among all social classes.[125] Some authorities recognized lactation as an effective means of birth spacing in the eighteenth and nineteenth centuries.[126] Women's diaries and letters written in the eighteenth or nineteenth centuries record their reliance on extended periods of breast feeding to space pregnancies.[127] American Indians apparently relied on prolonged lactation, along with ritualized sexual abstinence and infanticide, to maintain family sizes about half as large as their white neighbors.[128] Islamic law required a mother to suckle an infant for two years.[129] With such spacing, a woman, whether free or slave, white or non-white, could expect to be either pregnant or nursing a child (if she did not employ a wet nurse) for most of her adult life.[130]

Many of the historians who have already turned up in this study, when they were not focusing on supporting abortion rights, have concluded that lactation was the primary means of birth spacing until the twentieth century.[131] Others have sought to discredit the possibility that lactation was the secret to lower than expected birthrates, but their arguments are unpersuasive.

ogy of Human Reproduction: Lactation and Its Effects upon Birth Intervals in Eleven Punjab Villages, India, 18 J. CHRONIC DISEASES 1125 (1965); Virginia Vitzthum, Nursing Behavior and Its Relation to Duration of Post-Partum Amenorrhea in an Andean Community, 21 J. BIOSOCIAL SCI. 145 (1989).

125. BRODIE, supra note 9, at 46–47; JOHN DEMOS, A LITTLE COMMONWEALTH: FAMILY LIFE IN PLYMOUTH COLONY 133 (1970); PHILIP GREVEN, JR., FOUR GENERATIONS: POPULATION, LAND, AND FAMILY IN COLONIAL ANDOVER, MASSACHUSETTS 30, 112 (1970); LAUREL THATCHER ULRICH, GOODWIVES: IMAGE AND REALITY IN THE LIVES OF WOMEN IN NORTHERN NEW ENGLAND, 1650–1750, at 138–39, 141–44 (1983); Dorothy McLaren, Fertility, Infant Mortality, and Breast Feeding in the Eighteenth Century, 22 MED. HIST. 378 (1978); Sally McMillen, Mother's Sacred Duty: Breast-Feeding Patterns among Middle- and Upper-Class Women in the Antebellum South, 51 J. SOUTHERN HIST. 333 (1985). The possibility of developing a wet-nursing industry within the increasingly prosperous United States was preempted by the development of the nursing bottles. BRODIE, supra, at 47.

126. PIERRE DIONIS, TRAITÉ GÉNÉRAL DES ACCOUCHEMENTS, QUI INSTRUIT CE TOUT CE QU'IL FAUT FAIRE POUR ÊTRE HABILE ACCOUCHEUR 455 (1711); STORER, supra note 45, at 41–42. See also CATHERINE SCHOLTEN, CHILDBEARING IN AMERICAN SOCIETY 1650–1850, at 13–14 (1985).

127. See, e.g., CECIL DRINKER, NOT SO LONG AGO: A CHRONICLE OF MEDICINE AND DOCTORS IN COLONIAL PHILADELPHIA 54, 59–60 (1917) (quoting from the diary of Elizabeth Drinker); ULRICH, supra note 125, at 262 n.47 (analyzing the diary of Martha Ballard). See also EMMA ANGELL DRAKE, WHAT A YOUNG WIFE OUGHT TO KNOW 131–32 (1908); WOLLSTONECRAFT, supra note 123, at 315. See generally JUDITH SCHNEID LEWIS, IN THE FAMILY WAY: CHILDBEARING IN THE BRITISH ARISTOCRACY, 1760–1860, at 212–13 n.63 (1986); MARY BETH NORTON, LIBERTY'S DAUGHTERS: THE REVOLUTIONARY EXPERIENCE OF AMERICAN WOMEN 233 (1980); Klepp, supra note 56, at 102.

128. BRODIE, supra note 9, at 50–51; JOHN MACK FARAGHER, SUGAR CREEK: LIFE ON THE ILLINOIS PRAIRIE 114 (1986); JAMES MERRELL, THE INDIANS' NEW WORLD: CATAWBAS AND THEIR NEIGHBORS 140 (1989). In Japan, where infanticide appears to have been common, registered births on average were spaced between three and five years apart. See SUSAN HANLEY & KOZO YAMAMURA, ECONOMIC AND DEMOGRAPHIC CHANGE IN PREINDUSTRIAL JAPAN 1600–1868, at 241–46 (1977).

129. Sarah Rumage, Resisting the West: The Clinton Administration's Promotion of Abortion at the 1994 Cairo Conference and the Strength of the Islamic Response, 27 CAL. W. INT'L L.J. 1, 41–42 (1996).

130. 1 ANDERSON & ZINSSER, supra note 13, at 105.

131. See generally 1 ANDERSON & ZINSSER, supra note 13, at 109; BRODIE, supra note 9, at 17, 31–33, 45–49; D'EMILIO & FREEDMAN, supra note 9, at 5, 8, 13–14, 26, 48, 61, 118; GORDON, supra note 3, at 45, 49; MICHAEL GROSSBERG, GOVERNING THE HEARTH: LAW AND THE FAMILY IN NINETEENTH-CENTURY AMERICA 157, 159 (1985); JACQUES HENRIPIN, LA POPULATION CANADIENNE AU DÉBUT DU XVIIIe SIÈCLE 86–87 (1954); HRDY, MOTHER NATURE, supra note 8, at 104–05; HUNT, supra note 56, at 82–83; INGRAM, supra note 68, at 158; NORTON, supra note 127, at 232–34; SCHOLTEN, supra note 126, at 14; DANIEL BLAKE SMITH, INSIDE THE GREAT HOUSE: PLANTER FAMILY LIFE IN EIGHTEENTH-CENTURY CHESAPEAKE SOCIETY 36–37 (1980); ULRICH, supra note 125, at 135, 139, 262 n.47; L.F. Bouvier, The Spacing of Births among French Canadian Families: An Historical Approach, 5 CAN. REV. SOCIOLOGY & ANTHROPOLOGY 17 (1968); Jan Lewis & Kenneth Lockridge, "Sally Has Been Sick": Pregnancy and Family Limitation among Virginia Gentry Women, 1780–1830, 22 J.

British historian Angus McLaren noted that the effects of "long suckling children" on the birth rate were noted by the eighteenth century; he argued, however, that because women so obviously wanted to control the number and timing of their births, they must necessarily have had better means for doing so, basing his conclusion on the folk-beliefs of their medically primitive cultures in the effectiveness of magical rituals and procedures, with lactation at best serving to supplement the other methods that he assumed existed.[132] John Riddle claimed to consider every alternative to mechanical or medicinal contraceptives in order to discredit them and thereby to prove that safe and effective mechanical or medicinal contraceptives existed in times long past.[133] He did not bother, however, to consider lactation as a possible alternative.

The birth rate among women in America declined steadily during the late eighteenth century and throughout the nineteenth century, driven in part by economic and social changes although at different times and rates for various groups of women defined by class and race.[134] The rate of illegitimate pregnancies similarly declined sharply during the same period, both in America and

---

SOCIAL HIST. 5, 9–10 (1988); Dorothy McLaren, *Nature's Contraceptive: Wet-Nursing and Prolonged Lactation: The Case of Chesham, Buckinghamshire, 1578–1601,* 22 MED. HIST. 426 (1978).

132. MCLAREN, *supra* note 13, at 3–8, 107, 111.

133. RIDDLE, *supra* note 7, at 1–14.

134. CATHERINE CLINTON, THE PLANTATION MISTRESS: WOMAN'S WORLD IN THE OLD SOUTH 60–61, 152–56 (1982); DEGLER, *supra* note 9, at 178–209, 220–22; HASIA DINER, ERIN'S DAUGHTERS IN AMERICA: IRISH IMMIGRANT WOMEN IN THE NINETEENTH CENTURY 54 (1983); COLIN FORSTER & G.S.L. TUCKER, ECONOMIC OPPORTUNITY AND WHITE AMERICAN FERTILITY RATES, 1800–1860 (1972); PETCHESKY, *supra* note 3, at 73–74; ANNE SCOTT, THE SOUTHERN LADY: FROM PEDESTAL TO POLITICS, 1830–1930, at 38–39 (1970); RICHARD STECKEL, THE ECONOMICS OF U.S. SLAVE AND SOUTHERN WHITE FERTILITY 176 (1985); ROBERT WELLS, UNCLE SAM'S FAMILY: ISSUES AND PERSPECTIVES ON AMERICAN DEMOGRAPHIC HISTORY 28–56 (1985) ("WELLS, UNCLE SAM'S FAMILY"); STEPHANIE GRAUMAN WOLF, URBAN VILLAGE: POPULATION, COMMUNITY, AND FAMILY STRUCTURE IN GERMANTOWN, PENNSYLVANIA, 1683–1800, at 264–70 (1976); VIRGINIA YANS-MCLAUGLIN, FAMILY AND COMMUNITY: ITALIAN IMMIGRANTS IN BUFFALO, 1880–1930, at 105 (1977); Wendell Bash, *Changing Birth Rates in Developing America: New York State, 1840–1875,* 41 MILLBANK MEM. FUND Q. 163 (1963); Susan Bloomberg *et al., A Census Probe into Nineteenth Century Family History: Southern Michigan, 1850–1880,* 5 J. SOC. HIST. 28 (1971); Edward Byers, *Fertility Transition in a New England Commercial Center: Nantucket, Ma. 1680–1840,* 13 J. INTERDISCIPLINARY HIST. 17 (1982); Phillips Cutright & Edward Shorter, *The Effects of Health on the Completed Fertility of Non-White and White U.S. Women Born between 1867 and 1935,* 13 J. SOC. HIST. 191 (1979); Richard Easterlin, *Factors in the Decline of Farm Fertility in the United States: Some Preliminary Research Results,* 63 J. AM. HIST. 600 (1976); Michael Haines, *Fertility and Marriage in a Nineteenth-Century Industrial City: Philadelphia, 1850–1880,* 40 J. ECON. HIST. 151 (1980); Michael Haines, *Fertility Decline in Industrial America: An Analysis of the Pennsylvania Anthracite Region, 1850–1900,* 32 POPULATION STUD. 327 (1978); Tamara Hareven & Maris Vinovskis, *Marital Fertility, Ethnicity, and Occupation in Urban Families: An Analysis of South Boston and the South End in 1880,* 8 J. SOCIAL HIST. 464 (1975); Robert Higgs & H. Louis Stettler III, *Colonial New England Demography: A Sampling Approach,* 27 WM. & MARY Q. 289 (3rd ser. 1970); Klepp, *supra* note 56, at 93–107; Barbara Logue, *The Whaling Industry and Fertility Decline, Nantucket, Ma., 1680–1850,* 8 SOC. SCI. HIST. 427 (1983); Joseph McFalls, jr., & George Masnick, *Birth Control and the Fertility of the U.S. Black Population, 1880–1980,* 6 J. FAM. HIST. 89 (1981); Warren Sanderson, *Quantitative Aspects of Marriage, Fertility, and Family Limitation in Nineteenth Century America: Another Application of the Coale Specifications,* 16 DEMOGRAPHY 339 (1979); Xarifa Sallume & Frank Notestein, *Trends in the Size of Families Completed Prior to 1910 in Various Social Classes,* 38 AM. J. SOC. 404 (1932); Daniel Scott Smith, *The Demographic History of Colonial New England,* in THE AMERICAN FAMILY IN SOCIAL HISTORICAL PERSPECTIVE 397 (Michael Gordon ed. 1973); H. Temkin-Greener & A.C. Swedlund, *Fertility Transition in the Connecticut Valley, 1740–1850,* 32 POPULATION STUD. 40 (1978); Maris Vinovskis, *Socioeconomic Determinants of Interstate Fertility Differentials in the United States,* 6 J. INTERDISCIPLINARY HIST. 375 (1976); Robert Wells, *Family Size and Fertility Control in Eighteenth-Century America: A Study of Quaker Families,* 25 POPULATION STUD. 73 (1971); Lynne Withey, *Household Structure in Urban and Rural Areas: The Case of Rhode Island, 1774–1800,* 3 J. FAM. HIST. 38 (3rd ser. 1972).

across Europe.[135] Similarly, the rate of pregnant brides declined from a high of 30 percent at the beginning of the nineteenth century to about 10 percent by the middle of the century.[136] This period was marked by the emergence of a consumer economy in which many persons came to expect to be able to purchase what had only a few years before been seen as unobtainable luxury goods: lace curtains, imported teas, fine linens and china, silver tea services, and so on.[137] In such a setting, too many children could only impede a family's social advance. At the same time, new technologies and changing social arrangements made children an economic burden rather than a source of free labor.[138] Furthermore, the need to birth numerous children simply to maintain the population declined as life expectancy slowly rose throughout the nineteenth century[139]—a change that mostly reflected declines in infant mortality rather than improvement in the health of adults.[140] Women had the further incentive of limiting the risks to their lives and health from too frequent pregnancies.[141] Birthing in the early nineteenth century, without knowledge of analgesics, anesthetics, antiseptics, and antibiotics, remained painful, dangerous, and debilitating.[142]

Many women down through the centuries successfully spaced their infants at about two years apart.[143] The pattern is found widely through history, although with many exceptions. Our evidence does not reveal directly how women spaced their births. Birth spacing at two years could

---

135. D'EMILIO & FREEDMAN, *supra* note 9, at 76; TANNAHILL, *supra* note 13, at 333; Jaques Depauw, *Illicit Sexual Activity and Society in Eighteenth Century Nantes,* in FAMILY AND SOCIETY: SELECTIONS FROM THE AN-NALES ETC. 145 (Robert Forster & Orest Ranum eds. 1976).

136. *Id.* at 178–84.

137. BARBARA BERGMAN, THE ECONOMIC EMERGENCE OF WOMEN (1986); NEIL MCCORMICK *et al.,* THE BIRTH OF THE CONSUMER SOCIETY: THE COMMERCIALIZATION OF EIGHTEENTH CENTURY ENGLAND (1988); IVY PINCHBECK, WOMEN WORKERS AND THE INDUSTRIAL REVOLUTION, 1750–1850, at 282–83, 304–06 (1930); CAROLE SHAMAS, THE PRE-INDUSTRIAL CONSUMER IN ENGLAND AND AMERICA (1990); T.H. Breen, *An Empire of Goods: The Anglicization of Colonial America, 1690–1776,* 25 J. BRIT. STUD. 467 (1986).

138. *See generally* JOSEPH BANKS, VICTORIAN VALUES: SECULARISM AND THE SIZE OF FAMILIES (1981); JOSEPH & OLIVE BANKS, FEMINISM AND FAMILY PLANNING IN VICTORIAN ENGLAND (1964); JOSEPH BANKS, PROSPERITY AND PARENTHOOD: A STUDY OF FAMILY PLANNING AMONG THE VICTORIAN MIDDLE CLASSES (1954); MARY ANN MASON, FROM FATHER'S PROPERTY TO CHILDREN'S RIGHTS: THE HISTORY OF CUSTODY IN THE UNITED STATES (1994); Norman Himes, *The Birth Control Handbills of 1823,* LANCET, Aug. 6 1927, at 313. *See also* ANSLEY COALE & MELVIN ZELNICK, NEW ESTIMATES OF FERTILITY AND POPULATION IN THE U.S. 36 (1963); BROOKES, *supra* note 12, at 41–42; D'EMILIO & FREEDMAN, *supra* note 9, at 57–59; MYRA MARX FERREE & BETH HESS, CONTROVERSY AND COALITION: THE NEW FEMINIST MOVEMENT ACROSS THREE DECADES OF CHANGE 12 (rev. ed. 1994); GORDON, *supra* note 3, at 11, 48–49, 72–91, 150–54, 393–94; YASU-KICHI YASUBA, BIRTH RATES OF THE WHITE POPULATION IN THE UNITED STATES, 1800–1860: AN ECONOMIC STUDY (1962); Easterlin, *supra* note 134; Smith, *supra* note 89.

139. The life expectancy at birth for men in Massachusetts in 1850 was 38, and for women was 40.5; by 1900, the figure for men had reached 47, and for women 49. U.S. BUR. OF CENSUS, HISTORICAL STATISTICS OF THE UNITED STATES: COLONIAL TIMES TO 1970, at 37 (1975).

140. In 1850, in Massachusetts, 13% of children died during the first year of their life. *Id.* at 57. *See generally* POPULATION IN HISTORY: ESSAYS IN HISTORICAL DEMOGRAPHY (David Glass & David Eversley eds. 1965); FRANK LORIMER, CULTURE AND HUMAN FERTILITY(1954).

141. BRODIE, *supra* note 9, at 36–37; DEGLER, *supra* note 9, at 188–89, 195, 208; D'EMILIO & FREEDMAN, *supra* note 9, at 58–59; Smith, *supra* note 89.

142. DEGLER, *supra* note 9, at 59–63.

143. 1 ANDERSON & ZINSSER, *supra* note 13, at 133–37, 383; JEAN-LOUIS FLANDRIN, FAMILIES IN FORMER TIMES: KINSHIP, HOUSEHOLD AND SEXUALITY 59 (Richard Southern trans. 1979); M.W. FLINN, THE EURO-PEAN DEMOGRAPHIC SYSTEM 84 (1981); LASLETT, *supra* note 13, at xi; PETER LASLETT, THE WORLD WE HAVE LOST FURTHER EXPLORED 117–18 (1983); PETCHESKY, *supra* note 3, at 30–38; QUAIFE, *supra* note 5, at 133–34, 171–72; RIDDLE, *supra* note 7, at 15; RUSSELL, *supra* note 18, at 58–59; WRIGLEY, *supra* note 65, at 17–19, 93, 127; E.A. WRIGLEY & R.S. SCHOFIELD, THE POPULATION HISTORY OF ENGLAND, 1541–1871, at 230

reflect the patterns of prolonged lactation, a control that was in the hands of women. This remained, however, only a feeble control over the spacing of pregnancies. Yet, at we have seen, both mechanical and medicinal contraceptives were even feebler. There is another pattern that we need to explain: As we approach the nineteenth century, women began to stop having children at ever earlier ages.[144] Lactation cannot explain a woman's ceasing to bear children altogether.

# Abstinence

*It is surprising to what extent the laity believes that medical science knows how to control the birth-rate. Just let me say that I know of but one prescription which is both safe and sure—namely, that the sexes shall remain apart.*

    —H.S. Pomeroy[145]

The most telling evidence against successful use of contraceptives, and against common recourse to *coitus interruptus* in particular, is the considerable recourse by married couples to the far more drastic measure of spouses living separately, often apparently as a means of birth spacing.[146] Historians intent on showing that abortion and contraception must have been common and effective in the mid-nineteenth century have assumed that separate living simply did not occur. Generally, these historians have not bothered to examine the relevant evidence.[147] Janet Brodie assumed because it became common in mid-century for pamphleteers attempting to sell contraceptive or abortifacient devices to criticize sexual abstinence sharply, that separate living did not occur.[148] Brodie ignored both the contrary arguments by many nineteenth-century feminists and anti-feminists and also the contemporary evidence of living apart. Closely related to separate living patterns was a pattern of delayed marriage which appeared in region after region of the United States whenever open land became scarce.[149] A similar pattern was well entrenched

---

(1981); Philippe Ariès, *Interprétation pour une histoire des mentalités*, in LA PRÉVENTION DES NAISSANCES DANS LA FAMILLE 311, 314–19 (Hélène Bergues ed. 1960).

144. BRODIE, *supra* note 9, at 2–4; THE DECLINE OF FERTILITY IN EUROPE (Ansley Coale & Susan Cotts Watkins eds. 1986); DEMOS, *supra* note 125, at 68; JOAN JENSEN, LOOSENING THE BONDS: MID-ATLANTIC FARM WOMEN, 1750–1850, at 29, 119 (1986); J.E. KNODEL, THE DECLINE OF FERTILITY IN GERMANY, 1871–1939 (1974); NORTON, *supra* note 127, at 232–34; MICHAEL TEITELBAUM, THE BRITISH FERTILITY DECLINE: DEMOGRAPHIC TRANSITION IN THE CRUCIBLE OF THE INDUSTRIAL REVOLU TION (1984); WELLS, UNCLE SAM'S FAMILY, *supra* note 134, at 28–56 (1985).

145. H.S. POMEROY, THE ETHICS OF MARRIAGE 62 (1888) (emphasis in original).

146. BRODIE, *supra* note 9, at 10–11, 16, 18, 23, 24–27, 188; D'EMILIO & FREEDMAN, *supra* note 9, at 59, 62; FARAGHER, *supra* note 128, at 205; PAUL NAGEL, THE ADAMS WOMEN: ABIGAIL AND LOUISA, THEIR SISTERS AND DAUGHTERS 80, 96–97, 265–71 (1987); NANCY GREY OSTERUD, BONDS OF COMMUNITY: THE LIVES OF FARM WOMEN IN NINETEENTH-CENTURY NEW YORK 73 (1991); Klepp, *supra* note 56, at 72; Lewis & Lockridge, *supra* note 130, at 10–13. Not all of these separations were amicable, resulting in considerable litigation to enforce support obligations. *See* MARYLYNN SALMON, WOMEN AND THE LAW OF PROPERTY IN EARLY AMERICA 60–65 (1986); Joseph Ranney, *Anglicans, Merchants, and Feminists: A Comparative Study of the Evolution of Married Women's Rights in Virginia, New York, and Wisconsin*, 6 WM. & MARY J. WOMEN & L. 493, 500–01, 505 (2000).

147. *See, e.g.,* MOHR, *supra* note 39, at 282 n.100; QUAIFE, *supra* note 5, at 172.

148. BRODIE, *supra* note 9, at 188.

149. *See* HAL BARRON, THOSE WHO STAYED BEHIND: RURAL SOCIETY IN NINETEENTH-CENTURY NEW ENGLAND 26 (1984); DEGLER, *supra* note 9, at 182–86; D'EMILIO & FREEDMAN, *supra* note 9, at 5; FARAGHER, *supra* note 128, at 253–54; OSTERUD, *supra* note 146, at 72–80; YASUBA, *supra* note 138; Easterlin, *supra* note 134; Daniel Scott Smith, *"Early" Fertility Decline in America: A Problem in Family History*, 12 J. FAM. HIST. 73 (1987).

in England by the sixteenth century.[150] For the rising urban middle class, the seventeenth century saw the age of first marriage rise to levels never before seen—to the mid-twenties for women, and even older for men.[151]

Neither contraception nor abortion particularly appealed to most nineteenth-century feminists in the United States or the United Kingdom, although only abortion was condemned.[152] These women could hardly be described as timid or cautious. The very label "feminist" ought to suggest as much. Annie Besant, whose book on population control was widely read at the time, was a noted atheist who later fell under the influence of Henry Steel Olcott and Madame Blavatsky, becoming a Theosophist. Besant lived in India and became, despite her English birth, one of the major founders of the Indian National Congress.[153] Alice Stockham had become a physician at a time when that profession contained many men opposed the women becoming doctors at all. Susan B. Anthony and Elizabeth Cady Stanton abandoned the religions in which they were raised; Stanton went on to publish her own feminist version of the Bible.[154] Stanton was a figure of international stature who strongly influenced English suffragists as well as American, and had connections with suffragists in other European and Europeanized countries.[155] Her attempt to formulate her own version of sacred scripture came at a time when many women were finding religious fulfillment through increasing prominence in mainline Protestant churches rather than by attempting to break off on their own.[156]

American feminists of the nineteenth century were divided among many groups only loosely related to each other. One point on which they were remarkably consistent was in favoring "voluntary motherhood."[157] In a society where a dozen pregnancies and six or eight children were not unusual, "voluntary motherhood" was seen as the key to the improvement of women's lives.[158] Feminists often criticized marriage as bondage,[159] particularly before enact-

---

150. *See* Ingram, *supra* note 68, at 128–31, 135–36. We also find this pattern elsewhere in the world. *See, e.g.,* Hanley & Yamamura, *supra* note 128, at 227, 246–52, 257–58, 265–66, 324. *See generally* J. William Leasure, *Malthus, Marriage and Multiplication,* 16 Millbank Mem. Fund Q. 419 (1963). In European countries, dedicating superfluous sons or daughters to monasteries or convents often served the purpose of controlling population. *See* Hrdy, Mother Nature, *supra* note 8, at 341–42; James Boone III, *Parental Investment and Elite Family Structure in Preindustrial States: A Case Study of Late Medieval-Early Modern Portuguese Genealogies,* 88 Am. Anthropologist 859 (1986); Barbara Hager, *Get Thee to a Nunnery: Female Religious Claustration in Medieval Europe,* 13 Ethology & Sociobiology 385 (1992).

151. Tannahill, *supra* note 13, at 334; J. Hajnal, *European Marriage Patterns in Perspective,* in Population in History, *supra* note 140, at 101, 113–15. *See generally* 1 Fernand Braudel, Civilization and Capitalism, 15th–18th Century, at 31–103 (1979); Polgar, *supra* note 120.

152. *See, e.g.,* Besant, *supra* note 45; Stockham, *supra* note 81, at 246, 323–26; Victoria Claflin Woodhull, The Scare-Crows of Sexual Slavery 9–10 (1874). *See generally* Chapter 8.

153. Peter Washington, Madame Blavatsky's Baboon: A History of the Mystics, Mediums, and Misfits Who Brought Spiritualism to America 105–07 (1995). *See also* Edward Hower, *Spirited Story of the Psychic and the Colonel,* Smithsonian Mag., May, 1995, at 111, 127

154. Elizabeth Cady Stanton, The Women's Bible (1895).

155. *See* Elizabeth Cady Stanton as Revealed in Her Letters, Diary and Reminiscences (Theodore Stanton & Harriet Stanton Black eds. 1922); Sandra Stanley Holton, *From Anti-Slavery to Suffrage Militancy: The Bright Circle, Elizabeth Cady Stanton and the British Women's Movement,* in Suffrage and Beyond: International Feminist Perspectives 213 (Caroline Daley & Melanie Nolan eds. 1994).

156. *See* Ann Douglas, The Feminization of American Religion (1977); Smith-Rosenberg, *supra* note 120, at 129–64.

157. *See generally* Brodie, *supra* note 9, at 129–32; Gordon, *supra* note 3, at 95–135; Reva Siegel, *Abortion as a Sex Equality Right: Its Basis in Feminist Theory,* in Mothers in Law: Feminist Theory and the Legal Regulation of Motherhood 43, 50–51 (Martha Albertson Fineman & Isabel Karpin eds. 1995).

158. Gordon, *supra* note 3, at 95–120.

159. *See, e.g.,* 2 History of Woman Suffrage 642–44 (Elizabeth Cady Stanton, Susan B. Anthony, & Matilda Joslyn Gage eds. 1881); Victoria Woodhull, The Elixir of Life, or Why Do We Die? 8–9 (1873); Susan Anthony, *Editorial,* The Revolution, Oct. 27, 1870, at 264; M. Brinkerhoff, *Women and Motherhood,* The Revolution, Sept. 2, 1869, at 138. Apparently, a man wrote the earliest such criticism in the United

ment of the *Married Women's Acts*.[160] The movement for the reform of marriage was closely linked organizationally to the movement for the abolition of slavery before 1865, suggested by the common rhetorical reliance on the term "bondage."[161] The biographies of such feminist luminaries as Angelina Grimke (who married Theodore Weld), Abby Kelley (who married Stephen Foster), and Lucy Stone (who married Henry Blackwell) resonate with the modern reader because these women struggled to define an acceptable marriage relationship including economic and social equality, and then to design a marriage ceremony to express the relationship they were entering.[162]

Law professor Reva Siegel seeks to draw upon the tradition of the nineteenth-century feminist's denunciation of marriage as bondage to argue that the enactment of the abortion statutes in the nineteenth century was motivated by the desire to keep women in bondage.[163] The *Married Women's Acts* altered the terms of the struggle over marriage significantly, yet Siegel cavalierly mixed denunciations of marriage as bondage and theft from before the adoption of such acts with later criticisms focused more on the need for reproductive autonomy. She didn't even note the adoption of the *Married Women's Acts* or consider how the statutes, giving married women the right to control their own earnings and manage their own property, might have affected the discourse she quoted.[164] Siegel mentions the *Married Women's Acts* only in order to claim that the abortion statutes were meant to prevent women from acting on the rights conferred by these laws[165]—even though Siegel acknowledged that the questions of reforming marriage and of suppressing abortion "flowed from distinct conceptual premises."[166]

States. William Thompson, Appeal of One-Half of the Human Race, Women, against the Pretensions of the Other Half, Men, to Retain Them in Political, and Thence in Civil and Domestic Slavery (1825). *See generally* Degler, *supra* note 9, at 144–77; D'Emilio & Freedman, *supra* note 9, at 153–54; Joan Hoff, Law, Gender, and Injustice: A Legal History of U.S. Women 135–41 (1991); William Leach, True Love and Perfect Union: The Feminist Reform of Sex and Society (1980); Mary Roth Walsh, Doctors Wanted: No Women Need Apply 17–20 (1977); Ellen Carol DuBois, *Outgrowing the Compact of the Fathers: Equal Rights, Woman Suffrage, and the United States Constitution, 1820–1878,* 74 J. Am. Hist. 836 (1987). For the similar approach of English feminists, see Mary Lyndon Shanley, Feminism, Marriage, and the Law in Victorian England, 1850–1895 (1989).

160. *See generally* Mary Ritter Beard, Woman as a Force in History: A Study in Traditions and Realities 122–44, 158–66 (1946); Jean Donnison, Midwives and Medical Men: A History of the Struggle for the Control of Childbirth 74 (2nd ed. 1988); Hoff, *supra* note 159, at 121–35, 187–91; Salmon, *supra* note 146; Elizabeth Bowles Warbasse, The Changing Legal Rights of Married Women 1800–1861 (1987); Richard Chused, *Married Women's Property Law: 1800–1850,* 71 Geo. L.J. 1359 (1983); Ranney, *supra* note 146. For the parallel development of the law in England, see Shanley, *supra* note 159, at 49–78, 103–30.

161. *See* Ellen Carol DuBois, Feminism and Suffrage: The Emergence of an Independent Women's Movement in America, 1848–1869, at 32 (1978); Paula Giddings, When and Where I Enter: The Impact of Black Women on Race and Sex in America 55 (1984); Blanche Glassman Hersch, The Slavery of Sex: Feminist-Abolitionists in America (1978); Peggy Cooper Davis, *Neglected Stories and the Lawfulness of* Roe v. Wade, 28 Harv. C.R.-C.L. L. Rev. 299, 330–31 (1993); Holton, *supra* note 155.

162. Loving Warriors: Selected Letters of Lucy Stone and Henry B. Blackwell, 1853–1893 (Leslie Wheeler ed. 1981); Dorothy Sterling, Ahead of Her Time: Abby Kelly and the Politics of Anti-Slavery 60–62, 220–22 (1991); Benjamin Platt Thomas, Theodore Weld: Crusader for Freedom 159–64 (1950). *See also* Abigail Dunaway, *Liberty for the Married Woman,* New Northwest, Aug. 15, 1873, at 2. *See generally* Davis, *supra* note 161, at 324–31.

163. *See* Reva Siegel, *Reasoning from the Body: A (sic) Historical Perspective on Abortion Regulation and Questions of Equal Protection,* 44 Stan. L. Rev. 261 (1992). Justice Blackmun cited this article with approval in his last opinion in an abortion case. Planned Parenthood of S.E. Pa. v. Casey, 505 U.S. 833, 928 n.4 (Blackmun, J., partially concurring).

164. Siegel, *supra* note 163, at 306–08. *See also* Reva Siegel, *Home as Work: The First Women's Rights Claims Concerning Wives' Household Labor, 1850–1880,* 103 Yale L.J. 1073 (1994) ("Siegel, *Home as Work*").

165. Siegel, *supra* note 163, at 319–23. *See also* Petchesky, *supra* note 3, at 247–52, 262–76.

166. Siegel, *supra* note 163, at 320.

Some modern historians see the *Married Women's Acts* as designed to benefit male creditors rather than to emancipate women.[167] After all, the Indiana Supreme Court held in 1896 that the *Married Women's Acts* did not relieve married women of any duties owed to her husband or her family.[168] There is a certain irony here given that the earliest *Married Women's Acts* were a product of the Jacksonian and other political movements strongly hostile to creditors.[169] Siegel not only seems wholly ignorant of this history,[170] but she also ignored the fact that well before the end of the century feminists groups were condemning efforts to make divorce easier. In fact, the feminists of the nineteenth century generally supported marriage and the notion of women's unique responsibility for the home and the upbringing of children.[171] What they opposed was having to bear apparently unlimited pregnancies.

Feminist support for marriage during the nineteenth century should hardly surprise us. During the nineteenth century, fewer than five percent of white women in the United States worked outside the home after marriage.[172] In part as a result of the efforts of organized feminism, divorce was easier to obtain in the middle of the nineteenth century than at its end in many states.[173] Later, Susan B. Anthony was one of the few notable dissenters from the resolutions of women's groups favoring divorce reform—meaning divorce restrictions.[174] Orthodox feminist history today tends to support Anthony's view and to overlook the more complex reality of marriage and divorce in the nineteenth and early twentieth centuries.[175] In contrast, feminist groups

---

167. *See* NORMA BASCH, IN THE EYES OF THE LAW: WOMEN, MARRIAGE, AND PROPERTY IN NINETEENTH CENTURY NEW YORK (1982); BEARD, *supra* note 160, at 160–65; HOFF, *supra* note 159, at 120, 134–35, 187–91; DEBORAH RHODE, JUSTICE AND GENDER 24–26 (1989); CAROLE SHAMMAS, MARYLYNN SALMON, & MICHEL DAHLIN, INHERITANCE IN AMERICA FROM COLONIAL TIMES TO THE PRESENT 88–101 (1987); SHANLEY, *supra* note 159, at 104–09; Richard Chused, *Late Nineteenth-Century Married Women's Property Law: Reception of the Early Married Women's Acts by Courts and Legislatures,* 29 AM. J. LEGAL HIS. 24 (1985); Lawrence Friedman, *Rights of Passage: Divorce Law in Historical Perspective,* 63 OR. L. REV. 649, 655–56 (1984); John Johnston, *Sex and Property: The Common Law Tradition, the Law School Curriculum and Developments toward Equality,* 47 NYU L. REV. 1033 (1972); Suzanne Lebsock, *Radical Reconstruction and the Property Rights of Southern Women,* 43 J. SOC. HIST. 195 (1977); Isabel Marcus, *Locked In and Locked Out: Reflections on the History of Divorce Law in New York,* 37 BUFF. L. REV. 375, 399 (1988); Linda Speth, *The Married Women's Property Acts, 1839–1865: Reform, Reaction, or Revolution?,* in 2 WOMEN AND THE LAW: A SOCIAL HISTORICAL PERSPECTIVE 269 (D. Kelly Weisberg ed. 1982); Amy Dru Stanley, *Conjugal Bonds and Wage Labor: Rights of Contract in the Age of Emancipation,* 75 AM. J. LEGAL HIST. 471 (1988); Joan Williams, *Married Women and Property,* 1 VA. J. SOC. POL'Y & L. 383 (1994).

168. Arnold v. Rifner, 45 N.E. 618, 619 (Ind. Ct. App. 1896).

169. BASCH, *supra* note 167, at 135–42; Chused, *supra* note 160, at 1398–1401; Ranney, *supra* note 146, at 506–35. *See generally* PETER COLEMAN, DEBTORS AND CREDITORS IN AMERICA: INSOLVENCY, IMPRISONMENT FOR DEBT, AND BANKRUPTCY, 1607–1900 (1974).

170. *See, e.g.,* Siegel, *Home as Work, supra* note 164, at 1083–84.

171. DIO LEWIS, CHASTITY, OR OUR SECRET SINS 234 (1874); ABBA WOOLSON, WOMEN IN AMERICAN SOCIETY 82 (1873); *Women Discuss Divorce—Ways for Reform Suggested at the National Council [of Women],* N.Y. TIMES, Mar. 1, 1895, at 14, col.1; Emma Goldman, *Love and Marriage,* in WOMAN REBEL 1, 3 (Alex Baskin ed. 1976, original publication 1914). *See generally* DEGLER, *supra* note 9, at 362–94; PETCHESKY, *supra* note 3, at 41–42; SHANLEY, *supra* note 159; SMITH-ROSENBERG, *supra* note 120, at 243–44; Smith, *supra* note 89.

172. PETCHESKY, *supra* note 3, at 75; LYNN WEINER, FROM WORKING GIRL TO WORKING MOTHER 6 (1985).

173. GEORGE ELLIOTT HOWARD, A HISTORY OF MATRIMONIAL INSTITUTIONS 13, 17 (1904); Friedman, *supra* note 167, at 653–54. For an interesting analysis of the divorce reform movement at the turn of the century, see James J. White, *Ex Proprio Vigore,* 89 MICH. L. REV. 2096 (1991).

174. *Miss Anthony for Divorce—Objects to National Women's Council Resolution against It,* N.Y. TIMES, Apr. 15, 1905, at 1, col. 5.

175. *See, e.g.,* Norma Basch, *The Emerging Legal History of Women in the United States: Property, Divorce, and the Constitution,* 12 SIGNS 97 (1986); Mary Odem, *Fallen Women and Thieving Ladies: Historical Approaches to Women and Crime in the United States,* 17 LAW & SOC. INQUIRY 351, 351 (1992).

(including the Women's Christian Temperance Union—the largest and most influential women's organization to exist anywhere in the world at that point) often took on the role of "marriage enforcers" at this time, pressuring men to marry their pregnant paramours (and sometimes pressuring the women involved as well) unless they considered the marriage hopeless.[176]

One of the central realities of marriage (and of divorce) at the end of the nineteenth century remained the utter lack of an appropriate technology for contraception. Feminists (and others) at that time urged sexual abstinence even within marriage as the appropriate means to achieve the proper spacing of births.[177] In fact, "voluntary motherhood" seems to have been understood by many people as requiring sexual abstinence as late as the 1930s[178]—even though some 317,000,000 condoms by then were being sold in the United States annually.[179] Many of the advocates of abstinence appeared to their contemporaries, and even sometimes to us now, as hostile to sex. Feminist historian Linda Gordon has amply documented this aspect of even the "free love" wing of feminism.[180] As Carl Degler note, the "free love" movement of the nineteenth century was more devoted to giving women the right to say "no" within marriage than the right to say "yes" outside of marriage.[181] After all, sexual abstinence was still the only highly effective means of preventing pregnancy in the mid- to late-nineteenth century. The matter was summed up by Dr. H.S. Pomeroy in 1888:

> It is surprising to what extent the laity believes that medical science knows how to control the birth-rate. Just let me say that I know of but one prescription which is both safe and sure—namely, *that the sexes shall remain apart.* So thoroughly do I believe this to be a secret which Nature has kept to herself, that I should be inclined to question the

---

176. Linda Gordon, Heroes of Their Own Lives: The Politics and History of Family Violence, Boston, 1880–1960, at 297 (1988); Joan Jacobs Brumberg, *"Ruined" Girls: Changing Community Responses to Illegitimacy in Upstate New York, 1890–1920*, 18 J. Soc. Hist. 247, 254–57 (1984).On the WCTU generally, see Ruth Bordin, Women and Temperance: The Quest for Power and Liberty, 1873–1900, at 3–4 (1981); Barbara Epstein, The Politics of Domesticity: Women, Evangelism, and Temperance in Nineteenth-Century America (1981); David Pivar, Purity Crusade: Sexual Morality and Social Control, 1868–1900 (1973).

177. *See, e.g.,* Elizabeth Blackwell, The Human Element in Sex: Being a Medical Inquiry into the Relation of Sexual Physiology to Christian Morality 77 (2nd ed. 1884); Eliza Bisbee Duffey, The Relations of the Sexes 242–45 (1876) ("Duffey, Relations"); Eliza Bisbee Duffey, What Every Woman Should Know (1873); Elizabeth Cady Stanton, Eighty Years and More: Reminiscences, 1815–1897, at 297 (1898); Stockham, *supra* note 81, at 323–26; Goldman, *supra* note 171, at 3; *Our Book Tale,* Nat'l Citizen & Ballot Box, Nov. 1878, at 2. *See also* Henry Wright, Marriage and Parentage; or, The Protective Element in Man, as a Means to His Elevation and Happiness 117–18 (2nd ed. 1855). *See generally* Brodie, *supra* note 9, at 279–80; Degler, *supra* note 9, at 202–06, 215; D'Emilio & Freedman, *supra* note 9, at 154–55; Flandrin, *supra* note 65, at 221–25; Faye Ginsburg, Contested Lives: The Abortion Debate in an American Community 233–35 (1989); Gordon, *supra* note 3, at 100–11, 127–29, 144–45, 151, 238, 388–89; Hersch, *supra* note 161, at 209–11, 244–48; Petchesky, *supra* note 3, at 76–77; Reed, *supra* note 9, at 32; Rhode, *supra* note 167, at 204–05; Tannahill, *supra* note 13, at 408; Linda Gordon & Ellen DuBois, *Seeking Ecstasy on the Battlefield: Danger and Pleasure in Nineteenth-Century Feminist Century Sexual Thought,* 9 Feminist Stud. 7 (1983); Deborah Rhode, *Adolescent Pregnancy and Public Policy,* 108 Poli. Sci. Q. 635, 642–43 (1994); Siegel, *supra* note 163, at 305, 312–13 n.208; Smith, *supra* note 89, at 223–27.

178. Nanette Davis, From Crime to Choice 3 (1985). *See also* Leslie Reagan, When Abortion Was a Crime: Women, Medicine, and Law in the United States, 1867–1973, at 38, 58–59 (1997).

179. Himes, *supra* note 13, at 201. *See generally* Tone, *supra* note 14, at 183–200; Christopher Tietze & Clarence Gamble, *The Condom as a Contraceptive Method in Public Health Work,* 9 Hum. Fertility 97 (Dec. 1944); Grace Naismith, *The Racket in Contraceptives,* 71 Am. Mercury 12 (July 1950).

180. Gordon, *supra* note 3, at 103–07, 116–20, 123–26, 236–43.

181. Degler, *supra* note 9, at 277. *See also* Lucy Bland, Banishing the Beast: Sexuality and the Early Feminists (1995); Sheila Jeffreys, The Spinster and Her Enemies: Feminism and Sexuality 1880–1930 (1985); Kern, *supra* note 45, at 153.

ability or the honesty of any one professing to understand it so as to be able safely and surely to regulate the matter of reproduction.[182]

Historian Linda Gordon criticized this statement as indicating Pomeroy's blindness to the evidence before him because his "moralism" had overwhelmed his "scientific curiosity."[183] Yet Gordon herself had stated only two pages before her criticism that abstinence was the major form of birth control even as late as the turn of the twentieth century.[184] Later she described the diaphragm as the only effective means of "women's contraception" even while acknowledging that diaphragms were so tricky to use as to make failure highly likely, especially among the ill-educated or those without "privacy, running water, and full explanation."[185] Gordon also indicated that the diaphragm was annoying to use and often ended up abandoned in a drawer.[186]

Pomeroy wasn't blind; he was right, as a careful examination of the contraceptives available in 1888 shows. No wonder those who favored "voluntary motherhood"—the early equivalent of "planned parenthood"—focused on sexual abstinence in marriage as the recommended method of birth control. Even Dr. Horatio Storer, the leading campaigner against abortion among physicians, apparently contemplated the sensible use of contraception or the abstinence preferred by many feminists. Storer advocated spacing the births of children about three years apart in passages where he also argued for the necessity of occasional pregnancies for women's health.[187]

Sexual abstinence in or out of marriage is not easy to achieve, yet appeals to personal concerns about the risks and burdens of undergoing numerous pregnancies and raising numerous children would not always succeed in uniting *both* members of a married couple in a determination to limit these risks and burdens even to the point of accepting a great deal of sexual abstinence within a marriage. Linda Gordon found the preference for abstinence over sex with effective birth control to be an expression of the prevailing commitment to monogamy and marital fidelity[188]—as if sexual abstinence within marriage would foster fidelity and monogamy. Another branch of the nineteenth-century rhetoric of sexual abstinence in order to achieve voluntary motherhood was perhaps a response to this problem.

The nineteenth century saw the emergence of appeals for the betterment of future generations as part of the eugenics movement.[189] The idea here was for a woman to provide better opportunities for the children to whom she gave birth by limiting the total number of children that she would bear and hence for which she would be responsible. Historian Barbara Taylor went so far as to infer from the failure of nineteenth-century feminists to support contraception that women at that time did not seek to limit their families, but only to provide better lives for their children.[190] She did not see that the two goals were linked. The desire to limit the number of pregnancies and the number of children, however, too often would not unite *both* members of

---

182. POMEROY, *supra* note 145, at 62 (emphasis in original).

183. GORDON, *supra* note 3, at 161. *See also* PETCHESKY, *supra* note 3, at 76; MARY RYAN, WOMANHOOD IN AMERICA: FROM COLONIAL TIMES TO THE PRESENT 164 (2nd ed. 1979).

184. GORDON, *supra* note 3, at 159.

185. *Id.* at 308–11.

186. *Id.* at 309 n*.

187. HORATIO ROBINSON STORER, IS IT I? A BOOK FOR EVERY MAN 115–16 (1868).

188. GORDON, *supra* note 3, at 176–77.

189. *Id.* at 120–35. *See* NAPHEYS, *supra* note 45, at 75–77; Norman Himes, *Eugenic Thought in the American Birth Control Movement 100 Years Ago*, 2 EUGENICS No. 5, at 3 (May 1929); Edward Ill, *The Rights of the Unborn—The Prevention of Conception*, 40 AM. J. OBSTET. & DISEASES OF WOMEN 577 (1899). *See generally* Chapter 11, at notes 25–192.

190. BARBARA TAYLOR, EVE AND THE NEW JERUSALEM: SOCIALISM AND FEMINISM IN THE NINETEENTH CENTURY 216 (1983).

the married couple in agreeing on sexual abstinence. The burden and risks fell disproportionately on women. This reality is expressed in a slogan originally popularized by English suffragist Christabel Pankhurst and prominent among the nineteenth-century feminists: "Votes for Women and Chastity for Men."[191]

Today, the idea of sexual abstinence in marriage as a primary means of birth control takes some getting used to. Advocacy of sexual abstinence has a long and continuing history, but in recent decades that advocacy generally focused on sexual abstinence outside of marriage. Delayed marriage was long the most successful and most common form of birth control.[192] Whether consciously or not, such concerns played a role in the popularity of the convent life in the Middle Ages, a form of organized feminism that, like the Vestal Virgins of Roman times, eschews sexual activity altogether.[193] The rhetoric of sexual abstinence, particularly when calling for total abstinence, often appears openly hostile to sex and sexuality, whether propounded by priests, nuns, or modern feminists. Law professor Jeanne Schroeder has decried the tendency of feminist scholars to ignore this history, thereby producing an "essentialist feminism" with more in common with the "virginal feminism" of the medieval convent than most feminist scholars realize.[194] Arch feminists like Catharine MacKinnon turn out to have a great deal in common with that "father" of patriarchy, St. Augustine.[195] Schroeder is not alone in identifying much of late-twentieth century feminism as "neo-puritan."[196] One of the stronger manifestations of this modern "virginal feminism" is the attempt to prohibit pornography on the basis of its alleged subordination

---

191. *See* Nancy Cott, The Grounding of Modern Feminism 42–49 (1987). *See also* Alice Echols, Daring to Be Bad: Radical Feminism in America 1967–1975, at 13–15, 167–75, 240–41, 288–91 (1989).

192. 1 Anderson & Zinsser, *supra* note 13, at 135–36; K.H. Connell, Irish Peasant Society 117–18 (1968); Laslett, *supra* note 13, at 13–14. *See also* Tannahill, *supra* note 13, at 128.

193. Jeanne Schroeder, *Feminism Historicized: Medieval Misogynist Stereotypes in Contemporary Feminist Jurisprudence*, 75 Iowa L. Rev. 1135 (1990). *See generally* Jo Ann Kay McNamara, Sisters in Arms: Catholic Nuns through Two Millennia (1996); Daniel Bornstein & Roberto Rusconi, Women and Religion in Medieval and Renaissance Italy (1996); Fiona McCarthy, *The Power of Chastity*, N.Y. Rev. Books, Dec. 19, 1996, at 31.

194. Schroeder, *supra* note 193.

195. *See* Jeanne Schroeder, *The Taming of the Shrew: The Liberal Attempt to Mainstream Radical Feminist Theory*, 5 Yale J.L. & Fem. 123, 162–79 (1992). *See, e.g.*, Catharine MacKinnon, Only Words (1993); Carole Pateman, *Defending Prostitution: Charges against Ericson*, 93 Ethics 561 (1983); Laurie Shrage, *Should Feminists Oppose Prostitution?*, 99 Ethics 347 (1989); Sibyl Schwarzenbach, *Contractarians and Feminists Debate Prostitution*, 18 NYU Rev. L. & Soc. Change 103 (1990).

196. Against Sadomasochism: A Radical Feminist Analysis (Robin Linden ed. 1982); Kathleen Barry, Female Sexual Slavery (1979); Jessica Benjamin, The Bonds of Love: Psychoanalysis, Feminism and the Problem of Domination 91–92 (1988); Susan Bordo, Unbearable Weight: Feminism, Western Culture, and the Body (1993); Susan Brownmiller, Against Our Will: Men, Women, and Rape (1975); Lynn Chancer, Sadomasochism in Everyday Life: Dynamics of Power and Powerlessness (1992); Wendy Chapkis, Live Sex Acts: Women Performing Erotic Labor (1997); Kathy Davis, Reshaping the Body: The Dilemma of Cosmetic Surgery (1995); Shulamith Firestone, The Dialectic of Sex: The Case for Feminist Revolution (1970); Good Girls/Bad Girls: Feminists and Sex Trade Workers Face to Face (Laurie Bell ed. 1987); Cecelia Hoigard & Liv Finstad, Backstreets: Prostitution, Money, and Love (1992); Sex Work: Writings by Women in the Sex Industry (Frederique Delacoste & Priscilla Alexander eds. 1987); Kate Millett, Sexual Politics (1970); Pleasure and Danger: Female Sexuality 247, 248 (Carole Vance ed. 1984); Katie Roiphe, The Morning After: Sex, Fear and Feminism on Campus (1993); Naomi Wolf, Fire with Fire: The New Female Power and How It Could Change the Twenty-First Century (1993); Joanna Calne, *In Defense of Desire*, 23 Rutgers L.J. 305, 307, 336–40 (1992); Lynn Chancer, *From Pornography to Sadomasochism: Reconciling Feminist Differences*, 571 Annals Am. Academy Pol. & Soc. Sci. 77, 83–85 (2000); Duncan Kennedy, *Sexual Abuse, Sexy Dressing and the Eroticization of Domination*, 26 N. Eng. L. Rev. 1309, 1362–65 (1992) Kenneth Lasson, *Feminism Awry: Excesses in the Pursuit of Rights and Trifles*, 42 J. Legal Educ. 1, 11–12 (1992); Kathryn Pauly Morgan, *Women and the Knife: Cosmetic Surgery and the Colonization of Women's Bodies*, 6 Hypatia 25 (1991); Jeannie Sclafani Rhee, *Redressing for Success: The Liability of Hooters Restaurant for Customer Harassment of Waitresses*, 20 Harv. Women's

of women.[197] As one commentator has suggested, the authors of such arguments are obsessed with the visual aspects of human interaction, attributing this obsession to men rather than recognizing that such an obsession must arise within them and does not necessarily inhere in those upon whom they project it.[198]

The "reasoning" behind such an obsession is shown on the very first page of the book by Catharine MacKinnon that serves as the prime statement of virginal feminism. MacKinnon tells us that,

> You grow up with your father holding you down and covering your mouth so another man can make horrible searing pain between your legs. When you are older, your husband ties you to the bed and drops hot wax on your nipples and brings in other men to watch and make you smile through it.[199]

Based on her writings, MacKinnon seems incapable of realizing that such experiences are not universal, or that there is rather less evidence to link the viewing of pornography to such events than she imagines. No wonder some feminist scholars stress "the indistinguishability of prostitution, marriage, and sexual harassment."[200]

---

L.J. 163 (1997); Kenneth Schneyer, *Hooting: Public and Popular Discourse about Sex Discrimination*, 31 U. Mich. J.L. Reform 551 (1998); Laurie Schrage, *Should Feminists Oppose Prostitution?*, 99 Ethics 347 (1989).

197. *See, e.g.*, Julie Allison & Lawrence Wrightsman, Rape: The Misunderstood Crime (1993); Andrea Dworkin, Pornography: Men Possessing Women (1981); Susan Eaton, The Problem of Pornography: Regulation and the Right of Free Speech (1994); Susan Estrich, Real Rape (1987); In Harm's Way: The Pornography Civil Rights Hearings (Catharine MacKinnon & Andrea Dworkin eds. 1997); MacKinnon, *supra* note 195; Stephen Schulhofer, Unwanted Sex: The Culture of Intimidation and the Failure of Law (2000); Cassia Spohn & Julie Horney, Rape Law Reform: A Grassroots Revolution and Its Impact (1992); Martha Chamallas, *Consent, Equality, and the Legal Control of Sexual Conduct*, 61 S. Cal. L. Rev. 777 (1988); Chancer, *supra* note 196, at 81–83; Andrea Dworkin, *Against the Male Flood: Censorship, Pornography, and Equality*, 8 Harv. Women's L.J. 1 (1985); Catharine MacKinnon, *Not a Moral Issue*, 2 Yale L. & Pol'y Rev. 321 (1984); Catharine MacKinnon, *Pornography as Defamation and Discrimination*, 71 B.U. L. Rev. 793 (1991); Catharine MacKinnon, *Pornography, Civil Rights, and Speech*, 20 Harv. C.R.-C.L. L. Rev. 1 (1985); Morrison Torrey, *When Will We Be Believed? Rape Myths and the Idea of a Fair Trial in Rape Prosecutions*, 24 U.C. Davis L. Rev. 1013 (1991). *See generally* Donald Downs, The New Politics of Pornography (1989); Paul Brest & Ann Vandenberg, *Politics, Feminism, and the Constitution: The Anti-Pornography Movement in Minneapolis*, 39 Stan. L. Rev. 607 (1987); Margaret Bonilla, *What Feminists Are Doing to Rape Ought to Be a Crime*, Pol'y Rev., Fall 1993, at 22; Richard Delgado & Jean Stefanic, *Pornography and Harm to Women: "No Empirical Evidence?,"* 53 Ohio St. L.J. 1037 (1992); Donald Dripps, *Beyond Rape: An Essay on the Difference between the Presence of Force and the Absence of Consent*, 92 Colum. L. Rev. 1780 (1992); Alon Harel, *Bigotry, Pornography, and the First Amendment: A Theory of Unprotected Speech*, 65 S. Cal. L. Rev. 1887 (1992); Andrew Jacobs, *Rhetoric and the Creation of Rights: MacKinnon and the Civil Right to Freedom from Pornography*, 42 Kan. L. Rev. 785 (1994); Caryn Jacobs, *Patterns of Violence: A Feminist Perspective on the Regulation of Pornography*, 8 Harv. Women's L.J. 1 (1985); Kevin Saunders, *The United States and Canadian Responses to the Feminist Attack on Pornography: A Perspective from the History of Obscenity*, 9 Ind. Int'l & Comp. L. Rev. 1 (1998); Cass Sunstein, *Pornography and the First Amendment*, 1986 Duke L.J. 589; Symposium, *The Sex Panic: Women, Censorship and "Pornography,"* 38 N.Y.L.S. L. Rev. 1 (1993). Ironically, Canadian authorities thereafter seized copies of a book by Andrea Dworkin—who, along with Catharine MacKinnon, was the principal architect of these laws—for its "pornographic" content because of its vivid descriptions of male sexual oppression of women. Chancer, *supra*, at 81.

198. Brian Bendig, *Images of Men in Feminist Legal Theory*, 20 Pepperdine L. Rev. 991, 1004–12 (1993). *See also* Amy Miles, Comment, *Feminist Theories of Interpretation: The Bible and the Law*, 2 Geo. Mason U. L. Rev. 305, 317–30 (1995).

199. MacKinnon, *supra* note 195, at 1.

200. Catharine MacKinnon, Feminism Unmodified: Discourses on Life and Law 59 (1987) ("MacKinnon, F.U."). *See also* Catharine MacKinnon, Toward a Feminist Theory of the State 184–86 (1989). *See generally* Andrea Dworkin, Intercourse (1987); Gordon, *supra* note 3, at 17–19; MacKinnon, F.U., *supra*, at 144–45, 193, 227; Abigail Thernstrom, *Rough Justice*, New Rep., Nov. 11, 1991, at 14.

Such malebashing[201] did not prevent MacKinnon's marriage—to notorious womanizer Jeffrey Masson—any more than similar sentiments prevented the marriage of most nineteenth century feminists. (Historian Linda Gordon at least was consistent enough to announce that lesbianism was far superior to heterosexuality both as a form of sexual relief and as a form of human relationship.[202]) As Camille Paglia observed, "[l]eaving sex to feminists is like letting your dog vacation at the taxidermist."[203] While criticism of such essentialism may be "much more common among feminist historians than among feminist lawyers," numerous feminist historians are drawn to just such essentialism.[204] Yet as Jeanne Schroeder points out, medieval feminism fed into patriarchy rather than opposing it effectively.

Many nineteenth-century feminists embraced the rhetoric of hostility towards sex and sexuality.[205] Not all men and women, certainly not all married men and women, were susceptible to appeals based upon hostility towards sex and sexuality. Although calls for sexual abstinence served to refute the charge, heard often in the nineteenth century, that feminists supported "free love," it would hardly refute the claim that feminism was inimical to the family given that complete, or even substantial, abstinence virtually required separate households for husband and wife.[206] And we do indeed find couples that could afford it separating for long periods to avoid pregnancy.[207] Nor could sexual abstinence or separate households assure the fiscal security and moral power that women derived at the time from the actuality or prospect of motherhood.[208] Remember that at the time only five percent of married white women in the United States worked outside the home.[209]

The problem for married women (and unmarried women if they were sexually active) was how to obtain control over the frequency and timing of intercourse without alienating the man upon whom their well-being depended, without making both of their lives intolerable. Dr. Alice Stockham recommended that a woman who lacked the ability to refuse her husband should use sexual coldness as a birth control device.[210] That advice simply would not solve the problem. Instead, most women chose a very different strategy for enlisting their man's support for sexual abstinence, or at least great sexual restraint.

During the nineteenth century in the European cultural zone many women turned to physicians for assistance in giving birth, but not because physicians were particularly helpful in the birthing process when compared to midwives. The turn to physicians initially was part of a strategy (whether conscious or not) of persuading husbands that birthing was too debilitating (or that women were too frail) to undergo the process very often.[211] This belief in turn supported the

---

201. *See* Susan & David Williams, *A Feminist Theory of Malebashing*, 4 MICH. J. GENDER & L. 35 (1996).

202. GORDON, *supra* note 3, at 380–81, 410–13.

203. Camille Paglia, *The Joy of Presbyterian Sex*, NEW REP., Dec. 2, 1991, at 24. *See also* NANCY FRIDAY, WOMEN ON TOP (1991); ROIPHE, *supra* note 196; CAROL SMART, THE TIES THAT BIND: LAW, MARRIAGE AND THE REPRODUCTION OF PATRIARCHAL RELATIONS (1984); Calne, *supra* note 196; Ruth Colker, *Marriage*, 3 YALE J.L. & FEMINISM 321 (1991); Lasson, *supra* note 196, at 19–21.

204. *See* HOFF, note 147, at 43–48.

205. *Id.* at 103–07, 116–20, 123–26.

206. Lewis & Lockridge, *supra* note 130, at 10–11.

207. See the references collected *supra* at note 146.

208. *See generally* GORDON, *supra* note 3, at 109–12; PETCHESKY, *supra* note 3, at 74–77.

209. PETCHESKY, *supra* note 3, at 75; WEINER, *supra* note 171, at 6.

210. STOCKHAM, *supra* note 81, at 152–53. *See also* Nancy Cott, *Passionless: An Interpretation of Victorian Sexual Ideology, 1790–1850*, 4 SIGNS 219 (1978); Klepp, *supra* note 56, at 101–02. *But see* PETER GAY, THE NAKED HEART (1995); PETER GAY, THE TENDER PASSION (1986).

211. *See, e.g.*, ALCOTT, *supra* note 62, at 9–14; G.L. AUSTIN, PERILS OF AMERICAN WOMEN: OR, A DOCTOR'S TALK WITH MAIDEN, WIFE, AND MOTHER 94–95 (1883); CATHARINE BEECHER, LETTERS TO THE PEOPLE ON HEALTH AND HAPPINESS 14 (1855); CATHARINE BEECHER, PHYSIOLOGY AND CALISTHENICS FOR SCHOOLS AND FAMILIES 164 (1856); BLACKWELL, *supra* note 176, at 31; ELIZABETH BLACKWELL, 1 ESSAYS IN MEDICAL SOCIOLOGY 31, 78, 253–54 (1902) ("BLACKWELL, ESSAYS"); EDWARD CLARKE, SEX IN EDUCATION: OR A FAIR

growth of a pattern of sexual abstinence or infrequent intercourse with a frequent necessity for the couple actually to live apart.[212] After all, even reducing intercourse to three or four times per month was a highly effective, albeit imperfect, contraceptive.[213]

Literary and other images of feminine frailty that became common in the nineteenth century are evidence of the strategy.[214] Some modern observers have concluded that male authors invented such images as a means of the controlling emerging independent women.[215] Such observers do not discuss why such noted woman physicians as Elizabeth Blackwell and Alice Stockham also expressed the view that "excessive sexuality" in marriage was debilitating to women's health.[216] Nor do these arguments deal with the assertions that excessive sex was also harmful to men's health.[217] Women in New England had by 1850 organized their own "physiological societies" to explore women's medical needs and to propagandize for the solutions they preferred.[218]

Images of female frailty found receptive audiences among women for at least two reasons. First, women found the images socially functional.[219] Second, images of female frailty simply did not seem altogether inappropriate to many late nineteenth century women.[220] In particular, the

---

CHANCE FOR GIRLS 63 (1878); JOHN COWAN, THE SCIENCE OF A NEW LIFE 116–17 (1871); IRA CRADDOCK, LETTER TO A PROSPECTIVE BRIDE 6–9, 12–16 (1897); EDWARD DIXON, WOMEN AND HER DISEASES FROM THE CRADLE TO THE GRAVE 134, 140 (1857); DUFFEY, RELATIONS, *supra* note 176, at 96–97, 178, 208–09, 224, 281–82; ELIZABETH EDSON EVANS, THE ABUSE OF MATERNITY 47–48, 117–19, 128 (1875); ORSON FOWLER, SEXUAL SCIENCE, INCLUDING MANHOOD, WOMANHOOD, AND THEIR MUTUAL INTERRELATIONS ETC., AS TAUGHT BY PHRENOLOGY 682 (1870); KELLOGG, *supra* note 62, at 264; CHARLES KNOWLTON, THE FRUITS OF PHILOSOPHY 48 (Charles Bradlaugh & Annie Besant eds. 3rd ed. 1878); NAPHEYS, *supra* note 45, at 91; J. SOULE, THE SCIENCE OF REPRODUCTION AND REPRODUCTIVE CONTROL 12, 26–27 (1856); STOCKHAM, *supra* note 81, at 47–48, 153–55; HENRY WRIGHT, THE UNWELCOME CHILD, OR, THE CRIME OF THE UNDESIGNED AND UNDESIRED MATERNITY 80 (1860); *The American People Starved and Poisoned,* 32 HARPER'S NEW MONTHLY MAG. 771 (1866). *See generally* CHARLOTTE BORST, CATCHING BABIES: THE PROFESSIONALIZATION OF BIRTH, 1870–1920 (1995); BRODIE, *supra* note 9, at 65, 182–83; DEGLER, *supra* note 9, at 223, 257–58, 269–97; D'EMILIO & FREEDMAN, *supra* note 9, at 59; GORDON, *supra* note 3, at 160–62; HIMES, *supra* note 13, at 265–66; NAGEL, *supra* note 146, at 97; DAVID PIVAR, PURITY CRUSADE: SEXUAL MORALITY AND SOCIAL CONTROL, 1868–1900 (1973); SMITH-ROSENBERG, *supra* note 120, at 197–216; TANNAHILL, *supra* note 13, at 355; F.M.L. THOMPSON, THE RISE OF RESPECTABLE SOCIETY: A SOCIAL HISTORY OF VICTORIAN BRITAIN, 1830–1900, at 53–70 (1988); Klepp, *supra* note 56, at 99; Ann Douglas Wood, *"The Fashionable Diseases": Women's Complaints and Their Treatment in Nineteenth-Century America,* 4 J. INTERDISCPLINARY HIST. 25 (1971); Lewis & Lockridge, *supra* note 130, at 12–14.

212. Wood, *supra* note 211, at 35. See also the references collected *supra* at note 146.

213. DEGLER, *supra* note 9, at 215.

214. *See, e.g.,* NATHANIAL HAWTHORNE, OUR OLD HOME: A SERIES OF ENGLISH SKETCHES (1863); AUGUSTUS HOPPER, A FASHIONABLE SUFFERER: OR CHAPTERS FROM LIFE'S COMEDY (1883); S. WEIR MITCHELL, ROLAND BLAKE (1886).

215. TERRY CASTLE, CLARISSA'S CIPHERS (1982); TERRY EAGLETON, THE RAPE OF CLARISSA (1982); RITA GOLDBERG, SEX AND ENLIGHTENMENT: WOMEN IN RICHARDSON AND DIDEROT (1984); P. HOFFMAN, *LA FEMME DANS LA PENSÉE DE LUMIÈRES* (1977); WENDY MITCHINSON, THE NATURE OF THEIR BODIES: WOMAN AND THEIR DOCTORS IN VICTORIAN CANADA 47 (1991); REGINA MORANTZ-SANCHEZ, CONDUCT UNBECOMING A WOMAN: MEDICINE ON TRIAL IN BROOKLYN 115–19 (1999); ORNELLA MOSCUCCI, THE SCIENCE OF WOMAN: GYNECOLOGY AND GENDER IN ENGLAND, 1800–1929, at 102 (1990); RUTH PERRY, WOMEN, LETTERS AND THE NOVEL (1980); ELAINE SHOWALTER, THE NEW FEMINIST CRITICISM (1986). *See also* ELAINE SHOWALTER, THE FEMALE MALADY (1986).

216. BLACKWELL, *supra* note 177, at 31; 1 BLACKWELL, ESSAYS, *supra* note 211, at 31, 78, 253–54; STOCKHAM, *supra* note 81, at 47–48, 153–55.

217. *See* John Burnham, *The Progressive Era Revolution in American Attitudes toward Sex,* 59 J. AM. HIST. 901 (1973).

218. WALSH, *supra* note 159, at 39–43.

219. *See* TANNAHILL, *supra* note 13, at 349–50, 388–91.

220. *See, e.g.,* OLIVE SCHREINER, WOMEN AND LABOUR 288 (1911). For further examples of women who thought in such terms, see VINETTA COLBY, THE SINGULAR ANOMALY: WOMEN NOVELISTS IN THE NINETEENTH CENTURY 158 (1970); JOHN DODDS, THE AGE OF PARADOX: A BIOGRAPHY OF ENGLAND, 1841–1851,

genuine risks of death as a direct result of childbirth were still real, although the risks were declining markedly at the very time that images of female frailty were becoming most prominent in social discourse.[221]

If claims of frailty failed to achieve sexual abstinence or restraint, women could (and did) resort to "hysteria" as a means for avoiding sex and preventing pregnancy.[222] Historian Carroll Smith-Rosenberg has studied the then fairly common "choice" of hysteria as a means of managing a wide variety of women's problems,[223] although she described hysteria as "a stark caricature of femininity." Smith-Rosenberg, however, seems as unconscious of the birth-control aspects of the practice as the women of the nineteenth century appear to have been of the functional utility of hysteria.[224] The hysterical strategy, even if unconscious, fostered the notion of female frailty and was exploited to limit sexual relations and thereby to limit pregnancy. Physicians of the era even viewed sexual excess as a cause of hysteria.[225] The emergence of shoplifting as a common pattern after the Civil War also contributed to the image of women as "frail" as middle class women caught shoplifting sought refuge, again with the aid of physicians, in the "diagnosis" of "kleptomania."[226] "Kleptomania" too was exploited as evidence of female frailty.[227] Even the rise of excessively restrictive clothing that became fashionable as the nineteenth century wore on helped to debilitate women, along with Victorian attitudes towards sexuality generally.[228]

The core source of these changes was the "social purity" movement that affected the United States in the nineteenth century.[229] The "social purity" is now mostly remembered for its off-

---

at 71–72 (1953); KATHARYN KISH SKLAR, CATHARINE BEECHER: A STUDY IN AMERICAN DOMESTICITY 211 (1973); Johnny Farragher, *Women and Their Families on the Overland Trail, 1842–1867,* 2 FEMINIST STUD. 151 (1975). There were, of course, women's voices opposed this view. *See, e.g.,* SUSAN ANTHONY & IDA HUSTED HARPER, 4 THE HISTORY OF WOMEN'S SUFFRAGE xxii (1902).

221. *See* DEGLER, *supra* note 9, at 60; Charles Mann, *Women's Health Research Blossoms,* 269 SCI. 766, 767 (1995); James Trussell, Letter, *Women's Longevity,* 270 SCI. 719 (1995).

222. *See* ELAINE SHOWALTER, THE FEMALE MALADY: WOMEN, MADNESS AND ENGLISH CULTURE (1985); SMITH-ROSENBERG, *supra* note 120, at 197–216; WALSH, *supra* note 159, at 17–19; Carroll Smith-Rosenberg, *The Hysterical Woman: Sex Role Conflict in Nineteenth-Century America,* 39 SOC. RES. 652, 655 (1972) ("Smith-Rosenberg, *Hysterical Woman*").

223. SMITH-ROSENBERG, *supra* note 120, at 197–216.

224. *Id.* at 207.

225. *See, e.g.,* ROBERT CARTER, ON THE PATHOLOGY AND TREATMENT OF HYSTERIA 46, 90 (1853); GEORGE PRESTON, HYSTERIA AND CERTAIN ALLIED CONDITIONS 37 (1890); A.J. SKENE, MEDICAL GYNECOLOGY: A TREATISE ON THE DISEASES OF WOMEN FROM THE STANDPOINT OF THE PHYSICIAN 320 (1895); E.W. Cushing, *Melancholia; Masturbation; Cured by Removal of Both Ovaries,* 8 JAMA 441 (1887); Robert Edes, *Ovariotomy for Nervous Disease,* 130 BOS. MED. & SURGICAL J. 105 (1894); Henry MacNaughton-Jones, *The Correlation of Sexual Function with Insanity and Crime,* 92 BRIT. J. MED. SCI. 455 (1886); George Rohé, *The Relation of Pelvic Disease and Psychical Disturbance in Women,* 5 TRANS. AM. ASS'N OF OBSTET. & GYNECOLOGISTS 321 (1892); H.A. Tomlinson & Mary Bassett, *Association of Pelvic Diseases and Insanity in Women, and the Influence of Treatment of Local Diseases upon the Mental Condition,* 33 JAMA 827 (1899) (rejecting the theory). *See also* MITCHINSON, *supra* note 215, at 50; REGINA MORANTZ-SANCHEZ, SYMPATHY AND SCIENCE: WOMEN PHYSICIANS IN AMERICAN MEDICINE 215–16 (1985); Andrew Scull & Diane Fabeau, *"A Chance to Cut Is a Chance to Cure": Sexual Surgery for Psychosis in Three Nineteenth-Century Societies,* 8 RESEARCH IN LAW, DEVIANCE, AND SOCIAL CONTROL 17 (1986); Sally Shuttleworth, *Female Circulation: Medical Discourse and Popular Advertising in the Mid-Victorian Era,* in BODY/POLITICS: WOMEN AND DISCOURSES OF SCIENCE 47 (Mary Jacobus, Evelyn Fox Keller, & Sally Shuttleworth eds. 1990). *See generally* EDWARD SHORTER, FROM PARALYSIS TO FATIGUE: A HISTORY OF PSYCHOSOMATIC ILLNESS IN THE MODERN ERA 40–94 (1992).

226. *See* ELAINE ABELSON, WHEN LADIES GO A-THIEVING: MIDDLE-CLASS SHOPLIFTERS IN THE VICTORIAN DEPARTMENT STORE (1989); Odem, *supra* note 175.

227. *See* Odem, *supra* note 175, at 360.

228. HALLER & HALLER, *supra* note 45, at xiii–xiv (sexuality); KERN, *supra* note 45, at 10–20 (clothing and its reform).

229. *See generally* BARBARA BERG, THE REMEMBERED GATE: ORIGINS OF AMERICAN FEMINISM 181–84, 211 (1978); RUTH BORDIN, WOMEN AND TEMPERANCE: THE QUEST FOR POWER AND LIBERTY, 1873–1900 (1981);

shoot, the temperance movement, but it was equally concerned with prostitution, pornography, and other vices. Modern feminist historians have tended to see a link between the increasingly harsh criminal penalties applied to prostitution and the increasing legal activity directed against abortion, seeing both as attempts to control female sexuality.[230] Janet Brody would have us believe that the social purity movement began with Anthony Comstock and the YMCA, and that it was focused on "disempowering" women.[231] Comstock did not invent the attitudes he expressed. The "social purity" movement was from its inception mostly a women's movement which only later came under the influence of men such as Comstock. Nineteenth-century feminists almost uniformly condemned prostitution and made crusades against it a mainstay of their activities, often seeing this as necessary to achieve control over male sexuality rather than a surrender of their own sexuality to male control.[232] While the motive here appears to have been to eliminate competition for husband's affections, the movement forms part of the sustained effort to de-sexualize life that was essential if sexual abstinence were to be a successful strategy for controlling the frequency and number of births.

Such disparate aspects of nineteenth century life as clothing fashions, medical "discoveries" of new "diseases" and disabilities, literary styles, campaigns to end prostitution, and even the suddenly common need to faint all better fit a pattern that formed a woman's strategy for achieving control over the frequency of births rather than a pattern of male-imposed means of disabling women. At the center of this pattern was the transformation of the birthing process itself into a medical event requiring the attendance of a physician. The medicalization of birth apparently began even earlier in England and France than in the United States.[233] The medicalization on both sides of the Atlantic was accompanied by a decline in the age of marriage, substituting female frailty and sexual abstinence within marriage for delayed marriage (in earlier times, the most popular form of sexual abstinence) as a means of birth control.[234] Only after the medicalization of birth was well underway did women gain incentives to medicalize birthing on truly

PAUL BOYER, PURITY IN PRINT: THE VICE-SOCIETY MOVEMENT AND BOOK CENSORSHIP IN AMERICA (1968); D'EMILIO & FREEDMAN, *supra* note 9, at 69–73, 140–45, 148–60, 202–15; DONNISON, *supra* note 160, at 82; EPSTEIN, *supra* note 176; GORDON, *supra* note 3, at 116–35; GROSSBERG, *supra* note 131, at 47–48; BRIAN HARRISON, DRINK AND THE VICTORIANS (1971); PIVAR, *supra* note 211; RUTH ROSEN, LOST SISTERHOOD 112–36 (1982); SMITH-ROSENBERG, *supra* note 120, at 109–28; Elizabeth Hovey, *Obscenity's Meaning: Smut-Fighters, and Contraception: 1872–1936*, 29 SAN DIEGO L. REV. 13, 15–20 (1992); Kathi Kern, *"The Cornerstone of a New Civilization": The First International Council of Women and the Campaign for "Social Purity,"* 84 KY. L.J. 1235 (1996).

230. *See, e.g.,* D'EMILIO & FREEDMAN, *supra* note 9, at 64; Odem, *supra* note 175, at 352. *See also* Chapter 1, at note 31.

231. BRODIE, *supra* note 9, at 258–66. On Comstock's career, see D.M. BENNETT, ANTHONY COMSTOCK AND HIS CAREER OF CRIME AND CRUELTY (1880 as a chapter in THE CHAMPIONS OF THE CHURCH: THEIR CRIMES AND PERSECUTIONS; reprinted separately 1971); HEYWOUD BROUN & MARGARET LEECH, ANTHONY COMSTOCK: ROUNDSMAN OF THE LAW (1927); CHARLES TRUMBELL, ANTHONY COMSTOCK, FIGHTER (1913). *See also* NICOLA BEISEL, IMPERILED INNOCENTS: ANTHONY COMSTOCK AND FAMILY REPRODUCTION IN VICTORIAN AMERICA (1997); TONE, *supra* note 14, at 5–13, 16, 19–24.

232. *See, e.g.,* Ellen Battelle Dietrick, *Rescuing Fallen Women*, WOMEN'S J., May 27, 1893, at 162. *See generally* BERG, *supra* note 229, at 181–84, 211; BORDIN, *supra* note 229, at 110–11 (1981); BOYER, *supra* note 229; D'EMILIO & FREEDMAN, *supra* note 9, at 140–45, 148–56, 202–15; EPSTEIN, *supra* note 176, at 125–28; GORDON, *supra* note 3, at 116–35; GROSSBERG, *supra* note 131, at 47–48; PIVAR, *supra* note 211; ROSEN, *supra* note 229, at 112–36; SHANLEY, *supra* note 159, at 79–86, 92–93 (1989); SMITH-ROSENBERG, *supra* note 120, at 109–28; Elizabeth Pleck, *Feminist Responses to "Crimes against Women," 1800–1896*, 8 SIGNS 459 (1983).

233. RANDOLPH TRUMBACH, THE RISE OF THE EGALITARIAN FAMILY: ARISTOCRATIC KINSHIP AND DOMESTIC RELATIONS IN EIGHTEENTH-CENTURY ENGLAND 176 (1978).

234. On the prevalence of delayed marriage as a birth control arrangement, see 1 ANDERSON & ZINSSER, *supra* note 13, at 135–36; CONNELL, *supra* note 192, at 117–18; LASLETT, *supra* note 13, at 13–14. *See also* Chapter 7, at notes 259–304.

medical grounds as physicians gradually learned techniques for controlling pain and reducing danger.[235]

The rise of physicians to dominance over obstetric and gynecological medicine must be understood first as a social and political development, and only secondarily as one rooted in changes in medical technologies.[236] Rather than being seen as anti-woman as is so common today,[237] such social conventions as feminine frailty and sexual constraint—and the medicalization of birth—should be seen, in their time, as part of the movement "to enhance the autonomy of women, to give them a greater sense of their own self-interest" and the ability to act on it.[238] Women's gains in controlling birth patterns could only be obtained, however, at the cost of sub-

---

235. *See* Arturo Castiglioni, A History of Medicine 628–31 (2nd ed. 1947); Audrey Eccles, Obstetrics and Gynaecology in Tudor and Stuart England 124 (1982); Sherwin B. Nuland, The Doctors' Plague: Germs, Childbed Fever, and the Strange Story of Ignác Semmelweiss (2003); Tony Pensabene, The Rise of the Medical Practitioner in Victoria 33 (1980); Kerry Petersen, Abortion Regimes 16–17, 32–34 (1993); Paul Starr, The Social Transformation of American Medicine: The Rise of a Sovereign Profession and the Making of a Vast Industry 134–40 (1982); Regina Morantz-Sanchez, *Physicians*, in Women, Health & Medicine in America 477, 487 (Rima Apple ed. 1990). Some commentators insist that even today obstetricians endanger women and babies rather than help them; these studies must be evaluated carefully given that in contemporary societies midwives will, if possible, turn a birth over to a physician if there is, or are likely to be, "complications." *See* Suzanne Arms, Immaculate Deception: A New Look at Women and Childbirth 53–54 (1977); Donnison, *supra* note 160, at 192–93; Judy Barrett Litoff, The American Midwife Debate 83, 147 (1986); Barbara Katz Rothman, In Labor: Women and Power in the Birthplace 42 (1982); Lynn Silver & Sidney Wolfe, Unnecessary Cesarean Sections: How to Cure a National Epidemic (1989); Marjorie Tew, Safer Childbirth? 289 (1990); Dorothy & Richard Wertz, Lying In: A History of Childbirth in America 161 (1977); Robbie Davis-Floyd, *The Role of Obstetrical Rituals in the Resolution of Cultural Anomaly*, 31 Soc. Sci. Med. 175 (1990); A. Mark Durand, *The Safety of Home Birth: The Farm Study*, 82 Am. J. Pub. Health 450 (1992); Chris Hafner-Eaton & Laurie Pearce, *Birth Choices, the Law, and Medicine: Balancing Individual Freedoms and Protection of the Public's Health*, 19 J. Health Pol., Pol'y & L. 813, 815, 817–18, 822–23 (1994); Tamar Lewin, *Midwives Deliver Healthy Babies with Fewer Interventions*, N.Y. Times, Apr. 18, 1997, at A15; Kristin McIntosh, *Regulation of Midwives as Home Birth Attendants*, 30 B.C. L. Rev. 477, 492–96 (1989); Ken Nagaya *et al.*, *Causes of Maternal Mortality in Japan*, 283 JAMA 2661 (2000); Francis Notzon, *International Differences in the Use of Obstetric Interventions*, 263 JAMA 3286 (1990); Roger Rosenblatt, *The Perinatal Paradox: Doing More and Accomplishing Less*, 1989 Health Aff. 158; Suzanne Hope Suarez, *Midwifery Is Not the Practice of Medicine*, 5 Yale J. Law & Feminism 315, 317–21, 327–28, 335–55 (1993); Marjorie Tew, *Do Obstetric Intranatal Interventions Make Birth Safer?*, 93 Brit. J. Obstet. & Gynaecology 659 (1986); Marsden Wagner, *Infant Mortality in Europe: Implications for the United States, Statement to the National Commission to Prevent Infant Mortality*, 9 J. Pub. Health 473, 481 (1988).

236. *See* Evan Willis, Medical Dominance 69 (rev. ed. 1986).

237. *See, e.g.,* Arms, *supra* note 235; Brodie, *supra* note 9, at 287; Brookes, *supra* note 12, at 26, 52, 67, 134; Ginny Cassidy-Brinn, Francis Hornstein, & Carol Downer, Women Centered Pregnancy and Birth 92–101 (1984); Donnison, *supra* note 160; Gordon, *supra* note 3, at 160; Harrison, *supra* note 7, at 165–66; McLaren, *supra* note 13, at 123–24, 127–29; Ann Oakley, The Captured Womb: A History of the Medical Care of Pregnant Women (1986); Petchesky, *supra* note 3, at 71–73, 79–81; Petersen, *supra* note 235, at 10–11; Riddle, *supra* note 7, at 162; Barbara Katz Rothman, In Labor: Women and Power in the Birthplace (1982); Deborah Sullivan & Rose Weitz, Labor Pains: Modern Midwives and Home Birth 1–19 (1988); James Boyd White, Acts of Hope: Creating Authority in Literature, Law, and Politics 165–66 (1994); Jane Maslow Cohen, *A Jurisprudence of Doubt: Deliberative Autonomy and Abortion*, 3 Colum. J. Gender & Law. 175, 208–10 (1992); Hafner-Eaton & Pearce, *supra* note 235, at 816–19, 829–30; Dianne Martin, *The Midwife's Tale: Old Wisdom and a New Challenge to the Control of Reproduction*, 3 Colum. J. Gender & L. 417 (1992); Catherine Scholten, *On the Importance of the Obstetrick Art: Changing Customs of Childbirth in America, 1760–1825*, in Women and Health in America 142, 146–47 (Judith Walzer Leavitt ed. 1984); Siegel, *supra* note 163, at 283–84; Rickie Solinger, *"A Complete Disaster": Abortion and the Politics of Hospital Abortion Committees, 1950–1970*, 19 Feminist Stud. 241, 250–51, 257–58, 263–64 (1993); Suarez, *supra* note 235; Michael Thomson, *Women, Medicine and Abortion in the Nineteenth Century*, 3 Fem. Leg. Stud. 159, 175–77 (1995).

238. Degler, *supra* note 9, at 271–73.

ordinating their needs to that of their doctors, and also at the cost of their surrendering some of the physical intimacy that the nineteenth-century's cult of romantic love was awakening[239] as well as by their embracing an image of themselves as weak, frail, and delicate.

# Infanticide in Western Societies

*He who asks a question cannot avoid the answer.*

—Cameroonian proverb[240]

The recent "discovery" that childhood has a history has given rise to some rather bizarre interpretations of how childhood was experienced—by parents as well as children—in times past. Several prominent historians have argued that parents were unattached or even hostile toward their children until relatively recent times.[241] Such arguments greatly overstate the case.[242] Parents generally were attached to their children, driven as they were by a biological urge to reproduce. Yet no society has ever been free of unwanted children and of attempts to dispose of unwanted children. As we have seen, however, mechanical and chemical means of birth control began to be available in America and England to any large extent only after 1880, and then only over considerable public opposition. This reality meant that unplanned and unwanted pregnancies were more common through most of history than they are today. Furthermore, in chapter 1 we found that abortion was not a real option. Someone who was utterly determined to be rid of an unwanted child but was unwilling or unable to risk a near suicidal abortion could only "terminate" the child after it was born, rather than "terminate" the pregnancy before birth.

While western societies seem to suffer amnesia regarding the frequency of the practice of infanticide in their own pasts, in fact much evidence for infanticide or abandonment in England and throughout Europe shows these to have been common practices even during the Christian

---

239. Lewis & Lockridge, *supra* note 130, at 13. *See generally* D'Emilio & Freedman, *supra* note 9, at 42–53, 73–84; Karen Lystra, Searching the Heart: Women, Men, and Romantic Love in Nineteenth-Century America (1989); Smith-Rosenberg, *Hysterical Woman, supra* note 222, at 655, 678.

240. Rhoda Tripp, The International Thesaurus of Quotations 316 (1970).

241. *See, e.g.,* Philippe Ariès, Centuries of Childhood: A Social History of Family Life (Robert Baldick trans. 1962); Elisabeth Badinter, Mother Love: Myth and Reality (Frances du Plessix Grey trans. 1981); Philip Greven, The Protestant Temperament 37 (1977); Lawrence Stone, The Family, Sex, and Marriage in England 1500–1800, at 163–64 (1977); Valerie Polakow Suransky, The Erosion of Childhood (1982); The History of Childhood 51–54 (Lloyd de Mause ed. 1974). *See also* Nancy Scheper-Hughes, Death without Weeping: The Violence of Everyday Life in Brazil 400–01 (1992). This thought leads into the idea that "mothering"—the strong desire of most women to nurture their children (and often others' children as well)—is "socially constructed," rather than the result of genetically programmed biological processes. *See, e.g.,* Mothering: Essays in Feminist Theory (Joyce Trebilcot ed. 1983); Shari Thurer, The Myths of Motherhood: How Culture Reinvents the Good Mother (1994); Katharine Baker, *Taking Care of Our Daughters* (book rev.), 18 Cardozo L. Rev. 1495, 1509–25 (1997); Mary Becker, *Maternal Feelings: Myth, Taboo, and Child Custody,* 1 S. Cal. L. Rev. 133 (1992). For the contrary view, see Hrdy, *supra* note 8, at 388–92, 419–26, 431–38, 480–81, 488–96; Robert Karen, Becoming Attached: Unfolding the Mystery of the Infant-Mother Bond and Its Impact on Later Life (1994).

242. *See* Hrdy, Mother Nature, *supra* note 8, at 308–14, 535, 539; Hunt, *supra* note 56; Nicholas Orme, Medieval Children (2001); Steven Ozment, Ancestors: The Loving Family in Old Europe (2001); Linda Pollack, The Forgotten Children (1983); Edward Shorter, The Making of the Modern Family (1975); The History of the European Family: Volume 1, Family Life in Early Modern Times, 1500–1789 (David Kertzer & Marzio Barbagli eds. 2001); Wrightson, *supra* note 13, at 151; Patricia Crawford, *"The Suckling Child": Adult Attitudes in Child Care in the First Year of Life in Seventeenth Century England,* 1 Continuity & Change 23 (1986).

era.[243] Except during the later years of the nineteenth century, even abandonment at a foundling home was tantamount to infanticide. Only a few historians, most notably Barbara Hanawalt, have concluded that infanticide was rare during the Middle Ages.[244] Hanawalt herself, however, documented the relative frequency of prosecutions for infanticide compared to other crimes.[245] On the other hand, Jonathan Swift gained considerable notoriety in the early eighteenth century for satirically recognizing the link between infanticide and abortion in his (in)famous proposal to authorize parents to sell their unwanted children as meat—which, as he pointed out, would have "another great advantage...it will prevent those voluntary abortions, and that horrid practice of women murdering their bastard children...."[246]

---

243. *See generally* 1 ANDERSON & ZINSSER, *supra* note 13, at 30–31, 138–40, 403–05; DAVID BAKAN, SLAUGHTER OF THE INNOCENTS (1971); JOHN BOSWELL, THE KINDNESS OF OTHERS: THE ABANDONMENT OF CHILDREN IN WESTERN EUROPE FROM LATE ANTIQUITY TO THE RENAISSANCE (1988); GORDON, *supra* note 3, at 32–35; HARRISON, *supra* note 6, at 182–83; HOFFER & HULL, *supra* note 8; HRDY, MOTHER NATURE, *supra* note 8, at 288–317, 463–68, 517–19; INFANTICIDE: HISTORICAL PERSPECTIVES ON CHILD MURDER AND CONCEALMENT, 1550–2000 (Mark Jackson ed. 2002); LUKE LEE & ARTHUR LARSEN, POPULATION AND LAW 3–15 (1971); WILLIAM IAN MILLER, BLOODTAKING AND PEACEMAKING: FEUD, LAW, AND SOCIETY IN SAGA ICELAND 16 (1990); GEORGE PAYNE, THE CHILD IN HUMAN PROGRESS (1976); MARIA PIERS, INFANTICIDE: PAST AND PRESENT (1978); QUAIFE, *supra* note 5, at 22; DAVID RANSEL, THE FAMILY IN IMPERIAL RUSSIA 105 (1978); RUSSELL, *supra* note 17, at 222; THE HISTORY OF CHILDHOOD, *supra* note 241, at 25–32, 63 n.140, 245, 282–86, 306–11, 393–94; MICHAEL TOOLEY, ABORTION AND INFANTICIDE 315–22 (1983); BARBARA TUCHMAN, A DISTANT MIRROR: THE CALAMITOUS 14TH CENTURY 105, 366 (1978); Yves Brissaud, L'infanticide à la fin du moyen age, ses motivations psychologiques et sa repression, 50 REVUE HISTORIQUE DE DROIT FRAINÇAISE ET ÉTRANGER 229 (1972); Emily Coleman, L'infanticide dans le haut moyen âge, 29 ANNALES ECONOMIQUES-SOCIÉTÉS-CIVILISATIONS 315 (1974); Emily Coleman, *Infanticide in the Early Middle Ages*, in WOMEN IN MEDIEVAL SOCIETY 47 (Susan Mosher Stuard ed. 1976) ("Coleman, *Early Middle Ages*"); Catherine Damme, *Infanticide: The Worth of an Infant under Law*, 22 MED. HIST. 1 (1978); D.S. Davies, *Child-Killing in English Law*, 1 MOD. L. REV. 203, 216–18 (1937); Dellapenna, *supra* note 3, at 396–400; Catherine Demme, *Infanticide: The Worth of an Infant under Law*, 22 MED. HIST. 1 (1978); R.H. Helmholz, *Infanticide in the Province of Canterbury in the Fifteenth Century*, 2 HIST. CHILDHOOD Q. 379 (1975); Barbara Kellum, *Infanticide in England in the Late Middle Ages*, 1 HIST. CHILDHOOD Q. 367 (1974); John Krause, *Some Implications of Recent Work of Historical Demography*, 1 COMP. STUD. IN SOC'Y & HIST. 164 (1969); William Langer, *Infanticide: A Historical Survey*, 1 HIST. CHILDHOOD Q. 353 (1974); Kathryn Moseley, *The History of Infanticide in Western Society*, 1 ISSUES IN L. & MED. 345 (1986); Eugene Quay, *Justifiable Abortion—Medical and Legal Foundations (Pt. II)*, 49 GEO. L.J. 395, 406–25 (1961); Edward Shorter, *Infanticide in the Past*, 1 HIST. CHILDHOOD Q. 178 (1973); Richard Trexler, *Infanticide in Florence: New Sources and First Results*, 1 HIST. CHILDHOOD Q. 98 (1974) ("Trexler, *Florence*"); Richard Trexler, *The Foundlings of Florence*, 1 HIST. CHILDHOOD Q. 259 (1974); Laila Williamson, *Infanticide: An Anthropological Analysis*, in INFANTICIDE AND THE VALUE OF LIFE 61 (Marvin Kohl ed. 1978); Lawrence Wissow, *Editorial: Infanticide*, 339 NEW ENG. J. MED. 1241 (1998); Keith Wrightson, *Infanticide in Earlier Seventeenth Century England*, 15 LOCAL POP. STUD. 10, 11–12 (1975) ("Wrightson, *Earlier England*"); Keith Wrightson, *Infanticide in European History*, 3 CRIM. JUSTICE HIST. 1 (1982). *See also* INFANTICIDE AND PARENTAL CARE (Stefano Parmigiani & Frederick vom Saal eds. 1994); WILLIAM GRAHAM SUMNER, FOLKWAYS 272 (1906).

On the continuing reluctance of many today to accept the reality of infanticide even among animals, see HRDY, *supra*, at 293–94; A.I. Dagg, *Infanticide by Male Lions: A Fallacy Influencing Research into Human Behavior*, 100 AM. ANTHROPOLOGIST 940 (1999); Rosie Mestel, *Monkey "Murderers" May Be Falsely Accused*, NEW SCIENTIST, July 15, 1995, at 17; Glendon Schubert, *Infanticide by Usurper Hanuman Langur Males: A Sociobiological Myth*, 21 SOC. SCI. INFO. 199 (1982); Robert Sussman, James Cheverud, & Thad Bartlett, *Infant Killing as an Evolutionary Strategy: Reality or Myth?*, 3 EVOLUTIONARY ANTHROPOLOGY 149 (1995).

244. *See* B.A. HANAWALT, THE TIES THAT BOUND: PEASANT FAMILIES IN MEDIEVAL ENGLAND 95, 101–03 (1986); RIDDLE, *supra* note 6, at 10–15.

245. B.A. HANAWALT, FEMALE OFFENDERS AND CRIME IN FOURTEENTH-CENTURY ENGLAND 253–68 (1975).

246. Jonathan Swift, *A Modest Proposal for Preventing the Children of Ireland from Being a Burden to Their Parents or Country* (1729), reprinted in 5 ENGLISH MASTERPIECES: THE AUGUSTANS 82, 83 (Maynard Mack ed. 1950).

Throughout history until the emergence of abortion as a real alternative reduced the incidence of infanticide, making the latter a relatively minor legal problem, infanticide remained the most common crime in Europe, and probably in the rest of the world.[247] The evidence of such practices is both direct and indirect. Indirect evidence is perhaps the most conclusive as direct evidence in form of legal reports, church documents, and mentions of the practice in other documents tend to be particularized and hence debatable as to whether it represents an isolated, individual act or part of a general pattern of behavior. For the strongest indirect evidence, one can turn to skewed sex ratios and unnaturally low birth rates. While low rates of birth per woman might have had a number of explanations, the skewed sex ratios, absent any prenatal means of sex-selection, can only indicate female infanticide (including abandonment and neglect).[248]

Historical demographers have identified sex ratios as high as four-to-one in favor of male children in areas of medieval Europe.[249] This compares to a biologically normal sex ratio at birth

247. *See* D'EMILIO & FREEDMAN, *supra* note 9, at 65; GORDON, *supra* note 3, at 51; HARRISON, *supra* note 7, at 182–83; ROGER LANE, VIOLENT DEATH IN THE CITY: SUICIDE, ACCIDENT AND MURDER IN NINETEENTH-CENTURY PHILADELPHIA 99 (1979); PIERS, *supra* note 243, at 75; Constance Backhouse, *Desperate Women and Compassionate Courts: Infanticide in Nineteenth-Century Canada,* 34 U. TOR. L.J. 447, 447–48 (1984); La Sorte, *supra* note 13, at 172. Islam condemned infanticide in the strongest terms; one should not assume that this necessarily translated in effective prohibition of the practice. *See* Rumage, *supra* note 129, at 39–46.

248. 1 ANDERSON & ZINSSER, *supra* note 13, at 30; BOSWELL, *supra* note 243; HRDY, MOTHER NATURE, *supra* note 8, at 318–50; SARAH POMEROY, GODDESSES, WIVES, WHORES AND SLAVES: WOMEN IN CLASSICAL ANTIQUITY 91 (1975); Wrightson, *Earlier England, supra* note 243, at 19. As unlikely as it may seem, one study argued that such skewed sex ratios could have resulted from natural, biological causes. Vern Bullough & Cameron Campbell, *Female Longevity and Diet in the Middle Ages,* 55 SPECULUM 317 (1980). Other demographers have argued on the basis of this and other data that Asians are more prone to conceive sons than daughters. N.E. MORTON, C.S. CHUNG, & M.P. MI, GENETICS OF INTERRACIAL CROSSES IN HAWAII (1967); Pravin Visaria, *Sex Ratio at Birth in Territories with a Relatively Complete Registration,* 14 EUGENICS Q. 132 (1967). Such contentions ignore the rather considerable direct evidence for the practice of infanticide. Still others have occasionally simply questioned the validity of the claimed sex ratios despite the rather clear evidence for those male-favoring skewed sex ratios. DAVID HERLIHY, MEDIEVAL HOUSEHOLDS 63–65 (1985); RIDDLE, *supra* note 7, at 12–14. Less extreme but identifiably male-favoring skewed sex ratios are also found in Japan when infanticide was common. *See* HANLEY & YAMAMURA, *supra* note 128, at 238–41.
While the victims of such practices nearly always are girls, in some circumstances boys have been targeted for infanticide. *See* HRDY, *supra,* at 340–45; Tamas Bereczkei & R.I.M. Dunar, *Female-Biased Reproductive Strategies in a Hungarian Gypsy Population,* 264 PROC. ROY. SOC. OF LONDON, ser. B, at 17; Sam Clark *et al., Ten Thousand Tonga: A Longitudinal Anthropological Study from Southern Zambia, 1956–1991,* 49 POP. STUD. 91 (1995); Lee Cronk, *Parental Favoritism toward Daughters,* 81 AM. SCI. 272 (1993); Marina Faerman *et al., DNA Analysis Reveals the Sex of Infanticide Victims,* 385 NATURE 212 (1997); Georgia Dullea, *In Male-Dominated Korea, an Island of Sexual Equality,* N.Y. TIMES, July 9, 1987, at C1, C10; Paul Turke, *Helpers at the Nest: Childcare Networks on Ifaluk,* in HUMAN REPRODUCTIVE BEHAVIOR: A DARWINIAN PERSPECTIVE 173 (Laura Betzig, Monique ergerhoff, & Paul Turke eds. 1988). There has been no satisfactory explanation as to why Orthodox Jews produce more daughters than the normal ratio would suggest as neither abortion nor infanticide would appear to be common and the group does valorize sons; some have suggested that the pattern results from customs relating to the timing of sexual relations within the group. MARCIA GUTTENTAG & PAUL SECORD, TOO MANY WOMAN: THE SEX RATIO QUESTION 98 (1983); HRDY, MOTHER NATURE, *supra,* at 337; Susan Harlap, *Gender of Infants Conceived on Different Days of the Menstrual Cycle,* 300 NEW ENG. J. MED. 1445 (1979).

249. J.D. CHAMBERS, POPULATION, ECONOMY AND SOCIETY IN PRE-INDUSTRIAL ENGLAND 78 (1972); FLANDRIN, *supra* note 65, at 199; RUSSELL, *supra* note 243, at 148–49, 162, 167–68; TANNAHILL, *supra* note 13, at 30–31, 278; THE HISTORY OF CHILDHOOD, *supra* note 241, at 25–28; Carol Clover, *The Politics of Scarcity: Notes on the Sex Ratio in Early Childhood,* 60 SCANDINAVIAN STUD. 147 (1988); Coleman, *Early Middle Ages, supra* note 243, at 60–64; Kellum, *supra* note 243; Trexler, *supra* note 243, at 100–01; E.A. Wrigley, *Family Limitation in Pre-Industrial England,* 19 ECON. HIS. REV. (2d Ser.) 105 (1966). This ratio is far more skewed than the sex ratio of nineteenth century China, where, we are told, female infanticide was common. C.F. GORDON-CUMMINGS, WANDERINGS IN CHINA 134–37, 272–76 (1900); PING-TI HO, STUDIES ON THE POPULATION OF CHINA, 1368–1953, at 8–13, 56–59 (1959); 1 R.M. MARTIN, CHINA: POLITICAL, COMMERCIAL AND

of 106 boys/100 girls.[250] The ability to control the sex ratio was as much of an incentive to the use of infanticide in preference to abortion or contraception as was the certainty of outcome.[251] Skewed sex ratios appear to have been common at least as far back as ancient Greece and throughout the Roman Empire.[252] The lesser value placed on females in Greece and Rome persisted throughout their lives, and is reflected in their receiving lesser amounts of food and other indicia of lesser value placed on girls' and women's labor and lives.[253] Neglect of little girls no doubt contributed to the skewed sex ratios characteristic of Europe (and most non-European societies) throughout the pre-industrial era.[254] In short, as historian Josiah Russell summed the matter up, "[p]opulation control was control over the number of women in the population."[255]

The prevalence of infanticide was eased by the common belief that newborn children were not really human until they were baptized, and malformed children were the spawn of the devil.[256] The French experience with infanticide demonstrates directly the changing incidence of the practice without any need to rely on inferences from the history of abortion. In France, the prevalence of female infanticide was so pronounced that it gave rise to the earliest true feminist movement in western history—a social crusade seeking for baby girls the right simply to live.[257] The contemporary counterpart to female infanticide is the modern practice of sex-selective abortions, a practice that poses considerable difficulties for those who are dogmatically committed to abortion freedom.[258] The principal result of the earlier feminist moment was the opening

SOCIAL, IN AN OFFICIAL REPORT TO HER MAJESTY'S GOVERNMENT 48–49 (1847); A.H. SMITH, VILLAGE LIFE IN CHINA: A STUDY IN SOCIOLOGY 308–09 (1899); Terence Hull, *Recent Trends in Sex Ratios at Birth in China*, 16 POP. & DEV. REV. 63 (1990). *See also* HRDY, MOTHER NATURE, *supra* note 8, at 319–20, 325–27 (China & India); LALITA PANIGRAHI, BRITISH SOCIAL POLICY AND FEMALE INFANTICIDE IN INDIA (1976).

250. Gerald Markle, *Sex Ratio at Birth: Values, Variations and Some Determinants*, 11 DEMOGRAPHY 131, 133–37 (Feb. 1974); Susan Greenhalgh & Jiali Li, *Engendering Reproductive Policy and Practice in Peasant China: For a Feminist Demography of Reproduction*, 20 SIGNS 601 (1995).

251. GORDON, *supra* note 3, at 32, 34; SUMNER, *supra* note 243, at 273–74.

252. 1 ANDERSON & ZINSSER, *supra* note 13, at 30; OTTO KIEFER, SEX LIFE IN ANCIENT ROME 61 (1934); TANNAHILL, *supra* note 13, at 30, 70, 97, 125–26; Mark Golden, *Demography and the Exposure of Girls at Athens*, 35 PHOENIX 316 (1981). *See also* Moseley, *supra* note 243, at 351.

253. 1 ANDERSON & ZINSSER, *supra* note 13, at 30–31, 41, 125–26; TANNAHILL, *supra* note 13, at 126.

254. 1 ANDERSON & ZINSSER, *supra* note 13, at 138–39. *See also* Coleman, *Early Middle Ages*, *supra* note 243, at 60; Kellum, *supra* note 243, at 368; Moseley, *supra* note 243, at 357–58; Trexler, *Florence*, *supra* note 243, at 100–01.

255. Quoted in Gina Kolata, *In Ancient Times, Flowers and Fennel for Family Planning*, N.Y. TIMES, Mar. 8, 1994, at C1, C10. For a remarkable (and disappointing) defense of female infanticide as a rational and non-sexist approach to controlling reproduction in less developed societies, see RICHARD POSNER, SEX AND REASON 143–44 (1992). *See also* TANNAHILL, *supra* note 13, at 31–32. For contrasting views, see Sharon Hom, *Female Infanticide in China: The Human Rights Specter and Thoughts toward (An)other Vision*, 23 COLUM. HUM. RTS. L. REV. 249 (1991); Robin West, *Sex, Reason, and a Taste for the Absurd*, 81 GEO. L.J. 2413, 2441–46 (1993).

256. Carl Haffter, *The Changeling: History and Psychodynamics of Attitudes to Handicapped Children in European Folklore*, 4 J. HIST. BEHAVIORAL SCI. 57 (1968); Kellum, *supra* note 243, at 372–73, 380; Moseley, *supra* note 243, at 352–55.

257. THE HISTORY OF CHILDHOOD, *supra* note 241, at 284–85. *See also* HRDY, MOTHER NATURE, *supra* note 8, at 299; Richard Trexler, *Infanticide in Florence: New Sources and First Results*, 1 HIST. CHILDHOOD Q. 98 (1973).

258. *See* MARY ANNE WARREN, GENDERCIDE: THE IMPLICATIONS OF SEX SELECTION (1985); SEX SELECTION OF CHILDREN 47 (Heil Bennett ed. 1983); April Cherry, *A Feminist Understanding of Sex-Selective Abortion: Solely a Matter of Choice?*, 10 WIS. WOMEN'S L.J. 161 (1995); Helen Holmes & Betty Hoskins, *Prenatal and Preconception Sex Choice Technologies: The Impact on Women*, in MAN-MADE WOMEN 1 (Gena Corea ed. 1987); Owen Jones, *Sex Selection: Regulating Technology Enabling the Predetermination of a Child's Gender*, 6 HARV. J.L. & TECH. 1 (1992); Alison Dundes Renteln, *Sex Selection and Reproductive Freedom*, 15 WOMEN'S STUD. INT'L F. 405 (1992); Viola Roggencamp, *Abortion of a Special Kind: Male Sex Selection in India*, in TEST TUBE WOMEN 267 (Rita Arditti et al. eds. 1989); John Schaibley, *Sex Selection Abortion: A Constitutional*

of the first European orphanages for girls in seventeenth-century France, centuries after orphanages for boys had become common.[259] A similar process occurred at a slightly later time in England.[260]

Orphanages were important as a means for combating infanticide because a common form of infanticide at the time was abandonment. Infanticide by abandonment remained so common in seventeenth-century France that historian Maria Piers concluded that the society was engaged in an "all-out war against infants."[261] While there is undoubted hyperbole in this comment, it appears that in the eighteenth century as many as 40 percent of the children born in Paris were abandoned.[262] If parents were so offended by a child's presence (because of illegitimacy, malformation, or for some other reason) that the parent utterly neglected it, the infant would quickly become an unresponsive and passive creature, seemingly more vegetative than human, enabling the parent to abandon the child or otherwise dispose of it with greater psychological ease.[263] Jean-Jacques Rousseau, despite fame built in large measure on his supposed feeling for children, abandoned all five of his children, apparently without regret.[264] Rosalind Petchesky attempted to put the best light on this fact by claiming that generally parents saw foundling homes as a place of temporary refuge for the child until the parent could take the child back, even approving Rousseau for his abandonments.[265] She herself, however, admitted that most abandonments were anonymous, thus precluding a later matching of parent with child (as was the case with Rousseau), and that mortality rates were appallingly high in foundling homes.[266]

In order to facilitate abandonments, monasteries, convents, and foundling homes in Europe develop a device (called a *tour* or turnbox) that allowed one to leave a child without being identified.[267] In France, some 84,000 infants were abandoned through a *tour* in 1815, and 127,000 in

---

*Analysis of the Abortion Liberty and a Person's Right to Know*, 56 IND. L.J. 281 (1981); George Schedler, *Benign Sex Discrimination Revisited: Constitutional and Moral Issues in Banning Sex-Selection Abortion*, 15 PEPP. L. REV. 295 (1988); Robert Steinbacher & Faith Filroy, *Sex Selection Technology: A Prediction of Its Use and Effect*, 124 J. PSYCH. 283 (1990).

259. THE HISTORY OF CHILDHOOD, *supra* note 241, at 285–87. On the emergence of foundling homes for boys, see Moseley, *supra* note 243, at 358; Trexler, *Florence, supra* note 243, at 100.

260. *See* ELIZABETH COLLIER, A SCHEME FOR THE FOUNDATION OF A ROYAL HOSPITAL . . . FOR THE MAINTENANCE OF A CORPORATION OF SKILLFUL MIDWIVES, AND SUCH FOUNDLINGS OR EXPOSED CHILDREN AS SHALL BE ADMITTED THEREIN 1 (1687). *See also* HRDY, MOTHER NATURE, *supra* note 8, at 299–300.

261. PIERS, *supra* note 243, at 63.

262. Claude Delaselle, *Abandoned Children in 18th Century Paris,* 4 SELECTIONS FROM THE ANNALES 47 (Robert Forster & Orest Ranum eds. 1978). *See also* OLWEN HUFTON, THE POOR IN EIGHTEENTH CENTURY FRANCE 318, 332–33 (1974); PETCHESKY, *supra* note 3, at 47; TANNAHILL, *supra* note 13, at 337–38; van de Walle, *supra* note 120, at 147.

263. PIERS, *supra* note 243, at 17. Parents and others tended to persuade themselves that malformed infants were not really human and thus not deserving of attention (or worse), a pattern found in some quarters even today. Victor Rosenblum & Michael Budde, *Historical and Cultural Considerations of Infanticide,* in INFANTICIDE AND THE HANDICAPPED NEWBORN 1 (Dennis y & Melinda Delahoyde eds. 1982).

264. MAURICE CRANSTON, THE SOLITARY SELF: JEAN JACQUES ROUSSEAU IN EXILE AND ADVERSITY 182–83 (1997); PAUL JOHNSON, INTELLECTUALS 21–23 (1988). *See also* BADINTER, *supra* note 241, at 138; HRDY, MOTHER NATURE, *supra* note 8, at 313. A pattern of multiple abandonment of all or nearly all of a couple's children was not limited to Rousseau. HRDY, *supra,* at 307–08. Rousseau, however, had far less excuse than some.

265. PETCHESKY, *supra* note 3, at 63–64 n.79.

266. *Id.* at 48.

267. 31 LA GRANDE ENCYCLOPEDIE 224 (1886–1902); 7 NOUVEAU LAROUSE ILLUSTRÉ 1069 (Claude Augé ed. 1898–1909). *See also* HRDY, MOTHER NATURE, *supra* note 8, at 304–06; DAVID KERTZER, SACRIFICED FOR HONOR: ITALIAN INFANT ABANDONMENT AND THE POLITICS OF REPRODUCTIVE CONTROL 104–22 (1993); William Langer, *Europe's Initial Population Explosion,* 69 AM. HIST. REV. 1, 8 (1963).

1833.[268] As orphanages became more accessible to anonymous abandonment, the percentage of children abandoned rose to as high as 43 percent in some locales at certain times.[269] Yet, as Petchesky noted, the presence of foundling homes did not guarantee survival. In Dublin in 1775–76, for example, of 10,272 children received into a foundling home, only 45 survived the year.[270] While this figure was extreme, mortality rates in foundling homes across Europe were high, ranging from 70 percent to 90 percent annually.[271] Foundling homes often delayed an infant's death only long enough to assure her baptism before her death.[272] And this was the best recourse available for parents who could not quite bring themselves to kill their children directly. Simply put, the situation produced "unintended consequences on a massive scale."[273]

The late eighteenth century saw a serious effort across the Europe to reduce the incidence of formal and informal infanticide.[274] The ruling classes generally remained aloof from this movement, reflecting, according to Maria Piers, a psychological strategy of externalizing the practice and denying its reality among "good people."[275] Finally, reacting to the continued prevalence of infant abandonment in the early nineteenth century, Napoleon made the *tour* mandatory for all foundling homes in France.[276] The *tour*, however, was suppressed in 1838.[277] Should we infer, as some American scholars have, that the suppression of the *tour* merely represented a change in attitude toward illegitimacy that ended the practice of abandonment?[278] Or are we to infer that the social elites who made the law in question had made a decision to favor the direct killing of the child over its anonymous abandonment? This also seems unlikely. English physician Alfred Taylor noted 276 infanticide prosecutions just in France in the years between 1838 and 1841.[279] Or did the problem of infanticide decline as abortion became a more practical option?

The practice of abandonment of newborns has not been so thoroughly studied in England as in France, and English historians have noted it only in passing.[280] The disappearance of abandonment in England sometime during the nineteenth century raises the questions regarding the disappearance of the practice in France at about the same time. Yet infanticide, with its skewed sex ratios remained common in rural areas of Europe well into the nineteenth century,[281] often because rural mothers "suppressed" their daughters to leave themselves free to supplement the

---

268. Angus McLaren, *Abortion in France: Women and the Regulation of Family Size, 1800–1914*, 10 French Hist. Stud. 461, 464 (1978). Another scholar gives the figure for 1833 as 164,000. *See* Owen Jones, *Evolutionary Analysis in Law: An Introduction and Application of Child Abuse*, 75 N.C. L. Rev. 1117, 1197 (1997).

269. Hrdy, Mother Nature, *supra* note 8, at 304.

270. Kenny, *supra* note 8, at 181.

271. *See* D. Herlihy & C. Klapisch, The Tuscans and Their Families: A Study of the Florentine Castrati of 1427, at 147 (1985); Hrdy, Mother Nature, *supra* note 8, at 299–308, 369; Kertzer, *supra* note 267, at 139; David Ransel, Mothers of Misery: Child Abandonment in Russia (1988); Claude Delasselle, Les enfants abandonés à Paris au XVIIIe siècle, 30 Annales: économies, sociétés, civilisations 187 (1975); Langer, *supra* note 267, at 8–9. *See generally* A. Dupoux, Sur les pas de Monsieur Vincent: Trois Cents ans d'histoire Parisienne de l'enfance abandonée (1958).

272. Hrdy, Mother Nature, *supra* note 8, at 302–03.

273. Ransel, *supra* note 267, at 194–95. In a similar vein, the residents of Brescia, Italy, proposed in the early nineteenth century that the following be carved over the entrance to the town's orphanage: "Here children are killed at public expense." Hrdy, Mother Nature, *supra* note 8, at 304.

274. Oscar Helmuth Werner, The Unmarried Mother in German Literature 6–9 (1917).

275. Piers, *supra* note 243, at 122.

276. Loi de 19 Jan. 1811, [1811] Bulletin des Lois (4th ser.) pt. I, at 82.

277. *See* François Vidal, De la répartition des richesses 285 (1846).

278. Caleb Foote, Robert Levy, & Frank Sander, Cases & Materials on Family Law 633–34 (2nd ed. 1976). The authors cited no authority for the proposition that illegitimacy had become so acceptable a practice less than 30 years after the law of 1811 that abandonment ceased to be a social problem.

279. A.S. Taylor, Medical Jurisprudence 431 (2nd Am. ed. 1850).

280. *See, e.g.*, Stone, *supra* note 240, at 421.

281. 1 Anderson & Zinsser, *supra* note 13, at 138–39.

family income as wet nurses to urban families.[282] The number of infanticides actually grew across Europe during the middle years of the nineteenth century,[283] and then simply declined as a social problem, apparently because of growing resort to abortion.[284] Indeed, anthropologist Georges Devereux has concluded that the imposition of a foreign prohibition of infanticide on a culture where the practice is broadly accepted puts pressure on the culture to devise safer and effective means to abort.[285] We find corroboration for Devereux's theory in the recent history of Japan where, although there appear to have been few social restrictions on abortion, there too infanticide remained far more common than abortion until at least the late nineteenth century when abortion apparently replaced infanticide as the common practice.[286]

Abandonment, however, could not be so common in a small community where everyone knew everyone else, and would know who had abandoned the child. Potential wet nurses did have a means of disposal of unwanted children (their own or those of others) ready at hand, so much so that wet nursing itself often turned out to be just a "polite" form of infanticide.[287] So commonly did children die while in the care of wet nurses that English slang for wet nurse was "angelmaker," and the same slang term turns up in French (*"faiseuse d'ange"*) and German (*"Engelmacherin"*).[288]

The dangers of wet nursing were widely reported at the time.[289] The usually level-headed anthropologist Sarah Blaffer Hrdy, based upon her study of maternal behavior among monkeys and other primates, became so wedded to the importance of "allomothers" (persons who stand in the place of and assist mothers) that she would have us believe that the numerous criticisms of wet nursing as often being scarcely hidden infanticide were merely propaganda by people seeking

---

282. BRODIE, *supra* note 9, at 47; HRDY, MOTHER NATURE, *supra* note 8, at 359–60, 368; Trexler, *supra* note 243, at 270; Trexler, *supra* note 257, at 102.

283. KENNY, *supra* note 8, at 183–85; R. Sauer, *Infanticide and Abortion in Nineteenth-Century Britain*, 32 LOCAL POP. STUD. 81, 84–90 (1978).

284. *See* BROOKES, *supra* note 12, at 1, 53–54; GORDON, *supra* note 3, at 35; KENNY, *supra* note 8, at 181; L.A. PERRY, CRIMINAL ABORTION 95–96 (1932); LIONEL ROSE, MASSACRE OF THE INNOCENTS: INFANTICIDE IN GREAT BRITAIN 1800–1839, at 182 (1986); George Behlmar, *Deadly Motherhood: Infanticide and Medical Opinion in Mid Victorian England*, 34 J. HIST. MED. 403 (1979); Krause, *supra* note 243, at 177.

285. Devereux, *supra* note 8, at 108.

286. *See* STANDLEE, *supra* note 36, at 101; IRENE TAEUBER, THE POPULATION OF JAPAN 29–30 (1958); Lynn Wardle, *"Crying Stones": A Comparison of Abortion in Japan and the United States*, 14 N.Y.L.S. J. INT'L & COMP. L. 183, 187 (1993). For the assumption that abortion as well as infanticide were common in ancient times, based largely allusions by ancient poets, see BONSEN TAKAHASHI, DATAI MABIKI NO KENKYU (A STUDY OF INDUCED ABORTION AND INFANTICIDE) 1–10, 27–35 (1936). Takahashi concluded that the attempts by the Tokugawa Shoguns to prohibit abortion were only half-hearted and that enforcement was lax. TAKAHASHI, *supra*, at 35–46. What techniques might actually have been used remain remarkably obscure, however, even to those who believe that abortion was common. TAKAHASHI, *supra*, at 6–26. My thanks to Professor Lynn Wardle for making his copy of a partial English translation of this work available to me; the translation, by Douglas Hymas & Todd Koyama, was made in 1989.

287. PIERS, *supra* note 243, at 52.

288. HRDY, MOTHER NATURE, *supra* note 8, at 355; Langer, *supra* note 267, at 8.

289. See 2 LOUISE BOURGEOIS, *OBSERVATIONS DIVERSES SUR LA STÉRILITÉ, PERTE DE FRUIT FEOCONDITÉ, ACCOUCHEMENTS ET MALADIES DES FEMMES ET ENFANTS NOUVEAUX NAIZ* 65–66 (1626); JACQUES GUILLEMEAU, THE NURSING OF CHILDREN preface (1612); LAURENT JOUBERT, *PREMIÈRE ET SECONDE PARTIE DES ERREURS POPULAIRES ET PENSÉES VULGARES TOUCHANT LA MÉDECINE ET LE RÉGIME DE SANTÉ* 406–09 (1608); FRANÇOIS MEAURICEAU, *TRAITÉ DES MALADIES DES FEMMES GROSSES, ET CELLES QUI SONT ACCOUCHÉES... 496* (1681). *See also* VALERIE FILDES, BREASTS, BOTTLES AND BABIES 196 (1986); SARAH MATTHEWS GRIECO, BREASTFEEDING: WET NURSING AND INFANT MORTALITY IN EUROPE (1400–1800), at 44 (1984); HRDY, MOTHER NATURE, *supra* note 8, at 291, 354–55; GEORGE SUSSMAN, SELLING MOTHER'S MILK: THE WET-NURSING BUSINESS IN FRANCE, 1715–1914, at 80–83, 122–24 (1982); MARGARET YALOM, THE HISTORY OF THE BREAST 108–11 (1997); John Foote, *Ancient Poems on Infant Hygiene*, 2 ANN. MED. HIST. 213 (1919).

to confine mothers to their homes.[290] She never explained, however, why the reports should be so widely credited by the population at large if there were no truth behind the stories. Unlike the efficacy of reputed abortifacients, the frequency of mortality among infants in the care of wet nurses was not something that could be easily overestimated. Interestingly, Hrdy presaged her discussion by noting that French peasants were so inured to the death of infants being wet-nursed that they typically responded to the ringing of a church bell with a simple shrug on the theory that "It's nothing, a little Parisien died!," and also mentioned the quaint expression "an-gelmaker" in several languages.[291] Hrdy just seems unable to accept the idea that a wet nurse could have been employed for the purpose of disposing of an unwanted child rather than for nourishing the child.

In a sense, Professor Hrdy is right. Most of the children sent to wet nurses were not killed. In the late eighteenth century, some 95 percent of all children born in Paris were sent to wet nurses, and if most had been killed Paris quickly would have been depopulated.[292] Apparently some 80 percent of the children sent out from Paris to stay with wet nurses did eventually re-turn to their parents.[293] Yet that still leaves nearly 20 percent of the children born in Paris dying at the hands of their wet nurses—and Hrdy herself estimates the rate to have been as high as 40 percent.[294]

There are several techniques whereby an infant's wet nurse could be transformed into the in-fant's killer, of which "overlying" (smothering) was probably the most common. The sponsoring family, having sent an unwanted child to a wet nurse in a remote village, would simply stop pay-ing for an unwanted child's keep, and shortly thereafter the wet nurse would report the child had died through being overlain while sleeping with the wet nurse.[295] Overlying was so common that the Catholic Church in the early Middle Ages attempted to prohibit women from sleeping with the children in their care without protective devices to prevent overlying.[296] One study found 529 reported instances of overlying from 1639–1659 for London-born children.[297] The actual inci-dence of overlaying was presumably higher. After all, coroner's reports for London listed 3,900 deaths from overlying just between 1855 and 1860.[298] Several historians have suggested that re-ports of overlying were instances of "Sudden Infant Death Syndrome (SIDS)," unrecognized as such.[299] Of course, there is growing evidence that SIDS, a relatively modern malady, itself some-

---

290. Hrdy, Mother Nature, *supra* note 8, at 354–57, 367–69. On allomothering generally, see Thomas Weisner & Ronald Gallimore, *My Brother's Keeper: Child and Sibling Caretaking*, 18 Current Anthropology 169 (1977).

291. Hrdy, Mother Nature, *supra* note 8, at 354–55. *See also* Sussman, *supra* note 289, at 124.

292. Sussman, *supra* note 289, at 22–23.

293. *See also* Christiane Klapisch-Zuber, Family and Ritual in Renaissance Italy 136 (Lydia Cochrane trans. 1986) (about 83% of children sent out wet nurses in Renaissance Florence survived).

294. Hrdy, Mother Nature, *supra* note 8, at 369. *See also* Sussman, *supra* note 289, at 66–67.

295. 1 Anderson & Zinsser, *supra* note 13, at 140, 383; Badinter, *supra* note 241, at 109–12; Donnison, *supra* note 160, at 45; Flandrin, *supra* note 65, at 198–206, 236–37; Hrdy, Mother Nature, *supra* note 8, at 290–91; Hunt, *supra* note 56, at 101–03; Klapisch-Zuber, *supra* note 293, at 102–06; Shorter, *supra* note 241, at 169–90; The History of Childhood, *supra* note 241, at 29–30, 282–83, 308–11, 352–55; Kellum, *supra* note 243, at 367–69; William Langer, *Checks on Population Growth: 1750–1850*, 226 Sci. Am. 96, 97 (1972); Moseley, *supra* note 243, at 355–56, 359–60; Trexler, *Florence*, *supra* note 243, at 102, 107–08; Wright-son, *Earlier England*, *supra* note 243, at 16–18.

296. Fildes, *supra* note 289, at 196; Grieco, *supra* note 289, at 44; Hrdy, Mother Nature, *supra* note 8, at 291; Moseley, *supra* note 243, at 356.

297. John & Morwenna Rendle-Short, The Father of Child-Care: The Life of William Cadogan 26 (1966).

298. Hrdy, Mother Nature, *supra* note 8, at 291; Langer, *supra* note 287, at 97.

299. 1 Anderson & Zinsser, *supra* note 13, at 139; Todd Savitt, *Smothering and Overlying of Virginia Slave Children: A Suggested Explanation*, 49 Bull. His. Medicine 401 (1975); Laura Sessions Stepp, *Infants Now Murdered as Often as Teens: Actual Rate May Be Higher Experts Say*, Wash. Post, Dec. 10, 2002, at A3.

times involves deliberate infanticide.[300] Infants in the care of wet nurses also had a remarkable incidence of drowning or of "falling" into cooking fires.[301]

Killing by one means or another by wet nurses was so common that one study of renaissance Florence found that 58 percent of all children who died during their first year of life died while in the care of wet nurses, with a predominance of girls over boy among those who died.[302] Rosalind Petchesky prefers to see the pattern of infant deaths while in the "care" of a wet nurse as merely a "serious problem" of infant mortality due to the harsh conditions of the life at the time.[303] Petchesky finds contrary views to be "glazed with a heavy dose of high-minded retrospective moralizing."[304] Although we will perhaps never know with certainty the specifics of infant mortality in the care of wet nurses, the historical pattern of overlying and other infant deaths in the care of wet nurses—as they appear in the records—seems rather too convenient (predominantly girls, under circumstances where the family would benefit from one less child) to have been purely unintentional.[305]

While conditions improved somewhat in the nineteenth century, wet nursing remained a means of disposing of unwanted infants well into that century.[306] As a result, France enacted a statute in 1874 requiring all children sent to wet nurses to be registered with the state and to be regularly examined by representatives of the state.[307] Curiously, while mothers actually faced the death penalty for killing their own child, wet nurses were seldom punished.[308] England's Parliament adopted licensing requirements for wet nurses in 1872 precisely to reduce the incidence of infant deaths in a statute tellingly titled the *"Infant Life Preservation Act of 1872."*[309]

# Infanticide under English Law

*Go but one Circuit with the Judges here in England; observe how many*
*women are condemned for killing their Bastard Children.*

—William Walsh[310]

---

300. Hrdy, Mother Nature, *supra* note 8, at 291–93; Richard Firstman & Jamie Talan, The Death of Innocents (1997); Stuart Asch, *Crib Deaths: Their Possible Relationship to Post-Partum Depression and Infanticide,* 35 J. Mt. Sinai Hosp. 214 (1968); George Judson, *Mother Guilty in the Killing of 5 Babies: Infant Death Syndrome Is at Last Discounted,* N.Y. Times, Apr. 22, 1995, at 25; Julie Stoiber & Linda Loyd, *One Question Remains in Marie Noe Case: Why? A Controversial Plea Deal May Be the Only Way to Find Out Why She Killed Eight of Her Children,* Phila. Inquirer, July 4, 1999, at E1.

301. Moseley, *supra* note 243, at 355.

302. Trexler, *Florence, supra* note 243, at 100. *See generally* Klapisch-Zuber, *supra* note 293, at 132–64.

303. Petchesky, *supra* note 3, at 46.

304. *Id.* at 63 n.71. *See also* Shanley, *supra* note 159, at 87–93.

305. *See* Donnison, *supra* note 160, at 86–87; Langer, *supra* note 243. *See also* Iris Oigo, The Merchant of Prato 216 (1957) (reporting that a mother "vowed" to become a live-in wet nurse if her own child would die, followed by death from overlaying).

306. *See* J. Brandon Curgenven, On Baby-Farming and the Registration of Nurses 3 (1869); 2 Ambroise Paré, Ouevres complètes 684–86 (1840). *See generally* Langer, *supra* note 267, at 7–9. *Compare* George Sussman, *Parisian Infants and Norman Wet Nurses in the Early Nineteenth Century: A Statistical Study,* in Marriage and Fertility: Studies in Interdisciplinary History 249 (Robert Rotberg & Theodore Rabb eds. 1980), *with* Louis Adamic, The Story of One Man's Beginning 11, 45, 48 (1936).

307. M. Hewitt, Wives and Mothers in Victorian Industry 139 (1958).

308. Piers, *supra* note 243, at 51.

309. Infant Life Preservation Act of 1872, 37 & 38 Vict. c. 38. *See* Shanley, *supra* note 159, at 87.

310. William Walsh, *A Dialogue Concerning Women* (1699), in The Works of William Walsh, in Prose and Verse 156 (E. Curll pub. 1736).

The *Infant Life Preservation Act of 1872* was part of a tradition of English attempts to find effective means of preventing infanticide, in this instance by regulating those who cared for the infant at or shortly after birth (midwives and wet nurses). There is today some dispute regarding the purposes of the 1872 act. Historian Mary Shanley would have us believe that the real problem underlying persistently high infant mortality rates was the failure of fathers to provide for their illegitimate offspring.[311] She offers no suggestion how a statute regulating wet nurses and others offering in-home childcare might also have been thought to deal with the difficulties of illegitimate offspring in the care of their mothers. In her confusion, however, she merely echoed the arguments of some of the more extreme feminists of late nineteenth-century Britain.[312] So beside the point does this supposed purpose of the *Infant Life Preservation Act* appear to those who argue that it was directed at fathers of illegitimate children that one historian concluded that it was part of the "sexual purity" campaign of the time rather than as part of an argument about public health.[313] But not all English feminists agreed that the problem addressed was non-support by illegitimate fathers.[314] Shanley herself admitted that the practice of "baby-farming" (*i.e.*, taking in more infants than one could possibly care for) was often a covert form of infanticide.[315] Yet she insists on distinguishing this practice from wet-nursing on the grounds that a woman engaged in baby-farming could not possibly have intended to nurse them.

The real purpose of the *Infant Life Preservation Act of 1872* is suggested by its title, and by the remarkable number of infants (but never aborted foeti) recovered from the bottom of eighteenth-century London privies.[316] This led historian James Sharpe to conclude that there were virtual infanticide "factories" in London at the time.[317] Factories there were: the homes of wet nurses and the foundling institutions of the city.[318] The Reformation, the Enlightenment, and the Industrial Revolution, all failed to affect these patterns. English historian Keith Wrightson has estimated that in the seventeenth century about 6 percent of births resulted in stillborn infants or infants who died immediately after birth, including about 2 percent of all births that resulted in infanticide.[319] Dead babies remained a common sight in the streets of London as late as the middle of the nineteenth century.[320] Some 276 dead babies were reported found in London streets in 1870.[321] Infanticide accounted for perhaps six percent of all violent deaths in England as late as 1878.[322] What marks the nineteenth century as different from earlier times is not so

---

311. SHANLEY, *supra* note 159, at 87–93.

312. COMMITTEE TO AMEND THE LAW IN POINTS WHEREIN IT IS INJURIOUS TO WOMEN, INFANT MORTALITY: ITS CAUSES AND REMEDIES (1871).

313. F.B. SMITH, THE PEOPLE'S HEALTH, 1830–1910, at 70 (1979).

314. *See* Amelia Lewis, *Editorial*, WOMAN, July 20, 1872, at 450–51.

315. SHANLEY, *supra* note 159, at 88–89.

316. 1 PHILIP RAFFERTY, *ROE V. WADE*: THE BIRTH OF A CONSTITUTIONAL RIGHT 145–46 (1992; University Microfilms International Dissertation Information Service, Ann Arbor, MI).

317. J.A. SHARPE, CRIME IN SEVENTEENTH CENTURY ENGLAND: A COUNTY STUDY 137 (1983).

318. *See* Wrightson, *Earlier England, supra* note 243, at 17–18.

319. *Id.* at 18–19.

320. *See* IVY PINCHBECK & MARGARET HEWITT, CHILDREN IN ENGLISH SOCIETY 203 (1969); ROSE, *supra* note 284; GEORGE RUDE, CRIMINAL AND VICTIM: CRIME AND SOCIETY IN EARLY NINETEENTH-CENTURY ENGLAND 62–63 (1985); THE HISTORY OF CHILDHOOD, *supra* note 241, at 244–45; A.S. WOHL, ENDANGERED LIVES: PUBLIC HEALTH IN VICTORIAN BRITAIN 33–34 (1983); George Behlmer, *Deadly Motherhood: Infanticide and Medical Opinion in Mid-Victorian England*, 34 J. HIST. MED. & ALLIED SCI. 404 (1979); Maria White Greenwald & Gary Greenwald, *Coroner's Inquests: A Source of Vital Statistics: Westminster, 1761–1866*, 4 J. LEGAL MED. 51, 58–60, 65 (1983); C.H. Rolph, *A Backward Glance at the Age of "Obscenity"*, 32 ENCOUNTER 23 (June 1969).

321. 2 ANDERSON & ZINSSER, *supra* note 13, at 245–47.

322. Langer, *supra* note 267, at 96.

much the incidence of infanticide but the persistent public revulsion at, and incredulity at, the practice.[323]

Parliament apparently first addressed the problem of infanticide when it enacted the earliest known regulations of midwives in 1512. In addition to prohibiting midwives from practicing witchcraft in general, the regulations specifically dealt with infanticide and were in large measure directed at preventing the killing of infants.[324] A license from 1590 also included a promise that a midwife would not torture a woman in labor in order to extract additional fees.[325] On the other hand, midwives were also viewed as enforcers of community morals and were expected to interrogate women during birth to ascertain the father of bastard children and to investigate suspicions of concealment of the birth and death of a child.[326] It even became customary for many women to attend a birth—not to assist if problems were encountered (how many really could help at the same time?), but to witness that a stillborn baby had not been murdered.[327] Midwives were also required to promise to baptize all infants properly if the infant was unlikely to survive long enough for a priest to arrive.[328] Midwives only occasionally turn up in actual prosecutions for infanticide,[329] but their unsavory reputation as involved in infanticide and abortion helped "man midwives" (early obstetricians) in the competitive struggle for business in the eighteenth and nineteenth century.[330] As a result, the regulations applicable to midwives were repeatedly strengthened.[331] Yet by the middle of the eighteenth century the ecclesiastical licensing system was breaking down and had virtually disappeared in England and Scotland by 1800.[332]

During most of English history, interpersonal violence was endemic on a scale that would make the worse crime waive in the United States seem minor.[333] Infants were particularly vulnerable to homicide by means that made the cause of death difficult to prove and infant bodies were easy to hide or dispose of, vulnerabilities that increased if the fact of pregnancy itself had been concealed. Even pregnancy itself was easier to conceal in an age when women were expected to be considerably heavier than they generally are today. David Hume (nephew of the philosopher of the same name) described newborn bastards as the most common victim of murder.[334] Parlia-

---

323. Moseley, *supra* note 243, at 360–61.

324. 1 ANDERSON & ZINSSER, *supra* note 13, at 163, 168, 170–71, 419–21; DONNISON, *supra* note 160, at 19–20; PETERSEN, *supra* note 235, at 11.

325. James Hitchcock, *A Sixteenth-Century Midwife's License,* 41 BULL. HIST. MED. 76 (1967).

326. DONNISON, *supra* note 160, at 14–15. MARVIN OLASKY, ABORTION RIGHTS: A SOCIAL HISTORY OF ABORTION IN AMERICA 29–30 (1992); Mary Beth Norton, *Gender, Crime, and Community in Seventeenth-Century Maryland,* in THE TRANSFORMATION OF EARLY AMERICAN HISTORY: SOCIETY, AUTHORITY, AND IDEOLOGY 123, 144–48 (James Henretta, Michael Kammen, & Stanley Katz eds. 1991). Midwife Martha Ballard discovered the names of 13 reputed fathers (including her own son) for the 20 illegitimate children she helped deliver. LAUREL THATCHER ULRICH, THE MIDWIFE'S TALE: THE LIFE OF MARTHA BALLARD BASED ON HER DIARY, 1785–1812, at 151 (1991).

327. DONNISON, *supra* note 160, at 14, 19, 45; ROBERT ERICKSON, MOTHER MIDNIGHT: BIRTH, SEX, AND FATE IN EIGHTEENTH-CENTURY FICTION (DEFOE, RICHARDSON, AND STERNE) 11 (1986); KEITH THOMAS, RELIGION AND THE DECLINE OF MAGIC 40–41 (1971).

328. DONNISON, *supra* note 160, at 15–16; T.R. FORBES, THE MIDWIFE AND THE WITCH 141 (1966); THOMAS, *supra* note 327, at 40–41.

329. *See, e.g.,* Rex v. Parker, 73 ENG. REP. 410 (1560).

330. PETERSEN, *supra* note 235, at 13.

331. FORBES, *supra* note 327, at 144–47. *See, e.g.,* JANE SHARP, THE MIDWIVES BOOK 38 (1671).

332. JOAN DONEGAN, WOMEN AND MEN MIDWIVES: MEDICINE, MORALITY, AND MISOGYNY IN EARLY AMERICA 148 (1978); DONNISON, *supra* note 160, at 35, 51.

333. QUAIFE, *supra* note 5, at 25–29; P.E.H. Hair, *Deaths from Violence in Britain: A Tentative Secular Survey,* 25 POP. STUDIES 5 (1971); John Walter & Keith Wrightson, *Death and the Social Order in Early Modern England,* 71 PAST & PRESENT 22 (1976).

334. 1 DAVID HUME, COMMENTARIES ON THE LAW OF SCOTLAND, RESPECTING CRIMES 291 (1797). *See also* Wrightson, *Earlier England, supra* note 243.

ment's increasing concern about these problems culminated in a statute enacted in 1624, during the reign of James I, as a reaction to the famine of the year before.[335] This act, entitled "An Act to Prevent the Destroying and Murdering of Bastard Children," conclusively presumed murder from concealment of the death of a bastard in order to conceal its birth.[336] As the title suggests, the statute did not apply to infanticides by married women—they were not presumed to have murderous intent. Married women at the time the statute was enacted were being acquitted of murdering their child on what today we would call a defense of "post-partum psychosis."[337] Similar concealment statutes were enacted in France and Geneva and can be traced back to Anglo-Saxon England.[338]

The statute of 1624 has often been treated carelessly by historians, being variously (and inaccurately) described as prohibiting the concealment either of the birth or of the death of the bastard child.[339] Edward Shorter and Reva Siegel interpreted concealment statutes as applying to abortions as well as to infanticide, although neither the language of the statutes nor the prosecutions under them suggests such a reading.[340] It simply beggars imagination to see in this statute only contempt for the rights of women, as several historians have,[341] rather than an extraordinary effort to protect helpless infants from murder, an effort made necessary by the circumstances of the crime. Infanticide was considered a horrible crime. The social opprobrium for—and personal psychological dissonance from—acts of infanticide is suggested by the psychological ploy of externalizing the act, blaming it on outsiders such as Jews, or Gypsies, or the riffraff in cities.[342]

Evidence supporting the direct accounts of infanticide in Western Europe is found in the extensive legal activity directed at infanticide, in contrast with the sparsity of legal materials relating to abortion. In England, the legal activity began as far back as the Anglo-Saxon legal codes that presumed that any dead child had been killed by its parents![343] True enough, three centuries later the notorious *Mirror of the Justices*[344] did state that infanticide within one year of birth was cognizable only by ecclesiastical courts, but reputable historians dismiss this book as worthless as an historical source.[345] On the other hand, Sir William Staunford and William Lambard both cited a 1315 conviction as holding that infanticide was a common law felony in the same pas-

---

335. LASLETT, *supra* note 13, at 113–18, 123–27. For some unexplained reason, Susan Klepp attributes this law to 1623, and describes it as prohibiting abortion rather than infanticide, although she then goes on to describe the concealment statute accurately without attributing any date to its enactment. Klepp, *supra* note 56, at 73–76. Similar bills had been introduced into Parliament in 1606 and 1610, but were not enacted. *See* Joan Kent, *Attitudes of Members of the House of Commons to the Regulation of "Personal Conduct" in Late Elizabethan and Early Stuart England*, 46 BULL. INST. OF HIST. RESEARCH 69 (1973). On the recurring famines of that time, see INGRAM, *supra* note 68, at 72–74, 78–82.

336. 21 James I ch. 27, §3 (1624).

337. 1 NIGEL WALKER, CRIME AND INSANITY IN ENGLAND 127, 129 (1968).

338. THE HISTORY OF CHILDHOOD, *supra* note 241, at 285 (France); JOHN THRUPP, THE ANGLO-SAXON HOME 85 (1862); E. William Monter, *Women in Calvinist Geneva (1550–1800)*, 6 SIGNS 189 (1980).

339. *Compare* 4 W.S. HOLDSWORTH, A HISTORY OF ENGLISH LAW 501 (23 vols., 7th ed. 1956), *with* 13 HOLDSWORTH, at 390 n.9. *See also* TIM STRETTON, WOMEN WAGING LAW IN ELIZABETHAN ENGLAND 35 n.54 (1998); Ian Lambie, *Mothers Who Kill: The Crime of Infanticide*, 24 INT'L J. LAW & PSYCH. 71, 75 (2000). Susan Klepp seems to think the statute prohibited abortions, although she also recognizes that some law or other dealt with concealment. Klepp, *supra* note 56, at 73–76.

340. SHORTER, *supra* note 4, at 179; Siegel, *supra* note 163, at 285 n.85.

341. PETERSEN, *supra* note 235, at 19; STRETTON, *supra* note 339, at 35 n.54.

342. PIERS, *supra* note 243, at 122.

343. THRUPP, *supra* note 338, at 85.

344. ANDREW HORN(?), THE MIRROR OF JUSTICES (*ca.* 1285), 7 SELDEN SOC'Y 139 (William Joseph Whittaker ed. 1895).

345. *See* Chapter 3, at notes 63–66.

sages in which they denied that abortion was a common law felony.[346] Royal courts contemporary with Staunford and Lambard actively punished those found guilty of infanticide, even denying benefit of clergy to at least one defendant accused of infanticide.[347] By this time, benefit of clergy extended to literate laypersons, but by statute was no longer available for murder and other more serious felonies,[348] a limitation that gave rise to the many technical distinctions among similar felonies, such as murder and manslaughter.[349]

Prosecutions for infanticide were rare in royal courts before the sixteenth century,[350] but prosecutions had been common in the ecclesiastical courts.[351] Martin Ingram, despite his insistence that English tradition respected personal privacy to a much greater degree than now is generally thought, nonetheless ended up conceding that ecclesiastical courts were quite efficient at ferreting out "blatant sexual offenders, especially bastard-bearers."[352] By the sixteenth century, such prosecutions were becoming common in the royal courts.[353]

Once prosecutions in the English royal courts for infanticide became common, they continued unabated throughout the seventeenth and eighteenth centuries. The Old Bailey Session Papers list nine infanticide prosecutions from January, 1685, to January, 1688, and 17 from 1714 to 1722, including six in 1718 alone; another 61 prosecutions are listed from 1730–1774.[354] Nor were these prosecutions limited to immoral London: Essex had 60 infanticide prosecutions between 1601 and 1665, in which 53 of the 62 infants (two cases involved sets of twins) were bastards and 59 of the 60 defendants were the mothers of the dead children.[355] The one woman who was not the mother appears to have been the infant's nurse. Apparently only one of the mothers was married, and for that woman two indictments survive, one of which describes her as married and one as a "spinster." The period of Wrightson's study was hardly abberational in Essex. Another study found 29 infanticide prosecutions in Essex from 1558 to 1603, [356] and yet another study found 40 infanticide prosecutions between 1559 and 1630).[357] No wonder historian James Sharpe concluded that infanticide was "one of the most characteristic" offenses in seventeenth-

---

346. WILLIAM LAMBARD, OF THE OFFICE OF THE JUSTICE OF THE PEACE 217–18 (1st ed. 1581); WILLIAM STAUNFORD, LES PLEAS DEL CORON ch. 13 (1557).

347. Regina v. Parker, 73 ENG. REP. 410 (1560) (the defendant—father of the child—was convicted for arranging for a midwife to cut his daughter's throat at birth and was denied benefit of clergy despite his argument that the child was "not in existence" when he counseled its death, i.e., the child was not yet born; the mother and the midwife had already been hung) [a second report of this case is found at 109 SELDEN SOC'Y 427–28 (1994)]; Regina v. Page (Lincoln Assizes 1559), 109 SELDEN SOC'Y 422 (1994) [Reports from the Lost Notebooks of Sir James Dyer, 1580, John Baker ed.] (a women was indicted for felonious murder for leaving a child under a haystack where it died of hunger).

348. ROBERT RODES, JR., LAY AUTHORITY AND REFORMATION IN THE ENGLISH CHURCH: EDWARD I TO THE CIVIL WAR 86–87, 95 (1982).

349. J.H. BAKER, THE LEGAL PROFESSION AND THE COMMON LAW 292–93 (1986).

350. J.B. GIVEN, THE MEDIEVAL MURDERER: SOCIETY AND HOMICIDE IN THIRTEENTH CENTURY ENGLAND 61–62 (1977); BARBARA HANAWALT, CRIME AND CONFLICT IN ENGLISH COMMUNITIES, 1300–1348, at 154–56 (1979); McLAREN, supra note 13, at 129–30; Kellum, supra note 243.

351. See generally Helmholz, supra note 243.

352. INGRAM, supra note 68, at 329.

353. P.E.H. Hair, Homicide, Infanticide and Child Assault in Late Tudor Middlesex, 9 LOCAL POP. STUD. 44 (1972).

354. 1 RAFFERTY, supra note 316, at 441–51 nn.17–21. See also HANAWALT, supra note 245, at 253–68; HOFFER & HULL, supra note 8; 1 WALKER, supra note 337, at 125–29; R.W. Malcolmson, Infanticide in the Eighteenth Century, in CRIME IN ENGLAND: 1550–1800, at 191 (J.S. Cockburn ed. 1977).

355. Wrightson, Earlier England, supra note 243, at 11–12.

356. F.G. EMMISON, ELIZABETHAN LIFE: DISORDER 156–57 (1970).

357. JOEL SAMAHA, LAW AND ORDER IN HISTORICAL PERSPECTIVE: THE CASE OF ELIZABETHAN ESSEX 20 (1974).

century Essex.[358] Sharpe found that it also had the highest actual execution rates of the capital offenses of the time, with 30 of 83 defendants (plus one accomplice) being sent to the gallows between 1620 and 1680. In contrast, Sharpe found that only 88 of 309 general homicide defendants were convicted; of these, only 47 were actually executed.[359]

Historians have found similar records in other counties.[360] One study found 98 infanticide prosecutions in the eighteenth century Somerset.[361] J.M. Beattie found 62 infanticide prosecutions during a 95-year sample drawn from the period 1660–1802 in Surrey.[362] Cynthia Herrup found that the incidence of infanticide as a proportion of violent crime rose from 14 percent in the 1590s to 32 percent by the 1630s in Sussex.[363] Roy Hunnisett found 44 infanticide prosecutions from 1752 to 1796 in Wiltshire.[364] All of this occurred in a country without a police force and with a deep, abiding distrust of public law enforcement.[365]

The prosecution of infanticide was transformed by the enactment of the concealment statute of 1624—even though the ordinary homicide laws continued to apply to married mothers.[366] The presumption grew from the real difficulties in detecting and proving the crime as well as the strong social incentives for concealing the birth of a bastard that arose from the penalties and the strong social pressures applied to such mothers.[367] During most of English history, mothers, but generally not fathers or others involved, faced severe and varied legal and ecclesiastical, as well as social, punishments for having a bastard child.[368] So grave were the consequences of bearing an illegitimate child that an occasional historian has placed the responsibility for the widespread infanticide of the time squarely on the Church.[369]

Prosecutions under the statute were common as William Walsh noted at the end of the seventeenth century.[370] Modern research confirms Walsh's observation. Valerie Edwards found 15

---

358. Sharpe, *supra* note 317, at 135. *See also* J.A. Sharpe, Crime in Early Modern England 1550–1750, at 60–63, 109–10, 170, 220 n.8 (1984) (infanticide was the most prosecuted species of murder in Cheshire, with 33 defendants hung for infanticide in Cheshire between 1580 and 1709).

359. Sharpe, *supra* note 317, at 134. Conviction rates for serious crimes had been low throughout the Middle Ages. *See, e.g.,* Edward Powell, Kingship, Law, and Society: Criminal Justice in the Reign of Henry V, at 188–216, 231–32 (1989); Pat McCune, *Justice, Mercy, and Late Medieval Governance,* 89 Mich. L. Rev. 1661, 1661–62 (1991). *See generally* Frank McLynn, Crime and Punishment in Eighteenth-Century England 260–62 (1989).

360. *See* Hair, *supra* note 353 (collecting infanticide cases in Middlesex); Wrightson, *Earlier England, supra* note 243, at 16–17 (collecting infanticidal wet-nurses in Lancashire in the seventeenth century).

361. S. Pole, Crime, Society and Law Enforcement in Hanoverian Somerset 174 (unpub. Ph.D. dissertation, Cambridge U., 1983).

362. J.M. Beattie, Crime and the Courts in England, 1660–1800, at 114–15 (1986)

363. Cynthia Herrup, The Common Peace: Participation and the Criminal Law in Seventeenth-Century England 40 n.38 (1987) (Herrup's earlier, unpublished Ph.D. dissertation listed 15 infanticide prosecutions, with six convictions and five executions, in that period in Sussex).

364. R.F. Hunnisett, *The Importance of Eighteenth Century Coroners' Bills,* in Law, Litigants, and the Legal Profession 126, 127, 131 (E.W. Ives ed. 1983).

365. McLynn, *supra* note 359, at 22–35. At the time, without a public prosecutor, the Justice of the Peace functioned as manager of the preliminary investigation of felonies, and, apparently, the clerks of the court managed the actual prosecution. *See* Baker, *supra* note 349, at 259–66, 281, 286–89; Theodore Plucknett, A Concise History of the Common Law 432 (5th ed. 1956); John Langbein, *The Criminal Trial before the Lawyers,* 45 U. Chi. L. Rev. 263 (1978).

366. 21 James I ch. 27, §3 (1624). See the text *supra* at notes 335–42.

367. On the close relationship of bastardy and infanticide throughout the pre-modern period, see also Bastardy and Its Comparative History 77–78, 155–58 (Peter Laslett ed. 1980); MacFarlane, *supra* note 13, at 305; Quaife, *supra* note 5, at 59, 179, 245; Wrightson, *supra* note 13, at 85.

368. Ingram, *supra* note 68, at 338–40; Quaife, *supra* note 5, at 216–42.

369. Werner, *supra* note 274, at 25.

370. Walsh, *supra* note 310.

prosecutions (and five convictions) under the statute in a sampling of five years in late-seventeenth-century London.[371] Keith Wrightson estimated that probably 163 infant murders occurred during the seventeenth century in Essex, based on a careful analysis of the parish birth registries.[372] Incomplete court records for the county show 60 prosecutions for infanticide.[373] Even if some of those prosecutions were of women who had not actually killed their child but had merely concealed its birth and death, this suggests a fairly high rate of detection and prosecution given the circumstances of the crime.[374] Such enforcement was possible because the poor laws (which made local communities responsible for the care of illegitimate children and destitute families) and the strong role of the church in the community fostered a close attention to all illegitimate pregnancies and thus to the unexplained disappearance of an expected child.[375] Midwives were often charged to investigate and determine whether a woman had recently given birth when a putative mother could not account for the child.[376] These were communities, after all, that had little or no privacy as we presently understand the concept.[377] Perhaps as a result, illegitimacy rates in the seventeenth century were remarkably low by twentieth-century standards, whether one counts bastard births or early births after marriage.[378]

Prosecutions under the concealment statute of 1624 continued into the eighteenth century, yet with progressively less success. Attorney Philip Rafferty found 56 prosecutions under the statute between 1744 and 1803, and yet few convictions despite the statutory presumption.[379] Only rarely did acquittal result from a direct rebuttal of the presumption of infanticide.[380] The paucity of convictions is explained by at least three facts: the criminal process of the time; emerging problems of proving that the child was born alive; and changing social attitudes towards illicit sexuality and the consequent rise in illegitimacy in England.

In the seventeenth and eighteenth centuries, courts seldom accepted guilty pleas, and nearly everyone accused of a felony went before a jury.[381] Lawyers were seldom employed on the prose-

---

371. Valerie Edwards, *Criminal Equity in Restoration England and Middlesex*, in CUSTOM, COURTS AND COUNSEL: SELECTED PAPERS OF THE SIXTH BRITISH LEGAL HISTORY CONFERENCE, NORWICH, 1983, at 81, 87, 95 n.39 (Albert Kiralfy et al. eds. 1985) (the years were 1662, 1667, 1675, 1682, & 1688).

372. Wrightson, *Earlier England, supra* note 243, at 18–19.

373. *Id,*. at 11–12.

374. Angus McLaren, by focusing on isolated anecdotes from the time, creates a rather different impression. McLAREN, *supra* note 13, at 131–32.

375. D'EMILIO & FREEDMAN, *supra* note 9, at 5; QUAIFE, *supra* note 5, at 38–43, 98–105, 202–03, 206–24; Norton, *supra* note 326, at 127, 136–37; Wrightson, *Earlier England, supra* note 243, at 13. Historian Walter King, on the other hand, concluded that detection and prosecution actually was rather small, but he does not compare his inferred prosecution rate with the prosecution rates for other serious crimes. Walter King, *Punishment for Bastardy in Early Seventeenth-Century England*, 10 ALBION 130 (1978).

376. Norton, *supra* note 326, at 144–48.

377. CHRISTOPHER HILL, SOCIETY AND PURITANISM IN PRE-REVOLUTIONARY ENGLAND 305 (1967); INGRAM, *supra* note 68, at 238–45, 328–29; LASLETT, *supra* note 13, at 21; STONE, *supra* note 241, at 144–45, 170, 384; THOMAS, *supra* note 327, at 527. *See also* QUAIFE, *supra* note 5, at 16–17, 39, 48–56, 89–90, 105–07, 145–52, 188–89, 209–12; Linda Pszybyszewski, *The Right of Privacy: A* (sic) *Historical Perspective*, in ABORTION, MEDICINE, AND LAW 667, 670–72 (J. Douglas Butler & David Walbert eds., 3rd ed. 1986).

378. INGRAM, *supra* note 68, at 277–79; PETER LASLETT, FAMILY LIFE AND ILLICIT LOVE IN EARLIER GENERATIONS: ESSAYS IN HISTORICAL SOCIOLOGY 117–42 (1977); QUAIFE, *supra* note 5, at 56–58; P.E.H. Hair, *Bridal Pregnancy in Rural England Further Examined*, 24 POPULATION STUD. 67 (1970); Peter Laslett & Karla Oosterveen, *Long Term Trends in Bastardy in England*, 27 POPULATION STUD. 259 (1973).

379. 1 RAFFERTY, *supra* note 316, at 448–51 n.20. *See also* McLAREN, *supra* note 13, at 61, 131.

380. *See, e.g.,* Regina v. Halle, OLD BAILEY SESSION PAPERS, July 1717, at 4.

381. *See generally* BAKER, *supra* note 349, at 268–70, 284; BEATTIE, *supra* note 362, at 336–37; John Langbein, *Shaping the Eighteenth-Century Criminal Trial: A View from the Ryder Sources*, 50 U. CHI. L. REV. 1 (1983); Langbein, *supra* note 365, at 277–78. On guilty pleas, see 4 WILLIAM BLACKSTONE, COMMENTARIES ON THE LAWS OF ENGLAND *329 (1765); 2 MATTHEW HALE, HISTORY OF PLEAS OF THE CROWN 25 (1736); 2

cution side and could not be employed by the defense unless a point of law arose upon the evidence.[382] The denial of representation to the accused reflected Coke's *dictum* that requiring a prisoner to speak in his or her own defense would allow the jury to judge the truthfulness of the defense, a plausible attitude at a time when the accused could not testify under oath.[383] (So much for the privilege against self-incrimination.) There was almost no law of evidence. Jurors were neither queried about possible bias before trial nor given much judicial guidance during trial.[384] While jurors were subject to numerous peremptory challenges (as many as 36 on a side), such challenges were in fact seldom made.[385] Even the "reasonable-doubt" standard was neither precisely formulated nor routinely announced.[386] A single judge (and perhaps a single jury) might hear as many as a dozen felony jury trials in a single day.[387] Indeed, a grand jury often would be meeting in secret in an anteroom, returning fresh indictments during breaks in the trials being conducted in the public room of the building in which the court sat.[388] A petit jury from another set of trials might be meeting in yet another private room deliberating verdicts from earlier trials.[389] So rapidly were trials conducted that it was not established until the eighteenth century that a court could even adjourn a criminal trial over night.[390]

Most research relating to sixteenth- to eighteenth-century trials has centered on London; the county procedures, although in differently structured courts (oyer & terminer; assizes; quarter sessions), followed the same procedures as the common law courts in London except that rural proceedings were faster and the courts were even less careful.[391] In either setting, the proceedings

---

WILLIAM HAWKINS, TREATISE ON THE PLEAS OF THE CROWN ch. 31, §3 (1716); LAMBARD, *supra* note 346, at 522–23; STAUNFORD, *supra* note 346, f.142.

382. BAKER, *supra* note 349, at 286–88; D.R. BENTLEY, SELECT CASES FROM THE TWELVE JUDGES' NOTE-BOOKS 5 (1997); Langbein, *supra* note 365, at 282–83. The limitations on defendants did not apply to appeals of felony as opposed to indictments, nor to misdemeanors, but we are here concerned with indictments of felony; the prohibition began to break down in the eighteenth century, but was not formally repealed until 1836. John Beattie, *The Scales of Justice: Defense Counsel and the English Criminal Trial in the Eighteenth and Nineteenth Centuries*, 9 LAW & HIST. REV. 221 (1991). The transition to allowing lawyers to appear generally on behalf of criminal defendants was earlier in some of the American colonies than in England. *See* LOIS GREEN CARR, COUNTY GOVERNMENT IN MARYLAND, 1689–1709, at 146–47, 196–97, 261–62 (1987); James Rice, *The Criminal Trial before and after the Lawyers: Authority, Law, and Culture in Maryland Jury Trials, 1681–1837*, 40 AM. J. LEGAL HIST. 455 (1996).

383. 3 EDWARD COKE, INSTITUTES OF THE LAW 137 (1644) (criminal law). *See also* 4 BLACKSTONE, *supra* note 381, at 354–56. *See generally* J.M. BEATTIE, POLICING AND PUNISHMENT IN LONDON, 1660–1750: URBAN CRIME AND THE LIMITS OF TERROR 263–64 (2001); John Langbein, *The Prosecutorial Origins of Defence Counsel in the Eighteenth Century: The Appearance of Solicitors*, 58 CAMBRIDGE L. REV. 314 (1999).

384. BAKER, *supra* note 349, at 289–91; BEATTIE, *supra* note 362, at 348–50; 1 HOLDSWORTH, *supra* note 339, at 333; Langbein, *supra* note 365, at 263, 276, 284.

385. BAKER, *supra* note 349, at 285–86.

386. Langbein, *supra* note 365, at 284. *See generally* BARBARA SHAPIRO, BEYOND "REASONABLE DOUBT" AND "PROBABLE CAUSE": HISTORICAL PERSPECTIVES ON THE ANGLO-AMERICAN LAW OF EVIDENCE (1991); Anthony Morano, *A Reexamination of the Development of the Reasonable Doubt Rule*, 55 B.U. L. REV. 507 (1975); Barbara Underwood, *The Thumb on the Scales of Justice: Burdens of Persuasion in Criminal Cases*, 86 YALE L.J. 1299 (1977).

387. *Id.* at 277. *See also* BAKER, *supra* note 349, at 284–89; *See also* BEATTIE, *supra* note 383, at 259–77; BENTLEY, *supra* note 382, at 6. *See generally* TWELVE GOOD MEN AND TRUE: THE ENGLISH CRIMINAL TRAIL JURY, 1200–1800 (J.S. Cockburn & T.A. Green eds. 1988).

388. BAKER, *supra* note 349, at 282; BEATTIE, *supra* note 383, at 264–65.

389. BAKER, *supra* note 349, at 291; BEATTIE, *supra* note 383, at 265–77.

390. BAKER, *supra* note 349, at 289.

391. *Id.* at 273–79. *See generally* J.S. COCKBURN, A HISTORY OF ENGLISH ASSIZES 1558–1714 (1972); E.G. DOWDALL, A HUNDRED YEARS OF QUARTER SESSIONS (1932); EMMISON, *supra* note 356; SIDNEY & BEATRICE WEBB, ENGLISH LOCAL GOVERNMENT: PARISH AND COUNTY 421–79 (1906).

were more inquisitorial than adversarial. Only as the eighteenth century wore on did the judges gradually abandon the role of inquisitor and leave the parties to their proofs.[392]

In such proceedings, whether inquisitorial or adversarial, one could only expect convictions if there was definite proof of what the public, as represented in the jury, considered a clear wrong, particularly given the notoriously harsh penalties in English law at the time. It is also worth noting that jurors then were always men.[393] While this perhaps skewed the results,[394] it does not seem to have resulted in an extraordinary number of convictions of women accused of infanticide. One can only speculate whether having women on the juries might have made obtaining a conviction easier or more difficult. Special juries of "matrons" were often used to determine whether a woman was or had been pregnant—in these prosecutions and after the woman in question had been sentenced to death or in the probate of a will when the woman in question claimed that an heir was on the way.[395] Juries of matrons do not seem to have been particularly protective of the women they examined.[396]

At the very least, the prosecution in an infanticide case had to convince the jury that there had been a child who could have been killed before the jury would entertain the presumption of its murder. During much of the period of the concealment statute, doctors were often willing to testify to the live birth of the child by assaying whether the deceased infants lungs would float—presumably evidence that the child had breathed before death.[397] By the latter years of the eighteenth century, defendants were beginning to make extensive use of medical experts in criminal cases, particularly if the charge was murder.[398] By this time doctors and other medical witnesses were questioning the validity of the floating-lung test.[399] As a result, it had become possible in practice to rebut the presumption of murder by lack of evidence that the child had been born alive, particularly if the mother could show that she had taken steps to welcome the child—as by preparing clothing or bedding for it.[400] Under the circumstances, statutory presumptions cannot have replaced evidence for many juries; indeed, more than one commentator thought the

---

392. Stephen Landsman, *The Rise of the Contentious Spirit: Adversary Procedure in Eighteenth-Century England,* 75 CORNELL L. REV. 497 (1990).

393. 3 BLACKSTONE, *supra* note 381, at *362. *See* Judy Cornett, *Hoodwinked by Custom: The Exclusion of Women from Juries in Eighteenth-Century English Law and Literature,* 4 WM. & MARY J. WOMEN & L. 1 (1997).

394. *See generally* Barbara Allen Babcock, *A Place in the Palladium: Women's Rights and Jury Service,* 61 U. CIN. L. REV. 1139 (1993); Joanna Grossman, Note, *Women's Jury Service: Right of Citizenship or Privilege of Difference?,* 46 STAN. L. REV. 1115 (1994); Carole Hinchcliff, *Women Jurors: A Selected Bibliography,* 20 GA. L. REV. 299 (1986); Carol Weisbrod, *Images of the Woman Juror,* 9 HARV. WOMEN's L.J. 59 (1986).

395. BLACKSTONE, *supra* note 381, at *395. *See* 2 FREDERICK POLLOCK & FREDERICK MAITLAND, THE HISTORY OF ENGLISH LAW BEFORE THE TIME OF EDWARD I 484 (2nd ed. 1898). *See generally* James Oldham, *The Origins of Special Juries,* 50 U. CHI. L. REV. 137 (1983).

396. Cornett, *supra* note 393, at 17–34.

397. *See, e.g.,* Rex v. Allen, OLD BAILEY SESSION PAPERS, Oct. 1737, at 203. *See also* MCLAREN, *supra* note 13, at 134.

398. *See generally* Stephen Landsman, *One Hundred Years of Rectitude: Medical Witnesses in the Old Bailey, 1717–1817,* 16 LAW & HIST. REV. 445, 450–53 (1998);

399. Rex v. M'Carthy, OLD BAILY SESSION PAPERS, Sept. 1802, at 460, 461; Rex v. Russell, OLD BAILEY SESSION PAPERS, July 1782, at 483; Rex v. Field, OLD BAILEY SESSION PAPERS, Dec. 1766, at 45; Rex v. Church, OLD BAILEY SESSION PAPERS, Apr. 1762, at 99, 100; Rex v. Mullen, OLD BAILY SESSION PAPERS, May 1757, at 221, 225; Rex v. Wilson, OLD BAILEY SESSION PAPERS, Apr. 1737, at 91; WILLIAM HUNTER, ON THE UNCERTAINTY OF THE SIGNS OF MURDER IN THE CASE OF BASTARD CHILDREN (1784); John Beck, *An Examination of the Medico-Legal Question, Whether, in Cases of Infanticide, the Floating of Lungs in Water Can Be Depended on as a Certain Test of the Child's Having Been Born Alive,* 1 N.Y. MED. & PHYSICAL J. 441 (1822); *Letter of W.P.,* 44 GENTLEMAN's MAG. 462 (1774). *See also* Landsman, *supra* note 398, at 458–62, 469–70, 472–73, 475–77, 483.

400. Shelley Gavigan, *The Criminal Sanction as It Relates to Human Reproduction: The Genesis of the Statutory Prohibition of Abortion,* 5 J. LEGAL HIST. 20, 25 (1984). *See also* 4 BLACKSTONE, *supra* note 381, at *199.

statute, creating a presumption of guilt, was "un-English."[401] Still, one should not infer too much from the failure to convict under the concealment statute as even such unquestioned crimes as homicide and arson produced similarly declining rates of conviction in the seventeenth and eighteenth century. Nor should one make too much of the technical legal difficulties preventing conviction, as these difficulties had existed in the seventeenth century as well—yet conviction rates at that time had been much higher.

In general, conviction and execution rates for felonies fell sharply in England throughout the seventeenth and eighteenth centuries despite (or perhaps because of) the legendary harshness of the English criminal law. One study found that in the seventeenth century, only 28 percent of those accused of any sort of homicide in one county were convicted, and only 15 percent of those accused were actually executed.[402] Conviction and execution rates for rape were even lower, at least in the eighteenth century.[403] By 1800, only one-third of those sentenced to death were actually executed. Even as early as the fourteenth and fifteenth centuries, juries were convicting of lesser offenses to avoid the death penalty,[404] while acquittals for those accused of simple homicide ran as high as 80 percent and for those accused of murder as high as 50 percent.[405] In London, anyone indicted for a felony stood a one-in-four chance of being hung in 1600, and only a one-in-ten chance in 1710; overall 140 persons were hung in 1600, and only 20 in 1800 despite a vast increase in the Middlesex County's population.[406] In short, juries regularly nullified the famously harsh common law of crimes.[407]

So severe was the problem of jury nullification that during the sixteenth and seventeenth centuries severe measures were sometimes taken in an effort to coerce jurors into enforcing the law. Jurors were fined and imprisoned,[408] while justices of the peace undertook to gather the evidence for the court, displacing the jury's former role as sources of testimony and evidence.[409] Judges also began to give formal charges to the jury, summarizing the evidence and explaining the law.[410] Finally, the law itself was refined to provide juries with a wider range of possible crimes, so that a jury unwilling to convict a defendant of a capital crime could convict of a non-capital crime.[411] One of the prime examples is the development of the crime of manslaughter (non-capital) as an alternative to the crime of murder (capital).

Another factor affecting the conviction rate under the concealment statute was the prolonged change in English family life that occurred throughout the eighteenth century. This change cen-

---

401. SHARPE, *supra* note 317, at 136. *See also* Lord Ellenborough's Act, 43 Geo. III ch. 58, § 3 (1803); J. KEOWN, ABORTION, DOCTORS AND THE LAW 16–17 (1988).

402. SHARPE, *supra* note 317, at 134. *See generally* THOMAS GREEN, VERDICT ACCORDING TO CONSCIENCE: PERSPECTIVES ON THE ENGLISH CRIMINAL JURY TRIAL, 1200–1800 (1985).

403. Anthony Simpson, *Vulnerability and the Age of Female Consent: Legal Innovation and Its Effect on Prosecutions for Rape in Eighteenth-Century London,* in SEXUAL UNDERWORLDS OF THE ENLIGHTENMENT 181, 188–89 (G.S. Rousseau & Roy Porter eds. 1988).

404. GREEN, *supra* note 402, at 38–46.

405. *Id.* at 32–34. *See also* EDWARD POWELL, KINGSHIP, LAW, AND SOCIETY: CRIMINAL JUSTICE IN THE REIGN OF HENRY V, at 82 (1989) ("Available data from the thirteenth to the fifteenth centuries suggests that roughly 70 per cent of indicted felons were acquitted.").

406. Stephen Palmer, *Book Review,* 37 AM. J. LEGAL HIST. 499, 499–500 (1993). Middlesex is the county that included London before its nineteenth century growth spilled across county lines.

407. GREEN, *supra* note 402, at 26. *See generally* ALBION'S FATAL TREE: CRIME AND SOCIETY IN EIGHTEENTH-CENTURY ENGLAND (Douglas Hay, E.P. Thompson, & Peter Linebaugh eds. 1975); John Langbein, *Albion's Fatal Flaws* (book rev.), 98 PAST & PRESENT 96 (1983); Peter Linebaugh, *(Marxist) Social History and (Conservative) Legal History: A Reply to Professor Langbein,* 60 NYU L. REV. 212 (1985).

408. *Id.* at 106.

409. *Id.* at 109–11.

410. MORANO, *supra* note 386, at 510–11.

411. GREEN, *supra* note 402, at 106–07.

tered on the rise of the enlightenment notions of sexuality as natural, healthy, and a legitimate source of pleasure apart from procreation.[412] Changing social mores are hinted at by the sharp fall in the birth rate among the English aristocracy during the century of 1675–1775, although precisely how this was accomplished remains obscure.[413] These ideas, in turn, can be traced back to the discovery of sperm and the growth of the idea of the male as the "active" partner pursuing a "passive" female, leading into the demise of the theory that a woman could not become pregnant without experiencing orgasm and to the notorious double standard.[414] These changes also legitimated the hitherto suspect notion of love as the basis for marriage,[415] which sparked a significant growth in the incidence of premarital pregnancies, as shown both in a rising incidence of "early births" after marriage and an even greater rise in illegitimate births. The percentage of pregnant brides hovered around 20 percent of all brides in England from the sixteenth to the eighteenth centuries.[416] The illegitimacy rate in England was around 3 percent in 1600.[417] The rate then fell to less than 1 percent at the beginning of the seventeenth century, thereafter rising to 6 percent by 1780.[418] No wonder the first proposal to repeal or modify the concealment statute's presumption of murder was introduced into Parliament (by Edmund Burke and Charles James Fox) in 1772.[419]

The concealment statute's presumption was repealed in *Lord Ellenborough's Act of 1803*— which also contained the first statutory prohibition of abortion in England—and the crime of concealment was lessened to a misdemeanor by the same Act.[420] The repeal of the presumption of murder did not express a growing sense of leniency towards infanticide. *Lord Ellenborough's Act* itself explained that the change was made not to ameliorate the law but to make convictions easier in face of juries unwilling to convict a woman of murder in such circumstances.[421] This statutory change, as well as apparently changing social attitudes towards concealment, suggests that infanticide was already becoming less of a social problem as the number of abortions began

---

412. D'EMILIO & FREEDMAN, *supra* note 9, at 40–41; Ray Porter, *Mixed Feelings: The Enlightenment and Sexuality in Eighteenth-Century Britain,* in SEXUALITY IN BRITAIN IN THE EIGHTEENTH CENTURY 1 (Paul-Gabriel Bouce ed. 1985).

413. *See* STONE, *supra* note 241, at 260. For parallel changes in the American colonies, see D'EMILIO & FREEDMAN, *supra* note 9, at 42–48

414. D'EMILIO & FREEDMAN, *supra* note 9, at 40–41, 43–47; McLAREN, *supra* note 13, at 13–14, 26–28. *See also* Cott, *supra* note 211 (exploring the rise of the double standard as a form of social history but ignoring the role of scientific discoveries in this process).

415. Love matches appear throughout history, but until fairly recently such unions were viewed with considerable suspicion as likely to be socially disruptive. The transition of "love" from a somewhat aberrant basis for marriage to the primary reason for marrying was already underway by the time of the Reformation in England and was thus always prominent in the American colonies. *See* INGRAM, *supra* note 68, at 171–218.

416. *Id.* at 157, 162–63, 219–37; LASLETT, *supra* note 13, at 139–46; Hair, *supra* note 378; P.E.H. Hair, *Bridal Pregnancies in Rural England in Earlier Centuries,* 20 POPULATION STUD. 233 (1966).

417. INGRAM, *supra* note 68, at 158. On the shortcomings of the illegitimacy ratio as a demographic index, see Peter Laslett, *Introduction: Comparing Illegitimacy over Time and between Cultures,* in BASTARDY AND ITS COMPARATIVE HISTORY 1 (Peter Laslett et al. eds. 1980).

418. D'EMILIO & FREEDMAN, *supra* note 9, at 41. *See generally* WRIGHTSON, *supra* note 13, at 84–86; KEITH WRIGHTSON & DAVID LEVINE, POVERTY AND PIETY IN AN ENGLISH VILLAGE: TERLING, 1525–1700, at 126–33 (1979).

419. 17 PARLIAMENTARY HISTORY OF ENGLAND 452–53 (1771–72). *See generally* McLAREN, *supra* note 13, at 131–35.

420. Lord Ellenborough's Act, 43 Geo. III ch. 58, §§ 3, 4 (1803). The close linkage between the concealment statute and the crime of abortion is also demonstrated by Blackstone, who discussed the two crimes in tandem as two aspects of a single phenomenon. 4 BLACKSTONE, *supra* note 381, at *198–99.

421. *Id.* Ellenborough's Act, 43 Geo. III ch. 58, § 3 (1803). *See* 11 THE PARLIAMENTARY REGISTER 390 (William Woodfall ed. 1803). Lord Ellenborough's speech to this effect in the House of Lords was also reported in the press. THE TIMES OF LONDON, No. 5672, Mar. 29, 1803. *See also* KEOWN, *supra* note 401, at 16–17.

to increase.[422] While one can speculate how the industrial revolution and other general social changes might have driven an increase in either abortion or infanticide, an upsurge in abortion in place of infanticide had to await the perfection of the technical means for performing abortions with an acceptable degree of risk for mothers. Convictions for infanticide declined throughout the nineteenth century.[423] The decline in the importance of infanticide as abortion became more available is perhaps best shown by the fact that, in 1849, Rebecca Smith became the last woman executed in England for infanticide.[424]

While it was in effect, the concealment statute did prompt coroners to investigate nearly every death of an infant, complete with what was then the highly unusual step of—in those early times—of a primitive autopsy, without any of the usual indicia of wrongdoing normally required to set a coroner's inquest in motion and regardless of whether charges were brought against someone as a result.[425] This practice continued in the nineteenth century. In the middle of the nineteenth century there were approximately 5,000 coroner's inquests annually regarding children who died before their seventh birthdays, even though there were only 39 convictions for infanticide in the period 1849–1864.[426] Instead, during the nineteenth century women tended to be convicted of the related crime of failing to prepare responsibly for the birth of their child.[427]

English law provides more direct evidence that infanticide functioned as an alternative to the utterly ineffectual abortion techniques of the time. We find this evidence in the prosecution in 1679 of the Reverend Robert Foulkes. The full record of *Rex v. Foulkes*[428] reads as follows:

## The Rev. Robert Foulkes

*Executed 31st of January, 1679, for the Murder of his newly born Babe*

This unhappy gentleman was a divine of the Church of England, and had been very much esteemed for his learning and abilities. Few men were more capable of shining in a church, or had a greater share of that sacred eloquence so requisite in a preacher. He was minister of Stanton-Lacy, in the county of Salop, where he was exceedingly followed and admired till his crimes came to be known, and where he might have been beloved till death in a natural way had taken him hence, and then universally lamented, if his heart had been as well furnished with grace as his head was with knowledge and his tongue with expressions.

A young gentlewoman of a considerable fortune, who had been left an infant by her parents, was committed to his care by her executors, as to a man who, they trusted, would not only deal justly with her, but also instruct her betimes in the principles of religion, and her several duties as a Christian. But, alas! how weak is human nature, and how soon are we tempted aside from the ways of piety! Mr. Foulkes, instead of answering the purpose of the young woman's friends, was soon smitten with her charms, and took an opportunity of discovering a criminal passion for her, though he had at that time a virtuous wife and two children living. The young lady too easily consented to gratify his lust, and they continued their conversation together till she became pregnant.

---

422. Dellapenna, *supra* note 3, at 398. Taking a somewhat different view that also links the two provisions as functions of each other, Angus McLaren argued that Ellenborough introduced the provisions on abortion because of his chagrin over having to relax the law on infanticide. McLaren, *supra* note 13, at 136.

423. Davies, *supra* note 243, at 216–23.

424. Hoffer & Hull, *supra* note 8, at 87; McLaren, *supra* note 13, at 193–94, n.80.

425. See J.D.J. Harvard, The Detection of Secret Homicide 6–7, 39, 115 (1960).

426. Davies, *supra* note 243, at 218.

427. Lucia Zedner, Women, Crime, and Custody in Victorian England 38–39 (1991).

428. The Complete Newgate Calendar 274–75 (J.T. Rayner & G.T. Crook eds. 1926).

All the means he could think of to procure abortion were now tried, and they all proved ineffectual; so that they must both be exposed to scandal, unless she could be removed to some convenient place, remote from the eyes of the world, and from the jealousies of Mrs. Foulkes, where she might be delivered of her burden, which was not yet perceived. A plausible excuse for his going up to London was soon formed, and for his taking Miss along with him, who at that time was under twenty years of age. When they arrived in town they took a lodging in York Buildings in the Strand, where she lay in, and where (shocking to think of!) the child was privately murdered, to prevent the infamy that might follow.

But divine vengeance would not suffer this horrible deed to remain long concealed, for before Mr. Foulkes went out of town the girl was examined upon the suspicion of some women, when she confessed the whole, and charged Mr. Foulkes with the murder, who was thereupon apprehended and committed to Newgate; in a short time after which he was condemned at the sessions house in the Old Bailey, upon the evidence of the young woman. On the 31st of January, 1679, he was executed at Tyburn.

The intimate relationship between the rise of abortion and the decline of infanticide was demonstrated by *Lord Ellenborough's Act* which, in the section immediately before the section that reduced the penalty for concealment from death to a term of imprisonment constituted the first English statutory provision relating to abortion.[429] By 1866, the Social Science Association could stage a major debate on whether women who committed infanticide should be condemned in the strongest terms or be seen as deserving of sympathy and compassion.[430] Still, during the closing years of the nineteenth century, infanticide and failing to prepare responsibly for the birth of a child remained by far the most common crimes charged against women.[431]

By the early years of the twentieth century, infanticide had become so unusual in western societies that in England its occurrence came to be seen as evidence of mental disturbance rather than evil intent.[432] In 1849, the Rebecca Smith became last woman was hanged in England for

---

429. 43 Geo. III, ch. 58, §§ 2–4 (1803).

430. Transactions of the National Association for the Promotion of the Social Science 1866, at 293–94. *See* Zedner, *supra* note 427, at 29–30. A similar change had set in in Canada as well. Constance Backhouse, *Desperate Women and Compassionate Courts: Infanticide in Nineteenth Century Canada,* 34 U. Tor. L. Rev. 447 (1984).

431. Zedner, *supra* note 427, at 38–39.

432. *See generally* Brookes, *supra* note 12, at 31; Hrdy, Mother nature, *supra* note 8, at 170–73; Mason, *supra* note 104, at 382–94; Lita Linzer Schwartz & Natalie Isser, Endangered Children: Neonaticide, Infanticide, and Filicide (2000); Cheryl Miller *et al.,* Mothers Who Kill Their Children: Understanding the Acts of Moms from Susan Smith to the "Prom Mom" (2001); 1 Walker, *supra* note 337, at 125–30; Zedner, *supra* note 427, at 88–90; Dominique Bourget & Alain Labelle, *Homicide, Infanticide, and Filicide,* 15 Clinical Forensic Pscyh. 661 (1992); Constance Backhouse, *Involuntary Motherhood: Abortion, Birth Control and the Law in Nineteenth Century Canada,* 3 Windsor Y.B. of Access to Justice 61, 98–99 (1983) (Canada); P.T. d'Orban, *Women Who Kill Their Children,* 134 Brit. J. Psych. 560 (1979); Christine Fazio & Jennnifer Comito, Note, *Rethinking the Tough Sentencing of Teenage Neonaticide Offenders in the United States,* 67 Fordham L. Rev. 3109, 3137–42 (1999) (surveying England and several other Commonwealth countries); C.M. Green & S.V. Manohar, *Neonaticide and Hysterical Denial of Pregnancy,* 156 Brit. J. Psych. 121 (1990); Hopwood, *supra* note 434; Lambie, *supra* note 75 (surveying England and several other Commonwealth countries); Robyn Lansdowne, *Infanticide: Psychiatrists in the Plea Bargaining Process,* 16 Monash U. L. Rev. 41 (1990) (Australia); R.D. Mackay, *The Consequences of Killing Very Young Children,* 1993 Crim. L. Rev. 21; D. Maier-Katkin & R. Ogle, *A Rationale for Infanticide Laws,* 1993 Crim. L. Rev. 903; M.N. Marks, *Characteristics and Causes of Infanticide in Britain,* 8 Int'l Rev. Psych. 99 (1996); J.C. Matheson, *Infanticide,* 1941 Medico-Legal Rev. 135; Katherine O'Donovan, *The Medicalization of Infanticide,* 1984 Crim. L. Rev. 259; J. Osbourne, *The Crime of Infanticide: Throwing out the Baby with the Bathwater,* 6 Can. J. Fam. L. 47 (1987) (Canada); A. Wilczynski & A. Morris, *Parents Who Kill Their Children,* 1993 Crim. L. Rev. 31.

Infanticide has continued to be rather common in some non-western societies, such as China, where modern contraception and prenatal diagnosis are still rare and expensive. *See* John Aird, Slaughter of the Innocents: Coercive Birth Control in China (1990); Janet Hadley, Abortion: Between Freedom and

murdering her child; thereafter, although theoretically a capital crime, women were no longer hanged for the crime, although they continued to be imprisoned for concealment (which was no longer a capital crime since *Lord Ellenborough's Act*).[433] Increasingly the women involved were incarcerated in mental institutions rather than in prison. Between 1902 and 1927 some 48 percent of the women held at Broadmoor—the United Kingdom's facility for the criminally insane—had committed infanticide.[434] In England, the notion of "postpartum psychosis" (then called "puerperal mania") was even given statutory expression in the *Infanticide Act of 1922*.[435]

Despite (or perhaps because of) the decreasing incidence of infanticide in England, prosecutions for infanticide actually continued to outnumber prosecutions for abortion. Infanticide remained easier to detect than abortion if only because of the greater difficulty of disposing of the remains, and the act of infanticide by its very rarity came to be more shocking than the now relatively more common crime of abortion.[436] It remains true today in England that infants under one year of age are four times more likely to be murdered—generally by a parent—than the general public, but the rate (45 per million) is nonetheless minuscule compared to the abortion rate (about 1 in 3).[437] Nor was all of this a peculiarly English pattern. Despite frequent assertions that Japanese culture did not find infanticide troubling, in fact the practice was often illegal there and the government from time to time took strong steps to repress it, although with little apparent success in remoter areas of the country.[438] Yet only when abortion became common in Japan did infanticide become rare.[439]

# Infanticide in England's American Colonies

*Lawyers know dead men's thoughts too well.*

—Carl Sandberg[440]

Historians have done less research into the actual records regarding infanticide in England's American colonies than they have for England. Numerous historians have concluded that infanticide was not common in colonial America, both because of the relative scarcity of direct evidence of such activities or of records of prosecutions for abortion or infanticide and because of their supposition that children were a highly valuable resource in the sparsely peopled land.[441]

---

NECESSITY 99–105 (1996); Hom, *supra* note 256; Kay Johnson, *Chinese Orphanages: Saving China's Abandoned Girls,* 30 AUSTRAL. J. CHINESE AFF. 61 (1993). *See also* POSNER, *supra* note 256, at 143–44.

433. ZEDNER, *supra* note 427, at 90.

434. HRDY, MOTHER NATURE, *supra* note 8, at 289. *See generally* J.S. Hopwood, *Child Murder and Insanity,* 73 J. MENTAL SCI. 95 (1927).

435. 12 & 13 Geo. V, c. 18 (1922).

436. BROOKES, *supra* note 12, at 31–32.

437. *See* MASON, *supra* note 104, at 384; M.N. Marks & R. Kumar, *Infanticide in England and Wales,* 33 MED. SCI. & L. 329 (1993).

438. HANLEY & YAMAMURA, *supra* note 128, at 233, 238–41; STANDLEE, *supra* note 36, at 152–54; TAKAHASHI, *supra* note 286, at 35–46, 57–63.

439. See the references *supra* at note 286.

440. Carl Sandberg, *The Lawyers Know Too Much,* in CARL SANDBERG, SMOKE AND STEEL 85 (1963).

441. D'EMILIO & FREEDMAN, *supra* note 9, at 5, 16, 25–26, 32, 65; GORDON, *supra* note 3, at 33, 49–51; SCHOLTEN, *supra* note 126, at 9; Smith, *supra* note 134; THE HISTORY OF CHILDHOOD, *supra* note 241, at 327, 336 n.55, 352–55; Lorena Walsh, *"Till Death Do Us Part": Marriage and Family Formation in Seventeenth-Century Maryland,* in THE CHESAPEAKE IN THE SEVENTEENTH CENTURY: ESSAYS IN ANGLO-AMERICAN SOCIETY 126 (Thad Tate & David Ammerman eds. 1979). For a challenge to this conclusion, without supporting evidence, see BRODIE, *supra* note 9, at 39–41.

The argument is that there was an element of patriotism (or should we say chauvinism?) in all this breeding, fueled by the need to "populate" an "empty" continent.[442] This alone might account for the reputation that the colonists early developed as parents who were exceptionally attached to and caring of their children compared to European parents.[443] The pervasive lack of personal privacy also contributed to the relative rarity of infanticide, particularly in New England were "solitary living" was forbidden.[444] Finally, those who migrated to New England (if not to the other colonies) were on the whole more law abiding than people who remained in old England.[445] This was rooted in the strong religious feelings of the Puritans and the Pilgrims.[446]

Symptomatic of both the general lawfulness of most New Englander's behavior and of the temptations that regularly broke through the usual rigid adherence to official norms was that the relatively minor crime of fornication accounted for 57 percent of the crimes charged in Middlesex County, Massachusetts, between 1760 and 1774 (210 of 370 prosecutions).[447] On the other hand, only two married women were ever executed for adultery in Massachusetts.[448] (Men seem not to have faced death for adultery.) The dearth of such cases perhaps simply reflects the severity of the penalty. In other New England counties, fornication also generally was the most common category of case brought in the county courts until late in the eighteenth century; fornication cases frequently constituted a majority of all prosecutions.[449] As in Massachusetts, adultery was another matter; it would appear that only one woman was executed for adultery in Connecticut,[450] although several women were executed for "adultery and infanticide."[451]

Despite the frequency of prosecution for fornication, the rate of fornication for the general population in New England seems to have been rather low. Apparently less than 10 percent of New England brides were pregnant in the seventeenth century; in contrast, nearly one-third of brides went to the altar pregnant in Maryland and Virginia during the same period.[452] Furthermore, at least in Middlesex County in Massachusetts, such crime as there was, particularly sexual misbehavior, tended to run within particular families or identifiable groups, almost as part of a "counterculture."[453] Prosecutions for fornication and related crimes in New Haven Colony and

---

442. *See* Paul Carrington, *One Law: The Role of Legal Education in the Opening of the Legal Profession since 1776*, 44 FLA. L. REV. 501, 543–47 (1992).

443. ROGER THOMPSON, SEX IN MIDDLESEX: POPULAR MORES IN A MASSACHUSETTS COUNTY, 1649–1699, at 164–68, 195–96 (1986).

444. D'EMILIO & FREEDMAN, *supra* note 9, at 16–17, 29–30; DAVID FLAHERTY, PRIVACY IN COLONIAL NEW ENGLAND 42–43, 76–84, 175–79, 207 (1972); RAPHAEL SEMMES, CRIMES AND PUNISHMENT IN EARLY MARYLAND 182–83 (1938); THOMPSON, *supra* note 443, at 157–58; ULRICH, *supra* note 125, at 89–99; Pszybyszewski, *supra* note 377, at 672–75. *See generally* HELENA WALL, FIERCE COMMUNION: FAMILY AND COMMUNITY IN EARLY AMERICA (1990); Edmund Morgan, *The Puritans and Sex,* in THE AMERICAN FAMILY IN SOCIAL-HISTORICAL PERSPECTIVE 363, 367 (Michael Gordon ed., 3rd ed. 1983).

445. THOMPSON, *supra* note 443, at 194–95. *See also* DAYTON, *supra* note 62, at 29.

446. THOMPSON, *supra* note 443, at 198–202. *See also* DAYTON, *supra* note 62, at 22–34; DAVID HALL, WORLDS OF WONDER, DAYS OF JUDGMENT: POPULAR RELIGIOUS BELIEF IN EARLY NEW ENGLAND (1989); TANNAHILL, *supra* note 13, at 328–30.

447. Richard Green, *Fornication: Common Law Legacy and American Sexual Privacy,* 17 ANGLO-AM. L. REV. 226, 227 (1988).

448. PETER CHARLES HOFFER, LAW AND PEOPLE IN COLONIAL AMERICA 22 (rev. ed. 1998)

449. DAYTON, *supra* note 62, at 160 (New Haven Cty., Conn.); PAUL MARSELLA, CRIME AND COMMUNITY IN EARLY MASSACHUSETTS: ESSEX COUNTY, 1700–1785, at 14, 18 (1990).

450. DAYTON, *supra* note 62, at 165–66.

451. *Id.* at 166, 167 n.17.

452. D'EMILIO & FREEDMAN, *supra* note 9, at 10, 33; Daniel Scott Smith & Michael Hindus, *Premarital Pregnancy in America, 1640–1971: An Overview and Interpretation,* 5 J. INTERDISCIPLINARY HIST. 537 (1975).

453. THOMPSON, *supra* note 443, at 192–95. *See also* HOFFER, *supra* note 448, at 19–23; INGRAM, *supra* note 68, at 268–74, 354–56, 365; LASLETT, *supra* note 378, at 147–51; Eli Faber, *Puritan Criminals: The Economic, Social, and Intellectual Background to Crime in Seventeenth-Century Massachusetts,* 11 PERSP. ON AM.

later New Haven County, Connecticut, tended to involve repeat offenders.[454] Repeat prosecutions represented as much as 37.5 percent of all prosecutions during some decades—and the ratio would rise if one includes offenders who transgressed repeatedly, but were only prosecuted once.[455] In New Haven before 1740, however, a significant number of those prosecuted for fornication were from the propertied classes.[456] The non-repeaters were significantly younger than the repeat offenders and far were more likely to be involved in paternity proceedings rather than criminal prosecutions.[457] This pattern suggests that criminal prosecution were brought not just for having made a mistake that could have been concealed, but rather the flaunting of one's sexuality in a society that generally repressed overt sexuality.[458] Such flaunting served not only to single them out for prosecution, but also to propel the defendants further to the edges of society.[459]

Sexual repression in New England seems to have been remarkably effective, shown by the relatively low rates of birth for illegitimate children and for children born less than nine months after marriage. Making a precise estimate of patterns of illegitimacy and pregnancy at marriage at any time before 1900 is, of course, problematic, given the serious gaps and limitations in the available data.[460] Historian Judith Leavitt summarized the problem in these words:

> [W]e simply do not know how often women in the past found themselves pregnant or even how frequently women labored to give birth. It is only in the twentieth century that the recording of births (live and still) began to be noted reliably by local and state health departments, and even today we cannot calculate precisely the risks women face each time they become pregnant. Because we cannot be sure about the number of labors or pregnancies, our statistical conclusions have limited meaning.[461]

While the evidence is undoubtedly incomplete, gross changes in such patterns do emerge rather clearly from historical research and, despite concerns such as Levitt expressed, we can have considerable confidence in the general pattern of changes in illegitimacy and bridal pregnancies, even if we cannot be certain of details of such estimates.[462] For example, John Demos, in a study of one community in Rhode Island, found no births within eight months of marriage before 1720, a rate of 10 percent between 1720 and 1740, and a rate between 45 and 50 percent between 1740 and 1780.[463] In New Haven Colony and later New Haven County of Connecticut, rarely was there more than one illegitimate child born in any given year from its founding in 1638 down to 1690.[464] The rate at which brides went to the altar pregnant throughout New England apparently rose from under 10 percent at the beginning of the eighteenth century to as high

---

Hist. 85; Ellen Fitzpatrick, *Childbirth and an Unwed Mother in Seventeenth-Century New England*, 8 Signs 744 (1983); Carolyn Ramsey, *Sex and Social Order: The Selective Enforcement of Colonial American Adultery Laws in the English Context*, 10 Yale J.L. & Humanities 191, 207–09, 219–27 (1998) (book rev.).

454. Dayton, *supra* note 62, at 161, 169, 171 n.26, 175, 179, 181, 197, 201–03, 207, 209–10, 225 n.134.

455. *Id.* at 210 n.108.

456. *Id.* at 201–03.

457. *Id.* at 220–21.

458. *Id.* at 197 (reporting that after prosecutions of men for fornication had become rare, three men were prosecution in New Haven County, two after impregnating one woman and then marrying another, and one for apparent rape).

459. *Id.* at 161.

460. *See* Daniel Scott Smith, *The Long Cycle in American Illegitimacy and Prenuptial Pregnancy*, in Bastardy and Its Comparative History, *supra* note 367, at 364.

461. Judith Walzer Leavitt, Brought to Bed: Childbearing in America 1750–1950, at 24 (1986).

462. Ulrich, *supra* note 326, at 152, 156; Smith & Hindus, *supra* note 452, at 553–57.

463. John Demos, *Families in Colonial Bristol, Rhode Island: An Exercise in Historical Demography*, 25 Wm. & Mary Q. 40, 56 table 10 (3rd ser. 1968).

464. Dayton, *supra* note 62, at 174–75, 184, 188; R.W. Roetger, *The Transformation of Sexuality Morality in "Puritan" New England: Evidence from New Haven Court Records, 1639–1698*, 15 Can. Rev. Am. Stud. 243, 254 (1984).

as 33 percent early in the nineteenth century, only to fall to under 10 percent by the end of the nineteenth century.[465] The rates illegitimate births also fell sharply during the nineteenth century and early years of the twentieth century.[466]

Repression of extramarital sexuality in New England or in other colonies did not have a depressing effect on the overall colonial birthrate. Fertility rates in the American colonies were "markedly higher than that ever recorded for any European country."[467] Foreign travelers commented on the amazing fecundity of Americans. An historian summarized such comments thusly:

> Children swarmed everywhere: "like ants" or "like broods of ducks in a pond." In the size of families, it was observed, even "Irishmen are nothing to the Yankeys (sic) and Buckskins in that Way," although it was a thought that the Yankees custom of bundling gave them an advantage over the less resourceful Irish. Even the beauties of Virginia were found to be "great Breeders." ... [468]

The extraordinarily high birth rates in the English colonies in North America strongly influenced Thomas Malthus in his development of a theory of population growth.[469] Only around the time of American Revolution did American fertility rates begin the steady but slow decline that persisted without significant interruption until the post-World War II baby boom.[470]

Even with falling rates of birth, illegitimacy, and pregnant brides, there is rather less evidence of infanticide than one might guess. When we do discover the occasional lament over excessive childbearing, say in a note between spouses or a letter between women friends or a secret notation in a diary, the subject is treated as one of resigned inevitability rather than something that one could control.[471] Yet given the lack of effective contraceptives and means of accomplishing an abortion, one should not be surprised that the incidence of infanticide seems to have risen in the newly independent United States just as these other indicators of social disarray were falling. Infanticide became prominent in the United States throughout the nineteenth century.[472]

As valuable and as valued as were children to the English colonists in America, there still must have been children whom one or both parents did not want and sought to eliminate. Just as in Europe and Asia, the desire to prevent or eliminate an unwanted child usually resulted in infanticide rather than contraception or abortion, although sexual abstinence played a prominent role in contraception.[473] While the English and other "old world" legal records have not been exhaustively researched, the colonial legal records have been even less thoroughly developed, leaving even greater gaps in our knowledge about law in the colonies generally as well as regarding particular questions. Notwithstanding such limitations on our knowledge, such colonial court

---

465. Demos, *supra* note 463, at 43, 178–84; Deborah Rhode, *Adolescent Pregnancy and Public Policy,* 108 POL. SCI. Q. 635, 636–38 (1994).

466. D'EMILIO & FREEDMAN, *supra* note 9, at 76; WELLS, UNCLE SAM'S FAMILY, *supra* note 134, at 28–56.

467. COALE & ZELNICK, *supra* note 138, at 34–35. *See also* DEGLER, *supra* note 9, at 178–80; Klepp, *supra* note 56, at 96–98; Smith, *supra* note 134.

468. JOHN MILLER, ORIGINS OF THE AMERICAN REVOLUTION 433 (1943).

469. DEGLER, *supra* note 9, at 188.

470. See the text *supra* at notes 134–42.

471. BRODIE, *supra* note 9, at 41; NORTON, *supra* note 127, at 74–75; ULRICH, *supra* note 125, at 195.

472. THOMAS NICHOLS, HUMAN PHYSIOLOGY: THE BASIS FOR SANITARY AND SOCIAL SCIENCE 21–27 (1872). *See also* GORDON, *supra* note 3, at 51.

473. *See, e.g.,* Sharon Ann Burnston, *Babies in the Well: An Underground Insight into Deviant Behavior in Eighteenth-Century Philadelphia,* 106 PA. MAG. HIST. & BIOGRAPHY, No. 2, at 151 (April 1982). *See also* OLASKY, *supra* note 326, at 19–21; ULRICH, *supra* note 125, at 184–85, 195–201.

records as have been searched demonstrate that the colonies did take steps prohibit the murder of children unwanted by their parents.

As in England, more colonial legal activity was directed against infanticide than against abortion; infanticide, it turns out, was frequent enough to raise some question about whether the practice really was any rarer, relative to population şize, in the colonies than in England.[474] The most prominent of the historians to argue that infanticide was common in the colonies, Peter Hoffer, has proven, however, remarkably capable of indulging in contradictory propositions simultaneously. He has, for example, claimed that the English colonization of North America was driven by merchant capitalists who were both intent on casting off the past and also intent on securing conditions of settlement that were already antiquated in England.[475]

In one extreme example, three infanticides were reported in a single issue of a Maryland newspaper in 1761.[476] On the other hand, there appear to have been only 11 prosecutions for infanticide in colonial Maryland during the entire seventeenth century.[477] There appear to have been only three prosecutions for infanticide Connecticut before 1710.[478] There seems to have been an upsurge in infanticide prosecutions in Connecticut after 1740 — 19 of the twenty-five infanticide prosecutions in Connecticut before 1790 were brought after 1740.[479] Six were brought in the 1750s alone.[480] This does not seem to have been only a local pattern. Another study found 34 women indicted for infanticide in Pennsylvania between 1763 and 1790, with seven convictions, and five death sentences.[481] During this same period, only 48 women were indicted for murder in Pennsylvania — and that includes the 34 indicted for infanticide.[482] The number of infanticide prosecutions in Massachusetts, however, declined during this period.[483]

The Massachusetts records are particularly interesting as they reflect a society with little privacy, strong religious constraints, and a general pattern of conformity to the law. One study found 35 suspected infanticides in Massachusetts between 1620 and 1700.[484] These are clumped in the latter half of the seventeenth century, mirroring the small but notable rise in bastardy and fornication proceedings during the same period.[485] Only 11 people were executed in Massachusetts between 1630 and 1692 for any crime, yet three of the four women included in this group

---

474. *See generally* Hoffer & Hull, *supra* note 8, at 33–113; Dayton, *supra* note 62, at 210–13. For specific examples, see D'Emilio & Freedman, *supra* note 9, at 34; Semmes, *supra* note 444, at 195; Ulrich, *supra* note 125, at 196–201.

475. *Compare* Hoffer, *supra* note 448, at 11, *with* Liam Séamus O'Melinn, Note, *The American Revolution and Constitutionalism in the Seventeenth Century West Indies,* 95 Colum. L. Rev. 104, 121 n.90 (1995).

476. Julia Cherry Spruill, Women's Life and Work in the Southern Colonies 323–25 (1938).

477. Norton, *supra* note 326, at 135 (table 1).

478. Dayton, *supra* note 62, at 167 n.17.

479. *Id.* at 210.

480. *Id.*

481. G.S. Rowe, *Infanticide, Its Judicial Resolution, and Criminal Code Revision in Early Pennsylvania,* 135 Am. Phil. Soc'y 200 (1991); G.S. Rowe, *Women's Crime and Criminal Administration in Pennsylvania, 1763–1790,* 109 Pa. Magazine Hist. & Biog. 356, 359–60 (1985) ("Rowe, *Women's Crime*").

482. Rowe, *Women's Crime, supra* note 481, at 359.

483. Hoffer & Hull, *supra* note 8, at 115.

484. Lyle Koehler, A Search for Power: The "Weaker Sex" in Seventeenth-Century New England 200–01 (1980). *See also* D'Emilio & Freedman, *supra* note 9, at 34; Hoffer & Hull, *supra* note 8, at 45–48, 53, 58, 63.

485. Thompson, *supra* note 443, at 193–94.

were executed for infanticide.[486] At least 15 women were hung in Massachusetts for infanticide between 1693 and 1769.[487] Even the Salem Witchcraft Trials have been linked to infanticide.[488]

There are, of course, other credible explanations for the prosecution or persecution of witches, both in Salem[489] and across Europe.[490] As the possible link to witchcraft suggests, however, most women who were convicted of infanticide were people who lived on the margins of society: servants, slaves, or outcasts.[491] Colonial society tended to view the crime as signaling "a rejection of the entire social and human order."[492] Given the communal ritual that birthing was at the time, the failure to call a midwife was as clear a rejection of the community as was the killing of the child itself.[493] People at the time also caught a whiff of the odor of suicide in the very thought of killing the fruit of one's own body.[494]

Changing rates of pregnancy, miscarriage, and illegitimacy provide a means for estimating indirectly the probable rate of infanticide, given the lack of adequate alternatives for preventing or "terminating" unwanted pregnancies. We have already seen that rates for illegitimacy and pregnant brides were low in the seventeenth and early eighteenth centuries, and then rose steadily,

---

486. Edwin Powers, Crime and Punishment in Early Massachusetts, 1630–1692, at 287–90 (1966); Ulrich, *supra* note 125, at 195.

487. D.H. Fischer, Albion's Seed: Four British Folkways in America 194 n.18 (1989). *See also* Donna Spindel, Crime and Society in North Carolina: 1663–1776, at 49, 88–89, 108 (1989).

488. Hoffer & Hull, *supra* note 8, at 55–56.

489. Just in this century, our image of the Salem Witchcraft Trials has moved from a vision of Freudian hysteria to class struggle to the suppression of feminine independence. *See, e.g.,* Paul Boyer & Stephen Nissenbaum, Salem Possessed (1974); John Demos, Entertaining Satan: Witchcraft and the Culture of Early New England (1982); Carol Karlsen, The Devil in the Shape of a Woman: Women and Witchcraft in Colonial New England (1987).

490. *See* 1 Anderson & Zinsser, *supra* note 13, at 161–73; Julio Caro-Baroja, The World of the Witches (O.N.U. Glendenning trans. 1964); Norman Cohn, Europe's Inner Demons: An Inquiry Inspired by the Great Witch-Hunt (1975); Arthur Evans, Witchcraft and the Gay Counterculture (1978); Jeanne Favret-Saada, Deadly Words: Witchcraft in the Bocage (Catherine Cullen trans. 1980); T.R. Forbes, The Midwife and the Witch; Carlo Ginzberg, The Night Battles: Witchcraft and Agrarian Cults in the Sixteenth and Seventeenth Centuries (1983); Gordon, *supra* note 3, at 31–32; Gustav Henningson, The Witches' Advocate: Basque Witchcraft and the Spanish Inquisition (1980); Richard Kieckhefer, European Witch Trials: Their Foundations in Popular and Learned Culture, 1300–1500 (1976); G.L. Kittredge, Witchcraft in Old and New England (1929); Joseph Klaits, Servants of Satan (1985); Christine Larner, Enemies of God: The Witchhunt in Scotland (1981); Brian Levick, The Witch-Hunt in Early Modern Europe (1987); H.C. Erik Midelfort, Witch Hunting in Southwestern Germany 1562–1684: The Social and Intellectual Foundations (1972); E. William Monter, Witchcraft in France and Switzerland: The Borderlands during the Reformation (1976); Margaret Murray, The God of the Witches (1931); The Politics of Gender in Early Modern Europe 13–89 (Jean Brink, Allison Coudert, & Maryanne Horowitz eds. 1989); G.R. Quaife, Godly Zeal and Furious Rage: The Witch in Early Modern Europe (1987); J.B. Russell, Witchcraft in the Middle Ages (1972); Thomas, *supra* note 327; H.R. Trevor-Roper, The European Witch-Craze of the Sixteenth and Seventeenth Centuries, and Other Essays (1969); Vern Bullough, *Heresy, Witchcraft and Sexuality,* in Sexual Practices and the Medieval Church 206, 211–17 (Vern Bullough & James Brundage eds. 1982); Mary Nelson, *Why Witches Were Women,* in Women: A Feminist Perspective 346 (Jo Freeman ed. 1975); Ruthann Robson, *Lesbianism in Anglo-European Legal History,* 5 Wis. Women's L.J. 1, 31–36 (1990).

491. *See, e.g.,* Ulrich, *supra* note 125, at 196. *See also* Dayton, *supra* note 62, at 211–13; Stone, *supra* note 241, at 473–75; Thompson, *supra* note 443, at 166–67. See also the references collected *supra* at notes 450–59.

492. Ulrich, *supra* note 125, at 196.

493. *Id.* at 196–97.

494. *Id.* at 196.

only to fall again in the later years of the nineteenth century, although illegitimacy rates always remained very low by contemporary standards.[495] Parallel with the rise in illegitimacy was the general disappearance first of prosecutions of men and later of prosecutions of women for fornication.[496] Which was cause and which was effect is not clear, and in fact these changes were probably reciprocal or perhaps joint manifestations of deeper social changes.[497] Given the rising rates of illegitimacy, one can hardly credit the suggestion of historian Laurel Thatcher Ulrich that the disappearance of fornication cases from the courts was because prosecution was unnecessary given the strong social constraints available for regulating sexual conduct.[498] The changing attitudes towards fornication, whatever the causes, did not signal any greater willingness to countenance either infanticide or abortion. Apart from religious or moral constraints, there were practical reasons for attempts at strong community control over sexual behavior.

As in England, poor laws cast upon the community in which a poor or destitute person was legally settled the burden of supporting that person, although enforcement of these laws varied considerably in space and time.[499] Often a destitute family consisted of an unmarried woman with a child, with similar results as in England, namely social control of individual behavior that could result in such a social burden. Historian Mary Beth Norton has suggested that bastardy rates in the colonies are underestimated because no one bothered with prosecutions if the putative father was someone without financial means who could protect a community from this burden.[500] The resulting close attention to pregnancies that could become a burden on the community created a likelihood that infanticides of bastard would be discovered, and an incentive beyond social opprobrium for unmarried pregnant women to conceal both the pregnancy and the birth.

Given the pressures and punishments that faced women giving birth to illegitimate children, one is not surprised to discover that such children were more likely to be killed than were legitimate children. Only two percent of the children born in colonial Massachusetts were bastards, yet 90 percent of the infanticide prosecutions involved the murder of bastard children.[501] Historians have discovered 51 convictions for infanticide in Massachusetts, fifteen more in Connecticut, and scattered cases from other colonies.[502] Even folk ballads lamented the practice of infanticide.[503]

Responding to the difficulty of proving the cause of death, ten colonies or states enacted statutes to punish as murder either the concealment of the birth of a bastard or of its death before the state in question adopted an abortion statute, beginning with Massachusetts in 1696.[504]

---

495. See the text *supra* at notes 460–66.

496. WILLIAM NELSON, THE AMERICANIZATION OF THE COMMON LAW 110–11 (1975); ULRICH, *supra* note 326, at 147–51.

497. CATHY DAVIDSON, REVOLUTION AND THE WORD: THE RISE OF THE NOVEL IN AMERICA 106–09 (1986); D'EMILIO & FREEDMAN, *supra* note 9, at 42–52; NELSON, *supra* note 494, at 110, 251–53; ULRICH, *supra* note 326, at 148–55; Smith & Hindus, *supra* note 451.

498. ULRICH, *supra* note 326, at 149.

499. Norton, *supra* note 326, at 127, 136–37; Stefan Riesenfeld, *The Formative Era of American Public Assistance Law,* 43 CAL. L. REV. 175, 223–24 (1955). *See also* DAYTON, *supra* note 62, at 205–06; DAVID ROTHMAN, THE DISCOVERY OF ASYLUM: SOCIAL ORDER AND DISORDER IN THE NEW REPUBLIC 20–25, 46–48 (1971); James Ely, jr., *Poor Laws of the Post-Revolutionary South, 1776–1800,* 21 TOL. L. REV. 1, 17–18 (1985). For the English experience, see the authorities collected *supra* at note 375.

500. Norton, *supra* note 326, at 138. *See also* OLASKY, *supra* note 326, at 29–33.

501. HOFFER & HULL, *supra* note 8, at 38–39; OLASKY, *supra* note 326, at 26.

502. HOFFER & HULL, *supra* note 8, at 109; OLASKY, *supra* note 326, at 26–27; SEMMES, *supra* note 444, at 195.

503. OLASKY, *supra* note 326, at 27.

504. *An Act to Prevent the Murder of Bastard Children,* CHARTERS & GEN'L L. OF THE COLONY & PROV. OF MASS. BAY: CAREFULLY COLLECTED FROM THE PUBLIC RECORDS AND ANCIENT PRINTED BOOKS ch. 38, at 293 (Nathan Dane, William Prescott, & Joseph Story eds. 1814). *See also* POWERS, *supra* note 486, at 307; ULRICH, *supra* note 125, at 196. *See also* GA. PENAL CODE §§ 22–24 (1816), reprinted in Quay, *supra* note 243, at 460;

The need for such statutes in the colonies is attested by a report of a criminal investigation undertaken by Captain John Smith of Virginia, who was unable to prosecute Dorcas Howard, an "unmarried servant," whose dead bastard son was found concealed shortly after his birth in the earliest years of the first English colony. Without proof of the cause of death and without a concealment statute, nothing could be done.[505] When the cause of death was apparent, the colonials did not hesitate to punish infanticide as murder. Thus Mary Martin was executed in 1648 in Massachusetts for infanticide when her bastard child was found in her hope chest with a fractured skull.[506]

Several extant records of prosecutions of women for concealment even before a colonial concealment statute had been adopted show that the English concealment statute was received in the colonies as part of the common law.[507] We have only one report thus far, however, in which the evidence and the application of the English statute are set out at length. That case, *Rex v. Monro*, arose in the Quaker colonies.[508] The full record of the case is:

> Upon the Tryall of Jannett Monro, Grand Jury returned and Impanelled [names of jurors omitted]. Attested.
>
> Jury of Life and death. [Names of jurors omitted.] The Charge given. The presentment upon the Coroner's Inquest, given to the Grand Jury with the returne of the same Inquest also: The Grand Jury returne and ring in the Bill. *Billa Vera*.
>
> The Sheriffe required to bring the Prisoner to the Barre. The Prisoner Arraigned. And upon her Arraignment pleads not Guilty: And referrs her selfe to God and the Countrey. The Jury of life and death called being above named: And the Prisoner required as they are called to make her Challenges or Exceptions against any of them, if shee please. Shee saith they are strangers to her, but she freely accepts them whereupon they are Attested.
>
> The Kings Evidences against the Prisoner called for.
>
> Dugglas Ireton (the wife of Obadiah Ireton) Attested, Deposeth, that a Child was found in a Tubb of water by an Indian near John Bainbridge house: And that shee being

---

1801 KY. ACTS ch. 67, §2, at 117, reprinted in Quay, *supra*, at 475; 1817 LA. ACTS §3, at 182, reprinted in Quay, *supra*, at 477; MICH. CODE §9 (1815), reprinted in Quay, *supra*, at 482, reenacted, 1820 MICH. (TERR.) LAWS §8, reprinted in Quay, *supra*, at 483; 1 N.H. ORIGINAL ACTS 96 (enacted 1714) & 1716 N.H. LAWS at 42, reprinted in Quay, *supra*, at 494–95; N.H. COMPILED LAWS at 269 (1797), reprinted in Quay, *supra*, at 495; PA. STAT., 1712–1723, at 202 (enacted 1718); 3 VA. STAT. 516–17 (William Waller Hening ed. 1823; enacted 1710), quoted in OLASKY, *supra* note 326, at 86–87; 1839 WIS. (TERR.) STATUTES §6, at 365 (1839), reprinted in Quay, *supra*, at 519. *See also* Spruill, *supra* note 476, at 324 (quoting from a request for a pardon on behalf of a woman convicted of concealment under the Virginia statute). For a statute classifying infanticide as murder without any presumption from concealment, see 1797 DEL. LAWS ch. 22, §6, at 67 (enacted 1719), reprinted in Quay, *supra*, at 456.

505. *See* OLASKY, *supra* note 328, at 20.

506. 2 JOHN WINTHROP, HISTORY OF NEW ENGLAND 1630–1649, at 317–318 (James Kendall Hosmer ed. 1908). *See also* THOMPSON, *supra* note 443, at 23, 26, 57–58 (reporting four such cases between 1649 and 1699, but no convictions).

507. GORDON, *supra* note 3, at 50; ULRICH, *supra* note 125, at 198–201; Klepp, *supra* note 56, at 74–76. New York and New Jersey were originally under Roman-Dutch Law, but that gave way to the common law when the English took over the Dutch colony. *See generally* DENNIS SULLIVAN, THE PUNISHMENT OF CRIME IN COLONIAL NEW YORK: THE DUTCH EXPERIENCE IN ALBANY DURING THE SEVENTEENTH CENTURY (1997).

508. For general studies of law in the Quaker colonies (Delaware, Pennsylvania, and West Jersey), see WILLIAM OFFUTT, JR., OF "GOOD LAWS" AND "GOOD MEN": LAW AND SOCIETY IN THE DELAWARE VALLEY, 1680–1710 (1995); Alfred Brophy, *"For the Preservation of the King's Peace and Justice": Community and English Law in Sussex County, Pennsylvania, 1682–1696*, 40 AM. J. LEGAL HIST. 167 (1996). *See also* HOFFER, *supra* note 448, at 33–35.

informed thereof came and found it there: And further Deposeth that the Child had a kind of blackish spott on its neck: and further saith not.

Sarah Bainbridge (the Prisoners Mistress) Attested; Desposes that shee was never sure that said Jannett (the Prisoner) was with Child, but onely had supition thereof: And therefore shee asked her the question, And shee said Jannett Denyed shee was with Child, but said shee was dropsicall; And further that shee (this Deponent) knowes nothing of the Child ever being alive; further saith not.

John Bainbridge (the Prisoners Master) Attested; Deposeth that hee Saw the Child, and that hee saw it at first in the Well, And that hee looked on the Child and the Child bended a litle in the neck. And that there appeared a little blewish Circle on the Child's neck; But that hee did not apprehend it to be any thing of the Cause of the Childs death; And that hee put the Child in the ground and acquainted the Constable forthwith further saith not.

John Joyner (One of the Jury) saith hee tooke the Child up after it was by John Bainbridge Covered, And that hee washed the Child, And there was a black spott upon the neck of the Child, But that hee could not perceive anything of a wound or that it was the Cause of its death. And further saith not.

Daniel Wills (Coroner and Chyrurgeion) Attested, Deposeth that hee saw the Child after it was taken out of the Earth and washed. And that it had a small blackish Ring upon its neck; But that hee thinks it might be onely a Setleing of blood and further saith not.

Francis Davenport Attested, desposeth that hee being one of the Coroners Jury, Saw the Child, And that hee and others of the Jury saw a black spott or Ring on the Childs neck; And it was the opinion of him and others that the same spott or ring was a Signe of violence done to the Child.

John Bainbridge further said that hee did not know the Prisoner to be with Child, but did Suspect it, And therefore that hee gave his wife Charge to be carefull of said Prisoner.

Proclamation made for all the rest of the Kings Evidence to drawn neare and give their Evidence for the King. Kings Attorney Generall Pleads that the Prisoner by vertue of an Act of Parliament is Guilty unlesse shee can make it appeare the Child was dead borne: To this the Judge and other of the Justices say that Law was made Ad Terrorem.

Prisoner Pleads the Child was still borne in the night in bed, but that shee can give no Evidence thereof, there being none with her.

The Governour gives the Charge to the Jury, that if they finde what has been Evidenced is proofe Sufficient of the Prisoner's murdering of killing the Child, they are to find her Guilty, otherwise not guilty.

Adjourned untill five at night: Court opened, Jury appear and called over, the Prisoner set to the Barre. The Jury by Richard Stockton (their Foreman) say they are agreed of their Verdict: And that they find Jannett Monro (the Prisoner) not Guilty, and so they say all.

The prisoner is ordered to be passed over for such tyme to some person or persons for soe long time as may discharge the Charges of the Court which is 3£. 16s. 00d. And Satisfye her Master John Bainbridge for remainder of her time.

And Shee is cleared by proclamation.

Court dissolved.[509]

This case contains considerable information regarding the law and social attitudes regarding infanticide. The matter was thought to be serious enough that the Governor himself presided at the trial. When the Attorney General invoked the Act of Parliament (the concealment statute), all the justices of the court concurred in its applicability, yet the Governor charged to jury to determined whether the evidence proved Jannett Monro guilty of murdering the child, a child she admitted bearing and which bore evidence of a violent death. The jury then found her not guilty, although only after some hours of deliberation. What can we make of all this?

It seems clear that the English concealment statute was part of the law of the colony even without local reenactment. The only ambiguity might arise from the Governor's charge to the jury to consider the evidence, but there is no hint that he contradicted the statements of the Attorney General and all the Justices that the statute applied. Indeed, what had "been evidenced" included the acts of concealment. Still, the jury declined to convict despite what seems to have been a strong case even without taking the concealment statute into account.

Colonial and early American juries were accorded the right to determine the law independently of the instructions of the court.[510] After all, at this time colonial judges (including governors) often lacked formal legal education. Yet there is no hint here that the jury took a different view of the law than the Attorney-General. In particular, there is no record of an argument about the law to the jury, a characteristic feature of cases in which there was a serious question about the law. There is simply nothing, except perhaps modern speculations, to raise any question about the application of the concealment statute in colonial New Jersey without local enactment.

A similar case arose in Anglican East Jersey at about the same time, with the same outcome—acquittal with the defendant charged costs to assure her good behavior.[511] Such outcomes in prosecutions under the concealment statute became quite common in England as well at about the same time.[512] The Puritans of New England, who had put at least one woman to death for infanticide early in their history, might have explained these outcomes as evidence of the Quaker's moral laxity. Puritans, after all, claimed that Quaker men shared their women as if they were common property.[513] In Catholic Maryland, a woman was executed in the seventeenth century on the basis of the concealment law while it had not yet been reenacted in that colony.[514] Some years later an accused woman was acquitted, based on a petition by several midwives suggesting that although the defendant had concealed the birth of her child they doubted

---

509. Rex v. Monro (1694), in *The Burlington Court Book: A Record of Quaker Jurisprudence in West New Jersey 1680–1709*, 5 Am. Legal Rec. 166–67 (H. Clay Reed & George Miller eds. 1944).

510. *See generally* Bruce Mann, Neighbors and Strangers: Law and Community in Early Connecticut 69–81 (1987); Shannon Stimson, The American Revolution in Law: Anglo-American Jurisprudence before John Marshall (1990); David Millon, *Juries, Judges, and Democracy*, 16 Law & Soc. Inquiry 135 (1993). Acceptance of the power of juries to decide the law for themselves persisted for some time after the formation of the United States. *See, e.g.,* State v. Jones, 5 Ala. 666 (1843); Bartholomew v. Clark, 1 Conn. 472 (1816); Townsend v. State, 2 Blackf. 150 (Ind. 1828); Bostock v. Gasquet, 10 La. 80 (1836); People v. Croswell, 3 Johns Cas. 137 (N.Y. 1804); McGowan v. State, 9 Yerger 184 (Tenn. 1836); State v. Wilkinson, 2 Vt. 480 (1829). Two state constitutions still provide for juries to decide the law as well as the facts in criminal cases. Ind. Const. art. 1, § 19; Md. Const., Declaration of Rights, art. 23.

511. Rex v. Wainwright (1696), 1 Journal of the Court of Common Right and Chancery of East Jersey, 1683–1702, at 297–99 (Preston Edsall ed. 1937).

512. Sharpe, *supra* note 317, at 135–36.

513. H.S. Nourse, Early Records of Lancaster 17–19 (1884); Thompson, *supra* note 443, at 105–06.

514. Norton, *supra* note 326, at 144–45. *See also* Spruill, *supra* note 476, at 324–25 (reporting a petition for a pardon on behalf of a Maryland woman convicted under the concealment law). Apparently a woman was also executed in Virginia under that colony's concealment statute. Spruill, *supra*, at 325 n.44.

that she had killed it.[515] In Virginia, in a case in which its concealment statute was applied, the governor issued a reprieve from execution to Jane Ham, and she later received a pardon from London.[516]

Yet another prosecution from the Quaker colonies again demonstrates the reception of the concealment statute of James I as part of the common law of the colonies although the facts are unclear whether the actual crime involved infanticide or abortion. That case comes from Delaware when it too was subject to the Penn proprietorship and some 20 years before enactment of Delaware's earliest infanticide statute.[517] The record of *Rex v. Holland* tells the story:

> Grand Jury present Elisabeth Holland alias Oneale for haveing a bastard Child and murtheringe the same, to the great Terror of his Majesties liege people, John Foster, foreman. Whereupon the said Elizabeth Holland is brought to barr and being (Upon her oath) Examined denyes that Ever she had any Child, and says that she has lived all-most two years in this County, and Came hither from New Castle where she Lived a long time. William Nickolls being sworne saith that Anna Letort at Seuerall times, and particularly in the last week in Captain Dubrois Corne field told him that Elizabeth Holland had had two Children and had murdered them and that she Could prove the same. Whereupon it is ordered that the said Anna Letort be forthwith sent for, which being accordingly done by a Constable and she brought to the barr Upon her Examination saith that of her Owne knowledge she never Knew anything thereof, but only that one Mr. Reverdee told her that the said Elizabeth Holland, had miscarried two or three times. The Court having Considered the same doe order the said Anna Letort to pay all Cost and Charges that have Accrued both by means of the presentment against the said Elizabeth Holland as alsoe another presentment against John Dubrois, which by her means, and the said Anna Letort to remaine in the Sherifs Custody till the same be paid, alsoe the said Elizabeth Holland is discharged.
>
> John Dubrois, merchant, being presented by the grand Jury for feloniouslie takinge and bearinge away one Silver spoone from John Test of the County of Philadelpia Cord-wainer. Is upon the Examination of Anna Letort discharged.[518]

This brief record leaves one to speculate what, if anything, really was going on between Anna Letort, Elizabeth Holland, and John Dubrois. We cannot even be certain whether the John Dubrois of the silver spoon was the Captain Dubrois of the "Corne field," although that seems likely. Regardless of such speculations, however, it remains clear that the grand jury and the magistrate considered the charges serious and did not quibble about the applicability of the law of infanticide and abortion. That concealment was accepted as proof of murder is suggested by the utter unconcern about the ability to produce a corpse of the supposedly murdered infants. Nor does the magistrate intervene to suggest that there could not possibly have been a crime when the talk turns from murdering infants to "miscarriages"—a possible reference to late abortions, which might be what actually had happened in some concealment cases with the two crimes simply shading into each other. The case collapsed not because the relevant English laws did not apply, but because the evidence was hearsay piled on hearsay—as was confirmed by the dismissal of the theft charges against John Dubrois.

---

515. *Id.* at 147.

516. OLASKY, *supra* note 326, at 87–88.

517. 1797 DEL. LAWS ch. 22, §6, at 67 (enacted 1719), reprinted in Quay, *supra* note 243, at 456 (this statute classified infanticide as murder but did not include the concealment provisions).

518. Rex v. Holland (1698), in *Court Records of Kent County, Delaware 1680–1705*, 8 AM. LEGAL REC. 121 (Leon de Valinger, jr. ed. 1959).

At least 57 women in Pennsylvania were prosecuted between 1682 and 1800, of whom 24 were convicted, with eight executed.[519] Prosecutions under concealment statutes became more common throughout the colonies during and after the American Revolution,[520] again suggesting that infanticide (or late term abortions) were becoming more common at that time. At least eight women in Pennsylvania were convicted of concealment between 1779 and 1792, of whom three were hanged.[521] As in the *Monro* case,[522] judges and juries (all men) often were lenient in these cases, but they did not completely abandon this law as the executions (and other punishments) in Pennsylvania attest.[523] Pennsylvania's legislature enacted a concealment statute in 1786, and revised it in 1790 and 1794.[524] After all of this tinkering, the legislature left the death penalty for infanticide, but not for concealment without proof that the mother had killed the child. For concealment alone, the prescribed penalty was five years in prison.[525]

That colonial and state legislatures and other officials thought of concealment statutes (whether modified as in Pennsylvania or not) and abortion statutes in similar terms was further demonstrated by the 12 states that enacted a concealment statute as part of, or contemporaneously with, the state's first abortion statute.[526] Another three states incorporated concealment statutes into their abortion statutes, but sometime after their first abortion statute was adopted.[527] Altogether, 20 of the 22 of the states that had a concealment statute at one point or another codified the statutes together with their abortion statutes. Only Louisiana and Wisconsin never consolidated their infanticide, concealment, and abortion statutes. Both states had prohibited concealment of infanticide long before they adopted their first abortion statute. After this flurry of legislative activity in the early nineteenth century, however, concealment prosecutions seem largely to disappear in the later years of the century as abortion became a more realistic alternative.

With that we have come full circle. Before the nineteenth century, abortion was rare, contraceptives were ineffective, and sexual abstinence was the most effective means of preventing births. In such a context, infanticide appears to have been the most common means of disposing

---

519. Klepp, *supra* note 56, at 75 n.9.

520. *See* GORDON, *supra* note 3, at 50–51. *See, e.g.,* Paul Gilje, *Infant Abandonment in Early 19th-Century New York City: Three Cases,* 9 SIGNS 587 (1983).

521. William Bradford, *An Enquiry: How Far the Punishment of Death Is Necessary in Pennsylvania, with Notes and Illustrations* 39–40 (1793).

522. See the text *supra* at notes 508–10.

523. Susan Klepp indicates that the low conviction rates reflected the sympathies of all-male juries for women who presented themselves as helpless victims, with the convictions and executions falling on women who did not express remorse and otherwise acted defiantly. Klepp, *supra* note 56, at 76.

524. *Id.,* at 75–76.

525. 1 ALEANDER JAMES DALLAS, LAWS OF THE COMMONWEALTH OF PENNSYLVANIA . . . , at 135–36 (1797.

526. Combined enactments: 1887 COMPILED LAWS DAK. TERR. §§ 6538–40; 1868 FLA. LAWS ch. 1637, tit. VIII, §§ 9–11; HAWAII PENAL CODE §§ 1–3 (1850), reprinted in Quay, *supra* note 243, at 463; 1863–64 IDAHO (TERR.) LAWS §§ 33, 34, 42, at 435, reprinted in Quay, *supra*, at 464; ILL. REV. CODE §§ 40, 41, 46, at 130–31 (1827), reprinted in Quay, *supra*, at 466; ME. REV. STAT. ch. 160, §§ 11–14 (1840); 1861 NEV. (TERR.) LAWS §§ 34, 42, at 61, 63, reprinted in Quay, *supra*, at 493; OKLA. STAT. §§ 2187–89 (1890); 1860 PA. LAWS, No. 374, §§ 87–89, reprinted in Quay, *supra*, at 507; 1869 WYO. (TERR.) SESS. LAWS ch. 3, §§ 25, 26, at 104, reprinted in Quay, *supra*, at 520. Contemporaneous enactment: MINN. (TERR.) REV. STAT. ch. 100, §§ 10, 11, at 493, & ch. 107, § 7, at 519 (1851), reprinted in Quay, *supra*, at 486–87. Remember that Dakota Territory included two modern states.

527. MO. REV. STAT. art II, §§ 9, 10, 26, 40, at 168 (1855), reprinted in Quay, *supra* note 243, at 490; 1871–72 MONT. LAWS, CRIM. LAWS ch. IV, §§ 41, 42, at 269, reprinted in Quay, *supra*, at 491; 1845 N.Y. LAWS ch. 260, §§ 1–6, reprinted in Quay, *supra*, at 500. This is similar to William Blackstone's approach to treating the two crimes in tandem as two aspects of a single phenomenon. 4 BLACKSTONE, *supra* note 381, at *198–99.

of unwanted children. In any event, infanticide was more common down to the middle of the nineteenth century, only to become a rare practice thereafter. As in England, the modern rarity of infanticide in the United States makes its occurrence shocking—something that demands an explanation in a way that few would expect for abortion.[528]

Coincidentally, newly developed techniques for performing abortions made that procedure increasingly common after millennia during which, however much abortion might have been wanted and attempted, abortions were rare, or at least rarely successful. Beginning after the decision in *Roe v. Wade*, however, infanticide became an increasingly common crime in the United States.[529] Only a few weeks after the Court decided *Roe v. Wade*, Dr. James Watson—co-discover of DNA—went public with a proposal to redefine the point at which a child became human being until three days after birth, precisely in order to allow the parents to decide whether the

---

528. *See* State v. White, 456 P.2d 797 (Idaho 1969); People v. Skeoch, 96 N.E.2d 473 (Ill. 1951); Clark v. State, 588 P.2d 1027 (Nev. 1979). *See also* Martin Daly & Margo Wilson, Homicide 62–63 (1988); Recent Advances in Postpartum Psychiatric Disorders (David Inwood ed. 1985); Barbara Barton, Comment, *When Murdering Hands Rock the Cradle: An Overview of America's Incoherent Treatment of Infanticidal Mothers*, 51 SMU L. Rev. 591 (1998); Beth Bookwalter, Note, *Throwing the Bath Water Our with the Baby: Wrongful Exclusion of Expert Testimony on Neonaticide Syndrome*, 78 B.U. L. Rev. 1185 (1998); Dominique Bourget & John Bradford, *Homicidal Parents*, 35 Can. J. Psych. 233 (1990); Morris Brozovsky & Harvey Falit, *Neonaticide: Clinical and Pscyhodynamic Considerations*, 10 J. Child Psych. 673 (1971); Ann Damante Brusca, Note, *Postpartum Psychosis: A Way out for Murderous Moms?*, 18 Hofstra L. Rev. 1133 (1990); Lori Button, *Postpartum Psychosis: The Birth of a New Defense?*, 6 Cooley L. Rev. 323 (1989); Patricia Crittendon & Susan Craig, *Developmental Trends in the Nature of Child Homicide*, 5 J. Interpersonal Violence 202 (1990); Deborah Denno, *Who Is Andrea Yates? A Short Story about Insanity*, 10 Duke J. Gender L. & Pol'y 1 (2003); Paul Duggan, *Prosecutors in Yates Trial Sit Back in Penalty Phase*, Wash. Post, Mar. 15, 2002, at A4; Fazio & Comito, *supra* note 437; Jennifer Grossman, *Postpartum Psychosis—A Defense to Criminal Responsibility or Just Another Gimmick?*, 67 U. Det. L. Rev.311 (1990); Megan Hogan, Comment, *Neonaticide and the Misuse of the Insanity Defense*, 6 Wm. & Mary J. Women & L. 259 (1999); Barbara Kantorwitz, *Despite Recent Spate of Baby Killings, Cases Still Rare*, N.O. Times-Picayune, July 13, 1997, at A24; Mary Lentz, *A Postmortem of the Postpartum Psychosis Defense*, 18 Capital U. L. Rev. 525 (1989); Geoffrey McKee & Steven Shea, *Maternal Filicide: A Cross-National Comparison*, 54 J. Clinical Psych. 659 (1998); Amy Nelson, Comment, *Postpartum Psychosis: A New Defense?*, 95 Dick. L. Rev. 625 (1991); Michelle Oberman, *Mothers Who Kill: Coming to Terms with Modern American Infanticide*, 34 Am. Crim. L. Rev. 1 (1996); Mary Overpeck et al., *Risk Factors for Infant Homicide in the United States*, 339 New Eng. J. Med. 1211 (1998); G.B. Palermo, *Murderous Parents*, 46 Int'l J. Offender Therapy & Comp. Criminology 123 (2002); S.E. Pitt & E.M. Bale, *Neonaticide, Infanticide, and Filicide: A Review of the Literature*, 23 Am. Academy of Psych. & L. 375 (1995); Laura Reece, *Mothers Who Kill: Postpartum Disorders or Criminal Infanticide?*, 38 UCLA L. Rev. 699 (1991); Phillip Resnick, *Murder of the Newborn: A Psychiatric Review of Neonaticide*, 126 Am. J. Psych. 1414 (1970); Barbara Rosenberg, Comment, *Postpartum Psychosis as a Defense to Infant Murder*, 5 Tuoro L. Rev. 287 (1989); Rachel Simon, *Fear of Shame Carries Far too High a Price in the Grossberg Case*, Phila. Inquirer, July 24, 1998, at A29; Julie Stoiber & Linda Loyd, *One Question Remains in Marie Noe Case: Why? A Controversial Plea Deal May Be the Only Way to Find Out Why She Killed Eight of Her Children*, Phila. Inquirer, July 4, 1999, at E1; Symposium, *From Baby Blues to Mothers Who Kill: Responses to Postpatrum Disorders in the Crimi nal and Civil Law*, 10 Wm. & Mary J. Women & L. 1–68 (2003); Symposium, *Tenth Anniversary Issue: Women and Criminal Defenses*, 10 Duke J. Gender L. & Pol'y 1–172 (2003); Ian Wilkey et al., *Neonaticide, Infanticide and Child Homicide*, 22 Med. Sci. & L. 31 (1982); G. LaVerne Williamson, *Postpartum Depression Syndrome as a Defense to Criminal Behavior*, 8 J. Fam. Violence 151 (1993); R. Willie & K.M. Beier, *Denial of Pregnancy and Infanticide*, 1 Sexologie 75 (1994). *See also* Julio Arboleda-Florenz, *Infanticide: Some Medical-Legal Considerations*, 20 Can. Psych. Ass'n J. 55 (1975); E. Cherland & P.C. Matthews, *Attempted Murder of a Newborn: A Case History*, 34 Can. J. Psych. 337 (1989); Pik-To Cheung, *Maternal Filicide in Hong Kong, 1971–1985*, 26 Med. Sci. & L. 185 (1986); M. Logan, *Mothers Who Murder*, 28 Can. Soc'y Forensic Sci. J. 201 (1995); J.D. Marleau et al., *Homicide d'enfant commis par la mère*, 40 Can. J. Psych. 142 (1995); Divya Singh, *The Recognition of Postpartum Psychosis as a Defence in Crimes of Filicide*, 32 Comp. & Int'l L.J. S. Afr. 317 (1999).

529. Stepp, *supra* note 299.

child should live.[530] The murder of children before their fourth birthday rose from 2.4 percent of all murders in 1979 to 3.3 percent of all murders in 1995.[531] The rate of killing for infants before their first birth rose from 7.2/100,000 to 8.7/100,000 over the period from 1983 to 1991.[532] It continued to rise thereafter, reaching 9.1/100,000 in 2000.[533] In fact, homicide was the only leading cause of childhood death in the United States that increased during this period.[534] The result was increasingly common criminal prosecutions resulting of those crimes.[535]

The resurgence in infanticide was not limited to particular classes or racial or ethnic groups, but appears to have occurred across the board in American society.[536] In fact, a child's riskiest day for being murdered is the day he or she is born. The risk is at least 10 times higher on that day than on any other day of the child's life.[537] Such killings usually occur when a mother gives birth alone, or at least outside of the medical system.[538] At this point, and for the first week of life, the killers are nearly always the mother, although after the first week of life the killer is more

---

530. *Endorsing Infanticide?*, Time, May 28, 1973, at 104.

531. Martha Smithey, *Infant Homicide: Victim/Offender Relationship and Causes of Death*, 13 J. Fam. Violence 285, 285 (1998). *See also* Katherine Christoffel & Kiang Liu, *Homicide Death Rates in Childhood in 23 Developed Countries: U.S. Rate Atypically High*, 7 Child Abuse & Neglect 339 (1983); Phillip McLain et al., *Geographic Patterns of Fatal Abuse or Neglect in Children Younger than 5 Years Old in the United States, 1979–1988*, 148 Arch. Pediatric & Adolescent Med. 82 (1994); Colin Pritchard & Alan Butler, *A Comparative Study of Children and Adult Homicide Rates in the USA and Major Western Countries, 1974–1999: Grounds for Concern?*, 18 J. Fam. Violence 341 (2003); Murray Strauss, *State and Regional Differences in U.S. Infant Homicide Rates in Relation to Sociocultural Characteristics of the States*, 5 Behavioral Sci. & L. 61 (1987).

532. Lawrence Wissow, *Infanticide*, 339 N. Eng. J. Med. 1239 (1998). *See also* U.S. Advisory Board on Child Abuse and Neglect, A Nation's Shame: Fatal Child Abuse and Neglect in the United States, Executive Summary 19 (1995).

533. Stepp, *supra* note 299.

534. Bernard Ewigman & Coleen Kivlahan, *Child Maltreatment Fatalities*, 18 Pediatric Ann. no. 9, at 476, 476 (Aug. 1989). *See also* D.R. Hargrave & D.P. Warner, *A Study of Child Homicide over Two Decades*, 32 Med. Sci. & L. 247 (1992).

535. *See, e.g.*, United States *ex rel.* Jones v. Washington, 836 F. Supp. 502 (N.D. Ill. 1993), *aff'd mem.*, 32 F.3d 570 (7th Cir. 1994); Moffit v. Arkansas, No. CACR 92–444 (Ark. Ct. App. Mar 17, 1993), 1993 Ark. App. LEXIS 171; *In re* Sophia M., 234 Cal. Rptr. 698 (Ct. App. 1987), *rehearing granted*; People v. Ehlert, 781 N.E.2d 500 (Ill. App. Ct. 2002), *appeal allowed*, 787 N.E.2d 176 (Ill. 2003); People v. Doss, 574 N.E.2d 806 (Ill. App. Ct. 1991); State v. Kinsky, 348 N.W.2d 319 (Minn. 1984); Berg v. State, 557 N.W.2d 593 (Minn. Ct. App. 1996); State v. Doyle, 287 N.W.2d 59 (Neb. 1980); People v. Wernick, 674 N.E.2d 322 (N.Y. 1996); People v. Wang, 490 N.Y.S.2d 423 (Sup. Ct. 1985); State v. Hopfer, 679 N.E.2d 321 (Ohio Ct. App.), *appeal dismissed*, 673 N.E.2d 146 (Ohio 1996); Commonwealth v. Reilly, 549 A.2d 503 (Pa. 1988); Commonwealth v. Meder, 611 A.2d 213 (Pa. Super. 1992), *appeal denied*, 622 A.2d 1375 (1993); State v. Collington, 192 S.E.2d 856 (S.C. 1972); Lane v. Commonwealth, 248 S.E.2d 781 (Va. 1978); Corrales v. Commonwealth, No. 2797-01-02 (Va. Ct. App. Nov. 19, 2002), 2002 WL 31553222; Myers v. Commonwealth, No. 1780-92-1 (Va. Ct. App. July 26, 1998), 1998 WL 389748; Vaughn v. Virginia, 376 S.E.2d 801 (Va. Ct. App. 1989); State v. McGuire, 490 S.E.2d 912 (W. Va. 1997); State v. Leggate, 537 N.W.2d 435 (Wis. Ct. App.), 1995 WL 239625, *rev. denied*, 537 N.W.2d 574 (Wis. 1995). *See generally* Ania Wilczynski, Child Homicide 30 (1997); Fazio & Comito, *supra* note 435; Susan Gilbert, *Infant Homicide Found to Be Rising in the U.S.*, N.Y. Times, Oct. 27, 1998, at F10; Mauro Mendlowicz et al., *A Case-Control Study on the Socio-Demographic Characteristics of 53 Neonaticidal Mothers*, 21 Int'l J. Law & Psych. 209 (1998); Edward Saunders, *Neonaticides Following Secret Pregnancies: Seven Case Reports*, 104 Pub. Health Rep. 368 (1989); Barbara Whitaker, *Deaths of Unwanted Babies Bring Plea to Help Parents*, N.Y. Times, Mar. 6, 2000, at A1.

536. Stepp, *supra* note 299.

537. *Id.*

538. *See, e.g.*, Julia Brienza, *When the Bough Breaks: Can Justice Be Served in Neonaticide Cases?*, Trial, Dec. 1997, at 13; Barbara Ehrenreich, *Where Have All the Babies Gone?*, Life, Jan. 1998, at 68; Marie McCullough, *In Newborn Killings, a New Profile*, Phila. Inquirer, Nov. 23, 1997, at A21; Steven Pinker, *Why They Kill Their Newborns*, N.Y. Times Mag., Nov. 2, 1997, at 52.

likely to be male than female.[539] Some of these cases arise in bizarre circumstances, such as in a bathroom during a prom dance, and therefore received wide publicity.[540]

The press coverage of several dramatic instances of infant murder served to suggest a link between the resurgence of infanticide and the increasing public acceptance of abortion.[541] In response to such dramatic stories, legislatures in no less than 32 states have enacted, beginning in 1999, statutes providing a "safe haven" for a parent who turns a child over to a hospital, a medical worker, or a child welfare agency.[542] By these laws, the parent cannot be prosecuted for child abandonment or child neglect, if the parent acts within the time allowed. The time specified in these statutes range from 72 hours after birth in several states up to a full year after birth in North Dakota, effectively reviving the turnbox.[543] Yet the mothers who kill their child on the day of its birth either do not know of these laws or simply ignore them.[544]

Some, at least, see a link between the newfound acceptance of abortion and the sudden spate of mothers killing their infants within 24 hours of birth.[545] We actually do not know, however, whether such cases are actually more common or merely more widely reported.[546] With this question, the point has come to turn to consideration of the history of the law and practice of abortion.

---

539. Stepp, *supra* note 299.

540. *See* Ronald Smothers, *Guilty Plea by Mother, 20, in Prom Death*, N.Y. TIMES, Aug. 21,1998, at B1. *See also* MILLER *et al, supra* note 432.

541. *See, e.g., Full Birth Abortion*, WASH. TIMES, Dec. 1, 1996, at 37. *See also* Stepp, *supra* note 299. *See generally* HRDY, MOTHER NATURE, *supra* note 8, at 288–89; Bookwalter, *supra* note 528; Brienza, *supra* note 536; Brusca, *supra* note 528; James Dvorak, Comment, *Neonaticide: Less than Murder?*, 19 N. ILL. U. L. REV. 173 (1998); Fazio & Comito, *supra* note 435; Kantrowitz, *supra* note 528; Lentz, *supra* note 528; Mendlowicz *et al., supra* note 529; Nelson, *supra* note 528; Oberman, *supra* note 528; Rosenberg, *supra* note 528; Williamson, *supra* note 528.

542. Margaret Graham Tebo, *Texas Idea Takes off: States Look to Safe Haven Laws as a Protection for Abandoned Infants*, ABA J., Sept. 2001, at 30. *See also* Patrick Murphy, *Helping Parents Choose Wrong*, N.Y. TIMES, June 26, 2000, at A17.

543. See the text *supra* at notes 270–78.

544. Stepp, *supra* note 299.

545. *See* Bookwalter, *supra* note 528, at 1187; Kantrowitz, *supra* note 528.

546. *See* Stepp, *supra* note 299.

# Chapter 3

# Imagine There's No Heaven[1]

*Put me in remembrance, let us argue together...*

—Isaiah[2]

Until 1968, the history of abortion in English and American law was considered unproblematic. Sir James Fitzjames Stephen, the great historian of the English criminal law, wrote in 1883 that he could "pass over many sections punishing particular acts of violence to the person, and in particular the whole series of offenses relating to the abduction of women, rape, and other such crimes. Their history possesses no special interest and does not illustrate either our political or our social history."[3] At the time, Stephen was embroiled in a harsh debate with John Stuart Mill in which Stephen supported the propriety of the legal enforcement morality.[4] Under the circumstances, one would have expected Stephen to explore a topic like abortion if he had found any reason to question its historic status as a crime. Stephen barely mentioned abortion, however, merely indicating his conclusion that under pre-Norman law (*i.e.,* before 1066), abortion was a crime exclusively within the ecclesiastical jurisdiction.[5]

Such neglect of abortion is characteristic of historical writing until quite recently. We generally find abortion presented merely an adjunct to discussions to what clearly were seen as significant social problems rather than as a topic of importance in its own right.[6] Sir William Holdsworth hardly mentioned abortion in his 23-volume history of English law. Holdsworth was content simply to report the adoption of *Lord Ellenborough's Act,* the first English statutory prohibition of abortion.[7]

We shall explore in chapters 14 and 21 how the history of abortion and abortion law became politicized along with the general topic of abortion. The politicization of the history of abortion law reached its peak when the majority opinion in the landmark abortion decision of *Roe v. Wade* was given over to a history of abortion.[8] The Supreme Court used that history to inform its

---

1. John Lennon, *Imagine* (1972).
2. *Isaiah* 43:26.
3. 3 James Fitzjames Stephen, History of the Criminal Law of England 117–18 (1883).
4. *Compare* John Stuart Mill, On Liberty (1859), *with* James Fitzjames Stephen, Liberty, Equality and Fraternity (1873). The debate is reviewed in Stefan Petrow, *The Legal Enforcement of Morality in Late-Victorian England,* 11 U. Tasmania L. Rev. 60 (1992). On Stephen's life and thought generally, see James Colalaco, James Fitzjames Stephen and the Crisis of Victorian Thought (1983); Leon Radzinowicz, Sir James Fitzjames Stephen and His Contribution to the Development of the Criminal Law (1957); K.J.M. Smith, James Fitzjames Stephen, Portrait of a Victorian Rationalist (1988); Leslie Stephen, The Life of Sir James Fitzjames Stephen (1895); Allen Boyer, *The Antiquarian and the Utilitarian: Charles Dickens vs. James Fitzjames Stephen,* 56 Tenn. L. Rev. 595, 600–05 (1989).
5. 1 Stephen, *supra* note 3, at 54. He also mentions the ecclesiastical jurisdiction over abortion in the fifteenth century. 2 Stephen, *supra* note 3, at 411. One might add his mention that under Roman law abortion was an "extraordinary crime," but not homicide. 1 Stephen, *supra,* at 25.
6. Roger Rosenblatt, Life Itself: Abortion in the American Mind 58 (1992).
7. 11 W.S. Holdsworth, A History of English Law 537 (23 vols., 7th ed. 1956).
8. 410 U.S. 113, 129–52, 156–62 (1973).

view of the values at stake in the controversy.[9] Unfortunately, the Court largely got the history wrong, basing its views upon and contributing to a new orthodoxy on abortion history that forms a set of myths that are coherent with each other but are utterly false to the historical record as it has come down to us.

The new orthodox history of abortion is based upon two simple presumptions: that abortion was common throughout history; and that, despite routine denunciations by most or all members of contemporary ruling elites, abortion was in fact seldom punished.[10] At the time *Roe* was decided, only six cases widely scattered in time were known to have dealt with abortion in England before 1800, and several of those arguably appeared uncertain regarding whether a crime had actually been charged.[11] Indeed, historian Shelley Gavigan, writing as recently as 1984, described the common law sources on abortion "very close to non-existent."[12] Yet the history embraced in *Roe* could not withstand careful examination even when *Roe* was written.[13] Furthermore, research since *Roe* was decided demonstrates that both presumptions (frequency and non-punishment) are false. The question of how frequent abortion (as compared with unsuccessful attempts) really was depends on the techniques available at the time, and there simply were no reliable techniques available that were not tantamount to suicide before 1700.[14] The major alternative to abortion was infanticide, and the law did actively seek out and prosecute persons who committed infanticide.[15] Nor were courts uncertain whether the occasional abortion prosecution that came before them properly charged a crime.

Extensive research has turned up indictments or appeals of felony for abortions dating back more than eight centuries. Abortionists were punished by hanging, imprisonment, and outlawry for the killing of the child, admittedly for abortions without the consent of the mother, but also without any requirement that the child be born alive before dying.[16] In-

---

9. *Id.* at 156–62.

10. For the new orthodoxy, see JAMES MOHR , ABORTION IN AMERICA: THE ORIGINS AND EVOLUTION OF NATIONAL POLICY, 1800–1900 (1978); Cyril Means, jr., *The Law of New York Concerning Abortion and the Status of the Foetus, 1664–1968: A Case of Cessation of Constitutionality,* 14 N.Y.L.F. 411 (1968) ("Means I"); Cyril Means, jr., *The Phoenix of Abortional Freedom: Is a Penumbral Right or Ninth-Amendment Right About to Arise from the Nineteenth-Century Legislative Ashes of a Fourteenth-Century Common-Law Liberty?,* 17 N.Y.L.F. 335 (1971) ("Means II"); Reva Siegel, *Reasoning from the Body: A Historical Perspective on Abortion Regulation and Questions of Equal Protection,* 44 STAN. L. REV. 278 (1992).

11. *See* Means II, *supra* note 10.

12. Shelley Gavigan, *The Criminal Sanction as It Relates to Human Reproduction: The Genesis of the Statutory Prohibition of Abortion,* 5 J. LEGAL HIST. 20, 20 (1984).

13. J. KEOWN, ABORTION, DOCTORS AND THE LAW 3–11 (1988); Robert Byrn, *An American Tragedy: The Supreme Court on Abortion,* 41 FORDHAM L. REV. 807 (1973); Joseph Dellapenna, *The History of Abortion: Technology, Morality, and Law,* 40 U. PITT. L. REV. 359 (1979); Robert Destro, *Abortion and the Constitution: The Need for a Life-Protective Amendment,* 63 CAL. L. REV. 1250 (1975); Eugene Quay, *Justifiable Abortion— Medical and Legal Foundations (Pt. II),* 49 GEO. L.J. 395 (1961); James Witherspoon, *Reexamining* Roe: *Nineteenth-Century Abortion Statutes and the Fourteenth Amendment,* 17 ST. MARY's L.J. 29 (1985).

14. *See* Chapter 1, at notes 184–517.

15. *See* Chapter 2, at notes 240–546.

16. *Hanging:* Rex v. Haule, JUST 1/547A, m.20d (London Eyre 1321), quoted *infra* at notes 110–11; Rex v. Kyltavenan (Cork, Ireland 1311), CALENDAR OF JUSTICIARY ROLES OR PROC. IN THE CT. OF THE JUSTICIAR OF IRELAND I TO VII YEARS OF EDWARD II, at 193 (Dublin Stationary Off., n.d.) ["IRISH JUSTICIARY ROLES"]. *Imprisonment:* Rex v. Code, JUST 1/789, m.1 (Hampshire Eyre 1281), quoted *infra* at note 92. *Outlawry:* Rex v. Ragoun, JUST 1/547A, m.55d (London Eyre 1310); Rex v. Eppinge, JUST 1/547A, m.46 (ms. dated 1321) (London Eyre 1304); Rex v. Hervy, JUST 1/547A, m.40d (1300, ms. dated 1321); Rex v. Hokkestere, JUST 1/547A, m.3 (London Eyre 1298, ms. date 1321); Rex v. Scot, JUST 1/547A, m.22 (1291, ms. dated 1321); Rex v. Dada, JUST 1/547A, m.19d (1290, ms. dated 1321); Rex v. Cliston, JUST 1/1011, m.62 (Wiltshire Eyre 1288); Rex v. Mercer, JUST 1/710, m.45 (Oxford Eyre 1285), quoted *infra* at note 109; Rex v. Brente, JUST 1/186, m.30 (Devon Eyre 1281); Rex v. Scharp, THE LONDON EYRE OF 1276, at 23 (no. 76) (London Rec. Soc'y 1976) ("1276 EYRE"), quoted *infra* at note 108; Juliana's Appeal (1256?), SOMERSET PLEAS (CIV. & CRIM.) FROM THE ROLLS OF THE ITINERANT JUSTICES 321 (no. 1243) (C. Chadwyck-Healey ed. 1897) ("SOMERSET

cluded among these was at least one case that resulted in the imprisonment of two men for the abortion of an unborn child apparently of one month's gestation.[17] By the sixteenth century, abortionists were convicted for unequivocally voluntary abortions.[18] Some evidence suggests that abortion was covered by the law in England even before the Norman Conquest, through the required payment of a full *wergeld* if the child were "living", and a half-*wergeld* if not "living."[19]

As we come closer to the present, the legal record regarding abortion becomes even more certain — as we shall see in the next chapter. One thing is clear: The law of abortion does have a history, a history that involved controversy and contested legal claims. Early in the history of the law of abortion, controversy was not over the criminality of abortion or attempted abortion; rather the controversy was solely over which court was the proper forum for trial of the charge. The prosecution of abortion was one of the questions over which the centuries-long struggle between the church courts and the civil courts took place. This chapter covers those early centuries, when the struggle over the relation of the human to the divine held center stage.

# The Early Common Law Confronts Abortion by Injury Techniques

*Institutions are shaped by their beginnings.*

— Roscoe Pound[20]

---

PLEAS"), quoted *infra* at notes 89–90; Erneburga's Appeal, JUST 1/175, m.38 (1249). *See also* Rex v. Haunsard, JUST 1/548, m.4 (London Eyre 1329) (the defendant was convicted of causing an abortion while extorting money); Rex v. Clouet (Guernsey 1304) (pardon), CALENDAR CH. WARRANTS IN THE PUB. REC. OFF. PREPARED UNDER THE SUPERINTENDENCE OF THE DEPUTY KEEPER OF THE REC., A.D. 1244–1326, at 232 (London 1927); Rex v. Cheney, JUST 1/323, m.47d (Hertfordshire Eyre 1278) (the defendant was amerced in trespass for an accidental abortion caused by the defendant's horse); Rex v. Cordwaner, 1276 EYRE, *supra*, at 18 (no. 62) (the defendant was outlawed for causing the birth of a child; the record is unclear about whether child died). That abortions as such might not be punishable without the live birth of the child showing the signs of the abortion was later suggested in *Regina v. Sims,* 75 Eng. Rep. 1075 (K.B. 1601), quoted in Ch. 4, at notes 16–17. *See also* EDWARD COKE, THIRD INSTITUTE 50–51 (1644), quoted in Ch. 4, at notes 101–03.

17. Rex v. Code, JUST 1/789 (Hampshire Eyre 1281), m.1, quoted *infra* at note 92.

18. Regina v. Robynson, Q/SR 110/68 (Coroner's Inquest 1589); Rex v. Lichefeld, K.B. 27/974, Rex m.4 (1505), quoted *infra* at notes 386–89; Rex v. Wynspere (Coroner's Inquest 1503), KB 9/434/12, in CALENDAR OF NOTTINGHAMSHIRE CORONERS' INQUESTS 1485–1558, at 8 (no. 10) (R.F. Hunnisett ed., 25 THORNTON SOC'Y REC. SER. 1966).

19. *LEGES HENRI PRIMI* ch. LXX.14 (L.J. Downer ed. 1972). *See generally* GERMAIN GRISEZ, ABORTION: THE MYTHS, THE REALITIES, AND THE ARGUMENTS 186–87 (1970); STEPHEN, *supra* note 3, at 54; Marilyn Deegan, *Pregnancy and Childbirth in the Anglo-Saxon Medical Texts: A Preliminary Survey,* in MEDICINE IN EARLY MEDIEVAL ENGLAND 17 (M. Deegan & D.C. Scragg eds. 1989); Mark Scott, Note, *Quickening in the Common Law: The Legal Precedent* Roe *Attempted and Failed to Use,* 1 MICH. L. & POL'Y REV. 199, 218–23 (1996). *Wergeld,* literally "man gold," was money that anyone who killed another without justification would be ordered to pay to relatives of the slain person, as a merciful alternative to the blood feud. *See* A.W.B. Simpson, *The Laws of Ethelbert,* in ON THE LAWS AND CUSTOMS OF ENGLAND: ESSAYS IN HONOR OF SAMUEL E. THORNE 1, 7, 13–15 (Morris Arnold et al. eds. 1981); Charles Tucker, jr., *Anglo-Saxon Law: Its Development and Impact on the English Legal System,* 2 USAFA J. LEGAL STUD. 127, 145–55 (1991). *Leges Henri Primi* was a 12th-century (ca. 1118) compilation of Anglo-Saxon law as modified by the early Norman kings. *See* PERCY WINFIELD, THE CHIEF SOURCES OF ENGLISH LEGAL HISTORY 49 (1925). It is by no means clear how often the specified payments were actually enforced. Simpson, *supra,* at 15.

20. ROSCOE POUND, THE LAWYER FROM ANTIQUITY TO MODERN TIMES 13 (1953).

The origins of the common law are obscure. The traditional date for the beginning of the common law is 1066, when William the Bastard became William the Conqueror. The Norman Conquest today is seen as marking a clear break with the past and a new beginning for England, although at the time William was careful to preserve, insofar as possible, the appearance of legal and political continuity with the Saxon past.[21] It mattered little, for then and for another century the law administered by the kings of England was personal and situational. The law had no regular courts, no fixed procedures, and little or no formal substantive rules.

The common law as we now think of it emerged from the efforts of King Henry II to settle the numerous disputes over land titles created by nearly 20 years of civil war between Henry's mother and King Stephen.[22] The legal system that emerged bore the stamp of the personal and situational law that preceded its emergence—as the common law does to this day. The law focused largely on questions of land title, as ownership of land determined one's status, one's wealth, and one's right to receive (or obligation to perform) duties from (or to) others. Even the king's ability to raise an army depended on his ability to call upon the principle landowners to provide particular numbers and kinds of soldiers. Under the circumstances, it was more important—to kings, at least—that title be settled quickly and clearly than that titles be settled correctly. And in a society that believed in the active participation of the divine in the affairs of men, ordeal and battle seemed to be quick and certain ways to resolve disputes.[23]

The emergence of more or less regular courts was soon followed by the creation of a regular system of court records. Judges were accompanied by the only literate persons of the time, clerics (hence are word "clerks"), who made notations in handwritten Latin on parchment. This was a common pattern across western Europe at about the same time. In fact, most of the records that survive from the European Middle Ages are legal documents—charters, registers, writs, contracts, wills, instruments of civil administration, canons of councils and synods, compilations of church law, bishops' registers, formularies, monastic cartularies, chronicles recounting suits and legal claims among royalty or the aristocracy and the punishment of crimes, not to mention chronicles of marriage contracts, divorces, and the disposition of estates.[24]

Those studying English legal and social history are particularly fortunate. England has (by European standards) largely avoided wars on its soil and thus has largely escaped the destruction of its legal records. Thus, unlike many other European countries, English court records, while never fully complete, form a matchless treasure trove of materials not only on English law, but also on English society from the very end of the twelfth century down to today. But these records

---

21. *See generally* KURT KYNELL, SAXON AND MEDIEVAL ANTECEDENTS OF THE ENGLISH COMMON LAW (2000); H.G. RICHARDSON & G.O. SAYLES, LAW AND LEGISLATION FROM AETHELBERHT TO MAGNA CARTA (1966). *See also* Tucker, *supra* note 19; Patrick Wormold, *Frederic William Maitland and the Earliest English Law,* 16 LAW & HIST. REV. 1 (1998).

22. *See generally* J.H. BAKER, AN INTRODUCTION TO ENGLISH LEGAL HISTORY 15 (3rd ed. 1990); PAUL BRAND, THE MAKING OF THE COMMON LAW (1992); PAUL BRAND, THE ORIGINS OF THE ENGLISH LEGAL PROFESSION (1992); ARTHUR HOGUE, THE ORIGINS OF THE COMMON LAW 32–37 (1966); 2 HOLDSWORTH, *supra* note 7, at 185–86; S.F.C. MILSOM, HISTORICAL FOUNDATIONS OF THE COMMON LAW 421–28 (2nd ed. 1981); THEODORE PLUCKNETT, A CONCISE HISTORY OF THE COMMON LAW 15, 150, 257–58 (5th ed. 1956); 1 FREDERICK POLLOCK & FREDERICK MAITLAND, HISTORY OF ENGLISH LAW BEFORE EDWARD I, at 82–84 (2nd ed. 1898); MAX RADIN, HANDBOOK OF ANGLO-AMERICAN LEGAL HISTORY 8–9 (1936); R.C. VAN CAENEGEM, THE BIRTH OF THE ENGLISH COMMON LAW 1–4, 68–70 (2nd ed. 1988); WINFIELD, *supra* note 19, at 103–09, 126–36, 145–57. *But see* JOHN HUDSON, THE FORMATION OF THE ENGLISH COMMON LAW: LAW AND SOCIETY IN ENGLAND FROM THE NORMAN CONQUEST TO MAGNA CARTA (1996) (arguing that the common law emerged under William the Conqueror and his sons).

23. *See* 1 JOHN BALDWIN, MASTERS, MERCHANTS AND PRINCES 323–32 (1970; ROBERT BARTLETT, TRIAL BY FIRE AND WATER: THE MEDIEVAL JUDICIAL ORDEAL (1986); Paul Hyams, *Trial by Ordeal: The Key to Proof in the Early Common Law,* in ON THE LAWS AND CUSTOMS OF ENGLAND, *supra* note 19, at 90.

24. *See* JAMES BRUNDAGE, MEDIEVAL CANON LAW 1 (1995).

are not easy to read; nor do they lend themselves to easy understanding. The problem is not simply one of comprehending documents written in a different language and in a vastly different time. Legal documents in any age tend to be highly formulaic and terse. These qualities are even more pronounced in the early Middle Ages. Writing on parchment was an expensive and time-consuming process. Court clerks recorded only the most salient aspects of the legal proceedings. The typical records were "plea rolls" documents that John Baker, one of the leading current English legal historians, described in these words:

> [T]he record was highly formulaic, using stereotyped Latin phrases in place of detailed assertions, omitting the evidence, the arguments of counsel, and the reasons for judgments. The debates between serjeants[25] and judges, the tentative pleading and judicial rulings which obliquely revealed the assumptions of the common law,[] took place off the record, and only the results went down on parchment.[26]

Fictional recitals and pleadings pervaded English legal records until the nineteenth century.[27] For the first several centuries of the common law, plea rolls were seldom relied on explicitly in later proceedings and, as late as 1300, seem to have been little more than the personal notes of the judge involved, kept by him and turned over to the court only after he died.[28] As a result, the court records often omit much or most of the information that is of genuine historical interest. Yet the plea rolls quickly came to be the conclusive and only legally acceptable evidence of what had happened in an English court.[29]

More about the law than court records were primitive and undeveloped. Until the nineteenth century, England had no regular police force or other means of professional detection and prosecution of crime. England for many centuries largely depended on private suitors to bring even matters of public order before the courts. The prevalent form of private prosecution of major crimes was called an appeal of felony.[30] Appeal remained important until the Reformation, and did not entirely disappear until the English Civil War in the 1640s. It even had a brief revival under Chief Justice John Holt who held in 1699 that the appeal was "a noble prosecution, and a true badge of English liberties."[31]

The normal mode of trial of an appeal was by battle.[32] If the accused failed to appear for the battle, he would be "outlawed"—a process that antedated the Norman Conquest and can be

---

25. "Serjeant" was a term applied to the leading lawyers in England until late in the nineteenth century.

26. BAKER, *supra* note 22, at 204. *See also* J.H. Baker, *Records, Reports, and the Origins of Case-Law in England,* in JUDICIAL RECORDS, LAW REPORTS, AND THE GROWTH OF CASE LAW 15–21 (J.H. Baker ed. 1989) ("Baker, *Records*"). *See generally* VAN CAENEGEM, *supra* note 22, at 29–61.

27. *See, e.g.,* Donald Sutherland, *Legal Reasoning in the Fourteenth Century: The Invention of "Color" in Pleading,* in ON THE LAWS AND CUSTOMS OF ENGLAND, *supra* note 19, at 182.

28. SAMUEL THORNE, ESSAYS IN ENGLISH LEGAL HISTORY 243–54 (1985).

29. Baker, *Records*, *supra* note 26, at 16.

30. *See generally* J.H. BAKER, THE LEGAL PROFESSION AND THE COMMON LAW 262 (1986) ("BAKER, LEGAL PROFESSION"); POLLOCK & MAITLAND, *supra* note 22, at 470. *See also* Margaret Kerr, *Angevin Reform of the Appeal of Felony,* 13 LAW & HIST. REV. 351 (1995); David Seipp, *The Distinction between Crime and Tort in the Early Common Law,* 76 B.U. L. REV. 59, 61–68 (1996). The term "felony" denoted a crime justifying the end of the feudal relationship between the criminal and his lord, entailing the escheat of the felon's land to his lord and the forfeiture of the felon's life and goods to his king. 2 HENRY DE BRACTON, THE LAWS AND CUSTOMS OF ENGLAND 235 (George Woodbine ed., Samuel Thorne trans. 1977 & 1982) (2 vols. ca. 1256) ("BRACTON"). *See also* BAKER, *supra* note 22, at 572; Siepp, *supra*, at 62–63.

31. Stout v. Cowper, 12 Mod. 373, 375 (K.B. 1699).

32. 1 BRITTON: THE FRENCH TEXT CAREFULLY REVISED WITH AN ENGLISH TRANSLATION AND NOTES 104–05 (F.M. Nichols ed. 1865) (original *ca.* 1305); THE TREATISE ON THE LAWS AND CUSTOMS OF THE REALM OF ENGLAND COMMONLY CALLED GLANVILL 25, 55–58, 64, 126–32, 154 (G.D.G. Hall ed. & trans. 1965) (original *ca.* 1189) ("GLANVILL"). *See generally* BAKER, *supra* note 22, at 574–76, 602–03; 2 HOLDSWORTH, *supra* note 7, at 98–99; MILSOM, *supra* note 22, at 285, 406–10; GEORGE NEILSON, TRIAL BY COMBAT (1891);

traced back to Teutonic tribes in Roman times.[33] An outlaw was a declared enemy of the realm whose life and property were placed beyond the protection of the law. Outlaws could be killed without legal consequence by anyone who chose to do them in.[34] An outlaw's only recourse was a royal pardon, or to purge the outlawry by appearing before a court, or by seeking sanctuary in a church followed by leaving the realm in the quickest possible time. Although outlawry seems to have become highly formalized and largely ineffective by 1400, in the thirteenth century it still carried much of its original force. If one wanted to avoid outlawry and trial by battle, one's only other choice was to "carry the iron"—a form of trial by ordeal in which one's guilt or innocence was determined by one's physiological reaction to carrying a red-hot piece of iron.[35] Gradually, the defendant was allowed to defend an appeal by recourse to "the country"—by trial by a jury of 12 lawful men from the place where the alleged wrong occurred.[36]

The feudal structure of society reflected in trial by battle disadvantaged women in many respects. For example, a woman could not inherit in her own right because of the feudal services due the overlord, services that only a man could perform. The problem of providing for widows and unmarried daughters figured prominently in the difficulties that led to *Magna Carta*.[37] Women were forced to turn to some extent to the ecclesiastical courts for protection of their right to receive property and support.[38]

When it came to appeals of felony, women were generally unable to prosecute an appeal because they could not engage in combat. Women had to depend on their husbands, fathers, or brothers to bring an appeal on their behalf.[39] Rather than representing pure male misogyny, free-floating and without any material basis, such limitations on women, like the limits on female inheritance, arose from some very practical needs of the time. Trial by battle, however, was already undergoing severe criticism by canonical lawyers in the early twelfth century and was formally prohibited by the Church in 1215 along with the other forms of trial by ordeal.[40] Yet trial by battle was not formally abolished in England until 1819, and in the high Middle Ages was some-

PLUCKNETT, *supra* note 22, at 116–18, 121–24, 424–25, 427–28; 2 POLLOCK & MAITLAND, *supra* note 22, at 605–06; Hyams, *supra* note 23, at 90, 111–24.

33. BAKER, *supra* note 22, at 76–77; 3 HOLDSWORTH, *supra* note 7, at 303–05, 604–10; PLUCKNETT, *supra* note 22, at 430–31; RADIN, *supra* note 22, at 33, 191–92; Siepp, *supra* note 30, at 64–65.

34. *See* JOHN BELLAMY, ROBIN HOOD: A HISTORICAL ENQUIRY 61–62 (1985) (noting that, unlike the legendary Robin Hood, an outlaw would not dare appear in any community where he was known for fear of being attacked or killed).

35. Hyams, *supra* note 22, at 112.

36. 2 BRACTON, *supra* note 30, at 385–86, 390.

37. *See generally* S.F.C. Milsom, *Inheritance by Women in the Twelfth and Early Thirteenth Centuries,* in ON THE LAWS AND CUSTOMS OF ENGLAND, *supra* note 19, at 60.

38. *Id.* at 62.

39. 1 FLETA ch. 33 (ca. 1290), reprinted in 53 SELDEN SOC'Y 88–89 (H.G. Richardson & G.O. Sayles eds. 1953). In a similar vein, boys entitled to appeal a felony had to wait until they were 21 in order to be of age to engage in battle. Seipp, *supra* note 30, at 66.

40. 1 BALDWIN, *supra* note 23, at 323–32; BARTLETT, *supra* note 23; BRUNDAGE, *supra* note 24, at 140–42; VAN CAENEGEM, *supra* note 22, at 68–70; John Baldwin, *The Intellectual Preparation for the Canon of 1215 against Ordeals,* 36 SPECULUM 613 (1961); Charles Donohue, jr., *Proof by Witnesses in the Church Courts of Medieval England: An Imperfect Reception of the Learned Law,* in ON THE LAWS AND CUSTOMS OF ENGLAND, *supra* note 19, at 127, 128–34; Richard Fraher, *The Theoretical Justification for the New Criminal Law of the High Middle Ages:* Rei Publicae Interest ne Crimina Remaneant Impunita, 1984 U. ILL. L. REV. 577; Hyams, *supra* note 23, at 101–06. Although the ordeal persisted in some parts of Europe as a popular form of procedure even after the Church forbade priests to participate, it became rare in England rather quickly after 1215. *See* Heikki Pihlajamäki, *"Swimming the Witch, Pricking for the Devil's Mark": Ordeals in the Early Modern Witchcraft Trials,* 21 LEGAL HIST. no. 2, at 35 (Aug. 2000).

times described as "an essential liberty."[41] The possibility of battle, however, probably explains why appeals of felony began to decline sharply after the thirteenth century to give place to indictments for felony or for trespass.[42] Historian Paul Hyams has suggested that the influence of trial by battle lives on today in our adversarial process rooted in its forms and spirit.[43]

There appear to have been three situations in which the affront to a woman was so great that she was allowed to prosecute an appeal of felony in her own name—if she could find (or employ) a champion to battle on her behalf. The three grounds were the murder of her husband in her arms, rape, and abortion. At least, we have statements to that effect in no less than nine cases in which the court dismissed appeals by women for robbery, wounding, and breaches of the peace on the grounds that they could appeal only on the three grounds specified above.[44] Historian Margaret Kerr has also found at least two cases in which a woman was reported to have been an "approver"—a convicted felon whose life is spared if he (or, apparently, she) would appeal another felon and survive the ensuing battle.[45] Kerr, however, remained at a loss to explain how a woman could be an approver if she really was expected to fight a man for her life. Kerr also notes that during the reign of King John, about half of all appeals were brought by women![46] Kerr does not dwell on the fact that many of these were dismissed as improperly brought.

The sudden popularity with women of bringing appeals of felony perhaps explains the attempt in *Magna Carta* to limit the right of women to prosecute appeals to cases of involving the death of a husband in the woman's arms.[47] The two most prominent writers about the common law in the century straddling *Magna Carta* (1165–1265; *Magna Carta* was signed in 1215)—"Glanvill" and Bracton—both gave only two grounds on which a woman could bring an appeal in her own name: murder of her husband in her arms, and injury to her body.[48] "Injury to her body" went beyond the provision in *Magna Carta* and is more consistent with the judge's observations in cases reported over the next century to the effect that a woman could appeal in their own name for murder of her husband, rape, or abortion. Whether the authors meant by "in jury to her body" rape, or abortion, or other injuries, is not clear from the text, but is perhaps indicated by the judicial comments.

The earliest surviving writer on the common law was reputed to be Ranulph de Glanvill.[49] We actually do not even know who the author of the work attributed to "Glanvill" really was. His

---

41. Hyams, *supra* note 23, at 124. The ordeal of water appears to have been used informally as late as 1863, although it had by then been illegal for 648 years. BAKER, *supra* note 22, at 6 n.7.

42. Theodore Plucknett, *A Commentary on the Indictment,* in PROCEEDINGS BEFORE THE JUSTICES OF THE PEACE IN THE FOURTEENTH AND FIFTEENTH CENTURIES: EDWARD III TO RICHARD III, at xxxvi (Bertha Putnam ed. 1938); Seipp, *supra* note 30, at 72–80; Christopher Wittick, *The Role of the Criminal Appeal in the Fifteenth Century,* in LAW AND SOCIAL CHANGE IN BRITISH HISTORY 55 (J.A. Guy & H.G. Beale eds. 1984).

43. Hyams, *supra* note 23, at 91.

44. Taylor v. Asshenden, 1 EYRE OF KENT OF 1313–14 (39 SELDEN SOC'Y), at 114 [analyzed in the introduction to the volume, at lxxx–lxxxi] (William Craddock Bolland ed. 1922); Agnes's Appeal, JUST 1/1011, m.59d (Wiltshire Eyre 1289); Luch's Appeal, JUST 1/351A m.2 (Huntington Eyre 1285); Juliana's Appeal, JUST 1/1005, pt. 2, ms. 155, 155d (Wiltshire Eyre 1281); Anonymous Appeal, Coram Rege Roll no. 37, m.17 (1278) in 1 SELECTED CASES IN THE COURT OF KINGS BENCH UNDER EDWARD I (55 SELDEN SOC'Y) at 40 (G.O. Sayles ed. 1936–39) ("SELECTED CASES"); Grecia's Appeal, 1 JUST 1/82 m.32d (Wiltshire Eyre 1268); Anonymous Appeal, JUST 1/998A, m.29 (Wiltshire Eyre 1268); Alice's Appeal, JUST 1/82 m.22 (Cambridge Eyre 1261); Anonymous Appeal, m.40 (Cambridge Eyre 1260). For an analysis of most of these cases, see G.O. Sayles, *Introduction,* in 3 SELECTED CASES, *supra,* at lxii–lxxiv.

45. Kerr, *supra* note 30, at 356 n.14.

46. *Id.* at 373.

47. MAGNA CARTA ch. 54 (1215).

48. 2 BRACTON, *supra* note 30, at 403, 414–20; GLANVILL, *supra* note 32, at 173–74 (l. xiv, ch. 3).

49. GLANVILL, *supra* note 32. *See generally* GEORGE GROSSMAN, LEGAL RESEARCH: HISTORICAL FOUNDATIONS OF THE ELECTRONIC AGE 263–64 (1994); W.S. HOLDSWORTH, SOME MAKERS OF ENGLISH LAW 8, 13–15

work is generally dated as having appeared at the end of the reign of Henry II, around 1187–1189. "Glanvill" does not seem to have commented on the question of abortion. Other early authors, whose identities and origins are similarly obscure, did leave us comments on the topic.

While debate continues over who Henry de Bracton really was and therefore over what background influences shaped his work, most historians now believe he was an early judge and royal official who undertook in the middle of the thirteenth century to create a manual of the common law when it was barely a century old.[50] Bracton apparently invented the idea of precedent as a source of law, writing about what courts actually did rather than more abstractly about the "pure" Roman law on which scholars were focusing on the European continent.[51] His great work actually was never finished, the work apparently having begun in the 1230s and having stopped in 1256.[52]

Chief among the other early writers on the common law is known to us only as "Fleta," a name derived from the fact that the work bearing that name apparently was written while the author was incarcerated in the Fleet Prison.[53] Another early author is known as Britton, an indication of his nationality rather than his real name.[54] The book bearing the name "Britton" declares that it was written by King Edward I himself,[55] but few historians believe it.[56] While Edward I ("Longshanks") was called the English Justinian because of his interest in and support for the modernization of the common law, he could hardly have had the time to become adequately familiar with legal minutiae to have written the book. Nor is it likely that he had the time, between his many military campaigns (in Scotland and elsewhere) to write the book.

For centuries, historians thought that the only early discussions of the English law of abortion were the brief comments of these thirteenth and early fourteenth century authors. Bracton, writing around 1250, declared that "[i]f one strikes a pregnant woman or gives her a potion in order to procure an abortion, if the foetus is already formed or animated, especially if it is animated, he commits homicide."[57] If "animation" means "quickening" (as it would later be understood), then Bracton did not require "quickening" before there would be a "homicide"; the foetus merely must be formed even if it is not yet animated.[58]

Sometime around 1290, Fleta similarly reported that:

---

(1938); Charles Donahue, jr., Jus Commune, *Canon Law, and Common Law in England,* 66 Tul. L. Rev. 1745, 1751–52 (1992).

50. J.L. Barton, *The Mystery of Bracton,* 14 J. Legal Hist., No. 3, at 1 (1993). *See also* Baker, *supra* note 22, at 201; Grossman, *supra* note 49, at 264–65; Hogue, *supra* note 22, at 188–91; Holdsworth, *supra* note 49, at 17–18; Herman Kantorowicz, Bractonian Problems (1941); Plucknett, *supra* note 22, at 20, 258–67; 2 Pollock & Maitland, *supra* note 22, at 31–80; H.G. Richardson, Bracton: The Problem of His Text (1965); Thorne, *supra* note 28, at 75–110; Winfield, *supra* note 19, at 258–62; J.L. Barton, *Bracton as a Civilian,* 42 Tulane L. Rev. 555 (1968); David Seipp, *Bracton, the Year Books, and the "Transformation of Elementary Legal Ideas" in the Early Common Law,* 7 Law & Hist. Rev. 175 (1989); D.E.C. Yale, *"Of No Mean Authority": Some Later Uses of Bracton,* in On the Laws and Customs of England, *supra* note 19, at 383–96.

51. T. Ellis Lewis, *The History of Judicial Precedent,* 46 Law Q. Rev. 207, 209–13 (1930).

52. 2 Bracton, *supra* note 30, at 341. *See* Samuel Thorne, *Introduction,* in 1 Bracton, *supra,* at xiii–lii.

53. *See* Winfield, *supra* note 19, at 262–63.

54. 1 Britton, *supra* note 32, at 114.

55. *Id.* at 1–2.

56. *See* Winfield, *supra* note 19, at 263–65.

57. 2 Bracton, *supra* note 30, at 341.

58. Byrn, *supra* note 13, at 816; Means I, *supra* note 10, at 419 n.15; Quay, *supra* note 13, at 431; Scott, *supra* note 19, at 224–25. Bracton's language is too often referred to as if he had required quickening before it would be a homicide. *See, e.g.,* Caroline Morris, *Technology and the Legal Discourse of Fetal Autonomy,* 8 UCLA Women's L.J. 47, 73 (1997).

> He, too, in strictness is a homicide who has pressed upon a pregnant woman or has given her poison or has struck her in order to procure an abortion or to prevent conception, if the foetus is already formed and animated, and similarly he who has given or accepted poison with the intention of preventing procreation or conception. A woman also commits a homicide if, by potion or the like, she destroys a quickened child in her womb.[59]

Fleta, however, seems to equate "formation" with "animation," and thus could be considered the source of the later confusion of the common lawyers that fetuses deserved full legal protection only after quickening.

On the other hand, Britton specifically denied that a woman could appeal for abortion, on the grounds that she could not "set forth the name of the person against whom the felony was committed."[60] This statement not only contradicts what the cases already cited state, it ignores the possibility that the crime was an injury to the woman as well as to the child. Yet Britton's contention is hardly a refutation of Bracton and Fleta as Britton did not rule out a prosecution through the then new procedural device of indictment. An indictment was, then as now, a prosecution in the name of the king rather than a private prosecution such as the appeal of felony. Britton's rationale for denying a woman's right to appeal the felony—the inability to provide a baptismal name—did not apply to indictments. After all, Britton himself defined the term *"murdrum"* (from which our word "murder" is derived) as the indictable offense of killing "a person who could not be identified."[61] A century earlier, a claim of *murdrum* could still have proceeded by appeal.[62] The crime was invented as a response to the presumed murder of unknown Normans who turned up dead in remote corners of the still largely hostile Saxon countryside, so a suit for *murdrum* was against the hundred in which the deceased was found rather than against a specific culprit. The sense of *murdrum* as the killing of an unknown person persisted at least until 1340.

The curious book *The Mirror of Justices* provides a more direct contradiction of Bracton and Fleta. The unknown author of *The Mirror* stated that to kill a child in its mother's womb was not homicide because "none can judge whether it be child before it is seen, and known whether it be a monster or not."[63] We need not worry too much about the meaning of this passage, for the two great English legal historians, Frederick Pollock and Frederic Maitland, writing in general terms and without concern about abortion, dismissed *The Mirror* out of hand as "so full of fables and falsehoods that as an authority it is worthless."[64] Percy Winfield, writing about thirty years later, described *The Mirror* thusly:

> The book is not exactly a tissue of fables from beginning to end, but where it does incorporate matter which has been verified, one is led to suspect that this is cast in as ground-bait to attract credulity to the wild assertions that are made elsewhere. . . . The *Mirror* cannot be ignored in tracing our legal history, but it had better be used with a *presumptio juris* against its accuracy.[65]

---

59. FLETA, *supra* note 39, at 60–61.

60. 1 BRITTON, *supra* note 32, at 114.

61. 1 BRITTON, *supra* note 32, at 38. *See also* 2 BRACTON, *supra* note 30, at 379–82; FLETA, *supra* note 39, at 78–79. *See generally* BAKER, *supra* note 22, at 600–02; 1 HOLDSWORTH, *supra* note 7, at 65–77, 580–632; MILSOM, *supra* note 22, at 422; 1 POLLOCK & MAITLAND, *supra* note 22, at 67–68, 545; 2 POLLOCK & MAITLAND, *supra*, at 480–86; RADIN, *supra* note 22, at 175–76, 242. *See also* B.R. O'Brien, *From* Mordor *to* Murdrum: *The Preconquest Origin and Norman Revival of the Murder Fine*, 71 SPECULUM 321 (1996).

62. GLANVILL, *supra* note 32, at 174.

63. ANDREW HORN(?), THE MIRROR OF JUSTICES (*ca.* 1285), reprinted in 7 SELDEN SOC'Y 139 (William Joseph Whittaker ed. 1895).

64. 2 POLLOCK & MAITLAND, *supra* note 22, at 478 n.1. The book even states that it was written in French because that was the language best understood by the common people of England! HORN, *supra* note 63, at 3.

65. *See* WINFIELD, *supra* note 19, at 162, 254, 266–68.

Even Chaucer knew better than the compiler of *The Mirror of Justices;* Chaucer described one who "maketh a woman outher bareyne by drinkage venemouse herbes,...or sleeth a child by drinkes willfully,...yet it is homicyde."[66]

When Justice Blackmun wrote the majority opinion in *Roe v. Wade,*[67] he (and nearly everyone else who considered the matter) knew of no actual legal decisions to support any of the foregoing statements. Available in 1973, but largely ignored, was an older compilation of Anglo-Norman laws, *Leges Henri Primi,* which also indicated that abortion was a crime.[68] Also, an as yet unpublished doctoral dissertation in Medieval History was accepted in 1973 at the University of Iowa summarized many of the cases to be discussed in this section, although its author remained skeptical whether abortion truly was treated as a crime given the high rate of acquittals in the cases he found.[69] Historians and lawyers generally were not even aware of the cases in which the court stated that a woman could appeal felony for abortion in which no abortion had occurred. Many thought of the statements of Bracton and Fleta as simply the expression of religious ideas rather than a description of actual legal practice—disregarding the reality that such a distinction would have been quite alien to lawyers and judges in medieval England.[70] Nor was there as yet a well developed theory of precedent that would (as the common law does today) distinguish between the *holding* of the case that determines the outcome on the actual facts of the case and mere *dicta* that courts utter even though irrelevant to the outcome of the case. Furthermore, English jurists and lawyers, then and for centuries thereafter, took Bracton as the authority on the common law regardless of whether actual case precedent supported his opinions or not.[71]

# Prosecutions in the Royal Courts for Abortions

*Ideas have consequences and the ideas embedded in judicial opinions have...*
*direct and immediate consequences.*

—Alex Kozinski[72]

Our lack of knowledge of relevant cases came from a lack of the necessary research rather than because of lack of cases. Today, the statements of Bracton and Fleta are amply corroborated; Britton and *The Mirror* have been proven wrong about abortion by numerous recently discovered records or reports of appeals and indictments of felonious abortion. The lack of knowledge of the abortion decisions in early centuries is hardly surprising given the general inattention to the history of English criminal law relative to the history of commercial or other civil law topics. As a noted English legal historian commented, "The criminal law has hardly received generous attention from English legal historians."[73] Only recently, since *Roe* was de-

---

66. GEOFFREY CHAUCER, CANTERBURY TALES 604–05 (A.C. Cawley ed. 1960; original ca. 1387).

67. 410 U.S. at 134–36. Cyril Means, jr., whose work on the history of abortion formed the basis for Blackmun's history in *Roe,* largely ignored Bracton and Fleta. Means II, *supra* note 10, at 340–41, 346.

68. See the text *supra* at note 19.

69. HAROLD SCHNEEBECK, JR., THE LAW OF FELONY IN MEDIEVAL ENGLAND FROM THE ACCESSION OF EDWARD I UNTIL THE MID-FOURTEENTH CENTURY 232–43 (1973).

70. NORMAN DOE, FUNDAMENTAL AUTHORITY IN THE LATE MEDIEVAL ENGLISH LAW 6, 114 (1990).

71. Blundell v. Catherall, 106 Eng. Rep. 1190 (K.B. 1821). On the rise and fall and rise again of Bracton's authority in English courts, see PLUCKNETT, *supra* note 22, at 262–65; Yale, *supra* note 50.

72. Sanders v. Parker Drilling Co., 911 F.2d 191, 217 (9th Cir. 1990) (Kozinski, J., dissenting), *cert. denied,* 500 U.S. 917 (1991).

73. BAKER, LEGAL PROFESSION, *supra* note 30, at 325. *See also* BAKER, *supra* note 22, at 570; Albert Schmidt, *Perspectives on Crime in England,* 3 CRIM. L.F. 327, 327 (1992) ("[C]riminal justice history as we know it really began in the 1970s.").

cided, has the gap regarding the history of the criminal law been filled to a considerable extent, more through the efforts of social historians interested in criminal records because of the rich detail they reveal about ancient life than through the efforts of legal historians seeking insights into legal practices. Several persons have searched specifically for abortion cases since *Roe*, none more thoroughly or more successfully than attorney Philip Rafferty of the California Bar.[74]

The earliest common law, with its emphasis on appeals of felony, was poorly suited to respond to wrongs that were not done against a specific adult. Nor was the earliest common law prepared to respond to wrongs against women except in narrow circumstances. One therefore will search in vain during the period before 1400 for a record of a prosecution for abortion that was not also a crime against the mother in the most graphic terms. Nonetheless, it turns out that these numerous terse court records settle the uncertainties left by the early commentaries. And the courts in these cases spoke unequivocally in terms of the killing of a child, and not just in terms of a crime against the mother. The common law, in its early centuries, treated abortion as a crime in principle because it involved the killing of an unborn child—a tradition that continued with elaboration, but without interruption, until *Roe* changed it.

Probably the earliest recorded common law proceeding to address an abortion that is *Agnes's Appeal*, an appeal of felony brought in 1200. The entire record of that appeal is:

> Lincolnshire. Agnes, the daughter of Saxi, appeals John of Paris that whereas she was in labor, he came to her house and dragged her out by the feet and struck her with a certain pole in such a way that she lost her child. And the citizens of Lincoln came and showed a charter of the lord king which witnesses that they should not be impleaded outside the walls of Lincoln (except for their moneyers and officials), and that they ought not to make battle concerning any appeal but to deraign themselves[75] according to the liberties and laws of the city of London; and they prayed this liberty. A day is given to them before the lord king wheresoever he should then be in England on the morrow of St. Edmund to hear their judgment.[76]

There probably is no record of an abortion case significantly earlier than *Agnes's Appeal*. The royal courts were just then coming into existence as regularly constituted institutions.[77] The earliest known plea rolls from any court date from 1194.[78] And when, in 1275, Parliament resolved to enact a date from which English legal records began, it chose 1189—designated as the limit of "living memory"; the date needed no updating as English legal records thereafter were more or less complete.[79] The quoted record is typical of most such early abortion proceedings, whether by appeal or by indictment.[80] John Baker, who provided the translation for these and other legal records not in the English language, commented on *Agnes's Appeal* thusly:

---

74. Philip Rafferty, *Roe v. Wade: The Birth of a Constitutional Right* (University Microfilms International Dissertation Information Service, Ann Arbor, MI 1992).

75. That is, to vindicate themselves or to prove their innocence.

76. Agnes's Appeal (1200), Select Pleas of the Crown (1 Selden Soc'y) 39 (no. 82) (F.W. Maitland ed. 1887).

77. *See* Baker, *supra* note 22, at 14–16; 1 Holdsworth, *supra* note 7, at 4–5.

78. The Earliest English Law Reports (Paul Brand ed. 1996). *See also* Baker, *Records, supra* note 26, at 15; Hogue, *supra* note 22, at 143, 149, 170–71.

79. M.T. Clanchy, From Living Memory to Written Records: England 1066–1307, at 123 (1979); Grossman, *supra* note 49, at 4.

80. *See* Rex v. Garton, K.B. 27/354, Rex. m.66 (1348); Rex v. Houdydoudy (Coroner's Inquest 1326), Calendar of Coroner's Rolls of the City of London, A.D. 1300–1378, at 166 (1913) (outcome unknown) ("Coroner's Rolls"); Rex v. Botevylayn (K.B. 1305), Wiltshire Gaol Delivery & Trailbaston Trials 1275–1306, at 105, 126, 131 (nos. 576, 800, 854) (1978); Boleheved's Appeal, JUST 1/112, m.9d (Cornwall Eyre 1284); Rex v. le Petiprestre, The London Eyre of 1244, at 48 (no. 116) (London Rec. Soc'y 1970) ("1244

As is common for these early reports, the outcome of *Agnes's Appeal* has not been found, and probably has not survived. This might be because the appeal was abandoned before trial. About 50% of all appeals appear to have been abandoned before trial, perhaps suggesting that the goal in bringing an appeal was to obtain a financial settlement, or that the appellors were unwilling to test their case in battle. This was seen as a significant problem, a problem that had nothing to do with abortion as such, for appeals were then the major means of enforcing the King's peace. Eventually, the Kings of England felt it necessary to assess a fine for abandonment of an appeal. This in turn led to the practice of "amercement"—the requirement that sureties post a bond for the willingness of a party (here the plaintiff) to appear at the trial.[81]

The abortion alleged in *Agnes's Appeal* is typical for the time, involving a battering of the woman, against her will, but with no indication of the motive behind the attack. The report, and those of other appeals, supports the judicial *dicta* in several cases to the effect that a woman could bring an appeal for abortion at a time when she could bring few other appeals because trial would have been by battle.[82] *Agnes's Appeal* demonstrates one of the techniques whereby an appellant might avoid the obligation of battle which, for a woman's appeal, would have involved facing a champion (a professional if the woman or her family could afford one).[83] The defendant invoked the liberties and laws of the city of London, a claim to trial by "wager of law" instead of by battle.[84] No one questioned the propriety of the charge, only the method of trial.

When fines and amercements proved ineffectual for compelling appellors to prosecute their cases, the King began to put appeals before juries if the appellor defaulted.[85] Otherwise, the King could not get at the truth and enforce the King's Peace. This practice produced a body of

---

EYRE"); Sauter's Appeal, PLEAS OF THE CROWN FOR GLOUCESTER CNTY. 1221, at 16 (no. 69) (1884) ("GLOUCESTER PLEAS"); Sibil's Appeal (1203), SELECT PLEAS OF THE CROWN, *supra* note 76, at 32 (no. 73).

81. For the full text of the letter, see 1 RAFFERTY, *supra* note 74, at 172. On the abandonment of battles, and the assessment of fines for doing so, see Kerr, *supra* note 30, at 359–68. On amercement, see 2 BRACTON, *supra* note 30, at 335; GLANVILL, *supra* note 32, at 21, 171.

82. See the text *supra* at note 44.

83. *See* 1 HOLDSWORTH, *supra* note 7, at 308–11; PLUCKNETT, *supra* note 22, at 117.

84. "Wager of law" involved swearing oaths rather than fighting to the death. *See generally* BAKER, *supra* note 22, at 69, 87–88, 578; 1 HOLDSWORTH, *supra* note 7, at 305; J.E.A. JOLLIFFE, THE CONSTITUTIONAL HISTORY OF MEDIEVAL ENGLAND: FROM THE ENGLISH SETTLEMENT TO 1485, at 2–4, 9–10, 58–59 (4th ed. 1961); F.W. MAITLAND, THE CONSTITUTIONAL HISTORY OF ENGLAND 115–18 (H.A.L. Fisher ed. 1908); MILSOM, *supra* note 22, at 38–39, 67–68, 245–48, 285–86, 406–13; PLUCKNETT, *supra* note 22, at 115–16, 362–64, 399–400; RADIN, *supra* note 22, at 32–33, 193–94; Harold Berman, *The Background of the Western Legal Tradition in the Folklaw of the Peoples of Europe*, 45 U. CHI. L. REV. 533, 561–63 (1978). See also the text *infra* at notes 295–332.

One source of the jury was simply the systematization of this compurgation process at law, in turn influenced by the compurgation process of the ecclesiastical courts. R.H. HELMHOLZ, CANON LAW AND COMMON LAW 62–66 (1989); MILSOM, *supra* note 22, at 410–13; PLUCKNETT, *supra* note 22, at 108; RADIN, *supra* note 22, at 207–08; G.R. QUAIFE, WANTON WENCHES AND WAYWARD WIVES: PEASANTS AND ILLICIT SEX IN EARLY SEVENTEENTH CENTURY ENGLAND 190–91 (1979); Charles Donohue, jr., *Proof by Witnesses in the Church Courts of Medieval England: An Imperfect Reception of the Learned Law*, in ON THE LAWS AND CUSTOMS OF ENGLAND, *supra* note 19, at 127, 134–41; Hyams, *supra* note 23, at 120; Charles Wells, *The Origin of the Petty Jury*, 27 LAW Q. REV. 347 (1911). Wager of law was also common in manorial courts and survived there longer than in the royal courts. John Beckerman, *Procedural Innovation and Institutional Change in Medieval English Manorial Courts*, 10 LAW & HIST. REV. 197, 203–12 (1992). Apparently the prevalence of the wager of law in the manorial courts helped speed their decline during the fourteenth century and later as plaintiffs opted for the less manipulable jury system then emerging in the royal courts. *Id.* at 206–09. At least some of the oath-helpers testified more like witnesses rather than merely attesting to the defendant's character and propensity to tell the truth. *Id.* at 210–11. Juries did gradually become common in manorial courts as well. *Id.* at 212–19.

85. 2 BRACTON, *supra* note 30, at 402. *See* Kerr, *supra* note 30, at 369–73. We know fairly little about the composition of the juries of this time, although they appear to have been composed of pretty much the same

records of appeals of abortion that are only somewhat less terse than the records of appeals for which the outcome is not known. The most common result of the jury appeals was a judgment of "not guilty,"[86] producing a pattern similar to the records that did not record an outcome. One of the earliest recorded appeals that resulted in a decision of not guilty of abortion is *Amice's Appeal:*

> Amice, who was the wife of Ralph Gundwine, appeals Adam Warner, William Warner and Henry Warner that they came to the house of her the said Amice and broke her house, and took her the said Amice and beat her severely so that, by reason of that beating, she the said Amice lost her child which was in her belly. And that they did this to her wickedly and feloniously against the peace etc., she offers etc.
>
> And the aforesaid Adam and others come and deny the [breach of the peace], the beating, and the whole *etc.* and put themselves upon a jury of the township. And they offer the lord king 50 pounds for having the jury therein, by pledge of [12 names].
>
> And the jurors say upon their oath that in truth the aforesaid Adam and others beat the aforesaid Amice; but they say that she immediately went off, and walked about hither and thither, and afterwards when eight days had elapsed she aborted a certain child having the form of a male five inches long; but they believe that this was rather due to the labor and foolish behavior of the selfsame Amice than to the aforesaid beating.[87]

Records finding "not guilty," as in *Amice's Appeal,* often contain more detail than records for which we do not know the outcome, yet we still do not know the arguments that were made about the law or the theories which the court relied on in the case. At the least, however, these records indicate, even more clearly than the mere record of the initiation of a proceeding based upon an abortion, that such indictments and appeals were valid under the common law. The case proceeded to judgment without any apparent suggestion that it should be dismissed because

---

people from year to year, and they appear to have been people of some substance. *See* Anthony Musson, *Twelve Good Men and True? The Character of Early Fourteenth-Century Juries,* 15 Law & Hist. Rev. 115 (1997).

86. Rex v. Mondson, JUST 1/527, m.11d (Lincolnshire Gaol Delivery 1361–62); Rex v. Skotard, JUST 1/169, m.25 (Derbyshire Eyre 1330); Rex v. Cobbeham, JUST 1/547, m.19d (London Eyre 1321); Rex v. Godesman, JUST 1/383, mm.18d, 96 (Kent Eyre 1313); Rex v. le Raggede (Dublin, Ireland 1311), Calendar of Justiciary Roles or Proc. in the Ct. of the Justiciar of Ireland I to VII Years of Edward II, at 216 (Dublin Stationary Off., n.d.) ("Irish Justiciary Roles"); Isabel's Appeal, JUST 1/544, m.55d (Middlesex Eyre 1294); Rex v. Skel, JUST 1/1098, pt. 2, m.79 (Yorkshire Eyre 1293); Rex v. Wyntercote, JUST 1/303, m.69d (Hereford Eyre 1292); Rex v. Boleye, JUST 1/741, m.41 (Shropshire Eyre 1292); Rex v. Hore, JUST 1/1011, m.56 (Wiltshire Eyre 1289); Agnes's Appeal, JUST 1/1011, m.59d (Wiltshire Eyre 1289); Rex v. Reeve, JUST 1/924, m.60 (Sussex Eyre 1288); Rex v. Neubyr', JUST 1/924, m.73 (Sussex Eyre 1288); Beatrix's Appeal, JUST 1/579, m.10d (Norfolk Eyre 1286); Matilda's Appeal, JUST 1/579, m.72 (Norfolk Eyre 1286); Lenota's Appeal, JUST 1/833, m.7 (Suffolk Eyre 1286); Alexandra's Appeal, JUST 1/833, m.23d (Suffolk Eyre 1286); Hervest's Appeal, JUST 1/789, m.26d (Hampshire Eyre 1281); Rex v. Benetley, JUST 1/789, m.3 (Hampshire Eyre 1281); de Pekering's Appeal, JUST 1/369, m.36 (Kent Eyre 1279); Rex v. le Gaoeler, JUST 1/369, m.37d (Kent Eyre 1279); Rex v. Surgeon, JUST 1/369, m.37d (Kent Eyre 1279); Joan's Appeal, JUST 1/921, m.23 (Sussex Eyre 1279); Gras's Appeal, 1276 Eyre, *supra* note 16, at 73–74 (no. 261); Sorel's Appeal, *id.* at 61 (no. 222); Isabel's Appeal, *id.* at 62–64 (nos. 157, 158); Cecily's Appeal (1249), C.A.F. Meekings, Studies in 13th Century Justice and Administration 257 (no. 562) (1981); Swayn's Appeal, JUST 1/359, m.36 (1249); Margaret's Appeal, JUST 1/174, m.40d (1249?); Orscherd's Appeal, JUST 1/174, m.40d (1249?); Alice's Appeal, JUST 1/176, m.27d (1249); Amice's Appeal, JUST 1/274, m.14d (1247); Phina's Appeal, JUST 1/778, m.57 (1246), *summarized in* Meekings, *supra,* at 267; Sarah's Appeal, 1244 Eyre, *supra* note 80, at 50–51 (no. 124); St. Alban's Appeal (1244), *id.* at 36 (no. 84); Modi's Appeal (1221), Rolls of the Justices in Eyre for Gloucestershire, Warwickshire, & Staffordshire (59 Selden Soc'y) 560–61 (no. 1336) (Doris Mary Stanton ed. 1940) ("Rolls of the Justices in Eyre"); Burel's Appeal (1202), Select Pleas of the Crown, *supra* note 76, at 11 (no. 26).

87. Amice's Appeal, JUST 1/274, m.14d (1247). The translation from Latin is by John Baker.

of any supposed non-criminality of abortion. To the same effect are the occasional proceedings in which a trial was preempted by the successful invocation of a true benefit of clergy, *i.e.*, a privilege against trial at law then accorded only to clerics and only for capital offenses.[88]

Proceedings that ended in serious punishments are even more definite about whether criminal charges were properly brought for an abortion.[89] One of the earliest of records of such punishments is *Juliana's Appeal*:

> John de Rechich beat one Juliana, daughter of Maynard, so that he killed her boy in her womb, and fled. Therefore let him be exacted and outlawed. He was received at Stoke Curcy. Therefore [that township] is in mercy.[90] The jurors concealed that matter; therefore they are in mercy. He had no chattels.[91]

The appeal records a fine on the jury for concealing the event and another fine on the township in which the defendant was to have awaited trial for the failure to contain him. The last sentence, with its laconic report that the defendant had no chattels, suggests that he also would have been fined had he had the means to pay it. The similar case of *Rex v. Scharp* is noteworthy not only because it resulted in a fine (amercement) on the sheriff for a deceased defendant's failure to appear for trial, but also because the victim was the defendant's wife:

> Richard Scharp, wool-merchant, beat his wife, Emma, so that she gave birth to a still-born boy. Because Richard has died, nothing from the outlawry. The mayor and aldermen testify that Richard was arrested and handed over to Richard de Ewell, sheriff, who released him on the pledges of six men. Because according to the law of the City no one accused of a man's death should be released on bail except on the pledges of twelve men, any of whom should be able to answer to the king for 100s. as amercement if he should fail, *to judgment* on Richard de Ewelle.[92]

Note also in *Scharp* that the only actionable death mentioned is that of the still-born son, yet the record described that proceeding as being based upon "a man's death."

Just a few years later, in *Rex v. Code*, an abortionist and his accomplices were imprisoned after a conviction upon a royal indictment:

> ...Alice, the wife of Adam Prest, coming from the city of Winchester out the vill of Upham, met [Walter] Code, Richard the Potter, and Stephen his brother, and Herbert the Carpenter, who knocked her over and beat her and would have lain with her by force, so that by the violence which they committed against her she gave birth to a certain abortive child as if of the age of one month. Therefore let them be taken. William de Stratton, the coroner, did not [come?]; therefore to judgment of him. Afterwards the aforesaid Walter and the others come and deny the death, the felony, and all...[and thereof] they put themselves upon the country. And twelve jurors say upon their oath that the aforesaid Walter, Richard, and Stephen with force knocked over and beat the aforesaid Alice, as a result of which she gave birth to a certain abortive child of such an age that it was unknown whether it was male of female; which child was eight inches long. And they say that the aforesaid Herbert is not guilty thereof. Therefore [let him

---

88. Mabel's Appeal, JUST 1/741, m.33 (Shropshire Eyre 1292) (damaged roll); Philippa's Appeal (1276?), 1276 EYRE, *supra* note 16, at 51 (no. 187). Benefit of clergy is discussed in more detail *infra* at notes 234–36.

89. The cases are collected *supra* at note 16.

90. *I.e.*, to be amerced: to pay a fine in lieu of more serious punishment. BLACK'S LAW DICTIONARY 1001 (7th rev. ed. 1999).

91. Juliana's Appeal, SOMERSET PLEAS, *supra* note 16, at 321 (no. 1243, ca. 1256). The translation from Latin is by J John Baker.

92. Rex v. Scharp, 1276 EYRE, *supra* note 16, at 23 (no. 76).

be] quit thereof. And the aforesaid Walter, Richard, and Stephen are committed to prison.[93]

In this record, there is no question of the criminality of the abortion. Three men were convicted and imprisoned for a felonious killing of an unborn child, while one was acquitted. The three convicts won their release only by obtaining a pardon *de perdon, mortis hominis*—for the killing of a person. Such pardons were common in homicides when the killing was without, as the phrase later crystallized, "malice aforethought."[94]

The case also clearly indicates that the doctrine of quickening had not yet taken hold in the courts even it was endorsed by both Bracton and Fleta.[95] Today "quickening" is understood as fetal movement recognized as such by the mother.[96] The timing of the first quickening varies with the vigor of the fetus and with the experience of the mother, for more experienced mothers will recognized the "butterflies" in her belly as fetal movement while a less experienced woman often will not.[97] The Latin word they used that today is translated as "quickened" is "*animatum*" or "*aminatus*"—"animated" or "ensouled" (derived from the Latin *anima*, meaning "soul"). This word could just as well be translated as "alive." This turns out not to be a translation glitch. Philip Rafferty's research has suggested that the phrase "quick with child" always meant simply that the women bore a living child whenever life might be said to have begun.[98] Although the phrase has become confused over the centuries with the more specific phrase "with quick child," Rafferty's research persuaded the Oxford English Dictionary to change its former definition of "quick with child" as used historically from "pregnant with a quick child" to pregnant with a live fetus regardless of quickening.[99] Compare the modern phrase "the quick and the dead."

The confusion of the phrase "quick with child" with the phrase "with quick child" bedevils modern research into ancient writings. For example, British historian Angus McLaren quoted at length from numerous sources in which the term "quick" was used to mean "alive" or "healthy"; he assumed that as his sources all referred to a "quickened" fetus in contrast with an unquickened fetus and that they concluded the unquickened fetus was not considered alive.[100] Only a few of the quotations actually convey that sense, however. Most were simply ambiguous. For example, McLaren quotes Thomas Urquhart's vulgar pun of referring to a penis as a "quickening peg."[101] This could be seen as a suggestion that life ("quickening") began at conception as conception is when the "peg" would make its influence most felt, although perhaps Urquhart had in mind a possible quickening by a fetus disturbed by intercourse late in the pregnancy. Some of McLaren's quotations, however, seem rather more clearly to convey the sense that "quick" simply meant "alive" and that the life in question began well before the sensation of quickening—the

---

93. Rex v. Code, JUST 1/789, m.17 (Hampshire Eyre 1281). The translation from Latin is by John Baker; the elisions and suggested words reflect damage to the roll.

94. *See generally* BAKER, *supra* note 22, at 589–90, 600–03; 8 HOLDSWORTH, *supra* note 7, at 303–04; NAOMI HURNARD, THE KING'S PARDON FOR HOMICIDE BEFORE A.D. 1307, at 106–07 (1965); MILSOM, *supra* note 22, at 422–23; PLUCKNETT, *supra* note 22, at 444–46.

95. Both had indicated that abortion was homicide if the fetus was "formed and animated." See the quotations *supra* at notes 57, 61.

96. BLACK'S LAW DICTIONARY, *supra* note 90, at 1261; DAVID BUSS, THE EVOLUTION OF DESIRE: STRATEGIES OF HUMAN MATING 119 (1994); Scott, *supra* note 19, at 221–23.

97. HELEN MARGARET IRWIN LILEY, MODERN MOTHERHOOD 37–38 (rev. ed. 1969).

98. 1 RAFFERTY, *supra* note 74, at 64–76, 116–19, 136–86. *See also* John Connery, *The Ancients and the Medievals on Abortion: The Consensus Ignored*, in ABORTION AND THE CONSTITUTION: REVERSING ROE V. WADE THROUGH THE COURTS 123, 129–31 (Dennis Horan, Edward Grant, & Paige Cunningham eds. 1987).

99. *Letter from J.A. Simpson (co-editor of the Oxford English Dictionary) to Philip Rafferty*, 23 Nov. 1990, quoted in 1 RAFFERTY, *supra* note 74, at 172–73.

100. ANGUS MCLAREN, REPRODUCTIVE RITUALS 108–09 (1984).

101. THOMAS URQUHART, THE FIRST (SECOND) BOOK OF MR. FRANCIS RABELAIS(1653).

very opposite of what McLaren (and most others) assume today. Thus Dr. Christopher Hooke's observation during a lecture to midwives published in 1590: "[E]ither being conceived, they shall not be quickened: or being quickened, they shall not in the womb accomplish the just time of the birth."[102] Hooke, lamenting the loss of a child's life in the womb, described a progression from conception to quickening to birth, perhaps not indicating anything more than that the progression occurs, yet in fact lamented the loss of the embryo before quickening every bit as much as after. A century later, Richard Blackmore included the following lines in his epic poem *Prince Arthur:*

> Barren Night did pregnant grow,
>
> And quicken'd with the World in Embrio.[103]

It was customary at the time to use the term "embryo" to refer to the unborn child before it quickened, and the term "fetus" to refer to the unborn child thereafter.[104] Note how Blackmore equated "quicken'd" with "pregnant" and attributed that quality to a metaphorical "Embrio"—the earliest stages of pregnancy. The notion that a conceptus was a living human being "whilst the blood is in its first formation of a human body" and that those who deliberately killed it were guilty of murder has been traced back at least as far as Tertullian in the second century of the Common Era[105]—as McLaren knew.[106] This same theory turns up again and again thereafter, in England and throughout Christendom.[107] McLaren almost willfully misreads these and other statements, much as he misreads the comment of an anonymous midwife that "from the time a woman is quick then she will seldom fail to be brought to bed."[108] McLaren read this statement as asserting that the quality of the fetus's life changed with quickening,[109] yet the statement actually is simply and unambiguously descriptive without any evaluative component at all. The midwife's point seems at most to be that miscarriages seldom occurred after quickening.

Whatever might be the correct interpretation of *animatum* or *animatus* in Bracton and Fleta, *Rex v. Code* clearly indicates that "quickening" in the modern sense was not required. The child in the case is described as being of about a month's gestation. The evidence on the point is somewhat contradictory. The statement that the child was about eight inches long suggests a longer gestational age, but the statement that the child's development had not reached the point where its sex could be determined would seem to confirm an early, pre-quickening gestational age. Tellingly, none of the defendants made an issue of the gestational age of the dead child.

---

102. CHRISTOPHER HOOKE, THE CHILD-BIRTH OR WOMEN'S LECTURE (1590).

103. RICHARD BLACKMORE, PRINCE ARTHUR II:26 (1695).

104. *See, e.g.,* STEPHEN BLANCARD, PHYSICAL DICTIONARY 48 (1702). *See also* DANIEL DEFOE, CONJUGAL LEWDNESS: OR MATRIMONIAL WHOREDOM, A TREATISE CONCERNING THE USE AND ABUSE OF THE MARRIAGE BED 152 (1727).

105. TERTULLIAN, APOLOGY ¶9.6 (197 A.D.) (T.R. Glove trans. 1966). *See generally* JOSEPH BINGHAM, ORIGINES ECCLESASTICAE: OR, THE ANTIQUITIES OF THE CHRISTIAN CHURCH 210 (1843); MICHAEL GORMAN, ABORTION AND THE EARLY CHURCH: CHRISTIAN, JEWISH & PAGAN ATTITUDES IN THE GRECO-ROMAN WORLD 54–58 (1982).

106. BINGHAM, *supra* note 105, is quoted in McLAREN, *supra* note 100, at 115–16.

107. *See* CHAUCER, *supra* note 65, at 292; POPE SIXTUS V, *EFFRAENATUM* (a Papal bull), quoted in McLAREN, *supra* note 100, at 117

108. As quoted in DANIEL BLAKE SMITH, INSIDE THE GREAT HOUSE: PLANTER FAMILY LIFE IN EIGHTEENTH-CENTURY CHESAPEAKE SOCIETY 28 (1980)

109. McLaren's misreading of these sources is matched by the contradictory positions he embraced on the safety of abortion in medieval and early modern England. Repeatedly, he insisted that abortion was safe and effective pretty much throughout English history. McLAREN, *supra* note 100, at 5–7, 107, 111–12, 114. Yet he also claimed that Lord Ellenborough's Act was adopted to protect women from being coerced by "seducers" into undergoing the unreasonably dangerous procedures by which abortion was then achieved. *Id.* at 136–37.

In addition to cases in which defendants were made to pay a fine, we now know of many cases in which defendants chose not to appear for trial and were therefore "outlawed."[110] Fairly typical of such cases is *Rex v. Mercer,* despite its atypical aspects in that the child was born alive and died "immediately" from the injuries inflicted on him in the womb:

> Emma, the wife of Reynold the Mercer, and Alice, the daughter of Thomas of North-leigh, being pregnant, were fighting together in the field of Northleigh in such a way that the aforesaid Emma struck with a certain stone on the side, by which blow the same Alice on the second day following gave birth to a certain living male child having on its head a wound from the blow of the same stone; which child died immediately after it was baptized. And the aforesaid Emma fled immediately after it was aborted. And the jurors say upon their oath that the aforesaid Alice gave birth one month before the [due] time of birth, and that the child died from the aforesaid blow, in respect of which they suspect her of wrong. Therefore, let her be outlawed and waived.[111]

*Rex v. Mercer* does not record a judgment of guilt of a felony but rather a penalty imposed for failing to appear to answer a charge of felony. The process of outlawry, however, was rife with technicalities. One could not be outlawed without the proper allegation of a crime, and the record is careful to note that a jury was prepared to testify to the accused's guilt and to note a good deal of evidence to support the charge. Thus the numerous examples of outlawry for failing to answer for injurious abortions again demonstrate the criminality of the challenged conduct.

Finally, we have two instances, one from England and one from Ireland, in which people were hung for having committed an injurious abortion. The English case was *Rex v. Haule:*

> In the twelfth year of the aforesaid reign of King Edward [II], John of Gisors being coroner, Stephen of Cornhill and Robert de Rokesle then being sheriffs, a certain Maud de Haule and Agnes the Convert were fighting together in this ward, and a certain Joan of Hallynghurst came along and separated them from each other, by reason of which the aforesaid Maud threw the aforesaid Joan out of the house where she dwelt and she fell on the step of a solar of the same house so that on the fourth day following she gave birth to a certain child of the female sex ten weeks before the due time, which same child died immediately after birth. And the aforesaid Maud was taken immediately after the deed and led to Newgate prison in the time of the aforesaid sheriffs. Therefore [let them answer for what happened].[112] And Robert Gobba, John Braaz, and Richard atte Vyngne, three neighbors, did not come; but they are not suspected of wrong. The aforesaid Robert was attached by Walter le Ken; therefore [he is] in mercy. The other mainpernor has died. The aforesaid John was attached by Hugh Trigge and John de Haleford; therefore [they are] in mercy. The aforesaid Richard was attached by John Bardewyne and John le Kent; therefore [they are] in mercy. Afterwards William le Leyre and Henry atte More, tenants of part of the lands which were held of the aforesaid

---

110. Rex v. Ragoun, JUST 1/547A, m.55d (London Eyre 1310); Rex v. Eppinge, JUST 1/547A, m.46 Rex v. Hervy, JUST 1/547A, m.40d (1300, ms. dated 1321); Rex v. Hokkestere, JUST 1/547A, m.3 (London Eyre 1298, ms. date 1321); Rex v. Scot, JUST 1/547A, m.22 (1291, ms. dated 1321); Rex v. Dada, JUST 1/547A, m.19d (1290, ms. dated 1321); Rex v. Cliston, JUST 1/1011, m.62 (Wiltshire Eyre 1288); Rex v. Mercer, JUST 1/710, m.45 (Oxford Eyre 1285), quoted *infra* at note 109; Rex v. Brente, JUST 1/186, m.30 (Devon Eyre 1281); Rex v. Scharp, 1276 EYRE, *supra* note 16, at 23 (no. 76), quoted *supra* at note 97; Juliana's Appeal (1256?), SOMERSET PLEAS, *supra* note 16, at 321 (no. 1243), quoted *infra* at notes 108–09; Erneburga's Appeal, JUST 1/175, m.38 (1249). *See also* Rex v. Cordwaner, 1276 EYRE, *supra,* at 18 (no. 62) (the defendant was outlawed for causing the birth of a child; the record is unclear about whether child died).

111. Rex v. Mercer, JUST 1/710, m.45 (Oxford Eyre 1285). The translation from Latin is by John Baker.

112. Dr. Baker remains uncertain about the correct translation of this passage: *Ideo r' ipsa de ea quo devenit.*

sheriffs, come and fully admit that the aforesaid Maud de Haule was in the aforesaid prison in the time of the aforesaid sheriffs, and they say that the aforesaid Maud was hanged before Hamon Hauteyn and his fellows, justices assigned to deliver the gaol aforesaid etc. And that appears from the rolls of the same Hamon etc. She had no chattels etc.[113]

What is one to make of this report? It does not say directly that Maude was hung for the abortion, yet that seems to be import of the report which indicates that she was imprisoned immediately after the deed and no other crime is even hinted at in the report. Before one tries to make too much of the fact that the first person reported hung for an abortion was a woman, one should note that in an Irish case a decade earlier the defendant sentenced to hang was a man.[114] The Irish court in question was also applying the common law. The defendant, John of Kyltavenan, was also convicted of burglary and rape, but these were not then capital offenses.

One might suspect, particularly as the English court system evolved, that the recital of physical assault was merely a typical common law verbal formula not meant to be taken as the recital of real events. For example, the phrase *vi et armis* ("by force and arms") in the writ of trespass evolved over a rather short time from a description of actual facts into a jurisdictional fiction.[115] The freshness and specificity of the recited facts, limited as the recitals are, suggests, however, that we are not dealing with mere formula. If so, few of these cases can have represented voluntary abortions into which a woman had been pressured or which, for unstated reasons, the woman thereafter regretted enough to bring an appeal or to cooperate in a prosecution. As a result, some pro-abortion historians have recently taken to dismissing these early cases as involving crimes against the mother rather than prosecutions for causing an abortion.[116] This distorts both what the various authors wrote, and what the courts decided.

The language of the case reports, as with Bracton and Fleta,[117] focuses on the injury to the child, often terming the crime homicide regardless of the injury to the mother; even the usually terse language of the plea rolls demonstrates a focus on the unborn child itself, with the child's death repeatedly recited as the crime and not treated as a mere incident to a crime against the mother. The same can be said of early and medieval Christian condemnations of abortion.[118] Nor is it clear that any crime was committed against the mother.[119] The mother's right to bring an appeal did not represent anything more than the usual rule that the next of kin is the proper party to appeal a homicide.[120] At a time when neither rape nor mayhem were indictable felonies,[121] even a serious battery of a woman without her death would not have been indictable

113. Rex v. Haule, JUST 1/547A, m.20d (London Eyre 1321). The translation from Latin is by John Baker.

114. Rex v. Kyltavenan (Cork, Ireland 1311), Irish Justiciary Roles, *supra* note 16, at 193. The Irish courts applied the English common law. *See* G.J. Hand, English Law in Ireland, 1290–1324 (1967).

115. *See* Baker, *supra* note 22, at 71–75; 8 Holdsworth, *supra* note 7, at 421–22A; Milsom, *supra* note 21, at 61–65; Plucknett, *supra* note 22, at 369–73, 460–61.

116. *See, e.g.,* Beverly Wildung Harrison, Our Right to Choose: Toward a New Ethic of Abortion 124–25 (1983). Often these cases are dismissed in an off-hand remark rather than an actual analysis or argument. *See* Sylvia Law, *Conversations between Historians and the Constitution,* 12 The Pub. Historian 11, 13 (1990).

117. See the text *supra* at notes 57–61.

118. *See, e.g.,* Harrison, *supra* note 116, at 130–44; Donald Judges, Hard Choices, Lost Voices 87–90 (1993). *See generally* John Connery, Abortion: The Development of the Roman Catholic Perspective 33–167 (1977); Grisez, *supra* note 19, at 137–55; John Noonan, jr., *An Almost Absolute Value in History,* in The Morality of Abortion: Legal and Historical Perspectives 1, 7–16 (John Noonan, jr., ed. 1970).

119. 2 Bracton, *supra* note 30, at 388–89; 1 Britton, *supra* note 32, at 109; Fleta, *supra* note 39, at 80–81.

120. *See also* Glanvill, *supra* note 32, at 174.

121. Baker, *supra* note 22, at 603; 3 Holdsworth, *supra* note 7, at 316; Plucknett, *supra* note 22, at 426, 443, 451, 456; 2 Pollock & Maitland, *supra* note 22, at 490–91.

as a felony. Rape was made an indictable felony by a statute adopted in 1285,[122] but *Rex v. Code*[123] was prosecuted in 1281, and the case was not alone.[124] And in fact, fathers brought several appeals for abortion without the death of the mother.[125]

# Cyril Means, Jr., and the "Twinslayer's Case"

*"Religion!" she said angrily. "We have no need of it.... We have something far better. We have history."*

—Isaac Asimov[126]

At first, the purveyors of the current myths of abortion history did not seek to dismiss the cases as crimes against the mother rather than against the child. At the time the Supreme Court decided *Roe v. Wade,* only two of these early cases were known: *Rex v. de Bourton*[127] and *Rex v. Anonymous.*[128] Law professor Cyril Means, jr., in his attempt to demonstrate his claim that abortion was not a common-law crime, seized upon these two cases as proof that even violent abortions against the will of the mother were not crimes. Those cases deserve close attention if only because Means' reading of them has been so pivotal to creating the current myths and, indeed, to the formulation of Justice Blackmun's opinion in *Roe v. Wade.*[129] Today there can be little doubt that Bracton and Fleta were correct, and Means wrong.

Means designed his research to support the political task of changing the abortion laws; no wonder his history of abortion was neither objective nor accurate.[130] Means wrote his first history article as the lawyer member of the Governor's Select Committee to Review the State's Abortion Laws ("the Froesel Commission") appointed by Governor Rockefeller to review New York's abortion laws.[131] More importantly, he was then general counsel for the National Association for the Repeal of Abortion Laws (NARAL—later the National Abortion Rights Action League, and the National Abortion and Reproductive Rights Action League, and now NARAL Pro-Choice America), and was still devoted to the "movement" when he wrote his second article.[132] Means' research was funded by the Association for the Study of Abortion (ASA), another important

---

122. *Statute of Westminster II* ch. 34 (1285).

123. Quoted *supra* at note 93.

124. Rex v. Brente, JUST 1/186, m.30 (Devon Eyre 1281); Rex v. Cheney, JUST 1/323, m.47d (Hertfordshire Eyre 1278); Rex v. Scharp, 1276 EYRE, *supra* note 16, at 23 (no. 76); Rex v. Cordwaner, 1276 EYRE, *supra,* at 18 (no. 62).

125. Boleheved's Appeal, JUST 1/112, m.9d (Cornwall Eyre 1284); Hervest's Appeal, JUST 1/789, m.26d (Hampshire Eyre 1281) (joint appeal of husband and wife); de Pekering's Appeal, JUST 1/369, m.36 (Kent Eyre 1279); Gras's Appeal, 1276 EYRE, *supra* note 16, at 73–74 (no. 261) (joint appeal of husband and wife); Sorel's Appeal, *id.* at 61 (no. 222); Swayn's Appeal, JUST 1/359, m.36 (1249); Orscherd's Appeal, JUST 1/174, m.40d (1249?); St. Alban's Appeal (1244), 1244 EYRE, *supra* note 80, at 36 (no. 84); Modi's Appeal (1221), ROLLS OF THE JUSTICES IN EYRE, *supra* note 86, at 560–61 (no. 1336); Sauter's Appeal (1221), GLOUCESTER PLEAS, *supra* note 80, at 16 (no. 69); Burel's Appeal (1202), SELECT PLEAS OF THE CROWN, *supra* note 77, at 11 (no. 26).

126. ISAAC ASIMOV, PRELUDE TO FOUNDATION 199 (Bantam ed. 1989) (emphasis in the original).

127. Y.B. Mich. 1 Edw. 3, f. 23, pl. 28 (K.B. 1327), quoted *infra* at notes 140–41.

128. (K.B. 1348), ANTHONY FITZHERBERT, GRAUNDE ABRIDGEMENT tit. Corone, f. 268, pl. 263 (1st ed. 1516) [K.B. 1348], quoted *infra* at note 164.

129. 410 U.S. 113 (1973). See the text *supra* at notes 8–9.

130. KEOWN, *supra* note 13, at 3–11; Dellapenna, *supra* note 13.

131. Means I, *supra* note 10, at 411 n.\*. *See also* Means II, *supra* note 10, at 335 n.\*, 353.

132. MARIAN FAUX, *ROE V. WADE:* THE UNTOLD STORY OF THE LANDMARK SUPREME COURT DECISION THAT MADE ABORTION LEGAL 73, 81, 216–19, 222–23, 234, 237, 240, 289–92 (1988). Faux's book was written with the full cooperation of those who argued on behalf of Norma McCorvey (Roe) in *Roe v. Wade* and, as

branch of the "movement" for abortion reform.[133] Means, in fact, wrote as a highly committed advocate, not as a scholar engaged in even a minimally objective inquiry into the history of abortion. He revealed neither the funding nor his advocacy position in his published "scholarship."[134]

NARAL and ASA were both actively involved in preparing the pro-choice argument in *Roe v. Wade*, including coordinating *amicus* briefs supporting the claim of a constitutional freedom to abort.[135] Means presented his radical revision of the history of abortion—a history that had been unquestioned for centuries—to the Supreme Court in one of the *amicus* briefs. Sarah Weddington, the attorney who argued for "Jane Roe" in the case, has stated that the Justices had copies of Means' articles on the bench with them during the oral arguments.[136] The effort was successful. Justice Blackmun, in writing the majority opinion in *Roe*, relied heavily and uncritically on Means' history, citing Means some seven times (and no other legal historian).[137]

When Means began to investigate the original sources for the received common law tradition, few sources were known. Historian Shelley Gavigan, writing in 1984, described the common law sources on abortion "very close to non-existent."[138] Nor (judging by his results) did Means undertake any serious effort to discover additional early material.[139] Instead, he was content to reinterpret the six cases then known from the era before the adoption of the first abortion statute in England in 1803. Most of these cases had been standard references since the work of Sir Edward Coke in the seventeenth century.[140] Means anachronistically read this handful of cases as if they were written by and for modern day lawyers. He made no effort to discover what the documents would have meant to lawyers (or others) when they were written, and with a strong tendency to disregard rather than to explain anything inconvenient to his thesis.

Means dubbed the earliest and most important of the few cases then known, *Rex v. de Bourton*, the "The Twinslayer's Case." This text is considerably more complete than the plea rolls of the prior century, for *de Bourton* comes from what is known as a "Yearbook." The Yearbooks were a peculiarly English phenomenon purporting to be a verbatim report, in law

---

one admiring reviewer put it, her book exhibits a clear bias "in favor of the pro-choice decision in *Roe v. Wade*." Francine Adkins Tone, *Book Review*, 19 Lincoln L. Rev. 67, 69 (1990).

133. Faux, *supra* note 132, at 216–19.

134. This is a prime example of the sort of advocacy scholarship denounced by Mary Ann Glendon and Ronald Collins. *See* Mary Ann Glendon, A Nation under Lawyers: How the Crisis in the Legal Profession Is Transforming American Society 208 (1994); Ronald Collins, *A Letter on Scholarly Ethics*, 45 J. Legal Educ. 139 (1995). Skeptics of advocacy scholarship occasionally deride those who denounce such scholarship for not naming names. *See, e.g.,* Sanford Levinson, *Book Review* (of Glendon, *supra*), 45 J. Legal Educ. 143, 146 (1995); Michael Sean Quinn, *"Scholarly Ethics": A Response*, 46 J. Legal Educ. 110 (1996). Cyril Means more than satisfies their demand.

135. Faux, *supra* note 132, at 234–38.

136. Sarah Weddington, *Introduction*, in Abortion in the Seventies: Proceedings of the Western Regional Conference on Abortion, Denver, Colorado February 27–29, 1976, at 187, 189 (Dr. Warren Hern & Bonnie Andrikopoulos eds. 1977).

137. 410 U.S. at 136–39. *See also* Wolfgang Saxon, *Obituary: Cyril C. Means, 73, A Specialist in Laws Regarding Abortion*, N.Y. Times, Oct. 6, 1992, at A15. Edward Steegman noted the inbalance in Justice Blackmun's review of history without observing its source; instead, he suggested that the inbalance was a direct result of Blackmun's exaggerated distaste for "religious intolerance" to which the Justice would apparently attribute all historical prohibition of abortion. Edward Steegman, Note, *Of History and Due Process*, 63 Ind. L.J. 369, 390–94, 396–97 (1987).

138. Gavigan, *supra* note 12, at 20. *See also* Glanville Williams, The Sanctity of Life and the Criminal Law 209–13 (1957).

139. Compare Means' assertion that no legislative history existed for *Lord Ellenborough's Act*, 43 Geo. III, c. 59 (1803), the first statutory prohibition of abortion in the common law legal tradition, with John Keown's extensive and careful legislative history of the Act. Keown, *supra* note 13, at 12–25; Means II, *supra* note 10, at 358. *See also* Gavigan, *supra* note 12, at 30–34.

140. Coke, *supra* note 16, at 50–51.

French, of the legal discussions in the English royal courts.[141] The Yearbooks undoubtedly were not full transcripts of all that was said in a case, but their truncated accounts are one of the very few sources from anywhere in Europe in which we can hear "the cut and thrust of medieval debate between named people."[142] The Yearbooks appear to have been lawyers' notes of what they observed in court transcribed for the edification of the law students of the time, although there is some uncertainty about how precisely they came to be written.[143] The Yearbooks began in the later thirteenth century, and we have a continuous dated series from 1307. There is some doubt as to how they originally circulated, with the modern compilations that we now rely on being arranged centuries later.[144] From these often scant, but lively, records derives the common law tradition of case reporting that is such a central feature of the system today.[145]

Means made his methodology clear through his treatment of *de Bourton*. A full translation of the case as then known is:

> A writ issued to the sheriff of Gloucester to apprehend one D. who, according to the testimony of Sir G. Scrop, is supposed to have beaten a woman in an advanced state of pregnancy who was carrying twins, whereupon directly afterwards one twin died, and she was delivered of the other, who was baptized John by name, and two days afterwards, through the injury he had sustained, the child died: and the indictment was returned before Sir G. Scrop, and D. came, and pled Not guilty, and for the reason that the Justices were unwilling to adjudge this thing a felony, the accused was released to mainpernors,[146] and then the argument was adjourned *sine die*. Thus the writ issued, as before stated, and Sir G. Scrop rehearsed the entire case, and how he [D.] came and pled.
>
> Herle: to the sheriff: Produce the body, *etc.* And the sheriff returned the writ to the bailiff of the franchise of such place, who said, that the same fellow was taken by the mayor of Bristol, but of the cause of this arrest we are wholly ignorant.[147]

Means provided his readers with a virtually identical translation.[148] He made one significant change, however, which would likely affect a reader's perception of the case. Means dropped the last sentence of the first paragraph and the entire second paragraph to the very end of an eleven-paragraph-long footnote appended to the translation of the case.[149] Means somewhat lamely excused his omission of the remainder of the text from his analysis on the grounds that neither he nor Samuel Thorne (then Harvard's legal historian) could explain its significance.

Means' editing enabled him to present the case as having ended with a dismissal based on a judicial conclusion that there had been no felony.[150] Even the full, albeit imperfect, rendition of the case as then available indicates to the contrary that de Bourton pleaded "not guilty" to an in-

---

141. *See generally* BAKER, *supra* note 22, at 204–06; Baker, *Records, supra* note 26, at 18; Seipp, *supra* note 30, at 178–80. On the foibles and evolution of "law French," see J.H. Baker, *Le Brickbat que narrowly mist,* 100 L.Q. REV. 544 (1984); J.H. Baker, *The Three Languages of the Common Law,* 43 McGILL L.J. 5 (1998).

142. Baker, *Records, supra* note 26, at 18.

143. *Id.* at 8–10; J.H. Baker, *Records, Reports, and the Origins of Case-Law in England,* in JUDICIAL RECORDS, LAW REPORTS, AND THE GROWTH OF CASE LAW 15, 21, 25, 33–34 (J.H. Baker ed. 1989).

144. Baker, *Records, supra* note 26, at 19.

145. L.W. ABBOTT, LAW REPORTING IN ENGLAND, 1485–1585, at 18–20 (1973).

146. Persons who would guarantee a defendant's appearance in further proceedings, in effect an early form of bail called "mainprise." *See* BLACK'S LAW DICTIONARY, *supra* note 90, at 1105.

147. Rex v. de Bourton, Y.B. Mich. 1 Edw. 3, f. 23, pl. 28 (K.B. 1327). The translation from law French is by John Baker.

148. Means II, *supra* note 10, at 337.

149. *Id.* at 337–38 n.4.

150. *Id.,* at 338.

dictment for killing one or both children without challenging the legal sufficiency of the charge. The defendant was bound over for a later hearing that was never completed, apparently because the defendant had been taken to answer for another crime. Thus, at best, *Rex v. de Bourton* could be taken as an inconclusive report on whether abortion under the circumstances was a crime—not, as Means would have it, proof that abortion was never a crime.[151] Since Means wrote, additional research has further undermined his conclusion that abortion was not a crime. Not only do the many similar cases already described directly contradict Means' reading of *de Bourton*, but further research on that case has thrown doubt on the text of that case on which he relied.

Prominent English legal historian John Baker, of Cambridge University,[152] has turned up the surviving original court records of the case and four manuscript versions of the Yearbook report that are about two centuries older than the printed version on which everyone, including Means, heretofore has relied.[153] The manuscript versions of the Yearbook all agree with each other and differ in some significant respects from the printed version.[154] The level of agreement among the manuscripts is remarkable. After all, English legal historian Percy Winfield had noted some 70 years ago that the Yearbooks "differed from one another again and again" so that "[e]very citation would begin a new dispute."[155] That the manuscripts differ from the printed version is also not surprising. Winfield also noted that the Yearbooks were well-known to be full of "gross blunders," including spellings, pagination, and dates: "To find a page turned upside down is a cause not of criticism but of thankfulness that the error is nothing worse."[156] The printed Yearbook report was simply a corrupted text. The original text reads:

A writ issued to the sheriff of Gloucestershire to take one D., who, by the testimony of Sir Geoffrey Scrop, is supposed to have beaten a woman great with two children, so that immediately afterwards one of the children died, and she was delivered of the other, which was baptized by the name of Joan,[157] but died two days later from the injury which the child had; and the indictment was returned before Sir Geoffrey Scrop; and D. came and pleaded Not guilty; and because the justices were not minded to treat[158] this thing as a felony, the indictee was released on mainprise and then this matter remained with a day set, and so the writ was issued as above, and it said that [by testimony of] Sir Geoffrey Scrop [*etc.*, and] recited the whole of the case [as above], and how he came and pleaded *etc.*, [and that the sheriff should have caused his body to come *etc.*][159] And the sheriff returned the writ to the bailiffs of the franchise of such and such a place, who said that the person in question had been taken by the mayor of Bristol, but they

---

151. *See also* KEOWN, *supra* note 13, at 4; Dellapenna, *supra* note 13, at 368–70.

152. Dr. Baker did this work at the behest of Philip Rafferty; Mr. Rafferty kindly shared the results with me.

153. The earliest printings of the Yearbooks occurred sometime after 1481. WINFIELD, *supra* note 19, at 173–74. The edition that has become the standard version since its printing appeared between 1640 and 1678, although printed versions of the King's Bench trials of the reign of Edward III had appeared as early as 1516. *Id.* at 175.

154. Lincoln's Inn MS. Hale 72 at fo. 86v; Lincoln's Inn MS. Hale 116 at fo. 3; Lincoln's Inn MS. Hale 137(2) at fo. 11; Bodleian Library Oxford MS. Bodl. 363 at fo. 9v. Dr. Baker's letter describing his search is published in 1 RAFFERTY, *supra* note 74, at 520–23.

155. WINFIELD, *supra* note 19, at 150.

156. *Id.* at 177–78.

157. "John" in the printed version and in some of the manuscripts; the original court records show the name as Joan.

158. *"d'agarder"* ("to award") in all four MSS.; *"adjudge"* only in the printed version.

159. Garbled in the printed version. Note that the printed version here introduces the name of C.J. William Herle of the Common Pleas, apparently through error as the name appears in none of the manuscript versions. Means relies on the supposed presence of Herle to discredit the crucial last paragraph of the printed version of the Yearbook, a paragraph that entirely undermines his reading of the case.

were wholly unaware of the reason for the taking *etc.* [Therefore, a writ issued to the mayor of Bristol to cause the body to come, together with the cause *etc.*][160]

The original Yearbook texts make clear that the entire proceeding was an inquiry about why he did not appear for trial. Even the passage in the printed version in which the judges appear unwilling to consider the acts to be a felony appears in the original in a more ambiguous light. Here we are told that the judges were unwilling to treat the acts as a felony and therefore permitted mainprise—an early form of bail in which other persons took responsibility for the accused's appearance at trial, suffering forfeiture of a fine should the accused fail to appear.[161] The passage in context suggests that the judges were discussing whether de Bourton's acts were done with "felonious intent" (which would make the crime non-bailable),[162] rather than whether it was a crime. Such uncertainty about basic matters is only to be expected. The King's Bench had only begun to hear criminal cases in 1323,[163] a bare four years before de Bourton's case was considered. The original court records cast yet a different light on the matter:

Gloucestershire. The lord king has sent his writ to the sheriff of Gloucestershire in these words:

Edward by grace of God king of England, lord of Ireland and duke of Acquitaine, to the sheriff of Gloucestershire, greeting! Because we have learned by the certificate of our beloved and faithful Geoffrey le Scrop, our chief justice, that Richard de Bourton has been indicted for that he entered the house of William Carles, tailor, at Bristol, and assaulted Alice, wife of the same William, being there greatly pregnant with two children, and with his hands beat and ill treated her, and violently knocked her to the ground, and with his feat so trampled upon the ground [*sic*] that he feloniously killed one of the aforesaid children in the belly of the same Alice its mother, and broke the head and arm of the other of the same children so that it was forthwith born and baptized by the name of Joan, and immediately after receiving her baptism died from the injury aforesaid; and that the foregoing matters still remain undetermined before ourself; and that this Richard had a day before us at a certain day now past for hearing the jury of the country on which, for good and ill, he put himself concerning the felony aforesaid, by mainprise of John le Taverner of Bristol and others named in the said certificate, who mainprised to have him before us at the said term; and on behalf of the selfsame Richard we are given to understand that by reason of the foregoing he has been taken, since that mainprise, and detained in our prison of Bristol, on account of which he could not come before us on the aforesaid day to stand to right upon the foregoing according to the law and custom of our realm: We, willing what is just to be done upon the foregoing, command you (as we commanded before) that if the same Richard is detained in the aforesaid prison by reason of the foregoing and not otherwise, and if he

---

160. The bracketed language was omitted in the printed version, except for the one noted as garbled..

161. Black's Law Dictionary, *supra* note 90, at 1105.

162. *See generally* E. De Haas, Antiquities of Bail: Origin and Historical Development in Criminal Cases to the Year 1275, at 68–69 (1940); W.A. Morris, The Medieval English Sheriff 232–33 (1927); Hurnard, *supra* note 94, at 50, 78–84, 109–10, 265, 281 n.2., 341–52 (1965). *See, e.g.,* Rex v. Abbot (1329), 97 Selden Soc'y 181, 218 (1983). For an acquittal of a criminal charge based on an injurious abortion not done with felonious intent, see *Rex v. Cheney,* JUST 1/323, m.47d (Hertfordshire Eyre 1278) (the defendant was amerced in trespass for an accidental abortion caused by the defendant's horse). *See also* Rex v. Luvet (1329), 97 Selden Soc'y 181 (1983); Rex v. Bodekesham, 58 Selden Soc'y cxiii (1939). Murder remained an offense for which bail was not permitted until the nineteenth century and bail was exceptional for any capital case. Baker, Legal Profession, *supra* note 30, at 281; 4 William Blackstone, Commentaries on the Laws of England *296 (1765).

163. G.O. Sayles, *Scripta Diversa* 230 (1982). On the origins and early functions of the King's Bench, see *Id.* at 222–35.

finds you sufficient mainpernors who mainprise him before us in a fortnight from Michaelmas day wheresoever we should then be in England, to do and receive what our court should decide in the foregoing, then cause the selfsame Richard to be meanwhile delivered from prison by the mainprise aforesaid. And have you there the names of those mainpernors, and this writ. And if the same Richard is indicted for any other felonies or trespasses in your county, then without delay send us distinctly and openly under your seal the tenor of the aforesaid indictment at the aforesaid day, that we may do further therein what by the law and custom aforesaid should be done, or else signify unto us the reason why you will not or cannot carry out our command heretofore directed unto you. Witness my self at Northallerton, the 14th day of July in the first year of our reign [1327].

By virtue of which writ, the sheriff (namely, Thomas de Rodbergh) returns that he commanded Everard Fraunceys and Robert Grene, bailiffs of the liberty of the vill of Bristol, who answered him that Richard de Bourton, lately indicted for the death of Joan, daughter of William Carles, tailor, at Bristol, as is contained in the writ, has not been taken by them the said bailiffs nor is for that reason detained in prison, but that he has been taken and detained by Roger Rurtels the mayor of the aforesaid vill for certain reasons which are unknown to them the said bailiffs etc.

And, after inspection of the aforesaid writ and return etc., the mayor and bailiffs of the vill of Bristol are commanded that if the same Richard finds sufficient mainpernors to be before the king in a fortnight from St. Hilary wheresoever etc. to hear the aforesaid jury and to do further and receive what the king's court should decide for him, then they should cause the selfsame Richard to be meanwhile delivered from the aforesaid prison by the above-mentioned mainprise. And if he is indicted for any other felonies or trespasses before them in the vill aforesaid, then they should distinctly and openly under their seals send that indictment (if any there be) or else the cause for which he was taken, to the king at the day aforesaid upon the incumbent peril, so that the lord king further etc. what is to be done etc.

At which day the mayor and bailiffs of the vill of Bristol return that the aforesaid Richard de Bourton did not or would not find sufficient mainpernors for being before the lord king at this day, namely in the quindene of St. Hilary etc., and to do and receive what is commanded in the writ, as a result of which they did nothing further in executing the writ etc. And because the same mayor and bailiffs have not returned here before the king the names of themselves according to the form of the statute etc., and also have not answered etc. for what reason the aforesaid Richard de Bourton has been taken, as in the lord king's writ directed them therein was commanded, nor whether or not the aforesaid Richard is indicted for any other felonies or trespasses before them in the vill aforesaid, the same mayor and bailiffs (namely, John le Romeseie, mayor, and Hugh de Langebrigge and Stephan Lespcier, bailiffs etc.) are in mercy. And they are assessed by the justices at 40s. And the sheriff is commanded that he should not omit by reason of the liberty of the aforesaid vill to enter the same etc., and if the same Richard should find him sufficient mainpernors to mainprise to have him before the king in a fortnight from Easter day wheresoever etc. to hear the jury aforesaid etc. and further to do etc., then he should cause the selfsame Richard to be meanwhile delivered from the aforesaid prison by mainprise aforesaid etc. The sheriff is also commanded that he should not omit on account of the liberty to cause the aforesaid mayor and bailiffs to come before the king at the said term to answer the king for the return etc. Also the mayor and bailiffs are commanded that if the aforesaid Richard is indicted for any felonies and trespasses before them in the aforesaid vill, then they should distinctly and openly under their seals send that indictment (if any there be) or else the cause for which he was taken, to the king at the day aforesaid *etc.* so that further *etc.*[164]

This rather straightforward document contains no hint of doubt about the criminality of de Bourton's acts. De Bourton was charged with a felony, although the record is not clear whether the charged felony was the killing of the child Joan who died immediately after her birth or of both children.[165] The entire inquiry was directed at whether de Bourton could be found and brought to trial.

At the point the actual court record takes up the story, de Bourton has already pleaded "not guilty" and been mainprised (bailed). Chief Justice Scrop of the King's Bench issued a writ in the new king's name. Edward III had come to the throne in 1327 through a palace coup against Edward II. Although the new king was a teenager, he quickly asserted himself against the coup plotters and went on to become one of England's strongest monarchs. Whether he might have been strong enough so early in his reign as to have personally influenced the *de Bourton* proceeding is unclear, but unlikely.

Scrop ordered the sheriff of Gloucester to take a mainprise for de Bourton's appearance at the next term of court only to be told that de Bourton had been arrested by the Mayor of Bristol for some other, unspecified crime. Chief Justice Scrop was so intent on bringing de Bourton to trial that he ordered the Mayor to present de Bourton at the Hilary term of court in 1328 with the mayor's charges to be sent to Scrop's court for investigation and trial. When the Mayor failed to appear with de Bourton, Scrop ordered the sheriff to enter Bristol to take the mainprise himself, fining the mayor and his aids 40 shillings for failure to produce de Bourton for trial at the Easter term (April 1328). The next recorded proceeding against de Bourton carries on the same story:

> Gloucestershire. The jury at the suit of the lord king to make recognition *etc.* whether Richard de Bourton of Bristol is guilty of the death of Joan, daughter of William Carles, tailor of Bristol, feloniously slain in the suburbs of Bristol, whereof he has been indicted (as appears to the king by a certain indictment lately made thereof before the coroners of the vill of Bristol, and which the king caused to come before him), is put in respite until the octaves of St. John the Baptist wheresoever *etc.*, for want of jurors, because none [came] *etc.* Therefore, let the sheriff have the bodies of all the jurors before the king at the said term, *etc.* And let the aforesaid Richard meanwhile be released by the mainprise which heretofore found, from day to day until *etc.* And the sheriff is commanded that except for them *etc.* he should put in as many and such *etc.* and have them before the king at the said term *etc.*[166]

Again the royal agents were unable to bring de Bourton to trial, this time for the failure of the jury to attend the court. At the time of *de Bourton,* a jury still functioned more like a collective witness than like a modern trier of fact.[167] There still was no hint of any doubt of the validity of the criminal charge. The final record of the actual proceedings against de Bourton again

---

164. Rex v. de Bourton, K.B. 27/270, Rex m.9 (Mich. term 1327). The translation from Latin is by John Baker.

165. The original indictment apparently did not survive; at least no one thus far has found it despite considerable effort. Dr. Baker has expressed the opinion that the expressions in the reports of the later proceedings against de Bourton suggesting that only the death of the girl Joan was charged might have been clerical shorthand. *Letter from Dr. J.H. Baker to Mr. Philip Rafferty,* in 1 Rafferty, *supra* note 74, at 521.

166. Rex v. de Bourton, K.B. 27/242, Rex m.9 (Easter term 1328). The translation from Latin is by Dr. Baker.

167. *See generally* Baker, *supra* note 22, at 86–90, 579–82; 9 Holdsworth, *supra* note 7, at 131–32; Plucknett, *supra* note 22, at 81, 107–12, 120–31; Radin, *supra* note 22, at 204–16.

shows no conclusive outcome, but for reasons utterly divorced from any supposed defect in the charge:

> Gloucestershire. The jury at the suit of the lord king to make recognition of whether or not Richard de Bourton of Bristol is guilty of the death of Joan, daughter of William Carles, tailor of Bristol, feloniously slain in the suburbs of Bristol, whereof he is indicted—as appears to the king by a certain indictment lately made thereof before the coroners of the vill of Bristol, and which the king has caused to come before [himself] *etc.*—is put in respite until one month from Michaelmas day, wheresoever *etc.*, for want of jurors, because none [came] *etc.* Therefore let the sheriff have the bodies of all the jurors before the king at the said date *etc.* And let the aforesaid Richard meanwhile be released by the mainprise which he previously found, from day to day *etc.* Afterwards, the same term, the aforesaid Richard came and proffered a charter of the present lord king for pardon of the aforesaid felony, which is enrolled in Hilary term in the first year of the reign of our present king. Therefore he [is to go] thereof *sine die etc.*[168]

As this report indicates, the jurors were punished for failing to show up for the trial; de Bourton, on the other hand, had obtained a royal pardon that precluded further proceedings against him. At the time in question, pardons were being issued to many on condition that they agree to serve in the Scottish wars. De Bourton appears to have been exempted from such a condition,[169] perhaps indicating that he was well connected at court. Such a connection also would explain why both mainpernors and jurors were willing to face fines rather than take the responsibility of acting against de Bourton to bring him to trial. In any event, the king did not pardon persons who were not properly charged with crimes.

The original records in *de Bourton* indicate clearly that the matter was undoubtedly a felony, and neither the problems in producing de Bourton for trial nor the failure to convict in any way supports a claim that his acts were not considered criminal. The factual question of whether de Bourton had committed a felony was still open in 1328, well after the proceedings incompletely reported in the Yearbooks, yet no one seems to have expressed any doubt that if he had done what he was charged with, he was guilty of a felony. Means supposition that the case demonstrates that abortion was not a crime in the fourteenth century was not supported by printed version of *Rex v. de Bourton,* and is utterly inconsistent with the original records and reports of the case.

Means dubbed his second fourteenth-century case, *Rex v. Anonymous,* the "Abortionist's Case." As the actual name of the case indicates, we actually know very little this case. The brief report of the case reads in full:

> One was indicted for that he killed a child in its mother's belly, and the opinion [was] that he shall not be arraigned on this since no name of baptism was in the indictment, and also it is hard to know whether he killed it or not *etc.*[170]

This does look like a decision that abortion could not be prosecuted as a crime in 1348 for want of a baptismal name. This report harkens back to the opinion in *Britton* early in the century.[171] Cyril Means, jr., certainly argued that the "Abortionist's Case" proved conclusively that

---

168. Rex v. de Bourton, K.B. 27/273, Rex m.12d (Octave of St. John, 2 Edw. III, 1328). The translation from Latin is by John Baker.

169. Dr. Baker found the pardon in Calendar of Patent Rolls 1327–1330, at 113: Pat. 1 Edw. III, pt. 2, m.17 (May 29, 1327).

170. Rex v. Anonymous, Fitzherbert, *supra* note 128, tit. Corone, f. 268, pl. 263 (1st ed. 1516) [K.B. 1348]. The translation from law French by John Baker.

171. Britton, *supra* note 32, at 114 (quoted *supra* at note 62).

172. Means II, *supra* note 10, at 339–43.

this case is from a secondary source written nearly two centuries after the purported decision.[173] The standard source for modern researchers—Sir Anthony Fitzherbert—included the case in his collection of materials yet another century later. We know very little of how Fitzherbert's cases were assembled. In fact, there appears to be good reason to doubt that Fitzherbert had much to do with assembling the abridgment that bears his name.[174]

If Means had investigated, he would have found that the lack of a baptismal name did not preclude an indictment for murder for that crime originated as a prosecution for the killing of an unidentifiable person.[175] Indeed, a rule as suggested in this *Rex v. Anonymous* would have precluded prosecutions for the infanticide of unbaptized infants—which clearly was not the law, as was shown in yet another case denominated *Rex v. Anonymous* decided in the very same year.[176] "Readers" at the Inns of Court were still telling their students nearly two centuries later that indictments would lie for the murder of victims whose name could not be determined.[177]

The Readings are strong evidence of the real state of the criminal law of the time. Although Readings (lectures on the common law) have survived dating back to the late fourteenth century, they are rarely in good shape much before the middle of the fifteenth century.[178] More than 30 Readings on criminal law survive from the period 1485 to 1545, a time when the Readings played a central role in developing the common law of crimes during this period.[179] At a time when reports of actual cases were rare and unreliable, the Readings in the Inns of Court formed the major corpus of the *communis eruditio* (common learning) that was understood as the common law by bench and bar; indeed, one could not become a serjeant, and hence possibly a judge, unless one had been a Reader at an Inn.[180] Thomas Littleton, in his famous *Tenures,* did not cite cases but rather readings.[181]

In light of this evidence, the most the quoted case can stand for is a comment on the primitive state of forensic medicine in 1348 (or 1516), and not about the criminal nature of abortion. Indeed, the later Lord Chief Justice Mansfield[182] would state expressly, in 1808, that the difficulties encountered in prosecuting abortions before the nineteenth century had purely resulted from the difficulty of proving that the child was in fact alive at the time of the act.[183] Further-

---

173. The source appears to be NICHOLAS STATHAM, ABRIDGMENT fo. 58v, no. 91 (ca. 1490). Whether Statham actually assembled this abridgment is as uncertain as his personal name and the date of the book's publication. WINFIELD, *supra* note 19, at 206–20.

174. GROSSMAN, *supra* note 49, at 12–13; WINFIELD, *supra* note 19, at 224–32; THORNE, *supra* note 29, at 218 n.8.

175. See the text *supra* at notes 63–64.

176. Rex v. Anonymous, KB 9/156/79 (1348).

177. *See, e.g., John Baldwin's Reading at Grey's Inn on the Statute of Marlborough, c.25 (murdrum),* Camb. Univ. Lib. Ms. Hh. 2.6, fo. 92v (ca. 1460); *Thomas Morow's Reading at the Inner Temple on the Statute of Westminster I* (Inner Temple 1503), *in* B.H. PUTNAM, EARLY TREATISES ON JUSTICE OF THE PEACE IN THE FIFTEENTH AND SIXTEENTH CENTURIES 379 (7 Oxford Stud. in Soc. & Legal Hist. 1924).

178. BAKER, LEGAL PROFESSION, *supra* note 30, at 14–16, 19–22.

179. *Id.* at 313–15, 326, 471–74.

180. BAKER, *supra* note 22, at 182–85, 595; BAKER, LEGAL PROFESSION, *supra* note 30, at 124–50; J.H. BAKER, THE THIRD UNIVERSITY OF ENGLAND: THE INNS OF COURT AND THE COMMON LAW TRADITION 16–20 (1990) ("BAKER, THE THIRD UNIVERSITY"); 4 HOLDSWORTH, *supra* note 7, at 270–71; PLUCKNETT, *supra* note 22, at 225; RADIN, *supra* note 22, at 251; W.C. RICHARDSON, A HISTORY OF THE INNS OF COURT (1978); J.H. Baker, *Introduction: Moots as Exercises in Pleading: The Degrees of Bencher and Barrister,* in READINGS AND MOOTS AT THE INNS OF COURT IN THE 15TH CENTURY (105 SELDEN SOC'Y) liv–lvii, lxxii (Samuel Thorne & J.H. Baker eds. 1989).

181. T. LITTLETON, TENURES § 481 (1591). *See also* BAKER, THE THIRD UNIVERSITY, *supra* note 180, at 19; EDWARD COKE, FIRST INSTITUTE ("*Coke on Littleton*") § 280b (1628).

182. Chief Justice of Common Pleas; not the great Chief Justice of the King's Bench of the later eighteenth century.

183. Rex v. Pizzy (Suffolk Assizes 1808). *See* WILLIAM NOTCUTT, THE REMARKABLE TRIAL AT LARGE OF WILLIAM PIZZY AND MARY CODD AT THE ASSIZES HOLDEN AT BURY ST. EDMUNDS ON THURSDAY AUGUST 11,

more, the anomalous statements in *Rex v. Anonymous,* along with the utter lack of facts and the two centuries between its supposed occurrence and the first report of the case throw some doubt on whether it is even the report of an actual case. The actual source appears to have been a virtual identical passage in a collection of precedents published in 1348.[184] This book consists mostly of the "holdings" of various cases, but there is no authority provided for this particular passage. Instead the passage opens with the word "query," suggesting it was simply a speculation by the compiler of the precedents.[185]

# The Canon Law of Abortion

*Few discoveries are more irritating than those which expose the pedigree of ideas.*

—Lord Acton[186]

If credible evidence demonstrates that injurious abortions were serious crimes in the early Middle Ages, what of the ingestive abortions that Bracton and Fleta also described as homicides[187] but which simply do not appear in the records of the law courts? A large part of the answer is that ingestive abortions simply were not common during this early period.[188] Such a conclusion might suggest that records of appeals or indictments for such abortions exist but, being rarer, have not been found. This is a distinct possibility given the utter lack of known cases supporting Bracton and Fleta as recently as 1984.[189] One would be surprised if ingestive abortions were not at least attempted during this era, and even more surprised if those attempts had left no trace in the English legal system if such abortions were indeed illegal.

Ingestive abortions, when attempted, in fact were not ignored by the authorities. The ecclesiastical authorities prosecuted such abortions fairly routinely as witchcraft.[190] The clerical establishment was pervasively and persistently hostile to witchcraft throughout Europe, in the Orthodox east as well as the Catholic west, and continuing after the Reformation in the Protestant north as well.[191] As Bracton and Fleta both drew freely from Roman and Canon

---

1808 FOR FELONIOUSLY ADMINISTERING A CERTAIN NOXIOUS AND DESTRUCTIVE SUBSTANCE TO ANN CHENEY WITH INTENT TO PRODUCE A MISCARRIAGE (1808).

184. 22 *LIBER ASSISARUM* (BOOK OF ASSIZES) pl. 94 (1348). *See generally* WINFIELD, *supra* note 19, at 220–21.

185. The passage was found by John Baker and Philip Rafferty. 1 RAFFERTY, *supra* note 74, at 595, 600.

186. As quoted in Brian Bendig, *Images of Men in Feminist Legal Theory,* 20 PEPPARDINE L. REV. 991, 991 (1993).

187. See the text *supra* at notes 57–61.

188. See Chapter 1, at notes 252–467.

189. *See, e.g.,* Dellapenna, *supra* note 13, at 368; Gavigan, *supra* note 12, at 20–21.

190. *See generally* BEFORE THE BAWDY COURT: SELECTIONS FROM CHURCH COURT AND OTHER RECORDS RELATING TO THE CORRECTION OF MORAL OFFENCES IN ENGLAND, SCOTLAND, AND NEW ENGLAND, 1300–1800, at 81, 152, 172, 204, 238 (nos. 150, 369, 427, 531) (Paul Hair ed. 1972); HELMHOLZ, *supra* note 84, at 159–60; KEOWN, *supra* note 22, at 5; JOHN RIDDLE, CONTRACEPTION AND ABORTION FROM THE ANCIENT WORLD TO THE RENAISSANCE 109–10 (1992).

191. G.L. KITTREDGE, WITCHCRAFT IN OLD AND NEW ENGLAND 85–208 (1929); EVE LEVIN, SEX AND SOCIETY IN THE WORLD OF THE ORTHODOX SLAVS, 900–1700, at 175–78 (1989); KEITH THOMAS, RELIGION AND THE DECLINE OF MAGIC 253–79, 435–501 (1971); Allison Coudert, *The Myth of the Improved Status of Protestant Women: The Case of the Witchcraze,* in THE POLITICS OF GENDER IN EARLY MODERN EUROPE 61, 64 (Jean Brink, Allison Coudert, & Maryanne Horowitz eds. 1989); Mary Nelson, *Why Witches Were Women,* in WOMEN: A FEMINIST PERSPECTIVE 346 (Jo Freeman ed. 1975); Pihlajamäki, *supra* note 40.

Law to fill gaps in the common law as they described it,[192] perhaps this was the source of their statements. After all, Henry de Bracton was a cleric himself.[193] Furthermore, English judges occasionally cited Canon or Roman law as the basis of their decisions during the Middle Ages.[194]

Medieval canon law was in large measure an internationally uniform body of laws that were in principle applicable to all Christians regardless of social standing or national allegiance.[195] We know from many secondary sources that medieval canon law condemned abortion, particularly (but not only) after quickening.[196] Although there is no explicit reference to abortion in the New Testament, there are several condemnations of the illicit use of drugs[197]—condemnations that, when written, very likely were indirect references to abortifacients.[198] Certainly the medical writings of the times used the same Greek term (*pharmakeia*—the source of our word "pharmacy") as a pseudonym for abortifacient potions.[199]

Apart from the Bible, the earliest Christian writings explicitly condemn abortion as murder, a tradition that continues in some strains of Christianity down to today. Thus we find early in the *Didache,* a work written in the late first or early second century CE, a command *Ou phoneuseis teknon en phthora* ("Thou shalt not murder a child by abortion.")[200] The term *phthora* literally means destruction, but it was then commonly used to mean abortion, as shown

---

192. Baker, *supra* note 22, at 201; 2 Holdsworth, *supra* note 7, at 236–44, 267–77; Milsom, *supra* note 22, at 41–42, 150, 264–65, 267; Plucknett, *supra* note 22, at 261–65; 1 Pollock & Maitland, *supra* note 22, at 185–88; Radin, *supra* note 22, at 281–83; Winfield, *supra* note 19, at 60–61; John Barton, *Roman Law in England*, in Ius Romanum Medii Aevi 13–24 (*Société d'histoire des droits de l'antiquité* 1971); Donahue, *supra* note 49, at 1752–53.

193. 2 Holdsworth, *supra* note 7, at 232–34; Radin, *supra* note 22, at 280.

194. *See generally* 2 Holdsworth, *supra* note 7, at 202–06, 353–57; Plucknett, *supra* note 22, at 235–36; 1 Pollock & Maitland, *supra* note 22, at 110–14, 167–69; 2 Pollock & Maitland, *supra*, at 473–76; T.E. Scrutton, The Influence of the Roman Law on the Law of England (1885); Winfield, *supra* note 19, at 54–69.

195. Brundage, supra note 24; Jean Gaudermet, Église et cité: Historie du droit canonique (1994); R.H. Helmholz, The Spirit of the Classical Canon Law (1996); Stephan Kuttner, The History of Ideas and Doctrines of Medieval Canon Law (2nd ed. 1992); R.A. Marchant, The Church under the Law 1560–1640 (1969); R.C. Mortimer, Western Canon Law (1957); John Noonan, Canons and Canonists in Context (1997). See also E.R. Brinkworth, Shakespeare and the Bawdy Courts of Stratford (1972). Two of its earliest leaders were Englishmen teaching in Bologna in the twelfth and early thirteenth centuries, although English canonists seem to have little influence on Canon Law generally thereafter. See Donahue, supra note 49, at 1768–70; Stephen Kuttner & Eleanor Rathbone, Anglo-Norman Canonists of the Twelfth Century, 7 Traditio 279 (1949–51).

196. Connery, *supra* note 118, at 33–167; Grisez, *supra* note 19, at 137–55; Roger Huser, The Crime of Abortion in Canon Law 12–61 (1942); Noonan, *supra* note 118, at 19–22; Quay, *supra* note 13, at 426–30. *See also* Levin, *supra* note 191, at 175–78; McLaren, *supra* note 100, at 115–20; Riddle, *supra* note 190, at 110–12; A. Cameron, *The Exposure of Children and Greek Ethics,* 46 Classical Rev. 105, 109–14 (1932).

197. *Galatians* 5:20; *Revelations* 9:21, 18:23, 21:8, 22:15. These do not include the ambiguous reference in 1 *Corinthians* 15:8, in which Paul does perhaps speak directly against abortion. On the role of the Bible in ecclesiastical law, see R.H. Helmholz, *The Bible in the Service of the Canon Law,* 70 Chi.-Kent L. Rev. 1557 (1995).

198. Gorman, *supra* note 105, at 48; J.H. Waszink, *Abtreibung,* 1 Reallexikon für Antike und Christentum 55, 59 (1950).

199. *See, e.g.,* Soranus, Gynecology ¶ 1.59 (Oswei Temkin trans. 1956). *See* Gorman, *supra* note 105, at 48; Waszink, *supra* note 198, at 59.

200. *Didache* § 2.2 (J.A. Kleist trans. 1948). *See also* Apocalypse of Peter ¶ 26 (late 1st or early 2d century), in 2 New Testament Apocrypha 674 (Wilhelm Scneemelcher ed., R. McL. Wilson trans. 1965); Athenagoras, *Legatio* ¶ 35 (mid- to late 2d century); Epistle of Barnabas ¶ 19.5 (also late 1st or early 2d century); Tertullian, supra note 105, ¶ 9.6 (197 CE). Sociologist Kristin Luker's claim that Christians condemned abortion only if it followed another sexual crime is simply wrong. Kristin Luker, Abortion and the Politics of Motherhood 12–13 (1984).

by the use of the term *phthoreus* as a label for abortionists.[201] These condemnations are un-equivocal and without qualification. No exceptions were expressed based on the gestational age of the fetus or on the purpose of the abortion.[202] For those who do not believe that all this was a divine revelation, the question arises as to when and how did these views become dominant among Christians.

The most obvious potential candidate source would be the Jewish tradition. That tradition was apparently more favorable to the possibility of abortion than were the early Christians, but allowed abortion only if the fetus posed a threat to the mother's well-being and not simply because the child was not wanted.[203] The most relevant Biblical text is found in *Exodus:*

> And if men struggle and strike a pregnant woman and her giving birth proceeds thereby, and there is no injury, he shall pay a fine according as the woman's husband lays upon him, he shall surely pay according to the assessment. And if there is injury you will prescribe life for life, eye for eye, tooth for tooth, hand for hand, foot for foot, burn for burn, wound for wound, bruise for bruise.[204]

One reading of this text is that the "injury" is to the mother and not to the child.[205] This reading would suggest that an unborn child was valued less highly than the mother for the killing of the unborn child could only be remedied by assessing a fine, whereas injury to the mother required an equivalent injury to the wrongdoer ("*lex talionis*").[206] The text, however, does not indicate that the injury in question must be to the mother rather than to the child.[207] Furthermore, several other passages in the Bible prescribe the *lex talionis* for injuries to women.[208] Thus this passage might actually refer only to injury to the child.[209] Most rabbinical commentary on abortion took the latter line, but insisted that the injury must refer to a "fully formed" (fully developed) unborn child with only a fine for the loss of a less than fully developed unborn child.[210]

How to translate this passage into a set of precepts applicable to voluntary abortions is not obvious. Starting from the standard view that a fetus before it is "fully formed" is not fully human, one might conclude that Judaism would not condemn abortions, especially early abortions. Yet as the Jewish tradition has come down to us, it did not contemplate abortion simply at the election of one or both parents. For example, the dominant view in Orthodox Judaism prohibits abortion based on the probability of a deformity in the unborn child, but permits the

201. GORMAN, *supra* note 105, at 49–50.

202. St. Augustine, *Enchridion* ¶¶ 23.85, 23.86; St. Basil the Great, *Epistularum* § 188.2, in 2 FATHERS OF THE CHURCH 12–2 (Agnes Clare Way trans. 1947); St. Jerome, *Letter to Eustochium* ¶ 22.13 (quoted in GORMAN, *supra* note 105, at 68). *See generally* GORMAN, *supra*, at 47–90; HUSER, *supra* note 196, at 15–20; Cameron, *supra* note 196, at 111; Noonan, *supra* note 196, at 10.

203. *See generally* DAVID FELDMAN, MARITAL RELATIONS, BIRTH CONTROL AND ABORTION IN JEWISH LAW 288–94 (1974); GORMAN, *supra* note 105, at 33–45; HUSER, *supra* note 196, at 5–8.

204. *Exodus* 21:22–25.

205. NORMAN FORD, WHEN DID I BEGIN? 55–56 (1988); GORMAN, *supra* note 105, at 40–41; Roy Ward, *The Use of the Bible in the Abortion Debate,* 13 ST. L.U. PUB. L. REV. 391, 394–95 (1993).

206. *See, e.g.,* Morris, *supra* note 58, at 71.

207. CARL KEIL & FRANZ DELITZSCH, 2 BIBLICAL COMMENTARY ON THE OLD TESTAMENT 135 (J. Martin trans. 1986).

208. *Exodus* 21:12–14; *Leviticus* 24:19–20; *Numbers* 35:9–34; *Deuteronomy* 4:41–43.

209. LES MILLER, A CHRISTIAN VIEW OF IN VITRO FERTILIZATION 32–38 (1985). Apparently, a similar law prevailed in other areas of the Fertile Crescent. ANCIENT NEAR EASTERN TEXTS RELATING TO THE OLD TESTAMENT 181, 184 (J.D. Pritchard ed., 3rd ed. 1969) ("ANCIENT NEAR EASTERN TEXTS").

210. *See* PHILO JUDAEUS, DE SPECIALIBUS LEGIBUS ¶ 3.191.108–09 (1929). *See generally* CONNERY, *supra* note 118, at 11; HUSER, *supra* note 196, at 5–8; Viktor Aptowitzer, *Observations of the Criminal Law of the Jews,* 15 JEWISH Q. REV. 87, 111 (1924); John Huesman, *Exodus,* in 1 THE JEROME BIBLICAL COMMENTARY 47, 59 (Raymond Brown *et al.* eds. 1968); Scott, *supra* note 19, at 201–02, 204–09.

same abortion because of the anguish the deformity will inflict on the mother.[211] At least some readings of the Jewish tradition find it more restrictive towards abortion than this dominant reading suggests.[212] And in fact, there is no actual record even of a therapeutic abortion among Jews in biblical times[213]—hardly a surprise given the prevailing inability to do abortions safely at all at the time.[214] And there is no evidence to suggest that abortions were more common among Jews than among Christians during the medieval period.

The Greek, Roman, and other pagan traditions were closer to later Christian views than is now generally thought. Considerable evidence indicates that Assyrian, Babylonian, Egyptian, Greek, Hittite, Persian, and Sumerian law all prohibited abortion.[215] As with the Biblical passage quoted above, some modern commentators have tended to see in these records evidence that the life of the fetus was valued less highly than the life of the mother, and thus was considered as less than human.[216] Much the same conclusion, however, would have to be accepted regarding women and children as well; they too generally were valued less highly than men.

Such commentators also tend to dismiss the evidence regarding Greek law because it is clear that Greek law permitted and sometimes even required infanticide.[217] One estimate has it that 10 percent of more of Greek infants were killed shortly after their birth.[218] Roman historian Polybius would complain in the first century BCE that Greece was experiencing serious depopulation, in large measure because of a lack of living children in Greek families.[219] The prevalence of infanticide was undoubtedly a contributor to this situation, although the chronic warfare from the sixth to the fourth centuries BCE as well as the opportunities for Greeks to procure employment throughout the Hellenistic world and later the Roman Empire probably contributed as much or more to this situation.[220]

Modern commentators often see no reason why the Greeks would have prohibited abortion if they allowed infanticide. Their view ignores the risks to the mothers from abortion that did not pertain to infanticide and also the inability of the Greeks to make the necessary eugenic determinations prior to birth that controlled the legality of the exposure of infants. While Plato and Aristotle did advocate mandatory abortions in certain cases, they did so in the context of advo-

---

211. Adena Berkowitz, *Thinking about Women in Abortion Controversies*, 2 S'Vara No. 2, at 25 (1991).

212. *See, e.g.*, Flavius Josephus, Against Apion ¶ 2.202 (Henry St. John trans., G.P. Gould ed. 1997; original date 1266–73). *See generally* Gorman, *supra* note 105, at 42–44. For a contemporary view to this effect, see J. David Bleich, Judaism and Healing 96 (1981) (describing abortion as a serious moral offense permissible only for the gravest reasons); David Feldman, Birth Control in Jewish Law 259–60 (1968) (describing abortion as murder if performed by non-Jews).

213. Gorman, *supra* note 105, at 33–34.

214. *See* Chapter 1.

215. Ancient Near Eastern Texts, *supra* note 209, at 175; Gorman, *supra* note 105, at 19–20, 24; Huser, *supra* note 196, at 2–4; Russ VerSteeg, Early Mesopotamian Law 110–11 (2000); Cameron, *supra* note 196, at 110; Quay, *supra* note 13; Waszink, *supra* note 198, at 57. Similarly, abortion appears to have been a crime punishable by death among the Aztecs and Incas. Reay Tannahill, Sex in History 303, 305 (1980). *See also* 1 G.R. Driver & John Miles, The Babylonian Laws 366–67 (1952) (arguing that abortion was legal in Babylonia for temple priestesses who became pregnant in violation of their vows).

216. *See, e.g.*, Morris, *supra* note 58, at 70.

217. G.R. Driver & John Miles, The Assyrian Laws ¶ 21 (1935); Gorman, *supra* note 105, at 20–21, 24; Huser, *supra* note 196, at 4–5; Tannahill, *supra* note 215, at 69–70; A.C. van Geytenbeek, Mussonius Rufus and Greek Diatribe 78-78 n.1 (1963); Heinrich Zimmern, Gesetze aus dem Staatsarchiv von Boghazköi 17–18 (1946); R. Crahay, *Les moralistes anciens et l'avortement*, 10 L'Antiquité Classique 10, 11–12 (1941); Waszink, *supra* note 198, at 56.

218. Mark Golden, *Demography and the Exposure of Girls at Athens*, 35 Phoenix 316 (1981).

219. Polybius, The Rise of the Roman Empire 537–38 (Ian Scott Kilvert ed. 1979).

220. Peter Garnsey, Famine and Food Supply in the Graeco-Roman World: Responses to Risk and Crisis 63–68 (1988).

cating their vision of an "ideal" (and highly coercive) society, and not as a description of contemporary social reality.[221] On the other hand, their contemporary, Hippocrites, clearly prohibited at least some forms of abortion in his famous oath.[222] We even have a fragmentary record of a case of a woman being prosecuted by her husband for homicide for undergoing an abortion without his consent.[223] Furthermore, inscriptions from Greek temples indicate that having survived an abortion rendered the women involved ritually unclean, that is unfit to participate in temple services until they had undergone a process of purification meant to cleanse them of the sinful effects of the procedure.[224] Birth and miscarriage also rendered a woman "impure," but infanticide did not.

Like the Greeks, the early Romans treated abortion as a legal offense, and not merely a moral offense, but only against the husband if he neither commanded nor consented to the abortion.[225] Given the Roman view of the *patria potestas,* including the power of the father to order the death of a grown child or his spouse (*jus vitae necicae*),[226] the power of the father to order or permit an abortion is hardly surprising. (One should note that under what became the most common form of Roman marriage after the third century BCE—*usus*—a married woman actually remained under the authority of her—usually absent—*father* rather than coming under the authority of her husband, thus effectively emancipating them.[227]) Any qualms about the power of the father over his wife or children would, if anything, have been diminished regarding abortion as in the Roman view the fetus was not a living person separate from the mother until birth.[228] Roman law did treat a fetus as a person when it was to the benefit of the foetus: *Conceptus por jam nato habetur* ("a conceptus for this purpose having been born").[229]

Writers in the early Roman Empire claimed that abortion was common. There is no reason to believe, however, that it was more common in Rome than elsewhere in the ancient world.[230] One must infer that infanticide was still the predominant means for dealing with unwanted pregnancies in Rome. After all, the power of life and death of Roman fathers even over their grown children made it rather easy to go along with his decisions to dispose of unwanted infants. One his-

---

221. PLATO, REPUBLIC ¶ 5.9; ARISTOTLE, POLITICS ¶¶ 7.1.1, 7.14.10. *See generally* GORMAN, *supra* note 105, at 21–23; HUSER, *supra* note 196, at 5; Crahay, *supra* note 217, at 23; Waszink, *supra* note 198, at 56.

222. ARTURO CASTIGLIONI, A HISTORY OF MEDICINE 148 (2nd ed. 1947); LUDWIG EDELSTEIN, THE HIPPOCRATIC OATH 3 (1943); RIDDLE, *supra* note 190, at 7–10; HENRY SIGERIST, ON THE HISTORY OF MEDICINE 38 (Felix Marti-Ibañez ed. 1960); Martin Arbagi, Roe *and the Hippocratic Oath*, in ABORTION AND THE CONSTITUTION, *supra* note 98, at 159.

223. Arbagi, *supra* note 219, at 165–66. At least one scholar suggested that the surviving speech was an account of a fictional trial rather than a real trial. ANGELA DARKOW, THE SPURIOUS SPEECHES IN THE LYSIANIC CORPUS (1917). In any event, the Greeks seem to have considered the decision to abort to be prerogative of the father. A.R.W. HARRISON, THE LAW OF ATHENS 72 (1968); RUSS VERSTEEG, LAW IN THE ANCIENT WORLD 245, 263 (2002).

224. GORMAN, *supra* note 105, at 24; Arbagi, *supra* note 219, at 168–69, 179–80 n. 34 ; Cameron, *supra* note 196, at 108; Crahay, *supra* note 217, at 16–17; Wiszink, *supra* note 198, at 56.

225. *See, e.g.,* MARCUS TULLIUS CICERO, PRO CLUENTIO ¶ 11.32. *See generally* GORMAN, *supra* note 105, at 24–26; GRISEZ, *supra* note 19, at 185–86; HUSER, *supra* note 196, at 8–11; THEODOR MOMMSEN, RÖMISCHES STRAFRECHT 636–37 (1899); VERSTEEG, *supra* note 223, at 335, 363.

226. *See generally* MARRIAGE, DIVORCE, AND CHILDREN IN ANCIENT ROME (Beryl Rawson ed. 1991).

227. JANE GARDNER, WOMEN IN ROMAN LAW AND SOCIETY 5–22 (1986); TANNAHILL, *supra* note 215, at 107–09.

228. JUSTINIAN, DIGEST ¶ 25.4.1.1 (*ca.* 533).

229. *Id.* ¶ 1.5.7. *See also* CICERO, *supra* note 225; Arbagi, *supra* note 219, at 169–71.

230. *See* Chapter 2, at notes 12–19, 241–50.

torian has concluded the right of the father to dispose of a newborn as "the strongest aspect of his 'right of life and death'" over his children.[231]

The Roman government, however, deplored abortion and infanticide as weakening the state.[232] Decrees and laws dating from the *Lex Cornelia* of 81 BCE (during the Roman Republic) and reiterated by Augustus and other emperors prohibited the selling of "poisons," apparently including abortifacient potions.[233] The jurist Julius Paulus made this explicit in the second century CE.[234] The penalty was harsh, the abortionist facing a sentence of work in the mines or exile. If the mother died, the abortionist was to be executed. Undergoing an abortion rendered the mother ritually impure in the Roman religion just as in the Greek religion.[235] During the reigns of Antoninus Pius and Septimus Severus, at the end of the second century CE, women who committed self-abortion were made subject to the criminal law.[236] They were to be exiled.

Nothing in the *Lex Cornelia* or in the decrees on self-abortion made any reference to the stage of the pregnancy. Presumably the criminal sanctions applied to abortions at the earliest stage of pregnancy if it could be proven, as well as to late-term abortions.[237] Nor was harm to the mother relevant to whether an abortion was punishable, although it did bear on the penalty. The Hippocratic prohibition of abortions was picked up by Scribonius and the Stoics under the Roman Empire in the first century of the modern era and extended to all abortions.[238] The Stoics also opposed infanticide, warfare, and gladiatorial combats.[239] All in all, Roman law appears to disclose a culture in which abortion law was designed to protect the rights of the father rather than the fetus. Despite this somewhat mixed record regarding Roman practice, modern commenta-

---

231. PIERRE GRIMAL, LOVE IN ANCIENT ROME 22 (Arthur Train trans. 1980). *See also* EVA KEULS, THE REIGN OF THE PHALLUS 110–12, 146–47 (1985); MARY LEFKOWITZ & MAUREEN FANT, WOMEN'S LIFE IN GREECE AND ROME 57, 87, 91, 94–95 (2nd ed. 1992).

232. CORA LUTZ, MUSSONIUS RUFUS: THE ROMAN SOCRATES 3–30 (1947); van GEYTENBEEK, *supra* note 217, at 3–50; Arbagi, *supra* note 219, at 171–72; Cameron, *supra* note 196, at 109–11. *See generally* GILLIAN CLARK, WOMEN IN LATE ANTIQUITY: PAGAN AND CHRISTIAN LIFESTYLES 35–36, 46–50 (1993); GORMAN, *supra* note 105, at 26–32. Caroline Morris' comment that opposition to abortion surfaced only after the Christianization of the Empire and then only to strengthen the authority of the father is too absurd to merit further comment. Morris, *supra* note 58, at 70.

233. JUSTINIAN, *supra* note 228, ¶¶ 47.11, 48.8.8, 48.19.38.5, 48.19.39. *See also* SORANUS, *supra* note 199, ¶ 3.19. *See* GORMAN, *supra* note 105, at 25–26; GRISEZ, *supra* note 19, at 185–86; HUSER, *supra* note 196, at 9; MOMMSEN, *supra* note 225, at 637; JOHN NOONAN, JR., CONTRACEPTION 18, 21, 26–27 (1965).

234. JUSTINIAN, *supra* note 228, ¶ 5.8 (*Opinions of Julius Paulus*). *See also* GORMAN, *supra* note 105, at 31–32; Connery, *supra* note 98, at 128.

235. Crahay, *supra* note 217, at 16–17.

236. JUSTINIAN, *supra* note 228, ¶ 47.11.4. *See generally* HUSER, *supra* note 196, at 9–10; MOMMSEN, *supra* note 225, at 354.

237. The Aristotelian notion that abortion was criminal only after "animation" apparently was introduced into the Roman law tradition by Accursio in the thirteenth century, declaring abortion after animation homicide and therefore a capital offense, without mentioning pre-animation abortions; presumably, this left the old punishments (exile or the mines) applicable to pre-animation abortions. ACCURSIO, *DIGESTUM NOVUM PANDECTARUM* 949 (1557). The same distinction appeared in church penitentials as early as the seventh century. *See* Connery, *supra* note 98, at 129–30. See also the text *supra* at notes 95–109.

238. SCRIBONIUS LARGUS, *COMPOSITIONES Praef.* 5.20–23, at 2 (S. Sconocchia ed. 1983); Mussonius Rufus, *Discourse 15,* in LUTZ, *supra* note 232, at 97. *See* ETHICS IN MEDICINE: HISTORICAL PERSPECTIVES AND CONTEMPORARY CONCERNS 5, 10 (Stanley Reiser *et al.* eds. 1977); GORMAN, *supra* note 105, at 23–24, 28–30, 77–78; Arbagi, *supra* note 219, at 159; Edmund & Alice Pellegrino, *Humanism and Ethics in Roman Medicine: Translation and Commentary on a Text of Scribonius Largus,* 7 LITERATURE & MED. 22 (1988); Quay, *supra* note 13, at 413.

239. LUTZ, *supra* note 232, at 3–4, 14–17; van GEYTENBEEK, *supra* note 217, at 3–4.

tors continue to insist, as one pro-abortion attorney put it, that "abortion was common and completely legal."[240]

Stoic ideas are strikingly similar to those adopted by Christianity, and with the establishment of Christianity as the state religion of the Roman Empire more stringent laws were enacted prohibiting abortion explicitly based on the premise that the unborn child was a human being entitled to legal protection.[241] Among Christians, penances for the abortion (and for the use of contraceptives) were listed along homicide and violence rather than among penances for sexual transgressions.[242] Early Christians condemned abortion long before they condemned contraception and before the first Christian articulation of the "sex for procreation only" theme that later would be so prominent in their theology.[243] The first known Christian condemnation of contraceptives is found in the work of Hippolytus.[244] John Noonan, now a federal judge but then a law professor, traced the history of Christian ideas on contraception back to the first century CE.[245] Noonan, however, confused references to abortion with references to contraception.[246] Noonan concluded, however, that Christian opposition to contraception was an extension of the Christian opposition to abortion.[247] In view of the evidence that Christian opposition to abortion was conceived of as opposition to violence and predates Christian opposition to contraception, one cannot easily maintain that the condemnation of abortion arose simply out of a general hostility to sexuality rather than a concern for the life of the fetus.[248] Early Christian condemnations of abortion were part of the program of social amelioration characteristic of the Christian approach to Roman and Medieval society, illustrated by the attempts of the Church to moderate or eliminate slavery, to restrain the excesses of warfare, and to rationalize the pursuit of justice.[249]

The early Christian view of abortion was distorted by the eventual triumph among Christians of the Aristotelian view of gestation—a view that never had gained dominance in the pagan world. Aristotle propounded the view, known as "mediate animation," that a fetus became a living animal only after 40 days of gestation began for males and after 80 (or 90) days of gestation began for females, and a human being shortly before birth.[250] The gendered distinction apparently arose from the fact that all fetuses appear to develop male genitalia at about 40 days into gestation, with the "proto-phallus" differentiating into female or male genitalia after about 80

---

240. Diane Curtis, *Doctored Rights: Menstrual Extraction, Self-Help Gynecological Care, and the Law*, 20 Rev. L. & Soc. Change 427, 435 (1994). *See also* A History of Private Life from Pagan Rome to Byzantium 9 (Phillipe Ariès, Georges Duby, & Paul Veyne eds., Arthur Goldhammer trans., 1987).

241. Gorman, *supra* note 105, at 62–63.

242. Georges Duby, The Knight, the Priest, and the Lady 62 (1983). *See also* Gorman, *supra* note 105, at 80–90.

243. *See generally* Gorman, *supra* note 105, at 77–80.

244. Hippolytus, Refutation of All Heresies Bk. 9, ch. 7, at 344–45 (J.H. MacMahon trans. 1870; original date ca. 238 CE).

245. Noonan, *supra* note 233, at 92–102.

246. Gorman, *supra* note 105, at 113 n.22.

247. Noonan, *supra* note 233, at 85–91.

248. For examples of the confusion refuted in the text, see Gorman, *supra* note 105, at 80–82; Jane Hurst, The History of Abortion in the Catholic Church 15 (1983); Luker, *supra* note 200, at 12–13; Tannahill, *supra* note 215, at 152; Robert Hardaway, *Environmental Malthusianism: Integrating Population and Environmental Policy*, 27 Envtl. L. 1209, 1230 (1997); Robert Hardaway, Miranda Peterson, & Cassadra Mann, *The Right to Die and the Ninth Amendment: Compassion and Dying after* Glucksberg *and* Vacco, 7 Geo. Mason L. Rev. 313, 353 (1999).

249. *See* Brundage, *supra* note 24, at 14–15, 27, 41–43, 93–96, 117–53; Adolf von Harnack, *Militia Christi*: The Christian Religion and the Military in the First Three Centuries (David McInness Gracie trans. 1981); Helmholz, *supra* note 195, at 6–20.

250. Aristotle, *De Generatione Animalium*, in 5 The Works of Aristotle Translated into English 729a–736b (J.A. Smith & W.D. Ross eds., A. Platt trans. 1912).

days of gestation. Thus, an unsophisticated view of the gross appearances would suggest that the female is not "fully formed" until the later time while the "male" has emerged at the earlier time.[251]

Aristotle's theory provided Christians a coherent theory of gestational development that was consistent with the standard reading of the only passage in the Bible (*Exodus* 21:22–25) that spoke directly to abortion, as well as consistent with the then recent Jewish reading of that tradition.[252] As a result, Aristotle was widely followed by the early Church fathers and the later by the Canon Law.[253] This was not entirely so, however, for the prohibition of abortion in the *Didache* did not contain the Aristotelian qualification, and Tertullian expressly rejected mediate animation, holding that a fetus was fully human from the earliest embryo.[254] On the other hand, such early Church fathers as St. Clement and Origen did follow Aristotle.[255] St. Augustine's embrace of the theory of mediate animation, however, largely settled the question for medieval Christians in both its eastern and western traditions.[256]

Canon Law was effectively codified and modernized in the Twelfth Century under the influence of the rediscovered Roman law embodied in the Code of Justinian.[257] Thomas Aquinas explained the canonical rule in terms of mediate animation.[258] Yet even abortion before animation was condemned; only the quality of the sin differed based on the stage of pregnancy, for abortion before "animation" was considered contraception, which was also a sin. The focus was always on when the conceptus became a living human being, and there is a good deal of evidence that at times, at least, both church law and civil law treated fetuses as living human beings well before quickening, the Aristotelian 40/80 days notion, or any other proffered test of mediate animation.

# Ecclesiastical Jurisdiction over Abortion by Ingestion Techniques

*[All] cats may be black at night, but not to other cats.*

—Henry Louis Gates, jr.[259]

Research into formal codes of Canon Law cannot be the end of the inquiry as the practice of canonical courts often varied from the theory propounded by Rome or the Church councils, de-

---

251. Scott, *supra* note 19, at 210 n.40.

252. See the text *supra* at notes 204–17.

253. FORD, *supra* note 205, at 26–30; HUSER, *supra* note 196, at 1, 13–16, 37–54, 62–69, 75–76; Scott, *supra* note 19, at 209–18.

254. *DIDACHE, supra* note 200, § 2.2 (quoted at note 194); TERTULLIAN, *supra* note 105, ¶¶ 9.6, 26.5, 37.1, 37.2. *See* GORMAN, *supra* note 105, at 56–58. *But see* HUSER, *supra* note 196, at 13–14.

255. GORMAN, *supra* note 105, at 59; HUSER, *supra* note 196, at 13–16; Scott, *supra* note 19, at 212–14.

256. AUGUSTINE, *QUESTIONES DE HEPTATEUCHEUM* II:lxxx, in 34 *PATROLOGIAE CURSUS COMPLETUS* 626–27 (Jacques-Paul Migne ed. 1887). *See* GORMAN, *supra* note 105, at 70–73; HUSER, *supra* note 196, at 37–54, 68–69, 75–76; Scott, *supra* note 19, at 214–18; Quay, *supra* note 13, at 428.

257. *See* BRUNDAGE, *supra* note 24, at 45–54; CHARLES HASKINS, THE RENAISSANCE OF THE TWELFTH CENTURY 214 (1927); Helmholz, *supra* note 197, at 1558–60; S. Kuttner, *The Revival of Jurisprudence,* in RENAISSANCE AND RENEWAL IN THE 12TH CENTURY 299 (R.L. Benson & G. Constable eds. 1982).

258. THOMAS AQUINAS, 1 *SUMMA THEOLOGICA* I, Q. 76, art. 1, in INTRODUCTION TO SAINT THOMAS AQUINAS 293 (Anton Pegis ed. 1948; original date ca. 1274). *See* Scott, *supra* note 19, at 216–18.

259. HENRY LOUIS GATES, JR., FIGURES IN BLACK: WORDS, SIGNS, AND THE "RACIAL" SELF 41 (1987).

riving authority from local custom as much as from decretals.[260] Despite the now common view that the medieval Christian church was so hopelessly sexist that its historically held views ought to be dismissed out of hand,[261] in fact the medieval Christian church was for its time surprisingly evenhanded in relation to issues of sexual conduct—as even some sharp critics of modern church practice have acknowledged.[262] Unfortunately, rather less research has been done on the early ecclesiastical prosecutions and, without a centralized record office, the search for relevant data in England (or elsewhere) is vastly more difficult than such a search for the royal courts.[263] One modern historian has described the extant records as "among the more repulsive of all the relics of the past" because of the difficulty of reading and interpreting them.[264] As a result, we must be content with a sketchier picture of these proceedings than for pleas of the crown.

The only direct evidence we now have of ecclesiastical prosecutions in England for abortion from the thirteenth and fourteenth centuries are the occasional cases in which a clerical defendant invoked the original form of benefit of clergy.[265] At that time, benefit of clergy was not yet the expansive doctrine used to ameliorate the rigors of the common law for first offenders that it would become by the eighteenth century. In the thirteenth century, benefit of clergy was still limited to actual clerics and contemplated that a cleric invoking the right would be tried accord-

---

260. J.H. BAKER, MONUMENTS OF ENDLESSE LABOURS: ENGLISH CANONISTS AND THEIR WORK, 1300–1900 (1998); BRUNDAGE, *supra* note 24, at 22–24, 30–31, 39, 44–59, 73, 158–59; R.H. HELMHOLZ, ROMAN CANON LAW IN REFORMATION ENGLAND 4–20 (1990); MARTIN INGRAM, CHURCH COURTS, SEX AND MARRIAGE IN ENGLAND, 1570–1640, at 41 (1987); Charles Donahue, jr., *Introduction*, in SELECT CASES FROM THE ECCLESIASTICAL COURTS OF THE PROVINCE OF CANTERBURY, c. 1200–1301 (95 SELDEN SOC'Y), at xxiv (C. Donahue, jr., ed. 1981). Michael Sheehan, *Choice of Marriage Partner in the Middle Ages: Development and Mode of a Theory of Marriage*, in 1 STUD. MEDIEVAL AND RENAISSANCE HISTORY 8 (J.A.S. Evans ed. 1978). For a brief description of the formal sources of canon law, see BRUNDAGE, *supra*, at 121–24; F.W. KEMP, AN INTRODUCTION TO CANON LAW IN THE CHURCH OF ENGLAND (1957); William Bassett, *Canon Law and the Common Law*, 29 HASTINGS L.J. 1383 (1978).

261. *See, e.g.,* FREDERICK ARTZ, MIND OF THE MIDDLE AGES, 200–1500, at 293–94 (3rd ed. 1962); FRIEDRICH HEER, THE MEDIEVAL WORLD (1963); 2 C.W. PREVITÉ-ORTON, THE SHORTER CAMBRIDGE MEDIEVAL HISTORY 943–47 (1952).

262. Joel Rosenthal, *Introduction*, in MEDIEVAL WOMEN AND THE SOURCES OF MEDIEVAL HISTORY vii, xi–xii (Joel Rosenthal ed. 1990). *See generally* JAMES BRUNDAGE, LAW, SEX, AND CHRISTIAN SOCIETY IN MEDIEVAL EUROPE 348–64 (1987) ("BRUNDAGE, CHRISTIAN SOCIETY"); BRUNDAGE, *supra* note 24, at 72–75; HELMHOLZ, *supra* note 195, at 132–39; James Brundage, *Sexual Equality in Medieval Canon Law*, in MEDIEVAL WOMEN AND THE SOURCES OF MEDIEVAL HISTORY, *supra*, at 67; Charles Donohue, jr., *The Canon Law on the Formation of Marriage and Social Practice in the Later Middle Ages*, 1 J. FAM. HIST. 144 (1983); Charles Duggan, *Equity and Compassion in Papal Marriage Decretals to England*, in LOVE AND MARRIAGE IN THE TWELFTH CENTURY 59, 87 (Willy van Hoecke & Andries Welenhuysen eds. 1981); Edward Makowski, *The Conjugal Debt and Medieval Canon Law*, 3 J. MEDIEVAL HIST. 99 (1977); Michael Sheehan, *The Formation and Stability of Marriage in Fourteenth-Century England: Evidence from the Ely Register*, 32 MEDIEVAL STUD. 228 (1971); Michael Sheehan, *The Influence of Canon Law on the Property Rights of Married Women in England*, 25 MEDIEVAL STUD. 109 (1963).

263. *See generally* COLIN CHAPMAN, ECCLESIASTICAL COURTS, THEIR OFFICIALS AND THEIR RECORDS 57–68 (1992); HELMHOLZ, *supra* note 260, at 120 n.5; INGRAM, *supra* note 260, at 20–24, 35–40; DOROTHY OWEN, THE RECORDS OF THE ESTABLISHED CHURCH IN ENGLAND EXCLUDING PAROCHIAL RECORDS (1970); J.S. PURVIS, AN INTRODUCTION TO ECCLESIASTICAL RECORDS (1953); D.M. SMITH, A GUIDE TO THE ARCHIVE COLLECTION IN THE BORTHWICK INSTITUTE OF HISTORICAL RESEARCH (1973); E.R. Brinkworth, *The Study and Use of Archdeacons' Court Records: Illustrated from the Oxford Records (1566–1759)*, 25 TRANS. ROYAL HIST. SOC'Y (4TH SER.) 93 (1943).

264. G.R. ELTON, ENGLAND 1200–1640, at 105 (1969). It is not clear whether this comment reflects the only the difficulty in reading the documents, or the reality they portrayed; one observer has noted that the Sixteenth and early Seventeenth Centuries "was the most dismal in the history of the legibility of English handwriting." Charles Donohue, jr., *Book Review*, 11 L. & HIST. REV. 442, 444 (1993).

265. Mabel's Appeal, JUST 1/741, m.33 (Shropshire Eyre 1292) (damaged roll); Philippa's Appeal (1276?), 1276 EYRE, *supra* note 16, at 51 (no. 187).

ing to Canon Law.[266] If convicted, the cleric might be turned over to secular authorities for punishment, depending on the nature of the crime charged. Benefit of clergy was codified, strengthened, and extended in the *Ordinance for the Clergy* enacted in 1351.[267]

Thanks legal historian Richard Helmholz, we have access to proceedings in English ecclesiastical courts from the fifteenth and sixteenth centuries suggesting a well-developed jurisprudence dealing with abortion.[268] Church courts also dealt extensively with the problem of infanticide.[269] Earlier historians had assumed that the relevant evidence simply had not survived.[270]

Punishments were available to the church courts, although they were different from those applied by the law courts. Rather than fines, imprisonment, maiming, outlawry, or death,[271] the range of punishments available to church courts included humiliating public admonitions and penances, restitution, fees, public whipping, suspension from the church, and excommunication.[272] While different, there is ample evidence that, during the Middle Ages, the "spiritual sanctions" were as effective as (or no less ineffective than) the secular sanctions.[273] Fees, analogous to legal fines, generally were a compromise to one of the more strictly spiritual sanctions.[274] Additionally, in later centuries the participants had to pay onerous court costs.[275]

Excommunication (also called "shunning") was functionally equivalent to legal outlawry, forbidding all in the community from having anything to do with a person who was to be treated

---

266. *Cf.* The Rector of Leaden Rothing's Case (Essex 1574), in Peter Laslett, Bastardy and Its Comparative History 76 (1980). *See generally* Baker, *supra* note 22, at 148–49, 586–89; Brundage, *supra* note 24, at 71; C.R. Cheney, The English Church and Its Law: 12th–14th Centuries 215–37 (1982); Gaudermet, *supra* note 195, at 493–97; Helmholz, *supra* note 84, at 122, 125, 130; Helmholz, *supra* note 195, at 284–85; Hogue, *supra* note 22, at 43–44; 6 Holdsworth, *supra* note 7, at 293–302; Milsom, *supra* note 22, at 420–21; Plucknett, *supra* note 22, at 439–41 Radin, *supra* note 22, at 100–01, 230–32; Robert Rodes, jr., Lay Authority and Reformation in the English Church: Edward I to the Civil War 31–33, 86–87, 95 (1982); Goldwin Smith, A Constitutional and Legal History of England 78–79, 88 (1990).

267. 25 Edw. 3, chs. 1–9 (Eng. 1351). *See* Robert Palmer, English Law in the Age of the Black Death, 1348–1381: A Transformation of Governance and Law 52 (1993).

268. Helmholz, *supra* note 84, at 159–60. On the significance of Helmholz's role in developing our modern knowledge of medieval Canon Law, see Charles Reid, jr. & John Witt, jr., *In the Steps of Gratian: Writing the History of Canon Law in the 1990s* (book rev.), 48 Emory L.J. 647, 681 (1999).

269. Helmholz, *supra* note 84, at 157–68; Ralph Houlbrooke, Church Courts and the People During the English Reformation 1520–1570, at 78 n.76 (1979); Richard Wunderli, London Church Courts and Society on the Eve of the Reformation 78, 128–29 (1981). Richard Helmholz's study of infanticide was originally published as R.H. Helmholz, *Infanticide in the Province of Canterbury in the Fifteenth Century*, 2 Hist. Childhood Q. 379 (1975).

270. *See, e.g.,* Thomas, *supra* note 191, at 449.

271. See the text *supra* at notes 93–116, and the cases collected *supra* at note 16. *See generally* Baker, Legal Profession, *supra* note 30, at 295–96; Brundage, *supra* note 24, at 92.

272. Brundage, *supra* note 24, at 151–53; Chapman, *supra* note 263, at 53–56; 1 Holdsworth, *supra* note 7, at 630–32; Rosalind Hill, The Theory and Practice of Excommunication in Medieval England 312–13 (1957); Helmholz, *supra* note 195, at 275–77; Ingram, *supra* note 260, at 52–58, 334–61; Plucknett, *supra* note 22, at 409; 2 Pollock & Maitland, *supra* note 22, at 516–17, 542–43; Quaife, *supra* note 84, at 192–97; Radin, *supra* note 22, at 107; Rodes, *supra* note 266, at 179–83.

273. Helmholz, *supra* note 84, at 3, 77–99; Helmholz, *supra* note 195, at 370–83. *See generally* Robert Rodes, jr., *The Canon Law as a Legal System—Function, Obligation, and Sanction,* 9 Nat. L.F. 45 (1964). Commonly, historians declare ecclesiastical sanctions ineffective without bothering to compare their effectiveness to the secular sanctions of the same time. *See, e.g.,* Hill, *supra* note 272, at 10; Marchant, *supra* note 195, at 205, 237; Quaife, *supra* note 84, at 194–96.

274. Helmholz, *supra* note 260, at 115–16; Ingram, *supra* note 260, at 54–55, 336–37; Marchant, *supra* note 195, at 245; Rodes, *supra* note 266, at 181–83, 186–87.

275. Helmholz, *supra* note 84, at 108, 111; Ingram, *supra* note 260, at 55–58, 335–36; Marchant, *supra* note 195, at 138–39, 142, 145, 267; Quaife, *supra* note 84, at 196–97. Ingram provides a table of court costs from two sets of ecclesiastical courts. Ingram, *supra*, at 56.

"as if dead."[276] Even kings and emperors could be, and occasionally were, excommunicated.[277] The Church did exempt one's family, servants, and serfs from the obligation to shun the excommunicant.[278] Excommunication could be enforced by imprisonment (or worse) by the secular authorities, although the ecclesiastical authorities seldom requested secular intervention.[279] Even a royal pardon could not remove an excommunication without a formal submission by the excommunicant to the authority of the Church.[280]

Some church courts had the authority to impose temporal penalties that would be executed by lay authorities. The Court of High Commission, created by Elizabeth I to enforce the religious settlement that marked her reign, was given the power both to fine and to imprison.[281] In only one sort of case could ecclesiastical courts pass a sentence of death—for heresy; but they seldom did so in England.[282] One lawyer has written that abortion, while subject to an exclusively ecclesiastical concern before the Cromwellian period, was treated as a "capital charge."[283] Both statements cannot be correct.

Reports from the Courts Christian (as the English ecclesiastical courts were called) are even more terse and uninformative than the reports from the early common law proceedings. Furthermore, the known ecclesiastical cases from the first 75 years of the fifteenth century dealing with abortion include only inconclusive proceedings or acquittals.[284] None of the few records that have been found from that time record any punishment for abortion, in this regard very unlike infanticide, even negligent infanticide.[285] Yet no one in these proceedings questioned the propriety of the charge. Our experience in researching the more accessible records of common law prosecutions ought to caution us against too hastily assuming that the lack of known corroborating evidence means that no proceedings ended in punishment or that no evidence of such proceedings exists.[286]

There are reasons, however, why convictions for abortion might have been even more rare in ecclesiastical courts than in law courts. Initially, the procedure basically was accusatorial, *i.e.*, no proceeding could be initiated unless a private individual made a complaint regarding the wrongdoing.[287] The accusatorial nature of the proceeding assured that highly secret attempts to abort

---

276. *See generally* CHAPMAN, *supra* note 263, at 54–55; HELMHOLZ, *supra* note 84, at 101–17; HELMHOLZ, *supra* note 260, at 21; HELMHOLZ, *supra* note 195, at 371; HILL, *supra* note 272; F.E. HYLAND, EXCOMMUNICATION: ITS NATURE, HISTORICAL DEVELOPMENT AND EFFECTS (1928); INGRAM, *supra* note 260, at 52–53, 342–43; EDWARD MURRAY, EXCOMMUNICATION AND CONSCIENCE IN THE MIDDLE AGES (1991); ELISABETH VODOLA, EXCOMMUNICATION IN THE MIDDLE AGES 164–90 (1986); Richard Helmholz, *Excommunication in Twelfth Century England*, 11 J. LAW & RELIGION 235 (1995).

277. HELMHOLZ, *supra* note 195, at 382.

278. HELMHOLZ, *supra* note 84, at 110; HELMHOLZ, *supra* note 195, at 381.

279. JOHN AUYLIFFE, PARERGON JURIS CONONICI ANGLICANI 257–61 (1726). *See* CHAPMAN, *supra* note 263, at 55; HELMHOLZ, *supra* note 84, at 116; INGRAM, *supra* note 260, at 53, 344, 355; F. DONALD LOGAN, EXCOMMUNICATION AND THE SECULAR ARM IN MEDIEVAL ENGLAND (1966); RODES, *supra* note 266, at 183–84; Helmholz, *supra* note 276, at 236.

280. HELMHOLZ, *supra* note 260, at 163.

281. HELMHOLZ, *supra* note 260, at 46; INGRAM, *supra* note 260, at 37–40; RODES, *supra* note 266, at 158.

282. BAKER, LEGAL PROFESSION, *supra* note 30, at 279–80; 1 HOLDSWORTH, *supra* note 7, at 618.

283. BERNARD DICKENS, ABORTION AND THE LAW 19 (1966).

284. *Inconclusive proceedings:* Thomas Deneham's Case (Canterbury 1471), in HELMHOLZ, *supra* note 84, at 159 n.11; Joan Gibbe's Servant's Case (Canterbury 1469), in HELMHOLZ, *supra*, at 159 n.13. *Acquital:* Anonymous' Case (Canterbury 1416), in HELMHOLZ, *supra*, at 159 n.10.

285. *See also* ANDREW KNAPP, THE NEW CALENDAR OR MALEFACTOR'S BLOODY REGISTER 604 (1932); HELMHOLZ, *supra* note 84, at 160–61.

286. For just such a hasty assumption, see DICKENS, *supra* note 283, at 19–20; Gavigan, *supra* note 12, at 21. See also R.H. Helmholz's comment on the difficulty of finding evidence of prosecutions for infanticide. HELMHOLZ, *supra* note 84, at 157–58.

287. BRUNDAGE, *supra* note 24, at 142; Richard Helmholz, *Crime, Compurgation, and the Courts of the Medieval Church*, 1 LAW & HIST. REV. 1, 20–22 (1983).

by ingesting a potion—prototypical "occult crimes"—would be unlikely even to come before a church court.[288] Not only did a participant or chance witness have to be willing to make an accusation, but the accuser had to pay his or her own expenses and ran the risk of being required to pay the defendant's expenses if the charges were not proven.[289] The risks were compounded so long as the church courts required "full proof"—proof by two eye witnesses willing to testify.[290] The successful defendant could even sue the accuser—before the same church court—for defamation from the bringing of a false (unproven) accusation.[291]

A would-be accuser could avoid the risk of liability for a false accusation by "denouncing" the culprit to church authorities, but only if the denouncer first confronted the transgressor in person and in private, demanding that the transgressor mend her or his ways.[292] Such a private confrontation had its own risks and unpleasantries, and did not eliminate the problems of proof. By the end of the twelfth century, the Courts Christian had developed a short-cut that allowed conviction and punishment without an accuser or denouncer and without "full proof" if the crime and its perpetrator were "notorious," *i.e.,* known to the community at large.[293] Only somewhat less drastic was the development in the thirteenth century of the possibility of a full procedure being brought in the name of the church (*ex officio*) without a formal accuser and without "full proof" when the crime and criminal were thought to be known even though these could not be said to be "notorious."[294] Because proceeding *per notarium* or *per inquisitionem* were subject to obvious abuses, the Courts Christian allowed the defendant to make defense to either form of proceeding by "compurgation."[295]

"Compurgation," the equivalent to "wager of law" in the royal courts, consisted of a defendant's denial of the deed under oath corroborated by the sworn statements of "oath-helpers," persons who would swear (in the earliest times) to the truth of the defendant's oath or (in the later Middle Ages) to the general truthfulness of the defendant. Compurgation is the only mode of proof mentioned in the abortion cases.[296] Modern commentators tend to be extremely skeptical about the likelihood of such a process to achieve true results, and hence of the efficacy of church courts generally.[297] Some support for this view is provided by the Assize

---

288. BRUNDAGE, *supra* note 24, at 144; Helmholz, *supra* note 287, at 9–11.

289. BRUNDAGE, *supra* note 24, at 144; Helmholz, *supra* note 287, at 21–22.

290. BRUNDAGE, *supra* note 24, at 144–45; Helmholz, *supra* note 287, at 22–23. *See generally* Donahue, *supra* note 84; Frank Herrmann, *The Establishment of a Rule against Hearsay in Romano-Canonical Procedure,* 36 VA. J. INT'L L. 1 (1995).

291. BRUNDAGE, *supra* note 24, at 144; Helmholz, *supra* note 287, at 21–22.

292. BRUNDAGE, *supra* note 24, at 145; Helmholz, *supra* note 287, at 23–24.

293. BRUNDAGE, *supra* note 24, at 144–47; Helmholz, *supra* note 287, at 23–24.

294. BRUNDAGE, *supra* note 24, at 147–51; Helmholz, *supra* note 287, at 22–23.

295. BRUNDAGE, *supra* note 24, at 147; HELMHOLZ, *supra* note 195, at 296–97; Helmholz, *supra* note 287, at 18–20.

296. *See, e.g.,* Thomas Tyry's Case, HRO CB2, fo. 59v (Winchester, mid-1500s); Thomas Love's Case, HRO CB4, fo. 117v (Winchester 1534); John Hunt's Case (Hertfordshire 1530), in BEFORE THE BAWDY COURT, *supra* note 190, at 81 (no. 150); Margaret Sawnder's Case (London Dioc. 1527), in W.H. HALE, PRECEDENTS IN ECCLESIASTICAL COURTS 34 (no. 128) (1847); John Russell's Case (London Dioc. Ct. 1493), in HALE, *supra,* at 105 (no. 331); Anonymous' Case (Canterbury 1416), in HELMHOLZ, *supra* note 84, at 159 n.10. *See generally* HELMHOLZ, *supra,* at 131–38; HELMHOLZ, *supra* note 195, at 158–59; 1 HOLDSWORTH, *supra* note 7, at 605–11; 9 HOLDSWORTH, *supra,* at 199–200; INGRAM, *supra* note 260, at 51–52, 331–34; Donohue, *supra* note 84, at 127; Helmholz, *supra* note 287.

297. *See, e.g.,* J.G. BELLAMY, CRIME AND PUBLIC ORDER IN ENGLAND IN THE LATER MIDDLE AGES 144 (1973); F.G. EMMISON, ELIZABETHAN LIFE: MORALS AND THE CHURCH COURTS 294 (1973); LEONA GABEL, BENEFIT OF CLERGY IN ENGLAND IN THE LATER MIDDLE AGES 104 (1929); CHRISTOPHER HILL, SOCIETY AND PURITANISM IN PRE-REVOLUTIONARY ENGLAND 310 (1967); HILL, *supra* note 272, at 8; 1 POLLOCK & MAITLAND, *supra* note 22, at 443; QUAIFE, *supra* note 84, at 191; MARGARET STIEG, LAUD'S LABORATORY: THE DIOCESE OF BATH AND WELLS IN THE EARLY SEVENTEENTH CENTURY 279–80 (1982); Means I, *supra* note 10, at 439 n.63.

of Clarendon (1166), an early form of statute, in this case to limit the applications of compurgation in royal criminal proceedings.[298] And, by the sixteenth century, three-fourths of the accused put to the oath were able to clear their names;[299] indeed, by then there were professional oath helpers who simply hung around the courts to provide the necessary oaths for a fee.[300] At least one careful study has found, however, that ecclesiastical courts were relatively effective, even during the weakening of their authority during the stresses of the Reformation.[301]

To evaluate the compurgation process, begin by noting that juries (which some see as derived from the oath-helpers of the compurgation process)[302] were just as unlikely to convict someone of a serious crime, yet they have not been subjected to similar skepticism.[303] Juries convicted only 20–25 percent of those accused of a crime during the Middle Ages, even when the jury was composed largely or completely of the same men as the "presenting jury"—the body that brought the charge in the first place.[304] Rather than condemning juries as failures, modern commentators are likely to see their failure to convict as "humanizing" the otherwise harsh medieval law of crimes.[305] Juries' subjection to the prejudices and the influence of local magnates also might explain the propensity of jurors to change their mind between presentment and trial.[306]

The more central role that religious faith played in medieval lives might even have made the compurgation process more reliable than juries. In the early Middle Ages, religious faith was so strong that in a trial in 1050 a bishop apparently found himself unable to utter the standard clerical formula *"Gloria filio et patri et spiritu sancto"* in a court.[307] Further more, the oath-helpers were likely to be neighbors in small, tightly knit communities who would have to live with the perpetrator, the victim, and the parish priest afterwards.[308] Indeed, an accused could not even be required to take the oath unless there was first a showing that the community generally consid-

---

298. The relevant portions of the Assize are quoted in PLUCKNETT, *supra* note 22, at 112–13. *See also* HELMHOLZ, *supra* note 84, at 65–66, 136–37; H.C. LEA, SUPERSTITION AND FORCE 1–84 (2nd ed. 1971); G.B. Flahiff, *The Writ of Prohibition to Court Christian in the Thirteenth Century (Pt. II)*, 7 MEDIEVAL STUD. 229, 269 (1945).

299. EMMISON, *supra* note 297, at 296; HELMHOLZ, *supra* note 84, at 137; HOULBROOKE, *supra* note 259, at 45. Helmholz indicated that in earlier periods, the conviction rate was even lower, although he acknowledged that his opinion was based on rather slim samples.

300. BAKER, LEGAL PROFESSION, *supra* note 30, at 424–26. These "strawmen" (so called because they could be identified by a straw behind their ear) were also available as professional witnesses to speak on behalf of the parties who, as such, were barred from testifying at a trial. *Id.* at 426, 438. *See also* PLUCKNETT, *supra* note 22, at 160.

301. INGRAM, *supra* note 260, at 323–74.

302. See the authorities to this effect collected *supra* at note 84.

303. BELLAMY, *supra* note 297, at 157–61; J.B. GIVEN, SOCIETY AND HOMICIDE IN THIRTEENTH-CENTURY ENGLAND 7 (1979); HELMHOLZ, *supra* note 84, at 137–38; HILL, *supra* note 297, at 371; INGRAM, *supra* note 260, at 17, 34–35, 323, 344–45; R.B. PUGH, SOME REFLECTIONS OF A MEDIEVAL CRIMINOLOGIST 140 (1973).

304. Thomas Green, *The Jury and the English Law of Homicide, 1200–1600*, 74 MICH. L. REV. 414, 431 (1976) (20% conviction rate for all defendants); Barbara Hanawah, *Crime in East Anglia in the Fourteenth Century*, 46 NORFOLK RECORD SOC'Y 20 (1976) (30% conviction rate for larceny); Elizabeth Kimball, *A Cambridgeshire Gaol Delivery Roll, 1332–1334*, 4 CAMBRIDGE ANTIQUARIAN RECORDS 26 (1978) (25% conviction rate for all felonies). On the overlap between trial juries and presenting juries, see Musson, *supra* note 85, at 136–40.

305. BELLAMY, *supra* note 297, at 161; GIVEN, *supra* note 303, at 105.

306. G.R. ELTON, POLICY AND POLICE: THE ENFORCEMENT OF THE REFORMATION IN THE AGE OF THOMAS CROMWELL 310 (1972).

307. A. Stacpole, *Hugh of Cluny and the Hildebrandine Miracle Tradition*, 77 BENEDICTINE STUDIES 341, 356–58 (1967).

308. BAKER, *supra* note 22, at 87; HELMHOLZ, *supra* note 84, at 135–36, 139; INGRAM, *supra* note 260, at 248–49, 329–32; MILSOM, *supra* note 22, at 38–39, 67, 245, 408–12; PLUCKNETT, *supra* note 22, at 115–16; VON CAENEGEM, *supra* note 22, at 66–67; Hyams, *supra* note 23, at 92–93, 95. 98–99, 106–08.

ered the person guilty (*fama*—"common fame");[309] one could not be put to the oath simply by accusation by one's enemies.[310] During the Elizabethan era, the instructions to the parishes dropped the requirement of notoriety,[311] although "fame" regarding crimes was still admitted as evidence in criminal trials before juries as late as the early seventeenth century.[312] This suggests that the real function of compurgation was to publicize innocence (should that be established) rather than to determine guilt.[313]

Historian Paul Hyams has suggested that before the oath was administered, the judge often made clear whom he thought should win, thus affecting the outcome of the oathtaking.[314] In any event, during some periods as many as half the people offered compurgation in a church court failed the test.[315] Law courts took ecclesiastical compurgations seriously, treating the result as evidence and even referring cases to the church courts for compurgation before proceeding to the conclusion of a law trial.[316] These various circumstances perhaps reflect delays in the oath taking until all parties were willing to acquiesce in the proposed outcome. This practice would be less troubling than one might expect given the social pressures to accept a reasonable resolution[317]— except, of course, in cases that were the most troubled to begin with. Finally, one might note that compurgation continues today to be a vital form of legal process in France, Italy, Morocco, the Netherlands, and Spain.[318] These patterns hardly suggest an unreliable and ineffectual procedure.

The medieval constraints might well have made compurgation about as likely to produce true results as would modern trial processes, at least until the compurgation trials were removed to distant courts. Removal of trials from the community in which the witnesses lived to the centralized royal courts accounts for the decline of compurgation in lay courts long before a similar decline occurred in the still dispersed church courts.[319] The looming Reformation also tended to make spiritual threats from one cleric more likely to be an occasion to join another church than a source of fear for one's eternal soul.[320] This was particularly true in England, where Henry VIII

---

309. On the role of ill repute in justifying an *ex officio* investigation, see Fraher, *supra* note 40; Herrman, *supra* note 290, at 47–49; Mary Hume Maguire, *Attack of the Common Lawyers on the Oath ex Officio as Administered in the Ecclesiastical Courts of England,* in Essays in History and Political Theory in Honor of Charles Howard McIlwain 199, 203–06 (Carl Wittke ed. 1936).

310. Helmholz, *supra* note 84, at 131–33; Hill, *supra* note 297, at 310; Ingram, *supra* note 260, at 238–45, 328–29; Milsom, *supra* note 22, at 506–09. *See also* M. Patricia Hogan, *Medieval Villany: A Study in the Meaning and Control of Crime in an English Village,* 2 Stud. in Medieval & Renaissance Hist. (N.S.) 123 (1979); H.R.T. Summerson, *The Structure of Law Enforcement in Thirteenth Century England,* 23 Am. J. Legal Hist. 313 (1979).

311. Quaife, *supra* note 84, at 39, 48–50, 187–88; Rodes, *supra* note 266, at 137–40.

312. Ingram, *supra* note 260, at 332; Thomas, *supra* note 191, at 528.

313. Helmholz, *supra* note 84, at 138–41. *See also* R.B. Pugh, *The Writ de Bono et Malo,* 92 L.Q. Rev. 258 (1976).

314. Hyams, *supra* note 23, at 98.

315. Ingram, *supra* note 260, at 334. *See also* Houlbrooke, *supra* note 269, at 45–46.

316. Marchant, *supra* note 195, at 225.

317. Helmholz, *supra* note 84, at 33, 106–11, 115, 138–44; Houlbrooke, *supra* note 269, at 310–11.

318. Mauro Capolletti & Bryant Garth, 16 International Encyclopedia of Comparative Law 37–38 (1987); Herbert Liebesny, Foreign Legal Systems: A Comparative Analysis 318–19 (1981); Lawrence Rosen, The Antrhopolgy of Justice: Law as Culture in Islam 33 (1989); Thomas Glyn Watkin, The Italian Legal Tradition 103–04 (1997).

319. Helmholz, *supra* note 84, at 61–66.

320. J.H. Aveling, The Handle and the Axe: The Catholic Recusants in England from Reformation to Emancipation (1976); Baker, *supra* note 22, at 87–88; Patrick Collinson, The Elizabethan Puritan Movement 40–41 (1967); John Davis, Heresy and Reformation in the South-East of England, 1520–1559 (1983); Helmholz, *supra* note 260, at 34–41, 47–48; Hill, *supra* note 297, at 360–70; Houlbrooke, *supra* note 269, at 49–50, 267–69; Ingram, *supra* note 260, at 53, 84–86, 90–96, 107–24, 330–31, 340–63, 373–74; D.M. Loades, The Reign of Mary Tudor: Politics, Government and Religion in England, 1553–1558, at 153 (1979); Marchant, *supra* note 195, at 203–34, 243; Diarmaid MacCulloch, The

broke with Rome but attempted to preserve an English version of Catholicism, followed by his son Edward VI under whom the Anglican Church turned more Protestant, followed by Mary I who reverted to Roman Catholicism, and finally by Elizabeth I under whom the English church turned decidedly Protestant.[321]

The twists and turns at the top both tended to delegitimate the established church and to result in survival of vestigial groups of followers at each turn. Because the Protestants sought to defend their reforms against the institutionalized tradition of the Roman Catholic Church by appeals to Scripture as a direct source of authority, the very process of official religious rebellion legitimated even more splintering of new Protestant sects as different groups disagreed among themselves about how to read Scripture. In reaction to this splintering,[322] the leaders of the established Church undertook strenuous, yet unavailing, efforts to coerce adherence to the (official) Church of England. They established the High Commission as the principle organ, but also sought to strengthen the *ex officio* (criminal) side of the ordinary Courts Christian.[323] Thus, we find a prosecution for saying "Amen" too loudly (and hence scoffingly) after public prayers.[324] These efforts cannot have been very effective, for we find the first frequent appearance of prosecutions for consorting with excommunicants during the sixteenth century.[325] Also during this period, lawyers ("proctors") became common in the Courts Christian after having been rare before the Reformation.[326] And, during this period, both royal (prerogative) and ecclesiastical courts sought to shore up the efficacy of the procedure by adding torture to "test" the oaths.[327]

Already in the fourteenth century, if not earlier, compurgation too often turned simply into a swearing contest in which both parties could (and often did) attempt to win the contest by introducing ever larger numbers of witnesses, many of whom served only to impress the court with the number and importance of a party's support.[328] When, by the close of the fifteenth century, "oath-helpers" began to be merely hired "witnesses" tolerated for the trial of less serious issues, the efficacy of the procedure must have been of little further utility.[329] The use of profes-

---

LATER REFORMATION IN ENGLAND: 1547–1603, at 135 (1990); MILSOM, *supra* note 22, at 67–68, 245–48, 410–12; PLUCKNETT, *supra* note 22, at 116, 363–64; JASPER GODWIN RIDLEY, THE LIFE AND TIMES OF MARY TUDOR 173 (1973); ROLAND USHER, THE RISE AND FALL OF THE HIGH COMMISSION 99 (rev. ed. 1968); ROBERT WHITING, THE BLIND DEVOTION OF THE PEOPLE: POPULAR RELIGION AND THE ENGLISH REFORMATION (1989); KEITH WRIGHTSON & DAVID LEVINE, POVERTY AND PIETY IN AN ENGLISH VILLAGE: TERLING, 1525–1700 (1979); Michael deHaven Newsom, *The American Protestant Empire: A Historical Perspective,* 40 WASHBURN L.J. 187, 221–23 (2001); F.D. Price, *The Abuses of Excommunication and the Decline of Ecclesiastical Discipline under Queen Elizabeth,* 57 ENG. HIST. REV. 106 (1942).

321. *See generally* A.G. DICKENS, THE ENGLISH REFORMATION (2nd ed. 1964); T.M. PARKER, THE ENGLISH REFORMATION TO 1558 (2nd ed. 1976); LEO SOLT, CHURCH AND STATE IN EARLY MODERN ENGLAND, 1509–1640, at 44–80 (1990).

322. BARBARA SHAPIRO, PROBABILITY AND CERTAINTY IN SEVENTEENTH-CENTURY ENGLAND 78 (1983).

323. CHAPMAN, *supra* note 263, at 19–20; HELMHOLZ, *supra* note 260, at 39, 45–48, 77–78, 105–17, 160, 174; NORMAN JONES, FAITH BY STATUTE (1982); KENNETH PARKER, THE ENGLISH SABBATH 133–38 (1988); RODES, *supra* note 266, at 152–63, 170–74, 208–11, 236–37; USHER, *supra* note 320; Maguire, *supra* note 309, at 212–20; H. Gareth Owen, *The Episcopal Visitation: Its Limits and Limitations in Elizabethan London,* 11 J. ECCLESIASTICAL HIST. 179 (1960); J.A. Vage, *Ecclesiastical Discipline in the Early Seventeenth Century,* 7 J. SOC'Y ARCHIVISTS 86 (1982).

324. Maie's Case, in HELMHOLZ, *supra* note 260, at 108.

325. HELMHOLZ, *supra* note 260, at 113–14.

326. *Id.* at 117–19; INGRAM, *supra* note 260, at 61–62.

327. 1 HOLDSWORTH, *supra* note 7, at 609; 3 HOLDSWORTH, *supra,* at 301; JOHN LANGBEIN, TORTURE AND THE LAW OF PROOF: EUROPE AND ENGLAND IN THE *ANCIEN REGIME* (1977); 1 POLLOCK & MAITLAND, *supra* note 22, at 426–27; RADIN, *supra* note 22, at 194–95; HYAMS, *supra* note 23, at 125–26.

328. Donohue, *supra* note 40, at 148–53.

329. BAKER, *supra* note 22, at 87–88; MILSOM, *supra* note 22, at 245–48, 285–86; RODES, *supra* note 266, at 178.

sional witnesses (called "strawmen" because they loitered outside the courts with a straw behind an ear to identify themselves), became so common that occasional critics of church court officers could characterize the oaths taken in connection with their official duties as worth no more than "the taking up of a straw."[330] Still, such evidence as we have of strawmen as oath-helpers or false witnesses pertains to the law courts and not directly to the church courts.[331] Strawmen were all the more likely to be used in the prosecution of crimes like abortion for which there would be few witnesses other than the parties to the crime—parties who, by the fifteenth century, were considered incompetent to testify precisely because they were parties to the litigation.[332]

In church courts, a more developed system of proof by witnesses was introduced early on from the Roman law along with procedural requirements similar to modern notions of due process, both centuries before lay courts developed like requirements.[333] Witnesses in proceedings brought in the name of the church (*ex officio,* rather than based on an individual complainant)[334] were required to take an oath to answer all questions put to them—the dreaded *ex officio* oath that was also used in the Star Chamber. This oath eventually came to be understood as contrary to the liberties of Englishmen by denying the privilege against self-incrimination.[335]

With the decline of the efficacy of oaths, the ecclesiastical records that have been searched (mostly late fifteenth through sixteenth centuries) are precisely those in which the procedures followed in the church courts were least likely to have been effective in checking abortion (or any other transgression), while proceedings that might have been brought during earlier, more effective periods of ecclesiastical law remain virtually unresearched.[336] There is yet another reason for the lack of discovery of successful prosecutions of abortion in the church's courts: Researchers have been looking for the wrong kinds of cases.

In the fifteenth century, most ecclesiastical prosecutions for abortions denominated as such involved injury techniques. In this, church proceedings resembled contemporary royal proceedings which, regarding abortion, still exclusively involved injury techniques.[337] Two ecclesiastical prosecutions, however, involved ingestion techniques.[338] Attempted recourse to ingestion tech-

---

330. *See* THOMAS, *supra* note 191, at 67.

331. INGRAM, *supra* note 260, at 333.

332. Donohue, *supra* note 40, at 130–31.

333. BRUNDAGE, *supra* note 24, at 93–96, 129–34; CHAPMAN, *supra* note 263, at 43–47; HELMHOLZ, *supra* note 84, at 104–06, 113–14, 131–36; HELMHOLZ, *supra* note 260, at 179–80; INGRAM, *supra* note 260, at 47–51; LOGAN, *supra* note 279, at 116–20; Donohue, *supra* note 40; Richard Fraher, *Conviction According to Conscience: The Medieval Jurists' Debate Concerning Judicial Discretion and the Law of Proof,* 7 LAW & HIST. REV. 23 (1989). *See also* QUAIFE, *supra* note 84, at 191–92; RODES, *supra* note 266, at 178–79.

334. CHAPMAN, *supra* note 263, at 47–48; INGRAM, *supra* note 260, at 43–47.

335. *See* ROBERT BEALE, A BOOK AGAINST OATHS MINISTERED IN THE COURTS OF ECCLESIASTICAL COMMISSION FROM HER MAJESTY, AND OTHER COURTS ECCLESIASTICAL (1583). *See generally* HELMHOLZ, *supra* note 260, at 131–32, 156–57; HELMHOLZ, *supra* note 195, at 155–56; R.H. HELMHOLZ ET AL., THE PRIVILEGE AGAINST SELF-INCRIMINATION: ITS ORIGINS AND DEVELOPMENT 17–20 (1997); HILL, *supra* note 297, at 382–408; INGRAM, *supra* note 260, at 329; LEONARD LEVY, ORIGINS OF THE FIFTH AMENDMENT 266–79 (1968); RODES, *supra* note 266, at 186, 207–08; Maguire, *supra* note 309; John Henry Wigmore, *The Privilege against Self-Crimination (sic): Its History,* 15 HARV. L. REV. 610 (1902).

336. *See, e.g.,* HOULBROOKE, *supra* note 269; Price, *supra* note 320.

337. Rex v. Cokkes (Ch. 1415), 7 CALENDAR OF INQUISITIONS MISC. (CH.) PRESERVED IN THE PUB. REC. OFF. 1399–1422, at 296 (no. 523) (1968); Rex v. Portere (K.B. 1400), THE SHROPSHIRE PEACE ROLE 1400–1414, at 57–58 (no. 24) (1959).

338. George Hemery's Case (Rochester 1493), in HELMHOLZ, *supra* note 84, at 159 n.12; Joan Gibbe's Servant's Case (Canterbury 1469), in HELMHOLZ, *supra,* at 159 n.13.

niques struck the fifteenth century mind as a kind of witchcraft,[339] and was punishable as such. Accusations of witchcraft related to abortion continued in England down to the early years of the nineteenth century.[340]

Between 100,000 and 200,000 women were accused of witchcraft in England between 1450 and 1750, with about half being executed.[341] (Men were rarely accused; of 291 accused witches in Essex County between 1560 and 1680, only 23 were men, and 11 of those were accused in conjunction with a woman.[342]) Even with all the executions, the rate of acquittals in England actually was among the highest in Europe, particularly after trial moved from ecclesiastical courts into the law courts before a jury.[343] The number of witchcraft prosecutions peaked generally across Europe between 1550 and 1650.[344] England followed the general European pattern, with the number of trials peaking in the 1580s and the number of executions rising thereafter even as the number of trials declined.[345] King James (VI of Scotland, I of England) himself had written a book on witchcraft and sponsored a new law against witchcraft in his first English Parliament.[346]

Understanding the phenomenon of witchcraft trials is complex and problematic. Just in this century, our image of the Salem Witchcraft Trials has moved from a vision of Freudian hysteria to class struggle to the suppression of feminine independence.[347] Others have interpreted witchcraft prosecutions as having been directed at lesbians, although direct evidence to support such claims is rather slim.[348] Prosecutors on rare occasions did include accusations of lesbian practices in proceedings against particular accused witches, including Joan of Arc.[349] Yet others have in-

---

339. *Malleus Maleficarum* 66 (Montague Summers ed. 1966; originally published 1488); James Rueff, The Expert Midwife 61 (1637). *See also* C.H. L'Estrange Ewen, Witchcraft & Demonism 41, 52, 77, 145 (1953).

340. *See* Anonymous, Extraordinary Life and Character of Mary Bateman, the Yorkshire Witch 12 (1809).

341. Brian Levack, *Possession, Witchcraft, and the Law of Jacobean England,* 32 Was. & L. L. Rev. 1613, 1614, 1624 (1995). *See generally* Witchcraft and Hysteria in Elizabethan London (Michael MacDonald ed. 1990).

342. Norman Cohn, Europe's Inner Demons: An Enquiry Inspired by the Great Witch-Hunt 248 (1975); Tannahill, *supra* note 215, at 273.

343. Brian Levack, The Witch-Hunt in Early Modern Europe 85–90 (1987); Andrew MacFarlane, Witchcraft in Tudor and Stuart England 57–58 (1970); Levack, *supra* note 341, at 1624–25, 1633, 1637–39. For estimates of the incidence of witchcraft prosecutions throughout Europe during this period, see Anne Barstow, Witchcraft: A New History of the European Witch-Hunts 20–23, 179–81 (1994); Levack, *supra,* at 19–22.

344. H.C. Erik Midelfort, Witch Hunting in South-Western Germany 1562–1684: The Social and Intellectual Foundations 89, 96–98, 137, 187 (1972); E. William Monter, Witchcraft in France and Switzerland 60 (1977); Tannahill, *supra* note 215, at 274; Levack, *supra* note 341, at 1616.

345. C.H. L'Estrange Ewen, Witch Hunting and Witch Trials: The Indictments for Witchcraft from the Records of the 1373 Assizes Held for the Home Circuit A.D. 1559–1736, at 100–01 (1929); MacFarlane, *supra* note 343, at 26–27, 58; Levack, *supra* note 341, at 1616–17.

346. James VI, Deamonologie (G.B. Harrison ed. 1924; first ed. 1597); 1 Jam., Ch. 12 (1604).

347. *See, e.g.,* John Demos, Entertaining Satan: Witchcraft and the Culture of Early New England (1982); Chadwick Hansen, Witchcraft at Salem (1969); Peter Charles Hoffer, The Devil's Disciples: Makers of the Salem Witchcraft Trials (1996); Peter Charles Hoffer, The Salem Witchcraft Trials: A Legal History (1997); Carol Karlsen, The Devil in the Shape of a Woman: Women and Witchcraft in Colonial New England (1987); Salem Possessed: The Social Origins of Witchcraft (Paul Boyer & Stephen Nissenbaum eds.1974); Witchcraft in Early Modern Europe: Studies in Culture and Belief (J. Barry *et al.* eds. 1996).

348. *See* Arthur Evans, Witchcraft and the Gay Counterculture (1978); Vern Bullough, *Heresy, Witchcraft and Sexuality,* in Sexual Practices and the Medieval Church 206, 211–17 (Vern Bullough & James Brundage eds. 1982); Ruthann Robson, *Lesbianism in Anglo-European Legal History,* 5 Wis. Women's L.J. 1, 31–36 (1990).

349. Evans, *supra* note 348, at 6, 11, 77, 151; Andrea Dworkin, Intercourse 90–95 (1987); J.B. Russell, Witchcraft in the Middle Ages 76, 260–61 (1972).

sisted that witchcraft trials were used as a means of Christianizing the masses and disciplining them to the emerging absolutist state.[350] Thus midwives were occasionally prosecuted for nothing more than using pagan incantations rather than Christian prayers while assisting at child birth.[351] Nor should we overlook the fact that those accused of witchcraft were often the mundane personal enemies of the accusers.[352]

We need not resolve these questions. For our purposes, merely note that witchcraft generally was the practice of medicine in the sense that its usual goal was to prevent (or cause) death and to alleviate pain and "human misfortune."[353] Nor should we overlook that the women involved in the practice of folk medicine generally were midwives.[354] Historian Thomas Forbes was sufficiently impressed by the connection between midwifery in general and prosecutions for witchcraft that he entitled a major work *The Midwife and the Witch*.[355] This does not mean that midwives generally promoted abortion; we know of midwives who deliberately misled women seeking abortions in order to preclude it.[356] Forbes himself identified only one proceeding that unequivocally charged an abortion. One suspects, however, that more of the witchcraft prosecutions that he described involved similar concerns. If so, medieval authorities considered abortion by ingestive techniques to be a crime against God as well as against the law. The evidence for this becomes clearer as we examine the records of the take over of the prosecution of witchcraft by the royal courts.

---

350. Brian Levack, *State-Building and Witch Hunting in Early Modern Europe,* in WITCHCRAFT IN EARLY MODERN EUROPE, *supra* note 347, at 96

351. *See, e.g.,* Isabel Muir's Case (York 1481), 35 THE FABRIC ROLLS OF YORK MINSTER No. 1528, at 273 (James Raine ed. 1859). *See generally* JEAN DONNISON, MIDWIVES AND MEDICAL MEN: A HISTORY OF THE STRUGGLE FOR THE CONTROL OF CHILDBIRTH 15 (2nd ed. 1988).

352. DONNISON, *supra* note 351, at 17; MIREILLE LAGET, *NAISSANCES: L'ACCOUCHEMNET AVANT L'AGE DE LA CLINIQUE* 55 (1982); THOMAS, *supra* note 191, at 311; Levack, *supra* note 341, at 1619–21.

353. DONNISON, *supra* note 351, at 17–19; THOMAS, *supra* note 191, at 5–17. *See also* LINDA GORDON, WOMAN'S BODY, WOMAN'S RIGHT: A SOCIAL HISTORY OF BIRTH CONTROL IN AMERICA 31–32 (1976).

354. *See* BARBARA BROOKES, ABORTION IN ENGLAND 1900–1967, at 54 (1988); JOHN D'EMILIO & ESTELLE FREEDMAN, INTIMATE MATTERS: A HISTORY OF SEXUALITY IN AMERICA 145–50 (1988); JOAN DONEGAN, WOMEN AND MEN MIDWIVES: MEDICINE, MORALITY, AND MISOGYNY IN EARLY AMERICA (1978); DONNISON, *supra* note 351, at 12–17; BARBARA EHRENREICH & DEIDRE ENGLISH, WITCHES, MIDWIVES, & NURSES: A HISTORY OF WOMEN HEALERS 44–48 (1973); GORDON, *supra* note 353, at 163–66; HARRISON, *supra* note 116, at 165–66; JOSEPH KETT, THE FORMATION OF THE AMERICAN MEDICAL PROFESSION: THE ROLE OF INSTITUTIONS, 1780–1890, at 117–21 (1968); LUKER, *supra* note 200, at 3–19; ANGUS MCLAREN, BIRTH CONTROL IN NINETEENTH-CENTURY ENGLAND 240–41 (1978); MCLAREN, *supra* note 100, at 123; ANN OAKLEY, THE CAPTURED WOMB: A HISTORY OF THE MEDICAL CARE OF PREGNANT WOMEN (1986); ROSALIND POLLACK PETCHESKY, ABORTION AND WOMEN'S CHOICE: THE STATE, SEXUALITY, AND REPRODUCTIVE FREEDOM 80–83, 169–78 (rev. ed. 1990); KERRY PETERSEN, ABORTION REGIMES 36–42 (1993); BARBARA KATZ ROTHMAN, IN LABOR: WOMEN AND POWER IN THE BIRTHPLACE (1982); RICHARD SHRYOCK, MEDICINE AND SOCIETY IN AMERICA: 1680–1860, at 143–51 (1960); CARROLL SMITH-ROSENBERG, DISORDERLY CONDUCT: VISIONS OF GENDER IN VICTORIAN AMERICA 228–29 (1985); PAUL STARR, THE SOCIAL TRANSFORMATION OF AMERICAN MEDICINE: THE RISE OF A SOVEREIGN PROFESSION AND THE MAKING OF A VAST INDUSTRY 32–37, 49–50, 54–59, 124 (1982); LAUREL THATCHER ULRICH, THE MIDWIFE'S TALE: THE LIFE OF MARTHA BALLARD BASED ON HER DIARY, 1785–1812, at 254–61, 339–40 (1991); MARY ROTH WALSH, DOCTORS WANTED: NO WOMEN NEED APPLY 1–10 (1977); DOROTHY & RICHARD WERTZ, LYING IN: A HISTORY OF CHILDBIRTH IN AMERICA 55–59 (1977); Lesley Biggs, *The Case of the Missing Midwives: A History of Midwifery in Ontario from 1795–1900,* 75 ONT. HIST. 21 (1973); Dianne Martin, *The Midwife's Tale: Old Wisdom and a New Challenge to the Control of Reproduction,* 3 COLUM. J. GENDER & L. 417 (1992).

355. T.R. FORBES, THE MIDWIFE AND THE WITCH (1966). *See also* JANET FARRELL BRODIE, CONTRACEPTION AND ABORTION IN NINETEENTH-CENTURY AMERICA 39 (1994); EHRENREICH & ENGLISH, *supra* note 354, at 44–48; KARLSEN, *supra* note 347; TANNAHILL, *supra* note 215, at 273–74; THOMAS, *supra* note 191, at 177–211, 435–583; D. Seaborn Davies, *The Law of Abortion and Necessity,* 2 MODERN L. REV. 126, 132 (1938). For a criticism of the identification of midwives with witchcraft, see Margaret Connor Versluyen, *Old Wives Tales? Women Healers in British History,* in REWRITING NURSING HISTORY 175, 191–93 (Celia Davis ed. 1980).

356. BRODIE, *supra* note 355, at 54–55; MARIE CAMPBELL, FOLDS DO GET BORN 85 (1946).

# Royal Courts Capture the Ecclesiastical Jurisdiction

*The law which church courts administered was the same law that the royal courts administered when they took over the jurisdiction, and the same law that the American courts have always administered.*

—Robert Rodes, Jr.[357]

During the fifteenth century, there are almost no records of prosecutions for abortion in the royal courts, perhaps suggesting that the royal courts were surrendering their competence in the matter into churchly hands. After all, much of the law regulating sexuality was relinquished into ecclesiastical hands on the continent.[358] This does not seem to be an entirely convincing answer for England as the retreat by secular authority was not so pronounced there as on the continent. Besides, abortion insofar as it appeared in the royal courts was more a matter of violence and death, not a matter of sexuality.[359] More probably, the dearth of records regarding such cases arose from the pervasive civil strife known as "The War of the Roses" (1455–1485), producing both a breakdown in civil order and a breakdown in record keeping.[360] In fact, litigation before royal courts appears to have declined generally because of the near collapse of the social order.[361] The strife did help to give us the concept of the judge owing allegiance to an impersonal law rather than to a personal sovereign, and thus contributed to the growth of the ideal of the "rule of law" in England.[362] The disorders ended with the establishment of the Tudor dictatorship. The Tudors, for their part, set about to restore the authority of legal institutions and (eventually) to take ecclesiastical matters into royal hands. The result was a considerable increase in litigation generally, including litigation involving the rights and interests of women in particular.[363]

Overlap in ecclesiastical and lay jurisdiction was normal in England throughout most of the country's history.[364] According to the great English judge, Lord Hale, both temporal and ecclesiastical courts derived their authority from the Crown, and thus both together represented the "law of England."[365] Indeed, as one historian recently observed,

> [I]t would probably be misleading to say that they [church courts] continued to offer an alternative to the civil courts in handling certain types of cases. Rather, most notably in probate and matrimonial cases, they *were* the civil courts. The law which church courts administered was the same law that the royal courts administered when they took over the jurisdiction, and the same law that the American courts have always administered.[366]

---

357. Robert Rodes, jr., *Secular Cases in the Church Courts: A Historical Survey*, 32 CATH. LAW. 301, 305 (1989).

358. *See* BRUNDAGE, *supra* note 262, at 223–28, 319–24, 578–79.

359. See the cases described *supra* at notes 76–169. *See also* DUBY, *supra* note 243, at 62.

360. 1 HOLDSWORTH, *supra* note 7, at 490–92; RADIN, *supra* note 22, at 14–15, 283–84, 291–93.

361. J.M. SOSIN, THE ARISTOCRACY OF THE LONG ROBE 38, 44–45 (1989).

362. BAKER, *supra* note 22, at 190. Some see the rise of the idea of "rule of law" and of other fundamental constitutional ideals as having roots in ecclesiastical law as much or more than in any secular developments. *See* BERMAN, *supra* note 24, at 98–119; HAROLD BERMAN, LAW AND REVOLUTION: THE FORMATION OF THE WESTERN LEGAL TRADITION (1983); BRIAN TIERNEY, RELIGION, LAW, AND THE GROWTH OF CONSTITUTIONAL THOUGHT, 1150–1650 (1982).

363. *See generally* TIM STRETTON, WOMEN WAGING LAW IN ELIZABETHAN ENGLAND (1998).

364. HELMHOLZ, *supra* note 84, at 59–99, 124–26, 167–68, 187–210; KEOWN, *supra* note 13, at 3–5.

365. 1 MATTHEW HALE, HISTORY OF PLEAS OF THE CROWN *Proemium* (an unnumbered first page) (1736). nSee also EDWARD COKE, SECOND INSTITUTE 599–618 (1642); MATTHEW HALE, ANALYSIS OF THE LAW 75–78 (1713).

366. Rodes, *supra* note 357, at 305. *See also* INGRAM, *supra* note 260, at 27–30.

In earlier centuries (before the War of the Roses), it was not unusual for a successful advocate or jurist in the Courts Christian to serve in one or another legal capacity in the lay administration and then to return to the ecclesiastical domain.[367] The traditional link between church and crown was exemplified by the *Statute of Winchester* adopted in 1393 prohibiting appeals to Rome from English ecclesiastical courts.[368] The statute completed a process begun 40 years earlier in the *Statute of Praemunire* of 1353 which decreed punishment for anyone who initiated a legal proceeding before a foreign court that should have been brought before a court of the realm.[369] Appeals to Rome were expensive and time consuming, forming an important source of income for the Papacy, and forming an important source of the medieval prosperity of the city of Rome.[370] The expense and delays incumbent on such appeals made the prohibition of appeals to Rome politically popular with the upper classes, the only group able to afford such proceedings.

Royal links to ecclesiastical courts had appeared at least a century and a half before the *Statute of Westminster* through the ritual formula for excommunicating "breakers of the church's liberties, and of the liberties or other customs of the realm."[371] The ensuing struggle over the relationship of secular and religious courts in turn grew out of and fed into the ongoing struggle between the Crown and the Church epitomized by the murder of Thomas à Becket in Canterbury Cathedral in 1171. After the *Statute of Westminster,* secular courts occasionally issued writs of prohibition against proceeding in a Court Christian, but without great success before the Reformation; equivalent proceedings were brought in the church courts against the party seeking the prohibition, apparently with greater efficiency, but without greater effect.[372] The theory that Courts Christian were a branch of royal authority was finally firmly established by the acceptance of the supremacy of the English Crown over the clergy in 1534 with the separation of the Church of England from Rome.[373]

The division of responsibility between lay and church courts fell more or less, albeit imperfectly, along these lines: The royal courts focused on keeping the King's peace; the church courts focused on crimes against conscience that did not involve violence or a threat of major social disruption.[374] This division in itself would account for the royal courts' concern with violent injurious

---

367. For brief biographies of three such men, see BRUNDAGE, *supra* note 24, at 136–37.

368. 16 Ric. 2 ch. 5 (1393). *See* BAKER, *supra* note 22, at 150.

369. 27 Edw. III, St. 1, c.1 (1353). *See* RODES, *supra* note 266, at 27–28, 46–48, 59–65; RADIN, *supra* note 22, at 107–08.

370. *See* BRUNDAGE, *supra* note 24, at 123–27; I.S. ROBINSON, THE PAPACY, 1073–1198: CONTINUITY AND INNOVATION 3, 106–39 (1990).

371. 38 Hen. III (1253), as translated in RODES, *supra* note 266, at 1.

372. HELMHOLZ, *supra* note 84, at 77–99; RODES, *supra* note 266, at 23–27; BRIAN WOODCOCK, MEDIEVAL ECCLESIASTICAL COURTS IN THE DIOCESE OF CANTERBURY 89–92 (1952); J. ROBERT WRIGHT, THE CHURCH AND THE ENGLISH CROWN, 1305–1334 (1980); Norma Adams, *The Writ of Prohibition to Court Christian,* 20 MINN. L. REV. 272 (1936); G.B. Flahiff, *The Use of Prohibition by Clerics against Ecclesiastical Courts in England,* 3 MEDIEVAL STUD. 101 (1941); G.B. Flahiff, *The Writ of Prohibition to Court Christian in the Thirteenth Century,* 6 MEDIEVAL STUD. 261 (1944) (Pt. I), 7 MEDIEVAL STUD. 229 (1945) (Pt. II). *See also* Charles Donahue, jr., *Roman Canon Law in the Medieval English Church:* Stubbs vs. Maitland *Re-examined after 75 Years in the Light of Some Records from the Church Courts,* 72 MICH. L. REV. 647 (1974); William Epstein, *Issues of Principle and Expediency in the Controversy over Prohibitions to Ecclesiastical Courts in England,* 1 J. LEGAL HIST. 211 (1980); W.R. Jones, *Relations of the Two Jurisdictions: Conflict and Cooperation during the Thirteenth and Fourteenth Centuries,* 7 STUD. IN MEDIEVAL & RENAISSANCE HIST. 79 (1970).

373. 26 Hen. VIII, c.1 (1534). *See* HELMHOLZ, *supra* note 260, at 29; RODES, *supra* note 266, at 87–94, 157–63. *See also* 24 Hen. VIII, c.12 (1533); 25 Hen. VIII, c.21 (1534); BAKER, *supra* note 22, at 146–54; HELMHOLZ, *supra* note 84, at 77–99; HELMHOLZ, *supra* note 260, at 25–54, 158–95; MILSOM, *supra* note 22, at 23–35; PLUCKNETT, *supra* note 22, at 197, 485, 729–31; RADIN, *supra* note 22, at 98–109.

374. BAKER, LEGAL PROFESSION, *supra* note 30, at 279–80; HELMHOLZ, *supra* note 84, at 126–31; HELMHOLZ, *supra* note 260, at 1–3, 21; 1 HOLDSWORTH, *supra* note 7, at 616–21; QUAIFE, *supra* note 84, at 197–98; RODES, *supra* note 266, at 12–22. For a description of this division written when it was breaking

abortions, and the church courts' concern with the perhaps voluntary ingestive abortions. Indeed, the few apparently voluntary attempts at abortion through injury techniques were prosecuted in a church court rather than in a royal court.[375] In addition to the likelihood that an ingestive abortion was voluntary rather than coerced, when abortion was sought through ingesting a potion it seemed to smack of magic sufficiently to seem devil's work. This made it appear peculiarly appropriate to the Courts Christian rather than to be a concern of lay courts. In a similar vein, a married couple was prosecuted before a church court for witchcraft because of they kept an empty cradle next to their bed and acted as if there were a child in it in an effort to encourage the conception of an actual child.[376] Finally, the continuing ability of the church courts to put a defendant to his or her oath without the hindrance of the emerging privilege against self-incrimination might have convinced royal judges that ecclesiastical courts were better suited to trying voluntary abortions where no evidence could be obtained except through a confession from one of the wrongdoers.[377]

The frequently overlapping jurisdictions of the lay and ecclesiastical courts across a broad range of human activities, however, produced a prolonged struggle between the two systems.[378] As legal historian Frederic Maitland noted, there always a "debatable land which is neither very spiritual nor very temporal."[379] This uncertain realm featured as much cooperation as competition.[380] The struggle aspect, however, is what concerns us here. The *Statue of Winchester* of 1393 was merely an incident in this struggle, until the triumph of the Reformation in England established the primacy of temporal law over canon law.[381]

Much of the early history of the common law consists of attempts by one court to capture the jurisdiction of another court, beginning with the struggle between the royal courts and the Courts Christian. This process broadened in the seventeenth century into a struggle of Parliament against the Crown, in which a central arena of the struggle was the efforts of the common law courts to capture the jurisdiction of the courts exercising the royal "prerogative" to do justice; only the Chancery Court survived largely intact.[382] The prerogative courts included the Court of Chancery, the Council (the Star Chamber), the Court of Admiralty, the Court of the Constable and Marshall, and others. The Star Chamber, as well as some of the ecclesiastical courts, were permanently abolished in 1641; the Court of the Constable and Marshall largely ceased to function after 1689, although one case was reported as late as 1737. The Court of Admiralty survived only in a highly truncated form. The outcome of this struggle also settled the

---

down, see Christopher St. Germain, Doctor and Student (c. 1530) (91 Selden Soc'y) (T.F.T. Plucknett & J.L. Barton eds. 1974). On St. Germain, see Rodes, *supra* note 266, at 69–77.

375. *See, e.g.,* Thomas Deneham's Case (Canterbury 1471), in Helmholz, *supra* note 84, at 159 n.11 (a man was charged with inducing an abortion through imposing "inordinate labors" upon a woman).

376. John Phipps' Case, 70 Oxfordshire Archival Soc'y Rep. 95 (1925); Thomas, *supra* note 191, at 188–89.

377. *See* Keown, *supra* note 13, at 5; Dellapenna, *supra* note 13, at 369.

378. Brundage, *supra* note 24, at 73, 175–78; Charles Duggan, Canon Law in Medieval England 359–90 (1982); Helmholz, *supra* note 260, at 1–5, 20–54, 158–95; 3 Holdsworth, *supra* note 7, at 299–307; Robert Rodes, jr., Ecclesiastical Administration in Medieval England (1977); Rodes, *supra* note 266; Richard Helmholz, *Conflicts between Religious and Secular Law: Common Themes in the English Experience,* 12 Cardozo L. Rev. 707 (1991).

379. Frederic Maitland, Roman Canon Law in the Church of England 56 (1898).

380. Helmholz, *supra* note 84, at 19–20; Helmholz, *supra* note 260, at 20; Jones, *supra* note 372.

381. J.J. Scarisbrick, Henry VIII, at 241–304 (1968); Epstein, *supra* note 372; Christopher Haigh, *Anticlericalism and the English Reformation,* in The English Reformation Revised 64 (Christopher Haigh ed. 1987). See also the authorities collected *supra* at note 372.

382. *See generally* Baker, *supra* note 22, at 14–62, 112–54; 1 Holdsworth, *supra* note 7, at 218–31, 395–525, 544–632; 2 Holdsworth, *supra,* at 251–52, 266–67, 304–07, 457–59; 5 Holdsworth, *supra,* at 412–23; 9 Holdsworth, *supra,* at 249; Milsom, *supra* note 22, at 11–36, 60–70, 82–96; Plucknett, *supra* note 22, at 48–67, 157–63, 169–73, 191–98, 657–70; Radin, *supra* note 22, at 65–72, 88–111, 168–78, 422–39.

long-standing question of the relation of positive law to natural law, in England largely subsumed as a struggle of Parliamentary statutes against judge-made common and prerogative law.[383] The Courts Christian were abolished entirely during the Civil War and Protectorate period, from 1640 to 1660, and reemerged thereafter as rather pale reflections of their former selves.[384]

We shall return to the struggle against the prerogative courts in the next chapter. Here we focus entirely on the struggle between church courts and the royal courts. One of the issues disputed today regarding these struggles is the extent that we should disregard the canon law applied in the church courts as having been based on religion—a body of law the application of which is impermissible in a nation with a constitutional prohibition on the establishment of religion.[385] Others dismiss reliance on canon law as expressing (along with most traditional religions) a male conspiracy against women.[386] As a Unitarian, I share suspicion of a hidden establishment of religion or of unjust conspiracies. The absorption of the greater part of the canon law into the common law is rather more complex than Means or other critics would suppose, however. The general displacement of ecclesiastical courts from a major role in English life did not put an end to much, if any, law formerly made and applied in the church courts. Much modern law that today are unquestionably secular originated in the church courts, often passing through the prerogative courts into the common law courts as law or into the chancery courts as equity.[387]

During the seventeenth century, the common law courts captured jurisdiction over libel and slander from the Star Chamber, which in turn had taken those proceedings over from the ecclesiastical courts.[388] The common law courts also captured the law of attempts and conspiracies from the Star Chamber, which again had taken them from the ecclesiastical courts.[389] The privilege against self-incrimination arose out the struggle between the common law courts and the

---

383. *See generally* NORMAN DOE, FUNDAMENTAL AUTHORITY IN LATE MEDIEVAL ENGLISH LAW (1990).

384. HELMHOLZ, *supra* note 260, at 122.

385. Means II, *supra* note 10, at 346–48.

386. *See, e.g.,* Angela Padilla & Jennifer Winrich, *Christianity, Feminism, and the Law,* 1 COLUM. J. GENDER & L. 67 (1991).

387. *See* BAKER, *supra* note 22, at 146–53; BRUNDAGE, *supra* note 24, at 70–72; HELMHOLZ, *supra* note 84, at 291–305, 341–53; HELMHOLZ, *supra* note 255, at 51–54; 1 HOLDSWORTH, *supra* note 7, at 65–77, 455–57, 580–632 (1938); 3 HOLDSWORTH, *supra,* at 408–28, 441–54, 534–36; 5 HOLDSWORTH, *supra,* at 167–69, 197–218, 291–99; 8 HOLDSWORTH, *supra,* at 301–07, 324–417; 15 HOLDSWORTH, *supra,* at 198–208; Charles Donohue, jr., Jus Commune, *Cannon Law, and Common Law in England,* 66 TULANE L. REV. 1745, 1768–80 (1992); R.H. Helmholz, *Continental Law and Common Law: Historical Strangers or Companions?,* 1990 DUKE L.J. 1207; Jack Moser, Note, *The Secularization of Equity: Ancient Religious Origins, Feudal Christian Influences, and Medieval Authoritarian Impacts on the Evolution of Legal Equitable Remedies,* 26 CAPITAL U.L. REV. 483 (1997); Samuel Thorne, *Tudor Social Transformation and Legal Change,* 26 NYU L. REV. 10, 19–22.

388. BAKER, *supra* note 22, at 495–503; IRVING BRANT, THE BILL OF RIGHTS 113–30, 154–73 (1965); BRUNDAGE, *supra* note 24, at 91–92; HELMHOLZ, *supra* note 260, at 2–3, 6–7, 24, 30–33, 35, 51–52, 56–69, 127, 138–39, 163–64, 174, 190–91; R.H. HELMHOLZ, SELECT CASES ON DEFAMATION TO 1600 (101 SELDEN SOC'Y) (1985); 5 HOLDSWORTH, *supra* note 7, at 205–12; 8 HOLDSWORTH, *supra,* at 333–78; INGRAM, *supra* note 260, at 292–319; MARCHANT, *supra* note 195, at 72–75; MILSOM, *supra* note 22, at 23–24, 379–92, 418; PLUCKNETT, *supra* note 22, at 488–500; RODES, *supra* note 266, at 21, 204–06; SOSIN, *supra* note 361, at 42–45; Donohue, *supra* note 387, at 1776–77; R.H. Helmholz, *Canonical Defamation in Medieval England,* 15 AM. J. LEGAL HIST. 255 (1971); Helmholz, *supra* note 387, at 1215–16, 1218–21; Samuel Rezneck, *The Trial of Treason in Tudor England,* in ESSAYS IN HISTORY AND POLITICAL THEORY IN HONOR OF CHARLES HOWARD MCILWAIN, *supra* note 309, at 258.

389. HELMHOLZ, *supra* note 195, at 129; 5 HOLDSWORTH, *supra* note 7, at 197–205; MILSOM, *supra* note 22, at 418–19, 427; JAMES FITZJAMES STEPHEN, 2 HISTORY OF THE CRIMINAL LAW OF ENGLAND 221–25 (1883). leH

Star Chamber.[390] The law of informal contracts passed to the law courts at about this time, partly from the Court of Chancery and partly directly from the ecclesiastical courts.[391] The early ecclesiastical concern with informal contracts became the basis for enforcing wills generally, and provisions for the support and inheritance of widows and daughters specifically, not to mention bequests to ecclesiastical institutions.[392] The ecclesiastical enforcement of wills was well established in England by the end of the twelfth century.[393] There is also some evidence that bankruptcy proceedings originated in ecclesiastical courts, although whatever happened there was not simply transplanted into secular courts.[394] Apparently, bankruptcy grew out of the probate jurisdiction that remained vested in English ecclesiastical courts until the nineteenth century.[395] The ecclesiastical courts also were involved in the regulation of other aspects of economic activity, some of which regulations survive (often considerably modified) into modern law.[396] In a sense, each of the resulting new common law proceedings dealt with violations of conscience that did not rise to the level of a breach of the peace. Yet, as these examples show, one cannot simply assume that because a body of law originated in the Courts Christian that the resulting law was merely an expression of what we today consider to be an establishment of religion.

The Tudor era saw an apparent upsurge in the attention given abortion in both ecclesiastical and temporal courts, although that might merely reflect the better record keeping of the Tudor dictatorship. Before the Reformation, the frequency of all sorts of proceedings in the church courts declined sharply—as much as 85 percent in some dioceses as common lawyers set about to capture the business of the Courts Christian for themselves.[397] The decline largely occurred before the Reformation reached England and slowly reversed itself after 1570.[398]

---

390. HELMHOLZ, *supra* note 84, at 9; LEONARD LEVY, ORIGINS OF THE FIFTH AMENDMENT (2nd ed. 1986); THE PRIVILEGE AGAINST SELF-INCRIMINATION: ITS ORIGINS AND DEVELOPMENT (Richard Helmholz ed. 1997); Helmholz, *supra* note 387, at 1216–18; Richard Helmholz, *Origins of the Privilege against Self-Incrimination: The Role of the European* Ius Commune, 65 NYU L. REV. 962 (1990).

391. HELMHOLZ, *supra* note 84, at 77–78, 263–89, 323–39; HELMHOLZ, *supra* note 260, at 2, 25, 30–33; HELMHOLZ, *supra* note 195, at 391; 1 HOLDSWORTH, *supra* note 7, at 455–57; 3 HOLDSWORTH, *supra*, at 441–54; 5 HOLDSWORTH, *supra*, at 294–99; 2 POLLOCK & MAITLAND, *supra* note 22, at 201; KEVIN TEEVEN, A HISTORY OF THE ANGLO-AMERICAN COMMON LAW OF CONTRACT 4, 35–36 (1990); Donahue, *supra* note 49, at 1764–66. *See generally* BAKER, LEGAL PROFESSION, *supra* note 30, at 341–68; BERMAN, *supra* note 24, at 70–97; 5 HOLDSWORTH, *supra*, at 167–69, 183, 197–218, 291–99; 8 HOLDSWORTH, *supra*, at 301–07, 324–427; MILSOM, *supra* note 22, at 23–25, 87–91, 201–02, 336–38, 343, 357; 2 POLLOCK & MAITLAND, *supra* note 22, at 185–98; PLUCKNETT, *supra* note 22, at 455–62, 483–502, 651; RODES, *supra* note 260, at 13–14, 204; A.W.B. SIMPSON, A HISTORY OF THE COMMON LAW OF CONTRACT: THE RISE OF THE ACTION OF ASSUMPSIT 375–405 (1987 ed.); THORNE, *supra* note 29, at 206–10; WOODCOCK, *supra* note 372, at 89–92; Frederick Pollock, *Contracts in Early English Law*, 6 HARV. L. REV. 389 (1893); O.W. Holmes, jr., *Early English Equity*, 1 L.Q. REV. 162, 173–74 (1885). *See also* BRUNDAGE, *supra* note 24, at 79–80.

392. HELMHOLZ, *supra* note 195, at 116–44; Milsom, *supra* note 37, at 62.

393. GLANVILL, *supra* note 32, at ¶ 7.8. *See generally* BRUNDAGE, *supra* note 24, at 87–90; CHAPMAN, *supra* note 263, at 22–23, 48–51; HELMHOLZ, *supra* note 84, at 307–21; HELMHOLZ, *supra* note 260, at 7–8, 13–14, 23–24, 31, 39, 79–89, 126, 134, 144, 160, 166, 174, 191; 2 POLLOCK & MAITLAND, *supra* note 22, at 331–33; RODES, *supra* note 266, at 13, 19–20.

394. HELMHOLZ, *supra* note 260, at 11–15.

395. HELMHOLZ, *supra* note 84, at 291–321.

396. *See* JOHN BALDWIN, MEDIEVAL THEORIES OF THE JUST PRICE (1959); BRUNDAGE, *supra* note 24, at 75–87; JOHN GILCHRIST, THE CHURCH AND ECONOMIC ACTIVITY IN THE MIDDLE AGES (1969); HELMHOLZ, *supra* note 84, at 325–39; JOHN NOONAN, THE SCHOLASTIC ANALYSIS OF USURY (1957); John McGovern, *The Rise of New Economic Attitudes—Economic Humanism, Economic Nationalism—During the Later Middle Ages and the Renaissance*, 26 TRADITIO 217 (1970).

397. HELMHOLZ, *supra* note 260, at 31–32; WUNDERLI, *supra* note 269, at 81.

398. HELMHOLZ, *supra* note 260, at 43–45, 48. *See also* PETER CLARK, ENGLISH PROVINCIAL SOCIETY FROM THE REFORMATION TO THE REVOLUTION 280 (1977); INGRAM, *supra* note 260, at 69; MARCHANT, *supra* note 195, at 16–18, 62; WRIGHTSON & LEVINE, *supra* note 321, at 113–14; Ralph Houlbrooke, *The Decline of Eccle-*

Along with the decline of the business of the church courts was a decline in the quality of record keeping in those courts.[399] Again, this might be more a question of appearance than of reality. Entire record collections (called "Act Books") are missing, perhaps having been destroyed during one or another of the dramatic shifts in religious policy by the Crown during the sixteenth century.[400] Only after 1570 did the record-keeping improve, and improve dramatically.[401] The apparent upsurge in litigation after the Reformation thus might merely be a reflection of better record keeping, but one suspects there was a real change going on. After all, there was an upsurge in litigation across Western Europe during the Reformation era.[402] There is no reason to believe that England escaped this shift given that courts there as well as elsewhere in Europe were increasingly used to suppress dissent and to enforce the new religious orthodoxy.[403]

This period and the ensuing Jacobean period also saw a flowering of an English literature regarding ecclesiastical law[404] even though the church courts continued to apply the general Canon Law derived from the old religion in so far as it was consistent with the new official church.[405] As the Reformation progressed, the actual efficacy of church courts declined markedly, however, in part because the church courts became particular targets for enemies of the existing order (both religious and lay).[406] The decline of the church courts made those courts increasingly vulnerable to attack spurred by the growing dissension within English Protestantism (divided into Episcopalians, Presbyterians, Independents, and smaller groups).[407] The struggle was as much political as religious, both because of the royal involvement in church affairs and because the pulpit then provided the only organized means for influencing a still mostly illiterate population.[408] This would lead in the century after the Tudors to the Puritan Revolution of 1642–1649 and the Cromwellian dictatorship. We do not need to resolve the seemingly endless debate over the "deeper" causes of the Puritan Revolution, for regardless of those "deeper" causes the struggle focused on control of the pulpit and the subordination of the ecclesiastical courts to lay authority symbolized by the law courts.[409]

---

*siastical Jurisdiction under the Tudors,* in CONTINUITY AND CHANGE: PERSONNEL AND ADMINISTRATION OF THE CHURCH OF ENGLAND, 1500–1642, at 239, 244–48 (R. O'Day & F. Heal eds. 1976).

399. HELMHOLZ, *supra* note 260, at 34; WOODCOCK, *supra* note 372, at 3.

400. HELMHOLZ, *supra* note 260, at 38.

401. *Id.* at 42–43; WOODCOCK, *supra* note 372, at 3.

402. *See* RICHARD KAGAN, LAWYERS AND LITIGANTS IN GOLDEN AGE CASTILE, 1500–1700, at 3–20 (1981); Donohue, *supra* note 262, at 445–46.

403. HELMHOLZ, *supra* note 260, at 44–60, 74–77.

404. HELMHOLZ, *supra* note 260, at 121–57.

405. BRUNDAGE, *supra* note 24, at 183–84; HELMHOLZ, *supra* note 260, at 150.

406. *See generally* BAKER, *supra* note 22, at 150–52; HELMHOLZ, *supra* note 260, at 25–54; 1 HOLDSWORTH, *supra* note 7, at 588–96; 4 HOLDSWORTH, *supra,* at 3–54, 215–17, 232, 494–510; 5 HOLDSWORTH, *supra,* at 219–20, 273–94; MILSOM, *supra* note 22, at 380–84; MARCHANT, *supra* note 195; PLUCKNETT, *supra* note 22, at 39–47; H.R. TREVOR-ROPER, RELIGION, THE REFORMATION AND SOCIAL CHANGE (1967); Houlbrooke, *supra* note 398, at 239.

407. *See generally* HELMHOLZ, *supra* note 260, at 30–34, 171–88; 6 HOLDSWORTH, *supra* note 7, at 122–38.

408. MAURICE ASHLEY, THE GREATNESS OF OLIVER CROMWELL 42–44 (Collier Bks. ed. 1957); 6 HOLDSWORTH, *supra* note 7, at 133–36; Dellapenna, *supra* note 13, at 382–84.

409. *See* THOMAS COGSWELL, THE BLESSED REVOLUTION: ENGLISH POLITICS AND THE COMING OF WAR, 1621–1624 (1989); CONFLICT IN EARLY STUART ENGLAND: STUDIES IN RELIGION AND POLITICS, 1603–1642 (Robert Cust & Ann Hughes eds. 1989); CHRISTOPHER DURSTON, CHARLES I (1998); JACK GOLDSTONE, REVOLUTION AND REBELLION IN THE EARLY MODERN WORLD (1991); CHRISTOPHER HILL, THE ENGLISH BIBLE AND THE SEVENTEENTH CENTURY REVOLUTION (1993); MARGARET JUDSON, CRISIS OF THE CONSTITUTION (1949); L.J. REEVE, CHARLES I AND THE ROAD TO PERSONAL RULE (1989); CONRAD RUSSELL, THE CAUSES OF THE ENGLISH CIVIL WAR (1990); J.P. SOMERVILLE, POLITICS AND IDEOLOGY IN ENGLAND, 1603–1642 (1986); LAWRENCE STONE, THE CAUSES OF THE ENGLISH REVOLUTION, 1529–1642 (1972); MICHAEL YOUNG, CHARLES I (1997).

The struggle for and against the ecclesiastical courts eventually led to yet another assertion of lay authority at the expense of clerical authority over abortion. Such a transition was hardly surprising in a context in which vast amounts of formerly ecclesiastical law was transformed into common law. These transitions were not so much an establishment of religion as a secularization of legal processes. This is not to say that religious attitudes were irrelevant. The Church of England, contrary to some Protestant sects that simply did not pay much attention to the problem and consistent with the Anglican liturgical closeness to Catholicism, continued the church's strong moral condemnation of abortion.[410] Yet in the end, abortion by ingestive as well as by injurious techniques became a province of the common law courts and the role of canon law courts became utterly secondary.

Ecclesiastical court records include no less than ten prosecutions for abortion during the reign of the first two Tudor kings (1485–1547). These records, still terse and barely informative, include inconclusive proceedings[411] and acquittals,[412] but they also include cases involving a flight to avoid prosecution[413] and punishments.[414] Two things are noteworthy in this flurry of activity. First, as before in both lay and ecclesiastical courts, no one challenged the propriety of the prosecutions. Second, eight of these ten cases involved ingestive abortions,[415] removing any doubt about whether such abortions were included within the proscription of abortion already evident in the earlier cases involving injurious abortions. As final evidence of the determination of the English courts to exploit the ecclesiastical institutions to suppress witchcraft, infanticide, and abortion was the requirement enacted in 1512 requiring midwives to receive an ecclesiastical license issued only after the midwife took an oath not to engage in such practices.[416] Midwives were also required to commit themselves to baptize all infants properly.[417] These regulations were repeatedly strengthened over the centuries.[418]

---

410. HARRISON, *supra* note 116, at 148–50. *See generally* George Houston Williams, *Religious Residues and Presuppositions in the American Debate on Abortion*, 31 THEOLOGICAL STUD. 33, 42 (1970).

411. Elizabeth Fraunce's Case (July 26, 1556), in EWEN, *supra* note 339, at 318 (a witchcraft prosecution); Thomas Love's Case, HRO CB4, fo. 117v (Winchester 1534); Anonymous' Case (Canterbury 1521), in HELMHOLZ, *supra* note 84, at 159 n.13; John Wren's Case (London Dioc. Commissary Ct. 1487), in HELMHOLZ, *supra*, at 387 n.10. *See also* STRETTON, *supra* note 363, at 200.

412. Margaret Sawnder's Case (London Dioc. 1527), in HALE, *supra* note 296, at 34 (no. 128); John Russell's Case (London Dioc. Ct. 1493), in HALE, *supra* note 293, at 105 (No. 331).

413. George Hemery's Case (Rochester 1493), in HELMHOLZ, *supra* note 84, at 159 n.12.

414. Agnes Hobsen's Case, (York ca. 1550), in FORBES, *supra* note 355, at 149 ("expiation" reported); Thomas Tyry's Case, HRO CB2, fo. 59v (Winchester, mid-1500s) (a public penance was ordered for an abortion brought about by the defendant's son); John Hunt's Case (Hertfordshire 1530) (a public penance and marriage were ordered), in BEFORE THE BAWDY COURT, *supra* note 192, at 81 (no. 150). *See also* Joan Schower's Case (Buckinghamshire 1530), in BEFORE THE BAWDY COURT, *supra*, at 204 (no. 531) (a woman was punished for what the record describes as the "lesser crime" of giving birth to bastards, without any record of the resolution of an accompanying charge of abortion; as abortion was the only other charge reported, the description of birthing bastards as a "lesser crime" must mean that abortion was a more serious crime).

415. Agnes Hobsen's Case, (York ca. 1550), in FORBES, *supra* note 355, at 149; Thomas Tyry's Case, HRO CB2, fo. 59v (Winchester, mid-1500s); Thomas Love's Case, HRO CB4, fo. 117v (Winchester 1534); Joan Schower's Case (Buckinghamshire 1530), in BEFORE THE BAWDY COURT, *supra* note 190, at 204 (no. 531); John Hunt's Case (Hertfordshire 1530), in BEFORE THE BAWDY COURT, *supra*, at 81 (no. 150); Margaret Sawnder's Case (London Dioc. 1527), in HALE, *supra* note 296, at 34 (no. 128); Anonymous' Case (Canterbury 1521), in HELMHOLZ, *supra* note 84, at 159 n.13; George Hemery's Case (Rochester 1493), in HELMHOLZ, *supra*, at 391 n.12.

416. 1 BONNIE ANDERSON & JUDITH ZINSSER, A HISTORY OF THEIR OWN: WOMEN IN EUROPE FROM PREHISTORY TO THE PRESENT 163, 168, 170–71, 419–21 (1988); DONNISON, *supra* note 351, at 18–20; PETERSEN, *supra* note 354, at 11.

417. DONNISON, *supra* note 351, at 15–16; FORBES, *supra* note 355, at 141.

418. FORBES, *supra* note 355, at 144–47. *See, e.g.*, JANE SHARP, THE MIDWIVES BOOK 38 (1671).

Midwives did figure somewhat in the reported prosecutions in the sixteenth century.[419] Those who want to argue that abortion was always socially acceptable before the nineteenth century also admit, without any apparent recognition of the implications, that one reason midwives lost out to physicians was the unsavory reputation that arose from the linkage of midwifery to abortion.[420] Midwives were by no means always the nurturing mother figures exercising secret skills to alleviate pain and serve women that feminist historians conjure up. The midwife's license in 1590 even found it necessary to forbid explicitly the midwife's torturing a woman in labor in order to extort extra fees.[421]

The persistence of ecclesiastical proceedings against abortions without challenge to the ecclesiastical jurisdiction is all the more telling in light of the apparently dramatic declines in the frequency of ecclesiastical proceedings generally during the period before 1570.[422] The period also saw a decline in the enforcement of the ecclesiastical licensing of midwives.[423] Furthermore, the fact that few were charged with the crime of abortion without also being charged with other, related crimes led historian Angus McLaren to infer that no one really cared to prosecute abortion as such.[424] His inference ignores both the technical limitations of the time on the ability to induce abortion and the technical difficulties of proof in ecclesiastical courts. Despite these limitations and the temporary general decline of the ecclesiastical courts, the records of the abortion proceedings during this time puts the question of whether abortion was some sort of canonical crime in England beyond dispute.

The opening of sixteenth-century also finds a sudden spurt of lay proceedings; in these decisions, courts and other officers of the crown clearly held voluntary as well as injurious abortions to be crimes. One of the first was a coroner's inquest that held that Jane Wynspere's death through self-abortion was a "felonious suicide."[425] Intentional suicide was a crime at the time, punished by non-Christian burial and the forfeiture of the suicide's goods to the Crown.[426] In the aftermath of this death, the man who had aided her in the abortion was indicted as an accessory to felonious murder in a case reported as *Rex v. Lichefeld*:

> Nottinghamshire. Heretofore, namely on the vigil of the Epiphany of [our] Lord in the nineteenth year of the reign of the present lord king [Jan. 5, 1504], at Basford in the aforesaid county, before Richard Parker one of the said lord king's coroners in the aforesaid county upon the view of the body of Jane Wynspere of Basford aforesaid, it was presented by the oath of twelve jurors that the said Jane Wynspere of Basford in the county of Nottingham, single woman, being pregnant,[427] on the twelfth day of December in the year above mentioned [1503] at Basford aforesaid, being inspired by the

---

419. *See, e.g.,* Rex v. Parker, 73 Eng. Rep. 410 (1560). *See also* 1 Reports from the Lost Notebooks of Sir James Dyer (109 Selden Soc'y ) 45 (J.H. Baker ed. 1994) ("Lost Notebooks").

420. *See, e.g.,* Petersen, *supra* note 365, at 13.

421. James Hitchcock, *A Sixteenth-Century Midwife's License,* 41 Bull. Hist. Med. 76 (1967).

422. See the text *supra* at notes 396–402.

423. Petersen, *supra* note 354, at 11.

424. McLaren, *supra* note 100, at 119–20.

425. Rex v. Wynspere (Coroner's Inquest 1503), KB 9/434/12, in Calendar of Nottinghamshire Coroners' Inquests 1485–1558, *supra* note 18, at 8 (no. 10). *See also* Regina v. Robynson, Q/SR 110/68 (Coroner's Inquest 1589). That coroners' inquests served as indictments, see Calendar of Assize Records: Home Circuit Indictments, Elizabeth I and James I: Introduction 74 (J.S. Cockburn ed. 1985). *See generally* Keown, *supra* note 13, at 6.

426. Hales v. Petit, 75 Eng. Rep. 387 (Q.B. 1562). *See generally* Sue Woolf Brenner, *Undue Influence in the Criminal Offense of "Causing Suicide,"* 47 Alb. L. Rev. 62 (1982).

427. *puerpera*: perhaps means "in labor".

devil drank various bad[428] and [impure][429] potions in order to kill and destroy the child in her body, and took them into her body, as result of which the said Jane then and there died, and thus the same Jane in manner and form aforesaid feloniously and as a felo de se slew and poisoned herself and the child in her body; and that Thomas Lichefeld of Basford in the county aforesaid, cleric, knowing that the said Jane had committed said felony in form aforesaid, then and there feloniously harbored the said Jane....

On the Thursday after the quindent of Hilary [Jan. 30, 1505], Lichefeld comes in custody and demurs to the indictment on the ground that the principal is dead and that he cannot answer without her. The court adjudges that he is discharged *sine die*.[430]

Arguably, Jane Wynspere's actions amounted to two crimes—felonious suicide and abortion. Wynspere's crime of self-murder, however, was not accomplished until her death, at which time Lichefeld could not have become an accessory as charged.[431] Attempted suicide was only a misdemeanor at common law.[432] The crime of attempted suicide required the specific intent to commit suicide.[433] Thus, Jane Wynspere would not have committed a crime of attempted suicide if, as seems likely, she did not intend to kill herself in attempting to abort herself. After Wynspere's death, Lichefeld could not have been guilty of receiving or harboring a dead person.[434] Thus it appears that the only crime charged against Lichefeld is that he harbored Wynspere after her abortion but before her death. The proceeding was dismissed, but only on the ground that an accessory could not be tried without the principal and thus could never be prosecuted when the principal was already dead.

The proceeding against Lichefeld is also noteworthy as the first instance now known of a common law proceeding, rather than an ecclesiastical proceeding, based on an ingestive abortion instead of an injurious abortion. Not only does this appear to be a move into a domain hitherto left to the ecclesiastical courts, but the defendant himself was a cleric. By this time, benefit of clergy, rather than preventing trial, could be invoked (if at all) only after conviction to prevent punishment for first offenders.[435]

A few years later, a man who provided a potion to induce an abortion was saved from trial only by his own death. For *Rex v. Wodlake,* we actually have fairly complete records, including no less than three separate documents. First are the presentments (indictments) by a grand jury:

Middlesex. The jurors present that William Wodlake of the parish of St. Clement Danes in the county of Middlesex, net-maker, on the twentieth day of May in the seventh year of the reign of Henry VIII [1525], with force and arms (namely knives etc.) at the aforesaid parish of St. Clement, assaulted Katherine Alaund, then a girl of fourteen years of

---

428. *corupta*

429. *immaculata*: Dr. Baker suggests the word here should be translated as "polluted" although it normally means the opposite; perhaps, the *in-* refers here to putting something in the potion rather than functioning as a negative to *maculata*.

430. Rex v. Lichefeld, K.B. 27/974, Rex m.4 (1505). The translation from Latin is by John Baker. Note that the lack of the allegation "*contra pacem*" in the indictment would also have been sufficient grounds for dismissal.

431. *Cf.* Cooper v. The Hundred of Basingstoke (1702), 2 Ray. Rptr. 825, 827 (1775) (receivers of one who killed another are not thereby accessories to murder if the felon leaves before the victim dies).

432. Regina v. Burgess, 169 ENG. REP. 1387 (Q.B. 1862).

433. J.C. SMITH & BRIAN HOGAN, CRIMINAL LAW 252 (4th ed. 1965).

434. *See* 1 HALE, *supra* note 365, at 618–20.

435. BAKER, *supra* note 22, at 586–89; 3 HOLDSWORTH, *supra* note 7, at 293–300; MILSOM, *supra* note 22, at 420–21; PLUCKNETT, *supra* note 22, at 439–41; RADIN, *supra* note 22, at 230–31.

age, and then and there violently and against her will feloniously raped her and carnally knew her, against the peace of the lord king etc.

Middlesex. The jurors present that William Wodlake of the parish of St. Clement Danes in the county of Middlesex, net-maker, on the tenth day of November in the eighteenth year of the reign of King Henry VIII [1526], by the instigation of the devil, knowing that a certain Katherine Alaund was pregnant with a child, with dissembling words gave the same Katherine to drink a certain drink in order to destroy the child then being in the said Katherine's body, and desired and caused her the said Katherine to drink the selfsame drink, by reason of which drink the same Katherine was afterwards delivered of that child dead: so that the same William Wodlake feloniously killed and murdered the child with the drink in manner and form aforesaid, against the peace of the lord king etc.[436]

The indictments, as one would expect, are highly formulaic, with a real possibility that the factual content apparently recited in the indictment is pure formula and not factual at all except for the words that are specific to the particular individuals. Still, the indictment clearly charges William Wodlake with two independent crimes: rape of the mother and murder of an unborn child. With the lapse of eighteen months between the alleged rape and the alleged abortion, the aborted pregnancy could not have been a direct result of the rape. That fact suggests a more enduring relationship of some sort between William Wodlake and Katherine Auland than the mere recitals of the indictment indicate, but as to the nature of that relationship we can now only guess.

The indictments were made before justices of the peace for Middlesex County, but the matter was serious enough to prompt removal to the King's Bench, as shown by a writ, dated April 29, 1530, and sewn to the bill of indictment in the King's Bench file, ordering the justices of the peace for Middlesex to send all indictments concerning William Wodlake for appearance "before the king", *i.e.,* before the King's Bench:

TRUE BILL taken at St. John's Street in the county of Middlesex before Sir John More, knight, Robert Wroth, Robert Chesemen, John Brown, Richard Hawkes, and John Palmer, keepers of the peace of the lord king and the same king's justices assigned to hear and determine various felonies, trespasses, and misdeeds in the county of Middlesex, on the Thursday next after the feast of the Conception of the Blessed Virgin Mary in the twenty-first year of the reign of King Henry VIII [Dec. 9, 1529], by the oath etc. of...jurors[437] delivered before the lord king on the Saturday next after the quindene of St. John this same term [July 9, 1530], by the hand of the aforesaid John More, one of the aforesaid justices, in order to be determined.[438]

One would not want to emphasize this removal too strongly as it apparently was fairly routine to remove felony charges arising in Middlesex (the county that included London) to trial before the King's Bench in Westminster Hall. The endorsement provides one important further fact about this indictment, telling us that the writ was "tested" before Chief Justice John FitzJames and found to be legally sufficient. The writ was also endorsed by Sir John More to the effect that all indictments concerning Wodlake have been sent according to the tenor of the writ. The final entry was made by the clerk of the court indicating that the proceedings against Wodlake were terminated when he died:

Middlesex. William Wodlake (dead) of the parish of St. Clement Danes in the county aforesame, net-maker, is to be taken [and brought here] in the octave of Michaelmas [to answer] for various felonies, murders, and misdemeanors of which he is indicted....

---

436. Rex v. Wodlake, K.B. 9/513/m23 (1530). The translation from Latin is by John Baker.
437. This still refers to the grand jury; I have omitted the list of their names.
438. Rex v. Wodlake, K.B. 9/513/m.23d (1530). The translation from Latin is by John Baker.

Afterwards, in Hilary term 22 Henry VIII [1531] he is to be taken [and brought here] in the quindene of Easter: at which day he is dead. Therefore let the process against him here totally cease.[439]

The clerk's notation is worth quoting as it indicates that Wodlake was held to answer for "various felonies, murders, and misdemeanors." Even allowing for the formulaic nature of the entry (which explains why the charges are given in the plural), the inclusion of "murder" as one of the charges for which Wodlake was to answer can only refer to the abortion. At no point was there any suggestion that the indictment was in any way defective.

The next interesting cases even more clearly involved the incorporation of what had formerly been matters of exclusively ecclesiastical concern into the common law. In 1534, a Court Christian heard a defamation proceeding by Elizabeth Johnson against Agnes Cutter for charging Johnson with having used a potion to abort Johnson's daughter.[440] At that time, defamation was still largely relegated to the canon law, although it would shortly be taken over by the common law.[441] That a defamation proceeding should be permitted based on an allegation of abortion would hardly suggest that abortion was then socially acceptable, although the record does not indicate the outcome of the proceeding.

Some forty years later, in the case of *Cockaine v. Witnam,* [442] we find a similar proceeding before a lay court, signaling the take over of defamation proceedings by the royal courts. We actually have three slightly variant records of this proceeding, all of which agree that the court held that accusing a woman of offering abortifacients to another supported an action for slander because the words were sufficient grounds to require a judicial bond for good behavior. This conclusion reflects the emerging view that falsely alleging that another has committed a crime is a libel (if in writing) or a slander (if spoken).[443] By the eighteenth century, lawyer Giles Jacob could use abortion as a prime example of such a defamation when "a man reproach another with a heinous crime, as that he went about to get a poison to kill the child that such a woman goeth with, or lay in wait to rob another, or procured a person to murder him."[444] The most complete record of the proceeding against Witnam reads as follows:

> Action for words. At the Nisi Prius the defendant pleaded *concord puis le darraine* continuance, judgment *si al enquest, etc.* And by all the justices it was no plea, but he ought to conclude, judgment *si actio, etc.,* and so in all pleas pleaded since the last continuance.
>
> Then it was moved, if judgment shall be given upon this, or a new Nisi Prius be granted; and upon good advice judgment was given for the plaintiff, for it was a confession of the matter in issue.
>
> The words were "My Lady Cockaine did offer two shillings to a woman with child, to get her a drink to kill her child, because it was gotten by J.S., Sir Thomas Cockaine's butler." And it was moved the action did not lie for these words; but it was adjudged for the plaintiff, for by them the lady's credit is impaired; and, if true, there was cause to bind her to good behavior, although it was not said she did give money, or any hurt was

---

439. Rex v. Wodlake, K.B. 29/162/m.11d (1531). The translation from the Latin is by John Baker.

440. Johnson v. Cutter (Durham 1534), in BEFORE THE BAWDY COURT, *supra* note 190, at 172 (no. 427).

441. See the authorities collected *supra* at note 388. On sexual slanders in church courts, see INGRAM, *supra* note 260, at 292–319; J.A. SHARPE, DEFAMATION AND SEXUAL SLANDER IN EARLY MODERN ENGLAND: THE CHURCH COURTS AT YORK (1980).

442. Hil., 19 Eliz. 1 (1577).

443. *See* AUYLIFFE, *supra* note 278, at 212–15; WILLIAM VAUGHAN, THE SPIRIT OF DETRACTION 161–64 (1611).

444. GILES JACOB, A TREATISE OF LAWS: OR A GENERAL INTRODUCTION TO THE COMMON, CIVIL, AND CANON LAW IN THREE PARTS 74 (1721).

done, but that she offered *etc.* This case was adjudged Hill. 19 Eliz. Intratur, Mich. 17 & 17 Eliz. Rot. 183. *Ex relatione* Chamberlaine. *Vide* 4 Co. 16.b.[445]

The final interesting common law proceeding against abortion in the century not only involved a prosecution for witchcraft (formerly a charge cognizable only in Courts Christian), but also indicates that the defendant was sentenced to death for the abortion. The first statute to make witchcraft a crime at law was enacted in 1542.[446] It had made the practice witchcraft "for any unlawful purpose" a capital offense, but this statute was repealed in 1547. Apparently no prosecutions occurred under this statute.[447] In 1563, under Elizabeth I, Parliament enacted a statute that provided for the death penalty in its first section for witchcraft "whereby any person shall happen to be killed or destroyed" and in its second section for being twice convicted of any act of witchcraft that injures a person.[448] At times, the Elizabethan witchcraft statute accounted for as much as 13 percent of the criminal prosecutions in some counties. While the numbers went up with periodic witch hunts, the business of catching witches provided steady and unspectacular employment for all connected with the royal courts.[449] These statutes followed the pattern set by a French statute of 1490 prohibiting witchcraft, apparently the earliest lay prohibition in Europe.[450] The Elizabethan requirements that the witchcraft kill a person or that the witchcraft twice injure a person, and the punishing of witches by hanging rather than by burning show that witchcraft was prosecuted primarily as an anti-social activity rather than as a heresy.[451] Indeed, nearly all persons convicted of witchcraft were found guilty of having done some other forbidden act rather than merely having "entertained evil spirits"; most were found guilty of having killed a person through witchcraft.[452]

The record of *Regina v. Turnour* includes three indictments and three convictions. That record reads as follows:

> Joan Turnour of Stisted, spinster, on 1 July, 21 Eliz. [1579], at S., bewitched Anne Feast, wife of Richard F., who did despair of her life. [Endorsed:] *True Bill. Guilty, Judgment.*[453]

> _____, on 1 May, 22 Eliz. [1580], at S., bewitched George Sparrow, aged 7 years, who languished for half a year. [Endorsed:] *True Bill. Guilty, Judgment.*[454]

> Essex: The jurors for [our] lady the queen present that Jane Turnour of Stisted in the aforesaid county, spinster, being a common witch and enchantress, not having God before her eyes, but being seduced by the instigation of the devil, on the eight day of January in the twenty-second year of the reign of the Lady Elizabeth [1580], Queen of

---

445. Cro. Eliz. 49 (1586). *See also* Brit. Lib. Ms. Landsdowne 1067, fo. 97; Harv. L.S. Lib. Ms. 1180(1), fo. 387; Helmholz, *supra* note 84, at 85. Richard Helmholz also cited another case in which a contrary argument was made but not decided before an ecclesiastical court. Helmholz, *supra*, at 79–80.

446. 33 Hen. VIII, c.8 (1542). *See generally* Coke, *supra* note 19, at 44; 4 Holdsworth, *supra* note 7, at 507–11; 2 Pollock & Maitland, *supra* note 22, at 552–56; Rodes, *supra* note 263, at 237–38; Thomas, *supra* note 191, at 440–42, 450.

447. *See* 1 Ewen, *supra* note 339, at 11, 2 Ewen, *supra*, at 414. Catholic priests were prosecuted for witchcraft before the Star Chamber for the saying of masses, for the blessing of candles, and for the sprinkling of holy water. None of these charges were laid under Henry's statute, but on the basis of an obscure precedent from 1371. *See* J.H. Baker, *Introduction*, in 1 Lost Notebooks, *supra* note 419, at i, lxviii–lxxi.

448. 5 Eliz. I, ch.15 (1563).

449. Thomas, *supra* note 191, at 451–52.

450. 1 Anderson & Zinsser, *supra* note 416, at 166–67.

451. Thomas, *supra* note 191, at 443–44.

452. *Id.* at 444–49; R.G. Usher, The Presbyterian Movement in the Reign of Queen Elizabeth 70 (1905).

453. Calendar of Assize Rec.: Essex Indictments, Eliz. I, at 212 (no. 1225) (1975) ("Elizabethan Essex Indictments"). *See also* Ewen, *supra* note 339, at 141 (no. 143) (1929).

454. Elizabethan Essex Indictments, *supra* note 453, at 212 (no. 1225). *See also* Ewen, *supra* note 339, at 142 (no. 144).

England, France and Ireland, defender of the faith, devilishly and maliciously at Stisted aforesaid, on various days and occasions both before and since, maliciously and devilishly bewitched and enchanted a certain Helen Sparrowe, wife of John Sparrowe, in the body of the same Helen, being then great with a certain living child, by reason whereof not only was the same Helen then and there on various occasions gravely vexed in her body horribly troubled, to the greatest danger of her life, but also the aforesaid child (of which the same Helen was then and there great) then and there came to death. And thus the aforesaid jurors say upon their oath that the aforesaid Jane Turnour, in manner and form aforesaid, on the day and in the year aforesaid, at Stisted aforesaid, maliciously and devilishly bewitched and enchanted the aforesaid Helen Sparrowe, and deprived the living child (of which the aforesaid Helen was then pregnant) of his life by reason of these enchantments and bewitchings, contrary to the form of the statute made and provided for such cases, and to the bad and pernicious example of all other offending in such cases, and against the peace of the said present lady the queen.

[Note by the clerk:] Puts herself on the country;[455] guilty judgment.[456]

The record is not entirely clear on the sentence Turnour received, but two subsequent entries in the jail records indicate that she was twice reprieved for a year.[457] Turnour could only have been reprieved from a death sentence, and we do not know if she was ever executed. Turnour was convicted of several acts of witchcraft, only one of which involved abortion, so we also cannot be entirely certain whether the death sentence was for the abortion, although that appears to be the import of these records when one examines the relevant laws on witchcraft. Turnour was indicted under the Elizabethan witchcraft statute. With the successive indictments, it is possible that she was sentenced to death for multiple convictions under section 2 rather than for causing a death under section 1. As best we can determine, however, this was not the case. If she were convicted for causing a death, that can only have been for the death of the unborn child.

Another witchcraft statute was enacted in the first year of James I.[458] This statute made it a capital felony to kill or injure a person by witchcraft, or to take up a dead body for magical purposes, or to "consult, covenant with, entertain, employ, feed, or reward any evil or wicked spirit to or for any intent or purpose"; the statute preserved the requirement of two convictions before the death penalty could be imposed for witchcraft to find treasure or lost goods, to conjure an "unlawful love," to destroy cattle or goods, or to attempt without success to kill a person. No acts of witchcraft except killing a person or twice injuring a person had been capital under the Elizabethan statute. Although the Jacobean statute was more severe than the Elizabethan statute, it did not satisfy Puritans who wanted the death penalty for every sort of witchcraft.[459] The Jacobean witchcraft statute was repealed in 1736, to be replaced with a statute making it criminal

---

455. *I.e.*, accepted a trial by jury.

456. Essex Assizes 35/23/29 (Essex 1581). The translation from Latin by John Baker. *See also* ELIZABETHAN ESSEX INDICTMENTS, *supra* note 453, at 212 (no. 1225); EWEN, *supra* note 339, at 142 (no. 145). Dr. Cockburn erroneously translated this indictment as charging the murder of the mother, Helen Sparrowe. He has acknowledged his error in a letter to Philip Rafferty, dated May 18, 1990. 2 RAFFERTY, *supra* note 74, at 665.

457. EWEN, *supra* note 339, at 143 (Essex Gaol Delivery Roll, July 17, 1581), 146 (Essex Gaol Delivery Roll, Mar. 22, 1582). Philip Rafferty interprets these entries as indicating that Turnour was twice sentenced to death and that both times her sentenced was commuted to one year in prison. 2 RAFFERTY, *supra* note 74, at 863. The entries seem less conclusive to me.

458. 1 James I ch. 12 (1604).

459. *See* COKE, *supra* note 365, at 468; COKE, *supra* note 16, at 46. *See generally* THOMAS, *supra* note 191, at 440–44.

fraud to pretend to witchcraft. Witchcraft thereafter was not a statutory offense in England. Lynchings for witchcraft, however, continued into the later nineteenth century in rural England.[460]

Apparently the requirement of two convictions in order to be subject to the death penalty meant convictions at two separate trials.[461] We do know of instances in which a woman definitely was tried simultaneously on several indictments for witchcraft.[462] There is nothing in the records of the Turnour proceedings, however, to indicate whether she was tried concurrently or successively. The failure to plead an earlier conviction in the later indictments suggests a single trial on all three indictments, and therefore a conviction for only one capital offense.

If, as I am suggesting, a death sentence was imposed on Turnour under section 1 of the act authorizing death as the penalty for killing a person by witchcraft, the court must have concluded that the unborn child killed by Turnour was a "person." Indeed, if the prosecution did not seek the death penalty for the killing of the unborn child under section 1, but rather for the second (or third) conviction for injuring a person under section 2, the description of the child and the manner of its death would have been superfluous in the third indictment. Under the common law, it was murder (homicide, not abortion) if a child wounded in the womb died after being born alive.[463] The crystallization of this "born alive" rule will be addressed at length at the opening of the next chapter. For now, it is sufficient to note that Turnour's conviction cannot be seen as an early instance of the "born-alive" rule because the indictment did not allege that the child was born alive before it died. If, as apparently was the case, Turnour was sentenced to death for abortion, abortion by potion clearly was a capital felony at least by 1581 (and probably earlier), albeit under the label of witchcraft and not under the label of homicide.

The sixteenth-century legal activity directed at abortion involved, as the criminalization of witchcraft suggests, the secularization of ecclesiastical jurisdiction. Not surprisingly ecclesiastical judicial activity directed at abortion declined during the Reformation. After 1563 (when witchcraft became firmly established as a statutory offense in England), we find no ecclesiastical proceedings based on abortion except for occasional proceedings against clerics accused of involvement.[464] Such proceedings seem more concerned with ecclesiastical discipline than with the abortion itself. Conversely, prosecutions for sorcery before royal courts before 1563 were very rare.[465] There is little room to doubt that after 1563, if not before, the law courts took primary responsibility for abortions of all types and that abortion was unequivocally treated as a crime in the law courts. Whatever residual role church courts retained in policing abortion or other serious matters ended with the closing of the Courts Christian from 1641 to 1660. This did not pre-

---

460. THOMAS, *supra* note 191, at 452–53.

461. Sir Edward Coke, writing 30 to 40 years later, told us that a statutory prohibition of fraud was passed immediately before the witchcraft statute and required multiple convictions that had to occur in separate trials. 5 Eliz. I ch. 14 (1563); COKE, *supra* note 16, at 172. *See also* EDWARD WILLIAMS, PRECEDENTS OF WARRANTS, CONVICTIONS, AND OTHER PROCEEDINGS, BEFORE JUSTICES OF THE PEACE CHIEFLY ORIGINAL; AND CONTAINING NONE THAT ARE TO BE MET WITHIN DR. BURN'S JUSTICE 619 (1801). I am indebted to Philip Rafferty for sharing a letter from John Baker, dated June 30, 1987, in which Baker describes and analyses these sources and the sources in the next footnote. 2 RAFFERTY, *supra* note 74, at 666–67.

462. Rex v. Worman (1607), CALENDAR OF ASSIZE RECORDS: ESSEX INDICTMENTS, JAMES I, at 16 (no. 84) (J.S. Cockburn ed. 1982) (six indictments); Regina v. Mynnet (1593), in ELIZABETHAN ESSEX INDICTMENTS, *supra* note 453, at 407 (no. 2464) (four indictments).

463. *See* Regina v. Sims, 75 ENG. REP. 1075 (K.B. 1601), quoted in Ch. 4, at notes 34–35.

464. HOULBROOKE, *supra* note 269, at 78. *See, e.g.,* The Rector of Leaden Rothing's Case (Essex 1574), in LASLETT, *supra* note 266, at 76 (no. 29).

465. THOMAS, *supra* note 191, at 465–68.

vent local congregations, even among such "liberal" groups as the Quakers, from continuing to exert the moral judgment of the community to prevent or punish aborting members.[466]

---

466. *See* 2 THE FIRST MINUTE BOOK OF THE GAINESBOROUGH MONTHLY MEETING OF THE SOCIETY OF FRIENDS 116 (Harold Brace ed. 1949).

# Chapter 4

# Riders on the Storm[1]

*If the idea of a document of superior legal authority is to have meaning, terms which
have a precise, history-filled content to those who drafted and adopted the document
|must be held to that precise meaning.*

— J. Willard Hurst[2]

By the end of the sixteenth century, two broad classes of techniques were in use to attempt
abortion—injury techniques and ingestion techniques.[3] Legal records of the time indicate that
both forms of abortion were capital felonies regardless of consent or (more typically) lack of
consent by the women undergoing the abortion attempt. These same legal records indicate that
by the end of the sixteenth century, both sorts of crime were prosecuted in the royal (law)
courts, although at the beginning of the century ingestive abortions (considered witchcraft) had
usually been prosecuted the church courts. The ecclesiastical records are spotty and incomplete,
but they are entirely consistent with this summary.[4] The record thereafter becomes even clearer.

In the seventeenth century, we find a woman condemned for self-abortion,[5] as well as noteworthy cases in which a man was convicted of murder when the infant was born alive and subsequently died bearing the signs of the abortion[6] and in which it was held to be murder if the
woman died from an abortion even though she had consented to the procedure.[7] Later still, a
woman was convicted of aborting another (consenting) woman before the child quickened; the
abortionist was sentenced to three years imprisonment after exposure in the stocks.[8] The evidence leaves little room to believe that abortion was a common law liberty, contrary to the new
orthodoxy of abortion history. [9]

---

1. Jim Morrison, *Riders on the Storm* (1971).
2. J. WILLARD HURST, THE ROLE OF HISTORY, SUPREME COURT AND SUPREME LAW 57 (1954).
3. *See* Chapter 1.
4. *See* Chapter 2.
5. Regina v. Webb (Q.B. 1602), CALENDAR OF ASSIZE REC., SURREY INDICTMENTS, ELIZ. I, at 512 (no.
3146) (J. Cockburn ed. 1980) ("SURREY INDICTMENTS"), quoted *infra* at notes 56–57.
6. Regina v. Sims, 75 ENG. REP. 1075 (Q.B. 1601), quoted *infra* at notes 16–17.
7. Rex v. Anonymous (1670), 1 MATTHEW HALE, HISTORY OF PLEAS OF THE CROWN 429–30 (1736).
8. Rex v. Beare, 2 THE GENTLEMAN'S MAGAZINE 931 (Aug. 1732), quoted in Chapter 5, at note 28.
9. *See* Cyril Means, jr., *The Phoenix of Abortional Freedom: Is a Penumbral Right or Ninth-Amendment
Right about to Arise from the Nineteenth-Century Legislative Ashes of a Fourteenth-Century Common-Law Liberty?*, 17 N.Y.L.F. 335, 336, 351–54, 374–75, 409–10 n.175 (1971) ("Means II"). *See also* Roe v. Wade, 410 U.S.
113, 140 (1973); Beechem v. Leahy, 287 A.2d 836, 839 (Vt. 1972); *Amicus Brief of 250 American Historians in
support of Appellants in* Planned Parenthood of Southeastern Pennsylvania v. Casey, [505 U.S. 833 (1992)]
("*Casey Historians' Brief*"), at 5–6; *Amicus Brief of 281 American Historians supporting Appellees in* Webster v.
Reproductive Health Services [492 U.S. 490 (1989)] ("*Webster Historians' Brief*"), reprinted at 11 WOMEN'S
RTS. L. RPTR. 163, 170 (1989), and in 8 DOCUMENTARY HISTORY OF THE LEGAL ASPECTS OF ABORTION IN THE
UNITED STATES: WEBSTER V. REPRODUCTIVE HEALTH SERVICES 107 (Roy Mersky & Gary Hartman eds. 1990)
(hereafter pagination will be given only to the version in the *Women's Rts. L. Rptr.*); LINDA GORDON, WOMAN'S
BODY, WOMAN'S RIGHT: A SOCIAL HISTORY OF BIRTH CONTROL IN AMERICA 52–53, 57 (1976); JAMES MOHR,
ABORTION IN AMERICA: THE ORIGINS AND EVOLUTION OF NATIONAL POLICY, 1800–1900, at 128–29, 134–36,

The seventeenth century was among the stormiest in the history of European culture, with the Thirty Years War putting an end to the pretensions of the Vatican and the Holy Roman Empire to universal rule, and with it the loss of the Spanish-Portuguese monopoly of Europe's colonial expansion. These changes found their echoes in England and in England's American colonies. The English crown passed to the Scottish King James under whom England's first permanent colonies were founded across the Atlantic. Thereafter, England experienced a civil war culminating in the execution of King Charles I in 1649, followed by the Puritan Commonwealth under the dictatorship of Oliver Cromwell, Restoration in the person of Charles II, and finally the "Glorious Revolution" that drove the Catholic James II from the throne, placing James' daughter Mary and her husband William on the throne, and launching England into the first of a series of wars with France in the next century and a quarter.[10] Each change in England had its impact on England's dependencies, setting up the divisions in Ireland that so bedevil that island to this day. Similarly, the changes in England were reflected in its growing American colonies, with struggles between religious and political factions complicating struggles to build homes in an alien land and to drive off Dutch, French, and Spanish competitors.

Attempts to abort apparently were becoming more common, and were consistently treated as a serious crime in England and prosecuted as such, although some confusion was introduced regarding the point at which a fetus became a "person." In the story of these legal events, two men—Sir Edward Coke and Sir Matthew Hale—stand out as lawyers, judges and scholars who shaped the thinking of their societies about these and other legal matters. Given their prominence in the events of their century, they truly were riders on the storm. Under their influence, the common law regarding abortion did change, but abortion was not and did not become legal—as the legal scholars of the following century unanimously attest.[11] And these same legal patterns regarding abortion were replicated in England's American colonies.

# The Law near the End of the Reign of Queen Elizabeth

*The woman who commits an abortion on herself is regarded rather as the victim than the perpetrator of the crime.*

—Judge George Orlady[12]

---

144–45, 201, 208–11, 226, 229, 235–36 (1978); Reva Siegel, *Reasoning from the Body: A Historical Perspective on Abortion Regulation and Questions of Equal Protection*, 44 STAN. L. REV. 261, 278 (1992). On the various notions of "right" and "liberty" (neither relating to abortion) prevalent among Americans in 1791, see Philip Hamburger, *Natural Rights, Natural Law, and American Constitutions*, 102 YALE L.J. 907 (1993).

10. THE STRUGGLE FOR POWER: ENGLISH HISTORY, 1550–1720 (John Beattie & Michael Finalyson eds. 1987).

11. ANONYMOUS, THE LAWS RESPECTING WOMEN 348 (1777); 1 WILLIAM BLACKSTONE, COMMENTARIES ON THE LAWS OF ENGLAND *129–30 (1765); 4 BLACKSTONE, *supra*, at *198; RICHARD BURN, THE JUSTICE OF THE PEACE AND THE PARISH OFFICER 380 (3rd ed. 1756); 2 WILLIAM HAWKINS, TREATISE ON THE PLEAS OF THE CROWN 80 (1716)

12. Commonwealth v. Weible, 45 Pa. Super. 207, 209 (1911).

Curiously, given the frequent prosecutions of abortion before the law courts during the Tudor era,[13] the two best-known sixteenth-century writers (Sir William Staunford[14] and William Lambard[15]) on criminal pleadings denied that abortion was a felony. Lambard's passage is short and derivative from Staunford. Staunford's discussion is longer, the entire passage reading:

> It is required that the thing killed be *in rerum natura*.[16] And for this reason if a man killed a child in the womb of its mother: this is not a felony, neither shall he forfeit anything, and this is so for two reasons: First, because the thing killed has no baptismal name: Second, because it is difficult to judge whether he killed it or not, that is, whether the child died of this battery of its mother or through another cause. [Here Staunford cited to *Rex v. de Bourton*[17] and *Rex v. Anonymous*.[18]] If a man beats a woman in an advanced stage of pregnancy who was carrying twins, so that afterwards one of the children died at once and the other was born and given a name in baptism, and two days afterward through the injury he had received he died; and the opinion was, as previously stated, that this was not a felony. [Here Staunford gives an alternative citation to *Rex v. de Bourton*, followed by yet another citation to *Rex v. Anonymous*.] But it seems that this reason, that he had no baptismal name, is of no force, for you shall see [citing an infanticide case from 1314] that there was a presentment "That a certain woman whilst walking opposite a chapel gave birth to a son, and immediately she cut his throat and threw him in a pond of stagnant water and fled: on that account she shall be summoned by writ of *exigent* and shall be outlawed": for this was homicide inasmuch as the thing was *in rerum natura* before being killed: thus this case is in no wise like those above mentioned where the child is killed in the womb of its mother, *etc*. Which case Bracton affirmed as law in his division of homicide…But the contrary of this seems to be the law as above stated.[19]

Law professor Cyril Means, jr., in his revision of abortion history, simply ignored Staunford's discrediting of the lack of a baptismal name as grounds for the non-criminality of abortion.[20] Instead, Means seized Staunford's statement that "neither shall he forfeit anything" as proving that abortion was not even a misdemeanor.[21] In asserting that Staunford had indicated that abortion was not even a misdemeanor at common law, Means confused a misprision (for which a forfeiture could follow) with a misdemeanor for which a lesser penalty would be in order.[22] "Misprision" originally meant the concealment of treason or a felony; by the seventeenth century, the word had acquired an extended but vague meaning somewhere between felony and modern misdemeanor.[23] Forfeiture never applied to misdemeanors.[24]

---

13. *See* Chapter 3, at notes 357–466.

14. WILLIAM STAUNFORD, LES PLEAS DEL CORON ch. 13 (1557). Staunford's name was also spelled as Stanford and as Stamford; on his life and the history of his work, see PERCY WINFIELD, THE CHIEF SOURCES OF ENGLISH LEGAL HISTORY 324–25 (1925).

15. WILLIAM LAMBARD, OF THE OFFICE OF THE JUSTICE OF THE PEACE 217–18 (1st ed. 1581).

16. "among natural things," *i.e.*, in the natural world.

17. Quoted in Chapter 3, at notes 146–47.

18. Quoted in Chapter 3, at note 170.

19. STAUNFORD, *supra* note 14, ch. 13.

20. Means II, *supra* note 9, at 339–42.

21. *Id.* at 341–42.

22. *Id.* at 341–42. *See also* Shelley Gavigan, *The Criminal Sanction as It Relates to Human Reproduction: The Genesis of the Statutory Prohibition of Abortion*, 5 J. LEGAL HIST. 20, 23 (1984).

23. 3 W.S. HOLDSWORTH, A HISTORY OF ENGLISH LAW 389 n.1 (7th ed. 1956); 8 HOLDSWORTH, *supra*, at 322–24.

24. *See generally* J.H. BAKER, AN INTRODUCTION TO ENGLISH LEGAL HISTORY 274–75, 571–73 (3rd ed. 1990); THEODORE PLUCKNETT, A CONCISE HISTORY OF THE COMMON LAW 176–77, 430–31, 442–44, 455–59,

Lambard and Staunford both supported their questionable conclusions[25] only with the irrelevant claim that indictment was precluded by lack of a baptismal name and the same problem of forensic proof as reputedly troubled a court in *Rex v. Anonymous*.[26] In contrast, a formbook of the time, with four editions from 1506 and 1544 and prepared under the name of Sir Anthony Fitzherbert (a recognized authority on law at the time), included a form indictment for homicide of a child born dead because of an abortion through physical assault on the mother.[27] Readers at the Inns of Court were similarly divided. Some argued that abortion was no crime at all unless the child was born alive before dying;[28] some that abortion was a criminal trespass (misdemeanor);[29] and some that it was a felony.[30] John Baldwin indicated in his Reading only that killing the child in the womb is not a felony because one could not know the cause of death.[31]

Perhaps Staunford, Lambard, and those Readers who supported them merely reflected the inconclusiveness of the more widely, albeit inaccurately, reported decisions. Perhaps they simply meant that abortion was a crime less than a felony or that abortion properly belonged before a court other than the King's Bench. Whatever their ground, by the end of the century (and perhaps before) they clearly were wrong.

The books of William Lambard and Sir William Staunford raise some doubts in some minds about whether abortion was a crime in England. If so, several decisions at the opening of the seventeenth century dispel all doubts even while the first of the cases introduced a certain confusion regarding the law of abortion. In 1601, in *Regina v. Sims*,[32] two Justices of the King's Bench held an abortion in which a child dies after its live birth to be murder on grounds that the birth and subsequent death of the child permitted proof of the death and its cause, overcoming certain difficulties in proving either. Less than a year later, in March of 1602, an Assize in Surrey tried Margaret Webb for self-abortion without a live-birth before the child's death; she was pardoned, although it is not clear whether this was before or after a conviction.[33] The Worcestershire Quarter Session Records indicate a third case in this same time period, although the record is very brief and does not indicate the outcome of the legal proceedings.[34] The first two cases deserve extended analysis.

---

536 (5th ed. 1956); 2 Frederick Pollock & Frederick Maitland, The History of English Law Before the Time of Edward I, at 500 (2nd ed. 1898); Max Radin, Handbook of Anglo-American Legal History 234–41 (1936).

25. *See* Chapter 3. *See also* Mark Scott, Note, *Quickening in the Common Law: The Legal Precedent Roe Attempted and Failed to Use*, 1 Mich. L. & Pol'y Rev. 199, 229–32 (1996).

26. *See* Chapter 3, at notes 170–85.

27. Anthony Fitzherbert, Boke of the Justyces of the Peas ch. vi, fol. iii (1515). On Fitzherbert generally, see Winfield, *supra* note 14, at 302–03.

28. *William Wadham's Reading on the Statute of Westminster II*, reprinted in 94 Selden Soc'y 306 n.7 (Lincoln's Inn 1501); *John Hutton's Reading on the Statute of Westminster II*, Camb. U. L. Ms. Hh. 3.10, fo. 32v (Inner Temple ca. 1490). On the role and significance of "Readings" at the Inns of Court, see the Chapter 3, at notes 177–81.

29. *Thomas Morow's Reading at the Inner Temple on the Statute of Westminster I* (Inner Temple 1503), *in* B.H. Putnam, Early Treatises on Justice of the Peace in the Fifteenth and Sixteenth Centuries 379 (7 Oxford Stud. in Soc. & Legal Hist. 1924); *Anonymous Reading on the Statute of Gloucester*, Camb. U. L. Ms. Ee. 5.22, fo. 212 (15th century).

30. *Anonymous Reading*, *supra* note 29, fo. 213 (15th century).

31. *John Baldwin's Reading at Grey's Inn on the Statute of Marlborough, c.25 (murdrum)*, Camb. Univ. Lib. Ms. Hh. 2.6, fo. 92v (ca. 1460).

32. 75 Eng. Rep. 1075 (Q.B. 1601).

33. ASSI 35/44/7 m.18 (1602), in Surrey Indictments, *supra* note 5, at 512 (no. 3146). *See also* J. Keown, Abortion, Doctors and the Law 7 (1988).

34. Flicher v. Genifer (1601), 1 Worcestershire Calendar of the Quarter Session Papers, 1591–1643, at 44 (No. 111) (J.W. Willis Bund ed. 1900) ("Worcestershire Calendar"), quoted *infra* at notes 63–64.

The first of the three cases, decided in 1601, coupled with its championing by Sir Edward Coke, seemed clearly to indicate that abortion was a felony trespass if the acts resulted in a live birth followed by a death immediately attributable to the prenatal attack. The case, however, introduced (or reflected) some uncertainty regarding the criminality of abortion should the indicated facts not be found. The case, *Regina v. Sims,* reads in full:

> Trespasse and assualt was brought against one Sims by the Husband and the Wife for beating of the woman.
>
> Coke [Attorney-General]: the case is such, as appears by examination. A man beats a woman which is great with child, and after the child is born living, but hath signes, bruises in his body, received by the said batterie, and after dyed thereof, I say that this is murder.
>
> Fenner & Popham [JJ.], *absentibus caeteris,* clearly of the same opinion, and the difference is where the child is born living, for it be born dead it is no murder, for *non constat*[35] whether the child were living at the time of the batterie or not, or if the batterie was the cause of the death, but when it is born living, and the wounds appear in his body, and then he dye, the Batteror shall be arraigned of murder, for now it may be proved whether these wounds were the cause of the death or not, and for that if it be found, he shall be condemned.[36]

*Regina v. Sims* definitely disposed of and Lambard and Staunford. The two Justices in *Regina v. Sims* indicated that only the inability to prove the cause of death prevented convicting other abortionists of murder. This is a problem of forensic medicine, not a rejection of the criminality of abortion. *Sims* posed a serious problem to Cyril Means, jr., in his project of inventing a more useful history of English abortion law.[37] Even Means acknowledged the inference that the Justices treated the lack of a baptismal name as irrelevant, thereby disposing of *Rex v. Anonymous*[38] (Means' "Abortionist's Case").[39] *Sims* would also seem to dispose of his reading of *Rex v. de Bourton*[40] (Means' "Twinslayer's Case") as indicating that abortion was not properly chargeable as a crime. Rather than searching for additional records of the two cases that could have clarified the apparent contradictions,[41] Means chose to express perplexity while relying on his dubious reading of *de Bourton* as contradicting and therefore prevailing over *Regina v. Sims.*[42] Several commentators noted that a more careful reading of *de Bourton* would have shown it to be consistent with *Sims,* explaining why the two Justices in *Sims* did not bother to overrule the earlier case.[43] It did not seem to bother his admirers, including Justice Harry Blackmun, that Means distorted the meaning of *de Bourton* and, more obviously, reversed the usual temporal priority among precedents. Consider, for example, how a court would receive an argument that *Brown v. Board of Education*[44] and its progeny were not the law and should be ignored because they were so obviously based upon disregard of the earlier precedents, such as *Plessy v. Ferguson.*[45]

---

35. "[if] it cannot be proved"

36. Regina v. Sims, 75 ENG. REP. 1075 (Q.B. 1601).

37. Means' role and intentions are explored in Ch. 3, at notes 126–85.

38. (K.B. 1348), ANTHONY FITZHERBERT, GRAUNDE ABRIDGEMENT tit. Corone, f. 268, pl. 263 (1st ed. 1516) [K.B. 1348], quoted in Ch. 3, at notes 170.

39. Means II, *supra* note 9, at 344.

40. Y.B. Mich. 1 Edw. 3, f. 23, pl. 28 (K.B. 1327), quoted in Ch. 3, at notes 146–47.

41. *See* Ch. 3, at notes 148–70.

42. Means II, *supra* note 9, at 344, 351.

43. *See* KEOWN, *supra* note 33, at 4; Robert Byrn, *An American Tragedy: The Supreme Court on Abortion,* 41 FORDHAM L. REV. 807, 819 (1973); Joseph Dellapenna, *The History of Abortion: Technology, Morality, and Law,* 40 U. PITT. L. REV. 359, 368–70 (1979).

44. 347 U.S. 483 (1954).

45. 163 U.S. 537 (1896). The point was suggested in Dennis Horan & Thomas Balch, Roe v. Wade: *No Justification in History, Law, or Logic,* in ABORTION AND THE CONSTITUTION: REVERSING *Roe v. Wade* THROUGH

To sustain his claim that his reading of *de Bourton* stated the true law of England, Means sought to dismiss the court's language in *Regina v. Sims* regarding the criminality of abortion as an inconclusive *dictum*. By *dictum*, a lawyer means a statement by a court that is not pertinent to the case at hand and therefore does not count as a legal precedent. Means stressed that only two Justices (out of four) were present and expressed themselves,[46] but apparently recognized that the absence of two Justices was not enough to discredit the complete agreement of those present. Means went on to assert that *Regina v. Sims* was not a criminal proceeding at all because it was based on a writ of trespass.[47] If that were so, the statements about the criminality of abortion could not have been a holding. Means also sought to support this view by citing a book by Michael Dalton, published after *Sims* was decided, that quoted Stanford's views *verbatim*.[48] Because Dalton wrote 35 years before a report of *Regina v. Sims* was published, it proves nothing other than a likelihood that Dalton had not heard of the case.[49]

In order to argue that *Regina v. Sims* was not a criminal case, Means either had to be ignorant of, or chose to ignore, the origin of trespass as a royal proceeding to enforce the "king's peace" with civil damages tacked on only to enlist private enforcement in place of the nonexistent police.[50] In the early days, double or even treble damages were awarded as an incentive for private enforcement of the king's peace.[51] The practice of creating indictable trespasses continued well into the reign of Queen Elizabeth I.[52] To reduce the risk of confusion, criminal trespasses eventually came to be called misdemeanors.[53] Although trespass in 1601 was diverging into criminal and civil branches such as we know in modern law,[54] *Regina v. Sims* appears to have been a criminal proceeding. The case was brought on behalf of the Queen and was argued before the court by the Attorney General, Sir Edward Coke.[55] The only reported comments from the bench refer

---

THE COURTS 57, 66 (Dennis Horan, Edward Grant, & Paige Cunningham eds. 1987).

46. Means II, *supra* note 9, at 343–44.

47. *Id.* at 344.

48. MICHAEL DALTON, THE COUNTRY JUSTICE, CONTEYNING THE PRACTICE OF THE JUSTICES OF THE PEACE 213 (1618). For Dalton's source, see STAUNFORD, *supra* note 14.

49. Means II, *supra* note 9, at 345.

50. 2 HENRY DE BRACTON, THE LAWS AND CUSTOMS OF ENGLAND 438 (George Woodbine ed., Samuel Thorne trans. 1977 & 1982) (2 vols., original in Latin, 1256?) ("BRACTON"). *See generally* BAKER, *supra* note 24, at 71–73, 572–73; 2 HOLDSWORTH, *supra* note 23, at 364–65, 453–54; S.F.C. MILSOM, HISTORICAL FOUNDATIONS OF THE COMMON LAW 285–95 (2nd ed. 1981); PLUCKNETT, *supra* note 24, at 366–67, 455–59, 465–67; 2 POLLOCK & MAITLAND, *supra* note 24, at 165–66, 510–17, 523–26, 570–71, 617–18; RADIN, *supra* note 24, at 196, 236, 440–44; John Beckerman, *Adding Insult to* Injuria: *Affronts to Honor and the Origins of Trespass*, in ON THE LAWS AND CUSTOMS OF ENGLAND: ESSAYS IN HONOR OF SAMUEL E. THORNE 159 (Morris Arnold *et al.* eds. 1981); S.F.C. Milsom, *Trespass from Henry III to Edward III*, 74 L.Q. REV. 195 (Pt. I), 407 (Pt. II), 561 (Pt. III) (1958); David Seipp, *The Distinction between Crime and Tort in the Early Common Law*, 76 B.U. L. REV. 59, 68–72, 76–77, 80–83 (1996).

51. 2 HOLDSWORTH, *supra* note 23, at 453; 2 POLLOCK & MAITLAND, *supra* note 24, at 520–21.

52. *See, e.g.*, 35 Eliz. I c.6 (1593).

53. *See generally* Dellapenna, *supra* note 43, at 380–81.

54. *See, e.g.*, LAMBARD, *supra* note 15, at 66; CHRISTOPHER ST. GERMAN, DOCTOR AND STUDENT (c. 1530), reprinted in 91 SELDEN SOC'Y 266 (T.F.T. Plucknett & J.L. Barton eds. 1974); STAUNFORD, *supra* note 14, at 266. *See generally* 2 HOLDSWORTH, *supra* note 23, at 365; 3 HOLDSWORTH, *supra*, at 318, 609–11; 4 HOLDSWORTH, *supra*, at 512–15; MILSOM, *supra* note 50, at 283–313; PLUCKNETT, *supra* note 24, at 456–58; 2 POLLOCK & MAITLAND, *supra* note 24, at 510–11; RADIN, *supra* note 24, at 196–98, 442–47; Seipp, *supra* note 50, at 80–86.

55. On the significance of the presence of the Attorney General in the case, see 6 HOLDSWORTH, *supra* note 23, at 457–72; PLUCKNETT, *supra* note 24, at 228–30.

to a criminal charge of killing, and not to any civil remedy. Means described the case as a civil suit and referred to it only as *Sim's Case,* utterly disregarding the fact that the case was a criminal prosecution for homicide.

At the time, to prove that an abortional act caused the death of a child, one would have to prove both that the child was alive when the act was committed and that the act, rather than some supervening act or event, caused the abortion. Given the primitive state of gestational and forensic knowledge, both proofs could often be problematic. The problem is hardly surprising. Forensic medicine remained extremely primitive even three centuries later.[56] In 1601, no certain means of proving that a woman even was pregnant existed until the infant had "quickened," that is had begun to move so that the mother (and others) could feel this movement.[57] A relatively certain clinical test for pregnancy did not emerge until 1927.[58] Thus even the fact of pregnancy was virtually impossible to prove, unless the mother aborted and she (or someone else) preserved the remains of the abortus or if the mother died and an autopsy were performed. Even experienced mothers were often uncertain. From the nineteenth century, we find the diary of Mary Poor (husband of the founder of Standard and Poor's), who birthed seven children and had at least two miscarriages during a period of 22 years, yet her diary shows her frequently fretting for months even near the end of her childbearing years over whether a missed period signaled another pregnancy or some other problem.[59] Even after development of a test for detecting HCG (human chorionic gonadotropin) in a woman's blood to confirm pregnancy ("the rabbit test") in 1927 and its refinement through the 1930s, uncertainty remained as the test continued to yield a significant number of false results until it was further refined in the 1960s.[60] Before then, physicians and midwives simply had no certain basis for determining whether a woman was pregnant until the gestation is about half complete.[61] Such confusion still existed at least as recently as 1905.[62]

Uncertainty about the fact of pregnancy underlay the ancient common law practice of delaying the execution of a pregnant woman only if she were carrying a "quick child" as determined by an inspection by a "jury of matrons."[63] The matrons could not determine whether the woman was pregnant if they could not feel the child move. Physicians and jurists were so uncertain about the facts of early pregnancy that they were still actively debating in the early nineteenth

---

56. *See* T.R. Forbes, *Early Forensic Medicine in England: The Angus Murder Trial,* 36 J. Hist. Med. 296 (1981). *See also* Rex v. Pizzy (Suffolk Assizes 1808), in William Notcutt, The Remarkable Trial at Large of William Pizzy and Mary Codd at the Assizes Holden at Bury St. Edmunds on Thursday August 11, 1808 for Feloniously Administering a Certain Noxious and Destructive Substance to Ann Cheney with Intent to Produce a Miscarriage (1808). *See generally* Mohr, *supra* note 9, at 72–73, 230–33; James Mohr, Doctors and the Law: Medical Jurisprudence in Nineteenth-Century America 51–56, 94–108 (1993) ("Mohr, Doctors").

57. On the concept of "quickening" over the centuries, see Ch. 3, at notes 95–109.

58. Thomas Eden & Eardley Holland, A Manual of Midwifery 77–78 (7th ed. 1931)

59. *See* Janet Farrell Brodie, Contraception and Abortion in Nineteenth-Century America 21–25 (1994). *See generally* Carl Degler, At Odds: Women and the Family in America from the Revolution to the Present 235 (1980); Gordon, *supra* note 9, at 57; Michael Grossberg, Governing the Hearth: Law and the Family in Nineteenth-Century America 183 (1985); Lilian Wyles, A Woman of Scotland Yard 227 (1952); Byrn, *supra* note 43, at 817–19; James Witherspoon, *Reexamining* Roe: *Nineteenth-Century Abortion Statutes and the Fourteenth Amendment,* 17 St. Mary's L.J. 29, 31–32, 56–57 (1985).

60. Carl Pauerstein *et al.,* Clinical Obstetrics 110–14 (1987); Patricia Miller, The Worst of Times 19 (1993).

61. Wooster Beach, An Improved System of Midwifery 65 (1854); John Burns, The Principles of Midwifery 174–75 (4th Am. ed. 1817); Samuel Farr, Elements of Medical Jurisprudence 4 (1787); Valentine Seaman, The Midwives Monitor and the Mothers Mirror 25–26, 70–72 (1800).

62. 3 Francis Wharton & Moreton Stillé, Treatise on Medical Jurisprudence 11 (5th ed. 1905).

63. Bernard Dickens, Abortion and the Law 26 (1966); Kerry Petersen, Abortion Regimes 18 (1993).

century just how long human gestation lasted.[64] Nor could a midwife or a physician diagnose a pregnancy as involving twins until after the birth of the first child.[65]

If proving the fact of pregnancy were not daunting enough, proving a cause of death was also problematic. Given the limits of forensic medicine at the time, courts had difficulty coping with any claim that an act significantly in the past had caused an adult's death. This problem was epitomized by the common law rule that no homicide could be charged if the victim died more than a year and a day after the act that allegedly caused the death for it could not then be shown that there was not some other intervening cause of death.[66] Such problems were even more pronounced for infants, as shown by the statutory presumption (first enacted in England in 1624) that one who concealed the death of child in order to conceal its birth was guilty of murder.[67]

Detecting and proving a voluntary abortion was difficult and problematic. Voluntary abortion by its nature is a highly private activity in which all persons capable of speaking are involved in the crime. And, as some secondary authorities appear to have it, if abortion were a crime only after quickening,[68] it would be virtually impossible to prove if the mother died for generally she alone could give evidence regarding whether she had perceived the fetus moving.[69] Nor could anyone prove that an abortion had occurred without the testimony of the woman. The following passage, from the middle of the beginning of the twentieth century, illustrates the point:

> The signs of abortion, as obtained by an examination of the female, are not very certain in their character. It is seldom, indeed, that an examination of the living female is had, and especially at a period early enough to afford any valuable indications. When abortion occurs in the early months, it leaves but slight and evanescent traces behind it.[70]

These problems of proof, making it extraordinarily difficult to prove either the act of abortion or the requisite intent to commit the crime were at the heart of the concerns of the two justices in *Regina v. Sims*, let alone whether the acts of the alleged abortionist caused the death of the fetus. The *Sims* case did not involve a voluntary attempt at an abortion, so the mother was quite ready to testify about the pregnancy, and about quickening if that were necessary, and even about the abortional acts of the defendant. Still, the court indicated that conviction would not obtain if the child were stillborn as the court could not then determine whether the abortional

---

64. *See* "A Correspondent" (apparently Dr. T.R. Beck), *Contributions in Medical Jurisprudence and Police, No. IV: Duration of Human Pregnancy*, 6 N.Y. MED. & PHYSICAL J. 224 (1827).

65. SEAMAN, *supra* note 61, at 36, 96.

66. Statute of Gloucester, 6 Edw. 1, ch. 9 (1278); Rex v. Heydon, 76 ENG. REP. 631(K.B. 1586); 4 BLACKSTONE, *supra* note 11, at *197–98; EDWARD COKE, THIRD INSTITUTE 53 (1644). 3 HOLDSWORTH, *supra* note 23, at 315. The rule was long followed in the United States. Louisville, E. & St.L. R. Co. v. Clarke, 152 U.S. 230, 239 (1894); United States v. Jackson, 528 A.2d 1211, 1218 n.18 (D.C. 1987); Percer v. State, 103 S.W. 780 (Tenn. 1907). In recent decades, courts have abandoned the rule wholesale because "advances in medical and related sciences have so undermined the usefulness of the rule as to render it without question obsolete." Rogers v. Tennessee, 532 U.S. 451, 463 (2001). *See also* People v. Carillo, 646 N.E.2d 582 (Ill.), *cert. denied*, 515 U.S. 1146 (1995); Commonwealth v. Lewis, 409 N.E.2d 771 (Mass. 1980), *cert. denied*, 450 U.S. 929 (1981); People v. Stevenson, 331 N.W.2d 143 (Mich. 1982); State v. Hefler, 310 S.E.2d 310 (N.C. 1984); Edwin Klett, *Abolition of the Year and a Day Rule:* Commonwealth v. Ladd, 65 DICK. L. REV. 166 (1961); Roderick Terry, *Criminal Procedures: Homicide: The Viability of the Year and a Day Murder Rule*, 31 HOW. L.J. 401 (1988); Donald Walther, Comment, *Taming a Phoenix: The Year-and-a-Day Rule in Federal Prosecutions for Murder*, 59 U. CHI. L. REV. 1337 (1992).

67. 21 James I ch. 27, § 3 (1624). The evolution of this presumption over time is described in Ch. 2, at notes 326, 333–42, 366–435, 504–21.

68. *See, e.g.,* COKE, *supra* note 66, at 50–51, quoted *infra* at notes 119–21; 1 HALE, *supra* note 7, at 429–30, quoted *infra* at notes 188–89. On the ambiguity in the phrase they use ("quick with child"), see Ch. 3, at notes 96–106.

69. GLANVILLE WILLIAMS, THE SANCTITY OF LIFE AND THE CRIMINAL LAW 158–59 (1957, reprinted 1972).

70. WHARTON & STILLÉ, *supra* note 62, at 277. *See also* GROSSBERG, *supra* note 59, at 183; MOHR, DOCTORS, *supra* note 56, at 72.

acts actually caused the miscarriage. The court simply noted that certain facts—the birth alive of the child showing the signs of the attack followed by the death of the child from the effects of the attack—resolved the uncertainties and allowed the court to convict the responsible person of murder.[71]

If *Regina v. Sims* is interesting for presenting the problems of proof that were (and to some extent still are) routine in abortion prosecutions, the second major case, *Regina v. Webb*,[72] is interesting for quite another reason. *Webb* involved self-abortion, and its outcome sets to rest the claim that while abortion may have been a crime at common law when imposed on a woman, it was a woman's right under the common law as reflected in the long tradition that women were not subject to punishment for abortion.[73] The indictment of Margaret Webb for aborting herself lays to rest any claim that women had a "common law liberty" to abort as claimed by so many advocates of abortional freedom.[74] The *Regina v. Webb* record reads:

> Surrey. The Jurors for our Lady the Queen present that Margaret Webb, late of Godalming in the county aforesaid, spinster, on the tenth day of August in the forty-first year of the reign of our Lady Elizabeth [1599] by the grace of God Queen of England, France and Ireland, and defender of the faith, with force and arms, and at Godalming aforesaid in the aforesaid county, not having the fear of God before her eyes but seduced by the instigation of the devil, once ate a certain poison called "ratsbane" with the intention of getting rid of[75] and destroying the child in the womb of the said Margaret: and thus the aforesaid Margaret, by reason of eating the aforesaid poison, then and there got rid of and destroyed the same child in her womb, to the most pernicious example to all other wrongdoers in similar cases, against the peace of the said lady the Queen, her crown and dignity.
>
> Church[76]

> Pardoned by the general pardon.

This brief report leaves many questions unanswered. We cannot be certain whether Margaret Webb was charged with a felony or a misdemeanor, or whether she was pardoned before or after conviction. Nor does the nature of the record, just an indictment with a note of the pardon, lend itself to the citation of authority or the report of arguments. Still, as law professor John Keown has noted, the trial was held before a "strong bench" comprised on Justice Francis Grandy (who only three years later would be named Chief Judge of Common Pleas) and Serjeant William Daniel (who would be named to the Judge of the Common Pleas only two years later).[77] Regardless of what one might speculate about possible misunderstandings entertained by the grand and petit juries, there is little likelihood that these judges would have overlooked the problem of a legally insufficient indictment.

---

71. See the text *supra* at notes 35–36.

72. ASSI 35/44/7 m.18 (1602), in Surrey Indictments, *supra* note 5, at 512 (no. 3146) (translation as corrected by John Baker). *See also* Keown, *supra* note 33, at 7.

73. *See, e.g.,* Samuel Buell, Note, *Criminal Abortion Revisited,* 66 NYU L. Rev. 1774, 1790 (1991); Jean Rosenbluth, Note, *Abortion as Murder: Why Should Women Get Off? Using Scare Tactics to Preserve Choice,* 66 S. Cal. L. Rev. 1237, 1262–66 (1993). *See also* Kristin Luker, Abortion and the Politics of Motherhood 137–38, 159–75, 195, 224, 241 (1984); Laurence Tribe, Abortion: The Clash of Absolutes 52–53, 76, 115, 132, 213, 232–34, 237–38, 242 (1990); Faye Ginsburg, Contested Lives: The Abortion Debate in an American Community 1, 6–19, 140–45, 172–97, 212–21 (1989); Beverly Wildung Harrison, Our Right to Choose: Toward a New Ethic of Abortion 2–4, 32–49, 59–62, 67, 181–82, 189–90 (1983).

74. See the authorities collected *supra* at note 9.

75. *spoilare,* which Keown translates as "spoiling" and Baker translates as "getting rid of."

76. Church was the clerk of the assize. 2 Philip Rafferty, *Roe v. Wade:* The Birth of a Constitutional Right 643 (University Microfilms International Dissertation Information Service, Ann Arbor, MI 1993).

77. Keown, *supra* note 33, at 7. *See also* Edward Fox, Biographical Dictionary of the Judges of England 213 (Daniel—"a verie honest, learned, and discreat man"), 293 (Grandy) (1870).

Apparently Webb was saved from punishment for her self-abortion only by a general pardon granted to nearly all felons for most offenses (exceptions included murder) committed before August 7, 1601.[78] Webb might have avoided trial by pleading the pardoning statute before trial,[79] but the clerical notation does not indicate either that the pardon was so pleaded or that there was a trial. Such authorities on legal history as Roy Hunnisett and James Cockburn have surmised that the pardon came after Webb's conviction,[80] while Philip Rafferty has concluded just the opposite.[81] In any event, the pardon in no way undercuts the notion that self-abortion was a crime at common law at the very time settlement of the American colonies was about to begin.

The third case, *Flicher v. Genifer*, reads as follows:

> Articles exhibited by Richard Flicher against *John Genifer* sworn before the Bishop of *Worcester*. State Mrs. Flicher being with child Genifer put her and more of her neighbors also with child into fear and she being on Severn Bridge he told one of her neighbors to have her in.[82] Whereupon she fell into labor and continued in extremity till it pleased God she lost the burden which time of her travail was a week's pace. [83]

We cannot even determine from this record whether this case was a civil trespass suit by the Flichers, or whether it, having apparently been begun as an ecclesiastical proceeding, had been taken over by the royal authorities as a criminal proceeding. We are not even told how the case ended up before a royal court rather than a church court. Nor do we have any inkling of the outcome of the case. In short, *Flicher* is too brief and inconclusive to allow us to draw any firm conclusions about the state of the law or the general attitude towards abortion as a practice. What is interesting is to discover three abortion cases in a space of barely one year given the difficulties of detection and proof inherent in all such cases. Thereafter, English courts prosecuted abortions fairly routinely under the early Stuarts,[84] Cromwell's Commonwealth,[85] and the Restoration.[86]

---

78. 43 Eliz. I ch. 19 (1601).

79. Les Reportes del Cases in Camera Stellata 1593–1609, at 118, 334 (W.P. Baildon ed. 1894).

80. As reported by John Keown. Keown, *supra* note 33, at 7. Cockburn has been described as the first true historian of English criminal law. Albert Schmidt, *Perspectives on Crime in England*, 3 Crim. L.F. 327, 327 (1992). Cockburn, however, equivocated when queried about his conclusion by Philip Rafferty. 2 Rafferty, *supra* note 76, at 641–42.

81. 2 Rafferty, *supra* note 76, at 640–42.

82. To throw her into the river.

83. Flicher v. Genifer (1601), 1 Worcestershire Calendar, *supra* note 34, at 44 (No. 111).

84. *Misdemeanor convictions:* Rex v. Hallibred, ERO (Chelmsford) O/S/R 236/102 (1622), 19B Calendar of Essex Cnty. Rec. 1611–1624, at 474 (no. 102) ("Essex Calendar"); Rex v. Berry, MJ/GSR/SF79 (1617), 4 (N.S.) Cnty. of Middlesex Calendar of the Sess. Rec. 1615–1616, at 292 ("Middlesex Calendar"); Rex v. Rastone, MJ/SR/552/135, MJ/SBP/1, f. 75 (1616), 3 (N.S.) Middlesex Calendar, *supra*, at 277; Rex v. Whalley, MJ/SR/552/136 (1616), 3 (N.S.) Middlesex Calendar, *supra*, at 277; Rex v. Robinson (1615), 3 (N.S.) Middlesex Calendar, *supra*, at 175. *Indictments without a record of the outcome:* Rex v. Lagott, SRO (Somerset) Q/S 62 (1629), 2 Quarter Sess. Rec. for the Cnty. of Somerset, Charles I, 1625–1639, at 228 (no. 16) ("Somerset QSR"); Rex v. Fookes, ERO (Chelmsford), Q/S/R 222/73 (1618), 19 Essex Calendar, *supra*, at 328 (no. 73); Rex v. Turner, MJ/SR/543/143 (f. MSR 111.51), MJ/SR/544/44, MJ/SBR/2 (1615), 3 (N.S.) Middlesex Calendar, *supra*, at 51; Rex v. Hodges (1615), 2 Calendar of Middlesex Cnty. Sess. Rec. 1614–1615, at 345 (1936) ("Middlesex Cnty. Sess.").

85. *Acquittal:* Commonwealth v. Carter (1652), Calendar of Assize Rec.: Kent Indictments, 1649–1659, at 96 (nos. 534, 535) (J.S. Cockburn ed. 1989) ("Kent Indictments"). *Indictments without a record of the outcome:* Commonwealth v. Simpson (1659), 6 N. Riding Q. Sess. Rec. 23 (1888) ("N. Riding QRS"); Commonwealth v. Foxall (1651), 3 Warwick Cnty. Rec., Q. Sess.Order Book 50 ("Warwick QSR").

86. *Acquittal:* Rex v. Squire, Gaol Del., ref: MJ/SR 1720 (1687). *Indictments without record of the outcome:* Rex v. Willson, ERO (Chelmsford) QSR/459/1 (1688), 25 Calendar of Essex Cnty. Quarter Sess. Rec. 30 ("Essex QSR"); Rex v. Rolfe, ERO (Chelmsford) QSR/405/64, 160, 184, QSR/406/43, 110, 112–13 (1665), 23

# Sir Edward Coke and the Born Alive Rule

*You will recollect that before the Revolution, Coke on Littleton was the universal elementary book of law students, and a sounder Whig never wrote, nor of profounder learning in the orthodox doctrines of the British constitution, or in what are called English liberties.*

—Thomas Jefferson[87]

Sir Edward Coke (1552–1634) was the Attorney-General who appeared in *Regina v. Sims*. Coke had a long and distinguished career at the bar, including service as Reader at the Inner Temple (1589), Speaker of the House of Commons (1593), Solicitor General (1592–94), Attorney General (1594–1606), Chief Justice of Common Pleas (1606–1613), and Chief Justice and of the King's Bench (1613–1616).[88] He also played a small but important role in the colonization of North America when, as Attorney-General, he drafted the first charter of the Virginia Company under which, a year later, Jamestown was settled.[89] He is perhaps best known today for his quarrel with James I.[90] Coke openly challenged the King's claim to a royal prerogative to judge personally on the legal merits of a jurisdictional dispute between Chancery and the King's Bench. As a result of his denial of royal authority, Coke was dismissed from the King's Bench in 1616. Even though Coke's struggles with King James before his dismissal failed to prevent the triumph of equity over the law, his struggle did contribute to the near

---

Essex QSR, *supra*, at 65, 74, 76. John Baker has also traced a form indictment published in 1675 to a prosecution in the Gloucester Quarter Sessions, but no record of the prosecution itself seems to have survived. For the indictment, see Officium Clerici Pacis 240–41 (1675).

87. 12 Thomas Jefferson, The Works of Thomas Jefferson 456 (Paul Ford ed. 1905) (letter to James Madison, 1826).

88. *See generally* Catherine Drinker Bowen, The Lion and the Throne (1956); 1 John Campbell, The Lives of the Chief Justices 245–57 (1849); Richard Helgerson, Form of Nationhood: The Elizabethan Writing of England ch. 2 (1991); 5 Holdsworth, *supra*, at 425–26; W.S. Holdsworth, The Historians of Anglo-American Law 14–17, 139 (1966) ("Holdsworth, Historians"); Hastings Lyon & Herman Block, Edward Coke: Oracle of the Law (1929); J.M. Sosin, The Aristocracy of the Long Robe 37–84 (1989); Samuel Thorne, Essays in English Legal History 223–78 (1985) ("Thorne, Essays"); Samuel Thorne, Sir Edward Coke (1957); Stephen White, Sir Edward Coke and "The Grievances of the Commonwealth," 1621–1628, at 3–23 (1979); Winfield, *supra* note 14, at 333–37. These works range from the hagiographic (Bowen) to the downright hostile (Sosin); they all document Coke's role in terms similar to those described in this and the next several paragraphs.

89. 1 Charles Andrews, The Colonial Period in American History 85–86 (1936).

90. *See* Baker, *supra* note 24, at 112–13, 124–26, 135–45, 164–69, 190–92; J.H. Baker, The Legal Profession and the Common Law 205–29 (1986); Bowen, *supra* note 88; Catherine Drinker Bowen, The Temper of a Man: Francis Bacon 133–74 (1963); 5 Holdsworth, *supra*, at 428–29; Louis Knafla, Law and Politics in Jacobean England 155–81 (1977); Lyon & Block, *supra* note 88, at 175–84, 189–90, 194–210; Milsom, *supra* note 50, at 91–93; Radin, *supra* note 24, at 266–67, 436–37; Roland Usher, The Rise and Fall of the High Commission (rev. ed. 1968); White, *supra* note 88, at 6–7; Thomas Barnes, *A Cheshire Seductress, Precedent, and a "Sore Blow" to Star Chamber,* in On the Laws and Customs of England, *supra* note 50, at 359; Raoul Berger, Doctor Bonham's Case: *Statutory Construction or Constitutional Theory?,* 117 U. Pa. L. Rev. 521 (1969); Harold Berman, *The Origins of Historical Jurisprudence: Coke, Selden, Hale,* 103 Yale L.J. 1651, 1673–94 (1994); Allen Dillard Boyer, *"Understanding, Authority, and Will": Sir Edward Coke and the Elizabethan Origins of Judicial Review,* 39 B.C. L. Rev. 43 (1997); Harold Cook, *Against Common Right and Reason: The Royal College of Physicians versus Doctor Thomas Bonham,* 29 Am. J. Legal Hist. 301 (1985); Esther Cope, *Sir Edward Coke and Proclamations, 1610,* 15 Am. J. Legal His. 215 (1971); John Dawson, *Coke and Ellesmere Disinterred: The Attack on the Chancery in 1616,* 36 Ill. L. Rev. 127 (1941); Charles Gray, Bonham's Case *Reviewed,* 116 Proc. Am. Phil. Soc'y 35 (1972); T.E.F. Plucknett, *Bonham's Case and Judicial Review,* 40 Harv. L. Rev. 30 (1926); Samuel Thorne, *The Constitution and the Courts: A Reexamination of the Famous Case of Dr. Bonham,* in The Constitution Reconsidered 15 (Conyers Read ed., rev. ed. 1968); Roland Usher, *James I and Sir Edward Coke,* 18 Eng. Hist. Rev. 664 (1903).

demise of the other prerogative courts and began the continuing sharp decline of the church courts.

Coke's retirement gave him 18 years to work on his *Institutes* [91]—books that became the basic texts of the common law for the next two centuries. Coke did return to government for a time as a Privy Councilor, but upon his election to Parliament in the 1620s he became the leader of the opposition to the Crown and thereafter was the intellectual mentor of the Roundheads. He wrote the Petition of Right, the document that is the second basic constitutional document in England after Magna Carta.[92] Because of Coke's Parliamentary activities, the royal government suppressed the further publication of his *Institutes* after the Petition of Right was adopted (1628) for fear of possibly seditious matter.[93] As a result, the last three volumes were not published until after his death. The Parliamentary forces during the Civil War published the books, and made them the political bible for the Puritan revolutionaries who executed Charles I, establishing that (as Coke had argued to James I) even the King is bound by the law.[94] Ironically, one of Coke's best known opinions today was one in which he claimed authority as a judge to set aside acts of Parliament if he found them to be "against common right and reason" [95]—a source of the American practice of judicial review.

At the time they were written, as well as today, Coke's *Institutes* were recognized as the first comprehensive and systematic treatment of the common law since Bracton.[96] The *Intsitutes* promptly acquired standing as the final word on almost any point Coke discussed.[97] Similarly, Coke published case reports while he was still on the bench; they were so highly regarded that they were cited simply as *The Reports*.[98] Among Coke's more important achievements in his several works was the revival of interest in the *Magna Carta* after a century and a half (or more) of desuetude.[99] In the course of reviving the *Magna Carta*, Coke shaped the modern ideas of judi-

---

91. EDWARD COKE, FIRST INSTITUTE (1628) (also known as COKE ON LITTLETON, covering real property); EDWARD COKE, SECOND INSTITUTE (1642) (covering the leading statutes); COKE, *supra* note 66 (1644) (the THIRD INSTITUTE covers the criminal law); EDWARD COKE, FOURTH INSTITUTE (1644) (covering the jurisdiction and history of English courts). *See generally* BAKER, *supra* note 24, at 217–18; PLUCKNETT, *supra* note 24, at 281–84.

92. 5 HOLDSWORTH, *supra* note 23, at 444–454; WHITE, *supra* note 88; Berman, *supra* note 90, at 1677; Jess Stoddart Flemion, *The Struggle for the Petition of Right in the House of Lords: The Study of an Opposition Party Victory*, 45 J. MODERN HIS. 193 (1973); Clarke Forsythe, *The Historical Origins of Broad Federal Habeas Review Reconsidered*, 70 NOTRE DAME L. REV. 1079, 1089–94 (1995).

93. BAKER, *supra* note 24, at 217–18. *See also* THORNE, ESSAYS, *supra* note 87, at 254–68.

94. G.O. SAYLES, SCRIPTA DIVERSA 75–81, 133–49 (1982); SOSIN, *supra* note 88, at 75–81; WHITE, *supra* note 88, at 15–19; Berman, *supra* note 90, at 1678–79, 1688–89.

95. Dr. Bonham's Case, 77 ENG. REP. 646, 652 (K.B. 1610).

96. PLUCKNETT, *supra* note 24, at 281; THORNE, ESSAYS, *supra* note 88, at 225; Berman, *supra* note 90, at 1679–82. On Bracton, see Ch. 3, at notes 45–47, 52.

97. J.H. BAKER, THE THIRD UNIVERSITY OF ENGLAND: THE INNS OF COURT AND THE COMMON LAW TRADITION 209–10, 218 (1990); 5 HOLDSWORTH, *supra* note 23, at 456–93; PLUCKNETT, *supra* note 24, at 282–84; RADIN, *supra* note 24, at 285–86; THORNE, ESSAYS, *supra* note 88, at 223–38; WHITE, *supra* note 88, at 10–11.

98. EDWARD COKE, REPORTS (13 vols., 1600–1616). *See generally* BAKER, *supra* note 90, at 177–204; JOHN DAWSON, THE ORACLES OF THE LAW 65–79 (1968) GEORGE GROSSMAN, LEGAL RESEARCH: HISTORICAL FOUNDATIONS OF THE ELECTRONIC AGE 112–13 (1994); WINFIELD, *supra* note 14, at 188–89; T.E.F. Plucknett, *The Genesis of Coke's Reports*, 27 CORNELL L.Q. 190 (1942); Damian Powell, *Coke in Context: Early Modern Legal Observation and Sir Edward Coke's Reports*, 21 LEGAL HIST. no. 3., at 33 (Dec. 2000).

99. COKE, SECOND INSTITUTE, *supra* note 91, at 50. *See generally* BAKER, *supra* note 24, at 165–66, 538–40; DANIEL FARBER & SUZANNA SHERRY, A HISTORY OF THE AMERICAN CONSTITUTION 67–68 (1990); J.C. HOLT, MAGNA CARTA 3–4 (1965); PLUCKNETT, *supra* note 24, at 50–51, 243–44, 336–37; RADIN, *supra* note 24, at 157, 163–64; SOSIN, *supra* note 88, at 5, 13–15, 18, 45–46, 58–61, 91 n.13; WHITE, *supra* note 88, ch. 7; Louis Boudin, *Lord Coke and the American Doctrine of Judicial Power*, 6 NYU L.Q. 233 (1929); Theodore Plucknett, *Bonham's Case and Judicial Review*, 40 HARV. L. REV. 30 (1926); Robert Riggs, *Substantive Due Process in 1791*, 1990 WIS. L. REV. 941, 957–59, 968 n.124; D.O. Wagner, *Coke and the Rise of Economic Liberalism*, 6 ECON. HIST. REV. 30 (1935).

cial review and "due process," becoming perhaps the first to include in due process the substantive component that has come to play such a pivotal role in modern debates about the constitutionality of abortion statutes.[100] Coke focused on a phrase taken from the *Magna Carta: per legem terrae*—variously translated as "according to the law of the land" or "according to a law of the land," a fine distinction on which many an argument has turned. It was Coke's protégé John Selden who, in 1627, popularized the hitherto rare expression "due process of law" as an equivalent expression.[101]

Coke's analyses were not only central regarding the abstract idea of "due process," but also were central in developing the prohibition of self-incrimination, in particular in crystallizing the rejection of the *ex officio* oath as part of the common law.[102] Coke's motivation was not so much to protect the freedoms of Englishmen as it was to make the common law supreme over the Church courts by crippling the latter courts' most important trial procedure.[103] Coke as Chief Justice of Common Pleas and later of the King's Bench issued writs of prohibition against ecclesiastical use of the *ex officio* oath.[104] This was, of course, simply another instance Coke's attempt to make the common law supreme over the prerogative courts generally, over the King's personal exercise of the prerogative to do justice, and even over the Parliament.[105]

Coke delved deeply into the early precedents of the common law. His historicism served to crystallize the notion of precedent that has played such a large role in our law generally and now in the abortion context as well.[106] Before Coke, precedents were usually cited only for procedural points and then often without any examination of the facts of the prior case to determine the meaning or effect of the precedent, with no sense of holding and *dictum*.[107] Modern use of precedent only became possible with the publication of case reports, a process in which Coke was a pioneer.[108] In short, Coke, despite his historicism, was not so much a reactionary as a "radical conservative, who reached back into the past not only to strike down innovations of the preceding century of accumulating royal power but also to justify wholly new legal principles."[109]

---

100. Dr. Bonham's Case, 77 Eng. Rep. 646, 652 (K.B. 1610); Coke, Second Institute, *supra* note 91, at 46–47. *See also* Thorne, Essays, *supra* note 88, at 230–31, 237, 269–78; Riggs, *supra* note 99, at 948–63, 991–95. *See generally* Hermine Herta Meyer, The History and Meaning of the Fourteenth Amendment 137–40 (1977); John Orth, Due Process of Law: A Brief History 7–8 15–32 (2003); Edward Corwin, *The Doctrine of Due Process of Law before the Civil War*, 24 Harv. L. Rev. 366, 368 (1911); Keith Jurow, *Untimely Thoughts: A Reconsideration of the Origins of Due Process of Law*, 19 Am. J. Legal Hist. 265, 276–77 (1975). For an argument that the phrase "due process" (or its earlier equivalent, "the law of the land") was understood substantively even before Coke, see C.H. McIlwain, *Due Process in Magna Carta*, 14 Colum. L. Rev. 27 (1914).

101. *Habeas Corpus for Sir Thomas Darnel*, 3 Howells' State Trials 17, 18 (K.B. 1627). *See* Berman, *supra* note 90, at 1700–01.

102. Mary Hume Maguire, *Attack of the Common Lawyers on the Oath* ex Officio *as Administered in the Ecclesiastical Courts of England*, in Essays in History and Political Theory in Honor of Charles Howard McIlwain 199, 212, 219–28 (Carl Wittke ed. 1936); John Henry Wigmore, *The Privilege against Self-Crimination* (sic): *Its History*, 15 Harv. L. Rev. 610, 621–24 (1902).

103. Maguire, *supra* note 102, at 220–21.

104. *Id.* at 225–27.

105. See the text *supra* at notes 90–95; and Chapter 3, at notes 382–84.

106. Berman, *supra* note 90, at 1689–94, 1732–33.

107. The distinction between a holding (a statement in a judicial opinion that addresses the precise facts of a case, and which therefore counts as precedent) and mere *dictum* (any other statement in a judicial opinion, which does not count as precedent) was first formally recognized in *Bole v. Horton*, 124 Eng. Rep. 1113, 1124 (K.B. 1673), and remains a subtle and often uncertain distinction today. *See generally* T. Ellis Lewis, *The History of Judicial Precedent*, 48 L.Q. Rev. 230 (1932); J. Stanley McQuade, *Medieval "Ratio" and Modern Formal Studies: A Reconsideration of Coke's* Dictum That Law is in the Perfection of Reason, 38 Am. J. Juris. 359 (1993).

108. Berman, *supra* note 90, at 1732–33.

109. *Id.* at 1688.

Although Coke seldom distinguished between what a court actually said and what he thought it ought to have said, his prestige among lawyers was such that this confusion hardly seemed to matter. As Chief Justice Best summed the matter up nearly two centuries ago, "[t]he fact is, Lord Coke had no authority for what he states, but I am afraid we should get rid of a good deal of what is considered law in Westminster Hall, if what Lord Coke says without authority is not law."[110] Even when Coke was wrong about the law, his professional standing or the Parliamentary triumph made him correct.[111] No wonder Coke earned the sobriquet "Father of the Common Law,"[112] or that Charles Gray, in his edition of the works of Sir Matthew Hale, paused to describe Coke as "the greatest lawyer in English history."[113]

Coke's role in shaping the common law is particularly important in disputes about the true state of the law as applied in the American colonies, or in the early years of the Republic. A copy of *The Reports* was on the *Mayflower,* [114] and Coke himself drafted the Charter of (and invested in) the Virginia Company that founded Jamestown.[115] American legal historian Julius Goebel concluded that it was "upon the methods and constitutional views of Coke that the colonial lawyers were nurtured"[116]—a view shared by Thomas Jefferson in a letter to James Madison in 1826.[117] And legal historian Samuel Thorne noted that every American lawyer was familiar with Coke's *Institutes* well into the nineteenth century and that "more American than English law can be traced back to his books, and no further."[118]

Understanding who Coke was and what influence he had is important in the history of abortion because he played a central role in crystallizing the common law of abortion as it was applied over the seventeenth and eighteenth century, in both England and America. In addition to his argument in *Regina v. Sims,*[119] Coke discussed abortion in his *Third Institute.* Perhaps remembering imperfectly the still unreported *Regina v. Sims,* he wrote:

> If a woman be quick with childe, and by a Potion or otherwise killeth it in her wombe; or if a man beat her, whereby the childe dieth in her body, and she is delivered of a dead childe, this is a great misprision, and no murder: but if the childe be born alive, and dieth of the Potion, battery, or other cause, this is murder: for the law it is accounted a reasonable creature, in rerum natura, when it is born alive. And the Book in 1 E. 3 was never holden for law. And 3 Ass. p.2 is but a repetition of that case. And so horrible an offence should not go unpunished. And so was the law holden in

---

110. Garland v. Jekyll, 130 ENG. REP. 311, 320 (C.P. 1824). *See also* BAKER, *supra* note 24, at 209–10; 5 HOLDSWORTH, *supra* note 23, at 490–93; HOLDSWORTH, HISTORIANS, *supra* note 98, at 14–17; PLUCKNETT, *supra* note 24, at 281; RADIN, *supra* note 24, at 318; SOSIN, *supra* note 88, at 55–59; THORNE, ESSAYS, *supra* note 88, at 226–34, 254–78; WHITE, *supra* note 88, at 11–22; WINFIELD, *supra* note 14, at 188–89; Dellapenna, *supra* note 43, at 379–89; Powell, *supra* note 98. For a catalogue of Coke's "errors," see 5 HOLDSWORTH, *supra,* at 472–90.

111. PLUCKNETT, *supra* note 24, at 476–78; RADIN, *supra* note 24, at 286. *See also* Dellapenna, *supra* note 43, at 381–86. Courts cited Coke as authoritative in a variety of contexts. *See* Millar v. Turner, 1 Vesey 86 (K.B. 1748); Beale v. Beale, 24 Eng. Rep. 373 (K.B. 1713); KEOWN, *supra* note 33, at 10–11.

112. *See, e.g.,* 5 HOLDSWORTH, *supra* note 23, at 489 (quoting Maitland to the effect that Coke's books were "the great divide" between medieval and modern law). *See also* HOLDSWORTH, HISTORIANS, *supra* note 88, at 14–15; SAYLES, *supra* note 94, at 219–22; SOSIN, *supra* note 88, at 13; THORNE, ESSAYS, *supra* note 88, at 224; WHITE, *supra* note 88, at 3; Berman, *supra* note 90, at 1694–95.

113. Charles Gray, *Introduction,* in MATTHEW HALE, HISTORY OF THE COMMON LAW OF ENGLAND xii (Charles Gray ed. 1971).

114. THORNE, ESSAYS, *supra* note 88, at 223.

115. ANDREWS, *supra* note 89, at 85–86; THORNE, ESSAYS, *supra* note 88, at 225.

116. Julius Goebel, *Constitutional History and Constitutional Law,* 38 COLUM. L. REV. 555, 563 (1938).

117. JEFFERSON, *supra* note 87, at 456, quoted *supra* at note 87.

118. THORNE, ESSAYS, *supra* note 88, at 223.

119. 75 ENG. REP. 1075 (Q.B. 1601), quoted *supra* at notes 35–36.

Bractons time, *Si aliquis qui mulierem praegnanem percusserit, vel ei venenum dederit, per quod fecerit abortivum, si puerperium jam formatum fuerit; & maxime si fuerit animatum, facit homicidium.*[120] And herewith agreeth Fleta: and herein the law is grounded upon the law of God, which saith, *Quicumque effuderit humanum sanguinem, fundetur sanguis illius, ad imaginem quippe Dei creatus est homo.*[121] If a man counsell a woman to kill the childe within her wombe, when it shall be born, and after she is delivered of the childe, she killeth it; the counsellor is an accessory to the murder, and yet at the time of the commandement, or counsell, no murder could be committed of the childe in utero matris: the reason of which case proveth well the other case.[122]

Coke's statement contradicts those of Staunford and Lambard written within the previous century, but Coke is closer to what courts actually were deciding than either of the earlier authors.[123] With the exception of Sir Matthew Hale's holding that the death of a mother from an abortion was a felony homicide,[124] the later seventeenth-century cases produced convictions only for misdemeanors, lending credence to Coke's conclusion that abortion before quickening was only a misdemeanor.[125] This may have been part of the pattern of providing juries with less serious alternative paths to conviction in order to prevent outright acquittals when either the evidence was not strong enough or the punishment tended to strike juries as too harsh.[126]

Today we cannot determine whether Coke's greater accuracy in reporting what courts were actually doing was because Coke was more intent on reporting what courts were doing, or whether the courts where simply following Coke. All important later commentators on the criminal law followed Coke in describing the common law relating to abortions.[127] Only Sir Matthew Hale apparently did not accept Coke as authoritative on the matter, although an examination of all of Hale's writings casts some doubt on this conclusion.[128] As for this difference of opinion, the weight of authority was decidedly in Coke's favor.[129]

Remarkably, several modern supporters of abortion rights have seriously misconstrued what Coke had to say about abortion. These recent commentaries on the law of abortion have emphasized Coke's statement that "[in] the law [a child] is accounted a reasonable creature, *in rerum natura*, when it is born alive" as indicating that abortion (or "feticide") could never be classed as homicide under the common law.[130] This is rather remarkable as Coke himself indicated that the

---

120. "If anyone strikes a pregnant woman or gives her a poison in order to make an abortion, if the foetus is already formed, especially if it is quickened, he commits homicide." Note that Bracton seemed to consider abortion murder even before quickening to be homicide so long as the fetus is "formed." For analysis of Bracton's discussion of abortion, see Ch. 3, at notes 52, 67–71, 94–107.

121. "Whosoever spills human blood, his blood shall be spilled, for surely man is created in the image of God." For analysis of Fleta's discussion of abortion, see Ch. 3, at notes 53–59, 67–71, 95–109.

122. Coke, *supra* note 66, at 50–51.

123. *See* Ch. 3, at notes 425–41. For Staunford and Lambard's views, see the text *supra* at notes 14–19.

124. Rex v. Anonymous (Bury Assizes 1670), in 1 Hale, *supra* note 7, at 429–30, quoted *infra* at note 182. See also the discussion in the text *infra* at notes 186–88.

125. See the cases collected *supra* at notes 84–86.

126. Scott, *supra* note 25, at 239–40. *See* Chapter 2, at notes 336–62.

127. *See, e.g.,* Anonymous, *supra* note 11, at 348; 1 Blackstone, *supra* note 11, at *129–30; 4 Blackstone, *supra,* at *198; Burn, *supra* note 11, at 380; 1 Edward Hyde East, A Treatise on the Pleas of the Crown 227–30 (1803); 2 Hawkins, *supra* note 11, at 80; 1 William Russell, A Treatise on Crimes and Misdemeanors 617–18, 796 (1819).

128. See the text *infra* at notes 156–222.

129. Williams v. State, 561 A.2d 216 (Md. 1989).

130. Bicka Barlow, *Severe Penalties for the Destruction of "Potential Life"—Cruel and Unusual Punishment?*, 29 U.S.F. L. Rev. 463, 467 (1995); Mary Barrazatto, Note, *Judicial Recognition of Feticide: Usurping the*

only reason for not classifying abortion as homicide was an inability to prove the necessary elements of the crime—something we now have the technical ability to do in many cases.[131] In this
context, Coke's use of the word "account" seems rather clearly to indicate only that the law was
not able to reach a definite conclusion, rather than that the unborn child could never, under any
circumstances, qualify as a human being.[132]

If there is any uncertainty about Coke's meaning, however, modern research has established
that by the close of the seventeenth century, the criminality of abortion under the common law
was well established. Courts had rendered clear holdings that abortion was a crime, no decision indicated that any form of abortion was lawful, and secondary authorities similarly uniformly supported the criminality of abortion. The only differences among these authorities
had been about the severity of the crime (misdemeanor or felony), an uncertainty that, under
Coke's influence, began to settle into the pattern of holding abortion to be a misdemeanor unless the child were born alive and then died from the injuries or potions that led to its premature birth. Even Cyril Means, jr., initially had treated Coke's passage as the correct and indisputable statement of the common law regarding abortion.[133] Yet when, in 1971, Means
undertook to recreate the history of Anglo-American abortion law in an effort to bolster the
attempt to overturn the laws, he was forced to attempt to discredit Coke's discussion of abortion. Otherwise, Means would have had to admit that the common law accepted in England
and its American colonies did treat at least some abortions as murders, and others as misprisions (misdemeanors).

The only opening Means found in Coke's writings for criticizing Coke's reasoning was
Coke's omission of pre-quickening abortion from a list of misprisions "divers and severall"
later in the same *Institute*.[134] Rather than suggesting inconsistency on Coke's part, the omission could demonstrate that Coke was not obsessed with abortion (contrary to Means'
claims), and thus the topic simply did not come to mind when he wrote about the criminal
law generally. Indeed, Coke's devotion of a single paragraph to the topic of abortion in the
four long volumes he wrote indicates rather strongly that Coke was not at all obsessed with
the practice.

Apparently realizing the weakness of arguing on the basis of the omission of abortion from a
list of misprisions, Means met Coke's discussion of abortion with pure invective. Means described Coke's analysis as an "outrageous" "politico-religious" power-grab motivated by Coke's
struggles with the ecclesiastical Court of High Commission while Coke was on the King's
Bench.[135] Means went on to describe Coke's discussion of abortion as "a masterpiece of perversion."[136] Means probably could not have gotten away with such posturing but for the contemporary American ignorance of who Coke was. Professor Harold Berman provided a more scholarly
appraisal of Coke: "The main key to Coke's character as a public figure was his dedication to the
law."[137]

---

*Power of the Legislature?*, 24 J. Fam. L. 43, 45 (1985); Katharine Folger, *When Does Life Begin…of End? The
California Supreme Court Redefines Fetal Murder in* People v. Davis, 29 U.S.F. L. Rev. 237, 239 (1994).

131. Scott, *supra* note 25, at 232–40.

132. *Id.* at 235–36.

133. Cyril Means, jr., *The Law of New York Concerning Abortion and the Status of the Foetus, 1664–1968: A
Case of Cessation of Constitutionality,* 14 N.Y.L.F. 411, 420 (1968) ("Means I").

134. Coke, *supra* note 66, at 139–42.

135. Means II, *supra* note 9, at 346–48.

136. *Id.* at 359.

137. Berman, *supra* note 90, at 1675.

Means assaulted Coke's credibility without concern for either consistency or accuracy. Means asserted that Coke's view on abortion was never taken seriously in England,[138] although Means had noted only four pages earlier that two nineteenth century English cases expressly followed Coke,[139] and had noted another three pages earlier that Hawkins and Blackstone had also followed Coke.[140] Indeed, Blackstone, again contrary to Means, had correctly noted that Coke's view had made the law more tolerant of abortion than had formerly been the case.[141] Means went on to describe the authority relied on by Coke as isolated and ambiguous, while describing the authorities to the contrary as numerous and well established.[142] In fact, the authorities putatively on both sides of the question were the same authorities. Furthermore, Means was quite willing to approve of Coke's innovations when it suited him.[143] Means' bemoaning what he described as deliberate misstatements by Coke[144] thus is, at best, the proverbial pot describing the kettle.

Means' invective centered on declaiming that Coke's analysis was an establishment of religion, and, as such, impermissible in secular America.[145] Means' analysis did not consider the wholesale reception of canon law into the common law which was occurring at that time[146]—often through Coke's activities.[147] Few (probably even including Means) would find such other changes to be "masterpieces of perversion." Indeed, Jane Larson, one of the authors of the notorious "*Historians' Briefs*" presented to the Supreme Court in 1989 and 1992 cited the canon law approvingly as the "roots *(sic)* of the common law of sexual crimes" in focusing on seduction rather than abortion.[148] Lawyers, judges, and ordinary people at the time did not make a sharp distinction between the laws of God and the laws of England.[149]

The final irony in Means' assault on Coke is that while Means was right that Coke changed the law of abortion, he was completely wrong regarding how Coke changed the law. Means claimed that English courts did not treat abortion as a crime before Coke argued successfully for such an outcome in *Regina v. Sims* and subsequently enshrined his view in his *Third Institute*. Yet as we have seen in Chapter 3 and in this chapter, English courts before Coke's time entertained no doubts regarding the criminality of abortion, whether inflicted on a woman against her will,[150]

---

138. Means II, *supra* note 9, at 355.

139. *Id.* at 351 n.35.

140. *Id.* at 348–349.

141. 1 BLACKSTONE, *supra* note 11, at *129–30.

142. Means II, *supra* note 9, at 343–348, 351–352.

143. *Id.* at 374 (consent to mayhem).

144. *Id.* at 360.

145. Means II, *supra* note 9, at 346–48.

146. On the "capture" of ecclesiastical jurisdiction over such matters as informal contracts, libel, slander, and the law of attempts and conspiracies, see Chapter 3, at notes 346–55.

147. *See, e.g.,* 5 HOLDSWORTH, *supra* note 23, at 198, 464–65.

148. Jane Larson, "*Women Understand So Little, They Call My Good Nature 'Deceit'": A Feminist Rethinking of Seduction,* 93 COLUM. L. REV. 374, 382 n.26 (1993). For discussion of the "historians' briefs," see Chapter 17, at notes 39–58.

149. *See* ST. GERMAN, *supra* note 54; James Stoner, jr., *Common Law and Natural Law,* 5 BENCHMARK, No. 2., at 91 (Winter 1993).

150. *See, e.g.,* Flicher v. Genifer (1601), 1 WORCESTERSHIRE CALENDAR, *supra* note 34, at 44 (No. 111), quoted *supra* at notes 82–83; Rex v. de Bourton, Y.B. Mich. 1 Edw. 3, f. 23, pl. 28 (K.B. 1327), analyzed in Ch. 3, at notes 141–69; Rex v. Haule, JUST 1/547A, m.20d (London Eyre 1321), quoted in Ch. 3, at notes 112–13; Rex v. Mercer, JUST 1/710, m.45 (Oxford Eyre 1285), quoted in Ch. 3, at note 111; Rex v. Code, JUST 1/789, m.17 (Hampshire Eyre 1281), quoted in Ch. 3, at note 93; Rex v. Scharp, THE LONDON EYRE OF 1276, at 23 (no. 76) (London Rec. Soc'y 1976) ("1276 EYRE"), quoted in Ch. 3, at note 92; Juliana's Appeal, SOMERSET PLEAS (CIV. & CRIM.) FROM THE ROLLS OF THE ITINERANT JUSTICES 321 (no. 1243) (C. Chadwyck-Healey ed. 1897), quoted in Ch. 3, at notes 90–91; Amice's Appeal, JUST 1/274, m.14d (1247), quoted in Ch. 3, at note

induced at her request,[151] or even self-induced.[152] These decisions did not turn on the stage of pregnancy (pre- or post-quickening), nor on whether the abortus died before or after birth. And while Coke did contradict the apparent positions on the legality of abortion taken by Sir William Staunford and William Lambard in their books of the previous century,[153] neither Staunford nor Lambard were followed in other legal books and in "Readings" in the Inns of Court even during their own lifetimes.[154] Coke's view that abortion was a misprision if the women were "quick with child," and murder only if the child was born alive and subsequently died, thus changed the law by restricting the full reach of the criminal law to only certain abortions, and in so doing created the "born alive" rule that is still the test of whether a homicide statute applies to the killing of an infant during or immediately before its birth.[155]

87; Agnes's Appeal (1200), Select Pleas of the Crown (1 Selden Soc'y) 39 (no. 82) (F.W. Maitland ed. 1887), quoted in Ch. 3, at notes 75–76.

151. See, e.g., Regina v. Turnour, Essex Assizes 35/23/29 (Essex 1581), quoted in Ch. 3, at 453–56; Rex v. Wodlake, K.B. 29/162/m.11d (1531), K.B. 9/513/m23 (1530), quoted in Ch. 3, at notes 395–98; Rex v. Lichefeld, K.B. 27/974, Rex m.4 (1505), quoted in Ch. 3, at notes 427–30.

152. See, e.g., Regina v. Webb, Essex Assizes 35/23/29 (Essex 1581), quoted supra at notes 75–76. See also Regina v. Robynson, Q/SR 110/68 (Coroner's Inquest 1589); Cockaine v. Witnam, Cro. Eliz. 49 (1586), quoted in Ch. 3, at 445; Rex v. Wynspere (Coroner's Inquest 1503), KB 9/434/12, in Calendar of Notting-hamshire Coroners' Inquests 1485–1558, at 8 (no. 10) (R.F. Hunnisett ed., 25 Thornton Soc'y Rec. Ser. 1966).

153. Lambard, supra note 15, at 217–18; Staunford, supra note 14, ch. 13. See Ch. 3, at notes 425–35.

154. See Ch. 3, at notes 437–42.

155. For more modern applications of the "born alive" rule, see United States v. Spencer, 839 F.2d 1341 (9th Cir. 1988), cert. denied, 487 U.S. 1238 (1988); Singleton v. State, 35 So. 2d 375 (Ala. Ct. App. 1948); Vo v. Superior Ct., 836 P.2d 408 (Ariz. 1992); State v. Cotton, 5 P.3d 918 (Ariz. Ct. App. 2000), rev. denied; Meadows v. State, 722 S.W.2d 584 (Ark. 1987); Keeler v. Superior Ct., 470 P.2d 617 (Cal. 1970); State v. Courchesne, 757 A.2d 699 (Conn. Super. 1999); State v. McCall, 458 So.2d 875 (Fla. Ct. App. 1984); Ranger v. State, 290 S.E.2d 63 (Ga. 1982); State v. Hammett, 384 S.E.2d 220 (Ga. Ct. App. 1989); People v. Ehlert, 781 N.E.2d 500 (Ill. App. Ct. 2002), appeal allowed, 787 N.E.2d 176 (Ill. 2003); State v. Trudell, 755 P.2d 511 (Kan. 1988); Jones v. Commonwealth, 830 S.W.2d 877 (Ky. 1992); State v. Brown, 378 So. 2d 916 (La. 1979); Williams v. State, 561 A.2d 216 (Md. 1989); People v. Guthrie, 293 N.W.2d 775 (Mich. 1980), appeal denied, 334 N.W.2d 616 (Mich. 1983); State v. Soto, 378 N.W.2d 625 (Minn. 1985); State v. Kinsky, 348 N.W.2d 319 (Minn. 1984); State ex rel. A.W.S., 440 A.2d 1144 (N.J. Ct. App. 1981); State v. Willis, 652 P.2d 1222 (N.M. 1982); People v. Hall, 557 N.Y.S.2d 879 (App. Div.), appeal denied, 564 N.E.2d 679 (N.Y. 1990); State v. Beale, 376 S.E.2d 1 (N.C. 1989); State v. Dickinson, 275 N.W.2d 599 (Ohio 1979); Commonwealth v. Booth, 766 A.2d 843 (Pa. 2001); State v. Amaro, 448 A.2d 1257 (R.I. 1983); State v. Collington, 192 S.E.2d 856 (S.C. 1972); State v. Evans, 745 S.W.2d 880 (Tenn. Ct. Crim. App. 1987); Delgado v. Yandell, 468 S.W.2d 475 (Tex. Ct. Crim. App.), writ refused, no rev'ble error, 471 S.W.2d 569 (Tex. 1971); State v. Larsen, 578 P.2d 1280 (Utah 1978); State v. Oliver, 563 A.2d 1002 (Vt. 1989); Vaughn v. Virginia, 376 S.E.2d 801 (Va. Ct. App. 1989); State v. Maguire, 490 S.E.2d 912 (W. Va. 1997); State v. Cornelius, 448 N.W.2d 434 (Wis. 1989), rev. denied, 451 N.W.2d 298 (Wis. 1990). For British law, see In re Attorney-General's Reference No. 3 of 1994, [1998] A.C. 245 (H.L.); Regina v. Sullivan, 63 C.C.C.3d 97 (1991); Regina v. West, 175 Eng. Rep. 329 (1848); Rex v. Brown, 172 Eng. Rep. 1272 (1834); Rex v. Enoch, 172 Eng. Rep. 1089 (1833); Rex v. Senior, 168 Eng. Rep. 1298 (1832); Regina v. Kwok Chak Ming, 1963 H.K. L. Rep. 349; McCluskey v. H.M. Advocate, 1989 Scot. L. Times 175. See J.K. Mason, Medico-Legal Aspects of Reproduction and Parenthood 150–51 (2nd ed. 1998); Annotation, Proof of Live Birth in Prosecutions for Killing Newborn Child, 65 A.L.R.3d 413 (1975); Bicka Barlow, Note, Severe Penalties for the Destruction of "Potential Life"—Cruel and Unusual Punishment?, 29 U.S.F. L. Rev. 463 (1995); D. Brahams, Transplantation, the Fetus and the Law, 138 New L.J. 91 (1988); D. Searborne Davies, Child-Killing in English Law, 1 Modern L. Rev. 203 (1937); Clarke Forsythe, Homicide of the Unborn Child: The Born Alive Rule and Other Legal Anachronisms, 21 Val. L. Rev. 563 (1987); Mark Kende, Michigan's Proposed Prenatal Protection Act: Undermining a Woman's Right to an Abortion, 5 J. Gender & L. 247, 257–61 (1996); Sandra Locke, Note, Abortion Revived: Is the Fetus a Person? Can the Present Law Remain in Light of State v. Courchesne?, 23 Thom . Jeff. L. Rev. 291 (2001); K. Mark McCourt, Foetus Status after R. v. Sullivan and Lemay, 29 Alberta L. Rev. 916 (1991); Jenny Morgan, Foetal Imaginings: Searching for a Vocabulary in the Law and Politics of Reproduction, 12 Can. J. Women & L. 371, 394–401 (2000); John Shannon, Note, A Fetus Is Not a "Person" as the Term Is Used in the Manslaughter Statute, 10 U. Ark. L. Rev. 403 (1987); Aaron

Means' *ad hominem* assault on Coke fails utterly for anyone who is familiar with Coke's work in general, but such familiarity is not necessary to realize that Means simply failed to discredit Coke. A careful reader would have noted the inaccuracies and inconsistencies in Means' diatribe, and would have reached a different conclusion as to who was discredited. Unfortunately, Justice Harry Blackmun noticed neither Means' inconsistencies nor Means' inaccuracies when accepting Means' arguments that Coke's views of abortion were abberational and probably did not represent the law of England.[156] Means was no more even handed regarding others' innovations in the law of abortion.

# Sir Matthew Hale and the Second *Rex v. Anonymous*

*But if a woman be with child, and any gives her a potion to destroy the child within her, and she take it, and it works so strongly, that it kills her, this is murder, for it was not given to cure her of a disease, but unlawfully to destroy the child within her…*

—Matthew Hale[157]

---

Wagner, Comment, *Texas Two-Step: Serving up Fetal Rights by Side-Stepping* Roe v. Wade *Has Set the Table for Another Showdown on Fetal Personhood in Texas and Beyond*, 32 Tex. Tech. L. Rev. 1085 (2001); Celia Wells & Derek Morgan, *Whose Foetus Is It?*, 18 J. Law & Soc'y 431, 440–42 (1991).

Several recent decisions have rejected the rule, applying homicide laws to the killing of a viable fetus that died before its delivery. Smith v. Newsome, 815 F.2d 1386 (11th Cir. 1987) (applying Georgia law); People v. Apodaca, 142 Cal. Rptr. 830 (Ct. App. 1978); Brinkley v. State, 322 S.E.2d 49 (Ga. 1984); State v. Burrell, 699 P.2d 499 (Kan. 1985); Commonwealth v. Cass, 467 N.E.2d 1324 (Mass. 1984); State v. Knapp, 843 S.W.2d 345 (Mo. 1992); Hughes v. State, 868 P.2d 730 (Okla. Ct. Crim. App. 1994); State v. Horne, 319 S.E.2d 703 (S.C. 1984). Some of these decisions reflected specific legislative enactments in the states in question reversing the common law rule. *See, e.g.,* Ark. Code Ann. § 51-102(13)(i)(B) (Michie 1997); Cal. Penal Code § 187(a) (West 1999); Ga. Code Ann. § 16-5-80 (1999); Ind. Code Ann. § 35-42-1-1(1) (West 1997); Mich. Comp. Laws § 750.322 (2002); Minn. Stat. §§ 690.266 to 609.26691 (2003); Utah Code Ann. § 76-5-201(1)(a) (1999). Several courts have dropped the viability requirement, holding that any unjustified killing of a fetus is a homicide. People v. Davis, 872 P.2d 591 (Cal. 1994). *See also* State v. Bauer, 471 N.W.2d 363 (Minn. 1991); State v. Merrill, 450 N.W.2d 318 (Minn. 1990) (upholding a feticide conviction for the death of a fetus only 27 days after conception), *cert. denied*, 436 U.S. 931 (1990); Regina v. Henderson, [1990] N.Z.L.R. 174 (upholding the "born alive" rule but stating in *dictum* that a fetus of more than 20 weeks gestation was a child and upholding a feticide statute criminalizing the killing of a child of that age regardless of whether it was viable).

*See generally* Michael Davidson, *Fetal Crime and Its Cognizability as a Criminal Offense under Military Law,* Army Law., July 1998, at 23; Mary Lynn Kime, Hughes v. State: *The "Born Alive" Rule Dies a Timely Death*, 30 Tulsa L.J. 539 (1995); Murphy Klasing, *The Death of an Unborn Child: Jurisprudential Inconsistencies in Wrongful Death, Criminal Homicide, and Abortion Cases*, 22 Pepp. L. Rev. 933 (1995); Legal Correspondent, *Dr. Leonard Arthur: His Trial and Its Implications*, 283 Brit. Med. J. 1340 (1981); Paul Benjamin Linton, *Planned Parenthood v. Casey: The Flight from Reason in the Supreme Court*, 13 St. L.U. Pub. L. Rev. 15, 58–64 (1993); Stephanie Ritrivi McCavitt, *The "Born Alive" Rule: A Proposed Change to the New York Law Based on Modern Medical Technology*, 36 N.Y.L. Sch. L. Rev. 609 (1991); Jeffrey Parness, *Crimes against the Unborn: Protecting and Respecting the Potentiality of Human Life*, 22 Harv. J. Legis. 97 (1985); Jean Reith Schroedel, Pamela Fiber, & Bruce Snyder, *Women's Rights and Fetal Personhood in Criminal Law*, 7 Duke J. Gender L. & Pol'y 89 (2000); Craig Smith, *Legal Murder: The Intentional Killing of the Unborn*, 11 Crim. Just. J. 423 (1989); Alison Tsao, *Fetal Homicide Laws: Shield against Domestic Abuse or Sword to Pierce Abortion Rights*, 25 Hastings Const'l L.Q. 457 (1998); Louis Waller, *"Any Reasonable Creature in Being,"* 13 Monash L. Rev. 37 (1987).

156. Roe v. Wade, 410 U.S. 113, 135–36 (1973).

157. Rex v. Anonymous (1670), 1 Hale, *supra* note 7, at 429–30.

Even before the publication *Regina v. Sims* and Coke's *Third Institute,* convictions for the crime of abortion became common in Stuart England.[158] The records of cases decided under the Cromwellian Commonwealth and during the Restoration, when Coke's influence was already dominant, include frequent indictments, but no convictions, for abortion.[159] The authoritative legal scholars of the eighteenth and nineteenth century followed Coke's lead uniformly.[160] A form book survives from the later seventeenth century with a standard form indictment for abortion.[161] Collectively, these several sources leave little room for any conclusion but that Coke's view of the law of abortion rapidly became the law of England.

Cyril Means, jr., apparently knew nothing regarding the cases from seventeenth century England apart from *Regina v. Sims.* Nor did he know anything regarding a seventeenth century form book. As for the writings of the legal scholars in the eighteenth and nineteenth centuries, Means (believing that no actual cases supported Coke) dismissed them on the grounds that they were in error for following Coke.[162] Justice Harry Blackmun, in following Means while writing *Roe v. Wade,* was equally dismissive of these scholars.[163] During this period of two centuries, one man stood out whom even Means and Blackmun could not dismiss—Sir Matthew Hale. Means sought to interpret Hale's writings as rejecting the criminality of abortion, and as supporting Means' reading of *Rex v. de Bourton,* the earliest *Rex v. Anonymous,* and *Regina v. Sims.*[164] Means' response to Hale's apparently equally innovative views contrasted sharply to his treatment of Coke.

Sir Matthew Hale (1609–1676) was the dominant legal thinker in England during the second half from the seventeenth century just as Coke had been in the first half.[165] As legal historian Percy Winfield noted, "there is probably no judge in English history who has been held in more honorable estimation."[166] Hale, orphaned at five, was raised to be a Puritan minister. He was sent to Oxford to study for the clergy, but found himself drawn to partying, sports, and the theater rather than to fulfilling such a calling. Eventually he decided to go to the Netherlands to fight the Span-

---

158. Rex v. Hallibred, ERO (Chelmsford) O/S/R 236/102 (1622), 19B Essex Calendar, *supra* note 84, at 474 (no. 102); Rex v. Berry, MJ/GSR/SF79 (1617), 4 (N.S.) Middlesex Calendar, *supra* note 84, at 292; Rex v. Rastone, MJ/SR/552/135, MJ/SBP/1, f. 75 (1616), 3 (N.S.) Middlesex Calendar, *supra,* at 277; Rex v. Whalley, MJ/SR/552/136 (1616), 3 (N.S.) Middlesex Calendar, *supra,* at 277; Rex v. Robinson (1615), 3 (N.S.) Middlesex Calendar, *supra,* at 175. There are also several records of indictments without a record of the outcome: Rex v. Lagott, SRO (Somerset) Q/S 62 (1629), 2 Somerset QSR, *supra* note 84, at 228 (no. 16); Rex v. Fookes, ERO (Chelmsford), Q/S/R 222/73 (1618), 19 Essex Calendar, *supra,* at 328 (no. 73); Rex v. Turner, MJ/SR/543/143 (f. MSR 111.51), MJ/SR/544/44, MJ/SBR/2 (1615), 3 (N.S.) Middlesex Calendar, *supra,* at 51; Rex v. Hodges (1615), 2 Middlesex Cnty. Sess., *supra* note 84, at 345 (1936).

159. *Acquittal:* Rex v. Squire, Gaol Del., ref: MJ/SR 1720 (1687); Commonwealth v. Carter (1652), Kent Indictments, *supra* note 85, at 96 (nos. 534, 535). *Indictments without a record of the outcome:* Rex v. Willson, ERO (Chelmsford) QSR/459/1 (1688), 25 Essex QSR, *supra* note 84, at 30; Rex v. Rolfe, ERO (Chelmsford) QSR/405/64, 160, 184, QSR/406/43, 110, 112–13 (1665), 23 Essex QSR, *supra,* at 65, 74, 76; Commonwealth v. Simpson (1659), 6 N. Riding QSR, *supra* note 85, at 23 (1888); Commonwealth v. Foxall (1651), 3 Warwick QSR, *supra* note 85, at 50.

160. See the authorities collected *supra* in note 127.

161. Officium Clerici Pacis, *supra* note 86, at 240–41.

162. Means II, *supra* note 9, at 348–49.

163. 410 U.S. at 135–36.

164. Means II, *supra* note 9, at 349–51.

165. *See generally* Baker, *supra* note 24, at 218–19, 244–46; Alan Cromartie, Sir Matthew Hale (1609–1676): Law, Religion, and Natural Philosophy (1995); Edward Heward, Matthew Hale (1972); 6 Holdsworth, *supra* note 23, at 574–95; Plucknett, *supra* note 24, at 385; Mary Cotterell, *Interregnum Law Reform: The Hale Commission of 1652,* 83 Eng. Hist. Rev. 689 (1968); Gray, *supra* note 112, at xiii–xxxvii. The earliest account of Hale's life is Gilbert Burnet, The Life and Death of Sir Matthew Hale, Kt. (1682).

166. Winfield, *supra* note 14, at 327.

ish. Before leaving, he became embroiled in a lawsuit and became so fascinated by the law that he became a lawyer instead—an exemplary lawyer who gave up the distractions of youth after witnessing a classmate at Lincoln's Inn almost drink himself to death.[167] Hale's mentor in the law was John Selden, whose mentor had been Sir Edward Coke.[168] As Harold Berman observed, "[a]ll three men started their careers as practicing lawyers. All three were deeply involved in the great constitutional struggles of their times. All three were dedicated and prolific scholars."[169]

Hale was always described as a man of becoming modesty and absolute integrity.[170] He demonstrated his integrity by defending Royalists charged with treason during the Civil War despite being a Roundhead himself, and interceded on behalf of Puritans during the Restoration although he was already a royal judge.[171] William Holdsworth even concluded that Hale served as counsel to Charles I at his trial—although the King refused to participate in the trial for that would have acknowledged the proceedings as legitimate.[172] Hale also supported toleration for all Protestants, including the Quakers.[173] Such was his reputation for honesty and integrity that none of this interfered with his steady advancement on the bench. He served as Judge of the Common Pleas (1654–1658) under Cromwell, and Chief Baron of the Court of Exchequer (1660–1671) and Chief Justice of the King's Bench (1671–1676) during the reign of Charles II. He also chaired Cromwell's Commission on Law Reform in 1652 that proposed the creation of system of county courts and other changes the common law system.[174]

Hale was hardly a saint by modern standards, however, but rather a superlative example of a man of his times. During the Restoration, he helped bury the law reforms he had led during the Commonwealth. Whether he did so from political expediency or from a sincere conclusion that the reforms did not work could be debated endlessly. And, despite his noted tolerance, Hale believed in witchcraft and sentenced at least two "witches" to death in 1665.[175] This was hardly unusual for a judge in the seventeenth century despite the bad taste it leaves in our mouths.

In his spare time, Hale became the consummate scholar of the law, while also studying the natural sciences, philosophy, and theology.[176] At the time, scholars did not sharply distinguish between these several topics as they would today. All these topics were then considered to be forms of "natural philosophy".[177] Indeed, Hale's highly empirical legal thinking derived in large measure from the then ongoing revolution in the natural sciences.[178]

Hale published only two scientific articles during his lifetime and forbade posthumous publication of most of the rest of his writings—a desire that delayed, but did not prevent, their publication. Hale's legal writings were all published many years after his death. Why Hale never published in his own lifetime is not clear. A perfectionism that would leave him never satisfied with his efforts or an inability to complete projects both seem unlikely for a highly respected and accomplished judge, but neither does an exaggerated sense of privacy seem likely for a per-

---

167. CROMARTIE, *supra* note 165, at 42–44; Berman, *supra* note 90, at 1703.

168. Berman, *supra* note 90, at 1695, 1702.

169. *Id.*

170. 6 HOLDSWORTH, *supra* note 23, at 579; Berman, *supra* note 90, at 1703–05.

171. W.S. Holdsworth, *Sir Matthew Hale*, 39 L.Q. REV. 402, 403 (1923).

172. *Id.*

173. HEWARD, *supra* note 164, at 94–107; Berman, *supra* note 90, at 1704–05.

174. Cotterell, *supra* note 165.

175. The Trial of the Witches, 6 STATE TRIALS 697 (1665). *See* G. Geis, *Lord Hale, Witches, and Rape*, 5 BRIT. J.L. & SOC'Y 26, 30–35 (1978).

176. HEWARD, *supra* note 165, at 127–28, 133–34; 6 HOLDSWORTH, *supra* note 23, at 580–81; SOSIN, *supra* note 88, at 88, 96; Berman, *supra* note 90, at 1705–08; Gray, *supra* note 113, at xvi–xix.

177. *See* Robert McRae, *The Unity of the Sciences: Bacon, Descartes, and Leibnitz*, 18 J. HIST. IDEAS 27 (1957).

178. Berman, *supra* note 90, at 1724–31.

son with such success in the public sphere.[179] Despite the delays in their publication, Hale's writings on the common law transformed the way of writing about law and thereby transformed common law jurisprudence. Legal historian John Baker has described Hale's writings on the law as "a distinct advance in the quality of English literature" that gave us "the first English law books to possess a coherence and style with which the modern reader can feel at ease."[180]

Hale was particularly interested in studying the common law as a living historical process with greater fidelity to historical accuracy than Coke ever evinced—just as one might expect from Hale's Puritan upbringing.[181] Perhaps because Hale did not expect his works to be published, each of his works, taken by itself, is incomplete and fragmentary. Legal historian Harold Berman has comment that "no one of [Hale's] written works constitutes an adequate statement of his legal philosophy."[182] This is perhaps why, as with other writers before recent decades, Hale actually wrote very little about abortion. His only known ruling as a judge on abortion was his decision holding, in yet another *Rex v. Anonymous,* that an abortion causing the death of the mother is murder. He vaguely referred to this case in his posthumously published major treatise, *A History of the Pleas of the Crown:*

> But if a woman be with child, and any gives her a potion to destroy the child within her, and she take it, and it works so strongly, that it kills her, this is murder, for it was not given to cure her of a disease, but unlawfully to destroy the child within her, and therefore he, that gives a potion to this end, must take the hazard, and if it kill the mother, it is murder, and so ruled before me at the assizes of *Bury* in the year 1670.[183]

For more than two centuries after this passage was published in 1736, this case was taken as an innovation on Hale's part. The impression resulted in part from the fact that Hale did not cite any other authority for the proposition, and stated the case on the basis of his own ruling. Actually, there were at least six cases decided before 1670 that already supported his decision.[184] As astute a scholar as Hale might very well have known of these then unpublished cases, but, in writing notes for himself, might not have thought it important to cite them. On the other hand, he might not have come across them. We have no way of determining this now. As was his pattern, Cyril Means, jr., entertained no doubts about the innovative character of Hale's ruling. Means characterized Hale's decision as an "act of restoration gallantry," without disclosing the criteria for distinguishing between restoration gallantry and masterpieces of perversion (as Means described Coke's innovations).[185]

---

179. The problem is discussed in Gray, *supra* note 113, at xvii–xviii.

180. BAKER, *supra* note 24, at 218.

181. Berman, *supra* note 90, at 1722–24 (tracing in more detail the parallels between Hale's thought and Calvinist religious precepts).

182. *Id.* at 1707.

183. Rex v. Anonymous (1670), 1 HALE, *supra* note 7, at 429–30 (emphasis in the original).

184. Regina v. Adkyns, ASS. 35/43/1, m.1 (1600), reprinted in CALENDAR OF ASSIZE REC.: ESSEX INDICTMENTS, ELIZ. I, at 510 (no. 3054) (1975); Regina v. Meddowe, Ass. 35/32, m.34 (1591), reprinted in CALENDAR OF ASSIZE REC.: SUSSEX INDICTMENTS, ELIZ. I, at 233 (no. 1212) (1975); Regina v. Poope (1589), reprinted in CALENDAR OF ASSIZE REC.: KENT INDICTMENTS, ELIZ. I, at 289 (no. 1751) (1975); Rex v. Cliston, JUST 1/1011, m.62 (Wiltshire Eyre 1288); Rex v. Reeve, JUST 1/924, m.60 (Sussex Eyre 1288); Rex v. Brente, JUST 1/186, m.30 (Devon Eyre 1281). *See also* Commonwealth v. Carter (1652), reprinted in KENT INDICTMENTS, *supra* note 85, at 96 (nos. 534, 535) (acquitted); Rex v. Skotard, JUST 1/169, m.25 (Derbyshire Eyre 1330) (acquitted); Rex v. Houdydoudy (Coroner's Inquest 1326), reprinted in CALENDAR OF CORONER'S ROLLS OF THE CITY OF LONDON, A.D. 1300–1378, at 166 (1913) (outcome unknown); Rex v. Godesman, JUST 1/383, mm.18, 96 (Kent Eyre 1313) (acquitted); Rex v. Boleye, JUST 1/303, m.69d (Shropshire Eyre 1292) (acquitted); Philippa's Appeal, 1276 EYRE, *supra* note 150, at 51 (no. 187) (defendant escaped trial through benefit of clergy); Orscherd's Appeal, JUST 1/174, m.40d (ca. 1249) (acquitted).

185. The quotation is from Means II, *supra* note 9, at 362. Compare that to his characterization of Coke's position on abortion. Means II, *supra,* at 359, discussed *supra* at notes 135–49.

In fact, if one interprets Hale's *Anonymous* decision as expressing the felony murder rule, Hale's decision was the perversion of the law, not Coke's decision. Murder normally requires a particular mental state described as "malice aforethought"—basically, an intent to kill without legal justification.[186] Under the felony murder rule, if anyone (even a fellow criminal engaged in helping carrying out the crime) dies as a result of the commission of certain serious felonies, all persons involved in committing the felony are guilty of murder without regard to their mental state and without regard to whether a particular defendant did the actual killing.[187] If abortion was only a misdemeanor, not a felony (as Coke suggests and later courts seemed to accept), Hale's decision could be seen as a stretching of the law to an extent unprecedented then or now.[188]

Precisely what Hale meant by the passage remains obscure at best, and is not settled by the full text of Hale's discussion:

> If a physician gives a person a potion without any intent of doing him any bodily hurt, but with an intent to cure or prevent a disease, and contrary to the expectation of the physician it kills him, this is no homicide, and the like of a chiurgeon, *3 E. 3 Coron. 163.* And I hold their opinion to be erroneous, that think, if he be licensed physician, that occasioneth this mischance, that then it is felony, for physic and salves were before licensed physicians and chiurgeons; and therefore if they be not licensed according to the statute of *3 H.8 cap. 11 or 14 H.8 cap. 5.* they are subject to the penalties in the statutes, but God forbid that any mischance of this kind should make any person not licensed guilty of murder or manslaughter.
>
> These opinions therefore may serve to caution ignorant people not to be too busy in this kind with tampering with physic, but are no safe rule for a judge or jury to go by: we see the statute of *34 & 35 H.8 cap. 8* dispenseth with the penalty of those former statutes, as to outward applications and medicines for agues, stone, strangury, which may be administered by any person, and the preamble of the statute tells us, that if none but licensed chiurgeons should be used in many cases, many of the king's subjects were like to perish for want of help.
>
> But if a woman be with child, and any gives her a potion to destroy the child within her, and she take it, and it works so strongly, that it kills her, this is murder, for it was not given to cure her of a disease, but unlawfully to destroy the child within her, and therefore he, that gives a potion to this end, must take the hazard, and if it kill the mother, it is murder, and so ruled before me at the assizes of *Bury* in the year 1670.
>
> And certainly if that opinion should obtain, that if one not licensed a physician should be guilty of felony, if his patient miscarry, we should have many of the poorer sort of people, especially remote from *London,* die for want of help, lest their intended helpers might miscarry.
>
> This doctrine, therefore, that if any dies under the hand of an unlicensed physician, it is a felony, is apocryphal, and fitted, I fear, to gratify and flatter doctors and licentiates in physic, tho it may, as I said, have its use to make people cautious and wary, how they take upon them two much in this dangerous employment....
>
> If a woman be quick or great with child, if she takes, or another gives her any potion to make an abortion, or if a man strike her, whereby the child within her is *kild,* it

---

186. Rex v. Mackalley, 77 ENG. REP. 828, 832–33 (K.B. 1610); COKE, *supra* note 66, at 50; HALE, *supra* note 7, at 450–51. *See generally* 3 HOLDSWORTH, *supra* note 23, at 314–15; WAYNE LaFAVE, CRIMINAL LAW § 7.1 (3rd ed. 2000).

187. Rex v. Burton, 93 ENG. REP. 648 (K.B. 1721); Rex v. Plummer, 84 ENG. REP.1103, 1107 (K.B. 1701); Rex v. Chichester, 82 ENG. REP. 888 (K.B. 1646); COKE, *supra* note 66, at 56; HALE, *supra* note 7, at 475; HAWKINS, *supra* note 11, at 112. *See generally* LaFave, *supra* note 186, § 7.5.

188. Gavigan, *supra* note 22, at 26.

is not murder nor manslaughter by the law of *England,* because it is not yet *in rerum naturae,*[189] tho it be a great crime, and by the judicial law of *Moses* was punishable with death, nor can it legally be made known whether it were kild or not, *22 E.3. Coron. 263.* so it is, if after such child were born alive, and baptized, and after die of the stroke given to the mother this is not homicide. *1 E.3. 23. b. Coron. 146*

But if a man procure a woman with child to destroy her infant, when born, and the child is born, and the woman in pursuance of that procurement kill the infant, this is murder in the mother, and the procurer is acessary to murder, if absent, and this, whether the child were baptized or not. *7 Co. Rep. 9. Dyer 186.*[190]

At the time Hale wrote, the officially recognized practice of medicine, like the practice of law, was divided into several increasingly regulated branches. Hale distinguishes here between physicians and chiurgeons (surgeons), the two recognized branches of the profession. Physicians, holding licenses from the Royal College of Physicians after 1518, held university degrees and had a monopoly on the practice of "physik," the diagnosis and management of illness or injury.[191] They could not perform surgery or even dispense pharmaceuticals. Surgery was done by members of the College of Barbers and Surgeons, organized in 1540. Surgeons learned their profession through apprenticeship, and did not become independent of barbers until 1745.[192] Apothecaries, with a monopoly on dispensing drugs, were organized as a separate profession in 1617 (the Worshipful Society of Apothecaries).[193] Before then they were simple grocers, and thus easily the humblest of the organized healing professions. Each of these organizations excluded women, and thus did not include the midwives and "wise women" who continued to function as an alternative and somewhat unseen lowest rung of the profession.[194]

Generally physicians had nothing whatsoever to do with childbirth, while surgeons would be called in only if the woman giving birth had encountered extreme difficulties such that serious cutting was required either to save the mother's life or to recover a living child from the body of a woman who had died in the attempt to deliver naturally.[195] The first male midwives appeared in England early in the seventeenth century.[196] While the earliest male midwives were tailors and butchers,[197] by the end of the century some male midwives were licensed as apothecaries, physicians, or surgeons.[198]

In the context of both Hale's broader discussion of the practice of medicine and considering the realities of medical practice in Hale's time, Hale's decision in *Rex v. Anonymous* runs contrary

---

189. "in the realm of nature"

190. HALE, *supra* note 7, at 429–30, 433 (emphasis in the original). The first case cited in the penultimate paragraph is the earlier *Rex v. Anonymous.* See the text in Ch. 3, at notes 170–85. The second case is *Rex v. de Bourton.* See the text in Ch. 3, at notes 141–69.

191. JEFFREY BERLANT, PROFESSION AND MONOPOLY 139 (1975).

192. M. JEANNE PETERSON, THE MEDICAL PROFESSION IN MID-VICTORIAN LONDON 9–11 (1978).

193. PETERSON, *supra* note 192, at 17.

194. JEAN DONNISON, MIDWIVES AND MEDICAL MEN: A HISTORY OF THE STRUGGLE FOR THE CONTROL OF CHILDBIRTH 11–13 (2nd ed. 1988); PETERSEN, *supra* note 63, at 15. Midwives also were subject to regulation, although they were not organized as the physicians, surgeons, and apothecaries were. *See* Chapter 2, at notes 324–32.

195. DONNISON, *supra* note 194, at 2; PETERSEN, *supra* note 63, at 15.

196. DONNISON, *supra* note 194, at 23, 32–33, 212 n.51; PETERSEN, *supra* note 63, at 15.

197. Margaret Connor Versluysen, *Midwives, Medical Men and "Poor Women" Labouring of Child: Lying-In Hospitals in Eighteenth Century London,* in WOMEN, HEALTH AND REPRODUCTION 21, 25 (Helen Roberts ed. 1981).

198. DONNISON, *supra* note 193, at 23–24, 55–56; Ann Oakley, *Wisewoman and Medicine Man: Changes in the Management of Childbirth,* in THE RIGHTS AND WRONGS OF WOMEN 19, 33 (Ann Oakley & Juliet Mitchell eds. 1976).

to his generally protective view of those who meddle in "physik." As the quoted passage shows, Hale clearly accepted the practice of medicine by unlicensed, even amateur, physicians or surgeons and he sought to accord them the same legal protections as the law provided licensed practitioners. After all, when Hale wrote, there were at times as few as nine licensed physicians and a few more licensed surgeons in London, a city then approaching a population of 200,000.[199] No wonder "apothecaries" (druggists) provided as much as 95 percent of recorded medical care in the London of Hale's time.[200] Licensed physicians and surgeons sometimes were more common there or elsewhere in England,[201] but licensed practitioners were simply too costly (and too ineffective given their cost) for most people to resort to them.[202] The inability to employ a physician or a surgeon was solved by resort to apothecaries and "witches"—herbalists, midwives, and "wise women" (or, apparently less often, "wise men").[203] As William Perkins recorded in 1608, "[c]harming is in as great request as physic, and charmers more sought unto than physicians in time of need."[204]

This difference in Hale's attitude towards an unsuccessful attempt to abort and other unsuccessful medical interventions suggests that Hale saw abortion as qualitatively different from the other procedures that do not amount to homicide if they miscarry, whether administered by a licensed physician surgeon or anyone else.[205] Hale summarized precisely what this difference was when he declared that the abortive potion "was not given to cure her of a disease, but unlawfully to destroy the child within her."[206] Means foresaw that his critics would seize on the word "unlawfully" as indicating that Hale considered abortion a crime cognizable under the common law, although not murder.[207] Means' fear perhaps explains why he deferred discussing this word for a dozen pages after concluding that Hale did not consider abortion a temporal crime. In an apparent effort to make Hale's views more consonant with his own, Means seized upon Hale's reference to the law of Moses to insist that Hale must have meant that abortion was "only" an ecclesiastical crime, buttressing his view by noting that Hale elsewhere had divided crimes into temporal and ecclesiastical crimes.[208] Only later did Means concede that Hale considered both sorts of crimes as "emanations of the same sovereign"[209]—the King of England, after all, was also the head of the Church of England when Hale wrote. Indeed, it was still a common comment in the nineteenth century that Christianity was part of the common law—as even the Supreme Court of the United States declared in 1844.[210] Means provided no further basis for his

---

199. George Clark, A History of the Royal College of Physicians of London 636–45 (2 vols. 1964–66).

200. 1 C. Wall & C. Cameron, A History of the Worshipful Society of Apothecaries 77, 289, 394 (E.A. Underwood ed. 1963).

201. See J.H. Rauch, A Directory of English Country Physicians, 1603–1643 (1962).

202. See generally Keith Thomas, Religion and the Decline of Magic 10–14, 534–46 (1971).

203. See Reginald Scot, Discoverie of Witchcraft V, ch. ix (1584) (B. Nicholson ed. 1886) ("At this day it is indifferent to say in the English tongue, 'she is a witch' or 'she is a wise woman.'"). See W.G. Black, Folk-Medicine (1883); Donnison, supra note 193, at 12, 17; G.L. Kittredge, Witchcraft in Old and New England (1929); T.J. Pettigrew, On Superstitions Connected with the History and Practice of Medicine and Surgery (1844); Thomas, supra note 202, at 177–211, 435–586;

204. William Perkins, A Discourse on the Art of Witchcraft 153 (1608).

205. Gavigan, supra note 22, at 27–28.

206. Hale, supra note 7, at 429–30.

207. Means II, supra note 9, at 362.

208. Id. at 350, citing Hale, supra note 7, at Proemium (an unnumbered first page). See also Matthew Hale, Analysis of the Law 75–78 (1713).

209. Means II, supra note 9, at 370.

210. Vidal v. City of Philadelphia, 43 U.S. 127, 198 (1844). See also 4 Blackstone, supra note 11, at *59. See generally Stuart Banner, When Christianity Was Part of the Common Law, 16 Law & Hist. Rev. 27 (1998); Arthur William Barber, Christianity and the Common Law, 14 The Green Bag 267 (1902).

conclusion than his intuition about Hale's gallantry towards the hazards of abortion, and not (as Hale himself suggested) the criminality of abortion. All Means could put forth was an analogy to Hale's discussion of certain jurisdiction problems in admiralty.[211]

Hale's meaning can be clarified by considering something else he wrote regarding abortion. Apparently Cyril Means, jr., was unaware that Hale had discussed abortion not in one book, but in two. Hale's comment in the second book, published only two years after his death in 1676, is rather different from the better-known passage relied on Means and published 60 years after Hale's death. In his *Pleas of the Crown: or, A Methodical Summary of the Principal Matters relating to that Subject,* Hale wrote simply:

> 5. What is the *person killed*?
>
> It must be a person *in rerum natura.*[212]
>
> If a Woman quick with Child take a potion to kill it, and accordingly it is destroyed without being born alive, a great misprision, but no Felony; but if born alive, and after dies of that potion, it is Murder.
>
> The like if it dies of a stroke given by another in like manner.[213]

This passage is precisely the same as the passage in Coke's *Third Institute* that Hale apparently repudiated in his later-published work.[214] We have no way of determining which passage Hale actually considered correct. Both were published posthumously, and even publication of the *Methodical Summary* much closer to Hale's life (two years compared to 60) does not settle the matter. The difference simply could have been the result of inexpert editing of the manuscript. Even what Hale intended to be the relation of the two works remains unclear. As the quoted passage demonstrates, the *Methodical Summary* was a mere outline of the law and not a developed, detailed analysis. Percy Winfield, in his authoritative work on the written sources of the common law, saw the *Methodical Summary* as a preliminary sketch never meant to be published or to be taken as Hale's final word on any point.[215] On the other hand, P.R. Glazebrook, in the introduction to a facsimile edition of the *Methodical Summary* published in 1972, concluded that it was meant as a systematic summary of the more detailed *History.*[216]

Sixty years later, in another English decision, *Rex v. Hodgson,*[217] the King's Bench held that an accidental death was not a criminal homicide unless the accident occurred in the course of an illegal act. *Hodgson* did not involve an abortion, but expressed the same principle as in Hale's *Anonymous* decision. By the time *Hodgson* was decided, at least, the court clearly had in mind illegality under the common law. Means did not discuss *Hogdson*; after all, it was not an abortion case. Instead, Means cited Sir William Russell as supporting the theory that Hale's decision was based on the hazards of the procedure, apparently lending some support to Means' intuition.[218] Russell, however, in the same passage described abortion as "malicious,"[219] while elsewhere in the same volume Russell agreed with Coke that an abortion leading to death after a live birth of the abortus is murder and rejected the difficulty of proof rationale for holding abortion not to be criminal.[220] Characteristi-

---

211. Means II, *supra* note 9, at 369–70.

212. "in the realm of nature"

213. MATTHEW HALE, PLEAS OF THE CROWN: OR, A METHODICAL SUMMARY OF THE PRINCIPAL MATTERS RELATING TO THAT SUBJECT *53 (P.R. Glazebrook ed. 1972) (original date 1678).

214. Coke's passage is quoted *supra* at notes 120–22.

215. WINFIELD, *supra* note 14, at 327.

216. P.R. Glazebrook, *Introduction,* in HALE, *supra* note 213.

217. Rex v. Hodgson (K.B. 1730), 1 CASES IN CROWN LAW 6 (Thomas Leach ed., 4th ed. 1815).

218. Means II, *supra* note 9, at 371.

219. 1 RUSSELL, *supra* note 127, at 659–60.

220. *Id.* at 618.

cally, Means buried the troubling points of Russell's analysis in a footnote in which Means criticized Russell for basing conclusions on erroneous (*i.e.,* different from Means') readings of the relevant materials.[221] Taken as a whole, Russell's analysis hardly proves that Hale meant, in characterizing abortion as a "great crime," to indicate only an ecclesiastical crime. Nor do two nineteenth-century American cases that held the death of the mother from an abortion to be murder on the grounds that abortion has no "lawful purpose" help Means to clarify Hale's meaning.[222] While "without lawful purpose" perhaps is less emphatic than describing abortion as a "great crime," it hardly suggests that abortion was legal, let alone that it was a "common law liberty."

The survival of Hale's decision as good law would seem to have unequivocally resolved any ambiguities in Hale's use of the word "unlawful." On the other hand, his apparent rejection of the "born alive" rule was never followed in the English cases.[223] If we take Hale as unequivocally contradicting Coke, Hale stood alone and continues to stand alone in the history of English law on these points.

# The Reception of the Common Law on Abortion and Infanticide in the American Colonies

*But though the communication of ideas is important, the acceptance of ideas depends on the social circumstances and needs of the people.*

—Linda Gordon[224]

Researching the law applied in the English colonies is not an easy matter.[225] While most of the county court records have been published in Maryland,[226] in most states they are available—if they are available at all—only in the original records in the various county courthouses. Often these records are stored in unsorted (and unindexed) boxes that must be searched item by item in each county seat.[227] Furthermore, the records for some courts were lost or destroyed during the Revolutionary War or the American Civil War,[228] or simply lost over the years. Thus we must be wary of concluding that the relatively few published colonial cases (or studies of colonial cases) involving abortion or infanticide represent the full account of such prosecutions in the colonies. Yet a few points are clear through the uncertainty of the present stage of historical research in colonial court records. Foremost is the fact that the English colonists brought the common law with them to the American colonies.[229]

---

221. Means II, *supra* note 9, at 371 n.71.

222. Means II, *supra* note 9, at 371–72, citing Smith v. State, 33 Me. 48, 54–55 (1851); Commonwealth v. Parker, 50 Mass. (9 Met.) 263, 265–66 (1845).

223. Regina v. West, 175 Eng. Rep. 329 (1848); Rex v. Brown, 172 Eng. Rep. 1272 (1834); Rex v. Enoch, 172 Eng. Rep. 1089 (1833); Rex v. Senior, 168 Eng. Rep. 1298 (1832).

224. GORDON, *supra* note 9, at 82.

225. During part of the time, English law did not apply in some of the colonies. Roman-Dutch law applied in what is now New York, New Jersey, Delaware and Pennsylvania until 1664. Thereafter, the common law replaced Roman-Dutch law. DENNIS SULLIVAN, THE PUNISHMENT OF CRIME IN COLONIAL NEW YORK: THE DUTCH EXPERIENCE IN ALBANY DURING THE SEVENTEENTH CENTURY (1997).

226. *See* Edmund Morgan, *Subject Women,* N.Y. REV. BOOKS, Oct. 31, 1996, at 66, 66.

227. ROGER THOMPSON, SEX IN MIDDLESEX: POPULAR MORES IN A MASSACHUSETTS COUNTY, 1649–1699, at vii–x (1986);

228. Morgan, *supra* note 226, at 66.

229. *See generally* DAVID GRAYSON ALLEN, IN ENGLISH WAYS: THE MOVEMENT OF SOCIETIES AND THE TRANSFERRAL OF ENGLISH LOCAL LAW AND CUSTOM TO MASSACHUSETTS BAY IN THE SEVENTEENTH CENTURY (1982); BERNARD BAILYN, THE IDEOLOGICAL ORIGINS OF THE AMERICAN REVOLUTION (1967); PETER CHARLES HOFFER, LAW AND PEOPLE IN COLONIAL AMERICA (rev. ed. 1998); JOSEPH SMITH, APPEALS TO THE

Courts and writers after American independence would stress that the reception of the common law in the future United States was limited by the need to adapt the common law to American conditions,[230] and later historians of a "Whiggish" bent still emphasize this view.[231] The view, however, had little support before the American Revolution.[232] The colonists did have their own assemblies and they began early on to assert that acts of Parliament did not apply to them unless the colonial assembly approved the particular act, although approval did not necessarily have to be by a formal act of the colonial assembly.[233] Even Blackstone, after the Revolution, would conclude that the colonies only received so much of the common law as was adapted to colonial conditions, yet Blackstone still concluded that all the common law applied unless the colonial legislature chose to modify the common law—and even that power, he asserted, was subject to review and control by the government in London.[234]

In contrast with Blackstone, during the Revolutionary era and for decades thereafter, hostility to things English inclined many lawyers and judges (as well as others) to criticize the common law and to argue for the adoption of some other system.[235] Future president James Monroe even went so far

---

PRIVY COUNCIL FROM THE AMERICAN PLANTATIONS (1950); JOSEPH SMITH, THE ENGLISH LEGAL SYSTEM: CARRYOVER TO THE COLONIES (1975); Julius Goebel, jr., *King's Law and Local Custom in Seventeenth-Century New England*, 31 COLUM. L. REV. 416 (1931); David Thomas Konig, *A Summary View of the Law in British America*, 50 WM. & MARY Q. (3rd ser.) 42 (1993).

230. *See generally* BRADLEY CHAPIN, CRIMINAL JUSTICE IN COLONIAL AMERICA, 1606–1660 (1983); ESSAYS IN THE HISTORY OF EARLY AMERICAN LAW (David Flaherty ed. 1969); LAWRENCE FRIEDMAN, A HISTORY OF AMERICAN LAW 27–90 (1985); HOFFER, *supra* note 229, at 16–17; MORTON HORWITZ, THE TRANSFORMATION OF AMERICAN LAW 1780–1860, at 1–64 (1977); PAUL REINSCH, ENGLISH COMMON LAW IN THE EARLY AMERICAN COLONIES 7 (1899); RADIN, *supra* note 24, at 21–23; Richard Dale, *The Adoption of the Common Law by the American Colonies*, 30 AM. L. REG. 553, 554 (1882).

231. *See, e.g.,* 1 JAMES KENT, COMMENTARIES ON AMERICAN LAW 537–38 (O.W. Holmes, jr., ed., 12th ed. 1873). *See also* DAVID GRAYSON ALLEN, IN ENGLISH WAYS: THE MOVEMENT OF SOCIETIES AND THE TRANSFERAL OF ENGLISH LAW AND CUSTOM TO MASSACHUSETTS BAY IN THE SEVENTEENTH CENTURY 61 (1981); CHARLES JOSEPH HILKEY, LEGAL DEVELOPMENTS IN COLONIAL MASSACHUSETTS, 1630–1686, at 69 (1967); GEORGE HASKINS, LAW AND AUTHORITY IN EARLY MASSACHUSETTS (1960); HOFFER, *supra* note 229; HORWITZ, *supra* note 230, at 6; Alfred Brophy, *"For the Preservation of the King's Peace and Justice": Community and English Law in Sussex County, Pennsylvania, 1682–1696*, 40 AM. J. LEGAL HIST. 167, 190–207 (1996). This approach appears predominant in the territories created by the United States as a precursor to statehood in the years 1787 to 1912—often, even in territories in which a different European based legal culture was already established before it became part of the United States. *See, e.g.,* Richard Cox, *Law and Community in the New Nation: Three Visions for Michigan, 1788–1831*, 4 S. CAL. INTERDISCIPLINARY L.J. 161 (1995) (describing the reception of the common law in Michigan and the displacement of French law there).

232. *See, e.g.,* ACTS AND LAWS OF THE ENGLISH COLONY OF RHODE ISLAND AND PROVIDENCE PLANTATIONS IN NEW ENGLAND IN AMERICA 56 (1767); 1 BLACKSTONE, *supra* note 11, at *104–05; Connecticut v. Danforth, 3 Day 112, 119 (Conn. 1819). *See also* RICHARD WEST, THE ENGLISH STATUTES IN MARYLAND 18 (1903); Bernard Hibbitts, *Book Review*, 12 LAW & HIST. REV. 197 (1994); Stanley Katz, *The Politics of Law in Colonial America: Controversies over Chancery Courts and Equity Law in the Eighteenth Century*, 5 PERSPECTIVES IN AM. HIST. 257 (1971); Ernest Mayo, *Rhode Island's Reception of the Common Law*, 31 SUFFOLK U. L. REV. 609 (1998). *But see* 2 EARLIEST PRINTED LAWS OF NORTH CAROLINA 1669–1751, at 39 (1977) (a statute of 1715 incorporated the "laws of England" insofar as "compatible with our Way of Living…")." *See also* Julius Goebel, *King's Law and Local Custom in Seventeenth Century New England*, 31 COLUM. L. REV. 416 (1931) (finding that the colonists imported the practices and procedures of the borough and manorial courts rather than of the common law courts).

233. *See* Barbara Black, *The Constitution of Empire: The Case for the Colonies*, 124 U. PA. L. REV. 1157, 1201 (1976).

234. 1 WILLIAM BLACKSTONE, COMMENTARIES ON THE LAWS OF ENGLAND *108 (10th ed. 1787).

235. *See, e.g.,* Connor v. Shepherd, 15 Mass. 164 (1818); Parker & Edgarton v. Foote, 19 Wend. 309, 318 (N.Y. 1838); Hall v. Smith, 1 S.C.L. (1 Bay) 330 (S.C. Sup. Ct. 1793); Martin v. Bieglow, 2 Aik. 183 (Vt. 1827). *See generally* ROSCOE POUND, THE FORMATIVE ERA OF AMERICAN LAW 7 (1938); CHARLES WARREN, A HISTORY OF THE AMERICAN BAR 224–27 (1911); Ford Hall, *The Common Law: An Account of Its Reception in the United States*, 4 VAND. L. REV. 781, 805–06 (1951); R.H. Helmholz, *Use of the Civil Law in Post-Revolutionary*

as to write that "the application of the principles of the English Common Law to our constitution" should be "good cause for impeachment."[236] Yet even after the Revolution, when many people were explicitly considering whether to reject the common law in favor of some other system, a prominent lawyer could write "[w]e live in the midst of the common law, we inhale it at every breath, imbibe it at every pore . . . [and] cannot learn another system of laws without learning at the same time another language."[237] Despite the controversy, most states enacted statutes or constitutional provisions providing for the application of "the common law of England" as the law of the state, except as changed by statute or because inapplicable to local conditions.[238] Still, the exigencies of the American experience prevented full application of the common law system here,[239] so one must inquire whether any particular legal institution or rule of law was in fact received in the colonies.

Just as with infanticide,[240] less research has been done into the legal records of abortion in the colonies than has been done for England. Several historians have concluded that abortion was not common in colonial America, both because of the relative scarcity of the direct evidence of the activity or of records of prosecutions for abortion and because of their supposition that children were a highly valuable resource in a sparsely peopled land.[241] In this regard, it is worth recalling that total fertility rates in the American colonies were "markedly higher than that ever recorded for any European country,"[242] greatly influencing Thomas Malthus in the development of his theories of population growth.[243] Foreign travelers commented with amazement on the fecundity of Americans. Historian John Miller summarized such comments in these words:

---

*American Jurisprudence,* 66 TUL. L. REV. 1649 (1992); Stewart Jay, *Origins of Federal Common Law, Part Two,* 133 U. PA. L. REV. 1231 (1985).

236. James Monroe, *Letter to John Breckinridge* (Jan. 15, 1802), quoted in 3 ALBERT BEVERIDGE, THE LIFE OF JOHN MARSHALL: CONFLICT AND CONSTRUCTION 1800–1815, at 59 (1919). *See also* James Madison, *Letter to St. George Tucker* (Nov. 27, 1800), in Jay, *supra* note 235, App. A, at 1326; James Madison, *Report on Resolutions, House of Delegates, Session of 1799–1800, Concerning Alien and Sedition Laws* ("the Kentucky Resolutions"), in 6 WRITINGS OF JAMES MADISON 373 (Gaillard Hunt ed. 1900–1910).

237. PETER STEPHEN DU PONCEAU, A DISSERTATION ON THE NATURE AND EXTENT OF JURISDICTION OF COURTS IN THE UNITED STATES 91 (1824). *See generally* William Wirt Blume, *Civil Procedure on the American Frontier: A Study of the Statues and Court Records of the Northwest and Indian Territories (1796–1805),* 56 MICH. L. REV. 161, 209 (1957); Cox, *supra* note 231, at 188–89.

238. DEL. CONST. Art. 25 (1776); Act of Feb. 25, 1784, 1 FIRST LAWS OF THE STATE OF GEORGIA 290 (1981); M MATTHEW PAGE ANDREWS, HISTORY OF MARYLAND: PROVINCE AND STATE 227 (1929); MASS. CONST. Ch. VI, art. VI (1780); N.H. CONST. pt. II (1784); N.Y. CONST. art. XXXV (1777); 1 LAWS OF THE NORTHWEST TERR., 1788–1800, at 253 (Theodore Calvin Pease ed. 1925); Act of Jan. 28, 1777, 9 PA. STAT. AT LARGE 29–30 (James Mitchell & Henry Flanders eds. 1903); N.C. LAWS 1778, ch. V; R.I. DIGEST OF 1766, quoted in 1 RICHARD POWELL & PATRICK ROHAN, POWELL ON REAL PROPERTY §62, at 212 (1995); S.C. CONST. art. VII (1790); Act of June 1782, WILLIAM SLADE, VERMONT STATE PAPERS 450 (1823); Act of May 6, 1776, ch. V, §VI, in FIRST LAWS OF THE STATE OF VA. 37 (1982). *See also* Fitch v. Brainerd, 2 Conn. 163, 189 (1805); Commonwealth v. Churchill, 43 Mass. (2 Met.) 118, 123–24 (1840); Kirk v. Dean, 2 Binn. 341 (Pa. 1810).

239. Hall, *supra* note 235, at 798; Harry Jones, *The Common Law in the United States: English Themes and American Variations,* in POLITICAL SEPARATION AND LEGAL CONTINUITY (Harry Jones ed. 1976); William Stoebuck, *Reception of English Common Law in the American Colonies,* 10 WM. & MARY L. REV. 393, 406–07 (1968).

240. *See* Chapter 2, at notes 377–446.

241. JOHN D'EMILIO & ESTELLE FREEDMAN, INTIMATE MATTERS: A HISTORY OF SEXUALITY IN AMERICA 5, 16, 25–26, 32, 65 (1988); GORDON, *supra* note 9, at 33, 49–51; CATHERINE SCHOLTEN, CHILDBEARING IN AMERICAN SOCIETY 1650–1850, at 9 (1985); Paul Carrington, *One Law: The Role of Legal Education in the Opening of the Legal Profession since 1776,* 44 FLA. L. REV. 501, 543–47 (1992). For a challenging view, largely devoid of supporting evidence, see BRODIE, *supra* note 59, at 39–41.

242. ANSLEY COALE & MELVIN ZELNICK, NEW ESTIMATES OF FERTILITY AND POPULATION IN THE U.S. 34–35 (1963). *See also* DEGLER, *supra* note 59, at 178–80; Daniel Scott Smith, *Family Limitation, Sexual Conduct, and Domestic Feminism in Victorian America,* 1 FEMINIST STUD. 40 (1973).

243. DEGLER, *supra* note 59, at 188.

Children swarmed everywhere: "like ants" or "like broods of ducks in a pond." In the size of families, it was observed, even "Irishmen are nothing to the Yankeys (*sic*) and Buckskins in that Way," although it was a thought that the Yankee's custom of bundling gave them an advantage over the less resourceful Irish. Even the beauties of Virginia were found to be "great Breeders." ...[244]

The pervasive lack of personal privacy also probably contributed to the relative rarity of abortion, particularly in New England were "solitary living" was forbidden.[245] Finally, New Englanders, at least, on the whole were notably more law abiding than people who remained in old England.[246] Only around the time of American Revolution did American fertility rates begin the steady but slow decline that persisted without significant interruption until the post-World War II baby boom.[247] And when we do discover the occasional lament over excessive childbearing, say in note between spouses or a letter between women friends or a secret notation in a diary, the subject is treated as one of resigned inevitability rather than something one could control.[248]

Yet no society has ever been entirely free of unwanted children and of attempts to dispose of unwanted children, and colonial America was no exception.[249] To whatever extent abortion or infanticide existed in the colonies, one should not be surprised to learn that midwives were thought to be involved. The midwives thought to be involved were often charged with witchcraft by the pious Puritans rather than with the secular crime of infanticide or abortion. Thus the first person ever executed in colonial Massachusetts was a Charleston midwife hung as a witch in 1648.[250] The Salem witchcraft trials also involved charges against midwives.[251] But not only midwives were targeted by the colonial authorities when it came to infanticide and abortion.

Such colonial court records as have been researched demonstrate that the colonies did prohibit the murder of unwanted children by their parents whether by abortion or by infanticide. As in England, infanticide prosecutions were more frequent in the colonies than abortion prosecutions.[252] The greater frequency of infanticide prosecutions compared to abortion prosecutions in the colonies was probably a function of the same lack of a safe and effective technology for per-

---

244. JOHN MILLER, ORIGINS OF THE AMERICAN REVOLUTION 433 (1943).

245. D'EMILIO & FREEDMAN, *supra* note 241, at 16–17, 29–30; DAVID FLAHERTY, PRIVACY IN COLONIAL NEW ENGLAND 42–43, 76–84, 175–79, 207 (1972); THOMPSON, *supra* note 227, at 157–58 (1986); LAUREL THATCHER ULRICH, GOODWIVES: IMAGE AND REALITY IN THE LIVES OF WOMEN IN NORTHERN NEW ENGLAND, 1650–1750, at 89–99 (1983); Linda Pszybyszewski, *The Right of Privacy: A* (sic) *Historical Perspective*, in ABORTION, MEDICINE, AND LAW 667, 672–75 (J. Douglas Butler & David Walbert eds., 3rd ed. 1986). *See also* RAPHAEL SEMMES, CRIMES AND PUNISH MENT IN EARLY MARYLAND 182–83 (1938). *See generally* HELENA WALL, FIERCE COMMUNION: FAMILY AND COMMUNITY IN EARLY AMERICA (1990); Edmund Morgan, *The Puritans and Sex*, in THE AMERICAN FAMILY IN SOCIAL-HISTORICAL PERSPECTIVE 311, 314 (Michael Gordon ed. 1983).

246. THOMPSON, *supra* note 227, at 194–95. For a brief review of the evidence supporting this claim, see Chapter 2, at notes 441–46.

247. See Chapter 2, at notes 462–70.

248. BRODIE, *supra* note 59, at 41; MARY BETH NORTON, LIBERTY'S DAUGHTERS: THE REVOLUTIONARY EXPERIENCE OF AMERICAN WOMEN 74–75 (1980); ULRICH, *supra* note 245, at 195.

249. *See, e.g.,* Sharon Ann Burnston, *Babies in the Well: An Underground Insight into Deviant Behavior in Eighteenth-Century Philadelphia*, 106 PA. MAG. HIST. & BIOGRAPHY, No. 2, at 151 (April 1982). *See also* ULRICH, *supra* note 241, at 184–85, 195–201.

250. JOAN DONEGAN, WOMEN AND MEN MIDWIVES: MEDICINE, MORALITY, AND MISOGYNY IN EARLY AMERICA 90 (1978); DONNISON, *supra* note 193, at 17.

251. SANFORD FOX, SCIENCE AND JUSTICE: THE MASSACHUSETTS WITCHCRAFT TRIALS 84–85 (1968); RICHARD WEISMAN, WITCHCRAFT, MAGIC AND RELIGION IN 17TH CENTURY MASSACHUSETTS 86, 88, 102–03 (1984).

252. *See* Chapter 2, at notes 474–521.

forming abortions, just as in England, rather than because of any lenience towards the practice of abortion.[253] We know this because prosecutions for abortion did sometimes occur in the colonies.

The earliest prosecution now known is *Rex v. Powell*,[254] a case initiated in Virginia in 1635 because of an abortion by injury techniques. We do not know the outcome of the proceeding. In Maryland, no less than three prosecutions for criminal abortion arose before 1665.[255] In two of those cases, *Commonwealth v. Lambrozo*[256] and *Commonwealth v. Brooks*,[257] the defendants escaped conviction because, before trial, they married (and thereby disqualified) the principal witness against them. The third of the Maryland cases, *Commonwealth v. Mitchell*,[258] reached a more definite result. The record in *Mitchell* is extensive, with evidentiary depositions, the indictment, and an account of the trial. The record of the trial reads as follows:

> The Court this day took into Consideration a Peticon exhibited by Capt. William Mitchell who intended (as it Seems) to have preferred the Same to the Assembly had it gone on; The Peticon being as followeth vizt.:

> To the Honble the Assembly for regulateing the affairs of the Province of Maryland:

> The humble Peticon of Capt. Wm. Mitchell Humbling Shewing That your Peticoner was on Saturday last comitted prisoner to the Common Gaol upon a Warrant Signed by Robert Brooke Esq., In which your Peticoner Stands charged in general words with Murther, Atheisme, and Blasphemy, Crimes never in the least acted or within the Intention of your Peticoner. Your Peticoner therefore humbly prays he may be Speedily called to his Answer, and have his liberty restored in Case noe crime in Law be proved against him that warrants his Imprisonment upon the warrant before menconed, And that his Natural filing for which God hath pleased to afflict and humble your Peticoner, may not be pressed against your Peticoner in Cases wherein the Laws of England are Silent, And your Peticoner Shall ever pray.

> [Signed] Wm. Mitchell

> Upon reading of which Peticon the Court gave direction for a Speedy tryall whereupon his Lordships Attorney, Mr. Hatton, brought in his charge as followeth, viz.:

> May it please this Honble Court: It is fallen to my Lott upon the alteracon in the Government as Attorney to the Lord-Proprietary to be prosecutor against Capt. William Mitchell now prisoner here upon Mr. Brookes Warrant, I could have wished there been no Such occasion, The Crimes for which I am to charge him being Soe many and Soe heynous, that I have not known or heard of the like, It troubles me the rather in regard the Lord Baltemore hath been formerly Soe deceived in him as to place him here in the Seat of Judicature, which by his Scandolous course of life and gross haynous offences, he hath extreamly abused, Whereas he ought (especially Soe placed) to have given good example to others an to imploy that Talent and those abilities of witt and understanding (which almighty God hath indeed in a large measure bestowed on him) to his glory and the publick good, But by Common experience it is

253. *See* Chapter 1.

254. Rex v. Powell (1635), *Cnty. Ct. Records of Accomack-Northampton, Virginia, 1632–1640*, 7 Am. Legal Records 43 (Susie Ames ed. 1954).

255. *See also* Commonwealth v. Robins, 41 Md. Archives 20 (1658), *and* Robins v. Robins, 41 Md. Archives 85 (1658).

256. 53 Md. Archives 387–91 (1663). Lambrozo, a Sephardic Jew, had also been charged with blasphemy for his failure to espouse Christianity; the Governor, acting consistently with Maryland's policy of religious toleration, refused to allow prosecution for this charge. Andrews, *supra* note 238, at 96.

257. 10 Md. Archives 464–65, 486–88 (1656).

258. 10 Md. Archives 171–86 (1652; published 1891). *See also* Semmes, *supra* note 245, at 174–77.

apparent, that the chiefest use he hath made thereof hath been to colour over his Vil-lanous Courses, and to mock and deride all Religion and Civil Government, As the Court (in part) take notice by the particulars of his Charge being as followeth Vizt.:

The charge of the Lord Proprietary's Attorney by way of Indictment against Capt. William Mitchell in the name of the Keepers of the Liberties of England by Authority of Parliamt. ffirst: That by his expressions as well as practice (as will as I conceive appear by proofe) he hath not only professed himself to be an Atheist, but hath also endeavoured to draw others to believe there is noe God, Making a Common practice by blasphemous ex-pressions and otherwise to mock and deride God's Ordinances, and all Religion, thereby to open a way to all wicked lustfull licentious and prophane Courses. Secondly: That he hath Comitted Adultery with one Susan Warren. Thirdly: That he hath Murtherously en-deavoured to destroy or Murther the Child by him begotten in the Womb of the Said Susan Warren. And is much Suspected (if not known) to have brought his late wife to an untimely end in her late Voyage hitherward by Sea.[259] ffourthly: That (as I conceive will appear by proofe) he hath Since his late wife's death lived in fornication with his now pre-tended wife Joane.

And for these and other grosse Crimes and Misdemeanors (sufficiently I conceive) appearing by proofe, My humble request is that the prisoner may be brought to his An-swer, and upon a Speedy tryall may receive punishment according to Justice to God's glory and discharge of the Government in that particular.

To which Charge the Said Capt. Mitchell the prisoner by his Answer pleading not Guilty, made Choice to be tryed by a Jury Whereupon these persons following were warned to be of the Grand Jury for the tryall vizt:...,[260] who being all particularly called by name and attending the Court, The prisoner being demanded whether he could take any personal excepcon against any of them, expressed that he could not but was well Satisfied therein. Whereupon the Jurors were Sworn and their charge given them to bring in a Just and true verdict upon every branch of the Attorneys Charge aforesaid ac-cording to evidence to the best of their Skill who after much time Spend therein brought in their Joynt verdict in the words following vizt.:

Vera[261] to the first Soe far as one Deposition with Sundry Circumstances thereunto agreeing Shall be thought valid in Law. To the Second, third, and fourth: *Billa Vera.*

*After the bringing of which verdict the Court discharged the Jurors and the day being far Spent and by reason of other Occasions, the Governor adjourned the Court till the day following....*

Capt. William Mitchell this day referred himself wholly to the determination and Judgement of the Court for all matters charged against him upon which the Grand Jury had given in their verdict the day before not desiring that the Court Should be troubled with impannelling another Jury for the further tryall thereof.

This Court therefore takeing the matter into Serious Consideracon upon the pe-rusal of the proofs and in pursuance of the verdict of the Grand Jury for his Several Of-fenses of Adultery, fornication and Murtherous intention, and in respect of his lewd and Scandalous Course of life Sufficiently appearing upon the proofs doth Order that the Said Capt. Mitchell Shall forthwith pay ffive thousand pounds of Tobacco and Cask or the value thereof as a ffine to the Lord Proprietary, And to enter into bond for his good behavior. And that he and his now pretended wife Joane be Seperated till they be

---

259. Note that this suggestion is not charged as a crime in the indictment.
260. I have omitted the names of the jurors here.
261. "True bill" — *i.e.,* a good indictment.

Joyned together in Matrimony in the usual allowed Manner, And that paying the Court Charges and other ffees and Charges of imprisonment he is to be discharged of his Imprisonment in this particular.[262]

Historians John D'Emilio and Estelle Freedman have noted the relatively greater social disorder of the southern colonies, manifested in part by sexual misconduct rooted in a sex ratio of four men *per* woman among the English settlers.[263] Skewed sex ratios may well have played a role in the events leading to the three abortion prosecutions in the 1650s in Maryland—*Brooks, Lambrozo,* and *Mitchell.* The level of extramarital sexual relations indicated in these several cases perhaps was not unusual at the time in Maryland.[264] White women were rare and in high demand, so that loss of virginity and even the bearing of an illegitimate child did not disqualify them from making "respectable" marriages. Nor were extramarital affairs and even *ménages-à-trois* unknown. Captain Mitchell, however, seemed to enjoy more than a fair share of the women of the colony; the extent to which this played a role in his prosecution is unclear. A rather more direct explanation lies in the disorders apparent in the colonial judicial proceedings in mid-sixteenth century Maryland, however.

These prosecutions all arose against a backdrop of the struggle between the Puritans and the Catholics over the government of the colony. Only in *Mitchell* did the court advert directly to this struggle, mentioning the recent "alteracon" of the government. This appears to refer to the displacement of the colony's "Catholic" government by its first securely Protestant government in 1654 through a Puritan coup mirroring Cromwell's triumph in England, although Cromwell himself had sought to discourage the Puritan's from taking control of the colony.[265] One of the first acts of the new government was to repeal Maryland's famed "Act Concerning Religion" of 1649 that had decreed toleration to all varieties of Christianity. The Puritan government then set about to eliminate "popery" in a colony that had been founded as a refuge for Catholics. This led to armed conflict between the Puritans and their opponents (the latter led by the governor— himself a Protestant—appointed by Lord Baltimore and seconded by Oliver Cromwell). The brief civil war ended with the victory of the Puritans in the Battle of the Severn in 1655.[266]

---

262. 10 Md. Archives at 182–85.

263. D'Emilio & Freedman, *supra* note 241, at 9–14. *See generally* Semmes, *supra* note 245, at 188; Criminal Proceedings in Colonial Virginia (Peter Hoffer & William Scott eds. 1984); Donna Spindel & Stuart Thomas, jr., *Crime and Society in North Carolina, 1663–1740,* 49 J.S. Hist. 222 (1983); Lorena Walsh, *"Till Death Do Us Part": Marriage and Family Formation in Seventeenth-Century Maryland,* in The Chesapeake in the Seventeenth Century: Essays in Anglo-American Society 126 (Thad Tate & David Ammerman eds. 1979).

264. D'Emilio & Freedman, *supra* note 241, at 10–11; Ulrich, *supra* note 245, at 156–58; Mary Beth Norton, *Gender and Defamation in Seventeenth-Century Maryland,* 44 Wm. & Mary Q. 38 (1987). *See generally* Kathleen Brown, Good Wives, Nasty Wenches, and Anxious Patriarchs: Gender, Race, and Power in Colonial America (1996); Mary Beth Norton, Founding Mothers and Fathers: Gendered Power and the Forming of American Society (1996). For a searching critique of Norton's book, see Carolyn Ramsey, *Sex and Social Order: The Selective Enforcement of Colonial American Adultery Laws in the English Context,* 10 Yale J.L. & Humanities 191 (1998) (book rev.).

265. *See generally* E.S. Riley, Maryland—The Pioneer of Religious Liberty 51–55 (1917); Albert Warwick Werline, Problems of Church and State in Maryland during the Seventeenth and Eighteenth Centuries 6–12 (1948); Kenneth Lasson, *The Religious Freedom and the Church-State Relationship in Maryland,* in Constitutional Revision Study Documents of the Constitutional Convention Commission of Maryland 15, 22 (H. Vernon Eney ed. 1968).

266. Several other colonies resisted the Puritan government in England for as much as three years, claiming to recognize Charles II as the king even though Cromwell and the Rump Parliament had abolished the monarchy: Antigua, Barbados, Bermuda, St. Kitts, and Virginia. Liam Séamus O'Melinn, Note, *The American Revolution and Constitutionalism in the Seventeenth Century West Indies,* 95 Colum. L. Rev. 104, 134–39 (1995). Some see in this an early striving for colonial independence; rather, one should see in it a reaction to the extremely high-handed behavior of the "Roundheads." Cromwell's agent for New England, for example, attempted to persuade all New Englanders to relocate to the newly conquered island of Jamaica. *Id.* at 143

Nonetheless, the Puritans gave up the government even before the Restoration in England, in part because of Cromwell's support for the Lord Proprietor, but not until 1658. At the end of the century, the government passed into the hands of Anglican leaders who once again undertook to persecute the Catholics who had, except for the Puritan interlude, governed the province.[267]

William Mitchell had been an officer of the Catholic colonial government that was replaced after Cromwell came to power. Mitchell was also a captain in the colonial militia. Although the Governor in the new government was a Protestant, as was half of his appointed Council and a majority in the elected Assembly, the regime was still too Catholic for the Puritans.[268] We do not need to resolve whose interests the new government served, but these circumstances do prevent us from too casually assuming what Mitchell's true religious beliefs might have been. After the beginning of this governmental transition, Mitchell was prosecuted for "atheism" and sundry moral crimes by the new government. Perhaps "atheism" simply meant he was a Catholic, mocking Anglicanism or Puritanism, or both; possibly the entire matter was a political affair without factual substance. The prosecutor even threw in a suspicion that Mitchell had murdered his wife to make room for his mistress.[269] That charge must have been highly inflammatory. Captain Mitchell was also charged with fraud.[270]

The extensive factual depositions support the substance of the charge of abortion far more than they address other charges.[271] In particular, Susan Warren and another witness deposed that Mitchell forced Warren to ingest a "Phisick" after she told him she was pregnant, causing Warren to become very ill, breaking out in boils and losing her hair.[272] Sometime later Warren gave birth to a dead child. (The precise time sequence is not clearly spelled out.) The apparent delay between Warren's ingesting of the potion and the stillbirth of her child raises at least a question regarding whether the potion was indeed the cause of the death of the child. Another witness — Mary Clocker, the attending midwife — deposed that the baby was born dead although perfectly formed and with hair and fingernails already grown.[273] Clocker also testified in court that while attending the delivery she demanded that Warren confirm that Mitchell was the father and had given her a "phisick" to destroy the child, and that Warren had confirmed it.[274]

Mitchell accepted the Grand Jury as fairly constituted and waived a jury in favor of a judgment by the bench. He was convicted of attempted murder, which can only refer to the death of the unborn child; the suggestion that he had murdered his wife was not actually charged as a crime in the indictment. Presumably, Mitchell was only charged and convicted of attempted murder ("Murtherously endeavoured"; "Murtherous intention") because of the inability to prove the cause of death for the "fully-formed" stillborn child. Upon convicting Mitchell of attempted murder, adultery, and fornication, the Court imposed a substantial fine and ordered him to marry his mistress. Further research is necessary to determine whether this punishment was more lenient than might have been expected in colonial Maryland given the seriousness of the crimes for which Mitchell stood convicted. If so, one's suspicions of the political nature of the proceedings would only be confirmed. *Commonwealth v. Mitchell,* as it

---

n.200; ARTHUR WATTS, *UNE HISTOIRE DES COLONIES ANGLAISES AUS ANTILLES (DE 1649 À 1660),* at 261–64 (1924).

267. Lasson, *supra* note 264, at 23–25. *See also Proceedings of the Maryland Court of Appeals,* 1 AM. LEGAL REC. xxx–xxxiii (Carroll Bond ed. 1933).

268. 2 ANDREWS, *supra* note 238, at 314; WERLINE, *supra* note 267, at 8.

269. See the text *supra* at note 258.

270. 10 MD. ARCHIVES 178–82, 185–86 (1652).

271. *Id.* at 171–78. *See also Id.* at 80, 148–49 (related depositions).

272. *Id.* at 176 (deposition of Susan Warren), 177–78 (deposition of Martha Webb).

273. *Id.* at 171 (deposition of Mary Clocker).

274. *Id.* at 177.

stands, is entirely consistent with Coke's then recent analysis of the law of abortion in England.[275] The only possible difference is that no inquiry was made regarding whether the child had "quickened" when the potion was administered, a point that would have been relevant according to Coke's view. One suspects that this child must have quickened before it was stillborn given its hair and fingernails.

The *Mitchell* case poses a serious problem for those who seek to claim that abortion was legal in colonial American. It figures prominently in several "pro-choice" accounts of abortion history. Historian Linda Gordon was among the first to stress the *Mitchell* case. Gordon concluded that the charges were brought by the Susan Warren because of unhappiness over having been forced to drink the unsuccessful abortion potion: "It didn't work, and she brought charges against him!"[276] Gordon's remark suggests that Warren was displeased by the failure of the potion rather than by Mitchell's coercive attempt. Nothing in the depositions or the testimony indicates such a scenario. Gordon's surmise that Warren was the cause of the prosecution simply ignores the political and social context in which the prosecution occurred. Even if Gordon was correct in her surmise that Warren was the one pushing for the prosecution, however, the record would indicate that Warren's concern was over being forced into an attempted abortion and not over the failure of that attempt. Warren, after all, deposed regarding her pregnancy that "it was a great sin to get it, but a greater to make it away."[277]

Historian Mary Beth Norton also concluded that Susan Warren was the moving actor in the prosecution. Norton supposes that Warren was desperately seeking a court order of financial support, an issue that did not arise in the proceedings![278] Norton further curiously describes the *Lambrozo* prosecution as having been prosecuted "in the interests of abstract justice" even though the proceedings resulted not in conviction but in marriage of the complainant.[279]

Historians John D'Emilio and Estelle Freedman insist that the charge of abortion in the *Mitchell* case was thrown in as a make-weight, and that the real charge was mocking religion.[280] Their claim simply ignores that fully half (nearly four) of the seven pages of depositions on the charges against Mitchell were directed at proving the abortion.[281] Their claim also ignores that the judgment of the court found Mitchell guilty of "Adultery, ffornication, and Murtherous intention," without mention of the alleged atheism. The judgment suggests that the charge of atheism was the makeweight, rather than the charge of abortion.

Finally, *Commonwealth v. Mitchell* is the only colonial prosecution mentioned in either of the *Historians' Briefs*—two *amicus* briefs to the Supreme Court in which several hundred historians joined in an attempt to bolster the decision in *Roe v. Wade* from attacks directed at the history in *Roe*.[282] The *Historians' Briefs* merely followed the line advanced by D'Emilio and Freedman, without adding anything new that might overcome the deficiencies in D'Emilio and Freedman's analysis. Despite the efforts of these various "pro-choice" historians, there seems no escape from the conclusion that at least in Maryland in 1652 abortion was a crime just as it was in England, and perhaps was considered a crime (despite the difficulty of proving the necessary facts) even

---

275. Coke, *supra* note 66, at 50–51, quoted *supra* at notes 120–22.

276. Gordon, *supra* note 9, at 54.

277. 10 Md. Archives at 176.

278. Norton, *supra* note 264, at 129.

279. *Id.* at 132.

280. D'Emilio & Freedman, *supra* note 241, at 12.

281. 10 Md. Archives 173–77 (1652), including depositions from Susan Warren, Martha Webb (who aided Mitchell in forcing "phisick" on the 21-year old Warren), and Mary Clocker (the midwife who attended the stillbirth delivery).

282. *Casey Historians' Brief, supra* note 9, at 7 n.12; *Webster Historians' Brief, supra* note 9, at 171 n.15.

before quickening. At least twice men were charged with murder for inducing an abortion of a pre-quickening fetus only to escape conviction by marrying the woman and thereby disqualifying the principle witness against the accused.[283] Any supposed "common law liberty of abortion"[284] is as mythical on this side of the Atlantic as on the other side.

Maryland was not the only colony about which this point could be made. Prosecutions for abortion also arose in at least four other colonies before the American Revolution. Given the rather primitive state of the colonial courts at this time, the preservation of records of any prosecutions is actually somewhat remarkable.[285] Taken together with the Maryland cases, these records support the conclusion that abortion was a crime throughout England's American colonies.

In *Rex v. Allen*,[286] a Rhode Island woman received 15 lashes for fornication and attempted abortion. Whipping appears to have been used more frequently as punishment for women than for men, and particularly if the woman was convicted of a sex-related crime.[287] Men, as in *Mitchell*, were more likely to be fined. This difference might reflect the reality that men controlled property while women might control nothing by themselves except for their bodies.[288] Whipping was also more of a shaming punishment for a woman, particularly if she were stripped to the waist in order to receive the lash.[289]

Indictments survive from *In re the Stillbirth of Agnita Hendricks' Bastard Child* [290] in Delaware and from *Rex v. Powell* [291] in Virginia. We do not know the outcome of these cases, although there is no indication that either indictment was questioned on the basis that abortion was not a crime. Agnita Hendricks, in a separate proceeding, received 27 lashes "for having had three Bastard Children one after another."[292] And in New York in 1719, Anna Maria Cockin received 31 lashes and was banished from the colony after she gave birth to a bastard child.[293] Anna Maria confessed that she had been "half drunk" and had engaged in sex in exchange for a pair a shoes. The child was found dead, but the defendant was unable (or unwilling) to say whether the child had been born dead or alive; there was no proof of infanticide or abortion.

Were these several prosecutions simply a manifestation of a male animus against women, expressing itself some years after settlement had reached a stage where women were no longer a scarce commodity? It does not seem so. Puritans settled in families and struggled with maintaining their morality from the beginning. We have no reason to think that people in Catholic Maryland were less intent on maintaining their moral values. The urge to protect moral values was felt at least as much by the women of the colony as by the men. Susan Warren, after all, indicated that she considered abortion a more grievous wrong than becoming pregnant out of wedlock.[294]

---

283. Commonwealth v. Lambrozo, 53 MD. ARCHIVES 387–91 (1663); Commonwealth v. Brooks, 10 MD. ARCHIVES 464–65, 486–88 (1656).

284. See the authorities collected *supra* at note 9.

285. SOSIN, *supra* note 88, at 127–36.

286. Rex v. Allen, NEWPORT CNTY. GEN. CT. TRIALS: 1671–1724.A n.p. (Sept. 4, 1683 sess.). *See also* LYLE KOEHLER, A SEARCH FOR POWER: THE "WEAKER SEX" IN SEVENTEENTH-CENTURY NEW ENGLAND 329, 336 n.132 (1980); 1 RAFFERTY, *supra* note 76, at 101–13.

287. Norton, *supra* note 264, at 139–43 (reporting on the record of punishment in colonial Maryland).

288. *Id.* at 140.

289. *Id.* at 140–41.

290. *In re* the Stillbirth of Agnita Hendricks' Bastard Child (1679), CT. REC. OF NEW CASTLE ON DEL. 1676–1681, at 274–75 (1904).

291. Rex v. Powell (1635), *Cnty. Ct. Records of Accomack-Northampton, Virginia, 1632–1640*, *supra* note 254, at 43.

292. Rex v. Hendricks, CT. REC. OF NEW CASTLE ON DEL. 1676–1681, *supra* note 289, at 320.

293. DOUGLAS GREENBERG, CRIME AND LAW ENFORCEMENT IN THE COLONY OF NEW YORK, 1691–1776, at 117–18 (1976).

294. 10 MD. ARCHIVES at 176.

Furthermore, even such apparently "masculinist" enactments as the statute adopted in Barbados in 1649 barring women from owning property except upon their husband's deaths was not so much an expression of male hegemony over women as an attempt to prevent supporters of Cromwell from transferring their property to their wives while the Royalists were in control of the colony's government.[295] Finally, if one does conclude that all prosecutions for abortion were "masculinist" oppressions of women, that does not alter the conclusion that abortion was a treated as a serious crime in the colonies.

The fourth case from another state than Maryland—*Rex v. Hallowell*[296]—deserves special mention before turning away from the abortion prosecutions in the American colonies. *Hallowell* is noteworthy in part because the unpublished record (kept in a box among the records of the Connecticut Superior Court) contains a more detailed account of an attempted abortion in a colonial setting than one usually finds. The case was found by historian Cornelia Hughes Dayton, whose report of the case forms the basis of the account here.[297] Her analysis of *Hallowell* is interesting as illustrating, along with the peculiar readings of *Mitchell* by numerous historians,[298] the way in which some historians willfully misinterpret historical evidence relating to abortion.

In 1742, John Hallowell, a self-styled physician, undertook to abort Sarah Grosvenor. Hallowell had an unsavory past.[299] He had been charged with fathering a bastard child while his wife was pregnant with their first child, and had settled the case (after first fleeing the county) by agreeing to pay support. He also had been charged with counterfeiting, but the charges were dismissed when a witness disappeared. He also was involved in 46 civil suits over 15 years. Sarah was the daughter of Leicester Grosvenor, one of the most prominent men in the community, a captain of the local militia, selectman of the town, representative in the colonial assembly, and justice of the peace for the county.[300] At first, Hallowell provided an undisclosed potion to the lover of Sarah Grosvenor for him to attempt to induce an abortion. The lover, Amasa Sessions, was the son of Nathanial Sessions, another leading member of the community, only slightly less prominent than Leicester Grosvenor.[301]

Apparently Sarah did ingest several doses over a period of three months, but she resisted taking the another potion because she then "Thot it an Evil." Dayton repeatedly doubted Sarah's reluctance, although the depositions all agree on it and none contradicts it.[302] Amasa, Sarah's lover, sought to encourage her by expressing fear that "She would be greatly hurt by what was already done," and that "there was no life in the Child."[303] The potion did not succeed, so Hallowell attempted to bring on the abortion by a "manual operation," although we are not told precisely what he did. Hallowell then was brought to minister to Sarah in person, and told several women who entered the room after Sarah fainted (remember, no anesthetics) that he had "either knipt or Squeised the head of the conception."[304] Sarah would later recount to her closest confidant

---

295. O'Melinn, *supra* note 266, at 134–35.

296. 9 Super. Ct. Records Nos. 113, 173, 175 (Wyndham Cnty., Conn., Super. Ct. Files, box 172) (1745–47).

297. Cornelia Hughes Dayton, *Taking the Trade: Abortion and Gender Relations in an Eighteenth-Century New England Village*, 48 Wm. & Mary Q. 19, 19–20, 23 (1991). Curiously, Dayton only makes passing mention of the case in a footnote in her book on women and courts in Connecticut. *See* Cornelia Hughes Dayton, Women before the Bar: Gender, Law, and Society in Connecticut, 1639–1789, at 211–12 n.112 (1995).

298. See the text *supra* at notes 276–83.

299. Dayton, *supra* note 297, at 35–38.

300. *Id.* at 29–30.

301. *Id.* at 30.

302. *Id.* at 32, 33.

303. *Id.* at 25.

304. *Id.* at 27.

(Abigail Nightengale) what happened during that encounter—just before Sarah died. Abigail's deposition reporting the dying declaration reads in full:

> ...[Hallowell] said he wanted to Speake with her alone; and then they two went into a Room together; and then sd. Hallowell told her it was necessary that something more should be done or else she would Certainly die; to which she replyed that she was afraid they had done too much already, and then he told her that there was one thing more that could easily be done, and she asking him what it was; he said he could easily deliver her. but she said she was afraid there was life in the Child, then he asked her how long she had felt it; and she replyed about a fortnight; then he said that was impossible or could not be or ever would; for that the trade she had taken had or would prevent it; and the alteration she felt was owing to what she had taken. And he farther told her that he verily thought that the Child grew to her body to the Bigness of his hand, or else it would have Come away before that time. and that it would never Come away, but Certainly Kill her, unless other Means were used. On which she yielded to his making an Attempt to take it away; charging him that if he could perceive that there was life in it he would not proceed on any Account. And then the Doctor openning his portmantua took an Instrument out of it and Laid it on the Bed, and she asking him what it was for, replyed that it was to make way; and that then he tryed to remove the Child for Some time in vain putting her to the Utmost Distress, and that at Last she observed he trembled and immediately perceived a Strange alteration in her body and thought a bone of the Child was broken; on which she desired him (as she said) to Call in some body, for that she feared she was a dying, and instantly swooned away.[305]

Several features of this deposition are noteworthy. First, Sarah initially refused the procedure for fear that the child within her was alive; indeed, she appears to have referred to the conceptus consistently as "the Child." Sarah only consented to the procedure when Hallowell told her that without removal of the child she would certainly die. We can only speculate whether Hallowell sincerely believed that the child was dead and needed to be removed to protect Sarah (as he said), or whether he was saying whatever he thought necessary to persuade Sarah to submit to his ministrations so he could complete the job. He certainly had no scruple about promising that the procedure would be "easy" when he must have known that, without anesthetics and with primitive tools, the procedure would be painful and risky.

The precise procedure that Hallowell used remains uncertain. We are told only that he used an "Instrument" to "make way," that its use caused Sarah the "Utmost Distress," and that Sarah believed that it broke "a bone of the Child." These facts are consistent with Hallowell's insertion of an object into Sarah's uterus in order to prompt an abortion with a primitive dilation and curettage. The reported facts are also consistent with simply attempting to cut Sarah's cervix to open a path for the fetus and prompt the abortion. The report is also consistent with an external assault on Sarah's abdominal wall to prompt an abortion, a possibility that is reinforced when one discovers another deposition in which Hallowell was quoted as saying he had "either knipt or Squeisd the head of the Conception."[306] Thus we cannot be certain whether Hallowell used an intrusion technique or an injury technique, although both sorts of technique were known in England (and—probably—in the colonies) in 1742.[307]

---

305. *Deposition of Abigail Nightengale,* quoted *id.* at 26–27.

306. *Deposition of Ebenezer Grosvenor,* quoted in Dayton, *supra* note 297, at 27.

307. *See* Rex v. Beare, 2 THE GENTLEMAN'S MAGAZINE 931 (Aug. 1732) (a woman died from the insertion of an object into her uterus in an attempt to induce an abortion), quoted in Chapter 5, at note 28; Rex v. Ipsley, OLD BAILEY SESSION PAPERS, April 23–26, 1718, at 5–6 (Harvester Press Microform Collection) (a woman

Whatever technique Hallowell used, it apparently had the desired effect. Two days later, Sarah was delivered of a child variously reported by witnesses as "hurt and decaying," as a "perfect child," and as a "pritty child."[308] Sarah developed a fever, became delirious, and suffered convulsions, dying about a month after Hallowell's "operation."[309] Nothing in the record indicates whether Hallowell wanted Sarah's death, was unhappily surprised at Sarah's death, or was utterly indifferent to Sarah's well being.

Rumors began to spread soon after Sarah's death, but witnesses were not willing to speak publicly for about two years. A local legend speaks of a ghostly apparition by Sarah as explaining why the witnesses eventually became willing to testify.[310] One study of criminal prosecutions in colonial Maryland has found that it was routine for crimes against women to be prosecuted only after a delay, whereas crimes against men were prosecuted more promptly.[311] Apparently men felt comfortable going directly to court but most women felt it necessary to find a man to go to court on their behalf even when there was no legal barrier to the women going themselves. In one such case, three years elapsed between the injury and the suit, the woman having died in the interval. Such patterns provide a more credible explanation than ghost stories as to why two years elapsed between Sarah's death and the initiation of legal proceedings against Hallowell.

Eventually, a grand jury indicted "Dr." Hallowell for attempting to destroy the Sarah's "health" and attempting to destroy "the fruits of her womb."[312] The grand jury refused to indict Hallowell on the charge that he was responsible for "murdering Sarah...and a Bastard Female Child with which she was pregnant,"[313] but ultimately he was indicted for "endeavoring" to endanger the health of the mother and attempting to destroy the fetus, without any allegation of quickening.[314] This last suggests that even pre-quickening abortions were considered serious crimes in colonial Connecticut. Upon his conviction, Hallowell was sentenced 29 lashes and two-hours exposure on the gallows "with a rope visibly hanging about his neck," but he managed to flee the colony before the punishment was carried out.[315] The lover, Amasa Sessions, was not even indicted and lived a long and respected life in his community.[316]

Cornelia Dayton's prejudice repeatedly emerges in her account of the case. The two most central distortions concern the abortion and the proceedings against Hallowell. Dayton concluded that Hallowell must have undertaken an intrusive abortion,[317] although the record is ambiguous about what precisely Hallowell did. Dayton also insisted that Hallowell was charged only for the death of the mother[318] even though the actual indictment, even as she reports it, is quite different: attempting ("endeavoring") to endanger Sarah's health and attempting to destroy the fetus.

In part, Dayton justified her conclusion about the technique employed by her assumption, made without any evidence whatsoever, that intrusive abortions were common and socially ac-

---

died from cutting the vagina in an effort to induce an abortion), analyzed in Chapter 5, at notes 19–26; Regina v. Sims, 75 Eng. Rep. 1075 (Q.B. 1601) (a child was born dead after its mother was beaten while pregnant), quoted *supra* at notes 35–36.

308. Dayton, *supra* note 297, at 28.
309. *Id.*
310. *Id.* at 45.
311. Norton, *supra* note 264, at 128–30.
312. Dayton, *supra* note 297, at 21, 46.
313. *Id.* at 46 n.91.
314. *Id.* at 21, 46.
315. *Id.* at 21, 47.
316. *Id.* at 22.
317. *Id.* at 19–20.
318. *Id.* at 20–21.

cepted in the American colonies; she also assumed the same for other sorts of abortions.[319] The only reason she provides for her assumptions was that the witnesses used a euphemism for attempting an ingestive abortion: "taking the trade" (which she used as the title for her article reporting the case). What is interesting about this euphemism is its origin as signifying faulty goods or bad medicine, a meaning that she reports without realizing its significance even though she describes the phrase as signifying "rubbish," "unsafe," and "associated with destruction."[320]

Dayton's confusion about the charge against Hallowell reflects her concern to find evidence of the exploitation of women in the affair rather than to recover the actual history of abortion. Dayton thus saw it as highly symbolic that although Sarah died, the man who operated on her received what she considered to be a mild sentence (29 lashes and two hours exposure on the gibbet), and her lover, Amasa Sessions, received no formal punishment at all.[321] We can only speculate now whether Sessions suffered even so much as a guilty conscience, although some of the depositions suggest that he did (Dayton remains skeptical).[322] The 29 lashes ordered for Hallowell was hardly a light penalty. Whipping was not an appropriate penalty for murder, but Hallowell was never charged with murder, nor with abortion, nor even with endangering Sarah's health. Hallowell was charged with attempting to endanger Sarah's health and attempting an abortion. Twenty-nine lashes was a harsh penalty for those crimes. Such publicly humiliating punishments were unusual for men, tending to be reserved for women who, after all, did not have any property for paying a fine—the usual male punishment.[323]

Dayton used the actual charges against Hallowell, plus the fact that the first attempt to obtain an indictment against Hallowell and Sessions for murder was rejected by the local grand jury,[324] to conclude that the town really did not condemn abortion. Dayton concluded that Hallowell's real crime was going behind the parents' (particularly the father's) back.[325] It never seems to have occurred to her that the reason Hallowell was not prosecuted for murder or abortion was that the authorities (and the town) had sincere and significant doubts about whether Hallowell's actions had in fact caused either the miscarriage or the death. Given the technological realities of abortion at the time, such doubts are at least plausible.[326]

Dayton confessed to a certain puzzlement over why if, as she assumes, abortion was usually safe and not objectionable on grounds relating to the fetus, did it always seem to occur covertly in times past.[327] Dayton explicitly rejected any concern about the life of the unborn child,[328] even though she noted that Sarah "Thot [abortion] an Evil,"[329] and, in the above quoted deposition, Sarah expressed fear for the child's life and not for her own.[330] Dayton's answer to her own puzzlement was that the abortion was hidden because it was usually undertaken to hide what were unsavory activities: fornication and adultery.[331] Dayton apparently never considered whether an activity always (or nearly always) associated with unsavory activities would come to share those unsavory connotations.

---

319. *Id.* at 19–20.
320. *Id.* at 24.
321. *Id.* at 21.
322. *Id.* at 30–31, 42–43.
323. Norton, *supra* note 264, at 139–43.
324. Dayton, *supra* note 297, at 21.
325. *Id.* at 35, 44, 47–48.
326. See the text *supra* at notes 56–71. *See generally* Ch. 1.
327. Dayton, *supra* note 297, at 23, 40.
328. *Id.* at 23
329. *Id.* at 25, 32–33.
330. *Id.* at 26–27.
331. *Id.* at 23, 40–41.

We have other evidence that colonial Americans respected the unborn fetus as a living child. In Massachusetts, the Reverend Benjamin Wadsworth at least twice denounced abortion, stating that anyone who purposefully undertook "to destroy the Fruit of their Womb (whether they actually do it or not) they're guilty of Murder in God's account."[332] Wadsworth would later serve as President of Harvard College from 1725 to 1737.[333] (That such denunciations from the pulpit in colonial times are rare is yet further evidence that the practice was then rare, rather than being evidence that few preachers cared.[334]) The case of Bethesda Spooner indicates similar sentiments towards the life of the unborn child at the time of the American Revolution.

Bethesda Spooner was a daughter of Timothy Ruggles, a prominent Massachusetts lawyer who served as president of the Stamp Act Congress. Ruggles later left Massachusetts when he was unwilling to support organized resistance to the King.[335] Mrs. Spooner was convicted of conspiring with a lover to kill her husband in 1778; she was sentenced to death.[336] There seems little reason to doubt the outcome as the three male defendants confessed in considerable detail before their execution.[337] Spooner requested, and the state's Executive Council granted, a stay of execution because she was pregnant. A jury of "two men-midwives and twelve matrons" examined her and found that she was not pregnant, and the stay was lifted after about a month.[338] Spooner immediately petitioned again, claiming once again that she was in fact pregnant. Someone seeking to delay her death will use the terms most likely to move those to whom the words are addressed. The petition is therefore worth quoting in full for it discloses what people thought regarding the fetus:

> May it please your honors: with unfeigned gratitude I acknowledge the favor you lately granted me, of a reprieve. I must beg leave, once more, humbly to lie at your feet, and to represent to you, that though the jury of matrons, that were appointed to examine into my case, have not brought in in my favor, yet that I am absolutely certain of being in a pregnant state, and above four months advanced in it; and that the infant I bear was lawfull begotten. I am earnestly desirous of being spared, till I shall be delivered of it. I must humbly desire your honors, notwithstanding my great unworthiness, to take my deplorable case into your compassionate consideration. What I bear, and clearly perceive to be animated, is innocent wholly of the faults of her who bears it, and has, I beg leave to say, a right to the existence which God hath begun to give it. Your honors' humane *christian* principles, I am very certain, must lead you to desire to preserve life, even in its miniature state, rather than to destroy it. Suffer me, therefore, with all earnestness, to beseech your honors to grant me such a further length of time, at least, as that there may be the fairest and fullest opportunity to have the matter fully ascertained—and as in duty bound, shall, during my short continuance, pray.[339]

The Reverend Thaddeus Maccarty, the elderly minister of a Worcester church who had been attending the condemned in jail, argued forcefully for the reprieve.[340] Maccarty's letter to the council also makes interesting reading:

---

332. Benjamin Wadsworth, The Well-Ordered Family 45 (1712). *See also* Benjamin Wadsworth, An Essay on the Decalogue or Ten Commandments 89 (1719).

333. John Noonan, jr., A Private Choice: Abortion in America in the Seventies 59–60 (1979).

334. Marvin Olasky, The Press and Abortion, 1838–1988, at 3–4 (1988).

335. 2 American Criminal Trials 1, 5–8 (Peleg Chandler ed. 1844).

336. *Id.* at 11–34.

337. *Id.* at 35–43.

338. *Id.* at 48–49.

339. *Id.* at 49–50.

340. *Id.* at 47–48, 50.

The news arrived last evening to Mrs. Spooner that her petition [*i.e.,* the first petition] for a reprieve was not granted. People that are acquainted with her circumstances, are exceedingly affected with it. I am myself fully satisfied of her being in a pregnant state, and have been so for a considerable time, and it is with deep regret that I think of her being cut off, till she shall have brought forth, which will eventually, though not intentionally, destroy innocent life. An experienced midwife, belonging here, visited her this week, and examined her, and found her quick with child. Wherefore, though I think justice ought to take place upon her as well as the rest, yet I must beg leave earnestly to desire that she might be respited, at least for such a time as that the matter may be fully cleared up. And I have no doubt it will be fully cleared up. And I have no doubt it will be so satisfactorily to every one. I write this, may it please your honors, of my own accord, not at her desire, for I have not seen her since the news arrived. I should be very sorry if your honors should consider me as over officious in the matter. But principles of humanity, and a desire that righteousness may go forth as brightness, and judgment at the noon-day, have powerfully prompted me to make this application on her behalf.[341]

What is noteworthy about both Spooner's petition and Maccarty's letter is that they speak of the fetus as "life," not as something that will later become alive. What is more, both speak in terms of the unborn child as "innocent" of the mother's crime—a clear recognition that the fetus was a separate and distinct being from the mother. There is no nonsense about "potential life," nor any thought that the life of the child was socially insignificant, not properly of concern to anyone but the mother. And the council agreed that if Spooner were pregnant, she could not be executed. The council ordered the jury of matrons to undertake a second examination. At the second examination, the two male-midwives and one of the matrons concluded that Spooner was pregnant.[342] The others, however, remained firm in their conviction that Spooner was not pregnant. The council, perhaps swayed by the disgrace of her Tory father or considering Spooner's consistent calmness to be arrogance, apparently concluded that Spooner merely sought to trick them.[343] The council ordered her execution to be carried out.

When informed of the denial of her second petition for a reprieve, Spooner requested only that her body be examined after her death.[344] She was hung on July 2, 1778. Doctors performed an autopsy that evening, and "a perfect male fetus, of a growth of five months, was removed from her."[345] This discovery turned the woman, who was strongly disliked in the community and whose fortitude in facing death was seen as contemptuous of the public, into something of folk-hero whose calm demeanor and persistent attempts to protect the life of her unborn child were recalled "around the hearths of those who saw her die" for many years thereafter—or so we are told by an account dating from 1844.[346]

Finally, a few words about colonial New York are in order. New York had a somewhat more complex history regarding the reception of English law given its Dutch origins, yet by 1700 the law of New York was thoroughly Anglicized and its courts were described as the most "English" in the colonies.[347] Given the intense scrutiny of the history of New York regarding the law of abortion, surprisingly little has been found regarding abortion there in colonial

---

341. *Id.* at 51.
342. *Id.* at 50.
343. *Id.* at 53–54.
344. *Id.* at 50.
345. *Id.* at 53.
346. *Id.* at 53–54.
347. HOFFER, *supra* note 229, at 31–33, 35–36. *See generally* HERBERT JOHNSON, ESSAYS ON NEW YORK COLONIAL LEGAL HISTORY (1981).

times. Two sources do clearly indicate that abortion in colonial New York was also treated as a crime, with at least some measures being taken to suppress the practice to whatever extent it might have occurred. In 1716, a New York municipal ordinance forbade midwives to aid or counsel abortion:

> You [midwives] Shall not Give any Counsel or Administer any Herb Medicine or Potion, or any other thing to any Woman being with Child whereby She Should Destroy or Miscarry of that she goeth withall before her time.[348]

The antecedent law for the colony to regulate "chiurgions, midwives, physicians, or others" who would be "employed about the bed of Men, women (*sic*), or Children at any time" did not mention abortion, but did mention a need to "inhibit and restrain the presumptious arrogancy of such" to "dare bouldly attempt to Exercise any violence upon or toward the body of young or old one or other, to the prejudice or hazard of the Life or Limb of any man, woman, or child."[349] A similar ordinance regulating midwifery was enacted in Virginia at about the same time.[350] Such regulations of midwives have a long history in the common law world, going back in England at least two centuries before the New York ordinance.[351]

Any doubts about the criminality of abortion in colonial New York are resolved by the work of jurist James Parker. His *Conductor Generalis: Or, the Office, Duty, and Authority of Justices of the Peace* is one of the few secondary sources on the common law as applied in an American colony. Parker recited the common law of abortion as part of the law applied in New York:

> If a physician or surgeon gives a person a potion, without any intent of doing him any bodily harm, but with intent to cure or prevent a disease, and contrary to the physician or surgeon's expectation it kills him, this is no homicide. And lord Hale says, he holds their opinion to be erroneous, who think that if he be no licensed surgeon or physician, that occasioneth this mischance, that then it is a felony. These opinions (he says) may caution ignorant people not to be too busy in this kind of tampering with physick, but are no safe rule for a judge or jury to go by. *I H.H. 429.*

> But if a woman be with child and any gives her a potion to destroy the child within her, and she takes it, and it works so strongly that it kills her, this is murder; for it was not given to cure her of a disease, but unlawfully to destroy the child, within her; and therefor he that gives her a potion to this end, must take the hazard, and if it kills the mother it is murder,. *I H.H. 430.*

> Also if a woman be quick with child, and by a potion or otherwise, killeth it in her womb; or if a man beat her, whereby the child dieth in her body, and she is delivered of a dead child, this is a great misprision, but no murder: but if the child be born alive, and dieth of the potion, battery, or other cause, this is murder. *3 Inst. 50.*

> Lord Hale says, that in this case it cannot be legally known, whether the child were killed or not; and that if the child die, after it is born and baptized, of the stroke given to the mother, yet it is not homicide. I H.H. 433. And Mr. Dalton says, whether it die within her body, or shortly after her delivery, it maketh no difference. Dalt. 332. But

---

348. 3 MIN. OF THE COMMON COUNCIL OF N.Y. 122 (July 27, 1716). *See generally* MICHAEL GORDON, AESCULAPIUS COMES TO THE COLONIES: THE STORY OF THE EARLY DAYS OF MEDICINE IN THE THIRTEEN ORIGINAL COLONIES 174–75 (1949).

349. DUKE OF YORKE'S LAWS 20 (Sept. 22, 1676).

350. SAMUEL EVANS MASSENGILL, A SKETCH OF MEDICINE AND PHARMACY 294 (2nd ed. 1942).

351. *See, e.g.,* JANE SHARP, THE MIDWIVES BOOK 38 (1671). *See generally* 1 BONNIE ANDERSON & JUDITH ZINSSER, A HISTORY OF THEIR OWN: WOMEN IN EUROPE FROM PREHISTORY TO THE PRESENT 163, 168, 170–71, 419–21 (1988); DONNISON, *supra* note 193, at 18–20; T.R. FORBES, THE MIDWIFE AND THE WITCH 141–47 (1966); PETERSEN, *supra* note 63, at 11–13; Norton, *supra* note 264, at 144–48.

Mr. Hawkins says, that (in this latter case) it seems clearly to be murder, notwithstanding some opinions to the contrary. *I. Haw. 80.*

Also it seems agreed, that where one counsels a woman to kill her child when it shall be born, who afterwards doth kill in pursuance of such advice, he is an accessary to the murder. *I Haw. 80.*

By the *21 J. c. 27.* If a woman be delivered of a bastard child, and she endeavor privately, either by drowning or secret burying thereof, or any other way, either by herself, or the procuring of others, so to conceal the death thereof, as that it may not come to light, whether it were born alive or not, but be concealed; she shall suffer death as in the case of murder, except she can prove by one witness that it was born dead.[352]

Parker's treatise merely summarizes the points made by Edward Coke and Matthew Hale in their writings.[353] Parker himself refers directly to Hale ("*H.H.*") and Coke ("*Inst.*"), as well as to English legal scholars Dalton and Hawkins, as support for his conclusions. Parker also noted the close relationship between the law of abortion and the law on the concealment of the death of a bastard child—the major alternative to abortion given the still primitive state of abortion techniques when Parker wrote.[354] Following his English sources, Parker set forth a coherent and comprehensive view of the criminality of abortion in colonial New York, consistent with the law of England and based upon the protection of the life of the fetus insofar as the means of detection and proof allowed. While no cases have been found thus far that applied these principles to actual abortions (or attempts to abort) in colonial New York, there is no reason to doubt that they expressed the general understanding of the law of abortion in colonial New York and throughout colonial America. All cases found in any colony (thus far Connecticut, Delaware, Maryland, Rhode Island, and Virginia) support the points Parker made, or are more restrictive of abortion than Parker (and the English sources he relied on) were. No evidence has ever been produced to contradict this conclusion. James Wilson, one of the principle drafters of the Constitution of the United States and an early Justice of the Supreme Court, echoed these conclusions in the 1790s.[355] We are left then with the conclusion that the English law regard ing abortion was fully received in the colonies, and that the purported "common law liberty" to abort is a myth.[356]

---

352. James Parker, Conductor Generalis: Or, the Office, Duty, and Authority of Justices of the Peace 216–17 (1764). Joseph Engelhard, at the time a third-year law student at Fordham University, drew my attention to this book in 1991.

353. *See* Coke, *supra* note 66, at 50–51, quoted *supra* at notes 120–22; Hale, *supra* note 7, at 429–30, quoted *supra* at notes 189–90.

354. *See* Chapter 2, at notes 310–532.

355. 2 The Works of James Wilson 596–97 (Robert Green McCloskey ed. 1967).

356. See the authorities collected *supra* at note 9.

# Chapter 5

# Way Down Inside[1]

There is nothing worse than an idea whose time has come.

*—Linda Hunt*[2]

For millennia, contraceptive techniques had ranged from poor to worthless.[3] People confronting unwanted pregnancies searched, without success, for ways to terminate the pregnancy with acceptable pain or risk for the mother.[4] Lacking effective contraceptives and effective abortion techniques, infanticide was far more common than today, despite persistent legal and other efforts to suppress the practice.[5] A major technical innovation for doing abortions appeared in Europe sometime after 1700 and began to shift the balance away from infanticide and toward abortion. The innovation, which might have been involved in the *Hallowell* case discussed in the last chapter,[6] was the refinement of intrusion techniques to a point where a skilled practitioner could induce an abortion without undue risk and pain for the mother. This transition continues down to today, thereby reshaping the way we think and argue about abortion.

No doubt intrusive abortions were attempted at many times throughout history. No one has yet established where or when the first successful intrusive abortion was performed, and perhaps no one ever will. Dr. Alan Guttmacher argued that the necessary utensils were found at Pompeii, although this requires considerable conjecture on his part.[7] Apart from this, the historical record in Europe is void of references of such techniques for more than 1,000 years.[8] We also find Japanese references to intrusion techniques from the late sixteenth century, although the safety and effectiveness of these techniques (which are not carefully described) remains unclear.[9] What is

---

1. Jimmy Page, Robert Plant, John Bonham, & John Paul Jones, *Whole Lotta Love* (1969).

2. As quoted in John Hart Ely, *Another Such Victory: Constitutional Theory and Practice in a World Where Courts Are No Different from Legislatures,* 77 Va. L. Rev. 833, 833 (1991), quoting in turn from Cynthia Zarin, *A Part in the Play,* The New Yorker, July 30, 1990, at 39.

3. *See* Chapter 2, at notes 1–375.

4. *See* Chapter 1.

5. *See* Chapter 2, at notes 240–532.

6. Rex v. Hallowell, 9 Super. Ct. Records Nos. 113, 173, 175 (Wyndham Cnty. Super. Ct. Files, box 172) (1745–47). *See* Chapter 4, at notes 295–330. *See also* Cornelia Hughes Dayton, *Taking the Trade: Abortion and Gender Relations in an Eighteenth-Century New England Village,* 48 Wm. & Mary Q. 19 (1991).

7. Alan Guttmacher, *The Shrinking Non-Psychiatric Indications for Therapeutic Abortion,* in Therapeutic Abortion 12, 13 (Harold Rosen ed. 1954) (this book was reissued in 1967 under the title Abortion in America). *See also* Soranus, Gynecology ¶¶ 1.63–1.65, at 65–68 (Oswei Temkin trans. 1956).

8. For the single known medieval reference to intrusion techniques, see Norman Himes, Medical History of Contraception 138 (1936).

9. Mary Walker Standlee, The Great Pulse: Japanese Midwifery and Obstetrics through the Ages 111 (1959); Lynn Wardle, *"Crying Stones": A Comparison of Abortion in Japan and the United States,* 14 N.Y.L.S. J. Int'l & Comp. L. 183, 187–89 (1993); Hiromi Maruyama, *Abortion in Japan: A Feminist Critique,* 10 Wis. Women's L.J. 131, 132 (1995). We should also note that the introduction of intrusion techniques into Japan were followed by steadily increasing attempts to prohibit abortions. Susan Hanley & Kozo Yama-

229

clear is that the earliest report of a successful intrusive abortion in Europe appeared in Denis Diderot's *Encyclopedie*.[10] The author, noted French naturalist Philippe-Laurent de Joubert, considered the procedure (performed by a physician in Nuremberg in 1714) to have been a true medical oddity. In any event, intrusive abortions remained highly dangerous for about two centuries after they first definitely appear in the history of Europe. Even medical historian Edward Shorter, usually an unquestioning optimist about abortion techniques, concluded that intrusive abortions only became feasible in the later nineteenth century.[11] As Shorter noted, the rarity of septic abortions treated by physicians, a rarity that continued nearly to the end of the nineteenth century, argues strongly that intrusive abortions did not occur in significant numbers before then.[12]

Some historians insist that intrusive abortions were always common, but either were a "women's secret" that men simply did not know about or were not considered either remarkable enough or objectionable enough to appear in the historical record.[13] No evidence supports such claims, while such evidence as we have suggests that the claims are not correct. Too many records speak of women being forced into abortions by men to conclude that any major class of abortion techniques was peculiarly a women's secret.[14] A supposed social tolerance for intrusive abortions when ingestive and injurious abortions were actively prosecuted supposes that intrusive abortions were either safer for the mother than the others techniques or that some other reason existed for distinguishing between the different sorts of abortions. In fact, intrusive abortions remained highly dangerous for the mother well into the nineteenth century, and probably into the

---

MURA, ECONOMIC AND DEMOGRAPHIC CHANGE IN PREINDUSTRIAL JAPAN 1600–1868, at 234 (1977). *See also* Chapter 1, at notes 477–78.

10. Philippe-Laurent de Joubert, *Fausse couche*, in 6 ENCYCLOPÉDIE 452 (Denis Diderot ed. 1766).

11. EDWARD SHORTER, A HISTORY OF WOMEN'S BODIES 188–208 (Pelican Books ed. 1984). *See also* MALCOLM POTTS, PETER DIGGORY, & JOHN PEEL, ABORTION 282 (1977).

12. SHORTER, *supra* note 11, at 190–97. *See also* Estelle Freedman, *Historical Interpretation and Legal Advocacy: Rethinking the Webster Amicus Brief*, 12 PUB. HISTORIAN 27, 28–30 (1990). *See also* R. Sauer, *Infanticide and Abortion in Nineteenth-Century Britain*, 32 LOCAL POP. STUD. 81, 88 (1978) (concluding that abortion was still rare in England because of its danger, but, based on anecdotal sources, was much more common in America—without explaining why it would have been less dangerous). *See generally* Chapter 1.

13. *See, e.g.*, 1 BONNIE ANDERSON & JUDITH ZINSSER, A HISTORY OF THEIR OWN: WOMEN IN EUROPE FROM PREHISTORY TO THE PRESENT 136–37 (1988); CARL DEGLER, AT ODDS: WOMEN AND THE FAMILY IN AMERICA FROM THE REVOLUTION TO THE PRESENT 227–28 (1980); LINDA GORDON, WOMAN'S BODY, WOMAN'S RIGHT: A SOCIAL HISTORY OF BIRTH CONTROL IN AMERICA 28–30, 47 (1976); BEVERLY WILDUNG HARRISON, OUR RIGHT TO CHOOSE: TOWARD A NEW ETHIC OF ABORTION 162, 165–66 (1983); ANGUS MCLAREN, BIRTH CONTROL IN NINETEENTH-CENTURY ENGLAND 231–32, 240–42 (1978) ("MCLAREN, BIRTH CONTROL"); ANGUS MCLAREN, REPRODUCTIVE RITUALS 89–93 (1984) ("MCLAREN, REPRODUCTIVE RITUALS"); JAMES MOHR, ABORTION IN AMERICA: THE ORIGINS AND EVOLUTION OF NATIONAL POLICY, 1800–1900, at 82–85, 103, 106–7 (1978); ROSALIND POLLACK PETCHESKY, ABORTION AND WOMEN'S CHOICE: THE STATE, SEXUALITY, AND REPRODUCTIVE FREEDOM 29–33, 51–53, 71–73, 179 (rev. ed. 1990); KERRY PETERSEN, ABORTION REGIMES 2, 10–13, 18, 23 (1993); ABRAHAM RONGY, ABORTION: LEGAL OR ILLEGAL? 35–36 (1933); PATRICK SHEERAN, WOMEN, SOCIETY, THE STATE, AND ABORTION: A STRUCTURALIST ANALYSIS 51-10 (1987); CARROLL SMITH-ROSENBERG, DISORDERLY CONDUCT: VISIONS OF GENDER IN VICTORIAN AMERICA 226 (1985).

14. *See, e.g.*, John Wren's Case (London Dioc. Commissary Ct. 1487), in R.H. HELMHOLZ, CANON LAW AND COMMON LAW 387 n.10 (1989); George Hemery's Case (Rochester 1493), in HELMHOLZ, *supra*, at 159 n.12; John Russell's Case (London Dioc. Ct. 1493), in W.H. HALE, PRECEDENTS IN ECCLESIASTICAL COURTS 105 (no. 331) (1847); Rex v. Lichefeld, K.B. 27/974, Rex m.4 (1505); John Hunt's Case (Hertfordshire 1530), in BEFORE THE BAWDY COURT: SELECTIONS FROM CHURCH COURT AND OTHER RECORDS RELATING TO THE CORRECTION OF MORAL OFFENCES IN ENGLAND, SCOTLAND, AND NEW ENGLAND, 1300–1800, at 81 (no. 150) (Paul Hair ed. 1972); Thomas Love's Case, HRO CB4, fo. 117v (Winchester 1534); Thomas Tyry's Case, HRO CB2, fo. 59v (mid-1500s); Commonwealth v. Mitchell, 10 MD. ARCHIVES 171–186 (1652; published 1891); ANGUS MCLAREN, BIRTH CONTROL IN NINETEENTH-CENTURY ENGLAND 89–93, 111–12 (1978; JAMES MOHR, ABORTION IN AMERICA 106–7 (1978).

twentieth century.[15] And while injurious abortions undoubtedly were imposed on women against their will, one also cannot suppose that intrusive abortions were any more consensual than the typical ingestive abortion of the time—which also appear typically to have been imposed on women rather than some thing they willingly underwent. What other reasons there might be for distinguishing between the several sorts of abortion procedure is not evident.

At the time intrusive abortions were being introduced, society did not distinguish the new procedure from the earlier, prohibited procedures. The first English prosecution involving an intrusion technique took place only 18 years after the Nuremberg experiment reported in the *Encyclopedie*.[16] If *Rex v. Hallowell* involved an intrusive abortion, the first prosecution in England's American colonies occurred only 10 years after that. Further prosecutions followed, and the enactment of the abortion statutes throughout the world in the nineteenth century could be traced to the impact of the resulting technological revolution.[17]

The evidence seems irrefutable that around 1800 abortion was a serious common law crime in England, certainly after quickening and perhaps before quickening as well. Abortion's criminality did not depend upon the means employed, nor did it turn upon whether the abortion was at the mother's request or over her objections or resistance. Courts and other legal and social sources consistently described abortion as a crime against the unborn child, and not simply as a crime against the mother. Yet prosecutions for abortion remained relatively rare, certainly when compared with prosecutions for infanticide during the same time periods. There was as yet no statute directed against abortion in sharp contrast with a harsh and rigid statute presuming murder from concealing the death of a bastard infant. The evidence of a recent technical innovation (the development of rudimentary forms of intrusive abortions) coupled with the sudden appearance of abortions performed by the new techniques in a series of cases, however, suggest that abortions were becoming somewhat more common, concomitantly with a slow but steady decline in the legal attention given to infanticide which perhaps reflected a decline in the incidence of infanticide. This latter point is more than just an inference, however, as we shall see when we examine the legislation regarding abortion that became characteristic around the world during the nineteenth century.

In this chapter, we focus on the changes in the law of abortion in England in the eighteenth and nineteenth centuries, changes that appear to have been a direct response to the introduction of intrusive techniques into England in the eighteenth century. The following chapter focuses on the similar changes in the law regarding abortion in the United States. One should not suppose, however, that the two sets of changes happened merely coincidentally. The changes are presented separately only to allow a certain clarity of focus. In fact, these changes influenced each other, and were in turn part of a larger pattern of change in laws regarding abortion that occurred around the world at about the same time. The ubiquity of these changes itself suggests that the changes had some origin other than mere intellectual fashion. While the connections regarding such changes in many parts of the world remain somewhat speculative, the relationship between the changes in England and the United States are not speculative. This was a time when lawyers and judges in the United States routinely cited English legal authorities, when physicians in the two nations were already reading the same sources and learning from each other, and when Eng-

---

15. *See* Chapter 1, at notes 468–517.

16. Rex v. Beare, 2 The Gentleman's Magazine 931 (Aug. 1732). For the Nuremberg experiment, see de Joubert, *supra* note 10.

17. *See generally* Mary Kenny, Abortion: The Whole Story 183 (1986); Joseph Dellapenna, *The History of Abortion: Technology, Morality, and Law*, 40 U. Pitt. L. Rev. 359, 406–16 (1979); Bartha Maria Knoppers, Isabel Brault, & Elizabeth Sloss, *Abortion in Francophone Countries*, 38 Am. J. Comp. L. 889, 893–98 (1990); Cyril Means, jr., *The Law of New York Concerning Abortion and the Status of the Foetus, 1664–1968: A Case of Cessation of Constitutionality*, 14 N.Y.L.F. 411 (1968) ("Means I").

lish and American feminists often exchanged ideas and studied each other's tactics. Those connections will be explored in Chapter 6, for we begin with the changes in England that largely preceded the changes in the United States in the eighteenth and nineteenth centuries.

# The Emergence of Intrusion Techniques in Seventeenth-Century England

*I go on in the dark, lit from within; does day exist? Is this my grave? or the womb of my mother?*

—Miguel Hernàndez[18]

Intrusive abortions apparently evolved from injury techniques. We can date this event so far as England is concerned to the early years of the eighteenth century, at about the same time reports of intrusive abortions first appear on the European Continent. Attorney Philip Rafferty found a case from 1718, *Rex v. Ipsley*,[19] that seems to represent the bridge between the two techniques. In *Ipsley*, two women, one the owner of a lodging house (Mary Ipsley) and the other a nurse-midwife (Elizabeth Rickets), were charged with murder of an unknown woman who died in the lodging house. The woman died while bleeding from the ears and mouth, but also had a crude incision to her vagina and severe bruises to her abdomen. Several witnesses were explicit that the damage to the vagina was the result of a cut reaching to the rectum, and not the result of natural tearing in childbirth. The defendants denied this.

The victim in *Ipsley* had been buried with a full-term infant whose nose apparently had been cut off and head badly bruised, presumably during the procedure that killed the mother. This might have resulted from efforts to intrude into the uterus. The *Ipsley* indictment has survived only in a bad state of disrepair; so far as it has survived, it indicates only a charge of murder of the unknown woman, and does not refer to the deceased child. Thus apparently no indictment was brought for the death of the child, presumably because no one could prove that the infant had been born alive. Without such proof, there could be no charge of murder for the death of the child for, as another judge in the same court would put the matter only seven years later, "the Law supposes it impossible for a Child to be murdered before it was born."[20] Without proof of even momentary life after birth, the suspected abortion was only a misdemeanor while the death of the mother was a capital felony.[21] Defendants were tried on the more serious charge. There would have been no point in charging the lesser crime (abortion) as the jury could not logically acquit the defendants of the charge of murder and convict them of abortion.[22]

The indictment in *Ipsley* did open with a rather unusual formula (in Latin) that the two defendants had acted "not having God before their eyes, but moved and seduced at the instigation of the Devil." This phrase might indicate that the person who recorded the indictment consid-

---

18. As quoted in John Bayley, *Night Mail*, N.Y. Rev. Books, June 24, 1993, at 20.

19. Rex v. Ipsley, Old Bailey Session Papers, April 23–26, 1718, at 5–6 (Harvester Press Microform Collection).

20. Rex v. Evans, Old Bailey Session Papers, *supra* note 19, Dec. 4–9, 1725.

21. *See* Regina v. Sims, 75 Eng. Rep. 1075 (Q.B. 1601), quoted in Chapter 4, at notes 34–35. *See also* Edward Coke, Third Institute 50–51 (1644), quoted in Chapter 4, at notes 120–21; 1 Matthew Hale, History of Pleas of the Crown 429–30 (1736), quoted in Chapter 4, at note 182.

22. *See also* Rex v. Hallam, Old Bailey Session Papers, *supra* note 19, 1732 no. 10, at 34 (a husband was convicted of murder for throwing his wife from a window, killing her and full-term unborn infant; no charge was brought for the death of the infant).

ered the crime charged to be particularly hideous, or perhaps the phrasing echoes the link of abortion charges to witchcraft. Concern over witchcraft was still alive in England and elsewhere in the common law world, as shown by, among other events, the Salem witchcraft trials of barely 20 years earlier. Whatever the source of the phrase, it recurs in a 1786 indictment that produced a conviction for manslaughter in the course of an attempted abortion through injury techniques.[23]

Despite considerable testimony from numerous witnesses linking the defendants to the crime, they were acquitted. Either the jury believed the defendants' story that the woman died from convulsive fits that they testified had lasted nearly a week before the birth and that the fits had been the cause of the injuries to the mother and the child, or the jury simply was not convinced beyond a reasonable doubt. There was by then such ample primary and secondary authority for the proposition that killing a woman through abortion was murder that we can take that issue as settled.[24] Nothing in the record of *Ipsley* suggests to the contrary.[25] Much the same sad story appears in *Rex v. Hallowell* in colonial Connecticut about a quarter of a century later, but with the defendant—a physician—being convicted rather than acquitted.[26]

Fourteen years after *Ipsley*, in 1732, we find the first prosecution based upon an unequivocal instance of intrusive abortion. That case, *Rex v. Beare*,[27] presents a stark contrast to the difficulties the prosecutors encountered in proceeding against Mary Ipsley and Elizabeth Rickets. The difference arose largely because in *Baere* the court had the testimony of an eye-witness—the victim herself. The relatively advanced (and effective) technique recorded in *Beare* also contrasts with the crudity of the attempted intrusion (if that is what happened) in *Ipsley*. The *Beare* case was reported only in a magazine. Despite considerable searching by several historians, no one has yet found an official record of what was, after all, only a misdemeanor conviction in an outlying county. The report reads in full as follows:

> Derby, August 15, 1732. ELEANOR MERRIMAN, now the Wife of *Ebenezer Beare,* indicted for a Misdemeanor, in endeavouring to persuade Nich. Wilson to poison his Wife, and for giving him Poison to that End.

---

23. Rex v. Lewis, HODGSON'S MIDDLESEX GAOL DELIVERY REP. ("HODGSON'S") 627 (no. 402) (1786) (using an injury technique).

24. Rex v. Anonymous (1670), 1 HALE, *supra* note 21, at 429–30; Regina v. Adkyns, ASS. 35/43/1, m.1 (1600), reprinted in CALENDAR OF ASSIZE REC., ESSEX INDICTMENTS, ELIZ. I, at 510 (no. 3054) (1975); Regina v. Meddowe, Ass. 35/32, m.34 (1591), reprinted in CALENDAR OF ASSIZE REC., SUSSEX INDICTMENTS, ELIZ. I, at 233 (no. 1212) (1975); Regina v. Poope (1589), reprinted in CALENDAR OF ASSIZE REC., KENT INDICTMENTS, ELIZ. I, at 289 (no. 1751) (1975); Rex v. Cliston, JUST 1/1011, m.62 (Wiltshire Eyre 1288); Rex v. Reeve, JUST 1/924, m.60 (Sussex Eyre 1288); Rex v. Brente, JUST 1/186, m.30 (Devon Eyre 1281). *See also* Commonwealth v. Carter (1652), reprinted in CALENDAR OF ASSIZE REC.: KENT INDICTMENTS, 1649–1659, at 96 (nos. 534, 535) (1989) (acquitted); Rex v. Skotard, JUST 1/169, m.25 (Derbyshire Eyre 1330) (acquitted); Rex v. Houdydoudy (Coroner's Inquest 1326), reprinted in CALENDAR OF CORONER'S ROLLS OF THE CITY OF LONDON, A.D. 1300–1378, at 166 (1913) (outcome unknown); Rex v. Godesman, JUST 1/383, mm.18, 96 (Kent Eyre 1313) (acquitted); Rex v. Boleye, JUST 1/303, m.69d (Shropshire Eyre 1292) (acquitted); Philippa's Appeal, THE LONDON EYRE OF 1276, at 51 (no. 187) (London Rec. Soc'y 1976) (defendant escaped trial through benefit of clergy); Orscherd's Appeal, JUST 1/174, m.40d (1249?) (acquitted).

25. *See also* Rex v. Lewis, HODGSON'S, *supra* note 23, at 627 (No. 402) (1786); Rex v. Winship, Durham 16/2, 17/25 (1785) *and* NEWCASTLE CURRENT, July 30, 1785, at 4. *See also* 2 M.A. RICHARDSON, THE LOCAL HISTORIAN'S TABLE BOOK: HISTORICAL DIVISION 112, 270, 299 (1843).

26. Rex v. Hallowell, 9 SUPER. CT. RECORDS Nos. 113, 173, 175 (Wyndham Cnty. Super. Ct. Files, box 172) (1745–47). *See* Chapter 4, at notes 295–330.

27. Rex v. Beare, 2 THE GENTLEMAN'S MAGAZINE 931 (Aug. 1732), available at http://www.bodley.ox.ac.uk/cgi-bin/ilej/imagel.pl?item=page&seq=1&size=1&id-gm.1732.8x2.x.x.931. Perhaps the first widely available report of this case is in 2 THE NEWGATE CALENDAR 315–16 (Andrew Knapp & William Baldwin eds. 1825). *See also* Shelley Gavigan, *The Criminal Sanction as It Relates to Human Reproduction: The Genesis of the Statutory Prohibition of Abortion,* 5 J. LEGAL HIST. 20, 28–29 (1984).

Indicted a second time by the Name of *Eleanor Beare,* for a Misdemeanor, in destroying the Foetus in the Womb of *Grace Belfort,* by putting an iron Instrument up into her Body, and thereby causing her to miscarry. Indicted a third time, for destroying the Foetus in the Womb of a certain Woman, to the jury unknown, by putting an Iron Instrument up her Body, or by giving her something to make her miscarry. Pleaded Not Guilty.

Indicted a third time, for destroying the foetus in the womb of a certain woman, to the jury unknown, by putting an iron instrument up her body, or by giving her something to make her miscarry. Pleaded not guilty.

To the Second Indictment

COUNSEL [FOR THE KING]: Gentlemen, you have heard the Indictment read, and may observe, that the Misdemeanor for which the Prisoner stands indicted, is of a most shocking Nature; to destroy the Fruit in the Womb carries something in it so contrary to the natural Tenderness of the Female Sex, that I am amazed how ever any Woman should arrive at such a degree of Impiety and Cruelty, as to attempt it in such a manner as the Prisoner has done, it has really something so shocking in it, that I cannot well display the Nature of the Crime to you, but must leave it to the Evidence: It is cruel and barbarous to the last degree.

Call *Grace Belfort.*

GRACE BELFORD (*sic*): I lived with the Prisoner as a Servant about ten Days, but was not hired, and I was off and on with her about fourteen Weeks: When I had been with her a few Days there came Company into the House, and made me drink Ale and Brandy (which I was not used to drink) and it overcame me; my Mistress sent me unto the Stable to give Hay to some Horses, but I was not capable of doing it, so [I] laid me down in the Stable; and there came to me one Ch_____r, a young Man that was drinking in the House, and after some Time I feared I was with Child by Ch_____r; upon that, my Mistress asked me if I was with Child, I told her I thought I was; Then she said if I could get 30 shilling from Ch_____r, she would clear me from the Child, without giving me Physick. A little Time after, some Company gave me Cyder and Brandy, my Mistress and I were both full of Liquor, and when the Company was gone, we could scarce get up Stairs, but we did get up; then I laid me on the Bed, and my Mistress brought a kind of an Instrument, I took it to be like an Iron Skewer, and she put it up into my Body a great Way, and hurt me.

COURT: What followed upon that?

EVIDENCE: Some Blood came from me.

COURT: Did you miscarry after that?

EVIDENCE: The next Day after I went to *Allesiree,* where I had a Miscarriage.

COURT: What did the Prisoner do after that?

EVIDENCE: She told me the Job was done. I then lodged two or three Nights with one *Ann Moseley* (now *Ann Oldknowles*) and coming one Morning to see the Prisoner, I called for a Mug of Ale and drank it, and told her I was going home; then came in *John Clark,* and on the Prisoner's saying I was going home, he said he would give me a Glass of Wine to help me forward, which accordingly he did, out of a Bottle he had in his Pocket, then I took my leave of him; and when I was a little Way out of Town, I fell down at a Style, and was not well, I lay a little while, then got up, and went to *Nottingham* that night.

Call *Ann Oldknowles.*

COURT: Do you konw any Thing of *Grace Belford* having a Miscarriage?

EVIDENCE: I know nothing, but that when she lay with me, I saw all the Symptoms of Miscarriage on the Bed where she lay.

Call *John Clark.*

COURT: Do you know the Prisoner?

EVIDENCE: Yes, I have frequented her House.

COURT: Did you ever hear her say anything that she had used Means to make a Woman with Child miscarry, by putting any kind of Instrument up their Bodies, or by giving them any Thing to take inwardly?

EVIDENCE: Yes, I have.—

COURT: Have you seen her Instrument for that Purpose, or have you seen her use any Means to make any Woman with Child miscarry?

CLARK: No, but I have heard her say she had done it, and that she then had under her one *Hannah,* whose other Name I know not.

COURT: Have you heard her say she had been sent for for these wicked Practices, or had any Reward for causing any one to miscarry?

CLARK: I heard her say she had been once sent for to *Nottingham,* and, as I remember, she said she had five Pounds for the Journey.

PRISONER: Did you not say you never heard me say any thing of using any Means to cause Miscarriage in any Person, or saw me use any Means for that End?

CLARK: No, I said I never saw you do any thing that Way, but had heard you say you had done it. Would you have me forswear myself?

PRISONER: No, but I would have you speak the Truth.

CLARK: I do.

Then the Prisoner called several Persons to speak in her Behalf, but only two appeared, and they only gave her Friends a reputable Character, and said the prisoner had a good Education, but they knew nothing of the latter Part of her Life.

MR. MAYOR: The Prisoner at the Bar has a very bad Character, and I have had frequent Complaints against her for keeping a disorderly House.

Many evidences were ready in Court to have proved the Facts she stood charged with in the third Indictment; but his Lordship observing that the second Indictment was proved so plainly, he thought there was no Necessity for going upon the third.

His Lordship summed up the Evidence in a very moving Speech to the jury, wherein he said, he never met with a Case so barbarous and unnatural. The Jury, after a short Consultation, brought the Prisoner in Guilty of both Indictments, and she received sentence to stand in the Pillory, the two next Market-Days, and to suffer close Imprisonment for Three Years.

*Derby, August 18, 1732.* This day *Eleanor Beare,* pursuant to her Sentence, stood for the first Time in the Pillory in the Market place; to which Place she was attended by several of the Sheriff's Officers; notwithstanding which, the Populace, to show their Resentment of the horrible Crimes wherewith she had been charged, and the little Remorse she has shown since her Commitments, gave her no Quarter, but threw such quantities of Eggs, Turnips, etc. that it was thought she would hardly have escaped with her Life: she disengaged herself from the Pillory before the Time of her standing was expired, jumped among the Crowd, whence she was with Difficulty carried back to Prison.[28]

Eleanor Beare was sentenced to the pillory and to three years in prison for inducing an abortion at less than 14 weeks of gestation, well before quickening was likely.[29] Beare's case thus is not only the first known instance of a genuine intrusive abortion in England, but it also clearly demonstrates that abortion before quickening was a misdemeanor—as Coke had argued.[30] Moreover, the tone of the report suggests that intrusive abortions then were a recent phenomenon in England rather than a practice with a long, albeit underground, history. The prosecutor declared in his opening statement his incredulity as to the method by which the abortion was induced:

> [T]he Misdemeanor for which the Prisoner stands indicted, is of a most shocking Nature; to destroy the Fruit in the Womb carries something in it so contrary to the natural Tenderness of the Female Sex, that I am amazed how ever any Woman should arrive at such a degree of Impiety and Cruelty, as to attempt it in such a manner as the Prisoner has done, it has really something so shocking in it, that I cannot well display the Nature of the Crime to you, but must leave it to the Evidence....

We have less in the statement of the judge, but he too declared that he had never before met with such a case "so barbarous and cruel." These statements suggest that the attorney and judge were repelled by the abortion not just as contrary to "the tenderness of the female sex," but as relying on a hitherto unknown practice. Their statements advert directly to the method by which the abortion was carried out. The prosecutor, at least, found the abortion technique to be "so shocking" that he could not discuss it but had to leave it to the witnesses.

*Rex v. Beare* thus is not only interesting for what it tells us about the state of the law regarding abortion during the reign of King George II, but also as further evidence that successful intrusive abortions were, at that time, a novel procedure largely unknown in the European cultural zone. In *Beare,* we find men of the world, accomplished enough to have risen to Queen's Counsel or to the Bench, shocked beyond words by their confrontation with a technique of which we have no prior record in England, and almost no prior record elsewhere in Europe. The editors of *The Newgate Calendar* also wrote in a tone of shock and horror in introducing the case.[31]

One piece of evidence suggests intrusive abortions were a novelty even to the defendant, Eleanor Beare. The proceeding begins with testimony that Beare provided poisons to a man intent on ridding himself of a wife, although the jury did not reach a conclusion on that charge. The same magazine also reports, in an issue published the previous April, that at the end of March a man and woman were executed in Derby for conspiring to poison the man's wife. At their execution, they confessed that Eleanor Beare had provided the poison.[32] That the charges all related to the death of women, along with Beare's conviction as an abortionist, raises a suspicion that the

---

28. 2 The Gentleman's Magazine 931 (Aug. 1732).

29. The use of the term "fetus" would indicate that the fetus was fully formed, *i.e.,* had all its external forms, including limbs and digits. John Quincy, Lexicon Physico-Medicum or, A New Physical Dictionary 158 (1719); William Smellie, A Treatise on Midwifery 110 (4th ed. 1752). *See generally* Philip Rafferty, *Roe v. Wade:* The Birth of a Constitutional Right 677–79 (University Microfilms International Dissertation Information Service, Ann Arbor, MI 1992).

30. *See* Coke, *supra* note 21, at 50–51, quoted in Chapter 4, at notes 120–21. *See also* Rex v. Code, JUST 1/789, m.1 (Hampshire Eyre 1281), quoted in Chapter 3, at note 93.

31. 2 *The Newgate Calendar, supra* note 27, at 315.

32. 2 Gentlemen's Magazine 722 (April 1732).

"poisonings" were really meant to be abortions, but the report in fact indicate that the husband was already involved with other women (including Beare) and simply wanted to be rid of his wife. Anyone familiar with the technologies of abortion will recognize, however, how Beare had become so familiar with poisons even if the poisoned women were not pregnant at the time.

# The Common Law Regarding Abortion Around 1800

*A historian is a babbler who plays tricks upon the dead.*

—Voltaire[33]

Those who insist that abortion was a "common law liberty" focus their attention on the period 1790–1870, for during this period the Bill of Rights and the Fourteenth Amendment came into the Constitution of the United States.[34] This period is critical to constitutional lawyers because the understanding of the legal status of abortion during that time would go far towards determining the "original intent" of the drafters of those amendments to the Constitution. This leaves aside arguments over whether the historical status of abortion at any earlier time should determine the constitutionality of laws regarding abortion today. Here we are only concerned with what in fact was the legal status of abortion at that time.

Until law professor Cyril Means, jr., discovered the supposed liberty in 1968, however, no statement in any legal or other document expressed the claim that anyone had a liberty to abort.[35] The unanimous sense of the legal and the general community was that abortion was a crime because it involved the killing of a child—if one could prove that the child was alive at the time of the abortive act and died as a result. As the review of the common law of abortion down to this point shows, when courts encountered abortions by any technique they treated it as criminal without reservation. This left open only the often difficult questions of proving that there was a living child and that the child was killed as a result of the abortion.[36] The results

---

33. 82 THE COMPLETE WORKS OF VOLTAIRE 452 (Theodore Betterman *et al.* eds. 1968).

34. Roe v. Wade, 410 U.S. 113, 140 (1973); Beecham v. Leahy, 287 A.2d 836, 839 (Vt. 1972); *Amicus Brief of 250 American Historians in support of Appellants in* Planned Parenthood of Southeastern Pennsylvania v. Casey, [505 U.S. 833 (1992)] ("*Casey Historians' Brief*"), at 5–6; *Amicus Brief of 281 American Historians supporting Appellees in* Webster v. Reproductive Health Services [492 U.S. 490 (1989)] ("*Webster Historians' Brief*"), reprinted at 11 WOMEN'S RTS. L. RPTR. 163, 170 (1989), and in 8 DOCUMENTARY HISTORY OF THE LEGAL ASPECTS OF ABORTION IN THE UNITED STATES: *WEBSTER V. REPRODUCTIVE HEALTH SERVICES* 107 (Roy Mersky & Gary Hartman eds. 1990) (hereafter pagination will be given only to the version in the *Women's Rts. L. Rptr.*); GORDON, *supra* note 13, at 52–53, 57; MOHR, *supra* note 13, at 128–29, 134–36, 144–45, 201, 208–11, 226, 229, 235–36; Cyril Means, jr., *The Phoenix of Abortional Freedom: Is a Penumbral Right or Ninth-Amendment Right About to Arise from the Nineteenth-Century Legislative Ashes of a Fourteenth-Century Common-Law Liberty?*, 17 N.Y.L.F. 335, 336, 351–54, 374–75, 409–10 n.175 (1971) ("Means II"); Reva Siegel, *Reasoning from the Body: A Historical Perspective on Abortion Regulation and Questions of Equal Protection*, 44 STAN. L. REV. 261, 278 (1992). On the various notions of "right" and "liberty" (neither relating to abortion) prevalent among Americans in 1791, see Philip Hamburger, *Natural Rights, Natural Law, and American Constitutions*, 102 YALE L.J. 907 (1993).

35. *See* Chapter 3, at notes 3–19.

36. *See especially* Chapter 4, at notes 31–66, 118–28.

were aptly summarized in the work of American legal scholar Francis Wharton writing before 1860: [37]

> There is no doubt that at common law the destruction of an infant unborn is a high misdemeanor, and at an early period it seems to have been deemed murder.[38] If the child dies subsequently to birth from wounds received in the womb, it is clearly homicide,[39] even though the child is still attached to the mother by the umbilical cord.[40] It has been said that it is not an indictable offence to administer a drug to a woman, and thereby to procure an abortion, unless the mother is *quick* with child,[41] though such a distinction, it is submitted, is neither in accordance with the result of medical experience,[42] nor with the principles of the common law.[43]

Even a cursory review of the legal authorities available in the later years of the eighteenth and early years of the nineteenth century confirms Wharton's summary.

Several prosecutions arose for injurious and ingestive abortions in the eighteenth century,[44] as well as two further prosecutions for intrusive abortions in England within the 70 years following *Beare,*[45] all before the enactment of England's first statutory prohibition of abortion. Later English authors who wrote about the common law all concurred in Wharton's analysis,[46] as Wharton's citations indicate. William Blackstone, the foremost scholar of the common law in the eighteenth century, expressed the view developed by Coke and summarized by Wharton:

> 1. Life is the immediate give of God, a right inherent by nature in every individual, and it began in contemplation of law as soon as an infant was able to stir in the mother's womb. For if a woman is quick with child, and by a potion or otherwise, killeth in her womb, or if any one beat her whereby the child dieth in her body, and she is delivered of a dead child; this, though not murder, was by the ancient law homicide or

---

37. 1 Francis Wharton, The Criminal Law of the United States § 1220 (5th rev. ed. 1861).

38. [Renumbered footnote in the original] 1 Russ. on Cr. 671; 1 Vesey, 86; 3 Coke's Inst. 50; 1 Hawk. c. 13, s. 16; 1 Hale, 434; 1 East, P.C. 90; 3 Chitty C.L. 798.

39. [Renumbered footnote in the original] R. *v.* Senior, 1 Mood. C.C. 36; 3 Inst. 50; see ante, § 942.

40. [Renumbered footnote in the original] R. *v.* Trilloe, 2 Moody, C.C. 13.

41. [Renumbered footnote in the original] Com. v. Bangs, 9 Mass. 387.

42. [Renumbered footnote in the original] W. & S. Med. Jur. § 344–5. Guy's Med. Juris. tit. Abortion; 1 Beck. 172, 192; Lewis, C.L. 10.

43. [Renumbered footnote in the original] 1 Russ. on Crim. 661; 1 Vesey, 86; 3 Coke's Inst. 50; 1 Hawk. c. 13, s. 16; Bracton, l.3, c. 21.

44. Rex v. Lewis, Hodgson's Middlesex Gaol Delivery Report 627, 628 (No. 402) (1786) (convicted); Rex v. Winship, Durham 16/2, 17/25 (1785) *and* Newcastle Current, July 30, 1785, at 4 (convicted); Rex v. J.H. (1781) (indictment survives; outcome unknown), in W. Stubbs & G. Talmash, The Crown Circuit Companion 138 (Thomas Dougherty ed., 6th ed. 1790); Rex v. Turner (1755) (not guilty), in K. Tweedsdale Meekings, Nottinghshire County Records—Extracts from the Records of the Eighteenth Century 137 (1947). *See also* 2 M.A. Richardson, The Local Historian's Table Book: Historical Division 112, 270, 299 (1843).

45. Rex v. Anonymous (1802), 3 Joseph Chitty, Criminal Law 798–801 (1816); Rex v. Tinckler (1781), 1 Edward Hyde East, A Treatise on the Pleas of the Crown 354–56 (1803). There is no report that unequivocally indicates that an intrusive abortion was performed in colonial America, although one ambiguous report might indicate such an abortion in 1742. Rex v. Hallowell, 9 Super. Ct. Records Nos. 113, 173, 175 (Wyndham Cnty. Super. Ct. Files, box 172) (1745–47). *See* Chapter 4, at notes 295–330.

46. Anonymous, The Laws Respecting Women 348 (1777); 1 William Blackstone, Commentaries on the Laws of England *129–30 (1765); 4 Blackstone, *supra*, at *198; Richard Burn, The Justice of the Peace and the Parish Officer 380 (3rd ed. 1756); 1 East, *supra* note 45, at 227–30; 2 William Hawkins, Treatise on the Pleas of the Crown 80 (1716); 1 William Russell, A Treatise on Crimes and Misdemeanors 617–18, 796 (1819).

manslaughter. But the modern law doth not look upon this offence in quite so atrocious a light, but merely as a heinous misdemeanor.[47]

Murder is therefore now defined, or rather described, by sir Edward Coke; "when a person of sound memory and discretion, unlawfully killeth any reasonable creature in being, and under the king's peace, with malice aforethought, either express or implied." The best way of examining the nature of this crime will be by considering the several branches of this definition....

Further, the person killed must be *"a reasonable creature in being, and under the king's peace,"* at the time of the killing. Therefore to kill an alien, a Jew, or an outlaw, who are all under the king's peace and protection, is as much murder as to kill the most regular born Englishman, except he be an alien enemy in time of war. To kill a child in its mother' womb, is now no murder, but a great misprision; but if the child be born alive, and dieth by reason of the potion or bruises it received in the womb, it seems, by the better opinion, to be murder in such as administered or gave them. But, as there is one case where it is difficult to prove the child's being born alive, namely, in the case of the murder of bastard children by the unnatural mother, it is enacted by statute, 21 Jac. 1, ch. 27, that if any woman be delivered of a child which if born alive should by law be a bastard; and endeavors privately to conceal its death, by burying the child or the like; the mother so offending shall suffer death as in the case of murder, unless she can prove by one witness at least that the child was actually born dead. This law, which savors pretty strongly of severity, in making the concealment of the death almost conclusive evidence of the child's being murdered by the mother, is nevertheless to be also met in the criminal codes of many other nations of Europe; as the Danes, the Swedes, and the French. But I apprehend it has of late years been usual with us in England, upon trial for this offence, to require some sort of presumptive evidence that the child was born alive, before the other constrained presumption (that the child whose death is concealed, was therefore killed by its parent) is admitted to convict the prisoner.[48]

All the writers on the common law of the eighteenth and nineteenth centuries on both sides of the Atlantic repeated Blackstone's views in virtually identical words.[49] While not precisely reporting in all respects what courts were actually doing, it would influence legal developments in the nineteenth century, particularly attempts to codify the law of abortion into statutory form. Cyril Means, jr., however, dealt with Blackstone quite cavalierly. Means was intent on proving that abortion was not a crime at common law. He therefore chose to quote in full only one part of one sentence from Blackstone ("To kill a child in its mother' womb, is now no murder, but a great misprision"), rephrasing another sentence to the assure the reader would read it as reflecting the views of individual men rather than the legal tradition of England ("But [Sir Edward Coke] doth not look upon this offence [abortion after quickening] in quite so atrocious a light [as Bracton], but merely as a heinous misdemeanor.").[50] Means ignored Wharton altogether.

In addition to confirming the points made by Blackstone, Wharton, and others, the two intrusive abortion cases that arose within 25 years before the enactment of the *Lord Ellenborough's*

---

47. 1 Blackstone, *supra* note 46, at *129–30.

48. 4 Blackstone, *supra* note 46, at *195–98.

49. *See* Burn, *supra* note 46, at 380; 1 East, *supra* note 45, at 227–30; 2 Hawkins, *supra* note 46, at 80; James Parker, Conductor Generalis: Or, the Office, Duty, and Authority of Justices of the Peace 216–17 (1764); 1 Russell, *supra* note 46, at 617–18, 796.

50. Means II, *supra* note 34, at 349.

*Act*[51]—the first statutory prohibition of abortion in England—deserve careful consideration. These cases appear to have influenced the decision to enact that statute. The cases are also important because Means and those who follow his lead insist that the cases demonstrate serious doubts about the criminality of abortion at that time. The first of these cases was *Rex v. Tinckler.* The full report of the *Tinckler* case in Sir Edward Hyde East's treatise reads as follows:

> Margaret Tinckler was indicted for the murder of Jane Parkinson, by inserting pieces of wood into her womb. A second count charged her as accessary (*sic*) before the fact. It was proved by several witnesses, that from the first time of the deceased taking to her bed, which was on the 12th of July, she thought that she must die, making use of different expresses, as, *that she was going; that she was working out her last*; and exclaiming, *Oh! that Peggy Tinckler has killed me.* She lingered till the 23d, when she died. She never was up but once during that time, when on telling a friend who attended her that she thought herself better, she advised her to get up, which the deceased did, and walked as far as the passage going out of the room, but was forced to return and go to bed again. It appeared by the testimony of several witnesses, that from the moment of her taking to her bed till the time of her death she had declared, *that Tinckler had killed her and dear child*, (stating the particular means used, which agreed with the charge in the indictment.) And during the same period she had declared more particularly, "that she was with child by one P. a married man, who, being fearful lest his wife should hear of it if she were brought to bed, advised her to go to the prisoner, a midwife, to take her advice how she should get rid of the child, being then five or six months gone." "That the prisoner gave her the advice" in question, which she followed accordingly. It was proved by the testimony of a witness, that three days before the delivery, which was on the 10th of July, she saw the deceased in the prisoner's bed-chamber, when the prisoner took her round the waist and shook her in a very violent manner six different times, and tossed her up and down: and that she afterwards delivered at the prisoner's house. The deceased also declared during her illness, that after her delivery the prisoner gave her the child to take home; and bid her to go to bed that night and sleep, and get up in the morning and go about her business, and nobody would know anything of the matter; but that appearing very ill the next day at a relation's house, they had ordered her to go home and go to bed, which she did. The child was born alive, but died instantly; and the surgeons, who were examined, proved that it was perfect. There was no doubt but that the deceased had died by the acceleration of the birth of the child: and upon opening her womb it appeared that there were two holes caused by the skewers, one of which was mortified, and the other only enflamed; and other symptoms of injury appeared. A short time before her death she was asked whether the account she had from time to time given of the occasion of her death, and the prisoner's treatment of her were true; and she declared it was. It was objected that the above evidence of the deceased's declarations ought not to be admitted, as she herself was *particeps criminis*, and likewise as it appeared at the time of her declarations she was better, or thought herself so. But Nares J. was of opinion, that however this objection might hold with respect to the second count, in which the prisoner was charged as an accessory to the deceased, yet the deceased was not willingly or knowingly an accessary to her own death; and therefore it was like the common case of any other murder. And as to the objection that she once thought herself better, and tried to get up, yet the same declarations she then made had been made repeatedly before to persons whom in confidence she told that she never should survive, when she first took to her bed; and she had repeated the same declara-

---

51. 43 Geo. III ch. 58 (1803).

tions the day before she died, and within a few hours of her death. And as to the fact it-self, he was clearly of opinion it was murder on the authority of Lord Hale. The jury found the prisoner guilty on the first count, charging her as a principal in the murder, and execution being respited to take the opinion of the judges on the whole case, they all met to consider of it: and were unanimously of opinion that these declarations of the deceased were legal evidence: for though at one time the deceased thought herself bet-ter, yet the declarations before and after and home to her death were uniform and to the same effect. And as to her being *particeps criminis*, they answered, that if two persons be guilty of murder, and one be indicted and the other not, the party not indicted is a wit-ness for the crown. And though the practice be not to convict on such proof uncorrob-orated, yet the evidence is admissible; and here it was supported by the proof of the prisoner tossing the deceased in her arms in the manner stated. Most of the judges in-deed held that the declarations of the deceased were alone sufficient evidence to convict the prisoner; for they were not to be considered in the light of evidence coming from a *particeps criminis*; as she considered herself to be dying at the times, and had no view or intent to serve in excusing herself, or fixing the charge unjustly on others. But others of the judges thought that her declarations were to be so considered; and therefore re-quired the aid of confirmatory evidence.[52]

Margaret Tinckler's conviction, like Sir Matthew Hale's ruling in *Rex v. Anonymous*,[53] poses a problem for those who insist that abortion was, before 1800, a "common law liberty." How can the exercise of a legally protected liberty give rise to a claim of murder when that exercise, pre-sumably unintentionally and not maliciously, miscarries and results in what was far too normal an outcome? Lame excuses about Restoration gallantry simply do not explain the way such cases were decided.[54] While Hale was not entirely clear regarding the theory of the crime, Sir Edward East was in his report of *Rex v. Tinckler*. East discussed this case elsewhere in his treatise, explic-itly describing the charge of murder as depending on the doctrine of "transferred intent":

> In these cases the act done follows the nature of the act intended to be done. Therefore if the latter were founded in malice, and the stroke from whence death ensued fell by mistake or accident upon a person for whom it was not intended, yet the motive being malicious, the act amounts to murder.... Hither also may be referred the case of one who gives medicine to a woman; and that of another who put skewers in her womb, with a view in each case to procure an abortion; whereby the women were killed. Such acts are clearly murder; though the original intent, had it succeeded, would not have been so, but only a great misdemeanor: for the acts were in their nature malicious and deliberate, and necessarily attended with great danger to the person on whom they were practiced.[55]

Means, never one to grasp the obvious, could only react to these statements by stressing the temporal separation of their writing from the trial of the case (although Means was quite willing to accept the accuracy of East's report of the case).[56] He also described East's characterization of a nonfatal abortion as a "great misdemeanor" as "an exegetic dilemma so ambiguous as almost to defy solution."[57] Why Means should find East's position so puzzling is somewhat unclear as

---

52. 1 EAST, *supra* note 45, at 354–56 (emphasis in the original).

53. Rex v. Anonymous (1670), 1 HALE, *supra* note 21, at 429–30, quoted in Chapter 4, at note 182.

54. The phrase "Restoration gallantry" was Cyril Means' explanation for Hale's *Rex v. Anonymous* decision. Means II, *supra* note 34, at 362. *See* Chapter 4, at note 184.

55. 1 EAST, *supra* note 45, at 230.

56. Means II, *supra* note 34, at 363, 371.

57. *Id.* at 367.

Means was insisting in this same article that the sole purpose of all abortion prosecutions was to protect the life and health of the mother.[58] Means, however, insisted that East did not adopt Coke's view of abortion, and was simply confused about what Hale meant.[59] To substantiate his claim, Means emphasized the failure of both Sir George Nares (the Common Pleas Justice who presided at Margaret Tinckler's trial) and East to discuss whether Margaret Tinckler's case involved two murders or one.

Means claimed that the failure of Nares and East to discuss whether the death of a born child was murder demonstrated that they rejected Coke's view that an abortion which produced a live-birth after which the child died could be charged as murder, and hence that they rejected of all of Coke's views on abortion.[60] Means was content, as always, to rely only on his idiosyncratic reading of the few texts relating to abortion that were widely known before 1970 rather than to undertake original research that might actually clarify the meaning of what might have been slightly obscure.[61] Thus Means did not know of a contemporary press account of the execution of Margaret Tinckler "for a crime in acting or recommending certain means to destroy an infant, which was effected; and finally with the death of the mother."[62] Even if we excuse his failure to find this data, we cannot excuse him for the remarkably strained readings of the material he did find.

East's report of the case tells us that "[t]he child was born alive, but died instantly." The test for the separate existence for a child under both ancient (and most modern homicide laws) was whether its umbilical cord was cut.[63] The statement is not altogether clear on whether the child died before or after its umbilical cord was cut, but the phrase "born alive" normally means that an infant did have at least a few moments of life wholly separate from the mother. Thus, the failure of Nares and East to discuss the possibility of a murder charge for the death of the child might not be so much a rejection of Coke's views as a failure of proof of the necessary facts. This is hardly a novel situation for abortion prosecutions. Lord Chief Justice Mansfield would state expressly, in 1808 (a quarter century after the *Tinckler* case, but only five years after East published his treatise reporting and analyzing the case), that the difficulties encountered in prosecuting abortions before the nineteenth century had purely resulted from the difficulty of proving that the child was in fact alive at the time of the act.[64] Furthermore, East's discussion of the case appears more than 120 pages before his report of the case. One simply cannot be certain that East considered his discussion as exhausting all that might have been involved in the *Tinckler* case. In short, Means' entire argument regarding East, rather than supporting Means' reading of Hale, hinges on the validity of Means' dubious assertions regarding Hale's meaning.[65]

The final pre-statutory case which has been widely discussed in histories of abortion law is yet another *Rex v. Anonymous*,[66] this time from 1802. The defendant was indicted on four counts of abortion, the first three of which related to the same pregnancy. The primary pregnancy resulted

---

58. *Id.* at 336. *See also* Gavigan, *supra* note 27, at 27.

59. Means II, *supra* note 34, at 367–73.

60. *Id.* at 367–68.

61. Compare Means' failure to search for the original records of *Rex v. de Bourton*. *See* Chapter 3, at notes 141–69. Similarly, Means did not seek to trace the legislative history of *Lord Ellenborough's Act. See* the text *infra* at notes 118–38.

62. Newcastle Chronicle, Nov. 24, 1781, at 2.

63. *See* Chapter 4, at notes 118–54.

64. Rex v. Pizzy (Suffolk Assizes 1808). *See* William Notcutt, *The Remarkable Trial at Large of William Pizzy and Mary Codd at the Assizes Holden at Bury St. Edmunds on Thursday August 11, 1808 for Feloniously Administering a Certain Noxious and Destructive Substance to Ann Cheney with Intent to Produce a Miscarriage,* 6 Edinburgh Med. & Surgical J. 244, 245 (1810). This Chief Justice Mansfield was Chief Justice of the Common Pleas. He was not the great Chief Justice of the King's Bench of the late eighteenth century.

65. *See* Chapter 4, at notes 182–221.

66. Rex v. Anonymous (1802), 3 Chitty, *supra* note 45, at 798.

in a live birth, with mother and child becoming "weak, sick, diseased, and distempered in body as a result of the abortion" and with the mother suffering "great and excruciating pains, anguish and torture both of body and mind" for the next six months. The fourth count apparently relates to a different attempted abortion without indicating what the outcome was, but contains similar recitals about the long-term debilitation of the mother.

The indictments seem to indicate rather clearly that the Crown's law officers considered abortion to be a serious crime even without the death of either the mother or the child. Although the indictments did not aver quickening, one could infer quickening from the birth of the child and other facts.[67] Means was not satisfied with this concession. He sought to discredit the case by stressing that there was no report of whether the indictments had actually been prosecuted, and by noting that as the indictments did not charge the death of either the mother or the child, it did not prove that a successful abortion would have been a crime![68] Apparently, according to Means, the crime that was charged (but, Means would have us believe, without prosecution) was the mental and physical injury to the mother through an unsuccessful abortion. Would the stillbirth of the child then have immunized the abortionist from these charges?

Means apparently thought highly of his arguments about the significance of the indictments in the 1802 *Rex v. Anonymous*. At least he thought his arguments would serve to confuse matters regarding the 1781 prosecution of Margaret Tinckler, as he chose to discuss *Anonymous* before *Tinckler* in an article that otherwise discussed the cases in strict chronological order.[69] Means went on to argue that the enactment of *Lord Ellenborough's Act* only one year after the second of two intrusive abortion cases to appear in a period of 20 years after an apparent hiatus of more than 100 years since what he erroneously considered the most recent prior reported abortion case,[70] suggested that the Crown law officers were not confident that their indictment from the year before was valid.[71] There is simply no indication, however, that anyone (including the anonymous defendant) questioned the validity or adequacy of the indictment in question.

# The Statutory Prohibition of Abortion in England

*Tracing the gradual evolution of an idea over time is like trying to lasso smoke.*

—William Quinn, Jr.[72]

With the nineteenth century, we enter the age of statutes. The century opened with the first great modern codification of the law in the Napoleonic Empire. The century closed with the second great codification in the newly founded German Empire. Such codes, enacted during the nineteenth and early twentieth centuries, became characteristic of most non-common law countries. While most common law countries did not codify their law, common law countries did enact extensive statutes during this period. In particular, common law countries undertook to

---

67. *See, e.g.,* Commonwealth v. Parker, 50 Mass. (9 Met.) 263, 267 (1845); Gavigan, *supra* note 27, at 29.

68. Means II, *supra* note 34, at 357–58.

69. *Id.* at 355–59, 363–72.

70. Rex v. Anonymous, 1 HALE, *supra* note 21, at 429–30.

71. Means II, *supra* note 34, at 358.

72. William Quinn, jr., *Federal Acknowledgment of American Indian Tribes: The Historical Development of a Legal Concept,* 34 AM. J. LEGAL HISTORY 331, 331 (1990).

replace the common law of crimes with statutes in order to provide fair notice to the public of prohibited conduct.[73]

In the context of this pervasive shift to statutory law, it is hardly surprising that nearly every nation across the globe enacted a statutory prohibition of abortion in the nineteenth or early twentieth century.[74] Nor can this global pattern simply be explained in terms European colonialism. Even in Japan, a country that retained more of its independence during the nineteenth century than most non-European countries, enacted a statutory prohibition of abortion.[75] There appear to have been weak prohibitions of abortion in Japan at least as early as the seventeenth century, although there were no prohibitions of infanticide there.[76] The professed reason for including abortion in Japan's first modern criminal code was to protect fetal life, although feminist historians refuse to believe this was the true reason.[77] In the face of such universal prohibition of abortion, at least one unsympathetic observer was reduced to describing the proliferation of statutory prohibitions of abortion around the world as merely an "interesting coincidence."[78]

The nineteenth century statutes often were the first statute to address abortion in each nation. This no more "proves" that abortion was not a crime before the statute was enacted than it would prove that murder or rape were not crimes simply because, as in England and its colonies, there were no statutes specifically making murder, manslaughter, or rape crimes before the nineteenth century. While the evidence that murder, manslaughter, and rape were common law crimes is more extensive than the evidence for abortion as a common law crime, those several bodies of evidence are equally definite. Abortion prosecutions and convictions are more rare because the practice itself was, until well into the nineteenth century, rare.[79] In addition, abortion was difficult to detect in an age when even mothers could not be certain they were pregnant until well into the pregnancy and there was no method of forensic examination after the fact to determine that a woman had recently undergone a terminated pregnancy.[80]

Those who insist, in the face of all the evidence to the contrary, that abortion was largely free of legal restraint before the earliest nineteenth-century statutes see the inclusion of those statutes in the various criminal codes as evidence of an anticompetitive conspiracy to hide an important change, missing utterly the true significance of those codifications.[81] These anti-

---

73. *See generally* CHARLES COOK, THE AMERICAN CODIFICATION MOVEMENT: A STUDY OF ANTEBELLUM LEGAL REFORM (1981); LAWRENCE FRIEDMAN, A HISTORY OF AMERICAN LAW 289–91 (1985); MORTON HORWITZ, THE TRANSFORMATION OF AMERICAN LAW 1780–1860, at 1–30 (1977); WILLIAM NELSON, THE AMERICANIZATION OF THE COMMON LAW 10, 38–39, 110–11 (1975).

74. KENNY, *supra* note 17, at 183.

75. *See* Maruyama, *supra* note 9, at 132–33; Kinko Nakatani, *Japan,* in ABORTION AND PROTECTION OF THE HUMAN FETUS: LEGAL PROBLEMS IN CROSS-CULTURAL PERSPECTIVE 221, 224 (S.J. Frankowski *et al.* eds. 1987); Wardle, *supra* note 9, at 192–94.

76. Wardle, *supra* note 9, at 189–92.

77. Maruyama, *supra* note 9, at 133, 138–39, 151–53. *See also* WILLIAM LaFLEUR, LIQUID LIFE: ABORTION AND BUDDHISM IN JAPAN 88, 99, 103–9, 120 (1992); George De Vos & Hiroshi Wagatsuma, *Status and Role Behavior in Changing Japan,* in SEX ROLES IN CHANGING SOCIETY 334, 350 (Georgene Seward & Robert Williamson eds. 1970); Evy McElmeel, Comment, *Legalization of the Birth Control Pill in Japan Will Reduce Reliance on Abortion as the Primary Method of Birth Control,* 8 PAC. RIM L. & POL'Y REV. 681, 684–85 (1999); Yoshiko Miyake, *Doubling Expectations: Motherhood and Women's Factory Work under State Management in Japan in the 1930s and 1940s,* in RECREATING JAPANESE WOMEN, 1600–1945, at 267, 277–78 (Gail Lee Bernstein ed. 1991); Sara Walsh, *Liquid Lives and Liquid Laws,* 7 INT'L LEG. PERSPECTIVES 187, 189, 191–93, 196–97, 199–200 (1995).

78. J.K. MASON, MEDICO-LEGAL ASPECTS OF REPRODUCTION AND PARENTHOOD 101 (1990).

79. *See* Chapter 1.

80. *See* Chapter 4, at notes 55–70.

81. *See, e.g.,* GORDON, *supra* note 13, at 52–53; MCLAREN, REPRODUCTIVE RITUALS, *supra* note 13, at 122–23; Siegel, *supra* note 34, at 285.

competitive urges must have existed long before the nineteenth century. Why would physicians have waited until then to seek to prohibit abortion if it was not a legally and socially accepted practice? Or, if abortion were legally and socially accepted, why would the physicians seize upon it as a vehicle for obtaining a monopoly of the practice of medicine? Why would such a self-serving policy, which supporters of abortion rights describe as so contrary to the interests of the public generally and women in particular, secure sufficient popular support to be enacted into law? And finally, in what is perhaps even a more perplexing puzzle, why would women embrace the medicalization of birth and the prohibition of abortion if the only real reason supporting the enhancement of the physicians' role was to give male doctors power over women?

The global pattern of legislation did not merely codify the law of abortion, however. The new legislation tended to deal with abortion as a problem that was becoming more serious than had formerly been the case. Generally, this is signaled by statutes making the penalties for abortion harsher than under the earlier law. For example, abortion had been classed as a homicide punishable by death (for the abortionist) under French law at least since 1566; the Penal *Code Pénal* of 1791 made abortion a homicide punishable by up to 20 years in prison for the abortionist, but provided no punishment for the mother.[82] Authorities in France included an abortion prohibition in the *Code Pénal* of 1810 that made the mother as well as the abortionist punishable for homicide.[83] A similar pattern is found in the statutes enacted in the common law world. As the first statute in a common-law country was enacted in England, we shall begin there.

It is against this background of codification that one must read *Lord Ellenborough's Act*.[84] It is customary among those who write about the history of abortion to discuss the abortion provisions as if they were a freestanding statute that dealt only with abortion. Thus Eugene Quay, in his otherwise admirable study of the history of abortion laws, described Ellenborough's Act as "The Miscarriage of Women Act."[85] Some also include the infanticide provisions of the Act. Few, if any, have bothered to note that *Lord Ellenborough's Act* was the first codification of the law of crimes against persons in the common law, as was suggested by the title often ascribed to it by persons who are not focused on abortion: "The Offences against the Person Act."[86]

Before *Lord Ellenborough's Act*, much of the common law relating to offenses against persons was unsettled, being covered by precedents and statutes created over many centuries. The ancient statutes were quite specific and were narrowly construed.[87] The statutes tended to prohibit acts with a specific intent (e.g., assault with intent to disfigure) or of peculiar danger (e.g., shooting into a dwelling place). Apart from such statutes, considerable uncertainty had arisen about the criminality of even heinous mayhems (the mutilating of a person's body). English legal historian Sir William Holdsworth concluded that mayhem was no longer a com-

---

82. *See* J.P. Brissot de Warville, *Les moyens d'adoucir la rigeur des lois penales en France* 108 (1793); Bartha Maria Knoppers, Isabel Brault, & Elizabeth Sloss, *Abortion in Francophone Countries*, 38 Am. J. Comp. L. 889, 893–94 (1990).

83. Code Pénal §317 (1810).

84. 43 Geo. III ch. 58 (1803).

85. Eugene Quay, *Justifiable Abortion—Medical and Legal Foundations (Pt. II)*, 49 Geo. L.J. 395, 431 n.40 (1961). *See also* Petersen, *supra* note 13, at 19–20 Robert Byrn, *An American Tragedy: The Supreme Court on Abortion*, 41 Fordham L. Rev. 807, 824–35 (1973); Mark Scott, Note, *Quickening in the Common Law: The Legal Precedent Roe Attempted and Failed to Use*, 1 Mich. L. & Pol'y Rev. 199, 251–52 (1996).

86. 11 W.S. Holdsworth, A History of English Law 536–37 (23 vols., 7th ed. 1956); 13 Holdsworth, *supra*, at 390; 3 James Fitzjames Stephen, History of the Criminal Law of England 113 (1883).

87. J.H. Baker, An Introduction to English Legal History 319–24 (3rd ed. 1990); 3 Holdsworth, *supra* note 86, at 316–18; 4 Holdsworth, *supra*, at 512–14; 6 Holdsworth, *supra*, at 403–4; 11 Holdsworth, *supra*, at 536–37; 3 Stephen, *supra* note 86, at 109–13.

mon law crime after the fourteenth century.[88] Other legal historians disagree.[89] *Lord Ellenborough's Act* was designed to eliminate any uncertainty regarding the criminality of the activities included in the Act by systematizing and generalizing the increasingly ancient statutes and precedents.[90] In short, the Act was a "piece of legal tidying up."[91] In addition to abortion by poisons (drugs) and some abortions by instruments, *Lord Ellenborough's Act* included such crimes as assault with a weapon with intent to murder and the armed resisting of arrest. Before this Act, armed assault with intent to murder was only a misdemeanor while armed robbery was already a capital felony. As Lord Ellenborough himself remarked in the parliamentary debates, "[t]he crime surely was more atrocious in the case where it was now least punishable."[92]

Admittedly, no recorded public outcry against abortion accounts for the legislative action against the crime.[93] The technological changes of the eighteenth and nineteenth centuries set the stage for the inclusion of the crime in *Lord Ellenborough's Act*. Even Cyril Means, jr., agreed on this point. Means concluded that the abortion provisions in *Lord Ellenborough's Act* were based on technological changes, coming as a response to difficulties he presumed the authorities had encountered in framing an indictment the year before.[94] Not all pro-abortion historians agree with Means, however. In his survey of the enactment of *Lord Ellenborough's Act*, British historian Angus McLaren, who strongly favors a freedom to abort but did not place much emphasis of legal doctrine, does not even mention a supposed difficulty with that earlier indictment.[95] As we shall see, even if Means' conclusion that abortion was included in *Lord Ellenborough's Act* because of uncertainty about the criminality of abortion were true, that does not entirely explain the matter. What we know of Ellenborough's personality, along with the provisions on abortion themselves, strongly suggests that whatever the reason for his inclusion of certain abortions in the Act, there is little likelihood that he intended to change the law relating to abortions.

Edward Law, who would become Lord Ellenborough, was Chief Justice of the King's Bench from 1802 to 1818. He was probably the most insistently conservative Chief Justice ever.[96] Ellenborough's manner was "rough and sarcastic," and he occasionally spoke in the House of Lords with the "coarse violence of the demagogue."[97] The only significant English jurist who approached Ellenborough in his conservatism was his contemporary, Lord Eldon, who served as Chief Justice of the Common Pleas (1799–1801) and as Chancellor (1801–1806, 1807–1827).[98] Probably their extreme conservatism was a reaction to the French Revolution and the wars with Napoleon that occurred during most of their time as judge or Chancellor.

Ellenborough was exceptionally learned in the ancient statutes, precedents, and scholarship of the common law, and he developed soundly reasoned decisions when the existing law allowed it.[99]

---

88. 3 HOLDSWORTH, *supra* note 86, at 316–18.

89. *See, e.g.,* THEODORE PLUCKNETT, A CONCISE HISTORY OF THE COMMON LAW 456–58 (5th ed. 1956).

90. 36 PARL. HIST. 1245 (1803). *See also* 11 HOLDSWORTH, *supra* note 86, at 537; 3 STEPHEN, *supra* note 86, at 113.

91. POTTS, DIGGORY, & PEEL, *supra* note 11, at 278.

92. 35 PARL. HIST. 1246 (1803). *See also* J. KEOWN, ABORTION, DOCTORS AND THE LAW 16 (1988).

93. KEOWN, *supra* note 92, at 12.

94. Means II, *supra* note 34, at 336, 355–59, 373. *See also* KEOWN, *supra* note 92, at 15; and the text *supra* at notes 66–71.

95. McLAREN, REPRODUCTIVE RITUALS, *supra* note 13, at 135–37.

96. 13 HOLDSWORTH, *supra* note 86, at 502–4; PLUCKNETT, *supra* note 89, at 72. *See generally* 4 JOHN CAMPBELL, THE LIVES OF THE CHIEF JUSTICES 102–254 (1849); 13 HOLDSWORTH, *supra*, at 499–516.

97. 13 HOLDSWORTH, *supra* note 86, at 502.

98. *See generally* 7 JOHN CAMPBELL, LIVES OF THE LORD CHANCELLORS 3–555 (1848); 13 HOLDSWORTH, *supra* note 86, at 595–638.

99. *See generally* 4 CAMPBELL, *supra* note 96, at 164–81; 13 HOLDSWORTH, *supra* note 86, at 507–16.

Thus, he seconded Lord Mansfield's reception of international law into the common law[100] and created the "mailbox" rule for the acceptance of contracts.[101] He even invented the presumption of death from an unexplained absence for seven years, drawing from analogous statutes.[102] As a judge, however, Lord Ellenborough proved completely unwilling to go beyond existing precedents (judicial or legislative) and frequently championed archaic notions that even superficial analysis would have led a lesser judge to abandon. Ellenborough's most notorious insistence on an archaic legal institution was his upholding of a demand for trial by battle in 1818 in *Ashford v. Thornton*[103]—at least two centuries after the last actual trial by battle in England. He was also the judge who first held that there was no action for wrongful death at common law—in *Baker v. Bolton*,[104] decided in 1808—because of the complete lack of precedent for such an action. Ellenborough was simply unconcerned that the lack of precedents resulted from the common law forfeiture of a felon's goods to the crown that in 1808 had only recently been abolished by statute.[105] This unfortunate decision would not be reversed by Parliament for another 40 years, and was followed even later by many states in the United States.[106] Many of his other, lesser known decisions also had to be reversed by statute.[107] Ellenborough was even one of the few champions of the *Statute of Frauds*.[108]

When Edward Law became Lord Ellenborough, he took his place in the House of Lords. He was similarly unprogressive in his parliamentary role as in his judicial role. He successfully opposed the amelioration of the insolvent debtors' laws and the mitigation of the death penalty.[109] Ellenborough even opposed reform of the commission-fee system for judges despite its tendency to corrupt.[110] After initially supporting a statute to ban cruelty to animals, Ellenborough later helped Lord Eldon defeat the bill.[111] The Act that bears his name was the only bill he introduced in 18 years in the House of Lords, and, consistent with the existing law of crimes he was intent on codifying in the act, less than 50 years later it was described as of "revolting severity."[112] In his entire parliamentary career, the only reform that Ellenborough supported was the abolition of the slave trade—at a time when slavery itself was already illegal in England.[113]

---

100. Vineash v. Becker, 3 M. & S. 284 (K.B. 1814). *See* 13 HOLDSWORTH, *supra* note 86, at 508–9.

101. Adams v. Lindsell, 106 ENG. REP. 250 (K.B. 1818). *See* 13 HOLDSWORTH, *supra* note 86, at 511.

102. Hopewell v. de Pinna, 170 ENG. REP. 1096 (K.B. 1810); George v. Jeason, 6 East 80 (K.B. 1805). *See* 9 HOLDSWORTH, *supra* note 86, at 141.

103. 106 ENG. REP. 149 (K.B. 1818). *See* 4 CAMPBELL, *supra* note 96, at 180–81; 13 HOLDSWORTH, *supra* note 86, at 217, 405, 516, 527–28; GEORGE NEILSON, TRIAL BY COMBAT 322–24 (1890).

104. 170 ENG. REP. 1033 (K.B. 1808).

105. *See* 3 HOLDSWORTH, *supra* note 86, at 328–36; 13 HOLDSWORTH, *supra*, at 513.

106. *See* Lord Campbell's Act, 9 & 10 Vict. c. 93. *See generally* W. PAGE KEETON *et al.*, PROSSER AND KEETON ON TORTS § 127 (5th ed. 1984).

107. *See, e.g.*, Priestly v. Hughes, 103 ENG. REP. 903 (K.B. 1809) (bastards cannot marry); Bennett v. Farnell, 170 ENG. REP. 909, 921 (K.B. 1807) (bills payable to a fictitious payee are void); Godsall v. Boldero, 103 ENG. REP. 500 (1807) (a contract of life insurance is a contract of indemnity, *i.e.*, the beneficiary can recover only provable losses arising from the insured's death and not the face value of the policy); Elwes v. Maw, 102 ENG. REP. 510 (K.B. 1803) (agricultural fixtures become property of the landlord, unlike other trade fixtures, because agriculture is not a mere trade). *See generally* 7 HOLDSWORTH, *supra* note 86, at 284–86; 13 HOLDSWORTH, *supra*, at 421–23, 509–10, 514.

108. 4 CAMPBELL, *supra* note 96, at 164–73, 176–77; 6 HOLDSWORTH, *supra* note 86, at 394–96; 13 HOLDSWORTH, *supra*, at 511.

109. 13 HOLDSWORTH, *supra* note 86, at 264–86, 503. On the death penalty, see 17 PARL. DEB. H.L. 200 (1810).

110. 4 CAMPBELL, *supra* note 96, at 164 n.1; 13 HOLDSWORTH, *supra* note 86, at 503.

111. 13 HOLDSWORTH, *supra* note 86, at 266.

112. 4 CAMPBELL, *supra* note 96, at 241–43. *See generally* 1 LEON RADZINOWICZ, A HISTORY OF THE ENGLISH CRIMINAL LAW 258, 506 (1948).

113. 13 HOLDSWORTH, *supra* note 86, at 504. On the status of slavery in England at the beginning of the nineteenth century, see Somerset v. Stewart, 98 ENG. REP. 499 (K.B. 1772); Smith v. Brown & Cooper, 91 ENG.

Doctor Roger Rosenblatt, yet another attempt to reconstruct the history of abortion in order to support abortion rights, described Lord Ellenborough as "a conservative chief justice who was upset at the number of crimes that were no longer capital offenses, [who therefore] created as many capital felonies as he could imagine in his omnibus bill."[114] Rosenblatt's account certainly reflects the severity of *Lord Ellenborough's Act,* yet careful scrutiny of Ellenborough's entire record suggests just the opposite. Ellenborough was conservative in the literal sense. He opposed change simply because it was change. This does not prove that nothing in his Act was new or innovative, but it counsels strongly against a hasty conclusion that any particular point was an innovation. In fact, Lord Ellenborough was so conservative that law professor and medical ethicist John Keown concluded that the small changes in the law relative to abortion and infanticide in section 2 of the Act demonstrate that section 2 must have been authored by other Lords than Ellenborough—although there is in fact no direct evidence to support this conclusion.[115]

Just as Ellenborough's personality leaves little room to suppose that he intended the new statutory provisions on abortion to change the law, the actual provisions on abortion are entirely consistent with the common law as actually applied by the courts[116] even though it went beyond the common law of abortion as then understood by the leading commentators.[117] The first section of Ellenborough's Act, in the midst of a long list of other offenses against persons, provided:

> [I]f any person...shall wilfully, maliciously, and unlawfully administer to, or cause to be administered to or taken by any of his Majesty's subjects, any deadly poison, or other noxious and destructive substance or thing, with intent such his Majesty's subject or subjects to murder, or thereby to cause and procure the miscarrige of any woman then being quick with Child...that then and in every such case the person or persons so offending, their counsellors, aiders, and abettors, knowing of and privy to such offense, shall be and are hereby declared to be felons, and shall suffer death as in cases of felony without benefit of clergy:....[118]

The second section of the Act provided:

> And whereas it may sometimes happen that poison or some other noxious and destructive substance or thing may be given, or other means used, with intent to procure miscarriage or abortion where the woman may not be quick with child at the time, or it may not be proved that she was quick with child, be it therefore further enacted, That if any person or persons,...shall wilfully and maliciously administer to, or cause to be administered to, or taken by any woman, any medicines, drug, or other substance or thing whatsoever, or shall use or employ, or cause or procure to be used or employed, any instrument or other means whatsoever, with Intent thereby to cause or procure the miscarriage of any woman not being, or not being proved to be,

---

Rep. 566, 566 (K.B. 1701); William Wiecek, *The Origins of the Law of Slavery in British North America,* 17 Cardozo L. Rev. 1711, 1716, 1724–25 (1996).

114. Roger Rosenblatt, Life Itself: Abortion in the American Mind 70 (1992).

115. Keown, *supra* note 92, at 19. See the text *infra* at notes 124–42.

116. Rex v. Anonymous, 3 Chitty, *supra* note 45, at 798–801, analyzed *supra* at notes 66–71; Rex v. Tinckler (1781), 1 East, *supra* note 45, at 354–56, quoted *supra* at note 52; Rex v. Beare, 2 The Gentleman's Magazine 931 (Aug. 1732), quoted *supra* at note 28. See also the explanation for the Act provided by the Chief Justice of Common Pleas in *Rex v. Pizzy* (Suffolk Assizes 1808), in Notcutt, *supra* note 64.

117. Anonymous, *supra* note 46, at 348; 1 Blackstone, *supra* note 46, at *129–30 (1765); 4 Blackstone, *supra,* at *198; Burn, *supra* note 45, at 380 (3rd ed. 1756); Coke, *supra* note 21, at 49–50; 1 East, *supra* note 45, at 227–30; Hale, *supra* note 21, at 429–30; 2 Hawkins, *supra* note 46, at 80 (1716); Parker, *supra* note 49, at 216–17.

118. 43 Geo. III ch. 58, § 1 (1803). The elided portions relate to other crimes against the person and to the effective date (July 1, 1803).

quick with child at the time of administering such things or using such means, that then and in every such case the person or persons so offending, the counsellors, aiders, and abettors, knowing of and privy to such offence, shall be and are hereby declared to be guilty of felony, and shall be liable to be fined, imprisoned, set in and upon the Pillory, publickly or privately whipped or to suffer one or more of the said punishments, or to be transported beyond the Seas for any term not exceeding fourteen Years, at the discretion of the court before which such offender shall be tried and convicted.[119]

The two provisions make curious reading together. Section 1 deals with murders and similarly life-threatening crimes, and includes a narrowly defined crime of abortion of a quick child by "poison or other noxious or destructive substance or thing" as a felony without benefit of clergy. "Benefit of clergy" no longer had anything to do with whether a defendant was a clergyman. In 1803, a felony with benefit of clergy would be punished by death only on a second conviction regardless of who committed the crime, the former literacy test once required in order to invoke benefit of clergy having been abolished by Act of Parliament nearly a century before.[120] To withhold the benefit of clergy, then, was to make the crime punishable by death upon the first conviction. The placement of the prohibition of post-quickening abortions in the statute, its link to poisons and the like, and its severe punishment all suggest that the prohibition was meant to protect human life. British historian Angus McLaren has argued that this suggests that the statute was directed at protecting the life of the mother,[121] yet the only life that would be taken by the crime as defined was the unborn child's.[122] But then McLaren also claimed that that the "bill elicited no debate"[123]— which is simply not true. Perhaps McLaren meant that the bill elicited no opposition, which is telling indeed.

Section 2 was added during the Parliamentary debates, and its tenor is entirely different from the first section. Section 2 deals only with abortion, creating a broad crime covering most abortions or attempted abortions,[124] when quickening could not be proved, while providing for comparably mild punishments—if one considers the crime to be homicide. Section 2, however, does not actually address abortion, it addresses attempts to abort. It prohibits the provision "of any thing" or the "use of any means" with the intent to procure a miscarriage. The latter phrase was not limited to the "noxious potions" or "instruments" expressly mentioned in the statute, and eventually was extended to manipulations by hand in an attempt to induce an abortion.[125] Yet, as law professor Glanville Williams noted, in comparison to the penalties for other criminal attempts, the penalties are extraordinarily harsh. Those penalties only became harsher as the two sections in *Lord Ellenborough's Act* were merged in successive recodifications.[126] Ultimately, abortionists, including women guilty of attempting self-abortion, faced life in prison for mere attempts to abort.[127]

---

119. 43 Geo. III ch. 58, § 2 (1803). The formula for the effective date (July 1, 1803) is omitted.

120. 6 Anne, ch. 9 (1706); 4 BLACKSTONE, *supra* note 46 at 370. *See* BAKER, *supra* note 87, at 586–89, 602; 3 HOLDSWORTH, *supra* note 86, at 315; S.F.C. MILSOM, HISTORICAL FOUNDATIONS OF THE COMMON LAW 420–21 (2nd ed. 1981); PLUCKNETT, *supra* note 89, at 440–41, 445–46; MAX RADIN, HANDBOOK OF ANGLO-AMERICAN LEGAL HISTORY 230–31 (1936).

121. MCLAREN, REPRODUCTIVE RITUALS, *supra* note 13, at 136.

122. *See* KEOWN, *supra* note 92, at 20.

123. MCLAREN, REPRODUCTIVE RITUALS, *supra* note 13, at 129. *See also* Gavigan, *supra* note 27, at 30–34; Means II, *supra* note 34, at 358.

124. *See* Rex v. Coe, 6 C. & P. 403 (1834).

125. Rex v. Spicer, [1955] CRIM. L. REP. 772.

126. GLANVILLE WILLIAMS, THE SANCTITY OF LIFE AND THE CRIMINAL LAW 153 (1957).

127. 24 & 25 Vict. ch. 100, §§ 58, 59 (1861).

Law professor and medical ethicist John Keown has so masterfully investigated the legislative history and judicial interpretation of these later abortion provisions that I will not reexamine that history extensively here.[128] One conjecture that Keown makes is not, however, is not clearly established. So different is the second section of *Lord Ellenborough's Act* from the first section that John Keown inferred from the language of the two provisions alone that someone other than Ellenborough had written section 2.[129] Among other points, Keown suggested that if Ellenborough had written the provision he would have made the crime a non-clergiable capital felony. If someone other than Ellenborough had proposed section 2, Ellenborough's concern with abortion was shared, or even surpassed, by others in the House of Lords. In fact, *Lord Ellenborough's Act* was adopted by both houses of Parliament without significant dissent; the only reservations expressed about the Act was about the number of new capital offenses created by the Act.[130] Only after it was enacted did some physicians become critical of the Act as both too stringent in not expressly exempting doctors performing therapeutic abortions and too lenient regarding early abortions, ingestive abortions, and abortion advertising.[131]

Section 2's making of post-quickening abortion a more serious crime than abortions in which quickening could not be proven suggests an intent to protect fetal life as then popularly understood.[132] Indeed, why would pregnancy be an element of the more serious crime at all if the intent was to protect women ingesting (or made to ingest) poisonous, noxious, or destructive substances?[133] A further suggestion that section 2 was intended to prevent interference with human procreation is found in the different sweep of the two sections. Section 1 mentions only "miscarriage" and thus arguably applied only after implantation;[134] section 2 covers both miscarriage and abortion, and hence arguably applied at any point after conception. Yet section 2 made an intrusion abortion a non-capital felony if quickening could not be proven, but apparently left such abortions as no crime at all upon quickening.[135] A report to Parliament in 1819 even referred to Ellenborough's "injudicious framing" whereby "that which ought to be the more serious offence, should be more imperfectly provided for than the less serious offence"[136] — precisely the same comment Ellenborough himself had made in advancing other parts of the bill.[137] Still 14 years transportation cannot have been much of an advantage over the death penalty.[138]

Read together, the two sections can fairly be described as "a rather clumsy exercise."[139] The anomalies created by the two sections offer some corroboration of the diverse authorship the-

---

128. KEOWN, *supra* note 92, at 26–83.

129. *Id.* at 19.

130. *Id.* at 17, 19; Gavigan, *supra* note 27, at 32. Keown and Gavigan cite to articles in the *Times of London* as sources for the few adverse comments.

131. McLAREN, REPRODUCTIVE RITUALS, *supra* note 13, at 137–38.

132. GRISEZ, *supra* note 212, at 380–81; KEOWN, *supra* note 92, at 20; MASON, *supra* note 77, at 101; WILLIAMS, *supra* note 126, at 227–29; Noonan, *supra* note 216, at 226. Some see the emphasis on quickening as an evidentiary rule, rather than as expressing a judgment that a fetus was not a human being before quickening. *See* Dellapenna, *supra* note 17, at 377–79; Clarke Forsythe, *Human Cloning and the Constitution,* 32 VAL. U. L. REV. 469, 488–91 (1998).

133. *See* Rex v. Scudder, 168 ENG. REP. 1246 (1829) (no crime even under § 2 if it definitely appears that the woman was not pregnant). *See also* HENRY ROSCOE, DIGEST OF THE LAW OF EVIDENCE IN CRIMINAL CASES 192–93 (1835).

134. Andrew Grubb, *Abortion Law—An English Perspective,* 20 N. MEX. L. REV. 649, 653–54 (1990).

135. KEOWN, *supra* note 92, at 18; ROSCOE, *supra* note 133, at 191–92.

136. 1 REPORT FROM THE SELECT COMMITTEE ON CRIMINAL LAW RELATING TO CAPITAL PUNISHMENT IN FELONIES, WITH MINUTES OF EVIDENCE 43 (1819).

137. Quoted *supra* at note 92.

138. A point made in MASON, *supra* note 77, at 100.

139. PETERSEN, *supra* note 13, at 20.

ory. If section 2 did not reach post-quickening intrusive abortions, all a woman need do to protect her abortionist if instruments had been used was to testify that the child had quickened.[140] Not only would this anomalous provision not protect fetal life, by not discouraging intrusive abortions it would also not protect the mother's life if that were the goal. A sensible judge rather quickly resolved this anomaly by ruling that quickening was immaterial under section 2.[141] The correction of the statutory language in this respect was the only change made when the prohibition of abortion was included in the *Offences against the Person Act* of 1828.[142]

A similar apparent anomaly existed relative to ingestive abortions under the two sections. The crime in section 1 required that the substance ingested be "noxious," apparently independently of whether it might induce an abortion, and thus would be materially narrower than the prohibition of the ingestion of any "medicine" to attempt an abortion where quickening could not be proved.[143] Again, the same judge ruled otherwise in the same case, holding that section 1 reached any ingestive abortion.[144]

Curiously, neither section made it a crime to kill a child in the process of being born—after emergence from the womb, but before the cutting of the umbilical cord. By 1828, it was clear that any abortion before birth was well along was a felony and killing an infant after its completed birth was murder, yet Parliament did not deal with the non-criminality of a killing during the birthing process for more than a century. Finally, with the adoption of the *Infant Life (Preservation) Act* in 1929, Parliament made the killing of an infant in the process of being born a felony.[145] No one seems to have considered this lacuna to have been anything more than a drafting oversight, although the 1929 statute overlapped the earlier statutes because it covered all killings of infants "capable of being born alive" before the child's birth. The overlap was important because, for the first time, the *Infant Life (Preservation) Act* expressly provided a therapeutic exception permitting abortions if necessary to preserve the life of the mother. Despite continuing criticism by the medical professions, Parliament apparently only seriously considered enacting a therapeutic once before 1929, rejecting the proposal when it reenacted the abortion sections in yet another *Offences against the Person Act*. Apparently, Parliament rejected a proposed therapeutic exception in 1861 simply because "in 1861, it would have been ridiculous to call [abortion] therapy."[146]

Lord Ellenborough, moreover, did not include all offenses against persons in his Act despite its popular name as the "*Offences against the Person Act*" and even though the parliamentary history of *Lord Ellenborough's Act* described it as having "for its object to generalize the law regarding certain penal offences and to adapt it equally to every part of the United Kingdom."[147] For example, neither murder nor manslaughter was included in the *Offences against the Person Act* until its next codification in 1828 (*Lord Landsdowne's Act*).[148] In undertaking the 1828 codification, Parliament found it necessary to repeal 57 statutes ranging in date from 1224 to 1762. This

---

140. Roscoe, *supra* note 133, at 192.

141. Rex v. Phillips, 170 Eng. Rep. 1310 (N.P. 1811). *See also* Roscoe, *supra* note 133, at 192.

142. 9 Geo. IV ch. 31, § 13 (1828).

143. Roscoe, *supra* note 133, at 191–92.

144. Rex v. Phillips, 170 Eng. Rep. 1310 (N.P. 1811). *See also* Rex v. Coe, 6 C. & P. 403 (1834) (construing Lord Landsdowne's Act—the Offences against the Person Act of 1828—to reach any attempted abortion even by ineffective means).

145. 19 & 20 Geo. V ch. 34 (1929). *See generally* J. Keown, *The Scope of the Offence of Child Destruction*, 104 Law Q. Rev. 120 (1988).

146. Williams, *supra* note 126, at 160.

147. 11 Parliamentary Register 390 (William Woodfall ed. 1803).

148. 9 Geo. IV ch. 31 (1828).

fact raises the question of why Ellenborough chose to include any abortions, let alone the particular abortions he did include.

Despite Ellenborough's extreme conservatism, he was not entirely out of touch with what was happening in England during his lifetime. He himself spoke in the preamble to his Act of his reasons for including abortion, referring to the changing incidence of abortion resulting from the introduction of intrusive techniques. After describing the law of mayhems and assaults as ineffectual, the Act went on to state that "certain other heinous Offences committed…with Intent to procure the Miscarriage of Women…have been of late also frequently committed, but no adequate Means have been hitherto provided for the Prevention and Punishment of such Offences;…"[149] This perception was widely shared by legal and medical authors of the time despite the lack of any precise statistical basis for the impression.[150] Indeed, historian Lawrence Stone noted the appearance in eighteenth-century London of what he termed "abortionist surgeons" and "abortion chemists shops," although, of course, they did not give themselves any such names.[151] In fact, there is reason to believe that abortion did not become much more common than during earlier centuries until later in the nineteenth century.[152] At the least, abortion certainly was becoming more visible and this probably reflected at least some small degree of greater frequency.

Lord Ellenborough also adverted to his specific reasons for including a provision on abortions in which quickening could not be proven. He sought to prevent the "administering [of] poisonous drugs to women for the purpose, and with the intent, of procuring abortion, which, at present, is only punishable where actual abortion of the living child is effected."[153] Presumably the same reasoning applied to intrusion abortions that were included in the same section of the Act. *Lord Ellenborough's Act* relieved the prosecution of the burden of proving that the child actually was alive at the time of the attempt and that the attempted abortion actually caused the miscarriage.[154] The Act did not go far enough if its purpose was to protect the mother as the section was interpreted as inapplicable if it were proved that the mother was not pregnant at all.[155] The prohibited actions were, however, just as dangerous for the mother if she were not pregnant as they were if she were pregnant. The section makes perfect sense as interpreted if its purpose was to protect fetal life.

Sections 3 and 4 of *Lord Ellenborough's Act* also changed the law of infanticide. These sections repealed the statutory presumption of murder from a mother's concealment of the birth of a bastard in order to conceal the child's death.[156] A House of Commons committee recommended repeal as early as 1771, without success.[157] But *Lord Ellenborough's Act* did not simply

---

149. 43 Geo. III ch. 58, *preamble* (1803).

150. *See, e.g.,* Alexander Burnett, The Medical Advertiser 293 (1824); John Burns, The Anatomy of the Gravid Uterus 58 (1799); Samuel Farr, Elements of Medical Jurisprudence 71 (1788); Archer Ryland, Crown Circuit Companion 64 (10th ed. 1836). *See also* Brissot de Warville, *supra* note 82, at 108. *See generally* Keown, *supra* note 92, at 21–22; McLaren, Reproductive Rituals, *supra* note 13, at 32.

151. Lawrence Stone, The Road to Divorce: England, 1530–1987, at 423 (1990).

152. Potts, Diggory, & Peel, *supra* note 11, at 282.

153. 36 Parl. Hist. 1246 (1803).

154. Keown, *supra* note 92, at 16, 18–19. *See also* Notcutt, *supra* note 64, at 245.

155. Rex v. Scudder, 168 Eng. Rep. 1246 (1829). *See also* Roscoe, *supra* note 133, at 192–93; The Trial of Charles Angus, Esq., on an Indictment for the Wilful Murder of Margaret Burns (1808); McLaren, Reproductive Rituals, *supra* note 13, at 141; T.R. Forbes, *Early Forensic Medicine in England: The Angus Murder Trial,* 36 J. Hist. Med. 296 (1981). In later years, some courts in the United States would treat an abortion performed on a woman who was not pregnant as a criminal attempt rather than as the crime of abortion. *See, e.g.,* People v. Cummings, 296 P.2d 610 (Cal. 1956). *See generally* Arnold Enker, *Impossibility in Criminal Attempts: Legality and the Legal Process,* 53 Minn. L. Rev. 665 (1969); Jeffrey Ghert, Annot., *Impossibility of Consummation of Substantive Crime as Defense in Criminal Prosecution for Conspiracy or Attempt to Commit Crime,* 37 A.L.R.3d 375 (1971).

156. 43 Geo. III ch. 58, § 3 (1803).

157. 1 Radzinowicz, *supra* note 111, at 432–33.

repeal the presumption, however; it made concealment a misdemeanor punishable by imprisonment for up to two years.[158] The Act itself explained that the change was made not to ameliorate the law but to make convictions easier to obtain in face of juries unwilling to convict a woman of murder in such circumstances.[159] Lord Ellenborough's speech to this effect in the House of Lords was also reported in the press.[160] Yet convictions became rarer than ever.[161]

With conviction rates for all crimes in eighteenth century England plummeting sharply,[162] the rarity of convictions under the older concealment statute was not all that unusual. The change in the law regarding the concealment of the death of a bastard suggests some change in the social attitudes towards concealment, a belief that infanticide was becoming less of a social problem at the same time as the number of abortions was increasing.[163] Historian Angus McLaren chooses to see the new concealment law as having been forced on Ellenborough against his will[164]—a claim for which there is no evidence unless one reads such a motive into Ellenborough's professed goal of making convictions for concealment easier. McLaren went on to argue from this conclusion that Ellenborough introduced the provisions on abortion because of his chagrin over having to relax the law on infanticide. This remarkable argument ignores both the legal context (the Act codified certain crimes against persons) and the social and political context in which *Lord Ellenborough's Act* was approved. Even were McLaren's wholly unsubstantiated claim regarding Ellenborough's motives valid, it would not explain why a unanimous House of Lords and the House of Commons as well would vote to approve the bill if no one really opposed abortion.

Perhaps the industrial revolution and other general social changes drove an increase in abortion or infanticide, yet an upsurge in abortion rather than infanticide had to await the perfection of the technical means for performing abortions with acceptable risk to mothers. The decline in the importance of infanticide as abortion came to be more available is perhaps best shown by the fact that, in 1849, Rebecca Smith became the last woman executed in England for infanticide.[165] It appears then that certain abortions were included in *Lord Ellenborough's Act* to reaffirm the existing law in the face of changing social practices respecting abortion and infanticide—just as one would expect from one of Ellenborough's ilk. Law professor and medical ethicist John Keown, in his careful analysis of the legislative history of Ellenborough's Act, reached similar conclusions.[166] Keown also concluded that individual medical practitioners, as they came to recognize fetal life as human life irrespective of quickening, influenced the values embodied in the Act.[167]

Historian Angus McLaren saw in all this a conspiracy by physicians to take the abortion decision away from mothers (who alone could determine whether quickening had occurred) and confer it on themselves (the priests of the new knowledge of gestation).[168] He went so far as to argue that the physicians' concern was for "medical etiquette," that is the obligation of doctors to

---

158. 43 Geo. III ch. 58, § 4.

159. *Id.* § 3. *See also* 11 PARLIAMENTARY REGISTER, *supra* note 147, at 390.

160. TIMES OF LONDON, No. 5672, Mar. 29, 1803. *See also* KEOWN, *supra* note 92, at 16–17.

161. D. Searborne Davies, *Child-Killing in English Law,* 1 MODERN L. REV. 203, 216–23 (1937).

162. J.A. SHARPE, CRIME IN SEVENTEENTH CENTURY ENGLAND: A COUNTY STUDY 134 (1983); Stephen Palmer, *Book Review,* 37 AM. J. LEGAL HIST. 499, 499–500 (1993). *See* Chapter 2, at notes 336–62.

163. Dellapenna, *supra* note 17, at 398.

164. MCLAREN, REPRODUCTIVE RITUALS, *supra* note 13, at 136.

165. PETER HOFFER & N.E.H. HULL, MURDERING MOTHERS: INFANTICIDE IN ENGLAND AND NEW ENGLAND 1558–1803, at 87 (1981); MCLAREN, REPRODUCTIVE RITUALS, *supra* note 13, at 193–94, n.80.

166. KEOWN, *supra* note 92, at 12–22.

167. *Id.* at 22–25.

168. MCLAREN, REPRODUCTIVE RITUALS, *supra* note 13, at 138–43. For similar arguments regarding American physicians, see MOHR, *supra* note 13; Siegel, *supra* note 34. *See* Chapter 6, at notes 213–331.

consult other doctors before doing an abortion (or a Caesarean) to assure collegial (professional) control.[169] He dismissed the physicians' expressed concerns about fetal life as inconsistent with the physicians' support for therapeutic abortions—completely overlooking that therapeutic abortions were then thought proper only in order to save the mother's life.[170]

Organized medical societies could not have been involved in the enactment of *Lord Ellenborough's Act* (or its earliest counterparts in the United States) as no such organizations then existed either in England or in America.[171] The British Parliament created a General Medical Council in 1858, consolidating all formally recognized branches of the profession under its authority, and giving the Council authority over medical education, medical qualifications, and medical discipline.[172] Similar professional authority was not achieved in the United States for another half century.[173] Furthermore, individual English physicians began to criticize *Lord Ellenborough's Act* almost immediately—because its anomalous second section did not adequately protect fetal life before quickening.[174] Indeed, noted American physician and teacher Dr. T. Romeyn Beck described *Lord Ellenborough's Act* this harsh language: "They tempt to the perpetuation of the same crime at one time which at another they punish with death."[175] Other doctors were even more critical, describing the distinction as "arbitrary and absurd,"[176] or "extremely defective."[177]

Given the medical criticisms, one need not wonder why Parliament returned to the question of abortion repeatedly in the nineteenth century, although each time in the context of enacting an increasingly more comprehensive "*Offences against the Person Acts.*" Parliament enacted *Offences against the Person Acts* (as the statutes were officially styled after 1837) in 1828,[178] 1837,[179] and 1861.[180] Each later version included new provisions relating to abortion that gradually removed the various technical restrictions on the crime of abortion that had been introduced by the somewhat confused language of *Lord Ellenborough's Act*,[181] culminating in the Act of 1861 that made all abortions by any means for virtually any purpose clearly criminal.[182] Along the way, Parliament dropped the reference to "miscarriage and abortion" found in section 2 of Ellenborough's Act, using only "miscarriage." Arguably, as a result of this change, devices that prevented implantation of a conceptus were not prohibited but only steps to interfere after implan-

---

169. McLaren, Reproductive Rituals, *supra* note 13, at 142. *See also* Ivan Waddington, *The Development of Medical Ethics: A Sociological Analysis*, 19 Med. Hist. 38 (1975).

170. McLaren, Reproductive Rituals, *supra* note 13, at 142–44.

171. Keown, *supra* note 92, at 22.

172. Petersen, *supra* note 13, at 30–31.

173. Paul Starr, The Social Transformation of American Medicine: The Rise of a Sovereign Profession and the Making of a Vast Industry 78 (1982).

174. *See generally* McLaren, Reproductive Rituals, *supra* note 13, at 138–40.

175. T.R. Beck & W. Dunlop, Elements of Medical Jurisprudence 140 (1825).

176. Charles Severn, First Lines of the Practice of Midwifery 134 (1831).

177. Michael Ryan, A Manual of Midwifery 205 (1831).

178. *Lord Landsdowne's Act*, 9 Geo. IV ch. 31, § 13 (1828).

179. *Offences against the Person Act*, 7 Will. & 1 Vict. ch. 85, § 6 (1837).

180. *Offences against the Person Act*, 24 & 25 Vict. ch. 100, §§ 58, 59 (1861).

181. *See, e.g.,* Regina v. Fretwell, 9 Cox Crim. Cases 152 (Ct. Crim. App. 1862) (one who provides poison to a woman to induce an abortion resulting in the woman's death cannot be prosecuted as an accessory before the fact when she took the poison out of his presence); Regina v. Wright, 173 Eng. Rep. 1039 (1841) (no one can be prosecuted as an accessory to concealment); Rex v. Russell, 168 Eng. Rep. 1302 (K.B. 1832) (same as *Fretwell*); Rex v. Scudder, 168 Eng. Rep. 1246 Kent Assizes 1829 (no crime under *Lord Ellenborough's Act* if the woman was not pregnant); Rex v. Anonymous, 170 Eng. Rep. 1310 (N.P. 1811) (no need to prove the potion was itself noxious if it was administered with the intent to procure an abortion). *See generally* McLaren, Reproductive Rituals, *supra* note 13, at 142–43.

182. For a brief summary of the legislative changes between 1803 and 1861, see Petersen, *supra* note 13, at 19–21.

tation when, so this argument goes, the woman could be said to be "carrying" the fetus.[183] On the other hand, manipulation of the abdomen by hand in an attempt to induce abortion was covered by the later enactments.[184]

The 1828 Act eliminated the apparent anomaly in *Ellenborough's Act* regarding intrusion abortions. The 1837 Act eliminated all reference to quickening, making "unlawful" abortion at any stage of pregnancy and attempted abortion even without pregnancy a felony punishable by imprisonment for up to three years or by transportation "beyond the sea" for from 15 years to life.[185] Finally, the term "unlawful"—which had never been defined in any of these statutes—disappeared from the 1861 act, only to be revived by implication into the 1861 Act in the decision in *Rex v. Bourne*.[186] The judge in *Bourne* concluded that the statute made abortion a crime only if the abortion were either performed by someone other than a physician, or, if by a physician, without a good faith belief that the abortion was necessary to preserve the mother's life or health. This meaning was derived from the *Infant Life (Preservation) Act* of 1929, although that Act made "child destruction" justifiable only to preserve the life of the mother.[187] The 1861 Act also expressly made a woman culpable for attempted self-abortion if she were pregnant, and changed the punishment for the abortionist to imprisonment for any term of years up to life[188] and added a misdemeanor punishable by imprisonment up to five years for providing a drug or instrument knowing that it would be used for an abortion.[189] The only restriction on the criminality of abortion to survive the 1861 Act was that a woman could not be prosecuted for self-abortion if she was not pregnant, another distinction that made sense only if the purpose of the statute was to protect fetal life. Women were prosecuted thereafter, up to a dozen per year in the later years of the nineteenth century.[190] While women were seldom convicted for self-abortion,[191] they were convicted for conspiracy to abort or for aiding and abetting an attempted abortion for their own attempted abortion undertaken by another abortionist without proof of pregnancy.[192]

The English statutes found ready acceptance throughout the British Empire. Thus, New Brunswick enacted a statute derived from *Lord Elleborough's Act* as early in 1810, followed by Prince Edward Island in 1836.[193] Shortly thereafter, future Canadian provinces began enacting versions of the 1837 English statute that dropped the quickening requirement of *Lord Ellenborough's Act*. The first to do so was Newfoundland in 1837, followed by Upper Canada in 1841, and New Brunswick in 1842.[194] New Brunswick went on the criminalize self-abortion in 1849, followed by Nova Scotia in 1851.[195] These various enactments were consolidated and made nationally uniform by the enactment of the New Brunswick law by the Canadian Parliament in 1869.[196]

---

183. Grubb, *supra* note 134, at 653–54.

184. Rex v. Spicer, [1955] Crim. L. Rep. 772.

185. Regina v. Goodhall, 169 Eng. Rep. 205 (1846) (conviction upheld despite a failure to prove pregnancy).

186. [1939] 1 K.B. 687.

187. 19 & 20 Geo. V ch. 34, § 1 (1929).

188. 24 & 25 Vict. ch. 100, § 58 (1861).

189. *Id.* § 59.

190. Lucia Zedner, Women, Crime, and Custody in Victorian England 39 (1991).

191. *But see* Rex v. Peake, 97 J.P. 353 (1932). *See also* Williams, *supra* note 126, at 153–55.

192. Regina v. Whitchurch, 24 Q.B.D. 420 (1890) (conspiracy); Rex v. Scokett, 72 J.P. 428 (1908) (aiding and abetting). *See also* People v. Cummings, 296 P.2d 610 (Cal. 1956).

193. Caroline Morris, *Technology and the Legal Discourse of Fetal Autonomy*, 8 UCLA Women's L.J. 47, 73 n.113 (1997).

194. *Id.*

195. *Id.*

196. *Id.*

# The Policy Foundations of
# the English Abortion Statutes

*No normal human being ever wants to hear the truth. It is the passion of a small and aberrant minority..., most of whom are pathological.*

—H.L. Mencken[197]

The evolution of the English abortion statutes during the nineteenth century suggests that English abortion policy was primarily directed at the protection of fetal life. Law professor and medical ethicist John Keown reached the same conclusion in his masterful study of the legislative history of the statutes and of the physicians attitudes towards the statutes.[198] Keown accepted the claim that physicians were interested in using abortion laws to consolidate their status as a profession, and argument we shall examine in more detail regarding the evolution of the nineteenth century American statutes on abortion.[199] Keown, however, did not conclude that this meant the expressions of concern about fetal life were insincere or irrelevant.[200] An historian committed to defending abortion rights concluded that the greater organizational success of the English medical profession compared to the American profession made it unnecessary to use abortion as a tool for gaining control of the practice of medicine and that therefore the English statutes cannot be cast in this light.[201] In fact, nothing in the history of the several acts adopted in England in the nineteenth century suggests any policy basis other than the protection of fetal life. Even the substitution of harsh prison terms for the death penalty was not an abandonment of that policy—experience had shown that juries were increasingly reluctant to convict abortionists if the penalty were death.[202] (The increasing reluctance of juries to convict extended to all capital crimes, and was not a phenomenon limited to abortion.)[203] Nor can these statutes be attributed to some English form of Comstockery—the urge to use the police to regulate individual morality did not take hold in England until after 1870,[204] after the evolution of English abortion statutes was complete.

Modern commentators have concluded that *Lord Ellenborough's Act* and the later English enactments were designed in part to protect the mother from a dangerous procedure.[205] To reach this conclusion, they ignore the legislative history of the Acts and what English courts said of the Acts in construing it. Even if protection of the mother were a goal of these Acts, the 1861 revision makes it clear that the protection of fetal life by itself was a sufficient justification for the law. The provision making a woman guilty of the crime of self-abortion only if she is pregnant can only be justified analytically by a policy of protecting fetal life.[206] If the purpose were the paternalistic protection of maternal life from foolhardy risks, why not prohibit attempted abortion

---

197. As quoted in Arnold Ludwig, The Importance of Lying 18 (1965).
198. Keown, *supra* note 92, at 27–48.
199. *See* Chapter 6, at notes 213–331.
200. Keown, *supra* note 92, at 39–47.
201. *See* Petersen, *supra* note 13, at 36.
202. Keown, *supra* note 92, at 29–30.
203. Sharpe, *supra* note 152, at 134; Palmer, *supra* note 162, at 499–500. *See* Chapter 2, at notes 397–411
204. V.A.C. Gastrell, *Crime, Authority, and the Policeman-State*, in 3 The Cambridge Social History of Britain 1750–1950, at 289 (F.M.I. Thompson ed. 1990); Stefan Petrow, *The Legal Enforcement of Morality in Late-Victorian England*, 11 U. Tasmania L. Rev. 60 (1992).
205. Grubb, *supra* note 134, at 654; Means II, *supra* note 34, at 358.
206. Grubb, *supra* note 134, at 654.

when the woman was not pregnant, as was the law if a pregnant woman resorted to an abortionist rather than attempting to abort herself? The 1861 law apparently accepted the right of women to risk their own lives, which they could do without endangering another when she was not pregnant; when pregnant, however, her attempt put another life at risk.

The concern to protect fetal life, of course, had been expressed in even the earliest abortion prosecutions from the thirteenth century.[207] Yet there appeared to be some reticence about protecting fetal life in the earlier stages of gestation when English legal commentators came to speak in terms of criminality only after quickening.[208] If so, the nineteenth-century English abortion statutes expressed a newly enhanced concern for fetal life. The material basis for such an enhanced concern about fetal life is not hard to find.

A profound change occurred in our understanding of human gestation concurrently with the upsurge in abortion as a practice. Scientific theories that a distinct human being began at conception can be traced back at least to the sixteenth century. Scientists by then had engaged in strident debate over the nature of human (and other) gestation for centuries.[209] One school advanced the theory of epigenesis (that the parts of an embryo develop by gradual diversification from an initially undifferentiated source). Other schools advanced various theories of preformation (that an embryo was fully preformed in either the paternal or the maternal seed, development being purely a process of nutritionally driven growth).[210] Among the contending theories of preformation were pangenesis, panspermatism, and the "box theory." Supporters of pangenesis held that the gonads assembled cells from all parts of a parent's body to make a new miniature body. Supporters of panspermatism supposed that the "seeds of life" floated in the air, settling in the womb after coition. The box theory contended that all persons were packed, as if in boxes, inside a parental seed, boxes inside boxes all the way back to Adam and Eve. Mingled with this debate was a long-standing dispute about the possibility of spontaneous generation.[211] While everyone knew that sexual intercourse was central to human reproduction, each of these theories left considerable doubt about just what function intercourse played in the gestational process.

In the face of such doubt, one prevalent popular theory that continued well into the nineteenth century that human personhood began with "quickening."[212] "Quickening" refers to the

---

207. *See* Chapter 3, at notes 72–125.

208. *See* Chapter 4, and *supra*, at notes 37–54.

209. M. Anthony Hewson, Giles of Rome and the Medieval Theory of Conception (1975); Danielle Jacquart & Claude Thomasset, *Sexualité et savoir médical au moyen âge* 84–120 (1985); McLaren, Reproductive Rituals, *supra* note 13, at 16–19, 21–26; Arthur Meyer, The Rise of Embryology 54–97 (1939); Joseph Needham, A History of Embryology 213–25 (1959); John Riddle, Contraception and Abortion from the Ancient World to the Renaissance 141–42 (1992); Anthony Preus, *Science and Philosophy in Aristotle's Generation of Animals,* 3 J. Hist. of Biology 1 (1970); Anthony Preus, *Galen's Criticisms of Aristotle's Conception Theory,* 10 J. Hist. of Biology 65 (1977).

210. On the two theories, see 2 Howard Adelman, Marcello Malpighi and the Evolution of Embryology 733–77 (1966); Thomas Laqueur, Making Sex: Body and Gender from the Greeks to Freud 57–59 (1990); McLaren, Reproductive Rituals, *supra* note 13, at 22–26; Meyer, *supra* note 209, at 54–61; Needham, *supra* note 209, at 115–229; Sherwin Nuland, The Mysteries within: A Surgeon Reflects on Medical Myths 232–49 (2000); Clara Pinto-Correia, The Ovary of Eve: Egg and Sperm and Preformation (1997); Jacques Roger, *Les sciences de la vie dans le pensée française du XVIIIe siècle* (1963); Peter Bowler, *Preformation and Pre-Existence in the Seventeenth Century,* 4 J. Hist. of Biology 221 (1971); Michael Hoffheimer, *Maupertuis and the Eighteenth-Century Critique of Pre-Existence,* 15 J. Hist. of Biology 119 (1982).

211. Meyer, *supra* note 209, at 28–53, 92–97; Needham, *supra* note 209, at 206–13; Nuland, *supra* note 210, at 241–42, 247–48.

212. *See* Pierre Bayle, *Dictionnaire historique et critique* 452 (1820); Daniel Defoe, Conjugal Lewdness: or Matrimonial Whoredom, A Treatise Concerning the Use and Abuse of the Marriage Bed 152 (1727); Buel Eastman, Practical Treatise on Diseases Peculiar to Women and Girls: To

felt movement of the unborn child perceived as such by the mother.[213] Yet during the Middle Ages, the phrase "quick with child" was used to indicate a living child regardless of whether the mother had felt it quicken.[214] By the middle of the eighteenth century, some physicians and theologians began to argue that a new human life began at conception.[215] Such ideas were popularized by the spreading cult of the "Immaculate Conception," a doctrine implying that Mary was alive from the moment of conception.[216] The doctrine of the Immaculate Conception, however, did not become dogma in the Catholic Church until 1854—after the scientific discovery of how conception occurred.[217] A strain of early Christian theology—"traducianism"—held that ensoulment (and hence life) began at conception, although that does not appear to have been the dominant view among Catholic theologians until the nineteenth century.[218] Many Protestants embraced a similar view during the Reformation, led by Calvin and Luther, although other Protestants did not say very much about abortion until the nineteenth century.[219] These debates could hardly be resolved with the small achievements produced by the considerable experimentation on human gestation beginning in the seventeenth century.

Anton van Leeuwenhoek had observed spermatozoa as early as 1674,[220] but a century and a half later no one had yet actually found a mammalian ovum.[221] This failure led some scientists to conclude that the father generated the embryo and the mother merely provided a home for it.[222] Perhaps the most prominent physician who took this view was Sir William Harvey, the first physician to describe with reasonable accuracy the human circulatory system. Harvey's failure to find spermatozoa under his microscope drove him, in 1651, back to the theory of panspermatism.[223] Others strongly believed in the existence of ova, although ova had not been observed,

---

Which Is Added an Eclectic System of Midwifery;…Particulary Adapted to the Use of Heads of Families and Midwives 25–28, 83–84, 171–73, 193–221 (3rd ed. 1848); Journal of the Senate of the State of Ohio…, 1867, *App.*, at 233–35 (1867); John Todd, Serpents in the Doves' Nest 6–14 (1867); Homer Hitchcock, *Report on Criminal Abortion,* Fourth Ann. Rep. of the Sec'y of State Bd. of Health of the State of Michigan 60–61 (1876). *See generally* Germain Grisez, Abortion: The Myths, the Realities, and the Arguments 130–55 (1970); Roger Huser, The Crime of Abortion in Canon Law 16–36 (1942); H.M.I. Liley, Modern Motherhood 37–38 (rev. ed. 1969); McLaren, Reproductive Rituals, *supra* note 13, at 107–11; Mohr, *supra* note 13, at 3–6, 65, 73–74, 117, 189, 207.

213. Black's Law Dictionary 1122 (5th rev. ed. 1979); David Buss, The Evolution of Desire: Strategies of Human Mating 119 (1994).

214. *See* Chapter 3, at notes 95–107.

215. *See, e.g.,* K. Cangiamila, Abrégé de l'embryologie sacrée 11–12 (1745); M. Des-Essartz, Traité de l'education corporelle 18 (1760).

216. McLaren, Reproductive Rituals, *supra* note 13, at 117–18; John Noonan, jr., *An Almost Absolute Value in History,* in The Morality of Abortion: Legal and Historical Perspectives 1, 27 (John Noonan, jr., ed. 1970). *But see* Michael Coughlan, The Vatican, the Law and the Human Embryo 86–88 (1990) (arguing that Catholics should have considered Mary—in this respect as in so many others—the exception rather than the rule); Ronald Dworkin, Life's Dominion: An Argument about Abortion, Euthenasia, and Individual Freedom 45 (1993) (adopting Coughlan's argument).

217. Noonan, *supra* note 216, at 34.

218. *See* Harrison, *supra* note 13, at 134–44.

219. *Id.* at 144–51.

220. Meyer, *supra* note 209, at 138–47; Needham, *supra* note 209, at 175; Nuland, *supra* note 210, at 244–45.

221. Meyer, *supra* note 209, at 98–120.

222. *See, e.g.,* George Garden, *A Discourse Concerning the Modern Theory of Generation,* 196 Philos. Trans. of the Royal Soc'y 474 (1691). *See generally* Nuland, *supra* note 210, at 243–45; Reay Tannahill, Sex in History 341–42 (1980).

223. The Works of William Harvey 362 (Robert Willis trans. 1965). *See generally* Nuland, *supra* note 210, at 242–43.

because the "Graafian follicles" (which produce ova in the ovaries) had been described by Renier de Graaf before 1672.[224]

Discoveries early in the nineteenth century led to a new consensus among scientists on the nature of human gestation.[225] Some thinkers had already begun to apply the cell theory to embryology, beginning the triumph of a modern version of epigenesis.[226] In 1824, Jean Louis Prevost and Jean-Baptiste-André Dumas succeeded in fertilizing frogs' eggs and recognized what they had done.[227] (Lazaro Spallanzini had already achieved the fertilization of frogs' eggs, but he did not recognize it because of his preformationist convictions.)[228] Prevost and Dumas might even have isolated mammalian ova at this time, although they did not achieve recognition for this feat.[229] Karl Ernst von Baer accidentally discovered ova in dogs three years later.[230] Scientists apparently gave slight notice given to even earlier claims (dating at least as far back as 1778) to have observed the human ovum.[231]

Even after these discoveries, much work remained to be done. In particular, it was not until 1838 that Theodor Ludwig Wilhem von Bischoff actually demonstrated mammalian fertilization.[232] No wonder Dr. Alexander Draper, writing in 1839 on abortion, could state that he could only speculate on the topic of conception as he knew next to nothing about it.[233] The principles of genetics, among many other questions, also remained to be worked out. The first actual observation of a human sperm penetrating a human ovum was not until 1879 when Hermann Fol did so, while Edouard van Beneden and August Weismann independently discovered the process of mitosis in ova and sperm (the splitting of the chromosomes to leave each germ cell with only one-half of the normal complement) in 1887.[234] It is no wonder then that some conservative

---

224. *See, e.g.,* John Case, The Angelical Guide 53 (1697); Joseph Blondel, The Strength of Imagination in Pregnant Women Examan'd 42 (1727); Alexander Hamilton, A Treatise on Midwifery 40 (1781). *See generally* Elizabeth Gasking, Investigations into Generation, 1651–1828 (1967); Charles Bodemer, *Embryological Thought in Seventeenth Century England,* in Medical Investigations in Seventeenth Century England 1 (Lester King ed. 1968). Historian Reay Tannahill wrongly took this to indicate that de Graaf had observed ova. Tannahill, *supra* note 222, at 344–45.

225. *See generally* 3 A History of Science 456–69, 480–83 (René Taton ed. 1965); C.D. Darlington, Genetics and Man 31–44, 66 (1964).

226. *See, e.g.,* O.W. Bartley, A Treatise on Forensic Medicine 5 (1815); Beck & Dunlop, *supra* note 172, at 138; Burns, *supra* note 150, at 84; George Edward Male, An Epitome of Judicial or Forensic Medicine 206 (1816); John Gordon Smith, The Principles of Forensic Medicine 294 (1821). *See generally* Kristin Luker, Abortion and the Politics of Motherhood 23–25 (1984); Meyer, *supra* note 209, at 302–19; Needham, *supra* note 209, at 223–39.

227. 3 A History of Science, *supra* note 225, at 461.

228. Meyer, *supra* note 209, at 170–81; Nuland, *supra* note 210, at 247–49.

229. Meyer, *supra* note 209, at 120–21. Historian Reay Tannahill has the basic facts right, but provides a date that is off by 30 years (1854). Tannahill, *supra* note 222, at 345.

230. Karl Ernst von Baer, *De Ovi Mammalium et Hominis Genesi* (1827). *See* 3 A History of Science, *supra* note 225, at 460–61; C.D. Haagenson & Wyntham Lloyd, A Hundred Years of Medicine 299 (1943); Meyer, *supra* note 209, at 120–31.

231. Needham, *supra* note 209, at 217.

232. 3 A History of Science, *supra* note 225, at 461; Meyer, *supra* note 209, at 184–90. *See generally* 3 A History of Science, *supra,* at 461–64; Haagenson & Lloyd, *supra* note 230, at 299; Meyer, *supra,* at 182–94, 319–41.

233. Alexander Draper, Observations on Abortion: With an Account of the Means Both Medicinal and Mechanical, Employed to Produce that Effect 110 (1839). *See also* Walter Coles, *Abortion—Its Causes and Treatment,* 1875 St. L. Med. & Surgical J. 252, 253; J.M. Toner, *Abortion in Its Medical and Moral Aspects,* 5 Med. & Surgical Rptr. 443, 443–44 (1861).

234. Stephen Kern, Anatomy and Destiny: A Cultural History of the Human Body 126 (1975). Oskar Hertwig had successfully observed a sea urchin spermatozoon entered a sea urchin ovum in 1875. *See* Nuland, *supra* note 210, at 250.

physicians continued to express uncertainty about the contributions of the mother and father to the conception process.[235] Even so, for most scientists and physicians the discoveries of Dumas and Prevost and of von Baer alone were enough to revolutionize the prevailing conceptions of human reproduction.[236]

The new scientific consensus on the nature of human gestation required an educational process to convince many in the public. Thus we find Dr. Thomas Radford lamenting in 1848 that early abortions continued out of popular ignorance of the fact that a "living human being" existed from the moment of conception.[237] Some will find in Radford's description of that "living human being" as a "potential man" either proof of his sexism or proof that he really did not believe a conceptus was a "living human being."[238] While Radford did indeed exhibit a typical nineteenth-century focus on the masculine, his use of the term "potential" is no more inconsistent with accepting the conceptus as a living human being than would be the description of a ten-year-old girl as a potential woman.

The English law regarding abortion responded to this new scientific consensus without awaiting the reeducation of the public. *Lord Ellenborough's Act* had, after all, treated abortion of a quickened child as a capital felony, but abortion before quickening as merely a serious misdemeanor.[239] The English abortion laws were promptly amended to remove all distinctions based on quickening.[240] English judges were just as responsive.

In *Regina v. Wycherley*,[241] Baron John Gurney did not wait for legislative action (which in fact came during the same year) but reinterpreted the term "quick with child" in *Lord Ellenborough's Act* to mean after conception rather than after quickening. Philip Rafferty has demonstrated that the phrase "quick with child" originally simply meant "alive" regardless of whether the child had quickened and that courts did in fact punish abortions before quickening during the Middle Ages.[242] This does not entirely resolve the matter, for under the influence of Coke, courts had come to distinguish between abortions before and after the child quickened.[243] This distinction had been carried forward into *Lord Ellenborough's Act*.[244] English courts, in at least two decisions, had barred prosecutions under section one of *Lord Ellenborough's Act* (the felony section) because there was no evidence of that a life had been taken before quickening.[245] Baron Gurney's decision reflected then a major shift in the legal and medical understanding of when a foetus or embryo became alive. This same changing knowledge induced the Catholic Church to reconsider

---

235. B.L. Hill, Midwifery Illustrated 44 (1860).

236. *See, e.g.,* Ryan, *supra* note 173, at 206; Severn, *supra* note 172, at 134; Stephen Tracy, The Mother and Her Offspring 108–11 (1853); Thomas Stewart Traill, Outlines of a Course on Medical Jurisprudence 28 (1836).

237. Thomas Radford, The Value of the Embryonic and Foetal Life: Legally, Socially, and Obstetrically Considered 11 (1848).

238. Degler, *supra* note 13, at 240–41; Harrison, *supra* note 13, at 187–89; McLaren, Reproductive Rituals, *supra* note 13, at 138.

239. 43 Geo. III ch. 58, §§ 1, 2 (1803).

240. *See Offences against the Person Act,* 7 Will. & 1 Vict. ch. 85, § 6 (1837); *Offences against the Person Act,* 24 & 25 Vict. ch. 100, §§ 58, 59 (1861).

241. 173 Eng. Rep. 486 (N.P. 1838). *See also* Theodoric Romeyn Beck & John Beck, Elements of Medical Jurisprudence 113 (5th ed. 1835); 1 Joseph Chitty, A Practical Treatise on Medical Jurisprudence 402 (1834); *The Trial of William Russell at Huntingdon Assize, March 1832,* 2 Legal Examiner 10, 12 (1832) (anonymous comment).

242. Rafferty, *supra* note 29, at 163–74. *See also* Chapter 3, at notes 97–107.

243. *See* Chapter 4.

244. 43 Geo. III ch. 58, §§ 1, 2 (1803).

245. *Cf.* Rex v. Phillips, 170 Eng. Rep. 1310 (N.P. 1811) (no prosecution possible before quickening because there was then no evidence of life); Rex v. Anonymous, 170 Eng. Rep. 1310 (N.P. 1811).

its doctrine on abortion, resolving the long-standing debate over the full humanity of embryos and fetuses early in pregnancy in favor of personhood from conception.[246]

Advocates of abortion rights simply ignore the technological basis of the emerging knowledge of human gestation, treating the new paradigm of when a human life begins as an arbitrary social construction chosen for its potential to oppress women. Thus British historian Angus McLaren argued that nineteenth-century doctors rejected the quickening distinction simply as a means of taking power over pregnancy away from women. No longer would the word of the woman (whether the child had quickened) carry as much weight as the word of the physician.[247] And the new abortion laws could be used to drive women midwives out of business to give "regular" physicians and surgeons a monopoly on medical practice. American historian James Mohr wrote an entire book on this theme.[248] Law professor Reva Siegel recently recapitulated this argument in an article cited in a concurring opinion in the Supreme Court.[249] Yet the British Parliament, during the period under consideration, repeatedly rejected bills to require licenses for midwives as unnecessary and therefore as tending towards an unjustified monopoly.[250] And when, in 1858, Parliament did finally require formal licensing for all physicians, it pointedly excluded midwifery from the fields in which physicians were to prove themselves competent.[251] Are we to assume then that the Members of Parliament were astute enough to see through the licensing requirements as a subterfuge for gaining an economic monopoly but not quite quick enough to see the same ploy in the abortion statutes?

The unreality of such arguments is clear from a careful reading of the works in which they appear. One of the clearest instances is in one of the most political documents to make the argument. The authors of the *Webster Historians' Brief* argued that because advanced thinkers were already adopting the cell theory of gestation before the first observation of ova and fertilization, a correct understanding of human gestational processes was already widespread before those discoveries.[252] Yet elsewhere in the same brief these authors acknowledged the prevalence "through the nineteenth century" of popular and legal distinctions based on quickening.[253] These same critics tend to see the entire movement to medicalize the birthing process as a plot by male physicians to gain control over women.[254] The insupportable assumption that women were effec-

---

246. John Connery, Abortion: The Development of the Roman Catholic Perspective 189–224 (1977).

247. McLaren, Reproductive Rituals, *supra* note 13, at 138–39.

248. Mohr, *supra* note 13.

249. Siegel, *supra* note 34, at 283–84, cited in *Casey v. Planned Parenthood of S.E. Pa.*, 505 U.S. 833, 928 n. 4 (1992) (Blackmun, J., partially concurring).

250. *See* Jean Donnison, Midwives and Medical Men: A History of the Struggle for the Control of Childbirth 55–56, 66–67 (2nd ed. 1988).

251. *Id.* at 67.

252. *Webster Historians' Brief, supra* note 34, at 180.

253. *Id.* at 170.

254. *See, e.g.,* G.J. Barker-Benfield, The Horrors of the Half-Known Life: Male Attitudes toward Women and Sexuality in Nineteenth Century America 61 (1976); Janet Farrell Brodie, Contraception and Abortion in Nineteenth-Century America 287 (1994); Raymond DeVries, Making Midwives Legal: Childbirth, Medicine, and the Law 23–27, 39–46, 51, 112 (2nd ed. 1996); Donnison, *supra* note 250, at 28–29, 58–59; Barbara Ehrenreich & Diedre English, For Her Own Good: 150 Years of the Experts' Advice to Women (1982); Gordon, *supra* note 13, at 19–25; Harrison, *supra* note 13, at 36; Catharine MacKinnon, Toward a Feminist Theory of the State 192 (1989); Susan McCutcheon-Rosegg, Natural Childbirth the Bradley Way 130–31, 189, 211–12, 222–24 (1984); McLaren, Birth Control, *supra* note 13, at 231–32; Petchesky, *supra* note 13, at 49–55; Kerreen Reiger, The Disenchantment of the Home 94 (1985); Beverly Savage & Diana Simkin, Preparation for Birth 194–97 (1987); Susan Sherwin, No Longer Patient 193–96 (1992); Starr, *supra* note 14, at 81, 117, 123–26; Dorothy & Richard Wertz, Lying In: A History of Childbirth in America 257–63 (1977); Erin Daly, *Reconsidering Abortion Law: Liberty, Equality, and the New Rhetoric of* Planned Parenthood v. Casey, 45 Am. U. L. Rev. 77, 85–86, 108–9, 116 (1995); Regina Markell Morantz & Sue Zschoche, *Professionalism, Feminism,*

tive in controlling their fertility throughout the ages turns the successful application of medical technology to human reproduction around, leading to a conclusion that doctors were simply trying to take over this female activity rather than to provide heretofore unavailable medical options.

Historians who espouse medical monopoly theory are forced to conclude that women succumbed to the desires of male midwives and physicians to take control of the birthing process as a matter of mere fashion or pretension.[255] It has even become fashionable to demand that women "seize" back control through "demedicalizing" the practice of gynecology and obstetrics without careful regard to the effects such an approach would have on women's lives if the lessons of modern medicine really were to be excluded.[256] Women, of course, were not so naïve or foolish as to submit to the medicalization of birthing simply because it was fashionable even though the new technologies were life threatening and provided few or no countervailing medical benefits.

One need not rely on conjecture to conclude that women did not accept the medicalization of birth out of a misguided desire to be "modern." Plenty of evidence survives showing that women in the nineteenth century actively sought the medicalization of birth, as a contraceptive measure as well as a health measure.[257] Yet abortion remained highly dangerous for women, and, in the United States, it did help a nascent medical profession suppress midwives and other "irregular" competitors. To examine the role of these concerns in the crafting of nineteenth-century abortion statutes, one must turn to the American experience rather than focus on the English experience.

---

*and Gender Roles: A Comparative Study of Nineteenth-Century Medical Therapeutics*, 67 J. Am. Hist. 568 (1980); Regina Morantz-Sanchez, *Physicians*, in Women, Health & Medicine in America (Rima Apple ed. 1990); Charles Rosenberg & Carroll Smith-Rosenberg, *The Female Animal: Medical and Biological Views of Women and Her Role in Nineteenth-Century America*, 4 J. Interdisciplinary Hist. 25 (1973); Reva Siegel, *Abortion as a Sex Equality Right: Its Basis in Feminist Theory*, in Mothers in Law: Feminist Theory and the Legal Regulation of Motherhood 43, 48 (Martha Albertson Fineman & Isabel Karpin eds. 1995); Siegel, *supra* note 34, at 287–88, 314–15; Brenda Waugh, *Repro-Woman: A View of the Labyrinth (from the Lithotomy Position)*, 3 Yale J.L. & Feminism 5 (1991). *See also* David Smolin, *The Jurisprudence of Privacy in a Splintered Supreme Court*, 75 Marq. L. Rev. 975, 1005–13 (1992).

255. *See, e.g.*, Donnison, *supra* note 250, at 35–36, 40, 58–59.

256. An early and classic statement is Boston Women's Health Collective, Our Bodies, Our Selves (1971). This book has now been reissued in at least six editions. *See also* Suzanne Arms, Immaculate Deception: A New Look at Women and Childbirth in America (1975); Rebecca Chalker & Carol Downer, A Woman's Book of Choices: Abortion, Menstrual Extraction, RU 486 9 (1993); Federation of Women's Health Ctrs., How to Stay Out of the Gynecologist's Office (Carol Downer, Rebecca Chalker, & Lorraine Rothman eds. 1981); Myra Marx Ferree & Beth Hess, Controversy and Coalition: The New Feminist Movement across Three Decades of Change 107–8 (rev. ed. 1994); Adrien Rich, Of Women Born: Motherhood as Experience and Institution (1976); Barbara Katz Rothman, In Labor: Women and Power in the Birthplace (1982); Sheryl Burt Ruzek, The Women's Health Movement: Feminist Alternatives to Medical Control (1978); Marie Ashe, *Zig-Zag Stitching and the Seamless Web: Thoughts on "Reproduction" and the Law*, 13 Nova L. Rev. 355 (1989); Diane Curtis, *Doctored Rights: Menstrual Extraction, Self-Help Gynecological Care, and the Law*, 20 Rev. L. & Soc. Change 427 (1994).

257. *See* Chapter 2, at 192–217; Chapter 7, at notes 259–304.

# Chapter 6

# Live and Let Die[1]

*It is easy enough to say something new if you don't care whether it makes any sense.*

—Frank Kermode[2]

The status of abortion was much the same in the United States in 1800 as it was in England at that time. Abortion clearly was a crime before the American Revolution,[3] and, unlike attitudes towards slavery, no one has advanced any reason to suppose that public attitudes towards abortion changed during the course of the American Revolution or in the early years of the Republic. The revolutionaries embraced the importance of "virtue" for the success of the Republic—meaning, among other things, that persons should be ready and willing to sacrifice individual interest when necessary for the needs of society.[4] If this view had any bearing on abortion, it suggested that abortion was a social decision and not a purely individual decision.

The continuity of legal thought regarding abortion is born out by comparing what two of the leading authorities on the common law as found in the United States wrote about abortion before and after the revolution. James Parker wrote the following in 1765:

> If a physician or surgeon gives a person a potion, without any intent of doing him any bodily harm, but with intent to cure or prevent a disease, and contrary to the physician or surgeon's expectation it kills him, this is no homicide.... But if a woman be with child and any gives her a portion to destroy the child within her, and she takes it, and it works so strongly that it kills her, this is murder; for it was not given to cure her of a disease, but unlawfully to destroy the child, within her; and therefor he that gives her a potion to this end, must take the hazard, and if it kills the mother it is murder....

> Also if a woman be quick with child, and by a potion or otherwise, killeth it in her womb; or if a man beat her, whereby the child dieth in her body, and she is delivered of a dead child, this is a great misprision, but no murder: but if the child be born alive, and dieth of the potion, battery, or other cause, this is murder....

> Also it seems agreed, that where one counsels a woman to kill her child when it shall be born, who afterwards doth kill in pursuance of such advice, he is an accessory to the murder....[5]

---

1. Paul McCartney, *Live and Let Die* (1973).

2. Frank Kermode, *The High Cost of the New History*, N.Y. Rev. Books, June 25, 1992, at 43.

3. *See* Chapter 4, at notes 223–355.

4. Saul Cornell, *Moving beyond the Canon of Traditional Constitutional History: Anti-Federalists, the Bill of Rights, and the Promise of Post-Modern Historiography*, 12 Law & Hist. Rev. 1, 25–27 (1994). *See generally* Symposium, *Roads Not Taken: Undercurrents of Republican Thinking in Modern Constitutional Theory*, 84 Nw. U. L. Rev. 1 (1989); Symposium, *1787: The Constitution in Perspective*, 29 Wm. & Mary L. Rev. 1 (1987); Symposium, *The Republican Civic Tradition*, 97 Yale L.J. 1493 (1988).

5. James Parker, Conductor Generalis: Or, the Office, Duty, and Authority of Justices of the

And, writing about 90 years later, Francis Wharton described abortion in these terms:

> There is no doubt that at common law the destruction of an infant unborn is a high misdemeanor, and at an early period it seems to have been deemed murder. If the child dies subsequently to birth from wounds received in the womb, it is clearly homicide, even though the child is still attached to the mother by the umbilical cord. It has been said that it is not an indictable offence to administer a drug to a woman, and thereby to procure an abortion, unless the mother is *quick* with child, though such a distinction, it is submitted, is neither in accordance with the result of medical experience, nor with the principles of the common law.[6]

Even more direct evidence of this continuity — not only of legal thought, but social thought as well — is born out by a case involving the Randolphs of Virginia and the future Chief Justice, John Marshall.[7] The Randolphs were long a leading family of Virginia,[8] with ties by marriage to the other leading families. There were so many Randolphs in Virginia sharing the same personal names that it was then, and is now, necessary to identify them by the name of the plantation that was their principal residence. The branch that is of concern here included two sons of John Randolph of "Matoax" — Richard and Theodorick. This John Randolph had died when his sons were young, and their widowed mother remarried to St. George Tucker, judge and professor of law at William and Mary. Shortly thereafter, when Richard was 19 years old, he married his first cousin, Judith Randolph (then 17 years old), and together they took up residence at one of the deceased John Randolph's other plantations, known as "Bizarre." At Bizarre, they were joined by Judith's younger sister, Nancy, and Richard's younger brother, Theodorick.

Theodorick was 21 when he came to live at Bizarre, and Nancy was 16. They became engaged, but Theodorick died in February 1792 before they could be married. After Theodorick's death, Nancy discovered that she was pregnant. Years later, Nancy would confide in a letter to John Randolph of Roanoke that Theodorick had died only a few days after "the scene which began my sorrows" — presumably the consummation of the yet to be solemnized marriage.[9] Nancy stayed on with her sister and brother-in-law, apparently hoping to keep her condition secret.

Nancy, Judith, and Richard Randolph went together for an overnight visit to yet another cousin's plantation. That cousin was Randolph Harrison. While there, on October 1, 1792, Nancy lost the baby. Precisely how this happened became the talk of the slave quarters, with rumors circulating that the baby had been born alive and then murdered by Richard. Rumor soon added that the Richard was the father. Finally, in an effort to squelch the rumors, Richard Randolph announced, in letters published in several newspapers on or around March 29, 1793 (when he was 22 years old) that he would present himself before the county court when it convened in April in order "to answer in due course of law, any charge or crime which any person or persons whatsoever shall then and there think proper to allege against me."[10]

---

PEACE 216–17 (1764) (citations omitted). A complete quotation of this passage is given and analyzed in Chapter 4, at notes 351–55.

6. 1 FRANCIS WHARTON, THE CRIMINAL LAW OF THE UNITED STATES § 1220 (5th rev. ed. 1861). A complete quotation of Wharton's writings on abortion appears in Chapter 9, at notes 143–56.

7. The following account is from the summary provided by the editors in 2 THE PAPERS OF JOHN MARSHALL 161–68 (Charles Cullen & Herbert Johnson eds. 1974).

8. *See, e.g.,* WILLIAM CABELL BRUCE, JOHN RANDOLPH OF ROANOKE, 1773–1833 (2nd ed. 1922); JONATHAN DANIELS, THE RANDOLPHS OF VIRGINIA (1972); H.J. ECKENRODE, THE RANDOLPHS: THE STORY OF A VIRGINIA FAMILY (1946).

9. 2 BRUCE, *supra* note 8, at 283.

10. 1 BRUCE, *supra* note 8, at 116; 2 THE PAPERS OF JOHN MARSHALL, *supra* note 7, at 163. *See also* Richard Randolph , jun., *To the Public,* VA. GAZETTE & GEN'L ADVERTISER, Apr. 3, 1793, at 1.

When Richard appeared before the court, he was taken into custody and held in jail for several days. At that point, Richard appeared before the court for an "examination"—equivalent to a modern day pre-trial hearing—and all charges were dismissed.[11] Historians often call this proceeding a trial, perhaps not understanding the difference between a trial and an examination.[12] Patrick Henry appeared in the proceeding on behalf of Richard Randolph.[13] John Marshall, a cousin of Richard Randolph and of the two women, was also present, although his precise role is not entirely clear. Marshall's notes suggest he was there to represent Nancy should she be charged in the proceedings.[14] Marshall prepared a detailed summary of each witness's evidence and his own detailed analysis in the form of an argument to the court. Copies of each have survived and have now been published.[15]

Marshall's notes disclose that Martha Jefferson Randolph, daughter of Thomas Jefferson and sister-in-law to Judith and Nancy Randolph, had suggested a medicine (Gum Guiacum) to cure Nancy's "cholic," but warned her about the possible abortifacient effects of the drug.[16] As the warning suggests, Martha suspected Nancy's pregnancy, and when Martha provided some of the drug to Nancy about two weeks later, Martha was careful to provide only a small quantity to assure that it could not be used to provoke a miscarriage.[17] About two weeks after that, Nancy, Judith, and Richard went to visit Randolph Harrison.

Harrison recounted in his testimony how, upon Nancy's arrival, she immediately retired upstairs to bed, only to awaken the household during the night with her screams.[18] Richard and his wife were in the second upstairs bedroom, and Mr. Harrison and his wife later heard someone, whom they presumed to be Richard, descend from the upstairs and after a time return upstairs. Harrison "entertained no unfavorable suspicion concerning her [Nancy], until information was given by a "negro-woman," that she [Nancy] had miscarried."[19] Mrs. Harrison added that Nancy had said, in Mrs. Harrison's presence, that she [Nancy] had taken her Gum Guiacum "as usual."[20] Mrs. Harrison had also noted blood stains on the pillow, the bedclothes, and the back stairs. Mrs. Harrison's testimony was corroborated by another witness, a Mrs. Wood.[21] John Randolph of Roanoke, who was not present during these events, testified that he had visited Bizarre on several occasions and supposed Nancy not to be pregnant, but to suffering "under obstruction."[22]

In the face of this evidence, Marshall's notes do not disclose any argument about abortion being a matter of small importance, let alone a woman's right. Marshall prepared an argument that he built entirely around a denial that Nancy had been pregnant,[23] arguing that she had suf-

---

11. THE PAPERS OF JOHN MARSHALL, *supra* note 7, at 164 n.7.

12. *See* LEONARD BAKER, JOHN MARSHALL: A LIFE IN THE LAW 139–53 (1974); 1 BRUCE, *supra* note 8, at 107–21; DANIELS, *supra* note 8, at 135–49; ECKENRODE, *supra* note 6, at 171–87; 2 WILLIAM WIRT HENRY, PATRICK HENRY, LIFE, CORRESPONDENCE AND SPEECHES 490–93 (1891); DUMAS MALONE, JEFFERSON AND THE ORDEAL OF LIBERTY 172–74 (1962); ROBERT DOUTHAT MEADE, PATRICK HENRY, PRACTICAL REVOLUTIONARY 417–20 (1969); Francis Biddle, *Scandal at Bizarre,* 12 AM. HERITAGE 10 (Aug. 1961).

13. 2 HENRY, *supra* note 12, at 490; MEADE, *supra* note 12, at 419; THE PAPERS OF JOHN MARSHALL, *supra* note 7, at 165.

14. No direct evidence exists of this, but the circumstantial evidence is quite strong. THE PAPERS OF JOHN MARSHALL, *supra* note 7, at 164–68.

15. *Id.* at 168–78.

16. *Id.* at 168–69.

17. *Id.* at 169.

18. *Id.* at 170–71.

19. *Id.* at 171.

20. *Id.* at 171–72.

21. *Id.* at 173.

22. *Id.* at 174. On the prevalence of the belief in the possibility of menstrual obstructions not caused by pregnancy, see Chapter 1, at notes 141–83.

23. THE PAPERS OF JOHN MARSHALL, *supra* note 7, at 175–78.

fered from a menstrual obstruction.[24] Marshall argued that had Nancy sought an abortion, she would have taken a more certain drug than Gum Guiacum.[25] Marshall's argument suggests that the situation regarding abortion in America in 1793 was virtually identical with that in England at the time: Abortion was a crime, but difficult to accomplish and even more difficult to prove. As if to underscore this point, Judith Randolph felt impelled to publish a letter, along with copies of another letter, after the acquittal in an effort to justify the dismissal in the public mind.[26]

A final confirmation of the reality that abortion was not only generally condemned and illegal, but that abortion was also a rare event in American society is found in the diary of midwife Martha Ballard.[27] Mrs. Ballard began midwifing during the American Revolution, and continued into the early years of the nineteenth century. Her diary has survived, covering the period 1785–1812. Her diary includes accounts of incest, illegitimacy, child abuse, and other unsavory activities, but never mentions a single abortion. She even reported interrogating unmarried women under her care in an effort to discover (for the community) who the father was—and discovering in one case that the father was her own son whom she helped to force to marry the girl in question.[28] In this as in other matters, Ballard's diary is simply so detailed that it seems unlikely that she considered abortions so routine that she simply would *never* have bothered to mention them. Perhaps Ballard considered abortion even viler than the activities she recorded. A more likely explanation is that Ballard did not perform any abortions, and furthermore that she also did not know of any—for she recorded noteworthy events even when she was not personally involved.

Just as with the Parliament in England, shortly after the turn of the nineteenth century, state legislatures in the United States began to prohibit abortion by statute. This process has been much studied because of the importance of this period in the history of American abortion laws in the legal (and hence political) arguments about the constitutionality of these abortion statutes. The two best known and admired studies are the works of law professor Cyril Means, jr., and historian James Mohr.[29] The myths these two authors propounded have become the core of the modern orthodoxy of abortion history. These myths, their current importance, and the shortcomings of the two men's work have already been described in general terms in Chapter 1.[30] It is unnecessary to rehearse yet again the evidence suggesting that, contrary to Means and Mohr, abortion was in fact a rare activity and was not widely approved in society. In this chapter, we shall consider their claims that the nineteenth century abortion statutes were enacted in order to protect the lives of mothers rather than the lives of fetuses,[31] and also to promote the consolidation of the professional monopoly of the "regular" physicians.[32] Yet other

---

24. *Id.* at 176–77.

25. *Id.* at 177.

26. Judith Randolph, *To the Public*, Va. Gazette & Gen'l Advertiser, May 15, 1793, at 1.

27. Laurel Thatcher Ulrich, The Midwife's Tale: The Life of Martha Ballard Based on Her Diary, 1785–1812 (1991).

28. *Id.* at 151–55.

29. James Mohr, Abortion in America: The Origins and Evolution of National Policy, 1800–1900 (1978); Cyril Means, jr., *The Law of New York Concerning Abortion and the Status of the Foetus, 1664–1968: A Case of Cessation of Constitutionality*, 14 N.Y.L.F. 411 (1968) ("Means I"); Cyril Means, jr., *The Phoenix of Abortional Freedom: Is a Penumbral Right or Ninth-Amendment Right About to Arise from the Nineteenth-Century Legislative Ashes of a Fourteenth-Century Common-Law Liberty?*, 17 N.Y.L.F. 335 (1971) ("Means II").

30. *See* Chapter 1, at notes 59–117.

31. Means I, *supra* note 29.

32. Mohr, *supra* note 29, at 147–99. *See also Amicus Brief of 250 American Historians in support of Appellants in* Planned Parenthood of Southeastern Pennsylvania v. Casey, [505 U.S. 833 (1992)] ("*Casey Historians' Brief*"), at 5–6, 13–15; *Amicus Brief of 281 American Historians supporting Appellees in* Webster v. Reproductive Health Services [492 U.S. 490 (1989)] ("*Webster Historians' Brief*"), reprinted at 11 Women's Rts. L. Rptr. 163, 170, 174–75 (1989), and in 8 Documentary History of the Legal Aspects of Abortion in

reasons have been advanced to explain the near universal enactment of statutory prohibitions of abortion in the nineteenth century, including claims that the statutes were part of conspiracy to suppress a budding female sexuality in order to assure male control of women's reproductive capacity, [33] and a conspiracy to increase the birthrate of middle and upper class white women to assure continued white dominance in England and the United States.[34] Only in dispelling those myths can we begin to get at the true history of these early American abortion statutes.

The new orthodoxy of abortion history creates several puzzles—which are resolved if technological changes are factored into the analysis. The most central puzzle is why would nineteenth-century legislators criminalize abortion at all if, as the new orthodoxy asserts, abortion was widely practiced, socially accepted, and relatively safe. Almost as important a puzzle is why would the abortion statutes meet with little social resistance, and indeed why would the nineteenth-century statutes have been strongly supported by most feminists of the time, even the most militant, as will be developed in Chapter 8. These puzzles are central to the new orthodoxy in that they create an impression that the reasons for the legal attention to abortion were a mystery that could be solved only by supposing that the proponents of that attention were unwilling to discuss their reasons openly. The supposition of nefarious reasons, in turn, has become the core dogma of the new orthodoxy of the history of abortion.

For example, precisely these puzzles bedevil the work of British historian Angus McLaren. He concluded not only that the nineteenth-century statutes were contrary to popular attitudes, but also that the new medical technologies were less effective than the folk-medicines they displaced.[35] Cyril Means' claim that the procedure was criminalized because it posed a major threat to the lives or health of the women who underwent the procedure actually undercuts this version of the new orthodoxy. James Mohr therefore sought an alternative explanation, denigrating the claim that abortion in the early nineteenth century was dangerous for the mother.[36] Even some who share Mohr's support of a claimed freedom to abort found his disparagement of the dangers of abortion as medically "naïve."[37] Still, questioning the asserted dangers of abortion in the nineteenth century was necessary in order to make a case for abortion suddenly becoming a focus of legal activity in the nineteenth century for a reason other than its emerging technical feasibility.

The dubious claim that these statutes were primarily motivated by a drive by the organized "regular" (allopathic) medical profession to gain control of the practice of medicine certainly does not apply to *Lord Ellenborough's Act*—England was still decades away from having an organized medical profession.[38] England did not formally organize a medical profession until the Medical Act of 1858 unified the hitherto separate professions of physician, surgeon, and apothecary under the authority of the General Medical Council, which was given authority over med-

THE UNITED STATES: WEBSTER V. REPRODUCTIVE HEALTH SERVICES 107 (Roy Mersky & Gary Hartman eds. 1990) ("DOCUMENTARY HISTORY") (hereafter pagination will be given only to the version in the *Women's Rts. L. Rptr.*); Reva Siegel, *Reasoning from the Body: A Historical Perspective on Abortion Regulation and Questions of Equal Protection*, 44 STAN. L. REV. 261, 278 (1992).

33. MOHR, *supra* note 29, at 86–118; *Casey Historians' Brief*, *supra* note 32, at 15–26; *Webster Historians' Brief*, *supra* note 32, at 175–78; Siegel, *supra* note 32.

34. *See, e.g.*, MOHR, *supra* note 29, at 166–67. *See generally* Chapter 9, at notes 36–43.

35. ANGUS MCLAREN, REPRODUCTIVE RITUALS 8–9 (1984).

36. MOHR, *supra* note 29, at 29–31.

37. EDWARD SHORTER, A HISTORY OF WOMEN'S BODIES 191 n.* (Pelican Books ed. 1984). One might reach the same conclusion regarding historian Angus McLaren's belief that because women so desperately wanted to control their own fertility that the magical rituals and procedures they followed must necessarily have worked. MCLAREN, *supra* note 34, at 5–8.

38. J. KEOWN, ABORTION, DOCTORS AND THE LAW 22 (1988). *See also* KERRY PETERSEN, ABORTION REGIMES (1993).

ical education, qualifications, and professional discipline.[39] Nor do fears of ethnic and class suicide apply in England throughout the nineteenth century. England, after all, was not an immigrant country at the time and the prosecutions for abortion, both before and after *Lord Ellenborough's Act* was adopted, usually involved the abortion of lower class women.[40] The claim that
these statutes were directed at women in the battle of the sexes founders on the realities that
most persons punished as abortionists were men[41] while the leading feminists of the time were
virtually unanimous in *demanding* the criminalization of abortion as well as generally supporting the medicalization of the birthing process[42] and pressure from women in general played a
strong role in the medicalization of birth.[43]

We shall find that the abortion statutes enacted in the United States evolved the same pattern
as we find in England. The earliest statute in most states was part of a codification of the common law of crimes. As part of the codification process, the earliest statutes captured the extent of
the existing precedents with their technicality and (often) less than comprehensive approach to
the practice of abortion, treating only abortions undertaken by the classic modes of injury or ingestion. Subsequently, the statutes were reenacted to systematize, simplify, and extend the law as
a response to the advent of intrusion abortions leading to a strong sense that abortion was becoming more common. We open our study of the American abortion statutes then with a general examination of such statutes as enacted before the end of the American Civil War. I leave
Means' thesis that these statutes were focused primarily on protecting the health of the mother
for the section after next, in large measure because Means focused almost entirely on the history
of legislation in New York. New York makes an interesting case study, but it is not the whole
story. Understanding what happened in New York is in fact easier against a backdrop of what was
happening in the whole nation than by examining New York in isolation. The final section in
this chapter focuses on James Mohr's thesis that these statutes were enacted in large measure as
an attempt by "regular" physicians to suppress competition from "irregular" physicians.

# The Earliest American Statutes (1821–1840)

*The only valid tribute to thought … is precisely to use it, to deform it, to make it grown and protest.*

—Michel Foucault[44]

The first abortion statute in any of the United States was enacted in Connecticut in 1821. It
read in full:

> Every person who shall, willfully and maliciously, administer to, or cause to be adminis-
> tered to, or taken by, any person or persons, any deadly poison, or other noxious or de-
> structive substance, with an intention him, her, or them, thereby to murder, or thereby

---

39. J.K. Mason & R. Alexander McCall Smith, Law and Medical Ethics 7–9 (1983); Petersen, *supra* note 38, at 30–31.

40. *See* Chapter 5.

41. As even some supporters of abortion rights have recognized. Cass Sunstein, *Neutrality in Constitutional Law (with Special Reference to Pornography, Abortion, and Surrogacy)*, 92 Colum. L. Rev. 1, 33 (1992);
Stephen Veltri, *Book Rev.*, 18 Oh. N.L. Rev. 257, 266–67 (1991).

42. *See* Chapter 8. Even James Mohr acknowledged as much. Mohr, *supra* note 29, at 110–14.

43. *See* Chapter 2, at 192–217; Chapter 7, at notes 259–304.

44. Michel Foucault, Power/Knowledge: Selected Interviews and Writings 93 (Colin Gordon *et
al.* trans. 1980).

to cause or procure the miscarriage of any woman, then being quick with child, and shall be thereof duly convicted, shall suffer imprisonment, in Newgate prison, during his natural life, or for such other term as the court having cognizance of the offense shall determine.[45]

Professor Marvin Olasky, in his history of abortion laws, attempts to explain the particular features of this statute by reference to the trial and conviction of the Reverend Ammi Rogers of abortion in 1818 in Griswold, Connecticut.[46] Rogers, a controversial Episcopalian minister, was convicted of seducing and aborting a young woman, using "pernicious drugs."[47] He served two years in the local jail rather than the harsher Newgate prison,[48] and always maintained that his enemies had framed him.[49] Rogers insisted that a disease, defect, or accident caused the woman's miscarriage and that neither he nor the young woman ever knew that she was pregnant.[50]

If we assume that Connecticut's legislature waited three years to respond to the then notorious Rogers case, the statute did address the issues Rogers had raised. The statute only addressed abortions using drugs, required quickening as proof of pregnancy, and required proof of the intent to procure an abortion.[51] The statute also specified that imprisonment was to be in Newgate Prison, addressing the sentencing question that had erupted at Rogers' trial.[52] Yet, because no record of the discussions of the statute in the legislative assembly (or of any public debate outside the legislature) has survived, we have no direct proof that the legislature was simply responding to the Rogers case, even if Connecticut's legislature was prompted to action by that case.

On the other hand, comparison of this awkwardly drafted statute to section 1 of *Lord Ellenborough's Act* shows that the 1821 Connecticut Act closely tracked the 1803 English Act.[53] The differences are mostly superficial, although the Connecticut Act does provide for a lesser penalty (life in prison or less, compared to death without benefit of clergy). The Connecticut statute, like section 1 of *Lord Ellenborough's Act,* prohibited only the induced abortion of an unborn child or the killing of a woman through administration of a "potion" or other "noxious and destructive substance." Missing from the Connecticut Act is any reference to a "noxious or destructive... thing" that appears in Lord Ellenborough's section 1, apparently excluding from the scope of the Connecticut Act injurious or intrusive abortions that arguably were within the scope of *Lord Ellenborough's Act.* On the other hand, the Connecticut statute combines in a single provision the administration of "any deadly poison, or other noxious or destructive substance" with an intention to murder with the administration of "any deadly poison, or other noxious or destructive substance" with the intention of causing an abortion. This is just as in Lord Ellenborough's sec-

---

45. 1821 Conn. Pub. Acts tit. 22, §§ 14, 16, at 152–53, reprinted in Eugene Quay, *Justifiable Abortion— Medical and Legal Foundations (Pt. II)*, 49 Geo. L.J. 395, 453 (1961).

46. Marvin Olasky, Abortion Rights: A Social History of Abortion in America 90–93 (1992).

47. Ammi Rogers, Memoirs 118 (1826). *See also* Daniel Phillips, Griswold: A History 115–16 (1929).

48. Rogers, *supra* note 47, at 149.

49. *Id.* at 91.

50. *Id.* at 88, 120.

51. Olasky, *supra* note 46, at 92–93.

52. Rogers, *supra* note 47, at 149.

53. 43 Geo. III ch. 58, § 1 (1803), quoted in Chapter 5, at note 118. While there is no direct reference connecting Connecticut's Act of 1821 to *Lord Ellenborough's Act,* only seven years later the Revisers of New York's statutes did refer to it, albeit not by name. *See* 6 Revisers' Notes 74 (1828). Furthermore, one Canadian province, New Brunswick in 1810, had already followed the language of *Lord Ellenborough's Act* in enacting an abortion statutes. 1810 (N.B.), 50 Geo. III, c. 2. *See* Constance Backhouse, *Involuntary Motherhood: Abortion, Birth Control and the Law in Nineteenth Century Canada*, 3 Windsor Y.B. of Access to Justice 61, 67–68 (1983).

tion 1. The parallels between the two statutes are simply too great, given the other connections between the two legal systems, to suppose that the similarities are simply a coincidence.

Those who propagate the modern myths of abortion history would dismiss any lessons we might draw from the adoption of *Lord Ellenborough's Act* for understanding the ensuing American legislation on the basis that the earliest American statutes did not go so far as Ellenborough's Act in declaring abortion a crime.[54] The only early statute that even arguably was markedly more constricted in its treatment of abortion than *Lord Ellenborough's Act* was that of Connecticut adopted in 1821, which prohibited only ingestion abortions after quickening. Whatever the reasons for its differing scope, the Connecticut legislature extended the statute to cover "instrumental" abortions after quickening in 1830.[55] James Mohr hardly mentions this development or that the other early statutes included intrusive abortions in their earliest form.[56] The so-called *Historians' Briefs* before the Supreme Court tell us only that by the 1830 act "Connecticut became the first state to punish abortion after quickening."[57] The latter statement not only is false,[58] it is not even coherent—after all, what did the 1821 Connecticut statute, which the briefs discuss, do?

If one examines the 1821 Connecticut statute strictly on its own, the joining of the prohibition of poisoning with intent to murder with the prohibition of poisoning with intent to induce an abortion, along with the failure to address injury or intrusion abortions, could suggest that the statute was a poison control measure rather than a prohibition of abortion.[59] Such a reading simply ignores the technological context within which the statute was enacted. Injury abortions were not common in 1821. Abortions were dangerous, painful, and generally ineffective.[60] While there is some evidence that intrusion abortions occurred in Connecticut before 1821,[61] there is no reason to believe that such abortions were common. Almost certainly, intrusion abortions were rare compared to ingestion abortions in Connecticut in 1821.[62] Unfortunately jurists, lawyers, and legal historians seldom consider the role changing technology plays in the evolution of any legal doctrine or legal institution.[63] Just because the technological context is generally ignored by historians, however, does not mean that it had no effect. Is one to suppose that the technical reality of abortion was wholly unknown or wholly ignored by Connecticut's legislature in 1821?

Even if historians like James Mohr can be excused for overlooking the technological context of the enactment, can they be excused for ignoring the legal context of the law they are studying? The Connecticut abortion provision was not an isolated statute specifically enacted

---

54. MOHR, *supra* note 29, at 21–26; *Casey Historians' Brief, supra* note 32, at 11–13; *Webster Historians' Brief, supra* note 32, at 173.

55. 1830 Conn. Pub. Acts ch. 1, §16, at 255, reprinted in Quay, *supra* note 45, at 453.

56. MOHR, *supra* note 29, at 24–25.

57. *Casey Historians' Brief, supra* note 32, at 12; *Webster Historians' Brief, supra* note 32, at 173.

58. *See* N.Y. REV. STAT. pt. IV, ch. 1, tit. 2, §§ 8, 9, at 550 (1829), reprinted in Quay, *supra* note 45, at 499, (quoted *infra* at note 116). By 1830, Illinois, Missouri, and New York had also prohibited certain abortions before quickening. ILL. REV. CODE §§ 40, 41, 46, at 130–31 (1827), reprinted in Quay, *supra*, at 466; 1 Mo. Rev. Laws 283 (1825); N.Y. REV. STAT. pt. IV, ch. 1, tit. 6, § 21, at 578 (1829), reprinted in Quay, *supra*, at 499 (quoted *infra* at note 116).

59. *See* MOHR, *supra* note 29, at 21; LESLIE REAGAN, WHEN ABORTION WAS A CRIME: WOMEN, MEDICINE, AND LAW IN THE UNITED STATES, 1867–1973, at 10 (1997).

60. *See* Chapter 1, at notes 203–51.

61. Rex v. Hallowell, 9 SUPER. CT. RECORDS Nos. 113, 173, 175 (Wyndham Cnty. Super. Ct. Files, box 172) (1745–47). *See* Chapter 4, at notes 295–320. *See also* Cornelia Hughes Dayton, *Taking the Trade: Abortion and Gender Relations in an Eighteenth-Century New England Village*, 48 WM. & MARY Q. 19 (1991).

62. SHORTER, *supra* note 37, at 190–97; Estelle Freedman, *Historical Interpretation and Legal Advocacy: Rethinking the Webster Amicus Brief*, 12 PUB. HISTORIAN 27, 28–30 (1990).

63. For an example of one of the few such studies, see Kevin Casey, *The Barbed Wire Invention: An External Factor Affecting American Legal Development*, 72 J. PAT. & TRADEMARK OFFICE SOC'Y 417 (1990).

to deal with abortion. The 1821 Connecticut statute was part of an attempt at a comprehensive codification of the criminal law, just as *Lord Ellenborough's Act* had been. Mohr did note that the Connecticut statute, like nearly all the early American abortion statutes, was part of a codification, but he argued that state legislatures, by including abortion prohibitions in codifications of the criminal law rather than enacting the prohibition in special statutes directed at abortion, indicated a lack of public support for such laws.[64] The proponents, according to Mohr, felt the need to hide their "innovation" in a large of body of laws directed at other topics.

A careful study also would have discovered that abortion was in fact a crime whenever a "living child" was thought to be present. Furthermore, the nineteenth-century statutes enacted in 17 states (and the District of Columbia) denominated the crime against the unborn child as "manslaughter," "murder," or "assault with intent to murder."[65] Most nineteenth-century statutes referred to the unborn child as a "child," not as a fetus or some other term that might suggest a lesser status, and many states classified abortion with other crimes against persons, usually homicide.[66] After reviewing these statutes, one can only marvel at historians who conclude that "the destruction of the fetus never gained the standing either of infanticide or homicide."[67]

James Mohr's approach allowed him to assume the contrary, without examining the evidence. His history of abortion is more subtle and nuanced than the strident dogmatism of Means, but no less misleading. Mohr, by focusing his research on the political and social history of abortion in nineteenth-century America, at once broadened the range of materials he considered and narrowed its scope in time and space. This had a major impact (whether intended or not) on the appearance of the evidence to Mohr and his readers. The breadth of his study gave him many more, and much bulkier, sources to draw upon. The greater number of sources served to protect Mohr from the charges easily leveled against Means that he deliberately ignored significant sources relevant to a strictly legal history of abortion in England and America. The greater heft of Mohr's sources absolved him from quoting sources in full, in turn allowing him to hide from readers any blatant distortions through selective quotation that are so obvious in Means. Mohr, however, exhibits the same pattern of cavalierly assuming what needs to be proven. He is particularly prone to sweeping assumptions that the popular knowledge of abortion in times past and the particular knowledge of those who created the sources he preferred were virtually the same as ours.[68] Even more pronounced is Mohr's consistent assumption that any evidence contrary to his theses represents subterfuge by the persons who produced the evidence rather than an honest description of that persons' (or group's) goals or motives.[69]

---

64. Mohr, *supra* note 29, at 40–43, 129–30, 132–33, 139, 141–43, 202–05, 221–23, 226, 229.

65. James Witherspoon, *Reexamining* Roe: *Nineteenth-Century Abortion Statutes and the Fourteenth Amendment*, 17 St. Mary's L.J. 29, 42–44 (1985).

66. *Id.* at 48–50.

67. *See, e.g.,* Michael Grossberg, Governing the Hearth: Law and the Family in Nineteenth-Century America 186 (1985). *See also* Ronald Collins, *The Problem of Penalties Clouds Issue of Abortion*, Nat'l L.J., July 29, 1985, at 13 (arguing that "the law" never took seriously the claim that a fetus was a human being because abortion "always" carried a less severe penalty than "true" murder—as if there are not different penalties for different sorts of killings of adults).

68. *See, e.g.,* Mohr, *supra* note 29, at 4, 6–7, 10 (relieving "obstructed menses" must always have been understood as abortion), at 4–10 (the quickening distinction demonstrates that people did not believe that killing a fetus was wrong when Mohr himself acknowledged, at 6, 73–77, that women at the time consider the pre-quickening infant to be "inert non-beings"), at 11–14, 18 (relatively safe and effective pharmaceutical techniques available for abortion, although Mohr himself denies this at 53–58, 71–73), 78–84 (falling birth rates proves rising abortion rates), at 102–10 (the emergence of early feminism must have caused rising abortion rates despite the evidence, cited by Mohr at 111–14, of early feminist opposition to abortion).

69. *See, e.g., id.* at , at 32–37, 85–118, 128, 147–82.

The distorting effects of the temporal and spacial limits of Mohr's inquiry are clear and crucial. By beginning his history of abortion in the year 1800, Mohr established the social, political,
and technical realities of that year as an apparently immutable baseline against which to measure
the changes of the nineteenth century. This enabled Mohr to assume whatever he chose about
the history and traditions that led up to 1800 without justifying those assumptions through examination of evidence from even a few years before 1800. By limiting his inquiry to the United
States, he absolved himself from examining the even more voluminous records of the changes in
English law and policy in the nineteenth century.[70] This also provided an excuse for his failure to
search American records from before 1800—a task that would have been considerably more difficult given the scarcity of materials relating to abortion from colonial America.

Mohr made his technique clear on the very first page of his book. There he assumes that abortion after quickening was a crime in 1800 unless there was "due cause" for the abortion.[71] Although he stressed the then understanding of the common law that abortion before quickening
was not a crime, Mohr departed from that understanding in asserting that even post-quickening
abortions were legal if for "due cause." Mohr never attempted to define "due cause." His only authority for this assertion is the first Means article[72]—without intimating that Means himself had
repudiated his article's conclusions about the common law before 1800 seven years before Mohr's
book was published.[73] Instead, Mohr focused on the origins and significance of the quickening
distinction, only to note that quickening was abandoned as a factor of legal significance in England in 1803.[74] His discussion, such as it was, seemed to embrace the tradition of abortion's
criminality, yet his glib assertion that even abortion after quickening was legal if done for undefined "due cause" allowed a reader to project any meaning the reader might want onto Mohr's
statement—even that abortion was a "common law liberty" if one were so inclined.[75]

Apart from occasionally ameliorating the punishment, the codification process in early
nineteenth century America usually involved little innovation.[76] Statutes covered very few
crimes before these early codifications.[77] Jurists and political thinkers early on concluded that
in a republic crimes must be defined by statute both to assure popular assent and to provide
notice to the public.[78] The considerable legal confusion that followed independence also fed a

---

70. *See generally* KEOWN, *supra* note 38, at 16.

71. MOHR, *supra* note 29, at 3. *See also* GROSSBERG, *supra* note 67, at 159–62; CARROLL SMITH-ROSEN-
BERG, DISORDERLY CONDUCT: VISIONS OF GENDER IN VICTORIAN AMERICA 219–20 (1985).

72. Mohr cited Means I, *supra* note 29, at 418–26.

73. Means II, *supra* note 29, at 336–76, 409–10 n.175.

74. MOHR, *supra* note 29, at 3–5. Mohr somewhat overstated this point as quickening was not entirely
abandoned in England until the decision in *Regina v. Wycherley*, 173 ENG. REP. 486 (N.P. 1838). *See* Chapter 5,
at notes 235–40.

75. Roe v. Wade, 410 U.S. 113, 140 (1973); Beechem v. Leahy, 287 A.2d 836, 139 (Vt. 1972); *Casey Historians' Brief, supra* note 32, at 5–6; *Webster Historians' Brief, supra* note 32, at 170; LINDA GORDON, WOMAN'S
BODY, WOMAN'S RIGHT: A SOCIAL HISTORY OF BIRTH CONTROL IN AMERICA 52–53, 57 (1976); MOHR, *supra*
note 29, at 128–29, 134–36, 144–45, 201, 208–11, 226, 229, 235–36; Means II, *supra* note 29, at 336, 351–54,
374–75, 409–10 n.175; Siegel, *supra* note 32, at 278; Rickie Solinger, *"A Complete Disaster": Abortion and the
Politics of Hospital Abortion Committees, 1950–1970,* 19 FEMINIST STUD. 241, 243 (1993).

76. *See generally* CHARLES COOK, THE AMERICAN CODIFICATION MOVEMENT: A STUDY OF ANTEBELLUM
LEGAL REFORM (1981); LAWRENCE FRIEDMAN, A HISTORY OF AMERICAN LAW 289–91 (1985); MORTON HOR-
WITZ, THE TRANSFORMATION OF AMERICAN LAW 1780–1860, at 1–30 (1977); WILLIAM NELSON, THE AMERI-
CANIZATION OF THE COMMON LAW 10, 38–39, 110–11 (1975); Shael Herman, *The Fate and Future of Codifica-
tion in America,* 40 AM. J. LEGAL HIST. 407, 408–25 (1996); Gunther Weiss, *The Enchantment of Codification in
the Common-Law World,* 25 YALE J. INT'L L. 435 (2000).

77. *See* GROSSBERG, *supra* note 67, at 161–62, 168–69.

78. United States v. Hudson, 11 U.S. (7 Cranch) 32 (1812). *See generally* COOK, *supra* note 76, at 136–53;
FRIEDMAN, *supra* note 60, at 96–97, 289–91; HORWITZ, *supra* note 76, at ch.1; JAMES MOHR, DOCTORS AND
THE LAW: MEDICAL JURISPRUDENCE IN NINETEENTH-CENTURY AMERICA 78–83 (1993); WILLIAM NELSON,

desire to simplify and to systematize[79] — a desire that later would be identified with a move to professionalize the law. The inclusion of a particular crime in these codes thus hardly demonstrates innovation or subterfuge. The codification movement simply did not represent a desire for wholesale change in the law or a desire to hide particular, controversial laws in a body of non-controversial material — as Mohr himself recognized in his later study of medical jurisprudence generally.[80]

Mohr did not consider the possibility that the abortion prohibitions were included in the earliest codifications simply because no one saw anything controversial in carrying forward the existing law. In fact, Mohr wanted to have it both ways in his argument. Only in Ohio did the legislature enact an early (pre-1840) abortion statute as part of a scheme limited to regulating the practice of medicine rather than as part of a general codification of the criminal law.[81] Mohr saw this as direct evidence supporting his claim that these laws were enacted as a covert means for creating a medical monopoly enacted without broad popular support. He did not mention that the Ohio enactment undercut his argument that the prevalent pattern of inclusion in early criminal codifications indicated a lack of public support for the abortion prohibitions, or that by his reasoning the separateness of the Ohio statute was evidence of popular support for Ohio's attempt to suppress abortion.[82] Damned if you do and damned if you don't.

Instead of grappling with the implications of codification, Mohr chose to emphasize that the Connecticut statute did not make a criminal of the woman who sought or underwent an abortion.[83] He suggested that this, like the narrow specification of abortion techniques in the statute, showed that the legislature's target was the profit from the sale of dangerous drugs rather than the abortion itself. Mohr's suggestion simply ignores the common-law tradition of treating the woman as a victim of the abortion, a tradition based on both the rarity in practice of voluntary, elective abortions and the danger of the procedure when it did occur.[84] In fact, several legal commentators of the time argued that the dangers of abortion were punishment enough for the woman.[85] Nor did Mohr find it significant to his argument that these statutes

---

THE AMERICANIZATION OF THE COMMON LAW 10, 38–39, 110–11 (1975); Richard Cox, *Law and Community in the New Nation: Three Visions for Michigan, 1788–1831,* 4 S. CAL. INTERDISCIPLINARY L.J. 161, 220–22 (1995); Michael Hoeflich, Plus ça change, plus c'est la meme chose: *The Integration of Theory and Practice in Legal Education,* 66 TEMPLE L. REV. 123, 136–39 (1993).

79. *See, e.g.,* THOMAS GRIMKÉ, AN ORATION ON THE PRACTICABILITY AND EXPEDIENCY OF REDUCING THE WHOLE BODY OF THE LAW TO THE SIMPLICITY AND GOOD ORDER OF A CODE (1827). *See also* COOK, *supra* note 76, at 102–32; FRIEDMAN, *supra* note 76, at 289–91; PERRY MILLER, THE LIFE OF THE MIND IN AMERICA 220, 246–49 (1962).

80. MOHR, *supra* note 78, at 77–79.

81. Ohio Gen. Stat. §§ 111(1), 112(2), at 252 (1841) (enacted Feb. 27, 1834), reprinted in Quay, *supra* note 45, at 504.

82. MOHR, *supra* note 29, at 39–40.

83. *Id.* at 22.

84. *See, e.g.,* People v. Davis, 276 P.2d 801, 807 (Cal. 1954); Hatfield v. Gano, 15 Iowa 177, 178 (1863); Peoples v. Commonwealth, 9 S.W. 509, 510 (Ky. 1898); Commonwealth v. Boynton, 116 Mass. 343, 345 (1874); State v. Murphy, 27 N.J.L. 112, 114–15 (1858); Dunn v. People, 29 N.Y. 523, 527 (1864); Smartt v. State, 80 S.W. 586, 589 (Tenn. 1904); Watson v. State, 9 Tex. Crim. App. 237, 244–45 (1880); State v. Howard, 32 Vt. 380, 403 (1859). *See also In re* Vince, 67 A.2d 141 (N.J. 1949); Miller v. Bennett, 56 S.E.2d 217, 221 (Va. 1949); WM. L. CLARK, JR., HAND-BOOK OF CRIMINAL LAW 182 (1894); 3 JOHN WIGMORE, A TREATISE ON THE LAW OF EVIDENCE 2755–56 (1905). *See also* MARY BOYLE, RE-THINKING ABORTION, PSYCHOLOGY, GENDER, POWER AND LAW 44 (1997). Historian Leslie Reagan would have us ignore this tradition. Leslie Reagan, *Victim or Accomplice?: Crime, Medical Practice, and the Construction of the Aborting Woman in American Case Law, 1860s to 1970,* 10 COLUM. J. GENDER & L. 311 (2001). *See generally* Chapter 1.

85. *See* JEREMY BENTHAM, THE THEORY OF LEGISLATION 493–94 (C.K. Ogden ed. 1931); WILLIAM BUCHAN, DOMESTIC MEDICINE, OR A TREATISE ON THE PREVENTION AND CURE OF DISEASES BY REGIMEN AND SIMPLE MEDICINE 403 (1816 ed.).

were intended as poison-control measures that the Connecticut legislature extended its ban on abortions to "instrumental abortions" (what I have termed intrusion techniques and perhaps injury techniques as well) in 1830,[86] only nine years after the statute that on which he focused his attention.

The clearest indication of Mohr's determination to read the Connecticut statute as permissive towards abortion was his treatment of the quickening requirement in the statute. That only abortions after quickening were declared criminal, Mohr argued, indicates that the Connecticut statute was intended to protect the supposed right to abort. He pointed out that the Connecticut legislature had not followed *Lord Ellenborough's Act* of 1803, which had treated pre- quickening abortion as a crime—albeit a lesser crime than abortion after quickening.[87] Mohr adduced no direct evidence of such intent and did not consider any possible alternative explanation for the statutory adoption of the quickening doctrine in Connecticut. The limiting of criminality to post-quickening abortions could very well have been a response to the evidentiary problems of proving both the pregnancy and that the fetus had been alive before the abortion before quickening. Proof of either continued to be difficult problems early in the nineteenth century for a crime requiring proof of the specific intent to abort.[88] Evidentiary problems had featured in Coke's and Hale's analyses of the criminality of abortion in the seventeenth century.[89] The same problem was highlighted in what in 1821 was still the only legal treatise written in America that discussed the law of abortion.[90] The authors of a leading treatise on medical jurisprudence were complaining of the same problem in 1855.[91] So uncertain were physicians (and midwives) of the facts of pregnancy in the 1820s that they were still actively debating just how long human gestation took.[92] The intent provisions, however, allowed for the conviction of a would-be abortionist when the attempt failed to induce an abortion. Courts upheld convictions for failed attempts at abortion in seven reported cases in the second half of the nineteenth century.[93] Thus addition of an intent requirement, rather than being designed to protect abortionists, appears to have been designed to make more likely that abortionists would be convicted.[94]

Mohr did bring up the evidentiary problem posed in the requirement that the prosecution prove the specific intent to "procure the miscarriage of a woman," but only to argue that the rather differently worded laws adopted in Illinois and Missouri during the 1820s, with the their requirement that the prosecution prove the specific intent to abort, must be read as consistent with the more restrictively worded Connecticut act.[95] The Illinois and Missouri statutes did not

86. 1830 Conn. Pub. Acts ch. 1, §16, at 255, reprinted in Quay, *supra* note 45, at 453. For Mohr's discussion of this statute, see MOHR, *supra* note 29, at 24–25.

87. MOHR, *supra* note 29, at 22–25.

88. OLASKY, *supra* note 46, at 92–93, 99–102. *See generally* Chapter 4, at notes 55–70.

89. EDWARD COKE, THIRD INSTITUTE 50–51 (1644), quoted in Chapter 4, at notes 119–21; 1 MATTHEW HALE, HISTORY OF PLEAS OF THE CROWN 429–30 (1736), quoted in Chapter 4, at notes 188–89. *See also* Regina v. Sims, 75 ENG. REP. 1075 (K.B. 1601), quoted in Chapter 4, at notes 34–35.

90. PARKER, *supra* note 5, at 216–17, quoted in Chapter 4, at note 351.

91. FRANCIS WHARTON & MORETON STILLÉ, TREATISE ON MEDICAL JURISPRUDENCE 277 (1855).

92. "A Correspondent" (apparently Dr. T.R. Beck), *Contributions in Medical Jurisprudence and Police, No. IV: Duration of Human Pregnancy,* 6 N.Y. MED. & PHYSICAL J. 224 (1827).

93. State v. Fitzgerald, 49 Iowa 260 (1878); Bassett v. State, 41 Iowa 303 (1872); Commonwealth v. Morrison, 82 Mass. (16 Gray) 224 (1860); State v. Owens, 22 Minn. 238 (1875); State v. Van Houten, 37 Mo. 357 (1866); State v. Cave, 33 26 s.w. 503 (Tex. Ct. Crim App. 1894).

94. *See* GROSSBERG, *supra* note 67, at 363; OLASKY, *supra* note 46, at 100–02.

95. ILL. REV. CODE §§40, 41, 46, at 130–31 (1827), reprinted in Quay, *supra* note 45, at 466; 1 Mo. Rev. Laws 283 (1825).

mention quickening, and thus appeared to make abortion by ingestion techniques criminal at any stage of pregnancy. Mohr argued that they nonetheless implicitly preserved the quickening distinction because conviction as a practical matter was impossible before quickening.[96] At this point, Mohr has told us that a statute permits pre-quickening abortion if, as in Connecticut, the statute declares ingestive abortions to be criminal only after quickening and also if, as in Illinois and Missouri, the statute declares ingestive abortions criminal without reference to quickening.[97]

Abortion statutes were enacted in ten states and one territory by 1841.[98] Maine, in 1840, became the first state to prohibit all abortions by any means at any point of gestation.[99] Maine's statute brings us to the second phase of legislative activity directed at abortion, a phase considered in the next chapter. In the rest of this chapter, we focus on New York's statutory provisions enacted before 1840.

# The First Abortion Statutes in New York (1829)

*That the scholar has decided he prefers peace to war does not require him to distort his facts.*

—Howard Zinn[100]

New York was one of the earlier states to follow Connecticut's lead by enacting abortion statutes in its first criminal code. New York's legislature revisited the abortion laws five times between 1828 and 1873. This statutory experience merits close attention, both because of its probable influence on other state legislatures and because law professor Cyril Means, jr., used New York's legislative history to build his argument for the "new" history of abortion that he advanced in his influential work. Means focused on New York both because he was based in New York and because he was directly involved in the repeal of New York's abortion laws.[101] Historian James Mohr also gave more extensive attention to the early New York abortion statutes than to those of other states,[102] in part perhaps because, thanks to Means, information regarding the New York statutes is more readily available to an historian.

---

96. Mohr, *supra* note 29, at 26. Mohr persisted in this argument when he considered later statutes that also dropped the quickening requirement. *Id.* at 41–43, 124, 131–33, 138–40, 142, 144. Mohr's ludicrous "double-speak" was also noted by Marvin Olasky. *See* Olasky, *supra* note 46, at 104–05.

97. *See also* Grossberg, *supra* note 67, at 161–63; Deborah Rhode, Justice and Gender 203 (1989).

98. Ark. Rev. Stat. ch. 44, div. III, art. II, §6 (1838), reprinted in Quay, *supra* note 45, at 450; 1821 Conn. Stat. tit. 22, §14, at 152, reprinted in Quay, *supra*, at 453; 1830 Conn. Pub. Acts ch. 1, §16, at 255, reprinted in Quay, *supra*, at 453; Ill. Rev. Laws §46 (1827), reprinted in Quay, *supra*, at 466; 1835 Ind. Gen. Laws ch. XLVII, §3, at 66, *codified at* Ind. Rev. Stat. ch. XXVI, §3, at 224 (1838), reprinted in Quay, *supra*, at 468; 1838 Iowa (Terr.) Stat. §18, at 145, reprinted in Quay, *supra*, at 470–71; Me. Rev. Stat. ch. 160, §§13 & 14 (1840), reprinted in Quay, *supra*, at 478; 1839 Miss. Laws tit. III, art. 1, §9, at 113, *codified at* Miss. Code ch. LXIV tit. III, §9, at 958 (1848), reprinted in Quay, *supra*, at 489; Mo. Rev. Stat. art. II, §§9, 10, 36, at 168–69, 172 (1835), reprinted in Quay, *supra*, at 490; N.Y. Rev. Stat. pt. IV, ch. I, tit. II, §§8, 9, at 550, & pt. VI, §21, at 578 (1829), reprinted in Quay, *supra*, at 499; 1834 Ohio Laws §§1, 2, at 20–21, *codified at* Ohio Gen. Stat. ch. 35, §§111, 112, at 252 (1841), reprinted in Quay, *supra*, at 504.

99. Me. Rev. Stat. ch. 160, §§13 & 14 (1840), reprinted in Quay, *supra* note 45, at 478.

100. Howard Zinn, The Politics of History 10 (2nd ed. 1990).

101. *See* Chapter 1, at notes 60–68.

102. Mohr, *supra* note 29, at 27–39.

Means used his history of the successive New York statutes to develop a theory that nine-teenth-century abortion statutes were enacted solely to protect the health of the mother.[103] He failed to explain why alarm over the risks of abortion emerged so prominently in the early nineteenth century to prompt the criminalization of what he and his supporters contend was before then a "common law liberty,"[104] an omission that gravely undermines his thesis. He never attempted to explain why what he claimed was the relatively uncontroversial practice of abortion suddenly would have became a legal (and inferentially a social) issue in the period be-tween 1803 (with the adoption of *Lord Ellenborough's Act*[105] in England) and 1840 (when Maine adopted the first American statute to ban all abortions).[106] Means never even attempted to pre-sent evidence that any legislatures were aware of any proliferation of abortions or of new abor-tion techniques during that time or of the dangers such proliferations might have posed to women's' health.[107]

New York, like the other original 13 states, carried forward the common law as the law of the state after independence, except in so far as the common law might be repugnant to "Republi-can" principles or other features of life in the new land.[108] The codification movement in New York responded to the same two concerns as in other states. First was a sense that it was unde-mocratic (contrary to "Republican" principles) for unelected judges (and the legal profession generally) rather than elected legislatures to define criminal conduct.[109] Second came a desire to simplify and systematize the confused law of the post-Revolutionary era.[110] In 1824, New York's legislature created Commission on Law Reform composed of three "Revisers" with authority to "alter the phraseology of statutes" in order to harmonize them with the state's constitution.[111] In other words, the Revisers were to codify the law of the state in an effort to sort out what already existed rather than to create a new body of law. In 1826, the legislature, at the urging of Gover-nor DeWitt Clinton, further authorized the Revisers to "redesign, reformulate, and redevelop the whole body of New York statute law."[112] This seems like an open-ended invitation to the Re-visers to create an entirely new body of law. James Mohr would stress this power in his later study of the codification process,[113] but any changes the Revisers introduced had to fit both as logically defensible propositions within a coherent whole and as politically acceptable to a leg-islative majority. The Revisers worked during the rise of Jacksonian democracy, with its anti-elit-

---

103. For a similar argument regarding *Lord Ellenborough's Act* in England, see McLaren, *supra* note 35, at 135–37.

104. For the "common law liberty" thesis, see: Roe v. Wade, 410 U.S. 113, 140 (1973); Beecham v. Leahy, 287 A.2d 836, 839 (Vt. 1972); *Casey Historians' Brief, supra* note 32, at 5–6; *Webster Historians' Brief, supra* note 32, at 170; Gordon, *supra* note 75, at 52–53, 57; Mohr, *supra* note 29, at 20–21, 128–29, 134–36, 144–45, 201, 208–11, 226, 229, 235–36; Laura Flanders, *Abortion: The Usable Past,* The Nation, Aug. 7, 1989, at 175; Morton Kondracke, *The Abortion Wars,* New Rep., Aug. 28, 1989, 17, at 19, col. 2; Means II, *supra* note 29, at 336, 351–54, 374–75, 409–10 n.175; Siegel, *Reasoning from the Body, supra* note 32; Solinger, *supra* note 75, at 243.

105. 43 Geo. III ch. 58 (1803), quoted in Chapter 5, at notes 118–19.

106. Me. Rev. Stat. ch. 160, §§ 13 & 14 (1840), reprinted in Quay, *supra* note 45, at 478.

107. Means I, *supra* note 29, at 503–06.

108. N.Y. Const., art. 7 § xiii (1821).

109. *See, e.g.,* Jesse Higgins, Sampson against the Philistines, or the Reformation of Lawsuits (1805).

110. *See, e.g.,* Robert Rantoul, *Oration at Scituate* [1836], reprinted in Memoirs, Speeches, and Writ-ings of Robert Rantoul, Jr. (Luther Hamilton ed. 1981).

111. Cook, *supra* note 60, at 141.

112. *Id.,* at 142.

113. Mohr, *supra* note 78, at 79.

ist and anti-professional inclinations—a bias that was particularly directed at medicine[114] and law.[115]

In 1829, the New York legislature enacted the Revisers' proposals as the *New York Revised Statutes*. New York's legislature did not enact the entire code as proposed by the Revisers, rejecting specific proposals that ran afoul of its preferences. A prime example that we shall look at below was the proposal to limit the discretion of "physicians" (of whatever ilk) to perform surgeries generally on their own responsibility. The legislature did enact restrictions on abortion that carried forward the common law regarding the crime as the first New York statutes to address abortion. Three sections of the *New York Revised Statutes* as enacted spoke directly to abortion:

§ 8:   The willful killing of an unborn quick child, by any injury to the mother of such child, which would be murder if it resulted in the death of such mother, shall be deemed manslaughter in the first degree.

§ 9:   Every person who shall administer to any woman pregnant with a quick child, any medicine, drug or substance whatever, or shall use or employ any instrument or other means, with intent thereby to destroy such child, unless the same shall have been necessary to preserve the life of such mother, or shall have been advised by two physicians to be necessary for such purpose, shall, in case of death of such child or of such mother be thereby produced, be deemed guilty of manslaughter in the second degree.

§ 21: Every person who shall willfully administer to any pregnant woman, any medicine, drug, substance or thing whatever, or shall use or employ any instrument or other means whatever, with intent thereby to procure the miscarriage of any such woman, unless the same shall have been necessary to preserve the life of such woman, or shall have been advised by two physicians to be necessary for that purpose; shall, upon conviction, be punished by imprisonment in a county jail not more than one year, or by a fine not exceeding five hundred dollars, or by both such fine and imprisonment.[116]

The Revisers also proposed a section 10 that would have made the negligent killing of a quick fetus manslaughter "in the same degree as if the mother had been killed."[117] The legislature did not enact proposed section 10.

Sections 8 and 9 made abortion of a quick child manslaughter if the abortion produced the death of the child, regardless of the effect on the mother. Section 21 made abortion of an unquickened fetus a misdemeanor, again regardless of the effect on the mother. Proposed section

---

114.  GROSSBERG, *supra* note 67, at 171–72; JOSEPH KETT, THE FORMATION OF THE AMERICAN MEDICAL PROFESSION: THE ROLE OF INSTITUTIONS, 1780–1890 (1968); WILLIAM ROTHSTEIN, AMERICAN PHYSICIANS IN THE NINETEENTH CENTURY: FROM SECTS TO SCIENCE 39–174 (1972); RICHARD SHRYOCK, MEDICAL LICENSING IN AMERICA, 1650–1965, at 98–115 (1967); MARY ROTH WALSH, DOCTORS WANTED: NO WOMEN NEED APPLY 11–14 (1977); ALEXANDER WILDER, HISTORY OF MEDICINE: A BRIEF OUTLINE OF MEDICAL HISTORY AND SECTS OF PHYSICIANS, FROM THE EARLIEST HISTORIC PERIOD; WITH AN EXTENDED ACCOUNT OF THE NEW SCHOOLS OF THE HEALING ART IN THE NINETEENTH CENTURY, AND ESPECIALLY A HISTORY OF THE AMERICAN ECLECTIC PRACTICE OF MEDICINE, NEVER BEFORE PUBLISHED 499–511 (1901); Charles Coventry, *History of Medical Legislation in New York*, 4 N.Y. J. MED. 151 (1845); Reginald Fitz, *The Rise and Fall of the Licensed Physician in Massachusetts, 1781–1860*, TRANS. ASS'N AM. PHYSICIANS 9 (1894).

115.  MAXWELL BLOOMFIELD, AMERICAN LAWYERS IN A CHANGING SOCIETY, 1776–1876, at 32–58 (1978); ALFRED REED, TRAINING FOR THE PUBLIC PROFESSION OF THE LAW 75–77 (1921); Paul Carrington, *The Missionary Diocese of Chicago*, 44 J. LEGAL EDUC. 467, 507–10 (1994); James Robinson, *Admission to the Bar as Provided for in the Indiana Constitutional Convention of 1850–51*, 1 IND. L.J. 209 (1926).

116.  N.Y. REV. STAT. pt. IV, ch. 1, tit. 2, §§ 8, 9, at 550, pt. IV, ch. 1, tit. 6, § 21, at 578 (1829), reprinted in Quay, *supra* note 45, at 499.

117.  Proposed N.Y. Rev. Stat. pt. IV, ch. 1, tit. 2, § 10 (1829), 6 REVISERS' NOTES, *supra* note 53, at 13.

10 would have made even the negligent killing of a quick fetus manslaughter. Simply reading these provisions suggests that they were designed to protect the life of the fetus rather than to protect the life of the mother.[118] Furthermore, the therapeutic exceptions in sections 9 and 21 authorized abortions only if necessary to protect the mother's life; protecting her health was not sufficient justification for an abortion.[119] The strictness of the therapeutic exceptions also suggests that these statutes were not merely health measure for the protection of the mother. Even Cyril Means, jr., had to concede that the 1829 enactments in New York appeared to be designed to protect the fetus rather than the mother.[120] He insisted, however, that a careful reading disclosed that the provisions were designed solely to protect health of the mother and not the life of the fetus even while conceding that nothing in the statute or the Revisers' Notes accompanying the statutes declared his proposition directly.[121]

Means began his analysis by arguing that sections 8 and 9 merely codified the traditional common law of abortion and did not represent considered thought about what the policies governing post-quickening abortion ought to be.[122] Ironically, only three years later he would "discover" that abortion in fact had never been a common law crime.[123] This did not lead him to a reexamine his conclusions regarding the significance of New York's 1829 provisions, for he had not rested his case entirely on the supposed congruence of those provisions and the common law.

A claim that the 1829 statutory provisions were not designed to protect the life of the fetus seems rather unlikely given the consistent pattern of the common law commentators, not to mention the courts, of describing the crime of abortion as designed to do just that.[124] The most influential commentator available at the time of the Revisers' work—William Blackstone—had introduced his brief discussion of abortion by describing life as "the immediate gift of God, a right inherent by nature in every individual" that begins as soon as the infant quickens.[125] James Parker's treatise on the common law as followed in New York also spoke in terms of protecting the life of the fetus.[126] Means did not report these views, instead seeking to buttress his reading of the New York provisions through recourse to the 1828 *Revisers' Notes* that accompanied the proposed *Revised Statutes* to the legislature.[127] The Revisers, however, actually did not say much about the intended meaning of their several proposals and said nothing directly to suggest that these provisions were merely health measures, and in fact contradicted Means.

The Revisers wrote explicitly that they understood section 8 to change the law by making it more restrictive of abortion. They thought that "[t]he killing of an unborn quick child, by striking the mother is now only a misdemeanor...."[128] The phrasing, however, suggests again a focus on protecting the child, not the mother. Section 9 went to the legislature without any

---

118. *See* B. James George, jr., *Current Abortion Laws: Proposals and Movements for Reform*, in Abortion and the Law 1, 11 (David Smith ed. 1967).

119. This pattern was general in nineteenth-century and early twentieth-century therapeutic exceptions in abortion statutes. Witherspoon, *supra* note 65, at 45–47. For early cases construing American therapeutic exceptions, see: State v. Lee, 69 Conn. 186, 198 (1897); Willey v. State, 46 Ind. 363 (1874); State v. Fitzporter, 93 Mo. 390, 394 (1887); State v. Meek, 70 Mo. 355 (1879); Moody v. State, 17 Ohio St. 111 (1866); State v. Stokes, 54 Vt. 179 (1881).

120. Means I, *supra* note 29, at 445, 449.

121. *Id.* at 450–52.

122. *Id.* at 446.

123. Means II, *supra* note 29.

124. See Chapter 4, Chapter 5 at notes 35–55, and this Chapter, *supra* at notes 3–6.

125. 1 William Blackstone, Commentaries on the Laws of England *129 (1765), quoted in Chapter 5, at notes 47, 48.

126. Parker, *supra* note 5, at 216–17, quoted in Chapter 4, at note 351.

127. Means I, *supra* note 29, at 443–53.

128. 6 Revisers' Notes, *supra* note 53, at 12.

explanatory note whatsoever. Means found this silence "astounding"[129]—as it would be had the Revisers considered themselves to be introducing a significant change in the law that would repeal a common law liberty, rather than merely elevating an existing misdemeanor to a felony. As for section 21, the Revisers indicated explicitly that their work was "founded upon an English statute…but with the qualification which is deemed just and necessary."[130] The referenced English statute could only be *Lord Ellenborough's Act*.[131] In a note referring to the proposed section 10, the Revisers stated that "[a] child not born, is considered as not being in *rerum natura,* and therefore not subject of murder, so that the killing [of] such a child is not murder or manslaughter."[132] We find here an intent to modify the law, rather than merely unthinkingly carrying forward of the law as it had existed before. And nowhere did the legislature or the Revisers distinguish the goals of their new statute—even section 21 regarding the abortion of a pre-quickened fetus—from the goals of the traditional protections afforded the fetus after quickening. Indeed, the Revisers' phrase *in rerum natura* comes directly from Blackstone—who had indicated that the purpose of such statutes was to protect fetal life.[133]

Means sought to infer the purpose of protecting maternal health from the inclusion of a therapeutic exception in the New York statutes.[134] Pregnancies were considerably more dangerous in the early nineteenth century than they are today and once abortions became somewhat practical arguments in favor of therapeutic exceptions began. English physicians had advocated therapeutic abortions at least as early as 1756,[135] although no authorization was enacted in England for such abortions until 1929.[136] Arguments for these exceptions were grounded on appeals to a maternal right of self-defense, not on a rejection of fetal personhood. The "self-defense" argument was made explicitly in the United States at least as early as 1866.[137] If we are to speculate about the Revisers' unstated premises, this would appear a more likely idea than the claim that they simply were not concerned about the life of the fetus. Yet the notion that allowing abortions to save the mother's life implicitly rejects (or at least undercuts) the claim that the fetus is a person with legal rights is common today among abortion rights supporters.[138] Apparently some cannot comprehend the idea of balancing a fetal right to life against a maternal right to life.

Means relied even more strongly on an unenacted proposal to ban all surgery unless necessary to save the life of the patient, included in the same title as section 21:

> §28:   Every person who shall perform any surgical operation, by which human life shall be destroyed or endangered, such as the amputation of a limb, or of the breast, trepanning, cutting for the stone, or for hernia, unless it appear that the same was nec-

---

129. Means I, *supra* note 29, at 448.

130. 6 REVISERS' NOTES, *supra* note 53, at 74 (the section is numbered §24 in the notes; it was renumbered as §21 when enacted due to several earlier sections being omitted by the legislature, including proposed §10 that dealt with the negligent killing of a fetus).

131. 43 Geo. III ch. 58 (1803), reprinted in Chapter 5, at notes 118–19.

132. 6 REVISORS NOTES, *supra* note 53, at 74.

133. 1 BLACKSTONE, *supra* note 125, at *129, quoted in Chapter 5, at notes 47, 48 .

134. Means I, *supra* note 29, at 449–50.

135. William Cooper, *A Case of the Caesarian Section,* 4 MED. OBSERVATIONS & INQUIRIES 261 (1771). *See* L.A. PARRY, CRIMINAL ABORTION 9 (1932).

136. *The Infant Life (Preservation) Act,* 19 & 20 Geo. V ch. 34, §1 (1929). The Act permitted therapeutic abortions only to preserve the life of the mother. *See generally* J. Keown, *The Scope of the Offence of Child Destruction,* 104 LAW Q. REV. 120 (1988).

137. *See* HORATIO ROBINSON STORER, WHY NOT? A BOOK FOR EVERYWOMAN 23–27 (1866).

138. *See, e.g.,* FAYE GINSBURG, CONTESTED LIVES: THE ABORTION DEBATE IN AN AMERICAN COMMUNITY 32 (1989); KRISTIN LUKER, ABORTION AND THE POLITICS OF MOTHERHOOD 32–33 (1984); LAURENCE TRIBE, ABORTION: THE CLASH OF ABSOLUTES 228–30 (1990).

essary for the preservation of life, or was advised, by at least two physicians, shall be ad-judged guilty of a misdemeanor.[139]

There are several problems with Means' reading of the proposed therapeutic exceptions (sections 9 and 21) together with the ban on unnecessary surgery (section 28). The therapeu-tic exceptions differed significantly from the proposal to ban unnecessary surgery. The abor-tion provisions excepted from criminality abortions that "shall have been necessary to pre-serve the life of such mother, or shall have been advised by two physicians to be necessary for such purpose." The proposed surgery statute made unnecessary surgery a crime "unless it ap-pear that the same was necessary for the preservation of life, or was advised, by at least two physicians." The subtle change would have made the latter therapeutic exception considerably broader, covering any procedure thought advisable for any health reasons by two physi-cians.[140] The therapeutic exceptions for abortion are limited to the most extreme circum-stances—when the life of the mother was at stake. Claims today, as by historian Kerry Pe-tersen, that physicians and the law in the eighteenth and nineteenth centuries authorized therapeutic abortions when either the mother's life or her health was in danger misstate the law.[141]

Means dismissed the change in language as a drafting oversight. He inferred *from the differ-ence in phrasing* that the surgery ban was earlier and cruder than what he considered the more developed therapeutic exception relating to pharmacologically induced abortions.[142] Means never considered whether the difference in phrasing arose because the therapeutic exception for abortion was a self-defense rule while the therapeutic exception for surgeries generally served other purposes, as indicated clearly by the Revisers' themselves:

> The rashness of many young practitioners in performing the most important surgical operations for the mere purpose of distinguishing themselves, has been a subject of much complaint, and we are advised by old and experienced surgeons, that the loss of life occasioned by the practice is alarming. The above section furnishes the means in-demnity (*sic*), by a consultation, or leaves the propriety of the operation to be deter-mined by the testimony of competent men. This offense is not included among the mal-practices in manslaughter, because, there may be cases in which the severest punishments ought not to be inflicted. By making it a misdemeanor, and leaving the punishment discretionary, a just medium seems to be preserved.[143]

All surgical procedures in the early nineteenth century were highly dangerous. In the era be-fore analgesics, anesthesia, antiseptics, and antibiotics, surgery often merely served to open the body to infection and the pain of surgery could (and often did) induce fatal shock. Based on the deposition of Dr. William Ober who had studied the records in the early surgery registry of the New York Hospital, Means himself concluded that the death rate early in the nineteenth century from "major peripheral surgery" was 37.5 per cent, nearly all of which (involving 31.25 per cent of all surgeries) was the result of septic infection.[144] The Revisers indicate they were concerned with these risks in proposed section 28 and with a fear that young surgeons were trying to prove their mettle by unnecessary surgery. This passage suggests that, unlike the abortion provisions, the Revisers did indeed intend to authorize and regulate general surgery necessary for any rea-

---

139. Proposed N.Y. Rev. Stat. pt. IV, tit. 6, § 28 (1829), 6 REVISERS' NOTES, *supra* note 53, at 75.

140. Robert Byrn, *An American Tragedy: The Supreme Court on Abortion*, 41 FORDHAM L. REV. 807, 831–32 (1973).

141. PETERSEN, *supra* note 38, at 18.

142. Means I, *supra* note 29, at 451–52.

143. 6 REVISERS' NOTES, *supra* note 53, at 75.

144. Means II, *supra* note 29, at 384–85.

son, and not merely surgery necessary to save the patient's life. This is an entirely different problem from the concerns underlying the ban on abortion. Means passed over these questions glibly, without ever really coming to grips with the language in the *Revisers' Notes*.[145] He also never attempted to explain why the Revisers would propose a statute specifically addressing abortion if the purpose of the proposed ban on abortion would have been fulfilled by a second proposed statute covering the very same ground in a wider swath.[146]

Perhaps, as James Mohr suggested, Means might have argued that the existence of the two provisions suggests that the Revisers did not consider abortion to be major surgery, and therefore did not consider abortion as included within the proposed section 28.[147] While the proposed section 28 did not refer to "major surgery," the *Revisers' Notes* did refer to "the most important surgical operations" as the object of this proposed regulation. Even Mohr, despite his suggesting the possibility that section 28 was confined to "major surgeries," found Means' analysis "less than convincing."[148] But then Mohr embraced the policy of protecting maternal health only insofar as it could serve to discredit a policy he disliked even more—protecting fetal life.[149]

As it turned out, the proposed statutory provisions on the negligent killing of a quick fetus and unnecessary surgery were never enacted.[150] The failure to enact does not change the implications to be drawn about the Revisers' intent. We have no direct record of what the New York legislature might have intended in adopting the proposals to ban abortions and rejecting the proposal to punish the negligent killing of a fetus and to ban unnecessary surgery. The pervasive silence on the import of these sections leaves the field open to speculation on what the motives or goals of the legislators were, but the several therapeutic exceptions taken together can hardly be said to prove—or even to suggest—that the legislature intended only to protect maternal health.

Means did not discuss another tangentially related but unenacted proposed statutory provision that would have made it a crime to use instruments in an obstetrical delivery unless advised by two physicians.[151] Whether Means overlooked this proposal in his haste to construct a pro-abortion history, or whether even he could not bring himself to claim that a regulation of cesarean sections demonstrated attitudes towards abortion, we shall never know. James Mohr, however, chose to argue that the failure to enact this provision confirms the legislature's lack of concern for protecting fetal life.[152] Mohr too did not consider that the failure to enact might represent a legislative preference for the preservation of the mother's life as determined by the judgment of the attending physician, a decision that might often arise in emergencies where no second physician could readily be found.

One other provision in the 1829 *Revised Statutes* as enacted is also relevant to whether that code was equally protective of fetal life before or after quickening. The *Revised Statutes* provided for the reprieve of a woman from execution if she were "quick with child."[153] This provision is

145. Means I, *supra* note 29, at 451–53.

146. A problem noted in Byrn, *supra* note 140, at 832.

147. MOHR, *supra* note 29, at 30–31.

148. *Id.* at 29.

149. *Id.* at 135–38, 239–40. *See also* Siegel, *supra* note 32, at 278.

150. Proposed N.Y. Rev. Stat. pt. IV, ch. 1, tit. 2, § 10, pt. IV, ch. 1, tit. 6, § 28 (1828), REVISERS' NOTES, *supra* note 53, at 13, 75.

151. 3 REVISERS NOTES, *supra* note 53, at 829.

152. MOHR, *supra* note 29, at 270–71 n.19.

153. N.Y. REV. STAT. pt. IV, ch. 1, tit. 6, § 22, at 578 (1829). Curiously, Vice-President Gore espoused allowing the condemned women to choose whether to delay her execution. Gore, who supports the death penalty but has become a convert to a woman's right to choose, found that any other answer to the question would interfere with the woman's right to control her own body—as if the execution were not a more significant interference in that right. Katharine Seelye, *The Issues: Gore and Bush Duel on an Odd Death-Penalty*

not conclusive on the attitude towards the presence or absence of life in the womb before quickening. First, at this time it was virtually impossible to know whether a woman was pregnant before quickening.[154] The doubt that precluded even a temporary reprieve thus could have related to the very fact of pregnancy and not to whether there was a living human being in the womb. The English practice of allowing only one reprieve for proven pregnancy perhaps suggests less of an inclination to see the fetus as a human being,[155] but could also be interpreted as simply expressing a strong policy against cheating the executioner. Consider how a condemned woman held in prison could become pregnant repeatedly. Second, the term "quick with child" turns out to be ambiguous upon close examination.

We have already noted the dramatic changes in scientific theories about the nature of conception and the emergence of a new consensus on when a distinct human being began that were built upon the scientific discoveries of the early nineteenth century.[156] This new scientific consensus on the nature of human gestation required an educational process to convince many in the public.[157] The new consensus seems to have been quickly accepted by the more articulate and educated portions of American society without the need for the sort of educational campaign necessary to propagate this new thinking among the rest of society, for the new consensus produced immediate legal effects. As in England, laws were quickly amended to remove, in all but a few states, all distinctions based on quickening, and even in the few that retained the distinction, abortion before quickening came to be treated as a serious crime.[158] In one well-known English decision, *Regina v. Wycherley*,[159] Baron John Gurney did not wait for legislative action but reinterpreted the term "quick with child" to mean after conception rather than after quickening. This decision apparently returned the legal meaning of the phrase to what had been its meaning in the Middle Ages: bearing a living child regardless of how the fact that the child was alive was determined or how long the pregnancy had continued.[160] The *Wycherley* decision was followed widely, albeit not universally, in the United States.[161] The quickening distinction survive in some

---

*Question*, N.Y. Times, July 18, 2000, at A14. Of course, such a position will seldom make any practical difference. How often will a woman in that position choose not to delay the execution?

154. *See* Chapter 1, at notes 128–34.

155. Donald Judges, Hard Choices, Lost Voices 96–97 (1993). Islamic law was considerably more generous, not only reprieving a woman under death sentence until she gave birth, but extending the reprieve for two years after birth to allow her to suckle the child. Fazul Karim, 2 Al-Hadis 538–40 (1939). *But see* Maulana Muhammad Ali, The Religion of Islam 556–57 (1990) (treating this supposed ruling as apocryphal).

156. *See* Chapter 5, at notes 209–46.

157. See the discussion of the writings of Dr. Thomas Radford in Chapter 5, at notes 231–32.

158. *See* Chapter 5, at notes 178–92, 239–46 (England), and Chapter 7, at notes 5, 12, 19, 22–23, 81–112 (America).

159. 173 Eng. Rep. 486 (N.P. 1838). *See also* 1 Joseph Chitty, A Practical Treatise on Medical Jurisprudence 402 (1834); *The Trial of William Russell at Huntingdon Assize, March 1832*, 2 The Legal Examiner 10, 12 (1832) (anonymous comment).

160. Philip Rafferty, *Roe v. Wade: The Birth of a Constitutional Right* 163–74 (University Microfilms International Dissertation Information Service, Ann Arbor, MI 1992). *See* Chapter 3, at notes 97–107.

161. State v. Reed, 45 Ark. 333, 334–36 (1885); Lamb v. State, 10 A. 208, 208 (Md. 1887); Commonwealth v. Taylor, 132 Mass. 261, 262 (1882); State v. Slagle, 83 N.C. 630, 632 (1880); Mills v. Commonwealth, 13 Pa. 630, 632 (1850). *Contra:* Taylor v. State, 33 S.E. 190 (Ga. 1899); Mitchell v. Commonwealth, 78 Ky. 204, 206–10 (1879); Smith v. State, 33 Me. 48, 57–60 (1851); Commonwealth v. Parker, 50 Mass. (9 Met.) 263, 265–68 (1845) (overruled in Commonwealth v. Taylor, *supra*, at 263); Commonwealth v. Bangs, 9 Mass. 386, 387 (1812) (overruled in Commonwealth v. Taylor, *supra*, at 263); State v. Cooper, 22 N.J.L. 52 (1849) (promptly reversed by statute; *see infra*, at notes 188–89); Evans v. People, 49 N.Y. 86 (1872) (see Chapter 7, at notes 82–101). *See also* Commonwealth v. Tibbetts, 132 N.E. 910 (Mass. 1893); Commonwealth v. Wood, 77 Mass. (11 Gray) 85, 92 (1858); Powe v. State, 2 A. 662, 664 (N.J. 1886).

American statutes as a basis for determining punishment.[162] An early anti-abortion polemic was published in the United States only one year after Gurney's decision.[163]

All of this happened a decade after the Revisers completed their work, so we cannot use *Wycherley* or its effects to ascertain what the phrase "quick with child" meant to the Revisers or to the New York legislature in 1828 and 1829. But there is some evidence that suggests that they were thinking along the same lines as the English judge would more famously think in 1838. This requires us to seek further evidence regarding precisely what lay behind the proposed legislation regarding pregnancy and abortion.

The abortion provisions in the 1829 *Revised Statutes* were actually drafted by Dr. T. Romeyn Beck.[164] The principal draftsman overall of the 1829 *Revised Statutes* was an attorney named John Canfield Spencer.[165] Spencer, a former United States District Attorney and Congressman, went on to serve as Secretary of War and as Secretary of the Treasury of the United States.[166] James Mohr has turned up a letter from Spencer to Beck (then the president of the New York State Medical Society), dated Sept. 11, 1828.[167] The letter attributes the authorship of the medical sections of the code to Beck and asks Beck to shepherd them through the legislature:

> I have prepared various Sections against medical malpractice according to your Suggestions, particularly the improper use of instruments, capital operations in Surgery, selling poisons &c. which when examined by Mr. Butler[168] I will have it edited and sent to you. In the meanwhile I want you to prepare the public and particularly the Legislature, by communications in the different newspapers, by extracts from approved writers on such subjects, and by such other means as occur to you, for a favorable examination and discussion upon our provisions. I have neither the time nor ability to do it.[169]

The letter does not mention abortion as such, unless the reference to selling poisons is a reference to abortifacient potions. If so, the reference is incomplete as the provisions Beck apparently provided included intrusive and injurious abortions as well as ingestive abortions.[170]

Romeyn Beck was the author of *Elements of Medical Jurisprudence,*[171] a book published in New York that had made him the leading American authority on medical jurisprudence at the time.[172] Beck favored several innovations in the law relating to procreation, as he termed it, including liberalizing of the law of rape (making penetration with or without ejaculation the gist of the crime)[173] and was strongly opposed to abortion. The tenor of Beck's attitude towards

---

162. See the statutes collected in Chapter 7, at notes 12. *See also* State v. Reed, 45 Ark. 333, 334 (1885); State v. Watson, 1 P. 770 (Kan. 1883); People v. Abbott, 74 N.W. 529, 530 (Mich. 1898); State v. Emerich, 13 Mo. App. 492, 497–99 (1883), *aff'd*, 87 Mo. 110, 111 (1885).

163. Henry Hodge, An Introductory Lecture to a Course on Obstetrics (1839).

164. Mohr, *supra* note 78, at 81–82.

165. N.Y. Rev. Stat., preface at vi (1846).

166. Mohr, *supra* note 78, at 80.

167. *Id.* at 81.

168. Benjamin Butler was another member of the commission charged with drafting the new code. *Id.* at 79. A future Attorney-General of the United States, he was also the founder of the New York University School of Law. *See* David Muzzey, *Benjamin F. Butler,* in 2 Dictionary of American Biography 356–57 (1929); Hoeflich, *supra* note 78, at 130–32.

169. Quoted in Mohr, *supra* note 78, at 81.

170. N.Y. Rev. Stat. pt. IV, ch. 1, tit. 2, §§ 8, 9, at 550, pt. IV, ch. 1, tit. 6, § 21, at 578 (1829), *reprinted in* Quay, *supra* note 45, at 499.

171. 1 Theodoric Romeyn Beck, Elements of Medical Jurisprudence (1823).

172. *See generally* Frank Hamilton, Eulogy on the Life and Character of Theodoric Romeyn Beck (1856); Mohr, *supra* note 78, at 15–28, 42–49, 54–64, 69–70, 76–91, 94–100, 105–06.

173. 1 Beck, *supra* note 171, at 86–99.

abortion is indicated by his inclusion of the topic in his discussion of infanticide.[174] In the latter respect, Beck was strongly influenced by the work of his younger brother, Dr. John Beck, who had established himself, beginning with a study published in 1817, as an internationally recognized expert on abortion and infanticide.[175] Indeed, beginning with the fifth edition of the elder Beck's now standard treatise on medical jurisprudence, both Beck's were listed as co-authors, although there is reason to believe that John's only contribution was the 177-page chapter on "infanticide."[176] Over successive editions, the chapter on infanticide grew to several hundred pages.

Although the Revisers' Notes are virtually silent about the policy goals of the statutory prohibition of abortion, Romeyn Beck was explicit about his views in his treatise. He did indeed oppose abortion because it was dangerous for the mother,[177] yet he made it abundantly clear that his central concern in opposing abortion was because it involved the unjustified killing of a human being.[178] His and his brother's work on "infanticide" make it clear that they anticipated *Wycherley* in concluding that "quick with child" simply meant "alive"—and they had concluded that life began at conception.[179]

Mohr sought to explain this second posture away by pointing out that the Doctors Beck, like other "medical jurisprudes" of their era, stressed the importance of resolving doubtful cases of suspected "infanticide" in favor of the mother.[180] Several of the arguments that Mohr relies on depend on student notes taken at lectures on medical jurisprudence; those notes, of course, might not be accurate, as any professor who has discussed a student's notes with the student can attest. Still, they convey how some students perceived the lecturer's message. Nothing in those notes, however, contradicts the repeated and explicit endorsement by the Becks of the theory that a new human life came into being at the moment of conception. These notes indicate clearly and directly the purposes for the prohibition of abortion, and the apparent understanding of the Revisers (by way of the Becks) of the meaning of the term "quick with child" in the reprieve provisions.

It thus is probable, although not altogether certain, that the phrase "quick with child" meant pregnant at any stage of gestation even in 1829. If so, it hardly helps those who might cite the reprieve provision as demonstrating a lack of legislative concern to protect early fetal life. Curiously, Cyril Means did not mention the reprieve provision or its import at all in arguing that the purpose of the several provisions in the *Revised Statutes* were intended solely to protect the mother's health and life—although arguably it provided the strongest, albeit hardly conclusive, legal evidence for his position. Nor did Means cite any evidence that either the Revisers or the legislators were aware of the relative safety of childbirth compared to abortion when they adopted New York's first abortion statutes. The earliest publication cited by Means that actually made the relative safety argument was not published until 1866.[181] Apparently the earliest medical source indicating a rising incidence of abortion in America was published in 1831.[182] That work was not published until three years after the Revisers completed their work and two years after the legislature enacted the *Revised Statutes*. Furthermore, that work is the tract of an anti-

---

174. *Id.* at 276–77.

175. JOHN BECK, AN INAUGURAL DISSERTATION ON INFANTICIDE 140 (1817). *See generally* C.R. GILMAN, SKETCH OF THE LIFE AND CHARACTER OF JOHN BROADHEAD BECK, M.D., LATE PROFESSOR OF *MATERIA MEDICA* AND MEDICAL JURISPRUDENCE IN THE COLLEGE OF PHYSICIANS AND SURGEONS, NEW YORK (1851); MOHR, *supra* note 78, at 21–22, 43, 45, 55–56.

176. T. ROMEYN BECK & JOHN BECK, ELEMENTS OF MEDICAL JURISPRUDENCE ch. 8 (5th ed. 1835).

177. BECK, *supra* note 171, at 276–77.

178. BECK & BECK, *supra* note 175, at 113.

179. See the text *supra* at notes 159–61.

180. MOHR, *supra* note 78, at 31–34, 43.

181. Means II, *supra* note 29, at 386, *citing* STORER, *supra* note 137, at 36–37, 46–47. *See also* STORER, *supra*, at 12–13, 35–49, 52–61, 70–71.

182. JOHN MCDOWELL, FIRST ANNUAL REPORT OF THE NEW YORK MAGDALEN SOCIETY (1831).

prostitution league that probably did not reach a wide audience. Apparently, the next earliest such work, also a report on prostitution, was published in England, but not until 1857.[183]

There is some evidence demonstrating that physicians and jurists at the end of the eighteenth and the beginning of the nineteenth century were concerned about the threats recent innovations in abortion technology posed to the lives or health of pregnant women. Means had missed several early medical and legal sources dating back to 1799 that had made much of the medical risks to women of the emerging possibility of abortion, including the books by the Drs. Beck.[184] Means sought to find evidence of reliance on a relative safety argument through a quotation from the first American edition (1844) of Dr. Alfred Taylor's *Manual of Medical Jurisprudence* on the medical indications for inducing labor or performing a cesarean section late in pregnancies.[185] Taylor's argument in fact tells us nothing about his (or others') views on whether abortion should be legally suppressed; Means simply ignored that Taylor unequivocally condemned abortion elsewhere in the same book.[186] In any event, England (as well as 12 states) had already enacted statutes explicitly banning abortions by 1844.[187] Given the uncontradicted evidence from the Drs. Beck and the Revisers, as well as the language of the provisions, that the motive behind enactment of the abortion provisions was to protect fetal life, Means surmise that the "real motive" for these provisions was only to protect maternal health simply does not hold up.

James Mohr's supposition that the "real motive" was to allow allopathic physicians to impose a monopoly on the practice of medicine fares no better. Although Mohr brought the Spencer-Beck letter to light, he did not confront the all too obvious implications of the Beck's work for the meaning of these statutes. True enough, the Becks were concerned that there be clear proof of "infanticide" before someone could be convicted of criminal abortion or infanticide.[188] Mohr did not bother to explain how insistence on clear proof of wrongdoing in infanticide or abortion cases suggests solicitude for those acts, while similar demands for clear proof from these same authors for suspected murders of adults or rapes does not represent such solicitude.[189] Indeed, the Becks generally insisted on the duty of physicians to undertake to investigate, on their own, any suspected crime in order to seek the necessary proof[190]—as Mohr himself knew.[191] Furthermore, even in the unlikely event that these physicians were secret supporters of abortion as Mohr incredibly argues,[192] such secrecy would tell us much about how society as a whole viewed such practices. What we are left with, then, is a set of laws proposed and supported by physicians who strongly condemned abortion as immoral and as murder, who favored including it in the emerging criminal codes, and who, consistent with the usual legal standard in criminal prosecutions in the United States, demanded proof beyond a reasonable doubt of the crime. The pattern was not limited to New York. Mohr himself told us in his

---

183. WILLIAM ACTON, PROSTITUTION (1857).

184. O.W. BARTLEY, A TREATISE ON FORENSIC MEDICINE 3, 5 (1815); JOHN BURNS, THE ANATOMY OF THE GRAVID UTERUS 57–58 (1799); BECK, *supra* note 171, at 276–77; BECK & BECK, *supra* note 175, at 113; 1 EDWARD HYDE EAST, A TREATISE ON THE PLEAS OF THE CROWN 230 (1803); GEORGE EDWARD MALE, AN EPITOME OF JUDICIAL OR FORENSIC MEDICINE 116–17 (1816).

185. Means II, *supra* note 29, at 395, *citing* ALFRED TAYLOR, MANUAL OF MEDICAL JURISPRUDENCE 595 (1st Am. ed. 1844). The book was originally published in England in 1842.

186. TAYLOR, *supra* note 185, at 201–02.

187. Joseph Dellapenna, *The History of Abortion: Technology, Morality, and Law*, 40 U. PITT. L. REV. 359, 400 n. 255 (1979). For detailed state-by-state studies of abortion legislation in the United States, see Quay, *supra* note 45; Witherspoon, *supra* note 65.

188. See the text *supra* at note 180.

189. MOHR, *supra* note 78, at 23, 33–34.

190. 2 BECK, *supra* note 171, at 10.

191. MOHR, *supra* note 78, at 23, 31.

192. *Id.* at 31. Does this mean that Mohr believes they were also secret supporters of infanticide?

study of medical jurisprudence generally that this was the typical pattern across the young nation.[193]

Cyril Means knew nothing of this, but then he was not really interested in discovering the true history of abortion. He was intent on creating a legal argument that could be used to overturn state abortion laws, an argument that did not depend on its historical accuracy.[194] Thus, instead of seeking out further evidence that might actually have clarified the purpose of New York's 1829 abortion statutes, Means was content to report a dearth of supporting legislative evidence. His response to that supposed dearth was even more misleading than his treatment of the *Revisers' Notes.* Means, and his followers, turned to an 1858 case in which the court appeared to endorse his view of the purpose of the similar laws enacted in New Jersey—*State v. Murphy.*[195] In *State v. Murphy,* a unanimous state supreme court seemed to declare definitively and decisively that the sole purpose of that state's recently adopted abortion statute was to protect maternal health and not to protect the life of the fetus: "The design of the statute was not to prevent the procuring 'of abortions, so much as to guard the health and life of the mother against the consequences of such attempts."[196] The same assertion appears in a later New Jersey case, *State v. Gedicke.*[197]

*Murphy* and *Gedicke* were the only nineteenth century case in which a court appeared to reject the protection of fetal life as a purpose of the state's abortion statutes, while no less than 17 other nineteenth-century decisions (several decided before *Murphy* and *Gedicke*) indicated that the protection of fetal life as well as the health of the mother was a purpose of their state's recently adopted abortion statutes, including one from New Jersey and three that were decided closer to the time the *New York Revised Statutes* were enacted.[198] Yet Means insisted that *State v. Murphy* was the only more or less contemporaneous case in which a court considered the purposes of a state's abortion statute.[199] Nor did he consider other possible readings of the meaning of the New Jersey decisions.

In *Murphy* itself, the New Jersey Supreme Court indicated (in the passage immediately before that quoted by Means) that the common law as received in New Jersey made abortion a crime only to protect the child.[200] The court therefore described New Jersey's eight-year old abortion statute[201] merely as a supplement to the common law, adding protection for the mother:

---

193. *Id.* at 82.

194. *See* Chapter 1, at notes 64–67.

195. 27 N.J.L. 112 (1858). *See* Means II, *supra* note 29, at 389–90; Means I, *supra* note 29, at 452, 507. *See also* GROSSBERG, *supra* note 67, at 162–66; SMITH-ROSENBERG, *supra* note 71, at 220 (while Smith-Rosenberg does not cite either to Means or to the case, her reference to *State v. Murphy* is clear in the text).

196. 27 N.J.L., at 114–15.

197. 43 N.J.L. 86, 89 (1881).

198. Dougherty v. People, 1 Colo. 514 (1872); State v. Lee, 37 A. 75 (Conn. 1897); Earll v. People, 99 Ill. 123 (1881); State v. Moore, 25 Iowa 128 (1868); Abrams v. Foshee, 3 Iowa 274 (1856); State v. Watson, 1 P. 770 (Kan. 1883); Smith v. State, 33 Me. 48 (1851); Lamb v. State, 10 A. 208 (Md. 1887); People v. Sessions, 26 N.W. 291 (Mich. 1886); People v. Olmstead, 30 Mich. 431 (1874); State v. Cooper, 22 N.J.L. 52 (1849); Railing v. Commonwealth, 1 A. 314 (Pa. 1885); Commonwealth v. W., 3 Pitts. R. 462 (1871); State v. Crook, 51 P. 1091 (Utah 1898); State v. Howard, 32 Vt. 380 (1859); Hatchard v. State, 48 N.W. 380 (Wis. 1891); State v. Dickinson, 41 Wis. 299 (1871). *See generally* Byrn, *supra* note 140, at 828–29; Robert Destro, *Abortion and the Constitution: The Need for a Life-Protective Amendment,* 63 CAL. L. REV. 1250, 1273–78 (1975).

199. Means II, *supra* note 29, at 389; Means I, *supra* note 29, at 452, 507.

200. *See also* State v. Cooper, 22 N.J.L. 52 (1849) (abortion is a crime at common law only after quickening, a rule the court held was intended to protect fetal life). The court in *Cooper, id.* at 57, rejected the *Wycherley* holding that "quick with child" meant "pregnant" regardless of whether the child had quickened. *See* Chapter 5, at notes 241–46.

201. N.J. Laws 1849, at 266, *reprinted in* Quay, *supra* note 45, at 496.

At the common law, the procuring of an abortion, by the mother herself, or by another with her consent, was not indictable, unless the mother was quick with child. The act was purged of its criminality, so far as it affected the mother, by her consent. It was an offense only against the life of the child.... [T]he statute [does not] make it criminal for the woman to swallow the potion or consent to the operation or other means to procure an abortion.... Her guilt or innocence remains as at common law. Her offence at the common law is against the life of the child.[202]

It should not have been too difficult for Means to realize this as the New Jersey Supreme Court had endorsed this reading of *Murphy* 12 years before Means wrote his first article on the history of abortion.[203]

In its later *Gedicke* decision, the New Jersey Supreme Court emphasized that abortion "in almost every case endangers the life and health of the woman."[204] This conclusion was still correct in 1881 when the *Gedicke* court wrote.[205] If so, the New Jersey court's solicitude for the welfare of women was quite understandable and it rendered moot whether the law was also directed at protecting the life of the fetus. The abortionist was only to be punished once regardless of whether it was for endangering the life of the mother or for killing (or attempting to kill) the fetus. Additionally, the court in *Gedicke* pointed out that the New Jersey legislature had extended the state's abortion statute in 1872 "to protect the life of the child also, and inflict the same punishment, in case of its death, as if the mother should die."[206] Even in New Jersey, protection of fetal life seems to have been a prominent purpose of the law relating to abortion.

Turning to cases from other states only reinforces the notion that these laws were enacted primarily to protect fetal life. The Iowa Supreme Court, in its 1868 decision of *State v. Moore*, perhaps delivered the clearest statement that the abortion statutes were designed to protect fetal life. First, the court quoted, with strong approval, the following language from the trial judge's charge to the jury:

To attempt to produce a miscarriage, except when in proper professional judgment it is necessary to preserve the life of the woman, is an unlawful act. It is known to be a dangerous act, generally producing one and sometimes two deaths,—I mean the death of the unborn infant and the death of the mother.[207]

The court then summarized its own view of the matter in these words:

The common law is distinguished, and is to be commended, for its all-embracing and salutary solicitude for the sacredness of human life and the personal safety of every human being. This protecting, paternal care, enveloping every individual like the air he breathes, not only extends to persons actually born, but, for some purposes, to infants *in* (sic) *ventre sa mere*.[208]

The Iowa court could hardly have spoken more clearly, and, although the case rather obviously involved an infant after quickening, the court did not mention this fact in its opinion.[209]

---

202. 27 N.J.L., at 114.

203. State v. Siciliano, 121 A.2d 490, 495 (N.J. 1956). *See also* Gleitman v. Cosgrove, 227 A.2d 689, 699 (N.J. 1967) (Francis, J., concurring). *See generally* 1 RAFFERTY, *supra* note 160, at 75–78.

204. 43 N.J.L., at 96.

205. *See* Chapter 1. *See also* SHORTER, *supra* note 37, at 177.

206. 43 N.J.L. at 90.

207. 25 Iowa 128, 131–32 (1868).

208. *Id.* at 135–36.

209. The irrelevance of quickening in *State v. Moore* was emphasized in *State v. Harris*, 136 P. 264, 266 (Kan. 1913).

Means not only did not discuss possible variant readings of the New Jersey cases, he also ignored numerous cases contemporary to the New Jersey decisions that clearly contradicted his view. Anyone who has attempted to do original research in early English legal records will undoubtedly sympathize with the difficulties that might explain Means' failure to find additional cases there from centuries ago.[210] No excuse appears, however, for an American law professor to miss so many American decisions relevant to his analysis and decided only a century or so before he was writing. Nor does any excuse appear for misreporting, apparently willfully, the actual statements of the decisions he does discuss. Means' thesis that these statutes were not directed at protecting fetal life but only at protecting maternal health, upon close examination, turns out to be a clear and successful example of "law office history."[211] It will not be the only example we shall find, although, because of its impact on *Roe v. Wade,*[212] it is the most important.

# The Allopathic "Conspiracy"

> *[I]t certainly represents a perversion of the historical intention underlying the abortion legislation, which was passed for the protection of the unborn child and not as a form of control of unregistered medical practitioners.*
>
> —Glanville Williams[213]

Historian James Mohr hardly did better in reading the *New York Revised Statutes of 1829* than did law professor Cyril Means, jr. After disparaging Means' conclusion that the abortion provisions in the *Revised Statutes* reflected concerns to protect the health of mothers from unnecessary surgery, Mohr asserted that these prohibitions were anti-poisoning statutes, not anti-abortion statutes.[214] Mohr's conclusion, the same as his conclusion regarding the first Connecticut statute,[215] is actually similar to that of Means and just as wrong. Mohr even claimed that the New York statutory provisions did not indicate a concern about abortions induced by "mechanical methods"[216] despite the fact that the New York statutes expressly prohibited abortions by both injury techniques and intrusion techniques.[217]

Mohr did not stop with reading the New York abortion provisions as anti-poisoning statutes, for he was adopted yet a more all encompassing rationale for the enactment of these statutes, of-

---

210. *See generally* Chapter 3.

211. Alfred Kelly, *Cleo and the Court: An Illicit Love Affair,* 1965 Sup. Ct. Rev. 119, 125–28. *See also* Robert Palmer, *Akhl Amar: Elitist Populist and Anti-Textual Textualist,* 16 S. Ill. L.J. 397, 397 (1992); Paul Murphy, *Time to Reclaim: The Current Challenges of American Constitutional History,* 69 Am. Hist. Rev. 64, 75 (1965); John Phillip Reid, *Law and History,* 27 Loy.-L.A. L. Rev. 193, 198–200, 204–12 (1993); William Wiecek, *Cleo as Hostage: The United States Supreme Court and the Uses of History,* 24 Cal. W.L. Rev. 227, 230, 258–64 (1988).

212. Justice Blackmun cited Means' supposed history no less than seven times in the opinion in *Roe,* 410 U.S., at 136–39. Blackmun cited no other sources on legal history. *See also* Wolfgang Saxon, *Obituary: Cyril C. Means, 73, A Specialist in Laws Regarding Abortion,* N.Y. Times, Oct. 6, 1992, at A15.

213. Glanville Williams, The Sanctity of Life and the Criminal Law 191 (1957).

214. Mohr, *supra* note 29, at 27–31.

215. *See* Mohr, *supra* note 29, at 21. See generally the text *supra* at notes 59–63.

216. Mohr, *supra* note 29, at 22, 30–31, 270–71 n.19.

217. *Injury techniques:* N.Y. Rev. Stat. pt. 4, ch. 1, tit. 2, §8, at 550 (1829), *reprinted in* Quay, *supra* note 45, at 499. *Intrusion techniques:* N.Y. Rev. Stat. pt. 4, ch. 1, tit. 2, §9, at 550 (post-quickening), & tit. 6, §21, at 578 (pre-quickening) (1829), *both reprinted in* Quay, *supra,* at 499. The full texts of these provisions are quoted *supra* at note 109.

fering as a rationale for the New York legislature's decision to prohibit all elective abortions in the 1829 *Revised Statutes* that the prohibitions were directed at "irregular practitioners, greedy physicians, and folk women."[218] Mohr's list covered every conceivable abortionist except those relying purely on divine intervention, and introduced his major thesis—that nineteenth-century abortion laws reflected a conspiracy of the organized, allopathic medical profession to suppress competition from irregular practitioners.[219] This claim became the pervasive theme throughout Mohr's book, and is widely followed by those who seek to perpetuate the new orthodoxy regarding the history of abortion.[220] Such charges are found in the "histories" of abortion—but not in the histories of midwifery, which acknowledge that the suppression of midwifery involved concerns of class, ethnicity, and the professional interests of physicians of both sexes.[221]

Allopathic medicine is the form of medicine that became dominant in the nineteenth century and remains so today.[222] Allopathic medicine was based upon the emerging biological science of the time, and sought to reverse or override the effects of disease. Allopaths viewed the human body in mechanistic terms, seeing disease as caused by localized problems within the machinery of the human body that the physician treated by repairing or excising the defective parts.[223] Under this theory, the physician was the dominant actor in curing disease and the patient was assigned a passive role. Allopathic medicine became university centered, and eventually gave us the germ theory of disease, with treatment increasingly centered upon drugs for the killing of germs and surgery for the correction or removal of diseased or defective organs.

The growth of allopathic medicine—academic medicine—in the United States was largely a product of the nineteenth century. In 1770, there were only two medical schools in the American colonies, and only four in 1800.[224] By 1850, there were 42, and some 11,828 medical degrees were awarded by these schools in the 1840s.[225] Yet the early and middle years of the nineteenth century were in some ways similar to the closing years of the twentieth century when allopathic medicine had to contend with numerous rival schools of medical theory for survival and dominance.[226] Of all the men who held themselves out as physicians in New England during the pe-

---

218. MOHR, *supra* note 29, at 31.

219. *Id.* at 31–45

220. *See* JANET FARRELL BRODIE, CONTRACEPTION AND ABORTION IN NINETEENTH-CENTURY AMERICA 266–72 (1994); BARBARA BROOKES, ABORTION IN ENGLAND 1900–1967, at 54–56 (1988); RAYMOND DEVRIES, MAKING MIDWIVES LEGAL: CHILDBIRTH, MEDICINE, AND THE LAW 25–27 (2nd ed. 1996); GORDON, *supra* note 75, at 59–60, 160–72; MCLAREN, *supra* note 35, at 115; PATRICIA MILLER, THE WORST OF TIMES 314 (1993); REAGAN, *supra* note 59, at 10–11, 81–82, 90–112; SMITH-ROSENBERG, *supra* note 71, at 223–44; Jane Pacht Brickman, *Public Health, Midwives, and Nurses, 1880–1930,* in NURSING HISTORY: NEW PERSPECTIVES, NEW POSSIBILITIES 65, 69 (Ellen Condliffe Lagemann ed. 1983); Jane Maslow Cohen, *A Jurisprudence of Doubt: Deliberative Autonomy and Abortion,* 3 COLUM. J. GENDER & LAW. 175, 208–10 (1992); Elizabeth Karlin, *"We Called It Kindness": Establishing a Feminist Abortion Practice,* in ABORTION WARS: A HALF CENTURY OF STRUGGLE, 1950–2000, at 273, 279 (Rickie Solinger ed. 1998). *See also* Neal Devitt, *How Doctors Conspire to Eliminate the Midwife even though the Scientific Data Support Midwifery,* in COMPULSORY HOSPITALIZATION: FREEDOM OF CHOICE IN CHILDBIRTH? 345 (D. & L. Stewart eds. 1979); Frances Kobrin, *The American Midwife Controversy: A Crisis of Professionalization,* 40 BULL. HIST. MED. 350, 358 (1966).

221. Judy Barrett Litoff, *Midwives and History,* in WOMEN, HEALTH, AND MEDICINE IN AMERICA: A HISTORICAL HANDBOOK 443 (Rima Apple ed. 1990). *See also* Chapter 8, at notes 252–55, 336–43.

222. *See generally* JUDGES, *supra* note 155, at 100–06; KETT, *supra* note 107; ROTHSTEIN, *supra* note 114; SHRYOCK, *supra* note 114, at 143–51 (1960); SMITH-ROSENBERG, *supra* note 71, at 228–30; PAUL STARR, THE SOCIAL TRANSFORMATION OF AMERICAN MEDICINE: THE RISE OF A SOVEREIGN PROFESSION AND THE MAKING OF A VAST INDUSTRY 51–59 (1982).

223. DEVRIES, *supra* note 220, at 184 n.4.

224. WALSH, *supra* note 114, at 14.

225. *Id.*

226. KETT, *supra* note 114, at 100–31; ROTHSTEIN, *supra* note 114. On the situation in the late twentieth century, see Jane Brody, *Alternative Medicine Makes Inroads, but Watch Out for Curves,* N.Y. TIMES, Apr. 28,

riod 1790–1840, only 27 percent had graduated from medical colleges, and only 42 percent belonged to the nascent (allopathic) medical societies.[227]

The strongest rivals to the allopaths in the nineteenth century were the homeopaths, whose
primary form of treatment of disease was to provide small doses of drugs that induced symptoms similar to the symptoms of the disease sought to be cured.[228] Before 1840, the herbal ori-

---

1999, at F7 (reporting a survey showing that 42% of Americans have used "alternative medicine within the
previous year, and that a growing number of health insurance plans and hospitals are offering alternative
medicine); Claudia Dreifus, *Separating Remedies from Snake Oil*, N.Y. TIMES, Apr. 3, 2001, at F5; *Family Doctor Losing Out to Alternative Medicine*, PHILA. INQUIRER, Nov. 15, 1998 (reporting the 40% of people suffering
from chronic conditions choose alternative medicine, and that more money is spent annually on such "therapies" than on hospitalizations); Catherine Robbins, *In Southwest, Doctor Meets Medicine Man*, N.Y. TIMES,
Nov. 15, 1998, at F7 (1 in 3 patients turn to alternative medicine). *See generally* ALTERNATIVE MEDICINE AND
ETHICS (Jams Humber & Robert Almeder eds. 1998); ALTERNATIVE MEDICINE: EXPANDING MEDICAL HORI-
ZONS (Brian Berman & David Larson eds. 1994); BARRIE CASSILETH, THE ALTERNATIVE MEDICINE HAND-
BOOK (1998); MICHAEL CASTLEMAN, NATURE'S CURES (1996); DEEPAK CHOPRA, AGELESS BODY, TIMELESS
MIND (1993); MICHAEL COHEN, COMPLEMENTARY & ALTERNATIVE MEDICINE: LEGAL BOUNDARIES AND REG-
ULATORY PERSPECTIVES (1998); OFFICE OF TECH. ASSESS., UNCONVENTIONAL CANCER TREATMENTS (1990);
JULIE STONE & JOAN MATTHEWS, COMPLEMENTARY MEDICINE AND THE LAW (1996); ANDREW WEIL, EIGHT
WEEKS TO OPTIMUM HEALTH (1997); Lori Andrews, *The Shadow Health Care System: Regulation of Alternative
Health Care Providers*, 32 HOUS. L. REV. 1273 (1996); John Astin, *Why Patients Use Alternative Medicine: Re-
sults of a National Study*, 279 JAMA 1548 (1998); Brian Berman *et al.*, *Physicians' Attitudes toward Complimen-
tary or Alternative Medicine: A Regional Survey*, 8 J. AM. BD. FAM. PRACTICE 361 (1995); Barry Beyerstein, *Why
Bogus Therapies Seem to Work*, SKEPTICAL INQUIRER, Sept.–Oct. 1997, at 30; Kathleen Boozang, *Western Medicine Opens the Door to Alternative Medicine*, 24 AM. J.L. & MED. 185 (1998); Michael Carlston, Marian Stuart,
& Wayne Jonas, *Alternative Medicine Instruction in Medical Schools and Family Practice Residency Programs*, 29
FAM. MED. 559 (1997); Ronald Chez & Wayne Jonas, *The Challenge of Complementary and Alternative Medicine*, 177 AM. J. OBSTET. & GYNECOLOGY 1156 (1997); Margaret Colgate, *Gaining Insurance Coverage for Alternative Therapies*, 15 J. HEALTH CARE MKTG. 24 (1995); Richard Cooper & Sandi Stoflet, *Trends in Education
and Practice of Alternative Medicine Clinicians*, 15 HEALTH AFF. 226 (1996); David Eisenberg, *Advising Patients
Who Seek Alternative Medical Therapies*, 127 ANN. INTERNAL MED. 61 (1997); Ezard Ernst *et al.*, *Complementary Medicine*, 155 ARCHIVES INTERNAL MED. 2405 (1995); Wayne Jonas, *Alternative Medicine and the Conventional Practitioner*, 279 JAMA 708 (1998); Ted Kaptchuk & David Eisenberg, *Chiropratic: Origins, Contro-
versies, and Contributions*, 158 ARCH. INTERNAL MED. 2215 (1998); Betty Lay, *Healer-Patient Privilege:
Extending the Physician-Patient Privilege to Alternative Health Care Practitioners in California*, 48 HASTINGS
L.J. 633 (1997); *Managed Care Organizations Begin Covering Alternative Treatment*, 12 MED. MALPRACTICE L.
& STRATEGY 3 (1996); Robert Park, *Alternative Medicine and the Laws of Physics*, SKEPTICAL INQUIRER,
Sept.–Oct. 1997, at 24; Lawrence Schneiderman, *Medical Ethics and Alternative Medicine*, SCI. REV. ALTERNA-
TIVE MED., Spring–Summer 1998, at 63; Cynthia Starr, *Exploring the Other Health Care Systems—Alternative
Medicine, Part I*, PATIENT CARE, July 15, 1997, at 134; Lisa Vincler & Mary Nicol, *When Ignorance Isn't Bliss:
What Healthcare Practitioners and Facilities Should Know about Complementary and Alternative Medicine*, 30 J.
HEALTH & HOSP. L. 160 (1997); David Weber, *The Mainstreaming of Alternative Medicine*, HEALTHCARE
FORUM J., Nov./Dec. 1996, at 16; Miriam Wetzel, David Eisenberg, & Ted Kaptchuk, *Courses Involving Com-
plementary and Alternative Medicine at US Medical Schools*, 280 JAMA 784 (1998). The field even has its own
journal. *See* Wallace Sampson, *Why a New Alternative Medicine Journal?*, 1 SCI. REV. OF ALTERNATIVE MED. 4
(1997).

227. BARNES RIZNIK, MEDICINE IN NEW ENGLAND 1790–1840, at 23 (1965); WALSH, *supra* note 114, at 14.
*See also* Edward Atwater, *The Medical Profession in a New Society—Rochester, New York, 1811–1860*, 47 BULL.
HIST. MED. 221 (1974).

228. SAMUEL HAHNEMANN, ORGANON OF THE MEDICAL ART (1842); JAMES TYLER KENT, LECTURES ON
HOMEOPATHIC PHILOSOPHY (1900); JOHN TARBELL, HOMEOPATHY SIMPLIFIED: OR DOMESTIC PRACTICE
MADE EASY (1859). *See generally* TREVOR COOK, SAMUEL HAHNEMANN: THE FOUNDER OF HOMEOPATHIC
MEDICINE (1981); 3 HARRIS COULTER, DIVIDED LEGACY: A HISTORY OF SCHISM IN MEDIEVAL THOUGHT
(1973); LAURA JOHNSON, A HOMEOPATHIC HANDBOOK OF NATURAL REMEDIES (2003); MARTIN KAUFMAN,
HOMEOPATHY IN AMERICA: THE RISE AND FALL OF A MEDICAL HERESY (1971); OTHER HEALERS: UNORTHO-
DOX MEDICINE IN AMERICA (Norman Gevirtz ed. 1988); NAOMI ROGERS, AN ALTERNATIVE PATH: THE MAK-
ING AND REMAKING OF HAHNEMANN MEDICAL COLLEGE AND HOSPITAL OF PHILADELPHIA (1998); STARR,
*supra* note 222, at 30–144; WALSH, *supra* note 114, at 195; JULIAN WINSTON, THE FACES OF HOMEOPATHY: AN

ented Thomsonians emerged as major rivals to the allopaths.[229] In the 1840s and 1850s, both the allopaths and the homeopaths faced considerable competition from hydropaths, devoted to the "water cure" for virtually everything.[230] The water cure involved drinking large amounts of pure cold water, taking various baths, and wrapping oneself in wet sheets for hours on end daily. This naturally led to the advocacy of hygienic douching, sometimes consciously suggesting attempts at contraception, although more often any contraceptive effect appears to have been unconscious.[231] Indeed, the introduction of pure water into a vagina could have facilitated the movement of sperm deeper into the genital tract rather than prevented it.

Mohr described the eventually well-organized, well-educated allopathic physicians who were the culprits of his morality tale as "regulars." In another context, Mohr conceded that "'[r]egularism' itself, however, remains difficult to define with any historical precision."[232] Despite these uncertainties, Mohr's usage has been widely followed. Mohr, however, hardly noticed a point that others have stressed: Nearly all of the "regulars" were men, while the "irregulars," whether midwives, folk herbalists, or informally educated "physicians," were often (indeed, for midwives and herbalists, usually) women.[233] In fact, the categories herbalists, midwives, and informally educated physicians often were interchangeable terms for a single person. A clear instance of the gender-based struggle within medicine in the nineteenth century

---

ILLUSTRATED HISTORY OF THE FIRST 200 YEARS (1999); Ann Jerome Croce, *Another Medical Paradigm: The Case of Classical Homeopathy*, 4 THE LONG TERM VIEW no. 4, at 25 (Fall 1999).

Homeopathy has recently experienced something of a revival, with 5% of Americans had recourse to homeopathy in 1999. Brody, *supra* note 226, at F7. *See generally* PAOLO BELLAVITE, HOMEOPATHY: A FRONTIER IN MEDICAL SCIENCE (1995); JUDYTH REICHENBERG-ULLMAN & ROBERT ULLMAN, RITALIN-FREE KIDS (1996); GEORGE VITHOULKAS, THE SCIENCE OF HOMEOPATHY (1980); J. Kleijnen, P. Knipshild, & G. ter Riet, *Clinical Trials of Homeopathy*, 302 BRIT. MED. J. 315 (1991); Jennifer Jacobs *et al.*, *Treatment of Acute Childhood Diarrhea with Homeopathic Medicine: A Randomized Clinical Trial in Nicaragua*, 93 PEDIATRICS 719 (1994).

229. ROTHSTEIN, *supra* note 114, at 130–3; WALSH, *supra* note 114, at 22–24. Herbal medicine is on the rise again, although no longer linked to the Thomsonians. Some 17% of Americans had recourse to herbal medicine in 1999. Brody, *supra* note 226, at F7.

230. *See, e.g.,* R.T. TRALL, THE HYDROPATHIC ENCYCLOPEDIA: A SYSTEM OF HYDROPATHY AND HYGIENE (1852). *See generally* BRODIE, *supra* note 220, at 143–50.

231. *See, e.g.,* RUSSELL TRALL, SEXUAL PHYSIOLOGY: A SCIENTIFIC AND POPULAR EXPOSITION OF THE FUNDAMENTAL PROBLEMS IN SOCIOLOGY 207, 210–11, 213 (1866). *See generally* BRODIE, *supra* note 220, at 148–50.

232. MOHR, *supra* note 78, at 281 n.24. *But see id.* at 87–88.

233. *See* BROOKES, *supra* note 220, at 54; JOHN D'EMILIO & ESTELLE FREEDMAN, INTIMATE MATTERS: A HISTORY OF SEXUALITY IN AMERICA 145–50 (1988); DeVRIES, *supra* note 220, at 23–26, 39–46; JOAN DONEGAN, WOMEN AND MEN MIDWIVES: MEDICINE, MORALITY, AND MISOGYNY IN EARLY AMERICA (1978); JEAN DONNISON, MIDWIVES AND MEDICAL MEN: A HISTORY OF THE STRUGGLE FOR THE CONTROL OF CHILDBIRTH (2nd ed. 1988); BARBARA EHRENREICH & DEIDRE ENGLISH, WITCHES, MIDWIVES, & NURSES: A HISTORY OF WOMEN HEALERS 44–48 (1973); GORDON, *supra* note 75, at 163–65; BEVERLY WILDUNG HARRISON, OUR RIGHT TO CHOOSE: TOWARD A NEW ETHIC OF ABORTION 162, 165–66 (1983); KETT, *supra* note 114, at 117–21; JUDY BARRETT LITOFF, AMERICAN MIDWIVES: 1860 TO THE PRESENT 7–10 (1978); LUKER, *supra* note 138, at 3–19; ANGUS MCLAREN, BIRTH CONTROL IN NINETEENTH-CENTURY ENGLAND 240–41 (1978); McLAREN, *supra* note 35, at 123; ANN OAKLEY, THE CAPTURED WOMB: A HISTORY OF THE MEDICAL CARE OF PREGNANT WOMEN (1986); PETERSEN, *supra* note 38, at 36–42; ROSALIND POLLACK PETCHESKY, ABORTION AND WOMEN'S CHOICE: THE STATE, SEXUALITY, AND REPRODUCTIVE FREEDOM 80–82 (rev. ed. 1990); BARBARA KATZ ROTHMAN, IN LABOR: WOMEN AND POWER IN THE BIRTHPLACE (1982); SHRYOCK, *supra* note 114, at 116; SMITH-ROSENBERG, *supra* note 71, at 228–29; STARR, *supra* note 222, at 32–37, 49–50, 54–59, 124; ULRICH, *supra* note 27, at 254–61, 339–40; WALSH, *supra* note 114; DOROTHY & RICHARD WERTZ, LYING IN: A HISTORY OF CHILDBIRTH IN AMERICA 55–59 (1977); WILDER, *supra* note 114; Lesley Biggs, *The Case of the Missing Midwives: A History of Midwifery in Ontario from 1795–1900*, 75 ONT. HIST. 21 (1973); Dianne Martin, *The Midwife's Tale: Old Wisdom and a New Challenge to the Control of Reproduction*, 3 COLUM. J. GENDER & L. 417 (1992); Matthew Ramsey, *Medical Power and Illegal Medicine: Illegal Healers in Nineteenth-Century France*, in THE MEDICINE SHOW 183 (P. Branca ed. 1977).

was the invention of the word "obstetrician" to displace the female connotations of the word "midwife."[234]

The closest Mohr came to suggesting the male/female dimensions of the struggle came in his hinting that the struggle of allopathic physicians to control the practice of medicine was linked to struggles by men for dominance in the home—generalized sexism.[235] Other historians have been far more insistent both that allopathy amounted to a male usurpation of traditional female roles and that abortion was a particular focus of this struggle. Carroll Smith-Rosenberg made much of her Freudian interpretation of the writings of nineteenth-century physicians to show that their arguments, calling for the reader to identify with the fetus, demonstrate the fundamental misogyny of the anti-abortion movement because it sees abortion-seeking mothers as the enemy.[236] She did not explain why, if opposition to abortion through identification with the fetus was misogynistic, nineteenth-century feminists almost unanimously opposed abortion, using similar imagery as the men.[237] Angus McLaren and Rosalind Petchesky gave a Marxist twist to the competition between allopathic physicians and midwives. McLaren's arguments can best be described as muddled, asserting that "the masses" must have known how to perform safe abortions because they so desperately wanted them.[238] Petchesky was more coherent, viewing "regular" physicians as representing "capital intensive" medicine bent on driving out "petty craftswomen and tradesmen (sic)" from the market for medical services.[239]

Historian Linda Gordon was even more brazen in sifting her facts to make a case for misogyny in the enactment of the abortion laws. Gordon set out briefly, but emphatically, the feminine character of the irregular physicians.[240] When she turned to the rather high incidence of quackery among the irregulars, she found a collection of "dishonest, avaricious, and ignoble men."[241] Her prime example, "Dr." A.M. Mauriceau (Charles Lohman), was married to the most famous woman abortionist of nineteenth century America, "Madame Restell."[242] Gordon mentioned Lohman's wife, but did not bother to give us her name or to discuss whether her practices might also have involved quackery[243]—even though Gordon devoted four pages to Madame Restell in an earlier chapter, treating her as a legitimate medical practitioner and a martyr for women's rights.[244] Gordon was more willing to overlook exaggerated claims on behalf of Dr. Edward Bliss Foote, who claimed to have invented the "French article" while keeping secret just exactly what he was talking about. The usual meaning of a reference to a "French article" was a condom, which Foote clearly did not invent, so Gordon concludes that he must have meant something else: the cervical cap.[245] If so, Foote kept it a well guarded secret for Gordon conceded that the cervical cap did not come into general use until 50 years after Foote was active.[246]

---

234. Carl Degler, At Odds: Women and the Family in America from the Revolution to the Present 56 (1980).

235. See Mohr, supra note 29, at 187–88. One might also consider Mohr's analysis of the abortion statutes as designed to prevent "race suicide" (generalized racism). Mohr, supra, at 166–67.

236. Smith-Rosenberg, supra note 71, at 242, 341–42 n.74. See also Adrienne Rich, The Theft of Childhood, N.Y. Rev. Books, Oct. 2, 1973, at 25.

237. See Chapter 8.

238. McLaren, supra note 35, at 107–14.

239. Petchesky, supra note 233, at 81–83, 169–78.

240. Gordon, supra note 75, at 163–65.

241. Id. at 165.

242. On the careers of Mr. and Mrs. Lohman, see Chapter 7, at notes 141–53, and Chapter 9, at notes 198–216.

243. Gordon, supra note 75, at 165–66.

244. Id. at 54–58.

245. Id. at 169 n.*.

246. Id. at 179.

In truth, the nineteenth century in Europe and North America saw a dramatic transferal of responsibility for attending to births from the largely female midwives to the largely male allopathic physicians, although that process was not fully completed until the 1930s.[247] Until 1755, no "regular" physician in America routinely attended women in childbirth.[248] The practice slowly became common thereafter.[249] At first, it hardly made a difference. Allopathic and other physicians in 1800 could do little to diagnose or treat most maladies or to aid birth. In 1800, two-thirds of all "physicians" in the city of Philadelphia had no formal medical education and the degrees of the remainder often counted for little.[250]

To make diagnoses, physicians of the time would take the patients' history while viewing the external features of the patients—male or female—without asking them to remove any clothes.[251] This was especially true for men practicing midwifery or otherwise attending to women. Physicians and male midwives (who were not considered physicians and who began to appear in the seventeenth century in England and elsewhere in Europe) generally undertook to examine women or to aid in their delivery, and even to manipulate any necessary medical instruments, by touch rather than by sight, with the woman's genitals remaining covered, to avoid em-

---

247. Nanette Davis, From Crime to Choice 89 (1985); Degler, *supra* note 234, at 56–57; DeVries, *supra* note 220, at 16–19, 25, 38, 48–49; Gordon, *supra* note 75, at 172; Litoff, *supra* note 233, at 27, 136–42; Richard Meckel, Save the Babies: American Public Health Reform and the Prevention of Infant Mortality 174 (1990); Petersen, *supra* note 38, at 40; Ulrich, *supra* note 27, at 28, 179–80; Wertz & Wertz, *supra* note 233, at 215–17; Neal Devitt, *The Transition from Home to Hospital Birth in the United States, 1930–1960,* 4 Birth & Fam. J. 47 (1977); Paul Jacobson, *Hospital Care and the Vanishing Midwife,* 34 Millbank Mem. Fund Q. 253 (1956); Kobrin, *supra* note 220, at 362–63; Martin, *supra* note 233, at 418–22, 437–48; Gail Robinson, *Midwifery and Malpractice Insurance: A Profession Fights for Survival,* 134 U. Pa. L. Rev. 1001 (1986); Barbara Katz Rothman, *Childbirth Management and Medical Monopoly,* in Women, Biology, and Public Policy 117 (Virginia Sapiro ed. 1985); Dale Walker, Note, *A Matter of the Quality of Birth: Mothers and Midwives Shackled by the Medical Establishment and Pennsylvania Law,* 23 Duq. L. Rev. 171 (1984). Of course, midwives remained dominant in most other parts of the world.

248. Laurel Thatcher Ulrich, Goodwives: Image and Reality in the Lives of Women in Northern New England, 1650–1750, at 134 (1983) (identifying Dr. Edward Augustus Holyoke of Salem, Mass., as the first physician to attend childbirth on a regular basis). Carl Degler and Paul Starr have nominated Dr. William Shipping, jr., as the first such physician, but only after 1763. Degler, *supra* note 234, at 56; Starr, *supra* note 222, at 49. *See also* Catherine Scholten, *On the Importance of the Obstetrick Art: Changing Customs of Childbirth in America, 1760–1825,* 34 Wm. & Mary Q. 426 (3rd ser. 1977). There are occasional reports of men (not always physicians) who were called in to help with exceptionally difficult births before 1763, but these hardly amount to a routine practice. *See, e.g.,* Ulrich, *supra,* at 132–33 (describing two births attended by Hugh Adams in New Hampshire as early as 1724).

249. Litoff, *supra* note 233, at 7–10; Ulrich, *supra* note 27, at 59–60, 176–79; Wertz & Wertz, *supra* note 233, at 29–44.

250. Mohr, *supra* note 29, at 32–34. *See also* Kenneth Ludmerer, Learning to Heal: The Development of American Medical Education 12–13 (1985); William Frederick Norwood, Medical Education in the United States before the Civil War 380–86 (1944); William Rothstein, American Medical Schools and the Practice of Medicine 49–63 (1987); Walsh, *supra* note 114, at 1–15, 21–29; Wertz & Wertz, *supra* note 233, at 48–50. For the development (or lack thereof) of the medical profession in England just before 1800, see Bernice Hamilton, *The Medical Professions in the Eighteenth Century,* 4 Econ. Hist. Rev. 141 (1951); Roy Porter, *Medicine and the Enlightenment in Eighteenth-Century England,* 25 Bull. Soc'y for the Social Hist. of Med. 27 (1979).

251. Donnison, *supra* note 233, at 23–24; R.W. Johnstone, William Smellie: The Master of British Midwifery 204 (1957); Richard Lewinsohn, A History of Sexual Customs 268 (1971); Stanley Joel Reiser, Medicine and the Reign of Technology 7 (1978); Ulrich, *supra* note 27, at 53–55; W.F. Bynam, *Health, Disease and Medical Care,* in The Ferment of Knowledge 211 (G.S. Rousseau & Roy Porter eds. 1980); R. L. Engle & B.J. Davis, *Medical Diagnosis, Present, Past and Future,* 112 Bull. Hist. Med. 512 (1963); Iago Galdston, *Diagnosis in Historical Perspective,* 9 Bull. Hist. Med. 367 (1941); Roy Porter, *A Touch of Danger: The Man-Midwife as Sexual Predator,* in Sexual Underworlds of the Enlightenment 206, 212–13 (G.S. Rousseau & Roy Porter eds. 1988). *See also* Walsh, *supra* note 114, at 40–42.

barrassing her and exposing himself to accusations of impropriety.[252] One eighteenth-century physician omitted anatomical detail from his midwifery manual for fear off offending modest readers.[253] For some time it was even customary for a male midwife, when called by a female midwife for assistance, to sneak into the usually poorly lighted lying-in room and to conceal his presence from the parturient.[254] Some seventeenth-century male midwives even crawled into the room on all fours to avoid being seen.[255]

Nor were treatment techniques particularly helpful. Physicians still regularly used bleeding and leaches to relieve complications in childbirth, often with fatal results.[256] Thus the wife of Salmon P. Chase (Lincoln's Secretary of the Treasury and later Chief Justice of the United States) died from excessive bleeding undertaken to relieve childbed fever.[257] And more than a few physicians and male midwives were denounced for excessive reliance on their forceps and other instruments.[258] The capabilities of physicians to attend usefully to childbirth changed only slowly over the next 50 years.[259] As late as 1916, in Newark, New Jersey at least, women and children who were attended by an obstetrician were more likely to die at childbirth or within the next

---

252. *See, e.g.,* J.H. AVELING, ENGLISH MIDWIVES: THEIR HISTORY AND PROSPECTS 122–23 (1872); CATHARINE BEECHER, LETTERS TO THE PEOPLE ON HEALTH AND HAPPINESS 134–37 (1855); FREDERICK DYER, CHAMPION OF WOMEN AND THE UNBORN: HORATIO ROBINSON STORER, M.D. 96–97, 273–76, 298–306, 356 (1999); FRANCIS FOSTER, THOUGHTS ON THE TIMES BUT CHIEFLY ON THE PROFLIGACY OF OUR WOMEN 17–24, 29–31, 79 89–94, 120–22, 160–61, 178, 189–93, 200 (2nd ed.1779); SAMUEL GREGORY, MAN-MIDWIFERY EXPOSED AND CORRECTED TOGETHER WITH REMARKS ON THE USE AND ABUSE OF ETHER AND DR. CHANNING'S "CASES OF INHALATION OF ETHER IN LABOR" (1848); HARRIOT HUNT, GLANCES AND GLIMPSES: OR FIFTY YEARS SOCIAL, INCLUDING TWENTY YEARS PROFESSIONAL LIFE 177, 184, 271, 376 (1856); FRANK NICHOLLS, A PETITION OF THE UNBORN BABES TO THE CENSORS OF THE ROYAL COLLEGE OF PHYSICIANS 6 (1751); ELIZABETH NIHELL, A TREATISE ON THE ART OF MIDWIFERY 80–86 (1760); 5 THE DIARY OF SAMUEL PEPYS 275 (Robert Latham & William Matthews eds. 1970–83); SARAH STONE, A COMPLETE PRACTICE OF MIDWIFERY xix (1737); PHILIP THICKNESSE, A LETTER TO A YOUNG LADY 11 (1764); PHILIP THICKNESSE, MAN MIDWIFERY ANALYSED, AND THE TENDENCY OF THAT PRACTICE DETECTED AND EXPOSED (1765) ("THICKNESSE, MAN MIDWIFERY"). *See generally* BRODIE, *supra* note 220, at 129; DEGLER, *supra* note 234, at 58–59; DE-VRIES, *supra* note 220, at 24–25; DONNISON, *supra* note 233, at 23–24, 36, 41–42, 46, 59–60, 64, 78, 240; GORDON, *supra* note 68, at 164; RUTH FINLEY, THE LADY OF GODEY'S: SARAH JOSEPHA HALE 102–05 (1931); DAVID HUNT, PARENTS AND CHILDREN IN HISTORY: THE PSYCHOLOGY OF FAMILY LIFE IN EARLY MODERN FRANCE 83–85 (1970); DANIELLE JACQUART & CLAUDE THOMASSET, *SEXUALITÉ ET SAVOIR MÉDICAL AU MOYEN ÂGE* 241 (1985); STEPHEN KERN, ANATOMY AND DESTINY: A CULTURAL HISTORY OF THE HUMAN BODY 1–2 (1975); SMITH-ROSENBERG, *supra* note 71, at 228–29; STARR, *supra* note 222, at 40–47, 64; REAY TANNAHILL, SEX IN HISTORY 351–52 (1980); WALSH, *supra* note 114, at 6–7, 37–39; WERTZ & WERTZ, *supra* note 233, at 68; Porter, *supra* note 244; B.B. Schnorrenberg, *Is Childbirth Any Place for a Woman? The Decline of Midwifery in Eighteenth Century England,* 10 STUD. IN 18TH CENT. CULTURE 393 (1981); Margaret Connor Versluysen, *Midwives, Medical Men and "Poor Women" Labouring of Child: Lying-In Hospitals in Eighteenth Century London,* in WOMEN, HEALTH AND REPRODUCTION 21, 29 (Helen Roberts ed. 1981).

253. EDMUND CHAPMAN, A TREATISE ON THE IMPROVEMENT OF MIDWIFERY xx (1733).

254. DONNISON, *supra* note 233, at 23–24; WALSH, *supra* note 114, at 6–7.

255. PERCIVAL WILLUGHBY, OBSERVATIONS IN MIDWIFERY: AS ALSO THE COUNTREY MIDWIFES OPUSCULUM AND VADE MECUM 6 (Henry Blenkinsop ed. 1863; original pub. ca. 1663).

256. *See generally* STARR, *supra* note 222, at 42.

257. WERTZ & WERTZ, *supra* note 233, at 68.

258. *See, e.g.,* JOHN MAUBRAY, THE FEMALE PHYSICIAN 181–82 (1724); NICHOLLS, *supra* note 258, at 8-1; NIHELL, *supra* note 252, at 92–95, 158–59; MARGARET STEPHEN, THE DOMESTIC MIDWIFE 55–63 (1795); STONE, *supra* note 252, at xi–xii; THICKNESSE, MAN MIDWIFERY, *supra* note 252, at 22. *See generally* DONNISON, *supra* note 233, at 42–44, 50; H.R. SPENCER, THE HISTORY OF BRITISH MIDWIFER FROM 1650–1800, at 73 (1927).

259. NORWOOD, *supra* note 250; SMITH-ROSENBERG, *supra* note 71, at 228–29; STARR, *supra* note 222, at 40–47, 64.

year than were women and children attended by a midwife[260]—although modern historians who attempt to make much of this fact have no way of discounting the statistics for the probability that physicians were more likely to be called in cases involving serious (even life-threatening) complications.[261] In this context, the sexually-tinged suspicions of the motives and effects of male midwives seem both inevitable and unremarkable.[262]

The allopathic or "regular" physicians did indeed lead the charge to prohibit abortion, but they did not explain their actions as a means for eliminating competitors in the marketplace for medical services. Of course, if that were their purpose they might not have wanted to publicize the fact. If they were engaged such a conspiracy, it was remarkable successful. No one has ever turned up a smidgen of direct evidence (in a diary, a letter, or any other record) of such a plan or program, either in the early years of the nineteenth century or later, when the abortion statutes were first enacted or when progressively more severe prohibitions were imposed.[263] The closest we come to such direct evidence is the occasional complaints by physicians that midwives and other "quacks" were depriving honest physicians of a living. Such complaints were always embedded in much broader criticisms of the evils of the competing form of practice, such as this comment by two American physicians on a midwife licensing law enacted for England in 1902:

> ...[I]t has not instituted a new system, and in the light of modern medicine, it is of questionable advantage to the community, for it provides a double system in obstetrics, the midwife but scantily trained, depending upon the physician who is not certain to respond to her call. Some 30,000 women have taken enough practice away from physicians to obtain a livelihood. Unquestionably the field of physicians has been invaded and the community is the loser.[264]

Why would such a comment serve as proof that the "real" motive in opposing midwives was loss of income from their competition.[265] That concern appears almost as an afterthought in a critique that opens and closes with concerns about whether midwives can provide adequate care. Why insist that only one and not the other professed concern was genuine? In fact, such licensing laws were important instruments for suppressing midwifery for the licensing authority was given to boards dominated by allopathic physicians (including both men and women physicians) rather than by midwives themselves.[266] Such regulation was often characterized by outright hostility to the profession of midwifery, unlike the friendly regulation that physicians or lawyers received before licensing boards drawn from their own ranks.[267]

---

260. Neal Devitt, *The Statistical Case for the Elimination of the Midwife: Fact versus Prejudice, 1890–1935 (Part 2),* 4 WOMEN & HEALTH 169, 171 (1979). *See also* Neal Devitt, *The Statistical Case for the Elimination of the Midwife: Fact versus Prejudice, 1890–1935 (Part 1),* 4 WOMEN & HEALTH 81 (1979).

261. *See, e.g.,* DEVRIES, *supra* note 220, at 26–27; Alfred Yankauer, *The Valley of the Shadow of Birth,* 73 AM. J. PUB. HEALTH 635 (1983).

262. See the authorities collected *supra* at note 252.

263. *See* D'EMILIO & FREEDMAN, *supra* note 222, at 145–50; MOHR, *supra* note 29, at 32–37, 147–82; PETCHESKY, *supra* note 222, at 78–96; STARR, *supra* note 214; WALSH, *supra* note 107.

264. A. Emmons & J. Huntington, *A Review of the Midwife Situation,* 164 BOS. MED. & SURGICAL J. 251, 260 (1911).

265. As in DEVRIES, *supra* note 220, at 26.

266. *See id.* at 35–39; DONNISON, *supra* note 233, at 85–90, 94–95, 108–11, 115–18, 120–89; LITOFF, *supra* note 233, at 48–134; REAGAN, *supra* note 59, at 94–98; Kobrin, *supra* note 220, at 353–54. *See generally* I.H. Butter & B.J. Kay, *State Laws and the Process of Midwifery,* 78 AM. J. PUB. HEALTH 1161 (1988); Diana Korte, *Midwives on Trial,* 76 MOTHERING 52 (Fall 1995); Charles Wolfson, *Midwives and Home Birth: Social, Medical, and Legal Perspectives,* 37 HASTINGS L.J. 909 (1986).

267. *See* DEVRIES, *supra* note 220, at 55–87, 92–102, 119–54, 163–81, 188–89; DONNISON, *supra* note 233, at 55, 94–96, 116–17, 121, 126–28, 140, 142, 144–47, 151–56, 159–60, 165–71, 173–74, 176–82, 203–07;

Even assuming that a conspiracy to obtain a monopoly did occur, that cannot explain how allopaths succeeded in criminalizing abortion in the face of Jacksonian democracy's intense passion to democratize the professions by eliminating barriers to entry.[268] Allopaths were strong enough in New York to succeed in having the legislature make the unauthorized practice of medicine a misdemeanor in 1827; that merely served to provoke the "irregulars" to organize themselves in favor of "laissez-faire" medical practice.[269] The irregulars organized mass rallies and achieved some legislative success in modifying the restrictions on the practice of medicine enacted in 1827. The New York legislature reject the proposal to ban unnecessary surgery (part of the same package that included New York's abortion laws),[270] and it liberalized access to the practice of medicine so that the widespread practice of medicine by "irregulars" continued in New York throughout the period from 1820 to 1850—as Mohr himself conceded.[271] The New York legislature also refused to require county coroners to be trained and licensed physicians. Mohr himself would later attribute the failure of the "medical jurisprudence" movement to secure the professionalization of coroners' offices to the Jacksonian spirit of opposition to professional expertise.[272] The irregulars apparently did not see the prohibition of abortion as a threat. In the midst of the political struggle over the licensing of the practice of medicine, the irregulars did not attempt to prevent enactment of the abortion provisions in the 1829 *Revised Statutes*, nor did they attempt to modify them or to secure their repeal.

The nascent allopathic medical societies of the early to mid-nineteenth century and individual allopaths did not have the legislative influence that organized medicine and its leaders have today.[273] They were unable to prevent the chartering of professional organizations for competing forms of medicine in New York and other states—for forms of medical practice that allopaths considered rank quackery. Nor could allopaths take positions that were widely unpopular with potential patients without disastrous income loss when allopaths and other medical practitioners were openly and intensely competitive.[274] Allopaths working in the emerging specialties of obstetrics and gynecology could not even trade on the high esteem of a well-established medical profession, for they were still looked down upon as sexually-suspect intruders rather than respected as physicians.[275] In short, allopaths could achieve little legislatively unless their arguments were widely accepted as true.

But let us suppose that the allopaths were conspiring to suppress midwifery as well as other competitors in the medical marketplace with little real concern for the lives of unborn children. Even if allopathic physicians felt compelled to hide certain ulterior motives behind more publicly acceptable phrases in order to obtain some tools useful against competitors for the dollars of potential patients, they undoubtedly would have turned to arguments that would be widely accepted by the audience they sought to influence. The arguments used to justify the campaign against abortion at the very least tell us what a great many, perhaps most, people in the society thought about the procedure at the time. And that in turn suggests some degree of authenticity in the arguments advanced at the time regarding abortion regardless of whether a particular proponent of prohibiting abortion personally believed the argument or not.

---

LITOFF, *supra* note 233, at 107. *See generally* Lawrence Friedman, *Freedom of Contract and Occupational Licensing, 1890–1910: A Legal and Social Study,* 53 CAL. L. REV. 487, 494–97, 516 (1965).

268. See the sources collected *supra* at notes 114–15.

269. MOHR, *supra* note 29, at 37–39; WILDER, *supra* note 114, at 499–511.

270. See the text *supra* at notes 139–49.

271. MOHR, *supra* note 29, at 34.

272. MOHR, *supra* note 78, at 86–93.

273. *See* OLASKY, *supra* note 122–27.

274. *See, e.g.* George Smith, *Foeticide,* 10 DET. REV. MED. & PHARMACY 211 (1875). *See generally* OLASKY, *supra* note 55, at 123–24.

275. See the text *supra* at notes 251–62.

The proponents of abortion prohibitions always advanced the protection of fetal life as the primary reason for the statutes, and, if they even mentioned it, treated protection of maternal health as a secondary reason.[276] The physician who most influenced New York's earliest abortion legislation wrote about abortion as a form of infanticide.[277] Other physicians who campaigned against abortion termed the practice "foeticide" rather than abortion.[278] One doctor went so far as to suggest that the adverse health effects for the mother were simply a fitting punishment.[279] Rather than considering whether these sentiments reflected an increasingly general understanding of what abortion entailed, Mohr insisted on dismissing these explanations as only the peculiar ideology and moral scruples of the allopathic medical profession.[280]

Mohr and his devotees appear singularly untroubled that this left them (in Mohr's case, explicitly) denigrating as an idiosyncratic moral prejudice the allopathic physicians' dedication to the protection of human life.[281] Sociologist Kristin Luker went so far as to call the physicians' crusade against abortion an "ideological sleight of hand."[282] Beverly Harrison, showing some slight restraint, described such attitudes as a "rhetorical flourish."[283] Such disdain for the obligation of physicians to preserve life is hardly surprising if one embraces a "quality of life" ethic and rejects a "right to life" ethic. Mohr, at least, was willing to do so explicitly.[284]

Despite the evidence to the contrary, Mohr continued to insist that the "real motive" of the allopathic physicians and their friends in the legislature was to eliminate competition from "irregulars."[285] Mohr asked us to accept his surmise about the true goals of the allopaths without regard to their professed "moral prejudices" about fetal life. He contended that the quickening theory meant that no one, least of all doctors, really believed that early abortions involved fetal life despite the considerable evidence that he himself adduced directly to the contrary.[286] Mohr also argued that the inclusion of an exception for therapeutic abortions recommended by two physicians as necessary to preserve the mother's life signaled an intent to put allopathic physicians in control of the practice of abortion rather than to suppress the practice.[287] Finally, he argued that, as the statutes punished only the conduct of the abortionist and did not punish the conduct of

---

276. DEGLER, *supra* note 234, at 241–42; MOHR, *supra* note 29, at 35–36, 43–45; Jonathan Imber, *Abortion Policy and Medical Practice,* SOCIETY, July/Aug. 1990, at 27, 28. *See also* Herman v. Turner, 232 P. 864, 864 (Kan. 1925) ("[T]he abortion statute is not designed for the protection of the woman, only of the unborn child and through it society…"); Bowlan v. Lunsford, 54 P.2d 666, 668 (Okla. 1936) (same).

277. BECK, *supra* note 171, at 276–77; BECK & BECK, *supra* note 176, ch. 8. See the text *supra* at notes 171–87.

278. HUGH HODGE, FOETICIDE, OR CRIMINAL ABORTION (1869); J. Boring, *Foeticide,* 2 ATLANTA MED. & SURGICAL J. 257 (1857); Henry Gibbons, sr., *On Foeticide,* 21 PAC. MED. & SURGICAL J. 97, 111 (1878); H.C. Markham, *Foeticide and Its Prevention,* 11 J.A.M.A. 805 (1888); J.J. Mulheron, *Foeticide,* 10 PENINSULAR J. MED. 387 (1874); Montrose Pallen, *Foeticide,* 3 MED. ARCHIVES (St. L. n.s.) 201–02 (1869); John Stoddard, *Foeticide—Suggestions toward Its Suppression,* 10 DET. REV. MED. & PHARMACY 656 (1875); Smith, *supra* note 274.

279. John Trader, *Criminal Abortion,* 11 ST. L. MED. & SURGICAL J., N.S. 583, 589 (1874).

280. MOHR, *supra* note 29, at 34–37. *See also* LUKER, *supra* note 138, at 214; PETCHESKY, *supra* note 233, at 79–84; Rachel Pine & Sylvia Law, *Envisioning a Future for Reproductive Liberty: Strategies for Making the Rights Real,* 27 HARV. C.R.-C.L. L. REV. 407, 423–25 (1992).

281. MOHR, *supra* note 29, at 35–36, 85–118, 128, 167–68, 175–76, 182–96. *See also* BARBARA HINKINSON CRAIG & DAVID O'BRIEN, ABORTION AND AMERICAN POLITICS 40 (1993); DEGLER, *supra* note 234, at 242–43; GORDON, *supra* note 75, at 59–60; PETCHESKY, *supra* note 233, at 79–80.

282. LUKER, *supra* note 138, at 39.

283. HARRISON, *supra* note 233, at 128–29. *See also* LUKER, *supra* note 138, at 214; Pine & Law, *supra* note 280, at 423–25.

284. MOHR, *supra* note 29, at 252–53.

285. *Id.* at 34, 37–39.

286. *Id.* at 74–77.

287. *Id.* at 38.

the mother, the statutes' real concern was not with abortion but with the competition of unlicensed practitioners.[288] None of these reasons withstands close examination.

The quickening theory was quickly abandoned by nearly all physicians upon the discovery of new scientific evidence regarding the process of conception.[289] While the therapeutic exception was an innovation in the law of abortion, it appears to have been premised on a rather ordinary concept of self-defense (made necessary and feasible by evolving medical technologies) rather than on denial of the humanity of the fetus.[290] Furthermore, requiring two physicians to recommend the abortion rather than leaving it to the unbridled judgment of an individual physician appears to express the allopathic prejudice in favor of life rather than contradict it.[291] Finally, carrying forward the traditional criminal law relating to abortion, as was the general pattern in code after code, by itself simply represented the usual, but not universal, treatment of women having an abortion as a victim rather than as a criminal.[292] The question of whether the woman seeking an abortion should be deemed a criminal is a bit more complex than that, however.

The tradition that women seeking abortions were victims rather than criminals originated in the suicidal dangers that long attended abortion.[293] As the medical realities of abortion began to change and the procedure became somewhat less dangerous for women, some jurists began to criticize the old tradition.[294] Nineteen states ultimately made it a crime for a woman to participate in her own abortion (as did England and Wales).[295] New York enacted a statute in 1845 declaring a woman who solicited or underwent an abortion to be guilty of a misdemeanor,[296] and raised the crime to a felony in 1872.[297]

Means, Mohr, and their followers consistently underreport the number of states that made self-abortion a crime.[298] Mohr acknowledged that California, Connecticut, Indiana, New Hamp-

---

288. *Id.* at 43–44. *See also* D'Emilio & Freedman, *supra* note 233, at 66, 147; McLaren, *supra* note 35, at 137; Cohen, *supra* note 220, at 210–11.

289. See Chapter 5, at notes 209–46, and the text *supra* at notes 156–63, 176–79.

290. See the text *supra* at notes 119, 134–49.

291. *See* Rothstein, *supra* note 250, at 82–83.

292. See the authorities collected *supra* at note 84.

293. *See, e.g.,* Buchan, *supra* note 85, at 403; Grossberg, *supra* note 67, at 164–65. *See generally* Chapter 1.

294. *See, e.g.,* Smith v. State, 33 Me. 51, 54–55 (1833) (*dictum*). *See also* In re Vince, 67 A. 2d 141, 145 (N.J. 1949).

295. Ariz. Penal Code §455, at 711 (1887), reprinted in Quay, *supra* note 45, at 449; Cal. Pen. Code §275, at 69 (1872), reprinted in Quay, *supra*, at 450, [derived from Cal. Stat. ch. DXXI, at 588 (1861)]; Conn. Pub. Acts ch. LXXI, §3, at 65–66 (1860), reprinted in Quay, *supra*, at 454, *codified at* Conn. Gen. Stat. tit. XII, ch. II, §24, at 249 (1866); Del. Code Ann. tit. 11, §652 (1974 Rev.); Idaho Rev. Stat. §6975 (1887); Minn. Laws ch. IX, §3, at 118 (1873), reprinted in Quay, *supra*, at 487, *codified at* Minn. Gen. Stat. ch. 94, §18, at 885 (1878); Mont. Penal Code §481 (1895); Nev. Laws ch. IX, §3, at 64–65 (1869); N.H. Laws ch. 743, §4, at 709 (1848), *codified at* N.H. Comp. Stat. tit. XXVI, ch. 227, §§11–14, at 544–45 (1853), reprinted in Quay, *supra*, at 494; 1845 N.Y. Laws ch. 260, §3, at 285, reprinted in Quay, *supra*, at 500; Dak. Penal Code §338, at 459 (1877), *recodified at* N.D. Rev. Codes §7178, at 1272 (1895); Okla. Stat. §2188 (1890), *codified at* Okla. Rev. Laws §2437, at 604 (1910); S.C. Acts No. 354, §3, at 548 (1883), reprinted in Quay, *supra*, at 512, *codified at* S.C. Rev. Stat., Crim. Stat. §138, at 310 (1893); Dak. Penal Code §338, at 459 (1877), *recodified at* S.D. Ann. Stat. §7798, at 1919 (1899); Utah Rev. Stat. §4227, at 903 (1898); Wash. Laws ch. 249, §197, at 948 (1909), *codified at* Rev. Code Wash. §9.02.020 (1961); Wis. Rev. Stat. pt. IV, tit. XXVII, ch. CLXIX, §59, at 969 (1858), reprinted in Quay, *supra*, at 519; Wyo. Laws ch. 73, §32, at 131 (1890), reprinted in Quay, *supra*, at 520, *codified at* Wyo. Stat. §6–78 (1957), reprinted in Quay, *supra*, at 519–20. *See generally* Witherspoon, *supra* note 58, at 58–61. On England and Wales, see 24 & 25 Vict. ch. 100, §58 (Eng. 1861); Lucia Zedner, Women, Crime, and Custody in Victorian England 39 (1991).

296. 1845 N.Y. Laws ch. 260, §3, at 285, reprinted in Quay, *supra* note 45, at 500.

297. 1872 N.Y. Laws ch. 181, §2, at 71, reprinted in Quay, *supra* note 45, at 501. *See also* 1881 N.Y. Laws ch. 676, §§194, 295.

298. *See, e.g.,* Grossberg, *supra* note 67, at 174–75; Reagan, *supra* note 84, at 313–17.

shire, New Jersey, and New York all eventually declared the woman to be guilty of a crime for seeking or securing an abortion, but he did not see this as contradicting his argument that the general failure to treat the woman seeking the abortion as a criminal proved that the legislatures were not interested in protecting the life of the fetus.[299] The attitude that the woman was a victim rather than a criminal, however, continued to be dominant in the twentieth century and remained dominant when *Roe v. Wade* was decided.[300]

Courts rationalized their view of women as victims of abortion even after early abortion became safer, safer perhaps than childbirth, by declaring that a woman "was not deemed able to assent to an unlawful act against herself."[301] This attitude was reinforced by the reality that gener-

---

299. MOHR, *supra* note 29, at 125–29, 133–34, 201–02, 208–09, 222–23, 226, 228. Leslie Reagan dwelt on California and Minnesota as criminalizing the conduct of the woman, and barely noted six other states. Reagan, *supra* note 84, at 314–15, 317 n.24.

300. *See* United States v. Holte, 236 U.S. 140, 148 (1915) (*dictum*); United States v. Vuitch, 305 F. Supp. 1032, 1034 (D.D.C. 1969), *rev'd on other grounds,* 402 U.S. 62 (1971); Heath v. State, 459 S.W.2d 420, 422 (Ark. 1970); People v. Buffum, 256 P.2d 317, 325 (Cal. 1953); People v. Clapp, 151 P.2d 237, 240 (Cal. 1944) (but requiring corroboration); People v. Wilson, 129 P.2d 149, 155 (Cal. 1942); People v. Gibson, 166 P. 585, 586 (Cal. 1917); People v. Kramer, 66 Cal. Rptr. 638, 645 (Cal. Ct. App. 1968); People v. Reinard, 33 Cal. Rptr. 908, 912 (Cal. Ct. App. 1963) (but requiring corroboration); People v. Moore, 28 Cal. Rptr. 530, 535 (Cal. Ct. App. 1963); People v. Bowden, 25 Cal. Rptr. 368, 371 (Cal. Ct. App. 1962) (but requiring corroboration); People v. Kutz, 9 Cal. Rptr. 626, 630 (1961); State v. Carey, 56 A.2d 632, 636 (Conn. 1904) (self-abortion); Zutz v. State, 160 A.2d 727, 729 (Del. 1967); Thompson v. United States, 30 App. D.C. 352, 363 (1908); Maxey v. United States, 30 App. D.C. 63, 72 (1907); Gullatt v. State, 80 S.E. 340, 341 (Ga. Ct. App. 1913); State v. Rose, 267 P.2d 109, 110 (Idaho 1954); State v. Proud, 262 P.2d 1016, 1019 (1927); People v. Young, 75 N.E.2d 349, 353 (Ill. 1947); Seifert v. State, 67 N.E. 100, 103 (Ind. 1903); State v. Stafford, 123 N.W. 167, 168 (Iowa 1909); State v. Smith, 68 N.W. 428, 431 (Iowa 1896); Richmond v. Commonwealth, 370 S.W.2d 399, 400 (Ky. 1963); Peoples v. Commonwealth, 9 S.W. 509, 510 (Ky. 1888); Basoff v. State, 118 A.2d 917, 923 (Md. 1956); Meno v. State, 83 A. 759, 760 (1912); Doe v. Doe, 314 N.E.2d 128, 132 (Mass. 1974); Commonwealth v. Turner, 112 N.E. 864, 865 (Mass. 1916); Commonwealth v. Follansbee, 29 N.E. 471, 471 (Mass. 1892); *In re* Vickers, 123 N.W.2d 253, 254 (Mich. 1963) (self-abortion); People v. Nixon, 201 N.W.2d 635, 639 (Mich. Ct. App. 1972) (self-abortion); State v. Tennyson, 2 N.W.2d 833, 836 (Minn. 1942); State v. Pearce, 57 N.W. 652, 653 (Minn. 1894); State v. Owens, 22 Minn. 238, 242 (1875); State v. Miller, 261 S.W.2d 103, 106 (Mo. 1953); Haus v. State, 22 N.W.2d 384, 393 (Neb.), *vacated on other grounds,* 25 N.W.2d 35 (Neb. 1946); State v. Thompson, 153 A.2d 364, 369 (N.J. Super. 1959), *rev'd on other grounds,* 158 A.2d 333 (N.J. 1960); State v. Hyer, 39 N.J.L. 598, 600 (1877); State v. Murphy, 27 N.J.L. 112, 114 (1858); State v. Shaft, 81 S.E. 932, 933 (N.C. 1914); Cahill v. State, 178 P.2d 657, 660 (Okla. Crim. Ct. App. 1947); Wilson v. State, 252 P. 1106, 1108 (Okla. Crim. Ct. App. 1927); State v. Barnett, 437 P.2d 821, 822 (Ore. 1968); State v. Wilson, 230 P. 810, 811 (Ore. 1925); State v. Glass, 5 Ore. 73, 84 (1873); Commonwealth v. Fisher, 149 A.2d 670, 670 (Pa. Super. 1959), *aff'd mem.,* 157 A.2d 207, 670 (Pa. 1960); Commonwealth v. Sierakowski, 35 A.2d 790, 793 (Pa. Super. 1944); Commonwealth v. Bricker, 74 Pa. Super. 234, 239 (1920); State v. Burlingame, 198 N.W. 824, 826 (S.D. 1924); Smartt v. State, 80 S.W. 586, 589 (Tenn. 1904); Thompson v. State, 493 S.W.2d 913, 915 (Tex. Ct. Crim. App. 1971) *vacated after* Roe v. Wade, 410 U.S. 950 (1973); Bristow v. State. 128 S.W.2d 818, 821 (Tex. Ct. Crim. App. 1939); Crissman v. State, 245 S.W. 438, 438 (Tex. Ct. Crim. App. 1922); State v. Cragun, 38 P.2d 1071, 1072 (Utah 1934); State v. McCurtain, 172 P. 481, 483 (Utah 1918); Beecham v. Leahy, 287 A.2d 836, 838 (Vt. 1972); State v. Montifiore, 116 A. 77, 79 (Vt. 1921); Miller v. Bennett, 56 S.E.2d 217, 220 (Va. 1949). *See also* State v. Ashley, 701 So. 2d 338 (Fla. 1997). *See generally* WM. L. CLARK, JR., HAND-BOOK OF CRIMINAL LAW 182 (1894); OTTO POLLAK, THE CRIMINALITY OF WOMEN 45–46 (paperback ed. 1961); REAGAN, *supra* note 59, at 116–19; PAUL WOHLERS, WOMEN AND ABORTION: PROSPECTS FOR CRIMINAL CHARGES 1 (Am. Cntr. for Bioethics; undated); WILLIAMS, *supra* note 213, at 153–54; Susan Alford, Note, *Is Self-Abortion a Fundamental Right?,* 52 DUKE L.J. 1011 (2003); Paul Linton, *Enforcement of State Abortion Statutes after Roe: A State-by-State Analysis,* 67 U. DET. L. REV. 157, 163–64 n.31 (1990); Jim Stone, *Abortion as Murder? A Response,* 26 J. SOC. PHILOS. 129, 134–36 (1995). *Compare* Rex v. Tinckler, 1 EAST, *supra* note 184, at 354–56, quoted in Chapter 5, at note 52

301. State v. Farnam, 161 P. 417, 419 (Or. 1916). *See also* Miller v. Bayer, 68 N.W. 869 (Wis. 1896) (same); Hancock v. Hullett, 82 So. 522 (Ala. 1919) (allowing a malpractice action on behalf of the father of a woman who was injured in an illegal abortion); Andrews v. Coulter, 1 P.2d 320 (Wash. 1931) (an administrator of the estate of a woman who died from an allegedly negligent illegal abortion can recover for medical care and bur-

ally no conviction of the abortionist could be obtained without the testimony of the woman who underwent the abortion yet, then as now, a criminal could not be convicted by the uncorroborated testimony of an accomplice.[302] If the woman were a party to the crime of abortion, convictions generally would have been virtually impossible to obtain, even with a grant of immunity from prosecution to the woman to overcome any self-incrimination problems.[303] New York did enact a statutory grant of immunity to aborted women precisely in order to make prosecution of the abortionist possible, beginning with the 1869 *Abortion Act*.[304] The immunity provision was dropped from the 1872 and 1881 acts, but was reenacted in 1942.[305] The statute remained on the books until after the 1970 abortion reform.

A grant of immunity did not solve the corroboration problem; only holding that the woman was not an accomplice to the crime allowed her uncorroborated testimony to be the basis of a conviction of the abortionist. While a New York trial court had held that women undergoing an abortion were parties to the crime under the 1829 *Revised Statutes*,[306] New York's higher courts, like courts elsewhere, solved the corroboration problem by holding that a woman undergoing an abortion was not an accomplice of that crime.[307] The practical basis of the rule was repeatedly stressed during a 1908 debate in the American Medical Association on a proposal to support the criminalization of the woman's conduct.[308] Higher courts in only three states held that the woman was an accomplice to her own abortion.[309] New Jersey's Supreme Court held that a woman could be indicted as a principal after the child quickened.[310] Several courts held that the

---

ial expenses). Some courts barred tort actions for medical malpractice against abortionists because the claim derived from the plaintiff's participation in unlawful conduct. Hunter v. Wheate, 289 F. 604 (D.C. Ct. App. 1923); Castronovo v. Murawsky, 120 N.E.2d 871 (Ill. App. Ct. 1954); Goldnamer v. O'Brien, 33 S.W. 831 (Ky. 1896); Szadiwicz v. Cantor, 154 N.E. 251 (Mass. 1927); Larocque v. Conheim, 87 N.Y.S. 625 (N.Y. Sup. Ct. 1904); Martin v. Morris, 42 S.W.2d 207 (Tenn. 1931). Other courts took the opposite view, usually because the woman was not an accomplice at law. Wolcott v. Gaines, 169 S.E.2d 165 (Ga. 1970); Nash v. Meyer, 31 P.2d 273 (Idaho 1934); Gunder v. Tibbits, 55 N.E. 762 (Ind. 1899); Joy v. Brown, 252 P.2d 889 (Kan. 1953); Lembo v. Donnell, 101 A. 469 (Me. 1917); True v. Older, 34 N.W.2d 700 (Minn. 1949); Milliken v. Heddesheimer, 144 N.E. 264 (Ohio 1924); Bowlan v. Lunsford, 54 P.2d 666 (Okla. 1936); Miller v. Bennett, 56 S.E.2d 217 (Va. 1949). *See generally* Reagan, *supra* note 84, at 317–31.

302. *See, e.g.,* CAL. PENAL CODE § 1111 (West 2002). *See also* Maxey v. United States, 30 App. D.C. 63, 77–78 (1907); Richmond v. Commonwealth, 370 S.W. 399, 400–01 (Ky. Ct. App. 1963); State v. Reilly, 141 N.W. 720, 727 (N.D. 1913). *See generally* 2 FRANCIS WHARTON, EVIDENCE IN CRIMINAL CASES 1224–27 (11th ed. 1935); JOHN HENRY WIGMORE, A TREATISE ON THE ANGLO-AMERICAN SYSTEM OF EVIDENCE IN TRIALS AT COMMON LAW 312–34 (3rd ed. 1940).

303. *See* GROSSBERG, *supra* note 67, at 125; OLASKY, *supra* note 46, at 99; POLLAK, *supra* note 300, at 45–46.

304. 1869 N.Y. Laws ch. 631, § 3, at 1502.

305. 1942 N.Y. Laws ch. 791, § 1. For similar statutory grants of immunity, see George, *supra* note 118, at 382 nn.70–73.

306. Frazer v. People, 1 Cowen's Crim. 377 (N.Y. Sup. Ct. 1863).

307. People v. Blank, 29 N.E.2d 73 (N.Y. 1940); People v. McGonegal, 32 N.E. 616 (N.Y. 1892); People v. Vedder, 98 N.Y. 630 (1885); Dunn v. People, 29 N.Y. 523 (1864); People v. Lohman, 2 Barb. 216 (N.Y. Sup. Ct.), *aff'd on other grounds,* 1 N.Y. 379 (1848); People v. Costello, 1 Denio 83 (N.Y. Sup. Ct. 1845). *See generally* Annotation, *Woman upon Whom Abortion Is Committed as Accomplice for Purposes of Rule Requiring Corroboration of Accomplice Testimony,* 34 A.L.R.3d 858 (1970); Ellen Willis, *Putting Women Back into the Abortion Debate,* in FROM ABORTION TO REPRODUCTIVE FREEDOM: TRANSFORMING A MOVEMENT 135 (Marlene Gerber Fried ed. 1990).

308. Walter Dorsett, *Common Abortion In Its Broadest Sense,* 51 JAMA 958 (1908).

309. Dykes v. State, 1 So. 2d 754 (Ala. Ct. App. 1941); Steed v. State, 170 So. 489 (Ala. Ct. App. 1936); Trent v. State, 73 So. 834 (Ala. Ct. App. 1916); People v. Peyser, 44 N.E.2d 58 (Ill. 1942); State v. McCoy, 89 N.E. 316 (Ohio 1894); State v. Jones, 70 N.E.2d 913 (Ohio Ct. App. 1946); Waite v. State, 4 Ohio App. 451 (1915).

310. *In re* Vince, 67 A.2d 141 (N.J. 1949).

fact that the woman was neither a principal nor an accomplice did not prevent her from being a co-conspirator.[311] These latter cases did not involve indictments of a woman; the naming of the woman as a co-conspirator was designed to ease the admission of letters or statements of the woman as evidence against indicted abortionists.

That these cases were motivated largely by a desire to make the conviction of the abortionist easier is also shown by the pattern of denying recovery on life insurance policies for women who died as a result of an illegal abortion.[312] Courts recognized the moral guilt of the woman as the basis for denying recovery,[313] all the while denying her legal responsibility. Only a few courts found that the moral guilt was not an adequate basis for finding that upholding liability would violate public policy.[314] Several courts also upheld the right of a woman to sue for the negligence of the abortionist, something that would have been barred had she been an accomplice to the abortionist's crime.[315] Almost as many courts, however, denied such recovery.[316]

Apparently, no woman has ever been convicted in the United States of the crime of abortion as such, and only a few have been charged.[317] In England, in contrast with the American practice, women who underwent abortions were successfully prosecuted as both co-conspirators and as

---

311. Solander v. People, 2 Colo. 48 (1873); State v. Gilmore, 132 N.W. 53 (Iowa 1911); State v. Crofford, 110 N.W. 921 (1907); State v. Brown, 64 N.W. 277 (Iowa 1895); People v. Davis, 56 N.Y. 95 (1874); State v. Mattson, 206 N.W. 778 (N.D. 1925); State v. Reilly, 141 N.W. 720 (N.D. 1913); Commonwealth v. Fisher, 149 A.2d 670 (Pa. Super. 1959), *aff'd mem.*, 157 A.2d 207, 670 (Pa. 1960); State v. Adams, 43 N.W.2d 446 (Wis. 1950); State *ex rel.* Tingley v. Hanley, 22 N.W.2d 510 (Wis. 1946); State v. Timm, 12 N.W.2d 670 (Wis. 1944); Kraut v. State, 280 N.W. 327 (Wis. 1938); State v. Henderson, 274 N.W. 266 (Wis. 1937).

312. Hatch v. Mutual Life Ins. Co., 120 Mass. 550 (1876); Wells v. New Eng. Mut. Life Ins. Co., 43 A. 126 (Pa. 1899); McCreighton v. American Catholic Union, 71 Pa. Super. 332 (1919).

313. A number of courts made the same distinction between moral and legal guilt in criminal prosecutions. *See* Thompson v. United States, 30 App. D.C. 352, 364 (1908); Seifert v. State, 67 N.E. 100, 100 (Ind. 1903); State v. Miller, 261 S.W. 103, 106 (Mo. 1953); People v. Vedder, 98 N.Y. 630, 632 (1885); State v. Shaft, 81 S.E. 932, 933 (N.C. 1914); State v. McCurtain, 172 P. 481, 483 (Utah 1918).

314. Lundholm v. Mystic Workers, 164 Ill. App. 472 (1911); Rosen v. Louisiana State Bd. Med. Examiners, 318 F. Supp. 1217, 1227 (E.D. La. 1970) (*dictum*), *vacated after* Roe v. Wade, 412 U.S. 902 (1973); Payne v. Louisiana Indus. Life Ins. Co., 33 So. 2d 444 (La. Ct. App. 1948); Simmons v. Victory Indus. Life Ins. Co., 139 So. 2d 68 (La. Ct. App. 1932).

315. Wolcott v. Gaines, 169 S.E.2d 165 (Ga. 1969); Martin v. Hardesty, 163 N.E. 610 (Ind. 1928); Kimberly v. Ledbetter, 331 P.2d 307 (Kan. 1958); Richey v. Darling, 331 P.2d 281 (Kan. 1958); Joy v. Brown, 252 P.2d 889 (Kan. 1953); Lembo v. Donnell, 103 A. 11 (Me. 1918); True v. Older, 34 N.W.2d 200 (Minn. 1948); Milliken v. Heddesheimer, 144 N.E. 264 (Ohio 1924); Miller v. Bayer, 68 N.W. 869 (Wis. 1896).

316. Hunter v. Wheate, 289 F. 604 (D.C. Ct. App. 1923); Nash v. Meyer, 31 P.2d 273 (Idaho 1934); Castronovo v. Murawsky, 120 N.E.2d 871 (Ill. App. Ct. 1954); Herman v. Turner, 232 P. 864 (Kan. 1925) (*dictum*); Szadiwicz v. Cantor, 154 N.E. 251 (Mass. 1926); Reno v. D'Javid, 369 N.E.2d 766 (N.Y. 1977); Larocque v. Couneim, 87 N.Y.S. 625 (N.Y. Sup. Ct. 1904); Henrie v. Griffith, 395 P.2d 809 (Okla. 1965); Bowlan v. Lunsford, 54 P.2d 666 (Okla. 1936); Martin v. Morris, 163 S.W.2d 207 (Tenn. 1931); Miller v. Bennett, 56 S.E.2d 217 (Va. 1949). *See also* Sayadoff v. Wanda, 271 P.2d 140 (Cal. Ct. App. 1954) (the woman was not allowed to recover for her injuries in a suit against the person who urged her to have an abortion); Goldnamer v. O'Brien, 98 Ky. 569 (1896) (same); Symone T. v. Lieber, 613 N.Y.S.2d 404 (App. Div. 1994) (denying liability for an illegal abortion performed after *Roe v. Wade*); Andrews v. Coulter, 1 P.2d 320 (Wash. 1931) (recovery was allowed for negligent treatment after the abortion but denied for the abortion itself) *See generally* Gail Hollister, *Tort Suits for Injuries during Illegal Abortions: The Effects of Judicial Bias,* 45 Villa. L. Rev. 387, 407–47 (2000).

317. *See, e.g.,* State v. Ashley, 701 So. 2d 338 (Fla. 1997); Ann-Louise Lohr & Paul Benjamin Linton, *Abortion Victims,* Chi. Trib., Apr. 22, 1991, at C16. *See also* Edwin Schur, Crimes without Victims: Deviant Behavior and Public Policy 36 (1965); Tribe, *supra* note 138, at 122; Alford, *supra* note 300; Thomas Harris, Note, *A Functional Study of Existing Abortion Laws,* 35 Colum. L. Rev. 87, 90–91 (1935).

accomplices.[318] Nor did English courts begin to grant immunity from prosecution to the woman who underwent the abortion in order to procure her testimony until 1932.[319]

The difficulties of proving abortion without the woman as a cooperative witness seem often to elude modern observers of the abortion debate.[320] Those who favor abortion rights insist that the fact that women have not been treated as criminal for having undergone an illicit abortion is a logically incoherent compromise lacking any policy justification, based only on the evident political unpopularity of punishing the women themselves for aborting their children.[321] Such arguments seem wholly ignorant of the long history underlying this rule, wholly unaware of the need for corroborating testimony or of the long and fact-based tradition of abortion as a crime against women. These reasons might strike a modern observer as overly paternalistic, treating women as if they were too immature to make their own decisions as in the parallel rule that a woman cannot be a co-conspirator to violate the *Mann Act* prohibiting her transportation across state lines for immoral purposes.[322] Women are reduced to the level of immature girls who are not treated as accessories to statutory rape.[323] Paternalistic or not, the tradition of not treating the women undergoing an abortion (whether self-induced or otherwise) as a criminal does not contradict the desire to protect the life of the fetus. In fact, by increasing the chance of conviction for the abortionist, it was perhaps the most effective means for protecting that life. The Supreme Court, overlooking both the traditional view of the mother as a victim of the abortion and the modern need for her testimony, concluded in *Roe v. Wade* (like Means and Mohr) that the general pattern of not treating the mother as a criminal supported the notion that the statutes were enacted to protect the mother, not the child.[324]

Mohr's surmise of a power grab by physicians then is both unnecessary to explain the features of the laws that he asserts supports his surmise and fails to account for the enactment of the abortion statutes of the nineteenth century. At the root of Mohr's argument is the utter absence of the larger legal and medical historical context within which these statutes were enacted. The inclusion of the abortion prohibitions in the nineteenth-century codifications suggests not a desire to evade controversy, but rather a lack of controversy when the common law of abortion was clarified and carried forward as part of the general law of crimes with only those changes necessitated by changing medical technologies.[325] Perhaps in response to such criticisms, Mohr has now published a study of that larger nineteenth-century context of the interface of law and medicine, but he says little in that study about the practice or prohibition of abortion.[326]

---

318. Regina v. Whitchurch, 24 Q.B.D. 420 (1890) (conspiracy); Rex v. Scokett, 72 J.P. 428 (1908) (aiding and abetting).

319. Rex v. Peake, 97 J.P. 353 (1932); BROOKES, *supra* note 220, at 40; WILLIAMS, *supra* note 213, at 146, 153–54.

320. *See, e.g.,* Ronald Collins, *The Problem of Penalties Clouds Issue of Abortion*, NAT'L L.J., July 29, 1985, at 13.

321. MARK GRABER, RETHINKING ABORTION: EQUAL CHOICE, THE CONSTITUTION, AND REPRODUCTIVE POLITICS 44–45 (1996); Samuel Buell, Note, *Criminal Abortion Revisited*, 66 N.Y.U. L. REV. 1774, 1790 (1991); Collins, *supra* note 321; Jean Rosenbluth, Note, *Abortion as Murder: Why Should Women Get Off? Using Scare Tactics to Preserve Choice*, 66 S. CAL. L. REV. 1237, 1262–66 (1993); Michael Sands, *The Therapeutic Abortion Act: An Answer to the Opposition*, 13 UCLA L. REV. 285, 295–96 (1966); Howard Ziff, *Recent Abortion Law Reforms*, 60 J. CRIM. L. & CRIMINOLOGY 3, 17 (1969).

322. Gebardi v. United States, 287 U.S. 112 (1932).

323. POLLAK, *supra* note 300, at 2.

324. 410 U.S., at 151–52.

325. *See generally* Chapter 1. For a critique of medical historian Paul Starr's neglect of the role of changing medical technology in the transformation of American medicine, see Allan Brandt, *The Ways and Means of American Medicine*, HASTINGS CNTR. REP., June 1983, at 41. The same point could be made regarding the other historians as well.

326. MOHR, *supra* note 78.

Mohr sought to buttress his claim that self-serving competitive goals underlay the campaign to enact statutes prohibiting abortions by noting that the statutes relating to medical practice engendered protests by the "irregulars." Mohr focused on the mass rallies that resulted and indicated that the irregulars achieved some legislative success in modifying the restrictions on the practice of medicine enacted in New York in 1827,[327] but he did not bother to point out that the irregulars, in their efforts to counter those restrictions, did not even attempt to modify or repeal the abortion statutes. Indeed, by phrasing his observation in terms of the date of the enactment of the medical practice statutes (1827), he might very well have misled readers who did not recall that the abortion statutes were enacted in December of 1828 (coming into effect in 1829).[328] Rather, Mohr argued, apparently without evidence other than his own intuition, that the public protests against restrictions on access to the profession of medicine caused the New York authorities to forbear enforcing the statutory prohibitions on abortion.[329]

Mohr inferred the lack of prosecution in New York from the absence of *reported* cases. Of course, he did not indicate that he had researched original trial court records to verify his inference, and he himself cited several unreported cases from other states at this time.[330] In other contexts, Mohr himself attributed the failure to enforce the new abortion statutes to the difficulty of proving the specific intent required under these early statutes rather than to official tolerance of the practice.[331] This brings us to perhaps the central point of the new orthodoxy of abortion history: Was abortion an accepted social practice in the nineteenth century?

# The Realities of Abortion in the Mid-Nineteenth Century

*I am toiling uphill against that heaviest of all argumentative weights—the weight of a slogan.*

—Charles Black[332]

We have, of course, no direct records that might enable us to reconstruct accurate measures of the frequency of abortion at any time in the nineteenth century, although we have plenty of information about how abortions were done then. The new orthodoxy of abortion history has it that abortion in the mid-nineteenth century was common throughout the United States, openly advertised and practiced, and not socially condemned except by a few religious fanatics—and by the self-serving allopathic physicians.[333] These claims are unreal, particularly early in the century when abortion techniques were crude, painful, and dangerous.

---

327. MOHR, *supra* note 29, at 39.
328. *See also* MOHR, *supra* note 78, at 88–89.
329. MOHR, *supra* note 29, at 39.
330. *Id.* at 275 n.55.
331. *Id.* at 26, 41–43, 138–40, 142, 144.
332. CHARLES BLACK, THE PEOPLE AND THE COURT 88 (1960).
333. *See, e.g.,* 1 BONNIE ANDERSON & JUDITH ZINSSER, A HISTORY OF THEIR OWN: WOMEN IN EUROPE FROM PREHISTORY TO THE PRESENT 137–38 (1988); BRODIE, *supra* note 220, at 33, 41–44, 224–25; BROOKES, *supra* note 220, at 1, 24; REBECCA CHALKER & CAROL DOWNER, A WOMAN'S BOOK OF CHOICES: ABORTION, MENSTRUAL EXTRACTION, RU 486, at 9 (1993); CELESTE MICHELLE CONDIT, DECODING ABORTION RHETORIC: COMMUNICATING SOCIAL CHANGE 77 n.29 (1990); D'EMILIO & FREEDMAN, *supra* note 233, at 63, 145–50; GINSBURG, *supra* note 138, at 23–24, 30; GORDON, *supra* note 75, at 28–29, 35–39, 52–54; HARRISON, *supra* note 233, at 238–44; OLWEN HUFTON, THE POOR IN EIGHTEENTH CENTURY FRANCE 331 (1974); JUDGES,

Statistics are sparse for any nineteenth century medical procedure. For a procedure like abortion, which was widely disapproved and unquestionably illegal throughout most of the nineteenth century, contemporary statistics do not exist. Furthermore, like the sex act itself, even the most personally revealing diaries from earlier times tell us little or nothing that is relevant about what was, after all, a crime. As one historian pointed out, "[i]t is easier to know what [a diarist] dreamed than to speak with confidence about his pelvic thrust."[334] Such details we will never know, and cannot expect to know, although this did not stop the *New York Times* from describing abortion as "The Evil of the Age" in 1871.[335]

Contrary to the new orthodoxy, there actually is little direct evidence (apart from an occasional criminal prosecution) to suggest that abortions even occurred in the middle of the nineteenth century in England, in America, or anywhere else, let alone that it was common.[336] Nor do we find records of abortions in the private diaries of midwives of the time.[337] This utter lack of records of actual abortions suggests that the practice either was not common or was sufficiently socially disapproved that anyone engaged in the practice wanted to keep it a secret. Most telling in clarifying which explanation is correct is the near total absence in the medical records of the time of treatments for incomplete septic abortions. Even Cyril Means, jr., was aware that no abortions of any kind are recorded in the records of the New York Hospital for the period 1808–1833.[338] The necessity of treatment of septic abortions only became common after 1880,[339] well after nearly all the nineteenth century legislative activity directed at abortion had occurred. Unless we are to suppose that some truly remarkable folk remedies were available in the early years of the century that somehow mysteriously were abandoned in favor of far more dangerous (and far less effective) techniques later in the century, the absence of evidence of incomplete or septic abortions is irrefutable proof that abortions of all kinds were in fact rare. Careful review of the indirect evidence for abortion does not contradict this conclusion.

Those who insist that abortion was a common practice by the middle of the nineteenth century, and even before, generally turn to two sorts of sources to support the claim. First, they turn to the advertisements of those who began, rather openly but almost always through eu-

---

*supra* note 155, at 32, 83–84, 96–97, 101; McLaren, *supra* note 233, at 34, 241; McLaren, *supra* note 35, at 5–7, 107, 111–12, 114; Mohr, *supra* note 29, at 11–14, 18, 25–40, 85–118, 128, 147–82; Connie Paige, The Right to Lifers: Who They Are; How They Operate; Where They Get Their Money 32–33 (1983); Petchesky, *supra* note 233, at 1–2, 28–30, 48–57, 70–71, 76–78; Petersen, *supra* note 38, at 1, 12; Deborah Rhode, Justice and Gender 202–05 (1989); Patrick Sheeran, Women, Society, the State, and Abortion: A Structuralist Analysis 49–51, 54, 58, 73, 75 (1987); Shorter, *supra* note 37, at 177–91; Smith-Rosenberg, *supra* note 71, at 217; Tribe, *supra* note 138, at 30–34; Jeffrey Weeks, Sex, Politics and Society 72 (1981); Catherine Whitney, Whose Life? A Balanced, Comprehensive View of Abortion from Its Historical Context to the Current Debate 39–44 (1991); *Casey Historians' Brief*, *supra* note 32, at 4–10; *Webster Historians' Brief*, *supra* note 32, at 170–77; Dayton, *supra* note 61, at 19–20, 23; Sheila Dickinson, *Abortion in Antiquity*, 6 Arethusa 159 (1973); Siegel, *supra* note 32, at 318 n.235; Étienne van de Walle, *Motivations and Technology and the Decline of French Fertility*, in Family and Sexuality in French History 135, 144–45 (Robert Wheaton & Tamara Hareven eds. 1980); Ray Bowen Ward, *The Use of the Bible in the Abortion Debate*, 13 St. L.U. Pub. L. Rev. 391, 392–93 (1993).

334. G.S. Rousseau & Roy Porter, *Introduction*, in Sexual Underworlds of the Enlightenment, *supra* note 251, at 1, 7. *See also* David Vincent, *Love and Death and the Nineteenth Century Working Class*, 5 Social Hist. 223 (1980).

335. August St. Clair, *The Evil of the Age*, N.Y. Times, Aug. 23, 1871, at 6. *See also* Martin Luther Holbrook, Parturition without Pain: A Code of Directions for Escaping from the Primal Curse 16 (1871) (describing abortion as a common "addiction").

336. *See* Chapter 1.

337. *See, e.g.,* Ulrich, *supra* note 27. See also the text *supra* at notes 27, 28.

338. Means II, *supra* note 29, at 384–85.

339. Shorter, *supra* note 37, at 191–96.

phemisms, to peddle purported abortifacients in the middle years of the century.[340] Second, they look to the assertions in the anti-abortion polemics that began to appear at about the same time.[341] Both sources do indeed report that abortions are alarmingly rampant and growing in number. Finally, they note the demographic transition (with the average American woman having seven children in 1800 and only 3.5 children in 1900) as indirect evidence of the popularity of abortion.[342] Even James Mohr, however, has conceded that abortion could not have been the primary means by which this demographic transition took place.[343]

The public dissemination of information about abortion techniques and pervasive advertising of abortion services and abortifacients became common from the 1840s on.[344] Historians who support abortion rights also sometimes claim that nineteenth-century public schools, through instruction on anatomy and physiology, played a central role in popularizing abortion, without, however, providing any evidence of what those courses actually taught. They simply do not go beyond the highly general condemnations of committed opponents of any such education.[345] One wonders how future historians will evaluate contemporary sex education if they rely only on the attacks of its harshest critics.

These historians hardly provide better support for their reliance on the advertised products as proof of the growing availability of abortifacients. They seldom examine whether these advertised products would actually have worked as claimed. James Mohr is particularly puzzling in this regard. After citing the advertisement of pills, nostrums, douches, and pessaries as proof that knowledge of how to do abortions was widespread, he expressly acknowledged that the items in these advertisements would not have been effective except through grave danger to the life or health of the mother.[346] As late as 1939, the Federal Trade Commission undertook to ban the advertisement or sale of "abortifacient preparations" because of the risk to women's health, including such standard herbal remedies as aloes, apiol, ergot, hellebore, and savin.[347]

The advertising itself also reveals that the practice of abortion was not socially acceptable. Invariably, the advertisements used euphemisms and often included (sometimes in bold type) warnings of the need for care in use so as to avoid inducing a miscarriage.[348] Even if we assume that these "warnings" were actually meant to convey the information that the product could induce an abortion, this practice hardly suggests that abortion had become a practice that was widely thought in society to be unobjectionable. Furthermore, the advertisements appear in what media historian Frank Mott described as the "lower class of story papers"—cheap periodicals designed for "*sub rosa* circulation to resorts of questionable character."[349] The better class of magazines mostly did not begin to carry any type of advertising until the later years of the nineteenth century.[350] Furthermore, much of this advertising literature appeared under pseudonyms or anonymously. And the advertisements frequently promised to send the product in a plain

---

340. *See, e.g.,* MOHR, *supra* note 29, at 50–52, 61.

341. *Id.* at 68–76, 149–52; SMITH-ROSENBERG, *supra* note 71, at 220–21.

342. MOHR, *supra* note 29, at 82–85.

343. *Id.* at 83.

344. D'EMILIO & FREEDMAN, *supra* note 233, at 63–64; MOHR, *supra* note 29, at 48–72; Michael La Sorte, *Nineteenth-Century Family Planning Practices*, 31 J. PSYCHOHIST. 163, 167–69 (1976).

345. MOHR, *supra* note 29, at 69–70.

346. *Id.* at 55–58, 61. *See also id.* at 9, 21–22, 71–73; BRODIE, *supra* note 220, at 224–27.

347. *The Action of the Federal Commission against Abortifacient Preparations*, 4 J. CONTRACEPTION 198 (1939). Curiously, Janet Brodie, in discussing this action, describes the ban as applying to "medicines designed to induce a delayed menstruation." BRODIE, *supra* note 220, at 226.

348. *See* BRODIE, *supra* note 220, at 225, 228–29; OLASKY, *supra* note 46, at 94–96.

349. 2 FRANK MOTT, HISTORY OF AMERICAN MAGAZINES, 1741–1850, at 185 (1930).

350. *See generally* BRODIE, *supra* note 220, at 191, 194–201, 227; 3 MOTT, *supra* note 350, at 9.

wrapper with no distinguishing external marks.[351] All of these steps suggest that what was being advertised was socially disapproved or fraudulent, something that had to be marketed surreptitiously. Reputable doctors, when describing what appeared to be abortion techniques, consistently declared that they were merely providing information on how to unblock the menses and that their suggestions should not be attempted if there was any reason to suspect pregnancy.[352] Mohr knew this, but buried it in a distant endnote or near the end of the chapter in which he identified the dissemination of information by reputable doctors as a factor in making abortions, in his view, popular and socially accepted.[353]

In place of hard evidence of the frequency of abortion, we are given enormously varied "guestimates."[354] Mohr cites different sources written by the same author but containing guestimates that vary wildly.[355] The evident lack of information did not prevent Mohr from guestimating that abortions amounted to as much as 20 percent of the number of live births,[356] although he did concede (in an endnote 225 pages from the guestimates he presents) that there is no hard evidence to support his claim.[357] Historian Carl Degler presented evidence of a sudden increase in abortions after 1820, conceding (unlike Mohr) that abortion was rare in the United States before then.[358] Degler noted the temporal correlation between this change in behavior and the decision to include abortion in the early criminal codes beginning in 1821, but he did not consider whether this supposed rise in frequency explained the sudden spate of legislative activity.

While abortion was a crime in many states by 1840, rates of prosecution probably do not indicate the true incidence of the crime. Rates of prosecution tell us more about general or official public attitudes than about actual personal behavior.[359] Consider, for example, that sodomy was a commonly prosecuted crime in seventeenth-century France and almost unknown in the courts of that country in the eighteenth century when literary representations of sodomy had become more common.[360] Also recall the changing rates of prosecution for witchcraft over the centuries. Yet we also know that infanticide prosecutions were still fairly common in the United States in the years leading up to 1840—in contrast with the rarity of abortion prosecutions up to that time.[361]

At least four women were prosecuted for infanticide in South Carolina between 1794 and 1836,[362] and at least six women were convicted for infanticide under Pennsylvania's concealment

---

351. BRODIE, *supra* note 220, at 232–33.

352. *See, e.g.,* FREDERICK HOLLICK, DISEASES OF WOMEN, THEIR CAUSES AND CURE FAMILIARLY EXPLAINED; WITH PRACTICAL HINTS FOR THEIR PREVENTION, AND FOR THE PRESERVATION OF FEMALE HEALTH; FOR EVERY FEMALE'S PRIVATE USE 149–53 (1849); GEORGE GREGORY, MEDICAL MORALS, ILLUSTRATED WITH PLATES AND EXTRACTS FROM MEDICAL WORKS: DESIGNED TO SHOW THE PERNICIOUS SOCIAL AND MORAL INFLUENCE OF THE PRESENT SYSTEM OF MEDICAL PRACTICE, AND THE IMPORTANCE OF ESTABLISHING FEMALE MEDICAL COLLEGES, AND EDUCATING FEMALE PHYSICIANS FOR THEIR OWN SEX 13–16 (1853); G. LAMMERT, *VOLSKMEDIZIN UND MEDIZINISCHER ABERGLAUBE IN BAYERN* 252 (1869); STORER, *supra* note 137, at 26, 41, 48. *See generally* 1 ANDERSON & ZINSSER, *supra* note 334, at 29–30; BROOKES, *supra* note 220, at 3; SHORTER, *supra* note 37, at 180, 286–87. The practice is discussed at some length in Chapter 1, at notes 141–83.

353. MOHR, *supra* note 29, at 66, 68, 278 n.37. *See also id.* at 141–42.

354. *See, e.g., id.* at 74–82; R. Sauer, *Attitudes to Abortion in America, 1800–1973,* 28 POP. STUDIES 53, 54–55 (1974).

355. See the discussion of the estimates of Dr. Edwin Hale, discussed in Chapter 7, at notes 163–71.

356. *Id.* at 50. *See also* GORDON, *supra* note 75, at 45–53.

357. MOHR, *supra* note 29, at 275 n.12. *See also* Chapter 7, at notes 163–206.

358. DEGLER, *supra* note 234, at 228–29, 245–46.

359. *See* Théodore Tarczylo, *From Lascivious Erudition to the History of* Mentalités (George St. Andrews trans.), in SEXUAL UNDERWORLDS OF THE ENLIGHTENMENT, *supra* note 251, at 26, 29–30.

360. *See* MAURICE LEVER, LES BÛCHERS DE SODOME (1985).

361. OLASKY, *supra* note 46, at 37–38.

362. JACK KENNY WILLIAMS, VOGUES IN VILLAINY: CRIME AND RETRIBUTION IN ANTE-BELLUM SOUTH CAROLINA 54 (1959).

statute during the same era.[363] While five of these women were sentenced to prison, some 20,000 people turned out to watch the execution of Susanna Cox in Reading, Pennsylvania, on June 10, 1809, for infanticide.[364] We can only infer from the still common occurrence of infanticide and the still extraordinary dangers of abortion, coupled with the lack of actual records of abortions, that infanticide was still the rule and that, in 1840, abortion was still rare—albeit less rare than a century before. To support that inference, it is worth taking a closer look at the rate of mortality associated with abortion in America around 1840.

Given that criminal prosecutions are our only direct evidence that abortions were done in the early nineteenth century, we should not be surprised that this evidence usually shows that the woman involved nearly always died as a result.[365] Without the woman's death, the crime could too easily be concealed. These cases also illuminate the usual pattern of attempting (usually either fatally or unsuccessfully) to bring on the abortion by ingestive means, and then (if the woman was still alive) proceeding to intrusive techniques without either antiseptics or anesthesia. The results always were painful and all too often were fatal. The progression is well illustrated by the testimony of the owner of a boarding house in the prosecution of Dr. Henry Chauncey in the doctor's prosecution for the murder of Eliza Sowers in 1839:

> [Chauncey] brought a girl to my house…At breakfast, next morning, Dr. Chauncey came in. He made me make some tea of a powder that looked like black pepper…At 2 o'clock the next morning, she called me. She said she was very bad. She said, "I won't take any more of that doctor's medicine; it will kill me." [Chauncey returned later that morning.] He did to her what doctors do to women when they are confined. He then washed his hands. He picked up something off the washstand, which shined and looked like a knitting needle, and wiped it…Said she was the most difficult person he had ever operated on. Said the medicine he gave her was too powerful, and had acted too quick.[366]

Notice that in this report the doctor, who may or may not have been an experienced abortionist, sought to excuse himself by stating that the potion given to the girl had been too strong. We cannot now determine whether he meant that this happened because his instructions on how to prepare the tea were wrong, or because the boardinghouse operator made a mistake in following the instructions, or because of the inherent variability of the herbs used in the tea.[367] Strong or not, the potion apparently was ineffective, and the doctor had to perform an intrusive abortion. Notice that he did not wash himself or his instruments until after he had performed the abortion. No wonder the girl sickened and died.

Cyril Means, jr., actually turns out to be one of the best sources on this question, and his conclusion supports the notion that abortion, even if it was becoming somewhat more common, was still highly dangerous and relatively rare around 1840. Means, who was intent on demonstrating that the abortion statutes of the nineteenth century were enacted to protect the health of the mother rather than the life of the child, made the dangerousness of the procedure the centerpiece of this thesis.[368] Means work in this regard is in some respects not particularly contro-

---

363. Sharon Ann Burnston, *Babies in the Well: An Underground Insight into Deviant Behavior in Eighteenth-Century Philadelphia,* 106 Pa. Mag. Hist. & Biography, No. 2, at 151, 176–77 (April 1982).

364. Olasky, *supra* note 46, at 37.

365. *See* Abrams v. Foshee, 3 Iowa 274 (1856); Smith v. State, 33 Me. 48 (1851); Commonwealth v. Parker, 50 Mass. (9 Met.) 263 (1845); Commonwealth v. Bangs, 9 Mass. 386 (1812); State v. Murphy, 27 N.J.L. 112 (1858); State v. Cooper, 22 N.J.L. 52 (1848); Lohman v. People, 1 N.Y. 379, 382–83 (1848); Mills v. Commonwealth, 13 Pa. 630, 632 (1850); State v. Howard, 32 Vt. 380 (1859). *See also* D'Emilio & Freedman, *supra* note 233, at 64; Olasky, *supra* note 46, at 39–41.

366. As quoted in Olasky, *supra* note 46, at 39–40.

367. *See* Chapter 1, at notes 363–91.

368. Means I, *supra* note 29. *See also* Means II, *supra* note 29, at 382–401.

versial. Psychiatrist Jerome Kummer and lawyer Zad Leavy were the first to advance the argument that the nineteenth-century abortion statutes in England and America were adopted to protect the life and health of the mother.[369] Means' version of this proposition was accepted by the majority in *Roe v. Wade,*[370] and has been examined and accepted by some of his sharpest critics[371] as well as by his supporters.[372] On the other hand, supporters of freedom to abort, while accepting protection of maternal health as a legitimate purpose of the abortion statutes, have increasingly downplayed the factual importance of this purpose as they have found it necessary to claim that abortion historically was common and relatively safe.[373] Beverly Harrison is rare among abortion-right's supporters in conceding that "until recently any act of abortion *always endangered the life of the mother* every bit as much as it imperiled the prenatal life in her womb."[374]

The controversy over Means' work in this regard is not over his description of the dangers of abortion in the early nineteenth century; it is over his assertion that the protection of maternal health was the sole purpose for the nineteenth century statutes. Means actual research to support his widely accepted thesis is remarkably, if characteristically, thin. He wrote before any of the extensive recent efforts to recover the medical history of abortion, and he did not attempt to do so himself. He was content to infer that abortion was about as safe (or as dangerous) as most other surgery of the time[375]—a subject that had been studied.

Early in the nineteenth century, all surgical procedures were highly dangerous. Before analgesics, anesthesia, antiseptics, and antibiotics, surgery often merely served to open the body to infection, while the pain of surgery could (and often did) induce fatal shock. Means relied on the research of Dr. William Ober, a prominent physician of the 1960s and 1970s who had studied the records in the early surgery registry of the New York Hospital. Ober was also a noted activist in the abortion reform movement and one of the founders of the National Association for the Repeal of Abortion Laws (NARAL).[376] Based on the information provided by Ober, Means speculated that the death rate early in the nineteenth century from "major peripheral surgery" was 37.5 per cent, of which more than 80 per cent (causing deaths in 31.25 per cent of all surgeries)

---

369. Zad Leavy & Dr. Jerome Kummer, *Criminal Abortion: Human Hardship and Unyielding Laws*, 35 S. Cal. L. Rev. 123 (1962). Zad Leavy even presented this argument to a California court before Means seized upon it. David Garrow, Liberty and Sexuality: The Right of Privacy and the Making of Roe v. Wade 309–10 (2nd ed. 1998).

370. 410 U.S. 113, 141–42, 148–52, 156–62 (1973).

371. *See, e.g.,* Keown, *supra* note 38, at 35–38, 59–78; Dellapenna, *supra* note 187, at 393–95, 400–01, 406–7, 411–17; Shelley Gavigan, *The Criminal Sanction as It Relates to Human Reproduction: The Genesis of the Statutory Prohibition of Abortion*, 5 J. Legal Hist. 20, 36 (1984).

372. Mohr, *supra* note 29, at 25–30; Smith-Rosenberg, *supra* note 71, at 219–20; Tribe, *supra* note 138, at 29; David Walbert & J. Douglas Butler, Abortion, Society and the Law 327–28 (1973); *Amicus Brief of the United States supporting Appellants in* Webster v. Reproductive Health Services, at 16, reprinted in 5 Documentary History, *supra* note 32, at 25; Sarah Weddington, *Keynote Address: Reflections on the Twenty-Fifth Anniversary of* Roe v. Wade, 62 Alb. L. Rev. 811, 825 (1999).

373. *See, e.g., Casey Historians' Brief, supra* note 32, at 4–13; *Webster Historians' Brief, supra* note 32, at 173–77; D'Emilio & Freedman, *supra* note 233, at 145–50; Gordon, *supra* note 75, at 52–53; Mohr, *supra* note 29, at 25–40, 85–118, 128, 147–82, *particularly at* 29–31; Petchesky, *supra* note 233, at 49–55, 70–71, 77–78; Tribe, *supra* note 138, at 30–34; Siegel, *supra* note 77, at 318 n.235. Donald Judges seems to want to have it both ways. Judges, *supra* note 155, at 96–97, 101. *See also* Brookes, *supra* note 220, at 24.

374. Harrison, *supra* note 233, at 124, 167.

375. Means II, *supra* note 29, at 382–87, 391–92; Means I, *supra* note 29, at 418, 436–37, 511–13.

376. William Ober, *We Should Legalize Abortion*, Sat. Evening Post, Oct. 8, 1966, at 14. On his prominence in the abortion reform movement, see Garrow, *supra* note 370, at 308, 334, 346. After 1973, NARAL changed its name to the National Abortion Rights Action League, and in 1993 it changed it to the National Abortion and Reproductive Rights Action League, and in 2002 it changed it again to NARAL Pro Choice America).

was the result of septic infection.[377] Whether abortion, had the procedure been lawful, would have produced similar rates can never be known for Ober, in searching the records of New York Hospital, found no abortions recorded for the period 1808–1833.[378]

Given the likelihood that a uterine infection would close the cervical canal, preventing drainage and the healing of the uterus, mortality from abortions—even if they had been legal—might well have been higher than from general surgery, although not higher than for any surgery for which proper dressing and draining would be difficult.[379] With added risks being introduced by the illegality of the practice, the death rate from abortions no doubt would have been higher still. In the mid-nineteenth century, at a time when probably one-third or more of the women who underwent abortions apparently would die, less than three per cent of mothers died in childbirth.[380] Reaching a conclusion based on this assumed general mortality rate for abortions, legal or illegal, Dr. Ober concluded that the risk of death from abortion was 10 to 15 times higher than the risk from childbirth, suggesting death rates from abortion in the range of 30 to 45 per cent.[381]

Several books not cited by Means or Ober, written in the mid-nineteenth century, support their conclusion regarding the mortality risks of abortions.[382] Modern research also supports their conclusions.[383] Childbirth, a riskier procedure then than now, was widely feared even by women who had experienced successful births.[384] These fears and risks are sometimes magnified in the modern imagination due in part, perhaps, the penchant of novelists in the eighteenth and nineteenth centuries for disposing of unwanted characters through death in childbirth. A truer impression is created by the diary of Martha Ballard, a midwife active in Maine in the late eighteenth and early nineteenth century. Laurel Thatcher Ulrich's review of this detailed diary found that only 5.6 percent of over 800 births involved any complications at all, and that only five out of nearly 1,000 resulted in maternal death.[385]

One study did find that a century earlier about 30 percent of women died before age 45 in the Chesapeake Bay area; while many of these deaths might have resulted from increased morbidity due to childbearing, the number who actually died in childbirth was much lower.[386] Moreover, as malaria and similar diseases apparently played a major role in the increase of female morbidity in the Chesapeake area,[387] in places such as New York, where these diseases were rare, maternal morbidity probably was lower. This reality also suggests that

377. Means II, *supra* note 29, at 384–85.

378. *Id.*

379. *Id.* at 385.

380. *Id. See also* C.D. HAAGENSON & WYNTHAM LLOYD, A HUNDRED YEARS OF MEDICINE 296–97 (1943) (reporting that one-third of women undergoing hysterectomies before 1870 died); REGINA MORANTZ-SANCHEZ, CONDUCT UNBECOMING A WOMAN: MEDICINE ON TRIAL IN BROOKLYN 96 (1999) (34 percent of women undergoing ovarectomies at the hands of one prominent physician in 1858 died).

381. Means II, *supra* note 29, at 384–85.

382. *See, e.g.,* M.K. HARD, WOMAN'S MEDICAL GUIDE: BEING A COMPLETE REVIEW OF THE PECULIARITIES OF THE FEMALE CONSTITUTION AND THE DERANGEMENTS TO WHICH IT IS SUBJECT, WITH A DESCRIPTION OF SIMPLE YET CERTAIN MEANS FOR THEIR CURE 3–4, 34, 38, 90 (1848).

383. *See* JEROME BATES & EDWARD ZAWADSKI, CRIMINAL ABORTION 85–87 (1964); SHORTER, *supra* note 37, at 191–96; Dellapenna, *supra* note 187, at 394–95, 400–01. *See generally* Chapter 1.

384. *See generally* JUDITH WALZER LEAVITT, BROUGHT TO BED: CHILDBEARING IN AMERICA 1750–1950, at 20–35 (1986); Jan Lewis & Kenneth Lockridge, *"Sally Has Been Sick": Pregnancy and Family Limitation among Virginia Gentry Women, 1780–1830*, 22 J. SOCIAL HIST. 5, 6–9 (1988).

385. ULRICH, *supra* note 27, at 169–83.

386. *See generally* ALLAN KULIKOFF, TOBACCO AND SLAVES: THE DEVELOPMENT OF SOUTHERN CULTURE IN THE CHESAPEAKE, 1680–1800, at 63 (1986).

387. Darrett Rutman & Anita Rutman, *Of Agues and Fevers: Malaria in the Early Chesapeake*, 33 WM. & MARY Q. 51 (3rd ser. 1976).

much of the maternal morbidity in the Chesapeake area was not a result of having given birth. Although the rates of maternal death in childbirth in England appear to have been as much as six times higher,[388] Dr. Charles White, an eighteenth century English physician, still could observe that a healthy young woman could give birth alone on the town common and probably do well.[389] The children did not fare quite as well as the mothers. Ballard experienced 19 stillbirths (or deaths within an hour of birth) out of 814 deliveries.[390] Giving birth seems to have been far less risky to the mother than abortion; for the child, no discussion is necessary.

In comparing maternal deaths from childbirth to maternal deaths from abortion, one should note that Dr. Ober's estimates are only for deaths resulting directly from an abortion. If later morbidity were factored in, the deadly effects of abortion would have been much higher and thus still considerably higher than any reasonable calculation of the effects of childbirth. Given the rising social pressure on unmarried women to avoid illegitimate pregnancies in a time of virtually nonexistent contraceptives,[391] the proliferation of prostitution,[392] and the growing desire of married women to control their family size,[393] one can readily believe that significant numbers of women were prepared to undergo the risks attendant to abortion, especially when those risks began to decline later in the century. There is evidence from the later years of the nineteenth century for each of these factors as significant in the then rising incidence of abortion.[394] Only for prostitution do we have suggestions from the middle of the century that this might be linked to a rise in the rate of abortions.[395]

The abortion-prostitution link is particularly important to keep in mind because of modern assertions that abortion was not only legal in the middle of the nineteenth century, but that it

---

388. ULRICH, *supra* note 27, at 172–74; B.M. Willmott, *An Attempt to Estimate the True Rate of Maternal Mortality, Sixteenth to Eighteenth Centuries*, 26 MEDICAL HIST. 79 (1982). *See also* CHARLES WHITE, A TREATISE ON THE MANAGEMENT OF PREGNANT AND LYING-IN WOMEN 236–40 (1st Am. ed. 1793).

389. WHITE, *supra* note 389, at 76. Martha Ballard, the Maine midwife of the same era, did express considerable anxiety over unattended births. ULRICH, *supra* note 27, at 170.

390. *See also* Laurel Thatcher Ulrich, *The Living Mother and a Living Child: Midwifery and Mortality in Eighteenth-Century New England*, 46 WM. & MARY Q. 27 (1989).

391. MICHAEL GORDON, THE AMERICAN FAMILY: PAST, PRESENT, AND FUTURE 173 (1978); PETER HOFFER & N.E.H. HULL, MURDERING MOTHERS: INFANTICIDE IN ENGLAND AND NEW ENGLAND 1558–1803, at 55, 109 (1981); MOHR, *supra* note 29, at 17–19; OLASKY, *supra* note 46, at 37–44; ROBERT WELLS, REVOLUTIONS IN AMERICANS' LIVES 353 (1982); *Casey Historians' Brief*, *supra* note 32, at 7–8; *Webster Historians' Brief*, *supra* note 32, at 171; Daniel Scott Smith & Michael Hindus, *Premarital Pregnancy in America, 1640–1971: An Overview and Interpretation*, 5 J. INTERDISCIPLINARY HIST. 537, 553–57 (1975). On the ineffectiveness of the contraceptives in use during the mid-nineteenth-century, see Chapter 2.

392. *See generally* D'EMILIO & FREEDMAN, *supra* note 233, at 137; OLASKY, *supra* note 46, at 44–59, 133–48; TANNAHILL, *supra* note 252, at 355–57.

393. *See* HODGE, *supra* note 278, at 6; E..M. Buckingham, *Criminal Abortion*, 10 CIN. LANCET & OBSERVER 139 (1867); Gibbons, *supra* note 278, at 212; Smith, *supra* note 274, at 211. *See generally* DEGLER, *supra* note 234, at 244–46; MOHR, *supra* note 29, at 86–110; OLASKY, *supra* note 46, at 61–82; PETCHESKY, *supra* note 233, at 49–57, 73–78; John Mack Farragher, *History From the Inside-Out: Writing the History of Women in Rural America*, 33 AM. Q. 536, 549 (1981); Daniel Scott Smith, *Family Limitation, Sexual Conduct, and Domestic Feminism in Victorian America*, 1 FEMINIST STUD. 40 (1973).

394. *Lack of safe and effective contraceptives:* JOHN COWAN, THE SCIENCE OF A NEW LIFE 279 (1871); ELIZABETH EDSON EVANS, THE ABUSE OF MATERNITY 13 (1875); Mulheron, *supra* note 278, at 387. *The close link between the incidence of abortion and the needs of prostitutes:* Hays v. State, 40 Md. 633, 645 (1874); Cowan, *supra*, at 285; C.E. ROGERS, SECRET SINS OF SOCIETY 76, 144 (1881); JOHN WARREN, JR., THIRTY YEARS BATTLE WITH CRIME, OR THE CRYING SHAME OF NEW YORK AS SEEN UNDER THE BROAD GLARE OF AN OLD DETECTIVE'S LANTERN 37–38, 53 (1874); Mulheron, *supra*, at 387. *Desire to control family size:* Mulheron, *supra*, at 391; Smith, *supra* note 274, at 211.

395. ACTON, *supra* note 183, at 206; JOHN MCDOWELL, FIRST ANNUAL REPORT OF THE NEW YORK MAGDALEN SOCIETY 23 (1831); WILLIAM SANGER, THE HISTORY OF PROSTITUTION 482, 586 (1859).

was not morally condemned "by the vast majority of Americans, provided it was accomplished before quickening."[396] Instead, a link of abortion and prostitution would have added to the unsavory reputation in which abortion and its practitioners were so manifestly clothed—a reputation that doctors could exploit successfully in seeking to suppress competition from midwives by stressing the link between the practice of midwifery and infanticide and abortion.[397] In 1874, we even find a court in Maryland, in a prosecution for an abortion committed in a brothel, commenting that a "house of ill-fame [was] most fitted for the perpetration of a crime like this."[398]

The attitudes of the nineteenth feminists are suggestive of the attitudes of mainstream women. The feminists of that time almost uniformly condemned prostitution and made various crusades against it a mainstay of their activities, often seeing this as necessary to achieve control over male sexuality.[399] Current feminist historians have tended to link the increasingly harsh criminal penalties for prostitution and the increasing legal activity directed against abortion, seeing both as attempts to control female sexuality—without bothering to explain why such control should have come to the fore in the nineteenth century.[400] They have missed completely the empirical link between abortion and prostitution as well as the causes of the increasing activity directed at abortion because of their blind insistence that the anti-abortion activity was without precedent before 1840 or (for some) later in the century.

Marvin Olasky has studied the link between abortion and prostitution in considerable detail.[401] He found that prostitution was a rare phenomenon in the American colonies before the middle of the eighteenth century,[402] while a century later one doctor was estimating that there were 60,000 prostitutes working nationwide.[403] During the recurring crusades for "social purity,"

396. MOHR, *supra* note 29, at 16.

397. PETERSEN, *supra* note 38, at 13. *See generally* Chapter 2, at notes 324–30.

398. State v. Hays, 40 Md. 633, 645 (1874). *See also* OLASKY, *supra* note 46, at 49, 59.

399. *See, e.g.,* Ellen Battelle Dietrick, *Rescuing Fallen Women,* WOMEN's J., May 27, 1893, at 162. *See generally* BARBARA BERG, THE REMEMBERED GATE: ORIGINS OF AMERICAN FEMINISM 181–84, 211 (1978); RUTH BORDIN, WOMEN AND TEMPERANCE: THE QUEST FOR POWER AND LIBERTY, 1873–1900, at 110–11 (1981); D'EMILIO & FREEDMAN, *supra* note 233, at 140–45, 148–56, 202–15; BARBARA EPSTEIN, THE POLITICS OF DOMESTICITY: WOMEN, EVANGELISM, AND TEMPERANCE IN NINETEENTH-CENTURY AMERICA 125–28 (1981); GORDON, *supra* note 75, at 116–35; GROSSBERG, *supra* note 67, at 47–48; DAVID PIVAR, PURITY CRUSADE: SEXUAL MORALITY AND SOCIAL CONTROL, 1868–1900 (1973); MARY LYNDON SHANLEY, FEMINISM, MARRIAGE, AND THE LAW IN VICTORIAN ENGLAND, 1850–1895, at 79–86, 92–93 (1989); SMITH-ROSENBERG, *supra* note 71, at 109–28; Elizabeth Pleck, *Feminist Responses to "Crimes against Women," 1800–1896,* 8 SIGNS 459 (1983). *See also* Chapter 2, at notes 229–32.

400. *See, e.g.,* D'EMILIO & FREEDMAN, *supra* note 233, at 64; Mary Odem, *Fallen Women and Thieving Ladies: Historical Approaches to Women and Crime in the United States,* 17 LAW & SOC. INQUIRY 351, 352 (1992).

401. OLASKY, *supra* note 46, at 44–59.

402. OLASKY, *supra* note 46, at 44–45. *See also* CARL BRIDENBAUGH, CITIES IN THE WILDERNESS: THE FIRST CENTURY OF URBAN LIFE IN AMERICA, 1625–1742, at 71–73 (1968); D'EMILIO & FREEDMAN, *supra* note 233, at 49–52; DAVID FLAHERTY, PRIVACY IN COLONIAL NEW ENGLAND 160, 212 (1972); LYLE KOEHLER, A SEARCH FOR POWER: THE "WEAKER SEX" IN SEVENTEENTH-CENTURY NEW ENGLAND 208 (1980); MILTON RUGOFF, PRUDERY AND PASSION: SEXUALITY IN VICTORIAN AMERICA 252 (1971); ROGER THOMPSON, WOMEN IN STUART ENGLAND AND AMERICA 42 (1974).

403. SANGER, *supra* note 396, at 614. *See also* JAMES MCCABE, NEW YORK BY SUNLIGHT AND BY GASLIGHT 477–80 (1882); HIRAM KNOX ROOT, THE LOVER's MARRIAGE LIGHTHOUSE 389 (1859). *See generally* LOIS BANNER, AMERICAN BEAUTY 42, 75–76 (1983); ANN BUTLER, DAUGHTERS OF JOY, SISTERS OF MISERY: PROSTITUTES IN THE AMERICAN WEST, 1865–1890 (1985); D'EMILIO & FREEDMAN, *supra* note 233, at 132–45; MARION GOLDMAN, GOLD DIGGERS AND SILVER MINERS: PROSTITUTION AND SOCIAL LIFE ON THE COMSTOCK LODE (1981); JULIE ROY JEFFREY, FRONTIER WOMEN: THE TRANS-MISSISSIPPI WEST, 1840–1880, at 121–24 (1979); OLASKY, *supra* note 46, at 44–48; MARY RYAN, WOMANHOOD IN AMERICA: FROM COLONIAL TIMES TO THE PRESENT 49 (2nd ed. 1979); SANGER, *supra*; CHRISTINE STANSELL, CITY OF WOMEN: SEX AND CLASS IN NEW YORK, 1789–1860, at 181–88 (1986); Lucie Cheng Hirata, *Free, Indentured, Enslaved: Chinese Prostitution*

investigators found direct evidence that prostitutes had many pregnancies but few children.[404] Other observers, however, commented that infanticide was the common means of child limitation for prostitutes.[405] Given the absence of effective contraceptives, some resort to either abortion or infanticide might be necessary to explain why prostitutes had few children.[406] Still, many prostitutes would eventually be rendered sterile by the effects of gonorrhea and many other children (perhaps as many as 30 percent) would die before birth because of syphilis.[407] Another bit of evidence suggests a strong link between prostitution and abortion by mid-century. The best contemporary statistics show that fetal deaths in New York City rose from 1 in 376 pregnancies in 1805 to 1 in 13 in 1849.[408] These New York statistics probably reflect the particular prevalence of prostitution in that city, with 6,000 (10 percent) of the nation's estimated total prostitutes.[409]

While prostitutes might well have provided a secure market for the emerging professional abortionists of the time, the relative scarcity of prostitution before the nineteenth century is yet another reason to conclude that abortion was a rare phenomenon in those early times. A nineteenth century physician who treated a lot of these prostitutes might easily conclude, as Dr. Edwin Hale did in 1860, that 90 per cent of women had undergone abortions.[410] None of this would be representative of the millions of women who were not prostitutes. Furthermore, abortion no doubt contributed to the short life span (literally) of prostitutes. Prostitutes could expect to spend five years or less in the "trade" in the nineteenth century, with many prostitutes descending through disease and debilitation to an early grave.[411] Becoming a victim of murder also appears to have a risk of a trade characterized by alcoholism, drugs, beatings, and abortion.[412]

Given the state of abortion technology in the early and middle nineteenth century, one might also readily agree, as Means argued,[413] that the abortion statutes enacted at that time might have been adopted as a paternalistic measure to protect women, increasingly tempted by the slow but steady improvements of abortion technology, from themselves. One might even be tempted to

---

*in Nineteenth-Century America,* 5 SIGNS 3 (1979); Yuki Ichioka, *Ameyuki-San: Japanese Prostitutes in Nineteenth-Century America,* 4 AMERASIA J. 1 (1977); Richard Tansey, *Prostitution and Politics in Antebellum New Orleans,* 18 SOUTHERN STUD. 451 (1979).

404. MCDOWELL, *supra* note 182, at 23; ROGERS, *supra* note 395, at 76, 144; SANGER, *supra* note 396, at 482, 586; WARREN, *supra* note 395, at 37–38. *See also* OLASKY, *supra* note 46, at 48–49, 54–55.

405. ACTON, *supra* note 183, at 206; CHARLES ROBERT DRYSDALE, PROSTITUTION MEDICALLY CONSIDERED, WITH SOME OF ITS SOCIAL ASPECTS 10–11, 14 (1866) [infanticide prevalent along with prostitution]. *See generally* OLASKY, *supra* note 46, at 49 n.31; RUTH ROSEN, THE LOST SISTERHOOD: PROSTITUTION IN AMERICA, 1900–1918, at 99 (1982) (estimating 20,000 prostitution-related abortions in New York City annually during the period she studied); JUDITH WALKOWITZ, PROSTITUTION AND VICTORIAN SOCIETY: WOMEN, CLASS AND THE STATE 19 (1980) [prostitution leads to disease, abortion, and infanticide].

406. *See* OLASKY, *supra* note 46, at 49–52, 55–59. *See generally* Chapter 2.

407. OLASKY, *supra* note 46, at 52–54.

408. HORATIO ROBINSON STORER & FRANKLIN FISKE HEARD, CRIMINAL ABORTION: ITS NATURE, ITS EVIDENCE AND ITS LAW 24 (1868) (reporting the studies of Dr. Elisha Harris, Registrar of Vital Statistics for New York City during 1840s). *See also* MOHR, *supra* note 29, at 50–52, 71–73, 76–83; OLASKY, *supra* note 46, at 77–78; SMITH-ROSENBERG, *supra* note 71, at 221.

409. SANGER, *supra* note 396, at 579–680. Sanger's rather precise figure might not be entirely accurate, but it probably reflects the general relationship of prostitution in New York to prostitution nationwide. *See also* OLASKY, *supra* note 46, at 133–34.

410. EDWIN HALE, ON THE HOMEOPATHIC TREATMENT OF ABORTION, ITS CAUSES AND CONSEQUENCES; WITH SOME SUGGESTIONS, AND INDICATIONS FOR THE USE OF THE NEW REMEDIES 5–15 (1860).

411. *See* MCCABE, *supra* note 406, at 479–80; CLIFFORD GRIFFITH ROE, THE GREAT WAR ON WHITE SLAVERY 15 (1911); C.E. ROGERS, SECRET SINS OF SOCIETY 76 (1881); SANGER, *supra* note 396, at 614. *See also* OLASKY, *supra* note 46, at 47, 58, 189.

412. *See, e.g.,* PATRICIA CLINE COHEN, THE MURDER OF HELEN JEWETT: THE LIFE AND DEATH OF A PROSTITUTE IN NINETEENTH-CENTURY NEW YORK (1998).

413. Means I, *supra* note 29, at 418, 453, 511–15; Means II, *supra* note 29, at 382–91.

agree with Mohr that the emerging allopathic medical profession seized upon abortion as a useful weapon against its competitors, although hardly an important one given the rarity of the practice in the early and middle nineteenth century. Such conclusions, however, hardly suggest that legislatures could not also have had other purposes in mind in adopting those statutes. And the evidence is overwhelming that the protection of the life of the unborn child (as they termed it) was the primary purpose underlying these statutes.

# Chapter 7

# The Song Remains the Same[1]

*Conspiracy theory is the sophistication of the ignorant.*

—Richard Grenier[2]

By 1841, ten states and one territory had enacted statutes prohibiting abortions.[3] These statutes codified the common law of abortion with only minor refinements and clarifications.[4] These statutes often carried forward a distinction based upon quickening, and sometimes covered only certain abortion techniques. Maine, in 1840, became the first state to outlaw all abortions by any means at any point in gestation.[5] Tens years later, California became the first state to prohibit abortion advertising.[6] With these enactments, we enter the second phase of American legislative activity directed at abortion. The nineteenth century saw a steady broadening of abortion statutes to reach all abortions regardless of technique or stage of pregnancy[7] and to include in nineteen states statutory provisions for the punishment for the mother who underwent the abortion.[8] By 1868, when the Fourteenth Amendment was ratified, thirty of the thirty-seven states had abortion statutes on the books.[9] Just three of these states prohibited abortion only after quickening.[10] Twenty states punished all abortion equally regardless the stage of

---

1. Jimmie Page & Robert Plant, *The Song Remains the Same* (1973).
2. As quoted in John Leo, *Angels and Dead Mackerel*, U.S. NEWS & WORLD REP., Dec. 29, 1997, at 10.
3. ARK. REV. STAT. ch. 44, div. III, art. II, §6 (1838), reprinted in Eugene Quay, *Justifiable Abortion— Medical and Legal Foundations (Pt. II)*, 49 GEO. L.J. 395, 450 (1961); 1821 Conn. Stat. tit. 22, §14, at 152, reprinted in Quay, *supra*, at 453; 1830 Conn. Pub. Acts ch. 1, §16, at 255, reprinted in Quay, *supra*, at 453; ILL. REV. LAWS §46 (1827), reprinted in Quay, *supra*, at 466; 1835 Ind. Gen. Laws ch. XLVII, §3, at 66, *codified at* IND. REV. STAT. ch. XXVI, §3, at 224 (1838), reprinted in Quay, *supra*, at 468; 1838 Iowa (Terr.) Stat. §18, at 145, reprinted in Quay, *supra*, at 470–71; ME. REV. STAT. ch. 160, §§13 & 14 (1840), reprinted in Quay, *supra*, at 478; 1839 Miss. Laws tit. III, art. 1, §9, at 113, *codified at* MISS. CODE ch. LXIV tit. III, §9, at 958 (1848), reprinted in Quay, *supra*, at 489; MO. REV. STAT. art. II, §§9, 10, 36, at 168–69, 172 (1835), reprinted in Quay, *supra*, at 490; N.Y. REV. STAT. pt. IV, ch. I, tit. II, §§8, 9, at 550, & pt. VI, §21, at 578 (1829), reprinted in Quay, *supra*, at 499; 1834 Ohio Laws §§1, 2, at 20–21, *codified at* OHIO GEN. STAT. ch. 35, §§111, 112, at 252 (1841), reprinted in Quay, *supra*, at 504.
4. *See* Chapter 6.
5. ME. REV. STAT. ch. 160, §§13 & 14 (1840), reprinted in Quay, *supra* note 3, at 478.
6. Carried forward as CAL. PENAL CODE §317 (1915); People v. McKean, 243 P. 898 (Cal. Ct. App. 1925).
7. *See generally* Mark Scott, Note, *Quickening in the Common Law: The Legal Precedent Roe Attempted and Failed to Use*, 1 MICH. L. & POL'Y REV. 199, 253–63 (1996); James Witherspoon, *Reexamining* Roe: *Nineteenth-Century Abortion Statutes and the Fourteenth Amendment*, 17 ST. MARY'S L.J. 29, 34–36 (1985).
8. On the problem of whether to consider a woman who underwent an abortion to be a criminal or a victim, see Chapter 6, at notes 292–300.
9. *See* Scott, *supra* note 7, at 255–56; Witherspoon, *supra* note 7, at 32–34.
10. *Arkansas:* The first Arkansas abortion statute did not make abortion a crime before quickening. ARK. REV. STAT. ch. 44, div. III, art. II, §6 (1838), reprinted in Quay, *supra* note 3, at 450. Subsequently, Arkansas would make quickening relevant only to the punishment and not to whether the abortion was criminal. ARK. STAT. ANN. §§41-301, 41-302, 41-2223, 41-2224 (1947), reprinted in Quay, *supra*, at 449–50.

pregnancy.[11] In 1868, seven states still punished abortion less severely before quickening than

*Minnesota:* The first Minnesota abortion statute did not make abortion a crime before quickening. MINN. (TERR.) REV. STAT. ch. 100, §100, at 493 (1851), *reprinted in* Quay, *supra*, at 487. Subsequently, Minnesota would eliminate the quickening distinction. 1873 Minn. Stat. vol. 2, ch. 54, Sec. 29, §§1–4, *carried forward as* MINN. STAT. ANN. §§617.18 to 617.21 (1953), all reprinted in Quay, *supra*, at 485–88.

*Mississippi:* The first Mississippi abortion statute did not make abortion a crime before quickening. 1839 Miss. Laws tit. III, art. 1, §9, at 113, *codified at* MISS. CODE ch. LXIV tit. III, §9, at 958 (1848), reprinted in Quay, *supra*, at 489. Subsequently, Mississippi would make quickening relevant only to the punishment and not to whether the abortion was criminal. MISS. CODE ANN. §§2222, 2223, 2289, 8893 (1956), reprinted in Quay, *supra*, at 488–89.

11. *Alabama:* The first Alabama abortion statute did not include a quickening distinction. ALA. PENAL CODE ch. VI, §2, at 238 (Meek Supp. 1841), *carried forward as* ALA. CODE tit. 14, §9, reprinted in Quay, *supra* note 3, at 447.

*California:* The first California abortion statute did not include a quickening distinction. 1849–50 Cal. Statutes ch. 99, §45, at 233, reprinted in Quay, *supra*, at 451, *carried forward as* CAL. PEN. CODE §274 (1915).

*Connecticut:* The first Connecticut abortion statute made abortion a crime only after quickening. 1821 Conn. Stat. tit. 22, §14, at 152, reprinted in Quay, *supra*, at 453. Connecticut eliminated the quickening distinction in 1860 Conn. Pub. Acts ch. LXXI, §§1–3, at 65–66, *codified at* CONN. GEN. STAT. tit. XII, ch. II, §22, at 248 (1868), *carried forward as* CONN. GEN. STAT. §§52–29 to 53–31 (1958), all reprinted in Quay, *supra*, at 453–54.

*Illinois:* The first Illinois abortion statute did not include a quickening distinction. ILL. REV. LAWS §46 (1827), *carried forward as* ILL. REV. STAT. ch. 38, §3 (1959), both reprinted in Quay, *supra*, at 465–66.

*Indiana:* The first Illinois abortion statute did not include a quickening distinction. 1835 Ind. Gen. Laws ch. XLVII, §3, at 66, *codified at* IND. REV. STAT. ch. XXVI, §3, at 224 (1838), *carried forward as* IND. STAT. ANN. §10–105 (1956), all reprinted in Quay, *supra*, at 467–68.

*Iowa:* The first Iowa abortion statute did not include a quickening distinction. 1838 Iowa (Terr.) Stat. §18, at 145, reprinted in Quay, *supra*, at 470–71. Subsequently, Iowa made abortion a crime only after quickening. IOWA (TERR.) REV. STAT. §10 (1843), reprinted in Quay, *supra*, at 471. Abortion was omitted altogether from the 1851 Iowa Code. IOWA CODE tit. I, ch. 4, §28 (1851). Finally, Iowa enacted a new statute without a quickening distinction in 1858 Iowa Laws ch. 58, §1, at 93, *codified at* IOWA REV. LAWS pt. 4, tit. XXIII, ch. 165, art. 2, §4221, at 723–34, *carried forward as* IOWA CODE §701.1 (1946), *reprinted in* Quay, *supra*, at 470–71.

*Louisiana:* The first Louisiana abortion statute did not include a quickening distinction. 1855 La. Acts, Act 120, §24, at 132–33, *codified at* LA. REV. STAT., CRIMES & OFFENSES §24, at 138 (1856), *carried forward as* LA. REV. STAT. ANN. §§14:87, 14:88 (1950), both reprinted in Quay, *supra*, at 477.

*Maine:* The first Maine abortion statute did not include a quickening distinction. ME. REV. STAT. ch. 160, §§13, 14, at 686 (1840), *carried forward as* ME. REV. STAT. ch. 134, §9 (1954), both reprinted in Quay, *supra*, at 477–78.

*Maryland:* The first Maryland abortion statute did not include a quickening distinction. 1867 Md. Laws ch. 185, §11, at 342–43 (Quay reprints the version that was reenacted a year later, Quay, *supra*, at 479–80). This was carried forward as MD. ANN. CODE §27, §3 (1957), reprinted in Quay, *supra*, at 478–79.

*Massachusetts:* The first Massachusetts abortion statute did not include a quickening distinction. 1845 Mass. Acts ch. 27, at 406, *carried forward as* MASS. GEN. LAWS ANN. ch. 272, §19 (1959), *reprinted in* Quay, *supra*, at 481.

*Missouri:* The first Missouri abortion statute did not include a quickening distinction. MO. REV. STAT. art. II, §§10, 36, at 168–69, 172 (1835), *carried forward as* MO. REV. STAT. §559.100 (1949), both reprinted in Quay, *supra*, at 489–90.

*Nevada:* The first Nevada abortion statute did not include a quickening distinction. 1861 Nev. (Terr.) Laws ch. XXVIII, div. IV, §42, at 63, reprinted in Quay, *supra*, at 493.

*New Jersey:* The first New Jersey abortion statute did not include a quickening distinction. 1849 N.J. Laws at 266, *carried forward as* N.J. REV. STAT. ANN. §2A:87-1 (1953), both reprinted in Quay, *supra*, at 495–96.

*New York:* The first New York abortion statute turned the level of punishment on whether the child had quickened. N.Y. REV. STAT. pt. IV, ch. I, tit. II, §§8, 9, at 550, & pt. VI, §21, at 578 (1829), reprinted in Quay, *supra*, at 499. New York subsequently eliminated the quickening distinction. 1869 N.Y. Laws ch. 631, §§1, 2, at 1502, reprinted in Quay, *supra*, at 500–01. The latter statute was judicially construed, however, as carrying forward the quickening distinction. Evans v. People, 49 N.Y. 86 (1872).

*Ohio:* The first Ohio abortion statute made abortion a crime only after quickening. 1834 Ohio Laws §§1, 2, at 20–21, *codified at* OHIO GEN. STAT. ch. 35, §§111, 112, at 252 (1841), reprinted in Quay, *supra*, at 504. Ohio subsequently eliminated the quickening distinction. 1867 Ohio Laws at 135–36, *carried forward as* OHIO

after.[12] The seven states without abortion statutes in 1868 were Delaware, Georgia, Kentucky, North Carolina, Rhode Island, South Carolina, and Tennessee. None was particularly populous or politically significant in 1868. Each state subsequently adopted an abortion statute, all except

---

Rev. Code Ann. § 2901.16 (1953), reprinted in Quay, *supra,* at 504.

*Oregon:* The first Oregon statute made abortion a crime only after quickening. 1853–54 Or. (Terr.) Stat. ch. III, § 13, at 187, reprinted in Quay, *supra,* at 505. Oregon subsequently eliminated the quickening distinction. Or. Gen. Laws, Crim. Code ch. 43, § 509, at 528 (1864), *carried forward as* Or. Rev. Stat. § 163.060 (1959), both reprinted in Quay, *supra,* at 505–06.

*Texas:* The first Texas abortion statute did not include a quickening distinction. 1854 Tex. Gen. Laws ch. XLIX, § 1, at 58, *superseded and codified at* Tex. Gen. Stat. Dig. ch. VII, arts. 531–36, at 524, *carried forward as* Tex. Pen. Code ch. 9, arts. 1191 t0 1194 (1960), all reprinted in Quay, *supra,* at 513–14.

*Vermont:* The first Vermont abortion statute did not include a quickening distinction. 1846 Vt. Acts No. 33, § 1, at 34–35, *codified at* Vt. Comp. Stat. tit. XXVIII, ch. 108, § 8, at 560–61 (1850), *carried forward as* Vt. Stat. Ann. tit. 13, § 101 (1959), reprinted in Quay, *supra,* at 515.

*Virginia:* The first Virginia abortion statute did not include a quickening distinction. 1847–48 Va. Acts ch. 120, tit. II, ch. III, § 9, at 96, *codified at* Va. Code tit. 54, ch. CXCL, § 8, at 784 (1849), *carried forward as* Va. Code Ann. §§ 18.1-62, 18.1-63 (Supp. 1960), all reprinted in Quay, *supra,* at 516–17.

*West Virginia:* West Virginia received the Virginia abortion statute upon its separation from that state. W. Va. Const. art. XI, par. 8 (1863). The Virginia statute was carried the West Virginia Code. W. Va. Code Ann. § 5923 (1955), reprinted in Quay, *supra,* at 518.

12. *Florida:* 1868 Fla. Acts ch. 1637 [No. 13], subch. III, § 11, at 64, & subch. VIII, § 9, at 97, *codified at* Fla. Stat. Ann. §§ 782.09, 782.10, 782.16, 797.01, 797.02 (1944), reprinted in Quay, *supra* note 3, at 457–58.

*Kansas:* 1855 Kan. (Terr.) Stat. ch. 48, §§ 10, 39, at 238, 243, *superseded by* 1859 Kan. (Terr.) Laws ch. XXVIII, §§ 10, 37, at 232, 237, *codified at* Kan. Comp. Laws ch. XXXIII, §§ 10, 37, at 288, 293 (1862), *carried forward as* Kan. Gen. Stat. Ann. §§ 21-410, 21-437 (Supp. 1959), all reprinted in Quay, *supra,* at 473–74.

*Michigan:* Mich. Rev. Stat. ch. 153, §§ 33, 34, at 662 (1846), *carried forward as* Mich. Stat. Ann. § 28.555 (1954), all reprinted in Quay, *supra,* at 482–84.

*Nebraska:* 1866 Neb. (Terr.) Stat. pt. III, ch. IV, § 42, at 598–99 ("vitalized embryo"), *carried forward as* Neb. Rev. Stat. §§ 28-404, 28-405 (1956), *reprinted in* Quay, *supra,* at 491–92.

*New Hampshire:* 1848 N.H. Laws ch. 743, §§ 1–4, at 708, *codified at* N.H. Comp. Stat. tit. XXVI, ch. 227, §§ 11, 12, at 544–45 (1853), *carried forward as* N.H. Rev. Stat. Ann. §§ 585:12 to 585:14 (1955), all reprinted in Quay, *supra,* at 493–94.

*Pennsylvania:* 1860 Pa. Laws No. 374, tit. VI, §§ 87, 88, at 404–05, reprinted in Quay, *supra,* at 507. Pennsylvania subsequently eliminated the quickening distinction. Pa. Stat. Ann. tit. 18, §§ 4718–4720 (1945), reprinted in Quay, *supra,* at 506–07.

*Wisconsin:* The first Wisconsin abortion statute did not make abortion a crime before quickening. Wis. Rev. Stat. ch. 133, §§ 10, 11 (1849). Nine years later, Wisconsin made abortion before quickening a crime, but punished it less severely than after quickening. Wis. Rev. Stat. pt. IV, tit. XXVII, ch. CLXIV, §§ 10, 11, at 930, & ch. CLXIX, §§ 58, 59, at 969 (1858), *carried forward as* Wis. Stat. Ann. § 940.04 (1958). All of these laws are reprinted in Quay, *supra,* at 518–19.

Several states and territories created a separate crime of the killing of an unborn quick child by an injury to the mother that would have qualified as murder had the mother died, and treated that more seriously than simple abortion. Dak. Penal Code §§ 335 to 337, at 458–59 (1877), *codified at* N.D. Rev. Codes §§ 7175 to 7177, at 1271–72 (1895), *carried forward as* N.D. Rev. Code § 12-2503 (1943) (the modern version is reprinted in Quay, *supra,* at 503), *and at* S.D. Ann. Stat. §§ 7795-7797, at 1918–19 (1899), *carried forward as* (the modern version is reprinted in Quay, *supra,* at 512–13); 1868 Fla. Acts ch. 1637 [No. 13], subch. III, § 10, at 64, *codified at* Fla. Stat. Ann. §§ 782.09 (1944), reprinted in Quay, *supra,* at 457–58; 1876 Ga. Laws No. CXXX, §§ I, at 113, *codified at* Ga. Code Ann. § 26-1103 (1933), reprinted in Quay, *supra,* at 462; 1855 Kan. (Terr.) Stat. ch. 48, § 9, at 238, *superseded by* 1859 Kan. (Terr.) Laws ch. XXVIII, § 9, at 232, *codified at* Kan. Comp. Laws ch. XXXIII, § 9, at 288 (1862), all reprinted in Quay, *supra,* at 473–74; Mich. Rev. Stat. ch. 153, §§ 33, 34, at 662 (1846), reprinted in Quay, *supra,* at 483–84, *carried forward as* Mich. Stat. Ann. § 28.554 (1954), reprinted in Quay, *supra,* at 482; 1839 Miss. Laws tit. III, art. 1, § 8, at 113, *codified at* Miss. Code ch. LXIV tit. III, § 8, at 958 (1848), *carried forward as* Miss. Code Ann. § 2222 (1956), all reprinted in Quay, *supra,* at 488–89; Mo. Rev. Stat. art. II, §§ 9, at 168 172 (1835), *carried forward as* Mo. Rev. State. § 559.090 (1949), reprinted in Quay, *supra,* at 489–90; Nev. Rev. Stat. § 200.210 (1959), reprinted in Quay, *supra,* at 492.

Kentucky, between 1876 and 1896.[13] Kentucky's highest court declared abortion to be a common law crime during that period.[14] This decision perhaps explains why Kentucky did not adopt its first abortion statute until 1910.[15]

Territorial statutes reflected a similar consensus, with six of the eight territories having abortion statutes very similar to those in the states.[16] Only Dakota and Utah Territories had no abortion statutes in 1868, both enacting their first abortion statutes in the middle 1870s.[17] Alaska, Oklahoma and Wyoming did not exist as political entities in 1868; they enacted their first abor-

---

13. *Delaware:* Delaware's first abortion statute did not include a quickening distinction. 1883 Del. Laws ch. 226, §2, at 522, *carried forward as* DEL. CODE ANN. §302 (1953), all reprinted in Quay, *supra* note 3, at 455–56.

*Georgia:* Georgia's first abortion statute made quickening relevant to the punishment. 1876 Ga. Laws No. CXXX, §§I–IV, at 113, *codified at* GA. CODE ANN. §§26-1101 to 26-1106 (1933), reprinted in Quay, *supra*, at 462.

*North Carolina:* North Carolina's first abortion statute did not include a quickening distinction. 1881 N.C. Sess. Laws ch. 351, §§1, 2, *carried forward as* N.C. GEN. STAT. §§14-44, 14-45 (1953), both reprinted in Quay, *supra*, at 502.

*Rhode Island:* Rhode Island's first abortion statute did not include a quickening distinction. R.I. GEN. LAWS ch. 277, §22, at 977 (1896), *carried forward as* R.I. GEN. LAWS ANN. §§11-3-1 to 11-3-4 (1956), all reprinted in Quay, *supra*, at 509–10.

*South Carolina:* South Carolina's first abortion statute did not include a quickening distinction. 1883 S.C. Acts No. 354, §§1–3, at 547–48, *carried forward as* S.C. CODE §16-82 to 16-84, all reprinted in Quay, *supra*, at 510–12.

*Tennessee:* Tennessee's first abortion statute did not include a quickening distinction. 1883 Tenn. Acts ch. CXL, §§1, 2, at 188–89, *codified at* TENN. CODE ANN. §§39-301, 39-302 (1955), all reprinted in Quay, *supra*, at 513.

14. Mitchell v. Commonwealth, 78 Ky. 204 (1879).

15. *Kentucky:* Kentucky's first abortion statute did not make a quickening distinction. 1910 Ky. Acts ch. 58 §§1–4, at 189 (1910), *carried forward as* KY. REV. STAT. ANN. §§435.040, 436.020 (1955), both reprinted in Quay, *supra*, at 474–76.

16. *Arizona:* Arizona's first abortion statute did not include a quickening distinction. ARIZ. (TERR.) CODE ch. X, div. 5, §45, at 54 (1865), reprinted in Quay, *supra* note 5, at 448.

*Colorado:* Colorado's first abortion statute did not include a quickening distinction. 1861 Colo. (Terr.) Laws div. 4, §42, at 296–97, *codified at* COLO. (TERR.) REV. STAT. ch. XXII, §42, at 202 (1868), *carried forward as* COLO. REV. STAT. ANN. §40-2-23 (1953), all reprinted in Quay, *supra*, at 452.

*Idaho:* Idaho's first abortion statute did not include a quickening distinction. 1863–64 Idaho (Terr.) Laws ch. IV, §42, *carried forward as* IDAHO CODE ANN. §18-601 (1948), both reprinted in Quay, *supra*, at 464.

*Montana:* Montana's first abortion statute did not include a quickening distinction. 1864 Mont. (Terr.) Laws, Criminal Practice Act ch. IV, §41, at 184, *carried forward as* MONT. REV. CODE ANN. §94-401 (1947), both reprinted in Quay, *supra*, at 490–91.

*New Mexico:* New Mexico's first abortion statute did not make abortion a crime before quickening. 1854 N.M. (Terr.) Laws No. 28, ch. 3, §11, at 88, *codified at* N.M. REV. STAT. art. XXIII, ch. LI, §11, at 320 (1865). New Mexico subsequently eliminated the quickening distinction. 1907 N.M. (Terr.) Acts ch. 36, §§5, 6, at 41–42, *carried forward as* N.M. STAT. ANN. §§40-3-1 to 40-3-3 (1953), all reprinted in Quay, *supra*, at 498.

*Washington:* Washington's first abortion statute made quickening relevant to the punishment. WASH. (TERR.) STAT. ch. II. §§37, 38, at 81 (1854). Washington subsequently eliminated the quickening distinction. WASH. REV. CODE, §9.02.010 (1951). Both are reprinted in Quay, *supra*, at 517.

17. *North and South Dakota:* The Dakota Territory's first abortion statute did not include a quickening distinction. DAK. PENAL CODE §§335 to 337, at 458–59 (1877), *codified at* N.D. REV. CODES §§7175 to 7177, at 1271–72 (1895) *carried forward as* N.D. REV. CODE §§12-2501 to 12-2504 (1943), *and at* S.D. ANN. STAT. §§7795–7797 (1899), *carried forward as* S.D. CODE §13.3101 to 13.3103 (Supp. 1960). Quay reprinted only the modern versions of the statute. Quay, *supra* note 5, at 503, 512–13.

*Utah:* Utah's first abortion statute did not include a quickening distinction. UTAH COMP. LAWS tit. IX, ch. III, §§142 (1876), *carried forward as* UTAH CODE ANN. §76-2-1 (1953), both reprinted in Quay, *supra*, at 514–15.

tion statutes in the year they were created as territories.[18] Hawaii, then an independent nation, had also already enacted a statutory prohibition of abortion that varied the penalty depending on quickening.[19]

Statutes in seventeen states and the District of Columbia denominated the crime against the unborn child as "manslaughter," "murder," or "assault with intent to murder."[20] Most of these statutes referred to the victim as a "child," not as a fetus or some other term that might distance them from the status of born humans.[21] Similarly, many states classified abortion with other crimes against persons, usually homicide. Generally, the severity of the punishment turned on whether the unborn child was killed (or "destroyed") rather than on the stage gestation had reached. This pattern appears in twenty of the thirty-seven states in 1868; in fourteen states, the highest degree of punishment for destroying a child in the womb was available without proof of quickening. Such statutes often punished the killing of the child the same as the killing of the mother. In 1868, nine statutes expressly provided for punishment for attempted abortion that increased identically should either the mother or the unborn child die.[22] Other statutes left the punishment should the mother die undefined, leaving such abortions to be punished as homicide under other laws; in many, but not all, states, this resulted in the two crimes being punished similarly. The states that had not yet eliminated the quickening distinction (most did by the end of the century) might have been concerned about proof of causation or intent given that the statutes had often been authored by the most outspoken proponents of protecting fetal life.[23]

By 1883, 20 statutes provided for increased punishment if either the mother or the child died, and 14 of these statutes provided the same penalty for the death of either the mother or the child, while only five of the 14 required proof of quickening. Ultimately, 21 states provided for the same punishment for the death of either the mother or the child, while only 3 states (Kentucky, Texas, and West Virginia) provided expressly for a heavier punishment for the death of the mother than for the death of the unborn child.[24] The punishment for abortions

---

18. *Alaska:* Alaska's first abortion statute did not include a quickening distinction. 1899 Alaska Sess. Laws ch. 1, §8, *codified at* ALASKA COMP. LAWS ANN. §65-4-6 (1949), reprinted in Quay, *supra* note 3, at 448.

*Oklahoma:* Oklahoma's first abortion statute did not include a quickening distinction. 1890 Okla. Stat. §§2185 to 2187, *codified at* OKLA. REV. LAWS §§2435, 2436, at 604 (1910), *carried forward as* OKLA. STAT. ANN. tit. 21, §861 (1958). Quay reprints only modern versions of the statute. Quay, *supra*, at 504.

*Wyoming:* Wyoming's first abortion statute did not include a quickening distinction. 1869 Wyo. (Terr.) Laws ch. 3, §§25, 26, at 104, *carried forward as* WYO. STAT. ANN. §§6-77, 6-78 (1957), all reprinted in Quay, *supra*, at 519–20.

Congress did not get around to enacting an abortion statute for the District of Columbia until 1901. 31 Stat. 1901, *codified at* D.C. CODE ANN. §22-2001 (1951), reprinted at Quay, *supra*, at 457. This statute did not make a distinction based upon quickening. The first codes of laws in Puerto Rico and the Virgin Islands also prohibited abortion without regard to quickening. PORTO RICO COMP. REV. STAT. §5708 (1913), *carried forward as* PUERTO RICO LAWS ANN. tit. 33, ch. 81, §1053 (1956), reprinted in Quay, *supra*, at 509; V.I. CODE, tit. IV, ch. 6, §9 (1921), *carried forward as* V.I. CODE ANN. tit. 14, §151 (1957), reprinted in Quay, *supra*, at 516.

19. HAW. PENAL CODE §§1–3 (1850), reprinted in Quay, *supra* note 3, at 463, *carried forward as* HAW. REV. LAWS §§309-3 to 309-5 (1955).

20. Witherspoon, *supra* note 7, at 42–44.

21. *Id.* at 48–50.

22. 1868 Fla. Laws ch. 1367, no. 13, ch. 3, §11, at 64; MICH. REV. STAT. ch. 153, §33, at 662 (1846), reprinted in Quay, *supra* note 3, at 483; MINN. REV. STAT. ch. 100, §11, at 493 (1851), reprinted in Quay, *supra*, at 487; MO. REV. STAT., art. II, §9, 10 (1835), reprinted in Quay, *supra*, at 490; 1846 N.Y. Laws ch. 22, §1, reprinted in Quay, *supra*, at 500; 1867 Ohio Laws at 135–36; OR. GEN. LAWS, CRIM. CODE ch. 43, §509, at 528 (1864), reprinted in Quay, *supra*, at 505–06; 1860 Pa. Laws No. 374, tit. 6, §87, reprinted in Quay, *supra*, at 507; WIS. REV. STAT. ch. 164, §11 (1858), reprinted in Quay, *supra*, at 519.

23. Witherspoon, *supra* note 7, at 36–40.

24. *Id.* at 40–42.

that killed either the mother or the child were generally less than for other homicides, but this was as true for the mother as for the child. Whether this reflected a lesser opprobrium for killing through an abortion, or difficulties of proof of various aspects of the crime, or a notion that the state of mind of those involved in the abortion merited some leniency, or some other reason remains unclear. In any event, the penalties for an abortion killing the child were severe, ranging from five years to life in prison.[25] Finally, nearly all statutes containing therapeutic exceptions generally applied them only to protect the life of the mother—nothing less would justify killing the child.[26] Law professor James Witherspoon has noted the several instances in which a legislature rejected attempts to broaden the exception to include protection of the mother's health. Only Alabama (after 1951), Colorado (after 1868), the District of Columbia (after 1901), Illinois (from 1867 to 1874), Maryland (after 1867), New Mexico (after 1919), and Wyoming (from 1869 to 1890) authorized abortions to protect the mother's health or according to some lesser standard.[27] Some see in the therapeutic exception a contradiction to the policy of protecting fetal lives, yet the strictness with which the exception was applied actually suggests the contrary.[28]

When placed against the backdrop of reduced recourse to the death penalty and the gradual abandonment of torture and corporal punishment in criminal processes, the slow creation of only partly successful mechanisms for preserving international peace, and the emancipation of slaves, the steady expansion of the legal protection afforded a fetus is, as pro-abortion historian Carl Degler concluded, entirely consistent with "the broad canvas of humanitarian thought and practice in Western society from the 17th to the 20th century (sic)."[29] One might add to Degler's list the dramatic changes in attitudes towards children generally, a complex process from the sixteenth to the twentieth century that is still imperfectly understood and subject to intense debate among historians.[30] Abortion, all too obviously except to the most politically motivated historians, was not a "common law liberty" when the Fourteenth Amendment was adopted.[31] Justice

---

25. *Id.* at 51–56.

26. *Id.* at 45–47.

27. *Id.* at 45 n.49. *See generally* Herbert Packer & Ralph Gampell, *Therapeutic Abortions: A Problem in Law and Medicine,* 11 STAN. L. REV. 417 (1959).

28. *See* Chapter 6, at notes 119–21, 134–49.

29. CARL DEGLER, AT ODDS: WOMEN AND THE FAMILY IN AMERICA FROM THE REVOLUTION TO THE PRESENT 247 (1980). *See also* James Hitchcock, *Respect for Life and the Health Care Professions: A Historical Study,* in HUMAN LIFE AND HEALTH CARE ETHICS 37, 43–46 (James Bopp, jr., ed. 1985); R. Sauer, *Attitudes to Abortion in America, 1800–1973,* 28 POP. STUDIES 53, 57–59 (1974).

30. *See* PHILIPPE ARIÈS, CENTURIES OF CHILDHOOD: A SOCIAL HISTORY OF FAMILY LIFE (Robert Baldick trans. 1965); DAVID HUNT, PARENTS AND CHILDREN IN HISTORY: THE PSYCHOLOGY OF FAMILY LIFE IN EARLY MODERN FRANCE 83–85 (1970).

31. For the claim that abortion was a "common law liberty" in 1868, see Beechem v. Leahy, 287 A.2d 836, 139 (Vt. 1972); *Amicus Brief of 250 American Historians in support of Appellants in* Planned Parenthood of Southeastern Pennsylvania v. Casey, [505 U.S. 833 (1992)] ("*Casey Historians' Brief*"), at 5–6; *Amicus Brief of 281 American Historians supporting Appellees in* Webster v. Reproductive Health Services [492 U.S. 490 (1989)] ("*Webster Historians' Brief*"), reprinted at 11 WOMEN'S RTS. L. RPTR. 163, 170 (1989), and in 8 DOCUMENTARY HISTORY OF THE LEGAL ASPECTS OF ABORTION IN THE UNITED STATES: WEBSTER V. REPRODUCTIVE HEALTH SERVICES 107 (Roy Mersky & Gary Hartman eds. 1990) ("DOCUMENTARY HISTORY") (hereafter pagination will be given only to the version in the *Women's Rts. L. Rptr.*); LINDA GORDON, WOMAN'S BODY, WOMAN'S RIGHT: A SOCIAL HISTORY OF BIRTH CONTROL IN AMERICA 52–53, 57 (1976); JAMES MOHR, ABORTION IN AMERICA: THE ORIGINS AND EVOLUTION OF NATIONAL POLICY, 1800–1900, at 128–29, 134–36, 144–45, 201, 208–11, 226, 229, 235–36 (1978); Cyril Means, jr., *The Phoenix of Abortional Freedom: Is a Penumbral Right or Ninth-Amendment Right About to Arise from the Nineteenth-Century Legislative Ashes of a Fourteenth-Century Common-Law Liberty?,* 17 N.Y.L.F. 335, 336, 351–54, 374–75, 409–10 n.175 (1971) ("Means II"); Reva Siegel, *Reasoning from the Body: A Historical Perspective on Abortion Regulation and Questions of Equal Protection,* 44 STAN. L. REV. 261, 278 (1992); Rickie Solinger, *"A Complete Disaster": Abortion and the Politics of Hospital Abortion Committees, 1950–1970,* 19 FEMINIST STUD. 241, 243 (1993).

Blackmun's conclusion in *Roe v. Wade* that abortion did not generally become a crime, at least after quickening, until after the Fourteenth Amendment was adopted is simply wrong.[32]

The only place mentioned thus far in this chapter that was not then part of the United States was Hawaii, and the Hawaiian statute could be attributed to the influence of American missionaries.[33] Similar laws were being enacted around the world during that period.[34] Even Japan, a country that remained relatively independent of European control during the nineteenth century, enacted strict statutory prohibitions of abortion during this era.[35] As was true nearly everywhere, the professed reason for including abortion in Japan's first modern criminal code was to protect fetal life, although some modern commentators refuse to believe this was the true reason.[36] In the United States, as in Japan, numerous jurists described the purpose of this legislation as the protection of the unborn child from destruction.[37] Failure to allege the death

---

32. *See* Roe v. Wade, 410 U.S. 113, 140 (1973).

33. On the pervasive influence of American missionaries on Hawaiian statutory law, see McBryde Sugar Co. v. Robinson, 504 P.2d 1330 (Haw. 1973).

34. Mary Kenny, Abortion: The Whole Story 183 (1986); Bernard Dickens & Rebecca Cook, *Development of Commonwealth Abortion Laws*, 28 Int'l & Comp. L.Q. 424, 425–32 (1979); Bonnie Hertberg, *Resolving the Abortion Debate: Compromise Legislation, an Analysis of the Policies in the United States, France, and Germany*, 16 Suffolk Transnat'l L. Rev. 513, 545 (1993); Jeremy Telman, *Abortion and Women's Legal Personhood in Germany: A Contribution to the Feminist Theory of the State*, 24 Rev. L. & Soc. Change 91, 97–101 (1998). In the Islamic tradition, abortion was condemned in the strongest terms from the earliest times. *See generally* Mohamed Mekki Naciri, *A Survey of Family Planning in Islamic Legislation*, in Muslim Attitudes toward Family Planning 129, 129–45 (Olivia Schiefflin ed. 1973); Sarah Rumage, *Resisting the West: The Clinton Administration's Promotion of Abortion at the 1994 Cairo Conference and the Strength of the Islamic Response*, 27 Cal. W. Int'l L.J. 1, 46–49 (1996); Sherifa Zuhur, *Sexuality*, in Encyclopedia of Islam 35, 36 (John Esposito ed. 1995).

35. *See* Hiromi Maruyama, *Abortion in Japan: A Feminist Critique*, 10 Wis. Women's L.J. 131, 132–33 (1995); Kinko Nakatani, *Japan*, in Abortion and Protection of the Human Fetus: Legal Problems in Cross-Cultural Perspective 221, 224 (S.J. Frankowski *et al.* eds. 1987); Lynn Wardle, *"Crying Stones": A Comparison of Abortion in Japan and the United States*, 14 N.Y.L.S. J. Int'l & Comp. L. 183, 192–94 (1993).

36. Maruyama, *supra* note 35, at 133, 138–39, 151–53. *See also* William LaFleur, Liquid Life: Abortion and Buddhism in Japan 88, 99, 103–09, 120 (1992); George De Vos & Hiroshi Wagatsuma, *Status and Role Behavior in Changing Japan*, in Sex Roles in Changing Society 334, 350 (Georgene Seward & Robert Williamson eds. 1970); Evy McElmeel, Comment, *Legalization of the Birth Control Pill in Japan Will Reduce Reliance on Abortion as the Primary Method of Birth Control*, 8 Pac. Rim L. & Pol'y Rev. 681, 684–85 (1999); Yoshiko Miyake, *Doubling Expectations: Motherhood and Women's Factory Work under State Management in Japan in the 1930s and 1940s*, in Recreating Japanese Women, 1600–1945, at 267, 277–78 (Gail Lee Bernstein ed. 1991); Sara Walsh, *Liquid Lives and Liquid Laws*, 7 Int'l Leg. Perspectives 187, 189, 191–93, 196–97, 199–200 (1995).

37. Trent v. State, 73 So. 834, 836 (Ala. Ct. App. 1916); Dougherty v. People, 1 Colo. 514, 522–23 (1872); State v. Lee, 37 A. 75, 79 (Conn. 1897); State v. Magnell, 51 A. 606, 606 (Del. 1901); Weightnovel v. State, 35 So. 857, 858–59 (Fla. 1903); State v. Alcorn, 64 P. 1014, 1019 (Idaho 1901); Earll v. People, 99 Ill. 123, 132 (1881); State v. Moore, 25 Iowa 128, 131–32, 135–36 (1868); Abrams v. Foshee, 3 Iowa 274, 278 (1856); State v. Miller, 133 P. 878, 879 (Kan. 1913); State v. Watson, 1 P. 770, 771–72 (Kan. 1883); Smith v. State, 33 Me. 48, 57–59 (1851); Worthington v. State, 48 A. 355, 357 (Md. 1901); Lamb v. State, 10 A. 208, 208–09 (Md. 1887); People v. Sessions, 26 N.W. 291, 293 (Mich. 1886); People v. Olmstead, 30 Mich. 431, 432–33 (1874); Smith v. State, 73 So. 793, 794 (Miss. 1916), *overruled on other grounds*, Ladnier v. State, 124 So. 432 (Miss. 1929); State v. Gedicke, 43 N.J.L. 86, 89–90, 96 (1881); State v. Cooper, 22 N.J.L. 52, 57 (1849); State v. Bassett, 194 P. 867, 868 (N.M. 1921); State v. Powell, 106 S.E. 133 (N.C. 1921); State v. Tippie, 105 N.E. 75, 77 (Ohio 1913); State v. Ausplund, 167 P. 1019, 1022–23 (Ore. 1917); State v. Farnam, 161 P. 417, 419 (Ore. 1916); State v. Atwood, 102 P. 295, 297; *aff'd on reh'g*, 104 p.195 (Or. 1909); Railing v. Commonwealth, 1 A. 314, 315 (Pa. 1885); Commonwealth v. W., 3 Pitts. R. 462, 470–71 (1871); Moore v. State, 40 S.W. 287, 289, 295 (Tex. Ct. Crim. App. 1897); State v. Crook, 51 P. 1091, 1093 (Utah 1898); State v. Howard, 32 Vt. 380, 399–401 (1859); Hatchard v. State, 48 N.W. 380, 381 (Wis. 1891); State v. Dickinson, 41 Wis. 299, 309 (1871). *See also* Rosen v. Louisiana Bd. Med. Examiners, 318 F. Supp. 1217, 1222–32 (E.D. La. 1970), *vacated after* Roe v. Wade, 412 U.S. 902 (1973); Nelson v. Planned Parenthood Center of Tucson, Inc., 505 P.2d 580, 582 (Ariz.

or destruction of the fetus was a fatal defect in an indictment for an abortion in which the mother did not die.[38] (The would-be abortionist could be indicted for attempted abortion without proof of the death of the fetus and even without proof that the woman had been pregnant.)[39] The worldwide pattern of legislation, even in countries where European influence on such topics appears not to have been strong, suggests that something more significant was happening than what one pro-abortion observer has chosen to describe as merely an "interesting" coincidence.[40]

Proponents of these statutes in the legislature expressed themselves largely in terms of protecting fetal life. One could pick almost any anti-abortion tract from the nineteenth century, open it at random, and find the argument.[41] This gradual broadening of the reach of the abortion laws was led nearly everywhere by the medical profession, expressing itself most emphatically and most compellingly in terms of protecting fetal life. A number of resolutions of the fledgling American Medical Association and related state associations clearly express the sense of the medical profession at the time. Justice Blackmun in *Roe v. Wade* quoted from an 1859 report to the Twelfth Annual Meeting of the American Medical Association by the Association's Committee on Criminal Abortion appointed, as the Committee report indicated, "with a view to its general suppression."[42] The report identified three reasons for the growing frequency of abortion, a pattern that the committee found indicative of a "general demoralization" of society:

---

Ct. App. 1973), McClure v. State, 215 S.W.2d 524, 530 (Ark. 1949); People v. Belous, 458 P.2d 194, 209 (Cal.) (Burke, J., dissenting); Hall v. People, 201 P.2d 382, 383 (Colo. 1948); Scott v. State, 117 A.2d 831, 835–36 (Del. 1955); Urga v. State, 20 So. 2d 685, 687 (Fla. 1944); Territory v. Young, 37 Haw. 150, 159–60 (1945), *appeal dismissed,* 160 F.2d 289 (9th Cir. 1947); Nash v. Meyer, 31 P.2d 273, 280 (Idaho 1934); Amman v. Faidy, 114 N.E.2d 412, 416 (Ill. 1953); Cheaney v. State, 285 N.E.2d 265, 267–70 (Ind. 1972) Joy v. Brown, 252 P.2d 889, 892 (Kan. 1953); Sasaki v. Commonwealth, 485 S.W.2d 897, 901–03 (Ky. 1972), *vacated after* Roe v. Wade, 410 U.S. 951 (1973); State v. Rudman, 136 A.2d 817, 819 (Me. 1927); Keyes v. Construction Services, Inc., 165 N.E.2d 912, 914 (Mass. 1960); Rainey v. Horn, 72 So. 2d 434, 439 (Miss. 1954); Rodgers v. Danforth, 486 S.W.2d 258, 259 (Mo. 1972); Hans v. State, 22 N.W.2d 385, 389 (Neb. 1946); Bennett v. Humers, 147 A.2d 108, 109–10 (N.H. 1958); State v. Siciliano, 121 A.2d 490, 495 (N.J. 1956); Endresz v. Friedberg, 242 N.E.2d 901, 904 (N.Y. 1969); People v. Lovell, 242 N.Y.S. 2d 958, 959 (1963); Williams v. Marion Rapid Transit, 87 N.E.2d 334, 336 (Ohio 1949); Bowlan v. Lunsford, 54 P.2d 666, 668 (Okla. 1936); Mallison v. Pomeroy, 291 P.2d 225, 228 (Ore. 1955); Sylvia v. Gobeille, 220 A.2d 222, 223 (R.I. 1966); State v. Steadman, 51 S.E.2d 91, 93 (S.C. 1948); State v. Munson, 201 N.W.2d 123, 125–26 (S.D. 1972), *vacated after* Roe v. Wade, 410 U.S. 950 (1973); Thompson v. State, 493 S.W.2d 913, 917–20 (Tex. Ct. Crim. App. 1971), *vacated after* Roe v. Wade, 410 U.S. 950 (1973); Anderson v. Commonwealth, 58 S.E.2d 72, 75 (Va. 1950); Miller v. Bennett, 56 S.E.2d 217, 221 (Va. 1949); State v. Cox, 84 P.2d 357, 361 (Wash. 1938). Courts in a handful of cases—all but two during the agitation leading up to *Roe v. Wade*—have denied this purpose. Walsingham v. State, 250 So. 2d 857, 861 (Fla. 1971); People v. Nixon, 201 N.W.2d 635, 639–41 (Mich. Ct. App. 1972); State v. Millette, 299 A.2d 150, 154 (N.H. 1972); State v. Jordan, 42 S.E.2d 674 (N.C. 1947); Foster v. State, 196 N.W. 233, 235 (Wis. 1923) (but acknowledging that "[i]n a strictly scientific and physiological sense there is life in an embryo from the time of conception"). *See generally* Robert Byrn, *An American Tragedy: The Supreme Court on Abortion,* 41 Fordham L. Rev. 807, 828–29 (1973); Robert Destro, *Abortion and the Constitution: The Need for a Life-Protective Amendment,* 63 Cal. L. Rev. 1250, 1273–78 (1975).

38. *See, e.g.,* Smith v. State, 33 Me. 48, 60 (1851); People v. Davis, 56 N.Y. 95 (1874); Cobel v. People, 5 Park. Crim. 348 (N.Y. Sup. Ct. 1862); Lohman v. People, 1 N.Y. 379, 382–83 (1848).

39. People v. Axelson, 119 N.E. 708 (N.Y. 1918).

40. J.K. Mason, Medico-Legal Aspects of Reproduction and Parenthood 101 (1990).

41. *See, e.g.,* John Beck, An Inaugural Dissertation on Infanticide 140 (1817); John Streeter, Practical Observations on Abortion 5–6 (1840); Horatio Robinson Storer & Franklin Fiske Heard, Criminal Abortion: Its Nature, Its Evidence and Its Law 9–10 (1868); "D.H.", *On Producing Abortion: A Physician's Reply to the Solicitations of a Married Woman to Produce a Miscarriage for Her,* 17 Nashville J. Med. & Surgical J. 200, 200 (1876).

42. *The Report on Criminal Abortion,* 12 Trans. of the Am. Med. Assn. 73 (1859) ("*Report*"), quoted in *Roe v. Wade,* 410 U.S. 113, 141–42 (1973). The Court incorrectly gave the date as 1857, which was when the committee was appointed, not when it delivered its report. *See generally* Mohr, *supra* note 31, at 154–57.

The first of these causes is a wide-spread popular ignorance of the true character of the crime—a belief, even among mothers themselves, that the foetus is not alive till after the period of quickening.

The second of the agents alluded to is the fact that the profession themselves are frequently supposed careless of foetal life. . . .

The third reason of the frightful extent of this crime is found in the grave defects of our laws, both common and statute, as regards the independent and actual existence of the child before birth, as a living being. These errors, which are sufficient in most instances to prevent conviction, are based, and only based, upon mistaken and exploded medical dogmas. With strange inconsistency, the law fully acknowledges the foetus in utero and its inherent rights, for civil purposes; while personally and as criminally affected, it fails to recognize it, and to its life as yet denies all protection.[43]

Based on this report, the Association unanimously adopted resolutions protesting "against such unwarrantable destruction of human life," calling upon state legislatures to revise abortion laws, and requesting cooperation by state medical societies "in pressing the subject."[44]

Many state medical societies readily cooperated in the crusade to perfect abortion laws with resolutions and other activities expressed in very much the same terms as the national society.[45] The resolution of the New York Medical Society of 1867 that figured prominently in securing stricter abortion laws in that state in 1869 read as follows:

*Whereas,* from the first moment of conception, there is a living creature in process of development to full maturity; and whereas, any sufficient interruption to this living process always results in the destruction of life; and whereas, the intentional arrest of this living process, eventuating in the destruction of life (being an act with intention to kill), is consequently murder; therefore,

*Resolved,* That this society do express their abhorrence, and deprecate, in a most emphatic manner, the growing increase of that demoralizing aid given and practice rendered in procuring criminal or unnecessary abortion.

*Resolved,* That this society will hail with gratitude and pleasure, the adoption of any measures or influences that will, in part or entirely, arrest this flagrant corruption or morality among women, who ought to be and unquestionably are the conservators of morals and virtue.

*Resolved,* That the publication in newspapers, and of secret circulars, of ostensible remedies for female diseases, that suggest abortion, are highly detrimental to public health and morals; and that the Legislature ought, by enactment of a suitable law, to forbid such publications.

*Resolved,* That a copy of this preamble and resolutions be transmitted to both branches of the Legislature now in session.[46]

The American Medical Association also reiterated its stand and its reasons from time to time during the movement to codify abortion laws. Finally, in 1870 yet another Committee on Criminal Abortion of the American Medical Association issued a report that even Justice Blackmun characterized as "long and vivid."[47] The report concluded that: "We had to deal with human life.

---

43. *Report, supra* note 33, at 75–76.
44. *Id.* at 28, 78.
45. Mohr, *supra* note 31, at 147–70. *See also* Hugh Hodge, Foeticide, or Criminal Abortion 5 (1869).
46. 1867 N.Y. Assembly J. 443–44.
47. *Roe,* 410 U.S. at 142.

In a matter of less importance we could entertain no compromise. An honest judge on the bench would call things by their proper names. We could do no less."[48] The Association responded by adopting resolutions declaring it unlawful and unprofessional for any physician to induce premature labor or abortion without the concurring opinion of another physician and then "always with a view to the safety of the child if that be possible."[49] A separate resolution at the 1870 meeting of the American Medical Association called upon the clergy of American to recognize the immorality of abortion and to join the crusade against the practice.[50] Many religious and social leaders, whether in response to the physicians' call or otherwise, also supported treating abortion as a crime.[51] The press frequently supported this consensus both through editorials and through its often sensationalized reporting of criminal abortions.[52]

The medical campaign cannot easily be dismissed as a masculinist conspiracy. The leading feminists of the time were, if anything, more emphatic in demanding harsh punishment for abortion, and on precisely the same grounds as the male dominated organized medical profession.[53] What emerged from this agitation was a strong and consistent consensus that abortion was homicide, and should therefore be prohibited. Michael Grossberg has termed the discrediting of the quickening distinction as "[t]he most far-reaching legal victory of the antiabortion forces" that demonstrated "the physicians' power."[54] It was a victory of sorts for the physicians. Whether it was simply an exertion of their power or something else is another matter. The consensus persisted through the first-half of the twentieth century with remarkably little dissent among the medical profession or elsewhere throughout society. Even some who would later become well-known crusaders for abortion reform initially strongly asserted that abortion was murder.

One of the best examples is Dr. Alan Guttmacher, who ended as such a well-known crusader on behalf of legalized abortion that the name "Alan Guttmacher Institute" has been given to the major medical research arm of the abortion rights movement. As late as 1961, he had written that at the fertilization of an ovum "a baby has been conceived."[55] If this is not a clear enough indication of his attitude at the time (and one might well suspect that he was already reconsidering his position by 1961), one can find explicit condemnations of abortion in his earlier writings:

---

48. W.E. Atlee & D.A. O'Donnell, *Report of the Committee on Criminal Abortion*, 22 Trans. Am. Med. Ass'n 240, 258 (1871). *See also* Isaac Quimby, *Introduction to Medical Jurisprudence*, 9 A.M.A. J. 164 (1887).

49. *Minutes of the 22nd Annual Meeting* [1870], 22 Trans. Am. Med. Ass'n 39 (1871).

50. *Id.*, at 39.

51. *See, e.g.,* Arthur Cleveland Coxe, Moral Reforms Suggested in a Pastoral Letter with Remarks on Practical Religion 9–75, 101–11 (1869); John Todd, Serpent in a Dove's Nest 6–14 (1867); Nathan Allen, *Comparative Decrease of Children*, 54 Congregational & Bos. Recorder 39 (Feb. 4, 1869); *The Crime of Infanticide*, 47 N.Y. Observer 194 (June 24, 1869); I.T. Dana, *Report of the Committee on the Production of Abortion*, 46 Christian Mirror 1 (Aug. 4, 1868); John Todd, *Fashionable Murder*, 52 Congregational & Bos. Recorder 45 (1867). *See generally* Michael Grossberg, Governing the Hearth: Law and the Family in Nineteenth-Century America 170–72 (1985); Mohr, *supra* note 31, at 187–93; Carroll Smith-Rosenberg, Disorderly Conduct: Visions of Gender in Victorian America 218 (1985); Sauer, *supra* note 29, at 56, 58.

52. Mohr, *supra* note 31, at 125–28, 176–82, 196–97; Marvin Olasky, The Press and Abortion, 1838–1988, at 17–53 (1988); Leslie Reagan, When Abortion Was a Crime: Women, Medicine, and Law in the United States, 1867–1973, at 46–61, 101–06, 109, 125; Cyril Means, jr., *The Law of New York Concerning Abortion and the Status of the Foetus, 1664–1968: A Case of Cessation of Constitutionality*, 14 N.Y.L.F. 411, 457–59, 471–72 n.164 (1968) ("Means I"); Sauer, *supra* note 29, at 58.

53. *See* Chapter 8.

54. Grossberg, *supra* note 51, at 184–85.

55. Alan Guttmacher, Birth Control and Love: The Complete Guide to Contraception and Fertility 12 (1961).

"To extinguish the first spark of life is a crime of the same nature, both against our Maker and society, as to destroy an infant, a child, or a man."[56]

After reviewing the foregoing evidence, one again can only marvel at historians who conclude that "the destruction of the fetus never gained the standing either of infanticide or homicide."[57] Were it not for the sheer political convenience of the claim, one doubts that it would have found any audience at all. The remainder of this chapter reviews the evolution of the abortion statutes in the United States in the middle and later years of the nineteenth century, in particular the social forces that drove that evolution, with some emphasis on the role of women in shaping the debate and the outcome of that evolution. The chapter opens with a detailed examination of the evolution of the New York legislation from 1845 onwards as an example of the evolution of such statutes generally.

# New York's Later Abortion Laws (1845–1942)

*[T]he conventions of history always reflect those of fiction; the Beards owe as much to writers like Norris as they owe to Marx.*

—Mark Sagoff[58]

Focusing on a particular state as a model of the evolution of abortion laws in the United States in the nineteenth century allows one to follow a coherent time line and to develop an intelligible narrative. Such a focus risks, however, becoming tied up in the inevitable peculiarities that characterize the law of any given state. New York in some ways is atypical of events elsewhere in the United States. Nonetheless, it remains the prime example of American developments in the law of abortion for two reasons. First, it was the most legally influential state throughout most of the nineteenth and much of the twentieth centuries. Second, the New York experience was thoroughly studied by historians, making more information available on the New York experience than for any other state. These are reasons enough to focus attention on New York, but there is another reason for doing so. Cyril Means, jr., focused on the history of New York's abortion laws in his reconstruction of the history of abortion laws, a reconstruction that strongly influenced the decision in *Roe v. Wade*.[59] Getting the history of New York's abortion laws right thus bears on evaluating the reasoning in that pivotal decision. Careful examination of

---

56. Alan Guttmacher, Having a Baby: A Guide to Expectant Parents 15 (1947); Alan Guttmacher, Into This Universe: The Story of Human Birth 46 (1937).

57. Grossberg, *supra* note 51, at 186. *See also* Ronald Collins, *The Problem of Penalties Clouds Issue of Abortion*, Nat'l L.J., July 29, 1985, at 13 (arguing that "the law" never took seriously the claim that a fetus was a human being because abortion "always" carried a less severe penalty than "true" murder—as if there are not different penalties for different sorts of homicide of adults).

58. Mark Sagoff, *On Preserving the Natural Environment*, 84 Yale L.J. 205, 243 (1974) (commenting on the indebtedness of historians Charles and Mary Beard to Frank Norris and other American Realist novelists in the Beard's development of their economic analysis of the drafting of the Constitution). *See also* Allen Boyer, *Formalism, Realism, and Naturalism: Cross-Currents in American Letters and Law,* 23 Conn. L. Rev. 669 (1991).

59. Justice Blackmun cited Means' two law review articles on the history of abortion, focused on England and New York, seven times in the majority opinion in *Roe. Roe,* 410 U.S. at 136–39. Blackmun cited no other contemporary historical sources. *See also* Wolfgang Saxon, *Obituary: Cyril C. Means, 73, A Specialist in Laws Regarding Abortion,* N.Y. Times, Oct. 6, 1992, at A15. For the articles, see Means I, *supra* note 52; Means II, *supra* note 31.

the subsequent recodifications of New York's abortion laws during the nineteenth century reveals that the recodifications consistently and explicitly reinforced the policy of protecting fetal life.

After initially codifying the law of abortion in 1829, New York's legislature revisited the topic of abortion in 1845. The 1845 codification made three significant changes compared to the 1829 *Revised Statutes.* Sections 1 and 2 of the 1845 statute narrowed the therapeutic exceptions by requiring that the abortion actually be necessary to preserve the life of the mother, unlike the 1829 *Revised Statutes* that justified therapeutic abortions that were recommended by two physicians as necessary to preserve the life of the mother even if, in fact, the abortion turned out not to be necessary.[60] The same two sections of the 1845 statute also reduced the punishment for pre-quickening abortions. Section three of the 1845 act made any woman who solicited or used any abortifacient guilty of misdemeanor punished equally with the pre-quickening abortionist.[61]

The reasons for these changes are not clear. The first section of the 1845 act was reenacted in 1846 to make clear that abortion of a quick child was manslaughter only if the child, or the mother, died—a provision left out in 1845, apparently by oversight.[62] Two New York courts went on to hold that the 1845 recodification left the 1829 provisions in force for pre-quickening abortions by intrusion techniques even though the 1829 provisions were not included in the later codification.[63] As the 1845 act expressly saved only the provisions governing abortions through injury techniques, those courts could be accused of indulging in a strained reading of the 1845 statutes. The failure of the courts (or, apparently, anyone else) to record the reasons for continuing to enforce the earlier statutes prevents certainty about such a conclusion.

Whatever these somewhat contradictory developments might signify, the provision making a woman's solicitation of or performance of an abortion on herself a crime would seem to make it indisputably clear that the 1845 statutory scheme, like that of 1829, was designed to protect fetal life. Although one might argue that the crime of self-abortion simply represented excessive paternalism, a more natural reading suggests an intent to protect the fetus from the mother. Instead of considering what the legislature itself did, Means busied himself with suppositions about legislative proposals the text of which have not survived or insinuations he finds in utterly ambiguous judicial opinions.[64] He was even willing to infer a contemporary interpretation supporting the non-criminality of an abortion from a gap of three weeks between the impaneling of a Coroner's jury and the arrest of the abortionist.[65] Curiously, however, he did not even comment on the reduction of punishment for the abortionist, a change that might be exploited to raise a doubt about the equation of abortion with homicide. Of course, one might also conclude that the reduction in punishment was meant to make it easier to secure a conviction from jurors who could be more reluctant to convict under the more serious the punishment. While we have no direct evidence of this in the New York legislative record, such a motive was explicit for the reduction in punishment for infanticide in *Lord Ellenborough's Act* in England in 1803.[66] Without any evidence from New York, conclusions about the purpose of the change must remain tentative at best.

Means asserted that the change making therapeutic abortions more difficult to obtain resulted from poor drafting.[67] This was an all too typical response to evidence he did not like.

---

60. 1845 N.Y. Laws ch. 260, §§ 1, 2, at 285, reprinted in Quay, *supra* note 3, at 500. For the 1829 version, see Chapter 6, at note 116.

61. 1845 N.Y. Laws ch. 260, § 3, reprinted in Quay, *supra* note 3, at 500.

62. 1846 N.Y. Laws ch. 22, § 1, at 19, reprinted in Quay, *supra* note 3, at 500.

63. Frazer v. People, 1 Cowen's Crim. 377 (N.Y. Sup. Ct. 1863); Cobel v. People, 5 Park. Crim. 348 (N.Y. Sup. Ct. 1862).

64. Examples of both ploys appear Means I, *supra* note 52, at 456.

65. *Id.* at 457.

66. 43 Geo. III ch. 58, § 3 (1803). *See also* 11 PARLIAMENTARY REGISTER 390 (William Woodfall ed. 1803).

67. Means I, *supra* note 52, at 454.

Means did mention that an early version of the statute punished self-abortion equally regardless of whether the abortion came before or after quickening.[68] Yet he simply declared the proposal "anomalous"[69] and had nothing further to say about it despite its obvious import for those who thought that the laws were designed to protect women rather than fetuses from abortionists. Means responded to indictments under the 1829 statute seventeen years after the 1845 recodification with incredulity rather than with analysis of the courts' reasoning regarding the relation of the two statutory schemes.[70] Despite an express reference to the 1829 *Revised Statutes* in the second of the two cases, Means did not consider the possibility that New York courts were expressing a strong distaste for abortion by continuing to enforce the earlier statute.

The 1845 statutes created a technical distinction between the crime of abortion (sections 1 or 2) and the crime of self-abortion (section 3). Because of this distinction, a woman undergoing an abortion was not an accomplice of that crime, and her testimony therefore need not be corroborated by other, independent evidence.[71] Apparently, under the 1829 *Revised Statutes*, the woman was a party to the same crime of abortion as the abortionists,[72] making convictions virtually impossible to obtain even with a grant of immunity from prosecution to the woman to overcome self-incrimination problems.[73]

Despite the abortion statutes then on the books in New York and elsewhere, abortion was becoming more common and was becoming an increasingly open phenomenon by the middle of the nineteenth century.[74] Opposition was also growing to the practice, expressed most clearly by the resolution quoted above that was adopted by the Medical Society of New York at Albany on February 5, 1867.[75] The resolution was communicated to the state's legislature too late for action in that session. Although Means dismissed the resolution as "metaphysical romanticism,"[76] describing it as "one of the most remarkable communications ever sent by a medical society to a parliamentary body,"[77] the resolution, coupled with an extensive press campaign against abortion[78] and several highly visible criminal trials of abortionists,[79] carried the day in the next legislative session. New York's legislature adopted yet another abortion statute in 1869 that reflected the Medical Society's concerns:

§ 1: Any person who shall administer to any woman with child, or prescribe for any such woman, or advise or procure her to take any medicine, drug, substance or thing whatever, or shall use or employ any instrument or other means whatever, with intent thereby to procure the miscarriage of any such woman, unless the same shall have been necessary to preserve her life, shall in case the death of such child, or of such woman be thereby produced, be deemed guilty of manslaughter in the second degree.

§ 2: Whoever shall unlawfully supply or procure any medicine, drug, substance or thing whatever, knowing that the same is intended to be unlawfully used or employed

---

68. *Id.* at 454–55.

69. *Id.* at 462–63.

70. *Id.* at 462, 487.

71. People v. Blank, 29 N.E.2d 73 (N.Y. 1940); People v. McGonegal, 32 N.E. 616 (N.Y. 1892); People v. Vedder, 98 N.Y. 630 (1885); Dunn v. People, 29 N.Y. 523 (1864); People v. Lohman, 2 Barb. 216 (N.Y. Sup. Ct.), *aff'd on other grounds*, 1 N.Y. 379 (1848); People v. Costello, 1 Denio 83 (N.Y. Sup. Ct. 1845). On the problem of accomplice testimony generally, see Chapter 6, at notes 302–24.

72. Frazer v. People, 1 Cowen's Crim. 377 (N.Y. Sup. Ct. 1863).

73. Otto Pollak, The Criminality of Women 45–46 (1950).

74. See the text *infra* at notes 163–206.

75. See the text *supra* at note 46.

76. Means I, *supra* note 52, at 463, 470–71.

77. *Id.* at 459–60.

78. *See* Chapter 9, at notes 28–34.

79. Marvin Olasky, Abortion Rites: A Social History of Abortion in America 96–97 (1992).

with intent to procure the miscarriage of any woman, whether she be or be not pregnant, shall be deemed guilty of a misdemeanor, and shall upon conviction, be punished by imprisonment in the county jail not less than three months nor more than
one year, or by a fine not exceeding one thousand dollars, or by both such fine and
imprisonment.

§ 3: Every person offending against either of the provisions of this act, shall be a competent witness against any other person so offending, and may be compelled to appear
and give evidence before any magistrate or grand jury, or in any court, in the same
manner as other persons; but the testimony so given shall not be used in any prosecution or proceeding, civil or criminal, against the person so testifying.[80]

This new statute, particularly when read against the background of the press campaign
against abortion and resolutions such as those from the Medical Society of New York, seemed to
eliminate any difference based on quickening, substituting the phrase "any woman with child"
for the former phrase "any woman pregnant with a quick child" and making the crime
manslaughter in the second degree if the child died, apparently at any stage of pregnancy.[81] Completely ignoring the clear language of the statute, Means announced that the changes were intended to perfect the protection of the mother's life, making clear that any abortion in which the
mother died was manslaughter.[82] That the crime was only manslaughter, and not capital murder
as some supporters of the statute had advocated, reflected a realistic appraisal of the reluctance
of juries to impose the death penalty for abortion, but not a devaluation of fetal life.[83] After all,
the death of the mother was also be punished as manslaughter rather than the murder it would
be in the normal operation of the felony murder rule—does one concede that this was a devaluation of maternal life? Whether particular jurors were reluctant to impose the death penalty for
abortion because they thought that abortion was not the equivalent of murder we cannot say.

In *Evans v. People*,[84] the first prosecution under the 1869 statute, New York's highest court (the
Court of Appeals) remarkably read the new statute as applying only to the miscarriage of a quick
child,[85] despite the language in the statute that appeared to be directly contrary. Judge J. Grover
Allen, writing for the majority, adopted the theory that the child was not living before quickening and therefore could not have been killed by the abortion as the statute required:

There is a period during gestation when, although there may be embryo life in the foetus, there is no living child.... It was error to charge that the death of a child could be
caused or produced before it had given evidence of life, had become "quick" in the
womb, and that the crime of manslaughter under the statute could be predicated of the
destruction of the foetus before that period.[86]

Judge Allen's conclusion was unusual in the late nineteenth century. A large number of courts
in other states and in England had embraced the new learning regarding when human life began,
interpreting even statutes that appeared to contain a quickening requirement to apply to abor-

---

80. 1869 N.Y. Laws ch. 631, §§ 1–3, at 1502, reprinted in Quay, *supra* note 3, at 500.

81. *Compare* 1869 N.Y. Laws ch. 631, § 1, at 1502, reprinted in Quay, *supra* note 3, at 500, *with* 1846 N.Y.
Laws ch. 22, § 1, 1845 N.Y. Laws ch. 260, § 1, at 285, reprinted in Quay, *supra*, at 500, *and with* N.Y. Rev. Stat.
pt. 4, ch. 1, tit. 2, §§ 8, 9 (1829), quoted in Chapter 6, at note 105, reprinted in Quay, *supra*, at 499. *See generally* Witherspoon, *supra* note 7, at 61–69.

82. Means I, *supra* note 52, at 463–90. *See also* Witherspoon, *supra* note 7, at 65–68 nn. 125–26.

83. Olasky, *supra* note 79, at 97–99. *See also* J.C. Stone, *Report on the Subject of the Criminality of Abortion*, 1 Trans. Iowa Med. Soc'y 31 (1874).

84. 49 N.Y. 86 (1872).

85. *Id.* at 88–91.

86. *Id.* at 90–91.

tions before quickening.[87] As we shall see, this new thinking represented a consensus among attorneys, feminists, journalists, religious leaders, and many others in society, not only physicians. Yet Means, working from yet another incomplete legislative record, argued that the legislature endorsed Allen's reading of the 1869 Act in a new abortion statute adopted contemporaneously with the decision in *Evans*.[88] The New York legislature in 1871 and 1872 did fail to pass several proposals to make the punishment of the crime even more severe,[89] including a proposal classifying nontherapeutic abortions as murder.[90] When the legislature did act again, its 1872 *Abortion Act* can hardly be characterized as expressing less concerned for protecting unborn children than the 1869 Act. In fact, the 1872 Act closely followed the language of the 1869 act except for three textual changes in the 1872 Act that all seemed to reflect even greater concern for fetal life than the 1869 Act:

§ 1: Any person who shall hereafter willfully administer to any woman pregnant with child or prescribe for any such woman, or advise or procure her to take any medicine, drug, substance or thing whatever, or shall use or employ, or advise or procure her to submit to the use or employment of any instrument or other means whatever, with intent thereby to produce the miscarriage of any such woman, unless the same shall have been necessary to preserve her life, or that of such child, shall, in the case the death of such child or such woman be thereby produced, be deemed guilty of a felony, and upon conviction shall be punished by imprisonment in a State prison for a term not less than four or more than twenty years.

§ 2: Any woman pregnant with child who shall take any medicine, drug, substance or thing whatever, or shall use or employ, or suffer any other person to use or employ, or submit to the use of employment of any instrument or other means whatever, with the intent thereby to produce the miscarriage of the child of which she is so pregnant, unless the same shall have been necessary to preserve her life or that of such child, shall in case the death of such child be thereby produced, be deemed guilty of a felony, and upon conviction shall be punished by imprisonment in the State prison for a term not less than four years or more than ten years.

§ 3: Every person who shall administer to any pregnant woman, or prescribe for any such woman, or advise or procure any such woman to take any medicine, drug, substance or thing whatever, or shall use or employ[91] any instrument or other means whatever, with intent thereby to procure the miscarriage of any such woman, shall upon conviction be punished, by imprisonment in a county jail, or in a State prison, not less than one nor more than three years, in the discretion of the court.

§ 4: Whoever shall unlawfully supply or procure any advice, medicine, drug, substance or thing whatever, knowing that the same is intended to be unlawfully used or employed with intent to procure the miscarriage of any woman, whether she be or be not pregnant,

---

87. State v. Reed, 45 Ark. 333, 334–36 (1885); Lamb v. State, 10 A. 208, 208 (Md. 1887); Commonwealth v. Taylor, 132 Mass. 261, 262 (1882); State v. Slagle, 83 N.C. 630, 632 (1880); Mills v. Commonwealth, 13 Pa. 630, 632 (1850); Regina v. Wycherley, 173 Eng. Rep. 486 (N.P. 1838). *Contra:* Taylor v. State, 33 S.E. 190, 191 (Ga. 1899); Mitchell v. Commonwealth, 78 Ky. 204, 206–10 (1879); Smith v. State, 33 Me. 48, 57–60 (1851); State v. Cooper, 22 N.J.L. 52 (1849) (promptly reversed by statute; see Chapter 6, at notes 188–89). *See also* Commonwealth v. Tibbetts, 32 N.E. 910 (Mass. 1893); Commonwealth v. Follansbee, 29 N.E. 471, 474 (Mass. 1893); Commonwealth v. Wood, 77 Mass. (11 Gray) 85, 92 (1858); Powe v. State, 2 A. 662, 664 (N.J. 1886). *See generally* Chapter 5, at notes 207–46, and Chapter 6, at notes 156–63.

88. Means I, *supra* note 52, at 473–88.

89. *Id.* at 473–86.

90. *Id.* at 473–78.

91. Amended in 1880 to add "advise or procure." 1880 N.Y. Laws ch. 283.

shall be deemed guilty of a misdemeanor, and shall upon conviction, be punished by imprisonment in the county jail not less than three months nor more than one year, or by a fine not exceeding one thousand dollars, or by both such fine and imprisonment.[92]

The first change added "advising or procuring" to the prohibition of intrusion abortions. The second change added the induction of a miscarriage to save the unborn child's life (*i.e.*, a Cesarean section) to the defense of necessity. Finally, the term "felony" (with punishment of from four to twenty years in prison) was substituted for the earlier statute's more general treatment of the crime as manslaughter. Apart from these changes, the legislature again prohibited aborting "any woman with child," just as in the 1869 Act.

Means dismissed any possible reading of the statute as protective of fetal life. For example, he derisively described the broadening of the therapeutic exception to allow the saving of the child as well as the saving of the mother as a "bicephalic" change in the law that served no rational purpose and must, as he so often concluded regarding statutory provisions that he did not like, have resulted from a legislative oversight.[93] Even this stretch paled in significance when compared to his stretch in claiming that the legislature enacted the new law in 1872 in order to codify the decision in *Evans*. The 1872 act had already cleared the legislature before the *Evans* decision was announced and was signed into law by the governor on the same day that the Court of Appeals handed down its *Evans* decision. Means was left to claim, rather lamely, that the legislature must certainly have been so impressed by the defendant's argument in *Evans* as to have anticipated what the Court of Appeals would decide.[94] *Evans*, Means claimed, merely returned the law to what it was in from 1845 to 1869 when pre-quickening abortions through intrusion techniques were, he alleged, legal.[95] He chose to ignore two precedents indicating that such abortions were criminal—under the 1829 statutes rather than under the 1845 statutes.[96] Means argument regarding the correct interpretation of the 1872 *Abortion Act* was so lame that Roy Lucas declined to use Means' entire historical argument in preparing the principal brief for "Jane Roe" in *Roe v. Wade*.[97] If only Justice Blackmun had read Means' work as carefully.

If one did not start from a reading based on *Evans*, one would naturally read the change from "any woman pregnant with quick child" to "any woman with child" as broadening the reach of the statute to reach abortion throughout pregnancy. This was how the trial court and Judge J. Martin Grover of the Court of Appeals in dissent read the statute.[98] Even Means conceded that the legislature had intended this in enacting the 1869 Act.[99] The legislature's carrying forward of this latter phrase from the 1869 Act to the 1872 Act before *Evans* was decided could hardly signal an intent to narrow the reach of the abortion prohibition to post-quickening abortions.

Means seized upon section 3 of the 1872 act to support his claim that the legislature had anticipated the Court of Appeals' ruling.[100] Section 3 made the administering or advising of an abortifacient to "any pregnant woman" a less serious felony than under section one of the Act, punishable by imprisonment from one to three years in the county jail. This, Means argued, could only be read as a punishment for pre-quickening abortion in contrast to section 1 of the

---

92. 1872 N.Y. Laws ch. 181, § 1, at 71, reprinted in Quay, *supra* note 3, at 501.

93. Means I, *supra* note 54, at 488.

94. *Id.* at 485–87.

95. *Id.* at 487.

96. Frazer v. People, 1 Cowen's Crim. 377 (N.Y. Sup. Ct. 1863); Cobel v. People, 5 Park. Crim. 348 (N.Y. Sup. Ct. 1862).

97. David Garrow, Liberty and Sexuality: The Right of Privacy and the Making of *Roe v. Wade* 500–01, 891–92 n.41 (2nd ed. 1998).

98. 49 N.Y. at 91–97.

99. Means I, *supra* note 52, at 463–64, 486.

100. *Id.* at 487–88.

Act. If one reads the 1872 provisions as intended to prohibit abortions throughout pregnancy rather than only after quickening, however, the import of section 3 is not a prohibition of pre-quickening abortions—these were already covered by section 1. Instead, the textual difference between sections 1 and 3 suggests that section 3 was designed to reach attempted abortions rather than pre-quickening abortions. Section 1 requires for conviction the death of the child or of the mother; section 3 does not. The application of section 3 to pre-quickening abortions developed only in response to the peculiarly narrow reading the Court of Appeals announced in *Evans*.

Section 2 of the 1872 Act raises difficulties for those, like Means, who argue that the legislature in 1872 sought to narrow surreptitiously the reach and effect of New York's ban on elective abortions, presumably in order to protect maternal choice. Section 2 raised the crime of a woman participating in her own abortion from a misdemeanor to a felony, with punishment to range from four to ten years in prison. Means sought to dismiss this provision on the grounds that it was a dead letter[101]—because of the prevalent practice of granting immunity to the mother to procure her testimony against the abortionist.[102] Dead letter or not, the inclusion of the provision clearly indicates the legislature's intent unless one is ready to indulge, as Means was, in an inference of utter cynicism on the part of the legislature.[103]

As a result of *Evans*, pre-quickening abortion continued to be a misdemeanor in New York and the state's legislature never fully eliminated the distinction that so many now saw as obsolete. Because the legislature in 1881 did not attempt to do more than restate the existing law, the quickening distinction was made explicit in that year's recodification[104] that pulled together and systematized the by then somewhat scattered and not entirely consistent statutes surviving from the several prior codifications. For once Means accurately described the import of the legislature's enactment: "It must be admitted that the framers of the Penal Code of 1881 did an excellent job of eliminating redundancies and inconsistencies in the pre-Code statutory materials."[105] One anomaly and two interesting changes were introduced, however. The anomaly carried forward from past codifications was the omission of a therapeutic exception for the preservation of the life of a quick child for the crime by abortionists,[106] although not for the crime of the mother.[107] Similarly, the 1881 Code carried forward the lack of a therapeutic exception for the crime of aborting an unquickened child by either an abortionist or the mother.[108] The first change introduced by the 1881 recodification was to make clear that the abortionist is guilty of the crime of abortion even if the woman was not in fact pregnant.[109] A close reading of the 1881 Code also suggests that the criminalization of the administration or advising of abortifacients with intent to abort an unquickened child to a woman who is not actually pregnant applies only to ingestion techniques and not to intrusion or injury techniques.[110] Finally, the 1881 recodification introduced a new provision making it a felony to manufacture, give, or sell abortifacients.[111]

---

101. *Id.* at 487, 491.

102. *Id.,* at 493. *See also* B. James George, jr., *Current Abortion Laws: Proposals and Movements for Reform,* in ABORTION AND THE LAW 1, 13–14 (David Smith ed. 1967). The same practice was to make the crime of self-abortion virtually obsolete in England as well. GLANVILLE WILLIAMS, THE SANCTITY OF LIFE AND THE CRIMINAL LAW 153–55 (1957). *See generally* Chapter 6, at notes 302–24.

103. Means I, *supra* note 52, at 489, 492.

104. 1881 N.Y. Laws ch. 676, §§ 190, 191, 194, 294, 295, 297.

105. Means I, *supra* note 52, at 491.

106. 1881 N.Y. Laws ch. 676, § 191.

107. *Id.* § 294.

108. *Id.* §§ 294, 295.

109. *Id.* §§ 191, 294. *See* People v. Axelsen, 119 N.E. 708 (N.Y. 1918).

110. 1881 N.Y. Laws ch. 676, § 294(1), (2).

111. *Id.* § 297.

New York's abortion laws remained essentially unaltered after 1881, except for renumbering in various recodifications, until the reform of 1970.[112] The conclusion seems inescapable, however, that the New York statutes, like those in other states, were adopted both to protect fetal life and to protect the health of the mother. Concern for the dangers that elective abortions posed to mothers does not change the reality of the concern for fetal life, even early in gestation. Despite New York's continuation of the quickening distinction, New York treated abortion at all stages of pregnancy, at least after January 1, 1830, as a serious crime, only its degree varying with quickening. After 1845, unlike the law in some states, the mother herself was guilty of a crime for submitting to an abortion on a pre-quick as well as a quick child. Just as the controversy over the reform of abortion laws was beginning, a New York court finally expressly acknowledged the statutory purpose of protecting fetal life.[113] Only thereafter, 134 years after New York's first abortion statute was adopted, did some seek to deny the purpose of protecting fetal life in order to justify changing abortion laws, a denial unsustainable in the face of the clear historical record.

# Changes in the Practice of Abortions in the Late Nineteenth Century

*Suffering was the only thing that made me feel I was alive*
*Thought that's just how much it cost to survive in this world.*

—Carly Simon[114]

All abortions, and particularly intrusive abortions, were still highly dangerous and apparently rare events in 1840.[115] Intrusion abortions thereafter became steadily more common during the

---

112. Means I, *supra* note 54, at 491–92.

113. People v. Lovell, 242 N.Y.S.2d 958 (N.Y. Cty. Ct. 1963). *See also* Endresz v. Friedberg, 248 N.E.2d 901, 904 (N.Y. 1969) (same conclusion, but without reference to any particular statute). For similar decisions recognizing that abortion statutes were intended to protect fetal life and recognize fetal personhood from other states, see Rosen v. Louisiana Bd. Med. Examiners, 318 F. Supp. 1217 (E.D. La. 1970), *vacated after* Roe v. Wade, 412 U.S. 902 (1973); Trent v. State, 73 So. 834 (Ala. Ct. App. 1916); Nelson v. Planned Parenthood, 505 P.2d 580 (Ariz. 1973); Hall v. People, 201 P.2d 382 (Colo. 1948); Passley v. State, 21 S.E.2d 232 (Ga. 1942); Nash v. Meyer, 31 P.2d 273 (Idaho 1934); State v. Alcorn, 64 P. 1014 (Idaho 1901); Cheaney v. State, 285 N.E.2d 265 (Ind. 1972); Joy v. Brown, 252 P.2d 889 (Kan. 1953); State v. Miller, 133 P. 878 (Kan. 1913); Sasaki v. Commonwealth, 485 S.W.2d 897 (Ky. 1972), *vacated after* Roe v. Wade, 410 U.S. 951 (1973); Rodgers v. Danforth, 486 S.W.2d 258 (Mo. 1972); State v. Siciliano, 121 A.2d 490 (N.J. 1956); State v. Hoover, 113 S.E.2d 281 (N.C. 1960); State v. Powell, 106 S.E. 133 (N.C. 1921); Williams v. Marion Rapid Transit, 87 N.E.2d 334 (Ohio 1949) (*dictum*); State v. Tippie, 105 N.E. 75 (Ohio 1913); Bowlan v. Lunsford, 54 P.2d 666 (Okla. 1936); Mallison v. Pomeroy, 291 P.2d 225 (Or. 1955) (*dictum*); State v. Ausplund, 167 P. 1019 (Or. 1917); State v. Farnam, 161 P. 417 (Or. 1916); State v. Atwood, 102 P. 295, *aff'd on reh'g*, 104 P. 195 (Or. 1909); State v. Steadman, 51 S.E.2d 91 (S.C. 1948); State v. Munson, 201 N.W.2d 123 (S.D. 1972), *vacated after* Roe v. Wade, 410 U.S. 950 (1973); Thompson v. State, 493 S.W.2d 913 (Tex. Ct. Crim. App. 1971), *vacated after* Roe v. Wade, 410 U.S. 950 (1973); Anderson v. Commonwealth, 58 S.E.2d 72 (Va. 1950); Miller v. Bennett, 56 S.E.2d 217 (Va. 1949); State v. Cox, 84 P.2d 357 (Was. 1938). *See also* People v. Belous, 458 P.2d 194, 209 (Cal. 1969) (Burke, J., dissenting). *But see* State v. Jordan, 42 S.E.2d 674 (N.C. 1947) (indicating that abortion statutes were not intended to protect fetal life before quickening). For the nineteenth century cases, see Chapter 6, at note 186.

114. Carly Simon & Jacob Brackman, *Haven't Got Time for the Pain* (1974).

115. *See* Chapter 6, at notes 332–413.

nineteenth century.[116] The most telling indication of this is the advent of septic abortions from incomplete or incompetently performed abortions as a significant item in hospital medical records after 1880.[117] So long as the abortion techniques that were most likely to accomplish the desired goal were injurious or ingestive, however, abortion remained more dangerous than successful, and consequently rare.[118] Indeed, early in this period medical groups often condemned infanticide, not abortion, although Mohr and other pro-abortion historians generally interpret these condemnations to have been directed at abortion without considering whether the physicians might actually have meant infanticide.[119] Doctors and lawyers, of course, well knew how to express the idea of "ante-natal infanticide" if that is what they meant.[120] One might also pause to ask that if by "infanticide" nineteenth-century speakers and writers meant abortion, what does that tell us about their motives in opposing abortion?

Developments in medical technology in the nineteenth century combined to make intrusion abortions practical by the end of the century. Eventually—in the twentieth century—intrusion abortions apparently became physically safer for the mother than childbirth at least if the abortion were performed before the fifteenth week of gestation, although that statement remains controversial even today.[121] Two key sorts of development were those pertaining directly to the performance of abortions, and those pertaining to surgery generally.

Several significant improvements in the technique for intrusion abortion occurred in the nineteenth century. Joseph Récantier, an early French gynecologist, modified the curette (a kind of blunt-headed knife) by lengthening and thinning the handle, creating the first "uterine curette" purportedly for treatment of cysts and tumors.[122] Thereafter uterine curettes were steadily refined, and one was reported in use in France among "nonmedical abortionists" by 1878.[123] The real breakthrough, however, came with the invention in the 1880s of Thorolf Hager's dilator that made the dilation and curettage procedure (a "D & C") safe and accurate.[124] A D & C involved using dilators to force open the cervix to create a passage into the uterus and a curette to scrape the inside of the uterus. Ironically, Hager invented his dilator not for doing abortions, but rather to treat "septic abortions" after a partial miscarriage (spontaneous or induced). Sometime around 1890, the D & C began to be used to initiate abortions, but only around World War I did it become a common means inducing abortions, use by non-medical abortionists as well as by physicians.[125]

The doing of a D & C relied on the more general technologies of analgesics, anesthetics, antiseptics, and (eventually) antibiotics for safety and comfort. The application of analgesics, anesthetics, antiseptics, and antibiotics became the true key to the successful development of intrusion abortions, for otherwise the pain-induced shock and risk of infection would have kept

---

116. Mohr, *supra* note 31, at 48–85, 94–98, 149–52, 173–76; Joseph Dellapenna, *The History of Abortion: Technology, Morality, and Law*, 40 U. Pitt. L. Rev. 359, 411–13 (1979); Means II, *supra* note 52, at 382–92.

117. Edward Shorter, A History of Women's Bodies 191–96 (Pelican Books ed. 1984).

118. *See generally* Chapter 1.

119. *See, e.g.,* Emma Drake, What a Young Wife Ought to Know 130 (1901); *Editorial,* 30 Bos. Med. & Surgical J. no. 15, at 302 (May 15, 1844). *See also* Mohr, *supra* note 31, at 49, 192, 300 n.30; James Mohr, Doctors and the Law: Medical Jurisprudence in Nineteenth-Century America 21–22, 43, 55–56 (1993); Shorter, *supra* note 116, at 179; Lucia Zender, Women, Crime, and Custody in Victorian England 29–30, 38–39, 88–90 (1991); Siegel, *supra* note 31, at 285 n.85.

120. *See, e.g.,* Andrew Nebinger, Criminal Abortion: Its Extent and Prevention 25 (1870).

121. *See* Chapter 10, at notes 9–17. There is no disagreement over the effect of the procedure on the fetus.

122. Shorter, *supra* note 117, at 205.

123. *Id.* at 207.

124. Kenny, *supra* note 34, at 179–81; Kerry Petersen, Abortion Regimes 50 (1993); Shorter, *supra* note 117, at 203–07.

125. Shorter, *supra* note 117, at 205–06. *See, e.g.,* Davis Hart, Guide to Midwifery 415 (1912).

abortion, whether legal or illegal, akin to suicide. Morphine was the first truly successful anal-
gesic, reported in use by 1806.[126] Morphine was followed by a seemingly endless list of pain-sup-
pressing drugs in use today. Experiments with chloroform, ethyl ether, and nitrous oxide began
in Britain and America in the 1840s and came into general use as anesthetics gradually thereafter.[127] Joseph Lister published his findings in on the importance of antisepsis in 1867; antiseptic practices came into general use after 1884.[128] Even such a simple arrangement as the use of
surgical gloves, introduced by W.S. Halsted at Johns Hopkins University in 1899, was an important means of saving lives.[129] Antibiotics came on the scene considerably later. Sulfa drugs became available after 1930, penicillin in 1940, and the list continues to grow. Justice Blackmun
recognized the significance of antibiotics for the availability of abortion in his opinion in *Roe*.[130]

Developments in surgery generally were, of course, not directed at intrusion abortions, but
they were embraced with particular enthusiasm in the nascent practice of obstetrics. This is particularly true for Lister's antiseptic practices because of the dramatic impact it had on the earlier
rampant "childbed fever" that was the greatest fear of women giving birth.[131] The general medical
developments had similar impact on the safety of abortions, much as they did on all surgical procedures,[132] although the developments created risks of their own. Anesthetics in particular are
high-risk procedures as evidenced by the significantly higher costs of insurance for anesthesiolo-
gists than for most other medical specialties.[133] As the timing of these developments suggest, intrusion techniques did not become truly safe until the end of the nineteenth century or the middle of twentieth century. Even before then, however, intrusion techniques might have been safer
than other techniques for abortion. We can only guess at the precise timing of this transition.

Well into the nineteenth century, then, most of these developments lay in the future. The
practice of abortion remained dangerous and primitive. Historians who claim otherwise are

---

126. 3 A History of Science 301 (René Taton ed. 1965).

127. *Id.* at 499–500. *See, e.g.,* J.C. Atkinson, *Chloroform: The Successful Obliteration of the Senses during Inhalation*, The Lancet, Mar. 15, 1855, at 302.

128. 3 A History of Science, *supra* note 127, at 301, 394, 508–10; C.D. Haagenson & Wyntham Lloyd,
A Hundred Years of Medicine 296–97 (1943); Charles Rosenberg, The Care of Strangers: The Rise
of America's Hospital System 137–50 (1987); Gert Brieger, *American Surgery and the Germ Theory of Dis-
ease*, 40 Bull. Hist. Med. 135 (1966). Some would attribute the development of antiseptic theory to a Hungarian physician working in Vienna, Ignác Semmelweiss. *See* Sherwin Nuland, The Doctors' Plague:
Germs, Childbed Fever, and the Strange Story of Ignác Simmelweiss (2003); K. Codell Carter &
George Tate, *The Earliest-Known Account of Semmelweiss's Initiation of Disinfection at Vienna's Allgemeines
Krankenhaus*, 65 Bull. Hist. Med. 252 (1991); Owen Wangentseen, *Nineteenth-Century Wound Management
of the Parturient Uterus and Compound Fracture: The Semmelweiss-Lister Priority Controversy*, Bull. N.Y.
Acad. Med., Aug. 1970, at 565.

129. *Id.* at 510. *See generally* George Rosen, A History of Public Health 315–19 (1958).

130. 410 U.S. at 149.

131. *See, e.g.,* Christopher Lawrence, *Democratic, Divine, and Heroic: The Historiography of Surgery*, in
Medical Theory, Surgical Practice: Studies in the History of Surgery 1, 25–26 (Christopher
Lawrence ed. 1992) (quoting a John Erickson, writing in 1881, to the effect that antisepsis was invented by ob-
stetricians independently of Joseph Lister).

132. *See* Howard Kelly, *History of Gynecology in America*, in A Cyclopedia of American Medical Biography i, xxxiii–xl (1912). *See generally* Arturo Castiglioni, A History of Medicine 722–24, 844–45,
1062–64 (2nd ed. 1947); Elliot Friedson, The Profession of Medicine 16 (1970); Regina Morantz-
Sanchez, Conduct Unbecoming a Woman: Medicine on Trial in Brooklyn 98–99 (1999); Martin Pernick, A Calculus of Suffering: Pain, Professionalism and Anesthesia in Nineteenth-Century
America (1985); Kerry Petersen, Abortion Regimes 31–32 (1993); Irvine Loudon, *Maternal Mortality:
1880–1950. Some Regional and International Comparisons*, 1 Soc. Hist. Med. 183 (1988). "Postmodern" historians tend to assume that causation ran the other way, that anesthesia was discovered because physicians
wanted to do surgery rather than that physicians became more willing to do surgery because anesthesia was
available. *See, e.g.,* Lawrence, *supra* note 132, at 24.

133. *See generally* Jacob Pearl Greenhill, Analgesia and Anesthesia in Obstetrics (2nd ed. 1962).

dealing in delusion. James Mohr's quotation of a pharmacist, Ely Van de Warker, who wrote in the late-nineteenth century, is a good example of this remarkably consistent misreading of the evidence relating to abortion practices. Mohr quoted Van de Warker as evidence of the supposedly widespread marketing of abortifacients during the middle and later years of the century. The quoted passage actually reveals, rather more clearly than Mohr seems to have realized, the true nature of the ingestion techniques then being purveyed and the questionable ethics of the purveyors—even assuming that one approves of the free availability of abortion:

> The apothecary usually compounds from two to five drugs, which he regards as emmenagogues, in the form of a mixture, bolus, or pill. I have known of perfectly inert drugs being mixed and sold to women who applied for abortifacient drugs for a criminal purpose. But generally druggists do not thus trifle with their reputations as skillful abortionists. The temerity with which even respectable druggists will sell violent and noxious drugs to women far advanced in pregnancy forms one of the most alarming features of this trade.[134]

Van de Warker's comment indicates that, when he was writing (1873), most advertisements of abortion services (and presumably most attempts of abortion) still involved ingestion techniques rather than intrusion techniques. Van de Warker suggests that abortionists were ruthless con-artists rather than purveyors of a service to the public—as the evidence developed by Mohr and other pro-abortion historians amply demonstrates.[135] Much the same was true of those advertising contraceptives for sale, and remained true well into the twentieth century, in part because of the very illegality of the advertising of such devices.[136] Thus Norman Himes reports a thinly veiled advertisement for Lysol as a contraceptive douche,[137] while an exposé in 1934 disclosed the advertising of ineffective cervical caps.[138] When it came to abortion, these well-meaning citizens (as Mohr would have us consider them) were selling a penny's worth of ineffective and dangerous drugs for several dollars (when a dollar had real value) to desperate women.[139]

An excellent example of the unscrupulous nature of the emerging commercial abortionists of the mid-nineteenth century is Charles Lohman, who styled himself as "Dr. A.M. Mauriceau."[140] Lohman claimed in his book to impart knowledge of an abortion technique that was "perfectly safe...and will 'impart no pain.'"[141] Lohman, a printer by trade who worked for the *New York Herald* before he began to market purported abortifacients, wrote the book under an assumed name, that of a famous eighteenth century French obstetrician.[142] Lohman

---

134. MOHR, *supra* note 31, at 60, quoting from Ely Van de Warker, *The Criminal Use of Proprietary or Advertised Nostrums,* 17 N.Y. MED. J. 23–35 (1873).

135. ANGUS MCLAREN, BIRTH CONTROL IN NINETEENTH-CENTURY ENGLAND 232–40 (1978); MOHR, *supra* note 31, at 9, 21–22, 55–60, 71–73, 125. *See also* BRITISH MED. ASS'N, MORE SECRET REMEDIES: WHAT THEY COST AND WHAT THEY CONTAIN 184–206 (1912) ("SECRET REMEDIES").

136. *See* GORDON, *supra* note 31, at 317–20; RACHEL LYNN PALMER & SARAH GREENBERG, FACTS AND FRAUD IN WOMEN'S HYGIENE(1936);

137. NORMAN HIMES, MEDICAL HISTORY OF CONTRACEPTION 329 (1936);

138. Dorothy Dunbar Bromley, *Birth Control and the Depression,* HARPER'S MAG., Oct. 1934, at 363.

139. SECRET REMEDIES, supra note 135, at 184–86.

140. A.M. MAURICEAU [CHARLES LOHMAN], THE MARRIED WOMAN'S PRIVATE MEDICAL COMPANION, EMBRACING THE TREATMENT OF MENSTRUATION, OR MONTHLY TURNS, DURING THEIR STOPPAGE, IRREGULARITY, OR ENTIRE SUPPRESSION. PREGNANCY, AND HOW IT MAY BE DETERMINED; WITH THE TREATMENT OF ITS VARIOUS DISEASES. DISCOVERY TO PREVENT PREGNANCY; ITS GREAT AND IMPORTANT NECESSITY WHERE MALFORMATION OR INABILITY EXISTS TO GIVE BIRTH. TO PREVENT MISCARRIAGE OR ABORTION. WHEN PROPER AND NECESSARY TO EFFECT MISCARRIAGE WHEN ATTENDED WITH ENTIRE SAFETY (1847).

141. *Id.* at 169. *See also* MOHR, *supra* note 31, at 77 (quoting another source saying that skillful abortion rarely produced death).

142. Historian Janet Brodie has identified the psuedo-Mauriceau as Joseph Trow, Ann Lohman's brother, because Trow apparently held the copyright at one point. The truth of the matter does not affect the point in

was the husband of "Madame Restell" (Ann Lohman), the most notorious professional abortionist in the United States at the time.[143] Lohman not only used a pseudonym, but he also
falsely claimed in the book to be a "Professor of Diseases of Women" under a name meant to
indicate that the author was both European trained and famous in Paris for his skill.[144]
Lohman falsely claimed to have conducted many famous operations reported in the *Bulletin of
the Academy of Medicine*.[145] And Lohman was careful to indicate that the abortions he was
promoting were intended to protect the life of mothers whose only choice was between an
early miscarriage and a nearly always-fatal Caesarian section.[146] Finally, Lohman purportedly
was advising women on how to remove "blockages" to menstrual flow rather than how to induce an abortion.[147]

At the very least, Lohman's ruses suggests a fear of being publicly identified with advocating
abortion. More likely, it suggests that the entire work is a fraud designed to promote the sale of
ineffective or dangerous abortifacients rather than a reliable source on the qualities of the techniques described in the book. Lohman actually did not reveal very much about his supposedly
safe and effective methods for inducing abortions. Instead, he instructed readers that they
could obtain the necessary pills he ("Dr. Mauriceau") recommended by mail from yet another
fictitious character invented by Lohman—Portuguese physician M.M. Desomeaux—for the
sum of five dollars.[148] Five dollars then was the cost of a month's rent for a New York City apartment. An investigative report by the British Medical Society in 1912 found that the pills and
nostrums collected in the report were sold for from 30 to as much as 500 times their cost.[149] As
suggested by Van de Warker,[150] the report found that some pills then being advertised in Britain
for relieving "obstructed menses" had no active ingredient at all.[151] Historians who favor abortion rights, however, generally fail to question the efficacy of such advertised nostrums.[152]

Just as pro-abortion historians seldom consider the efficacy of the potions or other techniques
they find, they never discussed the possibility that the entire enterprise was pure bunkum. They
would be well advised to consider sociologist Nanette Davis' apt description of professional
abortionists in the twentieth century as "medical rejects"—persons who had failed as physicians

---

the text. JANET FARRELL BRODIE, CONTRACEPTION AND ABORTION IN NINETEENTH-CENTURY AMERICA 64,
231 (1994). On Lohman's working for the *Herald*, see OLASKY, *supra* note 52, at 4.

143. *See* BRODIE, *supra* note 142, at 229–31; GORDON, *supra* note 31, at 54–58; GROSSBERG, *supra* note 51,
at 167; ALAN KELLER, SCANDALOUS LADY: THE LIFE AND TIMES OF MADAME RESTELL, NEW YORK'S MOST FA-
MOUS ABORTIONIST (1981); BARBARA MILBAUER & BERT OBRENTZ, THE LAW GIVETH: LEGAL ASPECTS OF THE
ABORTION CONTROVERSY 138–42 (1983); MOHR, *supra* note 31, at 48–53, 88–89, 94, 96, 125–28, 182, 199;
OLASKY, *supra* note 79, at 111–12, 150–52, 158–61; OLASKY, *supra* note 52, at 4–13.

144. MAURICEAU, *supra* note 140, at 15–16. Ironically, French supporters of abortion in the later nineteenth century would identify the sources of their knowledge as "American." *See* SARAH BLAFFER HRDY,
MOTHER NATURE: A HISTORY OF MOTHERS, INFANTS, AND NATURAL SELECTION 21 (1999).

145. MAURICEAU, *supra* note 140, at 281.

146. *Id.* at 168, 181.

147. *Id.* at 15–16.

148. *Id.* at 104, 108, 118–19, 146, 169.

149. SECRET REMEDIES, *supra* note 135, at 184–85, 192–206.

150. Quoted *supra* at note 134.

151. SECRET REMEDIES, *supra* note 135, at 200–03. *See also* BARBARA BROOKES, ABORTION IN ENGLAND
1900–1967, at 29, 117–18 (1988); KENNY, *supra* note 34, at 186–87.

152. *See. e.g.,* BRODIE, *supra* note 142, at 71–72; DEGLER, *supra* note 29, at 199–201, 203, 216–17,
219–220, 243; ANGUS MCLAREN, REPRODUCTIVE RITUALS 106–07 (1984) ("MCLAREN, REPRODUCTIVE RITU-
ALS"); MOHR, *supra* note 31, at 65–66; MOHR, *supra* note 31, at 60–68. McLaren's confidence in the efficacy of
the potions he reports is all the more remarkable as he himself studied the late nineteenth-century London
frauds. Angus McLaren, *Abortion in England, 1890–1914,* 20 VICTORIAN STUDIES 379, 389–92 (Summer 1977).

for reasons ranging from drug addiction or alcoholism to senility to having been caught in other criminal activity.[153] Charles Lohman seems to have been a pure criminal.

The fraud itself might be explanation enough why those advertising abortifacients almost invariably resorted to euphemisms for the purposes the goods they sold were to achieve.[154] The advertisements may have been thinly veiled, but veiled they always were. The utter lack of direct reference to abortion suggests something more—that abortion was at least considered something not a subject of polite communication if not something subject to serious opprobrium. And in fact, the only people in the early nineteenth century who "openly" advocated abortion were professional abortionists—if one can consider a book published under an assumed name that served primarily as an advertisement for fraudulent abortifacient pills to be "open" advocacy.[155] Charles Lohman is hardly the only example of this "advocacy." Consider also the even earlier book of Charles Knowlton, a book that also contains an open advocacy of abortion on demand.[156] The book was a prolonged study of contraception and was written primarily to advocate contraception.[157] Even historian Janet Brodie, who saw Knowlton as a champion of women's rights in the struggle for reproductive control, had to concede that "Knowlton's understanding of the process of conception was largely inaccurate by today's knowledge."[158] Casting the best light on these books, one would have to describe them as the nineteenth-century equivalents of "infomercials"—the program-length commercials that proliferate on late night and cable television.[159] Brodie even conceded that "the lines were increasingly blurred between sober advice tracts and lengthy advertising booklets for birth control products and services."[160]

# How Many Abortions?

*Sometimes numbers tell us what adjectives and adverbs cannot.*

—Richard Neumann jr.[161]

The slow improvement in the safety and effectiveness of abortion techniques during the nineteenth century raises as a serious question, probably for the first time in history, the question of just how many abortions there were. Medical record keeping improved steadily during the nine-

---

153. Nanette Davis, From Crime to Choice 89 (1985).
154. Degler, *supra* note 29, at 230–31, 243; Olasky, *supra* note 79, at 94–95, 267–68; Olasky, *supra* note 52, at 4–17, 20–22, 40–42, 48–51.
155. Degler, *supra* note 29, at 243.
156. Charles Knowlton, The Fruits of Philosophy 97–98 (1832). *See also* W.C. Lispenard, Private Medical Guide 194 (1854).
157. *See generally* Brodie, *supra* note 142, at 94–106.
158. *Id.* at 98.
159. *See, e.g.*, Edward Bliss Foote, Medical Common Sense Applied to the Cause, Prevention, and Cure of Chronic Disease and Unhappiness in Marriage 378–80 (rev. ed. 1864); Hiram Knox Root, The People's Medical Lighthouse (1854); Russell Trall, Pathology of the Reproductive Organs; Embracing All Forms of Sexual Disorders (1862); Russell Trall, Sexual Physiology: A Scientific and Popular Exposition of the Fundamental Problems in Sociology (1866); E.M. Buckingham, *Criminal Abortion*, 10 Cin. Lancet & Observer 139 (1867); S.K. Crawford, *Criminal Abortion: A Special Report*, Trans. 22d Anniv. Meeting Ill. St. Med. Soc'y 74 (1872); Henry Gibbons, sr., *On Foeticide*, 21 Pac. Med. & Surgical J. 97, 212 (1878); William McCollum, *Criminal Abortion*, Trans. Vt. Med. Soc'y for 1865, at 40.
160. Brodie, *supra* note 142, at 181. *See also id.* at 185–86, 189–91, 237–41.
161. Richard Neumann jr., *Women in Legal Education: What the Statistics Show*, 50 J. Legal Educ. 313, 313 (2000).

teenth century, making possible modern statistical studies of at least certain aspects of medical practice in the later years of the century, but not for abortion. Abortion was a crime. Abortionists kept no records. Precise estimates of the incidence of abortion in the later years of the century remain as much a matter of guesswork as it was in 1840 or 1850 when all medical record keeping was inadequate. Modern historians nonetheless continue to guess as to how many abortions were performed, while providing as little reason for confidence in their "guestimates" in the later years of the century as in the middle of the century.

Knowledge of how dangerous abortion still was during most or all of the nineteenth century ought to make one very cautious about accepting supposed proofs of the commonness of abortion in times past. One should be especially wary of such "evidence" as casual accusations that another person is an abortionist found in a seventeenth-century diary, references by eighteenth-century novelists or poets to the "vast clienteles" of abortionists, or advertisements in eighteenth-century newspapers.[162] What then of occasional estimates of the incidence of abortion by observers in the nineteenth century. Such estimates prove, upon examination, to be as unreliable as modern studies, being based on nothing but a single observer's personal experience without any attempt by the observer to evaluate whether his (and nearly always it was a man) experience was actually representative of society at large.

Consider the guestimates of Dr. Edwin Hale. Hale wrote in 1860 that more than 90 percent of American women had had abortions and that as many as 50 percent of American pregnancies ended in abortion.[163] Only six years later, Hale wrote that 25 percent of pregnancies ended in abortion,[164] while a year after that he wrote that 67 percent of pregnancies ended in abortion.[165] Hale's attitude towards abortion is as elusive as his statistics. Hale was a homeopath, rather than an allopath, and there is some evidence that he was, according to Mohr, "much less ideologically opposed to abortion than members of the regular medical sect [allopathic physicians]."[166] Mohr also saw Hale as actually supporting the desirability of abortion for a variety of reasons and advocating tolerance for it "regardless of circumstances."[167] Indeed, Hale's references to his own first-hand knowledge of abortion suggest that he was, if not a professional abortionist, at least an experienced one.[168] Yet Mohr, on the very next page after describing Hale as sympathetic to abortion, dismissed Hale's estimate that 67 percent of pregnancies ended in abortion as "a hyperbole for public effect" by an anti-abortion crusader.[169] Indeed, the title of Dr. Hale's third book (The Great Crime of the Nineteenth Century[170]) suggests as much. A responsible historian could only conclude that Hale had no clue as to the true incidence of abortion. Mohr, after dutifully reporting Hale's gyrations, accepted Hale's low-end figure of 25 percent as accurate, without bothering to offer any reason for why it was more trustworthy than the figures Mohr rejected.[171]

Dr. Horatio Robinson Storer and attorney Franklin Fiske Heard, two leading anti-abortion advocates from the later middle nineteenth century, provided yet another often quoted set of

162. For one who seemingly takes such sources as irrefutable proof, see McLaren, Reproductive Rituals, *supra* note 152, at 99–100.

163. Edwin Hale, On the Homeopathic Treatment of Abortion, Its Causes and Consequences; with Some Suggestions, and Indications for the Use of the New Remedies 5–15 (1860).

164. Edwin Hale, A Systematic Treatise on Abortion 22, 29–30, 57 (1866).

165. Edwin Hale, The Great Crime of the Nineteenth Century, Why Is It Committed? Who Are the Criminals? How Shall They Be Detected? How Shall They Be Punished? 4 (1867).

166. Mohr, *supra* note 31, at 76, 79, 173–74. *See also* Brodie, *supra* note 142, at 278.

167. Mohr, *supra* note 31, at 77, 174.

168. Hale, *supra* note 163, at 29–30, 234–37, 290–308, 313–20.

169. Mohr, *supra* note 31, at 78, 173–76.

170. Hale, *supra* note 165.

171. Mohr, *supra* note 31, at 76–78.

guestimates at about the same time as Hale was writing.[172] In 1868, Storer and Heard estimated, through an elaborate compilation of national and international vital statistics, that 20 percent of American pregnancies ended in abortion.[173] For the United States, Storer and Heard used data from Boston, New York, and Philadelphia, as well as from Massachusetts generally. We have no way of determining whether the data were accurate for the localities where they originated or whether the data were representative of the nation as a whole. Other sources, while relying on the work of Storer and Heard, produced estimates ranging from 25 percent to "more than half" of pregnancies ending in abortion.[174] Yet another physician writing at about the same time estimated the rate to be as low as 10 percent.[175] Again, Mohr reported these several estimates, sticking to his support of the 20–25 percent range without offering any particular reason for his choice.[176] Mohr also claimed that the incidence of abortion was similar throughout the nation even while admitting that no real evidence supported that claim either.[177]

Which, if any, of these many guesses is correct? No one knows, but there are reasons to be skeptical of them all. One should not be surprised that a professional abortionist would believe that 90 percent or more of women have had abortions and that abortions accounted for 50 percent, 67 percent, or even more of all pregnancies.[178] That probably accurately represented the abortionist's personal experience. After all, how often does someone who works primarily as an abortionist encounter professionally a woman not seeking an abortion? Professional abortionists might also have exaggerated the incidence in an effort to justify their activities, as also would professional or strongly committed anti-abortion crusaders.[179] Whether either sort of claim was (or is) at all representative of the general population is another matter.[180]

Mohr recognized these reasons for exaggeration and, on that basis, discounted the more extreme estimates.[181] Other historians have been less skeptical of the extreme estimates.[182] Even after recognizing the reasons why the larger estimates could not be accepted, Mohr did not consider that similar experiential bias could taint even the more moderate guesses he preferred.[183] After all, even physicians without an economic or political stake in the numbers would also professionally encounter disproportionate numbers of women who were seeking or had undergone abortions; it's the nature of the job. No one was a more prominent anti-abortion crusader than

---

172. On Storer's career as an anti-abortion crusader, see *infra* at notes 338–470.

173. STORER & HEARD, *supra* note 41, at 1–136.

174. HORACE KNAPP, WOMEN'S CONFIDENTIAL ADVISER ON THE HEALTH AND DISEASES OF WOMEN 72 (1873); William Ashbury Hall, *Criminal Abortion and Its Treatment,* 8 NW. LANCET 113 (1888); George Smith, *Foeticide,* 10 DET. REV. MED. & PHARMACY 211 (1875); Morse Stewart, *Criminal Abortion,* 2 DET. REV. PHARMACY & MED. 7 (1867). *See also* MOHR, *supra* note 31, at 79–82.

175. J. Miller, *Criminal Abortion,* 1 K.C. MED. REC. 295, 296 (1884).

176. MOHR, *supra* note 31, at 78–82, 159.

177. *Id.* at 98–100.

178. HALE, *supra* note 163, at 5–7; HALE, *supra* note 165, at 4.

179. OLASKY, *supra* note 52, at 290; ROSALIND POLLACK PETCHESKY, ABORTION AND WOMEN'S CHOICE: THE STATE, SEXUALITY, AND REPRODUCTIVE FREEDOM 77–78 (rev. ed. 1990). For examples of such apparently exaggerated claims from anti-abortion crusaders, see Hall, *supra* note 174; Smith, *supra* note 174; Stewart, *supra* note 174.

180. For similar claims regarding France, see F. BROCHARD, LA VÉRITÉ SUR LES TROUVÉS 98–99 (1876); AMBROISE TARDIEU, ÉTUDE MÉDICO-LÉGALE SUR L'AVORTEMENT 5 (5th ed. 1898). *See also* Angus McLaren, *Abortion in France: Women and the Regulation of Family Size, 1800–1914,* 10 FRENCH HIST. STUD. 461, 479 (1978).

181. MOHR, *supra* note 31, at 78. *See also* DEGLER, *supra* note 29, at 229–32.

182. *See, e.g.,* REAGAN, *supra* note 52, at 24–25; SMITH-ROSENBERG, *supra* note 51, at 220–21.

183. MOHR, *supra* note 31, at 76–82.

Dr. Storer, yet he reported having been called upon to treat no less than 15 women in a space of six months for complications from criminal abortions.[184]

Marvin Olasky concluded from such incidents that the occurrence of abortion was common in the nineteenth century, giving us a figure of 160,000 per year in the 1860s.[185] This is smaller than Mohr's estimate. Although Mohr did not report an actual number, his percentage rates (17–20 percent of annual births)[186] would have amounted to 300,000 to 400,000 per year. Neither they, nor other historians who provided similar estimates,[187] ever consider the medical realities of abortion, and hence the small likelihood that any such numbers of abortions were actually achieved, regardless of how many abortions were attempted. In the end, Olasky admits that the figure could actually have been much lower and that he has no real basis for settling on the figure that he gives.[188] Furthermore, Olasky explicitly conflates abortion and infanticide until at least the mid-nineteenth century,[189] obscuring the actual incidence of abortion in a society where it remained a highly dangerous procedure with still unperfected techniques, largely in the hands of con artists.[190]

Discounting the claims of the abortionists, Olasky justifies his estimate by reliance on the impressionistic reports of doctors opposed to abortion.[191] Yet just as a personal-injury lawyer is likely to hold an exaggerated personal impression of the frequency of auto-accidents or exploding soft-drink bottles, a doctor, whether describing his own impressions or reporting the results of surveys of other doctors, is likely to overstate the incidence of abortion and of abortion's complications. The editors of Boston's leading medical journal of the middle of the nineteenth century made the same point in their review of one of Storer's other books, expressing their skepticism that criminal abortion could possibly be "so general as some, whose special practice is the most likely to bring them into cognizance of it, are led to believe."[192]

Olasky only recognized this problem in a footnote dealing with estimates for the early twentieth century rather than for the nineteenth century.[193] Mohr acknowledged the problem in discussing why many nineteenth-century physicians insisted that abortion was most widespread among the "better" classes—those were the classes from which physicians drew their patients.[194] Mohr also argued that abortions were too expensive for lower class women, not noting that this contradicted his assertion that abortions were widely available, safe, and effective.[195] What is probably reliable about the nineteenth-century guestimates is the consistent impression that abortion became more common after 1840 even if we have no basis for estimating the actual rate.[196]

Some find support for the notion that abortion was becoming more common in the demographic transition that would become a major emphasis in the abortion debates of the late nineteenth century.[197] The demographic transition began in the late eighteenth century, seeing

184. STORER & HEARD, *supra* note 41, at 56.
185. OLASKY, *supra* note 79, at 290–91.
186. MOHR, *supra* note 31, at 50.
187. *See, e.g.,* SMITH-ROSENBERG, *supra* note 51, at 220–21.
188. OLASKY, *supra* note 79, at 291–92.
189. *Id.* at 19–41, 48–49, 68, 85, 288, 293 n.31.
190. See the text *supra* at notes 134–60, and Chapter 6, at notes 332–413.
191. OLASKY, *supra* note 79, at 43–49, 57–58, 221–33.
192. *Review of* Why Not? A Book for Every Woman, 15 BOS. MED. & SURGICAL J. no. 3, at 74 (July 21, 1866).
193. OLASKY, *supra* note 79, at 293 n.31.
194. MOHR, *supra* note 31, at 94–95.
195. *Id.* at 95–98.
196. *Id.* at 74–76. *See, e.g.,* Atlee & O'Donnell, *supra* note 48, at 250–51; John Trader, *Criminal Abortion,* 11 ST. L. MED. & SURGICAL J., n.s. 583 (1874).
197. *See* Chapter 8, at notes 164–69; Chapter 9, at notes 36–43.

the average number of children per American woman go from 7 in 1800 to 3.5 in 1900.[198] The demographic transition varied widely in different regions of the United States. At first, it was largely a northern phenomenon, with southern women continuing to bear eight to ten children nearly until the Civil War.[199] The southern demographic transition, when it did occur, consistently lagged behind that of the North. The pattern of declining family size continued into the twentieth century despite the increasingly effective prosecution of abortion and the criminalization of the dissemination of information about contraception, driving both practices underground.[200] Even Mohr, however, conceded that abortion could not have been the primary means by which the transition took place.[201] In fact, the most probable techniques behind the demographic transition in the nineteenth century were extended lactation and sexual abstinence.[202]

The rarity of medical treatment of septic abortions before 1880 and the rising rates of bridal pregnancies and illegitimate births suggests that abortion was not, in absolute terms, such a common practice as Mohr, or his nineteenth-century sources, thought.[203] We have even less evidence about who was having these abortions although there is some evidence to suggest that the major market for abortion services was the growing corps of prostitutes found in all sizable settlements.[204] We are left then with the conclusion that while abortion was becoming more common, probably throughout the nineteenth century, it was not in absolute terms common, and it certainly was not seen as a matter of moral or social indifference. It is time to consider those who led the fight to suppress abortion in the face of technical advances that began to make it a feasible alternative for women for the first time in human history.

---

198. MOHR, *supra* note 31, at 82–85.

199. CATHERINE CLINTON, THE PLANTATION MISTRESS: WOMAN'S WORLD IN THE OLD SOUTH 152–53 (1982); JOHN D'EMILIO & ESTELLE FREEDMAN, INTIMATE MATTERS: A HISTORY OF SEXUALITY IN AMERICA 58 (1988); RICHARD STECKEL, THE ECONOMICS OF U.S. SLAVE AND SOUTHERN WHITE FERTILITY 176 (1985); BERTRAM WYATT-BROWN, SOUTHERN HONOR: ETHICS AND BEHAVIOR IN THE OLD SOUTH 205 (1982); Jan Lewis & Kenneth Lockridge, *"Sally Has Been Sick": Pregnancy and Family Limitation among Virginia Gentry Women, 1780–1830*, 22 J. SOCIAL HIST. 5, 13–14 (1988); Maris Vinovskis, *Socioeconomic Determinants of Interstate Fertility Differentials in the United States*, 6 J. INTERDISCIPLINARY HIST. 375 (1976).

200. D'EMILIO & FREEDMAN, *supra* note 51, at 173–75; PAULA FASS, THE DAMNED AND THE BEAUTIFUL: AMERICAN YOUTH IN THE 1920's, at 60–61, 66–67 (1977).

201. MOHR, *supra* note 31, at 83.

202. *See* Chapter 2, at notes 122–239.

203. SHORTER, *supra* note 117, at 190–97; Estelle Freedman, *Historical Interpretation and Legal Advocacy: Rethinking the* Webster *Amicus Brief*, 12 PUB. HISTORIAN 27, 28–30. *See also* R. Sauer, *Infanticide and Abortion in Nineteenth-Century Britain*, 32 LOCAL POP. STUD. 81, 88 (1978) (concluding that abortion was still rare in England because of its danger, but, based on anecdotal sources, was much more common in America—without explaining why it would have been less dangerous).

204. *See* WILLIAM ACTON, PROSTITUTION (1857); JOHN MCDOWELL, FIRST ANNUAL REPORT OF THE NEW YORK MAGDALEN SOCIETY (1831).

# The Professionalization of
# the Practice of Medicine

*The very word justice irritates scientists. No surgeon expects to be asked if an operation for cancer is just or not. No doctor will be reproached on the grounds that the dose of penicillin he has proscribed is less or more than justice would stipulate.*

— Karl Menninger[205]

In addition to the social consensus on protecting fetal and maternal lives, the drive to professionalize the still largely disorganized practices of law and medicine did play a role in the crafting of the abortion statutes.[206] The drive to professionalize nursing that was occurring at about the same time also played a role.[207] Some scholars have seen in this process of professionalization only a nefarious conspiracy to gain an economic monopoly.[208] The process of professionalization was more complex than a simple effort to stake out an economic monopoly. Most scholars now gravitate to the view that the process represented a drive to systematize knowledge and to codify practice, not only to exclude competition but also to permit a standardized product consistent with the fundamental premises of the profession.[209] The ability to provide abstract generaliza-

---

205. KARL MENNINGER, THE CRIME OF PUNISHMENT 17 (1968).

206. *Compare* CHARLOTTE BORST, CATCHING BABIES: THE PROFESSIONALIZATION OF BIRTH, 1870–1920 (1995); *and* MOHR, *supra* note 31; *with* J. KEOWN, ABORTION, DOCTORS AND THE LAW (1988). *See generally* JOSEPH KETT, THE FORMATION OF THE AMERICAN MEDICAL PROFESSION: THE ROLE OF INSTITUTIONS, 1780–1890 (1968); NOEL & JOSE PARRY, THE RISE OF THE MEDICAL PROFESSION (1976); WILLIAM ROTHSTEIN, AMERICAN PHYSICIANS IN THE NINETEENTH CENTURY: FROM SECTS TO SCIENCE 39–174 (1972); RICHARD SHRYOCK, MEDICAL LICENSING IN AMERICA, 1650–1965, at 98–115 (1967); PAUL STARR, THE SOCIAL TRANSFORMATION OF AMERICAN MEDICINE: THE RISE OF A SOVEREIGN PROFESSION AND THE MAKING OF A VAST INDUSTRY (1982); WILLIAM WHITE, PUBLIC HEALTH AND PRIVATE GAIN (1979); ALEXANDER WILDER, HISTORY OF MEDICINE: A BRIEF OUTLINE OF MEDICAL HISTORY AND SECTS OF PHYSICIANS, FROM THE EARLIEST HISTORIC PERIOD; WITH AN EXTENDED ACCOUNT OF THE NEW SCHOOLS OF THE HEALING ART IN THE NINETEENTH CENTURY, AND ESPECIALLY A HISTORY OF THE AMERICAN ECLECTIC PRACTICE OF MEDICINE, NEVER BEFORE PUBLISHED 499–511 (1901); Charles Coventry, *History of Medical Legislation in New York,* 4 N.Y. J. MED. 151 (1845); Reginald Fitz, *The Rise and Fall of the Licensed Physician in Massachusetts, 1781–1860,* TRANS. ASS'N AM. PHYSICIANS 9 (1894). On the professionalization of medicine in England generally, see ERNEST SACKVILLE TURNER, CALL THE DOCTOR: THE SOCIAL HISTORY OF MEDICAL MEN 191–244 (1959). On the urge to professionalize law, see the Chapter 9, at notes 70–156.

207. ISABEL STEWARD & ANNE AUSTIN, A HISTORY OF NURSING 51–97 (1962).

208. *See generally* ANDREW ABBOTT, THE SYSTEM OF THE PROFESSIONS: AN ESSAY ON THE DIVISION OF EXPERT LABOR (1988); THE AUTHORITY OF EXPERTS: STUDIES IN HISTORY AND THEORY (Thomas Haskell ed. 1984); JEFFREY BERLANT, PROFESSION AND MONOPOLY (1975); BURTON BLEDSTEIN, THE CULTURE OF PROFESSIONALISM: THE MIDDLE CLASS AND THE DEVELOPMENT OF HIGHER EDUCATION IN AMERICA (1978); THOMAS BENDER, COMMUNITY AND SOCIAL CHANGE IN AMERICA (1978); TERRENCE JAMES JOHNSON, PROFESSIONS AND POWER (1972); MAGALI SARFATI LARSON, THE RISE OF PROFESSIONALISM: A SOCIOLOGICAL ANALYSIS (1977); JETHRO LIEBERMAN, THE TYRANNY OF THE EXPERTS: HOW PROFESSIONALS ARE CLOSING THE OPEN SOCIETY (1980); WILBERT MOORE, THE PROFESSIONS: ROLE AND RULES 10–13 (1970); PARRY & PARRY, *supra* note 206; PETERSEN, *supra* note 124, at 28–42; SMITH-ROSENBERG, *supra* note 51, at 227–36; STARR, *supra* note 206; MARY ROTH WALSH, DOCTORS WANTED: NO WOMEN NEED APPLY 133–39 (1977); EVAN WILLIS, MEDICAL DOMINANCE (rev. ed. 1986).

209. *See, e.g.,* RAYMOND DEVRIES, MAKING MIDWIVES LEGAL: CHILDBIRTH, MEDICINE, AND THE LAW 3–15 (2nd ed. 1996); LARSON, *supra* note 208, at 14, 225–32; JAMES FOSTER, THE IDEOLOGY OF APOLITICAL POLITICS (1986); ELIOT FREIDSON, PROFESSIONAL POWERS (1986). For a much earlier expression of this view that was temporarily eclipsed by those seeking evidence of economic monopoly, see ALEXANDER MORRIS CARR-SAUNDERS & PAUL ALEXANDER WILSON, THE PROFESSIONS (1933).

tions of professional knowledge enabled the group to define itself as a profession and to delimit its problems and tasks during a period of considerable social flux in the course of rapid industrialization, to defend those tasks from interlopers, and to adapt to new situations.[210] And, like any important historical transition, the professionalization process spanned centuries and has roots that go back at least to the high Middle Ages.[211]

The creation of a coherent national profession of medicine in the United States was seriously impeded by the hostility of the Jacksonian era to elite groups[212] and by the vast distances and poor communications of the nineteenth century. These same variables made the organization and implementation of unified professional stance on almost any question difficult to achieve. That such a stance on abortion was achieved through the efforts of a few strong leaders and of the fledgling medical societies suggests that the efforts spoke to powerful needs felt nationally.

Current fashion has it that the nineteenth century abortion statutes resulted from an allopathic conspiracy to suppress competing medical fields, particularly fields staffed largely by women.[213] This theory dismisses the expressed concern for fetal life as either a smoke screen or as the peculiar ideology of a narrow, socially unrepresentative group seeking what were purely, or at least largely, economic ends.[214] This argument seriously distorts the process by which the abortion statutes were enacted and the role physicians played in bringing about their enactment.

Physicians and their allies made little secret about their concerns. They openly stated goals such as promoting proper female behavior in the home and elsewhere.[215] Supporters of proper female behavior certainly at the time were unashamed of such views.[216] The physicians also expressed concern to promote the right sort of population growth.[217] But the physicians

---

210. ABBOTT, *supra* note 208, at 8–9; ELLIOT FRIEDSON, THE PROFESSION OF MEDICINE 137 (1970); J.A. JACKSON, PROFESSIONS AND PROFESSIONALIZATION 7–12 (1970); JOHNSON, *supra* note 208, at 45; LARSON, *supra* note 208, at 8, 54–56, 220–23; MOORE, *supra* note 208, at 15–19; T.S. PENSABENE, THE RISE OF THE MEDICAL PRACTITIONER IN VICTORIA 51–53 (1980); PETERSEN, *supra* note 124, at 31–32; STARR, *supra* note 206, at 80; ROBERT WIEBE, THE SEARCH FOR ORDER, 1877–1920 (1967).

211. *See, e.g.,* HARRIS COULTER, DIVIDED LEGACY: A HISTORY OF SCHISM IN MEDIEVAL THOUGHT (1973). *See generally* LARSON, *supra* note 208, at 2–5.

212. *See* SAMUEL HABER, THE QUEST FOR AUTHORITY AND HONOR IN THE AMERICAN PROFESSIONS, 1750–1900, at 105 (1991). *See also* Chapter 6, at notes 114–15, 268–72.

213. *See* Chapter 6, at notes 213–331.

214. *Id.* at notes 263–84.

215. *See, e.g.,* AUGUSTUS GARDNER, CONJUGAL SINS AGAINST THE LAWS OF LIFE AND HEALTH AND THEIR EFFECTS UPON THE FATHER, MOTHER, AND THE CHILD 225 (1876); HODGE, *supra* note 45, at 32–33; HORATIO ROBINSON STORER, WHY NOT? A BOOK FOR EVERYWOMAN 27, 35, 80–81 (1866); T. GAILLARD THOMAS, ABORTION AND ITS TREATMENT, FROM THE STANDPOINT OF PRACTICAL EXPERIENCE 3 (1890); D.H., *supra* note 41, at 201; Gibbons, *supra* note 159, at 111; O'Donnell & Atlee, *supra* note 48, at 240–41; Montrose Pallen, *Foeticide,* 3 MED. ARCHIVES (St. L. n.s.) 195, 195, 202–03, 205–06 (1869); Smith, *supra* note 174, at 211. *See generally* THOMAS LAQUEUR, MAKING SEX: BODY AND GENDER FROM THE GREEKS TO FREUD 2–24, 59–61 (1990); MOHR, *supra* note 31, at 88–89, 131, 141–42, 163–66, 207–08, 214, 216–17, 238; Siegel, *supra* note 31, at 291–97.

216. *See, e.g.,* Bradwell v. Illinois, 83 U.S. (16 Wall.) 130, 141 (1873) (Bradley, J., concurring) (women were physiologically incapable of being lawyers).

217. NATHAN ALLEN, CHANGES IN NEW ENGLAND POPULATION (1866); EDWARD CLARKE, SEX IN EDUCATION, OR, A FAIR CHANCE FOR GIRLS 63 (1878); GARDNER, *supra* note 215, at 5; HALE, *supra* note 164, at 4–6; NEBINGER, *supra* note 120, at 6–9; H.S. POMEROY, THE ETHICS OF MARRIAGE 39 (1888); STORER, *supra* note 215, at 63–65, 85; STORER & HEARD, *supra* note 41, at 41–53; Gibbons, *supra* note 159, at 111; Pallen, *supra* note 215, at 195, 198–99; Horatio Robinson Storer, *On the Decrease of the Rate of Increase of Population Now Obtaining in Europe and America,* 43 AM. J. SCIENCE & ARTS 141 (1867) ("Storer, *Decrease*"); James Whitemore, *Criminal Abortion,* 31 CHI. MED. J. 385, 392 (1874). *See generally* BROOKES, *supra* note 151, at 30, 56–57, 63–64, 70, 123, 134–35; GORDON, *supra* note 31, at 140–42, 236–45; GROSSBERG, *supra* note 51, at 170–71; PETCHESKY, *supra* note 179, at 77–79, 82–89, 93–94, 116–25, 129–30; SMITH-ROSENBERG, *supra* note

always first made the case that abortion killed a living child.[218] The only purpose that these physicians did not dwell on was professionalizing medicine, but this can hardly be ascribed to embarrassment over that goal. They fought hard publicly for a medical monopoly in other legislative battles, often losing those battles in the same legislative sessions that tightened the law regarding abortion.[219] Physicians were careful, however, not to fight these battles in terms of the economic gains they might have expected but in terms of other, more praiseworthy goals.[220]

Abortion is a medical procedure even if performed by midwives. It is hardly surprising that allopathic physicians sought to gain control of it. Historian James Mohr argued that doctors did so in an effort to legitimate their claims to expertise by taking control of the birthing process while they were still largely helpless at fighting disease.[221] Allopaths, of course, sought to acquire business at the expense of other forms of medical practice. Even if we assume, however, that the nineteenth century abortion statutes were enacted as a result of a conspiracy by the allopaths to drive their competitors out of business, such a conspiracy could not have succeed if women generally—who would have to change from their allegiance from midwives to obstetricians—did not derive real benefits from the change.[222] How a crusade against abortion helped the allopaths capture control of birthing if midwives were providing a socially accepted and sought after service that physicians were unwilling to provide (abortions) is something Mohr and his followers have simply never explained.[223] The paradox is particularly troubling if the physicians were no better (and may well have been worse) at the service they sought to provide (birthing). Explanations are available that do not depend upon either the deception of, or hostility to, women.[224] If there was a conspiracy, it was between allopaths and women, not against women.

---

51, at 224–28, 238; Siegel, *supra* note 31, at 297–300; Michael Thomson, *Women, Medicine and Abortion in the Nineteenth Century,* 3 Fem. Leg. Stud. 159, 179–81 (1995).

218. For example, Dr. Horatio Storer and Franklin Heard devoted chapter 1 of their book to the question of fetal life and chapter 2 to a class and ethnic analysis of the practice of abortion. Storer & Heard, *supra* note 41, 1–64.

219. See, *e.g.,* the text *infra* at notes 305–10; Chapter 6, at notes 268–72.

220. *See, e.g.,* John Ware, *Success in the Medical Profession: An Introductory Lecture, Delivered at the Massachusetts Medical College [Harvard], Nov. 6, 1850,* 43 Bos. Med. & Surgical J. no. 26, at 520 (Jan. 29, 1851) (cautioning students that in opposing irregular practitioners they should not exhibit merely a "mean jealously of encroachment on a profitable field of labor").

221. Mohr, *supra* note 31, at 31–34. *See also* Kristin Luker, Abortion and the Politics of Motherhood 30–31 (1984).

222. *See* Chapter 2, at notes 211–39.

223. *See also* Barbara Ehrenreich & Diedre English, One Hundred Years of Advice to Women 97 (1979); Judith Walzer Leavitt, Brought to Bed: Childbearing in America 1750–1950, at 43–57, 62–63 (1986); Smith-Rosenberg, *supra* note 51, at 231–36; Siegel, *supra* note 31, at 284–85 n.83.

224. *See* Arturo Castiglioni, A History of Medicine 628–31 (2nd ed. 1947); Audrey Eccles, Obstetrics and Gynaecology in Tudor and Stuart England 124 (1982); Tony Pensabene, The Rise of the Medical Practitioner in Victoria 33 (1980); Petersen, *supra* note 124, at 16–17, 32–34; Starr, *supra* note 206, at 134–40; Regina Morantz-Sanchez, *Physicians,* in Women, Health & Medicine in America 477, 487 (Rima Apple ed. 1990).

Some commentators insist that even today obstetricians endanger women and babies rather than help them; these studies must be evaluated carefully given that in contemporary societies midwives will, if possible, turn a birth over to a physician if there is, or are likely to be, "complications." *See* Suzanne Arms, Immaculate Deception: A New Look at Women and Childbirth 53–54 (1977); Jean Donnison, Midwives and Medical Men: A History of the Struggle for the Control of Childbirth 192–93 (2nd ed. 1988); Judy Barrett Litoff, The American Midwife Debate 83, 147 (1986); Barbara Katz Rothman, In Labor: Women and Power in the Birthplace 42 (1982); Lynn Silver & Sidney Wolfe, Unnecessary Cesarean Sections: How to Cure a National Epidemic (1989); Marjorie Tew, Safer Childbirth? 289 (1990); Dorothy & Richard Wertz, Lying In: A History of Childbirth in America 161 (1977); Robbie Davis-Floyd, *The Role of Obstetrical Rituals in the Resolution of Cultural Anomaly,* 31 Soc. Sci. Med. 175

Allopaths did take the lead in pressing for more comprehensive and stringent laws against abortion in the mid-nineteenth century. Women—particularly the founding mothers of feminism—also took the lead in these nineteenth century legislative battles.[225] And women physicians in the nineteenth century took a particularly strong leading role in the "crusade" against abortion.[226] None of these groups appear to have been motivated primarily by economic concerns.

It is worth recalling that the entry of allopathic physicians into the business of assisting women in giving birth was in the middle of the nineteenth century still a relatively new phenomenon, dating back probably no earlier than 1755 in North America.[227] Physicians and others who did venture into the field of "male midwifery" initially had very little to offer their patients when compared with an experienced midwife. Diagnosis and delivery techniques were limited and crude and exaggerated notions of sexual propriety impaired the application of even such knowledge as physicians possessed.[228] The invention of forceps was perhaps the one advantage that

---

(1990); A. Mark Durand, *The Safety of Home Birth: The Farm Study*, 82 Am. J. Pub. Health 450 (1992); Chris Hafner-Eaton & Laurie Pearce, *Birth Choices, the Law, and Medicine: Balancing Indiviual Freedoms and Protection of the Public's Health*, 19 J. Health Pol., Pol'y & L. 813, 815, 817–18, 822–23 (1994); Tamar Lewin, *Midwives Deliver Healthy Babies with Fewer Interventions*, N.Y. Times, Apr. 18, 1997, at A15; Kristin McIntosh, *Regulation of Midwives as Home Birth Attendants*, 30 B.C. L. Rev. 477, 492–96 (1989); Ken Nagaya et al., *Causes of Maternal Mortality in Japan*, 283 JAMA 2661 (2000); Francis Notzon, *International Differences in the Use of Obstetric Interventions*, 263 JAMA 3286 (1990); Roger Rosenblatt, *The Perinatal Paradox: Doing More and Accomplishing Less*, 1989 Health Aff. 158; Suzanne Hope Suarez, *Midwifery Is Not the Practice of Medicine*, 5 Yale J. Law & Feminism 315, 317–21, 327–28, 335–55 (1993); Marjorie Tew, *Do Obstetric Intranatal Interventions Make Birth Safer?*, 93 Brit. J. Obstet. & Gynaecology 659 (1986); Marsden Wagner, *Infant Mortality in Europe: Implications for the United States, Statement to the National Commission to Prevent Infant Mortality*, 9 J. Pub. Health 473, 481 (1988).

225. *See* Chapter 8.

226. *Id.* at notes 307–22.

227. *See* Degler, *supra* note 29, at 56; Litoff, *supra* note 224, at 7–10; Starr, *supra* note 206, at 49; Laurel Thatcher Ulrich, Goodwives: Image and Reality in the Lives of Women in Northern New England, 1650–1750, at 132–34 (1983) ("Ulrich, Goodwives"); Laurel Thatcher Ulrich, The Midwife's Tale: The Life of Martha Ballard Based on Her Diary, 1785–1812, at 59–60, 176–79 (1991) ("Ulrich, Midwife's Tale"); Dorothy & Richard Wertz, Lying In: A History of Childbirth in America 29–44 (1977); Catherine Scholten, *On the Importance of the Obstetrick Art: Changing Customs of Childbirth in America, 1760–1825*, in Women and Health in America 142 (Judith Walzer Leavitt ed. 1984). *See also* Chapter 6, at notes 247–50.

228. *See, e.g.*, J.H. Aveling, English Midwives: Their History and Prospects 122–23 (1872); Catharine Beecher, Letters to the People on Health and Happiness 134–37 (1855); Frederick Dyer, Champion of Women and the Unborn: Horatio Robinson Storer, M.D. 96–97, 273–76, 298–306, 356 (1999); Francis Foster, Thoughts on the Times but Chiefly on the Profligacy of Our Women 17–24, 29–31, 79 89–94, 120–22, 160–61, 178, 189–93, 200 (2nd ed.1779); Samuel Gregory, Man-Midwifery Exposed and Corrected together with Remarks on the Use and Abuse of Ether and Dr. Channing's "Cases of Inhalation of Ether in Labor" (1848); Harriot Hunt, Glances and Glimpses: or Fifty Years Social, Including Twenty Years Professional Life 177, 184, 271, 376 (1856); Frank Nicholls, A Petition of the Unborn Babes to the Censors of the Royal College of Physicians 6 (1751); Elizabeth Nihell, A Treatise on the Art of Midwifery 80–86 (1760); 5 The Diary of Samuel Pepys 275 (Robert Latham & William Matthews eds. 1737); Sarah Stone, A Complete Practice of Midwifery xix (1737); Philip Thicknesse, A Letter to a Young Lady 11 (1764); Philip Thicknesse, Man Midwifery Analysed, and the Tendency of that Practice Detected and Exposed (1765) ("Thicknesse, Man Midwifery"). *See generally* Brodie, *supra* note 143, at 129; Degler, *supra* note 29, at 58–59; DeVries, *supra* note 209, at 24–25; Donnison, *supra* note 224, at 23–24, 36, 41–42, 46, 59–60, 64, 78, 240; Ruth Finley, The Lady of Godey's: Sarah Josepha Hale 102–05 (1931); Gordon, *supra* note 31, at 164; David Hunt, Parents and Children in History: The Psychology of Family Life in Early Modern France 83–85 (1970); Danielle Jacquart & Claude Thomasset, *Sexualité et savoir médical au moyen âge* 241 (1985); Stephen Kern, Anatomy and Destiny: A Cultural History of the Human Body 1–2 (1975); Smith-Rosenberg, *supra* note 51, at 228–29; Starr, *supra* note 206, at 40–47, 64; Reay Tannahill, Sex in History 351–52 (1980); Walsh, *supra* note 208, at 6–7, 37–39; Wertz & Wertz, *supra* note 226, at 68; Roy

physicians or male midwives had over traditional midwives. Forceps appear to have been invented in England within family of Huguenot doctors and male midwives (the Chamberlens) sometime around 1647, but they (and any others who might have independently invented such a device) kept it a trade secret for at least another century.[229] Some would place both their invention and their popularization in sixteenth century France.[230] Regardless of when forceps were invented, the latter part of the eighteenth century witnessed the rapid development of forceps by male midwives as the means for aiding in the difficult deliveries.[231] As a result, male midwives became increasingly common in England after 1720 and in the American colonies after 1755, and they were increasingly brought in for routine cases, and not merely for difficult births.[232]

By 1760, male midwives had become common enough in England to figure as a major object of jokes in *Tristam Shandy*.[233] Two "man midwives" were even knighted during the later eighteenth century.[234] Nonetheless, male midwives were not fully accepted by the English professional organizations of physicians or surgeons, both of which denied male midwives the right to be elected to their governing boards.[235] This policy did not change until 1851.[236]

The forceps was hardly a panacea. Numerous allegations that a male midwife killed a baby through hasty misuse of the forceps are proof enough of that.[237] Furthermore, physicians, male midwives, and traditional midwives did not wash themselves carefully until the germ theory of disease gave them a reason for washing.[238] No wonder well-to-do women paying a top price for the "best" assistance at their births, whether from male or female midwives, seem to have had

---

Porter, *A Touch of Danger: The Man-Midwife as Sexual Predator,* in Sexual Underworlds of the Enlightenment 206, 212–13 (G.S. Rousseau & Roy Porter eds. 1988); B.B. Schnorrenberg, *Is Childbirth Any Place for a Woman? The Decline of Midwifery in Eighteenth Century England,* 10 Stud. in 18th Cent. Culture 393 (1981); Margaret Connor Versluysen, *Midwives, Medical Men and "Poor Women" Labouring of Child: Lying-In Hospitals in Eighteenth Century London,* in Women, Health and Reproduction 21, 29 (Helen Roberts ed. 1981). *See also* Chapter 6, at notes 251–55.

229. J.H. Aveling, The Chamberlens and the Midwifery Forceps (1882); Walter Radcliffe, Milestones in Midwifery and the Secret Instrument (1947). *See also* Donnison, *supra* note 224, at 26; Petersen, *supra* note 124, at 15; Ann Sablosky, *The Power of the Forceps: A Comparative Analysis of the Midwife — Historically and Today,* 1 Women & Health 10 (1976).

230. Marie Ashe, *Law-Language of Maternity: Discourse Holding Nature in Contempt,* 22 N. Eng. L. Rev. 521, 558 (1988).

231. *See* Edmund Chapman, A Treatise on the Improvement of Midwifery xvi–xviii (1733). *See also* DeVries, *supra* note 209, at 23–24; Donnison, *supra* note 224, at 21–22; Litoff, *supra* note 224, at 7–14; Ulrich, Goodwives, *supra* note 227, at 134; Ulrich, Midwife's Tale, *supra* note 226, at 180; Walsh, *supra* note 208, at 6–7; Wertz & Wertz, *supra* note 226, at 39; Robert Rousch, *The Development of Midwifery — Male and Female, Yesterday and Today,* 24 J. Nurse-Midwifery No. 3, at 27, 34 (1979); Scholten, *supra* note 226, at 147.

232. Joan Donegan, Women and Men Midwives: Medicine, Morality, and Misogyny in Early America 45–47 (1978); Donnison, *supra* note 224, at 34–71; Julia Cherry Spruill, Women's Life and Work in the Southern Colonies 272–72 (1938); Walsh, *supra* note 208, at 7; Wertz & Wertz, *supra* note 227, at 29–46; Scholten, *supra* note 226, at 145–48.

233. 1 Laurence Sterne, The Life and Opinions of Tristam Shandy, Gentleman 48–54 (1760–67).

234. Donnison, *supra* note 224, at 53.

235. *Id.*; Cecil Wall, A History of the Surgeons' Company: 1745–1800, at 54 (1937); 2 George Clark, A History of the College of Physicians 588 (1966).

236. Donnison, *supra* note 224, at 54; Wall, *supra* note 235, at 206–10.

237. *See, e.g.,* John Maubray, The Female Physician 181–82 (1724); Nicholls, *supra* note 228, at 8–11; Nihell, *supra* note 228, at 92–95, 158–59; Margaret Stephen, The Domestic Midwife 55–63 (1795); Stone, *supra* note 228, at xi–xii; Thicknesse, Man Midwifery, *supra* note 228, at 22. *See generally* Donnison, *supra* note 224, at 42–44, 50; H.R. Spencer, The History of British Midwifer from 1650–1800, at 73 (1927).

238. *See generally* René Dubos, Louis Pasteur: Free Lance of Science (1950).

higher death rates than poor women served by illiterate and untutored rural midwives.[239] Yet it remained true, not so long ago, that a birth would be attended by virtually every married woman in the typically small American communities.[240] A dozen or more women would pitch in to help out or just to witness the event. The real question, however, is how effective that assistance was.

Recent feminist histories of midwifery exhibit a certain tendency to romanticize the practice of midwifery by women as a Golden Age of wonderfully effective sisterly support.[241] Midwives remained largely self-taught or (at best) learned as apprentices assisting more experienced midwives; there were no standard procedures.[242] The experience of giving birth was considered to be the most important part of a midwife's "training."[243] Sanitation was barely considered. It is worth recalling historian David Hunt's hope that a midwife "would cut her nails, wash, and remove the rings from her hands before beginning."[244] How many women and infants died because of the inadvertent introduction of infection, whether by a physician, a male midwife, or a traditional midwife, can only be guessed today, but the number must have been considerable.

A midwife could do little if there were major difficulties. Usually a midwife had no instruments other than her own hands, and only alcohol or crude folk concoctions for easing pain.[245] Caesarean sections were rarely attempted unless the mother was already dead; such surgery was fatal.[246] Feminist historians now insist that midwives were displaced through a professional power grab and not as a result of any significant technological breakthrough.[247] It hardly seems

---

239. *See* CHARLES WHITE, A TREATISE ON THE MANAGEMENT OF PREGNANT AND LYING-IN WOMEN 338–41 (1773). *See generally* DONNISON, *supra* note 224, at 46, 106–07; WERTZ & WERTZ, *supra* note 226, at 62–73.

240. *See* DONNISON, *supra* note 224, at 14, 19; KEITH THOMAS, RELIGION AND THE DECLINE OF MAGIC 40–41 (1971); ULRICH, GOODWIVES, *supra* note 227, at 136–35; Cecilia Benoit, *Traditional Midwifery Practice: Limits of Occupational Autonomy,* 26 CAN. REV. SOC'Y & ANTHROPOLOGY 633 (1989); Scholten, *supra* note 226, at 444–45.

241. *See, e.g.,* Dianne Martin, *The Midwife's Tale: Old Wisdom and a New Challenge to the Control of Reproduction,* 3 COLUM. J. GENDER & L. 417, 436–37 (1992). *See generally* DONNISON, *supra* note 224.

242. *See* Chapter 1, at notes 7–16. *See, e.g.,* PIERRE DIONIS, *TRAITÉ GÉNÉRAL DES ACCOUCHEMENTS, QUI INSTRUIT CE TOUT CE QU'IL FAUT FAIRE POUR ÊTRE HABILE ACCOUCHEUR* 414–15 (1711); NIHELL, *supra* note 228, at 217–18; STONE, *supra* note 228, at xv–xvii; ULRICH, MIDWIFE'S TALE, *supra* note 227, at 11–12. *See also* DONEGAN, *supra* note 232, at 12, 42–43; DONNISON, *supra* note 224, at 55, 60–67, 70, 77–78, 82–85, 96, 105, 111, 117–20; ULRICH, GOODWIVES, *supra* note 227, at 134; WALSH, *supra* note 208, at 5–6.

243. DONNISON, *supra* note 224, at 14, 28; ULRICH, THE MIDWIFE'S TALE, *supra* note 227, at 12 (referring to STONE, *supra* note 224, at xiv); WALSH, *supra* note 208, at 5–6.

244. DAVID HUNT, PARENTS AND CHILDREN IN HISTORY: THE PSYCHOLOGY OF FAMILY LIFE IN EARLY MODERN FRANCE 86 (1970).

245. *See, e.g.,* LOUISE BOURGEOIS, *RECUIL DES SECRETS DE LOUYSE BOURGEOIS* 115–30 (1635); DIONIS, *supra* note 242, at 206; JACQUES GUILLEMEAU, CHILDBIRTH, OR THE HAPPY DELIVERY OF WOMEN ... 115 (1635); 2 AMBROISE PARÉ, *OUEVRES COMPLÈTES* 704–06 (1840). *See generally* HUNT, *supra* note 244, at 87–88; ULRICH, GOODWIVES, *supra* note 227, at 134–38, 184, 190.

246. 1 LOUISE BOURGEOIS, *OBSERVATIONS DIVERSES SUR LA STÉRILITÉ, PERTE DE FRUIT FEOCONDITÉ, ACCOUCHEMENTS ET MALADIES DES FEMMES ET ENFANTS NOUVEAUX NAIZ* 189 (1626); GUILLEMEAU, *supra* note 245, at 185–88; FRANÇOIS MAURICEAU, *TRAITÉ DES MALADIES DES FEMMES GROSSES* ... 348 (1675).

247. *See, e.g.,* SUZANNE ARMS, IMMACULATE DECEPTION: A NEW LOOK AT WOMEN AND CHILDBIRTH 53–54 (1977); BRODIE, *supra* note 142, at 287; BROOKES, *supra* note 151, at 26, 52, 67, 134; DONNISON, *supra* note 224; GORDON, *supra* note 31, at 160; BEVERLY WILDUNG HARRISON, OUR RIGHT TO CHOOSE: TOWARD A NEW ETHIC OF ABORTION 165–66 (1983); McLAREN, *supra* note 152, at 123–24, 127–29; ANN OAKLEY, THE CAPTURED WOMB: A HISTORY OF THE MEDICAL CARE OF PREGNANT WOMEN (1986); PETCHESKY, *supra* note 179, at 71–73, 79–81; PETERSEN, *supra* note 124, at 10–11; JOHN RIDDLE, CONTRACEPTION AND ABORTION FROM THE ANCIENT WORLD TO THE RENAISSANCE 162 (1992); BARBARA KATZ ROTHMAN, IN LABOR: WOMEN AND POWER IN THE BIRTHPLACE (1982); DEBORAH SULLIVAN & ROSE WEITZ, LABOR PAINS: MODERN MIDWIVES AND HOME BIRTH 1–19 (1988); JAMES BOYD WHITE, ACTS OF HOPE: CREATING AUTHORITY IN LITERATURE,

likely that allopaths succeeded in taking over the obstetric practice through a mere matter of fashion or as another example of women being imposed upon by men, but then perhaps I just have greater respect for the abilities of women patients than do the historians who posit such theories.

Women themselves adopted the medical model of birthing as a strategy both for persuading their husbands of the need to limit family size and, later, to obtain access to anesthesia and other medical aids—as a good many historians, including feminist historians of birth (rather than abortion), have concluded.[248] Some historians have even noted that the entire Victorian ideology of female sexual passivity, rather than being an attempt to exclude women from sexual pleasure, actually served to empower women by providing them with regulatory control of sexual activity—women were at last authorized to "just say no."[249] Of course, many historians see Victorian passivity as oppressive rather than empowering.[250] Indeed, the feminists of the time saw Victorian morality as oppressive; as Harriet Martineau put it as early as 1839, men were giving women indulgence as a substitute for justice.[251] Today, many modern feminists are deeply suspicious of the notion of consent as empowering women because of the abiding social structures that constrain their exercise of the "power" of consent.[252]

Allopathic physicians might well have exploited women's desires in order to enhance the physicians' status, but physicians could not have done so without fulfilling some perceived need of the women involved. While women could not then vote or serve in legislatures, they were hardly without influence on legislatures where their interests were directly involved. Consider their successful drive to reform the law relating to the tort of seduction, a reform that appears to have been directed at male sexual license.[253] Whether particular male legislators identified with male license or with an ideology of protecting their wives and daughters from predatory males,

---

LAW, AND POLITICS 165–66 (1994); Jane Maslow Cohen, *A Jurisprudence of Doubt: Deliberative Autonomy and Abortion*, 3 COLUM. J. GENDER & LAW. 175, 208–10 (1992); Chris Hafner-Eaton & Laurie Pearce, *Birth Choices, the Law, and Medicine: Balancing Indiviual Freedoms and Protection of the Public's Health*, 19 J. HEALTH POL., POL'Y & L. 813, 815–16 (1994); Martin, *supra* note 241; Scholten, *supra* note 227, at 146–47; Siegel, *supra* note 31, at 283–84; Solinger, *supra* note 31, at 250–51, 257–58, 263–64; Suzanne Hope Suarez, *Midwifery Is Not the Practice of Medicine*, 5 YALE J. LAW & FEMINISM 315, 315–18, 325–31 (1993); Thomson, *supra* note 217, at 175–77.

248. JUDITH SCHNEID LEWIS, IN THE FAMILY WAY: CHILDBEARING IN THE BRITISH ARISTOCRACY, 1760–1860 (1986); REGINA MARKELL MORANTZ-SANCHEZ, SYMPATHY AND SCIENCE: WOMEN PHYSICIANS IN AMERICAN MEDICINE 26, 222–23 (1985); MARTIN PERNICK, A CALCULUS OF SUFFERING: PAIN, PROFESSIONALISM, AND ANESTHESIA IN NINETEENTH-CENTURY AMERICA 149–54 (1985); CATHERINE SCHOLTEN, CHILDBEARING IN AMERICAN SOCIETY 1650–1850, ch. 2 (1985); Lewis & Lockridge, *supra* note 199, at 11–14.

249. DEGLER, *supra* note 29, at 257–59, 279–97; D'EMILIO & FREEDMAN, *supra* note 199, at 71; TANNAHILL, *supra* note 228, at 355; Nancy Cott, *Passionless: An Interpretation of Victorian Sexual Ideology, 1790–1850*, 4 SIGNS 219, 233 (1978); Jane Larson, *"Women Understand So Little, They Call My Good Nature 'Deceit'": A Feminist Rethinking of Seduction*, 93 COLUM. L. REV. 374, 392–93 (1993).

250. *See, e.g.,* DONNISON, *supra* note 224, at 63–65; SMITH-ROSENBERG, *supra* note 51, at 22–25; TANNAHILL, *supra* note 228, at 348–57.

251. HARRIET MARTINEAU, SOCIETY IN AMERICA 291 (1839; reprinted 1962).

252. *See* CATHARINE MACKINNON, TOWARD A FEMINIST THEORY OF THE STATE 174 (1989); DEBORAH RHODE, JUSTICE AND GENDER 165–67 (1989); Kathryn Abrams, *Ideology and Women's Choices*, 24 GA. L. REV. 761 (1990); Lucinda Finley, *Choice and Freedom: Elusive Issues in the Search for Gender Justice*, 96 YALE L.J. 914 (1987); Larson, *supra* note 249, at 426–31; Robin West, *Authority, Autonomy, and Choice: The Role of Consent in the Moral and Political Visions of Franz Kafka and Richard Posner*, 99 HARV. L. REV. 384 (1986); Joan Williams, *Gender Wars: Selfless Women in the Republic of Choice*, 66 N.Y.U. L. REV. 1559 (1991). *See generally* LUKER, *supra* note 221.

253. *See* BARBARA BERG, THE REMEMBERED GATE: ORIGINS OF AMERICAN FEMINISM 209–13 (1978); D'EMILIO & FREEDMAN, *supra* note 199, at 145; GROSSBERG, *supra* note 51, at 47–48; MOHR, *supra* note 31, at 121–22; SMITH-ROSENBERG, *supra* note 51, at 227–28; Larson, *supra* note 249, at 390–91. *See also* CONSTANCE BACKHOUSE, PETTICOATS AND PREJUDICE: WOMEN AND LAW IN NINETEENTH-CENTURY CANADA 70 (1991).

their votes determined the fate of such legislation. Ironically, the tort of seduction and related "heart-balm" actions fell out of favor when women obtained the vote—often with the feminists of the time leading the charge to abolish the torts.[254] A similar story applies to nineteenth-century prostitution. Male physicians often argued unsuccessfully for its legalization and regulation and feminist leaders generally successfully insisted on its prohibition.[255] Today some feminists favor legalizing prostitution ("sex work"), usually with little or no regulation;[256] physicians are not particularly prominent in the debate.

Women's interests combined with the available technology to drive a desire for the medicalization of birth quite independently of any competitive goals of the allopathic physicians.[257] The gains to women were enough for them to tolerate for nearly a century the reorganization of the birthing process for the convenience of doctors and the considerable inconvenience of the woman giving birth.[258] Indeed, more than inconvenience resulted. Before antiseptic practices became standard in the last third of the nineteenth century the incidence of diseases transmitted from patient to patient by way of a physician's hands (principally puerperal or "child-bed" fever) apparently was actually higher than the incidence of transmission through midwives.[259] Early in the twentieth century in Australia, maternal mortality during birth rose slightly even while infant mortality fell.[260] The same pattern happened in other English-speaking countries.[261] Furthermore, women's gains in controlling birth patterns could only be purchased not only at the cost of subordinating their needs to that of their doctors, but also at the cost of their surrendering some of the physical intimacy that the nineteenth-century's cult of romantic love was awak-

---

254. Larson, *supra* note 249, at 393–401.

255. *See* D'Emilio & Freedman, *supra* note 199, at 139–56; David Pivar, Purity Crusade: Sexual Morality and Social Control, 1868–1900 (1973); John Burnham, *Medical Inspection of Prostitutes in America in the Nineteenth Century: The St. Louis Experiment and Its Sequel*, 45 Bull. Hist. Med. 203 (1971). Prostitution was also legalized and regulated in Victoria (Australia). Jocelynne Scutt, *The Economic Regulation of the Brothel Industry in Victoria*, 60 Austral. L.J. 399 (1986).

256. *See, e.g.*, Micloe Bingham, *Nevada Sex Trade: A Gamble for the Workers*, 10 Yale J.L. & Feminism 69 (1998); Joan Fitzpatrick, *The Use of International Human Rights Norms to Combat Violence against Women*, in Human Rights of Women: National and International Perspectives 532, 551–64 (Rebecca Cook ed. 1994).

257. Petersen, *supra* note 124, at 38.

258. *See* Judith Walzer Leavitt, *"Science" Enters the Birthing Room: Obstetrics in America since the Eighteenth Century*, 70 J. Am. Hist. 281 (1983).

259. Kern, *supra* note 228, at 37–38.

260. E.S. Morris, *An Essay on the Causes and Prevention of Maternal Morbidity and Mortality*, [1925] 2 Med. J. Australia 301, 309. *See also* R.M. Allan, *Report on Maternal Mortality and Morbidity in the State of Victoria*, [1928] 1 Med. J. Australia 668; J.S. Purdy, *Maternal Mortality in Childbirth*, [1921] 1 Med. J. Australia 39.

261. Martin, *supra* note 241, at 433–35. Some commentators insist that even today obstetricians endanger women and babies rather than help them; one must remember, however, that midwives turn difficult births over to physicians, thus skewing the statistics. *See, e.g.*, Arms, *supra* note 228, at 53–54; Donnison, *supra* note 224, at 192–94; Rothman, *supra* note 246, at 42; Lynn Silver & Sidney Wolfe, Unnecessary Cesarean Sections: How to Cure a National Epidemic (1989); Marjorie Tew, Safer Childbirth? 289 (1990); Wertz & Wertz, *supra* note 226, at 161; Robbie Davis-Floyd, *The Role of Obstetrical Rituals in the Resolution of Cultural Anomaly*, 31 Soc. Sci. Med. 175 (1990); A. Mark Durand, *The Safety of Home Birth: The Farm Study*, 82 Am. J. Pub. Health 450 (1992); Hafner-Eaton & Pearce, *supra* note 246, at 815, 817–18, 822–23; Tamar Lewin, *Midwives Deliver Healthy Babies with Fewer Interventions*, N.Y. Times, Apr. 18, 1997, at A15; Kristin McIntosh, *Regulation of Midwives as Home Birth Attendants*, 30 B.C. L. Rev. 477, 492–96 (1989); Ken Nagaya et al., *Causes of Maternal Mortality in Japan*, 283 JAMA 2661 (2000); Francis Notzon, *International Differences in the Use of Obstetric Interventions*, 263 JAMA 3286 (1990); Roger Rosenblatt, *The Perinatal Paradox: Doing More and Accomplishing Less*, 1989 Health Aff. 158; Suarez, *supra* note 246, at 317–21, 327–28, 335–55; Marjorie Tew, *Do Obstetric Intranatal Interventions Make Birth Safer?*, 93 Brit. J. Obstet. & Gynaecology 659 (1986); Marsden Wagner, *Infant Mortality in Europe: Implications for the United States, Statement to the National Commission to Prevent Infant Mortality*, 9 J. Pub. Health 473, 481 (1988).

ening as well as by their embracing an image of themselves as weak, frail, and delicate.[262] No wonder it is more fashionable to decry this pattern of behavior as male-imposed in order to debilitate women from competing with men.[263]

By the end of the nineteenth century physicians had acquired the necessary technology and skill to deal with many complications, including the technology and skill to perform cesarean sections successfully and safely.[264] These technologies were the very ones that made surgery generally, and not just abortion, relatively safe and effective: analgesics, anesthetics, antiseptics, and (eventually) antibiotics.[265] Allopathic physicians had already made significant inroads on the obstetrics market before they developed the necessary skill and technologies. The new skills and technologies simply confirmed the wisdom of deferring to the physicians, allowing them virtually to eliminate traditional midwives from any role in the birthing process.[266]

The emerging preference for male midwives capable of providing the necessary assistance led to a sharp and dramatic decline in the number of women who obtained professional stature as midwives, particularly in urban areas. In Philadelphia, for example, traditional (female) midwives who listed themselves in the business directory quickly after 1800. By 1815, male-midwives outnumbered them by 23 to 21, and by 1819 by 42 to 13; female midwives virtually disappeared from the directory by 1825.[267] A similar transformation took place in the Boston business directory at about the same time.[268] Most traditional midwives undoubtedly never listed themselves in such directories, so there probably were many more female midwives than the directories indicate. The directories do indicate that traditional midwives rapidly lost social standing and suggest that women who could afford male midwives chose them in preference to the higher-priced female midwives.[269] The listings also suggest the intense competition that arose, particularly in the cities, between the male midwives and the traditional female midwives.[270]

---

262. Lewis & Lockridge, *supra* note 199, at 13. *See generally* D'EMILIO & FREEDMAN, *supra* note 199, at 42–53, 73–84; KAREN LYSTRA, SEARCHING THE HEART: WOMEN, MEN, AND ROMANTIC LOVE IN NINETEENTH-CENTURY AMERICA (1989); Carroll Smith-Rosenberg, *The Hysterical Woman: Sex Role Conflict in Nineteenth-Century America*, 39 SOC. RESEARCH 652, 655, 678 (1972).

263. *See, e.g.,* Thomson, *supra* note 217, at 175–77.

264. CASTIGLIONI, *supra* note 132, at 726–27, 854–60; McLAREN, REPRODUCTIVE RITUALS, *supra* note 152, at 125–29; PETERSEN, *supra* note 124, at 37–38; MALCOLM POTTS, PETER DIGGORY, & JOHN PEEL, ABORTION 155–56, 282–83 (1977); L. Townsend, *Obstetrics through the Ages*, [1952] 1 MED. J. AUSTRALIA 557, 564.

265. See the text *supra* at notes 126–33.

266. *See, e.g.,* JAMES SIMPSON, REMARKS ON THE SUPERINDUCTION OF ANESTHESIA IN NATURAL AND MORBID PARTURITION 7–8 (1847). *See generally* DONNISON, *supra* note 224, at 65–66.

267. DEGLER, *supra* note 29, at 57.

268. *Id.*

269. G.J. BARKER-BENFIELD, THE HORRORS OF THE HALF-KNOWN LIFE: MALE ATTITUDES TOWARD WOMEN AND SEXUALITY IN NINETEENTH CENTURY AMERICA 61–62, 84–88, 255 (1976); BARBARA EHRENREICH & DIEDRE ENGLISH, FOR HER OWN GOOD: 150 YEARS OF THE EXPERTS' ADVICE TO WOMEN 54–63 (1982); LEAVITT, *supra* note 223, at 87–115 (1986); LITOFF, *supra* note 224, at 3–14; MOHR, *supra* note 31, at 168–69; CHARLES ROSENBERG & CARROLL SMITH-ROSENBERG, THE MALE MIDWIFE & THE FEMALE DOCTOR: THE GYNECOLOGY CONTROVERSY IN NINETEENTH-CENTURY AMERICA (1974); SMITH-ROSENBERG, *supra* note 51, at 231; SARAH STAGE, FEMALE COMPLAINTS: LYDIA PINKHAM AND THE BUSINESS OF WOMEN'S MEDICINE 77–82 (1979); STARR, *supra* note 206, at 47–51, 87, 117, 124; WERTZ & WERTZ, *supra* note 224, at 29–44. *See generally* ALICK BOURNE, A SYNOPSIS OF OBSTETRICS AND GYNECOLOGY (1949); HERBERT THOMS, CHAPTERS IN AMERICAN OBSTETRICS (1933); ULRICH, MIDWIFE'S TALE, *supra* note 227, at 59–60, 176–79; Frances Kobrin, *The American Midwife Controversy: A Crisis of Professionalization*, 40 BULL. HIST. MED. 350 (1966).

270. JUANNE NANCARROW CLARKE, HEALTH, ILLNESS, AND MEDICINE IN CANADA 277–79 (1990); DONNISON, *supra* note 224, at 53–93; PETERSEN, *supra* note 124, at 15–16; WERTZ & WERTZ, *supra* note 224, at 49–54; T.R. Forbes, *The Regulation of English Midwives in the Eighteenth and Nineteenth Century*, 15 MED. HIST. 352, 354–55 (1971); Martin, *supra* note 241, at 429–37; Margaret Connor Versluysen, *Midwives, Medical Men and "Poor Women" Labouring of Child: Lying-In Hospitals in Eighteenth Century London*, in WOMEN, HEALTH AND REPRODUCTION 21, 27–28 (Helen Roberts ed. 1981).

Listings in business directories by no means indicate the true rate of reliance on traditional (female) midwives. The majority of births in England and the United States appear to have been attended by informal (*i.e.*, self-taught and unorganized) midwives rather than by obstetricians at least until World War I, and probably, at least in some areas, until the 1930s.[271] Indicative of the gradual demise of the profession is the drop in the number of informal midwives practicing in New York City from 1,700 in 1919 to 170 in 1939.[272] Ironically, as in England, male midwives initially were usually not physicians or surgeons, if only because "regular" physicians looked down upon "midwifery" as an inferior activity.[273] One Australian physician writing as late as 1885 felt free to describe midwifery as a branch of practice "which any man can undertake without fear of failure" while noting the tendency of "operative gynaecology" to overshadow obstetrics in that field.[274] Only a few pioneering physicians entered the field until the second half of the nineteenth century when it had been renamed as the medical specialty of "obstetrics" and was no longer known as "midwifery," and the related field of "gynecology" had also emerged.[275] One of the more direct examples of this transition is found by comparing the teaching career of Dr. David Humphreys Storer (Professor of Midwifery at Harvard Medical School in the early nineteenth century) with that of his son, renowned anti-abortion crusader Dr. Horatio Robinson Storer (the first person to teach gynecology as such at Harvard Medical School in the middle of the nineteenth century).[276] Yet standards remained generally low in obstetrics until the 1930s.[277]

Midwives were losing ground even before male midwives or their later incarnation, the obstetric physician, could offer a better service. Female midwives simply could not validate for husbands the wives' needs for sexual abstinence or restraint as successfully as the midwives male counterparts could.[278] Physicians also had an advantage in the unsavory reputation attached to midwives because of their association with abortion and infanticide.[279] This association perhaps explains why even the earliest midwife regulatory acts included requirements that midwives demonstrate themselves to be "of good character" and prohibited them from certifying the cause

271. DAVIS, *supra* note 153, at 89; DEGLER, *supra* note 29, at 56–57; DEVRIES, *supra* note 209, at 25; DONNISON, *supra* note 224, at 85, 149–50, 190–91; GORDON, *supra* note 31, at 172; LEAVITT, *supra* note 223, at 12, 171–95, 269; LITOFF, *supra* note 224, at 27, 136–41; RICHARD MECKEL, SAVE THE BABIES: AMERICAN PUBLIC HEALTH REFORM AND THE PREVENTION OF INFANT MORTALITY 174 (1990); PETERSEN, *supra* note 124, at 40; REAGAN, *supra* note 52, at 281 n.77; ROSENBERG, *supra* note 128, at 316; ROSEMARY STEVENS, AMERICAN MEDICINE AND THE PUBLIC INTEREST 80–82, 145 (1971). *See also* LOUIS REED, MIDWIVES, CHIROPODISTS, AND OPTOMETRISTS: THEIR PLACE IN MEDICAL CARE 5–6, 67 (1932) (describing the national distribution of midwives in 1930); ULRICH, MIDWIFE'S TALE, *supra* note 227, at 28, 179–80; WERTZ & WERTZ, *supra* note 224, at 133; Grace Abbott, *The Midwife in Chicago*, 20 AM. J. SOC. 684, 685–86 (1915); Kobrin, *supra* note 269, at 362–63.

272. DEVRIES, *supra* note 209, at 25.

273. *See generally* DONNISON, *supra* note 224, at 53–55, 58–59, 67.

274. J. Jamieson, *A Sketch of the History of Midwifery*, [1885] AUSTRALIAN MED. J. 193, 206. *See generally* PETERSEN, *supra* note 124, at 16, 37; Versluysen, *supra* note 270, at 28.

275. CASTIGLIONI, *supra* note 132, at 658–59; DONNISON, *supra* note 224, at 67–68; HAAGENSON & LLOYD, *supra* note 128, at 295–96; JAMES MARTIN *et al.*, HISTORICAL REVIEW OF BRITISH OBSTETRICS AND GYNAECOLOGY, 1800–1850, at 296–98 (1954); PETERSEN, *supra* note 124, at 37–38; JAMES RICCI, ONE HUNDRED YEARS OF GYNAECOLOGY (1945).

276. *See* STORER, *supra* note 215, at 17–18. *See also* DYER, *supra* note 228, at 266, 308–09; WALSH, *supra* note 208, at 109–10; IRVING WATSON, PHYSICIANS AND SURGEONS OF AMERICA: A COLLECTION OF BIOGRAPHICAL SKETCHES OF THE REGULAR MEDICAL PROFESSION 25 (1896). On the younger Storer's career generally, see *infra* at notes 338–470.

277. DEVRIES, *supra* note 209, at 39–46; PETERSEN, *supra* note 124, at 38; Kobrin, *supra* note 269, at 352–53; J. Whitridge Williams, *Medical Education and the Midwife Problem in the United States*, 58 JAMA 1 (1912).

278. *See* Chapter 2, at 211–39.

279. LUKER, *supra* note 221, at 41–45; McLAREN, *supra* note 135, at 241; PETERSEN, *supra* note 124, at 13, 40–41.

of death of someone under their care (mother or child).[280] By the nineteenth century, the moral reputation of midwives had become so suspect that novelists often characterized them as "drunken incompetent slattern[s]."[281] Their unsavory reputation belies the claim of abortion rights activists that abortion was always socially accepted among women.

Traditional midwives were also disadvantaged by the increasing "privatization" of family life, that is, by the break down of the strong communal and public aspects of family life that had continued until the late eighteenth or the early nineteenth century, including the hitherto very public nature of labor and birth itself. As women moved into cities, they were increasingly cut off from the older tradition of communal support, and had to seek over forms of support for the birthing process.[282] In some settings, this transformation of birthing took the form of "lying-in" hospitals[283]—to women's detriment because these institutions were highly dangerous, becoming hotbeds for the transmission of "childbed fever" from parturient woman to parturient woman.[284] In other settings, the transformation took the form of a doctor traveling to isolated homes to officiate at a delivery. Cause and effect become thoroughly blurred in this privatization process as the century wore on because the women of the neighborhood came to have less and less to contribute compared to the emerging medical profession.

Despite their advantages, deep hostilities and suspicions at first greeted men seeking to take charge of the birthing room, hostilities and suspicions that survived well into the nineteenth century.[285] This, added to the relative expense and inconvenience of resorting to a lying in hospital or calling a doctor to one's home, slowed the process of physicians displacing midwives. As late as 1911, approximately 50 percent of births in the United States were still attended only by a midwife,[286] and the nearly complete displacement of midwives did not occur until the 1930s.[287] Ironically, given the current arguments of historians that this change represented a seizure of power by male physicians from female midwives, this final stage of this transition (from 1921–1929) occurred precisely through the actions of the suffragists who succeeded, once they obtained the vote, in enacting exactly one major social program—the Children's Bureau.[288]

The Children's Bureau, with the active support of organized women's groups and of the Left generally,[289] undertook with considerable success to accustom rural white women, particularly in

---

280. PETERSEN, *supra* note 124, at 41.

281. Martin, *supra* note 241, at 433. *See also* DONNISON, *supra* note 224, at 45, 54, 70, 103; Nancy Schrom Dye, *History of Childbirth in America*, 6 SIGNS 97, 102 (1980).

282. *See* MARY CHAMBERLAIN, OLD WIVES' TALES: THEIR HISTORY, REMEDIES, AND SPELLS 84–93 (1981); Martin, *supra* note 241, at 432–33.

283. Versluysen, *supra* note 270.

284. DONNISON, *supra* note 224, at 46, 106–07; WALSH, *supra* note 208, at 93–94; WERTZ & WERTZ, *supra* note 224, at 121–22, 126–28.

285. See the authorities collected *supra* at note 228.

286. Thomas Darlington, *The Present State of the Midwife*, 63 AM. J. OBSTET. & GYNAECOLOGY 870 (1911). Apparently 95% of births were not hospital births as late as 1900. WERTZ & WERTZ, *supra* note 224, at 133. The pattern was similar in England. DONNISON, *supra* note 224, at 68–70.

287. See the authorities collected *supra* at note 271.

288. DOROTHY BRADBURY, FIVE DECADES OF ACTION: A SHORT HISTORY OF THE CHILDREN'S BUREAU (1964); JAMES BURROW, AMA: VOICE OF AMERICAN MEDICINE 161–64 (1963); LELA COSTIN, TWO SISTERS FOR SOCIAL JUSTICE 130–47 (1983); MECKEL, *supra* note 271, at 174–77; SUSAN TIFFLIN, IN WHOSE BEST INTEREST? CHILD WELFARE REFORM IN THE PROGRESSIVE ERA 229–47 (1982); Molly Ladd-Taylor, *Hull House Goes to Washington: Women and the Children's Bureau*, in GENDER, CLASS, AND RACE: REFORM IN THE PROGRESSIVE ERA 110 (N. Frankel & N. Dye eds. 1991); Susan Waysdorf, *Fighting for Their Lives: Women, Poverty, and the Historical Role of United States Law in Shaping Access to Women's Health Care*, 84 KY. L.J. 745, 771–97 (1996).

289. *See, e.g.*, THE AUTOBIOGRAPHY OF FLORENCE KELLEY: NOTES OF SIXTY YEARS 31–32 (Kathryn Kish Sklar ed. 1986); MECKEL, *supra* note 271, at 175–77; MARTHA MINOW, MAKING ALL THE DIFFERENCE: INCLU-

the South, to prenatal medical care and hospital births, and to upgrade and professionalize the midwives who still attended most black women's births.[290] This, in fact, was the first meaningful involvement of the hitherto white progressive and women's movements (the "social feminists") with African-American health care providers and activists in the rural South.[291] Given a choice, poor women quickly abandoned folk medicine and midwives in favor of physicians and clinics.[292] When Federal agencies dropped their support for black midwifery after World War II and sought to promote physician-attended births for all Americans, segregation in hospitals preserved the racially defined differences in birthing in the South until it ended in the 1960s.[293]

Before concerns about abortion clouded the issue, women historians celebrated the work of the Children's Bureau as a victory for women's health and women's rights.[294] In view of the prominent role of the women's movement in promoting the Children's Bureau and its anti-midwifery policies, current feminist historians have chosen either to ignore the Bureau's role in suppressing midwives or have criticized it as a racist or as a middle-class institution oppressing poor women.[295] There is, of course, a counter-narrative that defends the Children's

SION, EXCLUSION, AND AMERICAN LAW 247–50 (1990); Molly Ladd-Taylor, *Women's Health and Public Policy,* in WOMEN, HEALTH, AND MEDICINE IN AMERICA 391 (Rima Apple ed. 1990).

290. *See Sheppard-Towner Maternity and Infancy Act,* ch. 135, 42 Stat. 224 (1921), *repealed by* Act of Jan. 22, 1927 (effective June 30, 1929), ch. 53, § 2, 4 Stat. 1024; Frothingham v. Mellon, 262 U.S. 447 (1923). *See generally* Bruce Bellingham & Mary Pugh Mathis, *Race, Citizenship, and the Bio-Politics of the Maternalist Welfare State: "Traditional" Midwifery in the American South under the Sheppard-Towner Act, 1921–1929,* 1 SOC. POL. 157 (1994); Molly Ladd-Taylor, *"Grannies" and "Spinsters": Midwife Education under the Sheppard-Towner Act,* 22 J. SOC. HIST. 255, 264 (1988). *See also* LINDA GORDON, PITIED BUT NOT ENTITLED: SINGLE MOTHERS AND THE HISTORY OF WELFARE, 1890–1935, at 88–96 (1994); Judy Litoff, *Midwives and History,* in WOMEN, HEALTH, AND MEDICINE IN AMERICA, *supra* note 289, at 443, 455; Waysdorf, *supra* note 290, at 776–79, 795–97. On the birthing practices of southern black women generally, see DEBRA SUSIE, IN THE WAY OF OUR GRANDMOTHERS: A CULTURAL VIEW OF TWENTIETH-CENTURY MIDWIFERY IN FLORIDA (1988).

291. GORDON, *supra* note 290, at 143. On the struggles of African-Americans for better health care, see generally Edward Beardsley, *Race as a Factor in Health,* in WOMEN, HEALTH, AND MEDICINE IN AMERICA, *supra* note 289, at 121; Barbara Bernier, *Class, Race and Poverty: Medical Technologies and Socio-Political Choices,* HARV. BLACKLETTER J. 115 (Spring 1994); Marianne Lado, *Breaking the Barriers to Access to Health Care: A Discussion of the Role of Civil Rights Litigation and the Relationship between Burdens of Proof and the Experience of Denial,* 60 BROOK. L. REV. 239 (1994); Vernellia Randall, *Does Clinton's Health Care Reform Proposal Ensure Equality of Health Care for Ethnic Americans and the Poor?,* 60 BROOK. L. REV. 167 (1994); Charlotte Rutherford, *Reproductive Freedoms and African American Women,* 4 YALE J.L. & FEMINISM 255 (1992); Waysdorf, *supra* note 288, at 790–94.

292. WAYNE FLINT, POOR BUT PROUD: ALABAMA'S POOR WHITES 348 (1989). Poor, rural women, who were the object of these efforts, were rather less welcoming to the idea of giving up child labor. *See* Ladd-Taylor, *supra* note 288.

293. Bellingham & Mathis, *supra* note 290, at 173.

294. Kobrin, *supra* note 269, at 350. *See, e.g.,* J. Stanley Lemons, *The Sheppard-Towner Act: Progressivism in the 1920s,* 55 J. AM. HIST. 776 (1968). *See also* EHRENREICH & ENGLISH, *supra* note 269, at 97; GORDON, *supra* note 290, at 95; Bellingham & Mathis, *supra* note 290, at 158; Nancy Dye, *History of Childbirth in America,* 1 SIGNS 97, 106 (1980); Waysdorf, *supra* note 288, at 788–97.

295. *See* GORDON, *supra* note 290, at 93–96; GWENDOLYN MINK, THE WAGES OF MOTHERHOOD: INEQUALITY IN THE WELFARE STATE, 1917–1942, at 72 (1995); ROBYN MUNCY, CREATING A FEMALE DOMINION IN AMERICAN REFORM, 1890–1935, at 162 (1991); THEDA SKOCPOL, PROTECTING SOLDIERS AND MOTHERS: THE POLITICAL ORIGINS OF SOCIAL POLICY IN THE UNITED STATES 510–24 (1992); Bellingham & Mathis, *supra* note 290; Eileen Boris & Peter Bardaglio, *The Transformation of Patriarchy: The Historic Role of the State,* in FAMILIES, POLITICS, AND PUBLIC POLICY: A FEMINIST DIALOG ON WOMEN AND THE STATE 20 (Irene Diamond ed. 1983); Wendy Brown, *Finding the Man in the State,* 18 FEMINIST STUD. 7 (1992); Patricia Cooper, *"A Masculinist Vision of Useful Labor": Popular Ideologies about Women and Work in the United States, 1820–1939,* 84 KY. L.J. 827, 840–42 (1996); Nancy Fraser, *Struggle over Needs: Outline of a Socialist-Feminist Critical Theory of Late Capitalist Political Culture,* in WOMEN, THE STATE, AND WELFARE 199 (Linda Gordon ed. 1990); Linda Gordon, *Black and White Visions of Welfare: Women's Welfare Activism, 1890–1945,* 78 J. AM. HIST. 559 (1991); Ladd-Taylor, *supra* note 291; Gwendolyn Mink, *The Lady and the Tramp: Gender, Race, and the Origins of the*

Bureau against such charges.[296] Indeed, the American Medical Association, the villain in contemporary feminist accounts of the suppression of midwifery, actively (and eventually successfully) opposed the activities of the Children's Bureau on the grounds that it amounted to "socialized medicine."[297] Some of the programs were restored in the *Social Security Act* of 1935.[298]

Long before the Children's Bureau, however, many women who might formerly have become professional midwives were transforming themselves into adjuncts to physicians rather than attempting to be physicians' rivals. This transition began by the by the end of the nineteenth century in the United States where the term "obstetrical nurse" appears at least as early as 1897.[299] The transition from relative independence to a structured dependence occurred even in England where the old professional title of midwife has been retained and where ostensibly midwives retain a more independent role.[300] A more dramatic example of this transition was the abolition in the State of Victoria, Australia, of the "Midwives Board" in 1928. The Victorian Nurses Board thereafter regulated midwives.[301] By the end of the 1930s, the profession of midwifery had virtually disappeared in English speaking countries even without legal prohibition.[302]

The evidence regarding women's interest in the medicalization of birth suggests there was rather less to the claims of an allopathic conspiracy than some modern historians would have us believe. We also find confirmation of the lack of evidence of an allopathic conspiracy driven by hope of economic gain in the extremes to which those historians who purport to discover such a conspiracy go in an effort to discover "evidence" of the conspiracy. So intent was James Mohr on twisting any scrap of evidence into support for his view of lack of popular support for the abortion statutes, or at least of deeply divisive public controversy, that he even insisted that an apparently routine two-week delay in the New Hampshire legislature's appointment of a conference committee to reconcile different versions of that state's first abortion statute to be proof of a "deadlock" between the houses.[303] Actually, as Mohr himself recorded, the conference committee seems to have functioned expeditiously after its appointment, leading to legislative adoption (less than a month after the committee's appointment) of the second law in the United States to declare a mother a criminal for securing an abortion.[304] The dispute in New Hamp-

---

*American Welfare State, in* WOMEN, THE STATE, AND WELFARE, *supra,* at 92; Barbara Nelson, *The Origins of the Two-Channel Welfare State, in* WOMEN, THE STATE, AND WELFARE, *supra,* at 125; Carole Pateman, *The Patriarchal Welfare State, in* DEMOCRACY AND THE WELFARE STATE 231 (Amy Gutmann ed. 1988).

296. *See* Ladd-Taylor, *supra* note 290.

297. *Proceedings of the St. Louis Session,* 78 JAMA 1613, 1709 (1922). *See* REAGAN, *supra* note 52, at 110–11; STARR, *supra* note 209, at 260–61; Ladd-Taylor, *supra* note 290, at 393; Lemons, *supra* note 296, at 779–81; Alice Sardell, *Child Health Policy in the U.S.: The Paradox of Consensus,* 15 J. HEALTH POL., POL'Y & L. 271, 275 (1990); Waysdorf, *supra* note 288, at 780–88.

298. *Social Security Act,* ch. 531, §§ 501–505, 49 Stat. 620, 629–31 (1935). *See* GORDON, *supra* note 290, at 96–98, 257; Beardsley, *supra* note 291, at 134; Ladd-Taylor, *supra* note 290, at 403–04; Lemons, *supra* note 294, at 786; Waysdorf, *supra* note 288, at 797–807.

299. F.M.C. FORSTER, PROGRESS IN OBSTETRICS AND GYNAECOLOGY 1049–50 (1967). *See also* LITOFF, *supra* note 224, at 142–45; PETERSEN, *supra* note 124, at 36; WERTZ & WERTZ, *supra* note 224, at 284–90; EVAN WILLIS, MEDICAL DOMINANCE: THE DIVISION OF LABOUR IN AUSTRALIAN HEALTH CARE 107–09 (rev. ed. 1986).

300. DONNISON, *supra* note 224, at 62; WENDY SAVAGE, SAVAGE ENQUIRY: WHO CONTROLS CHILDBIRTH? (1986); E.A. Bent, *The Growth and Development of Midwifery, in* NURSING, MIDWIFERY AND HEALTH VISITING SINCE 1900, at 180, 180–95 (Peter Allan & Moya Jolley eds. 1982); Martin, *supra* note 241, at 437–39; Sarah Robinson, *Career Intentions of Newly Qualified Midwives,* 2 MIDWIFERY 25 (1986); Sarah Robinson, *Normal Maternity Care: Whose Responsibility?,* 92 BRIT. J. OBSTETRICS & GYNECOLOGY 1, 1–3 (1985).

301. PETERSEN, *supra* note 124, at 41–42.

302. LITOFF, *supra* note 224, at 136–41.

303. MOHR, *supra* note 31, at 134.

304. *Id.* at 133–34.

shire, in fact, was not about whether to adopt an abortion statute, but about whether the statute should be unusually stringent for the time (the House version) or even more stringent (the Senate version).

Mohr claimed that New Hampshire's supposed legislative "deadlock" proved that the main legislative concern was to "regulate medical practice" rather than to regulate abortion.[305] He thought it significant that the legislature enacted a bill to incorporate the "New Hampshire Botanic Medical Society" while the conference committee was working on the abortion bill. Mohr's principal evidence for this claimed link, apart from the temporal one, was that the floor leader of the opposition to the Botanic bill and in support of the abortion bill was the same man,[306] overlooking that the "conspiring" allopathic physicians lost what must have been the main battle against competitors in the very same legislative session in which the abortion statute passed. Indeed, defeat on the Botanic bill came between the appointment of the conference committee on the abortion bill and its report. Mohr himself noted that the state's House of Representatives (which Mohr claimed was under the control of the "irregular" physicians),[307] initially passed its rather strict abortion bill without debate and without recorded vote.[308]

Mohr similarly recounts at length a legislative fight in Maryland when its legislature enacted a prohibition of abortion as part of a statute creating a comprehensive regulatory scheme for the practice of medicine, but promptly repealed all but the prohibition of abortion.[309] Much the same happened in South Carolina near the end of the nineteenth century.[310] Mohr noted that in Illinois in 1867 the vote on an abortion bill was unanimous in both houses of the legislature, without drawing a rather obvious conclusion regarding public opinion in that state.[311] In Michigan in 1873, the vote on an abortion law was recorded: 58 to 16 in the state House; and 25 to 2 in the state Senate.[312] For both states, Mohr again insisted the only concern behind the legislation was the allopaths' desire to suppress competition.

By Mohr's reasoning, if there is the least difficulty in getting an abortion bill through the legislature, this "proves" that the public opposed enactment of the statute and it could only be forced through by the allopathic conspiracy, but if the statute passes unanimously or at least without difficulty that also "proves" that there was an allopathic conspiracy. We are back in *la-la* land where we are damned if we do and damned if we don't.[313] Mohr's idea of evidence of an allopathic conspiracy becomes almost ludicrous when he cites the late-nineteenth century writings by "irregulars" (homeopaths) opposed to abortion as evidence of his supposed conspiracy of the "regulars" (allopaths) to suppress the irregulars.[314] Mohr also ignores the efforts of the "regulars" to weed out their own members who were doing abortions, evidence that again suggests that the concern was with abortion and not with who was doing it.[315]

There is no denying that allopathic physicians were in the lead in the fight for stricter abortion laws, including seeking to foster public recognition that non-allopathic medical practitioners were responsible for a good deal of the growing incidence of abortion. There was

---

305. *Id.* at 134–35.
306. *Id.* at 135, 140.
307. *Id.* at 135.
308. *Id.* at 134.
309. *Id.* at 211–15.
310. *Id.* at 228–29.
311. *Id.* at 205.
312. *Id.* at 221.
313. *See also* Chapter 6, at notes 81–82.
314. Mohr, *supra* note 31, at 173–76.
315. Dyer, *supra* note 228, at 329–32.

nothing secretive or conspiratorial about those efforts; nor did they evoke large-scale public opposition. Consider a report of a committee of the East River Medical Association in New York in 1871:

> Your committee deem the unrestricted practice of medicine as the main cause for the existence of professional abortionists, and the want of proper laws to regulate the practice of medicine as encouraging knaves to assume and practice under titles which institutions duly chartered by the State alone have the right to confer.[316]

Such statements do indicate the allopaths' belief that irregular physicians comprised the bulk of the professional abortionists; similar statements argued that these "irregulars" could exploit this practice to build a relationship that could allow the irregulars to obtain the entire medical business of the patients and their families.[317] Such statements do not show a feigned opposition to abortion invented to gain a competitive advantage over their irregular competition. The same reports often expressly condemned the spreading practice of abortion among the "regular" physicians (the allopaths) as well as its prevalence among irregulars.[318] For example, Dr. George Smith, who focused on the loss of business by law-abiding members of the medical profession, did not argue that the lost business went to irregulars rather than to less scrupulous regulars.[319]

These same sources also stressed the central concern of protecting fetal life as was most pointedly suggested by the very title (*"Foeticide"*) of no less than seven of these sources.[320] As the AMA campaign against abortion heated up, home medical guides were recast to withhold information about "emmenagogues" and filled with strong condemnations of abortion as the murder of unborn children.[321] Some of these books were quite popular; for example, Dr. George Naphey's *Transmission of Life* sold more than 150,000 copies in its first three years on the market.[322] Even the homeopaths—by the later years of the century, the major professional rivals to the al-

---

316. East River Med. Soc'y, Report of Special Committee on Abortion 3–4 (1871). *See also* Crawford, *supra* note 159, at 78; J.J. Mulheron, *Foeticide*, 10 Peninsular J. Med. 387, 389 (1874); Pallen, *supra* note 215, at 196; Augustus St. Clair, *The Evil of the Age*, N.Y. Times, Aug. 23, 1871, at 6; Smith, *supra* note 174, at 211–13. For Mohr's discussion of these sources, see Mohr, *supra* note 31, at 160–61, 179.

317. *See, e.g.*, Alexander Draper, Observations on Abortion: With an Account of the Means Both Medicinal and Mechanical, Employed to Produce that Effect 5–6 (1839); Storer, *supra* note 215, at 85; Walter Channing, *Effects of Criminal Abortion*, 60 Bos. Med. & Surgical J. no. 7, at 136, 139 (Mar. 17, 1859); E.P. Christian, *The Pathological Consequences Incident to Induced Abortion*, 2 Det. Rev. Med. & Pharmacy 147, 147 (1867); Mary Dixon-Jones, *Criminal Abortion—Its Evil and Its Sad Consequences*, 3 Women's Med. J. 61, 66 (pt. II) (1894); Denslow Lewis, *Facts Regarding Criminal Abortion*, 35 JAMA 35 (1900); W.W. Parker, *In Opposition to Women Doctors in Insane Asylums*, 22 JAMA 479 (1894); J.M. Toner, *Abortion in Its Medical and Moral Aspects*, 5 Med. & Surgical Rptr. 443, 443–46 (1861). *See generally* Mohr, *supra* note 31, at 160–61; Reagan, *supra* note 52, at 67–69; Smith-Rosenberg, *supra* note 51, at 232–33, 235.

318. Crawford, *supra* note 159; Christian, *supra* note 317, at 143. *See also* Gibbons, *supra* note 159, at 111; P.S. Haskell, *Criminal Abortion*, 4 Trans. Me. Med. Ass'n 463, 468–69 (1873). *See generally* Mohr, *supra* note 31, at 153, 156, 158, 162–63; Smith-Rosenberg, *supra* note 51, at 233.

319. Smith, *supra* note 174, at 213. *See also* Alfred Andrews, *On Abortion*, 7 Can. Lancet 289, 291 (1875).

320. Hodge, *supra* note 45; Jesse Boring, *Foeticide*, 2 Atlanta Med. & Surgical J. 257, 258 (1857); H.C. Markham, *Foeticide and Its Prevention*, 11 J.A.M.A. 805, 806 (1888); Mulheron, *supra* note 316; Pallen, *supra* note 215; Smith, *supra* note 174; John Stoddard, *Foeticide—Suggestions toward Its Suppression*, 10 Det. Rev. Med. & Pharmacy 656 (1875).

321. *See, e.g.*, James Jackson, The Sexual Organism, and Its Healthful Management 261–73 (1862); C. Morrill, The Physiology of Women 318–19 (1868); George Napheys, The Transmission of Life: Counsels on the Nature and Hygiene of the Masculine Function 123–24 (1878); S.Y. Richard, The Science of the Sexes, or How Parents May Control the Sex of Their Offspring 154–55, 248–49 (1870). *See generally* Mohr, *supra* note 31, at 171–73.

322. Mohr, *supra* note 31, at 173; Olasky, *supra* note 79, at 152.

lopaths—joined the chorus of increasingly strong condemnations of abortion.[323] And such occasional criticism as the anti-abortion crusade received among the allopathic medical profession often was made anonymously, as if the critic were afraid to be publicly identified with the practice they were defending.[324]

Unless, like Beverly Harrison, one is to dismiss all pro-life expressions as mere "rhetorical flourishes,"[325] one must conclude that the extant documents suggest an attempt to describe accurately the nature of the problem that foeticide posed to society and the means necessary to suppress efficiently the killing of unborn children rather than a mere desire to obtain a competitive advantage. Nor was this contradicted by the fact that much or most of the ant-abortion rhetoric was phrased in terms of "the profession"—professional organizations or a consensus of professional medical opinion.[326] Such statements undoubtedly were meant to enhance the weight of the opinions being expressed and perhaps even as a means of creating professional solidarity both behind the anti-abortion crusade and otherwise,[327] but they do not suggest that only professional advantage was in issue. After all, even Mohr conceded that the physicians' belief in the immorality of abortion was "no doubt sincere."[328] Mohr himself summed up the evidence in a statement that revealed more accurately than he realized its true import:

> As one historian of nineteenth-century physicians put it, the founding of the AMA had been "a time of hope...a time to gather the *righteous* under one banner, to seek out and destroy the foe." The anti-abortion crusade launched a decade later was one of the first manifestations of that spirit.[329]

Yet Mohr continued, in the face of the evidence he himself had gathered, to rely heavily on the evidence of a growing incidence of abortion from the mid-nineteenth century onwards to argue that abortion laws were enacted to respond to changing social mores which, by bringing business to the irregulars, created a professional threat that he alleges prompted the regular physicians to counterattack with increasingly stringent abortion statutes.[330] Mohr's story loses much of its little persuasiveness if one factors in the technological changes relating to abortion.[331]

Mohr wrapped up his history by acknowledging the efficacy of the "anti-abortion crusade" in sharply reducing the incidence of abortion.[332] He also conceded that the legalization of abortion in *Roe* had the effect of popularizing abortion.[333] Yet such effects seem to Mohr to be merely incidental to the elimination of competition to the regular (allopathic) medical profession,[334] and not the goal nor even a particular concern of the legal effort he recounted in such detail.[335] Mohr would have us believe that none of the participants in this process had any real concern for the

---

323. *See, e.g.,* HALE, *supra* note 165; G. Maxwell Christine, *The Medical Profession vs. Criminal Abortion,* 25 TRANS. HOMEOPATHIC MED. SOC'Y OF PA., 1889, at 70–72 (1890). *See generally* MOHR, *supra* note 31, at 173–76, 204.

324. OLASKY, *supra* note 80, at 117.

325. HARRISON, *supra* note 246, at 128–29.

326. A point stressed by Mohr. MOHR, *supra* note 31, at 162–64.

327. *Id.* at 163–64.

328. *Id.* at 164–65.

329. *Id.* at 161, quoting ROTHSTEIN, *supra* note 206, at 174 (emphasis added).

330. MOHR, *supra* note 31, at 160–64.

331. See the text *supra* at notes 121–33.

332. MOHR, *supra* note 31, at 239–44.

333. *Id.* at 261–63.

334. *Id.* at 312 n.41.

335. *Id.* at 237–39.

lives of the unborn—despite (as Mohr well knew) the pervasive and consistent recourse to the rhetoric of protecting unborn life by all those opposed to abortion.[336]

Mohr's mode of argument, if acceptable, will make the life of historians considerably easier. What is the need to invest years in researching original sources if one's intuition is a better guide to the truth of past events than anything shown in the evidentiary record? Historians could then write their tales in the manner of medieval monks writing the lives of saints, substituting intuition or divine revelation as the source for what happened hundreds of years earlier and thousands of miles away. But if, as the deconstructionists claim, all knowledge is merely a social construction between the writer and (preeminently) the reader with no possible reference to any objective external reality, this is what all scholarship has always consisted of anyway,[337] and the would-be Gibbons of the world are just wasting their time in dusty libraries. It is time to put the allopathic conspiracy theory off in the corner where it belongs, along with the theory that a Free-Mason conspiracy offers a full explanation of the French Revolution and the theory that the Air Force covered up an alien landing in Roswell, New Mexico.

# The Anti-Abortion Crusade: Horatio Robinson Storer and His Associates

*I really didn't say everything I said.*

—Yogi Berra[338]

Dr. Horatio Robinson Storer is the *bête noir* of the modern orthodoxy of abortion history.[339] Highly opinionated and stubbornly argumentative, Storer was the dominant personality in the

---

336. MOHR, *supra* note 31, at 87, 104, 110–11, 140, 143, 152–53, 156–59, 164–66, 207, 214, 216–17. *See also* Sauer, *supra* note 29, at 57–58.

337. *See, e.g.*, SANDÉ COHEN, HISTORICAL CULTURE: ON THE RECODING OF AN ACADEMIC DISCIPLINE (1986); JONATHAN CULLER, ON DECONSTRUCTION: THEORY AND CRITICISM AFTER STRUCTURALISM (1982); DECONSTRUCTION AND THE POSSIBILITY OF JUSTICE (Drucilla Cornell, Michael Rosenfeld, & David Gray Carlson eds. 1992); JACQUES DERRIDA, ON GRAMMATOLOGY (Gayatri Chakravorty Spivak trans. 1976); PETER DEWS, LOGICS OF DISENTEGRATION: POST-STRUCTURALIST THOUGHT AND THE CLAIMS OF CRITICAL THEORY (1987); MARY JOE FRUG, POSTMODERN LEGAL FEMINISM (1992); KLAUS GÜNTHER, HERO-POLITICS IN MODERN LEGAL TIMES—PRESUPPOSITIONS OF CRITICAL LEGAL STUDIES AND THEIR CRITIQUE (1990); DAVID HARVEY, THE CONDITION OF POSTMODERNITY (1989); DAVID KAIRYS, THE POLITICS OF LAW: A PROGRESSIVE CRITIQUE (1982); MARK KELMAN, A GUIDE TO CRITICAL LEGAL STUDIES (1987); DUNCAN KENNEDY, LEGAL EDUCATION AND THE REPRODUCTION OF HIERARCHY: A POLEMIC AGAINST THE SYSTEM (1983); JEAN-FRANÇOIS LYOTARD, THE POSTMODERN CONDITION: A REPORT ON KNOWLEDGE (Geoff Bennington & Brian Massumi trans. 1984); CHRISTOPHER NORRIS, THE CONTEST OF FACULTIES: PHILOSOPHY AND THEORY AFTER DECONSTRUCTION (1985); PAULINE MARIE ROSENAU, POST MODERNISM AND THE SOCIAL SCIENCES: INSIGHTS, INROADS, AND INTRUSIONS (1992); POLITICS, POSTMODERNITY, AND CRITICAL LEGAL STUDIES: THE LEGALITY OF THE CONTINGENT (Costas Dominas, Peter Goodrich, & Yifat Hachamovitch eds. 1994); MARK TUSHNET, RED, WHITE, AND BLUE: A CRITICAL ANALYSIS OF THE CONSTITUTION (1988); STEPHEN WHITE, POLITICAL THEORY AND POSTMODERNISM (1991); Arthur Austin, *Deconstruction Voice Scholarship*, 30 HOUS. L. REV. 1071 (1993); J.M. Balkin, *Understanding Legal Understanding: The Legal Subject and the Problem of Legal Coherence*, 103 YALE L.J. 105 (1993); Allan Hunt, *The Big Fear: Law Confronts Postmodernism*, 35 McGILL L.J. 507 (1990); Jane Larson & Clyde Spillenger, *"That's Not History": The Boundaries of Advocacy and Scholarship*, 12 PUB. HISTORIAN 33, 40–42 (1990). *See generally* Chapter 20, at notes 17–40.

338. DAVID NATHAN, BASEBALL QUOTATIONS 151 (1993).

339. *See* BRODIE, *supra* note 142, at 259–75; MOHR, *supra* note 31, at 148–59; REAGAN, *supra* note 52, at 82; SMITH-ROSENBERG, *supra* note 51, at 221–22; Siegel, *supra* note 31, at 283–85, 293–97, 303.

early stages of the American Medical Association's campaign against abortion, and thus perhaps the most important leader of the anti-abortion movement in nineteenth-century America.[340] He wrote the first AMA report on abortion in 1859,[341] published three books on the topic between 1865 and 1868,[342] co-authored another book on the topic with a prominent lawyer,[343] and advocated the enactment of stricter abortion laws in numerous articles, reports, and speeches.[344] Storer even took time to earn a law degree after he was established as both a physician and a significant political leader in the anti-abortion crusade—four years before he withdrew from an active leadership role in the crusade.[345] He was also an indefatigable joiner, a member of numerous medical societies on both sides of the Atlantic, who used his connections to press for the effective repression of the emerging practice of abortion.[346]

One should not exaggerate Storer's role. After 1870, Storer's name seldom appeared in publications relating to abortion. His contribution was not even mentioned in the 1871 *Report on Criminal Abortion* of yet another AMA committee,[347] a report that perhaps was even more influential than Storer's work on the topic. Justice Blackmun referred to the 1871 report in *Roe v. Wade*,[348] rather than to the 1859 AMA report that Storer had written and which Mohr and other pro-abortion historians prefer to stress.

Many modern historians, including James Mohr, in contrast to Justice Blackmun, see Storer as almost single-handedly responsible for the nineteenth century legislative activity in the United States.[349] Storer's modern critics see his campaign for the protection of fetal lives and maternal health as merely a means of personal advancement.[350] Some supporters of abortion rights go even further, seeing Storer as a narrow-minded crusader against abortion who must have had an abiding hostility to women, nothing short of the worst enemy of women in the mid-nineteenth century. Law professor Reva Siegel, for example, describes Storer as "antifeminist" in his "first principles" and sandwiched her most extended discussion of Storer's arguments against abortion between lengthy descriptions of the arguments of others calling on the bible as authority for their position.[351] Siegel infers from these facts that Storer desired

---

340. *See generally* DYER, *supra* note 228; FREDERICK CARPENTER IRVING, SAFE DELIVERANCE (1942). Frederick Dyer's book is a recent, detailed, and thorough recounting of Storer's activities.

341. *The Report on Criminal Abortion, supra* note 42. On Storer's role, see BRODIE, *supra* note 142, at 268.

342. HORATIO ROBINSON STORER, ON CRIMINAL ABORTION IN AMERICA 30 (1860) ("STORER, CRIMINAL ABORTION"); STORER, *supra* note 215; HORATIO ROBINSON STORER, IS IT I? A BOOK FOR EVERY MAN 94–95 (1868) ("STORER, EVERY MAN").

343. STORER & HEARD, *supra* note 41.

344. *See, e.g.,* Horatio Robinson Storer, *Criminality and Physical Evils of Forced Abortion*, 16 TRANS. AM. MED. ASS'N 709, 736 (1865); Storer, *Decrease, supra* note 217.

345. DYER, *supra* note 228, at 175 (noting that Storer earned a law degree from Harvard in 1868, perhaps in anticipation of teaching medical jurisprudence). *See also* IRVING, *supra* note 340, at 117 (explaining that Storer took a law degree in order to teach medical jurisprudence); James Walsh, *A Great Convert Physician*, AVE MARIA, Nov. 11, 1922, at 619, 622 (explaining that Storer took the law degree to further the struggle against abortion; Walsh was a close friend of Storer in his later years).

346. OLASKY, *supra* note 79, at 114–15; R. FRENCH STONE, BIOGRAPHIES OF EMINENT AMERICAN PHYSICIANS AND SURGEONS 495 (1894).

347. Atlee & O'Donnell, *supra* note 48. On the reasons for omitting Storer's name, see DYER, *supra* note 228, at 376.

348. *Roe*, 410 U.S. at 142.

349. *See* PATRICIA MILLER, THE WORST OF TIMES 315 (1993); MOHR, *supra* note 31, at 148–59, 169–70, 190, 201, 203, 206; SMITH-ROSENBERG, *supra* note 51, at 221–24, 234, 236–42; Cohen, *supra* note 246, at 207–08 n. 119. *But see* BRODIE, *supra* note 142, at 259–75 (blaming Storer and Anthony Comstock, although Comstock's activities did not begin until the legislative battles over abortion were largely concluded).

350. BRODIE, *supra* note 142, at 266–72; MOHR, *supra* note 31, at 148–49; SMITH-ROSENBERG, *supra* note 51, at 234–35.

351. Siegel, *supra* note 31, at 293–97, 303. *See also* GROSSBERG, *supra* note 51, at 171–72.

to establish his personal legitimacy and to displace midwives as competitors while he pioneered the new "sciences" of obstetrics and gynecology.[352] Perhaps because Mohr did not use explicitly condemnatory language in discussing Storer, Janet Brodie remarkably described Mohr's treatment of Storer and the "physicians' crusade" against abortion as "sympathetic."[353] Storer's critics simply do not mention that Storer worked during most of his career for and with women in ways that cost him standing among men physicians and income from potential patients.[354]

Storer's father, Dr. David Humphreys Storer, had been "Professor of Midwifery" at Harvard University.[355] Four years before his son was to emerge as the national leader of the medical crusade against abortion, the elder Storer became enmeshed in controversy when he devoted part of a lecture, given to inaugurate the academic year 1855 at Harvard Medical School, to the topic of abortion.[356] While the remainder of the lecture was published immediately,[357] the part of his lecture in which he claimed that a recent sharp increase in uterine disease was the result of an alarming rise of abortion was not published for 17 years.[358] The delay in publication appears to have been at least in part because at least some members of the Harvard medical faculty believed that abortion was not as common as the elder Storer had concluded.[359] The younger Storer shortly would allege that the offending part of the talk was suppressed because certain influential faculty members were afraid of a loss of income should abortion become an active concern in the profession.[360] One might see the suppressed part of the lecture, of which the son was aware, as a call for a champion to come forward to lead in the suppression of the growing practice.[361]

The younger Storer, following in his father's footsteps, became "the first in this country to teach gynecology proper, as contra-distinguished from obstetrics or midwifery, his separate courses on the diseases of women, unconnected with gestation, childbed, or the puerperal state, comprising not less than sixty lectures."[362] The bulk of his teaching, as with the teaching of other leading gynecologists down to the very end of the nineteenth century, occurred in the women's

---

352. Siegel, *supra* note 31, at 283–84.

353. BRODIE, *supra* note 142, at 349 n.43.

354. Malcolm Storer, *The Teaching of Obstetrics and Gynecology at Harvard*, 8 HARV. MED. ALUMNI ASS'N 439, 439–40 (1903). (Malcolm was Horatio's son.) *See also* DYER, *supra* note 228, at 166–69.

355. STORER, *supra* note 215, at 17–18. *See also* DYER, *supra* note·228, at 80–82, 387; WALSH, *supra* note 208, at 109; Storer, *supra* note 354. *See generally* IRVING, *supra* note 340, at 109–19.

356. *See generally* DYER, *supra* note 228, at 80–86.

357. DAVID HUMPHREYS STORER, AN INTRODUCTORY LECTURE BEFORE THE MEDICAL CLASS OF 1855–56 OF HARVARD UNIVERSITY (1855).

358. David Humphreys Storer, *Two Frequent Causes of Uterine Disease*, 6 J. GYNECOLOGICAL SOC'Y OF BOSTON 194 (1872).

359. *See* Horatio Robinson Storer, *Self Abuse in Women: Its Causation and Rational Treatment*, 1 W.J. MED. 449, 451 (1867). *See also* DYER, *supra* note 228, at 81, 101.

360. Horatio Robinson Storer, *Criminal Abortion: Its Prevalence, Its Prevention, and Its Relation to the Medical Examiner*, 7 N.H. J. MED. 208, 208 (1857). *See also* DYER, *supra* note 228, at 389–90.

361. DYER, *supra* note 228, at 81–84.

362. WALSH, *supra* note 208, at 109–10. *See also* DYER, *supra* note 228, at 387–88; WATSON, *supra* note 276, at 25. Curiously, sociologist Nanette Davis claims that gynecology as a specialty did not emerge until the 1930s. DAVIS, *supra* note 153, at 89. Some feminist historians have simply chosen to ignore the Storers—father and son—as pioneers in gynecology. Thus, Regina Morantz-Sanchez lists pioneers active in Chicago, New York, and Rome (Georgia) during the period from the 1840s to the 1870s without mentioning either Storer (who were from Boston). *See* MORANTZ-SANCHEZ, *supra* note 132, at 92. Morantz-Sanchez goes on to discuss the theory of "reflex insanity" without mentioning the younger Storer, despite his prominence in the creation and propagation of the theory. MORANTZ-SANCHEZ, *supra*, at 116–17, 121–22, 127–28. For Storer's role in the latter process, see HORATIO ROBINSON STORER, THE CAUSATION, COURSE AND TREATMENT OF REFLEX INSANITY IN WOMEN (1871).

hospitals with which he was affiliated.[363] Storer was probably the first male allopath to devote his practice exclusively to gynecology. As late as 1865, Storer could write that there was only one other such physician in the entire country.[364] He was co-founder and first secretary of the Gynaecological Society of Boston, as well as founding co-editor of the society's journal.[365] Storer's decision to become one of the earliest allopathic specialists in "women's diseases" attracted national attention—not all of it favorable given the suspicions then common regarding male physicians working with women patients.[366] One favorable result of this attention was that the appointment of Storer in 1864 to the first AMA committee to consider policies regarding the specialization of medical practice generally.[367]

Horatio Storer graduated from Harvard Medical School and then studied medicine in Europe.[368] Twenty years later, he became the first American physician to be included in the Register of Physicians of the British Medical Society.[369] Some have suggested that his time in Europe accounts for his concern about women's ills and perhaps also his attitude towards abortion,[370] but in fact he was interested in women's physical problems from early in his medical studies.[371] Perhaps his father's influence as much as his own inclination led him in this direction.[372] The son's inclination was strengthened when he came under the strong influence of the pioneering Scot gynecologist, James Young Simpson, during the younger Storer's two years abroad.[373]

Storer became noted for innovative, even if not always successful, operations that opened up the entire field of gynecological surgery.[374] Controversy attended his surgical experi-

---

363. *See* Ely Van De Warker, *How Gynecology Is Taught*, 11 JAMA 181 (1888). *See generally* MORANTZ-SANCHEZ, *supra* note 132, at 96.

364. Horatio Robinson Storer, *Specialism and Especialism: Their Respective Relations to the Profession*, 2 J. GYNAECOLOGICAL SOC'Y BOS. 39 (1870) (the publication of a report Storer presented in 1865 to the Annual Meeting of the AMA). Apparently Storer had in mind Dr. Thomas Addis Emmet as the other full-time gynecologist in the United States at that time. *See* STORER, EVERY MAN, *supra* note 342, at iii.

365. DYER, *supra* note 228, at 267–95. This position enabled Storer to be elected national president of the Association of the Editors of the American Medical Journals in 1870. *Id.* at 332. When Storer departed for Europe in 1872, the journal folded and one of Storer's bitterest rivals bought the plates for the back issues and had them destroyed. *Id.*

366. On general attitudes regarding early male gynecologists, see the authorities collected *supra* at note 228.

367. 15 TRANS. A.M.A. 52 (1864). *See also* Storer, *supra* note 360. *See generally* DYER, *supra* note 228, at 186, 198–203, 220–21.

368. DYER, *supra* note 228, at 41–79.

369. *Id.* at 405–06.

370. BRODIE, *supra* note 143, at 268, 274.

371. DYER, *supra* note 228, at 59–65.

372. On the close relationship between the Storer father and son, see *id.* at 3–16.

373. *Id.* at 70–79.

374. J.M. TONER, A SKETCH OF THE LIFE OF HORATIO R. STORER, A MEMORIAL VOLUME OF THE ROCKY MOUNTAIN MEDICAL ASSOCIATION 7–14 (1878); George Bixby, *Extirpation of the Puerperal Uterus by Abdominal Section*, 1 J. GYNAECOLOGICAL SOC'Y BOS. 223 (1869); Henry Marcy, *The Early History of Abdominal Surgery in America*, 54 JAMA 600, 602 (1910); J. Ford Prioleau, *Ovariotomy in which "Pocketing the Pedicle" Was Performed: Recovery*, 58 AM. J. MED. SCI. no. 115, at 80, 83 (1869). *See also* DYER, *supra* note 228, at 59–60, 78–79, 87–93, 203–06, 284-86, 289-90, 301–02, 346–48, 364–65; IRVING, *supra* note 340, at 114–16; WALSH, *supra* note 208, at 112–15. For examples of Storer's innovations, see Horatio Robinson Storer, *A New Operation for Umbilical Hernia*, 1 N.Y. MED. RECORD no. 3, at 73 (Apr. 2, 1866); Horatio Robinson Storer, *Cases Illustrative of Obstetric Disease*, 70 BOS. MED. & SURGICAL J. no. 4, at 69 (Feb. 25, 1864); Horatio Robinson Storer, *Operation for Intra-Mural Fibrous Tumor*, 55 BOS. MED. & SURGICAL J. no. 5, at 101 (Sept. 4, 1856); Horatio Robinson Storer, *Pocketing the Pedicle*, 55 AM. J. MED. SCI. no. 109, at 77 (Jan. 1868); Horatio Robinson Storer, *Protracted First Stage of Labor—Rigidity of the Os Uteri*, 54 BOS. MED. & SURGICAL J. no. 2, at 38 (Feb. 14, 1856); Horatio Robinson Storer, *Removal of a Large Horse-Shoe Pessary (Hodge's Open Lever) from within the Cavity of the Bladder without Incision*, 3 N.Y. MED. RECORD no. 9, at 220 (July 1, 1868); Horatio

ments,[375] although his surgical activities were restrained compared to the flamboyant activities of such unbridled egoists as Dr. J. Marion Sims in New York and Dr. Mary Dixon Jones in Brooklyn.[376] Sims favored clitoridectomies for numerous mental and "moral" disorders, including kleptomania and melancholy.[377] Remarkably little controversy seems to have attended another nineteenth-century gynecological practice—manual stimulation of a woman's "pelvic area" to the point of orgasm in order to relieve hysteria and other symptoms of unrelieved emotional, physical, sexual tension—a practice mechanized at the end of the nineteenth century with the invention of primitive vibrators.[378] Again, there is no record of Storer pursuing such dubious procedures.

Storer was affiliated with the Boston Lying-In Hospital in the 1850s.[379] His service there was critical to the hospital obtaining a "uterine ward" for gynecological problems, thus expanding it beyond being facility strictly for birthing.[380] This also gave him a site to teach other physicians

---

Robinson Storer, *Removal of the* Cervix Uteri *for Non-Malignant Hypertrophy,* 7 N.H. J. MED. no. 4, at 97 (April 1857); Horatio Robinson Storer, *Retained Placenta,* 54 Bos. MED. & SURGICAL J. no. 5, at 119 (Mar. 13, 1856); Horatio Robinson Storer, *Successful Removal of the Uterus and both Ovaries by Abdominal Section,* 51 AM. J. MED. SCIENCES no. 101, at 110 (Jan. 1866); Horatio Robinson Storer, *The Clamp Shield: An Instrument Designed to Lessen Certain Surgical Dangers, more Particularly Those of Excision of the Uterus by Abdominal Section,* 1 N.Y. MED. RECORD no. 16, at 385 (Oct. 15, 1866); Horatio Robinson Storer, *The Present Problems in Abdominal Section: Illustrated by a Successful Case of Double Ovariotomy,* 4 CAN. MED. J. 337 (1868); Horatio Robinson Storer, *The Propriety of Operating for Malignant Ovarian Disease,* 5 J. GYNAECOLOGICAL SOC'Y BOS. 158 (1871); Horatio Robinson Storer, *The Rectum in its Relation to Uterine Disease,* 1 AM. J. OBSTET. 66 (1868); Horatio Robinson Storer, *The Surgical Treatment of Hemorrhoids and* Fistual in Ano, *with Their Result,* 3 J. GYNAECOLOGICAL SOC'Y BOS. 221 (1870); Horatio Robinson Storer, *The Use and Abuse of Uterine Tents,* 37 AM. J. MED. SCIENCES no. 73, at 57 (Jan. 1859).

375. *See, e.g., Advisory Medical Boards for Insane Asylums,* 71 Bos. MED. & SURGICAL J. no. 23, at 451 (Jan. 5, 1865). *See generally* WALSH, *supra* note 208, at 112–15.

376. *See generally* HENRY CLARKE COE, THE OLD AND THE NEW GYNECOLOGY 3 (1887) (noting a *furor operandi*—a mania for operations—that swept gynecologists in the later nineteenth century, often at the expense of women's health). On Sims, see BARKER-BENFIELD, *supra* note 269, at 91–119; SEALE HARRIS, WOMEN'S SURGEON: THE LIFE STORY OF J. MARION SIMS (1950); DEBORAH KUHN MCGREGOR, SEXUAL SURGERY AND THE ORIGINS OF GYNECOLOGY: J. MARION SIMS, HIS HOSPITAL, AND HIS PATIENTS (1989); MORANTZ-SANCHEZ, *supra* note 132, at 91–99, 118, 125–26; JAMES RICCI, ONE HUNDRED YEARS OF GYNECOLOGY, 1800–1900, at 36–37, 46–47, 130 (1945); J. MARION SIMS, THE STORY OF MY LIFE (H. Marion Sims ed. 1886); WALSH, *supra* note 208, at 115–16; Isabelle Gunning, *Arrogant Perception, World-Traveling and Multicultural Feminism: The Case of Female Genital Surgeries,* 23 COLUM. H. RTS. L. REV. 189, 205–09 (1991); Henry Marcy, *Some Special Reasons Why the Laparotomist Should Consider the Medico-Legal Aspects of Abdominal Surgery,* 15 JAMA 174 (1890); Isabel McAslan, *Pornography or Misogyny? Fear and the Absurd,* in THE ANATOMY OF GENDER: WOMEN'S STRUGGLE FOR THE BODY 37 (Dawn Currie & Valerie Raoul eds. 1992); Anna Douglas Wood, *The Fashionable Disease: Women's Complaints and Their Treatment in Nineteenth Century America,* in CLIO'S CONSCIOUSNESS RAISED 1 (Mary Hartman & Lois Banner eds. 1974). On Dixon Jones, see MORANTZ-SANCHEZ, *supra.* On the similar behavior of early gynecologists in England, see CORAL LANSBURY, THE OLD BROWN DOG: WOMEN, WORKERS, AND VIVISECTION IN EDWARDIAN ENGLAND 83–87 (1985) (comparing experiment surgery on women with the vivisection of animals); MORANTZ-SANCHEZ, *supra,* at 99–100, 127–28.

377. Apparently the closest Storer came to such surgeries was an operation to cut a woman's cervix in order to dilate it, which he concluded relieved the woman's insanity. Horatio Robinson Storer, *The Relations of Female Patients to Hospitals for the Insane: The Necessity on their Account of a Board of Consulting Physicians to every Hospital,* 15 TRANS. AMA 125 (1864).

378. RACHEL MAINES, THE TECHNOLOGY OF ORGASM: "HYSTERIA," THE VIBRATOR, AND WOMEN'S SEXUAL SATISFACTION (1999); SHERWIN NULAND, THE MYSTERIES WITHIN: A SURGEON REFLECTS ON MEDICAL MYTHS 225–26 (2000).

379. IRVING, *supra* note 340, at 109–19.

380. DYER, *supra* note 228, at 87, 98–99. On the need for the ward, see Editorial, *The Boston Lying-in Hospital,* 54 Bos. MED. & SURGICAL J. no. 2, at 46 (Feb. 14, 1856).

and medical students the practice of gynecology. Storer also was prominent in the hospital's decision to begin to admit unmarried women to its maternity wards.[381] He perhaps supported this as an anti-abortion measure,[382] but it nonetheless remains a milestone in liberalizing reproductive rights. These several efforts to broaden the patient base of the hospital, however, were not enough to keep it open; it closed in November 1856 for want of funds.[383]

Storer thereafter became the only male physician to be on the staff of the New England Hospital for Women and Children ("Women's Hospital") before 1958.[384] Women's Hospital was founded by Dr. Marie Zakrzewska in 1862 as a teaching facility for women doctors and as a pioneering institution for providing gynecological, obstetric, and pediatric care in a setting run by women for women.[385] After the Lying-In Hospital closed, Women's Hospital and St. Elizabeth's were the only hospitals in Boston that allowed gynecological surgery until 1880.[386]

Storer practiced and taught at Women's Hospital for three years (1863–1866).[387] This was during the years in which he was leading the anti-abortion crusade. Storer referred to his experience at Women's Hospital in his joint work with attorney Franklin Fiske Heard on criminal abortion.[388] For two of those years, he was assisted by Dr. Anita Tyng is his private practice.[389] Storer continued to do pioneering work in gynecological surgery at St. Elizabeth's Hospital from 1866 to 1872, after his resignation from Women's Hospital, and later served as professor of obstetrics and medical jurisprudence at Berkshire Medical College.[390]

Storer's choice to specialize in gynecological disorders was criticized as unmanly, as was his agreeing to work under the direction of women physicians at Women's Hospital.[391] Further, he could expect to encounter considerable resistance from his intended patients as many women objected to male doctors conducting genital examinations. Such attitudes were common at the time towards male midwives, gynecologists, and obstetricians.[392]

Storer's career hardly paints a picture of a man hostile to women or looking for a shortcut to personal advancement. His one activity that can fairly be characterized as opposed to women's rights was his consistent public espousal, for some years, of the view that women were unfit by their nature to be physicians (or to perform other functions outside the home).[393] Storer argued

---

381. DYER, *supra* note 228, at 87.

382. *See* Editorial, *supra* note 380, at 47.

383. DYER, *supra* note 228, at 98–99; IRVING, *supra* note 340, at 123.

384. WALSH, *supra* note 208, at 109. *See generally* VIRGINIA DRACHMAN, HOSPITAL WITH A HEART: WOMEN DOCTORS AND THE PARADOX OF SEPARATISM AT THE NEW ENGLAND HOSPITAL, 1862–1969 (1984).

385. DRACHMAN, *supra* note 384, at 21, 38–39. On Zakrzewska's career, see DRACHMAN, *supra,* at 21–43, 114–18, 135–38, 154; AGNES VIETOR, A WOMAN'S QUEST: THE LIFE OF MARIE E. ZAKRZEWSKA (1924); WALSH, *supra* note 208, at 57–105, 108–09, 117–20, 148, 152. On the hospital generally, see DRACHMAN, *supra.* On Zakrezewska's remarkable career, see Chapter 8, at notes 263–68, 290.

386. WALSH, *supra* note 208, at 113. The second male doctor was appointed to the staff of Women's Hospital in 1958 as head the gynecological and obstetric division barely a decade before the hospital closed. *Id.* at 267.

387. DYER, *supra* note 228, at 169–70; TONER, *supra* note 374; WALSH, *supra* note 208, at 109–13.

388. STORER & HEARD, *supra* note 41, at 101.

389. Horatio Robinson Storer, *Letter of Resignation from the New England Hospital for Women and Children,* 75 BOS. MED. & SURGICAL J. no. 9, at 191 (Sept. 27, 1866). *See also* DYER, *supra* note 228, at 206–07. On Tyng's career, see WALSH, *supra* note 208, at 165–66.

390. WATSON, *supra* note 276, at 25.

391. SMITH-ROSENBERG, *supra* note 51, at 231, 233; WALSH, *supra* note 208, at 113, 136–39.

392. See the authorities collected *supra* at note 228.

393. STORER, *supra* note 362, at 79, 133, 148; STORER, *supra* note 215, at 74–75; STORER & HEARD, *supra* note 41, at 101; Horatio Robinson Storer, *The Gynecological Society of Boston and Women Physicians: A Reply to Mr. Wm. Lloyd Garrison,* 2 J. GYNAECOLOGICAL SOC'Y BOS. 95 (1870); *The Discussion on the Female Physi-*

that women are appendages of their reproductive systems, unlike men in whom, according to Storer, the reproductive system was "merely subsidiary."[394] He even quoted Dr. Charles Meigs to the effect that women have "a head almost too small for intellect but just big enough for love."[395] Storer was also a prominent advocate of the view that disorders in reproductive organs were a primary cause of insanity in women (and in men as well, although he was considerably less concerned about such cases).[396] Shocking as such comments are today, Storer's views reflected the widespread nineteenth century view (in both America and Britain) that because women's brains were, on average, measurably smaller than men's, they were incapable of higher education.[397] Nor should we overlook the effect on Storer of his first wife's severe mental illness that first disabled her and ultimately contributed to her early death.[398]

Storer's sharing of the general opinion regarding the ability of women to become physicians shows that he did not entirely rise above the prejudices of his time; it does not show that he was personally peculiarly misogynistic.[399] He also apparently shared the nativist fears that abortion among middle class (*i.e.,* white) American women would open the nation to settlement by foreigners (*i.e.,* darker skinned southern Europeans like my ancestors), and in this vein was not above the always fashionable Catholic-bashing.[400] Storer supported a resolution adopted by his

*cian Question in the American Medical Association,* 7 Bos. Med. & Surgical J. no. 22, at 371–72. *See also* Dyer, *supra* note 228, at 291–92, 302–6, 374–76.

394. Storer, *supra* note 362, at 150; Storer, *supra* note 215, at 74–75.

395. Storer, *supra* note 389, at 191, quoting C.D. Meigs, Lecture on Some of the Distinctive Characteristics of the Female, Delivered before the Class of the Jefferson Medical College, Jan. 1847, at 67 (1847). On theories of women's unfitness for higher education generally, see Clarke, *supra* note 220; Thomas Addis Emmett, The Principles and Practice of Gynecology 21–22 (1879); William Goodell, Lessons in Gynecology 355 (1879); William Warren Potter, How Should Girls Be Educated? A Public Health Problem for Mothers, Educators, and Physicians (1891); Univ. of Wis. Bd. Regents, Annual Report for the Year Ending September 30, 1877, at 45 (1877); Mary Colby, *Presidential Address,* 12 Women's Med. J. 154 (1902). *See generally* Morantz-Sanchez, *supra* note 248, at 54–55; Morantz-Sanchez, *supra* note 132, at 117, 121; Rosalind Rosenberg, Beyond Separate Spheres: Intellectual Roots of Modern Feminism 1–27 (1982); Sue Zschoche, *Dr. Clarke Revisited: Science, True Womanhood, and Female Collegiate Education,* 29 Hist. of Educ. Q. 545 (1989).

396. Storer, *supra* note 362. *See generally* Dyer, *supra* note 228, at 175–90, 296. On the belief that women's reproductive organs were a frequent cause of mental disorders, see Robert Carter, On the Pathology and Treatment of Hysteria 46, 90 (1853); George Preston, Hysteria and Certain Allied Conditions 37 (1890); A.J. Skene, Medical Gynecology: A Treatise on the Diseases of Women from the Standpoint of the Phsycian 320 (1895); E.W. Cushing, *Melancholia; Masturbation; Cured by Removal of Both Ovaries,* 8 JAMA 441 (1887); Robert Edes, *Ovariotomy for Nervous Disease,* 130 Bos. Med. & Surgical J. 105 (1894); Henry MacNaughton-Jones, *The Correlation of Sexual Function with Insanity and Crime,* 92 Brit. J. Med. Sci. 455 (1886); George Rohé, *The Relation of Pelvic Disease and Psychical Disturbance in Women,* 5 Trans. Am. Ass'n of Obstet. & Gynecologists 321 (1892); H.A. Tomlinson & Mary Bassett, *Association of Pelvic Diseases and Insanity in Women, and the Influence of Treatment of Local Diseases upon the Mental Condition,* 33 JAMA 827 (1899) (rejecting the theory). *See also* Wendy Mitchinson, The Nature of Their Bodies: Woman and Their Doctors in Victorian Canada 50 (1991); Morantz-Sanchez, *supra* note 248, at 215–16; Morantz-Sanchez, *supra* note 132, at 119–26; Andrew Scull & Diane Fabeau, *"A Chance to Cut Is a Chance to Cure": Sexual Surgery for Psychosis in Three Nineteenth-Century Societies,* 8 Research in Law, Deviance, and Social Control 17 (1986); Sally Shuttleworth, *Female Circulation: Medical Discourse and Popular Advertising in the Mid-Victorian Era,* in Body/Politics: Women and Discourses of Science 47 (Mary Jacobus, Evelyn Fox Keller, & Sally Shuttleworth eds. 1990). *See generally* Edward Shorter, From Paralysis to Fatigue: A History of Psychosomatic Illness in the Modern Era 40–94 (1992).

397. Steven Jay Gould, The Mismeasure of Man 105 (1981). *See also* Chapter 8, at notes 271–306.

398. Dyer, *supra* note 228, at 176–78, 352, 366, 390–91, 404.

399. *See* Walsh, *supra* note 208, at 139–40.

400. *See, e.g.,* Horatio Robinson Storer, *Contributions to Obstetric Jurisprudence—Criminal Abortion III: Its Victims,* 3 N. Am. Medico-Chirurgical Rev. 446 (1859); Storer, *supra* note 217. *See* Dyer, *supra* note 228,

classmates while a student at Harvard Medical School opposing the admission of women to the school, yet he had stood with the minority (the vote was 65 to 48) at the same meeting in opposing a resolution against the admission of African-American students.[401] Storer would long campaign against discrimination against African-Americans, sponsoring the resolution admitting the first African-American members of the American Medical Association,[402] writing caustically and at length about the history of slavery in his adopted community of Newport, Rhode Island,[403] and publicly condemning the publication of *The Clansman,* a notoriously racist novel,[404] and some years later the movie *The Birth of a Nation* based on that novel.[405]

A certain caution is necessary in judging a person from another time or place by historically contingent standards from a different time or place.[406] After all, even at Oberlin College, the first co-educational higher educational institution in the world, there was strong emphasis on maintaining gender roles and preparing women to be proper mothers.[407] Oberlin prohibited the reading of novels or dancing out of fear for the chastity of its women students.[408] Women students were required to clean the rooms of the men students as part of their education.[409] The women of Oberlin, however, seemed more concerned over whether they would be allowed to sing bass than over what today would strike us as more serious injustices.[410] In the end, one simply must be wary in "judg[ing] Moses by the standards of the Spartan Constitution."[411]

One of Storer's staunchest critics, historian Carroll Smith-Rosenberg, is quite ready to accept as an exculpatory rationale for Dr. Havelock Ellis's criticism of lesbianism that Ellis could not be expected to rise above this belief common in his time.[412] She does not excuse Storer in this fashion. One might compare the role of John Stuart Mill in England in the opening years of the women's suffrage movement at about the same time that Storer was leading the crusade against abortion in the United States. Mill, a great liberal champion of free thought and free speech, founded an early group for advocating the vote for women.[413] Mill even wrote a book that was a most important contribution to feminism.[414] Mill, however, blocked efforts to unify that movement under a shared leadership, and "any reader of the last years of his correspondence is likely to be shocked at his intolerance of disagreement, his rejection of public

---

at 137–39; Olasky, *supra* note 79, at 116; Smith-Rosenberg, *supra* note 51, at 238. No one seems to have accused Storer of Jew-baiting, although they were also "foreigners" in Storer's terms.

401. Dyer, *supra* note 228, at 43–45.

402. *Id.* at 324–25.

403. *Id.* at 434–36.

404. *Id.* at 474–75.

405. *Id.* at 491–92.

406. *See* Paul Carrington, *One Law: The Role of Legal Education in the Opening of the Legal Profession since 1776,* 44 Fla. L. Rev. 501, 502–03 (1992).

407. 1 Robert Fletcher, A History of Oberlin College: From Its Foundation through the Civil War 291 (1943).

408. *Id.* at 308.

409. *Id.* at 382.

410. 2 Fletcher, *supra* note 407, at 770.

411. 1 Francis Leiber, Manual of Political Ethics 311 (Theodore Woolsey ed. 2nd ed. 1911). *But see* Allen Buchanan, *Judging the Past: The Case of the Human Radiation Experiments,* 26 Hastings Ctr. Rep. no. 3, at 25 (May–June 1996).

412. Smith-Rosenberg, *supra* note 51, at 277.

413. *See generally* Barbara Caine, *John Stuart Mill and the English Women's Movement,* 18 Hist. Stud. 52 (1978). *See also* Andrea Nye, Feminist Theories and the Philosophies of Man 12–26 (paperback ed. 1989).

414. John Stuart Mill, The Subjection of Women (1869). On the impact of this book, see Jane Rendell, *Citizenship, Culture and Civilisation: The Languages of British Suffragists, 1866–1874,* in Suffrage and Beyond: International Feminist Perspectives 127, 135–36, 139 (Caroline Daley & Melanie Nolan eds. 1994).

campaigning, and his inability to work with any but womanly women."[415] Or compare the thinking of the first Justice Harlan about race. Justice Harlan is lauded for his dissent in *Plessy v. Ferguson*[416] and other cases dealing with race issues, but himself held strongly racist views that he felt private actors (as opposed to the state) should be free to act upon.[417] Such racist views were then commonly held even by the Radical Republicans who strongly favored the rights of former slaves during reconstruction.[418] In contrast, Storer seems to have behaved more openly and more liberally than Mill and to have been more clear and consistent about race than Harlan.

Horatio Robinson Storer was not the only male physician who reached a conclusion opposed to women as physicians even after extensive first hand experience working with educating women for the field.[419] The great majority of male physicians on both sides of the Atlantic considered women congenitally unfit to be physicians.[420] Although today we see such sentiments as absurd, just such ideas were expressed without embarrassment regarding university education generally as recently as 1962.[421] There were, of course, numerous women in the later nineteenth century who proved themselves as physicians, lawyers, soldiers, and virtually any other profession open to men. Unlike some of his contemporaries, Storer was not blind to this reality despite his expressed skepticism regarding the intellectual abilities of most women. He expressly recognized exceptions in Drs. Tyng and Zakrzewska, and thus implicitly that there could be others.[422] Tyng was one of the women turned down for admission by Harvard Medical School during the era when it did not admit women.[423] This did not prevent Storer, who was then on the faculty of the Harvard Medical School, from taking her on as an associate in his medical practice, or from working with Zakrzewska at Women's Hospital.

Storer associated himself with these women physicians in the face of a medical profession in Boston that was so hostile to women physicians that the Massachusetts Medical Society's journal failed to mention the Gynaecological Society of Boston in its annual list of "Medical Societies in Boston" and failed to list St. Elizabeth's hospital in its annual list of "Hospitals in Boston" as late as 1871.[424] The Massachusetts Medical Society, then as now, was dominated by the Harvard medical faculty. The Harvard medical faculty also refused in 1871 to appoint a "Professor of the Diseases of Women" when at least 14 other accredited medical schools already had done so.[425]

---

415. Rendell, *supra* note 414, at 130. *See also* TANNAHILL, *supra* note 228, at 392 (noting that Mill supported women's suffrage, but also demanded that voters demonstrate educational qualifications that most women — and many men — would not possess).

416. 163 U.S. 537, 552–64 (1896) (Harlan, J., dissenting).

417. *See, e.g.*, The Civil Rights Cases, 109 U.S. 3, 26–27 (1883) (Harlan, J., dissenting); *Plessy*, 163 U.S. at 561–62 (Harlan, J., dissenting). *See generally* TINSLEY YARBROUGH, JUDICIAL ENIGMA: THE FIRST JUSTICE HARLAN (1995).

418. YARBOROUGH, *supra* note 422, at 161–62; Herbert Hovenkamp, *Social Science and Segregation before Brown*, 1985 DUKE L.J. 624, 638–44.

419. *See* WALSH, *supra* note 208, at 119–30, 151–52 (reviewing the career of Dr. Edward Clarke).

420. *See* DONNISON, *supra* note 224, at 80–82, 89–92; PENINA GLAZER & MIRIAM SLATER, UNEQUAL COLLEAGUES: THE ENTRANCE OF WOMEN INTO THE PROFESSIONS, 1890–1940, at 1–23 (1987); MORANTZ-SANCHEZ, *supra* note 248, 9–27; WALSH, *supra* note 208, at 8–9, 27–32, 97–98, 106–46, 150–77.

421. FREDERICK RUDOLPH, THE AMERICAN COLLEGE AND UNIVERSITY: A HISTORY 324 (1962).

422. Storer, *supra* note 389, at 191. *See also* George Lyman, *The Interests of the Public and the Medical Profession*, MEDICAL COMMUNICATIONS OF THE MASSACHUSETTS MEDICAL SOCIETY 35 (1873).

423. WALSH, *supra* note 208, at 165–66.

424. The point was noted in *Editorial Notes*, 5 J. GYNAECOLOGICAL SOC'Y BOS. 306, 310–11 (1871). *See also* DYER, *supra* note 228, at 381–82.

425. *Editorial Notes*, *supra* note 424, at 380–81. *See also* DYER, *supra* note 228, at 383–84.

A few male doctors with female associates did come to accept the ability and right of women generally to become doctors.[426] Even Storer was able eventually to reach this conclusion. Storer's opposition to educating women generally arose in a context of certain difficulties he had, and he eventually came to support the opposite view. Storer did consistently strenuously attack claims that women were best treated by women, but then so did Dr. Zakrzewska.[427] In fact, all Storer would complain about when he resigned from women's hospital in 1866 was a decision, made some time earlier, to exclude male students from instruction by Storer at the hospital.[428]

The occasion for Storer's public announcement of his view that women were naturally unfit to be physicians was his resignation from Women's Hospital.[429] A complete record of his activities suggests something more was involved than fear of competition from women. He resigned during a time of deep personal difficulties. The conflict at Women's Hospital that led to his resignation arose from Storer's unwillingness to comply with a resolution of the board of the hospital that he consult with others on the staff before undertaking experimental surgery.[430] He had been dismissed earlier in the same year from the Harvard Medical School faculty after strenuous disagreements with senior faculty members there about similar questions.[431] Storer joined the staff of another women's hospital in Boston—St. Elizabeth's—within the year.[432] He also helped found a home for "deserted and destitute" infants early in 1867.[433]

Abdominal surgery was still a novel and controversial procedure in 1866. While one can only speculate now whether his continuing connection with Women's Hospital caused his troubles at Harvard,[434] we do know that Storer often was stubborn to the point of foolishness. For example, he insistently championed chloroform as superior to ether as an anesthetic in a city where most medical people were strongly committed to the other view.[435] His Harvard dismissal and the disputes with senior staff and the board of Women's Hospital that emerged immediately after his dismissal at Harvard appear to have affected his judgment on the abilities of women in general. These events did not seem to have affected his judgments of Drs. Tyng and Zakrzewska. Dr. Storer and Dr. Tyng were still corresponding cordially at least as late as 1893.[436] In the end, Storer did rise above the prejudices of his time even in his attitudes towards women physicians. He wrote to Harvard in 1878 (only a dozen years after strongly condemning the very idea of women physicians) to support the admission of women to study at Harvard

---

426. WALSH, *supra* note 208, at 148–51, 156–61.

427. *Id.* at 118. *See also* DRACHMAN, *supra* note 384, at 54–57; Richard Shryock, *Women in American Medicine,* 5 J. AM. MEDICAL WOMEN'S ASS'N 375 (1950).

428. Storer, *supra* note 389, at 191. DYER, *supra* note 228, at 170, 223–24.

429. Storer, *supra* note 389. Storer apparently had written to the same effect as early as 1856, but in an unsigned article. *Female Physicians,* 54 BOS. MED. & SURGICAL J. no. 9, at 169 (Apr. 3, 1856). *See* DYER, *supra* note 228, at 90. His letter has caused an historian to describe Storer as "the only real traitor" to Women's Hospital. DRACHMAN, *supra* note 384, at 56.

430. DYER, *supra* note 228, at 222–25; VIETOR, *supra* note 385, at 339–40; WALSH, *supra* note 208, at 112–14.

431. *See Editorial Notes,* 3 J. GYNAECOLGICAL SOC'Y BOS. 253, 259–63 (1870) (Storer was the editor the time); *Professional Criticism,* 74 BOS. MED. & SURGICAL J. no. 13, at 263 (Apr. 26, 1866). *See generally* DYER, *supra* note 228, at 210–19, 266, 342–44; WALSH, *supra* note 208, at 112.

432. DYER, *supra* note 228, at 225.

433. *Id.* at 232–33.

434. *See, e.g.,* SMITH-ROSENBERG, *supra* note 51, at 231.

435. HORATIO ROBINSON STORER, EUTOKIA: A WORD TO PHYSICIANS AND TO WOMEN UPON THE EMPLOYMENT OF ANAESTHETICS IN CHILDBIRTH (1863); Horatio Robinson Storer, *On the Employment of Anaesthetics in Obstetric Medicine and Surgery,* 69 BOS. MED. & SURGICAL J. no. 13, at 249 (Oct. 29, 1863). *See generally* DYER, *supra* note 228, at 88–90, 98–99, 170–75, 237, 306–10, 318–19, 356–57.

436. DYER, *supra* note 228, at 565 n.30.

Medical School without any distinction whatever between the women and the men students.[437] Those intent on seeing in Storer an incorrigible misogynist apparently have missed his turn-about completely.[438]

Storer apparently had been inspired by his father's controversial lecture in 1855 to undertake a crusade against the growing problem of abortion.[439] On February 28, 1857, he made his first public presentation on the topic at a meeting of the Suffolk District Medical Society.[440] He quickly emerged as the national leader of the allopathic physicians' campaign to suppress abortion.[441] From 1857 until he went abroad in 1872, Storer campaigned against abortion precisely to protect the life of the unborn infant[442] and also to protect the health of the mother. He considered maternal health to be at risk because of the dangers of the procedure[443] and because he believed that pregnancies were necessary for female health.[444] Storer warned the profession and the public about the dangers of abortifacients and about the dangers of the mechanical contraceptives of the day, attributing a wide range of disabilities to abortions, including abdominal problems, back problems, loss of bladder control, disabled limbs, headaches, neuralgic breasts, and changes of personality.[445] Those warnings appear grossly exaggerated to us, but in fact they reflected the very real dangers that the technologies then posed.[446]

As his opposition to the idea of women as doctors or his belief that a woman could not remain healthy if she never had any children amply demonstrated, Storer held a number of beliefs about women that today we would find laughable if there is no likelihood of persons in authority acting on them. On the other hand, Storer cannot be dismissed simply as one more narrow-minded prude; his entire career contradicts any attempt to paint him as unthinking, uncaring, or driven by reflexive hostility to women or to sexuality. Even his criticism of the idea of woman as a "mere plaything" for the gratification "of her own or her husband's desires"[447] hardly betokens hostility to women. Storer was an early champion of making convictions for rape easier, advocating the redefinition of the crime to eliminate any reference to force and to encompass any unwelcome "reciprocal contact between the generative organs of the two parties" as well as strongly supporting the idea of statutory rape as protection for "children of tender age."[448] Nearly

---

437. *Id.* at 419–20.

438. *See, e.g.,* ANDREA TONE, DEVICES AND DESIRES: A HISTORY OF CONTRACEPTIVES IN AMERICA 18 (2001); Rhoda Wynn, *Saints and Sinners: Women and the Practice of Medicine throughout the Ages,* 283 JAMA 668, 668 (2000).

439. *See, e.g.,* STORER & HEARD, *supra* note 41, at 2. *See generally* DYER, *supra* note 228, at 86–87. See the text *supra* at notes 355–61.

440. DYER, *supra* note 228, at 100–04. For a contemporary accounts of the talk, see Luther Parks, jr., *Minutes, Suffolk District Medical Society, Meeting of Feb. 28, 1857,* 56 BOS. MED. & SURGICAL J. no. 14, at 282 (May 7, 1857); "Student" (Charles Edward Buckingham), *Letter from Boston: Criminal Abortion,* 10 MED. & SURGICAL RPTR. 207 (1857).

441. *See generally* DYER, *supra* note 228, at 100–63, 190–98, 225–32, 236–50, 263–66, 296–97, 329–32, 339–40, 345–46, 390–91; IRVING, *supra* note 340, at 104–19.

442. STORER, *supra* note 215, at 29–35, 67–70, 73; *Report, supra* note 42, at 76 (Storer was the principal author of the report).

443. STORER, *supra* note 215, at 12–13, 35–49, 52–61, 70–71.

444. STORER, CRIMINAL ABORTION, *supra* note 342, at 115–16; STORER EVERY MAN, *supra* note 342, at 30; STORER, *supra* note 215, at 72–73, 75–76, 80. One might recall the similar notions permeating Aldous Huxley's *Brave New World,* Huxley being at the time a noted iconoclast and advocate of sexual freedom. ALDOUS HUXLEY, BRAVE NEW WORLD (1932).

445. *See* STORER, *supra* note 215, at 39–50.

446. See Chapter 1, and the text *supra* at notes 114–60.

447. STORER, *supra* note 215, at 80–81.

448. Horatio Robinson Storer, *A Medical-Legal Study of Rape,* 2 N.Y. MED. J. no. 8, at 81 (Nov. 1865); Horatio Robinson Storer, *The Law of Rape,* 2 Q.J. PSYCH. MED. & MED. JURISPRUDENCE no. 1, at 47 (Jan. 1868). *See generally* DYER, *supra* note 228, at 208–09.

alone among his contemporaries, he denounced marital rape[449] and seems to have contemplated the use of contraception of some sort, despite his belief that "occasional" pregnancy was a necessary condition to women's health. Storer described marriage without children as legalized prostitution,[450] but he also publicly advocated spacing children two-and-a-half to three years apart to permit the mother to "rest" as well as to provide adequate time for nurturing each infant.[451] He apparently believed in abstinence or the rhythm method of birth control.[452]

Storer certainly was not a feminist, but his thinking and advocacy were too complex to allow him to be dismissed merely as a misogynist. Storer was an upper middle class physician serving similarly upper middle class patients; he apparently did not encounter the prostitutes who formed a major part of the trade of the emerging professional abortionists, or the truly poor who relied on untrained midwives.[453] Storer himself reported that he had based his thinking about abortion on some 15 "respectable" married women who had asked him to perform abortions.[454] Given his experience as a physician, he saw abortion primarily as a problem among married, upper middle class women, and given his influence on the anti-abortion movement, he confirmed other, similar physicians in their like view.[455] The resulting class bias continues to distort the evidence we have today regarding the incidence of abortion in the mid- to late-nineteenth century as well as the social settings in which abortion occurred and the consequences of those abortions for society.[456]

In the midst of his professional difficulties, Storer developed a serious infection, apparently resulting from gynecological surgery.[457] Storer went to Europe for about five years to recover both from the infection and from the loss of his first wife.[458] There, he married for the second time—to the sister of his first wife—only to see her die about nine months after the wedding, four days after giving birth.[459] About two years later, he married a third time—to his long-time nurse.[460] Upon his return in 1877, Storer took up residence in Newport, Rhode Island.[461]

Mohr considerably overstates the matter when he claims that Storer retired in 1872.[462] While living in Newport, Storer was involved to some extent in the medical profession into the 1890s, although it appears that he only resumed an active practice of medicine for two years (1885 and 1886).[463] He even made a major public address on the problem of abortion as late as 1897.[464] By the time he passed away in 1922, Storer was a venerable old man who had made his peace even

---

449. STORER, EVERY MAN, *supra* note 342, at 89–95, 111.

450. *Id.* at 14, 83. *See also* STORER & HEARD, *supra* note 41, at 127; STORER, *supra* note 37, at 97; STORER, CRIMINAL ABORTION, *supra* note 342, at 101.

451. STORER, EVERY MAN, *supra* note 342, at 115–16.

452. STORER, *supra* note 215, pref. to 2nd ed. (1867). Such attitudes regarding birth control were widespread at the time. *See generally* TONE, *supra* note 438, at 16–19. Even Anthony Comstock shared the same view of contraception. Mary Alden Hopkins, *Birth Control and Public Morality: An Interview with Anthony Comstock,* HARPER'S WEEKLY, May 22, 1915, at 490.

453. OLASKY, *supra* note 79, at 115.

454. STORER & HEARD, *supra* note 41, at 56.

455. OLASKY, *supra* note 79, at 115.

456. *Id.* at 115 n.27.

457. *Editorial Note,* 6 J. GYNAECOLOGICAL SOC'Y BOS. 8 (1872). *See also* DYER, *supra* note 228, at 395; IRVING, *supra* note 340, at 118.

458. *Editorial Notes,* 7 J. GYNAECOLOGICAL SOC'Y BOS. 290 (1872). *See also* DYER, *supra* note 228, at 392–408. Storer seems to have suffered from a long history of ill health. *See* DYER, *supra,* at 66, 151.

459. DYER, *supra* note 228, at 397–401, 508–26.

460. *Id.* at 405.

461. *Id.* at 409–52.

462. MOHR, *supra* note 31, at 159.

463. DYER, *supra* note 228, at 441–42.

464. *Id.* at 463–68.

with Harvard, where he was honored for his many accomplishments — including being the oldest living alumnus for nearly a decade before his death at nearly 90.[465]

Storer was never the center of the anti-abortion movement after he returned from Europe. He did not have to be. Storer's most important contribution to the anti-abortion crusade was not his writings or his other steps to press the case against abortion; it was his gathering together of a committee of physicians who would in turn lead the crusade both nationally and in key states across the nation. These included Drs. Edward Barton of South Carolina, Thomas Blatchford of New York, Henry Brisbane of Wisconsin, Hugh Hodge of Pennsylvania, Charles Pope of Missouri, and Alexander Semmes of Louisiana.[466] These men and others recruited by Storer or by his disciples, served as presidents of state medical associations, and in the case of Pope as president of the American Medical Association. Other physicians, such as Joshua Taylor Bradford of Connecticut, Samuel Henry Eells and Homer Hitchcock of Michigan, P.S. Haskell and, Oren Horr of Maine, Addison Niles of Illinois, and Joseph Stone of Iowa, became active in the campaign against abortion as a reaction to the carnage they had seen during the Civil War.[467] Given the role the Civil War had played in their lives, one is hardly surprised to find that they saw in abortion an evil equivalent to the "curse of American slavery"[468] and compared the loss of life to abortion to "the broken ranks of…regiments during the late war."[469] Together, these men carried on where Storer left off; together, they succeeded in making the criminality of abortion abundantly clear throughout all stages of pregnancy.

---

465. *Id.* at 508–26.
466. *See* DYER, *supra* note 228, at 147–49; MOHR, *supra* note 31, at 151–55; OLASKY, *supra* note 79, at 118–19.
467. OLASKY, *supra* note 79, at 119–21, 128–29.
468. Haskell, *supra* note 318, at 471.
469. Stone, *supra* note 83, at 29.

# Chapter 8

# You're So Vain, I'll Bet You Think This Song Is about You[1]

*[E]ach generation gets the past it deserves.*

—Grant Gilmore[2]

The new orthodoxy of abortion history has it that the nineteenth-century legislatures debated the frequent statutory enactments in various states throughout the century that steadily closed gaps and fissures in the laws prohibiting abortions[3] primarily as a form of medical regulation.[4] The new orthodoxy also raises anti-foreign feeling, verging (among other prejudices) on anti-Semitism, as a major motive for the anti-abortion crusade of the late-nineteenth century.[5] Those who expound the new orthodoxy dismiss any professed concern of the leaders of the anti-abortion campaign for other values—such as the protection of fetal life,[6] the protection of the life or health of mothers,[7] or the protection of public morality[8]—as at best a mere "moral prejudice"[9] and at worst a subterfuge necessary to enlist others in the physicians' anticompetitive cam-

---

1. Carly Simon, *You're So Vain* (1972).

2. GRANT GILMORE, THE AGES OF AMERICAN LAW 102 (1977).

3. *See* Chapter 7, at notes 3–28.

4. *See, e.g.,* JAMES MOHR, ABORTION IN AMERICA: THE ORIGINS AND EVOLUTION OF NATIONAL POLICY, 1800–1900, at 119, 202 (1978). *See generally* Chapters 6 & 7.

5. ELLEN CHESLER, WOMEN OF VALOR: MARGARET SANGER AND THE BIRTH CONTROL MOVEMENT 60 (1992); DAVID GARROW, LIBERTY AND SEXUALITY: THE RIGHT OF PRIVACY AND THE MAKING OF ROE V. WADE 17, 96, 107–08, 129 (2nd ed. 1998); FAYE GINSBURG, CONTESTED LIVES: THE ABORTION DEBATE IN AN AMERICAN COMMUNITY 32 (1989); LINDA GORDON, WOMAN'S BODY, WOMAN'S RIGHT: A SOCIAL HISTORY OF BIRTH CONTROL IN AMERICA 140–42, 236–45 (1976); MARK GRABER, RETHINKING ABORTION: EQUAL CHOICE, THE CONSTITUTION, AND REPRODUCTIVE POLITICS 24 (1996); MICHAEL GROSSBERG, GOVERNING THE HEARTH: LAW AND THE FAMILY IN NINETEENTH-CENTURY AMERICA 170–71 (1985); DONALD JUDGES, HARD CHOICES, LOST VOICES 104 (1993); KRISTIN LUKER, ABORTION AND THE POLITICS OF MOTHERHOOD 27–28 (1984); MOHR, *supra* note 4, at 91–93, 180, 207–09; ROSALIND POLLACK PETCHESKY, ABORTION AND WOMEN'S CHOICE: THE STATE, SEXUALITY, AND REPRODUCTIVE FREEDOM 77–79, 82–89, 93–94, 116–25, 129–30 (rev. ed. 1990); CARROLL SMITH-ROSENBERG, DISORDERLY CONDUCT: VISIONS OF GENDER IN VICTORIAN AMERICA 224–28, 238 (1985); Jeannie Rosoff, *"The Politics of Birth Control,"* 20 FAM. PLANNING PERSPECTIVES 312, 313 (1988); Reva Siegel, *Reasoning from the Body: A Historical Perspective on Abortion Regulation and Questions of Equal Protection,* 44 STAN. L. REV. 261, 297–300 (1992).

6. *See, e.g.,* MOHR, *supra* note 4, at 87, 104, 110–11, 140, 143, 152–53, 156–59, 164–66, 207, 214, 216–17.

7. *Id.* at 120–22, 125–29, 207, 254–55.

8. *Id.* at 88–89, 131, 141–42, 163–66, 207–08, 214, 216–17, 238.

9. *Id.* at 140, 143–44, 147–54, 164–70, 196–99, 219–21, 238, 261–63, 307 n.69.

paign.[10] Only an occasional pro-abortion historian are more candid, admitting that virtually all the discussion of abortion in medical and other literature in the nineteenth century stressed the protection of fetal life (often even labeling the crime as "foeticide"), with other reasons being mentioned, if at all, merely in passing.[11]

The new orthodoxy holds that the public in general, and women in particular, were either duped or disregarded in the efforts of the allopathic physicians to gain economic control over the birthing process. The allopaths supposedly used abortion as a weapon to drive out the competition, particularly midwives. The historians of the new orthodoxy offer no direct evidence of such an allopathic conspiracy, substituting conjecture about the motives of individuals and groups. These conjectures do not hold up when one examines the evidence offered to support them.[12] Completely absent from the new orthodoxy is any sense of change in the methods or techniques by which abortions were performed,[13] yet these changes were central to professional responses to abortion throughout the nineteenth century. Nor does the new orthodoxy adequately address the role of women relative to abortion in the nineteenth century.

Historians of the new orthodoxy, particularly those who describe themselves as feminists, tend to project their notions of what women feel and think today onto women of the past, particularly American women of the nineteenth century. Such projections, often enough questionable regarding women the late twentieth century, are wholly insupportable for women in the late nineteenth century. Even James Mohr, intent as he was to demonstrate that the criminalization of abortion was an imposition by a medical conspiracy against society, cited a great deal of evidence of a broad social consensus in favor of the criminalization of abortion — including the near unanimous strong condemnation of abortion by nineteenth-century feminists. Mohr was reduced to describing the feminist attitudes towards abortion as "an anomaly."[14]

The historical record is clear. Only by impugning the integrity of innumerable social and professional leaders can one argue that protection of unborn children from the rising numbers of abortions was not a significant concern. Even charges of insincerity hardly explain the attitude of the nineteenth century feminists. Their attitude also belies the claims in the two so-called *Historians' Briefs*[15] that nineteenth-century abortion statutes were adopted by men in order to oppress women — in struggles between doctors and midwives for markets, or between husbands and wives for dominance in the home, or of men to use women to prevent "race suicide."[16] It is particularly important to discover what stand the emerging women's movement (the "first wave of feminism") took on these matters.

---

10. *Id.* at 134–35, 159–64, 220–21, 224–26, 228–29, 237–39, 244–45, 255–60. *See also* SMITH-ROSENBERG, *supra* note 5, at 236–44.

11. *See, e.g.,* CARL DEGLER, AT ODDS: WOMEN AND THE FAMILY IN AMERICA FROM THE REVOLUTION TO THE PRESENT 241 (1980).

12. *See* Chapter 6, at notes 213–331, and Chapter 7, at notes 205–470.

13. *See* Chapter 6, at notes 332–413, and Chapter 7, at notes 114–60.

14. MOHR, *supra* note 4, at 113.

15. *Amicus Brief of 250 American Historians in support of Appellants in* Planned Parenthood of Southeastern Pennsylvania v. Casey, [505 U.S. 833 (1992)], at 11–21 ("*Casey Historians' Brief*"); *Amicus Brief of 281 American Historians supporting Appellees in* Webster v. Reproductive Health Services [492 U.S. 490 (1989)] ("*Webster Historians' Brief*"), reprinted at 11 WOMEN'S RTS. L. RPTR. 163, 173–77 (1989), and in 8 DOCUMENTARY HISTORY OF THE LEGAL ASPECTS OF ABORTION IN THE UNITED STATES: WEBSTER V. REPRODUCTIVE HEALTH SERVICES 107 (Roy Mersky & Gary Hartman eds. 1990) ("DOCUMENTARY HISTORY") (hereafter pagination will be given only to the version in the *Women's Rts. L. Rptr.*).

16. See the text *infra* at notes 164–69; and Chapter 9, at 36–43; Chapter 11, at notes 5–24.

# The Nineteenth Century Feminists

*Our similarities are different.*

—Dale Berra[17]

The later nineteenth century was an era in which sexual roles were heavily contested. Growing numbers of women sought to enter what many considered to be "male" occupations, including medicine and law. Often men in those lines of work succeeded in organizing themselves to exclude women. This effort was largely successful in excluding women from the law; a few women fought stubbornly and eventually successfully to enter the profession against claims that women were inherently unsuited for such work.[18] Women were also largely excluded from the dominant (allopathic) medical profession at this time.[19] The women who fought these battles were among the feminist leaders and organizers of the later nineteenth century, the so-called "first wave" of feminism.[20] Most of these women generally were neither lawyers nor physicians and they were not representative of the hypothetical "average" woman of the time. The feminist leaders represent thoughtful and articulate women of the time. This section examines their attitudes, later sections of this chapter examining the specific experiences and attitudes of women physicians. The next chapter examines the specific experiences and attitudes of women lawyers.

Today it is fashionable for pro-abortion historians and lawyers to assert that the late nineteenth century feminists supported abortion rights and were simply unable to overcome the sexist oppression of the time to secure these rights for their sisters.[21] Several hundred historians

---

17. David Nathan, Baseball Quotations 153 (1993).

18. *See* Chapter 9, at notes 233–329.

19. *See* Chapter 6, at notes 213–67, Chapter 7, at notes 394–439, and *infra*, at notes 253–308.

20. On the use of this expression, see Cassandra Langer, A Feminist Critique: How Feminism Has Changed American Society, Culture, and How We Live from the 1940s to the Present 6 (1996). *See generally* Barbara Berg, The Remembered Gate: Origins of American Feminism (1978); Carrie Chapman Catt & Nettie Rogers Shuler, Woman Suffrage and Politics (1969); William Henry Chafe, The American Woman: Her Changing Social, Economic, and Political Roles, 1920–1970 (1972); Catherine Clinton, The Other Civil War: American Women in the Nineteenth Century (1984); Degler, *supra* note 11, at 328–61; Ellen Carol Dubois, Feminism and Suffrage: The Emergence of an Independent Women's Movement in America, 1848–1869 (1978); Ellen Carol Dubois, Harriot Stanton Blatch and the Winning of Woman Suffrage (1997); Eleanor Flexner, A Century of Struggle: The Woman's Rights Movement in the United States (rev. ed. 1975); Dolores Hayden, The Grand Domestic Revolution: A History of Feminist Designs for American Homes, Neighborhoods and Cities (1981); Aileen Kraditor, The Ideas of the Woman Suffrage Movement: 1890–1920 (1971); Suzanne Marilley, Women Suffrage and the Origins of Liberal Feminism in the United States, 1820–1920 (1996); Louise Michele Newmann, Men's Ideas/Women's Realities (1985); William O'Neill, Everyone Was Brave: A History of Feminism in America (1969); Deborah Rhode, Justice and Gender 12–50 (1989); Anne & Andrew Scott, One Half the People: The Fight for Women Suffrage (1975); Andrew Sinclair, The Better Half: The Emancipation of the American Woman (1966); The Selected Papers of Elizabeth Cady Stanton and Susan B. Anthony Volume One: The School of Anti-Slavery (Ann Gordon ed. 1997); Reay Tannahill, Sex in History 388–402 (1980); Nancy Woloch, Women and the American Experience (1984).

21. *See* Janet Farrell Brodie, Contraception and Abortion in Nineteenth-Century America xii 41–44, 253–72, 275–80 (1994); Barbara Brookes, Abortion in England 1900–1967, at 2–7, 14, 40, 57, 63–67, 70–71, 79–88, 105–6, 113–17 (1988); Gordon, *supra* note 5, at 97–111; Grossberg, *supra* note 5, at 155–95; Beverly Wildung Harrison, Our Right to Choose: Toward a New Ethic of Abortion 161–72 (1983); Petchesky, *supra* note 5, at 45–46, 54–56, 67–73, 82–84, 89–90, 188–92; Leslie Reagan, When

signed a brief for the Supreme Court making just such an assertion,[22] while in an earlier brief these same historians asserted that the nineteenth century abortion statutes resulted from a male conspiracy to oppress women.[23] Nothing could be further from the truth. Historian Estelle Freedman, who co-authored one of the leading histories of sexual practices in America,[24] candidly acknowledged that she signed the first brief even though it contradicts the history of women as she has found it.[25] Other historians signed those briefs without even reading them.[26] The briefs are more of a political manifesto than a serious attempt to develop the history of abortion in the United States.

Feminism was a major political and social force from the middle of the nineteenth century onward in the United States, its influence declining only in the middle years of the twentieth century.[27] Yet the feminists did not stand apart from the emerging scientific knowledge of their time. Indeed, perhaps the most impressive demonstration of the new consensus on the nature of human gestation[28] was its emphatic embrace by all leading feminists during the period when the abortion statutes were being enacted. Feminist leaders, as a result, were explicit and uncompromising, and virtually unanimous, in condemning abortion as "ante-natal murder," "child-murder," or "ante-natal infanticide."[29]

Explaining the underlying motives of the early feminists in opposing abortion is no easier than it is for others who opposed abortion during that time. While the leading feminists of the nineteenth century were rebelling in so many ways against the social conventions of the time, they were by no means free of those conventions. Some of the leading feminists of the time were notoriously racist, arguing that women should have the vote as a bulwark against the "brutish and ignorant Negro."[30] Such feminists might have opposed abortion out of fears of race suicide,[31]

---

ABORTION WAS A CRIME: WOMEN, MEDICINE, AND LAW IN THE UNITED STATES, 1867–1973, at 11–12 (1997); JAMES REED, FROM PRIVATE VICE TO PUBLIC VIRTUE: THE BIRTH CONTROL MOVEMENT AND AMERICAN SOCIETY SINCE 1830, at 34–35 (1978); RHODE, *supra* note 20, at 202; SMITH-ROSENBERG, *supra* note 5, at 220–525; Rachael Pine & Sylvia Law, *Envisioning a Future for Reproductive Liberty: Strategies for Making the Rights Real*, 27 HARV. C.R.-C.L. L. REV. 407, 455 n.219 (1992); Siegel, *supra* note 5, at 294–95, 302–14.

22. *Casey Historians' Brief, supra* note 15, at 18–20, & App. at 6.

23. *Webster Historians' Brief, supra* note 15, at 173–77.

24. *See* JOHN D'EMILIO & ESTELLE FREEDMAN, INTIMATE MATTERS: A HISTORY OF SEXUALITY IN AMERICA 67 (1988).

25. Estelle Freedman, *Historical Interpretation and Legal Advocacy: Rethinking the Webster Amicus Brief,* 12 PUB. HISTORIAN 27, 28–30. *See* Chapter 17, at notes 48–51. *See also* Chapter 17, at notes 52–66.

26. *See Remarks of Professor Joan Hollinger, AALS 1990 Conference Audio Tape No. 163* (available from Recorded Resources Corporation of Millersville, Md.) (proudly reciting how she personally recruited 38 members of the History Department at the University of Michigan to sign the *Webster Historians' Brief*—all signing without having read the brief they were subscribing to, let alone a brief on the other side).

27. See the authorities collected *supra* at note 20.

28. *See* Chapter 5, at notes 209–46.

29. *See, e.g.,* EMMA DRAKE, WHAT A YOUNG WIFE OUGHT TO KNOW 130 (1901); ELIZA BISBEE DUFFEY, THE RELATIONS OF THE SEXES 274–75 (1876); ALICE BUNKER STOCKHAM, TOKOLOGY 246–50 (1887); Susan B. Anthony, *Marriage and Maternity,* THE REVOLUTION, July 8, 1869, at 4; Ann Densmore, *Lectures,* THE REVOLUTION, Mar. 19, 1868, at 170; Matilda Gage, *Is Woman Her Own?,* THE REVOLUTION, April 9, 1868, at 215–16; Elizabeth Cady Stanton, *Child Murder,* THE REVOLUTION, March 12, 1868, at 146–47. *See generally* D'EMILIO & FREEDMAN, *supra* note 24, at 64; MARY KRANE DERR, MAN'S INHUMANITY TO WOMAN MAKES COUNTLESS INFANTS DIE (1991); GORDON, *supra* note 5, at 129; MARY LYNDON SHANLEY, FEMINISM, MARRIAGE, AND THE LAW IN VICTORIAN ENGLAND, 1850–1895, at 87–93 (1989).

30. *See, e.g.,* Ida Husted Harper, *Would Woman Suffrage Benefit the State, and Woman Herself?,* 178 N. AM. REV. 362, 373 (1904). *See generally* BELL HOOKS, TALKING BACK: THINKING FEMINIST, THINKING BLACK 130–31, 161–65 (1989); TANNAHILL, *supra* note 78, at 400; Deborah Rhode, *The "No-Problem" Problem: Feminist Challenges and Cultural Change,* 100 YALE L.J. 1731, 1741–42 (1991).

31. On the prominence of fears of race suicide among some opponents of abortion, see the text *infra* at notes 164–69; and Chapter 9, at 36–43; Chapter 11, at notes 5–24.

although no one has come forward with direct evidence of this motive among feminists. There might have been other unsavory motives for feminist opposition to abortion. But at least in part feminist opposition to abortion arose from a desire to protect women against the depredations of men. And regardless of what the motivations were, if the feminists and ordinary women all strongly opposed abortion, along with most men in society, the nineteenth century laws represented a clear social consensus regardless of the underlying motivations, and not simply a male conspiracy against women.

The authors of the *Casey Historians' Brief* would have us see early feminist opposition to abortion as based on Victorian hostility to sexuality or to "male license."[32] They mischaracterize the nineteenth-century feminist position on abortion as one of reluctance rather than opposition and attempted to conflate historical opposition to abortion with historical opposition to contraception.[33] The authors even claimed in that brief that the spousal notice requirement held unconstitutional in the *Casey* decision[34] was designed to carry forward the common-law tradition of subordination of a woman to her husband's control.[35] No one disputes that such traditions existed, and few would support those traditions as legal mandates today. Whether those traditions are relevant to the abortion controversy is another question. The answer is suggested by the fact that the same authors omitted any mention of nineteenth-century feminists in their earlier *Webster Historians' Brief* because it was simply too embarrassing for their argument.[36]

Susan B. Anthony and Elizabeth Cady Stanton both spoke in terms of child-murder.[37] To argue, as the authors of the *Casey Historians' Brief* do,[38] that such the nineteenth-century feminists' were merely seeking to protect women from exploitation by men and were not morally opposed to abortion is, at best, to focus narrowly on their stated goals to the exclusion of both how they explained their positions and what they themselves understood to be the practical effects of their efforts. Such women as Anthony and Stanton were hardly afraid of confronting male opinions on questions of basic morality. Numerous early feminists were actively engaged in working for the abolition of slavery, the imposition of temperance, and reforming of prisons as well as for development of women's rights.[39] Both Anthony and Stanton publicly abandoned the religions in which they were raised, and Stanton published her own feminist version of the Bible.[40] Stanton did so at a time when women, still excluded from formal political power, were a growing influence in mainstream Protestantism.[41] Stanton, like Anthony, was a figure of international stature who strongly influence English suffragists as well as American, and had connections with

---

32. *Casey Historians' Brief, supra* note 15, at 18–19.

33. *Id.* at 18–20.

34. Planned Parenthood of Southeastern Pennsylvania v. Casey, 505 U.S. at 911–22 (Stevens, J., partially concurring), 922–43 (Blackmun, J., partially concurring).

35. *Casey Historians' Brief, supra* note 15, at 17.

36. Sylvia Law, *Conversations between Historians and the Constitution,* 12 THE PUB. HISTORIAN 11, 15 (1990) (Sylvia Law was the principal author of the *Historians' Briefs*).

37. *See* Anthony, *supra* note 29; Stanton, *supra* note 29. *See also* DERR, *supra* note 29, at 24; ELIZABETH GRIFFITH, IN HER OWN RIGHT: THE LIFE OF ELIZABETH CADY STANTON 133 (1984).

38. *Casey Historians' Brief, supra* note 15, at 19.

39. Such wide-ranging activism had deep roots going back to Quaker women before the American Revolution. *See* REBECCA LARSON, DAUGHTERS OF LIGHT: QUAKER WOMEN PREACHING AND PROPHESYING IN THE COLONIES AND ABROAD, 1700–1775, at 94, 182, 185, 292–95, 302–03 (1999). *See also* JULIE ROY JEFFREY, THE GREAT SILENT ARMY OF ABOLITIONISM: ORDINARY WOMEN IN THE ANTISLAVERY MOVEMENT (1998); KATHRYN KISH SKLAR, WOMEN'S RIGHTS EMERGE WITHIN THE ANTISLAVERY MOVEMENT, 1830–1870 (2000). On the radicalism and influence of feminists in Europe on feminists in the United States, see BONNIE ANDERSON, JOYOUS GREETINGS: THE FIRST INTERNATIONAL WOMEN'S MOVEMENT, 1830–1860 (2000).

40. ELIZABETH CADY STANTON, THE WOMAN'S BIBLE (1895).

41. *See* ANN DOUGLAS, THE FEMINIZATION OF AMERICAN RELIGION (1977); SMITH-ROSENBERG, *supra* note 5, at 129–64.

suffragists in other European and Europeanized countries.[42] These were hardly women who backed off from an argument that they considered essential to women's lives because of fear of men's opinions.

Contemporary historians go further, conflating attitudes towards abortion and contraception in the nineteenth century.[43] This goes beyond merely draining the color out of our pictures of the past; it smacks of deliberate obfuscation. Some anti-feminists of the time did link abortion and contraception and blamed both on feminism.[44] One need look no further than the very nineteenth-century feminists that the authors of the *Casey Historians' Brief* discuss in claiming that such feminists opposed the abortion statutes[45] to discover that nineteenth-century feminists themselves distinguished sharply between the two practices, frequently and adamantly condemning abortion while supporting contraception.[46] Nineteenth century courts and legislatures also distinguished between abortion (a crime everywhere) and the use of contraceptives (a crime only in Connecticut).[47] Many male physicians of the time drew the same distinction.[48] Some anti-feminist moralists did condemn abortion and contraception in similar terms in the nineteenth century.[49] As Michael Grossberg noted, however, "they reserved their harshest condemnations and most zealous efforts for the antiabortion crusade."[50] Perhaps some men who supported the feminists also condemned contraception equally with abortion, but the principal example of this—Ezra Heywood—later defended the use of a contraceptive syringe.[51] Other pro-feminist

---

42. *See* ELIZABETH CADY STANTON, EIGHTY YEARS AND MORE: REMINISCENCES, 1815–1897 (1898); Elizabeth Cady Stanton, *Declaration of Sentiments,* reprinted in MARI JO & PAUL BUHLE, THE CONCISE HISTORY OF WOMAN SUFFRAGE: SELECTIONS FROM THE CLASSIC WORK OF STANTON, ANTHONY, GAGE, AND HARPER 94–95 (1978). *See also* GRIFFITH, *supra* note 37; ELIZABETH CADY STANTON AS REVEALED IN HER LETTERS, DIARY AND REMINISCENCES (Theodore Stanton & Harriet Stanton Black eds. 1922); Sandra Stanley Holton, *From Anti-Slavery to Suffrage Militancy: The Bright Circle, Elizabeth Cady Stanton and the British Women's Movement,* in SUFFRAGE AND BEYOND: INTERNATIONAL FEMINIST PERSPECTIVES 213 (Caroline Daley & Melanie Nolan eds. 1994).

43. *See, e.g.,* DEGLER, *supra* note 11, at 202–06, 215; HARRISON, *supra* note 21, at 161–72; RHODE, *supra* note 20, at 202; SMITH-ROSENBERG, *supra* note 5, at 220; PETCHESKY, *supra* note 5, at 25–35; Linda Gordon, *Voluntary Motherhood: The Beginnings of Feminist Birth Control Ideas in the United States,* 1 FEM. STUD. 5 (1973) ("Gordon, *Voluntary Motherhood*") (this became ch. 5 in GORDON, *supra* note 5); Linda Gordon, *Why Nineteenth Century Feminists Did Not Support "Birth Control" and Twentieth Century Feminists Do,* in RE-THINKING THE FAMILY 40 (Barrie Thorne & Marilyn Yalom eds. 1982) ("Gordon, *Nineteenth Century Feminists*"). This conflation pervades Gordon's major work. GORDON, *supra* note 5.

44. *See, e.g.,* H.S. POMEROY, THE ETHICS OF MARRIAGE 95–96 (1888); Montrose Pallen, *Foeticide,* 3 MED. ARCHIVES (St. L. n.s.) 195, 205–06 (1869). MOHR, *supra* note 4, at 107–08; MARY ROTH WALSH, DOCTORS WANTED: NO WOMEN NEED APPLY 145–46 (1977).

45. *Casey Historians' Brief, supra* note 15, at 18–20.

46. *See, e.g.,* ANNIE BESANT, THE LAW OF POPULATION: ITS CONSEQUENCES, AND ITS BEARING UPON HUMAN CONDUCT AND MORALS (1878). *See generally* D'EMILIO & FREEDMAN, *supra* note 24, at 50–63, 64–65; GROSSBERG, *supra* note 5, at 169–70.

47. Commonwealth v. Leigh, 15 PHILA. R. 376 (1881).

48. BRODIE, *supra* note 21, at 275–78.

49. *See, e.g.,* AUGUSTUS GARDNER, CONJUGAL SINS AGAINST THE LAWS OF LIFE AND HEALTH AND THEIR EFFECTS UPON THE FATHER, MOTHER, AND THE CHILD 31, 35, 101 (1876); DIO LEWIS, CHASTITY, OR OUR SECRET SINS 89–109, 183 (1874); WILLIAM WALLINGS, SEXOLOGY 74 (1876); JOHN TODD, SERPENT IN A DOVE'S NEST 23–24 (1867); William Goodell, *Clinical Lecture on Conjugal Onanism and Kindred Sin,* PHILA. MED. TIMES, Feb. 1, 1872, at 161, 162; Pallen, *supra* note 44, at 205.

50. GROSSBERG, *supra* note 5, at 193. *See generally* GROSSBERG, *supra,* at 175–78, 193–95; JOHN & ROBIN HALLER, THE PHYSICIAN AND SEXUALITY IN VICTORIAN AMERICA 114–15, 122–24 (1974).

51. EZRA HEYWOOD, CUPID'S YOKE; OR, THE BINDING FORCES OF CONJUGAL LIFE 20 (1887). *See* GORDON, *supra* note 5, at 107–09).

men openly advocated contraception while condemning abortion, a stance most feminists similarly embraced.[52]

Abortion rights advocates similarly attempt to obfuscate the distinction today.[53] Abortion has, and always has had, a different moral and legal quality compared to contraception or others forms of reproductive and sexual privacy, for abortion involves the killing of an embryo or a fetus regardless of how one morally evaluates the status of that being. The drawing of this distinction continues down to today,[54] and continued throughout the time that both abortion and contraception were becoming technologically feasible. For example, a survey of British physicians in 1922 found three-fourths of them supportive of birth control while very few supported the ready availability of abortion.[55] Even the Supreme Court in *Roe v. Wade* recognized that the evolving traditions regarding other forms of intimate privacy simply do not correspond to the abortion situation.[56] The joint plurality opinion of Justices Kennedy, O'Connor, and Souter made the same point in *Planned Parenthood of Southeastern Pennsylvania v. Casey*,[57] as did the two dissenting opinions representing four other justices.[58] Furthermore, the historical record itself demonstrates that the traditional condemnation of abortion in England and America was independent of the sometimes widespread opposition to contraception. As Dr. Alice Bunker Stockham put it in 1887, "[t]he remedy is in the prevention of pregnancy, not in producing abortion."[59] Yet at least one feminist historian, who noted this support for contraception, was so intent on conflating abortion and contraception that she never seemed to notice the differing professional response to the two procedures.[60]

Nor, when one fairly reads the record of what was said or written about abortion, can one fairly equate opposition to abortion in the nineteenth century to support for paternal dominance in the home. In fact, one of the stronger strands in the traditional condemnation of abortion has been the protection of the woman, even, if need be, against her husband.[61] The two *Historians' Briefs* admit as much, at least regarding the statutes adopted in the nineteenth century.[62]

---

52. *See* D.M. Bennett, Anthony Comstock and His Career of Crime and Cruelty 1068 (1878); Edward Bond Foote, The Radical Remedy in Social Science 89 (1886); Frederick Hollick, The Marriage Guide or Natural History of Generation 334 (1850). *See generally* Brodie, *supra* note 21, at 193–94; C. Thomas Dienes, Law, Politics and Birth Control 63 (1972); Degler, *supra* note 11, at 201–02; D'Emilio & Freedman, *supra* note 24, at 50–63, 64–65; Gordon, *supra* note 5, at 97–100; Grossberg, *supra* note 5, at 169–70, 187–95.

53. *See, e.g.,* Ronald Dworkin, Life's Dominion: An Argument about Abortion, Euthanasia, and Individual Freedom 32–34 (1993); Cheryl Meyer, The Wandering Uterus: Politics and the Reproductive Rights of Women 133–35 (1997); Susan Estrich & Kathleen Sullivan, *Abortion Politics: Writing for an Audience of One,* 138 U. Pa. L. Rev. 119, 128–30 (1989); Berta Hernàndez, *To Bear or Not to Bear: Reproductive Freedom as an International Human Right,* 17 Brooklyn J. Int'l L. 309, 323–24 (1991). *See generally* James Bopp, jr., & Richard Coleson, *What Does* Webster *Mean?,* 138 U. Pa. L. Rev. 157, 166–68 (1989).

54. *See* Nanette Davis, From Crime to Choice xiii, 3–4 (1985); Dworkin, *supra* note 53, at 10–24, 29–35, 50, 56–60, 67–101; Harrison, *supra* note 21, at 219–21, 225–26, 250–51.

55. Peter Fryer, The Birth Controllers 248 (1966).

56. Roe v. Wade, 410 U.S. 113, 159 (1973).

57. 505 U.S. 833, 851 (1992) (Kennedy, O'Connor, & Souter, JJ., joint plurality op.).

58. *Id.* at 951–52 (Rehnquist, C.J., dissenting, joined by Scalia, Thomas, & White, JJ.), 982 (Scalia, J., dissenting, joined by Rehnquist, C.J., & Thomas & White, JJ.).

59. Stockham, *supra* note 29, at 250. *See also* Anthony, *supra* note 29 (calling for an investigation into causes).

60. Brookes, *supra* note 21, at 65, 70–71.

61. *See, e.g.,* Rex v. Scharp, The London Eyre of 1276, at 23 (no. 76) (London Rec. Soc'y 1976) (a husband cannot compel his wife to have an abortion; therefore the husband's consent did not immunize the crime from prosecution) (quoted in Chapter 3, at note 92).

62. *Casey Historians' Brief, supra* note 15, at 11–13; *Webster Historians' Brief, supra* note 15, at 173.

This tradition views the woman undergoing an abortion as victim rather than culprit.[63] The tradition can be traced back to the very beginnings of the common law, when abortion, along with the rape of her virginity and the murder of her husband in her arms, were the only three personal invasions for which a woman could bring an appeal of felony without the consent of and representation by her husband or another appropriate male relative.[64] Also evidencing the policy of protecting the woman was the rule, which even law professor Cyril Means, jr., termed "an act or restoration gallantry," that an abortion causing the death of the mother is murder regardless of whether the killing of the fetus would be a punishable offense.[65] The nineteenth century feminists' opinion of abortion and abortion laws fell squarely within this tradition.

The notion that men were behind abortion has an ancient pedigree. Anthropologist Georges Devereux found that in pre-industrial societies around the world female attitudes towards pregnancy and abortion were largely determined by the attitudes of their men towards becoming a father.[66] Even when a woman chose to seek abortion on her own, including when she would abort out of spite against the man, her actions were largely a reaction to his attitudes rather than determined simply by her own desires.[67] And, of course, down through the ages more than a few women were literally coerced into attempting abortion—especially when abortion was tantamount to suicide.[68] The idea that abortion is solely a woman's concern, or solely of concern to the mother and to the fetus, is a distinctly modern view.[69]

Even today the father's attitude is likely to be extremely important to a woman who is seeking an abortion. A woman is far more likely to seek to abort if the father does not want the child, particularly if it is evident that she will receive no support or help from him.[70] Furthermore,

---

63. *See* Peoples v. Commonwealth, 9 S.W. 509, 510 (Ky. 1898); State v. Murphy, 27 N.J.L. 112, 114–15 (1858); Dunn v. People, 29 N.Y. 523, 527 (1864); Watson v. State, 9 Tex. Crim. App. 237, 244–45 (1880); State v. Howard, 32 Vt. 380, 403 (1859); Wm. L. Clark, jr., Hand-Book of Criminal Law 182 (1894); John Wigmore, A Treatise on the Law of Evidence 2755–56 (1905). *See also In re* Vince, 67 A.2d 141 (N.J. 1949); Mary Boyle, Re-Thinking Abortion, Psychology, Gender, Power and Law 44 (1997); Ellen Willis, *Putting Women Back into the Abortion Debate*, in From Abortion to Reproductive Freedom: Transforming a Movement 131, 135 (Marlene Gerber Fried ed. 1990). *See generally* Chapter 6, at notes 292–319.

64. See Chapter 3, at notes 30–46. At the time, the appeal of felony was the prevalent form of private prosecution of a felony. A woman's right to appeal a felony was limited because the normal mode of trial was by battle.

65. Rex v. Anonymous (1670), 1 Matthew Hale, History of Pleas of the Crown 429–30 (1736), quoted in Chapter 4, at note 164. See also the cases collected in Chapter 4, at note 157. On "restoration gallantry," see Cyril Means, jr., *The Phoenix of Abortional Freedom: Is a Penumbral Right or Ninth-Amendment Right About to Arise from the Nineteenth-Century Legislative Ashes of a Fourteenth-Century Common-Law Liberty?*, 17 N.Y.L.F. 335, 362 (1971) ("Means II").

66. Georges Devereux, A Study of Abortion in Primitive Societies 135–36 (1955).

67. *Id.* at 136.

68. *See* Chapter 1.

69. *See generally* George Harris, *Fathers and Fetuses*, 96 Ethics 594 (1986).

70. *See, e.g.,* Akinrinola Bankole et al., *Reasons Why Women Have Induce Abortions: Evidence from 27 Countries*, 24 Int'l. Fam. Plan. Persp. 117 (1998); Susan Davies, *Partners and the Abortion Decision*, in Abortion, Medicine, and the Law 223 (J. Douglas Butler & David Walbert eds., 3rd ed. 1986); Susan Fischman, *Delivery of Abortion to Inner-City Adolescents*, 47 Am. J. Orthopsychiatry 127 (1977); Malcolm Helper et al., *Life Events and Acceptance of Pregnancy*, 12 J. Psych. Research 183 (1968); Kristina Holmgren, *Time of Decision to Undergo a Legal Abortion*, 26 Gynelocogial & Obstet. Investigations 289 (1988); A. Kero et al., *The Male Partner Involved in Legal Abortion*, 14 Human Reproduction 2669 (1999); T. Kitamura et al., *Psychological and Social Correlates of the Onset of Affective Disorders among Pregnant Women*, 23 Psych. Med. 967 (1993); R. Kumar & Kay Mordecai Robson, *A Prospective Study of Emotional Disorders in Childbearing Women*, 144 Brit. J. Psych. 35 (1984); F. Lieh-Mak, *Husbands of Abortion Applicants: A Comparison with Husbands of Women Who Complete Their Pregnancies*, 14 Soc. Pscyh. 59 (1979); C.M. Lyon & G.J. Bennett, *Abortion—Whose Decision?*, 9 Fam. L. 35 (1979); M. Tornbom et al., *Evaluation of Stated Motives for Legal Abortion*, 15 J. Psychosomatic Obstet. & Gynecology 27 (1994).

even the Alan Guttmacher Institute—the research arm of the National Abortion Rights Action League as it was then known—found that in large measure a woman sought an abortion because of their man's attitude. In a 1987 survey of 1,900 women who had had abortion, the Institute found that 68 percent did so because they could not afford a baby at the time, 51 percent said they sought an abortion because they either had problems in their relationship with the father or had no relationship at all with the father, and 23 percent sought an abortion because the father insisted on it.[71] Some 29 percent of the women reported that they had sought an abortion because their partner would not, or could not, marry her, while another 32 percent indicated that they expected the relationship to break up soon.[72] No wonder so many women report that they felt isolated and alone when they underwent an abortion.[73] These feelings, and the attitude of the man generally, is even more important when abortion is illegal.[74]

The nineteenth century feminists often insisted that the criminal was either the abortionist (regardless of gender) or the man responsible for the pregnancy (who, they realized, often pressured an unwilling woman into an abortion), not the woman.[75] Some feminists reasoned from this view of the matter that only the man (or perhaps the abortionist regardless of gender) involved should be guilty of a crime, and not the mother. Dr. Stockham noted that "[a]n unmarried woman, seduced under false representations by a man who feels no responsibility for his own offspring, suffers alone all the shame and contumely of the act, and is tempted to cause miscarriage to shield her good name."[76] Matilda Gage expressed a stronger version of this view right after the Civil War:

> I hesitate not to assert that most of this crime of "child murder," "abortion," "infanticide," lies at the door of the male sex.... Many a woman has laughed a silent, derisive laugh at the decisions of eminent medical and legal authorities, in cases of crimes committed against her as a woman. Never, until she sits as a juror at such trials, will or can just decisions be rendered.[77]

Gage concluded that "[t]he crime of abortion is not one in which the guilt lies solely or chiefly with the woman" because the crime resulted from the denial of a woman's "right to her-

---

71. Aida Torres & Jacqueline Darroch Forrest, *Why Do Women Have Abortions?*, 20 Fam. Plan. Persp. 169, 170 (1988).

72. *Id. See also* Stanley Henshaw & K Kathryn Kost, *Abortion Patients in 1994–1995: Characteristics and Contraceptive Use*, 28 Fam. Plan. Persp. 140, 143 (1996) (finding that women who were never married or who were living with someone without being married to that person accounted for the great majority of abortions).

73. Eve Kushner, Experiencing Abortion xx (1997). *See also* Carol Gilligan, In a Different Voice: Psychological Theory and Women's Development 74 (1982).

74. O.A. Abiodun *et al.*, *Psychiatric Morbidity in a Pregnant Population in Nigeria*, 15 Gen. Hosp. Psych. 125 (1993); Augustine Ankomah, *Unsafe Abortions: Methods Used and Characteristics of Patients Attending Hospitals in Nairobi, Lima, and Manila*, 18 Health Care for Women Int'l 43 (1997); P.E. Bailey *et al.*, *A Hospital Study of Illegal Abortion in Bolivia*, 27 PAHO Bull. 27 (1988); Carole Browner, *Abortion Decision Making: Some Findings from Columbia*, 10 Stud. in Fam. Plan. 96 (1979); Helena Lutescia Coelho *et al.*, *Misoprostol: The Experience of Women in Fortaleza, Brazil*, 49 Contraception 101 (1994); Sarah Costa & Martin Vessey, *Misoprostol and Illegal Abortion in Rio de Janeiro, Brazil*, 341 Lancet 1261 (1993); Susan Pick de Weiss & Henry David, *Illegal Abortions in Mexico: Client Perceptions*, 80 Am. J. Pub. Health 715 (1990); V.M. Lema *et al.*, *Induced Abortion in Kenya: Its Determinants and Associated Factors*, 73 E. Afr. Med. J. 164 (1966).

75. *See, e.g.*, Anonymous, Why Not? A Book for Every Woman: *A Woman's View*, 75 Bos. Med. & Surgical J. no. 14, at 273 (Nov. 1, 1866). *See also* Derr, *supra* note 29, at 19; Percy Kammerer, The Unmarried Mother (1918); Mohr, *supra* note 4, at 111–14; Marvin Olasky, Abortion Rights: A Social History of Abortion in America 175–76, 187–88 (1992); Reagan, *supra* note 21, at 38, 58–59. There are a few lawsuits in which a woman sued her lover claiming he had pressured her into an abortion. Sayadoff v. Warda, 271 P.2d 140 (Cal. Ct. App. 1954); Goldnamer v. O'Brien, 98 Ky. 569 (1896).

76. Stockham, *supra* note 29, at 247.

77. Gage, *supra* note 29, at 215–16. James Mohr quoted only the first sentence of this passage. Mohr, *supra* note 4, at 112.

self," not as an exercise of that right.[78] She pointedly lay full responsibility for abortion on the machinations of men. Like most nineteenth century feminists,[79] Gage addressed the causes of abortion, including marital rape and exploitive relations between the sexes that left women vulnerable and, all too often, desperate. She, like other nineteenth century feminists who supported the criminal laws against abortion, did not suppose that the criminal statutes alone were sufficient, but also sought measures to eliminate the causes of abortion as well as the practice.

This feminist view neatly captured the long-standing tradition that the women who underwent abortions were victims of the crime rather than culprits. Such sentiments were not limited to women. For example, Dr. John Cowan wrote that "the licentiousness of the man and bondage of the woman...[produce] the monstrous crime...the murder of the unborn."[80] Even Horatio Robinson Storer, a leading campaigner against abortion among physicians whom modern abortion rights advocates assure us was utterly misogynistic,[81] recognized the guilt of husbands and lovers in encouraging or compelling abortions, although he did not excuse the mother for her share of responsibility.[82] Storer, the first true professor of gynecology, also denounced marital rape[83] and decried those who would treat a woman's body as a "mere plaything."[84]

The view that men were responsible for abortion was fully realized in the prosecution patterns as the nineteenth century turned to the twentieth century. Men involved with unmarried women who died from abortions were one of the more frequent targets of arrest, prosecution, and incarceration.[85] Only occasionally, however, did a more fortunate woman apparently exploit this feature of the abortion laws to make the responsible man "suffer for it."[86]

The "free love wing" of nineteenth-century feminists shared the same view of abortion of the more mainstream leaders.[87] The label "free love," when used by members of the "free love" movement in that century, did not have the salacious meaning ascribed to it by its enemies.[88] Those in the movement argued not that people should indulge in sexual relations without restraint, but that sexual relations should be based solely upon feelings of love—feelings that were not always present in marriage and sometimes were present outside of marriage.[89] As historian

---

78. *Id.*

79. *See, e.g.,* STOCKHAM, *supra* note 29, at 250; Anthony, *supra* note 29; Abigail Dunaway, *Liberty for the Married Woman*, NEW NORTHWEST, Aug. 15, 1873, at 2. *See generally* D'EMILIO & FREEDMAN, *supra* note 24, at 64; GORDON, *supra* note 5, at 108; MOHR, *supra* note 4, at 111–14.

80. JOHN COWAN, THE SCIENCE OF A NEW LIFE 275 (1871).

81. *See* Chapter 7, at notes 394–439.

82. HORATIO ROBINSON STORER, ON CRIMINAL ABORTION IN AMERICA 13 (1860); HORATIO ROBINSON STORER, WHY NOT? A BOOK FOR EVERYWOMAN 79 (1866) ("STORER, WHY NOT?").

83. STORER, WHY NOT?, *supra* note 82, at 11–13, 94–95.

84. *Id.* at 80–83. *See also* HORATIO ROBINSON STORER, THE CAUSATION, COURSE AND TREATMENT OF REFLEX INSANITY IN WOMEN 97 (1871) ("STORER, REFLEX INSANITY"); HORATIO ROBINSON STORER & FRANKLIN FISKE HEARD, CRIMINAL ABORTION: ITS NATURE, ITS EVIDENCE AND ITS LAW 127 (1868).

85. REAGAN, *supra* note 21, at 115, 122, 125, 128–30.

86. *See, e.g.,* People v. Patrick, 115 N.E. 390 (Ill. 1917); Dunn v. People, 50 N.E. 137 (Ill. 1898); Scott v. People, 30 N.E. 329 (Ill. 1892).

87. MOHR, *supra* note 4, at 112–13.

88. *See, e.g.,* DIARY OF GEORGE TEMPLETON STRONG: THE TURBULENT 50s, at 235 (entry for Oct. 17, 1855) (Allen Nevins & Miton Thomas eds. 1952); WILLIAM DIXON, SPIRITUAL LOVES 399 (1868); BENJAMIN HATCH, SPIRITUALISTS' INIQUITIES UNMASKED 16–24, 50–51 (1859); Pallen, *supra* note 44, at 217–28. *See generally* OLASKY, *supra* note 75, at 62–80; MAX RHEINSTEIN, MARRIAGE, STABILITY, DIVORCE, AND THE LAW 38–46 (1972).

89. STEPHEN PEARL ANDREWS, LOVE, MARRIAGE, AND DIVORCE, AND THE SOVEREIGNTY OF THE INDIVIDUAL (1889); R.D. CHAPMAN, FREELOVE A LAW OF NATURE (1881); TENNESSEE CLAFLIN, THE ETHICS OF SEXUAL EQUALITY (1873); ANDREW JACKSON DAVIS, THE GREAT HARMONIA (1856); DORA FORSTER, SEX RADICALISM AS SEEN BY AN EMANCIPATED WOMAN OF THE NEW TIME (1905); HEYWOOD, *supra* note 51; C.L. JAMES, THE FUTURE RELATION OF THE SEXES (1877); HARMON KNOX ROOT, LOVE'S MARRIAGE LIGHTHOUSE

Carl Degler noted, the "free love" movement of the nineteenth century was more devoted to giving women the right to say no within marriage than the right to say yes outside of marriage.[90]

Victoria Woodhull and Tennessee Claflin were sisters who led the "free love" wing of nineteenth-century feminism.[91] As their espousal of "free love" suggests, they were particularly independent in their thinking and in their actions. The sisters were the first women stockbrokers in New York, becoming millionaires.[92] Woodhull also became the first woman to run for President (with Frederick Douglas as her vice-presidential candidate),[93] under the guise of the "People's Party" some 15 years before the large scale Populist movement of the last fifteen years of the nineteenth century emerged. And Woodhull became the first woman ever to testify before a congressional committee—on January 11, 1871, on the vote for women, with Elizabeth Cady Stanton and Susan B. Anthony looking on.[94]

Victoria Woodhull and Tennessee Claflin had unsavory personal reputations, coming as they did from a family with a history of personal scandal.[95] Their political positions were also quite radical for their time. *Woodhull & Claflin's Weekly* printed the *Communist Manifesto* in English—more than 20 years after its initial appearance, but before any other press in the United States had done so.[96] Woodhull also served as honorary president of the American branch of Marx's First International.[97] They supported abolition of the death penalty, an international tribunal backed by an international military to settle disputes and to enforce peace, a national educational and welfare system, nationalization of mines, and progressive taxation—and "free love."[98] The two sisters were even jailed at the instigation of Anthony Comstock on the grounds that the journal they published was obscene, although they were released after one month.[99] No wonder historian Milton Rugoff described Woodhull as "in her life and loves as well as her views she was one of the most emancipated and uninhibited women of that or any other American time."[100]

The sisters Woodhill and Claflin did not support abortion rights. They published a journal in which they declared that any claim that abortion was not murder was so flimsy that those making such a claim "fully realize the enormity of the crime" and were not making a serious exculpa-

---

(1858); Victoria Claflin Woodhull, The Scare-Crows of Sexual Slavery (1874). *See generally* Martin Blatt, Free Love and Anarchism: The Biography of Ezra Haywood (1989); Brodie, *supra* note 21, at 125–30, 273–74, 279–80; Degler, *supra* note 11, at 198–99, 276–77; D'Emilio & Freedman, *supra* note 24, at 112–16, 156–57, 161–67; Barbara Goldsmith, Other Powers: The Age of Suffrage, Spiritualism, and the Scandalous Victoria Woodhull (1998); Gordon, *supra* note 5, at 95–117; M.M. Marberry, Vicky: A Biography of Victoria C. Woodhull (1967); Mary Marsh, Anarchist Women, 1870–1920, at 72–90 (1981); H.D. Sears, The Sex Radicals: Free Love in High Victorian America (1977); Taylor Stoehr, Free Love in America: A Documentary History (1979).

90. Degler, *supra* note 11, at 277. *See also* 4 Davis, *supra* note 89, at 426–45. *See generally* Stephen Kern, Anatomy and Destiny: A Cultural History of the Human Body 153 (1975).

91. *See generally* Mary Gabriel, Notorious Victoria: The Life of Victoria Woodhull (1998); Goldsmith, *supra* note 89; Emanie Sachs, The Terrible Siren (1928); Tannahill, *supra* note 20, at 397.

92. Goldsmith, *supra* note 89, at 162.

93. *Id.* at 320.

94. *Id.* at 247–48.

95. *Id.* at 14–16.

96. *Id.* at 305.

97. *Id.* at 273.

98. Gabriel, *supra* note 91, at 124–25; Goldsmith, *supra* note 89, at 303–06; Henryk Katz, The Emancipation of Labor: A History of the First International 121–22 (1992).

99. Nicola Beisel, Imperiled Innocents: Anthony Comstock and Family Reproduction in Victorian America 80 (1997); Heywood Broun & Margaret Leech, Anthony Comstock: Roundsman of the Lord 18 (1927); Andrea Tone, Devices and Desires: A History of Contraceptives in America 12 (2001). *See also* Goldsmith, *supra* note 89, at 344–45.

100. Milton Rugoff, The Beechers: An American Family in the Nineteenth Century 486 (1981).

tory argument.[101] The sisters also published in their journal the following statement of Sarah Norton:

> Perhaps there will come a time when the man who wantonly kills a woman and her babe [through abortion] will be loathed and scorned as deeply as the woman is now loathed and scorned who becomes his dupe; when the sympathy of society will be with the victim rather than the victimizer; when an unmarried mother will not be despised because of her motherhood; when unchastity in men will be placed on an equality with unchastity in women, and when the right of the unborn to be born will not be denied or interfered with...[102]

Men in the free love movement also condemned abortion.[103]

In contrast with the views of the nineteenth-century feminists, historian James Mohr somehow concluded that most nineteenth-century abortions resulted from mutual agreement between loving couples.[104] Remarkably, Mohr supported his claim by referring only to a diary that disclosed that the woman had undergone an abortion without bothering to tell her husband. Considerable evidence continues to suggest that even today men responsible for unwanted pregnancies often pressure unwilling women into having abortions, pressure that succeeds more easily without legal barriers to abortion.[105] Additional pressures can also come from the mother's parents, particularly if the mother is an adolescent[106]—or from the parents of the father if he also is an adolescent.[107] Even employers sometimes put intense pressure on pregnant women to abort.[108]

Curiously lacking in the writings of both the nineteenth-century feminists and their contemporary critics was any discussion of the role of prostitutes as providing a major market for the expanding abortion industry although there is some persuasive evidence of this in some medical

---

101. Victoria Woodhull & Tennessee Claflin, *The Slaughter of the Innocents,* Woodhull & Claflin's Weekly (June 20, 1874). *See generally* Mohr, *supra* note 4, at 112–13; Tone, *supra* note 99, at 16–18, 297 n.46.

102. Sarah Norton, *Tragedy, Social and Domestic,* Woodhull & Claflin's Weekly (Nov. 19, 1870).

103. *See, e.g.,* Bennett, *supra* note 119, at 1068; Foote, *supra* note 119, at 89 (1886); Heywood, *supra* note 118, at 20. *See generally* Tone, *supra* note 99, at 16–17, 297 n.46.

104. Mohr, *supra* note 4, at 114–17. *See also* Ginsburg, *supra* note 5, at 30; Daniel Scott Smith, *Family Limitation, Sexual Conduct, and Domestic Feminism in Victorian America,* 1 Feminist Stud. 40 (1973).

105. *See, e.g.,* Collins v. Thakker, 352 N.E.2d 507 (Ind. Ct. App. 1990), *appeal denied*; Gilligan, *supra* note 73, at 80–81, 90–91; Mary Ann Glendon, Hermeneutics, Abortion and Divorce: A Review of Abortion and Divorce in Western Law 52 (1989); Kathleen McDonnell, Not an Easy Choice: A Feminist Re-Examines Abortion 59 (1984); Daniel Callahan, *An Ethical Challenge to Prochoice Advocates: Abortion and the Pluralistic Proposition,* Commonweal, Nov. 23, 1990, at 681, 684; Kathleen Franco *et al., Psychological Profile of Dysphoric Women Postabortion,* 44 J. Am. Med. Women's Ass'n 113 (July/Aug. 1989).

106. *See* Nancy Heller Horowitz, *Adolescent Mourning Reactions to Infant and Fetal Loss,* 59 Social Casework 551, 557 (Nov. 1978) (only half of aborted adolescents approved of their abortion at the time and only one-fourth do so even years later). *See also* Linda Birde Francke, The Ambivalence of Abortion 178–206 (1978); Lucy Olson, *Social and Psychological Correlates of Pregnancy Resolution among Adolescent Women,* 50 Am. J. Orthopsychiatry 432, 437–41 (1980).

107. *See* Marie McCullough, *Abortion Case Taps Some of Parents' Deepest Fears,* Phila. Inquirer, Oct. 27, 1996, at A1; Marie McCullough, *For Young Teen's Mother, a Hollow Victory in Court,* Phila. Inquirer, Nov. 3,1996, at E2; David Stout, *Woman Who Took Girl for Abortion Is Guilty in Custody Case,* N.Y. Times, Oct. 31, 1996, at A15. *See also* Susan Dundon, *The Verdict Is in, but There's No Simple Answer When It Comes to Abortion,* Phila. Inquirer, Nov. 3, 1996, at E7.

108. *See* Mark Klebanoff *et al., Outcomes of Pregnancy in a National Sample of Resident Physicians,* 323 N. Eng. J. Med. 1040, 1041 (1990) (reporting that female resident physicians have three times as many abortions *per capita* as the general population); David Shulkin & Merlem Bari, *Letter to the Editor,* 323 N. Eng. J. Med. 630 (1991) (relating the intense pressures and even hostilities brought to bear on female residents when they become pregnant).

reports of the time.[109] Nineteenth-century feminists almost uniformly condemned prostitution and devoted considerable energy to crusading against it as something that had to be suppressed in order to achieve control over male sexuality.[110] Those early feminists coupled their condemnation of prostitution coupled with sympathy for the prostitute.[111] Ironically, modern feminist historians tend to see a link between the increasingly harsh criminal penalties applied to prostitution and the increasing legal activity directed against abortion, seeing both as attempts to control female sexuality—without bothering to explain why such control should have come to the fore in the nineteenth century and without noting that nineteenth century feminists strongly favored both sets of penalties.[112] The role of the early feminists in opposing both prostitution and abortion suggests some interesting speculations about how such a link might have affected their attitudes toward abortion.

Nineteenth century feminists did not simply talk about abortion as another form of male domination of women. Many feminists undertook to organize practical aid for pregnant, unmarried women and girls. Marvin Olasky has documented the efforts of women (sometimes with the help of sympathetic men) across the United States to provide shelter and medical care for those who had been seduced and abandoned, or at least who found themselves pregnant, homeless, and without financial resources.[113] By 1895, Chicago alone had at least a dozen shelters for the unmarried pregnant, with the most active of these shelters caring for 1,291 adults and 1,361 children in 1893.[114] These homes offered to place the children for adoption, offered education and job placement for the mothers, and provided personal counseling that it was hoped would enable the women and girls to avoid such problems in the future.[115] More than a few of the persons involved in these efforts were explicit that a major goal was to provide an alternative to abortion.[116]

---

109. *See* Hays v. State, 40 Md. 645 (1874); WILLIAM ACTON, PROSTITUTION 206 (1857); COWAN, *supra* note 80, at 275; JOHN MCDOWELL, FIRST ANNUAL REPORT OF THE NEW YORK MAGDALEN SOCIETY 23 (1831); C.E. ROGERS, SECRET SINS OF SOCIETY 76, 144 (1881); WILLIAM SANGER, THE HISTORY OF PROSTITUTION 482, 586 (1859); JOHN WARREN, JR., THIRTY YEARS BATTLE WITH CRIME, OR THE CRYING SHAME OF NEW YORK AS SEEN UNDER THE BROAD GLARE OF AN OLD DETECTIVE'S LANTERN 37–38, 53 (1874); J.J. Mulheron, *Foeticide*, 10 PENINSULAR J. MED. 387, 387 (1874). *See also* RUTH ROSEN, THE LOST SISTERHOOD: PROSTITUTION IN AMERICA, 1900–1918, at 99 (1982) (estimating 20,000 prostitution-related abortions in New York City annually during the period she studied). *See generally* D'EMILIO & FREEDMAN, *supra* note 24, at 137; OLASKY, *supra* note 75, at 43–59.

110. *See, e.g.,* Ellen Battelle Dietrick, *Rescuing Fallen Women*, WOMEN'S J., May 27, 1893, at 162. *See generally* BERG, *supra* note 20, at 181–84, 211; RUTH BORDIN, WOMEN AND TEMPERANCE: THE QUEST FOR POWER AND LIBERTY, 1873–1900, at 110–11 (1981); D'EMILIO & FREEDMAN, *supra* note 24, at 140–45, 148–56, 202–15; BARBARA EPSTEIN, THE POLITICS OF DOMESTICITY: WOMEN, EVANGELISM, AND TEMPERANCE IN NINETEENTH-CENTURY AMERICA 125–28 (1981); GORDON, *supra* note 5, at 116–35; GROSSBERG, *supra* note 5, at 47–48; DAVID PIVAR, PURITY CRUSADE: SEXUAL MORALITY AND SOCIAL CONTROL, 1868–1900 (1973); ROSEN, *supra* note 109, at 112–36; SHANLEY, *supra* note 29, at 79–86, 92–93; SMITH-ROSENBERG, *supra* note 5, at 109–28; Elizabeth Pleck, *Feminist Responses to "Crimes against Women," 1800–1896*, 8 SIGNS 459 (1983).

111. *See* D'EMILIO & FREEDMAN, *supra* note 24, at 149–56; GORDON, *supra* note 5, at 116–20.

112. *See, e.g.,* D'EMILIO & FREEDMAN, *supra* note 24, at 64; Mary Odem, *Fallen Women and Thieving Ladies: Historical Approaches to Women and Crime in the United States*, 17 LAW & SOC. INQUIRY 351, 352 (1992).

113. OLASKY, *supra* note 75, at 197–217, 242–45. *See also* WALTER BARRETT, THE CARE OF THE UNMARRIED MOTHER (1929); TIMOTHY HACSI, SECOND HOME: ORPHAN ASYLUMS AND POOR FAMILIES IN AMERICA (1998); REGINA KUNZEL, FALLEN WOMEN, PROBLEM GIRLS: UNMARRIED MOTHERS AND THE PROFESSIONALIZATION OF SOCIAL WORK, 1890–1945 (1993); REAGAN, *supra* note 21, at 28–29.

114. OLASKY, *supra* note 75 at 199.

115. *See* Joan Jacobs Brumberg, *"Ruined" Girls: Changing Community Responses to Illegitimacy in Upstate New York, 1890–1920*, 18 J. SOC. HIST. 247 (1984); Regina Kunzel, *The Professionalization of Benevolence*, 22 J. SOC. HIST. 21 (1988).

116. *See, e.g.,* Charles Reed, *Therapeutic and Criminal Abortion*, 7 ILL. MED. J. 26, 29 (1904).

As the foregoing demonstrates, feminist support for abortion laws that severely punished the men whom the feminists considered truly responsible for an abortion but did not punish the mother were based on a reality they well understood. Nineteenth century feminists saw abortion as something that was done to women, rather than as something done by women. This vision underlies the laws enacted in most states during the nineteenth century—under which the woman committed no crime.[117] Nonetheless, these laws did greatly restrict women's access to abortion.[118] The feminist concern to protect women from being pushed into an abortion by the men in their lives also serves to place the issue of abortion into the broader debate between the feminists and their critics over the institution of marriage.

The feminists of that time were critical (to varying degrees) of marriage as a form of bondage.[119] The first step taken to break the cruder forms of bondage in marriage was the *Married Women's Acts*, giving married women the right to own property and to manage their own incomes.[120] Before these laws, married women in common law countries were considered legally merged with their husband—who was vested with authority of the married women's property and incomes. While some modern feminist historians choose to see these acts as motivated by a desire to provide greater rights to creditors,[121] historian Jean Donnison is closer to the mark in concluding that nineteenth century feminism was born in the struggle for these statutes.[122]

---

117. *See* Chapter 6, at notes 292–319.

118. MOHR, *supra* note 4, at 239–44.

119. *See, e.g.,* 2 HISTORY OF WOMAN SUFFRAGE 642–44 (Elizabeth Cady Stanton, Susan B. Anthony, & Matilda Joslyn Gage eds. 1881); VICTORIA WOODHULL, THE ELIXIR OF LIFE, OR WHY DO WE DIE? 8–9 (1873); Susan Anthony, *Editorial*, THE REVOLUTION, Oct. 27, 1870, at 264; M. Brinkerhoff, *Women and Motherhood*, THE REVOLUTION, Sept. 2, 1869, at 138. *See generally* Chapter 2, at notes, 157–71; DEGLER, *supra* note 11, at 144–77; D'EMILIO & FREEDMAN, *supra* note 24, at 153–54; JOAN HOFF, LAW, GENDER, AND INJUSTICE: A LEGAL HISTORY OF U.S. WOMEN 135–41 (1991); WILLIAM LEACH, TRUE LOVE AND PERFECT UNION: THE FEMINIST REFORM OF SEX AND SOCIETY (1980); SHANLEY, *supra* note 29; WALSH, *supra* note 44, at 17–20; Ellen Carol DuBois, *Outgrowing the Compact of the Fathers: Equal Rights, Woman Suffrage, and the United States Constitution, 1820–1878*, 74 J. AM. HIST. 836 (1987).

120. *See generally* MARY RITTER BEARD, WOMAN AS A FORCE IN HISTORY: A STUDY IN TRADITIONS AND REALITIES 122–44, 158–66 (1946); JEAN DONNISON, MIDWIVES AND MEDICAL MEN: A HISTORY OF THE STRUGGLE FOR THE CONTROL OF CHILDBIRTH 74 (2nd ed. 1988); HOFF, *supra* note 119, at 121–35, 187–91; MARYLYNN SALMON, WOMEN AND THE LAW OF PROPERTY IN EARLY AMERICA (1986); ELIZABETH BOWLES WARBASSE, THE CHANGING LEGAL RIGHTS OF MARRIED WOMEN 1800–1861 (1987); Richard Chused, *Married Women's Property Law: 1800–1850*, 71 GEO. L.J. 1359 (1983). For the parallel development of the law in England, see SHANLEY, *supra* note 29, at 49–78, 103–30. *See also* Chapter 2, at notes 164–69.

121. *See* NORMA BASCH, IN THE EYES OF THE LAW: WOMEN, MARRIAGE, AND PROPERTY IN NINETEENTH CENTURY NEW YORK (1982); BEARD, *supra* note 120, at 160–65; HOFF, *supra* note 119, at 120, 134–35, 187–91; RHODE, *supra* note 20, at 24–26 (1989); CAROLE SHAMMAS, MARYLYNN SALMON, & MICHEL DAHLIN, INHERITANCE IN AMERICA FROM COLONIAL TIMES TO THE PRESENT 88–101 (1987); SHANLEY, *supra* note 29, at 104–09; Richard Chused, *Late Nineteenth-Century Married Women's Property Law: Reception of the Early Married Women's Acts by Courts and Legislatures*, 29 AM. J. LEGAL HIS. 24 (1985); Lawrence Friedman, *Rights of Passage: Divorce Law in Historical Perspective*, 63 OR. L. REV. 649, 655–56 (1984); John Johnston, *Sex and Property: The Common Law Tradition, the Law School Curriculum and Developments toward Equality*, 47 NYU L. REV. 1033 (1972); Suzanne Lebsock, *Radical Reconstruction and the Property Rights of Southern Women*, 43 J. SOC. HIST. 195 (1977); Isabel Marcus, *Locked In and Locked Out: Reflections on the History of Divorce Law in New York*, 37 BUFF. L. REV. 375, 399 (1988); Linda Speth, *The Married Women's Property Acts, 1839–1865: Reform, Reaction, or Revolution?*, in 2 WOMEN AND THE LAW: A SOCIAL HISTORICAL PERSPECTIVE 269 (D. Kelly Weisberg ed. 1982); Amy Dru Stanley, *Conjugal Bonds and Wage Labor: Rights of Contract in the Age of Emancipation*, 75 AM. J. LEGAL HIST. 471 (1988); Joan Williams, *Married Women and Property*, 1 VA. J. SOC. POL'Y & L. 383 (1994). *See also* Reva Siegel, *The Modernization of Marital Status Law: Adjudicating Wives' Rights to Earnings, 1860–1930*, 82 GEO. L.J. 2127 (1994) (arguing that the statutes weren't so much intended to benefit creditors as ineffectual at protecting women's interests); Reva Siegel, *Why Equal Protection No Longer Protects: The Evolving Forms of Status-Enforcing State Action*, 49 STAN. L. REV. 1111, 1116–19 (1997) (same).

122. DONNISON, *supra* note 120, at 74–75.

Feminist leaders of virtually every branch of the movement took a radical stance against the mistreatment of women in or out of marriage and most embraced a frank understanding and acceptance of female sexuality at a time when Victorian morality insisted that women were chaste beings who must subordinate their sexuality to nurturing and reproduction.[123] Dr. William Acton expressed the then prevalent view, against which the feminists were contending, in these words: "The majority of women (happily for them) are not very troubled with sexual feelings of any kind. What men are habitually, women are only exceptionally."[124] Despite Acton's double standard, the social strictures imposed on men during this same era were hardly less debilitating.[125]

Recently, some revisionist historians have argued that Victorians were not repressive about sexuality.[126] These "new histories" do demonstrate that many people of both genders gave considerable attention to their inner life back then—including their own personal sexual needs. (And when wasn't this true?) Yet these arguments serve more to highlight that the depth that separates us from Victorian times has become so great that some historians can no longer imagine a time so sexually repressive as the histories indicate that they feel impelled to try to persuade us that the Victorians were in fact happily unrepressed sexually.[127]

While the "free love" wing was at an extreme in the criticism of the institution of marriage, even the most mainstream feminists were comfortable comparing marriage with the chattel slavery abolished by the Thirteenth Amendment.[128] Interestingly, this point was first made, in writ-

---

123. CAROLINE DALL, THE COLLEGE, THE MARKET, AND THE COURT 293 (1867); 2 ELIZABETH CADY STANTON REVEALED, *supra* note 44, at 114; STOCKHAM, *supra* note 29, at 247–48; VICTORIA WOODHULL, THE HUMAN BODY THE TEMPLE OF GOD 38 (1890); Stanton, *supra* note 29.

124. WILLIAM ACTON, THE FUNCTIONS AND DISORDERS OF THE REPRODUCTIVE ORGANS IN YOUTH, IN ADULT AGE, AND IN ADVANCED AGE: CONSIDERED IN THEIR PHYSIOLOGICAL, SOCIAL AND PSYCHOLOGICAL RELATIONS 133 (1865). *See also* GARDNER, *supra* note 49; SYLVESTER GRAHAM, LECTURE TO YOUNG MEN ON CHASTITY (1834); SAMUEL GREGORY, LICENTIOUSNESS, ITS CAUSES AND EFFECTS (1846); GEORGE NAPHEYS, THE TRANSMISSION OF LIFE: COUNSELS ON THE NATURE AND HYGIENE OF THE MASCULINE FUNCTION 173–74 (1878); MICHAEL RYAN, PHILOSOPHY OF MARRIAGE (4th ed. 1843); EDWARD TILT, THE CHANGE OF LIFE IN HEALTH AND DISEASE 79, 93–94 (4th ed. 1882); HENRY WRIGHT, THE UNWELCOME CHILD, OR, THE CRIME OF THE UNDESIGNED AND UNDESIRED MATERNITY (1860); Goodell, *supra* note 49, at 162. *See generally* G.J. BARKER-BENFIELD, THE HORRORS OF THE HALF-KNOWN LIFE: MALE ATTITUDES TOWARD WOMEN AND SEXUALITY IN NINETEENTH CENTURY AMERICA (1976); D'EMILIO & FREEDMAN, *supra* note 24, at 50–63, 64–65, 70–72, 80–81; DEGLER, *supra* note 11, at 249–97; GORDON, *supra* note 5, at 16–25, 101–15, 174–81; GROSSBERG, *supra* note 5, at 45–49; HALLER & HALLER, *supra* note 50; KERN, *supra* note 81, at 1–9, 95–102, 109–13, 153–65; KAREN LYSTRA, SEARCHING THE HEART: WOMEN, MEN, AND ROMANTIC LOVE IN NINETEENTH-CENTURY AMERICA 50–59 (1989); STEVEN MARCUS, THE OTHER VICTORIANS (1964); PETCHESKY, *supra* note 5, at 74–77; MARY POOVEY, UNEVEN DEVELOPMENTS: THE IDEOLOGICAL WORK OF GENDER IN MID-VICTORIAN ENGLAND (1988); SMITH-ROSENBERG, *supra* note 5, at 182–216; LUCIA ZENDER, WOMEN, CRIME, AND CUSTODY IN VICTORIAN ENGLAND (1991); Ruth Bloch, *The Gendered Meanings of Virtue in Revolutionary America*, 13 SIGNS 37 (1987); Peter Cominos, *Late Victorian Sexual Repression and the Social System*, 7 INT'L REV. SOC. HIST. 18 (Pt. I), 216 (Pt. II) (1963); Nancy Cott, *Passionless: An Interpretation of Victorian Sexual Ideology, 1790–1850*, 4 SIGNS 219 (1978); Sondra Herman, *Loving Courtship or the Marriage Market? The Ideal and Its Critics, 1871–1911*, 25 AM. Q. 235 (1973); Jane Larson, *"Women Understand So Little, They Call My Good Nature 'Deceit'": A Feminist Rethinking of Seduction*, 93 COLUM. L. REV. 374, 388–93 (1993); Barbara Welter, *The Cult of True Womanhood*, 18 AM. Q. 151 (1966).

125. *See* KERN, *supra* note 90, at 102–11, 117–24, 139–52.

126. *See, e.g.*, PATRICIA ANDERSON, WHEN PASSION REIGNED: SEX AND THE VICTORIANS (1995); PETER GAY, THE NAKED HEART (1995); MICHAEL MASON, THE MAKING OF VICTORIAN SEXUALITY(1995).

127. A point made in reviews of these books. Noel Annan, *Under the Victorian Bed*, N.Y. REV. BOOKS, June 22, 1995, at 48; Richard Jenkyn, *Victoria's Secret*, N.Y. REV. BOOKS, Nov. 30, 1995, at 19.

128. *See* ELLEN CAROL DUBOIS, FEMINISM AND SUFFRAGE: THE EMERGENCE OF AN INDEPENDENT WOMEN'S MOVEMENT IN AMERICA, 1848–1869, at 32 (1978); PAULA GIDDINGS, WHEN AND WHERE I ENTER: THE IMPACT OF BLACK WOMEN ON RACE AND SEX IN AMERICA 55 (1984); Peggy Cooper Davis, *Neglected Stories and the Lawfulness of Roe v. Wade*, 28 HARV. C.R.-C.L. L. REV. 299, 330–31 (1993).

ing at least, by a man.[129] We have already seen the strained readings given these materials by such modern feminists as law professor Reva Siegel.[130] Yet the divorce reform movement of the late nineteenth-century was led by men such as Samuel Dike motivated more by eugenic concerns— the wrong people were marrying—than by any concern about individual liberation.[131] In contrast, by the end of the nineteenth century, most feminist leaders had joined in an attempt to make divorce more difficult to obtain.[132]

The truth is that most nineteenth century feminists, including even the "free love" wing, wanted to strengthen marriage rather than destroy it.[133] After all, fewer than five percent of white women in the United States worked outside the home after marriage during the nineteenth century[134]—and the feminist leaders of the time were predominantly white and married. No wonder the Women's Christian Temperance Union and other feminist groups often acted as "marriage enforcers" at this time, pressuring men to marry their pregnant paramours (and sometimes pressuring the women involved as well) unless they considered the marriage hopeless.[135]

Like Horatio Robinson Storer, the nineteenth-century feminists were strongly in favor of the rational spacing of children, speaking in terms of "voluntary motherhood."[136] Given the then technical incapacity to prevent conception mechanically or pharmacologically,[137] one is not surprised that nineteenth century feminists advocated the right to refuse a husband's sexual advances as the means to achieve the desired "voluntary motherhood."[138] If a woman lacked the ability to refuse her husband directly, Dr. Alice Bunker Stockham recommended sexual coldness

---

129. WILLIAM THOMPSON, APPEAL OF ONE-HALF OF THE HUMAN RACE, WOMEN, AGAINST THE PRETENSIONS OF THE OTHER HALF, MEN, TO RETAIN THEM IN POLITICAL, AND THENCE IN CIVIL AND DOMESTIC SLAVERY (1825).

130. *See* Chapter 2, at notes 163–71. For Siegel's work, see Reva Siegel, *Home as Work: The First Women's Rights Claims Concerning Wives' Household Labor, 1850–1880*, 103 YALE L.J. 1073 (1994) ("Siegel, *Home as Work*"); Siegel, *supra* note 5.

131. *See, e.g.,* NATIONAL DIVORCE REFORM LEAGUE, ANNUAL REPORT OF 1886, at 6 (1887) (decrying the significance of the foreign born in American cities); NATIONAL DIVORCE REFORM LEAGUE, ANNUAL REPORT OF 1888, at 12 (1889) (same); Samuel Dike, *Uniform Marriage and Divorce Laws*, 2 THE ARENA 399 (1890). *See also In re* McLaughlin's Estate, 4 Wash. 570, 590–91 (1892) ("All wise and healthful regulations...prohibiting such marriages as far as practicable would tend to the prevention of pauperism and crime, and the transmission of hereditary diseases and defects..."); George Elliott Howard, *Divorce and the Public Welfare*, 84 MC-CLURE'S MAG.232 (1909) (arguing that the functions of families should be transferred to the state); Elizabeth Scott Phelps, *Women's View of Divorce*, 150 N. AM. REV. 130 (1890) (arguing for an end of paupers begetting paupers). *See generally* GROSSBERG, *supra* note 5, at 83–95; Matthew Lindsay, *Reproducing a Fit Citizenry: Dependency, Eugenics, and the Law of Marriage in the United States, 1860–1920*, 23 LAW & SOC. INQUIRY 541, 553–54 (1998).

132. *See generally* DEGLER, *supra* note 11, at 362–94; PETCHESKY, *supra* note 5, at 41–42; Smith, *supra* note 103; James J. White, *Ex Proprio Vigore*, 89 MICH. L. REV. 2096 (1991).

133. *See* SMITH-ROSENBERG, *supra* note 5, at 243–44. *See also* Chapter 2, at notes 157–62.

134. PETCHESKY, *supra* note 5, at 75; LYNN WEINER, FROM WORKING GIRL TO WORKING MOTHER 6 (1985). For the similar pattern in England, see WENDY NEFF, VICTORIAN WORKING WOMEN (1966); IVY PINCHBECK, WOMEN WORKERS AND THE INDUSTRIAL REVOLUTION, 1750–1850 (1930).

135. LINDA GORDON, HEROES OF THEIR OWN LIVES: THE POLITICS AND HISTORY OF FAMILY VIOLENCE, BOSTON, 1880–1960, at 297 (1988); Constance Backhouse, *Involuntary Motherhood: Abortion, Birth Control and the Law in Nineteenth Century Canada*, 3 WINDSOR Y.B. OF ACCESS TO JUSTICE 61, 62 n.1 (1983); Brumberg, *supra* note 115, at 254–57. The WCTU was the largest and most influential women's organization anywhere in the world at that time. *See* RUTH BORDIN, WOMEN AND TEMPERANCE: THE QUEST FOR POWER AND LIBERTY, 1873–1900, at 3–4 (1981). *See also* EPSTEIN, *supra* note 110; DAVID PIVAR, PURITY CRUSADE: SEXUAL MORALITY AND SOCIAL CONTROL, 1868–1900 (1973).

136. *See* Chapter 2, at notes 157–58, 177–88

137. *See id.* at notes 12–121.

138. *See id.* at notes 145–240.

as a birth control device.[139] Although such advice refutes the charge that feminists in general supported "free love" in the salacious sense, the advice could hardly refute the claim that feminism was inimical to the family as total abstinence would require separate households for the wife and the husband.[140] Nor, for that matter, could a program of sexual abstinence and emotional withdrawal assure women the fiscal security and moral power that at the time derived from the actuality or prospect of motherhood.[141] What such women needed rather desperately was a technique that would allow them to prevent or terminate a pregnancy without reliance on crude sexual refusal. No wonder Victorian women generally seem to have opted not for coldness, but for the appearance of frailty as a device for limiting their husband's sexual access.[142]

Again we find Dr. Horatio Robinson Storer confounding his modern critics by taking the same line as nearly all feminists did. Storer apparently contemplated the sensible use of contraception or abstinence as preferred by many feminists, advocating the spacing children about three years apart in the very passages in which he argued for the necessity of pregnancy for women to retain their good health.[143] And the leading feminists, like Storer, condemned male complicity in the crime of abortion, but not as a means of excusing the abortion nor as a means of expressing hostility to sexual indulgence. All were uncompromising in their view of abortion.

Such attitudes persisted among feminists well into the twentieth century. For example, Margaret Sanger, famous as the founder of the birth control movement consistently and repeatedly condemned abortion as murder.[144] Dr. Marie Stopes, who played a similar role in England, also condemned abortion as murder.[145] As late as 1960, Dr. Mary Calderone, the medical director of Planned Parenthood and later one of the strongest supporters of the supposed freedom to abort, described abortion as "the taking of a life."[146] In short, until quite recently most feminists were strong opponents of abortion, and the farther back one goes in time the more nearly unanimous feminists become in their hostility to abortion.

# Obfuscating Nineteenth Century Feminist Attitudes

*Deconstruction is the banana peel on the sidewalk of language.*

—Sydney DeLong[147]

Reading the new orthodoxy of abortion history, one would never guess that the feminists of the nineteenth century were so consistently and so strongly opposed to abortion. This raises the intriguing question of why do feminist and other pro-abortion historians today seem incapable

---

139. STOCKHAM, *supra* note 29, at 152–53.

140. *See* Chapter 2, at notes 206–09.

141. *See generally* GORDON, *supra* note 5, at 109–12; PETCHESKY, *supra* note 5, at 74–77.

142. *See* Chapter 2, at notes 211–39.

143. STORER, REFLEX INSANITY, *supra* note 86, at 115–16.

144. MARGARET SANGER, MOTHERHOOD IN BONDAGE 394–96 (1928); MARGARET SANGER, MY FIGHT FOR BIRTH CONTROL 133 (1931); MARGARET SANGER, WOMEN AND THE NEW RACE 119–22, 129 (1920). *See also* Chapter 11, at notes 247–54.

145. MARIE STOPES, MOTHER ENGLAND: A CONTEMPORARY HISTORY 183 (1929). *See also* BROOKES, *supra* note 21, at 2–3, 5–8, 80; MARY KENNY, ABORTION: THE WHOLE STORY 188, 297–98 (1986).

146. Mary Calderone, *Illegal Abortion as a Public Health Problem*, 50 AM. J. PUB. HEALTH 948, 951 (1960).

147. Sidney DeLong, *Jacques of All Trades: Derrida, Lacan, and the Commercial Lawyer*, 45 J. LEGAL EDUC. 131, 133 (1995).

of realizing that until recently even the most militant feminists considered abortion an abominable crime against nature and against women, a crime that society should prohibit and attempt to stamp out. These historians, in crafting the new orthodox history of abortion, claim to have "deconstructed" the attitudes of the early feminists to discover hidden support for abortion for which there is no evidence except the historian's intuition. The thought is captured in historian James Mohr's comment that "the relationship between abortion and feminism in the nineteenth century nevertheless remained indirect and ironical."[148] No extended analysis of deconstruction theory is necessary to understand how it has affected the way we envision the history of abortion. It is only necessary to know that such theories embrace a thorough going skepticism that concludes that the only truth is that there is no truth,[149] overlooking the contradiction inherent in such a view.[150] Accepting this proposition often cause such scholars to miss the fact that although one might not be able to determine the truth in any ultimate sense, one often can recognize lies.[151] Yet, as Tatyana Tolstaya has written, "lying, perhaps humankind's primary weakness, is precisely what historians must overcome."[152] This turns out to be a serious problem for historians of abortion, although it is not always clear whether the historian is lying to her readers or to herself.

Historian Linda Gordon provides a prime example. While frankly acknowledging that nineteenth-century feminists opposed abortion, she sought to explain that reality away as representing a "false consciousness."[153] Gordon at least is honest about what she is attempting. She is one of the few historians of the new orthodoxy of abortion history to admit expressly that much of her work relating to the use and regulation of birth control techniques is "not a history but a schematic hypothesis [that] does not purport to describe what actually happened but offers a theoretical model of the way it might have happened."[154] In other words, Gordon writes her "history" of the lives of women in times past much like monks in medieval monasteries wrote of their "lives" of saints—works in which the imagination of the author filled in innumerable details in the absence of, or even in defiance of, relevant written records. Like those lives of

---

148. MOHR, *supra* note 4, at 109.

149. *See, e.g.* JONATHAN CULLER, ON DECONSTRUCTION: THEORY AND CRITICISM AFTER STRUCTURALISM (1982); JACQUES DERRIDA, ON GRAMMATOLOGY (Gayatri Chakravorty Spivak trans. 1976); MICHEL FOUCAULT, ARCHEOLOGY OF KNOWLEDGE AND THE DISCOURSE ON LANGUAGE (A.M. Sheridan Smith trans. 1972); DAVID HARVEY, THE CONDITION OF POSTMODERNITY (1989); JEAN-FRANÇOIS LYOTARD, THE POSTMODERN CONDITION: A REPORT ON KNOWLEDGE (Geoff Bennington & Brian Massumi trans. 1984); PAULINE MARIE ROSENAU, POST MODERNISM AND THE SOCIAL SCIENCES: INSIGHTS, INROADS, AND INSTRUSIONS(1992); STEPHEN WHITE, POLITICAL THEORY AND POSTMODERNISM (1991).

150. *See generally* REGIS DEBRAY, TEACHERS, WRITERS, CELEBRITIES: THE INTELLECTUALS OF MODERN FRANCE (David Macey trans. 1981); PETER DEWS, LOGICS OF DISINTEGRATION: POST-STRUCTURALIST THOUGHT AND THE CLAIMS OF CRITICAL THEORY (1987); ROGER KIMBALL, TENURED RADICALS: HOW POLITICS HAS CORRUPTED HIGHER EDUCATION (1990); CHRISTOPHER LASCH, THE TRUE AND ONLY HEAVEN: PROGRESS AND ITS CRITICS(1991). *See generally* Chapter 20, at notes 17–40.

151. *See* ADRIENNE RICH, ON LIES, SECRETS, AND SILENCE 185 (1979); Allan Hunt, *The Big Fear: Law Confronts Postmodernism*, 35 MCGILL L.J. 507, 525 (1990); Judith Lichtenberg, *Objectivity and Its Enemies*, 2 THE RESPONSIVE COMMUNITY 59 (1991); David Millon, *Objectivity and Democracy*, 67 NYU L. REV. 1, 23–35 (1992).

152. Tatyana Tolstaya, *The Golden Age*, N.Y. REV. BOOKS, Dec. 17, 1992, at 3 (James Gambrell trans.).

153. Linda Gordon, *Why Nineteenth Century Feminists Did Not Support "Birth Control" and Twentieth Century Feminists Do*, in RETHINKING THE FAMILY 40, 51 (Barrie Thorne & Marilyn Yalom eds. 1982). *See also* GORDON, *supra* note 5, at 108, 114–15; PETCHESKY, *supra* note 5, at 41–45; Linda Gordon, *The Struggle for Reproductive Freedom: Three Stages of Feminism*, in CAPITALIST PATRIARCHY AND THE CASE FOR SOCIALIST FEMINISM 110 (Zillah Eisenstein ed. 1979).

154. GORDON, *supra* note 5, at 4 n.*.

saints, Gordon's disclaimer has not prevented others from relying on Gordon's work as if it were divine revelation.[155] Excessive reliance on Gordon's work comes about in no small measure because Gordon never reverts to this point again and takes no steps to indicate which parts of her work represent historical data and which represents her imagination. Furthermore, Gordon's remarks about "false consciousness" play right into her predilection to invent what she cannot discover.

Some prominent feminist scholars have long argued that "consciousness raising" is the central feminist contribution to the intellectual enterprise, precisely because they consider the "consciousness" of most women—other than some feminists—to be "false."[156] Claims of "false consciousness," however, often are simply a ploy to enable one to claim as fact something that the women actually involved (and other witnesses) deny. No wonder even some feminist scholars have described the theory of "false consciousness" as off-putting and counterproductive,[157] or as simply a strategic ploy, not a truth about certain women's experiences.[158]

Given Gordon's attitude towards historical evidence, one is not surprised to discover that she seems unable to recognize evidence of the widespread acceptance among all classes of women of the idea that abortion involved the killing of the child. Thus, Gordon quotes a letter from 1916 in which a young mother laments having considered killing a child through abortion, and her happiness that she had not done so, yet Gordon sees only a mother who desires to control births.[159] Linda Gordon also quotes the following letter, written in 1859 by a woman schoolteacher in Massachusetts to her parents in New Hampshire:

> Alphens' wife has been up here with her mother all summer. Poor Alphens he has got so poor that he cant keep house so he sent his wife to live on his father all winter—her poor health was caused by getting rid of a child as I suppose Alphens didn't feel able to maintain another one you must not say anything as I have only guessed it she was very large when she came here and in a short time she shrank to her normal size.[160]

Gordon reads this barely literate letter as indicating a casual acceptance of abortion by persons of the writer's class ("rural, upper middle class, respectable" is Gordon's description of the writer, Elisa Adams), despite the writer's admonition not to mention the event to anyone and despite the rather evident fact that the woman involved ("Alphens' wife") did not want to advertise the event. This is similar to Gordon's insistence that knowledge of how to do safe and effective abortions was widespread even while she herself referred to numerous letters sent to birth control advocates in the early twentieth century that, directly or indirectly, indicated that numerous couples had not the foggiest notion of how to get an abortion.[161]

As we have seen, there is considerable warrant for believing that ignorance of how to do abortions prevailed throughout most of our history.[162] We find some confirmation of this in the re-

---

155. *See, e.g.,* CONNIE PAIGE, THE RIGHT TO LIFERS: WHO THEY ARE; HOW THEY OPERATE; WHERE THEY GET THEIR MONEY 33 (1983); Siegel, *supra* note 5, at 304–14.

156. CATHARINE MACKINNON, FEMINISM UNMODIFIED: DISCOURSES ON LIFE AND LAW 60–61, 217–18 (1987) ("MACKINNON, F.U."); CATHARINE MACKINNON, TOWARD A FEMINIST THEORY OF THE STATE 83–105, 172–83, 215–34 (1989). *See also* Chapter 21, at notes 68–82.

157. *See, e.g.,* Kathryn Abrams, *Ideology and Women's Choices,* 24 GA. L. REV. 761 (1990).

158. Frances Olsen, *Feminist Theory in Grand Style,* 89 COLUM. L. REV. 1147, 1175–79 (1989).

159. GORDON, *supra* note 5, at 229–30.

160. *Id.* at 51 (quoting a letter of Elisa Adams to her parents).

161. *Compare id.* at 28–29, 35–39, 52–54, *with id.* at 367–68.

162. *See* Chapter 1.

markably detailed diary of midwife Martha Ballard.[163] Ballard's diary covers the period from 1785 to 1812, when Mohr, Gordon, and others insist that midwives were commonly performing abortions, yet Ballard does not mention even a single abortion in her diary. We cannot assume that Ballard simply did not bother to report her participation in such activities; her diary includes accounts of incest, illegitimacy, child abuse, and other unsavory activities, as well as many routine and unremarkable activities. Either Ballard considered abortion even more vile than the things she recorded or she did nor know of any abortions.

James Mohr, archpriest of the new orthodoxy of abortion history, is perhaps the best exemplar of obfuscation of the attitudes of nineteenth century feminists toward abortion. Mohr introduced his discussion of feminist attitudes by attributing the rising incidence of abortion largely to changes in social mores among upper class, native born, Protestant women.[164] There is some support in the anti-abortion writings of the second half of the nineteenth and early twentieth century to support this claim, notably among those who feared "race suicide."[165] This conclusion might be partially correct, although it ignores the effects of changing technology on social mores. In other words, abortion had become possible by the later years of the nineteenth century because of changing medical technology, and not simply because a certain class of women now wanted abortions. And in fact, there actually is no evidence indicating whether upper class, native born, Protestant women were having abortions more often than lower class or immigrant or Catholic or Jewish women. The only indirect evidence that might support such a conclusion is that the birthrate for upper-class, native born, Protestant women was falling faster than for other groups of women—but even Mohr conceded elsewhere in his book that abortion cannot have been the primary means for creating this differential.[166]

The falling birthrate was indeed the root of the "race suicide" fears, and as the physicians writing the books served an upper-class, native born, Protestant clientele, it is not surprising that the women they encountered who sought abortions fit that description. It hardly proves that these women had more frequent abortions than the groups of women about which these physicians knew little or nothing. By focusing his discussion on who was having abortions rather than how abortions were being done, however, Mohr sought to link the rise of abortion to the simultaneous widespread emergence of feminism in the United States.[167] Mohr found his link in allegations by men opposed to feminism who often described women who sought abortion to be

---

163. Laurel Thatcher Ulrich, The Midwife's Tale: The Life of Martha Ballard Based on Her Diary, 1785–1812 (1991).

164. Mohr, *supra* note 4, at 86–118, 128–29, 166–70. *See also* Grossberg, *supra* note 5, at 170–71; Judges, *supra* note 5, at 104; Smith-Rosenberg, *supra* note 5, at 224–25, 235–39; R. Sauer, *Attitudes to Abortion in America, 1800–1973*, 28 Pop. Studies 53, 54–56, 59 (1974). Similar ideas were expressed in Canada during the same period. *See* Angus McLaren, *Birth Control and Abortion in Canada, 1870–1920*, 59 Can. Hist. Rev. 319, 319–21, 328, 333 (1978).

165. O.C. Beall, Racial Decay: A Compilation of Evidence from World Sources (1911); Lydia Kingsmill Commander, The American Idea: Does the National Tendency toward a Small Family Point to Race Suicide or Race Degeneration? (1907); Gardner, *supra* note 49, at 117; Samuel Holmes, The Trend of the Race 169 (1921); Andrew Nebinger, Criminal Abortion: Its Extent and Prevention 31 (1870); W.E. Atlee & D.A. O'Donnell, *Report of the Committee on Criminal Abortion*, 22 Trans. Am. Med. Ass'n 240, 241 (1871); H. Gibbons, sr., *On Foeticide*, 21 Pac. Med. & Surgical J. 97, 110–11 (1878); P.S. Haskell, *Criminal Abortion*, 4 Trans. Me. Med. Ass'n 463, 467 (1873); "Kit" (Kathleen Blake Watkins), *Race Suicide*, Daily Mail & Empire (Toronto), Mar. 21, 1908, at 21; W.S. Wallace, *The Canadian Immigration Policy*, 30 Can. Mag. 360 (1907).

166. Mohr, *supra* note 4, at 83. *But see* McLaren, *supra* note 164, at 323, 327–28, 337–38 (arguing that abortion was the primary technique driving declining birthrates in late nineteenth and early twentieth century Canada).

167. Mohr, *supra* note 4, at 103–10, 167–70.

selfish and fashion-driven.[168] Non-physician opponents of abortion sometimes made the same accusation.[169]

Some the nineteenth century critics of feminism depicted abortions as done by women to women.[170] The tone of such remarks suggests that the critics saw the feminists as engaged in a conspiracy against men.[171] Some physicians also suggested that the rising incidence of abortion came from growing fears on the part of some women of death or serious injury through giving birth.[172] And, as we have seen, complaints that midwives doubled as abortionists go back centuries, both in England and in America.[173] Male physicians in the mid-nineteenth-century also charged women physicians with doing abortions, but without presenting any evidence to support the claim.[174] Mohr was aware of these charges,[175] but for some reason did not mention them as relevant to whether the nineteenth century feminists supported abortion. Instead, Mohr was content with two male physicians who espoused what Mohr termed a "feminist" view of the matter.

Of Mohr's male "feminists," one was an anonymous male physician who did appear to support strongly what are now termed abortion rights.[176] Mohr buried in a distant endnote, however, an admission that the anonymous author drew his arguments from a feminist book that "itself was by no means pro-abortion."[177] In any event, the very anonymity of the article speaks eloquently of the authors' perception of the popular attitude. The other male "feminist" was Dr. Henry Wright, whose book seems to have been a regretful apology for the reality of abortion

---

168. GARDNER, *supra* note 49, at 17–18, 180–81, 224–30; EDWIN HALE, THE GREAT CRIME OF THE NINE-TEENTH CENTURY, WHY IS IT COMMITTED? WHO ARE THE CRIMINALS? HOW SHALL THEY BE DETECTED? HOW SHALL THEY BE PUNISHED? 7–15 (1867); JOHN HARVEY KELLOGG, PLAIN FACTS FOR OLD AND YOUNG 271 (1881); NEBINGER, *supra* note 165, at 11; POMEROY, *supra* note 44, at vii, 137–38; STORER, WHY NOT?, *supra* note 82, at 42, 63, 73, 81, 85; STORER & HEARD, *supra* note 86, at 61; J. Boring, *Foeticide*, 2 ATLANTA MED. & SURGICAL J. 257, 258 (1857); E.M. Buckingham, *Criminal Abortion*, 10 CIN. LANCET & OBSERVER 139, 141 (1867); Walter Channing, *Effects of Criminal Abortion*, 60 BOS. MED. & SURGICAL J. 134, 134–35 (1859); "D.H.", *On Producing Abortion: A Physician's Reply to the Solicitations of a Married Woman to Produce a Miscarriage for Her*, 17 NASHVILLE J. MED. & SURGICAL J. 200, 200 (1876); Gibbons, *supra* note 165, at 105–07, 111; H.C. Markham, *Foeticide and Its Prevention*, 11 J.A.M.A. 805, 806 (1888); J. Miller, *Criminal Abortion*, 1 K.C. MED. REC. 295, 296 (1884); Pallen, *supra* note 44, at 201, 205–06; J.C. Stone, *Report on the Subject of Criminal Abortion*, 1 TRANS. IOWA ST. MED. SOC'Y 29, 34 (1871); J.M. Toner, *Abortion in Its Medical and Moral Aspects*, 5 MED. & SURGICAL RPTR. 443, 445 (1861). *See* DEGLER, *supra* note 11, at 233–35; MOHR, *supra* note 4, at 107–08; REAGAN, *supra* note 21, at 12; Sauer, *supra* note 164, at 56; Michael Thomson, *Women, Medicine and Abortion in the Nineteenth Century*, 3 FEM. LEG. STUD. 159, 175–77 (1995).

169. E. FRANK HOWE, SERMON ON ANTE-NATAL INFANTICIDE DELIVERED AT THE CONGREGATIONAL CHURCH IN TERRE HAUTE, ON SUNDAY MORNING, MARCH 28, 1869, at 2–3 (1869). *See also* BARKER-BENFIELD, *supra* note 124, at 135–226; MOHR, *supra* note 4, at 87–88 (discussing the writings of the Rev. John Todd).

170. *See, e.g.*, HALE, *supra* note 168, at 17; STORER & HEARD, *supra* note 86, at 97–103; TODD, *supra* note 49, at 4. *See also* SYLVANUS STALL, WHAT A YOUNG MAN OUGHT TO KNOW 198 (1897) (similar claims in a Canadian setting). *See generally* E.R. NORMAN, CHURCH AND SOCIETY IN ENGLAND, 1770–1970, at 270 (1976); McLaren, *supra* note 164, at 319–20. For modern echoes of this theory, see Chapter 1, at notes 18–30.

171. *See* WALSH, *supra* note 44, at 72 n.86; Siegel, *Home as Work*, *supra* note 130, at 49–51; Siegel, *supra* note 5, at 300–01. *See generally* WALSH, *supra*, at 106–77.

172. *See, e.g.*, E.P. Christian, *The Pathological Consequences Incident to Induced Abortion*, 2 DET. REV. MED. & PHARMACY 147, 147 (1867); John Trader, *Criminal Abortion*, 11 ST. L. MED. & SURGICAL J., n.s. 583, 588 (1874). *See also* MOHR, *supra* note 4, at 108, 170.

173. *See* Chapter 1, at notes 15–17; Chapter 2, at notes 283–89; Chapter 4, at 308–11.

174. *See, e.g.*, HARRIOT KEZIA HUNT, GLANCES AND GLIMPSES; OR FIFTY YEARS SOCIAL, INCLUDING TWENTY YEARS PROFESSIONAL, LIFE 159 (1856; reprinted 1970). *See also* WALSH, *supra* note 44, at 145–46.

175. MOHR, *supra* note 4, at 86–90.

176. Anonymous, *Abortion*, 7 MEDICO-LEGAL J. 170 (1889). *See* MOHR, *supra* note 4, at 108–09, 113.

177. MOHR, *supra* note 4, at 288 n.81.

rather than an argument in its favor.[178] In an earlier book, Wright had castigated the medical profession for its apparent willingness to condone abortions when performed by allopathic physicians while prosecuting abortions when performed by others.[179] Such criticism hardly supports a view of Wright as a friend of abortion.[180]

Mohr's problem was that the leading feminists of the nineteenth century were virtually unanimous in supporting the prohibition of abortion as a crime because of a professed concern to protect prenatal human life.[181] This reality severely undercut Mohr's claim that only physicians were staking out such an "idiosyncratic" position.[182] Mohr and other researchers actually found only one undoubted feminist advocating a right to abort during the nineteenth century, and this not until 1893.[183] By that time, abortion laws had produced a situation where abortion no longer was, as Mohr himself put it, a "viable alternative."[184]

To buttress his claims, Mohr turned to this sole feminist who, before the very end of the century, actually seemed to support abortion rights in an anonymous letter written from Maine to *The Revolution,* a feminist journal, in 1868.[185] This "Conspirator," as the letter writer styled herself, did seem to endorse the practice of abortion, but she was hardly an unequivocal supporter. So intent was she on criticizing the evils of marriage (rather than on defending abortion) that her pseudonym seems to refer to a "conspirator against marriage" rather than a conspirator seeking an abortion for herself or others. Indeed, the anonymous writer acknowledged what was in fact the major disincentive to abortion—women knew that abortion endangered their lives, a risk they were willing to undergo to escape having further children "whom the brutal lusts of a drunken husband have forced upon them."[186] Mohr attempted to increase the impact of this letter by noting that the journal was owned by Susan B. Anthony and edited by Elizabeth Cady Stanton and Parker Pillsbury, as if their publication of the letter committed them to supporting abortion.[187] He did not bother to inform his readers that Anthony and Stanton had described abortion in signed articles in the same journal as the murder of children.[188]

To buttress his singular feminist advocate of abortion rights, Mohr quoted from several of the women quoted in Dr. Wright's book. Dr. Wright's book does demonstrate that women were beginning to have abortions by the 1850s and perhaps even before then, yet unless we are to infer from the mere existence of a practice that people accepted it as legitimate, we must ask what women who had abortions, and those who aided them, thought about what they were doing. This question is one that Mohr simply ignored. Dr. Wright quoted from several women describing their abortions, generally in the most remorseful terms and clearly indicating that they themselves considered the act to have killed a child.[189] Mohr translated these views into the la-

---

178. WRIGHT, *supra* note 124. See DEGLER, *supra* note 11, at 244; MOHR, *supra* note 4, at 109–11; OLASKY, *supra* note 75, at 68–71.

179. HENRY WRIGHT, MARRIAGE AND PARENTAGE; OR, THE PROTECTIVE ELEMENT IN MAN, AS A MEANS TO HIS ELEVATION AND HAPPINESS 133 (2nd ed. 1855).

180. *See generally* LEWIS PERRY, CHILDHOOD, MARRIAGE AND REFORM: HENRY CLARKE WRIGHT, 1797–1870 (1980).

181. That he recognized this problem, see MOHR, *supra* note 4, at 111–14, 253. See the text *supra* at notes 29–146.

182. MOHR, *supra* note 4, at 73–74, 182–96.

183. *Id.* at 113. *See also* Siegel, *supra* note 5, at 307 n.185, 312 nn.202–05.

184. MOHR, *supra* note 4, at 113.

185. *Id.* at 107, referring to "Conspirator," *Letter,* THE REVOLUTION, Mar. 19, 1868, at 170.

186. "Conspirator," *supra* note 185, at 170.

187. MOHR, *supra* note 4, at 288 n.73.

188. Anthony, *supra* note 29; Stanton, *supra* note 29.

189. WRIGHT, *supra* note 124, at 65–69, 101–11.

conic statement that the women involved "hated to have to do it."[190] Mohr undercut this summation, however, by immediately quoting at length from a woman who, after describing how "a woman, a friend in whom I trusted" and the friend's "family physician"[191] "labored" to convince the author that the child was not alive until birth, concluded her description of the experience thusly:

> My only trouble was, with God's view of the case, I could not get rid of the feeling that it was an outrage on my body and soul, and on my unconscious babe.... Though I determined to do the deed, my reason, my conscience, my self-respect, my entire nature, revolted against my decision. My Womanhood rose up in withering condemnation.[192]

Statements such as these hardly express support for a freedom to abort, or of claims that the fetus was not yet a person, or that abortion was widely accepted as morally neutral. Mohr, however, chose this very quotation to demonstrate that ordinary people in the nineteenth century did not believe that the fetus was a person and believed that abortion was morally neutral.[193] Mohr also saw such stories as supporting the quickening doctrine.[194] The quotation, to the contrary, explicitly indicates that while the "friend" and the "physician" rejected the recognition of fetal personhood at any point before birth, the mother did not express doubt about fetal personhood at any point of gestation. Mohr went on to claim that the views of the friend and the physician "became the basis of the official position of American feminists toward abortion after the Civil War,"[195] without indicating what made any nineteenth-century woman's position "official." Mohr chose instead to refer to several leading feminists as supporting his claim that feminists' viewed abortion as a tragic necessity.[196]

Mohr simply did not bother to quote a letter in which the writer described abortion as a response to abuse within marriage, the desperation of the response shown, as the writer acknowledged, by the willingness of women knowingly to risk death from the procedure. Nor did he consider the extensive evidence that women who underwent abortions often felt great guilt about the procedure even decades after the event. Elizabeth Evans gathered remembrances from women who had survived abortions in a book she published in 1875 under the name *The Abuse of Maternity.*[197] One woman recalled that she had "mourned for many years the sin committed in her youth,"[198] while another woman stated that her memory of an abortion "serves as an effectual damper upon whatever degree of pride or satisfaction I might otherwise feel in the more praiseworthy deeds of my career."[199] Numerous other women remembered terrible sorrow over the loss of a child never seen and lying in an unknown grave.[200] According to Evans, doctors already recognized what today we would call "post-abortion syndrome"—"remorse [over abortion]...causing nervous maladies."[201] Today many would argue that this was simply a "guilt trip"

---

190. Mohr, *supra* note 4, at 110–11.
191. The quotation marks around the term "family physician" are in the original letter. Wright, *supra* note 124, at 101.
192. *Id.* For similar stories from modern times, see Mary Zimmerman, Passage through Abortion: The Personal and Social Reality of Women's Experiences (1977). *See also* Gilligan, *supra* note 73, at 80; Susan Nathanson, Soul Crisis (1989).
193. Mohr, *supra* note 4, at 111–12.
194. *Id.* at 117–18.
195. *Id.* at 112–13. *See also* Siegel, *supra* note 5, at 50–51.
196. Mohr, *supra* note 4, at 112–13.
197. Elizabeth Edson Gibson Evans, The Abuse of Maternity (1875).
198. *Id.* at 31.
199. *Id.* at 67.
200. *See* Olasky, *supra* note 75, at 183–87.
201. Evans, *supra* note 197, at 70.

laid on women, a kind of "false consciousness," and not a genuine expression of their "true selves." [202]

Whatever one thinks of the idea of a "false consciousness," the fact remains that many women did internalize the belief that abortion was wrong and reacted predictably to the guilt that resulted from the collision of those beliefs with having an abortion. Whether such feelings derived from a false or a true consciousness, a great many people condemned abortion, even (or especially) after having undergone the procedure. None of this suggests that abortion was either common or widely accepted, by women or men. Nor does any shred of evidence suggest that the feminists of the time felt differently.

Mohr's "evidence" of a feminist link to abortion was based more on an effort by the anti-feminists of the time to smear feminists with the brush of a widely-abhorred practice than a genuine indication of the role of the emerging women's movement. Law professor Reva Siegel virtually conceded as much when she wrote: "The [medical] profession's antifeminist arguments imbued the practice of controlling birth with emancipatory significance, whether or not it had this meaning for women who sought abortions."[203] Mohr's argument[204] that only allopathic physicians really wanted the new laws and that the public generally was tolerant or even supportive of abortion and abortionists thus fails even in terms of his own report of the attitudes of such a significantly interested group as politically active nineteenth-century women. This fact returns us to the central puzzle that arises if we take Mohr's second thesis seriously: Why would such self-aware and active women[205] be so gullible when it came to male assertions of control over their

---

202. *See, e.g.,* RUTH COLKER, ABORTION & DIALOGUE—PRO-CHOICE, PRO-LIFE, AND AMERICAN LAW 6–9 (1992); ANDREA DWORKIN, INTERCOURSE 143 (1987); ANDREA DWORKIN, RIGHT-WING WOMEN 227–31 (1982); MACKINNON, F.U., *supra* note 156, at 70–77; PETCHESKY, *supra* note 5, at 76; Patricia Cain, *Feminist Jurisprudence: Grounding the Theories,* 4 BERKELEY L.J. 191, 193–95 (1989); Patricia Cain, *Feminist Legal Scholarship,* 77 IOWA L. REV. 19, 25–27 (1991); Mari Matsuda, *Pragmatism Modified and the False Consciousness Problem,* 63 S. CAL. L. REV. 1763 (1990); Olsen, *supra* note 158, at 1168; Jeanne Schroeder, *Abduction from the Seraglio: Feminist Methodologies and the Logic of Imagination,* 70 TEX. L. REV. 109, 193–94, 206–07 (1991); Jeanne Schroeder, *The Taming of the Shrew: The Liberal Attempt to Mainstream Radical Feminist Theory,* 5 YALE J.L. & FEM. 123, 158–60 (1992); Carol Weisbrod, *Practical Polyphony: Theories of the State and Feminist Jurisprudence,* 24 GA. L. REV. 985, 990–91 (1990); Joan Williams, *Gender Wars: Selfless Women in the Republic of Choice,* 66 NYU L. REV. 1559, 1561, 1564–72, 1612–15 (1991). *See also* Chapter 20, at notes 105–23.

203. Siegel, *supra* note 5, at 302. *See generally* BARKER-BENFIELD, *supra* note 124, at 84–88, 193, 284–85; HALLER & HALLER, *supra* note 50, at 76–87, 123; SARAH STAGE, FEMALE COMPLAINTS: LYDIA PINKHAM AND THE BUSINESS OF WOMEN'S MEDICINE 84–85 (1979); WALSH, *supra* note 44, at 70 n.86; Siegel, *supra,* at 301–04, 310–14.

204. MOHR, *supra* note 4, at 73.

205. *See, e.g.,* STANTON, *supra* note 41. *See also* LOIS BANNER, ELIZABETH CADY STANTON: A RADICAL FOR WOMEN'S RIGHTS (1980); BUHLE & BUHLE, *supra* note 41; MARI JO BUHLE, WOMEN AND AMERICAN SOCIALISM (1981); OLIVIA COOLIDGE, WOMEN'S RIGHTS: THE SUFFRAGE MOVEMENT IN AMERICA, 1848–1920 (1966); DEGLER, *supra* note 11, at 144–77, 279–97; MARJORIE HOUSEPIAN DOBKIN, THE MAKING OF AN AMERICAN FEMINIST: EARLY JOURNALS AND LETTERS OF M. CAREY THOMAS (1979); DUBOIS, *supra* note 128; SARA EVANS, BORN FOR LIBERTY: A HISTORY OF WOMEN IN AMERICA 67–81, 93–95, 101–07, 122–30, 147–56 (1989); ELEANOR FLEXNER, CENTURY OF STRUGGLE: THE WOMEN'S RIGHTS MOVEMENT IN THE UNITED STATES (rev. ed. 1975); ELIZABETH GRIFFITH, IN HER OWN RIGHT: THE LIFE OF ELIZABETH CADY STANTON (1984); BLANCHE GLASSMAN HERSCH, THE SLAVERY OF SEX: FEMINIST ABOLITIONISTS IN AMERICA (1978); NANCY HEWITT, WOMEN'S ACTIVISM AND SOCIAL CHANGE: ROCHESTER, NEW YORK, 1822–1872 (1984); MARY RYAN, CRADLE OF THE MIDDLE CLASS: THE FAMILY IN ONEIDA COUNTY, NEW YORK, 1790–1865, at 89–142 (1981); EMANIE SACHS, "THE TERRIBLE SIREN," VICTORIA WOODHULL (1838–1927) (1928); KATHRYN KISH SKLAR, CATHERINE BEECHER: A STUDY IN AMERICAN DOMESTICITY (1973); SMITH-ROSENBERG, *supra* note 5, at 88–89, 109–64, 173–78, 245–58, 262–64; Nancy Hewitt, *Feminine Friends: Agrarian Quakers and the Emergence of Women's Rights in America,* 12 FEMINIST STUD. 27 (1986); Mary Ryan, *The Power of Female Networks: A Case Study of Female Moral Reform in Antebellum America,* 5 FEMINIST STUD. 66 (1979).

reproductive processes, particularly given their own defiant criticism of "male sexual license."[206] It is worth recalling in this context the slogan coined by Christabel Pankhurst (a prominent English suffragist) that the feminists' goal was "Votes for women and chastity for men."[207]

Mohr was forced, somewhat reluctantly, to acknowledge the problem feminists posed for his thesis when he wrote "the relationship between abortion and feminism in the nineteenth century nevertheless remained indirect and ironical."[208] Only at the very end of his discussion of feminists and abortion, however, did Mohr acknowledge that all of the women whom he claimed supported a right to abort "found themselves in the anomalous position of endorsing the anti-feminist physicians' calls for anti-abortion legislation."[209] Indirect and ironical indeed.

Most other scholars writing on the history of abortion have taken the same or a similar line as Mohr. For example, sociologist Rosalind Petchesky preferred to dismiss feminist opposition to abortion as reflecting the pervasive influence of the patriarchal society in which these women lived.[210] In sharp contrast, historian Carl Degler did not find feminist opposition to abortion as so anomalous; he saw it as of a piece with the opposition of organized feminists to slavery, the death penalty, war, and corporal punishment for crimes.[211] Others, including the authors of the *Historians' Briefs,* preferred simply to misrepresent what the feminists of the time thought.[212]

Despite such clear and direct evidence of what feminist leaders, and even ordinary women, knew and believed about fetuses and abortion in the middle and later years of the nineteenth century, there actually is some evidence that ordinary people did not accept the personhood of the fetus during that period.[213] That evidence is, however, similar to the strategy of the anti-feminists of blaming abortion on the feminists. Long after a good many ordinary people had accepted the personhood of the fetus from conception onward and the view that even the earliest abortion was "child murder," many in the professions of law and medicine apparently continued to believe that ordinary people entertained no such ideas.[214] As late as 1923 the Wisconsin Supreme Court would justify that state's continued reliance on the quickening distinction as a practical necessity because of popular ignorance that a pre-quickening fetus was a living person in these words:

> In a strictly scientific and physiological sense there is life in an embryo from the time of conception, and in such sense there is also life in the male and female elements that unite to form the embryo. But law for obvious reasons cannot in its classifications fol-

---

206. *See, e.g.,* ELIZA BISBEE DUFFEY, WHAT EVERY WOMAN SHOULD KNOW (1873); EVANS, *supra* note 197. *See generally* GORDON, *supra* note 5, at 24–25; RUTH ROSEN, THE LOST SISTERHOOD: PROSTITUTION IN AMERICA, 1900–1918 (1982); SMITH-ROSENBERG, supra note 5, at 46, 109–28.

207. BROOKES, *supra* note 21, at 81. *See also* TANNAHILL, *supra* note 20, at 398–400 (noting the puritan streak among American feminists demanding a "harsh...rectitude").

208. MOHR, *supra* note 4, at 113. *See also* BROOKES, *supra* note 52, at 109; GINSBURG, *supra* note 5, at 29–30.

209. MOHR, *supra* note 4, at 113. *See generally* D'EMILIO & FREEDMAN, *supra* note 24, at 150–67; GORDON, *supra* note 5, at 106–20; SMITH-ROSENBERG, *supra* note 5, at 243.

210. PETCHESKY, *supra* note 5, at 44–45.

211. DEGLER, *supra* note 11, at 247.

212. See the text *supra* at notes 31–46.

213. EVANS, *supra* note 197, at 58.

214. *See, e.g.,* HUGH HODGE, FOETICIDE OR CRIMINAL ABORTION 32–33 (1869); O.A. Cannon, *Septic Abortion,* 12 CAN. MED. ASS'N J. 166 (1922); Mary Dixon-Jones, *Criminal Abortion—Its Evils and Its Sad Consequences,* 3 WOPMEN'S MED. J. 34, 34 (1894); Palmer Findley, *The Slaughter of the Innocents,* 3 AM. J. OBSTET. & GYNECOLOGY 35, at 36 (1922); Joseph Taber Johnson, *Abortion and Its Effects,* 33 AM. J. OSTET. & DISEASES OF WOMEN & CHILDREN 86, 91 (1895); Minnie Love, *Criminal Abortion,* 1 COLO. MED. 55, 58 (1903). *See generally* REAGAN, *supra* note 21, at 25, 80–85, 109–10; GLANVILLE WILLIAMS, THE SANCTITY OF LIFE AND THE CRIMINAL LAW 207–08, 215 (1957, reprinted 1972); McLaren, *supra* note 164, at 334–35.

low the latest or ultimate declarations of science. It must for purposes of practical efficiency proceed upon more everyday and popular conceptions, especially as to definitions of crimes that are *malum in se*. These must be of such a nature that the ordinary
normal adult knows it is morally wrong to commit them. That it should be less of an offense to destroy an embryo in a stage where human life in its common acceptance has
not yet begun than to destroy a quick child is a conclusion that commends itself to most
men.[215]

Similarly, Dr. Frederick Taussig, in his famous early (1936) study of abortion, reached much
the same conclusion regarding his experience with patients: "Every physician will testify that it is
without any feeling of guilt that most women speak of induced abortions in the consultation
room."[216] Perhaps such thinking had become more common in the early years of the twentieth
century, or perhaps such thinking commended itself to professionals (doctors as well as lawyers)
who encounter a rather select sample of those who are seeking or have obtained abortions, yet
(as Dr. Wright's informants demonstrate) there actually is little evidence that such beliefs were
still widely shared by "ordinary normal adults" in the nineteenth or twentieth centuries except in
the professionals' own impressions.[217]

Other modern historians indulge in even weaker arguments to explain why we must understand that the early feminists simply did not mean it when they said over and over again that
they considered abortion murder and wanted to put an end to it. Historian Janet Brodie contended that "social opprobrium" attached to abortion and contraception in the late nineteenth
century solely because these had suddenly (and apparently inexplicably) been made criminal.[218]
Brodie also tells us that the women organized in a crusade for social purity opposed abortion
only "in vague and general ways" as if this meant they did not really mean it.[219] But what can you
expect of an historian who tells us that Comstock's law was passed by an inattentive Congress
that really did not support the law[220]—a law that, as Judge John Noonan wrote, "[i]n penalizing
the possession of contraceptives,…went further than any Pope or Canonist."[221]

Historian Joan Hoff attempts much the same ploy when she attributes the failure of the
nineteenth-century feminists to oppose abortion to their supposed single-minded devotion to
securing the vote, completely ignoring their publicly and frequently stated opposition to abortion as child-murder.[222] Historian Cornelia Dayton actually admitted to a certain puzzlement
over why reported abortions were invariably covert, even in the first months of pregnancy
when (she presumed) it was legal, if abortion were widely known and socially accepted in eigh-

---

215. Foster v. State, 196 N.W. 233, 235 (Wis. 1923). *See also* BROOKES, *supra* note 21, at 26, 30 (quoting
Lord Darling to the same effect while presiding over a trial of two abortionists).

216. FREDERICK TAUSSIG, ABORTION: SPONTANEOUS AND INDUCED 403 (1936). *See also* BROOKES, *supra*
note 21, at 3–9, 14; REPORT OF THE INTERDEPARTMENTAL COMMITTEE ON ABORTION 5, 105 (1939) ("INTER-
DEPARTMENTAL COMM."); KERRY PETERSEN, ABORTION REGIMES 52 (1993); ABRAHAM RONGY, ABORTION:
LEGAL OR ILLEGAL? 90 (1933).

217. INTERDEPARTMENTAL COMM., *supra* note 216, at 45.

218. BRODIE, *supra* note 21, at 281.

219. *Id.* at 262–63, 272–75.

220. *Id.* at 263–66. *See also* TONE, *supra* note 99, at 3–4; C. Thomas Dienes, *The Progeny of
Comstockery—Birth Control Laws Return to Court*, 21 AM. U. L. REV. 1, 3–9 (1971). Tone, remarkably, goes on
to tell us that Congress had passed two similar laws in the preceding eight years, apparently without anyone
ever noticing. TONE, *supra*, at 4–5.

221. JOHN NOONAN, JR., CONTRACEPTION 412 (1986).

222. HOFF, *supra* note 119, at 182. *See also* Deborah Rhode, *The "No-Problem" Problem: Feminist Challenges and Cultural Change*, 100 YALE L.J. 1731, 1742 (1991).

teenth- and nineteenth-century America.[223] Her unlikely answer is that abortion was hidden because it signaled other acts that were socially condemned—fornication and adultery—even though everyone considered abortion itself unproblematic. There are two problems with her reasoning. First, did no married women seek an abortion when the child was not a result of adultery? Second, how, if abortion usually signaled unsavory conduct, would abortion avoid unsavory connotations?

Finally we come to the work of law professor Reva Siegel, whom Justice Blackmun adopted as his new primary source for the history of abortion in his separate opinion in the *Casey* decision.[224] Siegel virtually conceded that the only people who saw feminism at work in such limited resistance to abortion laws as there was were the very same male physicians whom she saw as campaigning against women generally. Her observation that the antifeminist's arguments "imbued the practice of controlling birth with emancipatory significance, whether or not it had this meaning for women who sought abortions"[225] reveals her strategy for obfuscating this fact. Siegel consistently chose to write about "controlling birth" or "voluntary motherhood" rather than about abortion as such.[226] Siegel also repeatedly insisted that the common law did not require a woman to secure her husband's consent to have an abortion.[227] That is a meaningless claim—after all, abortion was a serious crime to which no one could assent.

Siegel would have us believe that anyone advocating birth control in the nineteenth century supported the practice of abortion.[228] This same ploy was used in the *Casey Historians' Brief*[229] and in numerous other histories that seek to obfuscate the nineteenth century feminist position on abortion.[230] In fact, however, nineteenth-century feminists strongly condemned abortion as a crime[231] while many of the same feminists openly espoused contraception.[232] Siegel acknowledged both of these facts only indirectly. After first noting that some feminists criticized contraceptives as well as abortion,[233] she simply asserted that "focusing on [the refusal of the feminists to endorse abortion] obscures the extent to which feminists of the era tacitly condoned abortion."[234] At other points, Siegel noted several feminist tracts as "virtually condoning abortion."[235] These tracts describe abortion with such names as "child murder," hardly suggesting approval of the practice, tacit or otherwise.[236] In other words, Siegel found no evidence of nineteenth century feminist support for abortion; she presents us with a search for the lost meanings of not so lost voices, with nothing more to go on than the passionate certainty of her convictions.[237]

---

223. Cornelia Hughes Dayton, *Taking the Trade: Abortion and Gender Relations in an Eighteenth-Century New England Village*, 48 Wm. & Mary Q. 19, 23 (1991).

224. (Blackmun, J., partially concurring).

225. Siegel, *supra* note 5, at 302. *See also id.* at 304–14. The sentence is quoted in full *supra* at note 203.

226. Siegel, *supra* note 5, at 294–95, 302–14.

227. *Id.* at 287 n.94, 296–97, 320 n.242.

228. *Id.* at 318.

229. *Casey Historians' Brief, supra* note 15, at 18–20.

230. *See also* Degler, *supra* note 11, at 202–06, 215; Harrison, *supra* note 21, at 161–72; Rhode, *supra* note 20, at 202; Smith-Rosenberg, *supra* note 5, at 220; Gordon, *Voluntary Motherhood, supra* note 42; Gordon, *Nineteenth Century Feminists, supra* note 42. See the text *supra* at notes 42–60.

231. See the text *supra* at notes 75–125.

232. See the text *supra* at notes 42–60.

233. Siegel, *supra* note 5, at 304.

234. *Id.* at 305, 307.

235. *Id.* at 306 n.179, 307 n.184, 311 n.201.

236. *See, e.g.*, Stanton, *supra* note 97.

237. *Cf.* Kenneth Lasson, *Feminism Awry: Excesses in the Pursuit of Rights and Trifles*, 42 J. Legal Educ. 1, 18 (1992) (so describing the work of Catherine MacKinnon).

Siegel argued that the feminists were unwilling to express their support for abortion openly because women needed the hope for children to snare a husband and because the feminists were already marginalized as inimical to the family and as favoring "free love."[238] She relied on the work of historian Linda Gordon for "proof" of these conclusions regarding the nineteenth-century feminists.[239] We have already noted why there are serious problems in relying on Gordon's work.[240] Furthermore, Siegel acknowledged that the nineteenth-century feminists actually advocated the right to refuse a husband's sexual advances as the means to achieve "voluntary motherhood."[241] This entire argument collapses on itself when Siegel tells us that the argument for voluntary motherhood derived from a far-ranging and strident critique of marriage.[242]

The closest Siegel came to finding a feminist directly supporting abortion is the same anonymous letter from somewhere in Maine that Mohr had relied on.[243] Regarding this letter, Siegel can charitably be called confused. For some reason, Siegel miscited this letter by referring to an article, *Child Murder*,[244] written by Elizabeth Cady Stanton and published a week earlier than the anonymous letter.[245] Siegel dated the article nearly a month later than its actual publication date. Beyond this, Siegel, like Mohr, could only argue that the feminist focus on the causes of abortion and hence on the behavior of men involved indicated that feminists opposed enactment of the abortion statutes.[246] Yet she herself offered in support of this claim quotations from an editorial by Susan B. Anthony that feminists "wanted *prevention*, not merely punishment," that they wanted "to reach the root of *evil*, and destroy it," and that they considered the women who sought abortions to be "awfully guilty" even if their men were "thrice guilty."[247] Siegel's reliance on this as an endorsement of abortion rights sums up the quality of her "history."

Have we crossed such a divide that feminist historians simply cannot conceive of a genuine feminist who actually opposed abortion? Or shall we accuse modern historians of frankly misrepresenting the historical record for political purposes? Or is it perhaps a little of both? Trying to answer this question requires a closer look at the strained efforts of the historians of the new orthodox history of abortion to "prove" that the nineteenth century feminists secretly supported abortion and only said they opposed abortion as a tactical maneuver. The plain fact is that no historian can afford to ignore "the stubborn resistance of the raw materials."[248] Yet this is precisely what those who seek to obfuscate the attitudes of the nineteenth century feminists do. Their approach lends itself to the very sort of advocacy scholarship that has come to bedevil the legal enterprise.[249] As a result, even radically revisionist historians have been skeptical, if not downright hostile, to such "postmodern" history.[250]

---

238. Siegel, *supra* note 5, at 305 n.175.

239. Siegel referred to Gordon, *supra* note 5, at 70, 97–111.

240. See the text *supra* at notes 153–61.

241. Siegel, *supra* note 5, at 305, 312–13 n.208. *See generally* Chapter 2, at notes 157–91.

242. Siegel, *supra* note 5, at 305–08.

243. See the text *supra* at notes 185–88.

244. Stanton, *supra* note 97.

245. Siegel, *supra* note 5, at 307 n.185, 312 nn.202–5.

246. *Id.* at 312.

247. Anthony, *supra* note 29, at 4 (emphasis in the original).

248. J. Willard Hurst, Justice Holmes on Legal History 61 (1964).

249. Mary Ann Glendon, A Nation under Lawyers: How the Crisis in the Legal Profession Is Transforming American Society 208 (1994); Ronald Collins, *A Letter on Scholarly Ethics*, 45 J. Legal Educ. 139 (1995); Michael Sean Quinn, *"Scholarly Ethics": A Response*, 46 J. Legal Educ. 110 (1996).

250. *See, e.g.,* Bryan Stone, Descent into Discourse: The Reification of Language and the Writings of Social History (1990); Lawrence Stone, *History and Post-Modernism*, 135 Past & Present 189 (1992); Steven Watts, *The Idiocy of American Studies: Poststructuralism, Language, and Politics in the Age of Self-Fulfillment*, 43 Am. Q. 625 (1991).

# Women Physicians in the Nineteenth Century

*Two roads diverged in a wood, and I -*
*I took the one less traveled by.*
*And that has made all the difference.*

—Robert Frost[251]

Those who would paint the struggle between allopaths and other healthcare providers in starkly genderized terms stumble over certain facts from the late nineteenth century. Although most allopathic physicians harbored genuine hostility toward the idea of women providing medical services and particularly towards midwives (not all of whom were women),[252] women were by no means so thoroughly excluded from the medical profession as they later would be. In the second half of the nineteenth century, the period when the most restrictive abortion statutes were enacted, women achieved considerable success in entering the allopathic medical profession, far more success than they would in the first seventy years of the twentieth century.

Women have been heavily involved in the informal healing arts since time immemorial. The nineteenth century saw significant numbers of women enter the formal medical professions— allopathic, homeopathic, or other forms—for the first time.[253] While women undoubtedly chose a formal medical career for many different reasons, a commonly expressed reason for their choice was to provide an alternative for women patients who, with the increasing medicalization of birth and related health problems, would otherwise be forced to turn to male physicians for services previously provided by informal—usually female—healers.[254] This was the era, remember, when women patients were still reluctant to allow male physicians to conduct genital examinations or to examine them while disrobed, and when suspicions of sexual misbehavior by male physicians attending women patients were just beginning to subside.[255]

Women physicians were outspoken in criticizing the errors they believed male physicians made regarding women, women's physiology, and women's rights.[256] Some of the women physicians also argued that they related fundamentally differently to their patients—female or male—than did men physicians.[257] This era saw the opening of medical schools specifically to train women as

---

251. Robert Frost, *The Road Not Taken,* THE POCKET BOOK OF ROBERT FROST'S POEMS 223 (Louis Untermeyer ed. 1971).

252. *See generally* DEGLER, *supra* note 11, at 56–59; WALSH, *supra* note 44, at 37–39. On advent of male midwives, see Chapter 6, at notes 247–62, and Chapter 7, at notes 227–302.

253. *See generally* WALSH, *supra* note 44.

254. *See, e.g.,* HUNT, *supra* note 174, at 135–39, 156–58, 251; Harriet Martineau, *On Female Industry,* EDINBURGH REV., April 1859, at 293, 331–32. *See also* DONNISON, *supra* note 120, at 61–62, 91; REGINA MARKELL MORANTZ-SANCHEZ, SYMPATHY AND SCIENCE: WOMEN PHSYICIANS IN AMERICAN MEDICINE 47–65, 216–28 (1985); SMITH-ROSENBERG, *supra* note 5, at 231–32; WALSH, *supra* note 44, at 25; John Blake, *Women and Medicine in Ante-Bellum America,* 39 BULL. HIST. MED. 99 (1965).

255. *See* DONNISON, *supra* note 120, at 79–80; WALSH, *supra* note 44, at 40–42. *See also* Chapter 6, at notes 251–55, and Chapter 7, at notes 228, 285.

256. *See, e.g.,* SARAH STEVENSON, THE PHYSIOLOGY OF WOMAN, EMBRACING GIRLHOOD, MATERNITY AND MATURE AGE 68, 77, 79 (2nd ed. 1881); STOCKHAM, *supra* note 29, at 257. *See generally* SMITH-ROSENBERG, *supra* note 5, at 262–63.

257. The premise was put forward by Dr. Elizabeth Blackwell that women made better physicians generally because of their greater capacity for empathy and caring. *See* Regina Morantz-Sanchez, *Feminist Theory and Historical Practice: Rereading Elizabeth Blackwell,* 31 HIST. & THEORY 51 (1992). *See also* Regina Morantz-Sanchez, *Physicians,* in WOMEN, HEALTH & MEDICINE IN AMERICA 477, 487 (Rima Apple ed. 1990); Regina

physicians, in part because of the refusal of established medical faculties to accept women students. Samuel Gregory in Boston founded the first women's medical school in 1848.[258] The second was founded in 1850 in Philadelphia.[259] For one year (1851–52), the two schools even shared faculty, offering the fall semester in Philadelphia and the spring semester in Boston.[260]

These schools often also developed what were first termed "lying-in" hospitals, and later "women's and children's hospitals," attached both as teaching facilities and to provide for better supervised births. In the British Isles, lying-in hospitals were far older than in the United States, dating back to 1745 in Dublin, to 1747 in London, and to 1756 in Edinburgh.[261] The Gregory school, renamed the New England Medical College, took over the Boston Lying-In Hospital in 1858.[262] The original resident physician at the hospital under the college, Dr. Marie Zakrzewska, resigned in 1862 to found the New England Hospital for Women and Children ("Women's Hospital").[263] Dr. Zakrzewska was a woman of considerable distinction, having been appointed chief midwife and professor of midwifery at Charité Hospital, the largest hospital in Prussia, in 1852 at the age of 23, only to resign the position in the face of the intense resistance she encountered because of her gender and her youth.[264] Zakrzewska was also a co-founder, in 1857, of the New York Infirmary for Women and Children, the first hospital staffed entirely by women in the United States.[265] The Boston Lying-In Hospital closed one week after Zakrzewska's new hospital opened.[266] The New England Medical College failed a decade later, and merged with the homeopathic Boston University medical faculty in 1873.[267]

Women's Hospital survived and thrived as leading teaching institution for women in Boston and as a pioneering institution for providing gynecological, obstetric, and pediatric care in a setting run by women for women. Women's Hospital and St. Elizabeth's were the only hospitals in Boston that allowed gynecological surgery before 1880.[268] One of Zakrzewska's principal assistants was Dr. Anita Tyng, a women turned down for admission by Harvard Medical

---

Morantz-Sanchez, *The Gendering of Empathic Expertise: How Women Physicans Became More Empathic than Men*, in THE EMPATHIC PRACTITIONER 40 (Maureen Milligan & Ellen Singer More eds. 1994); Regina Markell Morantz & Sue Zschoche, *Professionalism, Feminism, and Gender Roles: A Comparative Study of Nineteenth-Century Medical Therapeutics*, 67 J. AM. HIST. 568, 569, 577–80, 584 (1980); Ann Shalleck, *Feminist Legal Theory and the Reading of* O'Brien v. Cunard, 57 MO. L. REV. 371, 391–96 (1992).

258. FREDERICK WAITE, HISTORY OF THE NEW ENGLAND FEMALE MEDICAL COLLEGE (1950); WALSH, *supra* note 44, at 35–75.

259. GUILIELMA FELL ALSOP, HISTORY OF WOMEN'S MEDICAL COLLEGE, PHILADELPHIA, PENNSYLVANIA, 1850–1950 (1950); CLARA MARSHALL, THE WOMEN'S MEDICAL COLLEGE OF PENNSYLVANIA: AN HISTORICAL OUTLINE (1897).

260. WALSH, *supra* note 44, at 53–54.

261. DONNISON, *supra* note 120, at 37–40, 50, 61–62. A proposal to found such an institution made in England in 1660 came to nothing. *Id.* at 31.

262. WALSH, *supra* note 44, at 57; FREDERICK IRVING, SAFE DELIVERANCE 121–23 (1942).

263. AGNES VIETOR, A WOMAN'S QUEST: THE LIFE OF MARIE E. ZAKRZEWSKA 281–84 (1924); WAITE, *supra* note 258, at 52, 237–39; WALSH, *supra* note 44, at 64–66, 82–85. *See also* Chapter 7, at notes 385–88. On Women's Hospital, see VIRGINIA DRACHMAN, HOSPITAL WITH A HEART: WOMEN DOCTORS AND THE PARADOX OF SEPARATISM AT THE NEW ENGLAND HOSPITAL, 1862–1969 (1984).

264. DRACHMAN, *supra* note 263, at 28–29; VIETOR, *supra* note 263, at 84–85; WALSH, *supra* note 44, at 77–78. On Zakrzewska's career generally, see DRACHMAN, *supra*, at 21–43, 114–18, 135–38, 154; VIETOR, *supra*; WALSH, *supra*, 57–105, 108–09, 117–20, 148, 152.

265. DRACHMAN, *supra* note 263, at 34–36; VIETOR, *supra* note 263, at 211; WALSH, *supra* note 44, at 81–82.

266. WALSH, *supra* note 44, at 66.

267. *Id.* at 68–71, 75, 195–99.

268. *Id.* at 113.

School.[269] Noted anti-abortion crusader Horatio Robinson Storer was the only male physician appointed to the staff of the Women's Hospital during the nineteenth century—in fact until 1958, barely a decade before Women's Hospital closed.[270]

Opposition to women entering the formal medical profession was strong in the United States from the beginning. Dr. Charles Meigs led the early attack with the observation, during a lecture to medical students, that women have "a head almost too small for intellect but just big enough for love."[271] This shocking comment reflected the widespread nineteenth century view, based in part on the then recent discovery that women's brains were, on average, measurably smaller than men's, that women were incapable of higher education.[272] Also widespread at the time was the notion that women were predisposed to mental disorders because of their periodic menses, especially if they avoided becoming pregnant, leading to criticism of higher education for women as posing a threat to their health or to the health of their children.[273] Dr. William Warren Potter expressed a common thought in these words: "Why spoil a good mother by making an ordinary grammarian?"[274] Dr. Withers Moore summed up this attitude with his observation that "women are made and meant to be not men, but the mothers of men."[275] Apparently confirming such attitudes was the fact that during the nineteenth century fewer than five percent of white women

---

269. *Id.* at 165–66. Harvard did not get around to admitting women as medical students until 1945. *Id.* at xiv.

270. *Id.* at 109.

271. C.D. Meigs, Lecture on Some of the Distinctive Characteristics of the Female, Delivered before the Class of the Jefferson Medical College, Jan. 1847, at 67 (1847).

272. *See, e.g.,* 558 (1871; reprint ed. 1981); Herbert Spencer, *Psychology of the Sexes,* 4 Popular Sci. Monthly 30 (Nov. 1873). *See also* Fernand Corcos, Les avocates 158 (1926). *See generally* Steven Jay Gould, The Mismeasure of Man 105 (1981); Sarah Blaffer Hrdy, Mother Nature: A History of Mothers, Infants, and Natural Selection 13–23 (1999); Cynthia Eagle Russett, Sexual Science: The Victorian Construction of Womanhood (1989); Carol Tavris, The Mismeasure of Woman: Why Women Are Not the Better Sex, the Inferior Sex, or the Opposite Sex (1992); Stephanie Shields, *The "Variability Hypothesis": The History of a Biological Model of Sex Differences in Intelligence,* 7 Signs 769 (1982).

273. *See* Edward Clarke, Sex in Education, or, A Fair Chance for Girls 63 (1878); Thomas Smith Clouston, Female Education from a Medical Point of View (1882); Thomas Addis Emmett, The Principles and Practice of Gynecology 21–22 (1879); William Goodell, Lessons in Gynecology 355 (1879); William Warren Potter, How Should Girls Be Educated? A Public Health Problem for Mothers, Educators, and Physicians (1891); Univ. of Wis. Bd. Regents, Annual Report for the Year Ending September 30, 1877, at 45 (1877); Christian, *supra* note 172, at 152–53; William Edgar Darnall, *The Pubescent Schoolgirl,* 18 Am. Gynecological & Obstetrics J. 490 (1901); Johnson Martin, *Injury to Health from the Present System of Public Education,* Brit. Med. J., Feb. 16, 1884, at 311; Withers Moore, *The Higher Education of Women,* Br. Med. J., Aug. 14, 1889, at 295; Willoughby Francis Wade, *On Some Functional Disorders of Females,* Brit. Med. J., June 5, 1886, at 1053 (Lecture I), Brit. Med. J., June 12, 1886, at 1095 (Lecture II). *See also* George Reid, *Legal Restraint upon Employment of Women before and after Childbirth,* Brit. Med. J., July 30, 1892, at 275; W. Stanley Jevons, *Married Women in Factories,* Brit. Med. J., Jan. 14, 1882, at 63. *See generally* Catharine Beecher, The Peculiar Responsibilities of American Women, in Root of Bitterness 171 (Nancy Cott ed. 1972); Virginia Drachman, Women Lawyers and the Origins of Professional Identity in America: The Letters of the Equity Club, 1887–1890, at 31–37 (1993); Barbara Ehrenreich & Diedre English, For Her Own Good: 150 Years of Advice to Women 108–16 (1978); Gould, *supra* note 272, at 105; Morantz-Sanchez, *supra* note 254, at 54–55; Regina Morantz-Sanchez, Conduct Unbecoming a Woman: Medicine on Trial in Brooklyn 117, 121 (1999) ("Morantz-Sanchez, Conduct"); Rosalind Rosenberg, Beyond Separate Spheres: Intellectual Roots of Modern Feminism 1–27 (1982); Smith-Rosenberg, *supra* note 5, at 258–61; Walsh, *supra* note 44, at 106–46; Charles Rosenberg & Carroll Smith-Rosenberg, *The Female Animal: Medical and Biological Views of Women and Her Role in Nineteenth-Century America,* 4 J. Interdisciplinary Hist. 25 (1973); Thomson, *supra* note 168; Sue Zschoche, *Dr. Clarke Revisited: Science, True Womanhood, and Female Collegiate Education,* 29 Hist. of Educ. Q. 545 (1989).

274. Potter, *supra* note 273, at 9.

275. Moore, *supra* note 273, at 299.

in the United States worked outside the home after marriage.[276] Most male medical authorities of the time shared the opinion that women were physiologically unsuited to be physicians.[277]

Feminist leaders of the time hotly contested such claims. One of the cleverer ripostes to the claim that women would be rendered unfit for marriage and motherhood by education was to point out that too many women were not adequately prepared to become mothers. As Helen Cameron Parker wrote:

> Society has seen and said—"the hand that rocks the cradle rules the world, and it is therefore a moral necessity that women should receive the best intellectual training which the State can give;"…Is it a small matter to the nation that each day scores of women become wives without one idea of the true duties of a wife, of the awful responsibility of a mother,…Would ignorance be tolerated in any other profession?[278]

To a degree, social institutions developed to respond to this argument, but separately from the general education system. A large industry emerged to provide instruction to women on the proper performance of their social roles—mostly through public lectures and books.[279] The separation of this program of instruction from the general education establishment served to protect against arguments that women were unfit to develop their intellects. As a result, throughout the nineteenth century and well into the twentieth century, the prejudice against women becoming doctors prevailed without serious challenge within the medical establishment.

Only a few male doctors who had female associates came to accept the ability and right of women generally to become doctors.[280] This is hardly surprising considering the prevailing sentiments of female frailty and of the limited functions in life appropriate to the female intellect pervasive throughout much of human history, and particularly in the nineteenth century. Even at Oberlin College, the first co-educational institution in the United States, the strong emphasis on maintaining gender roles extended to requiring "coeds" to clean the rooms of male students,[281] while they were prohibited from reading novels for fear that such an activity would threaten their chastity.[282] So widely shared was the notion that women were generally not capable of serving as physicians that the leading woman physicians of the time, including those at Women's Hospital, seldom publicly opposed the prevailing wisdom. Public opposition to the notion of feminine incapacity to be educated generally or as physicians was expressed by various feminists,[283] but seldom by women physicians—or by women lawyers, either.[284]

---

276. PETCHESKY, *supra* note 5, at 75; WEINER, *supra* note 134, at 6.

277. *See, e.g.*, CLARKE, *supra* note 273; 2 G. STANLEY HALL, ADOLESCENCE 569–70 (1904); Jonathon Hutchinson, *A Review of Current Topics of Medical and Social Interest*, BRIT. MED. J., Aug. 9, 1876, at 231, 232; Editorial, *Female Physicians*, BRIT. MED. J., July 26, 1862, at 96; Editorial, *The Female Doctor Question*, BRIT. MED. J., Nov. 22, 1862, at 537; Editorial, *Medical Education for Women*, BRIT. MED. J., Apr. 30, 1870, at 445; *Shall We Have Female Graduates in Medicine?*, BRIT. MED. J., Aug. 2, 1856, at 653.

278. Helen Cameron Parker, *Technical Schools for Women*, 1 CAN. MAG. 633, 634–37 (1893).

279. *See generally* BARBARA EHRENREICH & DEIDRE ENGLISH, FOR HER OWN GOOD: 150 YEARS OF EXPERTS' ADVICE TO WOMEN (1978).

280. WALSH, *supra* note 44, at 132, 148–50, 155–62, 170–71. Eventually, this would include Horatio Robinson Storer, although not before he had opposed the idea of women physicians for some years. *See* Chapter 7, at notes 394–439.

281. *See* 1 ROBERT FLETCHER, A HISTORY OF OBERLIN COLLEGE: FROM ITS FOUNDATION THROUGH THE CIVIL WAR 382 (1943). *See also* Chapter 7, at notes 408–12.

282. 1 FLETCHER, *supra* note 281, at 308.

283. *See, e.g.*, ELIZA BISBEE DUFFEY, NO SEX IN EDUCATION; OR AN EQUAL CHANCE FOR BOTH GIRLS AND BOYS (1874); THE EDUCATION OF AMERICAN GIRLS (Anna Callender Brackett ed. 1874); GEORGE FISK & ANNA MANNING COMFORT, WOMAN'S EDUCATION AND WOMAN'S HEALTH: CHIEFLY IN REPLY TO "SEX IN EDUCATION" (1874); JULIA WARD HOWE, SEX AND EDUCATION: A REPLY TO DR. CLARKE'S "SEX IN EDUCATION" (1874). *See generally* WALSH, *supra* note 44, at 128–32.

284. DRACHMAN, *supra* note 263, at 33.

One of the few female physicians to dispute publicly the claims about women's natural fitness to become doctors was Dr. Mary Putnam Jacobi, but she did so purely in terms of disputing whether menstruation periodically incapacitated them physically or intellectually.[285] The general silence even of women physicians on whether women in general had the intellectual capacity to become educated tells much about the temper of the times even if one concludes that the women failed to respond solely because they considered it impolitic.[286] Although today we see such sentiments as absurd, just such ideas were expressed regarding university education for women generally as recently as 1962.[287] There were, of course, numerous women in the later nineteenth century who proved themselves fit to become physicians, lawyers, soldiers, and virtually any other profession open to men. Historian Mary Walsh surmised that the reason so many male physicians denigrated the abilities of female physicians was simply to eliminate competition from a quarter likely to be able to appeal with particular effectiveness to the clientele for gynecological services.[288] If the claimed attraction of women patients to women physicians were real, it would have been devastating to men physicians—women were a clear majority of the patients in the nineteenth century.[289] And we do find that Dr. Horatio Robinson Storer—the favorite whipping boy of modern feminist historians—did strenuously attack claims that women were best treated by women, but then so did Dr. Marie Zakrzewska.[290]

Women physicians were not welcomed by their male counterparts, but the women physicians did achieve considerable success in entering the allopathic (and homeopathic) medical profession despite the male opposition.[291] By 1890, there were 13 allopathic medical schools (and one homeopathic medical school) specifically for women, and women, after prolonged and bitter struggles, were beginning to gain admission to the formerly all-male medical schools.[292] In that same year, 18 percent of the physicians in Boston were women, and they maintained their own hospital and their own medical school.[293] In 1890 there were more woman doctors in Boston alone (210) than there were woman lawyers in the entire United States (200).[294] By 1893, women were 19 percent of the students at the University of Michigan Medical School, 31 percent of the students enrolled at the Kansas Medical College, and 10 percent or more of the students at another 16 "regular" medical colleges across the United States.[295] The number of women physicians in the United States was also impressive by international standards. For example, there were only 95 woman physicians in France in 1900 compared to 7,387 in the United States (counting only those with medical degrees).[296] The situation in England was even more dismal than in France. Historian Mary Walsh's report that there were then some 258 women physicians in England in

---

285. MARY PUTNAM JACOBI, THE QUESTION OF REST FOR WOMEN DURING MENSTRUATION (1877). *See also* EMILY POPE, C. AUGUSTA POPE, & EMMA CALL, THE PRACTICE OF MEDICINE BY WOMEN IN THE UNITED STATES (1881).

286. WALSH, *supra* note 44, at 117–18, 127–28.

287. FREDERICK RUDOLPH, THE AMERICAN COLLEGE AND UNIVERSITY: A HISTORY 324 (1962).

288. WALSH, *supra* note 44, at 116–17, 133–36.

289. *Id.* at 135.

290. *Id.* at 118. *See also* DRACHMAN, *supra* note 263, at 54–57; Richard Shryock, *Women in American Medicine*, 5 J. AM. MEDICAL WOMEN'S ASS'N 375 (1950).

291. *See generally* WALSH, *supra* note 44.

292. PENINA GLAZER & MIRIAM SLATER, UNEQUAL COLLEAGUES: THE ENTRANCE OF WOMEN INTO THE PROFESSIONS, 1890–1940, at 1–23 (1987); MORANTZ-SANCHEZ, *supra* note 254, at 64–183; WALSH, *supra* note 44, at 147–92.

293. PAUL STARR, THE SOCIAL TRANSFORMATION OF AMERICAN MEDICINE: THE RISE OF A SOVEREIGN PROFESSION AND THE MAKING OF A VAST INDUSTRY 117 (1982); WALSH, *supra* note 44, at xvi–xvii, 107–08, 185–86.

294. WALSH, *supra* note 44, at 107–08.

295. *Id.* at 182, 193.

296. *Id.* at 186.

1900 ignores the fact that four-fifths of the woman physicians registered in England were then practicing in India![297]

Eventually the criticism of women as physicians succeeded, but not until they gained admission to coeducational medical schools. The admission of women to coeducational medical schools was the death-knell for the women's medical schools. Only three—Woman's Medical College in Baltimore, New York Woman's Medical College in New York City, and Woman's Medical College of Pennsylvania in Philadelphia—survived after 1903.[298] Still, as late as 1926, 75 percent of the women in the American College of Surgeons had graduated from women's medical colleges.[299] Unfortunately, the apparent acceptance of women into the male medical schools proved illusory, and after 1910 women students were admitted to the coeducational schools only in sharply reduced numbers (in some cases they were excluded altogether).[300] By 1914, nationally only four percent of all medical students were women.[301] As a result, women reached a peak of six percent of all physicians in the United States in 1910.[302] In fact, there were fewer women physicians in Boston in 1970 than in 1900.[303] The total number of woman physicians in the whole of the United States in 1910 (9,015) declined and was not equaled again until 1950.[304] Even as late as 1970, only eight percent of all physicians in the United States were women, as were 13 percent of the medical students in that year.[305] Black women in particular found it nearly impossible to enter the profession, particularly after the turn of the century.[306]

In short, after 1910 women were largely excluded from the medical profession except in the role of nurses. Only after 1970 did the number of women in medical schools begin to grow significantly, soon exceeding the numbers at the end of the nineteenth century.[307] Yet at no time in this process of exclusion did opposition to the claim that women were by their nature incapable of being physicians correlate with support for abortion.[308]

Women physicians stood at a special place in the history of the nineteenth century abortion statutes, being at the intersection of the two major groups most interested in the practice and legality of abortion. Yet given that the predominant attitudes among both women (or at least among feminist leaders—who alone have left extensive records of their thought) and physicians was decidedly hostile to abortion, we should not be surprised to discover that women physicians in the nineteenth century were also outspoken supporters of the criminality of abortion. The

---

297. *Compare id.* at 181, *with* DONNISON, *supra* note 120, at 225 n. 26.

298. WALSH, *supra* note 44, at 179–80.

299. *Id.* at 262.

300. *Id.* at 182–267; GLAZER & SLATER, *supra* note 292, at 76. *See generally* GLAZER & SLATER, *supra*, at 69–117; GLORIA MELNICK MOLDOW, WOMEN DOCTORS IN GILDED AGE WASHINGTON: RACE, GENDER, AND PROFESSIONALISM 48–74 (1987); STARR, *supra* note 293, at 124; Jodi Elgart Paik, *The Feminization of Medicine*, 283 JAMA 666, 667 (2000).

301. Paik, *supra* note 300, at 667.

302. WALSH, *supra* note 44, at 186. *See generally* CAROL LOPATE, WOMEN IN MEDICINE (1968); Lee Powers, Harry Weisenfedler, & Rexford Parmelee, *Practice Patterns of Women and Men Physicians*, 44 J. MED. EDUC. 481 (1969).

303. WALSH, *supra* note 44, at 186. There was a similar decline the number of women medical faculty in the United States. *See, e.g.,* Kathleen Farrell, Marlys Hearst Wills, & Miguel Holguin, *Women Physicians in Medical Academia*, 241 JAMA 2808 (1979).

304. WALSH, *supra* note 44, at 186.

305. Paik, *supra* note 300, at 666.

306. STARR, *supra* note 293, at 102–06, 116–25, 162–63; MOLDOW, *supra* note 300, at 94–113.

307. WALSH, *supra* note 44, at 268–83, 303. *See also* Farrell, Wills & Holguin, *supra* note 303.

308. *Compare, e.g.,* DUFFEY, *supra* note 283 (supporting equal educational opportunities for girls), *with* DUFFEY, *supra* note 29, at 274–75 (opposing abortion).

hostility of women physicians towards abortion began with Elizabeth Blackwell, the first formally licensed woman physician in the United States.[309] Blackwell abhorred abortion, although the evidence of her attitude is confined to private letters.[310]

Women physicians were among the strongest crusaders against abortion and provided us with some of the most rigorous defenses of the unborn child's right to life. For example, Dr. Charlotte Denman Lozier, a professor at the New York City Medical College for Women, won acclaim both in the popular press and in the feminist press for her personal crusade against abortion. Her crusade was cut short by an untimely death at the age of 26 in 1870. She was eulogized in an obituary published in *The Revolution*.[311] *The Revolution* was a leading feminist journal of the time, owned by Susan B. Anthony and edited by Elizabeth Cady Stanton and Parker Pillsbury.[312] The obituary was written by Paulina Wright Davis, an ardent advocate of women's rights who on another occasion chose to describe marriage as "legalized prostitution."[313] This attitude did not deter Ms. Davis, in her obituary of Dr. Lozier, from giving fulsome praise to the deceased young doctor's efforts of to suppress abortion.

The position taken by virtually all women physicians is illustrated by this passage from a book by Dr. Alice Bunker Stockham:

> When the female germ and male sperm unite, then is the inception of a new life; all that goes to make up a human being—body, mind, and spirit, must be contained in embryo within this minute organism. Life must be present from the very moment of conception. If there was not life there could not be conception. At what other period of a human being's existence, either pre-natal or post-natal, could the union of soul and body take place? Is it not plain that the violent or forcible removal of it from the citadel of life, is its premature death, and hence the act can be denominated by no more mild term than murder, and whoever performs that act, or is accessory to it, guilty of the crime of all crimes?[314]

Stockham was not some simpering woman currying favor with male practitioners. Stockham was a pioneer in women's health. She enjoyed inventing a new vocabulary to suggest that her ideas were not simply derived from past or current popular ideas, and she was not afraid to outrage public opinion. Thus Stockham was one of the earliest public advocates of family planning.[315] The term she invented for her preferred method of contraception was "karezza," by which she meant *coitus reservatus*—intercourse without male ejaculation.[316]

---

309. Blackwell was also the first woman officially recognized as a physician in England. BRODIE, *supra* note 21, at 14; DONNISON, *supra* note 120, at 79. The second in England was Elizabeth Garrett. *See* DONNISON, *supra*, at 81; Jo MANTON, ELIZABETH GARRETT ANDERSON (1966). Historian Mary Walsh identifies Harriot Hunt as the first actual female physician in the United States, although Dr. Hunt was never formally licensed. WALSH, *supra* note 44, at 1, 20–33. *See also* 1 ELIZABETH CADY STANTON, SUSAN ANTHONY, & MATILDA JOSLYN GAGE, HISTORY OF WOMEN SUFFRAGE 224 (1969); Ann Douglas Wood, *The Fashionable Diseases: Women's Complaints and Their Treatment in Nineteenth-Century America*, 4 J. INTERDISCIPLINARY HIST. 25, 44–47 (1973); Regina Markell Morantz, *The Perils of Feminist History*, 4 J. INTERDISCIPLINARY HIST. 649 (1973). *See generally* HUNT, *supra* note 254.

310. BRODIE, *supra* note 21, at 34, 82, 128, 228.

311. *See, e.g.,* Paulina Wright Davis, *Obituary*, THE REVOLUTION, Jan. 20, 1870, at 42.

312. MOHR, *supra* note 4, at 288 n.73.

313. Paulina Wright Davis, *Address to the National Women's Suffrage Association*, quoted in GORDON, *supra* note 5, at 104.

314. STOCKHAM, *supra* note 29, at 246. *See also* Mary Dixon-Jones, *Criminal Abortion—Its Evil and Its Sad Consequences*, 3 WOMEN'S MED. J. 28 (1894).

315. *See, e.g.,* ALICE DUNCAN STOCKHAM, KAREZZA: THE ETHICS OF MARRIAGE 53, 82–83 (1898).

316. *See* Chapter 2, at notes 79–81.

The book that I have quoted for Stockham's attitude toward abortion was yet another work in which she sought to challenge conventional thinking. Even its title, *Tokology: A Book for Every Woman,* would be a challenge to many potential readers. Nonetheless, that book was not merely a tract read by a few other physicians. As its title indicates, the book was intended for lay readers, and it enjoyed great popularity. The book went through 45 editions between its publication in 1883 and 1897—an average of better than three per year.[317]

Dr. Stockham's analysis illustrated the sharp contrast—even among women who had had abortions—between the horror feminists expressed for abortion and their accepting attitude towards contraception.[318] This contrast suggests that their attitude toward abortion was focused on abortion rather than on either sex or men. This conclusion is also supported by strong evidence that women themselves were the primary movers in the process of medicalizing birth.[319] Dr. Jennie Oreman, a contemporary of Stockham, expressed similar views in a journal targeted at women readers.[320] Dr. Anne Densmore lectured to the same effect a generation earlier.[321] In 1894, Dr. Mary Dixon Jones, perhaps the most prominent woman physician in Brooklyn (then a large and separate city), also eloquently and passionately condemned abortion.[322]

Feminist historians have responded to this reality by arguing that women physicians feared association with abortion because of their vulnerability to criticism by men physicians.[323] This seems unlikely given the general pattern of hostility to abortion by nineteenth century feminists—women who did not shy away from advocating the outrageous. Indeed, as we have seen, Stockham's denunciations of abortion were contained in writings that were medically and sexually radical. Arguments that these women physicians were simply afraid of criticism over abortion are not credible. Moreover, if these arguments are credible, they undercut the argument that abortion was socially acceptable: if abortion were considered socially acceptable, men physicians could not deploy accusations of support for abortion to discredit women physicians with the general public.

Dr. Horatio Robinson Storer, he of the Women's Hospital staff, has been accused of blaming the rise in abortions on the emergence of women physicians in the later nineteenth-century. Storer never said this, forcing his accusers to claim that he did so by innuendo.[324] Neither he nor others campaigning against abortion who also criticized the possibility of women becoming physicians made any rhetorical use of abortion against the women doctors. Nothing could more eloquently indicate the rarity of support for the practice of abortion among female physicians.

---

317. D'EMILIO & FREEDMAN, *supra* note 24, at 67.

318. *See, e.g., id.* at 50–63, 64–65. See also the text *supra* at notes 42–60.

319. *See* Chapter 2, at notes 211–39.

320. Jennie Oreman, *The Medical Woman's Temptation and How to Meet It,* 3 THE WOMEN'S MED. J. 87 (1901).

321. Densmore, *supra* note 29.

322. Mary Dixon Jones, *Criminal Abortion—Its Evils and Its Sad Consequences,* 3 WOMEN'S MED. J. 28 (1894). Like so many others mentioned in this chapter, Dixon Jones in other respects was a strong defender of women's interests even while she condemned abortion. *See* MORANTZ-SANCHEZ, CONDUCT, *supra* note 273, at 131–33.

323. REAGAN, *supra* note 21, at 57–58. MORANTZ-SANCHEZ, CONDUCT, *supra* note 273, at 180.

324. WALSH, *supra* note 44, at 145–46. One unidentified doctor did make such a claim at a meeting where Storer spoke in 1857, but as Storer is identified repeatedly in the same article and is not identified as the speaker in this instance, there seems to be no reason to assume that the doctor who made this statement was Storer. *See* "Medicus," *Communication—Suffolk District Medical Society,* 2 MED. WORLD 211 (1857).

# Did Feminist Opposition to Abortion Make a Difference?

*[K]nowledge and truth are always fragmentary.*

—Allan Hutchinson[325]

There remains the question of whether the feminist opposition to abortion was of any real significance given the "allopathic conspiracy" that we are told was the real force behind the increasingly stringent abortion statutes of the nineteenth century. This is akin to asking whether environmentalists or business interests better explain why modern environmental regulations exist, or have taken one particular form rather than another. The answer is, of course, that both are responsible to some degree, and that often the precise influences are difficult to assess—particularly as neither group is monolithic and each group sometimes finds closer allies in the other group than among its "like kind." Going back to the nineteenth century to compare the effects of feminist opposition to abortion with medical or other opposition to abortion is even more uncertain because, by and large each, of these groups (and many others) were on the same side.

We are also somewhat befuddled by the understandable tendency of modern historians to anachronism. We tend to think of the organized medical profession and the organized legal profession as having enormous and disproportionate influence back then if we perceive them as wielding such influence today. Whatever may be the truth today, those professions had no such influence through much of the nineteenth century. We have already noted the failure of the allopathic medical societies to block legislative recognition of competing medical organizations or professions in the face of Jacksonian democracy.[326] In the next chapter, we shall examine the similar deprofessionalization of the Bar.[327] The disorganization of the Bar was particularly pronounced; the American Bar Association was not even organized until 1878—a full generation after the organization of the American Medical Association in the 1850s—and it was decades before it had any real political influence.[328] In contrast, the nineteenth-century feminists were highly organized and were successful in such areas as the reform of property regimes, of divorce, and (in some states) of the franchise.[329]

We need not rely solely on inferences about the legislative clout of these several groups. In at least one political fight, the doctors and the feminists were on opposite sides—and the feminists won. In the 1870s, many members of the American Medical Association were strong supporters of the legalization of prostitution on the state and local level, arguing that legalization would allow for mandatory health inspections as well as providing some measure of protection against the exploitation and abuse that were common in that trade.[330] Dr. J. Marion Sims, president of

---

325. Allan Hutchinson, *Identity Crisis: The Politics of Interpretation*, 26 New Eng. L. Rev. 1173, 1185 (1992).

326. *See* Chapter 6, at notes 268–72.

327. *See* Chapter 9, at notes 78–82.

328. Colin Croft, Note, *Reconceptualizing American Legal Professionalism: A Proposal for Deliberate Moral Community*, 67 NYU L. Rev. 1256, 1287–98 (1992). *See generally* Maxwell Bloomfield, American Lawyers in a Changing Society, 1776–1876 (1978); Robert Stevens, Law School: Legal Education in America from the 1850s to the 1980s (1983); The Legal Profession: Major Historical Interpretations (Kermit Hall ed. 1987).

329. *See* Chapter 2, at notes 153–62.

330. *See, e.g.,* Samuel Gross, *Syphilis in Its Relation to Natural Health*, 25 Trans. Am. Med. Ass'n 249 (1874).

the American Medical Association in 1876 and notorious practitioner of dubious gynecological surgery, made the legalization and regulation of prostitution the theme of his year at the head of the organization.[331] In the fight to legalize prostitution, the physicians found themselves largely alone, and they lost.

Feminists, organized in the "social purity" crusade, were strongly opposed to the legalization of prostitution, even introducing the term "white slavery" in an effort to link their crusade to the recently successful abolition movement.[332] Historian Jean Donnison suggests that the "social purity" movement, with its escalating intense attention to the hitherto largely neglected issue of prostitution, reflected a rising incidence of prostitution fueled by the increasing difficulty of women to find work outside the home.[333] Whatever the causes of the feminist concern about prostitution, nearly everywhere the proposed statutes or ordinances were defeated, and in St. Louis, where such an ordinance was enacted in 1870, the social purists succeeded in obtaining its repeal in 1874.[334] The feminists, of course, were not alone in their effort. Among their allies was Anthony Comstock, who was neither a physician nor a lawyer.[335] In fact, nineteenth century feminists were strong supporters of the Comstockery that today's feminists love to decry,[336] while Comstock himself devoted only a brief period in his long career crusading against the vices of others to pursuing abortionists.[337] When the doctors, the feminists, and the lawyers (together with the clergy, journalists, and others) joined together to fight the emerging practice of abortion, they were nearly irresistible.

Ultimately, we might never be able to sort out whether feminist opposition to abortion was a significant factor in bringing about the enactment of the abortion statutes. In one area, the influence of the men and the women physicians strongly coincided, and that coincidence could indeed have been critical to the success of the legislative effort regarding abortion. Rather than expressing some sort of womanly solidarity with midwives, women physicians were in the fore front of the movement to eliminate midwives, charging midwives with being unsanitary and inadequately trained.[338] Elisabeth Crowell, a nurse, was also one of the persons who most vehe-

---

331. J. Marion Sims, *Address,* 27 Trans. Am. Med. Ass'n 100 (1876). On his career, see Barker-Benfield, *supra* note 124, at 91–119; James Ricci, One Hundred Years of Gynecology, 1800–1900, at 36–37, 46–47 (1945); J. Marion Sims, The Story of My Life (H. Marion Sims ed. 1891); Walsh, *supra* note 44, at 115–16; Isabelle Gunning, *Arrogant Perception, World-Traveling and Multicultural Feminism: The Case of Female Genital Surgeries,* 23 Colum. H. Rts. L. Rev. 189, 205–09 (1991); Isabel McAslan, *Pornography or Misogyny? Fear and the Absurd,* in The Anatomy of Gender: Women's Struggle for the Body 37 (Dawn Currie & Valerie Raoul eds. 1992).

332. *See, e.g.,* Dietrick, *supra* note 110. *See generally* Berg, *supra* note 20, at 181–84, 211; D'Emilio & Freedman, *supra* note 24, at 140–45, 148–56, 202–15; Epstein, *supra* note 110, at 125–28; Gordon, *supra* note 5, at 116–35; Pivar, *supra* note 110; Rosen, *supra* note 109, at 112–36; Shanley, *supra* note 29, at 79–86, 92–93; Smith-Rosenberg, *supra* note 5, at 109–28; Pleck, *supra* note 110.

333. Donnison, *supra* note 120, at 72–73.

334. Marvin Olasky, The Press and Abortion, 1838–1988, at 126–28 (1988); Neil Shumsky, *Tacit Acceptance: Respectable Americans and Segregated Prostitution, 1870–1910,* 19 J. Soc. Hist. 665, 669 (1986). Similar episodes occurred in England (1864–1883), and in New Orleans (1870–1874) and in San Francisco (1911–1913) in the United States. Tannahill, *supra* note 20, at 366–68. *See generally* Barbara Meil Hobson, Uneasy Virtue: The Politics of Prostitution and the American Reform Tradition (2nd ed. 1990); Judith Walkowitz, City of Dreadful Delight: Narratives of Sexual Danger in Late-Victorian London (1992); Jeffrey Weeks, Sex, Politics and Society: The Regulation of Sexuality since 1800 (1981); Mary Ryan, *The Power of Women's Networks: A Case Study of Female Moral Reform in Antebellum America,* 5 Feminist Stud. 66 (1979).

335. Broun & Leech, *supra* note 99, at 18.

336. *See, e.g.,* Brodie, *supra* note 21, at 263–66, 281–88; Gordon, *supra* note 5, at 164–66, 208–09.

337. *See* Olasky, *supra* note 75, at 190–92.

338. *See, e.g.,* Georgina Grothan, *Evil Practices of the So-Called Midwife,* 7 Omaha Clinic 175 (1895); Elizabeth Jarrett, *The Midwife or the Women Doctor,* 54 Med. Rec. 610 (1898); Ella Marble, *The First Pan-American Medical Congress—Some of the Women Who Took Part,* 1 Women's Med. J. 199 (1893); Eliza Root, *The*

mently denounced the word "midwife" as virtually synonymous with "abortionist."[339] Women physicians and nurses might have been especially sensitive to competition from midwives, so their criticism might indeed have been nothing more than an effort to eliminate competitors from the market place.[340] Still, this hardly marks such an effort as a "male conspiracy."[341]

The women physicians and nurses involved in this effort saw themselves as protecting other women from the incompetence and unsanitary practices of midwives rather than as putting these other women more firmly under the control of men.[342] Acting from this perspective, non-professional women's organizations like the Welfare League and the Women's City Club joined the call for suppressing abortion and regulating midwifery in turn of the century Chicago.[343] No wonder historians of midwifery do not explain the suppression of midwifery as a male conspiracy, but in terms of class, ethnicity, and professional interest.[344] The charges of male conspiracy come only from historians of abortion.[345] Neither set of historians bother to explain, however, how the charges of incompetence or worse could be sustained in a public forum in which, at the beginning at least, nearly every women hearing the claims would have had personal experience with a midwife, if there was no substance whatsoever to the charges—as some historians would apparently have us believe.

---

*Status of Obstetrics in General Practice,* TRANS. FIRST PAN-AM. MED. CONG., pt. I, at 901 (1895). *See generally* DONNISON, *supra* note 120, at 90–91, 121–24, 134, 140, 142, 144–49, 167, 169–70, 172; MORANTZ-SANCHEZ, *supra* note 254, at 232–33; REAGAN, *supra* note 21, at 92–93.

339. F. Elisabeth Crowell, *The Midwives of New York,* 17 CHARITIES & THE COMMONS 667 (1907).

340. DONNISON, *supra* note 120, at 122, 134, 140, 178–79; REAGAN, *supra* note 21, at 93–94.

341. *Id.* at 94.

342. *Id.* at 95–96.

343. *Id.* at 105–07.

344. ROBYN MUNCY, CREATING A FEMALE DOMINION IN AMERICAN REFORM, 1890–1935, at 115–19 (1990); Molly Ladd-Taylor, *"Grannies" and "Spinsters": Midwife Education under the Sheppard-Towner Act,* 22 J. SOC. HIST. 255 (1988); Judy Barrett Litoff, *Midwives and History,* in WOMEN, HEALTH, AND MEDICINE IN AMERICA: A HISTORICAL HANDBOOK 443, 446–47, 451 (Rima Apple ed. 1990). *See generally* CHARLOTTE BORST, CATCHING BABIES: THE PROFESSIONALIZATION OF BIRTH, 1870–1920 (1995).

345. *See* BRODIE, *supra* note 52, at 54–56; RAYMOND DEVRIES, MAKING MIDWIVES LEGAL: CHILDBIRTH, MEDICINE, AND THE LAW 25–27 (2nd ed. 1996); GORDON, *supra* note 5, at 59–60, 160–72; MCLAREN, *supra* note 46, at 115; REAGAN, *supra* note 80, at 10–11, 81–82, 90–112; SMITH-ROSENBERG, *supra* note 5, at 223–44; Jane Pacht Brickman, *Public Health, Midwives, and Nurses, 1880–1930,* in NURSING HISTORY: NEW PERSPEC-TIVES, NEW POSSIBILITIES 65, 69 (Ellen Condliffe Lagemann ed. 1983); Jane Maslow Cohen, *A Jurisprudence of Doubt: Deliberative Autonomy and Abortion,* 3 COLUM. J. GENDER & LAW. 175, 208–10 (1992). *See also* Neal Devitt, *How Doctors Conspire to Eliminate the Midwife even though the Scientific Data Support Midwifery,* in COMPULSORY HOSPITALIZATION: FREEDOM OF CHOICE IN CHILDBIRTH? 345 (D. & L. Stewart eds. 1979); Frances Kobrin, *The American Midwife Controversy: A Crisis of Professionalization,* 40 BULL. HIST. MED. 350, 358 (1966).

# Chapter 9

# The Sounds of Silence[1]

*There is hardly a political question in the United States that
does not sooner or later turn into a judicial one.*

—Alexis de Tocqueville[2]

The previous two chapters explored the role of physicians and of feminists regarding the enactment of the nineteenth century abortion statutes. Others besides doctors and women were affected by the changes involved in the enactment of the abortion statutes. The two professions that were impacted most directly by these changes were medicine and law. Medical professionals felt impelled to oppose the rising incidence of abortion on the professed ground that abortion killed innocent human lives.[3] Lawyers reacted similarly. As a result, these two professions played the leading role in crafting the nineteenth century abortion statutes. In this chapter, we examine the role of the legal profession in the evolving abortion laws of the nineteenth century. There is broader question that must be addressed first.

Even if we assume that the professions of medicine and law were driven largely by a desire to crystallize a coherent professional order and to carve an economic niche for themselves, there is still the puzzle of why the statutes were enacted with little or no legislative opposition if the public at large were in favor of some supposed freedom of abortion. Throughout the nineteenth century we find ever stricter abortion laws enacted by unanimous or near unanimous votes even in legislatures that were simultaneously rejecting efforts by the medical profession to impose restrictions on the rights of competing medical professions to practice or even to exist.[4] In an era when the nation was politically divided to the point of civil war, it strains credulity to suggest that those who were opposed to abortion were simply silenced by narrow, dominant elites. And with the most consistently dissident voices of the century—the feminists—supporting enactment of the abortion statutes, one must conclude that something more was going on than narrow professional conspiracies.

Based in large measure on his belief about the common incidence of abortion, historian James Mohr insisted that only the medical profession was opposed to abortion and that public opinion generally and other professional opinion did not oppose the practice.[5] Mohr, however, included numerous examples in his book of broad public opposition to the growing practice of abortion, including hardening consensus among the legal profession against abortion[6] and the

---

1. Paul Simon, *The Sounds of Silence* (1965).
2. ALEXIS DE TOCQUEVILLE, DEMOCRACY IN AMERICA 200 (George Lawrence trans., J.P. Mayer & Max Lerner eds. 1966).
3. *See* Chapter 6, at notes 164–69, 195–211, 276–84; Chapter 7, at notes 320–31.
4. *See* Chapter 6, at notes 268–77.
5. JAMES MOHR, ABORTION IN AMERICA: THE ORIGINS AND EVOLUTION OF NATIONAL POLICY, 1800–1900, at 111–13, 121–23, 130, 183–96, 261–63, 290–91 n.14 (1978).
6. *Id.* at 230–37.

near unanimous strong condemnation of abortion by nineteenth-century feminists—which Mohr described as "an anomaly."[7] All recognizable social groups in society—doctors, lawyers, clergy, journalists, feminists, and on and on—opposed abortion; only the emerging class of professional abortionists defended the social propriety of the procedures.[8] The legislative record, with little or no expressed opposition to the enactments, suggests broad popular support for the new abortion statutes. One cannot rest upon this inference, however. One must examine such direct evidence as survives of what the public in general actually thought about abortion and the new statutes.

# General Public Opposition to Abortion

*The historian is a prophet facing backwards.*

—Friedrich Schlegel[9]

Direct discovery of what ordinary people, people without a professional involvement in abortion, actually thought about abortion in the middle and later years of the nineteenth century today is virtually impossible. We cannot ask them. Nor do we find letters, diaries, or similar documents from ordinary people discussing at length the pros and cons of the new practices or the new statutes. Ordinary people apparently did not dwell on these matters, and if they did they left few or no records. We are left only with records of what certain articulate classes said about the thoughts or feelings of ordinary people. We can detect some evidence of popular feeling when we find public rallies where opposition to abortion was at least a partial rallying cry. Thus we find a rally of 5,500 people in Boston in 1845, organized by Samuel Elliott to press for the criminalization of seduction in order, in part, to discourage abortion.[10] Furthermore, two professions not directly involved in the practice or detection of abortion seem particularly well situated to tell us something about what ordinary people thought—the clergy and journalists. These two groups both shaped and reflected popular opinion. Mostly, they opposed abortion just as vehemently as did doctors and lawyers.

Pro-abortion historians seek to put the evidence in the light most favorable to their claim of a dearth of non-medical support for abortion laws. Thus, James Mohr and Carroll Smith-Rosenberg characterized the rally of 5,500 people in Boston in 1845 as proof of a lack of public support for the suppression of abortion because that rally did not speak to the abortion statutes as such.[11] Nor, apparently for the same reason, did Mohr see what he himself described as the contemporaneous (mid-1840s) "public disgust" with the "immoral and corrupting" public advertising of abortion, leading to the criminal prohibition of such advertisements, as qualifying his

---

7. *Id.* at 113.

8. *See, e.g.,* Carl Degler, At Odds: Women and the Family in America from the Revolution to the Present 243–44 (1980); Mohr, *supra* note 5, at 62–65, 76–79; Marvin Olasky, The Press and Abortion, 1838–1988, at 3–17 (1988); Andrea Tone, Devices and Desires: A History of Contraceptives in America 16 (2001).

9. Friedrich Schlegel, Lucinde and the Fragments 170 (Peter Firchon trans. 1971) (original date, 1798).

10. Mohr, *supra* note 5, at 121–22; Carroll Smith-Rosenberg, Disorderly Conduct: Visions of Gender in Victorian America 227–28 (1985).

11. Mohr, *supra* note 5, at 121–22; Smith-Rosenberg, *supra* note 10, at 227–28.

view that the public did not oppose abortion.[12] Mohr did not note that such advertisements almost invariably relied on euphemisms and rarely, if ever, directly mentioned abortion.[13] This fact by itself hardly suggests that people in general thought there was nothing wrong with abortion. Most of the historians of the new orthodoxy are loath to admit this. Beverly Harrison is among the few for she has acknowledged, albeit reluctantly, that the condemnation of abortion has predominated throughout Western culture since (at least) the year 300.[14]

The only persons who openly advocated abortion in the nineteenth century were the professional abortionists themselves.[15] Mohr was able to cite only one anonymous 1889 study prepared for the New York Medico-Legal Society;[16] because it was anonymous, we know nothing of the professional activities of its author. Mohr sought to buttress his claim of a broad public acceptance of abortion by counting the purported silence of the major religious denominations on abortion before the Civil War as evidence of support for the practice.[17] He did not consider the possibility that the silence reflected instead a lack of concern about a practice that was not a frequent occurrence among their congregants. Mohr moreover chose to limit his research to national publications by mainline denominations.[18] If Mohr had searched more widely, he would have found considerable religiously based material decrying abortion before the Civil War.[19]

After the Civil War, leaders even of mainline Protestant denominations began to denounce abortion and to support the enactment of more stringent statutes as strongly as any physician.[20] The position of the Catholic Church, involving new canonical legislation based on a different understanding of fetal personhood than had prevailed before the nineteenth century, also became more critical of abortion than before.[21] Ironically, at just the point that clergy in general began to focus a hostile light on the rising incidence of abortion, physicians began to criticize heavily what the physicians considered to be an attitude of neutrality among the clergy.[22] That

---

12. MOHR, *supra* note 5, at 131. *See also* MARVIN OLASKY, ABORTION RIGHTS: A SOCIAL HISTORY OF ABORTION IN AMERICA 189–96 (1992).

13. *See* DEGLER, *supra* note 8, at 231, 243; OLASKY, *supra* note 12, at 192–93; OLASKY, *supra* note 8, at 6.

14. BEVERLY WILDUNG HARRISON, OUR RIGHT TO CHOOSE: TOWARD A NEW ETHIC OF ABORTION 119–54 (1983).

15. MOHR, *supra* note 5, at 63. *See generally* Chapter 7, at notes 140–60.

16. MOHR, *supra* note 5, at 90, 94, 108–09.

17. *Id.* at 182–87, 192–96. *See also* DEGLER, *supra* note 8, at 239; FAYE GINSBURG, CONTESTED LIVES: THE ABORTION DEBATE IN AN AMERICAN COMMUNITY 31 (1989); HARRISON, *supra* note 14, at 150–51; LAWRENCE LADER, ABORTION 89–90 (1966); ROSALIND POLLACK PETCHESKY, ABORTION AND WOMEN'S CHOICE: THE STATE, SEXUALITY, AND REPRODUCTIVE FREEDOM 80 (rev. ed. 1990).

18. MOHR, *supra* note 5, at 300 n.29.

19. *See, e.g.,* JOHN McDOWELL, FIRST ANNUAL REPORT OF THE NEW YORK MAGDALEN SOCIETY (1831).

20. *See, e.g.,* ARTHUR CLEVELAND COXE, MORAL REFORMS SUGGESTED IN A PASTORAL LETTER WITH REMARKS ON PRACTICAL RELIGION 9–75, 101–11 (1869); JOHN TODD, SERPENT IN A DOVE'S NEST 6–14 (1867) ("TODD, SERPENT"); Nathan Allen, *Comparative Decrease of Children,* 54 CONGREGATIONAL & BOS. RECORDER 39 (Feb. 4, 1869); I.T. Dana, *Report of the Committee on the Production of Abortion,* 46 CHRISTIAN MIRROR 1 (Aug. 4, 1868); *The Crime of Infanticide,* 47 N.Y. OBSERVER 194 (June 24, 1869); John Todd, *Fashionable Murder,* 52 CONGREGATIONAL & BOS. RECORDER 45 (1867) ("Todd, Murder"). *See generally* MICHAEL GROSSBERG, GOVERNING THE HEARTH: LAW AND THE FAMILY IN NINETEENTH-CENTURY AMERICA 170–72 (1985); MOHR, *supra* note 5, at 187–93; OLASKY, *supra* note 12, at 161–64; SMITH-ROSENBERG, *supra* note 10, at 218; R. Sauer, *Attitudes to Abortion in America, 1800–1973,* 28 POP. STUDIES 53, 56, 58 (1974).

21. DANIEL CALLAHAN, ABORTION: LAW, CHOICE, AND MORALITY 410–61 (1970); GERMAIN GRISEZ, ABORTION: THE MYTHS, THE REALITIES, AND THE ARGUMENTS 177–81 (1970).

22. *See, e.g.,* WINSLOW AYER, THE GREAT CRIME OF THE NINETEENTH CENTURY AND PERILS OF CHILD LIFE 5 (1880); S.K. Crawford, *Criminal Abortion: A Special Report,* TRANS. 22D ANNIV. MEETING ILL. ST. MED. SOC'Y 74, 78 (1872); J.H. KELLOGG, LADIES' GUIDE TO HEALTH AND DISEASE 365 (1893); P.S. Haskell, *Criminal Abortion,* 4 TRANS. ME. MED. ASS'N 463, 467 (1873); J. Miller, *Criminal Abortion,* 1 K.C. MED. REC. 295, 297 (1884); Addison Niles, *Criminal Abortion,* TRANS. OF 21ST ANNIV. MEETING OF ILL. ST. MED. SOC'Y

attitude was summed up by Dr. Junius Hogue in an article in the same journal written as a reply to the anonymous article that Mohr found so significant: "The law is a constant monitor.... [T]he clergy and all other educators may fail in their duty to properly instruct the people, but we still have left instruction in the law."[23] The criticism was no more justified than the similar criticism the physicians were then directing at lawyers and judges.[24] James Mohr would have us attribute the change in mainstream Protestant clergy solely a response to pressure from the physicians rather than an expression of sincere concern.[25] Other historians, however, have been ready enough to ascribe an anti-feminist, indeed anti-female, conspiracy to the clergy as well.[26] Despite Mohr's intent to place responsibility solely on the nascent medical profession, he also hinted at such motives on the part of the clergy.[27]

Just as various strands of the clergy spoke out against abortion throughout the century, so also the popular press (ranging from the *National Police Gazette* in the 1840s to the *New York Times* in the 1860s and 1870s) used lurid stories about abortion and abortionists in order to gain circulation.[28] Mohr and his ilk did not see this as evidence of popular sentiments against abortion.[29] Law professor Cyril Means, jr., in particular insisted that the increasingly strong press campaign that culminated in the Abortion Act of 1869 was merely a means of selling newspapers.[30] Lurid stories about "child murder," however, leave little doubt as to where the journalists stood on abortion.[31]

The national press was led by the *New York Times* which, contrary to its present stance, went so far as to characterize the practice of abortion as "The Evil of the Age."[32] The New York newspapers continued to campaign against abortion after New York's 1869 statute was adopted.[33] The continuing press campaign in New York included frequent assertions that the fetus is a human being from conception murdered by the crime of abortion.[34] Even in the face of all this, modern historians never ask why sensational stories about abortion would sell papers if the practice of abortion were as widespread and accepted as they think.

Several themes run through the popular arguments against abortion, always beginning with reference to the protection of fetal life.[35] What was perhaps the most common secondary

---

96, 101 (1872); Montrose Pallen, *Foeticide*, 3 MED. ARCHIVES (St. L. n.s.) 196 (1869); John Trader, *Criminal Abortion*, 11 St. L. MED. & SURGICAL J., n.s. 583, 587 (1874).

23. Junius Hogue, *Abortion and the Law*, 8 MEDICO-LEGAL J. 126 (1890). For Mohr's reliance on the anonymous article, see the text *supra* at note 16.

24. See *infra* at notes 71–73.

25. MOHR, *supra* note 5, at 182, 184–89.

26. *See, e.g.*, G.J. BARKER-BENFIELD, THE HORRORS OF THE HALF-KNOWN LIFE: MALE ATTITUDES TOWARD WOMEN AND SEXUALITY IN NINETEENTH CENTURY AMERICA 135–226 (1976); GROSSBERG, *supra* note 20, at 171–72.

27. MOHR, *supra* note 5, at 187–88.

28. *See generally* OLASKY, *supra* note 8, at 149–72; OLASKY, *supra* note 12, at 3–54.

29. LINDA GORDON, WOMAN'S BODY, WOMAN'S RIGHT: A SOCIAL HISTORY OF BIRTH CONTROL IN AMERICA 51–57 (1976); GROSSBERG, *supra* note 20, at 172–74; MOHR, *supra* note 5, at 125–28, 176–82, 196–97; SMITH-ROSENBERG, *supra* note 10, at 225–27; Cyril Means, jr., *The Law of New York Concerning Abortion and the Status of the Foetus, 1664–1968: A Case of Cessation of Constitutionality*, 14 N.Y.L.F. 411, 457–59, 471–72 n.164 (1968) ("Means I").

30. Means I, *supra* note 29, at 457–59.

31. *See, e.g.*, *Child Murder*, N.Y. DAILY TRIBUNE, Jan. 27, 1868, at 3.

32. Augustus St. Clair, *The Evil of the Age*, N.Y. TIMES, Aug. 23, 1871, at 6. *See also Advertising Facilities for Murder*, N.Y. TIMES, Aug. 30, 1871, at 4; *The Least of the Little Ones*, N.Y. TIMES, Nov. 3, 1870, at 4.

33. 1869 N.Y. Laws ch. 631, §§ 1–3, at 1502, reprinted in Eugene Quay, *Justifiable Abortion — Medical and Legal Foundations (Pt. II)*, 49 GEO. L.J. 395, 500 (1961). *See* Chapter 7, at notes 74–92.

34. *See, e.g.*, *The Root of the Evil*, N.Y. DAILY TRIBUNE, Aug. 30, 1871, at 4.

35. *See* AYER, *supra* note 22; COXE, *supra* note 20; HUGH HODGE, FOETICIDE, OR CRIMINAL ABORTION 3 (1869); SAMUEL HOLMES, THE TREND OF THE RACE 169 (1921); KELLOGG, *supra* note 22; ANDREW NEBINGER, CRIMINAL ABORTION: ITS EXTENT AND PREVENTION 21, 25 (1870); HORATIO ROBINSON STORER, ON CRIMI-

argument can fairly be characterized as racist—a fear that whites in general, and middle class Anglo-Saxons in particular, would be outbred by lesser classes of persons.[36] Anti-abortion crusaders made the same sort of argument in Canada and England where concerns about declining population fueled heightened vigilance regarding abortion.[37] The phrase "race suicide," introduced in 1901, became a popular description for fears of the traditionally dominant culture that it was being swamped by faster-breeding "races" in the early years of the twentieth century.[38]

The notion of "race" at that time was applied broadly, linking prejudices against Jews and Catholics with prejudices against darker-skinned people in a grand fear of "race suicide"[39] and

---

NAL ABORTION IN AMERICA 42 (1860) ("STORER, CRIMINAL ABORTION"); HORATIO ROBINSON STORER, WHY NOT? A BOOK FOR EVERYWOMAN 63–65 (1866) ("STORER, WHY NOT?"); TODD, SERPENT, *supra* note 20; *Advertising Facilities for Murder, supra* note 32; Allen, *supra* note 20; Nathan Allen, *The New England Family,* 145 THE NEW ENGLANDER 147 (March 1882) ("Allen, *New England Family*"); *Child Murder, supra* note 31; Dana, *supra* note 20; St. Clair, *supra* note 32; *The Crime of Infanticide, supra* note 20; *The Least of the Little Ones, supra* note 32; *The Root of the Evil, supra* note 34; Todd, Murder, *supra* note 20. *See also* CRAWFORD, *supra* note 22; E.M. Buckingham, *Criminal Abortion,* 10 CIN. LANCET & OBSERVER 139, 141–42 (1867); H. Gibbons, sr., *On Foeticide,* 21 PAC. MED. & SURGICAL J. 97, 111 (1878); Haskell, *supra* note 22; Miller, *supra* note 22; J.J. Mulheron, *Foeticide,* 10 PENINSULAR J. MED. 387 (1874); Niles, *supra* note 22; Pallen, *supra* note 22; Horatio Robinson Storer, *Criminality and Physical Evils of Forced Abortion,* 16 TRANS. A.M.A. 709 (1865) ("Storer, *Physical Evils*"); Trader, *supra* note 22.

36. *See, e.g.,* NATHAN ALLEN, CHANGES IN NEW ENGLAND'S POPULATION (1866); ARTHUR CALHOUN, A SOCIAL HISTORY OF THE AMERICAN FAMILY FROM COLONIAL TIMES TO THE PRESENT 225–54 (1919); AUGUSTUS GARDNER, CONJUGAL SINS AGAINST THE LAWS OF LIFE AND HEALTH AND THEIR EFFECTS UPON THE FATHER, MOTHER, AND THE CHILD 5 (1876); EDWIN HALE, THE GREAT CRIME OF THE NINETEENTH CENTURY, WHY IS IT COMMITTED? WHO ARE THE CRIMINALS? HOW SHALL THEY BE DETECTED? HOW SHALL THEY BE PUNISHED? 4–6 (1867); NEBINGER, *supra* note 35, at 6–9; H.S. POMEROY, THE ETHICS OF MARRIAGE 39 (1888); THEODORE ROOSEVELT, THE FOES OF OUR OWN HOUSEHOLD 257 (1917); STORER, WHY NOT?, *supra* note 35, at 63–65, 85; HORATIO ROBINSON STORER & FRANKLIN FISKE HEARD, CRIMINAL ABORTION: ITS NATURE, ITS EVIDENCE AND ITS LAW 41–53 (1868); Gibbons, *supra* note 25, at 111; Pallen, *supra* note 22, at 198–99; Horatio Robinson Storer, *On the Decrease of the Rate of Increase of Population Now Obtaining in Europe and America,* 43 AM. J. SCIENCE & ARTS 141 (1867); James Whitemore, *Criminal Abortion,* 31 CHI. MED. J. 385, 392 (1874).

37. *See, e.g.,* EDWARD CLARKE, SEX IN EDUCATION, OR, A FAIR CHANCE FOR GIRLS 63 (1873). *See also* A.M. CARR-SANDERS, POPULATION (1925); ENID CHARLES, THE TWILIGHT OF PARENTHOOD (1934); EUSTACE CHESSER, FROM GIRLHOOD TO WOMANHOOD 122 (1914); D.V. GLASS, THE STUGGLE FOR POPULATION (1936). *See generally* BARBARA BROOKES, ABORTION IN ENGLAND 1900–1967, at 30, 56–57, 63–64, 70, 123, 134–35 (1988); Angus McLaren, *Birth Control and Abortion in Canada, 1870–1920,* 59 CAN. HIST. REV. 319, 319–21, 328, 333 (1978).

38. *See, e.g.,* O.C. BEALL, RACIAL DECAY: A COMPILATION OF EVIDENCE FROM WORLD SOURCES (1911); LYDIA KINGSMILL COMMANDER, THE AMERICAN IDEA: DOES THE NATIONAL TENDENCY TOWARD A SMALL FAMILY POINT TO RACE SUICIDE OR RACE DEGENERATION? (1907); EDWARD EAST, MANKIND AT THE CROSSROADS 297 (1928); M.S. ISEMAN, RACE SUICIDE 137 (1912); 3 THEODORE ROOSEVELT, PRESIDENTIAL ADDRESSES AND STATE PAPERS 282 (1910); Charles Emerick, *College Women and Race Suicide,* 24 POL. SCI. Q. 269 (1909); "Kit" (Kathleen Blake Watkins), *Race Suicide,* DAILY MAIL & EMPIRE (Toronto), Mar. 21, 1908, at 21; Edward Ross, *Western Civilization and the Birth-Rate,* 12 AM. J. SOCIOLOGY 616 (1907); Margaret Sanger, *Is Race Suicide Possible?,* COLLIER'S MAG., Aug. 25, 1925, at 25; W.S. Wallace, *The Canadian Immigration Policy,* 30 CAN. MAG. 360 (1907). *See generally* GORDON, *supra* note 29, at 53, 130–58; GROSSBERG, *supra* note 20, at 170–71; REGINALD HORSMAN, RACE AND MANIFEST DESTINY (1981); RUTH HUBBARD, THE POLITICS OF WOMEN'S BIOLOGY 182 (1990); LESLIE REAGAN, WHEN ABORTION WAS A CRIME: WOMEN, MEDICINE, AND LAW IN THE UNITED STATES, 1867–1973, at 13, 50, 102–04 (1997); Margaret Phillips, *Reproduction with Technology: The New Eugenics,* 11 IN THE PUB. INT. 1, 2–5 (1991); Alex Zwerdling, *Anglo-Saxon Panic: The Turn-of-the-Century Response to "Alien" Immigrants,* 1 IDEAS FROM THE NAT'L HUMAN. CENTER 32, 38 (No. 2, 1993).

39. *See* Phillips, *supra* note 38, at 3; Zwerdling, *supra* note 38. *See also* GENA COREA, THE MOTHER MACHINE 27 (1985) (reporting that in 1912 between 79% and 87% of Hungarians, Italians, Jews, and Russians tested as "feeble-minded" and thus were excludable according to immigration authorities).

"mongrelization."[40] Historian Dallas Blanchard has even suggested that a strong motivation behind the anti-abortion statutes was to prevent white women who had sexual relations with African-Americans from destroying the evidence of their "guilt."[41] As this last comment suggests, attitudes towards race were linked with notions of public morality. Women, by this view, were abandoning their "proper" role in life, both racially and domestically, with the newly discovered possibility of abortion as the means to accomplish this abandonment.[42] Yet, despite widespread charges that women seeking their own emancipation were responsible for the rising incidence of abortion in the later years of the nineteenth century, women were among the strongest supporters of effective laws and forceful action against abortion.[43]

# The Catholic Dimension

*Seen from the viewpoint of politics, truth has a despotic character.*

—Hannah Arendt[44]

The Catholic Church was rather subdued in the United States during the nineteenth century. While the Catholic Church never supported a right to abort,[45] the Church largely remained silent on abortion in the nineteenth century in the United States. In fact, one strand of anti-abortion rhetoric expressed a strong anti-Catholic feeling.[46] The deeply ingrained anti-Papism of American Protestantism was fueled in this context by the reality that Catholics did not practice abortion to any great extent, fostering a fear that Catholics would eventually come to outnumber Protestants. A more balanced view of the large Catholic families should have tempered the

---

40. MICHAEL GUYER, BEING WELL-BORN: AN INTRODUCTION TO EUGENICS 296–98 (1916).

41. DALLAS BLANCHARD, THE ANTI-ABORTION MOVEMENT AND THE RISE OF THE RELIGIOUS RIGHT: FROM POLITE TO FIERY PROTEST 128 n.10 (1994).

42. *See, e.g.,* CALHOUN, *supra* note 68, at 242; GARDNER, *supra* note 68, at 225; HODGE, *supra* note 41, at 32–33; STORER, WHY NOT?, *supra* note 41, at 27, 35, 80–81; T. GAILLARD THOMAS, ABORTION AND ITS TREATMENT, FROM THE STANDPOINT OF PRACTICAL EXPERIENCE 3 (1890); "D.H.", *On Producing Abortion: A Physician's Reply to the Solicitations of a Married Woman to Produce a Miscarriage for Her,* 17 NASHVILLE J. MED. & SURGICAL J. 200, 201 (1876); Gibbons, *supra* note 68; W.E. Atlee & D.A. O'Donnell, *Report of the Committee on Criminal Abortion,* 22 TRANS. AM. MED. ASS'N 240, 240–41 (1871); Pallen, *supra* note 68, at 195, 202–03, 205–06; George Smith, *Foeticide,* 10 DET. REV. MED. & PHARMACY 211 (1875). *See generally* THOMAS LAQUEUR, MAKING SEX: BODY AND GENDER FROM THE GREEKS TO FREUD 2–24, 59–61 (1990); Siegel, *supra* note 5, at 291–97.

43. *See* Chapter 8.

44. HANNAH ARENDT, BETWEEN PAST AND FUTURE: EIGHT EXERCISES IN POLITICAL THOUGHT 229, 233, 241 (1968).

45. EDWARD LePROHON, VOLUNTARY ABORTION, OR FASHIONABLE PROSTITUTION, WITH SOME REMARKS UPON THE OPERATION OF CRANIOTOMY (1867); MOHR, *supra* note 5, at 195.

46. *See, e.g.,* HODGE, *supra* note 35, at 169; NEBINGER, *supra* note 35, at 21, 25; STORER, CRIMINAL, *supra* note 35, at 42; STORER, WHY NOT?, *supra* note 35, at 63–65; TODD, SERPENT, *supra* note 20, at 6; Allen, *New England Family, supra* note 35; Buckingham, *supra* note 35, at 141–42 (1867); Mulheron, *supra* note 35, at 390–91; Storer, *Physical Evils, supra* note 35, at 736. *See generally* BLANCHARD, *supra* note 41, at 14–15; DEGLER, *supra* note 8, at 239; GINSBURG, *supra* note 17, at 28; KRISTIN LUKER, ABORTION AND THE POLITICS OF MOTHERHOOD 60 (1984); BARBARA MILBAUER & BERT OBRENTZ, THE LAW GIVETH: LEGAL ASPECTS OF THE ABORTION CONTROVERSY 131–33 (1983); MOHR, *supra* note 5, at 90–91, 128, 130–31, 166–68, 187–90; Sauer, *supra* note 20, at 54–55.

Protestant fear through a realization that significant numbers of Catholics elected to pursue a celibate life in the Church, thereby cutting the overall Catholic birthrate.[47]

Catholics generally were not involved in legislative efforts to craft legal prohibitions of abortion. In fact, Catholics were objects of curiosity (or hostility) in the states (and the Kingdom of Hawaii) when they enacted their first abortion statutes. Catholics were barred by the state constitution from serving in the state legislature in New Hampshire until 1877.[48] New Hampshire enacted its first abortion statute in 1848.[49] One can trace the role of anti-Catholic prejudice in discussions of abortion (or its close relative, the craniotomy during delivery) to eighteenth-century England.[50] There is a certain irony to this pattern given the current pervasive appeals to anti-Catholic prejudice by those who would legalize abortion.[51]

Anti-Papism has long been a tradition in American public life and continues largely unabated today.[52] It is one the few "respectable" prejudices left. The modern prejudice tries to attribute nearly everything related to the "right to life" movement to the action of the Catholic bishops,[53] or to "fundamentalist" Catholics,[54] utterly neglecting the opposition to abortion by Protestants, Unitarians, and the non-religious.[55] In short, the current rhetoric suggests that opposition to abortion is purely a function of Catholic "bigotry,"[56] while finding the prominent involvement of

---

47. *See* Susan Nicholson, Abortion and the Roman Catholic Church 3 (1978); Kathy Rudy, Beyond Pro-Life and Pro-Choice: Moral Diversity in the Abortion Debate 155 n.4 (1996).

48. N.H. Const. pt. II (adopted 1783).

49. Quay, *supra* note 33, at 445, 494 (1961). *See* Chapter 7, at 303–08.

50. 2 Thomas Denman, An Introduction to the Practice of Midwifery 172–175 (1794); Samuel Merriman, A Synopsis of the Various Kinds of Difficult Parturition 171 (1814); Fielding Ould, A Treatise of Midwifery 198 (1742). *See generally* Angus McLaren, Reproductive Rituals 124–28 (1984).

51. Richard Posner, *Legal Reform from the Top Down and from the Bottom up: The Question of Unenumerated Constitutional Rights*, 59 U. Chi. L. Rev. 433, 448 (1992).

52. *See, e.g.,* Donald Beschle, *Catechism or Imagination: Is Justice Scalia's Judicial Style Typically Catholic?*, 37 Villa. L. Rev. 1329 (1992). *See generally* Philip Jenkins, The New Anti-Catholicism: The Last Acceptable Prejudice (2004); Jane Eisner, *Mel Gibson Aside, This Bias Is Troubling*, Phila. Inquirer, Oct. 5, 2003, at C5.

53. *See, e.g.,* Dallas Blanchard & Terry Prewitt, Religious Violence and Abortion: The Gideon Project 257 (1993) (blaming Catholic bishops for the bombings of abortion clinics despite the bishops' open condemnation of such actions).

54. Blanchard & Prewitt, *supra* note 53, at 216, 225–30, 261–63;

55. *See, e.g.,* Paul Ramsey, *Reference Points on Abortion,* in The Terrible Choice: The Abortion Dilemma 60 (Robert Cooke & Andrew Hellegers eds. 1968).

56. *See, e.g.,* The Abortion Controversy: A Documentary History 46, 82, 140–43, 219 (Eva Rubin ed. 1994); Blanchard, *supra* note 41, at 10–12, 27; Janet Farrell Brodie, Contraception and Abortion in Nineteenth-Century America 81, 266, 290 (1994); Brookes, *supra* note 37, at 7, 26, 63, 86–87, 98 n.1, 114–15, 146, 154; James MacGregor Burns & Stewart Burns, A People's Charter: The Pursuit of Rights in America 354–58 (1991); Robert Burt, The Constitution in Conflict 346–47 (1992); The Catholic Church and the Politics of Abortion: A View from the States (Timothy Byrnes & Mary Segers eds. 1992); Celeste Michelle Condit, Decoding Abortion Rhetoric: Communicating Social Change 30, 47–53, 74 n.5, 76 n.17, 124, 126–27 (1990); Barbara Hinkinson Craig & David O'Brien, Abortion and American Politics 32, 43–47, 54, 254–56 (1993); Mary Daly, Beyond God the Father: Toward a Philosophy of Women's Liberation 106 (1973); Nanette Davis, From Crime to Choice 30–33, 101, 114–16, 120–21 (1985); Degler, *supra* note 8, at 233, 239; Ronald Dworkin, Life's Dominion: An Argument about Abortion, Euthanasia, and Individual Freedom 7, 30, 36, 39–50, 91–92, 245 n.6 (1993); Marian Faux, Crusaders: Voices from the Abortion Front xiii–xiv, 4–8, 57–58, 185, 227–28, 230–64 (1990); Myra Marx Ferree & Beth Hess, Controversy and Coalition: The New Feminist Movement across Three Decades of Change 153 (rev. ed. 1994); David Garrow, Liberty and Sexuality: The Right of Privacy and the Making of Roe v. Wade passim (2nd ed. 1998); Gordon, *supra* note 29, at 52–53 n.*, 268–70, 281, 315–17, 336–37, 350–51, 415–16; Janet Hadley, Abortion: Between Freedom and Necessity 157–58, 164–66, 171–72 217 n.2 (1996); Robert Hardaway, Population, Law, and

clergy of other denominations in the abortion reform movement to be a laudable effort to secure basic human rights.[57] Only rarely does one find supporters of abortion rights willing to concede that the general stress on a Catholic role is misplaced.[58]

Hostility toward Catholicism dominates law professor David Garrow's "history" of abortion reform. For example, he introduces a discussion of clinic bombings by describing the bishops' opposition to the Mondale-Ferraro ticket and never mentions that those convicted of bombings in Pensacola and Washington, D.C., were not even Catholics.[59] The epitome of this sort of attitude is captured in law professor Jeanne Schroeder's comment that "it is impossible for a woman to be *too* angry with the [Catholic] Church."[60] In a similar vein, Dr. Roger Rosenblatt claims that the Catholic attitude towards abortion parallels Nazi authoritarianism.[61]

One need not reject the pervasive anti-Catholic prejudice expressed in much pro-abortion rhetoric today, nor decry the pervasive prejudice against religion in general among the ruling elites of our society,[62] to note that these biases have had their hand in distorting our perceptions of the past. Thus historian Dallas Blanchard has described Connecticut and Massachusetts as "predominantly Catholic" in 1890 and therefore concluded that they then were following the "Vatican policy" towards abortion[63] — when in fact both states were still decades away from becoming predominantly Catholic. Similarly, law professor Mary Dudziak blamed Connecticut's historic prohibition of the sale of contraceptives on the Catholic Church, ignoring that the prohibition originated long before Catholic influence became important in Connecticut.[64] Or con-

---

THE ENVIRONMENT 23, 26–27, 86–90, 113–14 (1994); HARRISON, *supra* note 14, at 24–26, 65, 77, 127–32, 180, 184–86, 238–39, 264 n.9, 272 n.16; ANTHONY HORDERN, LEGAL ABORTION: THE ENGLISH EXPERIENCE 11, 13–14, 40–42 (1971); JIMMYE (*sic*) KIMMEY, LEGAL ABORTION: A SPEAKERS (*sic*) NOTEBOOK 15–18 (1975); ELIZABETH MENSCH & ALAN FREEMAN, THE POLITICS OF VIRTUE: IS ABORTION DEBATABLE? 11, 117–18, 123, 138, 229 n.97 (1993); BERNARD NATHANSON & RICHARD OSTUNG, ABORTING AMERICA 172 (1979); SUSAN TEFT NICHOLSON, ABORTION AND THE ROMAN CATHOLIC CHURCH (1978); DAVID O'BRIEN, STORM CENTER: THE SUPREME COURT IN AMERICAN POLITICS 36 (3rd ed. 1993); KAREN O'CONNOR, NO NEUTRAL GROUND? ABORTION POLITICS IN AN AGE OF ABSOLUTES 19–20, 31–32, 59–62 (1997); CONNIE PAIGE, THE RIGHT TO LIFERS: WHO THEY ARE; HOW THEY OPERATE; WHERE THEY GET THEIR MONEY (1983); PETCHESKY, *supra* note 17, at xiii, 118–22, 252–76, 335–38; DEBORAH RHODE, JUSTICE AND GENDER 209 (1989); EVA RUBIN, ABORTION, POLITICS, AND THE COURTS 19, 23, 25–26, 50, 72, 90–95, 100–07, 113 (rev. ed. 1987); SUSAN SHERWIN, NO LONGER PATIENT: FEMINIST ETHICS AND HEALTH CARE 72 (1992); JAMES BOYD WHITE, ACTS OF HOPE: CREATING AUTHORITY IN LITERATURE, LAW, AND POLITICS 163–64, 166 (1994); GLANVILLE WILLIAMS, THE SANCTITY OF LIFE AND THE CRIMINAL LAW 193–206, 225–33 (1957, reprinted 1972).

57. GARROW, *supra* note 56, at 289–92, 296, 400–01, 404–05, 431, 438, 462.

58. *See* DONALD JUDGES, HARD CHOICES, LOST VOICES 15–16 (1993); B. Drummond Ayres, jr., *Virginia Leader Apologizes for Remark on Inquiry,* N.Y. TIMES, July 8, 1991, at A6; Alice Rossi & Bhavani Sitaraman, *Abortion in Context: Historical Trends and Future Changes,* 20 FAM. PLANNING PERSP. 273, 276 (1988). *See also They Have No Excuse for Anti-Catholic Bias,* NEWSDAY, July 22, 1991, at 34.

59. GARROW, *supra* note 56, at 650–52.

60. Jeanne Schroeder, Abduction from the Seraglio: *Feminist Methodologies and the Logic of Imagination,* 70 TEX. L. REV. 109, 172 n.192 (1991).

61. ROGER ROSENBLATT, LIFE ITSELF: ABORTION IN THE AMERICAN MIND 80 (1992).

62. *See generally* KENT GREENAWALT, CONFLICTS OF LAW AND MORALITY 6 (1987); GARRY WILLS, UNDER GOD: RELIGION AND AMERICAN POLITICS 15–25 (1990); R. Randall Rainey, *Law and Religion: Is Reconciliation Still Possible,* 27 LOY.-L.A. L. REV. 147 (1993). For a living example of this prejudice, see Howard Vogel, *The Judicial Oath and the American Creed: Comments on Sanford Levinson's 'The Confrontation of Religious Faith and Civil Religion: Catholics Becoming Justices,'*39 DE PAUL L. REV. 1107, 1116 (1990).

63. BLANCHARD, *supra* note 41, at 15.

64. Mary Dudziak, *Just Say No: Birth Control in the Connecticut Supreme Court before* Griswold v. Connecticut, 75 IOWA L. REV. 915, 927–31 (1990). *See also* GORDON, *supra* note 29, at 315; DAVID KENNEDY, BIRTH CONTROL IN AMERICA: THE CAREER OF MARGARET SANGER 269 (1970); ARTHUR SCHLESINGER, THE CRISIS OF THE OLD ORDER, 1919–1933, at 425–26 (1956).

sider Karen O'Connor who insists that Connecticut was "heavily Catholic" in 1821 when it enacted the first American abortion statute.[65] In 1821, before the Irish potato famine, Catholics
were rare in the United States anywhere outside of Maryland. That was only three years after
Connecticut became the last state to disestablish its hitherto state-supported Protestant
church.[66] The modern prejudice also peeks through in James Mohr's work.[67] Mohr, however, was
so intent on laying the blame for the abortion statutes solely on the allopathic medical profession that he pointedly played down any opposition by the Catholic Church to abortion in the
nineteenth-century.[68]

While the Catholic Church as an institution was always opposed to abortion, it played at best
a negligible role in tightening the laws against abortion in England or the United States in the
later years of the nineteenth century. While some Catholic individuals perhaps were involved in
that process, none were prominent in that process. And while Catholics and the Catholic Church
certainly are at the center of the anti-abortion movement today, it is hardly alone there.[69]

# Abortion in the Professionalization of the Law

*Texts matter to lawyers, not because lawyers are now perhaps the only actors in the great
world who know how and are willing to read, but because without text there really is no
law.... For lawyers the question is not disobedience or obedience as such. It is how to read.*

—Joseph Vining[70]

James Mohr and his followers, in their zeal to blame male allopathic physicians exclusively for
the enactment of the nineteenth century abortion statutes, do not blame the public, the clergy
(Catholic as well as Protestant), and the journalists for the nineteenth century abortion laws.
They also do not blame the lawyers. They relied on the evidence of physicians who, in the nineteenth century, frequently criticized the legal profession in rather extreme terms for failing to
take effective action against the growing practice of abortion.[71] Such criticism continued into the
twentieth century.[72] In England, such criticisms were voiced by Justice (later Lord) Darling who,
beginning in 1899, argued that the English practice of commuting death sentences for abortion

---

65. Karen O'Connor, No Neutral Ground? Abortion Politics in an Age of Absolutes 26 (1997).

66. *See* John Noonan, jr., The Believer and the Powers that Are 190–93 (1987). Massachusetts continued to provide tax support for its churches until 1834, but the preferred church was determined town-by-
town rather than statewide. *Id.* at 113–17, 139–60.

67. Mohr, *supra* note 5, at 167, 290–91 n.14.

68. *Id.* at 185–87.

69. *See also* Chapter 16, at notes 82–105, 251–62.

70. Joseph Vining, *Legal Affinities*, 23 Ga. L. Rev. 1035, 1041, 1048 (1989).

71. *See, e.g.,* Storer & Heard, *supra* note 36, at 6–7 ("in the sight of the common law, and in most cases
of statutory law also, the crime of abortion, properly considered does not exist"); Haskell, supra note 22, at
463. *See also* Heywoud Broun & Margaret Leech, Anthony Comstock: Roundsman of the Lord 165
(1927); Frederick Taussig, The Prevention and Treatment of Abortion 78–80 (1910). *See generally*
Frederick Dyer, Champion of Women and the Unborn: Horatio Robinson Storer, M.D. 330–31
(1999); Grossberg, *supra* note 20, at 180, 183, 186–87.

72. Mark Graber, Rethinking Abortion: Equal Choice, the Constitution, and Reproductive
Politics 45 (1996); Edwin Schur, Crimes without Victims: Deviant Behavior and Public Policy 34
(1965); Harvey Adelstein, *The Abortion Law*, 12 W. Res. L. Rev. 74, 85–86 (1960); Marvin Moore, *Antiquated
Abortion Laws*, 20 Wash. & Lee L. Rev. 250, 253 (1963).

to terms of imprisonment was unseemly.[73] Darling, upon entering the House of Lords, instigated the *Infant Life (Preservation) Act of 1929* to close a gap in the law.[74]

The practice of lawyers and jurists generally did not justify such criticism.[75] The criticism was more of a demand for new legislation than a description of the actual state of the law. The physicians' attacks appear to have been colored by the rising hostility between the legal and medical professions that Mohr himself identified as marking the middle and later years of the nineteenth century.[76] According to Mohr, that hostility arose from the frustrated expectations of physicians regarding their authority as expert witnesses and the deference they expected for their professional judgments in the slowly spreading malpractice suits.[77] Yet remarkably in reconstructing the history of abortion, which is, after all, a history of a set of legal decisions, Mohr and his followers actually invested little effort into describing the role of the legal profession toward abortion or the significance of the issue to the profession. They failed to provide any extended consideration of the actual practices of lawyers and jurists relative to abortion.

The Anglo-American legal profession goes back a thousand years. The urge to professionalize the law in a modern sense originated by the seventeenth century, most notably in the work of Sir Edward Coke and Sir Matthew Hale.[78] Lawyers were especially prominent in American society, described by Alexis de Tocqueville as a virtual ruling aristocracy.[79] Yet law, like medicine, was nearly destroyed as a coherent profession in the United States by the Jacksonian impulse.[80] The creation of a coherent national legal profession in the United States was seriously impeded not only by the hostility of the Jacksonian era to elite groups but also by the vast distances and poor communications of the early and mid-nineteenth century.[81] By the middle of the nineteenth century, judges riding circuit were accompanied by lawyers who resembled a "troupe of actors" who

---

73. BROOKES, *supra* note 37, at 26.

74. *Id.* at 27. *See* Chapter 11, at notes 244–56.

75. *See, e.g.,* NEBINGER, *supra* note 35, at 29.

76. JAMES MOHR, DOCTORS AND THE LAW: MEDICAL JURISPRUDENCE IN NINETEENTH-CENTURY AMERICA 99–139, 180–212, 227–36, 247–49, 253–57 (1993).

77. *See, e.g.,* J. SNOWDEN BELL, THE USE AND ABUSE OF EXPERT TESTIMONY (1879); STANFORD CHAILLÉ, ORIGIN AND PROGRESS OF MEDICAL JURISPRUDENCE, 1776–1876, at 8–11, 25–27 (1876); Edward Cox, *Our Relations to Jurisprudence*, 2 DET. LANCET 273 (1879); Thomas Logan, *Physicians as Witnesses*, 2 CIN. LANCET & OBSERVER 149 (1859); M.A. McClelland, *The Medical Expert and Medical Evidence*, 32 CHI. MED. J. & EXAMINER 32 (1875); Jacob Miller, *Expert Testimony—Its Nature and Value*, 6 SANITARIAN 67 (1878); Samuel Parkman, *On the Relation of the Medical Witness with the Law and the Lawyer*, 23 AM. J. MED. SCI. 126 (n.s. 1852). *See generally* KENNETH ALLEN DE VILLE, MEDICAL MALPRACTICE IN NINETEENTH-CENTURY AMERICA: ORIGINS AND LEGACY (1990).

78. *See* Chapter 4. *See also* C.W. BROOKS, PETTYFOGGERS AND VIPERS OF THE COMMONWEALTH: THE "LOWER BRANCH" OF THE LEGAL PROFESSION IN EARLY MODERN ENGLAND (1986); 6 W.S. HOLDSWORTH, A HISTORY OF ENGLISH LAW 431–81 (23 vols., 7th ed. 1956); DAVID LEMMINGS, GENTLEMEN AND BARRISTERS: THE INNS OF COURT AND THE ENGLISH BAR: 1680–1730 (1990); DAVID LIEBERMAN, THE PROVINCE OF LEGISLATION DETERMINED: LEGAL THEORY IN EIGHTEENTH CENTURY BRITAIN (1989).

79. 1 DE TOCQUEVILLE, *supra* note 2, at 245–47, 253.

80. *See* MAXWELL BLOOMFIELD, AMERICAN LAWYERS IN A CHANGING SOCIETY, 1776–1876, at 32–58 (1978); ALFRED REED, TRAINING FOR THE PUBLIC PROFESSION OF THE LAW 75–77 (1921); ROBERT STEVENS, LAW SCHOOL: LEGAL EDUCATION IN AMERICA FROM THE 1850s TO THE 1980s, at 7–10 (1983); Paul Carrington, *One Law: The Role of Legal Education in the Opening of the Legal Profession since 1776*, 44 FLA. L. REV. 501, 507–10 (1992); Colin Croft, Note, *Reconceptualizing American Legal Professionalism: A Proposal for Deliberate Moral Community*, 67 N.Y.U. L. REV. 1256, 1284–87 (1992); James Robinson, *Admission to the Bar as Provided for in the Indiana Constitutional Convention of 1850–51*, 1 IND. L.J. 209 (1926).

81. RICHARD ABEL, AMERICAN LAWYERS 40 (1989); Maxwell Bloomfield, *David Hoffman and the Shaping of a Republican Legal Culture*, 38 MD. L. REV. 673, 679 (1979); Croft, *supra* note 80, at 1284; Fannie Memory Farmer, *Legal Practice and Ethics in North Carolina, 1820–1860*, in THE LEGAL PROFESSION: MAJOR HISTORICAL INTERPRETATIONS 285 (Kermit Hall ed. 1987) ("THE LEGAL PROFESSION"); E. Lee Shepard, *Breaking into the Profession: Establishing a Law Practice in Antebellum Virginia*, THE LEGAL PROFESSION, *supra*, at 595.

knew little law.[82] Thus in the middle and later years of the nineteenth century, American lawyers, like the doctors, struggled to define themselves as a profession and to carve out a niche for the profession in the society and the economy.[83]

A pivotal event in the professionalization of law in the United States was the organization of the American Bar Association in 1878 — a full generation after the organization of the American Medical Association in the 1850s.[84] As with the professionalization of medicine, some early (and a few recent) scholars have seen in the process of professionalization only a nefarious conspiracy to gain an economic monopoly.[85] For law and medicine, scholars recently have tended to view that the process of professionalization as more complex, representing a drive to systematize knowledge and to codify practice, not only to exclude competition but also to permit a standardized product consistent with the fundamental premises of the profession.[86] The ability to provide abstract generalizations of relevant knowledge enabled the group to define itself as a profession and to delimit its problems and tasks during a period of considerable social flux caused by rapid industrialization, to defend those tasks from interlopers, and to adapt to new situations.[87]

---

82. *See, e.g.,* Daniel Calhoun, *Branding Iron and Retrospect: Lawyers of the Cumberland River Country,* in PROFESSIONAL LIVES IN AMERICA: STRUCTURE AND ASPIRATIONS, 1750–1850, at 63 (Daniel Calhoun ed. 1965). *See also* R. CARLYLE BULEY, THE OLD NORTHWEST PIONEER PERIOD, 1815–1840, at 238 (1950); J. WILLARD HURST, THE GROWTH OF AMERICAN LAW: THE LAW MAKERS 276–85 (1950); WILLIAM JOHNSON, SCHOOLED LAWYERS: A STUDY IN THE CLASH OF CULTURES 27–28 (1978); STEVENS, *supra* note 80, at 25–26; Paul Carrington & Erika King, *Law and the Wisconsin Idea,* 47 J. LEGAL EDUC. 297, 307 (1997); Richard Cox, *Law and Community in the New Nation: Three Visions for Michigan, 1788–1831,* 4 S. CAL. INTERDISCIPLINARY L.J. 161, 188–89, 234–35 (1995).

83. *See generally* ABEL, *supra* note 81; JEROLD AUERBACH, UNEQUAL JUSTICE: LAWYERS AND SOCIAL CHANGE IN MODERN AMERICA (1976); BLOOMFIELD, *supra* note 80; MORTON HORWITZ, THE TRANSFORMATION OF AMERICAN LAW 1780–1860 (1977); MORTON HORWITZ, THE TRANSFORMATION OF AMERICAN LAW, 1870–1960: THE CRISIS OF LEGAL ORTHODOXY (1992) ("HORWITZ II"); WILLIAM LAPIANA, LOGIC AND EDUCATION: THE ORIGIN OF MODERN AMERICAN LEGAL EDUCATION (1994); REED, *supra* note 80; STEVENS, *supra* note 80; THE LEGAL PROFESSION, *supra* note 81; Carrington, *supra* note 80; Ronald Collins & David Skover, *Paratexts,* 44 STAN. L. REV. 509, 529–34 (1992); Criton Constantinides, *Professional Ethics in Court: Redefining the Social Contract between the Public and the Professions,* 25 GA. L. REV. 1327, 1328–40 (1991); Croft, *supra* note 80, at 1262–98; Michael Hoeflich, *Law and Geometry: Legal Science from Leibniz to Langdell,* 30 AM. J. LEGAL HIST. 95 (1986); G. Edward White, *The American Law Institute and the Triumph of Modernist Jurisprudence,* 15 LAW & HIST. REV. 1, 3–23 (1997). On rather different, but in some ways parallel, path to modern professionalism in the law in England and Wales, see RAYMOND COCKS, FOUNDATIONS OF THE MODERN BAR (1983); DANIEL DUMAN, THE ENGLISH AND COLONIAL BARS IN THE NINETEENTH CENTURY (1983); Daniel Duman, *Pathway to Professionalism: The English Bar in the Eighteenth and Nineteenth Centuries,* 13 J. SOC. HIST. 615 (1980).

84. Croft, *supra* note 80, at 1287–98.

85. *See* ABEL, *supra* note 81, at 48–71, 127 (1989); AUERBACH, *supra* note 83; STEVENS, *supra* note 80; Constantinides, *supra* note 83, at 1332, 1337; Croft, *supra* note 80, at 1266–67, 1287–89; Robert Gordon, *The Case for (and against) Harvard,* 93 MICH. L. REV. 1231, 1240–60 (1995); Wayne Hobson, *Lawyers and Power,* 39 J. LEGAL EDUC. 128 (1989); Richard Posner, *The Material Basis of Jurisprudence,* 69 IND. L.J. 1 (1993). For such a view of the medical profession, see the authorities collected in Chapter 7, at note 209.

86. LEE EPSTEIN & JOSEPH KOBYLKA, THE SUPREME COURT AND LEGAL CHANGE: ABORTION AND THE DEATH PENALTY (1992); TERENCE HALLIDAY, BEYOND MONOPOLY: LAWYERS, STATE CRISES, AND PROFESSIONAL EMPOWERMENT (1987); HORWITZ II, *supra* note 83, at 9–15; Carrington, *supra* note 80; Mark Osiel, *Lawyers as Monopolists, Aristocrats, and Entrepreneurs,* 103 HARV. L. REV. 2009 (1990); David Sugarman, *Simple Images and Complex Realities: English Lawyers and their Relationship to Business and Politics,* 11 LAW & HIST. REV. 257 (1993). For such a view of the medical profession, see the authorities collected in Chapter 7, at note 208.

87. AUERBACH, *supra* note 83, at 63; STEVENS, *supra* note 80, at 20, 191–99; Pierre Bourdieu & Richard Terdiman, *The Force of Law: Toward a Sociology of the Juridical Field,* 38 HASTINGS L.J. 805 (1987); Constantinides, *supra* note 83, at 1333; Croft, *supra* note 80, at 1265–79; Robert Gordon, *The Independence of Lawyers,* 68 B.U. L. REV. 1, 2–6 (1988); Hoeflich, *supra* note 83; David Millon, *Objectivity and Democracy,* 67 N.Y.U. L. REV. 1, 24–33 (1992). See also the authorities collected in Chapter 7, at note 209.

In the early nineteenth century, educational levels for lawyers were extremely low, almost non-existent.[88] As late as 1879, only 15 (of 38) states imposed any formal educational requirements on applicants for admission to the bar.[89] To professionalize the practice of law required finding issues that commanded sufficiently widespread allegiance among practitioners, overcome public hostility and regionalism, and would not divide the profession in competition for clients.[90]

Modern historians tend to exaggerate the importance of abortion for the medical profession's process of defining itself while neglecting its role in the professionalization of law in part because abortion played a less direct role for lawyers in this respect than it did for doctors. Yet abortion was not an issue that the legal profession could ignore if it were to hold its role as a major arbiter of public life. Abortion proved to be a particularly appropriate vehicle for the professionalization process, although not the only one that could help to overcome the problems of public hostility and regionalism. Then as now, abortion raised fundamental questions about life itself—that most central of the issues that, in their different ways, both the legal and the medical professions sought to make their own. Yet the law of abortion was still in some important respects unsettled at the opening of the nineteenth century, with unresolved questions relating to the newer techniques and, more importantly, to whether abortion was a crime before quickening.

Historians who today contend that abortion was not a crime at common law are simply wrong.[91] While nineteenth-century American courts were unanimous that post-quickening abortion was a crime, those courts had split over whether pre-quickening abortion was a common-law crime.[92] The persistence of these uncertainties so late in the development of the common law itself suggests that abortion had not been a common practice much before the codification process began. The persistent uncertainties, however, contributed to the rising incidence of a practice after relatively safe and effective procedures began to be developed in the nineteenth century. Under the circumstances, for abortion to have been omitted from the professionalization of the criminal law through its codification in the early nineteenth century would have been far more remarkable than was its inclusion.

Much of the evidence suggesting that an increase in abortions prompted the adoption and extension of abortion statutes in the nineteenth century comes from the records of the medical profession and from other non-legal sources.[93] These same sources demonstrate again and again

---

88. ABEL, *supra* note 81, at 5, 40–41; STEVENS, *supra* note 80, at 3–5, 11; Bloomfield, *supra* note 87, at 678–83; W. Hamilton Bryson, *The History of Legal Education in Virginia,* in THE LEGAL PROFESSION, *supra* note 81, at 153; Croft, *supra* note 80, at 1285–86.

89. STEVENS, *supra* note 80, at 41.

90. *See* DAVID LANDON, COUNTRY LAWYERS 51–52 (1982); Maxwell Bloomfield, *Law vs. Politics: The Self-Image of the American Bar,* in THE LEGAL PROFESSION, *supra* note 81, at 101; Farmer, *supra* note 87, at 293.

91. *See* Chapters 3 & 4. The so-called *Historians' Briefs* were content simply to assert, without any discussion of the evidence, that abortion was not a crime at common law. *Amicus Brief of 250 American Historians in support of Appellants in* Planned Parenthood of Southeastern Pennsylvania v. Casey, [505 U.S. Ct. 833 (1992)] ("*Casey Historians' Brief*"), at 5; *Amicus Brief of 281 American Historians supporting Appellees in* Webster v. Reproductive Health Services [492 U.S. 490 (1989)] ("*Webster Historians' Brief*"), reprinted at 11 WOMEN'S RTS. L. RPTR. 163, 170 (1989), and in 8 DOCUMENTARY HISTORY OF THE LEGAL ASPECTS OF ABORTION IN THE UNITED STATES: WEBSTER V. REPRODUCTIVE HEALTH SERVICES 107 (Roy Mersky & Gary Hartman eds. 1990) ("DOCUMENTARY HISTORY") (specific pagination will be given only to the version in the *Women's Rts. L. Rptr.*). Donald Judges, even while discussing *Mills v. Commonwealth,* 13 Pa. 630 (1850), the leading case contrary to his view, claimed that "nearly all" the early American cases found that pre-quickening abortion was not a crime at common law. DONALD JUDGES, HARD CHOICES, LOST VOICES 98–100 (1993).

92. *Crime before quickening:* State v. Reed, 45 Ark. 333 (1885); Lamb v. State, 10 A. 208 (Md. 1887); State v. Slagle, 83 N.C. 630 (1880); Mills v. Commonwealth, 13 Pa. 630 (1850). *No crime before quickening:* Mitchell v. Commonwealth, 78 Ky. 204 (1879); Smith v. State, 33 Me. 48, 57 (1851); Commonwealth v. Parker, 50 Mass. (9 Met.) 263 (1845); Commonwealth v. Bangs, 9 Mass. 387 (1812); State v. Cooper, 22 N.J.L. 52 (1849).

93. See Chapter 7, at notes 161–204.

that the primary focus was on the protection of fetal life, with other concerns — such as the protection of maternal health or the elimination of competing professions — being secondary at best.[94] The legal profession, both in England and in America, subscribed to the same concerns. Thus throughout the nineteenth century, lawyers, legislators, and judges all expressed concern over the rising incidence of abortion as a threat to human life.

The codifiers of the abortion laws occasionally were explicit that they were both aware of and concerned about the apparent increase of the incidence of the practice. Lord Ellenborough sounded the alarm over a rising incidence of abortion in the preamble to his famous act.[95] While there are few explicit statements to that effect in the legislative histories of the earlier American statutes, the drafters of the 1860 codification of the common law of crimes in Pennsylvania explained their inclusion of a prohibition of attempted abortion (not a common law crime) in these words: "This section, it is hoped, may tend to put a stop to a crime of too frequent occurrence."[96] The Pennsylvania codification included three sections relating to abortion and or the concealment of a death of an infant. The first recognized as a crime any abortion or attempted abortion resulting in the death of the woman or of a quick child; the second recognized as a crime any attempted abortion even if neither mother nor child died; and the third reaffirmed that concealing the death of an illegitimate child was a felony even without proof of murder.[97] Although there is no evidence that their expression of concern about a rising incidence of abortion was derived from the preamble to *Lord Ellenborough's Act,* the phrasing is virtually identical. Historian James Mohr quoted the Pennsylvania codifiers' statement, but neither noted its parallel to the preamble to *Lord Ellenborough's Act* nor saw any significance to it other than as confirmation of his dubious surmise that abortion was as common as childbirth.[98] Barely five years later, noted anti-abortion crusader Dr. Horatio Robinson Storer expressed himself in much the same vein:

> The…crime of abortion also dates back through all history, like every other form of fruit of wickedness, originating in those deeply lying passions coeval with the existence of mankind. Till of late, however, even physicians, who from time to time have accidentally become cognizant of an isolated instance, have supposed or hoped (and here the wish was father to the thought), that the evil was of slight and trivial extent, and therefore, and undoubtedly with the feeling that a thing so frightful and so repugnant to every instinct should be ignored, the profession have, until within a few years, preserved an almost unbroken silence upon the subject.[99]

Storer's comments are more tentative in part because he apparently had not undertaken an historical investigation into the possibilities of abortion in earlier times. Like so many modern commentators, he assumed that if people in his time knew how to do the procedure, then people in prior times must have known how to do so as well. Nonetheless, Storer does tell us that doctors "till of late" supposed that abortion was a rare event and something about which they need not be concerned. If Storer had undertaken the necessary historical research and experimented with the techniques available even a few decades earlier he would have found that this supposition was based on far more than a mere hope.

---

94. See Chapter 6, at notes 213–331, and Chapter 7, at notes 205–337.

95. *Lord Ellenborough's Act,* 43 Geo. III ch. 58, *preamble* (1803). *See* Chapter 5, at notes 149–52.

96. Pa. Daily Legis. Rec. no. 19, at 151 (Jan. 27, 1860).

97. 1860 Pa. Laws No. 374, tit. VI, §§ 87, 88, at 404–05, reprinted in Quay, *supra* note 33, at 507. Pennsylvania subsequently eliminated the quickening distinction. Pa. Stat. Ann. tit. 18, §§ 4718–4720 (1945), *reprinted in* Quay, *supra,* at 506–07.

98. Mohr, *supra* note 5, at 202.

99. Storer, Why Not?, *supra* note 35, at 17.

In 1901, James Pearce, a Maryland judge, clearly delineated the reasons driving the anti-abortion legislation in terms that Lord Ellenborough, the Pennsylvania codifiers, and Horatio Storer would have accepted. Judge Pearce's opinion in *Worthington v. State* noted the rising incidence of abortion and attributed the rise to the changing technology of abortions:

> It is common knowledge that death is not now the usual, nor, indeed, the always probable, consequence of an abortion. The death of the mother, doubtless, more frequently resulted in the days of rude surgery, when the character and properties of powerful drugs were but little known, and the control over their application more limited. But, in these days of advanced surgery and marvelous medical science and skill, operations are performed and powerful drugs administered by skillful and careful men without danger to the life of the patient. Indeed, it is this comparative immunity from danger to the woman which has doubtless led to great increase of the crime, to the establishment of a class of educated professional abortionists, and to the enactment of the severe statutes almost everywhere found to prevent and punish the offense.[100]

Judge Pearce tells us here that changing medical technology encouraged women to undergo dangerous, albeit no longer suicidal, procedures to rid themselves of unwanted pregnancies. Other courts reached the same conclusion at about the same time.[101]

The court opinions suggest that the abortion statutes were designed, at least in part, to protect women from taking foolish risks by undergoing what were becoming increasingly common procedures. All nineteenth-century surgery was dangerous for the same reasons as for intrusion abortions (principally shock and infection), yet only for abortion were social or other pressures likely to induce a woman to undergo the procedure without an already existing risk to life or limb. Abortion statutes thus can be seen, as Judge Pearce notes, as a response to the premature application of new medical technologies,[102] affirming that intrusion abortions were as criminal as injury or ingestion techniques.

The defendant in *Worthington* had been convicted of manslaughter after the woman died, but argued that the verdict was improper on the grounds that the death of a woman from an abortion must be prosecuted as murder and not as manslaughter.[103] Judge Pearce, however, noted that the prosecution of abortions, continuing even as the danger to women decreased, was directed at protecting the life of the unborn child rather than the life of the woman:

> The woman takes her life in her hands when she submits to an abortion, be she wife or maid, but her death is no necessary element in the procuring of an abortion; and the application of the harsh rule here contended for would have no effect in the repression of that abhorrent crime, which can only be efficiently dealt with by severity in the enactment and administration of the law punishing the attempt upon the life of the unborn child.... The corpus delicti of the offense of abortion is the destruction of the unborn infant....[104]

The new orthodoxy of abortion history would have it that courts and other manifestations of the legal profession were actively indifferent to the life of the unborn child. The fathers of the

---

100. Worthington v. State, 48 A. 355, 356–57 (Md. 1901).

101. Wilson v. Commonwealth, 60 S.W. 400 (Ky. 1901); Moore v. State, 40 S.W. 287 (Tex. Crim. 1897). *See also* Nash v. Meyer, 31 P.2d 273, 277 (Idaho 1934) (no evidence that legal abortions were safer than illegal ones).

102. *See also* State v. Gedicke, 43 N.J.L. 86, 96 (1881); Moore v. State, 40 S.W. 287 (Tex. Crim. 1897). *See generally* J. KEOWN, ABORTION, DOCTORS AND THE LAW 12–48 (1988); Joseph Dellapenna, *The History of Abortion: Technology, Morality, and Law*, 40 U. PITT. L. REV. 359, 392–96, 400–01 (1979).

103. This proposition had been adopted by a court in *Commonwealth v. Parker*, 50 Mass. (9 Met.) 263 (1845).

104. *Worthington*, 48 A. at 357.

new orthodoxy, Cyril Means, jr., and James Mohr focused on the passage in *State v. Murphy*[105] in which the court stated that the statutory crime in that state was directed solely at protecting the mother's health.[106] They not only ignored numerous cases from other states that indicated the purpose of their statutes to be the protection of fetal life, they both simply ignored the language in *Murphy* (actually quoted by Mohr) in which the court stated that the statute served to protect maternal life because the common-law crime of abortion, which continued as before, was directed at protecting fetal life.[107] Mohr even told us that the New Jersey statute construed in *Murphy* was not directed at well-done abortions before quickening as much as at the faulty practice of medicine—even though he had told us only three pages earlier that the statute had made it a crime even to attempt or advise an abortion at any stage of gestation.[108]

Judge Pearce's opinion is enough to disprove the claimed judicial indifference to fetal life. There is moreover considerable evidence from many sources to substantiate Pearce's conclusions, including nineteen states that made abortion a crime for the mother as well as for the abortionist.[109] The evidence then is consistent and unequivocal that concern over a rising incidence of abortion drove the nineteenth-century legislation directed at abortion even though there is reason to believe that abortion in absolute terms was not truly common until late in the century.[110] And the concern that largely drove the greater legal attention to abortion was a belief that abortions killed children—albeit unborn children, but children nonetheless.

At the time Lord Ellenborough, the Pennsylvania codifiers, Horatio Storer, or Judge Pearce wrote, no one had yet undertaken thorough research into the history of abortion and abortion laws. The great English historian of the common law, Sir James Fitzjames Stephen, felt free to pass over abortion in virtual silence, describing such crimes as possessing "no special interest."[111] On our side of the Atlantic, even as great a legal historian as Oliver Wendell Holmes, jr., apparently had access to fewer sources than Cyril Means, jr., at least judging from his one extended meditation on the subject in *Dietrich v. Inhabitants of Northampton.*[112] Even without a careful historical study, however, the authors of the century's two leading American treatises on the law of crimes (Joel Prentiss Bishop and Francis Wharton) both concluded that abortion at any stage of pregnancy was a common law crime.

In the late nineteenth and early twentieth centuries, Bishop and Wharton were the "two most frequently cited American writers" on substantive criminal law.[113] Each left us an extended discussion of abortion, including analysis of the leading nineteenth-century cases for and against their view, and their reasons for favoring the view that abortion was a crime at common law even before quickening. Their analyses are worth quoting at length as they sum up the tenor of legal opinion around the time the abortion statutes were adopted. They attempted to create a systematic and coherent, that is intellectually defensible, body of rules to govern the substantive criminal law of abortion just as they did for any other criminal law topic. Each incorporated up-

---

105. 27 N.J.L. 112, 114–15 (1858).
106. MOHR, *supra* note 31, at 137–38; Cyril Means, jr., *The Phoenix of Abortional Freedom: Is a Penumbral Right or Ninth-Amendment Right About to Arise from the Nineteenth-Century Legislative Ashes of a Fourteenth-Century Common-Law Liberty?*, 17 N.Y.L.F. 335, 389–90 (1971) ("Means II"); Means I, *supra* note 54, at 452, 507. *See also* Chapter 6, at notes 194–206.
107. 27 N.J.L. at 114, quoted in Chapter 6, at note 202.
108. MOHR, *supra* note 5, at 135, 138.
109. See Chapter 6, at notes 293–324.
110. See Chapter 7, at notes 161–203.
111. 3 JAMES FITZJAMES STEPHEN, HISTORY OF THE CRIMINAL LAW OF ENGLAND 117–18 (1883). *See* Chapter 1, at notes 53–58.
112. 138 Mass. 14 (1884). See Chapter 10, at notes 74–185.
113. WILLIAM BURDICK, THE LAW OF CRIMES (1946).

to-date medical knowledge in their attempt to systematize legal theory and to codify legal practice that represented the best of the professionalizing impulse. First is fairly brief discussion of
the question by Joel Prentiss Bishop:[114]

> § 386. Whether, before the foetus has quickened, an abortion procured with the
> mother's consent is an offence at the common law, the English books do not distinctly
> inform us; and the question for England has long been settled by statute in the affirma-
> tive. In this country, the tribunals of some of the States have decided in the negative;
> holding, that, until the woman is quick with child, if she consents, no indictment lies at
> the common law,—though, if she does not consent, the act is an aggravated assault.[115]
> The Pennsylvania court, however, discarded this doctrine of the necessity of a quicken-
> ing; and the learned judge who delivered the opinion remarked with great force: "It is
> not the murder of a living child which constitutes the offence, but the destruction of
> gestation by wicked means against nature. The moment the womb is instinct with em-
> bryo life, and gestation has begun, the crime may be perpetrated."[116] If we look at the
> reason of the law, we shall prefer the Pennsylvania doctrine; because the public and pri-
> vate mischiefs are the same, whether the abortion takes place just before or just after the
> first movings of the coming human existence are perceptible to the expectant mother.
> The phrase, "quick with child," has been defined to mean, that the woman has felt the
> child move within her;[117] and a distinction between this expression and "with quick
> child," once taken by a learned judge,[118] has been discarded.[119]

Bishop's position is particularly revealing of the attitudes of the legal profession in the middle
and later years of the nineteenth century. Bishop devoted himself to writing about the law, even
giving up his law practice to write full-time on legal subjects. He contributed not only his influential studies of criminal law and practice, but also the most influential studies of the law of domestic relations of the time.[120] He was widely recognized as one of the leading legal scholars of
his time.[121] When the University of Bern in Switzerland awarded medals to distinguished scholars to celebrate the university's fiftieth anniversary, Bishop was the only American honored. He
was, the University of Bern declared, among those "who by their learning and their works rendered great service to their land and to the science of law."[122] Despite Bishop's intellectual
achievements, legal historian Stephen Siegel has concluded that Bishop, a man with little formal
education who had risen from a birth in poverty, was more representative in his thinking of the
average lawyer than the upper class lawyers who were the faculty at the prestigious university law
schools and the judges on the state and federal supreme courts.[123]

---

114. 1 JOEL PRENTISS BISHOP, CRIMINAL LAW § 386 (2nd ed. 1858).

115. [Renumbered footnote in the original] Commonwealth v. Parker, 9 Metc. 263; Commonwealth v.
Bangs, 9 Mass. 387; The State v. Cooper, 2 Zab. 52.

116. [Renumbered footnote in original] Mills v. Commonwealth, 1 Harris, Pa. 631, 633, opinion by Coulter, J.

117. [Renumbered footnote in original] Goldsmith's Case, 3 Camp. 76; Reg. v. Phillips, 3 Camp. 76.

118. [Renumbered footnote in original] Reg. v. Wycherley, 8 Car. & P. 262; and see this case for an interesting note by the reporter, showing, on medical authority, that "the popular idea of quick or not quick with
child is founded in error."

119. [Renumbered footnote in original] The State v. Cooper, 2 Zab. 52, 57; and see the authorities there
cited; also Rex v. Russell, 1 Moody, 356, 360. See The State v. Smith, 32 Maine, 369.

120. See generally GROSSBERG, supra note 20, at 21–24.

121. Note, Mr. Bishop as a Law Writer, 21 CENT. L.J. 81 (1885). See also A.W. Brian Simpson, The Rise and
Fall of the Legal Treatise: Legal Principles and the Forms of Legal Literature, 48 U. CHI. L. REV. 632, 673–74
(1981).

122. Joel Bishop, Joel Prentiss Bishop, 20 CENT. L.J. 321, 322 (1885); Note, A Deserved Tribute, 18 AM. L.
REV. 853, 854 (1884); Stephen Siegel, Joel Bishop's Orthodoxy, 13 LAW & HIST. REV. 215, 215 (1995).

123. Siegel, supra note 122, at 217–18, 252–58.

Bishop was born on a farm in upstate New York in 1814. After an early career as an active abolitionist and journalist, he read the law from 1842 to 1844, and then entered into a successful practice in Boston.[124] His writings were so successful that he abandoned the practice of law after about 10 years for full-time scholarship and involvement in the social issues of the day.[125] His highly innovative writings on contracts, family law and on the "new" criminal law were suffused with a deep sense of morality and justice which only added to his fame and regard.[126]

Harvard shunned Bishop in favor of the upper-class legal theorist Oliver Wendell Holmes, jr., although Bishop lived just blocks from the Harvard campus.[127] Harvard's attitude exemplifies the prevailing class bias and arguably contributed to Bishop's relatively obscurity today compared to his prominence during his life. Harvard, of course, has a long exhibited a strong class bias in the realm of ideas.[128] Bishop's willingness to consider the moral dimension of law contributed to the Harvard's determination to ignore him, for Harvard's faculty then was intent on excluding all concerns regarding morality from the study and practice of law.[129]

Bishop, in fact, anticipated Holmes' work in several respects. Bishop was the first of the two to argue that one studies law in order to predict what courts will do.[130] Bishop also was the first of the two to observe that judges decide cases on the base of hunches that are only dimly articulated.[131] And Bishop originated the theory that the common law is founded on experience and not on logic or theory.[132] That Holmes, the elite Harvard-connected judge, did not acknowledge Bishop as a precursor, let alone an influence, could be attributed to Holmes' ego (he rarely cited any contemporary scholar) or to the general refusal of the Harvard crowd to recognize Bishop as significant. That Holmes might not have read Bishop is extremely unlikely.

Judging from his writings, Bishop was in the mainstream of the classical legal theory then dominant in American law.[133] The role of natural or revealed law was actually quite small in Bishop's writings, for such vague general notions yield few principles or rules from which one can derive decisions in actual cases—in contrast with the case precedents, with their commonly recurring fact patterns, that he exhaustively accumulated in his books.[134] In contrast, Christo-

---

124. *Id.* at 218–19. *See generally* Charles Bishop, *Joel Prentiss Bishop, LL.D.,* 36 Am. L. Rev. 1 (1902); Bishop, *supra* note 122; Note, *Death of Joel Prentiss Bishop,* 23 Nat. Corp. Rptr. 326 (1901).

125. *See, e.g.,* Joel Prentiss Bishop, The Common Law and Codification (1888) ("Bishop, Codification"); Joel Prentiss Bishop, Secession and Slavery (1864); Joel Prentiss Bishop, Strikes and their Related Questions (1888); Joel Prentiss Bishop, Thoughts for These Times (1863).

126. *See, e.g.,* Joel Prentiss Bishop, Commentaries on the Law of Contracts 1–6 (1887) ("Bishop, Contracts"); Bishop, *supra* note 114, at 1–2; Joel Prentiss Bishop, Commentaries on Non-Contracts Law 33–37 (1889) ("Bishop, Non-Contracts"). *See generally* Siegel, *supra* note 122, at 220–21, 232–59.

127. Siegel, *supra* note 122, at 215–16.

128. Gordon, *supra* note 85, at 1255, 1258, 1260.

129. *See generally* LaPiana, *supra* note 83, at 55–58, 77, 157, 169.

130. *Compare* Bishop, Contracts, *supra* note 126, at x, *and* Joel Prentiss Bishop, Commentaries on the Law of Marriage and Divorce vii (1852), *with* Oliver Wendell Holmes, jr., *The Path of the Law,* 10 Harv. L. Rev. 457, 457–48, 461, 465 (1897).

131. *Compare* Bishop, Non-Contracts, *supra* note 126, at 33–35, *with* Oliver Wendell Holmes, jr., The Common Law 1, 127 (Mark Howe ed. 1963) (original date 1881).

132. *Compare* Bishop, Contracts, *supra* note 126, at 171, *and* Bishop, Non-Contracts, *supra* note 126, at 612–13, *with* Holmes, *supra* note 131, at 77–78.

133. On the contours of classical legal thought in the late nineteenth century, see Horwitz II, *supra* note 83, at 9–63; LaPiana, *supra* note 83, at 100–03, 110–31, 136–37, 146–47; Thomas Grey, *Langdell's Orthodoxy,* 45 U. Pitt. L. Rev. 1 (1983); Hoeflich, *supra* note 83; Roscoe Pound, *Mechanical Jurisprudence,* 8 Colum. L. Rev. 605 (1908); Stephen Siegel, *Historicism in Late Nineteenth-Century Constitutional Thought,* 1990 Wis. L. Rev. 1431, 1515–47; Siegel, *supra* note 122, at 221–25.

134. LaPiana, *supra* note 83, at 60.

pher Columbus Langdell, the founder and leader of the Harvard crowd, cited very few cases, and then only those that supported his vision of the law.[135]

Bishop believed that law was found from examining actual decisions of courts in order to induce the principles that guided the resolution of disputes, rather than *a priori* from moral or other external roots.[136] Bishop was, in a word, a positivist.[137] But he was a positivist with a twist. Bishop strongly supported the role of judges as the architects of a common law that flexibly reflected the role of reason in society, and opposed legislative reforms as the replacement of reason by mere command.[138] He was also deeply skeptical of the ability to change human behavior through law, arguing that "experience proves that the habits make the law, and not the law habits; and that it is unnatural, and it tends to disturb to disturb the just repose of the community to press forward a reform in either of these directions much in advance of the other."[139] A good many American jurists in the later years of the nineteenth century agreed with Bishop in opposing codification.[140] This then prevalent view explains why the common law was not thoroughly codified in the nineteenth century at about the same time that the Romano-Germanic civil law largely was. Had his view prevailed earlier in the century, the history of abortion law in England and America might read very differently.

Yet given Bishop's background as an abolitionist and journalist as well as lawyer and scholar, he did not hesitate to indicate that he thought a particular rule of law was not moral.[141] Bishop's approach in this regard contrasted sharply with most other legal writers in his time. They generally insisted that "they were merely describing American law, but [they] never seemed to find instances of conflict between good morals and existing law."[142] Bishop's willingness to express his understanding of the moral sense of the community does not, of course, mean that he correctly accessed the public's sentiments regarding abortion, but it does suggest that be believed that the law he favored did reflect prevailing social mores.

Francis Wharton's analysis of the question of abortion was more extensive and detailed, but the analysis displayed similar concerns and reached similar conclusions:[143]

> § 1220. There is no doubt that at common law the destruction of an infant unborn is a high misdemeanor, and at an early period it seems to have been deemed murder.[144]

---

135. *Id.* at 69. On the formative influences in Langdell's life, see Bruce Kimball, *Young Christopher Langdell, 1826–1854: The Formation of an Educational Reformer,* 52 J. LEGAL EDUC. 189 (2002).

136. *See, e.g.,* 1 BISHOP, *supra* note 114, at ix.

137. Siegel, *supra* note 122, at 227–32.

138. BISHOP, CODIFICATION, *supra* note 125, at 3; 1 JOEL PRENTISS BISHOP, NEW COMMENTARIES ON THE LAW OF MARRIAGE AND DIVORCE 181, 420 (1891); Joel Prentiss Bishop, *The Common Law as a System of Reasoning—How and Why Essential in Good Government; What Its Perils, and How Averted,* 22 AM. L. REV. 1 (1888); Joel Prentiss Bishop, *Law in the United States,* 3 AM. L. REG. 60 (1854); Joel Bishop, *Legal Principles, No. VII,* 3 AM. L. REG. 634 (1855). Bishop wrote a series of articles on "legal principles" in 1854 and 1855; these are summarized in LaPIANA, *supra* note 83, at 527–28.

139. 1 JOEL PRENTISS BISHOP, THE LAW OF MARRIED WOMEN 74–75 (1871).

140. *See, e.g.,* ALBERT MATTHEWS, THOUGHTS ON CODIFICATION OF THE COMMON LAW 9 (3rd ed. 1882); William Ivins, *Is the Common Law a Proper Subject for Codification?,* N.Y. ST. B. ASS'N REP. 195 (1879); Isaac Redfield, *The Responsibilities of the Legal Profession,* 10 AM. L. REG. N.S. 547 (1871); George Smith, *The True Method of Legal Education,* 24 AM. L. REV. 216 (1890); Shelton Viele, *Is the Common Law a Proper Subject for Codification?,* N.Y. ST. B. ASS'N REP. 195 (1879). Redfield was Chief Justice of Vermont when he wrote his article; Ivins and Viele were first and second place winners in an essay competition sponsored by the New York State Bar. *See generally* LaPIANA, *supra* note 83, at 530–36.

141. *See, e.g.,* 1 BISHOP, *supra* note 114, at 7 (discussing the doctrine of *caveat emptor*).

142. Siegel, *supra* note 122, at 225 n.41.

143. 1 FRANCIS WHARTON, THE CRIMINAL LAW OF THE UNITED STATES §§ 1220–1230 (5th rev. ed. 1861).

144. [Renumbered footnote in original] 1 Russ. on Cr. 671; 1 Vesey, 86; 3 Coke's Inst. 50; 1 Hawk. c. 13, s. 16; 1 Hale, 434; 1 East, P.C. 90; 3 Chitty C.L. 798.

If the child dies subsequently to birth from wounds received in the womb, it is clearly homicide,[145] even though the child is still attached to the mother by the umbilical cord.[146] It has been said that it is not an indictable offence to administer a drug to a woman, and thereby to procure an abortion, unless the mother is *quick* with child,[147] though such a distinction, it is submitted, is neither in accordance with the result of medical experience,[148] nor with the principles of the common law.[149] The civil rights of an infant in *ventre sa mere* are equally respected at every period of gestation; and it is clear that no matter at how early a stage he may be appointed executor,[150] is capable of taking as a legatee,[151] or under a marriage settlement,[152] may take specifically under a general devise, as a "child;"[153] and may obtain an injunction to stay waste.[154] Such also, was the effect of a decision on the direct point in Pennsylvania in 1845.[155]

§ 1221. Since the publication of the first edition of this work, the position taken in the text has been the subject of much discussion. [Here follows an extended discussion of *Commonwealth v. Parker,* 50 Mass. (9 Met.) 263 (1845), *State v. Cooper,* 22 N.J.L. 53 (1849), and *Smith v. State,* 33 Me. 48, 57 (1851), all of which disagreed with Wharton's conclusion that pre-quickening abortion was a crime at common law, of the medical authorities on human gestation, and a French treatise on *Médecine Légale* dealing with the crime of abortion.]

§ 1226. It appears, then, that quickening is a mere circumstance in the physiological history of the foetus, which indicates neither the commencement of a new stage of existence, nor an advance from one stage to another—that it is uncertain in its periods, sometimes coming at three months, sometimes at five, sometimes not at all—and that it is dependent so entirely upon foreign influences as to make it a very incorrect index, and one on which no practitioner can depend, of the progress of pregnancy. There is as much vitality, in a physical point of view, on one side of quickening as on the other, and in a social and moral point of view, the infant is as much entitled to protection, and society is as likely to be injured by its destruction, a week before it quickens as a week afterwards. But if the common law in making foeticide penal, had in view the great mischief which would result from its qualified toleration, *e.g.,* the removal of the chief restraint upon illicit intercourse, and the shock which would thereby be sustained by the institution of marriage and its incidents—we can have no authority now for withdrawing any epoch in gestation from the operation of the principle. Certainly the restraints upon illicit intercourse are equally removed—the inducements to marriage are equally diminished—the delicacy of the woman is as effectually destroyed—no matter what may be the period chosen for the operation. Acting under these views, the legislatures of Massachusetts and New Jersey, in order to fill up the supposed gap, passed acts

---

145. [Renumbered footnote in original] R. <u>v.</u> Senior, 1 Mood. C.C. 36; 3 Inst. 50; see ante, § 942.

146. [Renumbered footnote in original] R. <u>v.</u> Trilloe, 2 Moody, C.C. 13.

147. [Renumbered footnote in original] Com. *v.* Bangs, 9 Mass. 387.

148. [Renumbered footnote in original] W. & S. Med. Jur. § 344-5. Guy's Med. Juris. tit. Abortion; 1 Beck. 172, 192; Lewis, C.L. 10.

149. [Renumbered footnote in original] 1 Russ. on Crim. 661; 1 Vesey, 86; 3 Coke's Inst. 50; 1 Hawk. c. 13, s. 16; Bracton, l.3, c. 21.

150. [Renumbered footnote in original] Bac. Ab. tit. Infants.

151. [Renumbered footnote in original] 2 Vernon, 710.

152. [Renumbered footnote in original] Swift *v.* Duffield, 6 Seg. & Rawle, 38; Doe *v.* Clark, 2 H. Bl. 399; 2 Ves. jr. 673; Thelluson *v.* Woodford, 4 Vesey, 340.

153. [Renumbered footnote in original] Fearne, 429.

154. [Renumbered footnote in original] 2 Vernon, 710.

155. [Renumbered footnote in original] Com. *v.* Demain, &c., 6 Penn. Law Jour. 29; Brightly, 441.

making ante-quickening-foeticide individually penal. If, however, as has been argued, no such gap exists, it will be worth while for the courts of those States which have not legislated on the subject, to consider how far an exploded notion in physics is to be allowed to suspend the operation of a settled doctrine of the common law.

§ 1227. It is remarkable that both in Massachusetts and New Jersey, a leading English case on this point was not referred to, where in an investigation before a jury of matrons, Gurney, B., said, after taking medical counsel, "Quick with child, is having conceived; with *quick* child is when the child is quickened."[156] This view disposes of all the common law authorities against the indictability of the offence.

[Wharton concluded his discussion with a brief comment on certain points about framing an indictment and proving the elements of the crime.]

# Nineteenth Century Prosecutions of Abortion

*I still haven't found what I'm looking for.*

—U2[157]

Discussions such as those of Bishop and Wharton could hardly take the place of precedent or statute if the law relating to abortion was to be codified and clarified. By 1861, 70 percent of the American states (with 85 percent of the American population) had adopted statutes.[158] By 1895 abortion was clearly a serious crime in every state,[159] but this was hardly an innovation. The statutes settled the somewhat uncertain law of abortion, making clear that the crime related to every technique for abortion and at every stage of pregnancy, solemnly reaffirming social policy in the face of changing social behavior. But legislators and scholars provide a rather abstract form of law. The "living" law is what happens in actual courtrooms and in people's lives; it is to the living law that we now turn.

Prosecutions began to appear with some frequency in the judicial records after 1840, just as one might expect given the slow but steady rise in the incidence of abortion during the same period. Generally, however, these prosecutions resulted in acquittal or in conviction for lesser crimes such as attempted abortion.[160] Scholars and others—on both sides of the abortion controversy—have inferred from this pattern that jurists or jurors were and are tolerant of the crime.[161] Yet there were convictions for abortion, and not just for lesser crimes, sometimes in-

---

156. [Renumbered footnote in original] R. *v.* Wycherley, 8 C. & P. 265.

157. Paul Hewson (Bono of U2), *I Still Haven't Found What I'm Looking for* (1987).

158. Dellapenna, *supra* note 102, at 389.

159. See the statutes collected in Chapter 7, at notes at notes 9–15. *See generally* Dellapenna, *supra* note 102, at 389–407; Quay, *supra* note 33; James Witherspoon, *Reexamining* Roe: *Nineteenth-Century Abortion Statutes and the Fourteenth Amendment*, 17 St. Mary's L.J. 29, 34–36 (1985).

160. Gordon, *supra* note 29, at 57; Mohr, *supra* note 5, at 48–49, 120–22, 125, 136–38.

161. Robert Bell, Social Deviance: A Substantive Analysis 126 (1971); Brookes, *supra* note 37, at 27–29, 35–39; James Burtchaell, Rachel Weeping and Other Essays on Abortion 244 (1982); Davis, *supra* note 56, at 103; John D'Emilio & Estelle Freedman, Intimate Matters: A History of Sexuality in America 66 (1988); Marian Faux, Roe v. Wade: The Untold Story of the Landmark Supreme Court Decision that Made Abortion Legal 88 (1988); Paul Gebhard et al., Pregnancy, Birth and Abortion 192 (1958); Grossberg, *supra* note 20, at 165–66, 181; Fowler Harper & Jerome Skolnick, Problems of the Family 184 (1962); Graber, *supra* note 72, at 45; Luker, *supra* note 46, at 53; Patricia Miller, The Worst of Times 132 (1993); Reagan, *supra* note 38, at 116; Schur, *supra* note 72, at 38; Smith-Rosenberg,

volving well-established allopathic physicians. Thus Dr. William Graves of Lowell, Massachusetts, was convicted in September, 1837.[162] Historians of the new orthodoxy either ignore such convictions altogether or dismiss them as insignificant when compared to the general tendency not to convict.

Still, acquittals or dismissals do predominate among reported cases.[163] No one, thus far, has actually dug into the unpublished judicial archives to determine whether those cases for which a judge's opinion or similar document happened to be published in the nineteenth century are actually representative of what was happening in the larger number of cases for which no report was published. For example, in one case that James Mohr relied on as demonstrating the purported social acceptance of abortion, the only published document is the defense summation.[164] Mohr didn't tell us what the outcome of the case was; apparently no one knows.

Assuming that the reported cases are representative, before making definite judgments about jury nullification, one would also like to know how conviction rates for abortion compared with conviction rates for other crimes by or against women, such as homicide, arson, rape, and so on, during the same era.[165] This was an era, after all, when even novelists were beginning to depict trials as generally hamstrung by formal rules of evidence[166]—a favorite theme of fiction ever since.[167] Mohr himself concluded (in a study not focused on abortion) that American juries were "legendarily reluctant to convict in [all] capital cases."[168] Nor should one overlook the punitive effects of police investigations or public disclosure even if no prosecution resulted.[169]

There are serious reasons for concluding that a low conviction rate for abortion in the nineteenth century is not evidence of social or legal tolerance for abortion. Consider, for example, a recent failure to indict a woman for causing the death of her two toddlers run over by a train

---

*supra* note 10, at 220; STORER, CRIMINAL ABORTION, *supra* note 35, at 44, 86, 97, 99; LAURENCE TRIBE, ABORTION: THE CLASH OF ABSOLUTES 35 (1990); WILLIAMS, *supra* note 56, at 206–07; Adelstein, *supra* note 72, at 85; Samuel Buell, Note, *Criminal Abortion Revisited,* 66 N.Y.U. L. REV. 1774, 1795, 1828 (1991); Robert Byrn, *An American Tragedy: The Supreme Court on Abortion,* 41 FORDHAM L. REV. 807, 817–19 (1973); T.R. Forbes, *Early Forensic Medicine in England: The Angus Murder Trial,* 36 J. HIST. MED. 296, 303–05 (1981); Shelley Gavigan, *The Criminal Sanction as It Relates to Human Reproduction: The Genesis of the Statutory Prohibition of Abortion,* 5 J. LEGAL HIST. 20, 20 (1984); Thomas Harris, Note, *A Functional Study of Existing Abortion Laws,* 35 COLUM. L. REV. 87, 90–91 (1935); Michael La Sorte, *Nineteenth-Century Family Planning Practices,* 31 J. PSYCHOHIST. 163, 167–69 (1976); James Mohr, *Patterns of Abortion and the Response of American Physicians, 1790–1930,* in WOMEN AND HEALTH IN AMERICA: HISTORICAL READINGS 117, 120 (Judith Leavitt ed. 1984); Marvin Moore, *Antiquated Abortion Laws,* 20 WASH. & LEE L. REV. 250, 252 (1963); James Ridgeway, *One Million Abortions: Its Your Problem, Sweetheart,* THE NEW REP., Feb. 9, 1963, at 14; Harold Rosen, *The Psychiatric Indications of Abortion: A Case Study in Hypocrisy,* in THERAPEUTIC ABORTION at 72, 92 (Harold Rosen ed. 1954) (this book was reissued in 1967 under the title ABORTION IN AMERICA); James Voyles, *Changing Abortion Laws in the United States,* 7 J. FAM. L. 496, 500 (1967); Witherspoon, *supra* note 158, at 31–32, 56–58; Howard Ziff, *Recent Abortion Law Reforms,* 60 J. CRIM. L. & CRIMINOLOGY 3, 8 (1969). *See also* Constance Backhouse, *Involuntary Motherhood: Abortion, Birth Control and the Law in Nineteenth Century Canada,* 3 WINDSOR Y.B. OF ACCESS TO JUSTICE 61, 82–110 (1983).

162. The transcript is quoted at length in GORDON, *supra* note 29, at 55–56.

163. *See, e.g.,* Horatio Robinson Storer, *Contributions to Obstetric Jurisprudence—Criminal Abortion III: Its Obstacles to Conviction,* 3 N. AM. MEDICO-CHIRURIGICAL REV. 833, 834 (1859) (lamenting that none of the 32 prosecutions for abortion in Massachusetts of which he knew had resulted in conviction).

164. MOHR, *supra* note 5, at 310 nn.19, 20.

165. Compare the conviction patterns for infanticide in England in the sixteenth and seventeenth centuries with those of other serious crimes. *See* Chapter 2, at notes 366–411.

166. *See, e.g.,* J.F. COOPER, THE WAYS OF THE HOUR 469 (1850).

167. *See* Allen Boyer, *Formalism, Realism, and Naturalism: Cross-Currents in American Letters and Law,* 23 CONN. L. REV. 669 (1991).

168. MOHR, *supra* note 76, at 126, 230, 237.

169. REAGAN, *supra* note 38, at 116–17.

after the mother showed traces of drugs in her blood but the prosecution had no means for proving when the drugs had been taken or how the drugs might have affected the mother's behavior at the time of the deaths.[170] Does this failure to indict indicate official tolerance for infanticide? Or could it merely indicate an unwillingness to spend resources on a trial when the prosecution recognized that it could not prove its case?

Criminal abortion by its nature is a highly private activity in which all persons who are capable of speaking are voluntarily (more or less) involved in the crime. This makes abortion an extremely difficult crime to detect and prove.[171] Abortion (and even the fact of pregnancy) was virtually impossible to prove by medical examination in the nineteenth century, unless the abortion seriously injured or killed the mother, and even then it would be difficult to prove.[172] Remember that there simply was no reliable clinical test for pregnancy until 1927.[173] Francis Wharton and Moreton Stillé identified these serious impediments to conviction in 1855:

> The signs of abortion, as obtained by an *examination of the female*, are not very certain in their character. It is seldom, indeed, that an examination of the living female is had, and especially at a period early enough to afford any valuable indications. When abortion occurs in the early months, it leaves but slight and evanescent traces behind it.[174]

A Chicago coroner, John Traeger, noted the problems in 1905 in these terms:

> Notwithstanding the prevalence of the crime there are few accusations or indictments for inducing abortion unless the death of the mother results when of course the indictment is for murder. In the few cases of indictment for producing abortion the action was brought because of the serious injury to the mother. Ordinarily it is very difficult to get satisfactory evidence against a professional abortionist. The relatives or others interested in the case are generally very anxious to prevent any publicity for obvious reasons and even in case of the death of the mother it is frequently impossible to get any member of the family to take action in the matter. Outside parties cannot be expected to interest themselves with such matters which can concern them only in a very indirect way and which would bring them only great annoyance and perhaps place them in a very embarrassing position. This difficulty of securing evidence and initiating an accusation is the reason why the abortion law is so much of a dead letter.[175]

Traeger was not the only person to note that when a woman died, her family might very well prove reluctant to publicize her "disgrace."[176] As attorney Robert Taylor summed the matter up in 1896,

---

170. *Girls' Mother Released in Train Deaths*, PHILA. INQUIRER, Nov. 8, 1997, at A28.

171. *See, e.g.*, Slattery v. People, 76 Ill. 217 (1875); Rhodes v. State, 27 N.E. 866, 867 (Ind. 1891); Commonwealth v. Leach, 30 N.E. 163, 164 (Mass. 1892); People v. Sessions, 26 N.W. 291, 298 (Mich. 1886); People v. Van Zile, 73 Hun. 534 (N.Y. Sup. Ct. 1893); Commonwealth v. W., 3 Pitts. R. 463 (Pa. C.P. 1871). *See generally* BROOKES, *supra* note 37, at 26–29, 34, 37; MOHR, *supra* note 5, at 26, 41–43, 72–73, 124, 138–40, 142, 144; STORER, WHY NOT?, *supra* note 35, at 51–52; FREDERICK TAUSSIG, ABORTION: SPONTANEOUS AND INDUCED 438 (1936); WILLIAMS, *supra* note 56, at 207; D.V Glass, *The Effectiveness of Abortion Legislation in Six Countries*, 2 MOD. L. REV. 97 (Pt.1), 227 (Pt. II) (1938).

172. *See, e.g.*, HORATIO ROBINSON STORER, HENRY INGERSOLL BOWDITCH, & CALVIN ELLIS, SUFFOLK DISTRICT MEDICAL SOCIETY, REPORT OF THE COMMITTEE ON CRIMINAL ABORTION (1857); C.S. Bacon, *The Duty of the Medical Profession in Relation to Criminal Abortion*, 7 ILL. MED. J. 18, 21 (Jan. 1905); John Traeger, *Criminal Abortion as It Comes before the Coroner's Office*, 7 ILL. MED. J. 35 (Jan. 1905). *See generally* GROSSBERG, *supra* note 20, at 183; MOHR, *supra* note 5, at 72; RICKIE SOLINGER, THE ABORTIONIST: A WOMAN AGAINST THE LAW 13–14 (paperback ed. 1996). On the difficulties of proving pregnancy, see Chapter 1, at notes 145–51.

173. THOMAS EDEN & EARDLEY HOLLAND, A MANUAL OF MIDWIFERY 77–78 (7th ed. 1931)

174. FRANCIS WHARTON & MORETON STILLÉ, TREATISE ON MEDICAL JURISPRUDENCE 277 (1855).

175. Traeger, *supra* note 172, at 35. *See also* St. Clair, *supra* note 32.

176. REAGAN, *supra* note 38, at 119, 125–28, 130; Bacon, *supra* note 172, at 21.

Every person involved in the affair…is, for her own sake, pledged to secrecy.…The explanation of the small number of convictions…lies in the secrecy with which this crime in its very nature is committed, and in the fact that such proofs as are attainable rarely do more than cast a strong suspicion of guilt upon the person charged with the offense.[177]

Finally, if abortion were a crime only after quickening, it would be virtually impossible to prove if the mother died for she alone could give evidence regarding whether she had perceived the fetus moving.[178] Those who suggest that how rare it was to obtain a conviction for abortion demonstrates a high degree of social tolerance for the practice simply overlook these difficulties in obtaining a conviction.[179] Given the difficulties involved, what is truly impressive even about the reported cases is how persistent lawyers were in searching out and prosecuting the crime, and how creative judges were in overcoming obstacles to proving the crime.

Prosecutors never abandoned attempts to enforce abortion laws.[180] Many, but not all, of the resulting prosecutions did involve the death or serious injury of the mother. The reported cases from New York illustrate the pattern.[181] Similarly, 37 of 43 abortion cases that reached the Supreme Court of Illinois between 1870 and 1940 involved a woman's death.[182] By the end of the nineteenth century, dying declarations became a central piece of evidence in many prosecutions for abortion, with coroner's inquests providing much of the rest of the evidence needed to convict abortionists.[183] Dr. Leonard Parry, who wrote extensively about abortion early in the twentieth century, concluded that abortions could seldom be prosecuted except if the mother died.[184]

If a conviction were to be obtained without the woman's death, it was imperative to obtain the testimony of the woman who had undergone the abortion. This reality explains the struggles over whether the woman was an accomplice to the crime, and the practice in those states where she was an accomplice of granting her immunity from prosecution.[185] Even so, she was not likely to testify against her abortionist without a change of heart about the abortion (or perhaps a new-found willingness to defy those who might have pressured her into having an abortion she had not wanted).[186] Even if a woman complained to authorities about an abortion, she might not be willing to testify at a trial for any number of reasons. As her word was often the only real

---

177. Robert Taylor, *Why Do Abortions Go Unpunished?*, 9 Am. Medico-Surgical Bull. 453, 453–54 (1896).

178. Williams, *supra* note 56, at 158–59.

179. See the authorities collected *supra* at note 161.

180. *See generally* D'Emilio & Freedman, *supra* note 51, at 66; Grossberg, *supra* note 53, at 166–69; Reagan, *supra* note 54, at 116–18.

181. People v. Van Zile, 38 N.E. 380 (N.Y. 1894); People v. McGonegal, 32 N.E. 616 (N.Y. 1892); People v. Davis, 56 N.Y. 95 (1874); Weed v. People, 56 N.Y. 628 (1874); Lohman v. People, 1 N.Y. 379 (1848) (injury); People v. Flaherty, 218 N.Y.S. 148 (App. Div. 1926); Bradford v. People, 20 Hun. 309 (N.Y. Sup. Ct. 1880); People v. Restell, 3 Hill 289 (N.Y. Sup. Ct. 1842). *See also* Larocque v. Conheim, 87 N.Y.S. 625 (N.Y. Sup. Ct. 1904); Olasky, *supra* note 12, at 154–57, 168.

182. Reagan, *supra* note 38, at 116.

183. *Id.,* at 113–31; Backhouse, *supra* note 161, at 99–103; William Durfor English, *Evidence—Dying Declaration—Preliminary Questions of Fact—Degree of Proof,* 15 B.U. L. Rev. 380, 381–82 (1935). The Supreme Court of Illinois commented on dying declarations in about one-third of the appeals of convictions for abortion-related deaths between 1870 and 1940. Reagan, *supra,* at 297 n.6 *See also* Chapter 11, at notes 391–99.

184. L.A. Parry, Criminal Abortion 41 (1932). *See also* Wilhelm Becker, *The Medical, Ethical, and Forensic Aspects of Fatal Criminal Abortion,* 7 Wis. Med. J. 619, 633 (1909); H.H. Hawkins, *The Colorado Law on Abortion,* 40 JAMA 1096, 1099 (1903). *See generally* Mohr, *supra* note 76, at 121; McLaren, *supra* note 38, at 334–37.

185. *See* Chapter 6, at notes 293–319.

186. *See* Jerome Bates & Edward Zawadski, Criminal Abortion 10 (1964); Davis, *supra* note 56, at 51; Graber, *supra* note 72, at 44–45; Eva Rubin, Abortion, Politics, and the Courts 87 (rev. ed. 1987); Buell, *supra* note 162, at 1789–90; Moore, *supra* note 162, at 252.

evidence, the prosecution's case would collapse. Thus, in *State v. Quinn*,[187] Rose Haughey initially complained to authorities that George Quinn had attempted to abort her but then refused to testify against him at trial. The resulted was an acquittal.

The necessary change of heart leading a woman to testify against an abortionist was most likely if the woman was dying or seriously injured. Many courts created an exception to the hearsay rule in order to admit the dying declarations of women who had had the abortion as evidence against the abortionist.[188] From the beginning, doctors played a central role in obtaining dying declarations, a task that by the middle of the twentieth century some doctors found demeaning or demoralizing.[189] Injury, however, was not an indispensable precursor to prosecution. In fact, in most cases prosecuted in New York and Philadelphia, the mother was not seriously injured as far as one can determine from the reports of the cases.[190] In several cases, there was not even an abortion because the at tempt failed,[191] or because the mother declined to ingest the recommended drug,[192] or even because the woman was not pregnant.[193] (The crime was likely to be only a misdemeanor if there was no pregnancy.)[194]

Nor was prosecutorial zeal a reaction to criticism or pressure from the allopaths. New York prosecutors denounced abortion in the strongest terms at least from the 1840s onward, giving the lie to those who claim that abortion was socially, morally, and legally accepted prior to the American Medical Association's anti-abortion campaign of the later 1850s. The more persistent professional abortionists, if they escaped conviction or were convicted of minor infractions early in their careers, faced repeated police investigations and prosecutions until the law achieved its purpose. In the nineteenth century, the most prominent abortionists, whose activities pro-abortion historians claim demonstrate a lack of public disapproval of their practice, ended up in jail. Philadelphia's Dr. Isaac Hathaway was sentenced to seven years at hard labor years in 1883—

187. 45 A. 544 (Del. 1899).
188. *See, e.g.,* Montgomery v. State, 80 Ind. 338 (1881); State v. Baldwin, 45 N.W. 297 (Iowa 1890); Smith v. State, 33 Me. 48 (Me. 1851); People v. Olmstead, 30 Mich. 431 (1874); State v. Pearce, 57 N.W. 652 (Minn. 1894); People v. Davis, 56 N.Y. 95 (1874); State v. Harper, 35 Ohio St. 78 (1878); Commonwealth v. Keene, 7 Pa. Super. 293 (1898); State v. Dickinson, 41 Wis. 299 (1877). *See also* State v. Carey, 56 A. 632 (Conn. 1904); Commonwealth v. Brown, 121 Mass. 69 (1876); Frazer v. People, 1 Cowen's Crim. 377 (N.Y. Sup. Ct. 1863). *See generally* Chapter 11, at notes 391–98.
189. *See generally* REAGAN, *supra* note 38, at 115–16, 120–24.
190. People v. Blank, 29 N.E.2d 73 (N.Y. 1940); People v. Murphy, 101 N.Y. 126 (1886); People v. Vedder, 98 N.Y. 630 (1885); Evans v. People, 49 N.Y. 86 (1872); Crichton v. People, 1 Cowen's Crim. 454 (N.Y. 1864); People v. Hager, 168 N.Y.S. 182 (App. Div. 1917); People v. Lovell, 242 N.Y.S.2d 958 (Sup. Ct. 1963); People v. Candib, 129 N.Y.S.2d 176 (N.Y. Sup. Ct. 1954); Cobel v. People, 5 Park. Crim. 348 (N.Y. Sup. Ct. 1862); People v. Stockham, 1 Park. Crim. 424 (N.Y. Sup. Ct. 1853); People v. Costello, 1 Denio 83 (N.Y. Sup. Ct. 1845). *See generally* ROGER LANE, VIOLENT DEATH IN THE CITY: SUICIDE, ACCIDENT, AND MURDER IN NINETEENTH CENTURY PHILADELPHIA 93 (1979).
191. Dunn v. People, 29 N.Y. 523 (1864); Frazer v. People, 1 Cowen's Crim. 377 (N.Y. Sup. Ct. 1863). *See also* State v. Reed, 45 Ark. 333 (1885); Dougherty v. People, 1 Colo. 514 (1872); State v. Magnell, 51 A. 606 (Del. 1901); State v. Montgomery, 33 N.W. 143 (Iowa 1887); State v. Fitzgerald, 49 Iowa 260 (1878); Bassett v. State, 41 Iowa 303 (1872); State v. Watson, 1 Kan. 770 (Kan. 1883); Commonwealth v. Morrison, 82 Mass. (16 Gray) 224 (1860); State v. Baldwin, 45 N.W. 297 (Iowa 1890); State v. Owens, 22 Minn. 238 (1875); State v. Van Houten, 37 Mo. 357 (1866); State v. Dean, 85 Mo. App. 473 (1900); State v. Cave, 26 S.W. 503 (Tex. Ct. Crim. App. 1894).
192. People v. Phelps, 30 N.E. 1012 (N.Y. 1892).
193. People v. Axelsen, 119 N.E. 708 (N.Y. 1918). *See* Witherspoon, *supra* note 158, at 57–58. *See also* Rex v. Anonymous, 170 ENG. REP. 1310 (1811); People v. Cummings, 296 P.2d 610 (Cal. Ct. App. 1956); Commonwealth v. Surley, 42 N.E. 502 (Mass. 1895); Commonwealth v. Tibbetts, 32 N.E. 910 (Mass. 1893); Commonwealth v. Follansbee, 29 N.E. 471 (Mass. 1892).
194. Smith v. State, 33 Me. 48, 55 (1851); People v. Abbott, 74 N.W. 529, 530 (Mich. 1898); State v. Emerich, 87 Mo. 110, 116 (1885); State v. Dickenson, 41 Wis. 299, 309–10 (1877).

when he was 83 years old.[195] New York City's Dr. Henry McGonegal was sentenced in 1892 to 14 years after a patient died.[196] If McGonegal's acquittal 30 years earlier is supposed to demonstrate that jury nullification protected abortionists, does his later conviction demonstrates the opposite? Means, who highlighted McGonegal's acquittal,[197] never mentioned the evidence of a strong desire to "get" the abortionist. Nor did he comment on what McGonegal's ultimate conviction might tell us about either popular or official attitudes.

The career of the notorious "Madame Restell" illustrates both the determination of prosecutors to bring abortionists to justice and the difficulties prosecutors had to overcome in order to accomplish the task. Ann Lohman, who operated under the pseudonym of "Madame Restell," was the most notorious professional abortionist in the United States during much of the nineteenth century.[198] She advertised openly and aggressively various abortifacient potions for sale—consistently using euphemisms for the effects to be achieved by her products.[199] We have already examined the fraudulent nature of this advertising in reviewing the career of her husband, Charles Lohman, a printer who operated under the pseudonym "Dr. A.M. Mauriceau."[200] Like her husband, she also falsely claimed a medical education in Europe.[201] Restell (Lohman) even had the temerity to charge her competitors with falsely advertising ineffective "counterfeit pills" under a fraudulent claim of false medical credentials![202]

Pro-abortion historians like to extol Madame Restell as a model of a woman providing a much needed service for women and as demonstrating the openness of abortion practice in the mid-nineteenth century.[203] Historian Linda Gordon, who found Restell's husband to be a paradigm of male exploitation of gullible women through the fraudulent sales of fake abortifacients,[204] failed utterly to make any connection between his practices those Madame Restell. Nor do the feminists extolling her virtues attend to the evidence that she frequently blackmailed her patients, asking them for "loans" under threat of disclosure, sometimes doing so years after the event, all fully understanding that the loan would never be repaid.[205]

Despite the claim that Ann Lohman—Madame Restell—was tolerated by society and by the police, she was prosecuted repeatedly, beginning in 1842.[206] A public demonstration in front of her house in February, 1846, drew as many as a thousand persons (quite a crowd for the time) to

---

195. OLASKY, *supra* note 12, at 170; OLASKY, *supra* note 8, at 34–35, 39.

196. People v. McGonegal, 32 N.E. 616 (N.Y. 1892). *See also* OLASKY, *supra* note 12, at 170–71; OLASKY, *supra* note 8, at 46.

197. Means I, *supra* note 54, at 457–58

198. *See* BRODIE, *supra* note 56, at 229–31; GORDON, *supra* note 29, at 54–58; GROSSBERG, *supra* note 20, at 167; ALAN KELLER, SCANDALOUS LADY: THE LIFE AND TIMES OF MADAME RESTELL, NEW YORK'S MOST FAMOUS ABORTIONIST (1981); MILBAUER & OBRENTZ, *supra* note 46, at 138–42; MOHR, *supra* note 5, at 48–53, 88–89, 94, 96, 125–28, 182, 199; OLASKY, *supra* note 12, at 150–52, 158–61; OLASKY, *supra* note 8, at 4–13. Indeed, Restell's notoriety was such that her prominence as a "female physician" tarnished the opportunities for more legitimate women doctors. *See* VIRGINIA DRACHMAN, HOSPITAL WITH A HEART: WOMEN DOCTORS AND THE PARADOX OF SEPARATISM AT THE NEW ENGLAND HOSPITAL, 1862–1969, at 34 (1984).

199. *See particularly* OLASKY, *supra* note 8, at 4–8, 14–16.

200. *See* Chapter 6, at notes 242–44, and Chapter 7, at notes 140–49. Some argue that the false "Mauriecau" was her brother rather than her husband.

201. OLASKY, *supra* note 8, at 8.

202. *Id.* at 15–16.

203. BRODIE, *supra* note 56, at 229; GORDON, *supra* note 29, at 64; GROSSBERG, *supra* note 20, at 167; KELLER, *supra* note 198, at 28; MILBAUER & OBRENTZ, *supra* note 46, at 138–39; MOHR, *supra* note 5, at 48–49.

204. GORDON, *supra* note 29, at 165.

205. OLASKY, *supra* note 12, at 159, quoting EDWARD MARTIN, THE SECRETS OF THE GREAT CITY 430 (1868). "Edward Martin" apparently was a pseudonym for journalist James McCabe. *See* OLASKY, *supra*, at 159 n.57.

206. People v. Restell, 3 Hill 289 (N.Y. Sup. Ct. 1842).

protest Restell (Lohman) as a "wholesale female strangler."[207] Subsequently arrested, a prosecuting attorney at the trial in 1847 described her as "one who disgraces her sex, forgetting that she is a mother, disregarding at once divine providence and human laws, who has amassed a fortune in the daily perpetuation of a crime which violates and annuls one of the most sacred ordinances of Almighty God."[208] The prosecutor also was able to find, at last, a patient who had survived the procedure and was willing to describe graphically the horror of an intrusive abortion without anesthesia.[209] Although Restell was only convicted of a misdemeanor, she was sentenced to one year in prison—the maximum penalty.[210] Restell did not suffer over much, however, being allowed to bring her own feather bed to the prison, as well as easy chairs, a rocker, and carpeting. She was even allowed conjugal visits by her husband.[211]

The language of the prosecutor and unwillingness of the Court of Appeals to consider evidence of jury tampering[212] hardly suggests a legal profession, or a society, that condoned her activities. This experience apparently did not deter her, as we find her back in court in 1848, shortly after leaving prison.[213] First, the *National Police Gazette* and later the *New York Times* launched press crusades against abortion generally, and against Madame Restell in particular.[214] For 35 years, Lohman/Restell apparently was willing to accept social opprobrium and frequent prosecutions as part of the cost of doing business.[215] When she was arrested and prosecuted by Anthony Comstock in 1878, however, she faced the possibility, given that she was 65 years old, of spending the rest of her life in prison. Rather than rely on the "jury nullification" that modern historians insist was routine in abortion prosecutions, she committed suicide in her ornate New York mansion the night before her trial was to begin.[216]

Courts as well as prosecutors took an increasingly dim view of abortion as its incidence increased. Courts upheld convictions under the abortion statutes when the attempt failed or when the woman was not even pregnant.[217] Courts also relaxed the rules of evidence in abortion cases, upholding convictions when the prosecution could not prove which drug was used in the abortion.[218] In other cases, courts approved the introduction of business cards and advertisements as

---

207. OLASKY, *supra* note 12, at 151; OLASKY, *supra* note 8, at 11.

208. Quoted in GROSSBERG, *supra* note 20, at 167.

209. OLASKY, *supra* note 12, at 151; OLASKY, *supra* note 8, at 11.

210. BRODIE, *supra* note 56, at 230; OLASKY, *supra* note 12, at 151; OLASKY, *supra* note 8, at 11.

211. OLASKY, *supra* note 12, at 151.

212. GROSSBERG, *supra* note 20, at 167.

213. Lohman v. People, 1 N.Y. 379 (1848).

214. OLASKY, *supra* note 12, at 150–72; OLASKY, *supra* note 8, at 10–11, 19, 22–47, 51–59, 62–66.

215. *See* OLASKY, *supra* note 54, at 11–12, 32.

216. *See* BROUN & LEECH, *supra* note 71, at 156–57; ANTHONY COMSTOCK, TRAPS FOR THE YOUNG 137 (1882); GROSSBERG, *supra* note 20, at 190, 192; MILBAUER & OBRENTZ, *supra* note 46, at 140–42; MOHR, *supra* note 5, at 199; OLASKY, *supra* note 12, at 161; OLASKY, *supra* note 8, at 32–33; Carol Flora Brooks, *The Early History of the Anti-Contraception Laws*, 18 AM. Q. 3, 4–5 (1966); Means II, *supra* note 106, at 455–56 n.102; James Morton, jr., *A Little Chapter of the Early History of Anti-Contraception Laws*, 20 MED. CRITIC & GUIDE 258 (1917).

217. Dougherty v. People, 1 Colo. 514 (1872); State v. Magnell, 51 A. 606 (Del. 1901); State v. Montgomery, 33 N.W. 143 (Iowa 1887); State v. Fitzgerald, 49 Iowa 260 (1878); Bassett v. State, 41 Iowa 303 (1872); State v. Watson, 1 P. 770 (Kan. 1883) (not pregnant); Commonwealth v. Morrison, 82 Mass. (16 Gray) 224 (1860); People v. Abbott, 116 Mich. 263 (1898) (not pregnant); State v. Owens, 22 Minn. 238 (1875); State v. Van Houten, 37 Mo. 357 (1866); State v. Dean, 85 Mo. App. 473 (1900); State v. Emerich, 87 Mo. 110 (1885) (not pregnant); People v. Phelps, 30 N.E. 1012 (N.Y. 1892); Dunn v. People, 29 N.Y. 523 (1864); Frazer v. People, 1 Cowen's Crim. 377 (N.Y. Sup. Ct. 1863); State v. Cave, 26 S.W. 503 (Tex. Ct. Crim. App. 1894).

218. State v. Vawter, 7 Blackf. 592 (Ind. 1845); State v. Sherwood, 75 Ind. 15 (1881); People v. Stockham, 1 Parker's Crim. 424 (N.Y. Sup. Ct. 1853); State v. Cave 26 S.W. 503 (Tex. Ct. Crim. App. 1894); Rex v. Anonymous, 170 ENG. REP. 1310 (1811). *See also* Hays v. State, 40 Md. 633 (1874); Commonwealth v. Blair, 126 Mass. 40 (1878); Commonwealth v. Brown, 121 Mass. 69 (1876); Commonwealth v. Harvey, 103 Mass. 451

proof of the intent to abort required under the statutes—even though these cards and ads spoke only in euphemisms.[219] As one judge reasoned, "[i]t is not to be expected that cards and circulars of this kind will state in precise terms, or that their meaning will not be more or less disguised."[220] Such cases flatly contradict assertions that courts applied strict burdens of proof in order to protect abortionists against a law that the judges did not want to enforce.[221]

So long as proof of quickening was required for conviction, courts also had to deal with women who were unable or unwilling to testify whether the fetus had quickened. Courts were willing to assume that a woman had perceived that a child had quickened based on fetal maturity when the woman was dead and could not testify to the matter.[222] One New York court also held that the accusation of a woman of having had a pre-quickening abortion was to charge such an immoral act as to be slander *per se.*[223] No proof of injury to her reputation was necessary for her to sue for the affront. Decisions to the contrary in several states[224] were promptly reversed by statutes making pre-quickening abortions a crime—the imputation of which would be slander *per se.*[225] We find a particularly dramatic instance of such a legislative reaction in Iowa. There, when the state's Supreme Court held that there was no libel because the alleged pre-quickening abortion was not a crime, the state legislature in its very next session enacted a statute to it a crime to abort "any pregnant woman"—by a vote of 27-0 in the Senate, and of 53-1 in the House.[226]

Not all judges were willing to relax the rules of evidence, however, helping to keep the conviction rate for abortions low, even with new and tighter statutory prohibitions of abortion.[227] While such decisions were common even in the later nineteenth century, the judges usually coupled the decision with a clear and unequivocal condemnation of the crime, and sometimes complained of the inadequacies of the statute.[228] Nor did these courts stretch legal rules in order to free abortionists guilty under normal rules of evidence and statutory construction.[229] Such judi-

---

(1869); Commonwealth v. Sholes, 95 Mass. (13 Allen) 554 (1866); People v. McDowell, 30 N.W. 68 (Mich. 1886); State v. McLeod, 37 S.W. 828 (Mo. 1896); Backhouse, *supra* note 161, at 103–08 (Canadian cases).

219. *See, e.g.,* United States v. Kelly, 26 Fed. Cas. 128 (D. Nev. 1876) (No. 15,514); Holliday v. People, 9 Ill. 111 (1847); Commonwealth v. Barrows, 56 N.E. 830 (Mass. 1900); Commonwealth v. Jackson, 81 Mass. (15 Gray) 187 (1860).

220. Commonwealth v. Barrows, 56 N.E. 830 (Mass. 1900).

221. *See, e.g.,* GRABER, *supra* note 72, at 45; SCHUR, *supra* note 72, at 55–56; Zad Leavy & Jerome Kummer, *Criminal Abortion: Human Hardship and Unyielding Laws*, 35 S. CAL. L. REV. 123, 130–31 (1962).

222. *See, e.g.,* Evans v. People. 49 N.Y. 86, 89–91 (1872). *See also* State v. Steadman, 51 S.E.2d 91, 94 (S.C. 1948).

223. Bissell v. Cornell, 24 Wend. 354 (N.Y. 1840).

224. Abrams v. Foshee, 3 Iowa 274 (1856); Smith v. Gaffard, 33 Ala. 168 (1858).

225. MOHR, *supra* note 5, at 144.

226. JOURNAL OF THE SEN. OF THE 7TH GEN. ASSEMBLY OF IOWA, 1858, at 284 (1858); JOURNAL OF THE H. REP. OF THE 7TH GEN. ASSEMBLY OF IOWA, 1858, at 612–13 (1858). For the votes on other such laws, see Witherspoon, *supra* note 158, at 69.

227. *See, e.g.,* Eggart v. State, 25 So. 144 (Fla. 1898); State v. Forsythe, 43 N.W. 548 (Iowa 1889); Crichton v. People, 1 Cowen's Crim. 454 (N.Y. Sup. Ct. 1864). For similar highly technical evidentiary and procedural rulings in England that saved abortionists from conviction, see Regina v. Fretwell, 9 Cox. CRIM. CASES 152 (Ct. Crim. App. 1862); Regina v. Wright, 173 ENG. REP. 1039 (1841); Rex v. Enoch, 172 ENG. REP. 1089 (1833); Rex v. Russell, 168 ENG. REP. 1302 (1832).

228. *See, e.g.,* Holland v. State, 31 N.E. 359 (Ind. 1891); State v. Young, 40 P. 659 (Kan. 1895); Lamb v. State, 10 A. 208 (Md. 1887); People v. Aiken, 33 N.W. 821 (Mich. 1887); People v. Olmstead, 30 Mich 431 (1874); State v. McIntyre, 19 Minn. 93 (1872); State v. Schverman, 70 Mo. App. 518 (1897); Cobel v. People, 5 Park. Crim. 348 (N.Y. Sup. Ct. 1862); State v. Drake, 1 Vroom 422 (N.J. 1863); Commonwealth v. Railing, 4 A. 459 (Pa. 1886).

229. *See, e.g.,* State v. Lee, 37 A. 75 (Conn. 1897); Hauk v. State, 47 N.E. 465 (Ind. 1897); State v. Moothart, 80 N.W. 301 (Iowa 1899); Jones v. State, 17 A. 89 (Md. 1889); Eckhart v. People, 22 Hun. 525 (N.Y. Sup. Ct. 1880); State v. Morrow, 18 S.E. 853 (S.C. 1893). *See generally* GROSSBERG, *supra* note 20, at 180–82.

cial patterns hardly demonstrate judicial resistance to the stricter abortion laws—especially when the judicial denunciations even influenced legislatures considering new statutes.[230] Yet non-lawyer crusaders against the rising incidence of abortion were predictably frustrated by a lawyerly caution that they tended to interpret it as subversion of the tighter laws.[231]

The nineteenth-century legal effort against abortion is too great to be denied. Given this evidence, the claim that the legal profession was indifferent to abortion collapses. The attitudes of the legal profession might, however, be dismissed as the efforts of a misogynistic profession that barred women from its ranks.[232] While we have seen that women in general and feminists in particular in fact were strongly supportive of the codification and strengthening of abortion laws, did the handful of women attorneys hold a different view?

# The Role of Women Lawyers in the Nineteenth Century

*For the master's tools will never dismantle the master's house. They may allow us temporarily to beat him at his own game, but they will never enable us to bring about genuine change.*

—Audrey Lorde[233]

The voices of women were notably absent from discussions or actions within the legal profession regarding abortion. Women in the second half of the nineteenth century who sought to become licensed as physicians could draw upon the long tradition of women healers. While they encountered intense resistance, they overcame the opposition and achieved considerable success before career paths closed for them at the turn of the century.[234] Women who sought to become lawyers during this same period had no such traditions to draw upon and encountered even more resistance.

In ancient times, on rare occasions, women actually served with distinction as advocates. In general, they were not permitted to do so. In ancient Rome, a woman named Carfania achieved some notoriety as an advocate, provoking a praetorian edit around 60 BCE[235] that prohibited women from serving as advocates.[236] The Roman praetor Ulpian explained the prohibition in a passage written around 210 CE that comes down to us through the *Digest* prepared in the early sixth century:

> Next comes an edict against those who are not to plead on behalf of others: In this edict the praetor debarred on grounds of sex and disability, and also persons in disrepute. On the ground of sex, it is prohibited to women to plead on behalf of others, the reason for the prohibition is to prevent women from mixing themselves in other people's cases

---

230. Grossberg, *supra* note 20, at 173–74.
231. See the authorities collected *supra* at note 71.
232. *See, e.g.,* Bradwell v. Illinois, 83 U.S. (16 Wall.) 130 (1871).
233. Audrey Lorde, Sister Outsider 111 (1984).
234. *See* Chapter 8, at notes 251–324.
235. On the dating of the edict, see Tony Honoré, Ulpian 48 (1982).
236. According to one Roman historian, Carfania died in 48 BCE. Valerius Maximus ¶ 8.3.2. Apparently other women also appeared as advocates in Roman proceedings to some extent before Ulpian's edict, but the evidence of such activity is sparse. *See generally* Richard Powell, Women and Politics in Ancient Rome 45–52 (1992); Anthony Marshall, *Ladies at Law: The Role of Women in the Roman Civil Courts,* in 5 Studies in Latin Literature and Roman History 35 (C. Deroux ed. 1989).

contrary the modesty that befits their gender, and lest women perform the duties proper to men. The origin comes from Carfania, a most shameless, woman who by brazenly bringing cases and disturbing the magistrate provided the cause for the edict.[237]

Roman historian Valerius Maximus was less kind. He described women's speech in public settings as "barking," and not as speaking at all.[238]

Only one woman appears to have served as a lawyer in colonial era—Margaret Brent, who settled in Maryland in 1638.[239] Brent was highly successful. Maryland court records refer to Brent in 124 cases between 1642 and 1650 and she served as attorney for the governor, Leonard Calvert, and as executor of Calvert's estate.[240] Yet she failed to obtain the right to vote and the right to sit on the governor's council.[241]

Margaret Brent was not the beginning of a tradition of women lawyers. Apparently no woman followed in her footsteps for about two centuries. As a result, a woman lawyer could write in 1890 that "there is probably no one that would have amazed our good ancestors of a century ago more than the woman lawyer as she exists today."[242] As a result, the erstwhile women lawyers achieved considerably less success than their medical counterparts.[243] In fact, law has been called "the most engendered" profession and, even today, the most closed to women.[244] The engendered nature of law created serious tensions in the first women lawyers as they sought to reconcile their personal and professional identities.[245] Women lawyers of the time cautioned each other not to be too forward in their manner less they make themselves "obnoxious."[246] On the other hand, in contrast with the medical profession, once women were accepted as lawyers their numbers did not decline in the first half of the twentieth century. Perhaps this was because the number of women lawyers always remained low, growing only slowly until 1970.

---

237. Justinian, Digest ¶3.1.1.5 (533 CE). *See generally* Nikolaus Benke, *Women in the Courts: An Old Thorn in Men's Sides,* 3 Mich. J. Gender & L. 195, 203–12 (1995). The second part of the passage, omitted here, prohibits pleading by blind persons. The following passage excluded persons condemned for capital crimes, men who had fought as gladiators, and men who had taken the passive role in homosexual intercourse. Justinian, *supra,* ¶3.1.1.6.

238. Valerius Maximus, *supra* note 234, ¶8.3.2. *See also* Justinian, *supra* note 237, ¶5.3.1.3.

239. *See* Anton-Hermann Chroust, 1 The Rise of the Legal Profession in America 49 (1965); Karen Berger Morello, The Invisible Bar: The Woman Lawyer in America 1638 to Present 6–8 (1986).

240. Chroust, *supra* note 239, at 49; Morello, *supra* note 239, at 6.

241. Morello, *supra* note 239, at 6–7.

242. Lelia Robinson, *Women Lawyers in the United States,* 2 The Green Bag 10 (1890) [reprinted in 2 Green Bag 2nd at 68 (1998)].

243. Robinson, *supra* note 242. *See generally* Virginia Drachman, Sisters in Law: Women Lawyers in Modern American History (1998); Rhode, *supra* note 56, at 19–24; Stevens, *supra* note 80, at 83–84 (1982); Janette Barnes, *Women and Entrance to the Legal Profession,* 23 J. Legal Educ. 283 (1970); Carrington, *supra* note 80, at 551–57; Kathleen LaZarou, *Fettered Portias: Obstacles Facing Nineteenth Century Women Lawyers,* 64 Women Law. J. 21 (1978); Frances Olsen, *From False Paternalism to False Equality: Judicial Assaults on Feminist Community, Illinois, 1869–1895,* 84 Mich. L. Rev. 1518, 1523–31 (1986); Isabella Pettus, *The Legal Education of Women,* 38 J. Soc. Sci. 234 (1990); D. Kelly Weisberg, *Barred from the Bar: Women and Legal Education in the United States 1870–1890,* 28 J. Legal Educ. 485 (1977). *See also* Ronald Chester, Unequal Access: Women Lawyers in a Changing America (1985); Barbara Harris, Beyond Her Sphere: Women and the Professions in American History (1978).

244. Drachman, *supra* note 243, at 2. *See generally* Daniel Calhoun, Professional Lives in America: Structure and Aspirations, 1750–1850, at 59–87 (1965); Michael Grossberg, *Institutionalizing Masculinity: The Law as a Masculine Profession,* in Meanings for Manhood: Constructions of Manhood in Victorian America 133 (Mark Carnes & Clyde Griffen eds. 1990).

245. Drachman, *supra* note 243, at 3–4, 64–117.

246. Robinson, *supra* note 242, at 10.

Until the American Civil War, there were virtually no women lawyers. Although undoubtedly some women would have liked to become lawyers, there actually is little evidence that any woman aspired to the profession before that war. After the Civil War, however, women did begin to press for admission to the bar. Their very attempt to enter the bar challenged masculine prerogatives in a way that women physicians never did.[247] Women had to gain admission to courts and bar associations, institutions that were exclusively male in membership and outlook. Unlike women doctors who established their own medical schools and hospitals, women lawyers could not simply set up their own courts, and until the very end of the century no one made any attempt to open a law school just for women.[248] And the very act of becoming a lawyer challenged the laws of the land that denied women equal citizenship (including the right to vote) and denied to married women (before the *Married Women's Acts*[249]) the right to own or manage property. It is small surprise that women lawyers, more than any other group of professional women in America, committed themselves to pressing for women's suffrage.[250]

The first woman formally admitted to the practice of law was Belle Babb Mansfield of Mt. Pleasant, Iowa. She was admitted to the state bar of Iowa in 1869.[251] Although Mansfield seems not to have encountered much resistance to her admission, she never actually practiced law, instead becoming a history professor at De Pauw University. Other women had more difficulty obtaining a legal education or admission to the Bar, or both.

The most famous woman's struggle to gain admission to the bar was that of Myra Bradwell of Chicago who sought admission to the practice law in Illinois shortly after the end of the Civil War. The state of Illinois carried the fight all the way to the United States Supreme Court. In *Bradwell v. Illinois*,[252] the Supreme Court held (by an 8-1 vote) against Mrs. Bradwell on the narrow ground that the constitutional clause she relied on—the "privileges and immunities" clause of the Fourteenth Amendment—did not apply to complaints against the state of which the complainant was a citizen. The Court reached this conclusion even though the State of Illinois did not bother to send an attorney to argue the case before the Court.[253]

Justice Joseph Bradley's highly misogynistic concurring opinion in *Bradwell* is better known than the simple and brief opinion of the Court.[254] Justice Bradley (joined by Justices Stephen Field and Noah Swayne) gratuitously described women as unsuited by their emotional nature to be legal advocates. Even with the endorsement of three justices of the Supreme Court, however, the determination of the male legal profession to keep out the even more determined women was unsuccessful.[255] Myra Bradwell herself, supported emotionally

---

247. DRACHMAN, *supra* note 243, at 2–3.

248. CHESTER, *supra* note 243, at 9–42, 53–86; DRACHMAN, *supra* note 243, at 121–30, 149–67; STEVENS, *supra* note 80, at 83, 90–91.

249. *See* Chapter 2, at notes 160–71.

250. DRACHMAN, *supra* note 243, at 2; JOAN HOFF, LAW, GENDER, AND INJUSTICE: A LEGAL HISTORY OF U.S. WOMEN 162–62 (1991); MORELLO, *supra* note 239, at 11–13.

251. Robinson, *supra* note 242, at 21. Apparently, Mary Magoon practiced law for some time in a small town in rural Iowa without ever being formally admitted to the bar. MORELLO, *supra* note 239, at 11.

252. 83 U.S. (16 Wall.) 130, 137–39 (1872).

253. *Id.* at 137.

254. *Id.* at 139–42. *See also In re* Lockwood, 154 U.S. 116 (1894); *In re* Lockwood, 8 Ct. Cl. 346 (1873); *In re* Maddox, 50 A. 487 (Md. 1901); *In re* Robinson, 131 Mass. 376 (1881); Attorney General v. Abbott, 80 N.W. 372 (Mich. 1899); *In re* Stoneman, 40 Hun. 638(N.Y. 1886); *In re* Leonard, 6 P. 426 (Ore. 1885); *Ex parte* Griffin, 71 S.W. 746 (Tenn. 1901); *In re* Goodell, 39 Wis. 232 (1875).

255. *See In re* Thomas, 27 P. 707 (Colo. 1891); *In re* Hall, 50 Conn. 131 (1882); *In re* Leach, 34 N.E. 641 (Ind. 1893); *In re* Ricker, 29 A. 559 (N.H. 1890); *In re* Kilgore, 18 AM. L. REV. 478 (Phila. C.P. 1884); Robinson, *supra* note 242. *See generally* DRACHMAN, *supra* note 243, at 13–36; JANE FRIEDMAN, AMERICA'S FIRST WOMAN LAWYER: THE BIOGRAPHY OF MYRA BRADWELL (1993); HOFF, *supra* note 168, at 151–91; WILLIAM NELSON, THE FOURTEENTH AMENDMENT: FROM POLITICAL PRINCIPLE TO JUDICIAL DOCTRINE 151–81 (1988);

by her husband (a lawyer and also her law teacher), founded the leading legal newspaper in the Midwest, and eventually was admitted to the Illinois Bar and became a highly respected practitioner.[256]

Remarkably, most states eliminated formal barriers to women practicing law by 1880—eight years after *Bradwell*.[257] Congress enacted in 1879 that women were to be admitted to the Bar of the Supreme Court regardless of what the Justices thought.[258] The clearest sign that women could not be excluded altogether from the legal profession was their relatively rapid acceptance into the law schools that were then establishing themselves as the gatekeepers for the profession.[259]

Despite *Bradwell* (or perhaps because of it), Union Law College in Chicago became the first law school to admit women on a regular basis, although it was quickly overtaken by the University of Michigan in the number of women students.[260] Boston University was not far behind.[261] Women were being admitted to most publicly funded law schools by 1880 despite opposition from the Bar.[262] Only a few public universities held out longer.[263] Women were first admitted into the private law schools in the 1880s, beginning with Cornell and New York University.[264] By the end of the nineteenth century, new law schools were opening as co-educational from the start.[265] In 1920, 102 of 129 accredited law schools admitted women.[266] Unaccredited law schools, willing to accept any paying customer, were even more welcoming to women law students than were the accredited schools.[267]

As with medical schools, the fight against the admission of women to law school was led by Harvard University which overruled a decision of the law faculty to admit a woman applicant in 1899.[268] Harvard Law School, in fact, has the distinction of being the last Ivy League law school to admit women, waiting until 1950 to take the step, long after the University as a whole would

---

Carol Ellen Dubois, *Outgrowing the Compact of the Fathers: Equal Rights, Women Suffrage, and the United States Constitution, 1820–1878*, 74 J. Am. Hist. 836 (1987); Olson, *supra* note 243, at 1523–31.

256. Robinson, *supra* note 242, at 14. *See also* Friedman, *supra* note 255, at 18, 29; Frederic Crossley, Courts and Lawyers of Illinois 264 (1916); Drachman, *supra* note 243, at 16; Halliday, *supra* note 86, at 79; Paul Carrington, *The Missionary Diocese of Chicago*, 44 J. Legal Educ. 467, 481–82 (1994).

257. Cynthia Fuchs Epstein, Women in Law 79 (1981); Barnes, *supra* note 243, at 276; Weisberg, *supra* note 243, at 494–95.

258. *An Act to Relieve Certain Disabilities of Women*, 20 Stat. 292 (1879). The initiative for the statute came from lawyer and activist Belva Lockwood. *See* Hoff, *supra* note 250, at 183–84; Morello, *supra* note 239, at 34–35.

259. *See generally* Morello, *supra* note 239, at 39–107.

260. Robinson, *supra* note 242, at 14–21.

261. *Id.* at 88–89.

262. Carrington, *supra* note 80, at 552 n.271. *See also* Drachman, *supra* note 243, at 47, 55–61; Barbara Babcock, *Clara Shortridge Foltz: "First Woman,"* 30 Ariz. L. Rev. 673, 701–05 (1988).

263. *See, e.g.,* Thomas Barnes, Hastings College of the Law: The First Century 47–57 (1978); Babcock, *supra* note 262, at 700–15.

264. Drachman, *supra* note 243, at 118, 120–38; Carrington, *supra* note 80, at 551; Pettus, *supra* note 243, at 234, 240.

265. *See, e.g.,* Nora Chaffin, Trinity College, 1839–1892: The Beginnings of Duke University 240–41 (1950) (Duke's law school opened as coeducational in 1904); Orrin Elliot, Stanford University 87–92 (1937) (Stanford's law school opened as coeducational in 1899); Richard Storr, Harper's University: The Beginnings 86, 109 (1960) (the University of Chicago's law school opened as coeducational in 1902). *See generally* Drachman, *supra* note 243, at 43–47.

266. Chester, *supra* note 243, at 8; Drachman, *supra* note 243, at 118 (giving the figure as 102 of 142 law schools, but not mentioning how many of these schools were accredited).

267. Mark Steiner, *The Secret History of Proprietary Legal Education: The Case of the Houston Law School, 1919–1945*, 47 J. Legal Educ. 341, 345 (1997).

268. Harvard Law School Ass'n, The Centennial History of the Harvard Law School, 1817–1917, at 55 (1918) ("Centennial History"); Drachman, *supra* note 243, at 42–43, 138–42; Carrington, *supra* note 80, at 552.

have accepted the change.[269] The Harvard Law Faculty's later resistance to admitting women was perhaps rooted in the isolation of so many of its faculty from real world concerns after Langdell and Ames enshrined the ideal of an academized and cloistered law professorate.[270]

Yale had a similar experience of having the University overrule an early decision to admit a woman.[271] Yale and Columbia also lead the resistance to the admission of Catholics, Jews, and Negroes.[272] Yale did graduate a woman (Alice Jordan) in 1886, but thereafter took steps to "prevent a repetition of the Jordan incident."[273] Harvard, Yale, and Columbia were schools that could afford to turn away a few students, a luxury most law schools at that time could not indulge. Yet even at some schools that experienced difficulty in filling their seats, resistance to admitting women was high. At George Washington University, the faculty long voted to refuse admission to women.[274] Washington and Lee, the last law school to admit women, held out to 1972.[275]

Unlike most of these schools, at first the law faculty at Harvard supported admitting women and the university blocked it. When the University's persistently resisted allowing the law faculty to admit women students, several members of the law faculty opened the Cambridge Law School for women.[276] This school, like the Portia Law School in nearby Boston, failed for want of demand—perhaps because the Boston area had coeducational law schools sufficient for the few women who actually undertook to study law.[277] Furthermore, some women, like Mary Agnes Mahan, former president of the Massachusetts Association of Lawyers, strongly objected sex-segregated law schools:

> The phrase, "First graduate law school in America exclusively for women" has no charms for me. The students will lose the benefit of contact with men's view and opinions, and that benefit, under the circumstances, is inestimable. There have been generations of men lawyers; it's a new field for women, in a way. There have been few Portias through the ages. I think coeducation in a graduate law course is almost an essential.[278]

A similar experiment at the University of Southern California also failed.[279]

The failure of several attempts to open law schools specifically for women, along with the small numbers of women who enrolled in the coeducational programs until after 1970, raises a question: Why? Some women were unfairly denied admission and many more did not apply for fear of discrimination in the educational process—fears and suspicions that persist today when women form close to half (in a growing number of schools, more than half) of the student body.[280] With so many women in law schools, they still often complain of considerable alienation

---

269. DRACHMAN, *supra* note 243, at 138; EPSTEIN, *supra* note 257, at 50. Harvard hardly did better for women seeking admission to the medical school, not admitting its first woman medical student until 1945. MARY ROTH WALSH, DOCTORS WANTED: NO WOMEN NEED APPLY xiv (1977).

270. *See generally* Carrington, *supra* note 256.

271. DRACHMAN, *supra* note 243, at 43, 47–48, 142–43; FREDERICK HICKS, YALE LAW SCHOOL: 1869–1894, INCLUDING THE COUNTY COURT HOUSE PERIOD 72–74 (1937).

272. AUERBACH, *supra* note 83, at 99–100; DRACHMAN, *supra* note 243, at 41–43, 130–31, 143–45; Carrington, *supra* note 80, at 555.

273. Robinson, *supra* note 242, at 13.

274. DRACHMAN, *supra* note 243, at 43; STEVENS, *supra* note 80, at 83.

275. Carrington, *supra* note 80, at 559; Weisberg, *supra* note 243, at 486.

276. CENTENNIAL HISTORY, *supra* note 268, at 84; DRACHMAN, *supra* note 243, at 162–67.

277. CENTENNIAL HISTORY, *supra* note 268, at 83; DRACHMAN, *supra* note 243, at 149–62; Carrington, *supra* note 80, at 552–53.

278. *Graduate Law School for Women*, 4 AM. L. SCH. REV. 54, 54 (1918) (quoting Mary Agnes Mahan).

279. DOROTHY BROWN & MABEL WALKER WILLEBRANDT: A STUDY OF POWER, LOYALTY AND LAW 30–31 (1984).

280. Paul Mattessich & Cheryl Heilman, *The Career Paths of Minnesota Law School Graduates: Does Gender Make a Difference?*, 9 LAW & INEQUALITY 59, 68 (1990). *See generally* AMERICAN BAR ASS'N COMM'N ON

from legal academic process, perhaps contradicting Mary Agnes Mahan's comments of a century ago.[281] Law school is a stressful experience, alienating to nearly all students, even those with the

WOMEN IN THE PROFESSION, THE UNFINISHED AGENDA: WOMEN AND THE LEGAL PROFESSION 27 (2001) ("THE UNFINISHED AGENDA").

281. ROBERT GRANFIELD, THE MAKING OF ELITE LAWYERS: VISIONS OF LAW SCHOOL AT HARVARD AND BE-YOND 94–108 (1992); THE UNFINISHED AGENDA, *supra* note 280, at 28–29, 36–37; LINDA WIGHTMAN, WOMEN IN LEGAL EDUCATION: A COMPARISON OF THE LAW SCHOOL PERFORMANCE AND LAW SCHOOL EXPERIENCE OF WOMEN AND MEN (1996); Marina Angel, *Women in Legal Education: What It's Like to Be Part of a Perpetual First Wave or the Case of the Disappearing Women*, 61 TEMPLE L. REV. 799 (1988); Tanya Lovell Banks, *Gender Bias in the Classroom*, 14 S. ILL. U. L. REV. 527 (1990); Katharine Bartlett, *Feminist Perspectives on the Ideological Impact of Legal Education upon the Profession*, 72 N.C. L. REV. 1259 (1994); Sari Bashi & Maryana Iskander, *Methodology Matters*, 53 J. LEGAL EDUC. 505 (2003); Kathleen Bean, *The Gender Gap in the Law School Classroom—Beyond Survival*, 14 VT. L. REV. 23 (1989); Melissa Cole, *Struggling to Enjoy Ourselves or Enjoying the Struggle? One Perspective from the Newest Generation of Women's Law Professors*, 10 UCLA WOMENS L.J. 321 (2000); Mary Irene Coombs, *Crime in the Stacks, or A Tale of a Text: A Feminist Response to a Criminal Law Textbook*, 39 J. LEGAL EDUC. 117 (1989); Peggy Cooper Davis & Elizabeth Ehrenfest Steinglass, *A Dialogue about Socratic Teaching*, 23 NYU REV. L. & SOC. CHANGE 249 (1997); Karen Czapanskiy & Jana Singer, *Women in the Law School: It's Time for More Change*, 7 LAW & INEQ. J. 135 (1988); Nancy Erickson, *Sex Bias in Law School Courses: Some Common Issues*, 39 J. LEGAL EDUC. 101 (1989); Christine Haight Farley, *Confronting Expectations: Women in the Legal Academy*, 8 YALE J.L. & FEMINISM 333 (1996); Mary Joe Frug, *Re-Reading Contracts: A Feminist Analysis of a Contracts Casebook*, 34 AM. U. L. REV. 1065 (1985); Paula Gaber, *"Just Trying to Be Human in This Place": The Legal Education of Twenty Women*, 10 YALE J.L. & FEMINISM 165 (1998); Kathy Garner, *Gender Bias in Legal Education: An Annotated Bibliography*, 14 S. ILL. L.J. 547 (1990); Marsha Garrison, Brian Tomko, & Ivan Yip, *Succeeding Law School: A Comparison of Women's Experiences at Brooklyn Law School and the University of Pennsylvania*, 3 MICH. J. GENDER & L. 515 (1996); Robert Granfield, *Contextualizing the Different Voice: Women, Occupational Goals, and Legal Education*, 16 LAW & POL'Y 1 (1994); Lani Guinier, *Lessons and Challenges of Becoming Gentlemen*, 24 N.Y.U. REV. L. & SOC. CHANGE 1 (1998); Lani Guinier, Michelle Fine, & Jane Balin, *Becoming Gentlemen: Women, Law School, and Institutional Change*, 143 U. PA. L. REV. 1 (1994); Cynthia Hill, *Sexual Bias in the Law School Classroom: One Student's Perspective*, 28 J. LEGAL EDUC. 603 (1988); Suzanne Homer & Lois Schwartz, *Admitted but not Accepted: Outsiders Take an Inside Look at Law School*, 5 BERKELEY WOMEN'S L.J. 1 (1989); Ann Iijima, *Lessons Learned: Legal Education and Law Student Dysfunction*, 48 J. LEGAL EDUC. 524 (1998); Joan Krauskopf, *Touching the Elephant: Perceptions of Gender Issues in Nine Law Schools*, 44 J. LEGAL EDUC. 311 (1994); Ira Lupu, *Gloria Steinem at the Harvard Law Review Banquet*, 2 GREEN BAG 2ND 15 (Autumn 1998); Paula Lustbader, *Teach in Context: Responding to Diverse Student Voices Helps All Students Learn*, 48 J. LEGAL EDUC. 402 (1998); Elizabeth Mertz et al., *What Difference Does Difference Make? The Challenge for Legal Education*, 48 J. LEGAL EDUC. 1 (1998); Margaret Montoya, *Máscaras, Trenzas, y Greñas: Un/Masking the Self While Un/Braiding Latina Stories and Legal Discourses*, 17 HARV. WOMEN'S L. J. 185 (1994); Mary Jane Mossman, *Gender Issues in Teaching Methods: Reflections on Shifting the Paradigm*, 6 LEGAL EDUC. REV. 129 (1995); Banu Ramachandran, Note, *Re-Reading Difference: Feminist Critiques of the Law School Classroom and the Problem of Speaking from Experience*, 98 COLUM. L. REV. 1757 (1998); Judith Resnik, *A Continuous Body: Ongoing Conversations about Women and Legal Education*, 53 J. LEGAL EDUC. 564 (2003); Deborah Rhode, *Missing Questions: Feminist Perspectives on Legal Education*, 45 STAN. L. REV. 1547 (1993); Jennifer Rosato, *The Socratic Method and Women Law Students: Humanize, Don't Feminize*, 7 S. CAL. REV. LAW & WOMEN'S STUD. 37 (1997); Jennifer Russell, *On Being a Gorilla in Your Midst, or, the Life of One Black Woman in the Legal Academy*, 28 HARV. C.R.-C.L. L. REV. 259 (1993); Anne Scales, *Surviving Legal De-Education: An Outsider's Guide*, 15 VT. L. REV. 139 (1990); Adrienne Stone, *The Public Interest and the Power of the Feminist Critique of Law School: Women's Empowerment of Legal Education and its Implications for the Fate of Public Interest Commitment*, 5 J. GENDER & L. 525 (1997); Ruta Stropus, *Mend It, Bend It, and Extend It: The Fate of Traditional Law School Methodology in the 21st Century*, 27 LOY. U. CHI. L.J. 449 (1996); Susan Sturm, *From Gladiators to Problem-Solvers: Connecting Conversations about Women, the Academy, and the Legal Profession*, 4 DUKE J. GENDER L. & POL'Y 119 (1997); Susan Sturm & Lani Guinier, *Learning from Conflict: Reflections on Teaching about Race and Gender*, 53 J. LEGAL EDUC. 515 (2003); Symposium, *Women in Legal Education: Pedagogy, Law, Theory, and Practice*, 38 J. LEGAL EDUC. 1 (1988); Janet Taber et al., *Gender, Legal Education, and the Legal Profession: An Empirical Study of Stanford Law Students and Graduates*, 40 STAN. L. REV. 1209 (1988); Lee Teitelbaum, Antonette Sedillo López, & Jeffrey Jenkins, *Gender, Legal Education, and Legal Careers*, 41 J. LEGAL EDUC. 443 (1991); Sarah Thiemann, Note, *Beyond Guinier: A Critique of Legal Pedagogy*, 24 NYU REV. L. & SOC. CHANGE 17 (1998); Morrison Torrey, Jennifer Ries, & Elaine

strongest pre-law credentials who achieve notable success in school.[282] The experience was recalled in a novel by a male lawyer and novelist, Scott Turow:

> Why did I bother? Why did I care? Why didn't I write [the law professor] off as a
> bully or a showman? Why was I afraid?

> Imagine, is all that I can answer.

> You are twenty-six of twenty-two, it makes little difference. Either way you have a
> stake. You have given up a job, a career, to do this. Or you have wanted to be a lawyer all
> your life.

> All your life you've been good in school. All your life it's been something you could
> count on. You know that it's a privilege to be here. You've studied hours on a case that is
> a half page long. You couldn't understand most of what you read at first, but you have
> turned the passage inside out, and drawn diagrams, written briefs. You could not be
> more organized.

> And when you get to class that demigod who knows all the answers finds another
> student to say things you never could have. Clearer statements, more precise. And
> worse—far worse—notions, concepts, whole constellations of ideas that never turned
> inside your head.

> Yes, there are achievements in the past. They're nice to bandage up your wounded
> self-esteem. But "I graduated college *magna cum laude*" is not the proper answer when
> the professor has just posed a question and awaits your response with the 140 other per-
> sons in the class.

> The feeling aroused by all of that was something near to panic, a ferocious, grasp-
> ing sense of uncertainty, and it held me, and I believe most of my classmates, often dur-

---

Spiliopoulos, *What Every First-Year Female Law Student Should Know*, 7 Colum. J. Gender & L. 267 (1998);
Catherine Weiss & Louise Melling, *The Legal Education of Twenty Women*, 40 Stan. L. Rev. 1299 (1988);
Stephanie Wildman, *The Classroom Climate: Encouraging Student Involvement*, 4 Berkeley Women's L.J. 326
(1990); Susan Williams, *Legal Education, Feminist Epistemology, and the Socratic Method*, 45 Stan. L. Rev. 1571
(1993);
    The assumption that women students in law schools face problems that are fundamentally different from
those faced by men students mirrors the assumption that girls in school generally face far greater difficulties
obtaining an education than do boys, an assumption that at least some observers think is similarly misplaced.
*See* Carey Goldberg, *After Girls Get the Attention, Focus Shifts to Boys' Woes*, N.Y. Times, Apr. 23, 1998, at A1.
    282. *See, e.g.*, Richard Kahlenberg, Broken Contract: A Memoir of Harvard Law School (1992);
James Bridges, The Paper Chase (1973); Note, *Making Docile Lawyers: An Essay on the Pacification of Law
Students*, 111 Harv. L. Rev. 2027 (1998); *The Special Sadness of Liberal Law Students*, Reptile, Mar. 18, 1987,
at 13. *See generally* Granfield, *supra* note 281, at 55–61, 75–79, 130; G. Andrew Benjamin et al., *The Role of
Legal Education in Producing Psychological Distress among Law Students and Lawyers*, 1986 Am. B. Found. Res.
J. 225; Paul Carrington & James Conley, *The Alienation of Law Students: A Republication of the Alienation and
Dissatisfaction Factors*, 75 Mich. L. Rev. 1036 (1978); Susan Daicoff, *Lawyer Know Thyself: A Review of Empir-
ical Research on Attorney Attributes Bearing on Professionalism*, 46 Am. U. L. Rev. 1337, 1375–80 (1997); B.A.
Glesner, *Fear and Loathing in the Law Schools*, 23 Conn. L. Rev. 627 (1991); Gerald Hess, *Heads and Hearts:
The Teaching and Learning Environment in Law School*, 52 J. Legal Educ. 75 (2002); Peter Kutulakis, *Stress
and Competence: From Law Student to Professional*, 21 Cap. U. L. Rev. 835 (1992); Stephen Shanfield & G. Andrew Benjamin, *Psychiatric Distress in Law Students*, 35 J. Legal Educ. 65 (1985); Jeffrey Stempel, *All Stressed
up But Not Sure Where to Go: Pondering the Teaching of Adversarialism in Law School*, 55 Brook. L. Rev. 165
(1989); Alan Stone, *Legal Education on the Couch*, 85 Harv. L. Rev. 392 (1971); James Taylor, *Law School Stress
and the "Déformation Professionelle,"* 27 J. Legal Educ. 251 (1975); Andrew Watson, *The Quest for Professional
Competence: Psychological Aspects of Legal Education*, 37 U. Cin. L. Rev. 91 (1968). Research has found that the
stress of studying law is greater than the stress experienced in studying medicine. Marilyn Heins, Shirley Nick-
ols Fahey, & Roger Henderson, *Law Students and Medical Students: A Comparison of Perceived Stress*, 33 J.
Legal Educ. 511 (1983).

ing that first week and for a long while after. On many occasions I discovered that I didn't even understand what I didn't know until I was halfway through a class. Nor could I ever see how anyone else seemed to arrive at the right answer. Maybe they were all geniuses. Maybe I was the dumbest guy around....

I made *mistakes,* in fact, silly blunders. If lucky, I was mediocre. And my conviction of mediocrity was sour and unhappy. I had given up a good career, some security and distinction, to be swallowed in the horde, to confront intelligence which overshadowed my own. The shame at what I'd lost and was incapable of doing had become acute; and the day I embarrassed myself by making that mistake in Mann's class, I was low enough that my feelings worsened into something harrowing.

Walking out of that session, I was as close to tears as I had been in a decade. I wanted to explain to Mann, to all my classmates, that I really wasn't dumb or indiscreet, that I was able to accomplish many things worth doing. But there was no way to prove that, to them or even to myself.

When I had recovered somewhat, I vowed that I wouldn't let that feeling overcome me again. But that didn't mean taking a more balanced view of my feelings or a broader perspective on what was going on in general. I was too caught up in all of it by then. I promised instead that I would not talk in class. That meant feeling distant and frustrated while I sat in each meeting; it meant that I was giving in to fear. But I suffered it all, rather than face that horrible shame again, for weeks I did not let myself be heard.[283]

While the alienation felt by women law students is only marginally worse than that felt by men law students, the women are likely to attribute their alienation to gender rather than to other causes.[284] One result of the marginally greater alienation of women than men from the law school experience is that although the women admitted to law schools in the United States have somewhat higher undergraduate grade point averages (3.27 for women compared to 3.16 for men), the average grades of women in their law studies is slightly lower than for men. Men did have, on average, higher scores on the Law School Admission Test (36.92 to 36.05 in 1991).[285]

While the experience of law school a century ago was even more difficult for women,[286] the women who attended in those early years did not meet only unremitting resentment or disdain by their fellow students or the faculty.[287] For example, John Wigmore, one of the most prominent legal scholars of his day and Dean of the Northwestern University School of Law, refused to attend a function jointly sponsored by the law students at the University of Chicago and Northwestern because the affair was not open to women students.[288] Wigmore also argued against the

---

283. Scott Turow, One L 55–56, 131 (1977).

284. *See* Granfield, *supra* note 281, at 97–99; Carrington, *supra* note 80, at 572; Guinier, Fine, & Balin, *supra* note 281, at 37, 43–45, 56–59, 64; Homer & Schwartz, *supra* note 281, at 33, 37–38; Robin West, *Jurisprudence and Gender,* 55 U. Cin. L. Rev. 1 (1988); Scales, *supra* note 281; Stone, *supra* note 281, at 543–45; Taber *et al., supra* note 281, at 1240; Thiemann, *supra* note 281, at 18–19; Weiss & Melling, *supra* note 281, at 1328, 1333, 1337–39, 1345–55. *See also* Janice Austin *et al., Results from a Survey: Gay, Lesbian, and Bisexual Students' Attitudes about Law School,* 48 J. Legal Educ. 157 (1998); Richard Devlin, *Legal Education as Consciousness-Raising or Paving the Road to Hell,* 39 J. Legal Educ. 213 (1989).

285. Linda Wightman, Women in Legal Education: A Comparison of the Law School Performance and Law School Experiences of Women and Men 11–12 (1996). *See also* Guinier, Fine, & Balin, *supra* note 281, at 3; Richard Neumann jr., *Women in Legal Education: What the Statistics Show,* 50 J. Legal Educ. 313, 320–21 (2000).

286. Drachman, *supra* note 243, at 49–55; Harris, *supra* note 243; Barnes, *supra* note 243; LaZarou, *supra* note 243; Mattessich & Heilman, *supra* note 280; Weisberg, *supra* note 243.

287. Drachman, *supra* note 243, at 53–55; Carrington, *supra* note 80, at 551.

288. William Roalfe, John Henry Wigmore: Scholar and Reformer 67 (1977).

notion that women were less reliable witnesses than men were or that black witnesses were less reliable than white witnesses.[289] Of course, not everyone appreciates today the novelty of Wigmore's thinking at the time he wrote.[290]

There were other factors that were perhaps as effective as male bias within the legal academy in discouraging women from seeking a legal education and hence from becoming lawyers. First was the still pervasive expectation that women should marry and devote their major efforts to "making a home" and raising children, goals that are still difficult to integrate with a legal career and even more so at an earlier time when few or no professional accommodations were made to the needs of mothers.[291] No wonder that well into the twentieth century most women attorneys remained dependent on their lawyer-husbands or lawyer-fathers for employment,[292] or gravitated towards those areas of practice which were less demanding of time and hence less remunerative.[293] Even the legendary Myra Bradwell might not have succeeded as a lawyer were her husband not also a lawyer and supportive of her efforts.[294] The Bradwells' daughter Bessie also became a lawyer married to a lawyer.[295] The same problems bedeviled African-American lawyers during this period.[296] African-American women suffered both sets of disabilities.

---

289. JOHN HENRY WIGMORE, TREATISE ON EVIDENCE 643–46(1904).

290. Leigh Bienen, *A Question of Credibility: John Henry Wigmore's Use of Scientific Authority in Section 924a of the Treatise on Evidence,* 19 CAL. W. L. REV. 235 (1983) (castigating Wigmore for not opposing the requirement of corroboration for charges of rape).

291. DRACHMAN, *supra* note 243, at 97–117, 178–81, 195–99, 241–48; Virginia Drachman, *"My Partner in Law and Life": Marriage in the Lives of Women Lawyers in Late 19th- and Early 20th-Century America,* 14 LAW & SOC. INQUIRY 221 (1989). For modern circumstances, see CYNTHIA FUCHS EPSTEIN, WOMEN IN LAW (2nd ed. 1993); JOHN HAGAN & FIONA KAY, GENDER IN PRACTICE: A STUDY OF LAWYER'S LIVES (1995); MONA HARRINGTON, WOMEN LAWYERS: REWRITING THE RULES 18–19 (1994); Joan Brockman, *"Resistance by the Club" to the Feminization of the Legal Profession,* 7 CAN. J.L. & SOC'Y 47 (1992); Cynthia Fuchs Epstein *et al., Glass Ceilings and Open Doors: Women's Advancement in the Legal Profession: A Report of the Committee on Women in the Profession, the Association of the Bar of the City of New York,* 64 FORDHAM L. REV. 291 (1995); Martha Freeman, *Writing Briefs & Changing Diapers,* 6 CAL. LAW. 36 (1986); Deborah Holmes, *Structural Causes of Dissatisfaction among Large-Firm Attorneys: A Feminist Perspective,* 12 WOMEN'S RTS. L. RPTR. 9 (1990); Wynn Huang, *Gender Differences in the Earnings of Lawyers,* 30 COLUM. J.L. & SOC. PROBLEMS 267 (1997); Kathleen Hull, *The Paradox of the Contented Female Lawyer,* 33 LAW & SOC'Y REV. 687 (1999); Mark Kende, *Shattering the Glass Ceiling: A Legal Theory for Attacking Discrimination against Women Partners,* 46 HASTINGS L.J. 17 (1994); Mary Jane Mossman, *Challenging "Hidden" Assumptions: (Women) Lawyers and Family Life,* in MOTHERS IN LAW: FEMINIST THEORY AND THE LEGAL REGULATION OF MOTHERHOOD 289 (Martha Albertson Fineman & Isabel Karpin eds. 1995); Sheila Nielson, *The Balancing Act: Practical Suggestions for Part-Time Attorneys,* 35 N.Y.L.S. L. REV. 369 (1990); Sherwin Rosen, *The Market for Lawyers,* 35 J.L. & ECON. 215 (1992); Lynn Hecht Schafran, *Credibility in the Courts: Why Is There a Gender Gap?,* JUDGES' J., Winter 1995, at 5; Lynn Hecht Schafran, *Women Shaping the Legal Process: Judicial Gender Bias as Grounds for Reversal,* 84 KY. L.J. 1153 (1996); Stephen Spurr & Glenn Syeyoshi, *Turnover and Promotion of Lawyers: An Inquiry into Gender Differences,* 29 J. HUM. RESOURCES 813 (1994); *The Income of Michigan Attorneys,* 76 MICH. BAR J. 1315 (1997); Robert Wood *et al., Pay Differences among the Highly Paid: The Male/Female Earnings Gap in Lawyers' Salaries,* 11 J. LAB. ECON. 417 (1993).

292. DRACHMAN, *supra* note 243, at 103–12; Carrington, *supra* note 80, at 553. *See also* Robinson, *supra* note 242.

293. CHESTER, *supra* note 243, at 82; DRACHMAN, *supra* note 243, at 84–93, 168–73, 181–90, 215–41; Weisberg, *supra* note 243, at 497. Much the same pattern pertained for women lawyers abroad. Christine Alice Corcos, *Portia Goes to Parliament: Women and Their Admission to Membership in the English Legal Profession,* 75 DEN. U. L. REV. 307, 314 (England), 326 (New Zealand) (1998); Mary Lilly, *The French Women Lawyers,* 21 CASE & COMMENT 431 (1914).

294. *See* CROSSLEY, *supra* note 256, at 264; FRIEDMAN, *supra* note 255, at 18; DRACHMAN, *supra* note 243, at 16; HALLIDAY, *supra* note 86, at 79; Carrington, *supra* note 256, at 481–82.

295. Robinson, *supra* note 242, at 14.

296. *See generally* J. CLAY SMITH, JR., EMANCIPATION: THE MAKING OF THE BLACK LAWYER, 1844–1914 (1993). Very few African-American lawyers of that time were women. *See* DRACHMAN, *supra* note 243, at 45,

With such limited career prospects and facing the possibility of a hostile learning and professional environment, many women who might have felt inclined towards the legal profession concluded that devoting three or four years in obtaining a legal education was an investment that simply could not pay off adequately relative to the costs to be incurred.[297] Such concerns were all the stronger when they considered the steadily rising academic standards they would encounter in law school, which made the real costs of obtaining admission to the bar significantly higher over the century.[298] Law professor Paul Carrington summarized the fiscal cost of obtaining a legal education before 1960 in these words:

> In purely economic, human-capitalistic terms, law school was for a person of any race or either gender a poor investment yielding a low rate of return until at least as late as 1960. There were no summer law jobs to speak of, and little part-time employment in law. Hence, full-time students essentially faced a full three years of foregone income; for this reason, many, and in some places most, students pursued law study in the evenings on a part-time basis. Professional salaries were incredibly low by present standards. If a graduate were one of the select few to find a salaried job on graduation in 1920, the salary was unlikely to exceed one hundred dollars a month. By 1955, there were somewhat more jobs, but the top Wall Street salary was merely four thousand dollars a year. People securing such positions were assigned work reflecting the low price and economic value of their services and included many duties now likely to be performed by paralegals. On the other hand, a diligent and loyal hand was very likely to achieve partnership and a working relationship that would endure for a career. The alternative, of course, was probably solo practice. In the cities, this was often grinding work, financially and morally, a far cry indeed from the uplifting experience shared by the partners of the legendary contemporary firm of McKenzie, Brackman [the TV law firm in "L.A. Law"]. Small town practice had its charm, but seldom was it remunerative, especially for beginners. More than one good lawyer practicing in the first half of this century has confided to me that for as long as a decade, he made more money playing cards than practicing law. Thus, prior to 1960, very few chose law school for the reasons that animate most law students in 1993.[299]

The revolution in legal education introduced by Dean Christopher Columbus Langdell at Harvard in 1870 and the gradual spread of his "case method" with its highly demanding "Socratic dialogue" teaching technique served to raise academic standards without altering career prospects. This is a story that has been told many times.[300] As part of this transition, Harvard introduced written examinations for its students in 1871, over the vehement protests of students.[301] The practice of examining students and only graduating those who exhibited sufficient skill (even at the best schools, then a minority of the student body) also spread slowly but steadily to the other law schools. Some believe the rising academic standards were deliber-

---

52, 66, 206–07, 220–21; Rebels in Law: Voice in History of Black Women Lawyers (J. Clay Smith ed. 1998).

297. *See* Carrington, *supra* note 243, at 553–60.

298. Robert Stevens attributes the decline in the number of women physicians to a similar rise in academic standards in the medical schools. Stevens, *supra* note 80, at 91 n.90.

299. Carrington, *supra* note 80, at 554–55. *See generally* Jerome Carlin, Lawyers on Their Own 17–18, 155 (1962); Jerome Carlin, Lawyers' Ethics: A Survey of the New York City Bar 168–69 (1966); Joel Handler, The Lawyer and His Community: The Practicing Bar in a Middle-Sized City 30 (1967); Alfred Reed, Present Day law Schools in the United States and Canada 287–316 (1928).

300. *See, e.g.,* Joel Seligman, The High Citadel: The Influence of Harvard Law School (1978); Arthur Sutherland, The Law at Harvard (1967). *See also* Grey, *supra* note 133; Hoeflich, *supra* note 83; Kimball, *supra* note 135.

301. Sutherland, *supra* note 298, at 171; Carrington, *supra* note 80, at 512–13, 556.

ately devised as a means of excluding Jews, Catholics, African-Americans, and women.[302] To hold this new orthodoxy regarding the motives of the legal profession in raising academic standards, one must suppose that the leaders of the profession expected Jews and Catholics (who were then the major fear)[303] to be unable to perform at the higher levels while expecting their own WASP sons not to be able do so. If their purpose was to use academic standards to exclude the disfavored groups, they chose what proved to be a peculiarly ill-suited technique.[304] The Catholics, alone of these groups, successfully responded by organizing their own law schools.[305]

Given these realities, few women applied to enter law schools before 1970, and even fewer graduated or entered the practice of law. During the decade 1956–1965, only about 2,600 women graduated from the 108 AALS-member law schools, an average of about two for each graduating class of each school.[306] In 1950, only 12 of 1239 law professors were women, although there were many women law librarians or clinical teachers, directors, or administrators who did not qualify as full faculty members.[307] Such ratios were consistent with the status of women generally in society at the time. (The ratio of women partners in law firms to men partners was actually higher at the time than the ratio of women law professors to men law professors.[308])

The situation for women who would be lawyers was even grimmer in England and Wales than in the United States.[309] While Shakespeare had given us Portia as an image of a successful advocate four centuries ago,[310] and although several British colonial systems admitted women to the practice of law during the second half of the nineteenth century,[311] women were barred from serving as barristers and solicitors in England until the twentieth century. English barristers and solicitors expressed a belief that women were unsuited for the practice of law, yet also expressed the inconsistent fear of competition from women for clients.[312] The rather uneventful admission of women to law practice in France apparently made little impression on the

---

302. *See, e.g.,* Abel, *supra* note 81, at 40–73; Auerbach, *supra* note 83, at 98–129; Stevens, *supra* note 80, at 98–103.

303. Auerbach, *supra* note 83, at 99–100. *See generally* How We Lived: A Documentary History of Immigrant Jews in America, 1880–1930 (Irving Howe & Kenneth Libo eds. 1977).

304. Carrington, *supra* note 80, at 555.

305. *See* Leonard Nelson III, *God and Man in Catholic Law School,* 26 Cath. Law. 127, 127–33 (1981).

306. James White, *Women in the Law,* 65 Mich. L. Rev. 1051, 1053 (1967).

307. Carrington, *supra* note 80, at 585.

308. *Id.* at 586; White, *supra* note 306, at 1112 n.107.

309. *See* Richard Abel, The Legal Profession in England and Wales 172–76 (1988); Michael Birks, Gentlemen of the Law 276–78 (1960); Albie Sachs & Joan Hoff Wilson, Sexism and the Law: A Study of Male Beliefs and Legal Bias in Britain and the United States 27–33 (1978); Corcos, *supra* note 293; Norman St. John-Stevas, *Women in Public Law,* in A Century of Family: 1857–1957, at 256 (R.H. Graveson & F.R. Crane eds. 1957).

310. William Shakespeare, The Merchant of Venice act 4, sc. 1.

311. Corcos, *supra* note 293, at 316 (listing New Brunswick, Newfoundland, Queensland, Tasmania, and Victoria). *See also Flotsam and Jetsam: Women as Lawyers—Modern View,* 51 Can. L.J. 79 (1915); G. Flos. Greig, *The Law as a Profession for Women,* 6 Commonwealth L. Rev. 145 (1909); William Renwick Riddell, *Women as Practitioners of Law,* 18 J. Contemp. Leg. & Int'l L. 200 (1918). *See generally* Constance Backhouse, *"To Open the Way for Others of My Sex": Clara Brett Martin's Career as Canada's First Woman Lawyer,* 1 Can. J. Women & L. 1 (1985); Corcos, *supra,* at 323–26; Mary Kinnear, *"That There Woman Lawyer": Women Lawyers in Manitoba, 1915–1970,* 5 Can. J. Women & L. 411 (1992).

312. Birks, *supra* note 309, at 276–77; *The Admission of Women to the Profession,* 146 Law Times 428 (1919). *See also* Christine Alice Corcos, *Lawyers for Marianne: The Nature of Discourse of the Entry of French Women into the Legal Profession, 1894–1926,* 12 Ga. St. U. L. Rev. 435, 449–67 (1996) (reporting similar concerns and fears among the French *avocats*).

English.[313] The same could also be said of the American admissions already discussed in this section.[314]

The women who sought to enter the legal profession in England and Wales initially centered their efforts on becoming solicitors, for the relevant statute seemed on their side. The *Solicitor's Acts* of 1877[315] and of 1888[316] had defined as eligible to be a solicitor any "person" who passed a qualifying exam administered by the Law Society. The *Interpretation Act* of 1889 had enacted the rule that the word "person" was to be interpreted as including both males and females, unless "it be otherwise specifically provided, or there be something in the subject or context repugnant to such construction."[317] A society was formed to promote the admission of women to "any of [the] branches" of the legal profession, but with little success.[318] Yet when the issue finally was decided by the courts in 1913, the learned judges simply could not believe that Parliament really meant to open the Law Society to women and therefore held that a more explicit enactment would be necessary to accomplish that change.[319] The woman involved in that case, Gwyneth Marjorie Bebb, had graduated from Oxford University with honors in jurisprudence,[320] and had found a practicing solicitor (Edward Bell) to take her for the required clerkship that was necessary to complete the statutory qualifications.[321] Bell had already sponsored an unsuccessful bill in Parliament to compel the admission of women to the Law Society.[322]

Many women also sought to attend lectures at the Inns of Court with the apparent intention of later applying for admission to the Bar, but when Bertha Cave was admitted by mistake to study at Gray's Inn in 1902, she was promptly expelled when the error was discovered.[323] Public reaction to these decisions ranged from enthusiastic support for the exclusion of women[324] to outraged criticism.[325] These setbacks only delayed matters a few years. Repeated efforts in Parliament finally succeeded in 1919, along with legislation enabling women to vote and to stand for office.[326] Ivy Williams became the first woman called him to the Bar and Carrie Morrison became the first woman solicitor, both in 1922.[327]

---

313. *See* Louis Frank, La femme-avocat au point de vue de la sociologie (1888); *Current Topics: The Admission of Women to the French Bar*, 60 Solic. J. & Wkly. Rep. 35 (1915); Lilly, *supra* note 293. *See also* Corcos, *supra* note 312; Corcos, *supra* note 293, at 326–32.

314. *See* Edward Bell, *Admission of Women*, 56 Solic. J. & Wkly. Gazette 814, 814 (1912)

315. 40 & 41 Vict., ch. 25 (Eng.).

316. 51 & 52 Vict., ch. 65 (Eng.).

317. 52 & 53 Vict., ch. 63, §48 (Eng.).

318. Corcos, *supra* note 293, at 336; St. John-Stevas, *supra* note 309, at 271–72.

319. Bebb v. Law Society, 29 T.L.R. 634 (Ch.), *aff'd*, 30 T.L.R. (C.A. 1913). *See* Corcos, *supra* note 292, at 361–79.

320. *Bebb*, 29 T.L.R. at 635.

321. The clerkship was required under the *Solicitors Act of 1843*, 6 & 7 Vict., ch. 73 §§6, 7 (Eng.).

322. Bell, *supra* note 314. *See also* Corcos, *supra* note 293, at 388.

323. Corcos, *supra* note 293, at 336; Helen Kennedy, *Women at the Bar*, in The Bar on Trail 148, 148 (Robert Hazell ed. 1978).

324. *See, e.g.,* Douglas Gane, *The Admission of Women to the Law*, 58 Solic. J. & Wkly. Rep. 468 (1914); *Notes: Women and the Profession*, 26 Jurid. Rev. 130 (1914).

325. *See, e.g.,* Bell, *supra* note 314; *Editorial: The Admission of Women as Solicitors*, 26 Green Bag 28 (1914); *The Admission of Women to the Profession*, *supra* note 312. *See generally* Corcos, *supra* note 293, at 375–79.

326. *See The Parliament (Qualification of Women) Act of 1918*, 8 & 9 Geo. 5, ch. 47; *Representation of the People Act of 1918*, 8 Geo. 5, ch. 64, §4(1); *The Sex Disqualification (Removal) Act of 1919*, 9 & 10 Geo. 5, ch. 71. *See also* Birks, *supra* note 309, at 277; Bell, *supra* note 314; *Law Society: Admission of Women as Solicitors*, 146 Law Times & Solic. J. 409 (1919); *Women as Barristers and Solicitors*, 9 Irish L. Times & Solic. J. 66 (1919). *See generally* Brian Abel-Smith & Robert Stevens, Lawyers and the Courts: A Sociological Study of the English Legal System 1750–1965, at 193 (1967); Corcos, *supra* note 293, at 337–61, 379–95.

327. Corcos, *supra* note 293, at 393–94.

Scotland had known an actual woman advocate in a case litigated in 1563, but the Scottish courts also rejected a lawsuit brought in 1901 by 18-year-old Margaret Hall to gain the right to sit for the first of two qualifying exams.[328] In Ireland, women were allowed to appear and plead for themselves, but they were not admitted to the bar until 1920.[329] The same statutes as had compelled the admission of women in England and Wales covered Scotland and Ireland. Admission, of course, did not eliminate all the prejudices against women lawyers anymore in Britain than it did in the United States.[330] Years of struggle were necessary to begin to overcome the resulting problems, some of which still persist to this day.[331]

Because of the absence of women lawyers in England and Wales, they could play no significant role for or against the enactment or enforcement of abortion laws, or any other laws. The handful of women lawyers in the United States in the nineteenth century, on the other hand, took a leading part in feminist causes from the earliest times. They helped organized the special juvenile or "family" courts that emerged at this time.[332] The woman lawyers, along with women doctors, attempted (sometimes successfully) to intercede to prevent the wrongful commitment as insane of women who were merely troublesome to their families.[333] The few women who were lawyers in the United States in the later years of the nineteenth century and the early years of the twentieth century, however, do not seem to have spoken out on abortion.

Unlike the medical profession, where women physicians spoke out forcefully and frequently against abortion, we have no comparable evidence that women attorneys opposed to abortion; we also have no evidence that they supported any supposed right to abort. Their silence, however, cannot be taken dissent from the prevailing professional mores of doctors and lawyers. Women lawyers usually were less prominent in addressing questions of professional ethics and social justice apart from the rights of women generally. Indeed, given their often vocal attention to issues of concern to women, their silence regarding abortion, if anything, suggests that they, like women physicians, did not see the prohibition of abortion as oppressive to women. Thus, the near unanimity among women physicians in condemning abortion and calling for stricter

---

328. Hall v. Incorporated Soc'y of Law-Agents of Scotland, 3 Fr. 1059 (1901). *See* Corcos, *supra* note 293, at 316–21.

329. Alpha Connelly & Betty Hilliard, *The Legal Profession*, in GENDER AND THE LAW IN IRELAND 212 (Alpha Connelly ed. 1993); Corcos, *supra* note 293, at 321–22.

330. Joan Brockman, *Bias in the Legal Profession: Perceptions and Experiences*, 30 ALBERTA L. REV. 747 (1992); Pauline Molyneux, *Association of Women Solicitors—Membership Survey*, 83 LAW SOC'Y GAZETTE 3082 (1986); Daniel Podmore & Anne Spencer, *Law as a Sex-Typed Profession*, 9 J. LAW & SOC'Y 21 (1982) ("Podmore & Spencer I"); Daniel Podmore & Anne Spencer, *Women Lawyers in England: The Experience of Inequality*, 9 WORK & OCCUPATION 337 (1982) ("Podmore & Spencer II").

331. Corcos, *supra* note 293, at 395–417. *See generally* ABEL, *supra* note 310; ABEL-SMITH & STEVENS, *supra* note 326; BIRKS, *supra* note 309; HAGAN & FOY, *supra* note 291; HARRINGTON, *supra* note 291; Molyneux, *supra* note 330; Podmore & Spencer I & II, *supra* note 330; St. John-Stevas, *supra* note 309. From an American point of view, a peculiar aspect of the struggles in Britain centered on whether women barristers would be required (or allowed) to wear the wig. *See* Corcos, *supra* note 293, at 399–404; Gervase Webb, *The Law Wants a Verdict on Wigs in Court*, EVENING STDD. (London), Apr. 28, 1992, at 14; *Wig Debate*, BARRISTERS & SOLIC. J., Apr. 1, 1922, at 81; *Women Barristers*, 66 SOLIC. J. & WKLY. REP. 411, 411 (1922); *Women Barristers and Wigs*, 66 SOLIC. J. & WKLY. REP. 401 (1922).

332. G. Hopkins, *Women's Work in the Courts in the United States*, 15 J. COMP. LEGIS. 198 (1915). This also happened in France. *See* Lilly, *supra* note 293, at 433.

333. *Editorial Comment: Women Physicians and Lawyers Set Good Example*, 22 CASE & COMMENT 63 (1915). *See generally* JOEL PETER EIGEN, WITNESSING INSANITY: MADNESS AND MAD-DOCTORS IN THE ENGLISH COURT (1995); SANDRA GILBERT & SUSAN GUBAR, THE MADWOMAN IN THE ATTIC (1979); HELEN SMALL, LOVE'S MADNESS: MEDICINE, THE NOVEL, AND FEMALE INSANITY 1800–1865 (1996); Jennifer Rebecca Levison, *Elizabeth Parsons Ware Packard: An Advocate for Cultural, Religious, Legal Change*, 55 ALA. L. REV. 985 (2003).

criminal laws should not lead one to expect that had there been numerous women attorneys the law might have developed differently than it did.

# Chapter 10

# Turn the Page[1]

*Listen up, because I've got nothing to say and I'm only going to say it once.*

—Yogi Berra[2]

The nineteenth-century abortion statutes in England and America emerged from intersection of a four variables. First and always foremost was the concern, originating among women at least as much or more than among men, was to protect unborn children.[3] Related to this was a concern to protect mothers from what was still a highly dangerous set of procedures.[4] These concerns fed into a drive to professionalize the practice of law and the practice of medicine.[5] All of these concerns came under increasing pressure to adapt to new circumstances created by steadily changing medical technologies tending to make abortion increasingly safe for pregnant women.[6]

The increasing safety of abortion for the woman at last began to create an opening to criticize the centuries-long traditional prohibition of abortion. During the nineteenth century there emerged a class of professional abortionists who began, at first with more than a little fraud in their claims, to denigrate the existing abortion laws.[7] At the same time, social behavior underwent fundamental changes on both sides of the Atlantic as first the United Kingdom and then the United States passed through the Industrial Revolution. Changes in social behavior created a greater demand for abortion services at the very time that abortion was becoming a far less risky choice for a woman. The overall result of these changes was that the arguments against the existing abortion laws began, at first very slowly, to reach a wider audience and to be espoused by others than the professional abortionists—and with far less need for misrepresentation. This Chapter examines these changes and the continuing efforts by the legal and medical professions to enforce the abortion laws in the later years of the nineteenth century and the early years of the twentieth century. The next several chapters will turn to the emergence of the movement in both the United Kingdom and the United States that succeeded in the overturning the abortion statutes and ushering the present era of abortion freedom.

---

1. Bob Seger, *Turn the Page* (1973).
2. David Nathan, Baseball Quotations 151 (1993).
3. *See* Chapter 8.
4. *See* Chapter 5, at notes 1–32, and Chapter 6, at notes 332–413.
5. *See* Chapter 6, at notes 213–331; Chapter 7, at notes 205–470; Chapter 9, at notes 70–331.
6. *See* Chapter 7, at notes 114–204.
7. *See* Chapter 6, at 240–46; Chapter 7, at notes 140–60.

# Abortion Becomes Safe—for the Mother

*And no man putteth new wine into old bottles....*

—Mark[8]

Technical progress did not end with the crude insertion device of the eighteenth century or the improved surgical techniques of the nineteenth century that figured in the legal developments of those times. The relevant medical technologies for performing abortions and for recognizing and caring for unborn children continued to evolve throughout the nineteenth and twentieth centuries, and thereby to reshape the several interests involved in setting policy on abortion. The combined effect of these several technical innovations was dramatic. At some point between 1865 and 1955, abortion became dramatically safer for a pregnant women than it had been before.[9] The change was noted as early as 1895.[10] Abortion apparently became safer than carrying a child to term, at least if the abortion were performed before the fifteenth week of gestation.[11] This claim remains controversial, but has wide support.[12] The studies on which these conclusions are based, however, exhibit serious flaws.

The studies compare a procedure that usually takes a few minutes and rarely more than a day (with any long-term complications rarely being traced back to the abortion) to a process that last

---

8. *Mark* 2:22.

9. Roe v. Wade, 410 U.S. 113, 148–50, 163 (1973); BARBARA BROOKES, ABORTION IN ENGLAND 1900–1967, at 42, 49 n.132, 58–59, 70–71, 122 (1988); COMMITTEE FOR PSYCHIATRY AND THE LAW, THE RIGHT TO ABORTION: A PSYCHIATRIC VIEW 33–37 (1970); REPORT OF THE INTERDEPARTMENTAL COMMITTEE ON ABORTION 18 (1939) ("INTERDEPARTMENTAL COMM."); J.G. Moore & J.H. Randall, *Trends in Therapeutic Abortion: A Review of 137 Cases,* 63 AM. J. OBSTET. & GYNECOLOGY 34 (1952); Malcolm Potts, *Postconception Control of Fertility,* 8 INT'L J. GYNECOLOGY & OBSTETRICS 957, 967 (1970); Christopher Tietze, *United States: Therapeutic Abortions, 1963–1968,* 59 STUD. IN FAM. PLAN. 5, 7 (1970).

10. George Phillips, *Criminal Abortion: Its Frequency, Prognosis, and Treatment,* 12 ME. MED. ASS'N MED. TRANS. 306 (1895–97). *See also* TAYLOR'S MEDICAL JURISPRUDENCE 150 (F.J. Smith ed. 1920).

11. *See* Willard Cates, jr. & David Grimes, *Morbidity and Mortality of Abortion in the United States,* in ABORTION AND STERILIZATION: MEDICAL AND SOCIAL ASPECTS 155 (Jane Hodgson ed. 1981); Willard Cates *et al., Mortality from Abortion and Childbirth: Are the Statistics Biased?,* 248 JAMA 192 (1992) (their answer was yes—against abortion); David Grimes & Kenneth Schultz, *Morbidity and Mortality from Second Trimester Abortions,* 30 J. REPRODUCTIVE MED. 505 (1985); Herschel Lawson *et al., Abortion Mortality, United States, 1972 through 1987,* 171 AM. J. OBSTET. & GYNECOLOGY 1365 (1994); Roger Rochat, *et al., Maternal Mortality in the United States: Report from the Maternal Mortality Collective,* 72 OBSTETRICS & GYNECOLOGY 91 (1988); Phillip Stubblefield & David Grimes, *Septic Abortion,* 331 N. ENG. J. MED. 310 (1994); John Thorp, jr. & Watson Bowes, jr., *Prolife Perinatologist—Paradox or Possibility?,* 326 N. ENG. J. MED. 1217, 1218 (1992); R.T. Burkman, M.F. Alienza, & T.M. King, *Morbidity Risk among Young Adolescents Undergoing Elective Abortion,* 30 CONTRACEPTION 99 (1984) (finding a 12% complication rate during later pregnancies). On the risks of giving birth, see IRVINE LOUDON, DEATH IN CHILDBIRTH: AN INTERNATIONAL STUDY OF MATERNAL CARE AND MATERNAL MORTALITY, 1800–1950 (1992); EDWARD SHORTER, A HISTORY OF WOMEN'S BODIES 130–38 (Pelican Books ed. 1984); Joyce Antler & Daniel Fox, *The Movement toward a Safer Maternity: Physician Accountability in New York City, 1915–1940,* 50 BULL. HIST. MED. 569 (1976); Charles King, *The New York Maternal Mortality Study: A Conflict of Professionalization,* 65 BULL. HIST. MED. 476 (1991); Irvine Loudon, *Maternal Mortality: 1880–1950: Some Regional and International Comparisons,* 1 SOC. HIST. MED. 183 (1988) ("Loudon, *Maternal Mortality*"). Apparently some historians simply extrapolate the current situation into times past; at least one historian has argued abortion must have been common in past because childbirth was so likely to cause the mother's death. Constance Backhouse, *Involuntary Motherhood: Abortion, Birth Control and the Law in Nineteenth Century Canada,* 3 WINDSOR Y.B. OF ACCESS TO JUSTICE 61, 63 (1983).

12. MAUREEN PAUL *et al.,* A CLINICIANS GUIDE TO MEDICAL AND SURGICAL ABORTION 108–9 (1999); Lawson *et al. supra* note 11, at 1368. *See also* DONALD JUDGES, HARD CHOICES, LOST VOICES 73–81 (1993).

nine months. The studies often compare complication and fatality rates to statistics drawn from all births within the general population of the region, state, or nation rather than to birthing-samples matched for maternal age, health, and similar variables that could well affect the relative safety of the two procedures.[13] The studies usually did not consider maternal morbidity, an effect that is more difficult to measure.[14] One apparently careful study of pregnancy-related deaths in Finland found the risk of maternal death to be four times as high when giving birth, but that included deaths from accidents, suicides, and homicides and not simply from the physical processes involved in abortion or giving birth.[15] In any event, assuming appropriate prenatal care, the differences in relative safety of abortion and childbirth for the mother are quite small, all the more remarkable given the great disparities in the duration of the processes involved. There is no disagreement over the usual effect of the procedure on the fetus.

Studies regarding the relative safety of abortion also omit consideration of risks other than to the life or health of the mother, such as whether having an abortion, especially multiple abortions, creates greater risks of spontaneous miscarriages or other problems in later pregnancies.[16]

---

13. *See, e.g.,* Cates & Grimes, *supra* note 11; Grimes & Schultz, *supra* note 11. *See generally* ANNE SPECK-HARD, PSYCHO-SOCIAL ASPECTS OF STRESS FOLLOWING ABORTION (1987); Paige Comstock Cunningham & Clarke Forsythe, *Is Abortion the "First Right" for Women?: Some Consequences of Legal Abortion,* in ABORTION, MEDICINE AND THE LAW 100, 125–53 (J. Douglas Butler & David Walbert eds., 4th ed. 1992); Editorial, *How Safe Is Abortion?,* THE LANCET, Dec. 4, 1971, at 1239; Editorial, *Latent Morbidity after Abortion,* BRIT. MED. J. 506 (Mar. 3, 1973); Thomas Hilgers et al., *Abortion Related Maternal Mortality: An In-Depth Analysis,* in NEW PERSPECTIVES ON HUMAN ABORTION 69 (Thomas Hilgers, Dennis Horan, & David Mall eds. 1981); Harold Klinger, *Demographic Consequences of the Legalization of Induced Abortion in Eastern Europe,* INT'L J. GYNE-COLOGY & OBSTETRICS 680 (Sept. 1970); Christopher Tietze, *Abortion Laws and Abortion Practices in Europe,* in PROC. AM. ASS'N PLANNED PARENTHOOD PHYSICIANS 198 (1969).

14. Michelle Allen et al., *Ascertainment of Maternal Mortality in New York City,* 81 AM. J. PUB. HEALTH 380 (1991); American Med. Ass'n Council of Sci. Aff., *Induced Termination of Pregnancy before and after* Roe v. Wade: *Trends in the Mortality and Morbidity of Women,* 268 JAMA 3231 (1992); Nancy Binkin, *Trends in Induced Legal Abortion Morbidity and Mortality,* 13 CLINICAL OBSTET. & GYNECOLOGY 83 (1986); R.T. Burkman et al., *Morbidity Risk among Young Adolescents Undergoing Elective Abortion,* 30 CONTRACEPTION 99 (1984); Willard Cates, jr., & David Grimes, *Morbidity and Morality in the United States,* in ABORTION AND STERILIZA-TION: MEDICAL AND SOCIAL ASPECTS 155 (Jane Hodgson ed. 1981); Janet Gans Epner, Harry Jonas, & Daniel Seckinger, *Late-Term Abortion,* 280 JAMA 724, 727–28 (1998); E. Hakin-Elahi, *Complications of First-Trimester Abortions: A Report of 170,000 Cases,* 76 OBSTET. & GYNECOLOGY 129 (1990); Jack Smith, *An Assessment of the Incidence of Maternal Mortality in the United States,* 74 AM. J. PUB. HEALTH 780 (1984).

15. Mike Gissler et al., *Pregnancy-Associated Deaths in Finland, 1987–1994—Definition Problems and Benefits of Record Linkage,* 76 ACTA OBSTETRICA GYNEOLCOGICA SCANDINAVIA 651 (1997); Mike Gissler et al., *Suicides after Pregnancy in Finland, 1987–1994: Register Linkage Study,* 313 BRIT. MED. J. 1431 (1996). *See also* AMERICAN COLL. OBSTET. & GYNECOLOGISTS, GUIDELINES FOR WOMEN'S HEALTH CARE 128 (1996) (claiming that maternal deaths from pregnancy and birth are 25 times higher than maternal deaths during abortions, but without reference to any research or other sources); Cynthia Berg et al., *Pregnancy Related Mortality in the United States, 1987–1990,* 88 OBSTET. & GYNECOLOGY 161 (1996) (reporting an 8:1 ratio); American Med. Ass'n Council for Sci. Aff., *supra* note 14, at 3232 (reporting a 15:1 ratio).

16. SEBASTIAN FARO & MARK PEARLMAN, INFECTION AND ABORTION (1992); RISKING THE FUTURE: ADO-LESCENT SEXUALITY, PREGNANCY, AND CHILDBEARING (Cheryl Hayes ed. 1987); WILLIAMS OBSTETRICS 506–07 (F. Gary Cunningham, Paul MacDonald, & Norman Grant eds., 18th ed. 1989); C.V. Ananth, J.C. Smulian & A.M. Vintzileos, *Abortion: A Meta-Analysis,* 177 AM. J. OBSTET. & GYNECOLOGY 1071 (1997); Brenda Eskenazi, Laura Fenster, & Stephen Sidney, *A Multivariate Analysis of Risk Factors for Preclampsia,* 266 JAMA 237 (1991); Peter Frank et al., *The Effect of Induced Abortion on Subsequent Fertility,* 100 BRIT. J. OBSTET. & GYNAECOLOGY 575 (1993); M. Germain, M. Krohn, & J. Daling, *Reproductive History and the Risk of Neonatal Sepsis,* 9 PAEDIATRIC & PERINATAL EPIDEMIOLOGY 48 (1995); Judith Gerthner & Karin Nelson, *Maternal Infection and Cerebral Palsy in Infants of Normal Birth Weight,* 278 JAMA 207 (1997); Lars Heisterberg, *Factors Influencing Spontaneous Abortion, Dyspareunia, Dysmenorrhea, and Pelvic Pain,* 81 OBSTET. & GYNECOLOGY 594 (1993); Lars Heisterberg & Mette Kringelbach, *Early Complications after Induced First-Trimester Abortion,* 66 ACTA OBSTET. & GYNECOLOGICA SCAND. 201 (1987); Claire Infante-Rivard & Robert Gauthier, *Induced Abortion as a Risk Factor for Subsequent Fetal Loss,* 7 EPIDEMIOLOGY 540 (1996); Manica Jansson et al., *The In-*

The active resistance of abortion rights activists to requirements for detailed reports by abortion clinics has impaired the ability to accumulate data since 1973, exacerbating the morbidity and sample-matching problems. The voluntary nature of the reporting of ensuing medical complications and deaths assure incomplete records. Because abortion is usually an out-patient procedure, an abortionist might never learn of a complication arising after the woman returns to her home, perhaps some distance away. In short, there are good reasons to believe the current statistics on maternal deaths or lesser complications from abortion are probably seriously understated.[17]

Even if abortion early in pregnancy is safer than childbirth today, not so long ago this was not true. In fact, one of the surest ways that we know that intrusive abortions only became common after 1880 is because it is only after 1880 that hospital admissions for septic abortions become a common statistical item.[18] This is not to suggest that intrusive abortions were generally fatal; the great majority of such abortions, while painful and unpleasant, were probably successful without being fatal. But maternal death remained a known and all too common risk. Thus historian Leslie Reagan, who would like us to believe that abortion was a nearly universal and common experience for women in Chicago at the beginning of the twentieth century, culled almost all of her specific information about abortions and abortionists from coroner's inquests.[19] Reagan herself concluded that about 14 percent of maternal deaths in rural areas were a result of criminal

---

*fluence of Sexual and Social Factors on the Risk of Chlamydia Trachomatis Infections: A Population-Based Serologic Study,* 22 Sexually Transmitted Diseases 355 (1995); Marijane Krohn et al., *Prior Pregnancy Outcome and the Risk of Intraamniotic Infection in the Following Pregnancy,* 178 Am. J. Obstet. & Gynecology 381 (1998); Per-Goran Larsson, et al., *Incidence of PID after First-Trimester Legal Abortion in Women with Bacterial Vaginosis after Treatment with Metronidazole: A Double-Blind Randomized Study,* 166 Am. J. Obstet. & Gynecology 100 (1992); P. Levallois et al., *Chlamydial Infection among Females Attending an Abortion Clinic,* 137 Can. Med. Ass'n J. 33 (1987); A. Lopes & P.A. King, *The Impact of Multiple Induced Abortions on the Outcome of Subsequent Pregnancy,* 31 Austral. & N.Z. J. Obstet. & Gynecology 41 (1991); Margaret Mandelson, Christopher Maden, & Janet Daling, *Low Birth Weight in Relation to Multiple Induced Abortions,* 82 Am. J. Pub. Health 391 (1992); F. Parazzini et al., *Induced Abortions and Risk of Ectopic Pregnancy,* 10 Hum. Reprod. 1841 (1995); David Savitz & Jun Zhang, *Pregnancy-Induced Hypertension in North Carolina,* 82 Am. J. Pub. Health 675 (1992); D Daniel Seidman et al., *The Effect of Abortion on the Incidence of Pre-Eclampsia,* 33 Eur. J. Obstet. & Gynecology & Reproductive Biol. 109 (1989); F.E. Skeldestad et al., *Sentinal Surveillance of Chlamydia Trachomitis Infection in Women Terminating Pregnancy,* 73 Genitourin Med. 29 (1997); Jette Sorensen et al., *Early and Late Onset Pelvic Inflammatory Disease among Women with Cervical Chlamydia Trachomatis Infection at the Time of Induced Abortion: A Follow-up,* 22 Infection 242 (1994); Jette Sorensen & Ingrid Thronow, *A Double-Blind Randomized Study of the Effect of Erythromycin in Preventing Pelvic Inflammatory Disease after First Trimester Abortion,* 99 Brit. J. Obstet. & Gynaecology 434 (1992); B. Stray-Pedersen, *Induced Abortion: Microbiological Screening and Medical Complications,* 19 Infection 305 (1991); Peter Sykes, *Complications of Termination of Pregnancy: A Retrospective Study of Admissions in Christchurch Women's Hospital, 1989 and 1990,* 106 N.Z. Med. J. 83 (Mar. 10, 1993); Victoria Taylor et al., *Placenta Previa in Relation to Induced and Spontaneous Abortion: A Population-Based Study,* 82 Obstet. & Gynecology 88 (1993); Catherine Tharaux-Deneux et al., *Risk of Ectopic Pregnancy and Previous Induced Abortion,* 88 Am. J. Pub. Health 401 (1998); Anastasia Tzonou et al., *Induced Abortions, Miscarriages, and Tobacco Smoking as Risk Factors for Secondary Infertility,* 47 J. Epidemiology & Community Health 36 (1993); See generally Elizabeth Ring-Cassidy & Ian Gentles, Women's Health after Abortion: The Medical and Psychological Evidence (2002).

17. W.A. Bachrach & W. Baldwin, *Abortion Underreporting,* Fam. Plan. Persp., Sept./Oct. 1991, at 233; Brian Clowes, *The Role of Maternal Deaths in the Abortion Debate,* 13 St. L.U. Pub. L. Rev. 327, 349–61, 372–81 (1993); J. Hopwood et al., *There Is More to a Test than Technology—Evaluation of Testing for Chlamydia Infection in a Charitable Sector Termination Service,* 23 Brit. J. Fam. Plan. 116 (1998); Karen Nichols & Sandra Rasmussen, *Postabortion Medical Care: Management of Delayed Complications,* 49 J. Am. Med. Women's Ass'n 165 (1994).

18. Shorter, *supra* note 11, at 191–96.

19. Leslie Reagan, When Abortion Was a Crime: Women, Medicine, and Law in the United States, 1867–1973 (1997).

abortions, and that "rate was higher in urban areas."[20] And as late as 1930, the death rate from abortion or childbirth once septicemia or peritonitis set in was 60–70 percent.[21]

We cannot say precisely when combining improved techniques for doing abortions with analgesics, anesthetics, antibiotics, and antiseptics, made abortion early in pregnancy possibly safer than carrying a child to term. All we can say for certain is that the transition to relative safety for early abortions occurred sometime between the discovery of antiseptics in 1867 and the relegalization of abortion in the USSR in 1955.[22] After 1955, complication rates throughout eastern Europe fell below complication rates for childbirth; Scandinavian complication rates remained considerably higher than in eastern Europe, probably because abortions in Scandinavia tended to be performed later in the pregnancy.[23] Notwithstanding the uncertainties about precisely how safe abortion became and when it became so safe, at some point in the early twentieth century abortion early in a pregnancy seems to have become the safe, effective, and fairly comfortable procedure for a pregnant woman that the modern mythmakers would have us believe it always was. The incidence of later abortions is too infrequent to allow firm statistical studies, but mortality rates for late-term abortions, at least in the United States, appear to have been higher than for carrying the child to term.

The safety gains in doing abortions appear certainly to have been true of legal abortions, and probably were true for illegal abortions as well, at least when performed by a physician or other trained health-care professional.[24] As a result, the interests of mothers, children, and the professions, which until sometime in the late nineteenth or early twentieth century converged on the criminalizing of abortion, now diverged, bringing controversy to an area where once all agreed that only evil could be found. As historian Beverly Harrison concluded, surgical advances and new knowledge of embryology "precipitated—for the first time—a deep, culture-wide debate on abortion."[25] Harrison gave a strongly pro-abortion slant to her history, arguing that society merely "assumed" abortion was wrong before "modern medical science, as opposed to institutionalized health care and the social practice of medicine" made safe abortion possible by developing new intrusive techniques and by exploiting new embryological knowledge easing the use of those techniques.[26] She completely ignored the fact that growing embryological knowledge strengthened opposition to abortion even while other medical advances were making the perfor-

---

20. *Id.* at 77, 284 n.110.

21. *Statement of Dr. Frederick Taussig*, in White House Conf. on Child Health & Protection, Fetal, Newborn, & Maternal Morbidity and Mortality 466–67 (1933).

22. *See* Daniel Callahan, Abortion: Law, Choice, and Morality 31–43 (1970); Paul Gebhard *et al.*, Pregnancy, Birth and Abortion 215–32 (1958); Germain Grisez, Abortion: The Myths, the Realities, and the Arguments 104–06 (1970); Judith Walzer Leavitt, Brought to Bed: Childbearing in America 1750–1950, at 184, 194, 268 (1986); H.M.I. Liley, Modern Motherhood 42 (rev. ed. 1969); Reagan, *supra* note 19, at 162; Henry Olson *eg al.*, *The Problem of Abortion*, 45 Am. J. Obstet. & Gynecology 677 (1943); W. Nicholson Jones & Eugene Howe, *The Role of Antibiotics in the Management of Incomplete Abortions*, 67 Am. J. Obstet. & Gynecology 825 (1954); Loudon, *Maternal Mortality*, *supra* note 11, at 196–200; Christopher Tietze, *Mortality with Contraception and Induced Abortion*, 45 Stud. in Fam. Plan. 6 (1969); Christopher Tietze & Sarah Lewit, *Legal Abortion*, 236 Sci. Am. 21, 26–27 (Jan. 1977); Augusta Webster, *Management of Abortion at the Cook County Hospital*, 62 Am. J. Obstet. & Gynecology 1327 (1951). *See generally* Loudon, *Maternal Mortality*, *supra* note 11.

23. Christopher Tietze & Hans Lehfeldt, *Legal Abortion in Eastern Europe*, 175 JAMA 1149, 1152 (1961).

24. *See* Abraham Rongy, Abortion: Legal or Illegal? 134–35 (1933); Percy Russell, *The Conservative Treatment of Abortion*, 107 JAMA 1527 (1936); Regine Stix, *A Study of Pregnancy Wastage*, 13 Milbank Mem. Fund Q. 347, 362–63 (1935); Raymond Watkins, *A Five-Year Study of Abortion*, 26 Am. J. Obstet. & Gynecology 161, 162 (1933). These findings are summarized in Reagan, *supra* note 19, at 138.

25. Beverly Wildung Harrison, Our Right to Choose: Toward a New Ethic of Abortion 168, 194, 201–30 (1983). *See also* Mary Kenny, Abortion: The Whole Story 179–81 (1986).

26. Harrison, *supra* note 25, at 169.

mance of abortions easier and more certain. Other historians have simply assumed that the rising frequency of abortions proves that abortion was in fact considered to an acceptable or morally unobjectionable practice by "silenced" "ordinary Americans."[27]

Sociologist Nanette Davis has given us a more forthright account of the twentieth century's abortion reform movement. Although Davis wrote her history in order to support "abortion rights," she candidly summarized popular attitudes toward abortion up nearly until *Roe v. Wade* was decided (1973), even among those who underwent the procedure, not as a "choice," but as a "necessary evil," a "lesser evil," an "act of desperation," or a "morally despicable act."[28] Strong evidence of this view is the near universal resort to euphemisms to describe abortions when talking or writing about it—even among persons on intimate terms with each other.[29] Most historians supporting abortion rights do not even mention this aspect of the historical record. Leslie Reagan did mention it, seeking to dismiss it merely as evidence that the women (and men) using such euphemisms simply were unfamiliar with the word "abortion."[30] This is not a credible claim. While we cannot determine whether the persons Reagan is quoting had ever read any of the nineteenth century books written to reach a popular audience that used the term "abortion" without any apparent need to translate the word into a different, more familiar term, the statements that Reagan quotes are clearly meant to avoid naming the deed, rather than providing a more familiar name for it. For example, Reagan quotes women as using such expressions as "can fix you up"[31] "had it done,"[32] "bring her around,"[33] or "been relieved."[34] The attitude appears to have been nearly universal in the nineteenth and first half of the twentieth centuries. Even in Japan, a place were Westerners believe that abortion is accepted as unproblematic by the public, people actually express considerable remorse over abortion, demonstrated most impressively by the thousands of religious statues dedicated to the souls of aborted fetuses.[35]

Despite the near universal disdain for abortion, growing numbers of women certainly obtained illegal abortions after the enactment of the abortion statutes as the abortion procedure itself became safer and easier to undergo. Anecdotal evidence abounds for the growing and eventually widespread practice of abortion during the era from 1880–1970.[36] Indirect, but ultimately

---

27. *See* REAGAN, *supra* note 19, at 19–22.

28. NANETTE DAVIS, FROM CRIME TO CHOICE xiii, 3–4 (1985). *See also* JOHN D'EMILIO & ESTELLE FREEDMAN, INTIMATE MATTERS: A HISTORY OF SEXUALITY IN AMERICA 64 (1988).

29. *See, e.g.,* REAGAN, *supra* note 19, at 19–20.

30. *Id.* at 23–24.

31. *Id.* at 19, 24, 29.

32. *Id.* at 19, 24.

33. *Id.* at 24.

34. *Id.*

35. Evy McElmeel, Comment, *Legalization of the Birth Control Pill in Japan Will Reduce Reliance on Abortion as the Primary Method of Birth Control,* 8 PAC. RIM L. & POL'Y REV. 681, 681 (1999); Lynn Wardle, *"Crying Stones": A Comparison of Abortion in Japan and the United States,* 14 N.Y.L.S. J. INT'L & COMP. L. 183, 183–84 (1993); Sheryl WuDunn, *In Japan, a Ritual of Morning for Abortions,* N.Y. TIMES, Jan. 25, 1996, at A1, A8. At least one American feminist insists that this shows a lack of guilt rather than some sense that a wrong had been committed. Sara Walsh, *Liquid Lives and Liquid Laws,* 7 INT'L LEG. PERSPECTIVES 187, 200 (1995). For yet another take on this practice by an American feminist, see HELEN HARDACRE, MARKETING THE MENACING FETUS IN JAPAN (1997).

36. *See, e.g.,* SIMONE DE BEAUVOIR, THE SECOND SEX 540–50 (Vintage Books ed. 1974); BROOKES, *supra* note 9, at 2, 5–6, 26–36; REBECCA CHALKER & CAROL DOWNER, A WOMAN'S BOOK OF CHOICES: MENSTRUAL EXTRACTION, RU 486 97–109 (1993); DAVIS, *supra* note 28, at 65–107; D'EMILIO & FREEDMAN, *supra* note 28, at 254–55; ELLEN FRANKFURT, VAGINAL POLITICS 51–83 (Bantam ed. 1973); EUROPEAN WOMEN: A DOCUMENTARY HISTORY, 1789–1945, at 207–09 (Eleanor Riemer & John Fouts eds. 1980); FROM ABORTION TO REPRODUCTIVE FREEDOM: TRANSFORMING A MOVEMENT 71–73, 87–100 (Marlene Gerber Fried ed. 1990); JOYCE JOHNSON, MINOR CHARACTERS 107–110 (1983); KENNY, *supra* note 25, at 200–24; NANCY HOWELL LEE, THE SEARCH FOR AN ABORTIONIST (1969); KRISTIN LUKER, ABORTION AND THE POLITICS OF

uncertain, evidence of a rising incidence of abortion are suggested by a small rise in the incidence of maternal mortality during the early years of the twentieth century in England, at a time when general health care and prenatal care were both improving, but when techniques for performing abortion were still highly dangerous and (before the advent of antibiotics in the 1940s) the mortality rate for abortions had probably not yet begun to turn down to any great extent.[37] Estimates at the end of the nineteenth century range as high as the unlikely figure of 2,000,000 abortions per year across the United States.[38] In the end, actual measurements of the rate of abortion, an illegal and therefore hidden act, must remain conjectural.[39] No one can have confidence in the statistical claims about the incidence of illegal abortions in either England or America.[40]

# Early Critics of the Abortion Statutes

*You may not know what you're doing, but you know that you're right.*

—Nancy Stearns[41]

Given the probable increase in the incidence of abortion after 1880, one is not surprised then to discover that criticism of and even resistance to the nineteenth-century abortion statutes never completely disappeared. Despite the spread of abortion in practice, however, very few criticisms of abortion's prohibition appeared in medical or other literature prior to 1920. This was, after all, the period that produced the *Mann Act* and then applied the Act's prohibition of a man

MOTHERHOOD 73–76, 105 (1984); ANGUS MCLAREN, BIRTH CONTROL IN NINETEENTH-CENTURY ENGLAND 226–28 (1978); ELLEN MESSER & KATHRYN MAY, BACK ROOMS: VOICES FROM THE ILLEGAL ABORTION ERA 1–170 (1988); ROSALIND POLLACK PETCHESKY, ABORTION AND WOMEN'S CHOICE: THE STATE, SEXUALITY, AND REPRODUCTIVE FREEDOM 52–55 (rev. ed. 1990); REAGAN, *supra* note 19, at 19–45; CAROLINE HADLEY ROBINSON, SEVENTY BIRTH CONTROL CLINICS 66 (1930); DIANE SCHULDER & FLORYNCE KENNEDY, ABORTION RAP 44–82 (1971); FREDERICK TAUSSIG, ABORTION: SPONTANEOUS AND INDUCED 403 (1936); CATHERINE WHITNEY, WHOSE LIFE? A BALANCED, COMPREHENSIVE VIEW OF ABORTION FROM ITS HISTORICAL CONTEXT TO THE CURRENT DEBATE 48–69 (1991); GLANVILLE WILLIAMS, THE SANCTITY OF LIFE AND THE CRIMINAL LAW 211–12 (1957, reprinted 1972); Jerome Bates, *The Abortion Mill*, 45 J. CRIM. L. & CRIMINOLOGY 157 (1954); Rickie Solinger, *Extreme Danger: Women Abortionists and Their Clients before* Roe v. Wade, in NOT JUNE CLEAVER: WOMEN AND GENDER IN POSTWAR AMERICA, 1945–1960, at 335 (Joanne Meyrowitz ed. 1994); *The 25th Anniversary of* Roe v. Wade: *Has It Stood the Test of Time, Hearings before the Subcomm. On the Const., Federalism, & Property Rts. of the Sen. Comm. on the Judiciary,* 100th Cong. 42–44 (statement of Carol Carter Wall).

37. *See* BROOKES, *supra* note 9, at 23, 43 n.6, 108–11; JANE LEWIS, THE POLITICS OF MOTHERHOOD: CHILD AND MATERNAL WELFARE IN ENGLAND, 1900–1939, at 36, 117–35 (1980).

38. LINDA GORDON, WOMAN'S BODY, WOMAN'S RIGHT: A SOCIAL HISTORY OF BIRTH CONTROL IN AMERICA 493 n.23 (1976); REAGAN, *supra* note 19, at 23.

39. For such estimates, see GEBHARD *et al.*, *supra* note 22, at 55, 93–94; FAYE GINSBURG, CONTESTED LIVES: THE ABORTION DEBATE IN AN AMERICAN COMMUNITY 33–35 (1989); GORDON, *supra* note 38, at 406–11; LUKER, *supra* note 36, at 40–65, 101–08; PETCHESKY, *supra* note 36, at 101–32; RAYMOND TATALOVICH & BYRON DAYNES, THE POLITICS OF ABORTION: A STUDY OF COMMUNITY CONFLICT IN PUBLIC POLICY MAKING 23–26 (1981); TAUSSIG, *supra* note 36, at 185; Leslie Reagan, *"About to Meet Her Maker": Women, Doctors, Dying Declarations, and the State's Investigation of Abortion, Chicago, 1867–1940,* 77 J. AM. HIST. 1240, 1245–47 (1991); R. Sauer, *Attitudes to Abortion in America, 1800–1973,* 28 POP. STUDIES 53, 60–63 (1974).

40. *See* Chapter 7, at notes 164–204.

41. As quoted in Amy Kesselman, *Women versus Connecticut: Conducting a Satewide Hearing on Abortion,* in ABORTION WARS: A HALF CENTURY OF STRUGGLE, 1950–2000, at 42, 43 (Rickie Solinger ed. 1998).

transporting a woman across state lines for immoral purposes to consensual relations between adults who were not married to each other.[42]

During such a free thinking era as the Enlightenment, it would have been surprising if no one had questioned the received wisdom regarding abortion, and several thinkers did do so.[43] John Locke compared the fetus before birth with a mere vegetable, as one would expect with Locke's theory that sensations were necessary to create ideas and knowledge and his insistence that an infant came into the world as a *tabula rasa* (a blank slate).[44] Locke, however, did not advocate elective abortions. That had to await another century of Enlightenment. Indeed, 50 years after Locke, a decision by the Royal College of Physicians not to investigate the death of two infants delivered by male midwives was vigorously protested by members of the Royal College.[45]

The first public endorsement of elective abortion in Europe, at least since the rise of Christianity to dominance there, appears to have been by the Marquis de Sade in his *La Philosophie dans le Boudoir*.[46] De Sade also believed that murder and the torture of adults were natural activities that were therefore morally neutral.[47] De Sade in particular despised women in particular and saw them mainly as objects of torture.[48] His views of women are of a piece with his views on abortion and infanticide. De Sade not only defended abortion, he also endorsed infanticide as a "very unimportant matter."[49] One commentator summarized de Sade's philosophy thusly:

> [De Sade] was a monster of self-centeredness. Lever speaks of his *"autisme"* and his *"isolisme,"* that is, his conviction—which, indeed, he himself presents as a law of nature in *La philosophie dans le boudoir*—that the individual's only duty is toward himself in order to ensure his own acutest sensation of enjoyment. In the hypocritical part of his correspondence, and in his nonclandestine, soft-porn works, such as *Aline et Valcour,* he can pour out streams of eighteenth-century *sensibilité larmoyante* at will, but that does not offset his basic pathological assumption that *le droit du seignour* is paramount. In my view, it is this single-minded expression of selfish dominance which, independently of the scabrous physical details, makes his most characteristic works so unpalatable. *Les cent vingt journées de Sodome* and *La philosophie dans le boudoir* are dreams of absolute, destructive power, manifesting itself through rape, mutilation, and murder and exercised by groups of seignours over their helpless victims.[50]

To see in de Sade a champion of personal freedom, as a few modern commentators would have us, one must overlook this "quirk" in his thinking.[51]

---

42. 18 U.S.C. § 2421 (2000); Caminetti v. United States, 242 U.S. 470 (1917). *See generally* DAVID LANGUM, CROSSING THE LINE: LEGISLATING MORALITY AND THE MANN ACT (1994). The Mann Act was repealed in 1986.

43. *See generally* ANGUS MCLAREN, REPRODUCTIVE RITUALS 187 n.96, 187 n.96 (1984).

44. 1 JOHN LOCKE, ESSAY ON HUMAN UNDERSTANDING 88 (1695). *See also* 2 WILLIAM ROWLEY, THE RATIONAL PRACTICE OF PHYSIC 41 (1793).

45. DRS. POCUS & MAULUS, PETITION OF THE UNBORN BABES TO THE CENSORS OF THE ROYAL COLLEGE OF PHYSICIANS OF LONDON (2nd ed. 1751).

46. DONATIEN FRANÇOIS ALPHONSE DE SADE, LA PHILOSOPHIE DANS LE BOUDOIR 59, 76–77, 266–68 (1970 reprint ed.; original date 1795).

47. DE SADE, *supra* note 46, at 97.

48. *See generally* LAURENCE BONGIE, SADE: A BIOGRAPHICAL ESSAY (1998). *See also* FRANCINE DU PLESSIS GRAY, AT HOME WITH THE MARQUIS DE SADE: A LIFE (1998).

49. *Id.* at 115–18.

50. John Weightman, *The Human Comedy of the Divine Marquis,* N.Y. REV. OF BOOKS, Sept. 23, 1993, at 6, 8.

51. Robert Darnton, *The Real Marquis,* N.Y. REV. BOOKS, Jan. 14, 1999, at 19.

De Sade's views on abortion, as well as on other matters, were not widely persuasive at the time, although at least one historian has insisted that they "sparked" the modern abortion reform movement.[52] Yet de Sade's views on abortion were to find a receptive audience in the twentieth century. Guillaume de Appollinaire predicted accurately how de Sade would be seen in our century: "Ideas that ripened in the infamous atmosphere of the 'hells' of libraries have now come into their own and that man who seemed to count for nothing during the nineteenth century could very well dominate the twentieth century."[53]

In England, William Godwin did make very similar arguments shortly after de Sade's writings appeared.[54] Godwin, one should note, had only a few years earlier argued that by exalting the life of the mind one could extend one's life, obviating the need to procreate.[55] This, Godwin concluded, would enable a life even more focused on the mind and less concerned with degraded corporeal concerns.[56] Goodwin was never accused of loving children.

Godwin's arguments provoked a pointed response from John Bowles.[57] About 20 years later, Jeremy Bentham endorsed elective abortions on strictly utilitarian grounds, but his views were not published until more than a century later.[58] Bentham, however, acknowledged that in his time the danger of the procedure would keep its incidence low regardless of the law.[59]

Hardly any voices publicly advocated the legality and morality of abortion in the nineteenth century—except those of the professional abortionists. Even the professional abortionists hid their wares behind euphemisms, and all too often their advertisements and publications were nothing short of fraudulent.[60] A similar story arises when one examines advertisements by the women's clinics of the time, which historian James Mohr infers were really nothing but abortion mills.[61] The women's clinics did not advertise abortion directly if abortion services were what they were selling. The employment of euphemisms by those clinics and by professional abortionists eloquently indicates the public attitudes towards abortion regardless of its incidence.

So anxious are the modern historians of abortion rights to find someone, anyone, from the nineteenth century who supported freedom to abort that they have indulged in the fantasy that the feminists of the last century advocated freedom of abortion when they most emphatically did not.[62] No feminist has been found who advocated abortional freedom until 1893, by which time the abortion statutes had long been on the books and legalizing abortion simply was not a "viable alternative."[63] Historians who favor abortion rights have been forced to turn to persons such as Thomas

---

52. A.D. Farr, *The Marquis de Sade and Induced Abortion,* 6 J. Med. Ethics 7 (1980).

53. As quoted in Darnton, *supra* note 51, at 19.

54. William Godwin, Thought Occasioned by the Perusal of Dr. Parr's Spital Sermon 65–66 (1801).

55. William Godwin, 2 Enquiry Concerning Political Justice 511 (1793).

56. *See* Don Locke, A Fantasy of Reason: The Life and Thoughts of William Godwin 108–09, 159–60 (1980).

57. John Bowles, Reflections on the Political and Moral State of Society at the Close of the Eighteenth Century 134 (1802).

58. Jeremy Bentham, The Theory of Legislation 264–65, 479–94 (C.K. Ogden ed. 1931).

59. *Id.* at 493–94.

60. *See* Chapter 7, at notes 140–60.

61. James Mohr, Abortion in America: The Origins and Evolution of National Policy, 1800–1900, at 70–71 (1978).

62. *See* Chapter 8, at notes 147–250.

63. Mohr, *supra* note 61, at 113; Reva Siegel, *Reasoning from the Body: A Historical Perspective on Abortion Regulation and Questions of Equal Protection,* 44 Stan. L. Rev. 261, 307 n.185, 312 nn.202–05 (1992).

Nichols who did indeed argue that abortion was the woman's decision alone.[64] Nichols, however, described abortion as "unnatural" and as an act that "may be very wicked." Historian Janet Brodie (who attributes the book to Thomas and Mary Nichols, although Mary's name does not appear as co-author) has singled his work out as one of the two most favorable advocacies of abortion rights in the nineteenth century.[65] Brodie also identifies a pamphlet by James Ashton as "providing dispassionate advice about when and how to bring about miscarriage."[66] Yet Ashton himself indicated that abortion "should never be resorted to except in extreme circumstances and then only under medical advice" and that abortions, as "collisions with Nature's laws," were always dangerous even as he acknowledged that women sometimes "get by without suffering harm."[67] Similarly, Dr. Henry Marcy seemingly endorsed abortion rights when he wrote that "the product of early impregnation is of so little importance that abortion will not be seriously established as a criminal offense."[68] Yet Marcy wrote this in an article advocating greater efforts to educate the public in order to prevent abortions.

Try as one might, one finds virtually no published criticism in the United Kingdom or in the United States of the idea that abortion was the killing of a child, and as such a serious crime "against Nature." There also was little questioning of the prevailing mores in private documents that have come down to us. A true social consensus appears to have existed in support of those statutes when they were enacted, which explains why the statutes were passed unanimously or nearly so.[69] One finds similarly unanimity among professional groups when they voted on resolutions regarding abortion.[70] One finds only slightly more criticism from Britain or Europe.

Such attitudes apparently prevailed throughout those parts of the world subject to European control or influence. Abortion statutes similar to those in the common law world were in force throughout Europe and in all countries subject to European-derived law.[71] This was true even in Japan, a country that retained more independence during the nineteenth century than most non-European countries.[72] As in Europe and North America, the professed reason for including

---

64. Thomas Low Nichols, Esoteric Anthropology: A Comprehensive and Confidential Treatise on the Structure, Functions, Passional Attractions and Perversions, True and False Physical and Social Conditions, and the Most Intimate Relations of Men and Women 190 (1853).

65. Janet Farrell Brodie, Contraception and Abortion in Nineteenth-Century America 128 (1994).

66. *Id.* at 186.

67. James Ashton, The Book of Nature; Containing Information for Young People Who Think of Getting Married, on the Philosophy of Procreation and Sexual Intercourse; Showing How to Prevent Conception and to Avoid Child-Bearing 61 (1860).

68. Henry Marcy, *Education as a Factor in the Prevention of Criminal Abortion and Illegitimacy,* 47 JAMA 1889 (1906).

69. *See, e.g.,* Chapter 7, at notes 308, 312.

70. *See, e.g., The Report on Criminal Abortion,* 12 Trans. of the Am. Med. Assn. 28, 78 (1859).

71. Kenny, *supra* note 25, at 183; Backhouse, *supra* note 11; Bernard Dickens & Rebecca Cook, *Development of Commonwealth Abortion Laws,* 28 Int'l & Comp. L.Q. 424, 425–32 (1979); Bonnie Hertberg, *Resolving the Abortion Debate: Compromise Legislation, an Analysis of the Policies in the United States, France, and Germany,* 16 Suffolk Transnat'l L. Rev. 513, 545 (1993); Jeremy Telman, *Abortion and Women's Legal Personhood in Germany: A Contribution to the Feminist Theory of the State,* 24 Rev. L. & Soc. Change 91, 97 (1998). In the Islamic tradition, abortion was condemned in the strongest terms from the earliest times. *See generally* Mohamed Mekki Naciri, *A Survey of Family Planning in Islamic Legislation,* in Muslim Attitudes toward Family Planning 129, 129–45 (Olivia Schiefflin ed. 1973); Sarah Rumage, *Resisting the West: The Clinton Administration's Promotion of Abortion at the 1994 Cairo Conference and the Strength of the Islamic Response,* 27 Cal. W. Int'l L.J. 1, 46–49 (1996); Sherifa Zuhur, *Sexuality,* in Encyclopedia of Islam 35, 36 (John Esposito ed. 1995).

72. Hiromi Maruyama, *Abortion in Japan: A Feminist Critique,* 10 Wis. Women's L.J. 131, 132–33 (1995); Kinko Nakatani, *Japan,* in Abortion and Protection of the Human Fetus: Legal Problems in Cross-Cultural Perspective 221, 224 (S.J. Frankowski *et al.* Eds. 1987); Wardle, *supra* note 33, at 192–94.

abortion in Japan's first modern criminal code was to protect fetal life, although modern Japanese champions of abortion rights refuse to accept this as the "true" reason.[73]

# Oliver Wendell Holmes, Jr.

*[T]ruth is never separable from politics.*

—Allan Hutchinson[74]

The moral and legal ideas underlying the abortion statutes were largely unquestioned in the nineteenth century. This was particularly true of the idea that gained wide currency by the middle of the century that a fetus is a living human being (a "person") from the moment of conception.[75] The closest one comes in the nineteenth century to a serious questioning of the underlying moral and legal notions was the introduction of the concept of viability into the law by Judge (later Justice) Oliver Wendell Holmes, jr., in the 1884 case of *Dietrich v. Inhabitants of Northampton.*[76] Because of his opinion in *Dietrich,* some have enlisted Holmes as a "closet" supporter of abortion rights,[77] although he actually appears never to have written (or said) anything directly on the topic. Both because of the prestige attached to anything written by Holmes and because of the importance of the concept of viability for the debates of the later twentieth century about abortion, Holmes' opinion in *Dietrich* deserves careful consideration.

The concept of viability emerged among physicians in the nineteenth century, although even in the second half of the century they did not see the concept as having a potential legal significance.[78] The noted English lawyer Joseph Chitty had argued early in the century that viability should be part of the test of whether the killing of a newborn infant was homicide, but he did not provide any legal authority for his opinion simply because there was none.[79] The earliest legal use of the concept, although not the term itself, was by Holmes in his *Dietrich* opinion.

*Dietrich* involved a tort suit on behalf of the estate of a child who died after the child's mother slipped on a defect in a highway maintained by the town. The mother promptly miscarried a child in the fourth or fifth month of pregnancy.[80] The child, born without sign of injury, was too premature to survive given the available medical technology, and died after 10 or 15 minutes.[81] Under the "born-alive" rule, applicable then as now in Massachusetts and most states, had the death been the result of a culpable intent rather than negligence, the killing would have been a criminal homicide (murder or manslaughter) and not criminal abortion.[82]

---

73. Maruyama, *supra* note 72, at 133, 138–39, 151–53.

74. Allan Hutchinson, *Identity Crisis: The Politics of Interpretation,* 26 New Eng. L. Rev. 1173, 1176 (1992).

75. *See* Chapter 5, at notes 205–46; and Chapter 6, at notes 149–79.

76. 138 Mass. 14 (1884).

77. Sheldon Novick, *Justice Holmes and* Roe v. Wade, Trial, Dec. 1989, at 58. *See also* Clarke Forsythe, *The Legacy of Oliver Wendell Holmes* (book review), 69 U. Det. Mercy L. Rev. 679, 685–91 (1992)

78. *See* A.S. Taylor, A Manual of Medical Jurisprudence 413 (7th Eng. ed. 1861).

79. Joseph Chitty, A Practical Treatise on Medical Jurisprudence 415 (1st Am. ed. 1835). For a more detailed analysis of Chitty's theory, see Clarke Forsythe, *Homicide of the Unborn Child: The Born Alive Rule and Other Legal Anachronisms,* 21 Val. L. Rev. 563, 570 n.35 (1987).

80. *Dietrich,* 138 Mass. at 14–15.

81. *Id.* at 15.

82. Regina v. Sims, 75 Eng. Rep. 1075 (K.B. 1601). *See* Chapter 4, at notes 15–54, 118–54. Recent American decisions reaffirming the born alive rule are collected in Chapter 4, at note 128. *See generally* 2 William

The born-alive rule, like many rules affecting fetal rights, originated as an evidentiary rule necessary because of the medical inability (and legal inability) to determine whether a fetus was alive (or had the "capacity to live") before the complete delivery of the child.[83] The rule was obsolete as soon as the physicians gained the technical ability to make such judgments, well before the *Dietrich* case was decided.[84] Once the child was fully delivered and maintained an independent circulation, however briefly, the person causing the death of the child was responsible for a homicide even when the child had had no prospect of surviving more than momentarily.[85] Usually proof of an independent circulation required proof that the umbilical cord had been cut; complete delivery of the placenta as well as the infant would also be sufficient.[86] Breathing was not essential to a finding that the child had lived briefly.[87] The unsophisticated nature of the born-alive rule is shown by the irrelevance of any idea of viability in the application of the rule.

The operation of the "born alive" rule is clear in the English case of *Regina v. West*.[88] West had inserted "a pin" into a woman's womb in order to abort a quick child but had induced a live birth instead. The child was born, however, at such a premature stage that a "medical witness" concluded that "[i]t was incapable of maintaining a separate and independent existence."[89] Judge William Maule instructed the jury that West, if responsible, was guilty of murder.[90]

There was in 1884, however, no precedent for a civil action for the negligently caused wrongful death of an unborn child at any stage of gestation.[91] The absence of any such precedent is hardly surprising. The statutes creating actions for the wrongful killing of any person, including adults, were at most (depending on the jurisdiction) 38 years old in 1884. *Lord Campbell's Act*, the first such statute in a common law jurisdiction, was enacted in England in 1846.[92] The nineteenth century was also a time when, for any number of reasons, civil litigation was far less com-

---

OLDNALL RUSSELL, A TREATISE ON CRIMES AND MISDEMEANORS 671–72 (8th ed. 1865); D. Searborne Davies, *Child-Killing in English Law,* 1 MODERN L. REV. 203 (1937); Forsythe, *supra* note 76; L. Waller, *"Any Reasonable Creature in Being,"* 13 MONASH L. REV. 37 (1987).

83. Rex v. Pizzy (Suffolk Assizes 1808), in WILLIAM NOTCUTT, THE REMARKABLE TRIAL AT LARGE OF WILLIAM PIZZY AND MARY CODD AT THE ASSIZES HOLDEN AT BURY ST. EDMUNDS ON THURS DAY AUGUST 11, 1808 FOR FELONIOUSLY ADMINISTERING A CERTAIN NOXIOUS AND DESTRUCTIVE SUBSTANCE TO ANN CHENEY WITH INTENT TO PRODUCE A MISCARRIAGE (1808); TAYLOR, *supra* note 78, at 411. *See generally* Forsythe, *supra* note 79, at 571–92.

84. *See* TAYLOR, *supra* note 78, at 530. *See also* Commonwealth v. Cass, 467 N.E.2d 1324, 1329 (Mass. 1984); People v. Guthrie, 293 N.W.2d 775, 778–81 (Mich. Ct. App. 1980) *Appeal denied*, 334 N.W. 2d 616 (Mich. 1983); State *ex rel.* A.W.S., 440 A.2d 1145, 1146–47 (N.J. App. Div. 1981); BONNIE STEINBOCK, LIFE BEFORE BIRTH 82–83, 105–14 (1992); Robert Byrn, *An American Tragedy: The Supreme Court on Abortion*, 41 FORDHAM L. REV. 807, 817–25 (1973); Joseph Dellapenna, *The History of Abortion: Technology, Morality, and Law*, 40 U. PITT. L. REV. 359, 377–79 (1979) Forsythe, *supra* note 74, at 685–86; Forsythe, *supra* note 79, at 563–67, 583–86; James Witherspoon, *Reexamining* Roe: *Nineteenth-Century Abortion Statutes and the Fourteenth Amendment*, 17 St. Mary's L.J. 29, 31–32 (1985).

85. Regina v. Wright, 173 ENG. REP. 1039 (1841); Rex v. Sellis, 173 ENG. REP. 370 (Cambridge Assizes 1837); Rex v. Crutchley, 173 ENG. REP. 355 (N.P. 1837); Rex v. Enoch, 172 ENG. REP. 1089 (N.P. 1833); Rex v. Poulton, 172 ENG. REP. 997 (N.P. 1832).

86. Regina v. Trilloe, 169 ENG. REP. 103 (Crown Cases II 1842); Regina v. Reeves, 173 ENG. REP. 724 (N.P. 1839).

87. Rex v. Brain, 172 ENG. REP. 1272 (N.P. 1834).

88. 175 ENG. REP. 329 (N.P. 1848).

89. *Id.* at 329–30.

90. *Id.* at 330.

91. *See, e.g.,* A.A. White, *The Right of Recovery for Personal Injuries,* 12 LA. L. REV. 383, 384 (1952).

92. *See, e.g.,* W. PAGE KEETON *et al.,* PROSSER AND KEETON ON TORTS §§ 55, 127 (5th ed. 1984). Lord Ellenborough had held in 1808 that "in a civil court the death of a human being could not be complained of as an injury." Baker v. Bolton, 170 ENG. REP. 1033 (K.B. 1808). *See* Chapter 5, at notes 104–06. Ellenborough is now chiefly known as the author of *Lord Ellenborough's Act,* 43 Geo. III ch. 58 (1803), the first abortion statute in the common law world.

mon than it is today. Nor should one overlook that then, and for many years afterwards, recovery was permitted for wrongful death only to the extent that the death imposed a pecuniary loss on the surviving relatives; no recovery was permitted for the anguish of losing a loved one.[93] Pecuniary loss was unusual in the death of any young child and would have been unthinkable for an unborn child.[94]

Holmes' response was characteristically definite yet revealed both ignorance of the relevant common law authorities and a serious misreading of the authorities with which he was familiar. Holmes cited only *Rex v. de Bourton*[95] and the usual litany of secondary authorities.[96] He gave extended discussion only to Coke's explication of the born-alive rule, suggesting that it was incorrect, based on the prevalent version of *de Bourton* and Hale's apparent questioning of it.[97] While we cannot fault Holmes for failing to dig out the original records of *de Bourton,* even the corrupted version Holmes' relied on does not support his conclusions.[98] In any event, Holmes overlooked *Regina v. Sims,*[99] assuming that only long after Massachusetts was settled did the born-alive rule become the law of England, citing *Regina v. West* for the rule.[100] Nor did Holmes find the earlier Hale text that clarifies Hale's meaning in the text Holmes relied on, suggesting that perhaps there was less conflict with Coke's thinking than the later text read alone would have lead one to believe.[101]

Holmes concluded that reliance on Coke or on the criminal law was foreclosed by a 39-year old Massachusetts' precedent, *Commonwealth v. Parker.*[102] Chief Justice Lemuel Shaw held in *Parker* only that pre-quickening abortion was not a common law crime in Massachusetts. Shaw had not considered the born-alive rule and he expressly stated that "to many purposes, in reference to civil rights, an infant *in* (sic) *ventre sa mere* is regarded as a person in being."[103] Shaw, who was Holmes' father-in-law, four years after *Commonwealth v. Parker* would invent the doctrine of "separate but equal" regarding the schooling of black children.[104]

Holmes recognized that quickening was no longer a meaningful test of personhood as evidenced both by the evolution of judicial thinking and by the gradual elimination of quicken-

---

93. Stuart Speiser & Stuart Malawer, *An American Tragedy: Damages for Mental Anguish of Bereaved Relatives in Wrongful Death Actions,* 51 Tulane L. Rev. 1 (1976).

94. *See* Graf v. Taggert, 204 A.2d 140 (N.J. 1964); Harry Poulos, Comment, *Is There Consortium before Birth?,* 24 Loy. U. L.J. 559 (1993).

95. Y.B. Mich. 1 Edw. 3, f. 23, pl. 28 (K.B. 1327), as quoted in Chapter 3, at notes 139–40.

96. 1 William Blackstone, Commentaries on the Laws of England *129–30 (1765), quoted in Chapter 5, at notes 47–48; Edward Coke, Third Institute 50–51 (1644), quoted in Chapter 4, at notes 119–21; Anthony Fitzherbert, Graunde Abridgement tit. Corone, f. 268, pl. 263 (1st ed. 1516), quoted in Chapter 3, at note 170; 1 Matthew Hale, History of Pleas of the Crown 429–30 (1736), quoted in Chapter 4, at notes 188–89; 2 William Hawkins, Treatise on the Pleas of the Crown 80 (1716).

97. *Dietrich,* 138 Mass. at 15.

98. *See* Chapter 3, at notes 141–69.

99. 75 Eng. Rep. 1075 (Q.B. 1601).

100. For a recent decision concluding that the "born alive" rule was in fact the medieval rule in England, see *Williams v. State,* 561 A.2d 216 (Md. 1989).

101. *See* Matthew Hale, Pleas of the Crown: or, A Methodical Summary of the Principal Matters relating to that Subject *53 (P.R. Glazebrook ed. 1972) (original date 1678), quoted in Chapter 4, at notes 211–12.

102. 50 Mass. (9 Met. 263) 263 (1845). Holmes also cited *State v. Cooper,* 22 N.J.L. 52 (1848), discussed in Chapter 6, in note 200.

103. *Parker,* 50 Mass. (9 Met.) at 266. The court made a similar distinction *State v. Cooper,* 22 N.J.L. 52, 56–57 (1848), the other case on which Holmes relied.

104. Roberts v. City of Boston, 59 Mass. (5 Cush.) 198 (1849). *See generally* J. Morgan Kousser, *"The Supremacy of Equal Rights": The Struggle against Racial Discrimination in Antebellum Massachusetts and the Foundations of the Fourteenth Amendment,* 88 Nw. U. L. Rev. 941 (1988).

ing from most abortion statutes which had come to punish abortion equally regardless of the stage of gestation. Yet he felt bound by his reading of *Parker* to a rule that in order for there to be a common law crime of abortion in Massachusetts the mother must be "more than pregnant."[105] Holmes simply ignored the fact that the Massachusetts legislature had reacted to *Parker* by enacting a statute in 1845 that removed the quickening distinction from the state's abortion law.[106] Holmes instead noted that the statute punished abortion more severely if the mother died than if only the infant died.[107] Holmes noted that the state's statutes punished abortion less severely than murder or manslaughter.[108] He apparently did not consider the possibility that severity of punishment could reflect evidentiary concerns not applicable if the mother died.

The two leading American scholars of the criminal law at the time reached conclusions contrary to Holmes regarding both the born-alive rule and abortion.[109] Holmes' own court had also decided that abortion was in fact a common law crime from the point of conception only two years before *Dietrich* reached the court.[110] Instead of adopting the increasingly prevalent point of conception, however, Holmes in *Dietrich* substituted for quickening the idea that "the child shall have reached some degree of quasi independent life at the moment of the [wrongful] act."[111]

Holmes could have rested his decision on the then prevalent rule denying recovery for purely emotional losses from a wrongful death, a rule that precluded recovery for the death of any unborn child (and all children too young to earn wages).[112] He did not. Instead, Holmes stated his conclusion in *Dietrich* in the following terms: "[T]he infant dying before it was able to live separated from its mother could [not] be said to have become a person recognized by law as capable of having *locus standi* in court, or of being represented there by an administrator."[113] In casting his decision in terms of "personhood," Holmes also overlooked the evidentiary nature of various rules restricting criminal and civil liability for actions against unborn children.[114] Holmes, after all, had at least passing acquaintance with the fact that medical opinion considered viability irrelevant to the personhood of the fetus.[115] Holmes had reviewed the leading book on "medical jurisprudence"—that of Alfred Taylor, some years after its first appearance—presumably could have refreshed his recollections had he so desired.[116] In *Dietrich*,[117] Holmes even cited without comment the case that book had relied on, *Regina v. West*.[118] But Holmes seldom, if ever, acknowledged the influences on his thinking.[119]

---

105. *Dietrich*, 138 Mass. at 16.

106. 1845 Mass. Acts ch. 27, at 406, *reprinted in* Eugene Quay, *Justifiable Abortion—Medical and Legal Foundations (Pt. II)*, 49 Geo. L.J. 395, 481 (1961). On the purposes of the statute, see 1 Francis Wharton, The Criminal Law of the United States § 1226 (5th rev. ed. 1861), quoted in Chapter 9, after note 156.

107. *Dietrich*, 138 Mass. at 17.

108. *Id.*

109. Joel Prentiss Bishop, Criminal Law § 386 (2nd ed. 1858), quoted in Chapter 9, at notes 115–19; 1 Wharton, *supra* note 103, §§ 1220–30, quoted in Chapter 7, at notes 144–56.

110. Commonwealth v. Taylor, 132 Mass. 261, 262 (1882).

111. *Dietrich*, 138 Mass. at 17.

112. Steinbock, *supra* note 84, at 101.

113. *Dietrich*, 138 Mass. at 16.

114. *See* Smith v. Brennan,157 A.2d 497, 500 (N.J. 1960); Beth Driscoll Osowski, Note, *The Need for Logic and Consistency in Fetal Rights*, 68 N.D. L. Rev. 171 (1992).

115. Taylor, *supra* note 78, at 413. *See also* Russell, *supra* note 82, at 671–72.

116. O.W. Holmes, jr., *A Manual of Medical Jurisprudence* (book review), 1 Am. L. Rev. 377 (1867).

117. 138 Mass. at 16.

118. 175 Eng. Rep. 329 (Nottingham Assizes 1848).

119. *See* Neil Duxbury, *The Birth of Legal Realism and the Myth of Justice Holmes*, 20 Anglo-Am. L. Rev. 81, 88 (1991); Robert Gordon, *The Case for (and against) Harvard*, 93 Mich. L. Rev. 1231, 1239 n.9 (1995); A.W. Brian Simpson, *The Elusive Truth About Holmes* (book rev.), 95 Mich. L. Rev. 2027, 2039 (1997).

Holmes recognized the obsolescence of the evidentiary requirement of quickening when he sought to recast the traditional distinction in different terms. Moreover, he was willing, at least in *dictum,* to support the innovative possibility of a wrongful death action for an unborn child after it was viable,[120] something for which there also was then no precedent. It was 75 years before this possibility was realized with the gradual abandonment of the pecuniary loss rule.[121]

---

120. *Dietrich,* 138 Mass. at 16.

121. No American case actually held that there was a cause of action for prenatal injuries for a viable fetus until 1946. Bonbrest v. Kotz, 65 F. Supp. 138 (D.D.C. 1946). The first such case in the British Commonwealth was in Canada. Montreal Tramways v. Leveille, [1933] 4 D.L.R. 337 (Queb.). The first decision allowing recovery for the wrongful death of a viable fetus followed only three years later. Verkennes v. Corniea, 38 N.W.2d 838 (Minn. 1949). The rule against recovery for the wrongful death of a viable fetus has now been abandoned nearly everywhere. Endo Laboratories, Inc. v. Hartford Ins. Group, 747 F.2d 1264 (9th Cir. 1984) (applying California law); Wade v. United States, 745 F. Supp. 1573 (D. Haw. 1990); Wolfe v. Isbell, 280 So. 2d 758 (Ala. 1973); Summerfield v. Superior Ct., 698 P.2d 712 (Ariz. 1985); Aka v. Jefferson Hospital Ass'n, Inc., 42 S.W.3d 508 (Ark. 2001); Snyder v. Michael's Stores, Inc., 945 P.2d 781 (Cal. 1997); Empire Cas. v. St. Paul Fire & Marine Ins., 764 P.2d 1191 (Colo. 1988); Greater S.E. Comm. Hosp. v. Williams, 482 A.2d 394 (D.C. Ct. App. 1984); Day v. Nationwide Mut. Ins. Co., 328 So. 2d 560 (Fla. 1976); Volk v. Baldazo, 651 P.2d 11 (Idaho 1982); Renslow v. Mennonite Hospital, 367 N.E.2d 1250 (Ill. 1977); Hale v. Manion, 368 P.2d 1 (Kan. 1962); Mitchell v. Couch, 285 S.W.2d 901 (Ky. 1955); Danos v. St. Pierre, 402 So. 2d 633 (La. 1981); State *ex rel.* Odham v. Sherman, 198 A.2d 71 (Md. 1964); Torigian v. Watertown News Co., 225 N.E.2d 926 (Mass. 1967); O'Neill v. Morse, 188 N.W.2d 785 (Mich. 1971); Rainey v. Horn, 72 So. 2d 434 (Miss. 1954); Connor v. Monkem Co., 898 S.W.2d 89 (Mo. 1995); White v. Yup, 458 P.2d 617 (Nev. 1969); Wallace v. Wallace, 42 A.2d 134 (N.H. 1980); Salazar v. St. Vincent Hosp., 619 P.2d 826 (N.M. 1980); Stetson v. Easterling, 161 S.E.2d 531 (N.C. 1966); Hopkins v. McBane, 359 N.W.2d 862 (N.D. 1985); Williams v. Marion Rapid Transit, Inc., 87 N.E.2d 334 (Ohio 1949); Evans v. Olson, 550 P.2d 924 (Okla. 1976); Mallison v. Pomeroy, 291 P.2d 225 (Ore. 1955); Coveleski v. Bubnis, 634 A.2d 608 (Pa. 1993); Hall v. Murphy, 113 S.E.2d 790 (S.C. 1960); Farley v. Mount Marley Hosp. Ass'n, Inc., 387 N.W.2d 42 (S.D. 1986); Shousha v. Matthews Drivurself Service, Inc., 358 S.W.2d 471 (Tenn. 1962); Vaillancourt v. Medical Center Hosp. of Vt., Inc., 425 A.2d 92 (Vt. 1980); Kalafut v. Gruver, 389 S.E.2d 681 (Va. 1990); Moen v. Hanson, 537 P.2d 266 (Was. 1975); Baldwin v. Butcher, 184 S.E.2d 428 (W. Va. 1971); Kwaterski v. State Farm Mut. Auto Ins. Co., 148 N.W.2d 109 (Wis. 1967), *overruled on other grounds, In re* Estate of Stromsten, 299 N.W.2d 226 (Wis. 1980); *See also Congenital Disabilities (Civil Liability) Act of 1976* (England & Wales); Martell v. Merton & Sutton Health Auth'y, [1992] 3 All E.R. 820 (Q.B.); Cohen v. Shaw, 1992 S.C.L.R. 182; K. v. T., [1983] Q.R. 396. *See generally* Keeton et al., *supra* note 92, § 55, at 367; J.K. Mason, Medico-Legal Aspects of Reproduction and Parenthood 144–51 (2nd ed. 1998); Murphy Klassina, *The Death of an Unborn Child: Jurisprudential Inconsistencies in Wrongful Death, Criminal Homicide, and Abortion Cases,* 22 Pepp. L. Rev. 933 (1995); Jeffrey Lenow, *The Fetus as a Patient: Emerging Rights as a Person?,* 9 Am. J.L. & Med. 1, 5–10 (1983); Paul Benjamin Linton, Planned Parenthood v. Casey: *The Flight from Reason in the Supreme Court,* 13 St. L.U. Pub. L. Rev. 15, 47–58 (1993); Michael McCready, *Recovery for the Wrongful Death of a Fetus,* 25 U. Rich. L. Rev. 391 (1991); Gary Meadows, *Wrongful Death and the Lost Society of the Unborn,* 13 J. Legal Med. 99 (1992);

Apparently only New Jersey and Texas, among the American states, reject this rule. Alexander v. Whitman, 114 F.3d 1392 (3rd Cir.) (applying New Jersey law), *cert. denied,* 522 U.S. 949 (1997); Langford v. Blackman, 795 S.W.2d 742 (Tex. 1990); S. Jeffrey Gately, *Texas Fetal Rights: Is There a Future for the Rights of Future Texans?,* 23 St. Mary's L.J. 305 (1991). Courts in New Jersey, and Texas, do allow recovery for prenatal injuries if the infant is subsequently born alive. Smith v. Brennan, 157 A.2d 497 (N.J. 1960); Delgado v. Yandell, 468 S.W.2d 475 (Tex. Ct. Crim. App.), *writ refused, no rev'ble error,* 471 S.W.2d 569 (Tex. 1971);

Courts have split over whether to recognize a wrongful death action for an injury to a stillborn nonviable fetus. *Recognizing the action:* Wolfe v. Isbell, 280 So. 2d 758 (Ala. 1973); Seef v. Sutkus, 583 N.E.2d 510 (Ill. 1991); Danos v. St. Pierre, 402 So. 2d 633 (La. 1981); Group Health Ass'n v. Blumenthal, 453 A.2d 1198 (Md. 1983); Connor v. Monkem Corp., 898 S.W.2d 89 (1995); White v. Yup, 458 P.2d 617 (Nev. 1969); Stetson v. Easterling, 161 S.E.2d 531 (N.C. 1966); Hopkins v. McBane, 359 N.W.2d 862 (N.D. 1985); Wiersma v. Maple Leaf Farms, 543 N.W.2d 787 (S.D. 1996); Farley v. Sartin, 466 S.E.2d 522 (W. Va. 1995); Kwaterski v. State Farm Mut. Auto Ins. Co., 148 N.W.2d 109 (Wis. 1967), *overruled on other grounds, In re* Estate of Stromsten, 299 N.W.2d 226 (Wis. 1980). *Denying the action:* Gentry v. Gilmore, 613 So. 2d 1241 (Ala. 1993); Summerfield v. Superior Ct., 698 P.2d 712 (Ariz. 1985); Ferguson v. District of Colum., 629 A.2d 15 (D.C. 1993); Humes v. Clinton, 792 P.2d 1032 (Kan. 1990); Kandel v. White, 663 A.2d 1264 (Md. 1995); Fryover v. Forbes, 446 N.W.2d 292 (Mich. 1989); Wallace v. Wallace, 421 A.2d 134 (N.H. 1980); Miller v. Kirk, 905 P.2d 194

Holmes was highly regarded for his erudite antiquarianism, something for which I can hardly fault him. Holmes expressed his view of the controlling force of historical custom in several cases involving allegations that the government had taken private property without compensation.[122] Among the legacies of Holmes' antiquarianism is his reintroduction of the wearing of judicial robes to the Massachusetts Supreme Judicial Court, a practice he promoted when he became Chief Judge of that court. Holmes was awarded an honorary degree from Oxford for his work on legal history, work that heavily influenced Sir Frederick Pollack, Sir William Holdsworth, and other English legal historians.[123] Still, he was not an academic in the usual sense of the term. He actually served only about three months as a full-time professor.[124] Instead, before becoming a judge, Holmes was a practicing lawyer of a somewhat bookish, some might say even dilettantish, bent.[125]

Unfortunately, Holmes' history too often was not reliable.[126] Furthermore, his love of the past and his relentless temperamental conservatism produced an extraordinary reluctance to overrule precedents even when he strongly disagreed with them.[127] Holmes provided his own characteristically skeptical reasons for his conservatism:

---

(N.M. 1995); Coveleski v. Bubnis, 634 A.2d 608 (Pa. 1993); Miccolis v. AMICA Mut. Ins. Co., 587 A.2d 67 (R.I. 1991); West v. McCoy, 105 S.E.2d 88 (S.C. 1958). Two states have authorized such actions by statute. ILL. Rev. Stat. ch. 70, ¶2.2 (1991) S.D. Cod. Laws Ann. § 21-5-1 (1987). *See generally* Keeton *et al., supra,* § 55, at 368; Jason Cuomo, *Life Begins at the Moment of Conception for the Purposes of W. Va. Code § 55-7-5: The Supreme Court of Appeals of West Virginia "Rewrites" Our Wrongful Death Statute,* 99 W. Va. L. Rev. 237 (1996); Thomas Hurney, jr., *A Practical View of* Farley v. Sartin, 99 W. Va. L. Rev. 263 (1996); Joyce Mc-Connell, *Relational and Liberal Feminism: The "Ethic of Care," Fetal Personhood and Autonomy,* 99 W. Va. L. Rev. 291 (1996); Sheryl Symonds, *Wrongful Death of the Fetus: Viability Is Not a Viable Distinction,* 8 U. Puget Sound L. Rev. 103 (1984). *See also* Nealis v. Baird, 996 P.2d 438 (Okla. 1999) (recognizing a wrongful death action caused by injuries to a nonviable fetus that live briefly after its premature birth).

122. Pennsylvania Coal Co. v. Mahon, 260 U.S. 393, 415–16 (1922); Jackson v. Rosenbaum Co., 260 U.S. 22, 31 (1922); Laurel Hill Cemetery v. City of San Francisco, 216 U.S. 358, 366 (1910). *See generally* Erin Rahne Kidwell, *The Paths of the Law: Historical Consciousness, Creative Democracy, and Judicial Review,* 62 Alb. L. Rev. 91 (1998) (describing the role of "historical consciousness" in Holme's thinking).

123. Sheldon Novick, Honorable Justice: The Life of Oliver Wendell Holmes 293–95 (1989). *See generally* G. Edward White, Justice Oliver Wendell Holmes: Law and the Inner Self 128–31, 145–50 (1993); Morton Horwitz, The Transformation of American Law, 1870–1960: The Crisis of Legal Orthodoxy 110–42 (1992); Daniel Ernst, *The Critical Tradition in the Writing of American Legal History,* 102 Yale L.J. 1019, 1046–57 (1993).

124. For a detailed examination of Holmes' career as an academic, see 2 Marc DeWolfe Howe, Justice Oliver Wendell Holmes: The Proving Years, 1870–1882, at 259–73 (1963).

125. *See* Howe, *supra* note 124, at 26–29; Duxbury, *supra* note 119, at 87, 90. Holmes seemingly couldn't help showing off his learning, however. One commentator even concluded that Holmes' famous *Lochner* dissent was "not a jibe at [Herbert] Spencer; it was Holmes' pointed grumble that, of all the Justices on the Supreme Court, only he understood (because only he could accurately name) what the majority had been talking about." *See* Allen Boyer, *Formalism, Realism, and Naturalism: Cross-Currents in American Letters and Law,* 23 Conn. L. Rev. 669, 680 (1991) (commenting on *Lochner v. New York,* 198 U.S. 45, 74–76 (1905) (Holmes, J., dissenting)). Boyer concluded that Holmes in fact did attempt to incorporate the basics of Spencer's thinking in a number of legal doctrines, including his view of the law a merely a prediction of how courts will apply force to the persons before them. Boyer, *supra,* at 680–83.

126. William Wiecek, *Clio as Hostage: The United States Supreme Court and the Uses of History,* 24 Cal. W.L. Rev. 227, 236 (1988).

127. *See generally* Liva Baker, The Justice from Beacon Hill: The Life and Times of Oliver Wendell Holmes 9–10 (1991); Novick, *supra* note 123, at 141; Sheldon Novick, *Justice Holmes and the Art of Biography* (book rev.), 33 Wm. & Mary L. Rev. 1219, 1240–43 (1992); Morris Cohen, *Justice Holmes,* 82 New Rep. 206 (1935); Duxbury, *supra* note 116, at 92; George Olshausen, *Aristocratic Critic of Capitalism,* Am. Socialist, July 1956, at 25; G. Edward White, *The Rise and Fall of Justice Holmes,* 39 U. Chi. L. Rev. 51, 56 (1971).

[W]e have a great body of law which has at least this sanction that it exists. If one does not affirm that it is intrinsically better than a different body of principles which one could imagine, one can see an advantage which, if not the greatest, at least is very great—that we know what it is. For this reason I am slow to assent to overruling a decision. Precisely my skepticism, my doubt as to the absolute worth of a large part of the system we administer, or of any other system, makes me very unwilling to increase the doubt as to what the court will do.[128]

As is fairly common for Holmes, one can quote him on the opposite side of the question of overruling precedent. He cautioned against mere antiquarianism in his famous observation that

It is revolting to have no better reason for a rule of law than that so it was laid down in the time of Henry IV. It is still more revolting if the grounds upon which it was laid down have vanished long since, and the rule simply persists from blind imitation of the past.[129]

Such contradictory statements suggest the complexity of Holmes' personal philosophy. That philosophy remains an often puzzling set of unsorted contradictions that one biographer described as the tension of a judge torn between "the rules of conduct imposed on the crowd, and the special duties of the gentleman judge."[130]

One of the best known examples of Holmes' misguided conservatism was his unwillingness, in a majority opinion in *United Zinc & Chemical Company v. Britt*,[131] to reconsider the rule that landowners owe no duty to trespassers even when children drown in an unfenced pool of poisonous chemicals in which they unsuspectingly chose to go for a swim as they walked along a public road.[132] Holmes was not, however, simply adhering mechanistically to obsolete or incomplete precedent. Holmes went out of his way to restrict the already developed law of "attractive nuisance" that would have allowed recovery for the families of the dead boys.[133] Characteristically, Holmes did not respond to all of the arguments of the four dissenters *United Zinc*, but "only [to] those to which he found substantively or stylistically convenient" to respond.[134] Indeed, Holmes often would distort facts and law for the sake of a memorable phrase, "a pithily expressed generality."[135] Thus in *United Zinc*, he dismissed any notion of attractive nuisance with the comment

---

128. Oliver Wendell Holmes, jr., *Twenty Years in Retrospect* (A Speech at a Banquet of the Middlesex Cnty. Bar Assoc., Dec. 3, 1902), in THE OCCASIONAL SPEECHES OF JUSTICE OLIVER WENDELL HOLMES 154, 156 (Mark DeWolfe Howe ed. 1962) ("OCCASIONAL SPEECHES").

129. Oliver Wendell Holmes, jr., *The Path of the Law*, 10 HARV. L. REV. 457, 469 (1897) ("Holmes, *Path of the Law*"). *See also* OLIVER WENDELL HOLMES, JR., THE COMMON LAW 31–32 (Mark Howe ed. 1963) ("HOLMES, COMMON LAW") (arguing that decisions justified on historical grounds are often in fact new, being based on "considerations of what is expedient for the community concerned").

130. Sheldon Novick, *Justice Holmes's Philosophy*, 70 WASH. U. L.Q. 703, 747–53 (1992). For a defense of Holmes' complexity, see Thomas Grey, *Molecular Motions: The Holmesian Judge in Theory and Practice*, 37 WM. & MARY L. REV. 19 (1995).

131. 258 U.S. 268 (1922).

132. See also the brief discussion of this case in WHITE, *supra* note 120, at 381–84; G. EDWARD WHITE, INTERVENTION AND DETACHMENT: ESSAYS IN LEGAL HISTORY AND JURISPRUDENCE 91–92 (1994) (a reprint of G. Edward White, *The Integrity of Justice Holmes' Jurisprudence*, 10 HOFSTRA L. REV. 633 (1982)) ("WHITE, INTERVENTION AND DETACHMENT"). For a more general discussion of Holmes' approach to liability for "accident," see DAVID ROSENBERG, THE HIDDEN HOLMES: HIS THEORY OF TORTS IN HISTORY 79–81 (1995). Rosenberg does not, however, discuss either *United Zinc* or *Dietrich*.

133. *See generally* Peter Karsten, *Explaining the Fight over the Attractive Nuisance Doctrine*, 10 LAW & HIST. REV. 45 (1992).

134. WHITE, *supra* note 123, at 382.

135. *Id,*. at 383, 410, 451. Holmes was notoriously uninterested in facts, preferring to focus on ideas. *See* GARY AICHELE, OLIVER WENDELL HOLMES, JR.: SOLDIER, SCHOLAR, JUDGE 155–56 (1989); EDMUND WILSON, PATRIOTIC GORE: STUDIES IN THE LITERATURE OF THE AMERICAN CIVIL WAR 792 (1962); Gerald Caplan, *Searching for Holmes among the Biographers*, 70 GEO. WASH. L. REV. 769, 795–96 (2002). *See also* Duxbury,

that "a road is not an invitation to leave it elsewhere but at its end"[136]—as if everyone customarily only entered a road at one end and traveled only to its other end.[137] Legal historian Ted White argues that Holmes' famous penchant for "epigrammatic terseness" was "consciously or unconsciously adopted as badge" to distinguish his style from that of his famously loquacious father.[138]

The patterns of Holmes' tort decisions suggests that he was intent on restricting tort liability as much as the precedents would allow, and in particular to take discretion out of cases by taking them away from juries unless the liability of a defendant was "patently evident."[139] And his style of opinion writing was designed more to cut off thinking at preliminary stages than to promote understanding and clarity.[140] Indeed, his very terseness enabled him to write opinions quickly, without agonizing over them, and gave his colleagues on the bench little opportunity to think through or to respond to his views.[141] As Mary Ann Glendon summarized Holmes' approach to legal analysis, "With its seemingly cavalier dismissal of reason, morality, and tradition, Holmes helped to prepare the way for the carnival of late-twentieth-century American legal theory."[142]

Even more startling was Holmes dissent in *Bailey v. Alabama*.[143] The Supreme Court in *Bailey* had found an Alabama statute unconstitutional for imposing criminal penalties for breach of employment contracts, creating a form of peonage mostly affecting African-American tenant farmers.[144] Holmes' dissent was remarkable coming as it did from a man who had once argued that one who makes a contract merely promises either to perform or to pay damages, at the promisor's election, expressly denying that a contract subordinated one's will to that of another as to do so would be a kind of limited slavery.[145] Another part of the Holmes pattern is found in his famous opinion for *Buck v. Bell*.[146]

---

*supra* note 119, at 98–99; Mathias Reimann, *Holmes' Common Law and German Legal Science,* in THE LEGACY OF OLIVER WENDELL HOLMES, JR. 72, 105 (Robert Gordon ed. 1992) ("LEGACY").

136. *United Zinc,* 258 U.S. at 276.

137. The point is made in G. Edward White, *Would You Like to Do Lunch with Holmes?,* 61 U. COLO. L. REV. 737, 743 (1990).

138. WHITE, *supra* note 123, at 183.

139. *Id.* at 383–85. *See also* HOLMES, COMMON LAW, *supra* note 129, at 126–28.

140. WHITE, INTERVENTION AND DETACHMENT *supra* note 132, at 96, 98–99, 122–25.

141. NOVICK, *supra* note 123, at xvii.

142. MARY ANN GLENDON, A NATION UNDER LAWYERS: HOW THE CRISIS IN THE LEGAL PROFESSION IS TRANSFORMING AMERICAN SOCIETY 190 (1994).

143. 219 U.S. 219, 245–50 (1911).

144. If one sees this opinion as anti-labor rather than anti-black, it was not unique in Holmes' record. Before becoming a judge, Holmes had also staked out a harsh position regarding striking workers, arguing that the "stronger interests" should prevail to assure "the survival of the fittest." O.W. Holmes, *The Gas Stokers' Strike,* 7 AM. L. REV. 582 (1873). Later Holmes would write one of the more extreme anti-union opinions for a unanimous Supreme Court. Moyer v. Peabody, 212 U.S. 78 (1909).

145. HOLMES, COMMON LAW, *supra* note 129, at 235–36, 299–301, 311–12. *See* WHITE, *supra* note 123, at 335–340.

146. 274 U.S. 200 (1926). *See* BAKER, *supra* note 127, at 602–03; ALBERT DEUTSCH, THE MENTALLY ILL IN AMERICA 365–67 (2nd ed. 1949); PETCHESKY, *supra* note 36, at 87–89; RICHARD POSNER, LAW AND LITERATURE: A MISUNDERSTOOD RELATION 289 (1988); J. DAVID SMITH & K. RAY NELSON, THE STERILIZATION OF CARRIE BUCK (1989); WHITE, *supra* note 123, at 404–10; Robert, jr., & Marcia Pearce Burgdorf, *The Wicked Witch Is Almost Dead: Buck v. Bell and the Sterilization of Handicapped Persons,* 50 TEMPLE L.Q. 995, 1001–13 (1977); Barbara Burnett, *Voluntary Sterilization for Persons with Mental Disabilities: The Need for Legislation,* 32 SYR. L. REV. 913, 921–923 (1981); Robert Cynkar, Buck v. Bell: *"Felt Necessities" v. Fundamental Values?,* 81 COLUM. L. REV. 1418 (1981); Peggy Cooper Davis, *Neglected Stories and the Lawfulness of* Roe v. Wade, 28 HARV. C.R.-C.L. L. REV. 299, 357–60 (1993); Mary Dudziak, *Oliver Wendell Holmes as a Eugenic Reformer: Rhetoric in the Writing of Constitutional Law,* 71 IOWA L. REV. 833 (1986); Elyce Zenoff Ferster, *Eliminating the Unfit—Is Sterilization the Answer?,* 27 OHIO ST. L.J. 591, 594–96 (1966); Forsythe, *supra* note 74, at 693–95; John Gest, *Eugenic Sterilization: Justice Holmes v. Natural Law,* 23 TEMPLE L.Q. 306 (1950); Harry Kalvin, *A Special Corner of Civil Liberties: A Legal View,* 31 NYU L. REV. 1223, 1230–34 (1956); Charles Kindregan, *Sixty*

In *Buck v. Bell*, Carrie Buck appealed to the Supreme Court in an effort to prevent her involuntary sterilization while in the custody of a home for the retarded in Virginia. Buck's mother reportedly was of below average intelligence, and she herself had already given birth to an illegitimate daughter who was also diagnosed as of below average intelligence. Modern research has raised considerable doubt about whether Carrie Buck and her child actually were of below average intelligence.[147] The problems of the mother and the daughter seemed to center more on a casual attitude towards sex with a variety of partners than on any lack in intelligence.[148] Holmes hardly seemed interested, writing a brief opinion fully summarized in his famous aphorism: "Three generations of imbeciles are enough."[149] The only precedent Holmes cited was *Jacobson v. Massachusetts*,[150] a case in which the Court had upheld the constitutionality of compulsory small pox vaccinations. In Holmes' view, "[t]he principle that sustains compulsory vaccination is broad enough to cover cutting the Fallopian tubes."[151]

Holmes himself was even more callous about the matter than his opinion in *Buck v. Bell* indicates, writing to Albert Einstein that he felt a "profound contempt" for "all socialisms not prepared to begin with life rather than with property and to kill everyone below the standard."[152] Holmes would have none of the notion, endorsed by the Supreme Court some 36 years earlier, that "[n]o right is held more sacred, or is more carefully guarded, by the common law, than the right of every individual to the possession and control of his own person...."[153] One can only understand *Buck v. Bell* as expressing Holmes' deep commitment to a Boston patrician's thinking about eugenics.[154] In fact, Holmes wrote to Einstein that the only decision he participated in

---

*Years of Compulsory Eugenic Sterilization: "Three Generations of Imbeciles" and the Constitution of the United States,* 43 CHI.-KENT L. REV. 123 (1966); Charles Murdock, *Sterilization of the Retarded: A Problem or a Solution?,* 62 CAL. L. REV. 917, 921–22 (1974); James O'Hara & T. Howland Sanks, *Eugenic Sterilization,* 45 GEO. L.J. 20, 29–32 (1956); Louis Wolcher, *The Many Meanings of "Wherefore" in Legal History,* 68 WASH. L. REV. 559, 615–19 (1993).

147. BAKER, *supra* note 127, at 603; R. MACKLIN & R. GAYLIN, MENTAL RETARDATION AND STERILIZATION 66–67 (1981); PETCHESKY, *supra* note 36, at 130, 159, 179–80; SMITH & NELSON, *supra* note 146, at 5; STEPHEN TROMBLEY, THE RIGHT TO REPRODUCE: A HISTORY OF COERCIVE STERILIZATION 88 (1988); Burgdorf & Burgdorf, *supra* note 146, at 1006–08; Dudziak, *supra* note 146, at 848–55; Stephen Jay Gould, *Carrie Buck's Daughter,* 2 CONST'L COMMENTARY 331 (1985); Paul Lombardo, *Three Generations, No Imbeciles: New Light on* Buck v. Bell, 60 N.Y.U. L. REV. 30 (1985); O'Hara & Sanks, *supra* note 146, at 31–32.

148. This appears to have been a frequent feature of women selected for sterilization. *See, e.g.,* HENRY GODDARD, THE KALLIKANS 71 (1912). *See also* MARK HALLER, EUGENICS: HEREDITARIAN ATTITUDES IN AMERICAN THOUGHT 106–10 (1963); TROMBLEY, *supra* note 147, at 88–89; Dudziak, *supra* note 146, at 845–46 n.88; Lombardo, *supra* note 147, at 39–55. Carrie Buck's modern defenders insist that she had been raped rather than promiscuous. SMITH & NELSON, *supra* note 146, at 5.

149. *Buck v. Bell,* 274 U.S. at 207. The phrase seems to have been inspired by an observation in a memorandum on the case by Chief Justice Taft, "The strength of the facts in three generations of course is the strongest argument." BAKER, *supra* note 127, at 602; NOVICK, *supra* note 123, at 352.

150. 197 U.S. 11 (1905). Several state court had declared such statutes unconstitutional. Haynes v. Lapeer, 166 N.W. 938 (Mich. 1918); Smith v. Board of Examiners, 88 A. 963 (N.J. 1913); Osborn v. Thomson, 169 N.Y.S. 638 (Sup. Ct.), *aff'd mem.,* 171 N.Y.S. 1094 (App. Div. 1918).

151. *Buck v. Bell,* 274 U.S. at 207.

152. THE HOLMES-EINSTEIN LETTERS 145 (James Bishop Peabody ed. 1964).

153. Union Pacific Ry. v. Botsford, 141 U.S. 250, 251 (1891).

154. Clarke Forsythe, *The Legacy of Oliver Wendell Holmes* (book rev.), 69 U. DET. MERCY L. REV. 677, 694–95 (1992). *See also* WHITE, *supra* note 123, at 392 ("His one enthusiasm for a legislative policy was that for family planning by the eugenics movement; eugenics made sense to him because it attacked the problem of overbreeding among the lower classes.... Holmes had some hope that through eguenics a 'master race' could be bred, one that could withstand Malthusian inevitabilities."); Yosal Rogat, *Mr. Justice Holmes: A Dissenting Opinion,* 15 STAN. L. REV. 254, 282 (1962) ("It is difficult to overestimate the importance of eugenicism in Holmes' social thought."). On eugenics in the late nineteenth and early twentieth centuries, see Chapter 11, at notes 25–113.

during 1927 that gave him pleasure was the case that upheld "the constitutionality of a law permitting the sterilization of imbeciles."[155] As a result of his vision of the rights and wrongs in the case, *Buck v. Bell* stands with *Jacobson* (the vaccination case) as the only cases in which the Supreme Court approved the right of a physician to perform a procedure against the wishes of a patient—and in *Buck,* unlike vaccinations, the procedure was one from which the patient would derive no benefit.[156] No wonder law professor Allan Boyer describes Holmes' writings as expressing a "willfully stupid philosophy."[157]

Holmes' patterns of thought and writing regarding torts and life first came together in *Dietrich.* Legal historian Ted White, in a recent biography of Holmes, summed up Holmes' approach to *Dietrich* in these words:

> The decision was something of a prototype for Holmes' majority opinions in tort cases. He took an apparently sympathetic claim, suggested that its resolution in favor of the plaintiff would create a wide potential field of expanded tort liability, gave summary treatment to sources supporting his position, and reached a result that limited the potential scope of tort claims. After *Dietrich* prenatal tort injuries were eliminated from the class of compensable tort claims [until 1949].[158]

Viewed in this light, *Dietrich* is one of the few opportunities Holmes had as a judge to express the juridical requisites for the "scientific infanticide" that he publicly supported on the lecture circuit. As he said in one speech, "I can imagine a future in which science shall have passed from the combative to the dogmatic stage, and shall have gained such catholic acceptance that it shall take control of life, and condemn at once with instant execution what is now left for nature to destroy."[159] Holmes also commented that he could "understand better legislation that aims rather to improve the quality than to increase the quantity of the population. I can understand saying, whatever the cost, so far as may be, we will keep certain strains out of our blood."[160]

Such comments were not mere intellectual games. As a man, Holmes found it difficult to be intimate with anyone from whom he was not separated by an ocean while he publicly proclaimed that he was glad that he and his wife had not had children.[161] Even his most laudatory recent biographer, Liva Baker, observed in describing his personal relationships, "[a]s was his custom then and later, he kept his distance, unable or unwilling to communicate on any but an intellectual level...."[162] Thus Holmes' rejection of a cause of action for the wrongful death of an premature infant in *Dietrich* presaged his rejection of a cause of action for the wrongful death of children drowned in a pool of acid wastes and his indifference to reproductive rights in *Buck v. Bell.*

---

155. The Holmes-Einstein Letters, *supra* note 152, at 267.

156. *See also* Paul Lombardo, *Medicine, Eugenics, and the Supreme Court: From Coercive Sterilization to Reproductive Freedom,* 13 J. Contemp. Health L. & Pol'y 1, 7–8 (1996).

157. Boyer, *supra* note 125, at 694.

158. White, *supra* note 123, at 266.

159. Oliver Wendell Holmes, jr., *The Soldier's Faith,* in Occasional Speeches, *supra* note 128, at 73, 75-76. *See generally* Baker, *supra* note 127, at 603; Cynkar, *supra* note 146, at 1451 n.178; Novick, *supra* note 130, at 726–29, 732. Novelist Jack London had a character in one of his novels trace this theory back to Herbert Spencer. Jack London, The Sea-Wolf 72 (1904).

160. Oliver Wendell Holmes, jr., *Law and Social Reform,* in The Mind and Faith of Justice Holmes: His Speeches, Essays, Letters and Judicial Opinions 399, 400–01 (Max Lerner ed. 1943) ("Mind and Faith").

161. Grant Gilmore, The Ages of American Law 49 (1977); 1 Marc DeWolfe Howe, Justice Oliver Wendell Holmes: The Shaping Years, 1841–1870, at 8 (1957); White, Intervention and Detachment, *supra* note 132, at 88, 124.

162. Baker, *supra* note 127, at 193. *See also* Aichele, *supra* note 135, at ix; Baker, *supra,* at 9; White, *supra* note 123, at 411. Holmes' father expressed similar views in a thinly veiled description of his son in one of the senior Holmes' published essays. Aichele, *supra,* at 98–99.

Holmes' admirers want to see in such decisions a strong desire for "objective standards."[163] Holmes wanted "[t]he standards of the law [to be] standards of general application."[164] His admirers would add that Holmes combined his faith in objective standards with a studied indifference to the policy consequences of his judgments.[165] Holmes himself insisted that law should be understood from the perspective of a "bad man"—one "who cares nothing for an ethical rule which is believed and practiced by his neighbors," a man who cares only "to avoid being made to pay money, and...to keep out of jail if he can."[166] His "objective standards" were purchased at the cost of serious miscarriages of justice. Rather than indifference, *Dietrich,* like the other cases, represented outright misanthropy or at least cynicism.

Holmes' inability to discover satisfactory resolutions for the questions he confronted in these cases illustrated his most serious limitation as a judge: "There was...a harshness in his judgments upon men of good will, a contempt of humanitarianism as an ingredient of public policy, and an expressed preference for the predatory type of individual that his friends usually managed to overlook with embarrassed silence."[167] Biographer Sheldon Novick, who attempted to cast Holmes in as positive a light as possible, reached an even more critical judgment, noting that Holmes "in personal letters seemed to espouse a kind of a fascist ideology."[168] Another biographer, Ted White, concluded that "Holmes' vision is one of a community wholly unsympathetic to the weaker—in this case, the accident-prone—individual; a community which would make no distinction between presence and absence of intent, but would rather condemn a person for their 'congenital defects.' Very simply, Holmes' community is a community of the fittest."[169]

Holmes hardly hid such feelings from his contemporaries. Consider this comment in a letter from Holmes: "I do not believe that a shudder would go through the sky if our whole ant heap were kerosened. But then it might—in short my only belief is that I know nothing about it."[170] In another letter, he wrote:

---

163. *See, e.g.,* HOLMES, COMMON LAW, *supra* note 129, at 108–13. *See generally* P.S. ATIYAH, ESSAYS ON CONTRACTS 57–72 (1986); NOVICK, *supra* note 123, at 272; ROSENBERG, *supra* note 132; WHITE, *supra* note 123, at 180–81, 259–63, 273–80; Robert Birmingham, *Holmes and "Peerless": Raffles v. Wickelhaus and the Objective Theory of Contract,* 47 U. PITT. L. REV. 183 (1985); Duxbury, *supra* note 119, at 93–99; Robert Gordon, *Holmes'* Common Law *as Legal and Social Science,* 10 HOFSTRA L. REV. 719 (1982); Morton Horwitz, *The Place of Justice Holmes in American Legal Thought,* in LEGACY, *supra* note 135, at 31, 32; William Lundquist, *Oliver Wendell Holmes and External Standards of Criminal and Tort Liability: Application of Theory on the Massachusetts Bench,* 28 BUFF. L. REV. 607 (1979); Simpson, *supra* note 116; Mark Tushnet, *The Logic of Experience: Oliver Wendell Holmes on the Supreme Judicial Court,* 63 VA. L. REV. 975 (1977).

164. HOLMES, COMMON LAW, *supra* note 129, at 108.

165. NOVICK, *supra* note 123, at 272.

166. Holmes, *Path of the Law, supra* note 129, at 461–62. *See also* LON FULLER, THE LAW IN QUEST OF ITSELF 92–95 (1940); Henry Hart, jr., *Holmes' Positivism—An Addendum,* 64 HARV. L. REV. 929 (1951).

167. STOW PERSONS, AMERICAN MINDS: A HISTORY OF IDEAS 265 (1958).

168. NOVICK, *supra* note 123, at xvii. Novick also described Holmes' thinking about eugenics as "worse than wrong, it is evil." *Id.* at 732. *See also* ALBERT ALSCHULER, LAW WITHOUT VALUES: THE LIFE, WORK AND LEGACY OF JUSTICE HOLMES 15, 204 nn.21–22 (2000); 8 OWEN FISS, HISTORY OF THE SUPREME COURT OF THE UNITED STATES: TROUBLED BEGINNINGS OF THE MODERN STATE, 1888–1910, at 143, 184 (1993); LON FULLER, THE LAW IN QUEST OF ITSELF 63 (1940); GILMORE, *supra* note 161, at 49–50; Duxbury, *supra* note 119, at 96; Neil Duxbury, *The Reinvention of American Legal Realism,* 12 OXFORD J. LEGAL STUD. 137, 159–64 (1992); Forsythe, *supra* note 77, at 681–83; Thomas Grey, *Bad Man from Olympus,* N.Y. REV. BOOKS, July 13, 1995, at 4; Novick, *supra* note 127; Sheldon Novick, *Justice Holmes's Philosophy,* 70 WASH. U. L.Q. 703 (1992); Ben Palmer, *Hobbes, Holmes, and Hitler,* 31 ABA J. 569 (1945); Saul Touster, *In Search of Holmes from Within,* 18 VAND. L. REV. 457 (1965).

169. WHITE, *supra* note 132, at 119, 124–25. *See also* Simpson, *supra* note 119, at 2029–30; White, *supra* note 127, at 76–77.

170. *Letter from Oliver Wendell Holmes, jr., to Morris R. Cohen, May 27, 1917,* in LEONORA ROSENFIELD, PORTRAIT OF A PHILOSOPHER: MORRIS R. COHEN IN LIFE AND LETTERS 316 (1962).

One can change institutions by a fiat but populations only by slow degrees and as I don't believe in millennia and still less in the possibility of attaining one by tinkering with property while propagation is free and we do all we can to keep the products, however bad, alive, I listen with skepticism to plans for fundamental amelioration. I should expect more from systematic prevention of the survival of the unfit.[171]

No wonder James Bradley Thayer, of the Harvard law faculty that Holmes briefly joined, described Holmes as a man "sadly lacking in the noblest region of human character—selfish, vain, thoughtless of others."[172] Or that William James found himself repelled by Holmes' "intellectual heartlessness."[173] As for Holmes' once celebrated liberalism, perhaps he was a committed democrat, or perhaps he was just a conservative who did not care enough about his political views to use his judicial office to advance those views.[174] In particular, Holmes' opinions regarding the rights of racial minorities to participate in the political process were distinctly unsupportive.[175] There really does not seem to have been much of a liberal in him.[176]

Holmes, who remained active on the Supreme Court of the United States until his retirement at the age of 92 some 48 years after he wrote the *Dietrich* opinion, became the most celebrated jurists of his time.[177] Despite the flaws in the *Dietrich* opinion, the great prestige of Holmes' name became attached to the concept of viability, making it the controlling point in tort suits for wrongful death for 65 years after *Dietrich* was decided.[178] Holmes' theory continues to mesmer-

---

171. *Letter from Oliver Wendell Holmes, jr., to Harold Laski, July 17, 1925,* in HOLMES-LASKI LETTERS 761 (M.D. Howe, ed., 1953). One biographer attributes this harsh view to a supposition that Holmes' sensed that his own parents sent him off to die in the Civil War. NOVICK, *supra* note 123, at 477–78 n.65. Holmes would later describe those opposing American entry into World War I in similarly harsh terms: "Doesn't this squashy sentimentality of a big minority of our people about human life make you puke?," quoted in NOVICK, *supra,* at 469 n.11.

172. As quoted in HOWE, *supra* note 161, at 282. *Cf.* Richard Posner, *Introduction,* in THE ESSENTIAL HOLMES: SELECTIONS FROM THE LETTERS, SPEECHES, JUDICIAL OPINIONS, AND OTHER WRITINGS OF OLIVER WENDELL HOLMES, JR. xxii (Richard Posner ed. 1992) (describing Holmes as looking "at his fellow man through the wrong end of the telescope"). *See also* ALSCHULER, *supra* note 168, at 31–32; Caplan, *supra* note 135, at 773–74; Paul Freund, *Dark Equanimity,* 59 AM. SCHOLAR 303 (1990).

173. As quoted in BAKER, *supra* note 127, at 197.

174. ALEXANDER BICKEL, THE UNPUBLISHED DECISIONS OF MR. JUSTICE BRANDEIS: THE SUPREME COURT AT WORK 221 (1957); HORWITZ, *supra* note 123, at 127; MIND AND FAITH OF JUSTICE HOLMES, *supra* note 160, at xxxv; WHITE, *supra* note 123, at 397–401; William LaPiana, *Victorian from Beacon Hill: Oliver Wendell Holmes's Early Legal Scholarship,* 90 COLUM. L. REV. 809, 832 (1990); Yosal Rogat, *The Judge as Spectator,* 31 U. CHI. L. REV. 213, 255 (1964). For a sustained critique of this view, and a defense of Holmes' as the nation's premier democratic judge, see Thomas Grey, *Holmes, Pragmatism, and Democracy,* 71 ORE. L. REV. 521 (1992).

175. *See* Giles v. Harris, 189 U.S. 475 (1903).

176. *See also* United States v. Reynolds, 235 U.S. 133, 150 (1914) (Holmes, J., concurring, describing persons who breach surety contracts as "impulsive people with little intelligence or foresight"); Bailey v. Alabama, 219 U.S. 219, 245–50 (1911) (Holmes, J., dissenting, voting for a presumption that a breach of an employment contract seeks to injure or defraud the employer). *See generally* WHITE, *supra* note 123, at 334–38; Michael Carrier, *Book Review,* 93 MICH. L. REV. 1894, 1904 (1995).

177. *See, e.g.,* SIDNEY ASCH, THE SUPREME COURT AND ITS GREAT JUSTICES 83 (1971) (selecting Holmes as one of the 15 greatest justices); MORTON FRISCH & RICHARD STEVENS, THE POLITICAL THOUGHT OF AMERICAN STATESMEN: SELECTED WRITINGS AND SPEECHES 254 (1973); CLARENCE MORRIS, THE GREAT LEGAL PHILOSOPHERS: SELECTED READINGS IN JURISPRUDENCE 418 (Pa. paperback ed. 1971); NOVICK, *supra* note 123, at xv; RICHARD POSNER, CARDOZO: A STUDY IN REPUTATION 20, 31 (1991); G. EDWARD WHITE, THE AMERICAN JUDICIAL TRADITION: PROFILES OF LEADING AMERICAN JUSTICES 150–77 (1976); CHRISTOPHER WOLFE, THE RISE OF MODERN JUDICIAL REVIEW: FROM CONSTITUTIONAL INTERPRETATION TO JUDGE-MADE LAW 223–30 (1986).

178. See the authorities collected *supra* at note 121.

ize British and Canadian courts.[179] The precedent, however, now has been generally disregarded, having been overruled even in Massachusetts.[180]

Given Holmes' continuing prestige, one is not surprised that some supporters of abortion rights have attempted to enlist him as a supporter of *Roe v. Wade* although, of course, he never wrote (or, as far as we can tell, said) anything directly on the topic of abortion.[181] This effort is part of what biographer Sheldon Novick has lamented as the tendency to recruit Holmes as a supporter of "nearly every movement or school of jurisprudence since his death in 1935," creating considerable confusion over "what his ideas were and what value they might have for us now."[182] Efforts to enlist him in support of *Roe* founder not only on the discrediting of *Dietrich*, but also on Holmes' explicit and emphatic rejection of a right of privacy in the constitution.[183] Holmes probably would have considered the claim of fetal personhood to be metaphysical nonsense on a par with the economic theories in *Lochner v. New York*[184] if only because he did not consider an ethical concern for individuality to be fundamental. If Holmes took that approach, he probably would have deferred to the legislative judgment on the matter, whichever way it went.[185]

# Changes in Social Behavior at the Turn of the Century

*[W]omen are made and meant to be not men, but the mothers of men.*

—Withers Moore[186]

The industrial revolution brought about a major transformation in work patterns. Before the industrial revolution, all adults (and most children) in a family worked as a unit on the land, each contributing to the collective economic output of the family as a whole. After the industrial revolution, white men mostly worked outside the home for wages, their wives cared for the home and children without separate monetary income, and the children spent an increasingly prolonged adolescence in school or delinquency.[187] (The experiences of non-whites—a distinct

---

179. *See* Borowski v. Attorney-General of Canada, 4 D.L.R.4th 121, 131 (Can. 1984); Regina v. Tait, [1989] 3 All E.R. 682 (C.A.); C. v. S., [1988] Q.B. 135; *In re* F (*in utero*), [1988] Fam. 122; Paton v. British Pregnancy Advisory Services Trustees, [1979] Q.B. 276; Kelly v. Kelly, 1997 Scot. L. Times 896; Mason, *supra* note 121, at 144, 148, 150–51; Kenneth Norrie, *Liability for Injuries Caused before Birth*, 1992 Scot. L. Times 65; J.P. Wadsworth, *The Courts and the Rights of the Unborn Child*, 110 Law & Just. 66 (1991); Adrian Whitfield, *Common Law Duties to Unborn Children*, 1 Med. L. Rev. 28 (1993).

180. Torigian v. Waterton News Co., 225 N.E.2d 926, 927 (Mass. 1967).

181. *See, e.g.,* Steinbock, *supra* note 83, at 106; Cyril Means, jr., *The Law of New York Concerning Abortion and the Status of the Foetus, 1664–1968: A Case of Cessation of Constitutionality,* 14 N.Y.L.F. 411, 422–23 (1968) ("Means I"); White, *supra* note 137, at 740.

182. Novick, *supra* note 130, at 703. *See also* Baker, *supra* note 127, at 412, 543–44; Novick, *supra*, at 736–45.

183. Olmstead v. United States, 277 U.S. 438, 469 (1928) (Holmes, J., dissenting).

184. 198 U.S. 45, 76 (1905) (Holmes, J., dissenting).

185. Novick, *supra* note 77, at 58.

186. Withers Moore, *The Higher Education of Women*, Br. Med. J., Aug. 14, 1889, at 295, 299.

187. *See generally* Jeanne Boydston, Home and Work: Housework, Wages, and the Ideology of Labor in the Early Republic (1990); Stephanie Coontz, The Social Origins of Private Life (1988); Eric Foner, Free Soil, Free Labor, Free Men: The Ideology of the Republican Party before the

minority—were considerably different.) One can make too much of this transition for the white majority. Even before the industrial revolution, women in intensive agricultural societies (including England and colonial America) made a large part of their contribution to the joint enterprise of the family through caring for children, cooking, making clothe and clothing, and other house-centered activities, with only part of their effort being outside the house. For millennia, men in those societies were primarily responsible for farming, animal husbandry, and other outside activities. While it was true that many of the home-centered activities of the women could and often did contribute cash income to the family, and that women could be called upon to help out in the fields, the main responsibility for providing for the family in the marketplace usually lay with the men. Thus we find that one of the most common of traditional, pre-industrial Chinese expressions for wife is *nei ren* ("inside person"), and for husband is *waizi* ("outside person").[188] We can trace the tradition of the women as keepers of the hearth back to ancient Greece (remember Penelope awaiting Odysseus),[189] and beyond to ancient Egypt.[190] Indeed, the convention in ancient Egyptian art was to depict women as having a pale skin and men as heavily tanned, reflecting their respective existences inside the home and out in the fields.[191] These patterns were as true in England and colonial America as elsewhere in the world.[192]

The industrial revolution tended to focus white women more exclusively within the house and men more exclusively outside the house than had been the case before industrialization. By 1890, only 5 percent of married white women in the United States worked outside the home while nearly all urban white men did.[193] Furthermore, at least half of the white women who worked outside the home did not earn enough to support themselves, let alone dependent children, except in abject poverty[194]—giving the lie to suggestions by some late-nineteenth-century anti-feminists that numerous women were undergoing abortions to avoid giving up lucrative jobs.[195] So engrained did this pattern become that white women who worked outside the home

---

CIVIL WAR (1970); N.E.S. GRIFFITHS, PENELOPE'S WEB: SOME PERCEPTIONS OF WOMEN IN EUROPEAN AND CANADIAN SOCIETY (1976); JUANITA KREPS & ROBERT CLARK, SEX, AGE, AND WORK: THE CHANGING COMPOSITION OF THE LABOR FORCE (1975); STEVEN MINTZ & SUSAN KELLOGG, DOMESTIC REVOLUTIONS (1988); DAVID ROEDIGER, THE WAGES OF WHITENESS: RACE AND THE MAKING OF THE AMERICAN WORKING CLASS (1991); CHRISTINE STANSELL, CITY OF WOMEN: SEX AND CLASS IN NEW YORK 1789–1860 (1986); REAY TANNAHILL, SEX IN HISTORY 350–51 (1980); THE PROPER SPHERE: WOMAN'S PLACE IN CANADIAN SOCIETY (Ramsey Cook & Wendy Mithinson eds. 1976); Joan Williams, *Domesticity as the Dangerous Supplement of Liberalism*, 2 J. WOMEN'S HIST. 69 (1991).

188. Herbert Agiles, Chinese-English Dictionary, 1012, 1552 (1967).

189. HOMER, THE ODYSSEY (W.H.D. Rouse trans. 1937). *See generally* SUE BLUNDELL, WOMEN IN ANCIENT GREECE, 47, 130 (1995).

190. *See, e.g.,* JOYCE TYLDESLEY, HATCHEPSUT: THE FEMALE PHARAOH 44–47, 55–56 (Penguin ed. 1998).

191. *Id.* at 133, 240 n.4. This has not kept some doctrinaire feminists from insisting that the view that women largely stayed home with the children while the men went hunting in pre-agricultural societies is a modern, sexist construct and not an accurate picture of ancient life—although there is virtually no evidence to support their view. *See, e.g.,* Joan Gero, *Sociopolitics and the Women-at-Home Ideology,* 50 AM. ANTIQUITY 342 (1985); Kelley Hays-Gilpin, *Feminist Scholarship in Archeology,* 571 ANNALS AM. ACADEMY POL. & SOC. SCI. 89, 96–98 (2000); Linda Hurcombe, *Our Own Engendered Species,* 69 ANTIQUITY no. 262, at 87 (1995).

192. *See generally* CAROL BELKIN, FIRST GENERATIONS: WOMEN IN COLONIAL AMERICA (1966).

193. PETCHESKY, *supra* note 36, at 75; LYNN WEINER, FROM WORKING GIRL TO WORKING MOTHER 6 (1985).

194. ALICE KESSLER-HARRIS, OUT TO WORK: A HISTORY OF WAGE-EARNING WOMEN IN THE UNITED STATES 230, 258, 262–63 (1982); JOANNE MEYEROWITZ, WOMEN ADRIFT: INDEPENDENT WAGE EARNERS IN CHICAGO, 1880–1930, at 33–38 (1988); REAGAN, *supra* note 19, at 29; TANNAHILL, *supra* note 187, at 354; Kathy Peiss, *"Charity Girls" and City Pleasures: Historical Notes on Working-Class Sexuality, 1880–1920,* in POWERS OF DESIRE: THE POLITICS OF SEXUALITY 80 (Ann Snitow *et al.* eds. 1983).

195. *See, e.g.,* Edward Bulloch, *Criminal Abortion,* 45 AM. J. OBSTET. & DISEASES OF WOMEN & CHILDREN 235, 238 (1902).

risked losing their children to charges of neglect.[196] This transition was well underway before 1835 on both sides of the Atlantic and was largely complete by the end of the century.[197] At the same time, the transition from a largely rural to a largely urban society assured that transformation of family life in the cities meant the transformation of family life for the nation as a whole.

State and federal courts during this time strong supported the confinement of women to the home, not only attempting to bar them from the professions[198] but also upholding "protective legislation" that would be struck down as violating freedom of contract if it had been directed at men.[199] Courts also upheld "protective legislation" directed at children, further tending to confine women to the home to care for the children also increasingly excluded from working.[200] By upholding this "protective legislation," the courts made women less attractive as potential employees, and undercut the price they might have been able to command in the market place.[201] In

---

196. LINDA GORDON, HEROES OF THEIR OWN LIVES: THE POLITICS AND HISTORY OF FAMILY VIOLENCE, BOSTON, 1880–1960, at 92–95, 98, 107–09, 112–13.

197. See NANCY COTT, THE BOND OF WOMANHOOD: "WOMEN'S SPHERE" IN NEW ENGLAND, 1780–1835, at 59–60 (1977).

198. See Bradwell v. Illinois, 83 U.S. (16 Wall.) 130 (1872) (upholding a state's refusal to admit women to the Bar).

199. Compare Muller v. Oregon, 208 U.S. 416 (1908) (upholding a statute that limited the commercial working day for women to 10 hours); with Lochner v. New York, 198 U.S. 45 (1897) (striking down a statute restricting the number of hours a male baker could work in a week). See also Goesaert v. Cleary, 335 U.S. 464 (1948) (upholding a statute barring women, except for the wives or daughters of the owners of the establishment, from being bartenders although women could be waitresses in such establishments). See generally JUDITH BEER, THE CHAINS OF PROTECTION: THE JUDICIAL RESPONSE TO WOMEN'S LABOR LEGISLATION (1978); WILLIAM FORBATH, LAW AND THE SHAPING OF THE AMERICAN LABOR MOVEMENT 1–9, 35–58 (1989); KESSLER-HARRIS, supra note 194; PROTECTING WOMEN: LABOR LEGISLATION IN EUROPE, THE UNITED STATES, AND AUSTRALIA, 1880–1920 (Ulla Wikander, Alice Kessler-Harris, & Jane Lewis eds. 1995); Eileen Boris, New Deal Reformers Use the Government to Protect Women Workers, in MAJOR PROBLEMS IN THE HISTORY OF AMERICAN WORKERS 449 (Eileen Boris & Nelson Licktenstein eds. 1991); Patricia Cooper, "A Masculinist Vision of Useful Labor": Popular Ideologies about Women and Work in the United States, 1820–1939, 84 KY. L.J. 827, 838–59 (1996); Nancy Erickson, Muller v. Oregon Reconsidered: The Origins of a Sex-Based Doctrine of Liberty of Contract, 30 LABOR HIST. 228 (1989); Julie Novkov, Liberty, Protection, and Women's Work: Investigating the Boundaries between the Public and Private, 21 LAW & SOCIAL INQUIRY 857 (1997); Michael Thomson, Employing the Body: The Reproductive Body and Employment Exclusion, 5 SOC. & LEGAL STUD. 243 (1996). See generally WILLIAM FORBACH, LAW AND THE SHAPING OF THE AMERICAN LABOR MOVEMENT (1991); HOWARD GILLMAN, THE CONSTITUTION BESIEGED: THE RISE AND DEMISE OF THE LOCHNER ERA POLICE POWERS JURISPRUDENCE (1993).

200. LINDA GORDON, PITIED BUT NOT ENTITLED: SINGLE MOTHERS AND THE HISTORY OF WELFARE, 1890–1935, at 145–49, 175–79 (1994) ("GORDON, PITIED"); Cooper, supra note 199, at 851–52; Linda Gordon, Putting Children First: Women, Maternalism, and Welfare in the Early Twentieth Century ("Gordon, Putting Children First"), in U.S. HISTORY AS WOMEN'S HISTORY: NEW FEMINIST ESSAYS 82 (Linda Kerber et al. ed. 1995); Novkov, supra note 199, at 861.

201. See JEAN DONNISON, MIDWIVES AND MEDICAL MEN: A HISTORY OF THE STRUGGLE FOR THE CONTROL OF CHILDBIRTH 95, 140 (2nd ed. 1988); ALICE KESSLER-HARRIS, A WOMAN'S WAGE: HISTORICAL MEANINGS AND SOCIAL CONSEQUENCES 33–56 (1991) ("KESSLER-HARRIS, A WOMAN'S WAGE"); KESSLER-HARRIS, supra note 194, at 185–88; GWENDOLYN MINK, THE WAGES OF MOTHERHOOD: INEQUALITY IN THE WELFARE STATE, 1917–1942 (1995); Eileen Boris, The Regulation of Homework and the Devolution of the Postwar Labor Standards Regime: Beyond Dichotomy, in LABOR LAW IN AMERICA 449 (C. Tomlins & A. King eds. 1992); Cooper, supra note 199, at 846–48; Gordon, Putting Children First, supra note 200, at 81; Sybil Lipschultz, Hours and Wages: The Gendering of Labor Standards in America, 8 J. WOMEN'S HIST. 114 (1996); Elizabeth Reilly, The Rhetoric of Disrespect: Uncovering the Faulty Premises Infecting Reproductive Rights, 5 J. GENDER & L. 147, 161–72 (1996); Lucy Williams & Phyllis Baumann, The Mythogenesis of Gender: Judicial Images of Women in Paid and Unpaid Labor, 6 UCLA WOMEN'S L.J. 457 (1996). This problem continues today even in countries that go to great lengths to assure women of "equality" in the workplace. See Linda Haas & Philip Hwang, Company Culture and Men's Use of Family Leave Benefits in Sweden, 44 FAM. REL. 28 (1995); Shailagh Murray, Job Split: How Sweden's Push for Gender Equality Ended in Segregation, WALL ST. J. EUR., Jan. 19, 1999, at 1;

this setting, social activists generally focused on securing a "family wage" for the husband rather than on the right of women to work.[202] Many activists, including many active feminists, stressed the "natural" inclination of women towards domesticity, nurturing, and self-sacrifice.[203] And most feminists strongly supported making divorce difficult as the best means of protecting women's and children's well-being.[204] Feminists also founded and led the "social purity movement" in an effort to suppress prostitution and other vices that threatened the security of the family.[205]

The widening separation of the area in which women worked from the area in which men worked created a new, "separate spheres" ideology that further solidified the ancient tradition of male dominance in the family.[206] Against the background of the separate spheres ideology, attorneys Louis Brandeis and Samuel Warren wrote their famous article inventing a "right of privacy."[207] According to the "separate spheres" ideology, the world was divided into a "public sphere" of work which was the sphere of men, and a "private sphere" of the home in which women were accorded a considerable measure of authority—but always subordinate the authority of a man. These ideas, in turn, can be traced back to the discovery of sperm and the growth

---

Karen Sandqvist, *Swedish Family Policy and the Attempt to Change Paternal Roles*, in REASSESSING FATHER-HOOD: NEW OBSERVATIONS ON FATHERS AND THE MODERN FAMILY 144 (Charlie Lewis & Margaret O'Brien eds. 1987).

202. GORDON, PITIED, *supra* note 200, at 54; KESSLER-HARRIS, A WOMAN'S WAGE, *supra* note 201, at 8–10; MINK, *supra* note 201, at 149–61; Boris, *supra* note 201, at 262; Cooper, *supra* note 199, at 846–56; Maurine Weiner Greenwald, *Working-Class Feminism and the Family Wage Ideal: The Seattle Debate on Married Women's Right to Work, 1914–1920*, 76 J. AM. HIST. 118 (1989).

203. EILEEN BORIS, HOME TO WORK: MOTHERHOOD AND THE POLITICS OF INDUSTRIAL HOMEWORK IN THE UNITED STATES (1994); COTT, *supra* note 197, at 46, 71, 91; GORDON, PITIED, *supra* note 200, at 38–40, 44–45, 54–57, 83, 99, 193; KESSLER HARRIS, A WOMAN'S WAGE, *supra* note 201, at 31, 59–60, 69–70; MOLLY LADD-TAYLOR, MOTHER-WORK: WOMEN, CHILD WELFARE, AND THE STATE, 1890–1930 (1994); MINK, *supra* note 201, at 36–43, 52, 62–63, 151, 162–64, 171; STEPHEN MINTZ & SUSAN KELLOGG, DOMESTIC REVOLUTIONS: A SOCIAL HISTORY OF AMERICAN FAMILY LIFE 59 (1988); MOTHERS OF A NEW WORLD: MATERNALIST POLITICS AND THE ORIGINS OF WELFARE STATES (Seth Koven & Sonya Michel eds. 1993); ROBYN MUNCY, CREATING A FEMALE DOMINION IN AMERICAN REFORM, 1890–1935 (1991); ANNELISE ORLECK, COMMON SENSE AND A LITTLE FIRE: WOMEN AND WORKING-CLASS POLITICS IN THE UNITED STATES, 1900–1965 (1995); ELIZABETH PAYNE, REFORM, LABOR, AND FEMINISM: MARGARET DREIER ROBINS AND THE WOMEN'S TRADE UNION LEAGUE 123–29 (1988); Joanne Goodwin, *An American Experiment in Paid Motherhood: The Implementation of Mothers' Pensions in Early Twentieth-Century Chicago*, 4 GENDER & HIST. 323 (1992); Cooper, *supra* note 199, at 847–49, 859–60; Barbara Nelson, *The Origins of the Two-Channel Welfare State: Workmen's Compensation and Mothers' Aid*, in WOMEN, THE STATE, AND WELFARE 123 (Linda Gordon ed. 1990).

204. *See* Chapter 2, at notes 172–76; Chapter 8, at notes 128–35.

205. *See* Chapter 2, at notes 229–32.

206. BOYDSTON, *supra* note 187, at 142–63; COTT, *supra* note 197; JEAN ELSHTAIN, PUBLIC MAN, PRIVATE WOMAN: WOMEN IN SOCIAL AND POLITICAL THOUGHT (1981); MINTZ & KELLOGG, *supra* note 203; SUSAN MOLLER OKIN, WOMEN IN WESTERN POLITICAL THOUGHT (1979); DEBORAH RHODE, JUSTICE AND GENDER: SEX DISCRIMINATION AND THE LAW 132–60 (1989); STANSELL, *supra* note 187, at 217–21; WIENER, *supra* note 193; Cooper, *supra* note 199; Nancy Fraser & Linda Gordon, *A Genealogy of Dependency: Tracing a Keyword of the U.S. Welfare State*, 19 SIGNS 309 (1994); Linda Kerber, *Separate Spheres, Female Worlds, Women's Place: The Rhetoric of Women's History*, 75 J. AM. HIST. 9 (1988); Novkov, *supra* note 199, at 887–99; Frances Olsen, *The Family and the Market: A Study of Ideology and Legal Reform*, 96 HARV. L. REV. 1497 (1983); Barbara Welter, *The Cult of True Womanhood: 1820–1860*, 18 AM. Q. 151 (1966).

207. Samuel Warren & Louis Brandeis, *The Right of Privacy*, 4 HARV. L. REV. 193 (1890). On the relation of this "right" to our thinking about abortion, see Carole Joffe, *Comments on MacKinnon*, 18 RADICAL AM. 68 (Mar.–June 1984); Catharine MacKinnon, *The Male Ideology of Privacy: A Feminist Perspective on the Right to Abortion*, 17 RADICAL AM. 23 (July–Aug. 1983); Rosalind Pollack Petchesky, *Abortion as "Violence against Women": A Feminist Critique*, 18 RADICAL AM. 64 (Mar.–June 1984).

of the idea of the male as the "active" partner pursuing a "passive" female.[208] This discovery led to the demise of the theory that a woman could not become pregnant without experiencing orgasm and to the further crystallization of the notorious double standard. Ironically, men were able to participate fully in the public sphere of work precisely because they were deemed to have unfettered capacity to enter into a "private" relationship, namely an employment contract, without public interference in the form of regulations of the sort that were applied to "protect" women and children.[209]

The Supreme Court's abandoned its presumption that women were a special class always in need of protection in *Adkins v. Children's Hospital*.[210] This did little to alter the conditions of women's lives.[211] Courts continued to uphold protective legislation for women when "special need" was shown.[212] "Special need" usually related to the women's reproductive capacity[213] or their responsibility to care for children in the home.[214]

A few strong-willed white women did struggle to create careers outside the home, including in law and medicine.[215] A small, but significant, number of these women did not marry, and a few married women chose not to have children.[216] Some poor white women and many non-white women had to work outside the home notwithstanding the social ideal of "separate spheres" and the legal and structural barriers to their finding adequately paid, satisfying jobs.[217] For the majority of women in England or the United States, however, the only role they could occupy safely and securely was that of wife and mother.

Yet around the time of American Revolution American fertility rates began a steady but slow decline that persisted without significant interruption until the post-World War II baby boom.[218] This decline was driven in part by economic and social changes although at different times and rates for various groups of women defined by class and race.[219] The rate of illegitimate pregnan-

---

208. D'EMILIO & FREEDMAN, *supra* note 28, at 40–41, 43–47; McLAREN, *supra* note 36, at 13–14, 26–28. *See also* Nancy Cott, *Passionless: An Interpretation of Victorian Sexual Ideology, 1790–1850*, 4 SIGNS 219 (1978) (exploring the rise of the double standard as a form of social history but ignoring the role of scientific discoveries in this process).

209. FORBACH, *supra* note 199, at 135, 168; Erickson, *supra* note 199, at 229; Novkov, *supra* note 199, at 865, 877, 884–85, 887–99; Lea Vander Velde, *Hidden Dimensions in Labor Law History: Gender Variations on the Theme of Free Labor*, in LABOR LAW IN AMERICA, *supra* note 201, at 118.

210. 262 U.S. 525 (1923).

211. GORDON, PITIED, *supra* note 200, at 83; KESSLER-HARRIS, A WOMAN'S WAGE, *supra* note 201, at 50–54; Boris, *supra* note 199, at 456; Cooper, *supra* note 199, at 858.

212. Novkov, *supra* note 199, at 870–85.

213. KESSLER-HARRIS, *supra* note 194, at 184–86; Erickson, *supra* note 199, at 230; Novkov, *supra* note 199, at 872–73.

214. *See, e.g.*, W.C. Ritchie & Co. v. Wayman, 91 N.E.2d 695, 697–701 (Ill. 1910). *See generally* Novkov, *supra* note 199, at 875–76, 881.

215. *See* Chapter 8, at notes 251–322; Chapter 9, at notes 233–331.

216. *See* Charles Emerick, *College Women and Race Suicide*, 24 POLI. SCI. Q. 269 (1909).

217. *See, e.g.*, TERESA AMOTT & JULIE MATTHAEL, RACE, GENDER, AND WORK RACE, GENDER, AND WORK: A MULTICULTURAL ECONOMIC HISTORY OF WOMEN IN THE UNITED STATES 323–34 (1991); GORDON, PITIED, *supra* note 200, at 12, 111–43; KESSLER-HARRIS, *supra* note 194, at 137, 188; MINK, *supra* note 201, at 51–59, 142; PATRICIA MORTON, DISFIGURED IMAGES 1–13, 102–o3 (1991); Boris, *supra* note 199, at 450; Cooper, *supra* note 199, at 836–39, 843, 846–48, 854–56; Tera Hunter, *Domination and Renaissance: The Politics of Wage Household Labor in New South Atlanta*, 34 LABOR HIST. 205, 214–16 (1993); Nelson, *supra* note 203, at 139; Novkov, *supra* note 199, at 885–86.

218. *See* Chapter 2, at notes 134–44, 460–70.

219. CATHERINE CLINTON, THE PLANTATION MISTRESS: WOMAN'S WORLD IN THE OLD SOUTH 60–61, 152–56 (1982); CARL DEGLER, AT ODDS: WOMEN AND THE FAMILY IN AMERICA FROM THE REVOLUTION TO THE PRESENT 178–209, 220–22 (1980); HASIA DINER, ERIN'S DAUGHTERS IN AMERICA: IRISH IMMIGRANT

cies similarly declined sharply during the same period.[220] The rate of pregnant brides appears to have declined from a high of 30 percent at the beginning of the nineteenth century to about 10 percent by the middle of the century.[221]

Making estimates of rates of illegitimacy and pregnancy at marriage before 1900 is given the gaps and limitations in the available data.[222] Historian Judith Leavitt summarized the problem:

> [W]e simply do not know how often women in the past found themselves pregnant or even how frequently women labored to give birth. It is only in the twentieth century that the recording of births (live and still) began to be noted reliably by local and state health departments, and even today we cannot calculate precisely the risks women face each time they become pregnant. Because we cannot be sure about the number of labors or pregnancies, our statistical conclusions have limited meaning.[223]

Despite such concerns, however, we can have considerable confidence in the general changes in illegitimacy and bridal pregnancies, even if we cannot be certain of details of such estimates.[224]

This period was marked by the emergence of a consumer economy in which many persons came to expect to be able to purchase what had only a few years before been seen as luxury goods: lace curtains, imported teas, fine linens and china, silver tea services, and so on.[225] Once families began to value such opportunities, too many children could only impede a family's social advance. This change drew upon an even earlier change, in the eighteenth century, in English family life centered on the rise of the enlightenment notions of sexuality as natural, healthy,

---

WOMEN IN THE NINETEENTH CENTURY 54 (1983); PETCHESKY, *supra* note 36, at 73–74; ANNE SCOTT, THE SOUTHERN LADY: FROM PEDESTAL TO POLITICS, 1830–1930, at 38–39 (1970); RICHARD STECKEL, THE ECONOMICS OF U.S. SLAVE AND SOUTHERN WHITE FERTILITY 176 (1985); ROBERT WELLS, UNCLE SAM'S FAMILY: ISSUES AND PERSPECTIVES ON AMERICAN DEMOGRAPHIC HISTORY 28–56 (1985); VIRGINIA YANS-MCLAUGLIN, FAMILY AND COMMUNITY: ITALIAN IMMIGRANTS IN BUFFALO, 1880–1930, at 105 (1977); Wendell Bash, *Changing Birth Rates in Developing America: New York State, 1840–1875*, 41 MILLBANK MEM. FUND Q. 163 (1963); Susan Bloomberg et al., *A Census Probe into Nineteenth Century Family History: Southern Michigan, 1850–1880*, 5 J. SOC. HIST. 28 (1971); Phillips Cutright & Edward Shorter, *The Effects of Health on the Completed Fertility of Non-White and White U.S. Women Born between 1867 and 1935*, 13 J. SOC. HIST. 191 (1979); Richard Easterlin, *Factors in the Decline of Farm Fertility in the United States: Some Preliminary Research Results*, 63 J. AM. HIST. 600 (1976); Michael Haines, *Fertility and Marriage in a Nineteenth-Century Industrial City: Philadelphia, 1850–1880*, 40 J. ECON. HIST. 151 (1980); Michael Haines, *Fertility Decline in Industrial America: An Analysis of the Pennsylvania Anthracite Region, 1850–1900*, 32 POPULATION STUD. 327 (1978); Tamara Hareven & Maris Vinovskis, *Marital Fertility, Ethnicity, and Occupation in Urban Families: An Analysis of South Boston and the South End in 1880*, 8 J. SOCIAL HIST. 464 (1975); Joseph McFalls, jr., & George Masnick, *Birth Control and the Fertility of the U.S. Black Population, 1880–1980*, 6 J. FAM. HIST. 89 (1981); Warren Sanderson, *Quantitative Aspects of Marriage, Fertility, and Family Limitation in Nineteenth Century America: Another Application of the Coale Specifications*, 16 DEMOGRAPHY 339 (1979); Xarifa Sallume & Frank Notestein, *Trends in the Size of Families Completed Prior to 1910 in Various Social Classes*, 38 AM. J. SOC. 404 (1932); Maris Vinovskis, *Socioeconomic Determinants of Interstate Fertility Differentials in the United States*, 6 J. INTERDISCIPLINARY HIST. 375 (1976); Robert Wells, *Family Size and Fertility Control in Eighteenth-Century America: A Study of Quaker Families*, 25 POPULATION STUD. 73 (1971).

220. D'EMILIO & FREEDMAN, *supra* note 28, at 76.

221. *Id.* at 178–84; Deborah Rhode, *Adolescent Pregnancy and Public Policy*, 108 POLI. SCI. Q. 635, 636–38 (1994).

222. *See* Richard Smith, *The Long Cycle in American Illegitimacy and Prenuptial Pregnancy*, in BASTARDY AND ITS COMPARATIVE HISTORY 364 (Peter Laslett ed. 1980).

223. LEAVITT, *supra* note 22, at 24.

224. LAUREL THATCHER ULRICH, THE MIDWIFE'S TALE: THE LIFE OF MARTHA BALLARD BASED ON HER DIARY, 1785–1812, at 152, 156 (1991); Daniel Scott Smith & Michael Hindus, *Premarital Pregnancy in America, 1640–1971: An Overview and Interpretation*, 5 J. INTERDISCIPLINARY HIST. 537, 553–57 (1975).

225. BARBARA BERGMAN, THE ECONOMIC EMERGENCE OF WOMEN (1986); CAROLE SHAMAS, THE PRE-INDUSTRIAL CONSUMER IN ENGLAND AND AMERICA (1990).

and a legitimate source of pleasure apart from procreation[226] as well as the creation of a consumer society in England during that same century.[227] Changing social mores are hinted at by the sharp fall in the birthrate among the English aristocracy during the century of 1675–1775, although precisely how this was accomplished remains subject to debate.[228]

These changes also legitimated the hitherto suspect notion of love as the basis for marriage. Of course, love matches appear throughout history, but for centuries such unions were viewed with suspicion as likely to be socially disruptive.[229] The transition of "love" from a somewhat aberrant basis for marriage to the primary reason for marrying was already underway by the time of the Reformation in England and was thus always prominent in the American colonies.[230]

At about the same time, new technologies made children an economic burden rather than a source of free labor.[231] The need to birth numerous children simply to maintain the population also declined as life expectancy slowly rose throughout the nineteenth century. The life expectancy at birth for men in Massachusetts in 1850 was 38, and for women was 40.5; by 1900, the figure for men had reached 47, and for women 49.[232] (The change mostly reflected declines in infant mortality rather than any improvement in the health care of adults—and thus had little, if any, effect on the likely duration of a marriage.[233])

Women thus had growing incentives for limiting the risks to their lives and health from too frequent pregnancies even while depending on the roles of wife and mother for their livelihood and their social status.[234] Birthing in the early nineteenth century, without knowledge of anal-

---

226. D'EMILIO & FREEDMAN, *supra* note 28, at 40–41; Ray Porter, *Mixed Feelings: The Enlightenment and Sexuality in Eighteenth-Century Britain,* in SEXUALITY IN BRITAIN IN THE EIGHTEENTH CENTURY 1 (Paul-Gabriel Bouce ed. 1985).

227. NEIL MCCORMICK et al., THE BIRTH OF THE CONSUMER SOCIETY: THE COMMERCIALIZATION OF EIGHTEENTH CENTURY ENGLAND (1988). *See also* T.H. Breen, *An Empire of Goods: The Anglicization of Colonial America, 1690–1776,* 25 J. BRIT. STUD. 467 (1986).

228. *See* LAWRENCE STONE, THE FAMILY, SEX, AND MARRIAGE IN ENGLAND 1500–1800, at 260 (1977). For parallel changes in the American colonies, see D'EMILIO & FREEDMAN, *supra* note 26, at 42–48.

229. *See generally* JOSEPH CAMPBELL, THE HERO WITH A THOUSAND FACES (1968).

230. *See* MARTIN INGRAM, CHURCH COURTS, SEX AND MARRIAGE IN ENGLAND, 1570–1640, at 171–218 (1987).

231. *See generally* JOSEPH BANKS, VICTORIAN VALUES: SECULARISM AND THE SIZE OF FAMILIES (1981); JOSEPH & OLIVE BANKS, FEMINISM AND FAMILY PLANNING IN VICTORIAN ENGLAND (1964); JOSEPH BANKS, PROSPERITY AND PARENTHOOD: A STUDY OF FAMILY PLANNING AMONG THE VICTORIAN MIDDLE CLASSES (1954); G.D.H. COLE, A SHORT HISTORY OF THE BRITISH WORKING CLASS MOVEMENT, 1789–1925, at 29–32 (1925); MARY ANN MASON, FROM FATHER'S PROPERTY TO CHILDREN'S RIGHTS: THE HISTORY OF CUSTODY IN THE UNITED STATES (1994); Norman Himes, *The Birth Control Handbills of 1823,* LANCET, Aug. 6 1927, at 313. *See also* ANSLEY COALE & MELVIN ZELNICK, NEW ESTIMATES OF FERTILITY AND POPULATION IN THE U.S. 36 (1963); BROOKES, *supra* note 9, at 41–42; D'EMILIO & FREEDMAN, *supra* note 28, at 57–59; MYRA MARX FERREE & BETH HESS, CONTROVERSY AND COALITION: THE NEW FEMINIST MOVEMENT ACROSS THREE DECADES OF CHANGE 12 (rev. ed. 1994); GORDON, *supra* note 38, at 11, 48–49, 72–91, 150–54, 393–94; YASU-KICHI YASUBA, BIRTH RATES OF THE WHITE POPULATION IN THE UNITED STATES, 1800–1860: AN ECONOMIC STUDY (1962); Easterlin, *supra* note 219; Daniel Scott Smith, *Family Limitation, Sexual Conduct, and Domestic Feminism in Victorian America,* 1 FEMINIST STUD. 40, 130–32 (1973).

232. U.S. BUR. OF CENSUS, HISTORICAL STATISTICS OF THE UNITED STATES: COLONIAL TIMES TO 1970, at 37 (1975).

233. In 1850, in Massachusetts, 13% of children died during the first year of their life. *Id.* at 57. *See generally* DAVID GLASS & DAVID EVERSLEY, POPULATION HISTORY: ESSAYS IN HISTORICAL DEMOGRAPHY (1965); FRANK LORIMER, CULTURE AND HUMAN FERTILITY (1954).

234. BRODIE, *supra* note 65, at 36–37; DEGLER, *supra* note 219, at 188–89, 195, 208; D'EMILIO & FREEDMAN, *supra* note 28, at 58–59; Sheila Ryan Johansson, *Status Anxiety and Demographic Contraction of Privileged Populations,* 13 POP. & DEV. 439 (1987); Smith, *supra* note 222. *See generally* SARAH BLAFFER HRDY, MOTHER NATURE: A HISTORY OF MOTHERS, INFANTS, AND NATURAL SELECTION 365–66 (1999); HUMAN REPRODUCTIVE DECISIONS (R.I.M. Dunbar ed. 1995); J.H. Barlow & N. Burley, *Human Fertility, Evolutionary Bi-*

gesics, anesthetics, antiseptics, and antibiotics, remained painful, dangerous, and debilitating.[235] Women jumped upon the opportunity to medicalize birth, creating an image of female frailty and delicacy and indicating a need for sexual restraint or even abstinence within marriage.[236] After all, abstinence remained the best means of gaining control over the number and spacing of their pregnancies until well into the twentieth century.[237]

Another social change that followed from industrialization was the emergence of a large number of young men and women who left home to work in the factories, or elsewhere in cities, before marriage.[238] Historian Carl Degler estimates that the percentage of unmarried white women working outside the home grew from only 10 percent in 1800, to 20 percent in 1850, and to 50 percent by 1900.[239] Many factory owners and other employers did undertake to police the activities of women workers to assure their chastity if only to ease the fears of families that might preclude sending their daughters to work.[240] Yet there emerged for the first time in Western history a large class of young, sexually mature women who were living independently of the families into which they had been born and by which they had been raised without having come under the authority of a husband. By 1900, 5,000,000 women were working for pay—about 20 percent of the labor force, and some consider this a serious undercount.[241] As already noted, most of these women were either unmarried or non-white or both, for only five percent of married white women worked for wages outside the home at this time.[242]

This situation produced the predictable results. The growing economic emancipation of women, along with removing them from their birth homes, made them more open to (or at least more available for) sexual experimentation.[243] Indirect evidence of such changes in sexual

*ology, and the Demographic Transition*, 1 ETHOLOGY & SOCIOBIOLOGY 163 (1980); Monique Borgerhoff Mulder, *The Demographic Transition: Are We Any Closer to an Evolutionary Explanation?*, 13 TRENDS IN ECOL. & EVOLUTION 266 (1998).

235. DEGLER, *supra* note 219, at 59–63; DONNISON, *supra* note 201, at 106–07, 191.

236. *See* Chapter 2, at notes 145–239.

237. *Id.* at notes 12–144.

238. *See generally* BOYDSTON, *supra* note 187; KESSLER-HARRIS, *supra* note 194, at 37–44; KREPS & CLARK, *supra* note 187; MARY RYAN, CRADLE OF THE MIDDLE CLASS: THE FAMILY IN ONEIDA COUNTY, NEW YORK, 1790–1865, at 201–02 (1981); STANSELL, *supra* note 187, at 93–96; Angus McLaren, *Birth Control and Abortion in Canada, 1870–1920*, 59 CAN. HIST. REV. 319, 320–21 (1978).

239. DEGLER, *supra* note 219, at 155–56.

240. *See generally* FARM TO FACTORY: WOMEN'S LETTERS, 1830–1860 (Thomas Dublin ed., 2nd ed. 1993). *See also* VICTORIA BYNUM, THE POLITICS OF SEXUAL AND SOCIAL CONTROL IN THE OLD SOUTH (1992); JENNIE RUTTY, LETTERS OF LOVE AND COUNSEL FOR "OUR GIRLS" 236–52 (1899).

241. AMOTT & MATTHAEL, *supra* note 217, at 316.

242. PETCHESKY, *supra* note 36, at 75; WEINER, *supra* note 187, at 6 (1985). This pattern held true for immigrant women as well as for native-born women. Bina Kalola, *Immigration Laws and the Immigrant Woman: 1885–1924*, 11 GEO. IMMIGRATION L.J. 553, 567–73 (1997).

243. D'EMILIO & FREEDMAN, *supra* note 28, at 44, 73–78, 199–200, 272–73; FAYE DUDDEN, SERVING WOMEN 215–16 (1983); MEYEROWITZ, *supra* note 194; MARY ODEM, DELINQUENT DAUGHTERS: PROTECTING AND POLICING ADOLESCENT FEMALE SEXUALITY IN THE UNITED STATES, 1885–1920 (1986); MARVIN OLASKY, ABORTION RIGHTS: A SOCIAL HISTORY OF ABORTION IN AMERICA 38–41, 173–83 (1992); KATHY LEE PEISS, CHEAP AMUSEMENTS: WORKING WOMEN AND LEISURE IN TURN-OF-THE-CENTURY NEW YORK 62, 70–71, 108–10 (1986); PETCHESKY, *supra* note 36, at 110–12; STANSELL, *supra* note 187, at 178–86; Jane Larsen, *"Even a Worm Will Turn at Last": Rape Reform in Late Nineteenth-Century America*, 9 YALE J.L. & HUMANITIES 1 (1997); Jane Larson, *"Women Understand So Little, They Call My Good Nature 'Deceit'": A Feminist Rethinking of Seduction*, 93 COLUM. L. REV. 374, 384–87 (1993); Elizabeth Lunbeck, *"A New Generation of Women": Progressive Psychiatrists and the Hypersexual Female*, 13 FEMINIST STUD. 513 (1987); Mary Morton, *Seduced and Abandoned in an American City: Cleveland and Its Fallen Women*, 11 J. URBAN HIST. 443 (1985). *See also* RUTH ALEXANDER, THE GIRL PROBLEM: FEMALE SEXUAL DELINQUENCY IN NEW YORK, 1900–1930 (1995).

behavior is found in the rising rate of premarital pregnancy leading to births shortly after marriage late in the nineteenth century in the United States (from 10 percent of brides in 1850 back up to as much as 30 percent of brides in 1900).[244] The reported rising rate of premarital pregnancy suggests that abortion might actually have declined—perhaps sharply—as the laws against abortion became more stringent. The changing rates of premarital pregnancy, as much as the purported concern about "white slavery" (coerced prostitution), perhaps fueled the enactment in 1910 and fitful enforcement thereafter of the *Mann Act* prohibiting the transportation of women across state lines for "immoral purposes."[245]

This era also saw the transformation of seduction suits from proceedings on behalf of a woman's father for the loss of her services to a proceeding on behalf of a woman for the loss of her chastity.[246] Furthermore, the changes in employment patterns raised the real costs of having a child even among married women for if they could bring additional income into the home, staying barefoot, pregnant, and in the kitchen could only be "bought" by foregoing that income.[247] But few white women were willing to leave the home for work after marriage—something still rare in the beginning of the twentieth century.

People living in the closing years of the twentieth century might wonder why widespread sexual experimentation would necessarily lead to premarital pregnancies, but this overlooks the reality that until quite recently there were no effective contraceptives, and no truly safe means of aborting.[248] Only after 1880 did mechanical and chemical means of birth control begin to become available in America and England to any large extent[249] and then only over considerable public opposition.[250] The first public birth control clinic was established in the Netherlands in 1882.[251] One only can find the first indirect evidence of rising rates of abortion in the emergence of hospital admissions for septic abortions from incompletely or incompetently performed abortions, also after 1880.[252]

Ultimately, the preferred method of preventing conception remained, as it had for millennia, sexual abstinence, difficult as it might be to achieve. The prudential ethic that counseled abstinence was captured in the ditty about a lady

---

244. D'EMILIO & FREEDMAN, *supra* note 28, at 199; Rhode, *supra* note 221, at 639.

245. *See generally* LANGUM, *supra* note 41. The Mann Act was repealed in 1986.

246. *See* Mary Frances Berry, *Judging Morality: Sexual Behavior and Legal Consequences in the Late Nineteenth Century South*, 78 J. AM. HIST. 835 (1991); Larson, *supra* note 243; M.B.W. Sinclair, *Seduction and the Myth of the Ideal Woman*, 5 LAW & INEQUALITY 33 (1987); Lea VanderVelde, *The Legal Ways of Seduction*, 48 STAN. L. REV. 817 (1996).

247. PETCHESKY, *supra* note 36, at 103–10, 114–17; Lois Wladis Hoffman & Martin Hoffman, *The Value of Children to Parents*, in PSYCHOLOGICAL PERSPECTIVES ON POPULATION 65 (James Fawcett ed. 1973); Harris Presser & Wendy Baldwin, *Child Care as a Constraint on Employment: Prevalence, Correlates, and Bearing on the Work and Fertility Nexus*, 85 AM. J. SOC. 1202 (1980).

248. Deborah Dawson, Denise Meny, & Jeanne Ridley, *Fertility Control in the United States before the Contraceptive Revolution*, 12 FAM. PLAN. PERSP. 76 (1980). *See also* Chapters 1 & 2.

249. BRODIE, *supra* note 65, at 205–24; STEPHEN KERN, ANATOMY AND DESTINY: A CULTURAL HISTORY OF THE HUMAN BODY 155 (1975); PETCHESKY, *supra* note 36, at 34–35; CARROLL SMITH-ROSENBERG, DISORDERLY CONDUCT: VISIONS OF GENDER IN VICTORIAN AMERICA 224 (1985); Vivian Walsh, *Contraception: The Growth of a Technology*, in ALICE THROUGH THE MICROSCOPE: THE POWER OF SCIENCE OVER WOMEN'S LIVES 182, 182–83 (Lynda Birke *et al.* eds. 1980). *See generally* GORDON, *supra* note 38, at 159–390.; Steven Polgar, *Population History and Population Policies from an Anthropological Perspective*, 13 CURRENT ANTHROPOLOGY 203 (1972); Étienne van de Walle, *Motivations and Technology and the Decline of French Fertility*, in FAMILY AND SEXUALITY IN FRENCH HISTORY 135 (Robert Wheaton & Tamara Hareven eds. 1980).

250. *See generally* BRODIE, *supra* note 65, at 87–288; DAVID GARROW, LIBERTY AND SEXUALITY: THE RIGHT OF PRIVACY AND THE MAKING OF *ROE v. WADE* 1–269 (2nd ed. 1998).

251. GORDON, *supra* note 38, at 172.

252. SHORTER, *supra* note 12, at 191–96.

Who kept herself undefiled

By thinking of Jesus

And loathsome diseases

And the bother of having a child.[253]

The resources of families, churches, schools, and juvenile courts were marshaled to impress these concerns on young, particularly young female, minds.[254] Young men, on the other hand, were not so much concerned about their own virginity as about the virginity of a potential wife.[255]

Abortion's very illegality leaves us with no means of determining its actual incidence. The only careful statistical study of the incidence of abortion before World War II found an abortion rate of barely one per cent of pregnancies.[256] Most historians and other modern commentators believe this to have been a serious undercount.[257] One practicing physician in 1904 estimated the abortion rate for Chicago at 10–13 percent of all pregnancies.[258] At the other extreme, a Stanford University study that estimated in 1921 that about 50 percent of pregnancies ended in "abortions" including spontaneous abortions, with 25 percent being illegal abortions, was probably a gross overestimate.[259] Numerous doctors crusading against abortion in the opening decades of the twentieth century made similar assertions that illegal abortion was common, even pervasive.[260] On the other hand, various observers in the later years of the nineteenth century and the early years of the twentieth century reported that the incidence of illegal abortion had declined sharply.[261] One can only wonder, however, whether such claims are any more reliable than the estimates of enormous numbers of abortions.

---

253. Quoted in John Ayer, *The Last Butskellite* (book rev.), 93 Mich. L. Rev. 1805, 1810 (1995). Remarkably, Alfred Kinsey's study of the sexual behavior of the white, middle-class American women found that they expressed their fears somewhat differently—moral concerns, risk of loss of reputation, and concern over pregnancy. Alfred Kinsey et al., Sexual Behavior in the Human Female 315 (1953). *See also* Beth Bailey, Sex in the Heartland 76–78 (1999).

254. *See* Patricia Campbell, Sex Education Books for Young Adults, 1892–1979 (1979); Karen DeCrow, Sexist Justice 268–79 (1974); Harry Krause, Illegitimacy: Law and Social Policy (1971); Rickie Solinger, Wake Up Little Susie: Single Pregnancy and Race before *Roe v. Wade* 168–86 (1992); David Tyack & Elizabeth Hansot, Learning Together: A History of Coeducation in American Schools 223 (1990); Rhode, *supra* note 221, at 640–41.

255. Alfred Kinsey, Wardell Pomeroy, & Clyde Martin, Sexual Behavior of the Human Male 364 (1948).

256. Raymond Pearl, The Natural History of Population 222, 237 (1939).

257. *See, e.g.,* Williams, *supra* note 36, at 207–09.

258. C.S. Bacon, *The Duty of the Medical Profession in Criminal Abortion,* 7 Ill. Med. J. 18, 18 (1905).

259. Arthur Meyers, *The Frequency and Cause of Abortion,* 2 Am. J. Obstestrics & Gynecology 138 (1921).

260. *See, e.g.,* M.S. Iseman, Race Suicide 141–43, 153–55, 158, 199 (1912); C.S. Bacon, *Chicago Medical Society: Regular Meeting, Held Nov. 23, 1904,* 43 JAMA 1889 (1904); J. Henry Barbat, *Criminal Abortion,* 9 Cal. St. J. Med. 69 (1911); Robert Thrift Ferguson, *Abortion and Abortionist,* 93 S. Med. & Surgery 889 (1931); Rudolph Holmes, *The Methods of the Professional Abortionist,* 10 J. Surgery, Gynecology, & Obstet. 540, 542–43 (1910); Robert McNair, *Status of the Abortionist in the Modern Social Order,* 107 N.Y. Med. J. 503 (1918); G.D. Royston, *A Statistical Study of the Causes of Abortion,* 76 Am. J. Obstet. & Diseases of Women 582 (1917). *See generally* Olasky, *supra* note 243, at 222–23, 228–33; Reagan, *supra* note 19, at 23.

261. *See, e.g.,* William Parish, *Criminal Abortions,* 68 Med. Surgical Rptr. 646 (1893); James Scott, *Criminal Abortion,* 33 Am. J. Obstet. & Diseases of Women & Children 72 (1896); John Stoddard, *Foeticide—Suggestions toward Its Suppression,* 10 Det. Rev. Med. & Pharmacy 655 (1875). *See* Mohr, *supra* note 61, at 241–43; Olasky, *supra* note 243, at 221–22.

# After World War I

*The War was another Black Death that came upon the world.... And it*
*brought with it not the Dance of Death but the Dance of Priapus.*

— V.F. Calverton[262]

The various social forces pressing towards freer sexual experimentation came together in the wake of World War I. The war certainly contributed to the dissemination of information about contraceptives (particularly condoms) and to a certain loss of faith in the existing moral system.[263] Even historian Linda Gordon, who trenchantly denies that sexual behavior is driven by technological developments, has admitted that the spread of information about contraception correlated highly with changes in sexual practice.[264] The driving force of change, however, was not just what the men learned while in uniform, but also—during the war—the entry of even more unmarried women (and a good many married women as well) into the world of work outside the home, a process that had begun before the war.[265] Another technological development—the automobile—brought on changes in sexual mores by making privacy possible for young people who still lived with their parents.[266] The 1920s also were a period of unprecedented prosperity allowing economic emancipation for the young of both sexes even while they confronted a certain disillusionment with traditional values fostered by the experience of the war and the promotion of newer values by the new media of radio and motion pictures.

As a result, there appears to have been a jump in the rate of premarital sexual experimentation during the 1920s.[267] Premarital sexuality continued thereafter at a more or less stable rate until the next big jump after 1960.[268] The most direct evidence for this change in sexual behavior is found in the famous *Kinsey Report* on the sexual behavior of white, middle-class American

---

262. V.F. Calverton, The Bankruptcy of Marriage 18 (1928).

263. Gordon, *supra* note 38, at 200–01, 204–06; Andrea Tone, Devices and Desires: A History of Contraceptives in America 91–115 (2001).

264. *Id.* at 206. *See* Katherine Bement Davis, Factors in Sex Life 19–20 (1929).

265. Gordon, *supra* note 38, at 202–04.

266. *See, e.g.,* Helen & Robert Lynd, Middletown 137, 258–69 (1929). *See also* Beth Bailey, From Front Porch to Back Seat: Courtship in Twentieth-Century America (1988); David Lewis, *Sex and the Automobile: From Rumble Seats to Rockin' Vans,* in The Automobile and American Culture 19 (David Lewis & Laurence Goldstein eds. 1980). *See generally* Beverly Donofrio, Riding in Cars with Boys (1990); Peter Ling, America and the Automobile: Technology, Reform and Social Change (1990); John Rae, The Road and the Car in American Life (1971); Virginia Schafff, Taking the Wheel: Women and the Coming of the Motor Age (1991); Carol Sanger, *Girls and the Getaway: Cars, Culture, and the Predicament of Gendered Space,* 144 U. Pa. L. Rev. 705 (1995); Marianne Whatley, *Raging Hormones and Powerful Cars: The Construction of Men's Sexuality in School Sex Education and Popular Adolescent Films,* 179 B.U. J. Educ. 100 (1988).

267. *See generally* Paula Fass, The Damned and the Beautiful: American Youth in the 1920s (1977); John Modell, Into One's Own: From Youth to Adulthood in the United States, 1920–1975 (1989); Kevin White, The First Sexual Revolution: The Emergence of Male Heterosexuality (1993); Pamela Haag, *In Search of "The Real Thing": Ideologies of Love, Modern Romance, and Women's Sexual Subjectivity in the United States, 1920–1940,* 2 J. Hist. Sexuality 547 (1992). *See also* Wini Brienes, Young, White, and Miserable: Growing up Female in the Fifties (1992).

268. On the somewhat smaller changes that occurred during World War II, see Bailey, *supra* note 253, at 13–38; Beth Bailey & David Farber, The First Strange Place: The Alchemy of Race and Sex in WWII Hawaii (1992); John Costello, Virtue under Fire: How World War II Changed our Social and Sex-

women.[269] There was also a new openness to the idea of divorce,[270] an openness that had begun to emerge even before the war.[271] The new openness to the idea of divorce produced, however, only incremental changes in the incidence of divorce,[272] while changing behavior behind closed doors did not lead to challenges to the publicly professed moral code that still condemned non-marital sex in general and particular sexual practices within marriage.[273]

Following hard on the "roaring '20s," the Great Depression resulted in unprecedented levels of unemployment and underemployment, forcing whole families and individuals into abject poverty.[274] As a result, there was a further sharp decline in the birthrate, particularly among those without jobs or the prospect of jobs.[275] Yet there is no evidence that the rate of premarital sexual activity characteristic of the 1920s declined during the 1930s. The pattern of delaying marriage until one's economic circumstances could justify taking on the responsibility of a family increased, however, as shown by a sharp rise in the age of first marriages.[276] This pattern perhaps even increased the rate of premarital sexual activity.

Clearly Depression-inspired changes in marriage and pregnancy patterns, like the baby boom that followed World War II, were not merely technologically determined but resulted from choices people made in the face of a then grim (and after the war, extraordinarily favorable) economic reality.[277] Given the role of human choice, political scientist Rosalind Petchesky

---

UAL ATTITUDES (1985); D'EMILIO & FREED MAN, *supra* note 28, at 261; RICHARD POLENBERG, WAR AND SOCIETY: THE UNITED STATES 1941–1954, at 149–53 (1972).

269. KINSEY *et al.*, *supra* note 253, at 321–26. *See also* COTT, *supra* note 197, at 154–62; D'EMILIO & FREEDMAN, *supra* note 28, at 256, 262–65, 333; MYRA MARX FERREE & BETH HESS, CONTROVERSY AND COALITION: THE NEW FEMINIST MOVEMENT ACROSS THREE DECADES OF CHANGE 10–11 (rev. ed. 1994); JOSEPH KETT, RITES OF PASSAGE: ADOLESCENCE IN AMERICA, 1790 TO THE PRESENT 258–60 (1977); Rhode, *supra* note 221, at 640; B.K. Singh, *Trends in Attitudes toward Premarital Sexual Relations*, 42 J. MARRIAGE & FAM. 387 (1980).

270. *See, e.g.*, BEN LINDSEY & WAINWRIGHT EVANS, COMPANIATE MARRIAGE (1927); Bruce Barton, *Do Too Many People Marry?*, 82 GOOD HOUSEKEEPING 19 (Feb. 1926); Clarence Darrow, *The Divorce Problem: A Plea for the Application of Rational Principles to the Question of Domestic Relations*, 28 VANITY FAIR 31 (Aug. 1927); Robert Grant, *A Call to a New Crusade*, 73 GOOD HOUSEKEEPING 42 (Sept. 1921); Ruth Hale, *Freedom in Divorce*, 76 FORUM 333 (Sept. 1926); Rollin Lynde Hartt, *The Habit of Getting Divorces—II: Its Growth since the War*, 48 WORLD'S WORK 519 (Sept. 1924); George Koehn, *Is Divorce a Social Menace?*, 16 CURRENT HIST. 294 (MAY 1922); Gustavus Myers, *The Rapid Increase in Divorce*, 14 CURRENT HIST. 816 (Aug. 1921). *See generally* J. HERBIE DIFONZO, BENEATH THE FAULT LINE: THE POPULAR AND LEGAL CULTURE OF DIVORCE IN TWENTIETH-CENTURY AMERICA 13–36 (1997).

271. *See, e.g.*, Rheta Childe Dorr, *The Problem of Divorce*, 45 FORUM 68 (Jan. 1911); E.B. Harrison, *A Woman's View of Divorce*, NINETEENTH CENTURY 329 (Feb. 1911); E.A. Ross, *The Significance of Increasing Divorce*, CENTURY MAG., May 1909, at 151; Anita Garlin Spencer, *Problems of Marriage and Divorce*, 48 FORUM 188 (Aug. 1912).

272. DIFONZO, *supra* note 270, at 43–66.

273. BAILEY, *supra* note 253, at 30–31, 49, 73, 75–80, 119.

274. *See generally* LIZABETH COHEN, MAKING A NEW DEAL: INDUSTRIAL WORKERS IN CHICAGO, 1919–1939 (1990); JOHN KENNETH GALBRAITH, THE GREAT CRASH (1955); H.V. HODSON, SLUMP AND RECOVERY, 1929–1937 (1938); WILLIAM LEUCHTENBURG, FRANKLIN D. ROOSEVELT AND THE NEW DEAL, 1932–1940 (1963); BROADUS MITCHELL, DEPRESSION DECADE (1947); LIONEL ROBBINS, THE GREAT DEPRESSION (1934).

275. BROOKES, *supra* note 9, at 109; DONNISON, *supra* note 201, at 184; FERREE & HESS, *supra* note 231, at 11; GORDON, *supra* note 38, at 305, 307–08; TONE, *supra* note 263, at 85; Norman Hines, *The Birth Rate of Families on Relief: A Summary of Recent Studies in the U.S.A.*, MARRIAGE HYGIENE, Aug. 1935, at 60; Edward Sydenstricker & Frank Notestein, *Differential Fertility According to Social Class*, J. AM. STATISTICAL ASS'N, March 1930, at 25.

276. DAPHNE SPAIN & SUZANNE BIANCHI, BALANCING ACT: MOTHERHOOD, MARRIAGE, AND EMPLOYMENT AMONG AMERICAN WOMEN 27 table 2.2 (1996). *See also* Lois Rita Helmbold, *Beyond the Family Economy: Black and White Working-Class Women during the Great Depression*, 13 FEMINIST STUD. 629 (1987).

277. RICHARD EASTERLIN, BIRTH AND FORTUNE 55–57 (1980); GORDON, *supra* note 38, at 301–40; PETCHESKY, *supra* note 36, at 112–13.

has vehemently insisted that recourse to contraception and abortion simply are not technologically determined.[278] Even she has admitted, however, that the advent of oral contraceptives around 1960 induced major changes in women's expectations regarding pregnancy and birth and thus contributed to the choices that women (and their men) made regarding life styles in innumerable ways, including the desirability of abortions.[279] It would be very surprising if other changes in the availability of contraceptives or the changing realities of abortion did not have similar impacts.

People responded to the need to limit the number of their children during the Depression to a significant degree by the ancient techniques of delayed marriage and family separation. By 1940, over 1,500,000 married couples in the United States were living apart from each other while and some hundreds of thousands of children (many, but certainly not all, in their teens) wandered the country on their own.[280] Curiously, these shattered families did not lead to much of a rise in the divorce rate, suggesting that at least some of the people involved hoped at some point to reconstitute their families. And, although many women were forced into the workforce in an effort to keep bread on the table and to try to hold their families together, this generated considerable opposition aimed at confining women to the home.[281]

Assuming that premarital (and extramarital) sexual experimentation continued unabated during the Depression, family separation and delayed marriage cannot fully account for the sharp decline in the birthrate—and the rate at which babies were conceived.[282] The choices women and men made in the 1930s would have been impossible without the recently developed technologies of the condom, the diaphragm, and surgical sterilization, along with the older techniques of abstention (including delayed marriage) and withdrawal.[283] The newer techniques were then at most 50 years old, truly effective condoms and diaphragms having become possible with the perfection of galvanized rubber, while surgical sterilization was perfected through the controversial efforts of such pioneers in gynecological surgery as Horatio Robinson Storer.[284] One result of the pressures for family limitation created in response to the Depression was the decision of the American Medical Association in 1937 formally to abandon its long-standing opposition to doctors prescribing contraceptives in the absence of medical reasons for limiting pregnancies.[285]

Unlike earlier periods of declining birthrates, we can infer that abortion played a role in the decline of the birthrate in the United States because of the increasing safety of the procedure[286] and because of a small rise in the incidence of hospital performed "therapeutic" abortions de-

---

278. Petchesky, *supra* note 36, at 112–13, 172–73, 195–96.

279. *Id.* at 169–70. *See also* Celeste Michelle Condit, Decoding Abortion Rhetoric: Communicating Social Change 69–70 (1990); Susan Scrimshaw, *Women and the Pill: From Panacea to Catalyst*, 13 Fam. Plan. Perspectives 260 (1981).

280. DiFonzo, *supra* note 270, at 30; Mintz & Kellogg, *supra* note 203, at 136.

281. *See, e.g.,* Elisabeth Cushman, *Office Women and Sex Antagonism*, Harper's, March, 1940, at 356. *See generally* Cohen, *supra* note 274, at 213–49; DiFonzo, *supra* note 270, at 30–31; Gordon, Pitied, *supra* note 200, at 184–85, 193–98; Kessler-Harris, *supra* note 194, at 250–72; Elaine Tyler May, Homeward Bound: American Families in the Cold War Era 37–57 (1988); Mink, *supra* note 201, at 126–27, 154–62; Winifred Wandersee, Women's Work and Family Values, 1920–1940, at 84–102 (1981); Susan Ware, Holding Their Own: American Women in the 1930's, at 21–53 (1982); Boris, *supra* note 199, at 452–53; Cooper, *supra* note 199, at 856–59.

282. Gebhard et al., *supra* note 22, at 113–14, 140.

283. Dawson, Meny, & Ridley, *supra* note 248. *See also* Chapter 2.

284. *See* Chapter 2, at notes 95–121; Chapter 7, at notes 375–78.

285. D'Emilio & Freedman, *supra* note 28, at 244–48; David Kennedy, Birth Control in America: The Career of Margaret Sanger 214–71, 246–61 (1970); James Reed, From Private Vice to Public Virtue: The Birth Control Movement and American Society since 1830, at 239–41 (1978).

286. See the text *supra* at notes 8–40.

spite a sharp decline in the frequency of strictly medical indications for an abortion.[287] A study by the Children's Bureau in the United States had already found that 14 percent of maternal deaths were the result of illegal abortions in 1927 and 1928.[288] A study by the New York Academy of Medicine reached a similar result.[289] Furthermore, the early years of the depression saw a sharp rise in hospital admissions in the United States for septic abortions.[290] In Britain, reported maternal death rates from criminal abortions also increased somewhat after 1920, leveling off at between 500 and 600 per year during the 1930s.[291]

For the first time, abortion was a more common cause of maternal death than childbirth.[292] Given the historic dangers of abortion, this is yet further confirmation that abortion had heretofore been a rare procedure—even assuming a significant undercount in maternal deaths from abortion. Whether the reported increases in maternal death resulted from increased incidence or simply from greater vigilance by the authorities remains unclear.[293] Historian Leslie Reagan would have us believe that such statistics simply reflect the medicalization of birth generally, that is, the removal of all aspects of birthing from the home to the hospital, and has no bearing on the incidence of abortion.[294] Reagan, however, also suggests that doctors were more willing in the 1930s to do abortions to supplement incomes damaged by the Depression.[295]

Apparently an insistent and growing demand for abortion did begin only a decade or two after the most stringent statutes against abortion were enacted. The Kinsey survey of the late 1940s confirmed that, for the educated urban white women sampled for the survey, there was indeed a rise in the frequency with which pregnancies were aborted in the 1930s, with 24 percent

---

287. BROOKES, *supra* note 9, at 60–62, 133, 137; D'EMILIO & FREEDMAN, *supra* note 28, at 253; GINSBURG, *supra* note 39, at 34–35; ANTHONY HORDERN, LEGAL ABORTION: THE ENGLISH EXPERIENCE 226–27 (1971); KERRY PETERSEN, ABORTION REGIMES 54–61 (1993). On the declining medical indications for abortion, see TAUSSIG, *supra* note 34, at 278–82, 320–21; Thomas Watts Eden, *The Indications for Induction of Abortion*, [1926] 2 BRIT. MED. J. 237; R. Finlay Gayle, *The Psychiatric Considerations for Abortion*, 91 S. MED. & SURGERY 251 (1929); *Indications for Premature Termination of Pregnancy*, [1931] 2 BRIT. MED. J. 750; Irving Perlmutter, *Analysis of Therapeutic Abortions: Bellevue Hospital 1935–1945*, 53 AM. J. OBSTET. & GYNECOLOGY 1012 (1947); H. Douglas Singer, *Mental Disease and the Induction of Abortion*, 91 JAMA 2042 (1928).

288. U.S. DEP'T OF LABOR, CHILDREN'S BUREAU, MATERNAL MORTALITY IN FIFTEEN STATES 100–15, 133 (Bureau pub. no. 223). *See also* Frederick Taussig, *Abortion in Relation to Fetal and Maternal Welfare*, 22 AM. J. OBSTET. & GYNECOLOGY 729 & 868 (1931); Frederick Taussig, *Abortion in Relation to Fetal and Maternal Welfare*, in WHITE HOUSE CONF. ON CHILD HEALTH & PROTECTION, *supra* note 21, at 446.

289. RANSOM HOOKER, MATERNAL MORTALITY IN NEW YORK CITY: A STUDY OF ALL PUERPERAL DEATHS, 1930–1932, at 51 (1933). *See* REAGAN, *supra* note 19, at 138–39.

290. *See, e.g.,* HOOKER, *supra* note 289, at 54; Henry Sangmeister, *A Survey of Abortion Deaths in Philadelphia from 1931–1940 Inclusive*, 46 AM. J. OBSTET. & GYNECOLOGY 755 (1943); J. Thornwell Witherspoon, *An Analysis of 200 Cases of Septic Abortion Treated Conservatively*, 26 AM. J. OBSTET. & GYNECOLOGY 367 (1939). *See generally* REAGAN, *supra* note 19, at 134–35; TAUSSIG, *supra* note 38, at 363–64.

291. BROOKES, *supra* note 9, at 49 n.132, 51–52.

292. *Abortion as a Cause of Maternal Mortality*, [1930] 4 BRIT. MED. J. 566.

293. BROOKES, *supra* note 9, at 72 n.7; Irvine Loudon, *Deaths in Childbed from the Eighteenth Century to 1935*, 30 MED. HIST. 1 (1986).

294. REAGAN, *supra* note 19, at 138. On the medicalization of birth and what some see as its negative effects on women, see generally CHARLOTTE BORST, CATCHING BABIES: THE PROFESSIONALIZATION OF BIRTH, 1870–1920 (1995); BRODIE, *supra* note 65, at 287; BROOKES, *supra* note 9, at 26, 67, 134; DONNISON, *supra* note 201; GORDON, *supra* note 38, at 160; HARRISON, *supra* note 25, at 165–66; ANGUS McLAREN, REPRODUCTIVE RITUALS 123–24, 127–29 (1984); ANN OAKLEY, THE CAPTURED WOMB: A HISTORY OF THE MEDICAL CARE OF PREGNANT WOMEN (1986); PETCHESKY, *supra* note 36, at 71–73, 79–81; PETERSEN, *supra* note 287, at 10–11; BARBARA KATZ ROTHMAN, IN LABOR: WOMEN AND POWER IN THE BIRTHPLACE (1982); Dianne Martin, *The Midwife's Tale: Old Wisdom and a New Challenge to the Control of Reproduction*, 3 COLUM. J. GENDER & L. 417 (1992); Rickie Solinger, *"A Complete Disaster": Abortion and the Politics of Hospital Abortion Committees, 1950–1970*, 19 FEMINIST STUD. 241 (1993).

295. REAGAN, *supra* note 19, at 147.

of pregnancies aborted in 1930 and 18 percent aborted in 1935.[296] The Great Depression itself also was the time when direct studies of abortion patterns began to be based on more careful survey techniques than had been the case in earlier decades. Perhaps best study of abortion in the United States under modern conditions was by Dr. Frederick Taussig in 1936.[297] Dr. Regine Stix, in another study published in 1935, found that perhaps as many as 10 percent of first pregnancies were aborted, a rate considerably higher than any rate we can confirm from any earlier period.[298] This pattern was particularly pronounced among unmarried women, especially among unmarried white women who frequently chose to abort rather than to marry in a time when many men were unemployed and had few prospects for work.[299] Hurried marriage had been probably the most common response to premarital pregnancies in economically happier times.[300]

Many women also gave birth to illegitimate children during this era, with perhaps 90 percent of unmarried mothers opting for adoption at this time.[301] This alone suggests either that a significant number of women did not have access to abortion or did not find it to be an acceptable option. The unpleasant implications of the sudden rush of illegitimate births perhaps explains why Dr. Stix herself repudiated the high end estimates of her own 1935 study only three years later.[302] Even her lower figures might well be an exaggeration as Stix had studied the case histories of women who had voluntarily gone to a birth control clinic in the Bronx—hardly a representative sample, and probably one that exhibited a higher rate of abortions than the general population.

Further clouding the picture of various attempts to research the frequency of abortions in the United States are inconsistent reports regarding the fate of abortionists. We are continually regaled by tales of the horrors of illegal abortions, yet we are also informed of doctors (and occasionally others) who had long careers as abortionists and for whom large communities of former patients rallied to support when those careers were ended by police action.[303] Both

---

296. GEBHARD et al., supra note 22, at 109–10, 113–14, 120, 140.

297. TAUSSIG, supra note 36.

298. Stix, supra note 24, at 358.

299. KESSLER-HARRIS, supra note 194, at 256–57; REAGAN, supra note 19, at 133; Helmbold, supra note 276, at 640–41.

300. See LEONTINE YOUNG, OUT OF WEDLOCK (1954).

301. Maris Vinovskis, An "Epidemic" of Adolescent Pregnancy? Some Historical Considerations, 6 J. FAM. HIST. 205 (1981); Rhode, supra note 221, at 639.

302. Regine Stix & Dorothy Wiehl, Abortion and the Public Health, 28 AM. J. PUB. HEALTH 621, 623–24 (1938).

303. Perhaps the best collect of the horror stories is found in MESSER & MAY, supra note 36, although most of those stories are from a period much later than examined here. See also PATRICIA MILLER, THE WORST OF TIMES 10, 93, 114–15, 217–18, 252, 275 (1993); REAGAN, supra note 19, at 19–21, 30, 33–36, 38–38. For accounts, also mostly later than the period under study here, of underground abortionists with well appointed clinics and few medical complications for the women they served, see NINIA BAEHR, ABORTION WITHOUT APOLOGY: A RADICAL HISTORY FOR THE 1990s 7–30 (1990); RUTH BARNETT, THEY WEEP ON MY DOORSTEP (1969); LINDA FREEMAN, THE ABORTIONIST (1962); Garrow, supra note 250, at 307–08, 318, 333–34, 349–51, 361–64, 376–77, 384–86, 391–93, 422, 428–31, 438, 445, 466–68, 486–87, 539; GEBHARD et al., supra note 22, at 198–99; MARK GRABER, RETHINKING ABORTION: EQUAL CHOICE, THE CONSTITUTION, AND REPRODUCTIVE POLITICS 46–49 (1996); CAROL JOFFE, DOCTORS OF CONSCIENCE: THE STRUGGLE TO PROVIDE ABORTION BEFORE AND AFTER ROE V. WADE (1995); LAWRENCE LADER, ABORTION 42–47 (1966); MILLER, supra, at 122–28, 135; REAGAN, supra, at 46–49, 53–56, 67–69; EDWIN SCHUR, CRIMES WITHOUT VICTIMS: DEVIANT BEHAVIOR AND PUBLIC POLICY 27 (1965); KATE SIMON, BRONX PRIMITIVES: PORTRAITS IN A CHILDHOOD 68–70 (1982); RICKI SOLINGER, THE ABORTIONIST: A WOMAN AGAINST THE LAW (paperback ed. 1996); RAYMOND TATALOVICH & BYRON DAYNES, THE POLITICS OF ABORTION: A STUDY OF COMMUNITY CONFLICT IN PUBLIC POLICY MAKING 43 (1981); Bates, supra note 36; Linda Greenhouse, Dr. Milan Vuitch, 78, Fighter for Abortion Rights (Obituary), N.Y. TIMES, Apr. 11, 1993, at A30; Jerome Kummer & Zad Leavy, Therapeutic Abortion Law Confusion, 195 JAMA 96, 97 (1966). See also JEROME BATES & EDWARD ZAWADSKI, CRIMINAL

claims are plausible, although the claims of public acceptance of abortionists would be more plausible if those who made such claims did not undercut their own case by, for example, hiding the identity of the abortionists they write about under pseudonyms.[304] We will actually never know the precise numbers of women who had either sort of experience, yet reasonably good care by trained health-care professionals (operating underground) was probably more common if only because prosecutions, which usually followed botched abortions, steadily became rarer during the twentieth century. Confirming this, Dr. Kinsey, in a sample that included women who had had abortions in the closing years of the period examined in this chapter, found that 87 percent of the women who admitted to having had abortions (about 45 percent of his entire sample) reported that the abortion had been performed by a physician.[305]

Despite the claims of official toleration of abortion, prosecutions were common in the major metropolitan areas throughout every decade of the second half of the nineteenth century.[306] The data regarding the number of prosecutions is far from complete. At best, historians and others (myself included) have only surveyed the prosecutions that resulted in published court opinions plus occasional trial transcripts or newspaper accounts. This undoubtedly leaves a large number of prosecutions that have never been tallied in the attempt to assess the total number of prosecutions in any century—including the twentieth. Even assuming the accuracy of the count of prosecutions, it still gives us only the barest glimmer of the incidence of abortion. The data might simply represent those who failed to pay off the police or the prosecutors adequately or who so botched the operation that no one could ignore the results.[307]

Finally, one cannot discount the indirect evidence of the continuing opposition by most physicians to abortion. Sociologist Jonathan Imber has pointed out that well into the twentieth century the phrase "*early* termination of pregnancy" was not a reference to abortion during the first trimester of pregnancy (as it would be today), but to an abortion or a cesarean section during the last trimester of pregnancy.[308] In other words, the great majority of physicians sought to maintain even a problematic pregnancy as long as possible in the hope of achieving a live birth, and turned to abortion or a cesarean section only as a last resort if the situation were truly life-threatening to the mother or child.[309]

---

ABORTION 48 (1964) (claiming that every "sub-community" in New York County—Manhattan—has its resident abortionist); Ferguson, *supra* note 260, at 889, 892; Holmes, *supra* note 260, at 542–43; McNair, *supra* note 260, at 503; John Murphy, *Are Municipal Hospitals Unwitting Aids to Abortionists?*, 45 MED. TIMES 103 (Apr. 1917); Royston, *supra* note 260, at 582. *See also* Chapter 12, at notes 165–251.

304. *See, e.g.,* JOFFE, *supra* note 303; LAURA KAPLAN, THE STORY OF JANE: THE LEGENDARY UNDERGROUND FEMINIST ABORTION SERVICE (1996).

305. *See* ABORTION IN THE UNITED STATES 53 (Mary Calderone ed. 1958).

306. Thomas Harris, Note, *A Functional Study of Existing Abortion Laws*, 35 COLUM. L. REV. 87, 91 n.18 (1935). *See also* MARVIN OLASKY, THE PRESS AND ABORTION, 1838–1988, at 16, 25–30, 34–40, 45–46, 51–54 (1988).

307. For reports of bribes to law enforcement personnel, see OLASKY, *supra* note 306, at 58, 73–75.

308. Jonathan Imber, *Abortion Policy and Medical Practice*, SOCIETY, July/Aug. 1990, at 27, 29 (emphasis in the original).

309. *Id.*

# Chapter 11

# Look What They've Done to My Song[1]

*[L]egal theories are not an evasion of ideology, but a re-location of it.*

—Allan Hutchinson[2]

The last Chapter outlined how the increasing safety of abortions for the pregnant woman, along with increasing pressures to limit the number of children in a family and the rather inadequate contraceptives available for doing so, combined to create a growing demand for abortion in the United States and the United Kingdom. Much the same was happening in other industrialized countries. The precise numbers of abortions remain entirely speculative for no accurate statistics could be assembled for an illegal procedure like abortion.[3] What is certain is that women in industrialized countries succeeded in limiting their births through a new accessibility to abortion, or through improved contraceptives, or even through sexual abstinence through feigned frailty and living apart from their husbands.[4]

Middle and upper class white women in both England and America were more successful in limiting their births than were lower class women before and during the Depression. Yet falling birth rates were common across the whole industrial world, with birthrates falling so rapidly in some places that demographers were predicting that whole nations (France, for example) would become extinct within a half-century.[5] One study gave the following birthrates per 1,000 population for the following countries or parts of countries during the last quarter of the nineteenth century:[6]

|  | 1876 | 1901 |
|---|---|---|
| Austria | 40.0 | 36.9 |
| France | 26.2 | 22.0 |
| Germany | 40.9 | 35.7 |
| Prussia | 40.7 | 36.2 |
| Sweden | 30.8 | 26.8 |
| Switzerland | 33.0 | 29.1 |
| United Kingdom | 34.8 | 28.0 |
| England & Wales | 36.3 | 18.5 |

1. Melanie Safka, *What Have They Done to My Song, Ma* (1970).
2. Allan Hutchinson, *Identity Crisis: The Politics of Interpretation*, 26 New Eng. L. Rev. 1173, 1177 (1992).
3. *See* Chapter 10, at notes 256–61.
4. *Id.* at notes 280–85.
5. James Garner, *The Decreasing Population of France*, 85 Pop. Sci. Monthly 247 (1914); Emile Zola, *The Dwindling Population of France*, 17 Rev. of Reviews 336 (1898); Walter Weyl, *Depopulation of France*, 195 N. Am. Rev. 343, 352–53 (1912).
6. Edward Wheeler, *General Decline of Fertility in Western Countries*, 40 Current Lit. 295, 295 (1906).

Such changes were part of the demographic transition that occurred as societies industrialized.[7] Demographers initially were baffled as to why—and how—it was happening. Early twentieth century demographic studies concluded that the cause was rising sterility caused by increasing alcoholism, smoking (cigarettes being a relatively new invention), rampant venereal disease, and even the stress of life in an industrial society.[8] One demographer laid the blame on the entry of women into the workforce and the subsequent decision of some working women not to marry.[9] The number of women choosing not to marry or not to have children, however, was too small to account for the sharp decline in the general birthrate.

Concerns about falling birthrates became near panic when carnage in the trenches in World War I left European states fearing that they would not produce enough sons to indulge in another war.[10] Germany was so anxious to raise its birthrate that it offered financial incentives to women who had babies even if they were not married even before the Nazis came to power.[11] Benefits for mothers were considerably strengthened in Germany while abortion remained a crime except in cases of strict medical necessity in order to save the live of the mother.[12] Prosecutions and convictions for illegal abortions became increasingly common in Germany, especially after the war. One study found the following number of convictions in Germany in representative years:[13]

| | |
|---|---|
| 1882 | 191 |
| 1890 | 411 |
| 1910 | 760 |
| 1914 | 1,678 |
| 1921 | 4,248 |

Early demographers did not identify easy access to abortion as a cause of the decline in birthrates. Not until nearly a century later did historians, intent on claiming that abortion was common in the late nineteenth century, suddenly discover that abortion was widely use as the primary means for family control.[14] Such later studies ignored both alternative explanations for falling birthrates and the continuing staggeringly high rates of infant mortality.[15]

In the United States, the nineteenth-century opponents of the emerging practice of abortion did raise the demographic transition as a reason for banning both abortion and contraception. Their arguments expressed fear that whites in general, and middle class Anglo-Saxons in particular, would be outbred by the lesser classes.[16] The phrase "race suicide" came into use after 1901

---

7. *See* Chapter 7, at notes 197–202.

8. John Billings, *The Diminishing Birth Rate in the United States,* 15 Forum 4567, 475 (1893); Charles Franklin Emerick, *Is the Diminishing Birth Rate Volitional?,* 78 Pop. Sci. Monthly 71, 78 (1911); Robert Giffen, *Decline in Rate of Growth of Population,* 52 Sci. Am. Supp. 21633 (1901).

9. Frederick Bushee, *The Declining Birth Rate and its Cause,* 63 Pop. Sci. Monthly 355, 357–59 (1903).

10. *See generally* When Biology Became Destiny: Women in Weimar and Nazi Germany (Renate Bridenthal, Atina Grossman, & Marion Kaplan eds. 1984); Cornelie Usborne, The Politics of the Body in Weimar Germany: Women's Reproductive Rights and Duties (1992).

11. Usborne, *supra* note 10, at 182.

12. Jeremy Telman, *Abortion and Women's Legal Personhood in Germany: A Contribution to the Feminist Theory of the State,* 24 Rev. L. & Soc. Change 91, 106–07 (1998).

13. Telman, *supra* note 12, at 100 n.49. Telman's source was Hilde Benjamin, *Mittelungen der juristischen Arbeitskommission im Zentralen Frauenausschuss,* in Ende der Selsbtverstandlichkeit? Die Abschaftung des § 218 in der DDR Dokumente 41–42 (Kirsten Thietz ed. 1992).

14. *See, e.g.,* Angus McLaren, *Abortion in France: Women and the Regulation of Family Size, 1800–1914,* 10 French Hist. Stud. 461, 462, 472, 477, 479 (1978).

15. M. Hewitt, Wives and Mothers in Victorian Industry 139 (1958).

16. *See, e.g.,* Nathan Allen, Changes in New England Population (1866); A.M. Carr-Sanders, Population (1925); Arthur Calhoun, A Social History of the American Family from Colonial Times to the Present 225–54 (1919); Enid Charles, The Twilight of Parenthood (1934); Eustace Chesser, From Girlhood to Womanhood 122 (1914); Edward Clarke, Sex in Education, or, A Fair Chance for

to describe a fear in the traditionally dominant culture of being swamped by faster-breeding "races."[17] The notion of race at that time was applied broadly to link prejudices against Jews and Catholics with prejudices against darker-skinned people in a grand fear of "mongrelization."[18]

Fueling these fears in the United States were not only the falling birthrates of upper and middle class whites, but also an enormous influx of eastern and southern Europeans. Between 1900 and 1915, some 13,000,000 immigrants entered the United States—23 percent from Italy (nearly all Catholics), another 23 percent from "Hungary" (including what is now Croatia and Slovakia and a good part of Romania and Serbia, as well as modern Hungary; a majority of these were Catholic), and 19 percent from Russia (then including Poland; most of the Russo-Polish immigrants were Jewish)—immigrating to a country with a total population of less than 100,000,000.[19] Even Woodrow Wilson, the great champion of the freedom of peoples, someone whom we seldom think of as narrow minded, wrote at this time that

Throughout the [nineteenth] century men of the sturdy stock of the north of Europe had mad up the main strain of foreign blood which was every year added to the vital working force of this country...but now there came multitudes of men of the lower class from the south of Italy and men of the meaner sort out of Hungary and Poland—men out of the ranks where there was neither skill nor energy nor any initiative of quick intelligence—and they came in numbers which increased from year to year, as if the countries of the south of Europe were disburdening themselves of the more sordid and

---

GIRLS 63 (1873); AUGUSTUS GARDNER, CONJUGAL SINS AGAINST THE LAWS OF LIFE AND HEALTH AND THEIR EFFECTS UPON THE FATHER, MOTHER, AND THE CHILD 5 (1876); D.V. GLASS, THE STUGGLE FOR POPULATION (1936); EDWIN HALE, THE GREAT CRIME OF THE NINETEENTH CENTURY, WHY IS IT COMMITTED? WHO ARE THE CRIMINALS? HOW SHALL THEY BE DETECTED? HOW SHALL THEY BE PUNISHED? 4–6 (1867); ANDREW NEBINGER, CRIMINAL ABORTION: ITS EXTENT AND PREVENTION 6–9 (1870); H.S. POMEROY, THE ETHICS OF MARRIAGE 39 (1888); THEODORE ROOSEVELT, THE FOES OF OUR OWN HOUSEHOLD 257 (1917); HORATIO ROBINSON STORER, WHY NOT? A BOOK FOR EVERYWOMAN 63–65, 85 (1866) HORATIO ROBINSON STORER & FRANKLIN FISKE HEARD, CRIMINAL ABORTION: ITS NATURE, ITS EVIDENCE AND ITS LAW 41–53 (1868); H. Gibbons, sr., On Foeticide, 21 PAC. MED. & SURGICAL J. 97, 111 (1878); Seth Humphrey, *Parenthood and Social Consciousness,* 49 THE FORUM 257, 258 (1913); Edward Manson, *Eugenics and Legislation,* 19 J. SOC'Y OF COMP. LEGISLATION 123, 126 (1914); Montrose Pallen, *Foeticide,* 3 MED. ARCHIVES (St. L. n.s.) 195, 198–99 (1869); Karl Pearson, *The Scope and Importance to the State of the Science of National Eugenics,* 71 POP. SCI. MONTHLY 385, 407–08 (1907); Horatio Robinson Storer, *On the Decrease of the Rate of Increase of Population Now Obtaining in Europe and America,* 43 AM. J. SCIENCE & ARTS 141 (1867); W.C.D. & C.D. Wetham, *The Extinction of the Upper Classes,* 60 THE NINETEENTH CENTURY 95 (1909); James Whitemore, *Criminal Abortion,* 31 CHI. MED. J. 385, 392 (1874).

17. *See, e.g.,* O.C. BEALL, RACIAL DECAY: A COMPILATION OF EVIDENCE FROM WORLD SOURCES (1911); LYDIA KINGSMILL COMMANDER, THE AMERICAN IDEA: DOES THE NATIONAL TENDENCY TOWARD A SMALL FAMILY POINT TO RACE SUICIDE OR RACE DEGENERATION? (1907); JAMES HERBERT CURLE, OUR TESTING TIME: WILL THE WHITE RACE WIN THROUGH (1926); EDWARD EAST, MANKIND AT THE CROSSROADS 297 (1928); M.S. ISEMAN, RACE SUICIDE (1912); 3 THEODORE ROOSEVELT, PRESIDENTIAL ADDRESSES AND STATE PAPERS 282 (1910); Charles Emerick, *College Women and Race Suicide,* 24 POLI. SCI. Q. 269 (1909); "Kit" (Kathleen Blake Watkins), *Race Suicide,* DAILY MAIL & EMPIRE (Toronto), Mar. 21, 1908, at 21; Edward Ross, *Western Civilization and the Birth-Rate,* 12 AM. J. SOCIOLOGY 616 (1907); Margaret Sanger, *Is Race Suicide Possible?,* COLLIER'S MAG., Aug. 25, 1925, at 25; W.S. Wallace, *The Canadian Immigration Policy,* 30 CAN. MAG. 360 (1907). *See generally* BARBARA BROOKES, ABORTION IN ENGLAND 1900–1967, at 30, 56–57, 63–64, 70, 123, 134–35 (1988); LINDA GORDON, WOMAN'S BODY, WOMAN'S RIGHT: A SOCIAL HISTORY OF BIRTH CONTROL IN AMERICA 53, 130–58 (1976); MICHAEL GROSSBERG, GOVERNING THE HEARTH: LAW AND THE FAMILY IN NINETEENTH-CENTURY AMERICA 170–71 (1985); Angus McLaren, *Birth Control and Abortion in Canada, 1870–1920,* 59 CAN. HIST. REV. 319, 319–21, 328, 333 (1978); Alex Zwerdling, *Anglo-Saxon Panic: The Turn-of-the-Century Response to "Alien" Immigrants,* 1 IDEAS FROM THE NAT'L HUMAN. CENTER 32, 38 (No. 2, 1993).

18. *See, e.g.,* MICHAEL GUYER, BEING WELL-BORN: AN INTRODUCTION TO EUGENICS 296–98 (1916).

19. U.S. STATISTICAL ABSTRACT OF 1915, no. 15 at 90.

hapless elements of their population, men whose standards of life and work were such as American workmen had never dreamed hitherto.[20]

Fear of race suicide played a role in the tightening of the abortion statutes and the strengthening of the enforcement efforts behind those statutes. Concern about race suicide was not confined to concerns about the effects of immigration on the gene pool. Historian Dallas Blanchard has suggested that a strong motive for the anti-abortion statutes was a desire to prevent white women who had had sexual relations with blacks from destroying the evidence of their "guilt."[21] Blanchard's "insight," however, is another in of reliance on intuition rather than evidence.

Contrary to these fears, the increase in abortion does not seem to have been greater among unmarried white women than among non-white women. African-American women in particular seemed more accepting of births out of wedlock—whether before marriage or after widowhood, divorce, or abandonment.[22] Nonetheless, African-American women apparently had a greater rise in their abortion rate than did white women. After all, African-Americans lost their jobs more often than did whites.[23] The rise in abortions among African-American women was so great that Harlem Hospital (which served mostly poor African-Americans) felt impelled to open a special "Abortion Service" solely for treating women who came to the hospital suffering from botched abortions.[24] Thus, while fear of race suicide in the face of a flood of Jews and Catholics might well have rested on real numbers, fear of persons of color seems to have been based on illusion more than reality. And during this time there emerged a movement that would turn the "race suicide" concept on its head regarding both the having of children and the acceptability of abortion.

---

20. T. Woodrow Wilson, History of the American People 212–13 (5th ed. 1908). *See also* Harry Laughlin, Conquest by Immigration (1939).

21. Dallas Blanchard, The Anti-Abortion Movement and the Rise of the Religious Right: From Polite to Fiery Protest 128 n.10 (1994).

22. Paul Gebhard *et al.*, Pregnancy, Birth and Abortion 162 (1958); Paula Giddings, When and Where I Enter: The Impact of Black Women on Race and Sex in America 151–52 (1984); Leslie Reagan, When Abortion Was a Crime: Women, Medicine, and Law in the United States, 1867–1973, at 136–37 (1997); Virginia Clay Hamilton, *Some Sociological and Psychological Observations on Abortion*, 39 Am. J. Obstet. & Gynecology 919, 922–23 (1940).

23. Lois Rita Helmbold, *Beyond the Family Economy: Black and White Working-Class Women during the Great Depression*, 13 Feminist Stud. 629, 642–43 (1987); Ruth Milkman, *Women's Work and the Economic Crisis: Some Lessons from the Great Depression*, 8 Rev. Radical Pol. Econ. 73 (1976).

24. *See* Peter Marshall Murray & L.B. Winkelstein, *Incomplete Abortion: An Evaluation of Diagnosis and Treatment of 727 Consecutive Cases of Incomplete Abortions*, 3 Harlem Hosp. Bull. 31 (1950). *See also* Charles Garvin, *The Negro Doctor's Task*, 16 Birth Control Rev. 269 (1932). *See generally* Jesse Rodrique, *The Black Community and the Birth Control Movement*, in Passion and Power: Sexuality in History 138, 140–41 (Kathy Peiss, Christina Simmons, & Robert Padgug eds. 1989). Such apparently racial differences might have had more to do with social class than with race—several researchers at the time concluded that women of the same social class tended to have similar abortion rates regardless of their race or ethnic group. *See* Endre Brunner & Louis Newton, *Abortions in Relation to Viable Births in 10,609 Pregnancies: A Study Based on 4,500 Clinic Histories*, 38 Am. J. Obstet. & Gynecology 82, 83 (1939); Hamilton, *supra* note 22, at 923; George Kosmak, *The Responsibility of the Medical Professional in the Movement for "Birth Control,"* 113 JAMA 1553, 1559 (1939). Special abortion wards were common at other public hospitals as well. *See generally* Reagan, *supra* note 22, at 135–36, 138.

# The Eugenics Movement

*We only wish to raise quality of life for all species.*

— "Locutus of Borg"[25]

The Great Depression might have been explanation enough for the rising incidence of abortion during the 1930s.[26] Yet the slowly increasing acceptance of abortion was driven by more than just unhappy economic conditions joining with a gradual perfection of the necessary technologies. Concerns about "race suicide," long prominent among those seeking to eliminate abortion from society, also began to appear among those who encouraged abortion as a means of preventing the "wrong" people from having "too many" children. Concern about the "wrong" people having most of the babies was not an isolated phenomenon relating only to abortion. The concern to improve the human stock was powerful and widespread and took a technological turn at the very end of the nineteenth century and soon became very influential internationally.[27] The resulting eugenics movement was concerned to see that only those who would be "well-born" (the meaning of the Greek word *eugenios*) in the genetic sense would be born.[28] As Mar-

---

25. Michael Piller, *The Best of Both Worlds*, from *Star Trek: The Next Generation* (Sept. 22, 1990).

26. *See, e.g.,* FREDERICK TAUSSIG, ABORTION: SPONTANEOUS AND INDUCED 372 (1936).

27. *See, e.g.,* A DECADE OF PROGRESS IN EUGENICS: SCIENTIFIC PAPERS OF THE THIRD INTERNATIONAL CONGRESS OF EUGENICS (1934); FRANCIS GALTON, INQUIRIES INTO HUMAN FACULTY AND ITS DEVELOPMENT (1883); WILLIAM ROBINSON, FEWER AND BETTER BABIES, OR THE LIMITATION OF OFFSPRING (1915); LOTHROP STODDARD, THE REVOLT AGAINST CIVILIZATION: THE MENACE OF THE UNDERMAN (1922); JAMES WATSON, WHO ARE THE PRODUCERS OF HUMAN DAMAGED GOODS? (1913); SYDNEY WEBB, THE DECLINE OF THE BIRTH RATE (1909); A.B. Atherton, *The Causes of the Degeneracy of the Human Race,* 41 CAN. LANCET 97 (1907); Charles Davenport, *Eugenics: The Science of Human Improvement by Better Breeding,* 31 (1910); Norman Himes, *Eugenic Thought in the American Birth Control Movement 100 Years Ago,* 2 EUGENICS No. 5, at 3 (May 1929); Edward Ill, *The Rights of the Unborn — The Prevention of Conception,* 40 AM. J. OBSTET. & DISEASES OF WOMEN 577 (1899); H.E. Jordan, *Eugenics: The Rearing of the Human Thoroughbred,* 11 CLEV. MED. J. 875 (1912); R.W. Bruce Smith, *Mental Sanitation, with Suggestions for the Care of the Degenerate, and Means for Preventing the Propagating of the Species,* 40 CAN. LANCET 969 (1907).

28. The name was invented by Dr. Francis Galton. GALTON, *supra* note 27, at 17. *See also* GUYER, *supra* note 18, at 413–14. *See also* ALBERT DEUTSCH, THE MENTALLY ILL IN AMERICA 357–58 (2nd ed. 1949); J.H. LANDMAN, HUMAN STERILIZATION: THE HISTORY OF THE SEXUAL STERILIZATION MOVEMENT 3 (1932); LAUGHLIN, *supra* note 20, at 31–32. *See generally* BROOKES, *supra* note 17, at 38, 58, 66–68, 70; ELLEN CHESLER, WOMEN OF VALOR: MARGARET SANGER AND THE BIRTH CONTROL MOVEMENT 214–17 (1992); ANGELA DAVIS, WOMEN, RACE AND CLASS 210–19 (1981); R. MACKLIN & R. GAYLIN, MENTAL RETARDATION AND STERILIZATION (1981); NANCY GALLAGHER, BREEDING BETTER VERMONTERS: THE EUGENICS PROJECT IN THE GREEN MOUNTAIN STATE (1999); MARK HALLER, EUGENICS: HEREDITARIAN ATTITUDES IN AMERICAN THOUGHT (1963); RUTH HUBBARD, THE POLITICS OF WOMEN'S BIOLOGY 182–92 (1990); DAVID KENNEDY, BIRTH CONTROL IN AMERICA: THE CAREER OF MARGARET SANGER 115–21 (1970); MARY KENNY, ABORTION: THE WHOLE STORY 190–91 (1986); DANIEL KEVLES, IN THE NAME OF EUGENICS: GENETICS AND THE USES OF HUMAN HEREDITY (1985); KENNETH LUDMERER, GENETICS AND AMERICAN SOCIETY: A HISTORICAL APPRAISAL (1972); MARVIN OLASKY, ABORTION RIGHTS: A SOCIAL HISTORY OF ABORTION IN AMERICA 254–59 (1992); DIANE PAUL, CONTROLLING HUMAN HEREDITY: 1865 TO PRESENT (1995); ROSALIND POLLACK PETCHESKY, ABORTION AND WOMEN'S CHOICE: THE STATE, SEXUALITY, AND REPRODUCTIVE FREEDOM 87–93 (rev. ed. 1990); DAVID PICKENS, EUGENICS AND THE PROGRESSIVES (1968); G.R. SEARLE, EUGENICS AND POLITICS IN BRITAIN, 1900–1914 (1976); GEORGE SMITH II, THE NEW BIOLOGY: LAW, ETHICS, AND BIOTECHNOLOGY 69–72 (1989); THE WELL-BORN SCIENCE: EUGENICS IN GERMANY, FRANCE, BRAZIL, AND RUSSIA (Mark Adams ed. 1990); STEPHEN TROMBLEY, THE RIGHT TO REPRODUCE: A HISTORY OF COERCIVE STERILIZATION 15–17, 40–44, 53–55 (1988); Robert Cynkar, *Buck v. Bell: "Felt Necessities" v. Fundamental Values?,* 81 COLUM. L. REV.

garet Sanger put it, the goal in promoting birth control was "nothing more or less than the process of weeding out the unfit, of preventing the birth of defectives or those who will become defectives."[29]

Today, many think of the eugenics movement as reactionary or worse, but back then it was supported by the many who considered themselves "progressives" seeking to escape the limits of the past.[30] The eugenics movement became possible only with the perfection of medically safe procedures for abortion and sterilization at the end of the nineteenth century coupled with the new (and woefully incomplete) knowledge of the just emerging and mysterious science of genetics. On the one hand, new techniques for vasectomies and salpingectomies made surgical sterilizations more palatable to a wider public than older-style castrations and hysterectomies.[31] On the other hand, a common reaction to the beginnings of genetics was to conclude that genes determined at least a predisposition towards "degenerate" behavior, whether criminal, immoral, or a result of "feeble-mindedness."[32]

---

1418 (1981); Elyce Zenoff Ferster, *Eliminating the Unfit—Is Sterilization the Answer?*, 27 OHIO ST. L.J. 591 (1966); Paul Lombardo, *Medicine, Eugenics, and the Supreme Court: From Coercive Sterilization to Reproductive Freedom*, 13 J. CONTEMP. HEALTH L. & POL'Y 1 (1996); Michael Malinowski, *Choosing the Genetic Makeup of Children: Our Eugenics Past—Present, and Future?*, 36 CONN. L. REV.125 (2003); James O'Hara & T. Howland Sanks, *Eugenic Sterilization*, 45 GEO. L.J. 20 (1956); Margaret Phillips, *Reproduction with Technology: The New Eugenics*, 11 IN THE PUB. INT. 1 (1991); William Vukowich, *The Danwing of the Brave New World—Legal, Ethical and Social Issues*, 1971 U. ILL. L.F. 189; Michael Willich, *The Two-Percent Solution: Eugenic Jurisprudence and the Socialization of American Law, 1900–1930*, 16 LAW & HIST. REV. 63 (1998).

29. MARGARET SANGER, WOMEN AND THE NEW RACE 229 (1920). *See generally* GALLAGHER, *supra* note 28, at 3; KEVLES, *supra* note 28, at 145–47.

30. *See, e.g.,* J. EWING MEARS, THE PROBLEM OF RACE BETTERMENT (1910). *See generally* GALLAGHER, *supra* note 28, at 4; HALLER, *supra* note 28, at 76, 124; KEVLES, *supra* note 28, at 56, 61, 101; LUDMERER, *supra* note 28, at 15–18; PICKENS, *supra* note 28; Stephanie Hyatt, Note, *A Shared History of Shame: Sweden's Four-Decade Policy of Sterilization and the Eugenics Movement in the United States*, 8 IND. INT'L & COMP. L. REV. 475, 475–76 (1998). For a contemporary expression of this view, see FRANCIS FUKUYAMA, OUR POSTHUMAN FUTURE 88 (2002).

31. DOROTHY DUNBAR BROMLEY, BIRTH CONTROL: ITS USE AND MISUSE 159–63 (1934); ROBERT DICKINSON, CONTROL OF CONCEPTION 258–59 (1938); MEARS, *supra* note 30, at 27; JAMES RICCI, ONE HUNDRED YEARS OF GYNAECOLOGY 539–40 (1945). *See also* HALLER, *supra* note 28, at 132; KEVLES, *supra* note 28, at 92–93; LANDMAN, *supra* note 28, at 52, 208–12; JOHN LORAINE, SEX AND THE POPULATION CRISIS 407–21 (1970); PETCHESKY, *supra* note 28, at 84–89, 93, 159–60, 178–82; TROMBLEY, *supra* note 28, at 50; Robert, jr., & Marcia Pearce Burgdorf, *The Wicked Witch Is Almost Dead: Buck v. Bell and the Sterilization of Handicapped Persons*, 50 TEMPLE L.Q. 995, 999 (1977); T.N. Evans, *Sterilization of Women*, in HUMAN REPRODUCTION: CONCEPTION AND CONTRACEPTION 393 (Elsayed Saad Eldin Hafez & T.N. Evans eds. 1973); Ferster, *supra* note 28, at 592; J.F. Hulka & Joseph Davis, *Sterilization of Men*, HUMAN REPRODUCTION, *supra*, at 427; Charles Murdock, *Sterilization of the Retarded: A Problem or a Solution?*, 62 CAL. L. REV. 917, 920 (1974); O'Hara & Sanks, *supra* note 28, at 20; Edmund Overstreet, *Techniques of Sterilization*, 7 CLINICAL OBSTET. & GYNECOLOGY 109 (1964). The acceptability of the new techniques led to their increasing acceptance as voluntary means of contraception; by the late 1980s, as many as 40 percent of married couples in the United States had had one or both partners surgically sterilized, a percentage that remained stable for the next decade. Marie McCullough, *Surgical Birth Control Grows, Then Levels off: In a Survey, 41% of Women—about the Same as in '88—Said It's the Route They or Their Husbands Took*, PHILA. INQUIRER, July 16, 1998, at A2.

32. *See* RICHARD DUGDALE, THE JUKES: A STUDY IN CRIME, PAUPERISM, DISEASE, AND HEREDITY (1877); FRANCIS GALTON, ENGLISH MEN OF SCIENCE: THEIR NATURE AND NURTURE (1874); FRANCIS GALTON, HEREDITARY GENIUS (1869); GALTON, *supra* note 27. *See also* CHARLES BENEDICT DAVENPORT, HEREDITY IN RELATION TO EUGENICS (1911); HENRY GODDARD, THE CRIMINAL IMBECILE: AN ANALYSIS OF THREE REMARKABLE MURDER CASES (1915); HENRY GODDARD, THE KALLIKAK FAMILY: A STUDY IN THE HEREDITY OF FEEBLE-MINDEDNESS (1912); 3 GEORGE ELLIOTT HOWARD, THE HISTORY OF MATRIMONIAL INSTITUTIONS 258 (1904); S.A.K. STRAHAN, MARRIAGE AND DISEASE: A STUDY OF HEREDITY AND THE MORE IMPORTANT FAMILY DEGENERATIONS (1892); ALBERT EDWARD WIGGAM, THE NEW DECALOGUE OF SCIENCE 15–22 (1922); Humphrey, *supra* note 16; Manson, *supra* note 16; Adolf Meyer, *The Right to Marry: What Can a Democratic Civilization Do about Heredity and Child Welfare*, 36 THE SURVEY 243 (1916); Pearson, *supra* note 16; Jesse

The nineteenth century saw the rise of large institutions to care for, or at least to warehouse, mentally challenged people, raising an expectation that such behavior could be eliminated from or minimized in society.[33] The term "feebleminded" gained currency as an apparently objective concept after the introduction of IQ testing at the beginning of the twentieth century.[34] Many physicians, expecting that "deficient" persons could be identified and eliminated from society, supported eugenics as a public health measure, introducing a relatively simple and inexpensive medical model into what had formerly been seen as an intractable and expensive legal or moral question.[35]

Harry Laughlin, director of the "Eugenics Record Office" from its founding in 1910 until 1940 (he died in 1943), was the most important leader of the eugenics movement in the United States. The Eugenics Record Office, located in Cold Spring Harbor, New York, was a privately funded institution that served as a clearing house for information within the eugenics movement.[36] Laughlin admitted that "[t]he classification of the socially inadequate is obviously partly legal and partly medical, but in most part biological."[37] Laughlin went on to define the "socially inadequate" (and therefore deserving of compulsory sterilization) as including than ten classes of persons:

1. the feeble-minded;
2. the insane;
3. the "criminalist" ("including the delinquent and wayward");
4. epileptics;

---

Spaulding Smith, *Marriage, Sterilization, and Commitment Laws Aimed at Decreasing Mental Deficiency,* 5 J. CRIM. L. & CRIMINOLOGY 364 (1914). *See generally* C.P. BLACKER, EUGENICS, GALTON, AND AFTER (1952); STEPHEN JAY GOULD, THE MISMEASURE OF MAN (1981); KEVLES, *supra* note 28, at 1–56, 70–84; DAVID SMITH, MINDS MADE FEEBLE: THE MYTH AND LEGACY OF THE KALLIKAKS (1985); Cynkar, *supra* note 28, at 1420–22; Philip Jenkins, *Eugenics, Crime and Ideology: The Case of Progressive Pennsylvania,* 51 PA. HIST. 64, 72 (1984); Lombardo, *supra* note 28, at 2–5; Philip Reilly, *Eugenic Sterilization in the United States,* in GENETICS AND THE LAW III, at 227, 228–29 (Aubrey Milunsky & George Annas eds. 1985); Gail Rodgers, Comment, *Yin and Yang: The Eugenic Policies of the United States and China: Is the Analysis that Black and White?,* 22 HOUS. J. INT'L L. 129, 133–34 (1999).

33. RICHARD SCHEERENBERGER, A HISTORY OF MENTAL RETARDATION 109–36 (1983). *See generally* MICHEL FOUCAULT, DISCIPLINE AND PUNISH (A.M. Sheridan trans. 1977); Willich, *supra* note 28.

34. KEVLES, *supra* note 28, at 83–84. *See generally* STEVEN NOLL, FEEBLE-MINDED IN OUR MIDST: INSTITUTIONS FOR THE MENTALLY RETARDED IN THE SOUTH, 1900–1940 (1995); PSYCHOLOGICAL TESTING IN AMERICAN SOCIETY, 1890–1930 (Michael Sokal ed. 1987); JAMES TRENT, JR., INVENTING THE FEEBLE-MINDED: A HISTORY OF MENTAL RETARDATION IN THE UNITED STATES (1994); Willich, *supra* note 28, at 92–98.

35. *See, e.g.,* William Allen, *The Relationship of Eugenics to Public Health,* 21 EUGENICAL NEWS 73 (July–Aug. 1936); H.E Jordan, *The Place of Eugenics in the Medical Curriculum,* in PROBLEMS IN EUGENICS 396 (Eugenics Educ. Soc'y 1912). *See generally* GOULD, *supra* note 28, at 122–45; HALLER, *supra* note 28, at 21–25; KEVLES, *supra* note 28, at 70–84; PICKENS, *supra* note 28, at 85–87; PHILIP REILLY, THE SURGICAL SOLUTION: A HISTORY OF INVOLUNTARY STERILIZATION IN THE UNITED STATES (1991); Cynkar, *supra* note 28, at 1423–25; Ferster, *supra* note 28, at 619; Lombardo, *supra* note 28, at 6–7; Willich, *supra* note 28, at 83–92.

36. Garland Allen, *The Eugenics Record Office at Cold Spring Harbor, 1910–1945: An Essay in Institutional History,* 2 OSIRIS, 2ND SERIES 225 (1986). The seed money came from a $10,000,000 grant from the Carnegie foundation, more than the combined total of all endowments for research at American universities at the time, with support from Mary Harriman, a philanthropic socialite. KEVLES, *supra* note 28, at 45, 55–56.

In 1937, Laughlin was a founder of the Pioneer Fund to finance research on "heredity and genetics" and "race betterment"; it is still financing such research. *See* WILLIAM TUCKER, THE FUNDING OF SCIENTIFIC RACISM: WICKLIFFE DRAPER AND THE OF PIONEER FUND (2002); Paul Lombardo, *"The American Breed": Nazi Eugenics and the Origins of the Pioneer Fund,* 65 ALB. L. REV. 743 (2002). For a defense of the Pioneer Fund's activities, see J. Philippe Rushton, *The Pioneer Fund and the Scientific Study of Human Difference,* 66 ALB. L. REV. 207 (2002). For answers to Rushton, see Paul Lombardo, *Pioneer's Big Lie,* 66 ALB. L. REV. 1125 (2003); William Tucker, *A Closer Look at the Pioneer Fund: Response to Rushton,* 66 ALB. L. REV. 1145 (2003).

37. Harry Laughlin, *Report of the Committee to Study and to Report on the Best Practical Means of Cutting off the Defective Germ-Plasm in the American Population,* EUGENICS REC. OFF. BULL. No. 10A, at 17 (1914).

5.    inebriates (including drug users);
6.    those suffering from diseases such as leprosy, syphilis, tuberculosis, and other chronic contagious diseases subject to compulsory segregation;
7.    the blind (including those who merely suffered from seriously impaired vision);
8.    the deaf (including those who merely suffered from seriously impaired hearing);
9.    the deformed or crippled; and
10.    the dependent (including orphans, ne'er do wells, the homeless, tramps, and paupers).[38]

Laughlin's line of reasoning, of course, simply overlooked that 80 to 90 percent of those who are born with subnormal mental abilities are born to normal parents, while mentally subnormal parents often give birth to infants without genetic defect, including without abnormally low mental capacities.[39] As several items on Laughlin's list suggest, supporters of the eugenics movement initially saw surgical sterilization as only a more extreme form of the isolation in institutions already common for such "failings." At first, supporters of eugenic improvement of humankind often feared that advocating sterilization would increase resistance to their goals rather than further them.[40] Eventually surgical intervention to prevent the passing on of such characteristics seemed to many to be a relatively benign approach.[41] Certainly, the argument went, it was preferable to institutionalization and especially to Herbert Spencer's then popular doctrine of Social Darwinism that consigned such "defective" persons to destruction (through social processes) as unfit even while they continued to be a drain on society as a whole—which perhaps explains Julian Huxley's remarkable proposal that long-term unemployment should be grounds for sterilization.[42]

Linking notions of race to notions of Social Darwinism produced a supposedly "scientific" racism" that permeated western societies in the first half of the twentieth century.[43] This perspec-

---

38. HARRY LAUGHLIN, THE LEGAL STATUS OF EUGENICAL STERILIZATION 65 (1929). *See also* HALLER, *supra* note 28, at 41–43, 47–50, 73. On the effort to include the blind among those to be sterilized or forbidden to marry, see Lucien Howe, *The Relation of Hereditary Eye Defects to Genetics and Eugenics,* 70 JAMA 1994 (1918); *Nearsightedness Could Be Wiped out by Genetics,* 1942 SCI. NEWS LETTER 387. On efforts to include the deaf, see David Fairchild, *Alexander Graham Bell: Some Characters of His Greatness,* 13 J. HEREDITY 195, 195–98 (1922). *See generally* Paul Lombardo, *Taking Eugenics Seriously: Three Generations of ??? Are Enough,* 30 FLA. ST. U. L. REV. 191, 205–08 (2003).

39. ROBERT BLANK, FERTILITY CONTROL: NEW TECHNIQUES, NEW POLICY ISSUES 60–61 (1991); Sandra Coleman, Comment, *Involuntary Sterilization of the Mentally Retarded: Blessing or Burden?,* 25 S.D.L. REV. 55, 60 (1980); Kathryn Ann Calihey, Comment, *Involuntary Sterilization of the Mentally Retarded—Analysis of Standards o f Judicial Determination,* 3 W. NEW ENG. L. REV. 689, 696 (1981); Joe Zumpano-Canto, *Nonconsensual Sterilization of the Mentally Disabled in North Carolina: An Ethics Critique of the Statutory Standard and Its Judicial Interpretation,* 13 J. CONTEMP. HEALTH L. & POL'Y 79, 83 (1996).

40. John Radford, *Sterilization versus Segregation: Control of the "Feeble-Minded," 1900–1938,* 33 SOC. SCI. MED. 449, 453 (1991).

41. *See* E.S. GOSNEY & PAUL POPENOE, STERILIZATION FOR HUMAN BETTERMENT (1929).

42. *See* Mary Cawte, *Craniotomy and Eugenics in Australia: R.J.A. Berry and the Quest for Social Efficiency,* 22 HIST. STUD. 35 (1986). *See also* RICHARD DUGDALE, THE JUKES IN 1915, at 69–70 (1916); HERBERT SPENCER, SOCIAL STATISTICS 44 (1851); Laughlin, *supra* note 37, at 15–16; Pearson, *supra* note 32; Elizabeth Scott Phelps, *Women's View of Divorce,* 150 N. AM. REV. 130 (1890).

43. *See* REGINALD HORSMAN, RACE AND MANIFEST DESTINY 116–57 (1981); STODDARD, *supra* note 27; LOTHROP STODDARD, THE RISING TIDE OF COLOR AGAINST WHITE WORLD SUPREMACY (1920) ("STODDARD, TIDE OF COLOR"); WEBB, *supra* note 27, at 39–40; Samuel Batten, *The Redemption of the Unfit,* 14 AM. J. SOC. 233 (1908); Ernest Cox, *Repatriation of the American Negro,* 21 EUGENICAL NEWS 138 (1936); Pearson, *supra* note 32, at 412. *See generally* ALAN CHASE, THE LEGACY OF MALTHUS: THE SOCIAL COST OF THE NEW SCIENTIFIC RACISM (1977); CARL DEGLER, IN SEARCH OF HUMAN NATURE: THE DECLINE AND REVIVAL OF DARWINISM IN AMERICAN SOCIAL THOUGHT (1991); OLASKY, *supra* note 28, at 255–56; SEARLE, *supra* note 28, at 50; Willich, *supra* note 28, at 98–100.

tive informed the fear of "race suicide" in the first two decades of the century.[44] As a result, eugenics became popular in England, being embraced by such luminaries as Winston Churchill, Havelock Ellis, J.B.S. Haldane, Julian Huxley, Harold Laski, George Bernard Shaw, birth control campaigner Marie Stopes, and the Fabian Society leaders, Sydney and Beatrice Webb.[45] Dr. Marie Stopes, the "mother" of the English birth control movement, named her organization "The Society for Constructive Birth Control and Racial Progress."[46] Egyptologist Flinders Petrie wrote quite openly of what he hoped the movement would achieve. He advocated

> encouraging the "best stocks" to breed by means of grants and privileges and penalizing the "lower class of the unfits" with compulsory work: their women would be encouraged to seek voluntary sterilization. The higher the social organization and reward of ability, the more intense will be the weeding of the less capable, and the more highly sustained will be the general level of ability.[47]

Despite this widespread support, the British Parliament never enacted a compulsory sterilization statute.[48] Yet even without compulsory sterilization, the eugenics movement did have considerable impact in Britain. One British judge declined to sentence abortionists to prison on the grounds that their activities tended to improve the race.[49] Lord Riddell, the first proponent of abortion reform to receive wide attention in Britain, was also active in the eugenics movement.[50] The eugenics movement also found support in Australia, Canada, and New Zealand.[51]

The eugenics movement was even more successful in the United States.[52] Organizationally, the American Eugenics Society grew out of the Eugenics Section of the American Breeders Associa-

---

44. See the text *supra* at notes 5–24; and Chapter 8, at notes 164–69; Chapter 9, at notes 36–43.

45. KENNY, *supra* note 28, at 190. *See, e.g.,* HAVELOCK ELLIS, THE TASK OF SOCIAL HYGIENE (1912); WEBB, *supra* note 27. *See generally* SEARLE, *supra* note 28.

46. SANDRA FRIEDMAN, WOMEN AND THE LAW 120 (1997). *See also* REAY TANNAHILL, SEX IN HISTORY 415–16 (1980).

47. MARGARET DROWER, FLINDERS PETRIE: A LIFE IN ARCHEOLOGY 303 (1985).

48. *See* Alastair Bissett-Johnson & Ann Everton, *Preserving the Status Quo: Re D (a Minor)*, 126 NEW L.J. 104 (1976).

49. BROOKES, *supra* note 17, at 38.

50. George Riddell, *The Ethics of Abortion, Sterilization and Birth Control*, 39 J. OBSTET. & GYNAECOLOGY OF BRIT. EMPIRE 1 (1932).

51. *See, e.g.,* W.E. AGAR, EUGENICS AND THE AUSTRALIAN POPULATION (1939); W.A. CHAPPLE, THE FERTILITY OF THE UNFIT (1904); F.R. Beasley, *Sterilisation of the Unfit: The Legal Aspect*, 1935 MED. J. AUSTRALIA 295; Angela Booth, *Negative Eugenics: How Shall We Deal with Feeble-Mindedness*, THE ARGUS, Jan. 12, 1934, at 6; Paul Dane, *Sterilization of the Unfit*, 1936 MED. J. AUSTRALIA 707; Jean Devanny, *Eugenic Reform and the Unfit*, STEAD'S REV., May 1, 1930, at 21; Frank Robinson Kerr, *The Sterilization of Mental Defectives*, in REPORT OF THE SIXTH SESSION OF THE FEDERAL HEALTH COUNCIL, COMMONWEALTH OF AUSTRALIA, app. II (1933); D.M. McWhae, *Sterilisation of the Unfit: The Medical Aspect*, 1935 MED. J. AUSTRALIA 298; E.J.T. Thompson, *Sterilization of the Unfit: The Psychiatric Point of View*, 1935 MED. J. AUSTRALIA 301. *See generally* LAW REFORM COMM'N OF CANADA, STERILIZATION (working paper no. 24, 1979); Cawte, *supra* note 42; Ann Curthoys, *Eugenics, Feminism, and Birth Control: The Case of Marion Piddington*, 15 HECATE no. 1, at 73 (1989); Bernard Dickens, *Eugenic Recognition in Canadian Law*, 13 OSGOODE HALL L.J. 547 (1975); Stephen Garton, *Sir Charles Mackellar: Psychiatry, Eugenics and Child Welfare in New South Wales, 1900–1914*, 22 HIST. STUD. 21 (1986); Jeff Goldhar, *The Sterilization of Women with an Intellectual Disability*, 10 TASMANIA L. REV. 157 (1991); K.G. McWhirter & J. Weijer, *The Alberta Sterilization Act: A Genetic Critique*, 19 U. TOR. L.J. 424 (1969); Marcia Rioux, *The Right to Control One's Own Body: A Look at the "Eve" Decision*, 2 ENTOURAGE 26 (1987).

52. *See generally* MARCIA MOBILIA BOUMIL, LAW, ETHICS AND REPRODUCTIVE CHOICE 93–104 (1994); DEUTSCH, *supra* note 28, at 355–70; GOULD, *supra* note 28; HALLER, *supra* note 28; KEVLES, *supra* note 28; LUDMERER, *supra* note 28, PICKENS, *supra* note 28; REILLY, *supra* note 32; WOLF WOLFENSBERGER, THE ORIGIN AND NATURE OF OUR INSTITUTIONAL MODELS 33–41 (1975); Burgdorf & Burgdorf, *supra* note 31, at

tion—an association of cattle breeders.[53] Counted among the American supporters were major entrepreneurs, including Alexander Graham Bell, George Eastman, Samuel Fels, Mary Harriman, Dr. Harvey Kellogg, and John D. Rockefeller, along with Justice Oliver Wendell Holmes, jr.[54] Every president from Theodore Roosevelt to Herbert Hoover supported the eugenics movement to some extent.[55] With such support, the American movement was unwilling to rely upon voluntary sterilization for "improvement of the race."[56]

The American eugenics movement achieved extraordinary success along several fronts, beginning with the enactment of a statute in Connecticut in 1895 forbidding "epileptics, imbeciles, and feebleminded persons" to marry or to have non-marital sexual relations before the age of 45, subject to three years imprisonment for violations.[57] By 1929, 29 states had enacted similar statutes.[58] During this same period, states made venereal disease a bar to marriage, introducing a requirement of a health certificate as a predicate to a marriage license.[59] In one of the first cases to construe such statutes, a Connecticut court awarded a divorce to a woman who complained that her husband had concealed epilepsy from her before their marriage—a marriage that was therefore in violation of the 1895 statute.[60] All of this signaled the transformation of marriage from a largely private contractual relationship to one permeated by public policy concerns focused strongly, but not exclusively, on eugenic concerns.[61] One court, discussing the requirement of ceremonial marriage and the abolition of common law marriage, stated that "prohibiting such marriages as far as practicable would tend to the prevention of pauperism and crime, and the transmission of hereditary diseases and defects...."[62]

---

995–1013; Cynkar, *supra* note 28; O'Hara & Sanks, *supra* note 28; Reilly, *supra* note 32; Rodgers, *supra* note 32, at 135–40; Vukowich, *supra* note 28; Willich, *supra* note 28.

53. Burgdorf & Burgdorf, *supra* note 31, at 999.

54. *See, e.g.,* Alexander Graham Bell, *How to Improve the Race,* 5 J. Heredity 1 (1914). *See generally* Kenny, *supra* note 28, at 190; Lombardo, *supra* note 38, at 208–14; Philip Reilly, *Involuntary Sterilization in the United States: A Surgical Solution,* 62 Q. Rev. Bio. 153 (1987). On Holmes' eugenicist views, see Chapter 10, at notes 146–57.

55. Chase, *supra* note 43, at 15, 19–20, 126; Lombardo, *supra* note 28, at 1; Lombardo, *supra* note 38, at 209 n.114.

56. Harry Laughlin, Eugenical Sterilization in the United States (1922).

57. Act of July 4, 1895, 1895 Conn. Pub. Acts ch. 325. Such a law had been enacted in Michigan as early as 1846, barring marriage by "idiots" well before the eugenics movement began. *See* Marsha Churchill, *Marriage Laws Discriminate against the Disabled,* 80 Mich. B.J., no. 3, at 12 (Mar. 2001).

58. Grossberg, *supra* note 17, at 150; Haller, *supra* note 28, at 142; Chester Vernier, American Family Law 191–95 (1931); Note, *A Sterilization Statute for Kentucky,* 23 Ky. L.J. 168, 168 (1934). *See also* Matthew Lindsay, *Reproducing a Fit Citizenry: Dependency, Eugenics, and the Law of Marriage in the United States, 1860–1920,* 23 Law & Soc. Inquiry 541, 542 (1998).

59. *See* Fred Hall, Medical Certification for Marriage (1925); Prince Morrow, Social Diseases and Marriage: Social Prophylaxis (1904); Vernier, *supra* note 58, at 200–02. For litigation under one of these statutes, see Peterson v. Widule, 147 N.W. 966 (Wis. 1915). *See generally* Lindsay, *supra* note 58, at 575–76.

60. Gould v. Gould, 61 A. 604 (Conn. 1905). The law was repealed in 1969. 1969 Conn. Pub. Acts, ch. 828, §214. *See* Grossberg, *supra* note 17, at 149; Lindsay, *supra* note 58, at 573–74. *Accord:* Schoolcraft v. O'Neil, 123 A. 828 (N.H. 1923). *Contra:* Allan v. Allan, 95 A. 363 (N.J. 1915); Meekins v. Kinsella, 136 N.Y.S. 806 (App. Div. 1912); Roether v. Roether, 191 N.W. 576 (Wis. 1923).

61. *See, e.g.,* Elsie Clews Parsons, The Family 344 (1906); Vernier, *supra* note 58, at 171; Meyer, *supra* note 32; Smith, *supra* note 32; Edward Spencer, *Some Phases of Marriage Law and Legislation from a Sanitary and Eugenic Standpoint,* 25 Yale L.J. 58 (1915); Hiram Stanley, *Our Own Civilization and the Marriage Problem,* 2 The Arena 94 (1890); Albert Swindlehurst, *Some Phases of the Law of Marriage,* 30 Harv. L. Rev. 124 (1916). *See generally* Peter Bardaglio, Reconstructing the Household: Families, Sex, and Law in the Nineteenth Century South 183 (1995); Grossberg, *supra* note 17, at 150; Lindsay, *supra* note 58.

62. *In re* McLaughlin's Estate, 4 Wash. 570, 590–91 (1892).

Perhaps the purest expression of the eugenic perspective was the *Immigration Act of 1924*, which sharply restricted immigration from southern or eastern Europe, while leaving the door open to immigration from northern and western Europe.[63] After all, Congress was told that between 79 percent and 87 percent of all immigrant Hungarians, Italians, Jews, and Russians tested as "feeble-minded" on the recently introduced IQ tests.[64] The *Immigration Act's* principal draftsman was Harry Laughlin, the director of the "Eugenics Records Office."[65]

The American eugenics movement also succeeded in securing the enactment of compulsory sterilization statutes in at least 23 states between 1907 and 1931.[66] The first such statute was enacted in Indiana in 1907.[67] In a number of states, penal and mental institutions began the systematic sterilizations even without statutory authorization.[68] Just as at the federal level, these laws were prompted in some states by the immigration of "less desirable" types of people—such as California, where the statutes were a reaction to the influx of Mexicans and Orientals.[69]

Sterilization statutes and the eugenics movement encountered strong opposition from the start.[70] Clarence Darrow in 1926 described the "eugenics cult" as "the most senseless and impudent that has ever been put forward by irresponsible fanatics to plague the long-suffering [human] race."[71] In America, this resistance came to center on legal arguments about the constitutionality of the statutes. A few state courts early on declared these statutes unconstitutional on

---

63. *Immigration Act of 1924,* ch. 190, 43 Stat. 153. *See, e.g.,* J.S. DeJarnette, *Eugenics in Relation to the Insane, the Epileptic, the Feeble-Minded and Race Blending,* VA. MED. MONTHLY, Apr. 1925–Mar. 1926, at 290–91. *See generally* HUBBARD, *supra* note 28, at 84; KEVLES, *supra* note 28, at 97; ALAN KRAUT, SILENT TRAVELERS: GERMS, GENES, AND THE "IMMIGRANT MENACE" (1994); LUDMERER, *supra* note 28, at 89–114; Phillips, *supra* note 28, at 4.

64. GENA COREA, THE MOTHER MACHINE 27 (1985). On the testimony before Congress, see ALLAN CHASE, THE LEGACY OF MALTHUS: THE SOCIAL COSTS OF THE NEW SCIENTIFIC REVOLUTION 291–95 (1977); SMITH, *supra* note 32, at 6.

65. Lombardo, *supra* note 28, at 5.

66. HALLER, *supra* note 28, at 142; J.K. MASON, MEDICO-LEGAL ASPECTS OF REPRODUCTION AND PARENTHOOD 69 (2nd ed. 1998). Various historians give other numbers ranging from 17 to 32. *See* GORDON, *supra* note 17, at 311 (27 states); PETCHESKY, *supra* note 28, at 87 (32 states); SMITH, *supra* note 32, at 139 (30 states by 1938); SMITH, *supra* note 28, at 71–72 (25 states in 1925, 31 states in 1931); ANDREA TONE, DEVICES AND DESIRES: A HISTORY OF CONTRACEPTIVES IN AMERICA 144 (2001) (at least 26 states by 1932); Burgdorf & Burgdorf, *supra* note 31, at 1000 (28 states in 1930); Mary Dudziak, *Oliver Wendell Holmes as a Eugenic Reformer: Rhetoric in the Writing of Constitutional Law,* 71 IOWA L. REV. 833, 846–48 (1986) (17 states); Ferster, *supra* note 28, at 591 (31 states by 1937); Goldhar, *supra* note 51, at 163 (28 in 1931); Hyatt, *supra* note 30, at 490 (27 states); O'Hara & Sanks, *supra* note 28, at 20, 22–23 (32 states and Puerto Rico); Phillips, *supra* note 28, at 4 (30 states by 1938); Rodgers, *supra* note 32, at 136 (23 states by 1925); Richard & Robert Sherlock, *Sterilizing the Retarded: Constitutional, Statutory and Policy Alternatives,* 60 N.C. L. REV. 943, 945 (1982) (30 states); Judy Scales-Trent, *Racial Purity Laws in the United States and Nazi Germany,* 23 HUM. RTS. Q. 259, 291 (2001) (28 states). *See generally* GOULD, *supra* note 28, at 158–74; HALLER, *supra,* at 125–43; KEVLES, *supra* note 28, at 76–80, 100–01; TRENT, *supra* note 34, at 131–224; TROMBLEY, *supra* note 28, at 51–59.

67. Act of Mar. 9, 1907, 1907 Ind. Acts. Ch. 215. An effort to enact a sterilization act in Michigan in 1897 failed to pass the legislature. *See* Burgdorf & Burgdorf, *supra* note 31, at 999–1000; Ferster, *supra* note 28, at 593. A sterilization act passed by the Pennsylvania legislature in 1907 was vetoed by the governor. Burgdorf & Burgdorf, *supra* note 31, at 1000; Ferster, *supra* note 28, at 593; O'Hara & Sacks, *supra* note 28, at 22.

68. TONE, *supra* note 66, at 142–43; Burgdorf & Burgdorf, *supra* note 31, at 999; Cynkar, *supra* note 28, at 1432; O'Hara & Sanks, *supra* note 28, at 22; Rodgers, *supra* note 32; Ferster, *supra* note 28, at 592.

69. Reilly, *supra* note 32, at 231; Rodgers, *supra* note 32, at 136.

70. *See* DEGLER, *supra* note 43, at 59–211; GERALD GROB, MENTAL ILLNESS AND AMERICAN SOCIETY, 1875–1940, at 108–78 (1983); ELIZABETH LUNBECK, THE PSYCHIATRIC PERSUASION: KNOWLEDGE, GENDER, AND POWER IN MODERN AMERICA 117–20 (1994); TRENT, *supra* note 34, at 198–206; Willich, *supra* note 28, at 87, 103–09.

71. Clarence Darrow, *The Eugenics Cult,* AM. MERCURY, June 1926, at 137.

equal protection grounds.[72] Most state courts upheld the constitutionality of these laws as reasonable measures to protect public health and to improve the "race."[73] State litigation was shortly preempted by three notable Supreme Court decisions: *Buck v. Bell*,[74] which upheld the constitutionality of such statutes; *Skinner v. Oklahoma*,[75] in which a particular compulsory sterilization statute was struck down as a denial of equal protection of the laws; and *Loving v. Virginia*,[76] in which the Court declared a statute prohibiting interracial marriage to be a denial of equal protection of the laws. This book has already examined the reasoning involved in *Buck v. Bell*.[77]

The statute in *Skinner* authorized the sterilization of "habitual criminals."[78] "Habitual criminal" was defined in the statute as anyone who had twice been convicted of a crime involving "moral turpitude."[79] White collar crimes were exempted, including violation of prohibition, embezzlement, tax evasion, and political offenses.[80] The equal protection problem in *Skinner* arose from the differential treatment of different classes of criminals rather than from gender or race.

Jack Skinner was convicted three times for theft or robbery of items of relatively small value (Oklahoma law then defined any theft of more than $20 value as a felony).[81] He had lost a foot in an accident when he was 19, and claimed to be unable to hold a job because of the mishap. Apparently he stole to support himself and his wife. There was no evidence in the legal record that Skinner was predisposed by heredity to criminal activity because the only relevant question under the statute was whether he had been convicted twice for included crimes.[82]

Justice William Douglas wrote for the majority in *Skinner*. Unlike Justice Holmes in *Buck v. Bell*, Douglas concluded that compulsory sterilization involved "one of the basic civil rights of man. Marriage and procreation are fundamental to the very existence and survival of the race."[83] Some found Justice Robert Jackson's concurrence in *Skinner*, in which he appealed to personal autonomy rather than equal protection as the grounds for decisions, more to the point: "There are limits to the extent to which a legislatively represented majority may conduct biological experiments at the expense of the dignity and personality and natural powers of a minority—even

---

72. Mickle v. Hendricks, 262 F. 687 (D. Nev. 1918); Davis v. Perry, 216 F. 413 (S.D. Iowa 1914); *In re* Opinion of the Justices, 162 So. 123 (Ala. 1935); Williams v. Smith, 131 N.E. 2 (1921); Haynes v. Lapeer, 166 N.W. 938 (Mich. 1918) [overruled in Smith v. Wayne Probate Judge, 204 N.W.2d Ind. 140 (Mich. 1925)]; Smith v. Board of Examiners, 88 A. 963 (N.J. Sup. Ct. 1913); Osborn v. Thomson, 169 N.Y.S. 638 (Sup. Ct.), *aff'd*, 171 N.Y.S. 1094 (App. Div. 1918). *See generally* KEVLES, *supra* note 28, at 109–10; Burgdorf & Burgdorf, *supra* note 31, at 1000–01; O'Hara & Sanks, *supra* note 28, at 23–28.

73. *See,* State *ex rel.* Smith v. Schaffer, 270 P. 604 (Kan. 1928); Smith v. Wayne Probate Judge, 204 N.W.2d 140 (Mich. 1925).

74. 274 U.S. 200 (1926).

75. 316 U.S. 535 (1942).

76. 388 U.S. 1 (1967).

77. See Chapter 10, at notes 146–57.

78. *Sterilization of Habitual Criminals Act*, 1935 Okla. Sess. Laws ch. 26, art. I. For a detailed history of the Oklahoma legislation, see Lombardo, *supra* note 28, at 12–15. *See generally* Burgdorf & Burgdorf, *supra* note 31, at 1010–11, 1013–14.

79. *Sterilization of Habitual Criminals Act, supra* note 79, art. I.

80. *Id.*

81. Lombardo, *supra* note 28, at 15–16.

82. *Id.*

83. 316 U.S. at 541. For a more complete analysis of Douglas' opinion, see Lombardo, *supra* note 28, at 15–18. *See also* Gerber v. Hickman, 264 F.3d 882 (9th Cir. 2001) (finding that an inmate of a prison has a fundamental constitutional right to inseminate his wife artificially that the state can prevent only if it can show that its refusal to allow artificial insemination is reasonably related to a legitimate penological interest).

those who have been guilty of what the majority defines as crimes."[84] (Jackson would soon become chief American prosecutor at the Nuremberg trials.) All the justices were careful, however, to distinguish *Buck v. Bell*, rather than to overrule it.[85] Jackson, in particular, expressly approved *Buck v. Bell* on the grounds that a State has the right to prevent an "imbecile" from transmitting her defect to another generation.[86] In the 1980s and 1990s, debate about compulsory sterilization for crimes resurfaced, but in terms of castrating incorrigible sex-offenders or child abusers; whether this will hold up in light of *Skinner* is unclear.[87]

Finally, while *Loving* is generally thought of as a race discrimination case, a eugenic theory underlay the statute.[88] Indeed, Virginia's *Racial Integrity Act* was enacted by the same legislature on the same day as it enacted the *Eugenical Sterilization Act*.[89] Furthermore, physicians took the lead in pressing for enactment of the miscegenation law on eugenics grounds.[90] Dr. Walter Plecker, director of the Bureau of Vital Statistics of the [Virginia] State Board of Health from

---

84. 316 U.S. at 546 (Jackson, J., concurring). *See* Doug Comer, *Sterilization of Mental Defectives: Compulsion and Consent,* 27 BAYLOR L. REV. 174 (1975); Lombardo, *supra* note 28, at 18–19; John Robertson, *Genetic Selection of Offspring Characteristics,* 76 B.U. L. REV. 421, 473–74 (1996).

85. 316 U.S. at 539–40 (Douglas, J., for the majority), 544 (Stone, C.J., concurring), 546 (Jackson, J., concurring).

86. *Id.* at 546 (Jackson, J., concurring).

87. *See, e.g.,* Briley v. California, 564 F.2d 849 (9th Cir. 1977); People v. Blankenship, 61 P.2d 352 (Cal. 1936); People v. Pointer, 199 Cal. Rptr. 357 (Ct. App. 1984); State v. Estes, 821 P.2d 1008 (Idaho Ct. App. 1991); People v. Gauntlett, 352 N.W.2d 310 (Mich. Ct. App. 1984); State v. Brown, 326 S.E.2d 410 (S.C. 1985); William Baker, Comment, *Castration of the Male Sexual Offender: A Legally Impermissible Alternative,* 30 LOY. L. REV. 377 (1984); Fred Berlin & Carl Meineke, *Treatment of Sex Offenders with Antiandrogenic Medication: Conceptualization, Review of Treatment Modalities, and Preliminary Findings,* 138 AM. J. PSYCH. 601 (1981); Douglas Besharov & Andrew Vachhs, *Sex Offenders: Is Castration an Acceptable Punishment,* 78 ABA J. 42 (July 1992); John Bradford, *Organic Treatments for the Male Sexual Offender,* 3 BEHAV. SCI. & L. 355 (1985); Linda Demsky, *The Use of Depo-Provera in the Treatment of Sex Offenders,* 5 J. LEGAL MED. 295 (1984); Edward Fitzgerald, *Chemical Castration: MPA Treatment of the Sexual Offender,* 18 AM. J. CRIM. L. 1 (1990); Kenneth Fromson, Note, *Beyond an Eye for an Eye: Castration as an Alternative Sentencing Measure,* 11 N.Y. L. SCH. J. HUM. RTS. 311 (1994); Janet Ginzburg, *Compulsory Contraception as a Condition of Probation: The Use and Abuse of Norplant,* 58 BROOK. L. REV. 979 (1992); William Green, *Depo-Provera, Castration, and the Probation of Rape Offenders: Statutory and Constitutional Issues,* 12 U. DAYTON L. REV. 1 (1986); Nickolaus Heim & Carolyn Hursch, *Castration for Sex Offenders: Treatment of Punishment? A Review of Recent European Literature,* 8 ARCHIVES OF SEXUAL BEHAV. 281 (1979); John Melella *et al., Legal and Ethical Issues in the Use of Antiandrogens in Treating Sex Offenders,* 17 BULL. AM. ACAD. PSYCH. 223 (1989); Jim Rees, *"Voluntary" Castration of Mentally Disordered Sex Offenders,* 13 CRIM. L. BULL. 30 (1977); Stacy Russell, Comment, *Castration of Repeat Sexual Offenders: An International Comparative Analysis,* 19 HOUS. J. INT'L L. 425 (1997); Kari Vanderzyl, Comment, *Castration as an Alternative to Incarceration: An Impotent Approach to the Punishment of Sex Offenders,* 15 N. ILL. U. L. REV. 107 (1994). *See also* People v. Dominguez, 64 Cal. Rptr. 290 (Ct. App. 1967) (barring a probation condition that a woman not becoming pregnant again); State v. Livingston, 372 N.E.2d 1335 (Ohio Ct. App. 1976) (same); Carl Cannon, *Sterilization Could Alter Her Sentence,* PHILA. INQUIRER, Oct. 18, 1981, at 17A.

88. *See, e.g.,* MADISON GRANT, THE PASSING OF THE GREAT RACE OR THE RACIAL BASIS OF EUROPEAN HISTORY (1916); STODDARD, TIDE OF COLOR, *supra* note 43; STODDARD, *supra* note 27; DeJarnette, *supra* note 63. *See generally* Lombardo, *supra* note 28, at 19–20. For a more overtly racial interpretation of the growing fears of miscegenation, see MARTHA HODES, WHITE WOMEN, BLACK MEN: ILLICIT SEX IN THE NINETEENTH-CENTURY SOUTH (1997); Judy Scales Trent, *Racial Purity Laws in the United States and Nazi Germany,* 23 HUM. RTS. Q. 259 (2001).

89. *Racial Integrity Act,* Act of Mar. 20, 1924, ch. 371, 1924 Va. Acts 534; *Eugenical Sterilization Act,* Act of Mar. 20, 1924, ch. 394, 1924 Va. Acts 569.

90. Phillip Reilly, *The Virginia Racial Integrity Act Revisited: The Plecker-Laughlin Correspondence: 1928–1930,* 16 AM. J. MED. GENETICS 483 (1983). *See generally* Keith Sealing, *Blood Will Tell: Scientific Racism and the Legal Prohibitions against Miscegenation,* 5 MICH. J. RACE & L. 559 (2000).

1914 to 1942, was particularly effective in providing statistics to "prove" that interracial breeding was a serious cause of public health problems.[91] Similar arguments are advanced even today.[92]

Virginia's *Racial Integrity Act* made it a felony for any "white person" to marry anyone other than another "white person."[93] "White person" was defined as any person who had "no trace whatever of any blood other than Caucasian" except that persons who had one-sixteenth or less of "American Indian blood" would be deemed to be "white persons" if they had no other "non-Caucasic blood."[94] The Lovings, an interracial couple who had married in the District of Columbia (where there was no such legal barrier) and had lived there during most of their marriage until moving to Virginia in 1963, challenged the constitutionality of the law in a case that reached the Supreme Court in 1967. The Court declared the statute unconstitutional on equal protection grounds that echoed the decision in *Skinner*.[95]

As *Loving* suggests, the political leaders of the eugenics movement were even explicitly racist, with the movement's academic leaders justifying both compulsory sterilization and public funding of contraceptive services on the basis that African-Americans, compared to European-Americans, were disproportionately mentally unfit and yet were reproducing at higher rates.[96] One leader of the American movement declined an invitation to attend a White House conference on children's issues because Booker T. Washington had also been invited.[97] In England, Fabian socialist Sydney Webb, in arguing for eugenics, found time to inject comments on what he considered to be the alarming population increase among the Irish and the Jews.[98]

As a result of the American sterilization statutes, as many as 64,000 persons (mostly marginally retarded or poor women) were sterilized involuntarily in the United States by 1964 — 60 percent of them in California alone.[99] Moreover, another 200,000 may have been sterilized through ostensibly voluntary federally funded programs by 1972.[100] All of these statutes were applied primarily to institutionalized persons, and although initially most the persons were sterilized were men, after 1930 most were women.[101] Some 43 percent of the latter 200,000 were

---

91. *See, e.g.*, WALTER PLECKER, THE NEW FAMILY AND RACE IMPROVEMENT (1925). *See generally* Lombardo, *supra* note 28, at 20–21; Paul Lombardo, *Miscegenation, Eugenics, and Racism: Historical Footnotes in* Loving v. Virginia, 21 U.C. DAVIS L. REV. 421, 425–28 (1988).

92. *See, e.g.*, RICHARD HERRNSTEIN & CHARLES MURRAY, THE BELL CURVE: INTELLIGENCE AND CLASS STRUCTURE IN AMERICAN LIFE (1994).

93. VA. CODE ANN. § 20-54-59 (1950).

94. *Id.*

95. 388 U.S. at 12.

96. GORDON, *supra* note 17, at 329–34, 353–54. Some see *Loving* as implicitly overriding all laws limited marriage based on mental abilities. *See* Churchill, *supra* note 57.

97. Kathryn Kemp, *Jean and Kate Gordon: New Orleans Social Reforms, 1898–1933*, 24 LA. HIST. 389, 392 (1983); Edward Larson, *"In the Finest, Most Womanly Way:" Women in the Southern Eugenics Movement*, 39 AM. J. LEG. HIST. 119, 128–29 (1995).

98. WEBB, *supra* note 27, at 39–40.

99. HALLER, *supra* note 28, at 138; MASON, *supra* note 66, at 69; PETCHESKY, *supra* note 28, at 87; PICKENS, *supra* note 28, at 88. *See generally* J. RALPH LINDGREN & NADINE TAUB, THE LAW OF SEX DISCRIMINATION 413–18 (1988); THOMAS SHAPIRO, POPULATION CONTROL POLITICS: WOMAN, STERILIZATION AND REPRODUCTIVE CHOICE (1985); Eric Jaegers, Note, *Modern Judicial Treatment of Procreative Rights in Developmentally Disabled Persons: Equal Rights to Procreation and Sterilization*, 31 U. LOUISVILLE J. FAM. L. 947 (1993); Paul Lombardo, *Three Generations, No Imbeciles: New Light on* Buck v. Bell, 60 NYU L. REV. 30, 31 (1985). Nearly half of these — 27,000 — were sterilized between and 1907 and 1938. KEVLES, *supra* note 106–07; SMITH, *supra* note 32, at 139; Phillips, *supra* note 28, at 4.

100. Angela Davis, *Racism, Birth Control and Reproductive Rights*, in ALL AMERICAN WOMEN 239, 252 (Johnetta Cole ed. 1986).

101. Reilly, *supra* note 32, at 235–36.

African-American women, and nearly as many were Hispanic women.[102] The rather sorry history subsumed within these statutes and the cited cases has been described by law professor Harry Kalvin in these terms: "The legal career of sterilization is…a useful example, first, of the law too quickly adopting a popularized scientific premise without exposing it to adequate scrutiny, and second, of the law's consequent difficulty in keeping abreast of the revisions of scientific hypotheses."[103]

Eugenicists nonetheless were disappointed. After all, Paul Poponoe, an early demographer, had argued in 1928 that 10,000,000 Americans "needed" to be sterilized.[104] As late as 1938, Dr. J.S. Jarnette, director of the hospital where Carrie Buck had been sterilized, was reporting that some 12,000,000 defectives were in need of sterilization in the United States.[105] So blatant was the racist content of the eugenics and birth control movements that even some contemporary Americans decried the racism of the movements.[106] By the 1930s, the eugenics movement was losing ground in the United States and the number of sterilizations on eugenic grounds was already declining.[107] Finally, the American Medical Association concluded in 1937 that "there appears to be very little scientific basis to justify limitation of conception for eugenic reasons."[108] Even after this condemnation, however, the sterilization laws remained on the books, with nearly half of the sterilizations under these laws taking place after 1937.[109] Many courts continued to apply involuntary sterilization statutes without any apparent hesitation right up through the 1970s.[110] Only in the wake of the discovery of a right of privacy relating to procreative choice in *Griswold v.*

---

102. *Id. See also* Edward Spriggs, jr., *Involuntary Sterilization: An Unconstitutional Menace to Minorities and the Poor,* 4 NYU Rev. L. & Soc. Change 127 (1974).

103. Harry Kalvin, *A Special Corner of Civil Liberties: A Legal View,* 31 NYU L. Rev. 1223, 1234 (1956).

104. Paul Popenoe, *Number of Persons Needing Sterilization,* 19 J. Heredity 405–10 (1928).

105. Western State Hospital (Va.), 1938 Annual Report 110, as quoted in Lombardo, *supra* note 28, at 12.

106. *See, e.g.,* Lawrence Dublin, *The Fallacious Propaganda for Birth Control,* Atlantic Monthly, Feb. 1926, at 189. *See generally* Gordon, *supra* note 17, at 277–87, 303–12, 316–17, 395–402; Larson, *supra* note 97, at 128–29, 131.

107. Cynkar, *supra* note 28, at 1454–56; Reilly, *supra* note 32, at 235. *See generally* Gallagher, *supra* note 28, at 142–43.

108. Comm. to Study Contraceptive Practices & Related Problems, AMA Proc., May 1937, at 54. *See* Ferster, *supra* note 28, at 602–03; Charles Kindregan, *Sixty Years of Compulsory Eugenic Sterilization: "Three Generations of Imbeciles" and the Constitution of the United States,* 43 Chi.-Kent L. Rev. 123, 136–37 (1966); O'Hara & Sanks, *supra* note 28, at 35–41.

109. Reilly, *supra* note 32, at 235.

110. *See* Stump v. Sparkman, 435 U.S. 349 (1978); North Carolina Ass'n for Retarded Children v. North Carolina, 420 F. Supp. 451 (M.D.N.C. 1976); *In re* Susan S., No. 7764 (Del. Ct. Ch. Feb. 8, 1996), 1996 WL 75343; *In re* Guardianship of Matejski, 419 N.W.2d 576 (Iowa 1988); *In re* Moe, 432 N.E.2d 712 (Mass. 1982); *In re* Cavitt, 159 N.W.2d 566 (Neb. 1968), *appeal dismissed,* 396 U.S. 996 (1970); *In re* Penny N., 414 A.2d 541 (N.H. 1980); *In re* Grady, 426 A.2d 467 (N.J. 1981); *In re* Sallmaier, 378 N.Y.S.2d 989 (Sup. Ct. 1975); *In re* Sterilization of Moore, 221 S.E.2d 307 (N.C. 1976); *In re* Simpson, 180 N.E.2d 206 (Ohio Prob. 1962); Cook v. State, 495 P.2d 768 (Or. Ct. App. 1972); *In re* Terwilliger, 450 A.2d 1376 (Pa. Super. 1982); Frazier v. Levi, 440 S.W.2d 393 (Tex. Ct. Civ. App. 1969), *writ denied; In re* Marcia R., 383 A.2d 630 (Vt. 1978); *In re* Guardianship of Hayes, 608 P.2d 635 (Wash. 1980); *In re* Guardianship of Eberhardy, 307 N.W.2d 881 (Wis. 1981). *See generally* Medora Bass, *Surgical Contraception: A Key to Normalization and Prevention,* 16 Mental Retardation 399 (1978); Burgdorf & Burgdorf, *supra* note 31, at 1014–23; James Varner, *Rights of Mentally Ill—Involuntary Sterilization—Analysis of Recent Statutes,* 78 W. Va. L. Rev. 131 (1975); Vukowich, *supra* note 31.

*Connecticut*[111] did states begin to reexamine or repeal their compulsory sterilization laws.[112] No move was ever made to compensate the victims of those laws.[113]

# Eugenics in Germany

*Victims are entitled to insist on others' attention not because they can offer virtue to a fallen world, but because they are experts on their own lives.*

—Patricia Williams[114]

The eugenics movement was international, reaching well beyond the English speaking countries. Democratic countries such as those of Scandinavia early enacted forced sterilization laws and aggressively enforced compulsory sterilization of the unfit for many years.[115] Sweden enacted its sterilization law in 1935 and enforced it until its repeal in 1976[116]—more than 30 years after the end of the Nazi experiment that effectively discredited compulsory sterilization, not to men-

---

111. 381 U.S. 479 (1965).

112. *See* Stump v. Sparkman, 435 U.S. 349 (1978); Downs v. Sawtelle, 574 F.2d 1 (1st Cir.), *cert. denied*, 439 U.S. 910 (1978); Ruby v. Massey, 452 F. Supp. 361 (D. Conn. 1978); Relf v. Weinberger, 372 F. Supp. 1196 (D.D.C. 1974), *vacated as moot*, 565 F.2d 722 (D.C. Cir. 1977); Wyatt v. Aderholt, 368 F. Supp. 1383 (M.D. Ala. 1973); Wade v. Bethesda Hosp., 356 F. Supp. 380 (S.D. Ohio 1973); Hudson v. Hudson, 373 So. 2d 310 (Ala. 1979); *In re* C.D.M., 627 P.2d 607 (Alaska 1981); *In re* Valerie N., 707 P.2d 760 (Cal. 1985); *In re* A.W., 637 P.2d 366 (Colo. 1981); *In re* S.C.E., 378 A.2d 144 (Del. Ch. 1977); A.L. v. G.R.H., 325 N.E.2d 501 (Ind. Ct. App. 1975), *cert. denied*, 425 U.S. 936 (1975); Holmes v. Powers, 439 S.W.2d 579 (Ky. Ct. App. 1968); *In re* Debra B., 495 A.2d 781 (Me. 1985); Wentzel v. Montgomery Gen. Hosp., Inc., 447 A.2d 1244 (Md. 1982), *cert. denied*, 459 U.S. 1147 (1983); *In re* M.K.R., 515 S.W.2d 467 (Mo. 1974); *In re* M.R., 638 A.2d 1274 (N.J. 1994); *In re* D.D., 408 N.Y.S.2d 104 (App. Div. 1978), *appeal dismissed*, 405 N.E.2d 233 (N.Y. 1980); *In re* Estate of C.W., 640 A.2d 427, *stay granted*, 640 A.2d 445 (Pa. Super. 1994), *cert. denied*, 513 U.S. 1183 (1995). *See generally* TROMBLEY, *supra* note 28, at 199–201; Burgdorf & Burgdorf, *supra* note 31, at 1022–34; Comer, *supra* note 85; Deborah DuBois Davis, *Addressing the Consent Issue Involved in the Sterilization of Mentally Incompetent Females*, 43 ALB. L. REV. 322 (1979); Gary Dodge, Comment, *Sterilization, Retardation, and Parental Authority*, 1978 BYU L. REV. 380; Ferster, *supra* note 28; Jan Charles Gray, *Compulsory Sterilization in a Free Society: Choices and Dilemma*, 41 U. CIN. L. REV. 529 (1972); Bernard Green & Renal Paul, *Parenthood and the Mentally Retarded*, 24 TOR. L.J. 117 (1974); Hyatt, *supra* note 30, at 494–96; Jaegers, *supra* note 99, at 959; William Matoush, Note, *Eugenic Sterilization—A Scientific Analysis*, 46 DEN. L. REV. 631 (1969); Murdock, *supra* note 31; Gloria Neuwith, Phyllis Heisler, & Kenneth Goldrich, *Capacity, Competence, Consent: Voluntary Sterilization of the Mentally Retarded*, 6 COLUM. HUM. RTS. L. REV. 447 (1975); Eve Paul, *Sterilization of Mentally Retarded Persons: The Issues and Conflicts*, 3 FAM. PLANNING POP. REP. 96 (1974); Rodgers, *supra* note 32, at 146–54; Benjamin Schoenfield, *A Survey of the Constitutional Rights of the Mentally Retarded*, 32 SW. L.J. 605 (1978); Elizabeth Scott, *Sterilization of Mentally Retarded Persons: Reproductive Rights and Family Privacy*, 1986 DUKE L.J. 806 (1986); Jeffrey Shaman, *Persons Who Are Mentally Retarded: Their Right to Marry and Have Children*, 12 FAM. L.Q. 61 (1978); Symposium, *Sterilization of the Retarded: In Whose Interest?*, 8 HASTINGS CTR. REP. no. 3, at 28 (1978); S. John Vitello, *Involuntary Sterilization: Recent Developments*, 16 MENTAL RETARDATION 405 (1978). *See also* LAW REFORM COMM'N OF CANADA, *supra* note 51; Cawte, *supra* note 42; Ann Curthoys, *supra* note 50; McWhirter & Weijer, *supra* note 51.

113. *See* J. DAVID SMITH & K. RAY NELSON, THE STERILIZATION OF CARRIE BUCK 251–53 (1989); TROMBLEY, *supra* note 28, at 235–38; Hyatt, *supra* note 30, at 501–03.

114. Patricia Williams, *Dissolving the Sameness/Difference Debate: A Post-Modern Path beyond Essentialism in Feminist and Critical Race Theory*, 1991 DUKE L.J. 296, 307 n.112.

115. *See generally* EUGENICS AND THE WELFARE STATE: STERILIZATION POLICY IN DENMARK, SWEDEN, NORWAY, AND FINLAND (Gunnar Broberg & Nils Roll-Hansen eds. 1996).

116. Hyatt, *supra* note 30, at 476–87.

tion the eugenics movement generally, in most other countries.[117] Altogether 62,888 people (nearly all women) were sterilized in Sweden during the 40 years the law was on the books.[118] During much of this time, the policies in Sweden were frankly racist, seeking to eliminate those exhibiting "gypsy features" and otherwise to purify the "Nordic race," as well as to eliminate persons with demonstrated mental defects or even "vagabond" lifestyles.[119] Sweden's government in 1921 created what was perhaps the first national institute on racial biology headed by Herman Lundberg, a move supported by all shades of political opinion in the Parliament.[120] Sweden's Institute for Race Biology became a model for similar institutions in Africa, Central America, France, and Germany.[121] In the 1990s, the Swedish government suddenly found itself confronted with demands by about 20,000 survivors of the forced sterilizations for compensation for having been denied their fundamental rights.[122]

Compulsory sterilization of the unfit found a ready audience in Germany long before the Nazis became a political force.[123] As in Sweden, the first public manifestation eugenics policies was the creation of the Institute for Racial Hygiene in Berlin.[124] In line with their racial politics, the Nazis embraced eugenics from their earliest years, speaking in terms of "cleansing" and "regeneration" of the "Aryan race" rather than using the term "eugenics" itself.[125] Adolf Hitler explicitly endorsed eugenics in *Mein Kampf:* "The demand that for defective people the propagation of an equally defective offspring be made impossible is a demand of clearest reason and... the most humane act of mankind."[126] In Nazi hands, the term "defective" quickly proved to be a political, even genocidal, concept.[127] Nazi officials declared in 1934 that as many as 20 percent of the German population were defective and would have to be prevented from having children.[128]

The Nazi enacted *"The Law for the Prevention of Progeny with Hereditary Diseases"* on July 14, 1933 (less than six months after Hitler became Chancellor of Germany).[129] That law not only au-

---

117. Sterilizations peaked in Sweden in 1949, and were more common in 1960 than in 1940. EUGENICS AND THE WELFARE STATE, *supra* note 115, at 108.

118. *Id.* at 10, 108–10.

119. *Id.* at 81–87; Hyatt, *supra* note 30, at 480, 485 n.68, 487.

120. EUGENICS AND THE WELFARE STATE, *supra* note 115, at 86–91, 95–96, 101; Hyatt, *supra* note 30, at 481, 498–99.

121. EUGENICS AND THE WELFARE STATE, *supra* note 115, at 88–90.

122. Hyatt, *supra* note 30, at 478–80, 499–500.

123. GALLAGHER, *supra* note 28, at139; KEVLES, *supra* note 28, at 114–18; BENNO MÜLLER-HILL, MURDEROUS SCIENCE: ELIMINATION OF SCIENTIFIC SELECTION OF JEWS, GYPSIES AND OTHERS, GERMANY 1933–1945, at 7–9, 22–23, 28, 76, 88–90 (1988); MICHAEL KATER, DOCTORS UNDER HITLER 7–9 (1989); PAUL, *supra* note 28, at 86; Claudia Koonz, *Eugenics, Gender, and Ethics in Nazi Germany: The Debate about Involuntary Sterilization, 1933–1936,* in REEVALUATING THE THIRD REICH 66, 68–69, 77–79 (Thomas Childers & Jane Caplan eds. 1993); Malinowski, *supra* note 28, at 142–43.

124. ROBERT JAY LIFTON, THE NAZI DOCTORS: MEDICAL KILLING AND THE PSYCHOLOGY OF GENOCIDE 349, 357, 360–61, 369 (1986). *See also* EUGENICS AND THE WELFARE STATE, *supra* note 115, at 90. The Institute was partly funded by the Rockefeller Foundation. Malinowski, *supra* note 28, at 141. On the intellectual indebtedness of German eugenicists to the American experience, see ROBERT PROCTOR, RACIAL HYGIENE MEDICINE UNDER THE NAZIS 99–101, 349 n.115 (1988); Scales-Trent, *supra* note 66, at 291–92.

125. Koonz, *supra* note 123, at 68. *See generally* HUBBARD, *supra* note 28, at 184–91.

126. ADOLF HITLER, *MEIN KAMPF* 439 (John Chamberlain *et al.* trans. & eds. 1939).

127. LIFTON, *supra* note 124, at 116–18; INGO MÜLLER, HITLER'S JUSTICE: THE COURTS OF THE THIRD REICH 121–24 (Deborah Lucas Schneider trans. 1991); MÜLLER-HILL, *supra* note 123; PROCTOR, *supra* note 124; Leo Alexander, *Medical Science under Dictatorship,* 241 N. ENG. J. MED. 39 (1949); Matthew Lippman, *They Shoot Lawyers, Don't They? Law in the Third Reich and the Global Threat to the Independence of the Judiciary,* 23 CAL. W. INT'L L.J. 257, 287–88 (1993).

128. LIFTON, *supra* note 124, at 26; MÜLLER-HILL, *supra* note 123, at 28–29; Koonz, *supra* note 123, at 68.

129. The law is reprinted in 3 TRIALS OF WAR CRIMINALS BEFORE THE NUREMBERG MILITARY TRIBUNALS UNDER CONTROL COUNCIL LAW NO. 10, at 243 (1951). *See generally* HANS PETER BLEUEL, STRENGTH THROUGH JOY: SEX AND SOCIETY IN NAZI GERMANY 192 (1973); MICHAEL BURLEIGH & WOLFGANG WIPPERMAN, THE

thorized compulsory sterilization in order to eliminate "human imperfection" on a national scale, but it also authorized abortions before viability if the fetus was likely to be "defective."[130] The law established special "Health Courts" that approved 56,244 sterilizations in their first year, denying only 3,692.[131] The number of denials declined steadily. In the 12 years of their operation, the Health Courts approved well over 90 percent of the applications for sterilization, authorizing around 360,000 sterilizations that directly resulted in 17,500 deaths.[132] Additional sterilizations occurred without judicial authorization, with estimates ranging as high as 3,500,000[133]— which, if accurate, would be about five percent of the entire population of Germany, Austria, and the other lands that Hitler incorporated into the Greater Germany. No one knows the actual number.

Remarkably, only five percent of the 360,000 or so processed through the Health Courts were sterilized after 1939.[134] Some have suggested that the low-incidence of sterilization after 1939 reflected growing resistance within the medical profession to compulsory sterilizations.[135] This overlooks that at the beginning of World War II, the government ordered that sterilizations be performed only when there was "exceptionally great danger," presumably out of concern about interfering with the war effort.[136] It also overlooks the growing recourse to extermination rather than sterilization as a means of removing "undesirables" from society. Extermination had its eugenic as well as its overtly political form. Early on, the government implemented the "T4" program, involving "euthanasia" of the physically and mentally disabled.[137] About 70,000 persons were executed in the "T4" program.[138] Today, Holocaust imagery is often

---

RACIAL STATE: GERMANY 1933–1945, at 140–41 (1991); STEPHEN KERN, ANATOMY AND DESTINY: A CULTURAL HISTORY OF THE HUMAN BODY 232 (1975); MÜLLER-HILL, *supra* note 123, at 28; FRANZ NEUMANN, BEHEMOTH: THE STRUCTURE AND PRACTICE OF NATIONAL SOCIALISM 111–12 (1942); PAUL, *supra* note 28, at 86–87; PROCTOR, *supra* note 124, at 102; Koonz, *supra* note 123, at 69–70.

130. ROGER ROSENBLATT, LIFE ITSELF: ABORTION IN THE AMERICAN MIND 75 (1992); Albin Eser, *Reform of German Abortion Law: First Experience*, 34 AM. J. COMP. L. 369, 371 (1986); Nanette Funk, *Abortion Counselling (sic) and the 1995 German Abortion Law*, 12 CONN. J. INT'L L. 33, 35 (1996); Sabine Klein-Schonnefeld, *Germany*, in ABORTION IN THE NEW EUROPE: A COMPARATIVE HANDBOOK 113, 114 (Bill Rolston & Anna Eggert eds. 1994); Koonz, *supra* note 123, at 70; Lippman, *supra* note 127, at 287–88.

131. PROCTOR, *supra* note 124, at 102. See also MÜLLER-HILL, *supra* note 123, at 29, 32; Matthew Lippman, *Law, Lawyers, and Legality in the Third Reich: The Perversion of Principle and Professionalism*, 11 TEMPLE INT'L & COMP. L.J. 199, 257–60 (1997).

132. REILLY, *supra* note 34, at 109. See also MICHAEL BURLEIGH, DEATH AND DELIVERANCE: EUTHANASIA IN GERMANY 1900–1945, at 56 (1994); BURLEIGH & WIPPERMAN, *supra* note 129, at 138; ATINA GROSSMAN, REFORMING SEX: THE GERMAN MOVEMENT FOR BIRTH CONTROL AND ABORTION REFORM, 1920–1950, at 149 (1995); MÜLLER-HILL, *supra* note 123, at 31–32; PROCTOR, *supra* note 124, at 106–08; Lippman, *supra* note 131, at 259. Estimates for the number of deaths vary widely. See BURLEIGH & WIPPERMAN, *supra* note 129, at 253 (estimating 480 deaths); PROCTOR, *supra*, at 109 (estimating 2,000 deaths).

133. REILLY, *supra* note 34, at 109. See also MÜLLER-HILL, *supra* note 123, at 31 (reporting an estimate of 200,000 sterilizations annually).

134. Lippman, *supra* note 131, at 259.

135. PROCTOR, *supra* note 124, at 114–17; Lippman, *supra* note 131, at 259.

136. PROCTOR, *supra* note 124, at 117.

137. GOTZ ALY, PETER CHROUET, & CHRISTIAN PROSS, CLEANSING THE FATHERLAND: NAZI MEDICINE AND RACIAL HYGIENE (1994); BURLEIGH, *supra* note 132; BURLEIGH & WIPPERMAN, *supra* note 129, at 136–67; HENRY FRIEDLANDER, THE ORIGINS OF NAZI GENOCIDE: FROM EUTHANASIA TO THE FINAL SOLUTION (1995); HUGH GALLAGHER, BY TRUST BETRAYED: PATIENTS AND PHYSICIANS IN THE THIRD REICH (1990); MICHAEL KATER, DOCTORS UNDER HITLER 80–81 (1989); LIFTON, *supra* note 132; MÜLLER, *supra* note 127, at 126–28; MÜLLER-HILL, *supra* note 123, at 39–65; PAUL, *supra* note 28, at 90–91; Lippman, *supra* note 127, at 288; Friedemann Pfallin, *The Connection between Eugenics, Sterilization and Mass Murder in Germany from 1933 to 1945*, 5 MED. & LAW 1 (1986). See generally CHASE, *supra* note 43.

138. BURLEIGH & WIPPERMAN, *supra* note 129, at 142; MÜLLER-HILL, *supra* note 123, at 13, 15; Malinowski, *supra* note 28, at 145.

invoked in pro-life arguments because of the parallels they see in a policy favoring abortion to laws such as these.[139] There is more truth to such analogies than those who use them perhaps realize.

In contrast, "Aryans" who sought to be sterilized or to have an abortion seldom got them.[140] The Nazis strongly supported motherhood as the proper role for German women.[141] The Nazis extended the German policy of subsidizing motherhood even to unmarried women—if the parents were "Aryan."[142] The Nazis suppressed both independent and left-wing women's organizations.[143] They shut down birth control centers and increased the number of convictions annually for criminal abortion by 50 percent over the already high Weimar figures while the number of medical referrals for therapeutic abortions dropped from about 44,000 in 1932 to only 4,131 in 1937.[144] The Nazis persecuted pro-abortion activists, forcing many of them to flee abroad.[145] Despite these efforts, the birthrate under the Nazis actually fell to lower levels than under the Weimar Republic.[146] This drop is only partly explained by the large number of women whom the Nazis deemed "unfit" to reproduce and therefore sterilized, compelled to abort, or perhaps simply a general demoralization that rendered women unwilling to become mothers.[147]

Racism directly connects eugenics in the United Kingdom and the United States with the Nazi eugenics law. At the time, the Nazi law was widely approved in Australia, England, and the United States, as well as neighboring countries such as Sweden.[148] In fact, the number of sterilizations rose sharply in the United States during the 1930s, arguably in emulation of the Nazis.[149] And we have noted the 63,000 Swedes who were sterilized as racially or socially inferior under a law enacted in 1934.[150] Even today one can find a feminist historian such as Barbara Brookes praising the Nazi law because it was less restrictive regarding abortions than was the law in England at that time.[151] Some eugenics enthusiasts in England, the United States, and Australia also supported abortion on eugenic grounds, but they found little support in either the medical or the legal professions generally, or in the population at large.[152]

---

139. *See, e.g.,* James Burtchaell, Rachel Weeping and Other Essays on Abortion (1982).

140. Koonz, *supra* note 123, at 70.

141. *See* Proctor, *supra* note 124, at 116; David Schoenbaum, Hitler's Social Revolution: Class and Status in Nazi Germany, 1933–1939, at 179 (1966); Harry Shaffer, Women in the Two Germanys: A Comparative Study of a Socialist and a Non-Socialist Society 6 (1981).

142. Claudia Koonz, Mothers in the Fatherland: Women, the Family, and Nazi Politics 149–50, 186–87 (1987); Telman, *supra* note 12, at 109–10.

143. Koonz, *supra* note 142, at 141.

144. Grossman, *supra* note 132, at 149; Telman, *supra* note 12, at 109.

145. Grossman, *supra* note 132, at 136.

146. Telman, *supra* note 12, at 110.

147. Grossman, *supra* note 132, at 153.

148. *See, e.g.,* Agar, *supra* note 51, at 1; C.G Campbell, *The German Racial Policy,* 21 Eugenical News 1 (1936). *See generally* Kenny, *supra* note 28, at 191; Stefan Kuhl, The Nazi Connection: Eugenics, American Racism, and German National Socialism (1994); Edward Larson, Sex, Race, and Science: Eugenics in the Deep South 146 (1995); Olasky, *supra* note 28, at 256–57; Diane Paul, Controlling Human Heredity: 1865 to the Present (1995); Proctor, *supra* note 124, at 50, 58, 187; Lombardo, *supra* note 28, at 11–12; Paul Lombardo, *Involuntary Sterilization in Virginia: From Buck v. Bell to Poe v. Lynchburg,* 3 Dev. Mental Health L. 13, 20 (1983); Lombardo, *supra* note 36; Lombardo, *supra* note 38; Scales-Trent, *supra* note 66, at 291–92. *See also* Andres Horacio Reggiani, *Alexis Carrel, the Unknown: Eugenics and Population Research under Vichy,* 25 French Hist. Stud. 300 (2000).

149. Reilly, *supra* note 55, at 154–60.

150. *Sweden Plans to Pay Sterilization Victims,* N.Y. Times, Jan. 27, 1999, at A8.

151. Brookes, *supra* note 17, at 59, 74–75 n.54

152. *See, e.g.,* Report of the Interdepartmental Committee on Abortion 89–90 (1939) ("Interdepartmental Comm.") (rejecting eugenic grounds for abortion). *See generally* Kerry Petersen, Abortion Regimes 60–61 (1993).

Japan enacted a law similar to that of Nazi Germany in 1940.[153] The Japanese law did not authorize eugenic abortions, but did legalize "medically necessary" abortions and eugenically beneficial sterilizations, generally requiring physicians to apply to a governmental agency in advance of the operation and to consult a second physician. In Japan, however, the law was used less to compel sterilizations than to limit them in order to promote population increase.[154]

The major resistance to the ethos of the eugenics movement came from the Catholic Church.[155] The Pope issued an encyclical expressly denouncing sterilization and abortion in 1931.[156] The Catholic Church, so reviled for its opposition to abortion, has gotten little credit for having been the first significant organization actively to oppose the eugenics movement and compulsory sterilization. The Nazi experience, however, succeeded in discrediting the entire eugenics movement. The Supreme Court of the United States alluded to the Nazi programs in declaring unconstitutional an Oklahoma statute authorizing the sterilization of habitual criminals.[157] The World Medical Association adopted the *Declaration of Geneva* (also known as the "Nuremberg Code") in 1948 setting forth a "universal" standard for medical ethics:

> I will not permit considerations of religion, nationality, race, party politics or social standing to intervene between my duty and my patient. I will maintain the utmost respect for human life, from the time of conception; even under threat, I will not use my medical knowledge contrary to the laws of humanity.[158]

The eugenics movement did not disappear in the aftermath of the Nazi experience. Instead, it transformed itself from "eugenics" to "genetics," the *Eugenics Quarterly* becoming the *Journal of Social Biology*, and the *Annals of Eugenics* becoming the *Annals of Human Genetics*.[159] Supporters stopped talking about improving the "human stock" and began to talk about improving the

---

153. Hiromi Maruyama, *Abortion in Japan: A Feminist Critique*, 10 WIS. WOMEN'S L.J. 131, 133–34 (1995); Kinko Nakatani, *Japan*, in ABORTION AND PROTECTION OF THE HUMAN FETUS: LEGAL PROBLEMS IN CROSS-CULTURAL PERSPECTIVE 221, 225 (S.J. Frankowski *et al*. Eds. 1987).

154. Maruyama, *supra* note 153, at 134.

155. *See, e.g.,* HALLER, *supra* note 28, at 82–83, 131; KEVLES, *supra* note 28, at 118–21, 168; MÜLLER-HILL, *supra* note 123, at 15, 29, 41; REILLY, *supra* note 35, at 118–22; Larson, *supra* note 97, at 129–35.

156. Pope Pius XII, *Casti Canubii* (1931). *See also* KENNY, *supra* note 28, at 191; Koonz, *supra* note 123, at 69–76, 79–81.

157. Skinner v. Oklahoma, 316 U.S. 535, 541 (1942). *See also* Davis, *supra* note 100, at 363–64; O'Hara & Sanks, *supra* note 28, at 36–37.

158. World Med. Ass'n, *Declaration of Geneva*, 1 WORLD MED. ASS'N BULL. 109 (1949). *See generally* ELAZAR BARKAN, THE RETREAT OF SCIENTIFIC RACISM (1992); THE NAZI DOCTORS AND THE NUREMBERG CODE: HUMAN RIGHTS IN HUMAN EXPERIMENTATION (George Annas & Michael Grodin eds. 1992); WHEN MEDICINE WENT MAD: BIOETHICS AND THE HOLOCAUST (Arthur Caplan ed. 1992); Jay Katz, *Human Sacrifice and Human Experimentation: Reflections on Nuremberg*, 22 YALE J. INT'L L. 401 (1997); Malinowski, *supra* note 28, at 149–64; Jonathan Moreno, *"The Only Feasible Means": The Pentagon's Ambivalent Relationship with the Nuremburg Code*, 26 HASTINGS CTR. REP. no. 5, at 11 (Sept.–Oct. 1996); HHT.C. Routley, *Aims and Objects of the World Medical Association*, 1 WORLD MED. ASS'N BULL. 18 (1949). Although the problem of how to treat Nazi doctors themselves is presumably nearing an end as few of them can any longer be alive or practicing medicine, the World Medical Association itself continues to struggle with that legacy. In 1993, its president-elect (Hans-Joachim Sewering) resigned shortly before his inauguration after it was revealed that as a young doctor he had participated in the Nazi euthanasia program. Michael Grodin, George Annas, & Leonard Glantz, *Medicine and Human Rights: A Proposal for International Action*, HASTING CNTR. REP., July–Aug., 1993, at 8, 10. On the other hand, the *Declaration of Geneva* never had much direct impact on American medicine. *See* Jonathan Moreno, *Reassessing the Influence of the Nuremberg Code on American Medical Ethics*, 13 J. CONTEMP. HEALTH L. & POL'Y 347 (1997).

159. *See, e.g.,* L.C. Dunn, *Cross Currents in the History of Human Genetics*, 14 AM. J. HUM. GENETICS 1 (1962). *See generally* Phillips, *supra* note 28, at 5.

"gene pool."[160] Talk of DNA and genes replaced talk of race and hereditary traits.[161] The movement transformed itself from an avowedly discriminatory movement focused on "racial hygiene" to an apparently non-discriminatory movement focused on population growth—which just coincidentally targeted non-white countries as the ones primarily at risk from the "population explosion."[162] In fact, Dr. Gregory Pincus undertook his successful development of a contraceptive pill in part out of his concerns over the necessity of population control.[163]

The legal legacy of the eugenics movement also survived the Nazi debacle. Laws based on discredited eugenics theories were not repealed in many countries, including the United States, and the *Declaration of Geneva's* emphasis on the sanctity of life and equal right to live of human beings today is under attack.[164] In fact, Leon Kass has gone so far as to wonder "whether the development of amniocentesis and prenatal diagnosis may represent a backlash against…humanitarian and egalitarian tendencies in the practice of medicine."[165] Today, we are witnessing pressure for the revival of compulsory sterilization and contraception even in Western democracies.[166]

---

160. *See, e.g.,* DONALD CRITCHLOW, INTENDED CONSEQUENCES: BIRTH CONTROL, ABORTION, AND THE FEDERAL GOVERNMENT IN MODERN AMERICA 14–24 (1999); JAMES CROW, BASIC CONCEPTS IN POPULATION, QUANTITATIVE, AND EVOLUTIONARY GENETICS 6–10 (1986); Ira Carmen, *Human Gene Therapy: A Biopolitical Overview and Analysis,* 4 HUM. GENE THERAPY 187 (1993); John Fletcher, *Ethical Aspects of Genetic Controls: Designed Genetic Changes in Man,* 285 NEW ENG. J. MED. 776 (1971); E. Joshua Rosenkranz, *Custom Kids and the Moral Duty to Genetically Engineer our Children,* 2 HIGH TECH. L.J. 1 (1987); Robert Wilson, *Environmental Regulation of the Human Gene Pool as a Genetic Commons,* 5 NYU ENVTL. L.J. 833 (1996). PATRICIA SPALLONE, BEYOND CONCEPTION: THE NEW POLITICS OF REPRODUCTION 135, 141–42 (1989).

161. SPALLONE, *supra* note 160, at 143. *See, e.g.,* RICHARD HERRNSTEIN & CHARLES MURRAY, THE BELL CURVE: INTELLIGENCE AND CLASS STRUCTURE IN AMERICAN LIFE (1994). *See generally* MAREK KOHN, THE RACE GALLERY: THE RETURN OF RACIAL SCIENCE (1996); WILLIAM TUCKER, THE SCIENCE AND POLITICS OF RACIAL RESEARCH (1994); Lombardo, *supra* note 36, at 809–24; Larry Palmer, *Genetic Health and Eugenics Precedents: A Voice of Caution,* 30 FLA. ST. U. L. REV. 237 (2003); Rushton, *supra* note 36; Paul Weindling, *The Survival of Eugenics in 20th-Century Germany,* 52 AM. J. HUM. GENETICS 643 (1993).

162. COREA, *supra* note 62, at 19–20; Phillips, *supra* note 28, at 5. *See, e.g.,* JOEL COHEN, HOW MANY PEOPLE CAN THE EARTH SUPPORT? (1995); FORD FOUNDATION, REPRODUCTIVE HEALTH: A STRATEGY FOR THE 1990s—A PROGRAM PAPER OF THE FORD FOUNDATION (1991); AL GORE, EARTH IN BALANCE: ECOLOGY AND THE HUMAN SPIRIT 307 (1992); ROBERT HARDAWAY, POPULATION, LAW, AND THE ENVIRONMENT (1994); STANLEY JOHNSON, WORLD POPULATION—TURNING THE TIDE: THREE DECADES OF PROGRESS (1994); DONALD KAUFMAN & CECILIA FRANZ, BIOSPHERE 2000: PROTECTING OUR GLOBAL ENVIRONMENT 138–39 (1993); GEORGE MOFFETT, CRITICAL MASSES: THE GLOBAL POPULATION CHALLENGE (1994); POPULATION—THE COMPLEX REALITY: A REPORT OF THE POPULATION SUMMIT OF THE WORLD'S SCIENTIFIC ACADEMIES (Francis Graham-Smith ed. 1994); NAFIS SADIK, THE STATE OF WORLD POPULATION: CHOICES FOR THE NEW CENTURY (1990); UNITED NATIONS POPULATION FUND, POPULATION AND SUSTAINABLE DEVELOPMENT: FIVE YEARS AFTER RIO (1997); Diana Babor, *Population Growth and Reproductive Rights in International Human Rights Law,* 14 CONN. J. INT'L L. 83 (1999); John Hall, *Negative Population Growth: Why We Must, and How We Could, Achieve It,* POPULATION & ENVT., Sept. 1996, at 65; Julie Mertus & Simon Heller, *Norplant Meets the New Eugenicists: The Impermissibility of Coerced Contraception,* 11 ST. L.U. L. REV. 359 (1992).

163. SPALLONE, *supra* note 160, at 141; TONE, *supra* note 66, at 211–12. Pincus, of course, was not the only person involved in developing the contraceptive pill. *See* CARL DJERASSI, THE PILL, PYGMY CHIMPS, AND DEGAS' WHORES (1992); LARA MARKS, SEXUAL CHEMISTRY: AN INTERNATIONAL HISTORY OF THE PILL (2001); TONE, *supra* note 66, at 203–31; Irwin Winter, *Industrial Pressure and the Population Problem—The FDA and the Pill,* 212 JAMA 1067 (1970). Many of the others involved in developing the pill were also driven by concern over the "population explosion." PAUL VAUGHAN, THE PILL ON TRIAL 9 (1972); TONE, *supra,* at 207–08; ELIZABETH SIEGEL WATKINS, ON THE PILL: A SOCIAL HISTORY OF ORAL CONTRACEPTIVES, 1950–1970, at 19 (1998).

164. *See generally* JUDITH BOSS, THE BIRTH LOTTERY: PRENATAL DIAGNOSIS AND SELECTIVE ABORTION 139–42 (1993).

165. LEON KASS, TOWARD A MORE NATURAL SCIENCE 85 (1985).

166. *See* Stump v. Sparkman, 435 U.S. 349 (1978); Hudson v. Hudson, 373 So. 2d 310 (Ala. 1979); *In re* C.D.M., 627 P.2d 607 (Alaska 1981); *In re* Valerie N., 707 P.2d 760 (Cal. 1985); *In re* A.W., 637 P.2d 366 (Colo. 1981); *In re* S.C.E., 378 A.2d 144 (Del. Ch. 1977); *In re* Guardianship of Matejski, 419 N.W.2d 576 (Iowa 1988); Wentzel v. Montgomery Gen. Hosp., Inc., 447 A.2d 1244 (Md. 1982), *cert. denied,* 459 U.S. 1147 (1983)

While many American courts today often are reluctant to order the sterilization of the mentally retarded even when a person has requested it, other American courts seem willing to order sterilizations even, in some cases, without statutory authorization.[167] The eugenics move ment is still with us. It made a significant contribution to the emergence of more widespread criticism of the abortion laws as the twentieth century wore on. Before turning to that criticism, however, we pause to consider the relationship of the eugenics movement to women.

# Women and the Eugenics Movement

*I speak in sexual drag.*

—Mary Joe Frug[168]

Today it is customary to decry involuntary sterilization laws as particularly focused on deny-ing reproductive autonomy to women.[169] The overwhelming majority of those subjected to gov-ernment sponsored sterilizations were women or girls, and most of the people making specific

---

; *In re* Moe, 432 N.E.2d 712 (Mass. 1982); *In re* M.K.R., 515 S.W.2d 467 (Mo. 1974); *In re* Penny N., 414 A.2d 541 (N.H. 1980); *In re* Grady, 426 A.2d 467 (N.J. 1981); *In re* D.D., 408 N.Y.S.2d 105 (App. Div. 1978), *appeal dismissed*, 405 N.E. 2d. 233 (N.Y. 1980); *In re* Moore, 221 S.E.2d 307 (N.C. 1976); *In re* Estate of C.W., 640 A.2d 427 (Pa. Super.), *stay granted*. 640 A. 2d. 445 (Pa. Super. 1994), *cert. denied*, 513 U.S. 1183 (1995); *In re* Terwilliger, 450 A.2d 1376 (Pa. Super. 1982); Frazier v. Levi, 440 S.W.2d 393 (Tex. Ct. Civ. App. 1969), *writ denied*; *In re* Guardianship of Hayes, 608 P.2d 635 (Wash. 1980); *In re* Guardianship of Eberhardy, 307 N.W.2d 881 (Wis. 1981). *See generally* MENTAL RETARDATION AND STERILIZATION (Ruth Macklin & Willard Gaylin eds. 1981); Catherine Albiston, *The Social Meaning of the Norplant Condition: Constitutional Consider-ations of Race, Class, and Gender*, 9 BERKELEY WOMEN'S L.J. 9 (1994); American Acad. of Pediatrics, *Steriliza-tion of Women Who Are Mentally Handicapped*, 85 PEDIATRICS 868 (1990); Tracy Ballard, *The Norplant Condi-tion: One Step Forward or Two Steps Back?*, 16 HARV. WOMEN'S L.J. 139 (1993); Darci Elaine Burrell, *The Norplant Solution: Norplant and the Control of African-American Motherhood*, 5 UCLA WOMEN'S L.J. 401 (1995); Janet Ginzberg, *Compulsory Contraception as a Condition of Probation: The Use and Abuse of Norplant*, 58 BROOK. L. REV. 979 (1992); Robert Lee & Derek Morgan, *Sterilization and Mental Handicap: Sapping the Strength of the State?*, 15 J. LAW & SOC'Y 229 (1988); Gerard Letterie & William Fox, *Legal Aspects of Involun-tary Sterilization*, 53 FERTILITY & STERILITY 391 (1990); Rodgers, *supra* note 32, at 145–54; Toni Driver Saun-ders, *Banning Motherhood: An Rx to Combat Child Abuse*, 26 ST. MARY'S L.J. 203 (1994); Scott, *supra* note 112; Steven Spitz, *The Norplant Debate: Birth Control of Women Control?*, 25 COLUM. HUM. RTS. L. REV. 131 (1993); Symposium, *Long-Acting Contraception: Moral Choices, Policy Dilemmas*, 25 HASTINGS CNTR. REP., Jan.–Feb. 1995, at S1; Zumpano-Canto, *supra* note 39, at 107–11.

167. *See* Robert Randal Adler, Note, *Estate of C.W.: A Pragmatic Approach to the Involuntary Sterilization of the Mentally Disabled*, 20 NOVA L. REV. 1323 (1996); Steven Cleveland, Note, *Sterilization of the Mentally Dis-abled: Applying Error Cost Analysis to the "Best Interest" Inquiry*, 86 GEO. L.J. 137 (1997); Judy Derouin, Note, In re Guardianship of *Eberhardy: The Sterilization of the Mentally Retarded*, 1982 WIS. L. REV. 1199; Richard Estacio, Comment, *Sterilization of the Mentally Disabled in Pennsylvania: Three Generations without Legislative Guidance Are Enough*, 92 DICK. L. REV. 409 (1988); Alan Munro, Note, *The Sterilization Rights of Mental Re-tardates*, 39 WASH. & LEE L. REV. 207 (1982); Scott, *supra* note 112, at 817–24; Sherlock & Sherlock, *supra* note 66; P. Marcos Sokkapa, *Sterilization Petitions: Developing Judicial Guidelines*, 44 MONT. L. REV. 127 (1983).

168. MARY JOE FRUG, POSTMODERN LEGAL FEMINISM 229 (1992).

169. *See, e.g.*, MARTHA WARD, POOR WOMEN, POWERFUL MEN: AMERICA'S GREAT EXPERIMENT IN FAMILY PLANNING (1986); Roberta Cepko, *The Involuntary Sterilization of Women*, 8 BERKELEY WOMEN'S L.J. 122 (1993); Goldhar, *supra* note 51; Lucille Wolf & Donald Zarifas, *Parents' Atittudes toward Sterilization of Their Mentally Retarded Children*, 87 AM. J. MENTAL DEFICIENCY 122, 126 (1982); Zumpano-Canto, *supra* note 39, at 103–07.

decisions about whom to sterilize were men. Yet historically, both in Britain and in the United States, the eugenics movement was strongly linked with those who supported women's equality over a broad range of issues.[170] And the eugenics movement was also strongly linked to the more radical feminists of the early twentieth century. Half of the members and one-fourth of the officers of the British Eugenics Society were women,[171] as were as many as three-fourths of the "field workers" of the American movement.[172] These women came to the eugenics movement out of organized opposition to child labor, out of involvement in organized movements for promoting better institutional care for the retarded and mentally ill or of orphans, from the birth control movement, and from similar activities.[173] Even blind and deaf Helen Keller supported eugenics to some extent.[174] Furthermore, women predominated among the significant researchers who provided the "scientific" evidence supporting the eugenics movement,[175] in sharp contrast with the near exclusion of women from other areas of scientific research.[176] Apparently, many considered women particularly suited to investigate the mysteries of birth, and besides they would work for less pay.

The American eugenics movement played a dominant role in shaping the birth control movement in the United States, helping to define the activities of Margaret Sanger's then illegal birth control clinics.[177] The Arizona clinics were typical. Those clinics, founded by Barry Goldwater's mother, were explicitly targeted at Mexican-Americans.[178] As the Arizona experience suggests, the Anglo-American eugenics movement was overtly racist, with its academic leaders postulating that different ethnic groups were genetically distinct and could only deteriorate through "interbreeding."[179] Nationally, Sanger's American Birth Control League welcomed Lothrop Stoddard as a member of its Board of Directors.[180] Stoddard was a Harvard eugenicist whose wrote books on *The Rising Tide of Color against White World Supremacy* and *Revolt against Civilization: The Menace of the Underman..*[181]

Margaret Sanger, admired by many as the founding mother of the American birth control

170. GORDON, *supra* note 17, at 110, 126; KEVLES, *supra* note 28, at 39, 54–55, 64; Garland Allen, *Eugenics Record Office at Cold Springs Harbor, 1910–1940,* 2 OSIRIS 2d 225, 234–36 (1986); Larson, *supra* note 97, at 119; Nicole Hahn Rafter, *Introduction,* in WHITE TRASH: THE EUGENIC FAMILY STUDIES, 1877–1913, at 1, 20–26 (Nicole Hahn Rafter ed. 1988).

171. KEVLES, *supra* 28, at 64.

172. Allen, *supra* note 35, at 241; Rafter, *supra* note 170, at 20–21.

173. *See, e.g.,* JANE ADDAMS, A NEW CONSCIENCE AND AN ANCIENT EVIL 130–31 (1912). *See generally* CARMIN LINDIG, THE PATH FROM THE PARLOR: LOUISIANA WOMEN, 1829–1920, at 60–62, 110–18 (1985); Larson, *supra* note 97, at 122–28.

174. MATTHEW PERNICK, THE BLACK STORK: EUGENICS AND THE DEATH OF "DEFECTIVE" BABIES IN AMERICAN MEDICINE AND MOTION PICTURES SINCE 1915, at 55 (1996).

175. *See* H.H. Goddard, *The Binet Tests in Relation to Immigrants,* 18 J. PSYCHO-AESTHETICS 105, 106 (1913). *See generally* KEVLES, *supra* note 28, at 39, 220; Allen, *supra* note 35, at 241; Larson, *supra* note 97, at 121; Rafter, *supra* note 170, at 21.

176. *See* DANIEL KEVLES, THE PHYSICISTS: THE HISTORY OF A SCIENTIFIC COMMUNITY IN MODERN AMERICA 202–07 (1987); Margaret Rossiter, *"Women's Work" in Science, 1880–1910,* 71 ISIS 381 (1980).

177. *See, e.g.,* Margaret Sanger, *Birth Control and Racial Betterment,* BIRTH CONTROL REV., Feb. 1919, at 11; Sanger, *supra* note 17. *See generally* GORDON, *supra* note 17, at 207, 273–90, 303–12; PICKENS, *supra* note 28, at 85, 93; TONE, *supra* note 69, at 139–48; Larson, *supra* note 97; Davis, *supra* note 100; Edward Larson, *The Enactment of Eugenic Legislation in Georgia,* 46 J. HIST. MED. 44 (1991); Phillips, *supra* note 28, at 4–5.

178. ROBERT ALAN GOLDBERG, BARRY GOLDWATER 52 (1995).

179. *See, e.g.,* GUYER, *supra* note 18, at 296–98; PAUL POPPENOE & ROSWELL JOHNSON, APPLIED EUGENICS 294–97 (1925); R. Mcg. Carruth, *Race Degeneration: What Can We Do to Check It?,* 7 N. ORLEANS MED. & SURGICAL J. 188 (1919). *See generally* KENNY, *supra* note 28, at 190–91; TONE, *supra* note 66, at 211–12.

180. Davis, *supra* note 100, at 247.

181. STODDARD, *supra* note 27, at 21; STODDARD, TIDE OF COLOR, *supra* note 43.

movement, was as racist as any other leader of the birth control and eugenics movements.[182] She considered poor people unfit to be part of society, particularly if they were of a different race. She favored mandatory sterilization of the unfit, lamenting only that the practice would be too seldom used to rid society of the offspring of such persons.[183] Her attitude towards the "unfit" was caught in her statement that "[t]he most merciful thing that the large family does to one of its infant members is to kill it."[184] Two years after writing that charming comment, she wrote:

> Organized charity is itself the symptom of a malignant social disease. Those vast, complex, interrelated organizations aiming to control and to diminish the spread of misery and destitution and all the menacing evils that spring out of this sinisterly fertile soil, are the surest sign that our civilization has bred, is breeding and is perpetuating constantly increasing numbers of defectives, delinquents, and dependents. My criticism, therefore, is not directed at the "failure" of philanthropy, but rather at its success.... Such philanthropy...encourages the healthier and more normal sections of the world to shoulder the burden of unthinking and indiscriminate fecundity of others; which brings with it, as I think the reader must agree, a dead weight of human waste. Instead of decreasing and aiming to eliminate the stocks that are most detrimental to the future of the race and the world, it tends to render them to a menacing degree dominant.[185]

Sanger's attitude permeated the whole birth control movement. We have already noted the motivation behind the Arizona birth control clinics.[186] The first publicly funded birth control clinics in the United States were established in the South in the 1930s in order to lower the birthrate among African-Americas.[187] The Birth Control Federation of America (the predecessor to Planned Parenthood) established a "Negro Project" in 1939.[188] This project was designed to reach a group whom even W.E.B. Dubois described as "the mass of ignorant Negroes [who] still breed carelessly and disastrously, with the result that the increase among Negroes, even more than among whites, is from that portion of the population least intelligent and fit, and least able to rear children properly."[189]

At about the same time, the Tuskegee program began. The program left poor African-American men, who been infected with syphilis, untreated so the attending physicians could research the progress of the disease.[190] The program, under which the men were not informed that they were not being treated, lasted from 1932 to 1972, leading to sterility and death. At the same time, many African-American women were being pressured or even coerced into "consenting" to sterilization. Yet even in the 1970s, Planned Parenthood (and NARAL) opposed the efforts of the Committee to End Sterilization Abuse.[191] Perhaps as many as 100,000 to 150,000 poor women

---

182. *See, e.g.,* Margaret Sanger, The Pivot of Civilization 114–16, 177–78 (1922) ("Sanger, Pivot"); Sanger, *supra* note 29, at 34, 89. *See generally* Gordon, *supra* note 17, at 274–90, 304, 332–33; George Grant, Grand Illusions: The Legacy of Planned Parenthood (1988); Olasky, *supra* note 28, at 257–59; Tannahill, *supra* note 46, at 415; Davis, *supra* note 100, at 248; Dorothy Roberts, *Racism and Patriarchy in the Meaning of Motherhood,* 1 J. Gender & L. 1, 31–32 (1993).

183. Sanger, Pivot, *supra* note 181, at 101–02.

184. Sanger, *supra* note 29, at 63.

185. Sanger, Pivot, *supra* note 181, at 108, 116–17.

186. See the text *supra* at notes 177–78.

187. Gordon, *supra* note 17, at 314–29.

188. Ward, *supra* note 169; Loretta Ross, *African-American Women and Abortion,* in Abortion Wars: A Half Century of Struggle, 1950–2000, at 161, 168–72 (Rickie Solinger ed. 1998).

189. W.E.B. DuBois, *Black Folk and Birth Control,* Birth Control Rev., June 1932, at 166.

190. James Jones, Bad Blood: The Tuskegee Syphilis Experiment (1981); Larry Palmer, Susceptible to Kindness: Miss Evers' Boys and the Tuskegee Syphilis Study (1994).

191. Roberts, *supra* note 181, at 33. *See generally* Downs v. Sawtelle, 574 F.2d 1 (1st Cir.) (alleged conspiracy to sterilize a deaf mute against her will), *cert. denied,* 439 U.S. 910 (1978); Walker v. Pierce, 560 F.2d 609 (4th Cir. 1977) (alleged conspiracy to sterilize a woman because of her race and number of children); Cox v. Stanton, 529 F.2d 47 (4th Cir. 1975); Committee to End Sterilization Abuse, Sterilization Abuse: The

were sterilized in Alabama alone in the 1970s.[192] Today, voluntary sterilization is probably our most common form of birth control.[193] Our history, however, cautions us to take care to assure that such sterilizations really are voluntary.

FACTS (1976); CRITCHLOW, *supra* note 160, at 144–46; THOMAS LITTLEWOOD, THE POLITICS OF POPULATION CONTROL 107–33 (1977); THOMAS SHAPIRO, POPULATION CONTROL POLITICS: WOMEN, STERILIZATION, AND REPRODUCTIVE CHOICES (1985); Herbert Aptheker, *Sterilization, Experimentation, and Imperialism,* 53 POL. AFF. 48 (1974); Joseph Baker, Note, *Sexual Sterilization—Constitutional Validity of Involuntary Sterilization and Consent Determinative of Voluntariness,* 40 MO. L. REV. 509 (1975); Nadine Brozan, *The Volatile Issue of Sterilization Abuse: A Tangle to Accusations and Remedies,* N.Y. TIMES, Dec. 9, 1977, at B14; Patricia Donovan, *Sterilization and the Poor: Two Views on the Need for Protection from Abuse,* 5 FAM. PLANNING PERSPECTIVES 28 (1976); Claudia Dreifus, *Sterilizing the Poor,* THE PROGRESSIVE, Nov. 1975, at 13; Dick Grosboll, *Sterilization Abuse: Current State of the Law and Remedies for Abuse,* 10 GOLDEN GATE U. L. REV. 1147 (1980); Bertha Hernandez, *Chicanas and the Issue of Involuntary Sterilization: Reforms Needed to Protect Informed Consent,* 3 CHICANO L. REV. 3 (1976); Emily Diamond, Note, *Coerced Sterilization under Federally Funded Family Planning Programs,* 11 NEW ENG. L. REV. 589 (1976); Rosalind Pollack Petchesky, *Reproduction, Ethics, and Public Policy: The Federal Sterilization Regulations,* 9 HASTINGS CTR. REP. no5, at 29 (Oct. 1979); Jack Slater, *Sterilization: Newest Threat to the Poor,* EBONY, Oct. 1973, at 150. As is so often the case, this is not just an American problem. *See* Stephan Buckley, *Second Thoughts on Sterilization: Many Anguished Brazilian Women Want to Reverse Once Popular Procedure,* WASH. POST, Dec. 23, 2000, at A16.

192. *See* Relf v. Weinberger, 372 F. Supp. 1196, 1199 (D.D.C. 1974), *vacated,* 565 F.2d 722 (D.C. Cir. 1977). *See also* William Raspberry, *"Agonizing Questions" on Sterilization,* WASH. POST, July 13, 1973, at A29; George Will, *Sterilization and "Population Improvement,"* WASH. POST, July 23, 1973, at A22.

193. *Off the Pill: Sterilization Now First in Birth Control, Study Says,* PHILA. INQUIRER, Sept. 14, 1983, at 3A. *See also* Peter Cooney, *Birth Control: In Canada, Sterilization Is Preferred,* PHILA. INQUIRER, Apr. 20, 1986, at 9F. This represents a dramatic turn around, for less than a decade earlier voluntary sterilization was still illegal in some states and the law also often gave one's spouse a veto over one's decision to sterilize oneself. *See* Holton v. Crozer-Chester Med. Ctr., 560 F.2d 575 (3rd Cir. 1977) (ordering trial of claim that a hospital's refusal to perform sterilization without spousal consent violates the affected persons civil rights); Taylor v. St. Vincent's Hosp., 523 F.2d 75 (9th Cir. 1975) (a hospital that refuses to perform sterilizations on religious or moral grounds does not violate the civil rights of someone seeking a voluntary sterilization), *cert. denied,* 424 U.S. 948 1976; Chrisman v. Sisters of St. Joseph, 506 F.2d 308 (9th Cir. 1974) (same); Allen v. Sisters of St. Joseph, 490 F.2d 81 (5th Cir. 1974) (court declined to order the defendant's hospital to perform a sterilization); Hathaway v. Worcester City Hosp., 475 F.2d 701 (1st Cir. 1973) (a hospital violates constitutional rights when it refuses do perform sterilizations while performing other surgeries no more dangerous than sterilization); McCabe v. Nassau Cty. Med. Ctr., 453 F.2d 698 (2nd Cir. 1971) (trial allowed for constitutional claim against a county hospital that denied sterilizations through an age-parity formula); Voe v. Califano, 434 F. Supp. 1058 (D. Conn. 1977) (no constitutional violation from a denial of Medicaid coverage for a sterilization for someone under 20 years of age even though the petitioner had already had 10 pregnancies); Doe v. Temple, 409 F. Supp. 899 (E.D. Va. 1976) (doctors' refusal to perform sterilization without spousal consent violates the affected persons civil rights); Padin v. Fordham Hosp., 392 F. Supp. 447 (S.D.N.Y. 1975) (no constitutional violation from rescheduling a sterilization operation so long as this did not amount to a refusal to do the operation); Jessin v. Shasta Cty., 79 Cal. Rptr. 359 (Ct. App. 1969) (voluntary sterilization is legal); Ponter v. Ponter, 342 A.2d 574 (N.J. Ch. 1975) (a woman has a constitutional right to obtain a sterilization without the consent of her husband); Murray v. Vandevander, 522 P.2d 302 (Okla. 1974) (no liability to a husband for sterilizing of wife without the husband's consent); Parker v. Rampton, 497 P.2d 848 (Utah 1972) (voluntary sterilization is not prohibited). *See also* ADVANCES IN VOLUNTARY STERILIZATION (Marilyn Schima *et al.* ed. 1974); BEHAVIORAL-SOCIAL ASPECTS OF CONTRACEPTIVE STERILIZATION (Sidney Newman & Zanvel Klein eds. 1978); EVAN MCLEOD WYLIE, ALL ABOUT VOLUNTARY STERILIZATION: THE REVOLUTIONARY NEW BIRTH-CONTROL METHOD FOR MEN AND WOMEN (1977); Baker, *supra* note 191, at 520–26; Phyllis Beck & Carole Soskis, *Sterilization in Pennsylvania,* 54 TEMPLE L.Q. 213 (1981); William Challener, jr., *The Law of Sexual Sterilization in Pennsylvania,* 57 DICK. L. REV. 298 (1953); Rebecca Citron, *A Spouse's Right to Marital Dissolution Predicated on the Partner's Contraceptive Surgery,* 23 N.Y.L. SCH. L. REV. 99 (1977); Hulane Evans George, *Sterilization: Who Says No?,* 29 MERCER L. REV. 821 (1978); Jaroslav Hulko, *Current Status of Elective Sterilization in the United States,* 28 FERTILITY & STERILITY 515 (1977); Kathleen Davison Lebeck, *Voluntary Sterilization in New Mexico: Who Must Consent?,* 7 N.M. L. REV. 121 (1976); Kent Greenawalt, *Criminal Law and Population Control,* 24 VAND. L. REV. 465, 475–79 (1971); Charles Kindegran, *State Power over Human Fertility and Individual Liberty,* 23 HASTINGS L.J. 1401 (1972); Robert Kouri, *The Legality of Purely Contraceptive Ster-*

# Early Criticism of Abortion Laws
# and the Soviet Reform

*[A]ll sane and intelligent men and women agree that anything even approaching infanticide is nothing short of a crime, and that abortion, except for the purpose of saving the life of the mother, is practically murder.*

—H.W. Long[194]

The eugenics movement provided the first widespread and sustained espousal of abortion as a positive good. The eugenics movement did not, however, advocate individual choice regarding abortion, but social choice regarding who should and should not have children. Even in Nazi Germany, where compulsory sterilization and compulsory abortion were more common than anywhere else in the world, voluntary abortion remained generally illegal and difficult to obtain.[195] Advocacy of voluntary abortion remained almost unknown at the opening of the twentieth century, at least in the English speaking world.

A criticism of abortion restrictions appeared as early as 1865 in a posthumous edition of Taylor's *The Principles and Practice of Medical Jurisprudence*.[196] Taylor himself, however, had always strongly and unequivocally condemned abortions.[197] Other physicians in Britain and America also emerged in the early years of the twentieth century as supporters of an easing of restrictions on abortion, but without attracting a great deal of attention.[198] Dr. William Robinson in 1911 gave one of the first public talks in the United States by a physician openly supporting freedom of choice for abortion. His talk, however, was not published for more than 20 years after he delivered it.[199] His earlier published work had argued that abortion was "one of the

---

*ilization*, 7 REVUE DE DROIT DE UNIVERSITÉ DE SHERBROOKE 1 (1976); John Lombard, *Vasectomy*, 10 SUFFOLK L. REV. 25 (1975); W. Douglas Myers, *A Constitutional Evaluation of Statutory and Administrative Impediments to Voluntary Sterilization*, 14 J. FAM. L. 14 (1975); James McKenzie, *Contraceptive Sterilization: The Doctor, the Patient, and the U.S. Constitution*, 25 U. FLA. L. REV. 327 (1973); Peter Paterson, *Sterilization—His or Hers?*, 2 MED. J. AUSTRAL. 571 (1977); Harriet Pilpel, *Voluntary Sterilization: A Human Right*, 7 COLUM. HUM. RTS. L. REV. 105 (1975); G. Sharpe, *Consent and Sterilization*, 118 CAN. MED. ASS'N J. 591 (1978); Richard & Robert Sherlock, *Voluntary Sterilization: The Case for Regulation*, 1976 UTAH L. REV. 115; Elliott Siegall, *The Medical File: Surgical Sexual Sterilization*, 8 TRIAL no. 4, at 57 (July–Aug. 1972); Peter Tierny, *Voluntary Sterilization: A Necessary Alternative?*, 4 FAM. L.Q. 373 (1970). *See also* Edmund Kellogg, *The World's Laws Concerning Voluntary Sterilization for Family Planning Purposes*, 5 CAL. W. INT'L L.J. 72 (1974); Jan Stepan & Edmund Kellogg, *The World's Laws Concerning Voluntary Sterilization for Family Planning Purposes*, 5 CAL. W. INT'L L.J. 72 (1974); Charles Westoff & Elise Jones, *Contraception and Sterilization in the United States, 1965–1975*, 9 FAM. PLANNING PERSPECTIVES 153 (1977).

194. H.W. LONG, SANE SEX LIFE AND SANE SEX LIVING 120 (1919)

195. PETCHESKY, *supra* note 28, at 243; ROSENBLATT, *supra* note 130, at 80; Karen Crabbs, *The German Abortion Debate: Stumbling Block to Unity*, 6 FLA. J. INT'L L. 213, 217 (1991); Funk, *supra* note 130, at 35–36; Michael Mattern, Note, *German Abortion Law: The Unwanted Child of Reunification*, 13 LOY. L.A. INT'L & COMP. L.J. 643, 655–56 (1991). *See also* Koonz, *supra* note 123, at 70 (voluntary sterilizations difficult to obtain in Nazi Germany).

196. A.S. TAYLOR, THE PRINCIPLES AND PRACTICE OF MEDICAL JURISPRUDENCE 790–94 (8th ed. 1865).

197. ALFRED TAYLOR, MANUAL OF MEDICAL JURISPRUDENCE 594–95 (1st Am. ed.1844).

198. 6 HAVELOCK ELLIS, STUDIES IN THE PSYCHOLOGY OF SEX 588, 601–10 (1913); CHARLES MERCIER, CRIME AND CRIMINALS 196–97 (1918); Louis Blanchard, *The Business of Abortion*, 100 COLLIERS 37 (July 1938). *See generally* GORDON, *supra* note 17, at 173–78; KERN, *supra* note 129, at 165; OLASKY, *supra* note 28, at 234–40.

199. W.J. ROBINSON, THE LAW AGAINST ABORTION (1933) ("ROBINSON, AGAINST ABORTION"). *See also* William Robinson, *Abortion and Infanticide*, 39 AM. MED. 70 (1933).

most terrible evils of our society" because it remained so inordinately dangerous for the woman.[200] In the same passage, Robinson had favored contraception as a preventative for abortion. Thus his early published comments on abortion as a potential benefit to women remained ambiguous.[201]

More typical was the attitude expressed in popular medical books advocating liberal attitudes towards sexuality, including support for contraception (also an illegal activity at the time), while strongly condemning abortion. For example, Dr. H.W. Long wrote in his *Sane Sex Life and Sane Sex Living*:

> On this point, let it be said that all sane and intelligent men and women agree that anything even approaching infanticide is nothing short of a crime, and that abortion, except for the purpose of saving the life of the mother, is practically murder. But, while this is all true, to prevent the contact of two germs which, if permitted to unite, would be liable to result in a living human form, is *quite another affair*.[202]

Long advocated family planning and sex for pleasure, hardly a conservative position at the time. Furthermore, the book was published by the Eugenics Publishing Co., again suggesting that one could be a "liberal" on sexual and reproductive issues and still adamantly oppose abortion. Such an attitude had been quite common in the later years of the nineteenth century and appears to have continued well into the twentieth century.[203] Some commentators have concluded that this set of attitudes prevailed among Americans until the 1960s.[204]

The common therapeutic exceptions did give doctors some measure of control over authorizing abortions, although that authority was used sparingly in England and America before the 1930s.[205] The challenge to the consensus on abortion policy mostly came not from the medical profession nor from women's movements, but from the political left. The nearly worldwide consensus on the prohibition of abortion broke apart on November 18, 1920, when the Soviet government in Russia legalized abortion on demand.[206]

---

200. ROBINSON, *supra* note 27, at 121–22.

201. *Id.* at 133, 224–25. *See also* M. Rabinowitz, *End Results of Criminal Abortion: With Comments on Its Present Status,* 100 N.Y. MED. J. 897 (1914). *See generally* OLASKY, *supra* note 28, at 235.

202. LONG, *supra* note 193, at 120 (emphasis in the original).

203. *See* ANNIE BESANT, THE LAW OF POPULATION: IT CONSEQUENCES, AND ITS BEARING UPON HUMAN CONDUCT AND MORALS (1878); D.M. BENNETT, ANTHONY COMSTOCK AND HIS CAREER OF CRIME AND CRUELTY 1068 (1878); EDWARD BOND FOOTE, THE RADICAL REMEDY IN SOCIAL SCIENCE 89 (1886); MARGARET SANGER, MOTHERHOOD IN BONDAGE 394–96 (1928); Gretta Palmer, *Not to Be Born,* 38 PICTORIAL REV. 24 (Feb. 1937).

204. *See* NANETTE DAVIS, FROM CRIME TO CHOICE xiii, 3–4 (1985).

205. JOSEPH DELEE, THE PRINCIPLES AND PRACTICES OF OBSTETRICS 1045 (2nd ed. 1916); FOOTE, *supra* note 202, at 24–25; STORER & HEARD, *supra* note 16, at 102–03; HENRY WRIGHT, MARRIAGE AND PARENTAGE; OR, THE PROTECTIVE ELEMENT IN MAN, AS A MEANS TO HIS ELEVATION AND HAPPINESS 133 (2nd ed. 1855); H.J. Boldt, *The Treatment of Abortion,* 46 JAMA 791 (1906); W.C. Bowers, *Justifiable Artificial Abortion and Induced Premature Labor,* 33 JAMA 568 (1899); Frank Higgins, *The Propriety, Indications and Methods for the Termination of Pregnancy,* 43 JAMA 1531 (1904); Christian Johnson, *Therapeutic Abortion,* 9 ST. PAUL MED. J. 240 (1907); E.S. McKee, *Abortion,* 24 AM. J. OBSTET. & DISEASES OF WOMEN & CHILDREN 1331, 1333–34 (1891); Paul Titus, *A Statistical Study of a Series of Abortions Occurring in the Obstetrical Department of the John Hopkins Hospital,* 65 AM. J. OBSTET. & DISEASES OF WOMEN & CHILDREN 960 (1912). *See also* Clarke v. People, 16 Colo. 511 (1891); Scott v. People, 30 N.E. 329 (Ill. 1892); Beasley v. People, 89 Ill. 571 (1878); State v. Moore, 25 Iowa 128 (1868); Bradford v. People, 20 Hun. 309 (N.Y. Sup. Ct. 1880); State v. Clements, 14 P. 410 (Or. 1887); Hatchard v. State, 48 N. W. 380 (Wis. 1891). *See generally* GROSSBERG, *supra* note 17, at 183–84; ANGUS McLAREN, BIRTH CONTROL IN NINETEENTH-CENTURY ENGLAND 240–41, 244–45 (1978); REAGAN, *supra* note 22, at 61–70; Judith Walzer Leavitt, *The Growth of Medical Authority, Technology, and Morals in Turn-of-the-Century Obstetrics,* 1 MED. ANTHROPOLOGY Q. 230 (1987).

206. *See generally* DANIEL CALLAHAN, ABORTION: LAW, CHOICE, AND MORALITY 220–23 (1970); GERMAIN GRISEZ, ABORTION: THE MYTHS, THE REALITIES, AND THE ARGUMENTS 194–200 (1970); TAUSSIG, *supra* note

The Russian action expressed the views of "feminists of the Left."[207] Feminism with a distinctly Marxist cast originated in Germany, seeking—among other goals—to free women from enforced motherhood with its resulting virtual incarceration in the home.[208] Some early American socialists—including the aforementioned Dr. Robinson—argued that birth control was a necessary defense against the exploitation of the working classes under capitalism because the oversupply of workers depressed wages and overly large families overburdened the capacity of workers to support their families in the face of the depressed wages and also served to "imprison" mothers in childcare.[209] Socialism, however, never had much of an impact on the United States, at least not directly. Furthermore, at the time most feminist leaders then favored strengthening the position of women in the home rather than making it possible for them to work outside the home.[210] The notion that a goal of social reform should be to free women to work outside the home broke dramatically with mainstream social thought among reformist groups of the time.

The belief that women should be liberated from confinement to the home spread quickly throughout the international socialist movement,[211] finding its principal representative in the United States in Margaret Sanger.[212] Sanger was strongly influenced by the immigrant anarchist Emma Goldman ("Red Emma"). Goldman was prominent in promoting birth control in the

---

26, at 405–20; RICHARD STITES, THE WOMEN'S LIBERATION MOVEMENT IN RUSSIA 367–69, 374, 386–87 (1978); Andrej Popov, *The USSR*, in ABORTION IN THE NEW EUROPE, *supra* note 130, at 267, 269–70, 274–76; Mark Savage, *The Law of Abortion in the Union of Soviet Socialist Republics and the People's Republic of China: Women's Rights in Two Socialist Countries*, 40 STAN. L. REV. 1027 (1988); Eleanora Zielinska, *Recent Trends in Abortion Legislation in Eastern Europe, with Particular Reference to Poland*, 4 CRIM. L.F. 47, 48–51 (Regina Gorzkowska trans. 1993).

207. *See Abolishing Penalties for Abortion*, 74 JAMA 1656 (1920); *Bill to Legalize Abortion in Basel*, 73 JAMA 1095 (1919); *Independent Social Democrats that the Penalties for Abortion Be Removed*,75 JAMA 1283 (1920); *Proposed New Legislation Concerning Abortion*, 78 JAMA 208 (1922). *See generally* GROSSMAN, *supra* note 132; McLAREN, *supra* note 204; ANDREA NYE, FEMINIST THEORIES AND THE PHILOSOPHIES OF MAN 31–72 (paperback ed. 1989); REAGAN, *supra* note 22, at 139–41; USBORNE, *supra* note 10, at 166–67, 217–19; Telman, *supra* note 12, at 101–07.

208. *See* AUGUST BEBEL, WOMEN UNDER SOCIALISM (1904); FRIEDRICH ENGELS, THE ORIGIN OF THE FAMILY, PRIVATE PROPERTY AND THE STATE (1884; reprinted 1972). *See also* EDWARD CARPENTER, LOVE'S COMING OF AGE 60 (1911); 6 ELLIS, *supra* note 197, at 607–09. *See generally* CALLAHAN, *supra* note 205, at 460–68; FLOYD DELL, HOMECOMING 287–88 (1933); RICHARD EVANS, THE FEMINIST MOVEMENT IN GERMANY, 1894–1933 (1976); GORDON, *supra* note 17, at 187–89, 197–236, 249, 266–68; GROSSMAN, *supra* note 132; USBORNE, *supra* note 10, at 159, 180–81; Ann Taylor Allen, *Mothers of the New Generation, Adele Schreiber, Helene Stöcker, and the Evolution of a German Idea of Motherhood*, 20 SIGNS 418 (1985); Nancy Cott, *Early-Twentieth-Century Feminism in Political Context: A Comparative Look at Germany and the United States*, in SUFFRAGE AND BEYOND: INTERNATIONAL FEMINIST PERSPECTIVES 234, 236–37, 241–46 (Caroline Daley & Melanie Nolan eds. 1994); Atina Grossman, *Abortion and Economic Crisis: The 1931 Campaign against 218 in Germany*, 14 NEW GERM. CRITIQUE 119 (1978); Amy Hackett, *Helene Stöcker: Left-Wing Intellectual and Sex Reformer*, in WHEN BIOLOGY BECAME DESTINY, *supra* note 10, at 109; Klein-Schonnefeld, *supra* note 130, at 113–14.

209. *See, e.g.*, VIRGINIA BUTTERFIELD, PARENTAL RIGHTS AND ECONOMIC WRONGS 87 (1906); William Robinson, *The Birth Strike*, 14 INT'L SOCIALIST REV. 404 (Jan. 1914). *See generally* NANCY COTT, THE GROUNDING OF MODERN FEMINISM 60–61 (1987); GORDON, *supra* note 17, at 245–47; J. STANLEY LEMONS, THE WOMAN CITIZEN: SOCIAL FEMINISM IN THE 1920s, at 209–27 (1973); CAROLE McCANN, BIRTH CONTROL POLITICS IN THE UNITED STATES, 1916–1945, at 26–53 (1994); REAGAN, *supra* note 22, at 141–42.

210. *See* Chapter 2, at notes 171–76; Chapter 8, at notes 128–35; and Chapter 10, at notes 198–214.

211. ABORTION IN THE NEW EUROPE, *supra* note 130, at 2, 31, 102; REAGAN, *supra* note 22, at 37.

212. MARGARET SANGER, AUTOBIOGRAPHY 83–96, 108–22 (1938). *See generally* CHESLER, *supra* note 28, at 85–88, 97–99; DAVID GARROW, LIBERTY AND SEXUALITY: THE RIGHT OF PRIVACY AND THE MAKING OF *ROE v. WADE* 10–11 (2nd ed. 1998); GORDON, *supra* note 17, at 213–15, 220–32.

United States until she was deported during the Red Scare of 1920.[213] Despite the socialist origins of the birth control movement, that movement in the United States remained largely composed of professional and propertied people, as the participants themselves recognized in private moments.[214] The failure of birth control to capture the imagination of the working classes mirrored the failure of socialism to wean American workers away from the American dream.

The socialist goal of limiting the number of children a woman would bear so she could be liberated from confinement to the home fit neatly into the need for an enlarged labor force necessary to undertake the industrialization envisaged by the Communists in Russia, although the decree from the Commissariats of Health and Justice legalizing abortion on demand also mentioned improvements in women's health as a goal.[215] The Commissariats further described the decree as a temporary expedient to be repealed as soon as safe, effective, and convenient contraceptive devices could be made widely available. The Soviet government, however, never invested funds in research for such contraceptives and never made such contraceptives available even after they were developed in the West.[216]

Early Soviet support for abortion on demand did not last long. The government and Party began a campaign of anti-abortion propaganda in 1927, and even went so far as to deny anesthesia for abortions.[217] The clinical experience was rather gruesome. While mortality was modest, morbidity rates were high.[218] Abortion enthusiasts tended to ignore morbidity levels, as they often still do.[219] Finally, in 1936 the Soviet government prohibited abortions outright, except to protect the life or health of the mother or to prevent the transmission of hereditary disease.[220] The decree announced two reasons for this change: unhealthy side effects to the mother and the need to strengthen the family. Western commentators, on the other hand, generally concluded that the new decree sought to increase the national population for economic and military reasons.[221]

The 1920 Soviet decree on abortion had a lasting effect internationally, far more so than the decree recriminalizing it, becoming a model praised by leftists and feminists around the world. Most Baltic and Scandinavian nations—with elected left-wing governments—adopted moderately permissive abortion statutes in the 1930s.[222] In Germany, the issue of abortion was wrapped

---

213. ROBERT DRINNON, REBEL IN PARADISE 67, 166–68 (1961); GORDON, *supra* note 17, at 212–13, 217–21, 226, 232–33; NYE, *supra* note 206, at 42, 49–53.

214. GORDON, *supra* note 17, at 235–36, 239–45, 284, 294–302, 316; RICKIE SOLINGER, WAKE UP LITTLE SUSIE: SINGLE PREGNANCY AND RACE BEFORE *ROE V. WADE* 26 (1992).

215. Mark Field, *The Re-Legalization of Abortion in Soviet Russia*, 255 N. ENG. J. MED. 421 (Aug. 30, 1956); Zielinska, *supra* note 205, at 49.

216. Popov, *supra* note 205, at 271–74.

217. GRISEZ, *supra* note 205, at 196; TAUSSIG, *supra* note 26, at 418–20.

218. TAUSSIG, *supra* note 26, at 413–18.

219. *See* BROOKES, *supra* note 17, at 58.

220. Law of May 26, 1936, SBORNIK ZAKONOV SSSR, no. 34, at 309 (1936). *See* HENRY SIGERIST, MEDICINE AND HEALTH IN THE SOVIET UNION 322–23 (1947). *See also* CALLAHAN, *supra* note 205, at 223; GRISEZ, *supra* note 205, at 197–200; GLANVILLE WILLIAMS, THE SANCTITY OF LIFE AND THE CRIMINAL LAW 200 (1957, reprinted 1972); Louis Fisher, *New Soviet Abortion Law*, THE NATION, July 18, 1936, at 65–67, & THE NATION, July 25, 1936, at 97–99; Popov, *supra* note 205, at 270–71, 276–77.

221. HAROLD BERMAN, JUSTICE IN RUSSIA 246, 286 (1950); CALLAHAN, *supra* note 205, at 223; GRISEZ, *supra* note 205, at 198–99; WILLIAMS, *supra* note 219, at 219; Zielinska, *supra* note 205, at 49–50.

222. CALLAHAN, *supra* note 205, at 185–217; GEBHARD *et al.*, *supra* note 22, at 221–32; GRISEZ, *supra* note 195, at 203–06; KENNY, *supra* note 28, at 188–89; ROSENBLATT, *supra* note 130, at 74–76; WILLIAMS, *supra* note 219, at 236–47; Katarina Lindahl, *Sweden*, in ABORTION IN THE NEW EUROPE, *supra* note 130, at 237; Jolanta Plakwicz & Eleonora Zielinska, *Poland*, in ABORTION IN THE NEW EUROPE, *supra*, at 199; Nell Rasmussen, *Denmark*, in ABORTION IN THE NEW EUROPE, *supra*, at 69.

up in the eugenics policies, resulting in a combination of restrictions for "Aryans" and compulsory procedures of "*untermenschen.*"[223] Two Scandinavian nations did not go along with the changes for several decades. Finland did not liberalize its abortion law until 1950.[224] In Norway, the debate opened in 1935, but no new law was enacted until 1960.[225]

In England and the United States, a few recently enfranchised feminists and a few left-leaning physicians, such as Dr. William Robinson,[226] took up the issue of abortion reform during the period between the two World Wars, but with very limited success.[227] The American movement sponsored the studies of Dr. Frederick Taussig, which eventually became highly influential.[228] In the United States, Dr. Robinson finally published his speech calling for reform of the law to allow abortions for limited reasons other than the preservation of the life of the mother.[229] Dr. Abraham Rongy published a similar book, arguing for expansion of the indications for therapeutic abortions.[230] A law student at Columbia University also raised questions about reform of the abortion statutes.[231]

The influence of the Russian example in all this was clear. Robinson and Rongy were both immigrants from Russia who were active in politics.[232] Robinson specifically pointed to the relative safety of abortions in Russia compared to the dangers in the United States as a ground for legalization.[233] Yet even these authors described abortion as a decided evil, albeit a lesser evil than the economic or social destruction of the mother or her family.[234]

Publication of the Robinson and Rongy books failed to provoke any widespread public discussion in the United States. The *New York Times* even refused to allow advertisements for Rongy's book.[235] When Dr. George Glenn introduced a bill in the Colorado legislature in 1939 to legalize abortion in that state, the proposal died quietly, apparently finding little public support even in the birth control movement.[236] The proposal was met with such indifference that historian Leslie Reagan could find no records pertaining to it in the Colorado State Archives.[237]

While sexual role changes became widespread and came unhinged from their origins in the Left both in England and in America, the abortion reform movements in both countries re-

---

223. See the text *supra* at notes 123–47.

224. Marketta Ritamies, *Finland,* in ABORTION IN THE NEW EUROPE, *supra* note 130, at 85.

225. Britta Gulli, *Norway,* in ABORTION IN THE NEW EUROPE, *supra* note 130, at 187, 187–91; Jorun Wiik, *The Abortion Issue, Political Cleavage and the Political Agenda in Norway,* in THE NEW POLITICS OF ABORTION 139 (Joni Lovenduski & Joyce Outshoorn eds. 1986).

226. *See* ROBINSON, AGAINST ABORTION, *supra* note 197; Robinson, *supra* note 208.

227. CARL DEGLER, AT ODDS: WOMEN AND THE FAMILY IN AMERICA FROM THE REVOLUTION TO THE PRESENT 246–47 (1980); GRISEZ, *supra* note 205, at 208–20, 224–29; LAWRENCE LADER, ABORTION 103–08 (1966); PETERSEN, *supra* note 152, at 56–57; R. Sauer, *Attitudes to Abortion in America, 1800–1973,* 28 POP. STUDIES 53, 60–63 (1974).

228. TAUSSIG, *supra* note 22. *See generally* GORDON, *supra* note 17, at 258–59; GRISEZ, *supra* note 205, at 226–28; JONATHAN IMBER, ABORTION AND THE PRIVATE PRACTICE OF MEDICINE 3–12 (1986); OLASKY, *supra* note 28, at 261–62; MARVIN OLASKY, THE PRESS AND ABORTION, 1838–1988, at 70–71 (1988) ("OLASKY, THE PRESS"); REAGAN, *supra* note 22, at 142–43. On Dr. Taussig's advocacy of abortion reform, see TAUSSIG, *supra,* at 444–49.

229. ROBINSON, AGAINST ABORTION, *supra* note 198, at i, 115–19.

230. ABRAHAM RONGY, ABORTION: LEGAL OR ILLEGAL? 200–09 (1933).

231. Thomas Harris, Note, *A Functional Study of Existing Abortion Laws,* 35 COLUM. L. REV. 87 (1935).

232. GORDON, *supra* note 17, at 173–78; REAGAN, *supra* note 22, at 139–40.

233. ROBINSON, AGAINST ABORTION, *supra* note 198, at 26.

234. ROBINSON, *supra* note 27, at 121–22; RONGY, *supra* note 229, at 85, 97–98.

235. A.J. Rongy, *Abortion: The $100,000,000 Racket,* 40 AM. MERCURY 145 (Feb. 1937).

236. REAGAN, *supra* note 22, at 141.

237. *Id.* at 309 n.47.

mained minuscule and, even when—as in England—somewhat successful, remarkably diffident about precisely what reforms they were seeking.[238] Such statements as "Russia is the only
country that has faced abortion intelligently"[239] served to link the idea of abortion reform to the
Left even among moderate feminists in the two countries.[240] Some also linked birth control generally with Soviet Russia.[241] Rather more successful innovations, such as the creation of the
"Children's Bureau" in the federal government of the United States, also came to be seen as
"leftist."

The Children's Bureau was created in the 1920s to promote child welfare in poor areas of the
nation. This office was instrumental in the final displacement of midwives by physicians as well
as in popularizing the need for pre-natal care and knowledge of contraceptives.[242] Physicians
nonetheless often were hostile to the program from fear that the government would take control
of their practice of medicine.[243] The office's most ambitious programs were abolished in 1929
amidst rhetoric appealing to fears of Bolshevism, although some parts of the program were revived during the Depression.[244]

Interest in possible changes in abortion laws was not helped by the steep decline of the
women's movement as a political force in the United States during the years immediately after
women secured the vote.[245] Women's suffrage movements in other countries, upon achieving the
vote, also generally failed to carry on their momentum, and thus often failed to implement their
broader social agendas.[246] In the United States, suffragists who remained active continued to
draw a sharp line between abortion and contraception, opposing abortion even while supporting the dissemination of information about contraceptives and of the contraceptives themselves.

---

238. *See, e.g.,* CLAUD MULLINS, MARRIAGE, CHILDREN AND GOD 150–53 (1933). *See generally* GORDON,
*supra* note 17, at 226; WILLIAMS, *supra* note 219, at 216–19.

239. RACHEL LYNN PALMER & SARAH GREENBERG, FACTS AND FRAUD IN WOMEN'S HYGIENE 163 (1936).
*See also* Louis I. Dublin, *Ten Years of Legalized Abortion in the Soviet Union,* Vol. 21 AM. J. PUB. HEALTH 1043
(1931); S.A. Cosgrove & Patricia Carter, *A Consideration of Therapeutic Abortion,* 48 AM. J. OBSTET. & GYNE-
COLOGY 299, 305 (1944); Paul Lublinsky, *Birth Control in Soviet Russia,* 12 BIRTH CONTROL REV. 142 (1931);
Evelyn Pierce, *Real Rights for Women,* NEW REP., April 11, 1934, at 245; B.B. Tolnai, *Abortions and the Law,*
148 NATION 424 (1939). *See generally* BROOKES, *supra* note 17, at 68; GORDON, *supra* note 17, at 240–41;
GRISEZ, *supra* note 205, at 225; OLASKY, THE PRESS, *supra* note 228, at 69; REAGAN, *supra* note 22, at 142,
163–64, 171–72, 180.

240. BROOKES, *supra* note 17, at 58–60.

241. *See* GORDON, *supra* note 17, at 306, 324.

242. *See* Chapter 7, at notes 286–302.

243. REAGAN, *supra* note 22, at 110–11.

244. *See* THE AUTOBIOGRAPHY OF FLORENCE KELLEY: NOTES OF SIXTY YEARS 31–32 (Kathryn Sklar ed.
1986); DOROTHY BRADBURY, FIVE DECADES OF ACTION: A SHORT HISTORY OF THE CHILDREN'S BUREAU 6–11,
13–14 (1964); LELA COSTIN, TWO SISTERS FOR SOCIAL JUSTICE 130–47 (1983); RICHARD MECKEL, SAVE THE
BABIES: AMERICAN PUBLIC HEALTH REFORM AND THE PREVENTION OF INFANT MORTALITY (1990); MARTHA
MINOW, MAKING ALL THE DIFFERENCE: INCLUSION, EXCLUSION, AND AMERICAN LAW 247–50 (1990); SUSAN
TIFFLIN, IN WHOSE BEST INTEREST? CHILD WELFARE REFORM IN THE PROGRESSIVE ERA 229–47 (1982).

245. *See* MYRA MARX FERREE & BETH HESS, CONTROVERSY AND COALITION: THE NEW FEMINIST MOVE-
MENT ACROSS THREE DECADES OF CHANGE 17–23 (rev. ed. 1994).

246. *See* Johanna Alberti, *Keeping the Candle Burning: Some British Feminists between Two Wars,* in SUF-
FRAGE AND BEYOND: INTERNATIONAL FEMINIST PERSPECTIVES 295 (Caroline Daley & Melanie Nolan eds.
1994); Rawewyn Dalziel, *Presenting the Enfranchisement of New Zealand Women Abroad,* in SUFFRAGE AND BE-
YOND, *supra,* at 42, 52–58; Asunción Lavrin, *Suffrage in South America: Arguing a Difficult Cause,* in SUFFRAGE
AND BEYOND, *supra,* at 184; Susan Margarey, *Why Didn't They Want to Be Members of Parliament? Suffragists
in South Australia,* in SUFFRAGE AND BEYOND, *supra,* at 67; Yukiko Matsukawa & Kaoru Tachi, *Women's Suffrage and Gender Politics in Japan,* in SUFFRAGE AND BEYOND, *supra,* at 171; Karen Offen, *Women, Citizenship,
and Suffrage with a French Twist, 1789–1993,* in SUFFRAGE AND BEYOND, *supra,* at 151, 163–66; Martin Pugh,
*The Impact of Women's Enfranchisement in Britain,* in SUFFRAGE AND BEYOND, *supra,* at 313.

Despite the few isolated calls for abortion reform in the United States, the question of abortion reform in fact largely remained outside of public discourse; it simply did not come up even during the Depression.[247] No less a supporter of women's reproductive choice than Margaret Sanger repeatedly advance her abhorrence of abortion as a major reason for her founding of the organization that evolved into the Planned Parenthood Federation of America.[248] Sanger, a committed socialist, even went so far as to chide Soviet officials regarding their permissive abortion policies when she visited the USSR.[249] Modern feminist historians have been reduced to decrying Sanger's stand on abortion as a sell-out to the prejudices of the male doctors with whom she worked in her birth control activities.[250] More typically, pro-abortion historians praise the politics of Margaret Sanger's work for birth control without mentioning her opposition to abortion.[251] Lawrence Lader, the founder of NARAL and a confidant of Sanger, has contended that Margaret Sanger opposed abortion because she failed to realize that it had become safe for mothers since she had stopped practicing as a nurse some 30 or 40 years before she died.[252] Lader simply ignored Sanger's own statements that abortion was the murder of the infant.

Sanger's opposition to abortion did not arise from the lack of a model for championing abortion as a woman's right. After all, the first issue of the first magazine that she edited included an article arguing for abortion as a woman's right.[253] Even if one were to suppose that Sanger's opposition to abortion arose because she was remarkably ignorant or a dupe (neither in keeping with her character), one then must ask why was her pattern so general among the pioneers of the birth control movement on both sides of the Atlantic. The principal leader of the birth control movement in England, Dr. Marie Stopes, also adamantly opposed abortion, and for the same stated reasons as did Sanger.[254] Even in Germany, birthplace of the left-wing opposition to abortion laws, the great majority of women—or at least of women's associations—opposed any change in the abortion laws.[255]

---

247. GARROW, *supra* note 211, at 273–76; GRISEZ, *supra* note 205, at 225–26; OLASKY, THE PRESS, *supra* note 228, at 68–70.

248. SANGER, *supra* note 211, at 394–96; MARGARET SANGER, MY FIGHT FOR BIRTH CONTROL 133 (1931) ("SANGER, BIRTH CONTROL"); SANGER, *supra* note 29, at 119–22, 129; Margaret Sanger, *Why Not Birth Control Clinics in America?*, 3 BIRTH CONTROL REV. 5, 10 (1919). *See also Birth Control and Abortion*, 8 BIRTH CONTROL REV. 202 (1924); *Prevention or Abortion—Which?*, 7 BIRTH CONTROL REV. 181 (1923); John Vaughan, *Birth Control Not Abortion*, 6 BIRTH CONTROL REV. 183 (1922). *See generally* GARROW, *supra* note 211, at 30–31; REAGAN, *supra* note 22, at 36–37, 134, 141.

249. Joseph Imber, *Abortion Policy and Medical Practice*, SOCIETY, July–Aug. 1990, at 27, 29.

250. *See* DAVIS, *supra* note 28, at 210–19; GORDON, *supra* note 17, at 222–23, 325–26, 368; KENNEDY, *supra* note 28, at 115–21; PETCHESKY, *supra* note 28, at 89–96; DEBORAH RHODE, JUSTICE AND GENDER: SEX DISCRIMINATION AND THE LAW 204–05 (1989); Martha Minow, *Breaking the Law: Lawyers and Clients in Struggles for Social Change*, 52 U. PITT. L. REV. 723, 728–29 (1991). *See also* TONE, *supra* note 66, at 106–09, 117–49.

251. *See, e.g.*, JANET FARRELL BRODIE, CONTRACEPTION AND ABORTION IN NINETEENTH-CENTURY AMERICA 286–91 (1994); BROOKES, *supra* note 17, at 81; JOHN D'EMILIO & ESTELLE FREEDMAN, INTIMATE MATTERS: A HISTORY OF SEXUALITY IN AMERICA 222–23, 231–33, 243–46 (1988); BARBARA MILBAUER & BERT OBRENTZ, THE LAW GIVETH: LEGAL ASPECTS OF THE ABORTION CONTROVERSY 142–56 (1983); CATHERINE WHITNEY, WHOSE LIFE? A BALANCED, COMPREHENSIVE VIEW OF ABORTION FROM ITS HISTORICAL CONTEXT TO THE CURRENT DEBATE 46–48 (1991). When, in 2001, the Virginia legislature enacted a resolution expressing "profound regret" for the state's compulsory sterilizations, the legislature rejected a proposal to link Margaret Sanger to the practice. Pamela Stallsmith, *House "Regrets" Eugenics*, RICHMOND TIMES-DISPATCH, Feb. 3, 2001, at A1.

252. *See* ELLEN MESSER & KATHRYN MAY, BACK ROOMS: VOICES FROM THE ILLEGAL ABORTION ERA 190 (1988) (interview with Lawrence Lader).

253. Dorothy Kelly, *Prevention and the Law*, THE WOMEN REBEL, Apr. 1914, at 10, 10.

254. MARIE STOPES, MOTHER ENGLAND: A CONTEMPORARY HISTORY 183 (1929). *See also* BROOKES, *supra* note 17, at 2–3, 5–8, 80; KENNY, *supra* note 28, at 188, 297–98. On Stopes' career, see RUTH HALL, PASSIONATE CRUSADER: THE LIFE OF MARIE STOPES (1977).

255. KOONZ, *supra* note 142, at 104; USBORNE, *supra* note 10, at 92–93; Telman, *supra* note 12, at 104–05.

All of this was not simply window dressing. In 1928, Chicago birth control clinics turned away 201 clients—16 percent of the women who came to them that year—because the women were seeking abortions, and the clinics would have nothing to do with them.[256] Women going to birth control centers often were greeted with antiabortion messages delivered both by the staff and by posters on the clinic walls.[257] Later still, Dr. Mary Calderone, then the medical director of Planned Parenthood and later one of the strongest supporters of the freedom to abort, described abortion as "the taking of a life" as late as 1960.[258] A pamphlet published by Planned Parenthood came to the same conclusion in 1963.[259]

Morris Ernst and Harriet Pilpel, two attorneys who jointly served as legal counsel to the Planned Parenthood Federation in the 1950s and 1960s, also were on record as seeing abortion as the antithesis of birth control.[260] Yale law professor Tom Emerson, in arguing *Griswold v. Connecticut*[261] on behalf of the Planned Parenthood League of Connecticut (a branch of the Planned Parenthood Federation of America), took care to insist that the claimed right of privacy in that case would have no bearing on constitutionality of abortion laws.[262] In his argument in *Griswold*, Emerson agreed both that abortion involved the taking of a human life while contraception did not, and that abortions took place outside the home and thus did not implicate marital privacy as the prohibition of the marital use of contraceptives did. Emerson's clients, however, raised the possibility of overturning abortion laws with Emerson as soon as the decision in *Griswold* was announced (June 7, 1965).[263] Emerson endorsed that suggestion barely a week later (June 15).[264]

In the space of just a few years, a profound change took place in the legal understanding of *Griswold*. *Griswold* had involved a Connecticut statute banning the sale or use of contraceptives that applied even to married couples. In *Griswold*, the Court spoke of the family as a unit, with collective rights and responsibilities: "Marriage is a coming together for better or worse, hopefully enduring, and intimate to the degree of being sacred. It is an association that promotes a way of life, not causes; a harmony in living, not political faiths; a bilateral loyalty, not commercial or social projects."[265] The centerpiece of the Court's reasoning in *Griswold* was the "notions of privacy surrounding the marital relationship."[266] Barely six years later, the same court spoke not of families, but of individuals: "[T]he marital couple is not an independent entity with a mind and heart of its own, but an association of two individuals each with a separate intellectual and emotional make-up. If the right of privacy means anything, it is the right of the individual, married or single, to be free from unwarranted governmental intrusion into matters so fundamentally affecting a person as the decision whether to bear or beget a child."[267] Gone was any concern about protecting a person as a part

---

256. Rachelle Yarros, *Birth Control Clinics in Chicago*, 2 BIRTH CONTROL REV. 354 (1928).

257. KENNEDY, *supra* note 28, at 191; REAGAN, *supra* note 22, at 85.

258. Mary Calderone, *Illegal Abortion as a Public Health Problem*, 50 AM. J. PUB. HEALTH 948, 951 (1960).

259. H. Ratner, *Is It a Person or a Thing?*, 20, 22 (1963), cited in Charles Rice, *The Dred Scott Case of the Twentieth Century*, 10 HOUS. L. REV. 1059, 1071 n.64 (1973). *See also* PATRICK SHEERAN, WOMEN, SOCIETY, THE STATE, AND ABORTION: A STRUCTURALIST ANALYSIS 75–76 (1987); Neal Devins, *The Countermajoritarian Paradox*, 93 MICH. L. REV. 1433, 1441–42 (1995).

260. Morris Ernst & Harriet Pilpel, *Release from the Comstock Era*, BIRTH CONTROL REV., Dec. 1939, at 24–25.

261. 381 U.S. 479 (1965) (declaring Connecticut's ban on the use of contraceptives by a married couple to be an unconstitutional violation of the "right of privacy").

262. GARROW, *supra* note 211, at 240, citing to *Transcript of Proceedings, Griswold v. Connecticut*, U.S.S.C., Oct. term 1964, # 496.

263. GARROW, *supra* note 211, at 258–59. Chief Justice Warren, at least, foresaw the potential impact on abortion rights of striking down the Connecticut statute in issue, and was troubled by it. *Id.* at 241.

264. *Id.* at 260.

265. 381 U.S. at 486.

266. *Id.*

267. Eisenstadt v. Baird, 405 U.S. 438, 453 (1972).

of a relationship. With this transformation, it would become very easy to conclude that every consideration would be irrelevant apart from the mother's choice whether to abort. In this context, we are now told that freedom to choose abortion is a necessary implication of the *Griswold* decision.[268]

As early as 1942, Dr. Alan Guttmacher, then chief of obstetrics at Baltimore's Sinai Hospital, had called for small changes in the abortion laws in a speech to the annual meeting of the Birth Control Federation of America (the predecessor to the Planned Parenthood Federation) to allow abortions on eugenics grounds.[269] Even his modest call received little support, although a conference on "the abortion problem" in that same year at the New York Academy of Medicine featured several calls for rethinking abortion policy.[270] Several magazine articles appeared about this time suggesting a similar need to reconsider the abortion laws.[271] Planned Parenthood did not change its formal position until 1968,[272] while Betty Friedan was barely able to prevail when she proposed to include support for women's control for their "reproductive lives" in the Women's Bill of Rights drafted by the National Organization of Women in 1967.[273] When even committed activists in the birth control movement would characterize abortion as "murder"[274] or "the antithesis of contraception,"[275] there simply was no room in the United States for open discussion of the possibility of legalizing the practice.

## Attempts at Reform in England and Wales

*Always know, sometimes think its me*
*But you know, I know when its a dream*
*I mean I think I know*
*Ah yes, but its all wrong*
*That is, I think I disagree*

—John Lennon[276]

During the early years of the twentieth century, the English abortion reform movement achieved considerable success, especially compared to the United States. The English movement's most outspoken leader was Canadian-born F.W. Stella Browne, who advocated outright repeal of abortion laws as early as 1915 on the basis of sexual freedom.[277] Feminist historians, like Barbara

---

268. *See, e.g.*, Pro-Life Wisconsin, *PLW Marks Anniversary of Griswold v. Connecticut: Court Decision on Contraception Paved Way for Legalized Abortion*, Pro-Life Wisconsin News, June 7, 2004, available at http://www.prolifewisconsin.org/news_story.asp?id=78.

269. Alan Guttmacher, *The Genesis of Liberalized Abortion in New York: A Personal Insight*, 23 Case-W. Res. L. Rev. 756, 757–58 (1972). *See also* Garrow, *supra* note 211, at 271.

270. The Abortion Problem: Proceedings of the Conference Held under the Auspices of the Committee on Maternal Health, Inc. 50–52, 100–04 (Williams & Wilkins eds. 1944). *See* Olasky, *supra* note 28, at 262–63; Olasky, The Press, *supra* note 228, at 77–78.

271. Vera Connelly, *Death before Birth*, Colllier's, Jan. 22, 1944, at 11; Jane Ward, *What Everyone Should Know about Abortion*, Am. Mercury, Aug. 1941, at 194.

272. American Friends Service Committee, Who Shall Live? 102 (1970).

273. Rosenblatt, *supra* note 130, at 89.

274. *See, e.g.*, Alan Guttmacher, Having a Baby: A Guide to Expectant Parents 15 (1947); Alan Guttmacher, Into This Universe: The Story of Human Birth 46 (1937); Sanger, Birth Control, *supra* note 247, at 133.

275. Ernst & Pilpel, *supra* note 259, at 24–25.

276. John Lennon, *Strawberry Fields Forever* (1967).

277. F.W. Stella Browne, *The Right to Abortion*, in Sexual Reform Congress 178 (Norman Haire ed. 1930) (the proceedings of the Third Congress of the World League for Sexual Reform, held in London, Sept.

Brookes, are fond of making a great deal of Stella Browne's activities,[278] but the fact is that for nearly 20 years thereafter there is very little evidence that anyone was listening. Even Browne's closest supporters on other issues disassociated themselves from her embarrassing stand on abortion.[279]

At the time, many feminists were more hostile to sexuality than supportive of its unencumbered exercise. Christabel Pankhurst summarized this view in her slogan "Votes for women and chastity for men."[280] Stella Browne criticized this attitude as seeking "the reduction, almost the extirpation, of the sex impulse in men."[281] Yet she fared no better with feminists of the older "free love" wing of the movement. Dr. Marie Stopes, one of the leaders of the "free love" movement in England, for example, worked to legalize contraceptives while strongly opposing abortion.[282] Only a few other English left-wing feminists joined Browne's cause.[283]

Browne had no more success outside the feminist movement. Despite the Soviet example, both the British Communist Party and the Labour Party refused to include abortion repeal, or even reform, in their political programs.[284] The leadership of both parties considered birth control to be a "bourgeois" issue. A good many ordinary workers in the Labour party objected because they identified birth control with the eugenics movement, a movement that they saw as devoted to reducing their numbers or even eliminating them from the gene pool.[285] In 1924, a Labourite Minister of Health (John Wheatley) issued a directive forbidding welfare centers and public health clinics from providing birth control under any circumstances.[286] The ban remained in effect until lifted by another Labourite Minister of Health in 1930.[287] Thereafter, the birth control program had a highly varied effect depending largely on local opinion.[288] The situation was worsened by the common policy of dismissing woman doctors from the clinic staffs when they married. Browne's advocacy in England also had almost no impact on the United States.[289]

Finally, even though some physicians performed abortions surreptitiously, the medical profession as a whole, led by its most notable woman physicians, worked to suppress abortion rather than to legitimate it.[290] Doctors who performed abortions did so in shame and fear. Five Ministry of Health reports on maternal mortality between 1918 and 1937 never even mentioned abortion.[291] Finally, the report for 1937 did consider the matter and concluded that 15 percent of the maternal deaths between 1924 and 1933 had resulted from abortions.[292] These deaths arose out of an estimated 90,000 abortions per year (according to abortion proponents).[293] One should note, however, that no attempt was made in this study to distinguish between spontaneous and

---

8–14, 1929). *See generally* COLIN FRANCOME, ABORTION FREEDOM: A WORLDWIDE MOVEMENT 64–65, 68 (1984); SHEILA ROWBOTHAM, A NEW WORLD FOR WOMEN — STELLA BROWNE: SOCIALIST FEMINIST 27, 64, 105, 110, 113–14 (1977).

278. BROOKES, *supra* note 17, at 81–95, 122–23.

279. *Id.* at 87, 90–91; KENNY, *supra* note 28, at 188.

280. BROOKES, *supra* note 17, at 81.

281. F.W. Stella Browne, *Some Problems of Sex,* 27 INT'L J. ETHICS 468 (1917).

282. STOPES, *supra* note 253, at 183. *See also* BROOKES, *supra* note 17, at 2–3, 5–8, 80; KENNY, *supra* note 28, at 188, 297–98. *See generally* HALL, *supra* note 253.

283. *See* JANET CHANCE, THE COST OF ENGLISH MORALS 43 (1931); DORA RUSSELL, THE TAMARISK TREE: MY QUEST FOR LIBERTY AND LOVE 174 (1975).

284. BROOKES, *supra* note 17, at 80, 85–87, 92, 111.

285. *Id.* at 86.

286. *Id.*

287. *Id.* at 88, 113.

288. *Id.* at 113–15.

289. GARROW, *supra* note 211, at 272–73.

290. *Id.* at 53–67, 98 n.1.

291. *Id.* at 88.

292. *Id.* at 103–04 n.120, 105, 108.

293. *Id.* at 111.

induced abortions, regarding either the number of abortions or the number of deaths.[294] A fairly accurate count of spontaneous abortions might have been possible. Years later, the Royal Commission on Population estimated that total "wastage" from abortion to be between 9 percent and 16 percent, of which 2 percent to 5 percent was from induced abortions.[295]

Eventually Browne's advocacy did help to build pressure for reform, but not repeal, in England.[296] She, along with Dora Russell (one Bertrand Russell's wives) and Janet Chance, organized and led a succession of organizations made up largely of left-wing women devoted to working for the free availability of both birth control and abortion.[297] Many of the women who joined these organizations experience conflict between their left-wing commitments and their feminism, particularly after the USSR prohibited abortions in 1936. The new Soviet prohibition came in the very month the Abortion Law Reform Association organized its first national conference to publicize the cause of abortion reform in Britain.[298] Abortion was the only issue on which the women criticized the British Communist Party, the Labour Party, or the Soviet Union.

Under pressure from the eugenics movement, Parliament enacted in 1929 the sole legislative innovation that did take place during this time in England—the *Infant Life (Preservation) Act*.[299] By 1828, English statutes had made clear that any abortion before birth was well along was a felony and the killing of an infant after its birth was murder,[300] yet a killing during the birth process was not covered by the criminal statutes for a another century, until the adoption of the *Infant Life (Preservation) Act*. No one seems to have considered this to have been anything more than a drafting oversight. The 1929 statute, as drafted, overlapped the earlier statutes because it covered all killings of infants before birth if the child were "capable of being born alive" as well as the killing of a child during the birthing process.[301] The importance of the overlap arose from the inclusion in an English statute, for the first time, of a explicit therapeutic exception permitting abortions if necessary to preserve the life of the mother.[302] The 1861 *Abortion Act* that still governed in England omitted any mention of a therapeutic exception. After all, in 1861 the necessary technologies did not exist to enable a physician to perform an abortion for the benefit of a mother's life or health. As law professor Glanville Williams explained, "in 1861, it would have been ridiculous to call [abortion] therapy."[303] The *Infant Life (Preservation) Act* applied, however, only in England and Wales. The Act did not, does not, apply to Scotland, and was not extended to Northern Ireland until 1945.[304]

The *Infant Life (Preservation) Act* introduced the concept of viability into English law. The statute has been interpreted as creating a presumption of viability after 28 weeks of pregnancy.[305]

---

294. *Id.* at 109–10.

295. *Report of the Biological and Medical Committee,* Papers of the Royal Commission on Population 4 (1950).

296. *See also* Riddell, *supra* note 50.

297. *See* Chance, *supra* note 281; Russell, *supra* note 281. *See generally* Brookes, *supra* note 17, at 86–93.

298. Brookes, *supra* note 17, at 80, 86–87, 95.

299. 19 & 20 Geo. V ch. 34 (1929). *See generally* Petersen, *supra* note 152, at 22–23; Williams, *supra* note 219, at 38, 58, 66–68, 70.

300. *See Lord Landsdowne's Act,* 9 Geo. IV ch. 31, § 13 (1828).

301. Brookes, *supra* note 17, at 27; Mason, *supra* note 66, at 112, 157.

302. *See generally* Mason, *supra* note 66, at 112; J. Keown, *The Scope of the Offence of Child Destruction,* 104 Law Q. Rev. 120 (1988).

303. Williams, *supra* note 219, at 160.

304. Mason, *supra* note 66, at 114, 118.

305. *See* 19 & 20 Geo. V ch. 34, § 1(2) (1929); Brookes, *supra* note 17, at 67; Mason, *supra* note 66, at 114; A.E. Munir, *Perinatal Rights,* 24 Med. Sci. & L. 31, 32 (1984). The presumption was lowered in 1990 to 24 weeks.

The statute does not actually use the term "viable," a point that has led some scholars to conclude that in England the concept of "viability" is not a legal concept, but a medical one.[306] Parliament ignored this pedantic difference in 1967 when it referred to the *Infant Life (Preservation) Act* as serving to preserve "the life of the viable fetus."[307]

The reason for providing special protection to unborn children "capable of being born alive" is not at all clear. Some suggestion of just how quickly and carelessly the act was drafted is suggested, however, by the anomalous limitation of the therapeutic exception to post-viability abortions. The model that Parliament apparently had in view in adopting the therapeutic exception in the *Infant Life (Preservation) Act* was a once common procedure known as a "craniotomy"—the crushing of an impacted fetal head when normal birth proved impossible and failure to extract the fetus would doom both mother and child to death.[308] That procedure was virtually obsolete by 1929 due to the general availability of the Cesarean section as an alternative that made the survival of both mother and child probable. Cesarean sections, however, remained dangerous enough to justify at least some physicians in taking the position that a woman could refuse the procedure and insist on a craniotomy.[309] No one has ever advanced a rationale for limiting the protection of the Act so that it requires a physician to let both mother and child die if some serious problem develops and the child is not viable, yet allows the physician to kill a viable child in order to save its mother's life. Subsequently, English courts extended the therapeutic exception to the abortion of pre-viable fetuses based on an honest belief by a physician of a threat to either the physical or the mental health of the mother.[310] The problems with the therapeutic exception underlines that the entire *Infant Life (Preservation) Act* was hardly a carefully considered response to a medical-legal problem.[311]

In 1932 and 1933, motions were brought forward at the annual meeting of the British Medical Association to form a committee to reconsider the law of abortion.[312] As with the *Infant Life (Preservation) Act,* eugenics enthusiasts, not feminists, sponsored these motions.[313] The Ministry of Health did issue a report in 1933 that noted the failure of maternal mortality to decline as most other death rates had declined, suggesting that the reason was the marked increase in abortions over the previous two decades.[314] The British Medical Association finally appointed a committee in 1935, and issued a report in July of 1936 that declined, however, to recommend changes in the law on the grounds that these were moral issues of concern to the whole community and not just to the medical profession.[315] The report did conclude that, if

---

306. MASON, *supra* note 66, at 108–09, 137 n.29, 166; DAVID MEYERS, THE HUMAN BODY AND THE LAW 27–28 (2nd ed. 1990); Andrew Grubb, *Abortion Law—An English Perspective,* 20 N. MEX. L. REV. 649, 656–58 (1990); Kenneth Norrie, *Abortion in Great Britain: One Act, Two Laws,* 1985 CRIM. L. REP. 475; Gerald Wright, *Capable of Being Born Alive?,* 131 NEW L.J. 188 (1981). *But see* Tony Smith, *Late Abortions and the Law,* 296 BR. MED. J. 446 (1988); Victor Tunkel, *Late Abortion and the Crime of Child Destruction,* 1985 CRIM. L. REP. 133.

307. *Abortion Act of 1967,* § 5(1). *See also* C. v. S., [1988] Q.B. 135, [1987] 1 ALL. ENG. REP. 1230. *See generally* Grubb, *supra* note 305.

308. MASON, *supra* note 66, at 112.

309. THOMAS EDEN & EARDLEY HOLLAND, A MANUAL OF MIDWIFERY 624 (7th ed. 1931).

310. Regina v. Davidson, [1969] V.R. 667; Regina v. Newton, [1958] Crim. L. Rep. 469; Rex v. Bergmann, [1948] 1 BRIT. MED. J. 1008; Rex v. Bourne, [1939] 1 K.B. 687. *See generally* MASON, *supra* note 66, at 114; WILLIAMS, *supra* note 219, at 161–67, 187–91; Grubb, *supra* note 305, at 660–62; Keown, *supra* note 301.

311. WILLIAMS, *supra* note 219, at 160.

312. *Id.* at 67.

313. *Id.* at 38, 58, 66–68, 70.

314. CHIEF MEDICAL OFFICER, ON THE STATE OF THE PUBLIC HEALTH: ANNUAL REPORT 1933, at 261 (the report also noted that approximately 560 women died from abortion or "abortion-related" causes). *See also* Madeleine Simms, *Britain,* in ABORTION IN THE NEW EUROPE, *supra* note 130, at 31, 31–32.

315. BRITISH MEDICAL ASSOCIATION, REPORT OF THE COMMITTEE ON MEDICAL ASPECTS OF ABORTION 18 (1936).

legal abortion were available, there would be definite improvements in women's mortality and morbidity.[316]

The British Medical Association report proved controversial, and was narrowly approved for publication. The opposition, led by Dr. Louise McIlroy, argued that despite the refusal to take a stand, the report's conclusion would encourage those favoring abortion.[317] The three most prominent woman physicians of the time were all vocal critics of the report and strong opponents of abortion reform.[318] English historian Barbara Brookes concluded that the report did indeed spark the formation of the Abortion Law Reform Association in England.[319] The Association actually was organized a few months before the vote on the publication of the report, in part to push for a favorable outcome of the vote.[320] Brookes pointed out, however, that the people who organized the Abortion Law Reform Association had been actively working on the issue for as much as two decades.[321]

At the founding of the Abortion Law Reform Association, Janet Chance held the chair, Stella Browne became vice-chair, Alice Jenkins was secretary, and the all-female board included Beryl Henderson, Frida Laski, Bertha Lorsignol, and Dora Russell.[322] (The restriction to women did not extend to honorary vice-presidents.) Janet Chance remained the financial angel of the organization until her death in 1953.[323] Stella Browne lived until 1955, but became decidedly less active after moving to Liverpool during World War II.[324] The new association, composed of only about a dozen women and a few men,[325] was devoted to the repeal of the abortion laws. At about the same time (1934), the feminists succeeded in obtaining an overwhelming vote (1,360 to 20) of support for abortion reform from the Women's Co-Operative Guild.[326] Several books were also published arguing for abortion reform or more.[327]

The women leading the Abortion Law Reform Association failed to get the National Council of Women to endorse reform or repeal of the abortion laws. The Council did twice petition the Ministry of Health to establish a committee of inquiry into the operation of the abortion laws.[328] While a narrow majority of the National Council for Equal Citizenship did endorse the liberalization of the abortion law in 1936, in the same meeting the Council, by a four-fifths majority, also called for restricting the advertising and sale of contraceptives.[329]

These various pressures culminated in the government's appointment of a blue-ribbon commission ("The Interdepartmental Committee").[330] In the event, the handful of women and men who were the Abortion Law Reform Association seriously overestimated the support for their cause.[331] From the Association's point of view, the Committee was seriously compromised by the

---

316. *Id.* at 23.
317. BROOKES, *supra* note 17, at 68–69.
318. *Id.* at 98 n.1.
319. *Id.* at 69. *See generally Id.* at 93–98, 120–24.
320. *Id.* at 95.
321. *Id.*
322. *Id.* at 95.
323. *Id.* at 146–47, 160 n.93.
324. *Id.* at 147.
325. *Id.* at 96.
326. *Id.* at 93; MADELEINE SIMMS & KEITH HINDELL, ABORTION LAW REFORMED 62 (1971).
327. *See* F.W.S. BROWNE, A.M. LUDOVICI, & H. ROBERTS, ABORTION (1935); ALEC CRAIG, SEX AND REVOLUTION (1934); EDWARD GRIFFITH, MODERN MARRIAGE AND BIRTH CONTROL (1935); ALICE JENKINS, CONSCRIPT PARENTHOOD (1939).
328. BROOKES, *supra* note 17, at 93–94.
329. *Id.* at 98.
330. *Id.* at 94–95, 105–28.
331. *Id.* at 98.

charge given it: "To inquire into the prevalence of abortion and the present law relating thereto and to consider what steps can be taken by more effective enforcement of the law or otherwise to secure the reduction of maternal mortality and morbidity arising from this cause."[332] Additionally, the Committee consisted of 10 men, four titled women of upper-class background, and a woman (Dorothy Thurtle) who was an active social worker whose husband was a Labour Member of Parliament.[333] Most members were professionals in medicine and law. The chair was held by Norman Birkett, a judge (hence the occasional reference to the Committee as the "Birkett Committee").[334] Other men on the Committee included another judge, a prosecuting solicitor, five doctors who were veterans of earlier studies of abortion, and two secretaries of relevant Ministries (Health and the Home Office).

The Birkett Committee betrayed a certain naïveté in its work. For example, the Committee concluded that the majority of abortions in the country were spontaneous and that criminal abortions were declining[335] when all the evidence, even then, seemed to the contrary. The Committee received evidence from 55 witnesses, paying the greatest attention to their fellow professionals.[336] In the end, the Committee merely recommended an amendment to the abortion laws to recognize explicitly the right of doctors to perform abortions if two physicians believed in good faith that continuation of the pregnancy would pose a danger to the mother's life or health.[337] Reversing the pattern of the then recently enacted *Infant Life (Preservation) Act,* the Committee indicated that its proposal for recognizing and broadening a therapeutic exception to the prohibition of abortion would only apply before the 28th week of pregnancy.[338] The Committee told us that it assumed that once the fetus was "viable," no physician would seek to perform an abortion but would instead induce "premature labor," that is, would attempt to deliver a live child and thereafter to assure its survival. The British Medical Association and the Interdepartmental Committee both opposed legislation to specify the indications appropriate for an abortion. Only Dorothy Thurtle dissented, focusing on the class discrimination that would effectively result from the Committee's recommendations.[339]

Nothing happened in Parliament after the Birkett Committee's report was published, in part because of the linkage of abortion reform to the Soviet experiment.[340] The English movement for reform did successfully sponsor Dr. Aleck Bourne in a test case.[341] The time was ripe for such a challenge. By the 1930s at least one judge in England (Justice Henry Alfred McCardie) was declining to sentence women for aborting themselves or others.[342] Bourne had already performed at least one earlier questionable abortion[343] when a teen-age girl was brought to him, pregnant purportedly because of a gang rape. Bourne, by his own admission, saw the request

---

332. *Id.* at 105.

333. *Id.* at 107.

334. On Birkett's life, see H. MONTGOMERY HYDE, NORMAN BIRKETT (1964).

335. INTERDEPARTMENTAL COMM., *supra* note 152, at 13–14.

336. BROOKES, *supra* note 17, at 106–07.

337. INTERDEPARTMENTAL COMM., *supra* note 152, at 70–80, 122–23, recommendation 13. *See also* BROOKES, *supra* note 17, at 125–27; PETERSEN, *supra* note 152, at 51, 56; SIMMS & HINDELL, *supra* note 325, at 73.

338. INTERDEPARTMENTAL COMM., *supra* note 152, at 79.

339. *Id.* at 141–42. *See also* DOROTHY THURTLE, ABORTION—RIGHT OR WRONG? (1940). *See generally* BROOKES, *supra* note 17, at 126–28.

340. BROOKES, *supra* note 17, at 53.

341. Rex v. Bourne, [1939] 1 K.B. 687, [1938] 3 All Eng. Rep. 615.

342. BROOKES, *supra* note 17, at 37–39; COLIN FRANCOME, ABORTION FREEDOM: A WORLDWIDE MOVEMENT 66 (1984); PETERSEN, *supra* note 152, at 62; SIMMS & HINDELL, *supra* note 325, at 47, 66–67; WILLIAMS, *supra* note 219, at 161–62; Munir, *supra* note 304, at 32–33.

343. SIMMS & HINDELL, *supra* note 325, at 70.

for an abortion as an opportunity "to obtain a further definition of the present law."[344] He hoped to establish that mental health concerns were adequate reasons for a therapeutic abortion. His attorney, Gerald Thesiger, was also legal counsel to the British Abortion Law Reform Association.[345]

When Bourne came to trial, the only express statutory recognition of a defense to charges of criminal abortion on therapeutic grounds required the operation to be necessary to preserve the life of the mother and the fetus to be "capable of being born alive" at the time of the operation.[346] By 1938 (unlike 1861), not only could abortions be performed safely and easily, but fewer and fewer medical complications actually threatened the life of a mother, until by 1960 the incidence of truly therapeutic abortions had become virtually nil.[347] As the necessary technologies emerged, various commentators seized upon the word "unlawful" in the English statute to argue that there was an implicit exception for therapeutic abortions which were, they argued, not unlawful.[348]

Dr. Bourne informed the police in advance of his intent to perform the abortion, and then went ahead and did it. Bourne was tried for criminal abortion before Justice Macnaghten at the Old Baily. Macnaghten began from the premise that the prohibition of abortion was intended to protect the life of the unborn child and that goal could not be sacrificed for any reason less than preserving the life of the mother.[349] Still, Macnaghten chose to instruct the jury that "life depends on health" and that therefore Bourne was to be acquitted unless the prosecution had proven beyond a reasonable doubt that Bourne had not acted upon a good faith belief that the mental health of the mother

---

344. Aleck Bourne, *Abortion and the Law,* [1938] 2 Brit. Med. J. 254. *See also* Brookes, *supra* note 17, at 69.

345. Brookes, *supra* note 17, at 121.

346. *Infant Life (Preservation) Act,* 19 & 20 Geo. V ch. 34, § 1 (1929). See the text *supra* at notes 298–310.

347. *See* Sidney Bolter, *The Psychiatrist's Role in Therapeutic Abortion: The Unwitting Accomplice,* 119 Am. J. Psych. 312 (1962); John Ewing & Beatrice Rouse, *Is Therapeutic Abortion on Psychiatric Grounds Therapeutic?,* 1 Soc. Psych. 137 (1974); Howard Hammond, *Therapeutic Abortion: Ten Years Experience with Hospital Committee Control,* 89 Am. J. Obstet. & Gynecology 349 (1964); Robert Hall, *Therapeutic Abortion, Sterilization, and Contraception,* 91 Am. J. Obstet. & Gynecology 518, 524–25 (1965); J.A. Harrington, *Psychiatric Indications for the Termination of Pregnancy,* 185 Practitioner 654 (1960); Roy Hefferman & William Lynch, *What Is the Status of Therapeutic Abortion in Modern Obstetrics?,* 66 Am. J. Obstet. & Gynecology 335, 337 (1953); Arnold Levine, *The Problem of Psychiatric Disturbance in Relation to Therapeutic Abortion,* 6 J. Albert Einstein Med. Center 76 (1958); J.G. Moore & J.H. Randall, *Trends in Therapeutic Abortion: A Review of 137 Cases,* 63 Am. J. Obstet. & Gynecology 34 (1952); Kenneth Niswander, *Medical Abortion Practice in the United States,* in Abortion and the Law 242, 251–54 (David Smith ed. 1967); Kenneth Niswander & Manual Porto, *Abortion Practices in the United States: A Medical Viewpoint,* in Abortion, Medicine, and the Law 567, 570–78 (J. Douglas Butler & David Walbert eds., 3rd ed. 1986); Harold Rosen, *The Psychiatric Indications of Abortion: A Case Study in Hypocrisy,* in Therapeutic Abortion 72 (Harold Rosen ed. 1954) (this book was reissued in 1967 under the title Abortion in America); Keith Russell, *Changing Indications for Therapeutic Abortion: Twenty Years' Experience at Los Angeles County Hospital,* 151 JAMA J. 108, 108 (1953); Quentin Scherman, *Therapeutic Abortion,* 11 Obstet. & Gynecology 323 (1958).

348. *See* 2 Alfred Taylor, The Principles and Practice of Medical Jurisprudence 154 (Frederick Smith ed., 5th Am. ed. 1905); 1 William Russell, A Treatise on the Law of Crimes 830 (W.F. Craies & L.W. Kershaw eds., 7th ed. 1909); D.S. Davies, *The Law of Abortion and Necessity,* [1938] 2 Modern L. Rev. 126.

349. [1938] 3 All. Eng. Rep. at 620. As this page does not appear in the later-published King's Bench Reports version of the case, leading English law professor Glanville Williams concluded that Justice MacNaughten must have completely rewritten his ruling for the second report. Williams, *supra* note 219, at 161 n.5. Williams noted that in the second version, Justice Macnaghten only indicated that "there may be justification for the [abortion]" without mentioning preservation of the mother's life as the only grounds." [1939] 1 K.B. at 690.

would be impaired by the continuation of the pregnancy.[350] Indeed, Macnaghten indicated that had Bourne refused to perform the abortion, say on grounds of religiously based opposition to abortion, he would have charged with manslaughter had the girl committed suicide![351] Lord Diplock, in a case decided in 1981, criticized Macnaghten's analysis for its imprecise equating of life with health.[352]

Even though the ruling from the bench in Bourne's favor was merely a jury instruction at an Old Bailey trial, the case received wide publicity and the decision was widely cited as settling the matter in England and elsewhere in the Empire.[353] The *Bourne* case was even followed by at least one court in the United States.[354] The result in *Bourne* considerably liberalized the interpretation of England's abortion statute, even beyond the reforms proposed to Parliament and not enacted. While *Bourne* made prosecutions for abortion more difficult, the decision was sufficiently narrow that physicians would still need to worry about the possibility of a prosecution if they performed an abortion in less sympathetic circumstances. The luck of the draw in impaneling a jury would determine whether they were convicted. This concern could deter abortions by many physicians even if they were personally supportive of a liberalized approach to abortion.[355]

The war years in England saw a fourfold increase in reported criminal abortions, the number rising from 156 in 1939 to a high of 649 in 1944, with an average of 347 per year for the war years.[356] Fourteen physicians were convicted of procuring abortions in these five years.[357] That number represents more than 25 percent of all the physicians stuck from the medical register between 1900 and 1958.[358] There is no certain way of knowing whether such an increase represented an actual increase in the incidence of abortion or simply an increase in police vigilance. Probably the war years did yield an actual increase in the incidence of abortion given the general disruption of personal relations and the risks that had come to seem a normal part of life at that time, as well as because of the increasing safety of the procedure for the mother.[359]

Despite the apparently higher incidence, general public attitudes towards abortion hardly changed. Dr. Bourne resigned from the Abortion Law Reform Association in 1943 on the grounds that "the population problem [lack of growth in population] is so serious that public opinion will move away from easier abortion to tightening the law still further."[360] A year later, the Association could not get a single one of 25 newspapers to accept the Association's letter for publication.[361] The impetus for reform also never quite died out in the United States, but as World War II drew to a close, abortion was hardly an issue on the political horizon of either country.

---

350. [1939] 1 K.B. at 692.

351. *Id.* at 693.

352. Royal College of Nursing v. Department of Health & Soc. Sec'y, [1981] A.C. 800.

353. *See* Regina v. Wald, [1972] 3 D.C.R. (N.S.W.) 25; Regina v. Davidson, [1969] V.R. 667. *See generally* Brookes, *supra* note 17, at 69–70; Grisez, *supra* note 205, at 220–24; Anthony Hordern, Legal Abortion: The English Experience 8–9 (1971); Kenny, *supra* note 28, at 189; Mason, *supra* note 66, at 112–14; Petersen, *supra* note 152, at 61–65; Kerry Petersen, *Abortion Laws: Comparative and Feminist Perspectives in Australia, England and the United States,* 2 Med. L. Int'l 77 (1996).

354. Commonwealth v. Wheeler, 53 N.E.2d 4 (Mass. 1944).

355. *See generally* Brookes, *supra* note 17, at 149–53; Mason, *supra* note 66, at 114–15; Petersen, *supra* note 152, at 129–44; Simms, *supra* note 313, at 32–33.

356. Brookes, *supra* note 17, at 157 n.28, 158 n.68.

357. *Id.* at 65.

358. *Id.* at 142.

359. *Id.* at 137.

360. *Id.* at 144–45.

361. *Id.* at 144.

# Prosecutions of Abortion before 1940

*In abortion cases, the investigation procedures themselves*
*constituted a form of control and punishment.*

—Leslie Reagan[362]

We do not have complete figures for the total number of prosecutions for criminal abortion in the United States for any year in the period included in this chapter, or for the number of persons convicted of criminal abortion, let alone figures for the total number of persons prosecuted for the entire period from 1875 to 1945. Thus any assertion about the overall frequency or success of the efforts to detect and prosecute criminal abortion remains largely speculative. We do know that the press continued to crusade against abortionists, presenting them as well-to-do physicians who exploit, and all too often kill, vulnerable women.[363] And we know that prosecutions for illegal abortions occurred in every decade in every major metropolitan area throughout the nineteenth and first half of the twentieth century.[364]

In 1914, there were 47 arrests for criminal abortion in Chicago alone, with arrests for the decade 1910–1920 averaging 25 or 26 per year.[365] Coroner's inquests were even more common in Chicago.[366] Chicago's coroner sent an average of twelve suspected abortionists per year to the grand jury between 1905 and 1919.[367] The frequency with which coroner's inquests were conducted or prosecutions begun in Chicago increased steadily through the years.[368] Yet less than one-fourth of those arrested in Chicago were convicted, even though most of these prosecutions involved a woman's death as well as an abortion.[369] By the 1930s, prosecutions were common in all states, but convictions remained rare.[370] For example, one study found 44 convictions in 25 states over a period of 10 years in the first quarter of the century.[371]

Abortion rights advocates are prone to dismiss such prosecutions as occurred during this era as merely short-term crackdowns that always fizzled out within a year and therefore do not signify popular or even official perspectives.[372] These commentators further stress that convicted abortionists sometimes were promptly pardoned by the governor, without attempting to discover how general this practice might have been.[373] Other abortion rights advocates seem not even to notice

---

362. REAGAN, *supra* note 22, at 5.

363. OLASKY, *supra* note 28, at 265–73; OLASKY, THE PRESS, *supra* note 228, at 51–54, 58–59, 64–65, 72–74, 78–79; REAGAN, *supra* note 22, at 46–61, 101–06, 109, 125.

364. Harris, *supra* note 230, at 91 n.18. *See also* OLASKY, THE PRESS, *supra* note 228, at 16, 25–30, 34–40, 45–46, 51–54, 58, 60, 62–68, 71–75, 77, 80–84, 90.

365. REAGAN, *supra* note 22, at 107, 117.

366. *Id.* at 118–19.

367. *Id.* at 118.

368. *Id.*

369. *Id.* at 116–17; Harris, *supra* note 230, at 91 n.17.

370. ISEMAN, *supra* note 17, at 140–58; Palmer Findley, *The Slaughter of the Innocents*, 3 AM. J. OSTET. & GYNECOLOGY 35 (1922); Harris, *supra* note 230, at 91 n.17; N.W. Moore, *Abortion, Criminal and Inevitable*, 21 KY. MED. J. 332 (1923).

371. E.A. Ficklen, *Some Phases of Criminal Abortion*, 79 NEW ORLEANS. MED. & SURGICAL J. 884 (1927).

372. *See* MARK GRABER, RETHINKING ABORTION: EQUAL CHOICE, THE CONSTITUTION, AND REPRODUCTIVE POLITICS 44 (1996); James Mohr, *Patterns of Abortion and the Response of American Physicians, 1790–1930*, in WOMEN AND HEALTH IN AMERICA: HISTORICAL READINGS 117, 119–20 (Judith Leavitt ed. 1984).

373. GRABER, *supra* note 371, at 45; Mohr, *supra* note 371, at 121.

such events, simply asserting that abortion was not prosecuted.[374] Yet others have argued that prosecution rates declined during the Depression and climbed during the post-war era, all without statistical backing for this conclusion.[375] The actual record suggests a different story.

Abortion has always been a difficult crime to prove.[376] Abortions took place in secret and left little physical evidence. Abortionists were careful to perform the procedure with no one in the room except the woman undergoing the abortion (and the fetus, if one counts it as a person), so there would be no witness but the woman herself.[377] If the woman died, there could be no witness at all. Some abortionists entered the room already masked, so even if the woman were willing to testify, she would have difficulty identifying the abortionist. The *corpus delicti*, at least early in a pregnancy, was disposed of simply through flushing a toilet.

Without witnesses or evidence, the crime would be undetected and unpunished. Only if the mother died or was seriously injured by the procedure was it likely to come to light—if the family or paramour did not prefer silence to the shame of public disclosure. Prosecutors responded to the difficulties of proving abortion by resorting to dubious techniques of investigation. Numerous convictions of abortionists were reversed for entrapment, that is, on the theory that the government itself had instigated the crime (a crime that otherwise would not have happened) in order to entrap an individual in a crime not really of his or her doing.[378] While such results kept the abortionists out of prison, these practices did not betoken tolerance toward abortion.

As the entrapment decisions themselves demonstrate, police and prosecutors were going to extraordinary lengths to detect and eliminate abortionists. This pattern suggests that the police and prosecutors took the problem very seriously indeed, and were frustrated only by the difficulties of proving a case. Still, some modern historians continue to insist that the common failure to imprison abortionists demonstrates official as well as public tolerance toward abortion.[379]

Physicians, on the other hand, claimed to be able to distinguish between unlawful and medically justified abortions when a patient requested to be relieved of a pregnancy. This proved a slippery distinction and doctors increasingly found themselves caught "between the shore of extreme regard for religion and the law of the one hand, and sympathy and dishonesty on the

---

374. *See, e.g.,* GEBHARD *et al., supra* note 22, at 192; GRABER, *supra* note 371, at 44–45, 85–87; OTTO POLLAK, THE CRIMINALITY OF WOMEN 44 (1950); TAUSSIG, *supra* note 26, at 427; Samuel Buell, Note, *Criminal Abortion Revisited,* 66 NYU L. REV. 1774, 1798 (1991); Russell Fisher, *Criminal Abortion,* in THERAPEUTIC ABORTION, *supra* note 346, at 3, 6; Zad Leavy & Jerome Kummer, *Criminal Abortion: Human Hardship and Unyielding Laws,* 35 CAL. L. REV. 123, 125 (1962); James Voyles, *Changing Abortion Laws in the United States,* 7 J. FAM. L. 496, 510 (1967).

375. *See, e.g.,* GRABER, *supra* note 371, at 52–53 (as a perusal of the last several footnotes will disclose, Graber apparently never encountered any numerical assertion that supposedly demonstrates popular and official tolerance for abortion that he could not embrace).

376. *See* JOHN & J. COLLYER ADAM, CRIMINAL INVESTIGATION: A PRACTICAL TEXTBOOK 453 (1924); CHARLES O'HARA, FUNDAMENTALS OF CRIMINAL INVESTIGATION 477–89 (1956); HARRY SODERMAN & JOHN O'CONNELL, MODERN CRIMINAL INVESTIGATIONS 294–95 (1952); John Harlen Amen, *Some Obstacles to Effective Legal Control of Criminal Abortions,* in NATIONAL COMM. ON MATERNAL HEALTH, THE ABORTION PROBLEM 133, 135–36 (1944). *See also* OLASKY, *supra* note 28, at 224–31, 233. *See also* Ficklen, *supra* note 370, at 886.

377. Rudolph Holmes, *The Methods of the Professional Abortionist,* 10 J. SURGERY, GYNECOLOGY, & OBSTET. 542, 542–43 (1910).

378. *See, e.g.,* People v. Reed, 275 P.2d 633 (Cal. 1954). *See generally* GROSSBERG, *supra* note 17, at 179–88; PATRICIA MILLER, THE WORST OF TIMES 103 (1993).

379. *See, e.g.,* GRABER, *supra* note 371, at 45; REAGAN, *supra* note 22, at 59–60, 87, 116.

other."[380] Perhaps a third or more of illegal abortions were performed by licensed physicians.[381] Because of their ability to present arguably cogent justifications for an abortion—some lawful or at least moral excuse for the procedure—even if they were caught, doctors convicted of performing abortions often received less severe penalties even if the mother died.[382] Additionally, the penalty varied according to whether the physician-abortionist's activities appeared to be part of a commercial abortion enterprise or simply the offering of help to an occasional desperate woman.[383] Finally, a convicted physician would lose the license to practice medicine, which ironically could lead a physician to become a full-time abortionist upon release from prison as the only means left open for making a living from now-forbidden medical skills.[384]

In the nineteenth century, the most prominent abortionists in the United States, whose activities pro-abortion historians claim demonstrate public approval of their practice, ended up in jail. Philadelphia's Dr. Isaac Hathaway was sentenced to seven at hard labor years in 1883.[385] New York City's Dr. Henry McGonegal was sentenced in 1894 to 14 years after a patient died.[386] Even Madame Restell committed suicide when faced with yet another prosecution.[387] Other reports indicate the arrest of abortionists in police sweeps, although not all of those arrested were ultimately convicted.[388] Even in the last years of the prohibition of abortion, with widespread dissent from the enforcement of the laws, it remained true that virtually every professional abortionist had had "at least one brush with the law."[389]

Police training manuals also indicate substantial efforts to search out and arrest abortionists.[390] Obtaining proof of the crime continued to be particularly troublesome for abortion. Thomas Peters, an assistant district attorney in Queens County, New York, lamented in 1929 that "prosecutions are frequent, but in my experience convictions are seldom obtained."[391] Given the improbability of detection of a criminal abortion unless the mother died or was close to death, it is hardly surprising that criminal prosecutions in the United States depended to a large extent on the deathbed statements of aborted women. This led to what now appear to be unseemly efforts to pressure a dying woman into naming the abortionist.[392] While some doctors, at least by the middle of the

---

380. John Ellison et al., Sex Ethics: The Principles and Practice of Contraception, Abortion, and Sterilization 147 (1934). See also Iseman, supra note 17, at 140; C.S. Bacon, Chicago Medical Society: Regular Meeting, Held Nov. 23, 1904, 43 JAMA 1889 (1904); Frank Higgins, The Proper Indications and Methods for the Termination of Pregnancy, 43 JAMA 1531 (1904); Charles Jewett, Indication for Artificial Abortion in the First Three Months of Pregnancy, 8 N.Y. St. J. Med. 113 (1908); E.A. Weiss, Some Moral and Ethical Aspects of Foeticide, 67 Am. J. Obstet. 79 (1913). See generally Reagan, supra note 22, at 19–20, 46–61, 67–73.

381. Jerome Bates & Edward Zawadski, Criminal Abortion 202 (1964); Graber, supra note 371, at 48–49; Reagan, supra note 22, at 70–73; Carol Joffe, "Portraits of Three Physicians of Conscience:" Abortion before Legalization in the United States, 2 J. Hist. Sexuality 46, 47 (1991).

382. See, e.g., Rex v. Bourne, [1939] 1 K.B. 687, [1938] 3 All Eng. Rep. 615. See generally Brookes, supra note 17, at 36–37, 41; Graber, supra note 371, at 48–49; Messer & May, supra note 251, at 179–80; Bernard Nathanson & Richard Ostung, Aborting America 21–22 (1979); Joffe, supra note 380, at 54.

383. Brookes, supra note 17, at 37, 139–44; Bernard Dickens, Abortion and the Law 93–94 (1966).

384. Brookes, supra note 17, at 36–37.

385. Olasky, supra note 28, at 170–71.

386. Id.

387. See Chapter 9, at notes 198–216.

388. See generally Olasky, supra note 28, at 170–71; Harris, supra note 230, at 91 nn.17–18.

389. Miller, supra note 377, at 9.

390. John & J. Collier Adam, Criminal Investigation: A Practical Textbook 477 (1934); O'Hara, supra note 375, at 477–89; Harry Soderman & John O'Connell, Modern Criminal Investigation 298 (1952).

391. Quoted in Samuel Burke, The Development of the Law of Criminal Abortion, 57 Med. Times, 153, 158 (1929).

392. See generally Reagan, supra note 22, at 113–31. See Chapter 9, at notes 182–84.

twentieth century, found the task demeaning and demoralizing, many doctors and hospital administrators,[393] at least in the early decades of the century, apparently cooperated in this effort willingly.[394] In Chicago in 1917, the hospitals pledged to undertake to obtain dying declarations in a formal agreement with the coroner, the chief of police, and the state's attorney.[395] The editors of the *Journal of the American Medical Association* even recommended that physicians deny treatment to dying women until they named the abortionist, or at least exonerated the attending physician.[396]

Even efforts to obtain dying declarations from women suffering from septic abortions often did not produce evidence admissible in a court.[397] The dying woman had to be believe that she was about to die,[398] and, at least in some states, she had to consent to the use of the information in a court after her passing because a doctor would not be allowed to testify to something told him in confidence, particularly when it would "tend to blacken the character of the patient."[399] Yet while convictions remained rare relative to the number of crimes, police investigations in themselves could be a form of punishment and a serious deterrent even if no charges were ever brought—as some pro-abortion historians have conceded.[400]

While arrests continued to be common during the 1930s,[401] enforcement in the United States focused on the revocation of medical licenses.[402] Historian Leslie Reagan asserts that in Illinois medical licenses could be revoked for abortion only after a criminal conviction.[403] Even if she is right in this, in most states licenses could be revoked after a relatively simple civil procedure that

---

393. *See generally* REAGAN, *supra* note 22, at 115–16, 120–24.

394. *See, e.g.*, N.F. Thiberge, *Report of Committee on Criminal Abortion*, 70 N. ORLEANS MED. & SURGICAL J. 802, 807–08 (1918).

395. REAGAN, *supra* note 22, at 121, 131.

396. Editorial, *Criminal Abortion*, 39 JAMA 706 (1902). *See also* ROBINSON, *supra* note 27, at 105–11; Findley, *supra* note 379, at 37. *See generally* REAGAN, *supra* note 22, at 122–24, 301 n.34.

397. OLASKY, *supra* note 28, at 224–27; REAGAN, *supra* note 22, at 123–24; Constance Backhouse, *Involuntary Motherhood: Abortion, Birth Control and the Law in Nineteenth Century Canada*, 3 WINDSOR Y.B. OF ACCESS TO JUSTICE 61, 99–103 (1983).

398. *See, e.g.*, Winfrey v. State, 296 S.W. 82 (Ark. 1927); State *ex rel.* Johnson v. Clark, 232 S.W. 1031 (Mo. 1921). *See generally* GRAHAM LILLY, AN INTRODUCTION TO THE LAW OF EVIDENCE §7.25 (2nd ed. 1987); EDMUND MORGAN & JACK WEINSTEIN, BASIC PROBLEMS OF STATE AND FEDERAL EVIDENCE 281 (5th ed. 1976). For examples of this sort of interrogation in an abortion case, see People v. Cheney, 13 N.E.2d 171, 172–74 (1938); Hagenow v. People, 59 N.E. 242, 243–45 (Ill. 1901); OLASKY, *supra* note 28, at 266–67; REAGAN, *supra* note 22, at 113, 122.

399. W.S. Carroll, *The Rights of the Unborn Child*, 13 PA. MED. J. 941 (1910). *See also* Earnest Oakley, Jr., *Legal Aspects of Abortion*, 3 AM. J. OBSTET. & GYNECOLOGY 37, 37–41 (1922). *See generally* REAGAN, *supra* note 22, at 124–25.

400. MILLER, *supra* note 377, at 215–16; REAGAN, *supra* note 22, at 114–15, 121, 125–26, 130–31, 161, 164–72, 191–92. *See also* OLASKY, *supra* note 28, at 234.

401. OLASKY, *supra* note 28, at 68, 80; POLLAK, *supra* note 373, at 45.

402. Sos v. Board of Regents, 281 N.Y.S.2d 831 (N.Y. 1967) (revocation annulled for insufficient evidence); Walsh v. Board of Regents, 209 N.E.2d 821 (N.Y. 1965); Jablon v. Board of Regents, 73 N.E.2d 904 (N.Y. 1947); Friedel v. Board of Regents, 73 N.E.2d 545 (N.Y. 1947); Neshamkin v. Board of Regents, 66 N.E.2d 124 (N.Y. 1946); Epstein v. Board of Regents, 65 N.E.2d 756 (1946); Weinstein v. Board of Regents, 56 N.E.2d 104 (N.Y. 1944); Kasha v. Board of Regents, 48 N.E.2d 712 (N.Y. 1943); Kahn v. Board of Regents, 23 N.E.2d 16 (N.Y. 1939); Zimmerman v. Board of Regents, 294 N.Y.S.2d 435 (App. Div. 1968); Ciofalo v. Board of Regents, 258 N.Y.S.2d 881 (App. Div.), *appeal denied*, 261 N.Y.S. 2d 1025 (N.Y. 1965); Shapiro v. Board of Regents, 254 N.Y.S.2d 906 (App. Div. 1964), aff'd, 209 N.E. 2d 821 (N. Y. 1965); Robinson v. Board of Regents, 164 N.Y.S.2d 863 (App. Div. 1957); Genova v. Board of Regents, 74 N.Y.S.2d 729 (App. Div. 1947); Newman v. Board of Regents, 61 N.Y.S.2d 841 (App. Div. 1946); Rothenberg v. Board of Regents, 44 N.Y.S.2d 926 (App. Div. 1943), *appeal denied*, 47 N.Y.S.2d 284 (App. Div. 1944); Reiner v. Board of Regents, 6 N.Y.S.2d 356 (App. Div. 1938); Minton v. Board of Regents, 287 N.Y.S. 502 (App. Div. 1936). *See also* REAGAN, *supra* note 22, at 67, 280 n.68.

403. REAGAN, *supra* note 22, at 97, 120.

required a lower burden of proof than a criminal prosecution.[404] The necessary proof was often obtained by "testers," that is, by women who visited to suspected doctors posing as abortion seekers.[405] A license could be revoked if the doctor merely offered to perform an abortion even if the offer itself was not a crime.[406]

The license revocation process remained almost entirely in the hands of the medical profession itself, with courts becoming involved only in appeals by the accused physician after his license had been revoked. License revocations for offering to abort were frequent in New York between 1930 and 1970, and the cases upholding such revocations are numerous, in contrast with the sparsity of criminal prosecutions for abortions. License revocation proceedings are too numerous, at least in New York, to allow the claim that the medical profession as a whole was tolerant of abortion so long as performed by a licensed physician. Recurring campaigns by the medical profession to ferret out physicians performing abortions in order to revoke their licenses demonstrate that the organized profession was committed to stamping out abortion across the nation.[407] Physicians also occasionally turned abortionists into the police for criminal prosecution, as well as appearing as witnesses in coroner's inquests or criminal prosecutions.[408] In 1906, the American Medical Association even established its own "Bureau of Investigation" to pursue abortionists within the profession along with its pursuit of quacks.[409]

The American Medical Association or its local branches were also leaders in the effort to search out and convict midwives who were performing abortions.[410] For midwives, this effort took two forms—the imposition of licensing requirements intended both to upgrade the quality of care provided by midwives and to control their activities, and direct efforts to suppress abortion.[411] Additionally, while proving that a midwife had performed an abortion was no easier than proving that a physician had done so, midwives could rather easily be convicted of practicing medicine without a license—and 71 were in one five year period in New York City alone at the start of the century.[412]

The incidence of hospital performed "therapeutic" abortions declined sharply after 1940.[413] At one hospital in Los Angeles, the rate of therapeutic abortions dropped from 1/106 live births in 1931–1935, to 1/2,864 in 1946–1949, to 1/8,383 in 1950.[414] This happened at the same time that some physicians and lawyers were arguing for an increasingly expansive interpretation of what constitutes a therapeutic abortion.[415] The decline tells us little, however, about the incidence of illegal abortions during the same period. Nor are the prosecution or conviction rates particularly good evidence of the rate at which abortions were being performed illegally.

---

404. *See, e.g.,* Zimmerman v. Board of Regents, 294 N.Y.S.2d 435 (App. Div. 1968); Reiner v. Board of Regents, 6 N.Y.S.2d 356 (App. Div. 1938).

405. *See, e.g.,* Epstein v. Board of Regents, 65 N.E.2d 756 (N.Y. 1946); Rothenberg v. Board of Regents, 44 N.Y.S.2d 926 (App. Div. 1943), *appeal denied,* 47 N.Y.S.2d 284 (App. Div. 1944); Weinstein v. Board of Regents, 44 N.Y.S.2d 917 (App. Div. 1943), *rev'd,* 56 N.E.2d 104 (N.Y. 1944).

406. OLASKY, *supra* note 28, at 233–35 (1992).

407. *See, e.g.,* REAGAN, *supra* note 22, at 86–98. The periods of intense anti-abortion campaigns were interrupted by intervals when the profession seemed apathetic about abortion and did little. *Id.* at 89–90

408. *Id.* at 88.

409. *Id.* at 89.

410. *Id.* at 90–112.

411. *Id.* at 95–96.

412. F. Elisabeth Crowell, *The Midwives of New York,* 17 CHARITIES & THE COMMONS 667, 668 (1907).

413. D'EMILIO & FREEDMAN, *supra* note 250, at 253; FAYE GINSBURG, CONTESTED LIVES: THE ABORTION DEBATE IN AN AMERICAN COMMUNITY 34–35 (1989); WILLIAMS, *supra* note 219, at 167–69; Hammond, *supra* note 346.

414. Russell, *supra* note 347, at 111.

415. *See, e.g.,* WILLIAMS, *supra* note 219, at 160–83; Hefferman & Lynch, *supra* note 347, at 343; Levine, *supra* note 347; Rosen, *supra* note 347; Russell, *supra* note 347.

The 111 convictions in New York city between 1925 and 1950 can hardly have been more than a merest sample of the actual number of abortions performed there in that period.[416] We continue to know very little about the number of abortions in the United States or elsewhere before its legalization. The cautionary words of Judith Leavitt, already quoted, regarding statistical studies of childbirth (the study of which does not confront the added problem of active efforts to hide the records because the acts were illegal) remain compelling here.[417] One must keep this reality in mind in evaluating all estimates of the number of abortions. There is some reason to question even the apparently carefully developed statistics regarding legal abortions given the political uses of those statistics.[418]

Estimates for illegal abortions in the United States have generally ranged between 41,000 and 700,000 per year for the years 1935–1940.[419] The higher figure, derived from the work of Dr. Frederick Taussig, was based upon statistics gathered at a single birth control clinic in a poor section of the city of New York estimating 681,600 abortions nationally per year, without any attempt to determine whether the figures developed from this study were likely to be representative of the nation as a whole.[420] Taussig himself repudiated this figure as far too high six years after he published it.[421] Dr. Abraham Rongy, in his early polemic urging the legalization of abortion, estimated 2,000,000 induced abortions per year (5 percent therapeutic) in the early 1930s.[422] Modern supporters of abortion rights continue to cite Taussig's repudiated figure as authoritative without acknowledging the weakness of the data.[423] Law professor David Garrow has proposed the slightly higher figure of 800,000 per year, without providing a basis for it.[424]

In England, were detection was as difficult as in the United States, we appear to have somewhat harder data regarding the number of prosecutions and convictions than we have for the United States. The number of prosecutions increased steadily, doubling between 1900 and 1910, and doubling again between 1910 and 1930.[425] In contrast with the United States, conviction rates in these cases were not particularly low. In 1919, of 60 people charged with procuring abortions in England, 42 were convicted.[426] In what Barbara Brookes describes as a typical year (1934), 50 of 73 indictments went to trial and 33 of those resulted in convictions.[427] In any given

---

416. D'EMILIO & FREEDMAN, *supra* note 250, at 253–54.

417. JUDITH WALZER LEAVITT, BROUGHT TO BED: CHILDBEARING IN AMERICA 1750–1950, at 24 (1986), quoted in Chapter 2, at note 461; Chapter 10, at note 223.

418. GERALD ROSENBERG, THE HOLLOW HOPE: CAN COURTS BRING ABOUT SOCIAL CHANGE? 178 (1992); Paige Comstock Cunningham & Clarke Forsythe, *Is Abortion the "First Right" for Women?: Some Consequences of Legal Abortion,* in ABORTION, MEDICINE AND THE LAW 100, 100 (J. Douglas Butler & David Walbert eds., 4th ed. 1992).

419. D'EMILIO & FREEDMAN, *supra* note 250, at 252–53; WILLIAMS, *supra* note 219, at 191, 209.

420. TAUSSIG, *supra* note 219, at 26, 388. *See also,* KATHARINE BEMENT DAVIS, FACTORS IN THE SEX LIFE OF TWENTY-TWO HUNDRED WOMEN xi–xiii, 20–21 (1929); GILBERT VAN TASSEL HAMILTON, A RESEARCH IN MARRIAGE 133–34 (1929); MARIE KOPP, BIRTH CONTROL IN PRACTICE 121–23 (1934); Regine Stix, *A Study of Pregnancy Wastage,* 13 MILBANK MEM. FUND Q. 347 (1935). *See generally* OLASKY, *supra* note 28, at 70; OLASKY, THE PRESS, *supra* note 228, at 70.

421. *Statement of Dr. Frederick Taussig,* NATIONAL COMM. ON MATERNAL HEALTH, THE ABORTION PROBLEM 28 (1944). *See also Statement of Dr. Hermann Bundesan, Id.* at 155; Jerome Bates, *The Abortion Mill,* 45 J. CRIM. L. & CRIMINOLOGY 157, 158 (1954). Regine Stix also repudiated her estimate. Regine Stix & Dorothy Wiehl, *Abortion and the Public Health,* 28 AM. J. PUB. HEALTH 621, 623 (1938).

422. RONGY, *supra* note 219, at 89. *See also* ROBINSON, AGAINST ABORTION, *supra* note 27, at 114.

423. *See, e.g.,* GRABER, *supra* note 371, at 44–45; EDWIN SCHUR, CRIMES WITHOUT VICTIMS: DEVIANT BEHAVIOR AND PUBLIC POLICY 25 (1965); Alfred Kinsey, *Illegal Abortions in the United States,* in THE UNWED MOTHER 196–97 (Robert Roberts ed. 1966). *See generally* GEBHARD *et al., supra* note 29, at 189–214.

424. GARROW, *supra* note 211, at 272.

425. BROOKES, *supra* note 17, at 28, 45 n.46.

426. *Id.* at 28.

427. *Id.*

year, about three-quarters of the abortionists charged were likely to be women.[428] Two statistics show the vigor with which the crime of abortion was prosecuted in England. There appear to have been only 40 convictions in the state of Michigan during the 40 years from 1910–1940, yet in England (with a population about six to ten times as large) there were 52 prosecutions in 1955 alone, with 49 convictions.[429]

In England as in the United States, the women who had undergone the abortion usually was deceased. Her death was the event the led to the uncovering of the abortion. Prosecutor generally were successful in cases that went to trial in England even though the trial judge would routinely remind women who had undergone an abortion before testifying that by giving evidence they could incriminate themselves. Yet, immediately after providing the figures indicating the high degree of prosecutorial success in England, Brookes concluded that "[j]uries, usually sympathetic to the abortionist and appreciative of the heavy sentences, were reluctant to convict."[430] Brookes does not explain her remarkable conclusion.

Penalties for conviction of abortion remained severe even in England where, although the death sentence imposed by statute was routinely commuted to terms ranging from seven to ten or more years for physicians or even to life in prison for professional abortionists if they had no formal medical training.[431] Neighborhood women who did not charge a fee or despairing husbands, either of which were seen as acting from motives that justified mercy, were often given briefer jail terms even if the woman undergoing the abortion died.[432] What Brookes describes as the "harsh sentences" in such cases, in fact, averaged less than one year in prison.[433] Such a result, however, hardly suggests that the acts were not considered criminal. In England, women continued to be charged for procuring their own abortions, usually serving sentences of days or months, however, rather than years.[434]

With the apparently sharp rise in criminal abortions in England during World War II, prosecutions rose dramatically.[435] Despite the insistence of pro-abortion historians that there was no serious effort to enforce the prohibition of abortion, we find that at least 14 physicians were convicted in England between 1939 and 1944 of procuring abortions.[436] This represents more than 25 percent of all physicians struck from the medical register between 1900 and 1958.[437] Early abortion activist Stella Browne was no doubt exaggerating when she estimated that someone was convicted of abortion in England "every fortnight."[438] Browne was, however, closer to the truth that those who deny today that any serious steps were taken to enforce the abortion laws.

It is noteworthy that many of the doctors who were prosecuted for abortion in England after World War II, were foreigners who were, perhaps, outside the shield of professional solidarity that to some extent protected English doctors.[439] Prison sentences for foreign physicians also tended to be more harsh.[440] This pattern is harder to discern, however, before the war.

---

428. *Id.* at 28–29.
429. WILLIAMS, *supra* note 219, at 209–10.
430. BROOKES, *supra* note 17, at 29.
431. *Id.* at 26, 35–37, 138–39.
432. *Id.* at 137–39; WILLIAMS, *supra* note 219, at 146–47.
433. BROOKES, *supra* note 17, at 29.
434. *Id.* at 139.
435. See the text *supra* at notes 355–58.
436. BROOKES, *supra* note 17, at 65.
437. *Id.* at 142.
438. *Id.* at 91.
439. *Id.* at 140–41.
440. *Id.*

# Chapter 12

# Close the Wound,
# Hide the Scar[1]

*Past the open windows on the darker streets*
*Where unseen angry voices flash and children cry*
*Past the phony posers with their worn out lines*
*The tired new money dressed to the nines*
*The low life dealers with their bad designs*
*And the dilettantes with their open minds*

— Bob Seger[2]

At the end of World War II, abortion generally was illegal across the planet, usually condemned as the murder of unborn children.[3] In almost every nation, abortion was allowed only to protect the life or health of the mother. Denmark and Sweden were exceptions, allowing abortion based upon "social indications"—indications that ostensibly justified abortions only under limited circumstances, but which could encompass a broad range of abortion.[4] Abortion had been legal from 1920 to 1936 in the Soviet Union, but abortion was a serious crime there in 1945.[5] Over the next thirty years, this situation changed profoundly. Abortion became legal to some degree in many countries, ranging from laws providing for abortion only if narrowly defined "indications" were found to the United States where the Supreme Court discovered that virtually any restriction on a woman's right to choose abortion if she found a willing physician violated a constitutional right of privacy.[6]

Japan was the first nation to break away in the post-war period from the near universal condemnation of abortion—while it was under American occupation. Japan had promoted large families before and during the war to provide the manpower needed for industry and to staff the military, and therefore had made abortion a serious crime.[7] The Japanese government, however, explained the abortion prohibition not as necessary to increase the population but as

---

1. Carly Simon, *That's the Way I've Always Heard It Should Be* (1971).
2. Bob Seger, *The Fire Inside* (1991).
3. Mary Kenny, Abortion: The Whole Story 183 (1986).
4. Katarina Lindahl, *Sweden, in* Abortion in the New Europe: A Comparative Handbook 237 (Bill Rolston & Anna Eggert eds. 1994); Nell Rasmussen, *Denmark, in* Abortion in the New Europe, *supra,* at 69
5. Law of May 26, 1936, Sbornik Zakonov SSSR, no. 34, at 309 (1936). *See* Henry Sigerist, Medicine and Health in the Soviet Union 322–23 (1947); Andrej Popov, *The USSR, in* Abortion in the New Europe, *supra* note 4, at 267, at 270–71, 274–76.
6. Roe v. Wade, 410 U.S. 113 (1973).
7. Hiromi Maruyama, *Abortion in Japan: A Feminist Critique,* 10 Wis. Women's L.J. 131, 132–34 (1995); Kinko Nakatani, *Japan, in* Abortion and Protection of the Human Fetus: Legal Problems in Cross-Cultural Perspective 221, 224 (S.J. Frankowski *et al.* Eds. 1987); Lynn Wardle, *"Crying Stones": A Comparison of Abortion in Japan and the United States,* 14 N.Y.L.S. J. Int'l & Comp. L. 183, 192–94 (1993).

necessary to protect unborn children, a claim that modern feminists find impossible to believe.[8] Japan had also enacted a eugenics law in 1940 providing for "medically necessary" abortions as well as eugenically beneficial sterilizations, although physicians were generally required to apply to a governmental agency in advance of the operation and to consult with a second physician.[9]

Japan came out of World War II impoverished, unable even to raise enough rice to feed its population. Poverty, starvation, and fear of the creation of a large class of Amerasian children during the American occupation created pressures to introduce effective family planning measures.[10] Many Japanese were also fearful of radiation induced birth defects after Hiroshima and Nagasaki.[11] Japan, with a history of tolerance towards infanticide, adopted an "indications" policy in 1948 under the guise of revising the *Eugenics Protection Law*[12] and gradually broadened it over the next four years to eliminate virtually all restraints on abortion.[13] The new statute authorized abortion for pregnancies that threatened the life or health of the mother, resulting from rape, or likely to produce a child suffering from a hereditary disease or leprosy. Before the abortion could be performed, a local "Eugenics Committee" had to determine that the existence of one of the specified indications. Responding the widespread economic destitution after the war, economically based threats to maternal health were added as an "indication" for abortion in 1949.[14] Finally, in 1952, the approval of the local Eugenics Committee was eliminated, leaving it to each individual physician to determine whether a particular indication existed.[15]

At present, Japanese law requires spousal or parental consent in addition to a physician's finding of one of the specified indications,[16] but the required consent is easily forged because of the universal use of a family seal as the husband's or father's signature.[17] No abortion is allowed if the fetus is "viable."[18] Originally, "viability" was defined by administrative regulation as a fetus in the eighth month of gestation; since 1991, it has been defined as 22 weeks gestation.[19]

In Japan, maternal health remains the most common reported "indication" for abortion, with economic concerns a close second.[20] The qualifications of the physician and the quality of the facilities are regulated by the Medical Association of Japan, a requirement imposed on no other

---

8. Maruyama, *supra* note 7, at 133, 138–39, 151–53.

9. *Id.* at 133–34; Nakatani, *supra* note 7, at 225.

10. Daniel Callahan, Abortion: Law, Choice, and Morality 253 (1970); William LaFleur, Liquid Life: Abortion and Buddhism in Japan 135 (1992); Evy McElmeel, Comment, *Legalization of the Birth Control Pill in Japan Will Reduce Reliance on Abortion as the Primary Method of Birth Control,* 8 Pac. Rim L. & Pol'y Rev. 681, 685–87 (1999); Sara Walsh, *Liquid Lives and Liquid Laws,* 7 Int'l Leg. Perspectives 187, 202–03 (1995).

11. Walsh, *supra* note 10, at 203.

12. Yuusei Hogo Ho (Eugenics Protection Law) (Japan).

13. *See* Samuel Coleman, Family Planning in Japan 19–20 (1983); Mary Standlee, The Great Pulse: Japanese Midwifery and Obstetrics through the Ages 156–58 (1959); McElmeel, *supra* note 10, at 686; Michiko Ishii, *The Abortion Problem and Family Planning Law in Japan: A Reconsideration of Legalized Abortion under the Eugenic Protection Law,* 26 Annals Inst. Soc. Sci. 64 (1985); Maruyama, *supra* note 7, at 134–40; Takishi Wagatsuma, *Induced Abortion in Japan,* in Basic Readings in Population and Family Planning in Japan 101 (M. Muramatsu ed., 3rd ed. 1985); Wardle, *supra* note 7, at 194–97.

14. Wagatsuma, *supra* note 13, at 102.

15. Yuusei Hogo Ho, *supra* note 12, art. 14.

16. *Id.* arts. 3, 14(2).

17. *See* Maruyama, *supra* note 7, at 137. *See also* Callahan, *supra* note 10, at 255; Walsh, *supra* note 10, at 205; Wardle, *supra* note 7, at 197.

18. Yuusei Hogo Ho, *supra* note 12, art. 2.

19. Maruyama, *supra* note 7, at 136, 139.

20. Coleman, *supra* note 13, at 74–75.

medical procedure.[21] One effect of these various reforms was to eliminate any need for criminal abortion. Prosecutions for illegal abortions fell from 427 in 1948 (when there were still some real restrictions in place), to 76 in 1955, to only five in 1965.[22] (Criminal abortion has become so rare in Japan that no separate statistics are kept on this crime today.) Japan, however, continued to ban the contraceptive pill until June 1999,[23] and there remains considerable cultural resistance to using the pill even after it was finally approved.[24]

No change has occurred in the language of the Japanese Eugenics Protection Law since 1952. Several attempts to repeal the economic indication for abortion while adding as an indication the likelihood of fetal "defect" have failed, largely due to the opposition of the Medical Association of Japan.[25] Some observers believe this is because the power given the individual physician to interpret and apply the authorized indications gives them the power to extract excessive fees (US$600–$1,400) for an abortion.[26] Indeed, some saw these concerns as driving the long-continued ban of the contraceptive pill in Japan.[27] (The massive cultural resistance among Japanese women—and of Japanese men—to use of the pill suggests something more is at stake. Significant controversy arose in Japan because of the speed with which Viagra was approved by the Ministry of Health and Welfare at a time when the Ministry still had not approved low-dose—and safer—birth control pill after 10 years of study.[28]) In fact, the evolution of legal and medical practice in Japan resulted in abortion on demand because of the government's tolerance for a highly flexible interpretation of the requisite "indications." Still, some Japanese feminists seek to discover a "constitutional right" to abort.[29]

Since 1949, abortion has been the primary means of birth control in Japan, with Japanese women having one of the highest abortion rates in the world.[30] Japanese women terminate about one in four pregnancies by abortion.[31] Abortion is not something the Japanese accept without qualms, however. The Japanese express deep sorrow over abortions even when they have them,

---

21. Maruyama, *supra* note 7, at 136–37

22. COLEMAN, *supra* note 13, at 25.

23. McElmeel, *supra* note 10; Sonni Efron, *Japan OKs Birth Control Pill after Decades of Delay*, L.A. TIMES, June 3, 1999, at A1. *See also* Mariko Jitsukawa & Carl Djerassi, *Birth Control in Japan: Realities and Prognosis*, 265 SCI. 1048 (1994); Hiromi Maruyama *et al.*, *Why Japan Ought to Legalize the Pill*, 379 NATURE 579 (1996).

24. Jitsukawa & Djerassi, *supra* note 23, at 1049; McElmeel, *supra* note 10, at 699–701; Chisato Nagato *et al.*, *Unapproved Use of High-Dose Combined Pills in Japan*, 26 PREVENTIVE MED. 565 (1997); Naohiro Ogawa & Robert Retherford, *Prospects for Increased Contraceptive Pill Use in Japan*, 22 STUD. IN FAM. PLANNING 378 (1991); Sheryl WuDunn, *Japan May Approve the Pill, but Women May Not*, N.Y. TIMES, Nov. 27, 1996, at A1. *See also* B.J. Oddens & A. Lolkema, *A Scenario Study of Oral Contraceptive Use in Japan*, 58 CONTRACEPTION 13 (1998).

25. Maruyama, *supra* note 7, at 140–42.

26. COLEMAN, *supra* note 13, at 24; Maruyama, *supra* note 7, at 141–42.

27. COLEMAN, *supra* note 13, at 35–37; Maruyama, *supra* note 7, at 142–44; Maruyama *et al.*, *supra* note 23, at 579; McElmeel, *supra* note 10, at 695–99; Gwen Robinson, *Ministry Reverses OK of Contraceptive Pill; Health Officials Cite Rising Incidence of AIDS, but Family Planners Blame Economic Factors*, NIKKEI WEEKLY, Mar. 28, 1992, at 9; Walsh, *supra* note 10, at 206–07.

28. McElmeel, *supra* note 10, at 687, 689–90, 696; Sheryl WuDunn, *Japan's Tale of Two Pills: Viagra and Birth Control*, N.Y. TIMES, Apr. 27, 1999, at F1; Michael Zielenziger, *Japan Again Blocks Birth-Control Pill; After Nine Years, the Health Ministry Did Say It Had Finished Its Evaluation. Future Approval Was Suggested.*, N.Y. TIMES, Mar. 4, 1999, at A4.

29. Maruyama, *supra* note 7, at 139–40, 145, 147–51, 153–60.

30. JANE CONDON, A HALF STEP BEHIND: JAPANESE WOMEN TODAY 85 (1985); STANLEY HENSHAW, INDUCED ABORTION: A WORLD VIEW 406, 428 (1990); LaFleur, *supra* note 10, at 136; Maruyama *et al.*, *supra* note 23, at 579; McElmeel, *supra* note 10, at 686–87; Walsh, *supra* note 10, at 206–09; Wardle, *supra* note 7, at 234; Sheryl WuDunn, *In Japan, a Ritual of Morning for Abortions*, N.Y. TIMES, Jan. 25, 1996, at A1, A8.

31. McElmeel, *supra* note 10, at 681; Sheldon Segal, *Contraceptive Update*, 23 NYU REV. L. & SOC. CHANGE 457, 457 (1997).

most tellingly through the dedication of innumerable religious statues (*"mizuko-jizo"* — "crying stones") to the spirits of aborted fetuses.[32] The view of abortion as immoral even when it is not illegal dates back as far as we can trace abortion in Japan.[33] One can explain the apparent contradiction between mourning, even fear of, aborted fetuses on the one hand and social tolerance of large, albeit declining, numbers of abortion through the Buddhist belief in reincartion — abortion does not deprive a fetus of life; it merely delays the birth to a more propitious time. In Hiromi Murayama's words, the fetus is "put on hold until some later date."[34] Maruyama would prefer to see the "mourning" and fear of "cursing" as simply the commercial exploitation of an artificially created women's guilt.[35] Finally, one might note that the Japanese national health plan does not pay for either abortion or childbirth, and abortions are subject to the national consumption tax.[36]

Shortly after Japan, the Soviet Union reversed course, relegalizing abortion in 1955.[37] This decision was promptly emulated throughout the Soviet zone of eastern Europe.[38] Finland (in 1950) and Norway (in 1960) also joined the movement towards an indications policy.[39] The legalization of abortion in the USSR, and the general unavailability of contraceptives, made abortion more common there than even in Japan. As many as 80 percent of pregnancies were being terminated by abortion, with a typical woman undergoing nine abortions in her lifetime.[40] Despite the legality and commonness of abortion in the Soviet Union, the requirement of counseling by a midwife before undergoing the abortion so frightened first-time abortees that most (70–90 percent) underwent an illegal abortion rather than discuss their sexuality with a stranger.[41]

Even with all this legal change and experimentation going on in Northern and Eastern Europe and Japan, for many years there seemed to be only the barest stirrings of interest in changing

---

32. LaFleur, *supra* note 10, at 4–6, 44, 126; McElmeel, *supra* note 10, at 681; Wardle, *suprai* note 7, at 183–84; WuDunn, *supra* note 30. At least one American feminist insists that this shows a lack of guilt rather than some sense that a wrong had been committed. Walsh, *supra* note 10, at 200.

33. *See* Coleman, *supra* note 13, at 62; LaFleur, *supra* note 10, at 126–27, 155; Maruyama, *supra* note 7, at 132.

34. Maruyama, *supra* note 7, at 147. *See also* LaFleur, *supra* note 10, at 23–24.

35. Maruyama, *supra* note 7, at 147. *See also* Helen Hardacre, Marketing the Menacing Fetus in Japan (1997).

36. *Id.* at 137–38.

37. Vedomsti Verkovnogo Sovieta SSSR, no. 22, item 425 (1955). *See generally* Mark Field, *The Re-Legalization of Abortion in Soviet Russia*, 255 N. Eng. J. Med. 421 (Aug. 30, 1956); Mark Savage, *The Law of Abortion in the Union of Soviet Socialist Republics and the People's Republic of China: Women's Rights in Two Socialist Countries*, 40 Stan. L. Rev. 1027, 1060 (1988).

38. Ádám Balogh & Lászlo Lampé, *Hungary*, in Abortion in the New Europe, *supra* note 4, at 139; Tomas Frejka, *Induced Abortion and Fertility: A Quarter Century of Experience in Eastern Europe*, 9 Population & Dev. Rev. 494, 495–96 (1983); Nanette Funk, *Abortion Counselling* (sic) *and the 1995 German Abortion Law*, 12 Conn. J. Int'l L. 33, 39 (1996); Gail Kligman, *The Politics of Reproduction in Ceaucescu's Romania: A Case Study in Political Culture*, 6 E. Eur. Pol. & Soc'y 364 (1992); Nicki Negrau, *Listening to Women's Voices: Living in Post-Communist Romania*, 12 Conn. J. Int'l L. 117, 122–23 (1996); Terri Owens, Note, *The Abortion Question: Germany's Dilemma Delays Unification*, 53 La. L. Rev. 1315, 1322–25 (1993); A. Pricopi, *Romania: Before and after the Revolution*, 31 U. Louisville J. Fam. L. 431, 437–42 (1993); Jeremy Telman, *Abortion and Women's Legal Personhood in Germany: A Contribution to the Feminist Theory of the State*, 24 Rev. L. & Soc. Change 91, 121–26 (1998); Radim Uzel, *Czech and Slovak Republics*, in Abortion in the New Europe, *supra*, at 55, 55–56; Dimiter Vassilev, *Bulgaria*, in Abortion in the New Europe, *supra*, at 43, 43–45; Eleanora Zielinska, *Recent Trends in Abortion Legislation in Eastern Europe, with Particular Reference to Poland*, 4 Crim. L.F. 47, 50–51 (Regina Gorzkowska trans. 1993).

39. Britta Gulli, *Norway*, in Abortion in the New Europe, *supra* note 4, at 187, 187–91; Marketta Ritamies, *Finland*, in Abortion in the New Europe, *supra*, at 85

40. Owens, *supra* note 38, at 1323; Savage, *supra* note 37, at 1063.

41. Susan Gluck Mezey, *Civil Law and Common Law Traditions: Judicial Review and Legislative Supremacy in West Germany and Canada*, 32 Int'l & Comp. L.Q. 689, 707 (1983); Savage, *supra* note 37, at 1062.

abortion laws in either England or the United States—or most of the rest of the world. The abortion laws remained on the books, and abortion remained a mostly illegal and underground proceudre. Enforcement of the abortion laws remained difficult, uncertain, and inconsistent. And remarkably little was said about the possibility of reforming or repealing those laws.

# Intensifying the Prosecution of Abortion

*Lawyers and law are what hold us together. There is no ethos.*

—Joseph Campbell[42]

Prosecutions for illegal abortions continued in the United States during the 1940s and 1950s.[43] In 1956, *Time* magazine listed prominent abortionists in Akron, Ashland (Pennsylvania), Baltimore, Cincinnati, Sacramento, St. Louis, San Diego, and Wichita, who were convicted in the preceding five years.[44] The number of prosecutions actually increased in the 1950s compared to the 1930s,[45] perhaps reflecting a greater demand for illegal abortions in prosperous times, or perhaps reflecting campaigns against corruption in the police or prosecutors' offices.[46] Dr. Russell Fisher estimated in 1954 that about 1,000 abortionists were convicted annually, which, if true, hardly demonstrates disinterest in enforcing the law.[47]

New York launched an intensive investigation into methods for improving the enforcement of abortion laws in the early 1940s.[48] This probe, led by state Assistant Attorney General John Henry Amen (1898–1960), grew out of a probe of municipal corruption that had uncovered the bribery of several assistant district attorneys to obstruct the prosecution of abortionists.[49] The *Amen Report* noted three serious problems that impeded successful prosecutions of abortion.[50] First was the difficulty of obtaining evidence if the woman did not die.[51] Second was a certain lack of zeal in prosecuting abortions reflecting a tolerant public attitude. And third was the difficulty of "securing punishment sufficiently severe to act as an effective deterrent," particularly as conviction required proof that an abortion had actually been performed or attempted. Amen's comments on public attitudes are worth quoting at greater length:

---

42. As quoted in GEORGE ANNAS, STANDARD OF CARE: THE LAW OF AMERICAN BIOETHICS 12 (1993).

43. *See, e.g., Four Seized in Alleged Illegal Operation Raids*, L.A. TIMES, Sept. 30, 1948, at 2. *See* MARVIN OLASKY, THE PRESS AND ABORTION, 1838–1988, at 68 (1988).

44. TIME, Mar. 12, 1956, at 46.

45. *See, e.g., In re* Application of Grand Jury, 143 N.Y.S.2d 501 (App. Div. 1955); *In re* Abortion in King's County, 135 N.Y.S.2d 381 (App. Div. 1954).

46. On the prevalence of official corruption in the abortion business, see Jerome Bates, *The Abortion Mill*, 45 J. CRIM. L. & CRIMINOLOGY 157, 166 (1954).

47. Russell Fisher, *Criminal Abortion*, in THERAPEUTIC ABORTION 3, 10–11 (Harold Rosen ed. 1954) (this book was reissued in 1967 under the title ABORTION IN AMERICA).

48. John Harlan Amen, *Some Obstacles to Effective Legal Control of Criminal Abortions*, in NATIONAL COMM. ON MATERNAL HEALTH, THE ABORTION PROBLEM 133 (1944).

49. *In re* Lurie, 34 N.Y.S.2d 247 (App. Div. 1942); *In re* Madden, 24 N.Y.S.2d 127 (App. Div. 1940); OLASKY, *supra* note 43, at 72–77. *See also* Weinstein v. Board of Regents, 44 N.Y.S.2d 917, 919 (App. Div. 1943), *rev'd on other grounds*, 56 N.E.2d 104 (N.Y. 1944); RICKIE SOLINGER, THE ABORTIONIST: A WOMAN AGAINST THE LAW 15, 56–105, 150–54, 159–60, 164–65, 179–80, 195–96 (paperback ed. 1996); Bates, *supra* note 46, at 163–66.

50. Amen, *supra* note 48, at 135–36.

51. *See generally* CHARLES O'HARA, FUNDAMENTALS OF CRIMINAL INVESTIGATION 477–89 (1956); HARRY SODERMAN & JOHN O'CONNELL, MODERN CRIMINAL INVESTIGATIONS 294–95 (1952).

We all know that public opinion plays a large part, not only in placing laws on the statute books, but also in their enforcement. When the moral and common sense of the community are in accord that some particular kind of behavior is wrong, the problem of enforcement becomes relatively simple. Violations are infrequent since there are few who wish to commit them. When committed, the violators are dealt with promptly, vigorously and efficiently.

On the other hand, when public opinion is lukewarm or divided, the problem of law enforcement is tremendously increased.... [A] more complete solution of the problem lies in a still further aroused public opinion. Therefore, I think it is safe to say that the greatest obstacle so far encountered to the legal control of abortions is public indifference. So long as there is a widespread public feeling that under some circumstances an induced abortion should be permissible or justified, certain results inevitably follow. There will be a large market for the services of the criminal abortionist. This practice will remain a profitable field of medical activity. These facts will aid certain doctors in convincing themselves that they are performing a useful public service. The enormous number of abortions performed and the secrecy naturally surrounding them, will impose an insurmountable burden upon the State's investigative and enforcement agencies.[52]

If the authors of the *Amen Report* considered public opinion to be generally against enforcing the abortion laws (rather than only "under some circumstances"), they produced some peculiar recommendations. The *Amen Report* recommended that the state legislature make enforcement easier by making it a crime for someone to offer to perform an abortion.[53] A bill was introduced to that effect, with the crime to be triable by the Court of Special Sessions, a court for the trial of misdemeanors before a panel of three judges sitting without a jury. The bill was not enacted. Instead, a law was enacted to provide immunity from prosecution for the woman who underwent an abortion—as a means of encouraging her to give testimony against the abortionist.[54]

An enforcement crackdown accompanied the Amen study in New York. Police raided several abortion "mills," effectively putting them out of business.[55] Similar crackdowns occurred across the country, beginning around this time and continuing through the 1950s.[56] Police in San Francisco arrested a well-known San Francisco abortionist in 1945,[57] and the Chicago police in 1941 raided the abortion mill that formed the basis of historian Leslie Reagan's study of the referral of patients to abortionists in Chicago during the 1930s.[58] Long-time abortionists were arrested (with their offices raided) in Akron, Baltimore, Brooklyn, Cincinnati, Covington (Kentucky), Detroit, Los Angeles, Portland (Oregon), Sacramento, San Diego, San Fran-

---

52. Amen, *supra* note 48, at 135.

53. *Id.* at 136.

54. 1942 N.Y. Laws, ch. 791, §1. The failure to enact Amen's proposal might simply reflect Amen's enlistment in the Army in 1942, thus making him unavailable to argue for his proposals. *See* OLASKY, *supra* note 43, at 75–76.

55. LESLIE REAGAN, WHEN ABORTION WAS A CRIME: WOMEN, MEDICINE, AND LAW IN THE UNITED STATES, 1867–1973, at 160–61, 164, 167, 181 (1997).

56. ED KEEMER, CONFESSIONS OF A PRO-LIFE ABORTIONIST 163–64 (1980); LAWRENCE LADER, ABORTION 48–51 (1966); REAGAN, *supra* note 55, at 160–75; SOLINGER, *supra* note 49, at 161–68; Loretta Ross, *African-American Women and Abortion,* in ABORTION WARS: A HALF CENTURY OF STRUGGLE, 1950–2000, at 161, 172–74 (Rickie Solinger ed. 1998) ("ABORTION WARS").

57. Morton Sontheimer, *Abortion in America Today,* WOMEN'S HOME COMPANION, Oct. 1955, at 96.

58. REAGAN, *supra* note 55, at 148–55. See the text *infra* at notes 175–83.

cisco, St. Louis, Trenton, and Wichita.[59] In Los Angeles, six police officers were devoted solely to pursuing abortion cases.[60] Perhaps some of these arrests were staged in order to extort bribes from abortionists—as several observers inferred.[61] Still, many of the arrests resulted in convictions, an unlikely outcome if bribery were the goal. In fact, this effort was so intense that a journalist, writing in *Ebony* magazine in 1951, could write that "Ten years ago, reform movements and law enforcement drives drove practically all the competent abortionists out of business."[62]

New York introduced at this time "paid investigators" posing as women seeking abortions in order to obtain evidence against abortionists.[63] While many former patients were unwilling to testify, enough could be persuaded or pressured into testifying to bring about numerous convictions.[64] As in New York, states in which women were also criminals for having abortions enacted immunity statutes at about this time to protect women from prosecution if they would testify against their abortionists.[65] This highlighted the importance of the view in most states that women were victims of the crime of abortion rather than accomplices, removing any possible impediment to their testifying against the abortionist.[66] And while prosecutors were somewhat more reticent about pursuing doctors who had referred women to abortionists, this too began.[67]

With the use of paid investigators, willingness to bring intense pressure on women to force them to testifying, and use of abortionists' records seized in raids to track down former patients, prosecutions were no longer limited to cases in which the woman died.[68] So zealous were the police and prosecutors that some cases were overturned on appeal for violations of legal technicalities.[69] Even so, abortionists were out of business, at least for a time. The intensity of the pressure on abortionists is suggested by the murder of witnesses and by defendants committing suicide.[70] None of this suggests that prosecutions were simply an effort to extort money from abortionists.

The practice of using paid investigators, later to be a common feature of civil rights litigation, had long been used in professional disciplinary proceedings in New York.[71] Detection of illegal abortions in terms of professional disciplinary proceedings was no easier than for criminal prosecutions, but in a civil proceeding for the revocation of a license to practice medicine

---

59. Reagan, *supra* note 55, at 164. *See also* Keemer, *supra* note 56, at 163–64; Solinger, *supra* note 49, at 71–73, 117–21, 169–75, 201, 209, 211, 214; Ross, *supra* note 56, at 172–73.

60. David Garrow, Liberty and Sexuality: The Right of Privacy and the Making of *Roe v. Wade* 279 (2nd ed. 1998).

61. Jerome Bates & Edward Zawadski, Criminal Abortion 68–70 (1964). *See also* Reagan, *supra* note 55, at 164; Solinger, *supra* note 49, at 179–80.

62. *The Abortion Menace*, Ebony, Jan. 1951, at 24, as quoted in Reagan, *supra* note 55, at 164, 197. *See also* Abortion in the United States: A Conference Sponsored by the Planned Parenthood Federation of America, Inc. at Arden House and the New York Academy of Medicine 40 (statement of Dr. Alfred Kinsey) (Mary Calderone ed. 1958).

63. Amen, *supra* note 48, at 139. *See also* Solinger, *supra* note 49, at 166–67, 220.

64. Amen, *supra* note 48, at 164–71.

65. 1942 N.Y. Laws ch. 791, § 1. For other states with similar statutory grants of immunity, see B. James George, jr., *Current Abortion Laws: Proposals and Movements for Reform*, in Abortion and the Law 1, 12–14 nn.70–73 (David Smith ed. 1967).

66. *See* Chapter 6, at notes 303–19.

67. Reagan, *supra* note 55, at 166, 171–72.

68. *Id.* at 164, 170, 172; Solinger, *supra* note 49, at 195–96.

69. *See, e.g.*, People v. Stanko, 95 N.E.2d 861 (Ill. 1951), 84 N.E.2d 839 (Ill. 1949); People v. Martin, 46 N.E.2d 997 (Ill. 1943). *See* Patricia Miller, The worst of Times 215–16 (1993); Reagan, *supra* note 55, at 166–67, 171.

70. Reagan, *supra* note 55, at 167.

71. Amen, *supra* note 48, at 139.

the finding of a violation needed only be proven by preponderance of the evidence rather than, as in a criminal prosecution, beyond a reasonable doubt.[72] The result was a significant difference in success rates between the two sorts of proceedings. Although we have no reason to believe that disciplinary proceedings were more common than criminal prosecutions, we do know that the State of New York regularly revoked or suspended licenses to practice medicine based upon the performance of criminal abortions, attempts to perform criminal abortions, or offers to perform criminal abortions.[73] In New York, such proceedings were a more

---

72. Zimmerman v. Board of Regents, 294 N.Y.S.2d 435 (App. Div. 1968). *See also* Jordan v. Alderson, 192 P. 170 (Cal. Ct. App. 1920); Rutledge v. Department of Registration, 222 N.E.2d 195 (Ill. App. Ct. 1966); Knight v. Louisiana St. Bd. of Med. Examiners, 211 So. 2d 433 (La. Ct. App. 1968); Younge v. State Bd. of Registration for Healing Arts, 451 S.W.2d 346 (Mo. 1969). *But see* Shively v. Stewart, 421 P.2d 65 (Cal. 1966).

73. Friedel v. Board of Regents, 73 N.E.2d 545 (N.Y. 1947); Jablon v. Board of Regents,73 N.E.2d 904 (N.Y. 1947); Neshamkin v. Board of Regents, 66 N.E.2d 124 (N.Y. 1946); Epstein v. Board of Regents, 65 N.E.2d 756 (N.Y. 1946); Weinstein v. Board of Regents, 56 N.E.2d 104 (N.Y. 1944); Kasha v. Board of Regents, 48 N.E.2d 712 (N.Y. 1943); Neshamkin v. Board of Regents, 23 N.E.2d 16 (N.Y. 1939); Kahn v. Board of Regents, 23 N.E.2d 16 (N.Y. 1939); Mascitelli v. Board of Regents, 299 N.Y.S.2d 1002 (App. Div. 1969); Zimmerman v. Board of Regents, 294 N.Y.S.2d 435 (App. Div. 1968); Scardaccione v. Allen, 280 N.Y.S.2d 716 (App. Div. 1967); Sos v. Board of Regents, 272 N.Y.S.2d 87 (App. Div. 1966) (annulled based on lack of sufficient evidence), *aff'd*, 281 N.Y.S.2d 831 (App. Div. 1967); Ciofalo v. Board of Regents, 258 N.Y.S.2d 881 (App. Div.), *appeal denied*, 261 N.Y.S.2d 1025 (N.Y. 1965); Shapiro v. Board of Regents, 254 N.Y.S.2d 906 (App. Div. 1964), *aff'd*, 209 N.E.2d 821 (N.Y. 1965); Schacht v. Board of Regents, 248 N.Y.S.2d 65 (App. Div. 1964); Jones v. Allen, 168 N.Y.S.2d 42 (App. Div. 1957); Robinson v. Board of Regents, 164 N.Y.S.2d 863 (App. Div. 1957); Genova v. Board of Regents, 74 N.Y.S.2d 729 (App. Div. 1947); Newman v. Board of Regents, 61 N.Y.S.2d 841 (App. Div. 1946); *In re* Herschman, 56 N.Y.S.2d 241 (App. Div. 1945); Rothenberg v. Board of Regents, 44 N.Y.S.2d 926 (App. Div. 1943), *appeal denied*, 47 N.Y.S.2d 284 (App. Div. 1944); Reiner v. Board of Regents, 6 N.Y.S.2d 356 (App. Div. 1938); Minton v. Board of Regents, 287 N.Y.S. 502 (App. Div. 1936); Lefferts v. Wilson, 112 N.Y.S.2d 512 (Sup. Ct. 1952).

For a sampling of such proceedings in other states, see: Ladrey v. Commission on Licensure, 261 F.2d 68 (D.C. App. 1958); Schoenen v. Board of Med. Examiners, 54 Cal. Rptr. 364 (App. 1966); Randle v. State Bd. of Pharmacy, 49 Cal. Rptr. 485 (App. 1966); Marlo v. State Bd. of Med. Examiners, 246 P.2d 69 (Cal. Ct. App. 1952); Bogart v. Board of Med. Examiners, 233 P.2d 100 (Cal. Ct. App. 1951); Stuck v. Board of Med. Examiners, 211 P.2d 389 (Cal. Ct. App. 1949) (merely offering to do an abortion justifies revocation of a medical license); Bartosh v. Board of Osteopathic Examiners, 186 P.2d 984 (Cal. Ct. App. 1947); Murphy v. Board of Med. Examiners, 170 P.2d 510 (Cal. Ct. App. 1946); Minaker v. Adams, 203 P. 806 (Cal. Ct. App. 1921); Jordan v. Alderson, 192 P. 170 (Cal. Ct. App. 1920); Lanterman v. Anderson, 172 P. 625 (Cal. Ct. App. 1918); State Bd. of Med. Examiners v. Noble, 177 P. 141 (Colo. 1918); Thompson v. State Bd. of Med. Examiners, 151 P. 436 (Colo. 1915); Kemp v. Board of Med. Supervisors, 46 App. D.C. 173 (1917) (merely mailing information promoting abortions is grounds for revoking a license); State Bd. of Med. Examiners v. James, 158 So. 2d 574 (Fla. Ct. App. 1964); Grimes v. Kennedy, 152 So. 2d 509 (Fla. Ct. App. 1963); Rutledge v. Department of Registration, 222 N.E.2d 195 (Ill. App. Ct. 1966); Knight v. Louisiana St. Bd. of Med. Examiners, 211 So. 2d 433 (La. Ct. App. 1968); Kudish v. Board of Registration in Med., 248 N.E.2d 264 (Mass. 1969); Lawrence v. Briry, 132 N.E. 174 (Mass. 1921); Younge v. State Bd. of Registration for Healing Arts, 451 S.W.2d 346 (Mo. 1969); State *ex rel.* Johnson v. Clark, 232 S.W. 1031 (Mo. 1921) (insufficient evidence); Spriggs v. Robinson, 161 S.W. 1169 (Mo. 1913) (merely offering to do an abortion without doing it is not grounds for suspending a licence); Bridges v. State Bd. of Registration for Healing Arts, 419 S.W.2d 278 (Mo. Ct. App. 1967); Wasem v. Dental Bd., 405 S.W.2d 492 (Mo. Ct. App. 1966); State v. Kellogg, 36 P. 957 (Mont. 1894) (insufficient evidence); Mathews v. Hedlund, 119 N.W. 17 (Neb. 1908); Walker v. McMahan, 116 N.W. 528 (Neb. 1908); Munk v. Fink, 116 N.W. 525 (Neb. 1908); State *ex rel.* Kassabian v. State Bd. of Med. Examiners, 235 P.2d 327 (Nev. 1951); Blumberg v. State Bd. of Med. Examiners, 115 A. 439 (N.J. Super. 1921); *In re* Mintz, 378 P.2d 945 (Or. 1963); *In re* Buck, 258 P.2d 124 (Or. 1953); Board of Med. Examiners v. Eisen, 123 P. 52 (Or. 1912) (insufficient evidence); State v. Estes, 55 P. 25 (Or. 1898) (same); Martinez v. State Bd. of Med. Examiners, 476 S.W.2d 400 (Tex. Ct. Civ. App. 1972); Sherman v. McEntire, 179 P.2d 796 (Utah 1947); Rodermund v. State, 168 N.W. 390 (Wis. 1918). *See also* ROBERT DERBYSHIRE, MEDICAL LICENSURE AND DISCIPLINE IN THE UNITED STATES 78, 85 (1969) (collecting 71 such cases brought between 1963 and 1967).

successful tool against illicit abortions than criminal prosecutions, despite the fact that the *Education Law* required any recommendation of discipline by the investigating committee to be unanimous.[74] Remarkably, historian Leslie Reagan dismisses this reality by writing only that "physicians could imagine the state revoking physicians' medical licenses"—as if this seldom happened.[75]

Amen's proposals to streamline medical disciplinary process also were not enacted. Given the apparently greater success of such proceedings compared to criminal proceedings, failure to enact these proposals might have been because they were felt to be unnecessary rather than out of a concern to protect abortionists. After all, offers to perform an abortion, if made by a doctor, were already grounds for professional discipline under the state's licensing procedures.[76] It wasn't necessary to prove that the physician actually performed an abortion. When reliance on paid investigators was introduced into criminal trials, however, courts initially worried about the possibility of entrapment, and thus required independent corroborative evidence to sustain a conviction.[77] Eventually, the use of paid investigators was upheld by New York's highest court, and their testimony alone was then adequate to support a conviction.[78] At the other end of the country, the California legislature restricted the ability of defendant-physicians to delay proceedings to gather evidence in their defense.[79]

The *Amen Report* sought to strengthen the medical disciplinary rules and the criminal penalties as well as the procedures. The *Amen Report* proposed to make referrals for abortions subject to professional and criminal penalties.[80] The bill to amend the *Education Law* to subject a referring physician to disciplinary proceedings was enacted and signed into law on May 8, 1942.[81] A second bill to make it a misdemeanor to provide any information "as to where or by whom an abortion could be performed" died in the legislature,[82] a failure that would prove significant 25 years later when a group of clergy initiated an open abortion referral service in New York City that seriously undermined the state's abortion laws.[83]

The *Amen Report* proposed to strengthen enforcement of the abortion law and of educating the public about the seriousness of the wrong committed through violating the abortion statutes of the State. While the legislature did less to change New York's abortion laws than the *Amen Report* suggested, what changes the legislature did enact were all designed to strengthen rather than weaken enforcement. Yet even while these efforts were underway, the practice of abortion was changing in ways that would make enforcement of the abortion laws increasingly difficult.

---

74. Amen, *supra* note 48, at 142.

75. REAGAN, *supra* note 55, at 171.

76. *Id.* at 139; Thomas Harris, Note, *A Functional Study of Existing Abortion Laws*, 35 COLUM. L. REV. 87, 91 n. 18 (1935).

77. Rothenberg v. Board of Regents, 44 N.Y.S.2d 926 (App. Div. 1943), *appeal denied*, 47 N.Y.S.2d 284 (App. Div. 1944); Weinstein v. Board of Regents, 44 N.Y.S.2d 917 (App. Div. 1943), *rev'd on other grounds*, 56 N.Y.S.2d 104 (N.Y. 1944). *See also* MILLER, *supra* note 69, at 35 (reporting a similar practice in Baltimore).

78. Epstein v. Board of Regents, 65 N.E.2d 756 (N.Y. 1946).

79. *See* Keneally v. California Med. Bd., 32 Cal. Rptr. 2d 504 (Ct. App. 1994), *rev. denied*.

80. Amen, *supra* note 48, at 137–38. *Cf.* People v. Buffum, 256 P.2d 317 (Cal. 1953) (overturning a conviction for conspiracy to abort through referrals to a Mexican abortionist).

81. Codified at N.Y. EDUC. LAW §6530 (McKinney 1953).

82. Amen, *supra* note 48, at 142.

83. GARROW, *supra* note 60, at 333–34, 364; LOUIS LADER, ABORTION II: MAKING THE REVOLUTION 42–47 (1973); ROSALIND POLLACK PETCHESKY, ABORTION AND WOMEN'S CHOICE: THE STATE, SEXUALITY, AND REPRODUCTIVE FREEDOM 127–29 (rev. ed. 1990).

# The Incidence of Abortion
# between 1950 and 1970

*The plural of* anecdote *is not* data.

—Edith Greene[84]

Even while prosecutorial efforts intensified in the 1940s, abortion itself—whether legal or illegal—was becoming dramatically safer. The advent of antibiotics (sulfa drugs in the 1930s, and penicillin in 1940) reduced the incidence of the heretofore fatal infections and completed a dramatic reduction in the risk of death or injury from an abortion that had begun 75 years earlier.[85] This became apparent when statistics from the countries in eastern Europe that legalized abortion virtually on demand after 1955 were published.[86] Statistics in the United States told a similar story. The recorded number of women who died from septic abortions in New York City declined from 140 in 1931 to 48 in 1941 to only 15 in 1951.[87] As a result, a study by the pro-abortion Alan Guttmacher Institute concluded, some 30 years later, that

> reported rates of abortion mortality are more closely associated with the availability of modern methods of contraception (including surgical sterilization), with the general level of health services, and with the adequacy of the registration system than with the legal status of abortion or the presumed incidence of illegal abortions by untrained operators.[88]

Between 1945 and 1960, abortion finally became the safe, effective, and reasonably comfortable procedure for the mother that the new abortion history claims that it always was.[89] This cer-

---

84. Edith Green, *A Love-Hate Relationship*, 18 Just. Sys. J. 99, 100 (1995) (emphasis in the original).

85. Roe v. Wade, 410 U.S. 113, 148–50, 163 (1973); Barbara Brookes, Abortion in England 1900–1967, at 42, 49 n.132, 58–59, 70–71, 122 (1988); Committee for Psychiatry and the Law, The Right to Abortion: A Psychiatric View 33–37 (1970); Report of the Interdepartmental Committee on Abortion 18 (1939) ("Interdepartmental Comm."); Jerome Legge, Abortion Policy: An Evaluation of the Consequences for Maternal and Infant Health 150–55 (1985); J.G. Moore & J.H. Randall, *Trends in Therapeutic Abortion: A Review of 137 Cases*, 63 Am. J. Obstet. & Gynecology 34 (1952); Malcolm Potts, *Postconception Control of Fertility*, 8 Int'l J. Gynecology & Obstetrics 957, 967 (1970); Christopher Tietze, *United States: Therapeutic Abortions, 1963–1968*, 59 Stud. in Fam. Plan. 5, 7 (1970). *See also* Chapter 10, at notes 6–23.

86. Harold Klinger, *Demographic Consequences of the Legalization of Induced Abortion in Eastern Europe*, Int'l J. Gynecology & Obstetrics 680 (Sept. 1970); Christopher Tietze, *Abortion Laws and Abortion Practices in Europe*, in Proc. Am. Ass'n Planned Parenthood Physicians 198 (1969).

87. Solinger, *supra* note 49, at 140.

88. Christopher Teitze & Stanley Henshaw, Induced Abortion: A World Review 1986, at 127 (1986). *See also* Kerry Petersen, Abortion Regimes 50–51 (1993).

89. For historians who have assumed that abortion was always readily available to women through techniques that presumably were reasonably safe, effective, and comfortable, see 1Bonnie Anderson & Judith Zinsser, A History of Their Own: Women in Europe from Prehistory to the Present 137–38 (1988); Janet Farrell Brodie, Contraception and Abortion in Nineteenth-Century America 33, 41–44, 224–25 (1994); Brookes, *supra* note 85, at 1, 24; Rebecca Chalker & Carol Downer, A Woman's Book of Choices: Abortion, Menstrual Extraction, RU 486, at 9 (1993); Celeste Michelle Condit, Decoding Abortion Rhetoric: Communicating Social Change 77 n.29 (1990); John D'Emilio & Estelle Freedman, Intimate Matters: A History of Sexuality in America 63, 145–50 (1988); Audrey Eccles, Obstetrics and Gynaecology in Tudor and Stuart England 67 (1982); Marie-Thérèse Fontanille, Abortement et contraception dans la médecine grèco-romaine (1977); Faye Ginsburg, Contested Lives: The Abortion Debate in an American Community 23–24, 30 (1989); Linda Gordon, Woman's Body, Woman's Right: A Social History of Birth Control in America 28–29, 35–39, 52–54 (1976); Michael Gorman, Abortion and the Early Church: Christian, Jewish & Pagan Attitudes in the Greco-Roman World

tainly was true of legal abortions, and probably was true for illegal abortions as well, at least when performed by a physician or other trained health-care professional. And contemporaries were telling us that licensed physicians did most illegal abortions. Dr. Mary Calderone, national medical director of the Planned Parenthood Federation in 1960, estimated in that year that physicians performed 90 percent of illegal abortions.[90] Dr. Alan Guttmacher, a leader of the legalization movement whose memory is commemorated in the name of the pro-abortion research institute already mentioned, estimated in 1967 that physicians performed 80 percent of illegal abortions.[91] Guttmacher also mentioned an unnamed physician in Baltimore who in the 1930s performed 12,000 abortions with "only 4 deaths"—meaning, of course, maternal deaths.[92]

Today, abortion can be less painful for the mother than a trip to the dentist, and less anxiety producing—if the woman accepts emotionally what is happening.[93] Yet so long as abortion re-

---

14–15, 18–19, 25–28, 94 (1982); JANET HADLEY, ABORTION: BETWEEN FREEDOM AND NECESSITY 33–34 (1996); BEVERLY WILDUNG HARRISON, OUR RIGHT TO CHOOSE: TOWARD A NEW ETHIC OF ABORTION 238–44 (1983); OLWEN HUFTON, THE POOR IN EIGHTEENTH CENTURY FRANCE 331 (1974); MARTIN INGRAM, CHURCH COURTS, SEX AND MARRIAGE IN ENGLAND, 1570–1640, at 159 (1987); RALPH JACKSON, DOCTORS AND DISEASES IN THE ROMAN EMPIRE 105–09 (1988); DONALD JUDGES, HARD CHOICES, LOST VOICES 32, 83–84, 96–97, 101 (1993); ANGUS MCLAREN, BIRTH CONTROL IN NINETEENTH-CENTURY ENGLAND 34, 241 (1978) ("MCLAREN, BIRTH CONTROL"); ANGUS MCLAREN, REPRODUCTIVE RITUALS 5–7, 107, 111–12, 114 (1984); J.S. MILNE, SURGICAL INSTRUMENTS IN GREEK & ROMAN TIMES 81–82 (1907); JAMES MOHR, ABORTION IN AMERICA: THE ORIGINS AND EVOLUTION OF NATIONAL POLICY, 1800–1900, at 11–14, 18, 25–40, 85–118, 128, 147–82 (1978); PETCHESKY, *supra* note 83, at 1–2, 28–30, 48–57, 70–71, 76–78; PETERSEN, *supra* note 88, at 1, 12; G.R. QUAIFE, WANTON WENCHES AND WAYWARD WIVES: PEASANTS AND ILLICIT SEX IN EARLY SEVENTEENTH CENTURY ENGLAND 118–20 (1979); REAGAN, *supra* note 55, at 6–8; DEBORAH RHODE, JUSTICE AND GENDER 202 (1989); PATRICK SHEERAN, WOMEN, SOCIETY, THE STATE, AND ABORTION: A STRUCTURALIST ANALYSIS 49–51, 54, 58, 73, 75 (1987); EDWARD SHORTER, A HISTORY OF WOMEN'S BODIES 177–91 (Pelican Books ed. 1984); CARROLL SMITH-ROSENBERG, DISORDERLY CONDUCT: VISIONS OF GENDER IN VICTORIAN AMERICA 217 (1985); VERA ST. ERLICH, FAMILY IN TRANSITION: A STUDY OF 300 YUGOSLAV VILLAGES 257, 295 (1966); LAURENCE TRIBE, ABORTION: THE CLASH OF ABSOLUTES 30–34 (1990); JEFFREY WEEKS, SEX, POLITICS AND SOCIETY 72 (1981); CATHERINE WHITNEY, WHOSE LIFE? A BALANCED, COMPREHENSIVE VIEW OF ABORTION FROM ITS HISTORICAL CONTEXT TO THE CURRENT DEBATE 39–44 (1991); *Amicus Brief of 250 American Historians in support of Appellants in* Planned Parenthood of Southeastern Pennsylvania v. Casey, [505 U.S. 833 (1992)], at 4–10; *Amicus Brief of 281 American Historians supporting Appellees in* Webster v. Reproducive Health Services [492 U.S. 490 (1989)], reprinted at 11 WOMEN'S RTS. L. RPTR. 163, 170–77 (1989), and in 8 DOCUMENTARY HISTORY OF THE LEGAL ASPECTS OF ABORTION IN THE UNITED STATES: *WEBSTER V. REPRODUCTIVE HEALTH SERVICES* 107 (Roy Mersky & Gary Hartman eds. 1990) ("DOCUMENTARY HISTORY"); Jane Maslow Cohen, *A Jurisprudence of Doubt: Deliberative Autonomy and Abortion*, 3 COLUM. J. GENDER & LAW. 175, 206–07 (1992); Diane Curtis, *Doctored Rights: Menstrual Extraction, Self-Help Gynecological Care, and the Law,* 20 REV. L. & SOC. CHANGE 427, 435 (1994); Cornelia Hughes Dayton, *Taking the Trade: Abor tion and Gender Relations in an Eighteenth-Century New England Village,* 48 WM. & MARY Q. 19, 19–20, 23 (1991); Sheila Dickinson, *Abortion in Antiquity,* 6 ARETHUSA 159 (1973); James Hitchcock, *Respect for Life and the Health Care Professions: A Historical Study,* in HUMAN LIFE AND HEALTH CARE ETHICS 37, 37–38, 46 (James Bopp, jr., ed. 1985); John Noonan, jr., *An Almost Absolute Value in History,* in THE MORALITY OF ABORTION: LEGAL AND HISTORICAL PERSPECTIVES 1, 3–7 (John Noonan, jr., ed. 1970); Elizabeth Karlin, *"We Called It Kindness": Establishing a Feminist Abortion Practice,* in ABORTION WARS, *supra* note 56, at 273, 273; Ross, *supra* note 56, at 164–65; Reva Siegel, *Reasoning from the Body: A Historical Perspective on Abortion Regulation and Questions of Equal Protection,* 44 STAN. L. REV. 261, 318 n.235 (1992); Étienne van de Walle, *Motivations and Technology and the Decline of French Fertility,* in FAMILY AND SEXUALITY IN FRENCH HISTORY 135, 144–45 (Robert Wheaton & Tamara Hareven eds. 1980); Ray Bowen Ward, *The Use of the Bible in the Abortion Debate,* 13 ST. L.U. PUB. L. REV. 391, 392–93 (1993).

90. Mary Calderone, *Illegal Abortion as a Public Health Problem*, 50 AM. J. PUB. HEALTH 948, 949 (1960).

91. THE CASE FOR LEGALIZED ABORTION NOW 69, 71–72 (Alan Guttmacher ed. 1967) ("ABORTION NOW"). *See also* BERNARD NATHANSON & RICHARD OSTUNG, ABORTING AMERICA 21–22 (1979); REAGAN, *supra* note 56, at 70–73.

92. ALAN GUTTMACHER, BABIES BY CHOICE OR CHANCE 216 (1959).

93. KENNY, *supra* note 3, at 274–88.

mained in the shadows, a criminal act done in sleazy surroundings by secretive people, the procedure continued to be a source or guilt and shame for most women, as well as a source of actual danger because short cuts were taken to speed the procedure in the effort to avoid discovery.[94] As a result, many women came to see abortion's prohibition, rather than its possibility, as the threat to their well being.[95] These technological changes simply enabled social expression of the natural, inherent physiological conflict between a mother and her unborn child, a conflict the outcome of which determines whether a child is miscarried or born alive.[96] But many women seeking an abortion are ambivalent about having the child, and many women and abortion providers continue to feel guilt and shame about having an abortion, even with abortion legal and praised by prominent opinion leaders as a responsible and appropriate means of solving social, economic and physiological problems.[97] As Carole Joffe, a pro-abortion activist, reported after taking a job at an abortion clinic, "[b]efore I came here I don't remember any ambivalence—abortion was safe and legal, and I looked at it in terms of feminist platitudes....Working here, the rhetoric doesn't protect you from the implications of abortion, the moral issues."[98]

Nothing illustrates the increasing safety of abortions for the mothers in the twentieth century than the sharp decline in maternal deaths from induced abortions.[99] Maternal deaths annually almost certainly were less than 1,000 throughout the post-war years, and by the 1960s was probably less than 100 and perhaps as few as 25 per year after 1970.[100] No one can be quite sure precisely what the actual figure was. Thus, one study in Michigan found 286 maternal

---

94. *See* Nanette Davis, From Crime to Choice xiii, 3–4 (1985); D'Emilio & Freedman, *supra* note 89, at 64; Frederick Taussig, Abortion: Spontaneous and Induced 403 (1936); Caroline Hadley Robinson, Seventy Birth Control Clinics 66 (1930). *See generally* Simone de Beauvoir, The Second Sex 540–50 (2nd ed. H.M. Parshley trans. 1974); Brookes, *supra* note 85, at 2, 5–6, 26–36; Chalker & Downer, *supra* note 89, at 97–109; Davis, *supra*, at 65–107; D'Emilio & Freedman, *supra*, at 254–55; European Women: A Documentary History, 1789–1945, at 207–09 (Eleanor Riemer & John Fouts eds. 1980); Linda Bird Francke, The Ambivalence of Abortion (1978); Ellen Frankfurt, Vaginal Politics 51–83 (Bantam ed. 1973); From Abortion to Reproductive Freedom: Transforming a Movement 71–73, 87–100 (Marlene Gerber Fried ed. 1990); Joyce Johnson, Minor Characters 107–110 (1983); Kenny, *supra* note 3, at 200–24; Nancy Howell Lee, The Search for an Abortionist (1969); Kristin Luker, Abortion and the Politics of Motherhood 73–76, 105 (1984); McLaren, Birth Control, *supra* note 89, at 226–28; Ellen Messer & Kathryn May, Back Rooms: Voices from the Illegal Abortion Era (1988); Miller, *supra* note 69; Petchesky, *supra* note 83, at 52–55; Reagan, *supra* note 56, at 196–200; Diane Schulder & Florynce Kennedy, Abortion Rap 44–82 (1971); The Choices We Made (Angela Bonavoglia ed. 1991); Rita Townsend & Ann Perkins, Bitter Fruit: Women's Experience of Unplanned Pregnancy, Abortion, and Adoption (1991); Whitney, *supra* note 89, at 48–69; Glanville Williams, The Sanctity of Life and the Criminal Law 211–12 (1957, reprinted 1972); Bates, *supra* note 46.

95. *See* Brookes, *supra* note 85, at 58–60; Davis, *supra* note 94, at 3–14; Harrison, *supra* note 89, at 167–68; Petchesky, *supra* note 83, at 113–16; Donald & Beth Wellman Granberg, *Abortion Attitudes, 1965–1980: Trends and Determinants,* 12 Fam. Plan. Persp. 250 (1980).

96. *See* Marc Lipsitch, *Genetic Tug-of-War May Explain Many of the Troubles of Pregnancy: Study Depicts Conflict between Fetus and the Pregnant Woman,* N.Y. Times, July 20, 1993, at C3.

97. *See, e.g.,* Warren Hern, Abortion Practice 69–73 (2nd ed. 1990); Diane Gianelli, *Abortion Providers Share Inner Conflicts,* Am. Med. News, July 12, 1993, at 3; Nancy Kaltreider *et al., The Impact of Midtrimester Abortion Techniques on Patients and Staff,* 135 Am. J. Obstet. & Gynecology 235 (1979); Cleo Kocol, *Let's Take the Guilt Away,* 48 The Humanist 33 (May/June 1988); Bernard Nathanson, *Deeper into Abortion,* 291 N. Eng. J. Med. 1189 (1974); David Smolin, *Cultural and Technological Obstacles to the Mainstreaming of Abortion,* 13 St.L. U. Pub. L. Rev. 261, 270–74 (1993). *See also* James Burtchaell, Rachel Weeping and Other Essays on Abortion (1982).

98. Carole Joffe, The Regulation of Sexuality 112 (1986);

99. Kenny, *supra* note 3, at 195; Miller, *supra* note 69, at 327; John Noonan, Jr., A Private Choice: Abortion in America in the Seventies 65 (1979) (estimating between 250 and 500 maternal deaths per year); Preventing Maternal Deaths 109–10 (Erica Royston & Sue Armstrong eds. 1989).

100. Ian Gentles, *Good News for the Fetus: Two Fallacies in the Abortion Debate,* Policy Rev., Spring 1987, at 50 (finding evidence of only 20 to 25 maternal deaths per year in the United States, less than five per year in

deaths from abortions in Michigan spread over 22 years—an average of 13 per year.[101] This figure would indicate a national total for the United States of well under 1,000. The American Public Health Association gave the figure of 193 deaths for the entire United States in 1965.[102] Dr. Christopher Tietze, the leading statistician among the supporters of abortion freedom, estimated the number of maternal deaths in 1967 as between 500 and 1,000 nationwide.[103] Two decades later, Tietze apparently thought the real number was only 150 per year.[104] Others have estimated the number of maternal deaths as several hundred per year.[105] The Centers for Disease Controls estimated 39 maternal deaths from illegal abortions and 24 from legal abortions in 1972—the year before *Roe* was decided.[106] The Centers for Disease Control later estimated that abortion-related deaths after *Roe* averaged about 15 per year.[107] Indeed, Dr. Mary Calderone, medical director of Planned Parenthood, wrote in 1960, before she concluded that legalizing abortion was possible:

> Abortion is no longer a dangerous procedure. This applies not just to therapeutic abortions as performed in hospitals, but also to so-called illegal abortions as done by physicians. In 1957 there were only 260 deaths in the whole country attributed to abortions of any kind.... Two corollary factors must be mentioned here: First, chemotherapy and antibiotics have come in, benefiting all surgical procedures as well as abortion. Second, and even more important, the [1955 Planned Parenthood] conference estimated that 90 percent of all illegal abortions are presently done by physicians. Call them what you will, abortionists or anything else, they are still physicians, trained as such; and many of them are in good standing in their communities. They must do a pretty good job if the death rate is as low as it is. Whatever trouble arises usually comes after self-induced abortions, which comprise approximately 8 percent, or with the very small percentage that go to some kind of nonmedical abortionist.... Abortion, whether therapeutic or illegal, is in the main no longer dangerous, because it is being done well by physicians.[108]

Dr. Alan Guttmacher noted at about the same time, "[t]he technique of the well-accredited criminal abortionist is usually good. They have to be good to stay in business, since otherwise they would be extremely vulnerable to police action."[109]

---

Britain and in Canada "shortly prior to legalization"; attributing these low figures to the widespread use of antiseptics and antibiotics).

101. DAVIS, *supra* note 94, at 117.

102. JUDGES, *supra* note 89, at 78.

103. Christopher Tietze & Sarah Lewit, *Abortion*, 220 SCIENTIFIC AM. 220 (Jan. 1969).

104. Christopher Tietze, *The Public Health Effects of Legal Abortion in the United States*, 16 FAM. PLANNING PERSPECTIVES 26 (1984) (concluding that legalizing abortion saved 1,500 women's lives in its first decade).

105. BURTCHAELL, *supra* note 97, at 65 (estimating 133 deaths nationally in 1967); GERMAIN GRISEZ, ABORTION: THE MYTHS, THE REALITIES, AND THE ARGUMENTS 35–42 (1970) (estimating several hundred maternal deaths per year from abortions); DAVID REARDON, ABORTED WOMEN: SILENT NO MORE 282–84 (1987) (at most several hundred per year); Robert Hall, *Commentary*, in ABORTION AND THE LAW, *supra* note 65, at 224, 228 (estimating less than 500 deaths from abortion per year). Former Surgeon General C. Everett Koop has stated that the greatest number of maternal deaths from illegal abortions before *Roe* was 373, but without indicating what period he had in mind. *Koop Makes Abortion Prediction*, N.Y. TIMES, Jan. 20, 1989, at A5.

106. U.S. PUB. HEALTH SERV., CENTERS FOR DISEASE CONTROL, ABORTION SURVEILLANCE 61 (Nov. 1980). The Centers for Disease Control annual statistics for maternal deaths for the years 1970–85 are summarized in MAUREEN MULDOON, THE ABORTION DEBATE IN THE UNITED STATES AND CANADA: A SOURCE BOOK 9 (1991); Jack Smith, *Public Health Implications of Abortion: Statistics Compiled by the Centers for Disease Control*, in ABORTION AND THE STATES 81, 86–87, 98–99 (Jane Wishner ed. 1993).

107. Hanik Atrash *et al.*, *Legal Abortion in the United States: Trends and Mortality*, 35 CONTEMP. OBSTETRICS & GYNECOLOGY 58 (Feb. 1990); H.W. Lawson *et al.*, *Abortion Mortality, United States, 1972 through 1987*, 171 AM. J. OBSTET. & GYNECOLOGY 1365 (1994).

108. Calderone, *supra* note 90, at 949. *See also* ABORTION IN THE UNITED STATES, *supra* note 62, at 65–68.

109. GUTTMACHER, *supra* note 92, at 216.

The actual number of recorded maternal deaths from illegal abortions undoubtedly are an undercount given the incentives for the abortionist, and the dead woman's family, to hide the true cause of death. Just how much higher the real figures are must remain a mystery. In 1964, Jerome Bates and Edward Zawadski estimated at least 5,000 maternal deaths from illegal abortions annually without providing any basis for their figure.[110] They apparently took their figure from the similarly undocumented estimates that Dr. Russell Fisher made in 1954; Fisher estimated 8,000 maternal deaths per year in the 1930s and 5,000 per year in the 1950s.[111]

These figures were transmuted into a figure of 10,000 maternal deaths annually when abortion was illegal.[112] So firmly rooted has this figure become among abortion rights supporters, that today it is almost a mantra. Even this figure is inadequate for Nanette Davis who tells us that annual maternal deaths were "far in excess" of 10,000 per year—without attempting to tell us what that higher number might be.[113] Celeste Condit pushed the rhetoric to an even higher level by estimating that in the 1960s abortion cause about half of the maternal deaths in the United States annually without putting a precise number on this claim.[114] What Condit is counting as a "maternal death" is not clear, but if she means deaths resulting from pregnancy, her estimate that half were caused by illegal abortions cannot be true if abortion was safer than pregnancy. All in all, a figure as high as 1,000 seems highly unlikely.

Some advocates of abortion rights have candidly conceded that the higher estimates that are quoted as gospel by supporters of *Roe v. Wade* were severely inflated for political purposes. Thus, Christopher Tietze, of the Alan Guttmacher Institute, has called the figure of 10,000 abortion-induced deaths annually "unmitigated nonsense."[115] Tietze himself put the actual figure at under 1,000 per year.[116] Interestingly, one careful study intended to verify the "coat hangers" legend

---

110. BATES & ZAWADSKI, *supra* note 61, at 3. *See also* REAGAN, *supra* note 55, at 222; Jerome Kummer & Zad Leavy, *Therapeutic Abortion Law Confusion*, 195 JAMA 96, 144 (1966); *The 25th Anniversary of* Roe v. Wade: *Has It Stood the Test of Time, Hearings before the Subcomm. On the Const., Federalism, & Property Rts. of the Sen. Comm. on the Judiciary*, 100th Cong. 4 (statement of Senator Edward Kennedy) ("Kennedy Statement").

111. Fisher, *supra* note 47, at 8–9.

112. MARIAN FAUX, CRUSADERS: VOICES FROM THE ABORTION FRONT xiii–xiv, 4 (1990) (5,000 to 10,000 maternal deaths per year from abortion); MARK GRABER, RETHINKING ABORTION: EQUAL CHOICE, THE CONSTITUTION, AND REPRODUCTIVE POLITICS 43 (1996) (same); LADER, *supra* note 56, at 3 (same); EDWARD LAZARUS, CLOSED CHAMBERS: THE FIRST EYEWITNESS ACCOUNT OF THE EPIC STRUGGLES INSIDE THE SUPREME COURT 343 (1998) (8,000 to 15,000 maternal deaths per year); MILLER, *supra* note 69, at 13 (5,000 to 10,000 maternal deaths per year); PETCHESKY, *supra* note 81, at 113 (10,000 maternal deaths per year); RICHARD POSNER, SEX AND REASON 277 (1992) (same); RHODE, *supra* note 89, at 207 (between 1,000 and 10,000 deaths per year); RICHARD SCHWARZ, SEPTIC ABORTION 7 (1968) (10,000 maternal deaths per year); WILLIAMS, *supra* note 94, at 213 (8,000 maternal deaths for 1935); *Amicus Brief of the Am. Med. Ass'n supporting Appellants in* Webster v. Reproductive Health Services, 492 U.S. 490 (1989), at 9, *reprinted in* 11 WOMEN'S RTS. L. REP. 443, 454 (1989), and in 5 DOCUMENTARY HISTORY, *supra* note 89, at 341, 363 (10,000 maternal deaths per year); Don Mills, *A Medicolegal Analysis of Abortion Statutes*, 31 S. CAL. L. REV. 181, 182 (1958) (same); Kenneth Niswander, *Medical Abortion Practice in the United States*, in ABORTION AND THE LAW, *supra* note 65, at 242, 247 (between 5,000 and 10,000 deaths annually); Cass Sunstein, *Neutrality in Constitutional Law (with Special Reference to Pornography, Abortion, and Surrogacy)*, 92 COLUM. L. REV. 1, 37 (1992) (10,000 maternal deaths per year); James Voyles, *Changing Abortion Laws in the United States*, 7 J. FAM. L. 496, 497 (1967) (same); Howard Ziff, *Recent Abortion Law Reforms*, 60 J. CRIM. L. & CRIMINOLOGY 3, 6 (1969) (same).

113. DAVIS, *supra* note 94, at 99. One hardly needs to mention one doctor's estimate that 2,000,000 women died in 1972 alone from illegal abortions; it is so completely unreal that one suspects that it was not really what he meant to say. Timothy Vinceguerra, *Notes of a Footsoldier*, 62 ALB. L. REV. 1167, 1167 (1999).

114. CONDIT, *supra* note 89, at 189, 197 n.16. *See also* REAGAN, *supra* note 55, at 213–14 (estimating that abortion cause 42.1% of maternal deaths in New York City in "the early 1960s").

115. Fred Graham, *Fetus Defects Pose Abortion Dilemma*, N.Y. TIMES, Sept. 7, 1967, at 38.

116. Christopher Tietze & Sarah Lewit, *Legal Abortion*, 236 SCIENTIFIC AM. 21, 23 (Jan. 1977).

found that "the only known fatalities reported here involved abortions done by doctors...."[117] Patricia Miller, the author of the study, also acknowledged that coroners were encountering fewer and fewer deaths from abortion. Still she insisted (without evidence) that this was merely the tip of an iceberg.[118] In fact, it would appear that anecdotes of horrible deaths from illegal abortions are hardly more numerous than anecdotes of similarly horrible deaths from legal abortions,[119] and that without considering the gruesome stories of what was happening to the fetus. Trading anecdote for anecdote unfortunately does not take us very far.

The persistence of figure of 10,000 deaths annually from illegal abortions in the face of virtually no evidence of widespread mortality lies in the figure's political utility. Dr. Bernard Nathanson, one of the early leaders of the movement to legalize abortion and was once described as the "Abortion King" of New York City for the many abortions he was performing there, later admitted that his use of the 5,000 to 10,000 per year figure was a conscious lie. He wrote:

> How many deaths were we talking about when abortion was illegal? In N.A.R.A.L. we generally emphasized the drama of the individual case, not the mass statistics, but when we spoke of the latter, it was always "5,000 to 10,000 deaths a year." I confess that I knew the figures were totally false, and I suppose the others did too, if they stopped to think of it. But in the "morality" of our revolution, it was a *useful* figure, widely accepted, so why go out of our way to correct it with honest statistics? The overriding concern was to get the laws eliminated, and anything within reason that had to be done was permissible.[120]

Similarly unsubstantiated estimates of maternal deaths from illegal abortions still circulate without serious examination. Dr. Allen Rosenfield recently estimated that as many as 100,000 women still die annually in countries scattered around the world ("Africa, Latin America, and Asia") where abortion is illegal or at least frequently unavailable from medically qualified personnel.[121] Planned Parenthood bandies about the figure of 200,000 deaths per year.[122] Despite the claim that this figure is derived from "hospital records" worldwide (a most unlikely proposition), the actual figure is more likely in the neighborhood 1 or 2 percent of the asserted figure.[123] There has even been a claim that 400,000 women die annually from illegal abortions in Brazil alone.[124] In fact, less than 100,000 Brazilian women between the ages of 14 and 50 died from all causes in

---

117. MILLER, *supra* note 69, at 10.

118. *Id.* at 13.

119. *See, e.g.*, Estate of Ravenell v. Eastern Women's Center, 1990 WL 467656 (N.Y. Sup. Ct.) (a $1,200,000 judgment for the wrongful death of 13-year-old Dawn Ravenell, who died from an abortion in January 1985).

120. NATHANSON & OSTUNG, *supra* note 91, at 193. *See also* GORDON, *supra* note 89, at 52; SISTERHOOD IS POWERFUL 260 (Robin Morgan ed. 1970). This entire question is thoroughly explored in Brian Clowes, *The Role of Maternal Deaths in the Abortion Debate*, 13 ST. L. U. PUB. L. REV. 327, 349–61, 372–81 (1993).

121. Allen Rosenfield, *Maternal Mortality in Developing Countries: An Ongoing Neglected Epidemic*, 262 JAMA 376 (1989). *See also* Howard French, *In Africa's Back-Street Clinics, Illicit Abortions Take Heavy Toll*, N.Y. TIMES, June 3, 1998, at A1.

122. PLANNED PARENTHOOD FEDERATION OF AMERICA, THE BUSH ADMINISTRATION: DRAGGING US BACK TO THE BACK ALLEY (pamphlet, 1989). *See also* HADLEY, *supra* note 89, at 39–43, 53–58; HEALTH OF WOMEN: A GLOBAL PERSPECTIVE 133 (Marjorie Koblinsky ed. 1993); JODI JACOBSON, THE GLOBAL POLITICS OF ABORTION: STATE OF THE WORLD 1991, at 114–31 (1991); Ruth Macklin, *Women's Health: An Ethical Perspective*, 21 J. LAW, MED. & ETHICS 23, 28 (1993).

123. Clowes, *supra* note 120, at 361–64.

124. *Some 400,000 Women Die Annually during Abortions in Brazil*, REUTERS, Nov. 13, 1991, *available in* LEXIS, Nexis Lib., Reuters File. For more serious studies of abortion complication rates in Brazil, see H.L. Coelho *et al.*, *Misopostrol and Illegal Abortion in Fortaleza, Brazil*, 49 CONTRACEPTION 101 (1994); S.H. Costa & M.P. Vesey, *Misopostrol and Illegal Abortion in Rio de Janeiro, Brazil*, 341 LANCET 1258 (1993); S. Singh & G. Sedgh, *The Relationship of Abortion to Trends in Contraception and Fertility in Brazil, Colombia, and Mexico*, 23 INT'L FAM. PLANNING PERSPECTIVES 4, 5–9 (1997).

any given year.[125] Studies for the developing world as a whole suggest that of the women who die from pregnancy related causes only 13 percent died from unsafe abortions.[126] Others provide similarly high figures for the numbers of women seriously, but not fatally, injured by illegal abortions, generally centering around the number 350,000 annually.[127] This fabricating of statistics is hardly unique to the abortion controversy, although it seems particularly disturbing when engaged in by people who claim to be speaking from the moral high ground. Such fabrications appear all too common among certain radical feminists.[128]

The pervasive uncertainty over just how many abortions were performed annually when abortion was illegal allows the wild estimates of maternal deaths just reviewed. Given the consistent, and often successful, efforts to hide abortions, we have no certain way to determine just how common abortions were. The increasing number of prosecutions, as well as the increasing safety of the procedure, both suggest that the number of abortions was increasing during the years immediately before reform became a major political issue. Dr. Marie Kopp had estimated 1,000,000 illegal abortions annually in the 1930s, without providing any evidence for her claim.[129] James Mohr relied on an estimate of between 200,000 to 1,200,000 by the late 1960s.[130] This estimate in turn derived from the work of the Alfred Kinsey Foundation and from an estimate by Dr. Russell Fisher, both estimates being reworked for the Planned Parenthood Conference of 1955. The Kinsey Report found that among its subjects (upper-middle class, urban white women) the abortion rate declined significantly after 1930, yet still yielded the high-end estimate of 1,200,000 annually.[131] This figure apparently originated in the estimate of Dr. Russell Fisher, who estimated 1,300,000 abortions per year in the United States in the 1950s.[132] Fisher, however, was using the term in its correct medical sense to mean any premature interruption of a pregnancy, and went on to note that about two-thirds of that number were spontaneous abortions, along with a negligible number of therapuetic abortions (including abortions for "neuropsychiatric" reasons). Dr. Mary Calderone, then national medical director for the Planned Parenthood Federation, prepared a statistical report for the 1955 Conference on "Abortion in the United States," in which she acknowledged that the Kinsey study was skewed by including only upper-middle class white women. She concluded that the Kinsey Report figures "do not provide an ad-

---

125. Clowes, *supra* note 120, at 362. For a review of maternal mortality in "developing countries" from all causes, see Deobrah Maine et al., Guidelines for Monitoring Progress in the Reduction of Maternal Mortality: A Work in Progress (1992); World Health Organization & UNICEF, Revised 1990 Estimates of Maternal Mortality: A New Approach (1996); Alicia Ely Yamin & Deborah Maine, *Maternal Mortality as a Human Rights Issue: Measuring Compliance with International Treaty Obligations*, 21 Hum. Rts. Q. 563 (1999).

126. Yamin & Maine, *supra* note 125, at 569 (Table 2). Apparently the largest contributor to pregnancy-related deaths in Brazil has been the popularity of Cesarean sections as a preferred method of birth (44 % of all births); that in turn has been linked to the popularity of sterilizing a woman in connection with the Cesarean section. Stephan Buckley, *Second Thoughts on Sterilization: Many Anguished Brazilian Women Want to Reverse Once Popular Procedure*, Wash. Post, Dec. 23, 2000, at A16. The popularity of sterilization in turn has led to unprotected sex that some see as a cause of the AIDS epidemic ravaging Brazil. *Id.*

127. Condit, *supra* note 89, at 37, 189; Graber, *supra* note 112, at 43; Jack Star, *1,000,000 a Year: The Growing Tragedy of Illegal Abortion*, Look, Oct. 19, 1965, at 150; Voyles, *supra* note 112, at 496; Glanville Williams, *Euthanasia and Abortion*, 38 U. Colo. L. Rev. 178, 194 (1966).

128. *See, e.g.*, Marie McCullough, *Feminists Debate Comes to Swarthmore*, Phila. Inquirer, Apr. 29, 1994, at D2 (reporting that radical feminists often cite the figure of 150,000 deaths annually from anorexia and bulimia, when the actual recorded figure for 1991 was only 54). *See generally* Christina Hoff Sommers, Who Stole Feminism? How Women Have Betrayed Women (1994).

129. Marie Kopp, Birth Control in Practice 121–22 (1934).

130. Mohr, *supra* note 89, at 254.

131. Paul Gebhard et al., Pregnancy, Birth and Abortion 112, 140 (1958).

132. Fisher, *supra* note 47, at 3–5.

equate basis for reliable estimates of the incidence of induced abortion in the urban white population of the United States, much less for the total population."[133] Calderone came up with the range of 200,000 to 1,200,000 that Mohr uses, while acknowledging that "[t]here is no objective basis for the selection of a particular figure between those two estimates as an approximation of the actual frequency."[134] Other Conference Participants repeatedly indicated that there was no reliable figure for the incidence of abortion.[135] Nonetheless, Calderone ultimately concluded that about 10 percent of married women had had an abortion by the age of 25, and 22 percent by age 45, offering no better basis than the Kinsey study that she herself had cast into doubt.[136]

Again and again, others routinely refer to the high end of such estimates without any acknowledgment of the inadequacies of the basis for the estimates by Calderone, Fisher, Kinsey, and Mohr.[137] Only a few scholars attempted to provide any backing at all for the figure they report so confidently. Thus, Nanette Davis found that abortions constituted between 1 and 1.5% of all medical procedures in certain Detroit hospitals in 1971.[138] From this and similar research, she concluded that 1,000 abortions per hospital was a common figure in the 1950s, which would suggest at least 1,000,000 per year annually across the nation.[139] Based on her

---

133. Abortion in the United States, *supra* note 62, at 179. *See also* Robert Potter, *Abortion in the United States,* 37 Milbank Mem. Fund Q. 92, 94 (Jan. 1959).

134. Abortion in the United States, *supra* note 62, at 180.

135. *Id.* at 18 (statement of Dr. Bard Brekke), 37 (statement of Dr. Harold Rosen), 50 (statement of Dr. Alan Guttmacher), 70 (Dr. Carl Erhardt), 110 (Dr. Sophia Kleegman). *See also* Therapeutic Abortion, *supra* note 45, at 3–6 (statement of Dr. Russell Fisher), 180 (statement of Dr. Manfred Guttmacher).

136. Abortion in the United States, *supra* note 62, at 55.

137. *See* Bates and Zawadski, *supra* note 61, at 3 (1,000,000 illegal abortions per year); Boston Women's Health Book Collective, The New Our Bodies, Ourselves 310 (1984); Condit, *supra* note 89, at 37 n.4 (between 200,000 to 2,000,000 illegal abortions annually, with 350,000 as a "minimum" for the 1960s); Davis, *supra* note 94, at 5, 213 (1,200,000 illegal abortions per year); Faux, *supra* note 112, at 217 (same); Graber, *supra* note 112, at 23 (1,000,000 illegal abortions per year); Harrison, *supra* note 89, at 179 (650,000 abortions per year); Anthony Hordern, Legal Abortion: The English Experience 234 (1971) (1,200,000 illegal abortions per year); Kenneth Karst, Law's Promise, Law's Expression: Visions of Power in the Politics of Race, Gender, and Religion 50 (1993) (same); Lader, *supra* note 56, at 68 (1,500,000 per year); Petchesky, *supra* note 83, at 113 (1,200,000 illegal abortions per year); Reagan, *supra* note 55, at 240 (over 1,000,000 illegal abortions per year); Rhode, *supra* note 89, at 207 (1,200,000 illegal abortions per year); Hyman Rodman, Betty Sarvis, & Joy Bonar, The Abortion Question 23 (1987) (same); Gerald Rosenberg, The Hollow Hope: Can Courts Bring About Social Change? 355 (1992) (1,000,000 illegal abortions per year); Eva Rubin, Abortion, Politics, and the Courts 17 (rev. ed. 1987) (1,200,000 illegal abortions per year); Solinger, *supra* note 55, at ix, 197 (1,000,000 illegal abortions annually); Rickie Solinger, Wake Up Little Susie: Single Pregnancy and Race before *Roe v. Wade* ix (1992) (same); Tribe, *supra* note 89, at 41 (same); Jean van der Tak, Abortion, Fertility, and Changing Legislation: An International Review 72–73 (1974) (same); Mary Zimmerman, Passage through Abortion: The Personal and Social Reality of Women's Experiences 9, 17 (1977) (1,200,000 illegal abortions per year); Barbara Cox, *Refocusing Abortion Jurisprudence to Include the Woman: A Response to Bopp and Coleson and* Webster v. Reproductive Health Services, 1990 Utah L. Rev. 543, 545 n.13 (same); Robert Hall, *Abortion in American Hospitals,* 57 Am. J. Pub. Health 1933, 1934 (1957) (same); John Hebert, *Is Legalized Abortion the Solution to Criminal Abortion?,* 37 U. Colo. L. Rev. 283, 285 (1965) (same); Kennedy Statement, *supra* note 110, at 4 (1,200,000 abortions per year); Zad Leavy & Jerome Kummer, *Criminal Abortion: Human Hardship and Unyielding Laws,* 35 S. Cal. L. Rev. 123, 124 (1962) ("more than 1 million" per year, with one in five pregnancies ending in abortion); Marvin Moore, *Antiquated Abortion Laws,* 20 Wash. & Lee L. Rev. 250, 251 (1963) (same); James Ridgeway, *One Million Abortions: Its Your Problem, Sweetheart,* New Rep., Feb. 9, 1963, at 14, 16 (1,000,000 illegal abortions per year); Ross, *supra* note 54, at 175 (between 200,000 to 1,000,000 illegal abortions annually); Star, *supra* note 127, at 150 (1,000,000 illegal abortions per year); Rickie Solinger, *Pregnancy and Power before* Roe v. Wade, *1950–1970,* in Abortion Wars, *supra* note 56, at 15, 16 ("up to one million" abortions per year); Sunstein, *supra* note 112, at 38 (1,000,000 to 1,500,000 illegal abortions per year).

138. Davis, *supra* note 94, at 86 n.3.

139. *Id.* at 70.

hospital figures, she embraced the overall figure of about 1,200,000 per year.[140] Notwithstanding these claims, she also announced that there were only 8,000 hospital abortions nationwide "[t]hroughout the 1960s," having declined from "at least 30,000" twenty-five years earlier.[141] Others have also provided evidence that Davis' hospital figures are wholly unreliable.[142] Gerald Rosenberg was less troubled by a search for the correct figure. While Rosenberg acknowledged that the figures were inflated "for obvious reasons of partisanship" and that there was no hard data, he settled on a figure of 1,000,000 abortions per year for no particular reason.[143]

At the opposite extreme are estimates of an average of less than 100,000 illegal abortions per year in the 1950s and 1960s.[144] Historian Ian Gentles argued that, as the steady decline in maternal deaths from abortion is irrefutable even if one assumes that such deaths are seriously underreported, the steep decline of such deaths in the 1960s must indicate a steep decline in the number of abortions.[145] Gentles went on to estimate 135,000 abortions per year in the United States before 1973 — without proving his number any more satisfactorily than those who inflate the numbers.[146] Gentles and the others who estimate on the low side are probably nearer the mark than those who estimate on the high side. After all, if there were a vast number of illegal abortions across the United States before the operation was legalized, one might have expected to see a sudden and dramatic flood of the operations upon legalization. Nothing of the sort occurred.

In California, where early abortions were legalized in November 1967, 1968 saw only 5,000 legal abortions, not the 100,000 or more one might have expected had there been 1,000,000 nationally.[147] Indeed, in some states legalization actually was accompanied by an initial decrease in the number of reported abortions.[148] Generally when abortion was legalized, the number of abortions increased steadily over several years until a more or less stable level was reached. Legal abortions nationally in the year *Roe* was decided reached a total of only 615,000, a small increase (barely 5 percent) over the 586,000 legal abortions the year before when the procedure was legal to some degree in 19 states.[149] If we assume even a modest increase in the incidence of abortion as it gradually became legal in various states in the years between 1967 and 1973, the data then

---

140. *Id.* at 5, 213.

141. *Id.* at 98.

142. Alan Guttmacher, *The Shrinking Non-Psychiatric Indications for Therapeutic Abortion,* in THERAPEUTIC ABORTION, *supra* note 45, at 14–15 (reporting that abortions in hospitals vary relative to live births from 1:106 to 1:3,383 , and reporting only 301 abortions in one year in 61 hospitals); David Wilson, *The Abortion Problem in the General Hospital,* in THERAPEUTIC ABORTION, *supra,* at 191, 190–91 (reporting that therapeutic abortion relative to live births ranged from 1:76 to 1:285 in four widely scattered "general" hospitals in the 1930s and 1940s, totaling about 50 per year for the four hospitals combined, with the rates falling in the later years to as low as 1:337 in one hospital).

143. ROSENBERG, *supra* note 137, at 353–55.

144. Clowes, *supra* note 120, at 330–32; Barbara Syska *et al., An Objective Model for Estimating Criminal Abortions and Its Implications for Public Policy,* in NEW PERSPECTIVES ON HUMAN ABORTION 178 (Thomas Hilgers et al. eds. 1981). *See also* REARDON, *supra* note 105, at 291 (between 100,000 and 200,000 illegal abortions annually before 1973); Fisher, *supra* note 47, at 6 (330,000 illegal abortions per year in the 1950s).

145. Gentles, *supra* note 100, at 51.

146. *Id.* at 53.

147. Alan Guttmacher, *The Genesis of Liberalized Abortion in New York: A Personal Insight,* 23 CASE-W. RES. L. REV. 756, 763 (1972).

148. RUBIN, *supra* note 137, at 23; Neal Devins, *The Countermajoritarian Paradox,* 93 MICH. L. REV. 1433, 1434–35, 1447 (1995).

149. The Centers for Disease Control's annual reports are summarized in MULDOON, *supra* note 106, at 7. Remember that *Roe* was decided on January 22 of 1973, making the figures for that year in effect the figures for a full year of legal abortion.

suggest that illegal abortions were almost certainly less than 500,000 per year before the first re-form of an abortion law and that by the time *Roe* was decided there were few illegal abortions at all.[150] The Centers for Disease Control's figures for abortion rates indicate the sharp break in re-ported abortion practice occurred between 1970 and 1971 (when the first few states, including New York, legalized abortion on demand) and not after *Roe*.[151] Legal abortions did not reach 1,000,000 until 1975—two full years after *Roe* and eight years after the first reform of the abor-tion statutes.[152] All of this seems to point towards the low-end estimates, without, of course, giv-ing us anything like a precise figure.

Estimates for abortions in England and Wales before the loosening of the English law on abortion, effective in 1968, have ranged from 10,000 to 267,000 per year.[153] As one commentator on the English estimates summed the matter up (in terms equally applicable to figures suggested for the United States), "the breadth of the bracket testifies to its lack of authority."[154] Yet at a time when pathologists were taught to presume that any unexplained death of a young women had resulted from an abortion, 185 such deaths were the largest number ever actually recorded in any year in England and Wales between 1960 and 1966, while in 1966, 62 persons received prison sentences for committing illegal abortions.[155] And, as in the United States, the legalization of abortions did not bring on a sudden rush of abortion patients; it took several years for legal abortions to become fairly common in England and Wales.[156] Illegal abortion thus seems not to have been so common in England and Wales or in the United States as the reformers would have us believe.

Some Australians have claimed that the rate of abortion and infanticide was higher in Aus-tralia than in either England or the United States.[157] The claimed number is between 50,000 and 100,000 per year, but with a much smaller population base than in either the United Kingdom or the United States.[158] Whether these figures are any more reliable than those posited for the United Kingdom and the United States is doubtful.

Any estimate of the incidence of illegal abortion must remain largely a guess. The larger esti-mates have found an audience among those who favored the legalization of abortion as it allows them to claim that the abortion laws were a failure and therefore should have been repealed. They argued that the law merely made abortion dangerous without actually decreasing its inci-dence.[159] As law professor John Ely would comment, "it is a strange argument for the unconstitu-tionality of a law that those who evade it suffer."[160] If one were to apply the same premise to the

---

150. *Id.*

151. *Id. See also* Petchesky, *supra* note 94, at 113.

152. Statistical Abstract of the United States 70 (1989).

153. Brookes, *supra* note 85, at 154 (50,000 per year), 161 n.144 (115,000 to 125,000 per year); Hordern, *supra* note 137, at 1–2, 5; Interdepartmental Comm., *supra* note 83, at 9 (90,000 per year); Kenny, *supra* note 3, at 194 (between 10,000 and 15,000 per year). *See also* L.A. Perry, Criminal Abortion 18 (1932); Sydney Smith & F.S. Fiddes, Forensic Medicine 324 (10th ed. 1955); Williams, *supra* note 94, at 210–11; Eustace Chesser, *The Law of Abortion,* 72 Med. World 495 (1950); C.B. Goodhart, *On the Inci-dence of Illegal Abortion,* 27 Population Stud. 207 (1973); William James, *The Incidence of Illegal Abortions,* 25 Population Stud. 327 (1971).

154. J.K. Mason, Medico-Legal Aspects of Reproduction and Parenthood 115 (2nd ed. 1998).

155. *Id.*

156. Madeleine Simms, *The Abortion Act after Three Years,* 42 Pol. Q. 271 (1971).

157. Petersen, *supra* note 88, at 52–53; L. Finch & J. Stratton, *The Australian Working Class and the Prac-tice of Abortion,* 23 J. Australian Stud. 45 (1988).

158. John Bennett, Abortion Law Reform 3–4 (1968); Petersen, *supra* note 88, at 59 n.13; Paul Wil-son, The Sexual Dilemma 19–20 (1971).

159. *See, e.g.,* Leavy & Kummer, *supra* note 137, at 124–26.

160. John Hart Ely, *The Wages of Crying Wolf,* 82 Yale L.J. 920, 923 n.26 (1973).

rape laws, which deal with a crime that appears to be becoming steadily more common (according to reports to the police),[161] one would, I suppose, repeal those laws as well.

The problem of wildly varying estimates of the number of abortions persists in countries were abortions are still illegal. One recent survey of abortions in South America based its count on interviews with women who were hospitalized for complications arising from a miscarriage, and counted as a "probable abortion" the miscarriage of any woman who had either been using contraceptives when she became pregnant or who indicated that she had not wanted the baby. In this way, the surveyors succeeded in raising the percentage of abortions counted among the women from a reported 9 percent to an estimated 67 percent.[162] We have already noted reports that four times as many women died each year in Brazil from illegal abortions as the total number of women of child-bearing age who died from all causes in Brazil.[163] The pattern of statistical juggling makes credible a United Nations study that concluded in 1953 that abortion was not a significant means of limiting family size in most nations when compared to contraceptives.[164]

# Emergence of the Full Time Abortionist

*So you think you can tell heaven from hell, blue sky from pain.*
*Can you tell a green field from a cold steel rain?*

— Pink Floyd[165]

By the twentieth century, physicians, long in the forefront of those condemning abortion, were becoming the major providers of abortions (legal and illegal). Estimates are that as many as 90 percent of illegal abortions were performed by licensed physicians in good standing.[166] Dr. Alfred Kinsey, in a sample that included women who had had abortions from the 1920s to the 1950s, found that 87 percent of the women who admitted to having had abortions (about 45 percent of his entire sample) reported that the abortion had been performed by a physician.[167] No one knows whether such figures are close to the actual mark given the skewed nature of the sample, but increasingly those who were prosecuted for doing illegal abortions were physicians.[168]

We are now told that some physicians did abortions quite openly and with little trouble from the law or from the community.[169] An unknown number of physicians did earn handsome liv-

---

161. Jonathan D. Salant, *FBI: Murder and Rape Rates Increase*, THE BATTALION, June 17, 2003, at A1.

162. James Brooke, *High Rate of South American Abortion Ills Seen*, N.Y. TIMES, Nov. 23, 1993, at C5.

163. See the text *supra* at notes 124–26.

164. UNITED NATIONS, THE DETERMINANTS AND CONSEQUENCES OF POPULATION TRENDS 75 (Pop. Stud. no. 17, 1953).

165. Pink Floyd, *Wish You Were Here* (1975).

166. See the text *supra* at notes 89–92. Remarkably, strongly pro-abortion sociologist Kristen Luker has assumed that women did not obtain abortions from physicians before the legality of the procedure began to be debated. *See* LUKER, *supra* note 94, at 50–51.

167. ABORTION IN THE UNITED STATES, *supra* note 62, at 53.

168. See the sources collected *supra* at notes 43–45.

169. BACK ROOMS, *supra* note 94, at 218–24; NINIA BAEHR, ABORTION WITHOUT APOLOGY: A RADICAL HISTORY FOR THE 1990s, at 7–30 (1990); RUTH BARNETT & DOUG BAKER, THEY WEEP ON MY DOORSTEP (1969); BATES & ZAWADSKI, *supra* note 61, at 48; LINDA FREEMAN, THE ABORTIONIST (1962); GARROW, *supra* note 60, at 307–08, 318, 333–34, 349–51, 361–64, 376–77, 384–86, 391–93, 422, 428–31, 438, 445, 466–68, 486–87, 539; GEBHARD et al., *supra* note 128, at 198–99; GRABER, *supra* note 112, at 46–49; KEEMER, *supra* note 56; LADER, *supra* note 56, at 42–47; MILLER, *supra* note 69, at 32–33, 122–28, 135; REAGAN, *supra* note 55, at 132–33, 147–59; EDWIN SCHUR, CRIMES WITHOUT VICTIMS: DEVIANT BEHAVIOR AND PUBLIC POLICY

ings operating underground, performing abortions in particular communities with relatively little problem from the authorities for many years, although sooner or later they nearly always found themselves facing prosecution, often (but not always) after patients had died.[170] Only in one respect were physicians performing illegal abortions protected by the law—many courts would not allow women who consented to such operations to sue the physician because she had voluntary participated in the illegal activity.[171] Such "protection," however, was not meant to encourage abortion; rather, it was intended to prevent women from agreeing to undergo such procedures by withholding the law's protection should they be injured. This was clearly inconsistent with the view of women as the victim of abortion rather than as a criminal participant.[172] Whether deterrence would have been better served by allowing the suits and thus making the procedure riskier for the doctor is at least debatable. Such was the general disdain for abortion, however, that the courts usually did not delve into this question.[173]

27 (1965); SOLINGER, *supra* note 49; RAYMOND TATALOVICH & BYRON DAYNES, THE POLITICS OF ABORTION: A STUDY OF COMMUNITY CONFLICT IN PUBLIC POLICY MAKING 43 (1981); Bates, *supra* note 46; David Garrow, *Abortion before and after* Roe v. Wade: *An Historical Perspective*, 62 ALB. L. REV. 833, 834, 836 (1999); Linda Greenhouse, *Dr. Milan Vuitch, 78, Fighter for Abortion Rights* (Obituary), N.Y. TIMES, Apr. 11, 1993, at A30; Carol Joffe, *"Portraits of Three Physicians of Conscience:" Abortion before Legalization in the United States*, 2 J. HIST. SEXUALITY 46 (1991); Kummer & Leavy, *supra* note 110, at 97. This same idea is now being purveyed in fiction as well as in purported histories and biographies. *See, e.g.*, JOHN IRVING, THE CIDER HOUSE RULES (1985).

170. *See, e.g.*, People v. Peyser, 44 N.E.2d 53 (Ill. 1942); People v. Mitchell, 14 N.E. 2d 216 (Ill. 1938); Adams v. State, 88 A.2d 556 (Md. 1951); *Doctor Accused Second Time as an Abortionist*, CHI. DAILY TRIBUNE, Aug. 18, 1942, at 11; *Doctor Bares Abortion Ring, Then Kills Self*, CHI. DAILY TRIBUNE, Apr. 18, 1941, at 1; *Loop Physician Held in Abortion Conspiracy Case*, CHI. DAILY TRIBUNE, Nov. 21, 1940, at 5. *See also* BAEHR, *supra* note 169, at 7–30; BARNETT & BAKER, *supra* note 169; GARROW, *supra* note 60, at 307–08, 318, 333–34, 349–51, 361–64, 376–77, 384–86, 391–93, 422, 428–31, 438, 445, 466–68, 486–87, 539; KEEMER, *supra* note 56, at 163–74; LADER, *supra* note 56, at 48–51; REAGAN, *supra* note 55, at 148–49, 160–73; SOLINGER, *supra* note 49, at x; Isaac Jones, *Physicians Get 2-5 Jail Term*, MICH. CHRONICLE, Feb. 8, 1958, at 1.

171. Hunter v. Wheate, 289 F. 604 (D.C. Ct. App. 1923); Nash v. Meyer, 31 P.2d 273 (Idaho 1934); Castronovo v. Murawsky, 120 N.E.2d 871 (Ill. App. Ct. 1954); Herman v. Turner, 232 P. 864 (Kan. 1925) (*dictum*); Szadiwicz v. Cantor, 154 N.E. 251 (Mass. 1926); Reno v. D'Javid, 369 N.E.2d 766 (N.Y. 1977); Larocque v. Couneim, 87 N.Y.S. 625 (N.Y. Sup. Ct. 1904); Henrie v. Griffith, 395 P.2d 809 (Okla. 1965); Bowlan v. Lunsford, 54 P.2d 666 (Okla. 1936); Martin v. Morris, 42 S.W.2d 207 (Tenn. 1931); Miller v. Bennett, 56 S.E.2d 217 (Va. 1949). *See also* Sayadoff v. Wanda, 271 P.2d 140 (Cal. Ct. App. 1954) (the woman was not allowed to recover for her injuries in a suit against the person who urged her to have an abortion); Goldnamer v. O'Brien, 33 SW.W. 831 (Ky. 1896) (same); Symone T. v. Lieber, 613 N.Y.S.2d 404 (App. Div. 1994) (denying liability for an illegal abortion after performed *Roe v. Wade*); Androws v. Coulter, 1 P.2d 320 (Wash. 1931) (recovery was allowed for negligent treatment after the abortion but denied for the abortion itself). *But see* Wolcott v. Gaines, 169 S.E.2d 165 (Ga. 1969); Martin v. Hardesty, 163 N.E. 610 (Ind. 1928); Kimberly v. Ledbetter, 331 P.2d 307 (Kan. 1958); Richey v. Darling, 331 P.2d 281 (Kan. 1958); Joy v. Brown, 252 P.2d 889 (Kan. 1953); Lembo v. Donnell, 103 A. 11 (Me. 1918); True v. Older, 34 N.W.2d 200 (Minn. 1948); Milliken v. Heddescheimer, 144 N.E. 264 (Ohio 1924); Miller v. Bayer, 68 N.W. 869 (Wis. 1896).

172. *See, e.g.*, People v. Davis, 276 P.2d 801, 807 (Cal. 1954); Hatfield v. Gano, 15 Iowa 177, 178 (1863); Peoples v. Commonwealth, 9 S.W. 509, 510 (Ky. 1898); Commonwealth v. Boynton, 116 Mass. 343, 345 (1874); State v. Murphy, 27 N.J.L. 112, 114–15 (1858); Dunn v. People, 29 N.Y. 523, 527 (1864); Smartt v. State, 80 S.W. 586, 589 (Tenn. 1904); Watson v. State, 9 Tex. Crim. App. 237, 244–45 (1880); State v. Howard, 32 Vt. 380, 403 (1859); WM. L. CLARK, JR., HAND-BOOK OF CRIMINAL LAW 182 (1894); 3 JOHN WIGMORE, A TREATISE ON THE LAW OF EVIDENCE 2755–56 (1905). *See also In re* Vince, 67 A.2d 141 (N.J. 1949); Miller v. Bennett, 56 S.E.2d 217, 221 (Va. 1949); MARY BOYLE, RE-THINKING ABORTION, PSYCHOLOGY, GENDER, POWER AND LAW 44 (1997); Ellen Willis, *Putting Women Back into the Abortion Debate*, in FROM ABORTION TO REPRODUCTIVE FREEDOM: TRANSFORMING A MOVEMENT 131, 135 (Marlene Gerber Fried ed. 1990). *See generally* Chapter 6, at notes 84, 292–319.

173. Gail Hollister, *Tort Suits for Injuries during Illegal Abortions: The Effects of Judicial Bias*, 45 VILLA. L. REV. 387, 407–47 (2000). *See also* Francis Bohlen, *Consent as Affecting Civil Liability for Breaches of the Peace*, 24 COLUM. L. REV. 819, 832 (1924). For cases in which the court dismissed the deterrence question out of

Proponents of abortion rights now tend to treat these abortionists as heroes, exaggerating the openness of their practices and ignoring the substantial profits these supposedly high-minded individuals invariably made from their illegal practices. Proponents of abortion rights insist that any time an official looked the other way it was because he or she secretly supported abortion rights.[174] These proponents completely overlook the role of bribery or other forms of corruption.

Historian Leslie Reagan also insists that many physicians who would not do abortions frequently referred patients to the physicians who would do abortions, suggesting that the organized profession's opposition to abortion was rank hypocrisy.[175] The evidence for the claims of a widespread referals of patients for abortions, however, is rather thin. Reagan proves to be no more reliable a guide to this evidence than are Cyril Means or James Mohr. Thus Reagan tells us that "over two hundred doctors, including some of Chicago's most prominent physicians and AMA members, referred patients...for abortions."[176] In the footnote to this statement, 162 pages later, she tells us that in the records of the abortion clinic which apparently forms the basis of this claim she found referrals from only 18 doctors, only 11 of whom can be identified by name.[177] While all 11 were members of the American Medical Association, and eight were certified specialists, that hardly supports a claim that 200 prominent physicians routinely referred women for abortions. The careful reader would also have noted that the entire set of files which Reagan was able to examine amounted to only 70 patient records,[178] which itself would make the claim of referrals by 200 physicians most unlikely. Indeed, Reagan tells us in another footnote that a referral was recorded in only 38 instances (out of 70 patient records and seven other witnesses), and in only 18 of those (47 percent of recorded referrals, 26 percent of all patient records) was referral by a physician.[179] In other cases, the referral was by pharmacists, nurses, and even beauticians.[180]

These referrals were recorded because the abortionists in question paid a referral fee of $15[181]—suggesting that in the other 32 instances there had been no referral. (The fees charged to patients ranged from $35 and $300 depending on what the patient could pay, how far along the pregnancy was, and how successfully the patient could bargain, with a mean charge of $67—more than three weeks wages for the average working woman.)[182] Such referral fees were themselves considered unethical by the organized medical profession.[183]

Press coverage did gradually become sympathetic towards "reputable" physicians on trial for illegal abortions, presenting them as misguided or unfortunate, while remaining adamantly hos-

---

hand, see Sayadoff v. Warda, 271 P.2d 140, 143–44 (Cal. Ct. App. 1954); Castronovo v. Murawsky, 120 N.E.2d 871, 875 (Ill. App. Ct. 1954).

174. *See, e.g.,* BATES & ZAWADSKI, *supra* note 61, at 78–82; GEBHARD *et al.*, *supra* note 131, at 192; GRABER, *supra* note 112, at 46–47; SCHUR, *supra* note 169, at 34; Moore, *supra* note 137, at 253; Rickie Solinger, *"A Complete Disaster": Abortion and the Politics of Hospital Abortion Committees, 1950–1970,* 19 FEMINIST STUD. 241 (1993). *See also* NANCY HOWELL LEE, THE SEARCH FOR AN ABORTIONIST (1969); Peter Manning, *Fixing What You Feared: Notes on the Campus Abortion Search,* in STUDIES IN THE SOCIOLOGY OF SEX 137 (James Henslin ed. 1971); B.B. Tolnai, *The Abortion Racket,* 94 FORUM 176, 176 (Aug. 1935).

175. REAGAN, *supra* note 55, at 149–50.

176. *Id.* at 149. *See also* Virginia Clay Hamilton, *Abortion,* 117 JAMA 216 (1941).

177. REAGAN, *supra* note 55, at 311 n.78.

178. *Id.* at 149.

179. *Id.* at 311 n.79.

180. *Id.* at 150.

181. *Id. See also* George Wright, *Tells Bribe behind Killing,* CHI. DAILY TRIBUNE, May 2, 1941, at 1.

182. *Id.* at 154–55.

183. PAUL STARR, THE SOCIAL TRANSFORMATION OF AMERICAN MEDICINE: THE RISE OF A SOVEREIGN PROFESSION AND THE MAKING OF A VAST INDUSTRY 136, 358 (1982); ROSEMARY STEVENS, IN SICKNESS AND IN WEALTH: AMERICAN HOSPITALS IN THE TWENTIETH CENTURY 54, 114 (1989).

tile to "disreputable midwives, disgraced nurses, and quack doctors" caught doing abortions.[184] Yet, contrary to what the modern mythmakers assert, even "reputable" physicians who did abortions were at constant risk of apprehension and incarceration, not to mention loss of their medical license. For example, Dr. Milan Vuitch of Washington, D.C., is often cited as an example of a physician who openly did abortions and got away with it.[185] His 16 arrests hardly suggest official tolerance of his actions.[186] On the other hand, he never went to prison, in part because the United States Supreme Court itself overturned one conviction at a time when the abortion reform movement was already strong and growing stronger.[187] Even after *Roe v. Wade* was decided, Dr. Vuitch could not keep out of trouble. A jury found him liable in 1983 for negligently performing an abortion that necessitated a total hysterectomy for the unfortunate woman.[188] Rather than proving tolerance for abortion throughout the twentieth century, his personal history suggests that real resistance to abortion laws only began to emerge after 1950. Those who insist that abortion was tolerated by law enforcement institutions make no attempt to compare the rate of non-prosecutions for abortion against other serious crimes that also were not always prosecuted.[189]

The case of Ruth Barnett is particularly interesting as an example of someone who maintained a long-term career as an abortionist during the pre-*Roe* era and who, after her death, became something of a folk hero to those who support abortion rights. Barnett wrote a self-justifying and privately published autobiography "as told to Doug Baker," and has been the object of a hagiographic biography by historian Rickie Solinger.[190] The story is somewhat difficult to evaluate because Barnett herself is not fully reliable and Solinger's book contains only a sparse bibliography. Solinger did not attempt to document her specific claims by citations to authorities, references, or sources; her book even lacks an index. What is more, Solinger admits in her "bibliographic" note that several parts of the book—not clearly identified—are "composites" of actual persons or events.[191] In other words, a goodly part of the Solinger book is fiction, not history. On the whole, it reads like a novel and not like a serious attempt to recapitulate what can be discovered in the records of Barnett's life.[192]

"Dr." Barnett claimed to have performed 40,000 abortions altogether between 1918 and 1968.[193] Barnett, however, was not a physician; she learned her trade as an abortionist as a receptionist in the office of Dr. Alys Griff in her office in Portland, Oregon.[194] Griff was a woman physician who eventually specialized in abortion. Solinger attempts to put the best light on Barnett's background, describing Barnett as an "apprentice" for 11 years to Dr. Griff, but an apprentice who did abortions—"including the most difficult cases."[195] After leaving Dr. Griff, Barnett

---

184. Marvin Olasky, Abortion Rights: A Social History of Abortion in America 273–78 (1992) ("Olasky, Abortion Rights"); Olasky, *supra* note 43, at 88–89, 108–09, 119–20; Solinger, *supra* note 49, at 175–85, 195; Ross, *supra* note 56, at 173.

185. *See* Baehr, *supra* note 169, at 7–20; Garrow, *supra* note 60, at 318, 333; Solinger, *supra* note 49, at 175; Tatalovich & Byron Daynes, *supra* note 169, at 26–29; Greenhouse, *supra* note 169.

186. Garrow, *supra* note 60, at 382–83, 386, 494, 504, 509, 539, 561, 608, 646; Greenhouse, *supra* note 169.

187. United States v. Vuitch, 402 U.S. 62 (1971). The Court did so even though the case reached the Court "unilluminated by facts or record." *Id.* at 73 (White, J., concurring).

188. Vuitch v. Furr, 482 A.2d 811 (D.C. Ct. App. 1984).

189. *See generally* Albert Reiss, The Public and the Police (1971).

190. Barnett & Baker, *supra* note 169; Solinger, *supra* note 49.

191. Solinger, *supra* note 49, at 239–40.

192. For critical reviews of Solinger's book by reviewers who are sympathetic to her goals, see Garrow, *supra* note 60, at 955 n.1; Regina Morantz Sanchez, *Book Review* N.Y. Times Book Rev., Nov. 6, 1994, at 29.

193. Solinger, *supra* note 49, at 5, 145.

194. *Id.* at 9.

195. *Id.* at 27.

got a job for five years as a nurse-receptionist and assistant abortionist to Dr. George Watts, another Portland abortionist.[196] Watts died in prison after his conviction for criminal abortion.[197]

At Watt's suggestion, Barnett attended chiropractic school, focusing on naturopathic (herbal) medicine.[198] In Portland, most full-time abortionists were chiropractors rather than physicians.[199] Barnett, however, used neither chiropracty nor herbal medicine in her abortion practice. She later boasted, "I don't know anything from the waist up, but from the waist down, I do."[200]

Barnett finally set off on her independent abortion practice in 1934, buying out the practices of other established abortionists and practicing under their name rather than under her own.[201] Apart from a brief stint in Reno, Nevada, Barnett operated in Portland, Oregon, from 1934 to 1951 without prosecution.[202] Police corruption, including conventional bribes, has always been a problem with victimless crimes, and (without debating whether there is or isn't a victim) that has been true for abortion as well.[203] In the case of the Chicago abortion clinic that Leslie Reagan studied so carefully, a police officer (Daniel Moriarity) even attempted to kill the owner of the clinic (Ada Martin—the former receptionist at the clinic, not a physician) in order silence her.[204] He mistakenly killed her daughter.[205]

Barnett's career made her awash with funds that could be used to pay off police or others who might try to stop her activities. Although Solinger sought to present Barnett as a selfless servant of the women she aborted,[206] Barnett earned $17,000,000 (pre-1970 dollars) as an abortionist.[207] Solinger denigrates any suggestion that Ruth was just after the money with the lame comment that "[n]or did she organize her life in such a way as to dispel the townspeople's suspicions that she was one of those criminal practitioners who was in it for the money."[208]

Ruth Barnett in fact spent lavishly on herself, her husbands, her lovers, and her daughter Maggie.[209] Maggie reportedly was the result of Ruth's adulterous affair with Ruth's husband's older brother.[210] Ruth never married the older brother, but did marry and divorce four times altogether. Maggie married nine times, and was apparently always supported by her mother.[211] Ruth also served as the daughter's abortionist on numerous occasions.[212]

Barnett's selfless spirit and her profligate spending could not buy her acceptance in Portland society—she and her daughter remained social pariahs.[213] Even her own sister openly disap-

---

196. *Id.* at 28–29.

197. *Id.* at 121.

198. *Id.* at 29.

199. *Id.* at 175, 179. On allopathic medicine (what most of us think of as modern, scientific medicine), see Chapter 6, at notes 222–27.

200. SOLINGER, *supra* note 49, at 32.

201. *Id.* at 29–30, 55–56.

202. *Id.* at 10, 21.

203. *See, e.g.*, George Wright, *Fires Assistant Prosecutor*, CHI. DAILY TRIBUNE, May 3, 1941, at 3. *See also* OLASKY, *supra* note 43, at 72–77; REAGAN, *supra* note 55, at 155; SOLINGER, *supra* note 49, at 15, 56–105, 150–54, 159–60, 164–65, 179–80, 220; Bates, *supra* note 46, at 163–66. *See generally* SCHUR, *supra* note 169.

204. REAGAN, *supra* note 55, at 155.

205. *Id.* at 155, 167; Wright, *supra* note 181.

206. SOLINGER, *supra* note 49, at 4, 9, 22, 28, 31, 37–38, 42–46, 56, 162, 219–20, 228.

207. *Id.* at 37.

208. *Id.* at 37–40.

209. *Id.* at 30–31, 37–38, 40–41, 47–53, 157, 183, 221.

210. *Id.* at 8.

211. *Id.* at 21–22, 53, 221, 226, 228–29.

212. *Id.* at 33–34.

213. *Id.* at 26, 46–51.

proved of Barnett's activities.[214] Barnett's parents, while accepting her financial support, never wanted to hear about her business.[215] All in all, this hardly supports Solinger's—or Barnett's—claim that all Portland knew what she did and approved of it.[216]

Barnett's altruism did not prevent her from going to Reno in 1940 to undertake abortions on behalf of an organized crime syndicate.[217] Barnett, who worked on her autobiography from 1952 until her death in 1969, omitted any mention of the Reno episode.[218] Barnett apparently became the lover of Reg Rankin[219]—the head of the syndicate who had already served nearly four years in prison in California for his activities.[220] Barnett was hardly open for business in Reno before she was arrested after one of her patients was treated in a hospital for a septic abortion.[221] Ruth avoided serving time in jail by turning on her lover, becoming a leading witness for the state.[222]

Solinger presents Barnett as a victim of Reg Rankin and the other men involved in the conspiracy. Even as Solinger tells the tale, however, it is manifest that Barnett was a willing participant expecting big profits. Barnett went to Oakland, California, to order the paraphernalia for the Reno office in her own name;[223] she alone did abortions in Reno; and she readily betrayed her co-conspirators as soon as the legal troubles began. Finally, she chose to deny the entire Reno experience—even in her self-serving autobiography—than to present herself as a victim of men.

For a time things went better for Barnett back in Portland. Then things began to go seriously wrong. Barnett was prosecuted repeatedly in Oregon between 1951 and 1966.[224] The first raid on Barnett's establishment was at the behest of Portland's first woman mayor—a mayor who had been elected on an anti-vice platform.[225] Solinger tells us this was because of an ambitious District Attorney seeking easy marks for positive publicity.[226] Solinger would have us believe that district attorneys thought this would make them popular both because people were less sympathetic towards abortion now that the Depression was over and because of some mysterious spill over from the McCarthyite red scare.[227] Even Solinger admits that this explanation hardly seems adequate to explain why Barnett and others were arrested at that time.[228] As for the fact that Barnett was convicted by a jury of ordinary citizens, Solinger insists that it was only because she was a woman, and a person without proper medical credentials.[229] While Solinger's language drips with emotion, she simply ignores that goodly numbers of male abortionists were also being convicted all across the country, including some regularly licensed doctors,[230] and that some of the men who were prosecuted but not convicted lacked proper medical licenses.[231]

---

214. *Id.*
215. *Id.* at 41–42.
216. *Id.* at 131, 145, 149, 154–57.
217. *Id.* at 126–47.
218. *Id.* at 126, 144–47.
219. *Id.* at 131.
220. *Id.* at 121.
221. *Id.* at 137–43.
222. *Id.* at 142–44.
223. *Id.* at 132.
224. *Id.* at 195–218.
225. *Id.* at 157–64.
226. *Id.* at 170, 182, 197–98.
227. *Id.* at 160–61, 197. Historian Leslie Reagan makes similar claims in her study of the upsurge of prosecutions in the 1940s and 1950s. REAGAN, *supra* note 55, at 163–64, 172–73, 180–81. For an excellent short critique of the McCarthyite theory, see DONALD CRITCHLOW, INTENDED CONSEQUENCES: BIRTH CONTROL, ABORTION, AND THE FEDERAL GOVERNMENT IN MODERN AMERICA 269 n.68 (1999).
228. SOLINGER, *supra* note 49, at 197.
229. *Id.* at 195–218.
230. *See, e.g.,* KEEMER, *supra* note 56, at 48–51; REAGAN, *supra* note 55, at 160–61, 164, 167, 181.
231. SOLINGER, *supra* note 49, at 198–99.

In her first Oregon trial, in 1952, Barnett was convicted of "maintaining an establishment injurious to public morals."[232] She was arrested again while appealing this conviction.[233] Barnett was arrested yet again in 1953 while on probation from the second arrest.[234] In an effort to stop more patients from seeking her out, Barnett announced her retirement in 1953—a story that made the front page of the *Oregonian* newspaper.[235] In her announcement, Barnett admitted that 75 percent of her practice was the performing of abortions, but also claimed that she frequently talked women out of abortions and into having their babies—even buying layettes for them. Then she pleaded guilty to the charges stemming from the 1953 arrest, entering prison for the first time in 1954.[236] She served 120 days, one-third of her sentence of one year, being released early for good behavior.[237] Her early release was denounced in the pages of the *Oregon Journal,* and she returned to doing abortions promptly after her release.[238] Perhaps she needed money.[239]

Barnett was arrested again in 1956 and served three years in prison.[240] Upon her release, she again began doing abortions, this time finding a shield in a sexual liaison with a police captain and by hiring one of her former prosecutors as her attorney.[241] After her time in prison, however, "the number of women she was able to help [fell] to a 'relative trickle.'"[242] In 1965, another crusading district attorney brought pressure to bear, she lost her police captain and was arrested five times in the course of a year.[243] In the end, after one of her patients nearly died from a septic abortion,[244] Ruth Barnett was convicted at her trial in 1966—by an all woman jury.[245] This time she was convicted of manslaughter. The only person who had died was the unborn child.[246] She went back to prison after her conviction was upheld on appeal.[247]

All of this might serve to make Ruth Barnett a martyr in the struggle for abortion rights. It does not indicate, or even suggest, that the community in which she operated approved, or even tolerated, her activities. In fact, Barnett's philanthropic impulses were amply demonstrated by her legal argument that the women she had aborted thereby became criminals and therefore could not provide the sole basis for her conviction. Incidentally, Oregon was not a state that made a woman undergoing an abortion a criminal.[248] Ruth Barnett served five months of a two-year prison in 1968, as the oldest woman ever incarcerated in Oregon.[249] She then accepted the parole offered her on condition that she promise never to perform another abortion.[250] She died in 1969 of cancer at the age of 75.[251]

---

232. *Id.* at 219.
233. *Id.* at 220–21.
234. *Id.* at 221.
235. *Id.* at 221–23.
236. *Id.* at 223–25.
237. *Id.* at 225.
238. *Id.* at 225–27.
239. *Id.* at 226–29.
240. *Id.* at 227–28.
241. *Id.* at 228.
242. *Id.* at 4. *See also id.* at 228–29.
243. *Id.* at 230.
244. *Id.* at 230–31.
245. *Id.* at 232–33.
246. *Id.* at 233.
247. State v. Barnett, 437 P.2d 821 (Ore. 1968).
248. State v. Wilson, 230 P. 810, 811 (Ore. 1925).
249. SOLINGER, *supra* note 49, at 234–35.
250. *Id.* at 235.
251. *Id.*

# The Rise of the Hospital
# Abortion Committees

*"When I use a word," Humpty Dumpty said in a rather scornful tone, "it means just what
I choose it to mean—neither more nor less."*
*"The question is," said Alice, "whether you can make words mean so many different things."*
*"The question is," said Humpty Dumpty, "which is to be master—that's all."*

—Lewis Caroll[252]

At the time Ruth Barnett and Milan Vuitch were practicing abortion full time, ordinary physicians were empowered, with considerably less risk of arrest (and less chance to make substantial sums of money), to provide abortions to the favored few whom a particular physician found entitled to a therapeutic abortion. As the century proceeded, more and more such "therapeutic" procedures were justified on the basis of "psychiatric" indications.[253] Well before 1950, pregnancy itself was hardly ever life threatening for the mother.[254] Psychiatric indications, on the other hand, might mean no more than that a particular physician (who need not have any training in psychiatry or psychology) was sympathetic to the particular applicant for an abortion.[255] And that doctors, particularly younger doctors, were increasingly willing to do legal

---

252. Lewis Caroll, The Annotated Alice: Alice's Adventures in Wonderland and Through the Looking Glass 269 (Martin Gardner ed. 1980) (original date: 1871).

253. *See, e.g.,* Taussig, *supra* note 94, at 277–321; Hugo Ehrenfest, *Book Review,* 25 JAMA 463 (1933); R. Finlay Gayle, *The Psychiatric Considerations for Abortion,* 91 S. Med. & Surgery 251 (1929). *See generally* Graber, *supra* note 112, at 50–52; Miller, *supra* note 69, at 327; Nathanson & Ostung, *supra* note 91, at 147; Petchesky, *supra* note 82, at 124; Reagan, *supra* note 55, at 143–47, 201–03; Rodman, Sarvis, & Bonar, *supra* note 137, at 46, 74, 166–67; Betty Sarvis & Hyman Rodman, The Abortion Controversy 82, 95–96 (1973); Schur, *supra* note 169, at 16; Alex Barno, *Criminal Abortion Death: Illegitimate Pregnancy Deaths and Suicide in Pregnancy: Minnesota 1950–1965,* 98 Am. J. Obstet. & Gynecology 361 (1967); Daniel Callahan, *Abortion: Some Ethical Considerations,* in Abortion, Society, and the Law, *supra* note 102, at 89, 96; Fisher, *supra* note 47; Guttmacher, *supra* note 142; James Ingram et al., *Interruption of Pregnancy for Psychiatric Indications: A Suggested Method of Control,* 29 Obstet. & Gynecology 255 (1967); Leavy & Kummer, *supra* note 137, at 126; R.B. McGraw, *Legal Aspects of Terminations of Pregnancy on Psychiatric Grounds,* 56 N.Y. St. J. Med. 1605 (1965); Moore & Randall, *supra* note 85, at 39; Herbert Packer & Ralph Gampell, *Therapeutic Abortions: A Problem in Law and Medicine,* 11 Stan. L. Rev. 417, 425–26, 431–47 (1959); Allan Rosenberg & Emmanuel Silver, *Suicide, Psychiatrists and Therapeutic Abortions,* 102 Cal. Med. 103 (1965); Keith Russell, *Changing Indications for Therapeutic Abortion: Twenty Years' Experience at Los Angeles County Hospital,* 151 JAMA J. 108, 108 (1953); Quinten Scherman, *Therapeutic Abortion,* 11 Obstetrics & Gynecology 323 (1958); H. Douglas Singer, *Mental Disease and the Induction of Abortion,* 91 JAMA 2042 (1928); H.A. Stephenson, *Therapeutic Abortion,* 4 Obstet. & Gynecology 578 (1958). *See generally* Solinger, *supra* note 174, at 243–44, 246–48, 265 n.22.

254. Calderone, *supra* note 90, at 948–49; Roy Hefferman & William Lynch, *What Is the Status of Therapeutic Abortion in Modern Obstetrics?,* 66 Am. J. Obstet. & Gynecology 335 (1953); J.G. Moore & J.H. Randall, *Trends in Therapeutic Abortion: A Review of 137 Cases,* 63 Am. J. Obstet. & Gynecology 34 (1952); Keith Russell, *Changing Indications for Therapeutic Abortion: Twenty Years' Experience at Los Angeles County Hospital,* 151 JAMA J. 108, 108 (1953); Quentin Scherman, *Therapeutic Abortion,* 11 Obstet. & Gynecology 323 (1958).

255. Reagan, *supra* note 55, at 201–02; Taussig, *supra* note 94, at 296–97; Sidney Bolter, *The Psychiatrist's Role in Therapeutic Abortion: The Unwitting Accomplice,* 119 Am. J. Psych. 312 (1962); Peter Broeman & Jeannette Meier, *Therapeutic Abortion Practices in Chicago Hospitals—Vagueness, Variation, and Violation of the Law,* 4 Law & Soc. Order 757, 774 (1971); *Queries and Minor Notes: Abortions or Removal of Pregnant Uterus,* 96 JAMA 1169 (1931); Harold Rosen, *The Psychiatric Indications of Abortion: A Case Study in*

abortions was shown rather dramatically by a 1939 survey of medical students that found 68 percent of all medical students to be ready to perform an abortion if the procedure were legal.[256]

In order to make abortions safer for the mother, however, physicians moved the therapeutic procedure (like many other minor forms of surgery) out of their offices and into hospitals. This made it impossible for individual doctors to conceal the extent to which he or she individually undertook to perform therapuetic abortions.[257] Nor could they conceal that many of these abortions were, strictly speaking, illegal—as many commentators on abortion have concluded, although again without a single careful study of the question.[258] As doctors became aware of the practices of their colleagues, many became increasingly uncomfortable with the power they had achieved. In part, discomfort arose because of the evident inequities they encountered because some women could easily obtain abortions from reputable doctors under safe conditions (whether in a hospital or otherwise), while other women were maimed or killed by unqualified practitioners using unsafe techniques or operating in unsanitary circumstances.[259] Discomfort also arose because of the growing pressure on them from their woman patients seeking abortions.[260]

Changes in medical practice had by 1950 produced remarkable differences in the patterns of hospital abortions. Some hospitals during the 1950s or early 1960s recorded an abortion for every 20 live births; other hospitals recorded no abortions at all against thousands of live births.[261] A 1965 study found that at Women's Hospital in New York the abortion rate on ward service was one abortion per 900 live births, but in the private wards the rate was 1:20, while at

---

*Hypocrisy,* in THERAPEUTIC ABORTION, *supra* note 47, at 76, 82–87, 95–98, 105; Richard Schwartz, *Abortion on Request: The Psychiatric Implications,* in ABORTION, MEDICINE, AND THE LAW 323 (J. Douglas Butler & David Walbert eds., 4th ed. 1992); Gerald Webb, *Clinical Aspects of Tuberculosis,* in THE CYCLOPEDIA OF MEDICINE 244 (George Morris ed. 1935).

256. Norman Fielder, *Study of Attitudes, Personality, Social Adaptability, Character, and Motivation of Medical Students,* 113 JAMA 2003, 2005 (1939).

257. BARBARA HINKINSON CRAIG & DAVID O'BRIEN, ABORTION AND AMERICAN POLITICS 40 (1993); REAGAN, *supra* note 55, at 162; Moore & Randall, *supra* note 85; Solinger, *supra* note 174, at 243–44.

258. DAVIS, *supra* note 94, at 4–5; GRABER, *supra* note 112, at 49–50; RODMAN, SARVIS, & BONAR, *supra* note 137, at 190; SARVIS & RODMAN, *supra* note 253, at 65; SCHUR, *supra* note 169, at 14–18; Harvey Adelstein, *The Abortion Law,* 12 W. RES. L. REV. 74, 86 (1960); Alan Guttmacher, *The Law that Doctors Often Break,* READER'S DIGEST, Jan. 1960, at 51, 53; Hall, *supra* note 137, at 1933; Jerome Kummer, *A Psychiatrist Views Our Abortion Enigma,* in ABORTION NOW, *supra* note 91, at 114, 121; Kummer & Leavy, *supra* note 169, at 97; Leavy & Kummer, *supra* note 137, at 126; Zad Leavy & Jerome Kummer, *Criminal Abortion: A Failure of Law,* 50 ABA J. 52, 52 (1964) ("Leavy & Kummer, *Failure*"); Roy Lucas, *Federal Constitutional Limitations on the Enforcement and Administration of State Abortion Statutes,* 46 N.C. L. REV. 730, 748–49 (1968); Packer & Gampell, *supra* note 253, at 430, 444, 447; Harriet Pilpel, *The Abortion Crisis,* in ABORTION NOW, *supra,* at 98, 104; Rosen, *supra* note 255, at 87; Monroe Trout, *Therapeutic Abortion Laws Need Therapy,* 37 TEMPLE L.Q. 172, 173 (1964); Ziff, *supra* note 112, at 9.

259. *See, e.g.,* ABRAHAM RONGY, ABORTION: LEGAL OR ILLEGAL? 170–71 (1933); Jane Hodgson, *The Twentieth-Century Gender Battle: Difficulties in Perception,* in ABORTION WARS, *supra* note 56, at 290, 300. *See generally* CONDIT, *supra* note 89, at 33–34, 61–63, 189–90; GRABER, *supra* note 112, at 50–64; KENNY, *supra* note 3, at 192–94; LADER, *supra* note 56, at 56–57; REAGAN, *supra* note 55, at 146–47, 214, 216–17; Guttmacher, *supra* note 257.

260. *See, e.g.,* RONGY, *supra* note 259, at 134. *See generally* CONDIT, *supra* note 89, at 22–23; REAGAN, *supra* note 55, at 147–48.

261. DAVIS, *supra* note 94, at 61; GRABER, *supra* note 112, at 50–51; LUKER, *supra* note 94, at 45–46; S.A. Cosgrove & Patricia Carter, *A Consideration of Therapeutic Abortion,* 48 AM. J. OBSTET. & GYNECOLOGY 299, 305 (1944); Robert Hall, *Therapeutic Abortion, Sterilization, and Contraception,* 91 AM. J. OBSTET. & GYNECOLOGY 518, 524–25 (1965); Niswander, *supra* note 112, at 54; Packer & Gampell, *supra* note 253, at 427.

George Washington University Hospital in the District of Columbia, the rates were 1:4,324 vs. 1:218.[262]

The availability of hospital abortions was largely a matter of luck, clustering along class and racial lines. Older, upper or middle class white women often could obtain a hospital abortion, while younger women generally and poor or minority women of any age were often relegated to the "back alley."[263] Approximately 80 percent of recorded hospital abortions either took place in private hospitals or were performed upon private patients in public hospitals.[264] While private and ward patients had similar abortion rates when a pregnancy threatened their physical survival, private patients were 5.5 times more likely to receive an abortion for psychiatric indications, and 28 times more likely to have an abortion if they had had rubella.[265] One might have thought that objectively these problems would be more common among ward patients than among private patients.[266] Of course, we do not know how many procedures were performed on either class of patient but recorded as something other than an abortion, but in all likelihood the recorded discrimination carried over there as well.[267]

As a result, abortion-related mortality for black women rose sharply, soaring from a level twice as great as for white women to a rate six times as great between 1933 and 1966.[268] In the 1950s, over 90 percent of New York City's hospital abortions were per formed on white women, but nonwhite women suffered over 94 percent of the deaths from illegal abortions in the city.[269] Physicians frequently were willing to incur the minuscule risk of prosecution for aborting a private patient, but were unwillingly to incur even a small, albeit greater, risk for aborting a clinic

262. Hall, *supra* note 261, at 519–25. *See also* Edwin Gold *et al.*, *Therapeutic Abortions in New York City: A Twenty-Year Review*, 55 AM. J. PUB. HEALTH 964, 968 (1965); Keith Russell, *Therapeutic Abortion in California in 1950*, 60 WEST. J. SURGICAL OBSTET. & GYNECOLOGY 497 (1952).

263. ROBERT BELL, SOCIAL DEVIANCE: A SUBSTANTIVE ANALYSIS 134 (1971); DAVIS, *supra* note 94, at 5–6, 8; GRABER, *supra* note 112, at 6, 19, 52–55; GINSBURG, *supra* note 89, at 33; NANCY LEE, THE SEARCH FOR AN ABORTIONIST 163–64 (1969); LEGGE, *supra* note 85, at 117; LUKER, *supra* note 94, at 36; MILLER, *supra* note 69, at 4–5, 110–14; REAGAN, *supra* note 55, at 119–20, 193–94, 204–05; RODMAN, SARVIS, & BONAR, *supra* note 137, at 17, 149–154, 172; SCHUR, *supra* note 169, at 21; Willard Cates, jr., *Legal Abortion: The Public Health Record*, 215 SCIENCE 1586, 1588 (1982); Alan Charles & Susan Alexander, *Abortions for Poor and Non-white Women: A Denial of Equal Protection*, 23 HASTINGS L.J. 147 (1971); Gold *et al.*, *supra* note 262, at 966–71; Alan Guttmacher, *Abortion—Yesterday, Today & Tomorrow*, in ABORTION Now, *supra* note 91, at 8–9; Theodore Irwin, *The New Abortion Laws: How Are They Working?*, TODAY'S HEALTH, Mar. 1970, at 22, 23; Lucille Newman, *Between Ideal and Reality*, in ABORTION NOW, *supra*, at 54, 55; Niswander, *supra* note 112, at 39–40; Kenneth Niswander & Manual Porto, *Abortion Practices in the United States: A Medical Viewpoint*, in ABORTION, MEDICINE, AND THE LAW, *supra* note 255, at 567, 579; Roger Rochat, Carl Tyler, & Albert Schoenbucher, *An Epidemiological Analysis of Abortion in Georgia*, 61 AM. J. PUB. HEALTH 543, 548 (1971); Rosen, *supra* note 255, at 73. James Mohr has asserted that a similar pattern existed in the late nineteenth century, but, as is typical of Mohr, without bothering to present any evidence to support his claim. *See* MOHR, *supra* note 92, at 94–98.

264. GRABER, *supra* note 112, at 53–54; RODMAN, SARVIS, & BONAR, *supra* note 137, at 154; Gold *et al.*, *supra* note 262, at 968–71; Hall, *supra* note 137, at 1934; Niswander, *supra* note 112, at 39.

265. BELL, *supra* note 263, at 135; GRABER, *supra* note 112, at 53–54; Charles & Alexander, *supra* note 263, at 153–54; Gold *et al.*, *supra* note 262, at 970–71; Hall, *supra* note 261, at 1935; Hall, *supra* note 137, at 520–21.

266. GRABER, *supra* note 112, at 54; Gold *et al.*, *supra* note 262, at 970.

267. GRABER, *supra* note 112, at 55.

268. FREDERICK JAFFE, BARBARA LINDHEIM, & PHILIP LEE, ABORTION POLITICS 24 (1981). *See generally* Roger Rochat *et al.*, *Maternal Mortality in the United States: Report from the Maternal Mortality Collective*, 72 OBSTET. & GYNECOLOGY 91 (1988).

269. GRABER, *supra* note 112, at 54; REAGAN, *supra* note 55, at 205–06; SOLINGER, *supra* note 49, at 36; ROBERT STAPLES, BLACK WOMEN IN AMERICA 146 (1974); Gold *et al.*, *supra* note 262, at 966; Pilpel, *supra* note 259, at 101; Ross, *supra* note 55, at 173.

patient.[270] Private patients also found sympathetic psychiatrists more easily than ward patients, allowing in "therapeutic abortions" on highly suspect grounds.[271] Private patients were also more likely to receive comprehensive contraceptive services than ward patients.[272] Poor women, on the other hand, were often required to accept sterilization as the "price" of receiving a "legal" abortion, something generally not demanded of paying patients.[273] One study found that between 1931 and 1950, 75.6 percent of "legal" abortion patients were sterilized, with all the sterilized patients being indigent.[274] These same hospitals were, at the same time, sharply restricting access to sterilization by middle and upper class patients who sought voluntary sterilizations.[275]

After 1950, the discomfort of physicians with this situation came to be expressed in two contrary directions. The first was the transfer of authority to decide whether to perform hospital abortions to hospital committees to take it out of the sometimes too accommodating hands of individual doctors.[276] And second, doctors began to express their misgivings in conferences,

---

270. GRABER, *supra* note 112, at 52–54; SARVIS & RODMAN, *supra* note 253, at 172–73; Charles & Alexander, *supra* note 263, at 165; Guttmacher, *supra* note 263, at 11; Sophia Kleegman, *Planned Parenthood: Its Influence on Public Health and Family Welfare*, in THERAPEUTIC ABORTION, *supra* note 47, at 254, 256; Arthur Mandy, *Reflections of a Gynecologist*, in THERAPEUTIC ABORTION, *supra*, at 284, 288–89.

271. LUKER, *supra* note 94, at 260–62; REAGAN, *supra* note 55, at 207; Hall, *supra* note 261, at 519–22, 527; Moore & Randall, *supra* note 85, at 35.

272. RODMAN, SARVIS, & BONAR, *supra* note 137, at 17; Kleegman, *supra* note 270, at 256–58.

273. COMMITTEE FOR ABORTION RIGHTS AND AGAINST STERILIZATION ABUSE, WOMEN UNDER ATTACK: VICTORIES, BACKLASH, AND THE RIGHT TO REPRODUCTIVE FREEDOM (Susan Davis ed. 1988); DAVIS, *supra* note 94, at 54; GRABER, *supra* note 112, at 55; REAGAN, *supra* note 55, at 207–08, 231–32; RODMAN, SARVIS, & BONAR, *supra* note 137, at 151; SARVIS & RODMAN, *supra* note 253, at 188–93; SCHUR, *supra* note 169, at 22; SOLINGER, *supra* note 49, at 189–90; John Elliot et al., *The Obstetrician's View*, in ABORTION IN A CHANGING WORLD 85, 93 (Robert Hall ed. 1970); Manfred Guttmacher, *The Legal Status of Abortion*, in THERAPEUTIC ABORTION, *supra* note 47, at 175, 182; Hall, *supra* note 137, at 519, 522, 526–27; Bob Herbert, *Life before Roe*, N.Y. TIMES, May 7, 2001, at A17; Theodore Lidz, *Reflections of a Psychiatrist*, in THERAPEUTIC ABORTION, *supra*, at 276, 281–82; Mandy, *supra* note 270, at 289–90; Elizabeth Mensch & Alan Freeman, *The Politics of Virtue: Animals, Theology and Abortion*, 24 GA. L. REV. 923, 1119, 1124–25 (1991); Henry Myers, *The Problem of Sterilization: Sociologic, Eugenic, and Individual Considerations*, in THERAPEUTIC ABORTION, *supra*, at 87, 93–94; Harold Rosen, *The Hysterectomized Patient and the Abortion Problem*, in THERAPEUTIC ABORTION, *supra*, at 47; Nathan Simon, Audrey Sentura, & David Rothman, *Psychiatric Illness Following Therapeutic Abortion*, 124 AM. J. PSYCHIATRY 59, 59–60 (1967); David Wilson, *The Abortion Problem in the General Hospital*, in THERAPEUTIC ABORTION, *supra* note 47, at 189, 194. *See generally* ANGELA DAVIS, WOMEN, RACE, AND CLASS 215–21 (1981); PETCHESKY, *supra* note 83, at 84–89, 159–60, 178–81.

274. Russell, *supra* note 253, at 109–11. *See also* H. Close Hesseltine, F.L. Adair, & M.W. Boynton, *Limitations of Human Reproduction: Therapeutic Abortion*, 39 AM. J. OBSTET. & GYNECOLOGY 549, 551 (1940) (67% of the women who received abortions in one Chicago hospital also had sterilizations, 1932–1939); Hall, *supra* note 261, at 522 (33% of the women who receive abortions also had sterilizations).

275. *See, e.g.*, Hesseltine, Adair, & Boynton, *supra* note 274, at 561; Harry Pearse & Harold Ott, *Hospital Control of Sterilization and Therapeutic Abortion*, 60 AM. J. OBSTET. & GYNECOLOGY 285, 290–96 (1950). *See also* MILLER, *supra* note 69, at 80–91; REAGAN, *supra* note 55, at 208.

276. *See* Stewart v. Long Island Hosp., 313 N.Y.S.2d 502 (App. Div. 1970); WILLIAMS, *supra* note 94, at 168; Charles Dahlberg, *Abortion*, in SEXUAL BEHAVIOR AND THE LAW 379, 384 (Ralph Slovenko ed. 1965); Alan Guttmacher, *Therapeutic Abortion: The Doctor's Dilemma*, 21 J. MT. SINAI HOSP. 111 (1954); Howard Hammond, *Therapeutic Abortion: Ten Years' Experience with Hospital Committee Control*, 89 AM. J. OBSTET. & GYNECOLOGY 349 (1964); Arnold Levine, *The Problem of Psychiatric Disturbance in Relation to Therapeutic Abortion*, 6 J. ALBERT EINSTEIN MED. CENTER 76 (1958); Moore & Randall, *supra* note 85, at 36; Pearse & Ott, *supra* note 275; Lewis Savel, *Adjudication of Therapeutic Abortion and Sterilization*, in THERAPEUTIC ABORTION AND STERILIZATION 14 (Edmund Overstreet ed. 1964); Lewis Savel & Irving Perlmutter, *Therapeutic Abortion and Sterilization Committees: A Three-Year Experience*, 80 AM. J. OBSTET. & GYNECOLOGY 1192 (1960); Scherman, *supra* note 253, at 323. *See generally* FAUX, *supra* note 112, at 58–59; GRABER, *supra* note 112, at 55–56; LADER, *supra* note 56, at 27–28; MILLER, *supra* note 69, at 37; REAGAN, *supra* note 55, at 173–81, 190–91; WILLIAMS, *supra* note 94, at 167–69, 183–84; Peter Broeman & Jeannette Meier, *Therapeutic Abortion Practices in Chicago Hospitals—Vagueness, Variation, and Violation of the Law*, 4 LAW & SOC. ORDER

books, and discussions in which they began to question the legitimacy of existing abortion practices and laws.[277] The papers of one of the earliest and most important of these conferences were collected and published in 1954 under the title *Therapeutic Abortion;* the book was reissued in 1967 under the title *Abortion in America.*[278] The papers delivered at another conference, organized by Planned Parenthood in 1955, appeared in print under the title *Abortion in the United States.*[279]

At this time, very few people challenged the basic premises of the abortion laws.[280] Especially few doctors seriously questioned the existing laws, except for the occasional "hardship" case, such as rape or proven deformity of the fetus.[281] Physician support for the abortion laws was so obvious at the time that at least one abortionist attributed his conviction to the medical profession rather than to the police, the lawyers, or the jury.[282] And those few doctors who were prepared at least to question whether changes were needed in the existing abortion regime were so reluctant to do so in a public setting that they insisted that these early conferences be staged quietly.[283] The organizers of these conferences, in keeping with their desire to keep matters quiet, did not invite persons known to support the existing legal and regulatory regime to participate in these conferences. Furthermore, Dr. Mary Calderone, the medical director of the Planned Parenthood Federation during the 1950s and 1960s, went so far as to promise participants that they would not be quoted without their permission and could choose to have their "participation deleted" from the published proceedings.[284]

So widespread was the hostility to abortion in the 1950s, that even Dr. Calderone clearly and unequivocally condemned abortion as murder.[285] Dr. Alan Guttmacher, eventually such a prominent leader in the fight for abortion rights that the major research arm of the abortion rights movement now bears his name (the Alan Guttmacher Institute), in 1959 wrote that he "would vigorously oppose" any proposal for the unrestricted legalization of abortion.[286] Even as late as 1969, Guttmacher was writing that once "[f]ertilization has taken place[,] a baby has been conceived."[287] Thirty-two years earlier, Guttmacher had written that "[t]o extinguish the first spark of life is a crime of the same nature, both against our Maker and society, as to de-

---

757 (1971); Ingram, *supra* note 253; Leavy & Kummer, *supra* note 137, at 128; McGraw, *supra* note 253; Packer & Gampell, *supra* note 253, at 418, 429–30; Russell, *supra* note 262, at 497; Solinger, *supra* note 174, at 244–54. A similar transformation took place in England at about the same time. *See, e.g.,* J.V. O'Sullivan & I. Fairfield, *The Case against Termination on Psychiatric Grounds,* 20 MENTAL HEALTH 97 (Aug. 1961).

277. *See, e.g.,* Gold *et al., supra* note 262, at 965–66; Myrna Loth & H. Close Hesseltine, *Therapeutic Abortion at the Chicago Lying-In Hospital,* 72 AM. J. OBSTET. & GYNECOLOGY 304 (1956); Moore & Randall, *supra* note 85, at 28; Russell, *supra* note 253. *See generally* OLASKY, *supra* note 43, at 85–88; REAGAN, *supra* note 55, at 219–20; RUBIN, *supra* note 137, at 17–18; Scherman, *supra* note 253, at 325; Solinger, *supra* note 174, at 244–46.

278. THERAPEUTIC ABORTION, *supra* note 47.

279. ABORTION IN THE UNITED STATES, *supra* note 62.

280. DAVIS, *supra* note 94, at xiii, 3–4; LUKER, *supra* note 94, at 41; REAGAN, *supra* note 55, at 143, 175–76, 181.

281. *See, e.g.,* Roy Heffernan & William Lynch, *What Is the Status of Therapeutic Abortion in Modern Obstetrics?,* 66 AM. J. OBSTET. & GYNECOLOGY 535 (1953); Moore & Randall, *supra* note 85, at 34, 39; Pearse & Ott, *supra* note 275, at 299–300; Rosen, *supra* note 272; Rosenberg & Silver, *supra* note 253; Scherman, *supra* note 253, at 330–31; Morton Sontheimer, *Important Facts about Abortion,* 68 READERS' DIGEST 53 (Feb. 1956). *See generally* CONDIT, *supra* note 89, at 33, 35, 59; LUKER, *supra* note 94, at 107; Packer & Gampell, *supra* note 253, at 447–51; Solinger, *supra* note 174, at 258–59.

282. ABORTION IN THE UNITED STATES, *supra* note 62, at 63 (statement of Dr. George Timanus).

283. REAGAN, *supra* note 55, at 219 (citing to Dr. Mary Calderone's papers in the Schlesinger Library; Calderone).

284. *Id.*

285. Calderone, *supra* note 90, at 951.

286. GUTTMACHER, *supra* note 92, at 51–54.

287. ALAN GUTTMACHER, BIRTH CONTROL AND LOVE 12 (2nd rev. ed. 1969).

stroy an infant, a child, or a man."[288] Guttmacher, from his post as Director Obstetrics and Gy-necologist at New York's Mount Sinai Hospital, favored an indications policy allowing abortions on eugenics as well as maternal health grounds.[289] (This was in keeping with Guttmacher's service as Vice-President of the American Eugenics Society.) Such expressions of concern about, and even hostility to, abortion were more than mere rhetorical flourishes designed to cover a genuine, albeit covert, support for abortion on demand. The hospital abortion committees saw to that.

The first such committee appears to have been created in Harper Hospital (a large public hospital in Detroit) in 1939.[290] Such committees had become virtually universal by 1950.[291] Historian Leslie Reagan has suggested that doctors established the abortion committees to provide a legal "cover" for the abortions they wanted to do.[292] Yet it appears that no physician had ever been prosecuted for performing an abortion in a hospital in the United States.[293] This at least in part was because prosecutors believed, perhaps correctly, that any such prosecution would fail to persuade a jury to convict.[294] Reagan argued that doctors' feared prosecution because of the prosecution of Dr. Alec Bourne in England for a hospital abortion—a prosecution that was widely publicized in the United States.[295] If so, the American physicians must have overlooked that *Rex v. Bourne*[296] was a test case staged between the prosecutor and the defendant to achieve a liberalization of the interpretation of the English abortion laws.[297] If the doctors who created the abortion committees were genuinely afraid of being prosecuted, they succeeded. Certainly, no physician was prosecuted for performing an abortion approved by a hospital abortion committee.[298] Yet the tightened controls established by the committees simply were not necessary to preclude criminal prosecutions for abortions in a hospital.

While some doctors might have seen the committees as a means of protecting themselves for the doing of abortions, the professed goals of the founders of the committees were different.[299] Dr. Albert Catherwood of Detroit's Harper Hospital, for example, stated that the committee was formed because abortions had become too easy to obtain—the committee was to protect doctors not from the law, but their own errors in judgment in being too ready to perform an abortion[300] Doctors Harry Pearse and Harold Ott made similar comments regarding the motives behind the creation of the abortion committee at Florence Crittendon Hospital in Detroit

---

288. ALAN GUTTMACHER, INTO THIS UNIVERSE: THE STORY OF HUMAN BIRTH 46 (1937).

289. GUTTMACHER, *supra* note 92, at 116, 197–99, 215. *See also* ABORTION IN THE UNITED STATES, *supra* note 60, at 181–84.

290. Hesseltine, Adair, & Boynton, *supra* note 274, at 561.

291. Pearse & Ott, *supra* note 275.

292. REAGAN, *supra* note 55, at 174–75. *See also* Hesseltine, Adair, & Boynton, *supra* note 274, at 561; Pearse & Ott, *supra* note 275, at 290.

293. ABORTION IN THE UNITED STATES, *supra* note 62, at 34, (statement of Edwin Schur), 35–36 (statement of Dr. Milton Halperin), 164 (statement of Dr. Sophia Kleeman); DAVIS, *supra* note 91, at 57, 72; GRABER, *supra* note 112, at 48–50; LADER, *supra* note 56, at 26; REAGAN, *supra* note 55, at 175; RODMAN, SARVIS, BONAR, *supra* note 137, at 190–91; George, *supra* note 66, at 25; Leavy & Kummer, *Failure*, *supra* note 258, at 52; Lucas, *supra* note 258, at 749; Packer & Gampell, *supra* note 253, at 449; Solinger, *supra* note 174, at 250. *See also* GUTTMACHER, *supra* note 92, at 11.

294. *See, e.g.*, GEBHARD *et al.*, *supra* note 131, at 192; LADER, *supra* note 112, at 26.

295. REAGAN, *supra* note 53, at 175–76.

296. Rex v. Bourne, [1939] 1 K.B. 687, [1938] 3 All Eng. Rep. 615.

297. *See* Chapter 11, at notes 341–55.

298. Leavy & Kummer, *supra* note 137, at 128.

299. *See generally* Herbert Packer & Ralph Gampell, *Therapeutic Abortion: A Problem in Law and Medicine*, 11 STAN. L. REV. 417, 429 (1959).

300. Hesseltine, Adair, & Boynton, *supra* note 274, at 561 (comments of Dr. Catherwood).

in 1940.[301] Even Dr. Guttmacher was on record as having founded the abortion committee at Mt. Sinai Hospital in New York in the early 1950s with the apparent intent of restricting the too easy access to abortion then evident at the facility.[302] And the introduction of the committees generally did lead to a sharp reduction in the number of abortions performed in a hospital.[303] For example, medically indicated abortions at the University of Virginia Hospital fell from 128 such abortions between 1941 and 1950 to 11 from 1951 to 1955 after its committee was created.[304]

The introduction of the hospital abortion committees helped move therapeutic abortions out of the practitioners' offices and into the realm of hospital based specialists in obstetrics.[305] The committees' generally narrow approach to what could qualify as a therapeutic abortion in turn helped narrow the legal test of whether an abortion was therapeutic under the criminal law — if one could not get approval from a hospital abortion committee, the abortion was probably illegal and could be prosecuted.[306] Under the regime of the hospital abortion committees then, access to abortion became more a result of medical advocacy skills than of medical judgment.[307]

Abortion review committees, by reducing the availability of legal hospital abortions and increasing the risks of physicians performing abortions outside of a hospital setting, pushed desperate women into an illegal abortion market staffed by abortionists of dubious qualifications.[308] Admissions to hospitals for septic abortions soared.[309] Poor and minority women were less likely to have had the consultations and to have the recommendations from well-respected physicians that were likely to sway the review committee.[310] In New York City, under the committee regime, abortions for white women declined by 40 percent, for black women by 65 percent, and for Puerto Rican women by 90 percent.[311] In other words, the drop in abortions was particularly steep for minority women who had already found it difficult to obtain a hospital abortion.

The pervasive hostility of the medical profession towards abortion was also demonstrated by the common practice of linking abortion with sterilization, both being reviewed by a single hospital committee. Sterilization frequently was performed along with an abortion.[312] A woman re-

---

301. Pease & Ott, *supra* note 208, at 290.

302. Gold *et al.*, *supra* note 195, at 966; Guttmacher, *supra* note 195, at 118; Savel, *supra* note 276, at 16; Christopher Tietze, *Therapeutic Abortions in New York City, 1943–1947*, 60 AM. J. OBSTET. & GYNECOLOGY 146 (1950). *See also* REAGAN, *supra* note 53, at 180, 204–08; Solinger, supra note 174, at 248–50.

303. REAGAN, *supra* note 55, at 178–79, 200; Guttmacher, *supra* note 263, at 118–19; Hall, *supra* note 261, at 520–21; Pearse & Ott, *supra* note 275, at 299; Savel & Perlmutter, *supra* note 276, at 1194, 1198; Solinger, *supra* note 174, at 250–51.

304. Hebert, *supra* note 137, at 289 n.44.

305. REAGAN, *supra* note 55, at 177–78.

306. *Id.* at 181–90.

307. GRABER, *supra* note 112, at 56–57; MILLER, *supra* note 69, at 37–38; REAGAN, *supra* note 55, at 202, 218–19; Mandy, *supra* note 270, at 285.

308. REAGAN, *supra* note 55, at 179–80, 200, 209–10; Solinger, *supra* note 174, at 249–51, 261.

309. MILLER, *supra* note 69, at 72–74, 285–87; REAGAN, *supra* note 55, at 209–11; Mills, *supra* note 112, at 182–83 n.11.

310. DAVIS, *supra* note 94, at 77–79; GINSBURG, *supra* note 263, at 55; GRABER, *supra* note 112, at 56; LADER, *supra* note 56, at 8, 29–30; LUKER, *supra* note 94, at 57; MOHR, *supra* note 92, at 225; PETCHESKY, *supra* note 83, at 126–27; REAGAN, *supra* note 55, at 204–07, 213; Charles & Alexander, *supra* note 263, at 165–66; Pilpel, *supra* note 258, at 101; Rosen, *supra* note 258, at 89–90.

311. Gold *et al.*, *supra* note 195, at 966.

312. DAVIS, *supra* note 94, at 54; GRABER, *supra* note 112, at 55; RODMAN, SARVIS, & BONAR, *supra* note 137, at 151; SARVIS & RODMAN, *supra* note 253, at 188–93; SCHUR, *supra* note 169, at 22; Elliot *et al.*, *supra* note 267, at 93; Guttmacher, *supra* note 270, at 182; Hall, *supra* note 137, at 519, 526; Lidz, *supra* note 270, at 281–82; Mandy, *supra* note 270, at 290; Mensch & Freeman, *supra* note 270, at 1119, 1124–25; Myers, *supra* note 270, at 93–94; Rosen, *supra* note 270; Simon, Sentura, & Rothman, *supra* note 270, at 59–60; Wilson, *supra* note 270, at 194.

ceiving an abortion did not always consent to, or even know of, the sterilization.[313] One estimate in the 1940s and 1950s was that as many as 40 percent of abortions nationally were accompanied by sterilization.[314] In one hospital in Chicago the rate was 69 percent.[315] As many as 100,000 to 150,000 poor women were sterilized in Alabama alone in the 1970s.[316]

A good deal of the "voluntary" sterilizations were funded by the federal government. By 1972, as many as 200,000 women might have been sterilized through such federally funded programs.[317] Some 43 percent of those 200,000 were African-American women, and nearly as many were Hispanic women.[318] Nor were the white, middle class women who were leading the birth control movement and would eventually find themselves drawn to support of abortion rights put off by such disparities. Even in the 1970s, Planned Parenthood (and NARAL) openly opposed the efforts of the Committee to End Sterilization Abuse, a group working to eliminate the practice of pressuring (even coercing) African-American women into "consenting" to sterilization.[319]

More and more, the most desperate young, poor, and minority women were driven towards illegal abortions.[320] The illegal market posed serious risks for women seeking an abortion. Without state regulation, the quality of the abortionists varied dramatically. Given the illegality of their activity, information about a prospective abortionist was difficult and expensive to obtain and highly unreliable.[321] At bottom, the illegality of the procedure had "the effect of raising the risk and reward for the illegal practitioner and also of depressing the quality of service offered."[322] Few women left the abortionist's "office" with anything more than cabfare, if that much.[323] The extorted price might even include sex before the abortion.[324]

All this was very hit-or-miss: "poor women sometimes put themselves deeply in debt to pay for expensive abortions, while wealthy women are sometimes unable to find the highly skilled practitioners they can afford to pay."[325] Women with enough money would even travel to a country were abortion was legal, or at least easy to obtain.[326] At the extreme, one study concluded that about 1,000 women traveled from the United States to England in both 1969 and 1970 to obtain legal abortions that were not available at home.[327] The best known example of such an "abortion tourist" was Sherri Finkbine who traveled to Sweden to abort a baby damaged by thalidomide.[328]

---

313. DAVIS, *supra* note 94, at 72–73, 77–78; REAGAN, *supra* note 55, at 208; TAUSSIG, *supra* note 94, at 79; Elliot *et al.*, *supra* note 270, at 93; Moore & Randall, *supra* note 253, at 37; Pearse & Ott, *supra* note 275, at 296; Solinger, *supra* note 174, at 259–61.

314. Niswander, *supra* note 112, at 57.

315. Loth & Hesseltine, *supra* note 277, at 306.

316. *See* Relf v. Weinberger, 372 F. Supp. 1196, 1199 (D.D.C. 1974), *vacated*, 565 F.2d 722 (D.C. Cir. 1977).

317. Angela Davis, *Racism, Birth Control and Reproductive Rights*, in ALL AMERICAN WOMEN 239, 252 (Johnetta Cole ed. 1986).

318. *Id.*

319. Dorothy Roberts, *Racism and Patriarchy in the Meaning of Motherhood*, 1 J. GENDER & L. 1, 33 (1993).

320. See the authorities collected *supra* at note 263.

321. LEE, *supra* note 94, at 77, 154, 166; LUKER, *supra* note 94, at 74–75.

322. HERBERT PACKER, THE LIMITS OF THE CRIMINAL SANCTION 343–44 (1968). *See also* GEBHARD *et al.*, *supra* note 131, at 199; GRABER, *supra* note 112, at 59–60; LUKER, *supra* note 94, at 74–75; MILLER, *supra* note 69, at 10, 101; Bates, *supra* note 46, at 159–60.

323. Bates, *supra* note 46, at 160.

324. MILLER, *supra* note 69, at 59, 63.

325. LEE, *supra* note 94, at 13–14. *See also* MESSER & MAY, *supra* note 94, at 5–7.

326. CONDIT, *supra* note 89, at 34; DAVIS, *supra* note 94, at 61, 119; GRABER, *supra* note 112, at 62; MESSER & MAY, *supra* note 94, at 9, 72–73, 113–14; MILLER, *supra* note 69, at 33, 172; NATHANSON & OSTUNG, *supra* note 91, at 23, 26; George, *supra* note 65, at 1, 23; Pilpel, *supra* note 258, at 101.

327. William Liu, *Abortion and the Social System*, in ABORTION: NEW DIRECTIONS FOR POLICY STUDIES 137, 146 (Edward Manier, William Liu, & David Solomon eds. 1977).

328. *See* Chapter 13, at notes 214–23.

Others traveled to places were illegal abortions were apparently easy to obtain, including Mexico and Puerto Rico.[329] Apparently only one travel agent was ever prosecuted—in Massachusetts—for arranging such a trip.[330] Yet conditions could be very bad in places like Mexico.[331]

Some illegal abortions performed in the United States were done under highly dangerous conditions that led to infection, pain, and, rarely, death.[332] While many insist that any woman, or at least "any knowledgeable woman,"[333] could obtain an abortion, at least some women who wanted abortions did not obtain them either for lack of funds or for fear of subjecting themselves to the risks of the "back alley" procedure.[334] And, even when older affluent white women did resort to illegal abortion, they had an easier time than did younger, poor, or minority women.[335] The initial response to this changed reality was an intensification of the enforcement of the abortion laws. We have already noted efforts such as that of the Amen Commission to strengthen enforcement of the criminal penalties.[336] The 1940s and 1950s also saw an upsurge in the revocation of medical licenses from physicians who were caught offering or performing abortions.[337] The creation of the hospital abortion committees expressed the same urge to make the enforcement of the abortion laws more effective. Rather than seeking reform of the abortion laws, what doctors wanted at that time was to perfect their professional control over the abortion decision.[338] In attempting to perfect physician control over the abortion decision, differences emerged between those who wanted discretion vested in individual physicians and those who wanted discretion vested in hospital committees as representing the collective sense of the profession. While a few physicians reacted to this split by favoring some "liberalization" of the law, they did little to organize politically.[339] In either event, doctors generally wanted to exercise their own individual discretion to decide whether to do an abortion. It apparently never seemed to occur to them that women seeking abortions should control the decision. The doctors simply did not seek to address the larger social questions that were generating their discomfort.[340] Instead of organizing to oppose those who led the pressure for the creation of hospital abortion committees, doctors who favored liberalization tended to blame lawyers for the apparent impasse regarding changes in the abortion laws—while lawyers of the same persuasion in turn blamed doctors and clerics.[341]

---

329. Jaffe, Lindheim, & Lee, *supra* note 268, at 22; Star, *supra* note 127, at 154.

330. Graber, *supra* note 112, at 62.

331. *See* Gloria Elena Bernal, *The Story of Paulina—The Issue of Induced Abortion in Mexico: A Personal Point of View*, available at http://www.natverkstan.net/peripeti/artiklar/artikel_en/paulinas.html; Heather Rosman, Legalized Abortion, 25 Years After Roe v. Wade, The Online Daily, Jan. 22 1998, http://archives.thedaily.washington.edu/1998.012298/25_roe.html.

332. *See* Messer & May, *supra* note 94, at 11–12.

333. Garrett Hardin, *Abortion and Human Dignity,* in Abortion Now, *supra* note 91, at 69, 84.

334. Gebhard *et al.*, *supra* note 131, at 199–203.

335. Graber, *supra* note 112, at 59–62; Lader, *supra* note 112, at 23, 65–66; Lee, *supra* note 263, at 166–68; Luker, *supra* note 94, at 74–75; Miller, *supra* note 69, at 76, 209; Rodman, Sarvis, & Bonar, *supra* note 137, at 150; Sarvis & Rodman, *supra* note 253, at 170; Schur, *supra* note 169, at 32, 46; Charles & Alexander, *supra* note 263, at 155; Gold *et al.*, *supra* note 262, at 964–66; Newman, *supra* note 263, at 67; Niswander, *supra* note 112, at 39; Rochat, Tyler, & Schoenbucher, *supra* note 263, at 543–44; Rosen, *supra* note 258, at 92.

336. See the text *supra* at notes 42–83.

337. See the text *supra* at notes 71–75.

338. *See, e.g.*, Guttmacher, *supra* note 258, at 54; Irwin, *supra* note 263, at 230; W. Joseph May, *Therapeutic Abortion in North Carolina*, 23 N.C. Med. J. 548 (1962). *See generally* Condit, *supra* note 89, at 22–28; Luker, *supra* note 94, at 78,82; Rodman, Sarvis, & Bonar, *supra* note 137, at 30; Rubin, *supra* note 137, at 28–29; Tribe, *supra* note 137, at 43–44; Solinger, *supra* note 174, at 250–51, 257–58, 263–64; Voyles, *supra* note 112, at 511.

339. Ginsburg, *supra* note 263, at 35.

340. Condit, *supra* note 89, at 23.

341. *See, e.g.*, Kleegman, *supra* note 270, at 256–57.

# Chapter 13

# Girls Just Want to Have Fun[1]

*Hello. I love you. Won't you tell me your name?*

—The Doors[2]

As World War II ended, an increasing incidence of abortion in the United States was met by intensified efforts by the legal and the medical professions to suppress what most members of both professions seemed to consider a social evil.[3] On the legal side, the *Amen Report,* signaled an intent to strengthen enforcement of the abortion law and of educating the public about the seriousness of the wrong committed through violating the abortion statutes of the State.[4] While the legislature did less to change New York's abortion laws than the *Amen Report* suggested, what changes the legislature did enact were designed to strengthen, not weaken enforcement.[5] The medical profession also stepped up its efforts to detect doctors who were performed abortions without legal justification, revoking their licenses to practice medicine.[6] Finally, the establishment of hospital abortion committees effectively cut off the young, the poor, and minorities from access to legal abortion even while older, middle class white women often were able to obtain an ostensibly therapeutic abortion in a hospital.[7]

Yet barely 30 years after the publication of the *Amen Report* and 25 years after abortion committees became a near universal feature of American hospitals, the United States Supreme Court declared abortion laws to be an unconstitutional deprivation of women's and physicians' liberty.[8] The overturn of abortion laws in England and Wales was nearly as dramatic during the same time period. In fact, most industrialized countries made access to abortion significantly easier in the 1960s and 1970s.[9] This Chapter examines how the laws England and Wales and in the United States came to be transformed so radically. We begin with England and Wales, for the first halting steps had occurred there before the war,[10] and because when reform came it was simple statutory enactment. There could be no theory of unconstitutionality for the British.

---

1. Robert Hazard, *Girls Just Want to Have Fun* (1983) (performed by Cindy Lauper).
2. Jim Morrison, *Hello I Love You* (1968).
3. *See* Chapter 12.
4. John Harlen Amen, *Some Obstacles to Effective Legal Control of Criminal Abortions,* in NATIONAL COMM. ON MATERNAL HEALTH, THE ABORTION PROBLEM 133 (1944). *See generally* Chapter 12, at notes 46–50.
5. *See* Chapter 12, at notes 51, 52, 74–80.
6. *Id.* at notes 69–73.
7. *Id.* at notes 267–333.
8. Roe v. Wade, 410 U.S. 113 (1973).
9. *See* Chapter 15, at notes 141–361.
10. *See* Chapter 11, at notes 267–300.

# Reform in England and Wales

*You got to be very careful if you don't know where you're going, because you might not get there.*

—Yogi Berra[11]

The end of World War II brought Labour its first parliamentary majority in Britain. The resulting Labour government embarked upon a massive restructuring of British society, nationalizing industries and introducing the National Health Service system.[12] None of the changes seem to signal any change in abortion policy. Under Labour, police vigilance regarding abortion appears actually to have heightened.[13] As a result, the number of known criminal abortions declined slightly during the immediate post-war years from an average of 347 per year during the war to an average of 271 per year in the latter 1940s and 244 per year in the years 1950–54.[14]

The small decline in known criminal abortions is considerably less than one would have expected given the sudden and dramatic "baby boom" in England during these years.[15] Still, most institutions kept their distance from those who advocated abortion reform. This included institutions that today we would expect to take the lead in pressing for reform of the abortion laws. The Family Planning Association kept its distance from abortion, refusing any cooperation with or support for the Abortion Law Reform Association.[16] The Family Planning Association would continue to distance itself from any association with abortion until the mid-1970s, some years after the English law regarding abortion was liberalized in 1967.[17] The Socialist Medical Association also declined to support abortion reform, holding out until the late 1950s.[18]

In England, feminist women became active in large numbers in the movement for abortion reform at an earlier time than they would in the United States, but not until the late 1930s.[19] They were prominent in the founding of the Abortion Law Reform Association in 1936, and thereafter were active, albeit without much success, in pressing for parliamentary reform.[20] The more advanced position of the English feminists regarding abortion arose from the greater role of socialism in English politics in general and among English feminists in particular.[21] This made the earlier (1920–1935, and later, after 1955) Soviet example more attractive

---

11. DAVID NATHAN, BASEBALL QUOTATIONS 152 (1993).
12. COLM BROGAN, SOCIALISM CONQUERS LABOUR (1949); MICHAEL BERRY, PARTY CHOICE: THE REAL ISSUE BETWEEN THE PARITES (1948); A.P. FRANKLIN, PARTY OR COUNTRY? AN ARGUMENT AGAINST SOCIALISM (1947); HARRY LAIDLER, BRITISH LABOR AS GOVERNMENT AND AS OPPOSITION (1950); HERBERT TRACY, BRITISH LABOUR PARTY: ITS HISTORY, GROWTH, POLICY AND LEADERS (1948). *See generally* ROGER EATWELL, 1945–1951 LABOUR GOUVERMENTS (1979); MARK JENKINS, BEVANISM, LABOUR'S HIGH TIDE: THE COLD WAR AND THE DEMOCRATIC MASS MOVEMENT (1979); D.N. PRIT, LABOUR GOVERNMENT, 1945–1951 (1963). On the creation and evolution of the National Health Service, see BRITAIN'S HEALTH SYSTEM: FROM WELFARE STATE TO MANAGED MARKETS (Donald Light & Annabelle May eds. 1993).
13. BARBARA BROOKES, ABORTION IN ENGLAND 1900–1967, at 139–40 (1988).
14. *Id.* at 159 n.68.
15. *Id.* at 157 n.18.
16. *Id.* at 145.
17. *Id.* at 148, 159 n.88.
18. *Id.* at 148.
19. *Id.* at 79. *See also* Chapter 11, at notes 221–42.
20. BROOKES, *supra* note 13, at 79, 94–98; Madeleine Simms, *Britain*, in ABORTION IN THE NEW EUROPE: A COMPARATIVE HANDBOOK 31, 35 (Bill Rolston & Anna Eggert eds. 1994).
21. BROOKES, *supra* note 13, at 80.

than it ever was in the United States—although both the Labour Party and the British Communist Party refused to endorse abortion reform until after the passage of the 1967 reform act.[22]

The post-war Labour government lasted six years in England. During this period, the English abortion reform movement worked diligently to extend its appeal, moving away somewhat from its Leftist and feminist origins.[23] The movement appears to have been orchestrated initially by literary critic Cyril Connolly who, in an editorial published in 1946, linked abortion reform to such issues as ending racial discrimination, protecting natural beauty, subsidies for the arts, and ending the death penalty.[24] As Connelly's leadership suggests, leadership was passing out of the hands of highly isolated leftist women[25] and into the hands of somewhat more mainstream men. While two-thirds of the members of the Abortion Law Reform Association continued to be women,[26] even top leadership positions were opened to men after the passing of the founding generation. In the 1950s, Glanville Williams, Professor of Criminal Law at Cambridge, became president of the Association and continued to lead it into the successful push for reform in the 1960s.[27] From the beginning, Williams personally favored the complete repeal of abortion laws, but his views were still a distinct minority in the British association.[28]

The broadening of the movement was well enough along that the last Churchill government (Conservative, 1951–55) saw two unsuccessful private bills in Parliament in an attempt to enact abortion reform.[29] Separation from the Left was helped by the fact that abortion was then a crime in Communist eastern Europe—until a wave of statutes authorizing abortion on request were adopted after the Soviets did so in 1955.[30] Nonetheless, in Britain in the 1950s, abortion remained an issue that was largely tied to the labor unions and the Labour Party.[31] Even today members of the Labour Party continue to be more supportive of the "freedom to choose" than members of the Conservative Party, a support that troubles some Labourites because the freedom is couched in individualist terms that contradict their generally collectivist ethics.[32]

The efforts of the Abortion Law Reform Association to educate the public achieved considerable success. By 1956, a survey in the *Women's Sunday Mirror* found that 52 percent of the 2,000

---

22. *Id.* at 80, 85–87; Simms, *supra* note 20, at 33–35.

23. *Id.* at 144–49.

24. Paul Johnson, Intellectuals 316 (1988). On Cyril Connolly's life generally, *see id.* at 312–19; Jeremy Lewis, Cyril Connolly: A Life (1999).

25. *See* Chapter 11, at 222–34.

26. Brookes, *supra* note 13, at 153.

27. Anthony Hordern, Legal Abortion: The English Experience 11, 14 (1971); John Noonan, jr., A Private Choice: Abortion in America in the Seventies 35 (1979).

28. Madeleine Simms, *Abortion—A Note on Some Recent Developments in Britain,* 4 Brit. J. Criminology 495 (1964).

29. Brookes, *supra* note 13, at 147–48; Johnson, *supra* note 24, at 229–31; Glanville Williams, The Sanctity of Life and the Criminal Law 220–21 (1957, reprinted 1972); Simms, *supra* note 20, at 33.

30. Vedomsti Verkovnogo Sovieta SSSR, no. 22, item 425 (1955). *See also* Chapter 12, at notes 35–39.

31. Joyce Gelb, Feminism and Politics: A Comparative Analysis 39–41, 57, 73–74, 115–18, 182–83 (1989).

32. Brookes, *supra* note 13, at 89. *See also* Celeste Michelle Condit, Decoding Abortion Rhetoric: Communicating Social Change 104, 118 n.3, 120 n.20 (1990); Elizabeth Kingdom, What's Wrong with Rights?: Problems for Feminist Politics and Jurisprudence 46–62 (1991); Eugene Genovese, *Secularism in the General Crisis of Capitalism,* 42 Am. J. Juris. 195, 202 (1997); Nicholas Johnson, *Principles and Passions: The Intersection of Abortion and Gun Rights,* 50 Ariz. L. Rev. 97, 181–91 (1997); Linda McLain, *"Atomistic Man" Revisited: Liberalism, Connection, and Feminist Jurisprudence,* 65 S. Cal. L. Rev. 1171, 1187–88, 1242 (1992); Richard Stith, *A Critique of Fairness,* 16 Val. L. Rev. 459 (1982); Robin West, *The Nature of the Right to an Abortion,* 45 Hastings L.J. 961, 963–66 (1994).

women questioned favored a right to abort "at the request of the mother-to-be."[33] The BBC broadcast the first televised appeal for abortion reform, including graphic descriptions of "back-street butchery," in 1958.[34] Many prominent women, however, were opposed to abortion reform, including the three most prominent women physicians in England.[35] Dr. Marie Stopes, the leader of the birth control movement in England, was an outspoken critic of abortion who argued, much like Margaret Sanger in the United States, that contraceptives should be used in order to reduce or eliminate abortion.[36] Stopes did more than simply preach against abortion; she actively campaigned to ban the advertising of abortifacients, and achieved some informal success.[37]

The women Members of Parliament, even if they did not actively oppose abortion reform, played a negligible role in the repeal of 1967 and did not become active on the issue until nearly a decade later when attempts began to repeal the 1967 reforms.[38] David Steel, a Labourite MP, introduced the reform bill and shepherded it through Parliament; the still all-male House of Lords provided strong support.[39] From these facts, historian Barbara Brookes inferred that women MPs were beguiled by the ability of upper class British women to obtain abortions with the aid of cooperative physicians giving an ever-broadening interpretation of the notion of "therapeutic abortion."[40] While such a reality might have impeded the impetus for change in the law, historians such as Brookes overlook the possibility that some these women, like Stopes, were genuinely convinced that abortion was murder—just as they said.[41]

The Abortion Law Reform Association, reinvigorated by a new generation of feminists in the 1960s, continued to be led by Glanville Williams.[42] The Association promoted a reform statute in the 1960s, but the popular attitudes is shown by the Association's careful avoidance of any claim that abortion was a woman's right.[43] Instead, the Association fostered an "indications" approach whereby society set the standards for abortion. This essentially eugenic argument would let society decide whether "defective" fetuses should be born and sought to assure the "best" childcare by allowing abortions based upon "social" indications.

The impact of the thalidomide tragedy was very strong in Britain and elsewhere in Europe. Thalidomide was a tranquilizer frequently taken for morning sickness, but which produced terrible deformities in fetuses.[44] Children were born with hands or feet, but without legs or arms, or

---

33. BROOKES, *supra* note 13, at 148. Historian Brookes inflates these already impressive results by adding the 23% who favored abortion to protect a woman's health to the 52% favoring abortion on demand to arrive at a figure of 75% favoring abortion "on some grounds." *Id.*

34. *Id.* at 149.

35. *Id.* at 98 n.1.

36. MARIE STOPES, MOTHER ENGLAND: A CONTEMPORARY HISTORY 183 (1929). *See also* BROOKES, *supra* note 13, at 80.

37. BROOKES, *supra* note 13, at 99 n.9.

38. GELB, *supra* note 27, at 105–06; ELIZABETH VALLANCE, WOMEN IN THE HOUSE 75, 88 (1979); Alvin Cohan, *Abortion as a Marginal Issue: The Use of Peripheral Mechanisms in Britain and the United States,* in THE NEW POLITICS OF ABORTION 27, 33–34 (Joni Lovenduski & Joyce Outshoorn eds. 1986).

39. DAVID MARSH & JOANNA CHAMBERS, ABORTION POLITICS 19–20 (1981).

40. BROOKES, *supra* note 13, at 137.

41. *See, e.g.,* STOPES, *supra* note 36, at 183.

42. BROOKES, *supra* note 13, at 149; Simms, *supra* note 20, at 35. *See generally* HORDERN, *supra* note 27, at 11–14; MADELEINE SIMMS & KEITH HINDELL, ABORTION LAW REFORMED (1971).

43. BROOKES, *supra* note 13, at 154. For telling analyses of the rhetoric employed in the Parliamentary debates over the English Abortion Act, see Cohan, *supra* note 38, at 34; Sally Sheldon, *"Who Is the Mother to Make the Judgment?": The Constructions of Woman in English Abortion Law,* 1 FEMINIST LEG. STUD. 3 (1993).

44. *See generally* MICHAEL GREEN, BENEDICTIN AND BIRTH DEFECTS: THE CHALLENGES OF MASS TOXIC SUBSTANCES LITIGATION 64–69, 73 (1996); T.V.N. PERSAUD, ENVIRONMENTAL CAUSES OF HUMAN BIRTH DEFECTS 39–40 (1990); Kenneth Kaitin, *Thalidomide Revisited: New Clinical Uses for an Old Drug,* 3 PHARM.

with other grotesque rearrangements of body parts. The use of thalidomide had been more widespread in Britain and Europe than it was in the United States.[45] At least 349 thalidomide babies were born in the United Kingdom.[46] The British Ministry of Health went so far as to order "every possible effort" to prevent the birth of malformed children as a result of thalidomide, thus authorizing an unknown number of abortions that arguably were not legal at the time.[47] Ironically, notwithstanding their handicaps, "many thalidomide babies grew up very sane people."[48]

The discovery of the connection between rubella and birth defects also influenced the abortion debate in England.[49] In contrast to British medical groups won over by fear of birth defects, German medical associations—recalling the Nazi experience—continue staunchly to oppose abortion reform.[50] The erosion of family life and fears of a "population explosion," fueled by the rise of the "managerial class," provided further support in Britain for changes in the abortion laws.[51] Eventually the Abortion Law Reform Association arranged for David Steel to introduce a

---

MED. 203, 203–04 (1988); Sylvia Law, *Tort Liability and the Availability of Contraceptive Drugs and Devices in the United States,* 23 NYU REV. L. & SOC. CHANGE 339, 360–62 (1997).

45. BROOKES, *supra* note 13, at 133, 151–53; MARY KENNY, ABORTION: THE WHOLE STORY 196–98 (1986); SIMMS & HINDELL, *supra* note 42, at 108–09; Simms, *supra* note 20, at 34.

46. BROOKES, *supra* note 13, at 151. *See* S. v. Distillers Co. (Biochemicals) Ltd., [1969] All E.R. 1412.

47. BROOKES, *supra* note 13, at 152–53.

48. KENNY, *supra* note 3, at 198. *See generally* ETHEL ROSKIES, ABNORMALITY AND NORMALITY: THE MOTHERING OF THALIDOMIDE CHILDREN (1972). One further irony is that Thalidomide recently has been reintroduced as a therapy for a wide variety of conditions, including leprosy, rheumatoid arthritis, and certain AIDS-related diseases. *See* Kaitin, *supra* note 44, at 204–07; Kimberly McLarin, *Thalidomide: Old Horrors Clash with New Hope,* N.Y. TIMES, Dec. 28, 1995, at A1; Sheryl Gay Stolberg, *37 Years Later, A Second Chance for Thalidmide,* N.Y. TIMES, Sept. 23, 1997, at A1; Sheryl Gay Stolberg, *Thalidomide: Once Banned, Is in Demand,* N.Y. TIMES, Nov. 17, 1997, at A1.

49. BROOKES, *supra* note 13, at 150–51.

50. Julie George, *Political Effects of Court Decisions on Abortion: A Comparison between the United States and the German Federal Republic,* 3 INT'L J.L. & FAM. 106, 122 (1989). On the Nazi experience regarding abortion, see Chapter 11, at notes 85–102.

51. *See, e.g.,* James Bolner & Robert Jacobson, *Right to Procreated: The Dilemma of Overpopulation and U.S. Judiciary,* 25 LOY. L. REV. 235 (1979); Edgar Chasteen, *The Case for Compulsory Population Control,* MADEMOISELLE, Jan. 1970, at 142; Donald Harting & Leslie Corsa, *The American Public Health Association and the Population Problem,* 59 AM. J. PUB. HEALTH 1927 (1969); Kent Greenawalt, *Criminal Law and Population Control,* 24 VAND. L. REV. 465, 479–83 (1971); Margery Shaw, *Procreation and the Population Problem,* 55 N.C. L. REV. 1165 (1977). *See generally* BETH BAILEY, SEX IN THE HEARTLAND 107–15, 124–25 (1999); BROOKES, *supra* note 13, at 9–13, 56–57; DONALD CRITCHLOW, INTENDED CONSEQUENCES: BIRTH CONTROL, ABORTION, AND THE FEDERAL GOVERNMENT IN MODERN AMERICA (1999); H.A. Finlay, *Abortion—Right of Crime?,* 10 U. TASMANIA L. REV. 1 (1990); Simms, *supra* note 20, at 35–36. On the theory that population growth is the most central crisis in today's world, see LARRY BARNETT & EMILY REED, LAW, SOCIETY, AND POPULATION: ISSUES IN A NEW FIELD (1985); PAUL & ANNE EHRLICH, THE POPULATION BOMB (1968); PAUL & ANNE EHRLICH, THE POPULATION EXPLOSION (1990); GARRET HARDIN, LIVING WITH LIMITS (1993); Nancy Birdsall, *Population Growth and Poverty in the Developing World,* 35 POPULATION BULL. 9 (1980); Deborah Castetter, Comment, *India's Compulsory Sterilization Laws: The Human Right of Family Planning,* 8 CAL. W. INT'L L.J. 342 (1978); Elizabeth Rohrbough, *On Our Way to Ten Billion Human Beings: A Comment on Sustainability and Population,* 9 COLO. J. INT'L ENVTL. L. & POL'Y 235 (1994); Omar Saleem, *Be Fruitful, and Multiply, and Replenish the Earth, and Subdue It: Third World Population Growth and the Environment,* 8 GEO. INT'L ENVTL. L. REV. 1 (1995).

Some groups continue to use fears of a "population explosion" to press for abortion rights on a global scale. *See* Diana Babor, *Population Growth and Reproductive Rights in International Human Rights Law,* 14 CONN. J. INT'L L. 83 (1999); Steven Holmes, *Global Crisis in Population Is Far from Over, a Group Warns,* N.Y. TIMES, Dec. 31, 1997, at A6; Michael Marcus, Note, *United States Foreign Population Assistance Programs: Antiabortion Propaganda?,* 15 BROOK. J. INT'L L. 843 (1989). Others are so obsessed with fears of population growth that they have become involved in activities that are highly questionable on ethical or legal grounds or both. *See, e.g.,* Judith Scully, *Maternal Mortality, Population Control, and the War in Women's Wombs,* 19 WIS.

"private member's bill" in Parliament—a bill on which the government took no stand. Its enactment represents one of the relatively rare instances in which private lobbying groups have succeeded in moving the British Parliament to act.[52] With less than half of the Commons voting, the bill passed by a vote of 167–83 (out of more than 600 members of parliament) after a 27-hour continuous debate—the longest Parliamentary debate in Britain since before World War II.[53]

The House of Lords played an unusually active role in the legislation. The bill received stronger support in the Lords than in the Commons—and also stronger opposition.[54] Opposition to the bill was strong enough in the Lords that it initially voted to amend the bill to eliminate "social indications" and otherwise to tighten restriction on abortion, but eventually backed off for fear of too direct a confrontation with the Commons.[55] Women Members of Parliament played a negligible role in the debate.[56] The primary opposition came from obstetricians and gynecologists, rather than from the religious groups usually blamed for resistance to abortion reform.[57]

The *Abortion Act of 1967* authorized abortions when two physicians certify that one of the statutory indications exists.[58] The indications are: (1) preserving the life or health of the pregnant woman (maternal indications); (2) preventing adverse effects on the family (social indications); or (3) eliminating hereditary defects (eugenic indications). The Act amended only the *Offences against the Persons Act of 1861* and not the *Infant Life (Preservation) Act of 1929.*[59] The 1967 Act did not alter the near absolute prohibition of the abortion of a child "capable of being born alive"; abortion of such infants is lawful only to preserve the life of the mother. Lord Diplock would comment in subsequent litigation over the Act, "[the Act] lacks that style and consistency of draftsmanship both internal to the Act itself and in relation to other statutes which one would expect to find in legislation that had its origin in the office of parliamentary counsel."[60]

The British "indications policy" would have been unconstitutional under the "strict scrutiny" regime of *Roe v. Wade,*[61] and probably would still be unconstitutional under the "undue burden" test of *Planned Parenthood of Southeastern Pennsylvania v. Casey.*[62] The supposed limits are in

---

INT'L L.J. 103 (2001).

On the rise of the managerial class, see the text *infra* at notes 256–321.

52. GELB, *supra* note 31, at 115; HORDERN, *supra* note 27, at 10–12; BRIDGETT PYM, PRESSURE GROUPS AND THE PERMISSIVE SOCIETY 91 (1974); PATRICK RIVERS, POLITICS UNDER PRESSURE 206 (1974); Cohan, *supra* note 38, at 32.

53. HORDERN, *supra* note 27, at 12.

54. MARSH & CHAMBERS, *supra* note 39, 19–20; Simms, *supra* note 20, at 34–35.

55. GELB, *supra* note 31, at 116; HORDERN, *supra* note 27, at 12; Joni Lovenduski, *Parliament, Pressure Groups, Networks and the Women's Movement: The New Politics of Abortion Law Reform in Britain,* in THE NEW POLITICS OF ABORTION, *supra* note 38, at 49, 53.

56. GELB, *supra* note 31, at 105–06; VALLANCE, *supra* note 38, at 75, 88; Simms, *supra* note 20, at 35.

57. BROOKES, *supra* note 13, at 154. Madeleine Simms, who prefers to blame resistance on Catholics, merely hints at the opposition role of obstetricians and gynecologists. Simms, *supra* note 20, at 35–36.

58. *Abortion Act of 1967,* ch. 87, §1. *See generally* HORDERN, *supra* note 27, at 69–79; J.K. MASON, MEDICO-LEGAL ASPECTS OF REPRODUCTION AND PARENTHOOD 115–17 (2nd ed. 1998); DAVID MEYERS, THE HUMAN BODY AND THE LAW 26–34 (2nd ed. 1990); KERRY PETERSEN, ABORTION REGIMES 109–23 (1993); SALLY SHELDON, BEYOND CONTROL: MEDICAL POWER AND ABORTION LAW (1997); Andrew Grubb, *Abortion Law—An English Perspective,* 20 N. MEX. L. REV. 649, 661–68 (1990); Kenneth Norrie, *Abortion in Great Britain: One Act, Two Laws,* 1985 CRIM. L. REP. 475; Simms, *supra* note 20, at 36–37.

59. 19 & 20 Geo. V ch. 34 (1929). *See* Chapter 11, at notes 244–56. *See also* Cohan, *supra* note 38, at 36–37.

60. Royal College of Nursing v. Department of Health & Soc. Security, [1981] A.C. 800, 824 (per Diplock, L.J.).

61. MASON, *supra* note 58, at 116; P.T. O'Neill & Isobel Watson, *The Father and the Unborn Child,* 38 MOD. L. REV. 174, 178 (1975). *See* Roe v. Wade, 410 U.S. 113 (1973).

62. 505 U.S. 833 (1992).

fact non-existent. Professor of Forensic Medicine John Mason summarized the maternal or social indications thusly:

> [A] moment's reflection reveals that the terms are, in fact extremely wide, particularly
> in relation to s.1(1)(a) where there is no indication of "serious" risk.... The test is sim-
> ply one of comparison with non-termination. Given that she is actively seeking termi-
> nation, it is difficult to see how the fact of motherhood could not have a *relatively* ad-
> verse mental effect on the woman concerned; and, in the absence of a cornucopian
> supply of plenty, it is inconceivable that the arrival of a sibling would not have a greater
> effect on the existing family than would its non-arrival.... [T]here would be few obste-
> tricians who would deny that, *in general,* the risks to the health of a woman who carries
> a baby to full term and undergoes labour are greater than are those of an early termina-
> tion; from which it follows that the mere *fact* of pregnancy is sufficient justification for
> its legal termination on social grounds.[63]

Mason went on to conclude that even sex-selective abortions were mandated by the 1967 Act
as having a child with the "wrong" sex would certainly disturb a woman's peace of mind and
could endanger her physical well-being as well if her spouse or other relatives were to behave op-
pressively.[64] "Abortion on the grounds of sex," Mason wrote, "may well be unethical, and ecolog-
ically unsound, but it is certainly not illegal."[65] It follows from Mason's reasoning that a refusal to
do an abortion requires explanation under the 1967 Act, and not the decision to abort.

Is Mason's analysis were not enough, Madeleine Simms, a pro-abortion scholar, has argued
that cost is justification enough for promoting abortions over births because an abortion costs
the taxpayer (*i.e.,* the National Health Service) less than one-fourth what a live birth costs (£250
compared to £1,170).[66] In very much the same vein, the British military long enforced a policy of
dismissing from service any woman who, upon becoming pregnant, refused to undergo an abortion.[67] The British military attempted to justify this policy on the grounds that "military efficiency" requires that military personnel be available to go anywhere in the world on 24 hours
notice (as if childcare were an impossibility), and because the military sought to prevent the
aborted children from being orphaned. No policy prohibited male service members from leaving
orphans. Eventually, the government had to pay out over £55,000,000 in compensation when an
industrial tribunal ruled that the policy was a form of sex discrimination.[68]

With a new openness of English and Welsh physicians to doing abortions, the number of
abortions performed legally for English and Welsh residents rose from 76,000 in 1970 to 129,000
in 1980 to 173,000 in 1990, at rates of 7 abortions/1000 births in 1970, 11/1000 in 1980, and
16/1000 in 1990).[69] When one adds in the abortions performed in England for Scots and for foreigners, the numbers performed were 92,000 (1970), 169,000 (1980), and 196,000 (1990).[70] As
these numbers indicate, the claim, frequently made, that legal abortions in England in the 30
years since abortion was made widely available have averaged 170,000 per year is a small exagger-

---

63. MASON, *supra* note 58, at 116–17 (emphasis in original). *See also* McKay v. Essex Area Health Auth'y,
[1982] Q.B. 1166; MASON, *supra,* at 157–58; SHELDON, *supra* note 58, at 2; Ellie Lee, *Tensions in the Regulation
of Abortion in Britain,* J. LAW & SOC'Y 532 (2003).

64. MASON, *supra* note 58, at 117.

65. *Id.*

66. Simms, *supra* note 20, at 40. *See generally* A. McGUIRE & D. HUGHES, THE ECONOMICS OF FAMILY
PLANNING (1995).

67. JANET HADLEY, ABORTION: BETWEEN FREEDOM AND NECESSITY 110–11 (1996).

68. *See* Ministry of Defence v. Mutton, [1996] I.C.R. 590 (finding that requirement of abortion in order to
continue in service is sexual discrimination).

69. MASON, *supra* note 58, at 124–25; Lee, *supra* note 63, at 538; Simms, *supra* note 20, at 37–38.

70. MASON, *supra* note 58, at 124–25.

ation, but not far off the mark.[71] The figures suggest that the claims of those who lobbied Parliament for the new law that 267,000 illegal abortions were occurring annually in England and Wales were considerably exaggerated.[72]

Nearly all legal abortions in England and Wales after 1967 were justified by risks to the mental health or the social situation of the woman. In 1990, nearly all abortions performed English and Welsh women (98.4 percent) were justified by social indications, with even more of the abortions of foreign women (99.85 percent) being justified by social indications.[73] In 1986, less than 2,000 abortions were justified by reference to "risks to the health of existing children in the family," and barely 1,000 were based upon fear of serious handicap in the unborn child, a number that rose to 1,824 in 1995.[74] Because genuine risks to a woman's physical health are extremely rare,[75] such threats hardly appear in the records of abortions in England.

The English experience demonstrates that the attitude of the medical profession probably has more to do with the actual availability of abortion than the state of the law.[76] Only one doctor has been prosecuted for violating the 1967 Act, and that prosecution was based on how, rather than why, he performed the abortion.[77] Courts in several other cases have construed the law, generally liberally, as urged by medical witnesses in the proceedings.[78] The Department of Public Prosecutions has even declined to take action against two physicians who wrote "none" into the space on the required reporting form that asked for the reason for an abortion.[79] And the military doctors doing coerced abortions of military women hardly had a "good faith" belief that the continuation of the pregnancy endangered the woman's mental health.[80] The English medical

---

71. *See* HORDERN, *supra* note 27, at 102–04; Grubb, *supra* note 58, at 665–66; Lee, *supra* note 63, at 533; William Schmidt, *U.S. Abortion Protesters Shunned by the British*, N.Y. TIMES, April 13, 1993, at A-2, col. 1, 2.

72. BROOKES, *supra* note 13, at 154 (estimating the true figure at 50,000 per year), 161 n.144 (115,000 to 125,000 per year); HORDERN, *supra* note 27, at 1–2, 5; REPORT OF THE INTERDEPARTMENTAL COMMITTEE ON ABORTION 9 (1939) (90,000 per year); KENNY, *supra* note 45, at 194–95 (100,000 to 200,000 per year). *See also* L.A. PERRY, CRIMINAL ABORTION 18 (1932); SYDNEY SMITH & F.S. FIDDES, FORENSIC MEDICINE 324 (10th ed. 1955); WILLIAMS, *supra* note 29, at 210–11; Eustace Chesser, *The Law of Abortion*, 72 MED. WORLD 495 (1950); C.B. Goodhart, *On the Incidence of Illegal Abortion*, 27 POPULATION STUD. 207 (1973); William James, *The Incidence of Illegal Abortions*, 25 POPULATION STUD. 327 (1971).

73. MASON, *supra* note 58, at 124–25.

74. MASON, *supra* note 58, at 169; Simms, *supra* note 20, at 37. On genetic indications, see Derek Morgan, *Abortion: The Unexamined Ground*, [1990] CRIM. L. REP. 687.

75. *See* Howard Hammond, *Therapeutic Abortion: Ten Years' Experience with Hospital Committee Control*, 89 AM. J. OBSTET. & GYNECOLOGY 349 (1964); Robert Hall, *Therapeutic Abortion, Sterilization, and Contraception*, 91 AM. J. OBSTET. & GYNECOLOGY 518, 524–25 (1965); Roy Hefferman & William Lynch, *What Is the Status of Therapeutic Abortion in Modern Obstetrics?*, 66 AM. J. OBSTET. & GYNECOLOGY 335 (1953); J.G. Moore & J.H. Randall, *Trends in Therapeutic Abortion: A Review of 137 Cases*, 63 AM. J. OBSTET. & GYNECOLOGY 34 (1952); Kenneth Niswander, *Medical Abortion Practice in the United States*, in ABORTION AND THE LAW 242, 251–54 (David Smith ed. 1967); Kenneth Niswander & Manual Porto, *Abortion Practices in the United States: A Medical Viewpoint*, in ABORTION, MEDICINE, AND THE LAW 567, 571 (J. Douglas Butler & David Walbert eds., 4th ed. 1992); Quinten Scherman, *Therapeutic Abortion*, 11 OBSTETRICS & GYNECOLOGY 323 (1958).

76. MASON, *supra* note 58, at 114–15, 124. *See also* Evart Ketting & Philip van Praag, *The Marginal Relevance of Legislation Relating to Induced Abortion*, in THE NEW POLITICS OF ABORTION, *supra* note 38, at 154. This reality has not prevented arguments that the English abortion law demeans women and should be amended to conform to the actual practice of allowing women free choice to abort. *See, e.g.*, MARY BOYLE, RE-THINKING ABORTION, PSYCHOLOGY, GENDER, POWER, AND THE LAW (1997); SHELDON, *supra* note 58; Lee, *supra* note 63.

77. Regina v. Smith, [1974] 1 ALL E.R. 376. *See also* MASON, *supra* note 58, at 125–26.

78. *See* Royal College of Nursing v. Department of Health & Soc. Security, [1981] A.C. 800; C. v. S., [1988] 1 Q.B. 135; Paton v. British Pregnancy Advisory Service Trustees, [1979] Q.B. 276.

79. KINGDOM, *supra* note 32, at 50.

80. HADLEY, *supra* note 67, at 111.

profession has been as reticent as the legal profession about enforcing the 1967 act, bringing only a handful of minor disciplinary proceedings since 1970.[81]

The British Medical Association, which opposed the free availability of abortion in 1967, now institutionally supports it despite its commitment to the principle of "maintaining respect for human life from the time of conception."[82] Initially many Britain physicians invoked the Act's conscience clause to refuse to do abortions even when clearly legal.[83] As a result, well into the 1980s about half of the abortions were performed in private clinics, outside the National Health Service.[84] The National Health Service also did not include contraceptive services until 1974, and then only over some real (and continuing) opposition from the physicians.[85] Yet the conscience clause in the English Act (allowing a doctor or nurse to decline to do an abortion which violates his conscience) is tightly circumscribed. The physician or nurse who invokes it must be able to "prove" her conscientious status, and the clause cannot be invoked if the pregnant woman's life is in danger.[86] A physician who declines to do an abortion must still advise the patient on how to obtain one; to do otherwise would be considered a violation of the duty to care for the patient.[87] And a physician's secretary is wholly unprotected by the conscience clause should she object to typing the letter of referral.[88] With the advent of RU-486 and the like, no one knows whether a pharmacist can invoke the conscience clause.[89]

Today, a physician who invokes the conscience clause is likely to encounter considerable social pressure from other physicians.[90] Nurses are even more vulnerable. Obstetric nurses as a group were sufficiently disturbed by their role in prostaglandin abortions—where the nurses administered and supervised the injection or infusion of abortifacient hormones and the subsequent delivery of the child—that their professional organization brought a suit to challenge the legitimacy of the procedure.[91] While the Court of Appeal agreed that this was an illegal abortion because it was not performed by a physician, the House of Lords reversed by a 3-2 vote on the grounds that so long as the nurse was working under the supervision of a licensed physician, it was the physician who "performed" the abortion, and not the nurse.[92] Nurses can personally escape participating in any abortion by invoking the conscience clause, but only at the cost of impairing their utility to their employer as they are expected to be mobile throughout the hospital system.[93]

Today two-thirds or more of British abortions are provided by the National Health Service, but abortion remains the most frequent medical procedure for which the patient herself pays at a

---

81. Tarnesby v. Kensington, Chelsea & Westminster Health Auth'y, [1980] I.C.R. 475 (C.A.), [1981] I.C.R. 615 (H.L.); Faridian v. General Med. Council, [1970] 3 W.L.R. 1065 (P.C.). *See* MASON, *supra* note 58, at 125–26.

82. *Id.* at 152–53, 198–99; KINGDOM, *supra* note 32, at 113–14; MASON, *supra* note 58, at 125.

83. HADLEY, *supra* note 67, at 153; MASON, *supra* note 58, at 127–29.

84. *Id.* at 153.

85. *Id.* at 153–56; ROBERT SHAPIRO, CONTRACEPTION: A PRACTICAL AND POLITICAL GUIDE 22 (1987); David Bromham, *Are Current Sources of Contraceptive Advice Adequate to Meet Changes in Contraceptive Practice?*, 19 BRIT. J. FAM. PLANNING 179 (1993); David Bromham, *Knowledge and Use of Secondary Contraception among Patients Requesting Termination of Pregnancy,* 306 BRIT. MED. J. 556 (1993).

86. *Abortion Act, supra* note 58, § 4(2).

87. MASON, *supra* note 58, at 128.

88. Janaway v. Salford Area Health Auth'y, [1989] A.C. 537. *See also* David Poole, Janaway: *A Comment,* 98/99 LAW & JUST. 82 (1988).

89. MASON, *supra* note 58, at 129; B.D. Weinstein, *Do Pharmacists have a Right to Refuse to Fill Prescriptions for Abortifacient Drugs?,* 20 LAW MED. HEALTH CARE 220 (1992).

90. MASON, *supra* note 58, at 128–29.

91. Royal College of Nursing v. Department of Health & Soc. Security, [1981] A.C. 800.

92. *Id.* at 829 (per Diplock, L.J.).

93. *Id.* at 804–05 (per Denning, M.R.).

private clinic.[94] A good many doctors, nurses, and social workers in Britain put considerable pressure on women to have abortions when the professional considers the woman unsuited to be a mother.[95] The category of "unsuited for motherhood" apparently includes many women with darker skins.[96] The eugenics supporters seem to have more influence on abortion policy in England than most people realize.[97]

The increase in the incidence of abortions in England and Wales were enough to fuel repeated and growing protests for and against abortion rights in the streets of London—although the British protesters have eschewed the extreme forms of direct action (blockades and violence) sometimes indulged by anti-abortion protesters in the United States.[98] The "All-Party Pro-Life Group" in Parliament has attempted at least 20 times since 1967 to repeal or amend the *Abortion Act*, without success.[99] Members of Parliament have been reluctant to address questions about the efficacy of the *Abortion Act*, preferring to avoid such questions through parliamentary ruses rather than confronting the questions and declaring their hand.[100] The only legislative change was the *Human Fertilization and Embryology Act of 1990*[101] that removed all time limits on abortions responding to risks to the woman's health while limiting abortions to other causes to 24 weeks.

*Human Fertilization and Embryology Act of 1990* amended the *Infant Life (Preservation) Act of 1929* to lower the presumed age of viability from 28 weeks to 24 weeks, and to authorize "therapeutic" abortions after viability if the threat to the mother's life from continuance of the pregnancy is greater than the threat to the mother's life from terminating the pregnancy. The 1990 Amendment contains no requirement of an attempt to save the infant's life even if that could be done without unduly endangering the mother. As threats to the mother's life include "psychological" threats as determined in the unbridled discretion of a single physician, this amendment introduced virtual abortion on demand even for late-term fetuses, at least for women who could afford a willing private doctor. The *Abortion Act of 1967* continues, however, to be a serious and effective restraint on women who depend on the National Health Service.[102]

The *Abortion Act of 1967* never extended to Northern Ireland or to Scotland.[103] Several recent unreported decisions have reaffirmed *Rex v. Bourne* as the law in Northern Ireland, meaning that

---

94. HADLEY, *supra* note 67, at 155; Wendy Savage, *Requests for Later Termination of Pregnancy—Tower Hamlets 1983*, 290 BRIT. MED. J. 621 (1985).

95. HADLEY, *supra* note 67, at 111–16.

96. *See* Ann Phoenix, *Black Women in the Maternity Services*, in THE POLITICS OF MOTHERHOOD (J. Garcia *et al.* eds. 1990). *See also* Ronald Bayer, *The Suitability of HIV-Positive Individuals for Marriage and Pregnancy*, 261 JAMA 993 (1989).

97. *See* Diane Paul, *Is Human Genetics Disguised Eugenics?*, in GENES AND HUMAN SELF-KNOWLEDGE 67 (Robert Weir *et al.* eds. 1994). For the role of the eugenics movement in early debates regarding abortion, see Chapter 11, at notes 25–192.

98. HADLEY, *supra* note 67, at 153–54, 164–67; Cohan, *supra* note 38, at 38–43; Lovenduski, *supra* note 55.

99. HADLEY, *supra* note 67, at 159–60; MASON, *supra* note 58, at 115, 126; Lovenduski, *supra* note 55, at 53–59; Simms, *supra* note 20, at 39–40.

100. MASON, *supra* note 58, at 126. *See generally* Grubb, *supra* note 58, at 661–68.

101. *See* MASON, *supra* note 58, at 126; Simms, *supra* note 20, at 40. The debates surrounding this Act are described in Caroline Morris, *Technology and the Legal Discourse of Fetal Autonomy*, 8 UCLA WOMEN'S L.J. 47, 76–77 (1997).

102. D. MORGAN & R.G. LEE, BLACKSTONE'S GUIDE TO THE HUMAN FERTILIZATION AND EMBRYOLOGY ACT 1990, at 36 (1990). *See also* BROOKES, *supra* note 13, at 155–56; MASON, *supra* note 58, at 125; Bernard Dickens & Rebecca Cook, *Development of Commonwealth Abortion Laws*, 28 INT'L & COMP. L.Q. 424, 443–49 (1979).

103. MASON, *supra* note 146, at 111–12, 114, 118; Anna Eggert & Bill Rolston, *Ireland*, in ABORTION IN THE NEW EUROPE, *supra* note 4, at 157, 161, 169–71; Eileen Fegan & Rachel Rebouche, *Northern Ireland's Abortion Law: The Morality of Silence and the Censure of Agency*, 2 FEMINIST LEG. STUD. 221 (2003).

an abortion is lawful if the physician determines in good faith that the abortion is necessary to protect the life or health (physical or mental) of the mother.[104] One report describes the two cases as "friendly" proceedings in which both the prosecution and the defense favored a finding that the abortions were lawful and no participant in the proceedings opposed that claim.[105] Considerable uncertainty remains over just what the law applicable in Northern Ireland requires. Estimates of the number of legal abortions in Northern Ireland in recent years have ranged between 10 and 500 per year.[106] As many as 2,000 women travel from there to England annually to obtain abortions.[107] The abortion rate for Scotland rose parallel to the rate in England and Wales, but the Scottish rate always remained at about one-half of that of England and Wales.[108]

# Reform Comes to America

*When you come to the fork in the road, take it.*

— Yogi Berra[109]

World War II was followed in the United States by the longest and most fecund "baby boom" in American history. The psychological effect of having survived a war in which many lives were lost often is a measurable increase in the birth rate for at least a short period. (This perhaps explains the curious fact that one in ten of the women who served in the Gulf War came home pregnant despite the availability of birth control and abortion while they were over seas.[110] ) The baby boom after World War II, however, lasted longer (18 years) and produced more children than any comparable post-war boom,[111] suggesting that other factors were also at work. These factors included a long period of unprecedented prosperity, a sense in many that they had unduly delayed having children because of the dozen years of the Great Depression and because of the enforced separation of spouses by five years of war, and pressures on women to resume traditional female roles after taking on factory work and other "male" roles in unprecedented numbers during the war.[112] Yet during the "baby-boom" era, abortion was in fact more available than

---

104. *See* Re A, [1994] 2 Med. L. Rev. 374; Re K, [1994] 2 Med. L. Rev. 371; Tony McGleenan, Bourne *Again: Abortion Law in Northern Ireland after Re* K *and Re* A, 45 N. Ire. Leg. Q. 389 (1994); J. Scott Tiedemann, Comment, *The Abortion Controversy in the Republic of Ireland and Northern Ireland and Its Potential Effect on Unification,* 17 Loy.-L.A. Int'l & Comp. L.J. 737, 746–55 (1995); Fegan & Rebouche, *supra* note 103, at 226–30. *See also* Mason, *supra* note 58, at 118; Colin Francome, *Abortion in Ireland,* 305 Brit. Med. J. 436, 436 (1992); Sharon Kingman, *Northern Ireland's Abortion Law Criticised as Unclear,* 307 Brit. Med. J. 284 (1993).

105. McGleenan, *supra* note 104, at 393.

106. *Id.* at 391 n.10. *See also* Fegan & Rebouche, *supra* note 103, at 232–52.

107. Marie Fox & Therese Murphy, *Irish Abortion: Seeking Refuge in a Jurisprudence of Doubt and Delegation,* 19 J.L. & Soc'y 454, 463 (1992).*See also* Mary Sexton & Ann Rossiter, The Other Irish Journey: A Survey Update of Northern Irish Women Attending British Abortion Clinics (2001); Fegan & Rebouche, *supra* note 103, at 227–28.

108. Simms, *supra* note 20, at 37–38.

109. David Nathan, Baseball Quotations 150 (1993).

110. Barbara Kantrowitz *et al., The Right to Fight,* Newsweek, Aug. 5, 1991, at 22, 23.

111. Cheryl Russell, The Master Trend: How the Baby Boom Generation is Remaking America 11 (1993).

112. *See, e.g.,* Ferdinand Lundberg & Marynia Farnham, Modern Women: The Lost Sex (1947). *See generally* Susan Hartmann, The Home Front and Beyond: American Woman in the 1940s (1982); Elaine Tyler May, Homeward Bound: American Families in the Cold War Era (1988); Not June

ever before in history. These contradictory realities make claims about the incidence of abortion during this era highly problematic. The desire for relatively large families perhaps also explains the lack of public pressure for changes in the abortion laws until the baby boom ended.

Yet another factor also important explains the lack of public pressure for reform of abortion laws during the 1940s and the 1950s. Just as after World War I, the impetus for social reform nearly disappeared in the United States after World War II. Public opinion swung strongly against left-wing ideas during the early Cold War.[113] Historian Leslie Reagan goes so far as to link the turn towards the family and any crackdown on abortion to McCarthyism, a convenient scapegoat for whatever one doesn't like from the 1940s and 1950s.[114] A tiny movement in favor of abortion reform never quite died in the United States, but then it had never been more than barely alive.[115] Little public controversy occurred over the issue while its proponents busied themselves in divorcing it from formally leftist rhetoric.[116] The separation from Leftist rhetoric does not mean that there is no continuing empirical link between views on abortion and affiliation with Left or Right, but only that the arguments used were not formally or logically linked to Left/Right issues. Many people took positions on abortion that would contradict their positions on Left/Right issues if such positions were logically linked rather than merely empirically linked.[117] Ironically, several scholars have argued recently that abortion rights are specifically Marxist.[118] Not only is this a claim that would have been counterproductive 50 years ago, it is a claim that runs counter to the strongly collectivist notions that characterize Marxist thinking.[119]

Just as with so much else relating to birth control, Margaret Sanger, originally a strident socialist, led the separation from the Left in the United States.[120] Sanger, however, focused on contraception and eschewed abortion.[121] The first real challenge in the United States to the centuries old tradition condemning abortion came from law professor Glanville Williams in the Carpentier Lectures given at Columbia University School of Law in 1956.[122] (Others would identify the *Kinsey Report* as the source that reopened discussion of the acceptability of abortion, a book by ethicist Joseph Fletcher, or the published proceedings of a conference held in 1955 sponsored by the Planned Parenthood Federation[123]—but the proceedings of the conference were not pub-

---

CLEAVER: WOMEN AND GENDER IN POST-WAR AMERICA, 1945–1960 (Joanne Meyerowitz ed. 1994); ROSALIND POLLACK PETCHESKY, ABORTION AND WOMEN'S CHOICE: THE STATE, SEXUALITY, AND REPRODUCTIVE FREEDOM 106–14 (rev. ed. 1990); LESLIE REAGAN, WHEN ABORTION WAS A CRIME: WOMEN, MEDICINE, AND LAW IN THE UNITED STATES, 1867–1973, at 162–64 (1997); MARY RYAN, WOMANHOOD IN AMERICA: FROM COLONIAL TIMES TO THE PRESENT 167–68, 198–209 (1975).

113. *See, e.g.,* LINDA GORDON, WOMAN'S BODY, WOMAN'S RIGHT: A SOCIAL HISTORY OF BIRTH CONTROL IN AMERICA 359–63 (1976); DEBORAH RHODE, JUSTICE AND GENDER 29–30 (1989).

114. REAGAN, *supra* note 112, at 163–64, 172–73, 180–81. For an excellent short critique of the McCarthyite theory, see CRITCHLOW, *supra* note 51, at 269 n.68.

115. *See* Chapter 11, at notes 175–220.

116. GERMAIN GRISEZ, ABORTION: THE MYTHS, THE REALITIES, AND THE ARGUMENTS 231–32 (1970); PETCHESKY, *supra* note 112, at 92–95.

117. *See, e.g.,* MARIAN FAUX, CRUSADERS: VOICES FROM THE ABORTION FRONT xiii–xiv, 199–229 (1990); PETCHESKY, *supra* note 112, at 3–18.

118. *See* GORDON, *supra* note 113, at xvi–xviii, 11–22; PETCHESKY, *supra* note 112; Allison Jaggar, *Abortion and a Woman's Right to Decide,* in WOMEN AND PHILOSOPHY 347 (Carol Gould & Marx Wartofsky eds. 1976).

119. BROOKES, *supra* note 13, at 89; KINGDOM, *supra* note 32, at 46–62; Stith, *supra* note 32.

120. GORDON, *supra* note 113, at 213–15, 220–45, 249, 257–59, 294–95.

121. *See* Chapter 11, at notes 197–204.

122. WILLIAMS, *supra* note 29. *See* ELIZABETH MENSCH & ALAN FREEMAN, THE POLITICS OF VIRTUE: IS ABORTION DEBATABLE? 129 (1993); MARVIN OLASKY, THE PRESS AND ABORTION, 1838–1988, at 85–86 (1988); EVA RUBIN, ABORTION, POLITICS, AND THE COURTS 18 (rev. ed. 1987).

123. NANETTE DAVIS, FROM CRIME TO CHOICE 4 (1985); KERRY JACOBY, SOULS, BODIES, SPIRITS: THE DRIVE TO ABOLISH ABORTION SINCE 1973, at 3 (1998); REAGAN, *supra* note 112, at 220. On the conference, see ABORTION IN THE UNITED STATES: A CONFERENCE SPONSORED BY THE PLANNED PARENTHOOD FEDERATION

lished until 1958, after Williams' lectures.) Williams was Professor of Criminal Law at Cambridge University, and also president of the [British] Abortion Law Reform Association.[124]

Williams already favored a complete repeal of abortion laws, but found his views to be in a distinct minority even in the Abortion Law Reform Association in Britain.[125] In his lectures at Columbia University, he took a more moderate line, inaugurating the first open debate on abortion within either the American or the English legal profession.[126] After the publication of his Carpentier Lectures in 1957,[127] the lectures brought the wider popularity of the idea of abortion reform in England to the United States and led directly to the American Law Institute's innovative response to the question.[128] Williams was invited to participate in the drafting of the Institute's *Model Penal Code* although he was not a member of the Institute.[129] While the Institute has no official standing as a law-making body, it is an important and influential body composed of the leading judges, lawyers, and legal scholars of the day.[130] The Institute's *Model Penal Code* would lead to legislative change.[131]

Unlike the position he had taken in England, Williams chose to argue for a limited reform that would legalize abortion before the 28th week of pregnancy if the pregnancy threatened the mother's life or health, or if it resulted from rape or incest, or if it presented a significant likelihood that the fetus would be born with a serious defect or deformity. He argued for these changes based upon the social costs of illegal abortions and on a rejection of fetal personhood before the 28th week of pregnancy.[132] While he argued (erroneously) that opposition to abortion was based upon the Christian desire to baptize the infant,[133] his arguments, like so much else relating to abortion, actually were grounded in his understanding of technology.

William's concern for the social costs of illegal abortions made sense only if one supposed that abortion did not involve the killing of a human being. He based his conclusion partly on his belief that a fetal electroencephalogram (EEG) was impossible before the 28th week of gestation.[134] Shortly after Williams' lecture, it was established that a fetal EEG was possible as early as the eighth week of pregnancy.[135] Ultimately, however, Williams concluded that a fetus was not a per-

---

OF AMERICA, INC. AT ARDEN HOUSE AND THE NEW YORK ACADEMY OF MEDICINE (Mary Calderone ed. 1958); and Chapter 12, at notes 270–75.

124. HORDERN, *supra* note 27, at 11, 14; NOONAN, *supra* note 27, at 35.

125. Simms, *supra* note 20.

126. *See* Herbert Packer & Ralph Gampell, *Therapeutic Abortions: A Problem in Law and Medicine*, 11 STAN. L. REV. 417 (1959).

127. WILLIAMS, *supra* note 29.

128. AMERICAN L. INST., MODEL PENAL CODE § 2320.3 (Proposed Official Draft 1962).

129. NOONAN, *supra* note 27, at 35. Dr. Alan Guttmacher, already emerging as the leading physician supporter of abortion reform, also was active in lobbying the Institute. JAMES RISEN & JUDY THOMAS, WRATH OF ANGELS: THE AMERICAN ABORTION WAR 11 (1998).

130. G. Edward White, *The American Law Institute and the Triumph of Modernist Jurisprudence*, 15 LAW & HIST. REV. 1 (1997). *See generally* Symposium, *"From the Trenches and Towers": The Case for an In-Depth Study of the American Law Institute*, 23 LAW & SOC. INQUIRY 621 (1998).

131. See the text *infra* at notes 195–255.

132. WILLIAMS, *supra* note 29, at 225–33.

133. *Id.* at 193. The argument is repeated in the American Law Institute's Model Penal Code. AMERICAN L. INST., *supra* note 128, Tent. Draft No. 9 (1959), at 148 n.12. This view in fact was never accepted by most Christians, with some theologians arguing that under some circumstances an infant should be aborted precisely in order to enable baptism to be performed. NOONAN, *supra* note 27, at 53.

134. WILLIAMS, *supra* note 29, at 231.

135. H.M.I. LILEY, MODERN MOTHERHOOD 28 (rev. ed. 1969). For arguments positing moral, and perhaps legal, significance to this fact, see Joseph Dellapenna, *Nor Piety Nor Wit: The Supreme Court on Abortion*, 6 COLUM. H. RTS. L. REV. 379, 406–09 (1974); André Hellegers, *Fetal Development*, 31 THEOLOGICAL STUDIES 3, 7–8 (1970); Paul Ramsey, *Reference Points in Deciding about Abortion*, in THE MORALITY OF ABORTION 69–79 (John Noonan ed. 1970).

son before the 28th week because it was convenient to those who wanted abortion. Williams' conclusion enabled the effect on the fetus to be ignored in calculating the social costs of abortion.[136] Williams seized upon Holmes' concept of "viability" to ground his arbitrary line.[137]

The term "viability" itself illustrates the "abortion distortion," that is, a kind of doublethink involving the giving of words special meanings in the context of abortion to justify the political outcome of one's choice. Justice Byron White publicly lamented this problem as early as 1976, when he wrote, "I am not yet prepared to accept the notion that normal rules of law, procedure, and constitutional adjudication suddenly become irrelevant solely because a case touches on the subject of abortion."[138] Williams and other supporters of abortion freedom have made this posture explicit when discussing the term "viability."[139] The normal medical meaning of "viability" means "the ability to live, grow, and develop."[140] This concept aptly fits the great majority of fetuses about to be aborted, excepting only the occasional fetus that suffers a congenital defect that will prevent survival to term or through infancy.

As law professor Ruth Colker noted, all fetuses should be considered viable after implantation in the uterus because 80 percent of them will be born if there is no deliberate intervention to prevent birth.[141] Yet, in the context of the abortion controversy as exemplified by Justice Harry Blackmun's opinion in *Roe v. Wade*,[142] the term has been used to signify the point at which a fetus has a reasonable chance of surviving outside a natural womb. In other words, as Clifford Grobstein explained, the concept of viability in the abortion context means the "capability to survive disconnected from the placenta."[143] By either Blackmun's or Grobstein's definition, incidentally, zygotes are viable although embryos and fetuses are not (until late in pregnancy).[144] The extent of the distortion is clarified when one recalls that the very same philosophers, ethicists, and lawyers who argue that the dependence of young (born) children and the elderly is what justifies their greater protection by the community turn around and argue that the dependence of the "unviable unborn" justifies denying them protection by the community.[145]

Even disregarding the consistency with which the term "viability" is used, there remain serious problems in trying to ground a significant body of law on the concept. "Viability" sounds definite, but is in fact highly variable, depending both on the current state of medical technology and on what is considered a "reasonable chance" of a "normal life"—a judgment is very much in the eye of the beholder.[146] Is a 50 percent survivability rate a "reasonable chance"? Is 20 per-

---

136. WILLIAMS, *supra* note 29, at 231–32.

137. On the role of Justice Oliver Wendell Holmes, jr., in lending legal significance to the concept of "viability," see Chapter 10, at notes 72–175.

138. Planned Parenthood of Mo. v. Danforth, 428 U.S. 98 (1976)(White, J., dissenting).

139. *See, e.g.,* WILLIAMS, *supra* note 29, at 231–32; H. Tristam Engelhardt, *Viability and the Use of the Fetus,* in ABORTION AND THE STATUS OF THE FETUS 183, 194–95 (William Dondeson *et al.* eds. 1983); Alan Zaitchik, *Viability and the Morality of Abortion,* 10 PHILOS. & PUB. AFF. 18 (1980).

140. TABER'S CYCLOPEDIC MEDICAL DICTIONARY 1992 (1989).

141. RUTH COLKER, ABORTION & DIALOGUE—PRO-CHOICE, PRO-LIFE, AND AMERICAN LAW 109–10 (1992).

142. 410 U.S. 113, 157–62 (1973).

143. CLIFFORD GROBSTEIN, SCIENCE AND THE UNBORN 109 (1988). *See also* Matthew Swyers, Note, *Abortion and Its Viability Standard: The Woman's Diminishing Right to Choose,* 8 GEO. MASON CIV. RTS. L.J. 87, 94–95 (1997).

144. Daniel Callahan, *How Technology Is Reframing the Abortion Debate,* 16 HASTINGS CENTER REP., Feb. 1986, at 33, 34–35.

145. *See* JUDITH BOSS, THE BIRTH LOTTERY: PRENATAL DIAGNOSIS AND SELECTIVE ABORTION 119–21 (1993); CONDIT, *supra* note 32, at 208–10; Karen Lebacqz, *Prenatal Diagnosis and Selective Abortion,* 40 LINACRE Q. 109, 120 (May 1973).

146. Boss, *supra* note 145, at 119–21; GROBSTEIN, *supra* note 143, at 109; MASON, *supra* note 58, at 108–09, 170; Marilee Allen *et al., The Limit of Viability—Neonatal Outcome of Infants Born at 22 to 25 Weeks'*

cent? 10 percent? Less?[147] The presumption of viability at 28 weeks might have been generous in 1929 when it was made a statutory presumption in England's *Infant Life (Preservation) Act.*[148] When Williams gave the Carpentier Lectures in 1956, drawing the line as late as 28 weeks was already open to challenge.[149] Professor Williams chose not to reexamine the 28-week presumption in his lectures, nor did he consider that the statute he relied on did not preclude a finding of viability at some earlier point in gestation. Indeed, elsewhere Williams has written that the *Infant Life (Preservation) Act* should be interpreted to prohibit the intentional killing of a fetus if it would have a "recognizably beating heart."[150] This standard, like brain function, would carry the notion of viability back to the early weeks of the pregnancy[151] — something Williams clearly did not intend, and English courts did not accept.[152]

Williams did not indicate in his Carpentier Lectures the precise chance of survival that he considered controlling, but he did indicate that he thought that a fetus with a 33 percent chance of survival was viable and a fetus with a 5 percent chance of survival was not.[153] English bureaucrats have ruled that a child with a "slightly less than 50-50" chance of survival is not viable.[154] And, whatever the criterion, viability is ever changing to an earlier point in pregnancy. Today, the British Medical Association opposes abortion, except in rare instances, after the twentieth week of gestation on the grounds viability occurs not later than that point in the gestation process.[155]

The Supreme Court indicated in *Roe* that viability occurs at about 28 weeks of gestation, but recognized that viability could occur as early as 24 weeks.[156] Dr. Robert Hall, president in 1973 of the Association for the Study of Abortion (which funded some aspects of the *Roe* litigation and otherwise promoted reform or repeal of the abortion laws), already believed then that the point of viability was 20 weeks.[157] The survival rate of small premature infants has improved dramati-

---

*Gestation,* 329 New Eng. J. Med. 1597 (1993); Janet Gans Epner, Harry Jonas, & Daniel Seckinger, *Late-Term Abortion,* 280 JAMA 724, 724–25 (1998); Susan FitzGerald, *The Tiniest Infants, Five Years Later: 17 Fragile Babies Left the Hospital, Many to Go to Troubled Homes. How Did They Fare?,* Phila. Inquirer, Dec. 3, 1995, at A1; Roland Poland & Bruce Russell, *The Limits of Viability: Ethical Considerations,* 11 Seminars Perinatology 257, 257 (1987); Nancy Rhoden, *The New Neonatal Dilemma: Live Births from Late Abortions,* 72 Geo. L.J. 1451, 1461–66 (1984); Saroj Saigal et al., *Self-Perceived Health Status and Health-Related Quality of Life of Extremely Low-Birth-Weight Infants at Adolescence,* 276 JAMA 453 (1996); V.Y.H. Yu et al., *Prognosis for Infants Born at 23 to 28 Weeks' Gestation,* 293 Brit. Med. J. 1200 (1986). *See generally* American Coll. Obstet. & Gynecologists Comm. on Obstet. Pract., Perinatal Care at the Threshold of Viability (Comm. Op. no. 163, 1995); Williams' Obstetrics ch. 34 (F. Gary Cunningham et al. eds. 20th ed. 1997).

147. *See generally* Donald Judges, Hard Choices, Lost Voices 62–65 (1993); Williams Obstetrics, *supra* note 146, at 151–55; Marilee Allen, Pamela Donohue, & Amy Dusman, *The Limit of Viability—Neonatal Outcome of Infants Born at 22 to 25 Weeks' Gestation,* 329 New Eng. J. Med. 1597 (1993).

148. *See* Chapter 11, at notes 244–56.

149. J.K. Mason, Medico-Legal Aspects of Reproduction and Parenthood 162 (1990) (Mason does not discuss the point in the second edition).

150. Glanville Williams, Textbook of Criminal Law 290 (2nd ed. 1983).

151. Mason indicates that the beating heart is "recognizable" at 18 weeks of gestation, although it might well be earlier. Mason, *supra* note 58, at 103.

152. C. v. S., [1988] Q.B. 135, [1987] 2 W.L.R. 1108 (adopting the ability to breathe independently as the standard of capable of being born alive).

153. Williams, *supra* note 29, at 147 n.5.

154. Hordern, *supra* note 27, at 131.

155. Mason, *supra* note 58, at 126; T. Smith, *Late Abortions and the Law,* 296 Brit. Med. J. 653 (1988). *See also* Swyers, *supra* note 143, at 96–97.

156. *Roe,* 410 U.S. at 160. *See also* Boss, *supra* note 145, at 120; Williams Obstetrics, *supra* note 146, at 585.

157. Robert Hall, *The Abortion Decision,* 116 Am. J. Obstet. & Gynecology 1 (May 1, 1973). *See also* David Garrow, Liberty and Sexuality: The Right of Privacy and the Making of *Roe v. Wade* 607 (2nd ed. 1998). On the role of the Association in the abortion movement, see Olasky, *supra* note 122, at 106; Robert Hall, *The Abortion Revolution,* Playboy, Sept. 1970, at 112.

cally in the past 50 years.[158] Sixteen years after *Roe*, in a plurality opinion in the Supreme Court observed that "there may be a 4-week error in estimating gestational age," suggesting continuing uncertainty regarding whether a particular fetus is viable even assuming that all agreed on when a fetus would become viable.[159]

Premature births can produce an "extremely low birth weight" infant, defined as one weighing less than 1,000 grams (2.2 lbs.). In the 1950s, such an infant had barely a 2 percent chance of survival and a high probability of serious defects such as blindness, deafness, cerebral palsy, and mental retardation if it did survive. By 1960, survival rates had for infants weighing at birth between 500 (probably born at 24 weeks) and 1,000 grams (probably born at 28 weeks) had risen to 10 percent, and to 20 percent by 1970.[160] Currently, that rate is at least 50 percent.[161] Only about one-third of the surviving infants have the serious detriments that once were nearly universal, although as many as two-thirds of the survivors may suffer significant educational deficits.[162] These survival and success rates would all be higher if health care workers in neonatal intensive care units did not shy away from caring for newborns whom they *perceive* as "unviable."[163]

---

158. Poland & Russell, *supra* note 146, at 257.

159. Webster v. Reproductive Health Services, 492 U.S. 490, 530–31 (1989) (plurality op. per Rehnquist, C.J.). *See also* Paul Benjamin Linton, Planned Parenthood v. Casey: *The Flight from Reason in the Supreme Court*, 13 ST. L.U. PUB. L. REV. 15, 40–42 (1993).

160. Poland & Russell, *supra* note 146, at 257.

161. Allen, *supra* note 146, at 1598 (15% survive at 23 weeks of gestation; 56% at 24 weeks; 79% at 25 weeks); William Dillon & Edmund Egan, *Aggressive Obstetric Management in Late Second-Trimester Deliveries*, 58 OBSTET. & GYNECOLOGY 685 (1981) (36% at 24 weeks; 76% at 25 weeks); T. Bruce Ferrar *et al.*, *Changing Outcome of Extremely Premature Infants: Survival and Follow-up at a Tertiary Center*, 161 AM. J. OBSTET. & GYNECOLOGY 1114, 1116 (1989) (more than 50% at 26 weeks); Larry Gilstrap, *Survival and Short-Term Morbidity of the Premature Neonate*, 62 OBSTET. & GYNECOLOGY 37 (1983) (28% at 25 weeks; 88% at 28 weeks); Robert Goldenberg, *Survival of Infants with Low Birth Rate and Early Gestational Age, 1979–1981*, 149 AM. J. OBSTET. & GYNECOLOGY 508 (1984) (18% 24 weeks; 67% at 28 weeks); Marguerite Herschel, *Survival of Infants Born at 24 to 28 Weeks' Gestation*, 60 OBSTET. & GYNECOLOGY 154 (1981) (28% 24 weeks; 92% at 28 weeks); Dennis Worthington, *Factors Influencing Survival and Morbidity with Very Low Birth Weight Delivery*, 62 OBSTET. & GYNECOLOGY 550 (1983) (37% 25 weeks; 82% at 29 weeks). *See also* KENNY, *supra* note 45, at 291; Erol Amon *et al.*, *Obstetric Variables Predicting Survival of the Immature Newborn(< 1,000 grams): A Five-Year Experience at a Single Perinatal Center*, 156 AM. J. OBSTET. & GYNECOLOGY 1380, 1382 (1987); David Orentlicher, Webster *and the Fundamental Right to Make Medical Decisions*, 15 AM. J.L. & MED. 184 (1989); Swyers, *supra* note 143, at 98–102; Victor Yu, *The Extremely Low Birth Weight Infant: Ethical Issues in Treatment*, 23 AUSTRALIAN PAEDIATRICS 97, 98 (1987). Apparently the smallest infant to survive without any obvious defects is Christopher Williams, who was born at 24 weeks weighing 1 lb. 5.5 oz. (603 grams); Christopher weighed over 9 lbs. when he left neonatal intensive care. *Smallest Baby*, THE TIMES (London), May 17, 2001, at 8; Ann Wason & Zoe Morris, *Christopher, World's Tiniest Premature Baby*, THE EVENING STANDARD, May 17, 2001, at 7.

162. Allen, *supra* note 146, at 1598; Linda Herskowitz, *Study: High-Risk Premature Babies Often Overcome Abnormalities*, PHILA. INQUIRER, Mar. 11, 1982, at 4B; Poland & Russell, *supra* note 145, at 257; Alec Samuels, *Born Too Soon and Born Imperfect: The Legal Aspects*, 38 MED. SCI. & L. 57 (1998); Richard Strauss, *Adult Functional Outcome of Those Born Small for Gestational Age: Twenty-Six-Year Follow-up of the 1970 British Birth Cohort*, 283 JAMA 625 (2000). *See also* Jane Brody, *A Quality of Life Determined by a Baby's Size*, N.Y. TIMES, Oct. 1, 1991, at A1; Peter Dunn & Ann Lashford, *Limit of Fetal Viability*, THE LANCET, May 12, 1984, at 1079; Gina Kolata, *Parents of Tiny Infants Find Care Choices Are Not Theirs*, N.Y. TIMES, Sept. 30, 1991, at A1; Lindsey Turner, *Learning Disabilities Persist for Premature Babies, Study Finds*, PHILA. INQUIRER, Feb. 8, 2000, at A16; Nicholas Wood *et al.*, *Neurologic and Developmental Disability after Extremely Preterm Birth*, 343 N. ENG. J. MED. 378 (2000). Even those who do experience educational difficulties, however, seem to perform better than average in avoiding alcohol or drug abuse or other behavioral problems. Sheryl Gay Stolberg, *Tiniest Babies Show Success as Youths in Spite of Hurdles*, N.Y. TIMES, Jan. 17, 2002, § 1, at 1. For a report of twins born at 22 weeks who recently survived without any of the usual complications. Beth Yanofsky, *Bortn 17 Weeks Early, They Thrived*, MAIN LINE TIMES, Feb. 13, 1997, at 1.

163. Allen, *supra* note 146; Marilyn Sanders *et al.*, *Impact of the Perception of Viability on Resource Allocation in the Neonatal Intensive Care Unit*, 18 J. PERINATOLOGY 347 (1998). In at least one maternity ward in the

Infants younger than 23 weeks (below 500 grams) have lungs that are too immature for a significant chance of survival.[164] Halea Maurer survived birth at 300 grams without serious defect—although she is thought to have been born at 25-27 weeks gestation.[165] Halea was the length of a ballpoint pen and weighed as much as a can of soda, so small that her father's wedding band slipped up her arm all the way to her shoulder.[166] Reportedly only five smaller babies had ever survived to leave a hospital.[167] Halea had surgery to correct two hernias and overcame two infections in neonatal intensive care, and suffered other medical problems, but she went home four months after her birth without monitors, oxygen equipment, or any medications.[168]

While we do not yet have the technology for artificial placentas, no one can accurately predict when such a breakthrough might occur. Even today, some early infants could perhaps be saved by a heart-lung machine (extracorporal membrane oxygenation) although that device is not usually employed on infants of less than 2,000 grams birth weight (probably born at about 35 weeks gestation) because of potential side effects.[169] Recently, tests have demonstrated that filling premature lungs with an oxygen-rich liquid can both help the infant survive and prevent the many side effects usual in extremely low-birth-weight infants.[170] There has been similar progress in preventing the blindness that many extremely premature infants suffered in the past.[171]

To date, the earliest reported birth where a child survived (and survived relatively unimpaired) is that of Kane Benoit who was born after 16 weeks of gestation.[172] The baby, whose twin sister died within hours of birth, weighed less than 500 grams. A reporter noted the despair that descended on his parents because of the enormous medical costs incurred in saving Kane. Would

---

former East Germany, the practice was to dispose of any infant born weighing less than 1,000 grams in a bucket of water without any attempt to save it. SARAH BLAFFER HRDY, MOTHER NATURE: A HISTORY OF MOTHERS, INFANTS, AND NATURAL SELECTION 457 (1999). Parents also sometimes react negatively to the appearance of a low-birth-weight baby, which can have adverse effects on parental care should the child survive. *See* MARTIN DALY & MARGO WILSON, HOMICIDE 72–73 (1988); HRDY, *supra*, at 457–58; T.R. Alley, *Head Shape and the Perception of Cuteness*, 17 DEVELOPMENTAL PSYCH. 650 (1981); A.M. Frodi *et al.*, *Fathers' and Mothers' Responses to the Faces and Cries of Normal and Premature Infants*, 14 DEVELOPMENTAL PSYCH. no. 5, at 40 (1978); K.A. Hildebrandt & H.E. Fitzgerald, *Facial Feature Determinants of Infant Attractiveness*, 2 INFANT BEHAVIOR & DEV. 329 (1979); Richard Maier *et al.*, *The Perceived Attractiveness of Preterm Infants*, 7 INFANT BEHAVIOR & DEV. 403 (1984); Lynn Singer *et al.*, *Maternal Psychological Distress and Parenting Stress after the Birth of a Very Low-Birth-Weight Infant*, 281 JAMA 799 (1999). *See also* C.M. Hill & H.L. Ball, *Abnormal Births and Other "Ill Omens": The Adaptive Case for Infanticide*, 7 HUMAN NATURE 381 (1996).

164. LANGMAN'S MEDICAL EMBRYOLOGY 218–29 (T.W. Sadler ed., 5th ed. 1985); WILLIAMS' OBSTETRICS, *supra* note 146, at 748–49; Orentlicher, *supra* note 161, at 185.

165. Dan Rozek, *Hospital's Tiniest Baby Beats the Odds; She Wieghed a Scant 12 Ounces at Birth—Now She's Home*, CHI. SUN-TIMES, Oct. 27, 2001, at 18; Diana Wallace, *Life Finds a Way: When Halea Was Born Weighing Only 12 Ounces, Few Expected Her to Live. But the Tiny Test of Modern Medicine Not Only Survived to Go Home, She's Expected to Live a Normal Life*, CHI. DAILY HAROLD, Oct. 27, 2001, at 1.

166. Rozek, *supra* note 165; Wallace, *supra* note 165.

167. Wallace, *supra* note 165.

168. Rozek, *supra* note 165; Wallace, *supra* note 165

169. M. Hack & A.A. Fanaroff, *How Small Is Too Small? Consideration in Evaluating the Outcome of the Tiny Infant*, 15 CLINICAL PERINATALOGY 773, 782 (1988); Eileen Stork, *Extracorporeal Membrane Oxygenation in the Newborn and Beyond*, 15 CLINICAL PERINATALOGY 815, 821 (1988).

170. *New Technique Saves Infants with Lung Ills*, N.Y. TIMES, Sept. 12, 1996, at A16; M.R. Wolfson *et al.*, *A New Experimental Approach for the Study of Cardiopulmonary Physiology during Early Development*, 65 APPLIED PHYSIOLOGY 1436 (1988).

171. Lawrence Altman, *The Doctor's World: Staving off Blindness in the Tiniest of Infants*, N.Y. TIMES, Mar. 2, 1999, at F6.

172. Gerald Goldstein, *Region's Tiniest Baby Brings His Parents Joy—and Growing Despair*, PROVIDENCE SUNDAY J., Jan. 10, 1988, at A-24.

the family have been better off had both twins been allowed to die? Perhaps.[173] But if one asks such children for their opinion after they grow up, even children who had to undergo multiple operations and endure suffering throughout their lives unanimously agree that they should have been allowed to die. Parents are not so unanimous, but are more supportive than not.[174]

Because of fear of ever earlier viability, it has become a standard part of the pro-abortion litany to insist not only that the point of viability has not changed since 1973, but that it cannot change in the foreseeable future.[175] As if scientific progress were so predictable. No one can predict when some technological breakthrough will (probably fortuitously) dramatically alter the point of viability. Does our current ability to "reimplant" an ovum (or, eventually, a fetus) in another woman's uterus make even a fertilized ovum "viable"?[176]

The difficulty in sustaining such confidence in the inability of science to push the point of viability back were illustrated in the work of Gina Kolata, a journalist who writes frequently in the *New York Times* on new developments in reproductive technologies. In April 1989, Ms. Kolata reported that an unbreachable barrier to earlier viability had been reached preventing the pushing of viability back to an earlier point in pregnancy.[177] Less than six months later she reported the invention of new techniques for providing oxygen to infants with premature lungs that pushed viability back to some yet to be determined younger gestational age.[178]

Some supporters of abortion rights have responded by insisting that "viability" must be understood as an ethical term describing the moral worth of a fetus and not as technological term describing the survivability of the fetus.[179] Viability is indeed, as law professor Ruth Colker noted, a point of moral significance for the medical community, but not for pregnant women.[180] No wonder Mark Tushnet, one of stronger supporters of a freedom to abort, has called the concept of viability "perverse" if only because it is arbitrary and irrelevant.[181] Surely even Justice

---

173. *See* Raymond Duff & A.G.M. Campbell, *Moral and Ethical Dilemmas in the Special-Care Nursery*, 289 N. Eng. J. Med. 890 (1973) (admitting that 14% of deaths in their special care neonatal unit over the preceding two years resulted from their joint decision with the parents to allow the deaths to occur). The first long-term study to follow extremely-low-birth-weight infants into their teen years found that they suffered physical health problems and learning disabilities more commonly than the general population. *See* Turner, *supra* note 162. Other studies have contradicted this finding. *See* Stolberg, *supra* note 162.

174. C. Everett Koop, *Ethical and Surgical Considerations in the Care of the Newborn with Congenital Abnormalities*, in Infanticide and the Handicapped Newborn 89, 94–96 (Dennis Horan & Melinda Delahoyde eds. 1982).

175. *See, e.g., Amicus Brief of the Am. Med. Ass'n supporting Appellants in* Webster v. Reproductive Health Services, 492 U.S. 490 (1989), at 9, *reprinted in* 11 Women's Rts. L. Rep. 443 (1989), and in 5 Documentary History of the Legal Aspects of Abortion in the United States: Webster v. Reproductive Health Services 341 (Roy Mersky & Gary Hartman eds. 1990); Nancy Rhoden, *Trimesters and Technology: Revamping* Roe v. Wade, 95 Yale L.J. 639, 661 (1986). *See also* Allen, *supra* note 146, at 1599. A very few supporters of abortion rights concede that the point of viability is become earlier and likely to continue to do so. *See* Timothy Vinceguerra, *Notes of a Footsoldier*, 62 Alb. L. Rev. 1167, 1180–81 (1999).

176. Allen Hunter, *In the Wings: New Right Ideology and Organization*, 15 Radical Am. 113, 140–41 (1981).

177. Gina Kolata, *Survival of the Fetus: A Barrier Is Reached*, N.Y. Times, April 18, 1989, at C1.

178. Gina Kolata, *For Babies, "Liquid Air" May Spare Fragile Lungs: Experimental Effort Could Shift the Age of Fetal Viability*, N.Y. Times, Aug. 29, 1989, at 20. *See also New Technique, supra* note 170; Wolfson *et al., supra* note 170.

179. Rhoden, *supra* note 175, at 671.

180. Colker, *supra* note 141, at 110.

181. Mark Tushnet, *Two Notes on the Jurisprudence of Privacy*, 8 Const. Commentary 75, 80–85 (1991). *See also* Mason, *supra* note 149, at 162 ("It is increasingly clear that the fundamental difficulty lies in the concept of viability, which is an undefinable term."); Mason, *supra* note 58, at 108 ("viability is an imprecise determinant of 'human' life, in that it depends not only on the maturity of the fetus but also on the technology that is available to support its extrauterine life—and on the motivation with which that technology is put to

Harry Blackmun would not apply a "viability" test to determine whether to recognize and protect the constitutional right to life of newborn infants, the mentally disadvantaged, persons suffering from severe physical disadvantages, or any of the others whose very physical survival depends on the intensive care by one or more other persons.[182] Viability, rather than being an "objective" test of independent existence, poses a difficult ethical problem for the conscientious physician because she must determine the point at which to stop attempting to save a low-birth weight infant[183]—not to mention the uncertainties in estimating the gestational age of a fetus about to be aborted.[184]

Before Williams' Carpentier Lectures, viability had played no significant role in the common law or statute law of abortion, nor had it played a role in medical or popular discourse on the subject in the United States. Professional and popular opinion had focused instead either on "quickening" or on "conception" as the critical events in establishing the legal and moral status of the fetus.[185] The concept of "viability" in any event could not have had a very long history— it would have been meaningless before the time when medical intervention before full-term birth could have a significant effect. That point came only in the second half of the nineteenth century.

Williams drew upon only two tangentially related legal sources for the notion that fetal viability should determine whether the life of a fetus is deserving of legal protection. One was Holmes' now discredited opinion in *Dietrich v. Inhabitants of Northampton*.[186] Judicial acceptance of *Dietrich* had already begun to erode before Williams' lectures, but the precedent survived as the majority rule until the 1970s. The opinion now has been overruled in Massachusetts and is rejected in nearly every other state.[187] The other source was the poorly drafted *Infant Life (Preservation) Act*,[188] which, in England and Wales after 1929, made it a crime to abort a child "capable of being born alive." This Act was amended in 1990 to allow virtual abortion on demand in England and Wales even late in the pregnancy.[189]

Within a decade of Williams' lectures, standard medical texts incorporated the viability into the definition of abortion: "the termination of a pregnancy at any time before the fetus has at-

---

use"). *See also* Francis Beckwith, *When You Come to a Fork in the Road, Take It?: Abortion, Personhood, and the Jurisprudence of Neutrality,* 45 J. CHURCH & STATE 485 (2003) (arguing against viability as a meaningful test); Paul Simmons, *Religious Liberty and Abortion Policy: Casey as "Catch-22,"* 42 J. CHURCH & STATE 69 (2000) (arguing for viability as a meaningful test).

182. *See* RICHARD SHERLOCK, PRESERVING LIFE 201–18 (1987).

183. Poland & Russell, *supra* note 145, at 260. *See generally* BONNIE STEINBOCK, LIFE BEFORE BIRTH 82–83 (1992); Catherine Pap Mangel, *Legal Abortion: The Impending Obsolescence of the Trimester Framework,* 14 AM. J.L. & MED. 69, 195 (1988); Swyers, *supra* note 143, at 102–10.

184. Israel Goldstein, Albert Reece, & John Hobbins, *Sonographic Appearance of the Fetal Heel Ossification Centers and Foot Length Measurements Provide Independent Markers for Gestational Age Estimation,* 159 AM. J. OBSTET. & GYNECOLOGY 923 (1988); Angie Kay Huxley & M.A. Sibley, *Alleged Forgery of Sonography Report Leads to Abortion of Late 23 Week-Old Foetus,* 43 J. FORENSIC SCI. 218 (1998); Uday Kumar & Pradeep Kumar, *Estimation of Gestational Age from Hand and Foot Length,* 33 MED. SCI. & L. 48 (1993); Samuels, *supra* note 162, at 58. This can be a problem even after the abortion. *See, e.g.,* Maurizio Amato, Petra Huppi, & Renier Claus, *Rapid Biometric Assessment of Gestational Age in Very Low Birth Weight Infants,* 19 J. PERINATAL MED. 367 (1991); Angie Kay Huxley, *Comparability of Gestational Age Values Derived from Diaphyseal Length and Foot Length from Known Forensic Foetal Remains,* 38 MED. SCI. & L. 42 (1998); Angie Kay Huxley & Susan Jimenez, *Error in Olivier and Pineau's Regression Formulae for Calculation of Statute and Lunar Age from Radial Diaphyseal Length in Forensic Fetal Remains,* 100 AM. J. PHYSICAL ANTHROPOLOGY 435 (1996).

185. *See* Chapter 3, at notes 52–56, 94–107, Chapter 5, at notes 204–40.

186. 138 Mass. 14 (1884). *See* Chapter 10, at notes 72–175.

187. See the cases collected in Chapter 10, at note 119.

188. 19 & 20 Geo. V ch. 34 (1929). *See* Chapter 9, at 244–56.

189. See the text *supra* at notes 101–02.

tained the stage of viability."[190] Soon the term would be given a increasingly prominent role in the Supreme Court's jurisprudence of abortion[191] despite the risk that continually advancing medical technology would erode the precious freedom to abort. No one had briefed or argued in favor of viability in the arguments of *Roe v. Wade*. The appellant in *Roe* specifically disavowed any point in the pregnancy as a point beyond which the state could regulate the practice.[192] The State had argued that its interest in protecting fetal life was compelling from the moment of conception onward.[193] The Supreme Court majority in *Roe* apparently chose viability as the critical point for finding a transition in the state's interest because of Thurgood Marshall's concern that any earlier point would effectively limit the availability of abortions to the better educated, older urban women given the likelihood of psychological denial of pregnancy that Marshall felt would particularly affect younger, poorly educated, and rural women.[194] Apparently, no one questioned these stereotypes. Are poor women, or women not in college, or younger women really more likely to deny the reality of an unwanted pregnancy than other women?

# The *Model Penal Code* and Limited Reform

*The large liberal center, always first to be second, is generally going along.*

—John Hart Ely[195]

When Glanville Williams' Carpentier Lectures were published as a book,[196] the lectures succeeded both in opening a legal debate on abortion in the United States and in separating the issue from its Left-leaning political sources. The Left continued to support abortion reform but the issue now proved to have considerable political appeal beyond the Left; it could no longer be dismissed merely by rejecting leftist premises generally.[197] Some even found in Japan a conservative model to be considered.[198] Yet the socialist impulse did not entirely disappear. Celeste Condit noted that the radical feminist objection to a privacy analysis for abortion rights and support for an equality analysis, both of which emerged after 1980, are rooted in socialism, reflecting a "basic displeasure with private property."[199] As Condit's comment sug-

---

190. WILLIAMS' OBSTETRICS 493 (Louis Hellman & Jack Pritchard eds., 14th ed. 1971).

191. *Roe*, 410 U.S. at 160–65.

192. *Id.* at 153.

193. *Id.* at 156.

194. GARROW, *Supra* note 157, at 582–86.

195. John Hart Ely, *Another Such Victory: Constitutional Theory and Practice in a World Where Courts Are No Different from Legislatures*, 77 VA. L. REV. 833, 835 (1991).

196. WILLIAMS, *supra* note 29.

197. *See, e.g.,* Manfred Guttmacher, *The Legal Status of Abortion*, in THERAPEUTIC ABORTION 175 (Harold Rosen ed. 1954).

198. DANIEL CALLAHAN, ABORTION: LAW, CHOICE, AND MORALITY 253–77 (1970); GRISEZ, *supra* note 116, at 253–56; HORDERN, *supra* note 27, at 223–24. See Chapter 12, at notes 7–34.

199. CONDIT, *supra* note 32, at 104, 118 n.3, 120 n.20. *See also* BROOKES, *supra* note 13, at 89; KINGDOM, *supra* note 32, at 46–62; Stith, *supra* note 32. For examples of such arguments, see COLKER, *supra* note 141, at 83–143; RUTH COLKER, PREGNANT MEN: PRACTICE, THEORY, AND THE LAW 19–31, 173–202 (1994); HARRISON, *supra* note 89; CATHARINE MACKINNON, FEMINISM UNMODIFIED: DISCOURSES ON LIFE AND LAW 93–102 (1987); CATHARINE MACKINNON, TOWARD A FEMINIST THEORY OF THE STATE 184–94 (1989); RUBIN, *supra* note 129, at 190–91; Anita Allen, *The Proposed Equal Protection Fix for Abortion Law: Reflections on Citizenship, Gender, and the Constitution*, 18 HARV. J.L. & PUB. POL'Y 419 (1995); Twiss Butler, *Abortion Law: "Unique Problem for Women?" or Sex Discrimination*, 4 YALE J.L. & FEM. 133 (1991); Rhonda Copelon, *From Privacy to Autonomy: The Conditions for Sexual and Reproductive Freedom*, in FROM ABORTION TO REPRODUCTIVE FREE-

gests, while certain strains of modern feminism have struggled for autonomy from "the Left" (New or Old, but definitely "male"), much feminist thought retains a strong affinity to leftist ideas.[200]

Williams' description of the social costs of illegal abortion (death, debilitation, and guilt inflicted on the women involved) quickly became a standard litany that acknowledged, before viability, no possible countervailing social gain. Law professor Frances Olsen gave us one of the most extreme versions of such thinking, insisting that fetal life is merely potential human life until the umbilical cord is cut after birth. She argued from this premise that one could oppose abortion consistently only by favoring similar regulations on preventing the ejaculation of sperm in circumstances precluding conception (or the wasteful discharge of ova?).[201]

Shortly after Williams' lectures were published, the American Law Institute completed the *Model Penal Code*.[202] Bernard Schwartz, the principal drafter of the *Code*, considered abortion to be a "morals offense" based upon religious beliefs rather than what he took as the only legitimate secular purpose for making something a crime—the protection of public peace and order.[203] Williams served as a consultant to the project,[204] and the *Code's* closely tracked his proposal for a limited reform of abortion laws.[205] Schwartz himself termed the result a "political compromise," arguing that the only principled response to critiques such as Williams' was complete legalization.[206] The Institute expressly rejected total legalization[207] along with a proposal to allow abortions in case of illegitimacy.[208] Schwartz indicated that more sweeping reforms were rejected for fear of offending Catholic sensibilities, as if they were the only possible opponents.[209]

Given the lack of public discussion of abortion law reform only a few years before the *Model Penal Code* was completed, discussions in the American Law Institute were remarkably free of disagreement about the need to reform abortion law, and even about the form reforms should

---

DOM: TRANSFORMING A MOVEMENT 27, 34–40 (Marlene Gerber Fried ed. 1990); Erin Daly, *Reconsidering Abortion Law: Liberty, Equality, and the New Rhetoric of* Planned Parenthood v. Casey, 45 AM. U. L. REV. 77 (1995); Susan Estrich & Kathleen Sullivan, *Abortion Politics: Writing for an Audience of One*, 138 U. PA. L. REV. 119, 150–54 (1989); Ruth Bader Ginsburg, *Speaking in a Judicial Voice*, 67 NYU L. REV. 1185, 1199–1202 (1992); Sarah Harding, *Equality and Abortion: Legitimizing Women's Experiences*, 3 COLUM. J. GENDER & L. 7, 31–41 (1992); Sylvia Law, *Rethinking Sex and the Constitution*, 132 U. PA. L. REV. 955, 1014–28 (1984); Mangel, *supra* note 487; Frances Olsen, *Unraveling Compromise*, 103 HARV. L. REV. 105, 117–35 (1989); Rachael Pine & Sylvia Law, *Envisioning a Future for Reproductive Liberty: Strategies for Making the Rights Real*, 27 HARV. C.R.-C.L. L. REV. 407, 416–17 (1992); Catherine Grevers Schmidt, *Where Privacy Fails: Equal Protection and the Abortion Rights of Minors*, 68 NYU L. REV. 597 (1993); Reva Siegel, *Reasoning from the Body: A Historical Perspective on Abortion Regulation and Questions of Equal Protection*, 44 STAN. L. REV. 261, 347–81 (1992); Lynn Smith, *An Equality Approach to Reproductive Choice*: R. v. Sullivan, 4 YALE J.L. & FEM. 93 (1991) (Canadian Charter of Rights).

200. *See generally* ALICE ECHOLS, DARING TO BE BAD: RADICAL FEMINISM IN AMERICA 1967–1975(1989); PETCHESKY, *supra* note 78, at 92–96.

201. Olsen, *supra* note 199, at 129–30. *See also* LAWRENCE LADER, ABORTION 21–25 (1966); DIANE SCHULDER & FLORYNCE KENNEDY, ABORTION RAP 6–88 (1971).

202. AMERICAN L. INST., *supra* note 128.

203. Bernard Schwartz, *Morals Offenses and the Model Penal Code*, 63 COLUM. L. REV. 669 (1963). Schwartz derived this view from the work of, among others, John Stuart Mill. *Id.*, at 670 n.1. *See* J.S. MILL, ON LIBERTY (1859).

204. NOONAN, *supra* note 27, at 35.

205. *Compare* AMERICAN L. INST., *supra* note 128, *with* WILLIAMS, *supra* note 13, at 163–76 233–36. *See also* REAGAN, *supra* note 112, at 220–22.

206. Schwartz, *supra* note 203, at 683–86.

207. 1959 PROC. AM. L. INST. 258 ("PROCEEDINGS"). *See also* REAGAN, *supra* note 112, at 221; Leonard Dubin, *The Antiquated Abortion Laws*, 34 TEMPLE L.Q. 146, 151 (1961).

208. PROCEEDINGS, *supra* note 207, at 274–75, 279–81.

209. Schwartz, *supra* note 203, at 686.

take. Only two members of the Institute spoke against changing law on abortion.[210] Besides Williams' lectures, recently published one-sided reports of the two doctors' conferences on abortion might have influenced the Institute.[211] Nothing in the record demonstrates such influence.

The *Model Penal Code* was the first significant step in the United States towards "abortion liberalization."[212] Completion of the *Code* touched off a growing debate and agitation for reform.[213] Before 1957, only one or two law review articles were published annually on abortion, and those were generally inconsequential; the number rose to 10 in the period 1958–61 (3.3/yr.), to 12 in 1961–64 (4/yr.), to 25 in 1964–67 (8.3/yr.), and to two full columns in the index to legal periodicals during 1967–70.[214] The articles in general also became increasingly critical of existing laws. Attorney Eugene Quay responded with a major defense of the existing laws built around a lengthy study of their origins.[215]

One important step in the reform process was a newfound willingness of the news media to report women's experiences of abortion in a sympathetic light.[216] The exception was television, which largely ignored the issue until well after the legal changes of the 1960s and 1970s. Both fictional and nonfictional presentations on television regarding abortion had to await the 1980s. Such presentations, when they finally came, generally supported the right to choose abortion but frequently questioned abortion as a choice.[217]

The best known early news story regarding abortion involved the inability of Sherri Finkbine to abort a fetus deformed by thalidomide[218] in her home state of Arizona, and her subsequent trip

---

210. PROCEEDINGS, *supra* note 207, at 259–62, 264.

211. ABORTION IN THE UNITED STATES, *supra* note 123; THERAPEUTIC ABORTION, *supra* note 197. Both conferences had deliberately excluded any supporters of the abortion laws. *See* Chapter 12, at notes 277–84.

212. GARROW, *supra* note 157, at 275; EDWARD LAZARUS, CLOSED CHAMBERS: THE FIRST EYEWITNESS ACCOUNT OF THE EPIC STRUGGLES INSIDE THE SUPREME COURT 343–44 (1998); OLASKY, *supra* note 122, at 91.

213. *See, e.g.,* CALLAHAN, *supra* note 198, at 25–116; GRISEZ, *supra* note 116, at 236–50; JUDITH HOLE & ELLEN LEVINE, REBIRTH OF FEMINISM 284 (1971); REAGAN, *supra* note 112, at 222; Harvey Adelstein, *The Abortion Law,* 12 W. RES. L. REV. 74, 85–86 (1960); Dubin, *supra* note 207; B. James George, jr., *Current Abortion Laws: Proposals and Movements for Reform,* in ABORTION AND THE LAW 1, (David Smith ed. 1967); Alan Guttmacher, *The Law that Doctors Often Break,* READER'S DIGEST, Jan. 1960, at 51; Jerome Kummer, *A Psychiatrist Views Our Abortion Enigma,* in THE CASE FOR LEGALIZED ABORTION NOW 114 (Alan Guttmacher ed. 1967) ("ABORTION NOW"); Zad Leavy & Jerome Kummer, *Criminal Abortion: Human Hardship and Unyielding Laws,* 35 S. CAL. L. REV. 123 (1962); Roy Lucas, *Federal Constitutional Limitations on the Enforcement and Administration of State Abortion Statutes,* 46 N.C. L. REV. 730 (1968); Packer & Gampell, *supra* note 126; Harriet Pilpel, *The Abortion Crisis,* in ABORTION NOW, *supra,* at 98. *See generally* DAVIS, *supra* note 123, at 209–36; MARIAN FAUX, ROE V. WADE: THE UNTOLD STORY OF THE LANDMARK SUPREME COURT DECISION THAT MADE ABORTION LEGAL 234–38 (1988); GARROW, *supra* note 157, at 275–85; FAYE GINSBURG, CONTESTED LIVES: THE ABORTION DEBATE IN AN AMERICAN COMMUNITY 35–37, 64–71 (1989); LADER, *supra* note 201; LOUIS LADER, ABORTION II: MAKING THE REVOLUTION 111–16 (1973). Inexplicably, ethicist Kathy Rudy sees the *Model Penal Code* as an attempt to tighten the law rather than to liberalize it. KATHY RUDY, BEYOND PRO-LIFE AND PRO-CHOICE: MORAL DIVERSITY IN THE ABORTION DEBATE 59–60 (1996).

214. RUBIN, *supra* note 122, at 18–19.

215. Eugene Quay, *Justifiable Abortion—Medical and Legal Foundations (Pt. I),* 49 GEO. L.J. 173 (1961); Eugene Quay, *Justifiable Abortion—Medical and Legal Foundations (Pt. II),* 49 GEO. L.J. 395 (1961).

216. *See, e.g.,* Marguerite Clark, *Abortion Racket: What Should Be Done?,* NEWSWEEK, Aug. 15, 1960, at 50; Muriel Davidson, *The Deadly Favor,* LADIES HOME J., Nov. 1963, at 53; John Bartlow Martin, *Abortion,* SATURDAY EVENING POST, May 20, 1961, at 19. *See generally* NGUYENPHUC BUUTAP, LEGISLATION, PUBLIC OPINION, AND THE PRESS: AN INTERRELATIONSHIP REFLECTED IN THE NEW YORK TIMES REPORTING OF THE ABORTION ISSUE (unpub. Dissertation, U. Chi. 1979); CONDIT, *supra* note 107, at 23–28, 173–74, 176–77, 188–89; NOONAN, *supra* note 93, at 69–79; OLASKY, *supra* note 39, at 85–117.

217. CONDIT, *supra* note 32, at 123–42.

218. On the effects of thalidomide, see the text *supra* at notes 44–48.

to Sweden for the abortion.[219] Finkbine was a married mother of four. She was locally prominent as the host of a popular toddler television show, "Romper Room." She defied the stereotype of the "loose woman" or naive teenager slinking into a back alley for an abortion to hide her shame regarding the "illicit act" that led to the pregnancy. Her story popularized the idea that there are "good reasons" for abortion other than preservation of the mother's life.[220] This incident even prompted the first public opinion poll ever taken on attitudes towards abortion.[221]

At first, there were considerable contradictions between and within the new narratives.[222] For example, initially newspapers referred to the Finkbine fetus as a "baby" or a "child."[223] Indeed, even Sherri Finkbine was quoted as referring to the fetus variously as "the baby" or "the child."[224] Only as the story wore on did the press begin to use the word "fetus" or even "creature."[225] And, instead of "abortion," the press began to write of an "interrupted pregnancy"[226]—as if Finkbine could resume the pregnancy later. Nor did the press inquire whether tests were performed before the abortion to determine whether the Finkbine baby was deformed, or consider the offers to adopt the baby if it were born deformed.[227]

The message that there were good reasons for having an abortion found a ready audience among those who had had abortions, and those who had felt impelled (by conscience, or circumstances, or a desire for profit) to perform abortions, and those those deeply involved with persons in these other groups.[228] People were also inclined favorably towards the new narratives

---

219. Sherri Finkbine, *The Baby We Didn't Dare to Have*, REDBOOK, Jan. 1963, at 50; Sherri Finkbine, *The Lesser of Two Evils*, in ABORTION NOW, *supra* note 213, at 12. *See also* MYRA MARX FERREE & BETH HESS, CONTROVERSY AND COALITION: THE NEW FEMINIST MOVEMENT ACROSS THREE DECADES OF CHANGE 150 (rev. ed. 1994); GARROW, *supra* note 157, at 285–88; JACOBY, *supra* note 123, at 4; KRISTIN LUKER, ABORTION AND THE POLITICS OF MOTHERHOOD 64 (1984); MARVIN OLASKY, ABORTION RIGHTS: A SOCIAL HISTORY OF ABORTION IN AMERICA 278–82 (1992); OLASKY, *supra* note 122, at 92–99; RISEN & THOMAS, *supra* note 129, at 11–14; RUDY, *supra* note 213, at 60–61; John Jonathan Imber, *Abortion Policy and Medical Practice*, SOCIETY, July/Aug. 1990, at 27, 30–31; Donald Kenney, *Thalidomide—Catalyst to Reform*, 5 ARIZ. L. REV. 105 (1963); Marvin Moore, *Antiquated Abortion Laws*, 20 WASH. & LEE L. REV. 250 (1963); Rickie Solinger, *"A Complete Disaster": Abortion and the Politics of Hospital Abortion Committees, 1950–1970*, 19 FEMINIST STUD. 241, 262 (1993); Willard Sorensen, *Abortion and the Crime-Sin Spectrum*, 70 W. VA. L. REV. 20 (1967); H.B. Taussig, *The Thalidomide Syndrome*, 207 SCI. AM. 29 (Aug. 1962); Monroe Trout, *Therapeutic Abortion Laws Need Therapy*, 37 TEMPLE L.Q. 172 (1964).

220. *See* THE GALLUP POLL: PUBLIC OPINION 1935–1971, at 1984 (1972). *See also* ROBERT BLANK & JANNA MERRICK, HUMAN REPRODUCTION, EMERGING TECHNOLOGIES, AND CONFLICTING RIGHTS 36 (1995); CONDIT, *supra* note 32, at 28–31, 177; BARBARA HINKINSON CRAIG & DAVID O'BRIEN, ABORTION AND AMERICAN POLITICS 41 (1993); FAUX, *supra* note 117, at 42–51, 59; GARROW, *supra* note 157, at 285–91; GINSBURG, *supra* note 213, at 35–37; MARK GRABER, RETHINKING ABORTION: EQUAL CHOICE, THE CONSTITUTION, AND REPRODUCTIVE POLITICS 175–76 n.55 (1996); HOLE & LEVINE, *supra* note 213, at 283 (1971); LAZARUS, *supra* note 212, at 344; LUKER, *supra* note 219, at 62–65; OLASKY, *supra* note 122, at 97–99; RISEN & THOMAS, *supra* note 129, at 14; RUBIN, *supra* note 122, at 22, 36; RAYMOND TATALOVICH & BYRON DAYNES, THE POLITICS OF ABORTION: A STUDY OF COMMUNITY CONFLICT IN PUBLIC POLICY MAKING 44–47 (1981); LAURENCE TRIBE, ABORTION: THE CLASH OF ABSOLUTES 37 (1990); R. Sauer, *Attitudes to Abortion in America, 1800–1973*, 28 POP. STUDIES 53, 53–54 (1974).

221. Robert Blendon, John Benson, & Karen Donelan, *The Public and the Controversy over Abortion*, 270 JAMA 2871, 2872 (1993).

222. CONDIT, *supra* note 32, at 30–34; JACOBY, *supra* note 123, at 4.

223. OLASKY, *supra* note 122, at 96.

224. *Id.*

225. *Id.*, at 96, 103–04.

226. *Id.* at 97.

227. *Id.* at 95–97.

228. *See, e.g.*, GINSBURG, *supra* note 213, at 37; BERNARD NATHANSON & RICHARD OSTUNG, ABORTING AMERICA 187–94 (1979); Sauer, *supra* note 220, at 65–66.

if they embraced the more relaxed sexual mores that were becoming popular in the 1960s, or if they feared overpopulation or supported sharply lower fertility rates from eugenic concerns.[229]

These concerns did not command universal acceptance. Later champions of abortion rights would distance themselves from the demographic and eugenic arguments as inconsistent with the goal of individual choice that became the justification for abortion rights: Demographic and eugenic arguments tended to support social control over reproduction, albeit in the direction of fewer children rather than more children.[230] Others came to see the eugenic concerns as representing a "devaluation" of children that is expressed both in the refusal to accept a fetus as a person and in the increasingly evident pathologies of American families.[231]

Joseph Sunnen, a manufacturer of contraceptive foams, became one the principal financial supporters both of the movement to legalize the advertising and sale of contraceptives and of the reform of abortion laws.[232] Other, less directly interested philanthropists, such as Stewart Mott (an heir of a founder of General Motors) and the Rockefeller establishment, gave substantial funds as well.[233] These funds helped the push for change in the abortion laws to succeed faster than most of its early supporters had dared hope. The extent to which the reform movement was financed by seeking to profit from performing abortions has never been investigated, although abortion was the third most lucrative illegal activity in the 1960s (following gambling and narcotics).[234] While much of the income went to small time abortionists, there were large-scale operators who earned millions, some of whom became prominent in the reform movement.[235]

---

229. CRITCHLOW, *supra* note 51, at 1–10; FERREE & HESS, *supra* note 219, at 11–13; GINSBURG, *supra* note 213, at 38; GORDON, *supra* note 113, at 386–96; GARRETT HARDIN, POPULATION, EVOLUTION, AND BIRTH CONTROL 278 (2nd ed. 1969); HOLE & LEVINE, *supra* note 213, at 285; THOMAS LITTLEWOOD, THE POLITICS OF POPULATION CONTROL 9 (1977); PETCHESKY, *supra* note 112, at 118; JAMES MOHR, ABORTION IN AMERICA: THE ORIGINS AND EVOLUTION OF NATIONAL POLICY, 1800–1900, at 250–51 (1978); OLASKY, *supra* note 122, at 103; PETCHESKY, *supra* note 112, at 116–25; REAGAN, *supra* note 112, at 230–31; JAMES REED, FROM PRIVATE VICE TO PUBLIC VIRTUE: THE BIRTH CONTROL MOVEMENT AND AMERICAN SOCIETY SINCE 1830, at 377–79 (1978); MARTHA WARD, POOR WOMEN, POWERFUL MEN: AMERICA'S EXPERIMENT IN FAMILY PLANNING 27–31, 59–68 (1986); George, *supra* note 50, at 109; Richard Lamm, *Odyssey: From Abortions to Sustainability*, 75 DEN. U. L. REV. 669, 669–73 (1998); Loretta Ross, *African-American Women and Abortion*, in ABORTION WARS: A HALF CENTURY OF STRUGGLE, 1950–2000, at 161, 175–78 (Rickie Solinger ed. 1998); Babor, *supra* note 51; Sauer, *supra* note 220, at 63, 66–67; Solinger, *supra* note 219.

230. *See* Rebecca Cook, *Human Rights and Reproductive Self-Determination*, 44 AM. U. L. REV. 975, 995–96 (1995); Mahoud Fathalla, *The Impact of Reproductive Subordination on Women's Health Family Planning Services*, 44 AM. U. L. REV. 1179, 1183 (1995); Peter Manus, *The Owl, the Indian, the Feminist, and the Brother: Environmentalism Encounters the Social Justice Movements*, 23 ENVT. AFF. 249, 289–91 (1996); Gita Sen, *The World Progamme of Action: A New Paradigm for Population Policy*, ENVIRONMENT, Jan.–Feb. 1995, at 10, 15.

231. Sauer, *supra* note 220, at 66–67. On the growing pathologies in American families, see the text *infra* at notes 256–337. Reference to American families is not meant to suggest that our social pathologies are more serious than in other highly industrialized societies.

232. *See generally* CRITCHLOW, *supra* note 51, at 134, 198; GARROW, *supra* note 157, at 139–40, 156, 305–07, 349, 354, 361, 370, 463, 504.

233. CRITCHLOW, *supra* note 51, at 196–200, 204; GARROW, *supra* note 157, at 310, 317, 345–47, 349, 358, 361, 364, 421, 463–64, 483, 495, 545–47, 578, 605, 809 n.25; NOONAN, *supra* note 27, at 42–46; OLASKY, *supra* note 122, at 180 n.25.

234. ROBERT BELL, SOCIAL DEVIANCE: A SUBSTANTIVE ANALYSIS 125, 142 (1971). *See also* GRABER, *supra* note 220, at 43–44; EDWIN SCHUR, CRIMES WITHOUT VICTIMS: DEVIANT BEHAVIOR AND PUBLIC POLICY 25 (1965); Jerome Bates, *The Abortion Mill*, 45 J. CRIM. L. & CRIMINOLOGY 157, 161 (1954); Lucas, *supra* note 213, at 751; James Voyles, *Changing Abortion Laws in the United States*, 7 J. FAM. L. 496 (1967). *See also* Tamar Lewin, *Massachusetts Abortion Practice under U.S. Fraud Inquiry*, N.Y. TIMES, Dec. 15, 1995, at A30.

235. *See* NINIA BAEHR, ABORTION WITHOUT APOLOGY: A RADICAL HISTORY FOR THE 1990s, at 7–30 (1990); RUTH BARNETT & DOUG BAKER, THEY WEEP ON MY DOORSTEP (1969); LINDA FREEMAN, THE ABORTIONIST (1962); GARROW, *supra* note 157, at 307–08, 318, 333–34, 349–51, 361–64, 376–77, 384–86, 391–93, 422, 428–31, 438, 445, 466–68, 486–87, 539; RICKIE SOLINGER, THE ABORTIONIST: A WOMAN AGAINST THE

Supporters of abortion rights seldom discuss the profit motive of abortion providers, preferring to describe them as selfless crusaders for human rights. So intent are those who support abortion rights to present abortion providers as selfless heroes working for the welfare of women that there is even a tendency to deny the existence of medical malpractice by abortionists. Apparently they fear that acknowledging the profit motive of abortion providers will undermine the political/legal campaign for abortion rights, fearing that any criticism of abortionists must be politically motivated, or concluding that even bad abortionists must be protected if abortion is to remain available.[236] Yet abortionists do commit malpractice, beginning with a rather common failure to inform the patient clearly about the procedure.[237] At the extreme, some abortionists—even after the procedure became legal—have been so indifferent to the welfare of their patients that several have been convicted of murder or other homicide crimes, prosecutions that rarely—if ever—occur for other types of medical malpractice.[238]

The first significant national institution to endorse the *Model Penal Code* was the Unitarian Universalist Association in its General Assembly in 1963.[239] (Ironically, the founding president of Americans United for Life was George Huntson Williams, a Unitarian minister who then held the Hollis Professorship of Divinity at Harvard Divinity School.[240]) The *New York Times* editorially endorsed the *Model Penal Code* approach in 1965.[241] At about the same time, CBS broadcast a documentary on "Abortion and the Law" that implicitly endorsed abortion reform, although it did not stake out a clear position on how far change should go.[242]

Just as these developments were occurring, an outbreak of rubella (German measles) produced a serious split in the California medical community. The California rubella epidemic resulted in the most serious legal crackdown on licensed physicians for performing abortions in the history of the United States—41 doctors were indicted.[243] The medical profession also split in New York, with some hospitals allowing abortions routinely after the mother con-

---

LAW (paperback ed. 1996); Carol Joffe, *"Portraits of Three Physicians of Conscience": Abortion before Legalization in the United States,* 2 J. HIST. SEXUALITY 46 (1991); Solinger, *supra* note 219, at 249–50.

236. For one of the rare discussions of this problem by a supporter of abortion rights, see COLKER, *supra* note 199, at 31–35.

237. Joseph Stuart, *Abortion and Informed Consent: A Cause of Action,* 14 OHIO N. L. REV. 1 (1987). *See generally* DAVID REARDON, ABORTION MALPRACTICE (1994).

238. *Abortion Doctor Sentenced to Year in Jail in Death of Barstow Patient,* L.A. TIMES, May 27, 2000, at A20; Carol Sowers, *Examiner Says Tool Cut Womb,* ARIZ. REP., Feb. 7, 2001, at B5; Lynette Holloway, *Abortion Doctor Guilty of Murder,* N.Y. TIMES, Aug. 9, 1995, at A1 (reporting first such conviction in New York state and also mentioning a 1989 conviction in California). *See also Doctor to Lose License over Late Abortion,* ARIZ. REP., May 8, 2001, at A9 (reporting that a doctor charged with murder after a botched abortion pleaded guilty to a lesser charge).

239. GARROW, *supra* note 157, at 291; MENSCH & FREEMAN, *supra* note 122, at 236 n.46; NOONAN, *supra* note 27, at 61.

240. NOONAN, *supra* note 27, at 62.

241. Editorial, *A New Abortion Law,* NEW YORK TIMES, Feb. 13, 1965, at 26. *See also* Editorial, *The Cruel Abortion Law,* NEW YORK TIMES, April 7, 1965, at 42.

242. GARROW, *supra* note 157, at 299–300, 332–33.

243. BLANK & MERRICK, *supra* note 220, at 36; FERREE & HESS, *supra* note 219, at 150; FAUX, *supra* note 117, at 58–62; GARROW, *supra* note 157, at 300–02, 305–07, 312; HORDERN, *supra* note 27, at 240–43; JONATHAN IMBER, ABORTION AND THE PRIVATE PRACTICE OF MEDICINE 22 (1986); RUDY, *supra* note 213, at 61; SCHUR, *supra* note 233, at 15; Niswander, *supra* note 75, at 53; Keith Russell & Edwin Jackson, *Therapeutic Abortion in California,* 105 AM. J. OBST. & GYNECOLOGY 757 (1970); Michael Sands, *The Therapeutic Abortion Act: An Answer to the Opposition,* 13 UCLA L. REV. 285, 286 (1966). *See also* LADER, *supra* note 201, at 68; PETCHESKY, *supra* note 112, at 124–25; RUBIN, *supra* note 122, at 22–23; PATRICK SHEERAN, WOMEN, SOCIETY, THE STATE, AND ABORTION: A STRUCTURALIST ANALYSIS 74–75 (1987); Sarah Weddington, *The Donohue Lecture Series: Roe v. Wade: Past and Future,* 24 SUFF. U. L. REV. 601, 602 (1990).

tracted rubella with other hospitals not allowing abortions at all in these same circumstances.[244] In response to these events, the American Medical Association dramatically reversed its century-old posture, adopting a resolution in 1967 favoring the *Model Penal Code* approach.[245] The American College of Obstetricians and Gynecologists followed a year later.[246]

Apart from the Unitarians, support for abortion reform initially centered among doctors and lawyers. After 1968, the movement quickly broadened out beyond such narrow professional groups. The late 1960s saw a growing list of national and international organizations endorse the reform of the abortion laws.[247] Several other liberal religious groups came on board only after the Planned Parenthood Federation changed its stand: the National Council of Jewish Women (1969); the American Friends Service Committee (1970); the Young Women's Christian Association of the U.S.A. (1970); and the United Church of Christ (1971).[248] Even the Southern Baptists endorsed limited abortion reform at this time, only to recant later.[249] Groups of mostly Protestant clergy organized a national counseling and referral service for abortions—not all of which were legal.[250] The largest such group, the New-York-based Clergy Consultation Service on Abortion, was largely funded by Stewart Mott, the General Motors heir.[251] There is a certain irony in the heavy involvement of Protestant clergy in challenging the abortion laws given the persistent criticism of the involvement of the Catholic clergy in the anti-abortion movement.

The movement for limited reform had some success. Thirteen states adopted legislation along the lines of the *Model Penal Code,* beginning with Colorado in 1967.[252] The Colorado statute, sponsored by Richard Lamm (who would later as governor advocate compulsory euthanasia for the elderly), was enacted without much lobbying by abortion activists.[253] The lack of lobbying for the bill might have caught opponents of reform off guard, for little organized opposition occurred either.[254] Yet the reform movement's success was limited. Abortion reform bills were in-

---

244. *See* Abortion in the United States, *supra* note 123, at 80 (statement of Carl Erhardt); Alan Guttmacher, *The Genesis of Liberalized Abortion in New York: A Personal Insight,* 23 Case-W. Res. L. Rev. 756, 764–70 (1972).

245. *AMA Policy on Therapeutic Abortion,* 201 JAMA 544 (1967). *See also* Risen & Thomas, *supra* note 129, at 14.

246. Garrow, *supra* note 157, at 350.

247. Ginsburg, *supra* note 213, at 37–39; Tatalovich & Daynes, *supra* note 220, at 66–67; Tribe, *supra* note 220, at 37–49.

248. Mensch & Freeman, *supra* note 122, at 236 n.46

249. Richard John Neuhaus, America against Itself: Moral Vision and the Public Order 129 (1992).

250. Blank & Merrick, *supra* note 220, at 36; Jacoby, *supra* note 117, at 34–35; Luker, *supra* note 219, at 123; Reagan, *supra* note 112, at 241–42; Risen & Thomas, *supra* note 129, at 20; Ward, *supra* note 229, at 58; Ross, *supra* note 229, at 175.

251. Garrow, *supra* note 157, at 333–34, 364; Ira Lupu, *When Cultures Collide,* 103 Harv. L. Rev. 951, 961–62 (1990). *See generally* Condit, *supra* note 32, at 191–94; Suzanne Gage, When Birth Control Fails: How to Abort Ourselves (1979).

252. Colo. Rev. Stat. §§ 40-2-50 to 40-2-53 (Cumm. Supp. 1967). Attorney Paul Linton has surveyed the details of the various state statutes enacted between 1967 and 1973. Paul Linton, *Enforcement of State Abortion Statutes after Roe: A State-by-State Analysis,* 67 U. Det. L. Rev. 157, 158–61, 255–59 (1990). *See also* Condit, *supra* note 32, at 60; Garrow, *supra* note 157, at 323–34, 341–42, 347–48, 367–71, 411–14, 418–23, 432, 482–85, 490–91, 538–41, 545–47, 576–79; Ginsburg, *supra* note 213, at 37, 258 n.21; Harrison, *supra* note 198, at 232–33, 239; Hordern, *supra* note 27, at 254–65; Sagar Jain & Steven Sinding, North Carolina Abortion Law 1967: A Study in Legislative Process (1968); Lader, *supra* note 201, at 109–15; Rubin, *supra* note 122, at 20–24; Tatalovich & Daynes, *supra* note 220, at 24; B. James George, jr., *The Evolving Law of Abortion,* in Abortion, Society and Law 3 (David Wahlbert ed. 1973).

253. Garrow, *supra* note 157, at 323–25.

254. *Id.* at 327, 329–30.

troduced in 28 states in 1967 alone, yet only two passed that year, and others followed slowly over the next five years.[255]

# The Rise of the Managerial Class and the Decline of the Family

*The Supreme Court can screw faggots, so why can't I?*

—Anonymous[256]

The sudden transformation in the 1950s and 1960s of public thinking regarding abortion was rooted a broad cultural change reflecting the political ascendance of a managerial elite that, in the United States, was committed to a pragmatic liberalism based on a political morality of rationality and efficiency.[257] Historian Eugene Genovese summarized the membership in the new class:

> [W]ho belongs to the managerial elite that increasingly dominates every aspect of our lives? Begin with the executives and bureaucrats of private corporations and add their sometimes rivals and sometime allies, the executives and bureaucrats of the federal, state, and local governments. Add the administrators of school systems, universities, large churches, and other institutions. Add the professionals of various kinds, most notably the lawyers, teachers and doctors, who command powerful lobbies. Add the media personnel who shape as well as serve the larger elite. And do not fail to include the university intellectuals, whom the American people…considered something of a joke until President Kennedy put them to use, and who now significantly influence policy-making. The list may be extended or reshaped, but probably to no great advantage.[258]

The rise of this new class was not an accident. It resulted from an unprecedented general economic expansion coupled with a restructuring of employment, particularly in the increase in information processing and government-funded employment.[259] Entrance into the new class was

---

255. Lucas, *supra* note 213, at 735 n.26.

256. Protest sign seen in Washington on Oct. 11, 1987, quoted in Mary Dunlap, *Gay Men and Lesbians Down by Law in the 1990's USA: The Continuing Toll of* Bowers v. Hardwick, 24 Golden Gate L. Rev. 1, 4 (1994).

257. *See generally* Andrew Abbott, The System of the Professions: An Essay on the Division of Expert Labor (1988); The Authority of Experts: Studies in History and Theory (Thomas Haskell ed. 1984); Burton Bledstein, The Culture of Professionalism: The Middle Class and the Development of Higher Education in America (1978); Alvin Gouldner, The Future of Intellectuals and the Rise of the New Class (1979); Jethro Lieberman, The Tyranny of the Experts: How Professionals Are Closing the Open Society (1980); Leslie Margolin, Under the Cover of Kindness: The Invention of Social Work (1996); Mensch & Freeman, *supra* note 122, at 84; Genovese, *supra* note 32.

258. Genovese, *supra* note 32, at 203.

259. Alfred Chandler, The Visible Hand: The Managerial Revolution in American Business (1977); Alvin Gouldner, The Future of the Intellectual and the Rise of the New Class (1979); Christopher Lasch, The True and Only Heaven: Progress and Its Critics 509–29 (1991); Mensch & Freeman, *supra* note 122, at 85; Genovese, *supra* note 32, at 201; Kingsley Davis, *Wives and Work: The Sex Revolution and its Consequences,* 10 Pop. & Dev. Rev. 397 (1984); Shirley Harkness, *Women's Occupational Experiences in the 1970's: Sociology and Economics,* 10 Signs 495 (1985); Mary King, *Occupational Segregation by Race and Sex, 1940–1988,* 115 Monthly Labor Rev. 30 (1992); Francois Nielsen & Arthur Alderson, *Income Inequality, Development, and Dualism: Results from an Unbalanced Cross-National Panel,* 60 Am. Soc. Rev. 674 (1995); William Rau & Robert Wazienski, *Industrialization, Female Labor Force Participation, and the Modern*

through a higher education that increasingly marginalized tradition (particularly religious tradition) as a basis for decision-making in the name of impartial and dispassionate expertise.[260]

The resulting ideology not only validated the managerial class's roles, it also justified a wide-range of life-style choices that facilitated two-career couples working the fast lane[261]—and often led to the break-up of traditional families.[262] One notable result during the 1950s and 1960s was the increasing popularity among young, unmarried women of giving up an unwanted baby for adoption rather than accepting hurried marriage under circumstances that would preclude one or both parents from pursuing their dreamed of careers.[263]

In short, the managerial class focused on self-fulfillment in ways that had not been generally expressed before, especially not by women, with the members of the managerial class proving all too willing to sacrifice others in order to achieve their self-expression.[264] The newly dominant class found its justificatory philosophy in the vulgarized notions of Freudian psychology that, in the wake of widespread recourse to psychiatric evaluations and treatment in the military during World War II, spread across English-speaking nations in the 1950s.[265] Many psychologists pro-

---

*Division of Labor by Sex,* 38 INDUS. REL. 504 (1999); Kathryn Ward & Fred Pampel, *Structural Determinants of Female Labor Force Participation in Developed Nations, 1955–1975,* 66 SOC. SCI. Q. 654 (1985).

260. *See* STEPHEN CARTER, THE CULTURE OF DISBELIEF: HOW AMERICAN LAW AND POLITICS TRIVIALIZE RELIGIOUS DEVOTION (1993); FERREE & HESS, *supra* note 219, at 6–9; JAMES DAVISON HUNTER, CULTURE WARS: THE STRUGGLE TO DEFINE AMERICA (1991); Van Harvey, *On the Intellectual Marginality of American Theology,* in RELIGION AND TWENTIETH-CENTURY AMERICAN INTELLECTUAL LIFE 180 (Michael Lacy ed. 1989).

261. FERREE & HESS, *supra* note 219, at 9–10; ARLIE RUSSELL HOCHSCHILD, THE SECOND SHIFT: WORKING PARENTS AND THE REVOLUTION AT HOME (1989); MENSCH & FREEMAN, *supra* note 122, at 85–86, 111; THE POLITICS OF HOUSEWORK (Ellen Malos ed. 1980); Belinda Bennett, *The Economics of Wifing Services: Law and Economics on the Family,* 18 J. LAW & SOC'Y 206 (1991); John Noonan, jr., *Introduction,* in THE MORALITY OF ABORTION, *supra* note 135, at ix–xvii. *See generally* JUDITH BUTLER, GENDER TROUBLE: FEMINISM AND THE SUPPRESSION OF IDENTITY (1990); ELIZABETH SPELMAN, INESSENTIAL WOMAN: PROBLEMS OF EXCLUSION IN FEMINIST THOUGHT (1988); Tracy Higgins, *"By Reason of Their Sex": Feminist Theory, Postmodernism, and Justice,* 80 CORNELL L. REV. 1536, 1541–54 (1995).

262. MARTHA FINEMAN, THE ILLUSION OF EQUALITY: THE RHETORIC AND REALITY OF DIVORCE REFORM (1991); HILDA SCOTT, WORKING YOUR WAY TO THE BOTTOM: THE FEMINIZATION OF POVERTY (1984); JUDITH WALLERSTEIN & SANDRA BLAKESLEE, SECOND CHANCE: MEN, WOMEN, AND CHILDREN: A DECADE AFTER DIVORCE (1989); LENORE WEITZMAN, THE DIVORCE REVOLUTION: THE UNEXPECTED SOCIAL AND ECONOMIC CONSEQUENCES FOR WOMEN AND CHILDREN IN AMERICA (1985); Lloyd Cohen, *Marriage, Divorce, and Quasi Rents, or, "I Gave Him the Best Years of My Life,"* 16 J. LEGAL STUD. 267 (1987); Saul Hoffman & Greg Duncan, *What Are the Economic Consequences of Divorce?,* 25 DEMOGRAPHY 641 (1988); Elizabeth Scott, *Rational Decisionmaking about Marriage and Divorce,* 76 VA. L. REV. 9 (1990); Julien Teitler, *Reconsidering the Effects of Marital Disruption—What Happens to Children of Divorce in Early Adulthood,* 5 J. FAM. ISSUES 173 (June 1994); Martin Zelder, *The Economic Analysis of the Effect of No-Fault Divorce Law on the Divorce Rate,* 16 HARV. J.L. & PUB. POL'Y 241 (1991).

263. ELLEN MESSER & KATHRYN MAY, BACK ROOMS: VOICES FROM THE ILLEGAL ABORTION ERA 31–62 (1988); PATRICIA MILLER, THE WORST OF TIMES 173 (1993); REAGAN, *supra* note 112, at 194–95; SOLINGER, *supra* note 234, at 103–86; Regina Kunzel, *White Neurosis, Black Pathology: Constructing Out of Wedlock Pregnancy in the Wartime and Post-War United States,* in NOT JUNE CLEAVER, *supra* note 112, at 304, 306–08.

264. Genovese, *supra* note 32, at 202–03, 206–07.

265. BAILEY, *supra* note 51, at 50–74. This trend towards relying on psychotherapy has continued to this day; the number of licensed psychotherapists of various stripes has more than tripled between 1970 and 1997, reaching about 550,000 practitioners in the latter year. Andrew Hacker, *The War over the Family,* N.Y. REV. BOOKS, Dec. 4, 1997, at 34, 36 n.3. Ironically given the instrumental role of Freudian psychology in the liberation of women, many feminists were archly critical of Freud because of his apparently dismissive attitude toward women. *See, e.g.,* NANCY CHODOROW, THE REPRODUCTION OF MOTHERING (1978); SIMONE DE BEAUVOIR, THE SECOND SEX 40–54 (2nd ed. H.M. Parshley trans. 1974); BETTY FRIEDAN, THE FEMININE MYSTIQUE 114–16 (1963); KATE MILLETT, SEXUAL POLITICS 292–300 (1970); JULIET MITCHELL, PSYCHOANALYSIS AND FEMINISM (1975); ANDREA NYE, FEMINIST THEORIES AND THE PHILOSOPHIES OF MAN 115–71 (paperback ed. 1989).

pounded the essentially flexible, arbitrary, and contingent nature of sexual roles and social mores.[266] Their psychology focused on the self almost to the exclusion of concern for the effects of the analysis on the family or others who might be affected.[267] Family came to be seen as the root of individual psychological problems, rather than as something that, if it could be made to function better, could help solve an individual's problems.[268] Growing out of this attitude, in the decades since abortion was legalized, we have seen innumerable forms of life-style and non-traditional families stake a claim for legitimacy.

In the later years of the twentieth century, non-traditional families in the United Kingdom, the United States, and other industrialized countries proliferated in almost uncountable ways. One of the first open breaks from the traditional family structure was the emergence of a large number of unmarried heterosexual couples openly living together.[269] The number of such cou-

---

266. *See, e.g.,* Benjamin Glover, *Observations on Homosexuality among University Students,* 113 J. NERVOUS & MENTAL DISEASE 377 (1951). *See generally* BAILEY, *supra* note 51, at 68–73; JACQUES LACAN, FEMININE SEXUALITY (Juliet Mitchell & Jacqueline Rose eds., Jacqueline Rose trans. 1982).

267. *See generally* ROBERT BELLAH *et al.,* HABITS OF THE HEART: INDIVIDUALISM AND COMMITMENT IN AMERICA (1985); JOHN GOTTMAN & NAN SILVER, SEVEN PRINCIPLES FOR MAKING A MARRIAGE WORK (1999); ELLEN HERMAN, THE ROMANCE OF AMERICAN PSYCHOLOGY: POLITICAL CULTURE IN THE AGE OF EXPERTS (1995); CHRISTOPHER LASCH, THE CULTURE OF NARCISSISM (1979); PHILIP RIEFF, THE TRIUMPH OF THE THERAPEUTIC: USES OF FAITH AFTER FREUD (1966); Suzanne Klonis *et al., Feminism as Life Raft,* 21 PSCYH. OF WOMEN Q. 233 (1997). *See also* MILTON REGAN, JR., ALONE TOGETHER: LAW AND THE MEANING OF MARRIAGE (1999); Christopher Slobogin, *Therapeutic Jurisprudence: Five Dilemmas to Ponder,* 1 PSYCH., PUB. POL'Y & L. 193 (1995).

268. JOSEPH GUTTMAN, DIVORCE IN PSYCHOSOCIAL PERSPECTIVE: THEORY AND RESEARCH (1993). *See also* GUSTAV MARIUS BRUCE, MARRIAGE AND DIVORCE: A SOCIOLOGICAL AND THEOLOGICAL PERSPECTIVE 127 (1930) (arguing that the "philosophy of individualism and selfishness" was responsible for the rising divorce rate of the early twentieth century). *See generally* DAVID POPENOE & BARBARA DAFOE WHITEHEAD, THE STATE OF OUR UNIONS: THE SOCIAL HEALTH OF MARRIAGE IN AMERICA (1999); BARBARA DAFOE WHITEHEAD, THE DIVORCE CULTURE (1997); WOMEN IN FAMILIES (Monica McGoldrick, Carol Anderson, & Froma Walsh eds. 1989); Heidi Hartmann, *The Family as the Locus of Gender, Class, and Political Struggle,* 6 SIGNS 366 (1981); Dena Targ, *Feminist Family Sociology: Some Reflections,* 22 SOC. FOCUS 151 (1989); Alexis Walker & Linda Thompson, *Feminism and Family Studies,* 54 J. FAM. ISSUES 545 (1984); Maxine Baca Zinn, *Feminism and Family Studies for a New Century,* 571 ANNALS AM. ACADEMY POL. & SOC. SCI. 42 (2000).

269. MARGARET JASPER, LIVING TOGETHER (2003); DAVID POPENOE & BARBARA WHITEHEAD, COHABITATION IN AMERICA: A REPORT TO THE NATION (2002); Marin Clarkberg *et al., Atitudes, Values, and Entrance into Cohabitational versus Marital Unions,* 74 SOC. FORCES 609 (1995); Jennifer Robbennolt, *Legal Planning for Unmarried Committed Partners: Empirical Lessons for a Preventive Therapeutic Approach,* 41 ARIZ. L. REV. 417 (1999); Symposium, *Unmarried Partners and the Legacy of* Marvin v. Marvin, 76 NOTRE DAME L. REV. 1261–63 (2001); *Unmarried Couples on Rise in U.S.,* PHILA. INQUIRER, May 20, 2001, at 3E. This change, of course, produced ripples in the legal world. Foray v. Bell Atlantic, 56 F. Supp. 2d 327 (S.D.N.Y. 1999) (upholding as nondiscriminatory a benefits policy that treated married couples and unmarried homosexual couples identically, but denied benefits to an unmarried heterosexual couple); Lasota v. Town of Topsfield, 979 F. Supp. 45 (D. Mass. 1997) (barring a school district from dismissing a woman for living with a man without marriage); Hann v. Housing Auth'y, 709 F. Supp. 605 (E.D. Pa. 1989) (striking down a blanket prohibition of unmarried couples in public housing); Foreman v. Anchorage Equal Rts. Comm'n, 779 P.2d 1199 (Alaska 1989) (refusal to rent to an unmarried heterosexual couple violates a law against discrimination based on marital status); Smith v. Fair Employment & Housing Comm'n, 913 P.2d 909 (Cal. 1996) (same); Marvin v. Marvin, 557 P.2d 106 (Cal. 1976) (allowing suit on a cohabitation agreement between a heterosexual couple); Cochran v. Cochran, 106 Cal. Rptr. 2d 899 (Ct. App. 2001) (ordering trial on *Marvin*-type suit); Butcher v. Superior Ct., 188 Cal. Rptr. 503 (Ct. App. 1983) (allowing recovery for loss of consortium by an unmarried heterosexual partner); Department of Indus. Rel. v. Workers' Comp. Bd., 156 Cal. Rptr. 183 (Ct. App. 1979) (allowing recovery of workers' compensation benefits by an unmarried woman whose life-partner died); Salzman v. Bachrach, 996 P.2d 1263 (Colo. 2000) (allowing unjust enrichment claims between unmarried cohabitants); Hewitt v. Hewitt, 394 N.E.2d 1204 (Ill. 1979) (disallowing a claim based upon a cohabitation agreement); Crawford v. City of Chicago, 710 N.E.2d 91 (Ill. App. Ct.) (upholding municipal ordinance authorizing benefits to unmarried cohabitants), *aff'd mem.,* 720 N.E.2d 1090 (Ill. 1999); Mister v. A.R.K.

ples grew in the United States from about 1.5 percent of all households (1,100,000 couples) in 1977 to about 4.8 percent of all households (4,900,000 couples) in 1997.[270] The rate of growth in such relationships was even higher in Western Europe.[271] Almost simultaneously some women began to demand greater equality within traditional marriages, leading to considerable restructuring of such relationships.[272] Some couples began to experiment with "open relationships," in-

---

Ptrnshp., 553 N.E.2d 1152 (Ill. App. Ct. 1990) (a landlord does not discriminate on the basis of marital status by refusing to rent to an unmarried couple when he landlord refuses to rent to any group of unrelated individuals), *appeal denied,* 561 N.E.2d 694 (Ill. 1990); Prince George's Cnty. v. Greenbelt Homes, 431 A.2d 745 (Md. Ct. Spec. App. 1991) (same); Worcester Hous. Auth'y v. Massachusetts Comm'n against Discrimination, 547 N.E.2d 43 (Mass. 1989) (refusal to rent to an unmarried heterosexual couple violates a law against discrimination based on marital status); McCready v. Hoffius, 564 N.W.2d 493 (Mich. Ct. App. 1997) (a landlord is liable for refusing to rent to unmarried heterosexual couple despite the landlord's religiously based objections to cohabitation), *vacated,* 593 N.W.2d 545 (Mich. 1999); State v. French, 460 N.W.2d 2 (Minn. 1990) (upholding a right to discriminate on the basis of marital status because of the state's anti-fornication law); Kurman v. Fairmount Realty Corp., 8 N.J. Admin. 110 (1985) (refusal to rent to an unmarried heterosexual couple violates a law against discrimination based on marital status); In re Miller, 824 A.2d 1207 (Pa. Super. Ct. 2003) (allowing a woman to change her family name to that of her cohabitant without marriage); Devlin v. City of Philadelphia, 809 A.2d 980 (Pa. Commw. Ct. 2002) (municipal ordinance extending benefits to unmarried cohabitants preempted by state law), *appeal granted,* 833 A.2d 1115 (Pa. 2003); McFadden v. Elma Country Club, 613 P.2d 146 (Wash. Ct. App. 1980) (a landlord does not discriminate on the basis of marital status by refusing to rent to an unmarried couple when he landlord refuses to rent to any group of unrelated individuals); Dane Cty. v. Norman, 497 N.W.2d 714 (Wis. 1993) (same); Watts v. Watts, 405 N.W.2d 303 (Wis. 1987) (allowing breach of contract and unjust enrichment claims between unmarried cohabitants); Baumgartner v. Baumgartner, 164 C.L.R. 137 (Australia 1987) (finding a "constructive trust" for heterosexual cohabitants).

For early studies on this development, see BAILEY, *supra* note 51, at 200–05; IRVING SLOAN, LIVING TOGETHER: UNMARRIEDS AND THE LAW (1980); Stacey Boyle, Note, *Marital Status Classifications: Protecting Homosexual and Heterosexual Cohabitors,* 14 HASTINGS CONST. L.Q. 111 (1986); Robert Casad, *Unmarried Couples and Unjust Enrichment: From Status and Back Again?,* 77 MICH. L. REV. 47 (1978); Martha Fineman, *Law and Changing Patterns of Behavior: Sanctions on Non-Marital Cohabitation,* 1981 WIS. L. REV. 275; Herma Hill Kay & Carol Amyx, Marvin v. *Marvin: Preserving the Options,* 65 CAL. L. REV. 937 (1977); Rebecca Melton, *Legal Rights of Unmarried Heterosexual and Homosexual Couples and Evolving Definitions of Family,* 29 J. FAM. L. 497 (1990); Kenneth Norrie, *Proprietary Rights of Cohabitants,* 1995 JURIDICAL REV. 209; Symposium, *Unmarried Partners and the Legacy of* Marvin v. Marvin, 76 NOTRE DAME L. REV. 1271 (2001); Linda White, *The Negative Effects of Cohabitation,* 10 RESPONSIVE COMMUNITY 31 (1999).

270. Eric Nagourney, *Study Finds Families Bypassing Marriage,* N.Y. TIMES, Feb. 15, 2000, at F8. *See also* US CENSUS BUREAU, STATISTICAL ABSTRACT OF THE UNITED STATES: 1991, at 44 (111th ed. 1991); Judith Waldrop, *Living in Sin,* AM. DEMOGRAPHICS, Apr. 1990, at 12.

271. Sarah Lyall, *Europeans Opting against Marriage,* N.Y. TIMES, Mar. 24, 2002, § 1, at 1. *See also* Carol Bruch, *Nonmarital Cohabitation in the Common Law Countries: A Study in Judicial-Legislative Interaction,* 29 AM. J. COMP. L. 217 (1981); Arlene Skolnick, *The Social Context of Cohabitation,* 29 AM. J. COMP. L. 339 (1981).

272. *See, e.g.,* Lind R. v. Richard E., 561 N.Y.S.2d 29 (App. Div. 1990) (awarding custody to a working mother); Hoover v. Hoover, 764 A.2d 1192 (Vt. 2000) (transferring custody to the father after the mother moved out of state); Lane v. Schenck, 614 A.2d 786 (Vt. 1992) (denying a custodial mother right to leave the state to attend law school because it would interfere with the father's visitation rights). *See generally* ROSALIND BARNETT & CARYL RIVERS, SHE WORKS, HE WORKS: HOW TWO INCOME FAMILIES ARE HAPPIER, HEALTHIER, AND BETTER OFF (1996); STEPHANIE COONTZ, THE WAY WE REALLY ARE: COMING TO TERMS WITH AMERICA'S CHANGING FAMILIES (1997); STEPHANIE COONTZ, MAYA PARSON, & GABRIELLE RALEY, AMERICAN FAMILIES: A MUTLICULTURAL READER (1999); FAMILY, SELF, AND SOCIETY: TOWARD A NEW AGENDA FOR FAMILY RESEARCH (Philip Cowan *et al.* eds. 1993); FEMINISM AND FAMILIES (Hilde Lindemann Nelson ed. 1997); LINDA BECK FENWICK, PRIVATE CHOICES, PUBLIC CONSEQUENCES: REPRODUCTIVE TECHNOLOGY AND THE NEW ETHICS OF CONCEPTION, PREGNANCY, AND FAMILY 254–87 (1998); SUSAN FERGUSON, SHIFTING THE CENTER: UNDERSTANDING CONTEMPORARY FAMILIES (1998); MARTHA ALBERTSON FINEMAN, THE NEUTERED MOTHER, THE SEXUAL FAMILY AND OTHER TWENTIETH CENTURY TRAGEDIES (1995); HANDBOOK OF FAMILY DIVERSITY (David Demo, Katherine Allen, & Mark Fine eds. 2000); HANDBOOK OF MARRIAGE AND THE FAMILY (Marvin Sussman & Suzanne Steinman eds. 1987); KAREN HANSEN & ANITA ILTA GAREY, FAMILIES IN THE U.S.: KIN-

volving multiple participants with varying degrees of involvement and diverse sexual orientation.[273] All of this contributed to a vast increase in the divorce, leaving behind large numbers of single-parent households as well as more complex familial structures.[274]

---

SHIP AND DOMESTIC POLITICS (1998); HOCHSCHILD, *supra* note 261; MOTHERS IN LAW: FEMINIST THEORY AND THE LEGAL REGULATION OF MOTHERHOOD 118 (Martha Albertson Fineman & Isabel Karpin eds. 1995); SUSAN MILLER OKIN, JUSTICE, GENDER, AND THE FAMILY (1989); SOURCEBOOK OF FAMILY THEORIES (William Doherty *et al.* eds. 1993); JUDITH STACEY, BRAVE NEW FAMILIES: STORIES OF DOMESTIC UPHEAVAL IN LATE TWENTIETH CENTURY AMERICA (1990); THE CENTER FOR A WOMAN'S OWN NAME: BOOKLET FOR WOMEN WHO WISH TO DETERMINE THEIR OWN NAMES AFTER MARRIAGE (1974); THE POLITICS OF HOUSEWORK, *supra* note 261; KATH WESTON, THE FAMILIES WE CHOOSE (1991); JOHN WITTE, JR., FROM SACRAMENT TO CONTRACT: MARRIAGE, RELIGION AND LAW IN WESTERN TRADITION (1997); Kif Augustine-Adams, *The Beginning of Wisdom Is to Call Things by Their Right Names*, 7 REV. LAW & WOMEN'S STUD. 1 (1997); June Carbone, *Income Sharing: Redefining the Family in Terms of Community*, 31 HOUS. L. REV. 359 (1994); Jonathan Cohn, *A Man's Place: When Feminism Meets At-Home Fatherhood*, THE NEW REP., Nov. 7, 1998, at 20; Roslyn Daum, *The Right of Married Women to Assert Their Own Surnames*, 8 J. LAW REFORM 64 (1974); Myra Marx Ferree, *Beyond Separate Spheres: Feminism and Family Research*, 52 J. MARRIAGE & FAM. 866 (1990); Julia Lamber, *A Married Woman's Surname: Is Custom Law?*, 1973 WASH. L. REV. 779; Sara McLanahan & Lynn Casper, *Growing Diversity and Inequality in the American Family*, in 2 STATE OF THE UNION: AMERICA IN THE 1990s 1 (Reynolds Farley ed. 1995); J. Mark Ramseyer, *Toward Contractual Choice in Marriage*, 73 IND. L.J. 511 (1998); Eric Rasmusen & Jeffrey Evans Stake, *Lifting the Veil of Ignorance: Personalizing the Marriage Contract*, 73 IND. L.J. 453 (1998); Amy Wax, *Bargaining in the Shadow of the Market: Is There a Future for Egalitarian Marriage?*, 84 VA. L. REV. 509 (1998); Lenore Weitzman, *Legal Regulation of Marriage: Tradition and Change*, 62 CAL. L. REV. 1169 (1974). *See also* Suzanne Daley, *French Couples Take Plunge that Falls Short of Marriage*, N.Y. TIMES, Apr. 18, 2000, at A1 (reporting that 40% of the French couples joining themselves in *Pacte civile de solidarité*—Civil Unions under a law designed to accommodate the needs of homosexual couples—were heterosexual).

273. *See, e.g.*, Schochet v. State, 580 A.2d 176 (Md. 1990); NENA & GEORGE O'NEILL, OPEN MARRIAGE (1972); JOHN HEIDENRY, WHAT WILD ECSTASY: THE RISE AND FALL OF THE SEXUAL REVOLUTION (1997); Joan Dixon, *Sexuality and Relationship Changes in Married Females Following the Commencement of Bisexual Activity*, 11 J. HOMOSEXUALITY 115 (1985); Richard Green, *Fornication: Common Law Legacy and American Sexual Privacy*, 17 ANGLO-AM. L. REV. 226 (1988); Robert Misner, *Minimalism, Desuetude, and Fornication*, 35 WILLAMETTE L. REV. 1 (1999); Dianne Post, *Why Marriage Should Be Abolished*, 18 WOMEN'S RTS. L. RPTR. 283 (1997); Kenji Yoshino, *The Epistemic Contract of Bisexual Erasure*, 52 STAN. L. REV. 353 (2000). *See also* Hazel Glenn Beh, *Sex, Sexual Pleasure, and Reproduction: Health Insurers Don't Want You to Do Those Nasty Things*, 13 WIS. WOMEN'S L.J. 119 (1998).

274. *See, e.g.*, Troxel v. Granville, 530 U.S. 57 (2000) (finding unconstitutional a statute authorizing a court to award visitation to "any person" at "any time" if it is in the best interests of the child); Roth v. Weston, 789 A.2d 431 (Conn. 2002) (denying visitation rights to maternal family members of children in custody of father when there is no "established parent-like relationship" and it was not shown that child would suffer from lack of visitation); V.C. v. M.J.B., 748 A.2d 539 (N.J.) (denying joint custody as disruptive to all concerned), *cert. denied*, 531 U.S. 926 (2000); *In re* Bonfield 780 N.E.2d 241 (Ohio 2002) (allowing a court to declare the legal rights of the lesbian partner of the biological mother); *In re* Sleeper, 929 P.2d 1028 (Or. Ct. App. 1996) (husband of the mother awarded custody although all conceded that he could not have been their father), *aff'd on other grounds*, 982 P.2d 1126 (Or. 1999); Shea v. Metcalf, 712 A.2d 887 (Vt. 1998) (awarding legal authority over and responsibility for the children's education and medical care to the father and all other matters to the mother).

*See generally* ALL OUR FAMILIES: NEW POLICIES FOR A NEW CENTURY (Mary Ann Mason *et al.* eds. 1998); TERRY ARENDALL, FATHERS AND DIVORCE (1995); DAVID BLANKENHORN, FATHERLESS AMERICA: CONFRONTING OUR MOST URGENT SOCIAL PROBLEM (1995); NANCY DOWD, IN DEFENSE OF SINGLE-PARENT FAMILIES (1997); JUNE CARDONE, FROM PARTNERS TO PARENTS: THE SECOND REVOLUTION IN FAMILY LAW (2000); MAGGIE GALLAGHER, THE ABOLITION OF MARRIAGE: HOW WE DESTROY LASTING LOVE (1996); MARY ANN GLENDON, THE NEW FAMILY AND THE NEW PROPERTY (1981); WILLIAM GOODE, WORLD CHANGES IN DIVORCE PATTERNS (1993); JOINT CUSTODY AND SHARED PARENTING (Jay Folberg ed. 1984); CARMEN MASSEY & RALPH WARNER, SEX, LIVING TOGETHER AND THE LAW—A LEGAL GUIDE FOR UNMARRIED COUPLES (AND GROUPS) (1974); ROSS PARKE & ARMIN BROTT, THROWAWAY DADS (1999); LILLIAN RUBIN, FAMILIES ON THE FAULT LINE (1994); JUDITH STACEY, IN THE NAME OF THE FAMILY: RETHINKING FAMILY VALUES IN THE POSTMODERN AGE (1996); WALLERSTEIN, *supra* note 262; WALTER WEYRAUCH & SANFORD KATZ, AMERICAN FAMILY

Statistics record the changing patterns of relationships in the United States. In 1970, 94 percent of all women between the ages of 30 and 34 had been married, and 92 percent had had at least one child.[275] By 1994, only 80 percent of such women had been married, and 74 percent had had a child.[276] Furthermore, 40 percent of the childless women in their early thirties indicated that they did not expect ever to have a child.[277] The expression "had been married" is telling, not only because millions had lived with a man only to have the relationship broken off without ever formalizing the relationship in a marriage. And marriages were becoming far more unstable. The number of actual divorces had risen from 9.2 per 1,000 married couples in 1960 to 22.8 in 1979, and then declined slightly to 20.5 by 1994—a rate that meant there were about half as many divorces in 1994 as recorded marriages (504:1,000).[278] Some attribute the rising divorce rate to the liberalization of the divorce laws, but which was cause which effect was far from clear.[279] If one adds the break-ups of couples who were living together without marriage, the pattern of marital instability was considerably greater. As a result, the percentage of men and

---

LAW IN TRANSITION (1983); Susan Apel, *Communitarianism and Feminism: The Case against the Preference for the Two-Parent Family,* 10 WIS. WOMEN'S L.J. 1 (1995); Kathryn Bartlett, *Rethinking Parenthood as an Exclusive Status: The Need for Legal Alternatives When the Premise of the Nuclear Family Has Failed,* 70 VA. L. REV. 879 (1984); Margaret Brinig, *Feminism and Child Custody under Chapter Two of the American Law Institute's Principles of the Law of Family Dissolution,* 8 DUKE J. GENDER & L. 301 (2001); Margaret Brinig & Steven Crafton, *Marriage and Opportunism,* 23 J. LEGAL STUD. 869 (1994); Jack Croft, *Setting Precedent: Baby Sitter in Delaware Wins Custody of Child over the Mother's Protests,* PHILA. INQUIRER, Mar. 13, 1982, at 3B; Janet Dolgin, *The Fate of Childhood: Legal Models of Children and the Parent-Child Relationship,* 61 ALB. L. REV. 345 (1997); Susan Gilbert, *Raising Grandchildren: Rising Stress,* N.Y. TIMES, July 28, 1998, at B8; Sally Goldfarb, *Visitation Rights for Nonparents after* Troxel v. Granville: *Where Should States Draw the Line?,* 32 RUTGERS L.J. 783 (2001); Richard Green et al., *Lesbian Mothers and Their Children: A Comparison with Solo Parent Heterosexual Mothers and Their Children,* 15 ARCHIV. SEXUAL BEHAV. 167 (1986); John DeWitt Gregory, *Blood Ties: A Rationale for Child Visitation by Legal Strangers,* 55 WASH. & LEE L. REV. 351 (1998); Janet Johnston et al., *On Going Post Divorce Conflict: Effects on Children of Joint Custody and Frequent Access,* 59 AM. J. ORTHOPSYCH. 576 (1989); Carolyn Wilkes Kaas, *Breaking up a Family or Putting It Back Together Again: Refining the Preference in Favor of the Parent in Third-Party Custody Cases,* 37 WM. & MARY L. REV. 1045 (1996); Siobhan Morrissey, *The New Neighbors: Domestic Relations Law Struggles to Catch up with Changes in Family Life,* ABA J., Mar. 2002, at 37, 40–41; Laurence Nolan, *Legal Strangers and the Duty of Support: Beyond the Biological Tie—But How Far Beyond the Marital Tie,* 41 SANTA CLARA L. REV. 1 (2000); J. Thomas Oldham, *Limitations Imposed by Family Law on a Separating Parent's Ability to Make Significant Life Decisions: A Comparison of Relocation and Income Imputation,* 8 DUKE J. GENDER & L. 333 (2001); Sarah Ramsey, *Constructing Parenthood for Stepparents:* Parents by Estoppel *and* De Facto Parents *under the American Law Institute's Principles of the Law of Family Dissolution,* 8 DUKE J. GENDER & L. 285 (2001); Philip Schuster II, *Constitutional and Family Law Implications of the* Sleeper *and* Troxel *Cases: A Denouement for Oregon's Psychological Parent Statute?,* 36 WILLAMETTE L. REV. 549 (2000); Barbara Bennett Woodhouse, *"It All Depends on What You Mean by Home": Toward a Communitarian Theory of the "Nontraditional" Family,* 1996 UTAH L. REV. 569.

275. *See* Hacker, *supra* note 265, at 34.

276. *Id.* The average age at first marriage has also risen to record highs. DAPHNE SPAIN & SUZANNE BIANCHI, BALANCING ACT: MOTHERHOOD, MARRIAGE, AND EMPLOYMENT AMONG AMERICAN WOMEN 26 (1996). The percentage of black women who had never married (over 50%) is much higher than for white women. POPENOE & WHITEHEAD, *supra* note 268, at 4 fig. 2. *See also* Anthony King, *African American Females' Attitudes towards Marriage: An Exploratory Study,* 29 J. BLACK STUD. 416 (1999).

277. Hacker, *supra* note 265, at 34 n.1. *See generally* MADELYN CAIN, THE CHILDLESS REVOLUTION (2000).

278. *Id.* at 34–35. The ratio of divorces to marriages in 1960 was 258:1,000.

279. WHITEHEAD, *supra* note 268; Margaret Brinig & F.H. Buckley, *No-Fault Laws and At-Fault People,* INT'L REV. L. & ECON. 325 (1998); Ira Mark Ellman & Sharon Lohr, *Dissolving the Relationship between Divorce Laws and Divorce Rates,* 18 INT'L REV. L. & ECON. 341 (1998). Some might suggest that the cause of the rise in divorce was the decreasing satisfaction in sexual relations among married couples. *See, e.g.,* MICHELE WEINER DAVIS, THE SEX-STARVED MARRIAGE (2003); CRISTINA FERRARE, OKAY, SO I DON'T HAVE A HEADACHE (2000); JUDY REICHMAN, I'M NOT IN THE MOOD (1998); THE BITCH IN THE HOUSE (Cathi Hanauer ed. 2002); Caitlin Flanagan, *The Wifely Duty: Marriage Used to Provide Access to Sex. Now It Provides Access to Celibacy,* ATLANTIC MONTHLY, Jan./Feb. 2003, at 171.

women over the age of 18 who were still married fell from 70.6 percent in 1970 to 52.8 percent in 2000.[280] By 2000, only 24 percent of all family households in America included both a heterosexual couple and one or more of their own children—down from 40 percent in 1970.[281] A study found in 1995 that only half of all children in the United States were being raised in two-parent households, and half of those included a stepparent.[282]

Not all the unmarried adults were unmarried because of divorce. Not only were millions living together, but millions more had never been in any sort of live-in relationship and were never likely to be in one.[283] Moreover, increasing numbers of unmarried adults were having children, with 31 percent of children being born "out-of-wedlock" in 1995 (compared to 5.3 percent in 1960).[284] No wonder courts began, after 1970, to recognize to some extent rights in unmarried fathers and similarly to proscribe long-standing discriminations against illegitimate children (and their fathers).[285] Before long, complicated parenting relationships were

---

280. Morrissey, *supra* note 274, at 39, Table. *See also* Hacker, *supra* note 265, at 36, Table A.

281. Morriseey, *supra* note 274, at 39, Table. *See also* Hacker, *supra* note 265, at 36, Table A.

282. Hacker, *supra* note 265, at 38.

283. *See* ANDREW CHERLIN, MARRIAGE, DIVORCE, REMARRIAGE (rev. ed. 1992); HOWARD CHUDACOFF, THE AGE OF THE BACHELOR: CREATING AN AMERICAN SUBCULTURE (1994); Barbara Stark, *Marriage Proposals: From One-Size-Fits-All to Postmodern Marriage Law,* 89 CAL. L. REV. 1479 (2001). The rate at which people remain "never married" in the United States, however is not higher than it was at the end of the nineteenth century. Peter Brimelow, *Too Many Bachelors?,* FORBES, Nov. 15, 1999, at 143. Furthermore, that rate is lower than it was in 1950 in the wake of the Depression. SPAIN & BIANCHI, *supra* note 276, at 27, table 2.2.

284. REBECCA BLANK, IT TAKES A NATION: A NEW AGENDA FOR FIGHTING POVERTY 33 (1997); Hacker, *supra* note 265, at 36, Table B. While many of these births are to teenage mothers, as many as 25% of births to women aged 20 to 24 are also outside of a marriage. BLANK, *supra. See generally Facts at a Glance,* CHILD TRENDS RESEARCH BRIEFS, *available at* www.childtrends.org/PDF/FAAG02002.pdf (Sept. 2002); Elizabeth Terry-Human, Jennifer Manlove, & Kristin Moore, *Births Outside of Marriage: Perceptions versus Reality,* in CHILD TRENDS RESEARCH BRIEFS, *available at* www.childtrends.org/PDF/rb_032601.pdf (April 2001).

285. *See, e.g.,* Lalli v. Lalli, 439 U.S. 259 (1978) (upholding a statute requiring proof of paternity for an illegitimate heir that would not be required from a legitimate heir); Quilloin v. Walcott, 434 U.S. 246 (1978) (requiring an unwed father to establish paternity in a court proceeding before being able to object to an adoption); Trimble v. Gordon, 430 U.S. 762 (1977) (holding unconstitutional a statute barring an illegitimate child from inheriting from the father's estate); Stanley v. Illinois, 405 U.S. 645 (1972) (recognizing the due process rights of an unwed father to have custody of his children); Adoption of Kelsey S., 823 P.2d 1216 (Cal. 1992); *In re* Baby Girl T., 715 A.2d 99 (Del. Fam. Ct. 1998); Regan v. Joseph P., 677 N.E.2d 434 (Ill. App. Ct. 1996); *In re* Unborn Child Bloomfield, 673 N.E.2d 461 (Ill. App. Ct. 1996), *appeal denied sub nom.* Broomfield v. Yard, 679 N.E.2d 378 (Ill. 1997); Kaiser v. Esswein, 564 N.W.2d 174 (Mich. Ct. App. 1997); *In re* Adoption of Child by P.F.R., 705 A.2d 1233 (N.J. Super. Ct. App. 1998); *In re* Raquel Marie X., 559 N.E.2d 418 (N.Y.), *cert. denied,* 498 U.S. 984 (1990); *In re* M.T.T.'s Adoption, 354 A.2d 564 (Pa. 1976); Abernathy v. Baby Boy, 437 S.E.2d 25 (S.C. 1993); *In re* Adoption of Baby Boy Doe, 717 P.2d 686 (Utah 1986); *In re* Adoption of Jameson, 432 P.2d 881 (Utah 1967). *But see* Tuan Anh Nguyen v. Immigration & Naturalization Service, 533 U.S. 53 (2001) (upholding a statute barring automatic citizenship to an out-of-wedlock child of an American father born outside the United States even though the same statute conferred automatic citizenship to an out-of-wedlock child born to an American mother regardless of the citizenship of the father); Miller v. Albright, 523 U.S. 420 (1998) (same); Pena v. Mattox, 84 F.3d 894 (7th Cir. 1996) (a father of a child born as a result of statutory rape has no standing to block adoption of the child).

*See generally* AM. L. INST., PRINCIPLES OF FAMILY DISSOLUTION ch. 6 (2000); JEFFREY LEVING & KENNETH DACHMAN, FATHER'S RIGHTS (1997); Scott Altman, *Should Child Custody Rules Be Fair?,* 35 U. LOUISVILLE J. FAM. L. 325 (1996); Jerome Barron, *Notice to the Unwed Father and Termination of Parental Rights: Implementing* Stanley v. Illinois, 9 FAM. L.Q. 527 (1975); Burks, *supra* note 274, at 240–44; Deborah Foreman, *Unwed Fathers in Context,* 72 TEX. L. REV. 967 (1994); Carol Gorenberg, *Fathers' Rights vs. Children's Best Interest: Establishing a Predictable Standard for California Adoption Disputes,* 31 FAM. L.Q. 169 (1997); Alexandra Maravel, *Intercountry Adoption and the Flight from Unwed Fathers' Rights: Whose Right Is It Anyway?,* 48 S.C. L. REV. 497 (1997); David Meyer, *Family Ties: Solving the Constitutional Dilemma of the Faultless Father,* 41 ARIZ. L. REV. 753 (1999); Jeffrey Parness, *Abortions of the Parental Prerogatives of Unwed Natural Fathers: Deterring Lost Paternity,* 53 OKLA. L. REV. 345 (2000).

being created by ordinary contract, bearing only the most tenuous relation to traditional reproductive relationships.[286]

At about the same time, homosexuals began to "come out of the closet," insisting that they be protected against discrimination based on their sexual orientation.[287] Homosexual rights became

---

Whether a man married to a woman when she gave birth should be able to disclaim the child if DNA testing proves he was not the father has proven more controversial. *See* Michael H. v. Gerald D., 491 U.S. 110 (1989); Miscovich v. Miscovich, 688 A.2d 726 (Pa. Super. 1997); Elizabeth Buchanan, *The Constitutional Rights of Unwed Fathers before and after* Lehr v. Robertson, 45 Ohio St. L.J. 313 (1984). *See also* Jill Schachner Chanen, *Dad for a Day: Men Who Previously Admitted Paternity Can Now Raise a Challenge through DNA Testing and Forego Child Support*, ABA J., Sept. 2000, at 25. There has been no serious consideration of whether fathers should be able to repudiate their children before birth in a male equivalent to abortion. *See* Melanie McCulley, *The Male Abortion: The Putative Father's Right to Terminate His Interest in and Obligations to the Unborn Child*, 7 J. Law & Pol'y 1 (1985). Nor does the sympathy of courts for putative fathers allow them any say in the abortion decision of the mother. Arthur Shostak, *The Role of Unwed Fathers in the Abortion Decision*, in Young Unwed Fathers: Changing Roles and Emerging Policies 292 (Robert Lerman & Theodora Oooms eds. 1993).

286. Jhordan C. v. Mary K., 224 Cal. Rptr. 530 (Ct. App. 1986) (awarding visitation rights to a sperm-donor father); Doe v. Doe, 710 A.2d 1297 (Conn. 1998) (recognizing litigable issue regarding custody of a child of the husband and a surrogate mother even though the wife had never adopted the child); In re Adoption of Swanson, 623 A.2d 1095 (Del. 1993) (allowing a man to adopt another adult man in order to formalize their gay relationship). *See also* Chapter 18, at notes 78–127. *See generally* Butler, *supra* note 261; Mary Ann Glendon, The Transformation of Family Law (1989); Mason, *supra* note 146, at 5–14; John Witte, jr., From Sacrament to Contract: Marriage, Religion and Law in the Western Tradition (1997); Janet Dolgin, *The Family in Transition: From Griswold to Eisenstadt and Beyond*, 82 Geo. L.J. 1519 (1994); Ann Laquer Estin, *Can Families Be Efficient? A Feminist Appraisal*, 4 Mich. J. Gender & L. 25 (1996); Marjorie Maguire Shultz, *Contractual Ordering of Marriage: A New Model for State Policy*, 70 Cal. L. Rev. 204 (1982); Jana Singer, *The Privatization of Family Law*, 1992 Wis. L. Rev. 1443.

287. Lawrence v. Texas, 539 U.S. 558 (2003) (state sodomy laws violate due process); Romer v. Evans, 517 U.S. 620 (1996) (a state constitutional amendment that prohibited according a protected status to persons of homosexual orientation violates the Fourteenth Amendment's guarantee of equal protection); Boy Scouts of Am. v. Wyman, 335 F.3d 80 (2nd Cir. 2003) (upholding the state's exclusion of the Boy Scouts from a workplace charitable campaign because the Scouts discriminate against homosexuals); Equality Fndtn. of Greater Cincinnati v. City of Cincinnati, 128 F.3d 289 (6th Cir. 1997) (limiting the application of *Romer v. Evans*), *cert. denied*, 525 U.S. 943 (1998); Shahar v. Bowers, 114 F.3d 1097 (11th Cir. 1997) (upholding the dismissal of a deputy [state] Attorney General against a claim of sex-based discrimination because she, as a lesbian, would create a "bad appearance" for the state and suffer a conflict of interest in enforcement of the state's sodomy laws), *cert. denied*, 522 U.S. 1049 (1998); Jegley v. Picado, 80 S.W.3d 332 (Ark. 2002) (holding the state's criminal sodomy statute unconstitutional as applied to private consensual activities); Powell v. State, 510 S.E.2d 18 (Ga. 1998) (same); State v. Smith, 766 So. 2d 501 (La. 1999) (upholding the constitutionality of the state sodomy statute); Goins v. West Group, 635 N.W.2d 717 (Minn. 2001) (denying a cause of action for refusal to assign biological male to the women's restroom because of his/her sexual orientation); Gryczan v. State, 942 P.2d 112 (Mont. 1997) (finding a criminal sodomy statute unconstitutional under the state constitution); People v. Onofre, 415 N.E.2d 936 (N.Y. 1980) (laws making consensual "sodomy" between unmarried adults a crime is unconstitutional as an invasion of the federal right of privacy), *cert. denied*, 451 U.S. 987 (1981); In re Lori M., 496 N.Y.S.2d 940 (Fam. Ct. 1985) (denying a mother's request that her 15-year-old daughter be declared a "person in need of supervision" because of the daughter's association with a 21-year-old lesbian); Campbell v. Sundquist, 926 S.W.2d 250 (Tenn. Ct. App. 1996) (finding a criminal sodomy statute unconstitutional under the state constitution).

*See generally* Bailey, *supra* note 51, at 50–68, 175–99; Bruce Bauer, A Place at the Table: The Gay Individual in American Society (1993); Alan Bérubé, Coming Out under Fire (1990); Bi by Any Other Name (Loraine Hutchins & Lani Kaahumanu eds. 1991); Chandler Burr, A Separate Creation: The Search for Biological Origins of Sexual Orientation (1996); James Button et al., Private Lives, Public Conflicts: Battles over Gay Rights in American Communities (1997); Martha Chamallas, Introduction to Feminist Legal Theory 156–72 (2003); Alba Conte, Sexual Orientation and Legal Rights (1998); John D'Emilio, The World Turned: Essays on Gay History, Politics, and Culture (2002); Bernard Duncan, Escaping God's Closet: The Revelations of a Queer Priest (2000); William Eskridge, Gaylaw: Challenging the Apartheid of the Closet (1999); Lillian Faderman, Odd Girls and Twilight Lovers:

a prominent theme in movies and literature during the 1970s.[288] It became apparent just how acceptable openly homosexual men had become when Billy Crystal rose to television stardom playing the homosexual "Jody Dallas" on the situation soap opera *Soap* from 1977 to 1981. Thereafter followed widespread political agitation demanding stronger government action against,

---

A HISTORY OF LESBIAN LIFE IN TWENTIETH CENTURY AMERICA (1991); FEAR OF A QUEER PLANET—QUEER POLITICS AND SOCIAL THEORY (Michael Warner ed. 1993); LESLIE FEINBERG, STONE BUTCH BLUES (1993); EVAN GERSTMANN, THE CONSTITUTIONAL UNDERCLASS: GAYS, LESBIANS, AND THE FAILURE OF CLASS-BASED EQUAL PROTECTION (1999); GEORGE GRANT & MARK HORNE, LEGISLATING MORALITY: THE HOMOSEXUAL MOVEMENT COMES OUT OF THE CLOSET (1993); HOMOSEXUALITY: IMPLICATIONS FOR PUBLIC POLICY (John Gonsiorek & James Weinrich eds. 1991); STEPHEN JEFFERY-POULTER, PEERS, QUEERS, & COMMONS: THE STRUGGLE FOR GAY LAW REFORM FROM 1950 TO THE PRESENT (1991); ELIZABETH LAPOVSKY KENNEDY & MADELINE DAVIS, BOOTS OF LEATHER, SLIPPERS OF GOLD: THE HISTORY OF A LESBIAN COMMUNITY (1993); LAMBDA LEGAL DEF. & EDU. FUND, NATIONAL OVERVIEW OF JURISDICTIONS AND COMPANIES THAT RECOGNIZE AND/OR PROVIDE BENEFITS TO DOMESTIC PARTNERS OF EMPLOYEES (1996); LESBIANS, GAY MEN AND THE LAW (William Rubenstein ed. 1993); ERIC MARCUS, MAKING HISTORY: THE STRUGGLE FOR GAY AND LESBIAN EQUAL RIGHTS, 1945–1990 (1992); RICHARD MOHR, A MORE PERFECT UNION: WHY STRAIGHT AMERICA MUST STAND UP FOR GAY RIGHTS (1994); LESLIE MORAN, THE HOMOSEXUAL(ITY) OF LAW (1996); MICHAEL NAVA & ROBERT NAWIDOFF, CREATED EQUAL: WHY GAY RIGHTS REALLY MATTER TO AMERICA (1994); GABRIEL NUGENT, EMPLOYMENT DISCRIMINATION BASED ON SEXUAL ORIENTATION (1998); SUSAN PHARR, HOMOPHOBIA: A WEAPON OF SEXISM (1988); RICHARD POSNER, SEX AND REASON 29, 101–08, 291–309 (1992); PREVENTING HETEROSEXISM AND HOMOPHOBIA (Esther Rothblum & Lynne Bond eds. 1996); RUTHANN ROBSON, LESBIAN (OUT)LAW: SURVIVAL UNDER THE RULE OF LAW (1992); EVE KOSOFSKY SEDGWICK, EPISTEMOLOGY OF THE CLOSET (1990); SEXUAL ORIENTATION AND HUMAN RIGHTS IN AMERICAN RELIGIOUS DISCOURSE (Saul Olyan & Martha Nussbaum eds. 1998); STIGMA AND SEXUAL ORIENTATION—UNDERSTANDING PREJUDICE AGAINST LESBIANS, GAY MEN AND BISEXUALS (Gregory Herek ed. 1998); CARL STYCHIN, LAW'S DESIRE: SEXUALITY AND THE LIMITS OF JUSTICE (1995); ANDREW SULLIVAN, VIRTUALLY NORMAL: AN ARGUMENT ABOUT HOMOSEXUALITY (1995); THE LIBERATION DEBATE: RIGHTS AT ISSUE (Michael Leahy & Dan Cohn-Sherbok eds. 1996); URVASHI VAID, VIRTUAL EQUALITY (1995); Kelli Kristine Armstrong, *The Silent Minority within a Minority: Focusing on the Needs of Gay Youth in Our Public Schools,* 24 GOLDEN GATE L. REV. 67 (1994); Christine Denys, *Homosexuality: A Non-Issue in Community Law?,* 24 EUR. L. REV. 419 (1999); Pierre De Vos, *On the Legal Construction of Gay and Lesbian Identity and South Africa's Transitional Constitution,* 12 S. AFR. J. HUMAN RTS. 265 (1996); William Eskridge, *Galegal Narratives,* 46 STAN. L. REV. 607 (1994); Joel Jay Finer, *Gay and Lesbian Applicants to the Bar: Even Lord Devlin Could Not Defend Exclusion, circa 2000,* 10 COLUM. J. GENDER & L. 231 (2001); Credence Fogo, *Cabining Freedom: A Comparative Study of Lesbian and Gay Rights in the United States and Canada,* 6 CARDOZO J. INT'L & COMP. L. 425 (1998); Robin Ingli, *Gays in the Military: A Policy Analysis of "Don't Ask, Don't Tell" and the Solomon Amendment,* 20 HAMLINE J. PUB. POL'Y & L. 89 (1997); Jeffrey Keller, *On Becoming a Fag,* 58 SASKATCHEWAN L. REV. 191 (1994); Christopher Kendall, *"Real Dominant, Real Fun!": Gay Male Pornography and the Pursuit of Masculinity,* 57 SASKATCHEWAN L. REV. 21 (1993); Andrew Koppelman, *Why Discrimination against Lesbians and Gay Men Is Sex Discrimination,* 69 NYU L. REV. 197 (1994); Astrid Mattijssen & Charlene Smith, *Dutch Treats: The Lessons the U.S. Can Learn from How the Netherlands Protects Lesbians & Gays,* 4 AM. U. J. GENDER & L. 303 (1996); Raymond Psonak, Note, *"Don't Ask, Don't Tell, Don't Discharge," at Least in Europe: A Comparison of the Policies on Homosexuals in the Military in the United States and Europe after Grady v. United Kingdom,* 33 CONN. L. REV. 337 (2000); Alexandra Purvis & Joseph Castellino, *A History of Homosexual Law Reform in Tasmania,* 16 U. TASMANIA L. REV. 13 (1997); Symposium, *Gay Identity,* 12 S. AFR. J. HUMAN RTS. 265 (1996); Symposium, *Re-Orienting Law and Sexuality,* 48 CLEVE. ST. L. REV. 1 (2000); Charles Trueheart, *Toronto Teacher Stirs Freedom Debate: Homosexual Teacher Suspended after Revealing Work as Prostitute,* WASH. POST, Dec. 11, 1995, at A20; James Wilets, *International Human Rights Law and Sexual Orientation,* 18 HASTINGS INT'L & COMP. L. REV. 1 (1994).

See also RUTH COLKER, HYBRID: BISEXUALS, MULTIRACIALS, AND OTHER MISFITS UNDER AMERICAN LAW (1996); Mary Anne Case, *Disaggregating Gender from Sex and Sexual Orientation: The Effeminate Man in the Law and Feminist Jurisprudence,* 105 YALE L.J. 1 (1995); Henry Finley, *Legal Recognition of Transsexuals in Australia,* 12 J. CONTEMP. HEALTH L. & POL'Y 503 (1996); Laura Gans, *Inverts, Perverts, and Converts: Sexual Orientation Conversion Therapy and Liability,* 8 PUB. INT. L.J. 219 (1999); Symposium, *"Family" and the Political Landscape for Lesbian, Gay, Bisexual and Transgender People (LGBT),* 64 ALB. L. REV. 853 (2001); Kenji Yoshino, *The Epistemic Contract of Bisexual Erasure,* 52 STAN. L. REV. 353 (2000)

288. *See, e.g., Midnight Cowboy* (1969); *The Boys in the Band* (1970); *Sunday, Bloody Sunday* (1971). *See generally* Marc Fajer, *Can Two Real Men Eat Quiche Together? Storytelling, Gender-Role Stereotyping, and Legal Protection for Lesbians and Gay Men,* 46 U. MIAMI L. REV. 511 (1992).

and public sympathy for, those suffering from AIDS—which in western countries initially largely afflicted gay men.[289]

A particularly serious form of discrimination was the unwillingness of courts to award custody to a homosexual parent against the wishes of a heterosexual former spouse or objecting grandparents.[290] Again, one of the first widely seen sympathetic portrayals of such a situation oc-

---

289. *See generally* RANDY SHILTS, AND THE BAND PLAYED ON: POLITICS, PEOPLE, AND THE AIDS EPIDEMIC (1987) (documenting the history of the AIDS epidemic and the dramatic lack of attention paid to it by society and government when it appeared that only gay men were being afflicted); David L. Chambers, *Gay Men, AIDS, and the Code of the Condom,* 29 HARV. C.R.-C.L. L. REV. 353 (1993). *See also* Bruce Lambert, *In Shift, Gay Men's Health Group Endorses Testing for AIDS Virus,* N.Y. TIMES, Aug. 16, 1987, at Al; William N. Eskridge, Jr., *Gadamer/Statutory Interpretation,* 90 COLUM. L. REV. 609, 677–78 (1990).

290. Hembree v. Hembree, 660 So. 2d 1342 (Ala. Ct. Civ. App. 1995) (awarding custody to a lesbian mother when challenged by the paternal grandparents); S.N.E. v. R.L.B., 699 P.2d 875 (Alaska 1985) (lesbianism of the mother is a factor to be considered in deciding custody); Thigpen v. Carpenter, 730 S.W.2d 510 (Ark. 1987) (denying custody to a lesbian mother); In re Marriage of Birdsall, 243 Cal. Rptr. 287 (Ct. App. 1988) (lesbianism of mother a factor to be considered in deciding custody), *rev. denied*; In re Marriage of Diehl, 582 N.E.2d 281 (Ill. 1991) (denying custody to a lesbian mother), *appeal denied,* 591 N.E.2d 20 (Ill. 1992); In re Marriage of Williams, 563 N.E.2d 1195 (Ill. 1990) (same); Lundin v. Lundin, 563 So.2d 1273 (La. Ct. App. 1990) (awarding custody to a lesbian mother so long as she did not live with her lover); Doe v. Doe, 452 N.E.2d 293 (Mass. 1983) (lesbianism of the mother is not a harm to the child); McGuffin v. Overton, 542 N.W.2d 288 (Mich. Ct. App. 1995) (*per curiam*) (denying custody to the former lesbian life-partner of the mother when the mother had designated the life-partner as guardian in her will, awarding custody to a father who had no on-going relationship with the child and was in arrears on child support), *certi denied,* 546 N.W.2d 256 (Mich. 1996); White v. Thompson, 569 So.2d 1181 (Miss. 1990) (awarding custody of the children of a lesbian parent to the paternal grandparents); T.C.H. v. R.M.H., 784 S.W.2d 281 (Mo. Ct. App. 1989) (removing children from the custody of a lesbian parent); J.P. v. P.W., 772 S.W.2d 786 (Mo. Ct. App. 1989) (requiring noncustodial father's lover—and any other male—to be absent during children's visits); S.E.G. v. R.A.G., 735 S.W.2d 164 (Mo. Ct. App. 1987) (denying custody to a lesbian mother); M.P. v. S.P., 404 A.2d 1256 (N.J. 1979) (lesbianism of the mother is not a harm to the child); In re Jacob, 660 N.E.2d 397 (N.Y. 1995) (approving adoption by lesbian mother's life partner); Guinan v. Guinan, 477 N.Y.S.2d 830 (App. Div. 1984) (lesbianism of the mother is not a harm to the child); Newsome v. Newsome, 256 S.E.2d 849 (N.C. Ct. App. 1979) (removing child from the custody of her lesbian mother and ordering that the mother's life-partner not be present during visits); Damron v. Damron, 670 N.W.2d 871 (N.D. 2003) (overruling an award of custody to the heterosexual father because of social disapproval of the lesbianism of the mother); M.J.P. v. J.G.P., 640 P.2d 966 (Okla. 1982) (same); A. v. A., 514 P.2d 358 (Ore. Ct. App. 1973) (granting custody of a gay father on condition that no other man live in the family house); In re Breisch, 434 A.2d 815 (Pa. 1981) (removing a child from the custody of a lesbian mother); Stronman v. Williams, 353 S.E.2d 704 (S.C. 1987) (lesbianism of the mother is not a harm to the child); Chicoine v. Chicoine, 479 N.W.2d 891 (S.D. 1992) (denying visitation rights to a lesbian mother); Bottoms v. Bottoms, 457 S.E.2d 102 (Va. 1995) (awarding custody to the paternal grandmother over the lesbian mother); Roe v. Roe, 324 S.E.2d 691 (Va. 1985) (denying custody to a gay father); Doe v. Doe, 284 S.E.2d 799 (Va. 1981) (upholding parental rights for a lesbian mother); Salgueiroda da Silva Mouta v. Portugal, Application No. 323290/96, available at http://www.echr.coe.int/Eng/Judgments.htm (finding a violation of the European Convention of Human Rights when a court denied custody to a homosexual father because he was living with a male partner). *See also* L. v. D., 630 S.W.2d 240 (Mo. Ct. App. 1982) (forbidding a woman from seeing children during their visits with her lesbian life-partner); In re Adoption of Charles B., 552 N.E.2d 884 (Ohio 1990) (allowing adoption of a boy by a gay man).

*See generally* AMERICAN PSCYCH. ASS'N, LESBIAN AND GAY PARENTING: A SOURCEBOOK FOR PSYCHOLOGISTS (1994); GAY AND LESBIAN PARENTS (Ferderick Bozett ed. 1987); HOMOSEXUALITY AND FAMILY RELATIONSHIPS (Frank Bozett & Marvin Sussman eds. 1990); APRIL MARTIN, THE LESBIAN AND GAY PARENTING HANDBOOK (1993); POLITICS OF THE HEART: A LESBIAN PARENTING ANTHOLOGY (Sandra Pollack & Jeanne Vaughn eds. 1987); Carlos Ball & Janice Farrell Pea, *Warring with Wardle: Morality, Social Science, and Gay and Lesbian Parents,* 1998 U. ILL. L. REV. 253; Phillip Belcastro *et al., A Review of Date Based Studies Addressing the Effects of Homosexual Parenting on Children's Sexual and Social Functioning,* 20 J. DIVORCE & REMARRIAGE 105 (1993); Nanette Gartrell *et al., The National Lesbian Family Study,* 66 AM. J. ORTHOPSYCHIATRY 272 (1996); Gollombok *et al., supra* note 274; Green *et al., supra* note 273; Ghazala Afzal Javaid, *The Children of Homosexual and Heterosexual Single Mothers,* 23 CHILD PSYCHIATRY & HUMAN DEV. 235 (1993); Katheryn Katz, *Majoritarian Morality and Parental Rights,* 52 ALB. L. REV. 405 (1988); M.B. King & P. Pattison, *Homosexuality and Parenthood,* 303 BRIT. MED. J. 295 (1991); Cynthia McNeely, *Lagging Behind the Times: Parenthood, Custody, and Gen-*

curred in *Soap*. "Jody Dallas," Billy Crystal's character, was presented from 1979 to 1981 as raising his illegitimate daughter for nearly a year after she was abandoned by her mother, only to see the mother demand the child back as soon as she found a more "masculine" boyfriend. The producers of *Soap* backed off from their portrayal of the problem, however, by having "Jody" discover that he was in fact attracted to women and suddenly unsure about his attraction to men.

Homosexual couples soon began to demand the privileges and responsibilities traditionally available only to married heterosexuals.[291] (Only a few commentators were willing to mention

---

*der Bias in the Family Court*, 25 FLA. ST. U. L. REV. 891 (1998); Ann O'Connell, *Voices from the Heart: The Developmental Impact of a Mother's Lesbianism of Her Adolescent Children*, 63 SMITH C. STUD. SOC. WORK 281 (1993); Amy Ronner, *Bottoms v. Bottoms: The Lesbian Mother and the Judicial Perpetuation of Damaging Stereotypes*, 7 YALE J. L. & FEMINISM 341 (1995); Douglas Steinberg, *Bottoms v. Bottoms: A Comment*, 1 WM. & MARY J. WOMEN & L. 257 (1994); Peter Nash Swisher & Nancy Douglas Cook, *Bottoms v. Bottoms: In Whose Best Interest? Analysis of a Lesbian Mother Child Custody Dispute*, 34 U. LOUISVILLE J. FAM. L. 843 (1996).

291. Shahar v. Bowers, 114 F.3d 1097 (11th Cir. 1997) (upholding the dismissal of a deputy [state] Attorney General against a claim of sex-based discrimination because she, as a lesbian, would create a "bad appearance" for the state and suffer a conflict of interest in enforcement of the state's sodomy laws), *cert. denied*, 522 U.S. 1049 (1998); Foray v. Bell Atlantic, 56 F. Supp. 2d 327 (S.D.N.Y. 1999) (upholding as nondiscriminatory a benefits policy that treated married couples and unmarried homosexual couples identically, but denied benefits to an unmarried heterosexual couple); *In re* Appeal in Pima Cnty. Juvenile Action B-10489, 727 P.2d 830 (Ariz. Ct. App. 1986) (denying adoption to homosexual couple); Whorton v. Dillingham, 248 Cal. Rptr. 405 (Ct. App. 1988) (allowing suit on a cohabitation agreement between a gay couple); Crooke v. Gilden, 414 S.E.2d 645 (Ga. 1992) (allowing suit on a cohabitation agreement between a gay couple); *In re* Estate of Gardner, 42 P.3d 120 (Kan.) (ordering a trial on whether to recognize a marriage involving a post-operative transsexual), *cert. denied*, 537 U.S. 825 (2002); Braschi v. Stahl Assoc., 543 N.E.2d 49 (N.Y. 1989) (finding the life-partner of a gay man to be "family" under a rent control statute); *In re* Adoption of Robert Paul P., 471 N.E.2d 424 (N.Y. 1984) (refusing to allow a man to adopt another adult man in order to formalize their gay relationship); Littleton v. Prange, 9 S.W.3d 223 (Tex. Ct. App. 1999), *writ denied* (barring marriage between a man and a transsexual woman—*i.e.*, a former man now become woman), *cert. denied*, 531 U.S. 872 (2000). *See also In re* Adoption of Swanson, 623 A.2d 1095 (Del. 1993) (allowing a man to adopt another adult man in order to formalize their gay relationship); *In re* Adoption of Charles B., 552 N.E.2d 884 (Ohio 1990) (allowing adoption of a boy by a gay man).

*See also* Mark Hansen, *Bolstering Benefits: Houston Law Firm's Decision to Offer Insurance to Domestic Partners May Spark a Trend*, ABA J., Jan. 1998, at 32. *See generally* WILLIAM ESKRIDGE, JR., THE CASE FOR SAME SEX MARRIAGE (1996); LESBIAN AND GAY MARRIAGE: PRIVATE COMMITMENTS, PUBLIC CEREMONIES (Suzanne Sherman ed. 1992); ON THE ROAD TO SAME-SEX MARRIAGE: A SUPPORTIVE GUIDE TO PSYCHOLOGICAL, POLITICAL, AND LEGAL ISSUES (Robert Cabaj & David Purcell eds. 19998); SAME-SEX MARRIAGE: THE MORAL AND LEGAL DEBATE (Robert Baird & Stuart Rosenbaum eds. 1997); SAME-SEX MARRIAGE: PRO AND CON (Andrew Sullivan ed. 1997); SEX, PREFERENCE, AND FAMILY: ESSAYS ON LAW AND NATURE (David Estlund & Martha Nussbaum eds. 1996); MARK STRASSER, LEGALLY WED: SAME-SEX MARRIAGE AND THE CONSTITUTION (1997); Mary Becker, *Family Law in the Secular State and Restrictions on Same-Sex Marriage: Two Are Better than One*, 2001 U. ILL. L. REV. 1; Darren Bush, *Moving to the Left by Moving to the Right: A Law & Economics Defense of Same-Sex Marriage*, 22 WOMEN'S RTS. L. RPTR. 115 (2001); Patricia Cain, *Taxing Lesbians*, 6 S. CAL. REV. L. & WOMEN'S STUD. 471 (1997); Dana Canedy, *Miami Facing New Challenge on Gay Rights*, N.Y. TIMES, Sept. 5, 2002, at A18; Mary Coombs, *Sexual Dis-Orientation: Transgendered People and Same-Sex Marriage*, 8 UCLA WOMEN'S L.J. 219 (1998); John Culhane, *A "Clanging Silence": Same-Sex Couples and Tort Law*, 89 KY. L.J. 911 (2001); Linda Echols, *The Marriage Mirage: The Personal and Social Identity Implications of Same-Gender Matrimony*, 5 MICH. J. GENDER & L. 353 (1999); Rhoda Howard-Hassman, *Gay Rights and the Right to a Family: Conflicts between Liberal and Illiberal Belief Systems*, 23 HUM. RTS. Q. 73 (2001); Mae Kuykendall, *Resistance to Same-Sex Marriage as a Story about Language: Linguistic Failure and the Priority of a Living Language*, 34 HARV. C.R.-C.L. L. REV. 385 (1999); Morrissey, *supra* note 274, at 38–40; Christopher Nixon, *Should Congress Revise the Tax Code to Extend the Same Tax Benefits to Same-Sex Couples as Are Currently Granted to Married Couples?: An Analysis in Light of Horizontal Equity*, 23 S. ILL. U. L.J. 41 (1998); Ruthann Robson, *Mostly Monogamous Moms?: An Essay on the Future of Lesbian Legal Theories and Reforms*, 17 N.Y. L. SCH. J. HUM. RTS. 703 (2000); Katrina Rose, *The Transexual and the Damage Done: The Fourth Court of Appeals Opens the Pandora's Box by Closing the Door on Transsexuals' Right to Marry*, 9 LAW & SEXUALITY 1 (1999); Edward Sadtler, *A Right to Same-Sex Marriage under International Law: Can It Be Vindicated in the United States?*, 40 VA. J. INT'L L. 405 (1999); Maura Strassberg, *Distinctions of Form or Substance: Monogamy, Polygamy, and Same-Sex Marriage*, 75

the oddity that while so many married couples wanted out of marriage, homosexuals were fighting strongly in order to gain the right to enter into marriage.[292]) Finally, some homosexual couples began to give birth to children by having one of two lesbian partners become pregnant through artificial insemination (or perhaps not so artificial insemination), or through two gay partners entering into "surrogacy" arrangements. In late twentieth century America, homosexual couples having babies became so common place that a law professor coined a new term to describe the resulting children—"gaybies."[293] This in turn led to custody fights between lesbian former life-partners over visitation rights after their relationship ended.[294]

---

N.C. L. Rev. 1502 (1997); Symposium, *Same-Sex Marriage: The Debate in Hawaii and the Nation*, 22 U. Haw. L. Rev. 1 (2000); Donna Thompson-Schneider, *The Arc of History: Or, the Resurrection of Feminism's Sameness/Difference Dichotomy in the Gay and Lesbian Marriage Debate*, 7 Law & Sexuality 1 (1997); Linda Waite, *Social Science Finds: "Marriage Matters,"* 6 Responsive Community no. 3, at 26 (Summer 1996).

292. *See, e.g.,* Michael Kinsley, *Abolish Marriage*, Wash. Post, July 3, 2003, at A23 ("[I]n the United States we are about to find ourselves in a strange situation where the principal demand of a liberation movement is to be included in the red tape of a government bureaucracy."). *See also* Caitlin Flanagan, *The Wifely Duty: Marriage Used to Provide Access to Sex. Now It Provides Access to Celibacy*, Atlantic Monthly, Jan./Feb. 2003, at 171; Clifford Krauss, *Free to Marry, Canada's Gays Say, "Do I?,"* N.Y. Times, Aug. 31, 2003, § 1, at 1.

293. Marla Hollandsworth, *Gay Men Creating Families through Surrogate Arrangements: A Paradigm for Reproductive Freedom*, 3 Am. U. J. Gender & L. 183, 186 (1995). *See also* Lofton v. Kearney, 157 F. Supp. 2d 1372 (S.D. Fla. 2001) (upholding the constitutionality of Florida's ban on gay adoptions); *In re* N.M.D., 662 A.2d 837 (D.C. Ct. App. 1995) (allowing adoption by the lesbian life-partner of the mother); Adoption of Tammy, 619 N.E.2d 315 (Mass. 1993) (same); *In re* Adoption of Luke, 640 N.W.2d 374 (Neb. 2002) (barring adoption by the lesbian life-partner of the mother); *In re* Adoption of Two Children, 666 A.2d 535 (N.J. Super. 1995) (allowing adoption by the lesbian life-partner of the mother); *In re* Jacob, 660 N.E.2d 397 (N.Y. 1995) (approving adoption by lesbian mother's life partner); Thomas S. v. Robin Y., 618 N.Y.S.2d 356 (App. Div. 1994) (a father—donor for artificial insemination, known to the daughter as the father—is entitled to visitation rights to his daughter who is being raised by the mother and her lesbian life partner), *appeal denied*, 655 N.E.2d 708 (N.Y. 1995); *In re* Bonfield, 780 N.E.2d 241 (Ohio 2002) (allowing a court to declare the legal rights of lesbian partner of biological mother); *In re* Adoption of B.L.V.B., 628 A.2d 1271 (Vt. 1993) (approving adoption by lesbian mother's life partner); *In re* Angel Lace M., 516 N.W.2d 678 (Wis. 1994) (denying adoption to the lesbian life-partner of the mother and rejecting her claim of denial of due process); *In re* Interest of Z.J.H., 471 N.W.2d 202 (Wis. 1991) (holding a co-parenting contract between lesbian life-partners to be void). *See also* Jane Brody, *Gay Families Flourish as Acceptance Grows*, N.Y. Times, July 1, 2003, at F7; Frank Bruni, *A Small-but-Growing Sorority Is Giving Birth to Children for Gay Men*, N.Y. Times, June 25, 1998, at A12; Mary Jane Fine, *The Lesbian Couple Becomes a Family*, Phila. Inquirer, Apr. 5, 1987, at 1A; Susan FitzGerald, *Adoption Rights for Partners Backed: A Leading Medical Group Says Children Stand to Gain Legal Protection. Family Planning Advocates Question Same-Sex Parenting*, Phila. Inquirer, Feb. 4, 2002, at A1; Erica Goode, *Group Backs Gays Who Seek to Adopt a Partner's Child*, N.Y. Times, Feb. 4, 2002, at A1; *Largest Pediatrician Group Backs Homosexual Adoption*, Wash. Post, Feb. 4, 2002, at A1.

*See generally* Cheri Pies, Considering Parenthood: A Workbook for Lesbians (1993); Stacey, *supra* note 274, at 110; Susan Becker, *Second-Parent Adoption by Same-Sex Couples in Ohio: Unsettled and Unsettling Law*, 48 Cleve. St. L. Rev. 101 (2000); Fred Bernstein, *This Child Does Have Two Mothers…And a Sperm Donor with Visitation*, 22 NYU Rev. L. & Soc. Change 1 (1996); Patricia Falk, *Second-Parent Adoption*, 48 Cleve. St. L. Rev. 93 (2000); Fogo, *supra* note 287, at 440–42; Theresa Glennon, *Binding the Family Ties: A Child Advocacy Perspective on Second-Parent Adoptions*, 7 Temple Pol. & Civ. Rts. L. Rev. 255 (1998); Melanie Jacobs, *Micah Has One Mommy and One Legal Stranger: Adjudicating Maternity for Nonbiological Lesbian Coparents*, 50 Buff. L. Rev. 341 (2002); Ryiah Lilith, *The G.I.F.T. of Two Biological and Legal Mothers*, 9 Am. U. J. Gender, Soc. Pol'y, & L. 207 (2001); David Orentlicher, *Beyond Cloning: Expanding Reproductive Options for Same-Sex Couples*, 66 Brook. L. Rev. 651 (2000); Lewis Silverman, *Suffer the Little Children: Justifying Same-Sex Marriage from the Perspective of a Child of the Union*, 102 W. Va. L. Rev. 411 (1999); Kyle Velte, *Towards Constitutional Recognition of the Lesbian-Parented Family*, 26 NYU L. Rev. L. & Soc. Change 245 (2000); Taya Williams, *Committed Partnership: The Legal Status of Committed Partnerships and Their Children*, 13 J. Suffolk Acad. L. 221 (1999); Lynn Wardle, *The Potential Impact of Homosexual Parenting on Children*, 1997 U. Ill. L. Rev. 833; Taya Williams, *Committed Partnership: The Legal Status of Committed Partnerships and Their Children*, 13 J. Suffolk Acad. L. 221 (1999);.

294. Nancy S. v. Michelle G., 279 Cal. Rptr. 212 (Ct. App. 1991) (denying visitation rights to lesbian life-partner of the child's mother); Curiale v. Reagan, 272 Cal. Rptr. 520 (Ct. App. 1990) (same); Music v. Rachford, 654 So. 2d 1234 (Fla. Ct. App. 1995) (*per curiam*) (same); A.C. v. C.B., 829 P.2d 660 (N.M. Ct. App.)

The rise of the managerial class is a global phenomenon, with global consequences. Even in relatively conservative societies as well as liberal societies across the planet, there is pressure to recognize homosexual rights.[295] Statutes establishing the institution of a "civil union" as an ana-

---

(recognizing an agreement between a lesbian couple to share the raising of a child as the most important factor in a custody dispute), *cert. denied,* 827 P.2d 837 (N.M. 1992); Allison D. v. Virginia M., 572 N.E.2d 27 (N.Y. 1991) (denying visitation rights to a former lesbian life-partner of the child's mother); L.S.K. v. H.A.N., 813 A.2d 872 (Pa. Super. Ct. 2002) (former same-sex partner who encourage her partner to bear children using artificial insemination during their marriage and has sought shared custody of the children is equitable estopped from denying an obligation to support the children); *In re* Custody of H.S.H.-K., 533 N.W.2d 419 (Wis.) (awarding visitation rights to a former lesbian life-partner of the mother), *cert. denied,* 516 U.S. 975 (1995). *See also Transsexual's Mate Gives up Custody Fight,* PHILA. INQUIRER, June 6, 1981, at 7A. *See generally* Mary Coombs, *Insiders and Outsiders: What the American Law Institute Has Done for Gay and Lesbian Families,* 8 DUKE J. GENDER & L. 87 (2001); Emily Doskow, *The Second Parent Trap: Parenting for Same-Sex Couples in a Brave New World,* 20 J. JUVENILE L. 1 (1999); Kathy Graham, *How the ALI Child Custody Principles Help Eliminate Gender and Sexual Orientation Bias from Child Custody Determinations,* 8 DUKE J. GENDER & L. 323 (2001); Gregory, *supra* note 274, at 355–61; Eileen Huff, *The Children of Homosexual Parents: The Voices the Courts Have Yet to Hear,* 9 AM. U. J. GENDER, SOC. POL'Y & L. 695 (2001); Polikoff, *supra* note 291; Nancy Polikoff, *The Impact of* Troxel v. Granville *on Lesbian and Gay Parents,* 32 RUTGERS L.J. 825 (2001); Williams, *supra* note 291.

295. *See* A.D.T. v. United Kingdom, Application No. 35765/97 (Eur. Ct. Hum. Rts. July 31, 2000), http://www.echr.coe.int/Eng/Judgments.htm (finding that criminalizing homosexual conduct among adults if more than two persons are involved violates the right of privacy in the *European Convention on Human Rights*); Smith v. United Kingdom, Application No. 33985/96 (Eur. Ct. Hum. Rts. Sept. 27, 1999), available at http://www.echr.coe.int/Eng/Judgments/htm (finding that to discharge military personnel based on their homosexuality violates the right of privacy in the *European Convention for the Protection of Human Rights and Fundamental Freedoms,* art. 8, opened for signature Nov. 4, 1950, 213 UNTS 222); Lustig-Prean v. United Kingdom, Application No. 31417/96 (Eur. Ct. Hum. Rts. Sept. 27, 1999), available at http://www.echr.coe.int/eng/Judgments.htm (same); Sheffield v. United Kingdom, [1998] 3 F.C.R. 141 (Eur. Ct. H.R.) (finding that member states are not obliged under the European Convention on Human Rights to recognize the "post-operative gender" of transsexuals); EGALE Canada v. Canada (A.G.), 255 D.L.R.4th 472 (B.C. C.A. 2003) (barring homosexual marriage violates the Canadian Charter of Rights and Freedom); Halpern v. Canada (A.G.), 225 D.L.R.4th 529 (Ont. C.A. 2003) (same); Hendricks c. Québec (P.G.), J.E. 2003–466 (Que. 2003) (same); Grant v. South-West Trains, Ltd., [1998] All. E.R. 193 (E.C.) (the Treaty of Rome's prohibition of pay discrimination does not reach differences in benefits between "legal spouses" and same-sex partners); Tinsley v. Milligan, [1993] 3 All E.R. 65 (H.L.) (applying a "constructive trust" to the intermingled assets of two lesbians); Harrogate Borough Council v. Simpson, [1986] 16 FAM. L. REP. 359 (C.A.) (deny ing legal recognition to a homosexual relationship); Attorney-General for Ontario v. M. & H., 171 D.L.R.4th 577 (Can. 1999) (finding a statute that denies the right a share of joint property and to spousal support after the break-up of a long-term homosexual relationship to be a denial of equal protection when those rights are extended to heterosexual couples whether married or not); Sorochan v. Sorochan, 29 D.L.R.4th 1 (Can. 1986) (same); Pettkus v. Becker, 117 D.L.R.3rd 257 (Can. 1980) (finding a "constructive trust" for heterosexual cohabitants); Vriend v. Alberta, 132 D.L.R. 4th 595 (Alberta 1996) (sexual orientation is not a prohibited ground of discrimination in the Individual Rights Protection Act); Everson v. Rich, 53 D.L.R.4th 470 (Saskatachewan 1988) (declining to find a "constructive trust" for heterosexual cohabitants, but awarding damages for the services provided in the relationship); Gillies v. Keogh, [1989] 2 N.Z. L.R. 327 (declining to find a "constructive trust" for heterosexual cohabitants); Dec. 14/1995/III. 13/AB Res. (Hungarian Const'l Ct. 1995) (recognizing "domestic partnerships" for homosexual couples); National Coalition for Gay & Lesbian Equality v. Minister of Home Aff., CCT 10/99 (S. Afr. Const'l Ct. 1999) available at http://www.law.wilts.ac.za/archive.html (finding unconstitutional provisions facilitating the immigration of spouses but not extending the same right to same-sex partners), . *See also* Corbett v. Corbett, [1970] 2 All E.R. 33 (Dec. 9, 1969) (refusing to recognize a purported marriage between a man and a "transsexual"—a man converted into a woman by surgery).

*See generally* Deneen Brown, *Canada's Parliament Endorses Gay Marriage: Narrow Defeat on Traditional Matrimony Underscores National Divide,* WASH. POST, Sept. 17, 2003, at A23 (the vote was 137–132); Deneen Brown, *Hundreds of Gay Couples Make Their Way to Ontario to Say "I Do,"* WASH. POST, June 22, 2003, at A15; Tom Cohen, *Dozens in Canada Follow Gay Couple's Lead: Same-Sex Partners Apply for Marriage Licenses after Landmark Court Ruling,* WASH. POST, June 12, 2003, at A25; William Eskridge, jr., *Comparative Law and the*

logue to marriage were enacted in several countries.[296] Hawaii (in 1997), California (in 1999), and Vermont (in 2000) all enacted statutes recognizing civil unions.[297] In Hawaii and Vermont,

---

*Same-Sex Marriage Debate: A Step-by-Step Approach toward State Recognition,* 31 McGeorge L. Rev. 641 (2000); Fogo, *supra* note 287; Forum, *Same Sex Unions and the Law,* 41 U. Alberta L. Rev. 569–655 (2003); *Judges Come out for Gays,* The Economist, June 21, 2003, at 50; Clifford Krauss, *Canada's Push to Legalize Gay Marriages Draws Bishops' Ire,* N.Y. Times, Aug. 10, 2003, at A7; Clifford Krauss, *Canadian Leaders Agree to Propose Gay Marriage Law,* N.Y. Times, June 18, 2003, at A1; Clifford Krauss, *Canadian Legislators Narrowly Reject Move against Gay Unions,* N.Y. Times, Sept. 17, 2003, at A9; Clifford Krauss, *Gay Wedding Bells. Why No Hubbub? It's Canada,* N.Y. Times, Sept. 24, 2003, at A4; Colin McClelland, *Same-Sex Marriage Endorsed in Canada,* Wash. Post, June 18, 2003, at A22; Cynthia Sgalla McClure, Note, *A Case for Same-Sex Marriage: A Look at Changes around the Globe and in the United States, Including* Baker v. Vermont, 29 Cap. U.L. Rev. 783 (2002); Shannon O'Byrne & James McGinnis, Case Comment: Vriend v. Alberta: Plessy *Revisited: Lesbian and Gay Rights in the Province of Alberta,* 34 Albta. L. Rev. 892 (1996); Keith Richburg, *Dutch Legalize Same-Sex Marriages,* Wash. Post, Sept. 13, 2000, at A28; Keith Richburg, *Gay Marriage Becomes Routine for Dutch: Two Years after Enacting Law, up to 8 Percent of Weddings Are Same-Sex Unions,* Wash. Post, Sept. 23, 2003, at A20; *Same-Sex Dutch Couples Gain Marriage and Adoption Rights,* N.Y. Times, Dec. 20, 2000, at A8; Ravina Shamdasani, *Gay "Newlyweds" Threaten Legal Action,* S. China Morning Post, Oct. 6, 2003; Kurt Siehr, *Family Unions in Private International Law,* 50 Netherlands Int'l L. Rev. 419 (2003). *See also* Seth Mydans, *Men Marry, with and without a Church Blessing,* N.Y. Times, Sept. 9, 2003, at A4.

 296. *See* Fogo, *supra* note 287, at 436–40; Stephen Graham, *German Gays Embrace Union Law: Registry Grants Couples Benefits Akin to Marriage,* Chi. Trib., Aug. 2, 2001, at 8; Warren Hoge, *Britain Announces Proposal for Same-Sex Partnerships,* N.Y. Times, Dec. 7, 2002, at A8; Jon Jeter, *Using New Law, Buenos Aires Men Celebrate Civil Union,* Wash. Post, July 19, 2003, at A22; Linda Nielsen, *Family Rights and "Registered Partnership" in Denmark,* 4 Int'l J.L. & Fam. 297 (1990); Marianne Hojgaard Pedersen, *Denmark, Homosexual Marriages and New Rules Regarding Separation and Divorce,* 30 J. Fam. L. 289 (1991); Nancy Polikoff, *Recognizing Partners but Not Parents/Recognizing Parents but Not Partners: Gay and Lesbian Family Law in Europe and the United States,* 17 N.Y. L. Sch. J. Hum. Rts. 711 (2000).

 297. Haw. Rev. Stat. Ann. §§ 323-2, 560:2-102, 572C-1 to 572C-7 (Michie 1999); Cal. Fam. Code §§ 297, 298 (West Supp. 2002); Cal. Gov't Code §§ 22687 to 22877 (West Supp. 2002); Cal. Health & Safety Code § 1261 (West 2000); Vt. Stat. Ann. tit. 15, §§ 1202, 1301–6 (2001). *See generally* David Chambers, *Vermont Civil Unions: The Baker Case, Civil Unions, and the Recognition of Our Common Humanity: An Introduction and Speculation,* 25 Vt. L. Rev. 5 (2000); Craig Christensen, *If Not Marriage? On Securing Gay and Lesbian Family Values by a "Simulacrum of Marriage,"* 66 Fordham L. Rev. 1699 (1998); Barbara Cox, *But Why Not Marriage: An Essay on Vermont's Civil Unions Law, Same-Sex Marriage, and Separate But (Un)Equal,* 25 Vt. L. Rev. 113 (2000); David Cruz, *"Just Don't Call It Marriage": The First Amendment and Marriage as Expressive Resource,* 74 S. Cal. L. Rev. 925 (2001); William Duncan, *Domestic Partnership Laws in the United States: A Review and Critique,* 2001 BYU L. Rev. 961; Mary Ertman, *The ALI Principles' Approach to Domestic Partnership,* 8 Duke J. Gender & L. 107 (2001); Paula Ettelbrick, *Domestic Partnership, Civil Unions, or Marriage: One Size Does Not Fit All,* 64 Alb. L. Rev. 905 (2001); Christopher Hargis, *Queer Reasoning: Immigration Policy,* Baker v. State of Vermont, *and the (Non)Recognition of Same-Gender Relationships,* 10 Law & Sex. 211 (2001); Tonja Jacobi, *Same Sex Marriage in Vermont: Implications of Legislative Remand for the Judiciary's Role,* 26 Vt. L. Rev. 381 (2002); Greg Johnson, *Vermont Civil Unions: The New Language of Marriage,* 25 Vt. L. Rev. 15 (2000); Symposium, *Civil Unions in Vermont: Where to Go from Here?,* 11 Widener J. Pub. L. 361, 373–76 (2002). Courts in other states have thus far declined to recognize Vermont's civil unions, sometimes even without express statutory authorization of such a rejection. Rosengarten v. Downes, 802 A.2d 170 (Conn. Super. Ct. 2002).

 Less sweeping "domestic partnership" statutes were enacted in other states even before Vermont's. Alaska Stat. §§ 18.80.220 (prohibiting employers from discriminating based upon marital status), 47.24.016(a)(2) (allowing a domestic partner to be a surrogate decision maker for vulnerable adults) (LexisNexis 2002); Ariz. Rev. Stat. Ann. § 36-843(a)(6) (including domestic partners on the list of people who can donate the body parts of a deceased person), 36-3231A.4 (including domestic partners on the list of persons who can make health care decisions for an incapacitated person) (West 2003); Colo. R. Cir. Proc.. § 251.7 (the effect on domestic partners to be considered in deciding on probation) (West 2003); Conn. Gen. Stat. Ann. § 46b-215a (child support guidelines) (West Supp. 2003); D.C. Code Ann. §§ 3-413(a) (giving domestic partners the right to control the remains of a deceased person) (2003), 32-701, 32-705 (public employee benefits available to domestic partners) (2001), 47-1893.03(a)(15) (allowing the deduction of health insurance premiums for a domestic partner) (2002); Minn. Stat. Ann. § 145C-09(2) (implicitly recognizing the right of domestic partners to make health care decisions for an incapacitated person) (West Supp. 2003); Or. Rev. Stat. §§ 23.170

the legislatures acted only after the states' Supreme Courts declared the states' denial of the benefits of state sanctioned relationships to homosexuals to be a violation of the states' constitution.[298] The vote in the Vermont House of Representatives was only 77-69 despite the state Supreme Court's mandate, and that was achieved through some questionable tactics.[299] Courts, however, were careful to indicate that the states did not have to recognize the relationship as a marriage as such.[300] Courts in other states were authorized by Congress to decline to recognize same-sex marriages and civil unions, as many states have chosen to do so.[301] Indeed, popular op-

---

(public employee retirement benefits authorized domestic partners), 238.005(I) (excluding insurance premiums paid for a domestic partner of a employee from the employee's taxable salary or "other advantages") (2003); R.I. GEN. LAWS §§ 15-8-26 (authorizing an action to declare a mother and child relationship for a domestic partner), 36-12-1(3) (recognizing a domestic partner as a dependent for tax purposes) (Supp. 2003). *See generally* Lynn Wardle, *Counting the Costs of Civil Unions: Some Potential Detrimental Effects on Family Law*, 11 WIDENER J. PUB. L. 401, 411–15 (2002).

298. Baehr v. Lewin, 852 P.2d 44 (Haw. 1993), *dismissal after remand aff'd sub nom.* Baehr v. Miike, 950 P.2d 1254 (Haw. 1997) (the power of the state to define marriage confirmed by amendment to the state constitution in 1998); Baker v. State, 744 A.2d 864 (Vt. 1999). *See also* Tanner v. Oregon Health Sci. Univ., 971 P.2d 435 (Ore. Ct. App. 1998) (requiring the state to give benefits comparable to those of married couples to homosexual domestic partners). *See also* Anne Burton, *Gay Marriage—A Modern Proposal: Applying* Baehr v. Lewin *to the International Covenant on Civil and Political Rights*, 3 IND. GLOBAL LEGAL STUD. J. 177 (1995); David Orgon Coolidge & William Duncan, *Beyond* Baker: *The Case for a Vermont Marriage Amendment*, 25 VT. L. REV. 61 (2000); William Duncan & David Orgon Coolidge, *Marriage and Democracy in Oregon: The Meaning and Implications of* Tanner v. Oregon Health Sciences University, 36 WILLAMETTE L. REV. 503 (2000).

299. Brady v. Dean, 790 A.2d 428, 429–30 (Vt. 1999) (upholding the constitutionality of the Vermont civil union statute despite questionable voting tactics in the state House of Representatives).

300. *See* David Chambers, *Unmarried Partners and the Legacy of* Marvin v. Marvin: *For the Best of Friends and Lovers of All Sorts, A Status Other than Marriage*, 76 NOTRE DAME L. REV. 1347 (2001); *See also* Carey Goldberg, *Forced into Action on Gay Marriage, Vermont Finds Itself Deeply Divided*, N.Y. TIMES, Feb. 3, 2000, at A16; Carey Goldberg, *Vermont Gives Final Approval to Same-Sex Unions*, N.Y. TIMES, Apr. 26, 2000, at A14. *See generally* AMERICAN LAW INST., PRINCIPLES OF FAMILY DISSOLUTION: ANALYSIS AND RECOMMENDATIONS § 6.03(a), at 14–17 (recommending that courts retroactively recognize homosexual and heterosexual civil unions) (Tent. Draft no. 4, 2000).

301. *The Defense of Marriage Act*, 1 U.S.C. § 7, 28 U.S.C. § 1738C (2000) (authorizing states to decline to recognize homosexual marriages legal in other states); Burns v. Burns, 560 S.E.2d 47 (Ga. Ct. App. 2002), *state cert. denied*. For state statutes barring the recognition of same-sex relationships legal in other states, see ALASKA STAT. § 25.05.013 (LexisNexis 2002); ARIZ. REV. STAT. ANN. § 25-101(c) (West 2000); ARK. CODE ANN. § 9-11-107 (LexisNexis 2002); FLA. STAT. ANN. § 741.212 (West Supp. 2003); GA. CODE ANN. § 19-3-3.1 (1999); IDAHO CODE § 32-209 (1996); 750 ILL. COMP. STAT. ANN. 5/216 (West 1999); IND. CODE ANN. § 31-11-1-1 (West 1999); KAN. STAT. ANN. § 23-115 (Cumm. Supp. 2003); MICH. COMP. LAWS ANN. § 551-272 (West Supp. 2003); N.D. CENT CODE § 14-03-08; 23 PA. CONS. STAT. ANN. § 1704 (same) (West 2001); S.C. CODE ANN. § 20-1-15 (West Supp. 2003); TENN. CODE ANN. § 36-3-113 (2001); TEX. FAM. CODE ANN. § 2.001 (West 1998); UTAH CODE ANN. § 30-1-2(5) (Supp. 2003); VA. CODE ANN. § 20-45.2 (Michie 1995). *See generally* Paige Chabora, *Congress' Power under the Full Faith and Credit Clause and the Defense of Marriage Act of 1996*, 76 NEB. L. REV. 604 (1997); Barbara Cox, *Same-Sex Marriage and the Public Policy Exception in Choice-of-Law: Does It Really Exist?*, 16 QUINNIPIAC L. REV. 61 (1996); George Dent, jr., *The Defense of Traditional Marriage*, 15 J. LAW & POL. 581 (1999); Michael Kanotz, *For Better or for Worse: A Critical Analysis of Florida's Defense of Marriage Act*, 25 FLA. ST. U. L. REV. 439 (1998); Ken Kersch, *Full Faith and Credit for Same-Sex Marriages?*, 112 POL. SCI. Q. 117 (1997); Andrew Koppelman, *Same-Sex Marriage, Choice of Law, and Public Policy*, 76 TEX. L. REV. 921 (1998); Larry Kramer, *Same-Sex Marriage, Conflict of Laws, and the Un constitutional Public Policy Exception*, 106 YALE L.J. 1965 (1997); Kafahni Nkrumah, *The Defense of Marriage Act: Congress Re-Writes the Constitution to Pacify Its Fears*, 23 THURGOOD MARSHALL L. REV. 513 (1998); Barbara Robb, *The Constitutionality of the Defense of Marriage Act in the Wake of* Romer v. Evans, 32 N. ENG. L. REV. 263 (1997); Linda Silberman, *"Can the Island of Hawaii Bind the World?" A Comment on Same-Sex Marriage and Federalism Values*, 16 QUINNIPIAC L. REV. 191 (1996); Leslie Silverman, *Vermont Civil Unions, Full Faith and Credit, and Marital Status*, 89 KY. L.J. 1075 (2001); Wardle, *supra* note 297, at 421–24. *See also* Clifford Krauss, *Married Gay Canadian Couple Barred from U.S.*, N.Y. TIMES, Sept. 19, 2003, at A4. One New York court did recognize a Vermont same-sex civil union as conferring the status of a spouse under New York's wrongful death statute. Langan v. St. Vin-

position to recognition of civil unions or gay marriages actually declined after the Supreme Court declared criminal sodomy laws unconstitutional as applied to consenting adults.[302] Yet in 2003, the Massachusetts Supreme Judicial Court chose to decide that not to allow homosexuals to marry was an unconstitutional denial of equal protection of the laws of the state.[303]

In actuality, in many countries a majority those entering into civil unions were heterosexual couples rather than homosexual couples[304]—suggesting again a general eroding of traditional relationships. If civil unions quickly became something other than just a homosexual question, several high profile developments inescapably pushed the issue of homosexual rights front and center. Perhaps the development that received the greatest publicity was the elevation of an openly gay man to be the Episcopal Bishop of New Hampshire.[305] This proposal proved explosive, generating a real possibility of a schism in the American branch of the church and a threat of withdrawing recognition from the American branch by other Anglican denominations around the world.[306]

All of this was welcomed in certain circles of society as a refreshing departure from the past. In fact, some critics of older forms of interpersonal relationships would make "straight" (heterosexual) relationships the only suspect relationships.[307] Such extremes, of course, have not found

---

cent's Hospital, 765 N.Y.S.2d 411 (N.Y. Super. 2003). *But see In re* Goodale, 298 B.R. 886 (W.D. Wash. 2003) (same-sex partner does not qualify as a spouse under the Bankruptcy Code). *See also* Siehr, *supra* note 291.

302. Alan Cooperman, *Sodomy Ruling Fuels Battle over Gay Marriage,* WASH. POST, July 31, 2003, at A1 (referring to the decision in *Lawrence v. Texas,* 539 U.S. 558 (2003)).

303. Goodridge v. Department of Pub. Health, 798 A.2d 941 (Mass. 2003). *Contra:* Standhardt v. Superior Ct., 77 P.3d 451 (Ariz. Ct. App. 2003), *rev. denied.*

304. *See, e.g.,* Paul Lynd, *Domestic Partner Benefits Limited to Same-Sex Couples: Sex Discrimination under Title VII,* 6 WM. & MARY J. WOMEN & L. 561 (2000).

305. *See also* Alan Cooperman, *Episcopal Church Confirms Gay Bishop: Last-Minute Changes Rejected before 62-43 Vote,* WASH. POST, Aug. 6, 2003, at A1; Alan Cooperman, *Episcopal Debate on Gay Rights Is Polite, Passionate,* WASH. POST, Aug. 3, 2003, at A8; Monica Davey, *Gay Bishop Wins Episcopal Vote, Split Threatened,* N.Y. TIMES, Aug. 6, 2003, at A1; Jonathan Finer, *Episcopalians Consecrate First Openly Gay Bishop,* WASH. POST, Nov. 3, 2003, at A1; Laurie Goodstein, *New Hampshire Episcopalians Choose Gay Bishop, and Conflict,* N.Y. TIMES, June 8, 2003, § 1, at 1; Laurie Goodstein, *Openly Gay Man Is Made a Bishop,* N.Y. TIMES, Nov. 3, 2003, at A1. The Episcopal Church's compromise on same-sex marriage received notably less publicity than one might have expected, perhaps because of its overshadowing by the bishop question. Alan Cooperman, *Episcopal Church Ratifies Compromise on Gay Unions,* WASH. POST, Aug. 8, 2003, at A2; Monica Davey, *Episcopal Leaders Reject Proposal for Same-Sex Union Liturgy,* N.Y. TIMES, Aug. 7, 2003, at A20 Richard Morin & Alan Cooperman, *Majority against Blessing Gay Unions: 60% in Poll Oppose Episcopal Decision,* WASH. POST, Aug. 14, 2003, at A1.

306. *See, e.g.,* Alan Cooperman, *Activist Expects Episcopal Schism: Churches May Switch Bishops, Conservative Leader Says,* WASH. POST, Oct. 18, 2003, at A5; Alan Cooperman, *Anglican Conservatives Warn of "Realignment,"* WASH. POST, July 24, 2003, at A2; Alan Cooperman, *Church's Unity Is at Risk,* WASH. POST, July 30, 2003, at A4; Alan Cowell, *Archbishop of Canterbury Calls Meeting of Anglican Leaders over Gay Bishop in U.S.: Issue Prompts Debate World over,* N.Y. TIMES, Aug. 9, 2003, at A7; Davey, *supra* note 304; Glenn Frankel, *Anglican Head Seeks "Middle Way": Issue of Gay Bishop Is Test for Williams,* WASH. POST, Nov. 8, 2003, at A1; Glenn Frankel, *Gay Bishop Appointment Splits Anglican Church,* WASH. POST, June 29, 2003, at A19; Glenn Frankel, *Top Anglicans Warn against Plan to Install a Gay Bishop: Global Communion Could Break Apart, Leaders Fear,* WASH. POST, Oct. 17, 2003, at A1; Laurie Goodstein, *Anglican Leaders Work to Avoid Split over Gay U.S. Bishop,* N.Y. TIMES, Oct. 16, 2003, at A5; Laurie Goodstein, *Homosexuality Issue Threatens to Break Anglicanism in Two,* N.Y. TIMES, July 19, 2003, at A1; Marc Lacey, *African Episcopal Bishops Attack Vote for Gay Bishop of New Hampshire,* N.Y. TIMES, Aug. 7, 2003, at A20; Marc Lacey & Laurie Goodstein, *African Anglican Leaders Outraged over Gay Bishop in U.S.,* N.Y. TIMES, Nov. 4, 2003, at A21; Richard Ostling, *Conservative Anglicans Rebel: Faction Formally Denounces Acceptance of Gay Relationships,* WASH. POST, Oct. 10, 2003, at A15; Richard Ostling, *Episcopal Faction Plans to Battle Action on Gays: Conservatives Considering Split from Church,* WASH. POST, Oct. 8, 2003, at A9.

307. *See, e.g.,* SUZANNE PHARR, HOMOPHOBIA: A WEAPON OF SEXISM 18 (1988); Mary Francis, *Pitfalls of Perks: Workers without Children May Resent Policies Favoring Parents,* INDIANAPOLIS STAR, Feb. 1, 1999, at D1; Sylvia Law, *Homosexuality and the Social Meaning of Gender,* 1988 WIS. L. REV. 187; Adrienne Rich, *Compul-*

a wide audience given that at least 90 percent of the people in the world are predominantly heterosexual in their orientation. But there have been enough abuses of the notions of sexual harassment and related concepts to give some credibility to fears that the extreme heterophobes might prevail.[308] And when even six-year old children are charged with sexual harassment for kissing a classmate,[309] one begins to wonder were we are headed as a society.

The rise of the managerial class, and of the non-traditional forms of relationships that were so popular with members of that class, produced the predictable backlash.[310] One of the more

---

*sory Heterosexuality and Lesbian Existence*, 5 SIGNS 631 (1980); Katie Roiphe, *Date Rape Hysteria*, N.Y. TIMES, Nov. 20, 1991, at A27; Kenji Yoshino, *Covering*, 111 YALE L.J. 769 (2002). *See also* JUDITH LEVINE, MY ENEMY, MY LOVE: MAN-HATING AND AMBIVALENCE IN WOMEN'S LIVES (1992); DAPHNE PATAI, HETEROPHOBIA: SEXUAL HARASSMENT AND THE FUTURE OF FEMINISM (1999); Mary Becker, *Women, Morality, and Sexual Orientation*, 8 UCLA WOMEN'S L.J. 165 (1998); Richard Collier, *After Dunblane: Crime, Corporality, and the (Hetero-)Sexing of the Bodies of Men*, 24 J. LAW & SOC'Y 177 (1997); Billie Wright Dziech, Robert Dziech II, & Donald Hordes, *"Consensual" or Submissive Relationships: The Second-Best Kept Secret*, 6 DUKE J. GENDER & L. 83 (1999); Steven Homer, *Against Marriage*, 29 HARV. C.R.-C.L. L. REV. 505 (1994); Adrienne Rich, *Compulsory Heterosexuality and Lesbian Existence*, 5 SIGNS 631 (1980); Francesco Valdes, *Upacking Hetero-Patriarchy: Tracing the Conflation of Sex, Gender and Sexual Orientation to Its Origins*, 8 YALE J.L. & HUMAN. 161 (1996); Robin West, *The Harms of Consensual Sex*, 94 AM. PHIL. ASS'N NEWSLETTERS 52 (1995); Susan & David Williams, *A Feminist Theory of Malebashing*, 4 MICH. J. GENDER & L. 35 (1996); Deborah Zalesne, *Sexual Harassment: Has It Gone too Far, or Has the Media?*, 8 TEMPLE POL. & CIV. RTS. L. REV. 351 (1999). *See generally* FATHERHOOD TODAY: MEN'S CHANGING ROLES IN THE FAMILY (Phyllis Bronstein & Carolyn Pape Cowan eds. 1988); KATHLEEN GERSON, NO MAN'S LAND: MEN'S CHANGING COMMITMENTS TO FAMILY AND WORK (1993); REASSESSING FATHERHOOD: NEW OBSERVATIONS ON FATHERS AND THE MODERN FAMILY (Charlie Lewis & Margaret O'Brien eds. 1987).

308. *See, e.g.,* KATIE ROIPHE, THE MORNING AFTER: SEX, FEAR, AND FEMINISM (1997); Camille Paglia, *Twenty Questions*, PLAYBOY, Oct. 1991, at 132.

309. Sarah Swisher, Comment, *"Georgie Porgie...Kissed a Girl and Cause an Outcry?,"* 26 CAP. U. L. REV. 619 (1997).

310. *See, e.g., The Defense of Marriage Act*, 1 U.S.C. §7, 28 U.S.C. §1738C (authorizing states to decline to recognize homosexual marriages legal in other states) (2000); *The Adolescent Family Life Act*, 42 U.S.C. §300z (2000) (authorizing the use of federal funds for, among other things, counseling teenagers on the perils of premarital sex and the preferability of adoption to abortion); ALASKA STAT. §25.05.013 (barring recognition of homosexual marriages legal in other states) (LexisNexis 2002); ARIZ. REV. STAT. ANN. §25-101(c) (same) (West 2000); ARK. CODE ANN. §9-11-107 (same) (LexisNexis 2002); FLA. STAT. ANN. §§63.042 (banning adoptions by homosexuals), 741.212 (barring recognition of homosexual marriages legal in other states) (West Supp. 2003); GA. CODE ANN. §19-3-3.1 (barring recognition of homosexual marriages legal in other states) (1999); IDAHO CODE §§32-207 (barring homosexual marriages), 32-209 (barring recognition of homosexual marriages legal in other states) (1996); 5 ILL. COMP. STAT. ANN. 750/216 (same) (West 1999); IND. CODE ANN. §31-11-1-1 (same) (West 1999); KAN. STAT. ANN. §23-115 (same) (Cumm. Supp. 2003); MICH. COMP. LAWS ANN. §551-272 (same) (West Supp. 2003); N.H. REV. STAT. §170-B:4 (banning adoptions by homosexuals) (West 2001 & Supp. 2003); N.D. CENT CODE §14-03-08 (barring recognition of homosexual marriages legal in other states) (Supp. 2003); 23 PA. CONS. STAT. ANN. §1704 (same) (West. 2001); S.C. CODE ANN. §20-1-15 (barring recognition of homosexual marriages legal in other states) (West Supp. 2003); TENN. CODE ANN. §36-3-113 (same) (2001); TEX. FAM. CODE ANN. §2.001 (same) (West 1998); UTAH CODE ANN. §30-1-2(5) (same) (Supp. 2003); VA. CODE ANN. §20-45.2 (same) (Michie 1995).

*See also* Boy Scouts of America v. Dale, 530 U.S. 640 (2000) (a state's prohibition a of private organization's exclusion of a gay scoutmaster violates the First Amendment freedom of association); Kendrick v. Bowen, 487 U.S. 589 (1988) (holding that the *American Family Life Act* is not an unconstitutional establishment of religion); Shahar v. Bowers, 114 F.3d 1097 (11th Cir. 1997) (upholding the dismissal of a deputy [state] Attorney General against a claim of sex-based discrimination because she, as a lesbian, would create a "bad appearance" for the state and suffer a conflict of interest in enforcement of the state's sodomy laws), *cert. denied*, 522 U.S. 1049 (1998); Standhardt v. Superior Ct., 77 P.3d 451 (Ariz. Ct. App. 2003) (statute barring same-sex marriage is rational and does not deny a fundamental right), *rev. denied*; Curran v. Mount Diablo Council of Boy Scouts, 952 P.2d 218 (Cal. 1998) (upholding refusal by the Boy Scouts to accredit an openly homosexual scout master); State v. Baxley, 656 So.2d 973 (La. 1994) (upholding a criminal sodomy statute); McGuffin v. Overton, 542 N.W.2d 288 (Mich. Ct. App. 1995) (*per curiam*) (denying custody to the former les-

troubling manifestations of this backlash was the national hysteria in the 1990s over allegations of child molestation in childcare centers widely scattered across the United States—many of which charges were unfounded.[311] Innocent lives were destroyed even when the persons charged were ultimately acquitted, while the prosecutors (including their psychiatrist allies) often presented themselves as on a sacred crusade to protect children from Satanic forces. Meanwhile, real problems of inadequate childcare remained underfunded and neglected.

Supporters of abortion rights have long identified the backlash against non-traditional life styles, especially against changes that liberate women, as the "real" cause of the continuing strident opposition to abortion.[312] In other words, opponents of legalized abortion, we are told end-

---

bian life-partner of the mother when the mother had designated the life-partner as guardian in her will, awarding custody to a father who had no on-going relationship with the child and was in arrears on child support), *cert. denied*, 546 N.W.2d 256 (Mich. 1996); Miller v. State, 636 So.2d 391 (Miss. 1994) (upholding a criminal sodomy statute); Opinion of the Justices, 530 A.2d 21 (N.H. 1987) (upholding the constitutionality of a statute prohibiting adoptions by homosexuals); Sawatzky v. Oklahoma City, 906 P.2d 785 (Okla. Ct. Crim. App. 1995), *cert. denied*, 517 U.S. 1156 (1996) (upholding a criminal sodomy statute); State v. Post, 715 P.2d 1105 (Okla. Ct. Crim. App.) (upholding a statute prescribing certain sex acts even as applied to married heterosexuals), *cert. denied*, 479 U.S. 890 (1986); State v. Lopes, 660 A.2d 707 (R.I. 1995) (same), *cert. denied*, 516 U.S. 1123 (1996); Henry v. City of Sherman, 928 S.W.2d 464 (Tex. 1996), *cert. denied*, 519 U.S. 1156 (1997) (upholding discharge of police office for adultery); State v. Morales, 869 S.W.2d 941 (Tex. 1994) (upholding a criminal sodomy statute).

*See generally* DIDI HERMAN, THE ANTIGAY AGENDA: ORTHODOX VISION AND THE CHRISTIAN RIGHT (1997); POPENOE & WHITEHEAD, *supra* note 268; WHITEHEAD, *supra* note 268; MILTON REGAN, JR., FAMILY LAW AND THE PURSUIT OF INTIMACY (1993); Joseph Berger, *The Psychotherapeutic Treatment of Male Homosexuality*, 48 AM. J. PSYCHOTHERAPY 251 (1994); David Orgon Coolidge & William Duncan, *Reaffirming Marriage: A Presidential Priority*, 24 HARV. J.L. & PUB. POL'Y 623 (2001); Stanley Cox, *DOMA and Conflicts Law: Congressional Rules and Domestic Relations Conflicts Law*, 32 CREIGHTON L. REV. 1063 (1999); Maria De Crisofaro & Tracy Wilkinson, *Vatican to Leaders: Fight Gay Marriage*, PHILA. INQUIRER, Aug. 1, 2003, at A1; Michael Fletcher, *Campus Romance, Unrequited: Dating Scene Fails Women, Study Says*, WASH. POST, July 26, 2001, at A3; Howard-Hassman, *supra* note 291; Kanotz, *supra* note 301; Nancy Knauer, *"Simply So Different": The Uniquely Expressive Character of the Openly Gay Individual after Boy Scouts of America v. Dale*, 89 KY. L.J. 997 (2001); G.F. Mancini & S. O'Leary, *The New Frontier of Sex Equality in the European Union*, 24 EUR. L. REV. 331 (1999); Marc Poirier, *Hastening the Kulturkampf: Boy Scouts of American v. Dale and the Politics of American Masculinity*, 12 LAW & SEXUALITY 271 (2003); Lynn Wardle, *A Critical Analysis of Constitutional Claims for Same-Sex Marriage*, 1996 BYU L. REV. 1. On the power of political correctness on such issues, leading to difficulties for lawyers or law firms that represent the "wrong side," see Terry Carter, *Sins of the Client: Disdain over Unpopular Causes often Brands Law Firms, Lawyers*, ABA J., Mar., 2001, at 20 (discussing, among others, the case of *Dale v. Boy Scouts of America*, *supra*).

311. *See* PHILIP JENKINS, MORAL PANIC: CHANGING CONCEPTS OF THE CHILD MOLESTER IN MODERN AMERICA (1998); JAMES KINCAID, EROTIC INNOCENCE: THE CULTURE OF CHILD MOLESTING (1998); Margaret Talbot, *Against Innocence: The Truth about Child Abuse and the Truth about Children*, NEW REP., Mar. 15, 1999, at 27.

312. *See, e.g.*, JOHN ARTHUR, THE UNFINISHED CONSTITUTION: PHILOSOPHY AND CONSTITUTIONAL PRACTICE 259–60 (1989); DALLAS BLANCHARD, THE ANTI-ABORTION MOVEMENT AND THE RISE OF THE RELIGIOUS RIGHT: FROM POLITE TO FIERY PROTEST 1–9 (1984); DALLAS BLANCHARD & TERRY PREWITT, RELIGIOUS VIOLENCE AND ABORTION: THE GIDEON PROJECT xii, 227–28, 231, 241 (1993); JAMES MACGREGOR BURNS & STEWART BURNS, A PEOPLE'S CHARTER: THE PURSUIT OF RIGHTS IN AMERICA 356–58 (1991); CONDIT, *supra* note 32, at 30, 61–63, 74 n.9, 127–28; CRAIG & O'BRIEN, *supra* note 220, at 46–47; DIANE EYER, MOTHERGUILT: HOW OUR CULTURE BLAMES MOTHERS FOR WHAT'S WRONG WITH SOCIETY (1996); MARILYN FRALIK, IDEOLOGY AND ABORTION POLITICS (1983); GARROW, *supra* note 157, at 633; ELIZABETH FOX GENOVESE, FEMINISM WITHOUT ILLUSIONS 2, 81–83 (1991); GINSBURG, *supra* note 213, at 1, 6–19, 140–45, 172–97, 212–21; HARRISON, *supra* note 201, at 2–4, 32–49, 59–62, 67, 181–82, 189–90; JUDGES, *supra* note 147, at 12–15; KENNETH KARST, LAW'S PROMISE, LAW'S EXPRESSION: VISIONS OF POWER IN THE POLITICS OF RACE, GENDER, AND RELIGION 52–57 (1993); LUKER, *supra* note 219, at 137–38, 159–75, 195, 224, 241; CONNIE PAIGE, THE RIGHT TO LIFERS: WHO THEY ARE; HOW THEY OPERATE; WHERE THEY GET THEIR MONEY (1983); PETCHESKY, *supra* note 112, at xiii, xvi–xviii, xx–xxi, 5, 82–84; RHODE, *supra* note 113, at 214–15; JOHN ROBERTSON, CHILDREN OF CHOICE: FREEDOM AND THE NEW REPRODUCTIVE TECHNOLOGIES 66–68 (1994); ROGER ROSENBLATT, LIFE ITSELF: ABORTION IN THE AMERICAN MIND 37–38, 109, 121–31 (1992); PATRICK SHEEHAN, WOMEN, SOCIETY, THE STATE, AND ABORTION 125–28 (1987);

lessly, are insincere about the claim that the fetus is a "person" from the moment of conception. That may be true for some people. It is not the whole truth. After all, some noted liberals continue to oppose the free availability of abortion.[313] We even have feminists against abortion.[314] The managerial class is by no means unanimous in its attitudes about abortion and fetal rights.

Making sense of the connection between the rise of the managerial class and the controversy over abortion is more complex than the foregoing might suggest. Abortion activist Faye Ginsburg's study of the struggle over abortion rights in Fargo, North Dakota, is particularly instructive. Ginsburg started from a presumption that the battle over abortion reflected a contest between sincere supporters of women's rights and insincere supporters of fetal rights who really were out to keep women in their place.[315] She also expected to find that the two sets of activists represented very different social groups expressed through very different religious orientations. Ginsburg found, however, that pro-abortion and anti-abortion activists in Fargo had very similar religious, educational, and social backgrounds.[316] Nonetheless, Ginsburg did find a difference in attitudes towards life. While both sets of activists emphasized the traditionally female role of "nurturance," pro-abortion rights activists tended to seek ways to extend women's interests into the wider culture.[317] Anti-abortion rights activists tended to emphasize the primacy of "nurturance" in a woman's biological reproductive

---

SUSAN SHERWIN, NO LONGER PATIENT: FEMINIST ETHICS AND HEALTH CARE 111–14 (1992); CARROLL SMITH-ROSENBERG, DISORDERLY CONDUCT: VISIONS OF GENDER IN VICTORIAN AMERICA 217–18 (1985); SOLINGER, *supra* note 235, at 237–38; TRIBE, *supra* note 220, at 52–53, 76, 115, 132, 213, 232–34, 237–38, 242; JAMES BOYD WHITE, ACTS OF HOPE: CREATING AUTHORITY IN LITERATURE, LAW, AND POLITICS 166–67 (1994); Copelon, *supra* note 199, at 27–29; Nancy (Ann) Davis, *The Abortion Debate: The Search for Common Ground, Part I,* 103 ETHICS 516, 526–39 (1993); Amy Fried, *Abortion Politics as Symbolic Politics: An Investigation into Belief Systems,* 69 SOC. SCI. Q. 137 (1988); Marilyn Frye, *Some Reflections on Separatism and Power,* 6 SINISTER WISDOM 30 (1975); Linda Gordon & Allen Hunter, *Sex, Family, & the New Right,* 11/12 RADICAL AM. 9 (Dec. 1977, Feb. 1978); Donald Granberg, *Pro-Life or Reflections of Conservative Ideology?—An Analysis of Opposition to Legalized Abortion,* 62 SOCIOLOGY & SOC. RES. 414 (1978); Molly Ivins, *Sex Bullies: What Do the Anti-Abortion, Anti-Gay, Anti-Porn Groups Want? Nothing Less than Sex Control,* PLAYBOY, June 1990, at 88; Sylvia Law, *Abortion and Compromise—Inevitable and Impossible,* 1992 U. ILL. L. REV. 921, 933–37; Mary Jo Neitz, *Family, State, and God: Ideologies of the Right to Life Movement,* 42 SOCIOLOGICAL ANALYSIS 265 (1981); Pine & Law, *supra* note 199, at 423–25; Stephen Schnably, *Beyond Griswold: Foucauldian and Republican Approaches to Privacy,* 23 CONN. L. REV. 861, 910–21 (1991); Suzanne Staggenborg, *Life-Style Preferences and Social Movement Recruitment: Illustrations from the Abortion Conflict,* 68 SOCIAL SCI. Q. 779 (1987); Ellen Willis, *Putting Women Back into the Abortion Debate,* in FROM ABORTION TO REPRODUCTIVE FREEDOM, *supra* note 199, at 131–38.

313. *See, e.g,* Sidney Callahan, *Abortion and the Sexual Agenda,* COMMONWEAL, April 25, 1986, at 236; Nat Hentoff, *Abortion: Seeking a Common Ground* (book rev.), BOSTON GLOBE, June 10, 1990, at B43. *See generally* NOONAN, *supra* note 27, at 66–67; PAIGE, *supra* note 312, at 100–04.

314. ABORTION: UNDERSTANDING DIFFERENCES 1, 12 (Sydney & Daniel Callahan eds. 1984) (containing articles by both pro-life and pro-choice feminists); GINSBURG, *supra* note 213, at 172–93, 227–47; HADLEY, *supra* note 67, at 194–97; JACOBY, *supra* note 123, at 50–51, 184–85; KATHLEEN McDONNELL, NOT AN EASY CHOICE: A FEMINIST REEXAMINES ABORTION (1984); MENSCH & FREEMAN, *supra* note 122, at 4; MAUREEN MULDOON, THE ABORTION DEBATE IN THE UNITED STATES AND CANADA: A SOURCE BOOK 146–47 (1991); PRO-LIFE FEMINISM 81–106 (Gail Grenier Sweet ed. 1985); SISTERLIFE (a quarterly newsletter published by Feminists for Life of America); Martha Bayles, *Feminism and Abortion,* ATLANTIC MONTHLY 83 (April 1990); Callahan, *supra* note 312; Paige Comstock Cunningham & Clarke Forsythe, *Is Abortion the "First Right" for Women?: Some Consequences of Legal Abortion,* in ABORTION, MEDICINE AND THE LAW, *supra* note 75, at 100, 114–17; Diane Krstulovich, *Disposing of Pro-Life Stereotypes,* JOURNAL MONTAGE, Dec. 11, 1991, at 47, 56; Mary Meehan, *Will Somebody Please Be Consistent?,* 9 SOJOURNERS 14 (Nov. 1980); Ruth Putnam, *Being Ambivalent about Abortion,* TIKKUN, Sept.–Oct. 1989, at 81; Janet Smith, *Abortion as a Feminist Concern,* in THE ZERO PEOPLE 77, at 81–84 (Jeff Lane Hensley ed. 1983); *Amicus Brief of Feminists for Life supporting petitioners in* Bray v. Alexandria Women's Health Clinic, 504 U.S. 970 (1992).

315. GINSBURG, *supra* note 213, at 1, 6–19, 140–45, 172–97, 212–21.

316. *Id.* at 169–71. *See also* Davis, *supra* note 312, at 528.

317. GINSBURG, *supra* note 213, at 169–71.

roles.[318] The difference in attitude is tied to the drive to manage society that is characteristic of the managerial class, as opposed to a focus on oneself and one's own—the family. Reformed or repealed abortion laws served the interests of the managerial class by freeing men and women alike of familial responsibilities so they could spend ever longer periods in educational settings or working at managing society and its institutions.[319] Ginsburg's findings do not justify a claim that either set of activists is insincere in their beliefs, or that attitudes towards abortion are merely instrumental, developed, perhaps intuitively, from other, more important goals, such as the pursuit of careers, family roles, and so on. Cognitive systems are too complex to be explained in such a simple fashion. Yet a certain correlation is clear.

The managerial class rose to dominance in the United States with the New Deal in the 1930s, and has continued to dominate ever since. The managerial class thereafter achieved considerable success in enacting laws to require employers to bear additional costs to accommodate their life styles.[320] They even achieved a reform of the *Internal Revenue Code* to remove the so-called penalty against unmarried persons, enacting in the process what came to be called a "marriage penalty," under which a married couple would pay higher taxes than if they were living together "without the benefit of matrimony."[321]

A major transition like the rise of the managerial class does not, of course, come about overnight. Evidence of the transition to social domination by a managerial class can be traced back to the nineteenth century, particularly in England.[322] Nor was this transition limited to western or capitalist nations. In a real sense, the rise of Communism and Socialism was nothing more (or less) than a rise of the managerial class.[323] The overall results could hardly have been a surprise: Many of these new forms of adult relationships seemed to have seriously negative effects on children who found themselves in increasing numbers being raised in impoverished single-parent households, or step-households, or in even more confusing and unsettling circumstances.[324]

---

318. *Id.* at 143, 172, 185–86.

319. Garrow, *supra* note 157, at 723–26.

320. *See, e.g., Family Medical Leave Act of 1993,* 29 U.S.C. §§ 2601–2654 (2000); Nevada Dep't of Hum. Resources v. Hibbs, 538 U.S. 721 (2003) (states not immune to suit under the Family Medical Leave Act); Schafer v. Board of Pub. Educ., 903 F.2d 243 (3rd Cir. 1990) (prohibiting the granting of women one-year leaves after bearing a child without granting fathers the same right). *See also* Department of Labor, *Balancing the Needs of Families and Employers* (2003), available at http://www.dol.gov/dol/asp/public/fmla/main.htm (finding that employers consider family leave to be a significant burden, but also finding that the policy has little effect on productivity and profit).

321. Richard Elbert, *Love, God, and Country: Religious Freedom and the Marriage Penalty Tax,* 5 Seton Hall Const. L.J. 1171 (1995). *See also* Edmund Andrews, *House Votes to Extend Popular Measure Providing Tax Relief From 'Marriage Penalty',* N.Y. Times, April 29, 2004, at A20.

322. *See, e.g.,* Thorsten Veblen, The Theory of the Leisure Class (1899). *See generally* Brookes, *supra* note 13, at 9–13.

323. *See* Milovan Djilas, The New Class (1957).

324. Paul Amato & Alan Booth, A Generation at Risk: Growing Up in an Era of Family Upheaval (1997); Christy Buchanan, Eleanor Maccoby, & Sanford Dornbusch, Adolescents after Divorce (1996); Hrdy, *supra* note 163, at 109–10; Eleanor Maccoby & Robert Mnookin, Dividing the Child: Social and Legal Dilemmas of Custody (1992); Redefining Families: Implications for Children's Development (Adele Eskeles Gottfried & Allen Gottfried eds. 1994); Judith Wallterstein, The Unexpected Legacy of Divorce: A 25-Year Landmark Study (2000); Tonya Brito, *Madonna to Proletariat: Constructing a New Ideology of Motherhood in Welfare Discourse,* 44 Vill. L. Rev. 415 (1999); W.D. Erickson *et al., The Life Histories and Psychological Profiles of 59 Incestuous Stepfathers,* 15 Bull. Am. Acad. Psychol. & L. 349 (1987); Kathryn Franklin *et al., Long-Term Impact of Parental Divorce on Optimism and Trust: Changes in General Assumptions or Narrow Beliefs?,* 59 J. Personality & Soc. Psychol. 743 (1990); Frank Furstenberg, jr., & Julien Teitler, *Reconsidering the Effects of Marital Disruption: What Happens to Children of Divorce in Early Adulthood?,* 15 J. Fam. Issues 173 (1994); William Galston, *Causes of Declining Well-Being among U.S. Children,* in Sex,

The effects of the new style relationships on children remain highly debatable.[325] Yet the statistical incidence of child abuse is indisputable evidence of the impact of such developments—a child is four times more likely to die at the hands of a stepparent than at the hands of her own parent.[326] Those who prefer the new style relationships felt little enough pressure within themselves to change. As anthropologist Sarah Hrdy noted, "the pressures to change are less intense when children can (literally) live with the consequences."[327] Or, as economist Kenneth Boulding

---

PREFERENCE, AND FAMILY 290 (David Estlund & Martha Nussbaum eds. 1997); Richad Gardner, *Should Courts Order PAS Children to Visit/Reside with the Alienated Parent? A Follow-up Study,* 19 J. FORENSIC PSYCH. no. 3, at 61 (2001); Norval Glenn & Kathryn Kramer, *The Marriages and Divorces of the Children of Divorce,* 49 J. MARRIAGE & FAM. 811 (1987); Matthew Johnson, Christine Baker, & Angelina Maceira, *The 1997 Adoption and Safe Families Act and Parental Rights Termination Consultation,* 19 AM. J. FORENSIC PSYCH. no. 3, at 15 (2001); Stephanie Kasen *et al., A Multi-Risk Interaction Model: Effects of Temperament and Divorce on Psychiatric Disorders in Children,* 24 J. ABNORMAL CHILD PSYCHOL. 121 (1996); Gay Kitson & Leslie Morgan, *The Multiple Consequences of Divorce: A Decade Review,* 52 J. MARRIAGE & FAM. 913 (1990); Sara McLanahan & Karen Booth, *Mother-Only Families: Problems, Prospects, and Politics,* 51 J. MARRIAGE & FAM. 557 (1989); Kristin Anderson Moore, Susan Jekielek, & Carol Emig, *Marriage from a Child's Perspective: How Does Family Structure Affect Children, and What Can We Do about It?,* in CHILD TRENDS RESEARCH BRIEFS, *available at* www.childtrends.org/PDF/Marriagerb602.pdf (June 2002); Laura Padilla, *Single-Parent Latinas on the Margin: Seeking a Room with a View, Meals, and Built-in Community,* 13 WIS. WOMEN'S L.J. 179 (1998); Toby Parcel & Elizabeth Menaghan, *Family Social Capital and Children's Behavior Problems,* 56 SOC. PSYCHOL. Q. 120 (1993); James Peterson & Nicholas Zeill, *Marital Disruption, Parent-Child Relationships, and Behavior Problems in Children,* 48 J. MARRIAGE & FAM. 295 (1986); David Popenoe, *American Family Decline, 1960–1990,* 55 J. MARRIAGE & FAM. 527 (1993); Diana Russell, *The Prevalence and Seriousness of Incestuous Abuse: Stepfathers vs. Biological Fathers,* 8 CHILD ABUSE & NEGLECT 15 (1984); Choi Wann *et al., The Relationship between Social Support and Life Satisfaction as a Function of Family Structure,*58 J. MARRIAGE & FAM. 502 (1996); Richard Warshak, *Current Controversies Regarding Parental Alienation Syndrome,* 19 AM. J. FORENSIC PSYCH. no. 3, at 29 (2001). *See also* Ireland v. Smith, 542 N.W.2d 344 (Mich. Ct. App. 1995) (custody given to the father when the mother placed the child in daycare while she attended college). *See generally* MIMI ABRAMOVITZ, UNDER ATTACK, FIGHTING BACK: WOMEN AND WELFARE IN THE UNITED STATES (1996); JOEL HANDLER & YEHESKEL HASENFELD, WE THE POOR PEOPLE: WORK, POVERTY & WELFARE (1997); ARTHUR KORNHABER, CONTEMPORARY GRANDPARENTING (1996); ARLENE SKOLNICK, EMBATTLED PARADISE: THE AMERICAN FAMILY IN AN AGE OF UNCERTAINTY (1991); MARINA WARNER, FROM THE BEAST TO THE BLONDE: ON FAIRY TALES AND THEIR TELLERS (1995).

325. *See, e.g.,* ATTACHMENT IN PRESCHOOL YEARS: THEORY, RESEARCH AND INTERVENTION (Mark Greenberg, Dante Cicchetti, & E. Mark Cummings eds. 1990); CLARE BERMAN, ADULT CHILDREN OF DIVORCE SPEAK OUT: ABOUT GROWING UP WITH—AND MOVING BEYOND—PARENTAL DIVORCE (1991); DOROTHY BLOCH, "SO THE WITCH WON'T EAT ME": FANTASY AND THE CHILD'S FEAR OF INFANTICIDE (1978); JOHN BOWLBY, ATTACHMENT (2nd ed. 1982); JOHN BOWLBY, A SECURE BASE: PARENT-CHILD ATTACHMENT AND HEALTHY HUMAN DEVELOPMENT (1988); DOWD, *supra* note 274; EYER, *supra* note 312; F. CAROLYN GRAGLIA, DOMESTIC TRANQUILITY: A BRIEF AGAINST FEMINISM (1998); JUDITH RICH HARRIS, THE NURTURE ASSUMPTION (1998); E. MAVIS HETHERINGTON, FOR BETTER OR FOR WORSE: DIVORCE RECONSIDERED (2002); SILVIA ANN HEWLETT, THE COST OF NEGLECTING OUR CHILDREN (1991); HRDY, *supra* note 163, at 506–10; MICHAEL LAMB *et al.,* INFANT-MOTHER ATTACHMENT: THE ORIGINS AND DEVELOPMENTAL SIGNIFICANCE OF INDIVIDUAL DIFFERENCES (1985); PARENTING ACROSS THE HUMAN LIFESPAN: BIOSOCIAL DIMENSIONS (Jane Lancaster *et al.* eds. 1987); BRIAN ROBERTSON, THERE'S NO PLACE LIKE WORK: HOW BUSINESS, GOVERNMENT, AND OUR OBSESSION WITH WORK HAVE DRIVEN PARENTS FROM HOME (2000); SOCIOBIOLOGICAL PERSPECTIVES ON HUMAN DEVELOPMENT (Kevin MacDonald ed. 1988); FRANK SULLOWAY, BORN TO REBEL (1996); SHARI THURER, THE MYTHS OF MOTHERHOOD: HOW CULTURE REINVENTS THE GOOD MOTHER (1994); WALLERSTEIN, *supra* note 324; Jay Belsky, Laurence Steinberg, & Patricia Draper, *Childhood Experience, Interpersonal Development, and Reproductive Strategy: An Evolutionary Theory of Socialization,* 62 CHILD DEV. 647 (1991); K. Alison Clarke-Stewart, *The "Effects" of Infant Care Reconsidered: Reconsidered,* 39 EARLY CHILDHOOD RESEARCH Q. 293 (1988); Theresa Glennon, *Expendable Children: Defining Belonging in a Broken World,* 8 DUKE J. GENDER & L. 269 (2001); Lynn Wardle, *The Potential Impact of Homosexual Parenting on Children,* 1997 U. ILL. L. REV. 833.

326. HRDY, *supra* note 163, at 236–37. *See generally* HRDY, *supra,* at 237–44; Herbert Wray, *The Evolution of Child Abuse,* SCI. NEWS, Nov. 28, 1982, at 24.

327. HRDY, *supra* note 163, at 109. *See also* HRDY, *supra,* at 114–17.

observed, we were witnessing the aristocratization of the middle class—"and aristocrats have always been sons of bitches."[328]

Enough people shared the negative evaluations of the effects of the new style of relationship on children that a reaction against the new value system set in, resulting strident attempts to use law to buttress the traditional family and "family values."[329] It also led to the *Family and Medical Leave Act of 1993*,[330] enacted in an attempt to better enable people (usually, in fact, women) to take limited leaves from their jobs to provide care to family members without suffering significant career disadvantages from their absence.[331] It also led to the enactment of a statute in Ari-

---

328. Robert Glasgow, *A Conversation with Kenneth Boulding*, PSYCH. TODAY, Jan. 1973, at 62. *See also* Midge Decter, *The Madness of the American Family*, POL'Y REV., Sept.–Oct. 1998, at 33.

329. *See, e.g.*, the statutes collected *supra* at note 297. *See also* Altman v. Minnesota Dep't Corrections, 251 F.3d 1199 (8th Cir. 1999) (ordering the Department to remove letters of reprimand from guards' files issued for their refusal, on religious grounds, to participate in a seminar on gay and lesbian rights); C.K. v. New Jersey Dep't of Health & Hum. Services, 92 F.3d 171 (3rd Cir. 1996) (upholding New Jersey's fixed maximum payments for families eligible for welfare); Jones v. Hallahan, 501 S.W.2d 588 (Ky. 1973) (refusing to recognize homosexual marriages); Baker v. Nelson, 191 N.W.2d 185 (Minn. 1971) (same); De Santo v. Barnsley, 476 A.2d 952 (Pa. Super. 1984) (refusing to recognize homosexual marriages); Singer v. Hara, 522 P.2d 1187 (Was. 1974) (same).

*See generally* BLANKENHORN, *supra* note 274, at 107–23; DANA MACK, THE ASSAULT ON PARENTHOOD: HOW OUR CULTURE UNDERMINES THE FAMILY (1997); GALLAGHER, *supra* note 274; EDWARD MCCAFFERY, TAXING WOMEN (1997); REBUILDING THE NEST: A NEW COMMITMENT TO THE AMERICAN FAMILY (David Blankenhorn ed. 1990); STACEY, *supra* note 274; WHITEHEAD, *supra* note 268; Susan Frelich Appleton, *When Welfare Reforms Promote Abortion: "Personal Responsibility," "Family Values," and the Right to Choose*, 85 GEO. L.J. 155 (1996); Chabora, *supra* note 301; Cox, *supra* note 301; Dent, *supra* note 301; Martha Fineman, *Masking Dependency: The Political Role of Family Rhetoric*, 81 VA. L. REV. 2181 (1995); John Finnis, *The Good Marriage and the Morality of Sexual Relations: Some Philosophical and Historical Observations*, 42 AM. J. JURIS. 97 (1997); Robert George & Gerard Bradley, *Marriage and the Liberal Imagination*, 84 GEO. L.J. 301 (1995); Kersch, *supra* note 301; Koppelman, *supra* note 301; Kramer, *supra* note 301; Nkrumah, *supra* note 301; Twila Perry, *Family Values, Race, Feminism and Public Policy*, 36 SANTA CLARA L. REV. 345 (1996); Robb, *supra* note 301; Silberman, *supra* note 301; Silverman, *supra* note 301; Symposium, *Covenant Marriage*, 12 REGENT U. L. REV. 1 (1999); Katherine Shaw Spaht, *Revolution and Counter-Revolution: The Future of Marriage and the Law*, 49 LOY. L. REV. 1 (2003); Brad Wilcox & John Bartkowski, *The Evangelical Family: Conservative Rhetoric, Progressive Practice*, 9 THE RESPONSIVE COMMUNITY 34 (1999). *See generally* STACEY, *supra* note 274.

330. 29 U.S.C. §§ 2601–2654 (2000).

331. *See* JAMES LEVINE & TODD PITTINSKY, WORKING FATHERS: NEW STRATEGIES FOR BALANCING WORK AND FAMILY (1997); Stephanie Armour, *Dad Is Job One: Paternity Leaves Increasingly Popular*, USA TODAY, Feb. 23, 1998, at 1B; Maggie Jackson, *Men Fight for the Right to Take Parental Leave*, CHI. SUN-TIMES, Feb. 7, 1999, at 49; Betsy Morris, *Is Your Family Wrecking Your Career (and Vice Versa): The Dirty Little Secret Is This: For All Its Politically Correct Talk, Your Company Doesn't Much Like Your Kids*, FORTUNE, Mar. 17, 1997, at 72. *See generally* Catherine Cloud Barré, *The Viability of Maternity Leave Policies under Title VII and the Equal Protection Clause*, 5 VA. J. SOC. POL'Y & L. 603 (1998); Ruth Colker, *Hypercapitalism: Affirmative Protections for People with Disabilities, Illness, and Parenting Responsibilities under United States Law*, 9 YALE J.L. & FEMINISM 213 (1997); Sabra Craig, *The Family and Medical Leave Act of 1993: A Survey of the Act's History, Purposes, Provisions, and Social Ramifications*, 44 DRAKE L. REV. 51 (1995); Cristina Duarte, *The Family and Medical Leave Act of 1993: Paying the Price for an Imperfect Solution*, 32 U. LOUISVILLE J. FAM. L. 833 (1994); Maxine Eichner, *Square Peg in a Round Hole: Parenting Policies and Liberal Theory*, 59 OHIO ST. L.J. 133 (1998); Mikel Glavinovich, *International Suggestions for Improving Parental Leave Legislation in the United States*, 13 ARIZ. J. INT'L & COMP. L. 147 (1996); Jonathan Gruber, *The Incidence of Mandated Maternity Benefits*, 84 AM. ECON. REV. 622 (1994); Jane Shibley Hyde et al., *Parental Leave: Policy and Research*, 52 J. SOC. ISSUES 91 (1996); Martin Malin, *Fathers and Parental Leave Revisited*, 19 N. ILL. U. L. REV. 25 (1998); Carol Dougherty Rasnic, *The United States' 1993 Family and Medical Leave Act: How Does It Compare with Work Leave Laws in European Countries*, 10 CONN. J. INT'L L. 105 (1994); Jane Rigler, *Analysis and Understanding of the Family and Medical Levae Act of 1993*, 45 CASE-W. RES. L. REV. 457 (1995); Michael Salmi, *The Limited Vision of the Family and Medical Leave Act*, 44 VILL. L. REV. 395 (1999); Andrew Shlarlach & Blanche Grosswald, *The Family and Medical Leave Act of 1993*, SOC. SERVICE REV., Sept. 1997, at 335; Holly Thompson & Jon Werner, *The Family and Medical Leave Act: Assessing the Costs and Benefits of Use*, 1 EMPLOYEE RTS. & EMPLOYMENT POL'Y J. 125 (1997);

zona and Louisiana creating "covenant marriage" whereby couples agree to forego the possibility of no-fault divorce, leaving possible only divorce for serious fault including adultery, conviction of a serious felony, abandonment for a year or more, or physical or sexual abuse of the spouse of a child of the parties.[332] And, at least in the United States, a clear majority—led by President George W. Bush—opposed recognizing same-sex marriage even if many were supportive of eliminating most discrimination against homosexuals.[333] Notwithstanding this backlash, the ideology of the managerial class spread through the general populace through an increasingly pervasive mass media.

The divisiveness of the same-sex marriage issue was perhaps most clearly shown in the considerable change in public opinion in the United States. A Gallup poll taken in May 2003 found that 54 percent of Americans considered homosexuality to be "an acceptable alternative lifestyle" compared to 43 percent who did not.[334] At the same time, some 49 percent of Americans were opposed to civil unions for homosexual couples, and 49 percent supported the idea.[335] After two months of publicity about the advent of "gay marriages" in Canada, the Gallup survey of July 2003 the support for civil unions for homosexuals fell to 40 percent, while the opponents of such unions climbed to 57 percent.[336] This shift in turn affected attitudes towards homosexuality generally. Those who found homosexuality to be "an acceptable alternative lifestyle" fell to 46 percent, while those who did not find it to be acceptable rose to 49 percent.[337] This dispute is far from over, and might very well end up with general recognition of civil unions if not of homosexual marriages.

---

Eileen Trzcinski & William Alpert, *Pregnancy and Parental Benefits in the United States and Canada*, 29 J. Hum. Resources 535 (1994); Joseph Wills, *The Family and Medical Leave Act of 1993: A Progress Report*, 36 J. Fam. L. 95 (1997); Angie Young, *Assessing the Family and Medical Leave Act in Terms of Gender Equality, Work/Family Balance, and the Needs of Children*, 5 Mich. J. Gender & L. 113 (1998).

332. Ariz. Rev. Stat. §§ 25-901, 25-902 (West 2000); La. Rev. Stat. § 9:273 (West 2000). *See generally* Jane Biondi, *Who Pays for Guilt? Recent Fault-Based Divorce Reform Proposals, Cultural Stereotypes and Economic Consequences*, 40 B.C. L. Rev. 611 (1999); Jeanne Carriere, *"It's Déjà Vu All Over Again": The Covenant Marriage Act in Popular Cultural Perception and Legal Reality*, 72 Tul. L. Rev. 1701 (1998); Cynthia Samuel, *Letter from Louisiana: An Obituary for Forced Heirship and a Birth Announcement for Covenant Marriage*, 12 Tul. Eur. & Civ. L.F. 183 (1997); Katharine Shaw Spaht, *Beyond* Baehr: *Strengthening the Definition of Marriage*, 12 BYU J. Pub. L. 277 (1998); Katharine Shaw Spaht, *For the Sake of the Children: Recapturing the Meaning of Marriage*, 73 Notre Dame L. Rev. 1547 (1998); Katharine Shaw Spaht, *Louisiana's Covenant Marriage: Social Analysis and Legal Implications*, 59 La. L. Rev. 63 (1998); Katharine Shaw Spaht & Symneon Symeonides, *Covenant Marriage and the Law of Conflicts of Laws*, 32 Creighton L. Rev. 1085 (1999); Symposium, *supra* note 329. *But see* Christine Whelan, *No Honeymoon for Covenant Marriage*, Wall St. J., Aug. 17, 1998, at A14. *See generally* Glenn Stanton, Why Marriage Matters: Reasons to Believe in Marriage in Post-Modern Society (1997). Professor Spaht, who was the principal drafter of Louisiana's covenant marriage act, was also the principal drafter of Louisiana's no-fault divorce statute. Spaht & Simeonides, *supra*, at 1086.

333. *See, e.g.*, Mike Allen, *Gay Marriage Looms as Issue: GOP Push for Amendment Is Dilemma for Bush*, Wash. Post, Oct. 25, 2003, at A1; Gary Bauer, *When Courts Reinvent Marriage*, Wash. Post, Oct. 1, 2003, at A23; Maureen Dowd, *Next up, The Gay Divorcée*, N.Y. Times, July 2, 2003, at A25; *Frist Backs Putting Gay Marriage Ban in Constitution*, Wash. Post, June 30, 2003, at A2; Neil Lewis, *Bush Backs Bid to Block Gays from Marrying*, N.Y. Times, July 31, 2003, at A1; Morin & Cooperman, *supra* note 302; Frank Rich, *And Now, the Queer Eye for Straight Marriage*, N.Y. Times, Aug. 10, 2003, at AR1. Only weeks before, Bush had passed on an opportunity to oppose same-sex marriages. David Von Drehle, *Bush Unsure Ban on Gay Unions Is Needed*, Wash. Post, July 3, 2003, at A2. *See also* Alan Simpson, *Missing the Point on Gays*, Wash. Post, Sept. 5, 2003, at A21 (opposing federal action).

334. Alfred Lubrano, *Supporting Gays, But Not Gay Marriage*, Phila. Inquirer, Oct. 12, 2003, at A1, A6.

335. *Id.*

336. *Id.*

337. *Id.*

# From Reform to Repeal

*Oh Lord, won't you buy me a Mercedes Benz?*
*My friends all drive Porsches, I must make amends,*
*Worked hard all my lifetime, no help from my friends,*
*So oh Lord, won't you buy me a Mercedes Benz?*

— Janis Joplin[338]

The abortion statutes that did pass, including Colorado's, made little actual change in existing abortion practices.[339] If the reformed laws were strictly construed, they applied to at most five percent of the women seeking abortions because they authorized abortions only for actual threats to a woman's health or life, or because of rape or incest, or because of genuine fetal defects.[340] As a result, only 289 legal abortions were performed in Colorado in the first year its reform statute was in effect.[341] As Howard Moody, the leader of the New-York-based Clergy Consultation Service on Abortion, noted, "our day-to-day work taught us how few women wanted abortions for the reasons most liberals conceded were justifiable."[342]

At least some local prosecutors seem to have stepped up enforcement efforts of whatever abortion laws were on the books in their state, rather than conceding the field to those who would defy the law.[343] The close scrutiny roused by the controversy over abortion reform may have caused some hospitals to decrease the number of abortions actually performed under the reformed statutes than had been true before their enactment.[344] The liberalization of abortion laws, particularly when combined with the then pervasive review by hospital abortion committees, actually seems to have made legal abortions less available to women who were young, or poor, or members of racial minorities. No wonder Governor Richard Lamm, a legislative sponsor of the Colorado reform bill, even commented that doctors and hospitals had taken "a bill that would help about five percent" of women seeking abortions and "turned it into a three percent bill."[345] Lamm called for a repeal of Colorado's reformed abortion law less than two years after it was enacted in order to provide women with "the right to control [their] fertility."[346]

---

338. Janis Joplin, *Oh Lord, Won't You Buy Me a Mercedes Benz* (1971).

339. Garrow, *supra* note 157, at 332, 374–76; Lader, *supra* note 201, at 85–86; Rubin, *supra* note 122, at 27–29. On the experience under the reformed laws in specific states, see Hordern, *supra* note 27, at 250–54; William Droegemueller *et al.*, *The First Year of Experience in Colorado in Colorado with the New Abortion Law*, 103 Am. J. Obstet. & Gyencology 694 (1969); Abraham Heller & H.G. Whittington, *The Colorado Story: Denver General Hospital Experience with the Change in the Law on Therapeutic Abortion*, 125 Am. J. Psychiatry 809 (1968); Edwin Jackson, *Therapeutic Abortions in California: First Year's Experience under New Legislation*, 105 Am. J. Obstet. & Gynecology 757 (1969); Jerome Kummer, *New Trends in Therapeutic Abortion in California*, 34 Obstet. & Gynecology 883 (1969); Richard Lamm *et al.*, *The Legislative Process in Changing Therapeutic Abortion Laws*, 39 Am. J. Orthopsychiatry 684 (1969); Keith Monroe, *How California's Abortion Law Isn't Working*, N.Y. Times Mag., Dec. 29, 1968, at 10; Clyde Stanfield, *Colorado's Abortion Law*, 54 Neb. St. Med. J. 745 (1969).

340. Garrow, *supra* note 157, at 332.

341. *Id.* at 351.

342. Quoted *id. See also* Arlene Carmen & Howard Moody, Abortion Counseling and Social Change 102–04 (1973). *See generally* Olasky, *supra* note 122, at 105–06.

343. Ed Keemer, Confessions of a Pro-Life Abortionist 224–28 (1980); Reagan, *supra* note 112, at 242–44.

344. Garrow, *supra* note 157, at 374–75; Reagan, *supra* note 112, at 233.

345. Quoted Garrow, *supra* note 157, at 375.

346. Richard Lamm, *Unwanted Child Births Forced by Law*, Den. Post, Feb. 2, 1969, at G1, G5.

The decline of genuine threats to maternal health eliminated the only indications for abortion to which disfavored groups had relatively equal access with more affluent white women.[347] The statutory reforms merely reinforced this pattern as women of means found it considerably easier than poor women to find and retain two physicians to certify that she met one or another of the less objective statutory qualifications.[348] Only gradually did physicians in some states (California, Maryland, New Mexico, North Carolina) develop the "mental health" indication into a back door for abortion on demand.[349] By 1970, more than 90 percent of the abortions performed under the reformed laws were on the grounds that two doctors (not necessarily psychiatrists) certified that continuation of the pregnancy was a threat to the mother's mental health.[350] The national rate of abortions based upon psychiatric indications rose from 0.57/1000 live births to 3.61/1000 after enactment of the reformed laws.[351]

Despite increased recourse to the mental health exception as an escape hatch for those seeking an abortion, many women still could not obtain a legal abortion in their home state. Most states still had highly restrictive nineteenth-century abortion laws on the books. In some states with reformed statutes, doctors, police, and prosecutors combined to make legal abortions difficult to obtain. These problems could be solved by travelling to another state where reformed statutes were liberally construed. Soon, there would be a few states where abortion restrictions had been altogether repealed. Thus Dr. James Kahn and his associates found that as many Georgians were having abortions in New York City (with no restrictions on elective abortion) in 1970 as were having abortions in Georgia (with an indications policy).[352]

Poor women, however, could not afford to travel to distant states for on abortion.[353] Jean Pakter and her associates found two years after New York repealed its restrictions on abortion that nearly two-thirds of abortions in New York were performed on nonresidents,[354] but that 88 percent of the nonresidents receiving abortions were white compared to only 44 percent of the residents.[355] Even the underground abortion referral services that sprang up in many states often

---

347. GRABER, *supra* note 220, at 55–58; LADER, *supra* note 201, at 22; BETTY SARVIS & HYMAN RODMAN, THE ABORTION CONTROVERSY 170–71 (1973). On the pre-reform inequalities, see Chapter 12, at notes 254–66, 312–27. *See also* Edwin Gold *et al., Therapeutic Abortions in New York City: A Twenty-Year Review,* 55 AM. J. PUB. HEALTH 964, 968 (1965); Niswander, *supra* note 75, at 53; Kenneth Niswander, Morton Klein, & Clyde Randall, *Changing Attitudes toward Therapeutic Abortion,* 196 JAMA J. 1140, 1143 (1966).

348. BELL, *supra* note 233, at 127; CONDIT, *supra* note 32, at 34; DAVIS, *supra* note 123, at 99; GRABER, *supra* note 123, at 56–59, 63–64; FREDERICK JAFFE, BARBARA LINDHEIM, & PHILIP LEE, ABORTION POLITICS 21, 25, 223 (1981); RUDY, *supra* note 293, at 61–62; SARVIS & RODMAN, *supra* note 347, at 167; Henry David, *The Abortion Decision: National and International Perspectives,* in ABORTION PARLEY 59, 87–88 (James Burtchaell ed. 1980); George, *supra* note 213, at 23; Harold Rosen, *The Psychiatric Indications of Abortion: A Case Study in Hypocrisy,* in THERAPEUTIC ABORTION, *supra* note 197, at 76, 89–90; Sara Seims, *Abortion Availability in the United States,* 12 FAM. PLANNING PERSPECTIVES 88, 93 (1980).

349. GARROW, *supra* note 157, at 410–11, 457, 490.

350. James Kahn *et al., Surveillance of Abortion in Hospitals in the United States, 1970,* 86 HSMHA HEALTH REP. 423, 425–26 (1971). *See also* GRABER, *supra* note 220, at 57; MESSER & MAY, *supra* note 263, at 143, 176; NATHANSON & OSTUNG, *supra* note 228, at 40–41; HERBERT PACKER, THE LIMITS OF THE CRIMINAL SANCTION 344 (1968); Theodore Irwin, *The New Abortion Laws: How Are They Working?,* TODAY's HEALTH, Mar. 1970, at 22; Joffe, *supra* note 234, at 54; Niswander, Klein, & Randall, *supra* note 347, at 1143.

351. GRABER, *supra* note 220, at 58. *See also* BELL, *supra* note 233, at 135; Sands, *supra* note 262, at 297.

352. Kahn *et al., supra* note 350, at 428

353. GRABER, *supra* note 220, at 62; JEROME LEGGE, ABORTION POLICY: AN EVALUATION OF THE CONSEQUENCES FOR MATERNAL AND INFANT HEALTH 98, 102, 126 (1985); SARVIS & RODMAN, *supra* note 347, at 52; Seims, *supra* note 347, at 93.

354. Jean Pakter *et al., Two Years Experience in New York City with the Liberalized Abortion Law—Progress and Problems,* 63 AM. J. PUB. HEALTH 524, 525 (1973).

355. *Id.* at 529.

served "women of means" rather than poor women.[356] The results of these several practical problems in the implementation of the reformed laws were too predictable. The abortion-related mortality rate for black women in Georgia, already four times greater than for whites for 1960–1964, rose to 14 times greater for the period 1965–1969.[357] In the face of such realities, some critics of limited reform termed the laws "middle-class reform."[358]

Even before it became evident that limited abortion reform would not accomplish the objectives of those who sought to change the law, a small group in San Francisco began to call for total repeal—and began to take matters into its own hands. Medical technician Patricia Maginnis founded and led the Society for Humane Abortions to press for reform of the abortion laws; the Society came out in favor of total repeal of all restrictions on abortion by 1965.[359] At the same time, Maginnis organized a parallel group to run classes on abortion and to provide information on abortionists in Japan, Mexico, and Sweden.[360]

There were also hints that support for the *Model Penal Code* was in some circles a compromise from what supporters of change really wanted. Evidence of this is found in the statement of a prominent player in the game of change, Dr. Alan Guttmacher (by then, President of Planned Parenthood). Guttmacher wrote in 1967 that it was premature to advocate "abortion on demand" in face of the "beliefs and sentiments of most Americans."[361] Only a year before, however, Guttmacher had written in a private letter that he opposed repeal and favored limited reform not only because reform was politically feasible and repeal was not, but also because repeal would cause people to be careless about contraceptives and would develop "in both the medical profession and the laity a lack of reverence for life."[362] Guttmacher's thinking apparently changed quickly as he already was editing a book entitled *The Case for Legalized Abortion Now.*[363] In 1968, he would write that "the fetus, particularly during its early intra-uterine life, is merely a group of specialized cells that do not differ materially from other cells."[364] Under his leadership, the Planned Parenthood Federation reversed its opposition to elective abortion in 1968.[365]

Between 1967 and 1969, two conferences convened in the hope of achieving a consensus on the increasingly divisive issue of abortion. The first of the conferences convened in Washington, D.C., in 1967 under the auspices of the Harvard Divinity School and the Joseph P. Kennedy Foundation.[366] The conference included a wide range of participants, with, as one might have expected given the sponsorship, fully one-third religiously affiliated.[367] The meeting

---

356. Jaffe, Lindheim, & Lee, *supra* note 348, at 22.

357. Roger Rochat, Carl Tyler, & Albert Schoenbucher, *An Epidemiological Analysis of Abortion in Georgia,* 61 Am. J. Pub. Health 543, 543–44 (1971). *See also* Jaffe, Lindheim, & Lee, *supra* note 348, at 24 (reporting the abortion-related death rate for black women nationally as six times greater than for white women for 1966).

358. Graber, *supra* note 220, at 57; Lader, *supra* note 201, at 83–86; Packer, *supra* note 348, at 344; Irwin, *supra* note 344, at 23.

359. Patricia Maginnis, The Abortees' Songbook (1969). *See generally* Baehr, *supra* note 235, at 7–18; Luker, *supra* note 219, at 95–102; Reagan, *supra* note 112, at 222–24.

360. Baehr, *supra* note 235, at 10; Reagan, *supra* note 112, at 224.

361. Alan Guttmacher, *Introduction,* in Abortion Now, *supra* note 213, at 1, 12–13. *See generally* Reagan, *supra* note 112, at 233–34.

362. Quoted in Garrow, *supra* note 157, at 305. *See also* Reagan, *supra* note 112, at 234; Neal Devins, *The Countermajoritarian Paradox,* 93 Mich. L. Rev. 1433, 1442 (1995).

363. Abortion Now, *supra* note 213.

364. Alan Guttmacher, *Law, Morality, and Abortion,* 22 Rutgers L. Rev. 415, 416 (1968).

365. Lader, *supra* note 201, at 84; Noonan, *supra* note 27, at 36–38.

366. Reports on this conference appear in The Morality of Abortion, *supra* note 135; The Terrible Choice: The Abortion Dilemma (Robert Cooke & Andrew Hellegers eds. 1968). *See also* Garrow, *supra* note 157, at 340; Mensch & Freeman, *supra* note 122, at 110–14; Risen & Thomas, *supra* note 129, at 17–19.

367. Mensch & Freeman, *supra* note 122, at 216–17 n.1.

did not represent a single point of view. Attitudes about abortion laws ranged from those supporting an absolute prohibition to those who favored full legalization.[368] Most participants expressed deep reservations about the morality of abortion under most circumstances.[369] Some, like James Gustafson, argued for the morality of abortion under some circumstances.[370] The authors of a recent book noted that it was obvious that Catholic as well as Protestant participants in the conference "were willing to engage in open-minded dialogue on the abortion issue."[371]

Those favoring the radical change in the abortion laws were not happy with the 1967 conference. They convened a second conference at Hot Springs, Virginia, in 1968 under the sponsorship of the Association for the Study of Abortion as a direct counter to the conference a year earlier.[372] Those invited were stacked in favor of freedom of choice by a ratio of 20 to 1.[373] As David Garrow observed, "virtually all professional supporters of abortion law liberalization gathered for ASA's long-planned International Conference in Hot Springs...."[374] The conferees were predominantly physicians and nurses (56 of 93), compared to less than one-fourth (15 of 72) at the 1967 conference.[375] Religiously affiliated participates made up less than one-eighth (11 of 93) of the participants in contrast with the one-third at the 1967 conference. There was, furthermore, virtually no overlap in participants in the two conferences. Only two of the 93 Hot Springs conferees participated in the Harvard Divinity Conference.

Theologian Joseph Fletcher was the intended focus of what religiously based discussions occurred at Hot Springs.[376] Fletcher had gained prominence as an advocate of situational ethics that did not rely on abstract moral claims of the sort generally associated with religion.[377] Although Fletcher's perspective was not unchallenged, the entire meeting was dominated by secular voices that treated any metaphysical discussion as out of bounds.[378] Most participants looked to the physicians participating in the conference for answers.[379] Even the "women's panel" deferred to the physicians.[380] In the end, the conference crystallized a consensus among large parts of the managerial class in favor of at least abortion reform or even of the total repeal of abortion laws.

The triumphant secularism of the Hot Springs conference was not simply a convenient means for furthering the abortion agenda; rather, it represented a broad cultural change coming to

---

368. *See* MENSCH & FREEMAN, *supra* note 122, at 220 n.26.

369. *See* Bernard Häring, *A Theological Evaluation,* in THE TERRIBLE CHOICE, *supra* note 366, at 123; John Noonan, jr., *An Almost Absolute Value in History,* in THE MORALITY OF ABORTION, *supra* note 135, at 1; Ramsey, *supra* note 135.

370. James Gustafson, *A Protestant Ethical Approach,* in THE TERRIBLE CHOICE, *supra* note 366, at 101.

371. MENSCH & FREEMAN, *supra* note 122, at 113.

372. The proceedings were published in ABORTION IN A CHANGING WORLD (Robert Hall ed. 1970). *See also* GARROW, *supra* note 157, at 357–59; LAZARUS, *supra* note 212, at 345; MENSCH & FREEMAN, *supra* note 122, at 118–22.

373. NOONAN, *supra* note 27, at 44.

374. GARROW, *supra* note 157, at 357.

375. MENSCH & FREEMAN, *supra* note 122, at 224–25 n.58.

376. *See* Joseph Fletcher, *A Protestant Minister's View,* in 1 ABORTION IN A CHANGING WORLD, *supra* note 372, at 1.

377. *See* JOSEPH FLETCHER, MORAL RESPONSIBILITY: SITUATION ETHICS AT WORK (1967); JOSEPH FLETCHER, SITUATION ETHICS: THE NEW MORALITY (1966); THE SITUATION ETHICS DEBATE (Harvey Cox ed. 1968).

378. MENSCH & FREEMAN, *supra* note 122, at 118–21, 123–24.

379. *Id.* at 121–22. *See also* Packer & Gampell, *supra* note 126.

380. 2 ABORTION IN A CHANGING WORLD, *supra* note 372, at 201–03, 209. *See* MENSCH & FREEMAN, *supra* note 122, at 227–29, n.89.

fruition in the 1960s.[381] These changes were driven in part by changing technology that in turn brought about structural changes in the economy and the development of new media of communication. The very process of professionalization that had played a role in perfecting the prohibitions of abortion in the middle of the nineteenth century became an engine driving the reform and even repeal of those prohibitions in the middle of the twentieth century. As the Hot Springs conference demonstrated, by 1968 the desire for flexibility in personal relations—implying sexual freedom, easy divorce, and few or no children—was moving the "abortion rights" movement beyond mere reform and in favor of outright repeal.

Biologist Garrett Hardin was the first prominent advocate of complete repeal of the abortion laws and the first to advance publicly the claim of "a woman's absolute right to control her body," doing so as early as 1963.[382] In 1966, the Americans for Democratic Action became the first significant national institution to endorse complete repeal of abortion laws.[383] Financier John D. Rockefeller III became one of the first public figures to call openly for the total repeal of abortion laws—which he did in the keynote speech at the Hot Springs conference.[384]

In early 1968, Governor Nelson Rockefeller appointed the Governor's Select Committee to Review the State's Abortion Laws (the Froesel Commission), a body that helped to crystallize support behind repeal in New York.[385] Yet when the board of the American Civil Liberties Union early in 1967 endorsed support for legislative protection of a woman's right to choose (during the first 13 weeks of pregnancy), it accepted a committee report which concluded:

> There was almost unanimous agreement that restrictive laws are not unconstitutional on their face.... The Committee felt that restrictive abortion laws...while unduly restrictive, are not so unreasonable as to unconstitutional.... The Committee felt that society could decide...to place such value on the life of the unborn child (*sic!*) as to render abortion possible only in a narrow range of circumstance."[386]

At about the same time, the Massachusetts branch of the ACLU was reluctant to defend activist Bill Baird after his arrest for distributing contraceptives to unmarried persons.[387] Instead, Planned Parenthood of Massachusetts was careful to disassociate itself from Baird.[388] Even Cyril Means indicated in 1967 that any claim that the prohibitions of abortion were unconstitutional were "so perspicuously absurd" that he would not join any suit to litigate such a claim.[389] At the time, Means considered the laws against abortion simply required persons to accept the consequences of their actions. A year later, both Means and the ACLU had changed their minds.[390]

---

381. *See* NOONAN, *supra* note 27, at 38; Alice Rossi & Bhavani Sitaraman, *Abortion in Context: Historical Trends and Future Changes,* 20 FAM. PLANNING PERSP. 273, 276 (1988).

382. HARDIN, *supra* note 229; Garrett Hardin, *The Case for Legalized Abortion* [1963], in GARRETT HARDIN, STALKING THE WILD TABOO 10 (1973); Garrett Hardin, *Abortion and Human Dignity,* in LEGALIZED ABORTION NOW, *supra* note 213, at 69. *See* GARROW, *supra* note 157, at 293–95, 340.

383. GARROW, *supra* note 157, at 312.

384. John Rockefeller III, *Abortion Law Reform: The Moral Basis,* in ABORTION IN A CHANGING WORLD, *supra* note 372, at xix. *See also* NOONAN, *supra* note 27, at 44–45.

385. GARROW, *supra* note 157, at 345–46; RISEN & THOMAS, *supra* note 129, at 15.

386. GARROW, *supra* note 157, at 313–14. The Committee report and the ensuing discussion of it by the board has not been published; the quoted language appears in *id.* at 313.

387. *Id.* at 321–22.

388. *Id.* at 322–23.

389. *Id.* at 318–19. For Means' original view, Cyril Means, jr., *The Law of New York Concerning Abortion and the Status of the Foetus, 1664–1968: A Case of Cessation of Constitutionality,* 14 N.Y.L.F. 411 (1968).

390. On the ACLU's change, see GARROW, *supra* note 157, at 349–50. For Means, see *id.* at 356–57; Cyril Means, jr., *The Phoenix of Abortional Freedom: Is a Penumbral Right or Ninth-Amendment Right About to Arise from the Nineteenth-Century Legislative Ashes of a Fourteenth-Century Common-Law Liberty?,* 17 N.Y.L.F. 335

These changing perceptions led to the displacement of the reform movement in the United States by a more radical movement for the total overthrow of all restrictions on abortion (at least before 20 weeks of gestation). The American Public Health Association joined the call for a complete repeal of all abortion laws in 1968.[391] Planned Parenthood followed in 1969.[392] The year 1969 also saw the founding of the National Association for the Repeal of Abortion Laws (NARAL—later the National Abortion Rights Action League, then the National Abortion and Reproductive Rights Actions League, and now NARAL-Pro Choice America) as an umbrella organization dedicated to complete repeal.[393] Journalist Lawrence Lader—a confidant of Margaret Sanger who had written a book in 1966 to popularize the arguments for abortion reform[394]—became the first president of NARAL. Various other groups joined the repeal campaign quite rapidly. Law student Roy Lucas then set about to provide a legal analysis that would show that all abortion restrictions were unconstitutional.[395] Finally, the American Medical Association once again changed its position, endorsing abortion for social and economic reasons in 1970.[396] By the time Daniel Callahan published his book, *Abortion: Law, Choice, and Morality,*[397] in 1970, his call for reform of the abortion laws had already become politically obsolete.

Hawaii and New York in 1970 repealed all prohibitions in early pregnancy—before "viability" in Hawaii and before the twenty-fourth week of gestation (soon changed to the twentieth week) in New York.[398] Similar legislation followed in the Alaska, the District of Columbia, and Washington state.[399] In each state, repeal provoked a storm of opposition within and without the state's legislature.[400] Repeal changed the controversy. Opposition gathered strength after the repeals, while the "second wave" of feminism finally brought large numbers of women into the abortion debate. For this story, we turn to the next chapter.

---

(1971). On Means' role in reshaping the perceived history of abortion, see Chapter 1, at notes 59–71. Means' theories are examined in depth in Chapters 3, 4, 5, and 6.

391. GARROW, *supra* note 157, at 357; George, *supra* note 50, at 110.

392. GARROW, *supra* note 157, at 357.

393. ECHOLS, *supra* note 200, at 140–43; OLASKY, *supra* note 122, at 104–05; RUBIN, *supra* note 122, at 25–27. On the rational for repeal rather than reform, see BAEHR, *supra* note 235, at 33; RUDY, *supra* note 213, at 64–66.

394. LADER, *supra* note 201. Funding Lader and NARAL came from Hugh Moore, who had made millions from Dixie Cups and then devoted himself and his money to a radical program of advocating population control. *See* CRITCHLOW, *supra* note 51, at 4–5, 16–33, 54–55, 66–68, 75, 93, 150–54.

395. Lucas, *supra* note 213.

396. GARROW, *supra* note 157, at 455–56; HORDERN, *supra* note 27, at 243–44; LADER, *supra* note 201, at 42; PAIGE, *supra* note 312, at 44; PETCHESKY, *supra* note 112, at 124.

397. CALLAHAN, *supra* note 198.

398. 1970 Haw. Sess. Laws ch. 1, §2, codified at HAW. REV. STAT. §453-16 (1993); 1970 N.Y. Laws, ch. 127, codified at N.Y. PENAL LAW §§125.05(3), 125.15(2), 125.20(3), 125.40-125.60 (McKinney 1997).

399. 1970 Alaska Sess. Laws ch. 103, codified at ALASKA STAT. 18.16.010 to 18.16.090 (LexisNexis 2002); D.C. CODE ANN. §22-201 (1973); 1970 Wash. Laws ch. 3, codified at WASH. REV. CODE ANN. §9.02.100 (West 1998).

400. For the story of Hawaii's repeal, see BLANCHARD, *supra* note 312, at 26–28. The story of the political struggle in New York is told in BAEHR, *supra* note 235, at 31–49; GARROW, *supra* note 157, at 297–99, 304–05, 308, 310–19, 344–47, 407–10, 418–21, 431–32, 465–66; LADER, *supra* note 201, at 130–37. On the several repeal statutes generally, see Linton, *supra* note 252, at 161–236. *See also* GARROW, *supra,* at 411–14; GINSBURG, *supra* note 213, at 40; Sauer, *supra* note 220, at 64. The Washington repeal significantly was achieved through a referendum. GARROW, *supra,* at 465–66.

# Chapter 14

# When the Music's Over[1]

*[D]octrines that live by the sword of concocted history can perish in the same way, and the current vulnerability of privacy and intimate association doctrine suggests that while good history cannot secure a doctrine, unsupported history can weaken it.*

—William Wiecek[2]

The 1960s saw a sudden turn in social consciousness on many levels. One of the most sudden of the changes was the sea-change in social attitudes towards abortion. Before 1960, abortion was not a topic for polite conversation. At the beginning of the decade, abortion was a crime and there were few significant advocates for the changing the law.[3] Only in a few Communist and socialist countries and in Japan was abortion legal and commonly available.[4] Yet there was a large and growing illegal trade in abortions, a trade wrapped in shame and guilt, but a trade increasingly attractive to profit-seeking abortionists and to desperate women seeking an end to an unwanted pregnancy.[5] And the law changed. In the 1960s, a broadly based movement for changing the law of abortion emerged in both the United Kingdom and the United States. That movement succeeded, in the three years between 1967 and 1970, in enacting an "indications" policy in England and Wales,[6] and in enacting similar statutes in 13 states[7] and total repeal of restrictions on abortion in four states and the District of Columbia.[8] These remarkable changes did not occur

---

1. Jim Morrison, *When the Music's Over* (1967).

2. William Wiecek, *Clio as Hostage: The United States Supreme Court and the Uses of History,* 24 Cal. W. L. Rev. 227, 247 (1988)

3. *See* Rosalind Pollack Petchesky, Abortion and Women's Choice: The State, Sexuality, and Reproductive Freedom 243 (rev. ed. 1990); Mary Kenny, Abortion: The Whole Story 183 (1986); Roger Rosenblatt, Life Itself: Abortion in the American Mind 80 (1992); Bernard Dickens & Rebecca Cook, *Development of Commonwealth Abortion Laws,* 28 Int'l & Comp. L.Q. 424, 425–32 (1979); Bonnie Hertberg, *Resolving the Abortion Debate: Compromise Legislation, an Analysis of the Policies in the United States, France, and Germany,* 16 Suffolk Transnat'l L. Rev. 513, 545 (1993); Jeremy Telman, *Abortion and Women's Legal Personhood in Germany: A Contribution to the Feminist Theory of the State,* 24 Rev. L. & Soc. Change 91, 97 (1998).

4. For the status of abortion around the world before 1960, see Daniel Callahan, Abortion: Law, Choice, and Morality 185–223, 253–57 (1970); Samuel Coleman, Family Planning in Japan 19–20 (1983); Paul Gebhard et al., Pregnancy, Birth and Abortion 221–32 (1958); Germain Grisez, Abortion: The Myths, the Realities, and the Arguments 194–206, 253–56 (1970); Kenny, *supra* note 3, at 183. *See generally* Chapter 12, at notes 3–41, 252–342.

5. *See* Chapter 12, at notes 165–251.

6. *Abortion Act of 1967. See* Chapter 13, at notes 52–68. On developments in other countries, see Chapter 15, at notes 141–361.

7. *See* Paul Linton, *Enforcement of State Abortion Statutes after Roe: A State-by-State Analysis,* 67 U. Det. L. Rev. 157, 158–61, 255–59 (1990). *See* Chapter 13, at notes 248–51.

8. 1970 Alaska Sess. Laws ch. 103, also codified at Alaska Stat. 18.16.010 to 18.16.090; 67 Stat. 93, ch. 159, §22-201 (1970), codified at D.C. Code Ann. §22-201; 1970 Haw. Sess. Laws ch. 1, §2, codified at Haw. Rev. Stat. §1-2; 1970 N.Y. Laws, ch. 127, codified at N.Y. Penal Law §§125.05(3), 125.15(2), 125.20(3),

without controversy, and accomplishing these changes generated more controversy—in the United States[9] and abroad.[10] Abortion proved to be the most divisive social issue of our time.[11]

In contrast with the statutes enacting an indications policy, the repeal statutes generated real controversy in state legislatures. The New York *Abortion Reform Act of 1970* passed by only one vote, through a last minute change by a legislator of his vote.[12] Its enactment made New York City a national abortion Mecca. Two-thirds of the women obtaining abortions in the city in 1971

---

125.40–125.60; 1970 Wash. Laws ch. 3, codified at WASH. REV. CODE § 9.02.100. *See generally* Chapter 13, at notes 377–79.

9. *See generally* DALLAS BLANCHARD, THE ANTI-ABORTION MOVEMENT AND THE RISE OF THE RELIGIOUS RIGHT: FROM POLITE TO FIERY PROTEST (1994); ETHAN BRONNER, BATTLE FOR JUSTICE: HOW THE BORK NOMINATION SHOOK AMERICA (1988); ELIZABETH ADELL COOK, TED JELEN, & CLYDE WILCOX, BETWEEN TWO ABSOLUTES: PUBLIC OPINION AND THE POLITICS OF ABORTION (1992); BARBARA HINKINSON CRAIG & DAVID O'BRIEN, ABORTION AND AMERICAN POLITICS (1993); MARIAN FAUX, CRUSADERS: VOICES FROM THE ABORTION FRONT (1990); FEDERAL ABORTION POLITICS: A DOCUMENTARY HISTORY (Neal Devins & Wendy Watson eds. 1995); FAYE GINSBURG, CONTESTED LIVES: THE ABORTION DEBATE IN AN AMERICAN COMMUNITY (1989); KENNETH KARST, LAW'S PROMISE, LAW'S EXPRESSION: VISIONS OF POWER IN THE POLITICS OF RACE, GENDER, AND RELIGION 31–66 (1993); KRISTIN LUKER, ABORTION AND THE POLITICS OF MOTHERHOOD (1984); STEPHEN MARKMAN, JUDICIAL SELECTION: MERIT, IDEOLOGY AND POLITICS—THE REAGAN YEARS (1990); PATRICK McGUIGAN & DAWN WEYRICH, NINTH JUSTICE: THE BATTLE FOR BORK (1990); MICHELLE McKEEGAN, ABORTION POLITICS: MUTINY IN THE RANKS OF THE RIGHT (1992); MICHAEL PERTSCHUK & WENDY SCHAETZEL, THE PEOPLE RISING: THE CAMPAIGN AGAINST THE BORK NOMINATION (1989); PETCHESKY, *supra* note 3, at 241–76; EVA RUBIN, ABORTION, POLITICS, AND THE COURTS (rev. ed. 1987); CATHERINE WHITNEY, WHOSE LIFE? A BALANCED, COMPREHENSIVE VIEW OF ABORTION FROM ITS HISTORICAL CONTEXT TO THE CURRENT DEBATE (1991); SUZANNE STAGGENBORG, THE PRO-CHOICE MOVEMENT: ORGANIZATION AND ACTIVISM IN THE ABORTION CONFLICT (1991); BARBARA YARNOLD, ABORTION POLITICS IN THE FEDERAL COURTS: RIGHT VERSUS RIGHT (1995); Carla da Luz & Pamela Weckerly, *Recent Development, Will the New Republican Majority in Congress Wage Old Battles against Women?*, 5 UCLA WOMEN'S L.J. 501, 511–17 (1995); Neil Devins, *Through the Looking Glass: What Abortion Teaches Us about American Politics*, 94 COLUM. L. REV. 293 (1994); Merrill McLaughlin, *America's New Civil War*, U.S. NEWS & WORLD REP., Oct. 3, 1988, at 23; Fawn Vrazo, *Conservative Ascendancy Propels Abortion to the Crossroads*, PHILA. INQUIRER, Nov. 13, 1994, at A15. Note that these sources often make no pretense of neutrality, generally being strongly biased against opponents of abortion rights. Thus Catherine Whitney's book, subtitled *A Balanced, Comprehensive View*, is typical in being neither balanced nor comprehensive.

10. *See, e.g.,* F.L. MORTON, *MORGENTHALER V. BOROWSKI: THE CHARTER AND THE COURTS* (1992) ("MORTON, *MORGENTHALER*"); F.L. MORTON, PRO-CHOICE VS. PRO-LIFE AND THE COURTS IN CANADA (1993) ("MORTON, PRO-CHOICE"); *Anti-Abortion Law Reimposed in Poland*, N.Y. TIMES, Dec. 12, 1997, at A6; Sabine Berghahn, *Gender in the Legal Discourse in Post-Unification Germany: Old and New Lines of Conflict*, 2 SOC. POL.: INT'L STUD. IN GENDER, STATE & SOC'Y 37, 43–45 (1995); Donald Beschle, *Judicial Review and Abortion in Canada: Lessons for the United States in the Wake of* Webster v. Reproductive Health Services, 61 U. COLO. L. REV. 537 (1990); David Cole, *"Going to England": Irish Abortion Law and the European Community*, 17 HASTINGS INT'L & COMP. L. REV. 113 (1993); *Despite Pope's Protest, Polish Deputies Vote to Ease Abortion Law*, N.Y. TIMES, Oct. 25, 1996, at A4; Julie George, *Political Effects of Court Decisions on Abortion: A Comparison between the United States and the German Federal Republic*, 3 INT'L J.L. & FAM. 106 (1989); Deborah Goldberg, *Developments in German Abortion Law: A U.S. Perspective*, 5 UCLA WOMEN'S L.J. 531 (1995); Ewa Maleck-Lewy, *Between Self-Determination and State Supervision: Women and the Abortion Law in Post-Unification Germany*, 2 SOC. POL.: INT'L STUD. IN GENDER, STATE & SOC'Y 62 (1995); Anna Thompson, *International Protection of Women's Rights: An Analysis of* Open Door Counselling Ltd. and Dublin Woman Centre v. Ireland, 12 B.U. INT'L L.J. 371 (1994); Susan Walther, *Thou Shalt Not (But Thou Mayest): Abortion after the German Constitutional Court's 1993 Landmark Decision*, 36 GERMAN Y.B. INT'L L. 385 (1993); Noel Whitty, *Law and the Regulation of Reproduction in Ireland, 1922–1992*, 43 U. TOR. L.J. 351 (1993); Eleanora Zielinska, *Recent Trends in Abortion Legislation in Eastern Europe, with Particular Reference to Poland*, 4 CRIM. L.F. 47 (Regina Gorzkowska trans. 1993).

11. *See* Chapter 16.

12. ROSENBLATT, *supra* note 3, at 92; LAURENCE TRIBE, ABORTION: THE CLASH OF ABSOLUTES 47–49 (1990).

and 1972 came from outside the state,[13] indicating less of a local constituency for abortion than the raw number of abortions suggest. This was true in other repeal states as well. And a political reaction against the liberalization or repeal movement became pronounced immediately after the pro-abortion movement's successes culminated in the five repeal statutes of 1970.

The New York legislator who changed his vote finished third in the next election later that year and never again sat in the legislature.[14] New York courts quickly struck down local regulations that might have restricted abortions in some communities in the state.[15] The courts made short work of attempts by several abortion opponents to be appointed "guardians *ad litem*" (pending litigation) for an unborn child.[16] Trial courts also took steps to make it more difficult to convict persons caught performing illegal abortions in the state.[17] And the one case in which the court upheld a conviction for unlawful abortion contained no statement of the facts or discussion of the law, making it unhelpful as a precedent.[18] This pattern represented an abrupt change from the time before the new abortion statute.[19]

Abortion opponents succeeded on a few points. The power of departments of health to collect data from the clinics was upheld, although the courts did require the departments to assure the confidentiality of the resulting records.[20] Abortion opponents also obtained injunctions against abortion referral services that split fees with the abortion clinic to which the service referred patients.[21] The injunctions were not granted, however, on the grounds that

---

13. Jean Pakter *et al.*, *Two Years Experience in New York City with the Liberalized Abortion Law—Progress and Problems*, 63 Am. J. Pub. Health 524, 524–25 (1973). *See also* Leslie Reagan, When Abortion Was a Crime: Women, Medicine, and Law in the United States, 1867–1973, at 241–42 (1997).

14. Ira Lupu, *When Cultures Collide*, 103 Harv. L. Rev. 951, 961 (1990).

15. Robin v. Village of Hempstead, 285 N.E.2d 285 (N.Y. 1972) (striking down a local ordinance requiring abortions to be performed in accredited—and highly regulated—hospitals); People v. Dobbs Ferry Med. Pavilion, Inc., 340 N.Y.S.2d 108 (App. Div. 1973) (finding a state statute regulating hospital-performed abortions to be unconstitutional); People v. Hatchamovitch, 334 N.Y.S.2d 565 (App. Div. 1972) (striking down a local ordinance requiring abortions to be performed in accredited—and highly regulated—hospitals); Kim v. Town of Orangetown, 321 N.Y.S.2d 724 (Sup. Ct. 1971) (same). *But see* People v. Wickersham, 329 N.Y.S.2d 627 (Sup. Ct. 1972) (enjoining a free standing clinic as an "unlicensed hospital" although the clinic had applied for a license and had been approved by the New York City Dep't of Health).

16. Ryan v. Beth Israel Hosp., 409 N.Y.S.2d 681 (Sup. Ct. 1978); *In re* Unborn Infant of Gweyndolyn Thomas, 460 N.Y.S.2d 716 (Surr. Ct. 1983); *In re* Klein, 538 N.Y.S.2d 274 (Sup. Ct. 1989). Where a mother sought a protective order against an abusive husband in order to protect her unborn child, however, the order was granted. Gloria C. v. William C., 476 N.Y.S.2d 991 (Fam. Ct. 1984).

17. People v. Williams, 411 N.Y.S.2d 630 (App. Div. 1979); People v. Miller, 320 N.Y.S.2d 255 (App. Div. 1971).

18. People v. Perel, 346 N.Y.S.2d 785 (App. Div. 1973).

19. *See* People v. Black, 306 N.Y.S.2d 720 (App. Div. 1970) (upholding the conviction of an abortionist on two counts of abortion for two separate abortion procedures performed on the same person within a week); People v. Pontani, 306 N.Y.S.2d 240 (App. Div. 1969) (upholding defendant's conviction for conspiracy to commit abortion even though he had not been indicted for conspiracy); Mascitelli v. Board of Regents, 299 N.Y.S.2d 1002 (App. Div. 1969) (upholding the revocation of a physician's license to practice medicine based upon his guilty plea to a charge of criminal abortion).

20. Short v. Board of Managers of Nassau Cty. Med. Ctr., 442 N.E.2d 1235 (N.Y. 1982); Schulman v. New York City Health & Hosp. Corp., 342 N.E.2d 501 (N.Y. 1975); Bell v. Elco Corp., 521 N.Y.S.2d 368 (Sup. Ct. 1987); State v. Jacobus, 348 N.Y.S.2d 907 (Sup. Ct. 1973). *See also* City of Akron v. Akron Ctr. for Reprod. Health, 462 U.S. 416, 426–31 (1983); Thornburgh v. American College of Obstetricians & Gynecologists, 476 U.S. 747, 765–68 (1986).

21. State v. Abortion Inf. Agency, Inc., 285 N.E.2d 317 (N.Y. 1972); State v. Mitchell, 321 N.Y.S.2d 756 (Sup. Ct. 1971). *See also* Montwill Corp. v. Lefkowitz, 321 N.Y.S.2d 975 (Sup. Ct. 1971) (barring investigators of an abortion referral service from learning the precise type of abortions performed in the clinic); Lefkowitz v. Women's Pavilion, 321 N.Y.S.2d 963 (Sup. Ct. 1971) (barring investigators of an abortion referral service from learning the identity of particular clients); *In re* Weitzner, 321 N.Y.S.2d 925 (Sup. Ct. 1971) (upholding a

the service had a financial incentive to encourage the women being counseled to have abortions, but because the fee splitting the service was actually functioning as a "doctor's office" without a license. Courts also upheld a decision by the state Commissioner of Social Services that only "medically indicated" abortions were entitled to Medicaid reimbursements in New York.[22]

No reform or repeal statutes were enacted in the United States in 1971. In 1971 (only a year after repealing all restrictions on early abortions), New York's legislature lowered the time period in which a woman's choice to abort would be controlling ("abortion on demand") from 24 weeks to 20 weeks, prohibited public funding for abortions for the indigent, and prohibited all for-profit abortion clinics.[23] Finally, in 1972 New York's legislature attempted to reinstate severe restrictions on the availability of abortion even early in pregnancy, voting by margins of 79-68 in the state house and 30-27 in the state senate to repeal the state's *Abortion Reform Act of 1970.*[24] Governor Rockefeller vetoed the bill after the legislature adjourned.[25] The decision in *Roe v. Wade*[26] intervened to preclude further action after the legislature reconvened—much to Governor Rockefeller's relief, for he did not relish having to face another legislative battle.[27]

By 1973, the legislative reform or repeal drive had stalled, with only one state having changed its law since 1970, and several proposed reform bills having been defeated.[28] Calculating that indications bills were the most they could secure from legislatures, most abortion rights activists did not even seek outright repeal.[29] Pennsylvania's legislature voted overwhelmingly (157-34 in the Assembly) to prohibit abortions except to save the mother's life and the Massachusetts legislature was similarly decisive (176-46 in the General Court) in enacting a bill to define human life as beginning at conception.[30] In Connecticut, after a court declared its abortion statute unconstitutional,[31] the legislature promptly adopted another restrictive statute.[32] Referenda in several states resulted in overwhelming defeats of proposals to legalize

---

subpoena of a physician as a witness in a state investigation of the financial dealings of an abortion referral service).

22. Hope v. Perales, 634 N.E.2d 183 (N.Y. 1994); New York City v. Wyman, 281 N.E.2d 180 (N.Y. 1972).

23. *See* DAVID GARROW, LIBERTY AND SEXUALITY: THE RIGHT OF PRIVACY AND THE MAKING OF *ROE V. WADE* 483, 495 ( 2nd ed. 1998).

24. GARROW, *supra* note 23, at 483, 497, 545–47, 566–67, 578.

25. William Farrell, *Governor Vetoes Abortion Repeal Act as Not Justified: Tells Legislature He Finds No Cause for "Condemning" Women to "the Dark Age,"* N.Y. TIMES, May 14, 1972, at 1.

26. Roe v. Wade, 410 U.S. 113 (1973).

27. GARROW, *supra* note 23, at 605.

28. DONALD CRITCHLOW, INTENDED CONSEQUENCES: BIRTH CONTROL, ABORTION, AND THE FEDERAL GOVERNMENT IN MODERN AMERICA 146–47 (1999); GINSBURG, *supra* note 9, at 40; EDWARD LAZARUS, CLOSED CHAMBERS: THE FIRST EYEWITNESS ACCOUNT OF THE EPIC STRUGGLES INSIDE THE SUPREME COURT 345–46 (1998); RAYMOND TATALOVICH & BYRON DAYNES, THE POLITICS OF ABORTION: A STUDY OF COMMUNITY CONFLICT IN PUBLIC POLICY MAKING 63 (1981); Julie George, *Political Effects of Court Decisions on Abortion: A Comparison between the United States and the German Federal Republic,* 3 INT'L J.L. & FAM. 106, 111 (1989). Gerald Rosenberg, intent on discrediting the Supreme Court as a force for social change, argued that the legislative route was well on the way to accomplishing the changes the Court would shortly introduce through *Roe v. Wade,* completely ignoring the anti-abortion movement's success in blocking further legislative action after 1970. *See* GERALD ROSENBERG, THE HOLLOW HOPE: CAN COURTS BRING ABOUT SOCIAL CHANGE 178–84 (1991).

29. GARROW, *supra* note 23, at 355, 374.

30. *Id.* at 547.

31. Abele v. Markele, 342 F. Supp. 800 (D. Conn. 1972), *vacated after* Roe v. Wade, 410 U.S.915 (1973).

32. CELESTE MICHELLE CONDIT, DECODING ABORTION RHETORIC: COMMUNICATING SOCIAL CHANGE 65 (1990); RUBIN, *supra* note 9, at 86; Amy Kesselman, *Women versus Connecticut: Conducting a Statewide Hearing on Abortion,* in ABORTION WARS: A HALF CENTURY OF STRUGGLE, 1950–2000, at 42 (Rickie Solinger ed. 1998).

elective abortions even early in pregnancy in Michigan (61 percent against) and North Dakota (77 percent against—and that in a state where Catholics were only 12 percent of the population).[33] Opponents of abortion continue down to today to win most similar referenda regularly, with only rare defeats.[34] One might argue that such ballots produce distorted and unreliable results.[35] Supporters of abortion rights, however, generally do not make such arguments. Instead, they maintain a studied silence regarding electoral defeats, noting only the rare victory as "proving" that they represent the majority.[36] Among feminist scholars, apparently only Robin West has frankly admitted that the political momentum had swung strongly against the abortion reform movement in the two years before *Roe v. Wade*.[37] As David Kirp would write in the *New Republic* some 20 years later, "[i]t is wishful thinking…to imagine that, had they simply stayed out of court, abortion proponents could have slipped the issue by the right-to-life contingent much longer."[38]

Even in states where abortion reform had succeeded, the effect varied widely depending on the degree of public acceptance of the reform laws. While the reform ("indications") statutes were all modeled after the American Law Institute's *Model Penal Code* and adopted strikingly similar lists of indications as legal justifications for abortions, the actual legal abortion rates varied dramatically from state to state. The Centers for Disease Control found in 1970 that, among the reform states, California had an abortion rate of 135 abortions/1,000 live births, Maryland had 102/1,000, Colorado had 41/1,000, Virginia had 13/1,000, and the two Carolinas each had rates of 7/1,000.[39] Furthermore, legal abortion rates varied widely in different parts of a state, often with virtually all legal abortions in a particular state being performed in one or a few major cities, or even in a single facility.[40] Thus, about 64 percent of all legal abortions in California took place in San Francisco in 1968,[41] while more than 90 percent of all legal abortions in Maryland were in Baltimore in 1969.[42] The special septic abortion units at hospitals in these cities were the basis for exaggerated estimates of the rates of illegal abortions before *Roe v. Wade*.[43]

The struggles over segregation and criminal procedure accustomed Americans seeking to change society to a special confidence in the ability of courts to succeed where legislatures and

---

33. GARROW, *supra* note 23, at 496, 538, 547, 562–63, 567, 576–77; GINSBURG, *supra* note 9, at 64–72; JOHN NOONAN, JR., A PRIVATE CHOICE: ABORTION IN AMERICA IN THE SEVENTIES 34 (1979); Robert Destro, *Abortion and the Constitution: The Need for a Life-Protective Amendment*, 63 CAL. L. REV. 1250, 1337–38 (1975); Russell Kirk, *The Sudden Death of Feticide*, NAT'L REV., Dec. 22, 1972, at 1407.

34. CRAIG & O'BRIEN, *supra* note 9, at 65, 292.

35. *Cf.* Judith Daar, *Direct Democracy and Bioethical Choices: Voting Life and Death at the Ballot Box*, 28 U. MICH. J.L. REFORM 799 (1995) (arguing the unreliability of referenda as measures of public support for the "right to die").

36. CONDIT, *supra* note 32, at 74 n.7. *See generally* MCKEEGAN, *supra* note 9.

37. Robin West, *Book Review*, 13 LAW & HIST. REV. 433, 435 (1995).

38. David Kirp, *How Now, Brown*, THE NATION, June 1, 1992, at 757, 759.

39. James Kahn *et al.*, *Surveillance of Abortion in Hospitals in the United States, 1970*, 86 HSMHA HEALTH REP. 423, 425 (1971).

40. MARK GRABER, RETHINKING ABORTION: EQUAL CHOICE, THE CONSTITUTION, AND REPRODUCTIVE POLITICS 42 (1996). *See also* Alan Guttmacher, *The Genesis of Liberalized Abortion in New York: A Personal Insight*, 23 CASE-W. RES. L. REV. 756, 760 (1972).

41. Keith Russell & Edwin Jackson, *Therapeutic Abortions in California: First Year's Experience under New Legislation*, 105 AM. J. OBSTET. & GYNECOLOGY 757, 760 (1969).

42. Theodore Irwin, *The New Abortion Laws: How Are They Working?*, TODAY'S HEALTH, Mar. 1970, at 22, 23.

43. *See* GRABER, *supra* note 40, at 43; FOWLER HARPER & JEROME SKOLNICK, PROBLEMS OF THE FAMILY 182 (1962); PATRICIA MILLER, THE WORST OF TIMES 74, 119, 157, 221, 285 (1993); FREDERICK TAUSSIG, ABORTION: SPONTANEOUS AND INDUCED 158–61, 175–79 (1936); Donald Swartz, *The Harlem Hospital Experience*, in THE ABORTION EXPERIENCE: PSYCHOLOGICAL AND MEDICAL IMPACT 94, 95–96 (Howard & Joy Orsofsky eds. 1973).

executives failed.[44] The Warren Court, during the years 1953–1968,[45] followed a program of "un-relieved judicial activism in which one 'liberal' principle after another was discovered in or writ-ten into the Constitution"[46]—as even the court's admirers admitted.[47] The Warren Court exem-plified what law professor Laura Kalman calls "legal liberalism"—"trust in the potential of courts, particularly the Supreme Court, to bring about 'those specific social reforms that affect large groups of people…policy change with national impact.'"[48] Clerks who served with, and bi-ographers of, several Warren Court justices have disclosed how indifferent the justices were to legal authority for their decisions.[49] As a result, the Warren Court functioned as "an element of Johnson's Great Society coalition."[50] Finally, the Warren Court gave the nation an extreme and unprecedented claim for unquestioning obedience to its every whim:

> [*Marbury v. Madison*] declared the basic principle that the federal judiciary is supreme in the exposition of the law of the Constitution, and that principle has ever been respected by this Court and the Country as a permanent and indispensable fea-ture of our constitutional system. It follows that the interpretation of the Fourteenth Amendment enunciated by this Court in the *Brown* case is the supreme law of the land….[51]

In other words, the Constitution is what the Court says it is, and no one can question that.[52]

The attitude of the Warren Court carried over for at least a decade after Earl Warren retired.[53] With the legislative drive stalling, pro-abortion activists turned to the courts. They could expect a sympathetic hearing before a Supreme Court that was notoriously unsympathetic to the gov-

---

44. *The Future of the Court*, N.Y. TIMES, April 12, 1970, at E12.

45. THE WARREN COURT IN HISTORICAL AND POLITICAL PERSPECTIVE (Mark Tushnet ed. 1993) ("THE WARREN COURT").

46. DAVID CURRIE, THE CONSTITUTION IN THE SUPREME COURT: THE SECOND CENTURY, 1888–1986, at 375 (1990).

47. *See, e.g.*, RONALD DWORKIN, TAKING RIGHTS SERIOUSLY 136, 147 (1976) (discussing the "moral virtue" of the Warren Court in constitutionalizing its values); 2 ALFRED KELLY *et al.*, THE AMERICAN CONSTITUTION: ITS ORIGINS AND DEVELOPMENT 612 (7th ed. 1991) (describing the "breathtaking boldness" of the Warren Court); BERNARD SCHWARTZ, A HISTORY OF THE SUPREME COURT 263 (1993) (concluding that the Warren Court behaved more like a legislature than like a court). *See also* LAURA KALMAN, THE STRANGE CAREER OF LEGAL LIBERALISM 56 (1996) ("Law professors, many of whom had clerked at the Court, celebrated the great-ness and courageousness of Warren and his colleagues when Earl Warren surrendered the Chief Justice-ship…."); PHILIP KURLAND, POLITICS, THE CONSTITUTION, AND THE WARREN COURT 172–74 (1970) (a critic of the Warren Court who described it as behaving more like a legislature than like a court). The Warren Court, however, did not act unless there were wide-spread support for its views. *See* Michal Belknap, *The Warren Court and the Vietnam War: The Limits of Legal Liberalism*, 33 GA. L. REV. 65 (1998); Michael Klar-man, *Rethinking the Civil Rights and Civil Liberties Revolutions*, 82 VA. L. REV. 1 (1996).

48. KALMAN, *supra* note 47, at 2.

49. KALMAN, *supra* note 47, at 2; G. EDWARD WHITE, EARL WARREN: A PUBLIC LIFE 229 (1982); Belknap, *supra* note 6, at 68–71; Mark Tushnet, *The Warren Court as History: An Interpretation*, in THE WARREN COURT, *supra* note 45, at 1, 17–18; G. Edward White, *Earl Warren's Influence on the Warren Court*, in THE WARREN COURT, *supra*, at 37, 44; G. Edward White, *The Anti-Judge: William O. Douglas and the Ambiguities of Individ-uality*, 74 VA. L. REV. 17, 79–80 (1988).

50. KALMAN, *supra* note 47, at 43. *See also* JOHN MORTON BLUM, YEARS OF DISCORD 135, 186, 216–17 (1991); Tushnet, *supra* note 49, at 20.

51. Cooper v. Aaron, 358 U.S. 1 (1958).

52. *See, e.g.*, DANIEL FARBER *et al.*, CASES AND MATERIALS ON CONSTITUTIONAL LAW: THEMES FOR THE CONSTITUTION'S THIRD CENTURY 68–71 (2nd ed. 1998); GERALD GUNTHER & KATHLEEN SULLIVAN, CONSTI-TUTIONAL LAW 26 (13th ed. 1997); GEOFFREY STONE *et al.*, CONSTITUTIONAL LAW 53 (3rd ed. 1996).

53. *See, e.g.*, Belknap, *supra* note 47, at 151–53. Some would attribute this carry over to the influence of Justice William Brennan, so much so that some commentators refer to the 1960s and 1970s as the era of the "Brennan Court." *See, e.g.*, Tushnet, *supra* note 49, at 33.

ernment in cases involving claims of civil liberties.[54] Symbolic of this change of strategy was the decision of the American Civil Liberties Union in 1968 to shift from endorsing abortion reform to embracing abortion on demand before viability, with this lawyers' club choosing to throw substantial resources into securing what it now discovered to be a fundamental liberty after ignoring it for the first 47 years of the its history.[55] Only a year earlier, the Union had endorsed a woman's right to choose only during the first thirteen weeks of pregnancy, and then with some misgivings about the life of the "unborn child."[56]

Litigation actually began almost as soon as the first legislative enactments. Lower state and federal courts split over the constitutionality of abortion statutes in the nearly six years between the adoption of the Colorado statute and *Roe's* consideration by the Supreme Court.[57] Most of these decisions were vacated and remanded by the Supreme Court in the wake of *Roe*. The cases striking down the statutes followed the trail blazed by a law student, Roy Lucas.[58] Lucas's work won important endorsement from retired Supreme Court Justice Tom Clark.[59] Only in 1994 did New York's highest court review the question and reject Lucas' conclusions.[60]

---

54. *See* S. Sidney Ulmer, *Governmental Litigants, Underdogs, and Civil Liberties in the Supreme Court: 1963–1968 Terms*, 47 J. Pol. 899, 903, 906 (1985) (finding that the government won in less than one-third of the civil liberties cases).

55. Noonan, *supra* note 33, at 36.

56. *See* Chapter 13, at notes 365–66.

57. *Holding abortion statutes constitutional:* Crossen v. Attorney General, 344 F. Supp. 587 (E.D. Ky. 1972), *vacated,* 410 U.S. 950 (1973); Corkey v. Edwards, 322 F. Supp. 1248 (W.D.N.C. 1971), *vacated,* 410 U.S. 950 (1973); Steinberg v. Brown, 321 F. Supp. 741 (N.D. Ohio 1970); Doe v. Rampton, No. C-234-70 (D. Utah 1970), *vacated,* 410 U.S. 950 (1973); Rosen v. Board in Medical Examiners, 318 F. Supp. 1217 (E.D. La. 1970), *vacated,* 412 U.S. 902 (1973); Cheaney v. State, 285 N.E.2d 265 (Ind. 1972), *cert. denied for lack of standing,* 410 U.S. 991 (1973); State v. Abodeely, 179 N.W.2d 347 (Iowa 1970), *appeal dismissed,* 402 U.S. 936 (1971); Sasaki v. Commonwealth, 485 S.W.2d 897 (Ky. 1972), *vacated after* Roe v. Wade, 410 U.S. 951 (1973); State v. Campbell, 270 So. 2d 506 (La. 1972); State v. Scott, 255 So. 2d 736 (La. 1971); State v. Shirley, 237 So. 2d 676 (La. 1970); State v. Pesson, 235 So. 2d 568 (La. 1970); Spears v. State, 257 So. 2d 876 (Miss. 1972), *cert. denied,* 409 U.S. 1106 (1973); Rodgers v. Danforth, 486 S.W.2d 258 (Mo. 1972); State v. Moretti, 244 A.2d 499 (N.J. 1968); State v. Kruze, No. 72-11 (Ohio Mar. 10, 1972), *vacated after* Roe v. Wade, 410 U.S. 951 (1973); State v. Munson, 201 N.W.2d 123 (S.D. 1972), *vacated after* Roe v. Wade, 410 U.S. 950 (1973); Thompson v. State, 493 S.W.2d 913 (Tex. Ct. Crim. App. 1971), *vacated after* Roe v. Wade, 410 U.S. 950 (1973); State v. Bartlett, 270 A.2d 168 (Vt. 1970). *Holding abortion statutes unconstitutional:* Abele v. Markele, 342 F. Supp. 800, 351 F. Supp. 224 (D. Conn. 1972), *vacated,* 410 U.S. 951 (1973); YWCA of Princeton v. Kugler, 342 F. Supp. 1048 (D.N.J. 1972) *vacated,* 475 F.2d 1398 (3rd Cir. 1973), *aff'd after remand,* 493 F.2d 1402 (3rd Cir. 1974); Poe v. Menghini, 339 F. Supp. 986 (D. Kan. 1972); Doe v. Scott, 321 F. Supp. 1385 (N.D. Ill. 1971), *vacated after* Roe v. Wade, 410 U.S. 950 (1973); Babbitz v. McCann, 310 F. Supp. 273 (E.D. Wis. 1970), *appeal dismissed,* 400 U.S. 1 (1970); Nelson v. Planned Parenthood Center of Tucson, Inc., 505 P.2d 580 (Ariz. Ct. App. 1973); People v. Barksdale, 503 P.2d 257 (Cal. 1972); People v. Belous, 458 P.2d 194 (Cal. 1969), *cert. denied,* 397 U.S. 915 (1970); State v. Barquet, 262 So. 2d 431 (Fla. 1972); State v. Nixon, 201 N.W.2d 635 (Mich. Ct. App. 1972), *on remand,* 212 N.W.2d 607 (Mich. Ct. App. 1973); Beecham v. Leahy, 287 A.2d 836 (Vt. 1972). *See also* Byrn v. New York City Health & Hosp. Corp., 286 N.E.2d 887 (N.Y. 1972), *appeal dismissed after* Roe v. Wade, 410 U.S. 949 (1973) (*dictum* upholding constitutionality of state's reformed abortion statute while denying standing to a guardian *ad litem* claiming to represent the class of unborn children); Lee Epstein & Joseph Kobylka, The Supreme Court and Legal Change: Abortion and the Death Penalty 164–66 (1992); Noonan, *supra* note 33, at 15–18. The behind-the-scenes details of many of these cases are found in Garrow, *supra* note 23, at 284–85, 296, 298–99, 304, 306–10, 313–14, 318–20, 335–40, 349, 351–59, 364–67, 370–74, 377–88, 407–11, 414–18, 423–33, 457–65, 473–82, 487–90, 496–97, 509, 513, 522–23, 538–44, 561–62, 565–66, 579–80.

58. Roy Lucas, *Federal Constitutional Limitations on the Enforcement and Administration of State Abortion Statutes,* 46 N.C. L. Rev. 730 (1968).

59. Tom Clark, *Religion, Morality and Abortion: A Constitutional Appraisal,* 2 Loy.-L.A. L. Rev. 1 (1969). *See also* Devins, *supra* note 9, at 1441–43.

60. Hope v. Perales, 634 N.E.2d 183 (N.Y. 1994).

Some courts were particularly pro-abortion. In *People v. Belous,*[61] the California Supreme Court not only held the state's restrictive abortion statute unconstitutional, but also held that any abortion performed by a licensed physician must be presumed to have been necessary under any statutory exceptions, with a difficult burden of proof on the state to overcome to prove the unlawfulness of the abortion.[62] Such a presumption would be a problem in any attempt to re-criminalize abortion in California. (The 1969 decision in *Belous* tells us nothing about the rules governing prosecutions earlier in the twentieth century, although some pro-abortion advocates attempt to use the precedent in precisely this fashion.)[63] Lower courts in New York overturned the legislature's 1971 funding ban as violating the state constitution.[64]

The movement's victory in *Roe* fundamentally transformed the politics of abortion. Instead of those supporting abortion rights being "outsiders" attempting to change society against the wishes of many of its members, suddenly those who opposed abortion were the "outsiders" attempting to deprive many people of what they quickly came to feel was a fundamental right. Legislatures were disempowered to address the issue in any but superficial ways. The decision in *Roe* provoked those who opposed abortion rights into organizing themselves nationally, while those who supported abortion rights continued to function in their national organizations. The division over abortion in the United States became deeper and increasingly bitter.

# Enter the Women

*I am woman, hear me roar, in numbers too big to ignore.*

—Helen Reddy[65]

After 1969, legislative debates about limited abortion reform were overtaken by a change in the rhetoric and goals of those supporting the legalization of abortion—from a demand for access to abortion in difficult circumstances to a demand for a "right of choice."[66] Celeste Condit has identified this change as the introduction of feminist discourse into mainstream public debate.[67] There is a certain irony here given the problematic nature of "choice" as a basis for a feminist jurisprudence.[68] Even after the abortion reform movement began, for more than a decade,

---

61. 458 P.2d 194 (Cal. 1969), *cert. denied,* 397 U.S. 915 (1970).

62. *See also* People v. Ballad, 335 P 2d 204 (Cal. 1959).

63. *See* GRABER, *supra* note 40, at 45.

64. City of New York v. Wyman, 321 N.Y.S.2d 695 (N.Y. Cnty.), *aff'd,* 322 N.Y.S.2d 957 (App. Div. 1971).

65. Helen Reddy, *I Am Woman* (1972).

66. JANET HADLEY, ABORTION: BETWEEN FREEDOM AND NECESSITY 61 (1996); ELIZABETH MENSCH & ALAN FREEMAN, THE POLITICS OF VIRTUE: IS ABORTION DEBATABLE? 123–25 (1993).

67. CONDIT, *supra* note 32, at 64–72. *See also* NINIA BAEHR, ABORTION WITHOUT APOLOGY: A RADICAL HISTORY FOR THE 1990s, at 31–50 (1990); JUDITH HOLE & ELLEN LEVINE, REBIRTH OF FEMINISM 283–301 (1971); LUKER, *supra* note 9, at 95–125; REAGAN, *supra* note 13, at 222–34.

68. *See, e.g.,* RUTH COLKER, ABORTION & DIALOGUE—PRO-CHOICE, PRO-LIFE, AND AMERICAN LAW 83–143 (1992) ("COLKER, ABORTION & DIALOGUE"); RUTH COLKER, PREGNANT MEN: PRACTICE, THEORY, AND THE LAW 9–31, 173–202 (1994) ("COLKER, PREGNANT MEN"); BEVERLY WILDUNG HARRISON, OUR RIGHT TO CHOOSE: TOWARD A NEW ETHIC OF ABORTION (1983); NANCY HIRSCHMANN, RETHINKING OBLIGATION: A FEMINIST METHOD FOR POLITICAL THEORY (1992); CATHARINE MACKINNON, FEMINISM UNMODIFIED: DISCOURSES ON LIFE AND LAW 93–102 (1987) ("MACKINNON, F.U."); CATHARINE MACKINNON, TOWARD A FEMINIST THEORY OF THE STATE 184–94 (1989) ("MACKINNON, FEMINIST THEORY"); RUBIN, *supra* note 9, at 190–91; Anita Allen, *The Proposed Equal Protection Fix for Abortion Law: Reflections on Citizenship, Gender, and the Constitution,* 18 HARV. J.L. & PUB. POL'Y 419 (1995); April Cherry, *Choosing Substantive Justice: A Dis-*

from Carpentier Lectures of Glanville Williams (1956) to the transition to a demand for unlimited freedom of choice (1968–1970), abortion simply had not been a feminist cause.[69] Upper-middle class white men provided the abortion reform movement's strongest and most consistent support.[70] This pattern that continues to this day.[71] Women in general, and feminists in particular, supported criminal penalties for abortion throughout the nineteenth century and well into the twentieth century.[72] As Mary Kenny concluded, "Every opinion poll taken on this issue has shown men to be more liberal than women on abortion, and indeed to be more dispassionate."[73] The same pattern was, and is, found around the world.[74]

For many years, the leadership of the movement to change the abortion laws in the United States and the United Kingdom was largely white and male. The most prominent leaders were William Baird, Dr. Alan Guttmacher, Dr. Robert Hall, Garrett Hardin, Dr. Jerome Kummer, Lawrence Lader, Roy Lucas, Cyril Means, Dr. Bernard Nathanson, Bernard Schwartz, David

---

cussion of "Choice," "Rights" and the New Reproductive Technologies, 11 Wis. Women's L.J. 431 (1997); Rhonda Copelon, Losing the Negative Right of Privacy: Building Sexual and Reproductive Freedom, 18 NYU Rev. L. & Soc. Change 15 (1990); Erin Daly, Reconsidering Abortion Law: Liberty, Equality, and the New Rhetoric of Planned Parenthood v. Casey, 45 Am. U. L. Rev. 77 (1995); Susan Estrich & Kathleen Sullivan, Abortion Politics: Writing for an Audience of One, 138 U. Pa. L. Rev. 119, 150–54 (1989); Ruth Bader Ginsburg, Some Thoughts on Autonomy and Equality in Relation to Roe v. Wade, 63 N.C. L. Rev. 375 (1985); Ruth Bader Ginsburg, Speaking in a Judicial Voice, 67 NYU L. Rev. 1185, 1199–1202 (1992) ("Ginsburg, Judicial Voice"); Sylvia Law, Rethinking Sex and the Constitution, 132 U. Pa. L. Rev. 955, 1014–28 (1984); Frances Olsen, Unraveling Compromise, 103 Harv. L. Rev. 105, 117–35 (1989); Rachael Pine & Sylvia Law, Envisioning a Future for Reproductive Liberty: Strategies for Making the Rights Real, 27 Harv. C.R.-C.L. L. Rev. 407, 416–17 (1992); Catherine Grevers Schmidt, Where Privacy Fails: Equal Protection and the Abortion Rights of Minors, 68 NYU L. Rev. 597 (1993); Reva Siegel, Abortion as a Sex Equality Right: Its Basis in Feminist Theory, in Mothers in Law: Feminist Theory and the Legal Regulation of Motherhood 43 (Martha Albertson Fineman & Isabel Karpin eds. 1995); Lynn Smith, An Equality Approach to Reproductive Choice: R. v. Sullivan, 4 Yale J.L. & Fem. 93 (1991) (Canadian Charter of Rights).

69. Suzanne Staggenborg, The Pro-Choice Movement: Organization and Activism in the Abortion Conflict 20 (1991); Emily Moore, Abortion and Public Policy: What Are the Issues?, 17 N.Y. L.F. 411, 420 (1971); Alice Rossi & Bhavani Sitaraman, Abortion in Context: Historical Trends and Future Changes, 20 Fam. Planning Persp. 273, 273 (1988).

70. See, e.g., Anthony Hordern, Legal Abortion: The English Experience 227–30 (1971); Noonan, supra note 33, at 49–51; Judith Blake, Abortion and Public Opinion: The 1960–1970 Decade, 171 Science 540 (1971).

71. The Connecticut Mutual Life Report on American Values in the 80's, at 92 (1981); Craig & O'Brien, supra note 9, at 245–77; George Gallup, The Gallup Poll: Public Opinion 1986, at 49 (1987); Donald Judges, Hard Choices, Lost Voices 39–40 (1993); Kenny, supra note 3, at 65–86, National Opinion Research Center, General Social Survey, 1972–1987: Cumulative Codebook 229–30 (1987); Noonan, supra note 33, at 34–35, 48–50; David O'Brien, Storm Center: The Supreme Court in American Politics 39 (3rd ed. 1993); Hyman Rodman, Betty Sarvis, & Joy Bonar, The Abortion Question 140–41 (1987); Rosenblatt, supra note 3, at 137–89; Americans and Abortion, Newsweek, Apr. 24, 1989, at 39; Judith Blake, The Supreme Court's Abortion Decisions and Public Opinion in the United States, 3 Population & Dev. Rev. 45 (1977); E.J. Dionne, Poll on Abortion Finds the Nation is Sharply Divided, N.Y. Times, Apr. 26, 1989, at A1; George Skelton, Most Americans Think Abortion is Immoral, L.A. Times, Mar. 19, 1989, at 3; Wirthlin Group Survey, Jan. 15–17, 1990, in Public Op., May/June 1990, at 36. See generally Mary Ann Glendon, A Nation under Lawyers: How the Crisis in the Legal Profession Is Transforming American Society 50–52 (1994); Susan Nathanson, Soul Crisis 40 (1989); Mark Baker, Men on Abortion, Esquire 114 (Mar. 1990); Samuel Calhoun & Andrea Sexton, Is It Possible to Take Both Fetal Life and Women Seriously? Professor Lawrence Tribe and his Reviewers, 49 Was. & Lee L. Rev. 437, 445–46 (1992) (book rev.); Ellen Goodman, Men and Abortion, Glamour 178 (July 1989); Michael McConnell, How Not to Promote Serious Deliberation about Abortion, 58 U. Chi. L. Rev. 1181, 1190 (1991); Lynn Wardle, Rethinking Roe v. Wade, 1985 B.Y.U. L. Rev. 231, 244–45.

72. See Chapter 8.

73. Kenny, supra note 3, at 226.

74. Id. at 196.

Steel, Dr. Christopher Tietze, and Glanville Williams.[75] The meetings of the American Law Institute that brought forth the highly influential *Model Penal Code* supporting an indications policy for abortion were composed entirely of men[76] (the Institute still remains predominantly male). Ironically, lawyers and the doctors both identified the root of the problem as the abortion statutes rather than the hospital abortion committees that many of these same doctors helped to create and which had proven the most effective means of repressing voluntary abortions.[77]

So many of the male activists were physicians that a case could be made that their motivation was not so much to benefit women as to become able to obtain insurance for their hitherto illegal acts and to eliminate the risk of criminal prosecution. In other words, they supported abortion reform as a sound business strategy.[78] Some physicians in the 1960s argued that they merely favored legally codifying what was already standard medical practice.[79] A better explanation is that business interest combined with genuine empathy for women and a desire to assure professional control over the practice of medicine through excluding lawyers and judges.

Despite the growing mythology that describes the entire birth control movement, as well as the abortion reform movement, throughout the twentieth century as a "woman's movement,"[80] both movements were largely led by men (especially doctors) until the late 1960s. In contrast to the abortion reform movement, however, the birth control movement did feature the leadership of a large coterie of women, the best known being Dr. Mary Calderone, Estelle Griswold, Harriet Pilpel, and Margaret Sanger.[81] Several years later—in 1970—a woman legislator would state that the absence of women from the abortion reform movement was because women were not interested in reform and would not fight for it, but they would for repeal.[82] Even if that were true in 1970, we have no way of knowing how true it was even a short time before. After all, in the early years, it was not unusual for the majority of women in state legislatures (where the battles were mostly fought) to vote against reform or repeal of laws prohibiting contraceptives.[83] The

---

75. Dallas Blanchard & Terry Prewitt, Religious Violence and Abortion: The Gideon Project 240–41 (1993); Garrow, *supra* note 23, at 270–85, 343; Luker, *supra* note 9, at 145–46.

76. Garrow, *supra* note 23, at 275.

77. Reagan, *supra* note 13, at 218–19 (1997). On hospital abortion committees, see Chapter 12, at notes 217–42.

78. Noonan, *supra* note 33, at 35–36; Brian Clowes, *The Role of Maternal Deaths in the Abortion Debate,* 13 St.L. U. Pub. L. Rev. 327, 339–45 (1993).

79. *See* Alan Guttmacher, *Abortion Laws Make Hypocrites of Us All,* 4 New Med. Materia 4 (1956); Leonard Kinsolving, *What about Therapeutic Abortion?,* 81 Christian Century 632, 634 (May 13, 1964).

80. *See, e.g.,* Baehr, *supra* note 67, at 31–50; Hole & Levine, *supra* note 67, at 295–301; Luker, *supra* note 9, at 95–125; Reagan, *supra* note 13, at 222–45; Kathy Rudy, Beyond Pro-Life and Pro-Choice: Moral Diversity in the Abortion Debate 63–81 (1996); Lucinda Cisler, *Abortion Repeal (Sort of): A Warning for Women,* in Radical Feminism 151 (Anne Koedt ed. 1973); Kevin Fagan, *Battle over Right to Choose: Abortion Clinic in Redding Stirs up Fervor on Both Sides of Issue,* S.F. Chronicle, May 4, 1999, at A1; Laura Kaplan, *Before Safe and Legal: The Lessons of Jane,* in Abortion Wars, *supra* note 32, at 33; Kessleman, *supra* note 32; Rickie Solinger, *Pregnancy and Power before* Roe v. Wade, in Abortion Wars, *supra* note 32, at 15; Marcy Wilder, *The Rule of Law, the Rise of Violence, and the Role of Morality: Reframing America's Abortion Debate,* in Abortion Wars, *supra,* at 73, 77–78.

81. *See generally* Garrow, *supra* note 23, at 1–269.

82. Colin Francome, Abortion Freedom: A Worldwide Movement 108 (1984) (quoting New York Assemblywoman Constance Cook).

83. Garrow, *supra* note 23, at 28 (10 women voted "no," while 9 voted "yes"), 292 (a woman activist complained that in a 1963 California legislative hearing "the men have given us the greatest support").

Connecticut League of Women Voters opposed the birth control movement for the first twenty years of the League's formal existence.[84]

The reality of who was leading the birth control and abortion reform movements might well lead one to ask, as has law professor Catharine MacKinnon, whether the movements were in fact created simply to make it harder for women to decline to have sex with men who were increasingly less willing to commit themselves beyond the evening of the encounter.[85] MacKinnon noted that *Playboy* magazine was the first large-circulation publication to endorse the repeal of abortion laws, doing so in 1965.[86] MacKinnon argued that the availability of abortion allows men to fill women up, vacuum them out, and fill them up again. Or, as one critic of abortion rights put it, the new ethics of abortion validates predatory men saying to the women they've gotten pregnant, "It's your problem. You take care of it."[87] Another woman critic noted that the freedom to abort "kills human relationships just as efficiently as [abortion] kills unborn children."[88] The Playboy Foundation became a prime financial source for several of the suits challenging the constitutionality of abortion statutes.[89] And the lack of a supportive or reliable relationship with a man became the most common reason for women to seek an abortion.[90]

Forces were at work to change all of this, particularly the rising ideology of the managerial class.[91] Modern feminism (the so-called second waive) emerged as one of the more important aspects of that ideology in the midst of the turmoil of the Civil Rights Movement and the protests against the Vietnam War.[92] It is not just that men in the managerial class believe that "liberated

---

84. *Id.* at 34.

85. MacKinnon, F.U. *supra* note 68, at 97–99, 144–45; MacKinnon, Feminist Theory, *supra* note 68, at 188, 190. *See generally* Rudy, *supra* note 80, at 68–74.

86. *See also* Garrow, *supra* note 23, at 352–53, 360. *Playboy* thereafter published many pro-abortion articles, most notably, Robert Hall, *The Abortion Revolution*, Playboy, Sept. 1970, at 112.

87. Lynn Wardle, *The Quandary of Pro-Life Free Speech: A Lesson from the Abolitionists*, 62 Alb. L. Rev. 853, 943, 948–51 (1999). *See also* Milton Regan, jr., *Getting our Stories Straight: Narrative Autonomy and Feminist Commitments*, 72 Ind. L.J. 449, 455 (1997). *See generally* Barbara Ehrenreich, The Hearts of Men: American Dreams and the Flight from Commitment (1983). For the historical foundation of such attitudes, see Chapter 8, at notes 65–81.

88. Camille Williams, as quoted in Wardle, *supra* note 87, at 950. *See generally* Arthur Shostak & Gary McLouth, Men and Abortion: Lessons, Losses and Love (1984); Susan Davies, *Partners and the Abortion Decision*, in Abortion, Medicine, and the Law 223 (J. Douglas Butler & David Walbert eds., 3rd ed. 1986); Peter Feaver *et al.*, *Sex as Contract: Abortion and Expanded Choice*, 4 Stan. L. & Pol'y Rev. 211 (1992); Martha Albertson Fineman, *A Legal (and Otherwise) Realist Response to "Sex as Contract,"* 4 Colum. J. Gender & L. 128 (1994); Vincent Rue, *Abortion in Relationship Context*, Int'l Rev. Nat. Fam. Plan., Summer 1985, at 95.

89. Garrow, *supra* note 23, at 352–53, 360.

90. Aida Torres & Jacqueline Darroch Forrest, *Why Do Women Have Abortions?*, 20 Fam. Planning Persp. 169, 170 (1988) (reporting that 51% of women having an abortion do so because of problems in their relationship or fear of becoming a single parent). *See also* Geraldine Faria *et al.*, *Women and Abortion: Attitudes, Social Networks, Decision-Making*, 11 Soc. Work in Health Care no. 1, at 85 (Fall 1985); Wardle, *supra* note 87, at 949–50. *See generally* Chapter 8, at notes 65–73.

91. Sara Evans, Personal Politics: The Roots of Women's Liberation in the Civil Rights Movement and the New Left (1979); Myra Marx Ferree & Beth Hess, Controversy and Coalition: The New Feminist Movement across Three Decades of Change 2–6, 53–75 (rev. ed. 1994); Jo Freeman, The Politics of Women's Liberation: A Case Study of an Emerging Social Movement and Its Relation to the Policy Process (1975); Hole & Levine, *supra* note 67; Mensch & Freeman, *supra* note 66, at 133; Louise Everett Graham & Geraldine Maschio, *A False Public Sentiment: Narrative and Visual Images of Women Lawyers in Film*, 84 Ky. L.J. 1027 (1996). *See* Chapter 13, at notes 252–316.

92. On the relation of modern feminism to other protests of the era, see Jo Freeman, *The Women's Liberation Movement: Its Origins, Structures, Impact, and Ideas*, in Women: A Feminist Perspective 448 (Jo Freeman ed., 2nd ed. 1979). *See generally* Terry Anderson, The Movement and the Sixties: Protest in America from Greensboro to Wounded Knee (1995); Beth Bailey, Sex in the Heartland 136–99

women" best serve the interests of managerial men—although that is true enough.[93] Modern feminism itself is impossible without a significantly large group of women who have alternatives to marriage or other forms of service to men for their economic well being. The managerial class generated just such self-supporting single women.[94] At the same time, women who were married began to devote less time to the bearing and rearing children by the simple expedient of having fewer children, allowing more and more of them to join the managerial class if they were so inclined and were able to develop the necessary skills.[95]

The women of the managerial class, however, discovered that men of the managerial class— even left-wing men struggling to overturn received patterns that inhibited the dominance of the managerial class—tended to treat women as inherently subordinate and primarily interesting as sex objects.[96] Late twentieth-century feminism emerged as a means for women in the managerial class to justify their role in society as well as a means for creating openings for these women to achieve their dreams—even while it tended to shatter the dreams of women who still preferred to be economically dependent on a man.[97] In particular, the managerial class embraced no-fault

(1999); David Farber, The Age of Great Dreams (1994); James Miller, Democracy in the Streets (1994); Milton Viorst, Fire in the Streets: America in the 1960s (1979). On the increasingly complex patterns of moder feminist thought, see Nancy Levit, The Gender Line: Men, Women, and the Law (1998); Christina Hoff Sommers, Who Stole Feminism: How Women Have Betrayed Women (1994); Mark Hager, *Sex in the Original Position: A Restatement of Liberal Feminism,* 14 Wis. Women's L.J. 181 (1999); Nancy Levit, *Feminism for Men: Legal Ideology and the Constitution of Maleness,* 43 UCLA L. Rev. 1037 (1996).

93. One might recall any of the innumerable articles published over the years as "The Playboy Philosophy" in *Playboy* magazine. *See generally* Richard Posner, Overcoming Law 191 (1995); Patricia Cooper, *"A Masculinist Vision of Useful Labor": Popular Ideologies about Women and Work in the United States, 1920–1939,* 84 Ky. L.J. 827 (1996).

94. *See* Julia Kirk Blackwelder, Now Hiring: The Feminization of Work in the United States, 1900–1995 (1997); Victor Fuchs, Women's Quest for Economic Equality 11 (1988); Claudia Goldin, Understanding the Gender Gap 10–57 (1990); Gerda Lerner, The Creation of Feminist Consciousness: From the Middle Ages to Eighteen-Seventy 276 (1993); Adrien Rich, Blood, Bread, and Poetry 147 (1986); P. & H. Armstrong, *Women, Family, and Economy,* in Reconstructing the Canadian Family: Feminist Perspectives 143 (Nancy Mandell & Ann Duff eds. 1988); Barbara Stark, *International Human Rights Law: Feminist Jurisprudence, and Nietzsche's "Eternal Return": Turning the Wheel,* 19 Harv. Women's L.J. 169, 176, 194–96 (1996).

95. Catherine Hoskins, Integrating Gender: Women, Law, and Politics in the European Union 25–31 (1996); Evelyne Sullerot, Women, Society and Change 75 (1971).

96. *See, e.g.,* Bailey, *supra* note 92, at 154–55, 169–74; Alice Echols, Daring to Be Bad: Radical Feminism in America 1967–1975, at 28–37, 248 (1989); Hoskins, *supra* note 95, at 35–36; Cassandra Langer, A Feminist Critique: How Feminism Has Changed American Society, Culture, and How We Live from the 1940s to the Present 29–31 (1996); Freeman, *supra* note 92, at 199–202; Frigga Haug, *The Women's Movement in West Germany,* 155 New Left Rev. 60 (1986); Robin West, *Deconstructing the CLS—Fem Split,* 2 Wis. Women's L.J. 85 (1986).

97. *See, e.g.,* Betty Friedan, The Feminist Mystique (1963). *See generally* Mimi Abramovitz, Under Attack, Fighting Back: Women and Welfare in the United States (1996); Rosalind Barnett & Caryl Rivers, She Works, He Works: How Two-Income Families Are Happier, Healthier, and Better off (1996); Eileen Boris, Home to Work: Motherhood and the Politics of Industrial Homework in the United States (1994); Wini Breines, Young, White, and Miserable: Growing up Female in the Fifties (1992); J. Herbie DiFonzo, Beneath the Fault Line: The Popular and Legal Culture of Divorce in Twentieth-Century America (1997); Martha Albertson Fineman, The Neutered Mother, the Sexual Family and Other Twentieth Century Tragedies (1995); Fuchs, *supra* note 94; Gender and Family Issues in the Workplace (Francine Blau & Ronald Ehrenberg eds. 1997); Linda Gordon, Pitied But Not Entitled: Single Mothers and the History of Welfare, 1820–1935 (1994); Joel Handler & Yeheskel Hasenfeld, We the Poor People: Work, Poverty & Welfare (1997); Hoskins, *supra* note 95, at 5–9, 27; Glenna Matthews, "Just a Housewife" (1987); Diana Pearce & Harriette McAdoo, Women and Children: Alone and in Poverty (1991); Deborah Rhode, Speaking of Sex: The Denial of Gender Inequality (1997); Ruth Sidell, Women and Children Last: The Plight of Poor Women in Affluent America (1986); Michelene Wandor, Once a Feminist—Stories of a Generation (1990); Lenore

divorce to facilitate their life choices, although, of course, no-fault divorce did not turn out to be the panacea its proponents predicted.[98] As Dean Herma Hill Kay, once a leading advocate of no-fault divorce, pointed out, "[d]ivorce by unilateral fiat is closer to desertion than to mutual separation."[99] No wonder one observer concluded that "feminism came to mean denigrating motherhood, pursuing selfish goals and wearing a suit."[100]

WEITZMAN, THE DIVORCE REVOLUTION: THE UNEXPECTED SOCIAL AND ECONOMIC CONSEQUENCES FOR WOMEN AND CHILDREN IN AMERICA (1985); Tonya Brito, *Madonna to Proletariat: Constructing a New Ideology of Motherhood in Welfare Discourse*, 44 VILL. L. REV. 415 (1999); Ann Laquer Estin, *Can Families Be Efficient? A Feminist Appraisal*, 4 MICH. J. GENDER & L. 1 (1996); Martha Albertson Fineman, *Fatherhood, Feminism, and Family Law*, 32 MCGEORGE L. REV. 1031 (2001); F. Carolyn Graglia, *Feminism Isn't Antisex; It's Only Antifamily*, WALL ST. J., Aug. 6, 1998, at A14; Saul Hoffman & Greg Duncan, *What Are the Economic Consequences of Divorce?*, 25 DEMOGRAPHY 641 (1988); John Jones & Janet Kodras, *Restructured Regions and Families: The Feminization of Poverty in the U.S.*, 80 ANNALS ASS'N AM. GEOGRAPHERS 163 (1990); Janet Kodras *et al.*, *Contextualizing Welfare's Work Disincentive: The Case of Female-Headed Family Poverty*, 26 GEOGRAPHICAL ANALYSIS 285 (1994); Jana Singer, *Alimony and Efficiency: The Gendered Costs and Benefits of the Economic Justification for Alimony*, 82 GEO. L.J. 2423 (1993); Ann Tickamyer, *Public Policy and Private Lives: Social and Spatial Dimensions of Women's Poverty and Welfare Policy in the United States*, 84 KY. L.J. 721 (1996); Lucy White, *No Exit: Rethinking "Welfare Dependency" from a Different Ground*, 81 GEO. L.J. 1961 (1997).

98. *See, e.g.*, Ryan v. Ryan, 277 So. 2d 266 (Fla. 1973) (upholding the constitutionality of no-fault divorce); MAX RHEINSTEIN, MARRIAGE, STABILITY, DIVORCE, AND THE LAW (1972); Charles Tenney, jr., *Divorce without Fault: The Next Step, a Model for Change*, 46 NEB. L. REV. 24 (1967). On the consequences of no-fault divorce, see DiFonzo, *supra* note 97, at 171–77; ECONOMIC CONSEQUENCES OF DIVORCE: THE INTERNATIONAL PERSPECTIVE (Lenore Weitzman & Mavis McLean eds. 1992); DIANE FASSEL, GROWING UP DIVORCED: A ROAD TO HEALING FOR ADULT CHILDREN OF DIVORCE (1991); MARTHA FINEMAN, THE ILLUSION OF EQUALITY: THE RHETORIC AND REALITY OF DIVORCE REFORM (1991); FINEMAN, *supra* note 97; MAGGIE GALLAGHER, THE ABOLITION OF MARRIAGE: HOW WE DESTROY LASTING LOVE (1996); SHEILA KAMERMAN & ALFRED KAHN, MOTHERS ALONE: STRATEGIES FOR A TIME OF CHANGE (1988); LANGER, *supra* note 96, at 173–79; ALLEN PARKMAN, NO-FAULT DIVORCE: WHAT WENT WRONG? (1992); MILTON REGAN, JR., FAMILY LAW AND THE PURSUIT OF INTIMACY (1993); RHODE, *supra* note 97, at 179–86; ARLENE SKOLNICK, EMBATTLED PARADISE: THE AMERICAN FAMILY IN AN AGE OF UNCERTAINTY (1991); JAMES SNELL, IN THE SHADOW OF THE LAW: DIVORCE IN CANADA (1991); JUDITH WALLERSTEIN & SANDRA BLAKESLEE, SECOND CHANCES: MEN, WOMEN, AND CHILDREN A DECADE AFTER DIVORCE (1989); LENORE WEITZMAN, THE DIVORCE REVOLUTION: THE UNEXPECTED SOCIAL AND ECONOMIC CONSEQUENCES FOR WOMEN AND CHILDREN IN AMERICA (1995); BARBARA DAFOE WHITEHEAD, THE DIVORCE CULTURE (1997); Gary Becker, *Finding Fault with No-Fault Divorce*, BUS. WEEK, Dec. 7, 1992, at 22; Magaret Brinig & F.H. Buckley, *No-Fault Laws and At-Fault People*, INT'L REV. L. & ECON. 325 (1998); Ira Mark Ellman & Sharon Lohr, *Dissolving the Relationship between Divorce Laws and Divorce Rates*, 18 INT'L REV. L. & ECON. 341 (1998); Allen Parkman, *Bringing Consistency to the Financial Arrangements of Divorce*, 87 KY. L.J. 51 (1999); Annamay Sheppard, *Women, Families, and Equality: Was Divorce Reform a Mistake?*, 12 WOMEN'S L. RPTR. 143 (1990); Barbara Stark, *Divorce Law, Feminism, and Psychoanalysis: In Dreams Begins Responsibilities*, 38 UCLA L. REV. 1483 (1991); Stephen Waldman, *Deadbeat Dads: Wanted for Failure to Pay Child Support*, NEWSWEEK, May 4, 1992, at 46; Lynn Wardle, *Divorce Violence and the No-Fault Divorce Culture*, 1994 UTAH L. REV. 741.

99. Herma Hill Kay, *Beyond No-Fault: New Directions in Divorce Reform*, in DIVORCE REFORM AT THE CROSSROADS 1,8 (Stephen Sugarman & Herma Hill Kay eds. 1990). *See also* ANDREA BELLER & JOHN GRAHAM, SMALL CHANGE: THE ECONOMICS OF CHILD SUPPORT (1993); DEMIE KURTZ, FOR RICHER, FOR POORER (1995); PAULA ROBERTS, ENDING POVERTY AS WE KNOW IT: THE CASE FOR CHILD SUPPORT ENFORCEMENT AND ASSURANCE (1994); SARA MCLANAHAN & GARY SANDEFUR, GROWING UP WITH A SINGLE PARENT: WHAT HURTS, WHAT HELPS (1994); WEITZMAN, *supra* note 97, at 323; Becker, *supra* note 97; Penelope Eileen Bryan, *Vacant Promises? The ALI Principles of the Law of Family Dissolution and the Post-Divorce Financial Circumstances of Women*, 8 DUKE J. GENDER & L. 167 (2001); Marsha Garrison, *The Economic Consequences of Divorce: Would Adoption of the ALI Principles Improve Current Outcomes?*, 8 DUKE J. GENDER & L. 119 (2001); Sheppard, *supra* note 98, at 146–49; Cynthia Lee Starnes, *Victims, Breeders, Joy, and Math: First Thoughts on Compensatory Spousal Payments under the Principles*, 8 DUKE J. GENDER & L. 137 (2001).

100. Nancy Gibbs, *The War against Feminism*, TIME, Mar. 9, 1992, at 50, 52. *See generally* DANIELLE CRITTENDEN, WHAT OUR MOTHERS DIDN'T TELL US: WHY HAPPINESS ELUDES THE MODERN WOMAN (1999); F. CAROLYN GRAGLIA, DOMESTIC TRANQUILLITY: A BRIEF AGAINST FEMINISM (1998); WENDY SHALLIT, A RETURN TO MODESTY: DISCOVERING THE LOST VIRTUE (1999). For examples of such antagonism toward the

The "first wave" of feminism in the late nineteenth century focused on obtaining the vote and other indicia of legal equality with men. Striving for legal equality included obtaining the right to contract and to own property, but these rights remained largely abstract for most women— so much so that some modern scholars see the rights as imposed upon nineteenth century women for the benefit of creditors rather than as won by and for the benefit of women.[101] The failure of the first wave to deal adequately with economic issues contributed to the failure of the first wave to go on to achieve the social reforms that were the concern of many of the leaders of the first wave.[102] The "second wave" of feminism, in the second half of the twentieth century, focused first on economic issues. Thus the earliest achievements of the second wave did not involve abortion, divorce reform, or the opening of political offices to women.

The earliest goals of the second waive, "job equity,"[103] fit nicely with the personal needs of the new managerial class men as well as managerial class women. The earliest legal successes for the second wave were new requirements for equal pay for men and women performing the same jobs,[104] and the inclusion of "sex" as a category of prohibited discrimination in employ-

---

homemaker model for women, see Ann Oakley, The Sociology of Housework 197 (1974); Wally Secombe, *The Housewife and Her Labour under Capitalism*, 83 New Left Rev. 3 (1974).

101. *See, e.g.*, Mary Ritter Beard, Woman as a Force in History: A Study in Traditions and Realities 160–65 (1946); Joan Hoff, Law, Gender, and Injustice: A Legal History of U.S. Women 120, 134–35, 187–91 (1991); Carole Shammas, Marylynn Salmon, & Michel Dahlin, Inheritance in America from Colonial Times to the Present 88–101 (1987); Mary Lyndon Shanley, Feminism, Marriage, and the Law in Victorian England, 1850–1895, at 104–09 (1989); Joseph Ranney, *Anglicans, Merchants, and Feminists: A Comparative Study of the Evolution of Married Women's Rights in Virginia, New York, and Wisconsin*, 6 Wm. & Mary J. Women & L. 493, 541–59 (2000); Linda Speth, *The Married Women's Property Acts, 1839–1865: Reform, Reaction, or Revolution?*, in 2 Women and the Law: A Social Historical Perspective 269 (D. Kelly Weisberg ed. 1982); Amy Dru Stanley, *Conjugal Bonds and Wage Labor: Rights of Contract in the Age of Emancipation*, 75 Am. J. Legal Hist. 471 (1988). *See generally* Chapter 2, at notes 163–72.

102. *See* Ferree & Hess, *supra* note 91, at 17–23; Petchesky, *supra* note 3, at 100–16; Suffrage and Beyond: International Feminist Perspectives (Caroline Daley & Melanie Nolan eds. 1994). *See* Chapter 11, at notes 241–45.

103. *See generally* Susan Becker, The Origins of the Equal Rights Amendment: American Feminism between the Wars (1981); Alice Kessler-Harris, A Woman's Wage: Historical Meanings and Social Consequences (1991); Gwendolyn Mink, The Wages of Motherhood: Inequality in the Welfare State, 1917–1942 (1995); June Neilson, Equal Opportunities for Women in the European Union: Success or Failure? (1998); Rhode, *supra* note 97, at 141–76; Patricia Zelman, Women, Work, and National Policy: The Kennedy-Johnson Years (1982); Barbara Brown et al., *The Equal Rights Amendment: A Constitutional Basis for Equal Rights for Women*, 80 Yale L.J. 871 (1971); Elizabeth Defeis, *The Treaty of Amsterdam: The Next Step towards Gender Equality?*, 23 B.C. Int'l & Comp. L. Rev. 1 (1999); Symposium, *Work and Family*, 19 N. Ill. L. Rev. 1 (1998). Some younger contemporary feminists are now calling themselves a "third waive" in order to indicate that they are moving beyond the concerns of their mothers—the "second waive." While they perhaps no longer feel a need to fight for the basic laws regarding economic equality, they have not yet clearly indicated how the agenda of the "third waive" differs from that of the "second waive." *See, e.g.*, Ravina Aggarwal, *Traversing Lines of Control: Feminist Anthropology Today*, 571 Annals Am. Academy Pol. & Soc. Sci. 14 (2000); Lynn Chancer, *From Pornography to Sadomasochism: Reconciling Feminist Differences*, 571 Annals Am. Academy Pol. & Soc. Sci. 77 (2000).

104. *Equal Pay Act*, Pub. L. No. 88-38, 77 Stat. 56 (1963), *codified at* 29 U.S.C. §206(d) (2000). *See* Francine Blau et al., The Economics of Women, Men, and Work (3rd ed. 1998); Neilson, *supra* note 103, at 64–67; Goldin, *supra* note 94; Hoskins, *supra* note 95, at 43–96, 212; Francine Blau & Lawrence Kahn, *Rising Wage Inequality and the U.S. Gender Gap*, 84 AEA Papers & Proc., No. 2, at 23 (1994); Mary Corcoran & Greg Duncan, *Work History, Labor Force Attachment, and Earnings Differences between Races and Sexes*, 14 J. Hum. Resources 3 (1979); Allen Wellington, *Accounting for the Male/Female Wage Gap among Whites: 1976 and 1985*, 59 Am. Soc. Rev. 839 (1994). *See also* Defeis, *supra* note 103, at 5–11; Brian Johnson, *Ensuring Equality: Pursuing Implementation of the Equal Pay Principle via the Institutions of the European Union, the North American Agreement on Labor Cooperation, and Corporate Codes of Conduct*, 38 Va. J. Int'l L. 849 (1998).

ment[105] and education.[106] Less successful were demands for pay according to "comparable worth."[107] As doors hitherto closed to women were pried open by suit or the threat of suit,

105. *Civil Rights Act of 1964*, 42 U.S.C. §2000e-2(a)(1) (2000) ("Title VII"); *Pregnancy Discrimination Act*, 42 U.S.C. §2000e(k) (2000); Price Waterhouse v. Hopkins, 490 U.S. 228 (1989); Los Angeles Dep't of Water v. Manhart, 435 U.S. 702 (1978); Phillips v. Martin Marietta Corp., 400 U.S. 542 (1971). *See also* Council Recommendations 84/365, 1984 O.J. (L331) 34; Kalanke v. Freie Hansestadt Bremen, 1 C.M.L.R. 175 (1995). *See generally* Mary Bateson, Composing a Life (1989); Hoskins, *supra* note 95, at 97–211; Jerry Jacobs, Revolving Doors: Sex Segregation and Women's Careers (1989); Susan Omilian, Sex-Based Employment Discrimination (1990); Dolores Leal, Litigating Sexual Harassment and Discrimination Cases (1997); Sacha Prechal & Noreen Burrows, Gender Discrimination: Law of the European Community (1990); Jill Andrews, *National and International Sources of Women's Right to Equal Employment Opportunities: Equality in Law versus Equality in Fact*, 14 Nw. J. Int'l L. & Bus. 413 (1994); Thomas Bach, *Gender Stereotyping in Employment Discrimination: Finding a Balance of Evidence and Causation under Title VII*, 77 Minn. L. Rev. 1251 (1993); Robert Bird, *More than a Congressional Joke: A Fresh Look at the Legislative History of Sex Discrimination of the 1964 Civil Rights Act*, 3 Wm. & Mary J. Women & L. 137 (1997); Defeis, *supra* note 103, at 11–33; Martha Chamallas, *Mothers and Disparate Treatment: The Ghost of* Martin Marietta, 44 Vill. L. Rev. 337 (1999); Ann Donahue, *The* Kalanke *Ruling: Gender Equality in the European Labor Market*, 18 Nw. J. Int'l L. & Bus. 730 (1998); Panos Koutrakos, *Community Law and Equal Treatment in the Armed Forces*, 25 Europ. L. Rev. 433 (2000); Candace Saari Kovach-Fleischer, *Litigating against Employment Penalties for Pregnancy, Breastfeeding, and Childcare*, 44 Vill. L. Rev. 355 (1999); Linda Hamilton Krieger, *The Content of Our Categories: A Cognitive Bias Approach to Discrimination and Equal Employment Opportunity*, 47 Stan. L. Rev. 1161 (1995); Rebecca Means, Kalanke v. Freie Hansestadt Bremen*: The Significance of the* Kalanke *Decision on Future Positive Action Programs in the European Union*, 30 Vand. J. Transnat'l L. 1087 (1997); Steve Mazurana, Thomas Trelogan, & Paul Hodapp, *European Community—Principle of Equal Treatment—Sex Discrimination—Positive Action in Employment of Women*, 96 Am. J. Int'l L. 455 (2002); Gabriel Moens, *Equal Opportunities, Not Equal Results: "Equal Opportunity" in European Law after* Kalenke, 23 J. Legis. 43 (1997); Mary O'Melveny, *Playing the "Gender" Card: Affirmative Action and Working Women*, 84 Ky. L.J. 863 (1996); Jendi Reiter, *Accommodating Pregnancy and Breastfeeding in the Workplace: Beyond the Civil Rights Paradigm*, 9 Tex. J. Women & L. 1 (1999); Carol Sanger, *M Is for Many Things*, 1 S. Cal. Rev. L. & Women's Stud. 15 (1992).

106. *Educational Amendments Act of 1972*, 20 U.S.C. §§1681–1688 (2000) ("Title IX"); Gebser v. Lago Vista Ind. Sch. Dist., 524 U.S. 274 (1998); United States v. Virginia, 518 U.S. 515 (1996). *See generally* Nadya Aisenberg & Mona Harrington, Women in Academe: Outsiders in the Sacred Grove (1988); Susan Lie *et al.*, The Gender Gap in Higher Education (1994); Barbara Solomon, In the Company of Educated Women: A History of Women in Higher Education in America (1985); Women in Higher Education: A Feminist Perspective (Judith Glazer *et al.* eds. 1993); Jon Gould, *Title IX in the Classroom: Academic Freedom and the Power to Harass*, 6 Duke J. Gender L. & Pol'y 61 (1999); Magda Lewis & Roger Simon, *A Discourse Not Intended for Her: Learning and Teaching within Patriarchy*, 56 Harv. Educ. Rev. 457 (1986); Jane Martin, *The Contradiction of the Educated Woman*, in Changing Education 13 (Joyce Antler & Sari Biklen eds. 1990); Shelley Park, *Research, Teaching, and Service: Why Shouldn't Women's Work Count?*, 67 J. Higher Educ. 46 (1996); Susan Scollay & Carolyn Bratt, *Reflections on the Limitations of Rational Discourse, Empirical Data, and Legal Mandates as Tools for the Achievement of Gender Equity in American Higher Education*, 84 Ky. L.J. 903 (1996); Jason Skaggs, *Justifying Gender-Based Affirmative Action under* United States v. Virginia's *"Exceedingly Persuasive Justification" Standard*, 86 Cal. L. Rev. 1169 (1998); Jane Waldfogel, *Understanding the "Family Gap" in Pay for Women with Children*, 12 J. Econ. Persp. 137 (1998).

107. *See* Washington County v. Gunther, 452 U.S. 161 (1981); EEOC v. Sears, 839 F.2d 302 (7th Cir. 1988); American Nurses Ass'n v. Illinois, 783 F.2d 716 (7th Cir. 1986); American Fed'n State, Cty., & Mun. Employees v. Washington, 770 F.2d 1401 (9th Cir. 1985); Plemer v. Parsons-Gilbane, 713 F.2d 1127 (5th Cir. 1983); Lemons v. City of Denver, 620 F.2d 228 (10th Cir.), *cert denied*, 449 U.S. 888 (1980). *See generally* Joan Acker, Doing Comparable Worth: Gender, Class, and Pay Equity (1989); Linda Blum, Between Feminism and Labor: The Significance of the Comparable Worth Movement (1991); Christine Bose, Jobs and Gender: A Study of Occupational Prestige (1985); William Bridges & Robert Nelson, Legalizing Gender Inequality: Courts, Markets, and Unequal Pay for Women in America (1999); Comparable Worth and Wage Discrimination (Helen Remick ed. 1984); Comparable Worth: New Directions for Research (Heidi Hartmann ed. 1985); Paula England, Comparable Worth: Theories and Evidence (1992); Paula England & George Farkas, Households, Employment and Gender: A Social, Economic and Demographic View (1986); Ingredients for Women's Employment Policy (Christine Bose & Glenna Spitze eds. 1987); Just Wages: A Feminist Assessment of Pay Equity (Judy Fudge & Patricia McDermott eds. 1991); Alice Kemp, Women's Work: Degraded and Devalued (1994); Mary Ann Mason, The Equality Trap: Why Working

managerial class women secured a greater measure of equality on the job while obtaining a growing financial base from which to support other goals.

Entry of women into the managerial class did not simply result from an ideological change in how women perceived themselves or were perceived by men, nor was it brought about by legislative fiat independently of the changing economy or workplaces. The rise of the managerial class heralded the emergence of an economy based upon knowledge and information rather than physical strength. This transition made possible the large-scale employment of women in jobs outside the home that paid incomes similar to those traditionally earned by men.[108] Changes in women's work had begun by the end of the nineteenth century, but accelerated considerably after 1960, with (among other changes) the entrance of many women into formerly all-male professions, particularly law and medicine. The changes were most visible in higher education. The percentage of bachelor degrees awarded to women rose from 38.5 percent in 1960 to 55.1 percent in 1996, the percentage of Ph.D.'s rose from 10.5 percent to 45.4 percent, with the percentages of professional degrees rising even more dramatically than for the Ph.D.s.—from 5.5 percent for medical doctorates to 40.9 percent and first law degrees rising from 2.5 percent to 43.5 percent.[109] Only in engineering did the percentage of women lag seriously behind—rising even there from 0.4 percent to 16.1 percent.[110]

---

WOMEN SHOULDN'T BE TREATED LIKE MEN (1988); BARBARA RESKIN & IRENE PADAVIC, WOMEN AND MEN AT WORK (1994); RHODE, *supra* note 97, at 171–76; SOC. PERSPECTIVES ON LABOR MARKETS (Ivar Berg ed. 1981); WOMEN, WORK, AND WAGES: EQUAL PAY FOR JOBS OF EQUAL VALUE (Donald Treiman & Heidi Hartmann eds. 1981); Kathryn Branch, *Are Women Worth as Much as Men?: Employment Inequities, Gender Roles, and Public Policy,* 1 DUKE J. GENDER L. & POL'Y 119 (1994); Jeanne Dennis, *The Lessons of Comparable Worth: A Feminist Vision of Law and Economic Theory,* 4 UCLA WOMEN'S L.J. 1 (1993); John Donohue III, *Employment Discrimination Law in Perspective: Three Concepts of Equality,* 92 MICH. L. REV. 2583 (1994); Judy Fudge, *The Paradoxes of Pay Equity: Reflections on the Law and the Market in Bell Canada and the Public Service Alliance of Canada,* 12 CAN. J. WOMEN & L. 313 (2000); Diane Furchtgott & Christine Stolbe, *Comparable Worth Makes a Comeback,* WALL ST. J., Feb. 4, 1999, at A22; Evelyn Nakano Glenn, *Cleaning up/Kept down: A Historical Perspective on Racial Inequality in "Women's Work,"* 43 STAN. L. REV. 1333 (1991); Gillian Hadfield, *Households at Work: Beyond Labor Market Policies to Remedy the Gender Gap,* 82 GEO. L.J. 89 (1993); Barbara Stanek Kilbourne et al., *Returns to Skill: Compensating Differentials, and Gender Bias: Effects of Occupational Characteristics on the Wages of White Women and Men,* 100 AM. J. SOC. 689 (1994); Judith Malveaux, *Comparable Worth and its Impact on Black Women,* 14 BLACK POL. ECON. 47 (1985); Solomon Polacheck, *Occupational Segregation and the Gender Wage Gap,* 6 POP. RESOURCES & POL'Y REV. 47 (1987); Jim Sidanius & Marie Crane, *Job Evaluation and Gender: The Case of University Faculty,* 19 J. APPLIED SOC. PSYCHOL. 174 (1989); Elaine Sorenson, *Measuring the Pay Disparity between Typically Female Occupations and Other Jobs: A Bivariate Approach,* 42 INDUS. & LAB. REL. REV. 624 (1989); Ronnie Steinberg, *Social Construction of Skill: Gender, Power, and Comparable Worth,* 17 WORK & OCCUPATIONS 449 (1990). Governments in Canada have been much more supportive of comparable worth than have governments in the United States. *See* ; M. Neil Browne & Michael Meuti, *Individualism and the Market Determination of Women's Wages in the United States, Canada, and Hong Kong,* 21 LOY.-L.A. INT'L & COMP. L.J. 355, 372–87 (1999); Patrick Cihon, *Comparable Worth: The Quebec Experience,* 17 J. COLLECTIVE NEGOTIATIONS 249 (1988); Morley Gunderson & W. Craig Russell, *Comparable Worth: Canada's Experience,* 10 CONTEMP. POL'Y ISSUES 89 (1992); Nancy Kubasik et al., *Comparable Worth in Ontario: Lessons the United States Can Learn,* 17 HARV. WOMEN'S L.J. 103 (1994); Aileen McColgan, *Legislating Equal Pay? Lessons from Canada,* 22 INDUS. L.J. 269 (1993).

108. *See generally* BARBARA BERGMANN, THE ECONOMIC EMERGENCE OF WOMEN (1986); BARBARA RESKIN & PATRICIA ROOS, JOB QUEUES, GENDER QUEUES: EXPLAINING WOMEN'S INROADS INTO MALE OCCUPATIONS (1990). This was a European as well as an American phenomenon. *See* HOSKINS, *supra* note 95, at 30–32; SULLEROT, *supra* note 95, at 17; G.H.S. KOK, REPORT ON THE POLITICAL, SOCIAL AND CIVIC POSITION OF WOMEN IN EUROPE 33 (1967).

109. Andrew Hacker, *The Unmaking of Men,* N.Y. REV. BOOKS, Oct. 21, 1999, at 25, 26 (Table A, derived from figures of the U.S. National Center for Educational Statistics).

110. *Id.* This change appears much earlier in lower-level schooling rather than at the university level. Girls considerably outnumber boys in high school among high achievers, take more challenging classes, have lower drop-out and disciplinary rates, and generally are more optimistic about the future. Suzanne Fields, *Hillary's Blind Trust,* WASH. TIMES, Jan. 18, 1999, at A19; Maggie Gallagher, *Gender Equality, Scholastic Imbalance,* WASH. TIMES, Dec. 3, 1998, at A14; Barbara Kantrowitz & Claudia Kelly, *Boys Will Be Boys,* NEWSWEEK, May 11, 1998, at 54.

Women's educational successes translated into entrance into more lucrative jobs, except at the highest levels. Women went from constituting 16.7 percent of managers and executives in 1970 to 44.4 percent in 1998, from 28.6 percent of college faculty to 42.3 percent, and 11.4 percent of economists to 46.3 percent, with similar gains in other fields.[111] As a result, the average woman's income rose during this period from $607 for every $1,000 of men's earnings in 1960 to $766/$1,000 in 2002 for full-time workers.[112] The persistence of the wage gap reflects complex variables. Women at younger ages tend to be paid closer to what men earn, with the youngest age group (women aged 16-24) earning better than 90 percent of what men of the same age earn.[113] Working women on average are better educated than working men (31 percent of working women are college graduates, compared to 27 percent of working men), and are more likely to work as managers or professionals than working men (38 percent compared to 28 percent), but they still earn less on average than men, in large measure because they work fewer hours than working men (39.8 hours per week, compared to 46.1 hours per week for working men).[114] Women are also notably less willing to undertake overnight business trips, diminishing their value to their employers.[115] Women also took pregnancy and family leaves more often than men took family leaves, and also changed jobs more often in order to accommodate their family obligations.[116] Finally, 93 percent of those who die from job related causes are men, which might have something to do with levels of compensation.[117] Yet even in 1970 never married women who had worked for 20 or more years on aver-

111. Hacker, *supra* note 109, at 27 (Table B, derived from the Bureau of Labor Statistics).

112. Institute for Women's Policy Research, *The Gender Wage Gap: Progress of the 1980's Fails to Carry Through* (Nov. 2003), *available at* htpp://www.iwpr.org. *See also* GARY BECKER, A TREATISE ON THE FAMILY 53–79 (1991); BLAU *et al.*, *supra* note 104, at 134–36; DIANE FURCHTGOTT-ROTH & CHRISTINE STOLBA, WOMEN'S PROGRESS: THE ECONOMIC PROGRESS OF WOMEN IN AMERICA (1996); JOYCE JACOBSEN, THE ECONOMICS OF GENDER (1994); James Albrecht & Susan Vroman, *The Gender Gap in Compensation: Evaluating Policies to Reduce the Gender Gap: An Economic Approach,* 82 GEO. L.J. 69 (1993); Danielle Crittenen, *Yes, Motherhood Lowers Pay,* N.Y. TIMES, Aug. 22, 1995, at A15; Jeffrey Gray, *The Fall in Men's Return to Marriage: Declining Productivity or Changing Selection?,* 32 J. HUM. RESOURCES 481 (1997); Hacker, *supra* note 109, at 27 (Table B); Jennifer Hersch & Leslie Stratton, *Housework, Fixed Effects and Wages of Married Women,* 32 J. HUM. RESOURCES 285 (1997); Michael Kidd & Michael Shannon, *Does the Level of Occupational Aggregation Affect Estimates of the Gender Wage Gap?,* 49 INDUS. & LAB. REL. REV. 317 (1997); Sanders Korenman & David Neumark, *Does Marriage Really Make Men More Productive?,* 26 J. HUM. RESOURCES 282 (1991); Sanders Korenman & David Neumark, *Marriage, Motherhood & Wages,* 27 J. HUM. RESOURCES 233 (1992); Eng Seng Loh, *Productivity Differences and the Marriage Wage Premium for White Males,* 31 J. HUM. RESOURCES 566 (1996); Margaret Mooney Marini & Pi-Ling Fan, *The Gender Gap in Earnings at Career Entry,* 62 AM. SOC. REV. 588 (1997); June O'Neill & Solomon Polachek, *Why the Gender Gap in Wages Narrowed in the 1980s,* 11 J. LABOR ECON. 205 (1993); Jane Waldfogel, *The Effect of Children on Women's Wages,* 62 AM. SOC. REV. 209 (1997); Jane Waldfogel, *The Family Gap for Young Women in the United States and Britain,* 16 J. LAB. ECON. 505 (1998); Waldfogel, *supra* note 106, at 144–45, tables 4, 5; Allison Wellington, *Changes in the Male/Female Wage Gap, 1976–1985,* 28 J. HUM. RESOURCES 383 (1993).

113. Institute for Women's Policy Research, *supra* note 112.

114. Kirstin Downey, *Women's Pay Tied to Fewer Work Hours: Study Says Men Also Travel More,* WASH. POST, Oct. 1, 2003, at E3. *See also* Leigh Strope, *Educated Women Flock to Usual Jobs,* PHILA. INQUIRER, May 5, 2003, at A12.

115. Downey, *supra* note 114.

116. Nancy Reichman & Joyce Sterling, *Recasting the Brass Ring: Deconstructing and Reconstructing Workplace Opportunities for Women Lawyers,* 29 CAP. U.L. REV. 923 (2002). *See also* Rebecca Korzic, *Working on the "Mommy-Track": Motherhood and Women Lawyers,* 8 HASTINGS WOMEN'S L.J. 117 (1997); Renee Landers, Jams Rebitzer, & Lowell Taylor, *Rat Race Redux: Adverse Selection in the Determination of Work Hours in Law Firms,* 86 AM. ECON. REV. 329 (1996); Mary Jane Mossman, *Lawyers and Family Life: New Directions for the 1990s,* 2 FEMINIST LEG. STUD. 61 (pt. 1), 159 (pt. 2) (1994); Marc Schenker, *Self-Reported Stress and Reproductive Health of Female Lawyers,* 39 OCCUPATIONAL & ENVTL. MED. 556 (1997); Stephen Spurr & Glenn Syeyoshi, *Turnover and Promotion of Lawyers: An Inquiry into Gender Differences,* 29 J. HUM. RESOURCES 813 (1994).

117. *See* Kingsley Browne, *Sex and Temperament in Modern Society: A Darwinian View of the Glass Ceiling and the Gender Gap,* 37 ARIZ. L. REV. 971, 979 n.30 (1995).

age earned more than never married men who had also worked for 20 or more years.[118]

Further complicating the picture is that much of the "rise" in women's incomes relative to men's resulted from a decline in the real income of lower and lower middle class men rather than in a rise in women's real income in the same social strata.[119] As a result, we have seen the rise of two income families even in social groups where the values of the managerial class have penetrated least. In the United States by the 1990s, 73 percent of women aged 25–34 worked outside the home, and 76 percent of women aged 35–44 worked outside the home,[120] and 53 percent of all married couples included two income earners.[121] This change in turn generated considerable resentment among men who lost their status as "bread winners"—a status often central to their own self-image as men.[122] Even after a generation of two-income families, however, about two-thirds of American women as well as two-thirds of American men would prefer the male bread-winner/female homemaker model if it did not cause a lowered standard of living.[123] Thus many of people involved in the changing women's roles felt pressed into it involuntarily. The resulting change in women's economic roles has to a meaningful extent thrust working class white men into positions comparable to those of black men at least since the end of slavery.[124]

------

118. THOMAS SOWELL, THE QUEST FOR COSMIC JUSTICE 92 (1999).

119. *See* DAPHNE SPAIN & SUZANNE BIANCHI, THE BALANCING ACT: MOTHERHOOD, MARRIAGE, AND EMPLOYMENT AMONG AMERICAN WOMEN 95 (1996). *See also* ELAINE SORENSEN, EXPLORING REASONS BEHIND THE NARROWING GENDER GAP IN EARNINGS (1991); Sylvia Nasar, *Statistics Reveal Bulk of New Jobs over Average*, N.Y. TIMES, Oct. 17, 1994, at A1; David Leonhardt, *Wage Gap between Men and Women Shrinks*, N.Y. TIMES, Feb. 17, 2003, at A1.

120. Paul Osterman, *Work/Family Programs and the Employment Relationship*, 50 ADMIN. SCI. Q. 681, 683 (1995) (reporting statistics from 1993). The economic boom of the 1990s saw a small rise in the proportion of women staying home; perhaps this pattern would have been different had there been jobs available. *See* Joan Williams, *Why Moms Stay Home*, WASH. POST, July 17, 2003, at A21.

121. Marion Crain, *"Where Have All the Cowboys Gone?" Marriage and Breadwinning in Postindustrial Society*, 60 OHIO ST. L.J. 1877, 1877–78 n.3 (1999) (reporting statistics from 1997); Tamar Lewin, *Now a Majority: Families with 2 Parents Who Work*, N.Y. TIMES, Oct. 24, 2000, at A20. According to Crain, some estimate the percentage of two-income families as even higher. *Id. See generally* WILLIAM BAUMOL, ALAN BLINDER, & EDWARD WOLFF, DOWNSIZING AMERICA: REALITY, CAUSES AND CONSEQUENCES (2003); SIMON HEAD, THE NEW RUTHLESS ECONOMY: WORK AND POWER IN THE DIGITAL AGE (2003); LOW-WAGE AMERICA: HOW EMPLOYERS ARE RESHAPING OPPORTUNITIES IN THE WORKPLACE (Eileen Appelbaum, Annette Bernhardt, & Richard Murnane eds. 2003).

122. R. WILLIAM BETCHER & WILLIAM POLLACK, IN A TIME OF FALLEN HEROES: THE RE-CREATION OF MASCULINITY (1993); PHILIP BLUMSTEIN & PEPPER SCHWARTZ, AMERICAN COUPLES: MONEY, WORK, SEX 31–38, 117–29 (1983); DAVID BUSS, THE EVOLUTION OF DESIRE: STRATEGIES OF HUMAN MATING 178 (1994); WARREN FARRELL, THE MYTH OF MALE POWER: WHY MEN ARE THE DISPOSABLE SEX 15 (1993); DEMIE KURZ, FOR RICHER, FOR POORER: MOTHERS CONFRONT DIVORCE 47–52 (1995); RHONA MAHONY, KIDDING OURSELVES: BREADWINNING, BABIES, AND BARGAINING POWER (1995); STEVEN NOCK, SOCIOLOGY OF THE FAMILY 155 (1987); KATHERINE KOHLER REISSMAN, DIVORCE TALK: MEN AND WOMEN MAKE SENSE OF PERSONAL RELATIONSHIPS 50–55 (1990); ROBERTA SIGEL, AMBITION AND ACCOMMODATION (1996); TWO PAYCHECKS: LIFE IN DUAL-EARNER FAMILIES (Joan Aldais ed. 1982); Crain, *supra* note 121; Michelle Fine et al., *(In)Secure Times: Constructing White Working Class Masculinities in the Late Twentieth Century*, 11 GENDER & SOC'Y 52 (1997); Linda Lacey, *As American as Parenthood and Apple Pie: Neutered Mothers, Breadwinning Fathers, and Welfare Rhetoric*, 82 CORNELL L. REV. 79 (1996); Jane Lewis, *The Decline of the Male Breadwinner Model: Implications for Work and Care*, 82 SOC. POL. 152 (2001). *But see* BARNETT & RIVERS, *supra* note 97.

123. FELICE SCHWARTZ, BREAKING WITH TRADITION: WOMEN AND WORK, THE NEW FACTS OF LIFE 51 (1992); Richard Morin & Megan Rosenfeld, *With More Equity, More Sweat: Poll Shows Sexes Agree on Pros and Cons of New Roles*, WASH. POST, Mar. 22, 1998, at A1.

124. FATHERHOOD TODAY: MEN'S CHANGING ROLES IN THE FAMILY (Phyllis Bronstein & Carolyn Pape Cowan eds. 1988); KATHLEEN GERSON, NO MAN'S LAND: MEN'S CHANGING COMMITMENTS TO FAMILY AND WORK (1993); MARK GERZON, A CHOICE OF HEROES: THE CHANGING FACE OF AMERICAN MANHOOD (1982); REASSESSING FATHERHOOD: NEW OBSERVATIONS ON FATHERS AND THE MODERN FAMILY (Charlie Lewis & Margaret O'Brien eds. 1987). On the roles of black men, see ELIJAH ANDERSON, STREET WISE 113–14 (1990); PATRICIA HILL COLLINS, BLACK FEMINIST THOUGHT 59 (1990); BELL HOOKS, AIN'T I A WOMAN? 178 (1981); JACQUELINE JONES, LABOR OF LOVE, LABOR OF SORROW (1985); Glenn, *supra* note 107, at 1337; Andrea

Greater economic independence brought about changes in marital relations.[125] The age at first marriage rose for both men and women (from 22.8 years and 20.3 years respectively in 1960 to 26.7 and 25.0 in 1998), the number of births per women fell dramatically (from 3.45 in 1960 to 2.03 in 1998), and the percentage of adults who were living outside of marriage also rose dramatically (from 18.4 percent of men in 1970 to 41.3 percent in 1998, and from 19.4 percent of women in 1970 to 36.6 percent of women).[126] And, for the first time, large numbers of highly educated and self-confident women were working closely with male peers, with predictable patterns of sexual tension. The result was the invention of a new legal concept—the tort of "sexual harassment."[127] The successful transformation of the notion of "sex discrimination" from a narrow concept of refusing opportunities to women as a class simply because they were women to the doing of something in the workplace or at school that offended a particular woman even

---

Hunter & James Earl Davis, *Constructing Gender: An Exploration of Afro-American Conceptualization of Manhood,* 6 GENDER & SOC'Y 464 (1992); H. Edward Ransford & Jon Miller, *Race, Sex, and Feminist Outlooks,* 48 AM. SOC. REV. 46, 46 (1983); Joan Williams, *Toward a Reconstructive Feminism: Reconstructing the Relationship of Market Work and Family Work,* 19 N. ILL. U. L. REV. 89, 122–23 (1998). *But see* Amy Christian, *The Joint Return Rate Structure: Identifying and Addressing the Gendered Nature of Tax Law,* 13 J. LAW & POL. 241, 280 (1997) (concluding that the tax laws still view the man as the breadwinner and the woman's income as secondary).

125. STEPHANIE COONTZ, THE WAY WE REALLY ARE: COMING TO TERMS WITH AMERICA'S CHANGING FAMILIES (1997); LILLIAN RUBIN, FAMILIES ON THE FAULT LINE (1994); Jennifer Roback Morse, *Beyond "Having It All,"* 18 HARV. J. LAW & PUB. POL'Y 565 (1995); Williams, *supra* note 124, at 114–24.

126. Hacker, *supra* note 109, at 28 (Table C, derived from the Bureau of the Census and the National Center for Health Statistics), 29 (Table D, derived from the Bureau of the Census) (neither Hacker nor I have attempted to account for the discrepancies in percentages between the sexes). *See also* SPAIN & BIANCHI, *supra* note 119, at 63.

127. *See* Louise Marie Roth, *The Right of Privacy Is Political: Power, the Boundary between Public and Private, and Sexual Harassment,* 24 LAW & SOC. INQUIRY 45 (1999). *See also* Burlington Indus. v. Ellerth, 524 U.S. 742 (1998); Harris v. Forklift Sys., Inc., 510 U.S. 17 (1993); Meritor Savings Bank v. Vinson, 477 U.S. 57 (1986); Ellison v. Brady, 924 F.2d 872 (9th Cir. 1991); Henson v. City of Dundee, 682 F.2d 897 (11th Cir. 1982). *See generally* RALPH BAXTER, JR., SEXUAL HARASSMENT IN THE WORKPLACE: A GUIDE TO THE LAW (rev. ed. 1985); JANA HOWARD CAREY, AVOIDING AND LITIGATING SEXUAL HARASSMENT CLAIMS (1997); ALBA CONTE, SEXUAL HARASSMENT IN THE WORKPLACE: LAW AND PRACTICE (1994); LIN FARLEY, SEXUAL SHAKEDOWN: THE SEXUAL HARASSMENT OF WOMEN ON THE JOB (1978); LOUISE FITZGERALD, THE LAST GREAT SECRET: THE SEXUAL HARASSMENT OF WOMEN IN THE WORKPLACE AND ACADEMIA (1993); BARBARA GUTEK, SEX AND THE WORKPLACE: THE IMPACT OF SEXUAL BEHAVIOR AND HARASSMENT ON WOMEN, MEN, AND ORGANIZATIONS (1985); LANGER, *supra* note 96, at 218–23; LEAL, *supra* note 105; BARBARA LINDEMANN & DAVID KADUE, SEXUAL HARASSMENT IN EMPLOYMENT LAW (1992); CATHARINE MACKINNON, SEXUAL HARASSMENT OF WORKING WOMEN (1979); RHODE, *supra* note 97, at 96–107; KERRY SEAGRAVE, THE SEXUAL HARASSMENT OF WOMEN IN THE WORKPLACE: 1600–1993 (1994); SEXUAL HARASSMENT IN AMERICA: A DOCUMENTARY HISTORY (Laura Stein ed. 1999); Deborah Epstein, *Can a "Dumb Ass Woman" Achieve Equality in the Workplace? Running the Gauntlet of Hostile Environment Harassing Speech,* 84 GA. L.J. 399 (1996); Susan Estrich, *Sex at Work,* 43 STAN. L. REV. 813 (1991); Michael Levy, Note, *Sex, Promotions, and Title VII: Why Sexual Favoritism Is Not Sexual Discrimination,* 45 HASTINGS L.J. 667 (1994); Jeffrey Rosen, *Men Behaving Badly,* NEW REP., Dec. 20, 1997, at 18; Susanna Sangres, *Title VII Prohibition against Hostile Environment Sexual Harassment and the First Amendment: No Collision in Sight,* 47 RUTGERS L. REV. 481 (1995); Symposium, *Sexual Harassment: Beyond the Myth & Media,* 6 DUKE J. GENDER & L. 1 (1999); Allan Weitzman, *Employer Defenses to Sexual Harassment Claims,* 6 DUKE J. GENDER L. & POL'Y 27 (1999). This is not to deny that genuine sexual harassment exists. *See* Nancy Hauserman, *Comparing Conversations about Sexual Harassment in the United States and Sweden: Print Media Coverage of the Case against Astra USA,* 14 WIS. WOMEN'S L.J. 45 (1999). One scholar has undertaken to demonstrate that sexual harassment law has roots in the earlier common law. To accomplish this, they choose to ignore the differences between the relatively specific laws relating to incest, rape, seduction, statutory rape, and "sexual defilement" on the one hand (all of which required actual coitus under varying circumstances) and the open-ended approach of contemporary sexual harassment law. *See* Sara McLean, *Confided to His Care or Protection: The Late Nineteenth-Century Crime of Workplace Sexual Harassment,* 9 COLUM. J. GENDER & L. 47 (1999).

though it did not affect the opportunities of women as a class converted discrimination bans into truly powerful weapons for altering employment and education to suit female preferences almost without regard to the impact on men.[128] Extending these same provisions to protect men

128. *See, e.g.,* Kolstad v. American Dental Ass'n, 527 U.S. 526 (1999); Faragher v. City of Boca Raton, 524 U.S. 775 (1998); Burlington Indus., Inc. v. Ellerth, 524 U.S. 742 (1998); Harris v. Forklift Systems, Inc., 510 U.S. 17 (1993); Meritor Savings Bank v. Vinson, 477 U.S. 57 (1986). *See generally* DANIELLE CRITTENDEN, WHAT OUR MOTHERS DIDN'T TELL US: WHY HAPPINESS ELUDES THE MODERN WOMAN (1999); SUSAN FALUDI, STIFFED: THE BETRAYAL OF THE AMERICAN MAN (1999); HELEN FISHER, THE FIRST SEX: THE NATURAL TALENTS OF WOMEN AND HOW THEY ARE CHANGING THE WORLD (1999); CAROLINE FORELL & DONNA MATTHEWS, A LAW OF HER OWN: THE REASONABLE WOMAN AS A MEASURE OF MAN (2000); STEPHEN MOREWITZ, SEXUAL HARASSMENT AND SOCIAL CHANGE IN AMERICA (1996); DAPHNE PATAI, HETEROPHOBIA: SEXUAL HARASSMENT AND THE FUTURE OF FEMINISM RETHINKING MASCULINITY—PHILOSOPHICAL EXPLORATIONS IN LIGHT OF FEMINISM (Larry May *et al.* ed. 1996); KATIE ROIPHE, THE MORNING AFTER: SEX, FEAR, AND FEMINISM (1993); LIONEL TIGER, THE DECLINE OF MALES (1999); Kathryn Abrams, *The State of the Union: Civil Rights: Gender Discrimination and the Transformation of Workplace Norms,* 42 VAND. L. REV. 1183 (1989); Steven Aden, *"Harm in Asking": A Reply to Eugene Scalia and an Analysis of the Paradigm Shift in the Supreme Court's Title VII Sexual Harassment Jurisprudence,* 8 TEMPLE POL. & CIV. RTS. L. REV. 477 (1999); J.M. Balkin, *Free Speech and Hostile Environments,* 99 COLUM. L. REV. 2295 (1999); Rebecca Brannan, *When the Pig Is in the Barnyard, Not the Parlor: Should Courts Apply a "Coarseness Factor" in Analyzing Blue-Collar Hostile Work Environment Claims,* 17 GA. ST. U. L. REV. 789 (2001); Deborah Brenneman, *From a Woman's Point of View: The Use of the Reasonable Woman Standard in Sexual Harassment Cases,* 60 U. CIN. L. REV. 1281 (1992); Naomi Cahn, *The Looseness of Legal Language: The Reasonable Woman Standard in Theory and Practice,* 77 CORNELL L. REV. 1398 (1992); Lynn Dennison, *An Argument for the Reasonable Woman Standard in Hostile Environment Claims,* 54 OHIO ST. L.J. 473 (1993); Louis DiLorenzo & Larua Harshbarger, *Employer Liability for Supervisor Harassment after Ellerth and Faragher,* 6 DUKE J. GENDER L. & POL'Y 3 (1999); Billie Wright Dziech, Robert Dziech II, & Donard Hordes, *"Consensual" or Submissive Relationships: The Second-Best Kept Secret,* 6 DUKE J. GENDER L. & POL'Y 83 (1999); Epstein, *supra* note 127; Estrich, *supra* note 127; Katherine Franke, *What's Wrong with Sexual Harassment?,* 49 STAN. L. REV. 691 (1997); Elizabeth Glidden, *The Emergence of the Reasonable Woman in Combating Hostile Environment Sexual Harassment,* 77 IOWA L. REV. 1825 (1992); Hacker, *supra* note 109; Toni Lester, *The Reasonable Woman in Sexual Harassment Law,* 26 IND. L. REV. 227 (1993); John Marks, *Title VII's Flight beyond First Amendment Radar: A Yin-to-Yang Attenuation of "Speech" Incident to Discriminatory "Abuse" in the Workplace,* 9 COLUM. J. GENDER & L. 1 (1999); Tzili Mor, *Law as a Tool for a Sexual Revolution: Israel's Prevention of Sexual Harassment Law—1998,* 7 MICH. J. GENDER & L. 291 (2001); Michael Noone, *Chimera or Jackalope? Department of Defense Efforts to Apply Civilian Sexual Harassment Criteria to the Military,* 6 DUKE J. GENDER L. & POL'Y 151 (1999); Juan Perea, *Strange Fruit: Harassment and the First Amendment,* 29 U.C. DAVIS L. REV. 875 (1996); Teresa Godwin Phelps, *Gendered Space and the Reasonableness Standard in Sexual Harassment Cases,* 12 NOTRE DAME L. REV. 265 (1998); David Pinkston, *Redefining Objectivity: The Case for the Reasonable Woman Standard in Hostile Environment Claims,* 1993 BYU L. REV. 364; Lucetta Pope, *Everything You Ever Wanted to Know about Sexual Harassment But Were Too Politically Correct to Ask (or, the Use and Abuse of "But for" Analysis in Sexual Harassment Law under Title VII),* 30 SW. U. L. REV. 253 (2001); Jeannie Sclafani Rhee, *Redressing for Success: The Liability of Hooters Restaurant for Customer Harassment of Waitresses,* 20 HARV. WOMEN'S L.J. 163 (1997); Wayne Lindsey Robbins, jr., *When Two Liberal Values Collide in an Era of "Political Correctness": First Amendment Protection as a Check on Speech-Based Title VII Hostile Environment Claims,* 47 BAYLOR L. REV. 789 (1995); Abigail Saguy, *Employment Discrimination or Sexual Violence? Defining Sexual Harassment in American and French Law,* 34 LAW & SOC'Y REV. 1091 (2000); Eugene Scalia, *The Strange Career of* Quid Pro Quo *Sexual Harassment,* 21 HARV. J.L. & PUB. POL'Y 307 (1998); Shira Scheindlin & John Elofson, *Judges, Juries, and Sexual Harassment,* 17 YALE L. & POL'Y REV. 813 (1999); Kenneth Schneyer, *Hooting: Public and Popular Discourse about Sex Discrimination,* 31 U. MICH. J.L. REFORM 551 (1998); Nadine Strossen, *The Tensions between Regulating Workplace Harassment and the First Amendment: No Trump,* 71 CHI.-KENT L. REV. 701 (1995); Michael Studd & Urs Gattiker, *The Evolutionary Psychology of Sexual Harassment in Organizations,* 12 ETHOLOGY & SOCIOBIOLOGY 249 (1991); Symposium, *Sexual Harassment in the Workplace: Fifteen Years after* Meritor Savings Bank, 27 OHIO N.U. L. REV. 439 (2001); Eugene Volokh, *How Harassment Law Restricts Free Speech,* 47 RUTGERS L.J. 563 (1995) ("Volokh I"); Eugene Volokh, *What Speech Does "Hostile Work Environment" Harassment Law Restrict?,* 85 GEO. L.J. 627 (1997) ("Volokh II"); Susan & David Williams, *A Feminist Theory of Malebashing,* 4 MICH. J. GENDER & L. 35 (1996); Deborah Zalesne, *Sexual Harassment: Has It Gone too Far, or Has the Media?,* 8 TEMPLE POL. & CIV. RTS. L. REV. 351 (1999). *See also* Mary Karr, *A Witch Reports, Post-Witch Hunt,* CIVILIZATION,

who do not fit the dominant paradigm of masculinity from harassment by other men does not alter conclusions regarding the effect on the relations between women and men.[129]

Despite the considerable theoretical attention to same-sex harassment or women harassing men, the function of sexual harassment law remains the protection of women from men. Some 94 percent of such claims involve women complaining about the behavior of men—nearly always women under the age of 45.[130] Younger women have always worked outside the home to some extent, and at least some them, when working outside their family settings, have experienced sexual harassment on the job throughout all that time. They could have brought criminal charges or sought monetary awards for rape or even offensive touching for centuries.[131] Only after 1980, however, could anyone sue based upon hostile environment claims—today, the controversial core of modern sexual harassment law. Courts have accepted the claim that "hostile environments" for women arise when men make sexual remarks to women, solicit sex verbally, post "pin-ups" on the walls of the workplace, or take any of the myriad other steps meant to demean women.[132] In other words, the concept of sexual harassment adds the possibility of suing for merely boorish behavior by men. Complicating the legal picture is the fact that workplaces have assumed an increasingly prominent place as a meeting ground for poten-

---

Feb.-Mar. 1999, at 42 (reporting on campus hysteria leading to sexual harassment charges against the author arising from words she used in class); Hauserman, *supra* note 127; Allyson Singer, *Sex Discrimination in the Hong Kong Special Administrative Region: The Sex Discrimination Ordinance, the Equal Opportunities Commission, and a Proposal for Change,* 11 Ind. Int'l & Comp. L. Rev. 215 (2000); Ryuichi Yamakawa, *We've Only Just Begun: The Law of Sexual Harassment in Japan,* 22 Hastings Int'l & Comp. L. Rev. 523 (1999).

129. Oncale v. Sundowner Offshore Services, Inc., 523 U.S. 75 (1998). *See also* Goins v. West Group, 635 N.W.2d 717 (Minn. 2001) (employer's refusal to assign a biological male to the women's restroom because of his/her sexual orientation did not create a hostile work environment). *See generally* Gabriel Nugent, Employment Discrimination Based on Sexual Orientation (1998); Mary Ann Case, *Disaggregating Gender from Sex and Sexual Orientation: The Effeminate Man in the Law and Feminist Jurisprudence,* 105 Yale L.J. 1 (1995); Jonathan Cohn, *A Man's Place: When Feminism Meets At-Home Fatherhood,* The New Rep., Nov. 7, 1998, at 20; Mary Coombs, *Title VII and Homosexual Harassment after* Oncale: *Was It a Victory?,* 6 Duke J. Gender L. & Pol'y 113 (1999); Kiren Dosanjh, *Calling on* Oncale: *Federal Courts Post-*Oncale *Approach to the "Evidentiary Routes" to Discriminatory Intent in Title VII Same-Sex Harassment Claims,* 33 Urban Law. 547 (2001); Katherine Franke, *The Central Mistake of Sex Discrimination Law: The Disaggregation of Sex from Gender,* 144 U. Pa. L. Rev. 1 (1995); L. Camille Hebert, *Sexual Harassment as Discrimination "Because of…Sex": Have We Come Full Circle?,* 27 Ohio N.U. L. Rev. 439 (2001); Toni Lester, *Protecting the Gender Nonconformist from the Gender Police—Why the Harassment of Gays and Other Nonconformists Is a Form of Sex Discrimination in Light of the Supreme Court's Decision in* Oncale v. Sundowner, 29 N.M. L. Rev. 89 (1999); Sandra Levitsky, *Footnote 55: Closing the "Bisexual Defense" Loophole in Title VII Sexual Harassment Cases,* 80 Minn. L. Rev. 1013 (1996); Steven Locke, *The Equal Opportunity Harasser as a Paradigm for Recognizing Sexual Homosexuals under Title VII,* 27 Rutgers L.J. 383 (1996); Tamanna Qureshi & Anthony Vaupel, *Should Sexual Harassment Based upon Sexual Orientation Be Covered by Title VII or Prohibited?,* 27 Ohio N.U. L. Rev. 679 (2001); Regina Stone-Harris, *Same-Sex Harassment—The Next Step in the Evolution of Sexual Harassment Law under Title VII,* 28 St. Mary's L.J. 269 (1996).

130. Buss, *supra* note 122, at 160. *See also* David Terpstra & Susan Cook, *Complaining Characteristics and Reported Behaviors and Consequences Associated with Formal Sexual Harassment Charges,* 38 Personal Psych. 559, 573 (1985).

131. *See, e.g.,* Skousen v. Nidy, 367 P.2d 248 (Ariz. 1961); Gates v. State, 138 S.E.2d 473 (Ga. Ct. App. 1964); Hatchett v. Blacketer, 172 S.W. 533 (Ky. 1915); Ragsdale v. Ezell, 49 S.W. 775 (Ky. 1899); Liljegren v. United Railways Co., 277 S.W. 925 (Mo. Ct. App. 925 (1921); Hough v. Iderhoff, 139 P. 931 (Or. 1914); Martin v. Jansen, 193 P. 674 (Wash. 1920); Craker v. Chicago & Nw. Ry., 36 Wis. 657 (1875).

132. Aden, *supra* note 128; Balkin, *supra* note 128; Kingsley Browne, *Zero Tolerance for the First Amendment: Title VII's Regulation of Employee Speech,* 27 Ohio N.U. L. Rev. 563 (2001); Richard Allen Olmstead, *In Defense of the Indefensible: Title VII Hostile Environment Claims Unconstitutionally Restrict Free Speech,* 27 Ohio N.U. L. Rev. 691 (2001); Robbins, *supra* note 128; Stroessen, *supra* note 128; Volokh I, *supra* note 128; Volokh II, *supra* note 128.

tial mates,[133] making it impossible to ban all social contact between the sexes as they work together. But why did younger women not demand legal protection from boorish behavior before 1980?

There are two usual explanations for the historical silence of women: First, men made the law for the benefit of men, leaving women unable to make their concerns known. Second, women generally worked in sex-segregated jobs, minimizing opportunities for sexual harassment.[134] After all, only in 1964 was an equal pay law enacted as the first step in obtaining workplace equality.[135] But women did not always work apart from men at anytime in history. And can anyone really believe that Susan B. Anthony, Elizabeth Cady Stanton, and the Claflin sisters, to name just a few, would have been silent on this topic if they thought that women needed legal protection from such behavior? Others are also dissatisfied by these explanations.[136]

Economist Gertrud Fremling and Judge Richard Posner have offered an explanation for the timing problem that suggests that the emergence of hostile-environment sexual harassment is linked to the rise of the managerial class. They contend that the wrong done to working women in the hostile environment harassment claims arises from working women perceiving that their status has been challenged, rather than from the solicitation of sexual favors or the offering of sexual insults as such.[137] A woman who is the object of the harassment is being treated as a lower status individual because in our society men feel free to affront only lower status women — particularly if others know of the affront.[138] Studies seem to verify this when they find that, although women may feel that a higher status man's advances are potentially coercive, women most resent the advances by men of lower status than the woman being affronted.[139] Men, on the other hand, are likely to find sexual advances from women stimulating rather than demeaning. Recall in this regard that, many men are willing to have sex even with a woman they would never date, but most women are unwilling to have sex even with some of the men they do date.[140]

In former times, women working outside the home generally held only lower status jobs. Men strove for status through competition in social hierarchies of wealth, power and prestige.

---

133. *See* Carol Hymowitz & Ellen Joan Pollack, *Corporate Affairs: The One Clear Line in Interoffice Romance Has Become Blaired,* WALL ST. J., Feb. 5, 1998, at A1 ("Offices have replaced bars, churches, parties and gyms as the dominant meeting ground.").

134. Janine Benedet, *Same-Sex Sexual Harassment in Employment,* 26 QUEEN'S L.J. 101,117 (2000).

135. See the authorities collected *supra* in note 104.

136. *See, e.g.,* Gertrud Fremling & Richard Posner, *Status Signaling and the Law, with Particular Application to Sexual Harassment,* 147 U. PA. L. REV. 1069 (1999).

137. *Id.* at 1081–86. *See also* Henson v. City of Dundee, 682 F.2d 897, 902 (11th Cir. 1982) ("Surely the requirement that a man or woman run a gauntlet of sexual abuse in return for the privilege of being allowed to work...can be as demeaning and disconcerting...as the harshest of racial epithets."). For a remarkably similar analysis by a radical feminist who, presumably, would object to drawing conclusions such as those of Fremling and Posner from her analysis, see DRUCILLA CORNELL, THE IMAGINARY DOMAIN: ABORTION, PORNOGRAPHY, AND SEXUAL HARASSMENT 167–205 (1995). *See also* Debra Baker, *Plague in the Profession: Success in the Legal World Is No Safeguard against Sexual Harassment,* ABA J., Sept. 2000, at 40.

138. Fremling & Richard Posner, *supra* note 136, at 1082.

139. *Id. See also* BUSS, *supra* note 122, at 160–61; Patricia Frazier *et al., Social Science Research on Lay Definitions of Sexual Harassment,* 51 J. SOC. ISSUES 21, 27–29 (1995).

140. EDWARD LAUMANN *et al.,* THE SOCIAL ORGANIZATION OF SEXUALITY: SEXUAL PRACTICES IN THE UNITED STATES 201 (1994); Paul Chara & Lynn Kuenne, *Diverging Gender Attitudes Regarding Casual Sex: A Cross-Sectional Study,* 74 PSYCH. REP. 57 (1994); Russell Clark III & Elaine Harfield, *Gender Differences in Receptivity to Sexual Offers,* 2 J. PSYCH. & HUM. SEXUALITY 39 (1989); Fremling & Posner, *supra* note 136, at 1087; Douglas Kenrick *et al., Evolution, Traits, and the Stages of Human Courtship: Qualifying the Parental Investment Model,* 58 J. PERSONALITY 97, 104–10 (1990).

Women—even working women—obtained social status primarily through marriage and motherhood.[141] While the highest status positions in societies were held by men (and derivatively by their women), the lowest status positions were also held by men. (The lowest status rungs are the insane and the retarded, criminals, and beggars—all groups in which men even today continue to outnumber women.) So long as working women held relatively low-status jobs, there was, according to Fremling and Posner, no challenge to their status in verbal or visual harassment.[142]

With their entrance into the managerial class, women who were moving into formerly all-male or predominantly male jobs often moved into higher status jobs, jobs requiring high levels of education and skill. Such women were extremely sensitive to any challenge to their newly found professional status—precisely what sexual harassment laws, particularly in the hostile environment cases, are all about. Fremling and Posner suggest, however, that the highest status women are actually hurt by sexual harassment laws because even women of moderate status can now pretend to high status through objecting to harassing behavior, thus denying higher status women of the "prerogatives" of their status.[143] This loss was compensated by the effect of harassment laws in discouraging dating across status lines, making high status men more likely to marry high status women rather than secretaries.[144] Women of the managerial class also were concerned about the ambiguity (even in their own minds) when they (and others) are not certain if their achievements or failures result from their receptiveness to or rejection of sexual advances rather than from their professional abilities.[145]

After 1970, women were moving into the learned professions in unprecedented numbers. For example, women comprised 7.8 percent of first-year law students in 1970 and 28.4 percent by 1976; steady increases since have brought the percentage to near 50 percent today.[146] As a result, about 80 percent of all women who have ever practiced law in North America are doing so today.[147] A similar increase in the number of women law professors also occurred, rising from 1.7 percent of the legal professorate in 1967 to 10 percent in 1979 to 25 percent in 1990, with the

---

141. Fremling & Posner, *supra* note 136, at 1075–77, 1096, 1101, 1109.

142. Fremling and Posner also posit that working women, who until fairly recently nearly always would expect to get married and have children, were more likely to be dependent on a man's income and therefore would not want to depress actual or potential husbands' wages as would result from sexual harassment litigation. *Id.* at 1089–90, 1095–97. I am not convinced that economic analyses by low-status working women in times past were so sophisticated.

143. *Id.* at 1093–95.

144. *Id.* at 1097.

145. *Id.* at 1083–84.

146. American Bar Ass'n Comm'n on Women in the Profession, The Unfinished Agenda: Women and the Legal Profession 27 (2001) ("The Unfinished Agenda"); Paul Carrington, *One Law: The Role of Legal Education in the Opening of the Legal Profession since 1776*, 44 Fla. L. Rev. 501, 572 (1992); Terry Carter, *It's Not Just a "Guy Thing" Anymore: Law School Programs Will Be Different because of Who's Attending, Teaching*, 85 ABA J., Apr. 1999, at 18; Richard Neumann jr., *Women in Legal Education: What the Statistics Show*, 50 J. Legal Educ. 313, 314–20 (2000). *See also* Marina Angel, *Women in Legal Education: What It's Like to Be Part of a Perpetual First Wave or the Case of the Disappearing Woman*, 61 Temple L. Rev. 799 (1988); Beth Goldstein, *Little Brown Spots on the Notebook Paper: Women as Law School Students*, 84 Ky. L.J. 983 (1996); Darlene Goring, *Silent Beneficiaries: Affirmative Action and Gender in Law School Academic Support Programs*, 84 Ky. L.J. 941 (1996).

147. Cynthia Fuchs Epstein, *Faulty Framework: Consequences of the Difference Model for Women in the Law*, 35 N.Y.L.S. L. Rev. 309, 309 (1990); Mary Jane Mossman, *Challenging "Hidden" Assumptions: (Women) Lawyers and Family Life*, in Mothers in Law, *supra* note 68, at 289, 290 ("Mossman, *Hidden Assumptions*"); Mary Jane Mossman, *Portia's Progress: Women as Lawyers: Reflections on Past and Future*, 8 Windsor Y.B. Access to Justice 252, 252 (1988). Women now hold about 30% of all judgeships in the United States, but only 15% of federal judgeships. 2001 ABA Comm'n, *supra* note 146, at 26. Only 5% of managing partners in law firms are women. *Id.*, at 23. These and similar percentages, however, might represent the fact that relatively few women have been in practice for the length of time that one would expect before a lawyer would rise to

percentage continuing to rise during the 1990s.[148] Women are "overrepresented" among lower levels of law school administrators (48 percent in 1990), among clinicians and legal writing instructors (59 percent in 1998) — both groups that generally are not eligible for tenure and often are considered lesser members of the faculty (with men being concentrated in such positions at institutions where they are eligible for tenure), and among professional law librarians (69 percent in 1998), and "underrepresented" among the teaching faculty. This pattern predates the large-scale entry of women into the legal profession.[149] Despite the numerical progress women have made in entering the legal profession, they continue to earn less than men attorneys, in part because they tend to gravitate towards less lucrative fields of law, in part because they more often interrupt or side-track their careers because of family obligations, and arguably in part because of wage and other forms of discrimination.[150] Such discrimination as there is could feed back to

---

such positions. *See* Denise Lavoie, *Women Overcoming Some Hurdles in Legal Profession,* Phila. Inquirer, Apr. 27, 2001, at A24.

148. The Unfinished Agenda, *supra* note 146, at 27; Carrington, *supra* note 146, at 592–93; Carter, *supra* note 146, at 18; Richard Chused, *The Hiring and Retention of Minorities and Women on American Law Faculties,* 137 U. Pa. L. Rev. 537, 557 (1988); Donna Fossum, *Women Law Professors,* 1980 Am. B. Fndtn. Res. J. 903, 904–06; Herma Hill Kay, *The Future of Women Law Professors,* 77 Iowa L. Rev. 5 (1991); Deborah Jones Merritt, *Are Women Stuck on the Academic Ladder? An Empirical Perspective,* 10 UCLA Women's L.J. 249, 250 (2000); Frances Olsen, *Affirmative Action: Necessaries but not Sufficient,* 71 Chi.-Kent L. Rev. 937, 938 (1996); Neumann, *supra* note 146, at 322–23, 325–26, 336–37, 340–42; Dan Subotnik, *Bah, Humbug to the Bleak Story of Women Law Faculty: A Response to Professor Neumann,* 51 J. Legal Educ. 141 (2001); Elyce Zanoff & Kathryn Lorio, *What We Know, What We Think We Know, and What We Don't Know about Women Law Professors,* 25 Ariz. L. Rev. 869, 870 (1983). *See also* Jo Anne Duranko, *Second-Class Citizens in the Pink Ghetto: Gender Bias in Legal Writing,* 50 J. Legal Educ. 562 (2000).

149. The Unfinished Agenda, *supra* note 146, at 27–28; Marina Angel, *The Glass Ceiling for Women in Legal Education: Contract Positions and the Death of Tenure,* 50 J. Legal Educ. 1 (2000); Maureen Arrigo, *Hierarchy Maintained: Status and Gender Issues in Legal Writing Programs,* 70 Temple L. Rev. 117 (1997); Carrington, *supra* note 146, at 593; Chused, *supra* note 148, at 548–56; Neumann, *supra* note 146, at , 313–14, 326–39, 345–51; Merritt, *supra* note 148, at 253–54; Deborah Rhode, *Midcourse Corrections: Women in Legal Education,* 53 J. Legal Educ. 475, 481–82 (2003). "Undrepresentation" among teaching faculty is particularly pronounced at the so-called better schools. Olsen, *supra* note 148, at 938 (noting that although women constituted 26% of all full-time law professors in 1994, they were only 15% of the faculty at Harvard and the University of Chicago, 16% at the University of Michigan, 22% at Columbia, and 23% at Yale; only Stanford, at 36%, was above the national average). *See also* Merritt, *supra,* at 253; Neumann, *supra,* at 342–45, 353–57. For a debate over the significance of these numbers, see Dan Subotnik, *Seeing through "the Glass Ceiling": A Response to Professor Angel,* 50 J. Legal Educ. 450 (2000); and Marina Angel, *Comments in Reply: It's Becoming a Glass House,* 50 J. Legal Educ. 454 (2000).

Subotnik, in another article, compiles statistics that show, however, that although women constitute only about 35% of the applicants for tenure track positions on law faculties, they capture about 50% of the positions. Subotnik, *supra* note 148, at 142–43. He also points out that although women make up 22% of the pool from which law school deans and tenured associate deans are drawn, they hold 30% of such positions. *Id.,* at 146.

Regarding the similar situation across academia generally, see Nancy Langton & Jeffrey Pfeffer, *Sources of Salary Variations in Academic Labour Markets,* 59 Am. Soc. Rev. 236 (1994); Joan Williams, *What Stymies Women's Academic Careers? It's Personal,* Chron. Higher Educ., Dec. 15, 2000, at B10.

150. *See, e.g.,* Catchpole v. Brannon, 42 Cal. Rptr. 2d 440 (Ct. App. 1995), *rev. denied* (case reversed because of gender bias). *See also* Barbara Curran & Clara Carson, The Lawyer Statistical Report: The U.S. Legal Profession in the 1990s (1994); Lorraine Dusky, Still Unequal: The Shameful Truth about Women and Justice in America (1996); Cynthia Fuchs Epstein, Women in Law (2nd ed. 1993); Susan Estrich, Sex and Power (2000); John Hagan & Fiona Kay, Gender in Practice: A Study of Lawyer's Lives (1995) (Canada); Mona Harrington, Women Lawyers: Rewriting the Rules (1993); Suzanne Nossel & Elizabeth Westfall, Presumed Equal: What America's Top Women Lawyers Really Think about Their Firms (2nd ed. 1998); Jennifer Pierce, Gender Trials: Emotional Lives in Contemporary Law Firms (1995); Kathryn Plonsky, Balancing Law and Parenthood: Part-Time Careers in the Law (1999); Margaret Thornton, Dissonance and Distrust: Women in the Legal Profession (1996) (Australia); The Unfinished Agenda, *supra* note 146, at 6–7, 14–29; Browne, *supra* note 123;

influence the other two reasons for women lawyers' lower earnings. Much the same pattern persists for women doctors who face a widening gap in pay compared to the men in practicing in the same specialties and other gender-linked difficulties.[151]

---

Charlotte Chiu & Kevin Leicht, *When Does Feminization Increase Equality? The Case of Lawyers*, 33 Law & Soc'y Rev. 557 (1999); Jo Dixon & Caroll Seron, *Stratification in the Legal Profession: Sex, Sector, and Salary*, 29 Law & Soc'y Rev. 381 (1995); Cynthia Fuchs Epstein *et al.*, *Glass Ceilings and Open Doors: Women's Advancement in the Legal Profession: A Report of the Committee on Women in the Profession, the Association of the Bar of the City of New York*, 64 Fordham L. Rev. 291 (1995); Elizabeth Foster, *The Glass Ceiling in the Legal Profession: Why Do Law Firms Still Have so Few Female Partners?*, 42 UCLA L. Rev. 1631 (1995); Grace Giesel, *The Business Client Is a Woman: The Effect of Women as In-House Counsel on Women in Law Firms and the Legal Profession*, 72 Neb. L. Rev. 760 (1993); Wynn Huang, *Gender Differences in the Earnings of Lawyers*, 30 Colum. J.L. & Soc. Problems 267 (1997); Kathleen Hull, *The Paradox of the Contented Female Lawyer*, 33 Law & Soc'y Rev. 687 (1999); Fiona Kay & John Hagan, *Cultivating Clients in the Competition for Partnership: Gender and the Organizational Restructuring of Law Firms in the 1990s*, 33 Law & Soc'y Rev. 517 (1999); Korzic, *supra* note 116; Landers, Rebitzer, & Taylor, *supra* note 116; Hugh Lena, Sharyn Roach, & Seymour Warkov, *Professional Status at Midcareer: The Influence of Social and Academic Origins on Lawyers' Achievement*, 8 Soc. F. 365 (1993); Mossman, *Hidden Assumptions*, *supra* note 147, at 291–97; Mossman, *supra* note 116; Ninth Circuit Gender Bias Task Force, *The Effects of Gender in the Federal Courts*, 67 S. Cal. L. Rev. 745 (1994); Reichman & Sterling, *supra* note 116; Judith Resnik, *Asking about Gender in the Courts*, 21 Signs 952 (1996); Schenker, *supra* note 116; Spurr & Syeyoshi, *supra* note 116; Symposium, *Women and the Law: Changes Achieved, Challenges Ahead*, ABA J., Sept. 2000, at 29; Lawrence Stiffman, *A Snapshot of the Economic Status of Attorneys in Michigan*, 82 Mich. Bar J. 20 (2003); Marilyn Tucker, *Will Women Lawyers Ever Be Happy?*, Law Pract. & Mgt., Jan./Feb. 1998, at 47; Robert Wood *et al.*, *Pay Differences among the Highly Paid: The Male/Female Earnings Gap in Lawyers' Salaries*, 11 J. Lab. Econ. 417 (1993); Elizabeth Ziewacz, *Can the Glass Ceiling Be Shattered? The Decline of Women Partners in Large Law Firms*, 57 Ohio St. L.J. 971 (1996). Women law teachers also replicate this pattern of concentrating in the glamorous fields of law. Angel, *supra* note 155; Merritt, *supra* note 148, at 254–55; Deborah Jones Merritt, *Who Teaches Constitutional Law?*, 11 Const. Commentary 145 (1994); Robert Seibel, *Do Deans Discriminate?: An Examination of Lower Salaries Paid to Women Clinical Teachers*, 6 UCLA Women's L.J. 541 (1996); Subotnik, *supra* note 149.

Whether for the same reasons or otherwise, in at least some schools women law professors have had to struggle to be paid equivalently to men with similar levels of experience. *See, e.g.*, Martha West, *Faculty Women's Struggle for Equality at the University of California Davis*, 10 UCLA Women's L.J. 259 (2000). They have also achieved tenure at a notably lower rate—61% to 72%—than men. Subotnik, *supra* note 148, at 143–44. *See also* Williams, *supra* note 149. Yet one must be wary of assuming that discrimination can be inferred solely from statistical inequalities—inferences that Thomas Sowell has described as "the reigning *non sequitur* of our times, both intellectually and politically." Sowell, *supra* note 118, at 62. *See generally* Thomas Sowell, Preferential Politics: An International Perspective 128–43 (1990); Sowell, *supra* note 118, at 34–39, 60–68; Subotnik, *supra* note 148, at 146–48.

151. Natalie Angier, *Among Doctors, Pay for Women Still Lags*, N.Y. Times, Jan. 12, 1999, at F7; Erica Frank *et al.*, *Career Satisfaction of U.S. Women Physicians: Results from the Women Physicians' Health Study*, 159 Arch. Internal Med. 1417 (1999); Lynn Nonnemaker, *Women Physicians in Academic Medicine: New Insights from Cohort Studies*, 342 New Eng. J. Med. 399 (2000); Jodi Elgart Paik, *The Feminization of Medicine*, 283 JAMA 666 (1999); S. Redman *et al.*, *Determinants of Career Choices among Women and Men Medical Students and Interns*, 28 Med. Educ. 361 (1994); Lynne Simpson & Linda Grant, *Sources and Magnitude of Job Stress among Physicians*, 14 J. Behav. Med. 27 (1991).

On the general problem of women's incomes and work experiences, see EEOC v. Sears, Roebuck & Co., 839 F.2d 302 (7th Cir. 1988); Becker, *supra* note 112; Federal Glass Ceiling Commission, Good for Business: Making Full Use of the Nation's Human Capital (1995); Kathleen Hall Jamieson, Beyond the Double Bind: Women and Leadership (1995) Latinas and African-American Women at Work (Irene Browne ed. 1999); Robert Nelson & William Bridges, Legalizing Gender Inequality (1999); Schwartz, *supra* note 123; Donald Tomaskovic-Devey, Gender and Racial Inequality at Work (1993); Virginia Valian, Why So Slow? The Advancement of Women (1998); Ann Bookman, *Flexibility at What Price? The Costs of Part-Time Work for Women Workers*, 52 Wash. & Lee L. Rev. 799 (1995); Diane Bridge, *The Glass Ceiling and Sexual Stereotyping: Historical and Legal Perspectives of Women in the Workplace*, 4 Va. J. Soc. Pol'y & L. 581 (1997); Browne, *supra* note 117; Tonya Brito, *Spousal Support Takes on the Mommy Track: Why the ALI Proposal Is Good for Working Mothers*, 8 Duke J. Gender & L. 151 (2001); William Darity & Patrick Mason, *Evidence on Discrimination in Employment: Codes of Color, Codes of Gender*, 12 J. Econ. Persp. 63

The movement of managerial-class women into the job market posed all sorts of new problems for themselves and others compared to the problems from excluding women from the job market. Women often found themselves still doing most of the housework while holding a full time job in the marketplace.[152] No wonder journalist Ann Quindlen exclaimed that "[w]hen I

---

(1998); Paula England, *The Failure of Human Capital Theory to Explain Occupational Sex Segregation*, 17 J. HUM. RESOURCES 358 (1988); Martha Foschi, *Double Standards in the Evaluation of Men and Women*, 59 SOC. PSYCH. 237 (1996); Jacqueline Dowd Hall, *Women's History Goes to Trial: EEOC v. Sears, Roebuck & Co.*, 11 SIGNS 751 (1986); Thomas Haskell & Stanford Levinson, *Academic Freedom and Expert Witnessing: Historians and the Sears Case*, 66 TEX. L. REV. 1829 (1988); B. Tobias Isbell, *Gender Inequality and Wage Differentials between the Sexes: Is It Inevitable or Is There an Answer?*, 50 WASH. U.J. URBAN & CONTEMP. L. 369 (1996); Linda Jackson, *Relative Deprivation and the Gender Wage Gap*, 45 J. SOC. ISSUES 117 (1989); Alice Kessler-Harris, *Academic Freedom and Expert Witnessing: A Response to Haskell and Levinson*, 67 TEX. L. REV. 429 (1989); Alice Kessler-Harris, *EEOC v. Sears, Roebuck & Company: A Personal Account*, 35 RADICAL HIST. REV. 57 (1986); Barbara Kilbourne, Paula England, & Kurt Beron, *Effects of Individual, Occupational, and Industrial Characteristics on Earnings: Intersection of Race and Gender*, 72 SOC. FORCES 1149 (1994); Jacqueline Landau, *The Relationship of Race and Gender to Managers' Rating of Promotion Potential*, 16 J. ORG. BEHAVIOR 391 (1995); Karyn Loscocco, *Reactions to Blue-Collar Work: A Comparison of Women and Men*, 17 WORK & OCCUPATIONS 152 (1990); Karyn Loscocco & Glenna Spitze, *The Organizational Context of Women's and Men's Pay Satisfaction*, 72 SOC. SCI. Q. 3 (1991); Debra Meyerson & Joyce Fletcher, *A Modest Manifesto for Shattering the Glass Ceiling*, HARV. BUS. REV., Jan.–Feb. 2000, at 127; Ruth Milkman, *Women's History and the Sears Case*, 12 FEMINIST STUD. 375 (1986); Martina Morris & Bruce Western, *Inequality in Earnings at the Close of the Twentieth Century*, 25 ANNUAL REV. SOC. 623 (1999); Clifford Mottaz, *Gender Differences in Work Satisfaction, Work-Related Rewards and Values, and the Determinants of Work Satisfaction*, 39 HUMAN RELATIONS 359 (1986); Cecily Neil & William Snizek, *Gender as a Moderator of Job Satisfaction*, 15 WORK & OCCUPATIONS 201 (1988); Trond Peterson & Laurie Morgan, *Separate and Unequal: Occupation-Establishment Sex Segregation and the Gender Wage Gap*, 101 AM. J. SOC. 329 (1995); Jo Phelan, *The Paradox of the Contented Female Worker: An Assessment of Alternative Explanations*, 57 SOC. PSYCH. Q. 95 (1994); Barbara Reskin & Catharine Roos, *Jobs, Authority, and Earnings among Managers: The Continuing Significance of Sex*, 19 WORK & OCCUPATIONS 342 (1992); Carroll Seron & Kerry Ferris, *Negotiating Professionalism: The Gendered Social Capital of Flexible Time*, 22 WORK & OCCUPATIONS 22 (1995); Ronnie Steinberg, *Gender on the Agenda: Male Advantage in Organizations*, 21 CONTEMP. SOC. 576 (1992); Marta Tienda et al., *Industrial Restructuring, Gender Segregation, and Sex Differences in Earnings*, 52 AM. SOC. REV. 195 (1987); Amy Wharton, *Feminism at Work*, 571 ANNALS AM. ACADEMY POL. & SOC. SCI. 167 (2000); Williams, *supra* note 149; Karen Winkler, *Two Scholars Conflict in Sears Sex Bias Case Sets Off War in Women's History*, CHRON. HIGHER EDUC., Feb. 5, 1986, at A-8; Alan Witt & Lendell Nye, *Gender and the Relationship between Perceived Fairness of Pay or Promotion and Job Satisfaction*, 77 J. APPLIED PSYCH. 910 (1992); Nadja Zalokar, *Male-Female Differences in Occupational Choice and the Demand for General and Occupation-Specific Human Capital*, 26 ECON. INQUIRY 59 (1988).

152. *See generally* MARY FRANCES BERRY, THE POLITICS OF PARENTHOOD: CHILD CARE, WOMEN'S RIGHTS, AND THE MYTH OF THE GOOD MOTHER (1993); SUSAN CHIRA, A MOTHER'S PLACE (1998); SCOTT COLTRANE, FAMILY MAN: FATHERHOOD, HOUSEWORK, AND GENDER EQUITY (1996); MARJORIE DEVAULT, FEEDING THE FAMILY: THE SOCIAL ORGANIZATION OF CARING AS GENDERED WORK (1991); LINDA HAAS, EQUAL PARENTHOOD AND SOCIAL POLICY (1992); ARLIE HOCHSCHILD, THE TIME BIND: WHEN WORK BECOMES HOME AND HOME BECOMES WORK (1997); SARAH BLAFFER HRDY, MOTHER NATURE: A HISTORY OF MOTHERS, INFANTS, AND NATURAL SELECTION 109–14, 205–17, 499 (1999); KATHLEEN HALL JAMIESON, BEYOND THE DOUBLE BIND (1995); MAHONY, *supra* note 122; JOAN PETERS, WHEN MOTHERS WORK: LOVING OUR CHILDREN WITHOUT SACRIFICING OURSELVES (1997); JOHN ROBINSON & GEOFFREY GODFREY, TIME FOR LIFE: THE SURPRISING WAY AMERICANS USE THEIR TIME 105 tbl. 3 (1997); SPAIN & BIANCHI, *supra* note 119; DEBORAH SWISS & JUDITH WALKER, WOMEN AND THE WORK/FAMILY DILEMMA (1993); THE WORK-FAMILY CHALLENGE: RETHINKING EMPLOYMENT (Suzan Lewis & Jeremy Lewis eds. 1996); JOAN WILLIAMS, UNBENDING GENDER: WHY FAMILY AND WORK CONFLICT AND WHAT TO DO ABOUT IT (2000); WOMEN, HOUSEHOLDS, AND THE ECONOMY, *supra* note 97; Denise & William Bielby, *She Works Hard for the Money: Household Responsibilities and the Allocation of Work Effort*, 93 AM. J. SOC. 1031 (1988); Julie Brines, *Economic Dependency, Gender, and the Division of Labor at Home*, 100 AM. J. SOC. 652 (1994); Liza Burby, *When a Child Is Sick, Who Stays Home?*, NEWSDAY, Jan. 18, 1997, at B1; Naomi Cahn, *Gendered Identities: Women and Household Work*, 44 VILL. L. REV. 525 (1999); Janet Saltzman Chafetz & Jaqueline Hagan, *The Gender Division of Labor and Family Change in Industrial Societies: A Theoretical Accounting*, 27 J. COMP. FAM. STUD. 187 (1996); Stephanie Coontz & Maya Parson, *Complicating the Contested Terrain of Work/Family Intersections*, 22 SIGNS 440 (1997); Downey, *supra* note 114;

had children, I felt like feminism had abandoned me,"[153] or that another woman could state that "all feminism ever got us was more work."[154] Yet changing employment patterns meant that large numbers of well-educated women no longer aspired to spend their days "barefoot, pregnant, and in the kitchen."[155] These employment changes fueled numerous changes in intra-family relationships because many women demanded a more equal relationship commensurate with their new economic roles. An outgrowth of these changes was an apparent increase in domestic violence by husbands (or boyfriends) unwilling to accept new gender relations,[156] and by wives re-

Jennifer Glass & Valarie Camarigg, *Gender, Parenthood and Job-Family Compatibility,* 98 AM. J. SOC. 131 (1992); Howard Hayghe & Suzanne Bianchi, *Married Mothers Work Patterns: The Job-Family Compromise,* 117 MONTHLY LAB. REV. 24 (1994); Hersch & Stratton, *supra* note 112; Karen Judd & Sandy Morales, *The New Job Squeeze: Women Pushed into Part-Time Work,* Ms., May/June 1994, at 86; Jacob Klerman & Arleen Leibowitz, *The Work-Employment Distinction among New Mothers,* 29 J. HUM. RESOURCES 277 (1994); Korzic, *supra* note 116, at 126; Julie Press & Eleanor Townsley, *Wives' and Husbands' Housework Reporting: Gender, Class, and Social Desirability,* 12 GENDER & SOC'Y 188 (1998); Sanger, *supra* note 105; Beth Anne Shelton & Daphne John, *The Division of Household Labor,* 22 ANN. REV. SOC. 299 (1996); Myra Stober & Agnes Chan, *Husbands, Wives, and Housework: Graduates of Stanford and Tokyo Universities,* 4 FEMINIST ECON. 97 (1998); Jessica Primoff Vistnes, *Gender Differences in Days Lost from Work Due to Illness,* 50 INDUS. & LAB. REL. REV. 304 (1997); Carol Wharton, *Finding Time for the "Second Shift": The Impact of Flexible Work Schedules on Women's Double Days,* 8 GENDER & SOC'Y 189 (1994); Erik Olin Wright *et al., The Non-Effects of Class on Gender Division of Labor in the Home: A Comparative Study of Sweden and the United States,* 6 GENDER & SOC'Y 252 (1992). *But see* Rosalind Barnett & Caryl Rivers, *The New Dad Works the "Second Shift" Too,* RADCLIFFE Q., Winter 1997, at 9; Richard Collier, *A Hard Time to Be a Father?: Reassessing the Relationship between Law, Policy, and Family (Practices),* 28 J. LAW & SOC'Y 520 (2001); Tamar Lewin, *Men Assuming Bigger Share at Home, Survey Shows,* N.Y. TIMES, Apr. 14, 1998, at A18.

153. Anna Quindlen, *Let's Anita Hill This,* N.Y. TIMES, Feb. 28, 1993, § 4, at 15. *See also* DEBORAH FALLOWS, A MOTHERS WORK 214 (1985); Martha Burk & Heidi Hartman, *Beyond the Gender Gap,* THE NATION, June 10, 1996, at 19; F. Carolyn Graglia, *The Housewife as Pariah,* 18 HARV. J.L. & PUB. POL'Y 509 (1995).

154. Steven Holmes, *Is This What Women Want?,* N.Y. TIMES, Dec. 15, 1996, § 4, at 1 (quoting Heidi Hartman).

155. Carrington, *supra* note 146, at 571. *See generally* BLACKWELDER, *supra* note 94, at 95; HRDY, *supra* note 152, at 488–96; Nancy Ehrenreich, *The Colonization of the Womb,* 43 DUKE L.J. 492 (1993). For one woman's discussion of how she coped with a highly successful career dealing with evolutionary theory and her ambivalence about being a working mother in the twentieth-century United States, see HRDY, *supra,* at xi–xvi, 113, 489–90, 492. *See generally* DIANE EYER, MOTHERGUILT: HOW OUR CULTURE BLAMES MOTHERS FOR WHAT'S WRONG WITH SOCIETY (1996); LOUIS GENEVIE & EVA MARGOLIS, THE MOTHERHOOD REPORT: HOW WOMEN FEEL ABOUT BEING MOTHERS (1987); SHARON HAYS, THE CULTURAL CONTRADICTIONS OF MOTHERHOOD (1996); HRDY, *supra,* at 109–17; SHARI THURER, THE MYTHS OF MOTHERHOOD: HOW CULTURE REINVENTS THE GOOD MOTHER (1994).

156. *See, e.g.,* R. EMERSON DOBASH & RUSSELL DOBASH, WOMEN, VIOLENCE AND SOCIAL CHANGE (1992); ANN JONES, NEXT TIME, SHE'LL BE DEAD: BATTERING AND HOW TO STOP IT (1994); MARY KOSS *et al.,* No SAFE HAVEN: MALE VIOLENCE AGAINST WOMEN AT HOME, AT WORK, AND IN THE COMMUNITY (1994); KURZ, *supra* note 122, at 52–68; ELIZABETH SCHNEIDER, BATTERED WOMEN AND FEMINIST LAWMAKING (2000); LAWRENCE SHERMAN, POLICING DOMESTIC VIOLENCE (1992); THE PUBLIC NATURE OF PRIVATE VIOLENCE (Martha Albertson Fineman & Roxanne Mykitiuk eds. 1994); VIOLENCE AGAINST WOMEN: PHILOSOPHICAL PERSPECTIVES (Stanley French ed. 1998); Marina Angel, *Abusive Boys Kill Girls Just Like Abusive Men Kill Women: Explaining the Obvious,* 8 TEMPLE POL. & CIV. RTS. L. REV. 283 (1999); Kimberle Crenshaw, *Mapping the Margins: Intersectionality, Identity Politics, and Violence against Women of Color,* 43 STAN. L. REV. 1241 (1991); Martha Davis & Susan Krahson, *Protecting Women's Welfare in the Face of Violence,* 22 FORDHAM URBAN L.J. 1141 (1995); Zanita Fenton, *Mirrored Silence: Reflections on Judicial Complicity in Private Violence,* 78 OR. L. REV. 995 (1999); Catherine Kline & Leslye Orloff, *Providing Legal Protection for Battered Women: An Analysis of State Statutes and Case Law,* 21 HOFSTRA L. REV. 801 (1993); Joan Meier, *Domestic Violence, Character, and Social Change in the Welfare Reform Debate,* 19 LAW & POL'Y 105 (1997); Symposium, *Domestic Violence,* 8 VA. J. SOC. POL'Y & L. 1 (2000); Symposium, *Integrating Responses to Domestic Violence,* 47 LOY. N.O. L. REV. 1 (2001); Donna Wills, *Domestic Violence: The Case for Aggressive Prosecution,* 7 UCLA WOMEN'S L.J. 173 (1997). *See generally* ELIZABETH HAFKIN PLECK, DOMESTIC TYRANNY: THE MAKING OF SOCIAL POLICY AGAINST FAMILY VIOLENCE FROM COLONIAL TIMES TO THE PRESENT (1987).

taliating for wrongs (real or imagined) by their husbands.[157] The violence within families appears to be "sex symmetrical" (as common by women against husbands/partners as by men against wives/partners), although many commentators overlook this.[158]

We don't know whether domestic violence has actually increased or merely appears to be increasing because of greater social attention to the problem; either way, legal authorities addressed the problem with new vigilance and new laws.[159] The drive to remove this impediment

---

157. *See, e.g.,* Regina v. Smith, [2000] 3 W.L.R. 654 (H.L.). *See also* Philip Cook, Abused Men: The Hidden Side of Domestic Violence (1997); Marina Angel, *Criminal Law and Women: Giving the Abused Women Who Kills* A Jury of Her Peers *Who Appreciates* Trifles, 33 Am. Crim. L. Rev. 229 (1996); Marina Angel, *Susan Glaspell's* Trifles *and* A Jury of Her Peers: *Women Abuse in a Literary and Legal Context,* 44 Buff. L. Rev. 779 (1997); Mandy Burton, *Intimate Homicide and the Provocation Defence—Endangering Women?* R v. Smith, 9 Feminist Leg. Stud. 247 (2001); Holly Maguigan, *Battered Women and Self-Defense: Myths and Misconceptions in Current Reform Proposals,* 140 U. Pa. L. Rev. 379 (1991); Suzanne Steinmetz, *The Battered-Husband Syndrome,* 2 Victimology 499 (1978); Wanda Teays, *Standards of Perfection and Battered Women's Self-Defense,* in Violence against Women, *supra* note 156, at 57; Kimberley White-Mair, *Experts and Ordinary Men: Locating* R. v. Lavallée, *Battered Woman Syndrome, and the "New" Psychiatric Expertise on Women within Canadian Legal History,* 12 Can. J. Women & L.406 (2000).

158. Anne Campbell, Men, Women and Aggression (1993); Murray Straus & Richard Gelles, Physical Violence in American Families (1990); Jo Dixon, *The Nexus of Sex, Spousal Violence, and the State,* 29 Law & Soc'y 359, 360–61 (1995); Steinmetz, *supra* note 157. *See also* David Island & Patrick Letellier, Men Who Beat the Men Who Love Them (1991); Naming the Violence: Speaking Out about Lesbian Battering (K. Lobel ed. 1986); Claire Renzetti, Violent Betrayal: Partner Abuse in Lesbian Relationships (1992); Mary Easton, *Abuse by Any Other Name: Feminism, Difference, and Intralesbian Violence,* in The Public Nature of Private Violence, *supra* note 156, at 195; Mac Hunter, *Homosexuals as a New Class of Domestic Violence Subjects under the New Jersey Prevention of Domestic Violence Act of 1991,* 31 U. Louisville J. Fam. L. 557 (1993); Nancy Knauer, *Same-Sex Domestic Violence: Claiming a Domestic Sphere while Risking Negative Stereotypes,* 8 Temple Pol. & Civ. Rts. L. Rev. 325 (1999); Ryiah Lilith, *Reconsidering the Abuse That Dare Not Speak Its Name: A Criticism of Recent Legal Scholarship Regarding Same-Gender Domestic Violence,* 7 Mich. J. Gender & L. 181 (2001); Sandra Lundy, *Abuse that Dare Not Speak Its Name: Assisting Victims of Lesbian and Gay Domestic Violence in Massachusetts,* 28 New Eng. L. Rev. 273 (1993). Feminist icon Betty Friedan has been accused by her former husband of having violently abused him, kicking, scratching, and attacking him with knives. She responded to the charges by retracting her earlier charges that he had beaten her without commenting on whether she had attacked him. W. Speers, *Newsmakers: Betty Friedan's Ex-Husband: Hey, She Hit Me,* Phila. Inquirer, July 6, 2000, at D2.

For representative studies that completely ignore the possibility that physical abuse is sex-symmetrical, see Schneider, *supra* note 156; The Public Nature of Private Violence, *supra* note 156; Aurelio José Figueredo, *Blame, Retribution and Deterrence among Both Survivors and Perpetrators of Male Violence against Women,* 8 Va. J. Soc. Pol'y & L. 219 (2000); Alberto Lopez, *Forty Yeas and Five Nays—The Nays Have It:* Morrion's *Blurred Political Accountability and the Defeat of the Civil Rights Provisions of the Violence against Women Act,* 69 Geo. Wash. L. Rev. 251 (2001); Jerry Phillips, *What Is a Good Woman Worth? Tort Compensation for Domestic Violence,* 47 Loy. L. Rev. 303 (2001); Reva Siegel, *"The Rule of Love": Wife Beating as Prerogative and Privacy,* 105 Yale L.J. 2117 (1996); Patricia Tjaden, *Extent and Nature of Intimate Partner Violence as Measured by the National Violence against Women Survey,* 47 Loy. L. Rev. 41 (2001). None of this even approaches the question of how courts should treat consensual sado-masochistic relationships. *See* People v. Jovanovic, 700 N.Y.S.2d 156 (App. Div. 1999), *appeal dismissed,* 735 N.E.2d 1284 (N.Y. 2000); Cheryl Hanna, *Sex Is Not a Sport: Consent and Violence in Criminal Law,* 42 B.C. L. Rev. 239 (2001).

159. *See, e.g.,* Thurman v. City of Torrington, 595 F. Supp. 1521 (D. Conn. 1984); Pleck, *supra* note 156; Richard Berk et al., *The Deterrent Effect of Arrest: A Bayesian Analysis of Four Field Experiments,* 57 Am. Soc. Rev. 698 (1992); Cynthia Grant Bowman, *The Arrest Experiments: A Feminist Critique,* 83 J. Crim. L. & Criminology 201 (1992); Dixon, *supra* note 158, at 363–64; David Ford, *Prosecutions as a Victim Power Resource: A Note on Empowering Women in Violent Conjugal Relationships,* 25 Law & Soc'y Rev. 313 (1991); Linda Lengyel, *Survey of State Domestic Violence Legislation,* 10 Leg. Reference Services Q. 59 (1990); Anthony Pate & Edwin Hamilton, *Formal and Informal Deterrents to Family Violence: The Dade County Spouse Assault Experiment,* 57 Am. Soc. Rev. 691 (1992); Elizabeth Schneider, *Particularity and Generality: Challenges of Feminist Theory and Practice in Work on Woman-Abuse,* 67 NYU L. Rev. 520 (1992); Lawrence Sherman et al., *Crime, Punishment and Stake in Conformity: Legal and Informal Control of Domestic Violence,* 57 Am. Soc. Rev.

to the full integration of women into the information economy culminated in 1994 in the *Violence against Women Act* making it a federal crime to commit a crime of violence against women and providing a federal civil cause of action for victims.[160] Because organized feminism succeeded in having studies of violence by women treated as anathema,[161] the statute did not address violence against men. The Supreme Court's recent declaration of parts of that statute as unconstitutional for exceeding the power of Congress under the commerce clause of the Constitution[162] moves the locus of concern back to the states, but otherwise probably will have little effect on the issue.

Some observers have concluded that all these changes served to fuel the increasing fragility of marriage as an institution. As women found the economic gains from marriage and specialization in homemaking to be less compared to the gains achievable through working in the marketplace, fewer women invested themselves in the skills necessary to be a successful "homemaker" rather than in the skills necessary for success in the marketplace.[163] As a result, contemporary marriage in industrialized societies shifted from an economically efficient model of specialized roles and towards an economically inefficient model in which both members share the roles of homemaker and breadwinner.[164] Yet as formerly specialized tasks around the home and in the family become shared between spouses, the interdependence of the spouses diminished, gender

---

680 (1992); Joan Zorza, *Mandatory Arrest for Domestic Violence: Why It May Prove to Be the Best First Step in Curbing Repeat Abuse,* 10 CRIM. JUST. 2 (1995). On this historical incidence of domestic violence, see Erin Masson, *The Women's Christian Temperance Union, 1874–1898: Combatting Domestic Violence,* 3 WM. & MARY J. WOMEN & L. 163 (1997).

Similarly, we do not know whether the increase in the reported incidence of violence against children represents a real change or only a change in social vigilance. *See* Marie Ashe & Naomi Cahn, *Child Abuse: A Problem for Feminist Theory,* in THE PUBLIC NATURE OF PRIVATE VIOLENCE, *supra* note 156, at 167; A.B. Bergnanm R.M. Larsen, & B.A. Mueller, *Changing Spectrum of Serious Child Abuse,* 77 PEDIATRICS 338 (1993); Michael Durfee & Deanne Tilton-Durfee, *Multiagency Child Death Review Teams: Experience in the United States,* 4 CHILD ABUSE REV. 377 (1995); Marcia Herman-Giddens, *Underrecording of Child Abuse and Neglect Fatalities in North Carolina,* 52 N.C. MED. J. 634 (1991); Marcia Herman-Giddens et al., *Underascertainment of Child Abuse Mortality in the United States,* 282 JAMA 463 (1999); Philip McClain et al., *Geographic Patterns of Fatal Abuse or Neglect in Children Younger than 5 Years Old, United States, 1979 to 1988,* 148 ARCH. PEDIATRIC ADOLESCENT MED. 82 (1994); Karen McCurdy & Deborah Daro, *Child Maltreatment: A National Survey of Reports and Fatalities,* 9 J. INTERPERSONAL VIOLENCE 75 (1994); Mary Overpeck et al., *Risk Factors for Infant Homicide in the United States,* 339 N. ENGLAND J. MED. 1222 (1998); Dorothy Roberts, *Motherhood and Crime,* 79 IOWA L. REV. 95 (1993); Anna Waller, Susan Baker, & Andrew Szocka, *Childhood Injury Deaths: National Analysis and Geographic Variations,* 79 AM. J. PUB. HEALTH 310 (1989).

160. 42 U.S.C. § 13981 (2000). *See* David Atkins et al., *Striving for Justice with the Violence against Women Act and Civil Tort Actions,* 14 WIS. WOMEN'S L.J. 69 (1999); David Frazee, *An Imperfect Remedy for Imperfect Violence: The Construction of Civil Rights in the Violence against Women Act,* 1 MICH. J. GENDER & L. 163 (1993); Julie Goldscheid & Susan Kraham, *The Civil Rights Remedy of the Violence against Women Act,* 29 CLEARINGHOUSE REV. 505 (1995); Tracy Hulsey, *Violence against Women Act,* S.C. LAW., JAN.–FEB. 1996, AT 40; Catherine Klein, *Full Faith and Credit: Interstate Enforcement of Protection Orders under the Violence against Women Act of 1994,* 29 FAM. L.Q. 253 (1995); Jenny Rivera, *The Violence against Women Act and the Construction of Multiple Consciousness in the Civil Rights and Feminist Movements,* 4 J. LAW & POL'Y 463 (1996); Siegel, *supra* note 158; Wendy Rae Willis, *The Gun Is Always Pointed: Sexual Violence and Title III of the Violence against Women Act,* 80 GEO. L.J. 2197 (1992).

161. Dixon, *supra* note 158, at 360. *See, e.g.,* JONES, *supra* note 156.

162. United States v. Morrison, 529 U.S. 598 (2000).

163. *See generally* BECKER, *supra* note 103; ANDREW CHERLIN, MARRIAGE, DIVORCE, REMARRIAGE (1981).

164. PARKMAN, *supra* note 98, at 36; Crain, *supra* note 121, at 1899–1900. Some commentators argue that traditional marriage is efficient only so long as women are denied equal opportunity in the marketplace. *See, e.g.,* Crain, *supra,* at 1900; Hadfield, *supra* note 107, at 97; Singer, *supra* note 97, at 2440–41; Williams, *supra* note 149, at 822–23, 831. *See generally* BLAU & FERBER, *supra* note 104; JEAN POTUCHEK, WHO SUPPORTS THE FAMILY: GENDER AND BREADWINNERS BY DUAL EARNER FAMILIES (1997). Others have objected to the "commodification" of family implicit in such economic analyses. *See, e.g.,* Estin, *supra* note 97, at 28–30. For a de-

conflict increased, and more couples found marriage to be an arrangement they could do without.[165] Reinforcing this tendency, unhappy spouses invested ever more of their time in careers—whether as a hedge against divorce or to escape the misery of their homes, but in either event adding further strain to the marriage.[166] With women working outside the home, both men and women also found themselves exposed to more "spousal alternatives" than was the case when families followed the more traditional structure.[167] The enactment of no-fault divorce laws responded to the felt need for easier exit from marriage and at the same time encouraged people to think and to plan their lives on the basis that marriage could be ended rather easily.[168]

The redefined economic roles of women also provided a further material basis for devaluation of children and a rising demand for contraception and abortion. The sudden technological breakthrough with the introduction of the birth control pill with its advertised claims of virtually certain effectiveness fueled the behavioral and legal changes of the 1960s.[169] The Food and Drug Administration ("FDA") approved the contraceptive pill in 1960, allowing the introduction of the first effective contraceptive in history that was completely reversible, entirely under the control of the woman alone, and temporally separable from the sex act. The effectiveness of oral contraceptives depends, of course, on correct daily usage; even small errors can result in failure, which accounts for the failure rate of 3 percent within the first year of usage. Still, this compares well to the failure rate of 15 percent for condoms, the diaphragm, and the rhythm method, and 26 percent for spermicides.[170] The pill initially also carried a small but measurable risk to the heart and had mixed effects on the risk of cancer.[171] These risks, as well as typical side effects of

---

fense of commodification, see Katherine Silbaugh, *Commodification and Women's Household Labor,* 9 YALE J.L. & FEMINISM 81 (1997).

165. CHERLIN, *supra* note 163, at 52–53; FINEMAN, *supra* note 97; Theodore Greenstein, *Gender Ideology, Marital Disruption, and the Employment of Married Women,* 57 J. MARRIAGE & FAM. 31 (1995).

166. CHERLIN, *supra* note 163, at 52–53; HOCHSCHILD, *supra* note 152, at 201; Crain, *supra* note 121, at 1902.

167. *See* Scott South & Kim Lloyd, *Spousal Alternatives and Marital Dissolution,* 60 AM. SOC. REV. 21 (Feb. 1995).

168. GALLAGHER, *supra* note 98, at 182–83; PARKMAN, *supra* note 98, at 31–32, 88, 96–100; Crain, *supra* note 121, at 1901–02; Estin, *supra* note 97, at 13. *See also* Lloyd Cohen, *Marriage, Divorce and Quasi-Rents; or, "I Gave Him the Best Years of My Life,"* 16 J. LEGAL STUD. 267 (1987).

169. *See* BERNARD ASBELL, THE PILL: A BIOGRAPHY OF THE DRUG THAT CHANGED THE WORLD (1995); CRITCHLOW, *supra* note 28, at 33–41; CARL DJERASSI, THE PILL, PYGMY CHIMPS, AND DEGAS' WHORES (1992); HORDERN, *supra* note 70, at 48–50, 173–79; JAMES REED, FROM PRIVATE VICE TO PUBLIC VIRTUE: THE BIRTH CONTROL MOVEMENT AND AMERICAN SOCIETY SINCE 1830, at 334–37 (1978); ANDREA TONE, DEVICES AND DESIRES: A HISTORY OF CONTRACEPTIVES IN AMERICA 203–59 (2001); ELIZABETH SIEGEL WATKINS, ON THE PILL: A SOCIAL HISTORY OF ORAL CONTRACEPTIVES, 1950–1970 (1998).

170. ROBERT HATCHER, CONTRACEPTIVE TECHNOLOGY 115 (16th ed. 1994); INSTITUTE OF MED., CONTRACEPTIVE RESEARCH AND DEVELOPMENT: LOOKING TO THE FUTURE 96, 98 (Polly Harrison & Allan Rosenfield eds. 1996); Rachel Gold & Cory Richards, *Securing American Women's Reproductive Health,* in THE AMERICAN WOMAN 1994–95, at 196, 203, 205 (Cynthia Costello & Anne Stone eds. 1994); Elise Jones & Jacqueline Darroch Forrest, *Contraceptive Failure in the United States: Revised Estimates from the 1982 National Survey of Family Growth,* 21 FAM. PLANNING PERSP. 103 (1990). On the risks that arise from incorrect usage and the steps taken to minimize those risks, see TONE, *supra* note 169, at 257–59; Patricia Peck Gossel, *Packaging the Pill,* in MANIFESTING MEDICINE: BODIES AND MADNESS 105 (Robert Budd, Bernard Finn, & Helmut Trischler eds. 1999).

171. BARBARA SEAMAN, THE DOCTORS' CASE AGAINST THE PILL (1969); PAUL VAUGHAN, THE PILL ON TRIAL (1972); Robert Hoover et al., *Oral Contraceptive Use: Association of Frequency of Hospitalization and Chronic Disease Risk Indicators,* 68 AM. J. PUB. HEALTH 335 (1978); Lois Chevalier & Leonard Cohen, *The Terrible Trouble with the Birth-Control Pill,* LADIES' HOME J., July 1967, at 44–45. *See generally* TONE, *supra* note 169, at 241–45; WATKINS, *supra* note 169, at 82–86; David Skegg, *Oral Contraception and Health,* 318 BRIT. MED. J. 7176 (1998).

Continuous use of low-dose oral contraceptives (without the placebos used to bring on periods at the end of each cycle) suppresses menstruation altogether, although the long-term health effects of such suppression

tenderness in the breasts, weight gain, and occasional nausea, were eventually largely eliminated by development of low-dosage pills that were more effective than the original high dosage pills.[172]

Notwithstanding the early problems with the pill, more than 1,000,000 women were on the pill within two years of its approval by the FDA in 1960, and more than 6,000,000 within five years; by 1969, some 8,000,000 women were on the pill.[173] For the first time, women had available a contraceptive that gave real assurance of control over the frequency and timing of their pregnancies. This breakthrough helped prepare the way for the displacement of the demand for limited abortion reform with a demand for the complete repeal of abortion laws. The pill not only created expectations of definite control over when to conceive, but it also created expectations in women that they, rather than their mates (as with withdrawal, condoms, and even—to some extent—diaphragms), would control the decision whether to bear a child. In short, the introduction of the pill made reproduction a medical choice rather than a moral choice—for the woman.[174]

With the realization that women had biological choices came the expectation that women should have social choices.[175] One manifestation of the new social choices for women was the

---

remain uncertain. *See* Susan Rako, No More Periods? The Risks of Menstrual Suppression (2003); Tina Kelley, *New Pill Fuels Debate over Benefits of Fewer Periods,* N.Y. Times, Oct. 14, 2003, at F5.

172. Tone, *supra* note 169, at 233–35, 238, 245–46; Watkins, *supra* note 169, at 100; B. Burt Gerstman *et al, Trends in the Content and Use of Oral Contraceptives in the United States, 1964–1988,* 81 Am. J. Pub. Health 90 (1991); Diana Pettit *et al., Stroke in Users of Low-Dose Oral Contraceptives,* 335 New Eng. J. Med. 8 (1996); Roberto Rivera, *Oral Contraceptives: The Last Decade,* in Contraceptive Research and Development, 1984–1994: The Road from Mexico City to Cairo and Beyond 24, 30–32 (Paul Van Look & G. Perez-Palacios eds. 1994).

173. Bailey, *supra* note 92, at 105; Tone, *supra* note 169, at 233, 239; Watkins, *supra* note 169, at 34. The IUD also soared in popularity at this time until the Dalkon Shield debacle made many women too fearful to use it. *See* Nicole Grant, The Selling of Contraception: The Dalkon Shield Case, Sexuality, and Women's Autonomy (1992); Morton Mintz, At Any Cost: Corporate Greed, Women, and the Dalkon Shield (1985); Richard Sobel, Bending the Law: The Story of the Dalkon Shield Bankruptcy (1991); Tone, *supra,* at 263–83; Jacqueline Darrosh Forrest, *The End of IUD Marketing in the United States: What Does It Mean for American Women?,* 18 Fam. Planning Persp. 52 (1986).

174. Barbara Brookes, Abortion in England 1900–1967, at 153 (1988); Reay Tannahill, Sex in History 406, 417–18 (1980); Tone, *supra* note 169, at 240–42.

175. *See* Blanchard, *supra* note 9, at 19–20; Condit, *supra* note 32, at 69–70, 174, 177–82, 185–90; Elizabeth Fox Genovese, Feminism without Illusions 113–38, 145–50 (1991); Ginsburg, *supra* note 9, at 173–97; Linda Gordon, Woman's Body, Woman's Right: A Social History of Birth Control in America 29 (1976); Kenneth Karst, Law's Promise, Law's Expression: Visions of Power in the Politics of Race, Gender, and Religion 52–57 (1993); Kenny, *supra* note 3, at 195; Rudy, *supra* note 80, at 62–63; Tone, *supra* note 169, at 234–35; Tribe, *supra* note 12, at 92–112, 129–38; Laurence Tribe, American Constitutional Law 1352–59, 1613 (2nd ed. 1988) ("Tribe, American Constitutional Law"); Laurence Tribe, Constitutional Choices 243 (1985); Sylvia Law, *Sex Discrimination and Insurance for Contraception,* 73 Wash. L. Rev. 363 (1998); Jed Rubenfeld, *The Right of Privacy,* 102 Harv. L. Rev. 737, 782–91, 802–07 (1989); Reva Siegel, *Reasoning from the Body: A Historical Perspective on Abortion Regulation and Questions of Equal Protection,* 44 Stan. L. Rev. 261, 273–74 (1992); Janet Smith, *Abortion as a Feminist Concern,* in The Zero People 77, at 81–84 (Jeff Lane Hensley ed. 1983); Cass Sunstein, *Neutrality in Constitutional Law (with Special Reference to Pornography, Abortion, and Surrogacy),* 92 Colum. L. Rev. 1, 33 (1992). This notion peaked when courts began to rule, in 2001, that employers and insurance companies violated the rights of women by denying them reimbursement for the cost of their oral contraceptives. Erickson v. Bartell Drug Co., 141 F. Supp. 2d 1266 (W.D. Wash. 2001).

Ironically, one of the social choices some women made was to criticize the Pill as burdening women, and demanding (unsuccessfully) that the burden of using contraceptives should fall on men instead. *See, e.g.,* Jennifer Macleod, *How to Hold a Wife: A Bridegroom's Guide,* Village Voice, Feb. 11, 1971, at 5; Sheldon Segal, *Contraceptive Research: A Male Chauvinist Plot?,* 4 Fam. Planning Persp. 22 (1972). *See generally* Tone, *supra,* at 246–54; Watkins, *supra,* at 100–23.

"sexual revolution"[176] — at bottom, a separation of sexual activity from reproduction in a way that had never possible before. Would-be musician and revolutionary John Sinclair would write that there were "three essential human activities of greatest importance to all persons" — "rock and roll, dope, and fucking in the streets."[177] In a more veiled way, Lorretta Lynn sang:

> All these years I've stayed at home while you had all your fun;
> And ev'ry year that's gone by another baby's come;
> There's gonna be some changes made right here on Nurs'ry Hill;
> You've set this chicken this last time, 'cause now I've got the Pill.[178]

Early efforts by some physicians to restrict access to the pill to married women was already failing when the Supreme declared legal restrictions on access to the pill by unmarried women to be unconstitutional in 1972.[179] Before long, some women would find that the sexual revolution was not entirely a blessing. Women had lost their best excuse for saying "no" until fear of AIDS would come along to replace the fear of pregnancy.

Along with expectations of social choice came an expectation by many women that a choice to have a baby would be theirs alone and that their choices would be made effective by any means necessary.[180] Such expectations arose almost naturally in a United States experiencing the apparent achievements of the civil rights movement that peaked in the 1960s,[181] an intellectual milieu in which the concept of *privacy* was increasingly promoted as a central legal and intellectual concept,[182] and a society becoming pervasively secularized, at least in its leadership.[183]

Since the introduction of the pill, contraceptive control has gotten better. The introduction of a new method, marketed under the name Norplant, promised to carry certain control forward to even higher levels, although that promise became snarled in litigation over alleged defects in the product, primarily over alleged serious side effects that consumers were not warned about.[184]

---

176. *See generally* BAILEY, *supra* note 92; BARBARA EHRENREICH *et al.*, RE-MAKING LOVE: THE FEMINIZATION OF SEX (1986); LINDA GRANT, SEXING THE MILLENNIUM: WOMEN AND THE SEXUAL REVOLUTION (1994); JOHN HEIDENRY, WHAT WILD ECSTASY: THE RISE AND FALL OF THE SEXUAL REVOLUTION (1997).

177. JOHN SINCLAIR, GUITAR ARMY: STREET WRITINGS/PRISON WRITINGS 67–69 (1972).

178. Lorene Allen, Don McHan, & T.D. Bayless, *The Pill* (1972).

179. Eisenstadt v. Baird, 405 U.S. 438 (1972). *See also* Pearl Buck, *The Pill and the Teen-Age Girl*, READER'S DIGEST, Apr. 1968, at 92. *See generally* BAILEY, *supra* note 92, at 105–35.

180. *See, e.g.,* JEAN BETHKE ELSHTAIN, POWER TRIPS AND OTHER JOURNEYS: ESSAYS IN FEMINISM AS CIVIC DISCOURSE 47 (1990); PETCHESKY, *supra* note 3, at 27–28; Catharine MacKinnon, *Reflections on Sex Equality under Law*, 100 YALE L.J. 1281, 1320–21 (1991).

181. *See* Ginsberg, *Judicial Voice*, *supra* note 68, at 1203–04; Charles Stanley Ross, *The Right of Privacy and Restraints on Abortion under the "Undue Burden" Test: A Juris prudential Comparison of* Planned Parenthood v. Casey *with European Practice and Italian Law*, 3 IND. INT'L & COMP. L. REV. 199, 202–03 (1993).

182. Ross, *supra* note 181, at 203–05. *See* Griswold v. Connecticut, 381 U.S. 479 (1965); Haelan-Laboratories, Inc. v. Topps Chewing Gum Inc., 202 F.2d 866 (10th Cir. 1953); Louis Brandeis & Samuel Warren, *The Right to Privacy*, 4 HARV. L. REV. 193 (1890).

183. *See, e.g.,* THOMAS ALTIZER, THE GOSPEL OF CHRISTIAN ATHEISM (1966); HARVEY COX, THE SECULAR CITY: SECULARIZATION AND URBANIZATION IN THEOLOGICAL PERSPECTIVE (1965); JOSEPH FLETCHER, SITUATION ETHICS: THE NEW MORALITY (1966); BISHOP JOHN ROBINSON, HONEST TO GOD (1963). *See generally* STANLEY HAUERWAS, AFTER CHRISTENDOM? (1991); JAMES DAVISON HUNTER, CULTURE WARS: THE STRUGGLE TO DEFINE AMERICA (1991); CHRISTOPHER LASCH, THE TRUE AND ONLY HEAVEN: PROGRESS AND ITS CRITICS 509–29 (1991); MENSCH & FREEMAN, *supra* note 66, at 66–73, 83–125; GARRY WILLS, UNDER GOD: RELIGION AND AMERICAN POLITICS (1990); ROBERT WUTHNOW, THE RESTRUCTURING OF AMERICAN RELIGION: SOCIETY AND FAITH SINCE WORLD WAR II (1988).

184. *In re* Norplant Contraceptive Prod. Liab. Litig., 215 F. Supp. 2d 795 (E.D. Tex. 2002); Laura Duncan, *Norplant: The Next Mass Tort*, 81 ABA J. 16 (Nov. 1995). *See generally* BARBARA MINTZES, ANITA HARDON, & JANNEMIEKE HANHART, NORPLANT: UNDER HER SKIN (1993); JOHN ROBERTSON, CHILDREN OF CHOICE: FREE-

The resulting demands for legalizing contraceptives and abortion, however, could also be construed as the liberation of male sexuality rather than female sexuality, of freeing women to available for male sexual demands. Thus *Playboy* magazine became the first large-circulation magazine to endorse repeal of abortion laws and the Playboy Foundation became a prime source of funds for several suits challenging the constitutionality of abortion statutes.[185] As another result, in part, of the enhanced expectations of reproductive control, the law of divorce was changed in remarkably short order in the 1970s by the introduction of no-fault divorce.[186] No-fault divorce, like the legalization of contraception and abortion, also was ambiguous as to whether its function was to liberate women from subordination to men or to liberate men from responsibility for families.

In the rapidly changing social milieu of the late 1960s, abortion rights activists came to see mere reform as regressive, sustaining the position of women as dependent on the decisions of others.[187] Completely disregarding the *Playboy* connection, radical feminists particularly embraced the argument that only "repeal" could truly "liberate" women.[188] There is thus both a certain social amnesia and a certain irony in reading, as one does so often today, that abortion's legalization was the result of efforts by leaders of the nascent women's movement.[189]

Women who did support abortion reform in those early years generally worked within predominantly male institutions, like the American Civil Liberties Union, the American Medical Association, and the American Public Health Association.[190] The arguments these women made did not differ from those of the men. Even groups committed to radical change for the benefit of women did not emphasize abortion before the late 1960s. The radical feminists were a varied collection of women who emerged largely out of the so-called New Left that had come to domi-

---

DOM AND THE NEW REPRODUCTIVE TECHNOLOGIES 69–93 (1994); TONE, *supra* note 169, at 288–89; Jacqueline Darroch Forrest & Lisa Kaeser, *Questions of Balance: Issues Emerging from the Introduction of the Hormonal Implants*, 25 FAM. PLANNING PERSP. 127 (1993); Jennifer Frost, *The Availability and Accessibility of the Contraceptive Implant from Family Planning Agencies in the United States, 1991–1992*, 26 FAM. PLANNING PERSP. 4 (1994); Margaret Polaneczky *et al.*, *The Use of Levonorgestrel Implants (Norplant) for Contraception in Adolescent Mothers*, 331 NEW ENG. J. MED. 1201 (1994). *See also* Julie Mertus & Simon Heller, *Norplant Meets the New Eugenicists: The Impermissibility of Coerced Contraceptives*, 11 ST. L.U.L. REV. 359 (1992).

On the availability and usage patterns for modern contraceptives in Europe and the United States generally, see Elof Johansson, *Comparison of the Availability of Contraceptive Methods in Selected European Countries and the United States*, 23 NYU REV. L. & SOC. CHANGE 471 (1997). Dr. Johansson found that while 41% of European women relied on the pill, only 28% of American women did so. *Id.* at 472. *See also* Micheal Galen, *Just Whose Fault Is It? Birth-Control Options Limited by Litigation*, NAT'L L.J., Oct. 20, 1986, at 3; Sylvia Law, *Tort Liability and the Availability of Contraceptive Drugs and Devices in the United States*, 23 NYU REV. L. & SOC. CHANGE 339 (1997); Hallie Levin, *The Most Effective Contraceptive Method You've Never Tried*, COSMOPOLITAN, Sept. 1, 1997, at 204; Anne Szarewski & John Guillebaud, *Contraception: Current State of the Art*, 302 BRIT. MED. J. 6787 (1991).

185. See the text *supra* at notes 86–90.

186. See the sources collected *supra* at note 97.

187. *See, e.g.,* Jerome Kummer, *New Trends in Therapeutic Abortion in California*, 34 OBSTET. & GYNECOLOGY 883 (1969); Clyde Stanfield, *Colorado's Abortion Law*, 54 NEB. ST. MED. J. 745 (1969).

188. *See, e.g.,* Lucinda Cisler, *Abortion Reform: The New Tokenism*, 9 RAMPARTS 19 (1970). *See generally* BAEHR, *supra* note 67, at 33–49; CONDIT, *supra* note 32, at 61–63; GINSBURG, *supra* note 9, at 39–42; HOLE & LEVINE, *supra* note 67, at 295–301; LOUIS LADER, ABORTION II: MAKING THE REVOLUTION 166–67 (1973); LUKER, *supra* note 9, at 95–125; PETCHESKY, *supra* note 3, at 125–32; REAGAN, *supra* note 13, at 222–34; ELLEN WILLIS, UP FROM RADICALISM 117–18 (1971).

189. *See, e.g.,* CRAIG & O'BRIEN, *supra* note 9, at 5, 9; RONALD DWORKIN, LIFE'S DOMINION: AN ARGUMENT ABOUT ABORTION, EUTHANASIA, AND INDIVIDUAL FREEDOM 50–51 (1993); KARST, *supra* note 175, at 51; KERRY PETERSEN, ABORTION REGIMES 1 (1993); KESSLEMAN, *supra* note 32.

190. GINSBURG, *supra* note 9, at 37–38; LUKER, *supra* note 9, at 92–93; MENSCH & FREEMAN, *supra* note 66, at 129.

nate the anti-war and civil rights movements of the 1960s.[191] The National Organization for Women ("NOW"), launched with funds and other support provided by the United Auto Workers,[192] was formally organized with its first Annual Convention beginning on Oct. 29, 1966.[193] Abortion did not even figure in the agenda of that first convention. NOW was bitterly divided over abortion at its Second Annual Convention.[194] Groups of women, including many woman lawyers, withdrew from NOW when it changed its position to endorse abortion on demand, with the dissenters organizing the Women's Equity Action League.[195] Other women withdrew to the left, claiming that NOW was not radical enough on the issue of abortion.[196] The "Redstockings" group in particular gained considerable notoriety for disrupting a New York state legislative hearing in Manhattan in February, 1969, and organized the first "speak out" on abortion in March, 1969.[197] The "speak out" involved women speaking openly—and without apparent shame—in a public forum about their own abortions. Yet as late as 1968, officers of NOW were denying that abortion was a "women's issue," arguing instead that it was a *human* issue (their emphasis).[198] That attitude seems to have been born out by the politics of abortion when the simple slogan "Who Decides?", playing to the pervasive anti-government sentiment of the Reagan years, proved far more effective than any appeal to women's rights had ever been.[199] Only after 1970 did women actually emerge as the leaders of even one significant facet of the movement to eliminate abortion laws.

When women did take the lead in pressing for repeal or reform of abortion laws, they drew upon the very career changes described in this section. The new leaders in the abortion movement were often far different from the radical feminists who now generally claim credit for the overturning of the abortion laws, being well-behave professionals rather than meeting trashing radicals. Radical or not, they began to take the lead in pressing for "abortion on demand," particularly after the primary forum of the controversy changed from the legislatures

---

191. *See* Stewart Burns, Social Movements of the 1960's: Searching for Democracy 116–35 (1990); Maren Lockwood Carden, The New Feminist Movement (1974); Echols, *supra* note 97; Zillah Eisenstein, Feminism and Sexual Equality: Crisis in Liberal America (1984); Zillah Eisenstein, The Radical Future of Liberal Feminism (1981); Evans, *supra* note 91; Shulamith Firestone, The Dialectic of Sex: The Case for Feminist Revolution (1971); Freeman, *supra* note 91; Leah Fritz, Dreamers & Dealers: An Intimate Appraisal of the Women's Movement (1980); Daniel Horowitz, Betty Friedan and the Making of The Feminist Mystique (1998); Doris Lessing, Walking in the Shade: Volume Two of My Autobiography, 1949–1962 (1998); Reagan, *supra* note 13, at 228–29; Sisterhood Is Powerful (Robin Morgan ed. 1979); Gayle Graham Yates, What Women Want: The Ideas of the Movement (1975); Wendy Clarke, *The Dyke, the Feminist, and the Devil,* 11 Fem. Rev. 30 (1982).

192. Freeman, *supra* note 91, at 50–56, 71–102.

193. M. Margaret Conway et al., Women and Public Policy: A Revolution in Progress 7 (1995).

194. Carden, *supra* note 191, at 104–35; Condit, *supra* note 32, at xi; Flora Davis, Moving the Mountain 52–59, 66–68 (1991); Freeman, *supra* note 91, at 71–102; Garrow, *supra* note 23, at 343–44; Ginsburg, *supra* note 9, at 39; Lader, *supra* note 188, at 34–36; Leila Rapp & Verta Taylor, Survival in the Doldrums 179–86 (1987); Rosenblatt, *supra* note 3, at 89; Sheila Rothman, Women's Proper Place 244–46 (1978); Rubin, *supra* note 9, at 25; Winifred Wandersee, On the Move 36–54 (1988).

195. Critchlow, *supra* note 28, at 136–37; Evans, *supra* note 91, at 278; Ferree & Hess, *supra* note 91, at 66; Garrow, *supra* note 23, at 343; Joyce Gelb, Feminism and Politics: A Comparative Analysis 34 (1989); Marvin Olasky, The Press and Abortion, 1838–1988, at 107 (1988); James Risen & Judy Thomas, Wrath of Angels: The American Abortion War 15 (1998); Rubin, *supra* note 9, at 25.

196. *See* Baehr, *supra* note 67, at 38–44; Barbara Deckard, The Women's Movement 332–36 (1975); Echols, *supra* note 191, at 139–42; Freeman, *supra* note 91, at 51, 59, 62, 82; Rubin, *supra* note 9, at 25–26; Staggenborg, *supra* note 9, at 20.

197. Garrow, *supra* note 23, at 367–68; Diane Schulder & Florynce Kennedy, Abortion Rap 3 (1971).

198. Garrow, *supra* note 23, at 849 n.35.

199. Tribe, *supra* note 12, at 174; Nancy (Ann) Davis, *The Abortion Debate: The Search for Common Ground (Part 2),* 103 Ethics 731, 735–36 (1993).

to the courts. A single individual, with good timing and a willingness to persevere to the end, could become a fulcrum for changing an entire field of law during the Warren Court era. Thus in Minnesota, the dominating spirit of the court challenge to the constitutionality of that state's abortion law was not the male attorney who argued the case, but Dr. Jane Hodgson, a fifty-year-old obstetrician, who was to become the only physician ever convicted of performing an illegal abortion in a hospital in the United States.[200] She was convicted in 1970. Twenty years later, she was still a leading abortion activist in Minnesota.[201] Hodgson's role turned out to be crucial to the success of the abortion repeal movement as she identified fellow Minnesotan Harry Blackmun as someone who could be influenced by his close friend, Dr. Joseph Pratt of the Mayo Clinic (where Justice Harry Blackmun had been in-house counsel for a time).[202]

Increasingly after 1970, the attorneys litigating the court challenges to the constitutionality of abortion statutes also were women, including in particular *Roe v. Wade* and *Doe v. Bolton*.[203] They made, however, no new arguments regarding abortion and relied heavily on the published arguments of Roy Lucas.[204] Nor did all the women attorneys who became active in the litigation strategy take the side of "choice." There is a certain irony, given the current mythology of women rising up to seize their liberty, that when *Roe v. Wade* and *Doe v. Bolton* were first argued to the Supreme Court on a morning in 1971, many observers considered that the best of the four arguments was by a woman attorney—Dorothy Beasley—who supported Georgia's restrictions on abortion on the basis of protecting fetal life.[205]

---

200. Jane Hodgson, *The Twentieth-Century Gender Battle: Difficulties in Perception,* in ABORTION WARS, *supra* note 32, at 290, 300–02. *See also* GARROW, *supra* note 23, at 428–31, 466–68; Carol Joffe, *"Portraits of Three Physicians of Conscience:" Abortion before Legalization in the United States,* 2 J. HIST. SEXUALITY 46, 62–65 (1991) ("Joffe, *Portraits*"); Carole Joffe, *The Unending Struggle for Legal Abortion: Conversations with Jane Hodgson,* 49 J. AM. MED. WOMEN'S ASS'N 160 (Sept./Oct. 1994); Bruce & Diane Rodgers, *Abortion: The Seduction of Medicine,* 2 LIFE LIBERTY & FAM. 285, 287 n. 6 (1995).

201. *See* Hodgson v. Minnesota, 497 U.S. 417 (1990); Hodgson, *supra* note 200, at 302–06. *See also* Hodgson v. Lawson, 542 F.2d 1350 (8th Cir. 1976).

202. GARROW, *supra* note 23, at 474. On Blackmun's work with the Mayo Clinic, see RISEN & THOMAS, *supra* note 195, at 29–31.

203. *See* MARIAN FAUX, *ROE V. WADE:* THE UNTOLD STORY OF THE LANDMARK SUPREME COURT DECISION THAT MADE ABORTION LEGAL (1988); GARROW, *supra* note 23, at 389–407, 423–28, 433–459, 462–65, 491–95, 497–510, 513–17, 520–28, 564–65, 567–73, 600–01; REAGAN, *supra* note 13, at 234–40; RUBIN, *supra* note 9, at 54; SARAH WEDDINGTON, A QUESTION OF CHOICE (1992).

204. GARROW, *supra* note 23, at 440, 446, 448; LAZARUS, *supra* note 28, at 345; REGAN, *supra* note 13, at 335 n.67. For Lucas' arguments, see Lucas, *supra* note 58.

205. GARROW, *supra* note 23, at 528, 602.

# The Impact of Developments
# in Abortion Techniques

*How reproduction is managed and controlled is inseparable from how women
are managed and controlled.*

—Ann Oakley[206]

Feeding into the movement to reform or repeal abortion laws were technological changes that
made abortions safer—for the mother—than ever before.[207] Earlier technological developments
that had made abortion safer had mostly been the result of improvements in surgery generally.[208]
Even as late as the 1950s, the specific techniques for doing abortions were still relatively primitive,
involving "dilation and curettage" ("D&C")—the prying open of the cervix and the blind
scraping of the uterine wall.[209] Then, around 1960, two new techniques for performing abortions
were perfected that made the procedure both safer and much simpler. Vacuum aspiration ("suction
curettage") quickly replaced D&C's for abortions up to the twelfth week of pregnancy,[210]
while saline amniocentesis ("salting out") replaced hysterotomies for abortions after the sixteenth
week of pregnancy.[211]

Vacuum aspiration is particularly attractive to women seeking abortions, taking only a few
minutes and generally causing little pain to the mother. The technique had antecedents traceable
back to 1873 in a procedure known as "dry-cupping."[212] A similar technique was widely imposed
by the Japanese in occupied China in the 1930s on unwilling Chinese women.[213] Historian Rickie
Solinger tells us that abortionist Ruth Barnett and her mentor in Portland, Oregon, used a form
of vacuum aspiration—relying on water flowing from a faucet to generate the vacuum—as
early as the beginning of the twentieth century, although they kept their method secret until
1934.[214] The current procedure is considered by some to have been invented by Harvey Karman,
a "lay psychologist" who falsely styled himself as "Dr."[215] Others attribute the invention to a Chinese
physician.[216] Yet others attribute the invention to unnamed European activists as improved

---

206. Ann Oakley, Subject Women 206 (1981).

207. Robert Castadet, *Pregnancy Termination: Techniques, Risks, and Complications and their Management,*
45 Fertility & Sterility 5 (1986); Joseph Dellapenna, *The History of Abortion: Technology, Morality, and
Law,* 40 U. Pitt. L. Rev. 359, 412–14 (1979); Madeleine Simms, *Britain,* in Abortion in the New Europe: A
Comparative Handbook 31, 38 (Bill Rolston & Anna Eggert eds. 1994).

208. *See* Chapter 7, at notes 122–33; Chapter 12, at notes 85–89.

209. *See* Chapter 6, at notes 332–413; Chapter 7, at notes 122–25.

210. Hordern, *supra* note 70, at 93–94; Janet Gans Epner, Harry Jonas, & Daniel Seckinger, *Late-Term
Abortion,* 280 JAMA 724, 726 (1998); Emil Vladov, *The Vacuum Aspiration Method for Interruption of Early
Pregnancy,* 99 Am. J. Obstet. & Gynecology 202 (1967).

211. Warren Hern, Abortion Practice 122–24 (2nd ed. 1990). *See also* Planned Parenthood of Ctr.
Mo. v. Danforth, 428 U.S. 52, 75–79, 95–99 (1976) (White, J., dissenting, joined by Berger, C. J. and Rehnquist,
J.).

212. Malcolm Potts, Peter Diggory, & John Peel, Abortion 182 (1977).

213. *Id.* at 183.

214. Rickie Solinger, The Abortionist: A Woman against the Law 34, 58, 62, 66, 77–78, 88, 90, 130
(paperback ed. 1996).

215. Agnes Wohl, *The Harvey Karman Controversy,* Ms., Sept., 1974, at 60.

216. Hordern, *supra* note 70, at 93; Kenny, *supra* note 3, at 180.

by American feminists.[217] Whoever invented it, vacuum aspiration today is the most common technique up to the twentieth week of gestation, accounting for 99.5 percent of all abortions during the first trimester (the first 13 weeks of pregnancy).[218] Because the great majority of abortions occur in the first twenty weeks, vacuum aspiration is the method of choice for a substantial majority of all abortions.[219]

Both new procedures are rather gruesome if one focuses on the effect on the fetus. Vacuum aspiration involves vacuuming the contents of the womb through a thin tube, removing the fetus by tearing it to pieces and suctioning it out.[220] The process has lent itself to a return to the euphemism of "menstrual extraction."[221] "Salting out" is as gruesome for the fetus and poses serious risks to the mother as well. The process involves the injection of a saline solution into the amniotic fluid to burn the fetus seriously and after an hour or more results in premature labor that expels the dead or injured fetus. References to injecting salt water to induce an abortion can be found back in the nineteenth century, without, however, any mention of the risks of such practices.[222] Salting out can burn the uterus if performed improperly, and could induce other problems for the mother as well.[223] More importantly, salting out can produce a "live-birth abortion"—a rare but serious embarrassment to those who favor abortion.[224]

---

217. Rebecca Chalker & Carol Downer, A Woman's Book of Choices: Abortion, Menstrual Extraction, RU 486, at 116 (1993); Diane Curtis, *Doctored Rights: Menstrual Extraction, Self-Help Gynecological Care, and the Law,* 20 Rev. L. & Soc. Change 427, 437–38 (1994).

218. Judith Boss, The Birth Lottery: Prenatal Diagnosis and Selective Abortion 95 (1993); Judges, *supra* note 71, at 68; Potts, Diggory, & Peel, *supra* note 212, at 184–85; Williams Obstetrics 598 (F. Gary Cunningham *et al.,* eds. 20th ed. 1997]; Philip Stubblefield, *Surgical Techniques of Uterine Evacuations in First- and Second-Trimester Abortions,* 13 Clinical Obstet. & Gynecology 53, 66 (1986).

219. Jack Smith, *Public Health Implications of Abortion: Statistics Compiled by the Centers for Disease Control,* in Abortion and the States 81, 86, 97 (Jane Wishner ed. 1993).

220. Hern, *supra* note 211, at 114; Kenny, *supra* note 3, at 147–52, 170–74; Williams Obstetrics, *supra* note 218, at 596–98; Irwin Kaiser, *Update,* in Abortion, Medicine, and the Law, *supra* note 88, at 552, 557–59.

221. Chalker & Downer, *supra* note 217, at 121–27, 167–82; Karst, *supra* note 9, at 55; Christopher Teitze & Stanley Henshaw, Induced Abortion: A World Review 1986, at 85 (1986); Anita Allen, *Tribe's Judicious Feminism* (book rev.), 44 Stan. L. Rev. 179, 188 (1992); Robert Byrn, *An American Tragedy: The Supreme Court on Abortion,* 41 Fordham L. Rev. 807, 859 (1973); Curtis, *supra* note 217; Laura Punnett, *The Politics of Menstrual Extraction,* in From Abortion to Reproductive Freedom: Transforming a Movement 101–10 (Marlene Gerber Fried ed. 1990). At present, other techniques, including some "home remedies" for abortion, are also sometimes called "menstrual extraction." Hern, *supra* note 211, at 122; Judges, *supra* note 71, at 68–69; Williams Obstetrics, *supra* note 218, at 598.

222. *See* Hordern, *supra* note 70, at 96–99. *See also* John D'Emilio & Estelle Freedman, Intimate Matters: A History of Sexuality in America 65 (1988).

223. Boss, *supra* note 218, at 97–98; Hern, *supra* note 211, at 124; Kaiser, *supra* note 220, at 561–62. *See also* Colautti v. Franklin, 439 U.S. 379, 398–99 (1979); Planned Parenthood of Ctr. Mo. v. Danforth, 428 U.S. 52, 95–99 (1976) (White, J., dissenting, joined by Berger, C.J., & Rehnquist, J.).

224. *See, e.g.,* Floyd v. Anders, 440 F. Supp. 535 (D.S.C. 1977), *vacated & remanded,* 440 U.S. 445 (1979); Boss, *supra* note 218, at 98; Garrow, *supra* note 23, at 617–18; Hordern, *supra* note 70, at 130–31; Noonan, *supra* note 33, at 128–45; Olasky, *supra* note 195, at 123–32; Connie Paige, The Right to Lifers: Who They Are; How They Operate; Where They Get Their Money 9–28 (1983); Rubin, *supra* note 9, at 121–26; Kaiser, *supra* note 220, at 557; Robert Linsey, *A Doctor on Coast Is Accused of Killing Baby in Abortion,* N.Y. Times, Apr. 10, 1978, at A1; B. Towers, *The Trials of Dr. Waddill,* 5 J. Med. Ethics 205 (1979); Mary Anne Wood, *The Legal Implications of Medical Procedures Affecting the Unborn,* in Human Life and Health Care Ethics 161, 164–65 (James Bopp, jr., ed. 1985). *See generally* Commonwealth v. Edelin, 359 N.E.2d 4 (Mass. 1976); Regina v. Stone, [1977] Q.B. 354; J.K. Mason, Medico-Legal Aspects of Reproduction and Parenthood 165–70 (2nd ed. 1998); Rebecca Cooper, *Delivery Room Resuscitation of the High-Risk Infant: A Conflict of Rights,* 33 Cath. Law. 325 (1990); *Doctor Found Guilty of Infanticide in Death of Fetus in an Abortion: Witnesses Indicate the Child Might Have Lived,* N.Y. Times, June 13, 1989, at A18; Nancy Rhoden, *The*

Apparently, no statistics are kept on the frequency of live births resulting from attempted abortions. Despite the efforts of the abortion industry to prevent them, as many as 500 live-birth abortions were estimated as occurring annually during the late 1970s according to Dr. Willard Cates.[225] Cates, then Chief of Abortion Surveillance at the Centers for Disease Control, noted that this made live-birth abortions "literally an every day occurrence" in the United States. Rather than taking a hard look at the implications of such experiences, abortion supporters responded by developing special training to minimize the risk of such an outcome.[226] Those efforts seem to have succeeded. One study estimated the event at a rate of slightly more than 1:10,000 abortions, based on 18 live births for 160,000 abortions in New York state in 1982.[227] Extrapolating from the rate of third-trimester abortions nationally, we should be experiencing about 150 live-birth abortions annually in the nation as a whole. The figure might well have declined since 1982, however, as abortionists "perfected" the means of assuring the death of the infant before its birth.[228] Moreover, these figures count as live births both "viable" and "non-viable" fetuses. Still, there are survivors now old enough to tell the tale—or to sue for their injuries inflicted during the failed abortion.[229] One survivor of such a procedure—suffering from cerebral palsy as a result—touchingly related her experience before a congressional subcommittee on April 22, 1996.[230] Her testimony was studiously ignored by the major media. But then, the mainstream press has long exhibited a pronounced bias in favor of abortion rights.[231]

Because of the risks of saline amniocentesis, by 1970 doctors were already turning to a different technique for second trimester abortions—prostaglandin induction.[232] This procedure involves injecting prostaglandin into the amniotic fluid. Prostaglandin is a non-caustic hormone that induces labor with less risk to the mother than salting out but with a much higher likelihood of a live-birth of an undamaged (apart from prematurity) child.[233] Furthermore, only 40

---

*New Neonatal Dilemma: Live Births from Late Abortions,* 72 GEO. L.J. 1451 (1984); Benjamin Sendor, *Medical Responsibility for Fetal Survival under* Roe *and* Doe, 10 HARV. C.R.-C.L. L. REV. 444 (1975).

225. Liz Jeffries & Rick Edmonds, *Abortion: The Dreaded Complication: When a Crying Baby Emerges Instead of a Lifeless Fetus, Doctors Have a Problem with No Easy Answer,* PHILA. INQUIRER MAG., Aug. 2, 1981, at 14. There were six such births in hospitals in Madison, Wisconsin, in one ten-month period in the early 1980s alone. Michael Beulow, *Abortion Failures Stir Concern,* PHILA. INQUIRER, Mar. 23, 1983, at 9A. *See also* HERN, *supra* note 211, at 124; DAVID MEYERS, THE HUMAN BODY AND THE LAW 32–33 (2nd ed. 1990); OLASKY, *supra* note 195, at 123–32 (1988); HUNH Jessica Shaver, Gianna: Aborted—and Lived to Tell about It (1995); Allen Hunter, *In the Wings: New Right Ideology and Organization,* 15 RADICAL AM. 113, 135 (1981); Dena Kleiman, *When Abortion Becomes Birth,* N.Y. TIMES, FEB. 15, 1984 AT B1.

226. LADER, *supra* note 188, at 164–66; Nelson Isada *et al., Fetal Intracardiac Potassium Chloride Injection to Avoid the Hopeless Resuscitation of an Abnormal Abortus: I. Clinical Issues,* 80 OBSTET. & GYNECOLOGY 296 (1992); Rhoden, *supra* note 224, at 1501–03.

227. Hunter, *supra* note 224, at 135.

228. Gwen Gentile & Richard Schwarz, *Elective Abortion Techniques, Risks, and Complications,* in GENETIC DISORDERS AND THE FETUS 723, 732 (Aubrey Milunsky ed. 2nd ed. 1986); TIETZE & HENSHAW, *supra* note 221, at 88.

229. *See, e.g.,* Cherry v. Borsman, 75 D.L.R.4th 668 (B.C.S. Ct. 1991).

230. Gianna Jessen, *"I Am the Person She Aborted. I Lived Instead of Died.,"* NAT'L RT. TO LIFE NEWS, May 7, 1996, at 23. *See also* OLASKY, *supra* note 195, at 189 n. 72; SHAVER, *supra* note 227.

231. *See* NGUYENPHUC BUUTAP, LEGISLATION, PUBLIC OPINION, AND THE PRESS: AN INTERRELATIONSHIP REFLECTED IN THE NEW YORK TIMES REPORTING OF THE ABORTION ISSUE (unpub. Dissertation, U. Chi. 1979); S. ROBERT LICHTER, STANLEY ROTHMAN, & LINDA LICHTER, THE MEDIA ELITE: AMERICA'S NEW POWER BROKERS 29 (1986). Many feminists complain that the media are biased against feminism. *See, e.g.,* LANGER, *supra* note 96, at 75–86, 144–47. *See generally* CONDIT, *supra* note 32, at 23–28, 173–74, 176–77, 188–89; NOONAN, *supra* note 33, at 69–79; OLASKY, *supra* note 195, at 85–119, 133–51; Joanmarie Kalter, *Abortion Bias,* TV GUIDE, Jan. 21, 1985, at 8–27.

232. WILLIAMS OBSTETRICS, *supra* note 218, at 598.

233. *See* Colautti v. Franklin, 439 U.S. 379, 399 (1979); Planned Parenthood of Ctr. Mo. v. Danforth, 428 U.S. 52, 95–99 (1976) (White, J., dissenting, joined by Berger, C.J., & Rehnquist, J.); HORDERN, *supra* note 70,

percent of prostaglandin abortions are "completed."[234] "Completion" is such a simple procedure for prostaglandin induction, however, that it is now the most common technique for second-trimester abortions. Fear of live births resulting from attempted abortions has proven strong enough to inhibit the use of prostaglandin inductions. The Planned Parenthood Federation so opposed this possibility that it fought all the way to the Supreme Court to overturn a Missouri law that would have required prostaglandin injection in place of saline injection except in the rare case where prostaglandin would be more dangerous for the mother.[235] While prostaglandin might appear humane even for the fetus in the middle of the second-trimester when the child born alive will almost certainly quickly die,[236] abortion supporters oppose the use of prostaglandin throughout pregnancy—even when the result is likely to be a viable fetus with good chances of survival.

The persisting fear of live births resulting from abortions led some doctors to favor dilation and evacuation ("D&E") procedures as late as the 28th week of pregnancy (into the third trimester).[237] This is essentially the same as vacuum aspiration in the first trimester, except that it is necessary to cut or pull the child apart in the womb or as it is brought through the cervix before it can be "evacuated."[238] Such a late use of vacuum aspiration has advantages. It eliminates any chance of a live birth and prevents the woman from having any sensation of "expelling" an infant.[239] This is not to suggest that there are never medical reasons for choosing D&E over labor induction, simply that "protection of the woman" is usually not the major motivating factor.[240] Unfortunately, the rare child who somehow survives this procedure (because of the failure to empty and crush the skull) is likely to be born badly mangled. Ana Rosa Rodriguez, for example, was born without one of her arms after a failed D&E abortion.[241]

The timing of these developments was not accidental. Legalization of abortion in a growing number of countries served to legitimate research on abortion techniques as such. No longer would progress merely be incidental to progress in general surgical techniques spilling over into illegal abortions.[242] Such technological changes in turn helped create predictable interest groups

---

at 100–01; Kenny, *supra* note 3, at 159–70; Mason, *supra* note 224, at 166–67; David Grimes, *Second Trimester Abortions in the United States,* 16 Fam. Plan. Persp. 260, 262 (1984); Allen Rosenfield, *The Difficult Issue of Second-Trimester Abortion,* 267 JAMA 324 (1994).

234. Rosenfield, *supra* note 233, at 325.

235. Planned Parenthood of Ctr. Mo. v. Danforth, 428 U.S. 52 (1976).

236. Grimes, *supra* note 233, at 263.

237. Hern, *supra* note 211, at 133; Epner, Jonas, & Seckinger, *supra* note 210, at 726; Kaiser, *supra* note 220, at 559–61; Nancy Kaltreider *et al., The Impact of Midtrimester Abortion Techniques on Patients and Staff,* 135 Am. J. Obstet. & Gynecology 235, 237 (1979); Judith Bourne Rooks & Willard Cates, jr., *Emotional Impact of D&E vs. Instillation,* 9 Fam. Planning Persp. 276, 277 (Nov/Dec. 1977). *See also* Planned Parenthood Ass'n v. Ashcroft, 462 U.S. 476, 483 n.7 (1983); Kenny, *supra* note 3, at 152–59; Rosenfield, *supra* note 233, at 324.

238. Boss, *supra* note 218, at 95–96; Hern, *supra* note 211, at 135, 139–42, 151; Judges, *supra* note 71, at 70–73; Willard Cates, jr., *et al., Dilation and Evacuation Procedures and Second Trimester Abortions,* 248 JAMA 559 (1982); Epner, Jonas, & Seckinger, *supra* note 210, at 726; Grimes, *supra* note 233, at 262.

239. Hern, *supra* note 211, at 133.

240. Willard Cates, jr., *Legal Abortion: The Public Health Record,* 215 Sci. 1586, 1588 (1982); Willard Cates, jr., & David Grimes, *Deaths from Second-Trimester Abortion by Dilation and Evacuation,* 58 Obstet. & Gynecology 401 (1981); Centers for Disease Control, *Abortion Surveillance—United States, 1990,* 42 MWWR Morbidity & Mortality Wkly. Rep. 290 (1993).

241. Lisa Belkin, *State Suspends Manhattan Doctor Accused of Botching Abortion,* N.Y. Times, Nov. 26, 1991, at B1. *See also* Marvin Olasky, *Another Year of Abortions: This Week Marks 26th Anniversary of* Roe v. Wade, *and We're Still Surprised with Some News,* Austin Am.-Statesman, Jan. 20, 1999, at A17 (telling the story of a full-term girl born with a fractured skull from an attempted abortion but who survived to be adopted, and of another girl born with severe disabilities after an attempted abortion who was also adopted).

242. Dellapenna, *supra* note 207, at 413.

seeking to change the law to allow widespread use of the new technology: Women would gain greater control over their lives,[243] and doctors would acquire a new, relatively easy and low-risk, source of income. Of course, not every woman or every physician favored abortion,[244] but many did. One of the more dramatic examples of the physician's profit motive in action was the commuter doctors who, during the several year interval between the legalization of abortion in New York and *Roe's* legalization of abortion nationwide, would fly to New York City from various other states where abortion was still illegal to do abortions for one or two days per week, and then return to their regular practice back home.[245] Some of these abortionists even set up apparently independent "women's centers" for the purpose of referring potential abortion patients solely to the sponsoring abortionists—without regard to whether some other physician might be more conveniently located or otherwise in the best interests of the patient.[246]

Another development that fed into the repeal movement was the emergence, in the late 1960s in several areas of the United States, of "underground" groups for performing abortions.[247] The first apparently was the Association for the Repeal of Abortion Laws that operated as an adjunct to the Society for Humane Abortions in San Francisco.[248] Best known was a women's collective in Chicago that styled itself "Jane" after the practice of each member hiding behind the pseudonym "Jane" to minimize the risk of being identified to the police.[249] The group operated between 1967 and 1973.[250] "Jane" reached its stride when the women involved decided they could do the abortions themselves and dispense with physicians except as a backup.[251] At its peak, between 1969 and 1973, "Jane" was doing 3,000 abortions a year, about

---

243. NANETTE DAVIS, FROM CRIME TO CHOICE 109–14, 121–28 (1985).

244. *See, e.g.,* MAGDA DIENES, IN NECESSITY AND SO'RROW (1985); KENNY, *supra* note 3; Anne Roiphe, *Confessions of a Female Chauvinist Sow,* 5 NEW YORK, Oct. 30, 1972, at 52.

245. DAVIS, *supra* note 243, at 122.

246. *See, e.g.,* Okereke v. State, 518 N.Y.S.2d 210 (App. Div. 1987).

247. BAEHR, *supra* note 67, at 7–30; ARLENE CARMEN & HOWARD MOODY, ABORTION COUNSELING AND SOCIAL CHANGE (1973); CHALKER & DOWNER, *supra* note 217, at 83–83, 114–17; DAVIS, *supra* note 243, at xiv, 33–34, 180–81; FERREE & HESS, *supra* note 91, at 108–09; SUZANNE GAGE, WHEN BIRTH CONTROL FAILS: HOW TO ABORT OURSELVES SAFELY (1979); GARROW, *supra* note 23, at 307–08, 318, 333–34, 349–51, 361–64, 376–77, 384–86, 391–93, 422, 438, 445, 486–87, 539; GINSBURG, *supra* note 9, at 37, 258–59 n.25; GRABER, *supra* note 40, at 47; HOLE & LEVINE, *supra* note 67, at 253–54, 295–96; LADER, *supra* note 188, at 42–47; LUKER, *supra* note 9, at 34; LAURA KAPLAN, THE STORY OF JANE: THE LEGENDARY UNDERGROUND FEMINIST ABORTION SERVICE (1995); PETCHESKY, *supra* note 3, at 127–29; REAGAN, *supra* note 13, at 222–26; ROSENBLATT, *supra* note 3, at 40–41; RUBIN, *supra* note 9, at 24; RUDY, *supra* note 80, at 66–68; SHERYL BURT RUZEK, THE WOMEN'S HEALTH MOVEMENT: FEMINIST ALTERNATIVES TO MEDICAL CONTROL (1978); Pauline Bart, *Seizing the Means of Reproduction: An Illegal Feminist Abortion Collective—How and Why It Worked,* 10 QUALITATIVE SOCIOLOGY 339 (1987); Pauline Bart & Melinda Bart Schlesinger, *The Effect of Working in a Feminist Illegal Abortion Collective,* in WORKPLACE DEMOCRACY AND SOCIAL CHANGE 139 (Frank Lindenfield & Joyce Rothchild Whitt eds. 1981); Clowes, *supra* note 78, at 376–79; Curtis, *supra* note 217, at 429, 436–37; Diane Elze, *Underground Abortion Remembered,* SOUJOURNER: THE WOMEN'S FORUM, APRIL, 1988, at 14; Julie George, *Political Effects of Court Decisions on Abortion: A Comparison between the United States and the German Federal Republic,* 3 INT'L J.L. & FAM. 106, 110–11 (1989); "Jane," *Just Call "Jane,"* in FROM ABORTION TO REPRODUCTIVE FREEDOM, *supra* note 221, at 93–100; Charles King, *Calling Jane: The Life and Death of a Women's Illegal Abortion Service,* 20 WOMEN & HEALTH 75 (1993); Martha Minow, *Breaking the Law: Lawyers and Clients in Struggles for Social Change,* 52 U. PITT. L. REV. 723, 737–38, 745–47 (1991); Loretta Ross, *African-American Women and Abortion,* in ABORTION WARS, *supra* note 32, at 161, 178–79; Anastasia Toufexis, *Abortions without Doctors,* TIME, Aug. 28, 1989, at 66; Lindsey Van Gelder, *The Jane Collective: Seizing Control,* Ms., Sept./Oct. 1991, at 83.

248. *See* BAEHR, *supra* note 67, at 7–18; LUKER, *supra* note 9, at 95–102; REAGAN, *supra* note 13, at 222–24. *See also* Chapter 13, at notes 338–39.

249. KAPLAN, *supra* note 247; "Jane," *supra* note 247; King, *supra* note 247.

250. REAGAN, *supra* note 13, at 225.

251. Bart, *supra* note 247.

70 percent of which were for "women of color" although most of the activists in "Jane" were white.[252]

The police raided "Jane," but, in the already politicized atmosphere of the time, charges were dropped against those arrested.[253] Members of "Jane," however, felt compelled to go underground with their activities rather than to continue to act in the open.[254] On the other hand, such groups sometimes cooperated with the police to turn in abortionists that the group considered dangerous.[255] All of this is reminiscent of the opening of illegal contraceptive clinics in the early years of the twentieth century.[256] Like those earlier clinics, "Jane" and many other such operations were as much a political education project as a provider of abortions as they sought to teach women about their bodies and to agitate for legal changes intended to eliminate what they saw as male control over their pregnancies.[257] Yet, many of those whom "Jane" aborted had negative memories of the experience, recalling it as dirty, disorganized, and dangerous.[258]

Yet another group that found reasons for active support for abortion reform, the clergy who chose to serve as abortion brokers. These were mostly "mainstream" (liberal) Protestant clergy whom Nanette Davis has termed "moral entrepreneurs."[259] These clergy were usually involved in campus ministry or in regional church units or serving as assistant pastors in affluent suburbs, all functions that provided little public surveillance and a maximum of personal freedom. They gravitated to a succession of social causes as a substitute for their own dying theologies and their growing sense of not having access to a transcendent reality and of not belonging to what had become effectively little more than a purely local organizational structure. The same clergy were often involved in the protest movements for civil rights, against the war, for women's rights, and against poverty, as well as in the abortion rights movement, all of which involved public and active opposition to existing laws and (frequently) to prevalent mores as well.[260] The clergymen often became "lay counselors" advising those seeking abortion where to go and what to do. The largest such group, the New-York-based Clergy Consultation Service on Abortion, was largely funded by Stewart Mott, an heir to one of the founders of General Motors.[261]

The counseling proved to have its own problems—"[t]oo brief for depth and too long for simple information exchange."[262] Nanette Davis summarized the process by noting that "[a]s a religiously inspired event, abortion counseling was probably a colossal failure," which the women experienced as a "prefabricated format" that was "bewildering or even idiotic."[263] This counseling format, now secularized, survives today as a standard part of the abortion clinic experience.[264] The counseling usually was, and generally still is, heavily biased in favor of abortion

---

252. Kaplan, *supra* note 247, at 267; Reagan, *supra* note 13, at 225–26; "Jane," *supra* note 247, at 93; Ross, *supra* note 247, at 178–79.

253. Reagan, *supra* note 13, at 243–44; Bart, *supra* note 247, at 346.

254. Reagan, *supra* note 13, at 243.

255. Davis, *supra* note 243, at 142; Frederick Jaffe, Barbara Lindheim, & Philip Lee, Abortion Politics 22 (1981); Lader, *supra* note 188, at 48.

256. *See* Gordon, *supra* note 179, at 230–36; Margaret Sanger, Autobiography 215–34 (1938); Margaret Sanger, My Fight for Birth Control 144–58 (1931).

257. Reagan, *supra* note 13, at 223, 225–26.

258. *Id.* at 226.

259. Davis, *supra* note 243, at 129–54.

260. *Id.* at 130–31. *See also* Condit, *supra* note 32, at 60; Nancy Lee, The Search for an Abortionist 1969); Charles Bayer, *Confessions of an Abortion Counselor*, Christian Century, May 20, 1970, at 628.

261. Garrow, *supra* note 23, at 333–34, 364. *See also* Lupu, *supra* note 14, at 961–62. *See generally* Condit, *supra* note 32, at 191–94; Gage, *supra* note 247.

262. Davis, *supra* note 243, at 138.

263. *Id. See generally* The Choices We Made (Angela Bonavoglia ed. 1991).

264. *See generally* Davis, *supra* note 243, at 157–60, 173–74.

and against other possible responses to an unwanted pregnancy.[265] One result of all this is that it generally takes longer to arrange and accomplish a legal abortion than it did to arrange and accomplish an illegal abortion before *Roe*, without necessarily costing less.[266]

It was not immediately self-evident that women would find the improved abortion technologies liberating. There is a certain discordance between abortion rhetoric and abortion practice. Women are described as empowered by the availability of abortion but find themselves lying supine and being entered by (usually) a man intent on determining whether she is to be pregnant or not, reenacting the classic model of feminine passivity from which abortion supposedly frees women.[267] Those providing abortion counseling and services set out deliberately to "shield" women from the "raw reality" of abortion,[268] including opposition to informed consent (fetal description) statutes,[269] the denial of ultrasound views of the fetus to women about to undergo abortion although ultrasound is now a routine part of the procedure,[270] and a choice of abortion technique to assure a dead (and unrecognizable fetus).[271] This "protection" of women not only demeans them, but it also suggests a negative view of abortion itself even by those who profess to embrace the practice as enhancing the dignity of women.[272] Nonetheless, a majority of politically active women did embrace abortion precisely for its potential to liberate them.[273] At first, it appeared that only fetuses, as inarticulate and powerless class as ever there was, did not agree.[274]

# *Roe v. Wade* and *Doe v. Bolton*

*There's something odd about taking sexual reproduction which requires two individuals to work, and then treating it theoretically as independent actions of separate individuals with separate interests.*

—Anne Fasutin-Sterling[275]

By 1971, those who sought to change abortion laws in the United States were seeking a total repeal of all abortion laws—"abortion on demand" as they then put it.[276] But, as Dr. Alan

---

265. *See* Terry Steinberg, *Abortion Counseling: To Benefit Maternal Health,* 15 Am. J.L. & Med. 483 (1989); Uta Landy, *Abortion Counseling-A New Component of Medical Care,* 33 Clinics in Obstet. & Gynecology 37 (1986).

266. *Id.* at 168–70, 176.

267. David Smolin, *Cultural and Technological Obstacles to the Mainstreaming of Abortion,* 13 St. L.U. Pub. L. Rev. 261, 263–64 (1993). *See also* Carole Joffe, The Regulation of Sexuality 112 (1986) (reporting that female abortion counselors spoke of this sexual aspect of abortion practice, at least among themselves).

268. *See generally* Olasky, *supra* note 195, at 142–47; David Reardon, Aborted Women: Silent No More 15–19 (1987); Smolin, *supra* note 267, at 268–77.

269. *Compare* Planned Parenthood of S.E. Pa. v. Casey, 505 U.S. 833, 881–83 (1992) (upholding fetal description statutes), *with* Thornburgh v. American College of Obstetricians & Gynecologists, 476 U.S. 747, 762 (1986) (striking down such statutes).

270. Hern, *supra* note 211, at 69–73; Diane Gianelli, *Abortion Providers Share Inner Conflicts,* Am. Med. News, July 12, 1993, at 3, 37.

271. Hern, *supra* note 211, at 132–33; Kaltreider, *supra* note 237, at 235; Rooks & Cates, *supra* note 237, at 276–77.

272. Smolin, *supra* note 267, at 271–72. *See also* David Smolin, *The Jurisprudence of Privacy in a Splintered Supreme Court,* 75 Marq. L. Rev. 975, 1001–5 (1992) ("Smolin, Jurisprudence").

273. *See generally* Tribe, *supra* note 12, at 101–05 and sources cited therein.

274. John Hart Ely, *The Wages of Crying Wolf,* 82 Yale L.J. 920, 933–35 (1973).

275. As quoted in Natalie Angier, *Feminists and Darwin: Scientists Try Closing the Gap,* N.Y. Times, June 21, 1994, at C1, C13.

276. *See* Victoria Greenwood & Jack Young, Abortion on Demand 99 (1976). *See also* Rosalind Baxandall, Women and Abortion: The Body as Battleground 12 (1992).

Guttmacher (by then president of the Planned Parenthood Federation) had feared early in the reform process, the goal of legalizing abortion on demand provoked "bitter dissension."[277] Despite the lack of a personal stake in the adults fighting on behalf of fetuses, champions for fetuses emerged who were articulate and not completely without political power.[278] And the prosecution of abortionists in states that had not liberalized or repealed their statutes continued.

Some of those propagandizing for the reform or repeal of abortion laws in the 1950s and 1960s claimed that the crime was never prosecuted.[279] Yet, even in a "liberal" state like Oregon, long-time abortionist Ruth Barnett was prosecuted successfully in 1966, her conviction being upheld in 1968.[280] Authorities arrested seven abortionists in Chicago in May 1972.[281] Massachusetts successfully prosecuted Dr. Benedict Kudish just a few months before the Supreme Court decided *Roe v. Wade*.[282] Other convictions were affirmed on appeal in Louisiana, New Hampshire, and North Carolina during the last year before *Roe*.[283] Despite the folkloric claims that abortionists practiced freely and openly for decades without legal problems, when these "former abortionists" were interviewed by an historian 20 years after *Roe v. Wade*, nearly every one them could recall "at least one brush with the law."[284] This reality disproves the claim that only incompetent abortionists were being prosecuted.[285]

The continuing prosecutions required some response by those who claimed that the law was already a dead letter and that reform or repeal would only make the law on the books consistent with what actually was happening in society. Some commentators explained the prosecutions as representing cases in which the abortionist was involved in other vice crimes such as drug trafficking, issuing false death certificates, or black market adoptions.[286] Others have asserted that abortionists were prosecuted only when their transgressions involved race or other matters that were considered highly offensive yet were not in themselves criminal.[287] Such assertions are based on the author's impressions rather than any systematic search of the relevant records. The actual records of reported cases do not support the excuses.

---

277. Alan Guttmacher, *Introduction,* in The Case for Legalized Abortion Now 1, 13 (Alan Guttmacher ed. 1967).

278. *See* Condit, *supra* note 32, at 59–63, 74 n.5; John Jeffries, jr., Justice Lewis F. Powell, Jr. 354–59 (1994); Paige, *supra* note 224; Rosenberg, *supra* note 28, at 188, 341–42; Rubin, *supra* note 9, at 89–113, 151–83; Craig Seaton, Altruism and Activism: Character Disposition and Ideology as Factors in Blockade of an Abortion Clinic (1990).

279. *See, e.g.,* Harvey Adelstein, *The Abortion Law,* 12 W. Res. L. Rev. 74, 85–86 (1960); Marvin Moore, *Antiquated Abortion Laws,* 20 Wash. & Lee L. Rev. 250, 253 (1963); Note, *The Law of Criminal Abortion: An Analysis of Proposed Reforms,* 32 Ind. L.J. 193, 200 (1957); Jack Star, *1,000,000 a Year: The Growing Tragedy of Illegal Abortion,* Look, Oct. 19, 1965, at 150, 156.

280. State v. Barnett, 437 P.2d 821 (Ore. 1968). On Barnett's career, see Chapter 12, at notes 190–251.

281. King, *supra* note 247.

282. Commonwealth v. Kudish, 289 N.E.2d 856 (Mass. 1972).

283. State v. Campbell, 270 So. 2d 506 (La. 1972); State v. Millette, 299 A.2d 150 (N.H. 1972); State v. Coleman, 193 S.E.2d 395 (N.C. Ct. App. 1972).

284. Miller, *supra* note 43, at 9.

285. For such claims, see Jerome Bates & Edward Zawadski, Criminal Abortion 5–6, 10–11, 134–35 (1964); Davis, *supra* note 243, at 49–51, 61, 89–90, 142; Graber, *supra* note 40, at 39, 45–50, 84–87, 108–17; Jaffe, Lindheim, & Lee, *supra* note 255, at 22; Lawrence Lader, Abortion 48, 70 (1966); Lee, *supra* note 260, at 6; Luker, *supra* note 9, at 36, 85; Miller, *supra* note 43, at 262; Petchesky, *supra* note 3, at 129; Rubin, *supra* note 9, at 18; Betty Sarvis & Hyman Rodman, The Abortion Controversy 65 (1973); Joffe, *Portraits, supra* note 200, at 60; Zad Leavy & Jerome Kummer, *Criminal Abortion: A Failure of Law,* 50 ABA J. 52, 52 (1964); James Mohr, *Patterns of Abortion and the Response of American Physicians, 1790–1930,* in Women and Health in America: Historical Readings 117, 121 (Judith Leavitt ed. 1984).

286. Bates & Zawadski, *supra* note 285, at 78–82; Graber, *supra* note 40, at 46–47.

287. Herbert Packer & Ralph Gampell, *Therapeutic Abortions: A Problem in Law and Medicine,* 11 Stan. L. Rev. 417, 426–55 (1959).

So difficult was the problem of continuing prosecutions for abortion activists that some of them, in struggling to come to grips with the phenomenon, wound up contradicting themselves. Thus Jerome Bates and Edward Zawadski argued at several points that abortionists were seldom prosecuted unless they botched the procedure, yet at another point conceding that the police were not lax in their attempts to enforce abortion laws.[288] Nor do the explanations consider that such "official tolerance" as there was was purchased; bribery was a regular cost of business for abortionists.[289] The need to pay off police or prosecutors hardly demonstrates widespread social acceptance of the practice. Less committed advocates of abortion reform concede that most abortionists found the police "far from cooperative."[290] As Carole Joffe concluded after studying the careers of "three physicians of conscience" (*i.e.*, professional abortionists), "you could get away with [abortion] unquestionably, as long as you didn't do it as a business."[291]

That most abortion prosecutions resulted from botched abortions that severely injured or killed the mother was more a function of the realities of gathering the evidence necessary for a prosecution than as a reflection of official tolerance for the practice.[292] While convicted abortionists frequently were given probation rather than being sent to prison,[293] many doctors would later recall refusing to perform abortions for fear of prosecution.[294] And we should recall that Norma McCorvey, the "Jane Roe" of *Roe v. Wade*, actually gave birth because she was unable to locate an abortionist on her own (and her attorneys would not help her for fear of losing their client's legal standing to challenge the constitutionality of the Texas abortion statute).[295]

In the United States, the change of the goal to repeal rather than reform led to a change in tactics. Proceeding state by state through legislatures was too slow, too expensive, and too uncertain.[296] Defeats in referenda in several states raised a question about whether the gains already achieved could be sustained.[297] Concluding that their goal would not be achieved quickly or nationally through legislation, supporters of the "right to choose" turned to a campaign of litigation rather than legislation.[298] The change was hardly a surprise given the appar-

---

288. Bates & Zawadski, *supra* note 285, at 94.

289. *Id.* at 66–70; Lader, *supra* note 285, at 71–74; Edwin Schur, Crimes without Victims: Deviant Behavior and Public Policy 34–35 (1965); Graber, *supra* note 40, at 57–62; Howard Ziff, *Recent Abortion Law Reforms*, 60 J. Crim. L. & Criminology 3, 6, 9 (1969).

290. Bates & Zawadski, *supra* note 285, at 94.

291. Joffe, *Portraits, supra* note 200, at 53. *See also* Ellen Messer & Kathryn May, Back Rooms: Voices from the Illegal Abortion Era 180 (1988).

292. Bates & Zawadski, *supra* note 285, at 94; Graber, *supra* note 40, at 46–47; Lader, *supra* note 285, at 70–71; Sarvis & Rodman, *supra* note 285, at 65. *See generally* Chapter 9, at notes 157–232; Chapter 11, at notes 361–439; Chapter 12, at notes 42–83.

293. D'Emilio & Freedman, *supra* note 218, at 253.

294. Miller, *supra* note 43, at 32.

295. Norma McCorvey & Andy Meisler, I Am Roe: My Life, Roe v. Wade, and Freedom of Choice 104–06 (1994); *The 25th Anniversary of* Roe v. Wade: *Has It Stood the Test of Time, Hearings before the Subcomm. On the Const., Federalism, & Property Rts. of the Sen. Comm. on the Judiciary*, 100th Cong. 44–46 (statement of Norma McCorvey) ("McCorvey Statement").

296. See the text *supra* at notes 12–32; Chapter 13, at notes 248–51, 317–79.

297. See the text *supra* at notes 33–38; Kirp, *supra* note 38, at 759.

298. Schulder & Kennedy, *supra* note 197, at 121–23; Clark, *supra* note 59; Ruth Cowan, *Women's Rights through Litigation: An Examination of the American Civil Liberties Union Women's Rights Project, 1971–1976*, 8 Colum. Hum. Rts. L. Rev. 373 (1976); Lucas, *supra* note 58; Heather Sigworth, *Abortion Laws in the Federal Courts: The Supreme Court as Platonic Guardian*, 5 Ind. L.F. 130 (1971); Pat Vergata *et al., Abortion Cases in the United States*, 1 Women's Rts. L. Rptr. 50 (1972). *See, e.g.,* United States v. Vuitch, 402 U.S. 62 (1971); YWCA of Princeton v. Kugler, 345 F. Supp. 1048 (D.N.J. 1972) *vacated,* 475 F. 2d 1398 (3rd Cir. 1973), *aff'd after remand,* 493 F. 2d 1402 (3rd Cir. 1974); Abramowicz v. Kugler, 342 F. Supp. 1048 (D.N.J. 1972); Abele v. Markele, 342 F. Supp. 800 (D. Conn. 1972) *vacated after* Roe v. Wade, 410 U.S. 951 (1973); Rosen v. Louisiana St. Bd. of Med. Examiners, 318 F. Supp. 1217 (E.D. La. 1970) *vacated,* 412 U.S. 902 (1973); Roe v. Wade, 314

ent successes of the litigation strategy of the civil rights movement. *Brown v. Board of Education*,[299] which ended *de jure* segregation in public education and soon other institutions in American society, remains best known example. Other examples relating to civil rights, criminal procedure, political activism, and state involvement in religion in the immediate aftermath of *Brown,* include *Mapp v. Ohio,*[300] *Baker v. Carr,*[301] *Engel v. Vitale,*[302] *Miranda v. Arizona,*[303] *Griswold v. Connecticut.*[304] The hope that one could overturn abortion laws through the judiciary despite failure in state legislatures was rather normal when optimism reigned about the power and effectiveness of courts to change society for the better.[305] Today, there is growing argument about how much really was accomplished in these cases.[306] Even *Brown* has been questioned, with one commentator going so far as to call its influence on race relations indirect and "perverse."[307]

In *Griswold,* the Supreme court held laws prohibiting the sale of contraceptives for use by married couples to be unconstitutional. This proved to be the legal key to a claim that there existes in the Constitution, lurking and undiscovered, a right to privacy "broad enough to encompass a woman's decision to abort."[308] The *Griswold* opinion is famous for Justice William Douglas' discovery of the right to privacy as emanating from "penumbras" of the specific provisions of the Constitution.[309] Justice Arthur Goldberg proposed the long-neglected Ninth Amendment as an alternate source of the constitutional right of privacy.[310] Justice John Mar-

---

F. Supp. 1217 (N.D. Tex. 1970), *aff'd,* 410 U.S. 113 (1973); Babbitz v. McCann, 310 F. Supp. 293 (E.D. Wis. 1970), *appeal dismissed,* 400 U.S. 1 (1970); Abramowicz v. Lefkowitz, 305 F. Supp. 1030 (S.D.N.Y. 1969); People v. Belous, 458 P.2d 194 (Cal. 1969). *See generally* GARROW, *supra* note 23, at 411; GRABER, *supra* note 40, at 121–23; RUBIN, *supra* note 9, at 31–88; STAGGENBORG, *supra* note 69, at 152.

299. 347 U.S. 483 (1954).

300. 368 U.S. 871 (1961) (excluding evidence seized in an illegal state search and seizure from use at trial).

301. 369 U.S. 186 (1962) (ordering judicially supervised redistricting for state legislative elections).

302. 370 U.S. 421 (1962) (prohibiting state prescribed prayers in public schools).

303. 384 U.S. 436 (1966) (requiring state and local police to provide a set of warnings to anyone undergoing "custodial interrogation").

304. 381 U.S. 479 (1965) (banning state restrictions on access to contraceptives by married couples).

305. JACK GREENBERG, JUDICIAL PROCESS AND SOCIAL CHANGE (1977); DONALD HOROWITZ, THE COURTS AND SOCIAL POLICY (1977); CLEMENT VOSE, CONSTITUTIONAL CHANGE: AMENDMENT POLITICS AND SUPREME COURT LITIGATION SINCE 1900 (1972).

306. *See generally* ARCHIBALD COX, THE ROLE OF THE SUPREME COURT IN AMERICAN GOVERNMENT (1976); ROSENBERG, *supra* note 278.

307. Michael Klarman, Brown, *Racial Change, and the Civil Rights Movement,* 80 VA. L. REV. 7 (1994). *See also* ROSENBERG, *supra* note 28; David Garrow, *Hopelessly Hollow History: Revisionist Devaluing of* Brown v. Board of Education, 80 VA. L. REV. 151 (1994); Michael Klarman, Brown v. Board of Education: *Facts and Political Correctness,* 80 VA. L. REV. 185 (1994); Gerald Rosenberg, Brown *Is Dead! Long Live* Brown: *The Endless Attempt to Canonize a Case,* 80 VA. L. REV. 161 (1994); Mark Tushnet, *The Critique of Rights,* 47 SMU L. REV. 23 (1993); Mark Tushnet, *The Significance of* Brown v. Board of Education, 80 VA. L. REV. 173 (1994). For an empirical study that demonstrates that *Brown* did in fact have a significant impact on the decisions of federal district judges regardless of putative extralegal variables, and through them on race relations in many aspects of American life, see Francine Sanders, Brown v. Board of Education: *An Empirical Reexamination of Its Effects on Federal District Courts,* 29 LAW & SOC'Y REV. 731 (1995). *See generally* Michael Giles & Thomas Walker, *Judicial Policy Making and Southern School Segregation,* 37 J. POL. 917 (1975).

308. *Roe v. Wade,* 410 U.S. at 129–30.

309. 381 U.S. at 485. *See also* Richard Dixon, jr., *The* Griswold *Penumbra: Constitutional Charter for an Expanded Law of Privacy?,* 64 MICH. L. REV. 197 (1965); Paul Kauper, *Penumbras, Peripheries, and Emanations: Things Fundamental and Things Forgotten: The* Griswold *Case,* 64 MICH. L. REV. 197 (1965); Robert McKay, *The Right of Privacy: Emanations and Intimations,* 64 MICH. L. REV. 259 (1965).

310. 381 U.S. at 516–21. *See also* William Bertelsman, *The Ninth Amendment and Due Process of Law—Toward a Viable Theory of Unenumerated Rights,* 37 U. CIN. L. REV. 777 (1968); R.H. Clark, *The Ninth Amendment and Constitutional Privacy,* 5 U. TOL. L. REV. 83 (1973); Thomas Emerson, *Nine Justices in Search of a Doctrine,* 64 MICH. L. REV. 219 (1965); Frank Goldstein, *The Constitutional Rights of Privacy: "A Sizable Hunk*

shall Harlan rooted the constitutional right of privacy in the "substantive due process" enshrined in the Fifth and Fourteenth Amendments.[311] The very idea that the constitution included an amorphous right of privacy broader than the specific mandates of the Constitution was a startling innovation at the time (either brilliant or arrogant as one sees it).[312] Justice Hugo Black's dissent in *Griswold* was particularly scathing on the question of whether anything in the Constitution granted courts a free-ranging commission to serve as Platonic guardians to society.[313] One commentator described Black's dissent as "soaked in acid and blood," concluding that "[i]f a single dissent filled with rapier-like verbal stiletting could have destroyed the constitutional right of privacy at its inception, Black's dissent in *Griswold* would have done so."[314]

Back in 1788, Anti-Federalists had expressed fear of federal usurpation of authority to regulate all aspects of private life—extending even to "ladies at their toilette"— during the ratification debates, with some of them focusing on the Supreme Court as the organ that would be most likely to usurp state authority.[315] Yet Black's arguments were strong enough that a majority of the Supreme Court explicitly rejected a claim of a "general constitutional right to privacy" in *Katz v. United States*,[316] a criminal procedure case decided only two years after *Griswold*. In the end, however, Black failed to convince the other justices not to recognize a right of privacy that Justice Harry Blackmun would rely upon less than six years after *Katz* to constitutionalize the law of abortion. Of the majority justices in *Roe*, all except Stewart simply ignored *Katz*.[317]

---

*of Liberty,*" 26 MD. L. REV. 249 (1966); Ernest Katin, Griswold v. Connecticut: *The Justices and Connecticut's "Uncommonly Silly Law,"* 42 NOTRE DAME L. REV. 680 (1967); James Kelley, *The Uncertain Renaissance of the Ninth Amendment,* 33 U. CHI. L. REV. 814 (1966); Louis Kutner, *Neglected Ninth Amendment: The Other Rights Retained by the People,* 51 MARQ. L. REV. 121 (1967); A.F. Ringold, *History of the Enactment of Ninth Amendment and Its Recent Development,* 8 TULSA L.J. 1 (1972). *See generally* THE RIGHTS RETAINED BY THE PEOPLE: THE HISTORY AND MEANING OF THE NINTH AMENDMENT (Randy Barnett ed. 1989); Sotirios Barber, *The Ninth Amendment: Inkblot or Another Hard Nut to Crack?,* 64 CHI.-KENT L. REV. 67 (1988); G. Sidney Buchanan, *The Right of Privacy: Past, Present, and Future,* 16 OHIO N.U. L. REV. 403 (1990); Saul Cornell, *Moving beyond the Canon of Traditional Constitutional History: Anti-Federalists, the Bill of Rights, and the Promise of Post-Modern Historiography,* 12 LAW & HIST. REV. 1, 12–18 (1994); Thomas Grey, *The Original Understanding and the Unwritten Constitution,* in TOWARD A MORE PERFECT UNION: SIX ESSAYS ON THE CONSTITUTION 245 (Niel Longley York ed. 1987); David Helscher, Griswold v. Connecticut *and the Unenumerated Right of Privacy,* 15 N. ILL. U. L. REV. 33 (1994); Russell Kaplan, *The History and Meaning of the Ninth Amendment,* 69 VA. L. REV. 223 (1983); Calvin Massey, *The Anti-Federalist Ninth Amendment and Its Implications for State Constitutional Law,* 1990 WIS. L. REV. 1229; Thomas McAfee, *The Original Meaning of the Ninth Amendment,* 90 COLUM. L. REV. 1215 (1990); Lawrence Mitchell, *The Ninth Amendment and the Jurisprudence of Original Intention,* 74 GEO. L.J. 1719 (1986); Norman Redlich, *The Ninth Amendment as a Constitutional Prism,* 12 HARV. J.L. & PUB. POL'Y 23 (1989); Suzanna Sherry, *The Founders' Unwritten Constitution,* 54 U. CHI. L. REV. 1127 (1987).

311. 381 U.S. at 524–26. Harlan reiterated the theory he had advanced in his famous dissent in *Poe v. Ullman,* 367 U.S. 497, 522–55 (1961). *Poe* also involved a constitutional challenge to Connecticut's contraception statute. *See* GARROW, *supra* note 23, at 190–200; LAZARUS, *supra* note 28, at 334–36.

312. LAZARUS, *supra* note 28, at 339–42.

313. 381 U.S. at 540–43.

314. Rodney Blackman, *Spinning, Squirreling, Shelling, Stiletting and Other Strategies of the Supremes,* 35 ARIZ. L. REV. 503, 513–14 (1993).

315. 2 THE COMPLETE ANTI-FEDERALIST 315–16, 396 (Herbert Storing 1981) ("Letters of Brutus"). *See also* 6 THE COMPLETE ANTI-FEDERALIST, *supra*, at 14 ("Cincinnatus"); William Jeffrey, jr., *The Letters of "Brutus"—A Neglected Element in the Ratification Campaign,* 40 U. CIN. L. REV. 643 (1971); Gary McDowell, *Were the Anti-Federalists Right?: Judicial Activism and the Problems of Consolidated Government,* 12 PUBLIUS 99 (1982); Anne Stuart Diamond, *The Anti-Federalist "Brutus,"* 6 POL. SCI. REV. 249 (1976).

316. 389 U.S. 347, 349–50 (1967). *See also* Paul v. Davis, 424 U.S. 693, 712 (1976) (there is no right of privacy implicit in the Fifth Amendment).

317. *Roe v. Wade,* 410 U.S. 113, 167 n.2 (Stewart, J., concurring).

Assuming there is a right to privacy implicit in the Constitution, that does not necessarily extend as far as a right to abort—as was explicitly recognized during the argument of *Griswold*. Chief Justice Earl Warren during the oral argument endorsed the proposition that the right of privacy would extend to abortion. Thomas Emerson, the lawyer who argued the challenge to the Connecticut law in *Griswold*, responded to Warren's suggestion by insisting that recognizing a constitutional right of access to contraceptives did not lead to a right to abort because abortion "does not occur in the privacy of the home" and also "involves the taking what has begun to be a life."[318] Warren, however, embraced the idea, for he proposed to include such a statement in an opinion that ultimately was not published by the Court.[319]

Emerson quickly abandoned the position he had taken in his argument. Almost immediately after the decision in *Griswold* was handed down, Emerson suggested the just such an extension of the right of privacy in passing remark in a law review article.[320] Emerson did not note his own denial of that proposition during the oral argument of *Griswold*. He privately suggested that it would take 20 years to build a bridge between the privacy right of contraception and his proposed privacy right of abortion.[321] It took only six years.

So commonplace has the notion become that a right to choose to abort derives from the right of privacy that it might now be difficult to realize just how unlikely this proposition appeared even to those who supported the right to choose some 30 years ago. The American Civil Liberties Union concluded in 1967, that "restrictive abortion laws..., while unduly restrictive, are not so unreasonable as to unconstitutional.... [S]ociety could decide...to place such value on the life of the unborn child as to render abortion possible only in a narrow range of circumstances."[322] Young attorney Roy Lucas, whose article first developed the arguments for a constitutionally protected freedom to abort,[323] later recalled that his professors "kind of laughed at me."[324] Norman Dorsen, Lucas's faculty advisor on his research paper and a noted civil libertarian, was distinctly unenthusiastic about Lucas' project.[325] As late as 1970, journalist Linda Greenhouse described the claim to a constitutional right to abortion as "fantastic, illusory. The Constitution is searched in vain for any mention of it."[326] Yet to the surprise even of the purveyors of the right-to-abortion rhetoric,[327] the Supreme Court of the United States largely embraced this extreme position almost immediately upon its first presentation to the Court in *Roe v. Wade*.[328] And without the decision in *Roe,* it remains far from clear whether, or when, the ordinary political processes in the United States would have recognized a right to choose to abort.[329]

---

318. GARROW, *supra* note 23, at 240.

319. BERNARD SCHWARTZ, THE UNPUBLISHED OPINIONS OF THE WARREN COURT 239 (1985). Chief Justice Warren initially expressed doubt about the privacy theory and expressly rejected the idea that the holding in *Griswold* could extend to abortion during the conference discussion of *Griswold*. THE SUPREME COURT IN CONFERENCE (1940–1985): THE PRIVATE DISCUSSIONS BEHIND NEARLY 300 SUPREME COURT DECISIONS 800 (Del Dickson ed. 2001).

320. Emerson, *supra* note 310, at 228–33.

321. LAZARUS, *supra* note 28, at 346.

322. Quoted in GARROW, *supra* note 23, at 313.

323. Lucas, *supra* note 58.

324. GARROW, *supra* note 23, at 337.

325. *Id.*

326. Linda Greenhouse, *Constitutional Question: Is There a Right to Abortion?*, N.Y. TIMES MAG., Jan. 25, 1970, at 30. *See also* KERRY JACOBY, SOULS, BODIES, SPIRITS: THE DRIVE TO ABOLISH ABORTION SINCE 1973, at 5 (1998); Devins, *supra* note 9, at 1433, 1441–42.

327. CONDIT, *supra* note 32, at 103–04, 112–17; D'EMILIO & FREEDMAN, *supra* note 222, at 315; FERREE & HESS, *supra* note 91, at 150; LADER, *supra* note 188, at 68; DAVID ROHDE & HAROLD SPAETH, SUPREME COURT DECISION MAKING 151, 170 n.33 (1976); RUBIN, *supra* note 9, at ix, 4–5.

328. 410 U.S. 113 (1973).

329. Devins, *supra* note 9, at 1437–38.

We know a good deal of the behind the scenes story of *Roe v. Wade.* Not only have several serious scholars interviewed most of the principal participants and published accounts based on that research,[330] but both "Jane Roe" and her lead attorney have published autobiographies.[331] Given the 20 or so years that elapsed between the events recounted and the various books recording those events, there is room to suspect distorted memories or worse in these accounts.[332] Still, the several accounts reported from the perspectives of now hostile people agree on enough particulars that we can be fairly confident in the following account.

Norma McCorvey (Jane Roe) was leading an unsettled, one might say unstable, life in Dallas, Texas; she would later write that she measured economic success by being able to "do a whole week's worth of grocery shopping in one trip."[333] An unwed mother, she had surrendered custody of her first daughter to her mother and had given up her second child for adoption.[334] Then she found herself pregnant again and sought an abortion.[335] McCorvey herself had come from a dysfunctional family,[336] and seemed unable to establish a family as an adult that would function better.[337] One reviewer of McCorvey's autobiography concluded that had abortions been legal when McCorvey was born, she herself probably would have been aborted.[338] McCorvey recalls that she became involved in the abortion litigation not because she held any particular opinions about the law, but because she "was simply at the end of my rope."[339]

In searching for an abortion, McCorvey began to claim that her pregnancy had resulted from a rape in the hope that this would make obtaining an abortion easier.[340] She confirmed in her recent autobiography that there was no rape.[341] Eventually, McCorvey became the client of Linda Coffee and Sarah Weddington. Coffee and Weddington were two of only five women students who entered the University of Texas School of Law in 1965 in a class with 120 men. They took on McCorvey's case a little over a year after their graduation from law school and with virtually no experience in the practice of law.[342] As women seeking legal employment in 1967, they had found it difficult to obtain positions with a law firm. It was their first contested case as lawyers; they saw the case as an opportunity to change the law, not as a source of of direct income.[343] Weddington got the major credit for the outcome because she twice argued the case before the Supreme Court.

---

330. *See* FAUX, *supra* note 203; GARROW, *supra* note 23; JEFFRIES, *supra* note 278, at 332–52; LAZARUS, *supra* note 28, at 345–72; BOB WOODWARD & SCOTT ARMSTRONG, THE BRETHREN: INSIDE THE SUPREME COURT (1979); Bob Woodward, *The Abortion Papers,* WASH. POST, Jan. 22, 1989, at D1.

331. MCCORVEY & MEISLER, *supra* note 295; WEDDINGTON, *supra* note 203.

332. *See* Kevin McMunigal, *Of Causes and Clients: Two Tales of* Roe v. Wade, 47 HASTINGS L.J. 779 (1996).

333. MCCORVEY & MEISLER, *supra* note 295, at 35.

334. *Id.,* at 69–86.

335. *Id.* at 117. *See also* HADLEY, *supra* note 66, at 2–3.

336. *Id.* at 150.

337. *See generally* GARROW, *supra* note 23, at 402–04; RISEN & THOMAS, *supra* note 195, at 24–26.

338. Fawn Vrazo, *The Story of Jane Roe: A Life of Abuse, Regrets,* PHILA. INQUIRER, June 5, 1994, at E3.

339. MCCORVEY & MEISLER, *supra* note 295, at 115.

340. *Id.* at 109–80; McCorvey Statement, *supra* note 295, at 44. *See also* CARL ROWAN, DREAM MAKERS, DREAM BREAKERS 323 (1993); WEDDINGTON, *supra* note 203, at 52; Sarah Weddington, *The Donohue Lecture Series:* Roe v. Wade: *Past and Future,* 24 SUFF. U. L. REV. 601, 603 (1990).

341. MCCORVEY & MEISLER, *supra* note 295, at 179–80.

342. On the careers of Weddington and Coffee generally and their involvement in *Roe* in particular, see WEDDINGTON, *supra* note 203. *See also* GARROW, *supra* note 23, at 393–407, 433–44, 462–63, 492–93, 498–509, 513–17, 521–28, 564–65, 567–71, 600–01; RISEN & THOMAS, *supra* note 195, at 23–24. *See generally* Joan Steinman, *Public Trial, Pseudonymous Parties: When Should Litigants Be Permitted to Keep Their Identities Confidential?,* 37 HASTINGS L.J. 1 (1985).

343. Weddington, *supra* note 340, at 603–04.

Weddington and Coffee filed suit on McCorvey's behalf, using a standard lawyer's pseudonym of "Jane Roe" to preserve her client's anonymity.[344] The anonymous name was aptly symbolic for McCorvey virtually disappeared as a real person in the proceedings. Indeed, Weddington would later admit that in her mind "Jane Roe" represented "all women, not just one," and that she considered McCorvey as merely "ancillary to the primary focus on all women," a "vehicle for presenting the larger issues."[345] Weddington reminds us that "the case was not for one person; it was not just for Jane Roe, it was a class action for all women who might become pregnant and want the option of legal abortion to be available."[346] This perhaps explains why Weddington referred to her client throughout her autobiography as "Jane Roe," although McCorvey had revealed her identity years earlier.

Weddington and Coffee kept McCorvey out of the loop; McCorvey had virtually no involvement in the litigation other than providing an almost fictional plaintiff.[347] McCorvey's lawyers never consulted her on any question regarding their strategy.[348] Indeed, Weddington would later comment that "All Jane Roe did was sign a one page affidavit. She was pregnant and didn't want to be. That was her total involvement in the case."[349] It never seemed to occur to Weddington that by focusing on the collective interests of all women, she was treating McCorvey exactly like the governmental institutions that Weddington was seeking to change—institutions that focus on the collective interests of society as a justification for ignoring the interests of individual women seeking an abortion.[350]

One might excuse the failure to consult McCorvey. McCorvey, 21 years old, knocked up for the third time, and spewing lies, was a client who could hardly make choices about her own life, let alone choices that would affect the fate of millions of women.[351] Still, failure to consult the client was a major failure according to the legal profession's ethical codes.[352] Nor did the attorneys attempt to help McCorvey obtain the abortion she sought. What excuse was there for Weddington or Coffee deciding not to help McCorvey in her immediate crisis? Weddington herself had obtained a Mexican abortion while she was in law school, only a couple of years before McCorvey sought Weddington's assistance.[353] Weddington never mentioned this to McCorvey; nor did Weddington offer to help McCorvey obtain the abortion she sought even though Weddington was a co-founder of an abortion referral service then active in Texas.[354] In fact, by her own account Weddington's involvement in the *Roe* case grew out of her involvement with the abor-

---

344. WEDDINGTON, *supra* note 203, at 61. *See also* RISEN & THOMAS, *supra* note 195, at 26. At least in this case there really was a "Jane Roe." It appears that, in at least some of the suits to secure abortion rights that were brought on behalf of plaintiffs named "Doe" and "Roe" and the like, there was in fact no actual person behind the name, which, if true, should render the suit invalid under American law. *See* JAMES TARSNEY, *DOE v. GOMEZ AND THE JURISPRUDENCE OF DECEIT* (1996).

345. WEDDINGTON, *supra* note 203, at 54. At times, McCorvey also seems to speak and write as if "Jane Roe" were someone else. MCCORVEY & MEISLER, *supra* note 295, at 155, 191, 195.

346. Sarah Weddington, *Keynote Address: Reflections on the Twenty-Fifth Anniversary of* Roe v. Wade, 62 ALB. L. REV. 811, 813 (1999).

347. *See* Devins, *supra* note 9, at 1444 n.42; McCorvey Statement, *supra* note 295, at 44–45.

348. MCCORVEY & MEISLER, *supra* note 295, at 137 (McCorvey never knew of the decision to file a class action suit instead a suit solely on her behalf). *See also* WEDDINGTON, *supra* note 203, at 51–53, 260. *See generally* McMunigal, *supra* note 332, at 802–03.

349. McMunigal, *supra* note 332, at 790.

350. *Id.* at 805–07. *See generally* KATHY FERGUSON, THE FEMINIST CASE AGAINST BUREAUCRACY (1984); Kenney Hegland, *Beyond Enthusiasm and Commitment*, 13 ARIZ. L. REV. 805, 812–13 (1971).

351. McMunigal, *supra* note 332, at 812.

352. AMERICAN BAR ASS'N, CODE OF PROFESSIONAL RESPONSIBILITY, Ethical Considerations EC 7-5, EC 7-7, EC-7-8 (1970) ("ABA CODE").

353. *See* WEDDINGTON, *supra* note 203, at 11–15 (recounting her own abortion).

354. *Id.,* at 35–36.

tion referral service.[355] Apparently, Weddington kept silent about this possibility because she feared losing the only plaintiff she had with the necessary legal standing to challenge the law. This is consistent with Weddington's view that the good of the cause trumps individual self-interest. She was also willing to sacrifice herself for the cause. Despite the considerable difficulty she had finding her first job after graduation, she quit the job when pressured to abandon the case.[356]

McCorvey waited naively and in some desperation for the abortion that she thought would follow the trial court's ruling.[357] She never knew Weddington had had an abortion until she read about it in Weddington's autobiography.[358] McCorvey was furious when she learned this truth, for she had to go through giving birth and giving up her child for adoption, an experience so traumatic that it drove McCorvey to attempt suicide.[359] Weddington dismissed the entire question with one cold, simple sentence: "It was too late for Jane Roe; she gave birth early in the summer and placed the baby for adoption."[360] And so, Weddington—crusader for women's right to choose whether to carry a pregnancy to term—dismissed the possibility of choice for Norma McCorvey.[361] It puts one in mind of Derek Bell's observation that although idealism is a rarer motivation for lawyers than greed, it is harder to control.[362]

Weddington sees no ethical problem in her concealing from McCorvey the information about how she could obtain an abortion or in not consulting McCorvey about the case. Another ethical problem arises from Weddington and Coffee's failure to use the rape story. This alone seems to raise an ethical question that Weddington has thought about, at least after the fact, but only in regard to having not revealed that part of her client's story was a lie. This, however, was not a major failing because Weddington and Coffee decided not to use the rape story in the litigation.

In her autobiography, Weddington treats the failure to use the story as more or less a matter of luck.[363] Weddington, moreover, insists that lawyers' ethics precluded her from challenging her client's story.[364] Weddington, in a later letter, went further, insisting that she prevented McCorvey from telling this story to a court because she knew the story was a lie.[365] Her claim thus at best skirts the truth, for lawyers' ethics clearly obligate her to refuse to present a factual claim to a court if she knew that the witness was lying.[366] More candidly, Weddington indicates in her autobiography, published before McCorvey began to criticize Weddington publicly, only that she could not prove the allegation while frankly admitting that using the rape story would undercut Weddington's goal of the total abolition of all abortion laws.[367]

Weddington never discussed with her client the decision to ignore the rape story. McCorvey was unaware of that strategy until 20 years later, during which time she fretted over the possible

---

355. *Id.* at 45.

356. *Id.* at 83.

357. McCorvey & Meisler, *supra* note 295, at 127.

358. Alex Witchel, *Of* Roe, *Dreams and Choices: At Home with Norma McCorvey,* N.Y. Times, July 28, 1994, at C1, C9. *See also* McCorvey & Meisler, *supra* note 295, at 127; McCorvey Statement, *supra* note 295, at 44.

359. McCorvey & Meisler, *supra* note 295, at 127–35.

360. Weddington, *supra* note 203, at 69.

361. McMunigal, *supra* note 332, at 806–07.

362. Derek Bell, jr., *Serving Two Masters: Integration Ideals and Client Interests in School Desegregation Litigation,* 85 Yale L.J. 470 (1976). *See also* McMunigal, *supra* note 332, at 808–12.

363. Weddington, *supra* note 203, at 257.

364. Weddington, *supra* note 340, at 604. *See also* Judges, *supra* note 71, at 139–40.

365. Sarah Weddington, *Sarah Weddington Responds,* 78 Nat. F. 47 (No. 1, winter 1998).

366. ABA Code, *supra* note 352, Disciplinary Rule DR 7-102(A)(5). *See also* American Bar Ass'n, Model Rules of Professional Conduct Rule 3.3(a)(4) (1994).

367. Weddington, *supra* note 203, at 52–53. *See* McMunigal, *supra* note 332, at 795–96.

consequences should her lie be found out.[368] Nowhere in her autobiography did Weddington mention whether she had ever considered at the time or later whether a more limited strategy of focusing on the alleged rape might have been in McCorvey's best interest. Indeed, Weddington has acknowledged knowing that there was an informal policy in Texas of allowing abortions in cases of rape although no such exception appears in the Texas abortion statute.[369] If so, it would have been imperative for Weddington to pursue the rape question rather than to ignore it. Weddington, however, comments on this informal policy more than 100 pages after indicating her choice to ignore the rape story; she seems not to connect the two items in any way.[370] It appears more likely that Weddington simply didn't care. In fact, Weddington was so unconcerned about the rape allegation that she confirms in her autobiography that she was "startled by many of the details" of McCorvey's story when she read a detailed recounting of the "rape" in a magazine three years later.[371] The rape story was simply inconvenient to Weddington's goal of overturning all abortion laws—including laws that allowed abortion in case of rape.[372]

In reviewing Weddington's approach to the case, even regarding the non-use of the rape story, one is drawn back to a more basic question about an attorney's relation to her client than the question that Weddington now seeks to raise. Did Sarah Weddington and her co-counsel, Linda Coffee, ignore the rape story (and the possibility of helping to arrange an abortion for Norma McCorvey) because they were too intent on using her for their own purposes rather than on serving the client's needs?[373] After all, focusing on the alleged rape probably had a greater chance of success, and thus probably could have been resolved more quickly—perhaps quickly enough to enable McCorvey to have her abortion.[374] Such a focus on the lawyer's desires or the needs of women generally, instead of on the needs of the client, is a clear violation of the most basic tenets of lawyers' ethics.[375] As a sympathetic observer summarized Weddington's decision to ignore the rape story,

> [u]ltimately, then, it was Weddington's choice not to pursue a reform strategy rather than the language of the Texas statute that rendered McCorvey's rape allegation irrelevant. Weddington's justification obscures this point with its suggestion that the terms of the Texas statute rather than the lawyer's choice of strategy dictated exclusion of the rape allegation from the *Roe* complaint. Here a façade of apparent legal inevitability masks Weddington's exercise of power and disregard of McCorvey's interests and insulates them from scrutiny of challenge.... In this story, the idea of service to an individual client has no particular significance.... The interests of the cause are given primary value, she views herself as representing the collective interests of women rather than McCorvey's interests, and the individual interests of McCorvey are subordinated to the collective interests of women.[376]

---

368. McCorvey & Meisler, *supra* note 295, at 155, 180. *See* McMunigal, *supra* note 332, at 799.

369. Weddington, *supra* note 203, at 163.

370. McMunigal, *supra* note 334, at 794.

371. Weddington, *supra* note 203, at 256. For the article, see Joseph Bell, *A Landmark Decision,* Good Housekeeping, June 1973, at 77. *See generally* McMunigal, *supra* note 332, at 797–98.

372. McMunigal, *supra* note 332, at 791–99.

373. *See, e.g.,* Garrow, *supra* note 23, at 404; Risen & Thomas, *supra* note 195, at 26–27; Margaret Farrell, *Revisiting* Roe v. Wade*: Substance and Due Process in the Abortion Debate,* 68 Ind. L.J. 269, 282–85 (1993); McMunigal, *supra* note 332, at 798–99, 808–10. For a brief account of another activist lawyer's efforts to recruit clients for an abortion suit to suit her needs rather than the client's (albeit for *amicus* briefs), see Colker, Pregnant Men, *supra* note 68, at 9–17, 31–35.

374. McMunigal, *supra* note 332, at 793–94.

375. ABA Code, *supra* note 352, Ethical Consideration EC 5-1. *See also* ABA Code, *supra* note 352, Disciplinary Rule DR-5-101(A). *See generally* Deborah Rhode, *Class Conflicts in Class Actions,* 34 Stan. L. Rev. 1183 (1982); Ann Southworth, *Lawyer-Client Decision Making in Civil Rights and Poverty Practice: An Empirical Study of Lawyers' Norms,* 9 Geo. J. Legal Ethics 1101 (1996).

376. McMunigal, *supra* note 332, at 796, 801, 803. *See also id.* at 809–19.

No wonder Norma McCorvey now angrily proclaims that Sarah Weddington was indifferent to McCorvey's needs.[377]

McCorvey's ultimate disaffection from the cause that she unwittingly came to symbolize reached the point that she underwent a religious conversion, was baptized by an Evangelical leader of "Operation Rescue" (a leading anti-abortion activist group), and declared "I'm pro-life. I think I have always been pro-life, I just didn't know it."[378] Three years later, she became a Catholic.[379] How to explain McCorvey's conversion would be something of a problem for those defending *Roe* if they cared enough to mention it. Most do not, and others dismiss it as simply another example of Norma McCorvey's weak personality and her tendency to allow others to dominate her.[380] David Garrow, on the other hand, suggests that McCorvey's conversion "actually had little to do with abortion and far more with how Benham gave her the warmth and respect she rarely had felt from *Roe's* supporters."[381] McCorvey indeed records incident after incident of being neglected or insulted by leaders of the "pro-choice" movement when she did attempt to become a public supporter of abortion rights.[382] And whether Garrow realizes it or not, his "excuse" for her defection is more damning of the pro-abortion activists than if McCorvey had converted out of a considered reaction to abortion itself. In any event, McCorvey now tours the country denouncing abortion rights. She even filed a motion in 2003 to undo the decision in *Roe v. Wade*[383]—something she was unlikely to achieve. Her conversion is not complete, however, as she apparently still supports a right to abort during the first 13 weeks of pregnancy.[384]

Weddington and Coffee's approach to McCorvey was consistent to the very end. When the Supreme Court ruled in McCorvey's favor, Weddington personally shared the news with her colleagues in the cause, but made only cursory attempts to call McCorvey.[385] McCorvey found out about the decision "just like everyone else"—by reading a newspaper.[386]

Weddington's behavior contrasts with the behavior of the attorneys (principally Margie Pitts Hames) in the case that was argued and decided along with *Roe* in the Supreme Court, *Doe v. Bolton*.[387] The attorneys for the plaintiff in *Doe* not only helped to arrange an abortion for Sandra Race Bensing ("Mary Doe," now Sandra Bensing-Cano), but also helped to finance it. In the end, however, Bensing chose not to have the abortion.[388] Despite the greater caring exhibited by Hames, Bensing-Cano has raised questions about Hames' behavior as well. Later Bensing-Cano would also become an ant-abortion activist who became involved with Operation Rescue.[389] She

---

377. McCorvey & Meisler, *supra* note 295, at 127; McCorvey Statement, *supra* note 295, at 44–45; Witchel, *supra* note 358, at C9.

378. *"Jane Roe" Switches Sides on Abortion*, N.Y. Times, Aug. 11, 1995, at A12. *See also* Jacoby, *supra* note 326, at 44–45, n.1; Norma McCorvey & Gary Thomas, Won by Love (1997); McCorvey Statement, *supra* note 295, at 44–45.

379. Richard Ostling, *"Roe" of Noted Case Becomes a Catholic: Norma McCorvey Believes a Message from God Propelled Her Back into the Church*, Phila. Inquirer, Nov. 8, 1998, at A7.

380. McMunigal, *supra* note 332, at 804.

381. Garrow, *supra* note 23, at 720.

382. McCorvey & Meisler, *supra* note 295, at 157–58, 194. *See generally* McCorvey & Thomas, *supra* note 378.

383. *"Roe" Plaintiff Files to Undo Landmark Case*, Phila. Inquirer, June 18, 2003, at A8.

384. Hadley, *supra* note 56, at 3; Steve Waldman & Ginny Carroll, *Roe v. Roe*, Newsweek, Aug. 21, 1995, at 22.

385. Weddington, *supra* note 203, at 148 ("I assumed she had heard or would see press reports.).

386. McCorvey & Meisler, *supra* note 295, at 140.

387. 410 U.S. 179 (1973).

388. Garrow, *supra* note 23, at 444–45; Lazarus, *supra* note 28, at 348; Mark Curriden, Doe v. Bolton: *Mary Doe Has a Change of Heart, Pickets Abortion Clinics*, ABA J., July 1989, at 26.

389. David Treadwell, *Abortion Plaintiffs Now on Opposite Sides: Similar Pasts, Different Viewpoints for* Roe, Doe, L.A. Times, June 15, 1989, at 1.

now claims that in fact she had never wanted an abortion and was pressured into agreeing to one by Margie Hames.[390] Taking into account Hames' misrepresentation to the court that "Doe" did not have the abortion because she was unable to obtain one, with no mention of her decision not to have an abortion, Bensing-Cano's claim that she never wanted an abortion just might be true.

In the trial of *Roe,* Weddington and Coffee were fortunate to come before a three-judge panel that included a judge (Sarah Hughes) for whom Coffee had clerked only the year before and who was herself openly lobbying the Texas legislature for repeal of the Texas abortion statute.[391] Judge Hughes and the other judges asked no questions about the alleged rape. As usually the facts of a case are not reviewed by an appellate court, this lie, repeated frequently in open court, was carried up without question and appears in the Supreme Court opinion as well.[392] Now that it is known to be a lie, a remarkable number of supporters of abortion rights are completely untroubled by the fact that *Roe* was based on a lie.[393] Several well-regarded defenses of *Roe* have even relied heavily on the emotional appeal of the supposed rape.[394] As we shall see, that was not the only lie in the case. As realization that the "rape" was a fiction has spread, however, defenders of *Roe* have tended simply to ignore it rather than confronting the question of what role this fictional allegation might have had in shaping the Court's reaction to the case.[395]

The centerpiece of the first article to argue at length the claim that there is a constitutionally protected right to abort was the claim that the abortion laws constituted an establishment of religion.[396] Roy Lucas, the author of that article, fancied himself the genius of the abortion reform movement, although others, including Sarah Weddington, apparently found him to be more of a bother than a help; Lucas, by then a practicing lawyer, did provide the first draft of the lead brief for the Supreme Court in *Roe.*[397] Lucas, by the way, allowed his personal animosities towards other would-be gurus of the abortion reform movement as well as his recognition of how weak Means' work actually was to lead him virtually to exclude from his draft of the lead brief in *Roe* any reference to Cyril Means' historical work.[398] David Tundermann, one of Lucas' law clerks, reviewed Means' article and noted that Means'

> own conclusions sometimes strain credibility: in the presence of manifest public outcry over fetal deaths just prior to the passage of New York's 1872 abortion law, Means disclaims any impact upon the legislature of this popular pressure (even though the statute itself copies the language of a pro-fetal group).

---

390. Curriden, *supra* note 387.

391. GARROW, *supra* note 23, at 484.

392. 410 U.S. at 142.

393. *See, e.g.,* O'BRIEN, *supra* note 71, at 23–24; TRIBE, *supra* note 12, at 4–5; Ruth Colker, *Feminist Litigation: An Oxymoron?—A Study of the Briefs Filed in* William L. Webster v. Reproductive Health Services, 13 HARV. WOMEN'S L.J. 137, 161–63 (1990).

394. *See, e.g.,* COLKER, ABORTION & DIALOGUE, *supra* note 68, at 102–04, 126 n.3; BARBARA MILBAUER & BERT OBRENTZ, THE LAW GIVETH: LEGAL ASPECTS OF THE ABORTION CONTROVERSY 14 (1983).

395. *See, e.g.,* CRAIG & O'BRIEN, *supra* note 9, at 5–14.

396. Lucas, *supra* note 58.

397. WEDDINGTON, *supra* note 203, at 84–98. *See also* FAUX, *supra* note 203, at 171–74, 216, 219–224, 229–36, 277–78; GARROW, *supra* note 23, at 334–39, 351–53, 365–67, 371–72, 374, 379–84, 386–88, 408–10, 416–17, 421, 432–33, 459–64, 467–71, 474–75, 491–510, 513–17, 522–23, 528, 539–41, 563–64, 573, 604–05, 617–20, 630, 640; RUBIN, *supra* note 9, at 43–44, 51, 54; Devins, *supra* note 9, at 1441, 1444.

398. GARROW, *supra* note 23, at 493–94, 500–01, 503, 514–15. *See* Cyril Means, jr., *The Law of New York Concerning Abortion and the Status of the Foetus, 1664–1968: A Case of Cessation of Constitutionality,* 14 N.Y.L.F. 411 (1968) ("Means I"); Cyril Means, jr., *The Phoenix of Abortional Freedom: Is a Penumbral Right or Ninth-Amendment Right About to Arise from the Nineteenth-Century Legislative Ashes of a Fourteenth-Century Common-Law Liberty?,* 17 N.Y.L.F. 335 (1971) ("Means II"). On the quality of Means' work, see Chapters 3–7.

Tundermann concluded his analysis of the Means article these terms:

> Where the important thing is to win the case no matter how, however, I suppose I agree
> with Means's technique: begin with a scholarly attempt at historical research; if it does-
> n't work, fudge it as necessary; write a piece so long that others will read only your in-
> troduction and conclusion; then keep citing it until courts begin picking it up. This pre-
> serves the guise of impartial scholarship while advancing the proper ideological goals.[399]

We can forgive Tundermann his candor as he was at the time a summer law clerk after completing the first year of law school at the University of Cincinnati.[400] None of this phased Sarah
Weddington who chose to rely heavily on Cyril Means' purported history, referring to it no less
than three times during her fist oral argument of *Roe* and deriving her concept of the evolution
of abortion laws from his work.[401] Margie Hames also referred to the Means article in her first
oral argument of *Doe v. Bolton*.[402] In turn, Justice Harry Blackmun would rely on the Means' articles in constructing his own spurious history of abortion laws.[403]

*Roe* was first argued to the Court in 1971. Weddington presented her argument strongly.[404]
Jay Floyd, arguing on behalf of the Dallas District Attorney, made a short and lame argument,
opening with a weak joke about arguing a case against women and then repeatedly answering
questions from the Court based upon his own admitted surmises, as if he had not done his
homework.[405] During the justice's discussion of the case after the argument, five of the seven
justices then on the Court supported declaring the Texas law unconstitutional, but they divided over the rationale for that holding.[406] Justices William Brennan and William Douglas

---

399. *Memorandum by David Tundermann to Roy Lucas, Aug. 5, 1971,* as quoted in Garrow, *supra* note 23,
at 891–92 n.41.

400. Garrow, *supra* note 23, at 498.

401. Roe v. Wade *Oral Arguments,* 8 Seton Hall Const. L.J. 315, 323–25 (1998). *See also* Garrow, *supra*
note 23, at 524–25.

402. Garrow, *supra* note 23, at 527.

403. *Id.* at 589–90. Blackmun would cite Mean's two articles a total of seven times, and no other source on
the history of abortion more than once. *Roe,* 410 U.S. at 136–52, 158 n. 54.

404. Roe v. Wade *Oral Arguments, supra* note 401, at 318–29.

405. *Id.* at 329–38.

406. Lazarus, *supra* note 28, at 349–50; The Supreme Court in Conference, *supra* note 319, at
806–09. Only the nine justices are present during the conferences in which they discuss and decide cases; no
clerk, secretary, stenographer, or any other observer is allowed in and no official transcript is kept. Several justices made their private papers public after their retirement or death, including the private notes on conferences kept by Justices Brennan, Douglas, and Marshall relating to *Roe. See* The Supreme Court in Conference, *supra,* at xix–xxvii, 3–7, 804–15. Lazarus's research included these records and disclosures from a
number of law clerks to the justices (including Lazarus). The disclosures by the law clerks has earned Lazarus
opprobrium for breaching the confidentiality of the Court even though several of the justices for which the
clerks worked had made their papers public and law clerks have been interviewed by other historians. *See, e.g.,*
Joan Biskopic, *Ex-Supreme Court Clerk's Book Breaks the Silence,* Wash. Post, Mar. 4, 1998, at A8; Adam
Cohen, *Courting Controversy: A New Book by an Insider Claims Law Clerks Have Inordinate Influence over the
Supreme Court,* Time, Mar. 30, 1998, at 31; Martha Davis, *Book Review:* Closed Chambers, 24 Thurgood
Marshall L. Rev. 219 (1998); Christopher Drahozal, *The Arrogance of Certainty: Trust, Confidentiality, and
the Supreme Court* (book rev.), 47 Kan. L. Rev. 121 (1998); David Garrow, *Dissenting Opinion: A Witness from
Inside the Supreme Court Is Not Impressed* (book rev.), N.Y. Times, Apr. 19, 1998, at 26; Gideon Kanner, *"Holy
Shit, I'm Going to Write the Law of the Land"* (book rev.), 1 Greenbag 2d 425 (1998); Sally Kenney, *Puppeteers
or Agents? What Lazarus's* Closed Chambers *Adds to Our Understanding of Law Clerks at the U.S. Supreme
Court,* 25 Law & Soc. Inquiry 185, 211–19 (2000); Alex Kozinski, *Conduct Unbecoming* (book rev.), 108 Yale
L.J. 835 (1999); David O'Brien, *Breaching Confidences, Court Bashing, and Bureaucratic Justice,* 1 Jurist 19
(1998); Richard Painter, *Open Chamber?* (book rev.), 97 Mich. L. Rev. 1430 (1999); Carter Phillips, *Looking
into Closed Chambers: A Lawyer View,* 42 Am. Law. 44 (May 1998); Gretchen Craft Rubin, *Betraying a Trust,*
Wash. Post, June 17, 1998, at A27; Kathleen Sullivan, *Behind the Crimson Curtain,* N.Y. Rev. Books, Oct. 8,
1998, at 15; Mark Tushnet, *Hype and History,* 1 Jurist 22 (1998).

concluded that the Texas statute was unconstitutionally vague. Justice Thurgood Marshall would prefer to find that the Texas statute unconstitutionally invaded Jane Roe's "liberty" under the Fourteenth Amendment. Justice Potter Stewart indicated that the Texas statute was unconstitutional without indicating a ground for his conclusion. Justice Blackmun concluded that the Texas statute was unconstitutional because it did not protect doctors' rights; he concluded that the Georgia statute whose constitutionality was argued the same day was a "fine statute." (All of the justices were much less critical of the Georgia statute than they were of the Texas statute.) Chief Justice Warren Berger and Justice Byron White would have found the statute constitutional.

The case was set over for reargument for the fall of 1972. Chief Justice Burger's order for reargument was strongly opposed by several of the justices who apparently feared they would lose the apparent majority in favor of constitutionalizing abortion rights.[407] Sarah Weddington's second argument was as strong as the first, focusing on fleshing out the details of her first argument.[408] The state's second argument—by Robert Flowers of the state Attorney General's office—was much stronger than Floyd's had been,[409] but the damage had already been done.

Even if the second round of arguments had not changed much, the delay occasioned by the reargument might actually have helped those who favored abortion rights. At the conference where the rearguments were discussed, the justices were in about the same position as in their discussion after the first arguments of the cases, except Blackmun who now wanted to hold both statutes unconstitutional.[410] The two new justices split—Lewis Powell, jr., agreed with Blackmun's approach, while William Rehnquist indicated that he agreed with White. Blackmun had at first written a much narrower opinion for *Roe*, striking down the Texas abortion statute as unconstitutionally vague, only to strike out in the broad directions of the ultimate opinion under pressure from Brennan, Douglas, and Stewart. Apparently Blackmun had rewritten his draft opinion even before the case was reargued in October 1972.[411]

---

Dean Anthony Kronman, who had written a laudatory "blurb" for the back cover of Lazarus' book describing it as "well-researched and wonderfully written," retracted it after coming under pressure from influential Yale alumni. Several newspapers criticized Kronman's reversal as well as the notion that the deliberations of the Court should be secret. *See, e.g.,* Tony Mauro, *Yale Dean Caught in Book Controversy: Head of Law School Apologizes for Blurb on High Court Tell-All,* U.S.A. Today, May 10, 19999, at 10A; Robert Reno, *Reno at Large: A Supreme Court Gag Order Quiets the Wrong Talkers,* Newsday, May 12, 1999, at A51. Apparently, the *New York Times* did not consider this story to be news "fit to print." For a favorable review, see Erwin Chemerinsky, *Opening* Closed Chambers (book rev.), 108 Yale L.J. 1087 (1999). Some have raised significant questions about the reliability of Lazarus's factual statements. *See* Garrow, *supra,* at 27; Kenney, *supra,* at 215–19; Kozinski, *supra,* at 851–55; David O'Brien, *A Disturbing Portrait,* 81 Judicature 214, 214–16 (1998). *See also* Risen & Thomas, *supra* note 195, at 29.

407. Faux, *supra* note 203, at 284–86; Garrow, *supra* note 23, at 552–60; Lazarus, *supra* note 201, at 350–55; O'Brien, *supra* note 71, at 28–29; Risen & Thomas, *supra* note 195, at 31–33; James Simon, The Center Holds: The Power Struggle inside the Rehnquist Court 106 (1995); The Supreme Court in Conference, *supra* note 319, at 809–10; Melvin Urofsky, The Douglas Letters 181–85 (1987); Woodward & Armstrong, *supra* note 329, at 271–84; Woodward, *supra* note 330, at B6.

408. Roe v. Wade *Oral Arguments, supra* note 401, at 339–49. *See also* May It Please the Court 344–50 (Peter Irons & Stephanie Guitton eds. 1993).

409. Roe v. Wade *Oral Arguments, supra* note 401, at 349–62. *See also* May It Please the Court, *supra* note 408, at 350–54.

410. The Supreme Court in Conference, *supra* note 319, at 810–12. *See also* Lazarus, *supra* note 28, at 355.

411. *See* Craig & O'Brien, *supra* note 9, at 18–24; Epstein & Kobylka, *supra* note 57, at 197–98; Faux, *supra* note 203, at 266–76, 289–302; Garrow, *supra* note 23, at 528–38, 547–61, 573–76, 580–87; Lazarus, *supra* note 28, at 351–57; O'Brien, *supra* note 71, at 29–36; Risen & Thomas, *supra* note 195, at 31–33; Rubin, *supra* note 9, at 64–66; Bernard Schwartz, The Ascent of Pragmatism: The Burger Court in

Newly appointed Justice Lewis Powell, jr., played a major role in firming up the pro-abortion coalition.[412] Some years earlier, Powell had himself helped cover up an illegal abortion involving a young office assistant in his law firm.[413] Powell and Blackmun were both close to several physicians who apparently helped influence their attitudes towards abortion laws, and both had outspoken daughters who had stressed to their fathers the need for change in the abortion laws.[414] Powell apparently was the source of the notion that "viability" should be the point at which a state had some, albeit a very limited, right to protect fetal life.[415] Powell's later recanting his support for *Bowers v. Hardwick*[416] (the case upholding the constitutionality of criminalizing consenting private homosexual conduct) has been widely noted,[417] but his later comment that the *Roe* and *Doe* opinions were "the worst opinions I ever joined"[418] has been more or less completely ignored. Powell seems to have been plagued by considerable self-doubt throughout his tenure on the Court and after his retirement.[419]

Justice Potter Stewart, on the other hand, insisted that the majority opinion declare explicitly that a fetus is not a person, at least under the Fourteenth Amendment, or he would refuse to join the opinion.[420] Blackmun dutifully included a whole paragraph to make the point.[421] Twenty-three years later, after he had retired, Blackmun would tell C-Span that this was the only part of the opinion that he would tamper with if he were in a position to rewrite it.[422] Stewart, on the other hand, still wrote a note to Blackmun in which he decried the Blackmun's trimester framework as being legislative: "I appreciate the inevitability and indeed wisdom of the dicta [*i.e.*, the trimester framework] in the Court's opinion, but I wonder about the desirability of the dicta being quite so inflexibly 'legislative.'"[423] Stewart's willingness to join the *Roe* majority mirrors his willingness, only three years later, to join Blackmun's majority opinion in *Planned Parenthood of Central Missouri v. Danforth*[424]—an opinion that Stewart found so distasteful that he told one of his clerks that "[t]his is one of those cases where I'll have to hold my nose and jump."[425]

Blackmun also privately acknowledged the arbitrariness of the trimester framework, defending it merely as no more arbitrary than any other point that might be selected during pregnancy.[426] No wonder most of the law clerks that term of Court were surprised to see the justices

---

ACTION 297–310 (1990); BERNARD SCHWARTZ, THE UNPUBLISHED OPINIONS OF THE BURGER COURT 95–101, 103–19 (1988); Woodward & Armstrong, *supra* note 329, at 170–75, 186–89, 230–34.

412. JEFFRIES, *supra* note 278, at 332–52; LAZARUS, *supra* note 28, at 355; Devins, *supra* note 9, at 1444–45.

413. JEFFRIES, *supra* note 278, at 347.

414. LAZARUS, *supra* note 28, at 367–68.

415. JEFFRIES, *supra* note 278, at 342; LAZARUS, *supra* note 28, at 357–59; RISEN & THOMAS, *supra* note 195, at 35.

416. 478 U.S. 186, 192 (1986).

417. JEFFRIES, *supra* note 278, at 530; Anand Agneshwar, *Ex-Justice Says He May Have Been Wrong*, NAT'L L.J., Nov. 5, 1990, at 3.

418. JEFFRIES, *supra* note 278, at 341.

419. *Id.* at 8; RISEN & THOMAS, *supra* note 195, at 33; Michael Gerhardt, *The Art of Judicial Review* (book rev.), 80 CORNELL L. REV. 1595, 1609, 1620, 1637 (1995).

420. WOODWARD & ARMSTRONG, *supra* note 329, at 233. *See also* MAY IT PLEASE THE COURT, *supra* note 408, at 350, 352.

421. 410 U.S. at 158.

422. Frank Scaturro, *Abortion and the Supreme Court:* Roe, Casey, *the Myth of* Stare Decisis, *and the Court as a Political Institution*, 3 HOLY CROSS J.L. & PUB. POL'Y 133, 149, 219 n.145 (1998).

423. SIMON, *supra* note 407, at 114.

424. 428 U.S. 52, 95–99 (1976)

425. WOODWARD & ARMSTRONG, *supra* note 329, at 415.

426. *Id.* at 112–13. *See also* Eric Lode, *Slippery Slope Arguments and Legal Reasoning*, 87 CAL. L. REV. 1469, 1498–1501 (1999).

"openly brokering their decisions like a group of legislators" in a process that seemed to some, at least, as "embarrassing and dishonest."[427] How, in other words, can the Court insist that the Constitution dictates that certain lines be drawn regarding abortion when the justices are bargaining among themselves over what those lines should be? Some clerks even took to referring to Blackmun's draft opinion as "Harry's abortion."[428]

The opinion that finally emerged from Justice Blackmun's efforts commanded the votes of seven of the nine justices. Only Justices William Rehnquist and Byron White dissented, and even their dissent was on narrow, technical grounds, not a ringing endorsement of the abortion laws.[429] But the Court at the time was not an institution that appreciated or fostered doubts, and the fact remains that no one on the Court, not even the dissenters, really had much to say against abortion as a social practice.[430] Despite the increasingly evident national divisions over the abortion issue, not one of the justices on the Court in 1972 (so far as the present record discloses) expressed anything like a "right-to-life" sentiment, either in a court opinion or in private. Perhaps if a single justice had expressed an anti-abortion perspective, it would have changed enough votes to lead to the opposite outcome in the case. Chief Justice Burger's concurrence always seemed more a tactical move on his part than the expression of his genuine conclusion. Justice Powell's biographer believes that Powell could have been won over had he been approached in the proper manner.[431] And Blackmun seemed so full of agonized reservations during the drafting process that he too might have been won over.[432] We shall never know.

Despite the inordinate length of time Blackmun took to produce the majority opinion, the opinion in *Roe* is so poorly written that defenders of its outcome usually begin their analysis by apologizing for the opinion.[433] Lawyers and scholars have advanced so many theories in

---

427. WOODWARD & ARMSTRONG, *supra* note 329, at 233.

428. *Id.*

429. 410 U.S. at 171–77 (Rehnquist & White, JJ., dissenting). For a critical analysis of Justice Rehnquist's dissent in terms of the technical grounds he used, see Peter Irons, *Opticians and Abortion: The Constitutional Myopia of Justice Rehnquist*, 22 NOVA L. REV. 695 (1998).

430. LAZARUS, *supra* note 28, at 368–69.

431. JEFFRIES, *supra* note 278, at 350.

432. LAZARUS, *supra* note 28, at 368.

433. *See, e.g.*, JOHN ARTHUR, THE UNFINISHED CONSTITUTION: PHILOSOPHY AND CONSTITUTIONAL PRACTICE 210 (1989); G. PHILIP BOBBIT, CONSTITUTIONAL FATE: THEORY OF THE CONSTITUTION 157–59 (1982); GUIDO CALABRESI, IDEALS, BELIEFS, ATTITUDES, AND THE LAW: PRIVATE LAW PERSPECTIVE ON A PUBLIC LAW PROBLEM 92 (1985); COLKER, ABORTION & DIALOGUE, *supra* note 68, at 104, 108–09; LAZARUS, *supra* note 28, at 362–67; O'BRIEN, *supra* note 71, at 37; RICHARD POSNER, SEX AND REASON 337 (1992); H. JEFFERSON POWELL, THE MORAL TRADITION OF AMERICAN CONSTITUTIONALISM 173–80 (1993); DEBORAH RHODE, JUSTICE AND GENDER 210–13 (1989); MARK TUSHNET, RED, WHITE, AND BLUE: A CRITICAL ANALYSIS OF THE CONSTITUTION 54–55 (1988); JAMES BOYD WHITE, ACTS OF HOPE: CREATING AUTHORITY IN LITERATURE, LAW, AND POLITICS 98 (1994); Paula Abrams, *The Tradition of Reproduction*, 37 ARIZ. L. REV. 453, 493 (1995); Allen, *supra* note 221, at 187; Mark Beutler, Comment, *Abortion and the Viability Standard—Toward a More Reasoned Determination of the State's Countervailing Interest in Protecting Prenatal Life*, 21 SETON HALL L.J. 347, 351–56 (1991); Victor Blasi, *The Rootless Activism of the Burger Court*, in THE BURGER COURT: THE COUNTER-REVOLUTION THAT WASN'T 198, 212 (Vincent Blasi ed. 1983); Alan Brownstein & Paul Dau, *The Constitutional Morality of Abortion*, 23 B.C. L. REV. 689, 745–49 (1992); George, *supra* note 10, at 112–13; Ginsburg, *Judicial Voice*, *supra* note 68, at 1198; Philip Heyman & Douglas Barzeley, *The Forest and the Trees:* Roe v. Wade *and Its Critics*, 53 B.U. L. REV. 765, 765, 784 (1973); Richard Gregory Morgan, Roe v. Wade *and the Lesson of the Pre-*Roe *Case Law*, 77 MICH. L. REV. 1724, 1724 (1979); Michael Perry, *Abortion, the Public Morals, and the Police Power: The Ethical Function of Substantive Due Process*, 23 UCLA L. REV. 689, 690–92 (1976); Donald Regan, *Rewriting* Roe v. Wade, 77 MICH. L. REV. 1569, 1569 (1979); Kermit Roosevelt, *Shaky Basis for a Constitutional "Right,"* WASH. POST, Jan. 22, 2003, at A15; Carl Schneider, *Moral Discourse and the Transformation of American Family Law*, 83 MICH. L. REV. 1803, 1869 (1985); Siegel, *supra* note 176, at 272–80, 348–49; Lawrence Solum, *Faith and Justice*, 39 DE PAUL L. REV. 1083, 1101 n.61 (1990); Laurence Tribe, *Foreword: Toward a Model of Roles in the Due Process of Life and Law*, 87 HARV. L. REV. 1, 2–7 (1973); Louise

defense of *Roe,* all without finding they can agree on, that one defender of the right to abortion, Judge Richard Posner, went so far as to call the decision the "Wandering Jew of constitutional law."[434] The difficulty in picking out a coherent argument in the *Roe* opinion derives the difficulty in devising an adequate constitutional argument to support abortion rights without also opening the door to all sorts of things that even the staunchest supporters of abortion rights would not accept. Thus, within three years of deciding *Roe,* the Supreme Court found it necessary to retreat from the overly broad language in *Roe* regarding even first trimester abortions.[435]

Thomas Jipping, a strong critic of abortion rights, has described the difficulties of defending the opinion as written at some length.[436] Yet one need not look to opponents of the outcome of the case to find devastating comments on the notion that the Constitution provides a right to choose to abort. Even a blatant supporter of women's freedom to abort like Mark Tushnet has conceded that while "[m]ost academic commentators probably believe that... access to abortion should be relatively unrestricted[,]...none has been able to provide conclusive arguments that the Supreme Court correctly found that policy in the Constitution."[437] Tushnet was an enthusiastic supporter of Blackmun's *Roe* opinion during its preparation while he (Tushnet) was a law clerk to Justice Thurgood Marshall,[438] yet he has described recent attempts to find an alternative rationale for *Roe* as "bizarre," ranging from theories derived from equal protection, to freedom of religion, to the prohibition of slavery.[439] Or compare Richard Morgan's critique of the decision:

> Rarely does the Supreme Court invite critical outrage as it did in *Roe* by offering so little explanation for a decision that requires so much. The stark inadequacy of the Court's attempt to justify its conclusions...suggests to some scholars that the Court, finding no justification at all in the Constitution, unabashedly usurped the legislative function.[440]

The late Mary Joe Frug, a noted feminist legal scholar, conceded that *Roe* "received uniformly negative criticism from legal commentators concerned about jurisprudential integrity" without, however, indicating whether she agreed with the criticism.[441] Noted feminist law professor Robin West used even stronger language, describing the defense of freedom to abort as "irrational" and "a little insane" because its proponents cannot distinguish abortion from infanticide or explain how they can describe women as nurturing by their nature when they disregard the needs and feelings of the fetus, concluding that

---

Wheeler & Shirley Kovar, Roe v. Wade: *The Right to Privacy Revisited,* 21 U. Kan. L. Rev. 527, 527 (1973). *See also* Henry Friendly, *The Courts and Social Policy: Substance and Procedure,* 33 U. Miami L. Rev. 21, 35 (1978).

434. Posner, *supra* note 93, at 180.

435. Connecticut v. Menillo, 423 U.S. 9, 9–11 (1975) (affirming the Connecticut statute that abortions must be performed only by physicians).

436. Thomas Jipping, *Informed Consent to Abortion: A Refinement,* 38 Case W. Res. L. Rev. 329, 329–43 (1988).

437. Mark Tushnet, *The Supreme Court on Abortion: A Survey,* in Abortion, Medicine, and the Law, *supra* note 88, at 165, 165.

438. Garrow, *supra* note 23, at 582.

439. Mark Tushnet, *The Left Critique of Normativity: A Comment,* 90 Mich. L. Rev. 2331 n.27 (1992). *See also* David Cruz, *"The Sexual Freedom Cases"? Contraception, Abortion, Abstinence, and the Constitution,* 35 Harv. C.R.-C.L. L. Rev. 299 (2000).

440. Morgan, *supra* note 433, at 1724. *See also* Frank Easterbrook, *Bills of Rights and Regression to the Mean,* 15 Harv. J.L. & Pub. Pol'y 71, 79 n.28 (1992); Farrell, *supra* note 372, at 295–306; Seth Kreimer, *Does Pro-Choice Mean Pro-Kevorkian? An Essay on* Roe, Casey, *and the Right to Die,* 44 Am. U. L. Rev. 803, 808 (1995); Lynn Stout, *Strict Scrutiny and Social Choice: An Economic Inquiry into Fundamental Rights and Suspect Classification,* 80 Geo. L.J. 1787, 1799 n.55 (1992).

441. Mary Joe Frug, Women and the Law 433–35 (1992). *See also* Joan Hoff, Law, Gender, and Injustice: A Legal History of U.S. Women 34–35 (1991).

In fact,...the abortion issue is increasingly used in ethics as well as constitutional law classrooms to exemplify the "irrationality" of individual moral commitment....[W]e have tried to explain feminist reform efforts through the use of analogies that don't work and arguments that are strained. The result...is internally inconsistent, poorly reasoned, weak, and then vulnerable legal doctrine.[442]

West's response is to call for a redefinition of what is "rational."

The best way to understand Justice Blackmun's opinion in *Roe* is as an argument from history. Blackmun devoted one-half of his opinion to the history of abortion laws,[443] deriving his version from Cyril Means' specious history of abortion law. Blackmun cited Means no less than seven times and no one else more than once.[444] Blackmun did not even bother to cite, let alone to discuss, the Court's prior decisions—at least five—in which it had upheld or assumed the constitutionality of banning abortion.[445] Few commentators noted the imbalance in Blackmun's account of the history of abortion, and those who have generally did not attempt either to trace the source or to consider whether Blackmun got his history right. For example, a commentator who noted the imbalance, law student Edward Steegman, instead of tracing the source of that imbalance, was content to suggest that it resulted from Blackmun's exaggerated distaste for "religious intolerance" which Steegman thought was behind all prohibitions of abortion.[446]

Following Means, Blackmun in *Roe* claimed that abortion was not a crime under English or American law except for an aberrational period in the late nineteenth and early twentieth centuries.[447] Blackmun concluded that "it now appear[s] doubtful that abortion was ever established as a common law crime."[448] He also concluded that abortion statutes in the United States were not generally adopted until after the Civil War (*i.e.,* after the Fourteenth Amendment was adopted).[449] Finally, he intimated that the nineteenth century abortion statutes were adopted solely to protect the life and health of mothers and not to protect the life or health of unborn children.[450] Like Means, Blackmun's conclusions were wrong on all points.[451]

Arguing that abortion was a common practice that, even when illegal, was seldom prosecuted, Means and his followers conclude that abortion was a common law "liberty" when the

---

442. Robin West, *Jurisprudence and Gender,* 55 U. Chi. L. Rev. 1, 69–70 (1988).

443. 410 U.S. at 130–53.

444. *Id.* at 136–52, 158 n. 54. *See also* Wolfgang Saxon, *Obituary: Cyril C. Means, 73, A Specialist in Laws Regarding Abortion,* N.Y. Times, Oct. 6, 1992, at A15.

445. Wolf v. Colorado, 338 U.S. 25 (1949) (upholding a conviction for conspiracy to commit abortions against challenges based on an allegedly illegal search), *overruled by* Mapp v. Ohio, 367 U.S. 643 (1961) (extending the Fourth Amendment protections against illegal searches to state proceedings); Missouri *ex rel.* Hurwitz v. North, 271 U.S. 40 (1926) (affirming the revocation of a doctor's license under state law for performing illegal abortions); United States v. Holte, 236 U.S. 140 (1915) (*dicta* indicating that abortion was a crime); Hawker v. New York, 170 U.S. 189 (1898) (affirming a state court indictment of a doctor for practicing medicine illegally after his license was revoked for performing a criminal abortion); *Ex Parte* Jackson, 96 U.S. 727 (1877) (finding "no doubt" regarding the Comstock Act that banned, among other things, the mailing of any item "designed or intended" for procuring abortions). Of all the people who have written about *Roe v. Wade,* no one seems to have noticed this omission until historian/lawyer Frank Scaturro wrote about it in 1998. Scaturro, *supra* note 422, at 145–46.

446. Edward Steegman, Note, *Of History and Due Process,* 63 Ind. L.J. 369, 390–94, 396–97 (1987).

447. 410 U.S. at 136–43.

448. *Id.* at 136.

449. *Id.* at 139.

450. *Id.* at 147–152, 158 n.54.

451. *See generally* J. Keown, Abortion, Doctors and the Law 3–25 (1988); Dellapenna, *supra* note 207. *See also* Eugene Quay, *Justifiable Abortion—Medical and Legal Foundations (Pt. II),* 49 Geo. L.J. 395 (1961); Scaturro, *supra* note 422, at 136–43.

Fifth and Fourteenth Amendments were adopted.[452] From this premise, it was an easy step to conclude that the "liberty" to abort is part of the "liberty" protected by the due process clauses of the Fifth and Fourteenth Amendments.[453] Few supporters of abortion rights flatly reject this claim.[454] One wonders if they would reach the same conclusion regarding father-daughter incest which, one would suppose, has been, at least at times, a widespread practice that was in fact rarely prosecuted in English and American society and the criminality of which was seldom directly declared in statute or precedent.[455]

Blackmun himself, at least at the time, seems to have been unusually fond of historical arguments in shaping constitutional law. Consider the following histrionic passage from his concurring opinion in a case upholding the conviction of an army doctor for "conduct unbecoming an officer" after he refused to train medics for service in Vietnam:

> [T]imes have not changed in the area of moral precepts. Fundamental concepts of right and wrong are the same now as they were under the Articles of the Earl of Essex (1642), or the British Articles of War of 1765, or the American Articles of War of 1775, or during the long line of precedents of this and other courts upholding general articles....The...moral horizons of the American people are not footloose....The law should, in appropriate circumstances, be flexible enough to recognize the moral dimensions of man and his instincts concerning that which is honorable, decent, and right.[456]

These views (written only a year or so after his opinion in *Roe*) could have been used as a brief for upholding the abortion laws—unless one concludes, as Blackmun did, that these laws were a recent innovation based upon misguided if not suspect motivations. For some reason, Blackmun chose not to rely so directly upon his reading of the history of abortion in *Roe* itself. Although Blackmun noted Means' claim that the constitutionality of abortion prohibitions would turn upon whether it was a "common law liberty,"[457] he did not rest his conclusion there. Instead, he used his history of abortion laws to inform his interpretation of the values involved in the case and thus ultimately to inform whether the statutory prohibition of abortion was constitutional.[458]

Blackmun's reliance on history to justify his conclusions is understandable given the problems in constructing a non-historical constitutional argument in favor of freedom to abort. The long-standing tradition that the open-textured language of "due process" and "liberty" is

---

452. Means II, *supra* note 398, at 351–54, 374–75, 409–10 n.175. *See also* Beechem v. Leahy, 287 A.2d 836, 139 (Vt. 1972); GORDON, *supra* note 175, at 52–53, 57; JAMES MOHR, ABORTION IN AMERICA: THE ORIGINS AND EVOLUTION OF NATIONAL POLICY, 1800–1900, at 128–29, 134–36, 144–45, 201, 208–11, 226, 229, 235–36 (1978); *Amicus Brief of 250 American Historians in support of Appellants in* Planned Parenthood of Southeastern Pennsylvania v. Casey, [505 U.S. 833 (1992)] (*"Casey Historians' Brief"*), at 5–6; *Amicus Brief of 281 American Historians supporting Appellees in* Webster v. Reproductive Health Services [492 U.S. 490 (1989)] (*"Webster Historians' Brief"*), reprinted at 11 Women's Rts. L. Rptr. 163, 170 (1989), and in 8 DOCUMENTARY HISTORY OF THE LEGAL ASPECTS OF ABORTION IN THE UNITED STATES: WEBSTER V. REPRODUCTIVE HEALTH SERVICES 107 (Roy Mersky & Gary Hartman eds. 1990); Siegel, *supra* note 175, at 278.

453. *See, e.g.,* MOHR, *supra* note 452, at 20–21; Laura Flanders, *Abortion: The Usable Past*, THE NATION, Aug. 7, 1989, at 175; Morton Kondracke, *The Abortion Wars*, NEW REP., Aug. 28, 1989, 17, at 19, col. 2; *Casey Historians' Brief, supra* note 452, at 28–30; *Webster Historians' Brief, supra* note 452, at 180.

454. *See, e.g.,* WHITE, *supra* note 433, at 155–56.

455. On the historical record of incest prosecutions, see MARTIN INGRAM, CHURCH COURTS, SEX AND MARRIAGE IN ENGLAND, 1570–1640, AT 245–49 (1987); 2 FREDERICK POLLOCK & FREDERICK MAITLAND, THE HISTORY OF ENGLISH LAW BEFORE THE TIME OF EDWARD I, at 543–44 (2nd ed. 1898); Keith Thomas, *The Puritans and Adultery: The Act of 1650 Reconsidered,* in PURITANS AND REVOLUTIONARIES: ESSAYS IN SEVENTEENTH-CENTURY HISTORY PRESENTED TO CHRISTOPHER HILL 257, 257–58, 278–80 (1978).

456. Parker v. Levy, 417 U.S. 733, 763–64 (1974) (Blackmun, J., & Burger, C.J., concurring).

457. *Roe,* 410 U.S. at 140.

458. *Id.,* at 152–55.

informed by the legal traditions that operated as the context within which the Constitution was written or as defining the aspirations towards which the Constitution is evolving combine to make the history of abortion relevant to current interpretation of the Constitution.[459] The aspirational view of the Constitution was first voiced by abolitionists before the Civil War, including Abraham Lincoln.[460] One of its best presentations comes from Oliver Wendell Holmes, jr.:

> [T]he provisions of the Constitution are not mathematical formulas having their essence in their form; they are organic, living institutions transplanted from English soil. Their significance is vital, not formal; it is to be gathered not simply by taking the words and a dictionary, but by considering their origin and their line of growth.[461]

The "originalist" approach to the Constitution calls upon judges and other interpreters to determine how those who wrote or ratified the document would have decided in the case at hand. This approach too has a long and distinguished history of support by the American judiciary.[462] The distinction between the aspirational and the originalist recourse to history is similar to the

---

459. *See generally* Michael Perry, Morality, Politics, and Law 134–57 (1988); Herman Belz, *History, Theory, and the Constitution,* 11 Const'l Commentary 45, 59–61 (1994); Rebecca Brown, *Tradition and Insight,* 103 Yale L.J. 177 (1993); Ronald Dworkin, *The Moral Reading of the Constitution,* N.Y. Rev. Books, Mar. 21, 1996, at 46; Sanford Levinson, *Parliamentarianism, Progressivism, and 1937: Some Reservations about Professor West's Aspirational Constitution,* 88 Nw. U. L. Rev. 283 (1993); C.M.A. McAuliffe, *Constitutional Jurisprudence of History and Natural Law: Complementary or Rival Modes of Discourse?,* 24 Cal. W.L. Rev. 287 (1988); Walter Murphy, *Constitutional Interpretation: The Art of the Historian, Magician or Statesman?,* 87 Yale L.J. 1752 (1978); Gene Nichol, jr., *The Left, the Right, and Certainty in Constitutional Law,* 33 Wm. & Mary L. Rev. 1181, 1197–99 (1992); Shannon Stewart, *The Art of Constitutional Interpretation,* 17 J. Contemp. L. 91, 110–26 (1991); Robin West, *Constitutional Skepticism,* 72 B.U. L. Rev. 765, 790–98 (1992).

460. *See, e.g.,* Abraham Lincoln, *Fragment on the Constitution and the Union* (Jan., 1861), in 4 Collected Works of Abraham Lincoln 169 (Ray Basler ed. 1953).

461. Gompers v. United States, 233 U.S. 604, 610 (1914). *See also* Missouri v. Holland, 252 U.S. 416, 433 (1920).

462. Harmelin v. Michigan, 501 U.S. 957 (1991); Stanford v. Kentucky, 492 U.S. 361 (1989); Michael H. v. Gerald D., 491 U.S. 110 (1989); Bowers v. Hardwick, 478 U.S. 186, 192 (1986); Roberts v. United States Jaycees, 468 U.S. 609, 619 (1984); United States v. Sioux Nation, 448 U.S. 371 (1980); Smith v. Organization of Foster Families, 431 U.S. 816, 845 (1977); Moore v. City of East Cleveland, 431 U.S. 497, 503 (1977) (plur. op. per Powell, J.); Abington School Dist. v. Schempp, 376 U.S. 203, 241 (1963) (Brennan, J., concurring); Meyer v. Nebraska, 262 U.S. 390, 399 (1923); McCulloch v. Maryland, 17 U.S. (4 Wheat.) 316 (1819).

*See also* 3 Albert Beveridge, The Life of John Marshall 223–73 (1919); Daniel Boorstin, The Genius of American Politics 84–94 (1953); Gerald Chapman, Edmund Burke: The Practical Imagination (1967); John Daly, The Use of History in the Decisions of the Supreme Court, 1900–1930 (1954); Charles Miller, The Supreme Court and the Uses of History 20–28, 36–38, 100–48 (1969); White, *supra* note 433, at 158–60, 166; H. Trevor Colbourn, *Thomas Jefferson's Use of the Past,* 15 Wm. & Mary Q. 56 (1958); Celeste Michelle Condit, *Within the Confines of the Law: Abortion and a Substantive Rhetoric of Liberty* (book review), 38 Buff. L. Rev. 903, 915–17 (1990); William Foran, *John Marshall as a Historian,* 43 Am. Hist. Rev. 51 (1937); Deborah Forhan, Harmelin v. Michigan: *Should the Existence of an Eighth Amendment Guarantee of Proportionate Prison Sentences Rest on the Fate of Titus Oates and the Dreaded Consequences of Overtime Parking?,* 22 Sw. U. L. Rev. 1133 (1993); Carl Friedrich, *Law and History,* 14 Vand. L. Rev. 1027, 1027 (1961); Edward Grant & Paul Benjamin Linton, *Relief or Reproach?: Euthanasia Rights in the Wake of Measure 16,* 74 Ore. L. Rev. 449, 481–501 (1995); Thomas Grey, *Do We Have an Unwritten Constitution?,* 27 Stan. L. Rev. 703 (1975); Alfred Kelly, *Clio and the Court: An Illicit Love Affair,* 1965 Sup. Ct. Rev. 119; Marie Carolyn Klinkheimer, *John Marshall's Use of History,* 6 Cath. U. L. Rev. 78 (1956); Marie Carolyn Klinkheimer, *The Use of History in the Supreme Court, 1789–1835,* 36 U. Det. L.J. 553 (1959); David Richards, *Constitutional Interpretation, History, and the Death Penalty: A Book Review,* 71 Cal. L. Rev. 1372, 1380 (1983); Robert Riggs, *Substantive Due Process in 1791,* 1990 Wis. L. Rev. 941; Gloria Valencia-Weber, *American Indian Law and History: Instructional Mirrors,* 44 J. Legal Educ. 251 (1994); Robin West, *Reconstructing Liberty,* 59 U. Tenn. L. Rev. 441 (1992); Wiecek, *supra* note 2, at 228–35.

distinction drawn by historian Jaroslav Pelikan between tradition ("the living faith of the dead") and traditionalism ("the dead faith of the living").[463] While some see the aspirational view of the Constitution in decline among today's judges,[464] it was the dominant view at the time *Roe v. Wade* was decided. Even those who reject "original intent" (or original meaning) as controlling modern interpretations, tend to find in the original meaning a starting point for further reasoning or a baseline from which departures must be justified.[465]

Blackmun concluded that the "right of privacy" was "broad enough to encompass a woman's decision to abort."[466] He also concluded that the state had a legitimate interest in protecting "potential life."[467] (Blackmun claimed that he was incapable of determining when a human life begins,[468] although his decision seemed clearly premised on the idea that human life did not begin until birth.[469]) Blackmun also stressed the importance of leaving medical decisions to physicians,[470] reflecting his background as an attorney for the Mayo Clinic. Indeed, the most persistent criticism of *Roe* among supporters of abortion rights (who often believe the decision did not go far enough in assuring complete freedom to abort) is that the decision really serves to consolidate the power of doctors over women seeking abortions.[471] One feminist critic went so far as to

---

463. Jaroslav Pelikan, The Vindication of Tradition 65 (1984). *See also* Powell, *supra* note 433; Harold Berman, *The Origins of Historical Jurisprudence: Coke, Selden, Hale*, 103 Yale L.J. 1651, 1693–94 (1994).

464. Gary Jacobsohn, The Supreme Court and the Decline of Constitutional Aspiration(1986).

465. Akhil Reed Amar, *A Neo-Federalist View of Article III: Separating the Two Tiers of Federal Jurisdiction*, 65 B.U. L. Rev. 205, 207–08 (1985); Michael Stokes Paulsen, *The Most Dangerous Branch: Executive Power to Say What the Law Is*, 83 Geo. L.J. 217, 227–28 n.24 (1994).

466. 410 U.S. at 157.

467. *Id.* at 160–62.

468. *Id.* at 159.

469. Blackmun realized from the beginning that if a fetus was a human being, the state could not allow its abortion without providing "due process" of law; he said as much during the Justices' conference after the first oral argument of *Roe v. Wade*. Simon, *supra* note 407, at 91. His refusal to declare when life began was a sham from the start—the clear import of his decision is that only "potential life" is at stake. *See* Steven Smith, *Natural Law and Contemporary Moral Thought: A Guide from the Perplexed*, 42 Am. J. Juris. 299, 302–03 (1997) (book rev.). *See also* Radhika Roe, *The Author of* Roe, 26 Hastings Const'l L.Q. 21, 23–24 (1998); Jed Rubenfeld, *On the Legal Status of the Proposition that "Life Begins at Conception,"* 43 Stan. L. Rev. 599 (1991). Conceding that potential life is present would seem lead to the conclusion that a state could ban or otherwise strictly limit access to abortion, for protecting "persons" is hardly the limit of state authority to regulate conduct. As John Hart Ely famously pointed out, we protect dogs from cruelty, and they certainly are not persons. Ely, *supra* note 273, at 926. *See also* Scaturro, *supra* note 422, at 151–52.

470. 410 U.S. at 160. *See generally* Reagan, *supra* note 13, at 238–39; Ann Alpers, *Justice Blackmun and the Good Physician: Patients, Populations, and the Paradox of Medicine*, 26 Hastings Const'l L.Q. 41 (1998).

471. *See* Baehr, *supra* note 67, at 4; Robert Blank & Janna Merrick, Human Reproduction, Emerging Technologies, and Conflicting Rights 32–33, 38 (1995); Colker, Abortion & Dialogue, *supra* note 68, at 104–06; Condit, *supra* note 32, at 102; Davis, *supra* note 239, at 10–12, 17–20, 179–206, 226–32; Raymond DeVries, Making Midwives Legal: Childbirth, Medicine, and the Law 149–50 (2nd ed. 1996); Garrow, *supra* note 23, at 408, 613–14; Ginsburg, *supra* note 9, at 41–42, 55–56; Greenwood & Young, *supra* note 275, at 99; Harrison, *supra* note 68, at 9–10; Jaffe, Lindheim, & Lee, *supra* note 254, at 9–10; Kenny, *supra* note 3, at 260–67; Catharine MacKinnon, Feminism Unmodified: Discourses on Life and Law 98, 100–01 (1987); Catharine MacKinnon, Toward a Feminist Theory of the State 189, 192 (1989); Milbauer & Obrentz, *supra* note 394, at 122–24; Petchesky, *supra* note 3, at 90–93, 123–25, 130–32, 192–97, 289–94; Petersen, *supra* note 189, at 15–17, 76–78, 101–2, 154–55; Carol Smart, Feminism and the Power of Law 90–113 (1989); White, *supra* note 433, at 165; Abrams, *supra* note 433, at 487; Susan Frelich Appleton, *Doctors, Patients and the Constitution: A Theoretical Analysis of the Physician's Role in "Private" Reproductive Decisions*, 63 Wash. U. L.Q. 183 (1985); Andrea Asaro, *The Judicial Portrayal of the Physician in Abortion and Sterilization Decisions: The Use and Abuse of Medical Discretion*, 6 Harv. Women's L.J. 51 (1983); Marie Ashe, *Zig-Zag Stitching and the Seamless Web: Thoughts on "Reproduction" and the Law*, 13 Nova L. Rev. 355 (1989); David Boldt, *Farewell to Justice Blackmun: He Blew It on the "Roe" Decision*, Phila. Inquirer, Apr. 10, 1994, at D7; Curtis, *supra* note 217, at 428–29; Daly, *supra* note 68, at 79, 83–102,

describe *Roe v. Wade* as "the case of the Incredible Disappearing Woman."[472] In balancing these several interests, Blackmun devised the most original proposition in *Roe v. Wade* and the proposition with the least grounding in the Constitution—the trimester framework.

Blackmun conceived of human gestation as being divided in three equal periods of 13 weeks ("trimesters"), and provided a different test for the constitutionality of laws regulating abortion depending upon the trimester targeted by the regulation.[473] He declared that the state could not regulate abortion during the first trimester except for ordinary safety standards applicable to all medical procedures. During the second trimester, the state could enact additional regulations for abortions, but only to protect the health of the mother. Finally, during the third trimester, the state could enact regulations for abortions designed to protect the life or health of a "viable" fetus, but these regulations must give way before the health concerns of the mother. One is hard pressed, however, to discover where this trimester scheme is expressed in the Constitution. Indeed, the trimester scheme read more "like a set of hospital rules and regulations, whose validity [will be] destroyed with new statistics upon the medical risks of childbirth and abortion or new advances in providing for the separate existence of a fetus"[474] than like a constitutional principle.

To demonstrate that abortion has nearly always been treated as a serious crime in our history, with the late twentieth century liberalization as the aberration, is to claim that the Ninth and Fourteenth Amendments do not include a freedom ("liberty") to abort. Blackmun's version of the history of abortion thus remains one of the central concerns in the abortion controversy. All

---

108–09, 126–28; J. Shoshanna Ehrlich, *Minors as Medical Decision Makers: The Pretextual Reasoning of the Court in the Abortion Cases,* 7 MICH. J. GENDER & L. 65, 69–71 (2000); Ruth Bader Ginsburg, *Some Thoughts on Autonomy and Equality in Relation to* Roe v. Wade, 63 N.C. L. REV. 375, at 376–83 (1985); Karen Booth Glen, *Abortion in the Courts: A Lay Woman's Historical Guide to the New Disaster Area,* 4 FEMINIST STUD. 1 (1978); Patricia Karlan & Daniel Ortiz, *In a Different Voice: Relational Feminism, Abortion Rights, and the Feminist Legal Agenda,* 87 NW. U. L. REV. 858, 877 (1993); Law, *supra* note 68, at 1020; Laura Punnett, *The Politics of Menstrual Extraction,* in FROM ABORTION TO REPRODUCTIVE FREEDOM, *supra,* at 101; Roe *Hearing, supra* note 294, at 17–19, 21–22 (statement of Ronald Rotunda). For similar comments by opponents of abortion rights, see NOONAN, *supra* note 33, at 35–40; Robert Araujo, *Abortion, Ethics, and the Common Good: Who Are We? What Do We Want? How Do We Get There?,* 76 MARQ. L. REV. 701, 707–10, 729–30 (1993); Mary Ann Glendon, *The Women of* Roe v. Wade, 134 FIRST THINGS 19, 20 (June 2003); Smolin, Jurisprudence, *supra* note 271, at 1016–25. For similar criticisms of the English abortion act, see SUSAN ATKINS & BRENDA HOGGETT, WOMEN AND THE LAW 86–90 (1984); MARY BOYLE, RE-THINKING ABORTION, PSYCHOLOGY, GENDER, POWER, AND THE LAW 45 (1997); GREENWOOD & YOUNG, *supra,* at 132–33; ELIZABETH KINGDOM, WHAT'S WRONG WITH RIGHTS?: PROBLEMS FOR FEMINIST POLITICS AND JURISPRUDENCE 52–53 (1991); MASON, *supra* note 224, at 127–34; MEYERS, *supra* note 225, at 28; RUBIN, *supra* note 9, at 75–77; SALLY SHELDON, BEYOND CONTROL: MEDICAL POWER AND ABORTION LAW (1997); Ellie Lee, *Tensions in the Regulation of Abortion in Britain,* 30 J. LAW & SOC'Y 532, 536–42 (2003); Sally Sheldon, *"Who Is the Mother to Make the Judgment?": The Constructions of Woman in English Abortion Law,* 1 FEMINIST LEG. STUD. 3 (1993).

A majority of the Supreme Court continues to endorse the importance of physician autonomy and physician control. Stenberg v. Carhart, 530 U.S. 914, 932, 938, 946–47, 966–72 (2000). Despite the prevalence of this rhetoric, supporters of a supposed freedom to abort have seldom challenged statutory requirements that abortions be performed only by licensed physicians, in stark contrast to their insistent opposition to virtually every other restriction on free access to abortion. Curtis, *supra,* at 429. *See* Connecticut v. Menillo, 423 U.S. 9 (1975) (per curiam). *But see* State v. Hultgren, 204 N.W.2d 197 (Minn. 1973). *But see* Lynne Marie Kohm & Colleen Holmes, *The Rise and Fall of Women's Rights: Have Sexuality and Reproductive Freedom Forfeited Victory?,* 6 WM. & MARY J. WOMEN & L. 381, 404 (2000) (noting that Janet Benshoof, director of the Center for Reproductive Law and Policy, has declared that a court's upholding of such a law was "a devastating acceptance of discrimination against abortion providers").

472. Lynne Henderson, *Legality and Empathy,* 85 MICH. L. REV. 1574, 1626 (1987).

473. 410 U.S. at 163–65.

474. Cox, *supra* note 305, at 113–14. *See also* City of Akron v. Akron Ctr. for Reprod. Health, 462 U.S. 416, 458 (1983) (O'Connor, J., dissenting) ("The *Roe* framework…is clearly on a collision course with itself.").

of this would have been no surprise to Blackmun himself; he described the standards announced in *Roe* to be arbitrary in an internal court memorandum written while he was preparing the opinion.[475] Advocates of a constitutionally protected freedom to abort have moved from an originalist argument to an aspirational argument.[476] Under either form of argument, however, the claim of a freedom to abort fails if the history fails—and the history does fail.

Chief Justice William Rehnquist, who dissented in *Roe*, later suggested (in an opinion joined by Justices Anthony Kennedy and Byron White) that the Court in *Roe* went wrong in attempting to elaborate a broad, abstract rule rather than responding to the precise facts before the Court.[477] Not only critics of the decision reached the same conclusion. Legal philosopher Ronald Dworkin also suggested that the *Roe* majority opinion went too far. Although Dworkin concluded that *Roe* was the ideal solution, Dworkin still argued that the Court would have done better not to announce the trimester scheme but should have developed the proper limits on state regulation of abortion on a case-by-case basis that would have allowed a more carefully calibrated weighing of the competing interests than *Roe's* trimester scheme permitted.[478] Many other pro-abortion scholars have reached the same conclusion.[479] Something of this view is beginning to seep into the general public consciousness. In the midst of all the gushing sentimentality over Justice Harry Blackmun on the occasion of his retirement,[480] one editorial writer more somberly blamed him for all the difficulties that ensued from *Roe v. Wade* because of its "sweeping and unnuanced decree."[481]

---

475. Woodward, *supra* note 329, at D2.

476. Compare the originalist argument of Cyril Means, jr. Means II, *supra* note 398, with the aspirationalist arguments used in the *Webster* and *Casey Historians' Brief, supra* note 452. *See generally* MILLER, *supra* note 462, at 25–28, 149–201.

477. Webster v. Reproductive Health Services, 492 U.S. 490, 518–21 (1989) (Rehnquist, C.J., with Kennedy & White, JJ., plurality op.).

478. Ronald Dworkin, *Unenumerated Rights: Whether and How* Roe *Should be Overruled*, 59 U. CHI. L. REV. 381, 427–32 (1992).

479. *See* ROBERT BURT, THE CONSTITUTION IN CONFLICT 358–62 (1992); COLKER, ABORTION & DIALOGUE, *supra* note 68, at 101–02, 114–25; LAZARUS, *supra* note 28, at 369–72; MENSCH & FREEMAN, *supra* note 66, at 126–28; TRIBE, AMERICAN CONSTITUTIONAL LAW, *supra* note 175, at 1359; LAURENCE TRIBE, GOD SAVE THIS HONORABLE COURT 16 (1985) ("TRIBE, HONORABLE COURT"); LAURENCE TRIBE & MICHAEL DORF, ON READING THE CONSTITUTION 63 (1991); WHITE, *supra* note 433, at 162; Blasi, *supra* note 433, at 212; Daniel Conkle, *Canada's* Roe: *The Canadian Abortion Decision and Its Implications for American Constitutional Law and Theory*, 6 CONST'L COMMENTARY 299, 308–18 (1989); Ruth Bader Ginsburg, *On Muteness, Confidence, and Collegiality: A Response to Professor Nagel*, 61 U. COLO. L. REV. 715, 718–19 (1990); Ginsburg, *Judicial Voice, supra* note 68, at 1198–99, 1205–09; Ian Shapiro, *Introduction*, in ABORTION: THE SUPREME COURT DECISIONS 1, 16–18 (Ian Shapiro ed. 1995).

480. *See, e.g.,* Ann Alpers, *Justice Harry A. Blackmun*, 47 STAN. L. REV. 1 (1994); Comment, *Justice Harry Blackmun: A Retrospective Consideration of the Justice's Role in the Emancipation of Women*, 25 SETON HALL. L. REV. 1176 (1995); Editorial, *Sensitivity for the Downtrodden Defines Legacy of Justice Blackmun*, CLEVE. PLAIN DEALER, Apr. 7, 1994, at 15A; Frank Holleman, *Striving to Get It Right*, CONN. L. TRIB., Apr. 18, 1994, at 27; Ruth Marcus, *Blackmun Set to Leave High Court*, WASH. POST, Apr. 6, 1994, at A1; Estelle Rogers, *Thank You Justice Blackmun*, 43 AM. U. L. REV. 734 (1994); Herman Schwartz, *Justice Blackmun*, 43 AM. U. L. REV. 737 (1994); Mark Schneider, *Justice Blackmun: A Wise Man Walking the Corridors of Power, Gently*, 83 GEO. L.J. 11 (1994); Symposium, *A Tribute to Justice Harry A. Blackmun*, 108 HARV. L. REV. 1 (1994); Symposium, *Justice Harry A. Blackmun*, 97 DICK. L. REV. 421 (1993); Symposium, *Justice Harry A. Blackmun*, 71 N.D.L. REV. 3 (1995); Nina Totenberg, *Harry A. Blackmun: The Conscientious Conscience*, 43 AM. U. L. REV. 745 (1994); Sarah Weddington, *Parting Praise for Justice Harry A. Blackmun*, 43 AM. U. L. REV. 750 (1994). Similar outpourings of personal reminiscence and praise occurred when he died. *See* Chai Feldman, *Former Law Clerk Recalls Justice Blackmun's Humility*, NAT'L L.J., Mar. 15, 1999, at A24; Linda Greenhouse, *Justice Blackmun, Author of Abortion Right, Dies: Judge, 90, Will Forever be Linked to Issue in* Roe v. Wade, N.Y. TIMES, Mar. 5, 1999, at A1; Charles Rothfield, *One Fried Egg and Rye Toast*, LEGAL TIMES, Mar. 8, 1999, at 11; Symposium, *In Memoriam: Harry A Blackmun*, 113 HARV. L. REV. 1 (1999); Symposium, *Justice Harry A. Blackmun*, 26 HASTINGS CONST'L L.Q. 1 (1998).

481. Boldt, *supra* note 471.

That writer, David Boldt, a self-described "Kennedy liberal," went on to recall Senator Roman Hruska's defense of another (unsuccessful) nominee to the Supreme Court by noting that "There's little doubt that…the mediocre were ably represented by Blackmun, and nowhere, perhaps, was that mediocrity better exemplified than in *Roe v. Wade*." Boldt retired from his position as editor-in-chief of the *Philadelphia Inquirer* immediately after he wrote the column.

*Roe* was argued and decided along with the less known case of *Doe v. Bolton.*[482] In *Doe,* the Court declared an indications policy derived from the *Model Penal Code*[483] to be unconstitutional in the face of the trimester scheme announced in *Roe.* Ironically, the attacks on the constitutionality of the Georgia statute were organized by the very groups that had pushed it through the legislature.[484] By striking down the Georgia statute as unconstitutional, the Supreme Court rendered any possible legislative compromise impossible.[485] Indeed, Blackmun's definition of a women's "health" in *Doe* as encompassing anything affecting her "well-being" virtually precluded any possible regulation of abortion during the entire months of pregnancy.[486]

---

482. 410 U.S. 179 (1973).
483. *See* Chapter 13, at notes 128–31, 191–251.
484. GARROW, *supra* note 23, at 360, 375, 422–28; NOONAN, *supra* note 33, at 59.
485. Glendon, *supra* note 471, at 19.
486. 410 U.S. at 191–92. *See also* Glendon, *supra* note 471, at 20.

# Chapter 15

# Freedom Is Just Another Word for Nothin' Left to Lose[1]

*We made too many wrong mistakes.*

—Yogi Berra[2]

The Supreme Court decisions in the cases of *Roe v. Wade*[3] and *Doe v. Bolton*[4] overturned the abortion laws in at least 46 states,[5] constitutionalizing what amounted to abortion on demand throughout pregnancy. Probably even the statutes in the four states (Alaska, Hawaii, New York, and Washington) and the District of Columbia that had repealed all restrictions for abortions early in pregnancy did not comply with the requirements of *Roe* and *Doe* for late-term abortions. The decisions in *Roe* and *Doe* unequivocally would have overruled statutes in every state if the two decisions had come only three years earlier. The decisions thus marked a sharp break from the history and traditions that were expressed by the common law and were implicit in the Constitution's guarantees of due process, equal protection, and a right of privacy.

Despite the apparently sweeping effect of the two decisions, no one actually knew just what effect the decisions would actually be in the experience of women seeking abortions. The reformed statutes enacted between 1967 and 1970 with such fanfare generally had only a marginal effect on the actual availability of legal abortion.[6] In some states legal abortion became

---

1. Kris Kristofferson & Fred Foster, *Me and Bobby McGee* (1970).
2. David Nathan, Baseball Quotations 151 (1993).
3. 410 U.S. 113 (1973).
4. 410 U.S. 179 (1973).
5. 410 U.S. at 118 n.2. *See also* Mark Graber, Rethinking Abortion: Equal Choice, the Constitution, and Reproductive Politics 122 (1996); Barbara Hinkinson Craig & David O'Brien, Abortion and American Politics 74–77 (1993); Roger Rosenblatt, Life Itself: Abortion in the American Mind 92–95 (1992); Matthew Wetstein, Abortion Rates in the United States: The Influence of Opinion and Policy 15–16 (1996); *A Stunning Approval for Abortion*, Time, Feb. 5, 1973, at 50; Denis Cavanagh, *Legal Abortion in America: Factors in the Dynamics of Change,* 2 Life Liberty & Fam. 309, 312 (1995); Paul Benjamin Linton, Planned Parenthood v. Casey: *The Flight from Reason in the Supreme Court,* 13 St. L.U. Pub. L. Rev. 15, 24–27 (1993); Jay Alan Sekulow & John Tuskey, *The "Center" Lies in the Eye of the Beholder,* 40 N.Y.L.S.L. Rev. 2, 12 n.62 (1996). *See generally* Marian Faux, Roe v. Wade: The Untold Story of the Landmark Supreme Court Decision that Made Abortion Legal (1988); David Garrow, Liberty and Sexuality: The Right of Privacy and the Making of Roe v. Wade 389–407, 423–28, 433–459, 462–65, 491–95, 497–510, 513–17, 520–28, 564–65, 567–73, 600–01 (2nd ed. 1998); Leslie Reagan, When Abortion Was a Crime: Women, Medicine, and Law in the United States, 1867–1973, at 234–40 (1997); James Risen & Judy Thomas, Wrath of Angels: The American Abortion War 36 (1998); Eva Rubin, Abortion, Politics, and the Courts 54 (rev. ed. 1987); Sarah Weddington, A Question of Choice (1992).
6. *See* Chapter 13, at notes 318–37.

more difficult to obtain than before the reforms were enacted.[7] The confusing trimester scheme announced in *Roe* might have been exploited, had the Supreme Court allowed it, to circumscribe abortion rights. Thus questions remained about what effect the decisions would actually have.

Sweeping as the change decreed in *Roe* and *Doe* was, it did not occur in a vacuum. Similar — albeit generally less sweeping — changes were underway in most other industrialized countries (and some non-industrialized countries as well) at about the same time. This alone is enough to suggest that the new rulings were more than just an historical accident dependent on the personalities who just happened to be on the supreme bench when it considered the case. The legal changes also occurred in the face of dramatic changes in the way we perceive and interact with the "products of conception." Medical research and applications changed how we perceive and interact with unborn children. These changes were also centered in the same industrialized countries that were intent on making the disposal of unwanted unborn children legal, usually for the first time in those countries' history.

Understanding the contrasting contexts — social forces tending to legitimate abortion, medical developments tending to legitimate a claim of fetal personhood — is necessary to understand both the legal and the social effects of *Roe* and *Doe*. Once one identifies the two contexts, the ensuing, enduring struggle over the legitimacy of abortion takes on an aura of inevitability. Only by placing *Roe* and *Doe* in the setting of these two contexts can we begin to understand the effects of the two decisions — and the difficulty of arriving at a social consensus that would resolve the controversy over abortion. After considering the immediate effects of *Roe* and *Doe*, this Chapter examines the global changes in approaches to abortion followed by an introduction to the emergence of the fetus as a counterpoint to the pressures to legalize abortion.

# The Aftermath of *Roe* and *Doe*

*No one said a word about the sorrow.*

*—The Bee Gees*[8]

The trimester system announced in *Roe* misleads many into believing that abortion on demand is available only during the first three months of pregnancy. The trimester rules in fact precluded a state from adopting direct legal restrictions on a woman's choice whether to abort until the last three months of pregnancy.[9] Even in the third trimester, legal restrictions had to give way if the woman's choice to abort implicates any health concern of the mother. The Supreme Court had already held, two years earlier, that "health concerns" in the abortion context must include mental health concerns, and in *Roe's* companion case, *Doe v. Bolton*, had made it clear that "mental health" included any concern the woman might have about her happiness or well-being.[10] Mental health thus is a means to justify any choice the woman might make, amounting to a rule of abortion on demand even during the third trimester, limited only by a woman's ability to locate a physician willing to acquiesce in her

---

7. *Id.* at notes 322–25.

8. Robin & Barry Gibb, *How to Mend a Broken Heart* (1971).

9. 410 U.S. at 164–66. For a readable discussion of the confusions arising from *Roe's* trimester analysis, see Mary Ann Glendon, *The Women of* Roe v. Wade, 134 FIRST THINGS 19, 19–20 (June 2003).

10. Doe v. Bolton, 410 U.S. 179, 191–92 (1973); United States v. Vuitch, 402 U.S. 62 (1971).

choice. The apparently graduated scheme thus actually amounted in law to abortion on demand throughout the entire pregnancy. One of the best examples comes from California where legal abortions rose from 5,000 per year—the first full year under the state's reformed abortion law—in 1968 to 100,000 per year in 1972, virtually all done for reasons of mental health.[11] And for about 15 years after *Roe* and *Doe*, the Supreme Court was intent on assuring that almost all significant state efforts to restrict access to abortion even in the third trimester could not be enforced.[12] As a result, between five and seven percent of abortions in the United States are performed after the twenty-first week of gestation—when a fetus is viable or very close to viable.[13]

What effect then did *Roe* and *Doe* have on the frequency of abortions in the United States? Supporters of abortion reform generally insist that by the 1960s (and perhaps for several decades earlier) 1,200,000 illegal abortions were done annually in the United States, with perhaps 10,000 women dying each year from these procedures.[14] Those opposed to abortion insist that the number of abortions were far fewer before *Roe* (or at least before the abortion reform movement got underway) and suggest that maternal deaths immediately before *Roe* were already as few as 25 per year and that abortions then were as few as 100,000 per year.[15]

A sharp break in recorded abortions occurred after 1970 when the first abortion-on-demand statutes were enacted rather than in 1973 with the decisions in *Roe* and *Doe*.[16] After *Roe* and *Doe*, women (or their men) in many communities in the United States could find abortionists by simply looking in the Yellow Pages. Abortion, however, was not readily accepted in American society. Many hospitals refused to perform the procedure, and not just the vilified Catholic institutions. By 1974, a full year after the two decisions, only 15 percent of all municipal hospitals—secular institutions that provided care subsidized at taxpayers' expense—provided abortions.[17]

The two decisions do seem to have encouraged a trend towards more abortions in society. Without firm figures on how many abortions were actually being done before 1965, we cannot be certain about the precise effect of abortion reform, abortion repeal, and the Supreme Court's decisions on abortion practices. Anti-abortion historian Ian Gentles concluded in a careful study

---

11. People v. Barksdale, 503 P.2d 257, 265 (Cal. 1972). *See also* Louis Lader, Abortion II: Making the Revolution 164–66, 178 (1973); John Noonan, jr., A Private Choice: Abortion in America in the Seventies 11–12 (1979); Joseph Dellapenna, *The History of Abortion: Technology, Morality, and Law,* 40 U. Pitt. L. Rev. 359, 383 (1979); Norman Viviera, Roe *and* Wade: *Substantive Due Process and the Right of Abortion,* 25 Hastings L. Rev. 867, 874–75 (1974).

12. Hodgson v. Minnesota, 497 U.S. 417 (1990); Thornburgh v. American College of Obstetricians and Gynecologists 476 U.S. 747 (1986); City of Akron v. Akron Center for Reproductive Health, Inc., 462 U.S. 416 (1983); H.L. v. Matheson, 450 U.S. 398 (1981); Colautti v. Franklin, 439 U.S. 379 (1979); Bellotti v. Baird, 443 U.S. 622 (1979); Planned Parenthood of Mo. v. Danforth, 428 U.S. 52 (1976). The Court did uphold restrictions on using public funds to pay for abortions and requirements that abortions be performed by licensed physicians. Simopoulos v. Virginia, 462 U.S. 508 (1983); City of Akron *supra,* 462 U.S. at 429–30 n.11; Harris v. McRae, 448 U.S. 297 (1980); Poelker v. Doe, 448 U.S. 297 (1979); Maher v. Roe, 432 U.S. 464 (1977); Beal v. Doe, 432 U.S. 438 (1977). *See generally* Philip Smith, *Abortion from* Roe *to* Webster, 102/103 Law & Just. 6 (1989).

13. Lynn Wardle, *The Quandary of Pro-Life Free Speech: A Lesson from the Abolitionists,* 62 Alb. L. Rev. 853, 943, 962 (1999).

14. *See* Chapter 12, at notes 110–43.

15. *See* Chapter 12, at notes 99–109, 144–52.

16. Celeste Michelle Condit, Decoding Abortion Rhetoric: Communicating Social Change 204 (1990); Maureen Muldoon, The Abortion Debate in the United States and Canada: A Source Book 7 (1991); Wetstein, *supra* note 5, at 41, 45–52; Susan Hansen, *State Implementation of Supreme Court Decisions: Abortion Rates since* Roe v. Wade, 42 J. Pol. 372, 375 (1980).

17. Reagan, *supra* note 5, at 339 n.1 (1997); Harold Speert, Obstetrics and Gynecology in America: A History 170 (1980).

that there most likely was a six-fold increase in abortions after *Roe*, but reported that the results could have ranged from a doubling to a twelve-fold increase.[18] Gentles arrived at his figures in part by a careful review of the experience of other countries (particularly England and Canada) in legalizing abortion.[19] Recorded legal abortions in the United States rose from about 586,000 in 1972 (the year before *Roe*) to about 650,000 in 1973, to more than 1,000,000 in 1975, to more than 1,300,000 per year by 1980, and to nearly 1,800,000 in 1978.[20] Since then the number of abortions has steadily, but slowly, declined, until today there are less than 1,500,000 abortions done annually in the United States.[21]

The leveling off and then the decline of the total number of abortions in the United States could be attributed to the graying of the baby boomers.[22] As they aged, fewer women were in the age cohorts that are most likely to seek an abortion. The recent declines now extend, however, to the rate of abortion, whether measured against the total number of women of childbearing age or against the total number of pregnancies. Abortion accounted for about 30 percent of all pregnancies in the United States in the years 1978–1986.[23] The recent declines have dropped that percentage to about 27.5 percent of all pregnancies, and dropped the rate per 1,000 women of reproductive age from 29 to 25.9.[24]

These declines would have been even greater but for the proliferation of repeat abortions. The percentage of women undergoing abortion who had already had one or more abortions rose from 15 percent in 1974 to 46 percent in 1997.[25] Hidden from view is the fact that the number of women undergoing a first abortion was nearly the same number as in 1974 — one year after *Roe v. Wade* was decided.[26] Another result of the rise of repeat abortions has been the steady decline

---

18. Ian Gentles, *Good News for the Fetus: Two Fallacies in the Abortion Debate*, Policy Rev., Spring 1987, at 50, 53.

19. *Id.* at 52–53.

20. Muldoon, *supra* note 16, at 7; Statistical Abstract of the United States 70 (1989); Jack Smith, *Public Health Implications of Abortion: Statistics Compiled by the Centers for Disease Control*, in Abortion and the States 81, 84, 89 (Jane Wishner ed. 1993).

21. Tamar Lewin, *Abortions Fell Again in 1995, but Rose in Some Areas Last Year*, N.Y. Times, Dec. 5, 1997, at A14; Tamar Lewin, *Fewer Abortions Performed in the United States: Variety of Factors Cited for Lowest Level since 1979*, N.Y. Times, June 16, 1994, at A1; Tamar Lewin, *Pause in Abortion's Decline*, N.Y. Times, Dec. 5, 1997, at A14; Barbara Vobejda, *Abortion Rate in U.S. Off Sharply*, Wash. Post, Dec. 5, 1997, at A1; Wardle, *supra* note 13, at 942, 961.

22. Wardle, *supra* note 13, at 940–41. *See also* Timothy Vinceguerra, *Notes of a Footsoldier*, 62 Alb. L. Rev. 1167, 1171 (1999).

23. *See generally ABORTION: The Future Is Already Here*, Time, May 4, 1992, at 26, 32; Joan Williams, *Gender Wars: Selfless Women in the Republic of Choice*, 66 NYU L. Rev. 1559, 1584 (1991).

24. Lewin, *supra* note 21, at A1.

25. Center for Disease Control, Abortion Surveillance — United States, 1997, at 49 (2000) (reporting 46% of all abortions were repeat abortions in 1997); Stanley Henshaw & Jane Silverman, *The Characteristics and Prior Contraceptive Use of U.S. Abortion Patients*, 20 Fam. Plan. Perspectives 156, 158 (July–August 1988) (43 percent of all abortions to be repeat abortions in 1987); Wardle, *supra* note 13, at 941 (47 percent of all abortions to be repeat abortions in 1992). On the characteristics of women who have repeat abortions, see Susan Fisher, *Reflections on Repeated Abortions: The Meanings and Motivations*, 2 J. Soc. Work Practice 70 (1986); Kathleen Franco *e al.*, *Dysphoric Reactions in Women after Abortion*, 44 J. Am. Med. Women's Ass'n 113 (1989); Ellen Freeman, *Emotional Distress Patterns among Women Having First or Repeat Abortions*, 55 Obstet. & Gynecology 630 (1980); D. Naziri & A. Tzavaras, *Mourning and Guilt among Greek Women Having Repeated Abortions*, 26 Omega 137 (1992); Pirkko Niemela *et al.*, *The First Abortion — and the Last? A Study of the Personality Factors Underlying Repeated Failure of Contraception*, 19 Int'l J. Gynaecology & Obstet. 193 (1981); Mogens Osler *et al.*, *Repeat Abortion in Denmark*, 39 Dan. Med. Bull. 89 (1992); Mary Jo Shephard & Michael Bracken, *Contraceptive Practice and Repeat Induced Abortion: An Epidemiological Investigation*, 11 J. Biosocial Sci. 289 (1979); M. Tornbom *et al.*, *Repeat Abortion: A Comparative Study*, 17 J. Psychosomatic Obstet. & Gynecology 208 (1996).

26. Wardle, *supra* note 13, at 941–42.

of the percentage of women who have abortions under 19 years of age—from a peak of 32.9 percent of all women having abortions in 1975, to only 23 percent in 1990.[27] But then, polls suggest that young adults in the United States—including college freshman—support the legality of abortion less strongly than does the adult population generally.[28]

Those engrossed in the debate over abortion sharply disagree, of course, about the effect of *Roe* on maternal and fetal lives. Abortion rights proponents often insist that abortions did not increase "dramatically" since *Roe*, although their own figures show an increase from about 1 million to about 1.6 million per year over a period of five years.[29] Antiabortion activists, in contrast, tend to exaggerate the effect of *Roe*. David Reardon, for example, estimated a 10- to 15-fold increase in the incidence of abortion following *Roe*.[30] Both claims are wrong.

The actual increase—somewhere between two and three times—is significant, as a few supporters of abortion rights have conceded.[31] The Alan Guttmacher Institute—the research arm of the abortion rights movement—follows the officially reported figures, showing an increase from about 600,000 in 1972 to somewhat over 1,500,000 by 1980.[32] One study further concluded that less than half (47 percent between 1977 and 1981) of all legal abortions are actually reported to the statistical centers.[33] Whatever the actual increase, abortion is now the second most common surgical procedure in the United States, with more than 30,000,000 having been performed since 1973. (Commentators often describe abortion as the most common surgical procedure in the

---

27. *Id.,* at 961.

28. Jules Irwin, *Most Young Adults Are Ambivalent on Abortion: Open Talks Haven't Brought Consensus,* Cin. Enquirer, Jan. 18, 1998, at A5, A16.

29. Cass Sunstein, *Neutrality in Constitutional Law (with Special Reference to Pornography, Abortion, and Surrogacy),* 92 Colum. L. Rev. 1, 38 (1992). *See also* Condit, *supra* note 16, at 22; Graber, *supra* note 5, at 65–66; Frederick Jaffe, Barbara Lindheim, & Philip Lee, Abortion Politics 21 (1981); Rosalind Pollack Petchesky, Abortion and Women's Choice: The State, Sexuality, and Reproductive Freedom 141–61 (rev. ed. 1990); Gerald Rosenberg, The Hollow Hope: Can Courts Bring About Social Change? 179–80, 200, 355 (1990); Laurence Tribe, Abortion: The Clash of Absolutes 41 (1990); Raymond Adamek, *Abortion Policy: Time for Reassessment,* in Abortion Parley 1, 21 (James Burtchaell ed. 1980); *Amicus Brief of National Coalition against Domestic Violence supporting Appellees in* Webster v. Reproductive Health Services, reprinted in 11 Women's Rts. L. Rep. 281, 292 (1989), and in 7 Documentary History of the Legal Aspects of Abortion in the U.S. 97 (Roy Mersky & Gary Hartman eds. 1990); Michael Bracken, Daniel Freeman, & Karen Hillebrand, *Hospitalization for Medical-Legal and Other Abortions (sic) in the United States, 1970–1977,* 72 Am. J. Pub. Health 30, 34 (1982); Willard Cates, jr., *The First Decade of Legal Abortion in the United States* ("Cates, *First Decade*") in Abortion, Medicine, and the Law 307, 308 (J. Douglas Butler & David Walbert eds. 3rd ed. 1986); Willard Cates, jr., *Legal Abortion: The Public Health Record,* 215 Sci. 1586, 1586 (1982) ("Cates, *Public Health*"); Willard Cates & Roger Rochat, *Illegal Abortions in the United States, 1972–1974,* 8 Fam. Planning Persp. 86, 91 (1976); Frank Easterbrook, *Bills of Rights and Regression to the Mean,* 15 Harv. J.L. & Pub. Pol'y 71, 76–77 (1992); Byron Fujita & Nathaniel Wagner, *Referendum 20—Abortion Reform in Washington State,* in The Abortion Experience: Psychological and Medical Impact 232, 256 (Howard & Joy Orsofsky eds. 1973); Jonathan Quick, *Liberalized Abortion in Oregon: Effects on Fertility, Prematurity, Fetal Death, and Infant Death,* 68 Am. J. Pub. Health 1003, 1007 (1978); Christopher Tietze & John Bongaarts, *The Demographic Effects of Induced Abortion,* 31 Obstet. & Gynecological Survey 699, 706–08 (1976).

30. David Reardon, Aborted Women: Silent No More 291 (1987).

31. Graber, *supra* note 5, at 42; Betty Sarvis & Hyman Rodman, The Abortion Controversy 55 (1973); Donald Judges, Hard Choices, Lost Voices 30 (1993); Petchesky, *supra* note 29, at 142–43; Margaret Farrell, *Revisiting* Roe v. Wade: *Substance and Due Process in the Abortion Debate,* 68 Ind. L.J. 269, 279–80 (1993); Peter Schuck, *Public Law Litigation and Social Reform,* 102 Yale L.J. 1763, 1777–80 (1993); Judith Sklar & Beth Berkov, *Abortion, Illegitimacy, and the American Birth Rate,* 185 Science 909 (1974). *See also* Condit, *supra* note 16, at 191–93.

32. Smith, *supra* note 20, at 84–85, 90; Wardle, *supra* note 13, at 941.

33. Jacqueline Darroch Forrest, *Unintended Pregnancy among American Women,* 19 Fam. Planning Persp. 76 (1987).

United States.[34] This overlooks both that not all abortions are surgical and the even more common incidence of male circumcision.)

Abortion rights activists tend to counter concerns about rising abortion rates by insisting that the number of maternal deaths from induced abortions has declined by at least 90 percent since *Roe* was decided, from an alleged 10,000 to less than 1,000.[35] Historian Leslie Reagan goes so far as to describe the improvement in maternal mortality from the legalization of abortion as "rank[ing] with the invention of antisepsis and antibiotics."[36] Reagan bases her conclusion on gross rates of maternal mortality (including deaths from causes other than abortion) in several states, does not mention how many lives these rates actually represent, does not consider whether any other changes might have contributed to changes in these rates.[37] A careful analysis of the data suggests that the effects of legalizing abortion were more modest than Reagan suggests. Even such a well-known abortion rights campaigner Dr. Willard Cates was less enthusiastic about the effect of legalizing abortion on maternal mortality, concluding that legalized abortion saved the lives of 1,500 mothers by 1984—less than 100 per year since abortion reform laws were first enacted.[38] The actual number probably was considerably smaller. In fact, the data suggest that there have been as many maternal deaths in the United States annually from legal abortions (estimates range from 15 to 35 per year) as there were maternal deaths from illegal abortions in the years immediately before *Roe v. Wade* was decided.[39] Abortion has real physical risks—even without negligence on the part of the physician performing the procedure.[40]

---

34. *See, e.g.,* Robert Blank & Janna Merrick, Human Reproduction, Emerging Technologies, and Conflicting Rights 27 (1995); Faye Ginsburg, Contested Lives: The Abortion Debate in an American Community 55 (1989); Wardle, *supra* note 13, at 940; *Legacy of Shame: Abortion "Common" but Not "Safe,"* Cin. Enquirer, Jan. 22, 1998, at A14.

35. Sunstein, *supra* note 29, at 37. *See also* Jerome Legge, Abortion Policy: An Evaluation of the Consequences for Maternal and Infant Health 129–31 (1985); Selig Neubardt & Harold Schulman, Techniques of Abortion ix (2nd ed. 1977); Rodman, Sarvis, & Bonar, *supra* note 31, at 62–63; Ronald Kahan, Lawrence Baker, & Malcolm Freeman, *The Effect of Legalized Abortion on Morbidity Resulting from Criminal Abortion,* 121 Am. J. Obstet. & Gynecology 114 (1975); Paul Seward, Charles Ballard, & Arthur Ulene, *The Effect of Legal Abortion on the Rate of Septic Abortion at a Large County Hospital,* 115 Am. J. Obstet. & Gynecology 335 (1973).

36. Reagan, *supra* note 5, at 246.

37. *Id.* at 339, n.4.

38. Willard Cates, jr., *The Public Health Effects of Legal Abortion in the United States,* 16 Fam. Planning Persp. 26, 26 (1984). *See also* Jaffe, Lindheim, & Lee, *supra* note 29, at 23; Petchesky, *supra* note 29, at 157; Hyman Rodman, Betty Sarvis, & Joy Bonar, The Abortion Question 46 (1987); Bracken, Freeman, & Hillebrand, *supra* note 29, at 31; Cates, *Public Health, supra* note 29, at 1586–87; Ruth Roemer, *Legalization of Abortion in the United States,* in The Abortion Experience, *supra* note 29, at 280, 296.

39. *See* Hani Atrash Herschel Lawson, & Jack Smith, *Legal Abortion in the United States: Trends and Mortality,* 35 Contemp. Obstet. & Gynecology 58 (1990) (213 legal abortion deaths between 1973 and 1985, about 18 per year); Hani Atrash, *et al., Legal Abortion Mortality and General Anesthesia,* 158 Am. J. Obstet. & Gynecology 420 (1988) (193 deaths between 1972 and 1985, about 15 per year); Willard Cates, jr., Jack Smith, & Roger Rouchet, *Assessment of Surveillance and Vital Statistics Data for Monitoring Abortion Mortality, United States, 1972–1975,* 108 Am. J. Epidemiology 200 (1978) (204 deaths between 1972 and 1975, 104 from legal abortions, about 35 per year); David Grimes *et al.,Fatal Hemorrhage from Legal Abortion in the United States,* 157 Surgical Gynecology & Obstet. 461 (1983) (194 deaths between 1972 and 1979, about 26 per year); Herschel Lawson *et al., Abortion Mortality, United States, 1972 through 1987,* 171 Am. J. Obstet. & Gynecology 1365 (1994); Scott LeBolt *et al., Mortality from Abortion and Childbirth,* 248 JAMA 188 (1982) (138 deaths between 1972 and 1978, about 23 per year). *See generally* Nat Hentoff, *Covering Up Destructive Abortions,* Village Voice, June 18, 1991, at 20; Joyce Price, *Statistics May Be Misleading on Deaths Caused by Abortion,* Wash. Times, June 4, 1994, at A5; Christopher Tietze, *The Public Health Effects of Legal Abortion in the United States,* 16 Fam. Planning Perspectives 26 (1984). *See also* Chapter 12, at notes 62–83, 117–25.

40. Sebastian Faro & Mark Pearlman, Infection and Abortion (1992); Risking the Future: Adolescent Sexuality, Pregnancy, and Childbearing (Cheryl Hayes ed. 1987); Williams Obstetrics 600–01 (F. Gary Cunningham *et al.* eds., 20th ed. 1989); D. Avonts & P. Piot, *Genital Infections in Women Un-*

Probably many of the continuing maternal deaths and other problems were caused by physician malpractice. Medical malpractice in the performance of abortion has become increasing common, as shown both by the rare criminal proceeding,[41] by somewhat more common professional disciplinary proceedings,[42] and by the even more common civil judgments.[43] A growing

*dergoing Therapeutic Abortion,* 20 Eur. J. Obstet., Gynaecology, & Reprod. Biol. 53 (1985); Elaine Belanger, Ronald Melzack, & Pierre Lauzon, *Pain of First Trimester Abortion: A Study of Psychosocial and Medical Predictors,* 36 Pain 339 (1989); David Grimes, Kenneth Schulz, & Willard Cates, jr., *Measures to Prevent Cervical Injury during Suction Curettage Abortion,* 321 The Lancet 1182 (1983); David Grimes, Kenneth Schulz, & Willard Cates, jr., *Prevention of Uterine Perforation during Curettage Abortion,* 251 JAMA 2108 (1984); E. Hakin-Elahi, *Complications of First-Trimester Abortions: A Report of 170,000 Cases,* 76 Obstet. & Gynecology 129 (1990); Lars Heisterberg, *Factors Influencing Spontaneous Abortion, Dyspareunia, Dysmenorrhea, and Pelvic Pain,* 81 Obstet. & Gyncecology 594 (1993); Lars Heisterberg, Soren Hebjorn, Lars Andersen, *Sequelae of Induced First-Trimester Abortion: A Prospective Study Assessing the Role of Postabortal Pelvic Inflammatory Disease and Prophylactic Antibiotics,* 155 Am. J. Obstet. & Gynecology 76 (1986); Lars Heisterberg & Mette Kringelbach, *Early Complications after Induced First-Trimester Abortion,* 66 Acta Obstet. & Gynecologica Scand. 201 (1987); Steven Kaali, Ivan Szigetvari, & George Bartfai, *The Frequency and Management of Uterine Perforations during First Trimester Abortions,* 161 Am. J. Obstet. & Gynecology 406 (1989); Andrew Kaunitz *et al., Reducing Risk for Unrecognized Failed Abortion,* 20 Obstet. & Gynecology News no. 3, at 8 (Feb. 1, 1985); Per Goren Larsson, *et al., Incidence of PID after First-Trimester Legal Abortion in Women with Bacterial Vaginosis after Treatment with Metronidazole: A Double-Blind Randomized Study,* 166 Am. J. Obstet. & Gynecology 100 (1992); Jette Sorensen & Ingrid Thronov, *A Double-Blind Randomized Study of the Effect of Erythromycin in Preventing Pelvic Inflammatory Disease after First Trimester Abortion,* 99 Brit. J. Obstet. & Gynaecology 434 (1992); Babill Stray-Pedersen, *Induced Abortion: Microbiological Screening and Medical Complications,* 19 Infection 305 (1991); Peter Sykes, *Complications of Termination of Pregnancy: A Retrospective Study of Admissions in Christchurch Women's Hospital, 1989 and 1990,* 106 N.Z. Med. J. 83 (Mar. 10, 1993); Nancy Wells, *Pain and Distress during Abortion,* 12 Health Care for Women Int'l 293 (1991).

41. *See, e.g.,* People v. Bickham, 431 N.E.2d 165 (Ill. 1982). *See also* Lisa Belkin, *State Suspends Manhattan Doctor Accused of Botching Abortion,* N.Y. Times, Nov. 26, 1991, at B1.

42. *See, e.g.,* Keneally v. California Med. Bd., 32 Cal. Rptr. 2d 504 (Ct. App. 1994), *rev. denied*; Sherman v. Board of Med., 557 A.2d 943 (D.C. 1989); Ticktin v. Department of Prof. Reg., 532 So. 2d 47 (Fla. 1988); Tauber v. State Bd. of Osteopathic Med. Examiners, 326 So. 2d 90 (Fla. Ct. App. 1978); Bickham v. Selcke, 576 N.E.2d 975 (Ill. 1991); Biogenetics, Ltd. v. Department of Pub. Health, 431 N.E.2d 1042 (Ill. 1982); Village of Oak Lawn v. Marcowitz, 427 N.E.2d 36 (Ill. 1982); Cabinet for Human Resources v. Women's Health Services, Inc., 878 S.W.2d 806 (Ky. Ct. App. 1994); Louisiana State Bd. Med. Examiners v. Golden, 645 So. 2d 690 (La. Ct. App. 1994), *writ denied,* 650 So. 2d 1184 (La. 1995); Schwalben v. De Buono, 696 N.Y.S.2d 262 (App. Div. 1999); Hachamovitch v. State Bd. for Prof. Misconduct, 614 N.Y.S.2d 608 (App. Div.), *appeal denied,* 645 N.E.2d 1218 (N.Y. 1994), *mandamus denied,* 641 N.Y.S.2d 757 (App. Div.), *appeal denied,* 673 N.E.2d 1243 (N.Y. 1996); Terra v. Department of Health, 604 N.Y.S.2d 644 (App. Div. 1993); Brown v. State Univ. of N.Y., 537 N.Y.S.2d 655 (App. Div. 1989); Okereke v. State, 518 N.Y.S.2d 210 (App. Div. 1987); Alizadeh v. Ambach, 515 N.Y.S.2d 315 (App. Div. 1987); Schwarz v. Board of Regents, 453 N.Y.S.2d 836 (App. Div. 1982); Skolnick v. Nyquist, 399 N.Y.S.2d 482 (App. Div. 1977); Davis v. Fieker, 952 P.2d 505 (Okla. 1997); S.R. v. City of Fairmount, 280 S.E.2d 712 (W. Va. 1981).

43. *See* David Reardon, Abortion Malpractice (1994); Paul Baldwin, *Local Lawyer Wins $10 Million Abortion Case—Specializes in Suits against Doctors over Injury, Death,* Courier-Journal, Dec. 11, 1996, at 5B; Thomas Eller, *Informed Consent Civil Actions for Post-Abortion Psychological Trauma,* 71 Notre Dame L. Rev. 639 (1996); Jesse Garza, *Negligence Finding Won't Benefit Family,* Mil. J. Sentinal, May 5, 2001, at 1B; Peter Hertlaub, *$672,000 S.F. Abortion Verdict Is Appealed; Second Fetus Found after Procedure,* S.F. Chron., Apr. 11, 2001, at A17; Ray Kerrison, *Horror Tale of Abortion,* N.Y. Post, Jan. 7, 1991, at 2; Ray Kerrison, *Abort Patients Naivete Leads to Another Death,* N.Y. Post, Aug. 5, 1991, at 2; Tamar Lewin, *Malpractice Lawyers' New Target,* Med. Econ., July 1995, at 21; Kathy Seward Northern, *Procreative Torts: Enhancing the Common-Law Protection for Reproductive Autonomy,* 1998 U. Ill. L. Rev. 489; Bruce & Diane Rodgers, *Abortion: The Seduction of Medicine,* 2 Liberty Life & Fam. 285, 307–08 (1995); Raymond Smith, *Abortion Doctor Faces More Claims: Dr. Joseph Durante, Who Operates a Clinic in Moreno Valley, Has Been on Medical Probation since 1996,* The Press-Enterprise (Riverside, CA), May 12, 2000, at B1; Raymond Smith, *Lawsuit Filed in Abortion Case: Woman Says She Suffered Severe Internal Injuries,* The Press-Enterprise (Riverside, CA), July 23, 1999, at B1; Thomas Strahan, *Negligent Physical or Emotional Injury Related to Induced Abortion,* 9 Regent U. L. Rev. 149 (1997); Joseph Stuart, *Abortion and Informed Consent: A Cause of Action,* 14 Ohio N. L. Rev. 1

number of the resulting cases have reached appellate courts for a full-blown legal analysis.[44] Beyond simply botched abortions, there are cases finding liability for abortions performed when the attending physician misdiagnosed the condition of the pregnancy in a way that persuaded a woman to have an abortion when, had the true facts been known, she definitely would not have

---

(1987). *See generally* Paige Comstock Cunningham & Clarke Forsythe, *Is Abortion the "First Right" for Women?: Some Consequences of Legal Abortion,* in ABORTION, MEDICINE AND THE LAW 100, 130–37 (J. Douglas Butler & David Walbert eds., 4th ed. 1992); Gary Roberts, *Medical Malpractice in Abortion Cases,* 3 AM. J. TRIAL ADV. 259 (1979); A.J. Stone, III, Comment, *Consti-Tortion: Tort Law as an End-Run around Abortion Rights after* Planned Parenthood v. Casey, 8 AM. U. J. GENDER, SOC. POL'Y & L. 471, 497–515 (2000). *See also* Keneally v. California Med. Bd., 32 Cal. Rptr. 2d 504 (Ct. App. 1994), *rev. denied* (upholding the streamlining of the procedure for disciplining physicians accused of gross negligence and gross incompetence); Albala v. New York City, 429 N.E.2d 786 (N.Y. 1981) (no liability to an infant injured as a result of an abortion botched before he was conceived).

44. *See* Gaydar v. Sociedad Instituto Gineco-Quirurigico, 345 F.3d 15 (1st Cir. 2003); Arnold v. Board of Educ. of Escambia Cnty., 880 F.2d 305 (11th Cir. 1989); Baker v. Edman, 719 F.2d 122 (5th Cir. 1983); Fowler v. Bickham, 550 F. Supp. 71 (N.D. Ill. 1982); Boykin v. Magnolia Bay, Inc., 570 So. 2d 639 (Ala. 1990); Williams v. Robinson, 512 So. 2d 58 (Ala. 1987); Perguson v. Tamis, 937 P.2d 347 (Ariz. Ct. App. 1996); Vuitch v. Furr, 482 A.2d 811 (D.C. 1984); Sponaugle v. Pre-Term, Inc., 411 A.2d 366 (D.C. 1980); Atlanta Obstetrics v. Coleman, 398 S.E.2d 16 (Ga. 1990); Miller v. Vitner, 546 S.E.2d 917 (Ga. Ct. App. 2001); Bryant v. Crider, 434 S.E.2d 161 (Ga. Ct. App. 1993); Lewis v. Family Planning Mgnt., Inc., 715 N.E.2d 743 (Ill. 1999); Adams v. Family Planning Assoc. Med. Group, 733 N.E.2d 766 (Ill. App. Ct. 2000), *appeal denied,* 744 N.E.2d 283 (Ill. 2001); Shirk v. Kelsey, 617 N.E.2d 152 (Ill. App. Ct.), *appeal denied,* 622 N.E.2d 1228 (Ill. 1993); Brown v. Moawad, 570 N.E.2d 490 (Ill. App. Ct.), *appeal dismissed,* 575 N.E.2d 112 (Ill. 1991); Kirby v. Jarrett, 545 N.E.2d 965 (Ill. App. Ct. 1989); Collins v. Thakkar, 552 N.E.2d 507 (Ind. Ct. App. 1990); Reynier v. Delta Women's Clinic, Inc., 359 So. 2d 733 (La. Ct. App. 1978); Hitch v. Hall, 399 A.2d 953 (Md. Ct. Spec. App.), *cert. denied,* 285 Md. 730 (1979); Blair v. Hutzel Hosp., 552 N.W.2d 507 (Mich. Ct. App. 1996), *rev'd mem.,* 569 N.W.2d 167 (Mich. 1997); Joplin v. University of Mich. Bd. of Regents, 433 N.W.2d 830 (Mich. Ct. App. 1988), *remanded on other grounds,* 450 N.W.2d 263 (Mich.), *dismissed on other grounds,* 459 N.W.2d 70 (Mich. Ct. App. 1990); Kiddy v. Lipscomb, 628 So. 2d 1355 (Miss. 1993); Eidson v. Reproductive Health Services, 863 S.W.2d 621 (Mo. Ct. App. 1993), *transfer denied;* Blackburn v. Blue Mt. Women's Clinic, 951 P.2d 1 (Mont.), *cert. denied,* 524 U.S. 905 (1998); Ferrara v. Bernstein, 613 N.E.2d 542 (N.Y. 1993); Jessamy v. Parkmed Assocs., 761 N.Y.S.2d 639 (App. Div. 2003); Negron v. State, 638 N.Y.S.2d 977 (App. Div.), *appeal denied,* 670 N.E.2d 226 (N.Y. 1996); Ganapolskaya v. VIP Med. Assoc., 644 N.Y.S.2d 735 (App. Div. 1996); Nehorayoff v. Fernandez, 594 N.Y.S.2d 863 (App. Div. 1993); Martinez v. Long Island Jewish-Hillside Med. Ctr., 519 N.Y.S.2d 538 (App. Div. 1987); Klusterman v. Glick, 484 N.Y.S.2d 31 (App. Div. 1985); Jean-Charles v. Planned Parenthood, 471 N.Y.S.2d 622 (App. Div. 1984); Delaney v. Krafte, 470 N.Y.S.2d 936 (App. Div. 1984); Mears v. Alhadeff, 451 N.Y.S.2d 133 (App. Div. 1982); Phillips v. A Triangle Women's Health Clinic, 573 S.E.2d 600 (N.C. Ct. App. 2002), *aff'd mem.,* 597 S.E.2d 669 (N.C. 2003); Sorina v. Armstrong, 589 N.E.2d 1359 (Ohio Ct. App. 1990), *jurisdictional motion overruled,* 569 N.E.2d 512 (Ohio 1991); Davis v. Fieker, 952 P.2d 505 (Okla. 1997); Grandelli v. Methodist Hospital, 777 A.2d 1138 (Pa. Super. Ct. 2001); Roddy v. Volunteer Med. Clinic, 926 S.W.2d 572 (Tenn. Ct. App. 1996), *appeal denied;* Hunte v. Hinkley, 731 S.W.2d 570 (Tex. Ct. App. 1987), *writ refused, n.r.e.;* Lake v. Northern Va. Women's Med. Ctr., Inc., 483 S.E.2d 220 (Va. 1997); Ott v. Baker, 53 Va. Cir. 113 (2000); Senesac v. Associates in Obstet. & Gynecology, 449 A.2d 900 (Vt. 1982); S.R. v. City of Fairmount, 280 S.E.2d 712 (W. Va. 1981). *See also* Okpalobi v. Foster, 244 F.3d 405 (5th Cir. 2001); Sherman v. Ambassador Ins. Co., 670 F.2d 251 (D.C. Cir. 1981); Broemmer v. Abortion Services of Phoenix, Ltd., 840 P.2d 1013 (Ariz. 1992); Blanton v. Womencare, Inc., 696 P.2d 695 (Cal. 1985); Dunmore v. Babaoff, 386 N.W.2d 154 (Mich. Ct. App. 1985); Baker v. Gordon, 759 S.W.2d 87 (Mo. Ct. App. 1988); Koehler v. Schwartz, 399 N.E.2d 1140 (N.Y. 1979); Perez v. Park Madison Prof. Labs., Inc., 630 N.Y.S.2d 37 (App. Div.), *appeal dismissed,* 663 N.E.2d 922 (N.Y. 1995); Rockefeller v. Chul Hwang, 484 N.Y.S.2d 206 (App. Div. 1984); Sanchez v. Sirmons, 467 N.Y.S.2d 757 (Sup. Ct. 1983); Powers v. Floyd, 904 S.W.2d 713 (Tex. Ct. App. 1995), *cert. denied,* 516 U.S. 1126 (1996).

had the abortion.[45] This includes several cases where the physician was found to have performed an "abortion" on a woman whom the physician knew was not pregnant.[46]

Efforts to obtain redress from such abusive abortionists remains significantly easier in civil that criminal proceedings for two reasons. First, civil proceedings follow a relaxed burden of proof ("preponderance of the evidence" rather than "beyond a reasonable doubt"). Second, various technical safeguards apply in criminal proceedings simply do not apply in civil proceedings whether in a tort suit or in a professional disciplinary hearing.[47] We have, however, no reliable statistics to indicate how common abortion malpractice is, let alone whether that incidence is more or less or about the same as the equivalent problems when abortions were illegal.

To put these figures into perspective, recall that nearly all abortions are for "social" reasons and extremely few because of genuine medical indications. Thus, even if deaths from abortion are rare, they are almost always unnecessary in the sense that there was no medical reason for incurring the medical risk of an abortion—except the fact of pregnancy itself.[48] This is particularly true when the death results from the occasional, albeit rare, illegal abortion. Yet, as Drs. Christopher Tietze and Stanley Henshaw of the Alan Guttmacher Institute concluded, "[i]t is entirely possible that the death-to-case ratio following illegal abortion in the United States is now higher, not lower, than it was 15-20 years ago [before *Roe*]." [49]

Those who argue that legalized abortion has saved women's lives point to the fact that the maternal death rate per 100,000 live births has dropped sharply since *Roe* was decided, and may now be 20 percent or less of the rate in 1973 (when *Roe* was decided). The American Medical Association reports a 90 percent decline in maternal deaths from childbirth in the 30 years since

---

45. Robak v. United States, 658 F.2d 471 (7th Cir. 1981) (liability for misdiagnosis when the woman would not have had the abortion had the true facts been known); Johnson v. United States, 810 F. Supp. 7 (D.D.C. 1993) (same), *aff'd mem.*, 1995 WL 418651 (D.C. Cir. 1995); Ticktin v. Department of Prof. Reg., 532 So. 2d 47 (Fla. 1988) (licensed revoked for failing to inform the woman of the stage the pregnancy had reached); Wall v. Pecaro, 561 N.E.2d 1084 (Ill. App. Ct.) (performance of unnecessary abortion, represented as necessary, held to constitute intentional infliction of emotional distress), *appeal denied*, 567 N.E.2d 343 (Ill. 1991); Reynier v. Delta Women's Clinic, 359 So. 2d 733 (La. Ct. App. 1978) (no liability because the woman would have had the abortion even had the diagnosis been correct); Shelton v. St. Anthony's Med. Ctr., 781 S.W.2d 48 (Mo. 1989) (liability for misdiagnosis when the woman would not have had the abortion had the true facts been known); Hogle v. Hall, 916 P.2d 814 (Nev. 1996) (same); Martinez v. Long Island Jewish-Hillside Med. Cntr., 512 N.E.2d 538 (N.Y. 1987) (liability for misdiagnosis when the woman would not have had the abortion had the true facts been known). *See also* Deutsch v. Shein, 597 S.W.2d 141 (Ky. 1980) (x-rays administered without diagnosis of pregnancy). *But see* Symone T. v. Lieber, 613 N.Y.S.2d 404 (App. Div. 1994) (denying recovery for a woman severely injured by an abortion she knew to be illegal when it was performed); Gail Hollister, *Tort Suits for Injuries during Illegal Abortions: The Effects of Judicial Bias*, 45 VILLA. L. REV. 387 (2000).

46. *See* Terra v. Department of Health, 604 N.Y.S.2d 644 (App. Div. 1993); Alizadeh v. Ambach, 515 N.Y.S.2d 315 (App. Div. 1987). *See also Risky Abortions: Chicago Clinics Are Exposed*, TIME, Nov. 27, 1978, at 60. On the other hand, New York Courts do not recognize liability when the abortion fails to "terminate the pregnancy." Koehler v. Schwartz, 399 N.E.2d 1140 (N.Y. 1979).

47. *See, e.g.*, Sherman v. District of Columbia Bd. of Med., 557 A.2d 943 (D.C. 1989) (approving the Commission on Licensure's decision to increase the severity of the defendant's punishment after the Commission's earlier decision was overturned on appeal and without a new hearing on the sanction); Terra v. Department of Health, 604 N.Y.S.2d 644, 646 (App. Div. 1993) (approving the hearing board's drawing of an adverse inference from the defendant's invocation of the Fifth Amendment right against self-incrimination—an inference that would not be allowed in a criminal proceeding).

48. Brian Clowes, *The Role of Maternal Deaths in the Abortion Debate*, 13 ST. L.U. PUB. L. REV. 327, 350 (1993).

49. CHRISTOPHER TIETZE & STANLEY HENSHAW, INDUCED ABORTION: A WORLD REVIEW 1986, at 132 (1986).

*Roe* was decided.[50] Today, the maternal death rate related to pregnancy and childbirth is around 8/100,000 live births in the United States, being about double that rate (15/100,000) for African-American women and around 5/100,000 for other women. The rate has remained at that level for the past 20 years.[51] These levels are quite low by global standards, but higher than in other industrialized countries. Note that the verifiable declines in the overall maternal death rates refer to deaths from pregnancy as well as abortion.

The overall decline in pregnancy-related deaths does not appear to have resulted from the availability of abortion. Consider that there have been greater declines in maternal mortality in the Irish Republic (where abortions are illegal and remain difficult to obtain) than in most areas of the United Kingdom (where abortion is available virtually on demand).[52] The maternal mortality rate in the Irish Republic now is 7:100,000, in England and Wales 11:100,000, in Scotland 14:100,000, and in Northern Ireland 7:100,000.

Contraception, it would seem, has more to do with saving mothers' lives than abortion. As a result, death rates from childbirth are now much closer to the death rates directly from abortion even though the childbirth rate is still higher. The most recent evidence indicates that abortion is safer than childbirth only if the abortion occurs before the 16th week of pregnancy; after the 16th week, abortion is more likely to result in maternal death than carrying the child to term, and abortion becomes steadily more dangerous as the pregnancy progresses.[53] In any event, death from pregnancy or childbirth, as well as from abortion, is so rare that the risk hardly enters into a woman's calculations in deciding to become pregnant.

On the other hand, there does seem to have been some increase in sexually transmitted diseases as a result of the legalization of abortion.[54] This change—shown by comparing the rates of such diseases in states with high incidences of abortion with the rates of such diseases in states with low incidences of abortion—does not show up as a complication of abortion, let alone as resulting in abortion related deaths. Not only does much of this increase in disease not cause death, but even the fatal diseases are not recorded as abortion related for the woman at risk need never have had an abortion herself. The increase seems simply to reflect the greater willingness of persons to engage in sexual relations with multiple partners because of the decreased fear of pregnancy.

Many abortion activists go considerably farther than claims about maternal health in arguing for the benefits of liberalized abortion laws—stressing that abortion has reduced infant mortality![55] That is true enough—if one considers only the mortality of infants after birth. It's like ar-

---

50. *Amicus Brief of the Am. Med. Ass'n supporting Appellants in* Webster v. Reproductive Health Services [492 U.S. 490 (1989)], at 9, *reprinted in* 11 Women's Rts. L. Rep. 443, 454 (1989), and in 5 Documentary History of the Legal Aspects of Abortion in the U.S., *supra* note 29, at 341, 363 (10,000 maternal deaths annually, a 90% reduction since *Roe v. Wade*).

51. *U.S. Pregnancy Deaths Hold at 15-Year Plateau,* N.Y. Times, Sept. 4, 1998, at A14.

52. Mary Kenny, Abortion: The Whole Story 121–22 (1986).

53. AMA Council on Scientific Affairs, *Council Report: Induced Termination of Pregnancy before and after—Trends in Mortality and Morbidity of Women,* 268 JAMA 3231 (1992).

54. Jonathan Klick & Thomas Stratman, *The Effect of Abortion Legalization on Sexual Behavior: Evidence from Sexually Transmitted Diseases,* 32 J. Legal Stud. 407 (2003).

55. *See, e.g.,* Graber, *supra* note 5, at 184 n.212; Beverly Wildung Harrison, Our Right to Choose: Toward a New Ethic of Abortion 171 (1983); Legge, *supra* note 35, at 130–40; Anita Allen, *Tribe's Judicious Feminism* (book rev.), 44 Stan. L. Rev. 179, 193–94 (1992); *Amicus Brief of the International Women's Health Organization supporting Appellees in* Webster v. Reproductive Health Services, reprinted in 11 Women's Rts. L. Rep. 191, 202–04 (1989), and in 7 Documentary History of the Legal Aspects of Abortion in the U.S., *supra* note 29, at 3, 30; Byllye Avery, *A Question of Survival/A Conspiracy of Silence: Abortion and Black Women's Health,* in Abortion to Reproductive Freedom: Transforming a Movement 75, 81 (Marlene Gerber Fried ed. 1990); Rebecca Cook, *U.S. Population Policy, Sex Discrimination, and Principles of Equality under International Law,* 20 NYU J. Int'l L. & Pol. 93, 103–04, 112–13 (1987); Hope Corman & Michael Grossman, *Determinants of Neonatal Mortality Rates in the U.S.: A Reduced Form Model,* 4 J. Health Econ.

guing that the Holocaust was justified because it reduced the number of Jewish deaths from heart attacks or cancer. One might go on to mention those who insist that denial of an abortion injures the resulting children as well as the women forced to deliver an unwanted child.[56]

The notion that abortion is good for the child underlies claims by law professor John Donohue III and economist Steven Levitt that the advent of legalized abortions in 1973 accounts for the decline in the crime rate after 1991.[57] The article garnered considerable media attention even before it was published.[58] They cannot contend that abortion specifically targets would-be criminals 15 or more years before they would commit their first serious crime, but they do claim that women who are most likely to have children who grow up to become criminals are also most likely to seek an abortion. Who are those women? "Teenagers, unmarried women, and the economically disadvantaged."[59] Earlier drafts had been more blunt: "Teenagers, unmarried women, and African Americans"[60] and the published version itself refers as well to how the greatest effects on lowering birth-rates was on "black women."[61]

Leaving the evident class and race biases aside, Donohue and Levitt's attitude would deal with a problem by eliminating the persons involved with the problem rather than by attempting to solve the problem and save the people. This is the eugenics movement once again in full flower.[62] Law professor John Lott, jr., and economist John Whitley, with much less fanfare, have raised se-

---

213 (1985); Michael Grossman & Steven Jacobowitz, *Variations of Infant Mortality Rates among Counties of the United States: The Roles of Public Policies and Programs*, 18 DEMOGRAPHY 695 (1981); Michael Grossman & Theodore Joyce, *Unobservables, Pregnancy Resolutions, and Birth Weight Production Functions in New York City*, 98 J. POL. ECON. 983 (1990); Berta Hernàndez, *To Bear or Not to Bear: Reproductive Freedom as an International Human Right*, 17 BROOK. J. INT'L L. 309, 335, 338–40 (1991); Theodore Joyce, *The Impact of Induced Abortion on Black and White Birth Outcomes in the United States*, 24 DEMOGRAPHY 229 (1987); Luke Lee, *International Status of Abortion Legalization*, in THE ABORTION EXPERIENCE, *supra* note 29, at 338, 340–41; Kenneth Meier & Deborah McFarlane, *State Family Planning and Abortion Expenditures: Their Effect of Public Health*, 84 AM. J. PUB. HEALTH 1468 (1994); Jon Merz, Catherine Jackson, & Jacob Klerman, *A Review of Abortion Policy: Legality, Medicaid Funding, and Parental Involvement, 1967–1994*, 17 WOMEN'S RTS. L. RPTR. 1, 2 (1995); Michael Miller *et al.*, *The Effect of Legalization and Public Funding of Abortion on Neonatal Mortality: An Intervention Analysis*, 7 POP. RES. & POL'Y REV. 79 (1988); *Policy Statement of the United States of America at the United Nations International Conference on Population (2d Sess.)*, 10 POP. & DEV. REV. 576, 583 (1984); Quick, *supra* note 29, at 1004–05. *See also* BORN UNWANTED: DEVELOPMENTAL EFFECTS OF DENIED ABORTION (Henry David *et al.* eds. 1988) (arguing that children born after the state denied them abortions were developmentally disadvantaged compared to wanted children); Sisela Bok, *Ethical Problems of Abortion*, 2 HASTINGS CTR. STUD. no. 1, at 74 (Jan. 1974) (arguing that abortion prevents the suffering of malformed infants); Paul Camenisch, *Abortion: For the Fetus's Own Sake?*, 6 HASTINGS CTR. REP. no. 2, at 38 (Apr. 1976) (arguing against Bok's view); P.K. Dagg, *The Psychological Sequelae of Therapeutic Abortion—Denied and Completed*, 148 AM. J. PSYCH. 578 (1991) (finding that women denied abortions generally kept their children, but were unloving mothers); Joseph Fletcher, *Who Has First Claim on Health Care Resources?*, 5 HASTINGS CTR. REP. no. 3, at 15 (Aug. 1975) (arguing that abortion prevents the suffering of malformed infants); Barbara Gottlieb, *Abortion-1995*, 332 N. ENG. J. MED. 532 (1995) (arguing that abortion prevents premature births, low birth weights, and other problematic births).

56. *See, e.g.*, Delaney v. Krafte, 470 N.Y.S.2d 936 (App. Div. 1984). *See also* BORN UNWANTED, *supra* note 55.

57. John Donohue & Steven Levitt, *The Impact of Legalized Abortion on Crime*, 116 Q.J. ECON. 379 (2001).

58. *See, e.g.*, Marie McCullough, *Study Links Crime Rate's Fall, Legalized Abortion*, PHILA. INQUIRER, Aug. 11, 1999, at A1; Carl Rowan, *Fighting Crime with Abortion?*, N.Y. POST, Aug. 13, 1999, at 29.

59. Donohue & Levitt, *supra* note 57, at 381–82.

60. As quoted in McCullough, *supra* note 58.

61. Donohue & Levitt, *supra* note 57, at 390.

62. *See* Chapter 11, at notes 25–192. *See also* Editorial, *Eugenics with a Happy Face*, WASH. TIMES, Aug. 18, 1999, at A16; Nicole Huberfeld, *Three Generations of Welfare Mothers Are Enough: A Disturbing Return to Eugenics in the Recent "Workfare" Law*, 9 UCLA WOMEN'S L.J. 97 (1998); Julian Savulescu, *Is Current Practice around Late Termination of Pregnancy Eugenic and Discriminatory? Maternal Interests and Abortion*, 27 J. MED. ETHICS 165 (2001).

rious questions about the statistical analysis in the Donohue and Levitt study.[63] Moreover, one wonders how many of the people lauding this study realize that this take on abortion implicitly embraces the death penalty for the crimes prevented by the abortion.

In an atmosphere where abortion is claimed to reduce infant mortality and the crime rate, one should not be surprised to see some abortion rights supporters arguing that the unborn child is an aggressor, invading the body of a defenseless woman. This argument received its best known expression in an article by philosopher Judith Jarvis Thomson in which she developed a widely applauded analogy between human gestation and the coerced attachment of any randomly selected person to a famous violinist to provide life-support for keeping the violinist alive.[64] Numerous scholars writing about abortion rights have cited her argument with approval.[65] Others have developed variations on this theme.[66] Probably the most recent—and probably the most extreme—extended attempt to make this argument is by Eileen McDonagh.[67] McDonagh argued length that neither the father nor the mother "caused" the pregnancy—the "ovum" did.[68] She argued that "from the very moment of conception, the fetus is in 'in charge of the pregnancy,' that is 'in charge of the woman's body' in which it 'organizes the pregnancy,' even to the point of deciding when to be born."[69] She went on in considerable detail to present the "harms" done by an "ovum" to the woman into whose body the ovum has "intruded."[70] From this perspective, McDonagh concludes that a woman has a right of self-defense to expel the invading body from her womb.[71] Even noted constitutional law scholar Laurence Tribe gave us a similar argument, sug-

---

63. John Lott, jr., & John Whitley, *Abortion and Crime: Unwanted Children and Out-of-Wedlock Births*, Program for Studies in Law, Economics, and Public Policy, Working Paper # 254 (2001). *See also* Philip Cook & John Laub, *After the Epidemic: Recent Trends in Youth Violence in the United States*, 29 CRIME & JUSTICE 1, 22–27 (2002); Theodore Joyce, *Did Legalized Abortion Lower Crime?*, 38 Journal of Human Resources 1–37 (2003). For Donohue & Levitt's response, see John Donohue & Steven Levitt, *Further Evidence that Legalized Abortion Lower Crime: A Reply to Joyce*, SSRN Paper (2003), *available at* http://papers.ssrn.com/paper.tal?abstract_id=385660.

64. Judith Jarvis Thomson, *A Defense of Abortion*, 1 PHILOS. & PUB. AFF. 47, 66 (1971).

65. MARIAN FAUX, CRUSADERS: VOICES FROM THE ABORTION FRONT 226 (1990); JANET HADLEY, ABORTION: BETWEEN FREEDOM AND NECESSITY 78–79 (1996); JOHN ROBERTSON, CHILDREN OF CHOICE: FREEDOM AND THE NEW REPRODUCTIVE TECHNOLOGIES 51 (1994); TRIBE, *supra* note 29, at 129–35; Patricia Karlan & Daniel Ortiz, *In a Different Voice: Relational Feminism, Abortion Rights, and the Feminist Legal Agenda*, 87 Nw. U. L. REV. 858, 873–76, 880–82 (1993); Elizabeth Patterson, *Human Rights and Human Life: An Uneven Fit*, 68 TULANE L. REV. 1527, 1550 n.117 (1994); Rachael Pine & Sylvia Law, *Envisioning a Future for Reproductive Liberty: Strategies for Making the Rights Real*, 27 HARV. C.R.-C.L. L. REV. 407, 415 n.31, 417 n.38 (1992); Steven Ross, *Abortion and the Death of the Fetus*, 12 PHILOS. & PUB. AFF. 232 (1982); Sunstein, *supra* note 29, at 31–34, 41.

66. FRANCES MYRNA KAMM, CREATION AND ABORTION: A STUDY IN MORAL AND LEGAL PHILOSOPHY 53, 78–123 (1992); Steven Gelman, *"Life" and "Liberty": Their Original Meaning, Historical Antecedents, and Current Significance in the Debate over Abortion Rights*, 78 MINN. L. REV. 585 (1994); Jeffrey Goldberg, *Involuntary Servitudes: A Property-Based Notion of Abortion-Choice*, 38 UCLA L. REV. 1597 (1991); Sarah Harding, *Equality and Abortion: Legitimating Women's Experiences*, 3 COLUM. J. GENDER & L. 7, 24–31 (1992); Andrew Koppelman, *Forced Labor: A Thirteenth Amendment Defense of Abortion*, 84 Nw. U. L. REV. 480, 484 (1990); Linda McClain, *"Atomistic Man" Revisited: Liberalism, Connection, and Feminist Jurisprudence*, 65 S. CAL. L. REV. 1171, 1242–64 (1992); Donald Regan, *Rewriting* Roe v. Wade, 77 MICH. L. REV. 1569 (1979); Sunstein, *supra* note 29, at 31–40; Alec Walen, *Consensual Sex without Assuming the Risk of Carrying an Unwanted Fetus; Another Foundation for the Right to an Abortion*, 63 BROOK. L. REV. 1051 (1997).

67. EILEEN MCDONAGH, BREAKING THE ABORTION DEADLOCK: FROM CHOICE TO CONSENT (1996).

68. *Id.* at 42, 51–54.

69. *Id.* at 54.

70. *Id.* at 70–77, 85.

71. *Id.* at 32, 93, 102–04. *See also* Eileen McDonagh, *From Pro-Choice to Pro-Consent in the Abortion Debate: Reframing Women's Reproductive Rights*, 14 STUD. LAW, POL'Y & SOC'Y 245, 245 (1994); Eileen McDonagh, *My Body, My Consent: Securing the Constitutional Right to Abortion Funding*, 62 ALB. L.J. 1057, 1066–78 (1999).

gesting that the mother and the fetus are strangers to each other in his attempt to contrast the duties a parent owes to her children with the imposition that pregnancy imposes on a woman.[72]

The very unreality of the analogy that Thomson devised, however, ought to suggest that something is wrong with the argument. No less a friend to the right to abort than medical ethicist Daniel Callahan aptly described Thomson's theory as "one of the great illustrations of rationalistic reductionism."[73] As law professor Michael McConnell observed, Thomson ignores that while one might defend a person's right to unplug the violinist,[74] one would not necessarily endorse a right to stab the violinist to death if that were necessary to extricate oneself.[75] Thomson herself accepted something like this distinction when she acknowledged that the right to "unhook" a fetus would not justify slitting the child's throat should it somehow survive the abortion.[76] Much the same sort of criticisms applies to McDonagh's theorizing.[77] And even radical feminist law professor Catharine MacKinnon observed that such theories treat a pregnant woman as if she had just happened on the fetus, rather than as being involved in a set of intimate, albeit unequal, relationships.[78] MacKinnon argues, in fact, that the fetus is "a human form

---

72. Tribe, *supra* note 29, at 130–35.

73. Daniel Callahan, *Book Rev.,* 37 UCLA L. Rev. 433, 436 (1989). For Callahan's earlier contributions to furthering the cause of freedom to abort, see Callahan, *supra* note 4.

74. For a strong argument that would implicitly reject even the contention that it is moral to unplug the violinist, see Susan James, *The Duty to Relieve Suffering,* 93 Ethics 4 (1982).

75. Michael McConnell, *How Not to Promote Serious Deliberation about Abortion,* 58 U. Chi. L. Rev. 1181, 1186 n.8 (1991). *See also* John Arthur, The Unfinished Constitution: Philosophy and Constitutional Practice 198–200 (1989); Baruch Brody, Abortion and the Sanctity of Human Life 27–30 (1975); Ronald Dworkin, Life's Dominion: An Argument about Abortion, Euthanasia, and Individual Freedom 111, 249 n.4 (1993); Judges, *supra* note 31, at 154–55; Nancy (Ann) Davis, *Abortion and Self-Defense,* 13 Philos. & Pub. Aff. 175 (1984) ("Davis, *Self-Defense*"); Nancy (Ann) Davis, *The Abortion Debate: The Search for Common Ground (Part 2),* 103 Ethics 731, 758–64 (1993) ("Davis II"); John Finnis, *The Rights and Wrongs of Abortion,* 2 Philos. & Pub. Aff. 117, 120–23 (1973); Frank Scaturro, *Abortion and the Supreme Court: Roe, Casey, the Myth of Stare Decisis, and the Court as a Political Institution,* 3 Holy Cross J.L. & Pub. Pol'y 133, 165–68 (1998); Jeanne Schroeder, Abduction from the Seraglio: *Feminist Methodologies and the Logic of Imagination,* 70 Tex. L. Rev. 109, 140 (1991); Ian Shapiro, *Introduction,* in Abortion: The Supreme Court Decisions 1, 3 n.7 (Ian Shapiro ed. 1995).

76. Thomson, *supra* note 64, at 66. *But see* Michael Tooley, Abortion and Infanticide 43–44 (1983).

77. *See* Judith Scully, *Book Rev.,* 8 UCLA L. Rev. 125, 145–47 (1997).

78. Catharine MacKinnon, Feminism Unmodified: Discourses on Life and Law 94, 98–99 (1987) ("MacKinnon, F.U."); Catharine MacKinnon, Toward a Feminist Theory of the State 184, 189–90 (1989). *See also* Arthur, *supra* note 75, at 200; Dworkin, *supra* note 75, at 54–55; J.K. Mason, Medico-Legal Aspects of Reproduction and Parenthood 111–12 (2nd ed. 1998); Adrienne Rich, On Lies, Secrets, and Silence 64 (1979); Tooley, *supra* note 76, at 45–49; Joan Bullock, *Abortion Rights in America,* 1994 BYU L. Rev. 63, 81–83; Samuel Calhoun & Andrea Sexton, *Is It Possible to Take Both Fetal Life and Women Seriously? Professor Lawrence Tribe and his Reviewers,* 49 Was. & Lee L. Rev. 437, 449–51, 471–74 (1992) (book rev.); Davis II, *supra* note 75, at 752; Mary Dunlap, *Mediating the Abortion Controversy: A Call for Moderation, or for One-Sided Etiquette While the Bombs Keep Flying?,* 30 Wash. L.J. 42, 48–50 (1990); Susan Himmelweit, *More than a "Woman's Right to Choose,"* 29 Fem. Rev. 38, 49 (1988); David Smolin, *Why Abortion Rights Are Not Justified by Reference to Gender Equality: A Response to Professor Tribe* (book review), 23 J. Marshall L. Rev. 621, 642–44 (1990). For more on the shortcomings of Thomson's theory, see also Harrison, *supra* note 55, at 215; Rosalind Hursthouse, Beginning Lives 181–94 (1987); Kenny, *supra* note 52, at 247–49; Elizabeth Mensch & Alan Freeman, The Politics of Virtue: Is Abortion Debatable? 130–31 (1993); Bernard Nathanson & Richard Ostung, Aborting America 218–26 (1979); Stephen Schwartz, The Moral Question of Abortion 113–24, 170–74 (1990); Bonnie Steinbock, Life before Birth 76–78 (1992); James Sterba, The Demands of Justice 126–50 (1980); L.W. Sumner, Abortion and Moral Theory 65–73, 111–27 (1981); Tooley, *supra* note 76, at 40–49; Stanley Benn, *Abortion, Infanticide, and Respect for Persons,* in The Problem of Abortion 92 (Joel Feinberg ed. 1973); Davis, *Self-Defense, supra* note 75, at 747–61; Finnis, *supra* note 75; Smolin, *supra,* at 641–47; David Strauss, *Abortion, Toleration, and Moral Uncertainty,* 1992 Sup. Ct. Rev. 1, 10–14; Mary Anne Warren, *On the Moral and Legal Status of Abortion,* in The Problem of Abortion 102, 108 (Joel Feinberg ed. 2nd ed. 1984). *See generally* Daphne Patal &

of life" that is experienced by the pregnant woman as both "me" and "not me," which makes the abortion decision troubling even to MacKinnon's intense feminism.

Many of these same commentators laud the effect of *Roe* in making safe and affordable abortions available for the first time to young, poor, or minority women who were least able to obtain abortions before *Roe* and *Doe*.[79] They point out that free standing abortion clinics offering inexpensive abortions proliferated after *Roe* and especially *Doe* (which limited the regulations that could be applied to clinics and hospitals doing abortions).[80] By 1985, free-standing clinics performed about 86 percent of all abortions in the United States, less than 15 percent of all abortions were performed in hospitals and less than 3 percent (compared to 52 percent in 1973) involved a hospital stay of two or more days.[81] Hospitals accounted for only 7 percent of all abortions in the United States by 1992.[82] This pattern itself accounts in significant measure for the greater availability of abortions in metropolitan areas than in rural areas. One estimate has it that at least 400 women must need an abortion each year to support a freestanding abortion clinic.[83]

Still, *Roe,* and especially *Doe,* do appear to have considerably evened out the availability of abortion services nationally. In 1972, 84 percent of reported abortions occurred in the four states that had legalized abortion on demand in early pregnancy—Alaska, Hawaii, New York, and Washington.[84] By 1976, those states accounted for only 35 percent of all reported abortions. Nonetheless, wide variations continued among states in the abortion rate, with New York reporting the high of 43 abortions per 1,000 women aged 15–44, and West Virginia reporting the low of 3 abortions per 1,000 such women.[85] Such disparities continue. In 1988, California had the highest rate, at 49/1,000 women aged 15–44, and Wyoming claiming the low at 3/1,000 such

---

Noretta Koertge, Professing Feminism: Cautionary Tales from the Strange World of Women's Studies 136–57 (1994) (discussing the "biodenial" prevalent in much feminist thought, a patter of denying that biology has any relevance whatsoever to social behaviors).

79. For cases striking down most restrictions on clinics, see City of Akron v. Akron Center for Reproductive Health, Inc., 462 U.S. 416 (1983); Arnold v. Sendak, 429 U.S. 968 (1976); Doe v. Bolton, 410 U.S. 179 (1973); Aware Women Clinic, Inc. v. City of Cocoa Beach, 629 F.2d 1146 (5th Cir. 1980); Mahoning Women's Ctr. v. Hunter, 610 F.2d 456 (6th Cir. 1979); Friendship Med. Ctr. v. Chicago Bd. of Health, 505 F.2d 1141 (7th Cir. 1974), *cert. denied,* 420 U.S. 997 (1975); Word v. Poelker, 495 F.2d 1349 (8th Cir. 1974); Birth Control Ctrs., Inc. v. Reizen, 508 F. Supp. 1366 (E.D. Mich. 1981); Florida Women's Med. Clinic, Inc. v. Smith, 478 F. Supp. 233 (S.D. Fla. 1979); Fox Valley Reproductive Health Care Ctr. v. Arft, 446 F. Supp. 1072 (E.D. Wis. 1978). On the proliferation, see Graber, *supra* note 5, at 66–68; Jaffe, Lindheim, & Lee, *supra* note 29, at 11, 98; Legge, *supra* note 35, at 24; Sarvis & Rodman, *supra* note 31, at 175; Willard Cates, jr., *Legal Abortion: Are Black Women Healthier because of It?,* 38 Phylon 267 (1977).

80. Graber, *supra* note 5, at 70–71; Jaffe, Lindheim, & Lee, *supra* note 29, at 25, 35–37; Sarvis & Rodman, *supra* note 31, at 55; Patrick Sheeran, Women, Society, the State, and Abortion: A Structuralist Analysis 30, 45 (1987); David Grimes, *Clinicians Who Provide Abortions: The Thinning Ranks,* 80 Obstet. & Gynecology 719, 721 (1992); Jane Hodgson, *The Twentieth-Century Gender Battle: Difficulties in Perception,* in Abortion Wars: A Half Century of Struggle, 1950–2000, at 301 (Rickie Solinger ed. 1998); Carole Joffe, Patricia Anderson, & Judy Steinauer, *The Crisis in Abortion Provision and Pro-Choice Medical Activism in the 1990s,* in Abortion Wars, *supra,* at 320, 321.

81. Graber, *supra* note 5, at 375; Muldoon, *supra* note 16, at 12; Stanley Henshaw, *Induced Abortion: A World Review, 1990,* 22 Fam. Plan. Persp. 76, 83 (March–April 1990), *reprinted in* Abortion, Medicine, and the Law, *supra* note 29, at 406; Stanley Henshaw & Jennifer Van Vort, *Abortion Services in the United States, 1991 and 1992,* 26 Fam. Planning Persp. 100, 107–08 (1994). See also Ginsburg, *supra* note 34, at 55–56; Petchesky, *supra* note 29, at 157; Rosenberg, *supra* note 29, at 195–98; Cates, *supra* note 29, at 314–15; Cates, *Public Health, supra* note 29, at 1587–88.

82. Henshaw & Van Vort, *supra* note 81, at 104; Hodgson, *supra* note 80, at 304; Joffe, Anderson, & Steinauer, *supra* note 80, at 321.

83. Sara Seims, *Abortion Availability in the United States,* 12 Fam. Planning Persp. 88, 95 (1980).

84. Hansen, *supra* note 16, at 381.

85. *Id.* at 381–82.

women.[86] Such variations correlate strongly with the degree to which a state is urbanized (and suburbanized), as well as with income and education levels, rather than with differing policy restrictions—including the availability of Medicaid funding for abortions.[87]

One result of the more numerous and more widespread appearance of abortion clinics has been that the cost of an abortion fell sharply in the first decade after *Roe,* declining from $500 to $150.[88] Even Gerald Rosenberg, who is intent on denigrating the impact of Supreme Court decisions in bringing about social change, has conceded this effect.[89] And, although the mere opportunity to do frequent abortions improved the skill of those doctors willing to perform abortions,[90] the proliferation of freestanding abortions also served to isolate politically those who strongly supported abortion rights within the medical profession. Abortion and those who do abortions remained largely outside of "mainstream" medicine—as was predicted by at least one pro-abortion advocate at the time.[91]

Nor did the clinics resolve the problems of unequal access to abortion that had played so prominent a role in driving the abortion reform and abortion repeal movements. "Women of color" continue to incur higher rates of morbidity and mortality from legal abortions, just as they apparently did from illegal abortions.[92] Nonetheless, the abortion rate for African-American women and other women of color rose sharply, until it was as much as three times higher than for white women.[93] Some 58 percent of all abortions in New York during the first two years after legalization were on minority women.[94] The increase of abortions among African-American women was so pronounced that some have seen the new abortion regime as part of a program of genocide against blacks or other "persons of color."[95]

---

86. Center for Disease Control, *Morbidity and Mortality Weekly Report 40* (No. 1SS), at 24–25 (1991).

87. WETSTEIN, *supra* note 5, at 43–44.

88. Cates, *Public Health, supra* note 29, at 1588.

89. ROSENBERG, *supra* note 29, at 198.

90. Kenneth Niswander & Manual Porto, *Abortion Practices in the United States: A Medical Viewpoint,* in ABORTION, MEDICINE, AND THE LAW, *supra* note 29, at 567, 580. *See also* NANETTE DAVIS, FROM CRIME TO CHOICE 226–27 (1985); SHEERAN, *supra* note 80, at 22, 45; Cates, *First Decade, supra* note 29, at 307–08, 311–14; Cates, *Public Health, supra* note 29, at 1587; Hansen, *supra* note 16, at 378–79.

91. Robert Hall, *Pregnancy Termination: The Impact of the New Laws,* J. REPRODUCTIVE MED. 45 (1971); Robert Hall, *Realities of Abortion,* N.Y. TIMES, Feb. 13, 1971, at 27. *See generally* GARROW, *supra* note 5, at 456, 483, 874; David Garrow, *Abortion before and after* Roe v. Wade: *An Historical Perspective,* 62 ALB. L. REV. 833, 837–40 (1999); Gottlieb, *supra* note 55.

92. Cates, *supra* note 79, at 277 (after discounting for several variables, finding that black women are twice as likely to die from a legal abortion as are white women). *See also* GRABER, *supra* note 5, at 67; RODMAN, SARVIS, & BONAR, *supra* note 31, at 66–67; Hani Atrash & Trent McKay, *Legal Abortion Mortality in the United States: 1972 to 1982,* 156 AM. J. OBSTET. & GYNECOLOGY 611 (1987); Cates & Rochat, *supra* note 29, at 88; L.M. Koonan *et al., Maternal Mortality Surveillance, United States, 1979–1986,* 40 CENTERS FOR DISEASE CONTROL MORBIDITY & MORTALITY WEEKLY REP. 1 (June 1991).

93. PETCHESKY, *supra* note 29, at 156 (indicating a rate three times as high for women on Medicaid compared to other women). *See also* MENSCH & FREEMAN, *supra* note 78, at 1107 n.692; RODMAN, SARVIS, & BONAR, *supra* note 38, at 153 (reporting 549 abortions per 1,000 live births for black women, and 329/1000 for white women); CHRISTOPHER TIETZE, INDUCED ABORTION: A WORLD REVIEW, 1981, at 39 (4th ed. 1981); Cates, *supra* note 79, at 267–71, 280 (indicating a rate twice as high as for white women); Hansen, *supra* note 16, at 375; Patricia Steinhoff, *Background Characteristics of Abortion Patients,* in THE ABORTION EXPERIENCE, *supra* note 29, at 206, 208.

94. LEGGE, *supra* note 35, at 101. *See also* Jean Pakter *et al., Two Years Experience in New York City with the Liberalized Abortion Law—Progress and Problems,* 63 AM. J. PUB. HEALTH 524, 528 (1973) (reporting that 53% of abortions in New York were on minority women in the first year of legalization).

95. AKUA FURLOW, ABORTION AND THE AFRICAN AMERICAN—A DEADLY SILENCE (1994); PAULA GIDDINGS, WHEN AND WHERE I ENTER: THE IMPACT OF BLACK WOMEN ON RACE AND SEX IN AMERICA 318 (1984); LAURA KAPLAN, THE STORY OF JANE: THE LEGENDARY UNDERGROUND FEMINIST ABORTION SERVICE 175 (1995); THOMAS LITTLEWOOD, THE POLITICS OF POPULATION CONTROL 69, 75, 97 (1977); REAGAN, *supra*

One inclined to believe that abortion liberalization was a disguised campaign of genocide against African-Americans did not need to look further than to the writings of journalist Lawrence Lader, founding president of NARAL (the National Association for the Repeal of Abortion Laws, later National Abortion Rights Action League, then the National Abortion and Reproductive Rights Action League, and now NARAL-Pro Choice America). Lader deployed frankly racist appeals in his first book attempting to popularize the repeal of abortion laws, noting the "grim relationship between unwanted children and the violent rebellion of violent minority groups."[96] And those attitudes are still with us. Consider the apparently warm reception that the views of Professors Levitt and Donohue on how abortion solved the crime problem in urban America.[97]

Perhaps because of such concerns, Alan Keyes—the only African-American candidate in the Presidential primaries in 1996—was solidly against abortion, drawing, as one commentator put it, "deeply from the well of African-American history" to explain his position.[98] Nor is it a surprise that Louis Farrakhan and the Nation of Islam is also strongly against abortion.[99] Although the difference in the incidence of abortion among African-American women and white women has narrowed, African-American women continue to have higher abortion rates.[100]

In sum, if we take the raw data on recorded legal abortions as accurately reflecting the actual incidence of abortion, we discover that the number of abortions approximately tripled between

---

note 5, at 231–32; Andrea Tone, Devices and Desires: A History of Contraceptives in America 254–63 (2001); Martha Ward, Poor Women, Powerful Men: America's Experiment in Family Planning 92–95 (1986); Erma Clardy Craven, *Abortion, Poverty and Black Genocide: Gifts to the Poor?*, in Abortion and Social Justice 231 (Thomas Hilgers & Dennis Horan eds. 1972); Greg Keath, *Abortion Is Not a Civil Right*, Wall St. J., Sept. 27, 1989, at A22; Van Keys, *Thoughts for Negroes*, Black Panther, Mar. 9, 1969, at 1; Loretta Ross, *African-American Women and Abortion*, in Abortion Wars, supra note 80, at 179–82; Cal Thomas, *Flight of Life's Priorities*, Wash. Times, Apr. 1, 1993, p. G1; Mary Treadwell, *Is Abortion Black Genocide?*, 4 Fam. Planning Perspectives 4 (1972); Castellano Turner & William Darity, *Fears of Genocide among Black Americans as Related to Age, Sex and Region*, 63 Am. J. Pub. Health 1029 (1973); Robert Weisbord, *Birth Control and Black Americans: A Matter of Genocide?*, 10 Demography 571 (1973). See also Toni Cade, *The Pill: Genocide or Liberation?*, in The Black Woman: An Anthology 162 (Toni Cade ed. 1970); Dick Gregory, *My Answer to Genocide*, Ebony, Oct. 1971, at 66; Mary Smith, *Birth Control and the Negro Woman*, Ebony, Mar. 1968, at 29. See also Shirley Chisholm, Unbought and Unbossed 113–22 (1970); Elizabeth Adell Cook, Ted Jelen, & Clyde Wilcox, Between Two Absolutes: Public Opinion and the Politics of Abortion 44–48 (1992); Donald Critchlow, Intended Consequences: Birth Control, Abortion, and the Federal Government in Modern America 141–44 (1999); Littlewood, supra, at 72; Ward, supra, at 63; William Arney & William Trescher, *Trends in Attitudes toward Abortion, 1972–1975*, 8 Fam. Planning Persp. 117 (1976); Ross Baker, Laurily Epstein, & Rodney Firth, *Matters of Life and Death: Social, Political, and Religious Correlates of Attitudes on Abortion*, 9 Am. Pol. Q. 89 (1981); Toni Cade Bambara, *The Pill, Genocide or Liberation*, in The Black Woman 162 (Toni Cade Bambara ed. 1970); Michael Combs & Susan Welch, *Blacks, Whites, and Attitudes toward Abortion*, 46 Pub. Opinion Q. 510 (1982); Elaine Hall & Myra Marx Ferree, *Race Differences in Abortion Attitudes*, 12 J. Pol'y Analysis & Mgt. 498 (1986); Linda LaRue, *The Black Movement and Women's Liberation*, in Words of Fire: An Anthology of African-American Feminist Thought 36 (Beverly Guy-Sheftall ed. 1995); Ross, supra, at 180–201; Clyde Wilcox, *Race Differences and Abortion Attitudes: Some Additional Evidence*, 54 Pub. Opinion Q. 248 (1990); Clyde Wilcox, *Race, Religion, Region, and Abortion Attitudes*, 53 Soc. Analysis 97 (1992).

96. Lawrence Lader, Abortion 156 (1966).

97. McCullough, supra note 59. See the text supra at notes 57–63.

98. Kerry Jacoby, Souls, Bodies, Spirits: The Drive to Abolish Abortion since 1973, at 182, 184 (1998).

99. Id. at 183.

100. Nancy Ezzard et al., *Race-Specific Patterns of Abortion Use by American Teenagers*, 72 Am. J. Pub. Health 809 (1982). See generally Laurie Nsiah-Jefferson, *Reproductive Laws, Women of Color, and Low-Income Women*, 11 Women's Rts. L. Rptr. 15 (1989); Dorothy Roberts, *The Future of Reproductive Choice for Poor Women and Women of Color*, 12 Women's Rts. L. Rptr. 59 (1990); Ross, supra note 95.

1972 and 1980, and thereafter settled down at a rate approximately twice as high as before the legal changes began. The ratio probably would be higher if we could establish a firm baseline number for illegal abortions in 1960 or 1965. On the other hand, given the new ideological embrace by many of abortion as a "woman's right" and the technical reality of abortion's safety for the mother, there probably would have been some increase regardless of what the law was. Whether these changes are a good or a bad outcome depends on whether one believes that abortion resolves serious problems in a pregnant woman's life or is the killing of a human being. Somewhere between 600,000 to 1,500,000 additional fetuses were being aborted annually after *Roe* than before.[101] Even without recognizing fetal personhood, this fact renders arguments like law professor Cass Sunstein's that "the principal effect of the decision [in *Roe*] was not to increase fetal deaths, but instead to produce a shift from dangerous to safe abortions" and that "restrictions on abortion do not materially advance the goal of protecting life at all" patent nonsense, contradicting even the figures on which he and his ilk rely.[102]

Sunstein is nothing if not committed to the cause. Having himself estimated between 100,000 and 600,000 additional fetal deaths after *Roe*, he not only made the arguments just quoted, but he also insisted that "the futility of antiabortion restrictions also suggests...the presence of a discriminatory purpose...stem[ming] from punitive goals rather than an interest in protecting fetal life."[103] That conclusion follows only if one has already decided that preventing one-half million abortions annually would not be a significant goal.

Some evidence also supports the conclusion that abortion had some significant negative effects on the women having the abortions. No clear evidence demonstrates whether these effects are more or less significant than the effects of non-access to abortion on the affected women before *Roe* and *Doe*. Most controversial in this regard have been the claims of pervasive psychological stress, particularly from grieving after the abortion that some women apparently experience for many years after the abortion.[104] There are even three organizations for women who feel deep

---

101. NOONAN, supra note 11, at 65–66. *See generally* Jane Murphy, Banu Ethan Symington, & Sheldon Jacobson, *Pregnancy Resolution Decisions: What if Abortion Were Banned?*, 28 J. REPRODUCTIVE MED. 789 (1983).

102. Sunstein, *supra* note 29, at 38–40, 42. *See also* KENNETH KARST, LAW'S PROMISE, LAW'S EXPRESSION: VISIONS OF POWER IN THE POLITICS OF RACE, GENDER, AND RELIGION 50–52 (1993).

103. Sunstein, *supra* note 29, at 38–39.

104. CATHERINE BARNARD, THE LONG TERM PSYCHOLOGICAL EFFECTS OF ABORTION (1990); THERESA BURKE & DAVID REARDON, FORBIDDEN GRIEF: THE UNSPOKEN PAIN OF ABORTION (2002); MAGDA DIENES, IN NECESSITY AND SORROW (1985); JACOBY, *supra* note 98, at 49–51; EVE KUSHNER, EXPERIENCING ABORTION: A WEAVING OF WOMEN'S WORDS (1997); POST-ABORTION SYNDROME (Peter Doherty ed. 1994); REARDON, *supra* note 30; DAVID REARDON, A SURVEY OF POST-ABORTION REACTIONS (1987) ("REARDON, REACTIONS"); KATHY RUDY, BEYOND PRO-LIFE AND PRO-CHOICE: MORAL DIVERSITY IN THE ABORTION DEBATE 131–32 (1996); ANNE SPECKHARD, PSCYHO-SOCIAL STRESS FOLLOWING ABORTION (1987); RITA TOWNSEND & ANN PERKINS, BITTER FRUIT: WOMEN'S EXPERIENCE OF UNPLANNED PREGNANCY, ABORTION, AND ADOPTION (1991); JEANETTE VOUGHT, POST ABORTION TRAUMA: 9 STEPS TO RECOVERY (1991); E. Joanne Angelo, *Psychiatric Sequelae of Abortion: The Many Faces of Post-Abortion Grief*, 59 LINACRE Q., No. 2, at 69 (1992); Dennis Bagarozzi, *Identification, Assessment and Treatment of Women Suffering from Posttraumatic Stress after Abortion*, 5 J. FAM. THERAPY 25 (1994); Daniel Bluestein & Carolyn Rutledge, *Family Relationships and Depressive Syndrome Preceding Induced Abortion*, 13 FAM. PRAC. RES. J. 149 (1993); Priscilla Coleman *et al.*, *State-Funded Abortions vs. Deliveries: A Comparison of Outpatient Mental Health Claims over Four Years*, 72 AM. J. ORTHOPSYCH. 141 (2002); G. Kam Congleton & Lawrence Calhoun, *Post-Abortion Perceptions: A Comparison of Self-Identified Distressed and Non Distressed Populations*, 39 INT'L J. SOC. PSYCH. 255 (1993); L.L. DeVeber, Janet Ajzzenstat, & Dorothy Chisholm, *Post-Abortion Grief: Psychological Sequelae of Induced Abortion*, 7 HUMANE MED. 203 (1991); R.C. Erickson, *Abortion Trauma: Application of a Conflict Model*, 8 PRE- AND PERINATAL PSCYH. J. 33 (1993); Wanda Franz & David Reardon, *Differential Impact of Abortion on Adolescents and Adults*, 27 ADOLESCENCE 162 (1992); Mika Gissler *et al.*, *Suicides after Pregnancy in Finland: Register Linkage Study*, 313 BRIT. MED. J. 1431 (1996); Brenda Major *et al.*, *Perceived Social Support, Self-Efficacy, and Adjust-*

grief over what many of them consider to have been abortions coerced by boyfriends (or parents) or induced by deception by abortion providers: Abortion Victims of America; Victims of Choice; and Women Exploited by Abortion (WEBA).[105] Psychiatrists who support abortion rights tend to denigrate claims that abortion leaves psychological scars on the women who undergo abortion.[106] Forty years earlier, when abortion was illegal, many psychiatrists supported the opposite claim.[107]

*ment to Abortion*, 59 J. PERSONALITY & SOC. PSYCH. 452 (1990); D. Naziri & A. Tzavaras, *Mourning and Guilt among Greek Women Having Repeated Abortions*, 26 OMEGA 137 (1992); Philip Ney *et al.*, *The Effects of Pregnancy Loss on Women's Health*, 38 SOC. SCI. & MED. 1193 (1994); David Reardon & Jesse Cougle, *Depression and Unintended Pregnancy in the National Longitudinal Survey of Youth: A Cohort Study*, 324 BRIT. MED. J. 151 (2002); Jo Ann Rosenfeld, *Emotional Responses to Therapeutic Abortion*, 45 AM. FAM. PHYSICIAN 137 (1992); H. Soderberg *et al.*, *Selection Bias in a Study on How Women Experienced Induced Abortion*, 77 EUR. J. OBSTET. & GYNECOLOGY 67 (1998); Anne Speckhard & Vincent Rue, *Complicated Mourning and Abortion*, 8 J. PRE- & PERI-NATAL PSYCH. 5 (1993); Anne Speckhard & Vincent Rue, *Postabortion Syndrome: An Emerging Public Health Concern*, 48 J. SOC. ISSUES 95 (1992); Marijo Tamburrino *et al.*, *Post-Abortion Dysphoria and Religion*, 83 S. MED. J. 736 (1990); T. Thomas *et al.*, *Psychosocial Characteristics of Psychiatric Inpatients with Reproductive Losses*, 7 J. HEALTH CARE FOR THE POOR & UNDERSERVED 15 (1996); M. Tornbom *et al.*, *Repeat Abortion: A Comparative Study*, 17 J. PSYCHOSOMATIC OBSTET. & GYNECOLOGY 208 (1996); D.R. Urquhart & A.A. Templeton, *Psychiatric Morbidity and Acceptability Following the Medical And Surgical Methods of Induced Abortion*, 98 BRIT. J. OBSTET. & GYNECOLOGY 396 (1991); G. Zolese & C.V.R. Blacker, *The Psychological Complications of Therapeutic Abortion*, 160 BRIT. J. PSYCH. 742 (1992).

105. *See* ROSENBLATT, *supra* note 5, at 25–26, 42–44 (Victims); Calhoun & Sexton, *supra* note 78, at 479–81 (WEBA). *See generally* PAULA ERVIN, WOMEN EXPLOITED: THE OTHER VICTIM OF ABORTION (1985); JACOBY, *supra* note 98, at 50; PAM KOERBEL, ABORTION'S SECOND VICTIM (1986); MICHAEL MANNION, ABORTION & HEALING: A CRY TO BE WHOLE (1986); NANCY MICHAELS, HELPING WOMEN RECOVER FROM ABORTION (1988); REARDON, REACTIONS, *supra* note 104; KATHLEEN WINKLER, WHEN THE CRYING STOPS: ABORTION, THE PAIN AND THE HEALING (1992); C. Husfeldt *et al.*, *Ambivalence among Women Applying for Abortion*, 74 ACTA OBSTETRICIA ET GYNECOLGIA SCANDINAVICA 813 (1995). Whether rightly or wrongly, most anti-abortion activists see women undergoing abortion precisely as subject to coercion or deception, either by the father of the child or by the abortionist. *See* JACOBY, *supra*, at 48–55. For an example of the extremes to which some parents might go to coerce a minor daughter into having an abortion, see *In re* Mary P., 444 N.Y.S.2d 545 (Fam. Ct. 1981).

106. *See, e.g.*, Nancy Adler *et al.*, *Psychological Factors in Abortion: A Review*, AM. PSCYHOLOGIST, Oct. 1992, at 1194; Nancy Adler *et al.*, *Psychological Responses after Abortion*, 248 SCIENCE 41 (1990); Brenda Major *et al.*, *Psychological Responses of Women after First-Trimester Abortion*, 57 ARCHIVES OF GEN. PSYCH. 777 (2000); Mary Conklin & Brian O'Connor, *Beliefs about the Fetus as a Moderator of Post-Abortion Well-Being*, 14 J. SOC. & CLINICAL PSYCH. 76 (1995); Paul Dagg, *The Psychological Sequelae of Therapeutic Abortion—Denied and Completed*, 148 AM. J. PSYCH. 578 (1991); David Evans & John Gusdon, jr., *Postabortion Attitudes*, 34 N.C. MED. J. 271 (1973); Arthur Lazarus, *Psychiatric Sequelae of Legalized Elective First Trimester Abortion*, 4 J. PSYCHOSOMATIC OBSTET. & GYNECOLOGY 141 (1985); Brenda Major & Catherine Cozzarelli, *Psychosocial Predictors of Adjustment to Abortion*, 48 J. SOC. ISSUES 121 (1992); Brenda Major, Pallas Mueller, & Katherine Hildebrandt, *Attributions, Expectations, and Coping with Abortion*, 48 J. PERSONALITY & SOC. PSYCH. 585 (1985); Warren Miller *et al.*, *Testing a Model of the Psychological Consequences of Abortion*, in THE NEW CIVIL WAR: THE PSYCHOLOGY, CULTURE, AND POLITICS OF ABORTION 235 (Linda Beckman & S. Marie Harvey eds. 1998); D.T. Moseley *et al.*, *Psychological Factors that Predict Reaction to Abortion*, 37 J. CLINICAL PSYCH. 276 (1981); Joy & Howard Osofsky, *The Psychological Reactions of Patients to Legalized Abortion*, 42 AM. J. ORTHOPSYCHIATRY 48 (1972); Elizabeth Smith, *A Follow-Up Study of Women Who Request Abortion*, 43 AM. J. ORTHOPSYCHIATRY 574 (1973); Sharon Gold Steinberg & Abigail Stewart, *Psychologies of Abortion: Implications of a Changing Context*, in ABORTION WARS, *supra* note 80, at 356; Nada Stotland, *The Myth of the Abortion Trauma Syndrome*, 268 JAMA 2078 (Oct. 21, 1992); George Walter, *Psychologic and Emotional Consequences of Elective Abortion*, 36 OBSTET. & GYNECOLOGY 482 (1970); Gregory Wilmoth, Martin de Alteriis, & Danielle Bussell, *Prevalence of Psychological Risks Following Legal Abortion in the U.S.: Limits of the Evidence*, 48 J. SOC. ISSUES 37 (1992); Laurie Zabin & Valerie Sedivy, *Among Adolescents: Research Findings and the Current Debate*, 62 J. SCHOOL HEALTH 319 (1992). *See also* Elizabeth Karlin, *"We Called It Kindness": Establishing a Feminist Abortion Practice*, in ABORTION WARS, *supra*, at 273.

107. ROBIN BADGLEY *ET AL.*, REPORT OF THE COMMITTEE ON THE ABORTION LAW 313–21 (Ottawa 1977); PAUL MARX, THE DEATH PEDDLERS: WAR ON THE UNBORN 28–29 (1971) (reporting the conclusions of pro-

Furthermore, we have seen that there are real physical dangers to women from undergoing abortions—dangers that are unnecessary if the abortion is unnecessary.[108] Some in the United States have even suggested that the resistance of abortion supporters to compulsory reporting of abortion statistics[109] reflects not so much a concern about maternal privacy as a fear of letting the truth be known about how safe (or unsafe) abortions really are.[110] Whether that is the case or not, supporters of abortion rights are reluctant to acknowledge the deficiencies of abortion providers. In fact, the defense of incompetent (or worse) abortion providers by the champions of abortion rights can be astonishing.

Consider Dr. Bruce Steir. Steir pleaded guilty to involuntary manslaughter and waived his right to appeal while facing a charge of murder for causing the death of Sharon Hamptlon.[111] Hamptlon, a 27-year old woman, bled to death on December 13, 1996, on her drive home from Riverside to Barstow, California, with her three-year old son at her side. Steir's attorneys claimed the prosecution was politically motivated by anti-abortion activists.[112] Abortion rights activists rallied to his support.[113] Steir, after all, was one of those peripatetic abortionists who fly from clinic to clinic around the country to provide abortions in "under-served areas." In so doing, he had performed an estimated 40,000 abortions over 25 years.[114] Even after Steir's guilty plea, well-known activist attorney Carol Downer reportedly said, "I'm incredibly sad. I

---

abortion psychiatrist Julius Fogel); Sidney Bolter, *The Psychiatrist's Role in Therapeutic Abortion: The Unwitting Accomplice,* 119 Am. J. Psych. 312 (1962); Henry David, Niels Rasmussen, & Eric Holst, *Postpartum and Postabortion Psychotic Reactions,* 13 Fam. Plan. Persp. 88 (1981); F.G. Ebaugh & K.D. Heuser, *Psychiatric Aspects of Therapeutic Abortion,* 2 Postgraduate Med. 325 (1947); Charles Ford, Pietro Castelnuovo-Tedesco, & Kahilla Long, *Women Who Seek Therapeutic Abortion: A Comparison with Women Who Complete Their Pregnancies,* 129 Am. J. Psych. 546 (1972); Bruce Jansson, *Mental Disorders after Abortion,* 41 Acta Pschiatrica Scandinavia 87 (1965); Cynthia Martin, *Psychological Problems of Abortion for the Unwed Teenage Girl,* 88 Genetic Psych. Monographs 23 (1973); Robert Mumford, *Interdisciplinary Study of Four Wives Who Had Induced Abortions,* 87 Am. J. Obstet. & Gynecology 865 (1963); Philip Ney, *Relationship between Abortion and Child Abuse,* 24 Can. J. Psych. 610 (1979); Maria Perez & Ruth Falk, *Follow-Up after Therapeutic Abortion in Early Adolescence,* 28 Arch. Gen. Psychiatry 120 (1973); N.M. Simon, A.G. Senturia, & D. Rothman, *Psychiatric Illness Following Therapeutic Abortion,* 15 Am. J. Psych. 378 (1967). *See also* Rickie Solinger, *"A Complete Disaster": Abortion and the Politics of Hospital Abortion Committees, 1950–1970,* 19 Feminist Stud. 241, 257 (1993).

108. See the text *supra* at notes 39–49.

109. On more than one occasion, various pro-abortion groups have carried their opposition even to the anonymous reporting of abortion statistics all the way to the Supreme Court. Planned Parenthood of Se. Pa. v. Casey, 505 U.S. 833, 900 (1992); Thornburgh v. American College of Obstet. & Gynecologists, 476 U.S. 747, 765–67 (1986); Planned Parenthood of Ctr. Mo. v. Danforth, 428 U.S. 52, 80 (1976). *See also* Brian Clowes, *The Role of Maternal Deaths in the Abortion Debate,* 13 St. Louis U. Pub. L. Rev. 327 (1993); Lynne Marie Kohm, *Sex Selection Abortion and the Boomerang Effect of a Woman's Right to Choose: A Paradox of the Skeptics,* 4 Wm. & Mary J. Women & L. 91, 123–24 (1997).

110. *See* Hentoff, *supra* note 39. *See also* Stone, *supra* note 43, at 497–515.

111. Julie Marquis, *Doctor Pleads Guilty in Death after Abortion: Court, in Deal with Prosecutors, Defendant Accepts Charge of Involuntary Manslaughter. He Had Been Charged with Murder after Finding of Negligence,* L.A. Times, Apr. 6, 2000, at A3; Raymond Smith, *Plea Changed to Guilty in Abortion Case: An Agreement to a Lesser Charge Is Reached as the Murder Trial Was About to Begin,* The Press-Enterprise (Riverside, CA), Apr. 6, 2000, at A1; Jaxon Van Derbeken, *Guilty Plea Entered in Fatal-Abortion Trial: Patient Bled to Death after Doctor Sent Her Home,* S.F. Chronicle, Apr. 7, 2000, at A7.

112. Mike Kataoka, *Physician Finds Help in State High Court: The Ruling Gives an Abortion Doctor Accused of Murder a Hearing on His Request for Medical Disciplinary Board Records,* The Press-Enterprise (Riverside, CA), Feb. 26, 1999, at B 3; Raymond Smith, *Doctor Accused of Murder Seeks State Records: Appeal Alleges Bias in Abortion Case,* The Press-Enterprise (Riverside, CA), Feb. 26, 1999, at B1.

113. Editorial, *A Case's Closure,* The Press-Enterprise (Riverside, CA), Apr. 7, 2000, at A8; Kevin Fagan, *Battle over Right to Choose: Abortion Clinic in Redding Stirs up Fervor on Both Sides of Issue,* S.F. Chronicle, May 4, 1999, at A1.

114. Van Derbeken, *supra* note 111.

feel there was no case against Dr. Steir."[115] She was "sure this will give heart to people who want to attack doctors."[116] They seem unfazed by the evidence that Steir had fully known that he had punctured Hamptlon's uterus and then had left for the airport without sending her to a hospital.[117]

Steir was hardly the saint his supporters made him out to be. He had been disciplined five times between 1984 and 1996 for serious infractions, although his medical license was never suspended.[118] One doctor who reviewed the records of Steir's disciplinary proceedings stated that Steir "never seems to be aware of the extensive damage he is causing these patients." Steir was on probation a the time of Hamptlon's abortion, and did not have a physician monitoring his activities as required by the terms of his probation.[119] He surrendered his medical license in March, 1997 when the investigation of Hamptlon's death began.[120] After his guilty plea, Steir was sentenced to six months in jail, five years of probation, and 1,000 hours of community service.[121] Steir also agreed to a settlement that paid Hamptlon's son $2,000,000.[122]

Legislative attempts inspired by Sharon Hamptlon's death to increase regulation of abortion clinics to assure their safety for the mother were defeated by supporters of abortion rights as covert attempts to make abortion less available.[123] Indeed, supporters of abortion rights have even argued — successfully in lower courts, at least — that a Louisiana statute that declares abortion providers to be liable for any injuries caused by the abortion to the "mother" is unconstitutional as an undue burden on the mother's right to an abortion.[124] It seems that nothing — certainly not the safety of the women undergoing the procedures — takes precedence over keeping access to abortion free from any impediment.

Certain other statistics might also be of interest. We in the United States have experienced steadily rising rates of births out of wedlock and also births to teenage mothers despite the large

---

115. Maquis, *supra* note 111.

116. Smith, *supra* note 111.

117. Maquis, *supra* note 111; Raymond Smith, *Abortion Doctor Victim of Bias, Study Claims: The Physician Was Accused on Murder after a Patient at a Moreno Valley Clinic Died in 1996,* The Press-Enterprise (Riverside, CA), May 25, 2000, at B1 (reporting a study released by the ACLU after Steir's guilty plea).

118. Bill Ainsworth, *Doctors' Group Battles Licensing Fee Increase: Money Sought to Speed up Investigations of Physicians,* San Diego Union-Tribune, Mar. 22, 1999, at A1 (reporting that representatives of the California Medical Board stated that Dr. Steir had "slipped through" the disciplinary system because it lacked the resources to investigate him properly).

119. Marquis, *supra* note 111.

120. Smith, *supra* note 111.

121. *Abortion Doctor Sentenced to Year in Jail in Death of Barstow Patient,* L.A. Times, May 27, 2000, at A20. Anti-abortion activists thought this too lenient. *See* Joseph Hachee, *Letter to the Editor,* The Press-Enterprise (Riverside, CA), June 3, 2000, at A12; John Schwab, *Letter to the Editor,* The Press-Enterprise (Riverside, CA), June 3, 2000, at A12.

122. Smith, *supra* note 111. A very similar sequence of events lead to the bleeding to death of 33-year old LouAnne Herron in 1998 in a Phoenix, Arizona, abortion clinic, and the subsequent conviction (by a jury) of Dr. John Biskind of manslaughter and of clinic administrator Carol Stuart-Schadoff of negligent homicide. Carol Sowers, *Examiner Says Tool Cut Womb,* Ariz. Rep., Feb. 7, 2001, at B5.

123. Sam Delson, *Abortion Clinic Bill Dies in Committee: It Is the Second Time the Senate Panel Has Rejected the Measure by Ray Haynes,* The Press-Enterprise (Riverside, CA), Feb. 26, 1999, at Apr. 15, 1999, at B3. *See also* Kohm, *supra* note 128, at 121–24 (1997); Lynne Marie Kohm & Colleen Holmes, *The Rise and Fall of Women's Rights: Have Sexuality and Reproductive Freedom Forfeited Victory?,* 6 Wm. & Mary J. Women & L. 381, 403–06 (2000). One result perhaps of such pressures is he notoriously lax enforcement of such few regulations as there are for abortion clinics. *See* Diane Rado, *Enforcement of Abortion Rules Is Lax, Records Show,* St. Petersburg Times, Dec. 6, 1989, at B4.

124. Okpalobi v. Foster, 190 F.3d 337 (5th Cir. 1999).

number of abortions; in fact, the United States for some time has had the highest rate of births to teenage mothers of any developed nation.[125] Many states, however, require parental notification and consent before a juvenile undergoes an abortion, most containing a "judicial by-pass" provision allowing a judge to approve an abortion without notifying a parent.[126] Whether these

---

125. Elise Jones *et al.*, *Pregnancy in Developed Countries: Determinants and Policy Implications,* 17 Fam. Planning Persp. 53 (1985). *See generally* Risking the Future, *supra* note 40; Alison Spitz *et al.*, *Pregnancy, Abortion, and Birth Rates among US Adolescents—1980, 1985, and 1990,* 275 New Eng. J. Med. 989 (1996).

126. Ala. Code §26-21-3 (1992); Ariz. Rev. Stat. Ann. §36-2152 (West 2003); Ark. Stat. Ann. §§20-16-901 to 20-16-908 (LexisNexis Supp. 2003); Cal. Health & Safety Code §123450 (West 1996); Fla. Stat. Ann. §390-0111(4) (West 2002); Ga. Code Ann. §15-11-112 (2001); 750 Ill. Comp. Stat. Ann. §70/25 (West 1999); Ind. Code Ann. §§16-34-2-1 to 16-34-2-7 (West 1997 & Supp. 2003); Iowa Code Ann. §135L.3 (West Supp. 2003); Kan. Stat. Ann. §§65-6704, 65-6705 (2002); Ky. Rev. Stat. Ann. §311.732 (Michie 2001); La. Rev. Stat. Ann. §40:1299.35.5 (West 2001); Mass. Gen. Laws Ann. ch. 112, §12S (West 2003); Mich. Comp. Laws Ann. §722.903 (West 2002); Minn. Stat. Ann. §144.343 (West Supp. 2003); Miss. Code Ann. §41-41-53 (1999); Mo. Ann. Stat. §188.028 (West 2000); Neb. Rev. Stat. §71-6903 (1996); Nev. Rev. Stat. Ann. §§442.255, 442.2555 (Michie 2000); N.J. Stat. Ann. §§9:17A-1.1 to 9:17A-1.12 (2002); N.C. Gen. Stat. §§90-21.6 to 90-21.10 (2003); N.D. Cent. Code §§14-02.1 to 14-03.1 (Michie Supp. 2003); Ohio Rev. Code Ann. §2919.12 (Anderson 2002); Pa. Stat. Ann. tit. 18, §3206 (West 2000); R.I. Gen. Laws §23-4.7-6 (1997); S.C. Code Ann. §44-41-31 (LexisNexis 2002); Tenn. Code Ann. §§37-10-301 to 37-10-307 (2001); W. Va. Code §16-2F-3 (2001); Wyo. Stat. Ann. §35-6-118 (LexisNexis 2003). Eleven other statutes do not allow for a judicial by-pass, and thus are of doubtful constitutionality: Alaska Stat. §18.16.010 (LexisNexis 2002); Colo. Rev. Stat. §18-6-101 (2003); Del. Code Ann. tit. 24, §1790(b)(3) (2003); Idaho Code §18-609(A)(6) (1997); Md. Health-Gen. Code Ann. §20-103 (Michie 2000); Mont. Code Ann. §50-20-212 (2003); N.M. Stat. Ann. §30-5-1(C) (Michie 1994); S.D. Codified Laws Ann. §34-23A-7 (Supp. 2003); Tex. Fam. Code Ann. §33.003 (West 2002); Utah Code Ann. §76-7-304 (2003); Va. Code Ann. §16.1-241 (LexisNexis 2003); Wash. Rev. Code §9.02.100 (West 1998). One court, however, upheld the constitutionality of a statute without a judicial bypass for parental notice, although the statute did include a judicial bypass for parental consent. Planned Parenthood of Blue Ridge v. Camblos, 155 F.3d 352 (4th Cir. 1998) *cert. denied,* 525 U.S. 1140 (1999). Three other states require that minors be counseled about discussing the planned abortion with a parent, without actually requiring notice: Conn. Gen. Stat. Ann. §19a-601 (West 2003); Me. Rev. Stat. tit. 22, §1597-A (West 1992); Wis. Stat. Ann. §48.375 (West 2003).

*See* Lambert v. Wicklund, 520 U.S. 292 (1997); Hodgson v. Minnesota, 497 U.S. 417 (1990); H.L. v. Matheson, 450 U.S. 398 (1981); Bellotti v. Baird, 443 U.S. 622 (1979); Planned Parenthood v. Danforth, 428 U.S. 52, 74 (1975); Planned Parenthood of the Rocky Mtns. Services Corp. v. Owens, 287 F.3d 910 (10th Cir. 2002); Blackard v. Memphis Area Med. Ctr. for Women, 262 F.3d 568 (6th Cir. 2001), *cert. denied,* 535 U.S. 1053 (2002); Planned Parenthood of S. Ariz. v. Lawall, 180 F.3d 1022, *modified,* 193 F.3d 1042 (9th Cir. 1999); Memphis Planned Parenthood, Inc. v. Sundquist, 175 F.3d 456 (6th Cir. 1999); Causeway Med. Suite v. Ieyoub, 123 F.3d 849 (5th Cir. 1997), *cert. denied,* 522 U.S. 923 (1997); Manning v. Hunt, 119 F.3d 254 (4th Cir. 1997); Planned Parenthood, Sioux Falls Clinic v. Miller, 63 F.3d 1452 (8th Cir. 1995), *cert. denied sub nom.* Janklow v. Planned Parenthood, 517 U.S. 1174 (1996) (Rehnquist, C.J., Scalia & Thomas JJ., dissenting); Casey v. Planned Parenthood of S.E. Pa., 14 F.3d 848 (3rd Cir.), *application for stay denied,* 510 U.S. 1309 (1994); Cleveland Surgi-Center, Inc. v. Jones, 2 F.3d 686 (6th Cir. 1993), *cert. denied,* 510 U.S. 1046 (1994); Eubanks v. Wilkinson, 937 F.2d 1118 (6th Cir. 1991); Glick v. McKay, 937 F.2d 434 (9th Cir. 1991); Planned Parenthood of Atlanta Area, Inc. v. Miller, 934 F.2d 1462 (11th Cir. 1991); Arnold v. Board of Educ. of Escambia Cty., 880 F.2d 305 (11th Cir. 1989); Planned Parenthood Lg. of Mass. v. Bellotti, 868 F.2d 459 (1st Cir. 1989); *Ex parte* Anonymous, 806 So. 2d 169 (Ala. 2001); State v. Planned Parenthood of Alaska, 35 P.3d 30 (Alaska 2001); American Academy of Pediatrics v. Lungren, 940 P.2d 797 (Cal. 1996); North Fla. Women's Health Services, Inc. v. State, 866 So. 2d 612 (Fla. 2003); Woman's Choice-East Side Women's Clinic v. Newman, 671 N.E.2d 104 (Ind. 1996); *In re* Jane Doe, 866 P.2d 1069 (Kan. 1994); Kelly v. Vote Know Coalition of Md., Inc., 626 A.2d 959 (Md. 1993); Planned Parenthood Lg. of Mass., Inc. v. Attorney-General, 677 N.E.2d 101 (Mass. 1997); Planned Parenthood of Cent. N.J. v. Farmer, 762 A.2d 620 (N.J. 2000); *In re* Doe, 19 S.W.3d 346 (Tex. 2000). *See generally* Wetstein, *supra* note 5, at 15-19; Suellyn Scarnecchia & Julie Kunce Field, *Judging Girls: Decision Making in Parental Consent to Abortion Cases,* 3 Mich. J. Gender & L. 75 (1995). The situation in England and Wales is much less clear. Re B, [1991] 2 F.L.R. 426 (Q.F.D.); Re P, [1986] 1 F.L.R. 272 (Q.F.D.); Mason, *supra* note 78, at 130-32. *See also* Detlev Belling & Christina Eberl, *Teenage Abortions in*

statutes are good or bad for the girls and their families is hotly debated,[127] as are the effects of adolescent pregnancy and abortions generally.[128]

---

*Germany: With Reference to the Legal System in the United States,* 12 J. CONTEMP. HEALTH L. & POL'Y 475 (1996).

127. PATRICIA DONOVAN, OUR DAUGHTERS' DECISIONS: THE CONFLICT IN STATE LAW ON ABORTION AND OTHER ISSUES (1992); CHARLOTTE EHRENGARD ELLERTSON, MANDATORY PARENTAL INVOLVEMENT IN MINORS' ABORTIONS: EFFECTS OF THE LAWS IN MINNESOTA, MISSOURI, AND INDIANA (1993); 1 DOCUMENTARY HISTORY OF THE LEGAL ASPECTS OF ABORTION IN THE U.S., *supra* note 29, at 249-340; HADLEY, *supra* note 65, at 49-51; GARY MELTON, THE DETERMINANTS OF ADOLESCENT ABORTION (1986); THE POLITICS OF PREGNANCY: ADOLESCENT SEXUALITY AND PUBLIC POLICY (Annette Lawson & Deborah Rhode eds. 1993); Robert Blum, Michael Resnick, & Patricia Stark, *Factors Associated with the Use of Court Bypass by Minors to Obtain Abortions,* 22 FAM. PLANNING PERSP. 158 (1990); Freddie Clary, *Minor Women Obtaining Abortions: A Study of Parental Notification in a Metropolitan Area,* 72 AM. J. PUB. HEALTH 283 (1982); Ruth Colker, *An Equal Protection Analysis of United States Reproductive Health Policy: Gender, Race, Age, and Class,* 1991 DUKE L.J. 324, 359-63; Erin Daly, *Reconsidering Abortion Law: Liberty, Equality, and the New Rhetoric of* Planned Parenthood v. Casey, 45 AM. U. L. REV. 77, 105-11 (1995); J. Shoshanna Ehrlich, *Minors as Medical Decision Makers: The Pretextual Reasoning of the Court in the Abortion Cases,* 7 MICH. J. GENDER & L. 65 (2000); Melody Embree & Tracy Dobson, *Parental Involvement in Adolescent Abortion Decisions,* 10 LAW & INEQUALITY 53 (1991); Mary Griffin-Carlson & Kathleen Macklin, *Parental Consent: Factors Influencing Adolescent Disclosure Regarding Abortion,* 28 ADOLESCENCE 1 (1993); Katheryn Katz, *The Pregnant Child's Right to Self-Determination,* 62 ALB. L. REV. 1119 (1999); Catherine Lewis, *Minors' Competence to Consent to Abortion,* 42 AM. PSYCHOL. 84 (1987); Jesse Lieberman, State v. North Florida Women's Health and Counseling Services, Inc.: *The Constitutionality of the Parental Notice of Abortion Act,* 26 NOVA L. REV. 545 (2002); Martin, *supra* note 104; Merz, Jackson, & Klerman, *supra* note 55, at 9-61 (1995); Maggie O'Shaughnessy, *The Worst of Both Worlds?: Parental Involvement Requirements and the Privacy Rights of Mature Minors,* 57 OHIO ST. L.J. 1731 (1996); Anita Pliner & Suzanne Yates, *Psychological and Legal Issues in Minors' Rights to Abortion,* 48 J. SOC. ISSUES 203 (1992); Michael Resnick, Linda Bearinger, & Patricia Stark, *Patterns of Consultation among Adolescent Minors Obtaining an Abortion,* 64 AM. J. ORTHOPSYCH. 310 (1994); Deborah Rhode, *Adolescent Pregnancy and Public Policy,* 108 POL. SCI. Q. 635, 661-69 (1994); Helena Silverstein, In the Matter of Anonymous, a Minor: *Fetal Representation in Hearings to Waive Parental Consent to Abortion,* 11 CORNELL J.L. & PUB. POL'Y 69 (2001); Symposium, *Unburdening the Right to Abortion:* Casey's *Undue Burden Standard,* 10 AM. U.J. GENDER SOC. POL'Y & L. 255–59 (2001); Suzanne Yates & Anita Pliner, *Judging Maturity in the Courts: The Massachusetts Consent Statute,* 78 AM. J. PUB. HEALTH 648 (1988); Laurie Zabin *et al., To Whom Do Inner-City Minors Talk about Their Pregnancies? Adolescents' Communication with Parents and Parent Surrogates,* 24 FAM. PLANNING PERSPECTIVES 148 (1992).

128. *See* ADOLESCENT ABORTION: PSYCHOLOGICAL AND LEGAL ISSUES (Gary Melton ed. 1986); JEANNE BROOKS-GUNN & S. PHILIP MORGAN, ADOLESCENT MOTHERS IN LATER LIFE (1987); STANLEY HENSHAW *et al.,* TEENAGE PREGNANCY IN THE UNITED STATES: THE SCOPE OF THE PROBLEM AND STATE RESPONSES (1989); RISKING THE FUTURE, *supra* note 118; HYMAN RODMAN, SUSAN LEWIS, & SARALYN GRIFFITH, THE SEXUAL RIGHTS OF ADOLESCENTS: COMPETENTS, VULNERABILITY, AND PARENTHOOD CONTROL (1984); Patricia Bailey *et al., Adolescent Pregnancy 1 Year Later: The Effects of Abortion vs. Motherhood in Northeast Brazil,* 29 J. ADOLESCENT HEALTH 223 (2001); Robert Blum, Michael Resnick, & Trisha Stark, *The Impact of a Parental Notification Law on Adolescent Decisionmaking,* 77 AM. J. PUB. HEALTH 619 (1987); Debra Boyer & David Fine, *Sexual Abuse as a Factor in Adolescent Pregnancy and Child Maltreatment,* 24 FAM. PLANNING PERSPECTIVES 4 (1992); Mary Buchanan & Cynthia Robbins, *Early Adult Psychological Consequences for Males of Adolescent Pregnancy and Its Resolution,* 19 J. YOUTH & ADOLESCENCE 413 (1990); Nancy Campbell, Kathleen Franco, & Stephen Jura, *Abortion in Adolescence,* 23 ADOLESCENCE 813 (1988); Willard Cates, jr., *The Risks Associated with Teenage Abortion,* 309 N. ENG. J. MED. 621 (1983); Marvin Eisen & Gail Zellman, *Factors Predicting Pregnancy Resolution Satisfaction of Unmarried Adolescents,* 145 J. GENETIC PSYCHOL. 231 (1984); Wanda Franz & David Reardon, *Differential Impact of Abortion on Adolescents and Adults,* 27 ADOLESCENCE 162 (1992); Mark Jacoby *et al., Rapid Repeat Pregnancy and Experience of Interpersonal Violence among Low Income Adolescents,* 16 AM. J. PREVENTIVE MED. 318 (1999); Theodore Joyce, *The Social and Economic Correlates of Pregnancy Resolution among Adolescents in New York City, by Race and Ethnicity: A Multivarient Analysis,* 78 AM. J. PUB. HEALTH 626 (1988); Lucy Olson, *Social and Psychological Correlates of Pregnancy Resolution among Adolescent Women,* 50 AM. J. ORTHOPSYCH. 432 (1980); Cameron Ortiz & Ena Vazquez Nutall, *Adolescent Pregnancy: Effects of Family Support, Education, and Religion on the Decision to Carry or Terminate among Puerto Rican Teenagers,* 22 ADOLESCENCE 897 (1987); Marcia Redmond, *Attitudes of Adolescent Males toward Pregnancy and Fatherhood,* 34 FAM. REL., J. APPLIED FAM. CHILD STUD. 337 (1985); Rhode, *supra* note 120, at 647–61;

It is not clear how much difference such statutes actually make. Most girls involve their parents in the abortion decision even without a legal requirement to do so.[129] The younger the girl is, the more likely she is to involve her parents, with around 90 percent of girls under 14 involving their parents (compared to only 51 percent of girls aged 17).[130] Nor are parents invariably opposed to an abortion. Some parents are so convinced that an abortion is the only acceptable path for their pregnant minor daughter that they have gone before juvenile courts to have their daughter declared "incorrigible" in an effort—usually unsuccessful—to have the court coerce her into having the abortion.[131]

One point is objectively established about the parental notice statutes. The rate of births to teenagers, which varies from state to state, drops (sometimes precipitously), along with the abortion rate, in states with notice statutes.[132] This pattern holds true in a geographically small state like Massachusetts, from which recourse to out-of-state abortions is easy, as well as in a large state like Minnesota.[133] While some unknown number of these women might obtain abortions in neighboring states where parental notification is not required, the statistics do suggest that reducing access to abortion either discourages sexual activity or encourages careful use of contraceptives (or both).

Pro-abortion groups, locking themselves into defending abortion under all circumstances (somewhat like the gun-lobby defending the free availability of assault weapons), have felt com-

---

Susheela Singh, *Adolescent Pregnancy in the United States: An Interstate Analysis,* 18 FAM. PLANNING PERSP. 210 (1986); Michael Sobol & Kerry Daly, *The Adoption Alternative for Pregnant Adolescents: Decision Making Consequences and Policy Implications,* 48 J. SOC. ISSUES 143 (1992); Carl Tishler, *Adolescent Suicide Attempts Following Elective Abortion: A Special Case of Anniversary Reactions,* 68 PEDIATRICS 670 (1981); Kazuo Yamaguchi & Dennise Kandel, *Drug Use and Other Determinants of Premarital Pregnancy and Its Outcome: A Dynamic Analysis of Competing Life Events,* 49 J. MAR. & FAM. 257 (1987); Laurie Zabin, *et al., When Adolescents Choose Abortion: Effects of on Education, Psychological Status and Subsequent Pregnancy,* 21 FAM. PLANNING PERPS. 248 (1989).

129. Tamar Lewin, *Study Finds Abortion Plans Are Known by Most Parents,* N.Y. TIMES, Oct. 21, 1992, at A16.

130. *Id.*

131. *See, e.g.,* In re Mary P., 444 N.Y.S.2d 545 (Fam. Ct. 1981) (case dismissed). *But see In re* Barbara C., 474 N.Y.S.2d 799 (Sup. Ct. 1984) (allowing application for an abortion of a 25-year-old retarded woman based upon the consent of her father without regard to whether it was in the woman's best interest).

132. *See, e.g.,* Virginia Cartoof & Lorraine Klerman, *Parental Consent for Abortion: Impact of the Massachusetts Law,* 76 AM. J. PUB. HEALTH 397 (1986); Freddie Clary, *Minor Women Obtaining Abortions: A Study of Parental Notification in a Metropolitan Area,* 72 AM. J. PUB. HEALTH 283 (1982); Patricia Donovan, *Judging Teenagers: How Minors Fare When They Seek Court-Authorized Abortions,* 15 J. FAM. PLANNING PERSP. 259 (1981); Theodore Joyce & Robert Kaestner, *State Reproductive Policies and Adolescent Pregnancy Resolution: The Case of Parental Involvement Laws,* 15 J. HEALTH ECON. 579 (1996); Thomas Kane & Douglas Staiger, *Teen Motherhood and Abortion Access,* 111 Q.J. ECON. 467 (1996); Robert Obsfeldt & Stephan Gohmann, *Do Parental Involvement Laws Reduce Adolescent Abortion Rates?,* 12 CONTEMP. ECON. POL'Y 65 (1994); James Rogers *et al., Impact of the Minnesota Parental Notification Law on Abortion and Birth,* 81 AM. J. PUB. HEALTH 294 (1991); Tishler, *supra* note 128; Susan Yates & Anita Pliner, *Judging Maturity in the Courts: The Massachusetts Consent Statute,* 78 AM. J. PUB. HEALTH 646 (1988). Nationally, the percentage of abortions performed on women or girls under the age of 20 declined slightly from around 28% in 1973 to around 25% in 1988. *A Correction,* N.Y. TIMES, July 2, 1992, at A16. *See also* Lynn Vincent, *The Parent Gap: The Number of Abortions among Teenagers Is Dropping Much Faster in States with Strong Parental Consent Laws,* THE WORLD, Jan. 18, 2003, at 22. One study postulated that states with parental notice statutes are states characterized by stronger "religious sentiment," and that this relatively stronger religious sentiment accounts for the lower rates of adolescent abortions. Annette Tomal, *The Effect of Religious Membership on Teen Abortion Rates,* 30 J. YOUTH & ADOLESCENCE 103116 (2001).

133. Blum, Resnick, & Stark, *supra* note 128; Vincent, *supra* note 132, at 23. *Compare* Cartoof & Klerman, *supra* note 132, *with* Rogers, *supra* note 132; James Rogers & Amy Miller, *Inner-City Birth Rates Following Enactment of the Minnesota Parental Notification Law,* 17 LAW & HUMA. BEHAV. 27 (1993).

pelled even to defend a woman who took a thirteen-year-old girl to another state for an abortion without the knowledge or consent of the girl's parents when the first woman's motive was to protect her son from statutory rape charges.[134] (As it turned out, the son was convicted of statutory rape anyway.) Until recently, these same groups generally had not challenged laws that make it difficult or impossible for a teenager to have a tooth extracted, or any other major or minor medical procedure performed, without the consent of her parents.[135] Nor do these groups object

---

134. Marie McCullough, *Abortion Case Taps Some of Parents' Deepest Fears,* PHILA. INQUIRER, Oct. 27, 1996, at A1.

135. *See* Bonner v. Moran, 126 F.2d 121 (D.C. Cir. 1941); *In re* B, 497 S.W.2d 831 (Mo. 1973); *In re* Seiferth, 127 N.E.2d 820 (N.Y. 1955); *In re* Tuttendario, 21 Pa. Dist. 561 (1911); Zosky v. Gaines, 260 N.W. 99 (1935); Rishworth v. Moss, 159 S.W.2d 122 (Tex. Ct. Civ. App. 1913), *aff'd,* 222 S.W.2d 225 (Tex. Comm'n Appeals 1920); *In re* Hudson, 126 P.2d 765 (Wash. 1942). *See also* ANGELA HOLDER, LEGAL ISSUES IN PEDIATRICS AND ADOLESCENT MEDICINE (2nd ed. 1985); JOSEPHINE GITTLER *et al.,* ADOLESCENT HEALTH CARE DECISION MAKING: THE LAW AND PUBLIC POLICY (1990); MASON, *supra* note 78, at 319–39; GARY MELTON & GERALD KOOCHER, CHILDREN'S COMPETENCE TO CONSENT (1983); JAMES MORRISON *et al.,* CONSENT AND CONFIDENTIALITY IN THE HEALTH CARE OF CHILDREN AND ADOLESCENTS: A LEGAL GUIDE (1986); William Adams, *"But Do You Have to Tell My Parents?" The Dilemma for Minors Seeking HIV-Testing and Treatment,* 27 J. MARSHALL L. REV. 493 (1994); J.A. Devereux , D.P.H. Jones, & D.L. Dickenson, *Can Children Withhold Consent to Treatment,* 306 BRIT. MED. J. 1459 (1993); Janet Dolgin, *The Fate of Childhood: Legal Models of Children and the Parent-Child Relationship,* 61 ALB. L. REV. 345 (1997); Ehrlich, *supra* note 127, at 71–80; Janine Felsman, *Eliminating Parental Consent and Notification for Adolescent HIV Testing: A Legitimate Statutory Response to the AIDS Epidemic,* 5 J. LAW & POL'Y 339 (1996); Andrew Fergusson, *"Child M" and Her Heart Transplant— A Christian Doctor's Reflections,* 140/141 LAW & JUSTICE 22 (1999); Rhonda Gay Hartman, *Adolescent Autonomy: Clarifying an Ageless Conundrum,* 51 HASTINGS L.J. 1265 (2000); Joan Margaret Kun, *Rejecting the Adage "Children Should Be Seen and Not Heard": The Mature Minor Doctrine,* 16 PACE L. REV. 423 (1996); Edward Mulvey & Faith Peeples, *Are Disturbed and Normal Adolescents Equally Competent to Make Decisions about Mental Health Treatments?,* 20 LAW & HUM. BEHAV. 273 (1996); Erin Nealy, *Medical Decision-Making for Children: A Struggle for Autonomy,* 49 SMU L. REV. 133 (1995); James O'Leary, *An Analysis of the Legal Issues Surrounding the Forced Use of Ritalin: Protecting a Child's Legal Right to "Just Say No,"* 27 NEW ENG. L. REV. 1173 (1993); Maggie O'Shaughnessy, *The Worst of Both Worlds? Parental Involvement Requirements and the Privacy Rights of Mature Minors,* 57 OHIO ST. L.J. 1731 (1996); Richard Redding, *Children's Competence to Provide Informed Consent for Mental Health Treatment,* 50 WASH. & LEE L. REV. 695 (1993); Jennifer Rosato, *The Ultimate Test of Autonomy: Should Minors Have a Right to Make Decisions Regarding Life Sustaining Treatment?,* 49 RUTGERS L. REV. 1 (1996); Lainie Friedman Ross, *Pediatric Bioethics: Reintroducing the Family,* 9 THE RESPONSIVE COMMUNITY 40 (1999); David Sherer, *The Capacities of Minors to Exercise Voluntariness in Medical Treatment Decisions,* 15 LAW & HUM. BEHAV. 431 (1991); Walter Wadlington, *Medical Decision Making for and by Children: Tensions between Parent, State, and Child,* 1994 U. ILL. L. REV. 311. *See generally* Elizabeth Cauffman & Laurence Steinberg, *(Im)maturity of Judgment: Why Adolescents May Be Less Culpable than Adults,* 18 BEHAV. SCI. & L. 741 (2000); Elizabeth Cauffman & Laurence Steinberg, *The Cognitive and Affective Influences on Adolescent Decision-Making,* 68 TEMPLE L. REV. 1763 (1995); Elizabeth Scott, *Judgment and Reasoning in Adolescent Decisionmaking,* 37 VILLA. L. REV. 1607 (1992); Laurence Steinberg & Elizabeth Cauffman, *Maturity of Judgment in Adolescence: Psycholosocial Factors in Adolescent Decision Making,* 20 LAW & HUM. BEHAV. 249 (1996).

On occasion, courts did order medical treatment over the objection of parents, but only when the child's life was at stake and the parents were behaving unreasonably. *See In re* Custody of a Minor, 379 N.E.2d 1053 (Mass. 1978); *In re* Vasko, 263 N.Y.S. 552 (App. Div. 1933); *In re* Carstairs, 115 N.Y.S.2d 314 (Dom. Rel. Ct. 1952); *In re* Rotkowitz, 25 N.Y.S.2d 624 (Sup. Ct. 1941); *In re* Heinemann's Appeal, 96 Pa. 112 (1880). Physicians were authorized to act without either court approval or parental consent only in cases of true emergencies in situations when obtaining such authorization would be impractical. *See* Jackovach v. Yocom, 237 N.W. 444 (Iowa 1931); *In re* Turner, 145 P. 871 (Kan. 1915); Wells v. McGehee, 39 So. 2d 196 (La. Ct. App. 1949); Luka v. Lowrie, 136 N.W. 1106 (Mich. 1912); Brooklyn Hosp. v. Torres, 258 N.Y.S.2d 621 (Sup. Ct. 1965); Sullivan v. Montgomery, 279 N.Y.S. 575 (N.Y. City Ct. 1935); *In re* Clark, 185 N.E.2d 128 (C.P. 1962). In the later years of the twentieth century, a growing number of courts allowed "mature minors" to consent to medical procedures; by this time, the decisions were being influenced by the abortion controversy even when the medical procedure in question was something else than an abortion. *See* Younts v. St. Francis Hosp., 469 P.2d 330 (Kan. 1970); Lacy v. Laird, 139 N.E.2d 25 (Ohio 1956); Cardell v. Bechtol, 724 S.W.2d 739 (Tenn. 1987); Smith v. Seilby, 431 P.2d 719 (Was. 1967) (emancipated minor); *In re* T (a minor), [1997] 1 All E.R. 906

to medical regulations of the birthing process that, for example, extend the time that a woman remains in the hospital after giving birth.[136]

Several studies have concluded that the denial of public funds for abortions has only a small effect on abortion rates.[137] Whether this is actually the case, and if so whether the pattern would hold true if significant restrictions were imposed on the access of adult women generally to abortion, remains far from clear. One study, by Dr. Willard Cates, jr., concluded that the denial of funding resulted in about 20 percent of the affected women carrying their pregnancy to term, and about 4 percent turning to illegal abortions, and the remaining 76 percent paying for legal, private abortions with their own money or money provided by charitable or feminist groups.[138] Dr. Cates estimated that some 15,000 unwanted births and some 3,000 illegal abortions resulted annually across the nation as a result of the cut-off of Medicaid funds, leaving some 57,000 privately funded legal abortions. Law professor Mark Graber concluded that the Medicaid cut-off had a smaller proportional effect based on a figure for the total number of women affected by the cut-off that is four times higher than Cates' figure. Graber estimated 18,000 additional live births along with 282,000 privately funded abortions for women denied Medicaid funds.[139] Graber did not distinguish between legal and illegal private abortions. Careful study has also shown almost no increase in deaths to women denied publicly-funded abortions. The Centers for Disease Control has found only "four deaths from indigent women from illegal or self-induced abortions [due] to the unavailability of Medicaid funding."[140] Dr. Cates found only three maternal deaths "associated to some degree" with funding restrictions.[141]

---

(C.A.); Gillick v. West Norfolk & Wisbeck AHA, [1985] All E.R. 402 (C.A.).

    In the 1960s, several parts of the British Commonwealth enacted a statute giving minors the right to consent to medical procedures at the age of 16 or higher. *Minors (Property and Contracts) Act of 1970*, § 49 (N.S.W.); *Guardianship Act of 1968*, § 25 (N.Z.); *Famliy Law Reform Act of 1969*, § 8 (U.K.). *See generally* P.D.G. Skegg, *Consent to Medical Procedures on Minors*, 36 MOD. L. REV. 370 (1973).

    136. *See The Newborns & Mothers' Health Protection Act of 1996*, 42 U.S.C. §§ 300gg-4 to 300gg-51 (2000). *See also* Beth Mandel Rosenthal, Note, *Drive-Through Deliveries, and* The Newborns and Mothers' Protective Health Protection Act of 1996, 28 RUTGERS L.J. 753 (1997); Tracy Wilson Smirnof, Note, *"Drive-Through Deliveries": Indiscriminate Postpartum Early Discharge Practices Presently Necessitate Legislation Mandating Minimum Inpatient Hospital Stays*, 44 CLEVE. ST. L. REV. 231 (1996).

    137. Sandra Balmer, *Legal Abortions for Poorer Women Common Even without Federal Funds*, PHILA. INQUIRER, Sept. 4, 1981, at 3-A; Rebecca Blank, Christine George, & Rebecca London, *State Abortion Rates: The Impact of Policies, Providers, Politics, Demographics, and Economic Development*, 15 J. HEALTH ECON. 513 (1996); Mark Evans *et al.*, *The Fiscal Impact of the Medicaid Abortion Funding Ban in Michigan*, 82 OBSTET. & GYNECOLOGY 555 (1993); Deborah Haas-Wilson, *Consent and Notification Laws and Medicaid Funding Restrictions*, 12 J. POL'Y ANAL. & MGT. 498 (1993); Hansen, *supra* note 16; Stanley Henshaw & Lynn Wallisch, *The Medicaid Cutoff and Abortion Services for the Poor*, 16 FAM. PLANNING PERSP. 170 (1984); Carol Korenbrot *et al.*, *Trends in Rates of Live Births and Abortions Following State Restrictions on Public Funding of Abortion*, 105 PUB. HEALTH REP. 555 (1990); Phillip Levine, Amy Trainor, & David Zimmerman, *The Effect of Medicaid Abortion Funding Restrictions on Abortions, Pregnancies and Birth*, 15 J. HEALTH ECON. 555 (1996); Kenneth Meier *et al.*, *The Impact of State-Level Restrictions on Abortion*, 33 DEMOGRAPHY 307 (1996); James Trussell *et al.*, *The Impact of Restricting Medicaid Financing for Abortion*, 12 FAM. PLANNING PERSP. 120 (1980). *See generally* Harris v. McRae, 448 U.S. 297 (1980); 1 DOCUMENTARY HISTORY OF THE LEGAL ASPECTS OF ABORTION IN THE U.S., *supra* note 29, at 3–186; MACKINNON, F.U., *supra* note 78, at 93, 96–97, 100–01; TRIBE, *supra* note 29, at 151–59; WETSTEIN, *supra* note 5, at 19–25.

    138. Willard Cates, jr., *The Hyde Amendment in Action: How Did the Restrictions on Federal Funds for Abortion Affect Low-Income Women?*, 246 JAMA 1109 (1982). *See also* Trussell *et al.*, *supra* note 137, at 121, 129.

    139. GRABER, *supra* note 5, at 68.

    140. *See* Trussell *et al.*, *supra* note 137, at 121, 129.

    141. Julian Gold & Willard Cates, jr., *Restriction of Federal Funds for Abortion: 18 Months Later*, 69 AM. J. PUB. HEALTH 929 (1979).

# *Roe* in Light of World Trends

*If you can't imitate him, don't copy him.*

— Yogi Berra[142]

Abortion reform occurred in many parts of the world at roughly the same time in a broadly similar pattern, generally through statutes rather than court decisions.[143] As we have seen, England removed most restrictions on a woman's right to choose early abortion in 1967.[144] British courts explicitly rejected the claim that the common law contains a "right of privacy," largely on the grounds that the supposed right is too vague and could not be predictably applied by courts.[145] British courts even declined to give domestic effect to article 8 of the *European Convention on Human Rights,* which announces a protected right of privacy and which has been ratified by the United Kingdom.[146] As a result, the United Kingdom has been found in violation of article 8 on several occasions.[147]

None of the British cases involved abortion rights in the American sense — rights with which the legislature cannot interfere. The right to abort in England is secured by a statute that makes no claim to address "privacy" as an abstract right and provides less protection to the freedom to choose to abort that do *Roe* and *Doe.*[148] While some have found the English abortion law too restrictive[149] and others have found the English abortion law too permissive,[150] the matter simply has not generated much sustained controversy in Britain. The one attempt to bring the matter before the European Commission on Human Rights challenged the British statute as insufficiently protective of the life of the fetus.[151] The Commission rejected the claim out of hand.

---

142. NATHAN, *supra* note 2, at 150.

143. ABORTION AND PROTECTION OF THE HUMAN FETUS: LEGAL PROBLEMS IN CROSSCULTURAL PERSPECTIVE (Stanislaw Frankowski & George Cole eds. 1987); ABORTION IN THE NEW EUROPE: A COMPARATIVE HANDBOOK (Bill Rolston & Anna Eggert eds. 1994); COLIN FRANCOME, ABORTION FREEDOM: A WORLDWIDE MOVEMENT (1984); INTERNATIONAL HANDBOOK ON ABORTION (Paul Sachdev ed. 1988); JODI JACOBSON, THE GLOBAL POLITICS OF ABORTION: STATE OF THE WORLD 1991 (1991); KENNY, *supra* note 52, at 177–99; B.J. George, jr., *State Legislatures versus the Supreme Court: Abortion Legislation into the 1990s,* in ABORTION, MEDICINE, AND THE LAW, *supra* note 29, at 3, 5–8 n.14; Henshaw, *supra* note 81, at 82.

144. *Abortion Act of 1967,* ch. 87, § 1. *See* Chapter 12, at notes 266–90; BARBARA BROOKES, ABORTION IN ENGLAND 1900–1967, at 153–56 (1988); DANIEL CALLAHAN, ABORTION: LAW, CHOICE, AND MORALITY 142–49 (1970); GERMAIN GRISEZ, ABORTION: THE MYTHS, THE REALITIES, AND THE ARGUMENTS 229–31, 239–40, 250–53 (1970); ANTHONY HORDERN, LEGAL ABORTION: THE ENGLISH EXPERIENCE 69–79, 239–74 (1971); J. KEOWN, ABORTION, DOCTORS AND THE LAW 110–37 (1988); Donald Kommers, *Abortion in Six Countries: A Comparative Legal Analysis,* in ABORTION, MEDICINE, & THE LAW, *supra* note 29, at 303, 316–20.

145. Malone v. Metropolitan Police Comm'r, [1979] 1 Ch. 334, 372–73.

146. *In re* K.D., [1988] 1 App. Cas. 806 (H.L.); Regina v. Chief Immigration Officer, [1976] 1 W.L.R. 976 (C.A.); Somasundarum v. Entry Clearance Officer, [1990] Imm. A.R. 16; Chundawadra v. Immigration Appeal Tribunal, [1988] Imm. A.R. 161.

147. Boyle v. United Kingdom, 10 Eur. Hum. Rts. Rep. 425 (1988); R v. United Kingdom, 10 Eur. Hum. Rts. Rep. 74 (1987). *See generally* Ronald Krotoszynski, jr., Note, *Autonomy, Community, and Traditions of Liberty: The Contrast of British and American Privacy Law,* 1990 DUKE L.J. 1398.

148. *Abortion Act,* 1967, ch. 87, § 1. *See* Chapter 12, at notes 266–90.

149. *See, e.g.,* Sally Sheldon, *"Who Is the Mother to Make the Judgment?": The Construction of Woman in the English Law,* 1 FEM. LEGAL STUD. 3 (1993).

150. Youssef M. Ibrhim, *Planned Abortion of One Twin Stirs Furor in Britain,* N.Y. TIMES, Aug. 6, 1996, at A3; Jo Knowsley, *Abortion Too Easy, Say Most Women: Poll Reveals New Mood as Hume Attacks Blair,* THE SUNDAY TELEGRAPH, Oct. 26, 1997.

151. Paton v. United Kingdom, 3 Eur. H.R. Rep. 408 (1980) (Comm'n Rep.).

In Australia, the law regarding abortion is state law, and thus varies, depending on the state, from reform statutes, to "liberal" judicial interpretations, to prohibitory statutes dating from the nineteenth century.[152] Australia thus presents a microcosm that includes features of the American and the English experience as well as experiences that those strongly opposed to abortion in either America or England hope to bring about.[153] In Canada, in contrast, the abortion law, like all Canadian criminal law, is federal rather than provincial. There was a long and often bitter political struggle over abortion in Canada.[154] Attempts by Canada's national parliament to prohibit or restrict abortions foundered on Supreme Court decisions mandating a high degree of autonomy for women and physicians under the *Canadian Charter of Rights* enacted in 1982.[155] The decisive Canadian litigation was brought on behalf of abortion providers who complained of the interruption of their business rather than on behalf of women who had been denied abortion, yet the Canadian Supreme Court turned its decision on the rights of women to the "equal protection of the laws" and to the "equal benefit of the laws."[156] Notwithstanding the victory in the courts, however, access to abortion in Canada remains problematic outside of the largest cities.[157]

---

152. *See* Regina v. Davidson, [1969] V.R. 667; Regina v. Wald, [1972] D.R.C. 25 (N.S.W. Dist.); *Criminal Law Consolidation Ordinance*, Act No. 2 of 1973 (Australia — N. Terr.); *Criminal Law Consolidation Act Amendment*, Act no. 109 of 1969 (S. Australia). *See generally* Kerry Petersen, Abortion Regimes 71–88 (1993); H.A. Finlay, *Abortion — Right of Crime?*, 10 U. Tasmania L. Rev. 1 (1990); Kommers, *supra* note 144, at 320–23; J.A. McMahon, *Abortion: Asking the Rights Question*, 18 Victoria U. Wellington L. Rev. 201 (1988).

153. Petersen, *supra* note 152, at 99–148, 187–98; Jonathan Kelley & M.D.R. Evans, *Should Abortion Be Legal: Australians' Opinions and Their Sources in Ideology and Social Structure*, in Australian Attitudes: Social and Political Analysis from the National Social Sciences Survey 10 (Jonathan Kelley & Clive Bean eds. 1988); Catriona Mackenzie, *Abortion and Embodiment*, 70 Australasian J. Legal Phil. 136 (1992); Lisa Teasdale, *Confronting the Fear of Being "Caught": Discourses on Abortion in Western Australia*, 22 U.N.S.W. L.J. 60 (1999). Australia has even had anti-abortion protesters and even the murder of a clinic security guard by a protester. Editorial, *Horror: "Pro-Life" Murder*, Charleston Gazette & Daily Mail, July 18, 2001, at 4A. For New Zealand, see Paul Perry & Andrew Trillin, *Attitudes toward Abortion in a Provincial Area of New Zealand: Differentials and Determinants*, 18 Australian & N.Z. J. Soc. 399 (1982); Solana Pyne, *A Different Choice: With RU-486 on the Market, Abortion Providers Aim for More Access*, Newsday, July 31, 2001, at C3.

154. F.L. Morton, *Morgenthaler v. Borowski: The Charter and the Courts* (1992) ("Morton, *Morgenthaler*"); F.L. Morton, Pro-Choice vs. Pro-Life and the Courts in Canada (1993); Nicolas Bala, *Canada: Struggling to Find a Balance on Gender Issues*, 33 U. Louisville J. Fam. L. 301, 313–14 (1995).

155. Regina v. Morgenthaler, 107 D.L.R.4th 537 (Can. 1993); Borowski v. Canada (Attorney-General), [1989] 1 S.C.R. 342 (Can.); Morgenthaler v. Regina, [1988] 1 S.C.R. 30 (Can.). *See* Can. Const. §15(1) (1982); Donald Beschle, *Judicial Review and Abortion in Canada: Lessons for the United States in the Wake of* Webster v. Reproductive Health Services, 61 U. Colo. L. Rev. 537 (1990); Douglas Camp Chaffey, *The Right to Privacy in Canada*, 108 Poli. Sci. Q. 117, 128–32 (1993); Lorenne Clark, *Abortion Law in Canada: A Matter of National Concern*, 14 Dalhousie L.J. 81 (1991); Daniel Conkle, *Canada's* Roe: *The Canadian Abortion Decision and Its Implications for American Constitutional Law and Theory*, 6 Const'l Commentary 299, 308–18 (1989); Raymond Michael Ferri & Terese Ferri, *Canadian Abortion Law*, 30 Cath. Law. 336 (1986); Mary Ann Glendon, A Beau Mentir Qui Vient de Loin: *The Canadian Abortion Decision in Comparative Perspective*, 83 Nw. U. L. Rev. 569 (1989); Donna Greschner, *Abortion and Democracy for Women: A Critique of* Tremblay v. Daigle, 35 McGill L.J. 633 (1990); Hester Lessard, *Relationship, Particularity and Change: Reflections on* R. v. Morgenthaler *and Feminist Approaches to Liberty*, 36 McGill L.J. 263 (1991); Kathleen Mahoney, *The Constitutional Law of Equality in Canada*, 44 Me. L. Rev. 229 (1992); Moira McConnell, Sui Generis: *The Legal Nature of the Fetus in Canada*, 70 Can. B. Rev. 548 (1991); A. Anne McLellan, *Abortion Law in Canada*, in Abortion, Medicine, and the Law, *supra* note 29, at 333; Martha Shaffer, *Foetal Rights and the Regulation of Abortion*, 39 McGill L.J. 58 (1994); Lynn Smith, *An Equality Approach to Reproductive Choice:* R. v. Sullivan, 4 Yale J.L. & Feminism 93 (1991); Lorraine Eisenstat Weinrib, *The* Morgenthaler *Judgment: Constitutional Rights, Legislative Intention and Institutional Design*, 12 U. Tor. L.J. 1 (1992); Bertha Wilson, *Women, the Family, and the Constitutional Protection of Privacy*, 17 Queen's L.J. 5 (1992).

156. Morton, *Morgenthaler*, *supra* note 154, at 123–293. *But see* Peter Westen, *The Empty Idea of Equality*, 95 Harv. L. Rev. 537 (1982).

157. Hamuda Ghafour, *Access Is Ontario's Abortion Issue — Abortion Is Safe and Legal, but Hard to Get Outside the GTA [Greater Toronto Area]*, Toronto Star, Jan. 12, 2001, at LI2/

In South Africa, indigenous customary law gave the husband complete control over his wife's reproductive life.[158] The South African Parliament enacted an "indications" statute in 1975 allowing an abortion for a threat to the life or mental health of the mother, for serious defect in the child, after rape or incest, or because of the mental incompetence of the mother.[159] The statute, however, was designed to restrict access to abortion rather than to broaden it.[160] Only in 1996 did the first legislature dominated by the African National Congress enact a statute allowing abortion on demand and at state expense during the first 12 weeks of pregnancy.[161] The same statute enacted a broad set of indications for the next eight weeks, without any mandatory parental notification or consent requirement for minors.[162] The bill passed the South African Senate, however, only through the African National Congress's imposition of strict party discipline on the issue, resulting in more than 20 percent of the Senators (all ANC members) abstaining.[163] The net result has been a rush of women to hospitals for abortions—including women from neighboring countries where abortion remains illegal—threatening to overwhelm many hospitals that simply lack the equipment and qualified staff to meet the demand.[164] A lower court rejected the first constitutional challenge to the law.[165] The question will remain open until it is resolved by South Africa's Supreme Court.[166]

Resistance to abortion was stronger in Ireland than elsewhere in the common law world. Ireland amended its constitution in 1983 to put the prohibition of abortion beyond judicial scrutiny:

> The state acknowledges the right to life of the unborn and, with due regard to the equal right to life of the mother, guarantees in its law to respect, and as far as practicable, by its laws to defend and vindicate the right.[167]

---

158. Fitnat Naa-Adjeley Adjetey, *Religious and Cultural Rights: Reclaiming the African Woman's Individuality: The Struggle between Women's Reproductive Autonomy and African Society and Culture*, 44 Am. U. L. Rev. 1351, 1359 (1995); Audrey Haroz, Note, *South Africa's 1996 Choice on Termination of Pregnancy Act: Expanding Choice and International Human Rights to Black South African Women*, 30 Vand. J. Transnat'l L. 863, 875–76 (1997).

159. *Abortion and Sterilization Act*, No. 2 (1975).

160. S. Talcott Camp, *Why Have You Been Silent? The Church and the Abortion Ban in South Africa*, 4 Colum. J. Gender & L. 143, 144–46 (1994); Desirée Hansson & Diana Russell, *Made to Fail: The Mythical Option of Legal Abortion for Survivors of Rape and Incest*, 9 S. Afr. J. Hum. Rts. 500 (1993); Haroz, *supra* note 158, at 879–83; Craig Lind, *Rape Thy Wife—Abort Thy Child?*, 18 Businessman's Law. 158 (1989); Najma Moosa, *A Descriptive Analysis of South African and Islamic Abortion Legislation and Local Muslim Community Response*, 21 Med. & L. 257 (2002); F.F.W. van Oosten & Monica Ferreira, *Republic of South Africa*, in International Handbook on Abortion, *supra* note 143, at 416; A. Richards et al., *The Incidence of Major Abdominal Surgery after Septic Abortion—An Indicator of Complications Due to Illegal Abortion*, 68 S. Afr. Med. J. 799 (1985); Jeremy Sarkin, *Patriarchy and Discrimination in Apartheid South Africa's Abortion Law*, 4 Buff. Hum. Rts. L. Rev. 141 (1998); Jeremy & Nancy Sarkin-Hughes, *Choice and Informed Request: The Answer to Abortion*, 1 Stellenbosch L. Rev. 372 (1990). Moosa reports that 60% of abortion applications were denied during the 1980s, and that most of those whose applications to abort were approved were white. Moosa, *supra*, at 260–61.

161. *Choice on Termination of Pregnancy Act*, Act No. 92 (S. Afr. 1996).

162. *See* Haroz, *supra* note 158, at 887–89.

163. *South Africa Adopts a Liberal Abortion Law*, N.Y. Times, Nov. 6, 1996, at A4. *See also* Haroz, *supra* note 158, at 883–87.

164. Haroz, *supra* note 158, at 889–92.

165. Christian Lawyers Assoc. v. Minister of Health, [1998] 4 S. Afr. 1113 (T), available at http://www.law.wits.ac.za.

166. *See* Joanna Birenbaum, *Contextualising Choice: Abortion, Equality and the Right to Make Decisions Concerning Reproduction*, 12 S. Afr. J. Human Rts. 485 (1996); Tjakie Naudé, Case & Comment, *The Value of Life: A Note on* Christian Lawyers Association of S.A. v. Minister of Health, 15 S. Afr. J. Hum. Rts. 541 (1999); M. Nöthling Sabbert, *The Position of the Human Embryo and Foetus in International Law and Its Relevance for the South African Context*, 32 J. Comp. & Int'l L. S. Afr. 336 (1999).

167. Irish Const. Art. 40.3.3. The actual statute criminalizing abortion remains the *Offences against the Person Act*, enacted by the U.K. Parliament in 1861. *Offences against the Person Act*, 24 & 25 Vict. Ch. 100,

This provision was upheld against a challenge by a student group for interfering with the dissemination of information about "services" within the European Community on grounds that the student group was not engaged in a commercial enterprise.[168] The decision leaves the Irish prohibition subject to relatively easy evasion through travel to England. According to some reports, as many as 7,000 Irish women go to England annually in order to obtain an abortion—ending about 10 percent of Ireland's annual pregnancies.[169] The Irish Supreme Court then, in *Attorney General v. X*,[170] discovered a right to abortion when the mother's life is in danger even when the

---

§§ 58, 59 (1861). *See* Tom Hesketh, The Second Partitioning of Ireland; The Abortion Referendum of 1983 (1990); Vicki Randall, *The Politics of Abortion in Ireland,* in New Politics of Abortion 67 (Joni Lovenduski & Joyce Outshoorn eds. 1986); Jeffrey Weinstein, *"An Irish Solution to an Irish Problem": Ireland's Struggle with Abortion Law,* 10 Ariz. J. Int'l & Comp. L. 165, 170–71 (1993). The Irish Supreme Court has recognized a right of privacy in the Constitution, and had extended it the right to obtain contraceptives, but had not extended it to abortion. McGee v. Attorney General, [1974] I.R. 284 (the right of marital privacy protects allows a married woman to import contraceptive jelly on the advice of a physician); Ryan v. Attorney General, [1965] I.R. 294 (the right to bodily includes the right to prevent the fluoridation of public water supplies). *See generally* Hadley, *supra* note 65, at 18–27; Anne Barron, *This Amendment Could Kill Women,* 7 Harv. Women's L.J.287 (1984); Anna Eggert & Bill Rolston, *Ireland,* in Abortion in the New Europe, *supra* note 143, at 157, 162–63; Ruth Fletcher, *Post-Colonial Fragments: Representations of Abortion in Irish Law and Politics,* 28 J. Law & Soc'y 568 (2001); Brian Givens, *Social Change and Moral Politics: The Irish Constitutional Referendum 1983,* 34 Pol. Stud. 61 (1986); Keith Koegler, Note, *Ireland's Abortion Information Act of 1995,* 29 Vand. J. Transnat'l L. 1117, 1119–26 (1996); Rory O'Connell, *Natural Law: Alive and Kicking? A Look at the Constitutional Morality of Sexual Privacy in Ireland,* 9 Ratio Juris 258, 271–74 (1996); John Quinlan, *The Right to Life—An Assessment of the Eighth Amendment to the Irish Constitution,* 1984 BYU L. Rev. 371; J. Scott Tiedemann, Comment, *The Abortion Controversy in the Republic of Ireland and Northern Ireland and Its Potential Effect on Unification,* 17 Loy.-L.A. Int'l & Comp. L.J. 737 (1995); Noel Whitty, *Law and the Regulation of Reproduction in Ireland, 1922–1992,* 43 U. Tor. L.J. 351 (1993).

168. Society for the Protection of Unborn Children Ltd. v. Grogan, [1991] 3 C.M. L. Rep. 849; Open Door Counseling, Ltd. v. Ireland, 246 Eur. Ct. H.R. 32 (1991). *See generally* Hadley, *supra* note 65, at 22; Emily O'Reilly, Masterminds of the Right 110–19 (1992); Reed Boland, *International Reproductive Policy: Abortion Law in Europe in 1991–92,* 21 J. Law, Med. & Ethics 72, 82–83 (1993); Ruth Fletcher, *"Pro-Life" Absolutes, Feminist Challenges: The Fundamentalist Narrative in Irish Abortion Law, 1986–1992,* 36 Osgoode Hall L.J. 1 (1998); Koegler, *supra* note 167, at 1126–32; Donald MacLean, Note, *Can the EC Kill the Irish Unborn?: An Investigation of the European Community's Ability to Impinge on the Moral Sovereignty of Member States,* 28 Hofstra L. Rev. 527 (1999); Peta-Gaye Miller, Note, *Member State Sovereignty and Women's Reproductive Rights: The European Union's Response,* 22 B.C. Int'l & Comp. L. Rev. 195, 199–203 (1999); Elizabeth Spahn, *Abortion, Speech, and the European Community,* 1992 J. Soc. Welfare & Fam. L. 17 (1992); Angela Thompson, *International Protection of Women's Rights: An Analysis of* Open Door Counselling Ltd. and Dublin Woman Centre v. Ireland, 12 B.U. Int'l L.J. 371 (1994). On the outcome of this and similar cases in the Irish courts, see Kristin Carder, Note, *Liberalizing Abortion in Ireland: In re* Article 26 *and the Passage of the Regulation of Information (Services Outside the State for Termination of Pregnancies) Bill,* 3 Tulsa J. Comp. & Int'l L. 253 (1996); O'Connell, *supra* note 167, at 272–74.

169. Brian Lavery, *Irish Voters Reject Broader Ban on Abortion,* N.Y. Times, Mar. 8, 2002, at A6; T.R. Reid, *Irish Voters Reject Measure to Tighten Abortion Law,* Wash. Post, Mar. 8, 2002, at A25. *See also* Hadley, *supra* note 65, at 18–19, 25–26, 47; Mason, *supra* note 78, at 118; David Cole, *"Going to England": Irish Abortion Law and the European Community,* 17 Hastings Int'l & Comp. L. Rev. 113 (1993); Fletcher, *supra* note 167, at 583–87; Fletcher, *supra* note 168, at 2 n.1; Sarah Lyall, *Increasingly, Irish Turn to Britain for Abortions,* N.Y. Times, Dec. 24, 2001, at A3.

170. [1992] 1 I.R. 1. *See* Attorney General v. X and Others: Judgments of the High Court and Supreme Court (S. McDonaugh ed. 1992); Hadley, *supra* note 65, at 19–23; Boland, *supra* note 168, at 83–84; Eggert & Rolston, *supra* note 167, at 164–65; Marie Fox & Therese Murphy, *Irish Abortion: Seeking Refuge in a Jurisprudence of Doubt and Delegation,* 19 J. Law & Soc'y 454, 455 (1992); Connor Gearty, *The Politics of Abortion,* 19 J. Law & Soc'y 441 (1992); Janet Hadley, *God's Bullies: Attacks on Abortion,* 48 Feminist Rev. 94 (1994); Ann Hilbert, Note, *The Irish Abortion Debate: Substantive Rights and Affecting Commerce Jurisprudential Models,* 26 Vand. J. Transnat'l L. 1117 (1994); Koegler, *supra* note 167, at 1132–34; MacLean, *supra* note 168; Miller, *supra* note 168, at 203–04; O'Connell, *supra* note 167, at 274–78; Albie Smith, *The "X" Case: Women and Abortion in the Republic of Ireland, 1992,* 1 Feminist Legal Stud. 163 (1993); Seth Stoffre-

supposed danger is the possibility (perhaps even a remote possibility) of suicide if the pregnancy continues.

The Irish government succeeded in obtaining a Protocol to the *Maastricht Treaty* (transforming the European Community into the European Union) pledging that the European Union would not interfere with Ireland's abortion policies.[171] Subsequently, the Irish electorate approved amendments to the national constitution legalizing the dissemination of information regarding abortions abroad and legalizing travel to obtain an abortion (by majorities of 60 percent), but rejected a proposed amendment to authorize abortions to save the life (but not to preserve the health) of a mother by 65 percent majority.[172] As a result, Irish family planning agencies can advise women where to travel if the women have already decided to obtain an abortion, but cannot advise women that it would be in their best interests to do so.[173]

The question of whether to further liberalize Ireland's abortion laws remains a live political issue there. The Irish government undertook yet another study of whether to introduce reforms into its abortion laws in 1998.[174] Then, despite the *Maastricht* protocol, five of Ireland's 12 members of the European Parliament voted in early 1999 in favor of authorizing abortions across Europe in cases of rape or when the woman's life or health was endangered.[175] After that motion failed, four of the five denounced the Irish government for hiding from the issue and neglecting women's needs because of the government's refusal to press for reformation of the nation's abortion laws even though a clear popular majority still supports the restrictive policy.

Instead of conceding to its critics, the Irish government in 2002 proposed an amendment to the national constitution to overturn the decision in *Attorney General v. X.* The government's proposal was a complicated four part proposal that made voters uncertain how to vote.[176] Antiabortion portions of the proposed amendment would eliminate the possibility of obtaining an abortion based on the risk of suicide and would have imposed a 12-year prison term on anyone who performed or induced an abortion—including women who performed an abortion on themselves. The proposed amendment, however, also defined the beginning of human life as being the implantation of a fertilized egg in the woman's womb. While this aspect was meant to assure the legality of the "morning-after" pill, it caused some anti-abortion activists to campaign against the proposal.[177] Even with these problems, the proposal failed only by a margin of 50.4

---

gen, Comment, *Abortion and the Freedom of Travel in the European Economic Community: A Perspective on* Attorney General v. X, 28 New Eng. L. Rev. 543 (1993); Tiedemann, *supra* note 167, at 756–60; Paul Ward, *Ireland: Abortion: "X" + "Y" = ?!,* 33 U. Louisville J. Fam. L. 385 (1995); Weinstein, *supra* note 167; Sabina Zenkich, *X Marks the Spot while* Casey *Strikes Out: Two Controversial Abortion Decisions,* 23 Golden Gate U. L. Rev. 1001, 1003–26 (1993).

171. Hadley, *supra* note 65, at 22–25; Boland, *supra* note 168, at 84–86; Fletcher, *supra* note 168, at 53–57; MacLean, *supra* note 168, at 558–59; Smith, *supra* note 167, at 171–74.

172. Hadley, *supra* note 65, at 24–27; Boland, *supra* note 168, at 86–87; Koegler, *supra* note 167, at 1134–37; MacLean, *supra* note 168, at 559–60; Smith, *supra* note 167, at 175–77.

173. [1995] *In re* Article 26 and the Regulation of Information (Services Outside the State for the Termination of Pregnancies) Bill, No. 87 (Irish S.Ct.). *See also* Kristin Carder, Casenote, *Liberalizing Abortion in Ireland: In re* Article 26 and the Regulation of Information (Services Outside the State for the Termination of Pregnancies) Bill, 3 Tulsa J. Comp. & Int'l L. 253 (1996); James Clarity, *4 Irish Legislators Accuse Dublin of Negligence on Abortion Policy,* N.Y. Times, Mar. 15, 1999, at A6; Koegler, *supra* note 167, at 1137–50; Patsy McGarry, *Passing of Abortion Information Is Welcome Step, Says Church Publication,* Ir. Times, Mar. 24, 1995, at 5.

174. Fletcher, *supra* note 168, at 5.; Maol Muire Tynan, *June 13 Deadline for Drafting of Abortion Green Paper,* Irish Times, Dec. 3, 1997, *available at* www.irish-times.com.

175. Clarity, *supra* note 173.

176. *Ireland Again Asks Its Divided Voters to Resolve Abortion Issues,* N.Y. Times, Mar. 7, 2002, at A5; Lavery, *supra* note 169.

177. *Id.*

percent to 49.6 percent—a difference of 10,556 votes out of 1,200,000 cast in the election.[178] Further complicating the interpretation of the result was the effect of bad weather, which held voter turnout to only 42 percent—an unusually low figure in Irish elections.[179]

In non-common law countries, we find the same pattern of a general opening of access to abortion in many countries, with occasional countries resisting change or rolling back access to abortion after a period of relatively open access. Communist countries generally enacted highly permissive abortion laws in the 1950s.[180] Bulgaria, Czechoslovakia, Hungary, and Romania had already introduced restrictive policies by the 1960s or 1970s for fear that their populations were not reproducing themselves.[181] In Bulgaria and Romania, enforcement was particularly intrusive and severe, including such measures as periodic compulsory gynecological exams to detect unreported pregnancies and illegal abortions.[182] Yet both states lacked adequate housing, schooling, and medical care for the infants that resulted, leading to some pretty grim consequences.[183]

Hungary reintroduced relatively open access to abortion by administrative order as early as 1974.[184] In Hungary, the *Alkotmánybíróság* (Constitutional Court) declared a ministerial regulation on abortion unconstitutional on procedural grounds, but suggested that the parliament could regulate abortion if, in doing so, it were to define a fetus as a "human being."[185] The court

---

178. Lavery, *supra* note 169; Reid, *supra* note 169.

179. Lavery, *supra* note 176.

180. *See* Chapter 12, at notes 37–41.

181. *See* Henry David & Robert McIntyre, Reproductive Behavior: Central and Eastern European Experience (1981); Alena Heitlinger, Reproduction, Medicine and the Socialist State 146–74 (1987); Alena Heitlinger, Women and State Socialism: Sex Inequality in the Soviet Union and Czechoslovakia 186–89 (1979); Helsinki Citizens' Assembly Women's Comm'n, Reproductive Rights in Central and Eastern Europe 15, 18–19, 31 (1992); Hilda Scott, Does Socialism Liberate Women? 132–33, 141, 144, 153 (1974); Ádám Balogh & Lászlo Lampé, in Abortion in the New Europe, *supra* note 143, at 139, 140–46; Doina Pasca Harsanyi, *Women in Romania*, in Gender Politics and Post-Communism: Reflections from Eastern Europe and the Former Soviet Union 39, 46 (Nanette Funk & Magda Mueller eds. 1993); Mariana Hausleitner (Kathleen LaBahn trans.), *Women in Romania*, in Gender Politics and Post-Communism, *supra*, at 53, 54–55; Alena Heitlinger, *The Impact of the Transition from Communism on the Status of Women in the Czech and Slovak Republics,* in Gender Politics and Post-Communism, *supra*, at 95, 101; Gail Kligman, *The Politics of Reproduction in Ceaucescu's Romania: A Case Study in Political Culture,* 6 E. Eur. Pol. & Soc'y 364 (1992); Angela Lambert, *The Misery of Women Denied a Basic Choice: Abortion Was a Crime in Romania for 20 Years,* The Independent (London), Feb. 7, 1990, at 15; Julie Mertus, *Human Rights of Women in Central and Eastern Europe,* 6 Am. U.J. Gender Soc. Pol'y & L. 369, 439–40, 443, 447, 452 (1998); Nicki Negrau, *Listening to Women's Voices: Living in Post-Communist Romania,* 12 Conn. J. Int'l L. 117, 122–23 (1996); Dimitrina Petrova, *The Winding Road to Emancipation in Bulgaria,* in Gender Politics and Post-Communism, *supra*, at 22, 23–24; A. Pricopi, *Romania: Before and after the Revolution,* 31 J. Fam. L. 431, 437–38 (1993); Radim Uzel, *Czech and Slovak Republics,* in Abortion in the New Europe, *supra*, at 55, 55–56; Dimiter Vassilev, *Bulgaria,* in Abortion in the New Europe, *supra*, at 43, 43–45; Eleanora Zielinska, *Recent Trends in Abortion Legislation in Eastern Europe, with Particular Reference to Poland,* 4 Crim. L.F. 47, 51–58 (Regina Gorzkowska trans. 1993). On the other hand, gypsy women are being sterilized in Slovakia without their consent. Peter Green, *Gypsies in Slovakia Complain of Sterilizations,* N.Y. Times, Feb. 28, 2003, at A3.

182. Helsinki Citizens' Assembly Women's Comm'n, *supra* note 181, at 31; Harsanyi, *supra* note 181, at 46; Hausleitner, *supra* note 181, at 55; Gail Kligman, *Women and Reproductive Legislation in Romania,* in Dilemmas of Transition in the Soviet Union and Eastern Europe 145, 152 (George Breslauer ed. 1991); Mertus, *supra* note 181, at 452.

183. Harsanyi, *supra* note 181, at 46; Hausleitner, *supra* note 181, at 54–57; Petrova, *supra* note 181, at 23–24.

184. Enikö Bollobás, *"Totalitarian Lib": The Legacy of Communism for Hungarian Women,* in Gender Politics and Post-Communism, *supra* note 181, at 201, 204–05; Mertus, *supra* note 181, at 447–48.

185. Dec. 64/1991/XII.17/AB (Hungarian Const'l Ct. 1991). The regulations in question were: *Ordinance No. 76 of the Council of Ministers* (Nov. 3, 1988), Magyar Közlöny 1185–86 (1988), summarized in translation in 40 Int'l Digest of Health Legis. 595 (1989); *Ordinance No. 15 of the Ministry of Social Aff. & Health*

indicated that any law to be enacted could neither prohibit all abortions nor allow abortion without restriction, but gave no more specific guidance. In the end, the Hungarian Parliament enacted a statute that allowed abortion based upon any "serious crisis" facing a woman during the first 12 weeks of pregnancy, and thereafter to protect the woman's health or as a response to fetal defect.[186] The only real restraint on abortion was mandatory counseling followed by a three-day waiting period before the abortion can be performed. A vocal anti-abortion movement has not been able thus far to move the law in a yet more restrictive direction.[187]

The other east European states returned to relatively open abortion policies between 1986 and 1990, stretching across the time when Communist governments fell from power.[188] Yugoslavia (Serbia and Montenegro) did not reintroduce restrictive measures after "liberalizing" its abortion laws, although various social pressures have arisen to make it more difficult in practice for women to obtain abortions.[189] Croatia and Slovenia enshrined the "right to life" in their constitutions when they withdrew from Yugoslavia.[190] Lithuania also banned abortions after becoming independent from the Soviet Union.[191] Albania, on the other hand, had always prohibited abortion except for narrowly defined medical reasons.[192] In 1991, the government in Albania liberalized its abortion law, although still requiring approval of a medical committee before the abortion could be performed.[193] The new regime in Romania repealed that country's restrictive law on abortion as one of its first acts after the 1989 revolution.[194] Bulgaria removed its restrictions in 1990.[195] Abortion is now legal in Romania at the request of the woman for the first 14 weeks of pregnancy, but restricted to therapeutic grounds thereafter.[196] In Bulgaria, abortion on request is

---

(Dec. 15, 1988), Magyar Közlöny 1379–87 (1988), summarized in translation in 40 Int'l Digest of Health Legis. 595 (1989). *See also* Maria Adamik, *Feminism and Hungary,* in Gender Politics and Post-Communism, *supra* note 181, at 207, 208; Balogh & Lampé, *supra* note 181, at 151–54; Boland, *supra* note 168, at 75–76; Jean-Marie Henckerts & Stefan van der Jeught, *Human Rights Protection under the New Constitutions of Central Europe,* 20 Loy. L.A. Int'l & Comp. L.J. 475, 481 (1998); Mertus, *supra* note 181, at 447–48; Kim Lane Schepple, *Women's Rights in Eastern Europe,* 4 East Eur. Const. Rev. 66, 68 (1995); László Sólyom, *The Hungarian Constitutional Court and Social Change,* 19 Yale J. Int'l L. 223, 229–30 (1994).

186. *Law on the Termination of Pregnancy* (Dec. 17, 1992), Magyar Közlöny no. 132 (1992). *See* Boland, *supra* note 168, at 76; Mertus, *supra* note 181, at 447–48; Schepple, *supra* note 185, at 68.

187. Helsinki Citizens' Assembly Women's Comm'n, *supra* note 181, at 24–25; Mertus, *supra* note 181, at 448.

188. Balogh & Lampé, *supra* note 181, at 146–54; Anthea Hall, *Deprived of Contraception by the Ceaucescu Regime, Women Are Queuing up for Newly Legalized Abortions,* Sunday Telegraph (London), Mar. 11, 1990, at 44; Harsanyi, *supra* note 181, at 49; Hausleitner, *supra* note 181, at 55–56; Heitlinger, *supra* note 181, at 102; Kligman, *supra* note 181, at 399–417; Negrau, *supra* note 181, at 123–26; Pricopi, *supra* note 181, at 438–42; Chuck Sudetic, *Romania Seeks to Reduce Abortions,* N.Y. Times, Jan. 17, 1991, at A3; Uzel, *supra* note 181, at 58–65; Vassilev, *supra* note 181, at 45–54; Zielinska, *supra* note 181, at 58–61.

189. Helsinki Citizens' Assembly Women's Comm'n, *supra* note 181, at 33–34; Da_a Duha_ek, *Women's Time in the Former Yugoslavia,* in Gender Politics and Post-Communism, *supra* note 181, at 131; Mertus, *supra* note 181, at 455–56.

190. Boland, *supra* note 168, at 88; Slavenka Drakulic, *Women and the New Democracy in the Former Yugoslavia,* in Gender Politics and Post-Communism, *supra* note 181, at 123, 124–26. *But see* Helsinki Citizens' Assembly Women's Comm'n, *supra* note 181, at 18 (arguing that the liberal law of the former Yugoslavia still applies in Croatia as of 1991); Mertus, *supra* note 181, at 441–43 (same, as of 1993).

191. Zielinska, *supra* note 181, at 63.

192. *See* Boland, *supra* note 168, at 76–77; Zielinska, *supra* note 181, at 53–54. The provisions in question are translated in 16 Ann. Rev. Pop. 25 (1989).

193. Boland, *supra* note 168, at 77–78.

194. *Decree Law No. 1,* Dec. 26, 1989. *See also* Helsinki Citizens' Assembly Women's Comm'n, *supra* note 181, at 31; Mertus, *supra* note 181, at 452.

195. Helsinki Citizens' Assembly Women's Comm'n, *supra* note 181, at 15. Mertus, *supra* note 181, at 440.

196. Helsinki Citizens' Assembly Women's Comm'n, *supra* note 181, at 31; Mertus, *supra* note 181, at 452; Negrau, *supra* note 181, at 122.

legal for the first ten weeks of pregnancy, with therapeutic abortions allowed up until 22 weeks.[197]

The German Democratic Republic was founded after the being "liberated" by a Red Army bent on revenge, including the systematic rape of German women.[198] As many as 500,000 women were raped in Berlin alone, and several million in the entire Soviet Zone.[199] When the Soviets began to set up local German authorities in their zone, the German authorities suspended the laws against abortion.[200] The German Democratic Republic, created in 1949, introduced a restrictive policy in 1950 allowing abortions only if the life or health of the mother was threatened by the pregnancy or if either parent suffered from an hereditary defect.[201] The change reflected a concern to rebuild the population after the ravages of Nazism and the Nazi war.[202]

While women in the eastern part of Germany no doubt continued to undergo illegal abortions, legal abortions dropped below 1,000 per year.[203] Democratic (East) Germany did not introduce a truly open abortion policy until 1972, but that policy, once introduced, was not changed so long as the Communist system survived in eastern Germany.[204] East German policies generally disappeared in favor of the more restrictive west German policies after reunification, abortion having been one of the few serious obstacles encountered in that process.[205]

Poland, which had enacted a relatively liberal abortion law as early as 1932 (allowing abortions if a pregnancy posed a threat to a woman's health) and had adopted an open abortion policy in 1956, did not act to restrict abortion so long as the Communist dictatorship continued.[206] In 1992, three years after the overthrow of the Communists, Poland's parliament repealed the permissive abortion law, replacing it with a statute creating tight restrictions on abortion.[207] The

---

197. Helsinki Citizens' Assembly Women's Comm'n, *supra* note 181, at 15. Mertus, *supra* note 181, at 440.

198. Norman Naimark, The Russians in Germany: A History of the Soviet Zone of Occupation, 1945–1949, at 69–140 (1995).

199. Anita Grossman, Reforming Sex: The German Movement for Birth Control and Abortion Reform, 1920–1950, at 193 (1995).

200. Donna Harsch, *Society, the State, and Abortion in East Germany, 1950–1972,* 102 Am. Hist. Rev. 53, 56–57 (1997); Jeremy Telman, *Abortion and Women's Legal Personhood in Germany: A Contribution to the Feminist Theory of the State,* 24 Rev. L. & Soc. Change 91, 122 (1998).

201. Telman, *supra* note 200, at 122–24.

202. Harsch, *supra* note 200, at 57–58.

203. Helsinki Citizens' Assembly Women's Comm'n, *supra* note 181, at 21; Harsch, *supra* note 200, at 59–60; Mertus, *supra* note 181, at 444; Telman, *supra* note 200, at 123–24.

204. *Gesetzblatt der Deutschen Demokratischen Republik,* Mar. 15, 1972, at 89. Nanette Funk, *Abortion and German Unification,* in Gender Politics and Post-Communism, *supra* note 181, at 194, 194–96; Telman, *supra* note 200, at 124–26.

205. See the text *infra* at notes 229–37.

206. *Law on Conditions for the Termination of Pregnancy,* Dziennik Ustaw, No. 12, 1956, entry 61, translated in 9 Int'l Digest of Health Legis. 319 (1958); *Ordinance of the Minister of Health of Dec. 19, 1959,* Dziennik Ustaw, No. 2, 1960, entry 15, translated in 13 Int'l Digest of Health Legis. 140 (1962); *Instruction No. 11/81 of Sept. 21, 1981, of the Ministers of Health, Transport, Nat'l Defense, & Interior,* Dziennik Urzedowy Ministerstwz Zdrowia i Opieki Solecznej, No. 11, 1981, entry 42. See Boland, *supra* note 168, at 72; Malgorzata Fuszara, *Abortion and the Formation of the Public Sphere in Poland,* in Gender Politics and Post-Communism, *supra* note 181, at 241, 241–42; Jolanta Plakwicz & Eleonora Zielinska, *Poland,* in Abortion in the New Europe, *supra* note 143, at 199; Wanda Stojanowska, *Poland: The New "Anti-Abortion" Law,* 33 U. Louisville J. Fam. L. 421 (1995); Zielinska, *supra* note 181, at 64–88, 91–93.

207. Hadley, *supra* note 65, at 43–46; Boland, *supra* note 168, at 73–74; John Darnton, *Tough Abortion Law Provokes Dismay in Poland,* N.Y. Times, Mar. 11, 1993, at A3; Stephen Engelberg, *Poland Faces New Battle on Abortion,* N.Y. Times, Apr. 21, 1992, at A3; Fuszara, *supra* note 206, at 242–51; Andrzej Kulczycki, *Abortion Policy in Postcommunist Europe: The Conflict in Europe,* 21 Pop. & Dev. Rev. 471 (1995); Mertus, *supra* note 181, at 450–51; Plakwicz & Zielinska, *supra* note 206, at 209–10; Schepple, *supra* note 185, at 67; Zielinska, *supra* note 181, at 64–93.

remodeled Communists regained control of the parliament and the presidency in Poland by 1995, and the parliament again legalized abortion before the twelfth week of gestation, but only after the *Sejm* (lower house) overrode a veto by the Senate.[208] Beginning before the enactment of the first restrictive abortion law, Polish physicians themselves adopted and enforced a set of professional ethics on abortion that were more restrictive than abortion laws themselves and remained highly restrictive even during the period of the "reformed" law after 1995.[209] This proved more effective than any law, resulting in a reduction of the number of abortions performed from about 150,000 per year to only 30,000 per year, with the cost rising to several months worth of the average wage.[210] With the return of *Solidarnocz* (Solidarity) to power in the 1997 elections, the parliament again enacted a restrictive law on abortion.[211] At about the same time, the Polish Constitutional Tribunal declared that abortion could only be allowed in cases of incest, rape, and gross fetal defects.[212] There has also emerged a strong right to life movement in the Czech and the Slovak Republics, which had returned to a policy of abortion on demand in 1987, although those movements have not been strong enough to enact restrictive legislation on abortion.[213]

In western Europe, the most interesting case is the German Federal Republic. Unlike eastern Germany, western Germany had not experienced systematic rape at the end of World War II.[214] Still women who indicated that a pregnancy resulted from a rape during or after the war were allowed an abortion notwithstanding the restrictive law then in force.[215] This practice was brief and exceptional. Guilt over the Nazi crimes against life, as well as the need to rebuild families and population after the Nazi excesses and the losses of the war, quickly led the Federal Republic to enforce rigorously the restrictive abortion law enacted under the Kaiser and carried forward through Weimar and the Nazi era.[216] Nearly 20 years passed before the *Bundestag* (federal parliament) considered revising the abortion law. Meanwhile, medical practice gradually liberalized the interpretation of the exception for a woman's health to include "mental health"—including her own sense of a threatened well-being from simply being pregnant when she did not want to be.[217] The number of abortions based upon "medical indications" thereafter rose from less than 3,000 in 1968 to nearly 18,000 in 1974.[218]

---

208. *Despite Pope's Protest, Polish Deputies Vote to Ease Abortion Law,* N.Y. Times, Oct. 25, 1996, at A4. *See also* Mertus, *supra* note 181, at 450.

209. Hadley, *supra* note 65, at 44, 46; Mary Battiata, *New Code in Poland Prompts Doctors to Refuse Abortions,* Wash. Post, May 29, 1992, at A26; Boland, *supra* note 168, at 73–74.

210. Boland, *supra* note 168, at 74; Stephen Engelberg, *Polish Limits on Abortion Create a New Clandestine Movement,* N.Y. Times, Dec. 28, 1992, at A10.

211. Mark F. Brzezinski, *Constitutionalism and Post-Communist Polish Politics,* 20 Loy. L.A. Int'l & Comp. L.J. 433, 442, 448 (1998); Ryszard Cholewinski, *The Protection of Human Rights in the New Polish Constitution,* 22 Fordham Int'l L.J. 236, 261–62 (1998); Henckerts & van der Jeught, *supra* note 185, at 481.

212. *See* Mertus, *supra* note 181, at 450.

213. On the Czech and Slovak right-to-life movements, see Hadley, *supra* note 65, at 101–03; Boland, *supra* note 168, at 88; Heitlinger, *supra* note 181, at 101–03; Henckaerts & van der Jeught, *supra* note 185, at 481; Mertus, *supra* note 181, at 443–44, 458. On the abortion laws in the Czech Republic and Slovakia, see Helsinki Citizens' Assembly Women's Comm'n, *supra* note 181, at 18–19; Mertus, *supra,* at 443, 458. Heitlinger reports that between one-third and one-half of Czech and Slovak pregnancies end in abortion. Heitlinger, *supra,* at 101.

214. For the Soviet policy towards rape in the aftermath of World War II, see Naimark, *supra* note 198, at 69–140.

215. Hermine de Soto, *"In the Name of the Folk": Women and Nation in the New Germany,* 5 UCLA Women's L.J. 83, 90 (1994).

216. Telman, *supra* note 200, at 126–27; Udo Werner, *The Convergence of Abortion Regulation in Germany and the United States: A Critique of Glendon's* Rights Talk *Thesis,* 18 Loy.-L.A. L. Rev. 571, 581–82 (1996).

217. Telman, *supra* note 200, at 141–45; Werner, *supra* note 216, at 582.

218. Albin Eser, *Reform of German Abortion Law: First Experience,* 34 Am. J. Comp. L. 369, 371 (1986).

The *Bundestag* enacted a "liberal" abortion law on June 18, 1974.[219] The *Bundesverfassungs-gericht* (Federal Constitutional Court), however, promptly declared the statute unconstitutional for failure to protect fetal life adequately.[220] As one German jurist noted, although he personally thought abortion was not immoral, "after the Nazi experience of genetic engineering and racial extermination, the German Constitution could not possibly be interpreted as permitting abortion."[221] (Democratic Germany's denial of any responsibility for the Nazi past in part accounts for the greater acceptance of abortion by the government and the people in eastern Germany.[222]) As if to underscore the point, the dissent in the case (dissents are unusual in Germany) accepted that the law in question violated a constitutionally protected right to life, but argued against the majority's view that abortion, with few exceptions, must be made a crime.[223]

Federal (west) Germany then enacted an "indications" policy with abortions allowed when the woman's health was endangered, the pregnancy resulted from criminal activity, the child suffered from an incurable defect, or when overall poor social conditions would adversely affect the pregnancy, within time limits that ranged (depending on the indication) from 12 to 22 weeks of gestation.[224] Even in these circumstances, an abortion other than for strictly medical indications was legal only after highly directive counseling against abortion received at least three days before the abortion was performed.[225] Criminal sanctions generally applied only to

---

219. *Fünftes Gesetz zur Reform des Strafrechts,* 1974 BGBl I 1297, StGB §218 (decriminalizing abortion up to 12 weeks of gestation, allowing abortion thereafter if there was a threat to the woman's life or health if she received specified counseling). On the debates leading up to the amendment, see Donald Kommers, *Abortion and the Constitution: United States and Germany,* 25 Am. J. Comp. L. 256, 261–62 (1977); Michael Mattern, Note, *German Abortion Law: The Unwanted Child of Reunification,* 13 Loy. L.A. Int'l & Comp. L.J. 643, 656–60 (1991); Joyce Mushaben, *Feminism in Four Acts: The Changing Political Identity of Women in the Federal Republic of Germany,* in The Federal Republic of Germany at Forty 76, 91 (Peter Mierk ed. 1989); Telman, *supra* note 200, at 127–28; Werner, *supra* note 216, at 582–83.

220. Decision of 25 Feb. 1975, 39 *Entscheiderungen des Bundesverfassungsgerichts* [BverfGE] 1 (*Bundesverfassungsgericht*), *translated in* John Gorby & Robert Jonas, *West German Abortion Decision: A Contrast to Roe v. Wade,* 9 J. Marshall J. Pract. & Proc. 551 (1976). *See also* Belling & Eberl, *supra* note 126, at 480–82; Winifried Brugger, *A Constitutional Duty to Outlaw Abortion? A Comparative Analysis of the American and German Abortion Decisions,* 36 Jahrbuch des Öffentlichen Rects der Gegenwart 49 (1987); Hartmut Gerstein & David Lowry, *Abortion, Abstract Norms, and Social Control: The Decision of the West German Federal Constitutional Court,* 25 Emory L.J. 849 (1976); Kommers, *supra* note 219; Florian Miedel, *Is West Germany's 1975 Abortion Decision a Solution to the American Abortion Debate?: A Critique of Mary Ann Glendon and Donald Kommers,* 20 Rev. L. & Soc. Change 471 (1994); Douglas Morris, *Abortion and Liberation: A Comparison between the Abortion Decisions of the Supreme Court of the United States and the Constitutional Court of West Germany,* 11 Hastings Int'l & Comp. L. Rev. 159 (1988); Telman, *supra* note 200, at 128–36; Werner, *supra* note 216, at 583–88. On German constitutional law generally, see Donald Kommers, The Constitutional Jurisprudence of the Federal Republic of Germany (1989); Donald Kommers, *German Constitutionalism: A Prolegomenon,* 40 Emory L.J. 387 (1991).

221. 39 BverfGE at 67. *See also* Harold Berman, Faith and Order 301 (1993); Boland, *supra* note 168, at 80; Telman, *supra* note 200, at 93, 129–31, 135.

222. Telman, *supra* note 200, at 93, 139. On the differing approaches to responsibility for Nazi crimes in the two Germanys, see Jeffrey Herf, Divided Memory: The Nazi Past in the Two Germanys (1997).

223. 39 BverfGE at 68–69 (Rupp-von Brünneck, J., dissenting, joined by Simon, J.). *See also* Morris, *supra* note 220, at 174–83; Telman, *supra* note 200, at 131–33, 135–36.

224. 15 StRÄndG, 1976 BGB I 1213, art. 1 (adding StGB §§218a, 219(1). *See* Helsinki Citizens' Assembly Women's Comm'n, *supra* note 181, at 22; Eser, *supra* note 218, at 375–79; Nanette Funk, *Abortion Counselling* (sic) *and the 1995 German Abortion Law,* 12 Conn. J. Int'l L. 33, 38–39 (1996); Ewa Maleck-Lewy, *Between Self-Determination and State Supervision: Women and the Abortion Law in Post-Unification Germany,* 2 Soc. Pol.: Int'l Stud. in Gender, State & Soc'y 62, 66–68 (1995); Mertus, *supra* note 181, at 444; Telman, *supra* note 200, at 91–92, 136–38; Werner, *supra* note 216, at 587–88.

225. StGB §218(b)(1). *See* Funk, *supra* note 204, at 195–96; Funk, *supra* note 224, at 36–39; Telman, *supra* note 200, at 138, 143–44; Werner, *supra* note 216, at 596–97.

the physician; a woman could be prosecuted only if she failed to obtain the required counseling, or if she was aborted after 22 weeks of gestation, or if she underwent abortion by a non-physician.[226]

Public reactions to the law were mixed. Some thought the law too strict; others too lax.[227] In practice, the policy amounted to abortion on demand in parts of Germany. Even teenagers could obtain abortions without great difficulty in parts of Germany—as 2,694 between the ages of 15 and 18 did in 1993 (96 below the age of 15).[228] Yet in southern Germany abortions remained rare.[229] The rarity of abortion in Bavaria might simply reflect the fact that pre-abortion counseling was largely in the hands of the Catholic Church. The frequency of abortions there might change because the Pope in 1998 ordered the Catholic Church out of pre-abortion counseling remains to be seen.[230] This possibility was to a certain extent counteracted, however, by a decision of the Bavarian legislature to prohibit doctors from earning more than 25 percent of their income from abortions.[231] Given the unpopularity of abortions in Bavaria, only a few doctors do them, and they tend to specialize. This law drives such abortion specialists out of business.

German politicians were unwilling to bring the issue of whether, given its actual implementation, the 1976 law is constitutional before the Constitutional Court and that court has consistently declined to hear private complaints on the question on the grounds of lack of standing in the complainant.[232] As a result, one scholar noted a considerable convergence between American and German law: "In practical terms, the situation in Germany now resembles the post-*Casey* situation in Pennsylvania. Abortion is available after burdensome preliminaries."[233] West German authorities did not, however, turn an entirely blind eye to violations. More than 100 prosecutions were brought annually in between 1976 and 1988 for criminal abortions.[234] In 1991, the *Bundesverfassunggericht* upheld the Federal abortion law against a doctor's challenge to the constitutionality of the abortion laws as violating the right of physician-patient confidentiality and as intruding on the medical judgment of the physician.[235]

When, finally, the *Land* of Bavaria sought "abstract" review of the constitutionality of the revised abortion law, the case was preempted by the process of German reunification.[236] Reunification encountered serious difficulties over abortion because the law in Democratic (east) Ger-

---

226. StGB § 218(3).

227. *See* Eser, *supra* note 218, at 380–82. *See also* Funk, *supra* note 224, at 52–54 (reporting on the similarly mixed reactions to the 1995 abortion statute); Malek-Lewy, *supra* note 224, at 70–72 (same).

228. Belling & Eberl, *supra* note 126, at 475 n.1.

229. *See generally* Mary Ann Glendon, Hermeneutics, Abortion and Divorce: A Review of Abortion and Divorce in Western Law 34–37 (1989); Karen Crabbs, *The German Abortion Debate: Stumbling Block to Unity*, 6 Fla. J. Int'l L. 213, 221–23 (1991); Eser, *supra* note 218, at 381; Funk, *supra* note 224, at 54–57; Sandra Goldbeck-Wood, *Bavaria Threatens to Reduce Abortion Access*, 312 Brit. Med. J. 1118 (1996); Sabine Klein-Schonnefeld, *Germany*, in Abortion in the New Europe, *supra* note 143, at 113, 123; Gerald Neuman, *Casey in the Mirror: Abortion, Abuse and the Right to Protection in the United States and Germany*, 43 Am. J. Comp. L. 273, 273–74, 276 (1995), Werner, *supra* note 216, at 600–02.

230. Roger Cohen, *German Bishops to Halt Abortion Certificates*, N.Y. Times, Nov. 24, 1998, at A12; Allan Cowell, *Obeying Pope, German Bishops End Role in Abortion System*, NY Times, Nov. 28, 1998, at A3.

231. Telman, *supra* note 200, at 148 n.354.

232. Neuman, *supra* note 229, at 276–77.

233. *Id.* at 273. *See also* Telman, *supra* note 200, at 92. *But see* Funk, *supra* note 224, at 57–65.

234. Hadley, *supra* note 65, at 29; Klein-Schonnefeld, *supra* note 229, at 121, 122–25; M. Prützel-Thomas, *The Abortion Issue and the Federal Constitutional Court*, 2 German Pol. 467 (1993); Susan Walther, *Thou Shalt Not (But Thou Mayest): Abortion after the German Constitutional Court's 1993 Landmark Decision*, 36 German Y.B. In'tl L. 385, 386–87 (1993).

235. Boland, *supra* note 168, at 78–79.

236. Neuman, *supra* note 229, at 277.

many was wholly permissive toward the practice.[237] In contrast with the small number of abortions performed in Federal Germany, as many as one-third of all pregnancies in Democratic (east) Germany ended in abortion.[238] Furthermore, as many as 4,500 west German women were going to the Netherlands annually to obtain cheaper (and more easily obtained) abortions.[239] In the end, the west German approach prevailed and the conditions previously found in Federal German law became applicable throughout the country.[240] The post-unification law did create a category of abortions that were considered as "unlawful" but not criminal, perhaps opening a small window for somewhat greater freedom of choice among women—but still subject to the mandatory counseling requirement.[241] The resulting unified law is "one of the world's most complex and confusing laws governing abortion."[242] Under that law, a woman who qualifies for an abortion, and persists through the counseling, can obtain an abortion.[243] Yet another ruling by the *Bundesverfassunggericht* was necessary to prevent enactment of a less restrictive statute.[244]

One reason that apparently restrictive abortion laws in Germany have survived is because unwanted pregnancies have become unusual in Germany. The combination of freely available contraceptives, lightly restricted abortion, and a sense that children are an economic burden have combined to collapse the German birth rate to 1.3 per woman—well below the replacement level of 2.1.[245] As a result, fewer babies are born annually in Germany than in Nepal—although

237. Peter Merkl, German Unification in the European Context 176–80, 226–27 (1993); Sabine Berghahn, *Gender in the Legal Discourse in Post-Unification Germany: Old and New Lines of Conflict*, 2 Soc. Pol.: Int'l Stud. in Gender, State & Soc'y 37, 43–45 (1995); Crabbs, *supra* note 229; Funk, *supra* note 204, at 196–99; Funk, *supra* note 224, at 39–65; Deborah Goldberg, *Developments in German Abortion Law: A U.S. Perspective*, 5 UCLA Women's L.J. 531 (1995); Elizbeth Kapo, Comment, *Abortion Law Reform: The Nexus between Abortion and the Role of Women in the German Democratic Republic and the Federal Republic of Germany*, 10 Dick. J. Int'l L. 137 (1991); Klein-Schonnefeld, *supra* note 229, at 114–17, 130–32; Donald Kommers, *The Constitutional Law of Abortion in Germany: Should Americans Pay Attention?*, 10 J. Contemp. Health L. & Pol'y 1 (1993); Ewa Maleck-Lewy, *Between Self-Determination and State Supervision: Women and the Abortion Law in Post-Unification Germany*, 2 Soc. Pol.: Int'l Stud. in Gender, State & Soc'y 62 (1995); Mattern, *supra* note 219; Neuman, *supra* note 229, at 277–78; Terri Owens, Note, *The Abortion Question: Germany's Dilemma Delays Unification*, 53 La. L. Rev. 1315 (1993); Telman, *supra* note 200, at 139–41; Rosemarie Will, *German Unification and the Reform of Abortion Law*, 3 Cardozo L.J. 399 (1996); Zielinska, *supra* note 181, at 89–90.

238. Hadley, *supra* note 65, at 28–29; Funk, *supra* note 204, at 195.

239. Funk, *supra* note 224, at 39 n.35. Jeremy Telman estimates that 110,000 German women go to the Netherlands annually to obtain abortion. Telman, *supra* note 200, at 137 n.284. These women were theoretically liable to prosecution for going abroad to evade the German abortion law, but such prosecutions seldom happen. *See* Klein-Schonnefeld, *supra* note 229, at 120. On the availability of abortion on demand in the Netherlands, see Joyce Outshoorn, *The Rules of the Game: Abortion Politics in the Netherlands,* in The New Politics of Abortion, *supra* note 167, at 5.

240. Hadley, *supra* note 65, at 27–32; Belling & Eberl, *supra* note 123, at 479–80; Boland, *supra* note 168, at 78–82; Funk, *supra* note 224, at 40–52.

241. Boland, *supra* note 168, at 81; De Soto, *supra* note 215, at 87; Goldberg, *supra* note 229, at 549–50; Mertus, *supra* note 181, at 445–46; Neuman, *supra* note 229, at 292; Telman, *supra* note 200, at 142–46; Walther, *supra* note 234, at 399–400.

242. Telman, *supra* note 200, at 91.

243. Funk, *supra* note 224, at 39 n.35.

244. *Schwangeren- und Familienhilfeänderungsgestz* (SFHÄndG), 1995 BGB I.1049; Decision of 28 May, 1993, 88 BVerfGE 203 (1993), reprinted in 29 Europäisches Grundrechte Zeitschrift 228 (1993). *See* Helsinki Citizens' Assembly Women's Comm'n, *supra* note 181, at 23; Mason, *supra* note 78, at 119; Belling & Eberl, *supra* note 126, at 482–84; Boland, *supra* note 168, at 79–81; Funk, *supra* note 204, at 196–98; Funk, *supra* note 224, at 40–52; H.L. Karcher, *New German Abortion Law Agreed*, 311 Brit. Med. J. 149 (1995); Maleck-Lewy, *supra* note 224, at 68–70; Mertus, *supra* note 181, at 444–45; Miedel, *supra* note 220; Neuman, *supra* note 229, at 279–300; Telman, *supra* note 200, at 141–47; Walther, *supra* note 234; Werner, *supra* note 216, at 590–98.

245. Peter Peterson, *Gray Dawn: The Global Aging Crisis*, 78 For. Aff., No. 1, at 42, 45 (Jan./Feb. 1999).

Germany has more than four times as many people.[246] In fact, the birth rate for women in western Germany was actually lower than the birthrate for women in eastern German despite the widespread resort to abortion in the east.[247] Consequently, the ratio of workers to pensioners in Germany will fall to 1:1 and will go even lower by 2030.[248] A major crisis can only be avoided through immigration—something that Germans are not yet ready to accept.[249]

Constitutional courts have figured prominently in abortion controversies in other European countries as well. We have already note the role of the *Alkotmánybíróság* (Constitutional Court) in Hungary.[250]    Spain's *Tribunal Constitucional* declared a fetus to be a human being from the moment of conception and therefore entitled to the protection of the state.[251] Judicial or quasi-judicial decisions in Austria,[252] France,[253] and Portugal,[254] on the other hand, upheld wide legislative authority to allow, restrict, or prohibit abortions. The European Commission on Human Rights also supported legislative discretion regarding abortion policies.[255] Italy's *Corte constituzionale,* however, found significant limitations on the power of the parliament to restrict access to abortion.[256] Belgium's courts simply refused to decide contests to the constitutionality of that country's liberalized abortion law.[257]

---

246. *Id. See also* Frank Bruni, *Persistent Drop in Fertility Reshapes Europe's Future,* N.Y. Times, Dec. 26, 2002, at A1.

247. Will, *supra* note 237, at 413–14.

248. Peterson, *supra* note 245, at 44; Stefan Thiel, *A Heavy Burden,* Newsweek, June 20, 2003, at 28 (int'l ed.).

249. Peterson, *supra* note 245, at 44.

250. See the text *supra* at notes 185–87.

251. Decision of 11 April 1985, STC 53/1985 (*Pleno*), 119 *Boletin Oficial del Estado* 10 (supp. 18 *mayo* 1985), *summarized in English in* Richard Stith, *New Constitutional and Penal Theory in Spanish Abortion Law,* 35 Am. J. Comp. L. 513 (1987), reprinted in Abortion, Medicine and the Law, *supra* note 29, at 368. For the law in question, see Organic Law No. 9, of July 5, 1985, translated in 36 Int'l Digest of Health Legis. 614 (1985). *See also* Audrey Brassiloff, Religion and Politics in Spain: The Spanish Church in Transition, 1962–1996, at 123–24, 518–19 (1998); Reshona Fleishman, *The Battle against Reproductive Rights: The Impact of the Catholic Church on Abortion Law in both International and Domestic Arenas,* 14 Emory Int'l L. Rev. 277, 289–300 (2000); Encarna Bodelon Gonzalez, *Spain* (Nuala McKeever trans.), in Abortion in the New Europe, *supra* note 143, at 229.

252. Decision of 11 Oct. 1974, [1974] *Erklärungen des Verfassungsgerichtshofs* [VfGH] 221, 234–35, G 8/74, *translated in* Mauro Capelletti & William Cohen, Comparative Constitutional Law 615, 620–21 (1979). *See generally* Oskar Lehner, *Austria,* in Abortion in the New Europe, *supra* note 143, at 1.

253. Decision of 15 Jan. 1975, [1975] A.J.D.A. 134, *translated in* Capelletti & Cohen, *supra* note 252, at 577.

254. Decision of 19 March, 1984, 344 *Boletim de Ministerio da Justica* 197 (March 1985). The resulting law is found at *Law No.6/84* of May 11, 1984, summarized in English at 35 Int'l Digest of Health Legis. 768 (1984).

255. Bruggerman v. Federal Rep. of Germany, 3 Eur. Hum. Rts. Rep. 244 (1977); Paton v. United Kingdom, 8 Eur. Hum. Rts. Rep. 19 (1980). *See generally* Miller, *supra* note 168.

256. Decision of 18 Feb. 1975 (*Corte const.*), [1975] 98 *Foro It. I* (*Giurisprudencia costituzionale e civile*) 515, *translated in* Capelletti & Cohen, *supra* note 252, at 612–14. *See also* Lesley Caldwell, *Femnism and Abortion Politics in Italy,* in The New Politics of Abortion, *supra* note 167, at 105; Ross, *supra* note 170, at 207–09. Recently, controversy erupted in Italy over a court's refusal to authorize an abortion for a retarded 13-year-old girl. Alessandra Stanley, *Abortion Is Rejected for a Girl, 13, Bitterly Dividing the Italians,* Dec. 17, 1999, at A19. Italy presently has the lowest birthrater in Europe and perhaps in the world. Bruni, *supra* note 246.

257. *Loi de 3 Avril 1990,* translated in 41 Int'l Digest of Health Legis. 447 (1990). The law was enacted when King Badouin temporarily abdicated to avoid having to sign it. *See* Boland, *supra* note 168, at 87–88; Reed Boland, *Recent Developments in Abortion Law,* 19 Law, Med. & Health Care 267, 270 (1991); Paul Montgomery, *Belgian King, Unable to Sign Abortion Law, Takes Day off,* N.Y. Times, Apr. 5, 1990, at A14. For a study of the politics that lead up to this confrontation, see Berengère Marques-Pereira, *Abortion in Belgium: Consensus and Conflict on the Political and Institutional Scene,* in The New Politics of Abortion, *supra* note 167, at 124.

Elsewhere in Western Europe, the issue was handled legislatively rather than through a legal challenge to the validity of the law. France enacted a statute in 1975 legalizing abortions when a woman's health was endangered, when the pregnancy resulted from rape or incest, and in cases of fetal defect.[258] The 1975 reform statute opens with a section which "guarantees" respect for life "from the beginning of life" but goes on to authorize "necessary" abortions—which includes "distress" to the mother within the first ten weeks of pregnancy.[259] After 10 weeks, abortion is allowed only for a serious threat to the mother's health or because the child is likely to be born with a serious disease or defect, certified by two physicians. The French law requires that information be given the distressed woman regarding the government's disapproval of abortion and the social supports available for mothers and children and requires a waiting period of one week from the woman's request for the abortion, counseling by a government approved counselor, and a two-day waiting period after counseling. The French law also bans "pro-abortion" advertising and requires that abortions be performed in government-approved facilities. Not more than 25 percent of the surgical and obstetrical procedures performed in such facility can be abortions.

Although there has been no serious legislative challenge to the French abortion statute, there have been challenges in the street to the law. As a result, the French government has felt it necessary to introduce legislation making it a crime to obstruct abortion clinics.[260] The French government apparently has encountered some difficulty in enforcing its abortion access law in the courts.[261] Still, women in France undergo about 220,000 abortions per year.[262] In 2000, the French government extended the period of choice from 10 to 12 weeks, dropped the requirement of parental consent for minors, and lifted the ban on abortion advertising.[263]

Switzerland, on the other hand, had not formally liberalized its abortion law up until 2001, but the law apparently was given widely varying interpretations in different cantons.[264] Finally, in March 2001, after eight years of debate, the Swiss Parliament voted to allow abortion at the choice of the women during the first twelve weeks of pregnancy.[265] While widely supported in the National Council (the lower house), where it passed by a vote of 107-69, it barely passed the Council of States, where the vote was 22-20. The centrist Christian Peoples Party forced a referendum on the issue, but the reformed law passed with 72 percent in favor.[266] If they had succeeded in forcing a referendum, that would assure at the least that the new law would not go into effect for several years.

In Russia, the dissolution of the Soviet Union did not lead to changes in the abortion laws applicable there.[267] On the other hand, the emergence from under the Communist yoke did allow the

---

258. GLENDON, *supra* note 229, at 146–53; MALCOLM POTTS, PETER DIGGORY, & JOHN PEEL, ABORTION 380–81, 399 (1977); Monique Drapier, *La loi rélative à la grossesse dix ans apres: Histoire d'un compromis,* 101 REVUE DROIT PUBLIC ET DE LA SCIENCE POLITIQUE EN FRANCE ET À L'ÉTRANGER 445 (1985); Colette Gallard, *France* (Elinor Neubert trans.), in ABORTION IN THE NEW EUROPE, *supra* note 144, at 101; Danielle Keats Morris, Note, Planned Parenthood v. Casey: *From U.S. "Rights Talk" to Western European Responsibility,* 16 FORDHAM INT'L L.J. 761, 781–87 (1993); Jannine Mossuz-Lavau, in THE NEW POLITICS OF ABORTION, *supra* note 167, at 86.

259. 1975 J.O. 739, No. 75-17, 1975 B.L.D. 48. *See generally* GLENDON, *supra* note 229, at 15–20; Mossuz-Lavau, *supra* note 258, at 98–99.

260. MASON, *supra* note 78, at 107.

261. A. Dorozynski, *Paris Court Attacks Abortion Law,* 311 BRIT. MED. J. 149 (1995).

262. Jim Hanley, *France to Extend Abortion Law,* THE GUARDIAN, July 28, 2000, at 16.

263. *Id.*

264. Anne-Marie Rey, *Switzerland,* in ABORTION IN THE NEW EUROPE, *supra* note 143, at 253.

265. Bettina Stadelmann, *Councils OK Abortion Law, National Vote Expected in Switzerland,* S. FLA. SUN-SENTINAL (Ft. Lauderdale), Mar. 24, 2001, at 30A.

266. Elizabeth Olson, *Swiss Voters Lift Restriction on Abortions,* N.Y. TIMES, June 3, 2002, at A4.

267. Larissa Lissyutkina, *Soviet Women at the Crossroads of Perestroika,* in GENDER POLITICS AND POST-COMMUNISM, *supra* note 181, at 274, 278–29; Mertus, *supra* note 181, at 453. *See also* Chapter 12, at notes 37–41.

entry of foreign pharmaceutical companies into Russia. This, along with the proliferation of the formerly discouraged family planning clinics, enabled Russian women for the first time to have easy and affordable access to oral contraceptives.[268] While many women—especially older women—refused to use "the pill" for fear of cancer, the readiness of younger women to use it saw the proportion of women on the pill rise from 1.7 percent to 6.8 percent between 1990 and 1998.[269] This might not seem like a big change, but it was the major contributing factor in a decline in the number of births, of abortions, and of maternal deaths. In Russia, the birth rate fell from 13.4 per 1,000 people in 1990, to 8.6, per 1,000 in 1997, and the number of abortions fell from 4,600,000 in 1988 to 2,500,000 in 1997.[270] In 1993, about 70 Russian women died for every 100,000 live births, while in 1998 about 50 Russian women died for every 100,000 live births.[271] While the latter figure is a marked improvement, it remains dramatically higher than in Western Europe or the United States.

Presumably, greater penetration of the market by effective contraceptives will continue the Russian trend toward fewer abortions. Even with the sharp drop in abortions, the abortion rate is still five times more higher than in the United States, with 1 birth per 1.7 abortions in Russia compared to 3 births per abortion in the United States in 2002.[272] The prevalence of crudely done abortions has left millions of Russian women sterile.[273] The spread of contraceptives further contributes the downward trend in births in that troubled land. Russian nationalists, alarmed by the falling birth rate and a death rate that has surged with the collapse of the economy and the perennial Communist neglect of the environment coming home to roost,[274] have become alarmed about the proliferation of family planning services. They joined with the reemerging Orthodox Church in 1998 to ban the use of federal funds for such purposes.[275] Whether this portends greater restrictions on legal abortions remains unclear. Some observers believe that abortion has been part of the culture for so long that it would be virtually impossible to restrict.[276]

Across Asia, abortion generally is legal. Japan was one of the first nations to legalize abortion under a broad and loosely applied indications policy.[277] Despite its abortion law, Japan is not socially supportive of abortion.[278] Physicians and the public alike mourn for aborted fetuses, even having miniature cemeteries for them[279]—even though, as Buddhists who believe in rebirth, they generally believe that abortion merely delays the birth of a soul and does not prevent its birth. Because of social disapproval, there has been a steady decline in the number (and therefore in the

---

268. Celestine Bohlen, *Russian Women Turning to Abortion Less Often,* N.Y. TIMES, Mar. 29, 1999, at A3. The situation is similar in Romania. *See* Gail Counsell, *Where the Pill Is Still Bitter,* THE INDEPENDENT (London), Apr. 3, 1992, at 18; Negrau, *supra* note 181, at 124–25.

269. Bohlen, *supra* note 268.

270. *Id;* Mertus, *supra* note 181, at 454.

271. Bohlen, *supra* note 268.

272. Sharon LaFraniere, *Russians Feel Abortion's Complications,* WASH. POST, Feb. 22, 2003, at A16.

273. *Id.*

274. Bohlen, *supra* note 268.

275. *Id.*

276. *Id. See also Birth Control in Russia,* N.Y. TIMES, Sept. 2, 2003, at A22; LaFraniere, *supra* note 272; Kim Murphy, *Russia Tries to Curtail Its High Abortion Rates,* PHILA. INQUIRER, Sept. 23, 2003, at A2.

277. *See* Chapter 12, at notes 7–36.

278. Lynn Wardle, *"Crying Stones": A Comparison of Abortion in Japan and the United States,* 14 N.Y.L.S. J. INT'L & COMP. L. 183 (1993); Sheryl WuDunn, *In Japan, a Ritual of Morning for Abortions,* N.Y. Times, Jan. 25, 1996, at A1.

279. WILLIAM LaFLEUR, LIQUID LIFE: ABORTION AND BUDDHISM IN JAPAN 4–5, 26–27, 155 (1992); Hiromi Maruyama, *Abortion in Japan: A Feminist Critique,* 10 WIS. WOMEN'S L.J. 131, 146–47 (1995); WuDunn, *supra* note 278. At least one American feminist insists that this shows a lack of guilt rather than some sense that a wrong had been committed. Sara Walsh, *Liquid Lives and Liquid Laws,* 7 INT'L LEG. PERSP. 187, 200 (1995). Others see the practice as representing commercial exploitation of an artfully created guilt. *See* HELEN HARDACRE, MARKETING THE MENACING FETUS IN JAPAN (1997); Maruyama, *supra,* at 147. *See generally* John Peek, *Buddhism, Human Rights, and the Japanese Style,* 17 HUM. RTS. Q. 527, 538–39 (1995).

rate) of abortions in Japan since its popularity in the wake of military defeat; by 1985 less than half as many abortions were occuring in Japan annually (somewhere around 500,000 per year) as occurred in the peak year of 1955 (1,170,143, with a much smaller population base).[280] By 1993, there were only 386,807 abortions.[281] On the other hand, births in Japan have also fallen sharply, so much so that since 1995 the number of births annually in Japan is less than in 1900.[282] The result is an aging population that will experience a sharp decline in the working population at the same time that their burden of caring for their aging parents will be markedly expanding.[283]

Japanese researchers have identified other problems from the relatively free availability of abortion in their country. Japanese women who have had abortions have notably higher incidences of *chlamydia trachomatis* and related complications in later pregnancies than women who have not had abortions.[284] More public concern, however, focuses on abortion as an encouragement of adolescent sexuality along with what many Japanese consider to be unacceptable levels of sexually transmitted diseases and frequent abortions.[285]

In mainland China, abortion virtually on demand during the first three months of a pregnancy was legalized in 1957, over the expressed opposition of the medical profession.[286] Medical resistance was all the more remarkable given the still militant Communist dictatorship then in place. The decision to legalize abortion was perhaps even more remarkable given the strongly pro-birth policies that the government was then pursuing.[287] Mao, who believed that a growing

280. Jane Condon, A Half Step Behind: Japanese Women Today 85 (1985); Maruyama, *supra* note 279, at 135, 144–46; Wardle, *supra* note 278, at 219–24.

281. Maruyama, *supra* note 279, at 144.

282. Peterson, *supra* note 245, at 45.

283. *Id.* at 44.

284. M. Nishimura *et al.*, *Epidemiological Study of Chlamydia Trachomatis Infection in Pregnant Housewives and Investigation on Its Influence on Outcome of Pregnancy and on Their Newborns* (English abstract), Y. Kusano, *Demographic and Reproductive Factors for High Serioprevalence of Chlamydia Trachomatis among Pregnant Women in Japan* (abstract), 190 Tohuku J. Experimental Med. 1 (2000); 64 Kansenshogaku Zasshi 179 (1990). Related complications include higher incidences of *placenta previa*, preterm delivery, and small size at birth. Nishimura, *supra*; L.H. Roht *et al.*, *The Association of Multiple Induced Abortions with Subsequent Prematurity and Spontaneous Abortion*, 23 Acta. Obstet. & Gynecologica Japan 140 (1976). The correlation between abortion and chlamydia infection is not limited to Japan. *See generally* Faro & Pearlman, *supra* note 128, at 73–74, 83; Marguerite Barbacci *et al.*, *Postabortal Endometritis and Isolation of Chlamydia Trachomatis*, 68 Obstet. & Gynecology 686 (1986); Birger Moller *et al.*, *Pelvic Infection after Elective Abortion Associated with Chlamydia Trachomatis*, 59 Obstet. & Gynecology 210 (1982); Stellan Osser & Kenneth Perrson, *Postabortal Pelvic Infection Associated with Chlamydia Trachomatis Infection and the Influence of Humoral Immunity*, 150 Am. J. Obstet. & Gynecology 699 (1984); Sorensen & Thronov, *supra* note 40; Lars Westergaard, *Significance of Cervical Chlamydia Trachomatis Infection in Post-Abortal Pelvic Inflammatory Disease*, 60 Obstet. & Gynecology 322 (1982).

285. A. Ishii *et al.*, *Disease and Pregnancy in Adolescent Girls*, 4 Adv. Contracept. 311 (1988); S. Matsumoto, *Sex Education and Sexual Behaviour of Adolescents in Japan* (abstract), 24 Ann. of the Acad. Med. of Singapore 696 (1995); T. Munakata & K. Fujisawa, *HIV Risk-Relevant Behaviors of Japanese Adolescents* (abstract no. TuD2701), 11 Int'l Conf. on AIDS 385 (1996); K. Yamamoto *et al.*, *Abortion in Japan* (English abstract), 191 Arch. Kriminol 177 (1993).

286. Tu Ping & Herbert Smith, *Determinants of Induced Abortion and Their Policy Implications in Four Counties in North China*, 26 Stud. in Fam. Planning 278 (1995); Mark Savage, *The Law of Abortion in the Union of Soviet Socialist Republics and the People's Republic of China: Women's Rights in Two Socialist Countries*, 40 Stan. L. Rev. 1027, 1066, 1072–79 (1988). *See also* Bernard Hun-Kay Luk, *Abortion in Chinese Law*, 25 Am. J. Comp. L. 372, 384–89 (1977); Xinzhong Qian, *China's Population Policy: Theory and Methods*, 14 Stud. in Fam. Planning 295, 296 (1983).

287. *See* Loren Fessler, *The People's Republic of China and Population Policy*, 20 Am. Universities Fieldstaff Rep., E. Asia Ser. no. 3 (May 1973). *See also* John Aird, Slaughter of the Innocents: Coercive Birth Control in China 20–25 (1990); Reed Boland, *The Environment, Population, and Women's Human Rights*, 27 Envtl. L. 1137, 1143 (1997); Savage, *supra* note 286, at 1068–69.

population was essential both to economic development and to assure that China could survive a nuclear war, launched the pro-birth program by announcing the slogan that "[t]he more babies, the more glorious are their mothers."[288] While abortion remained legal, its availability in practice varied dramatically with the twists and turns of Chinese politics over the next two decades.[289]

Today, the policy approach the People's Republic of China is entirely different. Abortion not only is legal in all circumstances, but it is at least promoted in efforts to conform to that nation's "one child" policy adopted in 1979.[290] Although this party policy was not formally enacted as law throughout most of the time it was applied,[291] it was always enforced as rigorously as any law or policy in China.[292] Reports persist that in at least some parts of China government officials physically coerce women into having abortions that the women do not want.[293] About 200,000,000

---

288. Xiaorong Li, *License to Coerce: Violence against Women, State Responsibility, and Legal Failures in China's Family-Planning Program*, 8 Yale J.L. & Feminism 145, 148 (1995). *See also* Judith Banister, China's Changing Population 17–18 (1987).

289. Anibal Faundes & Tapani Luukainen, *Health and Family Planning Services in the Chinese People's Republic*, 3 Stud. in Fam. Planning 165 (1972); Qian, *supra* note 286, at 296; Savage, *supra* note 286, at 1078–81.

290. Banister, *supra* note 288, at 183–226; China's One-Child Family Policy (Elisabeth Croll, Deila Davin, & Penny Kane eds. 1985); Hadley, *supra* note 65, at 99–106; Betsy Hartman, Reproductive Rights and Wrongs: The Global Politics of Population Control 163 (1995); Sulameth Heins-Potter, Birthplanning in Rural China: A Cultural Account (1985); Chang Choncan, *Keeping Population Growth in Check*, Beijing Rev., May 6, 1991, at 32; Cheng Gang, *Family Planning: The Way Out*, Beijing Rev., Mar. 11, 1991, at 27; Garcia Gomez, *China's Eugenics Law as Grounds for Granting Asylum*, 5 Pac. Rim L. & Pol'y J. 563 (1996); Susan Greenhalgh, *Controlling Births and Bodies in Village China*, 21 Am. Ethnologist 3 (1994); Ellen Keng, *Population Control through the One-Child Policy in China: Its Effects on Women*, 18 Women's Rts. L. Rptr. 205 (1997); Nicholas Kristoff, *China's Crackdown on Births: A Stunning and Harsh Success*, N.Y. Times, Apr. 25, 1993, at A1; Li, *supra* note 288; Xizhe Peng, *Population Policy and Program in China: Challenge and Prospective*, 35 Tex. Int'l L.J. 51 (2000); Savage, *supra* note 286, at 1067–69, 1081–93; Carmel Shalev, *China to CEDAW: An Update on Population Policy*, 23 HuHHum. Rts. Q. 119, 132–37 (2001); Wang Xin, *Population vs. Development: Challenge of the New Century*, Beijing Rev., May 1, 1995, at 12; Sheryl WuDunn, *To Punish Births: Fines, Beatings, Success*, N.Y. Times, Apr. 25, 1993, at A12.

291. Antonaneta Bezlova, *Population China: Formalizing One-Child Policy Due Soon*, Inter press Service, May 23, 2001, available at 2001 WL 4804003.

292. *See* H. Yuan Tien, China's Strategic Demographic Initiative (1991); *See also* Hartman, *supra* note 290, at 163; Bai Yan, *A Model Family-Planning Worker*, Beijing Rev., May 6, 1991, at 35; Cheng Gang, *CFPA's [China Family Planning Ass'n] Contribution to Population Control*, Beijing Rev., Nov. 19, 1990, at 24; Jiang Wandi, *Explaining China's Population Policy to the World*, Beij. Rev., Apr. 14, 1997, at 16; Peng Peiyun, *Population Control: Difficult, but a Must*, Beijing Rev., Jan. 29, 1996, at 11; *Visitors to the Middle Kingdom*, The Economist, Oct. 3, 1992, at 33, 34; Wu Naitao, *Family Planning: A Complicated Choice*, Beijing Rev., Jan. 29, 1996, at 12. *See generally* Lisa Gregory, Note, *Examining the Economic Component of China's One-Child Family Policy under International Law: Your Money or Your Life*, 6 J. Chinese Law 45 (1992).

293. Aird, *supra* note 287; Susan Greenhalgh & Jiali Li, Engendering Reproductive Practice in Peasant China (1993); HadleyHadley, *supra* note 65, at 100; Steven Mosher, A Mother's Ordeal (1994); Tibetan Women's Ass'n, Tears of Silence: Tibetan Women and Population Control 15–17, 38–49 (1994); Boland, *supra* note 287, a 1144–46; *Forced Abortion and Sterilization in China: The View from the Inside*, Hearing before the Subcomm. on Int'l Operations & Hum. Rts. of the House Comm. on Int'l Rel., 105th Cong., 2nd Sess., Jun 10, 1998; *China Forces Abortion on Woman Who Exceeds Official Birth Limit*, Chi. Trib., Aug. 28, 2000, at 14; Gomez, *supra* note 290, at 568–69; Eva Herzer & Sara Levin, *China's Denial of Tibetan Women's Right to Reproductive Freedom*, 3 Mich. J. Gender & L. 551, 559–66 (1996); Blake Kerr, *Tibetans under the Knife*, in Anguish of Tibet 96, 102–06 (Petra Kelly et al. eds. 1991); Li, *supra* note 288, at 152–55; Damien McElroy, *Chinese Region "Must Conduct 20,000 Abortions"; Hated Family Planning "Police" Crack down on Rural Area Where Families Average Five Children*, The Sunday Telegraph (London), Aug. 5, 2001, at 29; Damien McElroy, *Sterilisation Outcry in China*, Scotland on Sunday, Aug. 19, 2001, at 17; Philip Pan, *China's One-Child Policy Now a Double Standard: Limits and Penalties Applied Unevenly*, Wash. Post, Aug. 20, 2002, at A1; John Pomfret, *China's Bumpy Path to Justice: Victim of Birth Control Policy Struggles after Rare*

abortions were performed in China between 1971 and 1990, with a sharp jump in the numbers during and after 1979.[294] Many of the coerced abortions take place during the third trimester of pregnancy, including up to the point of birth.[295]

The abortion rate peaked at 76 abortions per 100 live births in 1984, and generally runs to around one-third of more of all pregnancies.[296] In some provinces, there apparently are more abortions than live births annually.[297] With such heavy reliance on abortion for birth control, most women in China can expect to have several abortions during their reproductive years.[298] Some women have as many as four or five abortions in a single year.[299] In some provinces as many as one-third of all women have had coerced, late-term abortions.[300] Coupling the limits on the number of children allowed with the social pressures to have a son produces a growing and serious imbalance in the sex ratios in China.[301] The extent to which this results from sex-selective abortion, from fail-

---

*Court Win,* WASH. POST, Mar. 27, 2001, at A1; Anika Rahman, *Towards Government Accountability for Women's Reproductive Rights,* 69 ST. JOHN'S L. REV. 203, 203 (1995); Gail Rodgers, Comment, *Yin and Yang: The Eugenic Policies of the United States and China: Is the Analysis that Black and White?,* 22 HOUS. J. INT'L L. 129, 141–42 (1999); Savage, *supra* note 286, at 1082, 1085–92, 1115–16; Shalev, *supra* note 290, at 130–32, 137–47.

294. Karen Hardee-Cleveland & Judith Banister, *Fertility Policy and Implementation in China, 1986–88,* 14 POP. & DEV. REV. 245 (1988); Ping & Smith, *supra* note 286, at 278. The government itself reports that there were 200,000,000 fewer births between 1971 and 1988, but does not directly link this to the incidence of abortion. *China's Population Down to Size,* BEIJING REV., Oct. 15, 1990, at 8; Jing Wei, *China Still Facing Population Problem,* BEIJING REV., Dec. 28, 1992, at 16. *See generally* Susan Rigdon, *Abortion Law and Practice in China: An Overview with Comparisons to the United States,* 31 SOC. SCI. & MED. 445 (1990).

295. BANISTER, *supra* note 288, at 208; MARGERY WOLF, REVOLUTION POSTPONED 245 (1985); Susan Greenhaugh, *Controlling Births and Bodies in Village China,* 21 AM. ETHNOLOGIST 543 (1996).

296. BANISTER, *supra* note 288, at 180, 221; Savage, *supra* note 286, at 1092–93, 1115.

297. Y. Wang *et al., Induced Abortion in Eight Provinces of China,* 5 ASIA-PAC. J. PUB. HEALTH 31, 32 (1991). This also seems to be true on Taiwan, even with its different legal system and without coerced abortions. *See Abortion Pill Leads to a Shortage of Stem Cells,* STRAITS TIMES (Singapore), Aug. 12, 2001, available at 2001 WL 26053248; Lawrence Chung, *Tenfold Increase in Taiwan Abortions,* STRAITS TIMES (Singapore), Sept. 9, 2001, available at 2001 WL 26054953.

298. Lin Luo *et al., A Follow-up Study of First Trimester Induced Abortions at Hospitals and Family Planning Clinics in Sichuan Province, China,* 53 CONTRACEPTION 267 (1996). A survey in 1994 found that more than 25% of married women in China (with higher percentages in urban areas) had had an abortion, with two-thirds of those admitting to having had an abortion choosing to keep it a secret from their friends and colleagues. *Survey: Quarter of Married Women Have Had Abortion,* translated in FOR. BROADCAST INF. SERVICE-CHINA 94-018, Jan. 21, 1994, at 32.

299. Susan Rigdon, *Abortion Law and Practice in China: An Overview with Comparisons to the United States,* 42 SOC. SCI. MED. 543 (1996).

300. AIRD, *supra* note 287, at 91–92; Mark Baker, *Still Booming Despite Harsh Measures,* FIN. TIMES, Oct. 19, 1983, §IV, at 2; Greenhalgh, *supra* note 290, at 23; Li Ching-Feng, *Direct Report from the Divine Land,* translated in FOR. BROADCAST INF. SERVICE-CHINA 94–187, Sept. 27, 1994, at 47. One is left to speculate whether these practices help to make China the only country where women have a higher suicide rate than men. SARAH BLAFFER HRDY, MOTHER NATURE: A HISTORY OF MOTHERS, INFANTS, AND NATURAL SELECTION 322 (1999); Robert Neal, *Female Suicides in China Point to Burden for U.S. Men,* FOCUS, Summer 1998, at 1, 6.

301. HRDY, *supra* note 300, at 318–20; Eric Eckholm, *Desire for Sons Drives Use of Prenatal Scans in China,* N.Y. TIMES, June 21, 2002, at A3; David Fang, *Hainan Has Worst Gender Ratio,* S. CHINA MORNING POST, July 3, 2003; Terence Hull, *Recent Trends in Sex Ratios of Births in China,* 16 POP. & DEV. REV. 63 (1990); Sten Johansson & Ola Nygren, *The Missing Girls of China: A New Demographic Account,* 17 POP. & DEV. 35 (1991); Nicholas Kristoff, *A Mystery of China's Census: Where Have the Girls Gone?,* N.Y. TIMES, June 17, 1991, at A1; Nicholas Kristoff, *Stark Data on Women: 100 Million Are Missing,* N.Y. TIMES, Nov. 5, 1991, at B9; Daniel Kwan, *Gender Imbalance Big Threat, Say Experts,* S. CHINA MORNING POST, Sept. 24, 2002; Li, *supra* note 288, at 166–67; Li Yongping, *Infant Sex Ratio and Its Relationship with Socio-Economic Variables: Results of Population Census and the Reflected Realities,* 4 POP. & ECON. 3 (1998); S. Light, *Female Infanticide in China: Response to the Victimization of Women and Children,* 8 J. CENTRE OF WOMEN & POL'Y STUD. 5 (1985); Mu Guangzong, *A Theoretical Explanation of Recent Rise in Sex Ratio at Birth in China,* 1 POP. & ECON. 50 (1995); John Pomfret, *In China's Countryside, "It's a Boy!" Too Often,* WASH. POST, May 29, 2001, at A1; Rodgers, *supra* note 293,

ure to register the births of daughters, from deliberate female infanticide, or from simple neglect remains uncertain.[302] Despite laws prohibiting the sex-screening of fetuses,[303] China is looking forward to millions of men of marriageable age who will never be able to find a wife.

Compelled sterilizations are also common in China. Couples in China are required to undergo premarital physical examinations that can lead to compulsory sterilization before they have any children if they are found to be eugenically undesirable.[304] Even without eugenics concerns, one study found that virtually all Chinese women over the age of 35 had been sterilized.[305] According to Chinese government figures, fully 38 percent of all adult Chinese women have been sterilized.[306] Despite official denials, reports still leak out of women, in particular, forced to undergo unwanted sterilizations. One such report, disputed by the Chinese government, has it that Sun Zhonghua, a 34-year-old mother of two boys aged 12 and 13 who had not been pregnant

---

at 144–45; Philip Shenon, *China's Mania for Baby Boys Creates Surplus of Bachelors,* N.Y. TIMES, Aug. 16, 1994, at A1; Robert Thomson, *Boy Bias Beats China Family Planners,* FIN. TIMES, Nov. 19, 1985, §I, at 4; S. Tuljapurkar, N. Li, & M.W. Feldman, *High Sex Ratios in China's Future,* 267 SCIENCE 874 (1995); Xinhua News Service, *Unbalanced Birth Rates Viewed,* translated in FOR. BROADCAST INF. SERVICE 93-075, 21 Apr. 1993, at 19; Zeng Yi, *Cause and Implications of the Recent Increase in the Reported Sex Ratio at Birth in China,* 19 POP. & DEV. REV. 283 (1993). Unlikely as it may seem, some demographers have argued on the basis of this and other data that Asians are more prone to conceive sons than daughters. *See* N.E. MORTON, C.S. CHUNG, & M.P. MI, GENETICS OF INTERRACIAL CROSSES IN HAWAII (1967); Pravin Visaria, *Sex Ratio at Birth in Territories with a Relatively Complete Registration,* 14 EUGENICS Q. 132 (1967).

302. HRDY, *supra* note 300, at 319–20; Sharon Hom, *Female Infanticide in China: The Human Rights Specter and Thoughts towards (An)Other Vision,* 23 COLUM. HUM. RTS. L. REV. 249 (1991); Li Ching-Feng, *supra* note 300. Female infanticide was common in China even before the advent of the one-child policy. *See* W.R. GEDDES, PEASANT LIFE IN COMMUNIST CHINA 12–17 (1963); C.F. GORDON-CUMMINGS, WANDERINGS IN CHINA 134–37, 272–76 (1900); HSIAO-T'UNG FEI, PEASANT LIFE IN CHINA: A FIELD STUDY OF COUNTRY LIFE IN THE YANGTZE VALLEY 33–34, 51–53 (1939); PING-TI HO, STUDIES ON THE POPULATION OF CHINA, 1368–1953, at 8–13, 56–59, 217 (1959); O. LANG, CHINESE FAMILY AND SOCIETY 150–51 (1946); Pomfret, *supra* note 301; Zhongwei Zhao, *Deliberate Birth Control under a High-Fertility Regime: Reproductive Behavior in China before 1970,* 23 POP. & DEV. REV.729, 749 (1997).

303. *New Chinese Law Prohibits Sex-Screening of Fetuses,* N.Y. TIMES, Nov. 15, 1994, at A5; Gao Yan, *Sex-Selection Abortions Banned to End Population Imbalance,* S. CHINA MORNING POST, Mar. 25, 2003. *See also* Agence France-Presse, *Three-Year Campaign Launched against Aborting Girls,* S. CHINA MORNING POST, Aug. 16, 2003. Given widespread resort to genetic screening in China to assure a healthy baby, preventing sex-screening there is almost impossible. *See* Stacy Klein, Note, *Prenatal Genetic Testing and Its Impact on Incidence of Abortion: A Comparative Analysis of China and Ireland,* 7 CARDOZO J. INT'L & COMP. L. 73, 78–84 (1999).

304. Law on Maternal Health Care (Oct. 27, 1994), available in FOR. BROADCAST INF. SERV.—CHINA, no. 94-211, Nov. 1, 1994, at 29. *See generally* Dinah Ashman, Editorial, *The Chinese Way,* NEW SCIENTIST, Oct. 24, 1998, at 58; Andy Coghlan, *Perfect People's Republic,* NEW SCIENTIST, Oct. 24, 1998, at 18; Daniel Gewirtz, Note, *Toward a Quality Population: China's Eugenic Sterilization of the Mentally Retarded,* 15 N.Y.L. SCH. J. INT'L & COMP. L. 139 (1994); Gómez, *supra* note 290; Linda Johnson, *Expanding Eugenics or Improving Health Care in China: Commentary on the Provisions of the Standing Committee of the Gansu People's Congress Concerning the Prohibition of Reproduction by Intellectually Impaired Persons,* 24 J. LAW & SOC'Y 199 (1997); Li, *supra* note 288, at 161–70; Rodgers, *supra* note 293, at 143–44, 154–61; *Western Eyes on China's Eugenics Law,* 346 THE LANCET 131 (1995). *But see* John Pomfret, *China Suspends Sterilization of People with Genetic Ills,* INT'L HERALD TRIB., Aug. 18, 1998, at 5.

305. Ping & Smith, *supra* note 286, at 279. Female sterilization accounts for at least 40 percent of all contraceptive measures in the People's Republic of China. Wu Naitao, *Science Contributes to Population Control,* BEIJING REV., Oct. 23, 1995, at 30. *See generally* JUDITH JACOBSEN, PROMOTING POPULATION STERILIZATION: INCENTIVES FOR SMALL FAMILIES (1983).

306. Edward Gargan, *Family Joy Leads to Jail; In China, Strict Enforcement of 1-Child-per-Family Policy,* CHI. TRIB., May 29, 2001, at 4. China, with far and away the world's largest population, only recently became the fourth-largest producer of condoms—and many of those are of dubious quality. *See* Bill Savadove, *Nation Becomes the World's Fourth Largest Producer of Condoms,* S. CHINA MORNING POST, Jan. 28, 2003.

since the birth of her second son, was beaten to death for resisting sterilization.[307] Social scientists from outside of China have found that all of these policies are very unpopular among the Chinese, many of whom still favor large families.[308] And, in fact, the Chinese pursue the goal of having a child through all the usual (and some unusual) techniques of modern reproductive medicine at the same time as their government seeks to limit them to a single child.[309]

Elsewhere in the Confucian orbit, Hong Kong and Singapore have indications policies similar to that of England.[310] Abortion is legal and common in Vietnam, with widespread adverse impacts on women's health.[311] Abortion is also common and legal in the Democratic People's Republic of Korea (North Korea); Democratic Korea does not have a formal one-child policy, but the extreme poverty and recurring famines produce much the same result with abortion as the primary means of birth prevention.[312] In contrast, in the Republic of Korea (South Korea) abortion remains a serious crime, punishable by up to 10 years in prison, except for threats to the health of the mother or to the health of the fetus or if the pregnancy resulted from rape or incest.[313] Even if these indications are present, the woman must obtain the consent of her husband or guardian.[314] Nonetheless, abortion in Republican Korea appears to be a common procedure that, among other things, is frequently used to select boys in preference to girls.[315] In 1987, Re-

---

307. *Chinese Woman Dies after Taken to Be Sterilized*, Milwaukee J. Sentinel, May 20, 2001, at 20A; Gargan, *supra* note 306; *Seized Chinese Woman Dead; Forced Sterilization Was to Happen, Her Relative Says*, Ariz. Rep., May 20, 2001, at A26; *Woman Taken for Sterilization Dies*, Hous. Chron., May 27, 2001, at 26. British newspapers speculated that Ms. Sun died when she was pushed or jump from a fourth-story window in resisting the sterilization. Damien McElroy, *Woman Killed in Sterilization Office Fall*, The Scotsman, May 21, 2001, at 11; Richard Sears, *Thrown to Her Death, Mother Who Refused to Be Sterilised*, The Daily Mail, May 21, 2001, at 34. For examples of similar abuses in other countries, promoted by American population activists, see Judith Scully, *Maternal Mortality, Population Control, and the War in Women's Wombs*, 19 Wis. Int'l L.J. 103 (2001).

308. Virginia Li *et al.*, *Characteristics of Women Having Abortion in China*, 31 Soc. Sci. Med. 445 (1990); Elisabeth Rosenthal, *Rural Flouting of One-Child Policy Undercuts China's Census*, N.Y. Times, Apr. 14, 2000, at A6. *But see* Nicholas Kristoff, *More in China Willingly Rear Just One Child*, N.Y. Times, May 9, 1990, at A1.

309. *See, e.g.*, Leigh Jenkins, *Single Women Win Right to Have Test-Tube Babies*, S. China Morning Post, Nov. 9, 2002;*"Test-Tube" Babies Fulfill Parents' Dreams*, Beijing Rev., June 1, 1998, at 21; *Test-Tube Baby First on Mainland*, China Daily (Beijing), Mar. 11, 1988, at 1; Rick Weiss, *U.S.-Banned Fertility Method Tried in China*, Wash. Post, Oct. 14, 2003, at A10.

310. *Offences against the Person Ordinance*, ch. 212, §47A (Hong Kong); *Abortion Act of 1974*, Act no. 24 of 1974 (Singapore). Singapore, in fact, suffers from a perceived baby shortage and has set up a program to promote births, but without revising its abortion law. Seth Mydans, *Singapore, Hoping for a Baby Boom, Makes Sex a Civic Duty*, N.Y. Times, Apr. 21, 2001, at A5. In Hong Kong, prosecutions of physicians for violations of the indications policy seem to depend on the death or serious injury of the woman rather than on whether the abortion was justified by the necessary indications. *See* Sara Bradford, *Abortion Doctor Is Imprisoned for Killing*, S. China Morning Post, Oct. 31, 2003. Non-physicians are prosecuted without regard to whether the woman undergoing the abortion was injured. Niki Law, *Police Arrest Two Women Suspected of Providing Illegal Abortion*, S. China Morning Post, June 5, 2002.

311. Daniel Goodkind, *Abortion in Vietnam: Measurements, Puzzles, and Concerns*, 25 Stud. in Fam. Planning 342 (1994); Pamina Gorbach, *Reproduction, Risk and Reality: Family Planning and Reproductive Health in Northern Vietnam*, 30 J. Bio. Sci. 393 (1998).

312. Steven Mufson, *The Pyongyang Albright Didn't See*, Wash. Post, Oct. 25, 2000, at A26. *See also* James Brooke, *Defectors from North Korea Tell of Prison Baby Killings*, N.Y. Times, June 10, 2002, at A1.

313. Korean Crim. Code arts. 269, 270; Korean Pub. Welfare Law, ch. 2, art. 14 (Limited Permission of Induced Abortions). *See generally* Pyong-Choon Hahm, *The Criminality of Abortion in Korea*, in The Korean Political Tradition and Law (Pyong-Choon Hahm ed. 1987); Naryung Kim, *Breaking Free from Patriarchy: A Comparative Study of Sex Selection Abortions in Korea and the United States*, 17 Pac. Basin L.J. 301, 310–15 (1999).

314. Korean Pub. Welfare Law, ch. 2, art. 14 (Limited Permission of Induced Abortions). *See also* Kim, *supra* note 313, at 313.

315. Kim, *supra* note 313, at 310 n.46.

publican Korea enacted a ban on sex-selective abortions.[316] Prosecutions for abortion are virtually unknown in Republican Korea, but doctors have been "administratively punished" for such performing sex-selective abortions.[317]

India, despite its long-standing emphasis on population control, also has an indications policy, and limits abortion to a few approved facilities.[318] The number of authorized facilities is inadequate to meet demand.[319] As a result, many abortions in India are illegal—one estimate has the number as four times greater than the number of legal abortions.[320] Parents also seek abortions for reasons that are not legal indications, in particular as a means of sex-selection.[321] One result of common recourse to illegal abortions is a continuing pattern of serious complications from abortions.[322] This pattern, however, does not result entirely from the inadequacies of the illegal facilities—some 92 percent of rural Indian women have one or more gynecological of sexual diseases when they become pregnant, with the average rural Indian woman having 3.6 such diseases.[323]

Bangladesh's situation is similar to India's, with its prohibition of abortion being evaded through a general acceptance of "menstrual regulation."[324] Abortion remains illegal in the Philippines, but reportedly is common.[325] Nepal, on the other hand, appears to enforce its law pro-

---

316. Public Welfare Law, ch. 2, art. 19-2 (Medical Practices Act). *See also* Kim, *supra* note 313, at 314–25.

317. Kim, *supra* note 313, at 310, 314.

318. *Medical Termination of Pregnancy Act,* Act no. 34 of 1971 (India). India stresses sterilization rather than abortion in its birth control policies. *See* Celia Dugger, *Relying on Hard and Soft Sells, India Pushes Sterilization,* N.Y. Times, June 22, 2001, at A1.

319. *See generally* Sunil Khanna, *Traditional and Reproductive Technology in an Urbanizing North Indian Village,* 44 Soc. Sci. & Med. 171 (1997).

320. Kurus Coyaji, *Early Medical Abortion in India: Three Studies and Their Implications for Abortion Services,* 55 J. Am. Med. Women's Assoc. 191 (2000).

321. *See, e.g.,* Radhik Balakrishnan, *The Social Context of Sex-Selection and the Politics of Abortion in India,* in Power and Decision: The Social Control of Reproduction 267 (Gita Sen & Rachel Snow eds. 1994); Celia Dugger, *Abortion in India is Tipping Scales Sharply against Girls,* N.Y. Times, Apr. 22, 2001, § 1, at 1; John Lancaster, *The Desperate Bachelors: India's Growing Population Imbalance Means Brides Are Becoming Scarce,* Wash. Post, Dec. 2, 2002, at A1; Jo McGovern, *In India, They Abort Females,* Newsweek, Jan. 30, 1989, at 17; Vibbuti Patel, *Sex-Determination and Sex Preselection Tests in India: Modern Techniques for Femicide,* 21 Bull. Concerned Asian Scholars 2 (No. 1, 1989); Viola Roggencamp, *Abortion of a Special Kind: Male Sex Selection in India,* in Test Tube Women: What Future for Motherhood? 267 (Rita Arditti, Renate Klein, & Shelley Minden eds. 1984); David Rohde, *India Steps up Effort to Halt Abortions of Female Fetuses,* N.Y. Times, Oct. 26, 2003, at A17.

322. R. Arora & A. Muthal-Rathore, *Ectopic Pregnancy—Changing Trends,* 96 J. Indian Med. Assoc. no. 2, at 53 (Feb. 1998); Jagdish Bhatia & John Cleland, *Self-Reported Symptoms of Gynecological Morbidity and Their Treatment in South India,* 26 Stud. in Fam. Planning 203 (1995).

323. R.A. Lang et al., *High Prevalence of Gynaecological Diseases in Rural Indian Women,* 333 The Lancet 85 (1989).

324. Ruhul Amin et al., *Menstrual Regulation Training and Service Programs in Bangladesh: Results from a National Survey,* 20 Stud. in Fam. Planning 102 (1989); Ruth Dixon-Mueller, *Innovations in Reproductive Health Care: Menstrual Regulation Policies and Programs in Bangladesh,* 19 Stud. in Fam. Planning 129 (1988); Roger Rochat & Halida Hanum Akhter, *Tetanus and Pregnancy-Related Mortality in Bangladesh* (letter), 354 The Lancet 565 (1999). Some estimates of maternal deaths from abortions range as high as 7,800 annually. Ruth Macklin, *Women's Health: An Ethical Perspective,* 21 J. Law, Med. & Ethics 23, 28 (1993).

325. Augustine Ankomah et al., *Unsafe Abortions: Methods Used and Characteristics of Patients Attending Hospitals in Nairobi, Lima, and Manila,* 18 Health for Women Int'l 43 (1997); Juan Flavier & Charles Chen, *Induced Abortions in Rural Villages of Cavite, the Philippines: Knowledge, Attitudes, and Practice,* 11 Stud. in Fam. Planning 65 (1980); Moria Gallen, *Abortion in the Philippines: A Study of Clients and Practitioners,* 13 Stud. in Fam. Planning 35 (1982).

hibiting abortion rigidly.[326] Traditional Islam opposed abortion,[327] but Turkey legalized abortion during the first twelve weeks of pregnancy in 1983.[328] The law requires the written consent of both spouses and of the parents for an adolescent woman.[329] Despite these restrictions, legal abortion appears to be a common method of birth control in Turkey.[330] Algeria and Israel have also enacted "indications" policies.[331]

In most of Africa and Latin America, there has been little formal change in the law and abortion is still generally prohibited. Abortion is illegal, except to save the mother's life, in francophone Africa, including Benin, Burkino Faso, Central Africa Rep., Chad, Gabon, Guinea, Ivory Coast, Malagasy (Madagascar), Mali, Niger, Senegal, and Togo.[332] The situation in several former British colonies is more permissive, but most are still restrictive with abortion illegal except to save the life of the mother in Gambia, Malawi, Mauritius, Nigeria, and Zambia.[333] Tanzania is one of the few former British African colonies to enact a genuinely permissive abortion statute.[334]

Efforts by feminists in various parts of Latin America generally have failed to achieve even limited reform except in Cuba.[335] In 1989, Chile amended its constitution and its criminal law to

---

326. *Penal Code of Nepal,* Pt. 4, §§ 10, 28–33 (1976). According to one report, 75% of the women who have been imprisoned in Nepal are there because of abortion. Laura Katzive & Katherine Hall Martinez, *Roe v. Wade* in the Global Context: International Recognition of Abortion Rights (published as a "fact sheet" by the Center for Reproductive Law and Policy, N.Y., 1998).

327. Moosa, *supra* note 160, at 268–72; Mohamed Mekki Naciri, *A Survey of Family Planning in Islamic Legislation,* in Muslim Attitudes toward Family Planning 129, 129–45 (Olivia Schiefflin ed. 1973); Sarah Rumage, *Resisting the West: The Clinton Administration's Promotion of Abortion at the 1994 Cairo Conference and the Strength of the Islamic Response,* 27 Cal. W. Int'l L.J. 1, 46–49 (1996); Sherifa Zuhur, *Sexuality,* in Encyclopedia of Islam 35, 36 (John Esposito ed. 1995).

328. *Law No. 2827,* May 24, 1983, translated in 10 Ann. Rev. Pop. L. 29 (1983). *See* Erdem Aydin, *Biomedical Regulations in Turkey,* 25 J. Med. Ethics 404 (1999); Akile Gursoy, *Abortion in Turkey: A Matter of State, Family or Individual Decision,* 42 Soc. Sci. & Med. 531 (1996).

329. *See also* Ergun Ozsunay & Teoman Akunal, *Informed Consent for Medical Interventions under Turkish Law,* 17 Med. Law 429 (1998).

330. Dale Huntington *et al., The Quality of Abortion Services in Turkey,* 53 Int'l J. Gynaecological Obstet. 41 (1996).

331. *Act No. 85-05* (Algeria), translated in 36 Int'l Digest of Health Legis. 909 (1985); Ze'ev Falk, *The New Abortion Law of Israel,* 13 Israel L. Rev. 103 (1978).

332. International Planned Parenthood Federation (Africa Region), Unsafe Abortion and Post-Abortion Family Planning in Africa 13 (1994) ("Unsafe Abortion").

333. Unsafe Abortion, *supra* note 332, at 13; Rebecca Cook & Bernard Dickens, *Abortion Laws in African Commonwealth Countries,* 25 J. African L. 60 (1981); Kommers, *supra* note 144, at 305–13; Mark Lacey, *Despite a Ban, Teaching Safe Abortions in Kenya,* N.Y. Times, Feb. 17, 2002, § 1, at 3; *Reports from the International Women's Rights Action Watch (IWRAW) 1990 Conference,* 1 Colum. J. Gender & L. 143, 150–51 (Zambia) (1991) ("*Reports*"). Nigeria has such provisions in its two separate criminal codes, one for the northern (Moslem) states, and another for the southern (non-Moslem) states. *Criminal Code of Nigeria* § 228 (southern states); *Penal Code of Nigeria* § 232 (northern States).

334. *Act no. 26 of 1972* (Tanzania). *See* Bernard Dickens & Rebecca Cook, *Development of Commonwealth Abortion Laws,* 28 Int'l & Comp. L.Q. 424, 425 (1979). For other recent enactments dealing with abortion that move at least somewhat in a permissive direction, see *Penal Code (Amendment) Act,* 1991 (Botswana); *Criminal Code (Amendment) Law,* 1985, reprinted in 12 Ann. Rev. Pop. L. 34 (1985) (Ghana).

335. Reed Boland, *The Current Status of Abortion Laws in Latin America: Prospects and Strategies for Change,* 21 J. Law, Med. & Ethics 67 (1993); Claudia Lima Marques, *Assisted Reproductive Technology (ART) in South America and the Effect on Adoption,* 35 Tex. Int'l L.J. 65, 69–71 (2000); María Isabel Plata, *Reproductive Rights as Human Rights: The Colombian Case,* in Human Rights of Women 515 (Rebecca Cook ed. 1994); *Reports, supra* note 332, at 149 (Argentina), 149–50 (Mexico), 152–53 (general). *See also* P.E. Bailey *et al., A Hospital Study of Illegal Abortions in Bolivia,* 22 PAHO Bull. 27 (1988); H.P. David & S. Pick De Weiss, *Abortion in the Americas,* in Reproductive Health in the Americas 323 (A.M. Omran *et al.* eds. 1992); S. Pick De Weiss & H.P. David, *Illegal Abortion in Mexico: Client Perceptions,* 80 Am. J. Pub. Health 715 (1990);

prohibit all abortion, apparently even an abortion to save the life of the mother.[336] The former British colonies in the Western Hemisphere are generally as restrictive regarding abortion as are the former French, Portuguese, and Spanish colonies,[337] although several island states—former British colonies—have enacted more permissive statutes.[338] As is usual when abortion is strictly illegal, no one really knows how common illegal abortions really are, although estimates (usually by abortion advocates) range into the millions.[339] Prosecutions do occur, although they occur in much smaller numbers than the estimates of the number of abortions might lead one to expect.[340] Despite the utterly ambiguous nature of the evidence, this leads abortion advocates to assert that there is widespread public toleration of illegal abortion.[341] These same advocates also complain that despite such "toleration," women suffer the usual litany of informal punishments—death or maiming from incompetent practitioners, access dependent on money, and disempowerment.[342]

With so much support worldwide for the opening of access to abortion, particularly in the industrialized nations, it is no surprise that the UN Cairo Conference on Population and Development (1994) and the UN Beijing Fourth World Conference on Women (1995) both approved resolutions asserting that the right to safe and legal abortions is a universal human right.[343] Support for these resolutions, as well as for the liberalization of abortion laws in some less developed countries after President Clinton took office, was bolstered by large flows of aid money from the United States ($595,000,000 government funds in 1994 alone).[344] So central was the issue of abor-

---

S. Singh & G. Sedgh, *The Relationship of Abortion to Trends in Contraception and Fertility in Brazil, Colombia, and Mexico*, 23 INT'L FAM. PLANNING PERSPECTIVES 4, 7–12 (1997).

336. *Act 18.826* of Aug. 24, 1989, *Diario Oficial* no. 33474 (Sept. 15, 1989).

337. *See, e.g.*, Frederick Nunes, *Legal Opinion on Abortion Law Reform in Guyana, A Study of Magistrates, Attorneys, Police, Law Clerks, and Law Students*, 5 CARIBBEAN L. REV. 589 (1995).

338. *Medical Termination of Pregnancy Act of 1983*, reprinted in 10 ANN. REV. POP. L. 63 (1983) (Barbados); *Criminal Code Amendment Act* of Aug. 2, 1983, reprinted in 10 ANN. REV. POP. L. 67 (1983) (Bermuda); *Penal Code Amendment Act* of July 1, 1984, reprinted in 14 ANN. REV. POP. L. 39 (1987) (Montserrat); *Criminal Code Amendment Act of Oct. 6, 1988*, reprinted in 15 ANN. REV. POP. L. 330 (1988) (St. Vincent & the Grenadines).

339. *See, e.g.*, Boland, *supra* note 335, at 67 (estimating 1,800,000 annually across Latin America).

340. *Id.* (reporting 20 prosecutions annually in Costa Rica against an estimated 70,000 illegal abortions annually for that tiny country).

341. *Id.*, at 67–68.

342. *Id.*, at 68.

343. *See Report of the Fourth World Conference on Women*, UN Doc. A/CONF.177/20, ¶ 91 (1995); *Report of the International Conference on Population and Development*, UN Doc. A/CONF.71/13, ¶ 7.3 (1994). *See also* UN POPULATION FUND, THE STATE OF WORLD POPULATION 1997—THE RIGHT TO CHOOSE: REPRODUCTIVE RIGHTS AND REPRODUCTIVE HEALTH (1997). *See generally* RUTH DIXON-MUELLER, POPULATION POLICY AND WOMEN'S RIGHTS: TRANSFORMING REPRODUCTIVE CHOICE (1993); POPULATION POLICIES RECONSIDERED— HEALTH, EMPOWERMENT AND RIGHTS POPULATION POLICIES RECONSIDERED—HEALTH, EMPOWERMENT AND RIGHTS (Gita Sen *et al.* eds. 1994); Diana Babor, *Population Growth and Reproductive Rights in International Human Rights Law*, 14 CONN. J. INT'L L. 83 (1999); Rebecca Cook, *International Human Rights and Women's Reproductive Health*, in WOMEN'S RIGHTS, HUMAN RIGHTS: INTERNATIONAL FEMINIST PERSPECTIVES 256 (Julie Peters & Andrea Wolper eds. 1995); Hernàndez, *supra* note 55; Peter Manus, *The Owl, the Indian, the Feminist, and the Brother: Environmentalism Encounters the Social Justice Movements*, 23 ENVTL. AFF. 249, 288–97 (1996); Aaron Michel, *Abortion and International Law: The Status and Possible Extensions of Women's Right to Privacy*, 20 J. FAM. L. 241 (1981); Mona Zulficar, *From Human Rights to Program Reality: Vienna, Cairo, and Beijing in Perspective*, 44 AM. U. L. REV. 1017 (1995). *See generally* Lori Ashford, *New Perspectives on Population: Lessons from Cairo*, POPULATION BULL., Mar. 1995, at 50; C. Allison McIntosh & Jason Finkle, *The Cairo Conference on Population and Development: A New Paradigm?*, 21 POPULATION & DEV. REV. 223 (1995).

344. John Goshko, *Planned Parenthood Gets AID Grant: Award Ends Long Ban on Funding Abortion-Related Programs Overseas*, WASH. POST, Nov. 23, 1993, at A12; Brad Knickerbocker, *U.S. Assuming Major Role at Cairo Population Talks*, CHRISTIAN SCI. MONITOR, Aug. 31, 1994, at 1. *See generally* Craig Lesher, *U.S. Population Policy since the Cairo Conference*, 4 WW ENVTL. CHANGE & SECURITY PROJECT REP. 16 (Spring 1998); Kim Murphy, *U.S. Population Team Has Changed Jerseys in the Last Decade: At '84 Conference, the Reagan Adminis-*

tion to President Clinton that he stubbornly refused to accept Congressional restrictions on the funding of abortion programs abroad even though every foreign policy expert in his administration had recommended accepting the restrictions in order to get Congressional approval of badly needed payments of overdue United Nations dues. He eventually settled on an arrangement that would release the funds he wanted with a face-saving compromise that would not seriously impede his desire to fund pro-abortion lobbying worldwide.[345] Hilary Clinton, who headed the American delegation to the Beijing Conference, adverted to the need to bolster women's access to abortion no less than four times in her short speech at the opening of the conference.[346]

The Clinton administration also undertook to exclude opposing voices from these conferences. It denigrated any delegation publicly opposed to abortion rights.[347] It stacked the American delegation, excluding anyone who might undermine the official line that population growth is the cause of most of the world's ills.[348] And it arranged for the arrest of some representatives of non-governmental organizations in order to have them expelled from the parallel

---

*tration Said Expanding Numbers Had No Bearing on Development. Now Washington Has Led the Way to Adoption of Strategies for Curbing Population Boom,* L.A. Times, Sept. 14, 1994, at A9; Sean Murphy, *U.S. Funding for the U.N. Population Fund,* 96 Am. J. Int'l L. 962 (2002). One of President Clinton's first actions upon taking office was to revoke the "Mexico City policy" whereby the United States would not provide funds to any agency or organization that performed abortions or advocating easing restrictions on abortion. *Memorandum on the Mexico City Policy,* 1 Pub. Papers 10 (1993). *See generally* Shanti Conly, J. Joseph Speidel, & Sharon Camp, U.S. Population Assistance: Issues for the Shanti Conly, J. Joseph Speidel, & Sharon Camp, U.S. Population Assistance: Issues for the 1990s (1991).

As much as $5,000,000,000 was funneled into these activities by the United Nations Fund for Population Activities in 1994—with a good deal of this money also coming from the United States. Brian Robertson, *Uncle Sam , the Population Control Bully? U.S. Agenda at Cairo Questioned,* Wash. Times, Aug. 26, 1994, at A8. Additional billions were loaned by the World Bank to support these activities—again with much of the money coming from the United States. Andrew Ringel, *The Population Policy Debate and the World Bank: Limits to Growth vs. Supply-Side Demographics,* 6 Geo. Int'l Envt. L. Rev. 213 (1993); Amrit Wilson, *Breeding Difficulties: Population Control Policies,* New Statesman & Soc'y, Sept. 2, 1994, at 20. *See also* Lesher, *supra,* at 17.

Just as U.S. government funds were becoming somewhat scarcer, Ted Turner stepped forward to donate $1,000,000,000, to be paid in 10 annual installments of $100,000,000. Considerable evidence suggests that these funds will be used to promote population control, which again leads into support for abortion and perhaps for coercive measures. Ann Bardach, *Turner in 2000?,* New Yorker, Nov. 23, 1998, at 36, 37; Barbara Crossette, *Turner Picks State Dept. Official to Allocate UN Fund,* Int'l Herald Trib., Nov. 21, 1997, at 4; Mary Ann Glendon, *Foundations of Human Rights: The Unfinished Business,* 44 Am. J. Juris. 1, 11 (1999); Colin Woodward, *Ted Turner Gift Poised to Boost UN,* Christ. Sci. Monitor, Apr. 22, 1998, at 1. The man Turner chose to administer the fund, Timothy Worth, had been so zealous in advocating population control that he even praised China's highly coercive one-child policy as a "very, very effective high-investment [in] family planning." Jeffrey Gedmin, *Clinton's Touchy-Feely Foreign Policy,* Weekly Standard, May 13, 1996, at 19, 22. On the nature of the Chinese investment, see the text *supra* at notes 290–309.

345. *Foreign Operations, Export Financing, & Related Programs Appropriations Act of 2000,* § 599D, H.R. 3422, as contained in the *Consolidated Appropriations Act of 2000,* § 1000(a)(2), Pub. L. No. 106–113, 113 Stat. 1501, 1535 (1999); U.S. Exec. Off. of the Pres., The Impact of Delaying USAID Population Funding from March to July 1997 (1997). *See also* Helen Dewar, *Dispute Imperils U.S. Vote at U.N.,* Wash. Post, Oct. 28, 1999, at A10; Lesher, *supra* note 344, at 21–22; Thomas Lippman, *Drive Seeks to Get U.N. Funding Approved on Hill without Strings,* Wash. Post, June 13, 1999, at A22; Eric Schmitt, *Abortion Discord Holds Up U.N. Dues and U.S. Budget,* N.Y. Times, Nov. 11, 1999, at A18; Katharine Seelye, *Lawmaker Predicts Success in Fight Against Abortion Overseas,* N.Y. Times, Feb. 6, 1997, at A22; Philip Shenon, *Senate Backs U.N. Payment, but More Hurdles Remain,* N.Y. Times, June 23, 1999, at A4; David Stott, *A Deal Is Reached on Family Planning Money,* N.Y. Times, Dec. 1, 1999, at A21.

346. *Remarks by the First Lady,* Sept. 5, 1995, reprinted in 6 For. Pol'y Bull. No. 3, at 39–40 (Nov./Dec. 1995).

347. Rumage, *supra* note 328, at 87.

348. Julian Simon, *The Population Distraction,* N.Y. Times, Aug. 21, 1994, at D15 (complaining that "mainstream population economists" were precluded from attending the Cairo conference). *See also* Julian

"NGO" meeting to which the delegates had credentials.[349] This pattern helped to convince some "Third World" women to describe these resolutions as the foisting of the concerns of "First World" women onto an unwilling and silenced "Third World" — a program that smacks of old-style colonialism and simply does not speak to the concerns "Third World" feminists.[350] In part because of this reaction, the pressure from "First World" feminists to make "reproductive rights" the defining issue of women's rights worldwide has, in some countries, contributed to activating resistance to abortion reform or pressure to repeal reform once achieved.[351]

As this brief survey of world trends indicates, there have been dramatic changes in abortion laws in many parts of the world. Even so, the efforts to repeal or reform abortion laws in some nations failed utterly, including countries in which there has been a rollback in abortion rights after they were initially achieved. According to one estimate, even now more than 20 million of the claimed 38 million abortions annually worldwide are illegal.[352] Such estimates are, of course, no more likely to be accurate than were the spurious estimates of the number of illegal abortions performed annually in the United Kingdom or the United States at various times in the twentieth century.[353] Still, approximately 25 percent of the world's population lives in countries were abortion is illegal except to save the woman's life, another 22 percent live in countries with somewhat broader medical indications, with 53 percent living in countries where abortion is generally available although even in these countries the actual language of the controlling statute is likely to appear more restrictive.[354] The worldwide legislative trend corresponds to a worldwide trend for abortions to become dramatically more common, suggesting, once again, that something in the nature of abortion has changed significantly during the twentieh century.[355] That something is the safety of the procedure for the mother.

Before turning to the roots of the growing resistance to abortion reform, it is instructive to compare the foreign experience of abortion reform with the route imposed on the United States by the Supreme Court in *Roe* and *Doe*. The Supreme Court's haste to decide these

---

SIMON, POPULATION MATTERS: PEOPLE, RESOURCES, ENVIRONMENT AND IMMIGRATION (1990); JULIAN SIMON, THE ULTIMATE RESOURCE (1981).

349. John Walter, *Pro-Life Writers Cite Harassment at Conference*, WASH. TIMES, Sept. 10, 1994, at A1. The move was thwarted by the intervention of other officials attending the conference. John Waller, *Congressman, Ambassador Help Win Release of Pro-Lifers*, WASH. TIMES, Sept. 11, 1994, at A9. *See also* Rumage, *supra* note 328, at 86.

350. Azizah al-Hibri, *Who Defines Women's Rights? A Third World Woman's Response*, 2 AM. UNIV. HUM. RTS. BRIEF 9 (1994); Hilary Charlesworth, Christine Chinkin, & Shelley Wright, *Feminist Approaches to International Law*, 85 AM. J. INT'L L. 613, 645 n.40 (1991); Marguerite Holloway, *Population Summit: Women's Health and Rights Shape Cairo Document*, SCI. AM., June 1994, at 14–15; E. Michael Jones, *Bela Does Cairo: The Great Satan Swings and Misses at the Cairo Conference on Population and Development*, 2 LIBERTY LIFE & FAM. 1 (1995); Judith Richter & Loes Keysers, *Towards a Common Agenda? Feminists and Population Agencies on the Road to Cairo*, 1 DEVELOPMENT 50 (1994); Rumage, *supra* note 328.

351. Al-Hibri, *supra* note 350, at 9. *See also* Rumage, *supra* note 328, at 70–89.

352. Adrienne Germain, *The Christopher Tietze International Symposium: An Overview*, 1989 INT'L J. GYNECOLOGY & OBSTET., Supp. 3, 4 (1989). *See also* Note, *International Child Health and Women's Reproductive Rights*, 14 N.Y.L.S. J. INT'L & COMP. L. 143, 162–63 (1993). John Kenyon Mason estimates that there are between 40 and 60 million abortions worldwide annually. MASON, *supra* note 78, at 143. *See also Medical News: Global Perspectives on Abortion*, 294 BRIT. MED. J. 1102 (1987).

353. *See* Chapter 12, at notes 129–58.

354. Henshaw, *supra* note 81, at 76; Note, *supra* note 352, at 171–73

355. CALLAHAN, *supra* note 144, at 285; GRISEZ, *supra* note 144, at 42–48; JUDGES, *supra* note 31, at 31–32; PREVENTING MATERNAL DEATHS 107 (Erica Royston & Sue Armstrong eds. 1989); Henshaw, *supra* note 81.

cases—epitomized by its rush to decide the companion *Doe* case without even awaiting a decision by the Fifth Circuit Court of Appeals—imposed a more extreme approach to abortion on the United States than is found in almost any other nation.[356] A number of commentators—including especially supporters of abortion rights—have concluded that the political difficulties encountered by the *Roe* decision were a result of the haste and extremity of the decision.[357] Even the then recently enacted New York abortion law, a law that created abortion on demand until the 24th week of gestation and made New York the "abortion capital" of the country, was too protective of the foetus for Justice Blackmun and his colleagues.[358]

Chief Justice Rehnquist suggested in the *Webster* case (decided 16 years after *Roe*) that the Court in *Roe* had gone wrong in attempting to elaborate a broad, abstract rule rather than responding to the precise facts before the Court.[359] Rehnquist did indeed eschew any attempt to go beyond the precise facts of the case before the Court, to the chagrin of those who had hoped for a complete overruling of *Roe* by the decision in *Webster*. Only Judge (now Justice) Ruth Bader Ginsberg, however, has commented on the even greater haste and extremity evidenced by the *Doe* decision.[360]

In contrast, the more moderate legislative solutions in Europe and elsewhere outside the United States generally did not provoke the intractable controversy that resulted from the decision in *Roe*.[361] The English *Abortion Act of 1967* is a good example. Parliament there enacted an "indications" policy that would be unconstitutional if England were a part of the United States.[362] Even when constitutional courts in several countries intervened to declare overly permissive or overly restrictive laws void,[363] they always left considerable discretion to the legislature to prescribe the precise conditions and procedures necessary to obtain an abortion. Even the Soviet Union and other "East Bloc" coun-

---

356. *See generally* GLENDON, *supra* note 229, at 13–15, & Table, 145–54; MASON, *supra* note 78, at 119–21; Michael Freeman, *Abortion—What Do Other Countries Do?*, 138 NEW L.J. 233 (1988); Gallard, *supra* note 258, at 106–11 (describing the "obstacle race of procedures" to be cleared in order to obtain an abortion); Bonnie Hertberg, Note, *Resolving the Abortion Debate: Compromise Legislation, an Analysis of the Abortion Policies of the United States, France, and Germany,* 16 SUFF. TRANSNAT'L L. REV. 513, 514–16 (1993).

357. ROBERT BURT, THE CONSTITUTION IN CONFLICT 358–62 (1992); RUTH COLKER, ABORTION & DIALOGUE—PRO-CHOICE, PRO-LIFE, AND AMERICAN LAW 101–02, 114–25 (1992); MENSCH & FREEMAN, *supra* note 78, at 126–28; LAURENCE TRIBE, AMERICAN CONSTITUTIONAL LAW 1359 (2nd ed. 1988) ("TRIBE, CONSTITUTIONAL LAW"); LAURENCE TRIBE, GOD SAVE THIS HONORABLE COURT 16 (1985) ("TRIBE, HONORABLE COURT"); LAURENCE TRIBE & MICHAEL DORF, ON READING THE CONSTITUTION 63 (1991); JAMES BOYD WHITE, ACTS OF HOPE: CREATING AUTHORITY IN LITERATURE, LAW, AND POLITICS 162 (1994); Vincent Blasi, *The Rootless Activism of the Burger Court,* in THE BURGER COURT: THE COUNTER REVOLUTION THAT WASN'T 198, 212 (Vincent Blasi ed. 1983); Conkle, *supra* note 154, at 308–18; Ruth Bader Ginsburg, *On Muteness, Confidence, and Collegiality: A Response to Professor Nagel,* 61 U. COLO. L. REV. 715, 718–19 (1990); Ruth Bader Ginsburg, *Speaking in a Judicial Voice,* 67 NYU L. REV. 1185, 1198–09, 1205–09 (1992) ("Ginsburg, *Judicial Voice*"); Shapiro, *supra* note 75, at 16–18.

358. Dennis Horan & Thomas Balch, Roe v. Wade*: No Justification in History, Law, or Logic,* in ABORTION AND THE CONSTITUTION: REVERSING *ROE V. WADE* THROUGH THE COURTS 57, 58 (Dennis Horan, Edward Grant, & Paige Cunningham eds. 1987).

359. Webster v. Reproductive Health Services, 492 U.S. 490, 518–21 (1989) (Rehnquist, C.J., with Kennedy & White, JJ., plurality op.).

360. Ginsburg, *Judicial Voice, supra* note 357, at 1199 n.83.

361. GLENDON, *supra* note 229, at 40–43; Ross, *supra* note 170, at 200–01; Gordon Van Kessel, *Adversary Excesses in the American Criminal Trial,* 67 NOTRE DAME L. REV. 403, 474 (1992). *But see* Funk, *supra* note 224, at 54–57.

362. *See* Chapter 13, at notes 58–65; P.T. O'Neill & Isobel Watson, *The Father and the Unborn Child,* 38 MOD. L.R. 174, 178 (1975); Andrew Grubb, *Abortion Law—An English Perspective,* 20 N. MEX. L. REV. 649 (1990); Madeleine Simms, *Britain,* in ABORTION IN THE NEW EUROPE, *supra* note 143, at 31, 36–38.

363. See the text *supra* at notes 185–213, 267–76.

tries in Europe imposed greater restrictions on abortion than were possible under *Roe*.[364] The relative easy acceptance of abortion reform in many countries was in part because the statutes often were enacted in an effort to contain the number of abortions already being performed, usually illegally. While the restrictive tenor of the English statute, for example, served to insulate it from the more extreme criticisms provoked in the United States by *Roe*,[365] the English statute, like most foreign statutes, actually had the opposite effect of increasing the total number of abortions.[366]

In light of the foreign experience, one inevitably confronts the question of whether *Roe* and *Doe* were correctly decided. This is not a question about their merits as legal documents. Merit is beside the point for decisions grounded on an historical argument when the history is entirely wrong.[367] Almost no one defends the two cases on legal grounds; even the defenders of the outcome of the decisions almost invariably begin by apologizing for the opinion and then go on to attempt to rewrite the opinion in *Roe* in what the "defender" considers more legally defensible grounds.[368] Rather, the question is whether the cases were decidedly rightly as a political move in the effort to overturn restrictive abortion laws.

If, as supporters of abortion rights would have it, a strong popular majority supported reform or repeal of the abortion laws then and now,[369] the foreign experience suggests that the turn to the courts was a mistake. Legislative solutions seem more stable and less controversial than judicial fiat. If this view is correct, the turn to the courts backfired, for it motivated a massive outpouring of grassroots opposition to abortion reform or repeal, an opposition that has seriously undermined the judiciary and poisoned the political climate for more the three decades since *Roe* and *Doe* were decided.[370]

There are good grounds, however, for thinking that popular majorities, at least in 1972, were not ready to repeal abortion laws, and not much more supportive of even limited reform.[371] Constitutional law guru Laurence Tribe concluded that legislative change in abortion laws would have been rejected in most states of the United States and that *Roe* therefore was essential to bringing about the change here that was occurring legislatively in most of the industrialized world.[372] Tribe's conclusion presupposes that abortion was important enough to be worth the difficulties for the judiciary and the disrespect for the legal order that resulted from the decisions in *Roe* and *Doe*. This point is one that Tribe, supposedly our foremost thinker on matters constitutional, seems never to have written about despite considerable attention he has given to abortion in articles and books.[373] But then, perhaps lawyer Mark Graber is right is suggesting that it

---

364. GLENDON, *supra* note 229, at 23–24; HADLEY, *supra* note 65, at 143–46; Andrej Popov, *The USSR,* in ABORTION IN THE NEW EUROPE, *supra* note 143, at 267, 271–74. *See also* Mary Ann Glendon, *U.S. Abortion Law: Still the Most Permissive on Earth,* WALL ST. J., July 1, 1992, at A15, col. 1.

365. *See, e.g.,* William Schmidt, *U.S. Abortion Protesters Shunned by the British,* N.Y. TIMES, April 13, 1993, at A-2, col. 1, 2.

366. MASON, *supra* note 78, at 124–25; Simms, *supra* note 363, at 31, 37–38. *See* Chapter 13, at notes 63–75.

367. See Chapter 14, at notes 435–57.

368. *Id.* at notes 425–34.

369. *Cf.* Judith Daar, *Direct Democracy and Bioethical Choices: Voting Life and Death at the Ballot Box,* 28 U. MICH. J.L. REFORM 799 (1995).

370. *See* Chapter 16.

371. See Chapter 14, at notes 23–38.

372. TRIBE, *supra* note 29, at 35–51.

373. *Id.*; TRIBE, CONSTITUTIONAL LAW, *supra* note 357, at 1352–59, 1613; LAURENCE TRIBE, CONSTITUTIONAL CHOICES 238–45 (1985); TRIBE, HONORABLE COURT, *supra* note 357, at 116–20; TRIBE & DORF, *supra* note 357; Laurence Tribe, *The Abortion Conundrum: Inalienable Rights, Affirmative Duties, and Dilemma of Dependence,* 99 HARV. L. REV. 330 (1985); Laurence Tribe, *The Abortion Funding Conundrum: Inalienable Rights, Affirmative Duties, and the Dilemma of Dependence,* 99 HARV. L. REV. 330 (1985); Laurence Tribe, *A Constitution We are Amending: In Defense of a Restrained Judicial Role,* 97 HARV. L. REV. 433 (1983); Laurence

really did not make much difference whether abortion was legalized by judges or legislators: "Members of Operation Rescue do not and will not distinguish abortion clinics that remain open by judicial decree from abortion clinics sanctioned by local legislation."[374] But we are getting ahead of ourselves. We will return to Operation Rescue in the next Chapter.[375]

# The Emergence of the Fetus

*I go on in the dark, lit from within; does day exist?*
*Is this my grave? or the womb of my mother?*

— Miguel Hernàndez[376]

We have already noted how the steadily changing technologies for doing abortions impacted on the political processes that determined the law applicable to abortion.[377] Simultaneously, the perceived interests of society in unborn children changed as new medical information and technologies emerged that focused on human reproduction. This transformation began early in the nineteenth century with the growing realization that a fundamental genetic transformation occurred at conception.[378] Just as with our understanding of how to do an abortion, developments in our understanding of, and ability to manipulate, the gestation process also did not cease early in the nineteenth century. Today we can trace the development from the fertilization of the ovum to the moment of birth in remarkable detail — detail that allows us to describe the emergence of nearly all the characteristics that most of us would characterize as human.[379]

We now know that from the start a conceptus drives the gestation process through its own evolution and differentiation into embryo, amniotic and chorionic sacs, umbilicus, and placenta, causing its own implantation and inducing the maternal hormonal changes necessary for a successful pregnancy (and for lactation after birth).[380] For many years, we have also known that limited fetal brain waves can be detected at about eight weeks after fertilization.[381] At this point,

---

Tribe, *Foreword: Toward a Model of Roles in the Due Process of Life and Law,* 87 HARV. L. REV. 1 (1973); Laurence Tribe, *The Curvature of Constitutional Space: What Lawyers Can Learn from Modern Physics,* 103 HARV. L. REV. 1, 38–39 (1989); Laurence Tribe, *Childhood, Suspect Classifications, and Conclusive Presumptions: Three Linked Riddles,* 39 L. & CONTEMP. PROB. 8 (Summer 1975); Laurence Tribe, *Structural Due Process,* 10 HARV. CIV. RTS.-CIV. LIB. L. REV. 269, 317–21 (1975).

374. GRABER, *supra* note 5, at 126.

375. *See* Chapter 16, at notes 218–79.

376. As quoted in John Bayley, *Night Mail,* N.Y. REV. BOOKS, June 24, 1993, at 20.

377. *See* Chapter 5, at 18–32; Chapter 6, at notes 332–413; Chapter 7, at notes 114–60; Chapter 12, at notes 84–164; Chapter 14, at notes 199–267.

378. *See* Chapter 5, at notes 206–74.

379. *See, e.g.,* HAROLD MOROWITZ & JAMES TREFIL, THE FACTS OF LIFE : SCIENCE AND THE ABORTION CONTROVERSY (1992); William Sly, *When Does Human Life Begin? Does Science Provide the Answer?,* in ABORTION AND PUBLIC POLICY: AN INTERDISCIPLINARY INVESTIGATION WITHIN THE CATHOLIC TRADITION 62 (R. Randall Rainey & Gerard Magill eds. 1996).

380. WILLIAMS OBSTETRICS, *supra* note 40, at 16–22. *See also* HRDY, *supra* note 300, at 388–92, 419–26, 431–38, 480–81; Robert Bridges, *The Genetics of Motherhood,* 20 NATURE GENETICS 108 (1998); David Haig, *Altercations of Generations: Genetic Conflicts of Pregnancy,* 35 AM. J. REPRODUCTIVE IMMUNOLOGY 226 (1996); David Haig, *Genetic Conflicts of Human Pregnancy,* 68 Q. REV. BIOLOGY 495 (1993); David Haig, *Prenatal Powerplays,* 104 NAT. HISTORY 39 (1995).

381. John Goldenring, *The Brain-Life Theory: Towards a Consistent Biological Definition of Humanness,* 11 J. MED. ETHICS 198, 200 (1985); Hannibal Hamlin, *Life or Death by EEG,* 190 JAMA, Oct. 12, 1964, at 112; Robert Sokol & Mortimer Rosen, *The Fetal Electroencephalogram,* 1 CLINICS OBSTET. & GYNAECOLOGY 123

all fetal organs, at least in rudimentary form and including the basics of the central nervous and circulatory systems, are in place[382] and physicians change their term for the unborn child from "embryo" to "fetus."[383] At eight weeks of gestation, then, the fetus clearly looks like a higher primate and could not be mistaken for the fetus of any other animal except an ape.[384]

Early fetal brain waves are characteristically human, although they do gradually mature and achieve a pattern fairly similar to an adult human only at about 30 weeks of gestation.[385] Some still insist that the immaturity of early fetal brain waves prevents classification of the fetus as a "person" until after the seventh month of gestation.[386] This ignores a good deal of what we know about fetal brain development. The neocortex of a human fetus first appears at about eight weeks, and the basic brain elements assume their final appearance (except for size) by the end of the first trimester of gestation (13 weeks).[387] The brain's size changes as neurons are added; the neurons usually are fully in place by 20 weeks.[388]

The neuromotor area of the fetal brain has developed enough to have full operational control over the arms and legs during the fourth month of pregnancy, control manifested in the regular and irregular fetal movements that are eventually perceived by the mother as "quickening."[389] Furthermore, experimentation during abortions has shown that fetal brains react to morphine, scopolamine, and tiopental in patterns characteristic of functioning brains as early as 10 weeks of gestation.[390] These reactions alone are enough to indicate that the fetal brain at this stage al-

---

(1974). *See also* LLOYD STEFFEN, LIFE/CHOICE: THE THEORY OF JUST ABORTION 107 (1994); Joel Cornwell, *The Concept of Brain Life: Shifting the Abortion Standard without Imposing Religious Values,* 25 DUQ. L. REV. 471, 476 (1987); Joseph Dellapenna, *Nor Piety Nor Wit: The Supreme Court on Abortion,* 6 COLUM. H. RTS. L. REV. 379, 401–09 (1974). Some claim that we are able to identify fetal brain waves a week earlier. *See* JUDITH BOSS, THE BIRTH LOTTERY: PRENATAL DIAGNOSIS AND SELECTIVE ABORTION 123–24 (1993); Baruch Brody, *The Morality of Abortion,* in CONTEMPORARY ISSUES IN BIOETHICS 240, 245 (Tom Beauchamp & LeRoy Walters eds. 1982).

382. Boss, *supra* note 381, at 113–14; KEITH MOORE, BEFORE WE ARE BORN: BASIC EMBRYOLOGY AND BIRTH DEFECTS 2–4 (1983); JAMES BLAKE THOMAS, INTRODUCTION TO HUMAN BIOLOGY 215–17 (1968); WILLIAMS OBSTETRICS, *supra* note 40, at 151–54; Roy Filly, *Sonographic Anatomy of the Normal Fetus,* in THE UNBORN PATIENT: PARENTAL DIAGNOSIS AND TREATMENT 92 (Mitchell Goldbus, Michael Harrison, & Roy Filly eds., 2nd ed. 1991); Donald Hope, *The Hand as Emblem of Human Identity: A Solution to the Abortion Controversy Based on Science and Reason,* 32 U. TOL. L. REV. 205 (2001). A fetus at six to eight weeks has "a full adult complement of about a half million dopamine-producing cells." Sandra Blakeslee, *In Careful Test, Parkinson's Patient Shows Gains after Fetal-Cell Implant: But Doctors Are Cautious Six Months after Surgery,* N.Y. TIMES, May 2, 1989, at C3.

383. THOMAS, *supra* note 382, at 213.

384. *See, e.g.,* MARJORIE ENGLAND, COLOR ATLAS OF LIFE BEFORE BIRTH 13, 18 (1983); GERALDINE LUX FLANAGAN, THE FIRST NINE MONTHS OF LIFE 16–17, 42–45 (1962).

385. Michael Flower, *Coming into Being: The Prenatal Development of Humans* ("Flower, *Coming into Being*"), in ABORTION, MEDICINE, AND THE LAW, *supra* note 29, at 437, 442–45; Michael Flower, *Neuromaturation and the Moral Status of Human Fetal Life,* in ABORTION RIGHTS AND FETAL PERSONHOOD 71, 79 (Edd Doerr & James Prescott eds. 1989); Gary Gertler, Note, *Brain Birth: A Proposal for Defining When a Fetus Is Entitled to Human Life Status,* 59 S. CAL. L. REV. 1061 (1986); D. Gareth Jones, *Brain Birth and Personal Identity,* 15 J. MED. ETHICS 173 (1989); Vinceguerra, *supra* note 22, at 1180–81.

386. DWORKIN, *supra* note 75, at 15–17; ROBERTSON, *supra* note 65, at 51–53. *See generally* R. Alta Charo, *Biological Determinism in Legal Decision Making: The Parent Trap,* 3 TEX. J. WOMEN & LAW 265, 278 (1994).

387. STEFFEN, *supra* note 381, at 107; THE UNBORN PATIENT, *supra* note 382, at 92–130.

388. Miguel Marin-Padilla, *Structural Organization of the Human Cerebral Cortex prior to the Appearance of the Cortical Plate,* 166 ANATOMICAL EMBRYOLOGY 21, 21 (1983).

389. Raymond Gasser, *The Beginning of Individual Human Life from a Biological Perspective,* in HUMAN LIFE AND HEALTH CARE ETHICS 3, 17–18 (James Bopp, jr., ed. 1985).

390. Nils Petter Jorgenson & Karel Marshall, *Influence of Tiopental Anesthesia on Fetal Motor Behavior in Early Pregnancy,* 17 EARLY HUM. DEV. 71 (1988).

ready has drug receptors and synaptic transmitters capable of reacting to stimuli and of transmitting those reactions throughout the central nervous system.

"Quickening" occurs with any fetal movement recognized as such by the mother.[391] The timing of this event varies with the vigor of the fetus and the experience of the mother, for more experienced mothers will recognized "butterflies" in her belly as fetal movement while a less experienced woman often will not.[392] Attorney Philip Rafferty's research has shown that the phrase "quick with child" always meant simply that the women bore a living child whenever life might be said to have begun.[393] In older times, "quickening" was often, although not always, considered to signal that a fetus had become a living human person.[394] Quickening actually is the culmination of a process of neuromuscular development that began at least two months earlier. And at least 45 years ago, doctors observed neuromuscular responses in the fetus to the light touch of a human hair to the fetus's face—to being tickled—as early as the second month of gestation.[395]

The neuromotor development of such a young fetus goes beyond mere reflex reaction. We now know that a fetus makes controlled, rhythmic movements well before viability and that the fetus will move to avoid pain—including an abortionist's scalpel or an vacuum aspirator—at least as early as the third month of pregnancy.[396] Indeed, we can compare the "fluent, coordinated patterns seen in the normal fetus" with the poorly developed movements of the anencephalic fetus (fetus without a developed brain) of the same gestational age.[397] The same motor region of the cortex controls movements of the fetal eyes, and rapid eye movements, characteristic of dreaming, have been observed as early as the seventeenth week of pregnancy—the very end of the fourth month.[398] A fetus "will bend [its] fingers round an object in the palm of his hand" by the ninth week of gestation.[399] Physicians have even observed unborn children of as few as nine weeks gestation covering their eyes to shield them from the bright lights to which they are exposed during surgery and covering their ears to avoid loud noises in the operating room.[400]

---

391. BLACK'S LAW DICTIONARY 1261 (5th rev. ed. 1979); DAVID BUSS, THE EVOLUTION OF DESIRE: STRATEGIES OF HUMAN MATING 119 (1994).

392. HELEN MARGARET IRWIN LILEY, MODERN MOTHERHOOD 37–38 (rev. ed. 1969).

393. 1 PHILIP RAFFERTY, *ROE V. WADE:* THE BIRTH OF A CONSTITUTIONAL RIGHT 64–76, 116–19, 163–178 (1992; University Microfilms International Dissertation Information Service, Ann Arbor, MI).

394. *See* Chapter 3, at notes 57–59, 96–109; Chapter 5, at notes 207–53.

395. STEFFEN, *supra* note 381, at 107; Typhena Humphrey, *The Relation between Fetal Mouth Opening Reflexes and Closure of the Palate,* 125 AM. J. ANATOMY 317 (1969).

396. THOMAS, *supra* note 381, at 174–76; WILLIAMS' OBSTETRICS, *supra* note 379, at 103; K.J.S. Anand & P.R. Hickey, *Pain and Its Effect in the Human Neonate and Fetus,* 317 NEW ENG. J. MED. 1321 (1987); Michael Flower, *Neuromaturation of the Human Fetus,* 10 J. MED. & PHIL. 237, 239, 245 (1988); H.B. Valman & J.F. Pearson, *What the Fetus Feels,* 1980 BRIT. MED. J. 233 (1980).

397. Boss, *supra* note 381, at 114–15; Johanna de Vries, Gerard Visser, & Heinz Prechtl, *Fetal Motility in the First Half of Pregnancy,* in CONTINUITY OF NEURAL FUNCTIONS FROM PRENATAL TO POSTNATAL LIFE 46, 61–63 (Dr. Heinz Prechtl ed. 1984) ("CONTINUITY OF NEURAL FUNCTIONS"). *See generally* FETAL BEHAVIOR: DEVELOPMENTAL AND PERINATAL ASPECTS (Jan Nijhuis ed. 1992); Johanna de Vries *et al., The Emergence of Fetal Behavior: I. Qualitative Aspects,* 7 EARLY HUM. DEV. 301 (1982); Flower, *supra* note 396, at 239, 245; Nobuo Okado & Tobuzo Kojima, *Ontogeny of the Central Nervous System, Neurogenesis, Fibre Connection, Synaptogenesis and Myelination in the Spinal Cord,* in CONTINUITY OF NEURAL FUNCTIONS, *supra,* at 31, 42.

398. Jason Birnholz, *The Development of Fetal Eye Movement,* 213 SCI. 679 (1981). *See also* CARL SAGAN, THE DRAGONS OF EDEN 156 (1977).

399. Valman & Pearson, *supra* note 396, at 234. *See also* STANISLAV REINIS & JERMEM GOLDMAN, THE DEVELOPMENT OF THE BRAIN 232 (1980); Charles Baron, *If You Prick Us, Do We Not Bleed? Of Shylock, Fetuses, and the Concept of Person in the Law,* 11 LAW, MED. & HEALTH CARE 52 (1982).

400. THOMAS VERNEY & JOHN KELLY, THE SECRET LIFE OF THE UNBORN CHILD 36–42 (1981); A. William Liley, *The Fetus as a Personality,* 1 FETAL THERAPY 8 (1986), *reprinted from* 6 AUSTRAL. & N.Z. J. PSYCH. 99 (1972).

We cannot verify absolutely that a fetus experiences "pain," if only because we cannot ask a fetus "where it hurts." Still, the growing body of evidence is strongly suggestive.[401] Because of fetal reactions, physicians anesthetize fetuses before performing surgery on them.[402] On the other hand, we should not be surprised that physicians generally have come to recognize that newborns experience pain only within the past decade.[403] After all, we are just beginning to understand a little about how an adult human experiences pain.[404] In the face of this evidence, it remains a standard tactic for those who support abortion rights to deny that a fetus can feel pain until shortly before birth or even later.[405]

The fetal brain is physiologically immature, but so are all human brains until puberty. Brain waves forming patterns similar to adult humans do not emerge until fairly late in a pregnancy, at about 25–30 weeks gestation.[406] That does not prevent the fetal brain from functioning at an appropriate level any more than a brain's continuing physiological immaturity prevents a preadolescent from functioning at an appropriate level. Monoclonal antibody techniques for studying the chemical and even the molecular brain reactions have confirmed the results of histological and functional observations.[407] At some still undetermined point, a fetus begins to learn in the womb—as shown by a newborn's ability to recognize its mother's voice upon birth.[408] This is not exactly a new idea. Three psychologists argued as long ago as 1963 that we should count children at birth as a year old because of the importance of their experiences before birth; no doubt, they failed to recognize the importance that justifying abortion would later assume for their profession.[409] Another recent study, by a psychoanalyst, has concluded that the "behavioral states" of neonates exhibit continuity with the similar states not only forward into childhood but also backwards through the fetal stage.[410]

---

401. VERNEY & KELLY, *supra* note 400, at 54–72; M. Fitzgerald & N. McIntosh, *Pain and Analgesia in the Newborn*, 64 ARCH. DISEASE IN CHILDHOOD 441 (1989); Anne Fletcher, *Pain in the Neonate*, 317 NEW ENG. J. MED. 1347 (1987); Zosia Kmietowicz, *Antiabortionists Hijack Fetal Pain Argument*, 313 BRIT. MED. J. 188 (1996); S. Leonard, *Feotuses "Feel Pain," as Young as Six Weeks*, SCOTLAND ON SUNDAY, Oct. 3, 1996, at 3; John Scanlon, *Appreciating Neonatal Pain*, 38 ADV. PEDIATRICS 317 (1991); *The 25th Anniversary of* Roe v. Wade: *Has It Stood the Test of Time, Hearings before the Subcomm. On the Const., Federalism, & Property Rts. of the Sen. Comm. on the Judiciary,* 100th Cong. 27–35 ("*Roe Hearings*") (statement of Jean Wright) ("Wright Statement").

402. THE UNBORN PATIENT, *supra* note 382, at 172–81; A.H. Levine, *Fetal Surgery*, 54 ACORN J. 17, 27, 30 (1991). Curiously, physicians usually do not anesthetize new borns while undergoing painful procedures in neonatal intensive care. *Easing the Pain of Tiniest Babies,* N.Y. TIMES, Nov. 18, 2003, at F6.

403. *See* Boss, *supra* note 381, at 116–17; Wright Statement, *supra* note 401.

404. P.D. Wall, *The Biological Function and Dysfunction of Different Pain Mechanisms,* in ADVANCES IN PAIN RESEARCH AND THERAPY 19 (Dr. Frederigo Sicuteri ed. 1992).

405. *See, e.g.,* CONDIT, *supra* note 16, at 213; DWORKIN, *supra* note 75, at 16–17, 41–42; CLIFFORD GROBSTEIN, SCIENCE AND THE UNBORN: CHOOSING HUMAN FUTURES 55, 130 (1988); HADLEY, *supra* note 65, at 64, 67. *See also* H. TRISTAM ENGELHARDT, THE FOUNDATIONS OF BIOETHICS 218 (1986) (conceding that a fetus experiences pain, but insisting that a fetus cannot experience "suffering"); Nancy Rhoden, *The New Neonatal Dilemma: Live Births from Late Abortions,* 72 GEO. L.J. 1451, 1493 n.322 (1984).

406. GROBSTEIN, *supra* note 405, at 129–30; Flower, *supra* note 396, at 246.

407. Gerald Fischbach, *An Introduction to Molecular Approaches in Studies of Neuronal Development and Synapse Formation,* in MOLECULAR NEUROBIOLOGY IN NEUROLOGY AND PSYCHIATRY 143 (Eric Kandel ed. 1987); D.T. Yew et al., *Development and Localization of Enkephalin and Substance P in the Nucleus of the Tractus Solitarius in the Medulla Oblongata of Human Fetuses,* 34 NEUROSCIENCE 491 (1990).

408. A.J. De Casper & W.P Fifer, *Of Human Bonding: Newborns Prefer Their Mother's Voices,* 208 SCI. 1174 (1980); A.J. De Casper & P.A. Prescott, *Human Newborns' Perceptions of Male Voices: Preference, Discrimination and Reinforcing Value,* 17 DEVELOPMENTAL PSYCH. 481 (1984); Gina Kolata, *Studying Learning in the Womb,* 225 SCI. 302 (1984); John O'Neil, *Enduring Memories, in the Womb,* N.Y. TIMES, Oct. 10, 2000, at F8.

409. PAUL HENRY MUSSEN, JOHN JANEWAY CONGAR, & JEROME KAGAN, CHILD DEVELOPMENT AND PERSONALITY 29, 57 (2nd ed. 1963).

410. ALESSANDRA PIONTELLI, FROM FETUS TO CHILD: AN OBSERVATIONAL AND PSYCHOANALYTIC STUDY (1992).

Supporters of abortion rights have seized upon the lack of dendritic spines in the fetal brain before 28 weeks of gestation as "proof" than a fetus cannot think or even feel pain.[411] Actually limited synaptogenesis begins at least as early as 19 weeks of gestation.[412] Early fetal brains also exhibit "transitory sensory neurons" that disappear at later stages of development.[413] And the fact that a fetus experiences rapid eye movement—apparently is dreaming[414]—seems definitely to belie any claim that fetal brains are incapable of "thinking" before 28 weeks of gestation. What a fetus thinks about, of course, remains as unknown as what a newborn thinks about.

In recent years, our ability to interact directly with a fetus has also advanced dramatically. Physicians now can diagnose and treat an unborn child as a being independent of the mother.[415]

---

411. *See, e.g.,* GARROW, *supra* note 5, at 681; KARST, *supra* note 101, at 55; SAGAN, *supra* note 398, at 209; Flower, *Coming into Being, supra* note 385, at 77. *See also* MASON, *supra* note 78, at 200.

412. Mark Molliver *et al., The Development of Synapses in Cerebral Cortex of the Human Fetus,* 50 BRAIN RES. 403 (1973).

413. Okado & Kojima, *supra* note 397, at 40.

414. Birnholz, *supra* note 398; Levi, *supra* note 398.

415. *In re Attorney-General's Reference No. 3 of 1994,* [1998] A.C. 245, 267 (H.L.) (per Hope, L.J.); BLANK & MERRICK, *supra* note 35, at 140–44; Boss, *supra* note 381, at 71–76; LINDA BECK FENWICK, PRIVATE CHOICES, PUBLIC CONSEQUENCES: REPRODUCTIVE TECHNOLOGY AND THE NEW ETHICS OF CONCEPTION, PREGNANCY, AND FAMILY 54–71 (1998); GENETIC DISORDERS AND THE FETUS: DIAGNOSIS, PREVENTION AND TREATMENT (Aubrey Milunsky ed., 4th ed. 1998); MASON, *supra* note 78, at 152; OBSTETRICS AND GYNECOLOGY 5 (David Danforth *et al.* eds., 5th ed. 1986); OBSTETRICS AND GYNECOLOGY CLINICS OF NORTH AMERICA: PRENATAL DIAGNOSIS (Karen Blakemore ed. 1993); PETER VOLPE, THE PATIENT IN THE WOMB (1984); THE UNBORN PATIENT, *supra* note 382; THE UNBORN PATIENT: THE ART AND SCIENCE OF FETAL DEVELOPMENT (Michael Harrison ed. 2001); WILLIAM'S OBSTETRICS, *supra* note 380, at vii, 277; *Baby with Rare Disease Is Treated, Cured in Womb,* PHILA. INQUIRER, May 15, 1981, at 5A; Sandra Blakeslee, *Fetus Returned to Womb Following Surgery,* N.Y. TIMES, Oct. 7, 1986, at C1; *Bone Marrow Transplant in Fetus Staves off Immune Disease,* N.Y. TIMES, Dec. 12, 1996, at A27; Joseph Bruner, *Fetal Surgery for Myelomeningocele and the Incidence of Shunt-Dependent Hydrocephalus,* 282 JAMA 1819 (1999); Frank Chervenak *et al., Advances in the Diagnosis of Fetal Defects,* 315 NEW ENG. J. MED. 305 (1986); Susan Cohen, *Rare Surgery on Fetus Uses Doll, Ultrasound,* PHILA. INQUIRER, Aug. 1, 1983, at 5A; Mark Evans *et al., Fetal Therapy: The Next Generation,* 1 WOMEN'S HEALTH ISSUES 31 (1990); T. Brettel Dawson, *First Person Familiar: Judicial Intervention in Pregnancy, Again:* G.(D.F.), 10 CAN. J. WOMEN & L. 213, 228 (1998); Judd Everhart, *A Medical Advance: Fetus' Kidney Drained,* PHILA. INQUIRER, May 16, 1982, at 12C; Alan Fleischman, *The Fetus Is a Patient,* in REPRODUCTIVE LAWS FOR THE 1990s, at 249 (Sherill Cohen & Nadine Taub eds. 1989); John Fletcher, *The Fetus as Patient: Ethical Issues,* 246 JAMA 772 (1981); Janet Gallagher, *Fetus as Patient,* in REPRODUCTIVE LAWS FOR THE 1990s, *supra,* at 190; Whitney Gonsoulin *et al., Serial Maternal Blood Donations for Intrauterine Transfusion,* 75 OBSTET. & GYNECOLOGY 158 (1990); Denise Grady, *Operation on Fetus's Heart Valve Called a "Science Fiction" Success,* N.Y. TIMES, Feb. 25, 2002, at A1; Michael Harrison, *Successful Repair in Utero of a Fetal Diaphragmatic Hernia after Removal of Herniated Viscera from the Left Thorax,* 332 NEW ENG. J. MED. 1582 (1990); Deborah Hornstra, *A Realistic Approach to Maternal-Fetal Conflict,* 28 HASTINGS CTR. REP. No. 5, at 7, 10–11 (Sept.–Oct. 1998); Mark Jacobs & Roderic Phibbs, *Prevention, Recognition, and Treatment of Perinatal Asphyxia,* 16 CLINICS IN PERINATALOGY 785 (1989); George Keckstein *et al., Intrauterine Treatment of Severe Fetal Erythrobastosis: Intravascular Transfusion with Ultrasonic Guidance,* 17 J. PERINATAL MED. 341 (1989); Lisa Levitt, *First Successful Operation on Unborn Saves Twin Boy,* PHILA. INQUIRER, July 28, 1981, at 10A; Susan Mattingly, *The Maternal Fetal Dyad: Exploring the Two-Patient Obstetric Model,* 22 HASTINGS CTR. REP. No. 1, at 13 (Jan.–Feb. 1992); David McCullough, *A History of the Treatment of Hydrocephalus,* 1 FETAL THERAPY 38 (1986); Marie McCullough, *Surgery in Womb Gives Baby a Hopeful Start: A Risky Procedure at a Philadelphia Hospital Gave a Michigan Family Reason to Celebrate,* PHILA. INQUIRER, July 3, 1998, at A1; Virginia Nichols & Diana Bianchi, *Prenatal Pediatrics: Traditional Specialty Definitions No Longer Apply,* 87 PEDIATRICS 729 (1996); Neil Pattison, *The Management of Severe Erythroblastosis Fetalis by Fetal Transfusion: Survival of Transfused Adult Erythrocytes in the Fetus,* 74 OBSTET. & GYNECOLOGY 901 (1989); Eugene Pergament, *In Utero Treatment: Fetal Surgery,* in 2 EMERGING ISSUES IN BIOMEDICAL POLICY 136 (Robert Blank & Andrea Bennicksen eds. 1993); Roe *Hearings, supra* note 401, at 22–25 (statement of Steven Calvin); Joseph Schulman, *Treatment of the Embryo and the Fetus in the First Trimester,* 35 AM. J. MED. GENETICS 197 (1990); Sally Sheldon, *The Law of Abortion and the Politics of Medicalisation,* in LAW AND BODY POLITICS: REGULATING THE FEMALE BODY 105 (Jo Bridgeman & Susan Millns eds. 1995); Roger Shinn, *The Fetus as Patient: A Philosophi-*

So recent is this development that one embryologist commented in 1982 that "[t]he concept that the fetus may be a patient, an individual whose maladies are a proper subject for medical treatment as well as scientific observation, is alarmingly modern."[416] Separate treatment of the fetus as a patient actually had begun as early as 1928.[417] As late as 1970, however, the only intrauterine procedure undertaken with some prospect of success was intrauterine transfusion because of Rh sensitization.[418] Such transfusions today have largely become unnecessary just at a time that the techniques for performing them have improved considerably.[419]

Matters have now progressed so far that the current position of the American College of Obstetricians and Gynecologists Ethics Committee is that "a physician treating a pregnant woman in effect has two patients, the mother and the fetus, and should assess the risk and benefits attendant to each in advising the mother on the course of treatment."[420] Medical testing occurs at increasingly earlier times in the gestation process. A child's sex can even be determined before it implants in the uterus, as can a short but growing list of defects.[421] While some of these technologies have not been scientifically validated,[422] many of these technologies do work—as shown, for example, by their use to diagnose when surgery is necessary. Unfortunately, for most

---

*cal and Ethical Perspective,* in 3 Genetics and the Law 318 (Aubrey Milunsky & George Annas eds. 1985); Joe Leigh Simpson, *Fetal Surgery for Myelomeningocele: Promise, Progress, and Problems,* 282 JAMA 1873 (1999); Leslie Sutton *et al., Improvement in Hindbrain Herniation Demonstrated by Serial Fetal Magnetic Resonance Imaging Following Fetal Surgery for Myelomeningocele,* 282 JAMA 1826 (1999); Stuart Weiner *et al., Antenatal Diagnosis and Treatment of a Fetal Goiter,* 24 J. Reprod. Med. 39 (1980); Paul Williams, *Medical and Surgical Treatment of the Unborn Child,* in Human Life and Health Care Ethics, *supra* note 389, at 67.

416. Michael Harrison, *The Unborn: Historical Perspective of the Fetus as a Patient,* 1982 The Pharos 19, 19 (Winter).

417. J.W. Dudenhausen, *Historical and Ethical Aspects of Direct Treatment of the Fetus,* 12 J. Perinatal Med. 17 (1984).

418. *Compare* A. William Liley, *Intrauterine Transfusion of Foetus in Haemolytic Disease,* 2 Br. Med. J. 1107 (1963) (successful intervention), *with* Vincent Freda & Karlis Adamsons, *Exchange Transfusion in Utero,* 89 Am. J. Obstet. & Gynecology 817 (1964) (unsuccessful intervention). *See generally* Karlis Adamsons, *Current Concepts in Fetal Surgery,* 275 New Eng. J. Med. 204 (1966); John Queenan, *Intrauterine Transfusion: A Cooperative Study,* 104 Am. J. Obstet. & Gynecology 397 (1969).

419. *See* H. William Clewell *et al., Fetal Transfusions with Real-Time Ultrasound Guidance,* 57 Obstet. & Gynecology 516 (1981).

420. American Coll. Obstet. & Gynecologists, Patient Choice: Maternal-Fetal Conflict (Oct. 1987), *cited in In re A.C.,* 573 A.2d 1235, 1246 n.13 (D.C. Ct. App. 1991). *See also* Genetic Disorders and the Fetus: Diagnosis, Prevention, and Treatment (Aubrey Milunsky ed., 4th ed. 1998); Harriett Hornick, *Mama vs. Fetus,* 39 Med. Trial Q. 536 (1993); Jeffrey Lenow, *The Fetus as a Patient: Emerging Rights as a Person?,* 9 Am. J.L. & Med. 1, 17–27 (1983); Caroline Morris, *Technology and the Legal Discourse of Fetal Autonomy,* 8 UCLA Women's L.J. 47, 68–69 (1997); Warren Murray, *The Nature and the Rights of the Foetus,* 35 Am. J. Juris. 149, 166 (1990).

421. *See* Doris Teichler Zallen, Does It Run in the Family? A Consumer's Guide to DNA Testing for Genetic Disorders (1997); Jeffrey Kuller & Steven Laifer, *Contemporary Approaches to Prenatal Diagnosis,* 52 Am. Fam. Physician 2277 (1995); Michael Malinowski, *Coming into Being: Law, Ethics, and the Practice of Prenatal Genetic Screening,* 45 Hastings L.J. 1435 (1994); John Meaney *et al., Providers as Consumers of Prenatal Genetic Testing Services: What Do the National Data Tell Us?,* Fetal Diagnosis & Therapy 8 (Spring Supp. 1993); Teri Randall, *Gene Scene: Earlier, Eventually more Specific, Prenatal Genetic Diagnosis in the Realm of Possibility,* 264 JAMA 3113 (1990); Juan Tarin & Alan Handyside, *Embryo Biopsy Strategies for Preimplantation Diagnosis,* 59 Fertility & Sterility 943 (1993).

422. *See* Mason, *supra* note 78, at 158–60; J.A. Boss, *First Trimester Prenatal Diagnosis: Earlier Is Not Necessarily Better,* 20 J. Med. Ethics 146 (1994); David Grimes, *Technology Follies: The Uncritical Acceptance of Medical Innovation,* 269 JAMA 3030 (June 16, 1993; N.M. Fisk & S. Bower, *Fetal Blood Sampling in Retreat,* 307 Brit. Med. J. 143 (1993); Karen Hsu, *Growing Fetal Tissue for Surgery at Birth,* N.Y. Times, July 29, 1997, at C8; R.J. Lilford, *The Rise and Fall of Chorionic Villus Sampling,* 303 Brit. Med. J. 936 (1991); J.R.W. Yates, *Medical Genetics,* 312 Brit. Med. J. 1021 (1996). Note also that a mother's birth defect itself is *not* a good "marker" of the likelihood of passing that defect along—the only major study of this question found that only 3.8% of the children born to such mothers exhibited the same defect; while the risk was higher than for

detectable defects, the only "cure" is abortion.[423] Some practitioners of "genethics" even argue that there is a "moral duty to genetically engineer (*sic*) our children."[424]

Recourse to abortion as a cure for fetal defects is more problematic than many seem to realize. It challenges our commitment to the noncontingent love to our children.[425] Nor is the concept of defect all that clear.[426] If parents are unwilling to abort a Downs syndrome child, are they doing a wrong to the child? Should it matter that although testing before birth can identify whether a child

---

"normal" mothers (2.4%), the risk is nowhere near high enough to suggest a policy of aborting all such pregnancies. *See* Denise Grady, *New Data on Babies of Women with Birth Defects*, N.Y. Times, April 8, 1999, at A20.

423. *See* William Ray Arney, Power and the Profession of Obstetrics 182–83 (1982); Embryos, Ethics, and Women's Rights (Elaine Hoffman Baruch, Amadeo D'Adamo, & Joni Seager eds. 1988); Hadley, *supra* note 65, at 130–37; Rudy, *supra* note 104, at 3–21; Eva Alberman *et al.*, *Down's Syndrome: Births and Pregnancy Terminations in 1989 and 1993: Preliminary Findings*, 102 Brit. J. Ostet. & Gynecology 445 (1995); Cara Dunne & Catherine Warren, *Lethal Autonomy: The Malfunction of the Informed Consent Mechanism within the Context of Prenatal Diagnosis of Genetic Variants*, 14 Issues in L. & Med. 165 (1998); Wendy Farrant, *Who's for Amniocentesis? The Politics of Prenatal Screening*, in The Sexual Politics of Reproduction 96 (Hilary Homans ed. 1985). *See also* Stacy Klein, Note, *Prenatal Genetic Testing and Its Impact on Incidence of Abortion: A Comparative Analysis of China and Ireland*, 7 Cardozo J. Int'l & Comp. L. 73 (1999).

424. E. Joshua Rosecrantz, *Custom Kids and the Moral Duty to Genetically Engineer our Children*, 2 High Technol. L.J. 1 (1987). *See also* David Heyd, Genethics: Moral Issues in the Creation of People (1992); Barbara Katz Rothman, The Tentative Pregnancy: Prenatal Diagnosis and the Future of Motherhood (1987); Test-Tube Women: What Future for Motherhood? (Rita Arditti, Renate Klein, & Shelley Minden eds. 1984); The Custom-Made Child: Women-Centered Perspectives (Helen Holmes, Betty Hoskins, & Michael Gross eds. 1981); Adrienne Asch, *Reproductive Technology and Disability*, in Reproductive Laws for the 1990s, *supra* note 415; at 82; Barbra Paula Bluestone, *How Perfect? A Case for Prenatal Diagnosis*, 63 Mt. Sinai J. Med. 213 (1998); Alexander Morgan Capron, *Which Ills to Bear? Reevaluating the "Threat" of Modern Genetics*, 39 Emory L.J. 665 (1990); John Harding, jr., Comment, *Beyond Abortion: Human Genetics and the New Eugenics*, 18 Pepp. L. Rev. 471 (1991); Vicki Norton, *Unnatural Selection: Nontherapeutic Preimplantation Genetic Screening and Proposed Regulation*, 41 UCLA L. Rev. 1581 (1994); John Robertson, *Genetic Selection of Offspring Characteristics*, 76 B.U. L. Rev. 421(1996); Gail Rodgers, Comment, *Yin and Yang: The Eugenic Policies of the United States and China: Is the Analysis that Black and White?*, 22 Hous. J. Int'l L. 129, 161–64 (1999); Marsha Sexton, *Disability Rights and Selective Abortion*, in Abortion Wars, *supra* note 80, at 374, 380–83.

In Hong Kong, Dr. Leung Kai-Hong's license to practice medicine was suspended for three months for professional misconduct after failing to detect a birth defect through ultrasound and failing to test the parents for the relevant defective gene. Mary Ann Benitez, *Doctor Struck off for Failing to Spot Defective Gene in Foetus*, S. China Morning Post, Sept. 13, 2001. Dr. Leung, who had practice medicine for 35 years, had already announced his retirement.

425. Michael Shapiro, *Illicit Reasons and Means for Reproduction: On Excessive Choice and Categorical and Technological Imperatives*, 47 Hastings L.J. 1081, 1134–40 (1996). *See also* Renée Esfandiary, Note, *The Changing World of Genetics and Abortion: Why the Women's Movement Should Advocate for Limitations on the Right to Choose in the Area of Genetic Technology*, 4 Wm. & Mary J. Women & L. 499, 508–09 (1998); Martha Field, *Killing "The Handicapped" — Before and after Birth*, 16 Harv. Women's L.J. 79, 123–24 (1993); Paul Freund, *Xeroxing Human Beings*, in Human Genetics: Readings in the Implications of Genetic Engineering 233 (Thomas Robert Mertens ed. 1978); Harding, *supra* note 424, at 498–99; Hornstra, *supra* note 415, at 8–11; Therese Powers, Note, *Race for Perfection: Children's Rights and Enhancement Drugs*, 13 J. Law & Health 141 (1998); Hans Reinders, *A Threat to Disabled Persons? On the Genetics Approach to Developmental Disabilities*, Bioethics F., Fall 1996, at 3; Lois Shepard, *Protecting Parents' Freedom to Have Children with Genetic Differences*, 1995 U. Ill. L. Rev. 761.

426. Asch, *supra* note 424, at 72–73; Peter Berkowitz, *Other People's Mothers: The Utilitarian Horrors of Peter Singer*, New Rep., Jan. 10, 2000, at 27, 35; Gina Kolata, *Researchers Report Success in Method to Pick Baby's Face*, N.Y. Times, Sept. 9, 1998, at A1; Kimberly Mills, Editorial, *Scientific Progress Again Outpaces Ethics*, Seattle Post Intelligencer, Sept. 13, 198, at E2 ("being short, being of average intelligence, or being homosexual" are not diseases); Diane Paul, *Is Human Genetics Disguised Eugenics?*, in Genes and Human Self-Knowledge 67, 68 (Robert Weir *et al.* eds. 1994); Margaret Phillips, *Reproduction with Technology: The New Eugenics*, 11 In the Pub. Int. 1, 10 (1991); Rodgers, *supra* note 293, at 162–64.

will be born with Down's syndrome, the testing cannot—yet—determine how severe the condition will be.[427] Perhaps we can all agree that we should routinely abort children with Tay-Sachs, a defect that leads to an agonizing death by the age of five or six.[428] Does a fetus who will suffer cystic fibrosis merit abortion—with a life expectancy of about 40 years?[429] What about a fetus destined to be a dwarf or likely to be obese? Or a normal fetus being carried by a dwarf woman who wants a child like herself?[430] And what if one were to identify a gene for homosexuality?[431]

Too often parental counseling after prenatal diagnosis is biased in favor of abortion regardless of the nature or extent of the "defect." Worst case scenarios are painted in great detail, while the prospective parents are seldom invited to meet parents of children with such problems—parents who might present a more positive picture of going through with the birth.[432] Ironically, the pressures to abort "deformed" fetuses come at a time when the opportunities for social acceptance and fulfilling lives for children born with severe problems are better than ever before.[433]

Today, for a small but growing list of defects, fetologists can remove a child from the womb for surgery and then return it to the womb to complete gestation, or the fetologist can even perform a medical procedure inside the womb—either way permitting intervention before irreversible injury to the fetus and when its regenerative powers are greater than they will ever be after birth.[434]

---

427. Asch, *supra* note 424, at 82; Ann Finger, *Claiming All of Our Bodies: Reproductive Rights and Disabilities*, in TEST TUBE WOMEN, *supra* note 424, at 281, 288.

428. ROBERTSON, *supra* note 65, at 152; Shapiro, *supra* note 425, at 1140–41.

429. Benjamin Wilfond & Norman Frost, *The Cystic Fibrosis Gene: Medical and Social Implications of Heterzygote Detection*, 263 JAMA 2777 (1990); Benjamin Wilfond & Norman Frost, *The Introduction of Cystic Fibrosis Carrier Screening into Clinical Practice: Policy Considerations*, 70 MILBANK Q. 629 (1992). The same question has been asked—and answered for at least one parent—in the case of a woman who could expect herself, and her offspring, to suffer from advanced Alzheimer's disease by age 40. Yuri Verlinsky, *Preimplantation Diagnosis for Early-Onset Alzheiimer Caused by V717L Mutation*, 287 JAMA 1018 (Feb. 27, 2002). *See also* Denise Grady, *Baby Spared Mother's Fate by Genetic Tests as Embryo*, N.Y. TIMES, Feb. 27, 2002, at A16; Rick Weiss, *Alzheimer's Gene Screened from Newborn*, WASH. POST, Feb. 27, 2002, at A1.

430. *See* Kathy Fackelmann, *Beyond the Genome: The Ethics of DNA Testing*, 146 SCI. NEWS 298 (1994); Kathy Fackelmann, *DNA Dilemmas: Readers and "Experts" Weigh in on Biomedical Ethics*, 146 SCI. NEWS 408 (1994). *See also* ROBERTSON, *supra* note 65, at 171; Amy Elizabeth Brusky, *Making Decisions for Deaf Children Regarding Cochlear Implants: The Legal Ramifications of Recognizing Deafness as a Culture Rather than a Disability*, 1995 WIS. L. REV. 235; William Ruddick, *Parents and Life Prospects*, in HAVING CHILDREN: PHILOSOPHICAL AND LEGAL REFLECTIONS ON PARENTHOOD 124 (Onoro O'Neill & William Ruddick eds. 1979); Oliver Sacks, *Foreword*, in TEMPLE GRANDIN, THINKING IN PICTURES AND OTHER REPORTS FROM MY LIFE WITH AUTISM 11, 16 (1995); Lois Shepard, *Protecting Parent's Freedom to Have Children with Genetic Differences*, 1995 U. ILL. L. REV. 761. Along similar lines, one might ask, along with law professor Peter Berkowitz, what about parents whose child is "merely ordinary" when they seek one who will excel? *See* Berkowitz, *supra* note 426, at 36.

431. Lawrence Crocker, *Meddling with the Sexual Orientation of Children*, in HAVING CHILDREN, *supra* note 430, at 145. *See also* Ruth Hubbard, *Personal Courage Is Not Enough: Some Hazards of Childbearing in the 1980s*, in TEST TUBE WOMEN, *supra* note 424, at 331, 349.

432. FENWICK, *supra* note 415, at 1145–54; ROTHMAN, *supra* note 424, at 40; Asch, *supra* note 424, at 89–91; A. Clarke, *Is Non-Directive Genetic Counseling Possible?*, 338 THE LANCET 998 (1991); Phillips, *supra* note 426, at 11; Bruce & Diane Rodgers, *Abortion: The Seduction of Medicine*, 2 LIBERTY LIFE & FAM. 285, 295 (1995); Barbara Katz Rothman, *Commentary: Women Feel Social and Economic Pressures to Abort Abnormal Fetuses*, 17 BIRTH 81 (1990). *See generally* WOMEN AND PRENATAL TESTING: FACING THE CHALLENGE OF GENETIC TECHNOLOGY (Karen Rothenberg & Elizabeth Thomson eds. 1994).

433. *See, e.g.,* Michael Bérubé, *Life as We Know It*, HARPER'S, Dec. 1994, at 41.

434. N.S. Adzick & M.R. Harrison, *Fetal Surgical Therapy*, 343 THE LANCET 897 (1994); Sandra Blakeslee, *Fetus Returned to Womb Following Surgery*, N.Y. TIMES, Oct. 7, 1986, at C1; *Disorder Is Fixed in Fetus*, N.Y. TIMES, Aug. 29, 1995, at C10; Mitchell Golbus *et al.*, *In Utero Treatment of Urinary Tract Obstruction*, 142 AM. J. OBSTET. & GYNECOLOGY 383 (1982); Michael Harrison *et al.*, *Correction of Congenital Diaphragmatic Hernia in Utero: V. Initial Clinical Experience*, 25 J. PEDIATRIC SURGERY 47 (1990); Michael Harrison *et al.*, *Fetal Hydroenphrosis: Se-*

Surgery is possible as early as 18 weeks of gestation.[435] In its most extreme form, physicians can sustain a woman's body after her brain has died in order to produce, with luck (good or ill?) a healthy child.[436]

The prospect of keeping a dead woman's body functioning at a minimal level in order to enable a fetus to survive and be born is remarkably controversial among those who favor abortion.[437] Nonetheless, some 19 states of the United States have made an exception to their statutes authorizing "living wills" to preclude or limit giving effect to a woman's "advance statement" opting for death if she is pregnant.[438] Another ten states preclude giving effect to such an advance

---

*lection and Surgical Repair,* 22 J. Pediatric Surgery 556 (1987); Michael Harrison *et al., Fetal Surgery for Congenital Hydronephrosis,* 306 New Eng. J. Med. 591 (1982); Harrison *et al., supra* note 415; Gina Kolata, *Surgery on Fetuses Reveals They Heal without Scars: Finding Suggests Advantages of Prenatal Plastic Surgery,* N.Y. Times, Aug. 16, 1988, at C1; Ronald Kotulak, *Fetus Removed, Operated on, Then Returned to he Womb,* Phila. Inquirer, Nov. 15, 1981, at 1A; Levine, *supra* note 402; M.T. Longaker *et al., Maternal Outcome after Open Fetal Surgery,* 265 JAMA 737 (1991); Pergament, *supra* note 415, at 141; Mark Peters *et al., Cordocentesis for the Diagnosis and Treatment of Human Fetal Parvovirus Infection,* 75 Obstet. & Gynecology 501 (1990); Kevin Pringle, *Fetal Surgery: It Has a Past, Has It a Future?,* 1 Fetal Therapy 25 (1986); Williams, *supra* note 415, at 69–77. *See also* Blank & Merrick, *supra* note 35; Cynthia Daniels, At Women's Expense: State Power and the Politics of Fetal Rights 36–39 (1993); Fenwick, *supra* note 415, at 65–68; Morris, *supra* note 420, at 61–62 (1997); Kathleen Rauscher, *Fetal Surgery: A Developing Legal Dilemma,* 31 St. L.U. L.J. 775 (1987).

435. M.R. Harrison & N.S. Adzick, *The Fetus as Patient,* 213 Ann. of Surgery 279, 281 (1991).

436. *In re* A.C., 533 A.2d 611 (D.C. 1987), *rev'd after the fact,* 573 A.2d 1235 (D.C. Ct. App. 1990); Arthur Caplan, Due Consideration: Controversy in the Age of Medical Miracles 21–22 (1998); Daniels, *supra* note 434; William Dillon *et al., Life Support and Maternal Brain Death during Pregnancy,* 248 JAMA 1089 (1982); David Field *et al., Maternal Brain Death during Pregnancy: Medical and Ethical Issues,* 260 JAMA 816 (1988); H.L. Karcher, *German Doctors Struggle to Keep 15 Week Fetus Viable,* 305 Brit. Med. J. 1047 (1992); D. Kennedy, *Father May Sue over Coma Baby,* The Times (London), July 4, 1996, at 5; Debra Cassens Moss, *Legal Labor of Love: "Dead" Mom Gives Birth,* ABA J., Dec. 1, 1986, at 32; *Out of Death, a New Life Comes,* Newsweek, April 11, 1983, at 65; J. Robertson, *Coma Woman's Baby Is Taken into Care,* The Scotsman, Apr. 18, 1996, at 3; Michael Shapiro, *Illicit Reasons and Means for Reproduction: On Excessive Choice and Categorical and Technological Imperatives,* 47 Hastings L.J. 1081, 1132–34, 1180, 1194–95 (1996); Christine Russell, *Fetus Kept Alive in Brain-Dead Woman in Buffalo, N.Y.,* Phila. Inquirer, Sept. 3, 1982, at 12A; Douglas Shrader, *On Dying More than One Death,* 16 Hastings Center Rep., Feb. 1986, at 12; C. Toomey & G. Lees, *Baby Row Divides Germany,* The Sunday Times (London), Nov. 1, 1996, pt. 1, at 16; Linda Yglesias, *Sad & Silent B'day for Mom in Coma,* N.Y. Daily News, Apr. 28, 1996, at 32. *See also* Mark Butler, *Judge Rules Comatose Woman Can Have Abortion,* Phila. Inquirer, Aug. 26, 1982, at 1A.

437. *See generally* Fenwick, *supra* note 415, at 63–65; Regina Graycar & Jenny Morgan, The Hidden Gender of the Law 220–27 (1990); Mason, *supra* note 78, at 170–71; Peter Singer, Rethinking Life and Death 9–11 (1995); George Annas, *She's Going to Die: The Case of Angela C.,* 18 Hastings Ctr. Rep., no. 1, at 23, 24–25 (1988); Margaret Diamond, *Echoes from the Darkness: The Case of Angela C,* 51 U. Pitt. L. Rev. 1061 (1990); Janet Gallagher, *Collective Bad Faith: "Protecting" the Fetus,* in Reproduction, Ethics, and the Law: Feminist Perspectives 343, 359–60 (Joan Callahan ed. 1995); Gallagher, *supra* note 415, at 193–95, 199–200; John Hasnas, *From Cannibalism to Cesareans: Two Conceptions of Fundamental Rights,* 89 Nw. U. L. Rev. 900 (1995); James Jordan III, Note, *Incubating for the State: The Precarious Autonomy of Persistently Vegetative and Brain-Dead Pregnant Women,* 22 Ga. L. Rev. 1103 (1988); Joan Mahoney, *Death with Dignity: Is There an Exception for Pregnant Women?,* 57 UMKC L. Rev. 221 (1989); Jenny Morgan, *Foetal Imaginings: Searching for a Vocabulary in the Law and Politics of Reproduction,* 12 Can. J. Women & L. 371, 382–86 (2000); Hilde Lindemann Nelson, *The Architect and the Bee: Some Reflections on Postmortem Pregnancy,* 8 Bioethics 247 (1994); Tom Spivack, *Abortion: Unsolicited Gratuitous, Third-Party Stranger Intervention: Freedom of Choice,* 40 Med. Trial Techn. Q. 363 (1995); Katherine Taylor, *Compelling Pregnancy at Death's Door,* 7 Colum. J. Gender & L. 85 (1997). The intervention of the state of Florida to block an abortion for a severely retarded woman evoked a similar controversy. Abby Goodenough, *Guardian Sought for Fetus of a Retarded Floridian,* N.Y. Times, Aug. 8, 2003, at A14; Jackie Hallifax, *Fla. House OK's Bill to Feed Woman,* The Commercial Appeal Oct. 21, 2003, at A6; *Husband in Fla. Case Challenges His In-Laws' Motives,* Wash. Post, Oct. 28, 2003, mat A9.

438. Ala. Code §22-8A-4(e) (Supp. 2003); Conn. Gen. Stat. Ann. §19a-574 (West 2003); Fla. Stat. Ann. §765.113, 765.305 (West Supp. 2003); Haw. Rev. Stat. §327D-6 (1993); Idaho Code §39-4504(4)

statement if it is probable or certain that the fetus will be born alive,[439] and three other states preclude giving effect to such an advance statement if it is possible the fetus will be born alive.[440] Two other states and Scotland have enacted such provisions if the fetus is viable.[441] And Minnesota requires that a woman's advanced directive for the withdrawal of treatment is presumed not to apply if the woman is pregnant with "a real possibility that…the fetus could survive to the point of live birth" unless the woman expressly mentioned pregnancy in the directive.[442]

Amniocentesis, amniography, embryoscopy, fetography, fetoscopy, radiography, ultrasound, and other techniques for detecting abnormalities in a pregnancy allow us to treat the problems of a fetus independently of the mother and almost compel us to think about the fetus as an independent being—while also impacting on maternal/fetal bonding.[443] Even such apparently innocuous technical developments as the ability to picture the unborn infant by a sonogram or to hear the child's heart beating (today a ubiquitous experience fairly early in pregnancy) alters our relationship to the fetus and thus our concept of the being with which we deal.[444] I have written

---

(1998); Ind. Code Ann. § 16-36-4-8 (West 1997); Mo. Ann. Stat. § 459.025 (West 1992); N.H. Rev. Stat. Ann. § 137-H:14 (1996); Ohio Rev. Code Ann. § 2133.06(B) (Anderson 2002); Okla. Stat. Ann. tit. 63, § 3101.4(b)(IV)(a) (West Supp. 2003); Or. Rev. Stat. § 127.540 (2003); S.C. Code Ann. § 44-77-70 (West 2002); Tex. Health & Safety Code Ann. § 166.050 (West 2001); Utah Code Ann. § 75-2-1109 (2003); Wash. Rev. Code Ann. § 70.122.030(1)(d) (West 2002); Wis. Stat. Ann. § 154.03 (West 1997); Wyo. Stat. Ann. § 35-22-102(b) (LexisNexis 2003). *See generally* Timothy Burch, *Incubator or Individual? The Legal and Policy Deficiencies of Pregnancy Clauses in Living Will and Advance Health Care Directive Statutes*, 54 Md. L. Rev. 528 (1995); Janice MacAvoy-Snitzer, Note, *Pregnancy Clauses in Living Will Statutes*, 87 Colum. L. Rev. 1280 (1987); Taylor, *Supra* note 437, at 93.

439. Alaska Stat. § 18.12.040(c) (LexisNexis 2002); Del. Code tit. 16, § 2503(j) (2003); Ky. Rev. Stat. Ann. § 311.629(4) (Michie 2001); Mont. Code Ann. § 50-9-202(3) (2003); Neb. Rev. Stat. § 20-408(3) (1997); Nev. Rev. Stat. Ann. § 449.624(4) (Michie 2000); N.D. Cent. Code § 23-06.4-07(3) (Supp. 2003); 20 Pa. Cons. Stat. Ann. § 541(a) (West 2000); R.I. Gen. Laws § 23-4.11-6(c) (1997); S.D. Codified Laws § 34-12D-10 (Michie 1994).

440. Ariz. Rev. Stat. Ann. § 36-3262(3) (West 2003); Ark. Stat. Ann. § 20-17-206(c) (LexisNexis 2002); 755 Ill. Comp. Stat. Ann. § 35/3(c) (West 1992).

441. Colo. Rev. Stat. § 15-18-104(2) (2003); Ga. Code Ann. § 31-32-8(a)(1) (2001); *Adults with Incapacity (Scotland) Act of 2000*, Asp 4, s.84. *See* Mason, *supra* note 78, at 157.

442. Minn. Stat. § 145C.10(g) (West Supp. 2003). *See also* Amy Lynn Jerdee, Note, *Breaking the Silence: Minnesota's Pregnancy Presumption and the Right to Refuse Medical Treatment*, 84 Minn. L. Rev. 971 (2000).

443. N. Caccia *et al., Impact of Prenatal Testing on Maternal-Fetal Bonding: Chorionic Villus Sampling Versus Amnioentesis*, 165 Am. J. Ostet. Gynecology 1122 (1991); M. Neil Macintyre, *The Impact of an Abnormal Fetus or Child on the Choice for Prenatal Diagnosis and Selective Abortion*, in Abortion, Medicine and the Law, *supra* note 29, at 524; Morris, *supra* note 420, at 60; J.P. Newnham *et al., Effects of Ultrasound during Pregnancy: A Randomised Controlled Trial*, 342 The Lancet 887 (1993). *See generally* Blank & Merrick, *supra* note 35, at 133–40; Fenwick, *supra* note 415, at 68; Rothman, *supra* note 424; Belinda Bennett, *Pregnant Women and the Duty to Rescue: A Feminist Response to the Fetal Rights Debate*, 9 Law in Context 71, 85–89 (1991); Robert Blank, *Reproductive Technology: Pregnant Women, the Fetus, and the Courts*, 13 Women & Pol. 1, 2–3, 15 (1993); Randi Hutter Epstein, *Advances, and Angst, in a New Era of Ultrasound*, N.Y. Times, May 9, 2000, at F7; John Fletcher, *Emerging Ethical Issues in Fetal Therapy*, in Research Ethics 187, 196 (Kare Berg & Knute Tranoy eds. 1983); Gail Goichman & Harold Hirsch, *The Expanding Rights of the Fetus: An Evolution Not a Revolution*, 30 Med. Trial Technique Q. 212 (1983); Kenneth Niswander & Manual Porto, *Abortion Practices in the United States: A Medical Viewpoint*, in Abortion, Medicine, and the Law, *supra*, at 567; Christine Overall, *Pluck a Fetus from Its Womb: A Critique of Current Attitudes toward the Embryo/Fetus*, 24 U. W. Ont. L. Rev. 1 (1986); E.A. Reece *et al., Embryoscopy: A Closer Look at First-Trimester Diagnosis and Treatment,*166 Am. J. Obstet. & Gynecology 775 (1992); Åke Saldeen, *Sweden: Changes in the Code on Marriage and Plans for Reform in the Areas of Adoption, Child Custody and Fetal Diagnostics*, 29 J. Fam. L. 431, 433–35 (1991); Jean Reith Schroedel, Pamela Fiber, & Bruce Snyder, *Women's Rights and Fetal Personhood in Criminal Law*, 7 Duke J. Gender & L. 89, 93–98 (2000).

444. For examples of such images, see Langman's Medical Embryology 80, 82–83 (T.W. Sadler ed. 5th ed. 1985); Leonard Nilsson, *The First Days of Creation*, Life 26, 40–43 (Aug. 1990); Kenneth Miller, *What Does It Mean to Be One of Us?*, Life, 38, 38–49 (Nov. 1996). For discussions of the power of such images, see,

elsewhere of the necessity to render the victim faceless in order to put more easily their shared humanness out of mind; consider the effect of removing (or re-imposing) the veil in Islamic countries.[445] These new technologies largely remove the veil of the woman's abdominal wall.[446]

The effects of fetal medicine and of fetal imaging on the meaning of pregnancy are, of course, not objective.[447] Far too many people have managed to convince themselves of the non-humanity of people face to face, as the Nazi extermination camps amply demonstrated, not to mention apartheid, slavery, and segregation, to believe that even direct perception of a fetus necessarily and universally alters others' perception of the unborn being.[448] Law professor Patri-

---

e.g., Boss, *supra* note 382, at 65–68, 119; Condit, *supra* note 16, at 86–87; Garrow, *supra* note 5, at 578–79; Kenny, *supra* note 52, at 293–94; Steven Maynard-Moody, The Dilemma of the Fetus 89 (1995); Ann Oakley, The Captured Womb 155–86 (1984); Janice Raymond, Women as Wombs: Reproductive Technologies and the Battle over Women's Freedom 65 (1993); Marie Ashe, *Law-Language of Maternity: Discourse Holding Nature in Contempt*, 22 N. Eng. L. Rev. 521, 539–40 (1988); Bruce Blumberg, *The Emotional Impact of Prenatal Diagnosis*, in Psychological Aspects of Genetic Counseling 201 (Alan Emery ed 1984); Deidre Condit, *Fetal Personhood: Political Identity under Construction*, in Expecting Trouble: Surrogacy, Fetal Abuse, and New Reproductive Technologies 25, 26–33 (Patricia Boling ed. 1995); John Fletcher & Mark Evans, *Sounding Boards: Maternal Bonding in Early Fetal Ultrasound Examinations*, 308 New Eng. J. Med. 392 (1983); Sarah Franklin, *Fetal Fascination: New Dimensions to the Medical-Scientific Construction of Fetal Personhood*, in Off-Centre Feminism: Feminism and Cultural Studies 190, 203 (Sarah Franklin, Celia Lury, & Jackie Stacy eds. 1992); Morgan, *supra* note 437, at 374–75; Morris, *supra* note 420, at 59–60; Rosalind Pollack Petchesky, *Fetal Images: The Power of Visual Culture in the Politics of Reproduction*, 13 Feminist Stud. 263, 279 (1987); Carl Stychin, *Body Talk: Rethinking Autonomy, Commodification and the Embodied Legal Self*, in Feminist Perspectives on Health Care Law 211, 225 (Sally Sheldon & Michael Thomson eds. 1998).

445. Dellapenna, *supra* note 381, at 404. *See also* Leila Ahmed, Women and Gender in Islam 14 (1992); Farzaneh Milani, Veils and Words: The Emerging Voices of Iranian Women Writers 231 (1992); Fergus Bordewich, *Where Women Are an Annoyance that Disturbs the Symmetry of Life*, N.Y. Times, Dec. 9, 1973, § 10, at 1, col. 1; Lama Abu-Odeh, *Post-Colonial Feminism and the Veil: Considering the Differences*, 26 New Eng. L. Rev. 1527 (1992); Haleh Bakhash, *Veil of Fears*, New Rep., Oct. 28, 1985, at 15. *See generally* Geraldine Brooks, Nine Parts of Desire: The Hidden World of Islamic Women (1995); Elize Sanasarian, The Women's Rights Movement in Iran: Mutiny Appeasement, and Repression from 1900 to Khomeini (1982); Wiebke Walther, Women in Islam (1982); Alison Graves, *Women in Iran: Obstacles to Human Rights and Possible Solutions*, 5 J. Gender & L. 57 (1996); Alexandra Zolan, *The Effect of Islamization on the Legal and Social Status of Women in Iran*, 7 B.C. 3rd World L.J. 183 (1987). *See also* John Noonan, Jr., Persons and Masks of the Law 21 (1976).

446. Note in this regard that the Arabic word for fetus, *janin*, literally means "that which is veiled or covered." H. Anthony Salmone, Arabic-English Dictionary 107 (1890).

447. *See* Condit, *supra* note 16, at 81–92, 206–08, 211–14; Daniels, *supra* note 434, at 185; Hadley, *supra* note 65, at 192–94; Harrison, *supra* note 55, at 188–89, 201–30; Kristin Luker, Abortion and the Politics of Motherhood 150–51 (1984); Carol Smart, Feminism and the Power of Law 147–50 (1989); Marie Ashe, *Law-Language of Maternity: Discourse Holding Nature in Contempt*, 22 New Eng. L. Rev. 521 (1988); Rochelle Cooper Dreyfuss & Dorothy Nelkin, *The Jurisprudence of Genetics*, 45 Vand. L. Rev. 313, 316–21 (1992); Allen Hunter, *In the Wings: New Right Ideology and Organization*, 15 Radical Am. 113, 132 (1981); Nan Hunter, *Time Limits on Abortion*, in Reproductive Laws for the 1990s, *supra* note 415, at 129, 131–32; Anne Morris & Susan Nott, *The Law's Engagement with Pregnancy*, in Law and Body Politics—Regulating the Female Body 53 (Jo Bridgman & Susan Mills eds. 1995); Morris, *supra* note 420, at 53–59, 62–67; Petchesky, *supra* note 444; Rayna Rapp, *Constructing Amniocentesis: Maternal and Medical Discourses*, in Uncertain Terms: Negotiating Gender in American Culture 28 (Faye Ginsburg & Anna Lowenhaupt Tsing eds. 1990); Robert Veatch, *Abnormal Newborns and the Physician's Role*, in Decision Making and the Physician's Role 178 (Chester Swinyard ed.).

448. Joseph Borkin, The Crime and Punishment of I.G. Farben 126 (1978); William Brennan, Dehumanizing the Vulnerable: When Word Games Take Lives (1995); Richard Drinnan, Facing West: The Metaphysics of Indian-Hating and Empire Building (1980); W.E.B. Du Bois, The Soul of Black Folk 3 (1953); Ralph Ellison, The Invisible Man 3–4 (1952); Winthrop Jordan, White over Black: American Attitudes toward the Negro (1968); John Noonan, Jr., The Antelope: The Ordeal of the Recaptured Africans in the Administrations of James Monroe and John Quincy Adams (1977); Al-

cia Williams, discussing the treatment of African-Americans, has summarized the problem in these terms: "To live so completely impervious to the one's own impact on others is a fragile privilege, which over time relies…on the inability of others…to make their displeasure heard."[449]

In the context of abortion rhetoric, it is commonplace to describe an aborted fetus as merely a "little blob" or as "no different than a plant," and in any event as not a person until born.[450] Those who favor abortion tend to dismiss the power of fetal images as entirely unpersuasive, apparently based on the refusal of the pro-abortion activists themselves to take such images seriously.[451] Rosalind Petchesky was not content simply to reject the significance of the fetal images in the film "*The Silent Scream*," but insisted on claiming that the entire project was built on "visual distortions and visual fraud."[452] Petchesky also had difficulty explaining why so many women experience ultrasound examinations of their child as "empowering" when "feminist decoding of male 'cultural dreamworks'" should lead them to feel only subordination to control by (male) obstetricians.[453] Most who engage in such "feminist decoding" argue that modern reproductive "engineering" has been imposed on women as a means of subordinating them to male control. Petchesky, at least, was willing to concede that women generated considerable demand for such technologies, just as they generated a demand for the birthing technologies that emerged in the nineteenth century.[454] Caroline Whitbeck has perhaps gone the furthest in denying the power to imagine the fetus, arguing that fetal imaging and fetal diagnosis leads the mother to distance herself psychologically from the fetus as she may have to decide to "terminate" its life.[455] While this may well be the case before the imaging, what effect does the woman's perception of the image have on her feelings about the unborn child or any pending decisions? If such imaging has no effect or only a distancing effect on the mother, why do abortionists who frequently use ultrasound to assist their procedure take steps to assure that the mother does not observe the images of the fetus and of the abortion?[456]

---

BERT SPEER, INSIDE THE THIRD REICH 519–21 (1970); Elizabeth Kingtson-Mann, *Marxism and Russian Rural Development: Problems of Evidence, Experience, and Culture*, 4 AM. HIST. REV. 739, 742 (1981); Warren Leary, *Exhibition Examines Scientists' Complicity in Nazi-Era Atrocities: Medical Historians Trace the Loss of Ethics to Devaluation of Life*, N.Y. TIMES, Nov. 10, 1992, at C3; Martha McCluskey, *Privileged Violence, Principled Fantasy, and Feminist Method: The Colby Fraternity Case*, 44 ME. L. REV. 261 (1992); Ruthann Robson, *Lesbianism in Anglo-European Legal History*, 5 WIS. WOMEN'S L.J. 1 (1990). For examples of such reasoning in the abortion context, see Sisela Bok, *Ethical Problems in Abortion*, in BIOETHICS 45, 54–55 (Thomas Shannon ed. 1981); Julia Hanigsberg, *Homologizing Pregnancy and Motherhood: A Consideration of Abortion*, 94 MICH. L. REV. 371 (1995). For critiques, see Samuel Calhoun, *Valuing Intrauterine Life*, 8 REGENT U. L. REV. 69 (1997); Dellapenna, *supra* note 381, at 409; Charles Dougherty, *The Right to Begin Life with Sound Body and Mind: Fetal Patients and Conflicts with Their Mothers*, 63 U. DET. L. REV. 89, 113 (1989); Celina Romany, *Ain't I a Feminist?*, 4 YALE J.L. & FEMINISM 23, 32–33 (1991).

449. PATRICIA WILLIAMS, THE ALCHEMY OF RACE AND RIGHTS 72 (1991).

450. *See, e.g.,* CONDIT, *supra* note 16, at 183, 212, 215; KATRINA MAXTONE-GRAHAM, PREGNANT BY MISTAKE: THE STORIES OF SEVENTEEN WOMEN 85, 96, 198 (1973).

451. *See, e.g.,* LUKER, *supra* note 447, at 150. *See also* MARVIN OLASKY, THE PRESS AND ABORTION, 1838–1988, at 139–40 (1988).

452. Petchesky, *supra* note 444, at 265–71. A proposal by antiabortion "crisis pregnancy centers" to offer free ultrasound imaging to women contemplating an abortion was similarly denounced. David Crary, *Abortion Foes Aim to Use Ultrasound as a Deterrent*, PHILA. INQUIRER, Feb. 2, 2002, at A5.

453. *Id.* at 279. *See also* REAGAN, *supra* note 5, at 85.

454. Petchesky, *supra* note 444, at 279–80.

455. Caroline Whitbeck, *Fetal Imaging and Fetal Monitoring: Finding the Ethical Issues*, in EMBRYOS, ETHICS, AND WOMEN'S RIGHTS: EXPLORING THE NEW REPRODUCTIVE TECHNOLOGIES 47 (Elaine Hoffman Baruch, Amadeo D'Adamo, jr., & Joni Seager eds. 1988).

456. *See generally* CONDIT, *supra* note 16, at 79–81, 91–92, 147, 201–02, 205, 213–15. *See also* Warren Hern, *Correlation of Fetal Age and Measurements between 10 and 26 Weeks of Gestation*, 63 OBSTET. & GYNECOLOGY 26 (1984).

Few prominent voices today overtly claim connection to racist or sexist ideologies, yet the language used often unwittingly discloses the true linkage of one's ideas. Thus, the term "childfree," which some of the more militant in the pro-abortion crowd insist on substituting for "childless,"[457] echoes Hitler's determination to make Europe *Judenfrei*—Jew free. Law professor Laurence Tribe, with his remarkable penchant for getting it backwards were abortion is concerned, chose to note only that the Nazi's prohibited abortion and to ignore Nazi policies of compelling certain abortions, apparently in an attempt to link the Nazis to the right-to-life movement, rather than to his friends.[458] On the other hand, the similarity of treatment of unborn children with slaves accounts to some extent for the resistance to supporting abortion rights by many persons of color who are otherwise allied with groups strongly committed to those rights. Among the most notable examples of this phenomenon was the Reverend Jesse Jackson, who opposed abortion rights until it became too politically inconvenient when he sought to run for President. But then Vice-President Al Gore voted to define "unborn children" as "persons" from the "moment of conception" in 1984 only to deny that he had ever voted that way when he later ran for Vice-President and for President.[459]

Despite the strong motives some feel for willfully resisting what is now there for all to see, removing (or at least communicating through) the veil of the abdominal wall has a power that cannot be denied completely.[460] When an ad agency uses ultrasound images of a fetus to sell cars ("Is there something inside telling you to buy a Volvo?"),[461] we know not only that those images have become part of the background knowledge of nearly everyone, but also that those images represent something more than an undifferentiated blob of maternal tissue. Such images have a peculiar power that rhetorician Celeste Condit has noted:

> Visual forms of persuasion present special problems of analysis. Visual images seduce our attention and demand our assent in a peculiar and gripping fashion. Many audiences are leery of verbal constructions, which only "represent" reality, but because we humans tend to trust our own senses, we take what we *see* to be true. Therefore our trust in what we

---

457. *See, e.g.,* Deirdre Bair, Simone de Beauvoir: A Biography 170 (1990); Carolyn Steedman, Landscape for a Good Woman 84–88 (1986); Nancy Miller, *Mothers, Daughters, and Autobiography: Maternal Legacies and Cultural Criticism,* in Mothers in Law: Feminist Theory and the Legal Regulation of Motherhood 3 (Martha Albertson Fineman & Isabel Karpin eds. 1995); Penny Mitchell, *One Can Be "Child-Free" and Very Happy, too,* U.S. Today, Oct. 15, 1999, at 18A (letter). *See also* James Burtchaell, Rachel Weeping and Other Essays on Abortion 141 (1982); Diane Eyer, Motherguilt: Mother-Infant Bonding: A Scientific Fiction (1993); Jacoby, *supra* note 98, at 55–58.

458. Tribe, *supra* note 29, at 59. *See also* David Granfield, The Abortion Decision 166 (1969); Maxtone-Graham, *supra* note 450, at 54, 96, 151.

459. Congressional Record, June 26, 1984, at H-7051 (Al Gore's vote); Critchlow, *supra* note 95, at 142 (Jackson) Connie Paige, The Right to Lifers: Who They Are; How They Operate; Where They Get Their Money 100–01, 103 (1983) (Jackson); *Meet the Press,* NBC-TV, Feb. 21, 1988 (Al Gore's first denial), Sept. 6, 1992 (Al Gore's second denial); *This Week,* ABC-TV, Oct. 31, 1999 (Al Gore's third denial).

460. Condit, *supra* note 16, at 80; Dienes, *supra* note 108, at 60; Hadley, *supra* note 65, at 194; Judges, *supra* note 31, at 58, 287–89; Kenny, *supra* note 52, at 227, 293–94; Noonan, *supra* note 11, at 3–4, 154–55; Frederick Taussig, Abortion: Spontaneous and Induced 79 (1936); Daniel Callahan, *How Technology Is Changing the Abortion Debate,* 16 Hastings Cent. Rep. 33 (No. 1 Jan.–Feb. 1986); Jason DeParle, *Beyond the Legal Right,* 21 Wash. Monthly no. 4, at 28 (Apr. 1989); Fletcher & Evans, *supra* note 444; E. Anne Kaplan, *Look Who's Talking Indeed: Fetal Images in Recent North American Visual Culture,* in Mothering: Ideology, Experience, and Agency 121 (Evelyn Nakano Glenn *et al.* eds. 1994); Roy Kerrison, *Backdrop to Bush's Court Selection: Pictures Show What Abortion Is All About,* N.Y. Post, July 25, 1990, at 2. *See also* Lois Shepherd, *Sophie's Choices: Medical and Legal Responses to Suffering,* 72 Notre Dame L. Rev. 103, 126–56 (1996) (discussing the transformative effects of modern medical technology regarding attitudes towards the right to be born free of defect and to die without prolonged suffering).

461. Referred to in Morris, *supra* note 420, at 67; Carole Stabile, *Shooting the Mother: Fetal Photography and the Politics of Disappearance,* Camera Obscura, Jan. 1992, at 179, 195.

see gives visual images particular rhetorical potency....It is in the translation of visual images into verbal meanings that the rhetoric of images operates most powerfully.[462]

Dr. Michael Harrison, a specialist in fetal surgery has described the impact of songraphy in particularly forceful terms:

> The fetus could not be taken seriously as long as he (*sic*) remained a medical recluse in an opaque womb; and it was not until the last half century that the prying eye of the ultrasonogram rendered the once opaque womb transparent, stripping the veil of mystery from the dark inner sanctum, and letting the light of scientific observation fall on the shy and secretive fetus. The sonographic voyeur, spying on the unwary fetus, finds him or her a surprisingly active little creature, and not at all the passive parasite we had imagined.[463]

We have ample evidence of just such an effect from a visual "encounters" with fetuses. Consider the story of "Claire" as reported by psychologist Carol Gilligan.[464] "Claire," an abortion counselor, was thrown into "moral turmoil" by observing an "evacuated" fetus, something that before then she had, as ordered, described as just a blob of "jelly." Others have become active in the anti-abortion movement after discovering fetuses or fetal parts in trash bins outside abortion clinics.[465] Or consider "Darla," a strongly pro-choice woman who found she could not abort her fetus after she had seen it on ultrasound.[466]

Contrary to extreme claims of the irrelevance of fetal imaging, feminist historians argue that only with such fetal imaging have doctors (and others) really begun to "construct" the fetus as an independent person.[467] Such arguments simply ignore their own arguments that the process of "constructing" the fetus as a person was the doing of Dr. Horatio Robinson Storer and his ilk in the later nineteenth century.[468] Mary Kenny has identified the practice of listening to a fetal heartbeat through a stethoscope (first recorded in Geneva in 1818) as having played a major role in

---

462. CONDIT, *supra* note 16, at 81.

463. Quoted in Timothy McDonald, *When Does a Fetus Become a Child in Need of an Advocate? Focusing on Fetal Pain*, 17 CHILDREN'S LEGAL RTS. J., Spring 1997, at 12.

464. CAROL GILLIGAN, IN A DIFFERENT VOICE: PSYCHOLOGICAL THEORY AND WOMEN'S DEVELOPMENT 58–59 (1982).

465. JACOBY, *supra* note 98, at 115. The issue of how properly to dispose of fetal tissue after an abortion has generated considerable controversy. *See* City of Akron v. Akron Center for Reproductive Health, Inc., 462 U.S. 416, 451–52 (1983) (holding a requirement of "healthy and sanitary" disposal of fetal remains to be an unconstitutional restraint on a woman's right to abortion); Planned Parenthood v. Minnesota, 910 F.2d 479, 481–82 (8th Cir. 1990) (same); Margaret S. v. Treen, 794 F.2d 994 (5th Cir. 1984) (holding that a Louisiana statute requiring a woman to be informed how fetal remains were to be disposed of imposed an unconstitutional psychological burden on a women's right to abortion); Margaret S. v. Edwards, 488 F. Supp. 181 (E.D. La. 1980) (holding that a statute requiring fetal remains to be disposed of in the same manner as other human remains imposed an unconstitutional psychological burden on a women's right to abortion); McCoy v. Georgia Baptist Hosp., 306 S.E.2d 746 (Ga. 1983) (allowing a tort action for a woman when she was informed that her fetus was being held in cold storage). *See generally* MASON, *supra* note 78, at 176–78; *Calif. Judge Allows Burial of Fetuses*, PHILA. INQUIRER, July 7, 1985, at 5A; *Judge Balks at Rites for Interring Fetuses*, PHILA. INQUIRER, Oct. 20, 1982, at 18G; Steve Twomey, *Shedding Light on Fetuses Found in a Box*, PHILA. INQUIRER, June 26, 1982, at 10A. In contrast, Sweden requires that the remains of any fetus aborted after 12 weeks gestation to be held for one month pending the mother's decision regarding proper disposal. Kjeil Kallenberg, Lars Forslin, & Olle Westerborn, *The Disposal of the Aborted Fetus—New Guidelines and Ethical Considerations in the Debate in Sweden*, 19 J. MED. ETHICS 32 (1993).

466. RITA TOWNSEND & ANN PERKINS, FRUIT: WOMEN'S EXPERIENCE OF UNPLANNED PREGNANCY, ABORTION, AND ADOPTION 39 (1991).

467. *See, e.g.*, Lisa Cody, *The Doctor's in Labour, or a New Whim Wham from Guilford*, 4 GENDER & HIST. 175 (1992); Julia Epstein, *The Pregnant Imagination, Fetal Rights, and Women's Bodies: A* (sic) *Historical Inquiry*, 7 YALE J.L. & HUMAN. 138, 140 (1995); Rickie Solinger, *"A Complete Disaster": Abortion and the Politics of Hospital Abortion Committees, 1950–1970*, 19 FEMINIST STUD. 241, 254–58 (1993).

468. *See* Chapter 7, at notes 338–470.

persuading the medical profession to crusade against abortion in the nineteenth century.[469] These phenomena are not simply cultural accidents in the United States. Human rights documents are explicit that human rights attach to unborn children as well as women.[470] Those who refer to international human rights law to support the supposed freedom of women to abort curiously ignore the provisions in this body of law that supports human rights for unborn children.[471]

No wonder, with all the advances in reproductive medicine since 1818, that obstetricians (whether male or female) on the whole are more opposed to abortion of any other class of physicians.[472] Two-thirds of gynecologists refuse to do abortions.[473] The attitude of obstetricians has

469. KENNY, *supra* note 52, at 182–83. She similarly notes the importance of ultrasound and real-time scanning in fueling modern resistance to abortion. *Id.* at 199.

470. *See, e.g., United Nations Convention on the Rights of the Child,* G.A. Res. 44/25, U.N. GAOR, U.N. Doc. A/44/736, *Preamble* (1989); Sanford Fox, *The United Nations Convention on the Rights of the Child and United States Abortion Law,* 2 ANN. SURVEY INT'L & COMP. L. 15 (1995); Note, *International Child Health and Women's Reproductive Rights,* 14 N.Y.L. SCH. J. INT'L & COMP. L. 143 (1993).

471. Gayle Binnion, *Human Rights: A Feminist Perspective,* 17 HUM. RTS. Q. 509 (1995); Reed Boland, *Population Policies, Human Rights, and Legal Choice,* 44 AM. U. L. REV. 1257 (1995); Rebecca Cook, *Human Rights and Reproductive Self-Determination,* 44 AM. U. L. REV. 975 (1995); Rebecca Cook, *International Protection of Women's Reproductive Choice,* 24 NYU J. INT'L L. & POLITICS 401 (1992); Fleishman, *supra* note 251; Lynn Freedman & Stephen Isaacs, *Human Rights and Reproductive Choice,* 24 STUDIES IN FAM. PLAN. 18 (Jan./Feb. 1993); Aart Hendriks, *Promotion and Protection of Women's Right to Sexual and Reproductive Health under International Law: The Economic Covenant and the Women's Convention,* 44 AM. U. L. REV. 1123 (1995); Hernàndez, *supra* note 55; Renee Holt, *Women's Rights and International Law: The Struggle for Recognition and Enforcement,* 1 COLUM. J. GENDER & L. 117, 126–29 (1991); Rahman, *supra* note 293; Barbara Stark, *International Human Rights and Family Planning: A Modest Proposal,* 18 DEN. J. INT'L L. & POL'Y 59 (1989); David Thomasma, *Bioethics and International Human Rights,* 25 J. LAW, MED. & ETHICS 295 (1997).

472. *See* RICHARD SELZER, MORTAL LESSONS: NOTES ON THE ART OF SURGERY 153–60 (1976) (describing the "horror" of abortion); David Boldt, *Not Many Doctors Like the "Dirty Business" of Abortion,* PHILA. INQUIRER, July 18, 1993, at D5 (cataloguing the many reasons that the number of doctors doing abortions is declining, including that they consider it "contract killing"). *See also* COLKER, *supra* note 357, at 113–14; CONDIT, *supra* note 16, at 126–34, 168 n.11; DAVIS, *supra* note 91, at 66–72, 203, 206; HORDERN, *supra* note 144, at 11–12, 17–23, 113–15, 121–25, 152–54, 212–18, 232–36; JUDGES, *supra* note 31, at 42–43; Bernard NATHANSON & RICHARD OSTUNG, ABORTING AMERICA 141 (1979); PETCHESKY, *supra* note 29, at 80, 158–59; PETERSEN, *supra* note 152, at 10, 101–06; REAGAN, *supra* note 5, at 82; THE UNBORN PATIENT, *supra* note 382, at 165; GLANVILLE WILLIAMS, THE SANCTITY OF LIFE AND THE CRIMINAL LAW 163–71 (1957, reprinted 1972); Thomas Cavanaugh *et al., Changing Attitudes of American Ob/Gyns on Legal Abortion,* 20 THE FEMALE PATIENT 48 (May 1995); Carole Joffe, Patricia Anderson, & Judy Steinauer, *The Crisis in Abortion Provision and Pro-Choice Medical Activism in the 1990s,* in ABORTION WARS, *supra* note 80, at 320; Walter Dellinger, *Abortion: The Case against Compromise,* in ABORTION, MEDICINE, AND THE LAW, *supra* note 29, at 90, 92–93; Jane Hodgson, *The Twentieth-Century Gender Battle: Difficulties in Perception,* in ABORTION WARS, *supra,* at 290, 302–03; Jonathan Imber, *Abortion Policy and Medical Practice,* SOCIETY, July–Aug. 1990, at 27, 31–33; Julie Johnson, Priscilla Painton, & Elizabeth Taylor, *Abortion: The Future is Already Here,* TIME, May 4, 1992, at 26, 29; Cleo Kocol, *Let's Take the Guilt Away,* 48 THE HUMANIST 33 (May/June 1988); C.A. Nathanson & M.H. Becker, *Obstetricians' Attitudes and Hospital Abortion Services,* 12 FAM. PLANNING PERSPECTIVES 126 (1980); C.A. Nathanson & M.H. Becker, *Professional Norms, Personal Attitudes, and Medical Practice: The Case of Abortion,* 22 J. HEALTH & SOC. BEHAV. 198 (1981); Perry & Trillin, *supra* note 153, at 404; Petchesky, *supra* note 444, at 271–78; Anna Quindlen, *A Very Loud Silence,* N.Y. TIMES, Aug. 3, 1994, at A21; Rodgers & Rodgers, *supra* note 432, at 286 n.5; Kathleen Roe, *Private Troubles and Public Issues: Providing Abortion Amid Competing Definitions,* 29 SOCIAL SCIENCE & MED. 1191, 1196–97 (1989); Sara Seims, *Abortion Availability in the United States,* 12 FAM. PLANNING PERSPECTIVES 88, 93 (1980); John Thorp, jr. & Watson Bowes, jr., *Prolife Perinatologist—Paradox or Possibility?,* 326 NEW ENG. J. MED. 1217, 1218 (1992); Vinceguerra, *supra* note 22, at 1174–75; David Wilson, *The Abortion Problem in the General Hospital,* in THERAPEUTIC ABORTION 189, 197 (Harold Rosen ed. 1954) (this book was reissued in 1967 under the title ABORTION IN AMERICA).

473. Jane Gross, *Opposing Abortion: More Doctors Seek Ethical Balance,* N.Y. TIMES, Sept. 8, 1991, at A1, A12 (1985). *See also* Roger Rosenblatt *et al., Abortions in Rural Idaho: Physicians' Attitudes and Practices,* 85 AM. J. PUB. HEALTH 1423, 1423–25 (1995) (finding that only 2 of 114 physicians surveyed were willing to perform abortions, and that 82% of physicians who decline to perform abortions do so for personal moral rea-

deep historical roots.[474] Obstetrical nurses, if anything, are even more resistant to doing abortions.[475] As of 1986, 13 years after the *Roe* decision, a majority of American hospitals had not yet performed their first abortion.[476] Jonathan Imber has gone so far as to describe the private practice of medicine as the principle barrier to a more equitable provision of abortion services.[477]

The resistance of obstetricians and obstetrical nurses to doing abortions has not prevented some doctors (including some obstetricians) from seeking lucrative careers as abortion providers. Abortion providers themselves, however, have reported their own ambivalence upon seeing a foot (or a face) torn off during an abortion.[478] Thus, Dr. Warren Hern, a strong supporter of abortion rights, has described the performance of abortions as "an emotionally stressful experience for many."[479] Carol Joffe, once a prominent abortion rights activist who eventually went to work as a counselor in an abortion clinic, described her transformation in these words: "Before I came here I don't remember any ambivalence—abortion was safe and legal, and I looked at it in terms of feminist platitudes.... Working here, the rhetoric doesn't protect you from the implications of abortion, the moral issues."[480] Journalist Diane Gianelli, after interviewing abortion providers, found that they ask each other "where does the soul go?" and exchange nightmares about revenge by aborted fetuses.[481] This pattern of abortion providers losing confidence in the act and feeling guilt over the consequences of an abortion can be traced back two-and-a-half centuries through rare documents that actually record the emotional reactions of those involved in the act.[482]

The contradiction in—power of—the experience of aborting another on the one hand, and of working to promote the health of unborn children on the other, is amply documented in the autobiographical works of Dr. Bernard Nathanson, a co-founder of NARAL.[483] Nathanson went from being the "Abortion King" of New York to an anti-abortion activist through his experi-

---

sons). *See generally* AMERICAN COLL. OBSTET. & GYNECOLOGIST, *supra* note 420; HADLEY, *supra* note 65, at 129; Denis Cavanagh *et al., Changing Attitudes of American Ob/Gyns on Legal Abortions,* 20 THE FEMALE PATIENT 48 (May 1995); Denis Cavanagh, *Legal Abortion in America: Factors in the Dynamics of Change,* 2 LIFE LIBERTY & FAM. 309, 313–15, 317 (1995) ("Cavanagh, *Legal Abortion"*); Barbara Katz Rothman, *The Abortion Problem as Doctors See It,* 17 HASTINGS CENT. REP. 36 (No. 1, Jan./Feb. 1987); Vinceguerra, *supra* note 22, at 1179–80.

474. BROOKES, *supra* note 144, at 51, 60–62, 117, 124–25, 154; Dellapenna, *supra* note 11, at 415.

475. *See* Larson v. Albany Med. Ctr., 662 N.Y.S.2d 224 (Sup. Ct. 1997), *aff'd mem.,* 676 N.Y.S.2d 293 (App. Div. 1998). *See also* DAVIS, *supra* note 91, at 244; Ulana Baluk & Patrick O'Neill, *Health Professionals' Perceptions of the Psychological Consequences of Abortion,* 8 AM. J. COMMUNITY PSYCH. 67, 72 (1980); Walter Char & John McDermott, *Abortion and Acute Identity Crisis in Nurses,* 128 AM. J. PSYCH. 952 (1972); W. Cole Durham, jr., *et al., Accommodation of Conscientious Objection to Abortion: A Case Study of the Nursing Profession,* 1982 BYU L. RE. 253; Thomas Kane *et al., Emotional Reactions of Abortion Services Personnel,* 28 ARCH. GEN. PSYCH. 409 (1973); Nancy Kaltreider *et al., The Impact of Midtrimester Abortion Techniques on Patients and Staff,* 135 AM. J. OBSTET. & GYNECOLOGY 235, 236–37 (1979); Vinceguerra, *supra* note 22, at 1178–79.

476. Henshaw & Van Vort, *supra* note 88, at 107–08. *See also* GINSBERG, *supra* note 81, at 55; JAFFE, LINDHEIM, & LEE, *supra* note 29, at 15; PETCHESKY, *supra* note 29, at 157; RUBIN, *supra* note 5, at 169; RAYMOND TATALOVICH & BYRON DAYNES, THE POLITICS OF ABORTION: A STUDY OF COMMUNITY CONFLICT IN PUBLIC POLICY MAKING 206 (1981).

477. JONATHAN IMBER, ABORTION AND THE PRIVATE PRACTICE OF MEDICINE 114–15 (1986).

478. *See* GARROW, *supra* note 5, at 717–18; David Smolin, *Cultural and Technological Obstacles to the Mainstreaming of Abortion,* 13 ST. L.U. PUB. L. REV. 261, 270–74 (1993). *See also* Tharpa Roberts, *Letter: Abortion Degrades Everyone Involved,* WASH. TIMES, Jan. 9, 2001, at A14 (quoting comments by abortionists about being outcasts in their profession).

479. WARREN HERN, ABORTION PRACTICE 104 (2nd ed. 1990). *See also* Kaltreider, *supra* note 475, at 235.

480. CAROLE JOFFE, THE REGULATION OF SEXUALITY 112 (1986).

481. Diane Gianelli, *Abortion Providers Share Inner Conflicts,* AM. MED. NEWS, July 12, 1993, at 3, 36–37.

482. *See, e.g.,* Cornelia Hughes Dayton, *Taking the Trade: Abortion and Gender Relations in an Eighteenth-Century New England Village,* 48 WM. & MARY Q. 19, 28, 40–42, 44–45 (1991).

483. GARROW, *supra* note 5, at 361; DON SLOAN & PAULA HARTZ, ABORTION: A DOCTOR'S PERSPECTIVE 183 (1992).

ences as an abortionist and a fetologist.[484] Nathanson was particularly affected by fetal imaging in his fetology practice.[485] Yet Nathanson is not the only abortionist to have a change of heart when confronted with ultrasound images and other evidence of what really was at stake. For example, Carol Everett, who operated several abortion clinics, later renounced and denounced the abortion industry.[486]

Resistance by obstetricians and obstetrical nurses to abortion is widespread around the world even in countries where abortions have long been largely legal.[487] The same pattern occurred in Soviet medicine despite apparently complete social acceptance of the procedure.[488] The Soviet experience is particularly instructive as, by the 1980s, about half of Soviet gynecologists were engaged exclusively in performing abortions and the Soviet Union alone accounted for about 25 percent of the world's abortions (with 6 percent of the world's population).[489] The cost of these abortions amounted to 20 percent of the Soviet public health budget.[490] And in Japan, where Buddhism teaches that abortion does not kill a soul but merely delays rebirth, physicians and the public are deeply affected by abortion and publicly mourn the unborn infants who are delayed.[491]

Psychiatrists, who are most removed from personal involvement with fetology and abortion, are the physicians who, in the aggregate, are most supportive of abortion rights.[492] Their support began early in the twentieth century.[493] Psychiatrists were disproportionately active compared to other physicians in campaigning for the reform or repeal of abortion laws in the 1960s and

---

484. BERNARD NATHANSON, THE ABORTION PAPERS (1983); NATHANSON & OSTUNG, *supra* note 78; Bernard Nathanson, *Deeper into Abortion,* 291 NEW ENG. J. MED. 1189 (1974).

485. NATHANSON & OSTUNG, *supra* note 78, at 117–24. *See also* GARROW, *supra* note 5, at 334, 361, 364, 376, 409, 456, 651; JACOBY, *supra* note 98, at 54–55; SLOAN & HARTZ, *supra* note 483, at 190–91; CATHERINE WHITNEY, WHOSE LIFE? A BALANCED, COMPREHENSIVE VIEW OF ABORTION FROM ITS HISTORICAL CONTEXT TO THE CURRENT DEBATE 65–66, 81–82, 99, 101, 105, 173, 215 (1991).

486. CAROL EVERETT, THE SCARLET LADY: CONFESSIONS OF A SUCCESSFUL ABORTIONIST (1991). *See* Chapter 16, at notes 77–81. *See also* GARROW, *supra* note 5, at 718; Gallagher, *supra* note 415, at 191; Roe, *supra* note 472.

487. Balogh & Lampé, *supra* note 176, at 150; Katarina Lindahl, *Sweden,* in ABORTION IN THE NEW EUROPE, *supra* note 143, at 237, 244; Ross, *supra* note 164, at 209–10, 224–26; Uzel, *supra* note 181, at 55, 62.

488. PAUL GEBHARD *et al.,* PREGNANCY, BIRTH AND ABORTION 217–18 (1958); GRISEZ, *supra* note 144, at 196–98; TAUSSIG, *supra* note 460, at 418; WILLIAMS, *supra* note 472, at 219–20; Popov, *supra* note 181, at 267, 269–70.

489. Zielinska, *supra* note 181, at 61.

490. *Id.* at 61–62.

491. WuDunn, *supra* note 278, at A8. *See also* HARDACRE, *supra* note 279; LaFLEUR, *supra* note 279, at 4–5, 26–27, 155; Maruyama, *supra* note 279, at 146–47.

492. REAGAN, *supra* note 5, at 201–03, 218; Michael Cleary, *From Roe to* Webster: *Psychiatric, Legal and Social Aspects of Abortion,* 9 AM. J. FORENSIC PSYCH. 51, 55–58 (1991); Dellapenna, *supra* note 11, at 415 n.353; Ellen Freeman *et al., Emotional Distress Patterns among Women Having First or Repeat Abortions,* 55 OBSTET. & GYNECOLOGY 630 (1980); Arthur Mandy, *Reflections of a Gynecologist,* in THERAPEUTIC ABORTION, *supra* note 472, at 284; Nancy Felipe Russo, *Psychological Aspects of Unwanted Pregnancy and Its Resolution,* in ABORTION, MEDICINE, AND THE LAW, *supra* note 29, at 593; Richard Schwartz, *Abortion on Request: The Psychiatric Implications,* in ABORTION AND MEDICINE, AND THE LAW, *supra,* at 323; James Wilson, *Compelled Hospitalization and Treatment during Pregnancy: Mental Health Statutes as Models for Legislation to Protect Children from Prenatal Drug and Alcohol Exposure,* 25 FAM. L.Q. 149, 193 (1991).

493. *See, e.g.,* J.R. Lord, *The Induction of Abortion in the Treatment and Prophylaxis of Mental Disorder,* 73 J. MENTAL SCI. 390 (1927). *See also* BROOKES, *supra* note 144, at 150 (at University College Obstetric Hospital, abortions for psychiatric indications grew from 21% of all abortions there in 1938 to 52% in 1953); DAVIS, *supra* note 91, at 65–66, 72–86; PETERSEN, *supra* note 152, at 54, 60–61; REAGAN, *supra* note 5, at 201–02 (abortions for psychiatric indications amounted to "nearly half" of all therapeutic abortions at six hospitals between 1951 and 1960, rising from 20% in 1947; 94% of unmarried women had their abortions based on psychiatric indications at one Buffalo hospital); WILLIAMS, *supra* note 472, at 124–25, 145–46, 151, 175; Solinger, *supra* note 467, at 265 n.22 (in one Buffalo hospital, "therapeutic" abortions done for psychiatric reasons rose from 13% in 1943 to 87.5% in 1965).

1970s.[494] Endorsement of repeal by the Committee on Psychiatry and the Law was an important step in mobilizing pressure for abortion on demand.[495] Psychiatric indications quickly became the basis of more than 90 percent of all abortions under the reformed laws of the 1960s.[496] Critics of "psychiatric indications" for abortion noted from the start that usually such "indications" really were a subterfuge for the true reasons, social or economic, for seeking an abortion.[497] While serving on abortion committees in the 1950s and 1960s, some psychiatrists did work against approval of abortions, "uncovering" hidden motives of applicants that were then used to deny the request.[498] Yet overall the support of psychiatrists for abortion has been clear and strong. Not that this prevented psychiatrists from becoming special targets of the supporters of abortion on demand who resented having to feign psychological symptoms in order to justify the abortion.[499]

Women physicians and medical students are somewhat more supportive of abortion rights than are men physicians and medical students.[500] Yet it is actually somewhat surprising that women physicians and medical students are not much more supportive of abortion rights than their male counterparts given the general pattern that women with higher levels of education

---

494. *See, e.g.,* John Ewing & Beatrice Rouse, *Is Therapeutic Abortion on Psychiatric Grounds Therapeutic?,* 1 Soc. Psych. 137 (1974); Jacob Friedman, *The Vagarity (sic) of Psychiatric Indications for Therapeutic Abortion,* 16 Am. J. Psychotherapy 251 (1962); Alan Guttmacher, *The Shrinking Non-Psychiatric Indications for Therapeutic Abortion,* in Therapeutic Abortion, *supra* note 29, at 12–21; James Ingram *et al., Interruption of Pregnancy for Psychiatric Indications: A Suggested Method of Control,* 29 Obstet. & Gynecology 255 (1967); John Johnson, *Termination of Pregnancy on Psychiatric Grounds,* 2 Med. Gynecology & Sociology 1 (1966); Howard Kibel, *Staff Reactions to Abortion: A Psychiatrist's View,* 39 Obstet. & Gynecology 131 (1972); Jerome Kummer, *A Psychiatrist Views Our Abortion Enigma,* in The Case for Legalized Abortion Now 114 (Alan Guttmacher ed. 1967); Arnold Levine, *The Problem of Psychiatric Disturbance in Relation to Therapeutic Abortion,* 6 J. Albert Einstein Med. Center 76 (1958); Theodore Lidz, *Reflections of a Psychiatrist,* in Therapeutic Abortion, *supra,* at 276; Richard Schwartz, *Psychiatry and the Abortion Laws: An Overview,* 9 Comprehensive Psychiatry 99 (1968). *See generally* Hordern, *supra* note 144, at 23–30, 80–90, 115–16, 162–63, 206–07, 236–40, 252–54, 258–61; Edwin Schur, Crimes without Victims: Deviant Behavior and Public Policy 16 (1965).

495. Committee for Psychiatry and the Law, The Right to Abortion: A Psychiatric View (1970). *See generally* Garrow, *supra* note 5, at 375–76, 386.

496. Graber, *supra* note 5, at 57; Alan Guttmacher, *The Genesis of Liberalized Abortion in New York: A Personal Insight,* 23 Case-W. Res. L. Rev. 756, 763 (1972); Theodore Irwin, *The New Abortion Laws: How Are They Working?,* Today's Health, Mar. 1970, at 22, 22; James Kahn *et al., Surveillance of Abortion in Hospitals in the United States, 1970,* 86 HSMHA Health Rep. 423, 425–26 (1971); Leon Marder, *Psychiatric Experience with a Liberalized Therapeutic Abortion Law,* 126 Am. J. Psych. 1230 (1970); J.R. Partridge *et al., Therapeutic Abortion: A Study of Psychiatric Applicants in a North Carolina Memorial Hospital,* 32 N.C. Med. J. 131 (April 1971).

497. Taussig, *supra* note 460, at 320–21; H. Flanders Dunbar, Psychiatry in the Medical Specialties 279–81 (1959); Sidney Bolter, *The Psychiatrist's Role in Therapeutic Abortion: The Unwitting Accomplice,* 119 Am. J. Psych. 312 (1962); W.S. Dawson, *The Induction of Abortion and Premature Labour in Mental Disorders,* [1930] 2 Med. J. Australia 147, 149; J.A. Harrington, *Psychiatric Indications for the Termination of Pregnancy,* 185 Practitioner 654 (1960); Roy Heffernan & William Lynch, *What Is the Status of Therapeutic Abortion in Modern Obstetrics?,* 66 Am. J. Obstet. & Gynecology 335, 335 (1953); J.G. Moore & J.H. Randall, *Trends in Therapeutic Abortion: A Review of 137 Cases,* 63 Am. J. Obstet. & Gynecology 34, 34 (1952); J.V. O'Sullivan & I. Fairfield, *The Case against Termination on Psychiatric Grounds,* 20 Mental Health 97 (Aug. 1961).

498. Bolter, *supra* note 497, at 314–15; Charles Dahlberg, *Abortion,* in Sexual Behavior and the Law 379, 384 (Ralph Slovenko ed. 1965); S.D. Israel, *Editorial: Therapeutic Abortion,* 33 Postgraduate Med. 620, 623–24 (1963); Hans Lehfeldt, *Willful Exposure to Unwanted Pregnancy,* 78 Am. J. Obstet. & Gynecology 665 (1959); Lewis Savel & Irving Perlmuter, *Therapeutic Abortion and Sterilization Committees: A Three-Year Experience,* 80 Am. J. Obstet. & Gynecology 1192, 1194 (1960); Solinger, *supra* note 467, at 253–54, 258–59.

499. Reagan, *supra* note 5, at 223.

500. Jaffe, Lindheim, & Lee, *supra* note 29, at 64; Joy Walker Bonar, James Allen Watson, & Lynne Sanford Koester, *Abortion Attitudes in Medical Students,* 38 J. Am. Med. Women's Ass'n 43, 44 (1983).

and income are more supportive of abortion rights than are women with less education and income.[501] And while women obstetricians are more supportive of abortion rights than are men obstetricians, they are less supportive of abortion rights than are other women physicians.[502] The experience of Dr. Carol Everett and the attitudes of obstetrical nurses demonstrates that such women are no more immune to the impact of the reality of fetal life than are the men.[503]

In 1965, *Life* magazine published photos by Lennart Nilsson documenting fetal development through all major stages, spreading the image of a fetus as a "little person" to the general public[504]—just when the abortion reform movement was picking up steam. The pictures helped fuel the anti-abortion movement.[505] Critics noted that the mother was totally absent from these pictures.[506] This was hardly a surprise. The pictures were from Sweden where abortion was freely available. The pictured fetuses had been aborted ("surgically removed") and were not connected to a mother when the photographs were taken.

The power of visual and other images of a fetus, particularly a fetus struggling to avoid being aborted, explains the pro-abortion movement's intense anger over the film *The Silent Scream*.[507] Their opposition to the showing of *The Silent Scream* is even more intense than their disapproval of images of aborted fetuses or similar visual aides used by the pro-life movement.[508] As Barbara Katz Rothman has observed, "the fetus in utero has become a metaphor for 'man' in space, floating free, attached only by the umbilical cord to the spaceship."[509] Rothman asserted that this reduces the mother to empty space, ignoring that her metaphor had already identified the mother

---

501. Graber, *supra* note 5, at 34–36; Hyman Rodman, Betty Sarvis, & Joy Bonar, The Abortion Question 141–42 (1987).

502. Carol Weisman *et al.*, *Abortion Attitudes and Performance among Male and Female Obstetricians-Gynecologists,* 18 Fam. Planning Perspectives 67, 68 (1986).

503. See the text *supra* at notes 485–86.

504. *The Drama of Life before Birth,* Life, Apr. 30, 1965, at 54.

505. Karen Newman, Fetal positions: Individuals, Science, Visuality 8–16 (1996).

506. Solinger, *supra* note 467, at 255–56.

507. *See, e.g.,* Condit, *supra* note 16, at 86–87; Petchesky, *supra* note 29, at x–xiii; Jacoby, *supra* note 98, at 56; Betty Cuniberti & Elizabeth Mehren, *"Silent Scream": Abortion Film Stirs Friend, Foe,* L.A. Times, Aug. 8, 1985, at 1; Paul Houston, *"Silent Scream" Called "Testament for Pro-Life": White House Showcases Abortion Film,* L.A. Times, Feb. 13, 1985, at 6; Patricia Jaworski, *Thinking about the Silent Scream,* in Abortion Rights and Fetal "Personhood" 51 (Edd Doerr & James Prescott eds. 1990); Petchesky, *supra* note 444, at 267; Rachael Pine & Sylvia Law, *Envisioning a Future for Reproductive Liberty: Strategies for Making the Rights Real,* 27 Harv. C.R.-C.L. L. Rev. 407, 424–25 (1992); Claudia Wallis, *Silent Scream: Outcry over Anti-Abortion Film,* Time, Mar. 25, 1985, at 62. *See also* Boss, *supra* note 382, at 65–68, 119; Garrow, *supra* note 5, at 578–79; Kenny, *supra* note 52, at 293–94; Olasky, *supra* note 451, at 139–40; Stephen Schwartz, The Moral Question of Abortion 125–28 (1990); Blumberg, *supra* note 444; Fletcher & Evans, *supra* note 444, Morris, *supra* note 420, at 66.

508. *See generally* Paige, *supra* note 459, at 107–09, 122–23. *See also* Blank & Merrick, *supra* note 35, at 29–30; Tribe, *supra* note 29, at 50; Wanda Ward, *The Matron Cell,* 6 Yale J.L. & Feminism 143 (1994).

509. Rothman, *supra* note 424, at 114. Rothman's concept, although not her precise phrasing, apparently originated in an article by biologist Ruth Hubbard. Ruth Hubbard, *The Fetus as Patient,* Ms., Oct. 1982, at 28, 32. *See also* Karen Newman, Fetal Positions: Individualism, Science, and Visuality (1998); Petchesky, *supra* note 29, at xii–xvi; Rickie Solinger, The Abortionist: A Woman against the Law 187 (paperback ed. 1996); Tribe, *supra* note 29, at 138, 230; Ruth Hubbard, *Legal and Policy Implications of Recent Advances in Prenatal Diagnosis and Fetal Therapy,* 7 Women's Legal Rts. Rptr. 201 (1983); Isabel Karpin, *Legislating the Female Body: Reproductive Technology and the Reconstructed Woman,* 3 Colum. J. Gender & L. 325, 333–35 (1992); Ray Kerrison, *Backdrop to Bush's Court Selection: Pictures Show What Abortion Is About,* N.Y. Post, July 25, 1990, at 2; Morgan, *supra* note 437, at 380; Petchesky, *supra* note 444, at 263–71; Pine & Law, *supra* note 507, at 424–25; Carol Sanger, *M Is for the Many Things,* 1 Rev. L. & Women's Stud. 15, 23–24 n.35 (1992); Reva Siegel, *Reasoning from the Body: A Historical Perspective on Abortion Regulation and Questions of Equal Protection,* 44 Stan. L. Rev. 261, 325–26 (1992).

as a spaceship, which is certainly something more than empty space. This has now become a standard pro-abortion argument.[510] Barbara Duden has written an entire book on this theme.[511] Historian Carroll Smith-Rosenberg claims the same process of rendering the mother metaphorically "inert, total objectified" occurred in the nineteenth century.[512] The anger expressed in such statements expresses resentment over the shift in medical and public attitudes away from the mother and towards the child as the star of the show, as it were.[513]

Critics of *The Silent Scream* have tended to ignore the technically superior and therefore even more disturbing film, *Eclipse of Reason*. *Eclipse of Reason* also shows ultrasound images of a fetus being aborted, but with much better resolution and in real time, leaving itself less open to the criticism of misleading editing. The result has been described in these graphic terms:

> To watch this film is in itself a near-traumatic experience. After describing and displaying the instruments that will be in use in the filmed abortion, Dr. Nathanson explains the process of abortion in clinical terms. Nathanson describes the instruments as "cold" and "sharp." With the ultrasound, the audience is shown the beating heart and moving limbs of the unborn child. As the instruments are introduced, the movements take on a desperate character. From outside the womb, we watch as tiny bloody limbs are pulled from the fetal body and deposited on a white-sheeted table. There is blood. There is tissue. There are unmistakable hands and feet. Although the film is not long, it is by no means easy to sit through. While it is tempting to find fault with the film, the direct visual evidence is difficult to answer.[514]

Those who favor abortion rights apparently prefer to ignore this film than to try to refute it. When procedures such as hearing an infant's heartbeat, or seeing a sonogram of the infant, or other means of interacting with an unborn child do occur in the course of ordinary prenatal treatment, it usually is done in the conscious presence of the mother. The presence and reality of the fetus hence is more immediate and therefore more compelling than any high-tech image of an abstract infant-in-general. If a mother seeking an abortion were to see this film or to see an image of the child she herself is carrying, she might find it impossible to go through with the abortion.

The technology continues to advance. Physicians now practice embryoscopy that enables them to observe and photograph an actual fetus in the womb as early as the sixth week of a preg-

---

510. *See* SUSAN FALUDI, BACKLASH 459 (1992); CONDIT, *supra* note 16, at 79–95; DANIELS, *supra* note 434, at 16–17; GINSBURG, *supra* note 34, at 104–09; HADLEY, *supra* note 65, at 161–62; KARST, *supra* note 102, at 55; Janet Benschoof, *Reasserting Women's Rights,* 17 FAM. PLANNING PERSPECTIVES 162 (1985); April Cherry, *Maternal-Fetal Conflicts, the Social Construction of Maternal Deviance,* 8 TEX. J. WOMEN & L. 245, 247–48 (1999); Gallagher, *supra* note 415, at 188–92; Julia Hanigsberg, *Power and Procreation: State Interference with Pregnancy,* 23 OTTAWA L. REV. 35, 40 (1991); Morris, *supra* note 420, at 50–52, 58, 63–67; Sheila Noonan, *Theorizing Connection,* 30 ALBERTA L. REV. 719, 723–24 (1992); Petchesky, *supra* note 444, at 268, 271; Lucinda Peach, *From Spiritual Descriptions to Legal Prescriptions: Religious Imagery of Women as "Fetal Container" in the Law,* 10 J. LAW & RELIGION 73 (1993); Schroedel, Fiber, & Siegel, *supra* note 443, at 110–11; Siegel, *supra* note 509, at 326; Stabile, *supra* note 461; Joan Williams, *Gender Wars: Selfless Women in the Republic of Choice,* 66 NYU L. REV. 1559, 1577–78 (1991); Laura Woliver, *Reproductive Technologies, Surrogacy Arrangements, and the Politics of Motherhood,* in MOTHERS IN LAW, *supra* note 457, at 346, 355.

511. BARBARA DUDEN, DISEMBODYING WOMEN: PERSPECTIVES ON PREGNANCY AND THE UNBORN (1993).

512. CARROLL SMITH-ROSENBERG, DISORDERLY CONDUCT: VISIONS OF GENDER IN VICTORIAN AMERICA 239–42, 341 n.66 (1985).

513. KENNY, *supra* note 52, at 294–95; Hornstra, *supra* note 415, at 10–11.

514. JACOBY, *supra* note 98, at 56–57. See also the sonogram of a "fetal yawn" published in the *New England Journal of Medicine* in 1991. Robert Egerman & Donald Emerson, *A Fetal Yawn,* 335 NEW ENG. J. MED. 1497 (1991).

nancy.[515] The process involves the insertion of a tiny camera through a thin needle inserted through the abdominal wall into the uterus.[516] It is similar to but considerably more refined than the older practice of fetoscopy. As has so often been the case, these developments were not directed at abortion; in fact, they are part of a larger set of wider developments that have been going on for some time in the practice of medicine.[517] No wonder some abortion foes have suggested that women about to undergo an abortion be required to view an ultrasound image of their infant before finally consenting to the procedure.[518] Supporters of "freedom of choice" adamantly oppose allowing a woman considering whether to have an abortion to see a fetal image for fear that it would discourage them from having abortions.[519] So much for informed choice.

---

515. Gina Kolata, *Miniature Scope Gives the Earliest Pictures of a Developing Embryo,* N.Y. Times, July 6, 1993, at C3; E. Albert Reece & Carol Homko, *Embryoscopy, Fetal Therapy, and Ethical Implications,* 57 Albany L. Rev. 709 (1994).

516. *See* Boss, *supra* note 382, at 55–56.

517. *See generally* David Lee Drotar, Micro-Surgery: Revolution in the Operating Room (1981).

518. Richard Wilkins, Richard Sherlock, & Stephen Clark, *Mediating the Polar Extremes: A Guide to Post-Webster Abortion Policy,* in Abortion and the State: Political Change and Future Regulation 139, 169–70 (Jane Wi shner ed. 1993).

519. *See* Woliver, *supra* note 510, at 354–55.

# Chapter 16

# Break on Through
to the Other Side[1]

*The trouble is, what stirs our blood may end up embarrassing our conscience.*

—Peter Green[2]

In 1973, the Supreme Court was understood to have the final word on any dispute it chose to resolve. Resistance might continue after the Supreme Court spoke, as with the racial segregation decisions, but resistance ultimately would be futile. Many people therefore assumed that the Court's decision in *Roe v. Wade*[3] ended all meaningful dispute over abortion.[4] No wonder the *New York Times* declared on January 24, 1973 (two days after *Roe* was decided) that the Supreme Court's decision would provide "a sound foundation for final and reasonable resolution of a debate that has divided America too long."[5] That assumption was wrong.

Today, nearly all scholars who have considered the matter see the abortion decisions as having produced controversy rather than having quelled it.[6] Justice Blackmun, the author of the majority opinion in *Roe,* would later acknowledge that abortion had become "the most politically divi-

---

1. Jim Morrison, *Break on Through to the Other Side* (1967).

2. Peter Green, *The King Is Dead* (book rev.), New Rep., Dec. 20, 1997, at 36, 39.

3. 410 U.S. 113 (1973).

4. James Risen & Judy Thomas, Wrath of Angels: The American Abortion War 69 (1998). A plurality of the Supreme Court endorsed this expectation as late as 1992. Planned Parenthood of Southeastern Pennsylvania v. Casey, 505 U.S. 833, 867 (1992) (plurality op. per Kennedy, O'Connor, & Souter, JJ.).

5. *Editorial,* N.Y. Time, Jan. 24, 1973, at 40. On the press reaction to *Roe v. Wade* generally, see Abortion: Freedom of Choice & the Right to Life 3–12 (Leonard Sass ed. 1978); Marvin Olasky, The Press and Abortion, 1838–1988, at 118–19 (1988). *See also* Charles Franklin & Liane Kosacki, *Republican Schoolmaster: The U.S. Supreme Court, Public Opinion, and Abortion,* 83 Am. Pol. Sci. Rev. 751 (1989) (arguing that the Supreme Court in *Roe* was merely ratifying a change in popular preferences that was already occurring). Sarah Weddington—who had argued the case before the Supreme Court—also assumed that debate over the issue was finished once *Roe* was decided. Sarah Weddington, *Being "Historic" and a "Leader-in-Training,"* 77 Nat'l F. no. 3, at 30, 30–31 (Summer 1997) (recalling that she had thought that the decision was "written in granite" only to find over the years that it was only "written in sandstone").

6. *See* Celeste Michelle Condit, Decoding Abortion Rhetoric: Communicating Social Change 102 (1990); Barbara Hinkinson Craig & David O'Brien, Abortion and American Politics 35 (1993); Ronald Dworkin, Life's Dominion: An Argument about Abortion, Euthanasia, and Individual Freedom 4, 6–7, 102, 123 (1993); John Jeffries, jr., Justice Lewis F. Powell, Jr. 354–59 (1994); Donald Judges, Hard Choices, Lost Voices 4, 11–12, 242 (1993); Edward Lazarus, Closed Chambers: The First Eyewitness Account of the Epic Struggles inside the Supreme Court 371–72 (1998); Earl Maltz, Rethinking Constitutional Law: Originalism, Interventionism, and the Politics of Judicial Review 1–8 (1994); Robert Nagel, Constitutional Cultures: The Mentality and Consequences of Judicial Review 204 n.26 (1989); John Noonan, jr., A Private Choice: Abortion in America in the Seventies 189–191 (1979); David O'Brien, Storm Center: The Supreme Court in American Politics 48–49, 61–62, 106–07, 382 (3rd ed. 1993); Karen O'Connor, No Neutral Ground? Abortion Politics in an Age of Absolutes 3 (1996); Benjamin Page & Robert Shapiro, The Rational Public 107 (1992);

sive legal issue of our time."[7] Law professor James Boyd White was even more pointed about the abortion controversy after *Roe:* "Abortion is not an issue on which public and shared thought of a high quality seems possible in our political world but one that divides us into opposed camps, creating a political situation having many of the features of a civil war."[8] The abortion decisions have been at the center of the crisis of legitimacy that has gripped the American legal system in the last quarter of the twentieth century.[9] In short, abortion is "a problem that will not go away and that is transforming our politics."[10]

The Supreme Court's decision in *Brown v. Board of Education,*[11] declaring racial segregation unconstitutional, sparked a similar debate, but ultimately with less divisiveness. *Brown* was accepted as unquestionably legitimate within 20 years after it was decided.[12] The controversy over abortion, on the other hand, has only grown more intense as time passed. Eventually, the "pro-life" movement achieved considerable success. Whether the successes of "pro-life" groups will prove enduring is impossible to determine at this time. Presidents Reagan and Bush, who

---

MICHAEL PERRY, THE CONSTITUTION IN THE COURTS: LAW OR POLITICS? 179–80 (1994); H. JEFFERSON POWELL, THE MORAL TRADITIONS OF AMERICAN CONSTITUTIONALISM: A THEOLOGICAL INTERPRETATION 173–81 (1993); RISEN & THOMAS, *supra* note 4, at 5–6; GERALD ROSENBERG, THE HOLLOW HOPE: CAN COURTS BRING ABOUT SOCIAL CHANGE? 188, 341–42 (1992); BERNARD SCHWARTZ, THE ASCENT OF PRAGMATISM: THE BURGER COURT IN ACTION 294, 409–10 (1990); LAURENCE TRIBE, ABORTION: THE CLASH OF ABSOLUTES 79–82 (1990); LAURENCE TRIBE & MICHAEL DORF, ON READING THE CONSTITUTION 60–64 (1991); 191 (1979); MATTHEW WETSTEIN, ABORTION RATES IN THE UNITED STATES: THE INFLUENCE OF OPINION AND POLICY 41–42 (1996); Paul Carrington, *A Senate of Five: An Essay on Sexuality and the Law,* 23 GA. L. REV. 859, 898–906 (1989); Erwin Chemerinsky, *Foreword: The Vanishing Constitution,* 103 HARV. L. REV. 43, 70 (1989); Jane Maslow Cohen, *Comparison-Shopping in the Marketplace of Rights,* 98 YALE L.J. 1235, 1236 (1989); Rhonda Copelon, *Losing the Negative Right of Privacy: Building Sexual and Reproductive Freedom,* 18 NYU REV. L. & SOC. CHANGE 15, 18 (1990); Peggy Cooper Davis, *Neglected Stories and the Lawfulness of* Roe v. Wade, 28 HARV. C.R.-C.L. L. REV. 299, 304 (1993); Frank Easterbrook, *Bills of Rights and Regression to the Mean,* 15 HARV. J. L. & PUB. POL'Y 71, 76–80 (1992); John Hart Ely, *Another Such Victory: Constitutional Theory and Practice in a World Where Courts Are No Different from Legislatures,* 77 VA. L. REV. 833, 873 n.132, 876 n.139 (1991); Margaret Farrell, *Revisiting* Roe v. Wade: *Substance and Due Process in the Abortion Debate,* 68 IND. L.J. 269, 270–76 (1993); Franklin & Kosacki, *supra* note 5; Andrew Grubb, *Abortion Law—An English Perspective,* 20 N. MEX. L. REV. 649, 649–50 (1990); Dennis Horan, Clarke Forsythe, & Edward Grant, *Two Ships Passing in the Night: An Interpretavist Review of the White-Stevens Colloquy on* Roe v. Wade, 6 ST. L.U. PUB. L. REV. 229, 229–31 (1987); Morton Horwitz, *The Meaning of the Bork Nomination in American Constitutional History,* 50 U. PITT. L. REV. 655, 656 (1989); Sanford Levinson, *"Veneration" and Constitutional Change: James Madison Confronts the Possibility of Constitutional Amendment,* 21 TEX. TECH. L. REV. 2443, 2457 (1990); Hans Linde, *On Inviting an Echo: Comments on Nagel, Political Pressure and Judicial Integrity,* 61 U. COLO. L. REV. 721, 724–25 (1990); Robert Nagel, *Political Pressure and Judging in Constitutional Cases,* 61 U. COLO. L. REV. 685 (1990); Suzanna Sherry, *The Founders' Unwritten Constitution,* 54 U. CHI. L. REV. 1127, 1176 n.223 (1987); Robin West, *Foreword: Taking Freedom Seriously,* 104 HARV. L. REV. 43, 84 n.177 (1990); Joan Williams, *Abortion, Incommensurability, and Jurisprudence,* 63 TULANE L. REV. 1651, 1655 (1989). For a dissent from this view, see DONALD CRITCHLOW, INTENDED CONSEQUENCES: BIRTH CONTROL, ABORTION, AND THE FEDERAL GOVERNMENT IN MODERN AMERICA 149–50 (1999).

7. Webster v. Reproductive Health Services, 492 U.S. 490, 559 (1989) (Blackmun, J., dissenting).

8. JAMES BOYD WHITE, ACTS OF HOPE: CREATING AUTHORITY IN LITERATURE, LAW, AND POLITICS 167, 177 (1994).

9. *See* LAZARUS, *supra* note 6, at 288–89, 336, 360–72, 378; Stephen Carter, *Constitutional Adjudication and the Indeterminate Text: A Preliminary Defense of the Imperfect Muddle,* 94 YALE L.J. 821 (1985); Erwin Chemerinsky, *Wrong Questions Get Wrong Answers: An Analysis of Professor Carter's Approach to Judicial Review,* 66 B.U. L. REV. 47 (1986); Archibald Cox, *Foreword: Freedom of Expression in the Burger Court,* 94 HARV. L. REV. 1, 72 (1980); Kenneth Karst, *Religion, Sex, and Politics: Cultural Counterrevolution in Constitutional Perspective,* 24 U.C. DAVIS L. REV. 677 (1991).

10. TRIBE, *supra* note 6, at 9.

11. 347 U.S. 483 (1954).

12. *See* MORTON HORWITZ, THE TRANSFORMATION OF AMERICAN LAW, 1870–1960: THE CRISIS OF LEGAL ORTHODOXY 258–68 (1992).

strongly opposed abortion rights,[13] were replaced by President Clinton, who strongly supported those rights. Clinton, in turn, replaced by the second President Bush, who opposed those rights.

# The Controversy Continues

*Violence is always an outgrowth of milder states of mind.*

—Gordon Allport[14]

Supporters of a broad freedom to abort tend to ignore the burgeoning opposition to abortion on demand in this country before *Roe* and *Doe* were decided. Many claim that the political tide in America ran only one way until the *Roe* decision provoked opposition to abortion, an opposition they now ascribe to the rise of religious fundamentalism worldwide.[15] Law professor Ali Khan went so far as to describe all legal regulation related to sexual activity as a "religious neurosis."[16] Their attitude can be traced to the increasingly pervasive rejection by America's ruling elite of any role for religious belief in public life.[17] Such disparagement of opposition to abortion as deriving entirely from religious fundamentalism ignores the many people who question or oppose abortion (myself included) on purely secular grounds.[18]

---

13. *See, e.g.,* Ronald Reagan, *Abortion and the Conscience of the Nation,* 30 CATH. LAW. 99 (1986).

14. GORDON ALLPORT, THE NATURE OF PREJUDICE 57 (1954).

15. *See* TRIBE, *supra* note 6, at 238–41; RUTH COLKER, ABORTION & DIALOGUE—PRO-CHOICE, PRO-LIFE, AND AMERICAN LAW 169 (1992). *See also* MICHAEL BARONE, OUR COUNTRY: THE SHAPING OF AMERICA FROM ROOSEVELT TO REAGAN 756 n.14 (1990); RISEN & THOMAS, *supra* note 4, at 43–77; ROSENBERG, *supra* note 6, at 339–41; Mary Dunlap, *Mediating the Abortion Controversy: A Call for Moderation, or for One-Sided Etiquette While the Bombs Keep Flying?,* 30 WASH. L.J. 42, 62–64 (1990); Cass Sunstein, *How Independent Is the Court?,* N.Y. REV. OF BOOKS, Oct. 22, 1992, at 47, 49 (reviewing ROSENBERG, *supra*).

16. Ali Khan, *The Hermeneutics of Sexual Order,* 31 STA. CLARA L. REV. 47, 52 (1990). (Khan subsequently told me that he now finds his article personally embarrassing.)

17. *See* CONDIT, *supra* note 6; ELIZABETH ADELL COOK, TED JELEN, & CLYDE WILCOX, BETWEEN TWO ABSOLUTES: PUBLIC OPINION AND THE POLITICS OF ABORTION (1992); SARAH DIAMOND, SPIRITUAL WARFARE: THE POLITICS OF THE CHRISTIAN RIGHT (1989); FAYE GINSBURG, CONTESTED LIVES: THE ABORTION DEBATE IN AN AMERICAN COMMUNITY (1989); KERRY JACOBY, SOULS, BODIES, SPIRITS: THE DRIVE TO ABOLISH ABORTION SINCE 1973, at 7–25, 65–74, 95–100, 118–29 (1988); CHRISTOPHER LASCH, THE TRUE AND ONLY HEAVEN: PROGRESS AND ITS CRITICS 487–96 (1991). *See generally* STEPHEN CARTER, THE CULTURE OF DISBELIEF: HOW AMERICAN LAW AND POLITICS TRIVIALIZE RELIGIOUS DEVOTION (1993); KENT GREENAWALT, RELIGIOUS CONVICTION AND POLITICAL CHOICE (1988); JAMES DAVISON HUNTER, CULTURE WARS: THE STRUGGLE TO DEFINE AMERICA (1991); PAUL KREEFT, BACK TO VIRTUE: TRADITIONAL MORAL WISDOM FOR MODERN MORAL CONFUSION (1992); CHRISTOPHER MOONEY, PUBLIC VIRTUE: LAW AND THE SOCIAL CHARACTER OF RELIGION (1986); A. JAMES REICHLEY, RELIGION IN AMERICAN PUBLIC LIFE (1985); F. LAGARD SMITH, WHEN CHOICE BECOMES GOD (1990); GARRY WILLS, UNDER GOD: RELIGION AND AMERICAN POLITICS (1990); WETSTEIN, *supra* note 6, at 59–74; ROBERT WUTHNOW, THE RESTRUCTURING OF AMERICAN RELIGION: SOCIETY AND FAITH SINCE WORLD WAR II (1988); Philip Converse & Gregory Markus, Plus ca change…: *The New CPS Election Study Panel,* 73 AM. POL. SCI. REV. 32 (1979); R. Randall Rainey, *Law and Religion: Is Reconciliation Still Possible,* 27 LOY.-L.A. L. REV. 147 (1993); Frauke Schnell, *The Foundations of Abortion Attitudes: The Role of Values and Value Conflict,* in UNDERSTANDING THE NEW POLITICS OF ABORTION 23 (Michael Goggin ed. 1993); Howard Vogel, *The Judicial Oath and the American Creed: Comments on Sanford Levinson's 'The Confrontation of Religious Faith and Civil Religion: Catholics Becoming Justices',* 39 DE PAUL L. REV. 1107, 1116 (1990).

18. Sidney Callahan, *Abortion and the Sexual Agenda,* COMMONWEAL, April 25, 1986, at 236; Joseph Dellapenna, *Nor Piety Nor Wit: The Supreme Court on Abortion,* 6 COLUM. H. RTS. L. REV. 379 (1974); Nat

If, in 1972, one had added up all of those who felt guilty enough about having had or participated in an abortion, those whose work as health care providers sensitized them to concerns about fetal life, and those who opposed abortion out of a deeply rooted sense of religious commitment, one would most likely still have had only a significant minority of the population at large. Yet those opposed to reform or repeal of abortion laws won significant electoral and legislative victories by wide margins in Connecticut, Massachusetts, Michigan, New York, North Dakota, and Pennsylvania in 1972.[19] Evidently many people across the United States, acting from a more limited knowledge base than committed activists and often from widely varied motives, continued to support rather strict abortion laws and were unwilling to tolerate even the sort of reform promoted by the *Model Penal Code.*[20] At the very least, a more extended political dialogue between supporters and opponents of reform or repeal of the abortion laws would have been necessary if those favoring change were to prevail through political processes.

The decisions in *Roe* and *Doe* are particularly surprising coming as they did at the point in time when the Court was already changing from a liberal activist direction to a conservative activist direction.[21] The Supreme Court, through its decisions in *Roe* and *Doe,* cut off the political processes just as those opposed to changing the abortion laws were beginning a successful mobilization.[22] Indeed, Justice Harry Blackmun intended to do just that, insisting on timing the release of the decision to coincide with the openings of most state legislatures, and insisting that a press statement be released with the opinion to control how the opinion would be reported.[23] (The Court declined to give Blackmun his unprecedented press release.) Ironically, the decision in *Roe* was more effective in cutting off the political organizing of supporters of the abortion reform movement than of the opponents. Supporters of abortion rights thought they had won decisively and that there was no further need to fight over the issue.[24]

*Roe* and *Doe* spurred the opponents of abortion rights. Starting with few resources and no obvious legal path to success, those opposed to abortion gradually attained sufficient political power to shift the political and legal winds in their direction. Despite years of hype claiming that the electorate overall was solidly "pro-choice," most elections produced more mixed results, with only occasional elections seeming to swing in one direction or the other. The election of 1994 generated particularly strong "pro-life" results summarized in the following:

> [N]ot a single pro-life governor or member of Congress of either party was defeated by a pro-choice challenger; pro-life challengers defeated 28 House and 2 Senate incumbents;

Hentoff, *Abortion: Seeking a Common Ground* (book rev.), Bos. GLOBE, June 10, 1990, at B43. On my views, see the "Personal Aside" that opens this book.

19. See Chapter 14, at notes 12–38.

20. AMERICAN L. INST., MODEL PENAL CODE § 2320.3 (Proposed Official Draft 1962). *See* Chapter 13, at notes 198–207.

21. CRAIG & O'BRIEN, *supra* note 6, at 3–5.

22. *Id.* at 41–42; DAVID GARROW, LIBERTY AND SEXUALITY: THE RIGHT OF PRIVACY AND THE MAKING OF ROE V. WADE 484, 506–07 (2nd ed. 1998); ELIZABETH MENSCH & ALAN FREEMAN, THE POLITICS OF VIRTUE: IS ABORTION DEBATABLE? 4 (1993); RISEN & THOMAS, *supra* note 4, at 38–40; ROGER ROSENBLATT, LIFE ITSELF: ABORTION IN THE AMERICAN MIND 34–35 (1992); Neal Devins, *The Countermajoritarian Paradox,* 93 MICH. L. REV. 1433, 1448–50 (1995); Ruth Bader Ginsburg, *Speaking in a Judicial Voice,* 67 NYU L. REV. 1185, 1205 (1992); Lino Graglia, *"Interpreting" the Constitution: Posner on Bork,* 44 STAN. L. REV. 1019, 1029 (1992); Geoffrey Hazard, *Rising above Principle,* 135 U. PA. L. REV. 153, 166 (1986); James Kelley, *Winning* Webster v. Reproductive Health Services*: The Crisis of the Pro-Life Movement,* AMERICA, Aug. 19, 1989, at 79.

23. GARROW, *supra* note 22, at 585–87; Devins, *supra* note 21, at 1445; Bob Woodward, *The Abortion Papers,* WASH. POST, Jan. 22, 1989, at D1, D2.

24. Rachael Pine & Sylvia Law, *Envisioning a Future for Reproductive Liberty: Strategies for Making the Rights Real,* 27 HARV. C.R.-C.L. L. REV. 407, 441–42 (1992); Cass Sunstein, *Three Civil Rights Fallacies,* 79 CAL. L. REV. 751, 766–67, 769 (1991).

of the 48 races for open House seats, pro-lifers took 34; of the 11 new senators, all but one are pro-life; and of the 26 percent of the electorate who said, according to a Wirthlin Group post-election survey, that the abortion issue affected the way they voted, two-thirds backed abortion foes while only one-third voted for pro-choice candidates.[25]

The 1994 shift was not complete. In 1996, Bill Clinton, the most solidly "pro-choice" president thus far, won a solid reelection despite numerous personal and political scandals while the electorate was also returning a solidly "pro-life" Congress.[26] Twenty-five years after *Roe* and *Doe*, state and national legislatures were enacting restrictive laws on abortion although they remained without the power to prohibit altogether any significant number of abortions.[27] Yet, while federal courts seemed less and less inclined to interfere in such legislative choices,[28] some state supreme courts found a "right of privacy" in their state constitution that was even more strongly pro-abortion than *Roe v. Wade*.[29] Legal and extra-legal pressure by "pro-life" groups contributed to a steady decline in the number of abortions.[30] Under Clinton, only the executive branch at the na-

---

25. *This Week,* Nat'l Rev., Dec. 1994, at 12.

26. Jacoby, *supra* note 17, at 180–82. *See also* Garrow, *supra* note 22, at 713; Mark Graber, *The Clintonification of American Law: Abortion, Welfare, and Liberal Constitutional Theory,* 58 Ohio St. L.J. 731 (1997).

27. *See* Kathryn Kolbert & Andrea Miller, *Legal Strategies for Abortion Rights in the Twenty-First Century,* in Abortion Wars: A Half Century of Struggle, 1950–2000, at 95 (Rickie Solinger ed. 1998); Katharine Seelye, *Advocates of Abortion Rights Report a Rise in Restrictions,* N.Y. Times, Jan. 15, 1998, at A16.

28. *See* Chapter 17.

29. Simat Corp. v. Arizona Health Care Cost Containment System, 56 P.3d 28 (Ariz. 2002); Committee to Defend Reproductive Rights v. Myers, 625 P.2d 779 (Cal. 1981); Doe v. Maher, 515 A.2d 134 (Conn. 1986); *In re* T.W., 551 So. 2d 1186 (Fla. 1989) (finding a right of a minor to an abortion without notice to or consent by parents); Roe v. Harris, 917 P.2d 403 (Idaho 1996); Moe v. Secretary of State Admin. & Fin., 417 N.E.2d 387 (Mass. 1981); Women of Minn. v. Gomez, 542 N.W.2d 17 (Minn. 1995); Pro-Choice Mississippi v. Fordice, 716 So. 2d 645 (Miss. 1998); Right to Choose v. Byrne, 450 A.2d 925 (N.J. 1982); Planned Parenthood Ass'n v. Department of Human Resources, 663 P.2d 1247 (Or. 1983), *aff'd on other grounds,* 687 P.2d 785 (Or. 1984); Planned Parenthood of Middle Tenn. v. Sundquist, 38 S.W.3d 1 (Tenn. 2000); Women's Health Ctr. of W. Va. v. Panepinto, 446 S.E.2d 658 (W. Va. 1993). *But see* Renee B. v. Florida Agency for Health Care Admin., 790 So. 2d 1036 (Fla. 2001) (rejecting a claimed right to public funding for abortions); Doe v. Department of Social Services, 487 N.W.2d 166 (Mich. 1992); Mahaffey v. Attorney General, 564 N.W.2d 104 (Mich. Ct. App. 1997), *rev. denied,* 616 N.W.2d 168 (Mich. 1998); Hope v. Perales, 634 N.E.2d 183 (N.Y. 1994); Rosie J. v. North Car. Dep't of Human Resources, 491 S.E.2d 535 (N. Car. 1997); Fischer v. Department of Pub. Welfare, 502 A.2d 114 (Pa. 1985); Bell v. Low Income Women of Texas, 95 S.W.3d 253 (Tex. 2002).

*See generally* Edward Alexander, *The Right to Privacy and the New York State Constitution: An Analytical Framework,* 8 Tuoro L. Rev. 725 (1992); Kimberley Chaput, *Abortion Rights under State Constitutions,* 70 Ore. L. Rev. 593 (1991); Kathryn Kolbert & David Gans, *Responding to* Planned Parenthood v. Casey: *Establishing Neutrality Principles in State Constitutional Law,* 66 Temple L. Rev. 1151 (1993); Janice Steinschneider, *State Constitutions: New Battlefield for Abortion Rights,* 10 Harv. Women's L.J. 284 (1987); Linda Vanzi, *Freedom at Home: State Constitutions and Medicaid Funding for Abortions,* 26 N.M. L. Rev. 433 (1996). *See generally* William Brennan, jr., *The Bill of Rights and the States: The Revival of State Constitutions as Guardians of Individual Rights,* 61 NYU L. Rev. 535 (1986); Daniel Gordon, *Upside Down Intentions: Weakening the State Constitutional Right to Privacy, A Florida Story of Intrigue and a Lack of Historical Integrity,* 71 Temple L. Rev. 579 (1998); Judith Kaye, *Dual Constitutionalism in Practice and Principle,* 61 St. John's L. Rev. 339 (1987); Ben Overton & Katherine Giddings, *The Right of Privacy in Florida in the Age of Technology and the Twenty-First Century: A Need for Protection from Private and Commercial Intrusion,* 25 Fla. St. U. L. Rev. 25 (1997); John Sanchez, *Constitutional Privacy in Florida: Between the Idea and the Reality Falls the Shadow,* 18 Nova L. Rev. 775 (1994); David Skovar, *Address: State Constitutional Law Interpretation: Out of "Lock Step" and beyond "Retroactive" Decisionmaking,* 51 Mont. L. Rev. 243 (1990); Symposium, *State Constitutional Law,* 63 Tex. L. Rev. 959 (1985); Vito Titone, *State Constitution Interpretation: The Search for an Anchor in a Rough Sea,* 61 St. John's L. Rev. 431 (1986).

30. Tamar Lewin, *Abortions Fell Again in 1995, but Rose in Some Areas Last Year,* N.Y. Times, Dec. 5, 1997, at A14; Tamar Lewin, *Fewer Abortions Performed in the United States: Variety of Factors Cited for Lowest Level since 1979,* N.Y. Times, June 16, 1994, at A1; Tamar Lewin, *Slight Increase in Abortions Is Reported,* N.Y. Times, Dec. 4, 1998, at A27; Barbara Vobejda, *Abortion Rate in U.S. Off Sharply,* Wash. Post, Dec. 5, 1997, at A1.

tional level was unequivocally committed to protecting the right to choose abortion.[31] The federal executive even brought suit to force states to provide Medicaid funding for abortions when pregnancy results from rape or incest—something not required by a federal statute until 1994.[32]

As a result of this controversy more than any other single factor, the judicial confirmation process became politicized to an extent unthinkable before *Roe* and *Doe.*[33] The abortion controversy has come to play an increasingly prominent role in political campaigns at all levels.[34] After

---

31. *See, e.g.,* Eric Schmitt, *Abortion Discord Holds Up U.N. Dues and U.S. Budget,* N.Y. TIMES, Nov. 11, 1999, at A18; Robin Toner, *Anti-Abortion Movement Prepares to Battle Clinton,* N.Y. TIMES, Jan. 22, 1993, at A1.

32. Little Rock Family Planning v. Dalton, 516 U.S. 474 (1996); Planned Parenthood Affiliates of Mich. v. Engler, 73 F.3d 634 (6th Cir. 1996); Hope Medical Group for Women v. Edwards, 63 F.3d 418 (5th Cir. 1995), *cert. denied sub nom.* Foster v. Hope Medical Group for Women, 517 U.S. 1104 (1996); Elizabeth Blackwell Health Ctr. for Women v. Knoll, 61 F.3d 170 (3rd Cir. 1995), *cert. denied,* 516 U.S. 1093 (1996); Orr v. Nelson, 60 F.3d 497 (8th Cir. 1995), *cert. denied,* 516 U.S. 1074 (1996); Utah Women's Clinic v. Graham, 892 F. Supp. 1379 (D. Utah 1995); Planned Parenthood of Missoula v. Blouke, 858 F. Supp. 137 (D. Mont. 1994). *See also* Unborn Child Amendment Comm. v. Ward, 943 S.W.2d 591 (Ark. 1997).

33. *See, e.g.,* ROBERT BORK, THE TEMPTING OF AMERICA: THE POLITICAL SEDUCTION OF THE LAW 133–34 (1988); ETHAN BRONNER, BATTLE FOR JUSTICE: HOW THE BORK NOMINATION SHOOK AMERICA (1988); CRAIG & O'BRIEN, *supra* note 6, at 63–65; 3 FEDERAL ABORTION POLITICS: A DOCUMENTARY HISTORY 71–230, 303–58 (Neal Devins & Wendy Watson eds. 1995); GARROW, *supra* note 22, at 668–71; ROBERT NAGEL, JUDICIAL POWER AND AMERICAN CHARACTER: CENSORING OURSELVES IN AN ANXIOUS AGE 20–27 (1994); STEPHEN MARKMAN, JUDICIAL SELECTION: MERIT, IDEOLOGY AND POLITICS—THE REAGAN YEARS (1990); PATRICK McGUIGAN & DAWN WEYRICH, NINTH JUSTICE: THE BATTLE FOR BORK (1990); O'BRIEN, *supra* note 6, at 44, 111–15; MICHAEL PERTSCHUK & WENDY SCHAETZEL, THE PEOPLE RISING: THE CAMPAIGN AGAINST THE BORK NOMINATION (1989); HERMAN SCHWARTZ, PACKING THE COURTS 42, 60–62, 64–66, 84–85, 87–88, 100–01 (1988); CHRISTOPHER SMITH, CRITICAL JUDICIAL NOMINATIONS AND POLITICAL CHANGE: THE IMPACT OF CLARENCE THOMAS (1993); BARBARA YARNOLD, ABORTION POLITICS IN THE FEDERAL COURTS: RIGHT VERSUS RIGHT (1995); Frank Guliuzza III, Daniel Reagan, & David Barrett, *Character, Competency, and Constitutionalism: Did the Bork Nomination Represent a Fundamental Shift in Confirmation Criteria?,* 75 MARQ. L. REV. 409 (1992); Stephen Lubet, *Confirmation Ethics: President Reagan's Nominees to the United States Supreme Court,* 13 HARV. J.L. & PUB. POL'Y 229 (1990); L.A. Powe, jr., *From Bork to Souter,* 27 WILLAMETTE L. REV. 781 (1991); Rodney Smith, *Justice Clarence Thomas: Doubt, Disappointment, Dismay, and Diminishing Hope,* 7 ST. L.U. J. LEGAL COMMENTARY 277 (1991); Symposium, *Gender, Race, and the Politics of Supreme Court Appointments: The Impact of the Anita Hill/Clarence Thomas Hearings,* 65 S. CAL. L. REV. 1279 (1992); Symposium, *The Bork Nomination,* 9 CARDOZO L. REV. 1 (1987).

Some see the crisis in legitimacy as deriving from judicial receptivity to the claims of racial minorities and other "outsiders," of which women are merely one group. *See* G. PHILIP BOBBITT, CONSTITUTIONAL INTERPRETATION 83–108 (1991); MARTHA MINOW, MAKING ALL THE DIFFERENCE: INCLUSION, EXCLUSION, AND AMERICAN LAW 356–62 (1990); Richard Friedman, *Tribal Myths: Ideology and the Confirmation of Supreme Court Nominations,* 95 YALE L.J. 1283 (1986); Graglia, *supra* note 22, at 1037–43; Karst, *supra* note 9.

34. For a detailed, but far from balanced, account of the role of the abortion controversy in American politics from 1973 to 1990, see CATHERINE WHITNEY, WHOSE LIFE? A BALANCED, COMPREHENSIVE VIEW OF ABORTION FROM ITS HISTORICAL CONTEXT TO THE CURRENT DEBATE 23–35, 77–91, 117–55, 160–66, 220–40 (1991). For an account of abortion politics throughout the twentieth century that is even less evenhanded, see GARROW, *supra* note 22. *See also* THE ABORTION DISPUTE AND THE AMERICAN SYSTEM (Gilbert Steiner ed. 1983); DALLAS BLANCHARD, THE ANTI-ABORTION MOVEMENT AND THE RISE OF THE RELIGIOUS RIGHT: FROM POLITE TO FIERY PROTEST (1994); ROBERT BLANK & JANNA MERRICK, HUMAN REPRODUCTION, EMERGING TECHNOLOGIES, AND CONFLICTING RIGHTS 39–57 (1995); COOK, JELEN, & WILCOX, *supra* note 17; CRAIG & O'BRIEN, *supra* note 6; CRITCHLOW, *supra* note 6, at 200–24; JOHN D'EMILIO & ESTELLE FREEDMAN, INTIMATE MATTERS: A HISTORY OF SEXUALITY IN AMERICA 347–50 (1988); SUSAN FALUDI, THE UNDECLARED WAR AGAINST AMERICAN WOMEN 400–53 (1991); MARIAN FAUX, CRUSADERS: VOICES FROM THE ABORTION FRONT (1990); FEDERAL ABORTION POLITICS, *supra* note 33; GINSBURG, *supra* note 17, at 43–57; CYNTHIA GORNEY, ARTICLES OF FAITH: A FRONTLINE HISTORY OF THE ABORTION WARS (1998); MARK GRABER, RETHINKING ABORTION: EQUAL CHOICE, THE CONSTITUTION, AND REPRODUCTIVE POLITICS 118–56 (1996); JANET HADLEY, ABORTION: BETWEEN FREEDOM AND NECESSITY 1–17 (1996); BEVERLY WILDUNG HARRISON, OUR RIGHT TO CHOOSE: TOWARD A NEW ETHIC OF ABORTION 238–44 (1983); JACOBY, *supra* note 17; KENNETH KARST, LAW'S

all, the abortion controversy has become a pivotal (some would say, "the pivotal") focal point in the culture wars between right and left,[35] as well as having sparked violence between the strongly committed over a longer period of time than any similar dispute except that over race relations.[36]

In an effort to cut off debate, most courts refused to accept as legitimate the arguments of the disfavored side. This has been particularly true for the Supreme Court, which, for example, has never really considered the evidence of fetal development. In *Roe* itself, the Supreme Court refused to consider the interests of the fetus, considering only the interest of the state in the fetus.[37] Even when confronting the question of whether employers could impose workplace policies designed for fetal protection, the Court refused to consider the interests of the fetus in deciding that such policies discriminated illegally against women who were pregnant.[38]

---

PROMISE, LAW'S EXPRESSION: VISIONS OF POWER IN THE POLITICS OF RACE, GENDER, AND RELIGION 31–66 (1993); KRISTIN LUKER, ABORTION AND THE POLITICS OF MOTHERHOOD (1984); MICHELLE MCKEEGAN, ABORTION POLITICS: MUTINY IN THE RANKS OF THE RIGHT (1992); O'BRIEN, *supra* note 6, at 39–43, 111–21, 405–06; KAREN O'CONNOR, NO NEUTRAL GROUND? ABORTION POLITICS IN AN AGE OF ABSOLUTES (1996); CONNIE PAIGE, THE RIGHT TO LIFERS: WHO THEY ARE; HOW THEY OPERATE; WHERE THEY GET THEIR MONEY (1983); ROSALIND POLLACK PETCHESKY, ABORTION AND WOMEN'S CHOICE: THE STATE, SEXUALITY, AND REPRODUCTIVE FREEDOM 241–76 (rev. ed. 1990); A. JAMES REICHLEY, RELIGION IN AMERICAN PUBLIC LIFE 319–28 (1985); RISEN & THOMAS, *supra* note 4; EVA RUBIN, ABORTION, POLITICS, AND THE COURTS (rev. ed. 1987); PATRICK SHEERAN, WOMEN, SOCIETY, THE STATE, AND ABORTION: A STRUCTURALIST ANALYSIS 1–10 (1987); ROBERT SPITZLER, THE RIGHT TO LIFE MOVEMENT AND THIRD PARTY POLITICS (1987); SUZANNE STAGGENBORG, THE PRO-CHOICE MOVEMENT: ORGANIZATION AND ACTIVISM IN THE ABORTION CONFLICT (1991); RAYMOND TATALOVICH & BYRON DAYNES, THE POLITICS OF ABORTION: A STUDY OF COMMUNITY CONFLICT IN PUBLIC POLICY MAKING (1981); UNDERSTANDING THE NEW POLITICS OF ABORTION, *supra* note 17; WETSTEIN, *supra* note 6; Julie George, *Political Effects of Court Decisions on Abortion: A Comparison between the United States and the Ger man Federal Republic,* 3 INT'L J.L. & FAM. 106 (1989); William Saletan, *Electoral Politics and Abortion: Narrowing the Message,* in ABORTION WARS, *supra* note 27, at 111.

35. See the authorities collected *supra* at note 17.

36. See the text *infra* at notes 111–14.

37. 410 U.S. at 159; Farrell, *supra* note 6, at 302–06.

38. UAW v. Johnson Controls, Inc., 499 U.S. 187 (1991); ROBERT BLANK, FETAL PROTECTION IN THE WORKPLACE: WOMEN'S RIGHTS, BUSINESS INTERESTS, AND THE UNBORN (1993); BLANK & MERRICK, *supra* note 38, at 153–75; MARCIA MOBILIA BOUMIL, LAW, ETHICS AND REPRODUCTIVE CHOICE 59–83 (1994); COLKER, *supra* note 15, at 154–57; CYNTHIA DANIELS, AT WOMEN'S EXPENSE: STATE POWER AND THE POLITICS OF FETAL RIGHTS 72–95 (1993); SUSAN FALUDI, BACKLASH 477–91 (1992); HADLEY, *supra* note 34, at 71–73, 137–41; SALLY KENNEY, FOR WHOSE PROTECTION? REPRODUCTIVE HAZARDS AND EXCLUSIONARY POLICIES IN THE UNITED STATES AND BRITAIN (1992); NANCY LEVIT, THE GENDER LINE: MEN, WOMEN, AND THE LAW 74–77 (1998); J.K. MASON, MEDICO-LEGAL ASPECTS OF REPRODUCTION AND PARENTHOOD 144–50 (2nd ed. 1998); CHERYL MEYER, THE WANDERING UTERUS: POLITICS AND THE REPRODUCTIVE RIGHTS OF WOMEN 108–30 (1997); JOHN ROBERTSON, CHILDREN OF CHOICE: FREEDOM AND THE NEW REPRODUCTIVE TECHNOLOGIES 173–94 (1994); BONNIE STEINBOCK, LIFE BEFORE BIRTH 127–63 (1992); Elaine Draper, *Reproductive Hazards and Fetal Exclusion Policies after* Johnson Controls, 12 STAN. L. & POL'Y REV. 117 (2001); Janet Gallagher, *Collective Bad Faith: "Protecting" the Fetus,* in REPRODUCTION, ETHICS, AND THE LAW: FEMINIST PERSPECTIVES 343 (Joan Callahan ed. 1995); Judith Greenberg, *The Pregnancy Discrimination Act: Legitimating Discrimination against Pregnant Women in the Workplace,* 50 ME. L. REV. 225 (1998); Jeffrey Phelan, *The Maternal Abdominal Wall: A Fortress against Fetal Health Care?,* 65 S. CAL. L. REV. 461 (1991); Carol Sanger, *M Is for the Many Things,* 1 REV. L. & WOMEN'S STUD. 15, 48, 56–62 (1992); Michael Thomson, *Employing the Body: The Reproductive Body and Employment Exclusion,* 5 SOC. & LEGAL STUD. 243 (1996); Christopher Yates & Corinne Beckwith Yates, *Fetal Rights: Sources and Implications of an Emerging Legal Concept,* in MEDICINE, ABORTION AND THE LAW 293 (J. Douglas Butler & David Walbert eds., 4th ed. 1992). The British have been more reluctant to pursue such theories than the Americans. See DAVID MEYERS, THE HUMAN BODY AND THE LAW 2–22 (2nd ed. 1990); Anne Morris & Susan Nott, *The Legal Response to Pregnancy,* 54 OX. J. LEGAL STUD. 54 (1992). *See also Declaration-Position Statement and Proposed Plan of action for Period up to 2000 and in 21st Century: On Worker's* (sic) *Reproductive Health Protection,* adopted Dec. 10, 1998, at a conference sponsored by the World Health Organization, reprinted in 8 TEX. J. WOMEN & L. 127 (1998); Ilise Feitshans, *Is There a*

Lower courts in America have only begun to struggle with the implications of modern medical technologies regarding the status of the fetus. Thus lower federal courts have split over whether a fetus is a "person" protected by the so-called *Ku Klux Klan Act* enacted in 1871 to protect "persons" from action taken under color of state law to deprive them of the protections of the Fourteenth Amendment.[39] Most courts have concluded that the Supreme Court's decision in the *Roe v. Wade* precludes finding that the *Ku Klux Klan Act* protects unborn children.[40] An occasional court, however, has concluded that, in light of modern medical knowledge, the statute must be interpreted to protect the unborn even if the constitution does not.[41]

Or consider the legal controversies related to human reproduction if a baby is born (or dies) showing the effects of prenatal abuse from the mother's conduct. Apparently more women than men use crack[42] — with all too predictable results.[43] One estimate (in the later 1980s) by the Na-

---

*Human Right to Reproductive Health?*, 8 Tex. J. Women & L. 93 (1998); Åke Saldeen, *Sweden: Rights of the Unborn Child and a Children's Ombudsman*, 31 J. Fam. L. 477 (1993).

39. 42 U.S.C. § 1983 (2000).

40. Bray v. Alexandria Women's Health Clinic, 506 U.S. 263 (1993); Arnold v. Board of Educ. of Escambia Cnty., 880 F.2d 305, 312 n.9 (11th Cir. 1989); Ruiz Romero v. Gonzales Caraballo, 681 F. Supp. 123 (D.P.R. 1988); Harman v. Daniels, 525 F. Supp. 798 (W.D. Va. 1981); Green v. Stanton, 451 F. Supp. 567 (N.D. Ind. 1978); Poole v. Endsley, 371 F. Supp. 1379 (N.D. Fla. 1974), *remanded mem.*, 561 F.2d 898 (5th Cir. 1975); McGarvey v. Magee-Womens Hospital, 340 F. Supp. 751 (W.D. Pa. 1972), *aff'd mem.*, 474 F.2d 1339 (3rd Cir. 1973).

41. Crumpton v. Gates, 947 F.2d 1418 (9th Cir. 1991); Doe v. Lukhard, 493 F.2d 54 (4th Cir. 1974), *vacated on other grounds*, 420 U.S. 999 (1975); Douglas v. Town of Hartford, 542 F. Supp. 1267 (D. Conn. 1982). *See also* Stuart v. Canary, 367 F. Supp. 1343 (N.D. Ohio 1973); Green v. Stanton, 364 F. Supp. 123 (N.D. Ind. 1973), *rev'd on other grounds sub nom.* Wilson v. Weaver, 499 F.2d 155 (7th Cir. 1974), *vacated mem.*, 420 U.S. 999 (1975); Wilson v. Weaver, 358 F. Supp. 1147 (N.D. Ill. 1972), *rev'd on other grounds*, 499 F.2d 155 (7th Cir. 1974), *vacated mem.*, 420 U.S. 999 (1975); Cape May Cty. Chapter, Inc. v. Macchia, 329 F. Supp. 504 (D.N.J. 1971). *See generally* Paul Czepiga, Note, *The Fetus under Section 1983: Still Struggling for Recognition*, 34 Syr. L. Rev. 1029 (1983); N.B.T., Note, Douglas v. Town of Hartford: *The Fetus as Plaintiff under Section 1983*, 35 Ala. L. Rev. 397 (1984).

42. Gina Kolata, *On Streets Ruled by Crack, Families Die*, N.Y. Times, Aug. 11, 1989, at A13 (reporting that women use crack more often than men in New York City); Gillian Walker *et al.*, *A Descriptive Outline of a Program for Cocaine Using Mother and Their Babies*, 3 J. Feminist Fam. Therapy 7, 7 (1991) (60% of crack addicts are women). *See generally* James Inciardi, Dorothy Lockwood, & Anne Pottieger, Women and Crack Cocaine (1993).

43. *See* Gerald Briggs, Roger Freeman, & Summer Yaffe, Drugs in Pregnancy (3rd ed. 1990); Mason, *supra* note 38, at 172; Ira Chasnoff, *Cocaine, Pregnancy, and the Neonate*, 15 Women & Helath 23 (1989); Ira Chasnoff *et al.*, *Cocaine Use in Pregnancy*, 313 New Eng. J. Med. 666 (1985); Ira Chasnoff *et al.*, *Temporal Patterns of Cocaine Use in Pregnancy: Perinatal Outcome*, 261 JAMA 1741 (1989); Committee on Substance Abuse, *Drug-Exposed Infants*, 96 Am. Acad. Pediatrics 364 (1995); Nancy Day, Carrie Cottreau, & Gale Richardson, *The Epidemiology of Alcohol, Marijuana, and Cocaine Use among Woman of Childbearing Age and Pregnant Women*, 36 Clin. Obstet. & Gynecology 232 (1990); Barbara Howard & Karen O'Donnell, *What Is Important about a Study of Within-Group Differences of "Cocaine Babies"?*, 149 Arch. Pediatrics & Adolescent Med. 663 (1995); Louis Keith *et al.*, *Substance Abuse in Pregnant Women: Recent Experience at the Perinatal Center for Chemical Dependence of Northwestern Memorial Hospital*, 73 Obstet. & Gynecology 715 (1989); Linda Mayes *et al.*, *Information Processing and Development Assessments in Three-Month-Old Infants Exposed Prenatally to Cocaine*, Pediatrics, Apr. 1995, T 539; Mark Neehof *et al.*, *Cocaine Abuse During Pregnancy: Peripartum Prevalence and Perinatal Outcome*, 161 Am. J. Obstet. & Gynecology 633 (1989); Amy Oro & Suzanne Dixon, *Perinatal Cocaine and Methamphetamine Exposure: Maternal and Neonatal Correlates*, 111 J. Pediatrics 571 (1987); Diane Petitti & Charlotte Coleman, *Cocaine and the Risk of Low Birth Weight*, 80 Am. J. Pub. Health 25 (1990); James Wood, jr., Mark Plessinger, & Kenneth Clark, *Effect of Cocaine on Uterine Blood Flow and Fetal Oxygenation*, 257 JAMA 957 (1987). *See also* Sandra Blakeslee, *Crack's Toll among Babies: A Joyless View, Even of Toys*, N.Y. Times, Sep. 17, 1989, at A1; Micheal de Courey Hinds, *The Instincts of Parenthood become Part of Crack's Toll*, N.Y. Times, Mar. 17, 1990, at A8; Anastasia Toufexis, *Innocent Victims: Damaged by the Drugs Their Mothers Took, Crack Kids Will Face Social and Educational Hurdles and Must Count on Society's Compassion*, Time, May 13, 1991, at 56.

tional Association for Prenatal Addiction Research and Education placed the number of drug exposed infants born yearly in the United States at 375,000.[44] Prosecutors around the country have initiated criminal prosecutions of women for "delivering" drugs to their infant through the umbilical cord in the several seconds between birth and the cutting of the cord.[45] There were more than 160 such prosecutions in the first year after the first case that received wide publicity, and several state child abuse statutes were amended to authorize such prosecutions explicitly.[46]

---

44. Jean Davidson, *Drug Babies Push Issue of Fetal Rights,* L.A. Times, Apr. 25, 1989, pt. I, at 3 (11% of infants at 36 hospitals were born affected by crack). *See also* Douglas Besharov, *Crack Babies: The Worst Threat Is Mom Herself,* Wash. Post, Aug. 6, 1989, at B1; Marty Jessup & Robert Roth, *Clinical and Legal Perspectives on Prenatal Drug and Alcohol Use: Guidelines for Individual and Community Response,* 7 Med. & Law 377 (1988).

45. *See* Johnson v. State, 602 So. 2d 1288 (Fla. 1992).

46. The number of prosecutions comes from Julia Epstein, *The Pregnant Imagination, Fetal Rights, and Women's Bodies: A (sic) Historical Inquiry,* 7 Yale J.L. & Human. 138, 141 (1995). While such prosecutions have been common, most courts have found them improper under the applicable criminal statutes. *Sustaining prosecution:* Kruse v. Hawai'i, 68 F.3d 331 (9th Cir. 1995); *In re* Baby Boy Blackshear, 736 N.E.2d 762 (Ohio 2000) (criminal child abuse); Whitner v. State, 492 S.E.2d 777 (S.C. 1997), *cert. denied,* 523 U.S. 1145 (1998). *Dismissing prosecution:* Reinesto v. Superior Ct., 894 P.2d 733 (Ariz. Ct. App. 1995); Reyes v. Superior Ct., 141 Cal. Rptr. 912 (Ct. App. 1977); State v. Ashley, 701 So. 2d 338 (Fla. 1997); State v. Johnson, 602 So. 2d 1288 (Fla. 1992); State v. Gethers, 585 So. 2d 1140 (Fla. Dist. 1991); State v. Luster, 419 S.E.2d 32 (Ga. Ct. App. 1992), *state cert. denied*; Commonwealth v. Welch, 864 S.W.2d 280 (Ky. 1993); People v. Hardy, 469 N.W.2d 50 (Mich. Ct. App.), *appeal denied,* 471 N.W.2d 619 (Mich. 1991); People v. Morabito, 580 N.Y.S.2d 843 (Geneva City Ct. 1992); Sheriff of Washoe Cnty. v. Encoe, 885 P.2d 596 (Nev. 1994); State v. Gray, 584 N.E.2d 710 (Ohio 1992) (criminal child neglect); Collins v. State, 890 S.W.2d 893 (Tex. Ct. App. 1994); State v. Dunn, 916 P.2d 952 (Wash. Ct. App.), *rev. denied,* 928 P.2d 413 (Wash. 1996); State v. Osmus, 276 P.2d 469 (Wyo. 1954). *See also* David Firestone, *Woman Is Convicted of Killing Her Fetus by Smoking Cocaine,* N.Y. Times, Mar. 18, 2001, at A12; Bob Herbert, *Stillborn Justice,* N.Y. Times, May 24, 2001, at A29. For examples of the amended statutes, see S.D. Codified Laws §§ 34-20A-63 to 34-20A-70 (Michie 1994); Wis. Stat. Ann. §§ 48.01 to 48.347 (West 1998). *See generally* 70 A.L.R.5th 461 (1999).

*See also* Daniels, *supra* note 38, at 2–3, 102–03, 121; Linda Beck Fenwick, Private Choices, Public Consequences: Reproductive Technology and the New Ethics of Conception, Pregnancy, and Family 129–31 (1998); Center for Reproductive Law & Policy, Reproductive Freedom in Focus: Punishing Women for Their Behavior during Pregnancy (1996); Laura Gómez, Misconceiving Mothers: Legislators, Prosecutors, and the Politics of Prenatal Drug Exposure (1997); Valery Green, Doped Up, Knocked Up, and...Locked Up? The Criminal Prosecution of Women Who Use Drugs during Pregnancy (1993); Mason, *supra* note 38, at 172–76; Cheryl Meyer, The Wandering Uterus: Politics and the Reproductive Rights of Women 85–99 (1997); Lawrence Nelson & Mary Faith Marshall, Ethical and Legal Analyses of Three Coercive Policies Aimed at Substance Abuse by Pregnant Women (1998); Lynn Paltrow, Criminal Prosecutions against Pregnant Women (1992); Proceed with Care: Final Report of the [Canadian] Royal Commission on New Reproductive Technologies 964–65 (1993); Rachel Roth, Making Women Pay: The Hidden Costs of Fetal Rights (1999); John Cloud, *Protecting the Unborn: How Far Can Police Go to Prevent a Mother from Harming Her Fetus? The Supreme Court Will Decide,* Time, Oct. 6, 2000, at 50; Kathryn Ann Farr, *Fetal Abuse and the Criminalization of Behavior during Pregnancy,* 41 Crime & Delinquency 235 (1995); Patrick Healy, *Statutory Prohibitions and the Regulation of New Reproductive Technologies under Federal Law in Canada,* 40 McGill L.J. 905, 937–42 (1995); Michael Higgins, *Protective Custody: A Ruling Barring Forced Drug Treatment for a Pregnant Woman May Not End the Legal Dispute,* ABA J., July, 1997, at 28; Robyn Kaufman, *Legal Recognition of Independent Fetal Rights: The Trend towards Criminalizing Prenatal Maternal Conduct,* 17 Children's Legal Rts. J., no. 2, at 20 (Spring 1997); Norra MacReady, *Fetal Homicide Charge for Drinking While Pregnant?,* 313 Brit. Med. J. 645 (1996); Sheila Martin & Murray Coleman, *Judicial Intervention in Pregnancy,* 40 McGill L.J. 947 (1995); Stephanie Hainer Ojeda, Comment, *Whitner v. State: Expanding Child Abuse and Endangerment Laws to Protect Viable Fetuses from Prenatal Substance Abuse,* 99 W. Va. L. Rev. 311 (1996); Jean Reith Schroedel, Pamela Fiber, & Bruce Snyder, *Women's Rights and Fetal Personhood in Criminal Law,* 7 Duke J. Gender & L. 89 (2000); Sandra Smith, Note, *Fetal Homicide: Women or Fetus as Victim? A Survey of Current State Approaches and Recommendations for Future State Application,* 41 Wm. & Mary L. Rev. 1845 (2000); Ruth Ann Strickland & Marcia Lynn Whicker, *Fetal Endangerment Versus Fetal Welfare,* in Expecting Trouble: Surrogacy, Fetal Abuse, and New Reproductive Technologies: Discretion of Prosecutors in

Even more frequently, women have lost custody of children who were born drug addicted.[47] Other drug-addicted women have been ordered to use birth control devices as a condition of probation or parole[48] or compelled to undergo unwanted cesarean sections or other medical treatments in order to maximize the chances of a live—and healthy—birth.[49] One court or-

---

DETERMINING CRIMINAL LIABILITY 55 (Patricia Boling ed. 1995); *See also* André Panossian, Vahé Panossian, & Nancy Doumanian, *Criminalization of Perinatal HIV Transmission,* 19 J. LEG. MED. 223 (1998).

47. *See, e.g., In re* Maricopa Cnty. Juvenile Action No. JS-501568, 869 P.2d 1224 (Ariz. Ct. App. 1994); *In re* Jessie G., 67 Cal. Rptr. 2d 811 (Ct. App. 1997); *In re* Troy D., 263 Cal. Rptr. 869 (Ct. App. 1989); Ernst v. Monk, 344 N.W.2d 39 (Mich. Ct. App. 1984); *In re* Baby X, 293 N.W.2d 736 (Mich. Ct. App. 1980); *In re* Guardianship of K.H.O., 736 A.2d 1246 (1999); *In re* Stefanel Tyesha C., 556 N.Y.S.2d 280 (App. Div.), *appeal dismissed,* 565 N.E.2d 1267 (N.Y. 1990); *In re* Fatima Ashanti K.J., 558 N.Y.S.2d 447 (Fam. Ct. 1990); *In re* Smith, 492 N.Y.S.2d 331 (Fam. Ct. 1985); *In re* "Male" R., 422 N.Y.S.2d 819 (Fam. Ct. 1979); *In re* Ruiz, 500 N.E.2d 935 (Ohio C.P. 1986); *In re* J.M., 749 A.2d 17 (Vt. 2000); *In re* D. (a minor), [1987] 1 All E.R. 20 (H.L.); Superintendent of Family & Child Service v. McDonald, 135 D.L.R.3rd 330 (B.C. 1982); *In re* Children's Aid Soc'y of Kenora, 134 D.L.R.3rd 249 (Ont. 1981). *But see* People *ex rel.* H., 74 P.3d 494 (Colo. Ct. App. 2003), *state cert. denied; In re* Valerie D., 613 A.2d 748 (Conn. 1992); *In re* Nassau Cnty. Dep't Soc. Services, 661 N.E.2d 138 (N.Y. 1995); *In re* Fletcher, 533 N.Y.S.2d 241 (Fam. Ct. 1988); *See also* FENWICK, *supra* note 46, at 114–18, 133–43; MASON, *supra* note 38, at 174–76; Michael Freeman, *England's Moral Quagmire,* 27 J. FAM. L. 101, 105–09 (1988); Tony & Julie Zitella, *Protecting our Children: A Call to Reform State Policies to Hold Pregnant Drug Addicts Accountable,* 29 J. MARSHALL L. REV. 765 (1996).

48. *See, e.g.,* People v. Zaring, 10 Cal. Rptr. 2d 263 (Ct. App. 1992); People v. Pointer, 199 Cal. Rptr. 357 (Ct. App. 1984). *See also* People v. Bedenkamp, 625 N.E.2d 123 (Ill. App. Ct. 1993) (a woman sentenced to prison "to prevent her from becoming pregnant); State v. Oakley, 629 N.W.2d 200, *clarified on rehearing,* 248 N.W.2d 760 (Wis. 2001) (a man's probation conditioned on his not fathering any children for five years), *cert. denied,* 537 U.S. 813 (2002). *See* MEYER, *supra* note 46, at 104–07; ROBERTSON, *supra* note 38, at 82–83; AMA Board of Trustees, *Requirements or Incentives by Government for the Use of Long-Acting Contraceptives,* 267 JAMA 1818 (1992); Stacey Arthur, *The Norplant Prescription: Birth Control, Woman Control, or Crime Control?,* 40 UCLA L. REV. 1 (1992); Thomas Barrum, *Birth Control as a Condition of Probation—A New Weapon in the War against Child Abuse,* 80 Ky. L.J. 1037 (1992); Meredith Blake, *Welfare and Coerced Contraception: Moral Implications of State Sponsored Reproductive Control,* 34 U. LOUISVILLE J. FAM. L. 311 (1995); Joan Callahan, *Contraception or Incarceration: What's Wrong with This Picture?,* 7 STAN. L. & POL'Y REV. 67 (1996); Emily Campbell, *Birth Control as a Condition of Probation for Those Convicted of Child Abuse: A Psycholegal Discussion of Whether the Condition Prevents Future Child Abuse or Is A Violation of Liberty,* 28 GONZAGA L. REV. 67 (1992); David Coale, *Norplant Bonuses and the Unconstitutional Conditions Doctrine,* 71 TEX. L. REV. 189 (1992); Scott Jebson, *Conditioning a Woman's Probation on Her Using Norplant: New Weapon against Child Abuse Backfires,* 17 CAMPBELL L. REV. 301 (1995); Jack Lipton & Colin Campbell, *The Constitutionality of Court-Imposed Birth Control as a Condition of Probation,* 6 J. HUM. RTS. 271 (1989); Julie Mertus & Simon Heller, *Norplant Meets the New Eugenicists: The Impermissibility of Coerced Contraception,* 11 ST. L.U. PUB. L. REV. 359 (1992); Rachel Roth, *"No New Babies?" Gender Inequality and Reproductive Control in the Criminal Justice and Prison System,* 12 AM. U. GENDER, SOC. POL'Y & L. 391 (2004); Janet Steverson, *Stopping Fetal Abuse with No-Pregnancy and Drug Treatment Probation Conditions,* 34 STA. CLARA L. REV. 295 (1994); Symposium, *Long-Action Contraception: Moral Choices, Policy Dilemmas,* 25 HASTINGS CTR. REP., No. 1, Supp. at S1 (Jan.–Feb. 1995). *See also* Judy Howard, *Chronic Drug Users as Parents,* 43 HASTINGS. L. REV. 645 (1992); Linda Kelly, *Reproductive Liberty under the Threat of Care: Deputizing Private Agents and Deconstructing State Action,* 5 MICH. J. GENDER & L. 81, 100–06 (1998). *See generally* Symposium, *Too Hard: Unconstitutional Conditions and the Chimera of Constitutional Consistency,* 72 DEN. U. L. REV. 989 (1995).

49. *See, e.g.,* MINN. STAT. ANN. § 518.131(i) (West Supp. 2003); *In re* Steven S., 178 Cal. Rptr. 525 (Ct. App. 1981); *In re* M.B., [1997] 8 BRIT. MED. L. REP. 217; *In re* L, [1996] 35 BRIT. MED. L. REP. 44 (F.D.); Norfolk & Norwich (NHS) Trust v. W, [1996] 2 FAM. 613; *In re* S, [1993] 1 FAM. 123; Tameside & Glossop Acute Services Trust v. CH, [1996] 1 FAM. 762; *In re* Baby P, [1995] N.Z.L.R. 577. *But see* Arkansas Dep't of Human Services v. Collier, 95 S.W.3d 772 (Ark. 2003); *In re* H, 74 P.3d 494 (Colo. Ct. App. 2003), *state cert. denied;* State *ex rel.* Angela M.W. v. Kruzicki, 561 N.W.2d 729 (Wis. 1997); *In re* A, 72 D.L.R.4th 722 (Ont. Fam. Ct. 1990). For representative cases in which a court ordered medical care for an unborn child not involving drugs, see: Pemberton v. Tallahassee Mem. Regional Med. Ctr., Inc., 66 F. Supp. 2d 1247 (N.D. Fla. 1999); *In re* President & Directors of Georgetown College, Inc., 331 F.2d 1000 (D.C. Cir. 1964), *cert. denied sub nom.* Jones v. President & Directors of Georgetown College, Inc., 377 U.S. 978 (1965); *In re* A.C., 533 A.2d 611 (D.C. 1987), *vacated on rehearing en banc after the birth,* 539 A.2d 203 (D.C. 1988), *vacation aff'd sub nom. In re* Maydun, 573 A.2d

dered an addicted woman taken into state custody during her pregnancy in order to protect the fetus from possible abuse.[50] And at least one state court has allowed tort actions on behalf of the

1235 (D.C. Ct. App. 1990); Jefferson v. Griffin Spalding Cnty. Hosp. Auth'y, 274 S.E.2d 457 (Ga. 1981); Raleigh Fitkin-Paul Morgan Mem. Hosp. v. Anderson, 201 A.2d 537 (N.J.), *cert. denied,* 377 U.S. 985 (1964); Crouse Irving Mem'l Hosp. v. Paddock, 485 N.Y.S.2d 433 (Sup. Ct. 1985); *In re* Jamaica Hosp., 491 N.Y.S.2d 898 (Sup. Ct. 1985). For representative cases in which a court refused to order medical care for an unborn child not involving drugs, see: *In re* Maydun, 573 A.2d 1235 (D.C. Ct. App. 1990); *In re* Dubreuil, 629 So. 2d 819 (Fla. 1993); *In re* Fetus Brown, 689 N.E.2d 397 (Ill. App. Ct. 1997), *appeal denied,* 698 N.E.2d 543 (Ill. 1998); *In re* Baby Boy Doe, 632 N.E.2d 326 (Ill. App. Ct. 1994); Mercy Hosp. Inc. v. Jackson, 489 A.2d 1130 (Md. Ct. Spec. App. 1985), *vacated as moot,* 510 A.2d 562 (Md. 1986); Taft v. Taft, 446 N.E.2d 395 (Mass. 1983); St. George's Healthcare NHS Trust v. S, [1998] 3 All E.R. 673 (C.A.). At least one court has issued a restraining order against the father of an unborn child, threatening him with jail if he continued to abuse his pregnant wife — expressly premising the order on protection of the child. Gloria C. v. William C., 476 N.Y.S.2d 991 (Fam. Ct. 1984).

*See generally* Fenwick, *supra* note 46, at 62–64, 68–71; Mason, *supra* note 38, at 153–56; Meyer, *supra* note 46, at 164–76; David Blickenstaff, *Defining the Boundaries of Personal Privacy: Is There a Paternal Interest in Compelling Therapeutic Fetal Surgery?,* 88 Nw. U. L. Rev. 1168 (1994); Jennifer Brown, *A Troublesome Maternal-Fetal Conflict: Legal, Ethical, and Social Issues Surrounding Mandatory AZT Treatment of HIV Positive Pregnant Women,* 18 Buff. Pub. Int. L.J. 67 (2000); James Filkins, *A Pregnant Mother's Right to Refuse Treatment Beneficial to the Fetus: Refusing Blood Transfusions,* 2 DePaul J. Health Care 361 (1998); Robert Francis, *Compulsory Caesarean Sections: An English Perspective,* 14 J. Contemp. Health L. & Pol'y 365 (1998); Jonathan Herring, *Compelling Caesarean Sections,* 140/141 Law & Justice 43 (1999); Harriett Hornick, *Mama vs. Fetus,* 39 Med. Trial Q. 536 (1993); Lisa Ikemoto, *The Code of Perfect Pregnancy: At the Intersection of the Ideology of Motherhood, the Practice of Defaulting to Science, and the Interventionist Mindset of the Law,* 53 Ohio St. L.J. 1205 (1992); Deborah Mathieu, *Mandating Treatment for Pregnant Substance Abusers: A Compromise,* 14 Pol. & Life Sci. 199 (1995); Diane Meulemans, *Approaching the Slope: Process and Outcomes of the Use of the Slippery Slope in Legal Opinions,* 14 Wis. Women's L.J. 105, 118–20 (1999); Caroline Morris, *Technology and the Legal Discourse of Fetal Autonomy,* 8 UCLA Women's L.J. 47, 88–89, 91–94 (1997); Alice Oullette, *New Medical Technology: A Chance to Reexamine Court-Ordered Medical Procedures during Pregnancy,* 57 Alb. L. Rev. 927 (1994); Charity Scott, *Resisting the Temptation to Turn Medical Recommendations into Judicial Orders: A Reconsideration of Court-Ordered Surgery for Pregnant Women,* 10 Ga. St. U. L. Rev. 615 (1994); John Seymour, *A Pregnant Woman's Decision to Decline Treatment: How Should the Law Respond?,* 2 J. Law & Med. 27 (1994); Lois Shepherd, *Protecting Parents' Freedom to Have Children with Genetic Difference,* 1995 U. Ill. L. Rev. 761; Ceri Widdett & Michael Thomson, *Justifying Treatment and Other Stories,* 5 Fem. Legal Stud. 77 (1997).

Recently, Canadian courts have declined to become involved in such cases. *See* Winnipeg Child & Fam. Services v. G, [1997] 3 S.C.R. 925 (Can.); *In re* Baby R, 53 D.L.R.4th 69 (B.C. 1988); *In re* Children's Aid Soc'y of Kenora, 134 D.L.R.3d 249 (1981). Earlier decisions had gone the other way. *In re* A. (*in utero*), 72 D.L.R.4th 722 (1990); *In re* Children's Aid Soc'y of Belleville, 59 O.R.2d 204 (1987). *See* T. Brettel Dawson, *First Person Familiar: Judicial Intervention in Pregnancy, Again:* G.(D.F.), 10 Can. J. Women & L. 213 (1998); Julia Hanigsberg, *Power and Procreation: State Interference with Pregnancy,* 23 Ottawa L. Rev. 35, 40 (1991); Martin & Coleman, *supra* note 46; Jenny Morgan, *Foetal Imaginings: Searching for a Vocabulary in the Law and Politics of Reproduction,* 12 Can. J. Women & L. 371, 379–94 (2000); Sanda Rodgers, *Winnipeg Child and Family Services v. D.F.G.: Juridical Interference with Pregnant Women in the Alleged Interest of the Fetus,* 36 Alta. L. Rev. 711 (1998); Laura Shanner, *Pregnancy Intervention and Models of Maternal-Fetal Relationship: Philosophical Reflections on the* Winnipeg v. CFS *Dissent,* 36 Alta. L. Rev. 751 (1998); Alison Harvison Young, *New Reproductive Technologies in Canada and the United States: Same Problems, Different Discourses,* 12 Temple Int'l & Comp. L.J. 43, 65–75 (1998).

50. State *ex rel.* Angela M.W. v. Kruzicki, 541 N.W.2d 482 (Wis. Ct. App. 1995), *rev'd,* 561 N.W.2d 729 (Wis. 1997). *See also* Kenneth Jost, *Mother v. Child,* ABA J., Apr. 1989, at 84. *See generally* Fenwick, *supra* note 46, at 119–29; Meyer, *supra* note 46, at 99–104; Sandra Anderson Garcia & Ingo Keilitz, *Involuntary Civil Commitment of Drug Dependent Persons with Special Reference to Pregnant Women,* 15 Mental & Physical Disabilities L. Rptr. 418 (1991); Barrie Becker, *Order in the Court: Challenging Judges Who Incarcerate Pregnant, Substance Dependent Defendants to Protect Fetal Health,* 19 Hastings Const'l L.Q. 235 (1991); David Chavkin, *"For Their Own Good": Civil Commitment of Alcohol and Drug-Dependent Pregnant Women,* 37 S.D. L. Rev. 224 (1992); Wendy Chavkin, *Jennifer Johnson's Sentence,* 1 J. Clinical Ethics 140 (1991); Michael Flannery, *Court-Ordered Prenatal Intervention: A Final Means to the End of Gestational Abuse,* 30 J. Fam. L. 519

injured child against the mother.[51] Interestingly, few such steps have been taken against women who smoke tobacco or drink alcohol or coffee whose behavior also threatens the life or health of their infants.[52] Some have argued that this disparity arises because "crack mothers" are likely to be black, while mothers who abuse alcohol or tobacco more often are white.[53] So far, apparently only one woman has been prosecuted for excessive alcohol consumption late in her pregnancy— charged with attempted intentional homicide and reckless endangerment.[54]

When the United States Supreme Court finally entered into this dispute, it did so only with respect to the constitutionality of requiring urine tests as a precondition to prenatal care at a

---

(1991); Susan Goldberg, *Of Gametes and Guardians: The Impropriety of Appointing Guardians ad Litem for Fetuses and Embryos,* 66 WASH. L. REV. 503 (1991); Lisa Ikemoto, *Furthering the Inquiry: Race, Class, and Culture in the Forced Medical Treatment of Pregnant Women,* 59 U. TENN. L. REV. 487 (1992); Bonnie Steinbock, *Maternal-Fetal Conflict and In Utero Therapy,* 57 ALBANY L. REV. 781 (1994); James Wilson, *Compelled Hospitalization and Treatment during Pregnancy: Mental Health Statutes as Models for Legislation to Protect Children from Prenatal Drug and Alcohol Exposure,* 25 FAM. L.Q. 149 (1991). English and Canadian courts have concluded that they have no power to control a pregnant woman's behavior for the benefit of an *unborn* child. *In re* F. (in utero), [1988] Fam. 122; *In re* Baby R, 53 D.L.R.4th 69 (B.C. 1989). *See* MASON, *supra* note 38, at 174; J.H. Tanne, *Jail for Pregnant Cocaine Users in US,* 303 BRIT. MED. J. 873 (1991).

51. Grodin v. Grodin, 301 N.W.2d 869 (Mich. 1981). The Canadian Supreme Court, however, refused to allow suits based upon a mother's negligence, rejecting a lower court's attempt to distinguish simple negligence (here negligent driving) from her "'lifestyle choices'…peculiar to parenthood." Dobson v. Dobson, [1999] 2 S.C.R. 753, 763. Two members of the court sought to base the decision on constitutional equality grounds. *Dobson,* 2 S.C.R. at 770. *See generally* Morgan, *supra* note 49, at 372–73.

52. *See, e.g., In re* Appeal in Pima Cnty. Juvenile Severance Action, 905 P.2d 555 (Ariz. Ct. App. 1995), *rev. denied,* 911 P.2d 1085 (Ariz. 1996). *See* Cloud, *supra* note 46, at 52; MacReady, *supra* note 46. For one of the few such attempts—one that was rejected by the courts—see State v. Deborah J.Z., 596 N.W.2d 490 (Wis. Ct. App.), *rev. denied,* 604 N.W.2d 570 (Wis. 1999). *See generally* Ben Armstrong, Alison McDonald, & Margaret Sloan, *Cigarette, Alcohol, and Coffee Consumption and Spontaneous Abortion,* 82 AM. J. PUB. HEALTH 85 (1992); Linda Carroll, *Alcohol's Toll on Fetuses: Even Worse than Thought,* N.Y. TIMES, Nov. 4, 2003, at F1; Seymon Ioffe & Victor Chernick, *Maternal Alcohol Ingestion and the Incidence of Respiratory Disease Syndrome,* 156 AM. J. OBSTET. & GYNECOLOGY 1231 (1987); Mark Klebbanoff *et al., Serum Cotinine and Self-Reported Smoking during Pregnancy,* 148 AM. J. EPIDEMIOLOGY 259 (1998); Jennie Kline *et al., Cigarette Smoking and Spontaneous Abortion of Known Karyotype: Precise Data but Uncertain Inferences,* 141 AM. J. EPIDEMIOLOGY 417 (1995); James Mills, *Cocaine, Smoking, and Spontaneous Abortion,* 340 N. ENG. J. MED. 380 (1999); Roberta Ness *et al., Cocaine & Tobacco Use and the Risk of Spontaneous Abortion,* 340 NEW ENG. J. MED. 333 (1999); Raoul Walsh, *Effects of Maternal Smoking on Adverse Pregnancy Outcomes: Examination of the Criteria of Causation,* 66 HUM. BIOL. 1059 (1994); Michelle Williams *et al., Cigarette Smoking during Pregnancy in Relation to* Placenta Previa, 165 AM. J. OBSTET. & GYNECOLOGY 28 (1991); Gayle Windham, Laura Swan, & Barbara Fenster, *Parental Cigarette Smoking and the Risk of Spontaneous Abortion,* 135 AM. J. EPIDEMIOLIGY 1394 (1992). *But see* Jon Anderson, Comment, *Parental Smoking: A Form of Child Abuse?,* 77 MARQUETTE L. REV. 360 (1994); Hornstra, *supra* note 46, at 9–10; John Kleinig, *Criminal Liability for Fetal Endangerment,* 9 CRIM. JUST. ETHICS 11, 11–13 (1990); Schroedel, Fiber, & Snyder, *supra* note 46, at 106–07; Renee Solomon, *Future Fear: Prenatal Duties Imposed by Private Parties,* 17 AM. J. LAW & MED. 411 (1991).

53. DOROTHY ROBERTS, KILLING THE BLACK BODY 172–76 (1997); Ira Chasnoff, Harvey Landress, & Mark Barrett, *The Prevalence of Illicit-Drug or Alcohol Use during Pregnancy and Discrepancies in Mandatory Reporting in Pinellas County,* 322 N. ENG. J. MED. 1202 (1990); Dwight Greene, *Abusive Prosecutors: Gender, Race & Class Discretion and the Prosecution of Drug-Addicted Mothers,* 39 BUFF. L. REV. 737 (1991); Dorothy Roberts, *Motherhood and Crime,* 79 IOWA L. REV. 95 (1993); Dorothy Roberts, *Punishing Drug Addicts Who Have Babies: Women of Color, Equality, and the Right of Privacy,* 104 HARV. L. REV. 1419 (1991); Schroedel, Fiber, & Snyder. *supra* note 46, at 110; Barry Siegel, *In the Name of Children,* L.A. TIMES MAG., Aug. 7, 1994, at 14; Renee Solomon, Note, *Future Fear: Prenatal Duties Imposed by Private Parties,* 17 AM. J.L. & MED. 411, 418 (1991).

54. Robyn Blummer, *"Drunk Fetus" Cases Endanger Abortion Choice,* MILWAUKEE SENTINEL, Sept. 22, 1996, at A1; Ann Marie O'Neill *et al., Under the Influence,* PEOPLE, Sept. 9, 1996, at 53. *See also* Marilyn Hakim, Comment, *Mother v. Fetus: New Adversaries in the Struggle to Define the Rights of Unborn Children,* 18 J. JUVENILE L. 99 (1997). *See also* MacReady, *supra* note 46.

state-run hospital.[55] The majority found that the tests were compelled by the state and that as the results were obtained as part of a program that was intended to lead to prosecutions, the tests violated the Fourth Amendment's prohibition of unreasonable searches. The majority might have intended its decision to force hospitals to turn to therapy rather than to punitive measures in an effort to control drug use among pregnant women. Its practical effect, however, might prove to be the elimination of the strongest threats, measures that might assure that pregnant women in need of drug therapy would actually conform their behavior to a therapeutic regime.[56]

Ironically, any of these women could have demanded an abortion, and would have had a constitutional right to receive one if they could pay for it. Additionally, some hospitals that operate detoxification programs for addicts and alcoholics have sought to exclude pregnant women because of the greater expense and risks in treating such people.[57] Furthermore, several physicians have recently questioned the long-term effects of drug-use on newborns.[58] And, in any event, serious questions arise whether prosecuting or otherwise repressing women for abusing their children by ingesting drugs is the best way to deal with the problem.[59] Such actions might deter

---

55. Ferguson v. City of Charleston, 532 U.S. 67 (2001). *See also* Brian Bornstein, *Seize This Urine Test: The Implications of* Ferguson v. City of Charleston *for Drug Testing during Pregnancy,* 6 Mich. St. U. Det. Coll. L. J. Med. & L. 65 (2001); Samantha Weyrauch, *The Fetus and the Drug Addicted Mother: Whose Rights Should Prevail?,* 5 Mich. St. U. Det. Coll. L. J. Med. & L. 95 (2001). For the background of the *Ferguson* case, see Philip Jos *et al., The Charleston Policy on Cocaine Use during Pregnancy: A Cautionary Tale,* 23 J. Law, Med., & Ethics 120 (1995).

56. *Ferguson,* 532 U.S. at 76–86. *See generally* Ellen Marrus, *Crack Babies and the Constitution: Ruminations about Addicted Pregnant Women after* Ferguson v. City of Charleston, 47 Villa. L. Rev. 299 (2002).

57. Elaine W. v. Joint Diseases North General Hospital, Inc., 613 N.E.2d 523 (N.Y. 1993) (allowing suit under the New York Human Rights Law against a hospital that excluded women from its detoxification program).

58. *See* Deborah Frank *et al., Maternal Cocaine Use: Impact on Child Health and Development,* 40 Advances in Pediatrics 65 (1993); Tanya Kne *et al., A Program to Address the Special Needs of Drug-Exposed Children,* 64 J. Sch. Health 251 (1994); G. Koren *et al., Bias against the Null Hypothesis: The Reproductive Hazards of Cocaine,* 2 The Lancet 1440 (1989); Scott MacGregor *et al., Cocaine Abuse during Pregnancy: Correlation between Prenatal Care and Perinatal Outcome,* 74 Obstet. & Gynecology 882 (1989); Linda Mayes *et al., The Problem of Prenatal Cocaine Exposure: A Rush to Judgment,* 267 JAMA 406 (1992); L. Ryan, S. Ehrlich, & L. Finnegan, *Cocaine Abuse in Pregnancy: Effects on the Fetus and Newborn,* 9 Neurotoxicology & Teratology 295 (1987); Barry Zuckerman & Deborah Frank, *Crack Kids: Not Broken,* 89 Pediatrics 337 (1992). *See also* Michael Isikoff, *The Nation's Alcohol Problem Is Falling through the Crack,* Wash. Post (Nat'l Weekly ed.), Apr. 9–15, 1990, at 30; Dana Kennedy, *Children Born Addicted to Crack Defy Experts,* L.A. Times, Dec. 27, 1992, at A16; Daniel Neuspiel, *Let's Not Call Cocaine-Exposed Children "Crack Babies,"* N.Y. Times, Mar. 9, 1993, at A18; Zitella & Zitella, *supra* note 47, at 769.

59. *See* Reproductive Freedom in Focus, *supra* note 46; Fenwick, *supra* note 46, at 129–31; Gómez, *supra* note 46, at 26; Green, *supra* note 46; Mason, *supra* note 38, at 172–76; Meyer, *supra* note 46, at 85–99; Nelson & Marshall, *supra* note 46; Paltrow, *supra* note 46; [Canada] Royal Comm'n on New Reproductive Technologies, Proceed with Care: Final Report of the Royal Commission on New Reproductive Technologies 964 (1993); The Criminalization of Women's Bodies (Clarice Feinman ed. 1992); The Politics of Pregnancy: Policy Dilemmas in the Maternal-Fetal Relationship (Janna Merrick & Robert Blank eds. 1993); David Brody & Heidee McMillan, *Combating Fetal Substance Abuse and Governmental Foolhardiness through Collaborative Linkages, Therapeutic Jurisprudence and Common Sense: Helping Women Help Themselves,* 12 Hastings Women's L.J. 243 (2001); April Cherry, *Maternal-Fetal Conflicts, the Social Construction of Maternal Deviance, and Some Thoughts about Love and Justice,* 8 Tex. J. Women & L. 245, 252–59 (1999); Kenneth De Ville & Loretta Kopelman, *Fetal Protection in Wisconsin's Revised Child Abuse Law: Right Goal, Wrong Remedy,* 27 J. Law, Med. & Ethics 332 (1999); Nancy Ehrenreich, *The Colonization of the Womb,* 43 Duke L.J. 492 (1993); Gallagher, *supra* note 38; Patrick Healy, *Statutory Prohibitions and the Regulation of New Reproductive Technologies under Federal Law in Canada,* 40 McGill L.J. 905, 937–45 (1995); Deborah Hornstra, *A Realistic Approach to Maternal-Fetal Conflict,* 28 Hastings Ctr. Rep. No. 5, at 7 (Sept.–Oct. 1998); Lisa Ikemoto, *The Code of Perfect Pregnancy: At the Intersection of the Ideology of Motherhood, the Practice of Defaulting to Science, and the Interventionist Mindset of the Law,* 53 Ohio St. L.J. 1266 (1992); Mark Kende, *Michigan's Proposed Prenatal Protection Act: Undermining a Woman's Right to an Abor-*

women from seeking prenatal care, drug rehabilitation services while pregnant, and even medical assistance during and after birth.[60] Fear of such actions might also pressure women into having abortions they might otherwise not have—and there is considerable evidence that having an abortion is a significant predictor of later drug or alcohol abuse and dependence.[61]

The right to abort—the right to autonomous decision making by a pregnant woman—underlies the determination of so many commentators to argue that legal intervention on behalf of fetuses at the expense of mothers is unjustifiable. Add in a real uncertainty about the effect of the supposed abuse, and it becomes difficult to justify state intervention to threaten or punish a pregnant woman who endangers her unborn child. Such concerns might well justify objections to charging women with murder for a failure to protect a child from death at the hands of an abusive mate.[62] These concerns hardly explain why some supporters of abortion rights go so far as to say that merely providing relevant information is oppressive to women. Some of these com-

---

*tion,* 5 Am. U. Gender & L. 247 (1996); Nancy Kubasek, *The Case against Prosecutions for Prenatal Drug Abuse,* 8 Tex. J. Women & L. 167 (1999); Martin & Coleman, *supra* note 46; Lynn Paltrow, *Pregnant Drug Users, Fetal Persons, and the Threat to* Roe v. Wade, 62 Alb. L. Rev. 999 (1999); Ken Peak & Frankie Sue Del Papa, *Criminal Justice Enters the Womb: Enforcing the "Right" to Be Born Drug Free,* 21 J. Crim. Just. 245 (1993); Loren Siegel, *The Pregnancy Police Fight the War on Drugs,* in Crack in America 249 (Craig Reinerman & Harry Levine eds. 1997); Zitella & Zitella, *supra* note 47, at 770–98.

60. Gómez, *supra* note 46, at 50–59, 75–91; Shelly Gehshan, *Missed Opportunities for Intervening in the Lives of Pregnant Women Addicted to Alcohol or Other Drugs,* 50 J. Am. Med. Women's Ass'n 165 (1995); Jana Merrick, *Caring for the Fetus to Protect the Born Child? Ethical and Legal Dilemmas in Coerced Obstetrical Intervention,* 13 Women & Pol. 63 (1993); Kristi Messer et al., *Characteristics Associated with Pregnant Women's Utilization of Substance Abuse Treatment Services,* 22 Am. J. Drug & Alcohol Abuse 403 (1996); Paltrow, *supra* note 46, at 1023–29; Jim Schachter, *Help Is Hard to Find for Addict Mothers,* L.A. Times, Dec. 12, 1996, at 1; Schroedel, Fiber, & Snyder, *supra* note 46, at 105.

61. *See* Moira Plant, Women, Drinking and Pregnancy (1985); David Reardon, Aborted Women: Silent No More (1987); Anne Speckhard, Pscyho-Social Stress Following Abortion 51 (1987); Jeanette Vought, Post-Abortion Trauma: 9 Steps to Recovery 111–12 (1991); H. Amaro, B. Zuckerman, & H. Cabral, *Drug Use among Adolescent Mothers: Profile of Risk,* 84 Pediatrics 144 (1989); D.A. Frank, *Cocaine Use during Pregnancy: Prevalence and Correlates,* 82 Pediatrics 888 (1988); L.G. Keith et al., *Substance Abuse in Pregnant Women: Recent Experience at the Perinatal Center for Chemical Dependence of Northwestern Memorial Hospital,* 73 Obstet. & Gynecology 715 (1989); Albert Klassen & Sharon Wilsnack, *Sexual Experience and Drinking among Women in a U.S. National Survey,* 15 Archives Sex. Behav. 363 (1986); E.R. Morrisey & M.A. Schuckit, *Stressful Life Events and Alcohol Problems among Women Seen at a Detoxification Center,* 39 J. Stud. Alcohol 1559 (1978); A. Oro & S.D. Dixon, *Perinatal Cocaine Use and Methamphetamine Exposure: Maternal and Neonatal Correlates,* 111 J. Pediatrics 571 (1987); Kazuo Yamaguchi & Denise Kandel, *Drug Use and Other Determinants of Premarital Pregnancy and Its Outcome: A Dynamic Analysis of Competing Life Events,* 49 J. Marriage & Fam. 257 (1987).

62. *See* Marie Ashe & Naomi Cahn, *Child Abuse: A Problem for Feminist Theory,* in The Public Nature of Private Violence 167 (Martha Albertson Fineman & Roxanne Myhituik eds. 1994); Roberts, *supra* note 53, at 111. On the apparently rising incidence of child abuse generally, see A.B. Bergman, R.M. Larsen, & B.A. Mueller, *Changing Spectrum of Serious Child Abuse,* 77 Pediatrics 338 (1993); Michael Durfee & Deanne Tilton-Durfee, *Multiagency Child Death Review Teams: Experience in the United States,* 4 Child Abuse Rev. 377 (1995); Bernard Ewigman, Colleen Kivlahan, & Garland Land, *The Missouri Child Fatality Study: Underreporting of Maltreatment Fatalities among Children Younger than 5 Years of Age, 1983 through 1986,* 91 Pediatrics 330 (1993); Marcia Herman-Giddens, *Underrecording of Child Abuse and Neglect Fatalities in North Carolina,* 52 N.C. Med. J. 634 (1991); Marcia Herman-Giddens et al., *Underascertainment of Child Abuse Mortality in the United States,* 282 JAMA 463 (Aug. 4, 1999); Philip McClain et al., *Geographic Patterns of Fatal Abuse or Neglect in Children Younger than 5 Years Old, United States, 1979 to 1988,* 148 Arch. Pediatric Adolescent Med. 82 (1994); Karen McCurdy & Deborah Daro, *Child Maltreatment: A National Survey of Reports and Fatalities,* 9 J. Interpersonal Violence 75 (1994); Mary Overpeck et al., *Risk Factors for Infant Homicide in the United States,* 339 N. England J. Med. 1222 (1998); J. Showers et al., *Fatal Child Abuse: A Two Decade Review,* 1 Pediatric Emergency Care 66 (1985).

mentators have even argued that the discouragement (without more) of the drinking of alcohol during pregnancy is an imposition on women.[63]

With the general refusal of American courts to confront the most controversial—and to many, most central—issue in the abortion dispute, the courts abandoned the opportunity to initiate a dialogue on the difficult question of the propriety of abortion in modern society.[64] A careful and nuanced exploration of the nature and significance of human life and the impacts of evolving medical technology might have led to a very different sort of decision in *Roe* and *Doe*— say, a declaration in *Roe* that the uncompromising Texas statute is unconstitutional and an affirmation of Georgia's moderate reform statute at issue in *Doe*. But the Court took a more extreme view, more extreme than virtually any other country.[65] The Court undertook to impose its view on a society that did not fully accept the Court's conclusions, declaring both statutes unconstitutional and embarking on a program of beating down every attempt to limit or regulate abortion virtually throughout pregnancy.[66] The only issues on which opponents of abortion won were the prohibition of abortions other than by licensed physicians,[67] and whether the state has a constitutional obligation to pay for abortions for those who cannot afford them.[68] (After declining

---

63. *See* FENWICK, *supra* note 46, at 65, 88, 131–34; MEYER, *supra* note 46, at 86–87; Charles Babington, *Proposed Alcohol Warning Becomes a Lesson in Lobbying*, WASH. POST, Feb. 28, 1994, at D1; Julia Hanigsberg, *Homolgizing Pregnancy and Motherhood: A Consideration of Abortion*, 94 MICH. L. REV. 371, 405–06 (1995); Hornstra, *supra* note 46, at 11–12; Kevin Sack, *Unlikely Union in Albany: Feminists and Liquor Sellers*, N.Y. TIMES, Apr. 5, 1991, at B1; Sanger, *supra* note 38, at 35–36. *See also U.S.: Drinking Increasing among Pregnant Women*, CHI. TRIB., Apr. 25, 1997, at 20. On the effects of alcohol early in pregnancy, see NATIONAL INST. ON ALCOHOL ABUSE & ALCOHOLISM, ALCOHOL AND BIRTH DEFECTS: THE FETAL ALCOHOL SYNDROME AND RELATED DISORDERS (1987); James Drago, *One for My Baby, One More for the Road: Legislation and Counseling to Prevent Prenatal Exposure to Alcohol*, 7 CARDOZO WOMEN'S L.J. 163 (2001); Joan Whitely, *Troubled Lives: People Born with Fetal Alcohol Syndrome Struggle to Fit into Society*, LAS VEGAS REV. J., Aug. 3, 1997, at J1. For the counter-argument, see Kristin Johnson, Comment, *An Argument for Consideration of Prenatal Smoking in Neglect and Abuse Determinations*, 46 EMORY L.J. 1661 (1997).

64. *See* DWORKIN, *supra* note 6, at 148–79; Dellapenna, *supra* note 18.

65. *See* Chapter 15, at notes 141–356.

66. Hodgson v. Minnesota, 497 U.S. 417 (1990); Thornburgh v. American College of Obstetricians 476 U.S. 747 (1986); City of Akron v. Akron Ctr. for Reproductive Health, Inc., 462 U.S. 416 (1983); H.L. v. Matheson, 450 U.S. 398 (1981); Colautti v. Franklin, 439 U.S. 379 (1979); Bellotti v. Baird, 443 U.S. 622 (1979); Planned Parenthood of Mo. v. Danforth, 428 U.S. 52 (1976). *See generally* Philip Smith, *Abortion from* Roe *to* Webster, 102/103 LAW & JUST. 6 (1989).

67. Simopoulos v. Virginia, 462 U.S. 508 (1983); City of Akron v. Akron Ctr. for Reproductive Health, Inc., 462 U.S. 416, 429–30 n.11 (1983). *See also* Women's Med. Ctr. Of Nw. Hous. v. Bell, 248 F.3d 411 (5th Cir. 2001); Greenville Women's Clinic v. Bryant, 222 F.3d 157 (4th Cir. 2000), *cert. denied*, 531 U.S. 1191 (2001), *further appeal*, 317 F.3d 357 (4th Cir. 2002), *cert. denied*, 538 U.S. 1008 (2003); People v. Bickham, 621 N.E.2d 86 (Ill. App. Ct. 1993); People v. Higuera, 625 N.W.2d 444 (Mich. Ct. App. 2001); Davis v. Fieker, 952 P.2d 505 (Okla. 1997). *But see* Armstrong v. State, 989 P.2d 364 (Mont. 1999) (the state constitutional prohibits limiting the performance of pre-viability abortions to licensed physicians).

68. Dalton v. Little Rock Family Planning Services, 516 U.S. 474 (1996); Harris v. McRae, 448 U.S. 297 (1980); Poelker v. Doe, 448 U.S. 297 (1979); Maher v. Roe, 432 U.S. 464 (1977); Beal v. Doe, 432 U.S. 438 (1977). *See generally* COLKER, *supra* note 15, at 106–07, 136–43; CRITCHLOW, *supra* note 6, at 201–07; 1 FEDERAL ABORTION POLITICS, *supra* note 33, at 3–186; CATHARINE MACKINNON, FEMINISM UNMODIFIED: DISCOURSES ON LIFE AND LAW 93, 96–97, 100–01 (1987); EILEEN MCDONAGH, BREAKING THE ABORTION DEADLOCK: FROM CHOICE TO CONSENT 105–53 (1996); NOONAN, *supra* note 6, at 90–118; LESLIE REAGAN, WHEN ABORTION WAS A CRIME: WOMEN, MEDICINE, AND LAW IN THE UNITED STATES, 1867–1973, at 251 (1997); Susan Frelich Appleton, *Standards for Constitutional Review of Privacy-Invading Welfare Reforms: Distinguishing the Abortion-Funding Cases and Redeeming the Undue-Burden Test*, 49 VAND. L. REV. 1 (1996); David Robert Baron, *The Racially Disparate Impact of Restrictions on the Public Funding of Abortion: An Analysis of Current Equal Protection Doctrine*, 13 B.C. 3D WORLD L. REV. 1 (1993); Joan Callahan & Dorothy Roberts, *A Feminist Social Justice Approach to Reproduction-Assisting Technologies: A Case Study on the Limits of Liberal*

during the first decade after *Roe* was decided to around $150 per abortion, the cost has since risen to around $300 per abortion.[69])

After *Roe* and *Doe,* abortion became the second most commonly performed surgical procedure in the United States.[70] The commonness of abortion has created a large pool of people who are deeply committed to the legitimacy of abortion. Many of those who have had abortions have no regrets. Moreover, some who feel guilty over having had an abortion have chosen to cope with their anxiety or feelings of guilt by becoming a determined defender of the practice.[71]

All of this would suggest that fetuses, out of sight and out of mind, would have no voice in the matter. Fetuses (and embryos), however, did find champions willing to devote considerable effort to protecting fetal (and embryonic) life. For one thing, not all those who have had an abortion (or have been involved with someone who has had an abortion) are without regrets or support the practice's continued availability.[72] There are even three organizations for women

---

*Theory,* 84 Ky. L.J. 1197 (1996); Willard Cates, jr., *The Hyde Amendment in Action: How Did the Restrictions on Federal Funds for Abortion Affect Low-Income Women?,* 246 JAMA 1109 (1981); David Daley & Rachel Gold, *Public Funding for Contraceptive, Sterilizations* (sic*), and Abortion Services, Fiscal Year 1992,* 25 FAM. PLAN. PERSP. 244 (1993); Erin Daly, *Reconsidering Abortion Law: Liberty, Equality, and the New Rhetoric of* Planned Parenthood v. Casey, 45 AM. U. L. REV. 77, 111–16 (1995); Graber, *supra* note 26; Rachel Gold & Jennifer Macias, *Public Funding of Contraception, Sterilization, and Abortion Services, 1985,* 18 FAM. PLAN. PERSP. 259 (1986); Sarah Harding, *Equality and Abortion: Legitimating Women's Experiences,* 3 COLUM. J. GENDER & L. 7, 16–20 (1992); Stanley Henshaw & Lynn Walisch, *The Medicaid Cutoff and Abortion Services for the Poor,* 16 FAM. PLAN. PERSP. 170 (July/Aug. 1984); Eileen McDonagh, *My Body, My Consent: Securing the Constitutional Right to Abortion Funding,* 62 ALB. L.J. 1057 (1999); Dorothy Roberts, *The Future of Reproductive Choice for Poor Women and Women of Color,* 12 WOMEN'S RTS. L. RPTR. 59 (1990); Catherine Grevers Schmidt, *Where Privacy Fails: Equal Protection and the Abortion Rights of Minors,* 68 NYU L. REV. 597 (1993); Kathleen Sullivan, *Unconstitutional Conditions,* 102 HARV. L. REV. 1415 (1989); Sarah Tankersley, *Reproductive Freedom: Abortion Rights of Incarcerated and Non-Incarcerated Women,* 85 KY. L.J. 219 (1996); Laurence Tribe, *The Abortion Funding Conundrum: Inalienable Rights, Affirmative Duties, and the Dilemma of Dependence,* 99 HARV. L. REV. 330 (1985).

To a limited extent, this case has been reversed by political action. *See* Edwards v. Hope Medical Group, 512 U.S. 1 (1994) (Scalia, J., in chambers). The issue was also fought out in state courts under the various provisions of state constitutions for several years. *See* Committee to Defend Reproductive Rights v. Myers, 625 P.2d 779 (Cal. 1981) (finding a right to funding); Doe v. Maher, 515 A.2d 134 (Conn. 1986) (finding a right to funding); Right to Choose v. Byrne, 450 A.2d 925 (N.J. 1982) (finding a right to funding); Hope v. Perales, 619 N.E.2d 646 (N.Y. 1993) (finding no right to funding); Fisher v. Department of Pub. Welfare, 501 A.2d 617 (1985) (finding no right to funding). A similar debate is now emerging within the European Union over whether the Union's constitutional treaties require member states to fund abortion notwithstanding the desire of any given state to pursue a different policy. John Nishi, *Funding of Medically-Necessary Abortions: A Reexamination of U.S. Law and a Call for EC Federalism,* 1992 U. CHI. LEG. F. 517.

69. David Grimes, *A 26-Year-Old Woman Seeking an Abortion,* 282 JAMA 1169, 1170 (1999).

70. *See* Chapter 15, at note 34.

71. J.M. Balkin, *Understanding Legal Understanding: The Legal Subject and the Problem of Legal Coherence,* 103 YALE L.J. 105, 146–50, 157–61 (1993); Abigail Stewart & Sharon Gold-Steinberg, *Women's Abortion Experiences as Sources of Political Mobilization,* in MYTHS ABOUT THE POWERLESS 275 (M. Brinton Lykes *et al.* eds. 1996).

72. *See* CATHERINE BARNARD, THE LONG TERM PSYCHOLOGICAL EFFECTS OF ABORTION (1990); MAGDA DIENES, IN NECESSITY AND SORROW (1976); POST-ABORTION SYNDROME (Peter Doherty ed. 1994); REARDON, *supra* note 61; DAVID REARDON, A SURVEY OF POST-ABORTION REACTIONS 23 (1987); RISEN & THOMAS, *supra* note 4, at 83; SPECKHARD, *supra* note 61; VOUGHT, *supra* note 61; E. Joanne Angelo, *Psychiatric Sequelae of Abortion: The Many Faces of Post-Abortion Grief,* 59 LINACRE Q. 69 (No. 2, 1992); G. Kam Congleton & Lawrence Calhoun, *Post-Abortion Perceptions: A Comparison of Self-Identified Distressed and Non Distressed Populations,* 39 INT'L J. SOC. PSYCH. 255 (1993); Wanda Franz & David Reardon, *Differential Impact of Abortion on Adolescents and Adults,* 27 ADOLESCENCE 162 (1992); Richard Henshaw *et al., Psychological Responses Following Medical Abortion (Using Mifeprestone and Gemepost) and Surgical Vacuum Aspiration,* 73 ACTA OBSTET. GYNECOL. SCAND. 812 (1994); Philip Ney *et al., The Effects of Pregnancy Loss on Women's Health,* 38 SOC. SCI. & MED. 1193 (1994); George Skelton, *Many in Survey Who Had Abortion Cite Guilt Feelings,* L.A. TIMES, Mar. 19, 1989, at 28; Anne Speckhard &

who feel deep grief over what many of them consider to have been abortions coerced by boyfriends or induced by deception by abortion providers: Abortion Victims of America, Victims of Choice, and Women Exploited by Abortion (WEBA).[73] And there were all those obstetricians and obstetrical nurses for whom the fetus was neither out of sight nor out of mind.[74] Finally, there were the members of the general public who were convinced of the humanity of the unborn child and willing to commit themselves to overturning *Roe v. Wade* without regard to personal cost or material reward.[75] Rather than settling the issue of the extent to which abortion should be available in the United States, the *Roe* decision actually fueled the great controversy that continues to bedevil political life in the United States today.[76]

Many of those who became anti-abortion activists—particularly those who were not professionally involved in abortions—were motivated by personal religious convictions.[77] Some of these convictions derived from dramatic conversions. For few was the transformation more dramatic than for Carol Everett. Ms. Everett partly owned an abortion clinic in which perhaps 35,000 abortions had been performed.[78] She also had had an abortion herself. One day, Everett entered a church to pray. Everett powerfully describes her reaction upon returning to the clinic.

> I noticed something was different. When I left, it had seemed all the women were dancing in through the door singing, "I'm pregnant. Do my abortion." But when I got back, all the women were coming in the front door crying. I had never noticed that before.
>
> I went up to the receptionist and the counselors on duty and asked, "What happened while I was gone?"
>
> "Nothing that I know of." The answer was unanimous.
>
> For some reason I was not comfortable in my normal working environment.[79]

The experience of Carol Everett and the attitudes of obstetrical nurses also demonstrate that women are no more immune to the impact of the reality of fetal life than are the men."[80] No

---

Vincent Rue, *Complicated Mourning and Abortion,* 8 J. Pre- & Peri-Natal Psych. 5 (1993); Anne Speckhard & Vincent Rue, *Postabortion Syndrome: An Emerging Public Health Concern,* 48 J. Soc. Issues 95 (1992).

73. *See* Rosenblatt, *supra* note 22, at 25–26, 42–44 (Victims); Samuel Calhoun & Andrea Sexton, *Is It Possible to Take Both Fetal Life and Women Seriously? Professor Lawrence Tribe and his Reviewers,* 49 Was. & Lee L. Rev. 437, 479–81 (1992) (book rev.) (WEBA). Political scientist Kerry Jacoby has estimated that 4.8% of the women who have had abortions are now anti-abortion activists. Jacoby, *supra* note 17, at 17. *See generally* Paula Ervin, Women Exploited: The Other Victim of Abortion (1985); Jacoby, *supra* note 17, at 49–50; Pam Koerbel, Abortion's Second Victim (1986); Michael Mannion, Abortion & Healing: A Cry to Be Whole (1986); Nancy Michaels, Helping Women Recover from Abortion (1988); Reardon, *supra* note 61; Kathleen Winkler, When the Crying Stops: Abortion, the Pain and the Healing (1992).

74. *See* Chapter 15, at notes 453–72.

75. *See* Jacoby, *supra* note 17, at 101–03.

76. Numerous commentators have asserted that *Roe* and *Doe* provoked the "Right to Life" movement into existence. Colker, *supra* note 15, at 115–25; Craig & O'Brien, *supra* note 6, at 32; Lee Epstein & Joseph Kobylka, The Supreme Court and Legal Change: Abortion and the Death Penalty 207, 292 (1992); Marian Faux, Roe v. Wade: The Untold Story of the Landmark Supreme Court Decision that Made Abortion Legal 179 (1988); Ginsburg, *supra* note 17, at 43, 72; Graber, *supra* note 34, at 21; Hadley, *supra* note 35, at 3–5; Jacoby, *supra* note 17, at 27–28, 95–96, 103–05; Lazarus, *supra* note 6, at 371–72; Luker, *supra* note 34, at 125–26, 137; Rubin, *supra* note 34, at 186–88; Marcy Wilder, *The Rule of Law, the Rise of Violence, and the Role of Morality: Reframing America's Abortion Debate,* in Abortion Wars, *supra* note 27, at 73, 79–81. It actually only energized a movement that had already begun to score victories in the legislative arena before *Roe* and *Doe* were decided. See the text *supra* at notes 6–13.

77. Jacoby, *supra* note 17, at 12–18, 88–92, 95–100, 112–18.

78. Carol Everett, The Scarlet Lady: Confessions of a Successful Abortionist 191 (1991).

79. *Id.* at 199.

80. *Id.* at 191.

matter how dramatic the conversion, the transformation to anti-abortion activist often has been enduring.[81]

Many early activists against abortion were Catholics, some 80 percent according to sociologist Kristin Luker.[82] The impression that this was largely a Catholic effort was reinforced by the decision of the Catholic Church institutionally to take a strong stand against abortion and to organize opposition to *Roe*.[83] Catholic predominance did not last. Today anti-abortion activists are only slightly more likely to be Catholic than Protestant, with over half of the total activists being non-Catholic.[84] Still, the prominence of Catholic clergy and laity in the opposition to legalized abortion enabled supporters of abortion rights to attempt to disparage the "Right to Life" movement as a mere appendage of the Catholic Church.[85]

---

81. *See, e.g.,* Joyce Show, *Correspondence,* 333 New Eng. J. Med. 876 (1995). *See generally* Jacoby, *supra* note 17, at 116–17.

82. Luker, *supra* note 34, at 137. *See also* Jacoby, *supra* note 17, at 28, 69, 167; Risen & Thomas, *supra* note 4, at 43–77.

83. *See* National Conference of Catholic Bishops, Documentation on the Right to Life and Abortion (1974); John Scholl, A New Catechism of the Catholic Faith 98 (1973). *See generally* Jacoby, *supra* note 17, at 28–37, 40–44, 68–69; Keith Cassidy, *The Right to Life Movement,* in The Politics of Abortion and Birth Control in Historical Perspective 128 (Donald Critchlow ed. 1996); S.L. Markson, *The Roots of Contemporary Anti-Abortion Activism,* in Perspectives on Abortion 33 (P. Sachdev ed. 1985); R. Randall Rainey, Gerard Magill, & Kevin O'Rourke, *Introduction: Abortion, the Catholic Church, and Public Policy,* in Abortion and Public Policy: An Interdisciplinary Investigation within the Catholic Tradition 1, 11–25 (R. Randall Rainey & Gerard Magill eds. 1996).

84. Jacoby, *supra* note 17, at 17. *See also* Risen & Thomas, *supra* note 4, at 120. Protestants as a group were nearly as opposed to abortion as Catholics right from the beginning, but they were less willing or able to organize their opposition until years later. *Tidings,* Time, May 28, 1973, at 62 (reporting that 67% of Catholics opposed abortion under all or nearly all circumstances, while 59% of Protestants did so).

85. *See, e.g.,* The Abortion Controversy: A Documentary History 46, 82, 140–43, 219 (Eva Rubin ed. 1994); Blanchard, *supra* note 34, at 10–12, 15, 27; Janet Farrell Brodie, Contraception and Abortion in Nineteenth-Century America 81, 266, 290 (1994); Barbara Brookes, Abortion in England 1900–1967, at 7, 26, 63, 86–87, 98 n.1, 114–15, 146, 154 (1988); James MacGregor Burns & Stewart Burns, A People's Charter: The Pursuit of Rights in America 354–58 (1991); Robert Burt, The Constitution in Conflict 346–47 (1992); Condit, *supra* note 6, at 30, 47–53, 74 n.5, 76 n.17, 124, 126–27; Craig & O'Brien, *supra* note 6, at 32, 43–47, 54, 254–56; Critchlow, *supra* note 6, at 113–47, 166–73, 197–202, 218; Mary Daly, Beyond God the Father: Toward a Philosophy of Women's Liberation 106 (1973); Nanette Davis, From Crime to Choice 30–33, 101, 114–16, 120–21 (1985); Carl Degler, At Odds: Women and the Family in America from the Revolution to the Present 233, 239 (1980); Dworkin, *supra* note 6, at 7, 30, 36, 39–50, 91–92, 245 n.6; Faux, *supra* note 34, at xiii–xiv, 4–8, 57–58, 185, 227–28, 230–64; Myra Marx Ferree & Beth Hess, Controversy and Coalition: The New Feminist Movement across Three Decades of Change 153 (rev. ed. 1994); Garrow, *supra* note 22 (*passim*); Linda Gordon, Woman's Body, Woman's Right: A Social History of Birth Control in America 52–53 n.*, 268–70, 281, 315–17, 336–37, 350–51, 415–16 (1976); Robert Hardaway, Population, Law, and the Environment 23, 26–27, 86–90, 113–14 (1994); Harrison, *supra* note 34, at 24–26, 65, 77, 127–32, 180, 184–86, 238–39, 264 n.9, 272 n.16; Anthony Hordern, Legal Abortion: The English Experience 11, 13–14, 40–42 (1971); Jimmye (*sic*) Kimmey, Legal Abortion: A Speakers (*sic*) Notebook 15–18 (1975); Lazarus, *supra* note 6, at 379, 381; Mensch & Freeman, *supra* note 22, at 11, 117–18, 123, 138, 229 n.97; Andrew Merton, Enemies of Choice: The Right to Life Movement and Its Threat to Abortion (1981); James Mohr, Abortion in America: The Origins and Evolution of National Policy, 1800–1900, at 167, 290–91 n.14 (1978); Bernard Nathanson & Richard Ostung, Aborting America 51–52, 172 (1979); Susan Teft Nicholson, Abortion and the Roman Catholic Church (1978); O'Brien, *supra* note 6, at 36; Paige, *supra* note 34; Petchesky, *supra* note 34, at xiii, 118–22, 252–76, 335–38; Deborah Rhode, Justice and Gender 209 (1989); Risen & Thomas, *supra* note 4, at 6–7, 16–22, 39–40; Rubin, *supra* note 34, at 19, 23, 25–26, 50, 72, 90–95, 100–07, 113; Susan Sherwin, No Longer Patient: Feminist Ethics and Health Care 72 (1992); Reagan, *supra* note 68, at 221–22; The Catholic Church and the Politics of Abortion: A View from the States (Timothy Byrnes & Mary Segers eds. 1992); White, *supra* note 8, at 163–64, 166; Glanville Williams, The Sanctity of Life and the Criminal Law 193–206, 225–33 (1957,

"Anti-Papism," of course, has a long history in England and the United States and appears in many contexts other than abortion.[86] Whatever one thinks of the prejudice, in the context of abortion it can only be sustained by seriously distorting the facts of the controversy. For example, the founding president of Americans United for Life was George Huntson Williams, a Unitarian minister who held the Hollis Professorship of Divinity at Harvard Divinity School[87]—about as far as one can get from the Catholic Church and still be within the western religious tradition. Or consider historian Dallas Blanchard, who tells us that Connecticut and Massachusetts were "predominantly Catholic" in 1890 and were then following the "Vatican policy"—when, in fact, neither state was yet predominantly Catholic.[88] Or consider Karen O'Connor who insists that Connecticut was "heavily Catholic" in 1821 when it enacted the first American abortion statute.[89] 1821 was before the Irish potato famine, a time when

---

reprinted 1972); Reshona Fleishman, *The Battle against Reproductive Rights: The Impact of the Catholic Church on Abortion Law in both International and Domestic Arenas,* 14 EMORY INT'L L. REV. 277, 300–04 (2000); David Garrow, *Abortion before and after* Roe v. Wade: *An Historical Perspective,* 62 ALB. L. REV. 833, 835 (1999); Gordon, *supra* note 30, at 579; Brenda Hofman, *Political Theology: The Role of Organized Religion in the Anti-Abortion Movement,* 28 J. CHURCH & STATE 225 (1986); Kolbert & Miller, *supra* note 27, at 97; Harriet Pilpel, *A Non-Catholic Lawyer's View,* in ABORTION IN A CHANGING WORLD 158 (Robert Hall ed. 1970); Alec Walen, *Consensual Sex without Assuming the Risk of Carrying an Unwanted Fetus; Another Foundation for the Right to an Abortion,* 63 BROOK. L. REV. 1051, 1052–53 (1997). *See also* ANDREW GREELEY, AN UGLY LITTLE SECRET: ANTI-CATHOLICISM IN NORTH AMERICA 21–23 (1977); NOONAN, *supra* note 6, at 53–63, 74–79; OLASKY, *supra* note 5, at 104–07, 109–10, 115, 120, 128–29, 137–38; *See generally* TIMOTHY BYRNES, CATHOLIC BISHOPS IN AMERICAN POLITICS (1991).

Blaming the Catholics for all resistance to the legalization of abortion antedates *Roe v. Wade* by many years. *See, e.g.,* Bernard Schwartz, *Morals Offenses and the Model Penal Code,* 63 COLUM. L. REV. 669, 686 (1963). Such claims obviously have greater credibility in nations or states where the population is overwhelmingly Catholic for in such a nation or state virtually anything that happens is likely to be the work of Catholics. *See* Ruth Fletcher, *"Pro-Life" Absolutes, Feminist Challenges: The Fundamentalist Narrative in Irish Abortion Law, 1986–1992,* 36 OSGOODE HALL L.J. 1 (1998).

86. *See, e.g.,* ROBERT BAIRD, RELIGION IN THE UNITED STATES OF AMERICA: OR AN ACCOUNT OF THE ORIGIN, PROGRESS, RELATIONS TO THE STATE, AND THE PRESENT CONDITION OF THE EVANGELICAL CHURCH IN THE UNITED STATES WITH NOTICES OF THE UNEVANGELICAL DENOMINATIONS (1844). *See also* JERALD BRAUER, PROTESTANTISM IN AMERICA: A NARRATIVE HISTORY 26, 128 (1953); MARTIN MARTY, RIGHTEOUS EMPIRE: THE PROTESTANT EXPERIENCE IN AMERICA (1970); GEORGE SELDES, CATHOLIC CRISIS (1939); GEORGE SELDES, YOU CAN'T PRINT THAT! THE TRUTH BEHIND THE NEWS (1929); JOSIAH STRONG, OUR COUNTRY 59–88 (Jurgen Herbst ed. 1963; original pub. 1890); Donald Beschle, *Catechism or Imagination: Is Justice Scalia's Judicial Style Typically Catholic?,* 37 VILLA. L. REV. 1329 (1992). *See generally* SYDNEY AHLSTROM, A RELIGIOUS HISTORY OF THE AMERICAN PEOPLE 558 (1972); CHARLES DONOVAN & ROBERT MARSHALL, BLESSED ARE THE BARREN: THE SOCIAL POLICY OF PLANNED PARENTHOOD 133 (1991); PHILIP GLEASON, SPEAKING OF DIVERSITY: LANGUAGE AND ETHNICITY IN TWENTIETH-CENTURY AMERICA 207–31 (1992); GREELEY, *supra* note 85; JACOBY, *supra* note 17, at 41–42; MARK NOLL, A HISTORY OF CHRISTIANITY IN THE UNITED STATES AND CANADA (1992); Thomas Berg, *Anti-Catholicism and Modern Church-State Relations,* 33 LOY. U. CHI. L.J. 121 (2001); Jon Butler, *Coercion, Miracle, Reason: Rethinking the American Religious Experience in the Revolutionary Age,* in RELIGION IN A REVOLUTIONARY AGE 1 (Ronald Hoffman & Peter Albert eds. 1994); George Dargo, *Religious Toleration and Its Limits in Early America,* 16 N. ILL. U. L. REV. 341 (1996); Michael deHaven Newsom, *The American Protestant Empire: A Historical Perspective,* 40 WASHBURN L.J. 187 (2001).

87. NOONAN, *supra* note 6, at 62.

88. BLANCHARD, *supra* note 34, at 15. *See also* DALLAS BLANCHARD & TERRY PREWITT, RELIGIOUS VIOLENCE AND ABORTION: THE GIDEON PROJECT 216 (1993) (distinguishing between "rigid Catholics" & other Catholics), 225–30, 261–63 (finding that "fundamentalist Catholics" tend toward violence), 257 (blaming bishops for bombings); Mary Dudziak, *Just Say No: Birth Control in the Connecticut Supreme Court before* Griswold v. Connecticut, 75 IOWA L. REV. 915, 927–31 (1990) (blaming Connecticut's longstanding prohibition of the sale of contraceptives on the Catholic Church, ignoring that the prohibition originated long before Catholic influence in that state). Historian James Mohr, on the other hand, was careful to play down the influence of the Catholic Church in the nineteenth century. MOHR, *supra* note 85, at 185–87.

89. O'CONNOR, *supra* note 34, at 26.

Catholics were rare in the United States anywhere outside of Maryland, and only three years after Connecticut became the last state to disestablish its hitherto state-supported Protestant church.[90] In a similar vein, Madeleine Simms attributed the defeat of early efforts at abortion reform in England in the twentieth century entirely to Catholic opposition[91]—as if the Catholic Church has had any real political influence in England since the death of Queen Mary I.

The exploitation of anti-Catholic prejudice in discussions of abortion (or its close relative, the craniotomy during delivery) can be traced back to eighteenth-century England.[92] Perhaps the most persistent modern effort to discredit opposition to abortion as a purely Catholic phenomenon is from the word processor of law professor David Garrow. Garrow traces the history of the birth control, the abortion reform, and the abortion repeal movements in the United States in the twentieth century in great detail. He makes no effort to hide either his pro-choice prejudices or his anti-Catholic prejudices, presenting all opposition to his favored views as an expression of Catholic bigotry without acknowledging the possibility that some people might oppose abortion on purely secular grounds.[93] Garrow, on the other hand, finds nothing remarkable about the major involvement of Unitarian groups in bringing about abortion reform or even in helping to make *Roe v. Wade* possible.[94] (Despite the prominence of George Huntson Williams in the opposition to abortion rights, many more Unitarians were active in support of abortion rights and the Unitarian Universalist Association was the first major institution after the American Law Institute to endorse the *Model Penal Code*.)[95] Garrow goes so far as to use innuendo to suggest that Catholic bishops are directly responsible for the clinic bombings that occurred in the 1990s. Garrow introduces his account of the spate of clinic bombings by describing the bishops' opposition to the Mondale-Ferraro ticket and never mentions that those convicted of bombings in Pensacola, Florida, and Washington, D.C., were Protestants, one and all.[96]

Many of the commentators who see a Catholic priest under every anti-abortionist bed apparently believe they know better what Catholicism actually teaches than do Catholics themselves (up to and including the Pope).[97] For such observers, Catholic opposition to abortion can only seem to be perverse bigotry. Dr. Roger Rosenblatt chose to see the Catholic attitude towards abortion as parallel to Nazi authoritarianism.[98] Such prejudices might very well have played a role in *Roe v. Wade*. Justice William Douglas (who voted with the *Roe* majority), did not directly display his disdain for Catholicism, but did quote approvingly from a notoriously vicious anti-

---

90. John Noonan, jr., The Believer and the Powers that Are 234–38 (1987).

91. Madeleine Simms, *Britain*, in Abortion in the New Europe: A Comparative Handbook 31, 33–34, 39–40 (Bill Rolston & Anna Eggert eds. 1994).

92. *See* 2 Thomas Denman, An Introduction to the Practice of Midwifery 172–175 (1794); Edward LeProhon, Voluntary Abortion, or Fashionable Prostitution, with Some Remarks upon the Operation of Craniotomy (1867); Samuel Merriman, A Synopsis of the Various Kinds of Difficult Parturition 171 (1814); Fielding Ould, A Treatise of Midwifery 198 (1742). *See generally* Angus McLaren, Reproductive Rituals 124–28 (1984); Mohr, *supra* note 85, at 195.

93. Garrow, *supra* note 22, at 270–599.

94. *Id.* at 289–92, 296, 400–01, 404–05, 431, 438, 462.

95. *See id.* at 291; Mensch & Freeman, *supra* note 22, at 236 n.46; Noonan, *supra* note 6, at 61

96. Garrow, *supra* note 22, at 650–52. *See also* Blanchard & Prewitt, *supra* note 88, at 257; Marlene Gerber Fried, *Abortion in the United States—Legal but Inaccessible*, in Abortion Wars, *supra* note 27, at 208, 209. In an epilogue that Garrow added in 1998 to the original edition of the book, he did acknowledge one Bishop who spoke out against the violence. Garrow, *supra*, at 714.

97. *See, e.g.*, Dworkin, *supra* note 6, at 7, 36, 39–50, 91–92, 245 n.6; Reagan, *supra* note 68, at 8 (1997).

98. Rosenblatt, *supra* note 22, at 80. Dr. Bernard Nathanson, an early leader in the abortion reform movement, describes this as a deliberate and cynical ploy used to discredit opposition to abortion reform. Bernard Nathanson & Richard Ostung, Aborting America 33, 51–52 (1979).

Catholic polemicist in *Lemon v. Kurtzman*.[99] Anti-Catholic prejudice has also been played upon by supporters of birth control more generally.[100]

With some irony, Irish feminist Mary Kenny has pointed out that Catholic opposition to abortion really expresses a Lutheran principle: "Here I stand, I cannot do otherwise."[101] One might also recall that situation ethics, or at least the notion that a moral obligation becomes optional when its burdens are disproportionate to the obligation's benefits, originated in Catholic thought.[102] The Catholic bishops were, in fact, rather restrained in their opposition to abortion compared to some lay activists of whatever religious faith.[103]

Few supporters of abortion rights have ever acknowledged the inappropriateness of the blaming all opposition on the Catholic Church.[104] More recently, abortion rights supporters have had to broaden their criticisms of religiously based opposition to abortion as other organized religious groups have become active on abortion. Hence the tendency today to speak of "religious fundamentalism" generally and not just of Catholicism.[105] The lingering anti-Papism shows through with the unblinking inclusion of all Catholics opposed to abortion within the broad rubric "fundamentalist"—a label that hardly fits many of the activists, Catholic or otherwise.

# Silencing the Opposition

*I know what causes abortion. Sperm causes abortion.*

—Elizabeth Karlin[106]

A major ploy in the ongoing abortion controversy has been for supporters of abortion rights to smear opponents as acting out of religious bigotry.[107] The more the supporters of abortion rights make the tag stick in the public mind, the more they cut off the public's careful consideration of the arguments against abortion rights. In effect, they declare political debate about abortion out of bounds. This particular ploy has won endorsement at the highest levels of the judiciary,[108] as well as in overtly political organs of government.

---

99. 403 U.S. 602, 635 n.20 (Douglas, J., concurring) [quoting Lorraine Boettner, Roman Catholicism 360 (1962)]. *See generally* Andrew Greeley, An Ugly Little Secret 21–23 (1977); Noonan, *supra* note 6, at 53–63, 74–79.

100. Gordon, *supra* note 85, at 315; David Kennedy, Birth Control in America: The Career of Margaret Sanger 269 (1970); Arthur Schlesinger, The Crisis of the Old Order, 1919–1933, at 425–26 (1956).

101. Mary Kenny, Abortion: The Whole Story 301 (1986). *See also* Steven Smith, *Natural Law and Contemporary Moral Thought: A Guide from the Perplexed*, 42 Am. J. Juris. 299, 303 n.14 (1997) (book rev.).

102. *See, e.g., In re* Quinlan, 355 A.2d 647 (N.J.), *cert. denied sub. nom.* Garger v. New Jersey, 429 U.S. 922 (1976); Alexander Morgan Capron & Vicki Michel, *Law and Bioethics*, 27 Loy.-L.A. L. Rev. 25, 32 n.38 (1993).

103. Risen & Thomas, *supra* note 4, at 148–55, 173, 367.

104. *See* Judges, *supra* note 6, at 15–16; B. Drummond Ayres, jr., *Virginia Leader Apologizes for Remark on Inquiry*, N.Y. Times, July 8, 1991, at A6; Alice Rossi & Bhavani Sitaraman, *Abortion in Context: Historical Trends and Future Changes*, 20 Fam. Plan. Persp. 273, 276 (1988); *They Have No Excuse of Anti-Catholic Bias*, Newsday, July 22, 1991, at 34.

105. See the text *supra* at notes 15–18.

106. Elizabeth Karlin, *"We Called It Kindness": Establishing a Feminist Abortion Practice*, in Abortion Wars, *supra* note 27, at 273, 274.

107. *See, e.g.,* Blanchard, *supra* note 34; Paige, *supra* note 34; Reagan, *supra* note 68, at 248.

108. *See, e.g.,* Planned Parenthood of S.E. Pa. v. Casey, 505 U.S. 833, 913–15 (Stevens, J., partially concurring) (1992).

More nuanced decisions than *Roe* and *Doe* could have invited political debate rather than declaring it out of bounds.[109] Admittedly, allowing further political debate would have been difficult and divisive. The widespread moral dissensus then existing over the propriety of abortion was very different than the social consensus that already existed on the propriety of contraceptives when *Griswold v. Connecticut*[110] was decided. In this respect the situation regarding abortion was similar to the situation when the Court decided in *Brown v. Board of Education*[111] that legally mandated segregation violated the constitutional guarantee of equal protection of the laws. Like *Brown*, the Court's declaration that one major perspective on the question of abortion was outside the bounds of political discourse was bound to breed frustration, anger, and political resistance. Comparisons to *Brown* are particularly telling as the champions of *Roe* often describe it as expressing a "basic truth"[112] that is the "legal and moral equivalent of *Brown v. Board of Education*."[113] But unlike *Brown*, resistance to *Roe* only intensified over the years. There was no accommodation by the nation to the Court's decision.

One can explain the different long-term reactions to the decisions in *Brown* and *Roe*, at least in part, by the differing roles of the two decisions. *Brown*, reaching back to the Civil War Amendments to seize the moral high ground, lifted a ban on black voices, inviting them and their allies into the political dialogue.[114] *Roe* and *Doe*, without any such clear constitutional mandate, sought to exclude those who spoke up on behalf of the unborn from public debate.[115] The decisions in *Roe* and *Doe*, by denying the very legitimacy of the views it rejected, served to catalyze opposition into a strident and uncompromising attitude where before there had been discussion, disagreement, and at least a possibility of compromise.[116] *Roe* and *Doe* were a political and sociological disaster for the Court and, arguably, for the society.[117] Law professors Elizabeth Mensch and Alan Freeman have even argued that abortion would probably be more widely available to poor women today had the political processes been allowed to proceed to their conclusion than is the case in the wake of *Roe* with its ensuing battles in the streets.[118] They might be right.

Supporters of abortion rights, believing in their moral righteousness in championing a fundamental human liberty against religious bigotry, came to see suppressing opposing speech as necessary to prevent personal oppression of those seeking abortions.[119] They set about to delegitimate any viewpoint opposed to abortion. They began by disparaging the right of physicians

---

109. COLKER, *supra* note 15, at 119–25; MENSCH & FREEMAN, *supra* note 22, at 126–28. *See also* Stenberg v. Carhart, 530 U.S. 914, 956–79 (Kennedy, J., dissenting); Planned Parenthood of S.E. Pennsylvania v. Casey, 505 U.S. 833, at 995–96 (Scalia, J., dissenting).

110. 381 U.S. 479 (1965).

111. 347 U.S. 483 (1954).

112. GARROW, *supra* note 22, at 705.

113. Michael Anderson, *From Civil Rights to Abortion Rights*, N.Y. TIMES, Feb. 20, 1994, § 7 (book review), at 7 (quoting David Garrow).

114. BURT, *supra* note 85, at 347–50.

115. MENSCH & FREEMAN, *supra* note 22, at 127, 130, 232–33 n.26; Calhoun & Sexton, *supra* note 73, at 459; Daniel Conkle, *Canada's* Roe: *The Canadian Abortion Decision and Its Implications for American Constitutional Law and Theory*, 6 CONST'L COMMENTARY 299, 316–17 (1989); Mary Ann Glendon, *The Women of* Roe v. Wade, 134 FIRST THINGS 19 (June 2003).

116. MENSCH & FREEMAN, *supra* note 22, at 127–28. *See also* BARONE, *supra* note 15, at 565, 610; BURT, *supra* note 85, at 346–47; GINSBURG, *supra* note 17, at 381, 383; HUNTER, *supra* note 17, at 90–92; MOONEY, *supra* note 17, at 16–17; REICHLEY, *supra* note 17, at 292, 327–28; ROSENBERG, *supra* note 6, at 342; WILLS, *supra* note 17, at 121; WUTHNOW, *supra* note 17, at 319–20; Devins, *supra* note 21, at 1446; Ginsburg, *supra* note 22, at 1208.

117. MENSCH & FREEMAN, *supra* note 22, at 126; NOONAN, *supra* note 6, at 1.

118. MENSCH & FREEMAN, *supra* note 22, at 129.

119. *See, e.g.*, Kelly, *supra* note 45; Pine & Law, *supra* note 24, at 412–13. *See generally* NAT HENTOFF, FREE SPEECH FOR ME—BUT NOT FOR THEE (1994).

who oppose abortion to continue to practice "sectarian medicine."[120] They brought lawsuits in an effort to silence medical critics, or perhaps even to compel the critics to admit that they were wrong. The lawsuits began immediately after *Roe* with attempts, largely unsuccessful, to compel hospitals or physicians to perform abortions against their will.[121] These efforts continue to this day, still without great success.[122] While the effort failed, supporters of abortion rights succeeded in persuading some medical schools to discriminate in admissions against persons who questioned or opposed abortion.[123]

It is perhaps only natural that winners in the Supreme Court would hope that the victory before the Court would silence debate. As law professor Michael Paulsen observed, "[t]oo often, the claim that 'law is for the courts to decide' is used to squelch constitutional debate, not further it…. [T]he…'fetishization' of the Court[124]…is all too often employed as a trump card with which to condemn as 'lawless' those critics who have the temerity to challenge judicial hegemony and thereby to avoid engaging the critics' arguments on the merits."[125] While various commentators might not embrace such strategies consciously, the debate is stifled nonetheless.

---

120. *See* Barbara Gottlieb, *Abortion-1995,* 332 New Eng. J. Med. 532 (1995); Pilpel, *supra* note 85, at 158; Harriet Pilpel & Dorothy Patten, *Abortion, Conscience, and the Constitution: An Examination of Federal Institutional Conscience Clauses,* 6 Colum. H. Rts. L. Rev. 278, 303 (1974). *See also* Lewis v. Pearson Fndtn., 908 F.2d 318, *aff'd en banc mem.,* 917 F.2d 1077 (8th Cir. 1990); (enjoining a "problem pregnancy center" run by anti-abortion activists from advertising information regarding abortion services). *See generally* Noonan, *supra* note 6, at 83–84.

121. *See, e.g.,* Holton v. Crozer-Chester Med. Ctr., 560 F.2d 575 (3rd Cir. 1977); Greco v. Orange Memorial Hospital, 513 F.2d 873 (5th Cir. ), *cert. denied,* 423 U.S. 1000 (1975); Doe v. Bellin Memorial Hospital, 479 F.2d 756 (7th Cir. 1973); 42 U.S.C. § 300-7(a)(2)(A) (2000). *See also* Taylor v. St. Vincent's Hosp., 523 F.2d 75 (9th Cir. 1975) (upholding the right of a Catholic hospital to refuse to perform voluntary sterilizations), *cert. denied,* 424 U.S. 948 (1976); Chrisman v. Sisters of St. Joseph of Peace, 506 F.2d 308 (9th Cir. 1974) (same); Allen v. Sisters of St. Joseph, 490 F.2d 81 (5th Cir. 1974) (same); Swanson v. St. John's Lutheran Hosp., 597 P.2d 702 (Mont. 1979) (barring a hospital from dismissing a nurse who refused to participate in sterilization operations). *But see* Doe v. Charleston Area Med. Ctr., Inc., 529 F.2d 638 (4th Cir. 1975) (public hospital); Doe v. Bridgeton Hospital Ass'n, 366 A.2d 641 (N.J. 1976) (nonsectarian, non profit hospital), *cert. denied,* 433 U.S. 914 (1977). *See generally* Noonan, supra note 6, at 80–89; Dennis Horan, *Abortion and the Conscience Clause,* 20 Cath. Law. 289 (1974); Martin McKernon, jr., *Compelling Hospitals to Provide Abortion Services,* 20 Cath. Law. 317 (1974); Pilpel & Patten, *supra* note 120; George Siedel III, *The Hospital and Abortion,* Case & Comment, July–Aug. 1974, at 24; Marc Stern, *Abortion Conscience Clauses,* 11 Colum. J.L. & Soc. Prob. 571 (1975); Lynn Wardle, *Protecting the Rights of Conscience of Health Care Providers,* 14 J. Legal Med. 177 (1993).

122. *See, e.g.,* Larson & Thornton v. Albany Med. Cntr., 676 N.Y.S.2d 293 (App. Div. 1998) (nurses dismissed for refusing to assist at an abortion held not to have a civil cause of action after the local prosecutor refused to enforce the criminal provisions of the "conscience clause"). *See* Kathleen Boozang, *Deciding the Fate of Religious Hospitals in the Emerging Health Care Market,* 31 Hous. L. Rev. 1429 (1995); Kathleen Boozang, *Developing Public Policy for Sectarian Providers: Accommodating Religious Beliefs and Obtaining Access to Care,* 24 J.L. Med. & Ethics 90 (1996); Tamar Lewin, *With Rise in Health Unit Mergers, Catholic Standards Face Challenge,* N.Y. Times, Mar. 8, 1995, at B7; Christopher Meyers & Robert Woods, *An Obligation to Provide Abortion Services: What Happens When Physicians Refuse?,* 22 J. Med. Ethics 115 (1996); Toni Nelson, *Threat to Women,* Atlanta J. & Const., July 22, 1995, at A19. *See also* Brownfield v. Daniel Freeman Marina Hosp., 256 Cal. Rptr. 240 (Ct. App. 1989) (upholding dismissal of a malpractice action by a woman who was not referred for "contraceptive" services after being treated at a Catholic hospital for rape).

123. Albert Gunn & George Zenner, jr., *Religious Discrimination in the Selection of Medical Students: A Case Study,* 11 Issues in L. & Med. 363 (1996); Bruce & Diane Rodgers, *Abortion: The Seduction of Medicine,* 2 Liberty Life & Fam. 285, 301 n.36 (1995). *See also* Noonan, *supra* note 6, at 86; Paul Ramsey, Ethics at the Edges of Life 61–71 (1978).

124. Paulson takes the phrase from Sanford Levinson, *Tiers of Scrutiny—From Strict through Rational Bases—And the Future of Interests: Commentary on Fiss and Linde,* 55 Alb. L. Rev. 745, 746–47 (1992).

125. Michael Stokes Paulsen, *The Most Dangerous Branch: Executive Power to Say What the Law Is,* 83 Geo. L.J. 217, 244 (1994). *See also* Burt, *supra* note 85, at 357–58; Mary Ann Glendon, A Nation under Lawyers: How the Crisis in the Legal Profession Is Transforming American Society 2, 45, 47

Did the champions of abortion rights really imagine that they could consolidate their victory so easily? Would they, who now demand that society must unite behind the Court's ruling, abandon their cause—in response to the same arguments—if *Roe* were fully reversed? That never happens for a controversial issue. Even *Brown v. Board of Education*,[126] which brought an end to legally mandated racial segregation, hardly ended debate over race relations in the United States.

Abraham Lincoln described the inability of the Supreme Court to end the political debate over slavery. For example, he argued during the Lincoln-Douglas debates thusly:

> We do not propose that when Dred Scott has been decided to be a slave by the court, we, as a mob, will decide him to be free. We do not propose that, when any other one, or one thousand, shall be decided by that court to be slaves, we will in any violent way disturb the rights of property thus settled; but we nevertheless do oppose that decision as a political rule which shall be binding on the voter to vote for nobody who thinks it wrong, which shall be binding on the members of Congress or the President to favor no measure that does not actually concur with the principles of that decision. We do not propose to be bound by it as a political rule in that way.... We propose to resist it as to have it reversed if we can, and a new judicial rule established upon the subject.[127]

Andrew Jackson was more direct: "The Supreme Court must...have only such influence as the force of their reasoning deserves."[128] Congress seems to have accepted Lincoln's idea that sometimes a President is not bound to enforce a law he considers unconstitutional.[129]

---

(1994); MICHAEL PERRY, MORALITY, POLITICS, AND LAW 177 (1988); *Amicus Brief of the United States supporting Appellants in* Webster v. Reproductive Health Services [492 S. Ct. 490 (1989)], *reprinted in* 11 WOMEN'S RTS. L. RPTR. 163, 171 n.15 (1989), and in 8 DOCUMENTARY HISTORY OF THE LEGAL ASPECTS OF ABORTION IN THE UNITED STATES: *WEBSTER V. REPRODUCTIVE HEALTH SERVICES* 107 (Roy Mersky & Gary Hartman eds. 1990) ("DOCUMENTARY HISTORY") (specific pagination will be given only to the version in the *Women's Rts. L. Rptr.*); Paul Brest, *Constitutional Citizenship,* 34 CLEVE. ST. L. REV. 175 (1986); Richard Epstein, *Substantive Due Process by Any Other Name: The Abortion Cases,* 1973 SUP. CT. REV. 159, 168; Susan Estrich & Kathleen Sullivan, *Abortion Politics: Writing for an Audience of One,* 138 U. PA. L. REV. 119, 150–55 (1989); Ginsburg, *supra* note 22, at 1198–99; Thomas Merrill, *Judicial Opinions as Binding Law and as Explanations for Judgments,* 15 CARDOZO L. REV. 43, 77 (1993); James Bradley Thayer, *The Origin and Scope of the American Doctrine of Constitutional Law,* 7 HARV. L. REV. 129 (1893); Lawrence Tribe, *A Nation Held Hostage,* N.Y. TIMES, July 2, 1990, at A13.

126. 347 U.S. 483 (1954).

127. *Sixth Debate with Stephen Douglas, at Quincy, Illinois (Oct. 13, 1858), in* 3 COLLECTED WORKS OF ABRAHAM LINCOLN 245, 255 (Ray Basler ed. 1953). *See also* Abraham Lincoln, *First Inaugural Address—Final Text (Mar. 4, 1861), in* 4 COLLECTED WORKS OF ABRAHAM LINCOLN, *supra,* at 262, 268. Lincoln's views are analyzed at length in JOHN AGRESTO, THE SUPREME COURT AND CONSTITUTIONAL DEMOCRACY 86–95 (1984).

128. Andrew Jackson, *Message Vetoing the Renewal of the Second Bank of the United States, July 10, 1832,* 2 MESSAGES AND PAPERS OF THE PRESIDENTS 582 (James Richardson ed. 1896). *See generally* LOUIS FISHER, CONSTITUTIONAL DIALOGUES: INTERPRETATION AS POLITICAL PROCESS 275–79 (1988); THE PRESIDENCY IN THE CONSTITUTIONAL ORDER (Joseph Besette & Jeffrey Tulis eds. 1980); JEFFREY TULIS, THE RHETORICAL PRESIDENCY (1987); Paul Colby, *Two Views on the Legitimacy of Nonacquiescence in Judicial Opinions,* 61 TULANE L. REV. 1041 (1987); Frank Easterbrook, *Presidential Review,* 40 CASE-W. RES. L. REV. 905 (1990); Christopher Eisgruber, *The Most Competent Branches: A Response to Professor Paulsen,* 83 GEO. L.J. 347 (1994); Christopher May, *Presidential Defiance of "Unconstitutional" Law: Reviving the Royal Prerogative,* 21 HASTINGS CONST'L L.Q. 865 (1994); Thomas Merrill, *Judicial Deference to Executive Precedent,* 101 YALE L.J. 969 (1991); Paulsen, *supra* note 125, at 272–76; Symposium, *Executive Branch Interpretation of the Law,* 15 CARDOZO L. REV. 21 (1993).

129. *See* Pub. L. No. 96-132, §21(a)(1), 93 Stat. 1040, 1050 (1979) (directing how the Department of Justice is to declare a law unconstitutional).

Instead of following Lincoln's and Jackson's admonitions, institutions claiming to be open forums for diverse points of view on issues of public concern succumbed to pressures on them to silence abortion's opponents rather than undertaking to convince them.[130] The pressures brought against pro-life advocates to prevent their free expression exceed the pressures brought against almost any other social movement in the twentieth century. One commentator concluded that the closest comparable attempts to suppress unwelcome speech are the attempts to suppress abolitionist sentiment in the early nineteenth century.[131]

The Federal Communications Commission has approved denial of access during "prime time" for political ads regarding abortion because of its "offensive content" (disturbing pictures).[132] Municipalities have denied pro-life groups permission to set up booths or otherwise advocate their beliefs in areas or by means that other organizations are routinely allowed to use.[133] State "campaign finance" laws have been enacted in an effort to limit "issue advocacy groups"—including prominently "pro-life" groups—from spending freely to influence elections.[134] The Clinton administration has even ordered military chaplains not to preach *against* abortion in church services.[135] In legislative debates, attempts to restrict access to abortion are typically met by a simple assertion that such a law would be unconstitutional rather than by a serious discussion of the merits (moral or otherwise) of such a law.[136]

Courts also play this game.[137] Justice Harry Blackmun, author of the majority opinion in *Roe,* apparently believed that abortion is too sensitive for public debate.[138] Like the Federal Commu-

---

130. *See* Tracy Craige, Note, *Abortion Protest: Lawless Conspiracy or Prohibited Free Speech,* 72 Den. U. L. Rev. 445 (1995); Jason DeParle, *Beyond the Legal Right,* Wash. Monthly, April, 1989, at 28; Kelly Faglioni, Note, *Balancing First Amendment Rights of Abortion Protestors with the Rights of Their "Victims,"* 48 Wash. & Lee L. Rev. 247 (1991); Note, *Safety Valve Closed: The Removal of Nonviolent Outlets for Dissent and the Onset of Anti-Abortion Violence,* 113 Harv. L. Rev. 1210 (2000); Lynn Wardle, *The Quandary of Pro-Life Free Speech: A Lesson from the Abolitionists,* 62 Alb. L. Rev. 853 (1999). *See generally* Bruce Ledewitz, *Perspectives on the Law of the American Sit-in,* 16 Whittier L. Rev. 499, 569 (1995). Professor Tribe has characterized statements such as mine as "blaming the victim in the most perverse way." *See* Anthony Flint, *Some Say Law Too Harsh on Abortion Foes,* Bos. Globe, Jan. 5, 1995, at 8. I develop my response to this comment in the remainder on this chapter.

131. Wardle, *supra* note 130, at 883, 936–39. Many commentators find more extensive parallels between abortion and slavery. *See, e.g.,* Michael Perry, *Liberal Democracy and Religious Morality,* 48 DePaul L. Rev. 1 (1998); Debora Threedy, *Slavery Rhetoric and the Abortion Debate,* 2 Mich. J. Gender & L. 3 (1994).

132. Becker v. FCC, 95 F.3d 75 (D.C. Cir. 1996). *See* Lili Levi, *The FCC, Indecency, and Anti-Abortion Political Advertising,* 3 Villa. Sports & Ent. L.J. 85 (1996); Douglas Melcher, *Delineating the Scope of a Licensee's Obligation to Broadcast Political Advertisements,* 66 Geo. Wash. L. Rev. 842, 848–49 (1998); Milagros Ribera-Sanchez & Paul Gates, jr., *Abortion on the Air: Broadcasters and Indecent Political Advertising,* 46 Fed. Communications L.J. 267 (1994).

133. Wardle, *supra* note 130, at 884–85.

134. *See, e.g.,* Vt. Stat. Ann. tit. 17, §§ 2881–2883 (2002).

135. Wardle, *supra* note 130, at 885.

136. Maltz, *supra* note 6, at 98–100.

137. *See, e.g.,* Carr v. Axelrod, 798 F. Supp. 168 (S.D.N.Y. 1992) (refusing to allow removal to federal court of a state proceeding to close a pregnancy counseling center for violation of consumer protection statutes for not advertising its anti-abortion attitudes), *aff'd mem.,* 996 F.2d 302 (2nd Cir.), *cert. denied,* 510 U.S. 531 (1993). *See also* Note, *supra* note 130; Wardle, *supra* note 130; James Weinstein, *Free Speech, Abortion Access, and the Problem of Viewpoint Discrimination,* 29 U.C. Davis L. Rev. 471 (1996). *See generally* Stanley Fish, There's No Such Thing as Free Speech (1994); Kathleen Sullivan, *Discrimination, Distribution, and Free Speech,* 37 Ariz. L. Rev. 439 (1995); Mark Tushnet, *"Shut up He Explained,"* 95 Nw. U. L. Rev. 907 (2001).

138. Richard Wilkins, Richard Sherlock, & Stephen Clark, *Mediating the Polar Extremes: A Guide to Post-Webster Abortion Policy,* in Abortion and the State: Political Change and Future Regulation 139, 146–47, 191–92 n.42 (Jane Wishner ed. 1993).

nications Commission, a federal district court barred anti-abortion advertising on local television except during the hours between 12:00 a.m. and 6:00 a.m. on the grounds that its illustration of dismembered fetal parts was "obscene."[139] Similarly, two anti-abortion protestors were arrested and charge with "child pornography" for displaying a picture of an aborted fetus[140]— ignoring the irony that such a charge validates the central claim of the protestors. In one extreme case, a state trial court in California incarcerated an attorney for contempt of court when he insisted on referring to aborted fetuses as "unborn children" during a trial of abortion protestors despite the judge's order that he not do so.[141] Other judges have forbidden the use of the words like "kill," "murder," or "holocaust" by anti-abortion protestors.[142] On the other hand, courts, at least, construed federal campaign finance laws narrowly to avoid the possibility of transgressing the First Amendment guarantee of freedom of speech.[143] These courts concluded that the statutes affect only direct advocacy of the election or defeat of particular candidates rather than the advocacy of ideas or policies. And one court surprisingly held that the Southeastern Pennsylvania Transportation Authority's removal of anti-abortion advertisements from the Authority's stations violated the sponsoring group's freedom of speech.[144]

Attempts to reform the financing of federal elections, culminating in the *Bipartisan Campaign Reform Act of 2002* (known generally as the "McCain-Feingold Act"), raised fears that its ban on the use of "soft money" in political campaigns[145] would become yet another tool for suppressing politi-

---

139. Gillett Commun. of Atlanta, Inc. v. Becker, 807 F. Supp. 757 (N.D. Ga. 1992), *appeal dismissed,* 5 F.3d 1500 (11th Cir. 1993). *See generally* Lili Levi, *The FCC, Indency, and Anti-Abortion Political Advertising,* 3 Villa. Sports & Ent. L.J. 85 (1996); Milagros Rivera-Sanchez, *Abortion on the Air: Broadcasters and Indecent Political Advertising,* 46 Fed. Comm. L.J. 267 (1994); Hille von Rosenvinge Sheppard, *The Federal Communications Act and the Broadcast of Aborted Fetus Advertisements,* 1993 U. Chi. L.F. 393. While pro-abortion groups sometimes have trouble getting a media outlet to run their advertisements, they do not encounter the legal problems thrown up against anti-abortion advertisements. James Hirsch, *Media Become Newest Weapons in Battle for Support on Abortion,* N.Y. Times, Apr. 26, 1989, at A26. *See also* Planned Parenthood of S.C., Inc. v. Rose, 236 F. Supp. 2d 564 (D.S.C. 2002) (a statute authorizing "Choose Life" automobile license plates without any pro-choice alternative violates the freedom of speech guaranteed in the First Amendment).

140. Wardle, *supra* note 130, at 885.

141. Zal v. Steppe, 968 F.2d 924 (9th Cir.), *cert. denied,* 506 U.S. 521 (1992).

142. *See, e.g.,* Bering v. Share, 721 P.2d 918, 921, 937–38 (Wash. 1986) (limiting the injunction to situations in which children were present), *cert. denied,* 479 U.S. 1050 (1987). *But see* OBGYN Ass'ns v. Birthright of Brooklyn & Queens, Inc., 407 N.Y.S.2d 903, 906 (App. Div. 1978) (overturning a trial judge's order that an attorney not use the words "murder" or "kill" in connection with abortion). *See generally* Sandra Lynn Jordan, Comment, Bering v. Share: *Abortion Protestors Lose Ground in the State of Washington,* 18 Cumb. L. Rev. 205 (1987); Carrie Miller, *Abortion, Protest, and Constitutional Protection—* Bering v. Share, 62 Wash. L. Rev. 311 (1987); Wardle, *supra* note 130, at 885–86.

143. *See, e.g.,* Federal Election Comm'n v. Massachusetts Citizens for Life, Inc., 479 U.S. 328 (1986); Minnesota Citizens Concerned for Life v. Federal Election Comm'n, 113 F.3d 129 (8th Cir. 1997); Federal Election Comm'n v. Christian Action Network, Inc., 110 F.3d 1049 (4th Cir. 1997). *But see* California Pro-Life Council, Inc. v. Getman, 328 F.3d 1088 (9th Cir. 2003); Kentucky Rt. to Life, Inc. v. Terry, 108 F.3d 637 (6th Cir.), *cert. denied sub nom.* Kentucky Rt. To Life, Inc. v. Stengel, 522 U.S. 860 (1997). *See generally* Buckley v. Valeo, 424 U.S. 1 (1976); Gable v. Patton, 142 F.3d 940 (6th Cir. 1998); C. Edwin Baker, *Campaign Expenditures and Free Speech,* 33 Harv. C.R.-C.L. L. Rev. 1 (1998); Joel Gora, *Campaign Finance Reform: Still Searching Today for a Better Way,* 6 J. Law & Pol'y 137 (1997); Frank Sorauf, *Politics, Experience and the First Amendment: The Case of American Campaign Finance Reform,* 94 Colum. L. Rev. 1348 (1994); David Strauss, *Corruption, Equality, and Campaign Finance Reform,* 94 Colum. L. Rev. 1369 (1994); Ralph Winter, *The History and Theory of* Buckley v. Valeo, 6 J. Law & Pol'y 93 (1997).

144. Christ's Bride Ministries, Inc. v. Southeastern Pa. Transp. Auth'y, 148 F.3d 242 (3rd Cir. 1998), *cert. denied,* 525 U.S. 1068 (1999). *See also* Henderson v. Stalder, 287 F.3d 374 (5th Cir. 2002) (finding that challengers to Louisiana's sale of "choose life" license plates lacked standing to bring their suit); Planned Parenthood of S.C. Inc. v. Rose, 236 F. Supp. 2d 564 (D.S.C. 2003) (holding the sale of "choose life" license plates to be unconstitutional).

145. 2 U.S.C. §441i (2000).

cal advertising by anti-abortion groups.[146] A divided Supreme Court upheld the constitutionality of the ban insofar as it precluded naming particular candidates or any coordination with a political party or an electoral campaign against challenges brought by a wide array of groups from all parts of the political spectrum, most of which groups were not focused on abortion.[147] This, however, did not prevent pro- or anti-abortion groups from continuing to advertise independently during political campaigns, leaving it to the candidates to spell out where they stood on the issue without the independent group specifically naming a candidate. This could, of course, reduce the effectiveness of such independent advertising, but it did not eliminate or seriously curtail such advertising.

Private institutions also attempted to silence debate within their ranks. Women have been fired from their jobs for wearing pro-life buttons to work[148]—with virtually no media attention given to the firing. (How would the media respond if someone were to be fired for wearing an "AIDS awareness" button?)[149] Today such apparently disinterested institutions as the McArthur Foundation, with its "genius award," openly and substantially underwrite the continuing efforts to keep abortion legal. For example, a "genius award" enabled Janet Benshoof to leave the American Civil Liberties Union to found her Center for Reproductive Law and Policy.[150]

Ironically, the news media, exhibiting their pro-abortion bias, generally portray anti-abortion groups as the threats to freedom of speech. These are, after all, the media for which "a five-day wait for a handgun is a 'regulation' but a one-day wait for an abortion is a 'restriction,' one of the 'barriers' and 'obstacles' that 'whittle away at the edge of *Roe v. Wade.*"[151] Television stations and newspapers routinely refuse to carry "pro-life" advertisements unless they are administratively or judicially compelled.[152] Supporters of abortion rights have particularly seized upon the "gag rule" imposed on birth control clinics during the Bush administration as evidence of the deprav-

---

146. *See, e.g.,* Alison Mitchell, *Foes of Abortion Split Sharply over Campaign Finance Bill,* N.Y. Times, Mar. 26, 1998, at A21; Robert Samuelson, *Muzzling Speech,* Wash. Post, Dec. 18, 2003, at A35. *See also* Arizona Rt. to Life Political Action Comm. v. Bayless, 320 F.3d 1002 (9th Cir. 2003); Florida Rt. to Life, Inc. v. Lamar, 273 F.3d 1318 (11th Cir. 2001); Yes for Life Political Action Comm. v. Webster, 84 F. Supp. 2d 150 (D. Me. 2000); Volle v. Webster, 69 F. Supp. 2d 171 (D. Me. 1999); Right to Life of Dutchess Cty., Inc. v. Federal Election Comm'n, 6 F. Supp. 2d 248 (S.D.N.Y. 1998); National Right to Life Comm. v. McGrath, 982 F. Supp. 694 (D. Mont. 1997).

147. McConnell v. Federal Election Comm'n, 540 U.S. 93 (2003).

148. *See, e.g.,* Wilson v. US West Communications, Inc., 58 F.3d 13376 (8th Cir. 1995). *See also* Wardle, *supra* note 130, at 884.

149. Consider the press's hostile reaction to Justice Antonin Scalia appearing before a prayer breakfast for law students and delivering a strongly Christian homily—that did not speak directly to any legal issues—while largely taking in stride Justice Harry Blackmun's appearing before a different group of law students and stating that "I want to hang around and prevent those jokers from overruling *Roe.*" *Compare* Joan Biskupic, *Scalia Makes the Case for Christianity,* Wash. Post, Apr. 10, 1996, at A1; Clay Chandler, *Scalia's Religion Remarks: Just a Matter of Free Speech?,* Wash. Post, Apr. 15, 1996, at A7; Robert Sirico, *Scalia's Dissenting Opinion,* Wall St. J., Apr. 19, 1996, at A12; *and* Stuart Taylor, jr., *Justice Scalia's Persecution Complex,* Am. Law., June 1996, at 37; *with* Jeff Bucholtz, *Justice Blackmun Brings Overflow Crowd to Its Feet,* Harv. L. Rec., Mar. 11, 1994, at 1. Apparently Blackmun's remarks were so unobjectionable that no reporter in the major media saw it as newsworthy. *See generally* Michael Stokes Paulsen & Steffen Johnson, *Scalia's Sermonette,* 72 Notre Dame L. Rev. 863 (1997).

150. Richard Rueben, *Called to Action: Grants Help Crusading Attorneys Continue Work,* ABA J., Oct. 1996, at 27.

151. John Leo, *Litmus Tests, Slippery Slopes,* U.S. News & World Rep., Jan. 28, 1998, at 16. *See generally* Hunter, *supra* note 14, at 174, 226; Jacoby, *supra* note 14, at 107–09; Risen & Thomas, *supra* note 4, at 298; S. Robert Lichter & Stanley Rothman, *The Media Elite,* 96 Pub. Opinion 117 (1981); David Shaw, *Abortion Foes Stereotyped, Some in the Media Believe: Abortion and the Media,* L.A. Times, July 2, 1990, at 1; David Shaw, *Can Women Reporters Write Objectively on Abortion Issues?,* L.A. Times, July 3, 1990, at 23.

152. Michael Bailey, *Censorship by Media Elites Will Ultimately Threaten the Republic,* 47 Fed. Comm. L.J. 159 (1994).

ity of the opponents of abortion rights.[153] The "gag rule," we are told, deprives doctors and other health workers of their freedom to talk about abortion.[154] Yet the most noteworthy silencing of a voice in the abortion controversy was the refusal of the Democratic National Convention to allow Governor Robert Casey of Pennsylvania to address the Convention in 1992.[155] Almost as significant was the decision of the American Civil Liberties Union to oust journalist Nat Hentoff from its national board of directors after he announced "pro-life" sentiments.[156]

Supporters of abortion rights have invoked several general statutes in order to suppress protests against, or even criticism of, abortion. Courts have found violations of antitrust laws,[157] the *Ku Klux Klan Act*,[158] and of the *Racketeer Influenced and Corrupt Organizations Act* ("*RICO*").[159] Large damages were awarded even against peaceful protestors. Nuisance and tres-

---

153. Rust v. Sullivan, 500 U.S. 173 (1991); 2 Federal Abortion Politics, *supra* note 14, at 369–486. *See also* DKT Memorial Fund Ltd. v. Agency for Int'l Dev., 887 F.2d 275 (D.C. Cir. 1989) (upholding the constitutionality of federal funds barring aid funds to foreign family planning agencies that actively promote abortions); Pathfinder Fund v. Agency for Int'l Dev., 746 F. Supp. 192 (D.D.C. 1990) (same).

154. *See* Cass Sunstein, Democracy and the Problem of Free Speech 114–18 (1993); Paula Berg, *Toward a First Amendment Theory of Doctor-Patient Discourse and the Right to Receive Unbiased Medical Advice*, 74 B.U. L. Rev. 201 (1994); David Cole, *Beyond Unconstitutional Conditions: Charting Spheres of Neutrality in Government-Funded Speech*, 67 NYU L. Rev. 675 (1992); Phillip Cooper, *Rusty Pipes: The* Rust *Decision and the Supreme Court's Free Flow Theory of the First Amendment*, 6 Notre Dame J.L. Ethics & Pub. Pol'y 359; Stephen Heyman, *State-Supported Speech*, 1999 Wis. L. Rev. 1119, 1163–74; Stanley Ingbar, *Judging without Judgment: Constitutional Irrelevancies and the Demise of Dialogue*, 46 Rutgers L. Rev. 1473 (1994); Thomas Mayo, *Abortion and Speech: A Comment*, 46 SMU L. Rev. 309 (1992); Robert Post, *Subsidized Speech*, 106 Yale L.J. 151, 168–76 (1996); Martin Redish & Daryl Kessler, *Government Subsidies and Free Expression* Martin Redish & Daryl Kessler, *Government Subsidies and Free Expression*, 80 Minn. L. Rev. 543 (1996); Dorothy Roberts, Rust v. Sullivan *and the Control of Knowledge*, 61 Geo. Wash. L. Rev. 587 (1993); Stephen Rohde, Rust v. Sullivan: *Subverting the Constitution and Abusing Judicial Power?*, 25 Beverly Hills B. Ass'n J. 155 (1991); Peter Shane, *The* Rust *that Corrodes: State Action, Free Speech, and Responsibility*, 52 La. L. Rev. 1585 (1992); William Van Alstyne, *Second Thoughts on* Rust v. Sullivan *and the First Amendment*, 9 Const. Commentary 5 (1992); Christina Wells, *Abortion Counseling as a Vice Activity: The Fee Speech Implications of* Rust v. Sullivan *and* Planned Parenthood v. Casey, 95 Colum. L. Rev. 1724 (1995). Since 2000, it has become common among liberals to decry a general conservative bias in the media. *See, e.g.,* Michael Kelly, *Left Everlasting*, Wash. Post, Dec. 11, 2002, at A33.

155. *See* Jacoby, *supra* note 17, at 185–86; Judges, *supra* note 6, at 282. *See also* Peggy Fletcher Stack, *Zero Tolerance*, Salt Lake Trib., Jan. 8, 1994, at D1 (reporting physical attacks on "pro-life" advocate Anne Maloney at the Democratic National Convention in 1992).

156. Jacoby, *supra* note 17, at 87.

157. National Org. for Women v. Scheidler, 968 F.2d 612 (7th Cir.), *cert. denied*, 513 U.S. 1058 (1992); Town of West Hartford v. Operation Rescue, 915 F.2d 92 (2nd Cir. 1990), *vacated in part*, 991 F.2d 1039 (2nd Cir.), *cert. denied sub nom.* Syverson v. Summit Women's Ctr. West, Inc., 510 U.S. 865 (1993).

158. 42 U.S.C. § 1985(3) (2000). *See* Libertad v. Welch, 53 F.3d 428 (1st Cir. 1995); National Abortions Fed. v. Operation Rescue, 8 F.3d 680 (9th Cir. 1993); Town of West Hartford v. Operation Rescue, 991 F.2d 1039 (2nd Cir.), *cert. denied sub nom.* Syverson v. Summit Women's Ctr. West, Inc., 510 U.S. 865 (1993); Lucero v. Operation Rescue of Birmingham, 954 F.2d 624 (11th Cir. 1992); Volunteer Med. Clinic, Inc. v. Operation Rescue, 948 F.2d 218 (6th Cir. 1991); Roe v. Operation Rescue, 919 F.2d 857 (3rd Cir. 1990); National Org. for Women v. Operation Rescue, 914 F.2d 582 (4th Cir. 1990), *rev'd sub nom.* Bray v. Alexandria Women's Health Clinic, 506 U.S. 263 (1993); New York St. Nat. Org. for Women v. Terry, 886 F.2d 1339 (2nd Cir. 1989), *cert. denied*, 495 U.S. 947 (1990); Mississippi Women's Clinic v. McMillan, 866 F.2d 788 (5th Cir. 1989); Roe v. Abortion Abolition Soc'y, 811 F.2d 931 (5th Cir.), *cert. denied*, 484 U.S. 848 (1987). *See also* Craige, *supra* note 130, at 451–57; Elizabeth Crane, Comment, *Abortion Clinics and Their Antagonists: Protection from Protestors under 42 U.S.C. § 1985(3)*, 64 U. Colo. L. Rev. 181 (1993); David Gardey, Note, *Federal Power to the Rescue: The Use of § 1985(3) against Anti-Abortion Protestors*, 67 Notre Dame L. Rev. 707 (1992); Elizabeth Roberge, Note, *Operation Rescue's Anti-Abortion Rescue Blockades and 42 U.S.C. § 1985(3) (A/K/A the Ku Klux Klan Act)*, 26 Ind. L. Rev. 333 (1993); Wardle, *supra* note 130, at 897–99.

159. 42 U.S.C. §§ 1961–1968 (2000). *See* National Org. for Women v. Scheidler, 510 U.S. 249 (1994); Feminist Women's Health Ctr. v. Codispoti, 63 F.3d 863 (9th Cir. 1995); Roe v. Operation Rescue, 54 F.3d 133 (3rd Cir. 1995); Libertad v. Welch, 53 F.3d 428 (1st Cir. 1995); Pearson v. Planned Parenthood Clinic, 41 F.3d 794 (2nd Cir. 1994); National Org. for Women v. Operation Rescue, 37 F.3d 646 (D.C. Cir. 1994); Lucero v. Oper-

pass judgments ranging from $200,000 to $500,000 were awarded in Oregon against 30 anti-abortion protestors who sat peacefully on the steps of an abortion clinic singing and praying, but causing no damage to any property or to any person.[160] A jury in Chicago awarded some $1,000,000 in punitive damages against Chicago protestors in a case in which the jury found only $85,296 in actual damages,[161] and a jury in Texas awarded some $8,650,000 against peaceful picketers.[162] Some judges have also taken to awarding exorbitant attorneys' fees against abortion rights activists, although these awards have been reduced or thrown out on appeal.[163] No such damage or fee awards would be tolerated against, for example, the protestors who stalk of Justice Clarence Thomas.[164] And courts and juries have imposed vicarious liability on unrelated organizations with deep pockets with only the flimsiest of evidence of a connection between them and the actual wrongdoers.[165]

The monetary damages awarded in these cases were virtually impossible to collect.[166] Still, the suits went on for, if nothing else, successful suits branded the protestors as "racketeers" or worse.

---

ation Rescue of Birmingham, 954 F.2d 624 (11th Cir. 1992); Volunteer Med. Clinic, Inc. v. Operation Rescue, 948 F.2d 218 (6th Cir. 1991); Roe v. Operation Rescue, 919 F.2d 857 (3rd Cir. 1990); Town of West Hartford v. Operation Rescue, 915 F.2d 92 (2nd Cir. 1990), *vacated in part,* 991 F.2d 1039 (2nd Cir.), *cert. denied sub nom.* Syverson v. Summit Women's Ctr. West, Inc., 510 U.S. 865 (1993); Northeast Women's Ctr. v. McMonigle, 939 F.2d 57 (3rd Cir. 1991); Lovejoy Specialty Hosp. v. Advocates for Life, 855 P.2d 159 (Ore. Ct. App. 1993), *rev. denied,* 863 P.2d 1267 (Ore.), *cert. denied,* 511 U.S. 1070 (1994). *See also* Sarah Diamond, The Road to Dominion: Right Wing Movements and Political Power in the United States 302–05 (1995); Risen & Thomas, *supra* note 4, at 115–16, 295–97; Craig Bradley, NOW v. *Scheidler: RICO Meets the First Amendment,* 1994 Sup. Ct. Rev. 129; Fay Clayton & Sara Love, Now v. Scheidler: *Protecting Women's Access to Reproductive Health Services,* 62 Alb. L. Rev. 967 (1999); Craige, *supra* note 130, at 457–68; Faye Ginsburg, *Rescuing the Nation: Operation Rescue and the Rise of Anti-Abortion Militance,* in Abortion Wars, *supra* note 27, at 227, 238; Jon Jeter, *Jury Says Abortion Opponents Are Liable; Efforts to Close Clinics Violate Racketeering Law,* Wash. Post, Apr. 21, 1998, at A1; Dirk Johnson, *Abortion Foes Are Held Liable for Harassment,* N.Y. Times, Apr. 21, 1998, at A1; Steven Soule & Karen Weinstein, *Racketeering, Anti-Abortion Protestors, and the First Amendment,* 4 UCLA Women's L.J. 365 (1994); Wardle, *supra* note 130, at 888–90, 899–902; Geri Yonover, *Fighting Fire with Fire: Civil RICO and Anti-Abortion Activists,* 11 Women's Rts. L. Rptr. 153 (1989).

In one case, one of the two threats required for a *RICO* suit was a statement by a protestor that an abortion provider was in danger of losing her soul. G. Robert Blakely, *Enlarged RICO Threatens Right of Free Speech,* Nat'l L.J., May 4, 1998, at A22. There were numerous other, more threatening remarks were attributed to the protestors in the same case, including middle-of-the-night telephone calls, threats to burn the clinic, and the wearing of lapel pins in the shape of sticks of dynamite. National Org. for Women v. Scheidler, 739 F. Supp. 1210, 1213–14 (N.D. Ill. 1990), *aff'd on other grounds,* 968 F.2d 612 (7th Cir.), *cert. denied,* 513 U.S. 1058 (1992).

160. Wardle, *supra* note 130, at 887–88.

161. Jill Schachner Chanen, *A Trial Twelve Years in the Making: After Victory against Anti-Abortion Group, NOW Lawyer Recalls the Long Battle,* ABA J., June 1998, at 38; Abdon Pallasch & Judy Peres, *Abortion Foes Suffer Big Setback,* Chi. Trib., Apr. 21, 1998, at 1.

162. Tompkins v. Cyr, 995 F. Supp. 664 (N.D. Tex. 1998). *See also Jury Awards $8.65 Million in Anti-Abortion Protests,* Wall St. J., Oct. 26, 1995, at A13.

163. *See, e.g.,* Planned Parenthood v. Williams, 898 P.2d 402 (Cal. 1995) (upholding a $100,000 attorneys' fee award against individual protestors), *cert. denied,* 520 U.S. 1133 (1997); Feminist Women's Health Ctr. v. Blythe, 22 Cal. Rptr. 2d 184 (Ct. App. 1993), *vacated & remanded sub nom.* Reali v. Feminist Women's Health Ctr., 512 U.S. 1249 (1994), *on remand sub nom.* Feminist Women's Health Ctr. v. Blythe, 39 Cal. Rptr. 2d 189 (Ct. App.) (vacating attorneys' fee awards against Operation Rescue), *cert. denied sub nom.* Reali v. Feminist Women's Health Ctr., 516 U.S. 987 (1995).

164. Wardle, *supra* note 130, at 888. *See also* Soule & Weinstein, *supra* note 159, at 386–98; Weinstein, *supra* note 137, at 474–90.

165. Sue Ellen Christian, *Abortion Advocates See Conspiracy: Violence, Fear Tactics Link Foes, Court Hears,* Chi. Trib., Mar. 5, 1998, at 3; Sue Ellen Christian, *Activists Called too Independent to Conspire,* Chi. Trib., Apr. 16, 1998, at 17; Pallasch & Peres, *supra* note 161; Wardle, *supra* note 130, at 888–90.

166. Garrow, *supra* note 22, at 718–19; *Abortion Foes Lose Property to Opponents,* N.Y. Times, Apr. 21, 1995, at A18; Ginsburg, *supra* note 159, at 238; Tamar Lewin, *Abortion Foes' Losses Are Frustrating the Victors,* N.Y. Times, June 11, 1994, at A1.

Such scarlet letters still carry weight in American society, delegitimating the efforts of the protestors to express their opinions.[167] And so intent were the supporters of abortion rights on using the threat of financial burdens to stifle dissent over abortion that they held up a broadly supported bankruptcy reform unless it contains language barring bankruptcy for debts arising from fines or damages for protests at abortion clinics.[168]

The common thread to these suits is the theory that the defendants engaged in a conspiracy to deprive those seeking to obtain or provide abortions of their civil rights.[169] No one was surprised when Janet Reno, as Attorney General of the United States, organized a federal task force and two grand juries to investigate whether anti-abortion activists formed a criminal conspiracy to close abortion clinics.[170] Chief William Justice Rehnquist has also characterized the leading, joint opinion in *Planned Parenthood of Southeast Pennsylvania v. Casey* as yet just such an attempt to silence opposition to *Roe*, albeit slightly more subtle than the Attorney General's.[171] Finally, in 2003, the Supreme Court decided in by an 8-1 vote that protesters against abortion clinics were not engaged in racketeering offenses under *RICO* because they were not seeking to extort property from the clinics.[172] The Court vacated both the money judgment against the protesters and the nationwide injunction against their protests. That still left open the possibility of suppressing dissent through actions based upon other statutes, as Justices Ruth Bader Ginsburg and Stephen Breyer indicated in joining the majority opinion barring *RICO* suits.[173]

Over the years, supporters of abortion rights have obtained numerous injunctions against abortion protests.[174] Such injunctions were enforced against protestors not named in the injunc-

---

167. *See* Mike Robinson, *Racketeer Verdict Angers Opponents of Abortion, Set Stage for More Claims*, BUFF. NEWS, Apr. 21, 1998, at A6 (quoting Joseph Scheidler, "We wanted to come out as a legitimate force in America and not as racketeers. There is no honor in being a racketeer, and we're not racketeers.").

168. Philip Shenon, *Abortion Issue Holds up Bill on Bankruptcy,* N.Y. TIMES, Apr. 30, 2002, at A1.

169. *See* United States v. Arena, 180 F.3d 380 (2nd Cir. 1999) (two defendants convicted of "extortion" and "conspiracy to commit extortion" for defacing an abortion facility). *See, also* Habiger v. City of Fargo, 80 F.3d 289 (8th Cir.), *cert. denied,* 519 U.S. 1011 (1996); Veneklase v. City of Fargo, 78 F.3d 1264 (8th Cir.), *cert. denied,* 519 U.S. 876 (1996); Radich v. Goode, 886 F.2d 1391 (3rd Cir. 1989); Dowling v. City of Philadelphia, 855 F.2d 136 (3rd Cir. 1988); Fischer v. City of St. Paul, 894 F. Supp. 1318 (D. Minn. 1995); United States v. Lindgren, 883 F. Supp. 1321 (D.N.D. 1995); State v. Ross, 889 P.2d 161 (Mont. 1995); Operation Rescue v. Planned Parenthood of Houston, 975 S.W.2d 546 (Tex. 1998). *See generally* GARROW, *supra* note 22, at 714–15; Jon & H. Elaine Lindgren, *Social Change within the "Establishment": A City's Response to National Antiabortion Protestors,* 31 J. APPLIED BEHAVIORAL SCI. 475 (1995).

170. Timothy Egan, *Conspiracy Is an Elusive Target in Prosecuting Foes of Abortion: Abortion Violence, a Special Report,* N.Y. TIMES, June 18, 1995, at A18 ("Egan I"); Timothy Egan, *Is Abortion Violence a Plot? Conspiracy Is Not Confirmed,* N.Y. TIMES, June 18, 1995, at 1 ("Egan II").

171. Planned Parenthood of S.E. Pa. v. Casey, 505 U.S. 833, 962–65 (1992) (Rehnquist, C.J., dissenting). *See generally* Note, *supra* note 130, at 1220; Kathleen Sullivan, *Foreword: The Justices of Rules and Standards,* 106 HARV. L. REV. 22, 102–03 (1992).

172. Scheidler v. National Org. for Women, 537 U.S. 393 (2003). *See also* Palmetto State Med. Ctr. v. Operation Lifeline, 117 F.3d 142 (4th Cir. 1997); Kaplan v. Prolife Action League of Greensboro, 493 S.E.2d 416 (N.C. 1997), *cert. denied sub nom.* Winfield v. Kaplan, 512 U.S. 1253 (1994).

173. *Scheidler,* 537 U.S. at 411–12.

174. *See, e.g.,* Schenck v. Pro-Choice Network of W.N.Y., 519 U.S. 357 (1997); Madsen v. Women's Health Ctr., 512 U.S. 753 (1994); Frisby v. Schultz, 487 U.S. 474 (1988); *In re* Crawford, 328 F.3d 131 (2nd Cir.), *cert. denied,* 540 U.S. 881 (2003); New York *ex rel.* Spitzer v. Operation Rescue Nat., 273 F.3d 184 (2nd Cir. 2001); Edwards v. City of Santa Barbara, 150 F.3d 1213 (9th Cir. 1998), *cert. denied,* 526 U.S. 1004 (1999); United States v. Lynch, 104 F.3d 357 (2nd Cir. 1996), 1996 WL 717912, *cert. denied,* 520 U.S. 1170 (1997); McKusick v. City of Melbourne, 96 F.3d 478 (11th Cir. 1996); Roe v. Operation Rescue, 54 F.3d 133 (3rd Cir. 1995); Abrams v. Terry, 45 F.3d 17 (2nd Cir. 1995); Women's Health Care Services v. Operation Rescue, 24 F.3d 107, *vacated on mem.,* 25 F.3d 1059 (10th Cir. 1994); United States v. Terry, 17 F.3d 575 (2nd Cir.), *cert. denied,* 513 U.S. 946 (1994); Pro-Choice Network v. Walker, 994 F.2d 989 (2nd Cir. 1993); Portland Feminist Women's Health Ctr. v. Advocates for Life, Inc., 859 F.2d 681 (9th Cir. 1988); Planned Parenthood of Shasta-Diablo v.

tion who apparently did not know they would be subject to arrest for violating an injunction.[175] Supporters of abortion rights also succeeded in enacting the *Freedom of Access to Clinic Entrances Act*[176] specifically designed to foreclose protests near any abortion facility as a means of suppressing views differing from their own. The *Freedom of Access Act* was upheld in the lower federal courts against repeated challenges to its constitutionality on various grounds.[177] One court held

---

Williams, 898 P.2d 402 (Cal. 1995), *cert. denied*, 520 U.S. 1133 (1997); Hirsh v. City of Atlanta, 401 S.E.2d 530 (Ga.), *cert. denied*, 501 U.S. 1221 (1991); Planned Parenthood Lg. of Mass. v. Blake, 631 N.E.2d 985 (Mass.), *cert. denied*, 513 U.S. 868 (1994); Robbinsdale Clinic v. Pro-Life Action Ministries, 515 N.W.2d 88 (Minn. 1994); Murray v. Lawson, 649 A.2d 1253 (N.J. 1994), *cert. denied*, 515 U.S. 1110 (1995); Horizon Health Ctr. v. Felicissimo, 638 A.2d 1260 (N.J. 1994); Operation Rescue v. Planned Parenthood of Houston, 975 S.W.2d 546 (Tex. 1998). *But see* Cheffer v. McGregor, 6 F.3d 705 (11th Cir. 1993), *vacated mem.*, 41 F.3d 1422 (11th Cir. 1994). *See also* Douglas v. Brownell, 88 F.3d 1511 (8th Cir. 1996) (requiring a permit to picket an abortion clinic); Planned Parenthood Lg. of Mass. v. Bell, 677 N.E.2d 204 (Mass.) (enjoining a single, long troublesome protester from approaching within 50 feet of his targeted clinic), *cert. denied*, 522 U.S. 819 (1997); Commonwealth v. Blake, 654 N.E.2d 64 (Mass. 1995) (same). *But see* Kirkeby v. Furness, 52 F.3d 772 (8th Cir. 1995), 92 F.3d 655 (8th Cir. 1996).

See generally *Hearings on H.R. 25 before the Subcom. on Civil & Const'l Rights of the Comm. on the Judiciary*, 102nd Cong., Mar. 4, 1992; 1 FEDERAL ABORTION POLITICS, *supra* note 33, at 657–741; GARROW, *supra* note 22, at 709, 726; Alan Brownstein, *Rules of Engagement for Cultural Wars: Regulating Conduct, Unprotected Speech, and Protected Expressions in Anti-Abortion Protests (Part I)*, 29 U.C. DAVIS L. REV. 553 (1996); Craige, *supra* note 130, at 468–81; Deborah Ellis & Yolanda Wu, *Of Buffer Zones and Broken Bones: Balancing Access to Abortion and Anti-Abortion Protestors' First Amendment Rights in* Schenck v. Pro-Choice Network, 62 BROOK. L. REV. 547 (1996); Tara Kelly, *Silencing the Lambs: Restricting the First Amendment Rights of Abortion Clinic Protestors in* Madsen v. Women's Health Center, 68 S. CAL. L. REV. 427 (1995); Bruce Ledewitz, *Civil Disobedience, Injunctions, and the First Amendment*, 19 HOFSTRA L. REV. 67 (1990); Michael Stokes Paulsen, *Captain James T. Kirk and the Enterprise of Constitutional Interpretation: Some Modest Proposals from the Twenty Third Century*, 59 ALBANY L. REV., 671 n.1, 677–82 (1995); William Plouffe, jr., Note, *Free Speech v. Abortion: Has the First Amendment Been Expanded, Limited, or Blurred?*, 31 TULSA L.J. 203 (1995); Amy Sneirson, *No Place to Hide: Why State and Federal Enforcement of Stalking Laws May Be the Best Way to Protect Abortion Providers*, 73 WASH. U. L.Q. 635 (1995); Wardle, *supra* note 130, at 892–97, 903–12; Weinstein, *supra* note 137, at 508–15; Christina Wells, *Of Communists and Anti-Abortion Protestors: The Consequences of Falling into the Theoretical Abyss*, 33 GA. L. REV. 1, 19–64 (1998).

175. *See, e.g.,* McKusick v. City of Melbourne, 96 F.3d 478 (11th Cir. 1996).

176. 18 U.S.C. § 248 (2000). *See* GARROW, *supra* note 22, at 706–07, 709–10, 726.

177. United States v. Gregg, 226 F.3d 253 (3rd Cir. 2000), *cert. denied*, 532 U.S. 971 (2001); United States v. Weslin, 156 F.3d 292 (2nd Cir. 1998), *cert. denied*, 525 U.S. 1071 (1999); United States v. Vazquez, 145 F.3d 74 (2nd Cir. 1998); Hoffman v. Hunt, 126 F.3d 575 (4th Cir. 1997), *cert. denied*, 523 U.S. 1136 (1998); United States v. Bird, 124 F.3d 667 (5th Cir. 1997), *cert. denied*, 523 U.S. 1006 (1998); Lucero v. Trosch, 121 F.3d 591 (11th Cir. 1997); Terry v. Reno, 101 F.3d 1412 (D.C. Cir. 1996), *cert. denied*, 520 U.S. 1264 (1997); United States v. Soderna, 82 F.3d 1370 (7th Cir.), *cert. denied sub nom.* Hatch v. United States, 519 U.S. 1006 (1996); United States v. Dinwiddie, 76 F.3d 913 (8th Cir.), *cert. denied*, 519 U.S. 1043 (1996); Cook v. Reno, 74 F.3d 97 (5th Cir. 1996), *cert. denied sub nom.* Skott v. United States, 519 U.S. 806 (1996); United States v. Wilson, 73 F.3d 675 (7th Cir. 1995), *cert. denied sub nom.* Skott v. United States, 519 U.S. 806 (1996); Pro-Choice Network v. Schenck, 67 F.3d 377 (2nd Cir. 1995), *modified on other grounds*, 519 U.S. 357 (1997); Cheffer v. Reno, 55 F.3d 1517 (11th Cir. 1995); Hoover v. Wagner, 47 F.3d 845 (7th Cir. 1995); Woodall v. Reno, 47 F.3d 656 (4th Cir.), *cert. denied*, 515 U.S. 1141 (1995); American Life League v. Reno, 47 F.3d 642 (4th Cir.), *cert. denied*, 516 U.S. 809 (1995).

See Alan Brownstein, *Rules of Engagement for Cultural Wars: Regulating Conduct, Unprotected Speech, and Protected Expressions in Anti-Abortion Protests (Part II)*, 29 U.C. DAVIS L. REV. 1163 (1996); Marie McCullough, *Inconclusive First Year for Abortion-Protest Law: Anti-Abortion Violence Has Risen, and There Have Been Only 15 Federal Prosecutions under the New Law. But Some Officials Say It Has Been a Deterrence* (sic), PHILA. INQUIRER, May 14, 1995, at E-3; Amy Nemko, *Saving FACE: Clinic Access under a New Commerce Clause*, 106 YALE L.J. 525 (1996); John Scheib, Cheffner v. Reno: *Is the Regulation of Abortion Clinic Protests the Regulation of Interstate Commerce?*, 41 VILLA. L. REV. 867 (1996); Kristine Sendak, *"FACE"-ing the Constitution: The Battle over the Freedom of Access to Clinic Entrances Shifts from Reproductive Health Facilities to the Federal Courts*, 46 CATH. U. L. REV. 165 (1996); Laurence Tribe, *The Constitutionality of the Freedom of Access to Clinic Entrances Act of 1993*, 1 VA. J. SOC. POL'Y & L. 291 (1994); Weinstein, *supra* note 137, at 515–21. *See generally*

that the penalties under the *Freedom of Access to Clinic Entrances Act*—six months in prison and $10,000 fine—make interference with abortion clinic access a "petty offense" for which no jury trial is available.[178] Other courts routinely denied defendants the opportunity even to argue to a jury the "necessity defense" (*i.e.,* that violating then law was necessary to save human life).[179] Another court even held that an employer's decision to dismiss a woman who was known to be considering an abortion (but did not have one) was prohibited under the *Pregnancy Discrimination Act.*[180]

The use of legal proceedings to suppress speech that one opposes is a growing practice not confined to the abortion controversy. It is so common that it has developed an acronym SLAPP (Strategic Lawsuit Against Public Participation).[181] The abortion clinic precedents thus present a considerably broader danger to freedom of speech than simply inhibiting speech against abor-

---

John Baker, jr., *State Police Powers and the Federalization of Local Crime,* 72 TEMPLE L. REV. 673 (1999).

In contrast, the Supreme Court found the *Violence against Women Act,* 42 U.S.C. § 13981 (2000), to be unconstitutional for exceeding congressional power under the commerce clause. United States v. Morrison, 529 U.S. 598 (2000). *See also* Michelle Anderson, *Women Do Not Report the Violence They Suffer: Violence against Women and the State Action Doctrine,* 46 VILLA. L. REV. 907 (2001); Daniel Atkins *et al., Striving for Justice with the Violence against Women Act and Civil Tort Action,* 14 WIS. WOMEN's L.J. 69 (1999); Craige, *supra* note 130, at 482–89; Martha Davis & Curt Levey, *Domestic Violence—A Proper Subject of National Legislation?* United States v. Morrison *and the Violence against Women Act,* 47 LOY. L. REV. 535 (2001); Julie Goldscheid, *Gender-Motivated Violence: Developing a Meaningful Paradigm for Civil Rights Enforcement,* 22 HARV. WOMEN's L.J. 123 (1999); Alberto Lopez, *Forty Yeas and Five Nays—The Nays Have It:* Morrion's *Blurred Political Accountability and the Defeat of the Civil Rights Provisions of the Violence against Women Act,* 69 GEO. WASH. L. REV. 251 (2001); Yvette Mabbun, *Title III of the Violence against Women Act: The Answer to Domestic Violence or a Constitutional Time Bomb?,* 29 ST. MARY's L. REV. 207 (1997); Reva Siegel, *She the People: The Nineteenth Amendment, Sex Equality, Federalism, and the Family,* 115 HARV. L. REV. 947 (2002); Symposium, *Redefining Violence against Women,* 8 TEMPLE POL. & CIV. RTS. L. REV. 273 (1999). As one student commentator noted, with only slight exaggeration, that there seem to have been more law review articles about the *Violence against Women Act* than there have been court cases brought under the Act. Christopher James Regan, Note, *A Whole Lot of Nothing Going on: The Civil Rights "Remedy" of the Violence against Women Act,* 75 NOTRE DAME L. REV. 797, 797 (1999); *See also* Atkins *et al., supra,* at 69 n.13 (noting how "ridiculously infrequent" cases under the Act are); Stephanie Weiler, *Bodily Integrity: A Substantive Due Process Right to Be Free from Rape by Public Officials,* 34 CAL. W. L. REV. 591, 607 (1998).

178. 18 U.S.C. § 248 (2000). *See* United States v. Soderna, 82 F.3d 1370 (7th Cir.), *cert. denied sub nom.* Hatch v. United States, 519 U.S. 1006 (1996).

179. *See, e.g.,* United States v. Turner, 44 F.3d 900 (10th Cir.), *cert. denied,* 515 U.S. 1104 (1995); City of Wichita v. Tilson, 855 P.2d 911 (Kan.), *cert. denied,* 510 U.S. 976 (1993); City of Missoula v. Asbury, 873 A.2d 936 (Mont. 1994); People v. Crowley, 538 N.Y.S.2d 146 (Just. Ct. 1989); Commonwealth v. Markum, 541 A.2d 347 (Pa. Super. 1988), *appeal denied,* 554 A.2d 507 (Pa. 1988), *cert. denied,* 489 U.S. 1080 (1989). *See also* Debbe Levin, Note, *Necessity as a Defense to a Charge of Criminal Trespass in an Abortion Clinic,* 48 CIN. L. REV. 501 (1979); Terry Pfeifer, Note, City of Wichita v. Tilson: *The Necessity Defense as Applied to Abortion Clinic Trespass,* 42 KAN. L. REV. 79 (1994); Timothy Reinig, *Abortion, Social Values, and the Limits of Legal Analysis: Towards A Substantive Rhetoric of Law,* 11 IN THE PUB. INT. 71, 73–80 (1991). *See generally* AMERICAN L. INST., *supra* note 20, § 2.09; SANFORD KADISH, BLAME AND PUNISHMENT 93–95 (1987); WAYNE LAFAVE & AUSTIN SCOTT, jr., HANDBOOK ON CRIMINAL LAW § 5.3 (2nd ed. 1986); RISEN & THOMAS, *supra* note 4, at 72–73, 140–41, 144, 146, 150, 290, 366–67; GLANVILLE WILLIAMS, CRIMINAL LAW: THE GENERAL PART § 237 (2nd ed. 1961); Edward Arnold & Norman Garland, *The Defense of Necessity in Criminal Law: The Right to Choose the Lesser Evil,* 65 J. CRIM. L. & CRIMINOLOGY 289 (1974); George Christie, *The Defense of Necessity Considered from the Legal and Moral Points of View,* 48 DUKE L.J. 975 (1999). For an account of a few of the rare cases in which the court accepted the "necessity" defense, see RISEN & THOMAS, *supra,* at 70–72.

180. Turic v. Holland Hospitality, Inc., 85 F.3d 1211 (6th Cir. 1996). *See also Pregnancy Discrimination Act,* 42 U.S.C. § 2000e(k) (2000).

181. *See generally* GEORGE PRING & PENELOPE CANAN, SLAPP's: GETTING SUED FOR SPEAKING OUT (1996); Alexandra Dylan Lowe, *The Price of Speaking Out,* ABA J., Sept., 1996, at 48.

tion—as even at least one officer of the American Civil Liberties Union has acknowledged.[182] This perhaps explains why, despite its general willingness to indulge the "abortion distortion" (the application, or misapplication, of ordinary rules in extraordinary ways when abortion is involved),[183] the Supreme Court held that suits against protestors interfering with clinic access are not maintainable under the *Ku Klux Klan Act*,[184] and cut back on the more extreme applications of the *Freedom of Access to Clinic Entrances Act*.[185] Specifically, the Court held that injunctions and other restrictions on speech could not burden speech "more than necessary" to assure reasonable access to clinics; anything more would be a violation freedom of speech.[186] Applying this standard, the Court struck down the lower court's order creating a "floating buffer zone" prohibiting protestors from approaching within 15 feet of persons seeking access to the clinic.[187]

Not satisfied with actions designed to make open dissent impossible, abortion rights activists set about to prevent their opponents from making the names or addresses of abortion

---

182. Rorie Sherman, *Courts Deal Blockaders Big Setbacks*, Nat'l L.J., Nov. 13, 1989, at 30, 32 (quoting Antonio Califa, Legislative Counsel for the ACLU, Washington, DC). *See also* Wells, *supra* note 174.

183. *See, e.g.*, Jeanne Schroeder, Abduction from the Seraglio: *Feminist Methodologies and the Logic of Imagination*, 70 Tex. L. Rev. 109, 138–40 (1991) (noting that feminists often support the recognition of an actionable duty to save—except in the context of abortion). *See also* Judges, *supra* note 6, at 226, 242; Alan Brownstein, *How Rights Are Infringed: The Role of Undue Burden Analysis in Constitutional Doctrine*, 45 Hastings L.J. 867, 925–29 (1994); Steven Gey, *The* Nuremberg Files *and the First Amendment Value of Threats*, 78 Tex. L. Rev. 541 (2000); David Smolin, *The Jurisprudence of Privacy in a Splintered Supreme Court*, 75 Marq. L. Rev. 975, 1013–16 (1992); Christy Wilhelm, Note, *If You Can't Say Something Nice, Don't Say Anything at All:* Hill v. Colorado *and the Antiabortion Protest Controversy*, 23 Campbell L. Rev. 117, 134–41 (2000). *See generally* Richard Erb, jr., & Alan Mortensen, Comment, *Wyoming Fetal Rights—Why the Abortion "Albatross" Is a Bird of a Different Color: The Case for Fetal Federalism*, 28 Land & Water L. Rev. 627 (1993).

184. Bray v. Alexandria Women's Health Clinic, 506 U.S. 263 (1993); Dianne Olivia Fischer, Comment, Bray v. Alexandria Women's Health Clinic: *Women under Siege*, 47 U. Miami L. Rev. 1415 (1993); Kelly, *supra* note 48, at 83–86; Tracy Higgins, *"By Reason of Their Sex": Feminist Theory, Postmodernism, and Justice*, 80 Cornell L. Rev. 1536, 1554–60, 1573–79 (1995); Wardle, *supra* note 130, at 897–99.

185. Schenck v. Pro-Choice Network of W.N.Y., 519 U.S. 357 (1997). *See also* Kelly, *supra* note 48, at 86–92.

186. 519 U.S. at 377–79. *See also* Hill v. Colorado, 530 U.S. 703 (2000) (upholding making it unlawful to "knowingly approach" within 8 feet of another person within 100 feet of any health care facility without that person's consent); Madsen v. Women's Health Ctr., Inc., 512 U.S. 753, 757–61 (1994) (approving a 36-ft. fixed buffer zone around the clinic; striking down 300-ft. and 36-ft. floating buffer zones); New York *ex rel.* Spitzer v. Operation Rescue Nat., 273 F.3d 184 (2nd Cir. 2001) (approving a 15-ft. buffer zone); United States v. Scott, 187 F.3d 282 (2nd Cir. 1999) (approving a 28-ft. buffer zone around the clinic and an 8-foot floating buffer zone around persons seeking to enter or leave the clinic); Edwards v. City of Santa Barbara, 150 F.3d 1213 (9th Cir. 1998) (approving an 8-ft. fixed buffer zone striking down a 100-ft. floating buffer zone), *cert. denied*, 526 U.S. 1004 (1999); Sabelko v. City of Phoenix., 120 F.3d 161 (9th Cir. 1997) (upholding a 100-ft. buffer zone); Planned Parenthood Ass'n v. Operation Rescue, 57 Cal. Rptr. 2d 736 (Ct. App. 1996) (approving a 15-ft. fixed buffer zone; striking down a 250-ft. fixed buffer zone around the abortionist's home and floating buffer zones around clinic staff members), *state rev. denied, cert. denied sub nom.* Cochrane v. Planned Parenthood Ass'n of San Mateo, 522 U.S. 811 (1997); Johnson v. Women's Health Ctr., Inc., 714 So. 2d 580 (Fla. Ct. App. 1998) (approving a 36-ft. fixed buffer zone), *rev. denied*, 719 So. 2d 893 (Fla. 1998); *In re* Opinion of the Justices, 723 N.E.2d 1 (Mass. 2000) (advisory opinion supporting the constitutionality of proposed statutory 25-ft. buffer zone); Horizon Health Ctr. v. Felicissimo, 659 A.2d 1387 (N.J. Super.), *cert. denied*, 667 A.2d 191 (N.J. 1995) (approving a 36-ft. "bubble" zone). *See generally* Alan Chen, *Statutory Speech Bubbles: First Amendment Overbreadth and Improper Legislative Purpose*, 38 Harv. Civ. Rts.-Civ. Lib. L. Rev. 31 (2003); Kristen Cowen, *The Tailoring of Statutory Bubble Zones: Balancing Free Speech and Patient Rights*, 91 Crim. L. & Criminology 385 (2001); Kevin Francis O'Neill, *Disentangling the Law of Public Protest*, 45 Loy. L. Rev. 411 (1999); David Savage, *First Amendment in Your Face: Aggressive Demonstrators Are No More than Free Speech in Action*, ABA J., Apr. 1997, at 42; Wardle, *supra* note 130, at 903–12; Wilhelm, *supra* note 183.

187. *Schenck*, 519 U.S. at 377–79.

providers public.[188] Abortion rights supporters claimed that they were seeking to make violence against abortion providers more difficult.[189] The best known instance of such litigation is the suit against *The Nuremberg Files*—a website that listed the names and addresses of 12 abortion providers along with "wanted" pictures of the select group (crossing out the pictures of providers who had been killed).[190] Ostensibly, Neal Horsley set up the *Nuremberg Files* website in order to keep track of the "baby killers" for a future trial of crimes against humanity. Horsley and his associates refused to pay a $107,000,000 judgment against them under the *Freedom of Access to Clinic Entrances Act,* although the Internet Service Provider shut down the website over their objections after the judge issued an injunction against its operation.[191]

As with the *Freedom of Access to Clinic Entrances Act* generally, the efforts to suppress speech went far beyond simply protecting the lives of those under threat.[192] After all, the *Nuremberg Files* actually contained very little useful information—and it did itself not call for anyone's death; the *Files* called for the arrest and prosecution of the named individuals.[193] The goal of the suit was not simply to protect abortion providers' lives; the goal was to suppress all forms of dissent, even dissent that would make abortion providers or abortion seekers merely uncomfortable. This becomes clear when even simple picketing is equated with terrorism.[194] In sum, proponents of abortions sought to imprison or to ruin financially all with the temerity to oppose abortion through any means that might have some actual effect on the provision of the services.[195]

---

188. *See* Christina Couch, *Wanted: Privacy Protection for Doctors Who Perform Abortions,* 4 Am. U. J. Gender & L. 361 (1996); Melanie Hagan, Note, *The Freedom of Access to Clinic Entrances Act and* The Nuremberg Files *Web Site: Is the Site Properly Prohibited or Protected Speech?,* 51 Hastings L.J. 412 (2000); Sam Howe Verhovek, *Anti-Abortion Site on Web Has Ignited Free Speech Debate,* N.Y. Times, Jan. 13, 1999, at A1.

189. On violence against abortion providers, see *infra* at notes 221–325.

190. Planned Parenthood of Columbia/Willamette, Inc.v. American Coalition of Life Activists, 945 F. Supp. 1355 (D. Or. 1996) (denying defendant's motion to dismiss), 23 F. Supp. 2d 1182 (D. Or.) (denying defendant's motion for summary judgment), 41 F. Supp. 2d 1130 (D. Or. 1999) (entering a judgment based upon the jury's verdict and issuing injunction against the defendants), *vacated,* 244 F.3d 1007 (9th Cir. 2001), *vacated rev'd en banc,* 290 F.3d 1058 (9th Cir. 2002), *cert. denied,* 539 U.S. 958 (2003). The files were formerly found at http://www.christiangallery.com. For a summary of the contents of the files, see 23 F. Supp. 2d at 1186–88. *See generally* Risen & Thomas, *supra* note 4, at 360–61; Gey, *supra* note 183; Ira Glasser, Letter, *Murder Threats Are Not "Free Speech,"* Wall St. J., Feb. 17, 1999, at A23; Hagan, *supra* note 188, at 413–15 l Nat Hentoff, *When "Pro-Lifers" Threaten Lives,* Wash. Post, Feb. 27, 1999, at A21; James Morrow, *Watching Web Speech: Conflicting Court Decisions on Pornography and Abortion Test the Rules of the E-Road,* U.S. News & World Rep., Feb. 15, 1999, at 32; Wardle, *supra* note 130, at 887; Sam Howe Verhovek, *Creators of Anti-Abortion Web Site Told to Pay Millions,* N.Y. Times, Feb. 3, 1999, at A9.

191. *Nation in Brief: Antiabortion Web Site Pulled,* Wash. Post, Feb. 7, 1999, at A15. The organizer of the website promptly posted the website through a different Internet service provider. Gey, *supra* note 183, at 553 n.70; Karen Kaplan, *Technology Shuttered Antiabortion Site Surfaces on Dutch Server,* L.A. Times, Feb. 23, 1999, at C3.

192. Gey, *supra* note 183, at 553–98; Michael Vitiello, *The Nuremberg Files: Testing the Limits of the First Amendment,* 61 Ohio St. L.J. 1175 (2000).

193. Gey, *supra* note 183, at 553–54, 557–65. *See also* Steven Gey, *Fear or Freedom: The New Speech Regulation in Cyberspace,* 8 Tex. J. Women & L. 183 (1999). This is not so surprising as some might think. One of the lawyers involved in another case found a letter describing her as "a hard core, militant feminist" to be such a personal threat that she consulted with experts on personal security after seeing a copy of the letter. Chanen, *supra* note 161, at 38–39 (reporting the reactions of attorney Fay Clayton).

194. See the remarks reported in *Jury Awards $8.65 Million in Anti-Abortion Protests, supra* note 162, discussed in Wardle, *supra* note 130, at 891.

195. *See, e.g.,* New York St. Nat. Org. for Women v. Terry, 159 F.3d 86 (2nd Cir. 1998), *cert. denied sub nom.* Pearson v. Planned Parenthood Margaret Sanger Clinic, 527 U.S. 1003 (1999); United States v. Unterburger, 97 F.3d 1413 (11th Cir. 1996), *cert. denied,* 521 U.S. 1122 (1997); McKusick v. City of Melbourne, 96 F.3d 478 (11th Cir. 1996); Douglas v. Brownell, 88 F.3d 1511 (1996); Roe v. Operation Rescue, 54 F.3d 133 (3rd Cir. 1995); People v. Terry, 45 F.3d 17 (2nd Cir. 1995); Planned Parenthood of San Mateo Cnty. v. Oper-

Opponents of abortion rights won occasional victories in seeking a right to be heard. Their most significant victory was the overturning of the judgment in the *Nuremberg Files* case by a three-judge panel of the Ninth Circuit because the judgment violated the defendants' right to express freely their opposition to abortion.[196] The court found that there was no evidence linking their actions to any violence against any abortion providers or clinics. This did not happen, however, until some two years after the initial judgment was entered and well after the initial judgment had chilled the willingness of abortion opponents to express their views. Even then the matter was not over. Some 14 months later, the appellate court, in an *en banc* rehearing, overruled its panel by a 5-4 vote.[197] The majority held that the *Nuremberg Files* constitute a "true threat" to the lives of the persons depicted on the website, and thus was not protected by the First Amendment's guarantee of freedom of expression. The dissenters, of course, disagreed. The plaintiff's victory was not complete, however, for the majority ordered the case remanded for the trial court to reconsider the possibly excessive damages award. And, of course, the defendants could still appeal the decision to the Supreme Court.

Through it all, Horsley managed to keep the *Nuremberg Files* webpage up and running.[198] Horsley also set up a new webpage that he called *Abortioncams.com*.[199] His webpage allows visitors to the webpage to view persons entering or leaving an abortion clinic through cameras in a public space mounted outside the clinic. Currently Abortioncam operates in at least 21 states.[200] Horsley not only intends to expand this service across the nation, he intends to make the images available on local cable television.[201] In another kind of victory, a federal court disallowed a Roman Catholic police officer's suit under the *Religious Freedom Restoration Act* for the refusal exempt him from protecting abortion clinics only because he was eligible to transfer to duty in a police district that did not contain abortion clinics.[202]

Injunctions barring protestors from approaching within specified distances of abortion clinics have been held to be unconstitutional when the distance was set at too great a remove from the target of the protest.[203] Many communities, however, still enforce unconstitutionally large buffer zones, forcing anti-abortion groups to expend resources on court proceedings rather than in expressing their views on the street.[204] On the other hand, a few lower federal courts declared the

---

ation Rescue of Cal., 57 Cal. Rptr. 2d 736 (Ct. App. 1996), *state rev. denied, cert. denied sub nom.* Cochran v. Planned Parenthood of San Mateo Cnty., 522 U.S. 811 (1997); Commonwealth v. Manning, 673 N.E.2d 73 (Mass. App. Ct. 1996), *rev. denied,* 676 N.E.2d 55 (Mass. 1997); Kaplan v. Prolife Action League of Greensboro, 493 S.E.2d 416 (N.C. 1997), *cert. denied sub nom.* Winfield v. Kaplan, 512 U.S. 1253 (1994).

196. American Coalition of Life Activists v. Planned Parenthood of Columbia/Willamette, Inc., 244 F.3d 1007 (9th Cir. 2001) *vacated en banc,* 290 F.3d 1058 (9th Cir. 2002), *cert. denied,* 539 U.S. 958 (2003).

197. Planned Parenthood of Columbia/Willamette, Inc. v. American Coalition of Life Activists, 290 F.3d 1058 (9th Cir. 2002), *cert. denied,* 539 U.S. 958 (2003).

198. Robyn Blumner, *Abortioncam May Be Disheartening, But It's Legally Sound,* St. Petersburg Times, Sept. 9, 2001, at 1D.

199. *Id.*

200. *Id.*

201. *Id.*

202. Rodriguez v. City of Chicago, 156 F.3d 771 (6th Cir. 1998), *cert. denied,* 525 U.S. 1144 (1999).

203. *See, e.g.,* Women's Health Care Services v. Operation Rescue, 24 F.3d 107, *vacated mem.,* 25 F.3d 1059 (10th Cir. 1994); Cheffer v. McGregor, 6 F.3d 705 (11th Cir. 1993), *vacated mem.,* 41 F.3d 1422 (11th Cir. 1994).

204. *See, e.g.,* Sabelko v. City of Phoenix, 120 F.3d 161 (9th Cir. 1997) (a 100-ft. "bubble"); United States v. Lindgren, 883 F. Supp. 1321 (D.N.D. 1995) (a 100-ft. floating zone); Planned Parenthood of Shasta-Diablo v. Williams, 898 P.2d 402 (Cal. 1995) (a 75-ft. fixed buffer zone), *cert. denied,* 520 U.S. 1133 (1997); Operation Rescue v. Planned Parenthood of Houston, 975 S.W.2d 546 (Tex. 1998) (a 100-ft fixed buffer zone around certain clinics, but no buffer zone for other clinics). *See also* Wardle, *supra* note 130, at 892–93; Weinstein, *supra* note 137, at 487–89, 521–43; Wells, *supra* note 174, at 27–28.

*Freedom of Access to Clinic Entrances Act* to be unconstitutional, exceeding Congressional power under the Commerce Clause of the Constitution, in decisions that were promptly reversed on appeal.[205] The opponents of abortion rights also won victories in cases where the supporters of abortion rights sought to revoke the tax-exempt status of the Catholic Church because of its public opposition to abortion.[206] Yet another court held that two protestors could not be convicted of "willfully" blocking access to a clinic when they had acted out of "conscience and sincere religious belief."[207]

Supporters of abortion rights particularly target acts of civil disobedience by "right-to-life" groups.[208] This does not prevent those same supporters from fondly recalling their own acts of civil disruption when they were seeking political repeal of abortion prohibitions.[209] Several of the street protest cases involved demonstrations in favor of abortion as well as against it, but only the protests against abortion were enjoined.[210] Indeed, the Supreme Court has approved allowing clinic workers to select who shall be arrested by identifying particular protestors as "pro-life."[211] Even the American Civil Liberties Union—an organization so devoted to freedom of speech that it supported the right of American Nazis to parade through a predominantly Jewish

205. Hoffman v. Hunt, 923 F. Supp. 791 (W.D.N.C. 1996), *rev'd,* 126 F.3d 575 (4th Cir. 1997), *cert. denied,* 523 U.S. 1136 (1998); United States v. Wilson, 880 F. Supp. 621 (E.D. Wis. 1995), *rev'd,* 73 F.3d 675 (7th Cir.), *cert. denied,* 519 U.S. 806 (1996). *See also* Michael Stokes Paulsen & Michael McConnell, *The Doubtful Constitutionality of the Clinic Access Bill,* 1 Va. J. Soc. Pol'y & L. 261 (1994).

206. *See, e.g.,* U.S. Catholic Conference v. Abortion Rights Mobilization, Inc., 487 U.S. 72 (1988). *See generally* Risen & Thomas, *supra* note 4, at 154–55; David Brooks, Note, *In re* United States Catholic Conference: *Considering Non-Party Rights,* 1988 BYU L. Rev. 89; Junji John Shimazaki, Note, *Abortion Politics: The Roman Catholic Church's Tax-Exempt Status in Jeopardy under Section 501(c)(3) of the Internal Revenue Code,* 1988 BYU L. Rev. 799. A court did reject the petition of an IRS agent who sought to block his agency's grant of tax-exempt status to organizations that promote abortion and homosexuality. Haring v. Blumenthal, 471 F. Supp. 1172 (D.D.C. 1979).

207. United States v. Lynch, 952 F. Supp. 167, 169 (S.D.N.Y. 1997), *appeal dismissed,* 162 F.3d 732 (2nd Cir. 1998). *See* Jan Hoffman, *Judge Acquits Abortion Protestors on Basis of Religious Beliefs,* N.Y. Times, Jan. 19, 1997, § 1, at 25; Kelly, *supra* note 48, at 92–94.

208. *See* Winfield v. Kaplan, 512 U.S. 1253 (1994) (Kennedy, Scalia, & Thomas, JJ., dissenting from denial of *certiorari*); Madsen v. Women's Health Ctr., Inc., 512 U.S. 753 (1994); Sabelko v. City of Phoenix, 120 F.3d 161 (9th Cir. 1997); Horizon Health Ctr. v. Felicissimo, 722 A.2d 621 (N.J. App. Div. 1999); Lawson v. Murray, 649 A.2d 1253 (N.J. 1994), *cert. denied,* 515 U.S. 1110 (1995) (Scalia, J., concurring in denial of *certiorari*). *See also* Cassandra Langer, A Feminist Critique: How Feminism Has Changed American Society, Culture, and How We Live from the 1940s to the Present 26 (1996); Risen & Thomas, *supra* note 4, at 213, 241, 283; Craige, *supra* note 130; Rebecca Eisenberg, *Beyond* Bray: *Obtaining Federal Jurisdiction to Stop Anti-Abortion Violence,* 6 Yale J.L. & Feminism 155 (1994); Laurence Eisenstein & Steven Semeraro, *Abortion Clinic Protest and the First Amendment,* 13 St. L.U. Pub. L. Rev. 221 (1993); Higgins, *supra* note 184, at 1556–60; Tamar Lewin, *Citing Violence, Abortion Clinics Sue Opponents over Threats,* N.Y. Times, Oct. 27, 1995, at A21; Henry Reske, *RICO's Free Speech Reach: Experts Differ over Effect of High Court Decision on Abortion Protests,* ABA J., Mar. 1994, at 19; John Whitehead, *Civil Disobedience and Operation Rescue: A Historical and Theoretical Analysis,* 48 Wash. & Lee L. Rev. 77 (1991). On the roots of the anti-abortion protest movement in the earlier anti-war and civil rights movements, see Risen & Thomas, *supra* note 4, at 43–77.

209. Ruth Colker, Pregnant Men: Practice, Theory, and the Law 4, 31–37, 92, 113–26 (1994); D'Emilio & Freedman, *supra* note 34, at 314–15; Judith Hole & Ellen Levine, The Rebirth of Feminism 298 (1971); Louis Lader, Abortion II: Making the Revolution 72–97 (1973); Luker, *supra* note 34, at 66–125; Reagan, *supra* note 68, at 248. *See also* Susan Faludi, *The Antiabortion Crusade of Randy Terry: Operation Rescue's Jailed Leader and his Feminist Roots,* Wash. Post, Dec. 23, 1989, at C1.

210. Madsen v. Women's Health Ctr., Inc., 512 U.S. 753, 785–90 (1994) (Scalia, J., dissenting, describing both sets of protests). *See also* David Smolin, *The Religious Root and Branch of Anti-Abortion Lawlessness,* 47 Baylor L. Rev. 119, 139–41, 145 (1995).

211. Madsen v. Women's Health Ctr., Inc., 512 U.S. 753, 815–20 (1994) (Scalia, J., dissenting). *See also* Cheffer v. McGregor, 6 F.3d 705, 711 n.11 (11th Cir. 1993).

suburb of Chicago[212]—has supported injunctions against anti-abortion protestors.[213] No wonder, despite occasional victories in litigation arising from their opposition to abortion rights, opponents of abortion rights generally felt that they have been excluded from presenting their case through peaceful debate or protest.[214] One commentator summarized the situation in these words: "In the past, one did not have to be fanatically committed to a cause in order to sit-in. The protestor (*sic*) did not face, by and large, serious fines and jail-time.... That situation is changing."[215]

Finally, the legal profession has undertaken to throw its official weight behind the pro-abortion movement. The American Bar Association has endorsed abortion rights, precluding any individual, committee, section, or other branch of the Association from questioning this position.[216] As John Curtin, jr., a former president of the American Bar Association, recently argued regarding that organization's decision to endorse "abortion rights," the vote serves to make those who disagree feel excluded rather than to resolve the debate: "Such a resolution does not help bring people together. It polarizes."[217] More importantly, Judge Richard Sanders of the Washington Supreme Court was investigated and reprimanded by the state's Commission on Judicial Conduct for publicly speaking against abortion and for wearing a red rose (a symbol of the anti-abortion movement) while no charges were even filed against Judge James Dolliver of the same court when he publicly boasted not only of supporting abortion rights but of encouraging "a member of his family" to have an abortion and paying for it.[218] Interestingly, this was the first time in its 16-year history that the Commission had any occasion to investigate a justice of the state's supreme court.[219]

Harvard law professor Martha Minow followed this approach to its logical conclusion, arguing that an attorney has an ethical obligation to counsel and aid the breaking of the law "on principle" if that law would impede a woman's access to abortion.[220] Minow would not excuse even a lawyer who disagrees with the point the law-breaker is trying to make. The conclusion that follows from Minow's argument is clear. Lawyers who actively oppose abortion rights should be disbarred. Attorney Janet Benshoof, then Director of the ACLU Reproductive Free-

---

212. Collin v. Smith, 578 F.2d 1197, 1210 (7th Cir.), *cert. denied,* 439 U.S. 916 (1978).

213. *See* Weinstein, *supra* note 137, at 489 n.62.

214. *See generally* Wardle, *supra* note 130, at 912–15.

215. Ledewitz, *supra* note 130, at 569.

216. *ABA Backs Abortion Rights, Right to Die, and Job Protection,* 58 U.S.L.W. 2474, 2474–75 (Feb. 20, 1990); Don DeBenedictis, *ABA Supports Abortion Rights: Leaders Urge Neutrality Forces to Stick with the Association Despite Loss in the House,* ABA J., Oct. 1992, at 32.

217. *Id. See also* Burt, *supra* note 85, at 349–51; Condit, *supra* note 6, at 164–66; Glendon, *supra* note 125, at 2, 18; Warren Burger, *The ABA Has Fallen Down on the Job,* Wall St. J., Aug. 10, 1994, at A9; Carrington, *supra* note 6, at 905–06; Devins, *supra* note 21, at 1451–53; Christopher Griffin, *The A.B.A. and Abortion: Should the A.B.A. Resind Resolution 106(c)? No: Protect Basic Human Rights,* ABA J., July 1990, at 36; Earl Maltz, *The Supreme Court and the Quality of Political Dialogue,* 5 Const'l Commentary 375, 389–90 (1988); Anthony Palermo, *The A.B.A. and Abortion: Should the A.B.A. Resind Resolution 106(c)? Yes: Don' t Divide the Membership,* ABA J., July 1990, at 36. *See generally* The ABA in Law and Social Policy: What Role? (The Federalist Soc'y 1994); David Leonard, Note, *The American Bar Association: An Appearance of Propriety,* 16 Harv. J.L. & Pub. Pol'y 537 (1993).

218. *See* Patti Epler, *Justice Sanders Reprimanded : Judge Stands by Remarks He Made at Anti-Abortion Rally,* News Trib. (Tacoma, Wash.), May 13, 1997, at A1; Richard John Neuhaus, *The Public Square,* First Things, Apr. 1997, at 17–18.

219. Eventually, the Supreme Court cleared Judge Sanders of wrongdoing. *See* Wardle, *supra* note 130, at 892 n. 211.

220. Martha Minow, *Breaking the Law: Lawyers and Clients in Struggles for Social Change,* 52 U. Pitt. L. Rev. 723, 737–38, 745–47 (1991).

dom Project, undertook civil disobedience herself in order to protest the Guam statutes adopted to impose strict restrictions on abortion in 1990.[221] Presumably neither Benshoof nor Minow would support the same position for an anti-abortion protester seeking a pro-abortion lawyer's counsel for a planned blockade of an abortion clinic.[222] What do you suppose they would say of the notion that judges under such a strong moral duty to refuse to allow the death of the "innocent lives" of unborn children even if they must defy the "law" to do so?[223]

If Minow's view were to prevail, it would be the lawyer's equivalent of the attempts to compel doctors and nurses to perform abortions against their will. No wonder the new ABA policy position produced a sharp spike in cancellations of membership, which for the first time in 20 years exceeded new memberships.[224] Some of those who withdrew even organization a rival organization—the National Lawyers' Association—based on "respect for life."

# The Turn to Violence

*Sue me, sue me, shoot bullets through me.*

— "Nathan Detroit"[225]

Often stifling debate provokes dissent rather than ending it, particularly in a society where discussion generally is free. Commentators have frequently noted that *Roe* provoked the "Right to Life" movement into existence rather than stifling debate.[226] The intense criticism and opposition to *Roe* remains in stark contrast to the broad consensus that surrounds issues of true gender discrimination, such as discrimination in pay or promotion or sexual harassment in various contexts.[227] While the notion that *Roe* prompted all of this is an exaggeration, the Courts and their supporters in the streets, by attempting to cut off the political dialogue, unwittingly did provoke a turn towards violence by some opposed to the new abortion regime.

Initial attempts to organize peaceful direct action against abortion clinics recruited few followers and had little impact on the activities of those seeking or providing abortions.[228] Randall

---

221. Kathryn Abrams, *Lawyers and Social Change Lawbreaking: Confronting a Plural Bar*, 52 U. Pitt. L. Rev. 753, 774–75 (1991). The Guam statute was invalidated by the Court of Appeals for the Ninth Circuit with other persons who agreed to be plaintiffs challenging the statute. Guam College of Obstetricians v. Ada, 962 F.2d 1366 (9th Cir.), *cert. denied,* 506 U.S. 1011 (1992).

222. *See* David Luban, *Conscientious Lawyers for Conscientious Lawbreakers*, 52 U. Pitt. L. Rev. 793, 810–13 (1991).

223. *See* Michael Stokes Paulsen, *Accusing Justice: Some Variations on the Themes of Robert M. Cover's Justice Accused*, 7 J.L. & Rel. 33 (1993).

224. James Podgers, *Head Count: ABA Membership Levels Remain Steady in Difficult Year*, ABA J., Aug. 1993, at 105.

225. Frank Loesser, *Adelaide's Lament,* from Guys and Dolls (1949).

226. See the authorities collected *supra* at note 76.

227. *See* Ferree & Hess, *supra* note 85, at 86–99, 150; Joyce Gelb, Feminism and Politics: A Comparative Analysis 79–80 (1989); Graber, *supra* note 34, at 124–28; E.J. Dionne, *Struggle for Work and Family Fueling Women's Movement*, N.Y. Times, Aug. 22, 1989, at A18; Susanne Fields, *Even Feminists Now Boost the Family,* Chicago Sun-Times, May 7, 1991, at 23; Lynn Wardle, *Rethinking* Roe v. Wade, 1985 BYU L. Rev. 231, 249–50. *See generally* Rene Denfeld, The New Victorians: A Young Woman's Challenge to the Old Feminist Order (1995).

228. *See, e.g.,* Joan Andrews & John Cavanaugh O'Keefe, I Will Never Forget You: The Rescue Movement and Joan Andrews (1989); John Cavanaugh O'Keefe, A Peaceful Presence (1978) ("O'-

Terry succeeded in organizing such protests on a massive scale. He was a "born again" Christian with a history of drifting from job to job, a former heavy drug user, and a part-time missionary when, at the age of 24, he took up the anti-abortion cause as his own in October 1983.[229] Terry and his wife Cindy first undertook "sidewalk counseling" in Binghamton, New York, on May 1, 1984.[230] Terry, coming on the scene just as anti-abortion militancy was about to catch fire,[231] proved effective at recruiting, organizing, and directing what eventually became a nationwide campaign of civil disobedience intended to disrupt and even close abortion clinics.

Terry christened his organization "Operation Rescue,"[232] building on the strategy of "rescuing" fetuses about to be aborted by blockading and invading abortion clinics, using tactics first developed by such activists as Joan Anderson, Michael Bray, John O'Keefe, John Ryan, and Joe Scheidler.[233] Through Operation Rescue, Terry undertook to lead a classic program of civil disobedience designed to increase social tension over abortion by flooding the jails with protestors and further taxing the police and courts by instructing the arrested protestors to refuse to disclose their identities.[234] Whereas earlier leaders had recruited tens or hundreds for demonstrations, Terry recruited thousands; whereas earlier movements could force a clinic to close for a day, Terry's movement could tie up a whole city for a week or more. In a period spanning about six years (1986–1992), more than 60,000 people were arrested in support of Operation Rescue, making it easily the largest social protest movement in the United States since the Civil Rights and Anti-War Movements of the 1960s.[235] And Terry's activities transformed the manner of protesting. As one clinic director who lived through the early protests by Operation Rescue sum-

---

KEEFE, PEACEFUL PRESENCE"); JOHN CAVANAUGH O'KEEFE, NO CHEAP SOLUTIONS (1984) ("O'KEEFE, NO CHEAP SOLUTIONS"); JOHN CAVANAUGH O'KEEFE, NON-VIOLENCE IS AN ADVERB (1985) ("O'KEEFE, NON-VIOLENCE"); JOSEPH SCHEIDLER, CLOSED: 99 WAYS TO STOP ABORTION (1985). *See generally* RISEN & THOMAS, *supra* note 4, at 43–74, 88–89, 91–92, 99–105, 108–19, 132–67, 190–200, 203–04, 208–10; KATHY RUDY, BEYOND PRO-LIFE AND PRO-CHOICE: MORAL DIVERSITY IN THE ABORTION DEBATE 44–45 (1996); Ginsburg, *supra* note 159. Most accounts of the anti-abortion protest movement are either hagiographic on the one hand or hostile or dismissive on the other. Perhaps the best account is that by journalists James Risen and Judy Thomas, which manages to avoid either extreme while doing a thorough job. The major shortcoming of their work is that they did not include a single source note or other specific reference to any particular source, although they do include a bibliography and a list of the people interviewed.

229. RISEN & THOMAS, *supra* note 4, at 114, 118–19, 126, 131, 175–76, 223–39; RUDY, *supra* note 228, at 45–47; Stephen Hedges, David Bowermaster, & Susan Headden, *Abortion: Who's Behind the Violence?*, U.S. NEWS & WORLD REP., Nov. 14, 1994, at 55; Susan Faludi, *Where Did Randy Go Wrong?*, MOTHER JONES, Nov. 1989, at 23; Charles Rice, *Issues Raised by the Abortion Rescue Movement*, 23 SUFFOLK L. REV. 15 (1989); R. Mary Suh & Lydia Denworth, *The Gathering Storm: Operation Rescue*, Ms., April 1989, at 92; John Wauck, *Operation Rescue*, NAT'L REV., Apr. 7, 1989, at 41; Francis Wilkinson, *The Gospel According to Randall Terry*, ROLLING STONE, Oct. 5, 1989, at 85.

230. RANDALL TERRY, OPERATION RESCUE: WHY DOES A NICE GUY LIKE ME KEEP GETTING THROWN IN JAIL? 17 (1988). *See also* RISEN & THOMAS, *supra* note 4, at 239–47.

231. RISEN & THOMAS, *supra* note 4, at 240–41, 258, 263–65.

232. Apparently David Long, an Evangelical leader in Rochester, New York, coined the term "Operation Rescue"; use of the term "rescue" to describe abortion sit-ins and other acts of civil disobedience actually had emerged some years earlier in protests in Philadelphia. *Id.* at 168, 256, 258.

233. *See* RANDALL TERRY, ACCESSORY TO MURDER: THE ENEMIES, ALIENS, AND ACCOMPLICES TO THE DEATH OF OUR CULTURE (1990). *See also* RANDY ALCORN, IS RESCUING RIGHT? BREAKING THE LAW TO SAVE THE UNBORN (1990); ANDREWS & O'KEEFE, *supra* note 228; O'KEEFE, NO CHEAP SOLUTIONS, *supra* note 228; O'KEEFE, NON-VIOLENCE, *supra* note 228; O'KEEFE, PEACEFUL PRESENCE, *supra* note 228; PAUL DE PARRIE, THE RESCUERS (1989); SCHEIDLER, *supra* note 228. *See generally* JACOBY, *supra* note 17, at 131–56; PHILIP LAWLER, OPERATION RESCUE: A CHALLENGE TO THE NATION'S CONSCIENCE (1992); RISEN & THOMAS, *supra* note 4, at 168, 180–84, 205–08, 213–39, 263.

234. TERRY, *supra* note 230, at 198. *See also* RISEN & THOMAS, *supra* note 4, at 258–61; Whitehead, *supra* note 208, at 99 n.108.

235. RISEN & THOMAS, *supra* note 4, at 220.

marized the change, "It went from the sort of mild-mannered Catholic older ladies to a very in-your-face, obnoxious, I'll do anything kind of tactic. And he did do anything."[236]

Terry's first actual attempt to stop an abortion clinic from operating involved a physical invasion of a clinic in the suburbs of Binghamton on January 8, 1986.[237] All the protestors were arrested, and they were rearrested as they repeated their sit-ins and other disruptions. Eventually, they were convicted and fined, but only Terry refused to pay the fine and went to jail.[238] Subsequently Terry would forbid Operation Rescue members from entering clinics, insisting that they only blockade clinics from the outside—fearing that stronger measures would be counterproductive for the movement.[239]

Critics have described Terry's tactics as distinctly "male."[240] Yet many women participated in the "rescues"—including housewives, schoolteachers, service workers, and technicians.[241] At a slightly lower level of intensity, activists who serve as "sidewalk counselors" at abortion clinics are nearly always women—with men staying in the background, being there in case the women activists need protection.[242] Additionally, "rescuers" are disproportionately elderly—if only because retired people can give the time necessary to blockade a clinic or to sit in jail. At Wichita, fully one-third of the "rescuers" were over sixty years of age.[243] Retirees and housewives (and teachers in the summer) could more easily take off to a distant site or a nearby site during normal working hours to join a protest action than could persons who employed at eight-hour-a-day jobs.

Terry's first truly big "rescue" operation brought around 400 protestors to blockade an abortion clinic in Cherry Hill, New Jersey, on November 28, 1987—easily the largest protest against a clinic up until then.[244] At the end of the day, 211 "mothers, fathers, grandmothers, grandfathers, and singles" had been arrested, but, as Terry noted, "[n]o babies died" that day.[245] In May 1988, Operation Rescue staged an even larger demonstration for a week of protests across greater New York City, resulting in 503 arrests in Manhattan on Monday, 422 arrests in Queens on Tuesday, and another 400 arrests in Long Island on Thursday, and another 320 arrests back in Manhattan on Friday.[246] By the summer of 1988, Operation Rescue was able to inspire thousands of protestors to clog Atlanta in an effort to disrupt the Democratic National Convention. More than 1,300 protestors were arrested from July to October in the "Siege of Atlanta."[247] The operation was too large to be tightly controlled, and there were numerous clinic invasions as well as physical confrontations with the police.[248] Eventually the po-

---

236. Dan Barry, *Icon for Abortion Protesters Is Looking for a Second Act*, N.Y. Times, July 20, 2001, at A1, B5.

237. Risen & Thomas, *supra* note 4, at 253–54; Faludi, *supra* note 229, at 61–62.

238. Terry, *supra* note 230, at 22. *See also* Risen & Thomas, *supra* note 4, at 255. Terry was released early when an anonymous donor paid his fine. Risen & Thomas, *supra*, at 256.

239. Risen & Thomas, *supra* note 4, at 260.

240. Risen & Thomas, *supra* note 4, at 219; Faludi, *supra* note 229, at 25; Ginsburg, *supra* note 159, at 233. Critics also like to accuse Terry of racism, although Terry and his wife had adopted and raised two mixed-race children. Risen & Thomas, *supra*, at 246.

241. Ginsburg, *supra* note 159, at 236.

242. Jacoby, *supra* note 17, at 24, 133–35; Lawler, *supra* note 233, at 12–13.

243. Ginsburg, *supra* note 159, at 236.

244. Hadley, *supra* note 34, at 163; Jacoby, *supra* note 17, at 131–32; Risen & Thomas, *supra* note 4, at 261–63; Rudy, *supra* note 228, at 46; Terry, *supra* note 230, at 24–25; Ginsburg, *supra* note 159, at 227.

245. Terry, *supra* note 230, at 25. *See also* Risen & Thomas, *supra* note 4, at 263 (in fact, abortions were performed that evening after the blockade ended and after the clinic decided to open after its normal operating hours).

246. Risen & Thomas, *supra* note 4, at 264–68. Many of those arrested on successive days were the same people arrested two and three times and quickly released after being assessed a modest fine.

247. *Id.* at 271–86; Ginsburg, *supra* note 159, at 231–32.

248. Risen & Thomas, *supra* note 4, at 276.

lice in Atlanta introduced what they euphemistically called "pain compliance" techniques to keep access to clinics clear.[249]

In some respects, the Atlanta operation was a failure. The number of arrests over four months was less than the number in New York in one week. None of the Atlanta clinics was blocked for more than an hour or two. And the National Organization for Women and other groups organized increasingly effective "escort" programs to aid patients in entering the clinics (a program that at first aroused suspicions at the clinics).[250] In part, the more limited success of Operation Rescue in Atlanta resulted from the lack of sympathy in the police and the courts, including keeping the arrested in jail for extended periods rather than releasing them after a few hours to enable them to be arrested again the next day.[251] Once again, Terry personally chose to go to jail over paying a fine.[252] Facing a year in jail, Terry again was released early when an anonymous donor paid his fine—something of a divisive scandal within the organization.[253]

Whatever its shortcomings, the "Siege of Atlanta" was a public relations success. Extensive television coverage nationalized (and internationalized) Operation Rescue to a degree hitherto unthinkable. Terry topped it off with a "National Day of Rescue" on October 29, 1988, and again on October 30, 1988. In those two days, there were more than 4,600 arrests in 27 cities across the United States and Canada.[254] The next year saw at least one local rescue operation somewhere in the United States every weekend, many in cities were Randall Terry or other officers of Operation Rescue had never appeared.[255] Operation Rescue even managed to become involved in the blockade of abortion clinics in New Zealand.[256]

Between 1987 and 1990, more than 55,000 people were arrested for participating in "rescues."[257] Operation Rescue, however, received little support and almost no recognition from the mainstream pro-life organizations, and could be seen as a reaction against the moderation of the mainstream groups as much as an extension of their efforts.[258] The very success of Operation Rescue, however, forced it to close its national office because of its exposure to liability for the legal expenses of those arrested and the legal damages of those interfered with by the rescues.[259] Operation Rescue, already organizationally distinct from mainstream pro-life organizations, became a loose confederation of local anti-abortion groups that Randall Terry strongly influenced but could no longer control.[260]

---

249. *Id.* at 282, 284–85.

250. *Id.* at 277–78, 283, 285.

251. *Id.* at 282.

252. Ronald Smothers, *Organizer of Abortion Protests Is Jailed in Atlanta*, N.Y. Times, July 12, 1989, at A10. Risen & Thomas, *supra* note 4, at 302–03.

253. Risen & Thomas, *supra* note 4, at 275, 283, 306–07.

254. *Id.* at 286.

255. *Id.* at 286–88, 294; Ginsburg, *supra* note 159, at 232; Suh & Denworth, *supra* note 229, at 92. *See also* Felicity Barringer, *Abortion Foes Clog Vermont Courts*, N.Y. Times, May 7, 1990, at A12; Maureen Dowd, *Bush Chides Protestors on "Excesses,"* N.Y. Times, Aug. 17, 1991, § 1, at 7; Lynne Duke & Michael Abramowitz, *Anti-Abortion Protestors Blockade Clinic in Va.*, Wash. Post, Oct. 30, 1988, at B1. *See generally* Peter Korn, Lovejoy: A Year in the Life of an Abortion Clinic (1996).

256. Wilcox v. Police, [1994] N.Z.L.R. 243; Police v. O'Neill, [1993] N.Z.L.R. 712; Police v. O'Connor, [1992] N.Z.L.R. 87.

257. Rudy, *supra* note 228, at 46. *See also* Randy Frame, *Rescue Theology*, Christianity Today, Nov. 17, 1989, at 46; Ginsburg, *supra* note 159, at 228.

258. Risen & Thomas, *supra* note 4, at 39–40, 57, 104–05, 113, 141–42, 174, 207–08, 220–21, 240–41, 288, 290–92, 294, 304–05; Rudy, *supra* note 228, at 164 n.6; Ginsburg, *supra* note 159, at 234–35; Constance Hays, *Abortion Foes Lose Appeal on Protest*, N.Y. Times, Sept. 21, 1989, at A1.

259. Blanchard, *supra* note 34, at 94; Risen & Thomas, *supra* note 4, at 295–97, 301–14; Rudy, *supra* note 228, at 46–47; Ginsburg, *supra* note 159, at 235; Tamar Lewin, *With Thin Staff and Thick Debt, Anti-Abortion Group Faces Struggle*, N.Y. Times, June. 11, 1990, at A16.

260. Risen & Thomas, *supra* note 4, at 299–301, 311–14, 319–20; Rudy, *supra* note 228, at 47.

The advent of Operation Rescue coincided with the entry of Christian evangelicals into American politics on the largest scale seen in decades.[261] Some observers have suggested that Operation Rescue was critical to politicizing fundamentalist Protestant, who before the late 1970s avoided the anti-abortion movement and politics generally while awaiting what some fundamentalists expected to be the imminent Second Coming of Christ.[262] One result of the abortion controversy that perhaps has lasting historical importance was a rapprochement of Catholics and evangelical Christians—two groups that historically were extravagantly hostile to each other.[263]

Doubtless many variables were involved in the Christian awakening besides Operation Rescue. Fueled by the writings of Francis Schaeffer, the preaching of "televangalists" like Jerry Falwell, and the Moral Majority, the Christian Coalition, and similar groups, the New Christian Right became major force in the Republican Party and a strong contender for influence in the Reagan administration.[264] These groups, and Randall Terry himself, sought nothing less than the "Christianization" of the United States through public prayer, the prohibition of sexuality immorality, and the prohibition of abortion.[265] Robert Wuthnow summarized their attitude in thusly:

---

261. George Grant, Third Time Around: A History of the Pro-Life Movement from the First Century to the Present 145 (1991); Jacoby, *supra* note 17, at 35, 71–74, 78–100; Risen & Thomas, *supra* note 4, at 6, 50, 78–101, 119–21, 195–200, 217–20; Rudy, *supra* note 228, at 47–57. *See generally* Harold Bloom, The American Religion: The Emergence of the Post-Christian Nation 218–33 (1992); Steve Bruce, Peter Kivisto, & William Swatos, jr., The Rapture of Politics: The Christian Right as the United States Approaches the Year 2000 (1995); Jeffrey Hadden & Anson Shupe, Televangelism, Power and Politics on God's Frontier (1988); Hunter, *supra* note 17; Martin Marty, Pilgrims in their own Land: 500 Years of Religion in America 471–72 (1984); Duane Murray Oldfield, The Right and the Righteous: The Christian Right Confronts the Republican Party (1996); Gerard Straub, Salvation for Sale: An Insider's View of Pat Robertson (1988); Clyde Wilcox, Onward Christian Soldiers? The Religious Right in American Politics (1996); Robert Wuthnow, The Restructuring of American Religion: Society and Faith since World War II (1988); Michael Johnston, *The "New Christian Right" in American Politics*, 8 Pol'y Stud. J. 698 (1980); Kenneth Wald, Dennis Owen, & Samuel Hill, jr., *Evangelical Politics and the Status Issue*, 28 J. Sci. Stud. Religion 1 (1989).

262. Risen & Thomas, *supra* note 4, at 68, 73, 81, 88–89, 181–84, 218–19, 232. *See also* Ginsburg, *supra* note 159, at 234, 240–41; Kim Lawton, *Can the Prolife Movement Succeed?*, Christianity Today, Jan. 15, 1988, at 36; Wilkinson, *supra* note 229, at 86.

263. Alister McGrath *et al.*, Roman Catholicism: Evangelical Protestants Analyze What Divides and Unites Us (1994). *See also* Jacoby, *supra* note 17, at 19–20, 59–60, 90–91; Lawler, *supra* note 229, at 9; Risen & Thomas, *supra* note 4, at 6, 101–31, 133, 142–43, 186–90, 195, 197, 210–11, 221–23, 231, 255, 258–59, 267, 282. Internationally, the abortion controversy also helped set up a rapprochement of sorts between Catholics and Muslims. *See* Rumage, *supra* note 85, at 87–89; John Tagliabue, *Vatican Seeks Islamic Allies in U.N. Population Dispute*, N.Y. Times, Aug. 18, 1994, at Al.

264. *See* Colonel Doner, The Samaritan Strategy: A New Agenda for Christian Activism (1988); Ralph Reed, Active Faith: How Christians Are Changing the Soul of American Politics (1996); Ralph Reed, Politically Incorrect: The Emerging Faith Factor in American Politics (1994); Francis Schaeffer, A Christian Manifesto (1981); Francis Schaefer & C. Everett Koop, What Ever Happened to the Human Race? (1979). *See generally* Diamond, *supra* note 17; Robert Booth Fowler & Allen Hertzke, Religion and Politics in America: Faith, Culture and Strategic Choices (1995); Jacoby, *supra* note 17, at 73–74, 78–82, 89–94, 105–07, 111–12; Alan Hertzke, Representing God in Washington: The Role of Religious Lobbies in the American Polity (1988); William Martin, With God on Our Side: The Rise of the Religious Right (1996); Risen & Thomas, *supra* note 4, at 119–31; Rudy, *supra* note 228, at 49–52; William McLaughlin, *The Illusions and Dangers of the New Christian Right*, 25 Foundations 128 (Apr.–June, 1982); Gary Wills, *Evangels of Abortion*, N.Y. Rev. Books, June 15, 1989, at 15.

265. William Abraham, The Coming Great Revival: Recovering the Full Evangelical Tradition (1984); Hunter, *supra* note 17; Jacoby, *supra* note 17, at 88, 139–55, 173–74, 187–98; Martin Lloyd-Jones, Revival (1987); Winkie Pratney, Revival: Principles to Change the World (1983); Terry, *supra* note 230, at 159–63; Terry, *supra* note 233, at 35, 175; Ginsburg, *supra* note 159, at 229, 242–42; Wilkinson, *supra* note 233, at 92; Wills, *supra* note 264, at 21.

If public morality was indeed the mainstay of national strength, evangelicals could hardly stand by, knowing God had given them both the answers and the opportunity to voice their answers, while the social fabric decayed. In the biblical prophets evangelicals found dramatic examples of persons who had been called to speak out against moral decay, and the new group of conservative spokesman who rose to national prominence consciously adopted these models.[266]

Falwell and others provided a certain legitimacy to Operation Rescue. They also gave direct support without ever formally joining the organization. For example, Falwell himself went to Atlanta with $10,000 in bail money for those arrested in the summer long protests in that city.[267]

There is another strand to Operation Rescue—the "evangelical left." These anti-abortion activists approach rescue not in order to impose Christian values on the nation, but in an effort to make the national and Christian ethos ever more inclusive: first slaves, then women, and now the unborn.[268] Such activists—Protestant and Catholic—are often involved in staffing soup kitchens for the homeless or in direct and indirect social action against war and nuclear weapons.[269] They also are likely to be heavily engaged in working with women caught in a "crisis" pregnancy.[270] They tend to support national health insurance, spending more money for AIDS prevention and treatment, and even education about contraception in schools (but not the distribution of contraceptives there).[271] And many of them are as adamantly opposed to the death penalty as they are to abortion—overall anti-abortion activists are nearly evenly split on the death penalty, in contrast with a general public that, in the United States, overwhelmingly supports it.[272]

Operation Rescue's next major effort was an attempt to close all abortion clinics in Wichita, Kansas. Keith Tucci, by 1991 administrative head of Operation Rescue, chose Wichita because George Tiller, the physician at the city's abortion clinic, was one of the few in the United States willing to perform late-term abortions.[273] "Killer" Tiller, as Tucci dubbed him, advertised nationally and internationally his willingness to perform abortions right up until birth.[274] The effort ultimately failed even though the governor, the mayor, the city manager, and the chief of police were pro-life.[275]

Initially the invasion of Wichita (dubbed the "Summer of Mercy") proved remarkably successful. Protesters succeeded in closing all abortion clinics in the city for the first week of the operation with few arrests.[276] Then things turned ugly. Over 46 days, more than 3,000 protestors were arrested in Wichita.[277] Furthermore, the massive demonstrations by thousands of rescuers

---

266. WUTHNOW, *supra* note 261, at 204. *See also* FRANCIS SCHAEFFER & C. EVERETT KOOP, WHATEVER HAPPENED TO THE HUMAN RACE 133 (1983).

267. RISEN & THOMAS, *supra* note 4, at 276, 279; RUDY, *supra* note 228, at 50.

268. JACOBY, *supra* note 17, at 20–21, 84–86; PAIGE, *supra* note 34, at 67–70; RISEN & THOMAS, *supra* note 4, at 58, 60–61, 159, 304; RUDY, *supra* note 228, at 54–57.

269. JACOBY, *supra* note 17, at 22; RISEN & THOMAS, *supra* note 4, at 43–53, 57, 63–65, 70, 134, 138, 171, 221–22; RUDY, *supra* note 228, at 55–56; Wills, *supra* note 264, at 19.

270. JACOBY, *supra* note 17, at 23; RISEN & THOMAS, *supra* note 4, at 84, 146–47, 248, 251–52, 266, 320.

271. JACOBY, *supra* note 17, at 21–22.

272. *Id.* at 22; RISEN & THOMAS, *supra* note 4, at 63–65, 134, 138.

273. RISEN & THOMAS, *supra* note 4, at 320.

274. *Id.* at 320–23.

275. GARROW, *supra* note 22, at 688; HADLEY, *supra* note 34, at 163; JACOBY, *supra* note 17, at 135–36; PEGGY JARMAN, THE SIEGE OF WICHITA (1994); RISEN & THOMAS, *supra* note 4, at 317–34; Ginsburg, *supra* note 159, at 228, 235–36.

276. *Id.* at 323–25.

277. Ginsburg, *supra* note 159, at 247 n.54. *See also* RISEN & THOMAS, *supra* note 4, at 318 (reporting "nearly 2,700 arrests").

from across the nation evoked a similar outpouring of activists from the other side who descended on Wichita determined to keep the clinics open.[278] The local police and federal marshals (their first intervention in a clinic protest) began to use "pain compliance" techniques in the arrests to assure that protestors would not soon return.[279] Federal District Judge Patrick Kelly also took strong steps against Operation Rescue, jailing its demonstrators and in assessing fines and damages against its organizers.[280] Courts routinely refused to consider the defendant's invocation of the "necessity" defense—that violating the law was necessary to save human life.[281]

The protests had a long-term effect. Gradually, all the clinics in the city except George Tiller's closed.[282] Tiller's clinic became increasing reliant on out-of-state customers seeking late-term abortions.[283] Yet Tiller hung on. He was shot and wounded in 1993. Finally in 2001, the protesters returned under the aegis of Operation Save America, determined to shut Tiller down, but also recognizing the need to operate more discretely because of the threat of prosecutions under the *Freedom of Access to Clinic Entrances Act*.[284]

Randall Terry was no longer leading demonstrations, finding himself instead ostracized as an unrepentant sinner.[285] He divorced his wife Cindy after 19 years of marriage and married a former assistant 16 years younger than he was, and he was accused of "repeated sinful relationships and conversations with both single and married women."[286] Terry denied the accusations of sexual immorality, but the damage to his image was devastating. He now has no formal connection with Operation Rescue. Instead, he enlarged his activities to include a broad range of conservative, "Christian" values and became involved with the right-wing United States Taxpayers Party.[287]

Operation Rescue and its successor groups have not again attempted to operate on such a grand scale. For activists of both the evangelical left and the New Christian Right, however, the punitive actions of the state directed at them merely confirm their self-image as followers of the militant Christ tortured and martyred by the Romans.[288] In keeping with this image, the "rescuers" generally remained determinedly non-violent. Indeed, during the three years or so that Operation Rescue was able to mount mass protests, the frequency of violent incidents directed at

---

278. *See* Sue Hertz, Caught in the Crossfire: A Year on Abortion's Front Line (1991); Susan Church, *Poll Shows Terry's Tactics Disliked*, Birmingham Press & Sun Bull., Nov. 20, 1989, at 1. *See generally* Risen & Thomas, *supra* note 4, at 321, 323, 332–34.

279. Blanchard, *supra* note 34, at 92; Risen & Thomas, *supra* note 4, at 282, 284–85, 288, 302, 325–26, 332.

280. Women's Health Care Services v. Operation Rescue, 773 F. Supp. 258 (D. Kan. 1991), *rev'd*, 24 F.3d 107, *vacated mem.*, 25 F.3d 1059 (10th Cir. 1994). *See* Blanchard, *supra* note 34, at 93–94; Diamond, *supra* note 159, at 252; Risen & Thomas, *supra* note 4, at 326–33; Ginsburg, *supra* note 159, at 235, 238; Wells, *supra* note 174, at 27–29. Even the federal Department of Justice opposed Judge Kelly's rulings. Risen & Thomas, *supra*, at 330–31.

281. See the authorities collected *supra* at note 177.

282. William Claiborne, *A Decade Later, Abortion Foes Again Gather in Wichita: City Has Changed since Protests of '91*, Wash. Post, July 16, 2001, at A3.

283. *Id.* at 281; Tim Jones, *Abortion Battle Back in Wichita, Kansas; City Tries to Avoid Repeat of 1991 Melee*, Chi. Trib., July 17, 2001, at 9.

284. Claiborne, *supra* note 282; Jones, *supra* note 283; Alexandra Marks, *In Abortion Fight, Lines Have Shifted Ten Years after a Historic Rally; The Anti-Abortion Cause Had Made Gains*, Christian Sci. Monitor, July 16, 2001, at 1.

285. Dan Barry, *Icon for Abortion Protesters Is Looking for a Second Act*, N.Y. Times, July 20, 2001, at A1.

286. *Id.* at B5. Besides the sexual scandals, Terry was dammed for using foul language and for drinking and smoking in front of children.

287. Terry, *supra* note 230; Ginsburg, *supra* note 159, at 229; John Goetz, *Randall Terry and the U.S. Taxpayers Party*, 1 Front Lines Res. no. 2 , at 1 (Aug. 1994).

288. Ginsburg, *supra* note 159, at 242. *See also* Jacoby, *supra* note 17, at 67–68, 109–11, 138, 145–47.

abortion clinics fell sharply.[289] This correlation is missed, of course, by those who insist on describing Operation Rescue's actions as a form of violence.[290]

Yet even while Operation Rescue was peaking, it proved to be too tame and too slow for some committed to ending abortion in America. Some frustrated opponents of abortion rights—including veterans of the "Siege of Atlanta"—turned to violence in an effort to close abortion clinics and to stop abortions.[291] In the mid-1980s, several abortion clinics were set on fire or bombed.[292] In 1985, someone shot through the window of Justice Blackmun's apartment, showering Dorothy Blackmun with splinters of glass.[293] After a marked hiatus between 1987 and 1990 corresponding to the prominent phase of Operation Rescue, the incidence of such violence rose dramatically in the early 1990s.[294] The most noted victims were Dr. David Gunn, shot and killed

289. Note, *supra* note 130, at 1218.

290. *See, e.g.,* BLANCHARD, *supra* note 34, at 91.

291. NATIONAL ABORTION FEDERATION, ANNUAL REPORT ON CLINIC VIOLENCE, available at www.pro-choice.org. *See, e.g.,* JOAN ANDREWS, YOU REJECT THEM, YOU REJECT ME: THE PRISON LETTERS OF JOAN ANDREWS (Richard Cowden-Guido ed. 1988); SCHEIDLER, *supra* note 228. *See generally* ROY McMILLAN, PREPARING FOR SECESSION 122, 132 (1997); RISEN & THOMAS, *supra* note 4, at 74–100, 114–16, 125–26, 194, 314, 339–71; Warren Hern, *Life on the Front Lines,* in ABORTION WARS, *supra* note 27, at 307; Kelly, *supra* note 174, at 434–37; Smolin, *supra* note 210, at 143–50; Wells, *supra* note 174, at 26–28.

292. *See In re* Newchurch, 807 F.3d 404 (5th Cir. 1986); Bering v. Share, 721 P.2d 918, 929 (Was. 1986), *cert. dismissed,* 479 U.S. 1050 (1987). *See also* JACOBY, *supra* note 17, at 157–78; RISEN & THOMAS, *supra* note 4, at 4, 86–98, 197–99, 321; Teresa Carpenter, *Four Who Bombed in God's Name,* VILLAGE VOICE, Aug. 27, 1985, at 19; Merrill McLaughlin, *America's New Civil War,* U.S. NEWS & WORLD REP., Oct. 3, 1988, at 23; Michele Wilson & John Lynxwiler, *Abortion Clinic Violence as Terrorism,* 11 TERRORISM 263 (1988).

293. RISEN & THOMAS, *supra* note 4, at 3. The police investigation concluded that the shooting was a random event not targeted at Justice Blackmun or his wife, but many remained skeptical of this conclusion. *Id.* at 4.

294. *See* United States v. Hill, 893 F. Supp. 1034, 893 F. Supp. 1039, 893 F. Supp. 1044, 893 F. Supp. 1048 (N.D. Fla. 1994); *ACOG Joins Call for an End to Clinic Violence, Harassment,* ACOG NEWSLETTER, Mar. 1995, at 1; Lisa Belkin, *Kill for Life,* N.Y. TIMES MAG., Oct. 30, 1994, at 47; *Bombs Damage Abortion Clinic in Oklahoma,* N.Y. TIMES, Jan. 20, 1997, at A15; Sandra Boordman, *Abortion Foes Strike at Doctors' Home Lives,* WASH. POST, Apr. 8, 1993, at A1; William Booth, *Jury Urges Death Sentence in Abortion Clinic Murders; Hill Speaks Starkly of "Responsibility,"* WASH. POST, Nov. 4, 1994, at A1; Rick Bragg, *2 Bomb Blasts Rock Abortion Clinic at Atlanta,* N.Y. TIMES, Jan. 17, 1997, at A15; William Claiborne & Hamil Harris, *Explaining Pensacola's Violent Reputation; Residents Have Many Theories about Why Their City Has Become Abortion's Battleground,* WASH. POST, Aug. 1, 1994, at A4; Seth Faison, *Abortion Doctor Wounded Outside Kansas Clinic,* N.Y. TIMES, Aug. 20, 1993, at A12; Ginsburg, *supra* note 159, at 236–37; Henry Goldman, *Sniper Kills Doctor Who Performed Abortions,* PHILA. INQUIRER, Oct. 25, 1998, at A2; Stephen Hedges *et al., Abortion: Who's Behind the Violence?,* U.S. NEWS & WORLD REP., Nov. 14, 1994, at 50; Lori Heise, *Freedom Close to Home: The Impact of Violence against Women on Reproductive Rights,* in WOMEN'S RIGHTS, HUMAN RIGHTS: INTERNATIONAL FEMINIST PERSPECTIVES 238, 249–50 (Julie Peters & Andrea Wolper eds. 1995); Hern, *supra* note 291, at 314–15; Bill Hewitt, *In Life's Name,* PEOPLE, Mar. 29, 1993, at 44; Dianne Klein, *The End Does Not Justify the Fanatical Means of Terrorism,* L.A. TIMES, Mar. 16, 1993, at A3; Verlyn Klinkenborg, *Violent Certainties: Abortion Politics in Milwaukee,* HARPER'S MAG., Jan. 1995, at 37; Kevin Merida, *Doctor's Slaying Spurs Abortion-Rights Lawmakers,* WASH. POST, Mar. 15, 1993, at A15; Katie Monagle, *How We Got Here,* Ms., May/June 1995, at 54; Paul Newell, *Bomb Explodes Outside N.C. Clinic,* PHILA. INQUIRER, Mar. 14, 1999, at A6; B. Radford & G. Shaw, *Antiabortion Violence: Causes and Effects,* 3 WOMEN'S HEALTH ISSUES 144 (1993); Larry Rohter, *Doctor Is Slain during Protest over Abortion,* N.Y. TIMES, Mar. 11, 1993, at A1; Eric Schaff, *Redefining Violence against Women: The Campaign of Violence and the Delay of RU-486,* 8 TEMPLE POL. & CIV. RTS. L. REV. 311 (1999); Ronald Smothers, *Death of a Doctor: The Overview—Abortion Doctor and Bodyguard Slain in Florida; Protester Is Arrested in Pensacola's Second Clinic Killing,* N.Y. TIMES, July 30, 1994, at 1; *Special Report: Abortion: Who's Behind the Terrorism?: A 25-Page Call to Action,* Ms., May–June 1995, at 12; *Special Report: Abortion: As the Terrorism Escalates, the Pro-Choice Struggle Continues,* Ms., May/June 1995, at 42; Eric Wee, *Clinic Slaying Suspect Caught; Shooting at Norfolk Abortion Center Tied to Massachusetts Attacks,* WASH. POST, Jan. 1, 1995, at A1. *See generally* BLANCHARD, *supra* note 34, at 51; BLANCHARD & PREWITT, *supra* note 88; FERREE & HESS, *supra* note 85, at 154, 163–64; GARROW, *supra* note 22, at 702–05, 710–14, 718, 728, 732, 736; HADLEY, *supra*

in Pensacola, Florida, in March 1993; Dr. George Tiller, shot and wounded in Wichita in August 1993; Dr. George Patterson, shot and killed in Mobile, Alabama, in August 1993 (although this was never tied to an anti-abortion activist; it might have been a random killing[295] ); Dr. John Britton, shot and killed along with his bodyguard (James Barrett) in Pensacola in July 1994; and Shannon Lowney and Leanne Nichols, two abortion clinic receptionists, murdered in Boston in December 1994. The killers, the bombers, and the arsonists, when they were identified, mostly were deeply religious working-class men below the age of 40 who were classic loners—social isolates unrestrained by relationships and fortified by their faith from fear of punishment.[296] These men (and the occasional woman)[297] are marginal even within the groups they claim to represent.[298] Indeed, the men involved often share more traits with other criminals than they do with other ant-abortion activists.[299]

Some anti-abortion activists who have not engaged in violence themselves have nonetheless argued that the murder of abortionists is justified because abortion itself is a form of murder.[300] This view is controversial, to say the least.[301] It is so controversial that Michael Hirsch, the author of such an article, was fired by his employer—the American Center for Law and Justice, a religiously based organization in Virginia Beach, Virginia.[302]

---

note 34, at 162–66; DEBORAH RHODE, SPEAKING OF SEX: THE DENIAL OF GENDER INEQUALITY 203–04 (1997); Note, *supra* note 130, at 1219–21; Smolin, *supra* note 210, at 143–50. An annual listing of specific acts of violence involving abortion providers or supporters (motivation is not always clear) is found in NATIONAL ABORTION FEDERATION, *supra* note 291.

295. GARROW, *supra* note 22, at 704.

296. BLANCHARD & PREWITT, *supra* note 88, at 274–75; JACOBY, *supra* note 17, at 159; RISEN & THOMAS, *supra* note 4, at 339–42, 349–52, 367–68. *See also* Steve Goldstein, *Killer at Abortion Clinic Believes His Act Was Right*, PHILA. INQUIRER, May 6, 1999, at A29; Abby Goodnough, *Florida Executes Killer of an Abortion Provider*, N.Y. TIMES, Sept. 4, 2003, at A16; Manuel Roig-Franzia, *"I Expect a Great Reward": Abortion Provider's Killer Is Unrepentant on Eve of Execution*, WASH. POST, Sept. 3, 2003, at A1.

297. *See, e.g.*, United States v. Arena, 180 F.3d 380 (2nd Cir. 1999), *cert. denied*, 531 U.S. 811 (2000). *See also* RISEN & THOMAS, *supra* note 4, at 349–60; Peter Korn, *The Mysterious Violence of Shelley Shannon*, SELF, March 1997, at 98.

298. BLANCHARD & PREWITT, *supra* note 88, at 215; JACOBY, *supra* note 17, at 163–64; RISEN & THOMAS, *supra* note 4, at 198–99, 340–42, 345–46, 359; Kevin Fagan, *Battle over Right to Choose: Abortion Clinic in Redding Stirs up Fervor on Both Sides of Issue*, S.F. CHRONICLE, May 4, 1999, at A1.

299. BLANCHARD & PREWITT, *supra* note 88, at 228; JACOBY, *supra* note 17, at 159–66; RISEN & THOMAS, *supra* note 4, at 194–97, 341–43.

300. MICHAEL BRAY, A TIME TO KILL: A STUDY CONCERNING THE USE OF FORCE AND ABORTION (1994); PAUL HILL, SHALL WE DEFEND BORN AND UNBORN CHILDREN WITH FORCE? (1991); CATHY RAMEY, IN DEFENSE OF OTHERS: A BIBLICAL ANALYSIS AND APOLOGETIC ON THE USE OF FORCE TO SAVE LIVES (1995); Goldstein, *supra* note 296; Michael Hirsch, *In Defense of Another: The Paul Hill Brief*, 5 REGENT U. L. REV. 31 (1995); William Rasberry, *A Case of Abortion by Gunshot*, WASH. POST, Sept. 14, 1994, at A21; Charles Rice & John Tuskey, *The Legality and Morality of Using Deadly Force to Protect Unborn Children from Abortionists*, 5 REGENTS U. L. REV. 83 (1995). *See also* GARROW, *supra* note 22, at 702–03; RISEN & THOMAS, *supra* note 4, at 345–48, 358, 365; Fawn Vrazo, *A Small Chorus of Vigilantes*, DETROIT FREE PRESS, Jan. 19, 1995, at 1F. Paul Hill, the author of one of these books, went on to kill Dr. John Britton, and was unrepentant when he was executed for the killing nine years later. *Antiabortion Militant Executed for Killings*, WASH. POST, Sept. 4, 2003, at A3; Goodnough, *supra* note 296; Roig-Franzia, *supra* note 296.

301. Shelby Moore, *Doing Another's Bidding under a Theory of Defense of Others: Shall We Protect the Unborn with Murder?*, 86 KY. L.J. 257 (1998).

302. Matthew Bowers, *CBN [Christian Broadcasting Network] Fires Hirsch over Conflicting Views, not Article*, VA. PILOT & LEDGER-STAR, Nov. 2, 1994, at B3; *"Theoretical" Article Tied to Killing at Clinic*, RICHMOND TIMES-DISPATCH, Dec. 25, 1994, at A14. *See also* FREDERICK CLARKSON, ETERNAL HOSTILITY 139–57 (1997); GARROW, *supra* note 22, at 711–12; RISEN & THOMAS, *supra* note 4, at 74–77; Mark Curriden, *An Unusual Theory Tested and Rejected, Law Review Article withdrawn by Author, Argues Killing of Abortionist Justified*, ABA J., Dec. 1994, at 26; Eric Lipton, *Law Review Cancels Abortion Article*, WASH. POST, Aug. 23, 1994, at B2.

Furthermore, the violence was counterproductive, generating sympathy for abortion providers even among those opposed to abortion.[303] The violence also justifies abortion providers in feeling personally threatened even by peaceful protests.[304] Pro-abortion groups exploit these fears to raise funds and to garner political support,[305] contributing to the political climate in which legislatures and courts feel empowered to restrict peaceful protest.[306] Many of those who support abortion rights insist on attributing the violence to all who oppose abortion, not just to those who actually espouse violence or even direct action.[307] Pro-abortion leaders continue to focus attention on the violence even though since 1994 there have been fewer abortion-related killings, fewer bombings, and fewer blockades of abortion clinics.

In contrast with the picture painted by supporters of abortion rights, most leaders of the anti-abortion movement publicly condemned the violence either as wrong or at least as counter-productive.[308] Some leaders have even helped with the investigations of the killings.[309] The violence is particularly inconsistent with traditional Catholic teaching on the sanctity of all life.[310] Yet pro-abortion writers like David Garrow insist on using innuendo to suggest that Catholic Bishops are directly responsible for the clinic bombings.[311] By blaming all who are opposed to abortion for the violence of a marginal few, those who support abortion rights make compromise more difficult for they cannot then negotiate with the opposition without appearing to be appeasing vio-

---

303. *See, e.g.*, Lyn Cryderman, *A Movement Divided*, CHRISTIANITY TODAY, Aug. 12, 1988, at 48; Carole Joffe, Patricia Anderson, & Judy Steinauer, *The Crisis in Abortion Provision and Pro-Choice Medical Activism in the 1990s*, in ABORTION WARS, *supra* note 27, at 320, 327–31; Charles Rice & John Tuskey, *The Legality and Morality of Using Deadly Force to Protect Unborn Children from Abortion Providers*, 5 REGENT U. L. REV. 83 (1995); Peter Steinfels, *The Moral Emotion of the Abortion Debate Finds a Parallel in the Domestic Conflict over Vietnam*, N.Y. TIMES, July 6, 1994, at A22. *See also* JACOBY, *supra* note 17, at 154, 174; RISEN & THOMAS, *supra* note 4, at 60–61, 68, 93–95, 202–03, 207–08, 297, 344, 357, 366; Ginsburg, *supra* note 159, at 238–39.

304. *See, e.g.*, Sandra Boordman, *A Tale of Two Dallas Abortion Doctors: One Surrendered, One Is Fighting on*, WASH. POST, Apr. 8, 1993, at A16; Curtis Boyd, *The Morality of Abortion: The Making of a Feminist Physician*, 13 ST. L.U. PUB. L. REV. 303, 310 (1993); Tamar Lewin, *Malpractice Lawyers' New Target*, MED. ECON., July 1995, at 21.

305. Planned Parenthood of S.E. Pa., *Rights and Freedoms: Emergency Appeal* (fundraising letter, dated Feb. 11, 1994, signed by Joan Cooms, Executive Director) (copy in author's files). *See also* Ginsburg, *supra* note 159, at 239; Sara Rimer, *Brookline Shows Fervor in Keeping Clinics Open*, N.Y. TIMES, Jan. 3, 1995, at A12; Rene Sanchez, *From Year of Promise to Year of Violence: Abortion Rights Advocates Decry Trend toward Militant Opposition*, WASH. POST, Dec. 31, 1994, at A14; Faye Wattleton, *Anti-Choice Terrorism: From Blockades to Bombs to Murder*, Ms., Nov./Dec. 1994, at 90. *See generally* RISEN & THOMAS, *supra* note 4.

306. JACOBY, *supra* note 17, at 174–75; RISEN & THOMAS, *supra* note 4, at 357, 361; Dana Gershon, Note, *Stalking Statutes: A New Vehicle to Curb the New Violence of the Radical Anti-Abortion Movement*, 26 COLUM. HUM. RTS. L. REV. 215 (1994). See also the text *supra* at notes 106–216.

307. *See, e.g.*, BLANCHARD & PREWITT, *supra* note 88, at 257, 270–71; GARROW, *supra* note 22, at 650–52, 703; Fischer, *supra* note 184, at 1431 n.116; Fried, *supra* note 96, at 209; Ginsburg, *supra* note 159, at 228–29; Ellen Goodman, *The New Domestic Terrorists*, BOS. GLOBE, Mar. 14, 1993, at A25; Korn, *supra* note 297; Wilder, *supra* note 76, at 81–84.

308. *See, e.g.*, Goldstein, *supra* note 296; John Kennedy, *Killing Distorts Pro-Life Message; Assassination of Pensacola Doctor John Bayard Britton and James Barrett*, CHRISTIANITY TODAY, Sept. 12, 1994, at 56; Tamar Lewin, *A Cause Worth Killing For? Debate Splits Abortion Foes*, N.Y. TIMES, July 230, 1994, at A18; Moore, *supra* note 301, at 259; Marvin Olasky, *Another Year of Abortions: This Week Marks 26th Anniversary of* Roe v. Wade, *and We're Still Surprised with Some News*, AUSTIN AM.-STATESMAN, Jan. 20, 1999, at A17; Rohter, *supra* note 294, at B10; Smolin, *supra* note 210, at 119–20; Cal Thomas, *Exploitation of the Clinic Killings: Pro Life Is Not Pro Death*, WASH. TIMES, Jan. 16, 1995, at A16; Wardle, *supra* note 130, at 881–82. *See generally* BLANCHARD & PREWITT, *supra* note 88, at 215; GINSBURG, *supra* note 17, at 46–54; RISEN & THOMAS, *supra* note 4, at 173–74.

309. Rorie Sherman, *Abortion Activists Aiding Federal Probe*, NAT'L L.J., Aug. 15, 1994, at A9.

310. JACOBY, *supra* note 17, at 167–70.

311. See the text *supra* at note 96. *See also* Steinbeck, *supra* note 6, at 806–07.

lence or selling out their endangered supporters.[312] Yet given the improbability of ultimate victory on either side, sooner or later compromise will be necessary.

The factual record suggests that even Operation Rescue itself was not involved in the violence. Operation Rescue required participants in its "rescues" to sign a pledge to remain peaceful, to behave politely, and to be passive when arrested, as well as to obey the on-site leadership.[313] Operation Rescue also publicly condemned killing as a technique for stopping abortion at a 1994 meeting.[314] While David Garrow did report the ensuing split in Operation Rescue over the question of violence, he did not report the Operation Rescue vote condemning violence, insisting that those opposed to violence were a minority at the meeting.[315] By this time, however, Operation Rescue was in steep decline as an organization. And in the place of Operation Rescue and Randall Terry, a new organization emerged—the American Coalition of Life Activists—that did openly condone violence.[316]

At the same time that those supporting abortion rights were getting favorable press because of the violence directed at their cause, abortion protestors also faced threats and attacks.[317] In some cases, the administrators of abortion clinics—loudly complaining that they were the targets of anti-abortion violence—were themselves promoting violence against peaceful anti-abortion protestors.[318] And police resort to "pain compliance" techniques was far more common at clinic demonstrations than violence by the protestors ever was.[319] This was largely ignored by the news media and "scholars" who support abortion rights.[320] The result is an unbalanced response seeking to punish abortion protestors for non-threatening as well as threatening actions while ignoring equivalent actions—including violence—on the other side.[321]

The enactment of repressive laws and the issuance of strongly phrased injunctions after 1994 had the effect of limiting peaceful protest at abortion clinics as well as potentially violent ones.[322] Yet after several relatively quiet years from 1995 to 1997, both the demonstrations and the violence began to increase again in 1998. After several (mostly non-fatal) bombings in the southern United States and several non-fatal shootings related to Canadian abortion clinics,[323] a sniper killed Dr. Barnett Slepian, who performed abortions in Buffalo, New York on October 23,

---

312. JACOBY, *supra* note 17, at 154–55.

313. *Id.* at 153.

314. ALCORN, *supra* note 233, at 207–08; RISEN & THOMAS, *supra* note 4, at 357–58, 360–61; Egan I & II, *supra* note 170; Ginsburg, *supra* note 159, at 236–37. *See also* Goldstein, *supra* note 296.

315. GARROW, *supra* note 22, at 711.

316. *See* BRAY, *supra* note 300; Philip Pan, *In the Name of Life, Defending Violence: Banquet Honors Abortion Foes Who Killed, Burned for Cause*, WASH. POST, Jan. 22, 1999, at B8. *See generally* GARROW, *supra* note 22, at 711–12, 714; Egan I & II, *supra* note 170; Ginsburg, *supra* note 159, at 237–38.

317. *See* RISEN & THOMAS, *supra* note 4, at 160–62, 170, 172, 245; Wardle, *supra* note 130, at 883–84 n. 156.

318. RISEN & THOMAS, *supra* note 4, at 245, 247, 249–50, 252, 267, 277.

319. BLANCHARD, *supra* note 34, at 92; RISEN & THOMAS, *supra* note 4, at 282, 284–85, 288, 302.

320. *See generally* BLANCHARD & PREWITT, *supra* note 88.

321. *See, e.g.*, New York St. Nat. Org. for Women v. Terry, 159 F.3d 86 (2nd Cir. 1998), *cert. denied sub nom.* Pearson v. Planned Parenthood Margaret Sanger Clinic, 527 U.S. 1003 (1999); United States v. Lynch, 104 F.3d 357 (2nd Cir. 1996), 1996 WL 717912, *cert. denied,* 520 U.S. 1170 (1997); Olga Rodriguez, Note, *Advocating the Use of California's Stalking Statutes to Prosecute Radical Anti-Abortion Protestors* (sic), 7 HASTINGS WOMEN'S L.J. 151 (1996). *See also* Michael O'Brien, Note, *Operation Rescue Blockades and the Misuse of 42 U.S.C. § 1985(3)*, 41 CLEVE. ST. L. REV. 145 (1993); Paulsen & McConnell, *supra* note 205.

322. GARROW, *supra* note 22, at 726, 729, 735–36; RISEN & THOMAS, *supra* note 4, at 365–68, 373–74; Garrow, *supra* note 85, at 846–47.

323. *See* NATIONAL ABORTION FEDERATION, *supra* note 291; Rick Bragg, *Bomb Kills Guard at an Alabama Abortion Clinic*, NY TIMES, Jan. 30, 1998, at A1.

1998.[324] It took six months to identify a suspect (James Charles Kopp) and another three years before he was located in France.[325] Kopp has been linked to four other shootings of doctors in Canada on or around November 11— "Remembrance Day" in Canada.[326] ("Remembrance Day" refers to remembering the Armistice that ended World War I, but has been appropriated by Canadian anti-abortion groups as a day to remember the slaughtered unborn.) When Eric Rudolph, accused of bombing several abortion clinics and the Atlanta Olympics in 1996, took to the Carolina hills pursued by an intense police manhunt, many people in the region seemed to have helped him evade capture for nearly seven years.[327]

Six months later, on April 19, 1999, a new group, Operation Save America, launched a week of protest against abortion clinics in Buffalo that resembled Operation Rescue's protests of a decade earlier.[328] Operation Save America, however, broadened its protests to include child pornography, school violence, and teen-age sex, investing as much in picketing book stores and schools as in blockading abortion clinics. Local authorities, who still had not caught Dr. Slepian's killer, responded by persuading a court to widen the "buffer zone" around the clinics and those entering or leaving the clinics from 15 feet to 50 feet.[329] While the leader of the protests, Rev. "Flip" Benham, vowed to defy the order,[330] in fact the demonstrations remained small and the local authorities in the end arrested nobody.

Even more recently, a construction contractor in Austin, Texas, successfully organized a boycott that blocked the construction of a proposed abortion clinic in that city.[331] The news report of the incident described Austin as "a liberal enclave whose politics are more akin to those in Berkeley, Calif., than those in the Bible Belt."[332] Construction was stopped by appeals to the contractors' consciences and to their pocket books—numerous local churches announced they would boycott any contractors who participated in the project. Whether this tactic will spread around the country and become a successful means of impairing access to abortion remains to be seen.

---

324. Joseph Berger, *His Beliefs Pushed Doctor to Keep Role at Abortion Clinic*, N.Y. TIMES, Oct. 26, 1998, at A1; Jim Yardley & David Rohde, *Abortion Doctor in Buffalo Slain: Sniper Attack Fits Violent Pattern*, N.Y. TIMES, Oct. 25, 1998, at 1. *See also* Ellen Goodman, *Antiabortion Terrorism Is No Surprise*, BOS. GLOBE, Oct. 29, 1998, at A27.

325. Rose Ciotta, *Warrant Reported in Slepian Case*, PHILA. INQUIRER, May 6, 1999, at A29; Keith Richburg, *Court in France Approves Extradition of U.S. Fugitive*, WASH. POST, June 29, 2001, at A33; James Risen, *Tracing the Path of a Hard-Line Foe of Abortion*, N.Y. TIMES, Nov. 6, 1998, at B5; David Samuels, *The Making of a Fugitive*, N.Y. TIMES MAG., Mar. 21, 1999, at 47. *See also* Randal Archibold, *Abortion Foe Fights Charges in Killing of Doctor*, N.Y. TIMES, June 6, 2002, at B5; Carolyn Thompson, *Suspect in Buffalo Doctor's Murder Returned to U.S.: Anti-Abortion Militant Pleads Innocent to Federal Charges*, WASH. POST, June 5, 2002, at A13.

326. James Brooke, *Security Fears Rise at Clinics for Abortions in Canada*, N.Y. TIMES, Nov. 11, 1999, at A9.

327. Michael A. Fletcher, *Police Scour Mountains for Clues: Searchers Seek Answer to How Rudolph Survived on Lam*, WASH. POST, June 2, 2003, at A1; Jeffrey Gettleman & David Halbfinger, *Suspect in '96 Olympic Bombing and 3 Other Attacks Is Caught*, N.Y. TIMES, June 1, 2003, § 1, at 1; Allan Gurganus, *Why We Fed the Bomber*, N.Y. TIMES, June 8, 2003, § 4, at 13; Anne Hull, *Olympics Bombing Suspect Caught: Also Sought in Attacks on Abortion Clinics and Gay Club, Fugitive His for 5 Years*, WASH. POST, June 1, 2003, at A1.

328. David Chen, *Abortion Protests Continue Peacefully: Police and Media Outnumber Demonstrators in Buffalo Suburbs*, N.Y. TIMES, Apr. 20, 1999, at B5; David Chen, *A Week of Abortion Protests in Buffalo Begins Loudly but Peacefully*, N.Y. TIMES, Apr. 19, 1999, at B6 ("Chen, *Week of Protests*").

329. Chen, *Week of Protests*, *supra* note 328.

330. *Id.* Benham had a long history in anti-abortion politics and had long been a local leader of Operation Rescue in Dallas. *See* RISEN & THOMAS, *supra* note 4, at 123. He is the person who persuaded Norma McCorvey ("Jane Roe") to come out against abortion. *See* JACOBY, *supra* note 17, at 44–45, n.1; NORMA MCCORVEY & GARY THOMAS, WON BY LOVE (1997); *"Jane Roe" Switches Sides on Abortion*, N.Y. TIMES, Aug. 11, 1995, at A12.

331. Karin Brulliard, *Abortion Clinics Targeted before They Are Built: Foes Threaten to Boycott Contractors*, WASH. POST, Nov. 30, 2003, A1.

332. *Id.*

# The Decline of the Abortion Industry

*How can I think and hit at the same time?*

—Yogi Berra[333]

The continuing opposition to abortion, ranging from quiet discussion to loud debates to noisy protests to fatal violence, eventually had some effect. Nationally, the number of abortion providers in the United States declined from about 2,908 in 1982 to 2,380 in 1992.[334] About 85 percent of the counties in the United States have no facilities for doing abortions.[335] This breaks down as 94 percent of non-metropolitan counties and 33 percent of metropolitan counties—the latter often being suburban counties, in which women have access to abortion providers in an adjacent, more urbanized county. In 1993, about 24 percent of women in the United States lived more than 50 miles from an abortion clinic.[336] In several states, there are no abortion providers at all, forcing about 10 percent of the women seeking abortions to travel out of state to obtain the procedure.[337] This is not always as bad as it sounds, out of state sometimes is simply across a bridge or a few miles down the road. One estimate is that 100,000 women annually cannot obtain abortions they want because of the lack of abortionists at a convenient location.[338] The persons making this estimate do not disclose how they arrived at the number.

Abortion rights activists see the reluctance of obstetricians to perform abortions as entirely or largely the result of anti-abortion harassment and violence.[339] This claim finds some support in

---

333. DAVID NATHAN, BASEBALL QUOTATIONS 149 (1993).

334. BLANK & MERRICK, *supra* note 34, at 28; David Grimes, *Clinicians Who Provide Abortions: The Thinning Ranks,* 80 OBSTET. & GYNECOLOGY 719 (1992); Stanley Henshaw & Jennifer Van Vort, *Abortion Services in the United States,* 26 FAM. PLAN. PERSP. 100, 103–05 (1994).

335. This rate has been remarkably constant over at least two decades; the figures given by various sources range from 82% to 87%. *See* BLANK & MERRICK, *supra* note 34, at 28–29; GINSBURG, *supra* note 17, at 56; GRABER, *supra* note 34, at 70–72; FREDERICK JAFFE, BARBARA LINDHEIM, & PHILIP LEE, ABORTION POLITICS 191–92 (1981); PETCHESKY, *supra* note 34, at xxiv; ROSENBERG, *supra* note 6, at 190–95; Cecil Connolly, *Abortion Providers Fewest in 30 Years: Hospital Mergers, Politics Are Cited,* WASH. POST, Jan. 22, 2003, at A8; Mark Cunningham, *The Abortion War,* NAT'L REV., Nov. 2, 1992, at 42; Grimes, *supra* note 96, at 1170; Fried, *supra* note 96; Stanley Henshaw, *Abortion Incidence and Services in the United States, 1995–1996,* 30 FAM. PLAN. PERSP. 263, 266 (1998); Stanley Henshaw, Jacqueline Dorroch Forrest, & Jennifer Van Vort, *Abortion Services in the United States, 1984 and 1985,* 19 FAM. PLAN. PERSP. 63, 64–65 (1987); Henshaw & Van Vort, *supra* note 334, at 107; Joffe, Anderson, & Steinaur, *supra* note 303, at 322; Nadine Strossen & Ronald Collins, *The Future of an Illusion: Reconstructing* Planned Parenthood v. Casey, 16 CONST'L COMMENTARY 587, 590 (1999); Raymond Tatalovich & Byron Daynes, *The Geographic Distribution of U.S. Hospitals with Abortion Facilities,* 21 FAM. PLAN. PERSPECTIVES 81 (1989); Christopher Tietze, *Demographic and Public Health Experience with Legal Abortion: 1973–80,* in ABORTION, MEDICINE, AND THE LAW 289, 292–93 (J. Douglas Butler & David Walbert eds. 3rd ed. 1986); Linda Villarosa, *Newest Skill for Future Ob-Gyns: Abortion Training,* N.Y. TIMES, June 11, 2002, at F6. Women seeking abortions in Canada face similar difficulties. Hamuda Ghafour, *Access Is Ontario's Abortion Issue—Abortion Is Safe and Legal, but Hard to Get Outside the GTA [Greater Toronto Area],* TORONTO STAR, Jan. 12, 2001, at LI2.

336. Grimes, *supra* note 69, at 1170.

337. CRAIG & O'BRIEN, *supra* note 6, at 78.

338. GRABER, *supra* note 34, at 19–20. *See also* Council of Sci. Aff., Am. Med. Ass'n, *Induced Termination of Pregnancy before and after Roe v. Wade: Trends in the Mortality and Morbidity of Women,* 268 JAMA 3237 (1992); Joffe, Anderson, & Steinauer, *supra* note 303, at 322, 324–25; Verlyn Klinkenborg, *Violent Certainties,* HARPER'S, Jan. 1995, at 51.

339. GLENNA HALVORSON BOYD, SURVIVING A HOLY WAR: HOW HEALTH CARE WORKERS IN U.S. ABORTION FACILITIES ARE COPING WITH ANTIABORTION HARASSMENT (1990); BETSY HARTMANN, REPRODUCTIVE RIGHTS AND WRONGS 262 (1995); FERREE & HESS, *supra* note 85, at 163; JUDGES, *supra* note 6, at 43–48,

the common stance of many obstetricians and gynecologists of being fashionably liberal on abortion in theory while declining to do them in practice.[340] While some doctors are proud of doing abortions,[341] the supposition that doctors decline to do abortions solely because of fear, ignores that reluctance to do abortions has a long historical pedigree stretching back at least two centuries.[342] Obstetric nurses tend to be even more hostile to abortion than are obstetric physicians.[343]

As for abortion providers, considerable research supports the conclusion that they are not demoralized by the abuse or harassment at the hands of anti-abortion protestors. Abuse and harassment have energized them, making them feel like champions in a struggle for personal freedom and women's liberation.[344] Nor have they been much affected by a possibility of liability for medical malpractice so spotty is the legal response to that problem.[345] What demoralized them was the sense of professional isolation and utter lack of encouragement from the vast majority in the health care professions who disdain the abortion providers' activities.[346]

---

264–70; Mason, *supra* note 38, at 107; Petchesky, *supra* note 34, at xi–xii; Reagan, *supra* note 68, at 248; Risen & Thomas, *supra* note 4, at 342, 345, 376; Tracy Sefl *et al.*, Feminist Majority Foundation: 1999 National Clinic Violence Survey Report (2000); Whitney, *supra* note 34, at 214–15; Janet Benshoof, *Planned Parenthood v. Casey: The Impact of the New Undue Burden Standard on Reproductive Health Care,* 269 JAMA 2249, 2256–57 (1993); Boyd, *supra* note 304, at 306–11; Connolly, *supra* note 335; Diane Curtis, *Doctored Rights: Menstrual Extraction, Self-Help Gynecological Care, and the Law,* 20 Rev. L. & Soc. Change 427, 431 (1994); *Editorial,* 342 The Lancet 939 (1993); Kathryn Ann Farr, *Shaping Policy through Litigation: Abortion Law in the United States,* 39 Crime & Delinquency 167, 168 (1993); Jacqueline Darroch Forrest & Stanley Henshaw, *The Harassment of U.S. Abortion Providers,* 19 Fam. Plan. Persp. 9 (1987); Stanley Henshaw, *Factors Hindering Access to Abortion Services,* 27 Fam. Plan. Persp. 54, 58–59 (1995); Stanley Henshaw, *The Accessibility of Abortion Services in the United States,* 23 Fam. Plan. Persp. 246 (1994); Katheryn Katz, *The Pregnant Child's Right to Self-Determination,* 62 Alb. L. Rev. 1119, 1124–26 (1999); Gina Kolata, *Under Pressure and Stigma, More Doctors Shun Abortion,* N.Y. Times, Jan. 8, 1990, at A1; Susan Mezey *et al., Keeping Abortion Clinics Open,* 13 Policy Stud. Rev. 111 (1994); Liza Mundy, *Notes from a Doctor,* Wash. Post, Feb. 17, 2002, Mag. at W18; Elizabeth Reilly, *The Rhetoric of Disrespect: Uncovering the Faulty Premises Infecting Reproductive Rights,* 5 J. Gender & L. 147, 148 n.3, 149 (1996); Sara Rimer, *Abortion Clinics Search for Doctors in Scarcity,* N.Y. Times, Mar. 31, 1993, at A14; Pablo Rodriguez, *The Doctor in the Bulletproof Vest,* N.Y. Times, Oct. 28, 1998, at A29; Elisabeth Rosenthal, *Finances and Fear Spurring Hospitals to Drop Abortions,* N.Y. Times, Feb. 20, 1995, at A1; Allen Rosenfield, *The Difficult Issue of Second-Trimester Abortion,* 267 JAMA 324, 325 (1994); Mandee Silverman, Note, *RU-486: A Dramatic New Choice or Forum for Continued Abortion Controversy,* 57 NYU Ann. Surv. Am. L. 247, 249–51 (2000); Strossen & Collins, *supra* note 335, at 590; Georgia Sullivan, *Protection of Constitutional Guarantees under 42 U.S.C. §1985(3): Operation Rescue's "Summer of Mercy,"* 49 Wash. & Lee L. Rev. 237 (1992); Villarosa, *supra* note 335; Timothy Vinceguerra, *Notes of a Footsoldier,* 62 Alb. L. Rev. 1167, 1180 (1999). The same excuse has been offered for the similar spotty availability of abortion clinics in Canada. Henry Morganthaler, *Some Canadian Women Are More Equal than Others,* Globe & Mail (Toronto), July 16, 2001, at A13.

340. Kenny, *supra* note 101, at 259–60.

341. *See, e.g.,* Sallie Tisdale, *We Do Abortions Here,* Harper's Mag., Oct. 1987, at 66.

342. *See* Chapter 15, at notes 453–72. *See generally* Chapters 6–8.

343. Kenny, *supra* note 101, at 267–73.

344. *See, e.g.,* Suzanne Poppema, Why I Am an Abortion Doctor (1996); Boyd, *supra* note 304; Hern, *supra* note 291; Jane Hodgson, *The Twentieth-Century Gender Battle: Difficulties in Perception,* in Abortion Wars, *supra* note 27, at 301; Elizabeth Karlin, *"We Called It Kindness": Establishing a Feminist Abortion Practice,* in Abortion Wars, *supra,* at 273; Tisdale, *supra* note 341. *See also* Boyd, *supra* note 339; Patricia Lunneborg, Abortion: A Positive Decision 177–94 (1992); Wendy Simonds, Abortion at Work: Ideology and Practice in a Feminist Clinic (1996); Warren Hern, *Proxemics: The Application of Theory to Conflict Arising from Antiabortion Demonstrations,* 12 Population & Envt. 379 (1991). *See generally* Catherine Cozzarelli & Brenda Major, *The Effects of Anti-Abortion Demonstrators and Pro-Choice Escorts on Women's Psychological Responses to Abortion,* 13 J. Soc. & Clinical Psych. 404 (1994).

345. *See* Chapter 15, at notes 41–47.

346. Garrow, *supra* note 22, at 717–18; Diane Gianelli, *Abortion Providers Share Inner Conflicts,* Am. Med. News, July 12, 1993, at 3, 36–37; Kathleen Roe, *Private Troubles and Public Issues: Providing Abortion Amid Competing Definitions,* 29 Soc. Sci. & Med. 1191 (1989); Wendy Simonds, *At an Impasse: Inside an Abor-*

Neither harassment nor distaste, however, provides the best explanation for the present pattern of the distribution of abortion services. The pattern is probably explained more by the economics of freestanding clinics (the primary source of abortion services) than by the disinclination of physicians or any program of opposition.[347] This was done to maximize profits. Thus from the earliest days of abortion clinics, many clinics went so far as to split fees with abortion referral services to assure a flow of paying clients.[348] Some clinics wound up suing clients or their spouses for unpaid fees—although at least one court has held that a husband was not liable to pay for his wife's legal abortion because the procedure was not necessary for her health.[349] At the same time clinic operators fought successfully against regulations requiring abortions to be performed in accredited (and highly regulated) hospitals.[350] Yet, as one study concluded, there must be at least 400 women "in need" annually to support a freestanding abortion clinic.[351] In most, if not all, of the many counties without abortion services, there simply are too few women seeking abortions to support an abortion clinic or an abortion unit in a hospital.

Some who favor abortion rights have already begun to argue that abortion simply is not lucrative enough as an explanation for the large number of doctors who do not want to do abortions and for the failure of sympathetic doctors to organize in earlier times.[352] One should not, however, overplay the role of economics in explaining the revision of abortion practices and laws. After all, abortion laws vary widely in other advanced capitalist countries, ranging from in-

---

*tion Clinic,* 6 CURRENT RES. ON OCCUPATIONS & PROFESSIONS 99 (1991); Wendy Simonds, *Feminism on the Job: Confronting Opposition in Abortion Work,* in FEMINIST ORGANIZATIONS 248 (Myra Marx Ferree & Patricia Yancey Martin eds. 1995).

347. JAFFE, LINDHEIM, & LEE, *supra* note 335, at 191–92; Jacqueline Dorroch Forrest, Christopher Tietze, & Ellen Sullivan, *Abortion in the United States, 1976–1977,* 10 FAM. PLAN. PERSP. 271, 272, 277 (1978); Michael Graber, *The Ghost of Abortion Past: Pre-Roe Abortion Law in Action,* 1 VA. J. SOC. POL'Y & L. 309, 372 (1994) (this article is substantially reprinted as Chapter 2 of Graber's book, GRABER, *supra* note 34; the point referenced here is omitted in the book); Henshaw, Forrest, & Van Vort, *supra* note 335, at 69.

348. *See, e.g.,* State v. Abortion Inf. Agency, Inc., 285 N.E.2d 317 (N.Y. 1972) (enjoining an abortion referral service that split fees with abortion clinics as the unlicensed practice of medicine and insurance); State v. Mitchell, 321 N.Y.S.2d 756 (Sup. Ct. 1971) (enjoining an abortion referral service as an unlicensed "doctor's office"). *See also* Montwill Corp. v. Lefkowitz, 321 N.Y.S.2d 975 (Sup. Ct. 1971) (barring investigators of an abortion referral service from learning the precise type of abortions performed in the clinic); Lefkowitz v. Women's Pavilion, 321 N.Y.S.2d 963 (Sup. Ct. 1971) (barring investigators of an abortion referral service from learning the identity of particular clients); *In re* Weitzner, 321 N.Y.S.2d 925 (Sup. Ct. 1971) (upholding a subpoena of a physician as a witness in a state investigation of the financial dealings of an abortion referral service).

349. Sharon Clinic v. Nelson R., 394 N.Y.S.2d 118 (Sup. Ct. 1977).

350. *See, e.g.,* Simopoulos v. Virginia, 462 U.S. 506 (1983); Doe v. Bolton, 410 U.S. 179 (1973); Ragsdale v. Turnock, 841 F.2d 1358 (7th Cir. 1988), *appeal dismissed,* 503 U.S. 916 (1992); Birth Control Ctrs., Inc. v. Reizen, 743 F.2d 352 (6th Cir. 1984); Aware Woman Clinic, Inc. v. City of Cocoa Beach, 629 F. 1146 (5th Cir. 1980); Mahoning Women's Center v. Hunter, 610 F.2d 456 (6th Cir. 1979), *vacated mem.,* 447 U.S. 918 (1980); Baird v. Department of Pub. Health, 599 F.2d 1098 (1st Cir. 1979); Hallmark Clinic v. North Car. Dep't Hum. Resources, 519 F.2d 1315 (4th Cir. 1975); Word v. Poelker, 495 F.2d 1349 (8th Cir. 1973); Robin v. Village of Hempstead, 285 N.E.2d 285 (N.Y. 1972). *See also* Roman Cath. Diocese of Albany v. New York Dep't of Health, 489 N.E.2d 749 (N.Y. 1985) (upholding the Department's determination allowing clinics to add nonhospital abortions services); Keogh v. New York Dep't of Health, 513 N.Y.S.2d 761 (App. Div. 1987) (same). This struggle continues. *See, e.g.,* Greenville Women's Clinic v. Commissioner, S.C. Dep't Health, 317 F.3d 357, *vacated en banc,* 2002 WL 31875112 (4th Cir. 2002), *cert. denied,* 538 U.S. 1008 (2003); Indiana Hosp. Licensing Council v. Women's Pavilion of South Bend, Inc., 424 N.E.2d 461 (Ind. 1981); Davis v. Fieker, 952 P.2d 505 (Okla. 1997).

351. Sara Seims, *Abortion Availability in the United States,* 12 FAM. PLAN. PERSP. 88, 95 (1980).

352. *See* Julie Johnson, Priscilla Painton, & Elizabeth Taylor, *Abortion: The Future Is Already Here,* TIME, May 4, 1992, at 28.

dications policies, to authorization by professional committees, to prohibitions of all but very early abortions,[353] and abortion practices vary almost as widely.[354] These patterns cannot be correlated with the economics of demand for abortions.

Further feeding the decline in the availability of abortion services is that only a few residency training programs in obstetrics and gynecology routinely include abortion in the training.[355] A commentator estimated in 1992 that only 25 percent of ob/gyn residency programs require abortion training, while 24 percent deny such training altogether.[356] Others have estimated that only 12 percent of ob/gyn residency programs in the 1990s routinely required training in first-trimester abortions[357]—the most common and simplest of abortion procedures. This pattern, reflecting the longstanding obstetrical prejudice against doing abortions, is somewhat ironic given the open discrimination in medical school admissions against applicants who object to abortion.[358] In part, the lack of training simply represents the fruits of the decision of abortion activists to support freestanding and largely unregulated clinics as the major site for performing abortions.[359] By moving abortions into clinics, the procedure was removed from teaching hospitals as well as other hospitals, and hence from residency training programs. The move to clinics served to minimize public attention and to maximize profits, but it had its costs particularly in terms of training future abortionists.

The Accreditation Council on Graduate Medical Education attempted to adopt a rule in February 1995 to make abortion training mandatory in all residency programs—subject to a narrowly defined conscience clause for residents who objected to such training and without any protection at all for religiously affiliated hospitals or physicians.[360] This proposal met

353. *See* Condit, *supra* note 6, at 199–200; Mary Ann Glendon, Abortion and Divorce in Western Law 10–39 (1987).

354. *See, e.g.,* Hadley, *supra* note 34, at 146–52; Tomas Frejka, *Induced Abortion and Fertility: A Quarter Century of Experience in Eastern Europe,* 9 Population & Dev. Rev. 494, 497–509 (1983); Ian Gentles, *Good News for the Fetus: Two Fallacies in the Abortion Debate,* Policy Rev., Spring 1987, at 50, 54; Evert Ketting & Philip van Praag, *The Marginal Relevance of Legislation Relating to Induced Abortion,* in The New Politics of Abortion 154 (Joni Lovenduski & Joyce Outshoorn eds. 1986); Joni Lovenduski & Joyce Outshoorn, *Introduction: The New Politics of Abortion,* in The New Politics of Abortion, *supra,* at 1.

355. Felice Belman, *Abortion Training Is Harder to Come by,* Bos. Globe, Jan. 12, 1995, at A1; Connelly, *supra* note 335; Helen Cooper, *Medical Schools, Students Shun Abortion Study,* Wall St. J., Mar. 12, 1993, at B1; Gottlieb, *supra* note 120, at 532; Deborah Lerner & Francesca Taylor, *Family Physicians and First-Trimester Abortion: A Survey of Residency Programs in Southern California,* 26 Fam. Med. 157 (1994); Rosenfield, *supra* note 72, at 325; Jody Steinauer *et al., Training Family Practice Residents in Abortion and Other Reproductive Health Care: A Nationwide Survey,* 29 Fam. Plan. Persp. 222 (1997); Pamela Talley & George Bergus, *Abortion Training in Family Practice Residency Programs,* 28 Fam. Med. 245 (1996); Carolyn Westhoff, *Abortion Training in Residency Programs,* 49 J. Am. Med. Women's Ass'n 150 (1994); Carolyn Westhoff, Frances Marks, & Allen Rosenfield, *Residency Training in Contraception, Sterilization, and Abortion,* 81 Obstet. & Gynecology 311 (1993).

356. Cunningham, *supra* note 335, at 42. Another study found that in 1995 about 45% of ob/gyn programs offer abortion training, generally without requiring it. Rene Almeling *et al., Abortion Training in the U.S. Obstetrics and Gynecology Residency Programs, 1998,* 32 Fam. Plan. Persp. 268, 270–71 (2000).

357. Reagan, *supra* note 68, at 252; James Baron, *More Prospective Obstetricians Will Be Taught Abortion Skills,* N.Y. Times, Feb. 15, 1995, at A1; Grimes, *supra* note 69, at 1173; Joffe, Anderson, & Steinauer, *supra* note 303, at 321, 324; H. Trent MacKay & Andrea Phillips MacKay, *Abortion Training in Ostetrics and Gynecology,* 27 Fam. Plan. Persp. 112 (1995); J.H. Marshall *et al., Outpatient Termination of Pregnancy: Experience in Family Practice Residency,* 14 J. Fam. Practice 245 (1982); Rodgers & Rodgers, *supra* note 123, at 302; Vinceguerra, *supra* note 12, at 1176–77.

358. Gunn & Zenner, *supra* note 123.

359. Almeling *et al., supra* note 356, at 268; Rodgers & Rodgers, *supra* note 123, at 300–02.

360. National Abortion Federation, Who Will Provide Abortions? Ensuring the Availability of Qualified Practitioners (1991); Garrow, *supra* note 22, at 717; James Baron, *Group Requiring Abortion Study,* N.Y. Times, Feb. 15, 1995, at A1; Gottlieb, *supra* note 120; Joffe, Anderson, & Steinauer, *supra* note 303,

strong resistance on several fronts. Moving abortions back into hospitals, particularly teaching hospitals, would drain significant profits from the free-standing clinics, yet without doing so there will be fewer and fewer fully qualified abortionists. More importantly, the teaching physicians and the residents alike appear not to want to get involved.[361] Their resistance, along with Congressional pressure, forced the Council to back down, requiring only that teaching hospitals "not impede" residents who seek such training.[362] Again, we find doctors fashionably endorsing abortion but refusing to involve themselves in what they consider "dirty work."[363]

The 1996 decision by the Accreditation Council apparently did increase the opportunities for abortion training.[364] It did not result in most residency programs including such training, however. In 2002, Mayor Michael Bloomberg of New York City chose to become involved in the issue, signing an executive order requiring all public hospitals in the city to include abortion training for all ob-gyn residents.[365] One in seven medical residents nationally received training in New York City annually,[366] making the gesture significant. Only 22 of the 164 residents covered by the order opted out of the training on "religious or moral grounds."[367] Matthew Suh, a fourth-year medical student at State University of New York, suggested that more wanted to opt out, but were deterred by fear of negative repercussions should they make their views known publicly.[368] In any event, how many of those trained as a result of Mayor Bloomberg's order will become practicing abortionists is not clear.[369]

The general refusal of obstetrician/gynecologists to perform abortions explains why the overwhelming majority of abortions are performed in only a few of the approximately 2,300 clinics still open, generally by physicians who specialize in abortions.[370] Many of these physicians now commute between widely separated clinics, sometimes in different states hundreds of miles apart.[371] The few abortions performed by physicians who do not specialize in abortions are gener-

---

at 323–27; Ellen Lazarus, *The Crisis in Abortion Provision and Pro-Choice Medical Activism in the 1990s*, in 44 Soc. Sci. & Med. 1417 (1997); MacKay & MacKay, *supra* note 357, at 112–15; Rodgers & Rodgers, *supra* note 123, at 301–04; Marjorie Shaffer, *Council Mandates Abortion Training*, Med. Tribune Obstet. & Gynecology, Mar. 9, 1995, at 1; Vinceguerra, *supra* note 12, at 1177.

361. Sandra Boordman, *The Dearth of Abortion Doctors: Stigma, Low Pay and Lack of Personal Commitment Erode Ranks*, Wash. Post, Apr. 20, 1993, Health sec. 7; Diane Gianelli, *Abortion Training Mandate Sparks Furor*, Am. Med. News, Mar. 6, 1995, at 3; Rodgers & Rodgers, *supra* note 123, at 302.

362. Mary Castle & Enayat Hakim-Elahi, *Abortion Education for Residents*, 87 Obstet. & Gynecology 626 (1996); Denis Cavanagh, *Legal Abortion in America: Factors in the Dynamics of Change*, 2 Life Liberty & Fam. 309, 315–16 (1995); Diane Gianelli, *Legislators Seek to Bypass ACGME Abortion Training Rule*, Am. Med. News, July 17, 1995, at 1; Diane Gianelli, *Anti-Abortion Votes Stack up in House*, Am. Med. News, Aug. 7, 1995, at 3; Jerry Gray, *Senate Approves Cutback in Current Federal Budget*, N.Y. Times, July 22, 1995, at A7; Joffe, Anderson, & Steinauer, *supra* note 303, at 327; Rodgers & Rodgers, *supra* note 123, at 304.

Efforts to compel teaching hospitals to train all medical students in abortion techniques continue. *See* Leah Platt, *Making Choice Real*, Am. Prospect, Oct. 1, 2001, at A29; Lenore Skenazy, *Editorial: Making Abortion Safer: Bloomberg Takes a Stand, but Albany Sits on Its Hands*, N.Y. Daily News, Jan. 13, 2002, at 41.

363. Jonathan Imber, *Abortion Policy and Medical Practice*, Society, July–Aug. 1990, at 27, 32.

364. Villarosa, *supra* note 335.

365. Connolly, *supra* note 335; Villarosa, *supra* note 335.

366. Connolly, *supra* note 335.

367. *Id.*

368. *Id.*

369. Villarosa, *supra* note 335.

370. Imber, *supra* note 363, at 31–34.

371. *See, e.g.*, Cynthia Gorney, *Hodgson's Choice: A Long, Cold Abortion Fight*, Wash. Post, Nov. 29, 1989, at B1. *See also* Joffe, Anderson, & Steinauer, *supra* note 303, at 322.

ally for "medical" or "eugenic" indications, not for "personal" or "social" considerations.[372] As sociologist Jonathan Imber concluded, while "abortions have been technically routinized,…physicians have not generally accommodated them to their practice of medicine. In other words, abortion has not been morally routinized within the profession of medicine."[373] Imber has gone so far as to describe the private practice of medicine as the principle barrier to a more equitable provision of abortion services.[374] No wonder several "bioethicists" have argued that physicians who are conscientiously opposed to abortion cannot morally practice obstetrics or "maternal-fetal medicine" because of their unwillingness to provide "appropriate" care—that is, abortions.[375]

Further complicating the lives of would-be abortionists are the consequences of the advances in neonatal care. These advances have presented the Supreme Court with a problem it has consistently refused to acknowledge—the possibility of separating the claimed right of a woman to free her body of an unwanted pregnancy from a right in the woman to kill the unborn child. This problem comes to a head in the acute embarrassment of abortionists and their supporters over the "problem" of the "live-birth" abortion.[376]

Supporters of abortion rights have seldom openly admitted that their goal was not simply to rid a woman of an unwanted pregnancy, but was to prevent a live child from being born. Dr. Robert Crist testified in an early abortion case that "the abortion patient has a right not only to be rid of the growth, called a fetus, in her body, but also has a right to a dead fetus."[377] A federal judge even defined an "unsuccessful abortion" as one in which the fetus did not die.[378] Such assertions, somewhat startling when stated directly, actually are implicit in decisions such as *Planned Parenthood of Central Missouri v. Danforth*[379] in which the Supreme Court declared unconstitutional a state law that required the use of abortion techniques most likely to produce a live birth if the techniques did not increase the risks for the mother.

Current medical technology does not allow us to distinguish fully the right of a woman to rid her body of an unwanted pregnancy from the right to a dead fetus, at least absent an army of volunteer surrogate wombs.[380] We are close enough to that point, particularly in the later stages of pregnancy, however, that Laurence Tribe, currently the leading scholar of constitutional law, recognized the problem and favored separating the two claimed rights without his realizing how close we have come on the technical side already.[381] In distinguishing those rights, Tribe virtually

---

372. Imber, *supra* note 363, at 32–33.

373. *Id.*

374. Jonathan Imber, Abortion and the Private Practice of Medicine 114–15 (1986).

375. Jeffrey Blustein & Alan Fleischman, *The Pro-Life Maternal-Fetal Medicine Physician: A Problem of Integrity,* 25 Hastings Cntr. Rep. 22 (Jan.–Feb. 1995). *See also* John Thorp *et al., Integrity, Abortion, and the Pro-Life Perinatologist,* 25 Hastings Cntr. Rep. 27 (Jan.–Feb. 1989).

376. *See* Lader, *supra* note 209, at 164–66; Olasky, *supra* note 5, at 123–32 (1988); Dena Kleiman, *When Abortion Becomes Birth,* N.Y. Times, Feb. 15, 1984 at B1, col. 1. *See generally* Chapter 14, at notes 128–43.

377. *As quoted in* Planned Parenthood of Kansas City v. Ashcroft, 462 U.S. 476, 483 n.6 (1983). *See also* Williams, *supra* note 85, at 172–73; Anita Allen, *Tribe's Judicious Feminism* (book rev.), 44 Stan. L. Rev. 179, 201–02 (1992); Marie Ashe, *Zig-Zag Stitching and the Seamless Web: Thoughts on "Reproduction" and the Law,* 13 Nova L. Rev. 355, 371–79 (1989); Allen Hunter, *In the Wings: New Right Ideology and Organization,* 15 Radical Am. 113, 122 (1981); Steven Ross, *The Death of the Fetus,* 11 Phil. & Pub. Aff. 232 (1982).

378. Abele v. Markle, 351 F. Supp. 224, 232 (D. Conn. 1972) *vacated after* Roe v. Wade, 410 U.S. 915 (1973). *But see* Wynn v. Scott, 449 F. Supp. 1302, 1321 (N.D. Ill.) ("It never could be argued that she has a constitutionally protected right to kill the fetus."), *appeal dismissed sub nom.* Carey v. Wynn, 439 U.S. 8 (1978), *aff'd,* 599 F.2d 193 (7th Cir. 1979).

379. 428 U.S. 52 (1976).

380. Steinbock, *supra* note 38, at 83–84; Tribe, *supra* note 6, at 220–22.

381. Tribe, *supra* note 6, at 220–28. *See also* Daniel Callahan, Abortion: Law, Choice, and Morality 35 (1970); Colker, *supra* note 15, at 110; Condit, *supra* note 6, at 209–10; Robertson, *supra* note 38, at 29;

conceded that abortion kills a living human.[382] The care and quality with which Tribe considered this point is demonstrated by his varying approaches to the last question. Elsewhere in the book, Tribe denied being able to decide whether a fetus, at least in early stages of gestation, is a person.[383] Tribe at yet other points insisted that a fetus is not a "person."[384] In the first edition of his treatise on constitutional law, however, he concluded that the fetus is a form of human life.[385] (Does Tribe ever read what his research assistants write for him?) Tribe's pro-choice critics saw immediately that his argument about separating the right of a woman to be rid of an unwanted pregnancy from the right to a dead fetus gave the game away,[386] notwithstanding Tribe's ultimate willingness to accept the mother's right to kill the child even if it were to be removed without risk to its or the mother's health.[387]

Fear of "live-birth abortions" continues to shape how abortions are done. To avoid just such a "complication," abortionists introduced new procedure known as "dilation and extraction" ("D&X") to its friends and "partial birth abortion" to its critics.[388] D&X is a late-term technique, in use from 20 weeks of gestation onward—usually when the child clearly is "viable." The procedure involves removing the child by pulling its feet until the entire body is delivered except for its head. As the mother is not going through labor, the cervix does not fully dilate and traps the baby's head. At that point, scissors are used to open the skull and a catheter is used to extract brain tissue: other tissue can be used for possible use in experiments or for transplants. A Registered Nurse—Brenda Shafer—described such an abortion in graphic terms:

> It was the most horrible experience of my life.... The baby's body was moving. His little fingers were clasping together. He was kicking his feet. All the while his little head was

---

REAGAN, *supra* note 68, at 1573–75; RUBIN, *supra* note 34, at 137–38; Calhoun & Sexton, *supra* note 73, at 453–63; Nancy (Ann) Davis, *The Abortion Debate: The Search for Common Ground (Part 2)*, 103 ETHICS 731, 755–56 (1993); Benjamin Sendor, *Medical Responsibility for Fetal Survival under* Roe *and* Doe, 10 HARV. C.R.-C.L. L. REV. 444 (1975); Margaret Somerville, *Reflections on Canadian Abortion Law: Evacuation and Destruction—Two Separate Issues*, 31 U. TOR. L.J. 1 (1981); Judith Jarvis Thomson, *A Defense of Abortion*, 1 PHIL. & PUB. AFF. 47, 66 (1971). This apparently already is the law in England, although, as with other "restrictions" in England's law on abortions, little has been done to enforce this obligation. MASON, *supra* note 38, at 123–24, 165–70; R. Donald Mackay, *The Relationship between Abortion and Child Destruction in English Law*, 7 MED. L. 177 (1988); G. Wright, *The Legality of Abortion by Prostaglandin*, 1984 CRIM. L. REP. 347.

382. TRIBE, *supra* note 6, at 1, 8, 114, 116–20, 129, 135, 137–38, 229–30.

383. *Id.* at 116–19.

384. *Id.* at 121–28.

385. LAURENCE TRIBE, AMERICAN CONSTITUTIONAL LAW 1348–49 (1978).

386. *See, e.g.*, Allen, *supra* note 377, at 195–96, 201–02; Jean Braucher, *Tribal Conflict over Abortion* (book review), 25 GA. L. REV. 595, 595–96, 602 (1991); Davis, *supra* note 381, at 743–47; Mary Dunlap, *Mediating the Abortion Controversy: A Call for Moderation, or for One-Sided Etiquette While the Bombs Keep Flying?*, 30 WASH. L.J. 42, 57–59, 61 (1990).

387. TRIBE, *supra* note 6, at 223–25.

388. WARREN HERN, ABORTION PRACTICE 132–33, 137–42 (1984); Janet Gans Epner, Harry Jonas, & Daniel Seckinger, *Late-Term Abortion*, 280 JAMA 724, 726–29 (1998); Martin Haskell, *Dilation and Extraction for Late Second Trimester Abortion*, in SECOND TRIMESTER ABORTION: FROM EVERY ANGLE 27 (Gary Berger ed. 1992); Thomas Kerenyi, *Medical and Surgical Aspects of Elective Termination of Pregnancy*, in COMPLICATIONS OF PREGNANCY: MEDICAL, SURGICAL, GYNECOLOGICAL, PSYCHOLOGICAL, AND PERINATAL 822 (Sheldon Cherry & Irwin Merkatz eds. 4th ed. 1991); Lee Shulman *et al.*, *Dilation and Evacuation for Second-Trimester Genetic Pregnancy Termination*, 75 OBSTET. & GYNECOLOGY 1037 (1990). *See also Hearing on Partial-Birth Abortion*, H. Comm. On the Judiciary, 104th Cong., 1st Sess., June 15, 1995; Diane Gianelli, *Abortion Providers Share Inner Conflicts*, AM. MED. NEWS, July 12, 1993, at 3, 21–22. *See generally* AMERICAN MED. ASS'N, LATE-TERM ABORTION TERMINATION TECHNIQUES (1997).

still stuck inside. Dr. Haskell[389] took a pair of scissors and inserted them into the back of the baby's head. Then he opened the scissors up. Then he stuck a high-powered suction tune into the hole and sucked the baby's brains out. Next, Dr. Haskell delivered the baby's head, cut the umbilical cord and delivered the placenta.[390]

"The difference," Congressman Charles Canady observed, "between the partial birth abortion and homicide is a mere three inches."[391] Indeed, if the baby's brains were not extracted before full delivery, this procedure would produce a live birth through induced labor.[392] No wonder then that even activists who otherwise strongly support abortion rights have found such procedures to be more than repellent, to be "traumatic" as Dr. Warren Hern has described it.[393]

There is a certain irony in the tendency of the press and others to lionize Justice Blackmun for his late second thoughts concerning the death penalty for adults.[394] There are between several hundred and several thousand D&X procedures performed per year depending on whose count you accept.[395] Regardless of the correct number, the number for any given year is many times the number of adults executed on Blackmun's watch.[396]

Just as the development of the D&X technique alters the debate over third trimester ("late term") abortions, the emergence of a drug (RU-486) promises to permit abortions with less visible destruction of the fetus and apparently small (but real) risk to the mother. Such drugs—already approved for use in at least six countries (China, France, New Zealand, Sweden, Taiwan, and the United Kingdom)[397]—would again transform debate over first trimester abortions.[398]

---

389. Shafer is referring to Dr. Martin Haskell, the plaintiff in the successful suit to declare Ohio's prohibition of such procedures unconstitutional. Women's Medical Prof'l Corp. v. Voinovich, 130 F.3d 187 (6th Cir. 1997), *cert. denied,* 523 U.S. 1036 (1998). Dr. Haskell apparently provided the first public description of the procedure at a medical conference in 1992. *See* Timothy McDonald, *When Does a Fetus Become a Child in Need of an Advocate? Focusing on Fetal Pain,* 17 Children's Legal Rts. J., Spring 1997, at 12, 17 n.23.

390. *Affidavit of Brenda Shafer, R.N., read at a Hearing on the Partial-Birth Abortion Ban Act of 1995 before the Senate Judiciary Committee,* 104th Cong., 2nd Sess. (1995). For another graphic description, see *Stenberg v. Carhart,* 530 U.S. 914, 958–60 (2000) (Kennedy, J., dissenting).

391. John Yang, *House Votes to Outlaw Abortion Procedure,* Wash. Post, Nov. 2, 1995, at A1, A12.

392. *Statement of Pamela Smith,* in *Hearings on H.R. 1833 before the Senate Committee on the Judiciary,* 104th Cong., 1st Sess., 1995), at 45.

393. Hern, *supra* note 388, at 134.

394. Callins v. Collins, 501 U.S. 1141, 1144–45 (1994) (Blackmun, J., dissenting from denial of *certiorari*). For praise of Blackmun for this stand, see Malcolm Stewart, *Justice Blackmun's Capital Punishment Jurisprudence,* 26 Hastings Const'l L.Q. 271 (1998).

395. Epner, Jonas, & Seckinger, *supra* note 388, at 725.

396. *See* David Boldt, *Farewell to Justice Blackmun: He Blew It on the "Roe" Decision,* Phila. Inquirer, Apr. 10, 1994, at D7.

397. Elizabeth Crighton & Martina Ebert, *RU 486 and Abortion Practices in Europe: From Legalization to Access,* 24 Women & Politics no. 3, at 13 (2002); Lawrence Chung, *Tenfold Increase in Taiwan Abortions,* Straits Times (Singapore), Sept. 9, 2001, available at 2001 WL 26054953; Amy Porter, *International Reproductive Rights: The RU-486 Controversy,* 18 B.C. Int'l & Comp. L. Rev. 179, 180, 192, 196–98 (1995); Silverman, *supra* note 339, at 253–54; Lois Watson, *Controversial Abortion Pill in NZ,* The Press (Christchuch, NZ), Sept. 1, 2001, at 4.

398. *See, e.g.,* Benten v. Kessler, 505 U.S. 1084 (1992); Marcia Mobilia Boumil, Law, Ethics and Reproductive Choice 38–43 (1994); 2 Federal Abortion Politics, *supra* note 33, at 549–595, 727; Michael Klitsch, RU-486: The Science and the Politics (1990); Garrow, *supra* note 22, at 708–09, 713, 737; Hadley, *supra* note 34, at 117–24; Louis Lader, RU-486: The Pill that Could End the Abortion Wars and Why American Women Don't Have It (1991); Cheryl Meyer, The Wandering Uterus: Politics and the Reproductive Rights of Women 144–63 (1997); Renate Klein, Janice Raymond, & Lynette Dumble, RU-486—Misconceptions, Myths and Morals (1991); Robertson, *supra* note 38, at 63–66; Marie Bass, *Toward Coalition: The Reproductive Health Technologies Project,* in Abortion Wars, *supra* note 27,

Such drugs could alter the moral struggles of obstetricians and gynecologists over the realities of abortion while considerably reducing its profitability.[399]

Nearly everyone who has examined the question assumes that the arrival of RU-486 places control more firmly in the hands of women and makes abortion, for the first time, a truly private act. Law professor David Smolin is a notable exception.[400] Smolin argues that the use of RU-486 will force women to confront directly the products of the abortion, a prospect likely to be as unsettling to the woman as it has been to abortion providers. Journalist Gina Kolata, who (unlike Smolin) supports abortion rights, has also concluded that the use of RU-486 to make abortion "emotionally more difficult" as the woman would see "the fetus she aborted.[401] Furthermore, abortion by RU-486 is neither so simple nor so complication free as its enthusiasts insist—even if Kolata and Smolin are wrong in their analyses. First, RU-486 requires several visits (generally two, but possibly as many as four) to a medical facility and more time for medical care than existing abortion procedures.[402] In fact, several sympathetic commentators on RU-486

at 251; Daniel Callahan, *How Technology Is Reframing the Abortion Debate*, HASTINGS CTR. REP., no. 1, at 33 (Feb. 1986); Mary Ann Castle & Francine Coeytaux, *RU-486 Beyond the Controversy: Implications for Health Care Practice*, 49 J. AM. MED. WOMEN'S ASSOC. 156 (1994); Mary Ann Castle et al., *Listening and Learning from Women about Mifepristone*, 5 WOMEN'S HEALTH ISSUES 130 (1995); Alta Charo, *A Political History of RU-486*, in BIOMEDICAL POLITICS 43 (Kathi Hanna ed. 1991); Ellen Chesler, *Ru-486: We Need Prudence, Not Politics*, N.Y. TIMES, July 28, 1992, at A27; Denise Chicoine, *RU-486 in the United States and Great Britain: A Case Study in Gender Bias*, 16 B.C. INT'L & COMP. L. REV. 81 (1993); Annette Clark, *Abortion and the Pied Piper of Compromise*, 68 NYU L. REV. 265, 302–08 (1993); A.P. Cole & J.G. Duddington, *Legal and Ethical Implications of the RU486 Abortion Pill*, 110 LAW & JUST. 62 (1991); Leonard Cole, *The End of the Abortion Debate*, 138 U. PA. L. REV. 217 (1989); Rebecca Cook, *Antiprogestin Drugs: Medical and Legal Issues*, 42 MERCER L. REV. 971 (1991); David Grimes & Rebecca Cook, *Mifepristone (RU-486)—An Abortifacient to Prevent Abortion?*, 327 NEW ENG. J. MED. 1088 (1992); Karin Hansen, *Approval of RU-486 as a Postcoital Contraceptive*, 17 U. PUGET SOUND L. REV. 163 (1993); Kristina Holmgren, *Women's Evaluation of Three Early Abortion Methods*, 71 ACTA OBSTETRICA ET GYNECOLOGICA SCANDINAVICA 616 (1992); Carol Joffe, *Reactions to Medical Abortion among Providers of Surgical Abortion*, 31 FAM. PLAN. PERSP. 35 (1999); Gina Kolata, *New Use Is Found for Abortion Pill: Study Says RU486 Is Effective as Morning after Method*, N.Y. TIMES, Oct. 8, 1992, at A1; Susan MacKensie & Seonae Yao, *Pregnancy Interruption Using Mifepristone (RU-486)*, 42 J. NURSE-MIDWIFERY 86 (1997); Lauren Picker, *Abortion to Go?*, HARPER'S BAZAAR, Oct. 1994, at 246; Amy Porter, *International Reproductive Rights: The RU-486 Question*, 18 B.C. INT'L & COMP. L. REV. 179 (1995); Gwendolyn Prothro, *RU-486 Examined: Impact of a New Technology on an Old Controversy*, 30 U. MICH. J.L. REFORM 715 (1997); Sarah Ricks, *The New French Abortion Pill: The Moral Property of Women*, 1 YALE J.L. & FEMINISM 75 (1989); Allan Rosenfield, *Mifespristone (RU-486) in the United States: What Does the Future Hold?*, 328 NEW ENG. J. MED. 1560 (1993); Schaff, *supra* note 291, at 311–13; at A1; Silverman, *supra* note 339; Louise Silvestre et al., *Voluntary Interruption of Pregnancy with Mifepristone (RU-486) and a Prostaglandin Analogue: A Large-Scale French Experience*, 332 NEW ENG. J. MED. 645 (1990); Symposium, *Antiprotestin Drugs*, 20 LAW, MED., & HEALTH CARE 149 (No. 3, 1992); André Uhlmann et al., *RU-486*, SCI. AM., June 1990, at 42; David Van Diema, *But Will It End the Abortion Debate?*, TIME, June 14, 1993, at 54; Beverly Winikoff, *Acceptability of First-Trimester Medical Abortion*, in MODERN METHODS OF INDUCING ABORTION 145 (David Baird et al. eds. 1995); Renee Wyser-Pratte, *Protection of RU-486 as Contraception, Emergency Contraception and as an Abortifacient under the Law of Contraception*, 79 OR. L. REV. 1121 (2000).

Some researchers have begun tests that indicate that RU-486 could be used as a contraceptive, preventing ovulation; first trials suggest a 2% failure rate. Barbara Feder, *RU-486 Is Tested as Birth Control: Initial Trials Home in on Effective Dosage*, SAN JOSE MERCURY, Feb. 5, 2002, at 1G.

399. *See* Roger Rosenblatt et al., *Abortions in Rural Idaho: Physicians' Attitudes and Practices*, 85 AM. J. PUB. HEALTH 1423 (1995).

400. David Smolin, *Cultural and Technological Obstacles to the Mainstreaming of Abortion*, 13 ST.L. U. PUB. L. REV. 261, 277–81 (1993). *See also* Crighton & Ebert, *supra* note 397.

401. Gina Kolata, *France and China Allow Sale of a Drug for Early Abortion*, N.Y. TIMES, Sept. 24, 1988, at A1, A8. *See also* Hanna Rosin, *Pain, Penance and RU-486: Pill Isn't Likely to Change the Difficult Emotional Calculus of Abortion*, WASH. POST, Oct. 14, 2000, at A4.

402. HADLEY, *supra* note 38, at 119–20; MEYER, *supra* note 38, at 147–48; KLEIN, RAYMOND, & DUMBLE, *supra* note 398, at 25–29, 48–55; Christine Gorman, *The Chemistry of Abortion*, TIME, Oct. 6, 2000, at 44;

have concluded that its use decreases, rather than increases, a woman's privacy.[403] Second, RU-486, in fact, is not so safe, simple, or effective, as its advocates would have us believe.[404]

One study reported that "[a]lmost all the women (99 percent) reported at least one adverse event during the study period."[405] In Canada, clinical trials were halted the summer of 2001after a woman died while following the prescribed regimen.[406] On the other hand, the Food and Drug Administration (FDA) in the United States did not interfere with the distribution of the drugs when three women died in the United States after using the regimen, declaring only that the situation called for careful monitoring of the situation because "it is unknown whether there is a causal relationship between any of the events and the use of Mifeprex or misoprostol."[407] These problems have continued in the ensuing three years, without anyone in authority taking steps to remove the product from the market or to determine whether the medication really is causing the deaths.[408] Nor is the recourse to the process likely to be as morally simple as its proponents seem to think.[409]

In any event, widespread introduction of RU-486 was impeded by the revelation that Joseph Pike, the man selected by The Population Council to head up its project to manufacture and dis-

---

Marc Kaufman, *For Woman, Drug Was Right Choice,* Wash. Post, Sept. 29, 2000, at A18; Gina Kolata, *Use of Mispristone in Abortion Is a Three-Step Procedure,* N.Y. Times, Sept. 29, 2000, at A18.

403. Klein, Raymond, & Dumble, *supra* note 398, at 29.

404. George Grant, The Quick and the Dead: RU-486 and the New Chemical Warfare against Your Family (1991); Hadley, *supra* note 38, at 121; Klein, Raymond, & Dumble, *supra* note 398, at 31–47; Meyer, *supra* note 38, at 148–50; Claire Ahern, *Drug Approval in the United States and England: A Question of Medical Safety or Moral Persuasion?—The RU-486 Example,* 17 Suffolk Transnat'l L. Rev. 93 (1994); Etienne-Emile Baulieu & Thanh-Van Ngoc Nguyen, *The Biology and Clinical Uses of the Antisteroid Hormone RU486,* in Abortion, Medicine, and the Law, *supra* note 335, at 499; Debora Fliegelman, Comment, *The FDA and RU-486: Are Politics Compatible with the FDA's Mandate of Protecting Public Health?,* 66 Temple L. Rev. 143 (1993); Gorman, *supra* note 402; Horan, Cunningham, & Forsythe, *supra* note 6, at 140–43; Imber, *supra* note 363, at 33; Michael Klitsch, *Antiprogestins and the Abortion Controversy: A Progress Report,* 23 Fam. Plan. Persp. 275 (1991); Picker, *supra* note 398, at 246–47; Jean-Claude Pons et al., *Development after Exposure to Mifepristone in Early Pregnancy,* 338 The Lancet 763 (1991); Porter, *supra* note 398, at 193; Leslie Rubin, *Confronting a New Obstacle to Reproductive Choice: Encouraging the Development of RU-486 through Reform of Products Liability Law,* 18 NYU Rev. L. & Soc. Change 131 (1990); Alan Riding, *Frenchwoman's Death Tied to the Use of Abortion Pill,* N.Y. Times, Apr. 10, 1991, at A10; Gary Samuelson, *DES, RU-486, and Déjà Vu,* 2 J. Pharmacy & L. 56 (1993); Silverman, *supra* note 339, at 254–55; Silvestre et al., *supra* note 399, at 646; Uhlmann, *supra* note 399, at 47–48; Fawn Vrazo, *Abortion Pill Is No Magic Bullet, Americans Learning,* Phila. Inquirer, June 12, 1994, at C1; Fawn Vrazo, *In Europe, "Abortion Pill" Has Not Met Expectations,* Phila. Inquirer, Aug. 25, 1996, at A1; Dorothy Wickenden, *Drug of Choice: The Side Effects of RU-486,* New Rep., Nov. 26, 1990, at 24.

405. Irving Spitz et al., *Early Pregnancy Termination with Mifepristone and Misoprostol in the United States,* 338 N. Eng. J. Med. 1241, 1243–44 (1998).

406. Sarah Schmidt, *Women's Death Sparks Abortion Pill Debate: Head of Clinical Trial Says Victim Had Rare Virus Infection,* Nat'l Post, Sept. 17, 2001, at A13; Nancy Walsh, *Woman Dies of Sepsis in Abortion Pill Study: First Known Occurrence; Trial Suspended,* Ob. Gyn. News, Oct. 15, 2001, at 4.

407. Lisa Richwine, *Doctors Alerted to Death, Heart Attack in 2 Abortion-Drug Users,* Phila. Inquirer, Apr. 18, 2002, at A7 (the article discusses three deaths, one from a bacterial infection, one from a heart attack, and one from a burst ectopic pregnancy). The Population Council, a sponsor of RU-486 in United States, took the same line regarding Canadian death. Shari Roan, *Abortion Pill Is Safe in First Year of Use in U.S., Proponents Say,* L.A. Times, Oct. 1, 2001, at S3. An earlier death, in 1994, from a woman involved in trials of the drug, drew even less attention. Stan Guthrie, *Update: Doctors Slow to Prescribe Abortion Pill,* Christianity Today, Nov. 12, 2001, at 24.

408. Marc Kaufman, *Death after Abortion Pill Reignites Safety Debate: Opponents Renew Drive to Ban Drug Woman Took,* Wash. Post, Nov. 3, 2003, at A3; Mielikki Org, *Woman Dies after Taking Abortion Pill,* Phila. Inquirer, Sept. 23, 2003, at A12.

409. Rosenblatt, *supra* note 22, at 41.

tribute the drug, was an ex-lawyer who had been disbarred after his conviction for fraud.[410] Even as this episode was dragging out, a financial dispute among those who hope to profit from the sale of RU-486 nearly caused the entire project to unravel.[411] None of the problems connected with RU-486 fazed its enthusiastic supporters in the least.[412] Finally, on September 28, 2000, the FDA approved the drug for general use as an abortifacient.[413]

Because the drug had been in use in other countries, when the FDA finally got around to reviewing RU-486 (to be marketed under the name MifeprexTM), the agency used its "accelerated approval" process under which the usual clinical trials are more limited than normal.[414] The FDA's approval of RU-486 for use for the abortion of pregnancies of not more than seven weeks gestation prompted a great outpouring of press reports singing the praises of the drug.[415] The abortion pill itself even made the cover of *Time*.[416] Approval also prompted immediate calls for legislative or administrative intervention to ban or limit the drug, efforts that thus far have not succeeded.[417]

----

410. GARROW, *supra* note 22, at 728. *See* Gayle Kirshenbaum, *The Stealth Operation to Market RU-486,* GEORGE, April, 1997, at 112.

411. Tamar Lewin, *Dispute May Delay Abortion Drug in the U.S.,* N.Y. TIMES, Nov. 6, 1996, at A16. *See also* GARROW, *supra* note 22, at 732–33; HADLEY, *supra* note 38, at 121–24; MEYER, *supra* note 38, at 150–63; Tamala Edwards, *The Company in the Line of Fire,* TIME, Oct. 6, 2000, at 49; Emily MacFaquhar, *The Case of the Reluctant Drug Maker,* US NEWS & WORLD REP., Jan. 23, 1989, at 54.

412. *See, e.g.,* Jennifer Barrs, *The Pill II,* TAMPA TRIB., Baylife, Nov. 26, 2000, at 1; Sharon Lerner, *RU Pissed off Yet?,* VILLAGE VOICE, Sept. 5, 2000, at 42. Martha Minow spoke specifically about bringing RU-486 to market illegally if necessary when she suggested that lawyers were unethical if they would not cooperate in such illegal activity. Minow, *supra* note 220, at 723, 737–38, 745–47.

413. *FDA News Release: FDA Approves Mifepristone for the Termination of Early Pregnancy,* Sept. 28, 2000; *Letter from The Center for Drug Evaluation and Research to Susan Arnold of the Population Council,* Sept. 28, 2000. *See also* Marc Kaufman, *Abortion Pill Gets Approval from FDA,* WASH. POST, Sept. 29, 2000, at A1; Gina Kolata, *U.S. Approves Abortion Pill; Drug Offers More Privacy, and Could Reshape Debate,* N.Y. TIMES, Sept. 29, 2000, at A1; Rachel Zimmerman & Sarah Lueck, *FDA Approves the RU-486 Abortion Pill—Decision Puts Few Curbs upon Access, Expected to Begin within Month,* WALL ST. J., Sept. 29, 2000, at A3.

414. *Inside the Industry—Mifeprisone: Danco Says FDA Approval Not Fast-Tracked,* AM. POL. NETWORK-HEALTH , Mar. 29, 2001, at 11. *See also* Theresa Wagner, *A Rush to Market, Not a Remedy,* WASH. TIMES, Dec. 2, 2000, at A12. Advocates for the pill accused the FDA of delaying approval—delays attributed to the problems the financial and other problems that the sponsors had. Luaran Neergaard, *FDA Disputes Claims of Slower Approvals: Fewer Breakthrough Drugs Make Agency Seem More Cautious,* CHI. SUN-TIMES, Aug. 20, 2001, at 19.

415. *See, e.g.,* David Garrow, *Now, Another Pill Promises a Revolution,* N.Y. TIMES, Oct. 1, 2000, §4, at 3; Nancy Gibbs, *The Pill Arrives: The FDA Gives Women a New Abortion Choice. But Will They Choose It? And Will Doctors Be Willing to Take the Heat,* TIME, Oct. 6, 2000, at 40; Dirk Johnson, *Pill Seen as Offering Privacy to Women,* N.Y. TIMES, Sept. 30, 2000, at A3; Kaufman, *supra* note 413; Mark Kaufman, *For One Woman, Drug Was the Right Choice: Sense of Control, Not Having to Wait Cited as Benefits,* WASH. POST, Sept. 29, 2000, at A18; Gina Kolata, *Ready in 4 Weeks: Women Will Be Able to End Early Pregnancy in Her Own Home,* N.Y. TIMES, Sept. 29, 2000, at A1; Anna Quindlen, *RU-486 and the Right to Chose,* NEWSWEEK, Oct. 9, 2000, at 86; Robin Toner, *RU-486: Joy and Outrage,* N.Y. TIMES, Sept. 29, 2000, at A1; David Whitman & Stacey Schultz, *A Little Pill but a Big Dispute: Approval of the Abortion Drug Changes the Medicine and Politics of the Issue,* U.S. NEWS & WORLD REP., Oct. 9, 2000, at 18; Rachel Zimmerman & Sarah Lucek, *FDA Approves the RU-486 Abortion Pill: Decision Puts Few Curbs upon Access, Expected to Begin within Month,* WALL ST. J., Sept. 29, 2000, at A3; Aaron Zitner, *FDA Approves Use of Abortion Pill,* L.A. TIMES, Sept. 29, 2000, at A1.

416. TIME, Oct. 6, 2000. This was the second time; the abortion pill also made the cover of TIME on May 24, 1993.

417. William Claiborne, *Abortion Foes Want States to Curb RU-486,* WASH. POST, Oct. 5, 2000, at A1; Jeffrey Collins, *RU-486 Needs OK from Parent: Many States Agree Pill Is under Same Rules as Surgical Abortions,* DET. NEWS, Oct. 11, 2000, at 8A; Trisha Flynn, *RU-486 Could Prompt a Medical McCarthyism,* DEN. POST, Oct. 8, 2000, at K2; Gibbs, *supra* note 415, at 48–49; Marc Kaufman, *GOP Bid to Restrict Use of Abortion Pill Gains on Hill,* WASH. POST, Sept. 30, 2000, at A4; Jennifer Lenhart, *Va. Curbs RU-486 Use by Minors: Law Appears Strictest in Area on Abortion Pill,* WASH. POST, Oct. 10, 2000, at B1; Sarah Lucek, *Abortion Foes Face Tough Battle against RU-486 Drug,* WALL ST. J., Feb. 12, 2001, at A28; Susan Okie, *Pulling Abortion Pill Would Not Be*

So intense was the opposition to the abortion pill that the approval process had actually taken 20 years.[418] Furthermore, the FDA approved importing the abortion pill from China rather than having it manufactured in the United States where its production could be disrupted by protesters.[419] Danco Laboratories, LLC, the company that undertook to market the drug, shrouded its activities and its very location in secrecy in an effort to insulate itself from anti-abortion protestors.[420] Whether because of the secrecy or because of fear for the profitability of the company, Danco had difficulty raising capital until it was rescued by a $10,000,000 loan, made on advantageous terms by the David and Lucille Packard Foundation.[421] Despite all the hype, however, the approval of the abortion pill initially made little difference because few doctors were enthusiastic about using it.[422] Availability is further curtailed in many states by requirements that the pill be

---

*Difficult: FDA Rules on "Fast-Track" Drugs Could Allow Bush Administration Quick Removal,* WASH. POST, Jan. 28, 2001, at A5; Robert Pear, *Thompson Says He Will Order a New Review of Abortion Drug,* N.Y. TIMES, Jan. 20, 2001, at A17; Silverman, *supra* note 339, at 263–74; Toner, *supra* note 415; Stephanie Simon, *Abortion Rights Group Challenges Mich. Health Law,* L.A. TIMES, Feb. 27, 2001, at A12; Bill Walsh, *Abortion Drug May Get New Rules: Bill Requires More Training for Doctors,* TIMES-PICAYUNE (New Orleans), Feb. 7, 2001, at A9.

418. Lerner, *supra* note 412; Daniel Levy, *A Long Journey,* TIME, Oct. 6, 2000, at 42–43; Silverman, *supra* note 339, at 252–65; *20 Years from Lab to U.S. Consumer,* N.Y. TIMES, Sept. 29, 2000, at A18.

419. Philip Pan, *Chinese to Make RU-486 for U.S.,* WASH. POST, Oct. 12, 2000, at A1. *See also* Edwards, *supra* note 411.

420. Maria Alvarez, *Lab Tries to Keep Things under Wraps,* N.Y. POST, Sept. 29, 2000, at 5; Michael Daly, *A Pill & a Tale of Two Cities,* N.Y. DAILY NEWS, Oct. 1, 2000, at 18; Tamala Edwards, *The Company in the Line of Fire,* TIME, Oct. 9, 2000, at 49; Robert O'Harrow, jr., *Drug's U.S. Marketer Remains Elusive; Fearing Abortion Foes, Danco Keeps Location, Phone Number Secret,* WASH. POST, Oct. 12, 2000, at A18.

421. Edwards, *supra* note 420; O'Harrow, *supra* note 420. *See also* Sharon Berstein, *Persistence Brought Abortion Pill to U.S.: Two Feminist Activists Culled Nonprofit Organizations and Dedicated Individuals to Do the Work That No Pharmaceutical Company Was Willing to Tackle,* L.A. TIMES, Nov. 5, 2000, at A1.

422. Brian Basinger, *Abortion Legal, Unused: Doctors, Women Stay with Surgery,* FLA. TIMES-UNION (Jacksonville, FL), Sept. 23, 2001, at B1; Phil Galewitz, *RU-486 Demand Debated; Physicians Say Surgery Is Quicker,* SAN ANTONIO EXPRESS-NEWS, Sept. 30, 2000, at 3A; Denise Gellene, *RU-486 Abortion Pill Hasn't Caught on in U.S.,* L.A. TIMES, May 31, 2001, at A1; Denise Gellene & Barbara Brotman, *Abortion Pill Falling Short of Revolutionary,* CHI. TRIB., July 4, 2001, at 1; Guthrie, *supra* note 407; Carol Joffe, *Reactions to Medical Abortion among Providers of Surgical Abortion: An Early Snapshot,* 31 FAM. PLAN. PERSP. 35 (1999); Susan Kinzie, *The RU-486 Revolution,* NEWS & OBSERVER (Raleigh, NC), Oct. 4, 2001, at E1; Gina Kolata, *Wary Doctors Spurn New Abortion Pill: Some Doctors Insist that a Surgical Abortion Remains a Better Alternative than the New Pill,* N.Y. TIMES, Nov. 14, 2000, at F7; Raj Mishra, *Doctors Avoiding RU-486,* BOS. GLOBE, Dec. 5, 2000, at A1; Sabin Russell, *Survey Shows Low Demand for RU-486: Many Doctors Say They Fear Violent Protests if They Prescribe Controversial Drug,* S.F. CHRON., Sept. 24, 2001, at A1.

This reluctance came as a surprise to enthusiasts for RU-486. *See* Claude Aguillaume & Louise Tyrer, *Current Status and Future Projections on the Use of RU-486,* CONTEMP. OB/GYN, June 1995, at 23; Jill Burcum, *Abortion Pill's Use Limited Mostly to Clinics,* STAR TRIB. (Minneapolis-St. Paul), Mar. 10, 2002, at 1E; Silverman, *supra* note 339, at 254–55, 258–61; Beverly Winikoff *et al., Acceptability and Feasibility of Early Pregnancy Termination by Mifepristone-Misoprostol: Results of a Large Multicenter Trial in the United States,* 7 ARCHIVES FAM. MED. 360 (1998). Some commentators insist that this was because of fear of antiabortion protesters rather than because of concern over the effects of the abortion pill. Julia Duin, *Just 7% (sic) of U.S. Doctors Prescribe "Abortion Pill": Poll Cites Controversy, Low Demand,* WASH. TIMES, Sept. 25, 2001, at A3; Craig Garretson, *Abortion Foes: Pill Our New Target,* CIN. POST, Dec. 8, 2001, at 1A; Gibbs, *supra* note 415, at 41–42, 45–48; Henerson, *supra;* Rita Rubin, *RU-486: One Year after FDA Approval, the Controversial Abortion Pill Is Being Prescribed by Relatively Few Doctors,* USA TODAY, Oct. 1, 2001, at D5; Russell, *supra.* Yet, as Gina Kolata notes and as has been true in Europe as well, reluctance to use the abortion pill is just as strong among doctors who specialize in doing abortions as it is among doctors who do not do abortions. Kolata, *supra;* Jeremy Manier, *RU-486 Access a Personal Issue for Many Doctors,* CHI. TRIB., Nov. 20, 2000, at 1. *See also* Denise-Marie Balona, *Doctors Snub Abortion Pill: Women May Have to Go out of the County to Obtain the Controversial Prescription that Ends Pregnancies,* ORLANDO SENTINAL, Jan. 12, 2001, at 1; Suzanne Daley, *Europe Finds Abortion Pill Is No Magic Cure-All,* N.Y. TIMES, Oct. 5, 2000, at A3; Stephanie Erickson, *Drug to End Pregnancies Could Be Scarce in Lake County: Some Area Doctors Don't Feel Comfortable Prescribing the Controversial Drug, Now Approved by the FDA,* ORLANDO SENTINAL, Dec. 14, 2000, at 1; Andrea Garlin, *Pill's Presence*

administered solely by physicians or in clinics that are fully qualified under the law to do surgical abortions.[423] As a result, one year after the pill's approval, only one percent of general practice physicians offered Mifeprex (RU-486) abortions, and only six percent of gynecologists did likewise.[424] Abortion clinics remain almost the only source for such abortions.[425] Even clinics have been slow to begin using the pill, finding it to be troublesome and expensive.[426]

Mifeprex abortions more expensive than surgical abortions—costs range from $400 to $700 per abortion.[427] Women also have seemed less than enthusiastic what is involved in a Mifeprix abortion—not to mention the cost.[428] After all, a Mifeprex abortion requires at least three visits to the physician or clinic, as well as several days of pain or at least discomfort, compared to one visit for a surgical abortion and relatively short recovery period. As one director of clinic coun-

---

*Makes Little Impact: The Availability of Abortion Pill RU-486 Has Not Led to More Abortions in Europe,* PHILA. INQUIRER, Oct. 15, 2000, at A3; Robyn Soriano, *New Abortion Pill Arrives This Week: However, Only a Few Offices in the Orlando Area Will Have RU-486 Available Immediately,* ORLANDO SENTINAL, Nov. 29, 2000, at A5.

Doctors in New Zealand were similarly reluctant to use RU-486. Antony Paltridge, *Clarification on Abortion Drug Use Sought,* EVENING POST (Wellington, NZ), Mar. 1, 2002, at 15; Solana Pyne, *A Different Choice: With RU-486 on the Market, Abortion Providers Aim for More Access,* NEWSDAY, July 31, 2001, at C3.

423. *See, e.g.,* Bernard Harris & Tom Murse, *Clinic Seeks Abortion Pill for Use Here: Foes to Fight RU-486 Plan,* LANCASTER NEW ERA (Lancaster, PA), Feb. 28, 2002, at A1; Lerner, *supra* note 412; David Wenner, *Abortion Pill Still Not Available in Area: State Regulations, Lack of Interest by Patients Are among Reasons Cited,* PATRIOT-NEWS (Harrisburg, PA), Oct. 7, 2001, at B10. Similar restrictions are blamed for the limited recourse to RU-486 in New Zealand. *Abortion Committee Goes to Court over Pill,* THE DOMINION (Wellington, NZ), Feb. 27, 2002, at 8. On the other hand, the British government has relented on such restrictions, leading to an upsurge in "home abortions" there. Beezy Marsh, *The Home Abortion: Pro-Lifers Protest as 700 Women Try out Scheme that Allows Bedroom Terminations,* DAILY MAIL (London), Sept. 13, 2001, at 41.

424. Karen Auge, *RU-486 Has Scant Effect on Abortions: Kaiser Study Finds Drug Is Rarely Used,* DEN. POST, Sept. 24, 2001, at B1; Mitsi Crane, *Area Clinic Provides Abortion Pill,* COLUMBUS DISPATCH, Oct. 8, 2001, at 1C; Duin, *supra* note 422; Guthrie, *supra* note 407; Evan Henerson, *"Abortion Pill" Not Yet a Frequent Choice,* L.A. DAILY NEWS, Nov. 12, 2002, at L6; Gina Kolata, *Abortion Pill Slow to Win Users among Women and Their Doctors,* N.Y. TIMES, Sept. 25, 2002, at A1; Ruth Padawer, *Abortion Pill Seeing Little Use a Year after Approval,* THE RECORD (Bergen Cty., NJ), Sept. 25, 2001, at A3; Sara Rimensnyder, *Weak Choice,* REASON, Feb. 1, 2002, at 14; Rubin, *supra* note 422; Russell, *supra* note 422; Liz Szabo, *RU-486 Hasn't Changed Much in First Year: Not Many Dispense Pill that Was Expected to Revolutionize Abortion,* VIRGINIAN-PILOT & LEDGER-STAR (Norfolk, VA), Sept. 24, 2001, at B1.

425. Burcum, *supra* note 422; Crane, *supra* note 424; Rimensnyder, *supra* note 424.

426. Gellene & Brotman, *supra* note 422; Kolata, *supra* note 424.

427. Auge, *supra* note 424; Basinger, *supra* note 422; Henerson, *supra* note 424; Barrs, *supra* note 412; Crane, *supra* note 424; Padawer, *supra* note 424; Silverman, *supra* note 339, at 261–62; Szabo, *supra* note 424. *See also* Rachel Zimmerman, *Insurers Are Likely to Cover Abortion Pill—Obstacles Such as Training and Laws Mean Impact Won't Be Immediate,* WALL ST. J., Oct. 2, 2000, at A2. The cost of Mifeprex abortions in the United States is three to five times the cost of a similar abortion in France, largely because of the higher price charged by the manufacturer of the pill in the two countries. Gellene & Brotman, *supra* note 422.

428. Susan Aschoff, *Abortion Pill Isn't No. 1 Choice,* ST. PETERSBURG TIMES, Nov. 13, 2001, at 3D; Basinger, *supra* note 422; Daley, *supra* note 420; Duin, *supra* note 422; Stephen Fielding, Emme Edmunds, & Eric Schaff, *Having an Abortion Using Mifepristone and Home Misoprostol: A Qualitative Analysis of Women's Experience,* 34 FAM. PLAN. PERSP. 34 (2002). Phil Galewitz, *A Year Later, Abortion Pill Proves No Panacea,* PALM BEACH POST, Sept. 9, 2001, at 1F; Garlin, *supra* note 422; Gellene & Brotman, *supra* note 422; Gibbs, *supra* note 412, at 48; Kinzie, *supra* note 422; Padawer, *supra* note 424; Szabo, *supra* note 424; Wenner, *supra* note 423. *But see* Chung, *supra* note 397 (reporting on a large and growing illegal, self-help use on RU-486 by women in Taiwan); Zitner, *supra* note 412, at A1 (reporting that 70% of abortions in France are done with RU-486). The National Abortion Federation in the United States took to advertising that Mifeprix provided safe abortions without any reference to possible side effects. The Federation successfully fought off a suit by several pro-life activists. Julia Duin, *Ad for Abortion Pill Challenged: 3 Chicago Residents' Lawsuit Claims Deception by Group,* WASH. TIMES, Aug. 8, 2001, at A3; Julia Duin, *Pro-Life Group Drops Abortion Pill Ad Suit,* WASH. TIMES, Jan. 11, 2002, at A2; Emily Gest, *Abort Foes Irate over Ads for Pills,* N.Y. DAILY NEWS, July 19, 2001, at 23; Lindsey Tanner, *RU-486 Ad Draws Protests: Promotion Makes Procedure Seem Routine, Foes Say,* CHI. SUN-TIMES, July 19, 2001, at 4.

seling summed it up, "There are two things women are looking for when they call: They want it done as quickly as possible, and they don't want to know about it. RU-486, by its very nature, is the opposite of that."[429] And then there is the cost.

Recent reports indicate that a second drug regime (methotrexate taken with misoprostol) has emerged as an alternative to Mifeprex.[430] Reports suggest that this other ingestive technique would induce abortions with a 90 percent success rate, compared to 92 percent for RU-486 and more than 99 percent for intrusive abortions.[431] Furthermore, the recent reports regarding the effectiveness of standard oral contraceptives for use as "morning-after" pills itself could cause a great deal of the controversy regarding abortion simply to fade from sight.[432] Already debate has

---

429. Gallene & Brotman, *supra* note 422.

430. Barrs, *supra* note 412; Esteve Carbonell *et al., The Use of Misopostrol for Abortion at <9 Weeks' Gestation,* 2 EUR. J. CONTRACEPTION & REPROD. HEALTH CARE 181 (1997); Esteve Carbonell *et al., The Use of Misoprostrol for Termination of Early Pregnancy,* 55 CONTRACEPTION 165 (1997); Mitchell Creinin & Anne Burke, *Methotrexate and Misoprostrol for Early Abortion: A Multicenter Trial. Acceptability,* 54 CONTRACEPTION 19 (1996); Mitchell Creinin *et al., Acceptability of Medical Abortion with Methotrexate and Misoprostrol,* 52 CONTRACEPTION 41 (1995); Mitchell Creinin *et al., Conception Rates after Abortion with Methotrexate and Misopostrol,* 65 INT'L J. GYNECOLOGY & OBSTET. 183 (1999); Mitchell Creinin *et al., Methotrexate and Misoprostrol for Early Abortion: A Multicenter Trial. I. Safety and Efficacy,* 53 CONTRACEPTION 321 (1996); Mitchell Creinin *et al., Oral Methotrexate and Vaginal Misoprostol for Early Abortion,* 54 CONTRACEPTION 15 (1996); Richard Hausknecht, *Methotrexate and Misoprostol to Terminate Early Pregnancy,* 333 N. ENG. J. MED. 537 (1993); Ann Pastuszak *et al., Use of Miseprostol during Pregnancy and Möbius' Syndrome in Infants,* 38 NEW ENG. J. MED. 1881 (1998); Luis Sanchez-Ramos *et al., Labor Induction with Prostaglandin E1 Misoprostol Compared with Dinoprostone Vaginal Insert: A Randomized Trial,* 91 OBSTET. & GYNECOLOGY 401 (1998); Eric Schaff *et al., Combined Methotrexate and Misoprostal for Early Induced Abortion,* 4 ARCH. FAM. MED. 774 (1995); Eric Schaff *et al., Methotrexate and Misoprostal for Early Abortion,* 28 FAM. MED. 198 (1996); Eric Schaff *et al., Methotrexate and Misoprostal When Surgical Abortion Fails,* 87 OBSTET. & GYNECOLOGY 450 (1996). *See also* GARROW, *supra* note 22, at 733; MEYER, *supra* note 38, at 156–58; Jane Brody, *Abortion Method Using Two Drugs Gains in a Study,* N.Y. TIMES, Aug. 31, 1995, at A1; Mitchell Creinin *et al., Early Abortion: Surgical and Medical Options,* 20 CURRENT PROB. OBSTET., GYNECOLOGY & FERTILITY 6 (1997); Mitchell Creinin *et al., Misoprostol for Medical Evacuation of Early Pregnancy Failure,* 89 OBSTET. & GYNECOLOGY 768 (1997); *Drug Found to Be Good for Abortions,* N.Y. TIMES, Oct. 20, 1994, at A21; Karen Freeman, *Planned Parenthood to Participate in a Test of Abortion Drugs,* N.Y. TIMES, Sept. 12, 1996, at A17; David Grimes, *Medical Abortion in Early Pregnancy: A Review of the Evidence,* 89 OBSTET. & GYNECOLOGY 790 (1997); John Jain & Daniel Mishell, jr., *A Comparison of Intravaginal Misoprostol with Prostaglandin E, for Termination of Second Trimester Abortion,* 331 N. ENG. J. MED. 290 (1994); Michelle Lynn Lakony, *A Meaningful Choice: Two FDA Approved Drugs Are Combined to Perform Medical Abortions,* 18 WOMEN'S RTS. L. RPTR. 49 (1996); Lerner, *supra* note 412; Susan Okie, *RU-486 Joining Methotrexate in Reshaping Abortion,* WASH. POST, Oct. 13, 2000, at A3; Eric Schaff *et al., Methotrexate: A Single Agent for Early Abortion,* 42 J. REPRODUCTIVE MED. 56 (1997); Eric Schaff *et al., Vaginal Misoprostal Administered at Home after Mifeprestone (RU-486) for Abortion,* 44 J. FAM. PRACTICE 353 (1997); Beverly Winikoff, *Acceptability of Medical Abortion in Early Pregnancy,* 27 FAM. PLAN. PERSP. 142 (1995). Misoprostol is also used in connection with mifepristone (RU-486) to "complete" the abortion that mifepristone initiates. Spitz *et al., supra* note 405. Searle, a division of Pharmacia Corporation, manufactures misoprostol and warns on its label against administering the drug to pregnant women, creating a risk of liability on the part of a doctor or clinic that uses the drug to help induce an abortion. *See* Rachel Zimmerman, *Clash between Pharmacia and FDA May Hinder the Use of RU-486,* WALL ST. J., Oct. 18, 2000, at B1.

431. The success rate of 92% RU-486 used with misoprostol was for pregnancies of 7 weeks or less, falling off to 83% during the eighth week of pregnancy, and to 77% during the ninth week. E.V. Gouk *et al., Medical Termination of Pregnancy at 63 to 83 Days,* 106 BRIT. J. OBSTET. & GYNECOLOGY 535 (1999); Spitz *et al., supra* note 405, at 1242–43; Winikoff *et al., supra* note 422, at 361–62. On comparative success rates and attendant risks for intrusive abortions or the use of oral contraceptives as a "morning after pill," see Anna Glasier, *Safety of Emergency Contraception,* 53 J. AM. MED. WOMEN'S ASS'N Supp. II, at 219 (1998); John Westfall *et al., Manual Vaccum Aspiration for First-Trimester Abortion,* 7 ARCHIVES FAM. MED. 559, 560 (1998).

432. *See* Jane Brody, *Personal Health: Within Days of Unprotected Sex, Pills Can Prevent Pregnancy,* N.Y. TIMES, Sept. 23, 1997, at F9; Ellen Chesler, *New Options, New Politics,* AM. PROSPECT, Oct. 10, 2001, at A12; Marlene Cimons, *"Morning After" Use of Pill Found Safe by FDA Panel,* L.A. TIMES, June 29, 1996, at A1; Ko-

begun on whether such "emergency birth control" should be available without the prescription normally required for the purchase of oral contraceptives.[433] One of the major issues in this debate, at least in the United States, is whether such pills should be made available to adolescent women or only to adults.[434]

Considerable evidence continues to suggest that women prefer established intrusive (surgical) procedures to these ingestive procedures. When women were offered methotrexate and misoprostol free of charge at one clinic in Wichita, they overwhelming chose to pay for a surgical procedure instead.[435] Intrusive procedures, after all, require fewer visits, have a higher success rate, and result in less vaginal bleeding. So it might be too early to announce the end of abortion clinics—even if their profit margins and their numbers continue to decline. And just to make sure that RU-486 remains available, researchers have begun to examine the possibility of using the drug for other conditions, ranging from fibroids (non-cancerous growths in the uterus) to brain and other cancers to psychotic depression.[436]

---

lata, *supra* note 402; Josephine Marcotty, *Morning-after Pill Use Is Increasing: Option Remains Controversial, but More Women May Be Told about It,* Star-Trib. (Minneapolis-St. Paul), Feb. 11, 2002, at 1A; Marie McCullough, *"Morning-After" Pill Wins Approval from FDA,* Phila. Inquirer, Sept. 6, 1998, at E2; Liz Szabo, *Emergency Birth-Control Pills Gain in Popularity,* Virginian Pilot-Ledger Star (Norfolk, VA), Jan. 26, 2002, at A1; Toner, *supra* note 415; James Trussell *et al., Emergency Contraceptive Pills: A Simple Proposal to Reduce Unintended Pregnancies,* 24 Fam. Plan. Persp. 269 (1992). *See also* Glasier, *supra* note 431; S. Marie Harvey *et al., Women's Experience and Satisfaction with Emergency Contraception,* 31 Fam. Plan. Persp. 237 (1999); Allan Rosenfield, *Emergency Contraception: A Modality Whose Time Has Come,* 53 J. Am. Med. Women's Ass'n Supp. II, at 212 (1998); Amy Weintraub, *Back-up Plan: Women Need to Know about Emergency Contraception,* Charleston Gazette & Daily Mail, Mar. 22, 2002, at P5A Elizabeth Westley, *Emergency Contraception: A Global Overview,* 52 J. Am. Med. Women's Ass'n Supp. II, at 215 (1998); Wyser-Pratte, *supra* note 398.

433. Alwyn Cohall *et al., Inner-City Adolescent's Awareness of Emergency Contraception,* 53 J. Am. Med. Women's Ass'n Supp. II, at 258 (1998); Sandi Doughton, *Contraception after the Act: State Law Allows Wide Availability of Morning-after Pill, but That Hasn't Happened,* News Trib. (Tacoma, WA), Aug. 20, 2001, at SL1; Holly Edwards, *Birth Control Option Opened: "Morning after" Contraception Pill Can Be Dispensed without Prescription,* L.A. Daily News, Jan. 6, 2002, at N4; Charlotte Ellertson *et al., Should Emergency Contraceptive Pills Be Available without Prescription?,* 53 J. Am. Med. Women's Ass'n Supp. II, at 226 (1998); Jane Hutchings, *When the Morning after Is Sunday: Pharmacists Prescribing of Emergency Contraceptive Pills,* 53 J. Am. Med. Women's Ass'n Supp. II, at 230 (1998); Mark Kaufman, *Nonprescription Sale Sought for Contraceptive,* Wash. Post, Apr. 21, 2003, at A2; Gina Kolata, *A Contraceptive Clears a Hurdle to Wider Access,* N.Y. Times, Dec. 17, 2003, at A1; Melanie Latham, *Deregulation and Emergency Contraception: A Way Forward for Women's Healthcare?,* 9 Feminist Leg. Stud. 221 (2001); Sarah Lyall, *Britain Allows over-the-Counter Sales of Morning-after Pill,* N.Y. Times, Jan. 15, 2001, at A4; Clarence Page, *Time to Bring Morning-after Pill out of the Shadows,* Chi. Trib., Mar. 24, 2002, at 9; Lisa Rein & Craig Timberg, *Emergency Birth Control Approved: Bill Calls for Access without Prescription,* Wash. Post, Feb. 21, 2001, at A1; Tammie Smith, *Contraception Bill Fails in House Committee,* Richmond Times-Dispatch (Richmond, VA), Feb. 6, 2002, at A1; Laura Sessions Stepp, *Pill Ban Gives Birth to Protest: Vote on Contraceptive Galvanizes Campus,* Wash. Post, Apr. 24, 2003, at C1; Jeff Stryker, *"Emergency" Birth Control: Access Issues,* N.Y. Times, Mar. 11, 2003, at F5; Cheryl terHorst, *Emergencies Happen, and This Project Wants You to Be Prepared,* Chi. Trib., Mar. 20, 2002, at 3; Cheryl Wetzstein, *In an Emergency: Advocates Push Access to 72-Hour Birth Control,* Wash. Times, Jan. 2, 2002, at A2; Prithi Yelaja, *Big Rush for Morning-after Pill: Demand Exceeds Expectations of Pilot Program,* Toronto Star, Dec. 14, 2001, at F2; Kate Zernike, *Morning-after Pill Rising & It May Go over the Counter,* N.Y. Times, May 19, 2003, at A1. *See also* Tara Parker-Pope, *New Push Hopes to Increase Use of Morning-after Pill: Group Is Urging Advance Prescriptions,* Wall St. J., Mar. 1, 2002, at B1.

434. Page, *supra* note 34; Susan Reimer, *People Should Know about Emergency Contraception,* Balt. Sun, Feb. 26, 2002, at 1E; Wetzstein, *supra* note 433; Trish Wilson, *Preventing Unwanted Pregnancy, Abortions,* News & Observer (Raleigh, NC), Mar. 21, 2002, at A1.

435. Creinin & Burke, *supra* note 430.

436. Judy Foreman, *Health Sense: Overlooked Benefits of RU-486,* Bos. Globe, Oct. 10, 2000, at E1; Susan Okie, *Researchers Waiting to Plumb Medical Potential of RU-486,* Wash. Post, Nov. 2, 2000, at A3.

# Chapter 17

# Honesty Is Such a Lonely Word[1]

*When regard for truth has broken down or even slightly weakened all things will remain doubtful.*

—Sisela Bok[2]

By 1987, the United States was a society badly divided over abortion. Law professor, later Judge, John Noonan aptly described the divisions over abortion as "a plague for the parties and the party professionals."[3] The Supreme Court was firmly committed to one of the most open approaches to abortion found anywhere on the planet.[4] Only two years earlier, the Court in its 5-4 decision in *Thornburgh v. American College of Obstetricians*[5] reaffirmed *Roe,* holding unconstitutional such relatively innocuous statutory requirements as that a woman seeking abortion be informed of the medical risks attendant on having an abortion, of medical assistance available if she chose to have the baby, and of the father's financially responsibility for the child. The Court, in the same case, also held that simple reporting requirements to enable the state to gather accurate data on abortions were unconstitutional, as were requirements that the physician performing the abortion select the means most likely to produce, when possible, a live birth, and a requirement that a second physician be in attendance when a live birth was a possible outcome.[6] Less than three years earlier, the Court in a 6-3 decision in *City of Akron v. Akron Center for Reproductive Health, Inc.,*[7] had also struck down state statutes that required second and third trimester abortions to be performed in a hospital, that the physician performing an abortion inform women seeking an abortion of the state of development of the fetus and alternatives to abortion, that the woman thereafter wait 24 hours after receiving counseling, and that fetal remains be disposed of in a "humane and sanitary manner." In short, despite its insistence to the contrary,[8] the Court seemed intent on assuring that governments have no influence—other than the denying of financial assistance to poor women—on the decision to abort.[9] Republican President Ronald Reagan was strongly "pro-life" and Congress somewhat "pro-life," but so long as the Supreme Court held firm there was little they could do to impair the right of a woman to choose to have an abortion. In 1987, a vacancy opened on the Court with the retirement of Justice Lewis Powell, jr. Reagan

---

1. Billy Joel, *Honesty* (1978).
2. Sisela Bok, Lying 15 (1989).
3. John Noonan, jr., A Private Choice: Abortion in America in the Seventies 189–91 (1979).
4. *See* Chapter 14, at notes 421–76; Chapter 15, at notes 346–65.
5. 476 U.S. 747, 759–64 (1986).
6. *Id.* at 764–72.
7. 462 U.S. 416 (1983).
8. *Id.* at 444 n.33.
9. *Thornburgh,* 476 U.S. at 759; *City of Akron,* 462 U.S. at 443–44.

proposed appointing Judge Robert Bork to fill the vacancy. Powell had been "pro-choice." Bork, strongly "pro-life," could shift the Court towards overruling *Roe v. Wade.*

Reagan's appointment of Bork set off an immense battle over his confirmation. The fight raised many questions, but it clearly centered on Bork's views on abortion.[10] Bork's opponents mobilized strong support among law professors. Law professors are overwhelmingly liberal and supporters of the Democratic Party[11] and were all too willing to testify (or to sign petitions) declaring Bork—an outright conservative—outside the "legal mainstream."[12] Ricki Seidman of People for the American Way and William Taylor of the Leadership Conference on Civil Rights recruited 2,000 law professors to oppose Bork.[13] Because the professors largely work and speak only within a narrow community in which they can largely avoid anyone who disagrees with their political views, they are able to present their views as "the work of reason itself."[14] Opposi-

---

10. *See* Robert Bork, The Tempting of America: The Political Seduction of the Law (1998); Ethan Bronner, Battle for Justice: How the Bork Nomination Shook America (1988); Barbara Hinkinson Craig & David O'Brien, Abortion and American Politics 63–65, 181–85 (1993); Donald Critchlow, Intended Consequences: Birth Control, Abortion, and the Federal Government in Modern America 214–15, 219–20 (1999); 3 Federal Abortion Politics: A Documentary History 71–230 (Neal Devins & Wendy Watson eds. 1995); David Garrow, Liberty and Sexuality: The Right of Privacy and the Making of *Roe v. Wade* 668–71 (2nd ed. 1998); Mark Gitenstein, Matters of Principle: An Insider's Account of America's Rejection of Robert Bork's Nomination to the Supreme Court (1992); Edward Lazarus, Closed Chambers: The First Eyewitness Account of the Epic Struggles inside the Supreme Court 221–50 (1998); Stephen Markman, Judicial Selection: Merit, Ideology and Politics—The Reagan Years (1990); Patrick McGuigan & Dawn Weyrich, Ninth Justice: The Battle for Bork (1990); David O'Brien, Storm Center: The Supreme Court in American Politics 44, 111–15 (3rd ed. 1993); Michael Pertschuk & Wendy Schaetzel, The People Rising: The Campaign against the Bork Nomination (1989); Herman Schwartz, Packing the Courts 42, 60–62, 64–66, 84–85, 87–88, 100–01 (1988); Laurence Tribe, God Save This Honorable Court 98–99 (1985); Norman Vieira & Leonard Gross, Supreme Court Appointments: Judge Bork and the Politicization of Senate Confirmations (1998); Matthew Wetstein, Abortion Rates in the United States: The Influence of Opinion and Policy 27–39 (1996); Paul Dimond, *Common Sense About an Uncommon Rejection,* 15 Law & Soc. Inquiry 767 (1990); Ronald Dworkin, *The Bork Nomination,* 9 Cardozo L. Rev. 101 (1987); Joel Grossman, *Bork's Law and the Closing of the Judicial Mind,* 15 Law & Soc. Inquiry 805 (1991); Frank Guliuzza III, Daniel Reagan, & David Barrett, *Character, Competency, and Constitutionalism: Did the Bork Nomination Represent a Fundamental Shift in Confirmation Criteria?,* 75 Marq. L. Rev. 409 (1992); Morton Horwitz, *The Meaning of the Bork Nomination in American Constitutional History,* 50 U. Pitt. L. Rev. 655 (1989); Philip Kurland, *Bork: The Transformation of a Conservative Constitutionalist,* 9 Cardozo L. Rev. 127 (1987); Stephen Lubet, *Confirmation Ethics: President Reagan's Nominees to the United States Supreme Court,* 13 Harv. J.L. & Pub. Pol'y. 229 (1990); Madeline Morris, *The Grammar of Advice and Consent: Senate Confirmation of Supreme Court Nominees,* 38 Drake L. Rev. 863 (1989); Gene Nichol, jr., *Bork's Dilemma,* 76 Va. L. Rev. 337 (1990); L.A. Powe, jr., *From Bork to Souter,* 27 Willamette L. Rev. 781 (1991); Carol Rose, *Judicial Selection and the Mask of Nonpartisanship,* 84 Nw. U. L. Rev. 929 (1990); Jeffrey Segal, *Senate Confirmation of Supreme Court Justices: Partisan and Institutional Politics,* 49 J. Pol. 998 (1987); Martin Shapiro, *Interest Groups and Supreme Court Appointments,* 84 Nw. U. L. Rev. 935 (1990); Suzanna Sherry, *Original Sin,* 84 Nw. U. L. Rev. 1215 (1990).

11. Deborah Jones Merritt, *Research and Teaching on Law Faculties: An Empirical Exploration,* 73 Chi.-Kent L. Rev. 765, 780 n.54 (1998) (reporting that only 10% of law teachers are "conservative to some degree). Some 80% of law professors are registered Democrats, a figure that rises to 99.5% for women law professors—although 15% of all full-time working women are registered Republican. Neal Devins, *Bearing False Witness: The Clinton Impeachment and the Future of Academic Freedom,* 148 U. Pa. L. Rev. 165, 172 n.36 (1999).

12. Gitenstein, *supra* note 10, at 161; Robert Nagel, Judicial Power and American Character: Censoring Ourselves in an Anxious Age 27–43 (1994); Devins, *supra* note 11, at 175–77.

13. Gitenstein, *supra* note 10, at 160–61. *See also* Viera & Gross, *supra* note 10, at 143–44; Devins, *supra* note 11, at 175–76, 179–80.

14. Pierre Schlag, The Enchantment of Reason 38 (1998).

tion in the academy was not the reason Bork was in trouble, but it did provide convenient cover for those determined to defeat him.[15]

Bork was narrowly defeated. The man whom Reagan ultimately appointed to the seat, Judge Anthony Kennedy, also was "pro-life," although not so strongly as Bork.[16] Kennedy would be followed by other appointments (David Souter and Clarence Thomas) in whose selection and confirmation process the abortion controversy figured just as prominently.[17] Curiously, while Bork was attacked for not believing in "natural law" as a basis of constitutional law, the very same people attacked Thomas for believing in "natural law" as a basis of constitutional law.[18]

The changes in the Court, along with the likelihood of similar changes in the Court in the near future as other justices who strongly supported *Roe* passed from the scene, raised a real possibility that the Supreme Court would overrule *Roe* and return authority over abortion to the

---

15. Devins, *supra* note 11, at 180–82; George Kannar, *Citizenship and Scholarship*, 90 Colum. L. Rev. 2017, 2041 (1990); Mary McGrory, *The Supreme Sacrifice*, Wash. Post, Oct. 6, 1987, at A2; Cass Sunstein, *Professors and Politics*, 148 U. Pa. L. Rev. 191, 192 n.5 (1999).

16. Garrow, *supra* note 10, at 672–73; Gitenstein, *supra* note 10, at 317–18; Lazarus, *supra* note 10, at 251–55, 381; David Savage, Turning Right: The Making of the Rehnquist Court 175–77 (1992).

17. *See* David Brock, The Real Anita: The Untold Story (1993); John Danforth, Resurrection: The Confirmation of Clarence Thomas (1994); 3 Federal Abortion Politics, *supra* note 10, at 303–58; Lazarus, *supra* note 10, at 437–43, 449–58; Jane Mayer & Jill Abramson, Strange Justice: The Selling of Clarence Thomas (1994); Elizabeth Mensch & Alan Freeman, The Politics of Virtue: Is Abortion Debatable? 1 (1993); Nagel, *supra* note 12, at 20–27; Race-ing Justice, Engendering Power: Essays on Anita Hill, Clarence Thomas, and the Construction of Social Reality (Toni Morrison ed. 1992); Savage, *supra* note 16, at 349–58, 429; Christopher Smith, Critical Judicial Nominations and Political Change: The Impact of Clarence Thomas (1993); B. Drummond Ayres, jr., *Virginia Leader Apologizes for Remark on Inquiry*, N.Y. Times, July 8, 1991, at A6; Bob Cohn, *The "Soon-to-Be" Supreme*, Newsweek, Sept. 24, 1990, at 27; Ann Coulter, *Teddy and Howie Are Back: The Return of the Judicial Nomination Procedure, Part VI*, 7 St. L.U. J. Legal Commentary 61 (1991); Ronald Dworkin, *Justice for Clarence Thomas*, N.Y. Rev. Books, Nov. 7, 1991, at 41; David Garrow, *Justice Souter Emerges*, N.Y. Times, Sept. 25, 1994, § 6, at 6; Hays Gorey, *Supreme Confidence*, Time, Sept. 24, 1990, at 46; Jane Mayer & Jill Abramson, *The Surreal Anita Hill*, New Yorker, May 24, 1993, at 90; Dan Rosen, *The Sound of Silence*, 7 St. L.U. J. Legal Commentary 263 (1991); Paul Reidinger, *Mr. Souter Goes to Washington*, ABA J., Dec., 1990, at 48; Rodney Smith, *Justice Clarence Thomas: Doubt, Disappointment, Dismay, and Diminishing Hope*, 7 St. L.U. J. Legal Commentary 277, 279–80 (1991); Symposium, *Gender, Race, and the Politics of Supreme Court Appointments: The Impact of the Anita Hill/Clarence Thomas Hearings*, 65 S. Cal. L. Rev. 1279 (1992); Jeffrey Toobin, *The Burden of Clarence Thomas*, N.Y. Rev. Books, Sept. 27, 1993, at 38; Garry Wills, *The Selling of Clarence Thomas*, N.Y. Rev. Books, Feb. 2, 1995, at 36.

18. Terry Eastland, *Clarence Thomas: The Anti-Holmesian Legal Positivist*, 5 Benchmark No. 2, at 71 (1993); Russell Kirk, *Natural Law and the Constitution of the United States*, 69 Notre Dame L. Rev. 1035 (1994); Stephen Presser, *Should a Supreme Court Justice Apply Natural Law? Lessons from the Earliest Judges*, 5 Benchmark, No. 2, at 103 (1993); Frederick Schauer, *Constitutional Positivism*, 25 Conn. L. Rev. 797, 807–09 (1993); Laurence Tribe, *"Natural Law" and the Nominee*, N.Y. Times, July 15, 1991, at A-15. For the attacks against Judge Bork based on his failure to recognized the pertinence of "natural law," see Senate Comm. of the Judiciary, Nomination of Robert H. Bork to Be an Associate Justice of the U.S. Supreme Court, Sen. Exec. Rep. No. 7, 100th Cong., 1st Sess. 8–11, 30, 34 (1987). *See generally* Bennett Patterson, The Forgotten Ninth Amendment (1955); The Rights Retained by the People: The History and Meaning of the Ninth Amendment (Randy Barnett ed. 1989); Terry Brennan, *Natural Rights and the Constitution: The Original "Original Intent,"* 15 Harv. J.L. & Pub. Pol'y 965 (1992); Thomas Grey, *Do We Have an Unwritten Constitution?*, 27 Stan. L. Rev. 703 (1975); Helen Michael, *The Role of Natural Law in Early American Constitutionalism: Did the Founders Contemplate Judicial Enforcement of "Unwritten" Individual Rights?*, 69 N. Car. L. Rev. 421 (1991); O. John Rogge, *Unenumerated Rights*, 47 Cal. L. Rev. 787 (1959); Suzanna Sherry, *The Founders' Unwritten Constitution*, 54 U. Chi. L. Rev. 1127 (1987); Eulis Simien, jr., *It Is a Constitution We Are Expounding*, 18 Hastings Const'l L.Q. 67 (1990); Thomas Towe, *Natural Law and the Ninth Amendment*, 2 Pepp. L. Rev. 270 (1975); Eugene Van Loan III, *Natural Rights and the Ninth Amendment*, 48 B.U. L. Rev. 1 (1968).

legislatures of the several states. In a society as divided over abortion as the United States, the prospect of a major change in the only institution that had consistently championed abortion rights energized both supporters and opponents of abortion rights to press the Supreme Court for decisive action in their favor.[19] The Supreme Court's decisions in *Webster v. Reproductive Health Services*[20] and in *Planned Parenthood of Southeastern Pennsylvania v. Casey* [21] failed to calm the furor—although the latter did shift the attention somewhat away from the Court. Even though the abortion controversy apparently played a minor role in the election of William Clinton as President, abortion was prominent in the debates shaping the major party platforms shortly after *Casey* was decided.[22] Abortion again was a prominent issue in the 1996 presidential election.[23]

Ultimately, while a majority of the Court was consistently careful not to overrule *Roe,* by its decisions in *Webster* and *Casey,* the Court abandoned much of the field to state legislatures. At the same time, medical technology continued to develop in ways that impacted strongly on the issues that were so divisive to the nation. The combination of these unfolding events created a situation in which it could fairly be said that the *Roe* regime of abortion rights was unraveling. What the future held, however, remained far from clear.

# The Supreme Court Turns Away

*Doctrinal limbs too swiftly shaped, experience teaches, may prove unstable. The most prominent example in recent decades is* Roe v. Wade.

—Ruth Bader Ginsburg[24]

State legislatures across the United States never quit attempting to discover restrictions on abortion that would pass muster before the Supreme Court. One observer described the process as "a spaghetti against the wall approach"—if you throw enough spaghetti against the wall, some will stick.[25] Before 1989, few regulations had stuck to the wall erected by the Supreme

---

19. *See* CRAIG & O'BRIEN, *supra* note 10, at 197–242; 2 FEDERAL ABORTION POLITICS, *supra* note 10, at 353–63; GARROW, *supra* note 10, at 673–93; LAZARUS, *supra* note 10, at 245–48, 374–84; SUZANNE STAGGENBORG, THE PRO-CHOICE MOVEMENT: ORGANIZATION AND ACTIVISM IN THE ABORTION CONFLICT 134–36 (1991); TRIBE, *supra* note 10, at 16–17; CATHERINE WHITNEY, WHOSE LIFE? A BALANCED, COMPREHENSIVE VIEW OF ABORTION FROM ITS HISTORICAL CONTEXT TO THE CURRENT DEBATE 83–96 (1991). Some considered appointments to the lower levels of the federal bench to be almost as important. *See, e.g.,* Lynn Wardle, *Judicial Appointments to the Lower Federal Courts: The Ultimate Arbiters of the Abortion Doctrine,* in ABORTION AND THE CONSTITUTION: REVERSING *ROE V. WADE* THROUGH THE COURTS 215 (Dennis Horan, Edward Grant, & Paige Cunningham eds. 1987).

20. 492 U.S. 490 (1989).

21. 505 U.S. 833 (1992).

22. CRITCHLOW, *supra* note 10, at 220–21; MENSCH & FREEMAN, *supra* note 17, at 148; Alan Abramowitz, *It's Abortion, Stupid: Policy Voting in the 1992 Presidential Election,* 57 J. POL. 176 (1995); Mary Segers, *The Pro-Choice Movement Post-Casey,* in ABORTION POLITICS IN AMERICAN STATES 225 (Mary Segers & Timothy Byrnes eds. 1995). On the significance of the issue in the way people actually vote in presidential races, see Robert Blendon, John Benson, & Karen Donelan, *The Public and the Controversy over Abortion,* 270 JAMA 2871, 2873–75 (1993).

23. CRITCHLOW, *supra* note 10, at 223; Greg Adams, *Abortion: Evidence of an Issue Evolution,* 41 AM. J. POL. SCI. 718 (1997). Such debates continued in the 2000 election. *See, e.g.,* Cathleen Decker, *Dole Opposes Both Abortion and Battle about It in the GOP,* PHILA. INQUIRER, Apr. 11, 1999, at A6.

24. Ruth Bader Ginsburg, *Speaking in a Judicial Voice,* 67 NYU L. REV. 1185, 1198 (1992).

25. LAZARUS, *supra* note 10, at 375.

Court. The state of Missouri enacted a statute regulating abortion in 1986. The Missouri statute declared that "[t]he life of each human being begins at conception" and required that all state laws be interpreted to provide unborn children the same rights as other persons.[26] The statute also required that physicians test for viability if the physician suspected that the pregnancy was at least 20 weeks along, and also prescribed the specific findings that would determine whether a fetus was viable.[27] These provisions flew in the face of the decisions in *Thornburgh, City of Akron*, and other cases. The statute also banned the use of state facilities or state funds for providing abortions,[28] a proposition that less clearly contradicted the Supreme Court's prior caselaw on abortion. This grab bag of provisions was internally inconsistent, proclaiming that the unborn child was a "human being" from the moment of conception, but predicating its specific requirements on the lawfulness of abortion before viability.[29] Whether these provisions would pass constitutional muster came before the Supreme Court in *Webster v. Reproductive Health Services.*[30]

A group of abortion providers challenged the constitutionality of the Missouri statute immediately after the governor signed it into law. The federal District Court for the Western District of Missouri and the federal Court of Appeals for the Eighth Circuit declared the statute unconstitutional in major respects, including all of the provisions outlined above.[31] The granting of *certiorari* by the Supreme Court set off a massive campaign by both sides to influence the Court.[32] Justice Blackmun, alone of all the justices, reportedly read every note, every letter, and every postcard praising or castigating him for his authorship of *Roe*.[33] The most tangible reflection of the effort to influence the Court in *Webster* was the record 85 *amicus* briefs in filed the Supreme Court for that case.[34]

*Amicus* briefs, literally briefs filed by a "friend of the court" (*amicus curiae*), have been used for centuries in the common law. *Amicus* briefs are filed by persons who have special knowledge or expertise relating to a particular legal proceeding to which they were not a party. The friends of the court originally were expected to provide disinterested information to enable a court to make a more informed decision. Today, however, such briefs often are orchestrated by the parties themselves and serve as a device for evading the space limits on their briefs to the court. Even when not orchestrated, they are filed by corporations, governments, groups, or individuals who are anything but disinterested. In the 1995–96 term of the Supreme Court, nearly 90 percent of

---

26. Mo. Rev. Stat. § 1.205 (West 2000).

27. *Id.* at §§ 188.029, 188.210, 188.215.

28. *Id.* at §§ 188.210, 188.215,.

29. Lazarus, *supra* note 10, at 377–78; James Risen & Judy Thomas, Wrath of Angels: The American Abortion War 289–92 (1998).

30. 492 U.S. 490 (1989).

31. Reproductive Health Services v. Webster, 662 F. Supp. 407 (W.D. Mo. 1987), *aff'd*, 851 F.2d 1071 (8th Cir. 1988). *See also* Lazarus, *supra* note 10, at 330–31; Savage, *supra* note 16, at 227.

32. Lee Epstein & Joseph Kobylka, The Supreme Court and Legal Change: Abortion and the Death Penalty 269–73 (1992); Garrow, *supra* note 10, at 674; Lazarus, *supra* note 10, at 331, 373, 378–80, 396.

33. Lazarus, *supra* note 10, at 379. Lazarus and others have suggested that the effect of the criticism and the praise over the years was to change Blackmun from one of the more conservative members of the Court to one of its most liberal. *Id.* at 380 n.*. As John Jeffries put it, "Blackmun's turn to the left was…not intellectual but psychological." John Jeffries, jr., Justice Lewis F. Powell, Jr. 364–69 (1994).

34. The *amicus* briefs are listed in *Webster,* 490 U.S. at 497. *See generally* Symposium, *The* Webster Amicus Curiae *Briefs: Perspectives on the Abortion Controversy and the Role of the Supreme Court,* 15 Am. J.L. & Med. 155 (1989). That this was a record, see Alexander Wohl, *Friends with Agendas: Amicus Curiae Briefs May Be More Popular than Persuasive,* ABA J., Nov. 1996, at 46. The previous record was the 57 *amicus* briefs that the Court received in *Regents of the University of California v. Bakke,* 438 U.S. 265 (1978), a case involving race-based preferential admissions to a medical school. *See also* Garrow, *supra* note 10, at 674; Lazarus, *supra* note 10, at 373–74; Risen & Thomas, *supra* note 29, at 292. These authors, however, report the number *amicus* briefs in *Webster* as 78, instead of 83.

the cases decided had *amicus* briefs, compared with only 35 percent thirty years earlier.[35] The briefs might better be described as "friend of the parties" briefs than "friend of the court" briefs.[36]

The *amicus* briefs in *Webster* covered an enormous range of topics, from arcane points of constitutional law to discussions of current medical technology to dissertations on law and morality. Most such briefs did not provide the Court with new information or novel arguments to which the Court might otherwise not have access. Instead, as one commentator who clerked at the Supreme Court during the term in which *Webster* was argued, most of these briefs were "numbingly redundant."[37] The purpose of such a deluge of briefs was to bring yet more political pressure on the Court, similar to organized letter writing campaigns and mass demonstrations.

The extent of the politicization of legal processes relating to abortion is well illustrated by the several *amicus* briefs, including my own,[38] dealing with the history of abortion. The most widely noticed of the *amicus* briefs filed for *Webster* was one prepared on behalf of "281 historians"— the *Webster Historians' Brief*.[39] Eventually over 400 historians actually signed onto the *Webster Historians' Brief*; the smaller number represents the number who had indicated their support by the time the brief went to the printers.[40] Some 250 historians signed on to a reworking of that brief for the *Casey* case.[41]

At least in part because of the apparently strong consensus among historians expressed in the *Webster Historians' Brief,* that brief was one of the few that was written about in the popular press as well as in scholarly journals.[42] The press simply ignored the other historical briefs, several of which contradicted the story told in the *Historians' Brief*.[43] We have encountered the sub-

---

35. Wohl, *supra* note 34.

36. Michael Rustad, *With Friends Like These…,* THE RECORDER, Apr. 4, 1994, at 8. *See also* Samuel Krislov, *The Amicus Brief: From Friendship to Advocacy,* in ESSAYS ON THE AMERICAN CONSTITUTION 77 (Gottried Dietze ed. 1964); Luther Munford, *Listening to Friends of the Court: Amicus Briefs Are under Fire, but Because Court Decisions Affect the Community as a Whole, It Deserves to Have Its Voice Heard,* ABA J., Aug. 1998, at 128; Paul Smith, *The Sometimes Troubled Relationship between Courts and Their "Friends,"* 24 LITIGATION, no. 4, at 24 (Summer 1998).

37. LAZARUS, *supra* note 10, at 374.

38. *Amicus Brief of the Ass'n for Public Justice & the Value of Life Comm. supporting Appellants in* Webster v. Reproductive Health Services, *reprinted as* Joseph Dellapenna, *The Historical Case Against Abortion,* 13 CONTINUITY: A JOURNAL OF HISTORY 59 (1989), *and in* 2 DOCUMENTARY HISTORY OF THE LEGAL ASPECTS OF ABORTION IN THE UNITED STATES: WEBSTER V. REPRODUCTIVE HEALTH SERVICES 269 (Roy Mersky & Gary Hartman eds. 1990) ("DOCUMENTARY HISTORY"). I have also filed similar briefs in *Hodgson v. Minnesota,* 497 U.S. 417 (1990), and *Planned Parenthood of S.E. Pa. v. Casey,* 505 U.S. 833 (1992), as well as in cases before lower courts.

39. *Amicus Brief of 281 American Historians supporting Appellees in* Webster v. Reproductive Health Services [492 U.S. 490 (1989)] ("*Webster Historians' Brief*"), *reprinted at* 11 WOMEN'S RTS. L. RPTR. 163 (1989), and in 8 DOCUMENTARY HISTORY, *supra* note 38, at 107 (hereafter pagination will be given only to the version in the *Women's Rts. L. Rptr.*).

40. Sylvia Law, *Conversations between Historians and the Constitution,* 12 THE PUB. HISTORIAN 11, 11 (1990).

41. *Amicus Brief of 250 American Historians in support of Appellants in* Planned Parenthood of Southeastern Pennsylvania v. Casey, [505 U.S. 833 (1992)] ("*Casey Historians' Brief*").

42. *See, e.g.,* Ronald Dworkin, *The Great Abortion Case,* N.Y. REV. BOOKS, June 29, 1989, at 49, 50 n.10; Laura Flanders, *Abortion: The Usable Past,* THE NATION, Aug. 7, 1989, at 175; Tim Stafford, *The Abortion Wars,* CHRISTIANITY TODAY, Oct. 6, 1989, at 16; George Will, *Abortion Is a State Question,* WASH. POST, June 18, 1989, at C7, col. 1.

43. *See Amicus Brief of the Ass'n for Public Justice & the Value of Life Comm., supra* note 37; *Amicus Brief of Certain State Legislators supporting Appellants in* Webster v. Reproductive Health Services [492 U.S. 490 (1989)], *reprinted in* 8 DOCUMENTARY HISTORY, *supra* note 38, at 473; *Amicus Brief of the United States supporting Appellants in* Webster v. Reproductive Health Services [492 U.S. 490 (1989)], *reprinted in* 5 DOCUMENTARY HISTORY, *supra,* at 32.

stance of the two *Historians' Briefs* as the points covered in them were reached in this book's recounting of the history of abortion. What is noteworthy here is the process whereby so many historians joined those briefs, and what that process teaches about the reliability of those documents as evidence of the history of abortion and how those processes illustrate the political pressures brought on the Supreme Court between 1987 and 1992.

The Supreme Court itself was seriously interested in the historical question. Of all the *amicus* briefs filed for *Webster,* the only one that any Justice asked about during the oral argument of the case was an unnamed brief challenging the history on which *Roe* was based.[44] The question, from Justice Antonin Scalia, was directed to the attorney arguing for the unconstitutionality of the abortion statutes. He sought to dismiss arguments contrary to that of the *Historians' Brief* as mere advocacy documents and not as true history. Ironically, the *Historians' Brief* was the advocacy document. Although the authors of the *Historians' Brief* were at pains to present it as expressing the objective judgment of the relevant experts, they themselves later candidly admitted that they lied to the Court.

Given the recent history of *amicus* briefs, it is no surprise that the historians did not seek to appear before the Supreme Court merely as public spirited citizens urging the Court to protect a fundamental freedom, nor even as advocates committed to a cause. They set themselves up as experts who by their very numbers demanded that their views be accepted as the truth regarding the history of abortion. Sylvia Law, an attorney who was the primary author of the two *Historians' Briefs,* rationalized the inclusion of historians who had never studied the history of abortion, or even the history of Anglo-American legal or social systems generally, in these words: "What historians not working in this area will be saying is, 'This brief is consistent with what I know, and the people who are actively involved in writing it and who are cited in it are people whose work is known and respected.'"[45] At least one version of the letter that solicited historians to join the brief also closed with an appeal to historians as experts, rather than as advocates: "Your name will help demonstrate to the Court that abortion has always been a complex issue in our culture. It will also go far in rebutting some of the misleading and erroneous arguments from history that non-historians and pseudo-historians have brought to this issue."[46]

Despite the claims of professional expertise, however, many of the historians who signed onto the *Webster Historians' Brief* abandoned any pretense of objectivity to a point that undermines their claim to the very expertise that could have made their participation significant. The great majority of the historians who signed either of the two briefs had no expertise at all regarding the history of abortion because they simply had never studied the history in question. In fact, many historians subscribed to the *Webster Historians' Brief* (and later to the *Casey Historians' Brief*) when they were in serious disagreement with its contents. More than a few of the historians who signed the briefs did so without ever having seen the one she or he signed.

At a session of the Section on Legal History at the 1990 Annual Meeting of the Association of American Law Schools, Professor Joan Hollinger of the University of Detroit School of Law proudly recited recruiting 38 members of the History Department at the University of Michigan (in which her husband taught) to sign the *Webster Historians' Brief*—all without having read the

---

44. *Transcript of the Oral Arguments in* Webster v. Reproductive Health Services, N.Y. Times, April 27, 1989, at B12.

45. Quoted in Karen Winkler, *Historians Prepare Brief for Supreme Court Arguing U.S. Has Long Supported Abortion,* Chronicle of Higher Educ., Mar. 15, 1989, at A5, A10. *See also* Jane Larson & Clyde Spillenger, *"That's Not History": The Boundaries of Advocacy and Scholarship,* 12 Pub. Historian 33, 40–42 (1990) (the authors are attorneys who are listed with Sylvia Law as co-authors of the *Historians' Briefs*).

46. This quotation is from a copy in my files of a letter used to solicit historians for signing the brief. Professor James Mohr, who figured prominently in the preparation of the *Webster Historians' Brief* and also in this book, sent me the letter, apparently without realizing how revealing the letter is.

brief they were subscribing to, let alone any brief on the other side.[47] The *Historians Briefs* do not provide a rationale for how historians who have not examined the purported evidence can be cast as experts whose judgment should control the determination of an important issue of public debate. Professor Estelle Freedman, a respected historian at Stanford University and co-author of a major study of the history of sexual practices in America,[48] went further.

Freedman, in a thoughtful and revealing discussion of her role in preparing and propagating the *Webster Historians' Brief,* admitted that her own research demonstrated a story diametrically opposed to the brief's version of eighteenth- and nineteenth-century American social and cultural practices, particularly practices relating to abortion.[49] Still, when the drafters of the *Webster Historians' Brief* rejected her views, she signed the brief and publicly supported it. Her rationalization of this decision probably reveals more than she intended:

> As an historian, my primary difficulty with the earlier[50] versions of the brief had to do with the selective view of evidence, or lack of evidence, to show continuity rather than change, in order to support a particular legal argument about original intent. As a feminist, I have a similar difficulty with the necessity of shaping one's politics to support a particular legal argument about rights. Yet I realize that for the practical purposes of writing this brief, it was necessary to suspend certain critiques to make common cause and to use the legal and political grounds that are available to us. My purpose in raising these problems today is to ask that we keep the alternative frameworks within our historical and political perspective, even as we must narrow our arguments to fit the case at hand....My comments today are not meant to establish the correctness of historical over legal interpretation, but rather to suggest that legal briefs or testimony may differ from our historical works. As long as we accept that each type of argument has a place within a larger political discourse, I think we may safely continue to collaborate.[51]

Historian James Mohr's work was the most influential in creating the new orthodoxy of abortion history and thus on the content of the *Historians' Briefs.* His book, *Abortion in America,*[52] has become so central to disputes over the history of abortion that *amicus* briefs on both sides of *Webster* relied on Mohr's work to advance their own claims about the significance of that history.[53] Mohr was not even as explicit as Freedman regarding his reaction to the *Webster Historians' Brief.* He has, however, publicly admitted that he signed the brief despite disagreements with its content, going so far as to state that the brief was a political document, "not history, as I understand the craft."[54] Mohr has since voiced concern over the spreading confu-

---

47. Hollinger's remarks are recorded on *AALS 1990 Conference Audio Tape No. 163* (available from Recorded Resources Corporation of Millersville, Md.). The tape is on file in libraries at many law schools. On the imbalance among law the law professorate that could lead this woman to feel comfortable making such a statement in a public setting, see Charles Fried, *A Diverse Association of Law,* WASH. POST, Jan. 7, 2000, at A22; Norah Vincent, *Higher Ed: Where Are the Pro-Life Law Profs?,* VILLAGE VOICE, June 27, 2000, at 14.

48. JOHN D'EMILIO & ESTELLE FREEDMAN, INTIMATE MATTERS: A HISTORY OF SEXUALITY IN AMERICA 145–47 (1988).

49. Estelle Freedman, *Historical Interpretation and Legal Advocacy: Rethinking the Webster Amicus Brief,* 12 PUB. HISTORIAN 27, 28–30 (1990), reprinted in 21 CONF. GROUP IN WOMEN'S HISTORY NEWSLETTER 34 (1990).

50. In the context of her entire talk, and after comparing her objections to the final version of the brief as filed with the Court with her comments, it is clear that her problems were not resolved in the final version.

51. Freedman, *supra* note 49, at 32. *See* Ramesh Ponnuru, *Aborting History,* NAT. REV., Oct. 23, 1995, at 29, 31.

52. JAMES MOHR, ABORTION IN AMERICA: THE ORIGINS AND EVOLUTION OF NATIONAL POLICY, 1800–1900 (1978).

53. *See Amicus Brief of the United States, supra* note 43; *Webster Historians' Brief, supra* note 39.

54. James Mohr, *Historically-Based Legal Briefs: Observations of a Participant in the Webster Process,* 12 PUB. HISTORIAN 19, 25 (1990), reprinted in 21 CONF. GROUP ON WOMEN'S HISTORY NEWSLETTER 28 (1990).

sion of objectivity with neutrality even while he has as much as admitted that his posture of a disengaged scholar is a pose designed to maximize the effect of his work rather than the actual situation:

> In other words, I believed I was more useful as a disengaged scholar than as stated partisan, since I assumed all along that the implications of the tale I told in my book were pretty obvious. Perhaps the latter assumption, which may have been less obvious than I thought, allowed me the luxury of my position.[55]

Mohr did not sign the virtually identical *Casey Historians' Brief*, prepared by the same attorneys and presenting essentially the same arguments.[56] Yet Mohr has declined to discuss, both publicly and privately, why he did not sign the second brief. I know; I have asked him.[57] His proffered excuse for not signing—lack of time—hardly seems credible. One is left to surmise the real reasons.

Other historians also signed one or both briefs even though the briefs flatly contradicted the conclusions they themselves had reached in their own published research without publicly discussing their reasons for signing, and also without retracting their adherence to their earlier conclusions. These include Carl Degler and Linda Gordon. The presence of Degler, Freedman, Gordon, and Mohr perhaps justified the confidence that historians without any expertise might have felt in the arguments and conclusions in the two briefs. The team of attorneys (principally Sylvia Law, Jane Larson, and Clyde Spillenger) and historians (principally Estelle Freedman, Linda Gordon, and James Mohr) as a result produced a brief that has been described as

> an utter fraud, riddled with scholarly abuses and inaccurate conclusions. The historians mischaracterize sources. They misreport facts. They support claims with citations that have no relevance to those claims. They rip quotations out of context. They rely on discredited sources—even on sources that signatories to the brief have themselves discredited. They contradict sources on which they rely heavily and which signatories wrote, without a word of explanation or any retraction by those authors elsewhere. Sylvia A. Law, one of the lawyers who submitted the brief, later declared in a forum that "there is tension between truth-telling and advocacy." An examination of the brief suggests how the drafters resolved that tension.[58]

Such a posture of special pleading is often expected, yet still troubling, when indulged in by lawyers and other professional advocates.[59] One expects from historians at least an attempt at ob-

---

In addition to his speech to the American Historical Association, Mohr gave a similar speech as a panelist at an Annual Meeting of the Association of American Law Schools (AALS). Statement of James Mohr, Program of the Section on Legal History at the 1990 Association of American Law Schools Annual Meeting, *AALS 1990 Conference Audio Tape No. 162* (available from Recorded Resources Corporation of Millersville, Md.). The tape is on file in the libraries of many law schools. Much the same comment was made by Alfred Kelly regarding his "historical" brief in *Brown v. Board of Education. See* Alfred Kelly, *The School Desegregation Case,* in QUARRELS THAT HAVE SHAPED THE CONSTITUTION 243, 263 (John Garraty ed. 1962). *See also* Alfred Kelly, *Clio and the Court: An Illicit Love Affair,* 1965 SUP. CT. REV. 119, 156 ("The objective of the process is not objective truth, historical or otherwise, but advocacy.... The premises, the processes of inquiry, and the results are all radically different from those of a historian or a social scientist.").

55. Mohr, *supra* note 54, at 23–24.

56. Ronald Dworkin, one of our most prominent legal philosophers, stressed the significance of Mohr's signing the *Webster Historians' Brief* as substantiating the validity of its arguments, but did not notice that Mohr declined the sign the virtually identical *Casey Historians' Brief.* RONALD DWORKIN, LIFE'S DOMINION: AN ARGUMENT ABOUT ABORTION, EUTHANASIA, AND INDIVIDUAL FREEDOM 249 n.8 (1993).

57. Personal communication (by telephone) with the author.

58. Ponnuru, *supra* note 51, at 32. For Sylvia Law's concerns about her difficulties in choosing between truth-telling and advocacy, see the text *infra* at note 89.

59. *See* CHARLES MILLER, THE SUPREME COURT AND THE USES OF HISTORY 22–23, 25, 159–60 (1969); Donald Boyle, jr., Note, *Philosophy, History, and Judging,* 30 WM. & MARY L. REV. 181, 192–96 (1988); J. Peter

jectivity (even conceding the ultimate futility of such attempts), the absence of which debilitates both the legal and the historical enterprise.[60] Jane Larson and Clyde Spillenger hardly resolve these difficulties through their assertion that all discourse is necessarily political and that therefore the distinction between scholarship and distortion is an illusion.[61] One would hardly accept such a disclaimer as an adequate response from a judge who had accepted a bribe or who had a significant financial interest in the outcome of a case.[62] Such a posture is hardly less troubling when the advocate consciously distorts the evidence because of political commitment rather than for pecuniary gain. The increasingly pervasive skepticism toward the very idea of truth that their comments suggest smacks of the characteristic attitudes that gave rise to Nazi jurisprudence: equating law and politics, ridiculing the concept of judicial impartiality, and extolling the need for a "healthy prejudice" to generate "correct decisions."[63] After all, German courts had announced, five years before the Nazi's took power, that thereafter their guiding principle would be "Whatever benefits the people is right."[64] Or as Nazi academic Carl Schmitt would observe, "[a]ll law is situational law."[65] A modern adherent of "Critical Legal Studies," "Critical Feminism," or "Critical Race Theory" could not have said it more succinctly.[66]

---

Byrne, *Academic Freedom and Political Neutrality in Law Schools: An Essay on Structure and Ideology in Professional Education*, 43 J. LEGAL EDUC. 315, 322, 324 (1993); Harry Edwards, *The Growing Disjunction between Legal Education and the Legal Profession*, 91 MICH. L. REV. 34, 68–70 (1992); Steven Lubet, *Ethics and Theory Choice in Advocacy Education*, 44 J. LEGAL EDUC. 81 (1994).

60. Even James Mohr concedes as much. *See* Mohr, *supra* note 54, at 31. As Stanley Fish has noted, law (and, presumably, he would add history) as a discipline has its job to do and the tools to do the job, and objectivity in a conventional sense is one of the necessary tools. Stanley Fish, *Almost Pragmatism: Richard Posner's Jurisprudence* (book review), 57 U. CHI. L. REV. 1447, 1457–63, 1469–75 (1990). *See also* MENSCH & FREEMAN, *supra* note 17, at 108–09; Allan Hunt, *The Big Fear: Law Confronts Postmodernism*, 35 MCGILL L.J. 507, 532–33 (1990); Michiko Kakutani, *Is It Fiction? Is It Nonfiction? And Why Doesn't Anyone Care?: The Issues Joe McGinnis Has Stirred Up Go Way Beyond His Book*, N.Y. TIMES, July 27, 1993, at C13; William Leuchtenberg, *The Historian and the Public Realm*, 97 AM. HIST. REV. 1 (Feb. 1992); Jonathan D. Martin, Note, *Historians at the Gate: Accommodating Expert Historical Testimony in Federal Courts*, 78 NYU L. Rev. 1518 (2003); William Wiecek, *Clio as Hostage: The United States Supreme Court and the Uses of History*, 24 CAL. W.L. Rev. 227, 266–68 (1988).

61. Larson & Spillenger, *supra* note 45. While working on the *Webster Historians' Brief* in 1989, both were practicing law in Washington, D.C.; both are now law professors, Jane Larson at Northwestern, and Clyde Spillenger at Wisconsin.

62. Rebecca Eisenberg, *The Scholar as Advocate*, 43 J. LEGAL EDUC. 391, 397 (1993).

63. INGO MÜLLER, HITLER'S JUSTICE: THE COURTS OF THE THIRD REICH 73–75, 92, 219–20, 293–94 (Deborah Lucas Schneider trans. 1991). *See also* Office of the U.S. High Comm'r for Germany v. Migo, 13 Ct. App. Rep. 178, 182 (U.S. Ct. App. of the Allied High Comm'n for Germany 1951); WILLIAM SCHEUERMAN, BETWEEN NORM AND THE EXCEPTION: THE FRANKFURT SCHOOL AND THE RULE OF LAW (1994); IAN WARD, LAW, PHILOSOPHY AND NATIONAL SOCIALISM: HEIDEGGER, SCHMITT AND RADBRUCH IN CONTEXT (1992); Markus Dubber, *Judicial Positivism and Hitler's Injustice* (book rev.), 93 COLUM. L. REV. 1807 (1993); Graham Hughes, *Book Review* (of HITLER'S JUSTICE), 24 VAND. J. TRANSNAT'L L. 845, 856 (1991); Matthew Lippman, *Law, Lawyers, and Legality in the Third Reich: The Perversion of Principle and Professionalism*, 11 TEMPLE INT'L & COMP. L.J. 199, 208, 241–44 (1997); Matthew Lippman, *They Shoot Lawyers, Don't They? Law in the Third Reich and the Global Threat to the Independence of the Judiciary*, 23 CAL. W. INT'L L.J. 257, 261, 271 (1993); William Scheuerman, *After Legal Indeterminacy: Carl Schmitt and the National Socialist Legal Order, 1933–1936*, 19 CARDOZO L. REV. 1743 (1998); William Scheuerman, *Legal Indeterminacy and the Origins of Nazi Legal Thought: The Case of Carl Schmitt*, 17 HIST. POL. THOUGHT 571 (1996). *See also* MARY ANN GLENDON, A NATION UNDER LAWYERS: HOW THE CRISIS IN THE LEGAL PROFESSION IS TRANSFORMING AMERICAN SOCIETY (1994); Ruti Teitel, *Paradoxes in the Revolution of the Rule of Law*, 19 YALE J. INT'L L. 239 (1994); Richard Weisberg, *Legal Rhetoric under Stress: The Example of Vichy*, 12 CARDOZO L. REV. 1371 (1991).

64. MÜLLER, *supra* note 63, at 24.

65. CARL SCHMITT, POLITICAL THEOLOGY: FOUR CHAPTERS ON THE CONCEPT OF SOVEREIGNTY 13 (George Schwab trans. 1985, orig. pub. 1922).

66. *See* ANDREW ALTMAN, CRITICAL LEGAL STUDIES 91 (1990); MARK KELMAN, A GUIDE TO CRITICAL LEGAL STUDIES 258 (1987); Lawrence Solum, *On the Indeterminacy Crisis: Critiquing Critical Dogma*, 54 U.

HONESTY IS SUCH A LONELY WORD

Expectations of a reexamination by the Supreme Court of the history of abortion and its significance for competing constitutional claims were disappointed. All of the Justices except Justice Antonin Scalia apparently concluded that *Webster* could be decided without a thorough reexamination of *Roe*.[67] Scalia had pressed the question of the accuracy of the historical claims in *Roe* during the oral argument, but made no mention of this point in his opinion.[68] He contented himself with castigating the plurality for not confronting *Roe* directly rather than presenting a thorough review of the errors on which the earlier opinion had been based.[69]

The Court chose not to overrule *Roe* directly.[70] The unprecedented publication of Justice Thurgood Marshall's papers shortly after his death revealed the internal politics of the Court in the *Webster* decision.[71] Justice William Brennan's papers have also been published. The deliberations were difficult and intense, and the release of the opinions in *Webster* were, at the last minute, delayed several days.[72] In the end, no opinion commanded majority support for a direct challenge to *Roe*. Justice Sandra Day O'Connor shied away from overruling *Roe*, receiving vitriolic criticism of her position by Justice Scalia. The evasive plurality opinion sought to bridge the difference between O'Connor and Scalia. The several opinions in *Webster* severely undermined *Roe* without reaching a definitive conclusion about what should replace *Roe*.

A majority in Webster, through the opening parts of Chief Justice William Rehnquist's opinion, easily upheld the provisions declaring human life to begin at conception, requiring all statutes to be interpreted favorably to protecting such unborn lives, and banning the use of state resources for counseling or performing abortions. The Court read the first provision as a mere declaration of legislative opinion that had no operative effect on abortion decisions.[73] The other provisions were consistent with the cases decided on the basis of *Roe*.[74] Four Justices (Blackmun, Brennan, Marshall, and Stevens) dissented, voting to declare every provision of the Missouri statute unconstitutional, except for the ban on funding.[75]

Rehnquist went on to conclude, in a part of his opinion that was joined only by Justices Byron White and Anthony Kennedy that the state's interest in fetal life extended throughout pregnancy.[76] On this basis, the three voted to uphold the Missouri statute's viability testing requirements and to scrap the trimester framework that was the most innovative feature of the *Roe* decision.[77] The three, however, explicitly declined to "engage in a 'great issues' debate" on whether

---

CHI. L. REV. 462, 500 (1987); Alexander Somek, *From Kennedy to Balkin: Introducing Critical Legal Studies from a Continental Perspective*, 42 KAN. L. REV. 759, 762–66 (1994).

67. *See generally* James Bopp, jr., & Richard Coleson, *What Does* Webster *Mean?*, 138 U. PENNA. L. REV. 157 (1989); Christopher Crain, Note, *Judicial Restraint and the Non-Decision in* Webster v. Reproductive Health Services, 13 HARV. J.L. & PUB. POL'Y 263 (1989).

68. *See Transcript of the Oral Arguments in* Webster v. Reproductive Health Services, *supra* note 44.

69. *Webster*, 492 U.S. at 532–37 (Scalia, J., concurring).

70. LAZARUS, *supra* note 10, at 381–84, 395–96, 398.

71. David Johnston, *Marshall Papers Reveal Behind the Scenes:* Roe v. Wade *Was Nearly Overturned, an Account Says*, N.Y. TIMES, May 24, 1993, at A10.

72. GARROW, *supra* note 10, at 675–77; LAZARUS, *supra* note 10, at 391–96, 399–419. Several Justices revised their opinions down to the last minute, and Justices Anthony Kennedy and John Paul Stevens abandoned their efforts to write separate opinions.

73. *Webster*, 492 U.S. at 504–07 (plurality op., per Rehnquist, C.J.). Supporters of abortion rights still argue that such clauses are unconstitutional notwithstanding the decision in *Webster*. See, e.g., Mark Kende, *Michigan's Proposed Prenatal Protection Act: Undermining a Woman's Right to an Abortion*, 5 J. GENDER & L. 247, 249–57 (1996).

74. *Webster*, 492 U.S. at 507–13.

75. *Id.* at 537–60 (Blackmun, Brennan, & Marshall, JJ., dissenting), 560–72 (Stevens, J., dissenting).

76. *Id.* at 519 (plurality op., per Rehnquist, C.J.).

77. *Id.* at 513–21.

there is a right to privacy implicit in the constitution, and declined to reach the question of whether *Roe* should be overruled completely.[78]

Justice O'Connor wrote a separate opinion. Observers on both sides of the abortion controversy waited for her opinion with considerable concern, both because she was the first, and in 1989 still the only, woman on the Court,[79] and because she had dissented in *Thornburgh* and in *City of Akron* in opinions that had strongly criticized *Roe*.[80] Her *City of Akron* dissent had even described the *Roe* trimester scheme as "unworkable" and "on a collision course with itself."[81] Thus many expected her to join a majority to overrule *Roe*. In a sense she did, but only in a sense, for O'Connor flatly refused to consider whether it was necessary to overrule *Roe* in order to uphold all provisions of the Missouri law.[82] Instead, she interpreted *Roe* and its progeny as holding abortion statutes unconstitutional only if the statute in question created an "undue burden" on a woman's right to choose to abort.[83] On this basis, she found that even the provisions relating to testing for viability and protection of viable fetuses were constitutional[84]—effectively overruling *City of Akron* and *Thornburgh*, and, despite her protestations to the contrary, seriously undermining *Roe* itself. O'Connor's evasive approach to *Roe* infuriated Justice Scalia. He wrote a scathing critique of her opinion in his concurrence.[85] Scalia alone expressed a willingness to reexamine and overrule *Roe*,[86] predicting that the apparent indecisiveness of the *Webster* decision would invite even more public pressure on the Court.[87]

# Orchestrating Yet Another Abortion Case

*It's déjà vu all over again.*

—Yogi Berra[88]

The Supreme Court decision in *Webster* left uncertain just what standard should be applied to test the constitutionality of abortion statutes. Uncertainty served to increase the already shrill abortion debate in electoral politics to an even higher pitch.[89] Electoral politics, however,

---

78. *Id.* at 520–22.

79. *See, e.g.,* Susan Estrich & Kathleen Sullivan, *Abortion Politics: Writing for an Audience of One,* 138 U. Pa. L. Rev. 119, 150–54 (1989).

80. 476 U.S. at 814–33 (O'Connor, J., & Rehnquist, C.J., dissenting); 462 U.S. at 452–75 (O'Connor, White, & Rehnquist, JJ., dissenting). *See* Lazarus, *supra* note 10, at 381–84; Susan Halatyn, Comment, *Sandra Day O'Connor, Abortion, and Compromise for the Court,* 5 Tuoro L. Rev. 327 (1989).

81. 462 U.S. at 454, 458.

82. *Webster,* 492 U.S. at 525–26 (O'Connor, J., concurring). *See* Lazarus, *supra* note 10, at 391–94, 422–23. This is consistent with O'Connor's generally minimalist approach to judging cases; she generally avoids deciding a question if she can, a style that is becoming more widespread in American courts today. *See generally* Cass Sunstein, One Case at a Time: Judicial Minimalism on the Supreme Court (1999).

83. *Webster,* 492 U.S. at 530–31.

84. *Id.* at 525–31.

85. *Id.* at 532–37 (Scalia, J., concurring).

86. *Id.* at 534–37.

87. *Id.* at 535.

88. Paul Dickson, Baseball's Greatest Quotations 44 (1991). This, the most famous quotation attributed to the great Yogi, has been quoted (with approval) in at least two judicial opinions. United States v. Manni, 810 F.2d 80, 81 (8th Cir. 1987); Claussen v. Aetna Casualty & Sur. Co., 754 F. Supp. 1576, 1577 (S.D. Ga. 1990).

89. Craig & O'Brien, *supra* note 10, at 65–68, 242; Sarah Diamond, The Road to Dominion: Right Wing Movements and Political Power in the United States 175 (1995); Lazarus, *supra* note 10, at 419; Laurence Tribe, Abortion: The Clash of Absolutes 9, 194–96 (1990); R.W. Apple, jr., *An Altered Political*

produced decidedly mixed results.[90] Fear that they were about to lose the Court's protection particularly energized the supporters of abortion rights, while those opposed to abortion rights felt confident that it was only a matter of time before the Court would unequivocally decide in their favor. Two cases presented the Court with narrow issues relating to abortion; in each, the court upheld more stringent regulations than in the past.[91] The opinions in these cases revealed a badly divided Court that could not produce a majority opinion, but only a series of separate opinions with differently constituted majorities on different specific issues in the case.[92] The result was, as lawyer and former Supreme Court law clerk, Edward Lazarus put it, was a "blizzard of writings" resulting in "scrambled egg" opinions that was "utterly blinding" to lower courts, the bar, and the public.[93] Forgotten was Justice Robert Jackson's admonition that "We must do our utmost to make clear and easily understandable the reasons for deciding these cases as we do. Forthright observance of rights presupposes their forthright definition."[94]

In none of those cases did the Court address the broad question of revising or reversing *Roe.* One case presented that opportunity in a way that the Court could not avoid. The Pennsylvania legislature, long a stronghold of anti-abortion politics, enacted a statute very similar to the one declared unconstitutional in *Thornburgh,* a statute designed to test just how far a legislature could go after *Webster.*[95] The Planned Parenthood Federation of Southeastern Pennsylvania challenged the statute immediately, and the federal District Court for the Eastern District of Pennsylvania enjoined its enforcement.[96] The injunction was reversed in most respects by the federal Court of Appeals for the Third Circuit. The court reasoned that Justice Sandra Day O'Connor's "undue burden" test was the "controlling rule" in the Supreme Court's *Webster* decision although that test had commanded only one vote on the Court.[97] The case that many thought would spell the end of *Roe* was on its way to the Supreme Court.

The lawyers who had brought the appeal to the Third Circuit were stunned by the court's decision.[98] Kathryn Kolbert, an attorney for the American Civil Liberties Union who was the lead attorney in *Casey,* concluded that *Roe* would be overturned the next time it came before the Supreme Court. She nonetheless decided to expedite the appeal as much as possible, hoping that

---

*Climate Suddenly Surrounds Abortion,* N.Y. TIMES, Oct. 13, 1989, at A1; Rita Ciolli, *Taking Abortion Fight to the States,* NEWSDAY, Dec. 26, 1989, at 15; Don DeBenedictis, *Abortion Battles,* 76 ABA J. 30 (Feb. 1990); Ted Gest, *The Abortion Furor,* U.S. NEWS & WORLD REP., July 17, 1989, at 18; Nancy Gibbs, *Keep the Bums in,* TIME, Nov. 19, 1990, at 32; Kannar, *supra* note 15, at 2034–55; Rachael Pine & Sylvia Law, *Envisioning a Future for Reproductive Liberty: Strategies for Making the Rights Real,* 27 HARV. C.R.-C.L. L. REV. 407, 441–45 (1992); Julie Rovner, *Hill Faces Trench Warfare over Abortion Rights,* CONG. Q. WEEKLY REP. 2713 (Aug. 25, 1990); Kathleen Sullivan, *Foreword: The Justices of Rules and Standards,* 106 HARV. L. REV. 22, 107–11 (1992); Mark Tushnet, *Understanding the Supreme Court,* 1 MD. J. CONTEMP. LEGAL ISSUES 179, 183–88 (1990).

90. *See, e.g.,* LAZARUS, *supra* note 10, at 430; William Saletan, *Electoral Politics and Abortion: Narrowing the Message,* in ABORTION WARS: A HALF CENTURY OF STRUGGLE, 1950–2000, at 111 (Rickie Solinger ed. 1998).

91. Rust v. Sullivan, 500 U.S. 173 (1991); Hodgson v. Minnesota, 497 U.S. 417 (1990).

92. LAZARUS, *supra* note 10, at 430–36.

93. *Id.* at 435.

94. Douglas v. Jeanette, 319 U.S. 147, 182 (1943). *See also* RICHARD POSNER, FEDERAL COURTS: CHALLENGES AND REFORM 357–59 (1996).

95. *Pennsylvania Abortion Control Act,* 18 PA. CONS. STAT. ANN. §§ 3203–3220 (West 2000). *See* LAZARUS, *supra* note 10, at 460. *See generally* David Smolin, *Abortion Legislation after* Webster v. Reproductive Health Services*: Model Statutes and Commentaries,* 20 CUMBERLAND L. REV. 71 (1989).

96. Planned Parenthood of S.E. Pa. v. Casey, 736 F. Supp. 633 (E.D. Pa. 1990).

97. Planned Parenthood of S.E. Pa. v. Casey, 947 F.2d 682 (3rd Cir. 1991). For the grounds for concluding that Justice O'Connor's opinion in *Webster* was controlling, see LAZARUS, *supra* note 10, at 459–60; Bopp & Coleson, *supra* note 67, at 159–61; Estrich & Sullivan, *supra* note 79, at 132–50. *See also* Evan Caminker, *Why Must Inferior Courts Obey Superior Court Precedents?,* 46 STAN. L. REV. 817 (1994).

98. LAZARUS, *supra* note 10, at 460.

a clear repudiation of *Roe* a few months before the 1992 presidential election would generate such a political backlash that not only the White House, but also Congress and many state legislatures would be captured by "pro-choice" forces for the first time since before *Roe* was decided.[99] When she filed her petition for *certiorari*, two months before the deadline for filing, she asked the Supreme Court to address only one question: "Has the Supreme Court overruled *Roe v. Wade,* holding that a woman's right to choose abortion is a fundamental right protected by the United States Constitution?" If she was going to loose, she wanted to loose clearly and decisively. Anything less could not have the desired effect.

Despite efforts by Chief Justice Rehnquist to delay the argument of the case until after the elections, the Court scheduled the case for argument for April 22, 1992 — the last day for arguments in the spring of that year.[100] Once again there were mass demonstrations in the streets, an immense letter-writing campaign, and a well-orchestrated group of *amicus briefs*.[101] Both sides decided to reduce the total number of briefs, however, both in order to keep control over the contents of the briefs and to assure that the Justices (or their clerks) could actually read all the briefs. As a result, the Court received only 34 *amicus* briefs in the *Casey* case — 11 "pro-choice" and 23 "pro-life." Once again these included a brief I wrote to present the Court with a more accurate version of the relevant history than the Court had relied on in *Roe* and an answering brief signed by 250 historians.[102] The *Casey Historians Brief,* written by the same lawyers and signed by many of the same historians (but not by James Mohr),[103] exhibited the same cavalier attitude towards the truth as the earlier *Webster Historians' Brief*.[104]

Kathryn Kolbert stuck to her game plan, both in her brief and in her oral argument. She made a spirited defense of *Roe,* and challenged the Court either to overrule it completely or to reaffirm it in its full, original rigor. She practiced over and over again how not to let the justices' questions budge her from the extreme position she was staking out.[105] Pennsylvania's Attorney General, Ernest Preate, jr., pitched his argument precisely to Justice Sandra Day O'Connor (apparently the most undecided member of the Court) and her "undue burden" test. Preate, like Missouri Attorney General William Webster in the earlier case, left it to the Solicitor General of the United States (Kenneth Starr) to argue for overturning Roe.[106]

Arguments before the Supreme Court are usually a forensic spectacle. In recent decades, each side is allotted 30 minutes to argue the case. In *Casey,* as in *Webster,* the state's Attorney General took 20 minutes, leaving the other ten to the Solicitor General. Justices freely interrupt the advocates with pointed and sometimes hostile questions. Advocates, far from resenting these interruptions, welcome them as providing clear indications of what is on the questioner's mind. This in turn allows an advocate to clarify a point or convince a doubter — if not the questioner, then perhaps a less hostile Justice with the same question or doubt. The best advocates relish questions both as an opportunity to persuade, and as the best example of the intellectual combat at which they excel. What advocates fear most is silence from the Bench.

---

99. *Id.* at 460–62; Cynthia Gorney, *End of the Line for* Roe v. Wade, WASH. POST MAG., Feb. 23, 1992, at 6.
100. LAZARUS, *supra* note 10, at 462–63, 465.
101. *Id.* at 463–64, 481–82.
102. *Amicus Brief of the American Academy of Medical Ethics Supporting Respondents in* Webster v. Reproductive Health Services, *reprinted in* 2 DOCUMENTARY HISTORY, *supra* note 38, at 285; *Casey Historian's Brief, supra* note 41.
103. See the text *supra* at notes 52–57.
104. See the text *supra* at notes 45–66.
105. LAZARUS, *supra* note 10, at 464–65
106. *Id.*

When Kathryn Kolbert opened her all-or-nothing argument in *Casey*, she was met with a remarkable seven minutes of silence from the Bench.[107] At that point, an exasperated Justice Sandra Day O'Connor interrupted with the first question, asking Kolbert if she would ever get to the various specific issues that the Court had indicated that it wanted to hear argument on when the Court the writ granted *certiorari*. When Kolbert evaded this question, O'Connor, joined by Justice Anthony Kennedy, repeatedly pressed her to consider other possible lines of argument. Kennedy practically accused Kolbert of irresponsible lawyering.[108] Kolbert would not budge.

In contrast, Ernie Preate barely opened his mouth before Justice Harry Blackmun was on him, asking if Preate had even read *Roe*.[109] The other justices joined in with other questions and Preate spent practically his entire argument attempting to defend the Pennsylvania statute's requirement that a woman notify her husband of her intent to obtain an abortion.[110] When Kenneth Starr got up to argue, he was peppered with questions about the legal implications of abandoning the recognition of a constitutional right to an abortion.[111]

Court watchers were convinced that *Roe* was doomed.[112] Four Justices (Anthony Kennedy, William Rehnquist, Antonin Scalia, and Byron White) had voted to eviscerate *Roe* in the *Webster* case. Even if Justice David Souter's skeptical questioning of Preate and Starr suggested that he might not join them, no one doubted that Justice Clarence Thomas—who had not asked a single question during the argument—would. As it turned out, however, the Supreme Court was even more divided in *Planned Parenthood of Southeastern Pennsylvania v. Casey*[113] than in *Webster*.

Two days later, the justices discussed the case to get a feel for how it would come out and to decide who should write the majority opinion. Remarkably little was said by anyone. Edward Lazarus quotes an unnamed but "well-informed" law clerk as reporting that he "doubted that any Justice 'said more than two sentences.'"[114] (Relying exclusively on Lazarus is somewhat risky, not because he breached the confidentiality traditionally expected of court clerks,[115] but because

---

107. *Id.* at 465; *Transcript of the Oral Arguments in* Planned Parenthood of Southeastern Pennsylvania v. Casey, N.Y. Times, April 23, 1992, at B10, B11. David Garrow, however, concluded that the extended silences from the Bench were because the Justices found Kolbert's argument so impressive that they hesitated to interrupt. Garrow, *supra* note 10, at 690–91.

108. Lazarus, *supra* note 10, at 465; *Transcript of the Oral Arguments, supra* note 107, at B10.

109. Garrow, *supra* note 10, at 691; Lazarus, *supra* note 10, at 465; *Transcript of the Oral Arguments, supra* note 107, at B10.

110. Garrow, *supra* note 10, at 691; Lazarus, *supra* note 10, at 465–66; *Transcript of the Oral Arguments, supra* note 107, at B11.

111. Garrow, *supra* note 10, at 691–92; Lazarus, *supra* note 10, at 466; *Transcript of the Oral Arguments, supra* note 107, at B11.

112. Garrow, *supra* note 10, at 692; Lazarus, *supra* note 10, at 466.

113. 505 U.S. 833 (1992).

114. Lazarus, *supra* note 10, at 466–67.

115. Lazarus's book has been widely criticized for breaching the confidentiality of the Court even though several of the justices had made their papers public and law clerks have been interviewed by other historians. *See, e.g.,* Joan Biskopic, *Ex-Supreme Court Clerk's Book Breaks the Silence*, Wash. Post, Mar. 4, 1998, at A8; Adam Cohen, *Courting Controversy: A New Book by an Insider Claims Law Clerks Have Inordinate Influence over the Supreme Court*, Time, Mar. 30, 1998, at 31; Martha Davis, *Book Review:* Closed Chambers, 24 Thurgood Marshall L. Rev. 219 (1998); Christopher Drahozal, *The Arrogance of Certainty: Trust, Confidentiality, and the Supreme Court* (book rev.), 47 Kan. L. Rev. 121 (1998); David Garrow, *Dissenting Opinion: A Witness from Inside the Supreme Court Is Not Impressed* (book rev.), N.Y. Times, Apr. 19, 1998, at 26; Gideon Kanner, *"Holy Shit, I'm Going to Write the Law of the Land"* (book rev.), 1 Greenbag 2d 425 (1998); Sally Kenney, *Puppeteers or Agents? What Lazarus's* Closed Chambers *Adds to Our Understanding of Law Clerks at the U.S. Supreme Court*, 25 Law & Soc. Inquiry 185, 211–19 (2000); Alex Kozinski, *Conduct Unbecoming* (book rev.), 108 Yale L.J. 835 (1999); David O'Brien, *Breaching Confidences, Court Bashing, and Bureaucratic Justice*, 1 Jurist 19 (1998); Richard Painter, *Open Chamber?* (book rev.), 97 Mich. L. Rev. 1430 (1999); Carter Phillips, *Looking into Closed Chambers: A Lawyer View*, 42 Am. Law. 44 (May 1998); Gretchen Craft Rubin, *Betraying a*

reviewers of the book have noted a number of clear factual errors in his book.[116]) Reports vary, but apparently between five and seven justices wanted to uphold the entire statute, with four ready to overturn *Roe* explicitly.[117] On the basis of the tally, Rehnquist undertook to write a majority opinion.

Justice David Souter agonized long and hard over the case, resolving on the day before the conference to reaffirm *Roe,* largely on the basis of the doctrine of *stare decisis.*[118] Edward Lazarus claims that Souter was influenced by a memorandum from one of his law clerks in which the clerk had argued that overturning *Roe* simply because of new judicial appointments would undermine the institutional integrity of the Court.[119] Souter quickly recruited Sandra Day O'Connor. Together, they sought to enlist Anthony Kennedy (the only other justice who might respond favorably).[120] That Kennedy was open to the possibility was suggested by his decision to entrust research on this case to Michael Dorf, a law clerk in Kennedy's office who had been a protégé of Harvard law professor Laurence Tribe.[121] Tribe is one of the leading academic defenders of *Roe.*[122] Kennedy instructed Dorf to keep his work secret from Kennedy's other law clerks.

The three justices kept their project secret for more than a month while William Rehnquist worked on what he still thought was to be a majority opinion.[123] On June 3, a week after Rehnquist circulated his draft opinion, the three justices circulated a draft of their opinion to the surprise of the other justices and the consternation of Rehnquist, Antonin Scalia, and Clarence Thomas.[124] Personal visits by Rehnquist and Scalia failed to sway Kennedy to return to his former position.[125] Kennedy, however, was hardly sure of himself. On the morning of June 29, 1992,

---

*Trust,* WASH. POST, June 17, 1998, at A27; Kathleen Sullivan, *Behind the Crimson Curtain,* N.Y. REV. BOOKS, Oct. 8, 1998, at 15; Mark Tushnet, *Hype and History,* 1 JURIST 22 (1998). In one instance, Anthony Kronman, Dean of Yale Law School, wrote a laudatory "blurb" for the back cover of Lazarus' book describing it as "well-researched and wonderfully written," but then retracted it after coming under pressure from influential Yale alumni. Several newspapers criticized Kronman's reversal as well as the notion that the deliberations of the Court should be secret. *See, e.g.,* Tony Mauro, *Yale Dean Caught in Book Controversy: Head of Law School Apologizes for Blurb on High Court Tell-All,* U.S.A. TODAY, May 10, 19999, at 10A; Robert Reno, *Reno at Large: A Supreme Court Gag Order Quiets the Wrong Talkers,* NEWSDAY, May 12, 1999, at A51. Apparently, the *New York Times* did not consider this story to be news "fit to print." For a favorable review, see Erwin Chemerinsky, *Opening* Closed Chambers (book rev.), 108 YALE L.J. 1087 (1999).

116. *See* Garrow, *supra* note 115, at 27; Kenney, *supra* note 115, at 215–19; Kozinski, *supra* note 115, at 851–55; O'Brien, *supra* note 115, at 214–16.

117. LAZARUS, *supra* note 10, at 467; Garrow, *supra* note 17, at 36; Jeffrey Rosen, *The Agonizer,* NEW YORKER, Nov. 11, 1996, at 82.

118. Garrow, *supra* note 17, at 38.

119. LAZARUS, *supra* note 10, at 468–69. There is a certain irony in this claim as the major theme of Lazarus's book is that too much power was exercised at the Court by a "Cabal" of conservative law clerks, particularly over Justices O'Connor and Kennedy.

120. *Id.* at 469–72.

121. *Id.* at 470, 472. Dorf is now a law professor at Columbia University.

122. *See* Chapter 16, at notes 370–77.

123. LAZARUS, *supra* note 10, at 472–73.

124. *Id.* at 473–74, 478. Several published reports indicate that Justice Kennedy "flipped" his vote after the justices' conference on the case, changing from support for upholding the entire Pennsylvania statute and overruling *Roe* to the position espoused by the troika. JAMES SIMON, THE CENTER HOLDS: THE POWER STRUGGLE INSIDE THE REHNQUIST COURT 157, 163 (1995); Joan Biskupic, *When Court Is Split, Kennedy Rules,* WASH. POST, June 11, 1995, at A14; Max Boot, *How Judges Can Make Friends in Washington,* WALL ST. J., July 13, 1998, at A15; Terry Eastland, *The Tempting of Justice Kennedy,* AM. SPECTATOR, Feb. 1993, at 32, 33; Rowland Evans & Robert Novak, *Professor Sways Justice Kennedy,* CHI. SUN-TIMES, Sept. 4, 1992, at 33; Richard Reuben, *Man in the Middle,* CAL. LAW., Oct. 1992, at 35, 103; David Savage, *The Court's Rescue of Roe v. Wade,* L.A. TIMES, Dec. 13, 1992, at A1, A22. Another published report denies this. Linda Greenhouse, *Liberal Giants Inspire Three Centrist Justices,* N.Y. TIMES, Oct. 25, 1992, at 1.

125. LAZARUS, *supra* note 10, at 478.

while waiting to enter the courtroom for the reading of the opinions in *Casey,* Kennedy stood at the window in his chambers looking out at the protestors—pro and con—on the steps of the Court building and mused aloud, "Sometimes you don't know if you're Caesar about to cross the Rubicon or Captain Queeg cutting your own tow line."[126]

The result came as a complete surprise to the public when it was announced on June 29.[127] While those who had hoped to see *Roe* overruled were dismayed, Kathryn Kolbert hardly felt any better.[128] She had been denied the clear repudiation of *Roe* that she had sought, and with it any hope of making the 1992 election a referendum on abortion rights.

# The Supreme Court Abandons the Fight

*"Shut up," he explained.*

—Ring Lardner[129]

Justices Sandra Day O'Connor and David Souter's success in recruiting Justice Anthony Kennedy ensured another badly fractured decision, featuring no less than five opinions with the opinion of Kennedy, O'Connor, and Souter qualifying as the "plurality" opinion only because it set out the outcome of the case, even though Chief Justice William Rehnquist and Justice Antonin Scalia each wrote opinions that were joined by four Justices (Rehnquist and Scalia were joined by Justices Clarence Thomas and Byron White). As in *Webster,* the disagreements in *Casey* were expressed publicly and in highly personal terms.[130] About the only point on which all nine justices agreed was that the history and traditions of the American people determined whether the right to choose to abort is part of the rights reserved to the people by the Ninth Amendment,[131] part of the liberty protected against deprivation without due process guaranteed by the Fifth and Fourteenth Amendments,[132] or a necessary component of the equal protection of the

---

126. Terry Carter, *Crossing the Rubicon,* Cal. Law., Oct. 1992, at 39, 40. Apparently Kennedy's choice to have a reporter in the room—only the second time he had spoken to a reporter on the record since joining the Court four years earlier—and his remark were designed to leave a record for posterity. Frank Scaturro, *Abortion and the Supreme Court:* Roe, Casey, *the Myth of Stare Decisis, and the Court as a Political Insitution,* 3 Holy Cross J.L. & Pub. Pol'y 133, 134 (1998).

127. Garrow, *supra* note 10, at 692–93; Lazarus, *supra* note 10, at 482–83.

128. *Id.* at 483.

129. Ring Lardner, *The Young Immigrants,* in The Ring Lardner Reader 411, 426 (Maxell Geismar ed. 1963) ("'Are you lost, Daddy?,' I asked tenderly. 'Shut up,' he explained.").

130. Scaturro, *supra* note 124, at 134–35.

131. U.S. Const. Amend. IX. For such a claim, see Cyril Means, jr., *The Phoenix of Abortional Freedom: Is a Penumbral Right or Ninth-Amendment Right About to Arise from the Nineteenth-Century Legislative Ashes of a Fourteenth-Century Common-Law Liberty?,* 17 N.Y.L.F. 335 (1971) ("Means II"). *See generally* James Bopp, jr., & Richard Coleson, Webster *and the Future of Substantive Due Process,* 28 Duq. L. Rev. 271, 281–83 (1990).

132. U.S. Const. Amends. V, XIV. For such claims, see *Roe v. Wade,* 410 U.S. 113, 140 (1973); Linda Gordon, Woman's Body, Woman's Right: A Social History of Birth Control in America 52–53, 57 (1976); Mohr, *supra* note 52, at 128–29, 134–36, 144–45, 201, 208–11, 226, 229, 235–36; Means II, *supra* note 131, at 336, 351–54, 374–75, 409–10 n.175; Reva Siegel, *Reasoning from the Body: A Historical Perspective on Abortion Regulation and Questions of Equal Protection,* 44 Stan. L. Rev. 261, 278 (1992); Rickie Solinger, *"A Complete Disaster": Abortion and the Politics of Hospital Abortion Committees, 1950–1970,* 19 Feminist Stud. 241, 243 (1993); *Casey Historians' Brief, supra* note 41, at 5–6; *Webster Historians' Brief, supra* note 39, at 170. *See generally* Edward Grant & Paul Benjamin Linton, *Relief or Reproach?: Euthanasia Rights in the Wake of Measure 16,* 74 Ore. L. Rev. 449, 491–94 (1995).

laws protected by the Fifth and Fourteenth Amendments.[133] The joint plurality opinion of Justices Kennedy, O'Connor, and Souter were particularly eloquent in describing the reasons for such a commitment by the Court:

> Our Constitution is a covenant running from the first generation of Americans to us and then to future generations. It is a coherent succession. Each generation must learn anew that the Constitution's written terms embody ideas and aspirations that must survive more ages than one. We accept our responsibility not to retreat from interpreting the full meaning of the covenant in light of all our precedents. We invoke it again to define the freedom guaranteed by the Constitution's own promise, the promise of liberty.[134]

Such a statement calls to mind the words Justice Oliver Wendall Holmes, jr.:

> [W]hen we are dealing with words that are also a constituent act, like the Constitution of the United States, we must realize that they have called into life a being the development of which could not have been foreseen completely by the most gifted of its begetters. It was enough for them to realize or to hope that they had created an organism; it has taken a century and has cost their successors must sweat and blood to prove that they created a nation. The case before us must be considered in the light of our whole experience and not merely in that of what was said a hundred years ago.[135]

The four dissenters also endorsed the historical technique of constitutional interpretation.[136] Even Justices Harry Blackmun and John Paul Stevens in their partial concurrences seemed implicitly to endorse this approach in their insistence on the nineteenth-century roots of *Roe*.[137] Blackmun's choice to limit himself to nineteenth-century Supreme Court precedents perhaps is an implicit acknowledgment that the extended history he wrote for *Roe* was gravely flawed.

---

133. U.S. Const. Amend. XIV. For such claims, see Guido Calabresi, Ideals, Beliefs, Attitudes, and the Law: Private Law Perspectives on a Public Law Problem 87–114 (1985); Ruth Colker, Abortion & Dialogue — Pro-Choice, Pro-Life, and American Law 83–143 (1992); Catharine MacKinnon, Feminism Unmodified: Discourses on Life and Law 93–102 (1987); Paula Abrams, *The Tradition of Reproduction*, 37 Ariz. L. Rev. 453, 491–94 (1995); Anita Allen, *The Proposed Equal Protection Fix for Abortion Law: Reflections on Citizenship, Gender, and the Constitution*, 18 Harv. J.L. & Pub. Pol'y 419 (1995); Rhonda Copelon, *Losing the Negative Right of Privacy: Building Sexual and Reproductive Freedom*, 18 NYU Rev. L. & Soc. Change 15, 18, 40–50 (1990); Estrich & Sullivan, *supra* note 79, at 150–54; Ginsburg, *Some Thoughts on Autonomy and Equality in Relation to* Roe v. Wade, 63 N.C. L. Rev. 375 (1985); Sarah Harding, *Equality and Abortion: Legitimating Women's Experiences*, 3 Colum. J. Gender & L. 7, 31–41 (1992); Kenneth Karst, *Foreword: Equal Citizenship under the Fourteenth Amendment*, 91 Harv. L. Rev. 1, 53–59 (1977); Sylvia Law, *Rethinking Sex and the Constitution*, 132 U. Pa. L. Rev. 955, 1014–28 (1984); Frances Olsen, *Unraveling Compromise*, 103 Harv. L. Rev. 105, 117–35 (1989); Pine & Law, *supra* note 89, at 416–17; Donald Regan, *Rewriting* Roe v. Wade, 77 Mich. L. Rev. 1569, 1570, 1621–45 (1979); Siegel, *supra* note 132, at 347–81; Stephanie Wildman, *The Legislation of Sex Discrimination: A Critical Response to Supreme Court Jurisprudence*, 63 Or. L. Rev. 265 (1984). *But see generally* Peter Westen, *The Empty Idea of Equality*, 95 Harv. L. Rev. 537 (1982).

134. *Casey*, 505 U.S. at 901.

135. Missouri v. Holland, 252 U.S. 416, 433 (1920). *See also* Edmund Burke, Reflections on the Revolution in France 193 (Connor O'Brien ed. rev. ed. 1969); Oliver Wendall Holmes, jr., Collected Legal Papers 139 (1920); Theodore Blumoff, *The Third Best Choice: An Essay on Law and History*, 41 Hastings L.J. 537, 540 (1990); Robert Burt, *Precedent and Authority in Antonin Scalia's Jurisprudence*, 12 Cardozo L. Rev. 1685, 1696 (1991); Anthony Kronman, *Foreword: Legal Scholarship and Moral Education*, 90 Yale L.J. 955, 1064–66 (1981).

136. *Casey*, 505 U.S. at 952–53 (Rehnquist, C.J., partially dissenting, joined by Scalia, Thomas, & White, JJ.), 980 n.1, 984, 995–96 (Scalia, J., partially dissenting, joined by Rehnquist, C.J, & Thomas & White, JJ.). *See also* David Stern, *Tradition, Precedent, and Justice Scalia*, 12 Cardozo L. Rev. 1699, 1705 (1991).

137. *Casey*, 505 U.S. at 912 (Stevens, J., partially concurring), 926–27 (Blackmun, J., partially concurring).

Critics of this perspective have noted that no one would suggest looking to this country's tradition of racial discrimination to analyze the validity of race-based laws.[138] Such commentators, however, miss the point when they assume that the Court, in applying privacy analysis to reproductive regulation, is viewing reproductive rights through a lens distorted by historical gender discrimination.[139] Not only does the express text of the Fourteenth Amendment disavow the tradition of racial inequality that has bedeviled this country since its founding,[140] but the laws prohibiting abortion were not part of a scheme of gender discrimination.[141] Furthermore, even critics of the central importance of history and tradition find themselves appealing to history and tradition to buttress their arguments regarding abortion. Jurisprude Ronald Dworkin translated his understanding of our national history and traditions into "the Constitution's structure and history" which he then argued should be controlling relative to abortion in an article written while *Casey* was pending and which foreshadowed a good deal of the plurality opinion.[142]

Despite the justices' insistence on the controlling importance of history and traditions in determining the central points at issue in *Casey*, however, not one of the five opinions undertook to reexamine the relevant history and traditions. As law professor Jane Cohen has pointed out, the Court's majority (the three justices who jointly authored the plurality opinion and Justices Blackmun and Stevens in their concurrences) treated "*Roe v. Wade* as history's furthest horizon" rather than a recent incident in an historical tradition stretching across millennia.[143] The three justices who joined the plurality opinion simply contented themselves with standing on the rule of *stare decisis* without an original examination of the relevant history and tradition.[144]

Confining an examination of history to a review of Supreme Court precedents relating to abortion and to reproductive privacy generally is more than myopic.[145] It contradicts the rationale in the plurality opinion that "liberty" and "due process" in the Fourteenth Amendment express an historic covenant across generations. Furthermore, justifying precedents on abortion through precedents relating to other forms of reproductive freedom is remarkable in an opinion that insists that abortion is *sui generis*, raising issues that are utterly different from other forms of procreative freedom.[146] At best, such an approach had the effect of leaving the Court's imprimatur on the faulty history recited in *Roe*.[147] Yet the dissenting opinions also did not analyze that history, simply announcing that the history on which *Roe* was based was wrong.[148]

---

138. Abrams, *supra* note 133, at 455.

139. *Id.* at 490–500; Ronald Dworkin, *The Center Holds!*, N.Y. REV. OF BOOKS, Aug. 13, 1992, at 29, 32.

140. *Casey*, 505 U.S. at 980 n.1 (Scalia, J., dissenting, joined by Rehnquist, C.J., & Thomas & White, JJ.).

141. *See particularly* Chapter 8.

142. Ronald Dworkin, *Unenumerated Rights: Whether and How* Roe *Should be Overruled*, 59 U. CHI. L. REV. 381, 419, 426 (1992).

143. Jane Maslow Cohen, *A Jurisprudence of Doubt: Deliberative Autonomy and Abortion*, 3 COLUM. J. GENDER & LAW 175, 243 (1992).

144. *Casey*, 505 U.S. at 854–69 (Kennedy, O'Connor, & Souter, JJ., joint plurality op.). For an incisive critique of precisely this point, see David Smolin, *The Jurisprudence of Privacy in a Splintered Supreme Court*, 75 MARQ. L. REV. 975 (1992).

145. Such myopia is not justified simply because it is common. For other examples, see DONALD JUDGES, HARD CHOICES, LOST VOICES 130–37 (1993); Philip Heyman & Douglas Barzeley, *The Forest and the Trees:* Roe v. Wade *and Its Critics*, 53 B.U. L. REV. 765 (1973).

146. *Casey*, 505 U.S. at 857–58 (Kennedy, O'Connor, & Souter, JJ., joint plurality op.). *See also* Thornburgh v. American College of Obstet. & Gynecologists, 476 U.S. 747, 792 (White, J., dissenting); Harris v. McRae, 448 U.S. 297, 325 (1980); Roe v. Wade, 410 U.S. 113, 159 (1973).

147. *See, e.g.*, JUDGES, *supra* note 145, at 142.

148. *Casey*, 505 U.S. at 952–53 (Rehnquist, C.J., partially dissenting, joined by Scalia, Thomas, & White, JJ.). Remarkably, Chief Justice Rehnquist's sole reference to historical authority for his conclusion is to the work of James Mohr. MOHR, *supra* note 52. Mohr, of course, reached the opposite conclusion in his book from that of Rehnquist.

Such a cavalier approach to the relevant history smacks of Chief Justice Roger Taney's historiography that led to his warped reading of the word "persons" in *Dred Scott v. Sanford*.[149] It also smacks of the Court's implicit decision that "history has stopped" regarding race relations—that is, the willful refusal to acknowledge the "ongoing presence of the past" in contemporary civil rights cases.[150] The dissenter's failure to develop the true history of abortion—if that truly is their basis for deciding the constitutionality of abortion statutes—also at the very least leaves the Court vulnerable to charges of being "as political and crass as the executive and legislative arms of the government,"[151] relying on "[p]ower, not reason," as the "new currency of th[e] Court's decisionmaking."[152] Nor are these charges defused by knowledge the Court's failings arise from its tendency to read all relevant authorities as pointing toward a "harmonious conjunction" leading to the same result by ignoring nuances and possible contradictions in an effort to "avoid trouble or tension within the law's justificatory narratives" through "shallow or simplistic historical, economic, or philosophical analyses."[153] This judicial effort to "smooth out" has often proven to be in vain, while undermining the judicial candor that underlies the effectiveness of any institution that depends on respect for its reasoning as the basis of its authority.[154] As Professor Leonard Levy noted in a different context, "[t]wo centuries of [Supreme] Court history should bring us to understand what really is a notorious fact: the Court has flunked history."[155]

Once we move beyond the judicial consensus on the central importance of history and tradition to the constitutionality of abortion statutes in *Casey*, the Supreme Court split produced a rather unusual (and somewhat surprising) set of opinions.[156] Three justices, Anthony Kennedy, Sandra Day O'Connor, and David Souter, jointly wrote a "joint opinion" instead of producing the usual opinion authored by a single justice and supported by others.[157] The opinion is thus presented in a fashion only somewhat less striking than the opinion in *Cooper v. Aaron*[158] which had listed all nine justices as co-authors in a case involving the open defiance of the federal courts by Governor Orville Faubus of Arkansas. The last joint opinion before *Casey* was one joined by Justices Harry Blackmun, William Brennan, Thurgood Marshall, and Byron White in *Regents of the University California v. Bakke*, another civil rights case.[159] There is, of course, a great difference between a unanimous joint opinion (as in *Cooper*), and a joint opinion of only three justices. Some observers have speculated therefore that the real purpose of the joint opin-

---

149. 60 U.S. (19 How.) 393, 403–32 (1857). *See* Michael McConnell, *The Fourteenth Amendment: A Second American Revolution or the Logical Culmination of the Tradition?*, 25 Loy. L.A. L. Rev. 1159, 1173–74 (1992). Others have noted parallels between *Roe* and *Dred Scott*. *See, e.g.,* Charles Rice, *The Dred Scott Case of the Twentieth Century*, 10 Hous. L. Rev. 1059 (1973).

150. Cheryl Harris, *Whiteness as Property*, 106 Harv. L. Rev. 1715, 1761 (1993). *See also* Aviam Soifer, *On Being Overly Discrete and Insular: Involuntary Groups and the Anglo-American Judicial Tradition*, 48 Wash. & Lee L. Rev. 381 (1991).

151. Thomas Blumenthal, *Judicial Activism—The Politicization of the Right of Privacy*, 11 St. L.U. Pub. L. Rev. 329, 330 (1992). Blumenthal, however, went on to assure us that the Court erred in assuming that controlling traditions have anything to do with history. *Id.* at 348.

152. Payne v. Tennessee, 501 U.S. 808, 844 (1991) (Marshall, J., dissenting).

153. Richard Fallon, jr., *Non-Legal Theory in Judicial Decisionmaking*, 17 Harv. J.L. & Pub. Pol'y 87, 94–95 (1994); Richard Fallon, jr., *A Constitutional Coherence Theory of Constitutional Interpretation*, 100 Harv. L. Rev. 1189 (1987). *See also* Owen Fiss, *Objectivity and Interpretation*, 34 Stan. L. Rev. 739 (1982).

154. *See* David Shapiro, *Judicial Candor*, 100 Harv. L. Rev. 731 (1987).

155. Leonard Levy, Original Intent and the Framers' Constitution 300 (1988). *See also* Eric Foner, *The Supreme Court's Legal History*, 23 Rutgers L.J. 243, 247 (1992).

156. *See* Judges, *supra* note 145, at 225; John Robertson, Children of Choice: Freedom and the New Reproductive Technologies 60 (1994); Bopp & Coleson, *supra* note 143, at 273–79.

157. *Casey*, 505 U.S. at 843–911.

158. 358 U.S. 1 (1958).

159. 438 U.S. 265 (1978).

ion in *Casey* was to prevent any one justice from becoming the target of protestors in the fashion that Justice Blackmun was after *Roe*.[160]

The joint plurality opinion poses a number of interesting problems quite apart from its theories. Readers of the opinion are divided as to whether the opinion holds together as a coherent document. Kathleen Sullivan described the spectacle of the three justices taking turns reading their joint opinion from the bench as a "striking" suggestion of "three minds in one robe."[161] Her analysis suggests a "troika"—three horses pulling a sleigh, functioning together or not functioning at all. James Boyd White, on the other hand, described the opinion as exhibiting three "distinct voices," having "the feel of a text written by three minds, with some of the cracks and chinks still showing."[162] One student commentator has concluded that the opinion, judging from the themes of its argument, was primarily the work of Justice David Souter.[163]

The status of the joint plurality opinion is yet another problem, both because the case the three justices relied on—*Webster*—was itself a set of several opinions, dominated by a plurality rather than a majority opinion, and because the troika's opinion in *Casey* is, of course, only a plurality of the Court. Plurality opinions have become common over the past two decades, as if the justices have forgotten that they are members of a court charged to act as a collective body rather than a set of "individual monads that collide only in the process of voting."[164] The proliferation of plurality opinions leaves the development of the law in a, to say the least, troubled state.[165]

The troika's opinion became the opinion of the Court because two justices (Harry Blackmun and John Paul Stevens) concurred (in two separate opinions) in the part that declared unconstitutional the part of the Pennsylvania statute requiring a woman to notify her husband (with certain exceptions) before she could have an abortion,[166] while the other four justices (William Rehnquist, Antonin Scalia, Clarence Thomas, and Byron White) concurred (also in two separate opinions) in the part of the joint plurality opinion upholding the remainder of the Pennsylvania statute as constitutional.[167] Each of the four separate opinions dissented from the points they did not join. Furthermore, while the group of four dissenting justices signed both of the dissenting opinions, the two opinions actually stake out different positions on what is perhaps the most fundamental question: Does a woman have a constitutionally protected "liberty interest" in obtaining an abortion?[168] The opinion by Chief Justice Rehnquist said yes, although he would find

---

160. LAZARUS, *supra* note 10, at 478 n.\*.

161. Sullivan, *supra* note 89, at 119.

162. JAMES BOYD WHITE, ACTS OF HOPE: CREATING AUTHORITY IN LITERATURE, LAW, AND POLITICS 168–69 n.19 (1994).

163. David Koehler, Comment, *Justice Souter's "Keep-What-You-Want-and-Throw-Away-the-Rest" Interpretation of* Stare Decisis, 42 BUFF. L. REV. 859 (1994).

164. Henry Paul Monaghan, Stare Decisis *and Constitutional Adjudication*, 88 COLUM. L. REV. 723, 755 n.184 (1988). *See also* Paul Bator, *What Is Wrong with the Supreme Court*, 51 U. PITT. L. REV. 673, 686 (1990); Thomas Merrill, *Judicial Opinions as Binding Law and as Explanations for Judgments*, 15 CARDOZO L. REV. 43 (1993).

165. On the precedential effect of such splintered decisions, see *City of Lakewood v. Plain Dealer Publ. Co.*, 486 U.S. 750 (1988); *Vasquez v. Hillery*, 474 U.S. 254 (1986); *Marks v. United States*, 430 U.S. 188 (1977); *Gregg v. Georgia*, 428 U.S. 153 (1976). *See generally* John Davis & William Reynolds, *Juridical Cripples: Plurality Opinions in the Supreme Court*, 1974 DUKE L.J. 59; Linda Novak, Note, *The Precedential Value of Supreme Court Plurality Decisions*, 80 COLUM. L. REV. 756 (1980); William Peterson, Note, *Splintered Decisions, Implicit Reversals and Lower Federal Courts:* Planned Parenthood v. Casey, 1992 BYU L. REV. 289.

166. *Casey*, 505 U.S. at 911–22 (Stevens, J., partially concurring), 922–43 (Blackmun, J., partially concurring).

167. *Id.* at 944–79 (Rehnquist, C.J., partially dissenting, joined by Scalia, Thomas, & White, JJ.), 979–1002 (Scalia, J., partially dissenting, joined by Rehnquist, C.J., & Thomas & White, JJ.).

168. *See generally* Rodney Blackman, *Spinning, Squirreling, Shelling, Stiletting and Other Strategies of the Supremes*, 35 ARIZ. L. REV. 503, 518 (1993).

a compelling state interest in protecting the fetus virtually from the moment of conception.[169] The opinion written by Justice Scalia denies that women have any such constitutionally protected interest.[170]

The importance of the joint plurality opinion is unfortunate as even a casual reading discloses its utter intellectual incoherence.[171] The troika first identified the right of a woman to choose to abort as constitutionally protected and thus not subject to state control, although subject to state regulation—this, they told us, was the "essential holding" of *Roe.*[172] The three went on to tell us that the "essential holding" of *Roe* must be reaffirmed lest the Supreme Court appear to be buckling under political pressure,[173] overlooking that not to reverse *Roe* created exactly the same impression of buckling to political pressure, except from the opposite direction.[174] This problem of pressure coming from both sides is precisely the problem with efforts, such as that of law professor Stephen Schnably, to save *Roe* under a theory of "mediated persuasion" that would root it in the needs of a "rising" women's movement rather than in legal theory as such.[175] The question posed by these political pressures remains, as law professor Robert Byrn put it nearly two decades ago, "Whose morality?"[176]

Law professors Ronald Dworkin and James Boyd White were rather more impressed with the joint opinion's concern for precedent, arguing that it demonstrated the commitment of the troika to a decision based on legal (and moral) principle rather than their individual biases.[177] Dworkin's reticence about the political pressure argument is somewhat out of character as he

---

169. *Casey*, 505 U.S. at 966.

170. *Id.* at 980.

171. *See also* LAZARUS, *supra* note 10, at 484–85; Alan Bigel, Planned Parenthood of Southeastern Pennsylvania v. Casey: *Constitutional Principles and Political Turbulence*, 18 U. DAYTON L. REV. 733, 756, 758–60 (1993). *See generally* Joseph Raz, *The Relevance of Coherence*, 72 B.U. L. REV. 273 (1992).

172. *Casey*, 505 U.S. at 871 (Kennedy, O'Connor, & Souter, JJ., joint plurality op.). *See also id.* at 912–14 (Stevens, J., partially concurring), 923–28 (Blackmun, J., partially concurring). For support of this reading of *Roe*, see WHITE, *supra* note 162, at 163, 169; Neal Devins, *The Countermajoritarian Paradox*, 93 MICH. L. REV. 1433, 1455–57 (1995); Tom Tyler & Gregory Mitchell, *Legitimacy and the Empowerment of Discretionary Legal Authority: The United States Supreme Court and Abortion Rights*, 43 DUKE L.J. 703 (1994); Sandra Lynne Tholen & Lisa Baird, Note, *Con Law Is as Con Law Does: A Survey of* Planned Parenthood v. Case *in the State and Federal Courts*, 28 LOY. L.A.L. REV. 971, 975–80 (1995).

173. *Casey*, 505 U.S. at 865–69 (Kennedy, O'Connor, & Souter, JJ., joint plurality op.). *See also* Linda Greenhouse, *Revealing View of the Court: The Ruling's Words Are about Abortion, but They Offer a Portrait of 3 Key Justices*, N.Y. TIMES, July 1, 1992, at A1; Mark Tushnet, *"Shut up, He Explained,"* 95 NW. U. L. REV. 907, 916–17 (2001). On the politicization of the courts generally in abortion litigation, see BARBARA YARNOLD, ABORTION POLITICS IN THE FEDERAL COURTS: RIGHT VERSUS RIGHT (1995).

174. *Casey*, 505 U.S. at 998–1001 (Scalia, J., partially dissenting, joined by Rehnquist, C.J., & Thomas & White, JJ.). Some of that pressure is described in Blumenthal, *supra* note 151, at 356–57. *See also* Madsen v. Women's Health Center, Inc., 512 U.S. 753, 785–90 (1994) (Scalia, J., dissenting, summarizing videotaped protests in favor of, as well as against, the *Roe* decision). *See generally* Sylvia Tesh, *In Support of "Single-Issue" Politics*, 99 POL. SCI. Q. 27 (1984).

175. Stephen Schnably, *Beyond* Griswold: *Foucauldian and Republican Approaches to Privacy*, 23 CONN. L. REV. 861 (1991). *See also* Karen Chiu, *Book Rev.*, 24 COMMENTARIES 9, 12 (1991); Annette Clark, *Abortion and the Pied Piper of Compromise*, 68 NYU L. REV. 265, 319–20 (1993); Koehler, *supra* note 163, at 888–89; Paul Benjamin Linton, Planned Parenthood v. Casey: *The Flight from Reason in the Supreme Court*, 13 ST. L.U. PUB. L. REV. 15, 73–74 (1993); David Smolin, *The Religious Root and Branch of Anti-Abortion Lawlessness*, 47 BAYLOR L. REV. 119, 136–41, 144–45 (1995); Brett Williamson, Note, *The Constitutional Privacy Doctrine after* Bowers v. Hardwick: *Rethinking the Second Death of Substantive Due Process*, 62 S. CAL. L. REV. 1297, 1321–24 (1989).

176. Robert Byrn, *Abortion on Demand: Whose Morality?*, 46 NOTRE DAME LAW. 5 (1970). Even some who defend the troika's opinion concede that this is the ultimate question. *See* Guido Calabresi, *Foreword: Antidiscrimination and Constitutional Accountability (What the Bork-Brennan Debate Ignores)*, 105 HARV. L. REV. 80, 146–50 (1991); Lawrence Joseph, *Theories of Poetry, Theories of Law*, 46 VAND. L. REV. 1227, 1241–49 (1993).

177. WHITE, *supra* note 162, at 176–80; Dworkin, *supra* note 139, at 31–32.

had three years earlier accused pro-life forces of distorting democracy with their "single-issue" politics without seeing any similar problem on the other side of the debate.[178] More than one commentator, on the other hand, has suggested that the authors of the joint opinion are simply too concerned about how they will be portrayed in the media.[179] In any event, this assertion that it is essential for the Court to stand fast against political pressure belies the fact that the Court has almost never succeeded in blocking a determined law-making majority from enacting its policies—if only because if the political majority holds together long enough, it will determine who sits on the Court.[180] One study concluded that the Court performs the "counter-majoritarian functions ascribed to it by traditional theory" only during transitional periods when the Court is still dominated by justices appointed by an earlier, and now defunct, political coalition.[181] As we all know, the Court in fact, as "Mr. Dooley" put it, "follows the election returns."[182] Certainly this appears true at the federal level, which perhaps explains why the Supreme Court has never struck down a federally enacted restriction on access to abortion.[183]

The troika's argument also fails to consider whether the Court's prestige suffers more from incoherent arguments made to sustain insupportable precedent than from overruling that precedent in the face of extraordinary political pressure.[184] Affirmation of the "essence" of *Roe* is incoherent once the troika overruled *Roe* on the fundamental nature of the right involved,[185] on the now familiar trimester scheme,[186] and on the standard of review applicable to state regulations.[187] All are points that some—including Justice Sandra Day O'Connor in her *Thornburgh* dissent—had thought made up the essence of *Roe.*[188] Indeed, as law professor Reva Siegel

178. Ronald Dworkin, *The Future of Abortion,* N.Y. Rev. Books, Sept. 28, 1989, at 47, 50–51. For a critique of the "single-issue" argument, see Mark Graber, Rethinking Abortion: Equal Choice, the Constitution, and Reproductive Politics 28–29 (1996).

179. *See, e.g.,* Bruce Fein, *Yes: The Press Loves Activists,* ABA J., Oct. 1992, at 48. *See also* Sullivan, *supra* note 89, at 100–03. For a discussion of the "Greenhouse" effect, see the text *infra* at notes 423–25.

180. Robert Dahl, *Decision-Making in a Democracy: The Supreme Court as a National Policy-Maker,* 6 J. Pub. L. 279, 285–86 (1957).

181. Richard Funston, *The Supreme Court and Critical Elections,* 69 Am. Pol. Sci. Rev. 795, 796 (1975). *See generally* Charles Black, The People and the Court (1960); Beverly Cook, *Public Opinion and Federal Judicial Policy,* 21 Am. J. Pol. Sci. 567 (1977); Louis Fisher, *Social Influences on Constitutional Law,* 15 J. Pol. Sci. 7, 8 (1987).

182. *See* Funston, *supra* note 181, at 796.

183. Devins, *supra* note 172, at 1455. *See* Harris v. McRae, 448 U.S. 297 (1980) (upholding a statute denying federal funding for most abortions), Bowen v. Kendrick, 487 U.S. 589 (1988) (upholding a statute authorizing federal funds for religious organizations providing adoption counseling), and Rust v. Sullivan, 500 U.S. 173 (1991) (upholding a statute barring federally-funded family planning centers from discussing abortion). *See* Christina Wells, *Abortion Counseling as a Vice Activity: The Free Speech Implications of* Rust v. Sullivan *and* Planned Parenthood v. Casey, 95 Colum. L. Rev. 1724 (1995).

184. Crain, *supra* note 67, at 304–07.

185. *Casey,* 505 U.S. at 869 (Kennedy, O'Connor, & Souter, JJ., joint plurality op.) (a woman has "some freedom to terminate her pregnancy"—rather a lesser claim than that the woman has a fundamental right that can be invaded only on a showing of a "compelling state interest").

186. *Id.* at 869–73.

187. *Id.* at 873–79.

188. *Thornburgh,* 462 U.S. at 453 (O'Connor, J., dissenting). *See also Casey,* 505 U.S. at 929–40 (Blackmun, J., partially concurring), 954–55 (Rehnquist, C.J., partially dissenting, joined by Scalia, Thomas, & White, JJ.), 993–94 (Scalia, J., partially dissenting, joined by Rehnquist, C.J., & Thomas & White, JJ.). *See generally* Bruce Cornblum, The Legal Rights of Women: Legal Subjects that Most Affect the Lives of Women 1 (1995); Craig & O'Brien, *supra* note 10, at 334–35, 337–38; Dworkin, *supra* note 56, at 103–06; Graber, *supra* note 178, at 171 n.142; O'Brien, *supra* note 10, at 59–61; Robertson, *supra* note 156, at 61; Anita Allen, *Autonomy's Magic Wand: Abortion and Constitutional Interpretation,* 72 B.U. L. Rev. 683 (1992); Janet Benshoof, *The Pennsylvania Abortion Case,* 9 Tuoro L. Rev. 217, 232–40 (1993); Clark, *supra* note 175, at 318–22; Cohen, *supra* note 143, at 178–81, 186–88; Colleen Connell, *The Supreme Court's Recent Abortion Decisions: A Pro-Choice Critique,* in Abortion and the States 13, 16–18 (Jane Wishner ed. 1993); Peggy

noted, "[i]f one removes the trimester framework from *Roe*, much of the opinion's reasoning seems to support, rather than constrain, abortion-restrictive regulation."[189] Siegel summarized the problem succinctly:

> If the Court abandons *Roe's* trimester framework or qualifies a pregnant woman's privacy rights without imposing meaningful restraints on the interest in potential life *Roe* recognized, *Roe* will have spawned a constitutionally "compelling" interest in regulating the conduct of pregnant women that is elaborated in terms wholly inattentive to the social judgments prompting state action against the pregnant woman or the impact of state action upon her.[190]

No wonder Sarah Weddington, the attorney who argued *Roe v. Wade* before the Supreme Court, had written, even before *Casey* was decided, that "in [her] mind *Roe* is already gone" because of judicial erosion of the protections she saw that case as establishing.[191] As Chief Justice William Rehnquist famously commented in his dissent, "*Roe* continues to exist, but only in the way a storefront in a western movie exists: a mere façade to give the illusion of reality,"[192] and that "*Roe v. Wade* stands as a sort of Potemkin Village, which may be pointed out to passers-by as a monument to the importance of adhering to precedent."[193]

Nor did the joint plurality opinion even mention the right of privacy that was so central to the reasoning of the Court in *Roe* except in a phrase ("[i]f the right of privacy means anything...") that seems to suggest that the concept is meaningless, at least in the abortion context.[194] This did not, however, amount to the adoption of an equal protection theory of abortion rights. The troika insisted that the right to choose to abort is an aspect of the "liberty" protected by the due process clauses of the Fifth and Fourteenth Amendments.[195] Law professor Philip

---

Cooper Davis, *Neglected Stories and the Lawfulness of* Roe v. Wade, 28 HARV. C.R.-C.L. L. REV. 299, 369–70 (1993); Frank Easterbrook, *Constitutional Law Conference*, 61 U.S.L.W. 2237, 2246 (1992); Mary Edwards & Brian Lee, *Casenote*, 23 SETON HALL L. REV. 255, 318–22 (1992); Ginsburg, *supra* note 24, at 1199; John Horan, *A Jurisprudence of Doubt:* Planned Parenthood v. Casey, 26 CREIGHTON L. REV. 479, 513–17, 523–24 (1993); Patricia Karlan & Daniel Ortiz, *In a Different Voice: Relational Feminism, Abortion Rights, and the Feminist Legal Agenda*, 87 NW. U. L. REV. 858, 883–85 (1993); Koehler, *supra* note 163, at 881–83, 889–90; Vanessa Laird, Planned Parenthood v. Casey: *The Role of* Stare Decisis, 57 MOD. L. REV. 461, 463 (1994); Sylvia Law, *Abortion and Compromise—Inevitable and Impossible*, 1992 U. ILL. L. REV. 921, 923, 928–30; Linton, *supra* note 175, at 34–37; Julie Mertus, *Beyond the Solitary Self: Voice, Community, and Reproductive Freedom*, 3 COLUM. J. GENDER & L. 247, 249–50 (1992); Pine & Law, *supra* note 89, at 426–27; Charles Stanley Ross, *The Right of Privacy and Restraints on Abortion under the "Undue Burden" Test: A Jurisprudential Comparison of* Planned Parenthood v. Casey *with European Practice and Italian Law*, 3 IND. INT'L & COMP. L. REV. 199, 210–14 (1993); Thomas Ross, *Despair and Redemption in the Feminist Nomos*, 69 IND. L.J. 101, 133 (1993); Scaturro, *supra* note 126, at 197–98; Shapiro, *supra* note 10, at 11–12; Mark Woltz, Note, *A Bold Reaffirmation?* Planned Parenthood v. Casey *Opens the Door to Enact New Laws to Discourage Abortion*, 71 N. CAR. L. REV. 1787, 1788–89 (1993); George Wooditch, jr., *A Woman's Right to an Abortion as Affected by the Conservative Ear of the 1980's*, 34 HOWARD L.J. 427, 428–29 (1991); Richard Wilkins, Richard Sherlock, & Stephen Clark, *Mediating the Polar Extremes: A Guide to Post-*Webster *Abortion Policy*, in ABORTION AND THE STATES, *supra*, at 151–52. Sabina Zenkich, *X Marks the Spot while* Casey *Strikes Out: Two Controversial Abortion Decisions*, 23 GOLDEN GATE U. L. REV. 1001, 1032–36 (1993).

189. Siegel, *supra* note 132, at 276 n.56.

190. *Id.* at 276–77 n.57.

191. SARAH WEDDINGTON, A QUESTION OF CHOICE 236 (1992).

192. *Casey*, 505 U.S. at 954 (Rehnquist, C.J., partially dissenting, joined by Scalia, Thomas, & White, JJ.).

193. *Id.* at 966.

194. Charles Stanley Ross, *supra* note 188, at 205–06.

195. *Casey*, 505 U.S. at 851–53 (Kennedy, O'Connor, & Souter, JJ.). *See also* David Strauss, *Abortion, Toleration, and Moral Uncertainty*, 1992 SUP. CT. REV. 1, 2.

Hamburger, however, located an equality argument in the liberty clause by referring back to arguments from the eighteenth century, well before the equal protection clause was added to the Constitution, and indeed before the American Revolution.[196] Thus, an equality theory might be lurking in the troika's opinion.

The troika did stick to the "potential life" characterization that originated in *Roe*. The troika was careful when it first introduced the term to appear even handed, stating that "depending on one's beliefs,…life or potential life…is aborted."[197] This appeared to accept the legitimacy of both perspectives—a distinct advance over the single-minded insistence of the Court in *Roe* and the cases following it that the fetus is only "potential life." The troika went on, however, to use the term "potential life" without qualification no less than 17 times without ever again coupling it with any sort of recognition of the legitimacy of a belief that fetal life was "life" and not merely potential life.[198] In this regard, the troika did reaffirm the essential holding of *Roe*.[199]

The joint plurality opinion in *Casey* might simply be expressing the oft-stated criticism that the Supreme Court got into trouble in Roe by announcing abstract rules rather than dealing with the precise facts before the Court.[200] Nothing in the opinion expresses this view directly, although both Justices Anthony Kennedy and Sandra Day O'Connor had embraced this idea three years earlier.[201] In fact, the joint plurality opinion in *Casey* seems to embrace just such an abstract approach as failed in *Roe*. Furthermore, the opinion, standing almost entirely on the obligation to follow precedent, contradicted itself by overruling two cases squarely based on *Roe*[202] even while citing these very cases as proving the continuing vitality of the "essence" of *Roe*.[203] Journalist Donald Judges described the contrast between the strongly announced general claims of the joint plurality opinion and the wholesale abandonment of what those principles require as "like a spectacularly successful football rally followed by a lost game."[204] Attorneys Bruce Fein was blunter, describing this twist as causing the opinion to "degenerate in comic opera."[205]

---

196. Philip Hamburger, *Equality and Diversity: The Eighteenth-Century Debate about Equal Protection and Equal Civil Rights,* 1992 Sup. Ct. Rev. 295.

197. *Casey,* 505 U.S. 852.

198. *Id.* at 859, 871–73, 875–78, 882, 886, 898.

199. Scaturro, *supra* note 126, at 154–55.

200. *See* Webster v. Reproductive Health Services, 492 U.S. 490, 518–21 (1989) (Rehnquist, C.J., with Kennedy & White, JJ., plurality op.); Robert Burt, The Constitution in Conflict 358–62 (1992); Colker, *supra* note 133, at 101–02, 114–25; Mensch & Freeman, *supra* note 17, at 126–28; White, *supra* note 162, at 162; Vincent Blasi, *The Rootless Activism of the Burger Court,* in The Burger Court: The Counter Revolution that Wasn't 198, 212 (Vincent Blasi ed. 1983); David Boldt, *Farewell to Justice Blackmun: He Blew It on the "*Roe*" Decision,* Phila. Inquirer, Apr. 10, 1994, at D7; Daniel Conkle, *Canada's* Roe: *The Canadian Abortion Decision and Its Implications for American Constitutional Law and Theory,* 6 Const'l Commentary 299, 308–18 (1989); Dworkin, *supra* note 142, at 427–32; Ginsburg, *supra* note 24, at 1198–99, 1205–09; Shapiro, *supra* note 10, at 16–18.

201. Webster v. Reproductive Health Services, 492 U.S. 490, 518–20 (Rehnquist, C.J., joined by Kennedy & White, JJ., plurality op.), 526 (O'Connor, J., partially concurring) (1989).

202. *Casey,* 505 U.S. at 876–87 (Kennedy, O'Connor, & Souter, JJ.), *overruling* Thornburgh v. American College of Obstetricians 476 U.S. 747 (1986), *and* City of Akron v. Akron Center for Reproductive Health, Inc., 462 U.S. 416 (1983).

203. *Casey,* 505 U.S. at 858 (Kennedy, O'Connor, & Souter, JJ., joint plurality op.).

204. Judges, *supra* note 145, at 233.

205. Bruce Fein, *Never-Ending Abortion Litigation,* in Abortion and the States, *supra* note 188, at 39, 46. *See also* Benshoof, *supra* note 188, at 220–30. *See generally* Ruth Burdick, Note, *The* Casey *Undue Burden Standard: Problems Predicted and Encountered, and the Split over the* Salerno *Standard,* 23 Hastings Const'l L.Q. 825, 829–32 (1996); Cohen, *supra* note 143, at 182–85; Christopher Cox, *The Sad Career of the Reagan Justices,* Wall St. J., July 1, 1992, at A14; Michael Gerhardt, *The Pressure of Precedent: A Critique of the Conservative Approaches to* Stare Decisis *in Abortion Cases,* 10 Const'l Commentary 67, 76–78 (1993); Horan, *supra*

For a new standard, the joint plurality opinion adopted Sandra Day O'Connor's theory that abortion regulations are valid if the regulations do not impose an "undue burden" on a woman's right to abort.[206] The phrase had been used in Chief Justice Warren Earl Burger's concurring opinion in *Doe v. Bolton*[207] — the companion case to *Roe v. Wade*. The phrase appeared in majority opinions in abortion cases in *Maher v. Roe,*[208] *Bellotti v. Baird,*[209] and *Harris v. McRae.*[210] In the earlier cases, however, the phrase was simply used in passing; no Justice before O'Connor considered it to be a constitutional standard in any sort of case, let alone in the context of abortion.[211] The earlier abortion cases had all turned on whether the state had a compelling interest to justify its regulatory intervention, not on whether the regulation unduly burdened the woman.[212]

The troika did not seriously explore the burdens that would be created by various regulations of abortion.[213] They did not even bother to explain why requirements regarding waiting periods and compulsory information are not an undue burden on a woman's choice to abort (at least absent an evidentiary showing on these matters) while the requirement that requiring a woman to notify her husband (with statutory exceptions for situations where this might result in threats or worse for a wife) is an undue burden on its face (that is, without any evidentiary showing whatsoever).[214] The plurality's upholding of the "facial challenge" to the requirement that husbands be notified simply ignored the general rule that "facial challenges" must fail if there is any conceivable set of facts to which the statute could be applied without violating the Constitution.[215] This is yet another example of the "abortion distortion" — the application, or misapplication, of ordinary rules in extraordinary ways when abortion is involved.[216] The troika indulged in its

---

note 188, at 516–17; Kathryn Kolbert & David Gans, *Responding to* Planned Parenthood v. Casey: *Establishing Neutrality Principles in State Constitutional Law,* 66 TEMPLE L. REV. 1151, 1154–55 (1994); Sullivan, *supra* note 89, at 22–23, 73–74.

206. *Casey,* 505 U.S. at 876–901 (Kennedy, O'Connor, & Souter, JJ., joint plurality op.).

207. 410 U.S. 179, 208 (1973) (Burger, C.J., concurring).

208. 432 U.S. 464, 473–74 (1977).

209. 443 U.S. 622, 640 (1979).

210. 448 U.S. 297, 314 (1980).

211. Justice Scalia reviewed, succinctly but accurately, the prior usage of the phrase in abortion cases in his dissent in *Casey,* 505 U.S. at 985 n.3 (Scalia, J., dissenting, joined by Rehnquist, C.J., & Thomas & White, JJ.).

212. *See* Thornburgh v. American College of Obstetricians 476 U.S. 747, 760–62 (1986); City of Akron v. Akron Center for Reproductive Health, Inc., 462 U.S. 416, 443–44 (1983); Planned Parenthood of Cent. Mo. v. Danforth, 428 U.S. 52, 65–67 (1976); Roe v. Wade, 410 U.S. 113, 155, 162–63 (1973).

213. LAZARUS, *supra* note 10, at 483–84. For a brief discussion of the relative burdens of some proposed or actual abortion regulations, see James Bowers & Ummuhan Turgut, *Classical Liberalism, the Constitution, and Abortion Policy: Can Government Be Both Pro-Choice and Anti-Abortion,* 17 U. DAYTON L. REV. 1 (1991).

214. *Casey,* 505 U.S. at 881–900 (Kennedy, O'Connor, & Souter, JJ., joint plurality op.). *See generally* COLKER, *supra* note 133, at 96–98; JUDGES, *supra* note 145, at 242–43; NAGEL, *supra* note 17, at 151–56; WHITE, *supra* note 162, at 180 n.23; Leonard Berman, Planned Parenthood v. Casey: *Supreme Neglect for Unemancipated Minors' Abortion Rights,* 37 How. L.J. 577 (1994); Alan Brownstein, *How Rights Are Infringed: The Role of Undue Bur den Analysis in Constitutional Doctrine,* 45 HASTINGS L.J. 867, 887–92 (1994); Burdick, *supra* note 205, at 832–38; Erin Daly, *Reconsidering Abortion Law: Liberty, Equality, and the New Rhetoric of* Planned Parenthood v. Casey, 45 AM. U. L. REV. 77, 103–05, 128–34 (1995); Kathryn Kolbert & Andrea Miller, *Legal Strategies for Abortion Rights in the Twenty-First Century,* in ABORTION WARS, *supra* note 90, at 95, 100–01.

215. *See generally* United States v. Salerno, 481 U.S. 739 (1987); Brockett v. Spokane Arcades, Inc., 472 U.S. 33 (1985); Michael Dorf, *Facial Challenges to State and Federal Statutes,* 46 STAN. L. REV. 235 (1994); Kurt Ebersbach, Comment, Women's Medical Professional Corp. v. Voinovich: *Applying Overbreadth Analysis to Post-Viability Abortion Regulations,* 30 GA. L. REV. 1151 (1996); Richard Fallon, *Making Sense of Overbreadth,* 100 YALE L.J. 853 (1991); John Ford, *The* Casey *Standard for Evaluating Facial Attacks on Abortion Statutes,* 95 MICH. L. REV. 1443 (1997).

216. *See, e.g.,* Jeanne Schroeder, Abduction from the Seraglio: *Feminist Methodologies and the Logic of Imagination,* 70 TEX. L. REV. 109, 138–40 (1991) (noting that feminists often support the recognition of an actionable duty to save — except in the context of abortion). *See also* Stenberg v. Carhart, 530 U.S. 914, 977–78

"abortion distortion" despite Sandra Day O'Connor herself having decried that distortion just six years before when she wrote, in dissent to *Thornburgh,* that "[n]o legal rule or doctrine is safe from *ad hoc* nullification by this Court when an occasion for its application arises in a case involving state regulation of abortion."[217]

As a result of the *Casey* decision, many states have now enacted "right-to-know" statutes that require abortionists to inform women of certain prescribed information regarding the development of the fetus, alternatives to the procedure, or risks to themselves, sometimes combined with a mandatory waiting period between the provision of the information and the abortion.[218] Several of these statutes have been upheld against constitutional challenge under the *Casey* "undue burden" standard.[219] Whether such statutes ultimately withstand constitutional scrutiny or not, many find these statutes demeaning to women. As attorney Janet Benshoof commented, the decision in *Casey* "codified into constitutional law the view that women seeking abortions are morally shallow and incapable of making decisions in their own best interests."[220] The resistance among those favoring abortion rights to regulations affecting the counseling of women

---

(Kennedy, J., dissenting) (2000); Madsen v. Women's Health Ctr., Inc., 512 U.S. 753, 783–85 (1994) (Scalia, J., dissenting); Thornborgh v. American College of Obstetricians & Gynecologists, 476 U.S. 747, 814 (1986) (O'Connor, J., dissenting); JUDGES, *supra* note 145, at 226, 242; Brownstein, *supra* note 214, at 925–29; Scaturro, *supra* note 126, at 189–93; Smolin, *supra* note 144, at 1013–16. *See generally* Richard Erb, jr., & Alan Mortensen, Comment, *Wyoming Fetal Rights — Why the Abortion "Albatross" Is a Bird of a Different Color: The Case for Fetal Federalism,* 28 LAND & WATER L. REV. 627 (1993).

217. *Thornburgh,* 476 U.S. at 814 (O'Connor, J., dissenting).

218. ALA. ADMIN. CODE §420-5-1-.03(1)(f) (LexisNexis 2002); ALA. CODE §§26-23A-1 to 26-23A-13 (Supp. 2003); ALASKA ADMIN. CODE §40.070 (LexisNexis 2002); CONN. GEN. STAT. ANN. §19a-601 (West 2003); DEL. CODE ANN. tit. 24, §1794 (1997); FLA. STAT. ANN. §390.0111(4) (West 2002); IDAHO CODE §18-609 (Supp. 2003); IND. CODE ANN. §16-34-2-1 (West Supp. 2003); KAN. STAT. §§65-6709, 65-6710 (2002); KY. REV. STAT. ANN. §§311.723, 311.725, 311.760 (Michie 2001); LA. REV. STAT. ANN. §§40.1299.35.6, 40.1299.35.14 (West 2001); ME. REV. STAT. ANN. tit. 22 §1596 (West 1992); MASS. GEN. LAWS ANN. ch. 112 §125 (West 2003); MICH. COMP. LAWS ANN. §333.17015 (West Supp. 2003); MINN. STAT. ANN. §§145.411 to 145.416 (West Supp. 2003); MISS. CODE ANN. §§41-41-31 to 41-41-39 (West 1999); MO. REV. STAT. ANN. §§188.039, 188.040 (West 2000); MONT. CODE ANN. §§50-20-104, 50-20-106 (2003); NEB. REV. STAT. §§28-325 to 28-327.05 (1995); NEV. REV. STAT. ANN. §§442.252 to 442.255 (Michie 2000); N.D. CENT. CODE §§14-02.1-02, 14-02.1-03 (1997); OHIO REV. CODE ANN. §2317.56 (Anderson 2001); 18 PA. CONS. STAT. ANN. §3205 (West 2000); R.I. GEN. LAWS §§23-4-7.2 to 23-4-7.4 (1997); S.C. CODE ANN. §§44-41-31, 44-41-310 to 44-41-380, 44-41-60 (West 2002); S.D. CODIFIED LAWS ANN. §§34-23A-7, 34-23A-10.1, 34-23A-10.3 (LexisNexis Supp. 2003); TENN. CODE ANN. §§39-15-201, 39-15-202 (2003); UTAH CODE ANN. §§76-7-305, 76-7-305.5 (2003); VA. CODE ANN. §18.2-76 (LexisNexis Supp. 2003); WIS. STAT. ANN. §253.10 (West 2002). *See generally* Paula Berg, *Toward a First Amendment Theory of Doctor-Patient Discourse and the Right to Receive Unbiased Medical Advice,* 74 B.U. L. REV. 201 (1994); Barry Bostrom, Karlin v. Frost, 14 ISSUES IN L. & MED. 377 (1999); Clarke Forsythe, *Abortion Laws: A Report from the States,* WALL ST. J., Aug. 9, 1995, at A9; Susan Refner, Randal Shaheen, & Michael Hegarty, *The Woman's Right to Know: A Model Applicable to the Informed Consent of Abortion,* 22 LOY. U. L. REV. 409 (1991).

219. Leavitt v. Jane L., 518 U.S. 137 (1996) (Utah); Woman's Choice — East Side Women's Clinic v. Newman, 305 F.3d 684 (7th Cir. 2002) (Ind.), *cert. denied,* 537 U.S. 1192 (2003); Karlin v. Foust, 188 F.3d 446 (7th Cir. 1999) (Wis.); Planned Parenthood, Sioux Falls v. Miller, 63 F.3d 1452 (8th Cir. 1995) (N.D.), *cert. denied sub nom.* Janklow v. Planned Parenthood, Sioux Falls, 517 U.S. 1174 (1996) (Rehnquist, C.J., Scalia & Thomas JJ., dissenting); Fargo Women's Health Org. v. Schafer, 18 F.3d 526 (8th Cir. 1994) (N.D.); Barnes v. Moore, 970 F.2d 12 (5th Cir. 1992) (Miss.), *cert. denied,* 506 U.S. 1013 (1993); Pro-Choice Miss. v. Fordice, 716 So. 2d 645 (Miss. 1998). *See also* Preterm, Inc. v. Voinovich, 627 N.E.2d 570 (Ohio Ct. App. 1993) (applying the federal standard under the state constitution), *appeal dismissed. But see* State v. Presidential Women's Ctr., 707 So. 2d 1145 (Fla. Ct. App. 1998) (enjoining a waiting period for violating the state's constitution); Planned Parenthood of Cent. Tenn. v. Sundquist, 38 S.W.2d 1 (Tenn. 2000) (same). *See generally* Burdick, *supra* note 205, at 838–40, 843–69; Tholen & Baird, *supra* note 172, at 996–99.

220. Janet Benshoof, *Revisiting the Fundamentals,* 18 CONSCIENCE 16 (1997). *See also* GARROW, *supra* note 10, at 736.

considering an abortion leads to a certain irony as many women who underwent illegal abortions apparently received better (and more extended) counseling than they do today in assembly-line legal clinics.[221] Indeed, by some accounts, contemporary abortion "counseling" is seriously misleading, being designed to market a product rather than to inform women about the physical and emotional reality of the procedure they are about to undergo.[222] Abortion foes are too optimistic, however, if they think that if women were only given the correct information they would refuse to go through with the abortion.[223]

Those opposed to the regulation of abortion counseling do not take into account the regrettable tendency of abortion to attract the less skilled and even less ethical physicians. Not only have gynecologists lost their licenses for botching abortions,[224] but they gone to prison when they continued to perform abortions while their medical licenses were suspended.[225] One professional abortionist—Dr. Suresh Gandrotra—continued to ply his trade after having been convicted of 17 felonies and misdemeanors growing out of the practice of medicine, including causing the death of at least one woman who during an abortion.[226] Even Dr. John Britton who was murdered in Pensacola, Florida, was under investigation at the time for improper medical practices.[227]

The utter rejection by courts of any right in a father even to receive information regarding a possible abortion, on the other hand, is consistent with the general hostility of the American, Australian, Canadian, English and Scottish judges to recognizing any rights of a father relative to a mother's decisions concerning an unborn child.[228] While abortions have no physical effect on a

---

221. *See, e.g.,* Ellen Curro, Caring Enough to Help: Counseling at a Crisis Pregnancy 50–51 (1990) (describing a contemporary counseling session); Patricia Miller, The worst of Times 15 (1993) (same). *See generally* Marvin Olasky, The Press and Abortion, 1838–1988, at 142–47 (1988) David Reardon, Aborted Women: Silent No More 15–19 (1987); David Smolin, *Cultural and Technological Obstacles to the Mainstreaming of Abortion,* 13 St.L. U. Pub. L. Rev. 261, 268–77 (1993).

222. Curro, *supra* note 221, at 50–51; Kerry Jacoby, Souls, Bodies, Spirits: The Drive to Abolish Abortion since 1973, at 48–49 (1998); Thomas Jipping, *Informed Consent to Abortion: A Refinement,* 38 Case-W. Res. L. Rev. 329, 379–80 (1987); Judith Leach, *The Repeat Abortion Patient,* 9 Fam. Plan. Persp. 37, 38 (1977); Terry Nicole Steinbeg, Note, *Abortion Counseling: To Benefit Maternal Health,* 15 Am. J.L. & Med. 483 (1989).

223. Jacoby, *supra* note 222, at 48–52.

224. *See, e.g., Abortion Doctor Loses License,* Chi. Trib., Apr. 24, 1994; Roger Signor, *Doctor's License Revoked,* St. L. Post-Dispatch, Dec. 15, 1993.

225. *See, e.g.,* Michael Alexander, *Unlicensed Gynecologist Given 2-to-4-Year Term,* N.Y. Newsday, Dec. 16, 1993, at 37; Ronald Smothers, *Abortion Doctor Is Linked to Complaints in 5 States,* N.Y. Times, Sept. 30, 1994, at A19.

226. Peter Dalton, *Doctor Probed after Abortion Causes Death,* San Diego Union, Dec. 13, 1994, at B-1.

227. Elizabeth Gleick, *Crossing the Line,* People Mag., Aug. 15, 1994, at 60, 63.

228. *See* Doe v. Smith, 486 U.S. 1308 (1988); Planned Parenthood of Cent. Mo. v. Danforth, 428 U.S. 52, 69–72 (1976); Coe v. Cook Cty., 162 F.3d 491 (7th Cir. 1998), *cert. denied,* 526 U.S. 1040 (1999); Planned Parenthood of Wis. v. Doyle, 162 F.3d 463 (7th Cir. 1998), *vacated mem. on other grounds,* 530 U.S. 1231 (2000); Scheinberg v. Smith, 550 F. Supp. 1112 (S.D. Fla. 1982); *In re* Interest of S.P.B., 651 P.2d 1213 (Colo. 1982); Shinall v. Pergeorelis, 325 So. 2d 431 (Fla. Ct. App. 1975); Rothenberger v. Doe, 374 A.2d 57 (N.J. Super. Ct. Ch. Div. 1977); Doe v. Roe, 551 N.Y.S.2d 75 (Sup. Ct. 1990); Steinhoff v. Steinhoff, 531 N.Y.S.2d 78 (Sup. Ct. 1988); Bell v. Elco Corp., 521 N.Y.S.2d 368 (Sup. Ct. 1987); Kessel v. Leavitt, 511 S.E.2d 720, 746 n.24, 752 n.33, 756 n.35 (W. Va. 1998), *cert. denied,* 525 U.S. 1142 (1999); Paton v. United Kingdom, 3 Eur. Hum. Rts. Rep. 408 (1980); Attorney-General for Queensland *ex rel.* Kerr v. T., 57 A.L.J.R. 285 (Austral. 1983); Tremblay v. Daigle, [1989] 2 S.C.R. 530 (Can.); Medhurst v. Medhurst, 9 D.L.R. 4th 252 (Ont. 1984); *In re* Unborn Child "H", 106 D.L.R. 3rd 435 (N.S. Fam. Ct. 1980); C. v. S., [1987] 1 All E.R. 1230 (Q.B.); Paton v. British Pregnancy Advisory Service Trustees, [1978] 2 All E.R. 987 (Q.B.); Kelly v. Kelly, 1997 Scot. L. Times 896. *See also* Janet Hadley, Abortion: Between Freedom and Necessity 80–82 (1996); J.K. Mason, Medico-Legal Aspects of Reproduction and Parenthood 126–27 (2nd ed. 1998); Eileen McDonagh, Breaking the Abortion Deadlock: From Choice to Consent 42, 51–54 (1996); White, *supra* note 162, at 165–66; Nicholas Bala & Martha Bailey, *Canada: Controversy Continues over Spousal Abortion and Support,* 29 J. Fam. L. 303, 303–06 (1991); J. Kodwo Bentil, *U.S. and Anglo-Australian Decisions on a Husband's Right to Prevent*

father, they do have psychological impacts[229]—and protection of mental health remains the most common reason given for a women's decision to abort when decisions are required.[230] And there is a certain irony in certain feminists arguing simultaneously that men must become more involved and responsible parents and that men can have no say in the decision to abort—as even an occasional feminist has noticed.[231] And what would these feminists say if men were to argue seriously that equality requires that they be given the right to renounce any interest in and obligation to the fetus, and thus any financial or other obligations to the woman or the child?[232] While it is true that less people support a requirement of notice to a woman's spouse than the other restrictions upheld in *Casey,* a substantial majority of 62–69 percent has consistently supported spousal notification requirements, compared to support for parental notification laws to range between 70–73 percent, and for the 24-hour waiting period to range between 69–81 percent.[233]

Few judges seem to have considered the extent to which such a denial of a recognized interest in the father in the unborn child also implies the denial of responsibility of the father to the unborn child. While such a connection might not follow from strict logical necessity, psychologically it has considerable force.[234] On the other hand, one trial court did restrain a woman from having an abortion based upon an alleged oral contract with her paramour not to abort the child.[235] The "contract" consisted of an exchange of his promise to support the child in exchange for her promise not to abort. Such an agreement would not hold up for a husband, however, as he is already under a legal duty to support the child and thus such a promise from husband could not count as consideration—an argument only a lawyer could make or understand.[236] A lover's promise of support could be interpreted as a promise not to contest paternity for, unlike a husband, an unmarried lover is not presumed to be the father.[237] If this unreported decision were to become the law of the land, it would result in the rather anomalous situation that un-

---

*Abortion,* 102/103 Law & Justice 68 (1989); Susan Davies, *Partners and the Abortion Decision,* in Abortion, Medicine, and the Law 223 (J. Douglas Butler & David Walbert eds., 3rd ed. 1986); Peter Feaver *et al., Sex as Contract: Abortion and Expanded Choice,* 4 Stan. L. & Pol'y Rev. 211 (1992); Martha Albertson Fineman, *A Legal (and Otherwise) Realist Response to "Sex as Contract,"* 4 Colum. J. Gender & L. 128 (1994); Michael Freeman, *England's Moral Quagmire,* 27 J. Fam. L. 101, 111–12 (1988); George Harris, *Fathers and Fetuses,* 96 Ethics 594 (1986); Michael Jackson, *Fatherhood and the Law: Reproductive Rights and Responsibilities of Men,* 9 Tex. J. Women & L. 53 (1999); C.M. Lyon & G.J. Bennett, *Abortion—Whose Decision?,* 9 Fam. L. 35 (1979); Caroline Morris, *Technology and the Legal Discourse of Fetal Autonomy,* 8 UCLA Women's L.J. 47, 86–88 (1997); Judith Peterson, *Whose Freedom of Choice? Sometimes It Takes Two to Untangle,* 46 The Progressive 42 (Apr. 1982); Vincent Rue, *Abortion in Relationship Context,* Int'l Rev. Nat. Fam. Plan., Summer 1985, at 95; Arthur Shostak, *The Role of Unwed Fathers in the Abortion Decision,* in Young Unwed Fathers, Changing Roles and Emerging Policies 292 (Robert Lerman & Theodora Oooms eds. 1993); Tholen & Baird, *supra* note 172, at 999–1001; *See generally* Melanie McCulley, *The Male Abortion: The Putative Father's Right to Terminate His Interest in and Obligations to the Unborn Child,* 7 J. Law & Pol'y 1 (1998).

229. Linda Bird Francke, The Ambivalence of Abortion 113–47 (1978); Pete Palmer, The Issue of Men and Abortion (1993); Arthur Shostak & Gary McLouth, Men and Abortion: Lessons, Losses and Love (1984); E. Joanne Angelo, *Psychiatric Sequelae of Abortion: The Many Faces of Post-Abortion Grief,* 59 Linacre Q. 69 (1992); Mark Baker, *Men on Abortions,* Esquire, Mar. 1990, at 114; George Harris, *Fathers and Fetuses,* 96 Ethics 594 (1986); Janet Mattinson, *The Effects of Abortion on a Marriage,* 115 Ciba Fndtn. Symposium 165 (1985).

230. *See* Chapter 10, at notes 268–71, 421–23; Chapter 11, at notes 293–95.

231. Hadley, *supra* note 228, at 81.

232. *See, e.g.,* Thomas Lynch, *A Man's Right to Choose,* N.Y. Times, July 5, 2000, at A17.

233. Blendon, Benson, & Donelin, *supra* note 22, at 2873.

234. *See* Paul Carrington, *A Senate of Five: An Essay on Sexuality and the Law,* 23 Ga. L. Rev. 859, 898–906 (1989); Totz, *supra* note 228, at 170–82.

235. Martha Bohn, Note, *Contracts Concerning Abortion,* 31 J. Fam. L. 515, 517–19 (1993). *See also* Totz, *supra* note 228, at 182–232.

236. Restatement (Second) of Contracts §73 (1981).

237. Michael H. v. Gerald D., 491 U.S. 110 (1989).

married fathers are in a stronger position than husbands to challenge the abortion of their children.[238]

So extreme is the current constitutional law regarding abortion that the few, largely symbolic, restrictions on abortion upheld in *Casey* are "some of the nation's most restrictive abortion provisions" on the books today.[239] As this brief analysis shows, the joint plurality opinion (and hence the Court's judgment) is incoherent.[240] The two dissenting/concurring blocks were able to play off the inconsistency in the joint plurality opinion in arguing for their positions either for or against abortion freedom.[241] No wonder journalist Donald Judges noted wryly that the troika was simply carrying forward the pattern in which the two sides in the abortion controversy seem to gain the most when their arguments are weakest.[242] These difficulties alone also suggest that keeping the final say on whether a particular regulation of abortion is socially acceptable in the hands of the Court would be fundamentally wrongheaded—or, as some have said, "lawless."[243]

Even more troubling than the lack of logical coherence is the joint plurality opinion's utter disregard of the merits of the matter. After all, the troika began their opinion by noting that they would not have supported *Roe* had they been on the Court when it was decided.[244] Yet they insisted that they were bound to adhere to *Roe* despite their conclusion that it was wrongly decided because of its importance to liberty and the humane values expressed in the Constitution.[245] Harvard law professor Laurence Tribe and Michael Dorf (Tribe's student and a clerk to Justice Anthony Kennedy when the *Casey* joint opinion was written, and now a law professor at Columbia University) argued for just such a mode of analysis in a recent book where they contended that the only proper method for deciding what are fundamental rights is by extrapolating from precedent without any inquiry into the correctness of those precedents.[246] Yet Tribe and Dorf applauded the overruling of many cases that they think were wrong,[247] for example, *Lochner v. New York*.[248] Somehow, one suspects that Tribe and Dorf would prefer the Court to reexamine any precedent with which they disagree. No wonder Bruce Fein characterized their argument as encouraging interpretive arbitrariness and unchecked whimsy.[249]

The troika did not rest entirely on *stare decisis*. They attempted to develop a rationale for supporting a continuing deference to the woman's personal judgment regarding whether to abort, in the process producing one of the more quoted passages in the joint plurality opinion:

> [P]ersonal decisions relating to marriage, procreation, contraception, family relationships, child rearing, and education...involving the most personal choices a person may make in a lifetime, choices central to personal dignity and autonomy, are central to the liberty protected by the Fourteenth Amendment. At the heart of liberty is the right to define one's own concept of existence, of meaning, of the universe, and of the mystery

---

238. Unmarried fathers, however, would have no greater rights without a contract. *See* Coe v. Cook Cty., 163 F.3d 491 (7th Cir 1998), *cert. denied,* 526 U.S. 1040 (1999).

239. Daly, *supra* note 214, at 80.

240. *Id.* at 80; Koehler, *supra* note 163, at 883–87, 891–92.

241. *See* Margaret Farrell, *Revisiting* Roe v. Wade: *Substance and Due Process in the Abortion Debate,* 68 IND. L.J. 269, 306–17 (1993).

242. JUDGES, *supra* note 145, at 7–8, 255.

243. Richard John Neuhaus, *The Dred Scott of Our Time,* WALL ST. J., July 2, 1992, at A8; Smolin, *supra* note 175, at 136–44. *See also* JUDGES, *supra* note 145, at 8, 227–29, 233, 242, 248, 254–57, 280.

244. 505 U.S. at 844–47 (Kennedy, O'Connor, & Souter, JJ., joint plurality op.).

245. *Id.* at 845–46.

246. LAURENCE TRIBE & MICHAEL DORF, ON READING THE CONSTITUTION 73–80 (1991).

247. *Id.* at 65–66.

248. 198 U.S. 45 (1905).

249. Bruce Fein, *On Reading the Constitution* (book rev.), 90 MICH. L. REV. 1225, 1232 (1992).

of human life. Beliefs about these matters could not define the attributes of personhood were they formed under compulsion of the State.[250]

There are several problems with this reasoning. First, it confuses a right to refuse measures that invade one's body with the right to demand or control intrusions into one's body or the bodies of others.[251] Related to this problem, as Justice John Paul Stevens pointed out in his concurrence, is the reliance of this argument on an unstated assumption that a fetus is not a human being.[252] After all, to compel one to associate with blacks or Jews imposes the state's view on deeply personal choices by those who do not choose to associate, choices central to personal dignity and autonomy, just as much as the law's protection of fetal life imposes similar views regarding fetal life. Personal associations are important aspects of liberty, yet their importance is far outweighed by the effects of such choices of other persons—the blacks or the Jews (or the unborn, if they are persons), discriminated against. By not giving reasons for their assumption, or even stating it explicitly, the authors of the joint plurality opinion avoid confronting a central issue of the controversy while assuming its resolution.

The authors of the joint opinion are not unique in their willingness to assume that which must be proven, or at least supported by argument. Ironically, jurisprude Ronald Dworkin, who wrote an article that was published while *Casey* was pending before the Court that anticipates the very language quoted above,[253] faults Chief Justice William Rehnquist for failing to argue in his dissent that the fetus is a person even though Dworkin had already praised, in the same article, the joint opinion for assuming that the fetus is not a person.[254] Not only does this line of reasoning hearken back to the discredited claim that abortion laws work an establishment of religion,[255] it also would seem to preclude legal regulation of the end of life as well as of life's beginning[256] and at least gives comfort to those who believe that some races or ethnic groups are not really (or fully) human. It is not in the least clear why beliefs about any of these matters

---

250. *Casey*, 505 U.S. at 851. *See also* DRUCILLA CORNELL, THE IMAGINARY DOMAIN: ABORTION, PORNOGRAPHY, AND SEXUAL HARASSMENT 31–94 (1995); ROBERTSON, *supra* note 156, at 4; Randall Bezanson, *Emancipation as Freedom in* Roe v. Wade, 97 DICK. L. REV. 485, 496–512 (1993); Daly, *supra* note 214, at 116–26, 135–42, 148–50; Warren Quinn, *Abortion: Identity and Loss*, 13 PHIL. & PUB. AFF. 24 (1984).

251. Seth Kreimer, *Does Pro-Choice Mean Pro-Kevorkian? An Essay on* Roe, Casey, *and the Right to Die*, 44 AM. U. L. REV. 803, 834–40 (1995).

252. *Casey*, 505 U.S. at 912–14 (Stevens, J., concurring). *See also* Dworkin, *supra* note 139, at 30; Farrell, *supra* note 241, at 315–16; Smolin, *supra* note 144, at 1033–35.

253. Dworkin, *supra* note 142, at 419–21.

254. Dworkin, *supra* note 139, at 30, 32.

255. *See* Thornburgh v. American College of Obstetricians & Gynecologists, 476 U.S. 747, 795 n.4 (1986) (White, J., dissenting); MENSCH & FREEMAN, *supra* note 17, at 132–48; LAURENCE TRIBE, AMERICAN CONSTITUTIONAL LAW 928 (1978); James Bopp, jr., *Will There Be a Constitutional Right to Abortion after the Reconsideration of* Roe?, 15 J. CONTEMP. L. 131, 147–61 (1989); Joseph Dellapenna, *Nor Piety Nor Wit: The Supreme Court on Abortion*, 6 COLUM. H. RTS. L. REV. 379, 384–89 (1974); Dworkin, *supra* note 142, at 418–27; Smolin, *supra* note 175. For general arguments in favor of relying on religious arguments in political decision-making, see MILNER BALL, THE WORD AND THE LAW (1993); STEPHEN CARTER, THE CULTURE OF DISBELIEF: HOW AMERICAN LAW AND POLITICS TRIVIALIZE RELIGIOUS DEVOTION (1993); KENT GREENAWALT, RELIGIOUS CONVICTION AND POLITICAL CHOICE (1988); George Freeman III, *The Misguided Search for the Constitutional Definition of "Religion,"* 71 GEORGETOWN L.J. 1519 (1983); Scott Idleman, Note, *The Role of Religious Values in Judicial Decision Making*, 68 IND. L.J. 433 (1993); Michael Perry, *Liberal Democracy and Religious Morality*, 48 DEPAUL L. REV. 1 (1998).

256. *See, e.g.,* Alan Bigel, *The Rehnquist Court on the Right to Life: Forecast for the 1990s*, 18 OH. N.U.L. REV. 515, 568 (1992); Ronald Dworkin, *The Right to Death*, N.Y. REV. BOOKS 14, 17 (Jan. 31, 1991); Farrell, *supra* note 241, at 324; Stephen Goldberg, *The Changing Face of Death: Computers, Consciousness, and Nancy Cruzan*, 43 STAN. L. REV. 659 (1991); Seth Kreimer, *Does Pro-Choice Mean Pro-Kevorkian? An Essay on* Roe, Casey, *and the Right to Die*, 44 AM. U. L. REV. 803 (1995); Elizabeth Mensch & Alan Freeman, *The Politics of Virtue: Animals, Theology and Abortion*, 24 GA. L. REV. 923, 1119 (1991); Philip Prygoski, *Abortion and the Right to Die: Judicial Imposition of a Theory of Life*, 23 SETON HALL L. REV. 67 (1992); Lynn Stout, *Strict*

would fail as constitutionally protected definitions of personhood in precisely the way the plurality considered disparate views on the status of the fetus. As law professor David Smolin pointed out, we could experience the ironic justice of a generation that aborted one-third of their children because they would be too inconvenient or too expensive would be slaughtered by the aborted generation because it finds caring for the aborting generation too expensive or too inconvenient.[257]

The joint plurality opinion went on to state, "the ability of women to participate equally in the economic and social life of the Nation has been facilitated by their ability to control their re productive lives."[258] Several commentators have seized upon this passage as proof that the Court has understood the symbolic function of *Roe* as expressing the equal status of women under the law.[259] The argument is similar to one penned by a clerk to Justice Robert Jackson to explain why the clerk thought the Justice should dissent from *Brown v. Board of Education:* "Where a whole way of life has grown up around such a prior error, then I say we are stuck with it."[260] Even on the most general level, the reliance claim is dubious. As the controversy over *Roe* was never resolved, people could hardly have relied on the decision as settled law.[261] Some indication of this can be found in the fact that *Roe* is rarely cited as a basis of women's rights in any area other than abortion. Attorney Paul Linton has carefully surveyed the more than two thousand cases in which a court has cited *Roe* by the time it decided *Casey.*[262] Aside from the numerous cases involving abortion rights and an occasional decision regarding the application of wrongful death or criminal homicide decisions to unborn children, none of these cases citing *Roe* would have been decided differently if *Roe* had been decided differently.

Women rights and social goals have changed dramatically in the 30 years since *Roe* was decided. These changes resulted from state and federal legislation enacted and judicial decisions taken independently of *Roe.*[263] Does anyone really believe that large numbers of women would have chosen to become housewives rather than to enter some other career had they believed that *Roe* would be overruled during their working lives?[264] Furthermore, reliance arguments work

---

*Scrutiny and Social Choice: An Economic Inquiry into Fundamental Rights and Suspect Classification,* 80 Geo. L.J. 1787, 1810–12 (1992).

257. Smolin, *supra* note 144, at 1036–37.

258. *Casey,* 505 U.S. at 856 (Kennedy, O'Connor, & Souter, JJ., joint plurality op.). *See also* Mertus, *supra* note 188, at 293–99; Amy Miles, Comment, *Feminist Theories of Interpretation: The Bible and the Law,* 2 Geo. Mason U. L. Rev. 305, 328 (1995); Monaghan, *supra* note 164, at 750–52.

259. *See, e.g.,* Kenneth Karst, Law's Promise, Law's Expression: Visions of Power in the Politics of Race, Gender, and Religion 195–202 (1993); White, *supra* note 162, at 174–75, 181–82; Abrams, *supra* note 133, at 488–90; Clark, *supra* note 175, at 317–18.

260. *A Few Expressed Prejudices on the Segregation Cases (Memorandum of Donald Cronson to Justice Jackson),* quoted in Richard Kluger, Simple Justice 605 (1976).

261. Crain, *supra* note 67, at 302–04, 312–15. For a remarkably glib assertion that *Roe* is settled law that in no way considers the on-going controversy over the legitimacy of that decision, see Frank Michelman, *Always under Law?,* 12 Const'l Commentary 227, 242 (1995).

262. Linton, *supra* note 175, at 78–102.

263. *See, e.g.,* UAW v. Johnson Controls, Inc., 500 U.S. 942 (1991); Newport News Shipbuilding Co. v. E.E.O.C., 462 U.S. 669 (1983); Kirchberg v. Feenstra, 450 U.S. 455 (1981); Caban v. Mohammed, 441 U.S. 380 (1979); Califano v. Goldfarb, 430 U.S. 199 (1977); Craig v. Boren, 429 U.S. 190 (1976); Stanton v. Stanton, 421 U.S. 7 (1975); Weinberger v. Weisenfeld, 420 U.S. 636 (1975); Cleveland Bd. of Educ. v. Le Fleur, 414 U.S. 632 (1974); Frontiero v. Richardson, 411 U.S. 677 (1973); Reed v. Reed, 404 U.S. 71 (1971). *See generally* Paige Comstock Cunningham & Clarke Forsythe, *Is Abortion the "First Right" for Women?: Some Consequences of Legal Abortion,* in Abortion, Medicine and the Law 154 (J. Douglas Butler & David Walbert eds., 4th ed. 1992); Sally Kenney, *Pregnancy Discrimination: Toward Substantive Equality,* 10 Wis. Women's L.J. 351 (1995); Linton, *supra* note 175, at 43–46.

264. *See* Earl Maltz, *Abortion, Precedent, and the Constitution: A Comment on* Planned Parenthood of Southeastern Pennsylvania v. Casey, 68 Notre Dame L. Rev. 11, 20 (1992).

quite nicely when the dispute is over long-settled property rights.[265] Arguments about reliance have little place in determining fundamental social policy.

The three justices, moreover, advanced the foregoing passage, their only discussion of the merits of the controversy, not as a reason for deciding in favor of a freedom to choose abortion, but as evidence that people have relied on *Roe,* and that therefore to overrule *Roe* would unfairly prejudice those who had relied. Given that the political processes necessary to reinstate pro-hibitory abortion statutes would take longer than two months, any prejudice though reliance seems unlikely. Those who were relying on abortion as their primary means of birth control would be able to abort at least as late as two months into any existing pregnancy and would thereafter be on notice to switch to some other means for effectuating their reproductive choice.[266] Nor did the extensive reliance by governments and individuals on *Lochner v. New York*[267] and *Plessy v. Ferguson*[268] prevent those cases from being overruled.[269] Finally, the troika seems wholly unaware that their heavy stress on supposed social reliance on the *Roe* decision contradicts their vision of the abortion choice as personal and not socially constructed.[270] Be-cause the claim to protect reliance is so patently absurd, Ronald Dworkin (a strong supporter of the *Casey* decision) chose to interpret this as a general appeal to the rule of law rather than an appeal to any actual reliance.[271]

Despite the evident unpersuasiveness of its position, the joint opinion offers the changing roles of women in our national life only as support for the obligation to follow precedent and not as a claim in favor of freedom to choose abortion as such. Abortion rights advocates have in-creasingly made the latter claim.[272] When even Betty Friedan, whom some would count as the founder of the modern women's movement, initially declined to criticize abortion laws,[273] it is hard to claim that abortion is a woman's "first right." The three justices did no better in explain-ing why particular regulations unduly burden a woman's right to abort.[274]

Instead of attempting to develop a real theory that would justify its decision on the merits, the troika rested its opinion largely on an appeal to the doctrine of precedent, the rule of *stare deci-*

---

265. *See, e.g.,* United States v. Title Ins. & Trust Co., 265 U.S. 472 (1924).

266. *Casey,* 505 U.S. at 956–57 (Rehnquist, C.J., partially dissenting, joined by Scalia, Thomas, & White, JJ.). *See also* Sojourner T. v. Edwards, 974 F.2d 27 (5th Cir. 1992) [holding that the overruling of *Roe,* as ar-guably occurred in *Webster v. Reproductive Health Services,* 492 U.S. 490 (1989), did not automatically rein-state Louisiana's pre-*Roe* abortion statute], *cert. denied,* 507 U.S. 972 (1993). *See also* Linton, *supra* note 175, at 42–46.

267. 198 U.S. 45 (1905).

268. 163 U.S. 537 (1896).

269. Brown v. Board of Education, 347 U.S. 483 (1954) (overruling *Plessy*); Bunting v. Oregon, 241 U.S. 426 (1917) (overruling *Lochner sub silentio*). *See generally* Fein, *supra* note 205, at 39, 44–45; Morton Horwitz, *Foreword: The Constitution of Change: Legal Fundamentality without Fundamentalism,* 107 HARV. L. REV. 30, 71–92 (1993).

270. Vanessa Laird, Planned Parenthood v. Casey: *The Role of* Stare Decisis, 57 MOD. L. REV. 461, 464 (1994).

271. Dworkin, *supra* note 139, at 31–32.

272. *See, e.g.,* KRISTIN LUKER, ABORTION AND THE POLITICS OF MOTHERHOOD 97 (1984); ROSALIND POL-LACK PETCHESKY, ABORTION AND WOMEN'S CHOICE: THE STATE, SEXUALITY, AND REPRODUCTIVE FREEDOM 5 (rev. ed. 1990); Eve Paul & Paula Schaap, *Abortion and the Law in 1980,* 25 N.Y.L. SCH. L. REV. 497, 498 (1980); Faye Wattleton, *Reproductive Rights Are Fundamental Rights,* THE HUMANIST, Jan./Feb. 1991, at 21, 22. *See generally* BEVERLY WILDUNG HARRISON, OUR RIGHT TO CHOOSE: TOWARD A NEW ETHIC OF ABORTION (1983).

273. LAWRENCE LADER, ABORTION II: MAKING THE REVOLUTION 36 (1973).

274. *Compare* 505 U.S. at 879–901 (Kennedy, O'Connor, & Souter, JJ., joint plurality op.), *with Id.* at 918–22 (Stevens, J., partially concurring), 934–40 (Blackmun, J., partially concurring), at 965–79 (Rehnquist, C.J., partially dissenting, joined by Scalia, Thomas, & White, JJ.), *and* 986–93 (Scalia, J., partially dissenting, joined by Rehnquist, C.J., Thomas, & White, JJ.). *See also* Dworkin, *supra* note 139, at 30–31.

*sis.*[275] That rule—what one wag, echoing Shakespeare and Swift, defined as a Latin expression meaning "we stand by our past mistakes"[276]—is basically a rule of judicial restraint, although, as law professor Michael Paulsen has shown, one might use the claim of judicial restraint to justify almost any decision one might prefer.[277] Paulsen even went so far as to describe the troika's opinion as a hoax designed to provide cover for their decision rather than an honest discussion of the reasons for their decision.[278] One need not go so far, for it remains axiomatic that *stare decisis* has always had considerably less importance for the interpretation of the constitution than in other contexts, and has steadily become less important through the years, precisely because the Supreme Court itself is, as a practical matter, the only institution capable of correcting the Court's errors of constitutional interpretation.[279] Perhaps Justice Louis Brandeis provided the most cogent statement of this reality in one of his better known dissents:

> *Stare decisis* is usually the wise policy, because in most matters it is more important that the applicable rule of law be settled than that it be settled right. This is commonly true even where the error is a matter of serious concern, provided correction can be had by legislation. But in cases involving the Federal Constitution where correction through legislative action is practically impossible, this Court has often overruled its prior decisions. The Court bows to the lessons of experience and the force of better reasoning,

---

275. *Casey,* 505 U.S. at 861–64 (Kennedy, O'Connor, & Souter, JJ.). *See generally* WHITE, *supra* note 162, at 174–75; Crain, *supra* note 67, at 300–18.

276. James Gordon III, *Humor in Legal Education and Scholarship,* 1992 BYU L. REV. 313, 314 n.7. *See also* Erin O'Hara, *Social Constraint or Implicit Collusion?: Toward a Game Theoretic Analysis of* Stare Decisis, 24 SETON HALL L.J. 736 (1994). For Shakespeare and Swift, see WILLIAM SHAKESPEARE, THE MERCHANT OF VENICE act 4, sc. 1 ("There is no power in Venice Can alter a decree established. 'Twill be recorded for a precedent, And many an error by the same example Will Rush into state."); JONATHAN SWIFT, GULLIVER'S TRAVELS AND OTHER WRITINGS 203 (Mod. Lib. ed. 1988) ("[S]pecial Care to record all the Decisions formerly made against common Justice and the general Reason of Mankind...under the Name of *Precedents*...as Authorities to justify the most iniquitous Opinions."). *See generally* Christopher Peters, *Foolish Consistency: On Equality, Integrity, and Justice in* Stare Decisis, 105 YALE L.J. 2031 (1996).

277. *See* Michael Stokes Paulsen, *Abrogating Stare Decisis by Statute: May Congress Remove the Precedential Effect of* Roe *and* Casey?, 109 YALE L.J. 1535 (2000); Michael Stokes Paulsen, *The Many Faces of "Judicial Restraint,"* 1993 BYU PUB. INTEREST L. REV. 3. *See also* Thomas Lee, *Stare Decisis in Historical Perspective: From the Founding Era to the Rehnquist Court,* 52 VAND. L. REV. 647, 655–703 (1999).

278. Michael Stokes Paulsen, *Captain James T. Kirk and the Enterprise of Constitutional Interpretation: Some Modest Proposals from the Twenty-Third Century,* 59 ALB. L. REV. 671, 679–81 (1995).

279. *See Casey,* 505 U.S. at 954–55 (Rehnquist, C.J., partially dissenting, joined by Scalia, Thomas, & White, JJ.). *See also* Payne v. Tennessee, 501 U.S. 808, 842 (1991) (Souter, J., concurring); Patterson v. McLean Credit Union, 491 U.S. 164, 172–73 (1989); Gliddon v. Zdanok, 370 U.S. 530, 543 (1962). *See generally* J.M. Balkin, *Constitutional Interpretation and the Problem of History,* 63 NYU L. REV. 911, 947 (1988); Raoul Berger, *A Study of Youthful Omniscience: Gerald Lynch on Judicial Review,* 36 ARK. L. REV. 215 (1982); Charles Collier, *Intellectual Authority and Institutional Authority,* 42 J. LEGAL EDUC. 151 (1992); Charles Cooper, Stare Decisis: *Precedent and Principle in Constitutional Adjudication,* 73 CORNELL L. REV. 401, 402 (1988); Michael Gerhardt, *The Role of Precedent in Constitutional Decisionmaking and Theory,* 60 GEO. WASH. L. REV. 68 (1991); Andrew Jacobs, *God Save This Postmodern Court: The Death of Necessity and the Transformation of the Supreme Court's Overruling Rhetoric,* 63 U. CIN. L. REV. 1119 (1995); Gary Lawson, *The Constitutional Case against Precedent,* 17 HARV. J.L. & PUB. POL'Y 23 (1994); Lee, *supra* note 277, at 703–33; Earl Maltz, *Some Thoughts on the Death of* Stare Decisis *in Constitutional Law,* 1980 WIS. L. REV. 467 ("Maltz, *Death of* Stare Decisis"); Earl Maltz, *No Rules in a Knife Fight: Chief Justice Rehnquist and the Doctrine of* Stare Decisis, 25 RUTGERS L.J. 669 (1994); Michael Stokes Paulsen, *The Most Dangerous Branch: Executive Power to Say What the Law Is,* 83 GEO. L.J. 217, 273–75, 318–19, 332–33 (1994); Sullivan, *supra* note 89, at 70–71; Michael Vitiello, Payne v. Tennessee: *A "Stunning* Ipse Dixit," 8 NOTRE DAME J.L. ETHICS & PUB. POL'Y 165 (1994). Law professor Henry Monaghan has argued to the contrary that the basis of constitutional law must be *stare decisis* even when the precedent flies in the face of the constitution's meaning. Monaghan, *supra* note 164, at 744–50. Monaghan presents this as a defense of *Brown v. Board of Education,* without, however, explaining why the Court in *Brown* was justified in overruling *Plessy v. Ferguson.*

recognizing that the process of trial and error, so fruitful in the physical sciences, is appropriate also in the judicial function.[280]

The Library of Congress confirmed the reality of the Brandeis observation in a study identifying 184 instances in which the Supreme Court has overruled its earlier decisions.[281] Attorney Bruce Fein has counted as many as 300 such overrulings.[282] Law professor David O'Brien has counted 157 overrulings just since 1937.[283] In contrast, only four decisions of the Supreme Court have been reversed by Constitutional Amendment.[284] Yet a majority of the Court has insisted that *Roe* stand solely because of *stare decisis,* giving no constitutional warrant whatsoever for the decision on the substantive merits of the question.[285] Moreover, these champions of *stare decisis* for *Roe* have been among the most notable critics of that notion in other contexts.

Justices Anthony Kennedy, Sandra Day O'Connor, and David Souter regularly vote to overrule other decisions without fretting over the overruling a constitutional precedent, let alone the elaborate agonizing they espoused in *Casey.*[286] In fact, Kennedy and O'Connor could better be described as generally following a kind of "personal *stare decisis*"—following their own previously expressed views—rather than "institutional *stare decisis*"—in which one who dissents from the original decision feels bound by that decision as a precedent in later cases.[287] Kennedy and O'Connor, only four years after their defense of *stare decisis* in *Casey,* helped to make a majority for an opinion by Chief Justice William Rehnquist containing the following passage:

---

280. Burnet v. Coronado Oil & Gas Co., 285 U.S. 393, 406–10 (1932) (Brandeis, J., dissenting).

281. CONGRESSIONAL RESEARCH SERVICE, THE CONSTITUTION OF THE UNITED STATES: ANALYSIS AND INTERPRETATION 2115–27 & Supp. (1987). *See also* Harper v. Virginia Dep't of Taxation, 509 U.S. 86, 108–09 (1993) (Scalia, J., dissenting); SAUL BRENNER & HAROLD SPAETH, *STARE INDECISIS:* THE ALTERATION OF PRECEDENT ON THE SUPREME COURT, 1946–1992, at 16 (1995); Albert Blaustein & Andrew Field, *"Overruling" Opinions in the Supreme Court,* 57 MICH. L .REV. 151, 167, 184–94 (1958); Gerhardt, *supra* note 279, at 156–59; Lee, *supra* note 277, at 648–49; Maltz, *supra* note 263, at 12–17; Maltz, *Death of* Stare Decisis, *supra* note 279, at 494–96; Michael Pearce Pfeifer, *Abandoning Error: Self-Correction by the Supreme Court,* in ABORTION AND THE CONSTITUTION, *supra* note 16, at 3. One could easily add numerous further cases decided since the congressional study; arguably *Roe* itself has been overruled silently. James Bopp, jr., *et al., Does the United States Supreme Court Have a Constitutional Duty to Expressly Reconsider and Overrule* Roe v. Wade?, 1 SETON HALL CONST. L.J. 55, 77 (1990); Bopp & Coleson, *supra* note 132, at 277–78; Pine & Law, *supra* note 89, at 409–12.

282. Fein, *supra* note 205, at 44.

283. O'BRIEN, *supra* note 10, at 225. The bulk of these have been between 1953 and 1985; the "Warren Court" explicitly overruled 63 decisions, and the "Burger Court" explicitly overruled 61 decisions. *See* Todd Freed, Comment, *Is* Stare Decisis *Still the Lighthouse Beacon of Supreme Court Jurisprudence?: A Critical Analysis,* 57 OHIO ST. L.J. 1767, 1779 n.74 (1996).

284. *See* Chisholm v. Georgia, 2 U.S. (2 Dall.) 419 (1793) (reversed by the 11th Am.); Dred Scott v. Sanford, 60 U.S. (19 How.) 393 (1857) (13th & 14th Ams.); Pollack v. Farmers' Loan & Trust, 158 U.S. 601 (1895) (16th Am.); Oregon v. Mitchell, 400 U.S. 112 (1970) (26th Am.). *See generally* TRIBE, *supra* note 10, at 123; Pfeifer, *supra* note 281, at 52.

285. *Casey,* 505 U.S. at 854–69 (Kennedy, O'Connor, & Souter, JJ., joint plurality op.), 912 (Stevens, J., partially concurring), 924–25 (Blackmun, J., partially concurring); Thornburgh v. American College of Obstetricians, 476 U.S. 747, 779–81 (1986); City of Akron v. Akron Center for Reproductive Health, 462 U.S. 416, 420 (1983). *See generally* CRAIG & O'BRIEN, *supra* note 10, at 339–41; Smolin, *supra* note 175, at 138–39.

286. *See, e.g.,* Adarand Contractors, Inc. v. Pena, 515 U.S. 200 (1995) [overruling *Metro Broadcasting, Inc. v. FCC,* 497 U.S. 547 (1990)]; Quill Corp. v. North Dakota, 504 U.S. 298 (1992) [overruling *National Bellas Hess, Inc. v. Department of Revenue,* 386 U.S. 753 (1967)]; Payne v. Tennessee, 501 U.S. 808 (1991) [overruling *Booth v. Maryland,* 482 U.S. 496 (1987), & *South Carolina v. Gathers,* 490 U.S. 805 (1989)]; Coleman v. Thompson, 501 U.S. 722 (1991) [overruling *Fay v. Noia,* 372 U.S. 391 (1963)]. *See also* LAZARUS, *supra* note 10, at 447–48 (describing a similar inconsistency on the part of Justice Thurgood Marshall).

287. Scaturro, *supra* note 126, at 201–03. *See generally* BRENNER & SPAETH, *supra* note 281, at 73, 85, 87, 109.

Generally, the principle of *stare decisis*, and the interests that it serves, *viz.*, 'the even-handed, predictable, and consistent development of legal principles,... reliance on judicial decisions, and... the actual and perceived integrity of the judicial process," counsel strongly against reconsideration of our precedent. Nevertheless, we always have treated *stare decisis* as a "principle of policy," and not as an "inexorable command." "[W]hen governing decisions are unworkable or are badly reasoned, 'this Court has never felt constrained to follow precedent.'" Our willingness to reconsider earlier decisions have been "particularly true in constitutional cases, because in such cases 'correction through legislative action is practically impossible.'" (citations omitted)[288]

Justice Harry Blackmun, despite recognizing a necessary reluctance to overrule recent precedent, found no reason to hesitate to overrule a precedent less than a decade old that he found "unsound in principle and unworkable in practice" in writing for a five-to-four majority.[289] Blackmun had foreshadowed this attitude during his confirmation hearings, stating:

Precedent, I think, is a very valuable thing in the law. A lawyer has to say, however, that it is not absolute. Judges, even Justices of the Supreme Court, are human and I suppose attitudes change as we go along. I have made statements before that the overruling by the Supreme Court of a prior precedent is not a matter of great alarm. I think this has happened throughout its history. As times have changed, Justices have changed. People take a second look.[290]

In a similar vein, Justice John Paul Stevens, who concurred and dissented in *Casey* on the basis of *stare decisis*, has endorsed overruling precedent when it is inconsistent with his "sense of justice," the needs of "social welfare," or "the *mores* of the day."[291] Stevens, writing for a plurality of the Court, has even disregarded the usually higher respect accorded *stare decisis* in statutory cases.[292] He argued in *Hubbard v. United States* for the overruling of a statutory interpretation established for 40 years that had seemed to be working rather well even if, as Stevens concluded, it was wrongly decided.[293] The only limitation that Stevens has acknowledged was that the court should refrain from overruling a precedent unless it was "egregiously incorrect."[294]

Another frequent champion of *stare decisis* when *Roe* was questioned, Justice William Brennan, told us in 1985, when he apparently did not have the *Roe* problem in mind, that:

[T]he unique interpretive role of the Supreme Court with respect to the Constitution *demands* some flexibility with respect to the call of *stare decisis*.... When a Justice perceives an interpretation of the text to have departed from its essential meaning, that Justice is bound, by a larger constitutional duty to the community, to expose the departure and point toward a different path.[295]

---

288. Seminole Tribe v. Florida, 517 U.S. 44, 57–73 (1996).

289. Garcia v. San Antonio Metropolitan Transit Auth'y, 469 U.S. 528, 546, 557 (1985).

290. *Hearings before the Sen. Comm. on the Judiciary on the Nomination of Harry A. Blackmun,* 91st Cong., 2d Sess. 43 (1970).

291. Johnson v. Transportation Agency, 480 U.S. 616, 645 n.4 (1987) (Stevens, J., concurring); Runyon v. McCrary, 427 U.S. 160, 191 (1976) (Stevens, J., concurring).

292. Square D Co. v. Niagara Frontier Tariff Bureau, Inc., 476 U.S. 409, 424 (1986); Illinois Brick Co. v. Illinois, 431 U.S. 720, 736 (1977). *See also* William Eskridge, jr., *Overruling Statutory Precedents,* 76 GEO. L.J. 1361 (1988); Thomas Lee, Stare Decisis *in Economic Perspective: An Economic Analysis of the Supreme Court's Doctrine of Precedent,* 78 N. CAR. L. REV. 643, 691–705 (2000); Lawrence Marshall, *Let Congress Do It: The Case for an Absolute Rule of Statutory* Decisis, 88 MICH. L. REV. 177 (1989);

293. Hubbard v. United States, 514 U.S. 695, 711–16 (1995) (plurality op. *per* Stevens, J.).

294. Florida Dep't of Health & Rehab. Services v. Florida Nursing Home Ass'n, 450 U.S. 147, 153 (1981) (Stevens, J., concurring).

295. William Brennan, jr., *The Constitution of the United States: Contemporary Ratification,* 27 S. TEX. L. REV. 433 444 (1986) (emphasis added). *See also* Cooper, *supra* note 279, at 408; William Douglas, Stare Deci-

Of course, Brennan also insisted on seeking the "*actual* legislative intent" found through the "use of all available materials"[296]—but only when the search would not frustrate his personal goals on the bench. But then, Brennan, in a private Court memorandum regarding his opinion in *Green v. New Kent County*[297]—the first school busing case to reach the Supreme Court—had declared that honesty simply was "not practical" in this area.[298]

The Court as a whole reaffirmed the proposition that the doctrine of *stare decisis* does not preclude overruling an erroneous interpretation of the Constitution in *Payne v. Tennessee*[299]—only a year before the *Casey* decision was handed down. Only Justice David Souter, among those voting to reaffirm *Roe* on the basis of *stare decisis,* seems truly committed by sentiment and practice to a strong notion of precedent even in constitutional cases.[300] Yet even he joined in overruling precedent in *Payne*.[301] The others all seem open to attorney Bruce Fein's conclusion that "[t]here should be no statute of limitations for constitutional truths."[302] As law professor Karl Llewellyn pointed out some 30 years earlier,

> No phase of our law is so misunderstood as our system of precedent. The basic false conception is that a precedent or the precedents will in fact (and in a "precedent-system" ought to) dictate the decision in the current case.... Now the truth is this: only in times of stagnation or decay does an appellate system even fairly resemble such a picture of detailed dictation by the precedents.[303]

Law professor Lawrence Tribe, when not writing on abortion, expressed the same point even more strongly when he compared Justices who view constitutional precedents as binding in any strong sense as lacking "a sufficient appreciation of the evolutionary nature of constitutional law. It is sometimes more important that the court be right than that it be consistent."[304] The end result, as Karl Llewellyn noted, is that an ignorant or unimaginative judge will not know how to avoid a precedent and thus will be bound by the past, but the creative and skillful judge ("whom we would make free") will find a way to dispose of bad precedents. In Llewellyn's view, this makes the doctrine of precedent largely a force for good rather than something that truly binds us to past mistakes.[305] It is no wonder, however, why some commentators conclude that the Justices simply manipulate the doctrine of *stare decisis* to achieve preconceived ends.[306]

Manipulation is a charge particularly suited to the abortion cases. The full Latin maxim from which the phrase "*stare decisis*" comes is "*stare decisis et quieta non movere*": "Stand by decisions

---

sis, 49 COLUM. L. REV. 735, 746 (1949); Herbert Wechsler, *Foreword: Toward Neutral Principles of Constitutional Law,* 73 HARV. L. REV. 1, 31 (1959).

296. Public Citizen v. United States Dep't of Justice, 491 U.S. 440, 454 (1989).

297. 391 U.S. 430 (1968).

298. Lino Graglia, *Do Judges Have a Policy-Making Role in the American System of Government?,* 17 HARV. J.L. & PUB. POL'Y 121, 127 (1994) ("Graglia, *Policy*"); Lino Graglia, *When Honesty Is "Simply Impractical" for the Supreme Court,* 85 MICH. L. REV. 1153, 1169 (1985). *See generally* BERNARD SCHWARTZ, SWANN'S WAY: THE SCHOOL BUSING CASE AND THE SUPREME COURT 29–90 (1986).

299. 501 U.S. 808, 826–29, 829–30 (1991). *See also* United States v. Scott, 437 U.S. 82, 101 (1978); West Virginia Bd. Educ. v. Barnette, 319 U.S. 624, 642 (1943); Erie R.R. v. Tompkins, 304 U.S. 64, 74–78 (1938).

300. *See* LAZARUS, *supra* note 10, at 468–69; Koehler, *supra* note 163; Wilkins, Sherlock, & Clark, *supra* note 188, at 155–56.

301. *Casey,* 501 U.S. at 836–42 (Souter, J., concurring).

302. Fein, *supra* note 207, at 44. *See generally* Paulsen, *supra* note 279, at 272–76.

303. KARL LLEWELLYN, THE COMMON LAW TRADITION 62 (1960).

304. TRIBE, *supra* note 10, at 123.

305. KARL LLEWELLYN, THE BRAMBLE BUSH 68 (1951). *See also* O'Hara, *supra* note 276, at 804 2n.26; Roger Traynor, *Transatlantic Reflections on Leeways and Limits of Appellate Courts,* 1980 UTAH L. REV. 255, 263.

306. *See, e.g.,* Cooper, *supra* note 279, at 404; Linda Meyer, *"Nothing We Say Matters": Teague and the New Rules,* 61 U. CHI. L. REV. 423, 423 (1994).

and do not disturb the calm."[307] The maxim commands respect for settled legal doctrine, but does not apply to decisions like *Roe* that never received general assent.[308] Moreover, not only conservatives or committed opponents of current abortion policy see *Roe* as deserving to be overruled. For example, law professor Arnold Loewy, a self-described supporter of the freedom to abort, nevertheless supports overruling *Roe* precisely because the case has "departed from [the] essential meaning" of the Constitution:

> For an academic to advocate the overruling of a case so firmly entrenched, at least according to the Court's most recent opinion on the subject [*Thornburgh v. American College of Obstetricians*, 476 U.S. 747 (1986)], requires more than a demonstration that the case is wrong. Academics think many cases are wrong, and a healthy respect for stare decisis requires that simple wrongness not be the predicate for overruling a decision that the Court recently and resoundingly endorsed. *Roe v. Wade*, however, is not simply wrong; it is *Wrong* in a fundamental way that few, if any, recent decisions of the Supreme Court can match. The unique *wrongness* of *Roe* lies in its utter lack of support from any source that is legitimate for constitutional interpretation, coupled with its wholesale denial to a substantial portion of the populace of a meaningful opportunity to effectuate legislative change.[309]

Legal scholars, however, also partake of the "abortion distortion"—the inability to apply concepts they generally support consistently if to do so would imperil the freedom to abort. Thus, Ronald Dworkin, probably the leading legal philosopher working in the English language today, defended reliance on the doctrine of *stare decisis* for sustaining *Roe*.[310] When not discussing abortion, however, Dworkin opposes a strong rule requiring the following of precedent, particularly in constitutional litigation.[311]

In other words, to reaffirm an egregiously erroneous decision for no better reason than an overly rigid adherence to *stare decisis* is both unprecedented and shortsighted. Based as *Roe* was on a deliberately falsified history[312] and faced with steadily growing knowledge about the development of a human fetus during gestation,[313] the reasoning in *Roe* was, and is, fundamentally flawed. After all, "a Constitution...would serve little purpose if all that it promised, like the elegantly phrased Constitutions of some totalitarian or dictatorial Nations, was an ideal to be worshipped when not needed and debased when crucial."[314] As Justice Douglas once reminded us, "[a] judge...remembers that it is the Constitution which he (*sic*) swore to support and defend, not the gloss which his predecessors may have put upon it."[315]

To insist on rigid adherence to precedent because departure from the precedent would be controversial, as the troika did, defeats the whole point of judicial review. Such a refusal is

---

307. Stanley Reed, Stare Decisis *and Constitutional Law,* 9 PA. BAR ASS'N Q. 131, 131 (April 1938). *See also* Turpin v. Locket, 10 Va. (6 Call.) 113, 185 (1804).

308. Crain, *supra* note 67, at 302–03.

309. Arnold Loewy, *Why Roe v. Wade Should Be Overruled,* 67 N. CAR. L. REV. 939, 939 (1989). On Loewy's attitude towards the freedom to abort, see *id.* at 944, 947 n.57. *See also* John Hart Ely, *The Wages of Crying Wolf,* 82 YALE L.J. 920, 947 (1973).

310. Dworkin, *supra* note 139, at 31–32; Dworkin, *supra* note 142, at 430.

311. *See* Dworkin, *Response to Letters,* N.Y. REV. BOOKS, Nov. 19, 1992, at 56–57; Dworkin, *supra* note 142, at 417–18.

312. See the text *supra* at notes 44–66; Chapter 14, at notes 390–95, 435–57.

313. *See* Chapter 15, at notes 357–400; Chapter 18, at notes 1–209.

314. Flushing Nat'l Bank v. Municipal Assistance, 358 N.E.2d 848, 854 (N.Y. 1976). *See also* SUSAN BURGESS, CONTEST FOR CONSTITUTIONAL AUTHORITY 48–52 (1992); Dworkin, *supra* note 142, at 417.

315. Douglas, *supra* note 295, at 736. *See also* Lawson, 17 HARV. J.L. & PUB. POL'Y 23 (1994).

based not upon constitutional principle but only on concern for the Court's own power.[316] As one observer noted, the argument in *Casey* seems to come down to this: "[T]he further a decision deviates from the Constitution, the more important it is for the Court to adhere to that decision, or else the public may conclude that the emperor has no clothes."[317] That cannot be correct reading of the law. Nor can adhering to that proposition be expected to buttress the institutional legitimacy of the Court in the manner that the troika sought.[318] After all, *stare decisis* simply is not a coherent theory of judicial interpretation; it is only an admonition that, given concerns of prudence and judicial economy, mere disagreement with a prior decision is not a good enough reason for overruling it.[319] When good enough reasons exist, it would be an abuse of discretion for the Court to decline to overrule a bad precedent on the basis of *stare decisis* alone.[320]

The *Casey* plurality's inconsistency in this regard was particularly dramatic. Not only is a standard depending on the quantum of interference with a right rarely relevant to constitutional jurisprudence, but such a standard had no prior basis in the jurisprudence of abortion apart from Justice Sandra Day O'Connor's lone voice in support of the "undue burden" standard.[321] Only Justices William Rehnquist and Byron White had joined O'Connor's opinion in *City of Akron v. Akron Center for Reproductive Health*,[322] where she first proposed the "undue burden" test. She alone supported this theory in *Thornburgh v. American College of Obstetricians*,[323] *Webster v. Reproductive Health Services*,[324] and *Hodgson v. Minnesota*.[325] Even O'Connor chose not to rely on the "undue burden" test in *Rust v. Sullivan*.[326] And O'Connor redefined the "undue burden" standard from case to case. She started with a rule that would rarely find a statutory regulation of abortion unconstitutional (an "absolute obstacle" or "severe limitation" on the exercise of the right to abort),[327] only to arrive in *Casey* at a test that could find many such statutes unconstitutional (a "substantial obstacle" to the exercise of the right to abort).[328] The joint opinion's authors thus found themselves insisting that the rule of *stare decisis* requires the Court to enforce an "undue burden" standard that had been explicitly rejected by large majorities on the Court at least four times in the context of abortion. Instead of explaining or justifying why a right to abort is to be found in the Constitution, the plurality (and to a lesser extent Justices Harry

---

316. Michael Stokes Paulsen, *Book Review*, 10 CONST'L COMMENTARY 221, 226–33 (1993).

317. Thomas Merrill, *A Modest Proposal for a Political Court*, 17 HARV. J.L. & PUB. POL'Y 137, 137 (1994).

318. LAZARUS, *supra* note 10, at 483.

319. Crain, *supra* note 67, at 315.

320. Burnet v. Coronado Oil & Gas Co., 285 U.S. 393, 405–06 (1932) (Brandeis, J., dissenting).

321. *See generally* Estrich & Sullivan, *supra* note 79, at 133–34, 140; Dorothy Roberts, *Sandra Day O'Connor, Conservative Discourse, and Reproductive Freedom*, 13 WOMEN'S RTS. L. RPTR. 95, 98–100 (1991); Stephen Wermiel, *O'Connor: A Dual Role—An Introduction*, 13 WOMEN'S RTS. L. RPTR. 129, 135–37 (1991); David Zampa, Note, *The Supreme Court's Abortion Jurisprudence: Will the Supreme Court Pass the "Albatross" Back to the States?*, 65 NOTRE DAME L. REV. 731, 760–80 (1990). For an argument that the "undue burden" standard is not an innovation but rather captures the analysis implicit in the jurisprudence of much of due process litigation, see Brownstein, *supra* note 214.

322. 462 U.S. 416, 458–67 (1983) (O'Connor, J., dissenting).

323. 476 U.S. 747, 828–32 (1986) (O'Connor, J., dissenting).

324. 492 U.S. 490, 523 (1989) (O'Connor, J., concurring).

325. 497 U.S. 417, 458–60 (1990) (O'Connor, J., concurring).

326. 500 U.S. 173, 222–23 (O'Connor, J., concurring).

327. *City of Akron*, 462 U.S. at 453 (O'Connor, J., dissenting). *See also Thornburgh*, 476 U.S. at 828 (O'Connor, J., dissenting).

328. *Casey*, 505 U.S. at 877 (Kennedy, O'Connor, & Souter, JJ., joint plurality op.). Justice Kennedy had earlier supported the "rational basis" standard of review, switching to the new "undue burden" standard in *Casey. See Webster*, 492 U.S. at 499 (plur. op. per Rehnquist, C.J., joined by Kennedy & Scalia, JJ.). *See generally* Horan, *supra* note 190, at 516–18; Richard Lacayo, *Inside the Court*, TIME, July 13, 1992, at 29.

Blackmun and John Paul Stevens) attempted to explain when, and why, constitutional precedent should be overruled, focusing particularly on the two most controversial instances of overruling in this century—the overruling of *Lochner v. New York*[329] and *Plessy v. Ferguson*.[330]

The Court's account of the overruling *Lochner*—a case declaring state regulation of economic activity unconstitutional—is remarkable. After *Dred Scott v. Sanford*,[331] *Lochner* is the most thoroughly discredited decision in the Court's history. Today, most theories of constitutional interpretation begins with an account of how *Lochner* was wrong,[332] so much so that "the ultimate… criticism of a constitutional decision is to say that it is 'like *Lochner*.'"[333] The need to explain *Lochner* is equally strong for justices of the Supreme Court as for attorneys and legal scholars.[334] Only rarely have recent accounts of *Lochner* attempted to explain rather than criticize that decision.[335] Yet all the troika on the Court could develop to explain the demise of *Lochner* was a rather lame assertion that the Depression had shown that the factual assumption underlying that decision (the assumption that laissez faire contractual freedom would promote "minimal levels of human welfare") was untrue.[336] The troika thus seemed to rely on two unlikely claims: that the "factual" assumption they attributed to 1905 was uncontested in 1905 and that the same assumption had no supporters in 1937. But then, the troika even misidentified (by 20 years) the decision that overruled Lochner.[337]

---

329. 198 U.S. 45 (1905).

330. 163 U.S. 537 (1896).

331. 60 U.S. (19 How.) 393 (1857).

332. John Hart Ely, Democracy and Distrust 4, 65 (1980); Paul Kens, Lochner v. New York: Economic Regulation on Trial (1998); Lazarus, *supra* note 10, at 337–39; Richard Posner, Law and Literature: A Misunderstood Relation 285–86 (1988); Bernard Schwartz, A History of the Supreme Court 202 (2nd ed. 1993); White, *supra* note 162, at 159; J.M. Balkin & Sanford Levinson, *The Canons of Constitutional Law,* 111 Harv. L. Rev. 963, 1019 (1998); David Berntsein, *Lochner's Legacy's Legacy,* 82 Tex. L. Rev. 1 (2003); Matthew Bewig, Lochner v. the Journeymen Bakers of New York: *The Journeyman Bakers, Their Hours of Labor, and the Constitution,* 38 Am. J. Legal Hist. 413 (1994); Horwitz, *supra* note 269, at 74; Paul Kens, Lochner v. New York: *Rehabilitated and Revised, but Still Reviled,* 1 J. Sup. Ct. Hist. 1 (1997); Gene Nichol, *Constitutional Judgment (book rev.),* 91 Mich. L. Rev. 1107, 1108 (1993); Gary Rowe, Lochner *Revisionism Revisited,* 24 Law & Soc. Inquiry 221, 222–23 (1999); Warren Sandmann, *The Argumentative Creation of Individual Liberty,* 23 Hastings Const'l L.Q. 637 (1996); Eileen Scallen, *Presence and Absence in* Lochner: *Making Rights Real,* 23 Hastings Const'l L.Q. 621 (1996); Stephen Siegel, Lochner *Era Jurisprudence and the American Constitutional Tradition,* 70 N.C. L. Rev. 1 (1991); Cass Sunstein, Lochner's *Legacy,* 87 Colum. L. Rev. 873 (1987); William Wiethoff, *Preaching the Constitution,* 23 Hastings Const'l L.Q. 627 (1996).

333. Grey, *supra* note 18, at 711.

334. *See, e.g.,* United States v. Lopez, 514 U.S. 549, 601 n.9 (1995) (Scalia, J., for the majority), 605 (Souter, J., dissenting). *See* Blackman, *supra* note 168, at 520; Rowe, *supra* note 332, at 223, n.3.

335. *See, e.g.,* 8 Owen Fiss, History of the Supreme Court of the United States: Troubled Beginnings of the Modern State, 1888–1910, at 12–21, 103–06, 158–59, 165 (1993); *See generally* Howard Gillman, The Constitution Besieged: The Rise and Demise of Lochner Era Police Powers Jurisprudence (1993); Morton Horwitz, The Transformation of American Law, 1870–1960: The Crisis of Legal Orthodoxy 27–30, 208–10, 272 (1987); Bernard Siegan, Economic Liberties and the Constitution 113–21 (1980); David Bernstein, Lochner *Era Revisionism, Revised:* Lochner *and the Origins of Fundamental Rights Constitutionalism,* 92 Geo. L.J. 1 (2003); Jonathan Macey, *Public Choice, Public Opinion, and the Fuller Court,* 49 Vand. L. Rev. 373, 384–86 (1996); Michael Phillips, *The Progressiveness of the* Lochner *Court,* 75 Den. U. L. Rev. 453 (1998); Jonathan Sullivan, Comment, Eastern Enterprises v. Apfel: *How Lochner Got It Right,* 60 Ohio St. L.J. 1104 (1999); Charles Warren, *The Progressiveness of the United States Supreme Court,* 13 Colum. L. Rev. 294 (1913). *See also* Stephen Siegel, Lochner *Era Jurisprudence and the American Constitutional Tradition,* 70 N. Car. L. Rev. 1 (1991).

336. 505 U.S. 861–62 (Kennedy, O'Connor, & Souter, JJ., joint plurality op.).

337. *Id.* (identifying *West Coast Hotel Co. v. Parrish,* 300 U.S. 179 (1937), as the case in which *Lochner* was overruled; *West Coast Hotel* did overrule cases that built on *Lochner,* but *Lochner* itself had been overruled on its facts in *Bunting v. Oregon,* 241 U.S. 426 (1917)].

The troika's explanation of the overruling of *Lochner* is woefully inadequate.[338] The three-some did not even take account of Justice Oliver Wendell Holmes' widely admired dissent in *Lochner*, a dissent that criticized the majority on the basis of their legal theories, not because of their factual assumptions.[339] The troika's rationale also missed a fundamental point. One's conclusion regarding whether "freedom of contract" really contributed to the achievement of "minimum levels of human welfare," in 1905 and in 1937 rested as much or more on moral judgments (about what constitutes human welfare and what constitutes minimum levels thereof) as on factual determinations.[340] The troika's steadfast refusal to recognize that the fault lay in the earlier Court's claim to make highly contested moral judgments helps to sustain the troika's refusal to confront the similar moral failing of the Court's *Roe* opinion. Nor did the troika even attempt to apply its theory of *Lochner's* failings to the *Roe* opinion. The troika simply refused to reexamine Justice Blackmun's conclusions regarding the history of abortion or when "life" begins.

Justice Harry Blackmun himself had relied in *Roe* on "substantive due process" as the basis for the alleged constitutional right to abort *à la Lochner,* following Justice John Marshall Harlan's opinion in *Griswold v. Connecticut.*[341] Blackmun expressly rejected two other approaches that underlay the discovery of a constitutional "right to privacy" in *Griswold*—Justice William Douglas' "penumbras"[342] and Justice Arthur Goldberg's reliance on the Ninth Amendment.[343] Apparently, Blackmun did so because the "due process" clause protects "persons," allowing him to argue rather easily that this protected the interests of women ("persons") but not the interests of fetuses (merely "potential life").[344] The troika said not one word about how their theory regarding *Lochner* might undercut the rationale in *Roe.*

The moral bankruptcy of the joint plurality opinion is even more embarrassingly evident when one compares *Casey* to *Brown*. *Plessy*, the case *Brown* overruled, is even more universally condemned than *Lochner* as the paradigm of an egregiously wrong decision.[345] The troika again explained the later decision as correcting a "factual assumption" that formed the basis of overruled decision: the assumption that legally enforced racial segregation did not brand people of color as inferior.[346] The troika, however, described *Plessy* as wrong the day it was decided.[347] After all, the first Justice John Marshall Harlan had identified the psychological "badge of inferiority" that segregation implied as the major fault in the majority opinion in his *Plessy* dissent.[348]

The troika's analysis suggests that *Brown* did not result from a change of circumstances justifying a new departure in constitutional law, but was the correction of a simple, albeit tragic, factual error by the earlier Court.[349] As with their analysis of *Lochner*, their analysis of *Plessy* pro-

---

338. Horwitz, *supra* note 269, at 75–82.
339. 198 U.S. at 75–76 (Holmes, J., dissenting). *See also* WHITE, *supra* note 162, at 175.
340. Horwitz, *supra* note 269, at 75, 91–92; Cass Sunstein, *On Analogical Reasoning,* 106 HARV. L. REV. 741, 773 n.113 (1993).
341. *Roe,* 410 U.S. at 153, relying on *Griswold,* 381 U.S. at 499–502 (Harlan, J., concurring).
342. *Griswold,* 381 U.S. at 484–86 (Douglas, J., plur. op.).
343. *Id.* at 487–99 (Goldberg, J., concurring).
344. Blackman, *supra* note 168, at 523–24.
345. *See* Shannon O'Byrne & James McGinnis, *Case Comment:* Vriend v. Alberta: Plessy *Revisited: Lesbian and Gay Rights in the Province of Alberta,* 34 ALBERTA L. REV. 892 (1996).
346. *Casey,* 505 U.S. at 862–64 (Kennedy, O'Connor, & Souter, JJ., joint plurality op.).
347. *Id.* at 863.
348. Plessy v. Ferguson, 163 U.S. 537, 562 (Harlan, J., dissenting).
349. WHITE, *supra* note 163, at 176–77 n.21; Daniel Morrissey, *Moral Truth and the Law: A New Look at an Old Link,* 47 SMU L. REV. 61, 63, 89–91 (1993).

vides at best a weak rationale for its overruling.[350] Legal historian Morton Horwitz aptly summarized the problem with the troika's analysis of *Plessy* in these words:

> If *Plessy* was "wrong the day it was decided," it was not because the Supreme Court had failed to inform itself about the "facts" that underlay racial segregation or because the Court was unaware of the social meaning of Jim Crow laws, but rather because, almost from the moment the Civil War ended, the Court's decisions constituted betrayal of the "one pervading purpose"—the underlying spirit—of the Civil War Amendments.[351]

Furthermore, the troika refused to apply their own analytical method to the *Roe* decision. This fault is a particularly striking as the joint opinion's authors repeatedly suggested that some (perhaps all) of them would not have joined in the *Roe* majority opinion had they been on the Court in 1973.[352] Ronald Dworkin finds the arguments in *Casey* so compelling that he finds this statement puzzling.[353] Others see this admission of moral bankruptcy as simply carrying forward the moral bankruptcy of the original *Roe* decision.[354]

The admission that the troika (or at least several of them) would not have joined *Roe* had they been on the Court in 1973 is not all that surprising when one finds even strong proponents of abortional freedom describing the *Roe* opinion as "insane," "irrational," and "poorly reasoned."[355] After all, what would we have said about the Warren Court had it written in *Brown v. Board of Education* that although the Court had been egregiously wrong in *Plessy v. Ferguson* when it announced the doctrine of "separate but equal" in race relations, the doctrine of *stare decisis* precluded a later Court from reconsidering *Plessy*? This question became the starting point for a parody of the *Casey* opinion, purported to be a "first draft" of a *Brown* opinion of three "centrist" justices, written in the style of the joint plurality opinion in *Casey* and reaffirming *Plessy* on the basis of *stare decisis* after noting that *Plessy*, although wrong when decided, had not proven unworkable, had not been undermined by doctrinal or factual developments, and had been heavily relied on by the public.[356] The purported opinion concludes with an appeal to the need for the Court not to appear to buckle to political pressure in such sensitive cases, and an appeal to the public to rally around the decision to end to the political divisiveness of the issue.

Neither fear to engage with the relevant social science in which the Court was not expert, nor the centrality of decisions about the meaning of "personhood," nor in intimate personal relations presented an impediment to *Brown* and its progeny.[357] While *Brown* was subject to similar criticisms of assuming that which needed to be demonstrated and failing to provide an adequate

---

350. *See Casey,* 505 U.S. at 960 (Rehnquist, C.J., dissenting) (describing the joint opinion's explanation of *Brown* as "at best a feebly supported, *post hoc* rationalization"), 962 (describing the joint opinion's rationale on *Brown* as "strange"); Horwitz, *supra* note 269, at 82–90; Linton, *supra* note 175, at 65–66.

351. Horwitz, *supra* note 269, at 88. *See also* Michael McConnell, *Originalism and the Desegregation Decisions,* 81 Va. L. Rev. 947 (1995).

352. *Casey,* 505 U.S. at 853, 861, 864, 871 (Kennedy, O'Connor, & Souter, JJ., joint plurality op.). *See generally* White, *supra* note 162, at 155, 169– 70, 180–82; Horwitz, *supra* note 269, at 82–91; Linton, *supra* note 175, at 18–19, 38, 73; Smolin, *supra* note 175, at 136–42.

353. Dworkin, *supra* note 139, at 31.

354. Wilkins, Sherlock, & Clark, *supra* note 190, at 149.

355. Robin West, *Jurisprudence and Gender,* 55 U. Chi. L. Rev. 1, 69–70 (1988). *See also* Chapter 14, at notes 425–34.

356. Michael Stokes Paulsen & Daniel Rosen, Brown, Casey-*Style: The Shocking First Draft of the Segregation Opinion,* 69 NYU L. Rev. 1287 (1994).

357. *See, e.g.,* Wechsler, *supra* note 290. *See also* Alan Tomkins & Kevin Oursland, *Social and Social Scientific Perspectives in Judicial Interpretations of the Constitution: A (sic) Historical View and Overview,* 15 Law & Behavior 101 (1991).

legal analysis to justify its results,[358] the ensuing decades have seen the nation confirm the practical wisdom of *Brown* in that collectively we have at least accepted its premises as irrefutable even if we still disagree about working out the details of its conclusions.[359] This acceptance was largely accomplished within the first two decades after the *Brown* decision. Indeed, just as discrediting *Lochner* is the ultimate test of any theory of constitutional interpretation, justifying *Brown* has become the ultimate test.[360] The first two decades after *Roe*, however, have seen nothing similar. One need only recall the mass demonstrations for and against abortion and the role the issue plays in our political life.[361]

Perhaps this difference arises from the fact that *Brown* was clearly rooted in the text of the Constitution's Fourteenth Amendment and arguably built upon the historical tradition of that text, whereas *Roe* does neither.[362] There is a clear textual basis in the Constitution for *Brown* and no textual basis for *Roe* whatsoever. Indeed, to the extent that the text of the Constitution is relevant, it would seem to support a right to life for the fetus rather than a right to choose to kill the fetus. Not only is "life" protected from federal and state action in the Fifth and Fourteenth Amendments, but the preamble to the Constitution (which at least ought to be relevant to interpreting the text proper) speaks of securing "the Blessings of Liberty to ourselves and our Posterity…"[363] Law professor David Smolin furthermore suggests that the difference results because *Brown* is justified by a moral principle, but that no such claim is made for *Roe*. Supporters of *Roe* do not claim that abortion is morally correct but that abortion is always a tragic event and that it must be a personal matter each woman should decide for herself.[364] *Brown* reached back to the Civil War Amendments to seize the moral high ground to invite blacks and their allies into the political dialogue.[365] *Roe,* without any such clear mandate, sought to exclude those who spoke on behalf of the unborn from political debate.[366] President Ronald Reagan, the first President George Bush, and Pennsylvania Governor Robert Casey—the most prominent political opponents of abortion rights when the Court decided *Casey*—simply are not the moral equivalent of racist leader David Duke.

Today we cannot imagine the Senate confirming a nominee to the Supreme Court if she were to indicate that she did not accept *Brown* and would work for its reversal, but we have seen a succession of justices confirmed by a Senate that believed that the nominees would vote to overturn *Roe*[367]—even if in the event some of them did not do so. Sitting Justices of the Supreme Court flatly reject the legitimacy of *Roe,* something quite unthinkable for *Brown* even immediately after it was decided. Consider, for example, this impassioned comment by Justice Byron White written 13 years after *Roe* was decided:

> Abortion is a hotly debated moral and political issue. Such issues, in our society, are to be resolved by the will of the people, either as expressed through legislation or

---

358. *See, e.g.,* HARVIE WILKINSON III, FROM *BROWN* TO *BAKKE* 35 (1979); Louis Pollak, *Racial Discrimination and Judicial Integrity: A Reply to Professor Wechsler,* 108 U. PA. L. REV. 1, 24–34 (1959); Wechsler, *supra* note 290, at 31–35.

359. BORK, *supra* note 10, at 75; LAZARUS, *supra* note 10, at 288–91; MICHAEL PERRY, THE CONSTITUTION IN THE COURTS: LAW OR POLITICS? 180 (1994); Gerald Gunther, *Some Reflections on the Judicial Role: Distinctions, Roots, and Prospects,* 1979 WASH. U. L.Q. 817, 819; Horwitz, *supra* note 269, at 71–73; Wilkins, Sherlock, & Clark, *supra* note 188, at 144.

360. Graglia, *Policy, supra* note 298, at 124. Compare the authorities collected *supra* at notes 332–35.

361. Wilkins, Sherlock, & Clark, *supra* note 188, at 144. *See generally* Chapter 16.

362. Smolin, *supra* note 144, at 1038–39.

363. *See* Raymond Marcus, *"Posterity" in the Preamble and a Positivist Pro-Life Position,* 38 AM. J. JURIS. 273 (1993).

364. Smolin, *supra* note 144, at 1027–29.

365. BURT, *supra* note 200, at 347–50.

366. MENSCH & FREEMAN, *supra* note 17, at 127.

367. *Id.* at 1025–27.

through the general principles they have already incorporated into the Constitution they have adopted. *Roe v. Wade* implies that the people have already resolved the debate by weaving into the Constitution the values and principles that answer the issue.... [I]t is clear that the people have never—not in 1787, 1791, 1868, or at any time since—done any such thing. I would return the issue to the people by overruling *Roe v. Wade*.[368]

The resistance to *Roe* is virtually unprecedented, growing with every extension of the doctrine rather than declining over the years as the nation becomes accustomed to it as even the *Casey* troika acknowledged.[369] The only parallel is the slavery controversy before the Civil War.[370] The joint plurality opinion, in fact, attempted to deal this question explicitly. The troika told us that *Plessy* was morally (and constitutionally) indefensible in 1896 and to refrain from overruling it in 1954 would have been even more so.[371] Supporters of abortion rights find this line of argument at best gratuitous and irrelevant.[372] Justice Ruth Bader Ginsberg, who was not on the Court when *Casey* was decided, has argued that the decision in *Roe* itself does not benefit from this line of argument. *Brown* resulted from several decades of public education and debate (political and legal) that prepared the way for the decision. *Roe* preceded rather than followed this process.[373] And to insist, as the troika, does that *Roe* was the most significant decision by the Supreme Court in the last 20 years but that it does not matter much if that decision was wrong seems rather a stretch.[374] In short, one simply does not avoid the moral issues by reasoning about such questions as the rightness of abortion in legalistic terms, such as *stare decisis*.[375] Such an approach brings to mind Karl Marx's warning that we should avoid legitimating "the baseness of today with the baseness of yesterday."[376]

The plurality attempted to bolster its defense of *Roe* by insisting that no decisions since *Roe* had weakened its doctrinal footing. It is true that a series of cases leading up to *Brown* had refused to follow *Plessy* and thus presaged the overruling of the latter case.[377] But if that is the test, then surely *Roe* had been undermined. While *Roe* has been widely cited in other cases as exemplifying a general "right of privacy,"[378] all of the points made in these cases could have been made

---

368. Thornburgh v. American College of Obstetricians & Gynecologists, 476 U.S. 747, 796–97 (1986) (White, J., dissenting).

369. 505 U.S. at 868–69. *See also* Smolin, *supra* note 144, at 1028–32. 1038.

370. This is the sense in which Justice Scalia refers to *Roe* as the *Dred Scott* of this era, not some close doctrinal comparability. *Casey*, 505 U.S. at 979–1002 (Scalia, J., dissenting in part, joined by Rehnquist, C.J., & Thomas & White, JJ.). *See also* Robert Cover, *The Bonds of Constitutional Interpretation: Of the Word, the Deed, and the Role*, 20 Ga. L. Rev. 815, 832 (1986) Rice, *supra* note 149; Smolin, *supra* note 144, at 1031–33, 1039–41. *But see* Christopher Eisgruber, Dred *Again: Originalism's Forgotten Past*, 10 Const'l Commentary 37 (1993) (arguing that *Dred Scott* has no bearing on *Roe* because the two cases are based on different parts of the Constitution's text and use different interpretive techniques).

371. *Casey*, 505 U.S. at 862–64 (Kennedy, O'Connor, & Souter, JJ.).

372. Sullivan, *supra* note 89, at 101–02.

373. Ginsburg, *supra* note 24, at 1205–07. *See also* Blasi, *supra* note 200, at 212; Maltz, *supra* note 264, at 27–28. *See generally* Kluger, *supra* note 260, at 256–84 (relating the legal strategies used by Thurgood Marshall and his associates to lay the groundwork for *Brown* over a period of several decades).

374. *Casey*, 505 U.S. at 866–69 (Kennedy, O'Connor, & Souter, JJ., joint plurality op.). *See also* Smolin, *supra* note 144, at 1044.

375. Nagel, *supra* note 214, at 6–22, 106–20.

376. Donald Kelley, The Human Measure: Social Thought in the Western Legal Tradition 257 (1990) (quoting Marx).

377. *See* McLaurin v. Oklahoma St. Regents for Higher Educ., 339 U.S. 642 (1950); Sweatt v. Painter, 339 U.S. 629 (1950); Shelly v. Kramer, 334 U.S. 1 (1948); Sipuel v. Board of Regents, 332 U.S. 631 (1948); Missouri *ex rel.* Gaines v. Canada, 305 U.S. 337 (1938).

378. For a brief summary of the cases citing *Roe*, generally for the proposition that there is a "right to privacy" (or even a "zone of privacy") implicit in the Constitution, see Wilkins, Sherlock, & Clark, *supra* note 188, at 201–03 nn.95–96.

just as well by citing *Griswold*,[379] the original "right to privacy" decision. *Griswold*, like *Brown* and unlike *Roe*, was accepted rather quickly by the nation as part of a national consensus on the meaning of the "liberty" protected by the Fourteenth Amendment.[380] *Roe*, on the other hand, has been question by the Supreme Court not only in *Webster*,[381] but also by such cases as *Bowers v. Hardwick*[382] in which Justice Sandra Day O'Connor joined an opinion that refused to apply *Roe's* "right of privacy" to insulate private consensual homosexual activities from state regulation and questioned the legitimacy of "judge-made constitutional law having little or no cognizable roots in the language or design of the Constitution."[383]

The response by the Supreme Court to these analytical problems is that abortion (and hence *Roe*) is *sui generis,* an issue unlike any other in the law.[384] Rather than strengthening its doctrinal ties to constitutional law generally, recognition of the uniqueness of abortion actually separates the decision in *Roe* from those cases that might be said to have relied on it. In short, "abortion now appears to occupy its own jurisprudential island, with no readily explainable relation to the remainder of the Court's substantive due process cases."[385] And abortion simply has never been treated as a wholly private matter in our history and traditions before *Roe*, and the claim of that status for abortion after *Roe* has all too clearly not been accepted in our society.

The utter failure of the troika to articulate an adequate rationale for its refusal to either sustain or overrule *Roe* makes the *Casey* decision morally bankrupt. No wonder the decision in *Casey* has been harshly criticized even by those politically sympathetic to *Roe* who feared a clear ruling on the merits of *Roe* by the Court. Thus, legal historian Morton Horwitz, a supporter of abortion rights, has found the *Casey* troika's opinion to be a "rigid denial of the possibility of constitutional change" pure and simple,[386] with virtually no vision of justice (or anything else) to animate the Court's quest for "timeless truths."[387] His went on to write:

> Although Supreme Court opinions from the time of Chief Justice Marshall have been the preeminent American State Papers through which it has been possible to study some unfolding visions of the American Experience, there is hardly a trace of wisdom concerning the meaning of the American past or the possibilities of its future to be found in the opinions of the current Court. There is no picture of American ideals or American destiny.... There is no recognition that the world is rapidly changing and that the Court's understanding of the role of law may be growing dangerously out of touch with American society. Instead, most of this Court's opinions are surrounded by a thick undergrowth of technicality. With three or four "prong" tests everywhere and for everything; with an almost medieval earnestness about classification and categorization; with a theological attachment to the determinate power of various "levels of scrutiny"; with amazingly fine distinctions that produce multiple opinions designated in Parts, sub-parts, and sub-sub-parts, this is a Court whose Justices appear caught in the throes of various methodological obsessions.[388]

---

379. Griswold v. Connecticut, 381 U.S. 479 (1965).

380. DWORKIN, *supra* note 56, at 106.

381. Webster v. Reproductive Health Services, 492 U.S. 490 (1989).

382. 478 U.S. 186 (1986).

383. *Id.* at 194. *See* LAZARUS, *supra* note 10, at 385–88.

384. *Casey,* 505 U.S. at 857 (Kennedy, O'Connor, & Souter, JJ., joint plurality op.).

385. Mark Chopko & Michael Moses, *Assisted Suicide: Still a Wonderful Life?*, 70 NOTRE DAME L. REV. 519, 549 (1995); Grant & Linton, *supra* note 132, at 511–13. *See generally* James Bopp, jr., & Richard Coleson, Roe v. Wade *and the Euthanasia Debate*, 12 ISSUES IN L. & MED. 343 (1997).

386. Horwitz, *supra* note 269, at 98.

387. *Id.* at 92–98.

388. *Id.* at 98–99.

That a judicial opinion is incoherent is no light matter. Coherence—intellectual integrity—is, as Ronald Dworkin expressed it, "the life of law as we know it."[389] Dworkin goes so far as to posit "integrity" as an independent value, on a par with justice and fairness.[390] The obligation to speak coherently "provides protection against partiality or deceit or other forms of official corruption" and avoids the need to provide detailed rules on everything as the necessary rules can be inferred from the rules that exist.[391] More importantly, coherence is the basis of the claim of a government to the obedience of its citizens. Coherence demonstrates respect for all citizens and provides a reason even for the losers in litigation to accept the outcome.[392] In short, "we insist that the state act on a single, coherent set of principles even when its citizens are divided about what the right principles of justice and fairness really are."[393] As Dworkin noted some years before the *Casey* decision, one would find an arbitrary "checkerboard" solution such as one that allowed abortions to women born in odd-numbered years but not to women born in even-numbered years intolerable—regardless of one's views on abortion.[394] Ironically, Dworkin, the apostle of coherence or integrity in contemporary jurisprudence, embraced the troika's reasoning as the most appropriate response to the abortion problem, in part because he adheres to the new orthodoxy regarding abortion history—without having even examined any alternative history.[395]

The nub of the matter was caught by the late Alexander Bickel's comment that "intellectual incoherence is not excusable."[396] Any other approach quickly reduces the posture of the court from deciding according to legal principle to deciding by fiat, according to mere expedience.[397] In other words, the "abortion distortion," whether in terms of *stare decisis* or otherwise,[398] will not resolve the problem—as the last 20 years should have been enough to demonstrate. And, as if intellectual incoherence were not problem enough, the moral bankruptcy of the *Casey* decision simply compounds these difficulties.

What then explains the desperation of the judicial troika such that they embraced such an obviously flawed approach to such a highly visible issue? The intended message of Justices Anthony Kennedy, Sandra Day O'Connor, and David Souter in their remarkable joint plurality opinion seems all too clear. One might paraphrase the message as: "Enough already. Let us find a formula that by according recognition to both sides will put this problem behind us and get it off the Court's agenda."[399] The troika virtually said that directly:

> Where, in the performance of its judicial duties, the Court decides a case in such a way as to resolve the sort of intensely divisive controversy reflected in *Roe* and those rare, comparable cases, its decision has a dimension that the resolution of the normal case does not carry. It is the dimension present whenever the Court's interpretation of the Constitution calls the contending sides of a national controversy to end their national division by accepting a common mandate rooted in the Constitution.[400]

---

389. RONALD DWORKIN, LAW'S EMPIRE 167 (1986).

390. *Id.* at 166.

391. *Id.* at 188–89.

392. *Id.* at 191–92, 208–15.

393. *Id.* at 166.

394. *Id.* at 178–84.

395. DWORKIN, *supra* note 56, at 171–76.

396. ALEXANDER BICKEL, THE SUPREME COURT AND THE IDEA OF PROGRESS 47 (1970).

397. HERBERT WECHSLER, POLITICS AND FUNDAMENTAL LAW 21 (1961).

398. See the authorities collected *supra* at notes 215–17, 310–11.

399. *See also* LAZARUS, *supra* note 10, at 485.

400. *See Casey,* 505 U.S. at 866–67 (Kennedy, O'Connor, & Souter, JJ., joint plurality opinion). Left-wing law professor Mark Tushnet has described this passage as the "most offensive" example of the Court "shouting down opposition." Tushnet, *supra* note 173, at 916–17.

The dissenters acknowledged this message in Justice Antonin Scalia words: "We are offended by these marches who descend upon us, every year on the anniversary of *Roe,* to protest our saying that the Constitution requires what our society has never thought the Constitution requires."[401]

If that was the message, no one was listening, at least in part because the plea was so incoherent.[402] That a court decision would not calm the disputants seems even clearer than when *Roe v. Wade* was decided in 1973. Back then, at least some abortion rights activist delighted in the *Roe* decision because they saw its detailed rules as serving to "prevent years of litigation."[403] Such a hope on the part of the troika in 1992 can charitably be described as naïve. Neither those who want to erect impassable barriers to state regulation of abortion nor those who have dedicated themselves to overturning *Roe* and to restoring the legal prohibition of abortion appear in the least happy with *Casey* compromise.[404] Not only must both groups continue to bring their claims to the Court, demanding recognition for their theory of the Constitution as applicable to abor-

---

401. *Casey,* 505 U.S. at 999 (Scalia, J., dissenting, joined by Rehnquist, C.J., and Thomas, J.) *See generally* Crain, *supra* note 67, at 309–12; James Stoner, jr., *Common Law and Constitutionalism in the Abortion Case,* 55 Rev. of Pol. 421, 428–29 (1993). *But see* Gerhardt, *supra* note 205, at 80–81.

402. Smolin, *supra* note 144, at 975.

403. Janice Goodman, Rhonda Copelon, & Nancy Stearns, Doe *and* Roe*: Where Do We Go from Here?,* 1 Women's Rts. L. Rptr. 20, 27 (1973) (observation of Jan Goodman). *See also* Eva Rubin, Abortion, Politics, and the Courts 73 (rev. ed. 1987).

404. *See* Ruth Colker, Pregnant Men: Practice, Theory, and the Law 94–102 (1994); Craig & O'Brien, *supra* note 10, at 325–27, 342; Lazarus, *supra* note 10, at 483; Leslie Reagan, When Abortion Was a Crime: Women, Medicine, and Law in the United States, 1867–1973, at 251–52 (1997); Reflections after *Casey:* Women Look at the Status of Reproductive Rights in America (Vicki Alexander ed. 1993); Dan Allison, *How Anti-Abortionists Lost the War,* St. Petersburg Times, Aug. 16, 1992, at 7D; *Another Blow Against* Roe, St. L. Post-Dispatch, June 30, 1992,a t 2B (editorial); Janet Benshoof, Planned Parenthood v. Casey*: The Impact of the New Undue Burden Standard on Reproductive Health Care,* 269 JAMA 2249 (1993); Alan Bigel, Planned Parenthood of Southeastern Pennsylvania v. Casey*: Constitutional Principle and Political Turbulence,* 18 U. Dayton L. Rev. 735, 756–62 (1993); *Both Sides See Defeat in Decision,* St. L. Post-Dispatch, July 5, 1992, at 1A; R. Alta Charo, *Life after* Casey*: The View from Rehnquist's Potemkin Village,* 21 J. Law, Med. & Ethics 59 (1993); Annette Clark, *Abortion and the Pied Piper of Compromise,* 68 NYU L. Rev. 265, 268–70, 316–17 (1993); Kim Cobb, *Both Sides in Abortion Case Claim Defeat,* Hous. Chronicle, June 30, 1992, at A1; Daly, *supra* note 214, at 80; B.J. Isaacson-Jones, *Sorting Out the Abortion Decision: Women's Rights Remain Threatened,* St. L. Post-Dispatch, July 5, 1992, at 3B; Frances Kissling, *Pro-Choice Must Widen Its Agenda: Reproductive Rights Are in Peril, Not Just Abortion Rights,* L.A. Times, June 30, 1992, at B7; Linton, *supra* note 175, at 15–16; Jeanne Mejeur, *Abortion: The Never Ending Controversy,* 19 State Legislation, Nov. 1993, at 27; Mertus, *supra* note 188, at 249–51; Jon Merz, Catherine Jackson, & Jacob Klerman, *A Review of Abortion Policy: Legality, Medicaid Funding, and Parental Involvement, 1967–1994,* 17 Women's Rts. L. Rptr. 1, 5–6 (1995); Nancy Myers, *What Happens Next in Abortion Rights Battle? For Opponents of Abortion, Fight to Change the Law Begins Anew,* USA Today, June 30, 1992, at 11A; William Neikirk & Glen Elasasser, *Ruling Weakens Abortion Right,* Chi. Tribune, June 30, 1992, at C1; *Reproductive Rights under Attack,* St. L. Post-Dispatch, July 2, 1992, at 2C (editorial); Deborah Rhode, *Adolescent Pregnancy and Public Policy,* 108 Pol. Sci. Q. 635, 647–49 (1994); Alexander Sanger, *What Victory for Abortion?,* Newsday, Sept. 5, 1992, at 41 (letter to editor); Jean Reith Schroedel, Pamela Fiber, & Bruce Snyder, *Women's Rights and Fetal Personhood in Criminal Law,* 7 Duke J. Gender & L. 89, 113–17 (2000); Sullivan, *supra* note 89, at 33, 102–03; Laurence Tribe, *Write* Roe *into Law,* Ny times, July 27, 1993, at A13; David Tuller, *The 2 Sides Agree—Ruling Settles Nothing,* S.F. Chronicle, June 30, 1992, at A5; Woltz, *supra* note 188, at 1788; Marcy Wilder, *The Rule of Law, the Rise of Violence, and the Role of Morality: Reframing America's Abortion Debate,* in Abortion Wars, *supra* note 90, at 73, 85–86. For more positive views of the plurality opinion, see Mensch & Freeman, *supra* note 17, at 148–50; Clark, *supra,* at 316–29; B.D. Cohen, *Abortion Rights Prevail,* Newsday, July 14, 1992, at 59; Devins, *supra* note 172, at 1453–55; David Savage, *How* Roe v. Wade *Survived: Dramatic Shift on Court Ended Years of War over Abortion,* Dallas Morn. News, Dec. 17, 1992, at 41A; Ellery Schempp, *Court Again Upholds Rights of the Individual,* Ny times, July 17, 1992, at A25 (letter to editor); Nadine Strossen & Ronald Collins, *The Future of an Illusion: Reconstructing* Planned Parenthood v. Casey, 16 Const'l Commentary 587 (1999); Kathleen Sullivan, *A Victory for* Roe, N.Y. Times, June 30, 1992, at A23; Sarah Weddington, *Being "Historic" and a "Leader-in-Training,"* 77 Nat'l F. no. 3, at 30, 33–34 (Summer 1997).

tion,[405] but, by changing the standard from *Roe's* "fundamental freedom" to *Casey's* "undue burden," the Supreme Court has made it necessary to relitigate virtually every question heretofore settled regarding abortion.[406] Even the issues apparently settled in *Casey* are subject to being relitigated based on the specific factual experience under the statutory restrictions that were upheld against what was only a facial challenge in *Casey*.[407] No wonder Kathryn Kolbert, who ar-

---

405. *See, e.g.,* Linda Greenhouse, *Both Sides in Abortion Argument Look Past Court to Political Battle,* N.Y. TIMES, Apr. 20, 1992, at A1. *See also* Pine & Law, *supra* note 89, at 426–31, 436–41 (although written before *Casey* was decided by the Supreme Court, the article predicted the outcome and called for an "inch-by-inch" and *"Roe by Roe"* legal and political struggle contesting every possible issue in order to "maximize reproductive choice"—for all except the unborn).

406. ROBERTSON, *supra* note 156, at 61–63; Susan Frelich Appleton, *Standards for Constitutional Review of Privacy-Invading Welfare Reforms: Distinguishing the Abortion-Funding Cases and Redeeming the Undue-Burden Test,* 49 VAND. L. REV. 1 (1996); Benshoof, *supra* note 188, at 235–37; Robert Bork, *Again, a Struggle for the Soul of the Court,* N.Y. TIMES, July 8, 1992, at A15, col. 2; Burdick, *supra* note 205, at 840–43; Cohen, *supra* note 143, at 188–89; Diane Curtis, *Doctored Rights: Menstrual Extraction, Self-Help Gynecological Care, and the Law,* 20 REV. L. & SOC. CHANGE 427, 433 (1994); Daly, *supra* note 214, at 142–48; Fein, *supra* note 205, at 39–50; Horan, *supra* note 188, at 518–23; Tamar Lewin, *States Expected to Enforce Abortion Restrictions,* July 1, 1992, at A12; Linton, *supra* note 175, at 68–72; Kevin Francis O'Neill, *The Road Not Taken: State Constitutions as an Alternative source of Protection for Reproductive Rights,* 11 N.Y.L.S. J. HUM. RTS. 1, 20–30 (1993); Ross, *supra* note 188, at 201; Scaturro, *supra* note 126, at 176–89; Julie Schrager, *The Impact of* Casey, 1992 WIS. L. REV. 1331; Ian Shapiro, *Introduction,* in ABORTION: THE SUPREME COURT DECISIONS 1, 12–13, 18–20 (Ian Shapiro ed. 1995). In actuality, the obligation of a lower court to follow the mandate of a higher court in any but the same case is rather more troublesome than the theory of *stare decisis* might lead one to suppose. *See* C. Steven Bradford, *Following Dead Precedent: The Supreme Court's Ill-Advised Rejection of Anticipatory Overruling,* 59 FORDHAM L. REV. 39 (1990); Maurice Kelman, *The Force of Precedent in the Lower Courts,* 14 WAYNE L. REV. 3 (1967); Margaret Kniffen, *Overruling Supreme Court Precedents: Anticipatory Action by United States Courts of Appeals,* 51 FORDHAM L. REV. 55 (1982); John Rogers, *Lower Court Application of the "Overruling Law" of Higher Courts,* 1 LEGAL THEORY 179 (1995).

407. *Casey,* 505 U.S. at 926 (Blackmun, J., concurring), *on remand,* 978 F.2d 74 (3rd Cir. 1992), *on remand,* 822 F. Supp. 227 (E.D. Pa. 1993), *rev'd,* 14 F.3d 848 (3rd Cir.), *stay denied,* 510 U.S. 1309 (1994) (Souter, J.); GARROW, *supra* note 10, at 708; Susan Hansen, *What Didn't Happen: The Implementation of the* Casey *Abortion Decisions in Pennsylvania,* 14 COMPARATIVE STATE POLITICS 9 (1993); Kathryn Kolbert & Andrea Miller, *Government in the Examining Room: Restrictions on the Provision of Abortion,* 49 J. AM. MED. WOMEN'S ASSOC. 153 (1994); Tholen & Baird, *supra* note 172, at 1017–22. *See also* Leavitt v. Jane L., 518 U.S. 137 (1996); Dalton v. Little Rock Fam. Plan. Services, 516 U.S. 474 (1996); Woman's Choice—East Side Women's Clinic v. Newman, 305 F.3d 684 7th Cir. 2002), *cert. denied,* 537 U.S. 1192 (2003); Planned Parenthood of the Rocky Mtns. Services Corp. v. Owens, 287 F.3d 910 (10th Cir. 2002) Greenville Women's Clinic v. Bryant, 222 F.3d 157 (4th Cir. 2000), *cert. denied,* 531 U.S. 1191 (2001); Karlin v. Foust, 188 F.3d 446 (7th Cir. 1999); Planned Parenthood of S. Ariz. v. Lawall, 180 F.3d 1022, *modified,* 193 F.3d 1042 (9th Cir. 1999); Memphis Planned Parenthood, Inc. v. Sundquist, 175 F.3d 456 (6th Cir. 1999); Planned Parenthood of the Blue Ridge v. Camblos, 155 F.3d 352 (4th Cir. 1998), *cert. denied,* 525 U.S. 1140 (1999); Women's Med. Prof'l Corp. v. Voinovich, 130 F.3d 187 6th Cir. 1997), *cert. denied,* 523 U.S. 1036 (1998); Manning v. Hunt, 119 F.3d 254 (4th Cir. 1997); Causeway Med. Suite v. Ieyoub, 109 F.3d 1096 (5th Cir.), *cert. denied,* 522 U.S. 1093 (1997); Jane L. v. Bangerter, 102 F.3d 1112 (10th Cir. 1996), *cert. denied,* 520 U.S. 1274 (1997); Northland Family Planning, Inc. v. Engler, 73 F.3d 634 (6th Cir. 1996); Planned Parenthood, Sioux Falls Clinic v. Miller, 63 F.3d 1452 (8th Cir. 1995), *cert. denied sub nom.* Janklow v. Planned Parenthood, 517 U.S. 1174 (1996) (Rehnquist, C.J., Scalia & Thomas JJ., dissenting); Fargo Women's Health Org. v. Schafer, 18 F.3d 526 (8th Cir. 1994); Barnes v. Mississippi, 992 F.2d 1335 (5th Cir.), *cert. denied,* 510 U.S. 976 (1993); Barnes v. Moore, 970 F.2d 12 (5th Cir.), *cert. denied,* 506 U.S. 1021 (1992); Ada v. Guam Soc'y of Obstet. & Gynecologists, 962 F.2d 1366 (9th Cir.), *cert. denied,* 506 U.S. 1011 (1992); State v. North Fla. Women's Health Services, Inc., 852 So. 2d 254 (Fla. Ct. App. 2001), *rev'd on state grounds,* 886 So. 2d 612 (Fla. 2003); Preterm, Inc. v. Voinovich, 627 N.E.2d 570 (Ohio Ct. App. 1993); *In re* Initiative Petition No. 349, 838 P.2d 1 (Okla. 1992), *cert. denied,* 506 U.S. 1071 (1993).

*See generally* COLKER, *supra* note 404, at 102–09; Peter Applebome, *Mississippi Law Fails to Reduce Abortion Strife: 24-Hour Waiting Period Offers Look at Future,* NY TIMES, Oct. 13, 1992, at A14; Burdick, *supra* note 205, at 846–69; Jesse Choper, *Constitutional Law Conference,* 61 U.S.L.W. 2237, 2239–40 (1992); Clark, *supra* note 175, at 272–73 n.25; Connell, *supra* note 188, at 24–25; Crain, *supra* note 67, at 285–87; Dworkin, *supra*

gued *Casey* on behalf of Reproductive Services, summed up the result as guaranteeing "full employment for reproductive lawyers."[408] Furthermore, "undue burden" is a "standardless standard"—meaning one that provides no guidance to lower courts at all and can be filled in only by continuous recourse to the Supreme Court.[409]

No one should be particularly concerned about the denial of *certiorari* for a decision of the Court of Appeals for the Ninth Circuit declaring Guam's abortion statute unconstitutional[410] as there would have been little point to granting *certiorari* if the voting structure on the case will not have changed from *Casey*.[411] The joint plurality opinion in *Casey* expressly declared that statutes such as Guam's, imposing highly restrictive prohibitions on abortions,[412] violate the constitutional rights of the mother[413] and the two additional justices who supported a stronger reading of *Roe* in *Casey* would certainly concur. This was the first time that the Court denied *certiorari* in a significant abortion case.[414] This denial was followed quickly by further denials of *certiorari* in other significant abortion cases from Louisiana, Mississippi, Oklahoma, and Utah that raised more varied issues.[415]

While the Court now consistently declined to hear appeals in abortion cases, the Court also resolutely left that door open. While it did not prove as easy to reopen the *Casey* case itself after it was remanded as the Third Circuit and later Justice David Souter held that all questions relating to a challenge of the statute on its face had been settled by the mandate of the Supreme Court, Souter did once again leave open the possibility of challenging even the *Casey* statute as it is applied to particular abortion seekers or providers.[416] And the Court made it increasingly clear

---

note 139, at 30–31; Fein, *supra* note 205, at 40–43; Ford, *supra* note 215; Law, *supra* note 188, at 931–32; Teresa Scott, Note, *Burying the Dead: The Case against Revival of Pre-*Roe *and Pre-*Casey *Abortion Statutes in a Post-Casey World,* 19 NYU Rev. L. & Soc. Change 355 (1991); Katherine Sheehan, *Toward a Jurisprudence of Doubt,* 7 UCLA Women's L.J. 201 (1997); Rorie Sherman, *The War to Heat Up: Anti-Abortion Activists Are Going to Reignite the Battles in the States,* Nat'l L.J., Nov. 30, 1992, at 1, 39; Tholen & Baird, *supra. See also* Stephen Anderer, Note, *Getting the Facts: Empirical Evaluation and the Constitutionality of Pre-Abortion Parental Notification Statutes,* 36 Vill. L. Rev. 1611 (1991); Bopp & Coleson, *supra* note 67, at 161–65.

408. Quoted in Craig & O'Brien, *supra* note 10, at 347. *See also* Kolbert & Miller, *supra* note 214, at 98–99.

409. Smolin, *supra* note 175, at 141–42. *See also* H. Dale Dixon III, Note, *Deciphering the Recent Abortion Plurality Decisions:* Coe v. Melahn, 26 Creighton L. Rev. 901 (1993); Skye Gabel, Note, Casey *"versus"* Salerno: *Determining an Appropriate Standard for Evaluating the Facial Constitutionality of Abortion Statutes,* 19 Cardozo L. Rev. 1825 (1998).

410. Ada v. Guam Soc'y of Obstetricians, 962 F.2d 1366 (9th Cir.), *cert. denied,* 506 U.S. 1011 (1992).

411. Justice Blackmun, in his separate opinion in *Casey,* took the highly unusual step of noting his advanced age (83) and indicating that short of electing a Democratic president in 1992 his leaving the Court in the not too distant future would probably bring about, at last, the demise of *Roe. Casey,* 505 U.S. 945–47 (Blackmun, J., partially concurring).

412. Guam Pub. L. No. 20-134 (1990), *codified at* 9 Guam Code Ann. §§ 31.20 to 31.23 (1991 Supp.) (prohibiting abortion except to save the life or health of the mother).

413. *Casey,* 505 U.S. at 879 (Kennedy, O'Connor, & Souter, JJ., joint plurality op.).

414. Woltz, supra note 188, at 1809. *See also* Benshoof, *supra* note 188, at 218.

415. Barnes v. Mississippi, 992 F.2d 1335 (5th Cir.), *cert. denied,* 506 U.S. 975 (1993) (Mississippi's definition of "medical emergency" upheld because the purpose of the statute was to protect women's lives and health rather than to prohibit abortion); Soujourner T. v. Edwards, 962 F.2d 27 (5th Cir. 1992) (Louisiana's abortion statute unconstitutional because the statute prohibited abortion except to save the life of the mother, or if the result of rape or incest); Utah Women's Clinic, Inc. v. Leavin, 844 F. Supp. 1482 (D. Utah 1994) (a 24-hour waiting period and required disclosures not an undue burden on the right to abort); *In re* Initiative Petition No. 349, 838 P.2d 1 (Okla. 1992), *cert. denied,* 506 U.S. 1071 (1993) (initiative is unconstitutional because of its absolute prohibition of pre-viability abortions).

416. Casey v. Planned Parenthood of S.E. Pa., 14 F.3d 848 (3rd Cir.), *application for stay denied,* 510 U.S. 1309 (1994) (Souter, J.).

that each particular regulation or restriction must be evaluated separately to determine whether it by itself imposes an undue burden on an individual woman's right to abort.[417]

Furthermore, to ground the Court's decision on an unwillingness to continue to receive the public protests regarding the *Roe* decision, as the plurality does, amounts to punishing people "for exercising their First Amendment rights."[418] Law professor Earl Maltz, a supporter of abortion rights, sees this aspect of the troika's argument as based on faulty factual assumption (namely that the public cares more about the Court's institutional integrity than about its substantive correctness) and "breathtaking" theoretical innovations (namely, turning on its head the maxim that constitutional rulings should be open to reconsideration because other branches of government cannot overrule them).[419] Another law professor, Michael Paulsen, has described this as the "Big Lie" approach to precedent: The bigger the lie, the less it is subject to reexamination.[420] Paulsen went on to suggest that the real motivation was to avoid being seen as paying off on secret promises to overturn *Roe* in exchange for appointment to the Court.[421] Paulsen's bottom line perhaps gets at the real root of the problem: "The problem is not that the Court has done a poor job of peacemaking but that it invariably will perform poorly a task that is not its job and for which it is not particularly well suited."[422]

Why did the plurality adopt such a self-defeating posture? Some find the Court, particularly the stand taken by Justice Anthony Kennedy, as simply pandering to the press, to predominantly liberal academic circles, or to the Washington cocktail circuit.[423] Some observers took to calling this the "Greenhouse effect" after Linda Greenhouse, the highly liberal Supreme Court correspondent of the *New York Times*.[424] Law professors Barbara Hinkinson Craig and David O'Brien intimate that the plurality consciously tailored its opinion to the public attitudes as expressed in opinion polls.[425] Yet slowly, academic commentary began to reconcile itself to the decision.[426] Indeed, law professor David Garrow has gone so far as to insist that the *Casey* decision

---

417. Leavitt v. Jane L., 518 U.S. 137 (1996); Dalton v. Little Rock Fam. Plan. Services, 516 U.S. 474 (1996). This conclusion was implicit in *Casey*, 505 U.S. at 879–901 (Kennedy, O'Connor, & Souter, JJ., joint plurality op.).

418. Fein, *supra* note 205, at 45.

419. Maltz, *supra* note 264, at 21–28.

420. Paulsen, *supra* note 316, at 231.

421. *Id.* at 232–33.

422. *Id.* at 230.

423. Lazarus, *supra* note 10, at 427–39; Eastland, *supra* note 124, at 32; Bork, *supra* note 406; Graglia, *Policy*, *supra* note 295, at 122–23; Lino Graglia, *"Interpreting" the Constitution: Posner on Bork*, 44 Stan. L. Rev. 1019, 1023 (1992); Smolin, *supra* note 144, at 1024–25, 1041–42. *See also* Richard Duncan, *Casey's Lesson: Confirmation Battles Matter*, Tex. Law., July 27, 1992, at S10 ("[T][hree accidental justices who were supposed to restore legitimacy to the Constitution blinked under fire. The court's decision in *Casey* was cowardice cloaked as courage.")

424. Lazarus, *supra* note 10, at 428; Eastland, *supra* note 124. *See also* Fein, *supra* note 173; Sullivan, *supra* note 89, at 100–03

425. Craig & O'Brien, *supra* note 10, at 328.

426. White, *supra* note 162, at 153–83; Brownstein, *supra* note 214; Burdick, *supra* note 205; Daly, *supra* note 214; Dworkin, *supra* note 139; David Garrow, *Abortion before and after* Roe v. Wade: *An Historical Perspective*, 62 Alb. L. Rev. 833, 843–45 (1999); Robert Goldstein, *Reading* Casey: *Structuring the Woman's Decision-Making Process*, 4 Wm. & Mary Bill of Rts. L. Rev. 787 (1996); Stephen Macedo, *In Defense of Liberal Public Reason: Are Slavery and Abortion Hard Cases?*, 42 Am. J. Juris. 1, 15–19 (1997); Gillian Metzger, *Unburdening the Undue Burden Standard: Orienting* Casey *in Constitutional Jurisprudence*, 94 Colum. L. Rev. 2025 (1994); Valerie Pacer, *Salvaging the Undue Burden Standard — Is It a Lost Cause?*, 73 Wash. U. L.Q. 295 (1995); Sarah Stroud, *Dworkin and* Casey *on Abortion*, 25 Phil. & Pub. Aff. 140 (1996); Patricia Sullivan & Steven Goldzwig, *A Relational Approach to Moral Decision-Making: The Majority (*sic*) Opinion in* Planned Parenthood v. Casey, 81 Q.J. Speech 167 (1995); Tyler & Gregory, *supra* note 172.

necessarily has resolved the constitutional status of abortion laws *"for all time"*[427] — as if some later Court could never dare to overrule the fractured opinion in *Casey*. Yet the apparent hope of at least the troika to be rid of this enormously difficult problem was not to be realized.

---

427. Garrow, *supra* note 426, at 845 (emphasis in original).

# Chapter 18

# Both Sides Now[1]

*It's not over 'til it's over.*

—Yogi Berra[2]

With the Supreme Court appearing to relinquish its role in the abortion controversy, the primary forum for the struggle over abortion moved from the courts to the legislatures and to the White House. Legislatures enacted the regulations upheld in *Planned Parenthood of Southeast Pennsylvania v. Casey* in most states, particularly the compulsory disclosure of information,[3] mandatory waiting periods,[4]

---

1. Joni Mitchell, *Both Sides Now* (1967).
2. David Nathan, Baseball Quotations 150 (1993).
3. *See, e.g.,* Ala. Code §§ 26-23A-1 to 26-23A-13 (Supp. 2003); Alaska Code § 18.16.060 (LexisNexis 2002); Ark. Code Ann. §§ 20-16-602, 20-16-901 to 20-16-908 (LexisNexis Supp. 2003); Conn. Gen. Stat. Ann. §§ 19a-116, 19a-601 (West 2003); Del. Code Ann. tit. 24, § 1794 (1997); Fla. Stat. Ann. § 390.0111(3) (West 2002); Idaho Code § 18-609 (2003); Ind. Code Ann. §§ 16-18-2-69 (West 1997), 16-34-2-1 to 16-34-2-1.2 (West Supp. 2003); Kan. Stat. §§ 65-6709 to 65-6714 (2002); Ky. Rev. Stat. Ann. §§ 311.723(2), 311.725 (Michie 2001); La. Rev. Stat. Ann. § 40.1299.35.6 (West 2001); Me. Rev. Stat. Ann. tit. 22 § 1599-A (West 1992); Mass. Gen. Laws Ann. ch. 112 § 125 (West 2003); Mich. Comp. Laws Ann. §§ 333.177014, 333.17015, 333.17515 (West Supp. 2003); Minn. Stat. Ann. §§ 145.4241 to 145.4249 (West Supp. 2003); Miss. Code Ann. §§ 41-41-31 to 41-41-39 (1999); Mo. Rev. Stat. Ann. §§ 188.027, 188.039 (West 1992); Mont. Code Ann. §§ 50-20-104(5), 50-20-106, 50-20-301 to 50-20-308 (2003); Neb. Rev. Stat. §§ 28-327 to 28-327.05 (1995); Nev. Rev. Stat. Ann. §§ 442.252, 442.253 (Michie 2000); N.D. Cent. Code § 14-02.1-02(5) (Michie 1997); Ohio Rev. Code Ann. § 2317.56 (Anderson 2001); Okla. Stat. Ann. tit. 63, § 1-736 (West 1996); 18 Pa. Cons. Stat. Ann. §§ 3205, 3208, 3217 (West 2000); R.I. Gen. Laws §§ 23-4.7.2 to 23-4.7.5 (1997); S.C. Code Ann. §§ 44-41-30, 44-41-31, 44-41-310 to 44-41-380, 44-41-60 (West 2002); S.D. Codified Laws Ann. § 34-23A-10.1 to 34-23A-10.4 (LexisNexis Supp. 2003); Tenn. Code Ann. § 39-15-202 (2003); Tex. Health & Safety Code §§ 171.011 to 171.018 (West Supp. 2003); Ann. Utah Code Ann. §§ 76-7- 305, 76-7-305.5 (2003); Va. Code Ann. § 18.2-76 (LexisNexis Supp. 2003); W. Va. Code §§ 16-2I-1 to 16-2I-9 (2001); Wis. Stat. Ann. §§ 46.245 (West 2003), 253.10 (West 2002).

*See also* Marie v. McGreevey, 314 F.3d 136 (3rd Cir. 2002), *cert. denied,* 539 U.S. 910 (2003); Woman's Choice—East Side Women's Clinic v. Newman, 305 F.3d 684 (7th Cir. 2002), *cert. denied,* 537 U.S. 1192 (2003); Karlin v. Foust, 188 F.3d 446 (7th Cir. 1999); Utah Women's Clinic, Inc. v. Leavitt, 136 F.3d 707 (10th Cir. 1998); Fargo Women's Health Org. v. Schafer, 18 F.3d 526 (8th Cir. 1994); Casey v. Planned Parenthood of S.E. Pa., 14 F.3d 848 (3rd Cir.), *application for stay denied,* 510 U.S. 1309 (1994); Barnes v. Moore, 970 F.2d 12 (5th Cir. 1992), *cert. denied,* 506 U.S. 1021 (1993); *In re* Ballot Title for 1999-2000 no. 200A, 992 P.2d 27 (Cal. 2000); Woman's Choice-East Side Women's Clinic v. Newman, 671 N.E.2d 104 (Ind. 1996); Pro-Choice Miss. v. Fordice, 716 So. 2d 645 (Miss. 1998); Hill v. Women's Med. Ctr. of Neb., 580 N.W.2d 102 (Neb. 1998); Wyant v. Myers, 81 P.3d 392 (Or. 2003); Planned Parenthood of Cent. Tenn. v. Sundquist, 38 S.W.2d 1 (Tenn. 2000).

4. *See, e.g.,* Ala. Code §§ 26-23A-1 to 26-23A-13 (Supp. 2003); Ark. Code Ann. § 20-16-903(b)(3) (Lexis-Nexis Supp. 2003); Conn. Gen. Stat. Ann. § 19a-601 (West 2003); Del. Code Ann. tit. 24, § 1794(b) (1997); Fla. Stat. Ann. § 390.0111(4) (West 2002); Idaho Code § 18-609 (2003); Ind. Code Ann. § 16-34-2-1.1(1) (West Supp. 2003); Kan. Stat. §§ 65-6709 (2002); Ky. Rev. Stat. Ann. § 311.725 (Michie 2001); La. Rev. Stat. Ann. § 40.1299.35.6 (West 2001); Me. Rev. Stat. Ann. tit. 22 § 1596 (West 1992); Mass. Gen. Laws Ann. ch. 112 § 125 (West 2003); Mich. Comp. Laws Ann. § 333.17014(h), (i) (West Supp. 2003); Minn. Stat. Ann.

parental notification or consent,[5] and that abortions be performed only by licensed physicians or

§ 145.4242 (West Supp. 2003); Miss. Code Ann. § 41-41-33(b) (1999); Mo. Rev. Stat. Ann. § 188.039 (West 1992); Mont. Code Ann. § 50-20-106, 50-20-305 (2003); Neb. Rev. Stat. §§ 28-327(1) (1995); Nev. Rev. Stat. Ann. §§ 442.255, 442.2555 (Michie 2000); N.D. Cent. Code §§ 14-02.1-2(5), 14-02.1-02, 14-02.1-03, 14-02.1-03.1 (1997); Ohio Rev. Code Ann. § 2317.56(B) (Anderson 2001); 18 Pa. Cons. Stat. Ann. § 3205 (West 2000); S.C. Code Ann. § 44-41-330(C) (West 2002); S.D. Codified Laws Ann. §§ 34-23A-10.1 (LexisNexis Supp. 2003); Tenn. Code Ann. § 39-15-202(d) (2003); Tex. Health & Safety Code §§ 171.012(b), 171.013(a), 171.017 (West Supp. 2003); Utah Code Ann. §§ 76-7-305 (2003); Va. Code Ann. § 18.2-76(B) (LexisNexis Supp. 2003); W. Va. Code § 16-2I-2(b) (2001); Wis. Stat. Ann. § 253.10(c)(1) (West 2002).

*See also* Woman's Choice—East Side Women's Clinic v. Newman, 305 F.3d 684 (7th Cir. 2002), *cert. denied*, 537 U.S. 1192 (2003); Planned Parenthood of the Rocky Mtns. Services Corp. v. Owens, 287 F.3d 910 (10th Cir. 2002); Karlin v. Foust, 188 F.3d 446 (7th Cir. 1999); Fargo Women's Health Org. v. Schafer, 18 F.3d 526 (8th Cir. 1994); Casey v. Planned Parenthood of S.E. Pa., 14 F.3d 848 (3rd Cir.), *application for stay denied*, 510 U.S. 1309 (1994); Barnes v. Mississippi, 992 F.2d 1335 (5th Cir.), *cert. denied*, 510 U.S. 976 (1993); Barnes v. Moore, 970 F.2d 12 (5th Cir. 1992), *cert. denied*, 506 U.S. 1021 (1993); Woman's Choice-East Side Women's Clinic v. Newman, 671 N.E.2d 104 (Ind. 1996); Pro-Choice Miss. v. Fordice, 716 So. 2d 645 (Miss. 1998); Wyant v. Myers, 81 P.3d 392 (Or. 2003); Planned Parenthood of Cent. Tenn. v. Sundquist, 38 S.W.2d 1 (Tenn. 2000).

5. Ala. Code §§ 26-21-1 to 26-21-8 (Supp. 2003); Alaska Stat. §§ 18.16.010(a)(3), 18.16.020, 18.16.030 (LexisNexis 2002); Ariz. Rev. Stat. Ann. § 36-2152 (West 2003); Ark. Stat. Ann. §§ 20-16-801 to 20-16-808 (LexisNexis Supp. 2003); Cal. Health & Safety Code § 123450 (West 1996); Colo. Rev. Stat. §§ 12-37.5-101 to 12-37.5-108 (2003); Del. Code Ann. tit. 10, § 921, tit. 13, § 710 (1999), tit. 24, §§ 1780-1789B (1997); Fla. Stat. Ann. § 390-0111(4), 390.01115, 390.0116 (West 2002); Ga. Code Ann. §§ 15-11-28(2)(D), 15-11-110 to 15-11-117 (2001); Idaho Code §§ 9-340G, 18-602, 18-609A, 18-614, 18-615 (2003); 750 Ill. Comp. Stat. Ann. §§ 70/1 to 70/99 (West 1999); Ind. Code Ann. §§ 16-18-2-267, 16-34-2-4 (West 1997 & Supp. 2003); Iowa Code Ann. §§ 135L.1 to 135L.8 (West Supp. 2003), 232.5 (2000); Kan. Stat. §§ 65-6704, 65-6705 (2002); Ky. Rev. Stat. Ann. § 311.732 (Michie 2001); La. Rev. Stat. Ann. § 40:1299.35.5 (West 2001); Md. Health-Gen. Code Ann. § 20-103 (Michie 2000); Mass. Gen. Laws Ann. ch. 112, § 12S (West 2003); Mich. Comp. Laws Ann. §§ 722.901 to 722.908 (West 2002); Minn. Stat. Ann. § 144.343 (West Supp. 2003); Miss. Code Ann. §§ 41-41-51 to 41-41-63 (1999); Mo. Rev. Stat. Ann. § 188.028 (West 1992); Mont. Code Ann. §§ 50-20-201 to 50-20-215 (2003); Neb. Rev. Stat. §§ 71-6901 to 71-6908 (1996); Nev. Rev. Stat. Ann. §§ 442.255, 442.256 (Michie 2000); N.J. Stat. Ann. §§ 9:17A-1.1 to 9:17A-1.12 (West 2002); N.M. Stat. Ann. § 30-5-1(C) (Michie 1994); N.C. Gen. Stat. §§ 90-21.5 to 90-21.10 (2003); N.D. Cent. Code §§ 14-02.1-03 to 14-02.1-03.2 (1997); Ohio Rev. Code Ann. §§ 2151.85, 2505.73 2919.12 (Anderson 2002); 18 Pa. Cons. Stat. Ann. § 3206 (West 2000); R.I. Gen. Laws § 23.4.7-6 (1997); S.C. Code Ann. §§ 44-41-31 to 44-41-37 (West 2002); S.D. Codified Laws Ann. §§ 26-1-1 (LexisNexis 1999), 34-23A-7, 34-23A-7.1, 34-23A-22 (LexisNexis Supp. 2003); Tenn. Code Ann. §§ 37-10-301 to 37-10-307 (2001); Tex. Fam. Code Ann. §§ 33.001 to 33.011 (West 2002); Utah Code Ann. §§ 15-2-1, 76-7-304(2) (2003); Va. Code Ann. § 16.1-241 (LexisNexis Supp. 2003); W. Va. Code §§ 16-2F-1 to 16-2F-9 (2001); Wis. Stat. Ann. §§ 46.24, 48.16, 48.235(1)(d), 48.257, 48.373, 48.375 (West 2003); Wyo. Stat. Ann. §§ 5-8-102 (LexisNexis 2003), 35-6-101(ix), 35-6-118 (LexisNexis 2003). Two states require that minors be counseled about discussing the planned abortion with a parent, without actually requiring notice: Conn. Gen. Stat. Ann. § 19a-601 (West 2003); Me. Rev. Stat. tit. 22, § 1597-A (West 1992 & Supp. 2003). Guam and Oklahoma make any person who performs an abortion on a minor without parental consent liable for the cost of any subsequent medical treatment required as a result of the abortion. 19 Guam Civ. Code Ann. § 1111 (1995); § Okla. Stat. tit. 63, §§ 1-740, 2601(c) (West 1996 & Supp. 2003).

*See also* Lambert v. Wicklund, 520 U.S. 292 (1997); Hodgson v. Minnesota, 497 U.S. 417 (1990); H.L. v. Matheson, 450 U.S. 398 (1981); Bellotti v. Baird, 443 U.S. 622 (1979); Planned Parenthood v. Danforth, 428 U.S. 52, 74 (1975); Planned Parenthood of the Rocky Mtns. Services Corp. v. Owens, 287 F.3d 910 (10th Cir. 2002); Blackard v. Memphis Area Med. Ctr. for Women, 262 F.3d 568 (6th Cir. 2001), *cert. denied*, 535 U.S. 1053 (2002); Planned Parenthood of S. Ariz. v. Lawall, 180 F.3d 1022, *modified*, 193 F.3d 1042 (9th Cir. 1999); Memphis Planned Parenthood, Inc. v. Sundquist, 175 F.3d 456 (6th Cir. 1999); Planned Parenthood of the Blue Ridge v. Camblos, 155 F.3d 352 (4th Cir. 1998), *cert. denied*, 525 U.S. 1140 (1999); Causeway Med. Suite v. Ieyoub, 123 F.3d 849 (5th Cir.), *cert. denied*, 522 U.S. 923 (1997); Manning v. Hunt, 119 F.3d 254 (4th Cir. 1997); Planned Parenthood, Sioux Falls Clinic v. Miller, 63 F.3d 1452 (8th Cir. 1995), *cert. denied sub nom.* Janklow v. Planned Parenthood, 517 U.S. 1174 (1996) (Rehnquist, C.J., Scalia & Thomas JJ., dissenting); Casey v. Planned Parenthood of S.E. Pa., 14 F.3d 848 (3rd Cir.), *application for stay denied*, 510 U.S. 1309 (1994); Cleveland Surgi-Center, Inc. v. Jones, 2 F.3d 686 (6th Cir. 1993), *cert. denied*, 510 U.S. 1046 (1994);

in approved facilities,[6] to mention only the most common restrictions on access to abortion. One or more of these requirements have been enacted in all but six states. Litigation challenging these and other laws as imposing "undue burdens" on a woman's right to choose abortion proceeded slowly, and with mixed results.[7]

---

Eubanks v. Wilkinson, 937 F.2d 1118 (6th Cir. 1991); Glick v. McKay, 937 F.2d 434 (9th Cir. 1991); Planned Parenthood of Atlanta Area, Inc. v. Miller, 934 F.2d 1462 (11th Cir. 1991); Arnold v. Board of Educ. of Escambia Cnty., 880 F.2d 305 (11th Cir. 1989); Planned Parenthood Lg. of Mass. v. Bellotti, 868 F.2d 459 (1st Cir. 1989); *Ex parte* Anonymous, 806 So. 2d 169 (Ala. 2001); State v. Planned Parenthood of Alaska, 35 P.3d 30 (Alaska 2001); American Academy of Pediatrics v. Lungren, 940 P.2d 797 (Cal. 1996); North Fla. Women's Health Services, Inc. v. State, 866 So. 2d 612 (Fla. 2003); Woman's Choice-East Side Women's Clinic v. Newman, 671 N.E.2d 104 (Ind. 1996); *In re* Jane Doe, 866 P.2d 1069 (Kan. 1994); Kelly v. Vote Know Coalition of Md., Inc., 626 A.2d 959 (Md. 1993); Planned Parenthood Lg. of Mass., Inc. v. Attorney-General, 677 N.E.2d 101 (Mass. 1997); Planned Parenthood of Cent. N.J. v. Farmer, 762 A.2d 620 (N.J. 2000); *In re* Doe, 19 S.W.3d 346 (Tex. 2000).

6. Ala. Code §26-23A-7 (1992); Alaska Stat. §18.16.010(a)(1), (2) (LexisNexis 2002); Ariz. Rev. Stat. Ann. §§36-449.01 to 36-449.03 (West 2003); Colo. Rev. Stat. §18-6-101(1) (2003); Fla. Stat. Ann. §§390.015 to 390.021 (West 2002), 797.03 (West 2000); Ga. Code Ann. §16-12-141 (2003); 9 Guam Civ. Code §31.20(b) (2003); Haw. Rev. Stat. §453-16 (1993); Idaho Code §§18-605, 18-608A (2003); 210 Ill. Comp. Stat. Ann. §5/6.1 (West 2000); Ind. Code Ann. §16-34-2-1(1)(A) (West Supp. 2003); Ky. Rev. Stat. Ann. §§216B.0431, 216B.990 (Michie 1999), 311.723(1), 311.750 (Michie 2001); La. Stat. Ann. §40.1299.35.2(A) (West 2001); Me. Rev. Stat. tit. 22, §1598 (West 1992); Mass. Gen. Laws Ann. ch. 112 §§12L, 12M (West 2003); Md. Health-Gen. Code Ann. §§20-207, 20-208 (Michie 2000); Mich. Comp. Laws Ann. §§333.20115, 333.22224 (West 2001); Minn. Stat. Ann. §144.412.1(1), (2) (West 1998); Miss. Code Ann. §§41-75-1, 41-75-29, 188.043 (1999); Mo. Rev. Stat. Ann. §§188.020, 188.025 (West 1992); Mont. Code Ann. §§50-20-109, 50-20-112 (2003); Neb. Rev. Stat. §28-328 (1995); Nev. Rev. Stat. Ann. §442.251(1)(a) (Michie 2000); N.C. Gen. Stat. §§14-45.1, 131E-269 (2003); N.D. Cent. Code §14-02.1-04 (Michie 1997); Ohio Rev. Code Ann. §2919.123 (Anderson 2002); Okla. Stat. Ann. tit. 63, §§1-731, 1-733, 1-737 (West 1996); 18 Pa. Cons. Stat. Ann. §3207 (West 2000); P.R. Laws Ann. tit. 33, §1051 (2001); S.C. Code Ann. §§44-41-20, 44-41-75 (West 2002); S.D. Codified Laws Ann. §§34-23A-3 to 34-23A-6 (LexisNexis 1994); Tenn. Code Ann. §68-11-223 (2001); Tex. Health & Safety Code Ann. §§170.002, 171.003 to 171.005 (West Supp. 2003), 245.001 to 245.022 (West 2001 & Supp. 2003); Utah Code Ann. §76-7-302(1) (2003); V.I. Code Ann. tit. 14, §§151(b), 156 (1994); Va. Code Ann. §§18.2-72 to 18.2-74.1 (LexisNexis Supp. 2003); Wash. Rev. Code Ann. §9.02.110 (West 1998); Wis. Stat. Ann. §940.15 (West Supp. 2003); Wyo. Stat. Ann. §35-6-111 (LexisNexis 2003).

*See* Mazurek v. Armstrong, 520 U.S. 968 (1997) (summary reversal without argument of an injunction against enforcement of Montana's requirement that abortions be performed by licensed physicians); Women's Med. Ctr. of Nw. Hous. v. Bell, 248 F.3d 411 (5th Cir. 2001) (finding abortion clinic regulations to be unconstitutionally vague); Greenville Women's Clinic v. Bryant, 222 F.3d 157 (4th Cir. 2000) (upholding state regulations of abortion clinics as consistent with due process and equal protection), *cert. denied,* 531 U.S. 1191 (2001), *further appeal,* 317 F.3d 357 (4th Cir. 2002), *cert. denied,* 538 U.S. 1008 (2003); Planned Parenthood of Greater Iowa Inc. v. Atchison, 126 F.3d 1042 (8th Cir. 1997) (striking down zoning restrictions on abortion clinics).

7. *See, e.g.,* Mazurek v. Armstrong, 520 U.S. 968 (1997); Lambert v. Wicklund, 520 U.S. 292 (1997); Leavitt v. Jane L., 518 U.S. 137 (1996); Woman's Choice—East Side Women's Clinic v. Newman, 305 F.3d 684 (7th Cir. 2002), *cert. denied,* 537 U.S. 1192 (2003); Karlin v. Foust, 188 F.3d 446 (7th Cir. 1999); Memphis Planned Parenthood, Inc. v. Sundquist, 175 F.3d 456 (6th Cir. 1999); Planned Parenthood of the Blue Ridge v. Camblos, 155 F.3d 352 (4th Cir. 1997), *cert. denied,* 525 U.S. 1140 (1999); Planned Parenthood of S. Ariz. v. Neely, 130 F.3d 400 (9th Cir. 1997); Planned Parenthood of Greater Iowa v. Atchison, 126 F.3d 1042 (8th Cir. 1997); Manning v. Hunt, 119 F.3d 254 (4th Cir. 1997); Causeway Medical Suite v. Ieyoub, 109 F.3d 1096 (5th Cir.), *petition for rehearing* en banc *denied,* 123 F.3d 849 (5th Cir. 1997); Planned Parenthood, Sioux Falls Clinic v. Miller, 63 F.3d 1452 (8th Cir. 1995), *cert. denied sub nom.* Janklow v. Planned Parenthood, Sioux Falls Clinic, 517 U.S. 1174 (1996); Fargo Women's Health Org. v. Schafer, 18 F.3d 526 (8th Cir. 1994); Barnes v. Moore, 970 F.2d 12 (5th Cir. 1992), *cert. denied,* 506 U.S. 1021 (1993); Valley Hosp. Assoc. v. Mat-Su Coalition for Choice, 948 P.2d 963 (Alaska 1997); American Academy of Pediatrics v. Lungren, 940 P.2d 797 (Cal. 1997); Planned Parenthood Lg. of Mass. v. Attorney-General, 677 N.E.2d 101 (Mass. 1997); Davis v. Fieker, 952 P.2d 505 (Okla. 1997) (upholding a requirement that all third-trimester abortions be performed in a hospital). *See generally* Janet Benshoof, *Abortion Rights and Wrongs,* Nation, Oct. 14, 1996, at 19; Ruth Burdick, *The Casey*

Yet one of President Bill Clinton's first acts upon taking office was to issue executive orders that removed restrictions on abortions in federal facilities or paid for with federal funds.[8] He also appointed Dr. Jocelyn Elders as the first supporter of abortion rights to serve as Surgeon General since President Ronald Reagan took office in 1981.[9] Clinton also insisted on including coverage for abortion in his proposed national health care program even though 70 percent of the public opposed that policy.[10] While Clinton's health plan was politically dead on arrival for other strong reasons, his inclusion of abortion funding didn't help matters.

With all the ups and downs politically, the rhetoric of the great national debate over abortion hardly changed up until 1994. In 1995, with a new Republican majority in Congress, a proposal emerged that significantly altered the rhetorical stance of those contending over the rights and wrongs of the law on abortion. Opponents of abortion proposed the *Partial-Birth Abortion Ban Act*, pursuing it in Congress and, after President Clinton vetoed it, in the states.[11] The proposed

---

*Undue Burden Standard: Problems Predicted and Encountered, and the Split over the* Salerno *Test,* 23 HASTINGS CONST. L.Q. 825 (1996); Charlene Carres, *Legislative Efforts to Limit State Privacy Rights,* 25 FLA. ST. U. L. REV. 273 (1998); Kenneth Meier *et al., The Impact of State-Level Restrictions on Abortion,* 33 DEMOGRAPHY 307 (1996); Sandra Lynne Tholen & Lisa Baird, *Con Law Is as Con Law Does: A Survey of* Planned Parenthood v. Casey *in the State and Federal Courts,* 28 LOY.-L.A. L. REV. 971 (1995).

8. Admin. Order, *Privately Funded Abortion at Military Hospitals,* 3 CFR 722 (1993); Admin. Order, *The Title X "Gag Rule,"* 3 CFR 723 (1993). *See also* Admin. Order, *Importation of RU-486,* 3 CFR 724 (1993); DONALD CRITCHLOW, INTENDED CONSEQUENCES: BIRTH CONTROL, ABORTION, AND THE FEDERAL GOVERNMENT IN MODERN AMERICA 221–22 (1999); DAVID GARROW, LIBERTY AND SEXUALITY: THE RIGHT OF PRIVACY AND THE MAKING OF *ROE V. WADE* 702 (2nd ed. 1998); Ann Devroy, *Clinton Cancels Abortion Restrictions of Reagan-Bush Era,* WASH. POST, Jan. 23, 1993, at A1; Robin Toner, *Anti-Abortion Movement Prepares to Battle Clinton,* N.Y. TIMES, Jan. 22, 1993, at A1. *See generally* JANET HADLEY, ABORTION: BETWEEN FREEDOM AND NECESSITY 11–17 (1996).

9. *See* Carl Cannon, *U.S. Catholics Becoming Disillusioned with Clinton,* BALT. SUN, Sept. 12, 1994, at A1.

10. Robin Toner, *Abortion and the Health Plan: Hard Questions in Both Camps,* N.Y. TIMES, Oct. 22, 1993, at A20; Robin Toner, *Clinton Would End Ban on Aid to Poor Seeking Abortions,* N.Y. TIMES, Mar. 30, 1993, at A1; Robin Toner, *Middle Ground on Abortion Shifting into Terra Incognita,* N.Y. TIMES, July 15, 1993, at A1; Robin Toner, *Success Spoils Unity of Abortion Rights Groups,* N.Y. TIMES, Mar. 30, 1993, at A1.

11. *Partial-Birth Abortion Ban Act,* H.R. 1102, 105th Cong., 1st Sess. (1997), *and* H.R. 1833, 104th Cong., 1st Sess. (1995); ALA. CODE §§ 26-23-1 to 26-23-6 (Supp. 1998); ALASKA CODE § 18.16.050 (LexisNexis 2002); ARIZ. REV. STAT. ANN. § 13-3603.01 (West 2001); ARK. CODE ANN. §§ 5-61-201 to 5-61-204 (Michie 1997); FLA. STAT. ANN. §§ 390.011, 390.0111(5), (11) (West 2002), 782.30 to 782.36 (West Supp. 2003); GA. CODE ANN. § 16-12-144 (2003); IDAHO CODE § 18-613 (2003); 720 ILL. COMP. STAT. ANN. §§ 513/1 to 513/20, 513/99 (West 1999); IND. CODE ANN. §§ 16-18-2-267.5, 16-34-2-1 (West 1997); IOWA CODE ANN. § 707.8A (West 2003); KAN. STAT. ANN. § 65-6721 (2002); KY. REV. STAT. ANN. §§ 311.720, 311.765 (Michie 2001); LA. REV. STAT. ANN. §§ 14:32.9, 32:9, 40.1299.35.16, 40.1299.35.18 (West 2001); MICH. COMP. LAWS §§ 333.17016, 333.17516 (Supp. 2003); MISS. CODE ANN. §§ 41-41-71, 41-41-73, 87.1 (1999); MO. ANN. STAT. § 565.300 (West Supp. 2003); MONT. CODE ANN. § 50-20-401 (2003); NEB. REV. STAT. § 28-328 (Supp. 2003); N.J. STAT. ANN. §§ 2A:65A-5 to 2A-65-A-7 (West 2000); N.M. STAT. ANN. §§ 30-5A-1 to 30-5A-5 (Michie 1994 & Supp. 2003); N.D. CENT. CODE. §§ 14-02.6-01 to 14-026-03 (Supp. 2003); OHIO REV. CODE ANN. §§ 2307.53 (Anderson 2001), 2919.151 (Anderson 2002); OKLA. STAT. ANN. tit. 21, § 684 (West 2002); R.I. GEN. LAWS §§ 23-4.12.1 to 23-4.12.6 (1997); S.C. CODE ANN. § 44-41-85 (West 2002); S.D. CODIFIED LAWS §§ 34-23A-27 to 34-23A-33 (LexisNexis Supp. 2003); TENN. CODE ANN. § 39-15-209 (2003); TEX. REV. CIV. STAT. ANN. art. 6.5, § 4512.5 (1976); UTAH CODE ANN. §§ 76-7-301(3), 76-7-326 to 76-7-329 (2003); VA. CODE ANN. § 18.2-71.1 (LexisNexis Supp. 2003); W. VA. CODE §§ 33-42-3, 33-42-8 (2003); WIS. STAT. ANN. §§ 895.038, 940.16 (West Supp. 2003).

*See Joint Hearing on Bills to Ban Partial-Birth Abortions before the House & Senate Committees on the Judiciary,* 105th Cong., 1st Sess. (Mar. 11, 1997); *Hearing on the Effects of Anesthesia during a Partial-Birth Abortion before the Senate Judiciary Committee,* 104th Cong., 2nd Sess. (March 21, 1996); *Hearing on the Partial-Birth Abortion Ban Act of 1995 before the Senate Judiciary Committee,* 104th Cong., 1st Sess. (Nov. 17, 1995); *Hearing on the Partial-Birth Abortion Ban Act of 1995 before the House Judiciary Committee,* 104th Cong., 1st Sess. (June 15, 1995); GARROW, *supra* note 8, at 719-22, 727-39; George Annas, *Partial-Birth Abortion, Congress, and the Constitution,* 339 N. ENG. J. MED. 279 (1998); James Bopp, jr., & Curtis Cook, *Partial-Birth Abortion: The Final Frontier of Abortion Jurisprudence,* 14 ISSUES IN L. & MED. 3 (1998); Allison Gough, *Ban-*

Act would ban the "dilation and extraction" procedure,[12] and generated the predictable controversy with usual suspects.[13] Nothing in the *Casey* joint plurality opinion even hinted at whether the proposed *Partial-Birth Abortion Ban Act*—with its requirement that abortions, insofar as possible without actually physically endangering a woman's life or health, be done in a manner that maximizes the chances that the child would survive—would "unduly burden" a woman's right to abort. True enough, similar requirements were declared unconstitutional in three earlier cases,[14] but those decisions were made under the strict scrutiny standard of *Roe v. Wade* rather than the undue burden standard of *Casey,* and the Court had upheld, even under the strict scrutiny standard, a requirement of a second physician to attend to a probably viable fetus.[15] Not only are all previously decided issues up for grabs and subject to relitigation after *Casey* adopted the undue burden standard, but one of the cases declaring fetal protection statutes unconstitutional had already been partially overruled in *Casey* itself.[16]

---

*ning Partial Birth Abortion: Drafting a Constitutionally Acceptable Statute,* 24 U. Dayton L. Rev. 187 (1998); David Grimes, *The Continuing Need for Late Abortions,* 280 JAMA 747 (1998); Melinda Henneberger, *House Approves Bill to Overturn Veto on Abortion; Push May Fail in Senate,* N.Y. Times, Sept. 20, 1996, at A1; Allison Mitchell, *Clinton Seeks to Loosen Bill's Ban on an Abortion Method,* N.Y. Times, Feb. 28, 1996, at A13; Todd Purdum, *President Vetoes Measure Banning Type of Abortion,* N.Y. Times, Apr. 11, 1996, at A1; David Rogers, *Ban on Late-Term Abortion Method Gets Veto-Proof House Majority Vote,* Wall St. J., Mar. 21, 1997, at A4; Katharine Seelye, *House, by Broad Margin, Backs Ban on a Type of Later Abortion; Lott Says Senate Lacks Votes to Override a Veto,* N.Y. Times, Mar. 21, 1997, at A1; Deborah Sontag, *"Partial Birth" Just One Way, Physicians Say,* N.Y. Times, Mar. 21, 1997, at A1; Lynn Wardle, *The Quandary of Pro-Life Free Speech: A Lesson from the Abolitionists,* 62 Alb. L. Rev. 853, 943–45 (1999); John Yang, *House Sends Clinton Curb on Abortions: Late-Term Method Would Be Banned,* Wash. Post, Mar. 28, 1996, at A1.

12. *See* Chapter 16, at notes 378–86.

13. *See, e.g.,* Sarah Blaffer Hrdy, Mother Nature: A History of Mothers, Infants, and Natural Selection 4–6 (1999); James Risen & Judy Thomas, Wrath of Angels: The American Abortion War 374–76 (1998); George Annas, *Partial-Birth Abortion, Congress, and the Constitution,* 339 New Eng. J. Med. 279 (1998); Byron Calhoun, James Reitman, & Nathan Hoeldtke, *Perinatal Hospice: A Response to Partial Birth Abortion for Infants with Congenital Defects,* 13 Issues in L. & Med. 125 (1997); Janet Gans Epner, Harry Jonas, & Daniel Seckinger, *Late-Term Abortion,* 280 JAMA 724 (1998); David Garrow, *Abortion before and after* Roe v. Wade*: An Historical Perspective,* 62 Alb. L. Rev. 833, 848–50 (1999); David Grimes, *The Continuing Need for Late Abortions,* 280 JAMA 747 (1998); Michael Gerson, *For Key Abortion Foes, A Sudden Pragmatism: "Partial-Birth" Issue Is Prompting a Major Shift,* U.S. News & World Rep., June 1, 1998, at 25; Thomas Ginsberg, *Override: Action in N.J. Shows Strength of the Anti-Abortion Campaign,* Phila. Inquirer, Dec. 21, 1997, at D4; Steven Grasz, *If Standing Bear Could Talk…Why There Is No Constitutional Right to Kill a Partially-Born Human Being,* 33 Creighton L. Rev. 23 (1999); Kathryn Kolbert & Andrea Miller, *Legal Strategies for Abortion Rights in the Twenty-First Century,* in Abortion Wars: A Half Century of Struggle, 1950–2000, at 95, 101–03 (Rickie Solinger ed. 1998); Richard Kopf, *An Essay on Precedent, Standing Bear, Partial-Birth Abortion and Word Games—A Response to Steve Grasz and Other Conservatives,* 35 Creighton L. Rev. 11 (2001); John Leo, *Litmus Tests, Slippery Slopes,* U.S. News & World Rep., Jan. 28, 1998, at 16; Ann MacLean Massie, *So-Called "Partial-Birth Abortion" Bans: Bad Medicine? Maybe. Bad Law? Definitely,* 59 U. Pitt. L. Rev. 301 (1998); Timothy McDonald, *When Does a Fetus Become a Child in Need of an Advocate? Focusing on Fetal Pain,* 17 Children's Legal Rts. J., Spring 1997, at 12; Rigel Oliveri, *Crossing the Line: The Political and Moral Battle over Late-Term Abortion,* Yale J.L. & Feminism 397 (1998); Michelle Román, *Topical Summary: The Partial-Birth Abortion Ban Act and the Undue Burden It Places on Women's Right to an Abortion: The Controversy over D&E, Dilation and Evacuation,* 18 Women's Rts. L. Rptr. 381 (1997); Katharine Seelye, *Senators Reject Democrats' Bill to Limit Abortion: Loopholes Cited by Foes,* N.Y. Times, May 16, 1997, at A1; M. LeRoy Sprang & Mark Neerhof, *Rationale for Banning Abortions Late in Pregnancy,* 280 JAMA 744 (1998); Sheryl Gay Stolberg, *Definition of Fetal Viability Is Focus of Debate in Senate,* N.Y. Times, May 16, 1997, at A13.

14. Thornburgh v. American College of Obstetricians, 476 U.S. 747, 768–71 (1986); Colautti v. Franklin, 439 U.S. 379, 397–401 (1979); Planned Parenthood of Cent. Mo. v. Danforth, 428 U.S. 52, 81–84 (1976).

15. Planned Parenthood Ass'n of Kansas City v. Ashcroft, 462 U.S. 476, 482–86, 505 (1983).

16. 505 U.S. at 881–87 (Kennedy, O'Connor, & Souter, JJ., joint plurality op.) (overruling *Thornburgh* & *Akron*).

In the inevitable challenges to state partial-birth abortion statutes, several lower courts concluded that the state statutes were "clearly" unconstitutional under the *Casey* undue burden standard if the statute did not allow the abortions for threats to a woman's "mental health" or because the court found that statute unconstitutionally "vague" or "overbroad,"[17] while other courts found similar statutes to be clearly constitutional.[18] By March of the year 2000, at least 14 of the state partial-birth statutes had been declared unconstitutional.[19] Supporters of the statutes were unwilling to accept the "mental health" exception because they saw "mental health" exceptions as operating as a covert license for abortion on demand.[20] Moreover, less than 10 percent of abortions performed after the 20th week of pregnancy—about half way through gestation—are done for health reasons, and then usually because of problems of the fetus rather than of the mother.[21]

As with so much else in the abortion controversy, the dispute over the *Partial-Birth Abortion Ban Act* is first of all a dispute over developments in medical technology—not over whether the procedure can be done technically, but about whether the procedure should be done at all. The question, in other words, is whether recourse to the procedure is morally acceptable in light of our cultural traditions, including how we talk about morality. Yet this is not just a debate over the technology for doing abortions. Dramatic changes in reproductive technologies have fueled the abortion controversy from its start. It is time to reexamine those developments once again.

---

17. Planned Parenthood of Greater Iowa, Inc. v. Miller, 195 F.3d 386 (8th Cir. 1999) (Iowa), *cert. denied,* 530 U.S. 1274 (2000); Carhart v. Stenberg, 192 F.3d 1142 (8th Cir. 1999) (Nebraska), *aff'd,* 530 U.S. 914 (2000); Little Rock Family Plan. Services v. Jegley, 192 F.3d 794 (8th Cir. 1999) (Arkansas); Planned Parenthood of Wis. v. Doyle, 162 F.3d 463 (7th Cir. 1998) (Wisconsin) [*overruled,* Hope Clinic v. Ryan, 195 F.3d 857 (7th Cir. 1999), *vacated mem.,* 530 U.S. 1271 (2000), *rev'd,* 249 F.3d 603 (7th Cir. 2001)]; Women's Med. Prof'l Corp. v. Voinovich, 130 F.3d 187 (6th Cir. 1997) (Ohio), *cert. denied,* 523 U.S. 1036 (1998); WomenCare of Southfield, PC v. Granholm, 143 F. Supp. 2d 827 (E.D. Mich. 2000); Rhode Island Med. Soc'y v. Whitehouse, 66 F. Supp. 2d 288 (D.R.I. 1999), *aff'd,* 239 F.3d 104 (1st Cir. 2001); Choice for Women v. Butterworth, 54 F. Supp. 2d 1148 (S.D. Fla. 1998); Causeway Med. Ctr. v. Foster, 43 F. Supp. 2d 604 (E.D. La. 1999), *aff'd,* 221 F.3d 811 (5th Cir. 2000); Planned Parenthood of Cent. N.J.v. Vernieo, 41 F. Supp. 2d 478 (D.N.J. 1998), *aff'd,* 220 F.3d 127 (3rd Cir. 2000); Eubanks v. Stengel, 28 F. Supp. 2d 1024 (W.D. Ky. 1998), *aff'd,* 224 F.3d 576 (6th Cir. 2000); Planned Parenthood of S. Ariz. v. Woods, 982 F. Supp. 1369 (D. Ariz. 1997); Evans v. Kelley, 977 F. Supp. 1283 (E.D. Mich. 1997); Armstrong v. State, 989 P.2d 364 (Mont. 1999).

18. Hope Clinic v. Ryan, 195 F.3d 857 (7th Cir. 1999) (Illinois & Wisconsin), *vacated mem.,* 530 U.S. 1271 (2000), *rev'd,* 249 F.3d 603 (7th Cir. 2001); Summit Med. Assocs., PC v. Pryor, 180 F.3d 1326 (11th Cir. 1999) (Alabama), *cert. denied,* 529 U.S. 1012 (2000); Richmond Med. Ctr. for Women v. Gilmore, 144 F.3d 326 (4th Cir. 1998) (Virginia); Midtown Hosp. v. Miller, 36 F. Supp. 2d 1360 (N.D. Ga. 1997).

19. *See* Donald Baker & Craig Timberg, *Va. Ban on Some Abortions Lifted: State Official Vows to Appeal Ruling,* WASH. POST, July 17, 1999, at A1, A11 (reporting that 20 of 28 state partial-birth abortion statutes had been declared unconstitutional). According to Baker and Timberg, the statutes had entered into effect in Indiana, Kansas, Mississippi, Oklahoma, South Carolina, South Dakota, Tennessee, and Utah. Baker and Timberg did not note that courts allowed such statutes in Alabama, Illinois, Virginia, and Wisconsin to go into effect, at least for the most part. Hope Clinic v. Ryan, 195 F.3d 857 (7th Cir. 1999) (Illinois & Wisconsin), *vacated mem.,* 530 U.S. 1271 (2000), *rev'd,* 249 F.3d 603 (7th Cir. 2001); Summit Med. Assocs., PC v. Pryor, 180 F.3d 1326 (11th Cir. 1999) (Alabama), *cert. denied,* 529 U.S. 1012 (2000); Richmond Med. Ctr. for Women v. Gilmore, 144 F.3d 326 (4th Cir. 1998) (Virginia); Midtown Hosp. v. Miller, 36 F. Supp. 2d 1360 (N.D. Ga. 1997). *See also* Todd Goudy, *Slouching towards Barbarism? The Quest to Limit Partial-Birth Abortion after* Stenberg v. Carhart, 103 W. VA. L. REV. 219, 220 n.4 (2000).

20. *See* Chapter 12, at notes 253–55, 265, 271, *and* Chapter 13, at 331–35.

21. Marianne Lavelle, *When Abortions Come Late in Pregnancy: Though Rare, Most Aren't for Medical Reasons,* US NEWS & WORLD REP., Jan. 19, 1998, at 31.

# More Medicine

*Millions of eyes can see, yet why am I so blind?*

—The Bee Gees[22]

Few areas of contemporary life have been revolutionized so completely in recent decades as the practice of medicine and the popular and professional attitudes engendered by those changes. We have learned how to keep bodies alive long after the person whom that body once was has irretrievably left the scene.[23] We have also developed techniques for creating fertile outcomes to human coupling and successful outcomes to high-risk pregnancies that were hardly dreamed of only 25 years ago.[24] And we have devised techniques for treating or overcoming all manner of diseases and defects between birth and death.[25] While we have by no means solved all, or even the most important, medical problems, we have achieved so much that we have overturned seemingly timeless attitudes about health, longevity, and our need to adapt to or live with

---

22. Robin & Barry Gibb, *Holiday* (1967).

23. PRESIDENT'S COMM'N ON THE STUDY OF ETHICAL PROBLEMS IN MEDICINE, DEFINING DEATH: MEDICAL, LEGAL, AND ETHICAL ISSUES IN THE DETERMINATION OF DEATH (1981); *Uniform Brain Death Act*, 12 UNIFORM LAWS ANN. 15 (Supp. 1980). *See generally* DANIEL CALLAHAN, WHAT KIND OF LIFE: THE LIMITS OF MEDICAL PROGRESS (1990); EZEKIEL EMANUEL, THE ENDS OF HUMAN LIFE: MEDICAL ETHICS IN A LIBERAL POLITY (1991); QUALITY OF LIFE: THE NEW MEDICAL DILEMMA (James Walter & Thomas Shannon eds. 1990); James Bernat, *How Much of the Brain Must Die in Brain Death?*, 3 J. CLINICAL ETHICS 21 (1992); Paul Byrne & Richard Nilges, *The Brain Stem in Brain Death: A Critical Review*, 9 ISSUES IN L. & MED. 3 (1993); Nancy Childs & Walt Mercer, *Late Improvement in Consciousness after Post-Traumatic Vegetative State*, 334 N. ENG. J. MED. 24 (1996); Charles Leibson, *The Role of the Courts in Terminating Life-Sustaining Medical Treatment*, 10 ISSUES IN L. & MED. 437 (1995); Margaret Lock, *Death in Technological Time: Locating the End of Meaningful Life*, 10 MED. ANTHRO. Q. 575 (1996); J.K. Mason & G.T. Laurie, *The Management of the Persistent Vegetative State in the British Isles*, 1996 JURIDICAL REV. 263; David Powner et al., *Medical Diagnosis of Death in Adults: Historical Contribution to Current Controversies*, 348 LANCET 1219 (1996); Alan Sherman, *"Brainstem Death," "Brain Death" and Death: A Critical Reevaluation of the Purported Equivalence*, 14 ISSUES IN L. & MED. 125 (1998); Nicholas Tonti-Filippini, *Revising Brain Death: Cultural Imperialism?*, LINACRE Q., May 1998, at 51; Samantha Weyrauch, *Acceptance of Whole-Brain Death Criteria for Determination of Death: A Comparative Analysis of the United States and Japan*, 17 PAC. BASIN L.J. 91 (1999).

24. ROBERT BLANK & JANNA MERRICK, HUMAN REPRODUCTION, EMERGING TECHNOLOGIES, AND CONFLICTING RIGHTS (1995); COUNCIL OF EUROPE, HUMAN ARTIFICIAL PROCREATION (1989); LINDA BECK FENWICK, PRIVATE CHOICES, PUBLIC CONSEQUENCES: REPRODUCTIVE TECHNOLOGY AND THE NEW ETHICS OF CONCEPTION, PREGNANCY, AND FAMILY (1998); JENNIFER GUNNING & VERONICA ENGLISH, HUMAN *IN VITRO* FERTILIZATION: A CASE STUDY IN THE REGULATION OF MEDICAL INNOVATION (1993); HUMAN CLONING (James Humber & Robert Almeder eds. 1998); GINA KOLATA, CLONE: THE ROAD TO DOLLY, AND THE PATH AHEAD (1998); NATIONAL BIOETHICS ADVISORY COMM'N, CLONING OF HUMAN BEINGS: REPORT AND RECOMMENDATIONS (1997); REPRODUCTION, TECHNOLOGY, AND RIGHTS (Joseph Imber & Robert Almeder eds. 1996); LEE SILVER, REMAKING EDEN: CLONING AND BEYOND IN A BRAVE NEW WORLD (1997); PAUL LAURITZEN, PURSUING PARENTHOOD: ETHICAL ISSUES IN ASSISTED REPRODUCTION (1993); THE ETHICS OF REPRODUCTIVE TECHNOLOGY (Kenneth Alpern ed. 1992).

25. CONTROL COMMUNICABLE DISEASE MANUAL (James Chin ed. 17th ed. 2000); ELLEN & JAMES STRAUSS, VIRUSES AND HUMAN DISEASES (2001); MARGARET SCHELL FRAZIER et al., ESSENTIALS OF HUMAN DISEASES AND CONDITIONS (2000); PETER SALGO & JOE LAYDEN, THE HEART OF THE MATTER: THREE KEY BREAKTHROUGHS TO PREVENTING HEART ATTACKS (2003). *See generally* ARNO KARLEN, MAN AND MICROBES: DISEASES AND PLAGUES IN HISTORY AND MODERN TIMES (1996).

disabilities. Such changes necessarily impacted upon the law, although courts often proved incapable of reacting wisely to the pressures for change in the law.[26]

The controversy over the *Partial-Birth Abortion Ban Act* arose in the highly politicized context of debates over the legal and moral implications of modern medical technologies. On the one side were the champions of traditional morality, arguing for prohibition of the procedure. On the other hand, were the champions of a new, technologically driven morality who were determined to keep the procedure legal regardless of cost. The debate over the *Partial-Birth Abortion Ban Act* highlighted the determination of those who favor "choice" to protect abortion rights to the uttermost extreme. The debate produced several surprises. For once, the media reported that certain claims by the supporters of abortion rights in opposing the proposed Act were lies. Ron Fitzsimmons, executive director of the National Coalition of Abortion providers, admitted that he had "lied through [his] teeth" when he testified that about the number of D&X procedures that occurred annually in the United States.[27] And the American Medical Association, for the first time since before *Roe v. Wade,* endorsed a measure that would prohibit a rare but noteworthy class of abortions.[28] Supporters of abortion rights attributed the AMA's defection to a short-term political deal relating to the then on-going debate over health care reform.[29] Abortion rights supporters seemed unable to comprehend the possibility that some supporters of abortion rights cannot accept the D&X procedure. After all, even Dr. George Tiller, internationally known for performing late-term abortions, refuses to do D&X procedures on ethical grounds.[30] Tiller is hardly a doctor who shies away from unpleasant situations; his Wichita clinic had been targeted by protesters and he himself was once shot because of abortion.[31]

The *Partial-Birth Abortion Ban Act* is largely symbolic in the sense that probably less than 5,500 D&X abortions (the precise numbers are in dispute) are performed in the United States annually—compared to the 1,000,000 or so total abortions in the United States annually.[32] Symbols, however, are important. The frequency of an event does not affect its moral importance.[33] Given that such abortions occur when the mother is ready (or nearly ready) to give birth, opponents of such statutes find it difficult to portray the statutes as burdening the mother at all,[34] let alone "unduly" burdening her. The community through the state could simply take responsibility

---

26. *See generally* Barbara Katz Rothman, Recreating Motherhood: Ideology and Technology in a Patriarchal Society (1989); Vincent Brannigan, *Biomedical Technology: A First Order Technico-Legal Revolution,* 16 Hofstra L. Rev. 545 (1988); Sandra Anderson Garcia, *Sociocultural and Legal Implications of Creating and Sustaining Life through Biomedical Technology,* 17 J. Leg. Med. 469 (1996).

27. David Stout, *An Abortion Rights Advocate Says He Lied about Procedure,* N.Y. Times, Feb. 26, 1997, at A12. *See also* Garrow, *supra* note 8, at 729–30; Joe Fitzgerald, *Abortion-Rights Activists Play Loose with Truth,* Bos. Herald, Jan. 31, 1998, at; Wanda Franz, *A Look at…the New Politics: Abortion Realities Overtake the Rhetoric,* Wash. Post, June 1, 1997, at C3; Wardle, *supra* note 11, at 952–53. At least one professional abortion counselor has also confessed that many abortion advocates will not admit publicly to their moral qualms about late-term abortions. Lavelle, *supra* note 21, at 32.

28. Garrow, *supra* note 8, at 731; Katharine Seelye, *Medical Group Supports Ban on a Type of Late Abortion,* N.Y. Times, May 20, 1997, at A1.

29. Garrow, *supra* note 8, at 731. *See also* Robert Pear, *Inquiry Criticizes A.M.A. Backing of Abortion Procedure Ban,* N.Y. Times, Dec. 4, 1998, at A27.

30. Risen & Thomas, *supra* note 13, at 323.

31. *Id.,* at 355–57; Seth Faison, *Abortion Doctor Wounded Outside Kansas Clinic,* N.Y. Times, Aug. 20, 1993, at A12.

32. Lavelle, *supra* note 21, at 31. *See also* Garrow, *supra* note 8, at 732, 738; Epner, Jonas, & Seckinger, *supra* note 13, at 725–26; Radliff, *supra* note 11, at 1558 n.22; John Robertson, *Reconciling Offspring and Maternal Interests during Pregnancy,* in Reproductive Laws for the 1990s 259, 268 (Sherill Cohen & Nadine Taub eds. 1989); Matt Trewhalla, *Coming Home to Roost,* Life Advocate, Jan.–Feb. 1998, at 12.

33. J.K. Mason, Medico-Legal Aspects of Reproduction and Parenthood 166 (2nd ed. 1998).

34. Mary Kenny, Abortion: The Whole Story 291–92 (1986); Laurence Tribe, Abortion: The Clash of Absolutes 43–51 (1990).

for the care and custody of the child after its birth if its parents were unwilling to care for it. Whether such a solution is best for the child or not, it eliminates all tangible maternal burdens arising from the survival of the child. Of course, the reach of the statute conceivably could expand considerably with further technological change, but opponents of the statutes insistently deny that any such change is possible.

It has become a standard part of the pro-abortion litany to insist not only that the point of viability has not changed since 1973, but that it cannot change in the foreseeable future[35]—as if scientific progress were so predictable. Despite confident claims by the American Medical Association that no significant advances in the technologies of neonatal care are possible,[36] technologies change unpredictably. Researchers are already achieving considerable, if sporadic, success in striving to help parents who seek to save a premature child.[37] No one can predict when a technological breakthrough will dramatically alter the point of viability. Thus we find Gina Kolata, a science reporter for the *New York Times*, writing about a radically new technique for providing oxygen to premature infants that could push the point of viability back many weeks[38] even though she herself had written, less than six months earlier, that an unbreachable barrier to earlier viability had been reached.[39] And arguably, the possibility of implantation in another woman's uterus makes even fertilized ova "viable."[40] If the *Partial-Birth Abortion Ban Act* were eventually to be upheld by the courts, the growing need for the necessary technology to implement that Act might further hasten the development of techniques for assuring viability to ever earlier points in the pregnancy. No wonder some supporters of abortion rights have responded by insisting that "viability" must be understood as an ethical term describing the moral worth of a fetus and not as technological term describing the survivability of the fetus.[41]

The *Partial-Birth Abortion Ban Act* is a powerful symbol because it focuses on abortions where it is almost impossible for anyone who actually looks at what is happening to deny that the physician is killing a baby—a baby only minutes, days, or (at most) weeks away from a natural birth. Even without further technological change, such a statute evokes the most intense controversy thus far. Mothers whose children are protected will have to confront the psychological costs that abortion is said to avoid compared to adoption as a solution to unwanted pregnancy.[42] Even for abortions that do not come within the purview of the statute, the psychic costs

---

35. *See, e.g., Amicus Brief of the Am. Med. Ass'n supporting Appellants in* Webster v. Reproductive Health Services [492 U.S. 490 (1989)], *reprinted in* 11 Women's Rts. L. Rep. 443, 454 (1989), *and in* 5 Documentary History of the Legal Aspects of Abortion in the U.S.341, 361 (Roy Mersky & Gary Hartman eds. 1995); Gina Kolata, *Survival of the Fetus: A Barrier Is Reached*, N.Y. Times, April 18, 1989, at C1; Dick Polman, *When Is a Fetus Viable?*, Phila. Inquirer, July 16, 1989, at 1J; Nancy Rhoden, *Trimesters and Technology: Revamping* Roe v. Wade, 95 Yale L.J. 639, 661 1986).

36. *Amicus Brief of the Am. Med. Ass'n, supra* note 35.

37. *See, e.g.,* Craig Anderson, *Modern Achievements in the Intact Salvage of Very Small Premature Infants, in* Infanticide and the Handicapped Newborn 65 (Dennis Horan & Melinda Delahoyde eds. 1982); Gina Kolata, *For Babies, "Liquid Air" May Spare Fragile Lungs: Experimental Effort Could Shift the Age of Fetal Viability*, N.Y. Times, Aug. 29, 1989, at 20. *See also Experimental Lung Treatments Offer Hope for Tiniest Patients: Drugs Help Babies of Low Birth Weight Develop Normally*, N.Y. Times, July 11, 1989, at C3; *New Technique Saves Infants with Lung Ills*, N.Y. Times, Sept. 12, 1996, at A16.

38. Kolata, *supra* note 37.

39. Kolata, *supra* note 35. *See also* Ann Wason & Zoe Morris, *Christopher, World's Tiniest Premature Baby*, The Evening Standard, May 17, 2001, at 7.

40. Robert Glass, *First Embryo-Transfer Pregnancies Reported*, Phila. Inquirer, July 22, 1983, at 3A; Allen Hunter, *In the Wings: New Right Ideology and Organization*, 15 Radical Am. 113, 140–41 (1981).

41. Rhoden, *supra* note 35, at 671. *See also* F. Sessions Cole, *Editorial: Extreme Preterm Birth—Defining the Limits of Hope*, 343 N. Eng. J. Med. 429 (2000).

42. *See, e.g.,* Nanette Davis, From Crime to Choice 220–21, 244 (1985) ("Davis, Choice"); Nancy (Ann) Davis, *The Abortion Debate: The Search for Common Ground (Part 2)*, 103 Ethics 731, 756–58, 761–64 (1993); Reva Siegel, *Reasoning from the Body: A Historical Perspective on Abortion Regulation and Questions of Equal Protection*, 44 Stan. L. Rev. 261, 371–72 (1992).

of abortion are likely to rise. Women who have persuaded themselves that the "products of conception"[43] are not really a child before birth will find it more difficult to do so.

Opposition to the statute casts the supporters of abortion rights in a similar light as the controversy over assault weapons has cast the National Rifle Association in the battle over gun control. So extreme is the position espoused out of a fear that if any regulation is accepted it will lead to regulation of the whole field that the credibility of arguments against regulation of more central aspects of the field are undercut.[44] The proposed statute, one supposes, is then an example of the "sustained and often brilliant (if at times unprincipled) techniques" that law professor Joan Williams has argued are used by the "right-to-life" movement to "convince a significant portion of the American public that the fetus is a child."[45] Williams' notion of "principled techniques" is apparently somewhat malleable depending on whether an argument supports or undermines abortion rights. She sees nothing wrong with historians signing the *Historians' Briefs* sight unseen.[46]

One can expect very much the same rhetorical ploys in the emerging struggle of the *Unborn Victims of Violence Act*.[47] This proposed statute would define fetuses and embryos as "persons" for purposes of federal criminal law, making acts by persons other than the mother against the unborn child (other than an abortion sought by the mother) potentially punishable as federal crimes. Again this is decried as a threat to the mother's right to be rid of an unwanted pregnancy.

Courts have proven unable or unwilling to grapple with the changes in attitudes towards pregnancy and abortion resulting from the changing medical technologies that impact on our perceptions of those processes. Medical techniques for doing abortions, of course, are not the only changes in medical practice that impact on the abortion controversy. In recent decades, reproductive technologies in general have been changing on a scale unprecedented in history and faster than most other areas of medical practice. The pace of change in reproductive technologies appears to be accelerating. The results are startling.[48] When we can fertilize a human ovum

---

43. On the origins and strategy of this euphemism, see DAVIS, CHOICE, *supra* note 42, at 184–85.

44. The point is made in Martin Miller, *L.A. Law*, NEW REP., Feb. 22, 1999, at 14. For examples of such arguments, see David Garrow, *When "Compromise" Means Caving in*, WASH. POST, June 1, 1997, at C3; Kolbert & Miller, *supra* note 13, at 102–03. *See generally* GARROW, *supra* note 8, at 729. For a more general comparison of the arguments of the proponents of the right to abort with the arguments of proponents of the right to bear arms, see Nicholas Johnson, *Principles and Passions: The Intersection of Abortion and Gun Rights*, 50 ARIZ. L. REV. 97 (1997).

45. Joan Williams, *Gender Wars: Selfless Women in the Republic of Choice*, 66 NYU L. REV. 1559, 1585 (1991) (citation omitted).

46. See Chapter 17, at note 34.

47. *Unborn Victims of Violence Act*, H.R. 2436, 106th Cong., 1st. Sess. (1999). *See also* Jeffrey Rosen, *A Viable Solution*, LEGAL AFF., Oct. 2003, at 20.

48. *See generally* BLANK & MERRICK, *supra* note 24; JUDITH BOSS, THE BIRTH LOTTERY: PRENATAL DIAGNOSIS AND SELECTIVE ABORTION (1993); MARCIA MOBILIA BOUMIL, LAW, ETHICS AND REPRODUCTIVE CHOICE 59–83 (1994); RUTH COLKER, ABORTION & DIALOGUE — PRO-CHOICE, PRO-LIFE, AND AMERICAN LAW 144–57 (1992); CONTEMPORARY ISSUES IN BIOETHICS (Tom Beauchamp & LeRoy Walters eds. 4th ed. 1994); COUNCIL OF EUROPE, *supra* note 24; WARREN FREEDMAN, LEGAL ISSUES IN BIOTECHNOLOGY AND HUMAN REPRODUCTION: ARTIFICIAL CONCEPTION AND MODERN GENETICS (1991); ANDREW KIMBRELL, THE HUMAN BODY: THE ENGINEERING AND MARKETING OF LIFE (1993); LAURITZEN, *supra* note 24; MASON, *supra* note 33; DAVID MEYERS, THE HUMAN BODY AND THE LAW 54–120 (2nd ed. 1990); MARTHA MINOW, MAKING ALL THE DIFFERENCE: INCLUSION, EXCLUSION, AND AMERICAN LAW 312–49 (1990); OVERALL, *supra* note 24; ROBERT POLLACK, SIGNS OF LIFE: THE LANGUAGE AND MEANING OF DNA (1993); JANICE RAYMOND, WOMEN AS WOMBS: REPRODUCTIVE TECHNOLOGIES AND THE BATTLE OVER WOMEN'S FREEDOM (1993); REPRODUCTION, ETHICS, AND THE LAW: FEMINIST PERSPECTIVES (Joan Callahan ed. 1995) ("FEMINIST PERSPECTIVES"); REPRODUCTION, TECHNOLOGY, AND RIGHTS, *supra* note 24; DEBORAH RHODE, JUSTICE AND GENDER 219–29 (1989); JOHN ROBERTSON, CHILDREN OF CHOICE: FREEDOM AND THE NEW REPRODUCTIVE TECHNOLOGIES (1994); ROTHMAN, *supra* note 26; SUSAN SHERWIN, NO LONGER PATIENT: FEMINIST ETHICS AND HEALTH

in a petri dish, test the resulting embryos for desirable traits, and freeze or discard those not immediately desired by the intended parents, both parents and courts find themselves struggling to interpret human reproduction consistently with the humane traditions of our society.[49]

Physicians now are able to diagnose some genetic defects in a human zygote with as few as four cells, discarding zygotes that fail the test (or even kicking out particular cells from an embryo).[50] The development of techniques for preserving and reimplanting slices of a woman's ovary create the technical possibility of a woman remaining fertile as long as she chooses regardless of menopause.[51] Such dramatic developments, including the already accomplished *in vitro* fertilization of a 62-year-old woman enabling her to bear a child, compels us to begin thinking about the making of babies as a technological process as much as a biological one.[52] While less dramatic, similar patterns are emerging in some countries regarding substitutions of grandfathers for fathers in human reproduction.[53] Such events change our thinking about the nature of human reproduction and of what it is to be human even if such practices occur only rarely, so long as the new practices are widely known. The legal consequences of such developments have only begun to be considered.[54] For example, are women who choose such means to become

---

CARE 117–36 (1992); GEORGE SMITH II, THE NEW BIOLOGY: LAW, ETHICS, AND BIOTECHNOLOGY (1989); THE ETHICS OF REPRODUCTIVE TECHNOLOGY, *supra* note 24; WOMEN AND PRENATAL TESTING: FACING THE CHALLENGES OF GENETIC TECHNOLOGY (Karne Rothenberg & Elizabeth Thompson eds. 1994).

49. *See* FENWICK, *supra* note 24; CHERYL MEYER, THE WANDERING UTERUS: POLITICS AND THE REPRODUCTIVE RIGHTS OF WOMEN 41–84 (1997); Vicki Norton, Comment, *Unnatural Selection: Nontherapeutic Preimplantation Genetic Screening and Proposed Regulation,* 41 UCLA L. REV. 1581 (1994); Sandra Tomkowicz, *The Disabling Effects of Infertility: Fertile Grounds for Accommodating Infertile Couples under the American with Disabilities Act,* 46 SYR. L. REV. 1051 (1996). *See also* Hecht v. Los Angeles Cnty. Super. Ct., 59 Cal. Rptr. 2d 222 (Ct. App. 1996), *rev. denied, opinion ordered not published* (a man has no power to bequeath his sperm); LA. REV. STAT. ANN. §§ 9:121 to 9:133 (West 2000) (classifying embryos as "persons"—not as "property").

50. A.H. Handyside *et al., Birth of a Normal Girl after* in Vitro *Fertilization and Preimplantation Diagnostic Testing for Cystic Fibrosis,* 327 N. ENG. J. MED. 905 (1992); Gina Kolata, *Scientists Face New Ethical Quandaries in Baby-Making,* N.Y. TIMES, Aug. 19, 1997, at 2. *See also* BOUMIL, *supra* note 48, at 14–15; MEYER, *supra* note 49, at 50–52; Jeffrey Botkin, *Prenatal Diagnosis and the Selection of Children,* 30 FLA. ST. L. REV. 265 (2003); Richard Tasca & Michael McCLure, *The Emerging Technology and Application of Preimplantation Genetic Diagnosis,* 26 J. LAW & MED. 7 (1998).

51. Gina Kolata, *New Surgery Saves Parts of an Ovary for Later Implant,* N.Y. TIMES, Jan. 2, 1996, at A1. *See also* MASON, *supra* note 33, at 242–44.

52. Sheryl Stolberg, *Science Helps Italian Woman Give Birth at 62,* L.A. TIMES, July 19, 1994, at A1. As many as 42 women between the ages of 50 and 63 gave birth through such procedures at one clinic at the University of Southern California between 1991 and 2001, producing 61 children. Rick Weiss, *Age Barriers to Pregnancy Ease: Study Says Donor Eggs Can Aid Women in Their 60s; Practice Still Questioned,* WASH. POST, Nov. 13, 2002, at A11. *See also* FENWICK, *supra* note 24, at 9–24, 177–206; MEYER, *supra* note 49, at 7–8, 31–32; John Battersby, *South African Woman Gives Birth to 3 Grandchildren,* N.Y. TIMES, Oct. 2, 1987, at A9; Ken Budd, *Health News: Egg Beaters: Good News for Older Wannabe Moms: It Ain't Ova til It's Ova,* MODERN MATURITY, May–June 2002, at 15; Mary Duenwald, *After 25 Years, New Ideas in the Prenatal Test Tube,* N.Y. TIMES, July 15, 2003, at F5, F8; Editorial, *Too Old to Have a Baby?,* 341 THE LANCET 344 (1993); Claudia Kalb, *Should You Have Your Baby Now?,* NEWSWEEK, Aug. 13, 2001, at 40; Gina Kolata, *A Record and Big Questions as Woman Gives Birth at 63,* N.Y. TIMES, Apr. 24, 1997, at A1; Gina Kolata, *Reproductive Revolution Is Jolting Old Views,* N.Y. TIMES, Jan. 11, 1994, at A1; Gina Kolata, *When Grandmother Is the Mother, until Birth,* N.Y. TIMES, Aug. 5, 1991, at A1. *See generally* Battersby, *supra* note 24; Tony Hope *et al., Should Older Women Be Offered* in Vitro *Fertilization? An Ethical Debate,* 310 BRIT. MED. J. 1455 (1995); Abby Lippman, *"Never too Late": Biotechnology, Women and Reproduction,* 40 McGILL L.J. 875 (1995); Michael Shapiro, *Illicit Reasons and Means for Reproduction: On Excessive Choice and Categorical and Technological Imperatives,* 47 HASTINGS L.J. 1081, 1126–27 (1996); Patricia Smith, *Selfish Genes and Maternal Myths: A Look at Postmenopausal Pregnancy,* in MENOPAUSE: A MIDLIFE PASSAGE 92 (Joan Callahan ed. 1953).

53. *See* Doug Struck, *When Grandfather Is also Father,* WASH. POST, Nov. 17, 2000, at A1.

54. For one of the first attempts to consider these consequences, see Joan Heifetz Hollinger, *From Coitus to Commerce: Legal and Social Consequences of Noncoital Reproduction,* 18 J. LAW REFORM 865 (1985).

pregnant subject to the protections of the *Pregnancy Discrimination Act* or the *Americans with Disabilities Act*?[55]

Many of the new reproductive technologies create considerable risk of multiple pregnancies, resulting in an unprecedented number of births of sextuplets, septuplets, octuplets, and even nonuplets.[56] Frequently some or all of these babies are stillborn or die shortly after birth. One result—reflecting the changes in our thinking about human reproduction—is the "transabdominal reduction" of healthy fetuses in order to improve the chances for survival of siblings sharing a multiple pregnancy. Transabdominal reduction involves injecting potassium chloride into selected fetuses to achieve a "complete standstill of the fetal heart," with the killed fetus remaining in the womb.[57] If done at the proper time, the dead fetal material apparently will be reabsorbed by the siblings, although many of these procedures result in the "birth" of dead children along with the survivors of the procedure. The same procedure has also been undertaken when chromosomal analysis disclosed that one twin had Down's syndrome and the other did not.[58]

Ethical qualms about transabdominal reduction do not begin to approach the concerns raised by the growing willingness to countenance publicly causing death by neglect (often through star-

---

55. *Americans with Disabilities Act,* 42 U.S.C. § 12102 (1994); *Pregnancy Discrimination Act,* 42 U.S.C. §§ 2000e to 2000e–17 (1994). For a case applying these statutes, see: LaPorta v. Wal-Mart Stores, Inc., 163 F. Supp. 2d 758 (W.D. Mich. 2001). For cases declining to apply these statutes, see: Saks v. Franklin Covey Co., 316 F.3d 337 (2nd Cir. 2003); Krauel v. Iowa Methodist Med. Ctr., 95 F.3d 674 (8th Cir. 1996); Cleese v. Hewlett-Packard Co., 911 F. Supp. 1312 (D. Ore. 1995); Clapp v. Northern Cumberland Mem. Hosp., 964 F. Supp. 503 (D. Me. 1997); Erickson v. Board of Governors of State Colleges, 911 F. Supp. 316 (N.D. Ill. 1995); Zatarian v. WDSU-Television, Inc., 881 F. Supp. 240 (E.D. La. 1995), *aff'd mem.,* 79 F.3d 1143 (5th Cir. 1996); Pacourek v. Inland Steel, 858 F. Supp. 1393 (N.D. Ill. 1994). *See also* Samuel Issacharoff & Elyse Rosenblum, *Women and the Workplace: Accommodating the Demands of Pregnancy,* 94 Colum. L. Rev. 2154 (1994).

   This issue arises primarily because of the expense of the procedure and the unwillingness of insurance companies to pay for the procedures. *See* M.J. Levy, *Fertility Center Describes Its Shared-Risk Program,* 7 Women's Health Issues no. 3, at 172 (1997); John Robertson & Theodore Schneyer, *Professional Self-Regulation and Shared-Risk Programs for* in Vitro *Fertilization,* 25 J. Law, Med. & Ethics 283 (1997).

56. *See, e.g.,* Ronald Chester, *Double Trouble: Legal Solutions to the Medical Problems of Unconsented Sperm Harvesting and Drug-Induced Multiple Pregnancies,* 44 St. Louis U. L.J. 451 (2000); Ezekiel Emanuel, *Eight Is too Many,* New Rep., Jan. 25, 1999, at 8; Rick Lyman, *As Octuplets Remain in Peril, Ethics Questions Are Raised,* N.Y. Times, Dec. 22, 1998, at A1, A22 (reporting 10 instances of births of from six to nine babies since 1985); Norbert Gleicher *et al., Reducing the Risk of High-Order Multiple Pregnancy after Ovarian Stimulation with Gonadotropins,* 343 N. Eng. J. Med. 2 (2000) (noting that 441 induced pregnancies resulted in 88 twins, 22 triplets, and 17 births of four to six babies). *See also* Siladitya Bhattacharya & Allan Templeton, *In Treating Infertility, Are Multiple Pregnancies Unavoidable?,* 343 N. Eng. J. Med. 58 (2000).

57. Boss, *supra* note 48, at 98–99; Fenwick, *supra* note 24, at 201–03; Mason, *supra* note 33, at 134; Meyers, *supra* note 48, at 60–62, 69–71; Richard Berkowitz *et al., Selective Reduction of Multifetal Pregnancies in the First Trimester,* 318 N. Eng. J. Med. 1043 (1988); Judith Daar, *Selective Reduction of Multiple Pregnancies: Lifeboat Ethics in the Womb,* 25 U.C. Davis L. Rev. 773 (1992); Clare Dyer, *Selective Abortions Hit the Headlines,* 313 Brit. Med. J. 380 (1996); Mark Evans *et al., Selective Termination: Clinical Experience and Residual Risks,* 162 Am. J. Obstet. & Gynecology 1568 (1990); Elizabeth Villiers Gemmette, *Selective Pregnancy Reduction: Medical Attitudes, Legal Implications, and a Viable Alternative,* 16 J. Health Pol'y & L. 383 (1991); Mary Osborn, *Selective Reduction in Multiple Gestation,* 3 Perinatal & Neonatal Nursing 14 (1989); Mary Rorty & JoAnn Pinkerton, *Elective Fetal Reduction: The Ultimate Elective Surgery,* 13 J. Contemp. Health L. & Pol'y 53 (1996); Stacey Pinchuk, *A Difficult Choice in a Different Voice: Multiple Births, Selective Reduction and Abortion,* 7 Duke J. Gender & L. 29 (2000); Khalil Tabsh, *Transabdominal Multifetal Pregnancy Reduction: Report of 40 Cases,* 75 Obstet. & Gynecology 739 (1990).

58. Usha Chitkara *et al., Selective Second-Trimester Termination of the Anomalous Fetus in Twin Pregnancies,* 73 Obstet. & Gynecology 690 (1989); Thomas Kerenyi & Usha Chitkara, *Selective Birth in Twin Pregnancy with Discordancy for Down's Syndrome,* 304 N. Eng. J. Med. 1525 (1981). The same technique is used to preclude the possibility of a "live-birth" abortion. Nelson Isada *et al., Fetal Intracardiac Potassium Chloride Injection to Avoid Hopeless Resuscitation of an Abnormal Fetus: I. Clinical Issues,* 80 Obstet. & Gynecology 296 (1992).

vation) of newborns who do not measure up to some standard or other.[59] Probably the first public acknowledgment of this practice in the United States was by doctors Raymond Duff and A.G.M. Campbell in 1973 in an article in which they admitted that 14 percent of the deaths in their special care unit over the preceding two years resulted from their joint decision with the parents to allow the infants to die.[60] Was it a mere coincidence that this article appeared in the same year that *Roe v. Wade* was decided? Feminist historian Mary Kenny, for one, has traced the new acceptance of infanticide directly back to the political acceptance of abortion, from which infanticide—particularly for late-term abortions—is morally indistinguishable.[61] This perception perhaps explains why in the 59 cases involving infanticide in the United Kingdom between

---

59. *See, e.g.,* Bowen v. American Hosp. Ass'n, 476 U.S. 610 (1986); *In re* Baby K., 16 F.3d 59 (4th Cir.), *cert. denied sub nom.* Baby K. v. Ms. H., 513 U.S. 825 (1994); Johnson v. Thompson, 971 F.2d 1487 (10th Cir. 1992), *cert. denied,* 507 U.S. 910 (1993); Marzen v. Department of Health & Hum. Services, 825 F.2d 1148 (7th Cir. 1987); United States v. University Hospital, 729 F.2d 144 (2nd Cir. 1984); Gerben v. Holsclaw, 692 F. Supp. 557 (E.D. Pa. 1988); American Council of Pediatrics v. Heckler, 561 F. Supp. 395 (D.D.C. 1983); *In re* Truselo, 846 A.2d 256 (Del. 2000); *In re* K.I., 735 A.2d 448 (D.C. 1999); *In re* Conroy, 486 A.2d 1209 (N.J. 1985); *In re* AMB, 640 N.W.2d 262 (Mich. Ct. App. 2001); Weber v. Stony Brook Hospital, 456 N.E.2d 1186 (N.Y.), *cert. denied,* 464 U.S. 1026 (1983); *In re* Cicero, 421 N.Y.S.2d 965 (Sup. Ct. 1979); Burks v. St. Joseph's Hosp., 596 N.W.2d 391 (Wis. 1999); *In re* T (a minor), [1997] 1 All E.R. 906 (C.A.); Regina v. Cambridge Health Auth'y, [1995] 23 Brit. Med. L. Rep. 1 (C.A.). *See also* Rideout v. Hershey Med. Ctr., 30 Pa. D&C 4th 57 (1995) (allowing suit by parents when a hospital unilaterally decided to cut off life support to a terminally ill two-year-old); Miller v. HCA, Inc., 118 S.W.3d 758 (Tex. 2003) (a physician is not liable for battery in resuscitating a premature baby without parental consent).

*See generally* Renée Anspach, Deciding Who Lives: Fateful Choices in the Intensive-Care Nursery (1993); Blank & Merrick, *supra* note 24, at 199–214; Infanticide and the Handicapped Newborn, *supra* note 37; Informed Consent in European Neonatal Research and the Work of Research Ethics Committees (Christopher Megone & Su Mason eds. 2000); Mason, *supra* note 33, at 281–318; Meyers, *supra* note 48, at 83–120; Smith, *supra* note 48, at 29–66; AMA Council on Ethical & Judicial Aff., *The Use of Anencephalic Neonates as Organ Donors,* 273 JAMA 1614 (1995); Ian Balfour-Lynn & Robert Tasker, *Futility and Death in Pediatric Medical Intensive Care,* 22 J. Med. Ethics 279 (1996); Janet Beausoleil *et al., The Influence of Education and Experience on Ethical Attitudes in Neonatal Intensive Care,* 14 Med. Decision Making 403 (1994); Philip Boyle, *Religious Reasoning in Health Care Resource Management: The Case of Baby K,* 25 Seton Hall L. Rev. 949 (1995); A.G.M. Campbell & H.E. McHaffie, *Prolonging Life and Allowing Death: Infants,* 21 J. Med. Ethics 339 (1995); Alexander Morgan Capron, *Baby Ryan and Virtual Futility,* 25 Hastings Ctr. Rep. no. 2, at 20 (Mar.–Apr. 1995); Ellen Wright Clayton, *Commentary: What Is Really at Stake in* Baby K?, 23 J. Law Med. & Ethics 13 (1995); Mary Crossley, *Infants with Anencephaly, the ADA, and the Child Abuse Amendments,* 11 Issues in L. & Med. 379 (1996); V.A. Entwistle *et al., Media Coverage of the Child B Case,* 312 Brit. Med. J. 1587 (1996); Ellen Flannery, *One Advocate's Viewpoint: Conflicts and Tensions in the* Baby K *Case,* 23 J. Law Med. & Ethics 7 (1995); Norman Fost, *Decisions Regarding Treatment of Seriously Ill Newborns,* 281 JAMA 2041 (1999); Garcia, *supra* note 26, at 509–22; Zosia Kmietowitz, *Premature Baby Was Not Put on Ventilator,* 313 Brit. Med. J. 963 (1996); John Warwick Montgomery, *Human Dignity in Birth and Death: A Question of Values,* 140/141 Law & Justice 65 (1999); E. Haavi Morrein, *Futilitarianism, Exoticare, and Coerced Altruism: The ADA Meets Its Limits,* 25 Seton Hall L. Rev. 883 (1995); Erin Nealy, *Medical Decision-Making for Children: A Struggle for Autonomy,* 49 SMU L. Rev. 133 (1995); Saroj Saigal *et al., Differences in Preferences for Neonatal Outcomes among Health Care Professionals, Parents, and Adolescents,* 281 JAMA 1991 (1999); Giles Scofield, *Medical Futility Judgments: Discrimination or Discriminatory?,* 25 Seton Hall L. Rev. 927 (1995); Tony Sheldon, *Dutch Appeal Court Dismisses Case against Doctor,* 311 Brit. Med. J. 1322 (1995); Zier Versluys & Richard de Leeuw, *A Dutch Report on the Ethics of Neonatal Care,* 21 J. Med. Ethics 14 (1995). Of course, for persons with Down syndrome such discrimination is not limited to survival problems discovered at birth. *See* Julian Savulescu, *Resources, Down's Syndrome, and Cardiac Surgery,* 322 Brit. Med. J. 875 (2001).

60. Raymond Duff & A.G.M. Campbell, *Moral and Ethical Dilemmas in the Special-Care Nursery,* 289 N. Eng. J. Med. 890 (1973). *See also Endorsing Infanticide?,* Time, May 28, 1973, at 104 (reporting Dr. James Watson—co-discover of DNA—proposed redefining the point at which a child became human being until three days after birth precisely in order to allow the parents to decide whether the child should live).

61. Kenny, *supra* note 34, at 234–38. *See also* Mason, *supra* note 33, at 108; Robyn Lansdowne, *Infanticide: Psychiatrists in the Plea Bargaining Process,* 16 Monash U. L. Rev. 41 (1990).

1979 and 1988, not one person went to prison.[62] The point is made particularly dramatically by highly reported instances of one or both parents killing a newborn immediately after birth.[63] Some who defend this practice even have taken to calling it "full-birth abortions."[64]

In the United States, at least, the willingness to kill an infant even after she goes home with her mother seems to be rising.[65] At least the number of reported homicides of children before their first birthday rose from 7.2/100,000 to 8.7/100,000 over the period from 1983 to 1991.[66]

---

62. Regina v. Salsbury, 11 Crim. App. 533 (1989). One commentator has suggested that the reason for such leniency is that a parent who kills her child is not a threat to others in the community—unlike, say, a "gun-toting gang member." *See* Laura Sessions Stepp, *Infants Now Murdered as Often as Teens: Actual Rate May Be Higher Experts Say*, WASH. POST, Dec. 10, 2002, at A3.

63. *See, e.g.,* United States *ex rel.* Jones v. Washington, 836 F. Supp. 502 (N.D. Ill. 1993), *aff'd mem.*, 32 F.3d 570 (7th Cir. 1994); Moffit v. Arkansas, No. CACR 92-444 (Ark. Ct. App. Mar 17, 1993), 1993 Ark. App. LEXIS 171; *In re* Sophia M., 234 Cal. Rptr. 698 (Ct. App. 1987), *rehearing granted*; People v. Ehlert, 781 N.E.2d 500 (Ill. App. Ct. 2002), *appeal allowed*, 787 N.E.2d 176 (Ill. 2003); People v. Doss, 574 N.E.2d 806 (Ill. App. Ct. 1991); State v. Kinsky, 348 N.W.2d 319 (Minn. 1984); Berg v. State, 557 N.W.2d 593 (Minn. Ct. App. 1996); State v. Doyle, 287 N.W.2d 59 (Neb. 1980); People v. Wernick, 674 N.E.2d 322 (N.Y. 1996); People v. Wang, 490 N.Y.S.2d 423 (Sup. Ct. 1985); State v. Hopfer, 679 N.E.2d 321 (Ohio Ct. App.), *appeal dismissed*, 673 N.E.2d 146 (Ohio 1996); Commonwealth v. Reilly, 549 A.2d 503 (Pa. 1988); Commonwealth v. Meder, 611 A.2d 213 (Pa. Super. 1992), *appeal denied*, 622 A.2d 1375 (1993); State v. Collington, 192 S.E.2d 856 (S.C. 1972); Lane v. Commonwealth, 248 S.E.2d 781 (Va. 1978); Corrales v. Commonwealth, No. 2797-01-02 (Va. Ct. App. Nov. 19, 2002), 2002 WL 31553222; Myers v. Commonwealth, No. 1780-92-1 (Va. Ct. App. July 26, 1998), 1998 WL 389748; Vaughn v. Virginia, 376 S.E.2d 801 (Va. Ct. App. 1989); State v. McGuire, 490 S.E.2d 912 (W. Va. 1997); State v. Leggate, 537 N.W.2d 435 (Wis. Ct. App.), 1995 WL 239625, *rev. denied*, 537 N.W.2d 574 (Wis. 1995); Anna Cekola, *Woman Gets 15 to Life for Killing her Baby Crime: Despite Evidence Fullerton Resident Had Mental Problems when She Delivered Boy, Judge Says He Had to Send Her to Prison*, L.A. TIMES, May 13, 1997, at B1; Rachel Simon, *Fear of Shame Carries Far too High a Price in the Grossberg Case*, PHILA. INQUIRER, July 24, 1998, at A29; Ronald Smothers, *Guilty Plea by Mother, 20, in Prom Death*, N.Y. TIMES, Aug. 21,1998, at B1.

*See generally* JAN BROCKINGTON, MOTHERHOOD AND MATERNAL HEALTH 430–38 (1996); ANIA WILCZYN-SKI, CHILD HOMICIDE 30 (1997); Dominique Bourget & John Bradford, *Homicidal Parents*, 35 CAN. J. PSYCH. 233 (1990); Julia Brienza, *When the Bough Breaks: Can Justice Be Served in Neonaticide Cases?*, TRIAL, Dec. 1997, at13; Barbara Ehrenreich, *Where Have All the Babies Gone?*, LIFE, Jan. 1998, at 68; C.M. Green & S.V. Manohar, *Neonaticide and Hysterical Denial of Pregnancy*, 156 BRIT. J. PSYCH. 121 (1990); R.D. Mackay, *The Consequences of Killing Very Young Children*, 1993 CRIM. L. REV. 21; D. Maier-Katkin & R. Ogle, *A Rationale for Infanticide Laws*, 1993 CRIM. L. REV. 903; J.D. Marleau *et al.*, *Homicide d'enfant commis par la mère*, 40 CAN. J. PSYCH. 142 (1995); M.N. Marks & R. Kumar, *Infanticide in England and Wales*, 33 MED. SCI. & L. 329 (1993); Marie McCullough, *In Newborn Killings, a New Profile*, PHILA. INQUIRER, Nov. 23, 1997, at A21; Mauro Mendlowicz *et al.*, *A Case-Control Study on the Socio-Demographic Characteristics of 53 Neonaticidal Mothers*, 21 INT'L J. LAW & PSYCH. 209 (1998); Michelle Oberman, *Mothers Who Kill: Coming to Terms with Modern American Infanticide*, 34 AM. CRIM. L. REV. 1 (1996); Steven Pinker, *Why They Kill Their Newborns*, N.Y. TIMES MAG., Nov. 2, 1997, at 52; Julie Stoiber & Linda Loyd, *One Question Remains in Marie Noe Case: Why? A Controversial Plea Deal May Be the Only Way to Find Out Why She Killed Eight of Her Children*, PHILA. INQUIRER, July 4, 1999, at E1; Symposium, *From Baby Blues to Mothers Who Kill: Responses to Postpartum Disorders in the Criminal and Civil Law*, 10 WM. & MARY J. WOMEN & L. 1–68 (2003); Symposium, *Tenth Anniversary Issue: Women and Criminal Defenses*, 10 DUKE J. GENDER L. & POL'Y 1–172 (2003); Barbara Whitaker, *Deaths of Unwanted Babies Bring Plea to Help Parents*, N.Y. TIMES, Mar. 6, 2000, at A1; G. LaVerne Williamson, *Postpartum Depression Syndrome as a Defense to Criminal Behavior*, 8 J. FAM. VIOLENCE 151 (1993).

64. *Full Birth Abortion*, WASH. TIMES, Dec. 1, 1996, at 37; Ronald Smothers, *Guilty Plea by Mother, 20, in Prom Death*, N.Y. TIMES, Aug. 21,1998, at B1.

65. Patricia Crittendon & Susan Craig, *Developmental Trends in the Nature of Child Homicide*, 5 J. INTER-PERSONAL VIOLENCE 202 (1990); Susan Gilbert, *Infant Homicide Found to Be Rising in the U.S.*, N.Y. TIMES, Oct. 27, 1998, at F10; D.R. Hargrave & D.P. Warner, *A Study of Child Homicide over Two Decades*, 32 J. MED. SCI. & L. 247 (1992); Wilkey *et al.*, *supra* note 63. *But see* Barbara Kantorwitz, *Despite Recent Spate of Baby Killings, Cases Still Rare*, N.O. TIMES-PICAYUNE, July 13, 1997, at A24.

66. Mary Overpeck, *Risk Factors for Infant Homicide in the U.S.*, 339 N. ENG. J. MED. 1211 (Oct. 22, 1998).

The number of children who were murdered before their fourth birthday rose from a little over 2.4 percent of all murders in 1979 to 3.3 percent in 1995.[67] Homicide was the only leading cause of childhood death in the United States that increased between 1960 and 1990.[68] Is this too merely a coincidence?

Arguments that legalizing abortion leads to the legalization of infanticide smack of the "slippery slope," which some denigrate as a spurious kind of argument.[69] That a slope might be slippery does not make it any less real. After all, the United States is now a society in which there are intense debates whether it is too costly to test newborns routinely for treatable birth defects.[70] One Canadian study concluded that the legalization of abortion not only tends to legitimate infanticide, but that it also leads to an increase in child abuse.[71] That these patterns have some connection is clear when one realizes that many cases of infanticide result from prolonged and escalating patterns of abuse.[72]

Similarly controversial is the "harvesting" of fetal tissue for medical experimentation or organ transplantation[73]—with the consent of the next of kin whom the law deems to "own" the ca-

---

67. Martha Smithey, *Infant Homicide: Victim/Offender Relationship and Causes of Death*, 13 J. FAM. VIOLENCE 285, 285 (1998). *See also* Philip McLain et al., *Geographic Patterns of Fatal Abuse or Neglect in Children Younger than 5 Years Old in the United States, 1979–1988*, 148 ARCH. PEDIATRIC & ADOLESCENT MED. 82 (1994); Murray Strauss, *State and Regional Differences in U.S. Infant Homicide Rates in Relation to Sociocultural Characteristics of the States*, 5 BEHAVIORAL SCI. & L. 61 (1987).

68. Bernard Ewigman & Colleen Kivlahan, *Child Maltreatment Fatalities*, 18 PEDIATRIC ANN. 9 (Spring 1989).

69. Diane Meulemans, *Approaching the Slope: Process and Outcomes of the Use of the Slippery Slope in Legal Opinions*, 14 WIS. WOMEN'S L.J. 105 (1999).

70. Francesca Lunzer Kritz & Sharon Mazel, *Too Much for Too Little? Costly Newborn Test Fuels Debate on Value*, WASH. POST, July 2, 2002, at HE1.

71. Philip Ney, *Relationship between Abortion and Child Abuse*, 24 CAN. J. PSCYH. 610 (1979).

72. U.S. ADVISORY BOARD ON CHILD ABUSE AND NEGLECT, A NATION'S SHAME: FATAL CHILD ABUSE AND NEGLECT IN THE UNITED STATES, EXECUTIVE SUMMARY (1995); Michael Durfee, *Fatal Child Abuse—Intervention and Prevention*, PROTECTION OF CHILDREN, Spring 1989, at 9; Richard Gelles, *Physical Violence, Child Abuse, and Child Homicide: A Continuum of Violence or Distinct Behaviors?*, 2 HUM. NATURE 59 (1991); Leslie Margolin, *Fatal Child Neglect*, 69 CHILD WELFARE 309 (1990); Susan Sorenson & Julie Peterson, *Traumatic Child Death and Documented Maltreatment History, Los Angeles*, 84 AM. J. PUB. HEALTH 623 (1994); Smithey, *supra* note 67.

73. *In re* T.A.C.P., 609 So. 2d 588 (Fla. 1992). *See also* BLANK & MERRICK, *supra* note 24, at 176–98; BOUMIL, *supra* note 48, at 85–93; EXPERIMENTS ON EMBRYOS (Anthony Dyson & John Harris eds. 1990); 2 FEDERAL ABORTION POLITICS, *supra* note 35, at 669–747; FENWICK, *supra* note 24, at 155–75; HUMAN FERTILISATION & EMBRYOLOGY AUTH'Y, DONATED OVARIAN TISSUE IN EMBRYO RESEARCH AND ASSISTED CONCEPTION— REPORT (1994); MASON, *supra* note 33, at 187–206; Paul Byrne et al., *Anencephaly—Organ Transplantation?*, 9 ISSUES IN L. & MED. 23 (1993); Diane Chun, *Fetal Tissue Implanted Safely, Doctors Say*, N.Y. TIMES, Sept. 11, 2001, at F12; Jon Cohen, *New Fight over Fetal Tissue Grafts*, 263 SCI. 600 (1994); John Fletcher, *Abortion Politics, Science, and Research Ethics: Take Down the Wall of Separation*, 8 J. CONTEMP. HEALTH L. & POL'Y 95 (1992); Gregory Gelfand & Toby Levin, *Fetal Tissue Research: Legal Regulation of Human Fetal Tissue Transplantation*, 50 WASH. & LEE L. REV. 647 (1993); Diane Gianelli, *AMA Organ Donor Opinion Sparks Ethics Debate: Should Anencephalic Infants Be "Living Donors"?*, AM. MED. ASS'N NEWS, July 25, 1994, at 1; Julie Koenig, *The Anencephalic Baby Theresa: A Prognosticator of Future Bioethics*, 17 NOVA L. REV. 445 (1992); Sheldon Krimsky & Ruth Hubbard, *The Business of Research*, 25 HASTINGS CTR. REP. no. 1, at 41 (Jan–Feb. 1995); Mary Mahowald, *As if There Were Fetuses without Women: A Remedial Essay*, in FEMINIST PERSPECTIVES, *supra* note 48, at 199; Carla McCauley, *Fetal Tissue: A Medicolegal Predicament*, 40 MED. TRIAL Q. 230 (1993); Elizabeth Patterson, *Human Rights and Human Life: An Uneven Fit*, 68 TULANE L. REV. 1527, 1553–56 (1994). Ironically, some who are strongly committed to abortion rights, and who would presumably see nothing objectionable in harvesting fetal organs, object to transplanting animal organs into humans as violations of animal rights. *See* Jack Kress, *Xenotransplantation: Ethics and Economics*, 53 FOOD & DRUG L.J. 353 (1998).

daver.[74] Further complicating an ethical review of the new attitudes toward pregnancy is the emergence of sex-selective abortions, practices that are already widespread in several countries.[75] The victims of such practices nearly always are girls, although in rare circumstances boys rather than girls have been targeted.[76] The increasing acceptance of such practices is a sharp break with historic practices in which infanticide, at least in the West, occurred with some frequency but was always condemned and frequently prosecuted.[77] The challenge of such practices to our thinking about human reproduction were presented dramatically in *Davis v. Davis*.[78]

Since the first successful *in vitro* fertilization occurred in England in 1978,[79] the practice has grown dramatically, with over 11,000 such births in the United States in 1996 alone, and over

---

74. Newman v. Sathyavaglswaran, 287 F.3d 786 (9th Cir.), *cert. denied*, 537 U.S. 1029 (2002); Whaley v. Tuscola Cnty., 58 F.3d 1111 (6th Cir.), *cert. denied sub nom.* Saginaw Cty. v. Whaley, 516 U.S. 975 (1995); *Uniform Anatomical Gift Act*, 8A U.L.A. 3 (1987). *See* MASON, *supra* note 33, at 191–95. *See also* Moore v. Board of Regents, 499 U.S. 936 (1991); Guido Calabresi, *An Introduction to Legal Thought: Four Approaches to Law and to the Allocation of Body Parts*, 55 STAN. L. REV. 2113 (2003); G. Dworkin & I. Kennedy, *Human Tissue: Rights in the Body and Its Parts*, 1 MED. L. REV. 291 (1993); Richard Gold, *Owning Our Bodies: An Examination of Property Law and Biotechnology*, 32 SAN DIEGO L. REV. 1167 (1995); S.R. Munzer, *An Uneasy Case against Property Rights in Body Parts*, 11 SOC. PHILOS. & POL'Y 259 (1994); Kermit Roosevelt III, *The Newest Property: Reproductive Technologies and the Concept of Parenthood*, 39 SANTA CLARA L. REV. 79, 80–84 (1998); P.D.G. Skegg, *Medical Uses of Corpses and the "No Property" Rule*, 32 MED. SCI. & L. 311 (1992). Whether this is so regarding an aborted fetus has not yet been litigated.

75. HRDY, *supra* note 13, at 318–50; SUSAN GREENHALGH & JIALI LI, ENGENDERING REPRODUCTIVE PRACTICE IN PEASANT CHINA: THE POLITICAL ROOTS OF THE RISING SEX RATIO AT BIRTH (1993); MAN-MADE WOMEN: HOW NEW REPRODUCTIVE TECHNOLOGIES AFFECT WOMEN (Gena Corea ed.1987); MASON, *supra* note 33, at 116–17; MARY ANNE WARREN, GENDERCIDE: THE IMPLICATIONS OF SEX SELECTION (1985); Joni Davis, *Sexism and "the Superfluous Female": Arguments for Regulating Pre-Implantation Sex Selection*, 18 HARV. WOMEN'S L.J. 219 (1995); Celia Dugger, *Abortion in India is Tipping Scales Sharply against Girls*, N.Y. TIMES, Apr. 22, 2001, §1, at 1; Nora Frenkel, *"Family Planning": Baby Boy or Girl?*, N.Y. TIMES, Nov. 11, 1993, at C1; Edward Gargan, *Ultrasound Skews India's Birth Ratio*, N.Y. TIMES, Dec. 13, 1991, at A13; John Gittelsohn, *Bad Year for Baby Girls in Korea: Births Likely to Drop, Abortions to Rise*, BALT. SUN, Jan. 16, 1990, at A2; Frederic Golden, *Boy? Girl? Up to You*, TIME, Sept. 21, 1998, at 82; K.S. Jayaraman, *India Bans the Use of Sex Screening Tests*, 370 NATURE 320 (1994); Owen Jones, *Sex Selection: Regulating Technology Enabling the Predetermination of a Child's Gender*, 6 HARV. J. LAW & TECHNOL. 1 (1992); Naryung Kim, *Breaking Free from Patriarchy: A Comparative Study of Sex Selection Abortions in Korea and the United States*, 17 PAC. BASIN L.J. 301 (1999); Claudia Lima Marques, *Assisted Reproductive Technology (ART) in South America and the Effect on Adoption*, 35 TEX. INT'L L.J. 65 (2000); Viola Reggencamp, *Abortion of a Special Kind: Male Sex Selection in India*, in TEST TUBE WOMEN, *supra*, at 266; Amartya Sen, *More than 100 Million Women Are Missing*, N.Y. REV. BOOKS, Dec. 20, 1990, at 61; Loane Skene, *An Overview of Assisted Reproductive Technology Regulation in Australia and New Zealand*, 35 TEX. INT'L L.J. 31 (2000); *South Asia Criticized for Bias before Birth*, N.Y. TIMES, Dec. 15, 2000, at A22; David Stoller, *Prenatal Genetic Screening: The Enigma of Selective Abortion*, 12 J. LAW & HEALTH 121 (1998); Trees te Braake, *Regulation of Assisted Reproductive Technology in the Netherlands*, 35 TEX. INT'L L.J. 93 (2000); S. Tuljapurkar, N. Li, & M.W. Feldman, *High Sex Ratios in China's Future*, 267 SCIENCE 874 (1995); Dorothy Wertz, *International Perspectives on Ethics and Human Genetics*, 27 SUFFOLK L. REV. 1411, 1432 (1993); Dorothy Wertz & John Fletcher, *Prenatal Diagnosis and Sex Selection in 19 Nations*, 37 SOC. SCI. OF MED. 1359 (1993). For a defense of the practice, see John Robertson, *Genetic Selection of Offspring Characteristics*, 76 B.U. L. REV. 421, 446–48, 454–68 (1996).

76. *See* HRDY, *supra* note 13, at 340–41; Tamas Bereczkei & R.I.M. Dunar, *Female-Based Reproductive Strategies in a Hungarian Gypsy Population*, 264 PROC. ROY. SOC. OF LONDON, ser. B, at 17; Marina Faerman *et al.*, *DNA Analysis Reveals the Sex of Infanticide Victims*, 385 NATURE 212 (1997).

77. *See* Chapter 2, at notes 218–438.

78. 842 S.W.2d 588 (Tenn. 1992), *cert. denied sub nom.* Stowe v. Davis, 507 U.S. 911 (1993).

79. *The First Test Tube Baby*, TIME, July 31, 1978, at 58. The first in the United States was born in 1981. R.D. Gersh, *"Test-Tube" Pregnancy Is Achieved at Clinic in Va., a U.S. First*, PHILA. INQUIRER, June 12, 1981, at 6A; Craig Timberg, *Va. Clinic Is on Embryonic Frontier—Again*, WASH. POST, July 16, 2001, at A1. *See also* Philip Elmer-DeWitt, *Making Babies*, TIME, Sept. 30, 1991, at 56, 58; *In Australia, First "Test-Tube" Twins Born*, PHILA. INQUIRER, June 6, 1981, at 26C; John Robertson, *Embryos, Families, and Procreative Liberty: The Legal Structure of the New Reproduction*, 59 S. CAL. L. REV. 939, 942 (1986).

14,000 such births in 1997—more than 60,000 altogether by 1999.[80] Worldwide, at least 300,000 children have been born through in vitro fertilization.[81] The procedure is now so well established that a "test-tube" baby in England has now grown up and given birth to her own child—conceived the old-fashioned way.[82]

Because success rates for the process are low, doctors commonly fertilize a number of ova in a glass dish ("*in vitro*") and then insert several of the fertilized ova into the woman's uterus while freezing any left over to allow for a later attempt.[83] As many as 10,000 embryos are frozen annually for possible later use.[84] A total of 400,000 frozen embryos had accumulated by 2003, with no end in sight.[85] In *Davis,* the mother sought to have embryos produced through *in vitro* fertilization implanted in her uterus without the father's consent after the two had decided to divorce. The Tennessee Supreme Court denied the mother's request.[86] Several of the participants con-

---

80. *Fertility Clinics' Boom in Babies,* N.Y. Times, Feb. 9, 1999, at F8; Carey Goldberg, *Just Another Girl, Unlike any Other,* N.Y. Times, Oct. 27, 1999, at A16. *See generally* Victor Caplan, Due Consideration: Controversy in the Age of Medical Miracles 63 (1998); Tough Choices: *In Vitro* Fertilization and the Reproductive Technologies (Patricia Stephenson & Marsden Wagner eds. 1993); Lori Andrews *et al., ART into Science: Regulation of Fertility Techniques: Assisted Reproductive Technologies,* 281 Sci. 651, 651 (1998); Keith Alan Byers, *Infertility and* in Vitro *Fertilization,* 18 J. Leg. Med. 265, 266–67 (1997); Duenwald, *supra* note 52; Victor Stempel, *Procreative Rights in Assisted Reproductivity Technology: Why the Angst?,* 62 Alb. L. Rev. 1187, 1187–88 (1999). As only around 20% of such treatment cycles produced live births, this indicates that about 70,000 or so such procedures were attempted in 1997. National Ctr. for Chronic Disease Prevention & Health Promotion, US Dep't Health & Hum. Serv., 1995 Assisted Reproductive Technology Success Rates—National Summary and Fertility Clinic Reports 35 (1997).

81. Andrews *et al., supra* note 80, at 651. *See also* Fertility Soc'y of Australia, In Vitro Fertilization Pregnancies, Australia and New Zealand, 1990 (1992); *In Vitro* Fertilisation in the 1990s: Toward a Medical, Social and Ethical Evaluation of IVF (Elizabeth Hildt & Dietmar Mieth eds. 1999); S. Friedler, S. Mashiach, & N. Laufer, *Births in Israel Resulting from* in-Vitro *Fertilization /Embryo Transfer, 1982–1989: National Registry of the Israeli Association for Fertility Research,* 7 Hum. Reprod. 1159 (1992); FIV-NAT, *Pregnancies and Births Resulting from* in Vitro *Fertilization: French National Registry, Analysis of Data, 1986–1990,* 64 Fertility & Sterility 746 (1995); Jean-Christophe Galloux, *Le Statut des gamètes humains en droit français contemporain,* 40 McGill L.J. 993 (1995). Despite how common the practice has become, a few voices are still raised to argue that the procedure is fundamentally immoral and ought to be outlawed. *See* Joseph Spoerl, *Making Laws on Making Babies: Ethics, Public Policy, and Reproductive Technology,* 45 Am. J. Jurisprudence 93 (2000).

82. Goldberg, *supra* note 80, at A16. The first American test-tube baby is now a college student. Timberg, *supra* note 79, at A1.

83. For a detailed description of the practice, see Robertson, *supra* note 48, at 97–99; Robin Rowland, Living Laboratories: Women and Reproductive Technologies 19–28 (1992). *See also* Stavey Burling, *Embryo Frozen for 8 Years Became Healthy Baby Here: The Birth in December Was Similar to a Recent One Announced in Calif.,* Phila. Inquirer, Feb. 18, 1998, at A1; R. Alta Charo, *And Baby Makes Three—or Four, or Five, or Six: Redefining the Family after the Reprotech Revolution,* 15 Wis. Women's L.J. 231 (2000); Emmanuel Dulioust *et al., Long-Term Effects of Embryo Freezing in Mice,* 92 Proc. Nat'l Acad. Sci. 589 (1995); Allan Templeton & Joan Morris, *Reducing the Risk of Multiple Births by Transfer of Two Embryos after* in Vitro *Fertilization,* 339 New Eng. J. Med. 573 (1998).

84. *First Frozen-Embryo Pregnancy,* Phila. Inquirer, May 3, 1983, at 10C; Seth Mydans, *Science and the Courts Take a New Look at Motherhood,* N.Y. Times, Nov. 4, 1990, §4, at 6; Peter O'Laughlin, *Australians Are Freezing Test Embryos,* Phila. Inquirer, Apr. 10, 1981, at 24A; *Science Watch: Pregnancy with Frozen Embryo Is Successful at 14th Week,* N.Y. Times, May 24, 1983, at C2. At this time, we cannot freeze ova for possible later fertilization, although that appears to be coming. *See* Gina Kolata, *Researchers Report Breakthrough Using Frozen Eggs to Create Pregnancy,* N.Y. Times, Oct. 17, 1997, at A1.

85. *400,000 Embryos and Counting,* N.Y. Times, May 15, 2003, at A34.

86. *See also* York v. Jones, 717 F. Supp. 421 (E.D. Va. 1989); Del Zio v. Columbia Presbyterian Med. Cntr., No. 74-3558 (S.D.N.Y. Nov. 14, 1978); Robert B. v. Susan B., 135 Cal. Rptr. 2d 785 (Ct. App. 2003); Jaycee B. v. Superior Ct., 49 Cal. Rptr. 2d 694 (Ct. App. 1996); Moschetta v. Moschetta, 30 Cal. Rptr. 2d 893 (Ct. App. 1994); *In re* Marriage of Witten, 672 N.W.2d 768 (Iowa 2003); A.Z. v. B.Z., 725 N.E.2d 1051 (Mass. 2000); Y.G. v. Jewish Hosp. of St.L., 795 S.W.2d 488 (Mo. 1990); J.B. v. M.B. 783 A.2d 707 (N.J. 2001); Kass v. Kass,

cluded that the decision could only spark further rounds of litigation, although the destruction of the embryos at least precluded that for the Davises themselves.

Even Charles Clifford (attorney for the father) admitted to ambiguous feelings about the outcome of the case, suggesting that "[m]aybe we should bury them in the tomb of the unknown embryos."[87] Such ambivalence highlights the problems with frozen embryos even better than the *Davis* litigation itself. In *Davis*, one of the parents at least wanted to implant the frozen embryos. What of the situation where neither parent wants to attempt an implantation yet neither is willing to take responsibility for destroying the embryos? Are fertility clinics to keep the embryos in frozen limbo forever? And would disposing of the embryos—through something as simple as flushing them down a drain—exhibit too callous an attitude towards human life to contemplate? Such questions have been addressed through comprehensive legislation abroad rather than through litigation as in *Davis*.[88]

---

696 N.E.2d 174 (N.Y. 1998); McDonald v. McDonald, 608 N.Y.S.2d 477 (App. Div. 1994); Belsito v. Clark, 644 N.E.2d 760 (Ohio C.P. 1994); *In re* O.G.M., 988 S.W.2d 473 (Tex. Ct. App. 1999); Litowitz v. Litowitz, 48 P.3d 261, 53 P.3d 516 (Was. 2002), *cert. denied*, 537 U.S. 1191 (2003); *Fertility Clinic Success & Certification Act of 1992*, 42 U.S.C. §§ 263a-2 to 263a-7 (2000); 720 ILL. COMP. STAT. ANN. § 5/9-1.2 (West 1999); LA. REV. STAT. ANN. §§ 9:129, 9:132 (West 2000); MINN. STAT. ANN. §§ 609:266 to 609:2665 (West 2003); *British Women Lose Court Fight over Possessing Frozen Embryos*, N.Y. TIMES, Oct. 2, 2003, at A5; Annot., 87 A.L.R.5th 253 (2001).

*See generally* BLANK & MERRICK, *supra* note 24, at 94–96; BOUMIL, *supra* note 48, at 1–14; FENWICK, *supra* note 24, at 187–94; GUNNING & ENGLISH, *supra* note 24; JEROME LEJEUNE, THE CONCENTRATION CAN (1992); MEYER, *supra* note 49, at 59–68; MEYERS, *supra* note 48, at 58–60, 66–69, 76–77; ROBERTSON, *supra* note 48, at 26–29, 97–118; SMITH, *supra* note 48, at 199–208; Ruth Colker, *Pregnant Men Revisited or Sperm Is Cheap, Eggs Are Not*, 47 HASTINGS L.J. 1063 (1996); Janet Dolgin, *The Law Debates the Family: Reproductive Transformation*, 7 YALE J.L. & FEMINISM 37, 65–83 (1995); Dennis Doherty, *Frozen Embryos: The Birth of a Legal Controversy*, 65 WIS. L. REV. 14 (1992); Jane Eisner, *Whose Life Is It, Anyway? A Divorced Couple's Frozen Embryo's Are at Stake*, PHILA. INQUIRER, Mar. 4, 2001, at E1; Kate Harrison, *Fresh or Frozen: Lesbian Mothers, Sperm Donors, and Limited Fathers*, in MOTHERS IN LAW: FEMINIST THEORY AND THE LEGAL REGULATION OF MOTHERHOOD 167 (Martha Albertson Fineman & Isabel Karpin eds. 1995); Hodges, *supra* note 81; Isabel Karpin, *Legislating the Female Body: Reproductive Technology and the Reconstructed Woman*, 3 COLUM. J. GENDER & L. 325, 343–45 (1992); Donna Katz, *My Egg, Your Sperm, Whose Preembryo? A Proposal for Deciding Which Party Receives Custody of Frozen Preembryos*, 5 VA. J. SOC. POL'Y & L. 623 (1998); Jill Madden Melchoir, *Cryogenically Preserved Embryos in Dispositional Disputes and the Supreme Court: Breaking Impossible Ties*, 68 U. CIN. L. REV. 921 (2000); Christina Misner, *What If Mary Sue Wanted an Abortion Instead? The Effect of* Davis v. Davis *on Abortion Rights*, 3 AM. U. J. GENDER & L. 265 (1995); Robert Muller, Davis v. Davis: *The Applicability of Privacy and Property Rights on the Disposition of Frozen Preembryos in Intrafamilial Disputes*, 24 U. TOL. L. REV. 763 (1993); Christine Overall, *Frozen Embryos and "Father's Rights": Parenthood and Decision-Making in the Cryopreservation of Embryos*, in FEMINIST PERSPECTIVES, *supra* note 48, at 178; Stephanie Owen, *Establishing Guidelines for Resolving Disputes over Frozen Embryos*, 10 J. CONTEMP. HEALTH & POL'Y 493 (1994); Larry Palmer, *Who Are the Parents of Biotechnological Children?*, 35 JURIMETRICS 17 (1994); Clifton Perry & L. Kristen Schneider, *Cryopreserved Embryos: Who Shall Decide Their Fate?*, 13 J. LEGAL MED. 463 (1992); Philip Prygoski, *The Implications of* Davis v. Davis *for Reproductive Rights Analysis*, 61 TENN. L. REV. 609 (1994); John Robertson, *Precommitment Strategies for Disposition of Frozen Embryos*, 50 EMORY L.J. 989 (2001); Roosevelt, *supra* note 74, at 127–35; Carol Sanger, *M Is for the Many Things*, 1 REV. L. & WOMEN'S STUD. 15, 48–55 (1992); Helen Shapo, *Frozen Pre-Embryos and the Right to Change One's Mind*, 12 DUKE J. COMP. & INT'L L. 75 (2002); Thomas Shevory, *Through a Glass Darkly: Law, Politics, and Frozen Human Embryos*, in ISSUES IN REPRODUCTIVE TECHNOLOGY I: AN ANTHOLOGY 231 (Helen Bequaert Holmes ed. 1992); Stempel, *supra* note 80; Daniel Strouse, *Egg Donation, Motherhood and State Law Reform: A Commentary on Professor Palmer's Proposals*, 35 JURIMETRICS 31 (1994); Symposium, *Disputes Concerning Frozen Embryos*, 8 TEX. J. WOMEN & L. 285 (1999); Gregory Triber, *Growing Pains: Disputes Surrounding Human Reproductive Interests Stretch the Boundaries of Traditional Legal Concepts*, 23 SETON HALL LEGIS. J. 103, 121–26, 129–31 (1998); Ellen Waldman, *King Solomon in the Age of Assisted Reproduction*, 24 T. JEFFERSON L. REV. 217 (2002); Debrah Kay Walther, *"Ownership" of the Fertilized Ovum in Vitro*, 26 FAM. L.Q. 235 (1992).

87. Mark Curriden, *No Forced Fatherhood*, ABA J., Sept. 1992, at 35.

88. COUNCIL OF EUROPE, *supra* note 24, at 23–25; MASON, *supra* note 33, at 228–39; DEREK MORGAN & ROBERT LEE, BLACKSTONE'S GUIDE TO THE HUMAN FERTILISATION & EMBRYOLOGY ACT 1990: ABORTION AND

Obviously, different persons will have different responses to such questions. An ethics panel of the American Society for Reproductive Medicine decided in 1997 that clinics could destroy unclaimed embryos after five years.[89] Yet when an Arizona clinic decided, upon the impending retirement of its founder, to destroy hundreds of frozen embryos accumulated over more than a decade, some patients objected—even though the objecting patients had no intention of using the embryos themselves.[90] As Carmen Knauss, a woman with 22 frozen embryos in storage at the clinic remarked, "Every fertility patient thinks of those embryos as their (*sic*) babies."[91] Mrs. Knauss admitted that she had no intention of having those embryos implanted in herself, but indicated that she and her husband were willing to donate them to infertile couples.[92]

To some extent, the problems with *in vitro* fertilization described here can be solved by improved technology. For example, recently published reports suggest that leaving the embryo to develop even one day longer than the now standard three days will increase the success rate, allowing the implantation of blastocysts rather than zygotes.[93] Even a delay of one day makes it practical to implant fewer embryos, with a consequent reduced risk of multiple pregnancies.[94]

---

EMBRYO RESEARCH; THE NEW LAW (1990); K. Dawson & P. Singer, *Should Fertile People Have Access to* in Vitro *Fertilisation?*, 300 BRIT. MED. J. 167 (1990); Heidi Forster, *Recent Development: The Legal and Ethical Debate Surrounding the Storage and Destruction of Frozen Human Embryos: A Reaction to the Mass Disposal in Britain and the Lack of Law in the United States*, 76 WASH. U. L.Q. 759 (1998); John Bologna Krentel, *The Louisiana "Human Embryo" Statute Revisited: Reasonable Recognition and Protection of the* in Vitro *Fertilized Ovum*, 45 LOY. L. REV. 329 (1999); Jonathan Montgomery, *Rights, Restraints and Pragmatism:* The Human Fertilisation & Embryology Act, 1990, 54 MOD. L. REV. 524 (1991); Derek Morgan & Linda Nielsen, *Prisoners of Progress or Hostages to Fortune?*, 21 J. LAW, MED. & ETHICS 30 (1993); Cynthia Reilly, *Constitutional Limits on New Mexico's* in Vitro *Fertilization Law*, 24 N.M. L. REV. 125 (1994). *See also* MASON, *supra*, at 244–46 (describing legal issues arising from embryo donation).

90. *Clinic Plans to Destroy Unclaimed Embryos*, N.Y. TIMES, July 13, 1999, at F14. *See also Doctors in Quandary over Orphaned Human Embryos*, PHILA. INQUIRER, June 18, 1984, at 12A; *Lawyer: Millionaire Not the Father of Frozen Embryos in Australia*, PHILA. INQUIRER, June 21, 1984, at 16A; George Smith II, *Australia's Frozen "Orphan" Embryos: A Medical, Legal and Ethical Dilemma*, 24 J. FAM. L. 27 (1985); Lynne Thomas, *Abandoned Frozen Embryos and Texas Law of Abandoned Personal Property: Should There Be a Connection?*, 29 ST. MARY'S L.J. 255 (1997); M. Trounson & K. Dawson, *Storage and Disposal of Embryos and Gametes*, 313 BRIT. MED. J. 1 (1996).

90. *Clinic Plans to Destroy Unclaimed Embryos*, *supra* note 89.

91. *Id.*

92. This is not so fanciful a solution as some might think. Sheryl Gay Stolberg, *Clinics Full of Frozen Embryos Offer a New Route to Adoption*, N.Y. TIMES, Feb. 25, 2001, § 1, at 1. At least eight babies have been born in this fashion into six different families. *Id.*, at 17. *See generally* Olga Batsedis, *Embryo Adoption: A Science Fiction or an Alternative to Traditional Adoption*, 41 FAM. CT. REV. 565 (2003).

93. David K. Gardner *et al.*, *Culture and Transfer of Human Blastocysts Increases Implantation Rates and Reduces the Need for Multiple Embryo Transfers*, 69 FERTILITY & STERILITY 84 (1998); *Time Lends Hand to Test-Tube Fertilization*, N.Y. TIMES, July 27, 1999, at F14. *See also* Eric Nagourney, *A Common Link in Failed Pregnancies*, N.Y. TIMES, June 15, 1999, at F14 (reporting on research on when an embryo attaches to the uterine wall).

94. AMERICAN SOC'Y FOR REPRODUCTIVE MED., GUIDELINES ON THE NUMBER OF EMBRYOS TRANSFERRED (1998); Mario Bustillo, *Imposing Limits on the Number of Oocytes and Embryos Transferred: Is It Necessary/Wise or Naughty/Nice?*, 12 HUM. REPRODUCTION 1616 (1997); Carlene Elsner *et al.*, *Multiple Pregnancy Rate and Embryo Number Transferred during* in Vitro *Fertilization*, 177 AM. J. OBSTET. & GYNECOLOGY 350 (1997); Yunxia Hu *et al.*, *Maximizing Pregnancy Rates and Limiting Higher-Order Multiple Conceptions by Determining the Optimal Number of Embryos to Transfer Based upon Quality*, 69 FERTILITY & STERILITY 650 (1998); Laura Schieve *et al.*, *Live-Birth Rates and Multiple-Birth Risk Using* in Vitro *Fertilization*, 282 JAMA 1832 (1999); C. Staessen *et al.*, *Avoidance of Triplet Pregnancy by Elective Transfer of Two Good Quality Embryos*, 8 HUM. REPRODUCTION 1650 (1993); C. Staessen *et al.*, *The Relationship between Embryo Quality and the Occurrence of Multiple Pregnancies*, 57 FERTILITY & STERILITY 626 (1992); Thor Svendsen *et al.*, *The Incidence of Multiple Gestations after* in Vitro *Fertilization Is Dependent on the Number of Embryos Transferred and Maternal Age*, 65 FERTILITY & STERILITY 561 (1996); Murat Tasdemir *et al.*, *Two Instead of Three Embryo Transfer in* in Vitro

Such developments, however, do nothing to alter the dilemma of what to do with unwanted embryos. Nor do such developments address the problem presented in *Davis v. Davis*. Technology simply does not give us the answers to moral questions.

*In vitro* and other procedures involving freezing sperm, ova, or embryos raise many unsettling possibilities. Freezing a man's sperm and thereafter using the sperm to fertilize a life-partner after the man has died has already generated litigation.[95] One Australian court has held that an embryo that had been frozen before the man died but later thawed and successfully implanted in his widow is his child for inheritance purposes.[96] And a woman, apparently desperate for a grandchild, used sperm from her deceased son to impregnate a "surrogate" mother.[97] The equivalent has already happened for a woman when her parents sought a surrogate mother for a de-

---

*Fertilization,* 10 Hum. Reproduction 2155 (1995); Allen Templeton & Joan K. Morris, *Reducing the Risk of Multiple Births by Transfer of Two Embryos after in Vitro Fertilization,* 339 New Eng. J. Med. 573 (1998).

95.  Greenberg v. Miami Children's Hosp. Research Inst., Inc., 264 F. Supp. 2d 1064 (S.D. Fla. 2003) (persons whose tissues and fluids were used without their consent to isolate patented gene are entitled to compensation for the institute's unjust enrichment); Gillett-Netting v. Barnhart, 231 F. Supp. 2d 961 (D. Ariz. 2002) (denying recognition to posthumously conceived children for purposes of obtaining social security benefits), *appeal pending*; Hecht v. Superior Ct., 59 Cal. Rptr. 2d 222 (Ct. App. 1996) (a man has no power to bequeath his sperm), *rev. denied, opinion ordered not published*; Woodward v. Commissioner of Soc. Sec., 760 N.E.2d 257 (Mass. 2002) (directing the recognition of posthumously conceived children for purposes of obtaining social security benefits). *See* Jane Allen, *Woman Impregnated with Sperm Collected after Husband's Death,* Phila. Inquirer, July 16, 1998, at A2; James Bailey, *An Analytical Framework for Resolving Issues Raised by the Interaction between Reproductive Technologies and the Law of Inheritance,* 47 DePaul L. Rev. 743 (1998); Gloria Banks, *Traditional Concepts and Nontraditional Conceptions: Social Security Survivor's Benefits for Posthumously Conceived Children,* 32 Loy.-L.A. L. Rev. 251 (1999); Diana Brahams, *Widow Appeals over Denial of Rights to Husband's Sperm,* 348 The Lancet 1164 (1996); E. Carrigan, S.E. Mumford, & M.G.R. Hull, *Posthumous Storage and Use of Sperm and Embryos: Survey of Opinion of Treatment Centres,* 313 Brit. Med. J. 24 (1996); Chester, *supra* note 56; Ronald Chester, *Freezing the Heir Apparent: A Dialogue on Postmortem Conception, Parental Responsibility, and Inheritance,* 33 Hous. L. Rev. 967 (1996); Christina Djalleta, *A Twinkle in a Decedent's Eye: Proposed Amendments to the Uniform Probate Code in Light of New Reproductive Technologies,* 67 Temple L. Rev. 335 (1994); Maura Dolan, *High Court Lets Stand Ruling Allowing Man to Will Sperm,* L.A. Times, Sept. 3, 1993, at B3; Jeff Kramer, *Progeny or Property?: Frozen Sperm Held in Limbo during Fight over Will,* L.A. Times, Sept. 27, 1992, at B1; Pam Lambert & Stanley Young, *Frozen Assets: A Millionaire's Suicide Leaves His Lover and His Family Battling over His Estate—and His Sperm,* People, Feb. 22, 1993, at 75; David Margolick, *15 Vials of Sperm: The Unusual Bequest of an Even More Unusual Man,* N.Y. Times, Apr. 29, 1994, at B18; Sabine Mabouche, *Life after Death: French Woman Wins Sperm Bank Decision,* Wash. Post, Aug. 2, 1984, at B1; Karin Mika & Bonnie Hurst, *One Way to Be Born? Legislative Inaction and the Posthumous Child,* 79 Marq. L. Rev. 993 (1996); Debra Cassens Moss, *Lawyer's Legacy: Heirs Fight over Frozen Sperm,* ABA J., Feb. 1993, at 23; Timothy Murphy, *Sperm Harvesting and Postmortem Fatherhood,* 9 Bioethics 380 (1995); David Rameden, *Frozen Semen as Property in* Hecht v. Superior Court: *One Step Forward, Two Steps Backward,* 62 U. Mo. K.C. L. Rev. 377 (1993); John Robertson, *Emerging Paradigms in Bioethics—Posthumous Reproduction,* 69 Ind. L.J. 1027 (1994); Roosevelt, *supra* note 74, at 135–38; Jamie Roswell, *Stayin' Alive,* 41 Fam. Ct. Rev. 400 (2003); Renee Sekino, *Posthumous Conception: The Birth of a New Class,* Woodward v. Commissioner of Social Security, 8 B.U. J. Sci. & Technol. L. 362 (2002); Monica Shah, *Modern Reproductive Technologies: Legal Issues Concerning Cryopreservation and Posthumous Conception,* 17 J. Leg. Med. 547 (1996); Shapiro, *supra* note 52, at 1127–32; Evelyne Shuster, *The Posthumous Gift of Life: The World According to Kane,* 15 J. Contemp. Health L. & Pol'y 401 (1999); Michael Soules, *Commentary: Posthumous Harvesting of Gametes—A Physician's Perspective,* 27 J. Law, Med. & Ethics 362 (1999); Carson Strong, *Ethical and Legal Aspects of Sperm Retrieval after Death or Persistent Vegetative State,* 27 J. Law, Med. & Ethics 347 (1999); Gladys White, *Commentary: Legal and Ethical Aspects of Sperm Retrieval,* 27 J. Law, Med. & Ethics 359 (1999). *See generally* Fenwick, *supra* note 24, at 195–98, 244–53; Atherton, *supra* note 88, at 380–84; Judith Lorber, *Choice, Gift or Patriarchal Bargain? Women's Consent to in Vitro Fertilization in Male Infertility,* in Feminist Perspectives in Medical Ethics 169 (Helen Holmes & Laura Purdy eds. 1992).

96.  *In re* K. (deceased), [1996] 5 T.R. 365.

97.  Scott Sonner, *Woman Hopes Sperm from her Dead Son Produces Grandchild,* Buffalo News, Oct. 2, 1998, at A6.

ceased, unmarried woman in order to realize the woman's "right" to be a mother—and the parents' "right" to become grandparents.[98] All of this reminds one of the fictional theft of a dying man's sperm in *The World According to Garp*.[99]

Problems also arise because of occasional birth defects in *in vitro* children. While rare, there is some suspicion that birth defects result from the *in vitro* process itself as well as from inherited genetic defects.[100] Attempts to manipulate the genes of *in vitro* children pose particular risks in his regard. A less extreme form of gene manipulation involves injecting a single, selected sperm directly into the ovum to produce a more precisely genetically tailored child—but with considerable risks of inducing birth defects as well.[101] The looming possibility of cloning humans promises yet another transformation in our thinking.[102]

---

98. Evelyne Shuster, *Dead Parent Cannot Parent*, CHI. TRIB., Jan. 1, 1998, at 21. *See also* Kurt Weir, *Italians Debate the Birth of a Baby from Egg of Woman Now Deceased*, PHIL. INQUIRER, Jan. 12, 1995, at A3. *See generally* Laura Shanner, *The Right to Procreate: When Rights Claims Have Gone Wrong*, 40 McGILL L.J. 823 (1995).

99. JOHN IRVING, THE WORLD ACCORDING TO GARP 4–6 (1978).

100. *See* Valerie Beral *et al.*, *Outcome of Pregnancies Resulting from Assisted Conception*, 46 BRIT. MED. BULL. 753 (1990); Pat Doyle, Valerie Beral, & Noreen Maconochie, *Preterm Delivery, Low Birthweight and Small-for-Gestational-Age in Liveborn Singleton Babies Resulting from* in-Vitro *Fertilization*, 7 HUM. REPROD. 425 (1992); Lene Koch, *Physiological and Psychological Risks of New Reproductive Technologies*, in TOUGH CHOICES, *supra* note 80, at 122; Norma Morin *et al.*, *Congenital Malformations and Psychosocial Development in Children Conceived by* in Vitro *Fertilization*, 115 J. PEDIATRICS 222 (1989); Jean-Pierre Relier, Michele Couchard, & Catherine Huon, *The Neonatologist's Experience of* in Vitro *Fertilization Risks*, in TOUGH CHOICES, *supra*, at 135; Botros Rizk *et al.*, *Perinatal Outcome and Congenital Malformation in* in-Vitro *Fertilization from the Bourn-Hallam Group*, 6 HUM. REPROD. 1259 (1991); Pierre Rufat *et al.*, *Task Force Report on the Outcome of Pregnancies and Children Conceived by* in Vitro *Fertilization (France 1987 to 1989)*, 61 FERTILITY & STERILITY 324 (1994); Gail Vines, *Shots in the Dark for Infertility*, 140 NEW SCI. 13 (1993); Ulla-Britt Wennerholm *et al.*, *Postnatal Growth and Health in Children Born after Cyropreservation as Embryos*, 351 THE LANCET 1085 (1998).

101. *See* Gerald Schatten *et al.*, *Cell and Molecular Biological Challenges of ICSI: ART before Science?*, 26 J. LAW & MED. 29 (1998).

102. Sarah Delaney, *Scientists Prepare to Clone a Human*, WASH. POST, Mar. 10, 2001, at A16; Ira Carmen, *Should Human Cloning be Criminalized*, 13 NYU J.L. & POL. 745 (1997); Helen Dewar, *Human Cloning Ban Sidetracked*, WASH. POST, June 19, 2002, at A4; Leon Kass, *How One Clone Leads to Another*, N.Y. TIMES, Jan. 24, 2003, at A23; Gina Kolata, *On Cloning Humans, "Never" Turns Swiftly into "Why Not?"*, N.Y. TIMES, Dec. 2, 1997, at A1; Robert Kotulak, *Move over Dolly: U.S. Firm Clones in New Way: Latest Breakthrough Enhances Possibility of Work on Humans*, CHI. TRIB., Aug. 8, 1997, at 1; Colum Lynch, *U.N. Postpones Debate on Human Cloning: Action Derails Bid for Vote on a U.S.-Backed Measure Calling for a Moratorium*, WASH. POST, Nov. 7, 2003, at A2; Sheryl Gay Stolberg, *Panel Recommends a Moratorium on Cloning Research*, N.Y. TIMES, July 11, 2002, at A21; Symposium, *Conceiving a Code for Creation: The Legal Debate Surrounding Human Cloning*, 53 HASTINGS L.J. 987 (2002); Roger Taylor, *The Fear of Drawing the Line at Cloning*, 9 B.U. J. SCI. & TECHNOL. L. 379 (2003); Rick Weiss, *An Uncertain Year for Cloning Laws: Ban on Embryo Research Seen as Unlikely*, WASH. POST, Dec. 26, 2002, at A1.

The cloning of animals has been much less controversial. Tim Beardsley, *The Start of Something Big? Dolly Has Become a New Icon for Science*, 276 SCI. AM., May 1997, at 15; Jane Bradbury, *First Dolly the Sheep, Then Multiple Monkeys*, 349 THE LANCET 705 (1997); Faye Flam, *Maybe She Ain't What She Used to Be: Dolly's Cells Hint at Premature Aging; It's Hard to Tell*, PHILA. INQUIRER, May 27, 1999, at A1; Justin Gillis, *Ailing Dolly, First Cloned Animal, Is Euthanized*, WASH. POST, Feb. 15, 2003, at A2; Ian Helmut *et al.*, *Viable Offspring Derived from Fetal and Adult Mammalian Cells*, NATURE, Feb. 27, 1997, at 810; M.J. Iozzio, *Science, Ethics, and Cloning Technologies*, LINACRE Q., Nov. 1997, at 46; *In Breakthrough, Rats Are Cloned in France*, N.Y. TIMES, Sept. 26, 2003, at A3; *Japan Scientists Produce Clone of a Cloned Bull*, N.Y. Times, Jan. 25, 2000, at F6; Gina Kolata, *Animals Cloned for Food No Longer Draw Collective Yawn: Is It Safe to Eat a Cloned Animal? And if it is, Will People Buy It?*, N.Y. TIMES, Nov. 4, 2003, at F5; Gina Kolata, *In Big Advance in Cloning, Biologists Create 50 Mice: Indicates More Rapid Progress than Imagined*, N.Y. TIMES, July 23, 1998, at A1; Gina Kolata, *Japanese Scientists Clone a Cow, Making Eight Copies*, N.Y. TIMES, Dec. 9, 1998, at A8; Gina Kolata, *Researchers Find Big Risk of Defect in Cloning Animals*, N.Y. TIMES, Mar. 25, 2001, at A1; Gina Kolata, *What Is Warm and Fuzzy Forever? With Cloning, Kitten*, N.Y. TIMES, Feb. 15, 2002, at A1; Gina Kolata, *With Cloning of Sheep, the Ethical*

Yet another *in vitro* procedure gone bad serves to suggest how far our thinking about human reproduction will have to change to cope with the emerging technologies. In this instance, clinicians inserted several embryos into the womb of Donna Fasano and two of them implanted. When the twins were born, however, one was white (like the Fasanos), and the other was black. Apparently the clinician had mixed the Fasano embryos with those of another couple.[103] Although the Fasanos began to raise both boys as their sons, they agreed to surrender the black baby to Deborah Perry-Rogers and Robert Rogers, his genetic parents, after the Rogers filed suit[104]—and after the Rogers were matched to the baby by DNA tests and agreed to allow the

---

*Ground Shifts*, N.Y. Times, Feb. 24, 1997, at A1; Angelika Shnieke *et al.*, *Human Factor IX Transgenic Sheep Produced by Transfer of Nuclei from Transfected Fetal Fibroblasts*, 278 Science 2130 (1997); Rick Weiss, *First Cloned Horse Created in Italy*, Wash. Post, Aug. 7, 2003, at A1; Ian Wilmut *et al.*, *Viable Offspring Derived from Fetal and Adult Mammalian Cells*, 385 Nature 810 (1997).

The several public claims of a successful cloning of a human embryo are questionable, but it seems only a matter of time before it happens. DeNeen Brown, *The Leader of UFO Land: His Holiness Explains the Origins of Life on Earth. Except for That Clone*, Wash. Post, Jan. 17, 2003, at C1; Denise Grady & Robert Pear, *Outrage over Cloning Claim*, N.Y. Times, Dec. 29, 2002, §1, ax 18; Gina Kolata, *Company Says It Produced Human Embryo Clones*, N.Y. Times, Nov. 26, 2001, at A1; Bill McKibben, *A Threat to Our Coherent Human Future*, Wash. Post, Jan. 6, 2003, at A15; Rick Weiss, *Cloned-Fetus Rumor Stirs Talk: Report on Italian Doctor's Claim Cannot Be Confirmed*, Wash. Post, Apr. 6, 2002, at A2.

See generally Cloning (Paul Winters ed. 1998); Cloning and the Future of Human Embryo Research (Paul Lauritzen ed. 2001); Cloning Human Beings: Report and Recommendations of the National Bioethics Advisory Commission (1997); Council of Europe, Draft Additional Protocol to the Convention on Human Rights and Biomedicine on the Prohibition of Cloning Human Beings, adopted Sept. 22, 1997, *reprinted in* 36 Int'l Legal Mat'ls 1415 (1997); Fenwick, *supra* note 24, at 290–98; God and the Embryo: Religious Voices on Stem Cells and Cloning (Brent Waters & Ronald Cole-Turner eds. 2003); Human Cloning, *supra* note 24; Human Cloning: Religious Responses (Ronald Cole-Turner ed. 1997); Human Cloning: Science, Ethics, and Public Policy (Barbara MacKinnon ed. 2000); Kolata, *supra* note 24; Leon Kass & James Wilson, The Ethics of Human Cloning (1998); National Bioethics Advisory Comm'n, *supra* note 24; Gregory Pence, Who's Afraid of Human Cloning? (1997); Silver, *supra* note 24; The Human Cloning Debate (Glenn McGee ed. 1998); Robert Blomquist, *Cloning Endangered Animal Species?*, 32 Val. L. Rev. 383 (1998); Michael Broyde, *Cloning People: A Jewish Law Analysis of the Issues*, 30 Conn. L. Rev. 503 (1998); at 25; Clarke Forsythe, *Human Cloning and the Constitution*, 32 Val. L. Rev. 469 (1998); Christine Gorman, *To Ban or Not to Ban? The Report of a Presidential Commission Sets the Stage for a National Debate on Human Cloning*, Time, June 16, 1997, at 66; John Robertson, *Liberty, Identity, and Human Cloning*, 76 Tex. L. Rev. 1371 (1998); John Robertson, *Oocyte Cytoplasm Transfers and the Ethics of Germ-Line Intervention*, 26 J. Law & Med. 211 (1998); Harold Shapiro, *Ethical and Policy Issues of Human Cloning*, 277 Science 195 (1997); Rick Weiss, *Bush Backs Broad Ban on Human Cloning: Prohibition Would Cover Embryos for Research*, Wash. Post, June 21, 2001, at A1; Stephen Werber, *Cloning: A Jewish Law Perspective with a Comparative Study of Other Abrahamic Traditions*, 30 Seton Hall L. Rev. 1114 (2000).

103. Jim Yardley, *After Embryo Mix-Up, Couple Say They Will Give Up Baby: A Possible Error at a Fertility Clinic Entangles the Lives of Two Families*, N.Y. Times, Mar. 30, 1999, at B1. *See also* Sarah Lyall, *Whites Have Black Twins in in-Vitro Mix-up*, N.Y. Times, July 9, 2002, at A12 (reporting on a similar mix-up in the United Kingdom and another in the Netherlands); Jill Smolowe & Tara Weingarten, *The Test-Tube Custody Fight—Victims of the Irvine Stolen-Egg Scandal Go after Twins*, Time, Mar. 18, 1996, at 80.

104. Perry-Rogers v. Fasano, 715 N.Y.S.2d 19 (App. Div. 2000), *appeal denied*, 754 N.E.2d 199 (N.Y. 2001). *See also* York v. Jones, 717 F. Supp. 421 (E.D. Va. 1989) (the court ordered a medical clinic to release frozen embryos to their parents to enable another medical clinic to implant them); Prato-Morrison v. Doe, 126 Cal. Rptr. 2d 509 (Ct. App. 2002) (best interests of the child preclude considering claims of genetic parents of child wrongfully implanted in a different patient at an *in vitro* clinic); Perry-Rogers v. Obasaju, 723 N.Y.S.2d 28 (App. Div.) (sustaining a malpractice action against the responsible physician), *appeal dismissed*, 759 N.E.2d 374 (2001); Leslie Bender, *Genes, Parents, and Assisted Reproductive Technologies: Arts, Mistakes, Sex, Race & Law*, 12 Colum. J. Gender & L. 1 (2003); Judith Fischer, *Misappropriation of Human Eggs and Embryos and the Tort of Conversion: A Relational View*, 32 Loy.-L.A. L. Rev. 381 (1999); Alice Noble-Allgire, *Switched at the Fertility Clinic: Determining Maternal Rights When a Child Is Born from Stolen or Misdelivered Genetic Material*, 64 Mo. L. Rev. 517 (1999); John Robertson, *The Case of the Switched Embryos*, 25 Hastings Ctr. Rep. no. 6, at 13 (Nov.–Dec. 1995); Roosevelt, *supra* note 74; Rebecca Snyder, *Reproductive Technology and Stolen Ova: Who*

Fasanos extensive visitation rights.[105] Thereafter, the two families became competitive in their relationship with the child, even insisting on giving him two different names. The result was protracted litigation over visitation and relationship issues.[106]

None of the foregoing exhausts the mind boggling potential of the new reproductive technologies. In the course of developing the technology of ovarian manipulation, doctors have developed the ability to recover immature ova from an aborted female fetus. These ova can then be brought to maturity, fertilized, and implanted in an otherwise infertile woman to produce a healthy baby.[107] This raises the startling prospect of a baby whose "biological mother" never existed, if we are to take the pro-abortion rhetoric seriously. As journalist Stephen Chapman pointed out, this also means that a woman can become a "grandmother" without ever having been a "mother"—unless, of course, one counts the aborted pregnancy itself as conferring the latter status on a woman.[108] In light of these developments, our former agonizing over the rights and wrongs of artificial insemination now seem quaint.[109]

---

*Is the Mother?*, 16 LAW & INEQ. J. 289 (1998); Walther, *supra* note 86. *See also* Kristi Ayala, *The Application of Traditional Criminal Law to Misappropriation of Genetic Material*, 24 AM. J. CRIM. L. 503 (1997); Sarah Lyall, *British Judge Rules Sperm Donor Is Legal Father in Mix-up Case*, N.Y. TIMES, Feb. 27, 2003, at A5.

105. Samuel Maull, *A "Very Emotional" Custody Switch after Embryo Mix-Up*, PHILA. INQUIRER, May 27, 1999, at A29.

106. Perry-Rogers v. Fasano, 715 N.Y.S.2d 19 (App. Div. 2000). *See also* William Macklin, *Court's Complex Issue: Just What Is a Mother? A Visitation Squabble for Baby with White, Black Mothers*, PHILA. INQUIRER, July 16, 1999, at A1; Kathleen Parker, *Baby Case Ends with Multiracial Scrambled Eggs*, CHI. TRIBUNE, June 23, 2000, § 1, at 17.

107. *See* HUMAN FERTILISATION & EMBRYOLOGY AUTH'Y, *supra* note 73; MASON, *supra* note 33, at 201–02, 242–44; Luisa Dilner, *Use of Fetal Eggs for Infertility Treatment Is Banned*, 309 BRIT. MED. J. 289 (1994); Bernard Gondos, Lars Westerbaard, & Anne Grete Byskov, *Initiation of Oogenesis in the Human Fetal Ovary*, 155 AM. J. OBSTET. & GYNECOLOGY 189 (1986); Roger Gosden, *Transplantation of Fetal Germ Cells*, 9 J. ASSISTED REPROD. & GENETICS 118 (1992); Andrew Grubb, *Use of Fetal Eggs and Infertility Treatment*, 3 MED. L. REV. 203 (1995); Shirley Senoff, *Canada's Fetal-Egg Use Policy, the Royal Commission's* Report on New Reproductive Technologies, *and Bill C-47*, 25 MAN. L. REV. 1 (1997). A female fetus has her full complement of ova—about 7,000,000 of them—by the sixth month of gestation; this is 14,000 times as many as will ever mature sufficiently to be ovulated, and more than a million times as many as she will need for the number of children she is likely to produce in today's world; human females begin to lose immature oocytes even before her own birth. HRDY, *supra* note 13, at 419–21.

108. Stephen Chapman, *Abortion Tolerance Can Lead the Way to an Unsettling Future*, CHI. TRIB., Jan. 9, 1994, at 3.

109. *See, e.g.*, Gerber v. Hickman, 264 F.3d 882 (9th Cir. 2001); People v. Sorensen, 437 P.2d 495 (Cal. 1968); Dunkin v. Boskey, 98 Cal. Rptr. 2d 44 (Ct. App. 2000); *In re* Marriage of Buzzanca, 72 Cal. Rptr. 280 (Ct. App. 1998), *rev. denied*; Alexandra S. v. Pacific Fertility Med. Ctr., Inc., 64 Cal. Rptr. 2d 23 (1997); Jhordan C. v. Mary K., 224 Cal. Rptr. 530 (Ct. App. 1986); *In re* R.C., 775 P.2d 27 (Colo. 1989); *In re* Ritaray Adams, 551 N.E.2d 635 (Ill. 1990); Doornbos v. Doornbos, 139 N.E.2d 844 (Ill. App. Ct. 1956); K.S. v. G.S., 440 A.2d 64 (N.J. Super. 1981); C.M. v. C.C. 377 A.2d 821 (N.J. Super. 1977); Thomas S. v. Robin Y., 618 N.Y.S.2d 356 (App. Div. 1994) *appeal denied*, 655 N.E.2d 708 (N.Y. 1995); Anonymous v. Anonymous, 246 N.Y.S.2d 837 (Sup. Ct. 1964); Gursky v. Gursky, 242 N.Y.S.2d 409 (Sup. Ct. 1963); Strnad v. Strnad, 78 N.Y.S.2d 390 (Sup. Ct. 1948); Leckie v. Voorhees, 875 P.2d 521 (Ore. Ct. App. 1994); McIntyre v. Crouch, 780 P.2d 239 (Ore. Ct. App. 1989); Orford v. Orford, 58 D.L.R. 251 (Ont. 1921); *In re* C.H., 1 FAM. L. REP. 569 (1996); MacLennan v. MacLennan, 1958 Sess. Cas. 105 (Scot.); *Uniform Parentage Act* § 5(a), 9B U.L.A. 301 (1987); *Uniform Status of Children of Assisted Conception Act* § 4, 9B U.L.A. 189 (West Supp. 1997) ("*Uniform Status of Children Act*"). *See also* Johnson v. Superior Ct., 95 Cal. Rptr. 2d 864 (Ct. App. 2000), *rev. denied* (holding that a contract limiting the discovery of the identity of the sperm donor is against public policy).

*See* ANNETTE BARAN & REUBEN PANNOR, LETHAL SECRETS: THE SHOCKING CONSEQUENCES AND UNSOLVED PROBLEMS OF ARTIFICIAL INSEMINATION (1989); COUNCIL OF EUROPE, *supra* note 24, at 25–28; FENWICK, *supra* note 24, at 258–72; MASON, *supra* note 33, at 207–26; Atherton, *supra* note 86, at 375–76; John Dewar, *Fathers in Law? The Case of AID*, in BIRTHRIGHT: LAW AND ETHICS AT THE BEGINNINGS OF LIFE 115 (Robert Lee & Derek Morgan eds. 1989); Y. Englert, *Artificial Insemination of Single Women and Lesbian Women with Donor Semen*, 9 HUM. REPRODUCTION 1969 (1994); Jean-Christophe Galloux, *Le statut des*

Sperm banks as such are much less troubling to society than arrangements that appear to challenge the very heart of society's traditional notions of parenting.[110] Single women (or two lesbians) seeking artificial insemination in significant numbers so they can have and raise a child without a man severely challenge the traditional family.[111] One can debate whether such challenges cause or result from the breakdown of families.[112] Yet this is small change compared to the challenges posed by other applications of medical technologies.

Modern reproductive technologies have made possible the widespread open acceptance of "surrogate" motherhood contracts[113]—an ancient practice now shorn of its formerly neces-

---

*gamètes humains en droit français contemporain,* 40 McGill L.J. 993 (1995); Karen Ginsberg, *FDA Approved? A Critique of the Artificial Insemination Industry in the United States,* 30 U. Mich. J.L. Reform 823 (1997); Mallory Levitt, *Artificial Insemination: A Comparison between Jewish and American Law,* 3 Transnat'l L. 277 (1992); Jason Mazzone, *Towards a Social Capital Theory of Law: Lessons from Collaborative Reproduction,* 39 Sta. Clara L. Rev. 1, 17–28 (1998); Joshua Plosker, *Privacy on Thin Ice? Considering the California Court of Appeal Decision in* Johnson v. Superior Court, 42 Jurimetrics 73 (2001); Jane Ross, *A Legal Analysis of Parenthood by Choice, Not Chance,* 9 Tex. J. Women & L. 29 (1999); Roosevelt, *supra* note 74, at 104–13; Anne Richman Schiff, *Frustrated Intentions and Binding Biology: Seeking AID in the Law,* 44 Duke L.J. 524 (1994); Shapiro, *supra* note 52, at 1119–20; Daniel & Nancy Wikler, *Turkey-Baster Babies: The Demedicalization of Artificial Insemination,* 69 Milbank Q. 5 (1991). Some controversial issues regarding articficial insemination still arise, however. *See* Daniel Pollack, Chaim Steinmetz, & Andrea Tellerman, Goodwin v. Turner: *A Comparison of American and Jewish Legal Perspectives on Procreation Rights of Prisoners,* 86 Ky. L.J. 367 (1998).

110. *See, e.g.,* Meyer, *supra* note 49, at 8–23, 26–30; Shaheena Ahmad, *Internet: Click Here for Donor No. 1,* US News & World Rep., Feb. 9, 1998, at 9; Roxane Arnold, *Still a Secret: Sperm Bank Babies,* Phila. Inquirer, Sept. 28, 1980, at 3E; Ronald Clarke, *For 100 Babies, a Nobel Father,* Phila. Inquirer, Mar. 2, 1980 at 5C; *Designer Genes: Nobel-Winning Donors Bank on Better Babies,* Phila. Inquirer, Mar. 1, 1980; Jim Detjen, *Sperm Bank Move Renews Controversy,* Phila. Inquirer, Oct. 24, 1982, at 1F; *First Birth: Nobel Sperm Bank Says Healthy Girl Born,* Phila. Inquirer, May 25, 1982, at 3A; Sharon Jones, *"Superior" Sperm Bank Remains Controversial: Founder Is Proud of 8-Year-Old Repository's Success—and Babies—but Detractors Still Question His Mission,* Phila. Inquirer, Aug. 14, 1988, at 1J. Apparently this is true of testicular transplants as well. *First Testicle Transplant Reported,* Phila. Inquirer, Oct. 19, 1977, at 7A; *Testicle Transplant Works,* Phila. Inquirer, July 27, 1980, at 4A (reporting that the recipient has become a father).

111. Fred Bernstein, *This Child Does Have Two Mothers—And a Sperm Donor with Visitation,* 22 NYU Rev. L. & Soc. Change 1 (1996); Susan Golombok & Fiona Tasker, *Donor Insemination for Single Heterosexual and Lesbian Women: Issues Concerning the Welfare of the Child,* 9 Hum. Reproduction 1972 (1994); Holly Harlow, *Paternalism without Paternity: Discrimination against Single Women Seeking Artificial Insemination by Donor,* 6 Rev. L. & Women's Stud. 173 (1996); Vickie Henry, *A Tale of Three Women: A Survey of the Rights and Responsibilities of Unmarried Women Who Conceive by Alternative Insemination and a Model for Legislative Reform,* 19 Am. J.L. & Med. 285 (1993); Barbara Kritchavsky, *The Unmarried Woman's Right to Artificial Insemination: A Call for an Expanded Definition of Family,* 4 Harv. Women's L.J. 1 (1981); Sandy McClure, *Detroit Clinic Allows Single Woman to Undergo Artificial Insemination,* Phila. Inquirer, Sept. 12, 1980, at 5B.

112. *See, e.g.,* Elizabeth Noble, Having Your Baby by Donor Insemination (1987); Julia Tate, Artificial Insemination and Legal Reality (1992).

113. *See* George Annas, *Using Genes to Define Motherhood—The California Solution,* 326 New Eng. J. Med. 417 (1992); Atherton, *supra* note 86, at 376–80; Lisa Behm, *Legal, Moral, & International Perspectives on Surrogate Motherhood: The Call for a Uniform Regulatory Scheme in the United States,* 2 DePaul J. Health Care L. 557 (1999); D.R. Bronham, *Surrogacy: The Evolution of Opinion,* 47 Brit. J. Hosp. Med. 767 (1992); Marsha Garrison, *Law Making for Baby Making: An Interpretive Approach to the Determination of Legal Parentage,* 113 Harv. L. Rev. 835 (2000); Denise Grady, *Surrogate Mothers Report Few Regrets,* N.Y. Times, Oct. 20, 1998, at F12; Lawrence Gostin, *Surrogacy from the Perspectives of Economic and Civil Liberties,* 17 J. Contemp. Health L. & Pol'y 429 (2001); Aditi Gowri, *Reproduction, Rights and Public Policy: A Framework for Assessment,* 35 Tex. Int'l L.J. 13 (2000); Hollinger, *supra* note 54, at 901–14; Ilana Hurwitz, *Collaborative Reproduction: Finding the Child in the Maze of Legal Motherhood,* 33 Conn. L. Rev. 127 (2000); Carol Krucoff, *Bearing a Child for Another,* Phila. Inquirer, Nov. 2, 1980, at 1K; Murray Manus, *The Proposed Model Surrogate Parenthood Act: A Legislative Response to the Challenges of Reproductive Technology,* 29 U. Mich. J.L. Reform 671 (1996); Lima Marques, *supra* note 75, at 84–91; Mazzone, *supra* note 109; Noble-Allgire, *supra* note 104, at 539–53; Maria Schwartz, *How Technology Has Affected the Legal System: Great Expectations: The Surrogacy Debate Continues,* 34 How. L.J. 169 (1991); Michael Shapiro, *How (Not) to Think about Surrogacy and Other Re-*

sary link to sexual infidelity. Such contracts have become remarkably common in a short period of time, with 750–1,000 such births in the United States in 1990 alone.[114] Less than a decade earlier, such contracts were front-page news.[115] Nonetheless, such contracts are troubling to our traditions, challenging our notions of maternity (and, sometimes, paternity), as well as long established strictures against "baby selling."[116] In one extreme case, a child ar-

*productive Innovations,* 28 U.S.F.L. REV. 647 (1994); Shapiro, *supra* note 52, at 1120–23; *Surrogate Mother Felt Regret "Only Once,"* PHILA. INQUIRER, Dec. 4, 1980, at 1A. For one of the more peculiar turns of such an arrangement, see Elizabeth Bumiller, *Surrogate Mother Is Convicted of Killing Her Own Daughter,* PHILA. INQUIRER, June 18, 1984, at 1A. In Japan, fathers have donated sperm to impregnate their daughters-in-law when the son proved infertile. *See* Stuck, *supra* note 52.

114. ROBERT BLANK, REGULATING REPRODUCTION 75 (1990). *See also* Andrea Sachs, *And Baby Makes Four,* TIME, Aug. 27, 1990, at 53 (estimating 2,000 such births between 1987 and 1990).

115. *See, e.g.,* Art Harris, *Stand-in Mother: An Unmarried Woman, 20, to Bear a Delaware Couple's Child,* PHILA. INQUIRER, Feb. 12, 1980, at 1A. *See also* Doe v. Kelley, 307 N.W.2d 438 (Mich. Ct. App. 1981), *cert. denied,* 453 U.S. 1183 (1983); Tim Kiska, *Right to Hire a "Surrogate" Mother Denied,* PHILA. INQUIRER, Feb. 3, 1980, at 4A; Lois Timnick, *Surrogate Mother Wants the Child: Impregnated Woman, N.Y. Couple Wage Custody Battle,* PHILA. INQUIRER, Mar. 22, 1981, at 3A.

116. Stiver v. Parker, 975 F.2d 261 (6th Cir. 1992); J.R. v. Utah, 261 F. Supp. 2d 1268 (D. Utah 2002); Doe v. Keane, 658 F. Supp. 216 (S.D. Mich. 1988); Soos v. Maricopa Cnty. Super. Ct., 897 P.2d 1356 (Ariz. Ct. App. 1994); Johnson v. Calvert, 851 P.2d 776 (Cal.), *cert. dismissed sub nom.* Baby Boy J. v. Johnson, 510 U.S. 938 (1993); *In* Moschetta v. Moschetta, 30 Cal. Rptr. 2d 893 (Cal. Ct. App. 1994); *In re* Adoption of Matthew B., 284 Cal. Rptr. 18 (Ct. App. 1991), *cert. denied sub nom.* Nancy B. v. Charlotte M., 503 U.S. 991 (1992); Sherwyn v. Department of Social Services, 218 Cal. Rptr. 778 (Ct. App. 1985); Doe v. Doe, 710 A.2d 1297 (Conn. 1998); Surrogate Parenting Assocs. v. Commonwealth *ex rel.* Armstrong, 704 S.W.2d 209 (Ky. 1986); Culliton v. Beth Israel Deaconess Med. Ctr., 756 N.E.2d 1133 (Mass. 2001); R.R. v. M.H., 689 N.E.2d 790 (Mass. 1998); Syrkowski v. Appleyard, 362 N.W.2d 211 (Mich. 1985); *In re* Baby M., 537 A.2d 1227 (N.J. 1988); Andres A. v. Judith N., 591 N.Y.S.2d 946 (Fam. Ct. 1992); *In re* Adoption of Paul, 550 N.Y.S.2d 815 (Fam. Ct. 1990); *In re* Adoption of Baby Girl L.J., 505 N.Y.S.2d 813 (Sur. Ct. 1986); Huddleston v. Infertility Ctr. of Am., Inc., 700 A.2d 453 (Pa. Super. Ct. 1997); *In re* Q, [1996] 2 All E.R. 369 (Ch. D.); *In re* P., [1987] 2 FAM. L. REP. 421; *In re* an Adoption, [1987] 2 All E.R. 826 (Fam. D.). *See also In re* R.C., 775 P.2d 27 (Colo. 1989) (deny ing paternal rights to a donor of sperm for artificial insemination); *In re* Adoption of Stephen, 645 N.Y.S.2d 1012 (Fam. Ct. 1996) (voiding contract to pay living expenses for mother surrendering her baby for adoption when the expenses were not related to the pregnancy); State v. Verde, 770 P.2d 116 (Utah 1989) (reversing a conviction for selling a baby).

*See generally* BLANK & MERRICK, *supra* note 24, at 109–32; BOUMIL, *supra* note 48, at 45–57; COMMERCIAL AND NONCOMMERCIAL SURROGATE PARENTING: A REPORT TO THE CALIFORNIA LEGISLATURE FROM THE JOINT COMMITTEE ON SURROGATE PARENTING (1990); COUNCIL OF EUROPE, *supra* note 24, at 27–30; JANET DOLGIN, DEFINING THE FAMILY: LAW, TECHNOLOGY AND REPRODUCTION IN AN UNEASY AGE 63–93 (1997); FENWICK, *supra* note 24, at 209–58; NOEL KEANE & DENNIS BREO, THE SURROGATE MOTHER (1981); ELAINE LANDAU, BLACK MARKET ADOPTION AND SALE OF CHILDREN (1990); RUTH MACKLIN, SURROGATES AND OTHER MOTHERS: THE DEBATES OVER ASSISTED REPRODUCTION (1994); MASON, *supra* note 33, at 251–79; MEYER, *supra* note 49, at 70–84; MEYERS, *supra* note 48, at 62–65, 73–75, 77; DEREK MORGAN, SURROGACY AND THE MORAL ECONOMY (1994); ON THE PROBLEM OF SURROGATE PARENTHOOD: ANALYZING THE "BABY M" CASE (Herbert Richardson ed. 1987); POLICY RECOMMENDATIONS ON SURROGACY, APPROVED IN PRINCIPLE BY THE NEW JERSEY BIOETHICS COMMISSION (1989); DEIDERIKA PRETORIUS, SURROGATE MOTHERHOOD: A WORLDWIDE VIEW OF THE ISSUES (1994); PROCEED WITH CARE: FINAL REPORT OF THE [CANADIAN] ROYAL COMMISSION ON NEW REPRODUCTIVE TECHNOLOGIES 690 (1993); SCOTT RAE, THE ETHICS OF COMMERCIAL SURROGATE MOTHERHOOD: BRAVE NEW FAMILIES (1993); HELENA RAGONE, SURROGATE MOTHERHOOD: CONCEPTION IN THE HEART (1994); RHODE, *supra* note 48, at 223–29; ROBERTSON, *supra* note 48, at 119–48, 197–219; SMITH, *supra* note 48, at 175–83; SURROGATE MOTHERHOOD: POLITICS AND PRIVACY (Larry Gostin ed. 1990); MARILYN WARING, IF WOMEN COUNTED: A NEW FEMINIST ECONOMICS 187–223 (1988); MARY BETH WHITEHEAD & LORETTA SCHWARTZ-NOBEL, A MOTHER'S STORY: THE TRUTH ABOUT THE BABY M CASE (1989); ACOG, *Ethical Issues in Surrogate Motherhood,* 37 INT'L J. GYNECOLOGY & OBSTET. 139 (1992); C. Dyer, *Surrogate Mother Refuses to Give Up Baby,* 314 BRIT. MED. J. 250 (1997); Martha Ertman, *What's Wrong with a Parenthood Market? A New and Improved Theory of Commodification,* 82 N.C.L. REV. 1 (2003); S. Fischer & I. Gillman, *Surrogate Motherhood—Attachments, Attitudes, and Social Support,* 54 PSYCHIATRY 13 (1991); Melanie Williams Havens,

guably had as many as eight "parents."[117]

To minimize the risk of running afoul of such strictures, the contract is usually between the father and the "surrogate" mother (the biological parents of the infant); the father's wife (the future adoptive mother) is not a formal party to the agreement.[118] This can create further problems should the father and his wife separate and thereafter fight over custody of the child.[119] And, if the fetus is found to be "unacceptable" to the intended parents, who should determine whether the gestational mother is to undergo an abortion?[120]

Largely absent from these discussions is what, if anything, the new practice implies about the "personhood" of the fetus.[121] Nor is the relationship of the adult participants entirely settled. Usually, the "gestational" mother is also the biological mother in these arrangements, providing the ovum as well as the womb. New technologies enable ovum donation as well as sperm donation—which some view as changing the moral (and hence legal) dynamic of the arrangement.[122]

---

*Womb with a View: Gestational Surrogacy and Legal Parenthood,* 40 MED. TRIAL TECHNOL. Q. 208 (1995); Patrick Healy, *Statutory Prohibitions and the Regulation of New Reproductive Technologies under Federal Law in Canada,* 40 McGILL L.J. 905, 934–37 (1995); Randy Frances Kandel, *Which Came First: The Mother or the Egg? A Kinship Solution to Gestational Surrogacy,* 47 RUTGERS L. REV. 165 (1994); E. Ann Kaplan, *The Politics of Surrogacy Narratives,* in FEMINISM, MEDIA, AND THE LAW 193 (Martha Fineman & Martha McCluskey eds. 1997); Christine Kerian, *Surrogacy: A Last Resort Alternative for Infertile Women or a Commodification of Women's Bodies and Children?,* 12 WIS. WOMEN'S L.J. 113 (1997); Alexa King, *Solomon Revisited: Assigning Parenthood in the Context of Collaborative Reproduction,* 5 UCLA L. REV. 329 (1995); Linda Lacey, *"O Wind, Remind Him that I Have no Child": Infertility and Feminist Jurisprudence,* 5 MICH. J. GENDER & L. 163 (1998); Pamela Laufer-Ukeles, *Gestation: Work for Hire or the Essence of Motherhood? A Comparative Legal Analysis,* 9 DUKE J. GENDER L. & & POL'Y 91 (2002); Justin Oakley, *Altruistic Surrogacy and Informed Consent,* 6 BIOETHICS 269 (1992); Margaret Jane Radin, *What, If Anything, Is Wrong with Baby Selling?,* 26 PAC. L. REV. 135 (1995); Roosevelt, *supra* note 74, at 113–27; Barbara Katz Rothman, *Reproductive Technologies and Surrogacy: A Feminist Perspective,* 25 CREIGHTON L. REV. 1599 (1992); Jean Sera, *Surrogacy and Prostitution: A Comparative Analysis,* 5 J. GENDER & L. 315 (1997); Mary Lyndon Shanley, *Surrogate Mothering and Women's Freedom: A Critique of Contracts for Human Reproduction,* 18 SIGNS 618 (1993); Shanner, *supra* note 98; Shapiro, *supra* note 52, at 1120–23, 1143, 1180–1221; Richard Storrow, *Parenthood by Pure Intention: Assisted Reproduction and the Functional Approach to Parentage,* 53 HASTINGS L.J. 597 (2002); J.G. Thornton, H.M. McNamara, & I.A. Montague, *Would You Rather Be a Birth or a Genetic Mother—If so, How Much?,* 20 J. MED. ETHICS 87 (1994); Rosemarie Tong, *Feminist Perspectives and Gestational Motherhood: The Search for a Unified Focus,* in FEMINIST PERSPECTIVES, *supra* note 48, at 55; Anton van Niekerk & Liezl van Zyl, *The Ethics of Surrogacy: Women's Reproductive Labour,* 21 J. MED. ETHICS 345 (1995); Laura Woliver, *Reproductive Technologies, Surrogacy Arrangements, and the Politics of Motherhood,* in MOTHERS IN LAW: FEMINIST THEORY AND THE LEGAL REGULATION OF MOTHERHOOD 346 (Martha Albertson Fineman & Isabel Karpin eds. 1995); Kevin Yamamoto & Shelby Moore, *A Trust Analysis of a Gestational Carrier's Right to Abortion,* 70 FORDHAM L. REV. 93 (2001).

117. *See In re* Marriage of Buzzanca, 72 Cal. Rptr. 2d 280 (Ct. App. 1998), *rev. denied*; Alexander Morgan Capron, *Too Many Parents,* 28 HASTINGS CTR. REP. no. 5, at 22 (Sept.–Oct. 1998); Marsha Garrison, *Law Making for Baby Making: An Interpretive Approach to the Determination of Legal Parentage,* 113 HARV. L. REV. 835 (2000).

118. Manus, *supra* note 113, at 672 n.2. *See* Katie Marie Brophy, *A Surrogate Mother Contract to Bear a Child,* 20 J. FAM. L. 263, 264 (1982).

119. Doe v. Doe, 710 A.2d 1297 (Conn. 1998) (denying the wife standing to challenge custody because she had no legal relationship to the child); Seymour v. Stotski, 611 N.E.2d 454 (Ohio Ct. App. 1992) (same), *appeal dismissed,* 608 N.E.2d 760 (Ohio 1993); Tamar Lewin, *Custody Case in Ohio Ends in Slaying and Prison Term,* N.Y. TIMES, Dec. 8, 1990, at A9.

120. *See* Radhika Rao, *Assisted Reproductive Technology and the Threat to the Traditional Family,* 47 HASTINGS L.J. 951, 955 (1996); Roosevelt, *supra* note 74, at 123; Kevin Yamamoto & Shelby Moore, *A Trust Analysis of a Gestational Carrier's Right to Abortion,* 70 FORDHAM L. REV. 93 (2001).

121. *But see* Cheryl Robinson, *Surrogate Motherhood: Implications for the Mother-Fetus Relationship,* 13 WOMEN & POL. 203 (1993); Walter Weber, *The Personhood of Unborn Children—A First Principle in Surrogate Motherhood Analysis,* 13 HARV. J.L. & PUB. POL'Y 125 (1990).

122. *See* Johnson v. Calvert, 851 P.2d 776 (Cal.), *cert. denied sub nom.* Baby Boy J. v. Johnson, 510 U.S. 874 (1993); Jaycee B. v. Superior Ct., 49 Cal. Rptr. 2d 694 (Ct. App. 1996); Anna J. v. Mark C., 286 Cal. Rptr. 369

Hence the child with as many as eight "parents" — egg and sperm donors, their spouses, a surrogate mother and her husband, and the parents who are to raise the child.[123]

In response to the resulting controversies, some states have enacted legislation to facilitate surrogacy arrangements[124] while other states, countries, and cultures have flatly prohibited such arrangements, even imposing criminal penalties.[125] The drafters of the *Uniform Status of Children of Assisted Conception Act* could not reach an agreement about the rights and wrongs of surrogacy contracts when they finished their work in 1988. They proposed two alternative sections, one prohibiting such contracts and the other allowing them under close judicial supervision.[126]

---

(Ct. App. 1991), *cert. granted,* 4 Cal. Rptr. 2d 170 (1992); A.H.W. v. G.H.B., 772 A.2d 948 (N.J. Super. Ct. Ch. Div. 2000); McDonald v. McDonald, 608 N.Y.S.2d 477 (App. Div. 1994); Belsito v. Clark, 644 N.E.2d 760 (Ohio C.P. 1994). *See also* Fenwick, *supra* note 24, at 9–14, 203, 262; Mason, *supra* note 33, at 240–42; Meyer, *supra* note 49, at 7–8, 23–25, 30–40; New Ways of Making Babies: The Case of Egg Donation (Cynthia Cohen ed. 1995); Kenneth Baum, *Golden Eggs: Towards the Rational Regulation of Oocyte Donation,* 2001 BYU L. Rev. 107; Laura Brill, *When Will the Law Catch up with Technology?* Jaycee B. v. Superior Court of Orange County: *An Urgent Cry for Legislation on Gestational Surrogacy,* 39 Cath. Law. 241 (1999); Dolgin, *supra* note 86, at 44–65; Dalia Dorner, *Human Reproduction: Reflections on the* Nachmani *Case,* 35 Tex. Int'l L.J. 1 (2000); Susan Feldman, *Multiple Biological Mothers: The Case for Gestation,* 23 J. Soc. Phil. 98 (Spring 1992); Galloux, *supra* note 109; Randy Frances Kandel, *Which Came First: The Mother or the Egg? A Kinship Solution to Gestational Surrogacy,* 47 Rutgers L. Rev. 165 (1994); Katheryn Katz, *Ghost Mothers: Human Egg Donation and the Legacy of the Past,* 57 Alb. L. Rev. 733 (1994); John Leeton & Jayne Hurman, *Attitudes towards Egg Donation of Thirty-Four Infertile Women Who Donated During Their* in Vitro *Fertilization Treatment,* 3 J. in Vitro Fertilization & Embryo Transfer 374 (1986); R. Brian Oxman, *Maternal-Fetal Relationships and Nongenetic Surrogates,* 33 Jurimetrics 387 (1993); C. Snowdon, *What Makes a Mother: Interviews with Women Involved in Egg Donation and Surrogacy,* 21 Birth — Issues in Perinatal Care 77 (1994); James Treppa, In Vitro *Fertilization through Egg Donation: A Prospective View of Legal Issues,* 22 Golden Gate L. Rev. 777 (1992).

123. Storrow, *supra* note 116, at 602 .

124. *See, e.g.,* Ark. Code Ann. § 9-10-201 (LexisNexis 2002); Fla. Stat. Ann. §§ 742.14 to 742.17 (West 1997) (if the "intended mother" is infertile); Nev. Rev. Stat. § 126.045 (1995); N.H. Rev. Stat. Ann. §§ 168-B:1 to B:32 (2001). *See also* J.R. v. Utah, 261 F. Supp. 2d 1268 (D. Utah 2002).

125. *See* Ala. Code § 26-10A-34 (1992); 9 Ariz. Rev. Stat. Ann. § 25-218 (West 2000); D.C. Code Ann. § 16-402 (2001); Fla. Stat. Ann. § 63.212(d) (West Supp. 2003); Ind. Code Ann. §§ 31-8-1-1 to 31-8-1-5 (West 1997), 31-20-1-1, 31-20-1-2 (Michie 1997); Ky. Rev. Stat. Ann. § 199.590(4) (Michie 1999); Kan. Stat. Ann. § 59-2121 (1994); La. Rev. Stat. Ann. § 9:2713 (West 1991); Mich. Comp. Laws Ann. § 722.855 (West 2002); Neb. Rev. Stat. § 25-21,200 (1995); N.Y. Dom. Rel. Law §§ 121-124 (McKinney 1999); N.D. Cent. Code §§ 14-18-01 to 14-18-07 (1997); Utah Code Ann. § 76-7-204 (2003); Va. Code Ann. §§ 20-156 to 20-165 (Michie 1995); Wash. Rev. Code Ann. §§ 26.26.210-26.26.270 (West 1997); W. Va. Code § 48-4-16 (1995).

 *See also* Abdul Fadl Mohsin Ebrahim, Abortion, Birth Control, and Surrogate Parenting: An Islamic Perspective 54–65 (1989); Erwin Bernat & Ulrike Straka, *Austria: A Legal Ban on Surrogate Mothers and Fathers?,* 31 J. Fam. L. 267 (1993); Casey Chisick & Darren Baccus, *Not Just a Human Incubator: Legal Problems in Gestational Surrogate Motherhood,* 25 Man. L. Rev. 49 (1997); Skene, *supra* note 75; Alison Harvison Young, *New Reproductive Technologies in Canada and the United States: Same Problems, Different Discourses,* 12 Temple Int'l & Comp. L.J. 43, 75–82 (1998); Noam Zohar, *Artificial Insemination and Surrogate Motherhood: A Halakhic Perspective,* 2 S'vara no. 1, at 14 (1991).

126. *Uniform Status of Children Act, supra* note 109, § 5. *See also* Model Surrogacy Act (Section of Family Law, ABA 1988). *See generally* Randall Bezanson *et al., Model Human Reproductive Technologies and Surrogacy Act: An Act Governing the Status of Children Born through Reproductive Technologies and Surrogacy Arrangements,* 72 Iowa L. Rev. 943 (1987); Weldon Havins & James Dalessio, *Reproductive Surrogacy at the Millennium: Proposed Model Legislation Regulating "Non-Traditional" Gestational Surrogacy Contracts,* 31 Mc-George L. Rev. 673 (2001); James Levitt, *Biology, Technology and Genealogy: A Proposed Uniform Surrogacy Legislation,* 25 Colum. J.L. & Soc. Probs. 451 (1992); Manus, *supra* note 113; Ann MacLean Massie, *Restricting Surrogacy to Married Couples: A Constitutional Problem? The Married-Parent Requirement in the Uniform Status of Children of Assisted Conception Act,* 18 Hastings Const'l L.Q. 487 (1991); John Sheldon, *Surrogate Mothers, Gestational Carriers, and a Pragmatic Adaptation of the Uniform Parentage Act of 2000,* 53 Me. L. Rev. 523 (2001).

The implications of the many technology-based changes in human reproductive processes are far from certain. Different persons react in different ways to the same technological innovation. Thus, in what appears to be a remarkable reversal of cause and effect, attorney Michele Beasley concluded that the legalization of abortion gave rise to a legal action for "wrongful life" because *Roe v. Wade* made abortion, and thus the avoidance of an "undesirable" life, possible unless a physician prevented the abortion.[127] She predicted that overruling *Roe* would lead to the end of these causes of action. Beasley completely overlooked the argument that because of the availability of abortion, the parents, rather than a physician or pharmacist (the usual defendants), are responsible for such births if the parents choose to forego an abortion. *Roe* therefore makes such causes of action more problematic rather than less. In fact, since *Roe* as well as before, courts rejected claims for wrongful life many more times than they accepted the claim.[128] A related prob-

---

127. Michele Beasley, *Wrongful Birth/Wrongful Life: The Tort Progeny of Legalized Abortion*, in Abortion, Medicine, and the Law 232 (J. Douglas Butler & David Walbert eds. 3rd ed. 1986). *See generally* Boumil, *supra* note 48, at 105–14; Mason, *supra* note 33, at 160–65; Robertson, *supra* note 48, at 75–76; Ann Belsky, *Injury as a Matter of Law: Is This the Answer to the Wrongful Life Dilemma*, 22 Bal. L. Rev. 184 (1993); Jeffrey Botkin & Maxwell Mehlman, *Wrongful Birth: Medical, Legal and Philosophical Issues*, 22 J. Law Med. & Ethics 21 (1994); Andrew Grubb, *"Wrongful Life" and Prenatal Injury*, 1 Med. L. Rev. 261 (1993); Anthony Jackson, *Action for Wrongful Life, Wrongful Pregnancy, and Wrongful Birth in the United States and England*, 17 Loy.-L.A. L. Rev. 535 (1995); Dana Wechsler Linden & Mia Wechsler Doron, *Eyes of Texas Fasten on Life, Death and the Premature Infant*, N.Y. Times, Apr. 30, 2002, at F5; Mary Ellen Pelligrino, *The Protection of Prenatal Life: Tort Claims of Wrongful Birth or Wrongful Life and Equal Protection Claims under Pennsylvania's Constitution*, 72 Temple L. Rev. 715 (1999); Lois Shepherd, *Sophie's Choices: Medical and Legal Responses to Suffering*, 72 Notre Dame L. Rev. 103, 107–15 (1996); Carel Stolker, *Wrongful Life: The Limits of Liability and Beyond*, 43 Int'l & Comp. L.Q. 521 (1994); Adrian Whitfield, *Common Law Duties to Unborn Children*, 1 Med. L. Rev. 28 (1993).

128. The term "wrongful life" first appeared, and the claim was rejected, in Zepeda v. Zepeda, 190 N.E.2d 849 (Ill. App. Ct. 1963). Since then, courts have considered such claims in many cases. *Claim rejected:* Walker v. Mart, 790 P.2d 735 (Ariz. 1990); Lininger v. Eisenbaum, 764 P.2d 1202 (Colo. 1988); 1992 WL 43525; Cauman v. George Wash. Univ., 630 A.2d 1104 (D.C. 1993); Kush v. Lloyd, 616 So. 2d 415 (Fla. 1992); Etkind v. Suarez, 519 S.E.2d 210 (Ga. 1999); Blake v. Cruz, 698 P.2d 315 (Idaho 1984); Williams v. University of Chi. Hosps., 688 N.E.2d 130 (Ill. 1997); Bader v. Johnson, 732 N.E.2d 1212 (Ind. 2000); Bruggeman v. Schimke, 718 P.2d 635 (Kan. 1986); Grubbs v. Barbourville Fam. Health Ctr., PSC, 120 S.W.3d 682 (Ky. 2003); Davis v. Board of Supervisors of La. St. Univ., 709 So. 2d 1030 (La. Ct. App.), *writ denied,* 719 So. 2d 1288 (La. 1998); Kassama v. Magat, 792 A.2d 1102 (Md. 2002); Taylor v. Kurapati, 600 N.W.2d 670 (Mich. Ct. App. 1999); Hickman v. Group Health Plan, Inc., 396 N.W.2d 10 (Minn. 1986); Wilson v. Kuenzi, 751 S.W.2d 741 (Mo. 1988), *cert. denied,* 479 U.S. 835 (1986); Smith v. Cote, 513 A.2d 341 (N.H. 1986); Canesi v. Wilson, 730 A.2d 805 (N.J. 1999); Bani-Esraili v. Lerman, 505 N.E.2d 947 (N.Y. 1987); Azzolino v. Dingfelder, 337 S.E.2d 528 (N.C. 1985), *cert. denied,* 479 U.S. 835 (1986); Simmerer v. Dabbas, 733 N.E.2d 1169 (Ohio 2000); Hester v. Dwivedi, 733 N.E.2d 1161 (Ohio 2000); Ellis v. Sherman, 515 A.2d 1327 (Pa. 1986); Nelson v. Krusen, 678 S.W.2d 918 (Tex. 1984); James G. v. Caserta, 332 S.E.2d 872 (W. Va. 1985); Dumer v. St. Michael's Hospital, 233 N.W.2d 372 (Wis. 1975); McKay v. Essex Area Health Auth'y, [1982] 2 All E.R. 771 (Q.B.). *Claim accepted:* Jorgensen v. Mead Johnson Labs., Inc., 483 F.2d 237 (10th Cir. 1973) (Oklahoma); Keel v. Banach, 624 So. 2d 1022 (Ala. 1993); M.A. v. U.S., 951 P.2d 851 (Alaska 1998); Thibeault v. Larson, 666 A.2d 112 (Me. 1995); Viccaro v. Milunsky, 551 N.E.2d 8 (Mass. 1990); Emerson v. Magendatz, 689 A.2d 409 (R.I. 1997); Estate of Amos v. Vanderbilt Univ., 62 S.W.3d 133 (Tenn. 2001); Glascock v. Laserna, 439 S.E.2d 380 (Va. 1994); Harbeson v. Parke-Davis, Inc., 656 P.2d 483 (Was. 1983). *See also* Greco v. United States, 893 P.2d 345 (Nev. 1995) (no cause of action on behalf of the infant for failure to abort, but a cause of action for the mother for resulting medical and other expenses).

For courts that have allowed recovery for the costs of treating prenatal injuries even while rejecting a claim for wrongful life, see: Turpin v. Sortini, 643 P.2d 954 (Cal. 1982); Lininger v. Eisenbaum, 764 P.2d 1202 (Colo. 1988); Heyman v. Wilkerson, 535 A.2d 880 (D.C. 1987); Blake v. Cruz, 698 P.2d 315 (Idaho 1984); Siemieniec v. Lutheran Gen. Hosp., 512 N.E.2d 691 (Ill. 1987); Walker v. Rinck, 604 N.E.2d 591 (Ind. 1992); Arche v. United States, 798 P.2d 477 (Kan. 1980); Pitre v. Opelousas Gen. Hosp., 530 So. 2d 1151 (La. 1988); Viccaro v. Milunsky, 551 N.E.2d 8 (Mass. 1990); Profitt v. Bartolo, 412 N.W.2d 232 (Mich. Ct. App. 1987); Shelton v. St. Anthony's Med. Ctr., 781 S.W.2d 48 (Mo. 1989); Lynch v. Scheininger, 744 A.2d 113 (N.J. 2000); Moreta v. New York City Health & Hosps. Corp., 655 N.Y.S.2d 517 (App. Div. 1997); Ehlinger v. Sipes, 454 N.W.2d 754

lem arises in the recurring disputes over whether the law should recognize actions for "wrongful birth" (and the related tort of "wrongful conception") when contraceptive failure leads burdens parents with the birth of a healthy, but unplanned child.[129] (Courts do not always use these terms, although the several concepts can be identified as done here in the text regardless of the precise terminology used by the particular court.)

The question of what to do about wrongful birth and wrongful life suits ties directly into the abortion debate. In several states, the legislative coalition that has repeatedly sought to restrict

---

(Wis. 1990).

*See generally* Alan Belsky, *Injury as a Matter of Law: Is This the Answer to the Wrongful Life Dilemma?*, 22 U. BAL. L. REV. 185 (1993); Herbert Harrar, *Aspects of Failed Family Planning in the United States of America and Germany*, 15 J. LEGAL MED. 89 (1994); Anthony Jackson, *Wrongful Life and Wrongful Birth: The English Conception*, 17 J. LEG. MED. 349 (1996); Michael Lauder, *In Defense of Wrongful Life: Bringing Political Theory to the Defense of a Tort*, 62 FORDHAM L. REV. 1675 (1994); Philip Peters, jr., *Rethinking Wrongful Life: Bridging the Boundary between Tort and Family Law*, 67 TUL. L. REV. 397 (1992); Mark Strasser, *Wrongful Life, Wrongful Birth, Wrongful Death, and the Right to Refuse Treatment: Can a Reasonable Jurisdiction Recognize All but One?*, 64 MO. L. REV. 29 (1999).

129. While nearly all courts to have considered wrongful birth claims have allowed the claim to go forward to recover the medical expenses and pain and suffering of the mother involved in the unplanned birth, most do not allow recovery of the costs of raising the unplanned child. Garcia v. von Micsky, 602 F.2d 51 (2nd Cir. 1979) (New York); LaPoint v. Shirley, 409 F. Supp. 118 (W.D. Tex. 1976); Boone v. Mullendore, 416 So. 2d 718 (Ala. 1982); Wilbur v. Kerr, 628 S.W.2d 568 (Ark. 1982); Lininger v. Eisenbaum, 764 P.2d 1202 (Colo. 1988); Coleman v. Garrison, 349 A.2d 8 (Del. 1975); Morgan v. Psychiatric Fndtn. of Was., 691 A.2d 417 (D.C. 1997); Fassoulas v. Ramey, 450 So. 2d 822 (Fla. 1984); Etkind v. Suarez, 519 S.E.2d 210 (Ga. 1999); Cockrum v. Baumgartner, 447 N.E.2d 385 (Ill.), *cert. denied sub nom.* Raja v. Michael Reese Hosp., 464 U.S. 846 (1983); Chaffee v. Seslar, 786 N.E.2d 705 (Ind. 2003); Nanke v. Napier, 346 N.W.2d 520 (Iowa 1984); Byrd v. Wesley Med. Ctr., 699 P.2d 459 (Kan. 1985); Schork v. Huber, 648 S.W.2d 861 (Ky. 1983); Smith v. Clement, 797 So. 2d 151 (La. Ct. App. 2001), *writ denied,* 807 So. 2d 249 (2002); Macomber v. Dilleman, 505 A.2d 810 (Me. 1986); Rinard v. Biczak, 441 N.W.2d 441 (Mich. Ct. App. 1989); Girdley v. Coats, 825 S.W.2d 295 (Mo. 1992); Szekeres v. Robinson, 715 P.2d 1076 (Nev. 1986) (as a breach of contract rather than a tort); Smith v. Cote, 513 A.2d 341 (N.H. 1986); O'Toole v. Greenberg, 477 N.E.2d 445 (N.Y. 1985); McAllister v. Khie Sem Ha, 496 S.E.2d 577 (N.C. 1998); Wofford v. Davis, 764 P.2d 161 (Okla. 1988); Mason v. Western Pa. Hosp., 453 A.2d 974 (Pa. 1982); Emerson v. Magendantz, 689 A.2d 409 (R.I. 1997); Smith v. Gore, 728 S.W.2d 738 (Tenn. 1987); Crawford v. Kirk, 929 S.W.2d 633 (Tex. Ct. App. 1996); Miller v. Johnson, 343 S.E.2d 301 (Va. 1986); McKernan v. Aasheim, 687 P.2d 850 (Wash. 1984); James G. v. Caserta, 332 S.E.2d 872 (W. Va. 1985); Flint v. O'Connell, 648 N.W.2d 7 (Wis. Ct. App. 2002) (failure to diagnose pregnancy in time to allow for an abortion); Beardsley v. Wierdsma, 650 P.2d 288 (Wyo. 1982). For cases in which courts allowed recovery for the costs of raising the unplanned child but not for emotional distress, see: University of Ariz. Health Sci. Ctr. v. Superior Ct., 667 P.2d 1294 (Ariz. 1983); Foy v. Greenblott, 190 Cal. Rptr. 84 (Ct. App. 1983); Morris v. Frudenfeld, 185 Cal. Rptr. 86 (Ct. App. 1982); Burns v. Hanson, 734 A.2d 964 (Conn. 1999); Jones v. Malinowski, 473 A.2d 429 (Md. 1984); Burke v. Rivo, 551 N.E.2d 1 (Mass. 1990); Lovelace Med. Ctr. v. Mendez, 805 P.2d 603 (N.M. 1991); Johnson v. University Hosps., 540 N.E.2d 1370 (Ohio 1989); Marciniak v. Lundberg, 450 N.W.2d 243 (Wis. 1990) (negligent sterilization); Walkin v. South Manchester Health Auth'y, [1995] 4 All E.R. 132 (Q.B.); Allen v. Bloomsbury Health Auth'y, [1993] 1 All. E.R. 651 (Q.B.); Emeh v. Kensington & Chelsea & Westminster Area Health Auth'y, [1984] 3 All E.R. 1044 (Q.B.); Thake v. Maurice, [1984] 2 All E.R. 513 (Q.B.); Udale v. Bloomsbury Area Health Auth'y, [1983] 2 All E.R. 522 (Q.B.).

*See generally* TERRENCE KIELY, MODERN TORT LIABILITY: RECOVERY IN THE '90's §8.18 (1990); Bruce Cleaver, *"Wrongful Birth"—The Dawning of a New Action*, 108 S. AFR. L. REV. 47 (1991); P.R. Glazebrook, *Capable of Being, but No Right to Be, Born Alive?*, 50 CAMBRIDGE L.J. 241 (1991); Andrew Grubb, *Damages for the Birth of a Healthy Child:* Allen v. Bloomsbury Health Authority, 1 MED. L. REV. 238 (1993); Harrar, *supra* note 128; Jackson, *supra* note 127, at 582–606; Jackson, *supra* note 128, at 370–81; David Kerrane, *Damages for Wrongful Pregnancy*, 11 J. CONTEMP. LEGAL ISSUES 467 (2000); Belinda Kimbell, *Wrongful Birth: A Practitioner's Guide to a New Arrival*, 55 ALA. LAW. 84 (1994); Michael Mogill, *Misconceptions of the Law: Full Recovery for the Birth of the Unplanned Child*, 1996 UTAH L. REV. 827; A.J. Stone, III, *Consti-Tortion: Tort Law as an End-Run around Abortion Rights after* Planned Parenthood v. Casey, 8 AM. U.J. GENDER SOC. POL'Y & L. 471 (2000); Mark Strasser, *Misconceptions and Wrongful Births: A Call for a Principled Jurisprudence*, 31 ARIZ. L.J. 161 (1999).

access to abortion succeeded in enacting legislation to bar such suits.[130] A court has now rejected a suit filed by a woman who alleged that this statute interfered with her right to choose abortion when the attending physician, relying on the protections of the statute, chose not to inform her of defects he discovered in the fetus until it was too late for her to seek an abortion.[131] The United Kingdom has also barred wrongful life suits by statute.[132]

The continuing controversy over the exploitation of fetal tissue for research or for therapy for other persons or of anencephalic neonates as organ donors similarly challenges our traditional notions of what it means to be a member of the human community.[133] Until recently, fetal tissue became available too rarely for anyone to consider undertaking systematic research with it. Now, there is considerable research with fetal tissue—harvested from aborted infants.[134] Fetal experi-

---

130. *See, e.g.,* IDAHO CODE § 5-334 (1997); ME. REV. STAT. ANN. tit. 24, § 2931 (West 2000); MINN. STAT. ANN. § 145.424 (West 2003); MO. REV. STAT. § 188.130 (West 1992); N.D. CENT. CODE § 32-03-043 (Michie 1997); 42 PA. CONS. STAT. ANN. § 8305(West 2001); UTAH CODE ANN. § 78-11-24 (2003). *See* Hickman v. Group Health Plan, Inc., 396 N.W.2d 10 (Minn. 1986) (upholding the constitutionality of the state's statute); Wood v. University of Utah Med. Ctr., 67 P.3d 436 (Utah 2002), *cert. denied,* 540 U.S. 946 (2003) (same). *But see* Musk v. Nelson, 647 A.2d 1198 (Me. 1995) (statutory ban on wrongful life actions does not bar action to recover medical expenses for baby born with Down's syndrome after a doctor's failure to diagnose the problem precluded a possible abortion); Sejpal v. Corson, Mitchell, Tomhave, & McKinley, M.D.'s, Inc., 665 A.2d 1198 (Pa. Super. Ct. 1995) (same). *See also* Thomas Warnock, *Scientific Adventures: Will Technology Make the Unpopular Wrongful Birth/Life Causes of Action Extinct,* 19 TEMP. ENVTL. L. & TECH. J. 173, 182 (2001).

131. Edmonds v. Western Pa. Hospital Radiology Assoc., 607 A.2d 1083 (Pa. Super. Ct. 1992), *appeal denied,* 621 A.2d 580 (Pa.), *cert. denied,* 510 U.S. 814 (1993).

132. *Congenital Defects (Civil Liability) Act of 1976,* ch. 28; McKay v. Essex Area Health Auth'y, [1982] 2 All E.R. 711 (Q.B.). *See also* ANDREW GRUBB, MEDICAL LAW 976 (2nd ed. 1994); MASON, *supra* note 33, at 163–64; Jackson, *supra* note 129; G.E. Jones & C. Perry, *Can Claims for "Wrongful Life" Be Justified?,* 13 J. MED. ETHICS 152 (1983); N.C. Liu, *Wrongful Life: Some of the Problems,* 13 J. MED. ETHICS 69 (1987); M. Slade, *The Death of Wrongful Life: A Case for Resuscitation?,* 132 NEW L.J. 874 (1982); H. Teff, *The Action for "Wrongful Life" in England and the United States,* 34 INT'L & COMP. L.Q. 423 (1985).

133. *See, e.g.,* American Hospital Ass'n v. Heckler, 476 U.S. 610 (1986); Forbes v. Napolitano, 236 F.3d 1009 (9th Cir. 2000); Doe v. Shalala, 862 F. Supp. 1421 (D. Md. 1994); Lifchez v. Hartigan, 735 F. Supp. 1361 (N.D. Ill.), *aff'd mem.,* 914 F.2d 260 (7th Cir. 1990), *cert. denied,* 498 U.S. 1069 (1991); *In re* T.A.C.P., 609 So. 2d 588 (Fla. 1992). *See also* ARIZ. REV. STAT. ANN. § 36-2302 (West 2003). *See generally* FENWICK, *supra* note 24, at 27–52; MASON, *supra* note 33, at 196–202; NATIONAL INST. HEALTH, REPORT OF THE HUMAN EMBRYO RESEARCH PANEL (1994) (Pub. No. 95-3916); PROCEED WITH CARE, *supra* note 116, at 637, 643; PETER SINGER, RETHINKING LIFE AND DEATH 46–56 (1995); AMA Council on Ethical & Jud. Aff., *The Use of Anencephalic Neonates as Organ Donors,* 273 JAMA 1614 (1995); American Academy of Pediatrics, Comm. on Bioethics, *Infants with Anencephaly as Organ Sources: Ethical Considerations,* 89 PEDIATRICS 1116 (1992); Brahams, *supra* note 73; Byrne *et al., supra* note 73; Neil Davis, *The Constitutionality of Fetal Experimentation Statutes: The Case of* Litchez v. Hartigan, 25 J. HEALTH & HOSP. L. 37 (1992); Gianelli, *supra* note 73; Healy, *supra* note 116, at 931–34; W.F. May, *Brain Death: Anencephalics and Aborted Fetuses,* 22 TRANSPLANTATION PROC. 885 (1990); Medical Task Force on Anencephaly, *The Infant with Anencephaly,* 322 NEW ENG. J. MED. 669 (1990); Charles Plows, *Reconsideration of AMA Opinion on Anencephalic Neonates as Organ Donors,* 275 JAMA 443 (1996); Gregory Rutecki, *Anencephalic Neonates as Organ Donors Revisited: A Response to the Council on Ethical and Judicial Affairs of the American Medical Association,* 13 ETHICS & MED. 28 (1997). *See generally* E. RICHARD GOLD, BODY PARTS: PROPERTY RIGHTS AND THE OWNERSHIP OF HUMAN BIOLOGICAL MATERIALS (1996).

134. ARTHUR BAUER, LEGAL AND ETHICAL ASPECTS OF FETAL TISSUE TRANSPLANTATION (1994); COUNCIL OF EUROPE, *supra* note 24, at 30–34; EMBRYO EXPERIMENTATION (Peter Singer *et al.* eds. 1990); FETAL ISLET TRANSPLANTATION (Charles Peterson, Lois Jovánovic-Peterson, & Brent Formbsy ed.1995); Lori Andrews, *Regulation of Experimentation on the Unborn,* 14 J. LEGAL MED. 25 (1993); Robert Cefalo *et al., The Bioethics of Human Fetal Tissue Research and Therapy: Moral Decision Making of Professionals,* 170 AM. J. OBSTET. & GYNECOLOGY 12 (1994); June Coleman, *Playing God or Playing Scientist: A Constitutional Analysis of State Laws Banning Embryological Procedures,* 27 PAC. L.J. 1331 (1996); Benvenito Costello *et al., An Improved Method of Isolating Fetal Human Retinal Pigment Epithelium,* 14 CURRENT EYE RESEARCH 677 (1995); Gregory Gelfand & Tony Lewis, *Fetal Tissue Research: Legal Regulation of Human Fetal Tissue Transplantation,* 50 WASH. & LEE L. REV. 647 (1993); Alan Fine, *Human Fetal Tissue Research: Practice, Prospects, and Policy,* 3 CELL TRANSPLAN-

mentation continues despite growing doubts about whether this line of research will bear much fruit and whether most abortions will generate usable tissue.[135]

Perhaps more promising than fetal tissue research, but certainly as controversial, is research on human stem cells.[136] Human stem cells are undifferentiated embryonic cells capable of evolving into any organ of the human body (or an entire human body) depending on the signals provided by — or to — the cell's DNA.[137] In other words, stem cells are pluripotent. Stem cells can be harvested from umbilical cords, so this research need not depend on abortions. The capacity of such cells to become fully formed human beings raises, however, some of the same issues as fetal research generally.[138] When it was announced that scientists had developed ova and sperm cells from stem cells,[139] stem cell research also began to raise the same issues as cloning.

---

TATION 113 (1994); Bryan Hainline *et al.*, *Fetal Tissue Derived from Spontaneous Pregnancy Losses Is Insufficient for Human Transplantation*, 135 OBSTET. & GYNECOLOGY 619 (1995); Carla McCauley, *Fetal Tissue: A Medicolegal Predicament*, 40 MED. TRIAL TECHNOL. Q. 230 (1995); Michelle Mullen *et al*, *Transplantation of Electively Aborted Human Fetal Tissue: Physicians' Attitudes*, 151 CAN. MED. ASS'N J. 325 (1994); Christie Seifert, *Fetal Tissue Research: State Regulation of the Donation of Aborted Fetuses without the Consent of the "Mother,"* 31 JOHN MARSHALL L. REV. 277 (1997); Cory Zion, *The Legal and Ethical Issues of Fetal Tissue Research and Transplantation*, 75 OR. L. REV. 1281 (1996).

135. Jamie Talan, *Fetal Tissue Suitability Is Seen as Limited: Tissue from Miscarriages and Ectopic Pregnancies Could Rarely Be Used in Therapies, a Study Says*, PHILA. INQUIRER, Jan. 4, 1995, at A2 (reporting only 7 of 1,500 spontaneous abortions produced usable tissue, and only 1 in 10 of induced abortions do so).

136. *See, e.g.*, CLONING AND THE FUTURE OF HUMAN EMBRYO RESEARCH, *supra* note 101; RONALD GREEN, THE HUMAN EMBRYO RESEARCH DEBATES: BIOETHICS IN THE VORTEX OF CONTROVERSY (2001); Sandra Blakeslee, *In Early Experiments, Cells Repair Damaged Brain: Huge Hurdles Remain for Humans to Benefit*, N.Y. TIMES, Nov. 7, 2000, at F1; Gregg Easterbrook, *Medical Evolution: Will* Homo Sapiens *Become Obsolete?*, N. REP., Mar. 1, 1999, at 20; Gena Kolata, *When a Cell Does an Embryo's Work, a Debate Is Born*, N.Y. TIMES, Feb. 9, 1999, at F2; Julian Savluescu, *Why Human Research Cannot Be Locked in a Cell*, SYDNEY (Austral.) MORNING HERALD, Aug. 27, 2001, at 10; Sheryl Guy Stolberg, *Stem Cell Debate in House Has Two Faces, Both Young*, N.Y. TIMES, July 18, 2001, at A1; Timberg, *supra* note 79; Nicholas Wade, *Embryo Cell Research: A Clash of Values*, N.Y. Times, July 2, 1999, at A13; Trefil, *supra* note 102, at 44–46; Nicholas Wade, *Findings Deepen Debate on Using Embryonic Cells*, N.Y. TIMES, Apr. 3, 2001, at F1; Nicholas Wade, *Panel Drafts Rules for Human Embryo Study*, N.Y. TIMES, Apr. 9, 1999, at A20; Nicholas Wade, *Stem-Cell Advances Are Likely to Heighten Ethics Debate*, N.Y. TIMES, Apr. 27, 2000, at A1.

137. *See, e.g.*, Nicholas Wade, *Mouse Cells Are Converted into Specialized Brain Cells*, N.Y. TIMES, July 30, 1999, at A13; Nicholas Wade, *Injection of Cells Aids Mice: Hints of a Way to Treat Diseases like Alzheimer's and M.S.*, N.Y. TIMES, June 8, 1999, at F4; Rick Weiss, *Stem Cell "Master Gene" Found*, WASH. POST, May 30, 2003, at A1. *But see* Rick Weiss, *Clone Study Casts Doubt on Stem Cells: Variations in Mice Raise Human Research Issues*, WASH. POST, July 6, 2001, at A1. *See generally* DANIEL MARSHAK, RICHARD GARDNER, & DAVIE GOTTLIEB, STEM CELL BIOLOGY (2000).

138. *Britain Aims to Ease Cloning Law: Research Has "Potential to Relieve Suffering and Treat Disease," Health Chief Says*, GLOBE & MAIL (Toronto), Aug. 17, 2000, at A9; James Chapman, *Experts Find How to Clone Embryos for "Spare Parts,"* DAILY MAIL (London), Aug. 16, 2000, at 13; David Cracknell, *British Parliament Takes on Cloning*, CHI. SUN-TIMES, Aug. 13, 2000, at 8; M.W. Guzy, *From Dolly to Dilemma*, ST. L. POST-DISPATCH, Jan. 31, 2001, at B7; Jenny Hope, *Scientists Demand the Right to Clone Human Embryos*, DAILY MAIL (London), Nov. 8, 2000, at 30; Beezy Marsh, *Human Embryos Can Be Cloned for Spare Parts*, DAILY MAIL (London), July 31, 2000, at 8; Maureen McTeer, *Why Should We Trust Ottawa with Our Clones?*, GLOBE & MAIL (Toronto), May 9, 2001, at A17; David Montgomery, *Cloning: The Life or Death Dilemma*, THE SCOTSMAN, Dec. 19, 2000, at 10; Emma Ross, *Britain Ponders Human Cloning; Measure Would Expand Types of Research Done on Embryos*, SAN ANTONIO EXPRESS-NEWS, Dec. 20, 2000, at 12A; Sheryl Gay Stolberg, *Scientists Create Scores of Embryos to Harvest Stem Cells*, N.Y. TIMES, July 11, 2001, at A1; Nicholas Wade, *Stem Cell Mixing May Form a Human-Mouse Hybrid*, N.Y. TIMES, Nov. 27, 2002, at A21; Rick Weiss, *British Panel Urges Allowing Human Embryo Cloning; Proposal Would Put Country in Forefront of Stem Cell Research—and at the Center of Controversy*, WASH. POST, Aug. 17, 2000, at A26; Rick Weiss, *Scientists Use Embryos Made Only for Research*, WASH. POST, July 11, 2001, at A1.

139. Rick Weiss, *In Laboratory, Ordinary Cells Are Turned into Eggs*, WASH. POST, May 2, 2002, at A1; Rick Weiss, *Sperm Made from Stem Cells: Development in Mice Raises Issues for Human Reproduction*, WASH. POST, Sept. 16, 2003, at A12.

Despite the controversy, the British Parliament voted to legalize such research late in 2000 by a vote of 366 to 174.[140] Some measure of the divisiveness of the issue is shown by the 76 members of the majority party—the Labour Party—who voted against the measure after Prime Minister Tony Blair authorized a "free vote" on the question.[141] In the United States, President Clinton issued an order authorizing government funding for such research in the United States.[142] The younger President Bush countermanded this order several months after his inauguration, without stilling the debate.[143]

In light of the varied effects of the many procedures already discussed on our attitudes and behaviors, one can only speculate whether the effect of the human genome project will be to enhance our images of fetuses as persons or to reduce the idea of the fetus to a scientifically described lump of protoplasm.[144] Particularly intriguing are the highly debatable claims to explain

---

140. Graeme Wilson, *Scientists Can Clone Human Embryos after Commons Vote,* DAILY MAIL (London), Dec. 20, 2000, at 2. The vote was more lopsided in the generally powerless House of Lords, 212–92. James Chapman & John Deans, *Human Embryo Cloning Gets the Go-Ahead,* DAILY MAIL (London), Jan. 23, 2001, at 1.

141. Wilson, *supra* note 140. A "free vote" is where the majority party authorizes its members to vote their conscience rather than according to the party's position on the issue; a loss for the government on a free vote does not cause the fall of the government.

142. *Clinton Backs Work on Human Embryos,* DAILY MAIL (London), Aug. 24, 2000, at 23;

143. GOD AND THE EMBRYO, *supra* note 102; JANE MAIENSCHEIN, WHOSE VIEW OF LIFE? EMBRYOS, CLONING, AND STEM CELLS (2003); Jane Brody, *Weighing the Rights of the Embryo against Those of the Sick,* N.Y. TIMES, Dec. 18, 2001, at F8; Frank Bruni, *Of Principles and Politics: Decision Helps Define the President's Image,* N.Y. TIMES, Aug. 10, 2001, at A1; Cecil Connolly, *Embryo Cells' Promise Cited in NIH Study: Call for More Research Toughens Bush Choice,* WASH. POST, July 18, 2001, at A1; Nancy Gibbs & Michael Duffy, *"We Must Proceed with Great Care": In a 21st Century Speech on Stem-Cell Funding, Bush Budges and Finds Compromise. Will It Work?,* TIME, Aug. 20, 2001, at 14; Goldstein, *supra* note 102; Judy Keen, *60% Back Bush on Stem-Cell Decision: President Vows Veto of Measures to Go Further,* U.S.A TODAY, Aug. 14, 2001, at 1A; Michael Kinsley, *Kabuki and Stem Cells,* WASH. POST, Oct. 31, 2003, at A25; Gina Kolata, *A Thick Line between Theory and Therapy, as Shown with Mice,* N.Y. TIMES, Dec. 18, 2001, at F3; Richard Lacayo, *How Bush Got There: Months of Debate—and One Lucky Break—Led to the President's Compromise. The Inside Story,* TIME, Aug. 20, 2001, at 17; Jay Lefkowtiz, *The Facts on Stem Cells,* WASH. POST, Oct. 30, 2003, at A23; Erik Parens, *Clear Thinking on Cloning,* WASH. POST, Feb. 1, 2003, at A23; Robert Pear, *Bush Administration Is Split over Stem Cell Research,* N.Y. TIMES, June 13, 2001, at A29; Andrew Pollack, *Use of Cloning to Tailor Treatment Has Big Hurdles, Including Cost,* N.Y. TIMES, Dec. 18, 2001, at F2; Katherine Seelye, *Bush Gives His Backing for Limited Research on Existing Stems Cells: No New Embryo Use: He Plans to Appoint an Ethics Committee to Oversee All Work,* N.Y. TIMES, Aug. 10, 2001, at A1; Sheryl Gay Stolberg, *Controversy Reignites over Stem Cells and Clones,* N.Y. TIMES, Dec. 18, 2001, at F1; Sheryl Gay Stolberg, *U.S. Rule on Stem Cell Studies Lets Researchers Use New Lines,* N.Y. TIMES, Aug. 7, 2002, at A1; Sheryl Gay Stolberg & David Sanger, *Bush Aides Seek Compromise on Embryonic Cell,* N.Y. TIMES, July 4, 2001, at A1; Lindsay Tanner, *AMA Backs Cloning for Research,* PHILA. INQUIRER, June 18, 2003, at A6; Robin Toner, *Conservatives Pressure Bush in Cell Debate,* N.Y. TIMES, July 12, 2001, at A1; Nicholas Wade, *Scientists Divided on Limit of Federal Stem Cell Money,* N.Y. TIMES, Aug. 16, 2001, at A1; Weiss, *supra* note 102. *See also* Colum Lynch, *U.S. Seeks to Extend Ban on Cloning: U.N. Proposal Would End Work Using Human Embryos,* WASH. POST, Feb. 27, 2002, at A8;, N.Y. TIMES, Mar. 27, 2002, at A23; Kevin Sack & Gustav Niebuhr, *After Stem-Cell Rift, Groups Unite for Anti-Abortion Push,* N.Y. TIMES, Sept. 4, 2001, at A1; Rick Weiss, *Cloning Debate Escalates with Appearance by Reeve,* WASH. POST, Mar. 6, 2002, at A2. *See generally* Roger Brownsword, *Bioethics Today, Bioethics Tomorrow: Stem Cell Research and the "Dignitarian Alliance,"* 17 NOTRE DAME J.L. ETHICS & PUB. POL'Y 15 (2003); Christopher Hazuka, *Supporting the Work of Lesser Geniuses: An Argument for Removing Obstructions to Human Embryonic Stem Cell Research,* 57 U. MIAMI L. REV. 157 (2002).

144. *See* Moore v. Board of Regents, 499 U.S. 936 [793 P.2d 479 (Cal. 1990)] (1991); Kenneth Chang, *Incomplete, Project Is Already Paying off,* N.Y. TIMES, June 27, 2000, at F1; Denise Grady, *Baby Spared Mother's Fate by Genetic Tests as Embryo,* N.Y. TIMES, Feb. 27, 2002, at A16; Yuri Verlinsky, *Preimplantation Diagnosis for Early-Onset Alzheimer Disease Caused by V717L,* 287 JAMA 1018 (Feb. 27, 2002); Nicholas Wade, *Genome's Riddle: Few Genes, Much Complexity; Humans Have only about Three Times as Many Genes as the Fly,* N.Y. TIMES, Feb. 13, 2001, at F1; Nicholas Wade, *Now, the Hard Part: Putting the Genome to Work,* N.Y. TIMES, June

27, 2000, at F1; Rick Weiss, *Alzheimer's Gene Screened from Newborn,* WASH. POST, Feb. 27, 2002, at A1; Rick Weiss, *Genome Project Completed: Findings May Alter Humanity's Sense of Itself, Experts Predict,* WASH. POST, Apr. 15, 2003, at A6.

On the Human Genome Project, see Int'l Human Genome Sequencing Consortium, *Initial Sequencing and Analysis of the Human Genome,* 409 NATURE 860 (2001). *See generally* WALTER BODNER & ROBIN MCKIE, THE BOOK OF MAN: THE HUMAN GENOME PROJECT AND THE QUEST TO DISCOVER OUR GENETIC HERITAGE (1995); DESIGNING LIFE? GENETICS, PROCREATION AND ETHICS (Maureen Junker-Kenny ed. 1999); ENGINEERING THE HUMAN GERMLINE: AN EXPLORATION OF THE SCIENCE AND ETHICS OF ALTERING THE GENES WE PASS TO OUR CHILDREN (Gregory Stock & John Campbell eds. 2000); ETHICAL EYE: THE HUMAN GENOME (Jean-François Mattei eds. 2001); FENWICK, *supra* note 24, at 80–111; GENETIC ETHICS: DO THE ENDS JUSTIFY THE GENES? (John Kilner ed. 1997); GERM-LINE INTERVENTION AND OUR RESPONSIBILITIES TO FUTURE GENERATIONS (Emmanuel Agius *et al.* eds. 1998); ELIZABETH FOX KELLER, THE CENTURY OF THE GENE (2000); PHILIP KITCHER, THE LIVES TO COME: THE GENETIC REVOLUTION AND HUMAN POSSIBILITIES (1996); RICHARD LEWONTIN, IT AIN'T NECESSARILY SO: THE DREAM OF THE HUMAN GENOME AND OTHER ILLUSIONS (2000); GLENN MCGHEE, THE PERFECT BABY: A PRAGMATIC APPROACH TO GENETICS (1997); ROBERTSON, *supra* note 48, at 149–72; MARTIN ROTHBLATT, UNZIPPED GENES: TAKING CHARGE OF BABY-MAKING IN THE NEW MILLENNIUM (1997); CARSON STRONG, ETHICS IN REPRODUCTIVE AND PERINATAL MEDICINE: A NEW FRAMEWORK (1997); THE HUMAN GENOME PROJECT AND THE FUTURE OF HEALTH CARE (Thomas Murray, Mark Rothstein, & Robert Murray, jr., eds. 1996); Dan Brock, *The Non-Identity Problem and Genetic Harm,* 9 BIOETHICS 269 (1995); Laura Churchill *et al., Genetic Research as Therapy: Implications of "Gene Therapy" for Informed Consent,* 26 J. LAW & MED. 38 (1998); Cynthia Cohen, *Wrestling with the Future: Should We Test Children for Adult-Onset Genetic Conditions?,* 8 KENNEDY INST. ETHICS J. 111 (1998); Dena Davis, *Genetic Dilemmas and the Child's Right to an Open Future,* 28 RUTGERS L.J. 549 (1997); Jennifer Fitzgerald, *Geneticizing Disability: The Human Genome Project and the Commodification of Self,* 14 ISSUES IN L. & MED. 147 (1998); Philippa Ganon, Tom Guthrie, & Graeme Laurie, *Patents, Morality and DNA: Should There Be Intellectual Property Protection of the Human Genome Project?,* 1 MED. L. INT'L 327 (1995); Glenys Godlovitch, *Moral Questions, Legal Answers, and Biotechnological Advances,* 28 VICTORIA U. WELLINGTON L. REV. 225 (1998); Henry Greely, *The Revolution in Human Genetics: Implications for Human Societies,* 52 S. CAR L. REV. 377 (2001); Elizabeth Hepburn, *Genetic Testing and Early Diagnosis and Intervention: Boon or Burden?,* 22 J. MED. ETHICS 103 (1996); Barbara Jasny & Donald Kennedy, *The Human Genome,* 291 SCIENCE 1153 (2001); Leon Kass, *Triumph or Tragedy? The Moral Meaning of Genetic Technology,* 45 AM. J. JURISPRUDENCE 1 (2000); William Kerr & James Mulé, *Gene Therapy: Current Status and Future Prospects,* 56 J. LEUKOCYTE BIOLOGY 210 (1994); Eric Lander, *Scientific Commentary: The Scientific Foundations and Medical and Social Prospects of the Human Genome Project,* 26 J. LAW & MED. 184 (1998); Jeffrey Leiden, *Gene Therapy—Promise, Pitfalls, and Prognosis,* 333 NEW ENG. J. MED. 871 (1995); M. Therese Lysaught, *Commentary: Reconstructing Genetic Research as Research,* 26 J. LAW & MED. 48 (1998); Sheila McLean, *Genetic Screening of Children: The U.K. Position,*12 J. CONTEMP. HEALTH L & POL'Y 113 (1995); Kathleen Miller & Lynne Marie Kohm, *Designer Babies: Are Test Tubes and Microbes Replacing Romance? Relevant Legal Issues and DNA,* 16 AM. J. FORENSIC MED. & PATHOLOGY 3 (1995); Susan Pauker, *Clinical Commentary: The Challenges of Genetic Medicine to the Patient-Physician Relationship,* 26 J. LAW & MED. 221 (1998); Mary Pelias & Margaret DeAngelis, *The New Genetic Technologies: New Options, New Hope, and New Challenges,* 45 LOY. L. REV. 287 (1999); Hans Reinders, *A Threat to Disabled Persons? On the Genetic Approach to Developmental Disabilities,* BIOETHICS F., Fall 1996, at 3; Eduardo Rodriguez, *The Human Genome Project and Eugenics,* LINACRE Q., May 1998, at 73; Shapiro, *supra* note 52, at 1123–26, 1182–83; Mark Rothstein, *Genetics and the Work Force of the Next Hundred Years,* 3 COLUM. BUS. L. REV. 371 (2000); J.M. Spectar, *The Fruit of the Human Genome Tree: Cautionary Tales about Technology, Investment, and the Heritage of Humankind,* 23 LOY. L.A. INT'L & COMP. L. REV. 1 (2001); Symposium, *Genetic Engineering and the Human Future,* 3 J. LAW & SOC. CHALLENGES 1–16 (1999); Symposium, *Implications of Genetic Mapping,* 3 J. MED. & L. 153–59 (1999); Symposium, *Law and Human Genetics on the Threshold of the New Millennium,* 49 EMORY L.J. 745–49 (2000); Symposium, *Promoting and Managing Genome Innovation,* 7 RISK 197–200 (1996); Julia Walsh, *Reproductive Rights and the Human Genome Project,* 4 S. CAL. REV. L. & WOMEN'S STUD. 145 (1994); Dorothy Wertz, *Society and the Not-so-New Genetics: What Are We Afraid of? Some Future Predictions from a Social Scientist,* 13 J. CONTEMP. HEALTH L. & POL'Y 299 (1997); Doris Teichler Zallen, *Genetic Medicine: Milestones and Myths,* 4 THE LONG TERM VIEW no. 4, at 3 (Fall 1999). There is even a journal devoted to gene therapy: *Human Gene Therapy.* For a cinematic vision of what the new genetics might bring, see *Gattaca* (Columbia Pictures 1997).

One consequence of our new genetic knowledge is the ability largely to resolve doubts regarding paternity—hitherto something that could not be resolved definitively if thrown into doubt. *See* Allen Litovsky & Kirsten Schults, *Scientific Evidence of Paternity: A Survey of State Statutes,* 39 JURIMETRICS 79 (1998).

complex human behaviors through genetic analysis.[145] The complexities of identifying a genetic basis for specific human behaviors are amply demonstrated by certain nasty experiments with pregnant monkeys, where the creation of high stress environments for the monkeys induced high levels of anxiety in the resulting children long after their births.[146] As with the monkeys, the issues raised here are not limited to genetic research on humans, as shown by potentially far reaching research in agricultural genetics or seeking the genetic roots of canine behavior.[147] Indeed, the advances in developing genetically modified foods have become the focal point of a

---

145. PAUL EHRLICH, HUMAN NATURE: GENES, CULTURES AND THE HUMAN PROSPECT (2000); TIMOTHY GOLDSMITH, THE BIOLOGICAL ROOTS OF HUMAN NATURE: FORGING LINKS BETWEEN EVOLUTION AND BEHAVIOR (1991); STEPHEN JAY GOULD, THE MISMEASURE OF MAN (1981); HRDY, *supra* note 13, at 55–78; INTELLIGENCE, GENES, AND SUCCESS (Bernie Devlin *et al.* eds. 1997); JEROME KAGAN, THREE SEDUCTIVE IDEAS (1998); R.C. LEWONTIN, BIOLOGY AS IDEOLOGY: THE DOCTRINE OF DNA (1992); JOHN MEDINA, THE GENETIC INFERNO: INSIDE THE SEVEN DEADLY SINS (2000); ROBERT PLOMIN, NATURE AND NURTURE: AN INTRODUCTION TO HUMAN BEHAVIORAL GENETICS (1990); MATT RIDLEY, THE RED QUEEN: SEX AND THE EVOLUTION OF HUMAN NATURE (1993); LEROY WALTERS & JULIE GAGE PALMER, THE ETHICS OF HUMAN GENE THERAPY (1997); JONATHAN WEINER, TIME, LOVE, MEMORY: A GREAT BIOLOGIST AND HIS QUEST FOR THE ORIGINS OF BEHAVIOR (1999); Sandra Blakeslee, *Researchers Track Down a Gene that May Govern Spatial Abilities: Discovery Constitutes the First Such Link to Human Cognition*, N.Y. TIMES, July 23, 1996, at C3; Kingsley Browne, *Sex and Temperament in Modern Society: A Darwinian View of the Glass Ceiling and the Gender Gap*, 37 ARIZ. L. REV. 971 (1995); Steven Friedland, *The Criminal Law Implications of the Human Genome Project: Reimagining a Genetically Oriented Criminal Justice System*, 86 KY. L.J. 303 (1998); J. Gelernter *et al.*, *Population Studies of Polymorphisms of the Serotonin Transporter Protein Gene*, 88 AM. J. MED. GENETICS 61 (1999); P.S. Greenspan, *Free Will and the Genome Project*, 21 PHILOS. & PUB. AFF. 31 (1993); Gina Grimshaw *et al.*, *Relations between Prenatal Testosterone and Cerebral Lateralization in Children*, 9 NEUROPSYCHOLOGY 68 (1995); Shirley Hill, *Alternative Strategies of Uncovering Genes Contributing to Alcoholism Risk: Unpredictable Findings in a Genetic Wonderland*, 16 ALCOHOL no. 1, at 53 (1998); K.P. Lesch *et al.*, *Association of Anxiety-Related Traits with a Polymorphism in the Serotonin Transmitter Gene Regulatory Region*, 274 SCIENCE 1527 (1996); Bobbi Low, *Human Sex Differences in Behavioral Ecological Perspective*, 16 ANALYSE & KRITIK 38 (1994); June Reinisch *et al.*, *Hormonal Contributions to Sexually Dimorphic Behavioral Development in Humans*, 16 PSYCHONEUROENDOCRINOLOGY 213 (1991); George Rice *et al.*, *Male Homosexuality: Absence of Linkage to Microsatellite Markers at Xq28*, 284 SCIENCE 665 (1999); Nancy Segal, *Behavioral Aspects of Intergenerational Human Cloning: What Twins Tell Us*, 38 JURIMETRICS 57 (1997); Symposium, *Biology and Sexual Aggression*, 39 JURIMETRICS 113–16 (Pt. I), 233–42 (Pt. II) (1999); John Tooby & Leda Cosmides, *On the Universality of Human Nature and the Uniqueness of the Individual: The Role of Genetics and Adaptation*, 58 J. PERSONALITY 17 (1990); Michael Wiederman & Elizabeth Allgeier, *Gender Differences in Mate Selection Criteria: Sociobiological or Socioeconomic Explanation?*, 13 ETHOLOGY & SOCIOBIOLOGY 115 (1992). *See also* Deborah Gentry, *Genetic Technology and Family Conflict*, 18 MEDIATION Q. 5 (2000).

146. *See* A.S. Clarke & M.L. Schneider, *Prenatal Stress Has Long-Term Effects on Behavioral Responses to Stress in Juvenile Rhesus Monkeys*, 26 DEVELOPMENTAL PSYCHOBIOLOGY 293 (1993); M.L. Schneider, *Prenatal Stress Exposure Alters Behavioral Expression under Conditions of Novelty Challenge in Rhesus Monkey Infants*, 25 DEVELOPMENTAL PSYCHOBIOLOGY 529 (1992).

147. *See, e.g.*, NATIONAL RESEARCH COUNCIL, GENETICALLY MODIFIED PEST-PROTECTED PLANTS: SCIENCE AND REGULATION (2001); MAMMALIAN PARENTING: BIOCHEMICAL, NEUROLOGICAL, AND BEHAVIORAL DETERMINANTS (Norman Krasnegor & Robert Bridges eds. 1990). *See also* HRDY, *supra* note 13, at 147–51; Jennifer Brown *et al.*, *A Defect in Nurturing in Mice Lacking the Immediate Early Gene fosB*, 86 CELL 297 (1996); Shannon Brownlee, *Dollars for DNA: Biotech Finally Seems near to Living up to Its Hype*, U.S. NEWS & WORLD REP., May 25, 1998, at 48; Jon Cohen, *Does Nature Drive Nurture?*, 273 SCI. 577 (1996); Barnaby Feder, *Geneticists Arm Corn against Corn Borer but Pest May Still Win*, N.Y. TIMES, July 23, 1996, at C1; Erica Goode, *Building a Better Racehorse, from the Genome up*, N.Y. TIMES, May 8, 2001, at F1; Herbert Jervis, *The Beneficial Aspects of Cloning: A View from the Plant World*, 38 JURIMETRICS 97 (1997); Albert Rosenfeld, *New Breeds Down on the Pharm: Plain Old Barnyard Animals—with Genes from Other Species Added—Are Producing Medicines that Keep People Alive*, SMITHSONIAN MAG., July 1998, at 23; Nicholas Wade, *Animal's Genetic Program Decoded, in a Scientific First*, N.Y. TIMES, Dec. 11, 1998, at A1; Nicholas Wade, *First Sequencing of Cell's DNA Defines Basis of Life*, N.Y. TIMES, Aug. 1, 1995, at C1; Nicholas Wade, *Sequencing the Malaria Protozoan*, N.Y. TIMES, Nov. 10, 1998, at F1; Carol Kaesuk Yoon, *Stalked by Deadly Virus, Papaya Lives to Breed Again*, N.Y. TIMES, July 20, 1999, at F3.

major controversy that has more to do with fear of cultural change and nostalgia for a world that never was than with any realistic appraisal of the risks and potential of the new technology.[148] Yet when even the Amish embrace genetic therapy for their children,[149] we know that thresholds have been crossed over which there can be no return. And once such possibilities arise, containing them within bounds that all would agree are purely therapeutic is likely to be impossible.[150] As biologist Robert Pollack recently told us, the answers we accept to the questions posed by such research "will determine not so much the medicine of the next century as the manner in which we will live with one another."[151]

Do the new found techniques for perfecting our offspring makes it immoral to give birth to less than perfect offspring?[152] This view, a contemporary expression of the eugenics ideal of the early twentieth century,[153] would require us to use amniocentesis, chorionic villius sampling, and other techniques to survey pregnancies and to abort those fetuses who do not measure up to some pre-established ideal.[154] Some obstetricians have refused to do prenatal testing

---

148. *See, e.g.,* Michael Fox, Superpigs and Wondercorn: The Brave New World of Biotechnology and Where It All May Lead (1992); Alan McHughen, Pandora's Picnic Baskett: The Potential and Hazards of Genetically Modified Foods (2000); Jane Rissler & Margaret Mellon, The Ecological Risks of Engineered Crops (1996); Vandana Shiva, Stolen Harvest: The Hijacking of the Global Food Supply (2000); A. Bryan Endres, *"GMO": Genetically Modified Organism or Gigantic Monetary Obligation? The Liability Schemes for GMO Damage in the United States and the European Union,* 22 Loy. L.A. Int'l & Comp. L. Rev. 453 (2000); Symposium, *Genetically Modified Organisms,* 8 NYU Envtl. L.J. 523 (2000); Lisa Tracy, *Does a Genetically Modified Rose Still Smell as Sweet?—Labeling of Genetically Modified Organisms under the Biosafety Protocol,* 6 Buff. Envtl. L.J. 129 (1999); Lara Beth Winn, *Special Labelling Requirements for Genetically Engineered Food: How Sound Are the Analytical Frameworks Used by FDA and Food Producers?,* 54 Food & Drug L.J. 667 (1999). *See generally* Richard Lewontin, *Genes in the Food!,* N.Y. Rev. Books, June 21, 2001, at 81.

149. Denise Grady, *At Gene Therapy's Frontier, the Amish Build a Clinic,* N.Y. Times, June 29, 1999, at F1. For the first steps in the research that led to the Amish story, see Harold Schmeck, *Patient Gets Altered Genes in First Approved Test,* N.Y. Times, May 23, 1989, at C3.

150. *See, e.g.,* James Gorman, *When Fish Fluoresce, Can Teenagers Be Far Behind?,* N.Y. Times, Dec. 2, 2003, at F3.

151. Pollack, *supra* note 48, at 173–77.

152. Hadley, *supra* note 8, at 130–37; Barbara Katz Rothman, The Tentative Pregnancy: Prenatal Diagnosis and the Future of Motherhood (1986); Kathy Rudy, Beyond Pro-Life and Pro-Choice: Moral Diversity in the Abortion Debate 3–21 (1996). *See generally* Embryos, Ethics, and Women's Rights (Elaine Hoffman Baruch, Amadeo D'Adamo, & Joni Seager eds. 1988); The Ethics of Genetics in Human Procreation (Hille Haker ed. 2000); Symposium, *Genes and Disability: Defining Health and the Goals of Medicine,* 30 Fla. St. U.L. Rev. 237–64 (2003). *But see* Kenneth Weaver, *Genetic Screening and the Right Not to Know,* 13 Issues in L. & Med. 243 (1997).

153. *See, e.g.,* Developments in Human Reproduction and Their Eugenic Implications: Proceedings of the Nineteenth Annual Symposium of the Eugenics Society 205 (C. O. Carter ed. 1983); Robert KlarkGraham, The Future of Mankind 69–79 (1981); Hermann Muller, Studies in Genetics 590 (1962); Martin Currie-Cohen, *Current Practices of Artificial Insemination by Donor in the U.S.,* 300 New Eng. J. Med. 585 (1979); Joseph Fletcher, *Ethical Aspects of Genetic Controls,* 285 New Eng. J. Med. 776 (1972); Charles Frankel, *The Specter of Eugenics,* Commentary, Mar. 1974, at 25; Michael Malinowski, *Choosing the Genetic Makeup of Children: Our Eugenics Past—Present, and Future?,* 36 Conn. L. Rev.125, 172–224 (2003); Linus Pauling, *Reflections on the New Biology,* 15 UCLA L. Rev. 267, 269 (1968); Charles Weigel, II, & Stephen Tinkler, *Eugenics and Law's Obligation to Man,* 14 S. Tex. L.J. 361 (1973). *See also* Chapter 11, at notes 21–142. *See generally* Gena Corea, The Mother Machine 20–22 (1985); Troy Duster, Backdoor to Eugenics 112–29 (1990).

154. Hadley, *supra* note 8, at 135–36; Rothman, *supra* note 152, at 4–5; Rudy, *supra* note 152, at 11–14; Eva Alberman *et al., Down's Syndrome: Births and Pregnancy Terminations in 1989 and 1993: Preliminary Findings,* 102 Brit. J. Ostet. & Gynecology 445 (1995); Barbra Paula Bluestone, *How Perfect? A Case for Prenatal Diagnosis,* 63 Mt. Sinai J. Med. 213 (1998); Brock Eide, *"The Least A Parent Can Do": Prenatal Genetic Testing and the Welcome of Our Children,* 13 Ethics & Med. no. 3, at 59 (1997); Philip Farrell, *Cystic Fybrosis Neonatal Screening: A Continuing Dilemma, Especially in North America,* 2 Screening 63 (1993); Josephine Green,

unless the mother agrees to abort a defective fetus *before* the test is performed.[155] After all, as one obstetrician put it, "It's a waste of money if she's not going to act on the information."[156]

Such a policy is problematic. After all, most persons born with serious disabilities still lead rich lives and would never agree that they would have been better off if they had not been born.[157] The notion of "disability" is as much a social construct of dominant groups in society imposed on those in a less favorable position, as is the notion of "gender."[158] Furthermore, most of us carry three to five "defective" genes that will not affect our own lives but could, depending on the luck of the gene draw in future generations, produce serious defects in the future.[159] If we were to abort all fetuses carrying potential defects that could surface in future generations, few children would ever be born.

As is so usual in disputes about reproductive technologies, the claimed need to perfect our offspring set off alarms of resurgent Nazism.[160] Yet such attitudes actually are deeply rooted in western culture, having become dominant early in the nineteenth century when families began

---

*Obstetricians' Views on Prenatal Diagnosis and Termination of Pregnancy: 1980 Compared with 1993,* 102 Brit. J. Obstet. & Gynecology 228 (1995); Neil Holtzman, *What Drives Neonatal Screening Programs?,* 325 New Eng. J. Med. 802 (1991); Abby Lippman, *Prenatal Genetic Screening and Geneticization: Mother Matters for All,* Fetal Diagn. Ther., Apr. 1993, at 175; Michael J. Malinowski, *Coming into Being: Law, Ethics, and Practice of Prenatal Genetic Screening,* 45 Hastings L.J. 1435 (1994); David T. Morris, *Cost Containment and Reproductive Autonomy: Prenatal Genetic Screening and the American Health Security Act of 1993,* 20 Am. J.L. & Med. 295 (1994); Vicki Norton, *Unnatural Selection: Nontherapeutic Preimplantation Genetic Screening and Proposed Regulation,* 41 UCLA L. Rev. 1581 (1994); Hans Reinders, *A Threat to Disabled Persons? On the Genetics Approach to Developmental Disabilities,* Bioethics F., Fall 1996, at 3; John Robertson, *Genetic Selection of Offspring Characteristics,* 76 B.U. L. Rev. 421 (1996); Marsha Sexton, *Disability Rights and Selective Abortion,* in Abortion Wars, *supra* note 13, at 374, 380–83; Lois Shepard, *Protecting Parents' Freedom to Have Children with Genetic Differences,* 1995 U. Ill. L. Rev. 761; Shapiro, *supra* note 52, at 1134–40; Briget Wilcken, *Newborn Screening for Cystic Fibrosis: Its Evolution and a Review of the Current Situation,* 2 Screening 43 (1993).

155. William Ray Arney, Power and the Profession of Obstetrics 183 (1982); Farrell, *supra* note 154, at 113; Barbara Katz Rothman, *Commentary: Women Feel Social and Economic Pressures to Abort Abnormal Fetuses,* 17 Birth 81 (1990).

156. Farrell, *supra* note 154, at 113.

157. For an eloquent statement of this reality, see Harriet McBryde Johnson, *Unspeakable Conversations,* N.Y. Times, Feb. 16, 2003, at section 6 Page 50. *See also* Rudy, *supra* note 152, at 14–15; Allison Davis, *Women with Disabilities: Abortion and Liberation,* 2 Disability, Handicap, & Soc. 275 (1987); Finger, *supra* note 152, at 288; Susan Wendell, *Toward a Feminist Theory of Disability,* 4 Hypatia 104 (1989).

158. *See, e.g.,* Bragdon v. Abbott, 524 U.S. 624 (1998) (holding that asymptomatic HIV makes one "disabled" for purposes of the Americans with Disabilities Act). *See also* Asch, *supra* note 154, at 72–73. *See generally* Ann Marie Girot, Note, *"Disability Status" for Asymptomatic HIV? Pondering the Implications, Unanswered Questions, and Early Application of* Bragdon v. Abbott, 1999 Utah L. Rev. 755; Gary Marchant, *Genetic Susceptibility and Biomarkers in Toxic Injury Litigation,* 41 Jurimetrics 67 (2000); Symposium, *Re-Defining Disability: Legal Protection for Individuals with HIV, Genetic Predispositions to Disease, or Asymptomatic Diseases,* 3 J. Health Care L. & Pol'y 225–37 (2000).

159. Arney, *supra* note 155, at 186.

160. Hadley, *supra* note 8, at 133–34; Leon Kass, Toward a More Natural Science 85 (1985); Rudy, *supra* note 152, at 15–16; Roger Cohen, *Clash on Use of Embryos in Germany Stirs Echos of Nazism,* N.Y. Times, May 30, 2001, at A3; Christiane Henau-Hublet, *Le projet de Convention de Bioéethique du Conseil de l'Europe: L'esprit d'une protection élévée des droits de l'homme,* 9 Tijdscrift voo Gzondheidsrecht/Revue du Droit de Santé 25 (1995); Jon Leffel, *Engineering Life: Defining "Humanity" in a Postmodern Age,* 13 Ethics & Med. no. 3, at 67 (1997); Sheila McLean & Sarah Elliston, *Bioethics, the Council of Europe and the Draft Convention,* 2 Eur. J. Health L. 5 (1995); Larry Palmer, *Genetic Health and Eugenics Precedents: A Voice of Caution,* 30 Fla. St. U.L. Rev. 237 (2003); Estaban Peralta Losilla, *The Council of Europe and Its Work in the Field of Genetics,* 2 Law & Hum. Genetics Rev. 205 (1995); J. Vollman, *Why Does Bioethics Develop Differently in Germany?,* 4 Bull. Eur. Soc'y for Phil. of Me.d & Health Care 13 (1996). *See also* Chapter 9, at notes 317–41.

to have fewer children in order to provide a better start in life for those children who were born into the family.[161] The attitude also corresponds with modern liberal theory acknowledging as members of the community only those who are fully capable of rational participation in the community.[162] It also represents the growing sense that too much is invested in creating a child—several thousand dollars for a routine, natural birth in the United States today, and as much as $50,000 in producing a child through *in vitro* fertilization—to produce a less than perfect child.[163] As such attitudes become more widespread in society, however, the attitudes foster a distancing between mother and child before birth, a distancing that undoubtedly contributes to a growing alienation between parents and their children throughout life.[164] Another consequence of the expense not only of *in vitro* procedures but also of reproductive medicine generally, is the pressure for the early discharge of newborn infants whose expenses are covered by Medicaid— as a means of economizing the cost to the government—with possible, but unproven, adverse health consequences for the infants.[165] And, as ethicist Kathy Rudy, a strong advocate of abortion rights, pointed out, "The way we relate to our fetuses becomes the way we relate to each other."[166]

Thus far, the most immediate impact of the new genetic knowledge has not been along the lines of *Brave New World*,[167] but rather legislation designed to protect "genetic privacy." Such legislation is designed to preclude employers, insurers, or others from gaining access to or discriminating on the basis of, genetic information about specific persons.[168] Judges are only

161. *See generally* Joseph Banks, Victorian Values: Secularism and the Size of Families (1981); Joseph & Olive Banks, Feminism and Family Planning in Victorian England (1964); Joseph Banks, Prosperity and Parenthood: A Study of Family Planning among the Victorian Middle Classes (1954); Mary Ann Mason, From Father's Property to Children's Rights: The History of Custody in the United States (1994); Norman Himes, *The Birth Control Handbills of 1823,* 1927 The Lancet 313. *See also* Linda Gordon, Woman's Body, Woman's Right: A Social History of Birth Control in America 11, 48–49, 72–91, 150–54, 393–94 (1976); Daniel Scott Smith, *Family Limitation, Sexual Conduct, and Domestic Feminism in Victorian America,* 1 Feminist Stud. 40, 130–32 (1973).

162. H. Tristam Englehardt, The Foundation of Bioethics 118, 242 (1986); Rudy, *supra* note 152, at 7–10, 16–19.

163. Rudy, *supra* note 152, at 10–11.

164. *Id.* at 20–21; Rothman, *supra* note 152, at 114.

165. *See* Uma Kotagal *et al., Safety of Early Discharge for Medicaid Newborns,* 282 JAMA 1150 (1999).

166. Rudy, *supra* note 152, at 21.

167. Aldous Huxley, Brave New World (1931). For a more contemporary fictional view of dangers of modern reproductive science, take a look at the film *Gattaca* (Columbia Pictures 1997).

168. Fenwick, *supra* note 24, at 105–11; Genetic Testing and the Use of Information (Clarisa Long ed. 1999); Ruth Hubbard & Elijah Ward, Exploding the Gene Myth: How Genetic Information Is Produced and Manipulated by Scientists, Physicians, Employers, Insurance Companies, Educators, and Law Enforcers (1993); Anita LaFrance Allen, *Genetic Testing, Nature and Trust,* 27 Seton Hall L. Rev. 887 (1997); Lori Andrews, *Public Choices and Private Choices—Legal Regulation of Genetic Testing,* in Justice and the Human Genome Project, *supra* note 144, at 46; Jon Beckwith & Joseph Alper, *Reconsidering Genetic Antidiscrimination Legislation,* 26 J. Law & Med. 205 (1998); Paul Billings *et al., Discrimination as a Result of Genetic Testing,* 50 Am. J. Human Genetics 476 (1992); Elizabeth Cooper, *Testing for Genetic Traits: The Need for a New Legal Doctrine of Informed Consent,* 58 Md. L. Rev. 347 (1999); Gail Geller *et al., Physicians' Attitudes toward Disclosure of Genetic Information to Third Parties,* 21 J. Law, Med. & Ethics 238 (1993); Alexandra Glazier, *Genetic Predispositions, Prophylactic Treatments and Private Health Insurance: Nothing Is Better than a Good Pair of Genes,* 23 Am. J.L. & Med. 45 (1997); Mark Hall, *Insurer's Use of Genetic Information,* 37 Jurimetrics 13 (1996); Alistair Iles, *The Human Genome Project: A Challenge to the Human Rights Framework,* 9 Harv. Hum. Rts. J. 27 (1996); Edward Imwinkelried & D.H. Kaye, *DNA Typing: Emerging and Neglected Issues,* 76 Wash. L. Rev. 413 (2001); Melinda Kaufman, *Genetic Discrimination in the Workplace: An Overview of Existing Protections,* 30 Loy. U. Chi. L.J. 393 (1999); Michelle King, *Physician Duty to Warn a Pa-*

beginning to become aware of the broader challenges posed by the new genetic information.[169]

Finally, into this mix come arguments about the comparative safety of abortion and childbirth for the mother.[170] Few seem to realize that the necessary implication of focusing on a comparison of maternal deaths from abortion to maternal deaths from childbirth as a criterion for the desirability of allowing ready access to abortion is a suggestion that abortion is preferable to childbirth. Dr. Willard Cates has, apparently seriously, described pregnancy as a disease.[171] Dr. Warren Hern caught the same point when he wrote, "abortion is the indicated treatment of choice for pregnancy."[172] Along a similar line, theologian Nancy Rockwell has argued that abor-

---

*tient's Offspring of Hereditary Genetic Defects: Balancing the Patient's Right to Confidentiality against the Family Member's Right to Know,* 4 QUINNIPIAC HEALTH L.J. 1 (2000); Wendy MacKinnon *et al., Predisposition Testing for Late-Onset Disorders in Adults: A Position Paper of the National Society of Genetic Counselors,* 278 JAMA 1217 (1997); Michael Malinowski & Robin Blatt, *Commercialization of Genetic Testing Services: The FDA, Market Forces, and Biological Tarot Cards,* 71 TUL. L. REV. 1211 (1997); Paul Steven Miller, *Genetic Discrimination in the Workplace,* 26 J. LAW & MED. 189 (1998); William Mulholland II & Ami Jaeger, *Genetic Privacy and Discrimination: A Survey of State Legislation,* 39 JURIMETRICS 317 (1999); John Naber & David Johnson, *Mandatory HIV Testing Issues in State Newborn Screening Programs,* 7 J. LAW & HEALTH 55 (1997); Marvin Natowicz *et al., Genetic Discrimination and the Law,* 50 AM. J. HUMAN GENETICS 465 (1992); Susan O'Hara, *The Use of Genetic Testing in the Health Insurance Industry: The Creation of a "Biologic Underclass,"* 22 SW. U. L. REV. 1211 (1993); Andrea Farkas Paternaude, *The Genetic Testing of Children for Cancer Susceptibility: Ethical, Legal, and Social Issues,* 14 BEHAV. SCI. & L. 393 (1996); T.R. Reid, *Britain Moves to Ban Insurance Gene Tests,* WASH. POST, Apr. 30, 2001, at A11; Patricia (Winnie) Roche, Leonard Glantz, & George Annas, *The Genetic Privacy Act: A Proposal for National Legislation,* 37 JURIMETRICS 1 (1996); Eduardo Rodriguez, *Genetic Discrimination and Health Care: Ethical Reflections,* LINACRE Q., Nov. 1996, at 30; Mark Rothstein, *Genetic Privacy and Confidentiality: Why They Are So Hard to Protect,* 26 J. LAW & MED. 198 (1998); Mendel Singer & Randall Cebul, *BRCAI: To Test or Not to Test, That Is the Question,* 7 HEALTH MATRIX 163 (1997); Natalie Anne Stepanik, *Genetic Information and Third Party Access to Information: New Jersey's Pioneering Legislation as a Model for Federal Privacy Protection of Genetic Information,* 47 CATH. U. L. REV. 1105 (1998); Symposium, *Is There a Pink Slip in Your Genes? Genetic Discrimination in Employment and in Health Insurance,* 16 J. LAW & HEALTH 1–64 (2001); William Tarnow, *Genetic and Mental Disorders under the ADA,* 2 DEPAUL J. HEALTH CARE L. 291 (1998).

169. Sandra Blakeslee, *Genetic Questions Are Sending Judges Back to the Classroom,* N.Y. TIMES, July 16, 1996, a C1; Judith Fischer, *Walling Claims in or out: Misappropriation of Human Gametic Material and the Tort of Conversion,* 8 TEX. J. WOMEN & L. 143 (1999); Henry Greely, *The Control of Genetic Research: Involving the "Groups between,"* 33 HOUS. L. REV. 1397 (1997); Mark Hansen, *The Great Detective: DNA Evidence, the Best Police Investigative Tool Since the Advent of Fingerprinting, Also Helps Free the Innocent. As Exonerations Mount, More Are Questioning Their Faith in the Criminal Justice System,* ABA J., Apr. 2001, at 37; Molly Holman & Stephen Munzer, *Intellectual Property Rights in Genes and Gene Fragments: A Registration Solution for Expressed Sequence Tags,* 85 IOWA L. REV. 735 (2000); Lisa Ikemoto, *The Racialization of Genomic Knowledge,* 27 SETON HALL L. REV. 937 (1997); Eric Juengst, *Groups as Gatekeepers to Genomic Research: Conceptually Confusing, Morally Hazardous, and Practically Useless,* 8 KENNEDY INST. ETHICS J. 183 (1998); Maxwell Mehlman, *The Law of Above Averages: Leveling the New Genetic Enhancement Playing Field,* 85 IOWA L. REV. 517 (2000); Gilbert Merritt, *From the Scopes Trial to the Human Genome Project: Where Is Biology Taking the Law?,* 67 U. CIN. L. REV. 365 (1999); Laura Shanner, *The Right to Procreate: When Rights Claims Have Gone Wrong,* 40 McGILL L.J. 823 (1995); Symposium, *Legal Liabilities at the Frontier of Genetic Testing,* 41 JURIMETRICS 1 (Pt. I), 145 (Pt. II) (2001); Dorothy Wertz, *Society and the Not-so-New Genetics: What Are We Afraid of? Some Future Predictions from a Social Scientist,* 13 J. CONTEMP. HEALTH L. & POL'Y 299 (1997).

170. *See* Chapter 10, at notes 9–21; Chapter 15, at notes 18–40. *See also* Eric Lander, *In Wake of Genetic Revolution, Questions about Its Meaning,* N.Y. TIMES, Sept. 12, 2000, at F5.

171. Willard Cates, David Grimes, & Jack Smith, *Abortion as a Treatment for Unwanted Pregnancy: The Number Two Sexually Transmitted Condition,* 12 ADVANCES IN PLANNED PARENTHOOD 115 (No. 3, 1978). *See also* Elizabeth Harman, *Creation Ethics: The Moral Status of Early Fetuses and the Ethics of Abortion,* 28 PHILOS. & PUB. AFF. 310 (2000) (concluding that early abortions are never morally significant and thus never need to be justified, but that the decision to continue a pregnancy is morally significant and therefore requires justification).

172. WARREN HERN, ABORTION PRACTICE 46 (2nd ed. 1990).

tion is not only natural but in fact a holy act while saying almost nothing in favor giving birth.[173] In fact, she included in her argument a quotation from John the Baptist: "Do you think God needs you to make children? God can raise up children from these stones!"[174] Such persons as Hern and Rockwell seem to forget that pregnancy is a natural process and not a medical procedure.[175] No wonder even Kate Michaelman, president of NARAL, admitted in an unguarded moment that "[w]e think abortion is a bad thing."[176]

There is, in fact, a physiological basis for the notion that pregnancy is a disease. Rather than the traditional idea that the relationship between a woman and an embryo she is carrying as one of harmonious mutual support, the embryo (and the fetus) engage in a hormonal struggle over the control of the woman's biological processes to provide a balance between the needs of the two organisms.[177] Yet realizing that a certain measure of conflict between mother and child is inevitable cannot be the end of our inquiry. For as pro-choice anthropologist Sarah Blaffer Hrdy noted, "[i]f we accept that the fetus is a dependent organism that happens also to have its own agenda, at what point in the process of gestation can we honestly declare that the life of an individual has still not begun?"[178]

# The Battle over Names

*Reality is a cliché from which we escape by metaphor.*

—Wallace Stephens[179]

Few supporters of abortion rights have been willing to deal forthrightly with the moral problem posed by the proposed *Partial-Birth Abortion Ban Act,* let alone the problems posed by the emerging new technologies of human reproduction. Feminist legal scholars supporting freedom of choice regarding abortion have seldom conceded that a fetus could ever be an independent being. Law professor Catharine MacKinnon is one of the rare exceptions. MacKinnon summarized the point rather pithily when she observed that "No other body part gets up and walks away on its own eventually."[180] Nonetheless she continues to reject the claim that this reality

---

173. Nancy Rockwell, *Lust and the Love of God,* 13 St. L.U. Pub. L. Rev. 427, 456–60, 465 (1993). *See generally* Brian Clowes, *The Role of Maternal Deaths in the Abortion Debate,* 13 St. L.U. Pub. L. Rev. 327, 365–68 (1993).

174. *Luke* 3:8.

175. Davis, *Part 2, supra* note 42, at 747–48.

176. Jodi Enda, *Abortion-Rights Leaders Changing Both Message and Methods Secure in Their Court Battles, They're Broadening Their Agenda, Altering Their Image. Foes Scoff,* Phila. Inquirer, Dec. 11, 1993, at A1. Kate Michaelman subsequently denied that she made this statement, but the *Inquirer* offered the reporter's tape recording as proof. *See also* Garrow, *supra* note 8, at 738–39; Hadley, *supra* note 8, at 59; Kathleen McDonnell, Not an Easy Choice: A Feminist Reexamines Abortion 28 (1984); Nancy "Ann" Davis, *Morality and Biotechnology,* 65 Cal. L. Rev. 355, 369 (1991).

177. Hrdy, *supra* note 13, at 388–92, 419–26, 431–38, 480–81; Robert Bridges, *The Genetics of Motherhood,* 20 Nature Genetics 108 (1998); David Haig, *Altercations of Generations: Genetic Conflicts of Pregnancy,* 35 Am. J. Reproductive Immunology 226 (1996); David Haig, *Genetic Conflicts of Human Pregnancy,* 68 Q. Rev. Biology 495 (1993); David Haig, *Prenatal Powerplays,* 104 Nat. History 39 (1995).

178. Hrdy, *supra* note 13, at 391.

179. Wallace Stephens, *Adagio,* in Opus Posthumous 168 (Milton Bates ed. 2nd ed. 1989).

180. Catharine MacKinnon, *Reflections on Sex Equality under Law,* 100 Yale L.J. 1281, 1315 (1991).

makes the fetus a "person"[181] — the sort of subtle distinction that gives lawyers a bad name.[182] Instead of attempting to sell that distinction, supporters of abortion rights undertook a calculated program of disinformation to defend the D&X procedure, including lies in testimony before congressional committees about the frequency of, and reasons for, to the procedure.[183] They simply have not attempted to develop any sustained argument that the procedure does not kill a baby, an argument that they usually make for other abortion procedures earlier in pregnancy. Rather, they have preferred to attempt to deflect criticisms of their position through massive resort to euphemisms.

Confucius told us that only by calling things by their right names could we find order in the universe and sustain order in society.[184] While we in the West tend to see this as exaggerated, there is some truth to it. If we cannot face (and name) squarely what it is we are doing, we ought at least to ask whether we are doing something profoundly wrong. And for no medical procedure are there more euphemisms and evasions than for abortion.[185] Resort to euphemisms regarding abortion is hardly new; professional abortionists have indulged in the practice for centuries. Dr. O.C. Turner, writing in 1870, noted this sort of thinking in his observation that "[i]n these days, when theft is called peculation, robbery of public funds financial irregularity, &c., how can we expect to recognize murder that which is called simply 'getting rid' of something, or being 'helped' out of 'trouble?'"[186]

Today we find obstetricians referring to a conceptus as a "baby" when the mother wants the child and as "a product of conception" when the mother does not.[187] Such patterns are pervasive on both sides of the Atlantic. Even Glanville Williams, who figured so prominently in the movement to change the abortion laws in both England and the United States, noted that pregnant women indulge in a less sophisticated form of doublethink: "Women who are happy with their pregnancy think of themselves as carrying a child, while unwilling mothers tend to use the unfriendly word 'it' ('getting rid of it')...."[188] Even a law journal that openly and strongly supports the right to abort has carried a moving account of a miscarriage.[189] The author wrote in very per-

---

181. *Id.* at 1313–17. *See also* Anita Allen, *Tribe's Judicious Feminism (book rev.)*, 44 Stan. L. Rev. 179, 193 (1992); Jean Braucher, *Tribal Conflict over Abortion (book rev.)*, 25 Ga. L. Rev. 595, 600, 615–16 (1991); Mary Dunlap, *Mediating the Abortion Controversy: A Call for Moderation, or for One-Sided Etiquette While the Bombs Keep Flying?*, 30 Wash. L.J. 42, 61 (1990); Cass Sunstein, *Neutrality in Constitutional Law (with Special Reference to Pornography, Abortion, and Surrogacy)*, 92 Colum. L. Rev. 1, 41–42 (1992).

182. For a survey of the numerous ways in which various arguments seek to characterize the moral and legal status of the fetus, as well as whether there is any necessary link between those statuses, see Wieslaw Lang, *The Status of the Human Fetus,* 3 Crim. L.F. 119 (1992).

183. Garrow, *supra* note 8, at 729–30.

184. Confucius, The Analects 3 (ca. 450 BCE) (author's translation): "If names are not correct, then language is not in accord with the truth of things. If language is not in accord with the truth of things, then affairs cannot be carried out successfully."

185. The euphemisms are summarized in Donald Judges, Hard Choices, Lost Voices 4–5 (1993); John Noonan, jr., A Private Choice: Abortion in America in the Seventies 146–62, 168–71 (1979).

186. O.C. Turner, *Criminal Abortion,* Boston Med. & Surgical J., April 21, 1870, at 299.

187. Rosalind Hursthouse, *Virtue Theory and Abortion,* 20 Philos. & Pub. Aff. 223, 237–41 (1991). *See also* Celeste Michelle Condit, Decoding Abortion Rhetoric: Communicating Social Change 128, 131–32 (1990); Davis, Choice, *supra* note 42, at 182–86; Elizabeth Mensch & Alan Freeman, The Politics of Virtue: Is Abortion Debatable? 14–16 (1993); Samuel Calhoun & Andrea Sexton, *Is It Possible to Take Both Fetal Life and Women Seriously? Professor Lawrence Tribe and his Reviewers (book rev.),* 49 Was. & Lee L. Rev. 437, 462–63 (1992); Virginia Riggs, *Regulating Abortion Services,* 302 N. Eng. J. Med. 350 (1980).

188. Glanville Williams, *The Fetus and the "Right to Life,"* 53 Cambridge L.J. 71, 72–73 (1994). On his role in the two pro-abortion movements, see Chapter 13, at notes 27–28, 42–43, 122–40, 149–53, 185–211.

189. Bobbi Carr, *Neither Sound nor Sight,* 3 Yale J.L. & Feminism 153 (1991).

sonal terms of the child as a person ("you"), even though she lost it at eight weeks gestation and derided the doctors who distanced themselves from her "loss of her expectations."

Pro-abortion activists seem to delight in even more distorting euphemisms.[190] Several have called a fetus or embryo a "parasite."[191] The term "spinal animal" is even more startling.[192] Carl Sagan described fetuses as "parasites," "worms," "reptiles," and "pigs" at different stages of development.[193] Other terms favored after an abortion includes the relatively bland terms "tissue,"[194] "waste product,"[195] or "medical waste."[196] Perhaps the most extreme euphemism was a journalist's description of aborted children as "just garbage."[197]

Supporters of abortion rights substitute the bland phrase "termination of pregnancy" for any words that remotely connote what is really happening.[198] As one pro-abortion writer commented, "[t]he difference, of course, could not be in the life forms, but in our attitudes toward them. To be knocked up is not the same as to be blessed, but biologically they are identical events."[199] The political basis of such language is made clear by reflecting on one simple point: Do happily pregnant women say, "I feel my fetus kicking"?[200] Or "Doctor, how is the product of conception doing?"[201] If you are or have been pregnant, did you say such things? Or did you feel the baby kicking and ask the obstetrician how the baby was doing? In fact, even women about to undergo an abortion often refer to the soon-to-be-killed fetus as their "baby."[202] Some women even have "rites of mourning" for their lost "child" after having had an abortion.[203] Indeed, some women consider their embryos frozen in fertility clinics to be their "babies" even though the women in question have no intention of ever bringing those

---

190. *See generally* William Brennan, Dehumanizing the Vulnerable: When Word Games Take Lives (1995).

191. *See, e.g.,* Hern, *supra* note 172, at 346; Rosalind Pollack Petchesky, Abortion and Women's Choice: The State, Sexuality, and Reproductive Freedom 346 (rev. ed. 1990); Carl Sagan & Ann Druyan, *Is It Possible to be Pro-life and Pro-Choice?,* Parade Mag., Apr. 22, 1990, at 6, 8

192. Howard Kibel, *Staff Reactions to Abortion: A Psychiatrist's View,* 39 Obstet. & Gynecology 131 (1972).

193. Sagan & Druyan, *supra* note 191, at 8.

194. *See, e.g.,* Amitai Etzioni, *A Review of the Ethics of Fetal Research,* Soc'y, Mar./Apr. 1976, at 71

195. *See, e.g., Forum: Ethics in Embryo Research,* Harper's Mag., Sept. 1987, at 38 (remarks of Lewis Lapham, then editor of *Harper's*).

196. *See, e.g.,* Nick Themmesch, *Bizarre Case of Abortions Gone Awry,* St. Louis Globe-Dispatch, June 19, 1982, at 5B.

197. Naomi Wade, *Aborted Babies Kept Alive for Bizarre Experiments,* Nat'l Examiner, Aug. 19, 1980, at 20.

198. The choices among "abortion," "miscarriage," and "termination of pregnancy" are discussed briefly in Kerry Petersen, Abortion Regimes 4–5 (1993). *See also* Glanville Williams, The Sanctity of Life and the Criminal Law 147 (1957, reprinted 1972) (describing the avoidance of the term "abortion" because of its unsavory connotations); Naomi Wolf, *Rethinking Our Pro-Choice Rhetoric: Our Bodies, Our Souls,* New Rep., Oct. 16, 1995, at 111.

199. Ann Roiphe, *Moment of Perception,* N.Y. Times, Sept. 19, 1996, at A27. *See also* Eileen McDonagh, Breaking the Abortion Deadlock: From Choice to Consent (1996); Katha Pollitt, Reasonable Creatures: Essays on Women and Feminism 75 (1994).

200. Robert Crumbow, *The Subverting of the Goeduck: Sex and Gender, Which and That, and Other Adventures in the Language of the Law,* 14 U. Puget Sound L. Rev. 755, 772 (1991). *See also* Kerry Jacoby, Souls, Bodies, Spirits: The Drive to Abolish Abortion since 1973, at 119–23 (1998); Donna Greschner, *Abortion and Democracy for Women: A Critique of* Tremblay v. Deigle, 35 McGill L.J.633, 649–50 (1990).

201. Noonan, *supra* note 185, at 154–55.

202. Deborah Hornstra, *A Realistic Approach to Maternal-Fetal Conflict,* 28 Hastings Ctr. Rep. no. 5, at 7, 7–8 (Sept.–Oct. 1998); Carol Joffe, *"Portraits of Three Physicians of Conscience": Abortion before Legalization in the United States,* 2 J. Hist. Sexuality 46, 94, 114 (1991).

203. John Leo, *Taking a Right Turn,* U.S. News & World Rep., Feb. 23, 1998, at 13.

"babies" to term.[204] Yet today, we find a resurgence of the terms "menstrual extraction," and "menstrual regulation," and "postcoital contraception" when what we are talking about is abortion.[205]

Those who rely on such euphemisms strenuously object to those who seek to call abortion by more direct names.[206] One California trial judge even jailed an attorney for contempt of court when he insisted on referring to aborted fetuses as unborn children during a trial of abortion protestors.[207] The judge had ordered the attorney not to use any of the following words or phrases in the presence of the jury:[208]

| | | | |
|---|---|---|---|
| aborticide | deathscort | homicide | murderer |
| abortion | decimation | infanticide | Nazi |
| abortuary | destroy | kill | Nazism |
| assassin | destruction | killers | parricide |
| baby killers | eradication | killing | rescuer |
| bloodbath | execution | killing centers | rights of the unborn |
| bloodletting | extermination | manslaughter | sacrifice |
| butcher | feticide | martyrdom | slaughter |
| butchery | fetus | massacre | slay |
| Cain | fratricide | mass destruction | slaying |
| carnage | genocide | monster | sororicide |
| childslaughter | gorilla | monstrosity | thug |
| cutthroat | Hitler | murder | unborn |
| death mill | holocaust | | |

The trial judge's orders were approved by a United States Court of Appeals for the Ninth Circuit when the attorney, having served his contempt sentence in jail but still facing attorney discipline proceedings before the state bar association, sought *habeas corpus* review of the constitutionality of the contempt citation. One pro-choice commentator describes such actions to suppress un-

---

204. See the text *supra* at notes 89–95.

205. REBECCA CHALKER & CAROL DOWNER, A WOMAN'S BOOK OF CHOICES: ABORTION, MENSTRUAL EXTRACTION, RU 486 (1993); HADLEY, *supra* note 8, at 124–27, 147; Milagros Atienza *et al., Menstrual Extraction,* 121 AM. J. OBSTET. & GYNECOLOGY 490 (1975); Diane Curtis, *Doctored Rights: Menstrual Extraction, Self-Help Gynecological Care, and the Law,* 20 REV. L. & SOC. CHANGE 427 (1994); Ruth Dixon-Mueller, *Innovations in Reproductive Health Care: Menstrual Regulation Policies and Programs in Bangladesh,* 19 STUD. IN FAM. PLAN. 129 (1988); A. Glasier *et al., Mifepristone (RU 486) Compared with High-Dose Estrogen and Progestogen for Emergency Postcoital Contraception,* 327 N. ENG. J. MED. 1041 (1992); D.A. Grimes & R.J. Cook, *Mifepristone (RU 486)—An Abortifacient to Prevent Abortion?,* 327 N. ENG. J. MED. 1088 (1992); Ann Japenga, *The New Abortionists,* IN HEALTH, Nov., 1991, at 51; Gina Kolata, *New Use Is Found for Abortion Pill: Study Says RU486 Is Effective as Morning after Method,* N.Y. TIMES, Oct. 8, 1992, at A1; F.M. Shattuck & N.R.E. Ferdall, *The Role of the Paramedical in Voluntary Male Sterilization and Menstrual Regulation,* 7 COLUM. HUM. RTS. L. REV. 140 (1975).

206. *See, e.g.,* Ellen Goodman, *Irony and Personhood in Florida,* WASH. POST, May 24, 2003, at A31.

207. Zal v. Steppe, 968 F.2d 924 (9th Cir.), *cert. denied,* 506 U.S. 1021 (1992).

208. *Id.* at 925.

pleasant words to be an instance of "mal-intentioned illiteracy" and "willful ignorance," which she went on to tell us is "always strategic" whether puerile or vituperative.[209]

Such euphemisms can backfire. A woman, who had been told that the abortion would produce "tissue," was shocked when she saw that the result was a baby; she was able to sue successfully for the misrepresentation.[210] Even a physician, accustomed to cold, clinical descriptions of human bodies and their parts, became outraged when another physician spoke of the need to remove the remaining "tissue" after the first physician's wife suffered a spontaneous miscarriage. As Dr. Dan Doriani put it, "'That's not tissue, that's my baby,' I thought, I shouted within. 'Why can't he say it!?' 'I'm sorry Mr. and Mrs. Doriani, your baby's dead.' He won't even call it a fetus! Doesn't he know what's happening here?"[211]

A women seeking an abortion does not go to a physician seeking detailed and accurate descriptions of the stage of development of the fetus and what will happen to the fetus during the abortion. In fact, a woman does not even go to her physician if by that we mean a doctor who has and will serve the woman in other contexts.[212] Unless required by law, she usually has no dialogue with any physician before the abortion; she does not even see the physician who will do the abortion until she is on the surgical table. Nor is the abortionist exercising "professional judgment," not having considered any alternatives to the procedure. In such a setting, euphemisms are inevitable.

One need not look far for evidence that the use of euphemisms regarding abortions have untoward consequences in our society regardless of one's attitude toward the procedure. A striking example arises from the administration of the *Social Security Act*. Immediately after the decision in *Roe*, the Department of Health, Education, and Welfare revised its regulations for administering assistance to dependent children of Social Security beneficiaries. For thirty years, the regulations had defined "child" as used in the *Social Security Act* to include both born and unborn children. After *Roe*, the Department decided that the term could only refer to born children, thereby cutting off payments for prenatal care under the *Social Security Act*. This interpretation was, of course, upheld against legal challenge by the same Supreme Court that decided *Roe*.[213]

Consider the phrase "abortion on demand." That phrase originated in the late 1960s among proponents of a freedom to abort as neatly encapsulating their political agenda.[214] Only later did the phrase come to be a term of opprobrium used, without great success, by abortion opponents. Still, most pro-abortion activists now shun the phrase, substituting the phrase "abortion on request" as somehow more neutrally descriptive of their position than "abortion on demand."[215] This is a euphemism that is very hard to distinguish from the discredited earlier slogan.

---

209. Mary Faith Marshall, *Commentary: Mal-Intentioned Illiteracy, Willful Ignorance, and Fetal Protection Laws*, 27 J. LAW, MED. & ETHICS 343, 343 (1999). *See also* KATHRYN ALLEN RABUZZI, MOTHER WITH CHILD: TRANSFORMATION THROUGH CHILDBIRTH 52 (1994) (describing the act of "naming" what happens in an abortion as "painful"); Naomi Wolf, *Pro-Choice* and *Pro-Life*, N.Y. TIMES, Apr. 3, 1997, at A21.

210. Ferrara v. Bernstein, 613 N.E.2d 542 (N.Y. 1993).

211. Dan Doriani, *Reflections on Miscarriage*, PCA MESSENGER, Apr. 1991, at 17, 18. This story is not isolated. *See, e.g.,* Bill Keller, *Charlie's Ghost*, N.Y. TIMES, June 29, 2002, at A15.

212. *See generally* JAMES BURTCHAELL, THE GIVING AND TAKING OF LIFE 247 (1989).

213. Burns v. Alcala, 420 U.S. 575 (1975).

214. *See* VICTORIA GREENWOOD & JACK YOUNG, ABORTION ON DEMAND (1976); BERNARD NATHANSON & RICHARD OSTUNG, ABORTING AMERICA 176–77 (1979); Lucinda Cisler, *Unfinished Business: Birth Control and Women's Liberation*, in SISTERHOOD IS POWERFUL 245, 273–74 (Robin Morgan ed. 1970); Williams, *supra* note 45, at 1584.

215. *See, e.g.,* JUDGES, *supra* note 185, at 41–42; PETERSEN, *supra* note 197, at 6.

# The Supreme Court Again

*[I]n the days when the judges ruled there was a famine in the land.*

—Book of Ruth[216]

For nearly eight years after the Supreme Court decided *Planned Parenthood of Southeastern Pennsylvania v. Casey,*[217] the Court routinely refused to hear appeals from cases challenging the proliferating state abortion regulations.[218] The only exceptions were cases involving clinic protests.[219] Even in most of clinic protest cases, the court refused to allow the appeal.[220] Thus, although President Bill Clinton was able to block federal action to restrict access to abortion, state regulations were gradually limiting that access. Political processes seemed to be working, slowly but inexorably, against abortion rights. Editorialists for the *New York Times* exaggerated slightly, if at all, in writing that "a woman's right to choose is becoming ever more fragile.... [I]ncreasing efforts by state legislatures to hinder abortion rights have taken an enormous toll."[221]

---

216. BOOK OF RUTH 1:1.

217. 505 U.S. 833 (1992).

218. Women's Med. Prof'l Corp. v. Voinovich, 130 F.3d 187 (6th Cir. 1997), *cert. denied,* 523 U.S. 1036 (1998); Planned Parenthood, Sioux Falls Clinic v. Miller, 63 F.3d 1452 (8th Cir. 1995), *cert. denied sub nom.* Janklow v. Planned Parenthood, 517 U.S. 1174 (1996); Barnes v. Mississippi, 992 F.2d 1335 (5th Cir.), *cert. denied,* 506 U.S. 975 (1993); Sojourner T. v. Edwards, 974 F.2d 27 (5th Cir. 1992), *cert. denied,* 507 U.S. 972 (1993); Barnes v. Moore, 970 F.2d 12 (5th Cir.), *cert. denied,* 506 U.S. 1021 (1992); Ada v. Guam Soc'y of Obstet. & Gynecologists, 962 F.2d 1366 (9th Cir.), *cert. denied,* 506 U.S. 1011 (1992); *In re* Initiative Petition No. 349, 838 P.2d 1 (Okla. 1992), *cert. denied,* 506 U.S. 1071 (1993).

219. Schenck v. Pro-Choice Network of W.N.Y., 519 U.S. 357 (1997); Madsen v. Women's Health Ctr., Inc., 512 U.S. 753 (1994); National Org. for Women v. Scheidler, 510 U.S. 249 (1994); Bray v. Alexandria Women's Health Clinic, 506 U.S. 263 (1993); Planned Parenthood of Shasta-Diablo v. Williams, 851 P.2d 774 (Cal. 1993), 873 P.2d 1224 (Cal.), *vacated,* 513 U.S. 956 (1994), 898 P.2d 402 (Cal. 1995), *cert. denied,* 520 U.S. 1133 (1997); Murray v. Lawson, 642 A.2d 338 (N.J.), *vacated,* 513 U.S. 802, *on remand,* 649 A.2d 1253 (N.J. 1994), *cert. denied,* 515 U.S. 1110 (1995).

220. Hoffman v. Hunt, 126 F.3d 575 (4th Cir. 1997), *cert. denied,* 523 U.S. 1136 (1998); United States v. Bird, 124 F.3d 667 (5th Cir. 1997), *cert. denied,* 523 U.S. 1006 (1998); United States v. Lynch, 104 F.3d 357 (2nd Cir. 1996), *cert. denied,* 520 U.S. 1170 (1997); Terry v. Reno, 101 F.3d 1412 (D.C. Cir. 1996), *cert. denied,* 520 U.S. 1264 (1997); United States v. Unterburger, 97 F.3d 1413 (11th Cir. 1996), *cert. denied,* 521 U.S. 1122 (1997); United States v. Soderna, 82 F.3d 1370 (7th Cir.), *cert. denied sub nom.* Hatch v. United States, 519 U.S. 1006 (1996); Habiger v. City of Fargo, 80 F.3d 289 (8th Cir.), *cert. denied,* 519 U.S. 1011 (1996); People v. Operation Rescue National, 80 F.3d 64 (2nd Cir.), *cert. denied sub nom.* Broderick v. United States, 519 U.S. 1011 (1996); Veneklase v. City of Fargo, 78 F.3d 1264 (8th Cir.), *cert. denied,* 519 U.S. 876 (1996); United States v. Dinwiddie, 76 F.3d 913 (8th Cir. 1995), *cert. denied,* 519 U.S. 1043 (1996); United States v. Turner, 44 F.3d 900 (10th Cir.), *cert. denied,* 515 U.S. 1104 (1995); United States v. Terry, 17 F.3d 575 (2nd Cir.), *cert. denied,* 513 U.S. 946 (1994); City of Upper Arlington v. Vittitow, 830 F. Supp. 1077 (S.D. Ohio), *rev'd,* 43 F.3d 1100 (6th Cir.), *cert. denied,* 515 U.S. 1121 (1995); Planned Parenthood of San Mateo Cnty. v. Operation Rescue of Cal., 57 Cal. Rptr. 2d 736 (Ct. App. 1996), *cert. denied sub nom.* Cochran v. Planned Parenthood of San Mateo Cnty., 522 U.S. 811 (1997); City of San Jose v. Superior Court, 38 Cal. Rptr. 2d 205 (Ct. App.), *cert. denied sub nom.* Thompson v. San Jose, 516 U.S. 932 (1995); Feminist Women's Health Ctr. v. Blythe, 22 Cal. Rptr. 2d 184 (Ct. App. 1993), *vacated sub nom.* Realit v. Feminist Women's Health Ctr., 512 U.S. 1249 (1994); Alf v. Florida, 651 So. 2d 691 (Fla.), *cert. denied,* 516 U.S. 813 (1995); Hirsh v. City of Atlanta, 401 S.E.2d 530 (Ga.), *cert. denied,* 502 U.S. 818 (1991); Planned Parenthood League of Mass. v. Blake, 631 N.E.2d 985 (Mass.), *cert. denied,* 513 U.S. 868 (1994); Horizon Health Ctr. v. Felicissimo, 659 A.2d 1387 (N.J. Super.), *cert. denied,* 667 A.2d 191 (N.J. 1995); Lawson v. Murray, 649 A.2d 1253 (N.J. 1994), *cert. denied,* 513 U.S. 802 (1994); Kaplan v. Prolife Action League of Greensboro, 431 S.E.2d 379 (N.C. 1993), *cert. denied sub nom.* Winfield v. Kaplan, 512 U.S. 1253 (1994).

221. *Editorial,* N.Y. TIMES, Oct. 11, 2000, at A-30.

The Court reentered the fray in a big way in 2000 and 2001, deciding four cases related to the abortion controversy. The first two decisions, in 2000, involved abortion directly.[222] The Court followed with two decisions in 2001 that, while not directly involving abortion, involved issues that had figured prominently in the abortion controversy in the previous decade.[223] As inside information regarding the deliberations of the justices has not yet been made public, we can only speculate why a majority of the Court changed direction with the end of the Clinton administration in sight to attempt to resolve some of the most disputed issues that had emerged after *Casey* relating to abortion. Whatever the reasons, a majority in favor of abortion rights emerged composed of Justices Stephen Breyer, Ruth Bader Ginsburg, Sandra Day O'-Connor, David Souter, and John Paul Stevens, and they could pick up a sixth vote for particular cases.

In the first of the cases, *Hill v. Colorado*,[224] the Court did not break new ground. A Colorado statute enacted in 1993 made it unlawful to "knowingly approach" within 8 feet of another person for the purpose of "oral protest, education, or counseling" without that person's consent if the approached person is within 100 feet of any health care facility.[225] Leila Jeanne Hill and two other self-characterized "sidewalk counselors," challenged the law as a violation of their freedom of speech. Colorado admitted virtually all of the plaintiffs' factual allegations, but the Colorado Supreme Court upheld the constitutionality of the statute.[226] The sort of "counseling" that the Colorado courts found so offensive including yelling "you are killing your baby," "flashing bloody fetus signs," and "talking about fetuses and babies being dismembered, [and] arms and legs torn off."[227] In the U.S. Supreme Court, the majority, in an opinion by Justice John Paul Stevens, held that the statute was constitutional, primarily on the grounds that it was not a regulation of speech, but a "regulation of the places where some speech may occur."[228] Stevens also found that the regulations were "narrowly tailored" to serve the important governmental interests in protecting the privacy and safety of persons approaching abortion (and other health) clinics with the least possible intrusion on the speech rights of protesters.[229]

Justices Anthony Kennedy, Antonin Scalia, and Clarence Thomas dissented because the regulations are content-based and because the state was regulating speech in a public place (a street or a sidewalk) more broadly than necessary to protect access to clinics.[230] Indeed, Scalia pointed out that the decision invited bullying, bullhorns and screaming, but ruled out quiet, albeit close-up, counseling, praying, and other peaceful means.[231] Kennedy alone invoked *Planned Parenthood of Southeastern Pennsylvania v. Casey*[232] in *Hill*. Kennedy, one of the troika that wrote the lead opinion in *Casey,* argued that the suppression of speech in *Hill* cut against the core idea of *Casey*—that the state should not take sides in the moral debate over abortion.[233]

---

222. Stenberg v. Cathart, 530 U.S. 914; Hill v. Colorado, 530 U.S. 703 (2000).

223. Ferguson v. City of Charleston, 532 U.S. 67 (2001); Legal Services Corp. v. Velazquez, 531 U.S. 533 (2001).

224. 530 U.S. 703 (2000).

225. Colo. Rev. Stat. § 18-9-122(3) (2003).

226. Hill v. Thomas, 973 P.2d 1246 (Colo. 1999).

227. *Id.*, at 1250–51. That such tragedies do occur, see Jessica Shaver, Gianna: Aborted—and Lived to Tell about It (1995).

228. *Hill v. Colorado,* 530 U.S. at 719. *See also id.,* at 735–41 (Souter, J., with O'Connor, Ginsburg, & Breyer, JJ., concurring).

229. *Id.*, at 725–30.

230. *Id.*, at 741–65 (Scalia, J., with Thomas, J. dissenting), 765–92 (Kennedy, J., dissenting).

231. *Id.*, at 763 (Scalia, J., with Thomas, J., dissenting).

232. 505 U.S. 833 (1992). For analysis of the *Casey* decision, see Chapter 17.

233. *Hill v. Colorado,* 530 U.S. at 791–92 (Kennedy, J., dissenting).

In *Stenberg v. Carhart*,[234] a decision issued on the same day as *Hill v. Colorado*, the Court undertook for the first time to apply its "undue burden" test from *Casey* to a new set of facts. By a 5-4 vote, the Court declared Nebraska's ban on partial-birth abortions to be unconstitutional by imposing an "undue burden" on a woman's decision to abort. Nebraska had enacted the statute by a vote of 99-1 in its unicameral legislature.[235] The statute provided:

> No partial birth abortion shall be performed in this state, unless such procedure is necessary to save the life of the mother whose life is endangered by a physical disorder, physical illness, or physical injury, including a life-endangering physical condition caused by or arising from the pregnancy itself.[236]

The statute defined a "partial birth abortion" as "an abortion procedure in which the person performing the abortion partially delivers vaginally a living unborn child before killing the unborn child and completing the delivery."[237] The section goes on to make clear that for the purposes of this statute, "delivers vaginally" means "deliberately and intentionally delivering into the vagina a living unborn child, or any part thereof…" for the purpose of killing it.[238] The statute made its violation a felony punishable by up to 20 years in prison, a fine of $25,000, and (if the perpetrator is a doctor) automatic revocation of the license to practice medicine.[239]

Leroy Carhart is a physician who operates abortion clinics in Nebraska and Ohio.[240] Reportedly, he is only the physician to do second- and third-term abortions in Nebraska.[241] He is not a certified in any medical specialty related to childbirth or abortion,[242] He had been an Air Force surgeon and emergency medicine specialist for 21 years before retiring to Nebraska.[243] More importantly, Carhart was without admitting privileges at any hospital.[244] He had been personally targeted by protestors, and the barn on his Nebraska farm had been burned by arsonists.[245] He also admitted to performing abortions throughout pregnancy without regard to viability, including the partial-birth procedure that both Nebraska and Ohio prohibited.[246] Carhart challenged the law as including within its broad language not only the D&X (dilation and extraction) procedure, but also the D&E (dilation and evacuation) procedure.[247]

For the D&E, the physician could dismember the unborn child inside the uterus, but with a significant risk of physical injury to the mother. The mother's uterus might be perforated and nearby organs might be cut by the sharp instruments used to vivisect the child, sharp fragments of fetal bone might do the same, and fetal tissue left behind in the uterus might become a source

---

234. 530 U.S. 914 (2000).

235. David Savage, *Bitter Decisions: Justices End Term Angrily in Abortion Rulings on Procedure, Protests*, ABA J., Aug. 2000, at 34.

236. Neb. Rev. Stat. § 28-328(1) (Supp. 2001).

237. *Id.*, § 28-326(9).

238. *Id.*

239. *Id.*, §§ 28-105 (fine and imprisonment for class III felonies), 28-328(2) (defining the crime as a class III felony), 28-328(4) (revocation of the license to practice medicine).

240. *Stenberg*, 530 U.S. at 958 (Kennedy, J., dissenting).

241. Savage, *supra* note 235, at 34.

242. *Stenberg*, 530 U.S. at 958 (Kennedy, J., dissenting).

243. Marie McCullough, *Name on "Partial-Birth" Case Belongs to a Former Area Man*, Phila. Inquirer, June 29, 2000, at A20.

244. *Stenberg*, 530 U.S. at 958 (Kennedy, J., dissenting).

245. McCullough, *supra* note 243.

246. *Stenberg*, 530 U.S. at 958 (Kennedy, J., dissenting). The Ohio statute is found at Ohio Rev. Code Ann. §§ 2919.15 to 2919.17 (Anderson 2002).

247. *Stenberg*, 530 U.S. at 925–26. For descriptions of the two procedures, see Chapter 14, at notes 230–34 (D&E), Chapter 16, at notes 361–69 (D&X). *See also Stenberg*, 530 U.S. at 984–89 (Thomas, J., dissenting).

of infection.[248] To avoid these risks, physicians pull a second trimester fetus into the cervix and dismember the living fetus ("disarticulate it" as Dr. Carhart described it) by pulling against the resistance of the mouth (*os*) of the cervix.[249] In fact, some physicians describe the D&X procedure as an "intact D&E," meaning that the whole (or nearly the whole) of the child is delivered intact through the cervix into the vaginal canal, "collapsing" the skull before it passes through the cervix.[250] Some see the phrase "intact D&E" as a euphemism invented relatively recently to obfuscate the dispute over partial-birth abortions.[251] The statutory language arguably was broad enough to cover both procedures.[252]

Justice Stephen Breyer, writing on behalf of the majority, first concluded that the Nebraska statute was unconstitutional because it did not allow use of the prohibited procedures to protect the "health" of the mother.[253] He was unimpressed by the arguments that alternatives to D&X procedures were available that were safe for the mother, because, in his view, the alternatives were not as safe as the D&X procedure. Justice Kennedy pointed out in dissent that to reach this conclusion Breyer relied on testimony by "experts" all of whom admitted that they had never actually performed a D&X procedure.[254] Kennedy noted that the D&X procedure was not "part of standard medical practice," and argued that this gave their evidence "uncertain reliability."[255] Breyer nonetheless insisted that it was necessary to strike down the Nebraska statute in order to protect the discretion of a physician to select the "best or most appropriate procedure" for protecting the health of a woman when "substantial medical authority" supports the choice.[256]

Breyer then used the potential application of the statute to the D&E procedure to find that the statute imposed and "undue burden" on the mother's choice whether to have an abor-

---

248. WILLIAMS OBSTETRICS 598 (F. Gary Cunningham *et al.* eds., 20th ed. 1997).

249. *Stenberg*, 530 U.S. at 925–26, 958–59. Carhart admitted that he had observed fetal heartbeats via ultrasound even after removing "extensive parts of the fetus." *Id.*, at 959 (Kennedy, J., dissenting).

250. *Id.*, at 927–28, 959–60.

251. *Id.*, at 987 n.5 (Thomas, J., dissenting).

252. The majority treated this broad application as beyond serious dispute. *Id.*, at 942–45. So did abortion rights activists. *See, e.g.*, Philip Hilts, *Doctors Express Relief over Decision; Foes of Abortion Vow to Continue Their Fight*, N.Y. TIMES, June 30, 2000, at A20. The Nebraska Attorney General made an extended argument that the statute's language did not reach D&E procedures. *Id.*, at 940–44. The dissenters in *Sternberg* agreed with the state's Attorney General. *Id.*, at 972–79 (Kennedy, J., dissenting), 984–1005 (Thomas, J., dissenting). *See also* Richard Collin Mangrum, Stenberg v. Carhart: *Poor Interpretivist Analysis, Unreliable Expert Testimony, and the Immorality of the Court's Invalidation of Partial-Birth Abortion Legislation*, 34 CREIGHTON L. REV. 549, 572–78 (2001). Some of the statutes banning partial-birth abortions contained language designed to exempt D&E procedures. *See, e.g.*, KAN. STAT. ANN. §65-6721(b)(2) (2002); MONT. CODE ANN. §50-20-401(3)(c)(ii) (2003); UTAH CODE ANN. §76-7-310.5(1)(a) (2003).

253. *Stenberg*, 530 U.S. at 930–38. *See also id.*, at 947–48 (O'Connor, J., concurring).

254. *Id.*, at 966–67 (Kennedy, J., dissenting).

255. The factual allegations that formed the basis for the majority's claims are rehearsed at greater length in the two district court opinions. Carhart v. Stenberg, 972 F. Supp. 507, 515–30 (D. Neb. 1997) (granting a preliminary injunction), *judgment entered*, 11 F. Supp. 2d 1099, 1102–16, 1122–23 (D. Neb.), *aff'd*, 192 F.3d 857 (8th Cir. 1999), *aff'd*, 530 U.S. 914 (2000). *See also* Mangrum, *supra* note 249, at 550–61, 578–95. In fact, almost no research has been done on the relative safety of D&X or D&E compared to other techniques for abortion in comparable circumstances. Goudy, *supra* note 19, at 227–30; Mangrum, *supra*, at 585–95; Nancy Romer, *The Medical Facts of Partial Birth Abortion*, 3 NEXUS: J. OPIN., Fall 1998, at 57, 58–61.

256. *Stenberg*, 530 U.S. at 932, 938. Justices Ginsburg and Stevens apparently would provide an even stronger endorsement of the physicians' individual discretion to choose the treatment. *Id.*, at 946–47 (Stevens, J., with Ginsburg, J., concurring). Justice O'Connor also supported the exercise of "appropriate medical judgment" to protect the health of the mother. *Id.*, at 951 (O'Connor, J., dissenting). Justice Kennedy pointed out, however, that O'Connor did so in supporting an opinion that validated the practice of a physician (Carhart) who indicated that he used D&X for every patient in every abortion after the 15th week of gestation. *Id.*, at 972 (Kennedy, J., concurring).

tion.[257] Once Breyer concluded that the statute prohibited the D&E procedure, he did not see a need to discuss how this created an *undue* burden on the mother's right to choose.[258] Only Justice Ruth Bader Ginsburg addressed this point, arguing that because the statute would not prevent any abortion but would force recourse to more dangerous methods of abortion, it had to be understood as an effort to chip away at abortion rights rather than as a method to protect fetal life, and as such as an undue burden.[259] Justice Sandra Day O'Connor also concurred separately.[260] O'Connor provided the swing vote who allowed the Court to announce both *Stenberg* and *Boy Scouts of America v. Dale*[261] (upholding the right of the Boy Scouts to exclude homosexuals by a 5-4 vote) on the same day. She undertook to explain how one might draft a partial-birth abortion statute that she would vote to uphold, both by including a clear exclusion of D&E procedures and by including a broad health exception to the prohibition of the statute.[262]

Four Justices—Chief Justice William Rehnquist, and Justices Anthony Kennedy, Antonin Scalia, and Clarence Thomas—each filed separate dissenting opinions. Scalia put in a brief but bitter critique of the undue burden standard, comparing the decision to the decisions in *Korematsu*[263] and *Dred Scott*.[264] He identified the decision in *Stenberg* as yet another instance of bending the rules to accommodate abortion that he saw at work in *Hill in Colorado* as well.[265] Rehnquist simply indicated in a single paragraph his concurrence in the dissents of Kennedy and Thomas.[266] The latter two argued at length that the Nebraska statute in fact did not impose an "undue" burden on a woman's right to choose abortion.[267]

Kennedy was one of the three Justices who made up the "troika" that was decisive in *Planned Parenthood of Southeastern Pennsylvania v. Casey*.[268] That case had established the undue burden test as the controlling constitutional standard for the validity of abortion laws. His purported "defection" from a pro-abortion majority made the decision closer than most observers had expected.[269] Kennedy pointed out that the majority simply ignored the lengthy discussion in the *Casey* plurality opinion of the state's interest in protecting "potential life,"[270] as well as the interests Nebraska advanced in preserving the integrity of the medical profession and in "erecting a barrier to infanticide."[271] Along the same line, Thomas would point out that the majority relied

---

257. *Id.,* at 938–46.

258. *See also id.,* at 948–51 (O'Connor, J., concurring). *See generally* Janeen Berkowitz, Note, Stenberg v. Carhart: *Women Retain Their Right to Choose,* 91 J. CRIM. L. & CRIMINOLOGY 337, 378–83 (2001).

259. *Stenberg,* 530 U.S. at 951–52 (Ginsburg, J., with Stevens, J., concurring).

260. *Id.,* at 947–51 (O'Connor, J., concurring).

261. 530 U.S. 640 (2000).

262. For an argument that O'Connor's proposal was mere window dressing that would preclude any effective statute from being enacted, see Dorinda Bordlee, *Abortion Reform for Now,* WASH. TIMES, July 13, 2000, at A13.

263. Korematsu v. United States, 323 U.S. 214 (1944) (upholding the imprisonment of Japanese-Americans in concentration camps during World War II).

264. Dred Scott v. Sandford, 60 U.S. 393 (1856) (African-Americans cannot be citizens of the United States).

265. *Id.,* at 953–56 (Scalia, J., dissenting).

266. *Id.,* at 952 (Rehnquist, C.J., dissenting).

267. *Id.,* at 956–79 (Kennedy, J., with Rehnquist, C.J., dissenting), 980–1020 (Thomas, J., with Rehnquist, C.J., and Scalia, J., dissenting).

268. 505 U.S. 833 (1992). For analysis of the *Casey* decision, see Chapter 17.

269. Linda Greenhouse, *Court Rules that Governments Can't Outlaw Type of Abortion: A Nebraska Case: 5-4 Vote against a Bar to a Procedure Foes Call Partial Birth,* N.Y. TIMES, June 29, 2000, at A1.

270. *Casey,* 505 U.S. at 872, 876–77.

271. *Stenberg,* 530 U.S. at 960–62. *See also Stenberg,* 530 U.S. at 980–82, 1005–08 (Thomas, J., dissenting) (noting the departure from *Casey's* recognition of the right of a state to protect its interest in "life or potential life," depending on one's point of view). Regarding the state's interest in the integrity of the medical profession, see also *Washington v. Glucksberg,* 521 U.S. 702, 730–34 (1997).

on language from *Thornburgh v. American College of Obstetricians & Gynecologists*[272] in appraising the degree of burden even though the Court's evaluation of the interests at stake in that case had been overruled in *Casey*.[273] Rather than examining the burdens created by the Nebraska and considering whether those burdens were "undue," however, Kennedy chose to focus on the effect of the majority opinion on once again excluding the executive and legislative branches from the abortion controversy in favor of judicial preclusion of even the most symbolic restrictions on abortion.[274] Like Scalia, Kennedy saw the decision as coupled with *Hill v. Colorado* in an attempt to muzzle dissent from the Supreme Court's abortion decisions.[275]

Although Thomas spent the greater part of his dissenting opinion attempting to establish the Nebraska statute covered only the D&X procedure and did not reach the D&E procedure,[276] he went on to consider whether any burden imposed by the statute on a woman's right to choose was "undue." Because he saw the statute as limited to the D&X procedure, a procedure that was rare in Nebraska and elsewhere across the nation, he concluded that any burden imposed by prohibiting the procedure was small and was justified by the significant state interests in the case.[277] Thomas noted that the majority's view that a physician's discretion must be respected unless the state can prove that the prohibited technique is not safer than readily available alternatives was a significant departure from the standard announced in *Casey*.[278] Indeed, Thomas cited testimony supported the conclusion that the D&X procedure actually increased the medical risks to the mother com pared to other methods that could be used.[279] Thomas went on to argue that the majority stretched the notion that state laws must make provision for decisions "necessary" to the health of the woman when they argued that "necessity" arose when there are any comparative health benefits, no matter how small.[280] He concluded that the need for a "health" exception to the partial-birth abortion statutes had not been demonstrated both because such statutes did not create a significant barrier to women obtaining abortions and because the number of women who might be affected were too few to justify striking down the statute "on its face."[281] After all, if a minuscule increase in risk to women or the barring of a rare woman from obtaining an abortion were all that was required to find an undue burden, the Court could not have upheld the regulations (such as mandatory waiting periods) that it approved in *Casey*.[282]

Public responses to *Stenberg* was entirely predictable. The press assumed that the decision in *Stenberg* meant that all state partial-birth abortion bans were unconstitutional,[283] although some of these statutes might in fact be upheld under the undue burden standard as inter-

---

272. 476 U.S. 747 (1986).

273. *Stenberg*, 530 U.S. at 1011 (Thomas, J., dissenting). For the relevant language in *Casey*, see 505 U.S. 882. This was even true for Sandra Day O'Connor, who not only had joined in the troika opinion in *Casey*, but had vociferously dissented in *Thornburgh* on precisely these grounds. *Stenberg*, 530 U.S. at 948–51; *Thornburgh*, 476 U.S. at 828–32. Of course, O'Connor cited neither the majority in *Thornburgh* nor her dissent in that case even while adopting the reasoning of the majority.

274. *Stenberg*, 530 U.S. at 962–79 (Kennedy, J., dissenting).

275. *Id.*, at 978–79.

276. *Id.*, at 984–1005 (Thomas, J., dissenting).

277. *Id.*, at 1005–20.

278. *Id.*, at 1009–11.

279. *Id.*, at 1015–17.

280. *Id.*, at 1012–13.

281. *Id.*, at 1013–20.

282. *Id.*, at 1014. For the relevant part of *Casey*, see 505 U.S. at 881–900.

283. *See, e.g.,* Thomas Fitzgerald & Suzette Parmley, *Doubt Is Cast on N.J. Law: That Ban, Passed in 1997, Got a Conditional Veto from Whitman*, Phila. Inquirer, June 29, 2000, at A20; William Glaberson, *Foes of Abortion Start New Effort after Court Loss: Fight to Ban One Method: Aim Is to Rewrite the Statutes So They Will Pass Muster with the Court*, N.Y. Times, June 30, 2000, at A1; Greenhouse, *supra* note 19; Goudy, *supra* note 19, at 247–59; Marie McCullough, *"Partial Birth" Ban Falls in Neb.*, Phila. Inquirer, June 29, 2000, at A1;

preted by Justice O'Connor.[284] Legislative leaders and anti-abortion activists immediately announced that they would review their laws to assure that they were, or could be made to, conform to the requirements of the *Stenberg* decision.[285] Abortion rights leaders were elated.[286]

Lower federal courts took different views of the effect of the decision on the application of the undue burden test to other abortion restrictions. For example, a federal district court in Delaware struck down that state's 24-hour waiting period requirement because it did not contain an exception for a woman's health.[287] The Court of Appeals for the Tenth Circuit similarly struck down Colorado's parental notification and waiting periods as unconstitutional for lack of an exception for a woman's health.[288] The Court of Appeals for the Seventh Circuit, on the other hand, upheld a statute requiring an 18-hour waiting period because of the lack of any actual proof that it imposed any burden, let alone an undue one, on a woman's choice.[289]

The decision placed the Supreme Court once again at the center of a hotly contested presidential election with talk of appointments to the Supreme Court a staple of the campaign.[290] Governor, soon-to-be President, Bush expressed his disappointment and his willingness to work to overturn the decision.[291] Vice-President Gore, also campaigning for President, praised the Court for upholding "a woman's right to choose," but declined to mention either the Nebraska law or partial-birth abortions.[292] The younger President Bush would later come through on his promise after his election, at least in part, by ending the role of the American Bar Association in screening judicial nominees.[293]

In contrast with the high drama in *Hill v. Colorado* and *Stenberg v. Carhart,* the two decisions in 2001 were only tangentially relevant to the abortion controversy. In both cases, the majority took the view that would be more supportive of abortion rights should either case be cited in litigation directly about abortion. In the first, *Legal Services Corporation v. Velazquez,*[294] the majority declared unconstitutional a law prohibiting attorneys employed by grantees from the Legal Services Corporation from representing clients in cases challenging the constitutionality of welfare laws. Although the case did not directly involve abortion laws, its restrictions seemed remarkably similar to the restrictions upheld on federal-funded pregnancy counseling in *Rust v.*

---

Lisa Rein, *Va. Passes Ban on Type of Abortion: Exception Allowed for Women's Health,* WASH. POST, Mar. 8, 2002, at A1.

284. See the text *supra* at note 262. *See also* Glidewell, *supra* note 19, at 1114–50; Mangrum, *supra* note 252, at 595–609.

285. Glaberson, *supra* note 283; Glidewell, *supra* note 19; Hilts, *supra* note 252; Mandy Joersz, Comment, *Abortion & Birth Control—Right to Abortion & Regulation Thereof: The United State Supreme Court Invalidates a Statute Banning Partial Birth Abortions,* 77 N.D. L. REV. 345, 370–72 (2001).

286. *See, e.g.,* Berkowitz, *supra* note 258; Hilts, *supra* note 252; McCullough, *supra* note 283, at A20. *See also* Melissa De Rosa, Note, *Partial Birth Abortion: Crime of Protected Right?,* 16 ST. JOHN'S J. LEGAL COMMENT. 199 (2002); Jeffrey Van Detta, *Constitutionalizing* Roe, Casey *and* Carhart: *A Legislative Due-Process Anti-Discrimination Principle That Gives Constitutional Content to the "Undue Burden Standard of Review Applied to Abortion Control Legislation,* 10 S. CAL. REV. L. & WOMEN'S STUD. 211 (2001).

287. Planned Parenthood of Del. v. Brady, 250 F. Supp. 2d 405 (D. Del. 2003).

288. Planned Parenthood of the Rocky Mt. Services Corp. v. Owens, 287 F.3d 910 (10th Cir. 2002). *See also* Planned Parenthood of N. New Eng. v. Heed, 296 F. Supp. 2d 59 (D.N.H. 2003), *appeal pending.*

289. Women's Choice-East Side Women's Clinic v. Newman, 305 F.3d 684 (7th Cir. 2002), *cert. denied,* 537 U.S. 1192 (2003). *See also* Summit Med. Ctr. of Ala., Inc. v. Siegelman, 227 F. Supp. 2d 1194 (M.D. Ala. 2002).

290. Greenhouse, *supra* note 269, at A1.

291. Richard Berke, *Contrasting Strategies Reflected in Reactions,* N.Y. TIMES, June 29, 2000, at A26; McCullough, *supra* note 283, at A20; Savage, *supra* note 235, at 34.

292. Berke, *supra* note 291; McCullough, *supra* note 283, at A20; Savage, *supra* note 235, at 34.

293. Terry Carter, *Squeeze Play: Bush Acts to Limit ABA Role in Screening Judicial Nominations,* ABA J., May 2001, at 18. *See also* Chapter 19, at notes 21–25.

294. 531 U.S. 533 (2001).

*Sullivan.*[295] *Rust* had upheld regulations restricting the ability of publicly funded physicians to discuss abortion with their patients. The majority distinguished *Rust* on the grounds that in that case the physicians were speaking on behalf of the government, whereas in *Velasquez* the attorneys were speaking on behalf of a client other than the government. This was a different theory than the theory actually announced in *Rust,* where the majority had held that the government was free to fund activities that it approved of without funding other activities that it did not approve of—as the four dissenters (all of whom had been in the majority in *Rust*) pointed out.[296]

The final case in which the Supreme had an opportunity to involve itself in controversies relating to human reproduction was *Ferguson v. City of Charleston.*[297] In *Ferguson,* the Court held that a routine urine test during prenatal treatment at a maternity clinic in the Medical University of South Carolina—a state facility—was an "unreasonable search" under the Fourth Amendment. The tests were used to determine that the mother was using cocaine. The evidence obtained from the test were used in criminal prosecutions against the women tested. The case was a relatively easy one in terms of Fourth Amendment law, although the majority did feel constrained to distinguish the "special needs" doctrine.[298] That doctrine had been developed in several cases in which the Court had held that a special need to protect the public (for example, drug testing for persons operating public transportation) could justify an otherwise unlawful search.[299] Justice John Paul Stevens, writing for the majority, concluded that the "special needs" theory did not apply because the purpose of the test was to obtain evidence for the police and not for the protection of the mother and child.[300]

Justice Antonin Scalia, joined by Chief Justice William Rehnquist and Justice Clarence Thomas, dissented not on the grounds of special need to protect unborn children, but because they saw the urine samples as having been given voluntarily by women who chose to go to the clinic for prenatal care.[301] The dissenters also argued that the majority was wrong to conclude that the urine tests were solely for use by the police. Rather, Scalia concluded, the tests were primarily for the purposes of devising appropriate treatment regimens for the patients.[302] Remarkably, neither the majority nor the dissent had much to say about the decision, rendered only four months before, that the police could set up random roadblocks to check for illegal drugs.[303]

---

295. 500 U.S. 173 (1991).

296. *Velasquez,* 531 U.S. at 549–63 (Scalia, J., with Rehnquist, C.J., & O'Connor & Thomas, JJ., dissenting).

297. 532 U.S. 67 (2001). *See generally* Brian Bornstein, *Seize This Urine Test: The Implications of* Ferguson v. City of Charleston *for Drug Testing during Pregnancy,* 6 MICH. ST. U. DET. COLL. L. J. MED. & L. 65 (2001); Samantha Weyrauch, *The Fetus and the Drug Addicted Mother: Whose Rights Should Prevail?,* 5 MICH. ST. U. DET. COLL. L. J. MED. & L. 95 (2001).

298. *Ferguson,* 532 U.S. at 75–86.

299. Skinner v. Railway Labor Executives' Ass'n, 489 U.S. 602 (1989). *See also* Vernonia School Dist. 47J v. Acton, 515 U.S. 646 (1995); Treasury Employees v. Von Raab, 489 U.S. 656 (1989).

300. *Ferguson,* 532 U.S. 75–86. Justice Anthony Kennedy concurred in the result but disagreed with the majority's distinction between the ultimate goal (protection of mothers and children) and the "immediate purpose" (obtain evidence for the police) as a basis for distinguishing the two lines of cases. *Id.,* at 86–91 (Kennedy, J., concurring). He argued that the "special needs" cases all involved consensual searches even though pressure was brought to secure the consent; he concluded that the question of consent was not before the Court in *Ferguson.*

301. *Id.,* at 1296–99 (Scalia, J., with Rehnquist, C.J., & Thomas, J., dissenting).

302. *Id.,* at 1299–1302.

303. City of Indianapolis v. Edmond, 531 U.S. 32 (2000) (drug-interdiction check points violate the Fourth Amendment).

# The Struggle in the Lower Courts

*[A] judicious reconsideration of precedent cannot be as threatening to public faith
in the judiciary as continued adherence to a rule unjustified in reason.*

—John Marshall Harlan[304]

Several prosecutions at the turn of the millennium, however, suggested that local government officials were beginning to take a harder line against abortionists. In Florida, Dr. James Pendergraft, who owns five abortion clinics across the state, and his real-estate adviser Michael Spielvogel were indicted for attempting to extort money after he unsuccessfully sued a county commission on grounds that its members had threatened him and one of his clinics.[305] The indictment accused Pendergraft and Spielvogel of lying about the alleged threats in their unsuccessful suit filed in 1998. Pendergraft was a long-time abortion activist who was among the first physicians willing to offer RU-486 when it was approved for general use as an abortifacient.[306] Significantly, the indictment was brought by prosecutors working under the pro-abortion Clinton administration and well before the outcome of the 2000 election.[307]

A representative of Pendergraft alleged that the area was a "hostile environment" for Pendergraft.[308] After all, two of his clinics had been burned during the nine years before the suit that led to the indictment.[309] He had filed an earlier suit against a different county that was settled in his favor in 1996 for $325,000.[310] Predictably, Pendergraft's attorney insisted that the charges were not about extortion, but were "all about abortion."[311] Abortion rights advocates rallied to Pendergraft's defense, alleging that the indictment was an attempt to "chill" abortion rights.[312]

As it turned out, the FBI had taped telephone conversations in which Pendergraft and Spielvogel sought to have the county or others buy their clinic for $1,000,000 and also to obtain

---

304. Moragne v. State Marine Lines, 398 U.S. 375, 405 (1970).

305. Lynne Bumpus-Hooper, *Orlando Abortion Doctor Indicted: James Pendergraft Is Accused of Trying to Extort Money from Marion County,* ORLANDO SENTINAL, June 22, 2000, at D1. The description of Michael Spielvogel as a "real estate adviser" comes from *Extortion Case Delayed,* ORLANDO SENTINAL, Dec. 12, 2000, at D2.

306. Denise-Marie Balona, *Doctors Snub Abortion Pill: Women May Have to Go out of the County to Obtain the Controversial Prescription that Ends Pregnancies,* ORLANDO SENTINAL, Jan. 12, 2001, at 1; Stephanie Erickson, *Drug to End Pregnancies Could Be Scarce in Lake County: Some Area Doctors Don't Feel Comfortable Prescribing the Controversial Drug, Now Approved by the FDA,* ORLANDO SENTINAL, Dec. 14, 2000, at 1; Robyn Soriano, *New Abortion Pill Arrives This Week: However, Only a Few Offices in the Orlando Area Will Have RU-486 Available Immediately,* ORLANDO SENTINAL, Nov. 29, 2000, at A5. On the resistance, both among physicians and among those seeking abortions, to RU-486, see Chapter 16, at notes 368–91.

307. Of course, this did not prevent abortion-rights advocates from attempting to use the prosecution to tar the Bush administration with responsibility for the prosecution as the trial carried over after Bush's inauguration. Patricia Ireland, *Roe v. Wade v. Bush,* S. FLA. SUN-SENTINEL (Ft. Lauderdale), Jan. 22, 2001, at 19A.

308. Bumpus-Hooper, *supra* note 305.

309. Lynne Bumpus-Hooper, *Doctor: "I'm Not a Criminal"; The Lawyer for the Abortion Provider Said the Federal Case Is "All about Abortion,"* ORLANDO SENTINAL, July 7, 2000, at D1.

310. Bumpus-Hooper, *supra* note 305.

311. Bumpus-Hooper, *supra* note 309.

312. John Bacon, *Baltimore Homicides under 300 for First Time in 11 Years,* USA TODAY, Jan. 2, 2001, at 3A; Bumpus-Hooper, *supra* note 305; Pedro Ruz Gutierrez, *Prosecutor: Abortion Doctor Tried to Get Payoff; Jurors Heard Recorded Conversations as Testimony begin in the Federal Extortion-Conspiracy Case,* ORLANDO SENTINAL, Jan. 4, 2001, at D1; Ireland, *supra* note 307.

other millions in settlement of their suit.[313] Pendergraft himself was heard to say, "It's not the building you're getting rid of. For $1 million you get me off your back."[314] The focus of Pendergraft's and Spielvogel's discussions with county officials was all about the income they would lose from not opening the clinic rather than on serving the needs of women.[315] He also boasted that he and Spielvogel would bankrupt the county for opposing his clinic.[316] Pendergraft nonetheless insisted on the stand that his suit was not over money but to gain protection for his clinic.[317]

The two defendants were found guilty on all charges, which had no effect on the insistence of abortion-rights advocates on Pendergraft's innocence.[318] Indeed, he would be given a place of honor at the National Organization for Women's rally for abortion rights in Washington, DC, several months later.[319] Pendergraft's supporters also attempted to introduce race as an issue because Pendergraft is an African-American.[320] Meanwhile, the Florida Board of Medicine indicated that it would have to consider whether the conviction should affect Pendergraft's license to practice medicine.[321] Pendergraft also found himself facing a suit by a woman who claims that an abortion he had botched had left her sterile.[322] A month later, Pendergraft was sentenced to 10 months in prison, plus probation and a fine, while Spielvogel was sentenced to three years and five months in prison, with more probation.[323]

In perhaps an even more portentous cases, Michigan undertook to prosecute Dr. Jose Higuera, a 61-year-old gynecologist, for performing a third-trimester abortion without any medical reason for it.[324] Michigan, like most other states, prohibits the abortion of a viable fetus except to preserve the life or health of the mother.[325] As prosecutor Mark Blumer explained the matter, "A woman went into the doctor's office and wanted an abortion for no good reason. And we have a doctor who was willing to give it. That's why this case is so different."[326] The Michigan Court of Appeals upheld the indictment, allowing the case to go to trial.[327] In the end, the prosecutor agreed to a plea bargain dropping the charge of illegal abortion in exchange for a guilty plea to a lesser offense that entailed the loss of Higuera's license.[328]

The decisive variable would have to remain the attitudes of the public generally regarding abortion. As both sides of the abortion debate were only too quick to insist, public support for one side or the other of the abortion debate—or for particular laws affecting abortion—could not guarantee success. Still those attitudes would remain a key variable as both groups locked in the debate and the political maneuvering struggled for authority and control.

---

313. Ruz Gutierrez, *supra* note 312.

314. Pedro Ruz Gutierrez, *Jury Hears Pitch to Make Deal: "For $1 Million You Get Me off Your Back, Dr. James Pendergraft Said to a Top Marion County Official,* Orlando Sentinal, Jan. 5, 2001, at A1

315. Ruz Gutierrez, *supra* note 314.

316. Ruz Gutierrez, *supra* note 312.

317. Frank Stanfield, *Clinic Needed Protection, Doctor Says; Tapes Did Not Confirm Testimony from the Doctor Charged with Attempted Extortion,* Orlando Sentinal, Jan. 27, 2001, at B3.

318. Frank Stanfield, *Verdict Won't Close Clinics, Doctor Vows,* Orlando Sentinal, Feb. 2, 2001, at A1.

319. Carol Leonnig, *Abortion Rights Are Rally's Cry,* Wash. Post, Apr. 23, 2001, at B1.

320. Stanfield, *supra* note 317.

321. *Id.*

322. *Abortion Doctor Faces Suit,* Orlando Sentinal, Feb. 15, 2001, at D2.

323. *Doctor Gets Prison for Extortion: James Pendergraft, Who Operates Five Abortion Clinics, Also Was Fined $25,000,* Orlando Sentinal, May 25, 2001, at B3.

324. Lisa Collins, *Michigan Charges Doctor over Abortion,* Mil. J. Sentinal, Apr. 18, 2001, at 3A.

325. Mich. Comp. Laws Ann. § 722.901 (West 2002).

326. Collins, *supra* note 324.

327. People v. Higuera, 625 N.W.2d 444 (2001).

328. *Doctor to Lose License over Late Abortion,* Ariz. Rep., May 8, 2001, at A9.

# Chapter 19

# The Beat Goes On[1]

*If nothing is happening, it is fairly easy to predict the future.*

—Kenneth Boulding[2]

Opponents and supporters of abortion rights took to the streets to mark the thirtieth anniversary of the decision in *Roe v. Wade*.[3] Much had changed over the intervening decades, but the basic division between the two sides remained as wide as ever. The struggle over abortion continues, affecting the language, the history, the politics, and the law as well as the lives of women, their mates and offspring, and their physicians.

The advent of the Clinton administration had brought a dramatic turn in the politics of abortion at the national level.[4] Yet the Clinton years did not settle matters, as the Republican dominated Congress locked itself in struggle with the White House over possible limited restrictions on abortion—just at a time that the Supreme Court itself had appeared to back out of the controversy.[5] The nation was deadlocked over the issue, and nothing seemed in the offing that could change this. The election of 2000—the last election of the twentieth century—offered the nation a rather clear choice on the question of abortion. Vice-President Al Gore, having long since shed his posture as an opponent of abortion, presented himself as strongly pro-choice.[6] Governor George W. Bush, on the other hand, presented himself as an opponent of abortion who would not press hard on the issue so long as the nation remained divided.[7] Still, Bush stated clearly that he would take small steps—and if the opportunity arose, large ones as well—to discourage abortion and to move the country away from support for the practice. Yet, if only because of Bush's caution on the issue, the election was a hardly a referendum on abortion.[8]

The election defied all predictions: a virtual tie in the balloting for president and in the make up of both houses of Congress. While it took the intervention of the Supreme Court to decide

---

1. Sonny Bono, *The Beat Goes on* (1965).

2. Kenneth Boulding, *The Fallacy of Trends: On Living with Unpredictability*, 64 Nat'l F., No. 3, at 19, 19 (Summer 1984).

3. *See, e.g.,* Sylvia Moreno, *Both Sides on Abortion Try a Youthful Drumbeat*, Wash. Post, Jan. 22, 2003, at A1; Kate Zernike, *30 Years after* Roe v. Wade, *New Trends but the Old Debate*, N.Y. Times, Jan. 20, 2003, at A1. *See also* Editorial, *The War against Women*, N.Y. Times, Jan. 12, 2003, § 4, at 14.

4. *See* Chapter 17, at notes 8–16.

5. *See* Chapter 17, at notes 129–427; Chapter 18, at notes 3–7.

6. Bill Reel, *Gore Flips and Then Flops on Abortion*, Newsday, June 18, 1999, at A53. On Gore's earlier shift, see Felicity Barringer, *Clinton and Gore Shift on Abortion*, N.Y. Times, July 20, 1992, at A10.

7. Robin Toner, *With Stakes High on Abortion, Bush Is Walking a Careful Line*, N.Y. Times, Oct. 27, 2000, at A1.

8. One observer estimated that Bush had a net gain of 2,500,000 votes over Al Gore on the abortion issue. While this is a small number given the total number of votes cast for each candidate, if the figure is correct its subtraction from the Bush totals would have given the election decisively to Al Gore. *See* Mark Shields, *The Abortion Debate: Life Does Not End at Birth*, Seattle Post-Intelligencer, Feb. 5, 2001, at B3.

the presidential race,[9] the election actually was more decisive than one might have expected given how close it was. For the first time since Lyndon Johnson, the executive, the legislative, and the judicial branches were briefly[10] all in the hands of one party, and that party was the Republicans for the first time since 1930. After the 2002 election, both houses of Congress as well as the White House and the Supreme Court were all in the hands of the Republicans.[11] This outcome potentially could have significant consequences for the abortion controversy, although the margins were so thin in each branch of Congress that one still could not predict with confidence what might happen regarding abortion.[12]

As with President Bill Clinton in the opening days of his administration, President Bush undertook significant steps designed to fulfill his pledge to move the nation slowly away from support for abortion. His most important steps were the appointment of two strongly pro-life men to positions in the cabinet that would play key roles in regard to abortion during the Bush administration — John Ashcroft as Attorney General and Tommy Thompson as Secretary of Health and Human Services. The Ashcroft nomination evoked a storm of controversy that centered precisely on abortion rights.[13] The Thompson nomination did not become so problematic for Bush, although it was Thompson's Department that made what arguably was the first actual move in a campaign to restrict the availability of abortions in the United States — the classification of fetuses as children for purposes of the federally funded Children's Health Insurance Program.[14] President Bush also appointed pro-life physicians to a special FDA panel to review the safety and efficacy of reproductive health drugs, such as RU-486.[15]

On his second full day in office (which was also the twenty-eighth anniversary of *Roe v. Wade*), Bush issued an executive order reversing President Clinton's executive order (also issued on his second full day in office) authorizing funds for foreign non-governmental organizations that do abortions or that advocate liberalized access to abortion.[16] While the expenditure of American funds for

---

9. Bush v. Gore, 531 U.S. 98 (2000).

10. The defection of Senator Jim Jeffers of Vermont from the Republican Party gave control of the Senate to the Democrats even though Jeffers became an independent rather than joining the Democrats. *See* Frank Bruni, *Balance of Power: As Senate Shifts, Bush is Expressing Optimism on Issues,* N.Y. TIMES, June 6, 2001, at A1.

11. Adam Nagourney, *Shift of Power to White House Reshapes Political Landscape,* N.Y. TIMES, Dec. 22, 2002, § 1, at 1.

12. *See, e.g., Affecting Women: The Fight for Reproductive Rights,* 39 TRIAL, Aug. 2003, at 48

13. Frank Bruni & Marc Lacey, *Bush Acts to Halt Overseas Spending Tied to Abortion,* N.Y. TIMES, Jan. 23, 2001, at A1, at A14; Dennis Byrne, *When the Shoe Is on a Democrat's Foot,* CHI. TRIB., Jan. 8, 2001, at 11; Dan Eggen, *Abortion Rights Key in Fight over Ashcroft,* WASH. POST, Jan. 9, 2001, at A1; Derrick Jackson, *What Happened to Bush the Uniter?,* BOS. GLOBE, Jan. 24, 2001, at A15; Robin Toner, *Interest Groups Set for Battle on a Supreme Court Vacancy,* N.Y. TIMES, Apr. 21, 2001, at A1, A10.

14. Jeff Bingaman & Jon Corzine, *Health of the Mother,* N.Y. TIMES, Feb. 7, 2002, at A29; Alan Cooperman & Amy Goldstein, *HHS Proposes Insurance for Fetuses: Opponents Call It a Ploy to Pave Way for Ban on Abortion,* WASH. POST, Feb. 1, 2002, at A1; Ellen Goodman, *Irony and Personhood in Florida,* WASH. POST, May 24, 2003, at A31; Robin Toner, *Administration Plans Care of Fetuses in a Health Plan,* N.Y. TIMES, Feb. 1, 2001, at A23. *See also* Aaron Wagner, Comment, *Texas Two-Step: Serving up Fetal Rights by Side-Stepping* Roe v. Wade *Has Set the Table for Another Showdown on Fetal Personhood in Texas and Beyond,* 32 TEX. TECH. L. REV. 1085 (2001).

Thompson also promised to review the approval of RU-486 by the FDA, but there was in fact little he could do. *See* Sarah Lucek, *Abortion Foes Face Tough Battle against RU-486 Drug,* WALL ST. J., Feb. 12, 2001, at A28; Susan Okie, *Pulling Abortion Pill Would Not Be Difficult: FDA Rules on "Fast-Track" Drugs Could Allow Bush Administration Quick Removal,* WASH. POST, Jan. 28, 2001, at A5; Robert Pear, *Thompson Says He Will Order a New Review of Abortion Drug,* N.Y. TIMES, Jan. 20, 2001, at A17.

15. *Abortion Opponent Is Names to Panel on Women's Health,* WASH. POST, Dec. 31, 2002, at A15.

16. Mike Allen, *Bush Reverses Abortion Aid: U.S. Funds Are Denied to Groups that Promote Procedure Abroad,* WASH. POST, Jan. 23, 2001, at A1; Bruni & Lacey, *supra* note 13. *See also Hearing on U.S. Funding for the U.N. Population Fund: The Effect on Women's Lives Hearing on U.S. Funding for the U.N. Population Fund:*

the doing of abortions has been illegal since 1973,[17] under Clinton and before Ronald Reagan, American family planning funds were given to organizations that did abortions so long as the American funds were not directly used to pay for the abortions. Congress had legislated along the lines of Bush's new executive order,[18] but had allowed Clinton to waive the restriction—which he promptly did.[19] Now no congressional action would be necessary, although Congress would be called upon, unsuccessfully, to overrule the executive order.[20] Critics insisted that by reducing funding to family planning agencies, there would be an increase in unwanted pregnancies and therefore an increase in abortions, whether legal or illegal.[21] This criticism, of course, completely ignores that the experience in the United States that elimination of government funding for abortions was effective in reducing both the number of pregnancies and the number of abortions.[22] It was notable that Bush did not seek to reverse the several other executive orders that Clinton had issued contemporaneously with his abortion funding order that had made abortions available at military facilities worldwide or paid for with federal funds.[23] Bush was taking only small, albeit significant steps.

President Bush's next step regarding abortion was to end the American Bar Association's role in screening judicial candidates, a role it had held for 48 years.[24] While there were more issues than abortion involved the disestablishment of the Association in the judicial selection process, abortion was one of the issues that the Association appeared to have taken strongly into account in evaluating judicial nominees. The Association was now so one-sided on the issue that when a resolution was introduced by petition in 2000 to amend the Association's constitution to commit the association "defend the right to life of all innocent human beings, including all those con-

---

*The Effect on Women's Lives, before* Subcomm. on Int'l Operations & Terrorism, Sen. Comm. On For. Relations, 107th Cong., 2nd Sess., Feb. 27, 2002; Nicholas Kristof, *Killing Them Softly,* N.Y. Times, Sept. 20, 2003, at A13; Colum Lynch & Juliet Eilperin, *Family Planning Funds Withheld: Administration Decides Not to Contribute to U.N. Effort,* Wash. Post, July 20, 2002, at A4; *U.S. Aid Cut off to Groups Backing Abortion,* Wash. Post, Aug. 30, 2003, at A26; *U.S. May Abandon Support of U.N. Population Accord,* N.Y. Times, Nov. 2, 2002, at A8. Efforts by the Bush Administration to get an Asian regional meeting on population to repudicate abortion were rejected. James Dao, *At U.N. Family-Planning Talks, U.S. Raises Abortion,* N.Y. Times, Dec. 15, 2002, § 1, at 4; James Dao, *Over U.S. Protest, Asian Group Approves Family Planning Goals,* N.Y. Times, Dec. 18, 2002, at A7. The Bush administration also pressed unsuccessfully for the UN General Assembly Special Session on Children to repudiate abortion counseling and services. *See* Somini Sengupta, *U.N. Forum Stalls on Sex Education and Abortion Rights,* N.Y. Times, May 10, 2003, at A3; Alan Sipress, *U.S. Draws Abortion Line at U.N.,* Wash. Post, Aug. 28, 2001, at A1.

17. 42 U.S.C. § 300a-6 (2000).

18. Juliet Eilperin, *House Blocks Family Planning Funds,* Wash. Post, July 16, 2003, at A2.

19. Steven Holmes, *Republicans Agree on Abortion Deal to Advance Budget,* N.Y. Times, Oct. 25, 2000, at A1.

20. Juliet Eilperin, *House Blocks Family Planning Funds,* Wash. Post, July 16, 2003, at A2.

21. Karen DeYoung, *Abortion Aid Ban's Global Impact Debated,* Wash. Post, Jan. 26, 2001, at A2.

22. Stanley Henshaw & Lynn Wallisch, *The Medicaid Cutoff and Abortion Services for the Poor,* 16 Fam. Planning Persp. 170 (1984). *See* Chapter 15, at notes 137–41.

23. Admin. Order, *Privately Funded Abortion at Military Hospitals,* 3 CFR 722 (1993); Admin. Order, *The Title X "Gag Rule,"* 3 CFR 723 (1993). *See also* David Garrow, Liberty and Sexuality: The Right of Privacy and the Making of *Roe v. Wade* 702 (2nd ed. 1998); James Bennet, *Abortion-Rights Backers Win High-Level Support,* N.Y. Times, Jan. 23, 1997, at A14; C. Lewis Borders, Note, *Rape and Incest Abortion Funding under Medicaid—Can the Federal Government Force Unwilling States to Pick up the Tab?,* 35 J. Fam. L. 121 (1996); Ann Devroy, *Clinton Cancels Abortion Restrictions of Reagan-Bush Era,* Wash. Post, Jan. 23, 1993, at A1; Robin Toner, *Anti-Abortion Movement Prepares to Battle Clinton,* N.Y. Times, Jan. 22, 1993, at A1. *See generally* Janet Hadley, Abortion: Between Freedom and Necessity 11–17 (1996).

24. Terry Carter, *Squeeze Play: Bush Acts to Limit ABA Role in Screening Judicial Nominations,* ABA J., May 2001, at 18. *See also* Martha Barnett, *A Special Report to ABA Members,* ABA J., May 2001, at SR1; James Lindgren, *Examining the American Bar Association's Ratings of Nominees to the U.S. Courts of Appeals for Political Bias, 1989–2000,* 17 J. Law & Pol. 1 (2001); Neil Vidmar & Michael Saks, *A Flawed Search for Bias in the American Bar Association's Ratings of Judicial Nominees: A Critique of the Lindgren/Federalist Society Study,* 17 J. Law & Pol. 219 (2001).

ceived but not yet born," the resolution failed because not a single member of the 540-member House of Delegates was willing to speak in favor of the resolution.[25] The Association announced that it would continue its evaluation process and would make its results available to the individual members of the Senate Judiciary Committee.[26] Although some expressed fears that the screening process for candidates after their nomination had been announced would encounter a lack of candor that arguably was not characteristic of the established pre-nomination screening process,[27] the Democrats on the Judiciary Committee (who would take control of the Committee as the majority party from July 2001 to January 2003) announced that they would not proceed on any nomination before receiving the Association's report.[28] None of this prevented courts from continuing to make decisions supportive of abortion rights.[29]

With many expecting that soon vacancies would need to be filled on the Supreme Court, and with many unfilled vacancies on lower federal courts left over from the Clinton administration, the stage was set for the younger Bush to have a profound impact on the judiciary. While the prospect was gratifying to conservatives, it was alarming to liberals in general and to abortion rights supporters in particular.[30] Given the overall pattern of Bush's actions regarding abortion, they concluded that he was "deeply, and cleverly, hostile to abortion."[31] But the younger President Bush encountered stiff, and successful, Democratic resistance in the Senate to confirming his nominations if they were too clearly hostile to abortion rights—even after the Republicans obtained a majority in the Senate in the 2002 elections.[32] Among other things, the Democrats set

---

25. *Policy and Activity Roundup: ABA 2000 Annual Meeting,* ABA WATCH, Feb. 2001, at 8.

26. Barnett, *supra* note 24, at SR1.

27. Carter, *supra* note 24, at 18.

28. *Id.* Thanks to the Supreme Court decision in *Minnesota v. White,* 536 U.S. 765 (2002), judges running for election to positions on state courts have had to declare their position on issues that might come before the court, including regarding abortion. *See, e.g.,* Molly McDonough, *Judges Opine on the Issues: Debate May Be Future of Judicial Campaigns,* 2 ABA JOURNAL REPORT, May 23, 2003, at 20.

29. *See, e.g.,* Planned Parenthood of Central N.J. v. Attorney-Gen., 297 F.3d 253 (3rd Cir. 2002) (awarding attorneys fees against a state legislature that intervened in a case to defend the constitutionality of an abortion statute); Britell v. United States, 204 F. Supp. 2d 182 (D. Mass. 2002) (the military policy against paying for abortions other than those that threaten the mother's life violates due process when applied to a woman who decides to abort an anencephalic fetus). *See also Abortion Not to Be "Vetoed," Pa. Judge Rules,* WASH. POST, Aug. 6, 2003, at A2 (reporting a Pennsylvania Common Please judge's refusal to allow a man to block his girlfriend's abortion).

30. Helen Dewar, *Bush's Use of Clout Intensifies Senate Split: GOP's Boldness Riles Democrats Who Think President Uses Hill as Rubber Stamp,* WASH. POST, Mar. 2, 2003, at A4; Stephen Gillers, *Make a List,* N.Y. TIMES, June 11, 2003, at A31; David Schkade & Cass Sunstein, *Judging by Where You Sit,* N.Y. TIMES, June 11, 2003, at A31; Toner, *supra* note 7; Robin Toner & Neil Lewis, *Lobbying Starts as Groups Foresee Supreme Court Vacancy,* N.Y. TIMES, June 8, 2003, § 1, at 1.

31. Carol Joffe, *Bush's Antichoice Assault,* THE NATION, May 28, 2001, at 5.

32. *See, e.g.,* Mike Allen, *Judicial Nominee Admits Mistake,* WASH. POST, June 12, 2003, at A37; Mike Allen & Charles Lane, *President Renominates Miss. Judge, 29 Others,* WASH. POST, Jan. 8, 2003, at A1; Helen Dewar, *Battle over Judges Continues: Michigan Senators Object to Four Nominees for Appeals Court,* WASH. POST, July 31, 2003, at A17; Helen Dewar, *Bush Calls for Limit to Senate Debates: Proposal Prompted by Month-Long Filibuster Blocking Estrada Nomination,* WASH. POST, Mar. 12, 2003, at A4; Helen Dewar, *Estrada Abandons Court Bid,* WASH. POST, Sept. 5, 2003, at A1; Helen Dewar, *GOP Presses for Votes on Judges,* WASH. POST, July 30, 2003, at A4; Helen Dewar, *Senate Democrats Block Bush Court Pick: Pickering Is Fourth Nominee to Be Rejected for Federal Judiciary This Year,* WASH. POST, Oct. 31, 2003, at A23; Helen Dewar, *Senate Panel Rejects Bush Court Nominee,* WASH. POST, Sept. 6, 2002, at A1; Helen Dewar **Bush, Daschle Trade Charges; Senate's Talkathon on Judicial Nominees Exceeds 30 Hours,** WASH. POST, Nov. 14, 2003, at A6; David Firestone, *Frist Forsakes Deal Making to Focus on Party Principles,* N.Y. TIMES, Mar. 13, 2003, at A1; Alberto Gonzales, *Double Standard Filibuster,* WASH. POST, June 2, 2003, at A17; Charles Lane, *Judicial Nominee Challenged on Abortion Views,* WASH. POST, July 24, 2002, at A4; Neil Lewis, *Bitter Senators Divided Anew on Judgeships,* N.Y. TIMES, Nov. 15, 2003, at A1; Neil Lewis, *Democrats Reject Bush Pick in Battle over Court Balance,* N.Y. TIMES, Sept. 6, 2002, at A1; Neil Lewis, *Stymied by Democrats in Senate, Bush Court Pick Gives up,* N.Y. TIMES, Sept. 5, 2002, at A1;

about to inquire more deeply into nominee's personal beliefs and history than has been custom-ary in the judicial nomination process.[33] This prompted charges that Democratic Senators—even Catholic Democratic Senators—were blocking nominations because the candidates were Catholic,[34] although presumably the Democrats would have supported a pro-choice Catholic.

Congressional Republicans (and anti-abortion Democrats, which is not the oxymoron that some in the press and the national party leadership seem to believe it is[35]) were not so cautious as President Bush. They proposed once again to enact a ban on partial-birth abortions,[36] despite the Supreme Court's decision the year before that such statutes would be unconstitutional unless drafted in such a way as to make them almost meaningless.[37] Congressional Republicans also seized upon a bill that would make it a crime to injure a fetus by attacks upon a pregnant woman—the *Unborn Victims of Violence Act*.[38] They also proposed to make it a crime to kill an abortus if it happened to be fully born alive (the *Born-Alive Infants Protection Act*),[39] for anyone except a parent to transport a teenager across a state line to obtain an abortion (the *Child Cus-tody Protection Act*),[40] and to restrict access to the recently approved abortion pill (the *RU-486 Patient Health and Safety Protection Act*).[41] There was even a proposal to provide federal funds to "crisis pregnancy centers" (centers to provide women who were experiencing a "crisis preg-nancy" with alternatives to abortion) to enable them to obtain ultrasound machines to provide images of unborn children to mothers who were contemplating abortion.[42] Given the closeness of division in the Congress (particularly the Senate), however, none of these would pass the 107th Congress (2001–02). With Republican majorities in both houses of Congress in 2003, the anti-abortion groups expected finally to enact some or all of these bills.[43]

Michael Stokes Paulsen, a leading anti-abortion theoretician, even proposed that Congress simply overrule *Roe v. Wade*[44] and *Planned Parenthood of Southeastern Pennsylvania v. Casey*[45] by

---

Molly McDonough, *Showdown over the Bench: Bush Is Dealing with Some Determined Opposition over His Fed-eral Court Nominees,* ABA J., Apr. 2002, at 22.

33. *See, e.g.,* Gonzales, *supra* note 32; Benjamin Wittes, *Silence Is Honorable,* WASH. POST, Feb. 25, 2003, at A23.

34. Helen Dewar, *Appeals Court Nominee Again Blocked: Senate Action Renews Angry Exchanges over Charges of Anti-Catholic Bias,* WASH. POST, Aug. 1, 2003, at A2; Helen Dewar, *In New Ads, Judicial Battle Is a Matter of Faith,* WASH. POST, July 22, 2003, at A3; Jonah Goldberg, *Should Judges Be Disqualified if Their Reli-gious Beliefs Impact Their Votes?,* PHILA. INQUIRER, Aug. 13, 2003, at A22.

35. *See, e.g.,* Jeb Byrne, *Life and My Party,* WASH. POST, Dec. 31, 2002, at A12.

36. Juliet Eilperin, *House GOP Pushes New Abortion Limits,* WASH. POST, Mar. 16, 2001, at A1.

37. Stenberg v. Carhart, 530 U.S. 914 (2000). *See* Chapter 18, at notes 227–82.

38. Eilperin, *supra* note 36. *See also* Julie Rovner, *Congress Considers Bill to Protect Fetuses,* THE LANCET, Sept. 25, 1999, at 1105. *See generally* Colleen Jolicoeur-Wonnacott, Comment, *The Unborn Victims of Violence Act: Friend or Foe to the Unborn?,* 17 THOS. COOLEY L. REV. 563 (2000); Jeffrey Rosen, *A Viable Solution: Why It Makes Sense to Permit Abortions and Punish Those Who Kill Fetuses,* LEGAL AFF., Sept./Oct. 2003, at 20; Rick Santorum & Zoe Lofgren, *Debating the Unborn Victims of Violence Act,* PHILA. INQUIRER, June 8, 2003, at C5; Mamta Shah, Note, *Inconsistencies in the Legal Status of an Unborn Child: Recognition of a Fetus as Potential Life,* 29 HOFSTRA L. REV. 931 (2001). Several states have already enacted such statutes. *See, e.g.,* FLA. STAT. §§ 782.34, 784.045 (West 2000).

39. *See Hearing on H.R. 4292 before the Subcommittee on the Constitution of the Committee on the Judiciary of the House of Representatives,* 106th Congress, 2nd Sess., July 20, 2000.

40. Jesse Holland, *House Tries Again on Abortion Consent,* PHILA. INQUIRER, Apr. 18, 2002, at A7.

41. Eilperin, *supra* note 36. On the approval of the abortion pill, see Chapter 16, at notes 372–95.

42. David Crary, *Abortion Foes Aim to Use Ultrasound as a Deterrent,* PHILA. INQUIRER, Feb. 2, 2002, at A5. *See also* Alan Cooperman & Amy Goldstein, *Rove to Group: Bush to Press for Conservative Judiciary,* WASH. POST, Mar. 20, 2002, at A9.

43. *See* Robin Toner, *Foes of Abortion Push for Major Bills in Congress,* N.Y. TIMES, Jan. 2, 2003, at A1.

44. 410 U.S. 113 (1973).

45. 505 U.S. 833 (1992).

statute on the basis that the rule of *stare decisis* is a rule of policy and not a constitutional command.[46] Given the Court's strong reaction to the *Religious Freedom Restoration Act*,[47] such a bold measure was unlikely to succeed. Even Paulsen expressed some doubt that Congress would do anything so bold.[48] Yet the *Partial-Birth Abortion Ban Act*, depending on how it was phrased, could in fact pose just that sort of challenge to the Court.

The first proposal to reach a vote, the *Unborn Victims of Violence Act*, passed the House of Representatives easily on April 26, 2001, by a vote of 252 to 172 (including the positive votes of 53 Democrats).[49] Supporters of abortion rights were outraged.[50] Prospects for the bill in the Senate, however, were not clear; one year before, faced with the prospect of a veto by President Clinton, a nearly identical bill never came to a vote in that body.[51] Even without the possibility of a veto, opponents in the Senate continued to block a vote on it for at least two years.[52] Despite the problems getting this bill passed, the anti-abortion groups did succeed in enacting the *Born-Alive Infants Protection Act* in 2002, the principal effect of which was to define as born any child who upon birth breathes, has a beating heart, pulsation of the umbilical cord, or definite movement of voluntary muscles, regardless of whether the umbilical cord had been cut or whether the birth was natural or induced.[53]

Congressional Republicans also injected abortion into numerous other issues, including some that one might not have expected to have any relation to abortion. Congress delayed funding for the international campaign against AIDS while debating whether the funds must be steered away from clinics that also perform abortions.[54] Congress also failed to enact a bankruptcy reform bill because it included a provision barring abortion protestors from discharging judgments against them through declaring bankruptcy.[55] While there were other reasons bankruptcy reform was controversial, the margin for the defeat was provided by Congressmen opposed to abortion.

Encouraged by the change at the highest levels of government, anti-abortion protesters decided to take to the streets in an attempt to shut down Dr. George Tiller's clinic in Wichita, Kansas.[56] Tiller's clinic was one of the few nationally to perform third-trimester abortions,[57] leading significant numbers of women to travel from other states to obtain abortions that could not be obtained locally.[58] Tiller and his clinic had been targeted before. During the "Summer of

---

46. Michael Stokes Paulsen, *Abrogating* Stare Decisis *by Statute: May Congress Remove the Precedential Effect of* Roe *and* Casey?, 109 YALE L.J. 1535 (2000).

47. *See* City of Boerne v. Flores, 521 U.S. 507 (1997).

48. Paulsen, *supra* note 46, at 1599–1601.

49. Juliet Eilperin, *Unborn Victims Act Wins in House; Foes Call It an Attack on Abortion Rights*, WASH. POST, Apr. 27, 2001, at A1; Alison Mitchell, *House Approves Bill Criminalizing Violence to Fetus*, N.Y. TIMES, Apr. 27, 2001, at A1.

50. Eilperin, *supra* note 49; Mitchell, *supra* note 49.

51. Eilperin, *supra* note 49.

52. *See, e.g.*, Santorum & Lofgren, *supra* note 38.

53. 1 U.S.C. §8. *See also* Mike Allen, *President Signs Bill on Abortion Procedures: Move on Pa. Visit Reopens Debate*, WASH. POST, Aug. 6, 2002, at A3.

54. Sheryl Gay Stolberg, *Politics of Abortion Delays $15 Billion to Fight Global AIDS*, N.Y. TIMES, Mar. 6, 2003, at A22.

55. Philip Shenon, *Abortion Issue Holds up Bill on Bankruptcy*, N.Y. TIMES, Apr. 30, 2002, at A1; Philip Shenon, *Ant-Abortion Lawmakers Kill House Bankruptcy Bill*, N.Y. TIMES, Nov. 15, 2002, at A28; Jim VandeHei & Kathleen Day, *With Bankruptcy Bill, A Surprise Show of Force: GOP Abortion Foes Object to Provision, Block Law*, WASH. POST, Nov. 16, 2002, at A2.

56. William Claiborne, *A Decade Later, Abortion Foes Again Gather in Wichita: City Has Changed since Protests of '91*, WASH. POST, July 16, 2001, at A3; Tim Jones, *Abortion Battle Back in Wichita, Kansas; City Tries to Avoid Repeat of 1991 Melee*, CHI. TRIB., July 17, 2001, at 9.

57. JAMES RISEN & JUDY THOMAS, WRATH OF ANGELS: THE AMERICAN ABORTION WAR 320–23 (1998).

58. Claiborne, *supra* note 56.

Mercy" campaign in 1991, as many as 30,000 people gathered in an attempt to shut all abortion clinics in Wichita.[59] Tiller himself had been shot and wounded in August 1993.[60] This campaign had to be smaller and more discreet than earlier demonstrations because of fear of prosecutions under the *Freedom of Access to Clinics Act*.[61] Attorney General John Ashcroft, despite his strong pro-life leanings, made it clear that he would enforce the Act vigorously.[62] Yet a federal judge turned aside an attempt to ban the protests altogether as a violation of their right of free speech.[63]

An increasing number of states were also becoming receptive to enacting restrictions on abortion,[64] notwithstanding the Supreme Court's decision invalidating state-enacted partial birth abortion acts.[65] Even such hitherto staunchly pro-abortion state legislatures as that in New Hampshire suddenly found itself in play, enacting a parental consent statute.[66] Abortion rights supporters found no consolation from the argument that the bill really was about parental rights, and not about abortion.[67] In short order, a federal judge held the law unconstitutional because of its lack of a health exception for the parental consent requirement.[68] In Maryland, another hitherto staunchly pro-abortion rights state, saw its new governor, elected in 2002, endorsed parental consent and partial-birth abortion bills.[69] In New Jersey, yet another state the politics of which was dominated by those who favor abortion rights, the a state appeals court in 2002 held that a woman could sue the doctor who performed her abortion for causing her emotional distress by failing to tell her, before the abortion, that "the fetus, although a person unborn, was a complete, separate, unique and irreplaceable human being."[70] Pressures to enact successful restrictions on abortion were building to such an extent that even the Supreme Court might eventually have to yield, although that prospect was certainly not in view yet.

Finally, in November 2003, the President signed into law the first federal *Partial-Birth Abortion Act*.[71] The law, passed by lopsided majorities of 281-142 in the House of Representatives

---

59. GARROW, *supra* note 23, at 688; HADLEY, *supra* note 23, at 163; KERRY JACOBY, SOULS, BODIES, SPIRITS: THE DRIVE TO ABOLISH ABORTION SINCE 1973, at 135–36 (1998); PEGGY JARMAN, THE SIEGE OF WICHITA (1994); RISEN & THOMAS, *supra* note 57, at 317–34. *See also* Chapter 16, at notes 262–70.

60. GARROW, *supra* note 23, at 704.

61. Claiborne, *supra* note 56; Alexandra Marks, *In Abortion Fight, Lines Have Shifted Ten Years after a Historic Rally; The Anti-Abortion Cause Had Made Gains,* CHRISTIAN SCI. MONITOR, July 16, 2001, at 1; For the statute, see 18 U.S.C. § 248 (1994). *See* Chapter 16, at notes 168–73.

62. *AG Orders Protection for Clinics during Protest Week,* DALLAS MORNING NEWS, July 13, 2001, at 11A; Dan Eggan, *U.S. Marshalls to Protect Abortion Doctor; Ashcroft Had Been Accused of Ignoring Requests Ahead of Protests in Kansas,* WASH. POST, July 13, 2001, at A11; Jones, *supra* note 56; Marks, *supra* note 61.

63. Jones, *supra* note 56.

64. *See, e.g.,* Steven Ginsberg, *5 Antiabortion Bills Advance in House,* WASH. POST, Feb. 1, 2003, at B1; Michael Shear, *Va. Lawmakers Uphold Limits on Abortions: Vetoes on Parental Notification, Late-Term Procedure Voided,* WASH. POST, Apr. 3, 2003, at B1.

65. Stenberg v. Carhart, 530 U.S. 914 (2000). *See* Chapter 18, at notes 227–82.

66. Pamela Ferdinand, *N.H. Approves Abortion Consent Bill,* N.Y. TIMES, May 30, 2003, at A5.

67. Pamela Ferdinand, *N.H. House Passes Abortion Bill,* WASH. POST, Apr. 23, 2003, at A5; Stephen Frothingham, *Abortion Shift May Happen in N.H.: In an Abortion-Rights Stronghold, a Bill on Parental Notification Has a Chance to Succeed,* PHILA. INQUIRER, Apr. 27, 2003, at A7.

68. Planned Parenthood of N. New Eng. v. Heed, 296 F. Supp. 2d 59 (D.N.H. 2003).

69. Lori Montgomery, *Ehrlich May Back Abortion Restraints: Tougher Consent Bill for Minors Possible,* WASH. POST, Dec. 10, 2002, at B1.

70. Acuna v. Turkish, 808 A.2d 149 (N.J. Super. Ct. 2002). The quoted language comes from the plaintiff's complaint; the court reasoned that the doctor's representation that the fetus was "just blood and tissue" imposed his values on the plaintiff and denied her the right to make to make her own decision in these matters.

71. Dana Milbank, *Bush Signs Ban on Late-Term Abortions into Effect: Civil Rights Agency to Enforce Law; Lawsuits Are Filed,* WASH. POST, Nov. 6, 2003, at A4; Richard Stevenson, *Bush Signs Ban on a Procedure for Abortions,* N.Y. TIMES, Nov. 6, 2003, at A1; Robin Toner, *For GOP, It's a Moment,* N.Y. TIMES, Nov. 6, 2003, at A1.

and 64-34 in the Senate,[72] contained "congressional findings" that the procedure was not necessary to protect a woman's health, and thus that no health exception was necessary for the
*Act*.[73] Because of the lack of an exception for women's health, the *Act* was arguably unconstitutional.[74] Federal District Judge Richard Kopf in Nebraska enjoined enforcement of the *Act* on
the day it was enacted on precisely those grounds.[75] Presumably the Supreme Court will be
called upon to revisit its decision barely three years after holding comparable state laws unconstitutional.[76] That appeared to be a vain hope absent some change in the composition of the
Court.

The hope that the Supreme Court would reconsider its precedent might prove not to be entirely in vain when one realizes that the bill passed with the support of 17 Democratic Senators, many of them normally strong supporters of abortion rights.[77] On the other hand, the
*New York Times* editorialized repeatedly that the law's passage was secured through misrepresentations by its supporters[78]—a curious twist, given that that very paper had reported on
confessions by opponents of prior versions of the *Act* that they, rather than its supporters, had
lied to Congress.[79] Presumably these same representations will be made—again—to the
Court. And the Court in 2003, by an 8-1 vote in *Scheidler v. National Organization of
Women*,[80] virtually reversed its decision of nearly a decade earlier, and found that abortion
protestors could not be sued or enjoined under the *Racketeer Influenced and Corrupt Organizations Act*.[81]

Abortion rights advocates saw no choice but to attempt to make abortion a central issue in
the 2004 election—despite the great attention being given to the war against terrorism, to the
war in Iraq, and to economic conditions.[82] In particular, Democratic presidential candidates

---

72. Helen Dewar, *Senate Passes Ban on Abortion Procedure: Bush Set to Sign Bills, Foes Plan Court Fight*,
WASH. POST, Oct. 22, 2003, at A1; Sheryl Gay Stolberg, *Senate Approves Bill to Prohibit Type of Abortion*, N.Y.
TIMES, Oct. 22, 2003, at A1.

73. *See Hearing on H.R. 4965 (the Partial Birth Abortion Act) before the Subcomm. on the Const.*, House Judiciary Comm., 107th Cong., July 9, 2002.

74. *See* Stenberg v. Carhart, 530 U.S. 914 (2000). One court upheld a state statute with a health exception
shortly after the federal law was enacted. Women's Med. Prof'l Corp. v. Taft, 353 F.3d 436 (6th Cir. 2003). *See
generally* Melissa de Rosa, Note, *Partial Birth Abortion: Crime or Protected Right?*, 16 ST. JOHN'S J. LEGAL COM-
MENTARY 199 (2002).

75. Stevenson, *supra* note 71. Three different suits had been filed to block enforcement of the statute even
before President Bush signed it—in New York, Omaha, and San Francisco; Judge Kopf was the first to act. *See
3 Federal Suits Filed to Prevent Ban on Late-Term Abortions*, WASH. POST, Nov. 1, 2003, at A12. The other two
courts followed the day after the President signed the law. *Abortion Ban Blocked Again*, WASH. POST, Nov. 7,
2003, at A2. Federal judges were still blocking new state partial-birth bans while the federal act was wending
its way through Congress. Michael Shear, *Judge Blocks Va. "Partial-Birth" Abortion Ban*, WASH. POST, July 2,
2003, at B1.

76. *See* Stenberg v. Carhart, 530 U.S. 914 (2000).

77. Sheryl Gay Stolberg, *Bill Barring Abortion Procedure Drew on Backing From Many Friends of Roe v.
Wade*, N.Y. TIMES, Oct. 23, 2003, at A22.

78. Editorial, *A Deceptive Abortion Ban*, N.Y. TIMES, Sept. 19, 2003, at A25; Editorial, *Challenging a Men-
dacious Law*, N.Y. TIMES, Nov. 6, 2003, at A32; Editorial, *Frank Talk about Abortion*, N.Y. TIMES, Nov. 30, 2003,
at WK-8; Editorial, *"Partial-Birth" Mendacity, Again*, N.Y. TIMES, June 4, 2003, at A30. *See also* Mary Duenwald, *Extent of Ban Is Questioned*, N.Y. TIMES, Nov. 6, 2003, at A18; Ruth Marcus, *"Partial Birth," Partial
Truths*, WASH. POST, June 4, 2003, at A27.

79. C. Everett Koop, *Why Defend Partial-Birth Abortion?*, N.Y. TIMES, Sept. 26, 1996, at A27.

80. 537 U.S. 393 (2003). For the earlier decision, see *National Org. for Women v. Scheidler*, 510 U.S. 249
(1994).

81. 42 U.S.C. §§ 1961–1968 (1994).

82. Jennifer Lee, *Abortion Rights Group Plans a New Focus*, N.Y. TIMES, Jan. 5, 2003, § 1, at 19; Stevenson,
*supra* note 71, at A18; Toner, *supra* note 71.

sought to make the Bush judicial appointments an issue in the 2004 election.[83] And in an effort to refocus the debate on choice, NARAL—long the leading institution for the promotion of abortion rights—once again changed its name. Having first been named the National Association for the Repeal of Abortion Laws, and then the National Abortion Rights Action League, and then the National Abortion and Reproductive Rights Action League, it renamed itself at the opening of 2003 as NARAL-Pro Choice America.[84]

Abortion rights advocates were alarmed when the younger President Bush announced a policy of allowing states to define "an unborn child" as a "targeted low-income child" eligible for medical coverage under the Children's Health Insurance Program.[85] Even though this change would significantly increase the opportunities for federally funded prenatal care and birthing for women not eligible for Medicaid or other federal programs, self-styled advocates of women's rights (including a group called the National Partnership for Women and Families) opposed the change for fear that it would lead to the undermining of abortion rights.[86] Such advocates were locking themselves into the most extreme positions for fear that the least compromise would unravel the whole structure of abortion rights.

So intent were abortion rights advocates on preventing any possible breach in the wall of legal protection for the right to choose to abort that they were prepared to insist that someone who physically attacks a woman bearing a wanted fetus in the ninth-month of pregnancy and kills the fetus while only mildly injuring the mother—physically, at least—should be punished only for assaulting the mother and not for killing the fetus.[87] Consider Dr. Stephen Pack's attack on his paramour, pediatric nurse Joy Schepis. When Schepis told Pack that she was pregnant with his child and would not have an abortion, Pack followed Schepis (who worked with him at Montefiore Hospital) into the parking garage where her care was parked, threw her to the ground, and injected with large doses of methotrexate into her legs and buttocks.[88] Methotrexate itself was unlikely to induce an abortion, but it could produce "horrible birth defects" in about one-third of the instances of its use.[89] The birth defects could in turn result in a miscarriage. The drug could also induce serious damage to various organs in the mother. As it turned out, Schepis was determined to have the baby,[90] and for some time the *New York Post* provided daily reports on the progress of the pregnancy.[91] The Pack-Schepis story was big

83. Dan Balz, *Bush's Rights Record Assailed: Democratic Hopefuls Tailor Message to Feminist Audience*, WASH. POST, May 21, 2003, at A2.

84. Lee, *supra* note 82; Peggy Loonan, *Don't Compromise on Abortion*, N.Y. TIMES, Jan. 15, 2003, at A21.

85. Jan Cienski, *Bush Plan to Treat Fetus as Unborn Child: Policy Aimed at Expanding Medicare, Not at Promoting Cause of Anti-Abortionists*, NAT'L POST, July 7, 2001, at A11; Robert Pear, *Bush Plan Allows States to Give "Unborn Child" Medical Coverage*, N.Y. TIMES, July 6, 2001, at A1. *See also* Rick Weiss, *New Status for Embryos in Research*, WASH. POST, Oct. 30, 2002, at A1.

86. Cienski, *supra* note 85; Pear, *supra* note 85, at A1, A12.

87. Eilperin, *supra* note 49.

88. Sarah Chalmers, *Assault by Syringe Doctor, Chases Pregnant Lover to Kill Their Unborn Child*, DAILY MAIL (London), Apr. 19, 2000, at 7; Kirsten Danis & Allen Salkin, *A Brief Affair Links Pair Forever in Infamy*, N.Y. POST, Apr. 20, 2000, at 8; Ikimulisa Sockwell-Mason *et al.*, *Doc-Attack Nurse: I'm Not Having an Abortion*, N.Y. POST, Apr. 17, 2000, at 4. *See also* Tom Farmer, *Melrose Neighbors Recall N.Y. "Needle Doc" as Kid*, BOS. HERALD, Apr. 20, 2000, at 2.

89. Rita Delfiner, *How Drug Can Affect the Embryo*, N.Y. POST, Apr. 18, 2000, at 3; Linda Stasi, *Family Rights a Front-Page Issue*, N.Y. POST, Apr. 23, 2000, at 16.

90. Kirsten Danis, *Needle Nurse Asks for City's Payers*, N.Y. POST, Apr. 18, 2000, at 3; Kirsten Danis *et al.*, *Ultrasound Detects Heartbeat of Needle Nurse's Baby*, N.Y. POST, Apr. 19, 2000, at 4; Sockwell-Mason *et al.*, *supra* note 88.

91. Danis, *supra* note 90; Danis *et al.*, *supra* note 90; Danis & Salkin, *supra* note 89; Laura Italiano & Erika Martinez, *Nurse's Rage: Needle Doc's a Vicious Animal*, N.Y. POST, Apr. 21, 2000, at 2; Ikimulisa Sockwell-Mason, *Needle-Nurse Baby's Heart Still Beating*, N.Y. POST, Apr. 25, 2000, at 22. *See also* Denise Buffa, *DA Plans Pscyh Exam for "Insane" Needle Doc*, N.Y. POST, Oct. 26, 2000, at 38; Rita Delfiner, *"Needle" Nurse: My*

news. It even crowded the Elián González child-custody saga off the front pages of the *New York Post.*[92]

Seven months after the attack, Schepis gave birth to a healthy baby boy who weighed 7 lbs. 15 oz on November 28, 2000.[93] Pack was indicted for assault on the mother and for attempted illegal abortion.[94] He pleaded guilty to attempted abortion.[95] Peck was sentenced to two years in prison.[96] If the abortion rights advocates had their way, the charge of illegal abortion could not exist. Applying their reasoning in the debate of the *Unborn Victims of Violence Act,* if Pack had succeeded in killing or inducing serious deformities in the unborn child, he could have been prosecuted only for a relatively minor assault on his paramour.

Finally, the supporters of abortion rights launched an attack aimed at closing down "crisis pregnancy centers."[97] Such centers, usually located in close proximity to abortion centers, advertise that they will help with unplanned pregnancies. Sometimes young women enter the facility seeking an abortion, only to find counselors who will provide various forms of assistance but will not countenance abortions. The centers are primarily staffed by volunteers and funded by church groups with the aim of providing moral support hope for those caught in a crisis pregnancy, and make no apologies for presenting the gruesome realities of abortion to the women who come in for counseling. Increasingly those centers have doctors and nurses on call to provide medical assistance, including sonograph machines to show the women their own babies.[98] Notwithstanding the presence of qualified medically personnel, Eliot Spitzer, Attorney General of New York, launched an investigation into the centers on grounds of suspicion of the unlicensed practice of medicine and false advertising.[99] Spitzer did not initiate similar investigations to abortion clinics despite the frequent problems they have in delivering quality care to their clientele.[100] Apparently some officials and abortion supporters believe that the practice of medicine, at least the provision of medical services to women facing a crisis pregnancy, without being willing to provide an abortion, simply is not a legitimate form of the practice of medicine.[101] A spokesman for Spitzer defended the decision to investigate crisis pregnancy centers, rather than

---

*Baby Is a Boy,* N.Y. Post, June 28, 2000, at 2; Laura Italiano, *Pregnant Nurse Jabs at Accused Needle Doc,* N.Y. Post, May 25, 2000, at 6; Ikimulisa Sockwell-Mason, *Doc's Possible Pscyho Plea Vexes Needle Nurse,* N.Y. Post, Oct. 27, 2000, at 22.

92. Stasi, *supra* note 89. Elián González was a six-year-old Cuban whose mother died attempting to bring her son to the United States and who thereafter was caught up in a highly-publicized custody fight between relatives in Miami and his father in Cuba before he was eventually returned there to live with his father. *See* González *ex rel.* González v. Reno, 86 F. Supp. 2d 1167 (S.D. Fla. 2000), *aff'd sub nom.* González v. Reno, 212 F.3d 1338 (11th Cir. 2000); Sean Murphy, *Contemporary Practice of the United States Relating to International Law: Return of Elián González to Cuba,* 94 Am. J. Int'l L. 516 (2000).

93. Ikimulisa Sockwell-Mason, *Needle Mom Brings Home Miracle Baby,* N.Y. Post, Dec. 1, 2000, at 3; Ikimulisa Sockwell-Mason & Laura Italiano, *Needle Stab Mom's Newborn Appears OK,* N.Y. Post, Nov. 30, 2000, at 24.

94. Danis *et al, supra* note 90.

95. Clemente Lisi & Ikimulisa Sockwell-Mason, *Doc Cops Plea in Needle-Abort Try,* N.Y. Post, Jan. 12, 2000, at 4; Ray Sanchez, *Doc Admits Assault: Guilty Plea for Trying to Inject Pregnant Lover with Abortion Drug,* Newsday, Jan. 12, 2001, at 5.

96. Dan Kadison, *Doc Gets 2 Yrs. for Needle Attack on Pregnant Gal Pal,* N.Y. Post, Apr. 21, 2001, at 6.

97. Alan Cooperman, *Abortion Battle: Prenatal Care or Pressure Tactics? "Crisis Pregnancy Centers" Expand and Draw Criticism,* Wash. Post, Feb. 21, 2002, at A1.

98. *Id.*

99. *Id.*

100. *See* Chapter 14, at notes 41–47.

101. Cooperman, *supra* note 97.

abortion clinics, on the grounds that the Attorney General was bound to follow up when his office receives serious complaints of wrongdoing—without indicating from whom the complaints came or whether there were equivalent complaints about the nearby abortion clinics.[102]

The struggle over abortion remains part of a larger "cultural war" that continued unabated during the second Bush presidency. One of the most central aspects of this struggle centered on the rights of homosexuals in society. The year 2003 saw the Episcopal Church of the United States elect Gene Robinson as its first openly homosexual bishop,[103] to the consternation of conservatives in the American branch of the church[104] and to the dismay of numerous other branches of the Anglican church globally.[105] A threatened schism within the church either nationally or globally did not happen (at least not in the short run),[106] but that possibility could not be ruled out. Massachusetts' Supreme Judicial Court, following on holdings in several Canadian courts,[107] held that the ban on same-sex marriages violated the state constitutional guarantee of equal protection of the laws.[108] This produced yet another storm of controversy in Massachusetts and across the country.[109] One casualty of these culture wars was Patricia Ireland, President of the National Organization of Women for 10 years, who in became chief executive of the YWCA in April 2003. She was suddenly dismissed in October 2003 under circumstances that suggested

102. *Id.*

103. Laurie Goodstein, *New Hampshire Episcopalians Choose Gay Bishop, and Conflict*, N.Y. Times, June 8, 2003, §1, at 11.

104. *See, e.g.,* Laurie Goodstein, *Changes in Episcopal Church Spur Some to Go, Some to Join*, N.Y. Times, Dec. 29, 2003, at A1.

105. Stephen Bates, *Anti-Gay Anglicans Turn Their Fire on US—Convention Warned of Schism if Homosexual Bishop Is Confirmed*, The Guardian, July 26, 2003, at 11; Kelly Burke, *Jensen Warns US Church over Gays*, Sydney Morn. Herald, July 26, 2003, at 9; Laurie Goodstein, *Homosexuality Issue Threatens to Break Anglicanism in Two*, N.Y. Times, July 19, 2003, at A1; Laurie Goodstein, *Conservative Anglican Leaders Warn of a Schism*, N.Y. Times, July 24, 2003, at A12; Laurie Goodstein, *Dissident Episcopal Bishops Form New Group*, N.Y. Times, Dec. 17, 2003, at A32; Michael Paulson, *Vote on NH Bishop Could Provoke Anglican Split: Bishop's Election Could Be Divisive*, Bos. Globe, July 20, 2003, at A1; David Usborne, *Vote on Gay Bishop May Split Anglican Church*, The Independent (London), Aug. 4, 2003, at 2.

106. Laurie Goodstein, *Episcopalians Back away from Break*, N.Y. Times, Dec. 19, 2003, at A28.

107. EGALE Canada v. Canada (A.G.), 255 D.L.R.4th 472 (B.C. C.A. 2003); Halpern v. Canada (A.G.), 225 D.L.R.4th 529 (Ont. C.A. 2003); Hendricks c. Québec (P.G.), J.E. 2003-466 (Que. 2003). The Canadian decisions were more important than simply as intellectual influences; some homosexuals went to Canada to marry, challenging their home governments to recognized their unions on their return. Clifford Krauss, *Gay Couples Follow a Trail North Blazed by Slaves and War Resisters*, N.Y. Times, Nov. 23, 2003, §4, at 7.

108. Goodridge v. Department of Pub. Health, 798 N.E.2d 941 (Mass. 2003). *See also* Citizens for Equal Protection, Inc. v. Bruning, 290 F. Supp. 2d 1004 (D. Neb. 2003) (Nebraska's ban on same-sex marriage is an unconstitutional bill of attainder). *Contra:* Standhardt v. Superior Ct., 77 P.3d 451 (Ariz. Ct. App. 2003), *rev. denied. And see In re* Blanchflower, 834 A.2d 1010 (N.H. 2003) (a married woman's lesbian affair does not constitute adultery for purposes of the state's divorce statute). *See generally* James Donovan, Comment, *Same-Sex Union Announcements: Précis on a Not so Picayune Matter*, 49 Loy. L. Rev. 171 (2003); Kathleen Hull, *The Cultural Power of Law and the Cultural Enactment of Legality: The Case of Same-Sex Marriage*, 28 Law & Soc. Inquiry 629 (2003).

109. *See, e.g.,* Pam Belluck, *Gays Respond: "I Do,""I Might," and "I Won't,"* N.Y. Times, Nov. 26, 2003, at A1; Pam Belluck, *Gays' Victory Leaves Massachusetts Lawmakers Hesitant*, N.Y. Times, Nov. 20, 2003, at A29; David Brooks, *Give Everyone Access to the Power of Marriage*, Int'l Herald Trib., Nov. 25, 2003, at 7; Richard Cohen, *This May Be Good for Marriage*, Wash. Post, Nov. 20, 2003, at A41; Alan Cooperman, *Catholic Bishops Oppose Legalizing Gay Marriage*, Wash. Post, Nov. 13, 2003, at A2; Alan Charles Raul, *Undermining Society's Morals*, Wash. Post, Nov. 28, 2003, at A41; William Safire, *On Same-Sex Marriage*, N.Y. Times, Dec. 1, 2003, at A23; Katharine Seelye, *Conservatives Mobilize against Ruling on Gay Marriage*, N.Y. Times, Nov. 20, 2003, at A29; David Von Drehle, *Same-Sex Unions Move Center Stage: After a Decade on Fringe, Gay Marriage Enters American Consciousness*, Wash. Post, Nov. 23, 2003, at A1.

that her stance on abortion and on homosexual rights lay behind the decision— although the YWCA board had expressly cited her prominence as an "aggressive" advocate on "women's empowerment and racial justice" as reasons for her appointment in the first place.[110]

# Contemporary Attitudes toward Abortion

*The keenest sorrow is to recognize ourselves as the sole cause of our adversitites.*

—Caitlin Flanagan[111]

Probably no aspect of the continuing controversy over abortion exhibits more evasions, euphemisms, and downright lies than the disparate claims over what is the "true attitude" of the general public towards abortion. Both sides of the abortion controversy indulge in distortions or worse, with both camps claiming to speak for the "majority." Over the years, the Gallup Poll and similar surveys consistently have shown that a substantial majority of all persons in the United States oppose abortion on demand, with a broad majority favoring an indications policy whereby abortion would be legal if certain conditions exist.[112] Despite the intense controversy, these numbers have been remarkably stable over time.[113] Slight shifts in favor of the legality of access to abortion in the two decades after *Roe* was decided were followed by similarly slight shifts against the legality of access in the third decade after *Roe* was decided.[114]

---

110. Alan Cooperman, *YWCA's Top Official Fired after Six Months*, WASH. POST, Oct. 21, 2003, at A17.

111. THE MOST BRILLIANT THOUGHTS OF ALL TIME 9 (John Shanahan ed.1999).

112. BEVERLY WILDUNG HARRISON, OUR RIGHT TO CHOOSE: TOWARD A NEW ETHIC OF ABORTION 163 (1983); EVERETT LADD & KARLYN BOWMAN, PUBLIC OPINION ABOUT ABORTION: TWENTY-FIVE YEARS AFTER *ROE v. WADE* 17 (1997); MAUREEN MULDOON, THE ABORTION DEBATE IN THE UNITED STATES AND CANADA: A SOURCE BOOK 37 (1991). *See also* BHAVANI SITARAMAN, THE MIDDLE GROUND: AMERICAN PUBLIC OPINION AND THE ABORTION DEBATE (1994); Raymond Adamek, *Public Opinion and* Roe v. Wade*: Measurement Difficulties*, 58 PUB. OPINION Q. 409 (1994); Judith Blake, *Abortion and Public Opinion: The 1960–1970 Decade*, 171 SCIENCE 540 (1971) ("Blake, *Public Opinion*"); Judith Blake, *The Supreme Court's Abortion Decisions and Public Opinion in the United States*, 3 POPULATION & DEV. REV. 45 (1977) ("Blake, *Abortion Decisions*"); Robert Blendon, John Benson, & Karen Donelan, *The Public and the Controversy over Abortion*, 270 JAMA 2871 (1993); Christopher Caldwell, *Pro-Lifestyle*, THE NEW REP., Apr. 5, 1999, at 14, 15; Stanley Henshaw & Greg Martire, *Abortion and the Public Opinion Polls: Morality and Legality*, 14 FAM. PLAN. PERSP. 53 (1982); Eun-Kyng Kim, *Abortion Poll Shows Many Feel Conflicted*, BOSTON GLOBE, Jan. 20, 1998, at A3; Joseph Mowbray, *Are You Pro-Choice? How the Stem Cell Debate Has Changed Perceptions*, WASH. TIMES, Aug. 24, 2001, at A19; Alissa Rubin, *Americans Narrowing Support for Abortion: Times Poll: Results Reveal a Conflicted Stance—They Think It's Murder Yet Lean toward Leaving the Choice to Women. Still, Support Increases for Limiting the Procedures Availability*, L.A. TIMES, June 18, 2000, at A1; Jacqueline Scott, *Conflicting Beliefs about Abortion: Legal Approval and Moral Doubts*, 52 SOC. PSYCH. Q. 319 (1989); *Snapshot: Americans Closer on Abortion Issue*, USA TODAY, Jan. 24, 2001, at 1A; Christopher Wlezian & Malcolm Goggin, *The Courts, Interest Groups, and Public Opinion about Abortion*, 15 POL. BEHAVIOR 381 (1993); David Zizzo, *Abortion Poll Finds Mixed State Support: Most Surveyed Back Some Allowances*, DAILY OKLAHOMAN, Jan. 21, 2001, at 1A; Eric Zorn, *O'Malley Stand on Abortion Is Politically Gutsy*, CHI. TRIB., Jan. 24, 2002, at 1.

113. LADD & BOWMAN, *supra* note 112, at 17; MATTHEW WETSTEIN, ABORTION RATES IN THE UNITED STATES: THE INFLUENCE OF OPINION AND POLICY 61–74 (1996). For an early report on American's generally low opinion of abortion, see *Tidings*, TIME, May 28, 1973, at 62.

114. Lynn Wardle, *The Quandary of Pro-Life Free Speech: A Lesson from the Abolitionists*, 62 ALB. L. REV. 853, 947, 964 (1999). *See also* E.J. Dionne, jr., *Poll on Abortion Finds the Nation Is Sharply Divided: Court Gets Issue Today*, N.Y. TIMES, Apr. 26, 1989, at A1; Carey Goldberg & Janet Elder, *Public Still Backs Abortion, but Wants Limits, Poll Says: A Notable Shift from General Acceptance*, N.Y. TIMES, Jan. 16, 1998, at A1; Anna Greenberg, *Will Choice Be Aborted?*, AM. PROSPECT, Sept. 24, 2001, at A25; Mimi Hall, *Polls: Shift in Support for*

While the percentages approving or disapproving of abortion under particular circumstances vary widely from state to state, in every state only a minority favors abortion on demand.[115] The range of support for abortion on demand ranges from a high of 48 percent in Colorado to a low of 12 percent in Kentucky.[116] Yet the numbers of those who disapprove of legalized abortion, in general or under particular circumstances, have only seldom been translated into effective political action against abortion.[117] Furthermore, by concentrating on responses to particular questions one might conclude that a "real" majority favors "abortion on demand."[118] Thus, in polls taken at the same time as polls indicating that nearly 70 percent oppose abortion on demand, more than 50 percent favor legislation that would, in effect, make abortion on demand the law of the state in which they lived.[119] In a similar vein, some 33 percent of one Gallup sample described themselves as "pro-choice" even though 74 percent of the same sample either consistently or often disapprove of abortion.[120] Some of the remaining 26 percent disapproved of abortions if used as a substitute for birth control or as a means for sex selection among children.[121] The problem is caught by the response of theologian Paul Lehman to a question (following a public lecture) on whether he was opposed to abortion: "Yes…and no, in that order."[122]

In short, the debate is within each person as much as it is between people. These internal confusions and uncertainties are resolved in varied ways. As a result, the external debate does not break down along strictly liberal and conservative lines, as the writings of Sydney Callahan, Margot Hentoff, Nat Hentoff, Eugène Ionesco, and Marshall McLuhan—all liberal intellectuals op-

*Abortion,* USA Today, Jan. 21, 1998, at 1A; Jules Irwin, *Most Young Adults Are Ambivalent on Abortion: Open Talks Haven't Brought Consensus,* Cin. Enquirer, Jan. 18, 1998, at A5, A16; Rubin, *supra* note 112; Lydia Saad, *A Slight, but Perceptible Shift in Abortion Opinion,* Orlando Sentinel, Mar. 15, 1998, at G1; Dick Williams, Roe v. Wade *at 25: Tide May Be Turning on Abortion,* Atlanta J. & Atlanta Const., Jan. 20, 1998, at A6. *See also* Blendon, Benson, & Donelan, *supra* note 112, at 2872; Mowbray, *supra* note 112.

115. *See generally* George Gallup, jr. & Jim Castelli, The People's Religion: American Faith in the 90's, at 172 (1989); Wetstein, *supra* note 113, at 75–90; Zizzo, *supra* note 112.

116. Wetstein, *supra* note 113, at 78–79. *See also* Robert O'Connor & Michael Berkman, *Religious Determinants of State Abortion Policy,* 76 Soc. Sci. Q. 607 (1995).

117. Wetstein, *supra* note 113, at 85–112; Clarke Forsythe, *First Steps: A New Strategy for Pro-Lifers,* 51 Nat'l Rev. 42 (Dec. 20, 1999); Goldberg & Elder, *supra* note 114, at A1, A16.

118. *See, e.g.,* Dionne, *supra* note 114; Greenberg, *supra* note 114. On the variability of results regarding abortion depending on the wording of the poll, see Celeste Michelle Condit, Decoding Abortion Rhetoric: Communicating Social Change 147–51 (1990); Gallup & Castelli, *supra* note 115, at 167; Blendon, Benson, & Donelan, *supra* note 112, at 2872.

119. Condit, *supra* note 118, at 167–68 n.9; Muldoon, *supra* note 112, at 37–38; Michael Alvarez & John Brehm, *American Ambivalence towards Abortion Policy…,"* 39 Am. J. Pol. Sci. 1055 (1995); Blendon, Benson, & Donelan, *supra* note 112, at 2872–73; Neil Nevitte et al., *The American Abortion Controversy: Lessons from Cross-National Evidence,* 12 Pol. & Life Sci. 19, 25 (1993); Rubin, *supra* note 112.

120. Americans United for Life, Abortion and Moral Beliefs: A Survey of American Opinion, *Executive Summary* at 21 (1991). This survey was conducted by the Gallup Organization and copies were filed with the Supreme Court simultaneously with the filing of an *Amicus Brief of Feminists for Life supporting petitioners in* Bray v. Alexandria Women's Health Clinic, 506 U.S. 263 (1992). The poll included 200 questions posed in 45-minute interviews with 2,174 adults, with a margin of error of not more than 3% for the entire sample; questions asked of subsamples might have a slightly higher margin of error. The poll is analyzed in detail in Paige Comstock Cunningham & Clarke Forsythe, *Is Abortion the "First Right" for Women?: Some Consequences of Legal Abortion,* in Abortion, Medicine and the Law 100, 103–09 (J. Douglas Butler & David Walbert eds., 4th ed. 1992).

121. Americans United for Life, *supra* note 120, *Executive Summary* at 21. *See also* Blendon, Benson, & Donelan, *supra* note 112, at 2872–73.

122. Quoted in Elizabeth Mensch & Alan Freeman, The Politics of Virtue: Is Abortion Debatable? 219 n.22 (1993). *See also* Barbara Hinkinson Craig & David O'Brien, Abortion and American Politics 264–70 (1993); Caldwell, *supra* note 112; Kim, *supra* note 112; Rubin, *supra* note 112; Victoria Sackett, *Between Pro-Life and Pro-Choice,* Pub. Op., Apr.–May 1985, at 53.

posed to abortion—adequately attest.[123] Such noted liberal political figures as Cesar Chavez, Jesse Jackson (for a time), and Jeremy Rifkin were also active in the pro-life movement.[124]

Jesse Jackson's eventual defection in the hope of winning the Democratic Party's nomination for President of the United States was mirrored by the defection of Missouri's pro-life Congressman Dick Gephardt when he decided to run for president in 1988, in Tennessee Senator Al Gore's defection from the pro-life ranks in the same year for the same reason, and in Arkansas' pro-life governor Bill Clinton becoming one of the strongest of pro-choice Presidents.[125] It is unclear whether Geraldine Ferraro (a prominent Catholic) changed her views regarding abortion when she became a candidate for vice-president, but her announcement that she would not seek to translate her personal disapproval of abortion into law—coupled with her claim that Catholic teaching was "divided" on the question[126]—provoked a storm of controversy, including a public rebuke by several bishops.[127] Of course, presidential politics works conversions in both directions. Republican George H. Bush converted from the pro-choice side in 1980 and more recently Republican Steve Forbes did the same.[128]

To demonstrate the distortions inherent in broad assertions about how groups feel or believe about abortion, and the ease with which those distortions are accepted, compare the actual attitudes of women in particular towards abortion with the perception of those attitudes fostered by the media. The claims that abortion is a "women's issue," and that women overwhelming support abortion rights, has been made and repeated so often that it is commonly assumed to be true.[129] Journalist Donald Judges even puts the word "feminists" in quotation marks when he

---

123. *See* CONNIE PAIGE, THE RIGHT TO LIFERS: WHO THEY ARE; HOW THEY OPERATE; WHERE THEY GET THEIR MONEY 102 (1983); Sidney Callahan, *Abortion and the Sexual Agenda*, COMMONWEAL, April 25, 1986, at 236; Nat Hentoff, *Abortion: Seeking a Common Ground* (book rev.), BOSTON GLOBE, June 10, 1990, at B43.

124. JOHN NOONAN, JR., A PRIVATE CHOICE: ABORTION IN AMERICA IN THE SEVENTIES 66–67 (1979); PAIGE, *supra* note 123, at 100–04.

125. *See* RISEN & THOMAS, *supra* note 57, at 143 (Gephardt); Barringer, *supra* note 6; Mark Graber, *The Clintonification of American Law: Abortion, Welfare, and Liberal Constitutional Theory*, 58 OHIO ST. L.J. 731 (1997). Unsurprisingly, Gore was willing to sell out his new friends if he saw political advantage in that direction. Eric Schmitt, *Deal on U.N. Dues Breaks an Impasse and Draws Critics: Abortion Rights Advocates See "Sellout" as Gore Splits with the White House*, N.Y. TIMES, Nov. 16, 1999, at A1

126. *See* Janet Perlez, *Mrs. Ferraro for Vice President*, N.Y. TIMES, Dec. 23, 1983, at A14.

127. *See* Kurt Anderson, *An Emotional Issue Arises: Where Is the Wall of Separation between Religion and Politics?*, TIME, Sept. 10, 1984, at 8; Alfred Boylan, *Of Ferraro, Cuomo, and Moral Issues Confused with Dogma*, N.Y. TIMES, Sept. 9, 1984, at D24 (letter to the editor); Fox Butterfield, *Archbishop of Boston Cites Abortion as "Critical Issue,"* N.Y. Times, Sept. 6, 1984, at B13; Editorial, *Enough of "Holier than Thou,"* N.Y. TIMES, Aug. 2, 1984, at A22; Sam Roberts, *Cuomo to Challenge Archbishop over Criticism of Abortion*, N.Y. TIMES, Aug. 3, 1994, at A1; Kenneth Woodward, *Politics and Abortion: "Family Issues" Play in the Race for the White House*, NEWSWEEK, Aug. 20, 1984, at 66. *See also* RISEN & THOMAS, *supra* note 57, at 107–08 (discussing Mario Cuomo's similar problems in reconciling his personal opposition to abortion with his political support for abortion rights.

128. CRAIG & O'BRIEN, *supra* note 123, at 191 (Bush's conversion in 1988 when running for president); **Richard L. Berke, *In Forbes Strategy, Religious Right Now a Friend*, N.Y. TIMES, Sept. 21, 1997, § 1, at 28;** Joshua Micah Marshall, *Can We Talk?*, May 17, 1999 www.Salon.com, (accessed Aug. 10, 2004) (Steve Forbes takes a sharp right turn just as the Republican Party is looking for a centrist path.); **Leslie Wayne, *The 2000 Campaign: the Issues, Forbes Emphasizes Position Against Abortion and Taxes*, N.Y. TIMES, Jan. 23, 2000, § 1, at 16; Adam Clymer with Alison Mitchell, 2000 Campaign: the Next Stage, Forbes is Forcing a Renewed Debate About Abortions, N.Y. Times, Jan. 26, 2000, at A1;** Dana Millbank, *The Conversion of Steve Forbes*, THE NEW REP., Apr. 27, 1998, at 21.

129. *See, e.g.,* ELIZABETH ADELL COOK, TED JELEN, & CLYDE WILCOX, BETWEEN TWO ABSOLUTES: PUBLIC OPINION AND THE POLITICS OF ABORTION 166 (1992); MARK GRABER, RETHINKING ABORTION: EQUAL CHOICE, THE CONSTITUTION, AND REPRODUCTIVE POLITICS 131–35 (1996); ROGER ROSENBLATT, LIFE ITSELF: ABORTION IN THE AMERICAN MIND 14–17 (1992); SUZANNE STAGGENBORG, THE PRO-CHOICE MOVEMENT: ORGANIZATION AND ACTIVISM IN THE ABORTION CONFLICT 138–46 (1991); Glen Halva-Neubauer, *Abortion*

discusses "'feminists' against abortion" (which, by the way, is not what those women call them-selves: Feminists for Life).[130] In addition to the divisions among women generally, anecdotal evi-dence suggests that younger women are less inclined to support abortion rights than older women.[131] A somewhat similar pattern of assuming a unified response regarding abortion in the face of actual diversity appears within the homosexual community as well.[132]

Why female opposition to abortion should surprise anyone is a puzzle—unless one supposes that all, or nearly all, women must necessarily take the same side on at least some issues, a most unlikely proposition. In fact, the division in society (and within ourselves) over abortion is gen-erally more true for women than for men. And, in fact, abortion is not the top political issue in most women's lives despite the intense continuing attention of the media and of organized femi-nism to the topic. For example, one poll found, during a period of intense media attention to what was presented as a threat to "abortion rights" only days before the *Webster* decision was an-nounced, that only 2 percent of women considered abortion to be the most important issue for women's organizations, compared to 27 percent who listed job equity and 5 percent who listed childcare, among other alternatives.[133] Moreover, reliable opinion survey results demonstrate consistently that women as a group remain more opposed to unlimited choice regarding abor-tion than men—who as a group are (and have been) more supportive when compared to women.[134]

---

*Policy in the Post-Webster Age,* 20 Publius 27 (1990); Jerome Himmelstein, *The Social Basis of Antifeminism: Religious Networks and Culture,* 25 J. Sci. Study of Religion 1 (1986); Kenneth Karst, *Religion, Sex, and Poli-tics: Cultural Counterrevolution in Constitutional Perspective,* 24 U.C. Davis L. Rev. 677, 681–83, 712–13, 715–17 (1991).

130. Donald Judges, Hard Choices, Lost Voices 27 (1993). *See also* Graber, *supra* note 129, at 35–36.

131. Jennifer Baumgardner, *The Pro-Choice PR Problem,* The Nation, Mar. 5, 2001, at 19; Ellen Chessler *et al., Letters,* The Nation, May 14, 2001, at 2; Jennifer Weiner, *Sliding Support: Abortion Rights Pulls in Fewer Young Adults,* Phila. Inquirer, Jan. 25, 1998, at E3.

132. Edward Damich & Terence Wolfe, *Out a Second Time: Gay Heterodoxy on the Question of Abortion,* 13 St. L.U. Pub. L. Rev. 253 (1993).

133. E.J. Dionne, *Poll Finds Ambivalence on Abortion Persists in U.S.,* N.Y. Times, Aug. 3, 1989, at A18. *See also* Susanne Fields, *Even Feminists Now Boost the Family,* Chicago Sun-Times, May 7, 1991, at 23; Tamar Lewin, *Equal Pay for Equal Work Is No. 1 Goal of Women: Findings in Survey Prompts Union Action,* N.Y. Times, Sept. 5, 1997, at A20. *See generally* Hadley, *supra* note 23, at 59; Kathleen McDonnell, Not an Easy Choice: A Feminist Reexamines Abortion 28 (1984); Rene Denfeld, The New Victorians: A Young Woman's Challenge to the Old Feminist Order (1995).

134. *See, e.g.,* Mary Kenny, Abortion: The Whole Story 65–86, 225–52, especially at 226 (1986) ("Every opinion poll taken on this issue has shown men to be more liberal than women on abortion, and in-deed to be more dispassionate."); Rubin, *supra* note 112 (72% of women support a ban on all abortions after the first trimester of pregnancy, compared to only 58% of men); Mark Shields, *Beltway Media Are out of Touch on Abortion,* Seattle Post-Intellingencer, July 23, 2001, at B3 (61% of women consider abortion to be murder, compared to 57% of men). *See also* Americans United for Life, *supra* note 120; The Connecti-cut Mutual Life Report on American Values in the 80s, at 92 (1981); Craig & O'Brien, *supra* note 123, at 246–64; E.J. Dionne, Why Americans Hate Politics 341–43 (1991); George Gallup, jr., The Gallup Poll: Public Opinion 1986, at 49 (1987); Graber, *supra* note 129, at 17, 34–36 131–42; Anthony Hordern, Legal Abortion: The English Experience 227–30 (1971); James Davison Hunter, Before the Shooting Begins: Searching for Democracy in America's Culture Wars 90–91 (1994); Judges, *supra* note 130, at 39–40; Kristin Luker, Abortion and the Politics of Motherhood 238 (1984); Na-tional Opinion Research Ctr., General Social Survey, 1972–1987: Cumulative Codebook 229–30 (1987); Noonan, *supra* note 124, at 48–50, 173; David O'Brien, Storm Center: The Supreme Court in American Politics 39 (3rd ed. 1993); Hyman Rodman, Betty Sarvis, & Joy Bonar, The Abortion Ques-tion 140–43 (1987); Rosenblatt, *supra* note 129, at 137–89; *Americans and Abortion,* Newsweek, Apr. 24, 1989, at 39; Ross Baker, Laurily Epstein, & Rodney Forth, *Matters of Life and Death: Social, Political, and Reli-gious Correlates of Attitudes on Abortion,* 9 Am. Pol. Q. 89, 94 (1981); Blake, *Abortion Decisions, supra* note 112, at 53, 58; E.J. Dionne, *Poll on Abortion Finds the Nation is Sharply Divided,* N.Y. Times, Apr. 26, 1989, at A1 ("Dionne, *Sharply Divided*"); Charles Franklin & Liane Kosaki, *Republican Schoolmaster: The U.S. Supreme*

The Gallup Organization, in a poll funded by Americans United for Life, found that only 17 percent of women (compared to 20 percent of men) considered abortion to be acceptable, even during the first trimester of pregnancy, if the abortion was sought for no other reason than to prevent the interruption of the woman's career.[135] Only 7 percent of women (compared to 11 percent of men) approve of first trimester abortions as a substitute means for birth control.[136] Women consistently are less approving than men regardless of the reason for the abortion, and some 53 percent of women (compared to 47 percent of men) agree that the child's right to be born outweighs the woman's right to choose at the moment of conception.[137] The Wirthlin Survey found similar overall numbers: 11 percent of married women believed that abortion should not be permitted at all, and 44 percent of married women believed that abortion should be permitted only in cases of rape, incest, or to save the life of the mother, for a combined total of 55 percent disapproving of a general "right to choose"; nine percent of unmarried women agreed that abortion should not be permitted at all, and 42 percent of unmarried women agreed that it should only be permitted for the limited reasons already mentioned, for a total of 51 percent disapproving complete freedom of choice.[138] And even ardent supporters of abortion rights are troubled when the freedom to abort is used selectively to abort unborn daughters because one or

---

*Court, Public Opinion, and Abortion,* 83 Am. Pol. Sci. Rev. 751, 758–59 (1989); Goldberg & Elder, *supra* note 114, at A16; Donald Granberg, *Pro-Life or Reflections of Conservative Ideology?—An Analysis of Opposition to Legalized Abortion,* 62 Sociology & Soc. Res. 414, 418 (1978); Donald & Beth Wellman Granberg, *Abortion Attitudes, 1965–1980: Trends and Determinants,* 12 Fam. Plan. Persp. 250, 254 (1980); George Skelton, *Most Americans Think Abortion is Immoral,* L.A. Times, Mar. 19, 1989, at 3; Lucy Tedrow & E.R. Mahoney, *Trends in Attitudes toward Abortion, 1972–1976,* 43 Pub. Op. Q. 181, 184–85 (1979); *Wirthlin Group Survey, Jan. 15–17, 1990,* in Public Op., May/June 1990, at 36. *See generally* Mary Ann Glendon, Hermeneutics, Abortion and Divorce: A Review of Abortion and Divorce in Western Law 50–52 (1989); Susan Nathanson, Soul Crisis 40 (1989); Samuel Calhoun & Andrea Sexton, *Is It Possible to Take Both Fetal Life and Women Seriously? Professor Lawrence Tribe and his Reviewers* (book rev.), 49 Was. & Lee L. Rev. 437, 445–46 (1992); Ellen Goodman, *Men and Abortion,* Glamour 178 (July 1989); Alice Rossi & Bhavani Ssiraraman, *Abortion in Context: Historical Trends and Future Changes,* 20 Fam. Plan. Persp. 273, 276 (1988); Lynn Wardle, *Protecting the Rights of Conscience of Health Care Providers,* 14 J. Legal Med. 177, 244–45 (1993); Richard Wilkins, Richard Sherlock, & Stephen Clark, *Mediating the Polar Extremes: A Guide to Post-Webster Abortion Policy,* in Abortion and the States: Political Change and Future Regulation 139, 144–45 (Jane Wishner ed. 1993).

135. Americans United for Life, *supra* note 120, *Executive Summary* at 20–21. *See also* Condit, *supra* note 118, at 123–41 (analyzing images of abortion as portrayed on television); Myra Marx Ferree & Beth Hess, Controversy and Coalition: The New Feminist Movement across Three Decades of Change 165 (rev. ed. 1994) (claiming that 43% approve right to abort "under any circumstances"); Carol Gilligan, In a Different Voice: Psychological Theory and Women's Development 71–105 (1982) (finding that even women who have abortions speak disapprovingly of abortions for career purposes); Hadley, *supra* note 23, at 86–88; Hunter, *supra* note 134, at 95–101; R.W. Apple, jr., *Limits on Abortion Seem Less Likely,* N.Y. Times, Sept. 29, 1989, at A1 (only 33% approve abortion for career purposes); Dionne, *supra* note 133 (56% disapprove of abortion for career purposes); Dionne, *Sharply Divided, supra* note 134, at A1 (only 26% of Americans approve of abortion for career purposes); Goldberg & Elder, *supra* note 114, at A1 (only 25% of Americans approve of abortion for career purposes).

136. Americans United for Life, *supra* note 120, *Executive Summary* at 20–21. *See also* National Opinion Research Ctr., *supra* note 134, at 230 (50% of all Americans oppose abortion if the only reason is that a married woman simply does not want any more children); *Americans and Abortion, supra* note 134 (66% opposed abortion if the only reason is that the woman simply does not want a child); Dionne, *Sharply Divided, supra* note 134, at A25 (65% opposed if the only reason is that the woman simply does not want a child). *See generally* Apple, *supra* note 135, at A13; Wilkins, Sherlock, & Clark, *supra* note 134, at 145.

137. Americans United for Life, *supra* note 120, *Executive Summary* at 21. *See also* Craig & O'Brien, *supra* note 122, at 46, 258; Faye Ginsburg, Contested Lives: The Abortion Debate in an American Community 6, 134–35 (1989); Luker, *supra* note 134, at 194; Donald Granberg, *The Abortion Activists,* 13 Fam. Plan. Persp. 157, 159 (1981); Blendon, Benson, & Donelan, *supra* note 112, at 2872.

138. *Wirthlin Group Survey, supra* note 134. *See also* Ferree & Hess, *supra* note 135, at 90–92.

both parents would rather have a son—certainly an egregiously sexist act if ever there was one.[139]

Although the numbers approving abortion increase for certain particular reasons, most abortions (perhaps as much as 80 percent) are performed for precisely those reasons most disapproved by the public generally and by women in particular.[140] One need not focus on the widely reported (and perhaps fictitious) stories of occasional women who want an abortion in order not to have to reschedule a skiing vacation to justify this conclusion.[141] Yet career choices (or at least job prospects) are involved in at least half of all abortions. One study found that 76 percent of women undergoing an abortion chose to do so because of the affect pregnancy would have on their lives, and the greater part of this group (67 percent) indicated that the unwanted changes would center on interrupting their careers.[142] The same patterns are true in Britain as well.[143]

One study found that around 30 percent of women who have abortions indicate that they are doing so because "they are not ready" to have a baby; 25 percent chose abortion because they

---

139. *See generally* HADLEY, *supra* note 23, at 94–109; SEX SELECTION OF CHILDREN 47 (Neil Bennett ed. 1983); MARY ANNE WARREN, GENDERCIDE: THE IMPLICATIONS OF SEX SELECTION (1985); April Cherry, *A Feminist Understanding of Sex-Selective Abortion: Solely a Matter of Choice?*, 10 WIS. WOMEN'S L.J. 161 (1995); Jodi Danis, *Sexism and the "Superfluous Female": Arguments for Regulating Pre-Implantation Sex Selection*, 18 HARV. WOMEN'S L.J. 219 (1995); Richard Delgado & Judith Keyes, *Parental Preferences and Selective Abortion: A Commentary on* Roe v. Wade, Doe v. Bolton, *and the Shape of Things to Come*, 1974 WASH. U. L.Q. 203; Mark Evans *et al.*, *Attitudes on the Ethics of Abortion, Sex Selection, and Selective Pregnancy Termination among Health Care Professionals, Ethicists, and Clergy Likely to Encounter Such Situations*, 164 AM. J. OBSTET. & GYNECOLOGY 1992 (1991); E.F. Fugger *et al.*, *Births of Normal Daughters after Microsort Sperm Separation and Intratuterine Insemination, in Vitro Fertilixation, or Intracytoplasmic Sperm Injection*, 13 HUM. REPRODUCTION 2367 (1998); Betty Hoskins & Helen Bequaert Holmes, *Technology and Femicide*, in TEST TUBE WOMEN: WHAT FUTURE FOR MOTHERHOOD? 237 (Rita Arditti, Renate Klein, & Shelley Minden eds. 1984); Owen Jones, *Sex Selection Regulation Technology Enabling the Predetermination of a Child's Gender*, 6 HARV. J.L. & TECHNOL. 1 (1992); Lynne Marie Kohm, *Sex Selection Abortion and the Boomerang Effect of a Woman's Right to Choose: A Paradox of the Skeptics*, 4 WM. & MARY J. WOMEN & L. 91 (1997); Peter Lui & G. Alan Rose, *Social Aspects of over 800 Couples Coming Forward for Gender Selection of Their Children*, 10 HUM. REPRODUCTION 968 (1995); David McCarthy, *Why Sex Selection Should Be Legal*, 27 J. MED. ETHICS 302 (2001); Alison Dundes Renteln, *Sex Selection and Reproductive Freedom*, 15 WOMEN'S STUD. INT'L F. 405 (1992); Julian Savulescu, *Sex Selection—The Case for*, 171 MED. J. AUSTRALIA 373 (1999); John Schaibley, *Sex Selection Abortion: A Constitutional Analysis of the Abortion Liberty and a Person's Right to Know*, 56 IND. L.J. 281 (1981); George Schedler, *Benign Sex Discrimination Revisited: Constitutional and Moral Issues in Banning Sex-Selection Abortion*, 15 PEPP. L. REV. 295 (1988); Joe Leigh Simpson & Sandra Ann Carson, *The Reproductive Option of Sex Selection*, 14 HUM. REPRODUCTION 870 (1999); Nora Kuckreja Sohoni, *Where Are the Girls?*, Ms., July/Aug. 1994, at 96; Robert Steinbacher & Faith Filroy, *Sex Selection Technology: A Prediction of Its Use and Effect*, 124 J. PSYCHOL. 283 (1990); Claude Sureau, *Gender Selection: A Crime against Humanity or the Exercise of a Fundamental Right*, 14 HUM. REPRODUCTION 867 (1999); Mary Warren, *The Ethics of Sex Preselection*, in THE ETHICS OF REPRODUCTIVE TECHNOLOGY 232 (Kenneth Alpern ed. 1992).

140. Victoria Sackett, *Between Pro-Life and Pro-Choice*, PUB. OP., Apr.–May 1985, at 55. *See also* CRAIG & O'BRIEN, *supra* note 122, at 253; Caldwell, *supra* note 112, at 15; Nancy Felipe Russo, *Psychological Aspects of Unwanted Pregnancy and Its Resolution*, in ABORTION, MEDICINE, AND THE LAW, *supra* note 120, at 593, 607–10; Brian Wassom, Comment, *The Exception that Swallowed the Rule? Women's Medical Professional Corporation v. Voinovich and the Mental Health Exception to Post-Viability Abortion Bans*, 49 CASE-W. RES. L. REV. 799, 837–42 (1999). Similar patterns are found in other countries. Augustine Ankomah *et al.*, *Unsafe Abortions: Methods Used and Characteristics of Patients Attending Hospitals in Nairobi, Lima, and Manila*, 18 HEALTH FOR WOMEN INT'L 43, 48–51 (1997).

141. Caldwell, *supra* note 112, at 15. (Caldwell, a supporter of abortion rights, remarkably insists that "[m]any ob-gyn specialists have stories like this….").

142. Aida Torres & Jacqueline Darroch Forrest, *Why Do Women Have Abortions?*, 20 FAM. PLAN. PERSP. 169, 170 (1988). *See also* JUDGES, *supra* note 130, at 37–38.

143. C.M. Langford, *Attitudes of British Women to Abortion: Trends*, 22 POPULATION TRENDS 11 (1980).

"had all the children they wanted."[144] Moreover, nearly half of the abortions in the United States were repeat abortions, *i.e.*, abortions of women who had already had one or more abortions.[145] These patterns suggest a widespread practice of using abortion as a means of birth control despite popular disapproval of using abortion for this purpose. One journalist concluded that of all the predictions made about the effect of *Roe* when it was decided (*e.g.*, rampant rise in numbers, immediate safety for a hitherto unsafe procedure, or no more unwanted births), the only prediction that came true was that "some women would rely on the procedure almost as a form of birth control."[146] Claims by the Alan Guttmacher Institute that abortion is not being used as a means of birth control because most women who have abortions have used contraception sometime within three months of becoming pregnant simply begs the question.[147]

Women are also more supportive of criminalizing fetal abuse (for example, through the ingestion of recreational drugs) than are men.[148] Support for abortion breaks down more on class lines than on gender lines. Some studies found that women are slightly more supportive of abortion rights than men if one controls for such variables as level of education, affluence, career orientation, religious devotion, and so on.[149] One cannot, however, ascribe the different attitudes between men and women towards abortion simply to their differing education levels. Women, regardless of education level, took the lead in the peace movement, hardly a conservative position.[150] Large majorities of poor and minority women (and men) oppose legalized abortion.[151] Similarly large majorities of the rich and powerful—men and women—favor abortion rights.[152]

---

144. Torres & Forrest, *supra* note 142, at 170.

145. Center for Disease Control, Abortion Surveillance—United States 2000 (Nov. 28 2003) (reporting 46% of all abortions were repeat abortions in 1997); Stanley Henshaw & Jane Silverman, *The Characteristics and Prior Contraceptive Use of U.S. Abortion Patients,* 20 Fam. Plan. Persp. 156, 158 (July–August 1988) (43 percent of all abortions to be repeat abortions in 1987); Wardle, *supra* note 114, at 941 (47% of all abortions were repeat abortions in 1992). On the characteristics of women who have repeat abortions, see Susan Fisher, *Reflections on Repeated Abortions: The Meanings and Motivations,* 2 J. Soc. Work Practice 70 (1986); Kathleen Franco e al., *Dysphoric Reactions in Women after Abortion,* 44 J. Am. Med. Women's Ass'n 113 (1989); Ellen Freeman, *Emotional Distress Patterns among Women Having First or Repeat Abortions,* 55 Obstet. & Gynecology 630 (1980); Pirkko Niemela *et al., The First Abortion—and the Last? A Study of the Personality Factors Underlying Repeated Failure of Contraception,* 19 Int'l J. Gynaecology & Obstet. 193 (1981); Merete Osler *et al., Repeat Abortion in Denmark,* 39 Dan. Med. Bull. 89 (1992); Mary Jo Shephard & Michael Bracken, *Contraceptive Practice and Repeat Induced Abortion: An Epidemiological Investigation,* 11 J. Bioscocial Sci. 289 (1979); M. Tornbom *et al., Repeat Abortion: A Comparative Study,* 17 J. Pscyhosomatic Obstet. & Gynecology 208 (1996).

146. Fawn Vrazo, *"Roe" Ruling Reverberates in the Clashing of Symbols,* Phila. Inquirer, Jan. 24, 1993, at C1, C4. *See also* Harrison, *supra* note 112, at 168, 178–79, 299–300 n.34.

147. *See* Judges, *supra* note 130, at 36–37; Henshaw & Silverman, *supra* note 145, at 166–67.

148. Mark Curriden, *Holding Mom Accountable,* 76 ABA J. 50, 51 (Mar. 1990).

149. Cook, Jelen, & Wilcox, *supra* note 129, at 121–24; Wetstein, *supra* note 113, at 79–85, 100–09; Jerome Legge, jr., *The Determinants of Attitudes toward Abortion in the American Electorate,* 36 W. Pol. Q. 479, 486, 489 (1983). *See generally* Robert Erikson, Gerald Wright, & John McIver, Statehouse Democracy: Public Opinion and Policy in the American States (1993).

150. Kenny, *supra* note 134, at 226.

151. Debra Dodson & Lauren Burnbauer, Election 1989: The Abortion Issue in New Jersey and Virginia 23 (1990): Graber, *supra* note 129, at 136–37, 144; Christopher Lasch, The True and Only Heaven: Progress and Its Critics 488–92 (1991); Luker, *supra* note 134, at 27–28, 138–41; Raymond Tatalovich & Byron Daynes, The Politics of Abortion: A Study of Community Conflict in Public Policy Making 6, 38, 84, 117, 124–25 (1981); Alan Abramowitz, *It's Abortion Stupid: Policy Voting in the 1992 Presidential Election,* 57 J. Pol. 176, 181–82 (1995); Baker, Epstein, & Forth, *supra* note 134, at 94–95; Blake, *Public Opinion, supra* note 112, at 544; Blake, *Abortion Decisions, supra* note 112, at 67–68, 78; Karen Dugger, *Race Differences in the Determination of Support for Legalized Abortion,* 72 Soc. Sci. Q. 570, 583 (1991); Granberg, *supra* note 134, at 417–18; Granberg & Granberg, *supra* note 134, at 253; Peter Skerry, *The Class Conflict over Abortion,* 52 Pub. Int. 69 (1978); Tedrow & Mahoney, *supra* note 134, at 185–86.

152. Graber, *supra* note 129, at 144–45, 147; Goldberg & Elder, *supra* note 114, at A16; Robert Lerner, Althea Nagai, & Stanley Rothman, *Abortion and Social Change in America,* 37 Society 8, 11–12 (Jan./Feb.

No wonder the judiciary—drawn, as it is from the well educated and the well off—predominantly supports abortion rights.[153] After all, as law professor Stephen Griffin noted, "[l]ike metal filings in a magnetic field, political outcomes would tend to flow along the lines of force established by the most powerful special interest groups."[154] As political scientist E.E. Schattsschneider observed, "[t]he flaw in the pluralist heaven is that the heavenly chorus sings with a strong upper-class accent."[155]

While the founders and early leadership of both those supporting and those opposing abortion rights were men,[156] women have, for better than two decades, provided the bulk of the committed workers in both camps. And, given the relative numbers of women in the differing social classes that tend to support or to oppose abortion rights, one should not be surprised to discover that the number of women who are committed to working to limit access to abortion far outnumbers the number of women who are similarly committed to working to secure access to abortion.[157] While it belies the popular image of woman's attitudes towards abortion, women opposed to abortion have long been the driving force behind the pro-life movement, often including women who have had abortions. The National Women's Coalition for Life counts 1,800,000 members; in contrast, the strongly pro-abortion National Organization for Women (NOW—still the primary organization for the feminist movement) counts only 250,000 members. More than 60 percent of the delegates to the 1990 Convention of the National Right to Life Committee were women. The Committee does not keep membership statistics by gender, so we cannot say how its membership breaks down. Organizations that do keep such statistics consistently show women in the majority. Women are a majority in the American Life League (140,000 of 270,000 members) as well as other gender-integrated organizations organized to oppose abortion. Concerned Women for America, which features opposition to abortion as a major concern, includes 646,000 women in a total membership of 755,000.

One measure of women's discomfort with abortion is the denial and grief that many women feel after having an abortion. As many as half of the women who undergo an abortion will deny having done so.[158] Depending on which study one credits, between seven and 40 percent of women who have had abortions suffer form post-abortion trauma.[159] There are no less than

---

1990). This difference has persisted for at least a century. *See* PAUL GEBHARD *et al.*, PREGNANCY, BIRTH AND ABORTION 150, 162 (1958); LESLIE REAGAN, WHEN ABORTION WAS A CRIME: WOMEN, MEDICINE, AND LAW IN THE UNITED STATES, 1867–1973, at 135–37 (1997).

153. GRABER, *supra* note 129, at 145. *See also* GARROW, *supra* note 23, at 473–74, 539; LEE EPSTEIN & JOSEPH KOBYLKA, THE SUPREME COURT AND LEGAL CHANGE: ABORTION AND THE DEATH PENALTY 190 (1992); JOHN CALVIN JEFFRIES, JR., JUSTICE LEWIS F. POWELL, JR. 317 (1994); BOB WOODWARD & SCOTT ARMSTRONG, THE BRETHREN: INSIDE THE SUPREME COURT 196, 205, 272 (1979); Greenberg, *supra* note 114, at A25.

154. Stephen Griffin, *Bringing the State into Constitutional Theory: Public Authority and the Constitution*, 25 LAW & SOC'Y REV. 659, 678 (1991).

155. E.E. SCHATTSCHNEIDER, THE SOVEREIGN PEOPLE 31–35 (1960).

156. *See* Chapter 11, at notes 321–50; Chapter 13, at notes 23–28, 42, 36–39, 52, 56, 122–37, 202–10, 232–35, 326–30, 345–81; Chapter 14, at notes 69–90.

157. *See generally* GINSBURG, *supra* note 137, at 6–11, 16–18, 45, 134–35; LUKER, *supra* note 134, at 94, 126–57; MENSCH & FREEMAN, *supra* note 122, at 130; PAIGE, *supra* note 123, at 65–70; Deirdre English, *The War against Choice: Inside the Anti-Abortion Movement,* MOTHER JONES, Feb./Mar., 1981, at 16.

158. C. EVERETT KOOP, MEDICAL AND PSYCHOLOGICAL EFFECTS OF ABORTIONS 15 (1989); ANNE SPECKHARD, THE PSYCHO-SOCIAL ASPECTS OF STRESS FOLLOWING ABORTION 74 (1987); Steven Waldman, Elise Ackerman, & Rita Rubin, *Abortions in America: So Many Women Have Them, so Few Talk about Them,* US NEWS & WORLD REP., Jan. 19, 1998, at 20.

159. *See, e.g.,* ABORTION—THE EMOTIONAL IMPLICATIONS 46 (Roberta Kalmar ed. 1977); Terry Nicole Steinbeg, Note, *Abortion Counseling: To Benefit Maternal Health,* 15 AM. J.L. & MED. 483, 488 n.42 (1989). *See also* CATHERINE BARNARD, THE LONG TERM PSYCHOLOGICAL EFFECTS OF ABORTION (1990); ANGELA BROWNE-MILLER, HOW TO DIE AND SURVIVE (1997); MAGDA DIENES, IN NECESSITY AND SORROW (1976); KOOP, *supra* note 158, at 2–3; NATHANSON, *supra* note 134; POST-ABORTION SYNDROME (Peter Doherty ed.

three organizations for women who feel deep grief over what many of them consider to have been abortions coerced by boyfriends or induced by deceptive abortion providers: Abortion Victims of America;[160] Victims of Choice,[161] and Women Exploited by Abortion (WEBA).[162] Even convinced feminists are not united in support of abortion rights;[163] some see in the celebration

---

1994); David Reardon, Aborted Women: Silent No More (1987) ("Reardon, Silent No More"); David Reardon, A Survey of Post-Abortion Reactions 23 (1987); Speckhard, *supra* note 158; Jeanette Vought, Post-Abortion Trauma: 9 Steps to Recovery (1991); Nancy Adler et al., *Psychological Responses after Abortion*, 248 Science 41 (1990); E. Joanne Angelo, *Psychiatric Sequelae of Abortion: The Many Faces of Post-Abortion Grief*, 59 Linacre Q. 69 (No. 2, 1992); Dennis Bagarozzi, *Identification, Assessment and Treatment of Women Suffering from Posttraumatic Stress after Abortion*, 5 J. Fam. Therapy 25 (1994); Dennis Bagarozzi, *Post Traumatic Stress Disorders in Women Following Abortion: Some Considerations and Implications for Marital/Couple Therapy*, 1 J. Fam. & Marriage 51 (1993); Patricia Conklin & Brian O'Connor, *Beliefs about the Fetus as a Moderator of Post-Abortion Psychological Well-Being*, 14 J. Soc. & Clinical Psych. 76 (1995); G. Kam Congleton & Lawrence Calhoun, *Post-Abortion Perceptions: A Comparison of Self-Identified Distressed and Non Distressed Populations*, 39 Int'l J. Soc. Psych. 255 (1993); Paul Dagg, *The Psychological Sequelae of Therapeutic Abortion—Denied and Completed*, 148 Am. J. Psych. 578 (1991); Kathleen Franco et al., *Psychological Profile of Dysphoric Women Postabortion*, 44 J. Am. Med. Women's Ass'n no. 4, at 113 (July/Aug. 1989); Wanda Franz & David Reardon, *Differential Impact of Abortion on Adolescents and Adults*, 27 Adolescence 162 (1992); Richard Henshaw et al., *Psychological Responses Following Medical Abortion (Using Mifepristone and Gemepost) and Surgical Vacuum Aspiration*, 73 Acta Obstet. Gynecol. Scand. 812 (1994); Janet Mattinson, *The Effects of Abortion on a Marriage*, 115 Ciba Fndtn. Symposium 165 (1985); Philip Ney et al., *The Effects of Pregnancy Loss on Women's Health*, 38 Soc. Sci. & Med. 1193 (1994); Jo Ann Rosenfeld, *Emotional Responses to Therapeutic Abortion*, 45 Am. Fam. Physician 137 (1992); David Sherman et al., *The Abortion Experience in Private Practice in Women and Loss*, in Psychobiological Perspectives 98 (William Finn et al. ed. 1985); George Skelton, *Many in Survey Who Had Abortion Cite Guilt Feelings*, L.A. Times, Mar. 19, 1989, at 28; Anne Speckhard & Vincent Rue, *Complicated Mourning and Abortion*, 8 J. Pre- & Peri-Natal Psych. 5 (1993); Anne Speckhard & Vincent Rue, *Postabortion Syndrome: An Emerging Public Health Concern*, 48 J. Soc. Issues 95 (1992); Nada Stotland, *The Myth of Abortion Trauma Syndrome*, 268 JAMA 2078 (1992); John Thorp, jr., Katherine Hartmann, & Elizabeth Shadigian, *Long-Term Physical and Psychological Health Consequences of Induced Abortion*, 58 Obstet. & Gynecological Survey 67 (2002); Wassom, *supra* note 140, at 842–56; M.C.A. White-Van Mourik et al., *The Psychosocial Sequelae of Second Trimester Termination of Pregnancy for a Fetal Abnormality over a Two Year Period*, 28 Birth Defects 61 (1992); Gregory Wilmuth et al., *Prevalence of Psychological Risks Following Legal Abortion in the U.S.: Limits of the Evidence*, 49 J. Soc. Issues 37 (1992); Charles Zeanah et al., *Do Women Grieve after Terminating Pregnancies because of Fetal Anomalies: A Controlled Investigation*, 82 Obstet. & Gynecology 270 (1993). *See generally* Linda Birde Francke, The Ambivalence of Abortion (1978); Jill Gerston, *On Abortion: Regret, Relief, Hatred, and Joy*, Phila. Inquirer, Apr. 16, 1978, at K1.

160. *See* Rosenblatt, *supra* note 129, at 25–26, 42–44

161. *See* Jacoby, *supra* note 59, at 49–50.

162. *See* Calhoun & Sexton, *supra* note 134, at 479–81. *See generally* Paula Ervin, Women Exploited: The Other Victim of Abortion (1985); Pam Koerbel, Abortion's Second Victim (1986); Michael Mannion, Abortion & Healing: A Cry to Be Whole (1986); Nancy Michaels, Helping Women Recover from Abortion (1988); Reardon, Silent No More, *supra* note 159; Kathleen Winkler, When the Crying Stops: Abortion, the Pain and the Healing (1992).

163. *See* Abortion: Understanding Differences 1, 12 (Sydney & Daniel Callahan eds. 1984) (containing articles by pro-life and pro-choice feminists); Ginsburg, *supra* note 137, at 172–93, 227–47; Hadley, *supra* note 23, at 194–97; Gail Hamilton, Feminism Reconsidered: How Women Are Exploited by Abortion (1994); Jacoby, *supra* note 59, at 50–51, 184–85; McDonnell, *supra* note 133, at 59; Mensch & Freeman, *supra* note 122, at 4; Muldoon, *supra* note 112, at 146–47; Pro-Life Feminism 81–106 (Gail Grenier Sweet ed. 1985); Sisterlife (a quarterly newsletter published by Feminists for Life of America); Martha Bayles, *Feminism and Abortion*, Atlantic Monthly 83 (April 1990); Calhoun & Sexton, *supra* note 134, at 445–46; Callahan, *supra* note 123; Cunningham & Forsythe, *supra* note 120, at 114–17; Jason DeParle, *Beyond the Legal Right*, 21 Wash. Monthly no. 4, at 28 (Apr. 1989); Stephen Goode, *A Feminist Who Takes a Pro-Life Stand*, Insight Mag, Oct. 1, 2001, at 37; Susan Himmelweit, *More than a "Woman's Right to Choose*,'" 29 Fem. Rev. 38 (1988); Diane Krstulovich, *Disposing of Pro-Life Stereotypes*, Journal Montage, Dec. 11, 1991, at 47, 56; Mary Meehan, *Will Somebody Please Be Consistent?*, 9 Sojourners 14 (Nov. 1980); Ruth Putnam, *Being Ambivalent about Abortion*, Tikkun, Sept.–Oct. 1989, at 81; Janet Smith, *Abortion as a Feminist Con-*

of abortion the denial of the very qualities that make women women, qualities that provide women with their distinct social function.[164] African-American women in particular are less supportive of abortion than are either white men or white women.[165] Today as always, the debate is as much (or more) between differing groups of women as it is between the sexes[166] — hardly a surprise given that many individuals struggle within themselves over the rights and wrongs of abortion. And these divisions hold true as much among young women as among older women.[167]

Similar divisions exist among women worldwide, both within particular national or ethnic groups and between different cultural groups. Differences over abortion are similar to divisions over clitoridectomy (amputating part or all of the clitoris, often along with part or all of the labia) or infibulation (sewing the vagina closed) or both — the practice of so-called female circumcision. Western feminists are usually quick to deny the existence of universal truths as a "male" imposition,[168] yet they often insist that female circumcision violates the

---

*cern,* in The Zero People 77, at 81–84 (Jeff Lane Hensley ed. 1983); Amicus *Brief of Feminists for Life, supra* note 120. For the situation historically, see Chapter 8; Chapter 11, at notes 276–328; Chapter 13, at 36–38, 56.

164. Callahan, *supra* note 123; Smith, *supra* note 163, at 81–87. *See generally* Patricia Karlan & Daniel Ortiz, *In a Different Voice: Relational Feminism, Abortion Rights, and the Feminist Legal Agenda,* 87 Nw. U. L. Rev. 858, 880–82 (1993).

165. Ferree & Hess, *supra* note 135, at 91; Akua Furlow, Abortion and the African American — A Deadly Silence (1994); Kay Coles James, Never Forget 125–26 (1992); Baker, Epstein, & Firth, *supra* note 134; Michael Combs & Susan Welch, *Blacks, Whites, and Attitudes toward Abortion,* 46 Pub. Op. Q. 510 (1982); Elaine Hall & Myra Marx Ferree, *Race Differences in Abortion Attitudes,* 50 Pub. Op. Q. 193 (1986); Clyde Wilcox, *Race Differences and Abortion Attitudes: Some Additional Evidence,* 54 Pub. Opinion Q. 248 (1990); Clyde Wilcox, *Race, Religion, Region, and Abortion Attitudes,* 53 Soc. Analysis 97 (1992). *But see* Laurie Nsiah-Jefferson, *Reproductive Laws, Women of Color, and Low-Income Women,* 11 Women's Rts. L. Rptr. 15 (1989); Dorothy Roberts, *The Future of Reproductive Choice for Poor Women and Women of Color,* 12 Women's Rts. L. Rptr. 59 (1990); Loretta Ross, *African-American Women and Abortion,* in Abortion Wars: A Half Century of Struggle, 1950–2000, at 161 (Rickie Solinger ed. 1998).

166. *See, e.g.,* Condit, *supra* note 118, at 199–201; Craig & O'Brien, *supra* note 122, at 46–48; Francke, *supra* note 159; Elizabeth Fox Genovese, Feminism without Illusions 81–86, 99–101 (1991); Ginsburg, *supra* note 137; Luker, *supra* note 134, at 94–160, 193–94; Mensch & Freeman, *supra* note 122, at 130; Pro-Life Feminism, *supra* note 163; Bayles, *supra* note 163, at 85; Callahan, *supra* note 163; Greenberg, *supra* note 114, at A25; Susan Harding, *Family Reform Movements: Recent Feminism and Its Opposition,* 7 Feminist Stud. 57 (1981); *Is Abortion the Issue?,* Harper's Mag., July, 1986, at 35; Joan Williams, *Gender Wars: Selfless Women in the Republic of Choice,* 66 N.Y.U. L. Rev. 1559, 1561, 1564–94, 1624–29 (1991) ("Williams, *Gender Wars*"). *See also* Linda Gordon, *Why Nineteenth Century Feminists Did Not Support "Birth Control" and Twentieth Century Feminists Do,* in Rethinking the Family 40, 51 (Barrie Thorne & Marilyn Yalom eds. 1982) (describing women with a "nineteenth-century" mindset as opposed to abortion, and women with a "twentieth-century" mindset as supporting abortion).

On the divisions among women regarding feminism generally, see F. Carolyn Graglia, Domestic Tranquility: A Brief against Feminism (1998); Harrison, *supra* note 112, at 32–34; Donald Mathews & Jane DeHart, Sex, Gender and the Politics of ERA (1990); Christina Hoff Sommers, Who Stole Feminism? How Women Have Betrayed Women (1994); Susan Marshall, *Who Speaks for American Women? The Future of Antifeminism,* 515 Annals Am. Academy Pol. & Soc. Sci. 50 (1991); Elizabeth Mehren, *Feminist vs. Feminist,* L.A. Times, April 30, 1992, at E1; Joan Williams, *Dissolving the Sameness/Difference Debate: A Post-Modern Path beyond Essentialism in Feminist and Critical Race Theory,* 1991 Duke L.J. 296, 302–05 ("Williams, *Sameness/Difference*"). A somewhat similar split has arisen between those feminists who would ban pornography and those (sometimes derided as "ACLU feminists") who oppose the proposed ban as an intrusion on free speech. *See, e.g.,* Carrie Menkel-Meadow, *Mainstreaming Feminist Legal Theory,* 23 Pac. L.J. 1493, 1508–09 (1992).

167. *See* Moreno, *supra* note 3.

168. *See, e.g.,* Mary Field Belenky *et al.,* Women's Ways of Knowing: The Development of Self, Voice, and Mind (1986); Scyla Benhabih, Situating the Self: Gender, Community and Postmodernism in Contemporary Ethics (1992); Rosi Braidotti, Patterns of Discourse: A Study of Women in Contemporary Philosophy (1991); Drucilla Cornell, Beyond Feminism: Ethical Feminism, De-

universal human rights of women.[169] Ironically, the Americans who are most sensitive to the divisions among women regarding such practices often are the most doctrinally conserva-

---

CONSTRUCTION, AND THE LAW (1991); MARY JOE FRUG, POSTMODERN LEGAL FEMINISM (1992); CAROL GILLI-GAN, IN A DIFFERENT VOICE: PSYCHOLOGICAL THEORY AND WOMEN'S DEVELOPMENT (1982); SANDRA HARD-ING, THE SCIENCE QUESTION IN FEMINISM (1986); NANCY HIRSCHMANN, RETHINKING OBLIGATION: A FEMI-NIST METHOD FOR POLITICAL THEORY (1992); BELL HOOKS, TALKING BACK: THINKING FEMINIST, THINKING BLACK (1989); HUMAN RIGHTS, CULTURE AND CONTEXT: ANTHROPOLOGICAL PERSPECTIVES (Richard Wilson ed. 1997); CATHARINE MACKINNON, TOWARD A FEMINIST THEORY OF THE STATE (1989); MARTHA MINOW, MAKING ALL THE DIFFERENCE: INCLUSION, EXCLUSION, AND AMERICAN LAW (1990); NEL NODDINGS, CARING: A FEMININE APPROACH TO ETHICS AND MORAL EDUCATION (1984); SUSAN MILLER OKIN, JUSTICE, GENDER, AND THE FAMILY (1989); SARA RUDDING, MATERNAL THINKING: TOWARDS A POLITICS OF PEACE (1989); SUSAN SHERWIN, NO LONGER PATIENT: FEMINIST ETHICS AND HEALTH CARE (1992); CAROL SMART, FEMINISM AND THE POWER OF LAW (1989); ELIZABETH SPELLMAN, INESSENTIAL WOMAN: PROBLEMS OF EXCLUSION IN FEMINIST THOUGHT (1988); DEBORAH TANNEN, YOU JUST DON'T UNDERSTAND (1990); JANET TODD, GENDER AND LITERARY VOICE (1980); WOMEN, KNOWLEDGE AND REALITY: EXPLORATIONS IN FEMINIST PHILOSOPHY (Ann Garry & Marilyn Pearsall eds. 1989); Hilary Charlesworth, Christine Chinkin, & Shelley Wright, *Feminist Approaches to International Law*, 85 AM. J. INT'L L. 613 (1991); Judith Lichtenberg, *Objectivity and Its Enemies*, 2 THE RESPONSIVE COMMUNITY 59 (1991); Elene Mountie, *Cultural Relativity and Universalism: Reevaluating Gender Rights in a Multicultural Context*, 15 DICK. J. INT'L L. 113 (1996); Williams, *Sameness/Difference*, supra note 166.

169. *See, e.g.*, Robin Morgan & Gloria Steinem, *The International Crime of Genital Mutilation*, in OUTRAGEOUS ACTS AND EVERYDAY REBELLIONS 29 (Gloria Steinem ed. 2d ed. 1995). *See also* Abankwah v. INS, 185 F.3d 18 (2nd Cir. 1999); *In re* Kasinga, Bur. Imm. Appeals, Interim Dec. 3278, 1996 BIA LEXIS 15 (June 13, 1996), reprinted in 35 INT'L LEGAL MAT'LS 1145 (1996). *See generally* RAQUIYA HAJI DUALEH ABDALLA, SISTERS IN AFFLICTION: CIRCUMCISION AND INFIBULATION OF WOMEN IN AFRICA (1982); MAHID AL DIRIE, FEMALE CIRCUMCISION IN SOMALIA: MEDICAL AND SOCIAL IMPLICATIONS (1985); EFUA DORKENDO, CUTTING THE ROSE: FEMALE GENITAL MUTILATION: THE PRACTICE AND ITS PREVENTION (1994); ASMA EL DAREER, WOMEN WHY DO YOU WEEP? (1982); FRAN HOSKEN, STOP GENITAL MUTILATION: WOMEN SPEAK: FACTS AND ACTION (1995); INTERSECTIONS BETWEEN HEALTH AND HUMAN RIGHTS: THE CASE OF FEMALE GENITAL MUTILATION (Elizabeth Kirberger *et al.* eds. 1995); OLAYINKA KOSO-THOMAS, THE CIRCUMCISION OF WOMEN: A STRATEGY FOR ERADICATION (1987); ANIKA RAHMAN & NAHID TOUBIA, FEMALE GENITAL MUTILATION: A GUIDE TO LAWS AND POLICIES WORLDWIDE (2000); SEXUAL MUTILATIONS: A HUMAN TRAGEDY (George Denniston & Marilyn Fayre Milos eds. 1997); SHERWIN, *supra* note 168, at 58–75; NAHID TOUBIA, FEMALE GENITAL MUTILATION: A CALL FOR GLOBAL ACTION (1993); ALICE WALKER & PATIBITA PARMAR, WARRIOR MARKS: FEMALE GENITAL MUTILATION AND THE SEXUAL BLINDING OF WOMEN (1993); Sami Aldeeb abu-Sahlieh, *To Mutilate in the Name of Jehovah or Allah: Legitimization of Male and Female Circumcision*, 13 MED. LAW. 575 (1994); Fitnat Naa-Adjeley Adjetey, *Reclaiming the African Woman's Individuality: The Struggle between Women's Reproductive Autonomy and African Society and Culture*, 44 AM. U. L. REV. 1351 (1995); Catherine Annas, *Irreversible Error: The Power and Prejudice of Female Genital Mutilation*, 12 J. CONTEMP. HEALTH L. & POL'Y 325 (1996); Lois Bibbings, *Female Circumcision: Mutilation or Modification?*, in LAW AND BODY POLITICS: REGULATING THE FEMALE BODY 151 (Jo Bridgemen & Susan Milns ed. 1995); Colloquium, *Bridging Society, Culture, and Law: The Issue of Female Circumcision*, 47 CASE-W. RES. L. REV. 263 (1997); Julie Dimauro, *Toward a More Effective Guarantee of Women's Human Rights: A Mutlicultural Dialogue in International Law*, 17 WOMEN'S RTS. L. REP. 333, 334–35 (1996); Anna Funder, *De Minimus Non Curat Lex: The Clitoris, Culture and the Law*, 3 TRANSNAT'L L. & CONTEMP. PROBS. 417 (1993); Pia Gallo & Fanco Viviani, *The Origin of Infibulation in Somalia: An Ethological Hypothesis*, 13 ETHOLOGY & SOCIOBIOLOGY 253 (1992); Daniel Gordon, *Female Circumcision and Genital Operations in Egypt and Sudan: A Dilemma for Medical Anthropology*, 5 MED. ANTHROPOLOGY Q. 3 (1991); Isabelle Gunning, *Arrogant Perception, World-Traveling and Multicultural Feminism: The Case of Female Genital Surgeries*, 23 COLUM. H. RTS. L. REV. 189 (1991); Phoebe Haddon, *All the Difference in the World: Listening and Hearing the Voices of Women*, 8 TEMPLE POL. & CIV. RTS. L. REV. 377 (1999); Karen Hughes, *The Criminalization of Female Genital Mutilation in the United States*, 4 J. LAW & POL'Y 3212 (1995); Stephen James, *Reconciling International Human Rights and Cultural Relativism: The Case of Female Circumcision*, 8 BIOETHICS 1 (1994); Eike-Henner Kluge, *Female Circumcision: When Medical Ethics Confronts Cultural Values*, 148 CAN. MED. ASS'N J. 288 (1993); Joanne Liu, *When Law and Culture Clash: Female Genital Mutilation, a Traditional Practice Gaining Recognition as a Global Concern*, 11 N.Y. INT'L L. REV. 71 (1998); Robin Maher, *Female Genital Mutilation: The Modern Day Struggle to Eradicate a Torturous Rite of Passage*, 23 HUM. RTS. 12 (1996); Melissa Morgan, *Female Genital Mutilation: An Issue on the Doorstep of the American Legal Community*, 18 J. LEGAL MED. 93 (1997); Khadijah Sharif, *Female Genital Mutilation: What*

tive.[170] Even these commentators, however, seldom consider that female genital surgeries are performed by, as well as on, women and in a strong sense often serve to empower women

---

*Does Federal Law Really Mean?*, 24 FORDHAM URBAN L.J. 409 (1997); Barbara Stark, *Crazy Jane Talks with the Bishop: Abortion in China, Germany, South Africa and International Human Rights Law*, 12 TEX. J. WOMEN & L. 287, 308–20 (2003); Joan Tarpley, *Bad Witches: A Cut on the Clitoris with the Instruments of Institutional Power and Politics*, 100 W. VA. L. REV. 297 (1997); Nahid Toubia, *Female Circumcision as a Public Health Issue*, 331 NEW ENG. J. MED. 712 (1994); Leigh Trueblood, *Female Genital Mutilation: A Discussion of International Human Rights Instruments, Cultural Sovereignty and Dominance Theory*, 28 DEN. J. INT'L L. & POL'Y 437 (2000); Laura Ziv, *The Tragedy of Female Circumcision: One Woman's Story*, MARIE CLAIRE, Mar. 1996, at 65. *See also* CATHARINE MACKINNON, FEMINISM UNMODIFIED: DISCOURSES ON LIFE AND LAW 68–69 (1987) (criticizing sexism among Pueblo Indians as a practice imposed by White males, describing sexism as the root of all modern oppression of American Indians, and calling on them to change their cultural practices); Sarah Lai & Regan Ralph, *Female Sexual Autonomy and Human Rights*, 8 HARV. HUM. RTS. J. 201 (1995) (describing virginity examinations in Turkey and child marriages in Nigeria as human rights abuses). *See generally* IS MULTICULTURALISM BAD FOR WOMEN? (Joshua Cohen *et al.* eds. 1999); WOMEN'S RIGHTS, HUMAN RIGHTS: INTERNATIONAL FEMINIST PERSPECTIVES 224 (Julie Peters & Andrea Wolper eds. 1995); Arvonne Fraser, *Becoming Human: The Origins and Development of Women's Human Rights*, 21 HUM. RTS. Q. 853 (1999); Rhoda Howard, *Cultural Relativism and The Nostalgia for Community*, 15 HUM. RTS. Q. 315 (1993); Holly Maguigan, *Cultural Evidence and Male Violence: Are Feminists and Multiculturalist Reforms on a Collision Course in Criminal Courts?*, 70 NYU L. REV. 36 (1995); Martha Nussbaum, *Human Functioning and Social Justice: In Defense of Aristotelian Essentialism*, 20 POL. THEORY 203 (1992); Leti Volpp, *Feminism versus Multiculturalism*, 101 COLUM. L. REV. 1181 (2001). Much less attention has been given to the mutilation involved in male circumcision. *See, e.g.,* Andrew Maykuth, *Manhood, at What Cost? Ritual Circumcision Is a Rite of Passage in South Africa's Xhosa Tribe. Its Modern Legacy Includes Death and Maiming*, PHILA. INQUIRER, Feb. 1, 2000, at D1; Geoffrey Miller, *Circumcision: Cultural-Legal Analysis*, 9 VA. J. SOC. POL'Y & L. 497 (2002).

170.  Karen Engle, *Female Subjects of Public International Law: Human Rights and the Exotic Other Female*, 26 N. ENG. L. REV. 1509, 1511–13 (1992). *See also* Nancy Kim, *Toward a Feminist Theory of Human Rights: Straddling the Fence between Western Imperialism and Uncritical Absolutism*, 25 COLUM. HUM. RTS. L. REV. 49 (1993); Hope Lewis, *Between* Irua *and "Female Genital Mutilation": Feminist Human Rights Discourse and the Cultural Divide*, 8 HARV. HUM. RTS. J. 1 (1995). *And see* Duncan Kennedy, *Sexual Abuse, Sexy Dressing and the Eroticization (sic) of Domination*, 26 N. ENG. L. REV. 1309, 1327 (1992) (arguing that the differing responses to allegations of sexual abuse are "more heavily contested between conservatives and liberals than between men and women"). *See generally* JOANNE BAUER & DANIEL BELL, THE EAST ASIAN APPROACH TO HUMAN RIGHTS (1999); DEMOCRACY, THE RULE OF LAW, AND ISLAM (Eugene Cotran & Abdel Omar Sherif eds. 1999); ELLEN GRUENBAUM, THE FEMALE CIRCUMCISION CONTROVERSY: AN ANTHROPOLOGICAL PERSPECTIVE (2000); HUMAN RIGHTS IN CROSS-CULTURAL PERSPECTIVES—A QUEST FOR CONSENSUS (Abdullah Ahmed An-Na'im ed. 1992); MICHAEL IGNATIEFF, HUMAN RIGHTS AS POLITICS AND IDOLATRY (2001); ANN ELIZABETH MAYER, ISLAM AND HUMAN RIGHTS: TRADITION AND POLITICS (1999); MAHMOUD MONSHIPOURI, ISLAMISM, SECULARISM, AND HUMAN RIGHTS IN THE MIDDLE EAST (1998); ALISON DUNDES RENTELN, INTERNATIONAL HUMAN RIGHTS: UNIVERSALISM VERSUS RELATIVISM (1990); José Lindgren Alves, *The Declaration of Human Rights in Postmodernity*, 22 HUM. RTS. Q. 478 (2000); Kay Boulware-Miller, *Female Circumcision: Challenges to the Practice as a Human Rights Violation*, 8 HARV. WOMEN'S L.J. 155 (1985); Michele Brandt & Jeffrey Kaplan, *The Tension between Women's Rights and Religious Rights: Reservations to CEDAW by Egypt, Bangladesh and Tunisia*, 12 J. LAW & RELIGION 105 (1996); Neil Englehart, *Rights and Culture in the Asian Values Argument: The Rise and Fall of Confucian Ethics in Singapore*, 22 HUM. RTS. Q. S48 (2000); Amanda Garay, *Women, Cultural Relativism, and International Human Rights: A Question of Mutual Exclusivity or Balance?*, 12 INT'L INSIGHTS 19 (1996); Elvin Hatch, *The Good Side of Relativism*, 53 J. ANTHROPOLIGAL RES. 371 (1997); Soheir Morsey, *Safeguarding Women's Bodies: The White Man's Burden Medicalized*, 5 MED. ANTHROPOLOGY Q. 19 (1991); David Smolin, *Will International Human Rights Be Used as a Tool of Cultural Genocide? The Interaction of Human Rights Norms, Religion, Culture and Gender*, 12 J. LAW & RELIGION 143 (1996); Boaventura de Sousa Santos, *Towards a Multiplicultural Conception of Human Rights*, in SPACES OF CULTURE: CITY, NATURE, WORLD 214 (Mike Featherstone & Scott Lash eds. 1999); Symposium, *East Asian Approaches to Human Rights*, 2 BUFF. J. INT'L L. 231 (1996); John Tilley, *Cultural Relativism*, 22 HUM. RTS. Q. S01 (2000); Leigh Trueblood, *Female Genital Mutilation: A Discussion of International Human Rights Instruments, Cultural Sovereignty and Dominance Theory*, 28 DEN. J. INT'L L. & POL'Y 437 (2000); Christine Venter, *Community Culture and Tradition: Maintaining Male Dominance in Conservative Institutions*, 12 J. LAW & RELIGION 61 (1996).

within the confines of the material and social conditions of their societies.[171] Indeed, on occasion village women have opposed male demands for the end of female circumcision as inappropriate intrusions in women's affairs.[172] Rather than coming to grips with such realities, Western feminists tend to dismiss such responses as instances of "false consciousness."[173] I personally am appalled by female circumcision—but I also acknowledge that the values implicated in the practice are more complex and conflicted than, and that the conflict is, at least on the practical level, more difficult to resolve than many doctrinaire feminists would have us believe.[174]

In a similar vein, many Western feminists conclude that the universally applicable principles of what some claim to be their "multicultural intersubjective and diverse" ethical universe include a woman's right to choose to abort at any time during pregnancy.[175] Such feminists insist

---

171. Janice Boddy, Women and Alien Spirits: Women, Men, and the Zan Cult of Northern Sudan 52–88 (1989); Ellen Gruenbaum, The Female Circumcision Controversy: An Anthropological Perspective 41, 50, 192 (2001); Hanny Lightfoot-Klein, Prisoners of Ritual: An Odyssey into Female Genital Circumcision in Africa 39–40, 216 (1989); Morayo Atoki, *Should Female Circumcision Continue to Be Banned?*, 3 Fem. Legal Stud. 223 (1995); Janice Boddy, *Womb as Oasis: The Symbolic Content of Pharaonic Circumcision in Rural Northern Sudan*, 9 Am. Ethnologist 682, 687 (1982); Kay Boulware-Miller, *Female Circumcision: Challenges to the Practice as a Human Rights Violation*, 8 Harv. Women's L.J. 155 (1985); Anna Funder, De Minimus Non Curat Lex: *The Clitoris, Culture and the Law*, 3 Transnat'l L. & Contemp. Prob. 417 (1993); Gunning, *supra* note 169, at 218–26, 228–30; Asma Mohamed Abdel Halim, *Rituals and Angels: Female Circumcision and the Case of Sudan*, in From Basic Needs to Basic Rights 249 (Margaret Schuler ed. 1995); Micere Githae Mugo, *Elitist Anti-Circumcision Discourse as Mutilating and Anti-Feminist*, 47 Case-W. Res. L. Rev. 461 (1997); L. Amede Obiora, *Bridges and Barricades: Rethinking Polemics and Intransigence in the Campaign against Female Circumcision*, 47 Case-W. Res. L. Rev. 275 (1997); Melissa Parker, *Rethinking Female Circumcision*, 65 Africa 506 (1995); Richard Reuben, *New Ground for Asylum: Threatened Female Genital Mutilation Is Persecution*, ABA J., July, 1996, at 36; Marie Angélique Savanne, *Why We Are against the International Campaign*, 40 Int'l Child Welfare J. 37 (1979); Trueblood, *supra* note 170, at 446–48. Only recently, have some women's groups in countries where the practice is common begun to denounce it. *See* Marc Lacey, *African Women Gather to Denounce Genital Cutting*, N.Y. Times, Feb. 6, 2003, at A6.

172. Ellen Gruenbaum, *Reproductive Ritual and Social Reproduction: Female Circumcision and the Subordination of Women in Sudan*, in Economy and Class in Sudan 313 (Norman O'Neill & Jay O'Brien eds. 1988). *See also* December Green, Gender Violence in Africa: African Women's Responses 15 (1999); Susan Dillon, *Healing the Sacred Yoni in the Land of Isis: Female Genital Mutilation Is Banned (Again) in Egypt*, 22 Hous. J. Int'l L. 289, 296 (2000).

173. *See, e.g.*, Engle, *supra* note 170, at 1518; Robyn Cerny Smith, *Female Circumcision: Bringing Women's Perspectives into the International Debate*, 65 S. Cal. L. Rev. 2449, 2486–88 (1992). *See generally* Kimberle Crenshaw, *Mapping the Margins: Intersectionality, Identity Politics, and Violence against Women of Color*, 43 Stan. L. Rev. 1241, 1257 (1991); Jenny Rivera, *Domestic Violence against Latinas by Latino Males: An Analysis of Race, National Origin and Gender Differentials*, 15 B.C. Third World L.J. 231, 234 (1994); Adrien Katherine Wing, *Custom, Religion and Rights: The Future Legal Status of Palestinian Women*, 35 Harv. Int'l L.J. 149, 157 (1994). On the problem of "false consciousness" generally, see Chapter 20, at notes 118–31.

174. *See also* Janice Boddy, *Body Politics: Continuing the Anti-Circumcision Crusade*, 5 Med. Anthropology Q. 15, 16 (1991); Michael Ignatieff, *The Attack on Human Rights*, 80 For. Aff. no. 6, at 102, 112–13 (Nov./Dec. 2000); L. Amede Obiora, *New Wine, Old Skin: (En)Gaging Nationalism, Traditionalism, and Gender Relations*, 28 Ind. L. Rev. 575 (1995); Nancy Scheper-Hughes, *Virgin Territory: The Male Discovery of the Clitoris*, 5 Med. Anthropology Q. 25, 27 (1991).

175. Gayle Binnion, *Human Rights: A Feminist Perspective*, 17 Hum. Rts. Q. 509 (1995); Reed Boland, *Population Policies, Human Rights, and Legal Choice*, 44 Am. U. L. Rev. 1257 (1995); Rebecca Cook, *Human Rights and Reproductive Self-Determination*, 44 Am. U. L. Rev. 975 (1995); Rebecca Cook, *International Protection of Women's Reproductive Choice*, 24 N.Y.U. J. Int'l L. & Politics 401 (1992) ("Cook, *International Protection*"); Reshona Fleishman, *The Battle against Reproductive Rights: The Impact of the Catholic Church on Abortion Law in both International and Domestic Arenas*, 14 Emory Int'l L. Rev. 277 (2000); Lynn Freedman & Stephen Isaacs, *Human Rights and Reproductive Choice*, 24 Studies in Fam. Plan. 18 (Jan./Feb. 1993); Aart Hendriks, *Promotion and Protection of Women's Right to Sexual and Reproductive Health under International Law: The Economic Covenant and the Women's Convention*, 44 Am. U. L. Rev. 1123 (1995); Berta Hernàndez, *To Bear or Not to Bear: Reproductive Freedom as an International Human Right*, 17 Brook. J. Int'l L. 309 (1991); Renee Holt, *Women's Rights and International Law: The Struggle for Recognition and Enforcement*, 1

on making "reproductive freedom" a central focus of several recent international conferences over the objections of many delegates, including women delegates from non-western nations. These conferences have included the International Women's Rights Action Conference (New York 1990), the United Nations Conference on Population and Development (Cairo 1994), the United Nations Conference on Human Rights (Vienna 1995), and the Fourth International Conference on Women (Beijing 1996)[176] — and even at a conference called to declare formally that rape is a war crime (Rome 1998).[177] They are attempting to use international law to achieve what they so often were unable to achieve through domestic law, "trying to insert their least popular ideas into UN documents for unveiling at home as 'international norms.'"[178]

---

COLUM. J. GENDER & L. 117, 126–29 (1991); Anika Rahman, *Towards Government Accountability for Women's Reproductive Rights,* 69 ST. JOHN'S L. REV. 203 (1995); Barbara Stark, *International Human Rights and Family Planning: A Modest Proposal,* 18 DEN. J. INT'L L. & POL'Y 59 (1989); David Thomasma, *Bioethics and International Human Rights,* 25 J. LAW, MED. & ETHICS 295 (1997).

176. *Beijing Declaration,* adopted Sept. 15, 1995, UN Doc. A/CONF.177/20, ¶¶ 44, 89, 93–97, reprinted in 35 INT'L LEGAL MAT'LS 401, 414, 423–24 (1996). *See generally* SONIA CORREA, POPULATION AND REPRODUCTIVE RIGHTS: FEMINIST PERSPECTIVES FROM THE SOUTH (1994); RUTH DIXON-MILLER, POPULATION POLICY & WOMEN'S RIGHTS: TRANSFORMING REPRODUCTIVE CHOICE (1993); HADLEY, *supra* note 23, at 167–73; BETSY HARTMANN, REPRODUCTIVE RIGHTS AND WRONGS: THE GLOBAL POLITICS OF POPULATION CONTROL (1995); CASSANDRA LANGER, A FEMINIST CRITIQUE: HOW FEMINISM HAS CHANGED AMERICAN SOCIETY, CULTURE, AND HOW WE LIVE FROM THE 1940s TO THE PRESENT 154–55 (1996); POPULATION POLICIES RECONSIDERED — HEALTH, EMPOWERMENT AND RIGHTS (Gita Sen ed. 1994); INES SMYTH, POPULATION POLICIES: OFFICIAL RESPONSES TO FEMINIST CRITIQUES (1995); UNITED NATIONS POPULATION FUND, THE STATE OF WORLD POPULATION 1997: THE RIGHT TO CHOOSE: REPRODUCTIVE RIGHTS AND REPRODUCTIVE HEALTH (1997); Diana Babor, *Population Growth and Reproductive Rights in International Human Rights Law,* 14 CONN. J. INT'L L. 83 (1999); Reed Boland, *The Environment, Population, and Women's Human Rights,* 27 ENVTL. L. 1137 (1997); Sharon Camp, *The Impact of Mexico City Policy on Women and Health Care in Developing Countries,* 20 NYU U. INT'L L. & POL. 35 (1987); Rebecca Cook, *International Human Rights and Women's Reproductive Health,* in WOMEN'S RIGHTS, HUMAN RIGHTS, *supra* note 169, at 265; Fleishman, *supra* note 175, at 283–89; Mary Ann Glendon, *Foundations of Human Rights: The Unfinished Business,* 44 AM. J. JURIS. 1, 9–10 (1999); Marshall Green, *The Evolution of U.S. International Population Policy 1965–92: A Chronological Account,* 19 POP. & DEV. REV. 303 (1993); Marguerite Holloway, *Population Summit: Women's Health and Rights Shape Cairo Document,* SCI. AM., June 1994, at 14–15; E. Michael Jones, *Bela Does Cairo: The Great Satan Swings and Misses at the Cairo Conference on Population and Development,* 2 LIBERTY LIFE & FAM. 1 (1995); Cynthia Kennedy, *Cairo, Beijing, and the Global Environmental Crisis: The Continuing International Dialogue on Population Stabilization and Sustainable Development,* 8 GEO. INT'L ENVTL. L. REV. 451 (1996); Sarah Lai & Regan Ralph, *Recent Development: Female Sexual Autonomy and Human Rights,* 8 HARV. HUM. RTS. J. 201 (1995); Luke Lee, *Population: The Human Rights Approach,* 6 COLO. J. INT'L ENVTL. L. & POL'Y 327 (1995); Peter Manus, *The Owl, the Indian, the Feminist, and the Brother: Environmentalism Encounters the Social Justice Movements,* 23 ENVT. AFF. 249, 288–97 (1996); Meredith Marshall, Comment, *United Nations Conference on Population and Development: The Road to a New Reality for Reproductive Health,* 10 EMORY INT'L L. REV. 441 (1996); Anika Rahman, *A View towards Women's Reproductive Rights: Perspectives on Selected Laws and Policies in Pakistan,* 15 WHITTIER L. REV. 981 (1994); Anika Rahman & Rachael Pine, *An International Human Right to Reproductive Health Care: Toward Definition and Accountability,* 1 HEALTH & HUM. RTS. 400 (1995); Elizabeth Reilly, *The Rhetoric of Disrespect: Uncovering the Faulty Premises Infecting Reproductive Rights,* 5 AM. U. J. GENDER & L. 147 (1996); *Reports from the International Women's Rights Action Watch (IWRAW) 1990 Conference,* 1 COLUM. J. GENDER & L. 143, 147–53 (1991); Judith Richter & Lois Keysers, *Towards a Common Agenda? Feminists and Population Agencies on the Road to Cairo,* 1 DEV. 50 (1994); Andrew Ringel, *The Population Policy Debate and the World Bank: Limits to Growth vs. Supply-Side Demographics,* 6 GEO. INT'L ENVTL. L. REV. 213 (1993); Sarah Rumage, *Resisting the West: The Clinton Administration's Promotion of Abortion at the 1994 Cairo Conference and the Strength of the Islamic Response,* 27 CAL. W. INT'L L.J. 1 (1996); Mona Zulficar, *From Human Rights to Program Reality: Vienna, Cairo, and Beijing in Perspective,* 44 AM. U. L. REV. 1017 (1995).

177. Alessandra Stanley, *Semantics Stalls Pact Labeling Rape a War Crime,* N.Y. TIMES, July 9, 1998, at A3.

178. Mary Ann Glendon, *What Happened in Beijing,* FIRST THINGS, Jan. 1996, at 30, 35. *See also* Glendon, *supra* note 176, at 9–12.

The issue is not so clear-cut as these western feminists would have it. Internationally, as well as within the United States, "multicultural diversity" often speaks with a western, white, upper-class voice.[179] Beyond the few who attend UN conferences, there is nowhere near the near universal consensus regarding the rightness of abortion or even freedom of choice regarding abortion that one would expect to find behind a purported universal human right.[180] The basic international human rights documents do guarantee the freedom of both parents to control their reproductive capacities, but they also guarantee the right to life.[181] The documents do not, however, indicate how these conflicting guarantees play out with regard to abortion. Even the conference declarations, dominated in this regard by pro-abortion feminists, found it necessary to substitute vague phrases like "reproductive health care" and "access" for "abortion" and "right to choose."[182] One international commission (not a court) construing such an ambiguous document did conclude (in a 4-2-1 split) that allowing abortions did not violate the guarantee of a right to life, but even that commission confirmed that "in general" the right to life applied from the moment of conception.[183] The few human rights documents that do not avoid the question of abortion, however, explicitly favor the right to life over any supposed right to abort.[184]

---

179. SCHATTSCHNEIDER, *supra* note 155, at 31–35. *See, e.g.,* Martha Nussbaum, *In Defense of Universal Values,* 36 IDAHO L. REV. 379 (2000). *See also* Glendon, *supra* note 176, at 9–11; Theodor Meron, *A Report on the N.Y.U. Conference on Teaching International Protection of Human Rights,* 13 NYU J. INT'L L. & POL. 881, 901 (comments of Peter Berger); Joel Armstrong Schoenmeyer, *Book Review,* 3 MICH. J. GENDER & L. 609, 615–16 (1996).

180. *See, e.g.,* Azizah al-Hibri, *Who Defines Women's Rights? A Third World Woman's Response,* 2 AM. U. HUM. RTS. BRIEF 9 (1994); Boschmann, *supra* note 176; Charlesworth, Chinkin, & Wright, *supra* note 168, at 619 n.40; Joan Fitzpatrick Hartman, *The Impact of the Reagan Administration's International Population Policy on Human Rights Relating to Health and Family,* 20 NYU J. INT'L L. & POL. 169 (1987); Holloway, *supra* note 176, at 14–15; Jones, *supra* note 176; Richter & Keysers, *supra* note 176; Brian Robertson, *Uncle Sam, the Population Control Bully? U.S. Agenda at Cairo Questioned,* WASH. TIMES, Aug. 26, 1994, at A8; Rumage, *supra* note 176, at 70–89.

181. *See, e.g., European Convention for the Protection of Human Rights and Fundamental Freedoms,* opened for signature Nov. 4, 1950, art. 2, 213 UNTS 221; *Interamerican Convention on Human Rights,* opened for signature Mar. 6, 1981, art. 4, 1144 UNTS 123; *International Covenant on Civil and Political Rights,* opened for signature Dec. 2, 1966, art. 6, 999 UNTS 171; *UN Convention on the Rights of the Child,* opened for signature Nov. 20 1989, preamble, arts. 1, 6(1), 37(a), 1577 UNTS 3; *American Convention on Human Rights,* adopted Nov. 22, 1969, art. 4(1), 1144 UNTS 123; *Declaration on the Rights of the Child,* preamble, GA Res. 1386, UN GAOR, 14th Sess., Supp. 16, at 19–20, UN Doc. A/4354 (1959). *See generally* M. Nöthling Sabbert, *The Position of the Human Embryo and Foetus in International Law and Its Relevance for the South African Context,* 32 J. COMP. & INT'L L. S. AFR. 336 (1999).

182. *See* Dick Kirschten, *Women's Day,* 26 NAT'L J. 1016, 1018 (1994); Rumage, *supra* note 176, at 78–83. A recent *Declaration-Position Statement and Proposed Plan of action for Period up to 2000 and in 21st Century: On Worker's (sic) Reproductive Health Protection,* adopted Dec. 10, 1998, at a conference sponsored by the World Health Organization, managed to avoid mention of abortion altogether, reprinted in 8 TEX. J. WOMEN & L. 127 (1998). *See also* Julia Ernst, *U.S. Ratification of the Convention on the Elimination of All Forms of Discrimination against Woman,* 3 MICH. J. GENDER & L. 299, 331–33 (1995); Cook, *International Protection, supra* note 175; Ilise Feitshans, *Is There a Human Right to Reproductive Health?,* 8 TEX. J. WOMEN & L. 93 (1998); Eva Herzer & Sara Levin, *China's Denial of Tibetan Women's Right to Reproductive Freedom,* 3 MICH. J. GENDER & L. 551, 564–65 (1996).

183. Protection of Life Prior to Birth/"Baby Boy" Abortion Case, Case 2141 (United States), OAS/Ser. L/V/II.52 doc. 48 (Inter-Am. Comm'n on Hum. Rts.) (Mar. 6, 1981), reprinted in 2 HUM. RTS. L.J. 110 (1981). *See also* Dinah Shelton, *Abortion and the Right to Life in the Inter-American System: The Case of "Baby Boy,"* 2 HUM. RTS. L.J. 309 (1981).

184. *See generally* Tracy Higgins, *Anti-Essentialism, Relativism, and Human Rights,* 19 HARV. WOMEN'S L.J. 89 (1996).

The abortion rights crowd carefully ignores most divisions among women within western so-cieties or between women from different societies, yet there is one division that they insist that we all notice—the divisions among Catholics in general and among Catholic women in particu-lar.[185] These divisions are fostered by various non-Catholic groups that provide substantial finan-cial support for Catholics for a Free Choice, an organization of Catholics opposed to the Church's position regarding abortion. For example, the Ford Foundation alone gave Catholics for a Free Choice $1,000,000 in 1996.[186] Moreover, one would hardly guess from what is written or said about Catholic divisions that such divisions actually exist in most denominations. As in-stitutions, "liberal" denominations generally support *Roe v. Wade,* while "conservative" denomi-nations generally oppose it. This statement is so often taken as true that one could use a denom-ination's position on *Roe* as a litmus test for a long list of attributes that characterize a denomination as "liberal" or "conservative." Nonetheless, as the divisions among Catholics sug-gest, the debate remains more of a struggle between traditional and non-traditional members of a particular religious denomination than it is between denominations as such.[187]

Occasional abortion rights activists concede that many or most women oppose permissive abortion laws. Often such advocates, for example Andrea Dworkin and Kristin Luker, dismiss women who oppose abortion as tradition bound (or "right wing") women who see the ready availability of abortion as easing the task of men in pressuring or coercing women into promiscu-ous (or at least unwanted) sex while avoiding marriage and the responsibility of supporting a family.[188] As Catharine MacKinnon, one of the foremost feminist legal theorists commented,

---

185. *See, e.g.,* Abortion and Catholicism: The American Debate (Patricia Beattie Young & Thomas Shannon eds. 1988); Craig & O'Brien, *supra* note 122, at 45–46, 254–56, 259–62; Ronald Dworkin, Life's Dominion: An Argument about Abortion, Euthanasia, and Individual Freedom 47–49, 245 n.6 (1993); Marian Faux, Crusaders: Voices from the Abortion Front 230–64 (1990); Barbara Ferraro, Patricia Hussey, & Jane O'Reilly, No Turning Back: Two Nuns' Battle with the Vatican over Women's Right to Choose (1990); Hadley, *supra* note 23, at 207; Ferree & Hess, *supra* note 135, at 91; Rachel Gold, Abortion and Women's Health: A Turning Point for America? 19 (1990) (reporting that Protestant and Jewish women have abortions less commonly than Catholic women); Langer, *supra* note 176, at 153–54; Hans Lotstra, Abortion: The Catholic Debate in America (1985); Reagan, *supra* note 152, at 6–7, 233, 234; Kathy Rudy, Beyond Pro-Life and Pro-Choice: Moral Diversity in the Abortion Debate 22–43 (1996); Garry Wills, Under God: Religion and American Politics 310 (1990); Reed Boland, *The Current Status of Abortion Laws in Latin America: Prospects and Strategies for Change,* 21 J. Law, Med. & Ethics 67, 68 (1993); Joseph Donceel, *A Liberal Catholic's View,* in The Problem of Abortion 15 (Joel Feinberg ed. 1984); Reshona Fleishman, *The Battle against Reproductive Rights: The Impact of the Catholic Church on Abortion Law in both International and Domestic Arenas,* 14 Emory Int'l L. Rev. 277, 308–10 (2000); Richard McCormick, *Abortion: The Unexplored Middle Ground,* 10 Second Op.: Health, Faith, & Ethics 41 (1989); Teresa Godwin Phelps, *The Sound of Silence Breaking: Catholic Women, Abortion, and the Law,* 59 U. Tenn. L. Rev. 547 (1992); Mary Segers, *The Loyal Opposition: Catholics for a Free Choice,* in The Catholic Church and the Politics of Abortion: A View from the States 172 (Timothy Byrnes & Mary Segers eds. 1992); Michael Welch *et al., Attitudes toward Abortion among U.S. Catholics: Another Case of Symbolic Politics?,* 76 Soc. Sci. Q. 142 (1995). Consider also the furor over vice-presidential candidate Geral-dine Ferraro's comments regarding abortion. See the authorities collected *supra* at notes 126–27.

186. *Which Foundations Help Fund the FJE?,* ABA Watch, Feb. 2001, at 9. Early on, Catholics for a Free Choice were largely funded by John D. Rockefeller, III. Donald Critchlow, Intended Consequences: Birth Control, Abortion, and the Federal Government in Modern America 175–76, 192–200 (1999).

187. *See* Mensch & Freeman, *supra* note 122, at 83–84, 103–07.

188. Andrea Dworkin, Right-Wing Women 102–04 (1982); Luker, *supra* note 134, at 192–215. *See also* Ruth Colker, Abortion & Dialogue—Pro-Choice, Pro-Life, and American Law 130–32 (1992); MacKinnon, *supra* note 168, at 188, 190; Catharine MacKinnon, *The Male Ideology of Privacy: A Feminist Perspective on the Right to Abortion,* Radical Am., July–Aug. 1983, at 23; Reva Siegel, *Reasoning from the Body: A Historical Perspective on Abortion Regulation and Questions of Equal Protection,* 44 Stan. L. Rev. 261, 360–61 (1992).

after noting the strong support for "abortion rights" by the Playboy Foundation, "[t]he availability of abortion removes the one remaining legitimized reason that women have had for refusing sex besides the headache."[189] Other abortion rights advocates implicitly concede the division among women regarding abortion when those advocates acknowledge the need to devise strategies to counter the guilt women who have had abortions often feel, both before and after the event.

Pro-abortion advocates tend to dismiss the guilt some women feel as a "false guilt" foisted on them by pro-life groups rather than as an expression of a legitimate sense of loss or of wrongdoing.[190] Fear of such guilt underlies, however, the adamant opposition of abortion rights activists to laws requiring abortionists to disclose information about the stage of development of the fetus ("informed consent laws") or mandatory waiting periods.[191] Slogans such as "abortion on demand and without apology" simply do not address the guilt and remorse adequately.[192] No wonder that while Americans frequently talk about abortion in the abstract, most women (and men) are so reticent about discussing their own personal experience of abortion.[193]

Contemporary fiction written by committed feminists sometimes explores the unhappiness, if not guilt and remorse, resulting from abortion decisions.[194] Even more telling are first-person accounts by strongly committed feminists of their own negative feelings during and after an abortion.[195] One of the most interesting of these accounts is by law professor Marie Ashe.[196] Ashe, who remains a committed supporter of abortion rights, nonetheless bemoans our willful separation of ourselves from the reality of death, particularly deaths for which we are responsible. She also reports her more intense reaction to her induced abortion than to several spontaneous ones she has undergone: "Although I have grieved, sometimes at length, over every lost pregnancy, it is only my hospital abortion that has never left me alone."[197] As Ashe's experience suggests, women often are ambivalent about their own abortions, which is a major cause of the grief and remorse so often felt. Anecdotal reports have it that some women have given up smoking so as not to hurt the baby they have already decided to abort.[198] Or, as one women summed up her experience after abortion, "I know it was right, but I still think it was wrong."[199] And, as

---

189. MacKinnon, *supra* note 168, at 97, 99.

190. *See, e.g.,* Catherine Cozzarelli & Brenda Major, *The Effects of Anti-Abortion Demonstrators and Pro-Choice Escorts on Women's Psychological Responses to Abortion,* 13 J. Soc. & Clnical Psych. 404 (1994); Gerston, *supra* note 159, at K1 (quoting an unnamed "health professional sympathetic to abortion"); Elizabeth Karlin, *"We Called It Kindness": Establishing a Feminist Abortion Practice,* in Abortion Wars, *supra* note 165, at 273; Russo, *supra* note 140, at 615–19. *See generally* Hadley, *supra* note 23, at 56–57, 173–76, 195–96.

191. *See, e.g.,* Loretta Ross, *Raising Our Voices,* in From Abortion to Reproductive Freedom 139, 140 (Marlene Fried ed. 1990); Uta Landy, *Abortion Counseling, A New Component of Medical Care,* 13 Clinics in Obstet. & Gynecology 33 (1986).

192. Julia Hanigsberg, *Homologizing Pregnancy and Motherhood: A Consideration of Abortion,* 94 Mich. L. Rev. 371 (1995); Williams, *Gender Wars, supra* note 166, at 1584.

193. Waldman, Ackerman, & Rubin, *supra* note 158, at 20.

194. *See, e.g.,* Gloria Naylor, Women of Brewster Place 91–98 (1980)

195. *See, e.g.,* Colker, *supra* note 187, at 50–56; McDonnell, *supra* note 133; Idell Kesselman, *Grief and Loss: Issues for Abortion,* 21 Omega: J. of Death & Dying 241 (1990); Williams, *Gender Wars, supra* note 166, at 1589–90. *See also* Reardon, Silent No More, *supra* note 159, at 282–84.

196. Marie Ashe, *Zig-Zag Stitching and the Seamless Web: Thoughts on "Reproduction" and the Law,* 13 Nova L. Rev. 355, 376–79 1989).

197. Ashe, *supra* note 196, at 377.

198. Kenny, *supra* note 134, at 226–27.

199. *Id.* at 226. *See also Who Gets Abortions and Why: The Effects on Women Are Often Surprising, even Profound,* US News & World Rep., Jan. 19, 1998, at 26, 26–28, 30–31.

already noted, these reactions are common enough that there are three organizations of women who feel guilt over their abortions.[200]

The belief that women who oppose abortion are simply out of touch with their own needs is matched by a similar belief by some women opposed to abortion that women who have abortions are merely the dupes of men who are exploiting them.[201] There are, of course, many women who chose abortions despite the opposition of their man, and many women who then and thereafter rejoice in the choice they made.[202] Dismissive attitudes towards the experiences and felt needs of women who differ with the writer or speaker regarding abortion—regardless of the side of the debate that the writer or speaker may take— simply preclude any real dialogue between the two groups of women. Recent successes in opening such dialogues generally have put these differences out of bounds for discussion[203]—which does nothing towards resolving the differences.

The differences between women over abortion are a manifestation of the ambivalence that also characterizes women's responses to institutionalized feminism in general.[204] After all, as recently as 1988, one-third of the women in Congress declined to join the "Congressional Caucus for Women's Issues."[205] While ambivalence about the proper roles for women in society (the major issue for institutionalized feminism) does feed resistance to permissive abortion laws, ambivalence about feminism itself results—in a complex feedback loop—in part because of the identification of institutionalized feminism with extreme positions on questions such as abor-

---

200. See the text *supra* at notes 160–62.

201. Abortion, Medicine, and the Law, *supra* note 120, at 341–48.

202. Ashe, *supra* note 196, at 378–79; Hanigsberg, *supra* note 192, at 391–92; Rosalind Pollack Petchesky, *Fetal Images: The Power of Visual Culture in the Politics of Reproduction*, 13 Feminist Stud. 263, 271 (1987).

203. *See* Nancy (Ann) Davis, *The Abortion Debate: The Search for Common Ground, Part I*, 103 Ethics 516 (1993); Fields, *supra* note 1133; Marks, *supra* note 61.

204. Dallas Blanchard, The Anti-Abortion Movement and the Rise of the Religious Right: From Polite to Fiery Protest 1–9 (1994); Dallas Blanchard & Terry Prewitt, Religious Violence and Abortion: The Gideon Project xii, 227–28, 231, 241 (1993); Condit, *supra* note 118, at 30, 61–63, 74 n.9, 127–28; Marilyn Fralik, Ideology and Abortion Politics (1983); Genovese, *supra* note 166, at 2, 81–83; Ginsburg, *supra* note 137, at 1, 6–19, 140–45, 172–97, 212–21; Graglia, *supra* note 166; Harrison, *supra* note 112, at 2–4, 32–49, 59–62, 67, 181–82, 189–90; Judges, *supra* note 130, at 12–15; Kenneth Karst, Law's Promise, Law's Expression: Visions of Power in the Politics of Race, Gender, and Religion 52–57 (1993); Luker, *supra* note 134, at 137–38, 159–75, 195, 224, 241; Paige, *supra* note 123; Rosalind Pollack Petchesky, Abortion and Women's Choice: The State, Sexuality, and Reproductive Freedom xiii, xvi–xviii, xx–xxi, 5, 82–84 (rev. ed. 1990); Deborah Rhode, Justice and Gender 214–15 (1989); John Robertson, Children of Choice: Freedom and the New Reproductive Technologies 66–68 (1994); Rosenblatt, *supra* note 129, at 37–38, 109, 121–31; Patrick Sheehan, Women, Society, the State, and Abortion 125–28 (1987); Sherwin, *supra* note 167, at 111–14; Laurence Tribe, Abortion: The Clash of Absolutes 52–53, 76, 115, 132, 213, 232–34, 237–38, 242 (1990); Anne Appelbaum, *Teeing up for the Wrong Cause*, Wash. Post, Dec. 10, 2002, at A29; Jean Braucher, *Tribal Conflict over Abortion* (book rev.), 25 Ga. L. Rev. 595, 597–606, 619–24 (1991); Davis, *supra* note 203, at 526–39; Amy Fried, *Abortion Politics as Symbolic Politics: An Investigation into Belief Systems*, 69 Soc. Sci. Q. 137 (1988); Granberg, *supra* note 134; Wendy Kaminer, *Feminism's Identity Crisis*, Atlantic Monthly, Oct. 1993, at 51; Sylvia Law, *Abortion and Compromise—Inevitable and Impossible*, 1992 U. Ill. L. Rev. 921, 933–37; Krisztina Morvai, *What Is Missing from the Rhetoric of Choice? A Feminist Analysis of the Abortion Dilemma in the Context of Sexuality*, 5 UCLA Women's L.J. 445, 446–49 (1995); Mary Jo Neitz, *Family, State, and God: Ideologies of the Right to Life Movement*, 42 Soc. Analysis 265 (1981); Suzanne Staggenborg, *Life-Style Preferences and Social Movement Recruitment: Illustrations from the Abortion Conflict*, 68 Soc. Sci. Q. 779 (1987); Ellen Willis, *Putting Women Back into the Abortion Debate*, in From Abortion to Reproductive Freedom, *supra* note 191, at 377, 131–38.

205. Cynthia Fuchs Epstein, Deceptive Distinctions: Sex, Gender and the Social Order 185 (1988).

tion.[206] The divisions among women over *Roe* contrasts starkly with the broad consensus that surrounds issues such as discrimination in pay or promotion or sexual harassment.[207]

# Public Confusion over
# Abortion Law and Policy

*It is naïve to assume—in a culture in which doubt lingers about the location*
*of the sun in the morning—that the public understands the law.*

—Rowland Miller[208]

The survey data regarding abortion discloses a glaring discrepancy—while the great majority of Americans oppose abortion on demand, nearly as large a majority supports permissive abortion laws that create what amounts to abortion on demand.[209] Those supporting abortion rights seek to explain the discrepancies in reported public attitudes as capturing the difference between personal and political attitudes towards abortion.[210] Were abortion not such a tragic choice, one might be bemused by this explanation coming most strongly from the very people who so insistently tell us (in other contexts) that the personal is political.[211] As historian Elizabeth Fox Gen-

---

206. Janet Saltzman Chafetz, Gender Equity: An Integrated Theory of Stability and Change 169–70 (1990); Joan Hoff, Law, Gender, and Injustice: A Legal History of U.S. Women 13–14 (1991); Mensch & Freeman, *supra* note 122, at 130; Rhode, *supra* note 204, at 75–79; Lynne Marie Kohm & Colleen Holmes, *The Rise and Fall of Women's Rights: Have Sexuality and Reproductive Freedom Forfeited Victory?*, 6 Wm. & Mary J. Women & L. 381 (2000). *See generally* Nicholas Davidson, The Failure of Feminism (1988); Langer, *supra* note 176, at 146–49, 183–89, 245–60.

207. *See* Ferree & Hess, *supra* note 135, at 86–99, 150; Joyce Gelb, Feminism and Politics: A Comparative Analysis 79–80 (1989); Graber, *supra* note 129, at 124–28; E.J. Dionne, *Struggle for Work and Family Fueling Women's Movement*, N.Y. Times, Aug. 22, 1989, at A18. See also the text *supra* at note 133. *See generally* Denfeld, *supra* note 133.

208. Rowland Miller, *Confusion and Consternation, Misperceptions and Misconceptions on the Public's Misunderstandings of the Law*, 40 S. Tex. L. Rev. 973, 981 (1999).

209. See the text *supra* at notes 118–22.

210. *See, e.g.,* Condit, *supra* note 118, at 148–50; Dworkin, *supra* note 185, at 13–16, 19–22; Harrison, *supra* note 112, at 266–67 n.23; Rosenblatt, *supra* note 129; Gavin Anderson, *Rights and the Art of Boundary Maintenance* (book rev.), 60 Mod. L. Rev. 120 (1997); Richard Lacayo, *Whose Life Is It?*, Time, May 1, 1989, at 20, 20–21. *See also* Caldwell, *supra* note 112, at 15–16 (arguing that the discrepancy arises from an unwillingness to sacrifice personal life-style in favor of an abstract good).

211. The point traces back to two books published in 1970: Kate Millett, Sexual Politics (1970); Shulamith Firestone, The Dialectic of Sex: The Case for Feminist Revolution (1970). *See also* Ulrike Boehmer, The Personal and the Political: Women's Activism in Response to the Breast Cancer and AIDS Epidemics (1999); Janet Farrell Brodie, Contraception and Abortion in Nineteenth-Century America 35 (1994); Challenging the Public/Private Divide (S.B. Byrd ed. 1997); Andrew Clapham, Human Rights in the Private Sphere 124–33 (1993); Zillah Eisenstein, Feminism and Sexual Equality: Crisis in Liberal America 14–30 (1984); Sara Evans, Born for Liberty: A History of Women in America 263, 279–80, 282–84, 287–90, 294, 294 (1989); Jane Flax, Disputed Subjects: Essays on Psychoanalysis, Politics and Philosophy 111 (1993); Linda Gordon, Woman's Body, Woman's Right: A Social History of Birth Control in America 409 (1976); Linda Gordon, Heroes of Their Own Lives 294 (1988); Harrison, *supra* note 112, at 54–56; Nancy Hirschmann, Rethinking Obligation: A Feminist Method for Political Theory 20–22, 58–60, 74–75, 113, 271–74 (1992); MacKinnon, *supra* note 169, at 99–102; MacKinnon, *supra* note 168, at 120–21, 163–65, 191–93; Okin, *supra* note 168, at 9–13, 19–40, 116–17, 124–33; Carole Pateman, The Sexual Contract 221–23 (1988); Petchesky, *supra* note 204, at 137–38 n.73; Public and Private in Social Life (S.I. Benn & Gerald Gaus eds. 1983); Reagan,

ovese summarized the point, "[t]he real lesson of the middle-class feminism of the 1960s and 1970s is that the personal is social—a proposition that conservative traditionalists and Marxists alike have always understood."[212] Feminist law professor Catharine MacKinnon at least acknowledges that the distinction these commentators seek to draw in the abortion context contradicts their general attitude towards claims that the law should refrain from regulating the "private sphere."[213] (Feminists in formerly Communist countries generally have a keener appreciation of the importance of the private sphere than feminists from Western countries who have never lived in a society that denied persons the right to have a private niche outside of the state's reach.[214]) The distinction between the public and the private also overlooks that the polls indicate not just personal opposition to abortion, but a willingness to see it made illegal under varied appropriate circumstances.[215]

Confusion over the public and the private dichotomy is not a wholly satisfactory explanation for the apparent confusion over abortion policy in the public mind. The pervasive ignorance regarding the Supreme Court's decisions reflects in part the effect of *Roe v. Wade* in cutting off the normal paths political debate.[216] In part, however, the failure to connect popular

---

*supra* note 152, at 1–3; CARROLL SMITH-ROSENBERG, DISORDERLY CONDUCT: VISIONS OF GENDER IN VICTORIAN AMERICA 217 (1985); THE PUBLIC NATURE OF PRIVATE VIOLENCE 167 (Martha Albertson Fineman & Roxanne Myhituik eds. 1994); GERALD TURKEL, DIVIDING PUBLIC AND PRIVATE: LAW, POLITICS, AND SOCIAL THEORY (1992); ROBERTO UNGER, SOCIAL THEORY: ITS SITUATION AND ITS TASK 10, 145, 172 (1987); JEFFREY WEEKS, SEXUALITY AND ITS DISCONTENTS 244 (1985); Belinda Bennett, *The Economics of Wifing Services: Law and Economics on the Family,* 18 J. LAW & SOC'Y 206, 206–09 (1991); Binnion, *supra* note 175, at 515–20; Charlesworth, Chinkin, & Wright, *supra* note 168, at 625–27, 638–43; Christine Chinkin, *A Critique of the Public/Private Dimension,* 10 EUR. J. INT'L L. 1887 (1999); Ruth Colker, *Marriage,* 3 YALE J.L. & FEMINISM 321 (1991); Davina Cooper, *An Engendered State: Sexuality, Governance, and the Potential for Change,* 20 J.L. & SOC'Y 257, 268–72 (1993); Ruth Gavison, *Feminism and the Public/Private Distinction,* 45 STAN. L. REV. 1 (1992); Allan Hunt, *Identity Crisis: The Politics of Interpretation,* 26 N. ENG. L. REV. 1173, 1197–99, 1209–13 (1992); Linda Kelly, *Reproductive Liberty under the Threat of Care: Deputizing Private Agents and Deconstructing State Action,* 5 MICH. J. GENDER & L. 81, 95–100 (1998); Jane Larson, *"Women Understand So Little, They Call My Good Nature 'Deceit'": A Feminist Rethinking of Seduction,* 93 COLUM. L. REV. 374, 438–44 (1993); Frances Olsen, *Constitutional Law: Feminist Critiques of the Public/Private Distinction,* 10 CONST'L COMMENTARY 319 (1993); Carole Pateman, *Feminist Critiques of the Private/Public Dichotomy,* in PUBLIC AND PRIVATE SOCIAL LIFE 281 (Stanley Benn & Gerald Gaus eds. 1983); Celina Romany, *Women as Aliens: A Feminist Critique of the Public/Private Distinction in International Human Rights Law,* 6 HARV. HUM. RTS. L. REV. 87 (1993); Louise Marie Roth, *The Right of Privacy Is Political: Power, the Boundary between Public and Private, and Sexual Harassment,* 24 LAW & SOC. INQUIRY 45 (1999); Elizabeth Schneider, *The Violence of Privacy,* in THE PUBLIC NATURE OF PRIVATE VIOLENCE: THE DISCOVERY OF DOMESTIC ABUSE 36 (Martha Albertson Fineman & Roxanne Mykitiuk eds. 1994); Reva Siegel, *"The Rule of Love": Wife Beating as Prerogative and Privacy,* 105 YALE L.J. 2117, 2150–2207 (1996); Donna Sullivan, *The Public/Private Distinction in International Human Rights Law,* in WOMEN'S RIGHTS, HUMAN RIGHTS, *supra* note 169, at 126; Margaret Thornton, *The Public/Private Dichotomy: Gendered and Discriminatory,* 18 OXFORD J.L. & SOC'Y 448 (1991). *See also* Peter Beinart, *Private Matters: How the Personal Became Political,* NEW REP., Feb. 15, 1999, at 21 (noting the similarities between organized feminism and the Christian right in conflating the personal with the political); James Taranto, *Who's a Hypocrite—and Who Cares?,* WALL ST. J., Aug. 4, 1998, at A18 (noting that the very same people who are so insistent that "the personal is political" chose to defend President Clinton during the Lewinsky scandal on the grounds that it was a personal matter, not a political matter).

212. GENOVESE, *supra* note 166, at 28

213. MACKINNON, *supra* note 168, at 187–94; MACKINNON, *supra* note 169, at 93–102. For other, more nuanced analyses of the relation between our public lives and our private lives, see CONDIT, *supra* note 118, at 172–96; John Garvey, *Private Power and the Constitution,* 10 CONST'L COMMENTARY 311 (1993); Gavison, *supra* note 211.

214. *See* Prue Chamberlain, *Gender and the Private Sphere: A Touchstone of Misunderstanding between Eastern and Western Germany?,* 2 SOC. POL.: INT'L STUD. IN GENDER, STATE & SOC'Y 25 (1995).

215. MULDOON, *supra* note 112, at 37.

216. *See* Chapter 16, at 37–38, 114–214.

disapproval of legalized abortion with specific legislative enactments occurs because of re-markably pervasive ignorance of what the Supreme Court actually decided in *Roe*. As many as 63 percent of Americans believe that *Roe* made abortions legal only during the first three months of pregnancy, with 24 percent believing that *Roe* protects the right to have an abortion even during the first three months only if the mother can demonstrate a threat to her life and health.[217] In fact, only 30 percent of Americans even recall that *Roe v. Wade* dealt with abortion rights unless prompted by the polltaker.[218] Misunderstanding—or misstatements—regarding the effect of *Roe v. Wade* appeared in the press beginning with the very first press reports of the case.[219] Even scholars who should be able to understand more clearly the import of the Court's decision represent it as legalizing abortion only during the first trimester.[220] The public simi-larly misunderstands the meaning and significance of such widely reported and debated abor-tion decisions.[221]

Journalist Christopher Caldwell has argued that the discrepancy arises from the simple fact that Americans, whom he admits generally acknowledge abortion as the killing of a person, put their personal convenience ahead of even the lives of others.[222] This is hardly the explanation given that large majorities of Americans support criminalizing abortion for reasons of mere con-venience.[223] Perhaps the best explanation is that the public sees the legislative choice as between legal abortion that is safe for the woman at least and a similar number of illegal abortions that would kill many women.[224] If so, this proposition—the "necessary evil" proposition—is also based on pervasive ignorance both because it presupposes that criminalizing abortion would not affect the frequency of the event (thus saving few or no fetal lives) and that criminalizing abor-tion would endanger the lives of many women. While both factual assumptions are widely held in the general public, both are wrong.[225]

This sort of misunderstanding is hardly unique to the abortion controversy. To some de-gree or other, misunderstanding seems characteristic of the public regarding most controver-sial legal questions.[226] Psychologist Rowland Miller assures us this is so because the public generally lacks necessary education to evaluate legal information properly, is inattentive to that information, and is not motivated to correct these deficiencies.[227] According to Miller, people in such a state do not undertake a thoughtful appraisal of complex matters, but re-main "credulous, impressionable, and gullible."[228] They are more influenced by the style than the substance of the information, leading them to believe even absurd and foolish things pre-sented by a famous or attractive (physically or otherwise) source.[229] In particular, they are eas-ily influenced by a straightforward, coherent story even if it does not fit the facts.[230] A good

---

217. Americans United for Life, *supra* note 120, *Executive Summary* at 21.

218. Blendon, Benson, & Donelan, *supra* note 112, at 2872.

219. *See* Warren Weaver, jr., *High Court Rules Abortion Legal*, N.Y. Times, Jan. 23, 1973, at 1.

220. *See, e.g.*, Wetstein, *supra* note 112, at 15. *See generally* Noonan, *supra* note 124, at 70–74.

221. Americans United for Life, *supra* note 120, *Executive Summary* at 21 [public misunderstanding of *Webster v. Reproductive Health Services*, 492 U.S. 490 (1989)].

222. Caldwell, *supra* note 112 (arguing that the choice is between the admitted evil of abortion and a sig-nificantly reduced life-style).

223. See the text *supra* at notes 135–39.

224. Clarke Forsythe, *Abortion Is not a "Necessary Evil*," Christianity Today, May 24, 1999, at 63; Clarke Forsythe, *First Steps: A New Strategy for Pro-Lifers*, Nat'l Rev., Dec. 20, 1999, at 42.

225. See the text *infra* at notes 233–343.

226. *See* Miller, *supra* note 208.

227. *Id.* at 977.

228. *Id. See also* Daniel Gilbert, *How Mental Systems Believe*, 46 Am. Psychologist 107, 111–15 (1991).

229. Miller, *supra* note 208, at 977.

230. *Id.* at 977–78. *See also* Reid Hastie, *Reflections in the Magic Mirror of Law: Meida Effects on Juror Deci-sions*, 40 S. Tex. L. Rev. 903 (1999).

story is far more striking than a mere compilation of facts and a good story will often have greater impact on future beliefs and thought than the facts even when the story is altogether false.[231]

Not surprisingly, then, we find the two camps locked in a struggle over the stories we tell ourselves about abortion. News reports tell of a community in Nebraska, strongly opposed to abortion, that banded together to seize and hold an unmarried pregnant teenager in order to prevent her from having an abortion.[232] As presented in the *New York Times,* the story is of the family of the putative father, conspiring with a doctor, the local sheriff's office and police, the County Attorney, and a local Juvenile Court judge to deprive the girl (and her family) of their freedom, both the freedom to choose abortion and broader freedoms, by kidnapping the girl pursuant to a court order. One could as easily cast the "conspirators" as heroes intervening to save the life of an unborn child of 23 weeks gestation—now an infant girl described in the article as a "darling little baby" being raised by the parents of the unnamed teenage girl. The two stories are not presented directly but through quotations attributed to the participants as well as the civil lawsuit filed against the "conspirators" by the parents of the mother and by the mother herself.

Pennsylvania provides a somewhat similar story, but with the intervenors on the side of "choice" rather than of "life." In northeastern Pennsylvania, Rosa Marie Hartford was convicted of interfering with the custody of a 13-year old girl by taking the girl to New York for an abortion without the knowledge or consent of the girl's mother—who did not even know that the girl was pregnant.[233] Hartford apparently sought to avoid a statutory rape conviction for her 19-year old son. Hartford's efforts were in vain as it turned out; the son soon faced a jail sentence of up to seven years. Many persons (including, apparently, the seven men and five women on the jury—and a majority in the U.S. House of Representatives[234]) see Hartford's actions as the selfish exploitation of a vulnerable child and a high-handed disregard of the right of the child's parent to determine the medical procedures and cultural values that should play a role in her daughter's life. Others, led by Kathryn Kolbert of the Center for Reproductive Law and Policy (Hartford's defense attorney), see Hartford as a heroine who facilitated a young woman's achievement of her lawful choice in the face of an uncaring or even hostile world. Also from Pennsylvania, we find parents suing a school district after the school's guidance counselor arranged for high school girls to travel to New Jersey for abortion without informing their parents.[235]

These several stories epitomize the two competing visions of what has happened regarding abortion in the United States and other industrialized democracies over the past 40 years. Some see the story of abortion as told by the abortion rights movement as "propagating a philosophy of extreme individualism, if not selfishness, that negates the conception of the family, although this comes about in a haphazard and unplanned fashion."[236] Others, however, tell a different story, seeing women gaining control of their reproductive capacity to become whole individuals, with

---

231. *See* Keith Stanovich, How to Think Straight about Psychology 59–61 (1996).

232. Tamar Lewin, *Nebraska Abortion Case: The Issue is Interference,* N.Y. Times, Sept. 25, 1995, at A8.

233. Marie McCullough, *Abortion Case Taps Some of Parents' Deepest Fears,* Phila. Inquirer, Oct. 27, 1996, at A1; Marie McCullough, *For Young Teen's Mother, a Hollow Victory in Court,* Phila. Inquirer, Nov. 3, 1996, at E2; David Stout, *Woman Who Took Girl for Abortion Is Guilty in Custody Case,* N.Y. Times, Oct. 31, 1996, at A15. *See also* Susan Dundon, *The Verdict Is in, but There's No Simple Answer When It Comes to Abortion,* Phila. Inquirer, Nov. 3, 1996, at E7.

234. David Rosenbaum, *House Passes Bill to Restrict Minors' Abortions,* N.Y. Times, July 1, 1999, at A17.

235. Vanessa Dea, *Abortion Debate: Do the Schools Have a Role in Counseling Girls?,* Educ. Week, Mar. 7, 2001, at 1.

236. Walter Otto Weyrauch, *Book Review,* 37 Am J. Comp. L. 832, 833 (1989) (reviewing Glendon, *supra* note 134). *See also* Glendon, *supra,* at 119–49.

family and governmental institutions as oppressors.[237] While anti-abortion activists see themselves as struggling the save the lives of the most vulnerable members of the human community (including both women and unborn children),[238] their critics see them as mean spirited people really only intent on holding women down and actually indifferent to the fate of the unborn.[239]

In a society where the stories about abortion are so contested, the power to shape the stories we tell about abortion becomes the power to shape the public's perceptions of abortion law and policy. The pervasive public ignorance about abortion law and policy reflects the pervasive bias of the media in favor of freedom to abort.[240] While many feminists decry what they see as the pervasive bias of the media against feminism in general,[241] the bias of the news media regarding

237. Weyrauch, *supra* note 236, at 836. *See also* Planned Parenthood of S.E. Pa. v. Casey, 505 U.S. 833, 852–57 (1992) (Kennedy, O'Connor, & Souter, JJ., joint plurality op.); Robin West, *Jurisprudence and Gender,* 55 U. Chi. L. Rev. 1 (1988); Williams, *Gender Wars, supra* note 166, at 1572–94.

238. *See, e.g.,* Randy Alcorn, Is Rescuing Right? Breaking the Law to Save the Unborn (1990); Paul de Parrie, The Rescuers (1989); Jacoby, *supra* note 163; Philip Lawler, Operation Rescue: A Challenge to the Nation's Conscience (1992); Noonan, *supra* note 124; Randall Terry, Accessory to Murder: The Enemies, Aliens, and Accomplices to the Death of our Culture (1990).

239. *See, e.g.,* Blanchard, *supra* note 204, at 1–9, 119; Blanchard & Prewitt, *supra* note 204, at xii, 227–28, 231, 241; Condit, *supra* note 118, at 30, 61–63, 74 n.9, 127–28; Cynthia Daniels, At Women's Expense 53 (1993); Ginsburg, *supra* note 137, at 1, 6–19, 140–45, 172–97, 212–21; Harrison, *supra* note 112, at 2–4, 32–49, 59–62, 67, 181–82, 189–90; Judges, *supra* note 130, at 12–15; Karst, *supra* note 204, at 52–57; Luker, *supra* note 134, at 137–38, 159–75, 195, 224, 241; Paige, *supra* note 123; Petchesky, *supra* note 204, at xiii, xvi–xviii, xx–xxi, 5, 82–84; Rhode, *supra* note 204, at 214–15; Robertson, *supra* note 204, at 66–68; Rosenblatt, *supra* note 129, at 37–38, 109, 121–31; Sheehan, *supra* note 204, at 125–28; Sherwin, *supra* note 168, at 111–14; Smith-Rosenberg, *supra* note 211, at 217–18; Tribe, *supra* note 204, at 231–41; Rebecca Andrews, *The Unconstitutionality of State Legislation Banning "Partial-Birth" Abortion,* 8 B.U. Pub. Int. L.J. 521, 523 (1999); Janet Gallagher, *Collective Bad Faith: "Protecting" the Fetus,* in Reproduction, Ethics and the Law: Feminist Perspectives 343 (Joan Callahan ed. 1995); Walter Dellinger & Gene Sperling, *Abortion and the Supreme Court: The Retreat from* Roe v. Wade, 138 U. Pa. L. Rev. 83, 106–07 (1989). *See also* Suzanne Uttaro Samuels, Fetal Rights, Women's Rights: Gender Equality in the Workplace 9 (1965).

Each side accuses the other of bad faith—the anti-abortion activist insisting that a fetus is separate being; and the pro-abortion activist insisting that the fetus is "just a lump of tissue." *See* Himmelweit, *supra* note 163, at 49; Jenny Morgan, *Foetal Imaginings: Searching for a Vocabulary in the Law and Politics of Reproduction,* 12 Can. J. Women & L. 371, 391 (2000). *See also* Isabel Karpin, *Legislating the Female Body: Reproductive Technology and the Reconstituted Woman,* 3 Colum. J. Gender & L. 325, 329 (1992) (describing a fetus of, say, 24 weeks gestation as constituting with its mother "a single organism with two aspects"); Morgan, *supra,* at 399–405; John Seymour, *A Pregnant Woman's Decision to Decline Treatment: How Should the Law Respond?,* 2 J. Law & Med. 27, 34 (1994).

240. Jacoby, *supra* note 161, at 105–07; S. Robert Lichter & Stanley Rothman, *The Media Elite,* 96 Pub. Opinion 117 (1981); David Shaw, *Abortion Foes Stereotyped, Some in the Media Believe: Abortion and the Media,* L.A. Times, July 2, 1990, at 1; David Shaw, *Can Women Reporters Write Objectively on Abortion Issues?,* L.A. Times, July 3, 1990, at 23.

241. *See, e.g.,* Charlotte Brunsdon, Julie D'Acci, & Lynn Spigel, Feminist Television Criticism (1997); Feminism, Media, and the Law (Martha Fineman & Martha McCluskey eds. 1997); Ann Kaplan, Rocking Around the Clock: Music Television, Postmodernism and Consumer Culture (1987); Lisa Lewis, Gender Politics and MTV (1990); Tania Modleski, Living with a Vengeance: Mass-Produced Fantasies for Women (1982); Laura Stempel Mumford, Love and Ideology in the Afternoon: Soap Opera, Women and Television Genre (1995); Ellen Seiter, Remote Control: Television, Audiences, and Cultural Power (1989); Jane Shattuc, The Talking Cure: TV Talk Shows and Women (1997); Denise & William Bielby, *Women and Men in Film: Gender Inequality among Writers in a Culture Industry,* 10 Gender & Soc'y 248 (1996); Deborah Hornstra, *A Realistic Approach to Maternal-Fetal Conflict,* 28 Hastings Ctr. Rep. no. 5, at 7, 12 (Sept.–Oct. 1998); Kim Fridkin Kahn & Edie Goldenberg, *The Media: Obstacle or Ally of Feminism?,* 515 Ann. Am. Ac. Pol. & Soc. Sci. 104 (1991); Susan Miller, *Opportunity Squandered—Newspapers' and Women's News,* 7 Media Stud. J. 167 (1993); Monica Morris, *Newspapers and the New Feminism: Blackout as Social Control,* 50 Journalism Q. 37 (1973); Kate Pierce, *A Feminist Theoretical Perspective on the Socialization of Teenage Girls through* Seventeen Magazine, 23 Sex Roles 491 (1990); H. Leslie Steeves, *Creating Imagined Communities: Development Communication and the Challenge of Feminism,* 43 J. Communica-

abortion has been widely acknowledged by both pro-choice and pro-life leaders.[242] After all, anyone who followed the media's treatment of the *Casey* decision found that the media generally presented the upholding of even modest regulations as a major defeat for women's right to choose.[243] Such a bias arises from the strong correlation between attitudes towards abortion and one's level of education and social class.[244] Ask yourself, by the time journalists are in a position actually to influence major news outlets, to which social classes do they belong?

Media bias has become so pronounced that some media have at last felt compelled to take steps to preserve at least the appearance of neutrality on the issue. The *New York Times,* notoriously pro-choice in its editorial policy and among its staff, had to admonish one of its reporters for marching in pro-choice demonstrations.[245] The paper did not, however, reassign the reporter from covering the abortion controversy or otherwise take steps to control her bias or her writing.

The public is not better served when it turns to supposedly reputable scholars for guidance about what the Supreme Court has decided and what those decisions signify. Law professor Ronald Dworkin, considered by many as the leading American jurisprude of the last third of the twentieth century, wrote several major articles for the *New York Review of Books* to analyze the latest developments in abortion law for a well-educated but not legally sophisticated general audience.[246] When *Casey* was decided, Dworkin too described the decision as a defeat for women, approving as it did various regulations that Dworkin described as unduly burdensome for women.[247] Dworkin did not bother to tell his readers that he himself had argued in favor of just such regulations in a law review article written while *Casey* was pending—an article that apparently influenced the troika's plurality opinion so closely did it track Dworkin's arguments.[248] While he might have had good reasons for reversing field after *Casey* was decided, he ought at least to have explained those reasons. He never has. In his recent book on abortion and euthanasia, he simply continued to argue that the specific regulations upheld in *Casey,* as well as the denial of funds for abortion, were "undue burdens."[249]

---

tions 218 (1993); S. Craig Watkins & Rana Emerson, *Feminist Media Criticism and Feminist Media Practices,* 571 Annals Am. Academy Pol. & Soc. Sci. 151 (2000).

242. Ginsburg, *supra* note 137, at 52, 116–19; Noonan, *supra* note 124, at 69–79, 115; Sandra Faucher, *The Best Kept Secret,* in To Rescue the Future 59 (David Andrusko ed. 1983). Some see a similar bias emerging in the hitherto more open book publishing world. David Bernstein, *Closed Books: Conservatism Benefited over the Last Decade from the Inroads It Made in the World of Publishing. No more.,* Nat'l Rev., May 18, 1998, at 24.

243. *See, e.g.,* Dan Allison, *How Anti-Abortionists Lost the War,* St. Petersburg Times, Aug. 16, 1992, at 7D; *Another Blow Against* Roe, St. L. Post-Dispatch, June 30, 1992,a t 2B (editorial); Steven Ginsberg, *Bill Seeks Stiffer Rules for Abortion Clinics in Va.,* Wash. Post, Jan. 22, 2003, at B1; B.J. Isaacson-Jones, *Sorting Out the Abortion Decision: Women's Rights Remain Threatened,* St. L. Post-Dispatch, July 5, 1992, at 3B; Frances Kissling, *Pro-Choice Must Widen Its Agenda: Reproductive Rights Are in Peril, Not Just Abortion Rights,* L.A. Times, June 30, 1992, at B7; William Neikirk & Glen Elasasser, *Ruling Weakens Abortion Right,* Chi. Tribune, June 30, 1992, at C1; *Reproductive Rights under Attack,* St. L. Post-Dispatch, July 2, 1992, at 2C (editorial); William Neikirk & Glen Elasasser, *Ruling Weakens Abortion Right,* Chi. Tribune, June 30, 1992, at C1; *Reproductive Rights under Attack,* St. L. Post-Dispatch, July 2, 1992, at 2C (editorial). *See also* John Leo, *Litmus Tests, Slippery Slopes,* U.S. News & World Rep., Jan. 28, 1998, at 16.

244. See the text *supra* at notes 153–63.

245. *See* Stephen Gillers, *Against the Wall,* 43 J. Legal Educ. 405, 408 (1993).

246. Ronald Dworkin, *Response to Letters,* N.Y. Rev. Books, Nov. 19, 1992, at 56; Ronald Dworkin, *The Center Holds!,* N.Y. Rev. of Books, Aug. 13, 1992, at 29 ("Dworkin, *Center Holds*"); Ronald Dworkin, *The Future of Abortion,* N.Y. Rev. Books, Sept. 28, 1989, at 47; Ronald Dworkin, *The Great Abortion Case,* N.Y. Rev. Books, June 29, 1989, at 49; Ronald Dworkin, *The Moral Reading of the Constitution,* N.Y. Rev. Books, Mar. 21, 1996, at 46.

247. Dworkin, *Center Holds, supra* note 246, at 30–31.

248. Ronald Dworkin, *Unenumerated Rights: Whether and How* Roe *Should be Overruled,* 59 U. Chi. L. Rev. 381, 427–32 (1992).

249. Dworkin, *supra* note 185, at 151–54, 172–76.

This misinformation from "reputable" sources, along with the reluctance of most people to invest themselves heavily into the abortion controversy, results in pervasive public ignorance about what the law is and what various advocacy groups would like it to be. Misinformation also explains why so many survey respondents can describe themselves as "pro-choice" despite the strong public disapproval of "abortion on demand"—disapproval so strong that there must be considerable overlap among the two groups."[250] With confusion and contradiction so widespread, both sides of the abortion controversy find it extremely difficult to move the nation or its governing institutions.

# What Might Be Expected of Legislatures?

*The world functions only through misunderstanding. It is through universal misunderstanding that everyone agrees. For if by misfortune people understood one another, they could never agree.*

—Charles Baudelaire[251]

So long as *Roe v. Wade* and *Doe v. Bolton* set the constitutional limits on possible legislative action, very little could be expected from legislatures, state or national. After *Casey,* however, there appeared to be few remaining constitutional limits on what legislatures might do regarding abortion.[252] After *Casey* was decided, state legislatures enacted numerous statutes relating to abortion, most of which impose modest limitations on the procedure.[253] Why, despite large majorities apparently condemning most abortions during the greater part of pregnancy,[254] have most legislatures not seriously considered enacting truly stringent restrictions on access to abortion?

We have already noted the pervasive public confusion and ignorance regarding abortion law and policy as a serious impediment to legislative and judicial action regarding abortion law and policy. Ignorance cannot be the sole explanation, however. The Canadian public even more strongly and consistently favors legal restrictions on abortion than the public in the United States and there is no focus of distortion in Canada comparable to *Roe.* Yet in Canada the national legislature also has failed to develop a coherent and effective regulatory policy towards abortion.[255]

---

250. See the text *supra* at notes 113–22.

251. Charles Baudelaire, *My Heart Laid Bare,* in MY HEART LAID BEAR AND OTHER PROSE WRITINGS 1 (Peter Quennell ed. 1950).

252. *See* Chapter 17, at notes 72–347.

253. *Id.* at notes 161–62, 334–40.

254. See the text *supra* at notes 134–37.

255. MULDOON, *supra* note 112, at 38–41, 173–81, 212–22. *See generally* Donald Beschle, *Judicial Review and Abortion in Canada: Lessons for the United States in the Wake of* Webster v. Reproductive Health Services, 61 U. COLO. L. REV. 537 (1990); Daniel Conkle, *Canada's Roe: The Canadian Abortion Decision and Its Implications for American Constitutional Law and Theory,* 6 CONST'L COMMENTARY 299 (1989); Martin Bouffard, *Pour une reforme du droit de l'avortement,* 31 LES CAHIERS DE DROIT 575 (1990); I.A. Hunter, *The Canadian Abortion Quagmire: The Way In and a Way out,* 6 CAN. FAM. L.Q. 57 (1990); Hester Lessard, *Relationship, Particularity, and Change: Reflections on* R. v. Morganthaler *and Feminist Approaches to Liberty,* 36 McGILL L.J. 264 (1991); Sheila Martin, *The New Abortion Legislation,* 1 CONST. F. 5 (1990); K.M. McCourt & D.J. Love, *Abortion and Section 7 of the Charter: Proposing a Constitutionally Valid Foetal Protection Law,* 18 MAN. L.J. 365 (1989); S. Poirier, *L'avortement et la liberté de conscience du médecin,* 31 LES CAHIERS DE DROIT 287 (1990).

Perhaps not much can be expected from legislatures in Canada and the United States because there is a strong and determined legislative block united behind a simple goal: that no laws be enacted. The popular majority, in contrast, remains divided over whether to permit abortions at all and, if so, under what circumstances.[256] Public choice theory teaches what the outcome of such a legislative struggle is almost certain to be.[257] If one indulges the assumption every legislator votes exactly as a majority of her constituents would want, opponents would need to command the support of barely more than 25 percent of the voters to block any legislation as long as the 25 percent was concentrated as a razor-thin majority in a group of legislative districts aggregating one more than half of the total number of legislators—even if voters in the remaining districts were nearly unanimous on the other side.[258] In Congress, with a Senate subject to control by a group of states with a minority of the total population and with filibusters possible so long as 40 percent of the Senate opposes cloture, the percentage of the population capable of blocking legislation is even smaller. And given political logrolling and vote trading, the number of members of either house of Congress necessary to block legislation is actually smaller than the foregoing examples suggest.[259]

Some who favor abortion freedom use similar arguments to explain why they were generally unable to obtain their goals through legislative reform before *Roe* was decided.[260] Writing against a background of intense political effort to overturn *Roe v. Wade* and relatively modest efforts to organize electoral majorities to defend the decision, two legal scholars who have examined public choice theory found *Roe* justified as redressing the imbalance in favor of "moralistic pressure groups."[261] Public choice theory suggests that after the *Webster* decision, the political mobilization by the pro-abortion camp meant that the actual legislative outcome was more likely to be stalemate than a clear-cut victory for either side and why, even after the pro-choice side seized a dominant political position in the national government in 1992, supporters of abortion rights too was unable to push their "*Freedom of Choice Act*" through Congress.[262] The

---

256. CONDIT, *supra* note 118, at 148–49. See also the text *supra* at notes 208–250.

257. KENNETH ARROW, SOCIAL CHOICE AND INDIVIDUAL VALUES (2nd ed. 1963); JERRY MARSHAW, GREED CHAOS, AND GOVERNANCE: USING PUBLIC CHOICE TO IMPROVE PUBLIC LAW (1997); Gary Becker, *Pressure Groups and Political Behavior,* in CAPITALISM AND DEMOCRACY: SCHUMPETER REVISITED 120 (Richard Coe & Charles Wilbur eds. 1985); Herbert Hovenkamp, *Arrow's Theorem: Ordinalism and Republican Government,* 75 IOWA L. REV. 949 (1990); Saul Levmore, *Parliamentary Law, Majority Decisionmaking, and the Voting Paradox,* 75 VA. L. REV. 971 (1989); Jonathan Macey, *Transaction Costs and the Normative Elements of the Public Choice Model: An Application to Constitutional Theory,* 74 VA. L. REV. 471 (1988); Michael Munger, *Pangloss Was Right: Reforming Congress Is Useless, Expensive, or Harmful,* 9 DUKE ENVTL. L. & POL'Y F. 133 (1998); Richard Posner, *Economics, Politics, and the Reading of Statutes and the Constitution,* 49 U. CHI. L. REV. 263 (1982); Kenneth Shepsle & Barry Weingast, *Institutionalizing Majority Rule: A Social Choice Theory with Political Implications,* 72 AM. ECON. REV. 367 (1982); Maxwell Stearns, *The Misguided Renaissance of Social Choice,* 103 YALE L.J. 1219 (1994); Robert Tollison, *Public Choice and Legislation,* 74 VA. L. REV. 339 (1988).

258. Erwin Chemerinsky, *Foreword: The Vanishing Constitution,* 103 HARV. L. REV. 43, 79 n.160 (1989).

259. *See* HADLEY ARKES, BEYOND THE CONSTITUTION 221–31 (1990) (reviewing the struggles within Congress over whether to exempt abortion issues from the *Civil Rights Restoration Act*); Daniel Conkle, *Compromising on Abortion,* 8 CONST'L COMMENTARY 353 (1991) (recounting the legislative paralysis in Canada producing by the implacable opposition of both pro-life and pro-choice legislators to any compromise legislation). *See generally* Adrianne G. Threatt, *The Impact of Term Limits on the Congressional Committee System,* 6 GEO. MASON. L. REV. 767 (1998).

260. *See, e.g.,* HARRISON, *supra* note 112, at 233; EVA RUBIN, ABORTION, POLITICS, AND THE COURTS 82 (rev. ed. 1987).

261. DANIEL FARBER & PHILIP FRICKEY, LAW AND PUBLIC CHOICE: A CRITICAL INTRODUCTION 145–53 (1991).

262. *See* Adam Clymer, *Bill to Prohibit State Restrictions on Abortion Appears to Be Dead,* N.Y. TIMES, Sept. 16, 1993, at A18. For the earlier stages of the struggle in Congress, see CRAIG & O'BRIEN, *supra* note 122, at 307–22.

willingness of President Clinton to veto pro-life legislation prevented the political reversal of 1994 from leading to a repeal of the gains of the pro-choice side despite dire predictions at the time.[263]

If a broad public consensus were to emerge, it could actually lead to legislation, although legislation itself would be less necessary if such a consensus actually arose. And, despite the efforts of the pro-choice advocates and the pro-choice media to claim that the emerging consensus is pro-abortion, there is at least as much evidence pointing in the other direction. The media gives a great attention to efforts to open the Republican Party to pro-choice candidates and pro-choice programs.[264] The leading Republican presidential candidates have chosen to express themselves as personally opposed to abortion but unwilling to attempt to take strong legal steps to change the law on the matter.[265] Yet popular opinion has never been as supportive of abortion as the ruling elites of the United States have been, particularly in the Democratic Party.[266]

The Democratic Party became notably more open to pro-life candidates as it attempted to move towards the political center.[267] The new openness resulted in a slow tightening of the modest restrictions now applicable to access to abortion even in states like New Jersey that traditionally have been consistently liberal on abortion.[268] The National Organization for Women (NOW), despite the brave front it tries to put on things, has suffered a sharp loss in membership and in income over the past decade.[269] Whether any of this opening in the political ranks would have occurred were there a real possibility of legislative change we cannot know for sure. Apathy can turn to energy quickly in the face of a real threat, and tolerance is far easier for points of view that you believe have no chance of success than for truly competitive views.

Given the likelihood of continuing legislative paralysis in the United States, one need not invest much time in considering the possibility of enacting a constitutional amendment to secure either extreme vision of what the law ought to be. The likelihood of obtaining support by a two-thirds majority of each house of Congress and thereafter of simple majorities in the legislatures of 38 states is simply too remote to be a realistic option. This would seem to suggest that any change in the law, if it were to come, would come from either the executive branch or from the judiciary. The Supreme Court is still willing to set outer limits on abortion policy, but it appar-

---

263. Fawn Vrazo, *Conservative Ascendancy Propels Abortion to the Crossroads*, PHILA. INQUIRER, Nov. 13, 1994, at A15. *See also* Lizette Alvarez, *G.O.P. Bill to Back Parental Consent Abortion Laws*, N.Y. TIMES, May 21, 1998, at A30.

264. Editorial Desk, *A Pro-Choice Chance for Mr. Bush*, N.Y. TIMES, July 19, 2000, at A24; Bob Hepburn, *Pro-life Marchers Win Support from Bush Adoption Morally Superior, U.S. President Tells Crowd*, TORONTO (ONT.) STAR, Jan. 23 1990, at A14; Dave Lesher, *New Pro-Choice Group to Center on Candidates; Politics: Largely Republican Organization Forms With Exclusive Aim of Electing Candidates Who Support Women's Right to Abortion*, Los Angeles Times, Nov 7, 1989, at B1.

265. Cathleen Decker, *Dole Opposes Both Abortion and Battle about It in the GOP*, PHILA. INQUIRER, Apr. 11, 1999, at A6 (referring to Liddy Dole, not Bob, and noting that George W. Bush has taken the same position).

266. See the text *supra* at notes 111–208.

267. Dana Milbank, *Party Crashers: The Democrats' New Right-Wing Recruits*, THE NEW REP., June 15, 1998, at 21.

268. Marie McCullough, *As Bastion of Abortion Rights, N.J. Is Slipping*, PHILA. INQUIRER, July 4, 1999, at E3; Katharine Seelye, *Advocates of Abortion Rights Report a Rise in Restrictions*, N.Y. TIMES, Jan. 15, 1998, at A16. *See also* Zoe Freirich, Topical Summary, *State Assembly Bill 24: An Affront to Women*, 19 WOMEN'S RTS. L. RPTR. 305 (1998).

269. *See* Deirdre Shaw, *NOW's Battle Shifts: New Enemy Is Apathy*, PHILA. INQUIRER, Aug. 1, 1999, at E1. On the brave front, with its claims of a "feminist majority," see Ginia Bellafonte, *Feminism: It's All about Me!*, TIME, June 29, 1998, at 54; Joan Williams, *Toward a Reconstructive Feminism: Reconstructing the Relationship of Market Work and Family Work*, 19 N. ILL. U. L. REV. 89, 138–39 (1998).

ently has left a broader field for executive or legislative action than before *Webster* and *Casey*.[270] The White House, with its abilities limited to appointing judges,[271] issuing executive orders,[272] influencing administrative regulations,[273] and vetoing legislation with which the President disagrees,[274] remains central to the future of abortion policy. Yet even from the White House, significant change is increasingly unlikely. Remember, the leading Republican contenders for the Presidential nomination have shied away from taking a strong stand on abortion, announcing that while they personally oppose to abortion, the stalemate in the electorate precludes doing anything effective to prevent change the situation.[275]

# Unraveling *Roe*

*If people don't want to come to the ballpark, nobody's going to stop them.*

—Yogi Berra[276]

Suppose, unlikely as it might seem, that *Roe, Doe, Casey* and *Stenberg* were more or less fully overturned, either by another decision of the Supreme Court or by Congress or many state legislatures actually (and surprisingly) managing to satisfy the Court while enacting sharply restrictive or even prohibitory statutes on abortion. Clearly such a turn of events could only happen if it were a strong expression of society's values,[277] although just what values were being expressed would be hotly contested. But would such a change actually affect the practical experiences of women seeking to end a pregnancy?

The simple fact that abortion was becoming more common when it was still illegal in most countries suggests that recriminalizing it would not put an end to the practice, and might not even reduce its incidence by much. At the high end, Daniel Callahan had estimated 30 to 35 million abortions worldwide in 1970, most of which were illegal, although other pro-abortion authors came up with smaller numbers.[278] In attempting to predict the effect of a repeal of the legal right to abortion, however, one would do better to revisit the effect of *Roe* and *Doe* on maternal and fetal lives in the years immediately after those cases were decided than simply to speculate on the basis of highly uncertain estimates of illegal activity.[279]

---

270. Stenberg v. Carhart, 530 U.S. 914 (2000); Planned Parenthood of Southeastern Pennsylvania v. Casey, 505 U.S. 833 (1992); Webster v. Reproductive Health Services, 492 U.S. 490 (1989). *See* Chapter 17, & Chapter 18, at notes 231–87.

271. 28 U.S.C. § 541.

272. 44 U.S.C. § 1605.

273. U.S. Const. art. 2, § 3.

274. U.S. Const. art. 3, § 7, cl. 3.

275. Decker, *supra* note 265.

276. David Nathan, Baseball Quotations 150 (1993).

277. *See* Cass Sunstein, *On the Expressive Function of Law,* 144 U. Pa. L. Rev. 2021 (1996). *See also* Joseph Dellapenna, *Nor Piety nor Wit: The Supreme Court on Abortion,* 6 Colum. H. Rts. L. Rev. 379, 389–98 (1974).

278. Daniel Callahan, Abortion: Law, Choice, and Morality 285 (1970). *See also* Chapter 12, at notes 81–159; Simone de Beauvoir, The Second Sex 135 (Vintage Books ed. 1974) (France); Bernard Dickens, Abortion and the Law 73–83 (1966) (England); Glanville Williams, The Sanctity of Life and the Criminal Law 210–11 (1957, reprinted 1972) (England). *See generally* Germain Grisez, Abortion: The Myths, the Realities, and the Arguments 35–48 (1970).

279. *See* Chapter 15, at notes 8–141.

Beginning with an initial steady rise in the number of reported legal abortions continued until the number had nearly tripled five years after *Roe* was decided to nearly 1,500,000/year.[280] The number of abortions, however, then leveled off and even began to decline after 1990 to around 1,200,000/year.[281] Several reasons undoubtedly contributed to this reversal. Among the reasons were the determined pressure by pro-life groups, the partial elimination of public funding for abortions, and the addition of requirements of parental consent for abortions for minors and waiting periods for adults.

Continuing pressure by antiabortion groups ranged from widely varied educational (or propaganda) efforts to demonstrations to violence.[282] These efforts succeeded in reinforcing the traditional distaste for abortion, as well as in generating fear in would-be abortion providers. The result was a sharp decline in the numbers of physicians who do abortions on a regular basis and in the availability of the procedure to women who seek elective abortions.[283] The complex interplay of ideology, pressure, and personal concerns that causes doctors to avoid doing abortions is suggested by the fact that while women physicians who practice obstetrics are more supportive of abortion rights than are men physicians who practice obstetrics, such women physicians are less supportive of abortion rights than other women physicians.[284]

The funding changes were particularly controversial.[285] Many predicted a major rise in abortion-related deaths among women unable to afford legal abortions.[286] Yet, while the abortion rate among women dependent on public funding for their medical care declined, the decline was small.[287] One study estimated that there were only 18,000 additional live births annually because of the denial of Medicaid funding, but that there were also 282,000 abortions annually by

280. *Id.* at notes 20–21.

281. Tamar Lewin, *Abortions Fell Again in 1995, but Rose in Some Areas Last Year,* N.Y. Times, Dec. 5, 1997, at A14; Tamar Lewin, *Fewer Abortions Performed in the United States: Variety of Factors Cited for Lowest Level since 1979,* N.Y. Times, June 16, 1994, at A1; Tamar Lewin, *Slight Increase in Abortions Is Reported,* N.Y. Times, Dec. 4, 1998, at A27; Barbara Vobejda, *Abortion Rate in U.S. Off Sharply,* Wash. Post, Dec. 5, 1997, at A1.

282. *See* Chapter 16.

283. *Id.* at notes 326–62.

284. Carol Weisman *et al., Abortion Attitudes and Performance among Male and Female Obstetricians-Gynecologists,* 18 Fam. Plan. Persp. 67, 68 (1986). *See also* Chapter 16, at notes 340–62.

285. *See, e.g.,* Colker, *supra* note 187, at 106–07, 136–41; Dworkin, *supra* note 185, at 52; Lee Epstein & Joseph Kobylka, The Supreme Court and Legal Change: Abortion and the Death Penalty 136 (1992); Graber, *supra* note 129, at 68; Robertson, *supra* note 204, at 47; Rubin, *supra* note 260, at 176; Anita Allen, *The Proposed Equal Protection Fix for Abortion Law: Reflections on Citizenship, Gender, and the Constitution,* 18 Harv. J.L. & Pub. Pol'y 419, 449–54 (1995); Willard Cates, jr., *The Hyde Amendment in Action: How Did the Restrictions on Federal Funds for Abortion Affect Low-Income Women?,* 246 JAMA 1109, 1110–12 (1981); Erin Daly, *Reconsidering Abortion Law: Liberty, Equality, and the New Rhetoric of* Planned Parenthood v. Casey, 45 Am. U. L. Rev. 77, 111–16 (1995); Rachel Gold & Jennifer Macias, *Public Funding of Contraception, Sterilization, and Abortion Services, 1985,* 18 Fam. Plan. Persp. 259 (1986); Sarah Harding, *Equality and Abortion: Legitimating Women's Experiences,* 3 Colum. J. Gender & L. 7, 16–20 (1992); Kenneth Meier & Deborah McFarlane, *State Policies on Funding of Abortions: A Pooled Time Series Analysis,* 73 Soc. Sci. Q. 690 (1992); Kenneth Meier & Deborah McFarlane, *The Politics of Funding Abortions: State Responses to the Political Environment,* 21 Am. Pol. Q. 81 (1993); Laurence Tribe, *The Abortion Funding Conundrum: Inalienable Rights, Affirmative Duties, and the Dilemma of Dependence,* 99 Harv. L. Rev. 330 (1985). *See generally* 1 Federal Abortion Politics: A Documentary History 3–186 (Neal Devins & Wendy Watson eds. 1995); Noonan, *supra* note 124, at 90–118.

286. *See, e.g.,* Lawrence Berger, *Abortion in America: The Effects of Restrictive Funding,* 298 N. Eng. J. Med. 1474, 1475 (1978); Diane Pettiti & Williard Cates, *Restricting Funds for Abortions: Projections of Excess Mortality for Women of Childbearing Age,* 67 Am. J. Public Health 860 (1977).

287. *See generally* MacKinnon, *supra* note 169, at 93, 96–97, 100–01; David Robert Baron, *The Racially Disparate Impact of Restrictions on the Public Funding of Abortion: An Analysis of Current Equal Protection Doctrine,* 13 B.C. 3d World L. Rev. 1 (1993).

women who would have had Medicaid funding were it available.[288] Another study concluded that there are only 15,000 unwanted births annually, with 3,000 illegal abortions annually because of denial of public funding.[289] One study even concluded that the birth rate for women denied public funds for abortions actually fell despite the apparent decrease in access to abortion.[290] Dr. Willard Cates, perhaps our leading statistician of abortion, gave us the claim for the greatest effect of the cutoff of abortion funding on women's behavior. He concluded that the denial of funding resulted in about 20 percent of the affected women carrying their pregnancy to term, and about 4 percent turning to illegal abortions, leaving the remaining 76 percent to pay for legal, private abortions with their own money or money provided by charitable or feminist groups.[291]

Nor did the mortality rates climb as a result of the cutoff of Medicaid funds. The Centers for Disease Control found only four deaths of indigent women from illegal or self-induced abortions due to the unavailability of Medicaid funding.[292] Dr. Willard Cates found only three maternal deaths "associated to some degree" with funding restrictions in the first 18 months of the cutoff.[293] In sum, the denial of funding has had a strictly marginal effect had on women's behavior and has produced little demographic impact.[294]

Nonetheless, fearing the effect of a denial of public funding, several state supreme courts found a right to public funding under their state constitutions.[295] Courts in states with "equal

---

288. GRABER, *supra* note 129, at 68.

289. Cates, *supra* note 285, at 1110–12.

290. WETSTEIN, *supra* note 113, at 52–58. *See also* Mark Evans *et al.*, *The Fiscal Impact of the Medicaid Abortion Funding Ban in Michigan*, 82 OBSTET. & GYNECOLOGY 555 (1993); Susan Hansen, *State Implementation of Supreme Court Decisions: Abortion Rates since* Roe v. Wade, 42 J. POL. 372 (1980); Stanley Henshaw & Lynn Wallisch, *The Medicaid Cutoff and Abortion Services for the Poor*, 16 FAM. PLAN. PERSP. 170 (1984); Carol Korenbrot *et al.*, *Trends in Rates of Live Births and Abortions Following State Restrictions on Public Funding of Abortion*, 105 PUB. HEALTH REP. 555 (1990); Susheela Singh, *Adolescent Pregnancy in the United States: An Interstate Analysis*, 18 FAM. PLAN. PERSP. 210 (1986); James Trussel *et al.*, *The Impact of Restricting Medicaid Financing for Abortion*, 12 FAM. PLAN. PERSP. 120 (1980).

291. Cates, *supra* note 285.

292. Trussel *et al.*, *supra* note 290, at 129.

293. Julian Gold & Willard Cates, jr., *Restriction of Federal Funds for Abortion: 18 Months Later*, 69 AM. J. PUB. HEALTH 929 (1979).

294. Trussel *et al.*, *supra* note 290, at 129.

295. State v. Planned Parenthood of Alaska, Inc., 28 P.3d 904 (Alaska 2001); Simat Corp. v. Arizona Health Care Cost Containment System, 56 P.3d 28 (Ariz. 2002); Doe v. Maher, 515 A.2d 134 (Conn. Super. Ct. 1986); Committee to Defend Reproductive Rights v. Myers, 625 P.2d 779 (Cal. 1981); Roe v. Harris, 917 P.2d 403 (Idaho 1996); Moe v. Secretary of Admin., 417 N.E.2d 387 (Mass. 1981); Women of Minn. v. Gomez, 542 N.W.2d 17 (Minn. 1995); Right to Choose v. Byrne, 450 A.2d 925 (N.J. 1982); New Mexico Right to Choose/NARAL v. Johnson, 975 P.2d 841 (N.M. 1998), *cert. denied sub nom.* Klecan v. New Mexico Right to Choose/NARAL, 526 U.S. 1020 (1999); Women's Health Ctr. of W. Va. v. Panepinto, 446 S.E.2d 658 (W. Va. 1993). *Contra:* Humphries Clinic for Women, Inc., 796 N.E.2d 247 (Ind. 2003); Doe v. Department of Soc. Services, 487 N.W.2d 166 (Mich. 1992); Hope v. Perales, 634 N.E.2d 183 (N.Y. 1993); Rosie J. v. North Carolina Dep't of Hum. Resources, 491 S.E.2d 535 (N.C. 1997); Fisher v. Department of Pub. Welfare, 502 A.2d 114 (Pa. 1985); Bell v. Low Income Women of Tex., 95 S.W.3d 253 (Tex. 2002). *See generally* Charlene Carres, *Legislative Efforts to Limit State Privacy Rights*, 25 FLA. ST. U. L. REV. 273 (1998); Kimberly Chaput, *Abortion Rights under State Constitutions: Fighting the Abortion War in the State Courts*, 70 OR. L. REV. 593 (1991); Paul Stam, *The End of the North Carolina Abortion Fund*, 22 CAMPBELL L. REV. 119 (1999).

Courts in other cases have also found a right of privacy in the state constitutions that protects other aspects of claimed abortion rights besides funding. State v. Planned Parenthood of Alaska, 35 P.3d 30 (Alaska 2003) (voiding a parental consent statute); Valley Hosp. Ass'n v. Mat-Su Coalition for Choice, 948 P.2d 963 (Alaska 1997) ("quasi-public" hospital cannot refuse to perform abortions); American Academy of Pediatrics v. Lungren, 940 P.2d 797 (Cal. 1997) (voiding a parental consent statute); North Fla. Women's Health & Counseling Services, Inc. v. State, 866 So. 2d 612 (Fla. 2003) (voiding a parental notice statute); *In re* T.W., 551 So. 2d 1186 (Fla. 1989) (voiding a parental consent statute); Planned Parenthood Lg. of Mass., Inc. v. At-

rights amendments" to their state constitutions—designed to eliminate discrimination against
women—generally did not choose to rest their funding decisions on those provisions, but instead on a supposed state constitutional right of privacy or on generalized equal protection
grounds.[296] The texts of the relevant state and federal constitutional provisions generally read
identically, yet there is no similar right under the federal Constitution.[297]

Changes in federal policy under President Bill Clinton regarding the funding of abortions not
necessary to save the mother's life brought a new round of litigation in federal courts. The change
in policy is grounded in a change in the language of the so-called *Hyde Amendment* that bars
Medicaid funding, but the Clinton administration read the altered language more aggressively
than others would read it.[298] The courts, however, were not so receptive to the legal claims. The
Supreme Court held that a state's denial of its own funds to pay for abortions was lawful so long
as it complied with federal law in administering federal funds.[299] A similar debate emerged within
the European Union over whether the Union's constitutional treaties require member states to
fund abortion notwithstanding the desire of any given state to pursue a different policy.[300]

The impact of parental consent requirements now found in most states is not entirely clear.[301]
An increasing number of states have enacted notification and consent statutes in recent years.

---

torney General, 677 N.E.2d 101 (1997) (same); Planned Parenthood of Cent. N.J. v. Farmer, 762 A.2d 620
(N.J. 2000) (same). Rhode Islands constitution expressly disclaims that its equal rights clause provides any
basis for a right to abortion or to funding for abortions. R.I. CONST. Art. 1, § 2 (2001).

296. *See* Andrea Faraone, *The Florida Equal Rights Amendment: Raising the Standard Applied to Gender
under the Equal Protection Clause of the Florida Constitution,* 1 FLA. COASTAL L.J. 421 (2000); Stanley Friedel-
baum, *State Equal Protection: Its Diverse Guises and Effects,* 66 ALB. L. REV. 599 (2003); Paul Benjamin Linton,
*State Equal Rights Amendments: Making a Difference or Making a Statement?,* 70 TEMPLE L. REV. 907, 922–23
(1997); Jeffrey Shaman, *The Evolution of Equality in State Constitutional Law,* 34 RUTGERS L.J. 1013 (2003);
Sandra Lynne Tholen & Lisa Baird, Note, *Con Law Is as Con Law Does: A Survey of* Planned Parenthood v.
Casey *in State and Federal Courts,* 28 LOY. L.A. L. REV. 971, 1037–44 (1995).

297. *See* Dalton v. Little Rock Fam. Plan. Services, 516 U.S. 474 (1996); Harris v. McRae, 448 U.S. 297
(1980); Poelker v. Doe, 448 U.S. 297 (1979); Maher v. Roe, 432 U.S. 464 (1977); Beal v. Doe, 432 U.S. 438
(1977).

298. *See generally* Lewis Borders, Note, *Rape and Incest Abortion Funding under Medicaid—Can the Federal Government Force Unwilling States to Pick up the Tab?,* 35 J. FAM. L. 121 (1996).

299. Dalton v. Little Rock Fam. Plan. Services, 516 U.S. 474 (1996).

300. John Nishi, *Funding of Medically-Necessary Abortions: A Reexamination of U.S. Law and a Call for EC
Federalism,* 1992 U. CHI. LEG. F. 517.

301. ADOLESCENT ABORTION: PSYCHOLOGICAL AND LEGAL ISSUES (Gary Melton ed. 1986); JEANNE
BROOKS-GUNN & S. PHILIP MORGAN, ADOLESCENT MOTHERS IN LATER LIFE (1987); CHARLOTTE EHRENGARD
ELLERTSON, MANDATORY PARENTAL INVOLVEMENT IN MINORS' ABORTIONS: EFFECTS OF THE LAWS IN MIN-
NESOTA, MISSOURI, AND INDIANA (1993); NOONAN, *supra* note 124, at 90–95; RISKING THE FUTURE: ADOLES-
CENT SEXUALITY, PREGNANCY, AND CHILDBEARING (Cheryl Hayes ed. 1987); Marcia Custer, *Adoption as an
Option for Unmarried Pregnant Teenagers,* 28 ADOLESCENCE 891 (1993); Wanda Franz & David Reardon, *Dif-
ferential Impact of Abortion on Adolescents and Adults,* 27 ADOLESCENCE 162 (1992); Deborah Haas-Wilson,
*The Impact of State Abortion Restrictions on Minors' Demand for Abortion,* 31 J. HUM. RESOURCES 140 (1996);
Theodore Joyce, *The Social and Economic Correlates of Pregnancy Resolution among Adolescents in New York
City, by Race and Ethinicity: A Multivarient Analysis,* 78 AM. J. PUB. HEALTH 626 (1988); Tamar Lewin,
*Parental Consent to Abortion: How Enforcement Can Vary,* N.Y. TIMES, May 28, 1992, at A1; Robert Obsfeldt &
Stephan Gohmann, *Do Parental Involvement Laws Reduce Adolescent Abortion Rates?,* 12 CONTEMP. ECON.
POL'Y 65 (1994); Maggie O'Shaughnessy, *The Worst of Both Worlds? Parental Involvement Requirements and the
Privacy Rights of Minors,* 57 OHIO ST. L.J. 1731 (1996); Deborah Rhode, *Adolescent Pregnancy and Public Pol-
icy,* 108 POL. SCI. Q. 635, 647–61 (1994); Suellyn Scarnecchia & Julie Kunce Field, *Judging Girls: Decision Making in Parental Consent to Abortion Cases,* 3 MICH. J. GENDER & L. 75 (1996); Helena Silverstein, *Road Closed:
Evaluating the Judicial Bypass Provision of the Pennsylvania Abortion Control Act,* 24 LAW & SOC. INQUIRY 73
(1999); Torres & Forrest, *supra* note 142. *See also* Detlev Belling & Christina Eberl, *Teenage Abortions in Germany: With Reference to the Legal System in the United States,* 12 J. CONTEMP. HEALTH L. & POL'Y 475, 480–82;
(1996).

Most of these statutes contain "judicial bypass" provisions authorizing a judge to approve an abortion without notifying a parent.[302] Eleven statutes do not allow for a judicial bypass, and thus are of doubtful constitutionality.[303] Three other states require that minors be counseled about discussing the planned abortion with a parent.[304]

302. ALA. CODE §§ 26-21-1, 26-21-3 to 26-21-4 (1992); ARIZ. REV. STAT. ANN. §§ 36-2152, 36-2153 (West 2003); ARK. STAT. ANN. §§ 20-16-801 to 20-16-808 (LexisNexis 2002); CAL. HEALTH & SAFETY CODE § 123450 (West 1996); FLA. STAT. ANN. § 390.0111(4) (West 2002); GA. CODE ANN. §§ 15-11-110 to 15-11-117 (2001); 750 ILL. COMP. STAT. ANN. § 70/5 (West 1999); IND. CODE ANN. §§ 16-34-2-1 to 16-34-2-7 (West 1997 & Supp. 2003); IOWA CODE ANN. § 135L.5 (West Supp. 2003); KAN. § 65-6705 (2003); KY. REV. STAT. ANN. § 311.732 (Michie 2001); LA. REV. STAT. ANN. § 40:1299.35.5 (West 2001); MASS. GEN. LAWS ANN. ch. 112, § 12S (West 2003); MICH. COMP. LAWS ANN. § 722.903 (West 2002); MINN. STAT. ANN. § 144.343 (West Supp. 2003); MISS. CODE ANN. §§ 41-41-51 to 41-41-63 (West 1999); MO. REV. STAT. ANN. § 188.028 (West 1992); NEB. REV. STAT. §§ 71-6901 to 71-6908 (2003); NEV. REV. STAT. ANN. §§ 442.255, 442.2555 (Michie 2000); N.J. STAT. ANN. §§ 9:17A-1.1 to 9:17A-1.12 (West 2002); N.C. GEN. STAT. §§ 90-21.6 to 90-21.10 (2003); N.D. CENT. CODE §§ 14-02.1 to 14-03.1 (Supp. 2003); OHIO REV. CODE ANN. §§ 2151.85 (Anderson 2002), 2919.12 (Supp. 2003); 18 PA. CONS. STAT. ANN. § 3206 (West 2000); R.I. GEN. LAWS § 23-4.7-6 (1997); S.C. CODE ANN. §§ 44-41-31 to 44-41-37 (West 2002); TENN. CODE ANN. §§ 37-10-301 to 37-10-307 (2001); TEX. FAM. CODE ANN. § 33.003 (West 2002); W. VA. CODE §§ 16-2F-1 to 16-2F-5 (2001); WYO. STAT. ANN. §§ 35-6-101, 35-6-118 (LexisNexis 2003). *See* Hodgson v. Minnesota, 497 U.S. 417 (1990); Bellotti v. Baird, 433 U.S. 622 (1979); Planned Parenthood v. Danforth, 428 U.S. 52, 74 (1975); Blackard v. Memphis Area Med. Ctr. for Women, 262 F.3d 568 (6th Cir. 2001), *cert. denied,* 535 U.S. 1053 (2002); Planned Parenthood of S. Ariz. v. Lawall, 180 F.3d 1022, *modified,* 193 F.3d 1042 (9th Cir. 1999); Memphis Planned Parenthood, Inc. v. Sundquist, 175 F.3d 456 (6th Cir. 1999); Manning v. Hunt, 119 F.3d 254 (4th Cir. 1997); Casey v. Planned Parenthood of S.E. Pa., 14 F.3d 848 (3rd Cir.), *application for stay denied,* 510 U.S. 1309 (1994); Cleveland Surgi-Center, Inc. v. Jones, 2 F.3d 686 (6th Cir. 1993), *cert. denied,* 510 U.S. 1046 (1994); Eubanks v. Wilkinson, 937 F.2d 1118 (6th Cir. 1991); Glick v. McKay, 937 F.2d 434 (9th Cir. 1991); Planned Parenthood of Atlanta Area, Inc. v. Miller, 934 F.2d 1462 (11th Cir. 1991); Arnold v. Board of Educ. of Escambia Cty., 880 F.2d 305 (11th Cir. 1989); Planned Parenthood Lg. of Mass. v. Bellotti, 868 F.2d 459 (1st Cir. 1989); *Ex parte* Anonymous, 806 So. 2d 169 (Ala. 2001); American Academy of Pediatrics v. Lungren, 940 P.2d 797 (Cal. 1996); North Fla. Women's Health Services, Inc. v. State, 866 So. 2d 612 (Fla. 2003); Woman's Choice-East Side Women's Clinic v. Newman, 671 N.E.2d 104 (Ind. 1996); *In re* Jane Doe, 866 P.2d 1069 (Kan. 1994); Planned Parenthood Lg. of Mass., Inc. v. Attorney-General, 677 N.E.2d 101 (Mass. 1997); Planned Parenthood of Cent. N.J. v. Farmer, 762 A.2d 620 (N.J. 2000); *In re* Doe, 19 S.W.3d 346 (Tex. 2000). *See generally* Robert Blum, Michael Resnick, & Trisha Stark, *Factors Associated with the Use of Court Bypass by Minors to Obtain Abortions,* 22 FAM. PLAN. PERSP. 158 (1990); Melody Embree & Tracy Dobson, *Parental Involvement in Adolescent Abortion Decisions,* 10 LAW & INEQUALITY 53 (1991); Marie McCullough, *A 15-Year-Old Anguishes over Abortion Decision: Since She Felt She Could Not Approach Her Mother, She Would Have to Convince a Judge She Was Mature Enough to Decide,* PHILA. INQUIRER, May 29, 2001, at A1; Christine Sensibaugh & Elizabeth Allgeier, *Abortion and Judicial Bypass: Factors Considered by Ohio Juvenile Court Judges in Judicial Bypass Judgments: A Policy Capturing Approach,* 15 POL. & LIFE SCI. 35 (1996).

303. ALASKA STAT. § 18.16.010 (LexisNexis 2002); COLO. REV. STAT. § 18-6-101 (2003); DEL. CODE ANN. tit. 24, § 1794 (1997); IDAHO CODE § 18-609(6) (1997); MD. HEALTH-GEN. CODE ANN. § 20-103 (Michie 2000); MONT. CODE ANN. § 50-20-212 (2003); N.M. STAT. ANN. § 30-5-1(C) (Michie 1994); S.D. CODIFIED LAWS ANN. §§ 26-1-1 (1999), 34-23A-7 (Supp. 2003); UTAH CODE ANN. §§ 15-2-1, 76-7-304(2) (2003); VA. CODE ANN. § 16.1-241 (LexisNexis Supp. 2003); WASH. REV. CODE ANN. § 9.02.100 (West 1998). *See* Lambert v. Wicklund, 520 U.S. 292 (1997); H.L. v. Matheson, 450 U.S. 398 (1981); Planned Parenthood of the Rocky Mtns. Services Corp. v. Owens, 287 F.3d 910 (10th Cir. 2002); Planned Parenthood of the Blue Ridge v. Camblos, 155 F.3d 352 (4th Cir. 1998), *cert. denied,* 525 U.S. 1140 (1999); Causeway Med. Suite v. Ieyoub, 109 F.3d 1096 (5th Cir.), *petition for rehearing* en banc *denied,* 123 F.3d 849 (5th Cir.) (with 7 judges dissenting from the denial of the petition for rehearing), *cert. denied,* 522 U.S. 923 61997; Planned Parenthood, Sioux Falls Clinic v. Miller, 63 F.3d 1452 (8th Cir. 1995), *cert. denied sub nom.* Janklow v. Planned Parenthood, Sioux Falls Clinic, 517 U.S. 1174 (1996) (Rehnquist, C.J., Scalia & Thomas JJ., dissenting); State v. Planned Parenthood of Alaska, 35 P.3d 30 (Alaska 2001).

304. CONN. GEN. STAT. ANN. § 19a-601 (West 2003); ME. REV. STAT. tit. 22, § 1597-A (West 1992); WIS. STAT. ANN. § 146.78 (West 1997). *See* CRAIG & O'BRIEN, *supra* note 122, at 85, 88; 1 FEDERAL ABORTION POLITICS, *supra* note 285, at 249–340; Ruth Colker, *An Equal Protection Analysis of United States Reproductive Health Policy: Gender, Race, Age, and Class,* 1991 DUKE L.J. 324, 359–63; Daly, *supra* note 285, at 105–11; Jon

The abortion rate and the unwed pregnancy rate for teenagers in the United States are much higher than in Europe or other industrialized countries[305]—even for industrialized countries with similar rates of premarital sexual activity among teenagers.[306] On the other hand, the rate of births to teenagers varies from state to state and actually drops along with the abortion rate in states that require parental notification before a juvenile undergoes an abortion.[307] In Minnesota, the addition of a requirement of parental consent was followed by both a 33 percent decline in abortions performed on minors and a 13 percent decline in illegitimate births.[308] Did adolescent women travel to another state to have an abortion, or did many take effective steps to preclude pregnancy? No one knows. In a geographically small state like Massachusetts, recourse to out-of-state abortions is easier than in a large state like Minnesota, yet the decline in unwed pregnancies and in abortions is similar in the two states.[309] Making abortions more accessible thus hardly seems a promising means for lowering teen abortion and unwed pregnancy rates, particularly when one recalls that abortions generally are less accessible in other industrialized countries than in the United States.

For various reasons, the birth rate in the United States fell sharply during the 1990s, reaching an all-time low of 14.5 births per 1,000 Americans in 1997[310]—101.6 pregnancies per 1,000 women between the ages of 15 and 44.[311] By comparison, in 1957 (at the height of the post-war baby boom) the birth rate was 25.3 per 1,000 Americans, about 181.7 pregnancies per 1,000 women age 15-44. Leading the decline has been a sharp drop in births among teens—particularly illegitimate births. The teen pregnancy rate fell from 116.5 pregnancies per 1,000 teens (age 15–19) in 1990 to 94.3 per 1,000 teens.[312] As a result, 1997 saw 52.3 births

Merz, Catherine Jackson, & Jacob Klerman, *A Review of Abortion Policy: Legality, Medicaid Funding, and Parental Involvement, 1967–1994,* 17 WOMEN'S RTS. L. RPTR. 1, 9–61 (1995); Rhode, *supra* note 301, at 661–69.

305. Elise Jones, Jacqueline Forrest, & Noreen Goldman, *Teenage Pregnancy in Developed Countries: Determinants and Policy Implications,* 17 FAM. PLAN. PERSP. 53 (1985). *See also* RISKING THE FUTURE, *supra* note 301; Stanley Henshaw, *Induced Abortion: A World Review, 1990,* 22 FAM. PLAN. PERSP. 76 (March–April 1990), reprinted in ABORTION, MEDICINE, AND THE LAW, *supra* note 120, at 406; Allen Rosenfield, *The Difficult Issue of Second-Trimester Abortion,* 267 JAMA 324, 324–25 (1994).

306. Rosenfield, *supra* note 305, at 324.

307. *See, e.g.,* Virginia Cartoof & Lorraine Klerman, *Parental Consent for Abortion: Impact of the Massachusetts Law,* 76 AM. J. PUB. HEALTH 397 (1986); Freddie Clary, *Minor Women Obtaining Abortions: A Study of Parental Notification in a Metropolitan Area,* 72 AM. J. PUB. HEALTH 283 (1982); Patricia Donovan, *Judging Teenagers: How Minors Fare When They Seek Court-Authorized Abortions,* 15 J. FAM. PLAN. PERSP. 259 (1981); James Rogers, *Impact of the Minnesota Parental Notification Law on Abortion and Birth,* 81 AM. J. PUB. HEALTH 294 (1991); Lynn Vincent, *The Parent Gap: The Number of Abortions among Teenagers Is Dropping Much Faster in States with Strong Parental Consent Laws,* THE WORLD, Jan. 18, 2003, at 22; Susan Yates & Anita Pliner, *Judging Maturity in the Courts: The Massachusetts Consent Statute,* 78 AM. J. PUB. HEALTH 646 (1988). *See generally* Stanley Henshaw & Dina Feivelson, *Teenage Abortion and Pregnancy Statistics by State,* 32 FAM. PLAN. PERSP. 272 (2000).

308. ARKES, *supra* note 259, at 214–15. *See generally* CONDIT, *supra* note 118, at 191–92.

309. *See* Robert Blum, Michael Resnick, & Trisha Stark, *The Impact of a Parental Notification Law on Adolescent Abortion Decision-Making,* 77 AM. J. PUB. HEALTH 620 (1987).

310. Stephanie Ventura, Joyce Abma, & William Mosher, *Revised Pregnancy Raters, 1990–1997, and New Rates for 1998–99: United States,* 52 NAT. VITAL STATISTICS REP. no. 1 (2003). *See also Birth Rate Drops for Teenagers, but Gains for Unmarried Teens,* WALL ST. J., Mar. 21, 1997, at B9A; Sheryl Gay Stolberg, *Birth Rate at New Low as Teen-Age Pregnancy Declines,* N.Y. Times, Apr. 29, 1999, at A26. These reductions were achieved even though many employers did not cover contraceptives in their drug benefit plans. *See* Erickson v. Bartell Co., 141 F. Supp. 2d 1266 (W.D. Wash. 2001) (declaring the exclusion of birth control from a drug benefit plan to violate Title VII of the 1964 Civil Rights Act).

311. Cheryl Wetzstein, *Pregnancy Rate for Teens Reached Record Low in 1997: Slide in Abortions, Birthrates Began Early in Decade,* WASH. POST, June 13, 2001, at A3.

312. *Id. See also* Henshaw & Feivelson, *supra* note 307; Marc Lacey, *Teen-Age Birth Rate in U.S. Falls Again: Trend Spans Ethnic Groups and Geographic Areas, Report Finds,* N.Y. TIMES, Oct. 27, 1999, at A16. *See generally* Elizabeth Terry-Humen, Jennifer Malove, & Kristin Moore, *Births Outside of Marriage: Perceptions vs. Reality* (Child Trend Research Brief, Apr. 2001), available at *www.childtrends.org/PDF/rb:032601.pdf.*

per 1,000 teens, 27.5 abortions per 1,000 teens, and 14.5 fetal losses per 1,000 teens.[313] Some observers concluded that improved contraceptives and a greater social willingness to assure teens of access to such devices drove this decline.[314] Especially helpful were Norplant (a contraceptive hormonal implant) and Depo-Provera (a contraceptive hormonal injection), both of which, if used at all, are difficult to use incorrectly.[315] Strategies to deter early and promiscuous sexuality seem to have had indifferent impact,[316] yet there has been a rise in the age at which teens first engage in sex and a decline in the frequency and number of partners.[317] These changes in behavior in turn reflect a complex interaction of advocacy of sexual abstinence or at least sexual restraint, fear of AIDS, changes in the availability of abortion, and perhaps other factors.

Less progress has been made than in introducing new, safer and more effective contraceptives than was confidently expected 20 or 30 years ago.[318] Product liability suits almost immediately challenged Norplant,[319] while Depo-Provera was held up for 20 years by FDA review.[320] The "female condom," introduced in the 1990s, is not as reliable as other new methods.[321] The use of the oral contraceptive pill as a "morning-after" pill was, until very recently, the "best-kept secret" in pharmacological medicine.[322] Because of the limited advances in contraceptive technology in recent decades, significant voices still insist that the law—particularly the law of product liability—has seriously impeded research for even better contraceptives.[323] Only in 2002 did

---

313. Wetzstein, *supra* note 311.

314. Stolberg, *supra* note 310 (quoting Dr. Jacqueline Darroch, a well-known researcher on birth, birth control, and abortion rates).

315. *Id. See also* George Brown, *Long Acting Contraceptives: Rationale, Current Development, and Ethical Implications,* 25 HASTINGS CTR. REP., no. 1, at S12 (Jan.–Feb. 1995).

316. *See, e.g.,* Kathryn Wexler, *California Cracks Down on Men to Curb Underage Pregnancies,* WASH. POST, Apr. 6, 1996, at A3.

317. Stolberg, *supra* note 310 (quoting Dr. Jacqueline Darroch again).

318. Michael Klitsch, *Still Waiting for the Contraceptive Revolution,* 27 FAM. PLAN. PERSP. 246 (1995). *See generally* Micheal Galen, *Just Whose Fault Is It? Birth-Control Options Limited by Litigation,* NAT'L L.J., Oct. 20, 1986, at 3; Sheldon Segal, *Contraceptive Development and Better Family Planning,* 73 BULL. NY ACAD. MED. 92 (1996).

319. *In re* Norplant Contraceptive Prod. Liab. Litig. 215 F. Supp. 2d 795 (E.D. Tex 2002); Perez v. Wyeth Labs. Inc., 734 A.2d 1245 (N.J. 1999). *See also* Terry Carter, *Setting the Ground Rules: Judge Controls Snacks and Wisecracks, Dismisses Norplant Bellwether Case,* ABA J., Aug. 1997, at 33; Gina Kolata, *Will the Lawyers Kill off Norplant?,* N.Y. TIMES, May 28, 1995, §3, at 1; Sylvia Law, *Tort Liability and the Availability of Contraceptive Drugs and Devices in the United States,* 23 NYU REV. L. & SOC. CHANGE 339, 385–90 (1997); Sheldon Segal, *Contraceptive Update,* 23 NYU REV. L. & SOC. CHANGE 457, 460–52 (1997).

320. Klitsch, *supra* note 318, at 246; Segal, *supra* note 318, at 461, 465–66. *See also* Stephen Isaacs & Renee Holt, *Drug Regulation, Product Liability, and the Contraceptive Crunch: Choices Are Dwindling,* 8 J. LEGAL MED. 533, (1987).

321. Law, *supra* note 318, at 382; Louis Zaneveld, *Vaginal Contraception since 1984: Chemical Agents and Barrier Devices,* in CONTRACEPTIVE RESEARCH AND DEVELOPMENT, 1984–1994: THE ROAD FROM MEXICO CITY TO CAIRO AND BEYOND 69 (Paul Van Look & G. Perez-Palacios eds. 1994)

322. Jane Brody, *Pregnancy Prevention, the Morning after,* N.Y. TIMES, Apr. 10, 2001, at F8; Bennie Currie, *Ill. Agency Offers Birth-Control Pill Online,* PHILA. INQUIRER, June 16, 2001, at A5; Mark Kaufman, *Nonprescription Sale Sought for Contraceptive,* WASH. POST, Apr. 21, 2002, at A2; Segal, *supra* note 318, at 463. *See also* Charlotte Ellertson, *History and Efficacy of Emergency Contraception beyond Coca-Cola,* 28 FAM. PLAN. PERSP. 44 (1996); Laura Sessions Stepp, *Pill Ban Gives Birth to Protest: Vote on Contraceptive Galvanizes Campus,* WASH. POST, Apr. 24, 2003, at C1; Jeff Stryker, *"Emergency" Birth Control: Access Issues,* N.Y. TIMES, Mar. 11, 2003, at F5; Albert Yuzpe & William Lancee, *Ethinylestadiol and Di-Norgestrel as a Postcoital Contraceptive,* 28 FERTILITY & STERILITY 932 (1977); Kate Zernike, *Morning-after Pill Rising & It May Go over the Counter,* N.Y. TIMES, May 19, 2003, at A1.

323. Symposium, *Special Issue on Law and Contraceptive Methods,* 23 NYU REV. L. & SOC. CHANGE 329 (1997); Kevin White, *Notebook: Contraceptive Makers Chilled by Court Challengers,* 4 J. WOMEN'S HEALTH 223 (1995). *See generally* Louis Lasagna, *The Chilling Effect of Product Liability on New Drug Development,* in THE

press reports begin to circulate about new, innovative contraceptive devices[324] or the reemergence of contraceptive sponges after an eight-year hiatus.[325]

To the extent the decline in the birth rate suggests a decline in the pregnancy rate, the decline reduces demand for abortion regardless of what abortion protesters do or what the law is. Declines in abortion rates have also been caused by various strategies deployed against abortion—ranging from negligible to significant. This in turn suggests that truly restrictive abortion laws would induce a further decline in the number of abortions[326]—which in turn could feed back to induce yet further declines in birth rates. We cannot predict the magnitude of these declines with any confidence, however, and the decline in abortions could well turn out to be smaller than the increase after *Roe* was decided. Such legal and behavioral changes would follow even if no pre-*Roe* statute were held to revive automatically by an overruling of *Roe*.[327]

A similar conclusion is suggested by the extraordinary variation in abortion rates from state to state, a variation greater than that found for any other medical procedure.[328] This variation correlates, almost entirely, with the local availability of abortion services.[329] As simple a step as prescribing a mandatory 24-hour waiting period has been estimated to have reduced the incidence of abortion by eight per 1,000 live births—about 10 percent.[330] Prohibit or even impede

---

LIABILITY MAZE 334 (Peter Huber & Robert Litan eds. 1991); W. Kip Viscusi & Michael Moore, *Rationalizing the Relationship between Product Liability and Innovation,* in TORT LAW AND THE PUBLIC INTEREST: COMPETITION, INNOVATION AND CONSUMER WELFARE 105 (Peter Schuck ed. 1991).

324. Leslie Berger, *After Long Hiatus, New Contraceptives Emerge,* N.Y. TIMES, Dec. 10, 2002, at F5; Sue Redfern, *A New Ring Cycle: Contraceptive Woos the Wary,* WASH. POST, Aug. 6, 2002, at HE1 ("NuvaRing"); Rob Stein, *Experimental Pill Puts Menstruation on Hold: Seasonale Expects FDA Approval Soon,* WASH. POST, Mar. 3, 2003, at A1.

325. *Contraceptive Sponge Back on the Market: Awaiting FDA Approval to Sell It in the U.S., Company Makes It Available Via Internet,* WASH. POST, Mar. 5, 2003, at A7; *Contraceptive Sponge Makes Return: Loyalists Epitomized by "Seinfeld" pal Elaine Are Expected to Buy in Bulk from the Net or in Canada,* PHILA. INQUIRER, Mar. 5, 2003, at A13.

326. *See* WETSTEIN, *supra* note 113, at 109–30.

327. The only court to consider a claim that another case had so far overruled *Roe* and *Doe* as to revive the state's pre-*Roe* abortion statute concluded that intervening legislation had repealed the pre-*Roe* statute. Weeks v. Connick, 733 F. Supp. 1036 (E.D. La. 1990). This solution will not fit every state. *See* Paul Linton, *Enforcement of State Abortion Statutes after* Roe: *A State-by-State Analysis,* 67 U. DET. L. REV. 157 (1990); Erica Frohman Plave, Note, *The Phenomenon of Antique Laws: Can a State Revive Old Abortion Laws in a New Era,* 58 GEO. WASH. L. REV. 111 (1989); Teresa Scott, Note, *Burying the Dead: The Case against Revival of Pre-*Roe *and Pre-*Casey *Abortion Statutes in a Post-*Casey *World,* 19 N.Y.U. REV. L. & SOC. CHANGE 355 (1991); David Smolin, *The Status of Existing Abortion Prohibitions in a Legal World without* Roe: *Applying the Doctrine of Implied Repeal to Abortion,* 11 ST. L.U. PUB. L. REV. 385 (1992); William Michael Treanor & Gene Sperling, *Prospective Overruling and the Revival of "Unconstitutional" Statutes,* 93 COLUM. L. REV. 1902 (1993).

328. GINSBURG, *supra* note 137, at 56–57; GRABER, *supra* note 129, at 71–72; FREDERICK JAFFE, BARBARA LINDHEIM, & PHILIP LEE, ABORTION POLITICS 16 (1981); Stanley Henshaw & Jennifer Van Vort, *Abortion Services in the United States, 1991 and 1992,* 26 FAM. PLAN. PERSP. 100, 104 (1994).

329. REBECCA BLANK *et al.,* ABORTION RATES: THE IMPACT OF POLICIES, PROVIDERS, POLITICS, DEMOGRAPHICS AND ECONOMIC ENVIRONMENT (1994). *See also* GINSBURG, *supra* note 137, at 57; GRABER, *supra* note 129, at 71; JAFFE, LINDHEIM, & LEE, *supra* note 328, at 34; Robert Brown & R. Todd Jewell, *The Impact of Provider Availability on Abortion Demand,* 14 CONTEMP. ECON. POL'Y 95 (1996); Jacqueline Dorroch Forrest, Christopher Tietze, & Ellen Sullivan, *Abortion in the United States, 1976–1977,* 10 FAM. PLAN. PERSP. 271, 273 (1978); Patricia Gober, *The Role of Access in Explaining State Abortion Rates,* 44 SOC. SCI. & MED. 1003 (1997); Stephan Goldmann & Robert Ohlsfeldt, *Effects of Price and Availability on Abortion Demand,* 11 CONTEMP. ECON. POL'Y 42 (1993); Deborah Haas-Wilson, *The Economic Impact of State Restrictions on Abortion,* 12 J. POL'Y ANAL. & MGT. 498 (1993); Stanley Henshaw, *The Accessibility of Abortion Services in the United States,* 23 FAM. PLAN. PERSP. 246 (1994); Henshaw & Van Vort, *supra* note 328, at 106, 112; James Shelton, Edward Brann, & Kenneth Schulz, *Abortion Utilization: Does Travel Matter?,* 8 FAM. PLAN. PERSP. 260, 262 (1976).

330. Michael Graber, *The Ghost of Abortion Past: Pre-*Roe *Abortion Law in Action,* 1 VA. J. SOC. POL'Y & L. 309, 374 (1994) (this article is substantially reprinted as chapter II of his book, GRABER, *supra* note 129; the

abortion locally, and there will be a decline in abortions, declines that are not simply the result of the improved availability or use of contraceptives.[331] Thus Missouri's few and limited restrictions on abortion, which were approved by the Supreme Court in *Webster v. Reproductive Health Services,*[332] apparently led to a decline of abortions in that state by 29 percent between 1988 and 1992.[333] While some of the apparent decline in abortions might actually have occurred off the record (*i.e.,* illegally) or in other states,[334] probably not all do so. One would expect the difficulty in obtaining an abortion bears most heavily on those with the least income.[335] The waiting periods enacted in the wake of *Casey,* however, did not affect poor or minority women differently than affluent, white, women, despite considerable propaganda claiming the opposite.[336]

The experience of other countries that have imposed restrictive abortion laws after periods when the procedure was legal and available also suggests that restrictive laws would have a significant impact here. General social conditions are so different in countries such as Czechoslovakia, Hungary, and Romania that one might discount the generally sharp declines in abortion in those countries when restrictive abortion laws were subsequently enacted.[337] On the other hand, New Zealand's experience is suggestive. New Zealand is a nation sufficiently isolated that few women are likely to leave the country to obtain an abortion. When New Zealand changed its formerly permissive law in 1976 to permit abortions only for "serious" dangers to the mother's life or health, the abortion rate fell from a 1:9 ratio of abortions to live births to a ratio of 1:14.[338] When New Zealand changed its law again in 1982 to remove the "seriousness" requirement, the abortion rate rose again, to a 1:7 ratio of abortions to live births.[339]

Precise projection of the effects of changing abortion laws remains impossible, however, because of the many variables besides the legal status of abortion laws that affect abortion rates. Thus, the Netherlands has long had relatively open access to abortion.[340] The authorities stopped enforcing the restrictive Dutch abortion law more than a decade before the current relatively permissive law was enacted in 1984.[341] Under the current Dutch law, the only real restriction on access to early abortion in the Netherlands is a five-day waiting period between the request for an abortion and the abortion itself, a period that does not apply during the

---

few deletions in the reprinted version, however, all relate to evidence that might suggest that abortion laws and regulations might actually be effective; Graber's references to these estimates is one of the deletions). *See also* GARROW, *supra* note 23, at 718, 722–23; Francis Althause & Stanley Henshaw, *The Effects of Mandatory Delay Laws on Abortion Patients and Providers,* 26 FAM. PLAN. PERSP. 228 (1994); Hansen, *supra* note 290, at 383, 386; Theodore Joyce *et al., The Impact of Mississippi's Mandatory Delay Law on Abortions and Births,* 278 JAMA 653 (1997); Kenneth Meier *et al., The Impact of State-Level Restrictions on Abortion,* 33 DEMOGRAPHY 307 (1996); Sara Seims, *Abortion Availability in the United States,* 12 FAM. PLAN. PERSP. 88, 99–100 (1980).

331. Henshaw & Van Vort, *supra* note 328, at 106.

332. 492 U.S. 490 (1989).

333. Henshaw & Van Vort, *supra* note 328, at 103.

334. *See* Alissa Rubin, *Throwing Babies,* THE NEW REP., Oct. 26, 1992, at 19.

335. GRABER, *supra* note 129, at 71; JAFFE, LINDHEIM, & LEE, *supra* note 328, at 34; REAGAN, *supra* note 152, at 249; Forrest, Tietze, & Sullivan, *supra* note 329, at 279.

336. Graber, *supra* note 330, at 95–96.

337. Ian Gentles, *Good News for the Fetus: Two Fallacies in the Abortion Debate,* POLICY REV., Spring 1987, at 50. *See generally* Tomas Frejka, *Induced Abortion and Fertility: A Quarter Century of Experience in Eastern Europe,* 9 POPULATION & DEV. REV. 494, 497–509 (1983).

338. Gentles, *supra* note 337, at 50, 53.

339. *Id.* at 53–54.

340. *See generally* HADLEY, *supra* note 23, at 146–52.

341. *Id.* at 147–48; Evert Ketting & Philip van Praag, *The Marginal Relevance of Legislation Relating to Induced Abortion,* in THE NEW POLITICS OF ABORTION 154 (Joni Lovenduski & Joyce Outshoorn eds. 1986); Joyce Outshoorn, *Introduction: The New Politics of Abortion,* in THE NEW POLITICS OF ABORTION, *supra,* at 1.

first 16 days after a missed onset of menstruation.[342] Abortions are not allowed after 22 weeks gestation except to save the mother's life. While a woman must be in a "severe emergency situation" even before the 22-week limit, doctors usually defer to the woman's determination of whether such an emergency exists.[343] No one in the Netherlands lives more than an hour's drive from a licensed clinic, and abortions are free for Dutch citizens under the national health plan.[344]

The policies of deferring to a woman's judgment about the necessity of an abortion and of not enforcing the potentially more restrictive mandates of the abortion law on the books make the Netherlands a favorite destination for women seeking abortions who come from elsewhere in Europe where there are more restrictive abortion laws.[345] The cost of a Dutch abortion to a foreign woman was reported in 1996 to be about $300 US.[346] German border police frequently investigate women returning from the Netherlands looking "pale and emotional" for possible evasion of German restrictions on abortion.[347] Despite the ease of access to abortion in the Netherlands, that country has one of the lowest abortion rates in the world. In the early 1990s, the Dutch abortion rate is about 6 abortions/1000 women of reproductive age, compared to 14/1000 in the United Kingdom, 28/1000 in the United States, and 111/1000 in Russia.[348] Even with such a low rate, the majority of abortions done in the Netherlands are performed on foreign women rather than on Dutch citizens.[349]

The Dutch achieve their low abortion rates through a strong emphasis on contraception and on sex education, with 80 percent of all women between the ages of 15 and 25 using the pill.[350] In fact, in many ways, the Dutch are far more accepting than Americans of contraceptive use.[351] And, while the Netherlands has its anti-abortion campaign, anti-abortion activists have little direct impact on the operation of the abortion clinics.[352] Nonetheless, the Dutch people have never been comfortable with abortion, and strive hard to avoid an unwanted pregnancy rather than to terminate it.[353] The absence of similar patterns in most of the United Kingdom or the United States, however, suggests that the Dutch approach will not translate across the seas.

A further complicating factor in attempting to predict the probable effect of overruling *Roe v. Wade* and *Doe v. Bolton* lies in the strong form of federalism found in the United States.[354] Because of that federalism, even the unlikely enactment of a national highly restrictive abortion law in the United States probably would not create a nationally uniform policy in fact. The social variables would be widely different in different states, as also would be enforcement policies.

Canada's experience, meticulously documented in legally required Canadian hospital records, suggests the potential effect of highly divergent administration of a single national abortion law. Canada enacted a permissive national law on abortion in 1969 and has had no law on abortion

---

342. HADLEY, *supra* note 23, at 147.
343. *Id.*
344. *Id.*
345. *Id.* at 27, 47–48.
346. *Id.* at 147.
347. *Id.* at 29.
348. *Id.* at 149; Henshaw, *supra* note 329; Evert Ketting, *Is the Dutch Abortion Rate Really that Low?*, 23 PLANNED PARENTHOOD IN EUROPE 29 (1994).
349. HADLEY, *supra* note 23, at 47.
350. *Id.* at 149–50.
351. Philip Hilts, *U.S. Is Decades behind Europe in Contraceptives, Experts Report*, N.Y. TIMES, Feb. 15, 1990, at A1.
352. *Id.* at 216 n.5.
353. *Id.* at 149, 151.
354. *See generally* HADLEY, *supra* note 23, at 182–86.

at all since *Morgenthaler v. Regina*[355] was decided in 1988. Despite national legal uniformity, however, abortion statistics range widely from province to province with no abortions in Prince Edward Island for many years after 1983 and very few in other provinces, with apparently almost no inter-provincial travel to secure abortions in more permissive provinces. Only 12 women from Prince Edward Island took the short boat ride to the mainland to obtain an abortion in 1984.[356] In the year 2000, Prince Edward Island still saw no abortions on the island and an abortion rate of 11:1000 live births (counting women who left the province to obtain an abortion), with the highest provincial rate being 43.2/1000 live births for women residing in Quebec and an average national rate of 32.2/1000 live births.[357]

In thinking about the likely consequences of enacting a highly restrictive abortion law, one must also keep in mind its contemporary politicized status — something that did not exist before the twentieth century and which today would seriously impair attempts to restrict or prohibit the practice. After all, some 30,000,000 women have had 39,000,000 abortions since *Roe v. Wade* was decided.[358] If a significant minority of those women are willing to become active resisters of restrictive abortion laws, the enforcement of such laws will be seriously weakened and might fail altogether.

Abortion rights activists have declared their determination to defy openly any laws prohibiting abortions.[359] A Dutch activist, Dr. Rebecca Gomperts, has gone so far as to attempt to organize a foundation ("Women on Waves") to support a ship for doing abortions off the coast of countries with restrictive laws.[360] Gomperts was careful to keep the targeted countries secret. Reports that the first target would be Malta produced outcries of outrage there.[361] As it turned out, the first target was Ireland.[362] In Ireland, even some feminist groups were reluctant to become involved in the effort,[363] whether because it would hurt their image at home or for concern about

355. 1 S.C.R. 30 (1988).

356. Gentles, *supra* note 337, at 54.

357. *Canadian Abortion Statistics,* available at *http://www.webhart.net/vandee/abortstat.shtml#Reported.*

358. *See* Ellen Goodman, *30 Years, 30 Million Women,* WASH. POST, Jan. 22, 2003, at A15.

359. BRIGITTE & PETER BERGER, THE WAR OVER THE FAMILY: CAPTURING THE MIDDLE GROUND 75–77 (1983); REBECCA CHALKER & CAROL DOWNER, A WOMAN'S BOOK OF CHOICES: ABORTION, MENSTRUAL EXTRACTION, RU 486, at 121–27, 167–82 (1993); GRABER, *supra* note 129, at 40–41, 73; HARRISON, *supra* note 112, at 5; PAIGE, *supra* note 123, at 245; Suzanne Alford, Note, *Is Self-Abortion a Fundamental Right?,* 52 DUKE L.J. 1011 (2003); Susan Brenna, *Women Turn to Self-Help Groups for Abortion Despite the Risks,* N.Y. TIMES, Sept. 9, 1992, at C13; Barbara Brotman, *Secret Abortion Group of '60s Prepares for Return,* CHI. TRIB., Aug. 28, 1989, at C1; Diane Curtis, *Doctored Rights: Menstrual Extraction, Self-Help Gynecological Care, and the Law,* 20 REV. L. & SOC. CHANGE 427, 428–29 (1994); Gina Kolata, *Self-Help Abortion Movement Gains Momentum,* N.Y. TIMES, Oct. 23, 1989, at A8; Lynn Paltrow, *Women, Abortion, and Civil Disobedience,* 13 NOVA L.J. 471 (1989); Andrea Peyser, *Do Your Own Abortion,* N.Y. POST, Jan. 27, 1992, at 1; Laura Punnett, *The Politics of Menstrual Extraction,* in FROM ABORTION TO REPRODUCTIVE FREEDOM, *supra* note 191, at 101; Fawn Vrazo, *Preparing for the End of Legalized Abortion,* PHILA. INQUIRER, Aug. 25, 1991, at 1-A.

360. Leslie Berger, *Doctor Plans Off-Shore Clinic for Abortions,* N.Y. TIMES, Nov. 21, 2000, at F7; Peter Ford, *Banned on Land, but Free at Sea? A Dutch Abortion Doctor, a US-Based Internet Team, Each Set up Shop beyond Government's Reach,* CHRIST. SCI. MONITOR, June 23, 2000, at 1; Marina Jiminez, *Doctor's Floating Clinic to Offer Offshore Abortions: Procedures Will Be Carried out in International Waters,* NATIONAL POST, June 12, 2000, a A1; Alissa Quart, *Life Line,* MS. MAG., Apr. 1, 2000, at 25; Charles Trueheart, *Doctor Plans Offshore Abortions; Ship Would Anchor Outside Territory Where Procedure Is Illegal,* WASH. POST, June 16, 2001, at A20; Richard Wilner, *Dutch Group Floats Abortion-Boat Idea,* N.Y. POST, Aug. 20, 2000, at 28.

361. Trueheart, *supra* note 360. A physician in Australia has proposed doing the same for performing euthanasia off the coast of his country. Andrew Osborn Brussels, *Floating Clinic Will Offer the Sick Offshore Euthanasia Offshore (sic),* THE OBSERVER, Apr. 8, 2001, at 19.

362. Andrea Gerlin, *Law, Logistics Stall Abortion Boat's Debut,* PHILA. INQUIRER, June 16, 2001, at A6; Marlise Simons, *Dutch Ship to Perform Abortion in International Waters,* N.Y. TIMES, June 11, 2001, at A9.

363. Margaretta D'Arcy, *Letter,* IRISH TIMES, May 11, 2001, at 15 (disassociating herself from the refusal of the National Women's Council of Ireland to meet with representatives of Gomperts).

the safety of doing the procedures in a ship rolling with the waves.[364] Thus the National Women's Council of Ireland refused to meet with Gomperts or her representatives, and refused to support her project.[365]

Some six months after announcing her plans, and about two-years after she first conceived the plan, Dr. Gomperts and her ship sailed off to Dublin, only to find themselves stymied by her own government. The Dutch government threatened prosecution if any abortions were performed because the vessel was not a licensed medical facility.[366] The entire project was so ineffectual that even some of its supporters described it as more of a publicity stunt than as a real attempt to provide abortion services.[367] Still, it wouldn't take a great effort to organize such an effort off American coasts. One must question, however, whether even several such ships would provide a significant alternative for women seeking abortions.[368]

The pervasiveness of abortion in America in itself suggests that there would also be a large pool of people who would continue to struggle for the continued availability of abortion. After all, there were at least 34,000,000 abortions in the United States between 1973 and 1996, and only around 90,000,000 women who were capable of bearing children during that period.[369] Nearly 20 percent of all American women will have had abortions by the time they are 45 years old.[370] As with the underground abortion movement that arose in the 1960s,[371] however, defiance might very well satisfy the needs of older, affluent white women rather than the needs of young, poor, or minority women—particularly if abortions are legal in some states and not in others.[372]

The continued intense opposition to a practice that has become so pervasive in society suggests not only the peculiarity of the tensions generated by the practice, but also that there is a large pool of people who would actively seek to enforce such laws.[373] That pool of strongly com-

---

364. Thomas Cole, *Letter*, WASH. TIMES, June 16, 2001, at A22; Jimenez, *supra* note 360; Wilner, *supra* note 360.

365. D'Arcy, *supra* note 363.

366. Gerlin, *supra* note 362.

367. Thomas Grose, *An Abortion Ship on the High Seas: The Uncertain Start of a New Medical Service*, U.S. NEWS & WORLD REP., June 25, 2001, at 30.

368. *Id.* (reporting that the vessel's brief stop in Dublin, "more than 80 women had phoned the Women on Waves Ireland hotline" asking for abortions—"more than could have been accommodated").

369. Caldwell, *supra* note 112, at 14.

370. Barbara Gottlieb, *Sounding Board: Abortion—1995*, 332 NEW ENG. J. MED. 532 (1995); Andreas Kielich & Veronica Ravnikar, *Better Primary Care for Women: The Numbers Show the Need*, 27 PATIENT CARE No. 18, at 10 (1993). Some estimates in this respect run as high as 45%. *See* CHERYL MEYER, THE WANDERING UTERUS: POLITICS AND THE REPRODUCTIVE RIGHTS OF WOMEN 133 (1997); Caldwell, *supra* note 112, at 15; Jacqueline Dorroch Forrest, *Unintended Pregnancy among American Women*, 19 FAM. PLAN. PERSP. 76, 77 (1987); Stanley Henshaw, *Freestanding Abortion Clinics: Services, Structure, Fees*, 14 FAM. PLAN. PERSP. 248, 253 (1982); Richard Lacayo, *Whose Life Is It?*, TIME, May 1, 1989, at 20, 27. Perhaps the discrepancy in these estimates arises from a failure of those who offer the higher figure to take into account that nearly one-half of the abortions in any given year are repeat abortions. *See* CENTER FOR DISEASE CONTROL, *supra* note 145, at 29 (reporting 46% of all abortions were repeat abortions in 1997); Henshaw & Silverman, *supra* note 145, at 158 (43 percent of all abortions to be repeat abortions in 1987); Wardle, *supra* note 113, at 941 (47 percent of all abortions to be repeat abortions in 1992).

371. *See* Chapter 14, at 241–52.

372. GUIDO CALABRESI & G. PHILIP BOBBITT, TRAGIC CHOICES 207 n.7 (1978); GRABER, *supra* note 129, at 3–4, 8–10, 73–75; LUKER, *supra* note 134, at 233, 242; Mark Cunningham, *The Abortion War*, NAT'L REV. Nov. 2, 1992, at 42, 44; Mary Ann Lemanna, *Social Science and Ethical Issues: The Policy Implications of Poll Data on Abortion*, in ABORTION: UNDERSTANDING DIFFERENCES, *supra* note 163, at 1, 12.

373. An excellent study of the conflict generated in one small community by the opening of an abortion clinic, see GINSBURG, *supra* note 137, at 61–76.

mitted supporters of restrictive abortion laws, however, would make the enforcement of laws to limit or prohibit abortion a more realistic possibility than some might think. Even pro-abortion activist Mark Graber concedes that the success of the pro-life movement cannot be explained simply by asserting that the pro-choice movement went to sleep after winning *Roe* and *Doe*.[374] Yet Graber would have us believe that pro-life electoral successes arose because many pro-choice supporters, confident that the courts would preserve their right to abort, chose to vote for candidates who favored lower taxes even when such a candidate was pro-life.[375] Graber's theory, which on close examination isn't so very different from the sleeping movement theory, is that this strategy backfired when it led to "packing" the courts with pro-life judges.

Finally, integral to any program of resistance to abortion restrictions is the revival of midwifery as a profession. Midwifery had virtually disappeared as an independent profession in the United States and Canada by the late 1930s and was under increasingly severe restraint in the United Kingdom.[376] Courts in the United States generally refused to hear constitutional challenges to these statutory prohibitions.[377] Ironically, the court in what is perhaps the leading case rested its

---

374. GRABER, *supra* note 129, at 126. For just such claims, see CRAIG & O'BRIEN, *supra* note 122, at 43; EPSTEIN & KOBYLKA, *supra* note 153, at 206–07; ROSENBLATT, *supra* note 129, at 16–17; STAGGENBORG, *supra* note 129, at 126–27, 149.

375. GRABER, *supra* note 129, at 126–28. This is one way to interpret opinion poll data that finds that only a small number of voters (ranging from 7–25%) voted on the basis of the candidate's position on abortion, and of those voters the overwhelming majority (60–70%) voted "pro-life." Robert Blendon, John Benson, & Karen Donelan, *The Public and the Controversy over Abortion*, 270 JAMA 2871, 2873–75 (1993).

376. *See, e.g.,* Regina v. Sullivan, 3 C.R.4th 277 (Can. 1981). *See generally* NANETTE DAVIS, FROM CRIME TO CHOICE 89 (1985); CARL DEGLER, AT ODDS: WOMEN AND THE FAMILY IN AMERICA FROM THE REVOLUTION TO THE PRESENT 56 (1980); RAYMOND DEVRIES, MAKING MIDWIVES LEGAL: CHILDBIRTH, MEDICINE, AND THE LAW 16–19, 25, 38, 48–49, 227 n.26 (2nd ed. 1996); JEAN DONNISON, MIDWIVES AND MEDICAL MEN: A HISTORY OF THE STRUGGLE FOR THE CONTROL OF CHILDBIRTH 161–91, 202–07 (2nd ed. 1988); JUDY BARRETT LITOFF, AMERICAN MIDWIVES: 1860 TO THE PRESENT 27, 136–42 (1978); RICHARD MECKEL, SAVE THE BABIES: AMERICAN PUBLIC HEALTH REFORM AND THE PREVENTION OF INFANT MORTALITY 174 (1990); ANN OAKLEY & SUSANNE HOUD, HELPERS IN CHILDBIRTH: MIDWIFERY TODAY (1990); KERRY PETERSEN, ABORTION REGIMES 40 (1993); LAUREL THATCHER ULRICH, THE MIDWIFE'S TALE: THE LIFE OF MARTHA BALLARD BASED ON HER DIARY, 1785–1812, at 28, 179–80 (1991); DOROTHY & RICHARD WERTZ, LYING IN: A HISTORY OF CHILDBIRTH IN AMERICA 215–19 (1977); Neal Devitt, *The Transition from Home to Hospital Birth in the United States, 1930–1960*, 4 BIRTH & FAM. J. 47 (1977); Paul Jacobson, *Hospital Care and the Vanishing Midwife*, 34 MILLBANK MEM. FUND Q. 253 (1956); Frances Kobrin, *The American Midwife Controversy: A Crisis of Professionalization*, 40 BULL. HIST. MED. 350, 362–63 (1966); Dianne Martin, *The Midwife's Tale: Old Wisdom and a New Challenge to the Control of Reproduction*, 3 COLUM. J. GENDER & L. 417, 418–22, 437–48 (1992); Francis Notzon, *International Differences in the Use of Obstetric Interventions*, 263 JAMA 3286 (1990); Gail Robinson, *Midwifery and Malpractice Insurance: A Profession Fights for Survival*, 134 U. PA. L. REV. 1001 (1986); Barbara Katz Rothman, *Childbirth Management and Medical Monopoly*, in WOMEN, BIOLOGY, AND PUBLIC POLICY 117 (Virginia Sapiro ed. 1985). As late as 1989, less than 1% of births in the United States were attended by a midwife. Suzanne Hope Suarez, *Midwifery Is Not the Practice of Medicine*, 5 YALE J. LAW & FEMINISM 315, 322 (1993).

377. *See, e.g.,* Bowland v. Municipal Ct., 556 P.2d 1081 (Cal. 1977); Board of Med. Qual. Assurance v. Andrews, 260 Cal. Rptr. 113 (Ct. App. 1989); People v. Rosburg, 805 P.2d 432 (Colo. 1991); People v. Cryns, 786 N.E.2d 139 (Ill.), *cert. denied*, 540 U.S. 818 (2003); Smith v. State *ex rel.* Medical Licensing Bd., 459 N.E.2d 401 (Ind. 1984); Leigh v. Board of Registration in Nursing, 506 N.E.2d 91 (Mass. 1987); State v. Southworth, 704 S.W.2d 219 (Mo. 1986). *But see* Peckman v. Thompson, 966 F.2d 295 (7th Cir. 1992); State Bd. of Nursing v. Ruebke, 913 P.2d 142 (Kan. 1996); Legett v. Tennessee Bd. of Nursing, 612 S.W.2d 476 (Tenn. Ct. App. 1980), *state cert. denied*. For arguments in favor of a constitutional right to choose a midwife over a physician, see Chris Hafner-Eaton & Laurie Pearce, *Birth Choices, the Law, and Medicine: Balancing Indiviual Freedoms and Protection of the Public's Health*, 19 J. HEALTH POL., POL'Y & L. 813, 821–31 (1994); Kristin McIntosh, *Regulation of Midwives as Home Birth Attendants*, 30 B.C. L. REV. 477 (1989); Joleen Susan Pettee, Note, *Midwifery: Do Parents Have a Constitutional Right to Choose the Site, Process, and Attendant for the Birth of Their Baby?*, 24 J. CONTEMP. L. 377 (1998); Michael Pike, Note, *Restriction of Parental Rights to Home Birth via State Regula-*

conclusion on *Roe v. Wade* because the Supreme Court in *Roe* had held that the state's regulatory interest outweighed the woman's right to privacy during the final trimester of pregnancy.[378]

Midwives continued to practice underground even when the independent practice of midwifery was illegal, and recently all three countries have seen the revival of midwifery as an independent profession for delivering children.[379] In a related move, nurses pressed successfully for the enactment of a *"Nurse Practice Act"* that authorizes nurses who have been approved by the state medical board to diagnose and treat certain illnesses—including prescribing certain drugs.[380] To the extent that midwives are willing to practice under as obstetric nurses, such statutes facilitate the revival of professional midwifery. In the United States, the tie of revived midwifery to the nursing profession is even more explicit through statutes in every state specifically authorizing diagnosis and treatment (including prescribing drugs) by "nurse-midwives."[381]

---

*tion of Traditional Midwifery*, 36 BRANDEIS J. FAM. L. 609 (1998); Suarez, *supra* note 376, at 357–60. *See generally* Annot., 59 A.L.R.4th 929 (1988).

378. Bowland v. Municipal Ct., 556 P.2d 1081, 1089 (Cal. 1977).

379. *See* SUZANNE ARMS, IMMACULATE DECEPTION: A NEW LOOK AT WOMEN AND CHILDBIRTH 202, 269–80, 304–05 (1977); DeVries, *supra* note 376, at 47–117; DONNISON, *supra* note 376, at 202–03, 206–09; INA MAY GASKIN, SPIRITUAL MIDWIFERY (1977); LITOFF, *supra* note 376, at 145–47 (the United States); JUDY BARRETT LITOFF, THE AMERICAN MIDWIFE DEBATE (1986); SHERYL BURT RUZEK, THE WOMEN'S HEALTH MOVEMENT: FEMINIST ALTERNATIVES TO MEDICAL CONTROL (1978) (the United States); DEBORAH SULLIVAN & ROSE WEITZ, LABOR PAINS: MODERN MIDWIVES AND HOME BIRTH 23–29 (1988) (Canada); THE MIDWIFE CHALLENGE 98 (Sheila Kitzinger ed. 1988) (the United Kingdom & Canada); WERTZ & WERTZ, *supra* note 376, at 285–89 (the United States); Ernest Boyer, *Midwifery in America: A Profession Reaffirmed*, 35 J. NURSE-MIDWIFERY 214 (1990); Eugene DeClercq, *Where Babies Are Born and Who Attends Their Births: Findings from the Revised 1989 US Standard Certificate of Live Birth*, 81 OBSTET. & GYNECOLOGY 997 (1993); Lee Anne Schienbein, *Midwifery: A Woman's Labour, a Woman's Choice*, 58 SASKATCHEWAN L. REV. 173 (1994); Helen Zia, *Midwives: Talking about a Revolution*, Ms., Nov./Dec. 1990, at 91. *See generally* Martin, *supra* note 376, at 418–19. For an example of a recent American statute regulating midwives, see FLA. STAT. ANN. § 467.006 (West 2003).

380. *See* ALASKA STAT. § 08.68.410(8)(F) (LexisNexis 2002); CONN. GEN. STAT. ANN. § 20-9 (West Supp. 2003); N.C. GEN. STAT. §§ 90.18(14), 90.18.1, 90.18.2 (2003); OR. REV. STAT. § 678.385(5) (2003); WASH. REV. CODE ANN. §§ 18.79.040 (West Supp. 2003). Several statutes are ambiguous about nurses' authority to diagnose, treat, or prescribe. *See* CAL. BUS. & PROF. CODE § 2836.1 (West 2003); COLO. REV. STAT. §§ 12-38-101 to 12-38-130 (2003); GA. CODE ANN. § 43-34-26.1(a)(7) (2001); KAN. STAT. ANN. § 65-5812 (Michie 2002). Other statutes authorize nurses to diagnose, treat, or prescribe, but only under the supervision of a physician. ARIZ. REV. STAT. ANN. § 32-1141(D), 32-2951(F) (West 2003); D.C. CODE ANN. §§ 3-1206.01 to 3-1206.07 (2001); FLA. STAT. ANN. § 464.003(3)(c) (West 2001); IDAHO CODE § 54-141 (Supp. 2003); ME. REV. STAT. ANN. tit. 32, § 2102 (West 1999 & Supp. 2003); MD. HEALTH OCC. CODE ANN. § 8-101(f) (Michie 2000); MASS. GEN. LAWS ANN. ANN. ch. 112, § 80E (West 2003); MISS. CODE ANN. § 73-15-5(2) (West Supp. 2003); NEB. REV. STAT. § 71-1721 (1996); NEV. REV. STAT. ANN. § 632.237.1 (Michie 2000); N.H. REV. STAT. ANN. § 326-B:10(II) (1995); N.M. STAT. ANN. § 61-3-3 (Michie Supp. 2003); N.Y. PUB. HEALTH LAW § 6902(3)(b) (McKinney 2002); PA. STAT. ANN. tit. 63, § 1212 (West 1996); S.D. CODIFIED LAWS ANN. §§ 36-9A-5 (1999), 36-9A-12 (Supp. 2003); TENN. CODE ANN. § 63-7-123 (1997); TEX. OCC. CODE ANN. §§ 157.051(2), 157.53(b), 157.054 to 157.060, 301.002(2)(F) (West 1999); UTAH CODE ANN. § 58-31B-301 (2003); VT. STAT. ANN. tit. 26, § 1572(E) (1998); WIS. STAT. ANN. § 441.16 (West 1998); OP. MICH. ATT'Y GEN. 5630 (Jan. 22, 1980). *See generally* Lori Andrews, *The Shadow Health Care System: Regulation of Alternative Health Care Providers*, 32 HOUS. L. REV. 1273 (1996); Mary Beck, *Improving America's Health Care: Authorizing Independent Prescriptive Privileges for Advance Practice Nurses*, 29 U.S.F. L. REV. 951 (1995); Richard Cooper, Prakash Laud, & Craig Dietrich, *Current and Projected Workforce of Non-Physician Clinicians*, 280 JAMA 788 (1998); Julie Fairman, *Playing Doctor? Nurse Practitioners, Physicians, and the Dilemma of Shared Practice*, 4 THE LONG TERM VIEW no. 4, at 39 (Fall 1999); Linda Pearson, *1995 Annual Update of How Each State Stands on Legislative Issues Affecting Advanced Nursing Practice*, 20 NURSE PRACTITIONER 51 (1995); Barbara Safriet, *Health Care Dollars and Regulatory Sense: The Role of Advanced Practice Nursing*, 9 YALE J. REGUL. 417 (1992).

381. ALA. CODE §§ 34-19-2 to 34-19-10 (2002); ALASKA STAT. §§ 08.68.010 to 08.68.410 (LexisNexis 2002); ARIZ. REV. STAT. ANN. § 36-752.2 (West 2003); ARK. STAT. ANN. §§ 17-86-501 to 17-86-507 (LexisNexis 2002); CAL. BUS. & PROF. CODE §§ 2746 to 2746.8 (West 2003); COLO. REV. STAT. § 12-36-106(1)(f) (2003); CONN.

Some midwives object to the concept of "nurse-midwife" as subordinating their profession to the doctors.[382] They have succeeded in getting a growing number of states to enact statutes authorizing and regulating practice by lay midwives.[383] Lay midwives are sometimes called "direct entry" midwives—meaning midwives who entered the profession of midwifery directly, without qualifying as a nurse.[384] A more radical approach, which has found little support in legislatures, has been the proposal to completely deregulate medical professions, leaving it entirely to the consumer to choose whom to trust without any official licensing.[385]

In contrast with their close attention to abortion rights, the law professorate have been almost entirely indifferent to the revival of midwifery even though non-lawyer feminists see an intimate

---

Gen. Stat. Ann. §§ 20-86a to 20-86h (West Supp. 2003); Del. Code Ann. tit. 16, § 122(3)(h) (2003); D.C. Code Ann. §§ 3-1206.01 to 3-1206.08 (2001); Fla. Stat. Ann. §§ 464.001 to 464.023 (West Supp. 2004); Ga. Code Ann. §§ 31-26-2 (2001), 43-26-1 to 43-2639 (2002); Haw. Rev. Stat. § 321-13 (Michie Supp. 2003); Idaho Code §§ 54-1401 to 54-1416 (Supp. 2003); 225 Ill. Ann. Stat. § 65/15-5 (Smith-Hurd 2004); Ind. Code Ann. § 25-23-1-13.1 (West 2001); Iowa Code Ann. §§ 152.1 to 152.10 (West Supp. 2003); Kan. Stat. Ann. §§ 65-1163 (Michie 2002); Ky. Rev. Stat. Ann. §§ 314.011 to 314.991 (Michie 2001 & Supp. 2003); La. Rev. Stat. §§ 37.911 to 37.931 (West 2000 & West Supp. 2003); Me. Rev. Stat. tit. 32, §§ 2101 to 2258 (West 1999 & West Supp. 2003); Md. Health Occ. Code Ann. §§ 8.601 to 8.603 (Michie 2000); Mass. Gen. Laws Ann. ch. 112, §§ 74 to 81C (West 2003); Mich. Comp. Laws Ann. § 333.17210 (West 2001); Minn. Stat. Ann. §§ 148.171 to 148.285 (West Supp. 2003); Miss. Code Ann. §§ 73-15-1 to 73-15-37 (West Supp. 2003); Mo. Rev. Stat. Ann. §§ 191.331, 197.032 (West 1998); Mont. Code Ann. §§ 37-8-101 to 37-8-444 (2003); Neb. Rev. Stat. §§ 71-1739 to 71-1765 (1996 & Supp. 2003); Nev. Rev. Stat. Ann. §§ 41A.041(2) 442.119(4)(b) (Michie 2000); N.J. Stat. Ann. § 45:10 (West 1991); N.M. Stat. Ann. § 24-4-4.1 (Michie 2000); N.Y. Pub. Health Law § 6951 (2002); N.C. Gen. Stat. §§ 90-178.1 to 90-178.7 (2003); N.D. Cent. Code § 43-12.1 (1997 & Supp. 2003); Ohio Rev. Code Ann. §§ 4731.31, 4723.41 to 4723.43 (Anderson 2002); Okla. Stat. Ann. tit. 59, § 567.3 (West Supp. 2003); Or. Rev. Stat. §§ 659A.150(5), 743.845(1)(b) (2003); Pa. Stat. Ann. tit. 63, §§ 171 to 176 (West 1996); R.I. Gen. Laws §§ 23-13-9, 23-13-10 (1997); S.C. Code Ann. § 40-33 (West 2002); S.D. Codified Laws Ann. § 36-9A-1(4) (1999); Tenn. Code Ann. §§ 63-7-101 to 63-7-209 (Supp. 2003); Tex. Occ. Code Ann. § 203.002 (West 1999); Utah Code Ann. § 58-44A-102 (2003); Vt. Stat. Ann. tit. 26, §§ 1571 to 1584 (1998); Va. Code Ann. § 54.1-2957.01 (LexisNexis 2002)); Wash. Rev. Code Ann. § 18.50 (West Supp. 2003); W. Va. Code §§ 30-15-1 to 30-15-8 (2002); Wis. Stat. Ann. § 441.15 (West Supp. 2003); Wyo. Stat. Ann. §§ 33-21-101 to 33-21-156 (LexisNexis 2003). *See generally* Judith Rooks, *Nurse-Midwifery: The Window Is Wide Open,* Am. J. Nursing, Dec. 1990, at 30.

382. *See, e.g.,* Frances Cowper-Smith, *Midwifery and Nursing: Apples and Oranges,* 5 The Birthing Gazette 20 (1989); Suarez, *supra* note 376, at 324–25.

383. Ala. Code § 34-19-3(b) (2002); Alaska Stat. §§ 18.05.040 to 18.05.070 (LexisNexis 2002); Ariz. Rev. Stat. Ann. §§ 36-751 to 36-757 (West 2003); Ark. Stat. Ann. §§ 17-85-101 to 17-85-108 (LexisNexis 2002); Cal. Bus. & Prof. Code §§ 2505 to 2515 (West 2003); Colo. Rev. Stat. §§ 12-36-106(1)(f), 12-37-101 to 12-37-105 (2003); Fla. Stat. Ann. §§ 467.001 to 467.207 (West 2003); Ga. Code Ann. § 31-26 (2001); 225 Ill. Ann. Stat. § 65/5-15 (West 2004); La. Rev. Stat. Ann. §§ 37.1277, 37.3240 to 37.3248 (West 2000); Mich. Comp. Laws Ann. § 333.17001 (West 2001); Minn. Stat. §§ 147D.03 to 147D.27 (West Supp. 2003); Miss. Code Ann. § 73-25-35 (West Supp. 2003); Mo. Rev. Stat. Ann. §§ 334.120, 334.190, 334.260 (Vernon 2001); Mont. Code Ann. §§ 37-3-103(1)(p), 37-27-101 to 37-27-325 (2003); N.H. Rev. Stat. Ann. §§ 326-D:2 to 326-D:4 (1995); N.J. Stat. Ann. § 45:10 (West 1991); N.M. Stat. Ann. §§ 24-1-3(R) (Michie Supp. 2003); N.C. Gen. Stat. §§ 90-178.1 to 90-178.7 (2003); Or. Rev. Stat. § 687.420 (2003); R.I. Gen. Laws § 23-13-9 (1997); S.C. Code Ann. §§ 40-33-50(7) (West Supp. 2003), 44-89-30 (1976); Tenn. Code Ann. §§ 63-7-101 to 63-7-209 (Supp. 2003); Tex. Stat. Ann. § 203 (Vernon 2004); Va. Code Ann. § 54.1-2957.01 (LexisNexis 2002); Wash. Rev. Code Ann. §§ 18.50 to 18.50.135 (West. Supp. 2003); Wis. Stat. Ann. § 448.10(5) (West Supp. 2003).

384. *See* Hafner-Eaton & Pearce, *supra* note 377, at 820-21; McIntosh, *supra* note 377; Suarez, *supra* note 376, at 352-64; Stephanie Wheeless, Recent Development, *Medical Liability Lay Midwives: Midwifery and the Practice of Medicine,* 19 Am. J. Trial Advoc. 233 (1995).

385. Lori Andrews, Deregulating Doctoring (1983); Charles Baron, *Licensure of Health Care Professionals: The Consumer's Case for Abolition,* 9 Am. J.L. & Med. 335 (1983); Harris Cohen, *Professional Licensure, Organizational Behavior, and the Public Interest,* 51 Millbank Memorial Fund Q. 89 (1973); Harris Cohen, *On Professional Power and Conflict of Interest: State Licensing Boards on Trial,* 5 J. Health Pol'y & L. 291 (1980).

connection between the two issues.[386] If physicians generally comply with a renewed prohibition of abortions, midwives and nurses will come under pressure to add abortion to the repertoire of their services to their patients.[387] As in earlier times, even midwives who do not perform abortions will come under suspicion.[388] Such patterns are likely so regardless of whether, in today's medical world, midwives provide better obstetrical care than physicians, as some already believe.[389] This conclusion stands even if, as one sees in comparing Canada, the United Kingdom, and the United States, the contemporary legal position of midwives does not correlate with the extent of abortion rights in the particular society.[390] Such a suspicion could be used to justify the creation in Canada and in the United States of the sort of elaborate control mechanisms already in place in the United Kingdom to subordinate midwives to supposedly more responsible doctors.[391] In fact, such controls are already emerging in the United States in the statutes referred to in the preceding paragraph.

386. David Smolin, *Praying for Baby Rena: Religious Liberty, Medical Futility, and Miracles*, 25 SETON HALL L. REV. 960, 1009-1011 (1995).

387. REAGAN, *supra* note 152, at 253; Patricia Donovan, *Vermont Physician Assistants Perform Abortions, Train Residents*, 24 FAM. PLAN. PERSP. 225 (1992); Katherine McKee & Eleanor Adams, *Nurse Midwives' Attitudes toward Abortion Performance and Radical Procedures*, 39 J. NURSE-MIDWIFERY 300 (1994).

388. *See* Chapter 2, at notes 283-89.

389. WAYNE FLINT, POOR BUT PROUD: ALABAMA'S POOR WHITES 198 (1989); GERMAIN GREER, SEX AND DESTINY: THE POLITICS OF HUMAN FERTILITY 11–15, 20–21 (1984); ANN OAKLEY, THE CAPTURED WOMB: A HISTORY OF THE MEDICAL CARE OF PREGNANT WOMEN 251–74 (1986); BARBARA KATZ ROTHMAN, IN LABOR: WOMEN AND POWER IN THE BIRTHPLACE 259–65 (1982); Martin, *supra* note 376, at 423–27; Walker, *supra* note 376, at 176–81.

390. Martin, *supra* note 376, at 422–23.

391. *Id.* at 437–48. *See also* PENNY ARMSTRONG & SHERYL FELDMAN, A MIDWIFE'S STORY (1986).

# Chapter 20

# I Don't Wanna Be a Lawyer Mama, I Don't Wanna Lie[1]

*Living is easy with your eyes closed, misunderstanding all you see.*

—The Beatles[2]

In a mere 15 years (1958–1973), abortion in the United States went from a practice shrouded in shame and guilt to a fundamental constitutional right. The struggle over abortion, however, continues and is waged on many fronts. One of the more intense arenas of struggle is over control of the stories we tell ourselves about abortion, consuming tons of paper and millions of gallons of ink in shaping the stories through which we conceptualize abortion as either a necessary option in personal, family, or medical planning, or as incompatible with a just or moral society.[3]

Disputes over the stories told about abortion are hardly surprising, particularly in a United States where cultural pluralism nearly precludes the possibility of generally shared collective narratives. These debates are not merely an academic dispute. Such arguments are a political instrument intended to have, and having, enormous consequences for the lives of women and their children—born and unborn. Story telling as a means of political or legal argument, however, is problematic. As one unidentified law student has noted, "[i]f a story is so open that the reader can extract any meaning from it whatsoever, the author has provided entertainment, not argument. But if the author tries to corral the reader into one interpretation, the story form loses its special advantages over traditional legal [or political] argument."[4] Despite such prob-

---

1. John Lennon, *I Don't Wanna Be a Soldier, Mama* (1972).
2. John Lennon & Paul McCartney, *Strawberry Fields* (1966).
3. *See* Chapter 19, at notes 179–84. *See also* CELESTE MICHELLE CONDIT, DECODING ABORTION RHETORIC: COMMUNICATING SOCIAL CHANGE (1990); FAYE GINSBURG, CONTESTED LIVES: THE ABORTION DEBATE IN AN AMERICAN COMMUNITY (1989); CHRISTOPHER LASCH, THE TRUE AND ONLY HEAVEN: PROGRESS AND ITS CRITICS 487–96 (1991); KATHY RUDY, BEYOND PRO-LIFE AND PRO-CHOICE: MORAL DIVERSITY IN THE ABORTION DEBATE (1996); Peggy Cooper Davis, *Neglected Stories and the Lawfulness of* Roe v. Wade, 28 HARV. C.R.-C.L. L. REV. 299 (1993); Sally Sheldon, *"Who Is the Mother to Make the Judgment?": The Constructions of Woman in English Abortion Law*, 1 FEMINIST LEG. STUD. 3 (1993); Joan Williams, *Gender Wars: Selfless Women in the Republic of Choice*, 66 NYU L. REV. 1559 (1991). *See generally* RONALD DWORKIN, LAW'S EMPIRE 228–250, 313 (1986); ROBIN WEST, NARRATIVE, AUTHORITY, AND LAW (1993); JAMES BOYD WHITE, JUSTICE AS TRANSLATION 89–112, 257–269 (1990); Robert Cover, *Forward: Nomos and Narrative*, 97 HARV. L. REV. 4 (1983); Richard Delgado & Jean Stefancic, *Norms and Narratives: Can Judges Avoid Serious Moral Error?*, 69 TEX. L. REV. 1929 (1991); Patricia Ewick & Susan Silbey, *Subversive Stories and Hegemonic Tales: Towards a Sociology of Narrative*, 29 LAW & SOC'Y REV. 197 (1995); James Lindermann Nelson, *Genetic Narratives: Biology, Stories, and the Definition of the Family*, 2 HEALTH MATRIX 71 (1992).
4. Note, *And We Will Not Be Saved*, 106 HARV. L. REV. 1358, 1363 (1993). *See also* Peter Brooks, *The Rhetoric of Constitutional Narratives: A Response to Elaine Scarry*, 2 YALE J.L. & HUMAN. 129, 130–31 (1990); Stephen Landsman, *The Perils of Courtroom Stories* (book rev.), 98 MICH. L. REV. 2154 (2000); Douglas Litowitz, *Some Critical Thoughts on Critical Race Theory*, 72 NOTRE DAME L. REV.503 (1997).

lems, story telling as a mode of legal argument has become popular in certain circles.[5] This is not so strange, for many of the practitioners of the new scholarship embrace what Michel Foucault termed "obscurantist terrorism."[6] They feel what law professor Arthur Austin has termed "an obligation—literally a duty—to avoid lucidity and transparent language."[7] For such writ-

---

5. *See, e.g.*, DEREK BELL, AND WE ARE NOT SAVED: THE ELUSIVE QUEST FOR RACIAL JUSTICE (1987); DEREK BELL, FACES AT THE BOTTOM OF THE WELL: THE PERMANENCE OF RACISM (1992); LAW'S STORIES: NARRATIVE AND RHETORIC IN THE LAW (Peter Brooks & Paul Gewirtz eds. 1996); L.H. LARUE, CONSTITUTIONAL LAW AS FICTION: NARRATIVE IN THE RHETORIC OF AUTHORITY (1995); LAW'S STORIES (Peter Brooks & Paul Gewirtz eds. 1996); JANET MALCOLM, THE CRIME OF SHEILA MCGOUGH (1998); MARTHA NUSSBAUM, POETIC JUSTICE (1995); PATRICIA WILLIAMS, THE ALCHEMY OF RACE AND RIGHTS (1991); Kathryn Abrams, *Hearing the Call of Stories*, 79 CAL. L. REV. 971 (1991); Anita Allen, *The Jurisprudence of Jane Eyre*, 15 HARV. WOMEN'S L.J. 173 (1992); Jane Baron, *Resistance to Stories*, 67 S. CAL. L. REV. 265 (1994); Jane Baron, *The Many Promises of Story-telling in Law: An Essay Review of Narrative and the Legal Discourse: A Reader in Storytelling and the Law*, 23 RUTGERS L.J. 79 (1991); Marijane Camilleri, Comment, *Lessons in Law from Literature: A Look at the Movement and a Peer at Her Jury*, 39 CATH. U. L. REV. 557 (1990); Mary Coombs, *Outsider Scholarship: The Law Review Stories*, 63 U. COLO. L. REV. 683 (1992); Cover, *supra* note 3; James McCristal Culp, jr., *Telling a Black Legal Story: Privilege, Authenticity, "Blunders," and Transformation in Outsider Narrative*, 82 VA. L. REV. 69 (1996); Richard Delgado, *Storytelling for Oppositionists and Others: A Plea for Narrative*, 87 MICH. L. REV. 2411 (1989); Richard Duncan, *Wigstock and the Kulturkampf: Supreme Court Storytelling, the Culture War, and Romer v. Evans*, 72 NOTRE DAME L. REV. 345 (1997); William Eskridge, *Gaylegal Narratives*, 46 STAN. L. REV. 607 (1994); Marc Fajer, *Can Two Real Men Eat Quiche Together? Storytelling, Gender-Role Stereotypes, and Legal Protection for Lesbians and Gay Men*, 46 U. MIAMI L. REV. 511 (1992); Peter Halewood, *White Men Can't Jump: Critical Epistemologies, Embodiment, and the Praxis of Legal Scholarship*, 7 YALE J.L.& FEMINISM 1 (1995); Alex Johnson, jr., *Defending the Use of Narrative and Giving Content to the Voice of Color: Rejecting the Imposition of Process Theory in Legal Scholarship*, 79 IOWA L. REV. 803 (1994); Lisa Kelly, *If Anybody Asks You Who I Am: An Outsider's Story of the Duty to Establish Paternity*, 3 AM. U. J. GENDER & L. 247 (1995); Duncan Kennedy, *Sexual Abuse, Sexy Dressing and the Eroticization of Domination*, 26 N. ENG. L. REV. 1309, 1351–58 (1992); Frank Michelman, *Law's Republic*, 97 YALE L.J. 1493, 1513 (1988); Martha Nussbaum, *Poets as Judges: Judicial Rhetoric and the Literary Imagination*, 62 U. CHI. L. REV. 1477 (1995); Thomas Rose, *The Richmond Narratives*, 66 TEX. L. REV. 381, 386 (1989) ("Judges, as storytellers, tell their audiences that something happened."); Jane Rutherford, *The Myth of Due Process*, 72 B.U. L. REV. 1 (1992) (comparing our recourse to "due process" to the story of Robin Hood); Kim Lane Scheppele, *Foreword: Telling Stories*, 87 MICH. L. REV. 2073 (1987); Symposium, *Legal Storytelling*, 87 MICH. L. REV. 2073 (1989); Mark Tushnet, *The Degradation of Constitutional Discourse*, 81 GEO. L.J. 251 (1992); Shauna Van Praagh, *Stories in Law School: An Essay on Language, Participation, and the Power of Legal Education*, 2 COLUM. J. GENDER & L. 111 (1992); Robin West, *Murdering the Spirit: Racism, Rights, and Commerce*, 90 MICH. L. REV. 1771 (1992). *See also* Milner Ball, *The City of Unger*, 81 NW. U. L. REV. 625 (1987); William Felstiner & Austin Sarat, *Enactments of Power: Negotiating Reality and Responsibility in Lawyer-Client Interactions*, 77 CORNELL L. REV. 1447 (1992); Lawrence Joseph, *Theories of Poetry, Theories of Law*, 46 VAND. L. REV. 1227 (1993); Lucie White, *Subordination, Rhetorical Survival Skills, and Sunday Shoes: Notes on the Hearing of Mrs. G.*, 38 BUFF. L. REV. 1 (1990); Nicholas Zeppos, *People's Court*, 44 VAND. L. REV. 847 (1991).

For critiques of the narrative turn, see ARTHUR AUSTIN, THE EMPIRE STRIKES BACK: OUTSIDERS AND THE STRUGGLE OVER LEGAL EDUCATION (1998); DANIEL FARBER & SUZANNA SHERRY, BEYOND ALL REASON: THE RADICAL ASSAULT ON TRUTH IN AMERICAN LAW (1997); Dennis Arrow, *"Rich," "Textured," and "Nuanced": Constitutional "Scholarship" and Constitutional Messianism at the Millennium*, 78 TEX. L. REV. 149, 157–60 (1999); Arthur Austin, *Storytelling Deconstructed by Double-Session*, 46 U. Miami L. Rev. 1155 (1992); Arthur Austin, *An Allegory on the Banks of the Nile*, 39 KAN. L. REV. 929 (1991) (satirizing story-telling as a "legal" method); Paul Campos, *Against Constitutional Theory*, 4 YALE J.L. & HUMAN. 279 (1992); Daniel Farber & Suzanna Sherry, *Telling Stories Out of School: An Essay on Legal Narratives*, 45 STAN. L. REV. 807 (1993); David Hyman, *Lies, Damned Lies, and Narrative*, 73 IND. L.J. 797 (1998); Randall Kennedy, *Racial Critiques of Legal Academia*, 102 HARV. L. REV. 1745 (1989); Michael McConnell, *The Fourteenth Amendment: A Second American Revolution or the Logical Culmination of the Tradition?*, 25 LOY. L.A. L. REV. 1159, 1174–76 (1992); Richard Posner, *Legal Narratology*, 64 U. CHI. L. REV. 737 (1997); Mary Sigler, *A Sneeze and a Cup of Sugar: A Cautionary Tale of Narrative and the Law* (book rev.), 16 LAW & PHIL. 617 (1997); Mark Tushnet, *The Degredation of Constitutional Discourse*, 81 GEO. L.J. 251 (1992).

6. As quoted in DAVID LEHMAN, SIGN OF THE TIMES: DECONSTRUCTION AND THE FALL OF PAUL DE MAN 77 (1991).

7. Arthur Austin, *The Top Ten Politically Correct Law Review Articles*, 27 FLA. ST. U. L. REV. 233, 237 (1999). *See also id.* at 253–54, 271.

ers, "clarity is the enemy of writers whose stylistic mannerisms serve to cover over difficult theoretical problems by making it hard to pin down what they are saying."[8]

A feature of using the narrative form for legal argument is the tendency to merge legal and political arguments. Conflating legal and political arguments is more than an argumentative convenience. In the United States, political arguments usually become legal arguments over the constitutionality of proposed measures—as de Tocqueville noted 170 years ago.[9] Thus, while the struggle over stories we tell ourselves about abortion has been waged in nearly every conceivable forum, courts in the United States generally, and the Supreme Court in particular, have played a crucial role in this struggle.[10] Courts have taken a battering over the stories they tell about abortion, with the consequent politicization of the judicial confirmation process to an extent unthinkable before the Supreme Court constitutionalized the law of abortion.[11] A casualty of the struggle over the stories courts tell about abortion has been respect for legal process and the rule of law.

---

8.  Raymond Tallis, *A Cure for Theorrhea* (book rev.), 3 CRITICAL REV. 7, 29 (1989). *See also* Gil Grantmore, *The Death of* Contra, 52 STAN. L. REV. 889 (2000).

9.  ALEXIS DE TOCQUEVILLE, DEMOCRACY IN AMERICA 200 (George Lawrence trans., J.P. Mayer & Max Lerner eds. 1966).

10.  *See* Kathryn Ann Farr, *Shaping Policy through Litigation: Abortion Law in the United States,* 39 CRIME & DELINQUENCY 167 (1993). We, of course, also tell stories about the Supreme Court and the function it plays in shaping our society. Thus Mary Ann Glendon has argued that courts are in the throes of "romantic judging" that is activist and adventurist rather than judicial. MARY ANN GLENDON, A NATION UNDER LAWYERS: HOW THE CRISIS IN THE LEGAL PROFESSION IS TRANSFORMING AMERICAN SOCIETY 151–53 (1994). *See also* Mark Tushnet, *The Possibilities of Interpretive Liberalism,* 29 ALBERTA L. REV. 276, 286–87 (1991) ("Tushnet, *Interpretive Liberalism*"); Mark Tushnet, *Public Law Litigation and the Ambiguities of Brown,* 61 FORDHAM L. REV. 23 (1992).

11.  *See, e.g.,* DAVID BROCK, THE REAL ANITA HILL: THE UNTOLD STORY (1993); ROBERT BORK, THE TEMPTING OF AMERICA: THE POLITICAL SEDUCTION OF THE LAW 133–34 (1988); ETHAN BRONNER, BATTLE FOR JUSTICE: HOW THE BORK NOMINATION SHOOK AMERICA (1988); LOUIS CAPLAN, THE TENTH JUSTICE: THE SOLICITOR GENERAL AND THE RULE OF LAW 105–07 (1987); 3 FEDERAL ABORTION POLITICS: A DOCUMENTARY HISTORY 71–230, 303–58 (Neal Devins & Wendy Watson eds. 1995); CHARLES FRIED, ORDER AND LAW 88 (1991); DAVID GARROW, LIBERTY AND SEXUALITY: THE RIGHT OF PRIVACY AND THE MAKING OF *ROE v. WADE* 668–71 (2nd ed. 1998); EDWARD LAZARUS, CLOSED CHAMBERS: THE FIRST EYEWITNESS ACCOUNT OF THE EPIC STRUGGLES INSIDE THE SUPREME COURT 245–48, 329–34, 420–24 (1998); ROBERT NAGEL, JUDICIAL POWER AND AMERICAN CHARACTER: CENSORING OURSELVES IN AN ANXIOUS AGE 20–27 (1994); STEPHEN MARKMAN, JUDICIAL SELECTION: MERIT, IDEOLOGY AND POLITICS—THE REAGAN YEARS (1990); PATRICK MCGUIGAN & DAWN WEYRICH, NINTH JUSTICE: THE BATTLE FOR BORK (1990); MICHAEL PERTSCHUK & WENDY SCHAETZEL, THE PEOPLE RISING: THE CAMPAIGN AGAINST THE BORK NOMINATION (1989); HERMAN SCHWARTZ, PACKING THE COURTS 42, 60–62, 64–66, 84–85, 87–88, 100–01 (1988); CHRISTOPHER SMITH, CRITICAL JUDICIAL NOMINATIONS AND POLITICAL CHANGE: THE IMPACT OF CLARENCE THOMAS (1993); Frank Guliuzza III, Daniel Reagan, & David Barrett, *Character, Competency, and Constitutionalism: Did the Bork Nomination Represent a Fundamental Shift in Confirmation Criteria?,* 75 MARQ. L. REV. 409 (1992); Stephen Lubet, *Confirmation Ethics: President Reagan's Nominees to the United States Supreme Court,* 13 HARV. J.L. & PUB. POL'Y. 229 (1990); Madeline Morris, *The Grammar of Advice and Consent: Senate Confirmation of Supreme Court Nominees,* 38 DRAKE L. REV. 863 (1989); Rodney Smith, *Justice Clarence Thomas: Doubt, Disappointment, Dismay, and Diminishing Hope,* 7 ST. L.U. J. LEGAL COMMENTARY 277 (1991); Symposium, *Gender, Race, and the Politics of Supreme Court Appointments: The Impact of the Anita Hill/Clarence Thomas Hearings,* 65 S. CAL. L. REV. 1279 (1992); Symposium, *The Bork Nomination,* 9 CARDOZO L. REV. 1 (1987).

Some see the resulting crisis in legitimacy as arising from judicial receptivity to the claims of racial minorities and other "outsiders." *See* G. PHILIP BOBBITT, CONSTITUTIONAL INTERPRETATION 83–108 (1991); MARTHA MINOW, MAKING ALL THE DIFFERENCE: INCLUSION, EXCLUSION, AND AMERICAN LAW 356–62 (1990); Richard Friedman, *Tribal Myths: Ideology and the Confirmation of Supreme Court Nominations,* 95 YALE L.J. 1283 (1986); Lino Graglia, *"Interpreting" the Constitution: Posner on Bork,* 44 STAN. L. REV. 1019, 1037–43 (1992); Kenneth Karst, *Religion, Sex, and Politics: Cultural Counterrevolution in Constitutional Perspective,* 24 U.C. DAVIS L. REV. 677 (1991). The decision in *Brown v. Board of Education,* 347 U.S. 483 (1954), did spark a similar debate, but ultimately was less divisive—*Brown* was accepted within 20 years as unquestionably legitimate. MORTON HORWITZ, THE TRANSFORMATION OF AMERICAN LAW, 1870–1960: THE CRISIS OF LEGAL ORTHODOXY 258–68 (1992).

The idea of the rule of law is in profound crisis in the United States.[12] Acerbic debate preoccupies judges, lawyers, and scholars over the proper role of the judiciary and the other branches of government, over the proper techniques for determining and applying law, and even over the possibility of law as anything other than the caprice of individual decision-makers and hence over the very legitimacy of the legal enterprise itself.[13] The intellectual crisis regarding the rule of law in the United States feeds on a growing sense that government is hopelessly out of touch with the people and also in large measure corrupts those who work with it or depend upon it.

This crisis also stands in sharp contrast to the attraction of the rule of law for people in nations newly emerging from dictatorship who know what it means to live in a society without the rule of law.[14] Moreover, debate over the rule of law produces a more severe crisis in the United States than it might in some other countries, for in the United States faith in law has been a primary instrument for creating a national identity.[15] This crisis has many causes. Numerous com-

---

12. *See, e.g.,* ROBERT COVER, JUSTICE ACCUSED (1975); MARK KELMAN, A GUIDE TO CRITICAL LEGAL STUDIES 26, 273–74 (1987); ANTHONY KRONMAN, THE LOST LAWYER: FAILING IDEALS OF THE LEGAL PROFESSION (1993); POLITICS, POSTMODERNITY, AND CRITICAL LEGAL STUDIES: THE LEGALITY OF THE CONTINGENT (Costas Dominas, Peter Goodrich, & Yifat Hachamovitch eds. 1994); JOSEPH RAZ, THE AUTHORITY OF LAW 211–26 (1979); THE RULE OF LAW (Ian Shapiro ed. 1994); GEOFFREY WALKER, THE RULE OF LAW: FOUNDATIONS OF A CONSTITUTIONAL DEMOCRACY (1988); Bobby Baldock, *Justice and the Rule of Law: A Contradiction in Terms?,* 15 S. ILL. U.L.J. 57 (1990); Jeffrey Blum, *Critical Legal Studies and the Rule of Law,* 38 BUFFALO L. REV. 59 (1990); Richard Epstein, *Beyond the Rule of Law: Civic Virtue and Constitutional Structure,* 56 GEO. WASH. L. REV. 149 (1987); Richard Fallon, jr., *"The Rule of Law" as a Concept of Constitutional Discourse,* 97 COLUM. L. REV. 1 (1997); Toni Massaro, *Empathy, Legal Storytelling, and the Rule of Law: New Words, Old Wound?,* 87 MICH. L. REV. 2099 (1989); Francis Mootz III, *Is the Rule of Law Possible in a Postmodern World?,* 68 WASH. L. REV. 249 (1992); Margaret Jane Radin, *Reconsidering the Rule of Law,* 69 B.U. L. REV. 781 (1989); Eric Segall, *Justice Scalia, Critical Legal Studies, and the Rule of Law,* 62 GEO. WASH. L. REV. 991 (1994); Laurence Tribe, *Revisiting the Rule of Law,* 64 NYU L. REV. 126 (1989). The problems the concept is now encountering in the United States was thoroughly aired in a volume of the *Nomos* series (no. 36) published by New York University Press. THE RULE OF LAW (Ian Shapiro ed. 1994).

13. *See* Robert Cover, *Violence and the Word,* 95 YALE L.J. 1601 (1986). *See also* ANDREW ALTMAN, CRITICAL LEGAL STUDIES: A LIBERAL CRITIQUE (1989); RONALD COLLINS & DAVID SKOVER, THE DEATH OF DISCOURSE (1996); DWORKIN, *supra* note 3; MARY ANN GLENDON, HERMENEUTICS, ABORTION AND DIVORCE: A REVIEW OF ABORTION AND DIVORCE IN WESTERN LAW 209–15 (1989); KENT GREENAWALT, LAW AND OBJECTIVITY (1992); ALLAN HUTCHINSON, DWELLING ON THE THRESHOLD: CRITICAL ESSAYS IN MODERN LEGAL THOUGHT (1988); DAVID KAIRYS, THE POLITICS OF LAW: A PROGRESSIVE CRITIQUE (1982); KELMAN, *supra* note 9; DUNCAN KENNEDY, LEGAL EDUCATION AND THE REPRODUCTION OF HIERARCHY: A POLEMIC AGAINST THE SYSTEM (1983); FRANZ NEUMANN, THE RULE OF LAW: POLITICAL THEORY AND THE LEGAL SYSTEM IN MODERN SOCIETY (1986); TIMOTHY O'HAGEN, THE END OF LAW? (1985); MARK TUSHNET, RED, WHITE, AND BLUE: A CRITICAL ANALYSIS OF THE CONSTITUTION (1988); ROBERTO UNGER, WHAT SHOULD LEGAL ANALYSIS BECOME? (1996); J.M. Balkin, *Deconstructive Practice and Legal Theory,* 96 YALE L.J. 743 (1987); Guyora Binder & Robert Weisberg, *Cultural Criticism of Law,* 49 STAN. L. REV. 1149 (1997); Philip Soper, *Legal Theory and the Claim of Authority,* 18 PHIL. & PUB. AFF. 209 (1989); Roberto Unger, *The Critical Legal Studies Movement,* 96 HARV. L. REV. 561 (1983); Steven Winter, *Bull Durham and the Uses of Theory,* 42 STAN. L. REV. 639, 679 (1990); Steven Winter, *Indeterminacy and Incommensurability in Constitutional Law,* 78 CAL. L. REV. 1441 (1990).

14. *See, e.g.,* Albert Casamiglia, *Law and Transition to Democracy,* 9 RATIO JURIS 396 (1996); George Fletcher, *Searching for the Rule of Law in the Wake of Communism,* 1992 B.Y.U. L. REV. 145; Martin Golding, *Transitional Regimes and the Rule of Law,* 9 RATIO JURIS 387 (1996); Mikhail Gorbachev, *The Rule of Law,* 28 STAN. J. INT'L L. 477 (1992); Matthias Hartwig, *The Institutionalization of the Rule of Law: The Establishment of Constitutional Courts in the Eastern European Countries,* 7 AM. U.J. INT'L L. & POL'Y 449 (1992); Herman Schwartz, *Taking the Heat: Judges in Eastern Europe Are Struggling against Still-Repressive Regimes to Uphold the Rule of Law,* A.B.A. J., May, 1996, at 66; Symposium, *Marxism and the Rule of Law,* 15 LAW & SOC. INQUIRY 633 (1990); Symposium, *Military Checkpoints and the Rule of Law,* 64 PHILIPPINES L.J. 189 (1989); Symposium, *Transitions to Democracy and the Rule of Law,* 5 AM. U.J. INT'L L. & POL'Y 965 (1990); Brian Tamanaha, *The Lessons of Law-and-Development Studies,* 89 AM. J. INT'L L. 470, 475 (1995).

15. ROBERT FERGUSON, LAW AND LETTERS IN AMERICAN CULTURE 10 (1984). The thought that law forms the civil religion of the United States can be traced back at least as far as de Tocqueville in 1834. 1 DE TOC-

mentators, however, have noted that the crisis regarding the rule of law in the United States is in large measure a direct response to the intense struggle over the legitimacy of the judiciary's role in imposing national rules regarding abortion.[16]

While the struggle over abortion is, narrowly speaking, the cause of the crisis in the rule of law, a loss of faith in the possibility of objective truth in postmodern society is the broadest cause of the crisis. Debunkers of the rule of law claim to "deconstruct" legal theory to understand how society operates, including by the use of legal rhetoric to accomplish and to conceal its operations.[17] Deconstruction, the interpretive relative in the "postmodern" family,[18] is popu-

---

QUEVILLE, *supra* note 9, at 96–103, 137–51. *See also* SANFORD LEVINSON, CONSTITUTIONAL FAITH (1988). *See generally* Allan Hutchinson, *Identity Crisis: The Politics of Interpretation,* 26 N. ENG. L. REV. 1173 (1992).

16. Webster v. Reproductive Health Services, 492 U.S. 490, 559 (1989) (Blackmun, J., dissenting) (describing abortion as "the most politically divisive legal issue of our time."); JAMES BOYD WHITE, ACTS OF HOPE: CREATING AUTHORITY IN LITERATURE, LAW, AND POLITICS 167, 177 (1994) ("[A]bortion is not an issue on which public and shared thought of a high quality seems possible in our political world but one that divides us into opposed camps, creating a political situation having many of the features of a civil war."); Michael McConnell, *The Right to Die and the Jurisprudence of Tradition,* 1997 UTAH L. REV. 665, 665 ("Like *Brown v. Board of Education* and *Lochner v. New York* before it, *Roe v. Wade* was the galvanizing constitutional decision of a generation."). *See also* BARBARA HINKINSON CRAIG & DAVID O'BRIEN, ABORTION AND AMERICAN POLITICS 35 (1993); JAMES MACGREGOR BURNS & STEWART BURNS, A PEOPLE'S CHARTER: THE PURSUIT OF RIGHTS IN AMERICA 350–51 (1991); CONDIT, *supra* note 3, at 102; RONALD DWORKIN, LIFE'S DOMINION: AN ARGUMENT ABOUT ABORTION, EUTHANASIA, AND INDIVIDUAL FREEDOM 4, 6–7, 102, 123 (1993); DONALD JUDGES, HARD CHOICES, LOST VOICES 4, 11–12, 242 (1993); EARL MALTZ, RETHINKING CONSTITUTIONAL LAW: ORIGINALISM, INTERVENTIONISM, AND THE POLITICS OF JUDICIAL REVIEW 1–8 (1994) ("MALTZ, RETHINKING"); NAGEL, *supra* note 11, at 113–15; DAVID O'BRIEN, STORM CENTER: THE SUPREME COURT IN AMERICAN POLITICS 48–49, 61–62, 106–07, 382 (3rd ed. 1993); MICHAEL PERRY, THE CONSTITUTION IN THE COURTS: LAW OR POLITICS? 179–80 (1994); H. JEFFERSON POWELL, THE MORAL TRADITIONS OF AMERICAN CONSTITUTIONALISM: A THEOLOGICAL INTERPRETATION 173–81 (1993); EVA RUBIN, ABORTION, POLITICS, AND THE COURTS ix–x, 7, 185–911 (rev. ed. 1987); BERNARD SCHWARTZ, THE ASCENT OF PRAGMATISM: THE BURGER COURT IN ACTION 294, 409–10 (1990); LAURENCE TRIBE, ABORTION: THE CLASH OF ABSOLUTES 79–82 (1990); LAURENCE TRIBE & MICHAEL DORF, ON READING THE CONSTITUTION 60–64 (1991); Paul Carrington, *A Senate of Five: An Essay on Sexuality and the Law,* 23 GA. L. REV. 859, 898–906 (1989); Davis, *supra* note 3, at 304; Frank Easterbrook, *Bills of Rights and Regression to the Mean,* 15 HARV. J. L. & PUB. POL'Y 71, 76–80 (1992); John Hart Ely, *Another Such Victory: Constitutional Theory and Practice in a World Where Courts Are No Different from Legislatures,* 77 VA. L. REV. 833, 873 n.132, 876 n.139 (1991); Margaret Farrell, *Revisiting Roe v. Wade: Substance and Due Process in the Abortion Debate,* 68 IND. L.J. 269, 270–76 (1993); Geoffrey Hazard, jr., *The Future of Legal Ethics,* 100 YALE L.J. 1239, 1278–79 (1991); Morton Horwitz, *The Meaning of the Bork Nomination in American Constitutional History,* 50 U. PITT. L. REV. 655, 656 (1989); Sanford Levinson, *"Veneration" and Constitutional Change: James Madison Confronts the Possibility of Constitutional Amendment,* 21 TEX. TECH. L. REV. 2443, 2457 (1990); Hans Linde, *On Inviting an Echo: Comments on Nagel, Political Pressure and Judicial Integrity,* 61 U. COLO. L. REV. 721, 724–25 (1990); Earl Maltz, *The Prospects for a Revival of Conservative Activism in Constitutional Jurisprudence,* 24 GA. L. REV. 629, 642–47 (1990); Suzanna Sherry, *The Founders' Unwritten Constitution,* 54 U. CHI. L. REV. 1127, 1176 n.223 (1987); Joan Williams, *Abortion, Incommensurability, and Jurisprudence,* 63 TULANE L. REV. 1651, 1655 (1989).

17. *See, e.g.,* ANTHONY CARTY, POST-MODERN LAW (1990); DECONSTRUCTION AND THE POSSIBILITY OF JUSTICE (Drucilla Cornell *et al.* ed. 1992); COSTAS DOUZINAS & RONNIE WARRINGTON, POSTMODERN JURISPRUDENCE (1991); STEVEN FELDMAN, AMERICAN LEGAL THOUGHT FROM PREMODERNISM TO POSTMODERNISM (2000); DOUGLAS LITOWITZ, POSTMODERN PHILOSOPHY AND LAW (1997); GARY MINDA, POSTMODERN LEGAL MOVEMENTS (1995); Leslye Huff, *Deconstructing Sodomy,* 5 J. GENDER & L. 553 (1997); David Jabbari, *Critical Legal Studies: A Revolution in Legal Thought?,* in REVOLUTIONS IN LAW AND LEGAL THOUGHT 153 (Zenon Bankowski & Neil MacCormick eds. 1991); Mark Kelman, *Trashing,* 36 STAN. L. REV. 293 (1984); E. Dana Neacsu, *CLS Stands for Critical Legal Studies, if Anyone Remembers,* 8 J. LAW & POL'Y 415 (2000); Barbara Stark, *Deconstructing the Framers' Right to Property:* Liberty's Daughters *and Economic Rights,* 28 HOFSTRA L. REV. 963 (2000); Christian Zapf & Eben Moglen, *Linguistic Indeterminacy and the Rule of Law: On the Perils of Misunderstanding Wittgenstein,* 84 GEO. L.J. 485, 486–98 (1996). *See also* DENNIS PATTERSON, LAW AND TRUTH (1992).

18. Hutchinson, *supra* note 15, at 1185. *See also* Stephen Feldman, *The Politics of Postmodern Jurisprudence,* 95 MICH. L. REV. 166 (1996).

lar in many academic fields today. All knowledge, deconstruction theorists claim, is a social construction between the writer and (preeminently) the reader without reference to any objective external reality.[19] But this theory also dethrones the reader for the reader's meaning can no more be fixed than can the author's. Logical consistency demands that there are in fact no "subjects" to do the reading and writing.[20] As law professor Allan Hutchinson observed, "[r]eading ends not in a final affixing of meaning, but in a temporary respite from a lasting undecidability." [21]

Hutchinson was not afraid of following this line of reasoning to the end. Thus, he could write, "Meaning is not transmitted through language by independent subjects, possessed of pre-linguistic thought, but the communicating subjects are themselves constituted in and through that discourse itself."[22] Such thorough going skepticism about the possibility of truth was caught by Hutchinson's conclusion that "meaning is always to be argued for and never to be argued from."[23] No wonder Jorge Luis Borges concluded that "[t]here is no intellectual exercise which is not ulti-

---

19. *See, e.g.* HANS BERTENS, THE IDEA OF POSTMODERNISM: A HISTORY (1995); STEVEN BEST & DOUGLAS KELLNER, THE POSTMODERN TURN (1999); ANDREW BOYD, LIFE'S LITTLE DECONSTRUCTION BOOK: SELF-HELP FOR THE POST-HIP (1998); SANDE COHEN, HISTORICAL CULTURE: ON THE RECODING OF AN ACADEMIC DISCIPLINE (1986); HARRY COLLINS & TREVOR PINCH, THE GOLEM: WHAT EVERYONE SHOULD KNOW ABOUT SCIENCE (1993); JONATHAN CULLER, ON DECONSTRUCTION: THEORY AND CRITICISM AFTER STRUCTURALISM (1982); JACQUE DERRIDA, ON GRAMMATOLOGY (Gayatri Chakravorty Spivak trans. 1976); PETER DEWS, LOGICS OF DISENTEGRATION: POST-STRUCTURALIST THOUGHT AND THE CLAIMS OF CRITICAL THEORY (1987); TERRY EAGLETON, THE ILLUSIONS OF POSTMODERNISM (1996); JOHN ELLIS, AGAINST DECONSTRUCTION (1989); STANLEY FISH, THE TROUBLE WITH PRINCIPLE (1999); MICHEL FOUCAULT, ARCHEOLOGY OF KNOWLEDGE AND THE DISCOURSE ON LANGUAGE (A.M. Sheridan Smith trans. 1972); LASCH, *supra* note 3; JEAN-FRANÇOIS LYOTARD, THE POSTMODERN CONDITION: A REPORT ON KNOWLEDGE (Geoff Bennington & Brian Massumi trans. 1984); CHRISTOPHER NORRIS, WHAT'S WRONG WITH POSTMODERNISM? (1990); PAULINE MARIE ROSENAU, POST MODERNISM AND THE SOCIAL SCIENCES: INSIGHTS, INROADS, AND INTRUSIONS (1992); JOHN SEARLE, THE CONSTRUCTION OF SOCIAL REALITY (1995); ROBERTO UNGER, SOCIAL THEORY: ITS SITUATION AND ITS TASK (1987); STEPHEN WHITE, POLITICAL THEORY AND POSTMODERNISM (1991); WRITING CULTURE: THE POETICS AND POLITICS OF ETHNOGRAPHY (James Clifford & George Marcus eds. 1986); Ravina Aggarwal, *Traversing Lines of Control: Feminist Anthropology Today,* 571 ANNALS AM. ACADEMY POL. & SOC. SCI. 14 (2000); Dennis Arrow, *Pomobabble: Postmodern Newspeak and Constitutional "Meaning" for the Unitiated,* 96 MICH. L. REV. 461 (1997); Jacques Derrida, *Force of Law: The "Mystical Foundation of Authority,"* 11 CARDOZO L. REV. 921 (1990) (Mary Quintance trans.); John Fiske, *Admissible Postmodernity: Some Remarks on Rodney King, O.J. Simpson, and Contemporary Culture,* 30 USF L. REV. 917 (1996); Dale Jamieson, *The Poverty of Postmodernist Theory,* 62 U. COLO. L. REV. 577 (1991); Joseph, *supra* note 5, at 1229–41; Martha Nussbaum, *Skepticism about Practical Reason in Literature and Law,* 107 HARV. L. REV. 714 (1994); Craig Palmer, David DiBari, & Scott Wright, *Is It Sex Yet? Theoretical and Practical Implications of the Debate over Rapists' Motives,* 39 JURIMETRICS J. 271 (1999); Charles Peirce, *The Paranoid Style in Contemporary Legal Scholarship,* 31 HOUS. L. REV. 873 (1994).

No wonder the number of citations of law review articles in judicial opinions has fallen precipitously over the last 10 years—since post-modernism has become common in legal scholarship. *See* Arrow, *supra* note 5, at 165–66. *See also* Ruth Bader Ginsberg, *On the Interdependence of Law Schools and Law Courts,* 83 VA. L. REV. 829 (1997); Michael McClintock, *The Declining Use of Legal Scholarship by Courts: An Empirical Study,* 51 OKLA. L. REV. 659 (1998). For a tongue-in-cheek discussion of why law reviews are increasingly irrelevant, see Kenneth Lasson, *Scholarship Amok: Excesses in the Pursuit of Truth and Tenure,* 103 HARV. L. REV. 926 (1990).

20. *See, e.g.,* James Boyle, *Is Subjectivity Possible? The Post-Modern Subject in Legal Theory,* 62 U. COLO. L. REV. 489 (1991); Jennifer Wicke, *Postmodern Identity and the Legal Subject,* 62 U. COLO. L. REV. 455 (1991).

21. Hutchinson, *supra* note 15, at 1186.

22. *Id.* at 1185.

23. *Id.* at 1188. *See also* STEVEN BEST & DOUGLAS KELLNER, POSTMODERN THEORY: CRITICAL INTERROGATIONS 9 (1991) (arguing that reality is unordered and unknowable); FISH, *supra* note 19, at 306 ("[C]ommuniciation is a competitive [enterprise], and the prize in the competition is the (temporary) right to label your way of talking "undistorting," a label you can claim only until some other way of talking, some other vocabulary elaborated with a superior force, takes it away from you."); DUNCAN KENNEDY, A CRITIQUE OF ADJUDICATION (*FIN DE SIÈCLE*) 361 (1997) (announcing that he was "giving up the expectation of rightness in doing").

mately useless."[24] Another critic concluded that "the culture of critical discourse must put its hands around its own throat, and see how long it can squeeze."[25] Regis Debray has observed that this particular vision is rooted in professors in France and the mass media generally, for whom "the objective world—the thing there is something to speak of—is what the other media are saying. Be it hell or heaven, from now on we are going to have to live in this haunted hall where mirrors reflect mirrors and shadows chase shadows."[26] One need only recall the Marshall McLuhan scene from Woody Allen's movie *Annie Hall,* however, to see the absurdity of any such a concept of textual meaning.[27]

Thoroughgoing skeptics conclude that the only truth is that there is no truth. Overlooking the contradiction inherent in such a position, such skepticism renders all generalizations impossible, including even generalizations that would destabilize the very social order that postmodernists want to destabilize. The supposed impossibility of generalizing makes each example wholly particular. No one, however, can glean any lessons from particular examples that are not instances of generalized categories.[28] Yet just because not every woman is either Catharine MacKinnon or Phyllis Schafly does not mean that we cannot say anything meaningful about women in general.[29]

Furthermore, "[t]hose who believe that 'reality' is constructed rather than found overlook that not every social construction is arbitrary."[30] After all, anyone who chooses to continue living cannot simply jump out a seventh-story window and decide nonetheless to live without injury— regardless of the person's culture, sex, or socio-economic background.[31] As David Hume noted more than two centuries ago, humans simply are not capable of such comprehensive doubt as deconstruction expresses and as jumping out a window would require—despite the posturing by certain philosophers and others to the contrary.[32]

---

24. Jorge Luis Borges, *Pierre Menard, Author of the Quixote,* in Labyrinths 36, 43 (Donald Yates & James Irby eds. 1964).

25. Alvin Gouldner, The Future of the Intellectual and the Rise of the New Class 59–60 (1979).

26. Regis Debray, Teachers, Writers, Celebrities: The Intellectuals of Modern France 118 (David Macey trans. 1981). *See also* Paul Gross & Norman Levitt, Higher Superstition: The Academic Left and Its Quarrels with Science (1994). For a delightful skewering of the foibles of deconstruction theory in literary criticism, see Bernard Knox, *Author, Author,* N.Y. Rev. Books, Nov. 16, 1995, at 16. For a feminist criticism of "postmodernism," see Pauline Johnson, Feminism as Radical Humanism (1994).

27. *Annie Hall* (United Artists 1977). In this scene, Alvy (Woody Allen) and Annie (Diane Keeton) are waiting in line to buy tickets for a movie only to overhear a man, apparently a professor, boring his date with a long discussion of Marshall McLuhan's theories on media. When Alvy challenges the professor's theories, the professor defends himself by informing Alvy that he teaches communications at Columbia University. Alvy steps out of line and returns almost instantly with the real Marshall McLuhan who promptly demolishes the astounded professor's theories. Alvy turns to the camera and comments, "Boy, if only life were like this...."

28. Susan Bordo, *Feminism, Postmodernism, and Gender-Scepticism,* in Feminism/Postmodernism 131, 151 (Linda Nicholson ed. 1990); Judith Butler, *Gender, Trouble, Feminist Theory, and Psychoanalytic Discourse,* in Feminism/Postmodernism, *supra,* at 324, 327; Edward Rubin, *The New Legal Process, the Synthesis of Discourse, and the Microanalysis of Institutions,* 109 Harv. L. Rev. 1393, 1401 (1996). *See generally* Searle, *supra* note 19. While postmodernism's primary appeal has been to those who were generally excluded from the dominant discourse, postmodernism's undermining of all meaning has caused some feminist scholars to take alarm, even arguing that postmodernism has been put forth by masculine hierarchies as a mechanism for defusing criticism and retaining their power. *See, e.g.,* Nancy Hartsock, *Rethinking Modernism: Minority vs. Majority Theories,* 7 Cultural Critique 187 (1987).

29. Hutchinson, *supra* note 15, at 1197. *See generally* Kingsley Browne, *Sex and Temperament in Modern Society: A Darwinian View of the Glass Ceiling and the Gender Gap,* 37 Ariz. L. Rev. 971, 981, 983–84, 1016–17 (1995); Alice Eagly, *The Science and Politics of Comparing Women and Men,* 50 Am. Psychologist 145 (1995).

30. Richard Posner, Overcoming Law 291 (1995).

31. James Allan, *A Doubter's Guide to Law and Natural Rights,* 28 Victoria U. Wellington L. Rev. 243, 246 (1998).

32. *See generally* David Hume, A Treatise of Human Nature bk. 1 (1740).

In fact, much the same holds true for texts. A contrary conclusion could only lead to the conclusion that texts have no meaning at all apart from what a reader chooses to impose on them.[33] Yet we all know that we do convey meaning through language and through texts. Just because we do not communicate perfectly does not mean that communication fails utterly.[34] Do we really find such expressions as "keep off the grass" or "drop dead" confusing?[35] If so, why do we bother putting anything on paper beyond the single word "TEXT" and allow the reader to infer from it anything the reader likes, from the Bible to Shakespeare, Henry James, James Joyce, or Alice Walker.[36] How we would imagine these authors at all if all they had produced were the single word "TEXT" is another question.

Nor should one forget that although one might not be able to determine truth in any ultimate sense, one often can recognize lies.[37] Some critics have concluded that the deconstructionists fully understand all this—they are simply intent on blurring the line between truth and fiction.[38] Whatever the truth of the matter, deconstructionists indulge in a paranoid mode of thought that both insulates deconstructionists from the views of their opponents and provides a private language to communicate with the initiated.[39] Yet, as Tatyana Tolstaya has written, "lying, perhaps humankind's primary weakness, is precisely what historians must overcome."[40] This, it turns out, has become the most serious problem for the historians of abortion.

---

33. Roland Barthes, *The Death of the Author,* in ROLAND BARTHES, IMAGE MUSIC TEXT 142 (Stephen Heath trans. 1977).

34. The point is made in Denis Brion, *Performing the Constitution,* 49 WAS. & LEE U. L. REV. 293, 310 (1992). *See generally* Zapf & Moglen, *supra* note 17, at 498–520.

35. Gerald Graff, *"Keep Off the Grass" "Drop Dead" and Other Indeterminacies: A Response to Sanford Levinson,* 60 TEX. L. REV. 405 (1982). Of course, in particular situations these expressions might be indeterminate. *See generally* H.L.A. HART, THE CONCEPT OF LAW 125–26 (1961); Jim Chen, *Law as a Species of Language Acquisition,* 73 WASH. U. L.Q. 1263, 1290–96 (1995).

36. Don Herzog, *As Many as Six Impossible Things before Breakfast,* 75 CAL. L. REV. 609, 629 (1987).

37. *See* ADRIENNE RICH, ON LIES, SECRETS, AND SILENCE 185 (1979); Allan Hunt, *The Big Fear: Law Confronts Postmodernism,* 35 McGILL L.J. 507, 525 (1990); Judith Lichtenberg, *Objectivity and Its Enemies,* 2 THE RESPONSIVE COMMUNITY 59 (1991); David Millon, *Objectivity and Democracy,* 67 NYU L. REV. 1, 23–35 (1992); Dan Subotnik, *"Sue Me, Sue Me, What Can You Do Me? I Love You" A Disquisition on Law, Sex, and Talk,* 47 FLA. L. REV. 311 (1995). *See generally* BERNARD WILLIAMSON, TRUTH AND TRUTHFULNESS: AN ESSAY IN GENEALOGY (2002). The notion that one can identify falsehoods even if one cannot prove truth lies at the heart of the "falsification theory" of scientific methodology. *See* KARL POPPER, CONJECTURES AND REFUTATIONS (1963); Jeanne Schroeder, *Just So Stories: Posnerian Economic Methodology,* 22 CARDOZO L. REV. 351 (2001).

38. *See* AUSTIN, *supra* note 19, at 138–40; POSNER, supra note 30, at 372–75; Austin, supra note 7, at 243–45, 281–84; Anne Coughlin, *Regulating the Self: Autobiographical Performances in Outsider Scholarship,* 81 VA. L. REV. 1229, 1290 (1995); Edward Rubin, *On Beyond Truth: A Theory for Evaluating Legal Scholarship,* 80 CAL. L. REV. 889 (1992).

39. FARBER & SHERRY, *supra* note 5, at 136. *See also* Austin, *supra* note 7, at 276–80; Richard Epstein, *Legal Education and the Politics of Exclusion,* 45 STAN. L. REV. 1607 (1993). For a virtual admission that this is what the "critical enterprise" is about, see Richard Delgado, *On Telling Stories in School: A Reply to Farber and Sherry,* 46 VAND. L. REV. 665, 670 (1993).

40. Tatyana Tolstaya, *The Golden Age,* N.Y. REV. BOOKS, Dec. 17, 1992, at 3 (James Gambrell trans.).

# Abortion History Then and Now

*An historian is a babbler who plays tricks upon the dead.*

—Voltaire[41]

Extended analysis of deconstruction theory is not necessary to understand how it has affected the way we address the history of abortion. We have already noted how, until 1968, the history of abortion in English and American law was considered unproblematic.[42] Abortion generally was presented as merely an adjunct to discussions of other significant social problems rather than as a topic of importance in its own right.[43] Sir William Holdsworth hardly mentioned abortion in his 23-volume history of English law.[44] Modern feminist scholars, however, are inclined to see such silences as a contemptuous dismissal of women's concerns as beneath the notice of serious students of the law.[45] Yet that silence instead might indicate either that such laws were largely uncontroversial in our history, or were relatively unchanging through time, or both. One point is certain: The lack of attention to abortion by legal historians both left the relevant historical materials largely undeveloped and left abortion history open to unfettered exploitation by all sides when the legal status of abortion became controversial. Since 1968, the history of Anglo-American abortion laws has been central to the stories we tell ourselves about abortion. Advocates have used these stories both to interpret the Constitution and to establish a contemporary social context for appraising the ongoing value debates surrounding abortion.

The late Cyril Means, jr., a law professor at New York Law School, was the first person to undertake to revise our notions of abortion history.[46] Means claimed to have discovered two hitherto unsuspected historical "facts"—really, the theses he set out to prove. Means' first thesis was that abortion was not criminal in England or America before the nineteenth century.[47] His second thesis was that abortion was criminalized during the nineteenth century solely to protect the life or health of mothers, and not to protect the lives or health of unborn children.[48] Regardless of how many times these claims are repeated, however, they are not facts. Nor is there any validity to Means' conclusion from these supposed facts that abortion was "a com-

---

41. "*Un historien est un babillard qui fait des tracasseries aux morts.*" 82 THE COMPLETE WORKS OF VOLTAIRE 452 (Theodore Besderman ed. 1968).

42. *See* Chapter 1, at notes 53–58; Chapter 3, at notes 3–7.

43. ROGER ROSENBLATT, LIFE ITSELF: ABORTION IN THE AMERICAN MIND 58 (1992).

44. Holdsworth was content simply to report the adoption of Lord Ellenborough's Act, the first statutory prohibition of abortion. 11 W.S. HOLDSWORTH, A HISTORY OF ENGLISH LAW 537 (23 vols., 7th ed. 1956).

45. *See, e.g.,* Catharine MacKinnon, *Reflections on Sex Equality under Law,* 100 YALE L.J. 1281, 1281–82 (1991.

46. Cyril Means, jr., *The Law of New York Concerning Abortion and the Status of the Foetus, 1664–1968: A Case of Cessation of Constitutionality,* 14 N.Y.L.F. 411 (1968) ("Means I"); Cyril Means, jr., *The Phoenix of Abortional Freedom: Is a Penumbral Right or Ninth-Amendment Right About to Arise from the Nineteenth-Century Legislative Ashes of a Fourteenth-Century Common-Law Liberty?,* 17 N.Y.L.F. 335 (1971) ("Means II").

47. Means II, *supra* note 46, at 336–76.

48. *Id.* at 382–92. *See also* Means I, *supra* note 46, at 511–15. Means did not bother to explain why a twentieth-century legislature would need to re-enact a statute that already serves its purposes simply because the purposes have changed. *See* BORK, *supra* note 11, at 113; Richard Epstein, *Substantive Due Process by Any Other Name: The Abortion Cases,* 1973 SUP. CT. REV. 159, 168 n.34 ("There is no reason to require a legislature to protect or rehabilitate an old statute with a new preamble.").

mon law liberty" in 1791 (when the Ninth Amendment was adopted),[49] or that whatever restrictions on that "liberty" were enacted between 1791 and 1868 (when the Fourteenth Amendment was adopted) did not displace that "liberty" because the statutes, like the "liberty," were designed to protect women, not to subordinate women's interests to the interests of others.[50]

Professor Means' history of abortion was neither objective nor accurate.[51] Means knew this. He wrote as an advocate to make a case for legal change, not as a historian investigating the past.[52] Means was general counsel for the National Association for the Repeal of Abortion Laws (NARAL — later the National Abortion Rights Action League, then the National Abortion and Reproductive Rights Action League, and now NARAL Pro-Choice America) when he wrote his first article and was still a devoted pro-abortion activist when he wrote his second article.[53] His research was funded by the Association for the Study of Abortion (ASA), another important branch of the "movement" for abortion reform.[54] He revealed neither the funding nor his advocacy position in his published "scholarship" — "scholarship" that was relied on by the Supreme Court and accepted by much of the public as redefining the history of abortion.[55]

NARAL and ASA were both actively involved in preparing the pro-choice argument in *Roe v. Wade*,[56] including coordinating *amicus* briefs supporting the claim of a constitutional freedom to abort.[57] Means presented his radical revision of the history of abortion to the Supreme Court in one of the *amicus* briefs. Sarah Weddington, the attorney who argued for "Jane Roe" in the case, reports that the Justices had copies of Means' articles on the bench with them during the oral arguments.[58] Weddington was fully aware that Means' work was deeply flawed, having received a memorandum laying out the weaknesses in Means' research and analysis.[59] Even while referring to Means' analysis three times during her oral argument, she said nothing that would call Means' brief into question.[60] The effort to deceive the Court was successful.

---

49. Means II, *supra* note 46, at 336, 351–54, 374–75, 409–10 n.175.

50. *Id.* at 376–410.

51. *See* Chapters 3–7. *See also* JOHN KEOWN, ABORTION, DOCTORS AND THE LAW 3–11 (1988); Joseph Dellapenna, *The History of Abortion: Technology, Morality, and Law,* 40 U. PITT. L. REV. 359 (1979).

52. *See* Chapter 3, at notes 130–40.

53. MARIAN FAUX, *ROE V. WADE*: THE UNTOLD STORY OF THE LANDMARK SUPREME COURT DECISION THAT MADE ABORTION LEGAL 73, 81, 216–19, 222–23, 234, 237, 240, 289–92 (1988). Faux's book was written with the full cooperation of those who argued on behalf of "Jane Roe" in *Roe v. Wade,* which is not surprising given, as one admiring reviewer aptly put it, that her book exhibits a clear bias "in favor of the pro-choice decision in *Roe v. Wade.*" Francine Adkins Tone, *Book Review,* 19 LINCOLN L. REV. 67, 69 (1990). Faux does not seem to grasp the implications of her revelations.

54. FAUX, *supra* note 53, at 216–19.

55. This is a prime example of the advocacy scholarship denounced by Mary Ann Glendon and Ronald Collins. *See* GLENDON, *supra* note 10, at 208; Ronald Collins, *A Letter on Scholarly Ethics,* 45 J. LEGAL EDUC. 139 (1995). Skeptics of claims of advocacy scholarship occasionally deride those who denounce such scholarship for not naming names. *See, e.g.,* Sanford Levinson, *Book Review* (of Glendon, *supra*), 45 J. LEGAL EDUC. 143, 146 (1995); Michael Sean Quinn, *"Scholarly Ethics": A Response,* 46 J. LEGAL EDUC. 110 (1996). Cyril Means is such a name.

56. 410 U.S. 113 (1973).

57. FAUX, *supra* note 53, at 234–38.

58. Sarah Weddington, *Introduction,* in ABORTION IN THE SEVENTIES: PROCEEDINGS OF THE WESTERN REGIONAL CONFERENCE ON ABORTION, DENVER, COLORADO FEBRUARY 27–29, 1976, at 187, 189 (Dr. Warren Hern & Bonnie Andrikopoulos eds. 1977).

59. GARROW, *supra* note 11, at 498, 891–92 n.41. *See* Chapter 14, at notes 390–95.

60. Roe v. Wade *Oral Arguments,* 8 SETON HALL CONST. L.J. 315, 323–25 (1998). *See also* GARROW, *supra* note 11, at 524–25. Margie Hames also referred to the Means article in her first oral argument of *Doe v. Bolton,* a companion case to *Roe v. Wade.* GARROW, *supra,* at 527.

Justice Harry Blackmun, in writing the majority opinion in *Roe v. Wade,* relied heavily and uncritically on Means' history, citing Means seven times—and no other historian except for his brief examination of the history of the Hippocratic oath.[61] Blackmun devoted fully half of the majority opinion in *Roe* to the history of abortion, using that history to inform his interpretation of the values involved in the case and thus ultimately whether the statutory prohibition of abortion was constitutional.[62] Unfortunately, but predictably given Blackmun's reliance on Means' work, his conclusions regarding the history of abortion were wrong on all points.

Opponents of abortion rights only began to respond directly to Means and Blackmun after the announcement of the *Roe* decision. These critics attempted to refute Means and Blackmun by referring to off-hand remarks by judges in the very few cases then known in which a court discussed abortion or the equally brief remarks of the leading text writers on the common law from centuries ago.[63] Occasionally they would also refer to condemnations by leading clerics and church councils. The critics did not discuss the fact that most of their sources spoke in abstract terms about abortion in a context of discussing some other problem—they simply did not focus on abortion.[64] Nor did the critics ask why apparent prosecutions were apparently so rare if abortion was as serious a crime as the critics insisted it was. The critics simply did not consider non-legal evidence that might have shown whether abortion was a common and tolerated practice despite official condemnation by the royal and clerical officialdom.

Perhaps Means' critics can be forgiven in the narrowness of their focus. They were attempting to refute Means and Blackmun directly. The critics therefore focused on precisely the same materials as Means had used to build his spurious history and on which Blackmun had relied in following Means. The critics thoroughly discredited Means. Yet their failure to do more than recite the occasional condemnations of abortion by jurists, clerics, and others in history hardly refuted Means' major point. Neither Means nor his critics had uncovered any evidence of systematic or sustained efforts to seek out and suppress abortion before the nineteenth century. Still, the inadequacies of Means' history were sufficiently disturbing that historian James Mohr undertook to recast the historical claims in a somewhat different form.

Without seriously challenging Means, Mohr presented an alternative explanation of the enactment of the nineteenth century abortion statutes by creating two further, somewhat overlapping, historical theses in his book *Abortion in America.*[65] Mohr's first thesis was that abortion was a generally accepted and common practice in American society at the opening of the nineteenth

---

61. 410 U.S. at 136–39. *See also* Wolfgang Saxon, *Obituary: Cyril C. Means, 73, A Specialist in Laws Regarding Abortion,* N.Y. Times, Oct. 6, 1992, at A15. Edward Steegman noted the inbalance in Justice Blackmun's review of history without revealing its source; instead, he suggests that the inbalance is a result of Blackmun's exaggerated distaste for "religious intolerance" to which the Justice would apparently attribute all historical prohibition of abortion. Edward Steegman, Note, *Of History and Due Process,* 63 Ind. L.J. 369, 390–94, 396–97 (1987).

62. *See* Chapter 14, at notes 435–50.

63. *See* John Noonan, jr., A Private Choice: Abortion in America in the Seventies 5–6 (1979); Robert Byrn, *An American Tragedy: The Supreme Court on Abortion,* 41 Fordham L. Rev. 807 (1973); John Connery, *The Ancients and the Medievals on Abortion: The Consensus the Court Ignored,* in Abortion and the Constitution: Reversing *Roe v. Wade* through the Courts ("Abortion and the Constitution") 123 (Dennis Horan, Edward Grant, & Paige Cunningham eds. 1987); Robert Destro, *Abortion and the Constitution: The Need for a Life-Protective Amendment,* 63 Cal. L. Rev. 1250 (1975); Dennis Horan & Thomas Balch, Roe v. Wade: *No Justification in History, Law, or Logic,* in Abortion and the Constitution, *supra,* at 55, 60–70; James Witherspoon, *Reexamining Roe: Nineteenth-Century Abortion Statutes and the Fourteenth Amendment,* 17 St. Mary's L.J. 29 (1985).

64. *See* Rosenblatt, *supra* note 43, at 58.

65. James Mohr, Abortion in America: The Origins and Evolution of National Policy, 1800–1900 (1978).

century.[66] Mohr's second thesis was that the nineteenth-century statutes were a device for men to oppress women, particularly for the "organized" (largely male) medical profession to suppress competition from disorganized (largely female) "irregular" practitioners.[67] Mohr's book has become so central to disputes over the history of abortion that *amicus* briefs on both sides of later abortion cases have relied on Mohr's work to advance their own claims about the significance of that history.[68] Mohr's theses, like those of Cyril Means, were also unfounded.[69]

The four theses propounded by Means and Mohr have become the new orthodoxy of abortion history on which the claim of a constitutionally protected liberty to abort is based. This new orthodoxy supplies the erroneous premises from which arguments are constructed that either the Ninth or the Fourteenth Amendments (or both) protect this purported "common law liberty."[70] The very political convenience of this new orthodoxy ought to have suggested a need for caution regarding its truth. Yet the acceptance of the new orthodoxy has become nearly universal in the scholarly world today.[71]

The Supreme Court's continuing imprimatur on *Roe's* version of abortion history makes the acceptance that history particularly strong among legal scholars. Thus we find law professor Donald Judges recounting the history as provided by both sides, but utterly failing to see the significance of the stories he retells, largely because he assumes that abortion was a common practice throughout history.[72] Laurence Tribe (the leading constitutional law scholar in the United States today) and Ronald Dworkin (our leading jurisprude today) do not even bother to discuss the possibility of an alternative history to the new orthodoxy.[73] Another law professor, Jane Maslow Cohen, acknowledges my own work in criticizing the claims of Blackmun, Means, and Mohr, but sees the two lines of work as mere expressions of different "interpretive spins" without seriously evaluating the evidence.[74] The quality of professor Cohen's analysis is suggested by her explanation of why she speaks of the intent of legislatures when her deconstructionist tech-

---

66. *Id.* at 6–19.

67. *Id.* at 32–37, 147–82. *See* Chapter 6, at notes 213–331; Chapter 7, at notes 205–470.

68. *Amicus Brief of 250 American Historians in support of Appellants in* Planned Parenthood of Southeastern Pennsylvania v. Casey, [505 U.S. 833 (1992)] ("*Casey Historians' Brief*"); *Amicus Brief of 281 American Historians supporting Appellees in* Webster v. Reproductive Health Services [492 U.S. 490 (1989)] ("*Webster Historians' Brief*"), reprinted at 11 WOMEN'S RTS. L. RPTR. 163 (1989), and in 8 DOCUMENTARY HISTORY OF THE LEGAL ASPECTS OF ABORTION IN THE UNITED STATES: *WEBSTER v. REPRODUCTIVE HEALTH SERVICES* 107 (Roy Mersky & Gary Hartman eds. 1990) ("DOCUMENTARY HISTORY") (pagination will be given only to the version in the *Women's Rts. L. Rptr.*); *Amicus Brief of the United States supporting Appellants in* Webster v. Reproductive Health Services, reprinted in 5 DOCUMENTARY HISTORY, *supra*, at 25.

69. *See* Chapters 6–8.

70. Roe v. Wade, 410 U.S. 113, 140 (1973); Beecham v. Leahy, 287 A.2d 836, 839 (Vt. 1972); LINDA GORDON, WOMAN'S BODY, WOMAN'S RIGHT: A SOCIAL HISTORY OF BIRTH CONTROL IN AMERICA 52–53, 57 (1976); MOHR, *supra* note 65, at 20–21, 128–29, 134–36, 144–45, 201, 208–11, 226, 229, 235–36; Laura Flanders, *Abortion: The Usable Past,* THE NATION, Aug. 7, 1989, at 175; Morton Kondracke, *The Abortion Wars,* NEW REP., Aug. 28, 1989, 17, at 19, col. 2; Means II, *supra* note 46, at 336, 351–54, 374–75, 409–10 n.175; Reva Siegel, *Reasoning from the Body: A Historical Perspective on Abortion Regulation and Questions of Equal Protection,* 44 STAN. L. REV. 278 (1992); Rickie Solinger, *"A Complete Disaster": Abortion and the Politics of Hospital Abortion Committees, 1950–1970,* 19 FEMINIST STUD. 241, 243 (1993); *Casey Historians' Brief, supra* note 68, at 5–6; *Webster Historians' Brief, supra* note 68, at 170.

71. *See* Chapter 1, at notes 59–97.

72. JUDGES, *supra* note 16, at 90–110.

73. DWORKIN, *supra* note 16, at 45, 112; TRIBE, *supra* note 16, at 30–34; LAURENCE TRIBE, AMERICAN CONSTITUTIONAL LAW 1355–56 (2nd ed. 1988).

74. Jane Maslow Cohen, *A Jurisprudence of Doubt: Deliberative Autonomy and Abortion,* 3 COLUM. J. GENDER & LAW. 175, 205–06 n.116 (1992).

nique precludes any such imputation: "Although I am uncomfortable with any such ascription, *I have allowed my text to behave similarly.*"[75]

As a result of the pervasive acceptance of the new orthodoxy of abortion history, even such strongly anti-abortion journalists as George Will have reiterated the new orthodoxy.[76] When that happens, one realizes that this spurious history has become so thoroughly embedded in the popular culture that it has taken on the aura of unquestionable truth. This new orthodoxy of abortion history relies heavily on the judicial embrace for its continuing authoritative status. This embrace—involving a the erroneous reference to legal authorities spread over more than six centuries—provides a prime example of legal historian Morton Horwitz's observation that the "common law is especially cruel to those whom it casts aside. It either ignores them, soon forgetting that they ever existed, or, more usually, uses them as authority for propositions they did not accept."[77] We have yet to learn that simply because the Supreme Court has the power to bind us to their law does not empower the justices to bind us to their history.[78]

# Truth vs. Advocacy

*History is bunk.*

—Henry Ford[79]

The spurious history of abortion endorsed by the Supreme Court in *Roe v. Wade* distorts both arguments over the claim of a constitutional freedom to abort and over the contemporary social context for appraising the ongoing value debates. These distortions account for the widespread popularity of *Roe's* history. Not only is there a strong tradition in American law linking the constitutionality of particular laws to the historical roots of that law,[80] but tradition also is a strong rhetorical weapon in popular culture. Controversy rages over the proper uses of history in legal argument, particularly centering around whether the only correct reading of the Constitution is

---

75. *Id.* at 206 n.116 (emphasis added).

76. George Will, *Abortion Is a State Question*, WASH. POST, June 18, 1989, at C7, col. 1.

77. MORTON HORWITZ, THE TRANSFORMATION OF AMERICAN LAW 1780–1860, at 38 (1977).

78. MARK DEWOLFE HOWE, THE GARDEN AND THE WILDERNESS: RELIGION AND GOVERNMENT IN AMERICAN CONSTITUTIONAL HISTORY 4–5 (1965).

79. OXFORD DICTIONARY OF QUOTATIONS 209 (2nd ed. 1955). Ford was testifying in court (he was suing the Chicago Tribune for libel) when he made this remark in July 1919. Ford seems to have struck some sort of nerve with this oft-quoted quip. The term "debunking" came into use in academic circles within three years of Ford's use of the word, first appearing in the work of historian W.E. Woodward. OXFORD ENGLISH DICTIONARY 748 (1972 Supp.). It stretches credulity to consider this a mere coincidence.

80. *See, e.g.,* U.S. Term Limits, Inc. v. Thornton, 514 U.S. 779 (1995) (holding state enacted term limits for members of Congress unconstitutional based on the "original intent" of the framers of the Constitution); Wilson v. Arkansas, 514 U.S. 927 (1995) (the meaning of the Fourth Amendment framed entirely in terms of the understanding of that amendment "[a]t the time of the framing"); Burnham v. Superior Court, 495 U.S. 604 (1990) (upholding the constitutionality of "tag" jurisdiction—jurisdiction based solely upon the service of process a person—based on a continuing historical tradition); Michael H. v. Gerald D., 491 U.S. 110 (1989) (upholding the constitutionality of a nearly irrebuttable statutory presumption that a child was fathered by the man to whom the mother was married at the time because of a continuing historical tradition); Sun Oil Co. v. Wortman, 486 U.S. 717 (1988) (upholding the treating of statutes of limitations as purely procedural based on a continuing historical tradition).

according to the "original intent" of the framers of the document.[81] We do not need to resolve this controversy to understand why history is important in legal rhetoric. The strength of the revival of historical reasoning is apparent when one finds that even some of the strongest critics of traditional jurisprudence accept historical reasoning for at least some purposes.[82] Yet this turn towards history and tradition is all the more surprising as the "postmodernism" that the most extreme critics embrace is, as Frederic Jameson has pointed out, built on a foundation of having "forgotten how to think historically in the first place."[83]

For lawyers, at least, this is no really a great mystery. Law, particularly in a precedent-based legal system like the common law, demands attention to the past.[84] Law could even be called applied history. Legal historian Carl Friedrich described law as "frozen history,"[85] and historian

---

81. *See generally* Gregory Bassham, Original Intent and the Constitution: A Philosophical Study (1992); Bork, *supra* note 11; Susan Burgess, Contest for Constitutional Authority (1992); Dworkin, *supra* note 3; Dworkin, *supra* note 16, at 118–47; Judges, *supra* note 16, at 114–23; Leonard Levy, Original Intent and the Framers' Constitution (1988); Maltz, Rethinking, *supra* note 16; Michael Perry, The Constitution in the Courts: Law or Politics? (1994); Jack Rakove, Original Meanings: Politics and Ideas in the Making of the Constitution (1996); The Bill of Rights: Original Meaning and Current Understanding (Eugene Hickok, jr., ed. 1991); Tushnet, *supra* note 13, at 21–45. One could add innumerable law review articles debating these points. Interestingly, some of the strongest critics of "originalism" in the intense judicial confirmation hearings of the Reagan and first Bush administrations professed shock or outrage when a court declined to follow the critic's intent (in the form of an alleged congressional or senatorial intent or understanding), using the very sort of arguments these same critics decry when applied to issues relating to constitutional interpretation. *See, e.g., Statement of Senator Joseph Biden*, Joint Hearings before Sen. Comm. on For. Rel. & Sen. Comm. on Judiciary, 100th Cong., 1st Sess. 130 (1987) (describing the statement of Abraham Sofaer, then Legal Advisor to the State Department, on the interpretation of the Anti-Ballistic Missile Treaty as "incredible" and "absolutely staggering" because the interpretation departed from the Senate's understanding of the treaty when the treaty was ratified). For a rejection of "originalism" by a court acting virtually contemporaneously with the drafting of the relevant constitution, see *In re Section 94(2) of the Motor Vehicle Act*, [1985] 2 S.C.R. 486, 507–09 (Can.); *Law Soc. of Upper Canada v. Skapinker*, [1984] 1 S.C.R. 357, 365–68 (Can.). *See generally* Daniel Conkle, *Canada's Roe: The Canadian Abortion Decision and Its Implications for American Constitutional Law and Theory*, 6 Const'l Commentary 299 (1989); Christopher Manfredi, *The Canadian Supreme Court and American Judicial Review: United States Constitutional Jurisprudence and the Canadian Charter of Rights and Freedoms*, 40 Am. J. Comp. L. 213 (1992); Steven Smith, *Idolatry in Constitutional Interpretation*, 79 Va. L. Rev. 583, 590–93, 601 (1993).

82. Roger Cotterrell, The Politics of Jurisprudence: A Critical Introduction to Legal Philosophy 22, 229 (1989); Hutchinson, *supra* note 13, at 49; Paul Kahn, Legitimacy and History: Self-Government in American Constitutional Theory (1992); Laura Kalman, The Strange Career of Legal Liberalism 152, 167–246 (1996); Tribe & Dorf, *supra* note 16, at 98 ("historical traditions are to be the criteria of fit"), 109–112; Charles Lawrence, III, *The Word and the River: Pedagogy as Scholarship as Struggle*, 65 S. Cal. L. Rev. 2231, 2282–83 (1992) ("If we are to bring fairness and justice to legal interpretation and discourse, those processes must be informed by the context of history and culture"); Frank Michelman, *Bringing the Law to Life: A Plea for Disenchantment*, 74 Cornell L. Rev. 256 (1989); Neil Richards, *Clio and the Court: A Reassessment of the Supreme Court's Uses of History*, 13 NYU J.L. & Pol. 809, 828–31 (1997). *See also* Herman Belz, *History, Theory, and the Constitution*, 11 Const'l Commentary 45 (1994); Owen Fiss, *The Law Regained*, 74 Cornell L. Rev. 245 (1989); John Orth, *Thinking about Law Historically: Why Bother?*, 70 N.C.L. Rev. 287 (1991); Richard Posner, *Legal Reform from the Top Down and from the Bottom Up: The Question of Unenumerated Constitutional Rights*, 59 U. Chi. L. Rev. 433 (1992); Gerald Postema, *On the Moral Presence of Our Past*, 36 McGill L. Rev. 1153, 1170–80 (1991); Robin West, *Constitutional Skepticism*, 72 B.U. L. Rev. 765, 789–90 (1992). *See generally* Robert Gordon, *The Struggle over the Past*, 44 Cleve. St. L. Rev. 123 (1996).

83. Frederic Jameson, Postmodernism, Or the Cultural Logic of Late Capitalism ix (1991). *See also* Robert Gordon, *The Past as Authority and as Social Critic: Stabilizing or Destabilizing Functions of History in Legal Argument*, in The Historic Turn in the Human Sciences 339 (Terence McDonald ed. 1996).

84. Harold Berman, *The Origins of Historical Jurisprudence: Coke, Selden, Hale*, 103 Yale L.J. 1651, 1676 (1994); Alfred Kelly, *Clio and the Court: An Illicit Love Affair*, 1965 Sup. Ct. Rev. 119, at 121.

85. Carl Friedrich, *Law and History*, 14 Vand. L. Rev. 1027, 1027 (1961).

Peter Hoffer has described law as "history made by judges."[86] Ignoring the ambiguity in the last quotation, both descriptions sound somewhat pejorative. Law professor Harold Berman presented the matter with a more positive spin, writing that "the English doctrine of precedent has embodied the theory that in English law historical experience has a normative character."[87] Regardless of whether one considers the law's fixation on the past a virtue or a defect, that fixation cannot be denied. Justice Oliver Wendell Holmes, jr., made the point repeatedly, most famously when he wrote that "[t]he life of the law has not been logic: it has been experience."[88]

As a result of the law's concern with justification through reference to past experience and past decisions, it is easier to justify changes in the law as a return to some supposed "Golden Age" of the legal past than as a revolutionary departure from the values and traditions that have long prevailed in society.[89] This attitude is not, however, confined to lawyers. Abortion is not even the prime example of this phenomenon, but it is an example involving many persons, from all conceivable backgrounds, who have rushed to embrace a new history even at the risk of losing sight of the substantive vision that demands the change they seek. Oscar Wilde hit that nail squarely when he declared that "the one duty we owe to history is to rewrite it."[90]

History as a discipline certainly has its ample share of skeptics. Historians often tell radically differing stories about the same events, and which version is deemed "correct" often seems more a question of fashion than of evidence.[91] For a particularly striking example of the malleability of

---

86. Peter Charles Hoffer, *"Blind to History": The Use of History in Affirmative Action Suits: Another Look at City of Richmond v. J.A. Croson, Co.,* 23 Rutgers L.J. 271, 275 n.11 (1992).

87. Berman, *supra* note 84, at 1733.

88. Oliver Wendell Holmes, jr., The Common Law (Mark Howe ed. 1963), at 1. *See also* New York Times Co. v. Eisner, 256 U.S. 345, 349 (1921) ("Upon this point a page of history is worth a volume of logic."); Holmes, *supra,* at 5 ("In order to know what [the law] is, we must know what it has been, and what it tends to become."), 33 ("The history of the law has been necessary to the knowledge of what the law is."); Oliver Wendell Holmes, jr., *The Path of the Law,* 10 Harv. L. Rev. 457, 469 (1897) ("The rational study of law is still to a large extent the study of history.") ("Holmes, *The Path of the Law*"); Benjamin Nathan Cardozo, The Nature of the Judicial Process 114 (1921) (tradition, the collective judgment of the bench and bar, and "the spirit of the law" circumscribe judicial decisions). *See generally* Anthony Kronman, *Precedent and Tradition,* 99 Yale L.J. 1029, 1032 (1990); Earl Warren, *Introduction,* 1 Am. J. Legal Hist. 1, 1 (1957).

89. *See, e.g.,* Bruce Ackerman, We the People (1991) (the New Deal's revolution in constitutional theory was passed off as a return to the original meaning of the commerce clause as interpreted by Chief Justice Marshall); Robert Palmer, *Akhil Amar: Elitist Populist and Anti-Textual Textualist,* 16 S. Ill. L.J. 397, 397 (1992) ("The pursuit of social policy aims by analysis under the guise of historical textualism is an attempt to bootstrap otherwise unacceptable policies into law by constitutional mandate, instead of by the wisdom of the proposals."). *See generally* Howe, *supra* note 78, at 4; Bradley Clanton, *Standing and the English Prerogative Writs: The Original Understanding,* 63 Brook. L. Rev. 1001 (1997); William Fisher III, *Texts and Contexts: The Application to American Legal History of the Methodologies of Intellectual History,* 49 Stan. L. Rev. 1065 (1997); Kelly, *supra* note 84, at 125–28; Rudolph Peritz, *History as Explanation: Annals of American Political Economy,* 22 Law & Soc. Inquiry 231 (1997); John Phillip Reid, *Law and History,* 27 Loy.-L.A. L. Rev. 193, 198–200, 204–12 (1993); Richards, *supra* note 82; Daniel Rodgers, *Republicanism: The Career of a Concept,* 79 J. Am. Hist. 11 (1992); William Wiecek, *Clio as Hostage: The United States Supreme Court and the Uses of History,* 24 Cal. W. L. Rev. 227, 230, 258–64 (1988). C. Vann Woodward commented that an historical truth "lives" 17 or 18 years, or "at the outside twenty, seldom longer." C. Vann Woodward, Thinking Back: The Perils of Writing History 3 (1986).

90. Quoted in Arthur Schlesinger, jr., *History as Therapy: A Dangerous Idea,* N.Y. Times, May 3, 1996, at A31.

91. *See, e.g.,* Norman Cantor, Inventing the Middle Ages: The Lives, Works, and Ideas of the Great Medievalists of the Twentieth Century (1991) (reviewing the varied and conflicting accounts of life in the Medieval Europe); Barry Cushman, Rethinking the New Deal Court: The Structure of a Constitutional Revolution (1998) (reinterpreting the "judicial revolution" of the 1930s); G. Edward White, The American Judicial Tradition: Profiles of Leading American Judges 50–69, 106–28 (expanded ed. 1988) (reviewing the changing attitudes towards the Marshall Court and Justice Holmes); Bruce

an historian's thinking, compare the two major works by legal historian Morton Horwitz, works that, while dealing with similar topics in the history of American law, adopt radically different methodological, research, and intellectual approaches.[92] These changes seem based upon nothing but changing intellectual fashions. Horwitz himself, in a chapter he contributed to a book tellingly titled *Toward a Usable Past,* warned against "the dangers of roaming through history looking for one's friends," although he himself seems to be a prime example of the practice.[93]

Because of the malleability of historical studies, lavish amounts of ink and paper have been invested in arguing whether history is a species of fiction or of something that approximates (more or less imperfectly) the past.[94] Historian Haydon White provided a post modern explanation of the relation of history to fiction. History, he wrote, depends on story forms prevalent in the culture in which it is written in order to be intelligible to the reader.[95] Without narratives, White concluded, our lives—and our histories—lack "coherence, integrity, fullness, and closure."[96] Some would claim more strongly that narratives correspond with how we live, and thus

---

Ackerman & David Golov, *Is NAFTA Constitutional?*, 108 HARV. L. REV. 799 (1995) (analyzing the invention of an appropriate history to support a change in the way we ratify international agreements); Saul Cornell, *Moving beyond the Canon of Traditional Constitutional History: Anti-Federalists, the Bill of Rights, and the Promise of Post-Modern Historiography,* 12 LAW & HIST. REV. 1 (1994) ("deconstructing" the history of the drafting of the Bill of Rights); Daniel Rodgers, *Republicanism: The Career of a Concept,* 79 AM. HIST. REV. 11 (1990) (reviewing changing views of the American Revolution among twentieth-century historians and the eventual impact of some of these changes on legal scholars); James Whitman, *Of Corporatism, Fascism, and the First New Deal,* 39 AM. J. COMP. L. 747 (1991) (summarizing the changing views of historians on the sources of the early New Deal and recognizing a considerable debt to Italian Fascism; the article is interesting to read despite grammatical and spelling errors numerous enough to raise questions about where or when those responsible learned English). *See generally* THE ANTISLAVERY DEBATE: CAPITALISM AND ABOLITIONISM AS A PROBLEM IN HISTORICAL INTERPRETATION (Thomas Bender ed. 1992); PAUL CONKLIN & ROLAND STROMBERG, HERITAGE AND CHALLENGE: THE HISTORY AND THEORY OF HISTORY (1989); 8 OWEN FISS, HISTORY OF THE SUPREME COURT OF THE UNITED STATES: TROUBLED BEGINNINGS OF THE MODERN STATE, 1888–1910, at 12–18 (1993); HANS KELLNER, LANGUAGE AND HISTORICAL REPRESENTATION: GETTING THE STORY CROOKED (1989); PETER NOVICK, THAT NOBLE DREAM: THE "OBJECTIVITY QUESTION" AND THE AMERICAN HISTORICAL PROFESSION (1988); MICHAEL STANFORD, THE NATURE OF HISTORICAL KNOWLEDGE (1986); TUSHNET, *supra* note 13, at 32–45; HOWARD ZINN, THE POLITICS OF HISTORY 10 (2nd ed. 1990); Morton Horwitz, *History and Theory,* 96 YALE L.J. 1825 (1987); Paul Horwitz, *The Past Tense: The History of Crisis—and the Crisis of History—in Constitutional Theory,* 61 ALB. L. REV. 459 (1997) (book rev.); Eban Moglen, *Holmes's Legacy and the New Constitutional History,* 108 HARV. L. REV. 2027 (1995) (book rev.); Théodore Tarczylo, *From Lascivious Erudition to the History of Mentalités* (George St. Andrews trans.), in SEXUAL UNDERWORLDS OF THE ENGLIGHTENMENT 26 (G.S. Rousseau & Roy Porter eds. 1988); James Viator, *Give Me That Old-Time Historiography: Charles Beard and the Study of the Constitution,* 36 LOY. L. REV. 981 (1991); Christopher Wolfe, *Give Me That Old-Time Historiography: Mark Tushnet on Constitutional Law,* 15 LAW & SOC. INQUIRY 831 (1990).

92. HORWITZ, *supra* note 77; HORWITZ, *supra* note 11, at 9–14.

93. Morton Horwitz, *Republican Origins of Constitutionalism,* in TOWARD A USABLE PAST LIBERTY UNDER STATE CONSTITUTIONS 148, 148–49 (Paul Finkelman & Stephan Gottlieb eds. 1991). *See also* Horwitz, *supra* note 92. For detailed critiques of Horwitz's works, see Robert Gordon, *The Elusive Transformation,* 6 YALE J.L. & HUMANITIES 137 (1994) (book rev.); G. Edward White, *Reflections on the "Republican Revival": Interdisciplinary Scholarship in the Legal Academy,* 6 YALE J.L. & THE HUMANITIES 1, 17–21 (1994) ("White, *Republican Revival*"); G. Edward White, *The Studied Ambiguity of Horwitz's Legal History,* 29 WM. & MARY L. REV. 101 (1987) ("White, *Studied Ambiguity*"); G. Edward White, *Transforming History in the Postmodern Era,* 91 MICH. L. REV. 1315 (1993) ("White, *Transforming History*"). In particular, White finds Horwitz's second book to be a "set up" to demonstrate that the Critical Legal Studies movement is the natural heir to the progressive tradition in American jurisprudential thought. White, *Transforming History, supra,* at 1345, 1350–51.

94. *See, e.g.,* Stuart Banner, *Legal History and Legal Scholarship,* 76 WASH. U. L.Q. 37 (1998); Gordon Wood, *Novel History,* N.Y. REV. OF BOOKS 12 (June 27, 1991).

95. HAYDON WHITE, TROPICS OF DISCOURSE: ESSAYS IN CULTURAL CRITICISM 60 (1978).

96. HAYDEN WHITE, THE CONTENT OF FORM 24 (1987).

express better than any other form of history the truth of what happened in the past.[97] We must be wary, however, that embrace of scholarly narrative does not substitute for a search for truth.[98]

Because post modern thought so often denies the possibility of historical accuracy, it seems in the end to abolish history altogether even while it, as it often does, appeals to history.[99] Michael Howard, then Oxford Regius Professor of History and later Lovett Professor of History at Yale, discussed such extreme views in these words:

> The trouble is that there is no such thing as "history." History is what historians write, and historians are part of the process they are writing about.... We know that our work, if it survives at all, will be read as evidence about our own *mentalité* and the thought processes of our own time rather than for anything we say about the times about which we write, however careful our scholarship and cautious our conclusions....None the less all this work must have some object, some aspiration in view. It cannot be the study of the past for "its own sake," for outside the minds and writings of historians the past has no independent reality.[100]

Friedrich Nietzsche explained the same phenomenon more abstractly. While one must be careful with Nietzsche, the source of both deconstruction and postmodernism, given the contradictions and malevolence that characterizes so much of his thought,[101] his analysis is worth pondering. Nietzsche described "critical histories" as attempts to "implant a new habit,...a second nature so that the first nature withers away. It is an attempt, as it were, *a posteriori* to give oneself a past from which one would like to be descended in opposition to the past from which one is descended—always a dangerous attempt because it is so difficult to find a limit in denying the past and because second natures are mostly feebler than the first."[102] In other words, Nietzsche argued that history and morality consist of stories by which individuals deny responsibility for their lives.[103]

Sarah Hrdy, a feminist biologist writing about the debate within biology over whether primate evolution was driven by masculine or feminine needs, made the same point, writing that "[w]idespread stereotypes devaluing the capacities and importance of women have not improved either their lot or that of human societies. But there is also little to be gained from coun-

---

97. Paul Ricoeur, *Narrative Time*, 7 CRIT. INQUIRY 165 (1980). *See generally* PAUL RICOEUR, TIME AND NARRATIVE (3 vols. 1984–86); Dominick LaCapra, *Intellectual History and Its Ways*, 97 AM. HIST. REV. 425 (1992).

98. WHITE, *supra* note 96, at 24. *See also* GEORGE MARCUS & JAMES CLIFFORD, WRITING CULTURE: THE POETICS AND POLITICS OF ETHNOGRAPHY (1986); JOHN VAN MAANEN, TALES OF THE FIELD: ON WRITING ETHNOGRAPHY (1988); KEITH WINDSCHUTTLE, THE KILLING OF HISTORY: HOW LITERARY CRITICS AND SOCIAL THEORISTS ARE MURDERING OUR PAST (1997).

99. Hunt, *supra* note 37, at 532. *See also* Mark Tushnet, *The Left Critique of Normativity: A Comment*, 90 MICH. L. REV. 2325, 2329–30 (1992) (historicism is a ploy for localizing claims of injustice in order to evade the obligation to provide a broad theory of justice).

100. MICHAEL HOWARD, THE LESSONS OF HISTORY 11–12 (1991). *See also* JOYCE APPLEBY, LYNN HUNT, & MARGARET JACOB, TELLING THE TRUTH ABOUT HISTORY (1994); GERTRUDE HIMMELFARB, ON LOOKING INTO THE ABYSS: UNTIMELY THOUGHTS ON CULTURE AND SOCIETY (1994); JOSEPH LEVINE, THE AUTONOMY OF HISTORY: TRUTH AND METHOD FROM ERASMUS TO GIBBON (1999); G. EDWARD WHITE, INTERVENTION AND DETACHMENT: ESSAYS IN LEGAL HISTORY AND JURISPRUDENCE 6 (1994); Louis Wolcher, *The Many Meanings of "Wherefore" in Legal History*, 68 WASH. L. REV. 559 (1993).

101. *See, e.g.*, WHY WE ARE NOT NIETZSCHEANS (Luc Ferry & Alain Renault eds. 1997).

102. FRIEDRICH NIETZSCHE, ON THE ADVANTAGES AND DISADVANTAGES OF HISTORY FOR LIFE 22 (Peter Preuss trans. 1980). *See also* Horwitz, *supra* note 92, at 1830; Shel don Wolin, *Hannah Arendt and the Ordinance of Time*, 44 SOCIAL RE search 96 (1977).

103. *See* Barbara Stark, *Urban Despair and Nietzsche's "Eternal Return": From the Municipal Rhetoric of Economic Justice to the International Law of Economic Rights*, 28 VANDERBILT J. TRANSNAT'L L. 185, 207–13 (1995).

termyths that emphasize women's natural innocence from lust for power, her cooperativeness and solidarity with other women...."[104] Nietzsche's and Hrdy's arguments explains why so many have been so willing to ignore the obvious errors and contradictions in the new history of abortion. If Nietzsche is right, however, the new history will falter as history, and perhaps the "second nature" built on that false history will falter as well. If so, the faltering likely will not occur for some time. Legal historian Frederic Maitland caught the point best when he wrote "if history is to do its liberating work it must be as true to fact as it can possibly make itself, and true to fact it will not be if it begins to think what lessons it can teach."[105]

The new orthodoxy regarding the history of abortion amply illustrates these concerns. Careful examination of the actual historical record reveals that neither Cyril Means nor James Mohr considered abundant evidence relevant to their inquiries. Even more troubling are the major methodological errors in their approach to the evidence. Means and Mohr both characteristically project our present knowledge onto persons writing or acting in prior centuries. Thus they riddled their works with contradictions.[106] Even more troubling is Means' and Mohr's pervasive pattern of dismissing any evidence inconsistent with their theses as a ruse to conceal the person's "true" motives—motives that support their theses, and for which, peculiarly, no evidence has survived except Means' or Mohr's own surmise.[107]

As historian Daniel Boorstin long ago noted, projecting our knowledge or ideas onto persons living in earlier times is an endemic problem in legal history if only because of the desire to use ancient materials as modern legal authority.[108] Even Justice Antonin Scalia, our most fervent judicial advocate of the central importance of history to the judicial craft, has warned us that such errors become quite common in the doing of legal history when, as is often the case, the historian is more interested in using ancient materials as modern legal authority than in actually attempting to recover the record of past events or ideas.[109] In a similar vein, we find feminist historians and theologians denouncing various parts of the *Bible* as misogynistic and claiming that those passages were part of a conspiracy by men to subordinate women—with-

---

104. SARAH BLAFFER HRDY, THE WOMAN THAT NEVER EVOLVED 190 (1981).

105. THE LETTERS OF FREDERIC WILLIAM MAITLAND no. 116 (P.N.R. Zutshi ed. 1995).

106. *See, e.g.,* MOHR, *supra* note 65, at 4, 6–7, 10 (insisting that "obstructed menses" was always understood as a euphemism), 11–14, 18 (insisting that effective and safe pharmacological techniques were available in the United States in 1800), 53–58, 71–73 (acknowledging that available pharmacological techniques were highly dangerous and ineffective), 73–77 (insisting that people saw nothing wrong with killing an unborn child while admitting that the people whom he quoted did not think that a living child was present early in pregnancy), 102–10 (insisting that nineteenth century feminism led to a rise in abortion rates), 111–14 (acknowledging that all early feminists strongly opposed abortion), 78–84 (insisting that falling birth rates in the late nineteenth century must indirectly prove that abortion was a common practice without considering any other possible explanations); Means II, *supra* note 46, at 337–38 n.4 (describing the presence of the Chief Justice of Common Pleas as "unconstitutional"—as if anyone at the time thought in such terms), 343–45 (describing a trespass proceeding from 1601 as a civil action when it was a mixed civil/criminal proceeding, and the decision as mere *dictum* when that concept had not yet been invented). These points are discussed at length in Chapters 3 to 8.

107. *See, e.g.,* MOHR, *supra* note 65, at 32–37, 86–118, 128, 147–82; Means II, *supra* note 46, at 346–47.

108. Daniel Boorstin, *Tradition and Method in Legal History,* 54 HARV. L. REV. 424, 428–29 (1941).

109. *See* Antonin Scalia, *Originalism: The Lesser Evil,* 57 U. CIN. L. REV. 849, 856–57 (1989). Scalia has been accused of doing precisely what he faults in others. *See, e.g.,* Evan Tsen Lee, *Deconstitutionalizing Justiciability: The Example of Mootness,* 105 HARV. L. REV. 603, 637–39 (1992); Gene Nichol, jr., *Justice Scalia, Standing, and Public Law Litigation,* 42 DUKE L.J. 1141, 1153 (1993); Cass Sunstein, *What's Standing after* Lujan? *Of Citizen Suits, "Injuries," and Article III,* 91 MICH. L. REV. 163, 214 (1992). Which side in this particular debate is distorting history, of course, is itself hotly debated. *See* Clanton, *supra* note 89.

out any concern for the original social setting of the passages or the likely attitudes of women (as well as men) at the time.[110] The practice has been aptly described by Moshe Greenberg:

> At bottom, what feminists criticize is not what the texts meant to those who composed and received them in their historical context, but what the text means in today's context. VanDijk-Hemmes would presumably not be consoled by evidence that the women in Ezekiel's audience were persuaded by his rhetoric and identified with the pillorying of the wanton sisters. She demands a text that reflects her identity; for that purpose Ezekiel is but a male countertext, whose male-centered agenda must be exposed and disarmed in terms of today's values, psychology, and anthropology. Whether aiming to savage Scripture or to salvage it, feminists are judgmental. They applaud or decry, approve or disapprove. They write to promote a new gender reality. Their project differs fundamentally from the (quixotic?) historical-philological search for the primary, context-bound sense of Scripture that is the project of this commentary.[111]

Nor do those who seek to redesign society limit their radically revisionist readings to ancient texts. This approach allows academics such as sociologist Kristin Luker and constitutional scholar Laurence Tribe to deploy the same strategy to dismiss as illegitimate the claim of those who oppose abortion today. Luker and Tribe claim that the "right-to-lifers" really are pursuing the subordination of women rather than protection of the lives of the unborn, but accept at face value statements by supporters of abortion rights.[112]

This turn reflects a rather too common ploy by contemporary liberals. As modern liberalism precludes liberals from saying that one person's conception of "the good" is better or worse than another's, the liberal instead sets about to explain to opponents not that they are wrong, but that they actually, deep down agree with the liberal's views.[113] Or at least, the liberal explains that what she advocates is inherent in the values that the opponent already has accepted. In other words, Luker, Tribe, and similar academics know better the thoughts of people they have never met and with whom they profoundly disagree than those people know themselves. No wonder some have concluded that such a ploy generally turns upon a mischaracterization of what the people being described believe or with which they agree.[114] Law professor Steven Smith caught the sense of such an attitude in the following words:

> When the strategy is seen for what it is, what at first appeared to be a modest exercise in cultural interpretation reveals itself as an act of monumental bravado. For a philosopher to tell me that my beliefs are mistaken may be irksome, but for him to assert that I am deceived about what my beliefs are is truly audacious. This strategy also seems un-

---

110. *See, e.g.,* GRACIA FAY ELLLWOOD, BATTER MY HEART (1988); JUDITH PLASKOW, STANDING AGAIN AT SINAI: JUDAISM FROM A FEMINIST PERSPECTIVE (1990); RENITA WEEMS, BATTERED LOVE: MARRIAGE, SEX, AND VIOLENCE IN THE HEBREW PROPHETS (1995); Rachel Adler, *The Battered Wife of God: Violence, Law and the Feminist Critique of the Prophets,* 7 S. CAL. REV. L. & WOMEN'S STUDIES 171 (1998); T. Drorah Setel, *Prophets and Pornography: Female Sexual Imagery in Hosea,* in FEMINIST INTERPRETATION OF THE BIBLE 86 (Letty Russell ed. 1985).

111. Moshe Greenberg, *Ezekiel 21–37,* in THE ANCHOR BIBLE 471 (David Freedman ed. 1997). *See also* Benjamin Edidin Scolnic, *Bible-Battering,* 45 CONSERVATIVE JUDAISM 43 (1992).

112. KRISTIN LUKER, ABORTION AND THE POLITICS OF MOTHERHOOD 137–38, 159–75, 195, 224, 241 (1984); TRIBE, *supra* note 16, at 231–41. *See also* JAMES RISEN & JUDY THOMAS, WRATH OF ANGELS: THE AMERICAN ABORTION WAR 297–98 (1998).

113. *See* Steven Smith, *Natural Law and Contemporary Moral Thought: A Guide from the Perplexed,* 42 AM. J. JURIS. 299, 304–05 (1997) (book rev.).

114. *Id.* at 305.

likely to succeed: how is it that John Rawls or Ronald Dworkin can know what I *really* believe better than I do?[115]

Thomas Nagel caught the same point: "Postmodernism's specifically academic appeal," he wrote, "comes precisely from its being another in the sequence of 'unmasking' strategies that offer a way to criticize the intellectual efforts of others not by engaging them on the ground, but by diagnosing them from a superior vantage point and charging them with inadequate self-awareness."[116] No wonder those on the receiving end of such arguments find the dismissal their beliefs demeaning and pernicious. Pro-life law professor (now federal judge) Michael McConnell has termed Tribe's claim that those who oppose abortion really do not care about the lives of the unborn to be the most unattractive of Tribe's arguments.[117] Nonetheless, a growing chorus of pro-choice academics and others have made this claim a standard rhetorical ploy among those who support abortion rights.[118]

# Why Search for "Lost Voices"?

*A man hears what he wants to hear and disregards the rest.*

—Paul Simon[119]

Dismissing rather than examining the views of others has become so widespread among certain historians, including many of those who support abortion rights, that they have developed a

---

115. *Id.* at 304–05 (emphasis in original).

116. Thomas Nagel, *The Sleep of Reason*, THE NEW REP., Oct. 12, 1998, at 32, 38.

117. Michael McConnell, *How Not to Promote Serious Deliberation about Abortion*, 58 U. CHI. L. REV. 1181, 1188–93 (1991).

118. *See, e.g.,* JOHN ARTHUR, THE UNFINISHED CONSTITUTION: PHILOSOPHY AND CONSTITUTIONAL PRACTICE 259–60 (1989); DALLAS BLANCHARD, THE ANTI-ABORTION MOVEMENT AND THE RISE OF THE RELIGIOUS RIGHT: FROM POLITE TO FIERY PROTEST 1–9 (1994); DALLAS BLANCHARD & TERRY PREWITT, RELIGIOUS VIOLENCE AND ABORTION: THE GIDEON PROJECT xii, 227–28, 231, 241 (1993); BURNS & BURNS, *supra* note 16, at 356–58; CONDIT, *supra* note 3, at 30, 61–63, 74 n.9, 127–28; CRAIG & O'BRIEN, *supra* note 16, at 46–47; MARILYN FRALIK, IDEOLOGY AND ABORTION POLITICS (1983); GARROW, *supra* note 11, at 633, 736; ELIZABETH FOX GENOVESE, FEMINISM WITHOUT ILLUSIONS 81–83 (1991); GINSBURG, *supra* note 3, at 1, 6–19, 140–45, 172–97, 212–21; JANET HADLEY, ABORTION: BETWEEN FREEDOM AND NECESSITY 4–9 (1996); BEVERLY WILDUNG HARRISON, OUR RIGHT TO CHOOSE: TOWARD A NEW ETHIC OF ABORTION 2–4, 32–49, 59–62, 67, 181–82, 189–90 (1983); JUDGES, *supra* note 16, at 12–15; KENNETH KARST, LAW'S PROMISE, LAW'S EXPRESSION: VISIONS OF POWER IN THE POLITICS OF RACE, GENDER, AND RELIGION 52–57 (1993); CASSANDRA LANGER, A FEMINIST CRITIQUE: HOW FEMINISM HAS CHANGED AMERICAN SOCIETY, CULTURE, AND HOW WE LIVE FROM THE 1940's TO THE PRESENT 26–28, 55, 151–61 (1996); CONNIE PAIGE, THE RIGHT TO LIFERS: WHO THEY ARE; HOW THEY OPERATE; WHERE THEY GET THEIR MONEY (1983); ROSALIND POLLACK PETCHESKY, ABORTION AND WOMEN'S CHOICE: THE STATE, SEXUALITY, AND REPRODUCTIVE FREEDOM xiii, xvi–xviii, xx–xxi, 5, 82–84 (rev. ed. 1990); DEBORAH RHODE, JUSTICE AND GENDER 214–15 (1989); DEBORAH RHODE, SPEAKING OF SEX: THE DENIAL OF GENDER INEQUALITY 207–09 (1997) ("RHODE, SPEAKING OF SEX"); JOHN ROBERTSON, CHILDREN OF CHOICE: FREEDOM AND THE NEW REPRODUCTIVE TECHNOLOGIES 66–68 (1994); ROSENBLATT, *supra* note 43, at 37–38, 109, 121–31; PATRICK SHEEHAN, WOMEN, SOCIETY, THE STATE, AND ABORTION 125–28 (1987); SUSAN SHERWIN, NO LONGER PATIENT: FEMINIST ETHICS AND HEALTH CARE 111–14 (1992); CARROLL SMITH-ROSENBERG, DISORDERLY CONDUCT: VISIONS OF GENDER IN VICTORIAN AMERICA 217–18 (1985); WHITE, *supra* note 16, at 166–67; David Garrow, *Abortion and the Future*, CHI. TRIB., Jan. 21, 1998, at I–13; Warren Hern, *Life on the Front Lines*, in ABORTION WARS: A HALF CENTURY OF STRUGGLE, 1950–2000, at 307, 315 (Rickie Solinger ed. 1998); Elizabeth Karlin, *"We Called It Kindness": Establishing a Feminist Abortion Practice*, in ABORTION WARS, *supra*, at 273; Sarah Rumage, *Resisting the West: The Clinton Administration's Promotion of Abortion at the 1994 Cairo Conference and the Strength of the Islamic Response*, 27 CAL. W. INT'L L.J. 1, 87 (1996).

119. Paul Simon, *The Boxer* (1969).

name for the process. They call it the recovery of "lost voices."[120] The search for loss voices allows the most obvious and basic errors that historians can make—the projection of modern knowledge and needs onto the past.[121] Such projections are not, of course, limited to legal historians; many historians in all fields today describe their enterprise as the recovery "lost voices."[122] Historians who research questions thought to have implications for current policy debates seem particularly inclined to this enterprise.

Historians now purport to uncover the beliefs, attitudes, and opinions of ordinary people lost to history due to the absence of a documentary record. They seek to do so through inferences drawn from bits and pieces of surviving material and from "deconstructing" the ideas actually expressed in the records of not so lost voices.[123] The "lost voices" approach starts from the premise that history (and law) are written from the top down, from the perspective of the oppressors, ignoring the views of those at the bottom of the social hierarchy who constituted an oppressed majority.[124] This is all very true, but silence tells us nothing about what the silenced group actually believed. Law professor Richard Delgado expressed the point bluntly: "Silence may indicate consent, but may just as easily signal that the silenced group has just plain given up or been browbeaten into silence."[125]

The search for lost voices attempts to go beyond the prevailing abstractions of the ruling elites in an effort to get at the actual experiences of "real" people.[126] The search draws much of its appeal from the effort to recover "different voices" suppressed in contemporary discourse. The best known example of the search for different voices is the work of psychologist Carol Gilligan, whose study of the moral development of boys and girls (entitled *In a Different Voice*) arguably discovered two different, gender-linked patterns.[127] Gilligan's work has found a ready reception

---

120. *See, e.g.,* SMITH-ROSENBERG, *supra* note 118, at 234 (1985).

121. *See, e.g.,* 1 BONNIE ANDERSON & JUDITH ZINSSER, A HISTORY OF THEIR OWN: WOMEN IN EUROPE FROM PREHISTORY TO THE PRESENT 108 (1988) (asserting that medieval midwives performed craniatomies and caesareans, but citing as the source for this "information" only an interview with nurse-midwives of the late twentieth century).

122. *See, e.g.,* LINDA KERBER, WOMEN OF THE REPUBLIC: INTELLECT AND IDEOLOGY IN REVOLUTIONARY AMERICA (1980); SEAN WILENTZ, CHANTS DEMOCRATIC: NEW YORK CITY AND THE RISE OF THE AMERICAN WORKING CLASS, 1788–1850 (1984); Cornell, *supra* note 91, at 20–28; Hendrik Hartog, *Pigs and Positivism,* 1985 WIS. L. REV. 899, 934–35; Hoffer, *supra* note 86, at 278–79; John Toews, *Intellectual History after the Linguistic Turn: The Autonomy of Meaning and the Irreducibility of Experience,* 92 AM. HIST. REV. 879 (1987); Laurence Veysey, *Intellectual History and the New Social History,* in NEW DIRECTIONS IN AMERICAN INTELLECTUAL HISTORY 3–26 (John Higham & Paul Conkin eds. 1979).

123. *See, e.g.,* CULLER, *supra* note 19; DOMINICK LACAPRA, HISTORY AND CRITICISM (1985); DOMINICK LACAPRA, RETHINKING INTELLECTUAL HISTORY: TEXTS, CONTEXTS, AND LANGUAGE (1983); CHRISTOPHER NORRIS, DECONSTRUCTION THEORY AND PRACTICE (1982).

124. *See, e.g.,* Arthur Austin, *Antitrust Deconstructed,* 22 STETSON L. REV. 1101, 1101 (1993); J.M. Balkin, *Understanding Legal Understanding: The Legal Subject and the Problem of Legal Coherence,* 103 YALE L.J. 105 (1993); Richard Devlin, *Nomos and Thanatos (Part A): The Killing Fields: Modern Law and Legal Theory,* 12 DALHOUSIE L.J. 298 (1989); Pierre Schlag, *Normativity and the Politics of the Subject,* 69 TEX. L. REV. 1627 (1991).

125. Richard Delgado, *Judicial Influences and the Inside-Outside Dichotomy: A Comment on Professor Nagel,* 61 U. COLO. L. REV. 711, 714 (1990).

126. SANDE COHEN, HISTORICAL CULTURE: ON THE RECODING OF AN ACADEMIC DISCIPLINE (1986); Kathryn Anderson *et al., Beginning Where We Are: Feminist Methodology in Oral History,* in FEMINIST RESEARCH METHODS 94 (Joyce McCarl Nielson ed. 1990); Kathryn Kolbert, *The Webster Amicus Curiae Briefs: Perspectives on the Abortion Controversy and the Role of the Supreme Court,* 15 AM. J. L. & MED. 153, 165 (1989).

127. CAROL GILLIGAN, IN A DIFFERENT VOICE: PSYCHOLOGICAL THEORY AND WOMEN'S DEVELOPMENT (1982). *See also* MAPPING THE MORAL DOMAIN (Carol Gilligan, Janie Ward, & Jill Taylor eds. 1988).

particularly among feminist scholars,[128] including many feminist lawyers as well as so-called critical race theorists.[129] A large body of argument even claims that the notion that women law students, lawyers, and judges experience law as a profession in a different manner than their male counterparts.[130] Evidence for the different voice theory, however, is actually rather thin, which

---

128. *See* Emily Abel, Who Cares for the Elderly? Public Policy and the Experiences of Adult Daughters (1991); An Ethic of Care: Feminist and Interdisciplinary Perspectives (May Jeanne Larrabee ed. 1993); Mary Field Belenky *et al.,* Women's Ways of Knowing: The Development of Self, Voice, and Mind (1986); Scyla Benhabib, Situating the Self: Gender, Community and Postmodernism' in Contemporary Ethics (1992); Rosi Braidotti, Patterns of Discourse: A Study of Women in Contemporary Philosophy (1991); Lyn Brown & Carol Gilligan, Meeting at the Crossroads: Women's Psychology and Girl's Development (1992); Eva Browning Cole & Susan Coultrap-McQuin, Explorations in Feminist Ethics (1992); Diemut Bubeck, Care, Gender, and Justice (1995); Circles of Care: Work and Identity in Women's Lives (Emily Abel & Margaret Nelson eds. 1990); Marilyn Freedman, What Are Friends for? Feminist Perspectives on Personal Relationships and Moral Theory (1993); Hadley, *supra* note 118, at 84–86; Sandra Harding, The Science Question in Feminism (1986); Susan Hekman, Moral Voices, Moral Selves: Carol Gilligan and Femnist Moral Theory (1995); Virginia Held, Feminist Morality: Transforming Culture, Society and Politics (1993); Nancy Hirschmann, Rethinking Obligation: A Feminist Method for Political Theory (1992); Bell Hooks, Talking Back: Thinking Feminist, Thinking Black (1989); Eva Feder Kittay & Diana Meyers, Women and Moral Theory (1987); Nel Noddings, Caring: A Feminine Approach to Ethics and Moral Education (1984); Sara Ruddick, Maternal Thinking: Towards a Politics of Peace (1989); Rudy, *supra* note 3, at 103–27; Science, Morality and Feminism (Kai Neilsen ed. 1994); Susan Sherwin, No Longer Patient: Feminist Ethics and Health Care 42–50 (1992); Deborah Tannen, You Just Don't Understand (1990); Janet Todd, Gender and Literary Voice (1980); Women and Moral Theory (Eva Kittay & Diana Myers eds. 1987); Women, Knowledge and Reality: Explorations in Feminist Philosophy (Ann Garry & Marylin Pearsall eds. 1989).

129. Minow, *supra* note 11, at 173–372; Leslie Bender, *From Gender Difference to Feminist Solidarity: Using Carol Gilligan and an Ethic of Care in Law,* 15 Vt. L. Rev. 1 (1990); Eloise Buker, *"Ladie" Justice: Power and Image in Feminist Jurisprudence,* 15 Vt. L. Rev. 69 (1990); Richard Delgado, *When a Story Is Just a Story: Does Voice Really Matter?,* 76 Va. L. Rev. 95 (1990); Lucinda Finley, *Breaking Women's Silence in Law: The Dilemma of the Gendered Nature of Legal Reasoning,* 64 Notre Dame L. Rev. 886 (1989); Angela Harris, *Race and Essentialism in Feminist Legal Theory,* 42 Stan. L. Rev. 581 (1990); Mari Matsuda, *When the First Quail Calls: Multiple Consciousness of Jurisprudential Method,* 11 Women's Rts. L. Rep. 7 (1989); Linda McClain, *"Atomistic Man" Revisited: Liberalism, Connection, and Feminist Jurisprudence,* 65 S. Cal. L. Rev. 1171 (1992); Carrie Menkel-Meadow, *Excluded Voices: New Voices in the Legal Profession Making New Voices in the Law,* 42 U. Miami L. Rev. 29 (1987); Carrie Menkel-Meadow, *What's Gender Got to Do with It? The Politics and Morality of an Ethic of Care* (book rev.), 22 NYU Rev. L. & Soc. Change 265 (1996); Frances Olsen, *The Family and the Market: A Study on Ideology and Legal Reform,* 96 Harv. L. Rev. 1497 (1983); Elizabeth Schneider, *The Dialectic of Rights and Politics: Perspectives from the Women's Movement,* 61 NYU L. Rev. 589 (1986); Suzanna Sherry, *Civic Virtue and the Feminine Voice in Constitutional Adjudication,* 72 Va. L. Rev. 543 (1986); Robin West, *Jurisprudence and Gender,* 55 U. Chi. L. Rev. 1 (1988); Williams, *supra* note 3, at 1564–72; Shelley Wright, *Patriarchal Feminism and the Law of the Father,* 1 Feminist Leg. Stud. 115 (1993). *See also* Ruth Colker, Abortion & Dialogue — Pro-Choice, Pro-Life, and American Law 3–18 (1992) (a Gilliganesque analysis without Gilligan).

130. *See* Feminist Contentions: A Philosophical Exchange (Seyla Benhabib *et al.* eds. 1995); Bender, *supra* note 129; David Chambers, *Accommodation and Satisfaction: Women and Men Lawyers and the Balance of Work and Family,* 14 Law & Soc. Inquiry 251 (1989); Stephen Ellman, *The Ethic of Care as an Ethic for Lawyers,* 81 Geo. L.J. 2665 (1993); Farber & Sherry, *supra* note 5; Lucinda Findley, *Transcending Equality Theory: A Way Out of the Maternity and Workplace Debate,* 86 Colum. L. Rev. 1118 (1986); Owen Flanagan, jr., & Kathryn Jackson, *Justice, Care, and Gender: The Kohlberg-Gilligan Debate Revisited,* in Feminism and Political Theory 37 (Cass Sunstein ed. 1990); Carol Gilligan & Catharine MacKinnon, *Feminist Discourse, Moral Values, and the Law — A Conversation,* 34 Buff. L. Rev. 11 (1985); Kit Kimports, *Evidence Engendered,* 1991 U. Ill. L. Rev. 413; Marjorie Kornhauser, *The Rhetoric of the Anti-Progressive Income Tax Movement: A Typical Male Reaction,* 86 Mich. L. Rev. 465 (1987); Carrie Menkel-Meadow, *Portia in a Different Voice: Speculations on a Women's Lawyering Process,* 1 Berkeley Women's L.J. 39 (1985); Carrie Menkel-Meadow, *Portia Redux: Another Look at Gender, Feminism and Legal Ethics,* 2 Va. J. Soc. Pol'y & L. 75 (1994); Student Project, *Gender, Legal Education, and the Legal Profession: An Empirical Study of Stanford Law Students and Graduates,* 40 Stan.

probably explains why Gilligan's different voice theory has been less welcomed in her own field of psychology than among political feminists.[131] Empirical evidence does not support the claim that women experience the law or function as lawyers differently—even if they feel they must work harder than men to get ahead.[132] Furthermore, what Gilligan and her followers describe as a feminine voice in mainstream American culture actually appears as a masculine voice in cultures at least as sexist as our own.[133] As a result, a growing number of feminist scholars have come to recognize the limitations or even failure of different voice theory.[134]

---

L. REV. 1209 (1988); Lee Teitelbaum, Antoinette Sedillo López, & Jeffrey Jenkins, *Gender, Legal Education, and Legal Careers,* 41 J. LEGAL EDUC. 443 (1991).

131. *See* CAROL TAVRIS, THE MISMEASURE OF WOMAN 79–92 (1992); John Broughton, *Women's Rationality and Men's Virtue: A Critique of Gender Dualism in Gilligan's Theory of Moral Development,* 50 SOC. RESEARCH 597 (1983); Alice Eagly & Blair Johnson, *Gender and Leadership Style: A Meta-Analysis,* 108 PSYCH. BULL. 233 (1990); Owen Flanagan, jr., & Jonathan Adler, *Impartiality and Particularity,* 50 SOC. RESEARCH 576 (1983); Catherine Greene & Eleanor Macoby, *How Different Is the "Different Voice"?,* 11 SIGNS 301 (1986); Rachel Hare-Mustin & Jean Marecek, *The Meaning of Difference: Gender Theory, Post-Modernism, and Psychology,* 43 AM. PSCYH. 3 (1988); Steven Karau & Mona Makhijani, *Gender and the Effectiveness of Leaders: A Meta-Analysis,* 117 PSYCH. BULL. 125 (1995); Linda Kerber *et al., On* In a Different Voice: *An Interdisciplinary Forum,* 11 SIGNS 304 (1986); Peter Lifton, *Individual Differences in Moral Development: The Relation of Sex, Gender, and Personality in Morality,* 53 J. PERSONALITY 306 (1985); Joan Miller & Donald Bersoff, *Culture and Moral Judgment: How Are Conflicts between Justice and Interpersonal Responsibility Resolved?,* 62 PERSONALITY & SOC. PSCYCH. 541 (1992); Carol Stack, *The Culture of Gender: Women and Men of Color,* 11 SIGNS 321 (1986); Debra Nails, *Social-Scientific Sexism: Gilligan's Mismeasure of Man,* 50 SOC. RESEARCH 643 (1983); Joan Tranto, *Beyond Gender to a Theory of Care,* 12 SIGNS 644 (1987); James Walker, *In a Diffident Voice: Cryptoseparatist Analysis of Female Moral Development,* 50 SOC. RESEARCH 665 (1983); Lawrence Walker, Brian de Vries, & Shelley Trevethan, *Moral Stages and Moral Orientation in Real Life and Theoretical Dilemmas,* 58 CHILD DEV. 842 (1987).

132. *See* Sue Davis, *Do Women Judges Speak "In a Different Voice?" Carol Gilligan, Feminist Legal Theory, and the Ninth Circuit,* 8 WIS. WOMEN'S L.J. 143 (1992) (finding, at 171, that some women judges sometimes speak "in a different voice," but that some men judges sometimes also do so); Zella Luria, *A Methodological Critique,* 11 SIGNS 316 (1986) (reporting that women actually perform better at rule-based reasoning—what Gilligan characterizes as the "masculine voice"—than men after social class is factored out of the comparison). *See also* AMERICAN BAR ASS'N COMM'N ON WOMEN IN THE PROFESSION, THE UNFINISHED AGENDA: WOMEN AND THE LEGAL PROFESSION 30–32 (2001); SUE THOMAS, HOW WOMEN LEGISLATE (1994); Michael Solomine & Susan Wheatley, *Rethinking Feminist Judging,* 70 IND. L.J. 891 (1995). This is not to suggest that women judges sometimes take a different view of certain substantive issues, such as civil rights, gender discrimination, or obscenity. Theresa Beiner, *What Will Diversity on the Bench Mean for Justice?,* 6 MICH. J. GENDER & L. 113 (1999); Sue Davis *et al., Voting Behavior and Gender on the U.S. Court of Appeals,* 77 JUDICATURE 129 (1993); Jennifer Segal, *The Decision Making of Clinton's Nontraditional Judicial Appointees,* 80 JUDICATURE 279 (1997). Such differences do not always fit the stereotypes. Thus one journalist found that women judges in Texas were harder on criminals in general, and more willing to impose the death penalty, than were men judges. Jeffrey Toobin, *Women in Black,* NEW YORKER, Oct. 30, 2000, at 48.

133. *See* ANTHONY CORTESE, ETHNIC ETHICS: THE RESTRUCTURING OF MORAL THEORY (1990); Martha Jean Baker, *The Different Voice: Japanese Norms of Consensus and "Cultural" Feminism,* 16 PAC. BASIN L.J. 133 (1997); Stephen Friedell, *The "Different Voice" in Jewish Law: Some Parallels to a Feminist Jurisprudence,* 67 IND. L. REV. 915, 918, 944 (1992). My own reaction to Carol Gilligan's work was not doubt affected by the fact that I had already become immersed in Chinese legal theory before I discovered Gilligan.

134. The best of these such recognitions is found in Jeanne Schroeder, Abduction from the Seraglio: *Feminist Methodologies and the Logic of Emagination,* 70 TEX. L. REV. 109 (1991). Schroeder was one of the subjects of Gilligan's original study. *See also* BIOLOGICAL WOMAN—THE CONVENIENT MYTH (Ruth Hubbard, Mary Sue Henefin, & Barabara Fried eds. 1982); CONDIT, *supra* note 3, at 179–80; CYNTHIA FUCHS EPSTEIN, DECEPTIVE DISTINCTIONS: SEX, GENDER AND THE SOCIAL ORDER 81–83 (1988); SUSAN FALUDI, BACKLASH: THE WAR AGAINST WOMEN 325–34 (1981); FEMINISM AND FOUCAULT: REFLECTIONS ON RESISTANCE (Irene Diamond & Lee Quinby eds. 1988); ELIZABETH FOX GENOVESE, FEMINISM WITHOUT ILLUSIONS 81–85, 117–19 (1991); ARLIE RUSSELL HOCHSCHILD, THE MANAGED HEART: THE COMMERCIALIZATION OF HUMAN FEELING (1983); RUTH HUBBARD, THE POLITICS OF WOMEN'S BIOLOGY (1990); MARIAN LOWE & RUTH HUBBARD, WOMEN'S NATURE: RATIONALIZATON OF INEQUALITY (1983); CATHARINE MACKINNON, TOWARD A FEMINIST

Oddly, the primary source of empirical support for different voice theory actually comes from the field of "sociobiology" and "evolutionary psychology." The two fields are so close that some consider them a single field of study, but others insist that they are separate and distinct.[135] What studies in these fields disclose are consistent patterns of differences in temperament between men and women rather than in thought as such.[136] Both fields are highly unpopular, however, among political feminists who take such analyses to be claims that stereotypical sex roles are bio-

THEORY OF THE STATE 51 (1989); SUSAN MILLER OKIN, JUSTICE, GENDER, AND THE FAMILY 14–17, 89–109 (1989); CAROL SMART, FEMINISM AND THE POWER OF LAW 72–76 (1989); ELIZABETH SPELLMAN, INESSENTIAL WOMAN: PROBLEMS OF EXCLUSION IN FEMINIST THOUGHT (1988); JOAN TRONTO, MORAL BOUNDARIES: A POLITICAL ARGUMENT FOR AN ETHIC OF CARE (1993); Sharyn Roach Anleu, *Critiquing the Law: Themes and Dilemmas in Anglo-American Feminist Legal Theory*, 19 J.L. & SOC'Y 423 (1990); Judith Baer, *Nasty Law or Nice Ladies? Jurisprudence, Feminism, and Gender Differences*, 11 WOMEN & POLITICS 1 (1991); Nitya Duclos, *Lessons of Difference: Feminist Theory on Cultural Diversity*, 38 BUFF. L. REV. 325 (1990); Ruth Bader Ginsberg, *Some Thoughts on the 1980's Debate over Special Versus Equal Treatment for Women*, 4 L. & INEQUALITY 143 (1986); Patricia Karlan & Daniel Ortiz, *In a Different Voice: Relational Feminism, Abortion Rights, and the Feminist Legal Agenda*, 87 NW. U. L. REV. 858 (1993); Rita Mae Kelly, Michelle Saint-Germain, & Jody Horn, *Female Public Officials: A Different Voice?*, 515 ANNALS AM. ACADEMY POLI. & SOC. SCI. 77 (1991); Sylvia Law & Patricia Hennessey, *Is the Law Male?: The Case of Family Law*, 69 CHI.-KENT L. REV. 345 (1993); Julie Mertus, *Beyond the Solitary Self: Voice, Community, and Reproductive Freedom*, 3 COLUM. J. GENDER & L. 247, 255–82 (1992); Michelle Moody-Adams, *Gender and the Complexity of Moral Voices*, in FEMINIST ETHICS 195 (Claudia Card ed. 1991); Martha Reineke, *The Politics of Difference: A Critique of Carol Gilligan*, 2 CAN. J. FEMINIST ETHICS 3 (1987); Deborah Rhode, *The "Woman's Point of View,"* 38 J. LEGAL EDUC. 39 (1988); Ann Scales, *The Emergence of Feminist Jurisprudence: An Essay*, 95 YALE L.J. 1373 (1986); Joan Shaughnessy, *Gilligan's Travels*, 7 LAW & INEQUALITY 1 (1988); Ronnie Steiner & Deborah Figart, *Emotional Labor since* The Managed Heart, 561 ANNALS AM. ACADEMY POL. & SOC. SCI. 8 (1999); Joan Williams, *Deconstructing Gender*, 87 MICH. L. REV. 797 (1989); Iris Marion Young, *Gender as Seriality: Thinking about Women as a Social Collective*, 19 SIGNS 713 (1994). Law professor Mary Joe Frug sought to bridge these conflicting views with her own "progressive" reading of Gilligan. MARY JOE FRUG, POSTMODERN LEGAL FEMINISM (1992) ("FRUG, POSTMODERN"); Mary Joe Frug, *Progressive Feminist Legal Scholarship: Can We Claim a "Different Voice"?*, 15 HARV. WOMEN'S L.J. 38 (1992).

135. *See* Linda Caporael, *Mechanisms Matter: The Difference between Sociobiology and Evolutionary Psychology*, 12 BEHAVIORAL & BRAIN SCI. 17 (1989).

136. RICHARD ALEXANDER, THE BIOLOGY OF MORAL SYSTEMS (1987); LARRY ARNHART, DARWINIAN NATURAL RIGHT: THE BIOLOGICAL ETHICS OF HUMAN NATURE (1998); BIOLOGY AND THE FOUNDATION OF ETHICS (Jane Maienschein & Michael Ruse eds. 1999); DONALD BROWN, HUMAN UNIVERSALS (1999); FRANS DE WAAL, GOOD NATURED: THE ORIGINS OF RIGHT AND WRONG IN HUMANS AND OTHER ANIMALS (1996); EVOLUTIONARY ETHICS (Matthew & Doris Nitecki eds. 1993); HELEN FISHER, THE FIRST SEX: THE NATURAL TALENTS OF WOMEN AND HOW THEY ARE CHANGING THE WORLD (1999); SCOTT FREEMAN & JON HERRON EVOLUTIONARY ANALYSIS (1998); STEVEN GOLDBERG, WHY MEN RULE: A THEORY OF MALE DOMINANCE (1993); TIMOTHY GOLDSMITH, THE BIOLOGICAL ROOTS OF HUMAN NATURE: FORGING LINKS BETWEEN EVOLUTION AND BEHAVIOR (1991); DIANE HALPERN, SEX DIFFERENCES IN COGNITIVE ABILITIES (2nd ed. 1992); HANDBOOK OF EVOLUTIONARY PSYCHOLOGY: IDEAS, ISSUES, AND APPLICATIONS (Charles Crawford ed. 1998); KATHARINE & KERMIT HOYENGA, GENDER-RELATED DIFFERENCES: ORIGINS AND OUTCOMES (1993); HRDY, *supra* note 104; INVESTIGATING THE BIOLOGICAL FOUNDATIONS OF HUMAN MORALITY (James Hurd ed. 1996); J.R. KREBS & N.B. DAVIES, AN INTRODUCTION TO BEHAVIOURAL ECOLOGY (3rd ed. 1993); ROBERT MCSHEA, MORALITY AND HUMAN NATURE: A NEW ROUTE TO ETHICAL THEORY (1990); ANNE MOIR & DAVID JESSEL, BRAIN SEX: THE REAL DIFFERENCE BETWEEN MEN AND WOMEN (1989); LOUIS PETRINOVICH, HUMAN EVOLUTION, REPRODUCTION, AND MORALITY (1995); ROBERT PLOMIN, NATURE AND NURTURE: AN INTRODUCTION TO HUMAN BEHAVIORAL GENETICS (1990); ROBERT POOL, EVE'S RIB: THE BIOLOGICAL ROOTS OF SEX DIFFERENCES (1994); R.J. RICHARDS, DARWIN AND THE EMERGENCE OF EVOLUTIONARY THEORIES OF MIND AND BEHAVIOR (1989); MATT RIDLEY, THE ORIGINS OF VIRTUE: HUMAN INSTINCTS AND THE EVOLUTION OF COOPERATION (1996); MICHAEL RUSE, TAKING DARWIN SERIOUSLY: A NATURALISTIC APPROACH TO PHILOSOPHY (1998); SOCIOBIOLOGY AND PSYCHOLOGY: IDEAS, ISSUES, AND APPLICATIONS (Charles Crawford *et al.* eds. 1987); SOCIOBIOLOGICAL PERSPECTIVES ON HUMAN DEVELOPMENT (Kevin MacDonald ed. 1988); THE ADAPTED MIND: EVOLUTIONARY PSYCHOLOGY AND THE GENERATION OF CULTURE (Jerome Barkow *et al.* eds. 1992); THE SENSE OF JUSTICE: BIOLOGICAL FOUNDATIONS OF LAW (Roger Masters & Margaret Gruter eds. 1992); ROBERT TRIVERS, SOCIAL EVOLUTION (1985); JONATHAN WEINER, TIME, LOVE, MEMORY: A GREAT BI-

logically based and immutable.[137] They refer to such studies dismissively as "essentialist."[138] Actually, the position of the social biologists is more subtle than that.

Sociobiologists and evolutionary psychologists identify group differences. These differences tell us little or nothing about particular individuals—recall my remarks about Catharine MacKinnon and Phyllis Schafly.[139] Yet the differences are nonetheless real for all that—we are talking about group differences, not individual differences, after all. And the sociobiologists and evolutionary psychologists both emphasize that particular personality traits result from the interaction of genetic predispositions with the environment, not as their critics would have it as being fully dictated by genes.[140] Compare, for example, how an individual's height is a complex interplay between genetic potential, diet, exercise, and perhaps other variables.

The contrary view, that behavioral differences between the sexes result solely from social construction, derives from deconstruction theory that in turn looks back to what has long been the orthodox position in the social sciences. As Émile Durkheim put it, "the determining cause of a social fact should be sought among the social facts preceding it."[141] Sociologist George Murdock went so far as to insist that the study of culture must be "independent of the laws of biology and psychology."[142] Such a view, however, smacks of medieval scholasticism—social constructs become the god of the deconstructionists, a cause that itself is uncaused.[143]

Sociobiologists and evolutionary biologists do not claim that societies must necessarily accede to biological predispositions. They claim only that such predispositions must be understood if social policy is to be made either wisely or effectively.[144] John Beckstrom summarized

---

OLOGIST AND HIS QUEST FOR THE ORIGINS OF BEHAVIOR (1999); JAMES WILSON, THE MORAL SENSE (1993); ROBERT WRIGHT, THE MORAL ANIMAL: THE NEW SCIENCE OF EVOLUTIONARY PSYCHOLOGY (1994).

137. *See, e.g.,* ANNE FAUSTO-STERLING, MYTHS OF GENDER: BIOLOGICAL THEORIES ABOUT WOMEN AND MEN (2nd ed. 1992); Ruth Bleier, *Biology and Women's Policy: A View from the Biological Sciences,* in WOMEN, BIOLOGY, AND PUBLIC POLICY 19 (Virginia Spiro ed. 1985); Ruth Hubbard, *The Political Nature of "Human Nature,"* in THEORETICAL PERSPECTIVES ON SEXUAL DIFFERENCE 63 (Deborah Rhode ed. 1990) ("THEORETICAL PERSPECTIVES"); Kathryn Abrams, *Social Construction, Roving Biologism, and Reasonable Women: A Response to Professor Epstein,* 41 DEPAUL L. REV. 102 (1992); Herma Hill Kay, *Perspectives on Sociobiology, Feminism, and the Law,* in THEORETICAL PERSPECTIVES, *supra,* at 74; Evelyn Fox Keller, *Genetics, Reductionism, and the Normative Uses of Biological Information: Response to Kevles,* 65 S. CAL. L. REV. 285 (1991). *See also* STEPHEN JAY GOULD, THE MISMEASURE OF MAN (1981); PHILIP KITCHER, VAULTING AMBITION: SOCIOBIOLOGY AND THE QUEST FOR HUMAN NATURE (1985); John Dupré, *Global versus Local Perspectives on Sexual Differences,* in THEORETICAL PERSPECTIVES, *supra,* at 47; Eagly, *supra* note 29; Jeffrey Rachlinski, *Comment: Is Evolutionary Analysis of Law Science or Storytelling?,* 41 JURIMETRICS J. 365 (2001); Donald Symons, *A Critique of Darwinian Anthropology,* 10 ETHOLOGY & SOCIOBIOLOGY 131 (1989); Michael Wiederman & Elizabeth Allgeier, *Gender Differences in Mate Selection Criteria: Sociobiological or Socioeconomic Explanation?,* 13 ETHOLOGY & SOCIOBIOLOGY 115 (1992).

138. *See, e.g.,* Kathryn Abrams, *Title VII and the Complex Female Subject,* 92 MICH. L. REV. 2479 (1994); Angela Harris, *Race and Essentialism in Feminist Legal Theory,* 42 STAN. L. REV. 581 (1990); Christine Littleton, *Does It Still Make Sense to Talk about "Women"?,* 1 UCLA WOMEN'S L.J. 15 (1991).

139. See the text *supra* at note 29. *See also* Steven Goldberg, *Statistics, Law, and Justice,* 39 JURIMETRICS J. 255 (1999).

140. *See, e.g.,* Auke Tellegen et al., *Personality Similarity in Twins Reared Apart and Together,* 54 J. PERSONALITY & SOC. PSYCH. 1031, 1036 (1988) (finding a genetic basis for various personality traits ranging from 39% to 58%—with achievement at the low end and self-control at the high end).

141. ÉMILE DURKHEIM, THE RULES OF SOCIOLOGICAL METHOD 110 (8th ed. 1938). *See also* JOHN WATSON, BEHAVIORISM 74–75 (1925). *See generally* Browne, *supra* note 29, at 1037, 1050–64.

142. George Murdock, *The Science of Culture,* 34 AM. ANTHROPOLOGIST 200, 200 (1932).

143. MICHAEL LEVIN, FEMINISM AND FREEDOM 67 (1987). Compare the position of the "deconstructionists" discussed *supra* at notes 17–41.

144. JOHN BECKSTROM, EVOLUTIONARY JURISPRUDENCE: PROSPECTS AND LIMITATIONS ON THE USE OF MODERN DARWINISM THROUGHOUT THE LEGAL PROCESS (1989); Kingsley Browne, *Biology, Equality, and the Law: The Legal Significance of Biological Sex Differences,* 38 SW. L.J. 617 (1984); Browne, *supra* note 29, at

the correct approach to using evolutionary psychology for designing legal policy by drawing an analogy to an airline ticket office: "It may be of little or no help in telling us where we ought to go, but it may help us estimate the costs of getting there and help us to make the journey."[145]

For our purposes, it really does not matter whether the different voice (as distinct from the lost voice) theory is correct. The historical enterprise is necessarily different from the enterprise of giving voice to groups excluded from contemporary social or political discourse. After all, unlike the silenced living, we cannot interview persons whose voices were not recorded centuries ago.[146] And the records of what "real" people were thinking gets awfully thin awfully quickly as we go back in history. Historians seeking lost voices therefore seek to "decode" the historical record to discover hidden "counter-meanings" to what was written or otherwise recorded. Decoding, as historian Carroll Smith-Rosenberg (one of its noted practitioners) has virtually admitted, is the projecting of one's subjective reactions to past events onto long-dead observers or actors:

> "Public language" exists to convey socially shared experiences in an affective but deliberately distorted manner. Driven to discuss what is too painful or too political to be discussed overtly, societies as a whole, or specific groups within them, develop metaphoric or mythic systems that cloak real meanings behind symbolic masks. The most "public language" thus can be decoded to reveal the interplay of social experience and emotional realities. Sociological realities and political motivations will then emerge, not stripped bare by analysis, but enveloped in the feelings that constitute one of their most central components.[147]

All historians engage in decoding the past. Traditionally, historians sought to do so by attempting to learn what particular words or phrases meant in particular times past. But a conclusion that such records as we have are "deliberately distorted" regarding all matters of significance would appear to make the study of history utterly impossible. Smith-Rosenberg and similar "postmodernist" historians, however, conclude that this lack of evidence empowers an "historian" by enabling her to project whatever meaning she wants onto the past.

To the extent that historians use lost voice theory to project by extrapolating from highly dubious contemporary visions, the results tell us a good deal about contemporary politics, but little about the past.[148] This pattern, found increasingly in many scholarly fields, has also begun to spread into other segments of society. For example, Joe McGinnis, among other supposedly "reputable" journalists or biographers, has taken to imagining the thoughts and words of living people without bothering to interview them or even in disregard of actual interviews.[149]

---

973–85; Owen Jones, *Law and Evolutionary Biology: Obstacles and Opportunities,* 10 J. CONTEMP. HEALTH L. & POL'Y 265 (1994); Owen Jones, *Evolutionary Analysis in Law: An Introduction and Application to Child Abuse,* 75 N.C. L. REV. 1117, 1160–70 (1997); Owen Jones, *The Evolution of Irrationality,* 41 JURIMETRICS J. 289 (2001); Jeffrey Evans Stake, *Comment: Can Evolutionary Science Contribute to Discussions of Law?,* 41 JURIMETRICS J. 379 (2001).

145. BECKSTROM, *supra* note 144, at 39.

146. *See* Stephen Daniels, *"You Can't Interview the Dead": McIntosh's* The Appeal of the Civil Law *and the Debate over Longitudinal Studies of Courts,* 17 LAW & SOC. INQUIRY 291 (1992); Lawrence Friedman, *Civil Wrongs: Personal Injury Law in the Late 19th Century,* 1987 A.B.F. RES. J. 351, 354–55.

147. SMITH-ROSENBERG, *supra* note 118, at 45. *See also* HARRISON, *supra* note 118, at 154–58; SMITH-ROSENBERG, *supra,* at 179–80; Gerda Lerner, *Placing Women in History: Problems and Challenges,* 3 FEMINIST STUD. 10 (1975).

148. For an example of where passionate feminism can lead in historical analysis, see R.H. Helmholz, *Book Rev.,* 44 J. LEGAL EDUC. 140 (1994) [reviewing EILEEN SPRING, LAW, LAND AND FAMILY: ARISTOCRATIC INHERITANCE IN ENGLAND, 1300 TO 1800 (1993)].

149. Michiko Kakutani, *Is It Fiction? Is It Nonfiction? And Why Doesn't Anyone Care?: The Issues Joe McGinnis Has Stirred Up Go Way Beyond His Book,* N.Y. TIMES, July 27, 1993, at C13. *See also* Masson v. New York Times, 501 U.S. 496 (1991).

For many historians, the model for this sort of history is Michel Foucault and his attempts to "deconstruct" the accepted history of western society over the past three centuries or so in order to substitute his own vision of the past.[150] Foucault's personal agenda appears to have been a desire to delegitimate the social and legal proscription of homosexuality in western societies. In order to do so, he was notoriously indifferent to facts, ignoring or distorting inconvenient details that might make his attempted reconstruction of the past less plausible.[151] As a sympathetic biographer noted, "Foucault definitely prefers ideological drama to the wayward contingencies of social history."[152] Many of Foucault's admirers seem unaware of his difficulty with facts, but a few have frankly embraced Foucault's wayward approach to facts, arguing that Foucault is theoretically or rhetorically correct even if he is empirically wrong.[153] It remains unclear how one can be "theoretically" or "rhetorically" correct if one must get major facts wrong in order to reach the conclusions one seeks.

The import of such arguments is all too clear. Facts must give way before political preferences. As Ruth Shalit summarized the results of such a "scholarly" enterprise:

> During the last decade feminist scholars have embarked on a campaign to uncover and to promote the timid exploits of "lesser lives," as revealed in the prayerful and humble diaries of unpaid wet nurses, hapless milkmaids, shy spinsters, and sweet domestics. Great claims are were made for the revolutionary potential of these "found narratives," which often amounted to little more than the daily record-keeping of genteel housewifery. "As feminists have insisted that battles for power, authenticity, moral stature, and survival occur as fiercely within the domestic as in the public arena of life, what was once seen as placidly domestic now offers the reader a world charged with great issues".... But too often, alas, the diaries of the widows and fishwives turn out to be something less than one would hope. These redoubtable women were reluctant to discuss personal emotions, or expose their lives, thoughts, and feelings in any meaningful way.... There is, in fact, a poignant gulf between the swaggering claims of the feminist

---

150. *See* FOUCAULT, *supra* note 19; MICHEL FOUCAULT, DISCIPLINE AND PUNISH: THE BIRTH OF THE PRISON (Alan Sheridan trans. 1979); MICHEL FOUCAULT, THE HISTORY OF SEXUALITY (Robert Hurley trans. 1980) ("FOUCAULT, SEXUALITY"); MICHEL FOUCAULT, POWER/KNOWLEDGE: SELECTED INTERVIEWS AND WRITINGS 119 (Colin Gordon *et al.* trans. 1980) ("FOUCAULT, POWER/KNOWLEDGE"). For an examination of the influence of Foucault on feminist history and feminist thinking generally, see ZILLAH EISENSTEIN, THE FEMALE BODY AND THE LAW (1988); FEMINISM AND FOUCAULT, *supra* note 134; SUSAN HEKMAN, GENDER AND KNOWLEDGE: ELEMENTS OF A POST-MODERN FEMINISM 175–88 (1990); CHRIS WEEDON, FEMINIST PRACTICE AND POSTSTRUCTURALIST THEORY 125 (1987); Annie Bunting, *Feminism, Foucault, and Law as Power/Knowledge,* 30 ALBERTA L. REV. 829 (1992); Jana Sawicki, *Foucault and Feminism: Toward a Politics of Discourse,* in FEMINIST INTERPRETATIONS AND POLITICAL THEORY 226 (Mary Lyndon Shanley & Carole Pateman eds. 1991); Carol Smart, *Law's Power, the Sexed Body, and Feminist Discourse,* 17 J. LAW & SOC'Y 194 (1990).

151. *See, e.g.,* JOHN LANGBEIN, TORTURE AND THE LAW OF PROOF: EUROPE AND ENGLAND IN THE ANCIEN REGIME 27–60 (1977); PIETER SPIERENBERG, THE SPECTACLE OF SUFFERING: EXECUTIONS AND THE EVOLUTION OF REPRESSION 64, 108–09 (1984); David Garland, *Foucault's* Discipline and Punish: *An Exposition and Critique,* 1986 ABF RES. J. 847; Harold Tanner, *Policing, Punishment, and the Individual: Criminal Justice in China,* 20 LAW & SOC. INQUIRY 277, 288–89 (1995). Some make similar comments about the "scholarship" of Jacques Derrida. For example, one scholar commented that "Jacques Derrida risks giving bad faith a bad name." Mark Lilla, *The Politics of Jacques Derrida,* N.Y. REV. BOOKS, June 25, 1998, at 36, 40. Another commented that Derrida is "the sort of scholar who gives bullshit a bad name. We cannot, of course, exclude the possibility that this may be an expression of praise in the deconstructionist vocabulary." John Searle, *The World Turned Upside Down* (book rev.), N.Y. REV. BOOKS, Oct. 27, 1983, at 74, 78 n.3.

152. J.G. MERQUIOR, FOUCAULT 97 (1985). *See generally* Vikki Bell, *"Beyond the 'Thorny Question'": Feminism, Foucault and the Desexualisation of Rape,* 19 INT'L J. SOC. OF LAW 83 (1991).

153. *See, e.g.,* Michael Dutton, *One Story, Two Readings: A Response to Harold Tanner,* 20 LAW & SOC. INQUIRY 305, 310 n.5 (1995); Nanette Funk, *Abortion Counselling* (sic) *and the 1995 German Abortion Law,* 12 CONN. J. INT'L L. 33, 62–63 (1996). *See also* Hutchinson, *supra* note 15, at 1190–91.

historiographers and the mild, matronly tone of the actual documents, which are often cloying paeans to the glowing hearth and the patter of little feet.[154]

George Orwell pointed out many years ago that such authors obfuscate their meanings in excess and obscure verbiage in an attempt—too often successfully—to sound profound and insightful when they really have nothing to say.[155] Or they seek to sound like they are making an argument when they are actually avoiding serious engagement with the ideas of others.[156] As Foucault's influence suggests, men historians can play this game as easily as women historians,[157] yet feminist historians seem particularly prone to rewriting the past based on a political vision rather than on an examination of the factual record.

Smith-Rosenberg has admitted as much about her own "decoding" of the past, writing that "[w]ithout question, our first inspiration was political.... The intricate relations between the construction of gender and the structure of power became our principal concern."[158] Smith-Rosenberg applied her approach by using pop-psychology terms to explain the appeal of the anti-abortion ideology that animated the enactment of the nineteenth-century statutes. After arguing that men were afraid that women would enter the "public realm" to compete with men for jobs, she went on to assert:

> The image of the lethally powerful aborting woman not only bespoke men's professional anxieties; it expressed far more universal and psychological primitive fears and projections. Indeed, the psychosexual is as revealing as the professional. Each constitutes one pole in a complex symbolic language. Both meanings were deeply appealing. We must decipher both if we are to understand the mass appeal the anti-abortion movement wielded.[159]

Smith-Rosenberg went on to posit a "new Oedipal triangle, linking the male physician with the male (*sic*) fetus against the mother. The mother was potentially lethal and insane.... When the physician actually prevented an abortion, it was he, not the mother, who gave the fetus life."[160]

Yet, as Marvin Olasky commented, Smith-Rosenberg's "psychohistory is too farfetched for all but the most avid proponents of abortion."[161] In fact, Smith-Rosenberg's psychobabble reveals far more about her projections onto men than about nineteenth-century male projections onto aborting mothers. In particular, Smith-Rosenberg's fantasies about "primitive male fears" ignores, indeed completely devalues, the ideas and importance of nineteenth century feminists who were virtually unanimous in their hostility to abortion and in their support of the abortion statutes.[162] No wonder feminist historians like Smith-Rosenberg have been intensely criticized by other women as too class-based (bourgeois") and race-based ("white") in their thinking.[163]

---

154. Shalit, *supra* note 134, at 38.

155. George Orwell, *Politics and the English Language*, in A COLLECTION OF ESSAYS BY GEORGE ORWELL 162 (a Doubleday Anchor Book 1954). *See also* RICHARD EVANS, IN DEFENSE OF HISTORY (1998); ALAN SOKAL & JEAN BRICMONT, FASHIONABLE NONSENSE: POSTMODERN PHILOSOPHERS' ABUSE OF SCIENCE (1998).

156. Nagel, *supra* note 116, at 38.

157. *See, e.g.*, G.R. QUAIFE, WANTON WENCHES AND WAYWARD WIVES: PEASANTS AND ILLICIT SEX IN EARLY SEVENTEENTH CENTURY ENGLAND (1979), and the critique of Quaife in MARTIN INGRAM, CHURCH COURTS, SEX AND MARRIAGE IN ENGLAND, 1570–1640, at 159–61 (1987).

158. SMITH-ROSENBERG, *supra* note 118, at 12. *See also* M.M. Slaughter, *The Legal Construction of "Mother,"* in MOTHERS IN LAW: FEMINIST THEORY AND THE LEGAL REGULATION OF MOTHERHOOD 73 (Martha Albertson Fineman & Isabel Karpin eds. 1995).

159. SMITH-ROSENBERG, *supra* note 118, at 239.

160. *Id.* at 242.

161. MARVIN OLASKY, ABORTION RIGHTS: A SOCIAL HISTORY OF ABORTION IN AMERICA 285 (1992).

162. *See* Chapter 8.

163. SMITH-ROSENBERG, *supra* note 118, at 16. *See also* Tarczylo, *supra* note 91, at 27–28.

Such approaches lend themselves to unbounded fantasies that too often end in unintentional silliness. The work of Janet Brodie provides an all too typical an example. Having searched without success for evidence that Henry Clarke Wright had lectured in the late nineteenth century about contraception, Brodie concluded that "[i]f Wright did not explicitly speak of contraception to the audiences attending his lectures he may well have done so quietly to smaller, more informal groups after the actual lecture."[164] He may well have had orgies with such groups, for all we know—or he might never have met with such groups at all. Or consider historian Susan Klepp, who insists that "a careful analysis of the language of eighteenth-century women, reinterpreting the now-hidden meanings of women's words in the light of twentieth century understandings, can recover the lost technology of fertility control."[165] The quality of her "recovery" is shown by her extended discussion of an English abortion statute of 1623.[166] The only the problem is that there is no such statute. Klepp apparently was confused about the provisions of a 1624 statute that was directed as suppressing infanticide by creating a presumption of murder from the concealment of the death of an infant.[167] The depth of Klepp's confusion—or indifference to facts—is indicated by her extended discussion of the latter presumption as if it derived from a different statute.[168]

Brody and Klepp are only slightly less silly than Umberto Eco in describing the whimsical decision of the protagonists of his novel, *Foucault's Pendulum*, to interpret a simple driver's manual as disclosing that an automobile exists "only to serve as a metaphor of creation."[169] The engine is "Omnia Movens," the ultimate source that "communicates its creative energy to the...higher wheels: the Wheel of Intelligence and the Wheel of Knowledge," while the clutch is "the Sefirah of grace that establishes or interrupts the flow of love that binds the rest of the tree [the drive shaft] to the Supernal Energy."[170] In a more strictly legal setting, law professor Sidney DeLong chose to illustrate the silliness of such "analyses" by reading a mandate for traditional gender roles into the following passage from the Uniform Commercial Code:

> (1) If a security interest in goods was perfected and subsequently the goods or a part thereof have become part of a product or mass, the security interest continues in the product or mass if
>
> (a) the goods are so manufactured, processed, assembled or commingled that their identity is lost in the product or mass....[171]

DeLong suggested that the commentary reveals the hidden meaning in the Code when it discusses the commingling of flour, sugar, and eggs (the female) into a cake and then the assembly of components into a machine (the masculine), an intent merely "emphasized" by the very absence of any mention of such concepts in the text of the Code itself.[172] De Long, like Eco, was writing with tongue firmly in cheek. One would presume that no one would ever take such assertions seriously. After all, lawyers do not confuse the Constitution with a recipe for key lime pie; nor do chefs discover that cooking recipes reveal insights into legal rights or the separation

---

164. Janet Farrell Brodie, Contraception and Abortion in Nineteenth-Century America 112 (1994).

165. Susan Klepp, *Lost, Hidden, Obstructed, and Repressed,* in Early American Technology: Making and Doing Things from the Colonial Era to 1850, at 68, 70 (Judith McGaw ed. 1994).

166. *Id.,* at 73–74, 76.

167. 21 James I ch. 27, §3 (1624). *See* Chapter 2, at notes 335–42, 366–424, 504–27.

168. Klepp, *supra* note 165, at 74–76.

169. Umberto Eco, Foucault's Pendulum 378 (William Weaver trans. 1989).

170. *Id.* at 378–79.

171. UCC §9-315.

172. Sidney DeLong, *Jacques of All Trades: Derrida, Lacan, and the Commercial Lawyer,* 45 J. Legal Educ. 131, 136 (1995).

of governmental powers.[173] If such parodies strike you as too extreme, however, consider the following from feminist icon Luce Irigaray:

> Is $E=MC^2$ a sexed equation? Perhaps it is. Let us make the hypothesis that it is insofar as it privileges the speed of light over other speeds that are vitally necessary to us. What seems to me to indicate the possible sexed nature of the equation is not directly its uses by nuclear weapons, rather it is having privileged what goes the fastest....[174]

Irigaray, however, is not joking, nor is she alone.[175] One would never guess from reading such a passage that the relationship between energy, mass, and the speed of light had an empirical basis. Rather than persuading us of the "privileging" of the speed of light, she and those who write like her simply display their ignorance. Such nonsense does serve a purpose, however. There is, after all, "no direct way to refute a fogbank."[176] As philosopher Thomas Nagel put it,

> The[se] writers...use technical terms without knowing what they mean, refer to theories and formulas that they do not understand in the slightest, and invoke modern physics and mathematics in support of psychological, sociological, political, and philosophical claims to which they have no relevance. It is not always easy to tell how much is due to invincible stupidity and how much to the desire to cow the audience with fraudulent displays of theoretical sophistication. Lacan and Baudrillard come across as complete charlatans, Irigaray as an idiot, Kristeva and Deleuze as a mixture of the two. But these are delicate judgments.[177]

Brodie, of course, is not so extreme as Irigaray, yet her arguments too are just plain silly. In fact, I suspect that Brodie herself knows how silly her argument is. After all, just a few pages onward she criticized unnamed historians for assuming without evidence that any woman who traveled the public lecture circuit in the nineteenth century must have lectured on reproductive control.[178] Another example of presumably unintended silliness is provided by the insistence of some feminist historians on using the word "herstory" instead of "history"—an insistence that merely betrays the "herstorians'" ignorance of the etymology of words.[179] In a like vein are such new, but already standard terms, as "malestream," meaning any form of moral reasoning that the author or speaker doesn't approve of and used largely as an attempt to silence opponents rather than to reason about points of disagreement.[180] Nor should one neglect contemporary

---

173. KIM SCHEPPLE, LEGAL SECRETS 89–90 n.13 (1988).

174. As quoted in Nagel, *supra* note 116, at 33.

175. *See generally* SOKAL & BRICMONT, *supra* note 155.

176. Nagel, *supra* note 116, at 34.

177. *Id.* at 33. *See also* Fernando Tesón, *Feminism and International Law: A Reply,* 33 VA. J. INT'L L. 647, 679–80 (1993) (discussing the abandonment of the scientific method by some strands of feminist thought).

178. BRODIE, *supra* note 164, at 119–21. Contrast this with Brodie's own assertions regarding Henry Clarke Wright, discussed *supra* at note 164.

179. *See, e.g.,* Janis McDonald, *The Need for Contextual ReVision: Mercy Otis Warren,* 5 YALE J.L. & FEMINISM 183, 214–15 (1992). *Cf.* Matthew Ritter, *The Penile Code: The Gendered Nature of the Language of the Law,* 2 N.Y.C. L. REV. 1 (1998). For more general arguments in favor of using "politically correct" language, see CHERIS KRAMARAE, WOMEN AND MEN SPEAKING (1981); SEXIST LANGUAGE: A MODERN PHILOSOPHICAL ANALYSIS (Mary Vetterling-Braggin ed. 1981); THE WOMEN AND LANGUAGE DEBATE: A SOURCE BOOK (Camille Roman *et al.* eds. 1994); Robin Barnes, *Standing Guard for the P.C. Militia, or, Fighting Hatred and Indifference: Some Thoughts on Expressive hate-Conduct and Political Correctness,* 1992 U. ILL. L. REV. 979; Fatemah Khoroshahi, *Penguins Don't Care, but Women Do: A Social Identity Analysis of a Whorfian Problem,* LANGUAGE SOC'Y, Fall 1989, at 505; Cheryl Preston, *This Old House: A Blueprint for Constructive Feminism,* 83 GEO. L.J. 2271, 2292–98 (1995).

180. *See, e.g.,* HARRISON, *supra* note 118, at 10; MARY O'BRIEN, THE POLITICS OF REPRODUCTION 5 (1981) (perhaps the first usage of the term); SHERWIN, *supra* note 118, at 37; Lisa Brush, *The Curious Courtship of Feminist Jurisprudence and Feminist State Theory: Smart on the Power of Law,* 19 LAW & SOC. INQUIRY 1059, 1066 (1994).

calls for a "mamafesta" (not *manifesto*) of women's rights, a term that was invented by a man (James Joyce) as something of a joke.[181] In a similar vein, a woman law professor recently substituted the term "womentoring" for "mentoring," without noticing that the new word still has the offending syllable.[182] The greatest absurdity comes in the attempt to portray "intimacy" among women as "natural" and the "privileging" of heterosexual relations as "artificial."[183] Silly, ludicrous, absurd, but hardly laughable when its practitioners attempt to gain coercive power to compel all to incorporate the neologisms into their vocabularies, and the agenda carried by the new words.

Such "historians" simply ignore "the stubborn resistance of the raw materials."[184] The approach poses "serious epistemological problems for historians...challeng[ing] the notion of contextualizing past events and documents" as the method for understanding the past and its meaning.[185] It lends itself to the sort of advocacy scholarship that bedevils the legal enterprise.[186] As a result, even radically revisionist historians are often skeptical, if not downright hostile, to "post modernist" history.[187]

Linda Gordon is one of the few of the new historians to admit that much of her work on the history of birth control is "not a history but a schematic hypothesis [that] does not purport to describe what actually happened but [that] offers a theoretical model of the way it might have happened."[188] Such an admission brings to mind the "lives" of saints written by medieval monks in which the imagination of the author filled in innumerable details in the absence of, or even in defiance of, the relevant written records. Gordon's disclaimer has not prevented others from relying on her work as if it were divine revelation.[189] Gordon promotes such reverence by never referring to the imaginative quality of her work after she first mentions it and by never indicating which parts of her work represent historical data and which are, shall we say, creative.

The pattern of believing what one wants and of disregarding or even fabricating evidence is not limited to feminist historians. Several mainstream historians have attracted considerable attention by writing works that read more like novellas than like history. Best known among these works probably are Natalie Zemon Davis' *The Return of Martin Guerre* (1983), or Simon Schama's *Dead Certainties*.[190] Both of these works feature invented dialogue and considerable

---

181. *See* Drucilla Cornell, Beyond Feminism: Ethical Feminism, Deconstruction, and the Law 1–2 (1991); Wright, *supra* note 129, at 117–18.

182. Leslie Bender, *For Mary Joe Frug: Empowering Women Law Professors*, 6 Wis. Women's L.J. 1, 2 (1991).

183. *See, e.g.,* Foucault, Sexuality, *supra* note 150; Adrienne Rich, Of Women Born (1976); Smith-Rosenberg, *supra* note 118, at 26–42, 53–76, 266–96; Sandra Gilbert, *Costumes of the Mind: Transvestism as Metaphor in Modern Literature*, Critical Inquiry, Winter 1980, at 391; Ellen Ross & Rayna Rapp, *Sex and Society: A Research Note from Social History and Anthropology*, 23 Comp. Stud. in Soc'y & Hist. 51 (1981).

184. J. Willard Hurst, Justice Holmes on Legal History 61 (1964).

185. Cornell, *supra* note 91, at 2. *See generally* R.H. Collingwood, The Idea of History (1946); Murray Murphy, Our Knowledge of the Historical Past (1973); Quentin Skinner, *Meaning and Understanding in the History of Ideas*, 8 Hist. & Theory 3 (1969).

186. Glendon, *supra* note 10, at 208; Collins, *supra* note 55; Quinn, *supra* note 55.

187. *See, e.g.,* Bryan Stone, Descent into Discourse: The Reification of Language and the Writings of Social History (1990); Lawrence Stone, *History and Post-Modernism*, 135 Past & Present 189 (1992); Steven Watts, *The Idiocy of American Studies: Poststructuralism, Language, and Politics in the Age of Self-Fulfillment*, 43 Am. Q. 625 (1991).

188. Gordon, *supra* note 70, at 4 n.*.

189. *See, e.g.,* Connie Paige, The Right to Lifers: Who They Are; How They Operate; Where They Get Their Money 33 (1983).

190. Natalie Zemon Davis, The Return of Martin Guerre (1983); Simon Schama, Dead Certainties (1991). The books are great reads and perhaps capture the essence of the times which they describe, but should we describe historical novels as "history."

speculative material not supported by the actual records on which the studies were based and without any guidance to the readers as to what in the book was taken more or less directly from the record and what was invented. All historical writings involve imaginative reconstruction to some extent,[191] but there remains a fundamental distinction between inductive inferences and pure invention or the introduction of anachronistic material from a different age.[192] Historians such as Davis, Gordon, and Schama simply break faith with audiences who look to them to discover the origins of contemporary social institutions and practices, or for the roots of their own identity.[193] Their inferences must be verifiable against the evidence.[194] And while streamlining a work by omitting footnotes or other attempts at verification might very well make the work more accessible to a general audience, it renders the work virtually useless to any serious student of the topic.[195] Without any attempt to distinguish between fact and fiction, the work undermines the credibility of the verifiable, rather than validating the unverifiable.[196]

We should not put too much blame on historians, feminist or otherwise. A fair number of feminist scholars besides historians seem to be even more prone to wishful versions of history or just plain nonsense.[197] A feminist law professor even felt it necessary to explain that the word "mother" is gendered (*i.e.,* does not include men—at least sometimes).[198] Or consider the tale that the phrase "rule of thumb" refers to an ancient common law rule that a husband was privileged to chastise his wife with a stick no thicker than his thumb. There were cartoons indicating such a rule in the eighteenth century, but no actual evidence of such a rule from judicial decisions—ever.[199] The linkage of this "folklaw" to the phrase "rule of thumb" apparently originated

---

191. JOHN DEMOS, THE UNREDEEMED CAPTIVE 22–23 (1994); Gordon, *supra* note 93, at 16.

192. *See generally* Bruce Kimball, *"Warn Students that I Entertain Heretical Opinions, Which They Are not to Take as Law": The Inception of Case Method Teaching in the Classrooms of early C.C. Langdell, 1870–1883,* 17 LAW & HIST. REV. 57, 78–84 (1999).

193. *Cf.* Robert Darnton, *Looking the Devil in the Face,* N.Y. REV. BOOKS, Feb. 10, 2000, at 14, 14:

> Of course, there are philosophical problems inherent in the notion of factuality, and no history can be written without resort to artifice, not merely in combining evidence but also in using words. Nonetheless, any historian who makes up evidence or presents fantasy as fact breaks the contract. He or she is guilty of bad faith.

194. *See* Robert Finley, *AHR Forum:* The Return of Martin Guerre, *The Refashioning of Martin Guerre,* 93 AM. HIST. REV. 553 (1988).

195. Kimball, *supra* note 192, at 82–83.

196. *Id.* at 83, n. 85.

197. *See* MARTHA NUSSBAUM, SEX AND SOCIAL JUSTICE 136 (1999) (conceding that many "factual" claims by fellow feminists cannot be substantiated); DAPHNE PATAI, HETEROPHOBIA: SEXUAL HARASSMENT AND THE FUTURE 61–62 (1998) (noting the "gender bias" in the purported statistics used to discuss harassment); CHRISTINA HOFF SOMMERS, WHO STOLE FEMINISM? HOW WOMEN HAVE BETRAYED WOMEN 225–26 (1994) (noting the tendency of self-proclaimed feminists to "alarm the public with inflated statistics"). *See also* Neil Gilbert, *The Phantom Epidemic of Sexual Assault,* 103 PUB. INTEREST 54 (1991); Edward Greer, *Tales of Sexual Panic in the Legal Academy: The Assault on Reverse Interest Suits,* 48 CASE-W.R. L. REV. 513 (1998); Edward Greer, *The Truth behind Legal Dominance Feminism's "Two Percent False Rape Claim" Figure,* 33 LOY.-L.A. L. REV. 947 (2000) ("Greer, *False Rape*"); M.Z. Rosaldo, *The Use and Abuse of Anthropology: Reflections on Feminism and Cross-Cultural Understanding,* 5 SIGNS 392 (1980).

198. Elizabeth Clark, *Love and Chicken Soup for Free: Goldstein's* Mother-Love and Abortion, 16 LAW AND SOC. INQUIRY 161, 161 n.2 (1991). *See also* MARTHA ALBERTSON FINEMAN, THE NEUTERED MOTHER: THE SEXUAL FAMILY AND OTHER TWENTIETH CENTURY TRAGEDIES 234–35 (1995); MOTHERING: ESSAYS IN FEMINIST THEORY (Joyce Trebilcot ed. 1983); Katharine Baker, *Taking Care of Our Daughters* (book rev.), 18 CARDOZO L. REV. 1495 (1997).

199. State v. Rhodes, 61 N.C. 453 (1868) (rejecting supposed then rule of thumb). *See generally* Henry Ansgar Kelly, *Rule of Thumb and the Folklaw of the Husband's Stick,* 44 J. LEGAL EDUC. 341 (1994). *See also* WILLIAM PROSSER, HANDBOOK OF THE LAW OF TORTS 136 (4th ed. 1971).

in the imagination of an English journalist—Terry Davidson.[200] The phrase "rule of thumb" is actually much older than those eighteenth-century cartoons and was always used in its modern sense of a rule developed from practice or experience rather than a description of a switch for beating a wife.[201] But the legend that the phrase referred to wife beating has now become thoroughly entrenched in feminist writings,[202] so much so that a feminist who uses the phrase in its ordinary sense has been accused of being "politically incorrect."[203] One suspects that the myth of

---

200. Terry Davidson, *Wifebeating: A Recurring Phenomenon throughout History,* in A PHENOMENOLOGICAL STUDY OF DOMESTIC VIOLENCE 2, 18 (Maria Roy ed. 1977). A whimsical use of the expression "rule of thumb" to describe the folklaw myth is found a year earlier in DEL MARTIN, BATTERED WIVES 31 (1976) (describing the folklaw rule as "a rule of thumb, so to speak"). These references and a discussion of the background of Terry Davidson is found in Kelly, *supra* note 199, at 343–44.

201. Kelly, *supra* note 199, at 342–43. Some have speculated that the phrase came originally from woodworking. SOMMERS, *supra* note 197, at 204–05.

202. The following cite Davidson and little, if anything else: LENORE WALKER, THE BATTERED WOMAN 12 (1979); Deborah Goelman, *Shelter from the Storm: Using Jurisdictional Stautes to Protect Victims of Domestic Violence after the Violence against Women Act,* 13 COLUMN J. GENDER J.L. 101, 104 (2004); Martha Fineman, *Dominant Discourse, Professional Language, and Legal Change in Child Custody Decisionmaking,* 101 HARV. L. REV. 727, 740 n.52 (1988); Victoria Mikesell Mather, *The Skeleton in the Closet, the Battered Woman Syndrome, Self-Defense, and Expert Testimony,* 39 MERCER L. REV. 545, 547–48 (1988); Jeanne Schroeder, *Using Battered Women Syndrome Evidence in the Prosecution of a Batterer,* 76 IOWA L. REV. 553, 555 n.17 (1991); Kerry Shad, *State v. Norman: Self-Defense Unavailable to Battered Women Who Kill Passive Abusers,* 68 N.C. L. REV. 1159, 1165 n. 43 (1990); Reva Siegel, *"The Rule of Love": Wife-Beating as Prerogative and Privacy,* 105 YALE L.J. 2117, 2207 (1996). *See also* Hope Keating, *Battered Women in Florida: Will Justice Be Served?,* 20 FLA. ST. U. L. REV. 679, 680–81 (citing Mather, *supra*); Lea VanderVelde, *The Legal Ways of Seduction,* 48 STAN. L. REV. 817, 820 n.8 (1996) (citing the then unpublished article by Reva Siegel). Others simply don't cite any source for the tale. *See, e.g.,* UNDER THE RULE OF THUMB: BATTERED WOMEN AND THE ADMINISTRATION OF JUSTICE: A REPORT OF THE UNITED STATES CIVIL RIGHTS COMMISSION 2 (1982); Nan Oppenheimer, *The Evolution of Law and Wife Abuse,* 3 LAW & POL'Y Q. 382, 387 (1981). Lawrence Stone, a distinguished historian, repeats the myth, supporting it with citations that do not refer to it. LAWRENCE STONE, THE ROAD TO DIVORCE: ENGLAND, 1530–1987, at 201 (1990). But then Stone, in another book, quoted a sermon as supporting the right of a husband to beat his wife when in fact the sermonist said exactly the opposite. LAWRENCE STONE, THE FAMILY, SEX, AND MARRIAGE IN ENGLAND 1500–1800, at 198 (1977). *See* Kelly, *supra* note 199, at 362–63. One source even cites Prosser for this use of the expression, although Prosser denied any privilege tested by the size of the husband's thumb ever existed. Pauline Gee, *Ensuring Police Protection for Battered Women: The* Scott v. Hart *Suit,* 8 SIGNS 554, 555 (1983). This entire question is explored in SOMMERS, *supra* note 197, at 205–07; Kelly, *supra,* at 344–49.

Similarly embedded in feminist folklore is the claim that only two percent of all rape charges are false. *See, e.g.,* JULIE ALLISON & LAWRENCE WRIGHTSMAN, RAPE: THE MISUNDERSTOOD CRIME 205 (1993); HELEN BENEDICT, VIRGIN OR VAMP: HOW THE PRESS COVERS SEX CRIMES 18 (1992); SUSAN BROWNMILLER, AGAINST OUR WILL: MEN, WOMEN AND RAPE 410 (1976); SEDELLE KATZ & MARY ANN MAZUR, UNDERSTANDING THE RAPE VICTIM: A SYNTHESIS OF RESEARCH FINDINGS 209 (1979); RHODE, SPEAKING OF SEX, *supra* note 118, at 125; Louise Fitzgerald, *Science v. Myth: The Failure of Reason in the Clarence Thomas Hearings,* 65 S. CAL. L. REV. 1399, 1404 (1992); Kathy Mack, *Continuing Barriers to Women's Credibility: A Feminist Perspective on the Proof Process,* 4 CRIM. L.F. 327, 336 (1993); Wendy Murphy, *Minimizing the Likelihood of Discovery of Victims' Counseling Records and Other Personal Information in Criminal Cases: Massachusetts Gives a Nod to a Constitutional Right to Confidentiality,* 32 NEW ENG. L. REV. 983, 1006–07 n.120 (1998); Roberta O'Neale, *Court Ordered Psychiatric Examination of a Rape Victim in a Criminal Rape Prosecution—or How Many Times Must a Woman Be Raped?,* 18 STA. CLARA L. REV. 119, 141 (1978); Elizabeth Pendo, *Recognizing Violence against Women: Gender and the Hate Crimes Statistics Act,* 17 HARV. WOMEN'S L.J. 157, 171 (1994); Beverly Ross, *Does Diversity in Legal Scholarship Make a Difference? A Look at the Law of Rape,* 100 DICK. L. REV. 795, 812 (1996); Eloise Salholz, *Sex Crimes: Women on Trial,* NEWSWEEK, Dec. 16, 1991, at 22; Lynn Hecht Schafran, *Writing and Reading about Rape: A Primer,* 66 ST. JOHN'S L. REV. 979, 1013 (1993); Morrison Torrey, *When Will We Be Believed? Rape Myths and the Idea of a Fair Trial in Rape Prosecutions,* 24 U.C. DAVIS L. REV. 1013, 1028 (1991). For the provenance of this undoubtedly false claim, see Greer, *False Rape, supra* note 197, at 954–60.

203. Martha Fineman & Anne Ople, *The Uses of Social Science Data in Legal Decisionmaking: Custody Determinations at Divorce,* 1987 WIS. L. REV. 107, 109 n.5. *See generally* Kelly, *supra* note 199, at 341–42.

the "rule of thumb" is now so well entrenched (and fits so nicely with the prejudices of the writers) that it will not go away even if these writers become aware of their error.

Such an approach to history is a part of the broader pattern of disparaging the significance of public discourse that has been a prime feature of twentieth-century intellectual life, a disparagement that is especially misleading relative to abortion even in purely modern contexts.[204] Historians like Carroll Smith-Rosenberg are ideologues. They deceive others only because they first deceive themselves.[205] Smith-Rosenberg projects a past in which women are oppressed victims, in which social processes are what happens to women rather than what women, as well as men, do. Law professor Catharine MacKinnon is even more insistent regarding such claims, insisting that we cannot discern a "woman's voice" because women are so systematically oppressed that they have no voice in which to speak.[206] Carol Smart even counsels against resort to law or the state in struggles to improve women's status because those institutions invariably victimize women.[207]

Some advocates of women's victimhood go even further. Simone de Beauvoir argued that women were doomed to be subordinated to men because of the very nature of the sexual act itself. In her view, heterosexual intercourse dooms women to a passive role with the man always playing the active role, man the subject penetrating women the object, as de Beauvoir put it.[208] (What might one speculate about her sex life?) Robin West is so committed to characterizing women as victims that she ascribes femininity to a male character in a novel without women characters simply on the basis that her favored male is a victim.[209] West also described childbirth as one of "women's distinctive, gender-specific injuries"—one that is dismissed (apparently arbitrarily) as "inevitable."[210]

---

204. CONDIT, *supra* note 3, at 2–3.

205. *Cf.* CLIFFORD GEERTZ, THE INTERPRETATION OF CULTURES 196 (1973); Russell Korobkin, *A Multi-Disciplinary Approach to Legal Scholarship: Economics, Behavioral Economics, and Evolutionary Psychology*, 41 JURIMETRICS J. 319, 350–51 (2001).

206. MACKINNON, *supra* note 134, at 135; Gilligan & MacKinnon, *supra* note 130. For a forceful statement of the same idea, see Mary Joe Frug, *A Postmodern Feminist Legal Manifesto (An Unfinished Draft)*, 105 HARV. L. REV. 1045, 1075 (1992) ("Only when the word 'woman' cannot be coherently understood, will oppression by sex be fatally undermined."). *See also* TI-GRACE ATKINSON, AMAZON ODYSSEY (1974); JESSICA BENJAMIN, THE BONDS OF LOVE: PSYCHOANALYSIS, FEMINISM AND THE PROBLEM OF DOMINATION (1988); BROWNMILLER, *supra* note 202; JUDITH BUTLER, GENDER TROUBLE: FEMINISM AND THE SUBVERSION OF IDENTITY (1990); MARY DALY, GYN/ECOLOGY: THE METAETHICS OF RADICAL FEMINISM (1978); ANDREA DWORKIN, PORNOGRAPHY: MEN POSSESSING WOMEN (1981); EVA FIGES, PATRIARCHAL ATTITUDES (1970); SHULAMITH FIRESTONE, THE DIALECTIC OF SEX: THE CASE FOR FEMINIST REVOLUTION (1970); GERMAIN GREER, THE FEMALE EUNUCH (1971); JOAN HOFF, LAW, GENDER, AND INJUSTICE: A LEGAL HISTORY OF U.S. WOMEN 3–12 (1991); CHERIS KRAMARAE, WOMEN AND MEN SPEAKING (1981); GUNTHER KRESS & ROBERT HODGE, LANGUAGE AND IDEOLOGY 78–82 (1979); ROBIN LAKOFF, LANGUAGE AND WOMEN'S PLACE (1975); GERDA LERNER, THE CREATION OF FEMINIST CONSCIOUSNESS: FROM THE MIDDLE AGES TO EIGHTEEN-SEVENTY 274 (1993); LISTENING TO SILENCES: NEW ESSAYS IN FEMINIST CRITICISM (Elaine Hedge & Shelley Fisher Fishkin eds. 1994); LUKER, *supra* note 112, at 40; PATRICIA MILLER, THE WORST OF TIMES 6–7 (1993); KATE MILLETT, SEXUAL POLITICS (1970); ANDREA NYE, FEMINIST THEORIES AND THE PHILOSOPHIES OF MAN 95–108 (paperback ed. 1989); PERCEIVING WOMEN (Shirley Ardener & A. Edwin Ardener eds. 1975); IRIS YOUNG, THROWING LIKE A GIRL AND OTHER ESSAYS IN FEMINIST PHILOSOPHY AND SOCIAL THEORY 150–56 (1990); Drucilla Cornell, *The Doubly-Prized World: Myth, Allegory and the Feminine*, 75 CORNELL L. REV. 644 (1990); Robin West, *Feminism, Critical Social Theory and Law*, 1989 U. CHI. LEGAL F. 59, 61–78.

207. SMART, *supra* note 134. For a critique of Smart's stance, see Brush, *supra* note 180, at 1071–75.

208. SIMONE DE BEAUVOIR, THE SECOND SEX 418 (2nd ed. H.M. Parshley trans. 1974). *See also* JACQUES LACAN, FEMININE SEXUALITY (Juliet Mitchell & Jacqueline Rose eds., Jacqueline Rose trans. 1982).

209. Robin West, *The Feminine Silence: A Response to Professor Koffler*, 1 CARDOZO STUDIES IN L. & LIT. 15 (1989). For an extended critique of West's vision of women as victims and her correspondingly negative, even hostile, vision of men, see Bendig, *supra* note 130, at 1022–42. *See also* Martha Minow, *Surviving Victim Talk*, 40 UCLA L. REV. 1411 (1993).

210. Robin West, *The Difference in Women's Hedonic Lives: A Phenomenological Critique of Feminist Legal Theory*, 3 WIS. WOMEN'S L.J. 81, 82 (1987). *See also* DE BEAUVOIR, *supra* note 208, at 553.

The view of women as victims rather than as shapers of their own destiny even has the imprimatur of the Supreme Court,[211] for whatever that is worth. Of course, some women really were victims in times past and some still are today.[212] But the same is true of men. Moreover, women were not, and are not, always and only victims, just as not all men were or are either victims or oppressors. Moreover, there is more than a little irony in the present claims of the victimhood of women as if it were an eternal and inflexible status. As Ian Buruma noted, "the more emancipated women become, the more some extreme feminists begin to define themselves as helpless victims of men."[213]

I suspect that women were rather more involved in working out their own fates than this model supposes.[214] If in fact women were lesser partners in many forms of social activity throughout the history of Anglo-American society, still they were partners.[215] Smith-Rosenberg at times intimates as much herself, although she never quite says so.[216] And at least one recent study concluded that the vision of women as victims rests on fabricated evidence.[217]

A significant part of this vision of women as victim is the assertion that law reflects male concerns and is structured, along with all of society, to reward male attributes—regardless of

---

211. United States v. Virginia, 518 U.S. 515, 531 (1996) ("Our Nation has had a long and unfortunate history of sex descrimination.").

212. See, e.g., Ustinia Dolgopol, *Women's Voice, Women's Pain,* 17 HUMAN RTS. Q. 127 (1995).

213. Ian Buruma, *The Joys and Perils of Victimhood,* N.Y. REV. BOOKS, Apr. 8, 1999, at 4, 6.

214. For criticisms of the tendency of feminist historians to present women purely as victims of a male conspiracy, see CONDIT, *supra* note 3, at 182–96; G.S. Rousseau & Roy Porter, *Introduction,* in SEXUAL UNDERWORLDS OF THE ENLIGHTENMENT, *supra* note 91, at 1, 15; Martha Minow, *Surviving Victim Talk,* 40 UCLA L. REV. 1411 (1993); Sherry, *supra* note 129, at 581; Tesón, *supra* note 177, at 668–70. For criticisms of the tendency of self-avowed feminists generally to embrace the ultimately disempowering role of victim, see MARTHA CHAMALLAS, INTRODUCTION TO FEMINIST LEGAL THEORY 97–101 (2003); COLKER, *supra* note 129, at 32–38; RENÉ DENFIELD, THE NEW VICTORIANS: A YOUNG WOMAN'S CHALLENGE TO THE OLD FEMINIST ORDER (1995); KATIE ROIPHE, THE MORNING AFTER: SEX, FEAR AND FEMINISM ON CAMPUS (1993); NAOMI WOLF, FIRE WITH FIRE (1993); Kathryn Abrams, *Complex Claim ants and Reductive Moral Judgments: New Patterns in the Search for Equality,* 57 U. PITT. L. REV. 337 (1996); Kathryn Abrams, *Sex Wars Redux: Agency and Coercion in Feminist Legal Theory,* 95 COLUM. L. REV. 304 (1995); Lillian BeVier, *Thoughts from a "Real" Woman,* 18 HARV. J.L. & PUB. POL'Y 457 (1995); Marianne LaFrance, *The Schemas and Schemes in Sex Discrimination,* 65 BROOK. L. REV. 1063 (1999); Martha Mahoney, *Whiteness and Women, in Practice and Theory: A Reply to Catharine MacKinnon,* 5 YALE J.L. & FEMINISM 217 (1993); Elizabeth Schneider, *Feminism and the False Dichotomy of Victimization and Agency,* 38 N.Y.L. SCH. L. REV. 387 (1993). *See generally* LANGER, *supra* note 118, at 34–48. A "Women's Freedom Network" criticizes such "victim talk" generally, and not just among historians. *See* LANGER, *supra,* at 32–33.

215. CATHERINE ALLGOR, PARLOR POLITICS: IN WHICH THE LADIES OF WASHINGTON HELP BUILD A CITY AND A GOVERNMENT (2000). *See also* Brush, *supra* note 180, at 1070 n.26; Edward Larson, *"In the Finest, Most Womanly Way:" Women in the Southern Eugenics Movement,* 39 AM. J. LEG. HIST. 119, 119 (1995); Joel Rosenthal, *Introduction,* in MEDIEVAL WOMEN AND THE SOURCES OF MEDIEVAL HISTORY vii, x (Joel Rosenthal ed. 1990). *See generally* BENJAMIN, *supra* note 206, at 4–6, 65; DAVID BUSS, THE EVOLUTION OF DESIRE: STRATEGIES OF HUMAN MATING (1994); FOUCAULT, POWER/KNOWLEDGE, *supra* note 150, at 119; JACQUELYN DOWD HALL, REVOLT AGAINST CHIVALRY: JESSIE DANIEL AMES AND THE WOMAN'S CAMPAIGN AGAINST LYNCHING (1979); CARMIN LINDIG, THE PATH FROM THE PARLOR: LOUISIANA WOMEN, 1829–1920 (1985); WILLIAM LINK, THE PARADOX OF SOUTHERN PROGRESSIVISM, 1880–1930, at 119–20, 134–42 (1992); MARY BETH NORTON, FOUNDING MOTHERS AND FATHERS: GENDERED POWER AND THE FORMING OF AMERICAN SOCIETY (1997); LINDA WILLIAMS, HARD CORE: POWER, PLEASURE AND THE "FRENZY OF THE VISIBLE" 23 (1989); Joanna Calne, *In Defense of Desire,* 23 RUTGERS L.J. 305, 325–28 (1992); Carol Rose, *Bargaining and Gender,* 18 HARV. J.L. & PUB. POL'Y 547 (1995). The complexities of this reality are explored in SHARON LAMB, THE TROUBLE WITH BLAME: VICTIMS, PERPETRATORS AND RESPONSIBILITY (1995).

216. SMITH-ROSENBERG, *supra* note 118, at 197–216.

217. SOMMERS, *supra* note 197. *See also* KRISTIN BUMILLER, THE CIVIL RIGHTS SOCIETY: THE SOCIAL CONSTRUCTION OF VICTIMS (1988).

whether those attributes are inherent or socially constructed.[218] Yet historians continue to identify situations were the law protected and rewarded female attributes, and not just in the form of protective legislation that had the effect of disabling women from competing with men.[219] Nor should we overlook that it was the early feminists who promoted "separate spheres" model of male/female relationships (which today's feminists find so disabling to women) as a means of protecting themselves from the often appalling conditions in early factories and as a means of promoting the "civilizing" of husbands and children.[220]

Even when women were denied the vote, they were not completely without political influence. Recall the influence of Harriet Beecher Stowe on the coming of the Civil War, or of Julia Ward Howe's *Battle Hymn of the Republic* on the course of the war, let alone the less well-known roles of women as nurses, as spies, and as producers on the "home front."[221] President Lincoln is said to have attributed the war's coming to Stowe, reportedly saying, on meeting her, "So you're the little woman who wrote the book that made this great war."[222]

One is rather bemused then to see a highly privileged modern American feminist legal academic bemoaning her "victimhood." How much of an outsider can one be with a six-figure salary from an Ivy League law school? An English law professor at an American law school (a real outsider, I suppose) summarized such claims of victimhood in these words:

> [T]he American translation of European social theory...seems predicated upon the belief that by supporting the marginal, the foreign, the peripheral, or the outsider, the intellectual within the institution becomes, presumably by projection, marginal or foreign— and so *ipso facto* politically radical himself. It is as if the greatest injustice known to the world were the indignity of being fired from Yale, refused tenure at Harvard, or barred from promotion at Stanford or Pennsylvania. As if a political biography which ends at the Georgetown Law Center in Washington, D.C., or at the University of Wisconsin-Madison, or at Cardozo in New York, or at Hampshire College in Amherst, the New School in San Francisco, Amsterdam, Earth, Mars, or Kansas somehow spells out in its entirety the injustice of the American polity, the marginal, the unloved, the ignored.[223]

Much the same comments could be made regarding "radical" historians, political scientists, or sociologists—male or female—although they have lower salaries than law professors.

Even if I am wrong in my view about the victimhood of women, it would perhaps be well for those who emphasize the victimhood of women in times past to ponder Nietzsche's comment that "[t]here is a degree of sleeplessness, or rumination, of 'historical sense' that (in the victim at least) injures the living thing, be it a person, or a people, or a system of culture."[224] Or, as historian Arthur Schlesinger would have it, it is time to stop using history as therapy to salve the

---

218. *See, e.g.,* EISENSTEIN, *supra* note 150; FRUG, POSTMODERN, *supra* note 134, at 125–31; DEBORAH RHODE, THEORETICAL PERSPECTIVES ON SEXUAL DIFFERENCE (1990); Sherry Colb, *Words That Deny, Devalue, and Punish: Judicial Responses to Fetus-Envy?*, 72 B.U. L. REV. 101 (1992); Elizabeth Reilly, *The Rhetoric of Disrespect: Uncovering the Faulty Premises Infecting Reproductive Rights*, 5 J. GENDER & L. 147 (1996).

219. *See, e.g.,* Barbara Welke, *When All the Women Were White, and All the Blacks Were Men: Gender, Class, Race, and the Road to* Plessy, *1855–1914*, 13 LAW & HIST. REV. 261, 292–95 (1995) (noting that black women were considerably more successful in challenging segregated transportation facilities than were black men).

220. Sandra Berns, *Women in English Legal History*, 12 U. TASMANIA L. REV. 26, 49–52 (1993).

221. *See generally* MARY CHESTNUT, MARY CHESTNUT'S CIVIL WAR (C. Vann Woodward ed. 1981); Paul Carrington, *One Law: The Role of Legal Education in the Opening of the Legal Profession since 1776*, 44 FLA. L. REV. 501, 546–47 (1992).

222. STEPHEN OATES, WITH MALICE TOWARD NONE 389 (1977).

223. Peter Goodrich, *Sleeping with the Enemy: An Essay on the Politics of Critical Legal Studies in America*, 68 NYU L. REV. 389, 399 (1993).

224. As quoted in Amos Elon, *The Politics of Memory*, N.Y. REV. BOOKS, Oct. 7, 1993, at 3, 5.

wounds of the past.[225] Yet the claims of victimhood persist and extend to ever widening circles of victims until there is hardly anyone left to be called an oppressor.

What we find in the feminist histories written in the past few decades is a classic instance of the "historian's fallacy," the error of believing that one who had an experience in times past "knows it, when [having] it, to be all that a historian would know it to be, with the advantage of historical perspective."[226] Consider, for example, the feminist historians' pervasive devaluing of the work of eighteenth-century historian, poet, playwright, and essayist Mercy Otis Warren because she did not dwell upon the oppressed status of women.[227] Our subjective reactions are conditioned by our contemporary experiences and current modes of thought. There is little reason to believe that anyone's modern response to studying an event is similar to the actual response of those who lived the event decades or centuries ago. Historians engaged in decoding the past must seek documentary and other evidence to support their suppositions; they cannot just intuit what people must have felt or done.

# Doing "Outsider" History

*Deconstruction is the banana peel on the sidewalk of language.*

—Sidney DeLong[228]

Lacking direct records of the experiences of historically mute classes, "outsider" historians have turned to the margins of the historical record to search for the "lost voices," knowing that some counter interpretation of what happened in the past (and, more importantly, why) can always be found in the margins.[229] For example, that there was a "counterculture" regarding sexual behavior even in Puritan New England is clear from the historical record, and at times that

---

225. Schlesinger, *supra* note 90.

226. DAVID HACKETT FISCHER, HISTORIANS' FALLACIES 209–13 (1970). *See also* Daniel Ernst, *The Critical Tradition in the Writing of American Legal History*, 102 YALE L.J. 1019, 1039–44 (1993); Tarczylo, *supra* note 91, at 35–43. *Cf.* WILLIAM JAMES, PRINCIPLES OF PSYCHOLOGY 129 (23rd prtg. 1980) (identifying a similar fallacy among psychologists); James Lindgren, *The Lawyer's Fallacy*, 68 CHI.-KENT L. REV. 109 (1992) (identifying a fallacy among lawyers and judges of assuming that people experience their lives in legal categories).

227. Janis McDonald, *The Need for Contextual ReVision: Mercy Otis Warren*, 5 YALE J.L. & FEMINISM 183 (1992). *See generally* BARBARA HANAWALT, THE TIES THAT BOUND 10 (1986); Jeanne Schroeder, *History's Challenge to Feminism*, 88 MICH. L. REV. 1889, 1889–92, 1905–06 (1990).

228. DeLong, *supra* note 172, at 133.

229. *See, e.g.,* HARRISON, *supra* note 118, at 119–53 (contending that the moral position of Christianity towards abortion is mixed rather than consistently condemnatory, based on a supposed—but unrecorded—opposition to the "malestream" theologians in ancient and medieval times); SMITH-ROSENBERG, *supra* note 118, at 18 (describing her search for the "excluded Other" in order to find a "more inharmonious" view of the past). The point is illustrated in Arthur Austin, *A Primer on Deconstruction's "Rhapsody of Word-Plays,"* 71 N. CAR. L. REV. 201, 219–28 (1992). *See also* DRUCILLA CORNELL, THE PHILOSOPHY OF THE LIMIT (1992); KERRY PETERSEN, ABORTION REGIMES 9–10 (1993); SMITH-ROSENBERG, *supra*, at 129–64, 242–44; Paul Campos, *That Obscure Object of Desire: Hermeneutics and the Autonomous Legal Text*, 77 MINN. L. REV. 1065 (1993); William Forbarth, Hendrik Hartog, & Martha Minow, *Introduction: Legal Histories from Below*, 1985 WIS. L. REV. 759; Peter Goodrich, *Gynaetopia: Feminine Genealogies of Common Law*, 20 J.L. & SOC'Y 276 (1993); Robert Gordon, *The Politics of Legal History and the Search for a Usable Past*, 2 BENCHMARK 269 (1990); Gordon, *supra* note 82, at 137–43; Hartog, *supra* note 122; Joan Scott, *History in Crisis? The Other Side of the Story*, 98 AM. HIST. REV. 680 (1989); Susan Last Stone, *In Pursuit of the Counter-Text: The Turn to the Jewish Legal Model in Contemporary American Theory*, 106 HARV. L. REV. 813 (1993); Lawrence Veysey, *The "New" Social History in the Context of American Historical Writing*, 7 REV. AM. HIST. 1 (1979); Joan Williams, *Culture and Certainty: Legal History and the Reconstructive Project*, 76 VA. L. REV. 713, 728–31, 743–46 (1990).

counterculture clearly represented different views of social ordering than the socially dominant view.[230] One should not seek to make more of this than the record allows, however. The "counterculture" in Puritan New England included such sexually free groups as the Quakers and the Baptists. I write ironically, of course, but in today's increasingly humorless world perhaps this needs to be explicit. The only riot in Middlesex County, Massachusetts between 1649 and 1699 was in support of the *status quo*.[231]

There is a more fundamental problem with doing history through the periphery than just the risk of getting the facts wrong. Formerly peripheral views of what is going on in society (and why) might very well prove more functional today than at the time the view originated. Such views might even have been more insightful (or even more functional) when they were peripheral. Nevertheless, it seems peculiar to seek a correct understanding of what "society" as a whole thought, valued, or did in such peripheral views.[232] Only when there is a serious contest between different worldviews, as regarding slavery before the Civil War, the Civil Rights Movement in the mid-twentieth century, or the current debates over feminism, do "counter meanings" have any real claim to recognition as a formative part of the legal or social order.

If one can get past the problem of whether "countertexts" are a legitimate means of recovering the past, particularly the past of the law, there remains the problem of how do we recover the voices that are lost now precisely because they were so marginalized in their own time that no records of those voices were preserved? Those searching for "lost voices" have turned to plays, poems, paintings, diaries, wills, letters, and so on, as their primary sources.[233] Such artifacts might be interesting and intriguing to historians, and I have referred to letters between women in colonial and early nineteenth-century America, as well as to poems, songs, movies, and other similar sources. Still, we are less able to evaluate the representativeness of an isolated letter or diary (or work of fiction such as a poem or play) than the far more voluminous "official" records, particularly if the latter presents a coherent and consistent picture and the former—grouped with similar documents from not too distant times—does not. And the "wealth of material"[234] on which feminist historians, in particular, have relied itself represents only an elite view of life and even that decreases sharply as one moves back before the nineteenth century.[235]

---

230. ROGER THOMPSON, SEX IN MIDDLESEX: POPULAR MORES IN A MASSACHUSETTS COUNTY, 1649–1699, at 98–109 (1986).

231. *Id.* at 105–06, 169

232. *See* Forbath, Hartog, & Minow, *supra* note 229; Thomas Haskell, *The Curious Persistence of Rights Talk in the "Age of Interpretation,"* 74 J. AM. HIST. 984, 1004 (1987); William Nelson, *The Role of History in Interpreting the Fourteenth Amendment*, 25 LOY. L.A. L. REV. 1177, 1269 (1992). *See also* Thomas Bender, *Wholes and Parts: The Need for Synthesis in American History*, 73 J. AM. HIST. 120 (1986); Robert Williams, jr., *Taking Rights Aggressively: The Perils and Promise of Critical Legal Theory for Peoples of Color*, 5 LAW & INEQ. J. 103 (1987); Wolcher, *supra* note 100, at 562–63. For a critique of this position, see Williams, *supra* note 229, at 721–35.

233. ANDERSON & ZINSSER, *supra* note 121, at xviii–xxi; SMITH-ROSENBERG, *supra* note 118, at 25–31. For use of a play to "prove" how "respectable" English doctors felt about abortion in 1906, see ANGUS MCLAREN, BIRTH CONTROL IN NINETEENTH-CENTURY ENGLAND 244 (1978). For a claim that fiction, even from centuries later, is a significant resource for determining what those who left no records actually thought, see Barry Schulter, *Getting the Stories Right: Reflections on Narrative Voice in State Constitutional Interpretation*, 26 CONN. L. REV. 671, 677–78 (1994).

234. 1 ANDERSON & ZINSSER, *supra* note 121, at xviii.

235. LAUREL THATCHER ULRICH, GOODWIVES: IMAGE AND REALITY IN THE LIVES OF WOMEN IN NORTHERN NEW ENGLAND, 1650–1750, at 127 (1983) ("Childbirth in early America was almost exclusively in the hands of women, which is another way of saying that its interior history has been lost."). *See also* Tarczylo, *supra* note 91, at 27.

How many letters did illiterate peasant women (the overwhelming majority of women before the late nineteenth century) write? Or illiterate urban housewives and laborers, for that matter?[236]

This is similar to the problem of historians who seek to discover what life was really like for slaves—with almost no first hand accounts from the slaves themselves. In addition to the few autobiographical accounts of slaves, there are some recollections of survivors of slavery collected 70 or so years after emancipation by the Federal Writers Project of the 1930s.[237] What we have that tell us what slaves in America thought or felt are records of the things people did to the slaves or wrote about them—including the slave owners.[238] While this might not be an insuperable barrier to recovering a "true vision" of what slavery was like from the slaves' perspective, one is not surprised to discover that the histories of slavery conflict so widely.[239] All too often, the results reflect "a projection of the current underclass African-Americans back onto their slave ancestors, another case of the long tail of implication wagging the dog...."[240] In other words, a perfectly fine analysis of a current situation (if such it is) could be a poor guide to the past.

Feminist historians, seeking to discover a "women's culture" as a "countertext" to the dominant (male) culture, face the same problem. They have dealt with it all too often by neglecting the very people who were most marginalized historically—slave, immigrant, and working class women—because they were marginalized within women's culture as well as men's.[241] With rare exceptions, these women simply left no records of their thoughts and feelings. Even for elite women or men, reliance on letters or diaries is particularly worrisome when used by someone attempting to recover the "true" history of sexual and reproductive practices from times past. As G.S. Rousseau and Roy Porter remind us, when we "[r]ead many eighteenth-century diaries,... it is possible to know what the diarist had for dinner almost every day of his life, but impossible to tell what he did in bed."[242] Even when someone finds a diary that records, perhaps in a code, the frequency of intercourse, the diary is likely to tell us nothing about modes or styles of performance, let alone whether contraceptive methods, if any, were used.[243] Nor do the diaries often tell us why something was done.[244] Similarly, working-class

---

236. *See* EDWARD SHORTER, A HISTORY OF WOMEN'S BODIES xiii–xiv (Pelican Books ed. 1984).

237. Edmund Morgan, *Plantation Blues*, N.Y. REV. BOOKS, June 10, 1999, at 30, 30.

238. *Id.*

239. *See, e.g.,* IRA BERLIN, MANY THOUSANDS GONE: THE FIRST TWO CENTURIES OF SLAVERY IN NORTH AMERICA (1998); JOHN BLASSINGAME, THE SLAVE COMMUNITY: PLANTATION LIFE IN THE ANTE-BELLUM SOUTH (1972); PAUL DAVID ET AL., RECKONING WITH SLAVERY: A CRITICAL STUDY IN THE QUANTITATIVE HISTORY OF AMERICAN NEGRO SLAVERY (1976); WILMA DUNAWAY, THE AFRICAN-AMERICAN FAMILY IN SLAVERY AND EMANCIPATION (2003); STANLEY ELKINS, SLAVERY: A PROBLEM IN AMERICAN INSTITUTIONAL LIFE (1959); ROGER FOGEL & STANLEY ENGERMAN, TIME ON THE CROSS: THE ECONOMICS OF AMERICAN SLAVERY (1974); JOHN HOPE FRANKLIN & LOREN SCHWENINGER, RUNAWAY SLAVES: REBELS ON THE PLANTATION (1999); HERBERT GUTMAN, THE BLACK FAMILY IN SLAVERY AND FREEDOM, 1750–1925 (1976); NORRECE JONES, BORN A CHILD OF FREEDOM YET A SLAVE: MECHANISMS OF CONTROL AND STRATEGIES OF RESISTANCE IN ANTEBELLUM SOUTH CAROLINA (1990); WINTHROP JORDAN, WHITE OVER BLACK (1968); ORLANDO PATTERSON, RITUALS OF BLOOD: CONSEQUENCES OF SLAVERY IN TWO AMERICAN CENTURIES (1999); ORLANDO PATTERSON, SLAVERY AND SOCIAL DEATH: A COMPARATIVE STUDY (1982); ORLANDO PATTERSON, THE SOCIOLOGY OF SLAVERY: AN ANALYSIS OF THE ORIGINS, DEVELOPMENT AND STRUCTURE OF NEGRO SLAVE SOCIETY IN AMERICA (1967).

240. Morgan, *supra* note 237, at 33.

241. *See* Nancy Hewitt, *Beyond the Search for Sisterhood: American Women's History in the 1980's*, 10 SOC. HIST. 299 (1985). *See generally* Sherene Razack, *Using Law for Social Change: Historical Perspectives*, 17 QUEEN'S L.J. 31 (1992); Williams, *supra* note 229, at 737–40.

242. Rousseau & Porter, *supra* note 214, at 7. *See generally* 1 ANDERSON & ZINSSER, *supra* note 121, at xix–xx; HARRISON, *supra* note 118, at 159–60; Rosenthal, *supra* note 215, at ix–x.

243. *See, e.g.,* BRODIE, *supra* note 164, at 9–25.

244. *Id.* at 36.

autobiographies from the nineteenth century proudly recount the author's reading life, but not his love life.[245]

Of course, the dearth of material from the unlettered mass of humanity from times past can itself be seen as evidence of the oppression and suppression of the masses. That still doesn't get us very far in figuring out what they would have wanted had they been in a stronger position. Supporters of the "lost voices" approach to legal history have never credibly explained how they could recover the lost voices of historically mute classes nor how the lost voices are to weighed against formal legal records to establish what the "real" law was. If, as Canadian law professor Allen Hunt has noted, we are to abandon attempts to ground knowledge in formal law and take to sailing the shifting uncharted sea of responsible moral judgment, as postmodernist legal scholars demand, those scholars owe us an obligation to demonstrate how to sail.[246]

The problem was caught rather pithily by English historian James Sharpe in describing his conclusion that infanticide was widely accepted in seventeenth century Essex: "Such attitudes, at least in the opinion of the present writer, were more common than the evidence suggests."[247] Sharpe based his conclusion on a single source, choosing to ignore the numerous executions for the crime[248] and explicit statements from numerous sources describing the crime as "unnatural" and "heinous."[249] Sharpe echoes the attitude expressed in a remark animators put in the mouth of the indomitable Foghorn Leghorn when the fictional rooster didn't like the answer another cartoon character gave him: "You got your signals crossed, boy, but *I* know what you mean."

American law professor David Millon provided an excellent example of the difficulties such claims pose to legal historians by publishing a sophisticated search for lost legal voices in a relatively uncontroversial context involving medieval civil litigation.[250] A more modern analogue of Millon's argument would be to attempt to assess, from general verdicts and other, similarly vague data presently available, the actual extent to which juries followed the rule of contributory negligence in the 1920s or 1930s—a rule that many lawyers, in conversations among themselves in the 1960s, doubted that juries had ever really followed. While Millon did not dwell upon his motives for seeking such knowledge about relatively non-controversial topics of medieval law, his later writings suggest a strongly political motive underlay his attempt.[251] Yet even Millon conceded that his theory of the irrelevance of formal legal doctrine to medieval law flies in the face of the elaborate formal doctrinal analyses developed in courts and elsewhere by medieval and early modern lawyers and jurists. Millon also conceded that the recovery of lost voices is, in any real sense, impossible.

---

245. David Vincent, *Love and Death and the Nineteenth Century Working Class,* 5 SOCIAL HIST. 223 (1980).

246. *Cf.* Hunt, *supra* note 37, at 525. *See also* John Elson, *The Case Against Legal Scholarship or, If the Professor Must Publish, Must the Profession Perish?,* 39 J. LEGAL EDUC. 343, 371–75 (1989); Robert Gordon, *Critical Legal Histories,* 36 STAN. L. REV. 57, 117–24 (1984).

247. J.A. SHARPE, CRIME IN SEVENTEENTH CENTURY ENGLAND: A COUNTY STUDY 137 (1983).

248. *Id.* at 135–36. *See also* Keith Wrightson, *Infanticide in Earlier Seventeenth Century England,* 15 LOCAL POP. STUD. 10, 11–12 (1975).

249. *See, e.g.,* WILLIAM GOUGE, OF DOMESTICATED DUTIES 499–500, 507 (1622). *See generally* Wrightson, *supra* note 248, at 10–11.

250. David Millon, *Positivism in the Historiography of the Common Law,* 1989 WIS. L. REV. 669. *See also* NORMAN DOE, FUNDAMENTAL AUTHORITY IN THE LATE MEDIEVAL ENGLISH LAW (1990); S.F.C. MILSOM, HISTORICAL FOUNDATIONS OF THE COMMON LAW 421–28 (2nd ed. 1981); PERCY WINFIELD, THE CHIEF SOURCES OF ENGLISH LEGAL HISTORY (1925); David Millon, *Book Review,* 12 LAW & HIST. REV. 181 (1994); Donald Sutherland, *Legal Reasoning in the Fourteenth Century: The Invention of "Color" in Pleading,* in ON THE LAWS AND CUSTOMS OF ENGLAND: ESSAYS IN HONOR OF SAMUEL E. THORNE 182 (Morris Arnold *et al.* eds. 1981).

251. *See* Millon, *supra* note 37, at 51–57.

The "lost voices" approach to the history of abortion turned up in the notorious *Historians' Briefs* given to the Supreme Court in the *Webster* and *Casey* cases.[252] The *Historians' Briefs* did not discuss the difficulties in applying that theory to the history of anything. There are more serious problems with the *Historians' Briefs* than reliance on "lost voices,"[253] but the "lost voices" create the opening for the introduction of those other failings of the briefs. Law professor Reva Siegal has given even fuller expression to the lost voices approach to the history of abortion than most other historians.[254] Her strenuous effort to "deconstruct" the historical record and to patch together a narrative of "lost voices" in fact eloquently exposes the reality that actually recorded voices do not support her thesis. Donald Judges, who even referred to "lost voices" in the title of his book on abortion, was no more successful than Siegel.[255]

Voices have indeed been lost from the historical record of abortion just as for every other aspect of the past. Furthermore, even if a more or less full record of a particular voice is found, full recovery of what the speaker or writer actually meant often is impossible.[256] History as written does depend to a large measure on a professional consensus on data and its relevance.[257] The cultural contingency of accepted history neither destroys the factual nature of what actually happened in the past nor the historian's obligation to attempt to recapture as much as possible of what actually happened.[258] Nor does the frequent indeterminacy of the historical record mean that nothing at all can be learned from its study.[259] As historian Carl Friedrich pointed out, "the perplexing paradox of all historical work is that what actually happened can never be recaptured, although historical research would lose its point without a belief that more of it can be recaptured than is presently known."[260]

Consider the events in China in 1989. Would any American historian claim that the apparent social consensus in today's China to pretend (at least in public rhetoric) that no students were killed in or near Tienanmen Square in June of 1989 changed the reality—or import—of what happened there, or that the answer would be different if the whole world were to join a conspiracy of silence on the matter? As Chinese poet and novelist Lu Xun wrote over 50 years ago, "Lies

---

252. *Webster Historians' Brief, supra* note 68, at 170. *See also* Sylvia Law, *Conversations between Historians and the Constitution,* 12 The Publ. Historian 11, 14 (1990); Statement of Kristen Luker at the Panel on Legal History at the Association of American Law Schools 1990 Annual Meeting, *AALS Tape No. 163 Conference Audio Tape No. 163* (available from Recorded Resources Corporation of Millersville, Md.). The tape is on file in libraries at many law schools. The *Casey* Historians' Brief does not expressly mention the theory of lost voices, but its claim to speak of the history of abortion "deeply and accurately" as well as its insistence that "the Court consult evidence of daily life as well as official and governmental action to uncover the beliefs and practices of a broad range of American society" represents the same sort of claim. *Casey Historians' Brief, supra* note 68, at 2, 4.

253. *See* Chapter 17, at notes 39–58.

254. Siegel, *supra* note 70.

255. Judges, *supra* note 16.

256. *See* Friedrich, *supra* note 85, at 1028–31, 1046–48.

257. Christopher Lasch, *Consensus: An Academic Question?,* 76 J. Am. Hist. 457 (1989). *See generally* Lasch, *supra* note 3.

258. *See generally* Edward Carr, What Is History? (1961); Bernice Carroll, Liberating Women's History (1976); W.E.B. DuBois, Black Reconstruction 1860–1880 (1935); Minow, *supra* note 11, at 239–46; Novick, *supra* note 91; Wolfe, *supra* note 91, at 856–67.

259. *See, e.g.,* Larry Kramer, *Judicial Asceticism,* 12 Cardozo L. Rev. 1789, 1792–93 (1991) (arguing that despite the indeterminacy of the scope of application of legal rules, the rules do constrain judges to some extent). *But see* Tribe & Dorf, *supra* note 16, at 98–109 (arguing that the indeterminacy of historical traditions render them incapable of resolving disputes about the Constitution); Tushnet, *supra* note 13, at 32–45 (arguing that the indeterminacy of history leaves originalist judges with "as much room to maneuver as nonoriginalist ones").

260. Friedrich, *supra* note 85, at 1031.

written in ink cannot obscure a truth written in blood."[261] The current conspiracy of silence in the People's Republic of China, its scope, and its effect are themselves, of course, interesting and important historical data.[262] But they are not the whole story. Or consider the point made by a distinguished historian referring to a European context: "If we cannot prove that the Holocaust revisionists are wrong in some inarguable way, we are clearly in deep trouble."[263] Even some who normally embrace a politically correct and casual attitude toward historical truth find the denial of the Holocaust troubling.[264] It must be possible to establish that Hitler was more than just some fellow with "unstandard tastes."[265]

The task of historians remains to attempt, as best they can, to report and interpret the past as it was and not as the historians wish it were.[266] Otherwise we would have no way of answering a claim that the fact that Columbus navigated the ocean in 1492, or that an American-led coalition went to war with Iraq with 1991, or that a nuclear incident occurred in Chernobyl in 1986, are "created" by a social consensus rather than objectively verifiable events.[267] For an outstanding example of such a manipulative approach, consider law professor Duncan Kennedy's argument that pants originated as the basic dress for men and skirts for women as a means of expressing (and realizing) sexual access and control.[268] One is put in mind of the comment in the movie *Shoot the Piano Player,* where one character speculates whether women experience continual sexual arousal because their naked thighs are rubbing together beneath their skirts. All that Kennedy was demonstrating, however, was his complete ignorance of the role of horse-back hunting and fight-

---

261. Quoted in Nicholas Kristoff, *How the Hardliners Won,* N.Y. TIMES MAG., Nov. 12, 1989, at 38, 71. Lu Xun was referring to an earlier massacre in Tiananmen Square. *See* Jonathan Mirsky, *Squaring the Chinese Circle,* N.Y. REV. OF BOOKS, Nov. 5, 1992, at 51, 52.

262. *See* ARTICLE 19, THE YEAR OF THE BIG LIE: CENSORSHIP AND DISINFORMATION IN THE PEOPLE'S REPUBLIC OF CHINA (1989) ("Article 19" is a human rights group in London; its address is 90 Borough High St., London SE1 1LL); James D'Amato, *How Regimes Profit by Curbing U.S. Television News,* 35 ORBIS 347, 357–63 (1991). *See also* ROBERT ROSENSTONE, VISIONS OF THE PAST: THE CHALLENGE OF FILM OVER OUR IDEA OF HISTORY (1995) (arguing that the "visual history" of movies is as valid as the "written history" of historians); Carol Greenhouse, *Revisiting Hopewell: A Reply to Neal Milner,* 17 LAW & SOC. INQUIRY 335, 338–40 (1992) (arguing that popular beliefs about the history of a community are at least as significant at the actual record of events); Thomas Doherty, *Seamless Matching,* 77 NAT'L F. no. 3, at 39 (1997) (exploring the impact of Oliver Stone's film, *JFK*). *Compare* ROBIN LANE FOX, THE UNAUTHORIZED VERSION: TRUTH AND FICTION IN THE BIBLE (1992). *See generally* Reid, *supra* note 89, at 205–17 (on the role of the fictive "ancient constitution" in English and American constitutional history).

263. George Frederickson, *Pioneer,* N.Y. REV. OF BOOKS, Sept. 23, 1993, at 30, 32. *See also* DEBORAH LIPSTADT, DENYING THE HOLOCAUST: THE GROWING ASSAULT ON TRUTH AND MEMORY (1993); MICHAEL SHERMER & ALEX GROBMAN, DENYING HISTORY: WHO SAYS THE HOLOCAUST NEVER HAPPENED AND WHY DO THEY SAY IT? (2000); PIERRE VIDAL-NAQUET, ASSASSINS OF MEMORY: ESSAYS ON THE DENIAL OF THE HOLOCAUST (Jeffrey Mehlmann trans. 1992); Eric Hobsbawm, *The New Threat to History,* N.Y. REV. OF BOOKS, Dec. 16, 1993, at 62 (referring similarly to the Armenian Massacres during World War I); Tony Judt, *Writing History, Facts Optional: If There Is No "Truth," Why Not Deny the Holocaust,* N.Y. TIMES, Apr. 13, 2000, at A31. *See generally* Thomas Haskell, *Objectivity Is Not Neutrality: Rhetoric vs. Practice in Peter Novick's That Noble Dream,* 29 HIST. & THEORY 129 (1990); Nelson, *supra* note 232.

264. *See, e.g.,* DIFFERENT VOICES: WOMEN AND THE HOLOCAUST (Carol Rittner & John Roth eds. 1993); R. RUTH LINDEN, MAK ING STORIES, MAKING SELVES: FEMINIST REFLECTIONS ON THE HOLOCAUST (1993); Vivian Grosswald Curran, *Deconstruction, Structuralism, Antisemitism and the Law,* 36 B.C. L. REV. 1 (1994); Stark, *supra* note 103, at 171 n.10.

265. Clifford Geertz, *Anti Anti-Relativism,* 86 AM. ANTHRO. 263, 264 (1984).

266. For an eloquent statement of the need to "validate memory" in the face of totalitarian (Communist) reconstruction of social reality, see Stanislaw Baranczak, *Memory: Lost, Retrieved, Abused, and Defended,* 1 IDEAS 3 (Summer 1992). *See also* PAST IMPERFECT: HISTORY ACCORDING TO THE MOVIES (Mark Carnes ed. 1995); BARBARA TUCHMAN, PRACTICING HISTORY 16 (1981); Kelly, *supra* note 84, at 157; Wiecek, *supra* note 89, at 266–68; Wolcher, *supra* note 100, at 587–88, 610.

267. Lichtenberg, *supra* note 37, at 66–68.

268. Kennedy, *supra* note 5, at 1369.

ing in creating a need for the more complex (in terms of sewing) pants for men (and for women among the horse-nomads)—needs epitomized by the pants-wearing Huns and Teutons who overthrew the toga-clad Roman empire. Nor does he consider the gradual effect of changing occupational patterns on the persistence and alteration of dress codes through the centuries.

We cannot abandon the notion that history is a search for the truth of what really happened. If, in the end, there is no referential fact in the study of history (or if such referential facts as might exist are always of no moment, which comes out about the same), then we are left only with stories. We shall have no place left for history. And we shall have no means left for testing those stories for any "truth value." Legal historian Morton Horwitz attempted to deal with this problem by insisting that skepticism and subjectivity are avoided if the historian strives to give the "best possible explanation" of their subjects of study.[269] Horwitz, however, never explains how one is to judge which possible explanation is "best" without any basis for testing an explanation against a real past.[270]

To better understand the difference between stories and history, consider whether Faulkner or Hemingway is "more true." The question cannot be answered if by the question we mean which conforms more nearly to real persons or events to which their stories refer. Their stories do not refer, at least not in any close way, either to real persons or to real events. All we can allege is that the one or the other is more interesting, a matter of individual taste. One cannot establish the truth either of their stories or of one's assertion that the one or the other is more interesting. And if I prefer neither, finding the stories of Thomas Bell or James Farrell more interesting, who is to say I am wrong. Reasoned argument becomes irrelevant, or at least inconclusive.

Stanley Fish recognized as much when he stated that deconstruction "relieves me [Fish] of the obligation to be right…and demands only that I be interesting."[271] Or consider historian Karl Popper's observation that "[t]here can be no history of 'the past as it actually did happen'; there can only be historical interpretations, and none of them final."[272] There is, after all, no such thing as "immaculate perception."[273] Is that really the end of our history or our law? Law professor Richard Bourne suggests an answer in his comments on the proper use of critical legal studies, critical race theory, and feminist "readings" in teaching the case of *O'Brien v. Cunard SS Co.*,[274] a case commonly used in first year torts classes:

> It may be that we all have points of view we cannot transcend and that a level of coercion is inevitable in education. To acknowledge these as true is not to argue that we shouldn't try to go beyond our personal limitations or not to coerce our students. To sin is human, but humans rightly try not to sin. Truly objective search for truth is beyond any journalist, but that some try harder than others and should continue to do so is something perusal of back issues of the *New York Times* and *Pravda* would readily reveal.[275]

---

269. HORWITZ, *supra* note 11, at viii.

270. *See* White, *Transforming History, supra* note 93, at 1351–52.

271. LEHMAN, *supra* note 6, at 75 (quoting Fish). *See also* JOHN ELLIS, AGAINST DECONSTRUCTION (1989); Peter Swan, *Critical Legal Theory and the Politics of Pragmatism,* 12 DALHOUSIE L.J. 349 (1989).

272. KARL POPPER, THE OPEN SOCIETY AND ITS ENEMIES 268 (4th ed. 1962). *See also* STANLEY FISH, IS THERE A TEXT IN THIS CLASS? 557–59 (1980); Belz, *supra* note 82, at 52–57; Paul Murphy, *Time to Reclaim: the Current Challenges of American Constitutional History,* 69 AM. HIST. REV. 64, 74–77 (1963).

273. Allan Megill, *Recounting the Past: "Description," Explanation, and Narrative in Historiography,* 94 AM. HIST. REV. 627, 632 (1989).

274. 28 N.E. 266 (Mass. 1891).

275. Richard Bourne, *A "Traditionalist" Approach to Teaching* O'Brien *and to Ideology in the Classroom,* 57 MO. L. REV. 455, 465 (1992). On the several different but related schools of thought that flourished (and to some extent declined) in the 1990s, see Robert Ellickson, *Trends in Legal Scholarship: A Statistical Study,* 29 J. LEGAL STUD. 517 (2000).

As lawyers turned to history to solve to the lawyers' crisis of legitimacy,[276] they found, as the foregoing discussion demonstrates, that historians face the same uncertainties about the sources and meaning of "truth" as have the lawyers. Some historians have even confused a desirable objectivity with what they see as undesirable neutrality.[277] One observer has termed this confusion the "postmodernist fallacy,"[278] although it can be traced back at least as far as Nietzsche.[279] Historians who suffer from this confusion have found it both difficult and inconvenient to concern themselves with the truth of their claims about history. Such historians have been tempted to follow the path prescribed by philosopher Richard Rorty: "to describe a past that the past never knew."[280]

The temptation to tamper with the truth in political arenas is neither new nor unique to academics, although academics sometimes seek to appear as if they are above such sordid realities. The tendency to fabricate convenient histories received considerable impetus from the tendency of the motion picture industry around the world to present blatant fictions as history, in the process often serving as the only sources of history for large numbers of people.[281] Yet the resulting confusion over the possibility, or even the desirability, of truth is most pernicious among professional scholars; scriptwriters and directors are far less problematic in comparison.

Consider the resolution adopted at an American Historical Association Annual Meeting condemning historian Rosalind Rosenberg for having testified for the defendant-employer in an employment discrimination suit. It read: "We believe as feminist scholars we have a responsibility not to allow our scholarship to be used against the interests of women struggling for equity in our society."[282] Singularly lacking from the resolution, sponsored by the Coordinating Committee of Women in the Historical Profession and the Conference Group in Women's History, was concern about whether Rosenberg's testimony was accurate or whether she had acted in good faith.

---

276. See the authorities collected *supra* at notes 79–118.

277. SANDRA HARDING, FEMINISM AND METHODOLOGY 9 (1987); Jeanne Schroeder, *Subject: Object,* 47 U. MIAMI L. REV. 1, 10–11 (1992).

278. Henry Hultquist, Comment, *Legal Philosophy and the Postmodernist Fallacy,* 2 GEO. MASON U. L. REV. 223, 228–29, 241–44 (1995).

279. See the text *supra* at notes 101–05.

280. RICHARD RORTY, CONTINGENCY, IRONY, AND SOLIDARITY 29 (1989).

281. *See* PAST IMPERFECT, *supra* note 266; ROSENSTONE, *supra* note 262.

282. COORDINATING COMMITTEE ON WOMEN IN THE HISTORY PROFESSION NEWSLETTER, Feb. 1986, at 8. *See also* NOVICK, *supra* note 91, at 502–10; JOAN SCOTT, GENDER AND THE POLITICS OF HISTORY 169–70 (1988); Mary Joe Frug, *Sexual Equality and Sexual Difference in American Law,* 26 N. ENG. L. REV. 665, 673–82 (1992); Jacqueline Dowd Hall, *Women's History Goes to Trial: EEOC v. Sears, Roebuck & Co.,* 11 SIGNS 751 (1986); Thomas Haskell & Stanford Levinson, *Academic Freedom and Expert Witnessing: Historians and the Sears Case,* 66 TEX. L. REV. 1829 (1988); Hoffer, supra note 86, at 272–73; Alice Kessler-Harris, *Academic Freedom and Expert Witnessing: A Response to Haskell and Levinson,* 67 TEX. L. REV. 429 (1989); Alice Kessler-Harris, EEOC v. Sears, Roebuck and Company: *A Personal Account,* 35 RADICAL HIST. REV. 67 (1986); Ruth Milkman, *Women's History and the Sears Case,* 12 FEMINIST STUD. 375 (1986); Deborah Rhode, *The "No-Problem" Problem: Feminist Challenges and Cultural Change,* 100 YALE L.J. 1731, 1768–70 (1991); Rosalind Rosenberg, *What Harms Women in the Workplace,* N.Y. TIMES, Feb. 27, 1986, at A23; Vicki Schultz, *Telling Stories about Women and Work: Judicial Interpretations of Sex Segregation in the Workplace in Title VII Cases Raising the Lack of Interest Argument,* 103 HARV. L. REV. 1750 (1990); Joan Scott, *Deconstructing Equality-Versus-Difference,* 14 FEMINIST STUD. 33 (1988); Carol Sternhell, *Life in the Mainstream,* Ms. MAG., July 1986, at 48; Joan Williams, *Dissolving the Sameness/Difference Debate: A Post-Modern Path beyond Essentialism in Feminist and Critical Race Theory,* 2 DUKE L.J. 296, 302–05 (1991); Karen Winkler, *Two Scholars Conflict in Sears Sex Bias Case Sets Off War in Women's History,* CHRON. HIGHER EDUC., Feb. 5, 1986, at A-8.

Social science scholars generally, and not just historians, have suffered similar difficulties in distinguishing between objectivity and neutrality.[283] Law professor George Kannar addressed the results of similar confusions among law professors during the Bork nomination. As he observed, "[o]ne need not believe blindly in the notion of objective truth to appreciate the psychological, moral, and political difficulties of maintaining under such conditions any strong distinction between knowledge and conviction, between detachment and engagement, or between benevolent paternalism and selfish mass manipulation."[284] Law professor Joan Williams also summarized the problem. While, she argued, "all histories are either presentist or boring," she also described as "bad history" any work that "cares so much about the present that it ceases to concern itself with a conscientious respect for the pastness of the past."[285] What such approaches produce might not be "nonsense, but neither is it history."[286]

We might try to excuse such historical distortions as an unremarkable examples of "postmodernism," because the reader is the "author" of the text, because a text takes its meaning from what the reader chooses to see in it rather than from what the person who created it put into the text.[287] "Historians" engaged in such exercises could deflect merely factual criticism by claiming to be engaged in a "creative misreading" of the texts in question or that the critic has missed the "postmodern irony" in her apparent error.[288] Each of these several rationalizations are rooted in the thinking of Paul de Man—the onetime guru of deconstruction in Yale's English department. Yet upon examining de Man more closely, however, we find a leading example of conscious falsification of the past in the whitewashing of his Nazi past by his deconstructionist admirers.[289]

Before De Man became an American academic, he was an ardently pro-Nazi journalist in occupied Belgium who wrote numerous anti-Semitic articles. In order to defend de Man, even his most ardent students felt a need to abandon indeterminacy and to insist that there is a single true version of the facts.[290] (De Man, once described as "the only man who ever looked into the abyss and came away smiling,"[291] was dead when the scandal broke). In a less dramatic vein, Stanley Fish, the guru of deconstruction among American law professors, has sought to defend his work by insisting that others have "misread" his text without reference to his own claims that the

---

283. *See generally* Mark Chesler, Joseph Sanders, & Debra Kalmuss, Social Science in Court: Mobilizing Experts in the School Desegregation Cases (1988); Lawrence Solan, The Language of Judges (1993); G.O. Sayles, Scripta Diversa 1–16, 133–49 (1982); Zinn, *supra* note 91, at 40–41; Donna Boswell, *Book Review,* 30 Jurimetrics J. 517 (1990); Patricia Falk, *The Prevalence of Social Science in Gay Rights Cases: The Synergistic Influences of Historical Context, Justificatory Citation, and Dissemination Efforts,* 41 Wayne L. Rev. 1 (1994); Friedrich, *supra* note 85; Haskell, *supra* note 263; Peter Irons, *Clio on the Stand: The Promise and Perils of Historical Review,* 24 Cal. W.L. Rev. 337 (1988); J. Morgan Kousser, *Are Expert Witnesses Whores? Reflections on Objectivity in Scholarship and Expert Witnessing,* 6 The Publ. Historian 5 (1984); James McClellan, *Commentary on the Papers Delivered by Professors Derrick Bell and Peter Charle Hoffer,* 23 Rutgers L.J. 297 (1992); Peyton McCrary & J. Gerald Hebert, *Keeping the Courts Honest: The Role of Historians as Expert Witnesses in Southern Voting Rights Cases,* 16 S.U. L. Rev. 101 (1989).

284. George Kannar, *Citizenship and Scholarship,* 90 Colum. L. Rev. 2017, 2058–59 (1990). *See generally Id.* at 2055–69. *See also* Tushnet, *supra* note 13, at 57–60; William Leuchtenberg, *The Historian and the Public Realm,* 97 Am. Hist. Rev. 1 (Feb. 1992).

285. Williams, *supra* note 229, at 719–20.

286. *Id.* at 720.

287. *See, e.g.,* Fish, *supra* note 272, at 557–59. *See* the text *supra* at notes 18–26.

288. DeLong, *supra* note 172, at 132 n.5 (1995).

289. David Hirsch, The Deconstruction of Literature: Criticism after Auschwitz (1991); Lehman, *supra* note 6; Norman Fruman, *Deconstruction, de Man, and the Resistance to Evidence: David Lehman's Signs of the Times,* Acad. Questions, Summer 1992, at 34.

290. *See* Responses: On Paul de Man's Wartime Journalism (Werner Hamacher, Neil Hertz, & Thomas Keenan eds., Peggy Kamuf trans. 1989).

291. Lehman, *supra* note 6, at 156.

meaning of a text is provided by the reader rather than by the author.[292] These efforts only did do to deconstruction what deconstruction had set out to do to meaning and certainty: "they left it in ruins."[293] Much the same occurred when the lies in Nobel laureate Rigoberta Menchu's so-called autobiography were disclosed.[294]

These are not just examples of individuals failing under pressure. Something more sinister is at work. Besides de Man and Menchu, consider the efforts of the French historian Lucien Febevre's promotion of a "radically structuralist and apolitical, even ahistorical" approach to history through the once internationally prominent *Annales* school.[295] No one seems to have asked whether Febevre's approach, developed after World War II, was a result of his betrayal to the Nazis of his Jewish colleague in the founding of the *Annales*, Marcel Bloch.[296] De Man and Febevre seem to have invented their approaches precisely to allow themselves to read back into their own past personal histories more to their liking. No wonder Thomas Nagel concluded that "[o]bjectivity should be valued by anyone whose policies are not supported by lies."[297]

Yet de Man and Febevre, along with Foucault's determination to delegitimate social condemnation of homosexuality,[298] are the models for the leading contemporary historians of abortion, homosexuality, and many other fields of historical inquiry. Lying about the history of homosexuality is hardly a surprise after the decision in *Bowers v. Hardwick.*[299] In *Bowers*, the Supreme Court's upheld state prohibitions of homosexual conduct as constitutional even when undertaken in private between consenting adults on the basis of long-established history and traditions banning such activities. While efforts to overturn *Bowers* might be politically correct, and even laudable, the stories being told simply have little or nothing to do with real history.[300] Ex-

---

292. Stanley Fish, *How Come You Do Me Like You Do? A Response to Dennis Patterson*, 72 Tex. L. Rev. 57 (1993). For the other side of the debate, see Dennis Patterson, *The Poverty of Interpretive Universalism: Toward the Reconstruction of Legal Theory*, 72 Tex. L. Rev. 1 (1993); Dennis Patterson, *You Made Me Do It: My Reply to Stanley Fish*, 72 Tex. L. Rev. 67 (1993).

293. Peter Shaw, *The Rise and Fall of Deconstruction*, Commentary, Dec. 1991, at 50, 51 (quoting J. Hillis Miller). *See also* Austin, *supra* note 229, at 210–14, 220, 234–36; Balkin, *supra* note 13, at 764–66; Norman Fruman, *Deconstruction, de Man, and the Resistance to Evidence: David Lehman's Signs of the Times*, Academic Questions, Summer 1992, at 34; Richard Warner, *Why Pragmatism? The Puzzling Place of Pragmatism in Critical Theory*, 1993 U. Ill. L. Rev. 535.

294. *Compare* Larry Rohter, *Nobel Winner Finds Her Story Challenged*, N.Y. Times, Dec. 15, 1998, at A1 (substantiating anthropologist David Stohl's disclosures about the lies Menchu told); *and Footnotes*, Chron. Higher Educ., Feb. 26, 1999, at A12 (reporting the Menchu has acknowledged some details in her "autobiography" were not accurate); *with* Hal Cohen, *The Unmasking of Rigoberta Menchu*, Lingua Franca, Jul.–Aug. 1999, at 48, 52 (arguing that we should credit the statements of a Nobel laureate with a "proven record" more than we do an "anthropologist who is male, white, tall, and gringo"); *and* Robin Wilson, *A Challenge to a Multicultural Icon*, Chron. Higher Educ., Jan. 15, 1999, at A14 (quoting Wellesley's Marjorie Agosin: "Whether her book is true or not, I don't care.").

295. Tony Judt, *France without Glory*, N.Y. Rev. Books, May 23, 1996, at 39, 42 n.19.

296. Philippe Burrin, La France à l'heure allemande 317–23 (1995).

297. Nagel, *supra* note 116, at 37. *See also* Adler, *supra* note 110, at 188:

Yet paradoxically, human beings wish to trust and to be trusted, and this is impossible without accountability. Only a cynic or a nihilist disclaims responsibility for yesterday's robbery on the grounds that he was a different person then. The rest of us struggle to bridge the discontinuities between who we were and who we are, what we did and what we do now, to compose a coherent narrative with which to extend ourselves into the future.

298. See the text *supra* at notes 150–53.

299. 478 U.S. 186 (1986).

300. The decision in *Romer v. Evans*, 517 U.S. 620 (1996), holding an amendment to the Colorado Constitution banning affirmative action for homosexuals to be a violation of equal protection, arguably overrules *Bowers* although the majority opinion never even mentions *Bowers* in a highly general analysis that relies on a conclusion that the amendment was motivated solely by animus against homosexuals for its conclusion. *See* Akhil Amar, *Attainder and Amendment 2:* Romer's *Rightness*, 95 Mich. L. Rev. 203 (1996); Thomas Grey,

amples include Martha Nussbaum's demonstrably false testimony before Congress regarding the history of homosexuality,[301] or the recent fabrication of a past by European historians in which gender roles were not defined and homosexuality was celebrated rather than condemned.[302] In fact, throughout most of European history, homosexuality was seen as demeaning to the pene-trated partner (seen as taking the "female" role) even if empowering to the penetrating partner (seen as behaving like a man). This pattern goes back at least as far as ancient Egypt.[303] And in America, one finds at least two men executed and a third severely whipped for "sodomy" in colonial Connecticut between 1646 and 1677.[304] One could go on and on.

Yet the manufactured history of homosexuality prevailed, at least in the courts, when the Supreme Court in *Lawrence v. Texas,*[305] by a vote of 6-3, overruled *Bowers.* Justice Anthony Kennedy, writing for the majority on the Court, specifically relied upon "academic writings, and...the scholarly *amicus* briefs filed to assist the Court in this case," to conclude that "there is no longstanding history in this country of laws directed at homosexual conduct as a distinct matter."[306] After all, he noted, the laws prohibited particular sexual acts without regard to whether they were undertaken between persons of the same sex or between persons of different sexes.[307] He then noted that the burden of proof made convictions of consenting adults ex-tremely difficult and that therefore prosecutions of consenting adults were rare in the nineteenth century.[308] From these facts, he concluded that laws targeting homosexual conduct as such did not emerge until the last third of the twentieth century![309] He then went on to conclude that in any event the emerging trend of legalizing homosexual conduct during that same last third of the twentieth century was most relevant to determining whether federal due process guarantees precluded criminalizing private homosexual conduct between consenting adults acting in pri-vate.[310] Building from this last conclusion and drawing on, among other cases, the abortion deci-sions about personal privacy, Kennedy concluded that the federal constitution did indeed pre-clude treating private consensual homosexual conduct as criminal.[311] Justice Sandra Day O'Connor, who had voted with the majority in *Bowers,* concurred in the result in *Lawrence* on

---

Bowers v. Hardwick *Diminished,* 68 U. Colo. L. Rev. 373 (1997); Janet Halley, Romer v. Hardwick, 68 *U. Colo. L. Rev.* 429 (1997); Richard Rueben, *Gay Rights Watershed? Scholars Debate whether Past and Future Cases Will Be Affected by Supreme Court's* Romer *Decision,* ABA J., July, 1996, at 30; Louis Michael Seidman, Romer's *Radicalism: The Unexpected Revival of Warren Court Activism,* 1996 Sup. Ct. Rev. 67. *See generally* Garrow, *supra* note 11, at 723–35.

301. Analyzed in John Finnis, *Law, Morality, and "Sexual Orientation,"* 69 Notre Dame L. Rev. 1049, 1055–63 (1994). She repeated her false testimony before a trial court in the first stage of *Romer v. Evans,* 517 U.S. 620 (1996). *See* Daniel Mendelsohn, *The Stand,* Lingua Franca, Sept.–Oct. 1996, at 34, 34–35. For Nussbaum's views, see Martha Nussbaum, *Platonic Love and Colorado Law: The Relevance of Ancient Greek Norms to Modern Sexual Controversies,* 80 Va. L. Rev. 1515 (1994).

302. Discussed in Keith Thomas, *As You Like It,* N.Y. Rev. Books, Sept. 22, 1994, at 9. For an example, see K.J. Dover, Greek Homosexuality (1978). For evidence of the condemnation and even punishment of ho-mosexuality during the era that the "new historians" tell us homosexuality was tolerated, see, *e.g.,* Jeffrey Mer-rick, *Commissioner Foucault, Inspector Noël, and the "Pederasts" of Paris, 1780–83,"* 32 J. Soc. Hist. 289 (1998) (reporting 111 arrests in three years, and one person broken on the rack and burned alive).

303. Joyce Tyldesley, Hatchepsut: The Female Pharaoh 188–90 (Penguin ed. 1998); Lise Manniche, *Some Aspects of Ancient Egyptian Sexual Life,* 38 Acta Orientalia, 11–23 (1977).

304. Cornelia Hughes Dayton, Women before the Bar: Gender, Law, and Society in Connecti-cut, 1639–1789, at 164 n.11 (1995).

305. 539 U.S. 558 (2003).

306. *Id.* at 567–68.

307. *Id.* at 568–69.

308. *Id.* at 569–70.

309. *Id.* at 570.

310. *Id.* at 570–73.

311. *Id.* at 573–79.

equal protection grounds, expressly refusing to question the history-based due process analysis in *Bowers*.[312]

Justice Antonin Scalia, writing in dissent on behalf of himself, Chief Justice William Rehnqist, and Justice Clarence Thomas, noted that the majority's decision to overrule *Bowers* only 17 years after it was decided was apparently based upon three premises: that the foundations of the "intensely divisive" opinion had been undermined by subsequent decisions (particularly *Romer v. Evans*[313]), that the opinion had been subject to "substantial and continuing criticism," and that it had not resulted in "individual or societal reliance."[314] He then pointed out that each of these premises applied equally to the decision in *Roe v. Wade*,[315] although the majority in *Lawrence* certainly would not overrule *Roe*.[316] Scalia went on to argue that it was Kennedy who had gotten the history wrong, rather than Justice Byron White in *Bowers*.[317]

I analyze *Lawrence* not in order to suggest that homosexual acts should remain crimes (personally, I'm against it[318]), but to illustrate the extent to which historical studies are distorted and even falsified in order to justify a particular legal outcome before the Supreme Court. Such distortions and falsifications of history also occur in the making of political or legal arguments in other forums—like legislatures. Radical historian Howard Zinn suggested the proper method for reconciling the reality that all historians work from a basis of personal values yet seek after truth: "Our values should determine the *questions* we ask in scholarly inquiry, but not the answers."[319] This is not so easy as its statement might suggest. Ted White, a leading legal historian, describes the process in thus:

> [An] historian's decision to study a particular segment of the past is never accidental; it is, at one level, a product of presentist concerns. Not only are the historian's choices of historical subject matter affected by the way he or she relates to contemporary culture, the historian's interpretations of the subjects chosen are likewise affected. The act of examining the past is thus a form of intervention, in which the historian brings a contemporary perspective to bear on the subjects of a past time, and necessarily casts those subjects in a different light.
>
> Here is the first of the professional quandaries inherent in writing history surfaces. There is a well-established difference between history and fiction. There is an equally well established, if less clear-cut, difference between history and polemics. If historical scholarship is primarily motivated by presentist concerns, how does the historian prevent those concerns from overwhelming historical subject matter? Or, put another way, why should it matter if they did? While generations of historians have wrestled with those questions, their answers have been remarkably similar: when the concerns of the present overwhelm the materials of the past, history ceases to exist.
>
> Thus along with the impulse to intervene a historian struggles with another impulse, the impulse to achieve detachment. In the initial meaning of the term, detachment refers to a distancing of the historian from the presentist concerns that impelled him or

---

312. *Id.* at 579–85 (O'Connor, J., concurring).
313. 517 U.S. 620 (1996).
314. *Lawrence,* 539 U.S. at 587 (Scalia, J., dissenting).
315. 401 U.S. 113 (1973).
316. *Lawrence,* 539 U.S. at 587–92 (Scalia, J., dissenting).
317. *Id.* at 594–998.
318. I would agree with Justice Clarence Thomas, who wrote a separate dissent to the holding in *Lawrence* simply in order to state that he considered the criminal statute in question to be "uncommonly silly." *Id.* at 605.
319. ZINN, *supra* note 91, at 10 (emphasis in the original).

her to seek out a particular subject from the past for study. As a professional goal, detachment in this sense requires that distancing: it requires an immersion by the historian in the mores and thought patterns of an alien culture. Only with this sort of detachment from one's subject…is one able to produce history, as distinct from fiction or polemics.…[At] the level of politics,…the only stance the historian can properly offer is that of detachment, which is [itself] a form of intervention.…[T]he paradox is that the most effective interventions are those that retain elements of the historian's initial passion.[320]

## The Stories Told about Abortion Past

*To trace the history of the Wilson administration is relatively simple;*
*to formulate that of the Debs' presidency requires a subtler intelligence.*

—Paul Campos[321]

Historian James Mohr and his followers have sought to avoid close scrutiny of their treatment of the evidence regarding the law of abortion by shifting the focus from the increasingly clear history of the law to the far less certain issue of the "true" social attitudes concerning abortion. Supposedly, the true attitudes regarding abortion are found in "lost voices"—in diaries, letters, published statements by non-legal professionals, newspaper reports, and almost anything else except judicial opinions or legislative records. The problem, as we have seen, is how to recover "voices" that left no trace in the actual records of their time.

In the attempt to recapture the "true" history of the law of abortion, Mohr would have us ignore all legal sources except for the few that tangentially, at best, support their position. He also discounts the records of attitudes with which he disagrees either in favor of other, similar records of attitudes he finds useful, or even in favor of presumed unrecorded opinions of historically mute classes.[322] Those who employ such purportedly sociological approaches to history never bother to explain why the formal institutions of a society would choose to express themselves in such unrepresentative terms if their publicly expressed attitudes did not connect in some significant way with values widely shared in the society. Nor do they bother to explain why the official story of abortion continued with only minor changes through numerous major changes of social and political structure. Mohr's approach does have the inestimable virtue of permitting him to infer at will what the "true" attitudes were.

Most remarkable about such an approach to abortion history is that so many accept it even when the evidence used for the various claims is internally inconsistent. The greatest inconsistency is the proposition that the best way to determine the *legal* tradition underlying the Constitution is to examine *non-legal* sources, with little or no attention to legal sources, a proposition

---

320. WHITE, *supra* note 100, at 3–4, 6. White included extensive discussion of this paradox in his book. *Id.* at 17–72. The three chapters are reprints of earlier articles. G. Edward White, *The Art of Revising History: Revisiting the Marshall Court,* 16 SUFFOLK L. REV. 659 (1982); G. Edward White, *The Text, Interpretation, and Critical Standards,* 60 TEX. L. REV. 569 (1982); G. Edward White, *Truth and Interpretation in Legal History,* 79 MICH. L. REV. 594 (1981).

321. Paul Campos, *Mirror for the Magistrate,* 9 CONST'L COMMENTARY 151, 157 (1992).

322. *See, e.g.,* MOHR, *supra* note 65, at 91–101, 115–18, 240–45.

explicit in the notorious *Historians' Briefs*[323] and underlying Mohr's much-admired book[324] as well as turning up in the work of others who argue that Anglo-American history supports a "liberty" to abort. Thus law professor Berta Hernàndez makes the same argument regarding the entire world, admitting that abortion has nearly always been condemned by law yet claiming that this fact is largely irrelevant to determining whether there is a *legal* right to abort because, despite its universal condemnation, abortion has been universally practiced.[325] It is equally true of that murder, mayhem, and rape are universals, found in every society, notwithstanding their formal, universal condemnation—even allowing for different definitions in different societies of what counts as murder, mayhem, and rape. No one supposes that we have a legal right to engage in those activities. To say that these crimes are different because they have non-consenting victims simply begs the question, for many people see abortion as involving a non-consenting victim.

Law professor Cyril Means, jr., aptly summarized the results of his and related attempts to rework history in a manner convenient to modern desires—in a criticism that he directed at some of his contemporary opponents. With typical understatement, he described those who criticized his history as "latter-day zealots,"[326] writing that "[a]fter all this, one can only conclude that Clio has many clients, and some of them are clowns."[327] There are, of course, zealots and clowns on both sides. Some might think Means was among the better examples of those qualities.[328]

The most prominent examples of historians who have sought to use history in the controversy over abortion without regard to the evidence available are the many historians who subscribed to the *Webster* and *Casey Historians' Briefs* despite their own serious disagreement with the contents of the briefs or without having studied the history in question.[329] We have encountered the substance of the *Historians' Briefs* at the points relevant to this book's recounting of the history of abortion. The two briefs themselves have been described as an "utter fraud, riddled with scholarly abuses and inaccurate conclusions."[330] We find the same indifference to truth in the historians who signed the *Historians' Briefs* sight unseen.[331]

A brief in a legal proceeding is not a work of history, but of advocacy. That alone might preclude any attempt to strike a balance between present political or legal concerns and concerns about recovering the truth of the past.[332] In any event, the problem of balancing involvement (what legal historian Ted White terms "intervention") with detachment obviously does not lend itself to incontestable outcomes.[333] Yet the goal of balancing involvement with detachment does

---

323. *Casey Historians' Brief, supra* note 68, at 4–5; *Webster Historians' Brief, supra* note 68, at 117–24.

324. MOHR, *supra* note 65, at 6, 43–45.

325. Berta Hernàndez, *To Bear or Not to Bear: Reproductive Freedom as an International Human Right,* 17 BROOK. J. INT'L L. 309, 335, 345–46 (1991). For a similar argument concerning the proper interpretation of the Constitution regarding race relations, see Paul Finkelman, *Book Review* (of ANDREW KULL, THE COLOR OF LAW), 87 NW. U.L. REV. 937, 959, 961 (1993) (denigrating a constitutional history of race relations as concerned with "legalistic" readings of the Constitution and evincing mere "lawyer's points" in argument).

326. Means II, *supra* note 46, at 362 n.12.

327. *Id.* at 362.

328. *See* Chapter 3, at notes 126–85; Chapter 4, at notes 11–222; Chapter 5, at notes 35–196; Chapter 6, at notes 100–212; Chapter 7, at notes 58–113.

329. *Casey Historians' Brief, supra* note 68, at 1; *Webster Historians' Brief, supra* note 68, at 169.

330. Ramesh Ponnuru, *Abortion History,* NAT. REV., Oct. 23, 1995, at 29, 32. The full passage is quoted in Chapter 17, at note 58. *See generally* Chapter 17, at notes 39–58.

331. *See* Chapter 17, at note 47.

332. *See* Kelly, *supra* note 84.

333. See the text quoted *supra* at note 314.

provide constraints within which respectable historians must operate—as even the lawyers who gave us the *Historians' Briefs* knew.

Thus, we find Jane Larson (one of the lawyers who wrote the *Historians' Briefs*) admitting in another context that the inability of determining "absolute truth" does not preclude her from identifying a "smaller set of untruths that result from knowing and intentional misrepresentations."[334] Sylvia Law—the lead attorney on the *Briefs*—candidly lamented the authors' collective "serious deficiencies as truth-tellers" in preparing the *Webster Historians' Brief*.[335] Despite these deficiencies, the *Historians' Briefs* rely on the expectations of detachment and objectivity in their audience to make their claims credible even when the claims are conscious falsehoods that served only presentist concerns rather a genuine attempt to recover the past.[336]

Despite Sylvia Law's admitted deficiencies as a truth-teller (or perhaps because of her deficiencies), she has argued that historians can do a better job of "telling the truth" by participating in briefs than by appearing as witnesses precisely because briefs are not subject to cross-examination.[337] No wonder law professor Ruth Colker (apparently without knowing of these comments) concluded after reading the *Webster Historians' Briefs* that "very few of the briefs reflected the aspirations that I believe we should hold as feminists. In particular, the aspiration of good faith dialogue often seems to be absent."[338] Such special pleading, even when expected, is still troubling when indulged by lawyers and other professional advocates.[339] One expects from historians at least an attempt at objectivity (even conceding the ultimate futility of such attempts), the absence of which debilitates both the legal and the historical enterprise. The emerging practice of some historians of disparaging the distinction between scholarship and advocacy as an illusion is hardly conducive to either neutrality or objectivity.[340] Ultimately, the number of historians who signed the two *Historians' Briefs* indicates far more about abortion's current political standing than about its history.[341]

---

334. Jane Larson, *"Women Understand So Little, They Call My Good Nature 'Deceit'": A Feminist Rethinking of Seduction,* 93 COLUM. L. REV. 374, 452 (1993). *See also* RICH, *supra* note 37, at 185.

335. Law, *supra* note 252, at 14–16.

336. *See* Chapter 17, at notes 45–46.

337. Law, *supra* note 252, at 14.

338. COLKER, *supra* note 129, at 129.

339. *See* CHARLES MILLER, THE SUPREME COURT AND THE USES OF HISTORY 22–23, 25, 159–60 (1969); R.P. Boast, *Lawyers, Historians, Ethics and the Judicial Process,* 28 VICTORIA U. WELLINGTON L. REV. 87 (1998); J. Peter Byrne, *Academic Freedom and Political Neutrality in Law Schools: An Essay on Structure and Ideology in Professional Education,* 43 J. LEGAL EDUC. 315, 322, 324 (1993); Harry Edwards, *The Growing Disjunction between Legal Education and the Legal Profession,* 91 MICH. L. REV. 34, 68–70 (1992); Steven Lubet, *Ethics and Theory Choice in Advocacy Education,* 44 J. LEGAL EDUC. 81 (1994).

340. *See, e.g.,* Jane Larson & Clyde Spillenger, *"That's Not History": The Boundaries of Advocacy and Scholarship,* 12 PUB. HISTORIAN 33, 40–42 (1990).

341. *Cf.* Gerard Bradley, *Academic Integrity Betrayed,* FIRST THINGS, Aug./Sept. 1990, at 10. Another brief in *Webster* was signed by 20% of the law professors in the United States, including "some of our nation's most respected constitutional theorists." *Amicus Brief for a Group of American Law Professors in Support of Appellee* in Webster v. Reproductive Health Services, *reprinted in* 6 DOCUMENTARY HISTORY, *supra* note 68, at 513. *See* Kathryn Kolbert, *The* Webster *Amicus Curiae Briefs: Perspectives on the Abortion Controversy and the Role of the Supreme Court,* 15 AM. J. L. & MED. 153, 164 (1989). One wonders how many of the law professors read the brief before signing.

A similar situation arose with the attempt to impeach President Clinton. Some 400 historians signed a letter and 430 law professors signed another letter, both addressed to Congress and both indicating that there were absolutely no grounds for impeachment. Nearly all of these professors signed the letter site unseen, and all purported to speak as experts on the question, even though few of the signers of either letter had any particular knowledge of the matters about which they claimed to speak. *See generally* Neal Devins, *Bearing False Witness: The Clinton Impeachment and the Future of Academic Freedom,* 148 U. PA. L. REV. 165 (1999); Michael Klarman, *Constitutional Fetishism and the Clinton Impeachment Debate,* 85 VA. L. REV. 631 (1999); John

Perhaps this experience counsels the wisdom of the suggestion that non-lawyer experts, in filing an *amicus* brief, should stick to presenting their field of expertise and not attempt to argue for a particular outcome in the case before the Court.[342] After all, if pervasive lying is necessary to justify a policy, can that policy possibly be right? Without honestly confronting our past how can we hope to understand, let alone, overcome it? Even if you think for abortion the ends justify the means, is not lying on such a scale likely, sooner or later, to result in a wrong turn on the policy road? Can lies really provide us with a correct reading of the Constitution? When, if ever, should a lawyer lie on behalf of client?[343] The record of the abortion controversy forces us to answer such questions.

While the past is, of course, not completely knowable, neither is the present. Just as the incomplete knowability of the present does not excuse us from attempting as best we can to reason through to sound answers about today's world and our relation to it, so too the incomplete knowability of the past does not absolve us from attempting to come to terms with it. Historian Herbert Muller made the point 50 years ago:

> [T]he admission of *ultimate* uncertainty does not mean *complete* uncertainty. The absolutist tradition of Christendom leads men (*sic*) to assume that if we don't have absolute standards we can't have any standards, and that if we are not standing on the Rock of Ages we are standing on nothing. Actually, we can and do know plenty of objective truths without knowing the whole or final Truth.... In general, the uniformities and continuities of human existence are what make significant thought possible; the manifold possibilities of experience are what make critical thought necessary. Hence a refusal on principle to say the last word about human history is not a refusal to say any word, or to pass any firm judgment. Rather, it defines conditions of judgment. Say that our most cherished beliefs are matters of opinion and it is then our business to get sound opinions, based on honest thought and the best available knowledge; only a fool will say that any opinion is as good as any other when he gets sick. Say that our final preferences are matters of taste and it is then our business to cultivate good taste.... [T]he most certain knowledge we do have about the history of [humankind] belies all pretense to absolute certainty. We must nevertheless have principles, standards, faiths; many... have been demoralized by a shallow relativism that denies us the right to judge anyone or anything, while we perforce keep judging.[344]

---

McGinnis, *Impeachable Defenses*, Pol'y Rev., June–July 1999, at 27. Judge Richard Posner has hinted that the signing of the letter represents a "sort of herd behavior" while not quite embracing that description. Richard Posner, An Affair of State 242 (1999). For a fairly lame defense of these letters, see Cass Sunstein, *Professors and Politics*, 148 U. Pa. L. Rev. 191 (1999). Sunstein openly discusses the extent to which he coordinated his efforts to recruit law professors with Democratic Congressional leaders, without apparently realizing how damning his admissions are. *See also An Open Letter to Congressman Gingrich*, 104 Yale L.J. 1539 (1995); *Constitutional Scholars' Statement on Affirmative Action after* City of Richmond v. J.A. Croson Co., 98 Yale L.J. 1711 (1989).

342. *See* Thomas Grisso & Michael Saks, *Psychology's Influence on Constitutional Interpretation*, 15 Law & Human Behavior 205 (1991).

343. *See, e.g.,* Carrie Menkle-Meadow, *Lying to Clients for Economic Gain or Paternalistic Judgment: A Proposal for a Golden Rule of Candor*, 138 U. Pa. L. Rev. 761 (1990); Frederick Miller, *Commentary: "If You Can't Trust Your Lawyer...,"* 138 U. Pa. L. Rev. 785 (1990); Geoffrey Peters, *The Use of Lies in Negotiations*, 48 Ohio St. L.J. 1 (1987); Thomas Shaffer, *On Lying for Clients*, 71 Notre Dame L. Rev. 195 (1996). *See generally* Sisela Bok, Lying: Moral Choice in Public and Private Life (1978).

344. Herbert Muller, The Uses of Past: Profiles of Former Societies 47–48 (Mentor Book ed. 1954).

# Could History Provide the Answers?

*Our Constitution is a covenant running from the first generation of Americans to us and then to future generations. It is a coherent succession. Each generation must learn anew that the Constitution's written terms embody ideas and aspirations that must survive more ages than one.*

—Anthony Kennedy, Sandra Day O'Connor, and David Souter[345]

A deconstructionist approach to the history of abortion leads to the conclusion either that the history has no real content or that it has whatever content we prefer to give it.[346] Indeterminacy in the law is an old problem, of course, having been recognized at least as early as the end of the eighteenth century.[347] For most of the past two centuries, lawyers, jurists, and others resolved the problem by recourse to the command of the actual lawmaker based on the supposition that legal and other texts mean what their authors intended the texts to mean.[348] As law professor Steven Smith noted, "[t]he practice of interpretation can seem to be a sensible one, and one essentially different from what we regard as nonrational or superstitious practices such as astrology, only on the premise that the text is the expression of a mindful author."[349]

Deconstruction theory, however, insists precisely that there is no discoverable authorial intent, having their greatest success in their arguments in the field of contemporary theories of constitutional interpretation.[350] Abandonment of the theory of original meaning in constitutional "interpretation" poses the problem of interpretation in such stark terms that jurisprude Ronald Dworkin has sought to resolve the ensuing crisis of authority by the rather peculiar notion that judges both receive authority from and are constrained by a supposed intent of a hypothetical author rather than on the intent of any actual author.[351] As this suggests, courts and scholars increasingly justify a claim to relative objectivity through recourse to history and tradition as the source of continuity and constraint in legal decisionmaking even when they reject the idea of seeking some sort of "original intent" or "original meaning."[352]

---

345. Planned Parenthood of S.E. Pa. v. Casey, 505 U.S. 833, 901 (1992) (Kennedy, O'Connor, & Souter, JJ., joint plurality op.).

346. Larson & Spillenger, *supra* note 326.

347. Walter Walsh, *Redefining Radicalism: A Historical Perspective*, 59 Geo. Wash. L. Rev. 636 (1991).

348. *See, e.g.*, John Norton Pomeroy, An Introduction to the Constitutional Law of the United States 11–12 (1868); Thomas Cooley, A Treatise on the Constitutional Limitations which Rest upon the Legislative Power of the States of the Union 37, 55, 59–61, 175 (1868). In his day Cooley was considered the foremost constitutional scholar in the United States. *See* Caryn Jacobs, Law Writers and the Courts: The Influence of Thomas M. Cooley, Christopher G. Tiedeman, and John F. Dillon upon American Constitutional Law 18, 29, 34–35 (1954); Alan Jones, The Constitutional Conservatism of Thomas McIntyre Cooley 1 (1987); Philip Paludan, A Covenant with Death: The Constitution, Law, and Equality in the Civil War Era 249, 252 (1975).

349. Smith, *supra* note 81, at 590. *See also* Steven Smith, *Law without Mind*, 88 Mich. L. Rev. 104 (1989).

350. *See, e.g.*, Arthur, *supra* note 118; Bobbit, *supra* note 11; Maltz, *supra* note 16; Tribe & Dorf, *supra* note 16, at 98–109; Tushnet, *supra* note 13, at 32–45; Stephen Macedo, *Originalism and the Inescapability of Politics*, 84 Nw. U.L. Rev. 1203 (1990); ' note 82; Winter, *supra* note 13.

351. *See* Dworkin, *supra* note 3. For a detailed critique of this theory, see Campos, *supra* note 5, at 288–89, 296–302; Smith, *supra* note 81.

352. *See* John Daly, The Use of History in the Decisions of the Supreme Court, 1900–1930 (1954); Dworkin, *supra* note 3; Glendon, *supra* note 10, at 251; Hutchinson, *supra* note 13, at 267, 281; Miller, *supra* note 339; Michael Perry, Morality, Politics, and Law 127, 136–42 (1988); Tribe & Dorf, *supra* note 16, at 13–19, 33, 52–53, 59–60, 70–71, 97–99 (1991); Walker, *supra* note 12, at 53–54; White, *supra* note 3, at 124–27, 172–74; Theodore Blumoff, *The Third Best Choice: An Essay on Law and History*, 41 Hast-

At bottom, law is applied history,[353] particularly in a system of law that accords explicit legal authority to precedents. No wonder historical justification is actually an old feature of the Anglo-American legal tradition. Patrick Henry said as much at the outbreak of the American Revolution: "I have but one lamp by which my feet are guided and that is the lamp of experience. I know of no way of judging the future but by the past."[354] Law professor Harold Berman traced recourse to historic justification in English law back to Sir Edward Coke in the seventeenth century.[355] Berman summarized his findings thusly: "Law…is the balancing of morality and politics in the light of history; it is the balancing of justice and order in the light of experience."[356] Law professor Jane Rutherford has found appeals to history going back to *Magna Carta*.[357]

The sense that history can provide some degree of certainty is not confined to the law. Even such a committed anarchist as Emma Goldman turned to history when she wrote, "History may be a compilation of lies; nevertheless, it contains a few truths, and they are the only guides we have for the future."[358] As this suggests, we have seen a turn to history (or at least to tradition) to resolve the absence of an absolute philosophical basis for knowledge. This turn also has its roots in certain forms of non-legal philosophy and study generally.[359]

Recourse to history as a source of legal or cultural certainty has generally been more problematic than those using the history seem to realize. Failure to realize the difficulties inherent in using history to interpret the present is exemplified by the lack of close attention to this process over most of the many centuries in which we have used history to interpret the law. Despite the antiquity of historical justification in the law, that process has seldom been studied and often has often been abused. Thus Theodore Dwight could note, barely a century ago, that Henry Sumner Maine's book was virtually the only work "in the English language in which general jurisprudence is regarded from the historical point of view."[360] There certainly were historians of the

---

INGS L.J. 537 (1990); Campos, *supra* note 5; Peggy Cooper Davis, *Contested Images of Family Values: The Role of the State*, 107 HARV. L. REV. 1348, 1350–51 (1994); Neil Duxbury, *Deconstruction, History and the Uses of Legal Theory*, 41 N. IR. LEGAL Q. 167 (1990); Frank Easterbrook, *Abstraction and Authority*, 59 U. CHI. L. REV. 349 (1992); E. Donald Elliott, *Against Ludditism: An Essay on the Perils of the (Mis)Use of Historical Analogies in Technology Assessment*, 65 S. CAL. L. REV. 279 (1991); Farrell, *supra* note 16, at 308–09; Friedrich, *supra* note 85; Peter Charles Hoffer, *"Blind to History": The Use of History in Affirmative Action Suits: Another Look at* City of Richmond v. J.A. Croson, Co., 23 RUTGERS L.J. 271 (1992); Horwitz, *supra* note 91; Hunt, *supra* note 37, at 529–40; Kelly, *supra* note 84; Kronman, *supra* note 88; McConnell, *supra* note 5; Nelson, *supra* note 232; Reid, *supra* note 89; Richards, *supra* note 37; Steegman, *supra* note 61, at 386–90; John Yoo, *Clio at War: The Misuse of History in the War Powers Debate*, 70 U. COLO. L. REV. 1169 (1999).

353. See the text *supra* at notes 84–90.

354. Patrick Henry, *Speech in the Virginia Convention, March 25, 1775, quoted in* Rita Marker *et al.*, *Euthanasia: A Historical Overview*, 2 MD. J. CONTEMP. LEGAL ISSUES 257, 298 (1991). *See also* EDMUND BURKE, REFLECTIONS ON THE REVOLUTION IN FRANCE 110–11 (1793).

355. Berman, *supra* note 84. Berman found some intimations of this approach even back to the fifteenth century, but was unpersuaded that this attitude was prevalent before the seventeenth century. *Id.* at 1658–67.

356. *Id.* at 1731.

357. Rutherford, *supra* note 5, at 28.

358. Quoted in NANCY COTT, THE GROUNDING OF MODERN FEMINISM vii (1987).

359. *See* ALISDAIR MCINTYRE, WHOSE JUSTICE? WHICH RATIONALITY? 6 (1988); THE HISTORIC TURN IN THE HUMAN SCIENCES (Terence McDonald ed. 1996).

360. Theodore Dwight, *Introduction*, in HENRY SUMNER MAINE, ANCIENT LAW at ix (3rd Am. ed. 1864). *See also* Stephen Utz, *Maine's* Ancient Law *and Legal Theory*, 16 CONN. L. REV. 821 (1984); Paul Vinogradoff, *The Teaching of Sir Henry Maine*, 20 L.Q. REV. 119 (1904). The most noted articulation of an historical approach to law, finding normative significance in law's history, remains the work of the German jurisprude von Savigny, first published in 1813. FRIEDRICH CARL VON SAVIGNY, OF THE VOCATION OF OUR AGE FOR LEGISLATION AND JURISPRUDENCE (Abraham Hayward trans. 1966). One can trace this approach back at least as far as Montesquieu. CHARLES DE SECONDAT MONTESQUIEU, 1 THE SPIRIT OF LAWS 31 (Thomas Nugent trans. 1899; original pub. date 1748). *See generally* GEORGE PEABODY GOOCH, HISTORY AND HISTORIANS IN THE NINE-TEENTH CENTURY 47–53 (1913).

common law before Maine, but they tended not to consider a possible role for their work beyond mere compilations of fact.[361] Matthew Hale and Edmund Burke provide major exceptions.[362]

Many twentieth-century legal scholars believe that the nineteenth century was the heyday of natural law thinking in the common law world, with jurists seeking to incorporate natural law into the law and into the Constitution.[363] Actually, the opposite is true. By the end of the nineteenth century, history had come to be understood as the key to a correct reading of precedent, to the understanding of law generally, and to the interpretation of the Constitution in particular.[364] As Albert Dicey, the great nineteenth-century English legal scholar, observed, "It were far better, as things now stand, to be charged with heresy, than to fall under the suspicion of lacking historical-mindedness, or of questioning the universal validity of the historical method."[365]

The Supreme Court has repeatedly endorsed recourse to history and tradition as the key to the correct interpretation of the Constitution of the United States. The passage in *Planned Parenthood of Southeast Pennsylvania v. Casey* quoted at the beginning of this section is only a particularly strong appeal to that notion. As legal historian Charles Miller observed,

> Neither the clinical destruction of the Court's use of history through legal scholarship nor outright advocacy of forward-looking decisions has been able to tear up traditions of constitutional and judicial thinking deeply rooted in the American political culture. The ties of the Constitution are to the past, and when history calls, the justices strain to listen.[366]

Justice Joseph Story first voiced this view of the Constitution more than a century ago.[367] The later nineteenth century commentators on constitutional law such as Cooley and Pomeroy pressed this same notion.[368] Yet despite their espousal of the historical approach to legal (particularly constitutional) reasoning, the Justices of the American Supreme Court do not seem to have become all that consciously historical in their reasoning until the rise of judicial activism in the 1930s required the Court to reexamine the original meaning of the Constitution and other texts and to explain the errors of interpretation which the Court was intent on repudiating.[369] The later Justice John Marshall Harlan, in his dissent to *Poe v. Ullman*, provided one of the best explanations of the role history and traditions ought to play in our legal system:

> Due process has not been reduced to any formula; its content cannot be determined by reference to any code. The best that can be said is that through the course of this Court's decisions it has represented the balance which our Nation, built upon postulates of respect for the liberty of the individual, has struck between that liberty and the

---

361. *See generally* W.S. HOLDSWORTH, THE HISTORIANS OF ANGLO-AMERICAN LAW 3–64 (1966); SAYLES, *supra* note 283, at 1–16, 133–49.

362. BRUCE FROHNEN, VIRTUE AND THE PROMISE OF CONSERVATISM: THE LEGACY OF BURKE AND TOCQUEVILLE (1993); Berman, *supra* note 84, at 1702–21.

363. *See, e.g.*, BENJAMIN WRIGHT, AMERICAN INTERPRETATION OF NATURAL LAW 280–81, 288–92, 298–300 (1931); Roscoe Pound, *Liberty of Contract*, 18 YALE L.J. 454, 460–68 (1909); Horwitz, *supra* note 16, at 657–58.

364. *See, e.g.*, Joseph Beale, *The Development of Jurisprudence during the Past Century*, 18 HARV. L. REV. 271, 283 (1905). *See generally* STEFAN COLLINS, DONALD WINCH, & JOHN BURROW, THAT NOBLE SCIENCE OF POLITICS: A STUDY IN NINETEENTH CENTURY INTELLECTUAL HISTORY 183–246 (1983); Stephen Siegel, *Historicism in Late Nineteenth-Century Constitutional Thought*, 1990 WIS. L. REV. 1431.

365. ALBERT VENN DICEY, INTRODUCTION TO THE STUDY OF THE LAW OF THE CONSTITUTION 14 (1885).

366. MILLER, *supra* note 339, at 51.

367. JOSEPH STORY, COMMENTARIES ON THE CONSTITUTION OF THE UNITED STATES §325 n.7 (3rd ed. 1858).

368. COOLEY, *supra* note 348, at 61, 85–129, 166, 175–76, 410–17; POMEROY, *supra* note 348, at 17–18, 103–05, 110–13.

369. Kelly, *supra* note 84, at 123; Murphy, *supra* note 272, at 75; Reid, *supra* note 89, at 197–201.

demands of organized society. If the supplying of content to this Constitutional concept has of necessity been a rational process, it certainly has not been one where judges have felt free to roam where unguided speculation might take them. The balance of which I speak is the balance struck by this country, having regard for what history teaches are the traditions from which it developed as well as the traditions from which it broke. That tradition is a living thing. A decision of this Court which radically departs from it could not long survive, while a decision which builds on what has survived is likely to be sound. No formula could serve as a substitute, in this area, for judgment and restraint.[370]

Justice Felix Frankfurter summarized the point more pithily, commenting that the Constitution is "a stream of history."[371] Justice Oliver Wendell Holmes, jr., even gave us one of his inevitable aphorisms from the bench, "A page of history is worth a volume of logic."[372] But even as Justices Felix Frankfurter and the younger John Marshall Harlan were speaking or writing, however, sophisticated historical justifications were becoming rarer in our courts. Some saw this drop of historical reasoning from juridical favor as the result of judges becoming more concerned with displacing traditional law than with preserving received values.[373] Two major alternatives to historical analysis emerged in contemporary legal philosophy: interpretive liberalism and communitarian thinking.[374] Neither theory has yet demonstrated much resonance in the thinking of judges and lawyers. In any event, both rely heavily on history if one is to talk about real communities or the interpretation or an actual moral tradition. As a result, the historical mode has made a strong comeback in recent years as those who seek to role back the changes of the Warren Court seek to present their changes as a return to prior law.[375]

Law professor Steven Siegel missed the point when he argued that the rise of legal positivism drew attention to history long before the advent of the Warren Court.[376] True enough, "historicism" (Siegel's term) is a corollary to legal positivism. How else could a jurist properly respectful of a duty to obey the law enacted by others resolve questions left open in necessarily ambiguous positive law? Yet while positivism reinforces the recourse to history, it does not necessarily display with any great concern for accuracy in that history. Judges often use spurious history as a device for justifying a break with unhappy precedent.[377] In the end, all this talk about the use of history on the Court only serves to remind us, as law professor Leonard Levy aptly noted in a

---

370. Poe v. Ullman, 367 U.S. 497, 542 (1961) (Harlan, J., dissenting).

371. *Quoted in* SANFORD LEVINSON, CONSTITUTIONAL FAITH 33 (1988).

372. New York Times Co. v. Eisner, 256 U.S. 345, 349 (1921). For related comments by Holmes, see the text *supra* at note 88.

373. MILLER, *supra* note 339, at 2–3, 17–20, 28–38; William Beaney, *Book Review,* 55 AM. POL. SCI. REV. 634 (1961). *See generally* MARTIN SHAPIRO, LAW AND POLITICS IN THE SUPREME COURT (1964); William Anderson, *The Intention of the Framers: A Note on Constitutional Interpretation,* 49 AM. POL. SCI. REV. 340 (1955).

374. *See, e.g.,* United States v. Verdugo-Urquidez, 494 U.S. 259 (1990); DWORKIN, *supra* note 3; JAMES FISHKIN, RECONSTRUCTING THE SOCIAL CONTRACT: TOWARDS A NEW LIBERAL THEORY (1991); WILLIAM GALSTON, LIBERAL PURPOSES: GOODS, VIRTUES, AND DIVERSITY IN THE LIBERAL STATE (1991); MARY ANN GLENDON, RIGHTS TALK: THE IMPOVERISHMENT OF POLITICAL DISCOURSE (1991); ALISDAIR MACINTYRE, A STUDY IN MORAL THEORY (1982); ROGER SMITH, LIBERALISM AND AMERICAN CONSTITUTIONAL LAW (1985); WILLIAM SULLIVAN, RECONSTRUCTING PUBLIC PHILOSOPHY (1982); MICHAEL WALZER, SPHERES OF JUSTICE (1983); John Rawls, *The Idea of an Overlapping Consensus,* 7 OX. J. LEGAL STUD. 1 (1987); Tushnet, *supra* note 10.

375. See the text *supra* at notes 88–90.

376. Siegel, *supra* note 364. *See also* Robert Gordon, *Historicism in Legal Scholarship,* 90 YALE L.J. 1017 (1981).

377. Kelly, *supra* note 84, at 125–28, 156; Murphy, *supra* note 272; Wiecek, *supra* note 89, at 228.

different context, that "[t]wo centuries of [Supreme] Court history should bring us to understand what really is a notorious fact: the Court has flunked history."[378]

In part, such errors arise because of the differing goals of lawyers and historians. Lawyers seek to determine the meaning of a statute or precedent in today's world and tend to assume that a statute or precedent always meant—"at least potentially"—what it means today.[379] This reflects a distinction between a lawyer's "logic of authority" and a historian's "logic of evidence."[380] Courts seek to read all relevant authorities as pointing toward a "harmonious conjunction" leading to the same result by ignoring nuances and possible contradictions in an effort to "avoid trouble or tension within the law's justificatory narratives" through "shallow or simplistic historical, economic, or philosophical analyses."[381] As legal historian John Phillip Reid noted,

> when grappling with the Rule in *Shelley's Case,* [a lawyer] is interested only in the latest interpretation of the rule—the last decision in the jurisdiction—and nothing else. Lawyers, in functioning as lawyers, do not have to learn anything of sixteenth-century law, or of the rule's subsequent historical evolution. All that lawyers need care about is the net result of that evolution, the latest judicial, *nonhistorical* appraisal or interpretation of the rule....Common lawyers tend to be anachronistic, not merely because they are advocates, but because of the way they think and speak about the past.[382]

Reid defends that practice as "forensic history."[383]

The lawyer's habit of mind gives rise to what historian Alfred Kelly called "law-office history"—history designed to win a case rather than to explore the historical record.[384] Kelly noted that law-office history was generally a signal that the jurist in question was seeking to break with precedent by finding a spurious "original intent" or similar historical basis for the result sought. Samuel Krislov has described law-office history as "a stark, crabbed, oversimplified picture of the past, developed largely to plead a case."[385] As John Phillip Reid cautions us,

---

378. LEVY, *supra* note 81, at 300. *See also* Eric Foner, *The Supreme Court's Legal History,* 23 RUTGERS L.J. 243, 247 (1992); Wilcomb Washburn, *The Supreme Court's Use and Abuse of History,* ORG. OF AM. HISTORIANS NEWSL., Aug. 1983, at 7, 9.

379. J.W. GOUGH, FUNDAMENTAL LAW IN ENGLISH CONSTITUTIONAL HISTORY 6–7 (1955).

380. Frederic Maitland, *Why the History of English Law Is Not Written,* in 1 THE COLLECTED PAPERS OF FREDERIC WILLIAM MAITLAND 480, 490–91 (H.A.L. Fisher ed. 1911)

381. Richard Fallon, jr., *Non-Legal Theory in Judicial Decisionmaking,* 17 HARV. J.L. & PUB. POL'Y 87, 94–95 (1994). *See also* Richard Fallon, jr., *A Constitutional Coherence Theory of Constitutional Interpretation,* 100 HARV. L. REV. 1189 (1987); Owen Fiss, *Objectivity and Interpretation,* 34 STAN. L. REV. 739 (1982).

382. Reid, *supra* note 89, at 194–95, 197. For a similar analysis of the Court's use of another discipline (linguistics), see SOLAN, *supra* note 283, at 27 ("The more difficult it is for a judge to state in the opinion what drove him to the decision[,] the more tempting independent noncontroversial argumentation becomes, such as arguments based on our knowledge of language."), 62 ("[J]udges do not make good linguists because they are using linguistic principles to accomplish an agenda distinct from the principles about which they write.").

383. Reid, *supra* note 89, at 204–23. *See also* Robert Gordon, *Foreword: The Arrival of Critical Historicism,* 49 STAN. L. REV. 1023 (1997); John Phillip Reid, *The Jurisprudence of Liberty: The Ancient Constitution in the Legal Historiography of the Seventeenth and Eighteenth Centuries,* in THE ROOTS OF LIBERTY: MAGNA CARTA, ANCIENT CONSTITUTION, AND THE ANGLO-AMERICAN TRADITION OF THE RULE OF LAW 147 (Ellis Sandoz ed. 1993).

384. Kelly, *supra* note 84, at 122 n.13. *See generally* HOWE, *supra* note 78, at 3–4; Blumoff, *supra* note 352, at 556–76; Leila Sadat Wexler, *Reflections on the Trial of Vichy Collaborator Paul Touvier for Crimes against Humanity in France,* 20 LAW & SOC. INQUIRY 191, 215–17 (1995); Murphy, *supra* note 272, at 77; White, *Republican Revival, supra* note 93, at 16–21; White, *Studied Ambiguity supra* note 93, at 105–06; Wiecek, *supra* note 89, at 230, 258–64; J.R. Wiggins, *Lawyers as Judges of History,* 75 PROC. MASS. HIST. SOC'Y 84 (1964).

385. Samuel Krislov, *The Amicus Brief: From Friendship to Advocacy,* in ESSAYS ON THE AMERICAN CONSTITUTION 77, 80 (Gottfried Dietze ed. 1964). *See also* Bruce Ackerman & David Golov, *Is NAFTA Constitutional?,* 108 HARV. L. REV. 799, 807 (1995) (critiquing what the authors see as an invented history regarding the constitutionality of using simple legislation to ratify an international agreement.)

"[l]awyer's history and law office history are really the same despite the variety of definitions they have been given."[386] Yet the use and abuse history to buttress a point has often failed even while undermining the judicial candor that underlies the effectiveness of any institution that depends on respect for its reasoning as the basis of its authority.[387]

Notwithstanding the evident weaknesses of "historicism" as an analytical and persuasive devise, the strength of the revival of historical reasoning is apparent when one finds that even some of the strongest critics of traditional jurisprudence accept it,[388] while no other mode has thus far been advanced that might serve better.[389] This turn is all the more surprising as the "post-modernism" that the extreme critics embrace is, as Frederic Jameson pointed out, built on a foundation of having "forgotten how to think historically in the first place."[390] The proper role of history in the law is summarized by Anthony Kronman in these words: "[T]he past is, for lawyers and judges, a repository of information and of value, with the power to confer legitimacy on actions in the present, and though its power to do so is not limitless, neither is it nonexistent."[391]

It matters little if a court, even the Supreme Court, misconstrues the historical circumstances of some arcane rule of law such as the Rule in *Shelly's Case*. The social consequences can be enormously significant, however, when the Court, either deliberately or through simple error, misstates the intellectual or social history of a major aspect of our culture.[392] Legal historian William Wiecek provided a rationale for the impact of the Court's decisions:

> The United States Supreme Court is the only institution in human experience that has the power to *declare* history: that is, to articulate some understanding of the past and then compel the rest of society to conform its behavior to that understanding. No Ministry of State Security, no Thought Police, has ever succeeded in establishing such authority. This power exists irrespective of the degree to which that judicial perception of the past conforms to reality.[393]

Even without fully agreeing with Wiecek's point, it brings us back to the abortion controversy.

---

386. Reid, *supra* note 89, at 197.

387. David Shapiro, *Judicial Candor,* 100 Harv. L. Rev. 731 (1987).

388. See the authorities collected *supra* at note 82.

389. Of course, many critics of legal objectivity have not been persuaded, although they offer little else to resolve the crisis of legitimacy resulting from their rejection of the possibility of objectivity. *See, e.g.,* Blum, *supra* note 12, at 149–51 (1990) (critical functionalism teaches that society should not shape constitutional law according to the wishes of a group of gentlemen who represented American upper classes two hundred years ago); Blumoff, *supra* note 352, at 539 ("Because historical determinacy is itself impossible to attain, the use of history as a device to constrain judges is impossible."); Rosemary Coombe, *"Same as It Ever Was": Rethinking the Politics of Legal Interpretation,* 34 McGill L.J. 603 (1989) (interpretation is a purely political process which can be evaluated only in terms of political desirability); Cover, *supra* note 3, at 53 (courts kill law; they do not create it); Richard Delgado, *Norms and Normal Science: Toward a Critique of Normativity in Legal Thought,* 139 U. Pa. L. Rev. 933, 937 (1991) (arguing that the indeterminacy thesis no more disadvantages would-be reformers than did earlier critiques of law).

390. Jameson, *supra* note 83, at ix. *See also* Robert Post, *Postmodern Temptations* (book rev.), 4 Yale J.L. & Human. 391 (1992).

391. Kronman, *supra* note 88, at 1032. *See also* Gerda Lerner, Why History Matters: Life and Thought (1997); Frederick Schauer, *Precedent,* 39 Stan. L. Rev. 571, 600 (1987).

392. *See* Howe, *supra* note 78, at 4.

393. Wiecek, *supra* note 89, at 227–28.

# Chapter 21

# Nobody's Right if Everybody's Wrong[1]

> *I still haven't found what I'm lookin' for.*
>
> —U2[2]

I, unlike some modern (or postmodern) commentators, do not consider the current or past predilection for founding legal conclusions on historical inquiries to be simply an intellectual fashion.[3] There are good reasons why history appeals to lawyers and judges. Yet despite the evident appeal of such claims, however, this understanding did not last. Consider the problem such "historical-mindedness" poses to a jurist—or to a society. The problem for the lawyer, the jurist, and the concerned citizen is to work out a suitable approach to using history to inform the interpretation of legal texts in a manner that, while true to the past, responds to the needs of the present and the future. The problem is particularly central in a legal system where the basic law is a 200-year old text, the writing of which is amply documented despite the inevitable gaps and uncertainties that one encounters in any such documentation. Nowhere has this problem been illustrated more clearly than in the legal and social controversy over abortion.

## Juridical Abuses of Abortion History

> *As lies spread,... trust is damaged. Yet, trust is a social good to be protected just as much as the air we breathe or the water we drink. When it is damaged the whole community suffers; and when it is destroyed, societies falter and collapse.*
>
> —Sisela Bok[4]

In the leading case in the abortion controversy, Justice Harry Blackmun devoted more than half of his majority opinion in *Roe* to a history of abortion.[5] He used his history of the laws relating to abortion to inform the values at stake in the controversy, and thus as the instrument for weighing the competing interests to arrive at his "trimester" formula of state power to regulate

---

1. Stephen Stills, *Something's Happening Here,* recorded by "Buffalo Springfield" (1967).
2. Paul Hewson (Bono of U2), *I Still Haven't Found What I'm Looking for* (1987).
3. *See, e.g.,* Stephen Siegel, *Historicism in Late Nineteenth-Century Constitutional Thought,* 1990 Wis. L. Rev. 1431, 1442–43.
4. Sisela Bok, Lying 26–27 (1989).
5. 410 U.S. at 129–52, 156–62.

abortion.[6] Such a situation is hardly unique in today's jurisprudence. The rise in importance of historical argument in legal cases has resulted in the incorporation of numerous "historical essays" in various Supreme Court opinions.[7] As far as courts are concerned, such "historical essays" are protected by the principle of *stare decisis,* making it extremely difficult to overturn such an "historical essay" as a legal matter.[8] Unfortunately, Blackmun, like most Supreme Court Justices, was not a thorough or objective historian.[9] In fact, his history of abortion was wrong in nearly all respects.

Scholars have seriously challenged Blackmun's uncritical adoption of the theories of law professor Cyril Means, jr., on abortion history.[10] The challenges have received small attention in the general and academic press or in subsequent opinions by the Supreme Court.[11] Blackmun would later criticize Justice Antonin Scalia for practicing law office history, for treating "history as a grab-bag of principles, to be adopted where they support the Court's theory, and ignored when they do not."[12] This, as one observer noted, "an extreme instance of the pot calling the kettle black."[13]

The historical status of abortion came up again in 1992 in *Planned Parenthood of Southeastern Pennsylvania v. Casey.*[14] In that case, all the Justices, to some degree or another, embraced history and tradition as controlling the constitutionality of state regulation of abortion. The "joint opinion" by Justices Anthony Kennedy, Sandra Day O'Connor, and David Souter referred to history and tradition to determine the scope of the liberty protected by the due process clause and gave us the eloquent model of the Constitution as a covenant running between the founding generation, the present generation, and future generations.[15] Chief Justice William Rehnquist's separate opinion (joined by Justices Antonin Scalia, Clarence Thomas, and Byron White) also explicitly embraced history and tradition as dispositive,[16] as did Scalia's separate opinion (also joined by Rehnquist, Thomas, and White).[17] While Blackmun and Justice John Paul Stevens, in their separate opinions, were not so direct about it, their emphasis on what they saw as the antiquity of the precedents supporting *Roe* seemed implicitly to adopt the same position.[18] Remarkably, how-

---

6. Celeste Michelle Condit, Decoding Abortion Rhetoric: Communicating Social Change 100–01 (1990).

7. *See* Neil Richards, *Clio and the Court: A Reassessment of the Supreme Court's Uses of History,* 13 NYU J.L. & Pol. 809, 834–83 (1997). *See also* Darrel Amundsen, *The Ninth Circuit's Treatment of the History of Suicide by Ancient Jews and Christians in* Compassion in Dying v. State of Washington: *Historical Naiveté or Special Pleading?,* 13 Issues in L. & Med. 365 (1998).

8. Richards, *supra* note 7, at 889.

9. This comment paraphrases a confession by Justice Robert Jackson, made at the time he was on leave from the Court to serve as the chief American prosecutor at Nuremberg. Robert Jackson, *Full Faith and Credit — The Lawyer's Clause of the Constitution,* 45 Colum. L. Rev. 1, 6 (1945).

10. *See* J. Keown, Abortion, Doctors and the Law 3–25 (1988); Joseph Dellapenna, *The History of Abortion: Technology, Morality, and Law,* 40 U. Pitt. L. Rev. 359 (1979). For Means views, see Cyril Means, jr., *The Law of New York Concerning Abortion and the Status of the Foetus, 1664–1968: A Case of Cessation of Constitutionality,* 14 N.Y.L.F. 411 (1968); Cyril Means, jr., *The Phoenix of Abortional Freedom: Is a Penumbral Right or Ninth-Amendment Right About to Arise from the Nineteenth-Century Legislative Ashes of a Fourteenth-Century Common-Law Liberty?,* 17 N.Y.L.F. 335 (1971) ("Means II"). On Blackmun's debt to Means, the Chapter 14, at notes 435–47.

11. See the authorities collected in Chapter 1, at notes 77–85.

12. Lucas v. South Carolina Coastal Council, 505 U.S. 1003, 1060 (Blackmun, J., dissenting).

13. John Phillip Reid, *Law and History,* 27 Loy.-L.A. L. Rev. 193, 198 (1993).

14. 505 U.S. 833 (1992).

15. *Id.* at 849–50, 901.

16. *Id.* at 952–53.

17. *Id.* at 980 n.1, 987, 995–96.

18. *Id.* at 913–18 (Stevens, J., partially concurring), 926–29 (Blackmun, J., partially concurring).

ever, none of the five *Casey* opinions gave more than passing mention to what the relevant history and traditions might actually be. *Roe's* history thus still stands without serious juridical reexamination, although the extent that Blackmun backed away from relying on the actual history and traditions regarding abortion suggests that even he realizes how deeply flawed his version of that history is.[19]

In this book, I have attempted to set forth as true an account as possible of the history of abortion in England and America. While many particulars remain obscure, the general character of that history is remarkably clear. We cannot now establish with absolute certainty everything that happened up to eight centuries ago regarding abortion, but we can recapture enough of the record to explain with some confidence how the law in those two countries came to be as it was in 1200, 1300, 1400, 1500, 1600, 1700, 1800, 1900, and 2000. Without exception, abortion was always illegal, throughout all or most stages of pregnancy, under the common law and later by statute—until reforms began on both sides of the Atlantic in 1967. That illegality expressed certain core values of the common law tradition. The similar treatment of abortion throughout Europe and many other nations during this same period expressed the same core values:

1.  the protection of fetal life;
2.  the protection of the mother's life and health; and
3.  the protection of mothers from being pressured or coerced into abortions they did not want and (until quite recently) were unlikely to survive.

This unbroken legal tradition, extending over at least eight centuries of Anglo-American social life, condemning abortion and other aggression against unwanted children, is the distillation—the witness and external deposit—of the moral sense of our communities.[20] In the United States, the role of legal history goes beyond providing insight to past social attitudes. It is, after all, a constitution we are expounding. Legal traditions must inform legal documents like the Constitution. Yet the precise contours of legal action regarding abortion changed as a result of the interplay between these core values, changing social roles for women, and changing medical technology for performing abortions. The interplay became particularly pronounced from the last part of the nineteenth century onward when the interest in protecting fetal life diverged from protection of the mother interests. This last point leads into consideration of the relevance of a correct view of the history of abortion has, or ought to have, in resolving the abortion controversy.

The precise historical tradition regarding abortion must be the primary referent in any examination of the constitutional power of governments to regulate or prohibit abortion if history is to play a role in that determination at all. This is not the sort of claim Scalia made in *Michael H. v. Gerald D.*[21] In a now famous footnote, Scalia stated that the Court must always base its analysis on the most specific relevant historical tradition. Here there is a particular reason for focusing on the specific historical tradition even if one believes that in other contexts more general historical traditions might be controlling. Abortion always has been and still is

---

19. *Id.* at 922–43.

20. Oliver Wendell Holmes, jr., *The Path of the Law,* 10 Harv. L. Rev. 457, 459 (1897). *See also* Davis, *supra* note 9, at 1351–61.

21. 491 U.S. 110, 127 n.6 (1989). *See generally* Edward Lazarus, Closed Chambers: The First Eyewitness Account of the Epic Struggles inside the Supreme Court 388–91 (1998); Frank Easterbrook, *Abstraction and Authority,* 59 U. Chi. L. Rev. 349 (1992). *See also* Laurence Tribe & Michael Dorf, On Reading the Constitution 97–98 (1991).

treated differently than other aspects of reproductive privacy, as the Supreme Court itself recognized in *Roe*[22] and *Casey*,[23] and as the continuing intense controversy demonstrates. Indeed, in an unguarded moment even Kate Michaelman, president of the National Abortion Rights Action League, admitted as much when she stated in an interview that "[w]e think abortion is a bad thing."[24]

What then can the true history of abortion teach us regarding the constitutionality of state regulation or prohibition of the practice? The simplest way of putting the matter is that abortion involves a public interest manifested in state policies as well as the private interests of the woman seeking an abortion, the physician providing the abortion, and others intimately involved in the decision and the activity. The history of abortion law disposes of any claim that abortion was a "common law liberty" when our Constitution was adopted or amended[25] and hence of the argument that therefore it is a liberty protected by the Fifth, Ninth, or Fourteenth Amendments, or some combination of those and other provisions.[26] Yet determining the "original intent" can hardly be the end of the matter, as the joint plurality opinion in *Casey* noted.[27]

---

22. *Roe,* 410 U.S. at 159.

23. *Casey,* 505 U.S. at 852 (Kennedy, O'Connor, & Souter, JJ., joint plurality op.). *See also* Harris v. McRae, 448 U.S. 297, 329–32 (1980).

24. Jodi Enda, *Abortion-Rights Leaders Changing Both Message and Methods,* PHILA. INQUIRER, Dec. 11, 1993, at A-1, A-4. Kate Michaelman has subsequently denied that she made this statement, but the *Inquirer* responded with the reporter's tape recording of the statement as proof. *See also* DAVID GARROW, LIBERTY AND SEXUALITY: THE RIGHT OF PRIVACY AND THE MAKING OF *ROE V. WADE* 738–39 (2nd ed. 1998); JANET HADLEY, ABORTION: BETWEEN FREEDOM AND NECESSITY 59, 157–58 (1996); KATHLEEN MCDONNELL, NOT AN EASY CHOICE: A FEMINIST REEXAMINES ABORTION 28 (1984); Peggy Cooper Davis, *Neglected Stories and the Lawfulness of* Roe v. Wade, 28 HARV. C.R.-C.L. L. REV. 299, 369 (1993). For some of the voices who have rejected the view of abortion as at best the lesser of two (or more) evils, see ANNE GAYLOR, ABORTION IS A BLESSING (1975); PATRICIA LUNNEBORG, ABORTION: A POSITIVE DECISION (1992); Elizabeth Karlin, *"We Called It Kindness": Establishing a Feminist Abortion Practice,* in ABORTION WARS: A HALF CENTURY OF STRUGGLE, 1950–2000, at 273, 278 (Rickie Solinger ed. 1998).

25. For this claim, see *Roe,* 410 U.S. 113, 140 (1973); LINDA GORDON, WOMAN'S BODY, WOMAN'S RIGHT: A SOCIAL HISTORY OF BIRTH CONTROL IN AMERICA 52–53, 57 (1976); JAMES MOHR, ABORTION IN AMERICA: THE ORIGINS AND EVOLUTION OF NATIONAL POLICY, 1800–1900, at 128–29, 134–36, 144–45, 201, 208–11, 226, 229, 235–36 (1978); Means II, *supra* note 10, at 336, 351–54, 374–75, 409–10 n.175; Reva Siegel, *Reasoning from the Body: A Historical Perspective on Abortion Regulation and Questions of Equal Protection,* 44 STAN. L. REV. 278, 278 (1992); Rickie Solinger, *"A Complete Disaster": Abortion and the Politics of Hospital Abortion Committees, 1950–1970,* 19 FEMINIST STUD. 241, 243 (1993); *Amicus Brief of 250 American Historians Amici Curiae in support of Appellants in* Planned Parenthood of Southeastern Pennsylvania v. Casey, [505 U.S. 833 (1992)], in LANDMARK BRIEFS AND ARGUMENTS OF THE SUPREME COURT OF THE UNITED STATES: CONSTITUTIONAL LAW, at 508 (*"Casey Historians' Brief"*); *Amicus Brief of 281 American Historians supporting Appellees in* Webster v. Reproductive Health Services [492 U.S. 490 (1989)] (*"Webster Historians' Brief"*), reprinted at 11 WOMEN'S RTS. L. RPTR. 163 (1989), and in 8 DOCUMENTARY HISTORY OF THE LEGAL ASPECTS OF ABORTION IN THE UNITED STATES: *WEBSTER V. REPRODUCTIVE HEALTH SERVICES* 107, 170 (Roy Mersky & Gary Hartman eds. 1990) ("DOCUMENTARY HISTORY") (pagination will be given only to the version in the *Women's Rts. L. Rptr.*). For one of the few retellings of this version of the abortion story to concede that the story does not indicate anything like a "cherished liberty," at least before the nineteenth century, see DONALD JUDGES, HARD CHOICES, LOST VOICES 97 (1993).

26. Means II, *supra* note 10, at 376–410.

27. *Casey,* 505 U.S. at 846–49 (Kennedy, O'Connor, & Souter, JJ., joint plurality op.). This notion goes back to the early days of the Republic. *See, e.g.,* McCulloch v. Maryland, 17 U.S. (4 Wheat.) 316, 415 (1819); Martin v. Hunter's Lessee, 14 U.S. (1 Wheat.) 304, 326 (1816). *See also* Home Bldg. & Loan Ass'n v. Blaisdell, 290 U.S. 398, 443 (1934); Ruth Bader Ginsburg, *Speaking in a Judicial Voice,* 67 NYU L. Rev. 1185, 1187 (1992).

# The Past as Paradigm

*To start fresh, we must forgive the past.*

— Randy Lee[28]

Because our situation — socially and medically — is different, can our response to abortion remain the same today as it was over the past eight centuries? With his penchant for pithy aphorisms, Justice Oliver Wendell Holmes, jr., summed up our conundrum regarding abortion in writing about more general problems of the proper use of history to resolve legal questions. He warned us that there must be some better reason for a rule of law than that some judge in the reign of Henry IV said so,[29] while also reminding us that "law is the witness and external deposit of our moral life."[30] The law serves as witness and deposit of our moral life even if we cannot now discern the reasons for it. Yet, although law might well be described as frozen history,[31] even honest history can be subversive of established law. History demonstrates the roots of our current problems and suggests where (and occasionally how) we need to rethink our situation. Friedrich Nietzsche summarized the point nicely: "Every past is worth condemning... [because] living and being unjust are one.... [W]hen [the] past is considered critically,... one puts the knife to its roots.... It is always a dangerous process...."[32] In other words, we must avoid legitimating the baseness of today by appeals to the baseness of yesterday.[33]

In fact, scholars often embrace history in an effort to justify legal reform[34] — even scholars who frequently use of history to justify what is.[35] After all, only something completely dead does

---

28. Randy Lee, *A Look at God, Feminism, and Tort Law,* 75 Marq. L. Rev. 369, 376 (1992).

29. Holmes, *supra* note 20, at 464–78.

30. *Id.* at 459.

31. Carl Friedrich, *Law and History,* 14 Vand. L. Rev. 1027, 1027 (1961).

32. Friedrich Nietzche, On the Advantages and Disadvantages of History for Life 15 (Peter Preuss trans. 1980). *See also* Robert Gordon, *Foreword: The Arrival of Critical Historicism,* 49 Stan. L. Rev. 1023 (1997); Robert Gordon, *The Past as Authority and as Social Critic: Stabilizing or Destabilizing Functions of History in Legal Argument,* in The Historic Turn in the Human Sciences 339 (Terence McDonald ed. 1996).

33. *See* Donald Kelley, The Human Measure: Social Thought in the Western Legal Tradition 257 (1990) (quoting Karl Marx).

34. *See, e.g.,* Santiago Dantas, 1 Programa de Direito Civil 30 (1977); Beverly Wildung Harrison, Our Right to Choose: Toward a New Ethic of Abortion 90 (1983); Howard Zinn, The Politics of History 281–83 (2nd ed. 1990); John Elson, *The Case Against Legal Scholarship or, If the Professor Must Publish, Must the Profession Perish?,* 39 J. Legal Educ. 343, 371–75 (1989); Robert Gordon, *Critical Legal Histories,* 36 Stan. L. Rev. 57, 124 (1984); Morton Horwitz, *The Historical Contingency of the Role of History,* 90 Yale L.J. 1057, 1058 (1981); Allan Hutchinson, *From Cultural Construction to Historical Deconstruction,* 94 Yale L.J. 209 (1984); John Orth, *Thinking about Law Historically: Why Bother?,* 70 N. Car. L. Rev. 287, 294–95 (1991); Cheryl Preston, *This Old House: A Blueprint for Constructive Feminism,* 83 Geo. L.J. 2271 (1995); Mark Tushnet, *Civil Rights and Social Rights: The Future of the Reconstruction Amendments,* 25 Loy. L.A. L. Rev. 1207, 1219 (1992); Walter Walsh, *Redefining Radicalism: A Historical Perspective,* 59 Geo. Wash. L. Rev. 636, 652–53 (1991); Deborah Widiss, Note, *Re-Viewing History: The Use of the Past as Negative Precedent in United States v. Virginia,* 108 Yale L.J. 237 (1998); Robert Williams, jr., *The Hermeneutics of Indian Law,* 85 Mich. L. Rev. 1012, 1018 (1987).

35. *See, e.g.,* Zinn, *supra* note 34, at 288–319; Gordon, *supra* note 34, at 124; Morton Horwitz, *The Conservative Tradition in the Writing of Legal History,* 17 Am. J. Legal Hist. 275, 276, 281 (1973).

not change.[36] Writing history is one way to liberate us from its grip.[37] To liberate ourselves, we must undertake to seek after the truth of the matter, and perhaps to mix wise remembering with wise forgetting,[38] but not merely to enslave ourselves to deliberate untruths. To accept untruths is to submit to a "new tyranny of the group, pretending to speak for individuals as it crushes them."[39]

Besides being important sources of legal insight, the records of legal proceedings are also evidence of social practices involved in the proceedings. Unfortunately, reliance on legal records as indicators of social patterns from times past can pose serious methodological problems. After all, in reading an ancient court record, one cannot determine whether persons appearing before a court are representative of the community or part of criminal subculture alienated from the community. Nor can one always sort out how the formalities of legal proceedings distort the account of who did what. Yet a sufficiently wide selection of court records to some extent overcomes these difficulties if the records display consistent patterns of criminal behavior and public response.[40]

Thus, while the social, medical, and moral contexts illuminate legal traditions, those contexts are in turn illuminated by the legal tradition.[41] Social contexts are not an independent, let alone overriding, source of legal right. In fact, in England and its American colonies, before the seventeenth century, the social and moral context of whole communities often is recorded only in legal records. Historian G.R. Quaife, a committed enemy of abortion prohibitions, put it thusly:

> [C]ontemporary court records cover a very small proportion of the population and a limited range of human activity. In the seventeenth century the secular and ecclesiastical courts between them covered almost every aspect of human endeavour and operated in such a miniscule world, especially in rural parishes, that in a number of cases the whole village appears to have given evidence. Such evidence, often from the most respectable members of the community, sheds as much light on prevailing village attitudes as it does on the specific matter in dispute.[42]

I do not argue that something is right simply because it is old.[43] There are two points to be made. First, we are attempting to interpret a legal document for which legal sources must be primary. Second, even for alternative approaches to "interpretation"—even in the search for lost voices—legal sources generally remain primary if only because often they are the only actual source of relevant data from times long past that we have. If one believes that actual data is preferable to the imaginings of modern ideologues, one must focus on what the legal record shows us. That the views of a few or even many perhaps dissented from the dominant views during the time a legal tradition was established or continued does not make the legal expression of

---

36. Harrison, *supra* note 34, at 85–88.

37. Elson, *supra* note 34, at 3–4.

38. Thomas Carlyle, Critical and Miscellaneous Essays 247–57 (1860). *See* Elson, *supra* note 4, at 5.

39. Camille Paglia, *The Joy of Presbyterian Sex*, The New Rep., Dec. 2, 1991, at 24.

40. Roger Thompson, Sex in Middlesex: Popular Mores in a Massachusetts County, 1649–1699, at xvii–xviii (1986).

41. Gordon, *supra* note 34, at 101–09, 117–24 (arguing that as law is constitutive of society, looking at legal elites is appropriate for understanding a society).

42. G.R. Quaife, Wanton Wenches and Wayward Wives: Peasants and Illicit Sex in Early Seventeenth Century England 5 (1979). *See also id.* at 42–43.

43. *See generally* Kevin Saunders, *Informal Fallacies in Legal Argumentation*, 44 S. Car. L. Rev. 343, 365–66 (1993).

the dominant views any less the law. After all, legal history is a winner's history.[44] This reality explains the prominence of history in the debate over abortion.

One might structure a recounting of the story of abortion in English and American society in a number of ways, and how one structures the story will determine much of its content. Rosalind Petchesky, who has been called "the major theorist of the reproductive rights movement,"[45] argues that ideology is the primary, indeed virtually the only, cause of changing attitudes toward, and laws regarding, abortion. Petchesky's major work, *Abortion and Women's Choice,* is an argument that attitudes toward and laws regarding abortion are a function of the prevalent ideology of male dominance and female subordination that she sees as solidifying only the nineteenth century.[46] Historian Carl Degler similarly explained changing birth spacings in American families over the last two centuries as caused by different ideas about the role of families and the needs of children.[47] Such stories begin (and end) by attempting to recover what people thought about abortion or related topics. These stories also allow one to dismiss the dominant view, as did Petchesky, as purely a method of capturing and maintaining power by one group in society over others in the same society.[48] In short, many historians, including in particular many self-styled feminist historians, seek to explain "sexism" in its many manifestations (including, in their view, the prohibition of abortion) entirely in ideological terms of dominance without any consideration of whether earlier practices might have been a reasonable response to the material conditions of the time.[49]

Reality is more complex than the ideologues would have it. Even radical law professor Robert Gordon, while arguing for space for alternative voices in the past, recognized that law expresses a vision of social reality that was not simply imposed on dissenters. The past, Gordon wrote, is:

> not…a single developmental path, but…multiple trajectories of possibility, the path actually chosen being chosen not because it had to be, but (where relevant) because the people pushing for alternatives were weaker and lost out in their struggle, and also (in part) because both winners and losers shared a common consciousness that set the agenda for all of them, highlighting some possibilities and suppressing some others completely.[50]

Petchesky and Degler's belief in the social construction of reality does not explain why one idea is seen as "better" than another, or why "new" theories displace earlier theories when they do. Theories that today are cornerstones of our notions of reality (*e.g.,* the atomic theory of matter) were around for decades or centuries, but were seen as marginalized or irrelevant until the theory displaced a previously dominant theory. No wonder "[t]racing the gradual evolution of

---

44. R.H. Helmholz, Canon Law and Common Law 1 (1989). *See also* Louis Wolcher, *The Many Meanings of "Wherefore" in Legal History,* 68 Wash. L. Rev. 559, 638–40 (1993). This point has only occasionally been conceded by feminist historians. *See, e.g.,* Carol Smart, Feminism and the Power of Law 3 (1989).

45. Kathy Rudy, Beyond Pro-Life and Pro-Choice: Moral Diversity in the Abortion Debate 92 (1996).

46. *See* Rosalind Pollack Petchesky, Abortion and Women's Choice: The State, Sexuality, and Reproductive Freedom (rev. ed. 1990). *See also* Caroll Smith-Rosenberg, Disorderly Conduct: Visions of Gender in Victorian America (1985); Rudy, *supra* note 45; Jane Maslow Cohen, *A Jurisprudence of Doubt: Deliberative Autonomy and Abortion,* 3 Colum. J. Gender & Law. 175, 194–217 (1992); Means II, *supra* note 10.

47. Carl Degler, At Odds: Women and the Family in America from the Revolution to the Present (1980).

48. *See also, Casey Historians' Brief, supra* note 25, at 520–49; *Webster Historians' Brief, supra* note 25, at 138–46.

49. Cassandra Langer, A Feminist Critique: How Feminism Has Changed American Society, Culture, and How We Live from the 1940's to the Present 53–70 (1996).

50. Gordon, *supra* note 34, at 112.

an idea over time is like trying to lasso smoke."[51] How ideas in general change and how law in particular changes is a complex amalgam of reasons, some technological, some social, some economic, some political, and so on.

When neighboring societies that are similar in most respects adopt very different legal rules, explaining that difference can be difficult and complex.[52] Nor can one entirely rule out chance. Yet when a broadly similar change is occurring across the globe, one must look for global reasons. Why attitudes and laws changed towards abortion lie not so much on the ebb and flow of ideas as in the material culture within which ideas arise, flourish, and dissipate. My argument superficially appears to be one of a materialistic or technological determinism, but it is not. Ideas are not simply the result of a technology that appears at a given moment, and sometimes the demand for a technology—a demand that might be itself be driven by the prevalent ideas of the time—might drive the development of a technology. Yet, just as there is no guarantee that the emergence of a new technology will cause most people to adopt the intellectual response that appears most natural to me, neither can anyone guarantee that the demand for a new technology will be met successfully—despite the apparent conviction of ideologues like Petchesky that if enough people want a technology, someone somehow will develop it.

My approach to resolving the tension between the role of ideas and the role of material conditions in changing attitudes and laws draws on the early work of Thomas Kuhn, a leading, if controversial, historian of science.[53] Many read Kuhn as arguing that scientific models are "arbitrary" because any particular scientific model (in Kuhn's snob word, a "paradigm") neither resolves all questions about the relevant experimental data that the model purports to address, nor can claim to be, in any ultimate sense, true.[54] Those who read Kuhn thus would have us conclude that any scientific paradigm is as good as any another. Kuhn himself seems to have supported this notion in some of his later writings.[55] This reading of Kuhn supports the notion that

---

51. William Quinn, jr., *Federal Acknowledgment of American Indian Tribes: The Historical Development of a Legal Concept,* 34 AM. J. LEGAL HIST. 331, 331 (1990)

52. Contrast the complexities explored by Charles Donohue regarding why England developed a "separate property" regime for marriage, while France developed a "community property" regime, with the rather more radically simplified views of Marxist historians. *Compare* MICHAEL TIGAR & MADELEINE LEVY, LAW AND THE RISE OF CAPITALISM (1977); *with* Charles Donohue, jr., *What Causes Fundamental Legal Ideas? Marital Property in England and France in the Thirteenth Century,* 78 MICH. L. REV. 60 (1979).

53. THOMAS KUHN, THE STRUCTURE OF SCIENTIFIC REVOLUTIONS (1962). *See also* THOMAS KUHN, THE ESSENTIAL TENSION 270–92 (1977) ("KUHN, ESSENTIAL TENSION"). For a simplistic, but extended, attempt to apply Kuhn's analysis to legal change, see Edward Conry & Caryn Beck-Dudley, *Meta-Jurisprudence: A Paradigm for Legal Studies,* 33 AM. BUS. L.J. 691 (1996).

54. *See, e.g.,* RICHARD BERNSTEIN, BEYOND OBJECTIVISM AND RELATIVISM 52–71, 86–93 (1983); PAUL FEYERABEND, AGAINST METHOD: OUTLINE OF AN ANARCHISTIC THEORY OF KNOWLEDGE (1975); STEVEN FULLER, THOMAS KUHN: A PHILOSOPHICAL HISTORY FOR OUR TIMES (2000); SHEILA JASANOFF, THE FIFTH BRANCH OF SCIENCE: ADVISERS AND POLICY MAKERS 12–14 (1990); RICHARD RORTY, CONTINGENCY, IRONY, AND SOLIDARITY 4 (1989); G. EDWARD WHITE, INTERVENTION AND DETACHMENT: ESSAYS IN LEGAL HISTORY AND JURISPRUDENCE 23–27, 35–36 (1994); WORLD CHANGES (Paul Horwich ed. 1993); Charles Collier, *Interdisciplinary Legal Scholarship in Search of a Paradigm,* 42 DUKE L.J. 840, 840–41, 845 nn. 20–21 (1993); Thomas Cotter, *Legal Pragmatism and the Law and Economics Movement,* 84 GEO. L.J. 2071, 2095–98 (1996); Paul Feyerabend, *Consolations for the Specialist,* in CRITICISM AND THE GROWTH OF KNOWLEDGE 197, 214–15 (Imre Lakatos & Alan Musgrave eds. 1970) ("*Feyerabend, consolations*"); D. Marvin Jones, *The Death of the Employer: Image, Text, and Title VII,* 45 VAND. L. REV. 349, 359–66 (1992); Jeanne Schroeder, *Subject: Object,* 47 U. MIAMI L. REV. 1, 20 n.44, 23–24, 26 n.65, 77–79, 91–93 (1992); Peter Schuck, *Multi-Culturalism Redux: Science, Law, and Politics,* 11 YALE L. & POL'Y REV. 1, 15–18, 37–38 (1995); G. Edward White, *Reflections on the "Republican Revival": Interdisciplinary Scholarship in the Legal Academy,* 6 YALE J.L. & THE HUMANITIES 1, 27–29 (1994).

55. *See* Thomas Kuhn, *Reflections on My Critics,* in CRITICISM AND THE GROWTH OF KNOWLEDGE, *supra* note 54, at 231, 260–65. Kuhn, however, was notorious for disavowing almost every reading of his writings by others. *See* FULLER, *supra* note 54, at xii–xiii, 3–4. He is even quoted as having shouted out from the audience

changes in society, and changes in science, are purely functions of intellectual fashion rather than a response to anything outside of capricious minds embracing new ideas.

Read in this way, Kuhn deserves the harsh criticisms sometimes addressed to his work, particularly by scientists and by other philosophers or historians of science.[56] I do not read Kuhn—at least early Kuhn—in this fashion. Rather, I posit that the material conditions of the time shape intellectual fashions at least as much as intellectual fashions shape material conditions.[57] Material conditions do not affect social and individual attitudes in a simple, deterministic way. Rather, the material conditions of life pose certain core problems to those living at the time just as particular experimental data pose certain core problems to scientists working with that data. Intellectual paradigms will be constructed to address the core problems and succeed in gaining adherents if the paradigm appears to resolve those core problems even while leaving unresolved (or perhaps exacerbating) problems seen as on (perhaps pushed to) the periphery.[58] The new intellectual paradigm in turn shapes further thought and at least some changes in future material conditions. In a sort of interactive loop, however, the changed material conditions—whatever the source of those changes—alters the core problems of the society and thus lead to the rise of new intellectual paradigms.[59]

Changing material conditions might exist for some time before their intellectual significance becomes clear, but once large numbers of people begin to ponder that significance, change in cultural paradigms can come rapidly. We did not take the existence of nuclear programs in India, Israel, North Korea, and Pakistan as a significant security problem even for some years after the end of the Cold War removed that distraction from our sight, but then, at the very end of the twentieth century, these "rogue states" came to be seen as a serious national threat. The Internet was around for more than 20 years before it began to have a major impact on the economy or on people's social lives, but then it spread very rapidly. Even before these events, however, the advent of computerization began to challenge the way we think about the mind, consciousness, and personhood.[60] And, of course, such changing material conditions did not

---

at one meeting, "One thing you people need to understand: I am not a Kuhnian." *See* Freeman Dyson, *Clockwork Science,* N.Y. Rev. Books, Nov. 6, 2003, at 42, 43.

56. *See, e.g.,* Imre Lakatos, *Falsification and the Methodologies of Scientific Research Programmes,* in Criticism and the Growth of Knowledge, *supra* note 54, at 91, 177–80; Thomas Nagel, *The Sleep of Reason,* The New Rep., Oct. 12, 1998, at 32, 35–36; Karl Popper, *Normal Science and Its Dangers,* in Criticism and the Growth of Knowledge, *supra,* at 57; Steven Weinberg, *The Revolution that Didn't Happen,* N.Y. Rev. Books, Oct. 8, 1998, at 48. *See generally* Paul Galison, Image and Logic (1997).

57. *See, e.g.,* Kuhn, Essential Tension, *supra* note 53, at 261. Compare Linda Gordon's analysis of the transition from a sexual ethic of repression and denial to one of expression and embrace as rooted in the life experiences of people in a changing economic structure. Gordon, *supra* note 25, at 180–82, 189–91. *See also* Daniel Rodgers, *Republicanism: The Career of a Concept,* 79 Am. Hist. Rev. 11, 20–30 (1990). *See generally* Jared Diamond, Guns, Germs, and Steel: The Fates of Human Societies (1996); Nancy Hartsock, Money, Sex, and Power: Toward a Feminist Historical Materialism (1983); Doreen Massey, Space, Place and Gender (1994); Cotter, *supra* note 54, at 2097; Lynn Staeheli & Patricia Martin, *Spaces for Feminism in Geography,* 571 Annals Am. Academy Pol. & Soc. Sci. 135 (2000); Symposium, *Standpoint Theory,* 18 Women & Pol. 73 (1997).

58. *See, e.g.,* White, *supra* note 54, at 41–43; Feyerabend, Consolations *supra* note 54, at 220; Lakatos, *supra* note 56, at 116–18; Schroeder, *supra* note 54, at 165–67, 175–81.

59. *See also* J. Herbie DiFonzo, Beneath the Fault Line: The Popular and Legal Culture of Divorce in Twentieth-Century America 1–12 (1997). *Cf.* Raymond DeVries, Making Midwives Legal: Childbirth, Medicine, and the Law 9–16 (2nd ed. 1996) (law and medicine as systems form an interactive system in which each affects the other).

60. *The Computer's Mental Grip,* N.Y. Times, July 22, 1984, at BR3; Edward B. Fiske, *Educator Assails Computer 'Hype',* N.Y. Times, April 19, 1985, at D19; Daniel Hatch, *Science Fiction Leapfrogs the Tough Stuff,* N.Y. Times, July 17, 1988, at CN3.

produce a single, unified interpretation of the import of the changes for our intellectual or cultural images of the world. For one thing, we must choose what counts as significant in the changing conditions, and what forms the physical-cultural background against which the change occurs.

Law professor David Luban has suggested an example that perhaps sets the distinction I am drawing more clearly:

> Causal relations are standpoint- and purpose-relative. A surge of electricity through a wire will not cause it to ignite unless oxygen is present, so in one sense the presence of oxygen has just as much a claim as the surge of electricity to be the cause of the wire's igniting. The electricity, like the oxygen and other factors such as the wire's conductivity, are *contributing conditions* of the wire igniting. Ordinarily, however, we would say that it was the electricity, not the oxygen, that caused the wire to ignite: if, in answer to the question, "What made the wire burn up?," someone replied "The air did it," we would treat the reply as a wisecrack. All contributing conditions are created equal, but for practical explanatory purposes we must inevitably distinguish background conditions (such as the presence of oxygen) from foreground conditions, such as the surge of electricity. The ones in which we are interested move to the foreground, and precisely these we dignify by calling them *causes* of events.[61]

Luban apparently considers the choice of foreground and background factors to be a matter of mere preference rather than a result of a particular fit between an aspect of the "contributing conditions" and the event that leads most people to ascribe that aspect as the cause. He does not mention that oxygen is seen as a background condition precisely because it is always present, while electricity is seen as the "cause" because it is a new variable the introduction of which precipitates the fire. In the context of abortion, the desire of significant numbers of women to be free of unwanted pregnancies was, like oxygen, always present. The historians of the new orthodoxy see changing attitudes towards abortion among various key groups (physicians, lawyers, politicians, and religious leaders) as the precipitating cause of the changes in abortion laws. They do not consider whether there was an immediate or precipitating cause for changes in attitudes towards abortion and hence for changes in abortion laws. While claims about the causation of any complex human action will remain controversial, to insist that only socially constructed attitudes count is arbitrary and shortsighted. I have sought to show in this book that the precipitating cause of changes in attitudes towards, and laws relating to, abortion was the changes of the medical technology for the doing of abortions—changes that mostly occurred in the nineteenth and twentieth centuries.

---

61. David Luban, *Getting the Word*, 91 Mich. L. Rev. 1247, 1259 (1993) (book rev.). Luban derives this example from two sources: H.L.A. Hart & Tony Honoré, Causation and the Law 34–35 (2nd ed. 1985); J.L. Mackie, *Causes and Conditions*, 2 Am. Phil. Q. 245 (1965). *See also* Joel Feinberg, Harm to Others 177 (1984).

# Consciousness — True or False?

*The faintest of all human passions is the love of truth.*

—A.E. Housman[62]

History simply does not often provide easy answers—either about the past or about how we should conduct ourselves in the future. Indeed, history often serves only to frame the questions we should ask.[63] Philosopher John Dewey summarized the problem in these words:

> The old and the new have forever to be integrated with each other, so that the values of old experience may become the servants and instruments of new desires and aims. We are always possessed by habits and customs, and this fact signifies that we are always influenced by the inertia and the momentum of forces temporally outgrown but nevertheless still present with us as a part of our being. Human life gets set in patterns, institutional and moral. But change is also with us and demands the constant remaking of old habits and old ways of thinking, desiring, and acting....In its large sense, this remaking of the old through union with the new is precisely what intelligence is. It is conversion of past experience into knowledge and projection of that knowledge in ideas and purposes that anticipate what may come to be...that indicate how to realize what is desired.[64]

If we are to be true to the traditions that define us as a people, even as we adapt those traditions to the needs of the present and the future, we must try to recapture as honestly as possible a sense of the choices we have made in the past, our "covenant across generations."[65] We must "translat[e] the majestic generalities of the Bill of Rights, conceived as part of the pattern of liberal government in the eighteenth century, into concrete restraints on officials dealing with the problems of the [twenty-first] century."[66] As we have seen, all groups in society (viewed collectively, even though some individuals dissented within any given group), including women, people of color, lawyers, doctors, clergy, journalists, and others, supported the prohibition of abortion until very recent times.[67] In such a case, the tradition must have been much more an instance of a common consciousness than of winners and losers.[68] Many modern feminist scholars simply dismiss any such earlier consensus regarding abortion as a "false consciousness."[69] This response is wholly inadequate.

---

62. A.E. Housman, *Introduction,* in M. Manilii, Astronomicon I, at xiii (1903).

63. John Wofford, *The Blinding Light: The Uses of History in Constitutional Interpretation,* 31 U. Chi. L. Rev. 502, 533 (1964). For an excellent example of the use of history in constitutional argument, see Charles Wilkinson, American Indians, Time, and the Law: Native Societies in a Modern Constitutional Democracy (1987). *See generally* Paul Kahn, Legitimacy and History: Self-Government in American Constitutional Theory (1992).

64. John Dewey, Liberalism and Social Action 49–50 (1935).

65. *Casey,* 505 U.S. Ct. at 901 (1992) (Kennedy, O'Connor, & Souter, JJ., joint plurality op.), quoted in Chapter 17, at 134. *See also* Edmund Burke, Reflections on the Revolution in France 110–11 (1793); Joseph Story, Commentaries on the Constitution of the United States § 325 n.7 (3rd ed. 1858); Bruce Ackerman, *Liberating Abstraction,* 59 U. Chi. L. Rev. 317, 328–38 (1992).

66. West Va. St. Bd. of Educ. v. Barnette, 319 U.S. 624, 639–40 (1943).

67. *See* Chapters 6–8.

68. *See* Gordon, *supra* note 34, at 112, quoted *supra* at note 50.

69. *See, e.g.,* Ruth Colker, Abortion & Dialogue—Pro-Choice, Pro-Life, and American Law 6–9 (1992); Andrea Dworkin, Intercourse 143 (1987); Andrea Dworkin, Right-Wing Women 227–31 (1982); Catharine MacKinnon, Feminism Unmodified: Discourses on Life and Law 70–77 (1987); Petchesky, *supra* note 46, at 76; Patricia Cain, *Feminist Jurisprudence: Grounding the Theories,* 4 Berkeley L.J. 191, 193–95 (1989); Patricia Cain, *Feminist Legal Scholarship,* 77 Iowa L. Rev. 19, 25–27 (1991) ("Cain, *Feminist Legal Scholarship*"); Mari Matsuda, *Pragmatism Modified and the False Consciousness Problem,* 63 S.

The theory of false consciousness can be traced back to Karl Marx and was developed in the current century by Antonio Gramsci.[70] "Second-wave" feminist groups picked up "consciousness raising" as a technique for analyzing their situation and how to change it. The technique involves examining things for deeper or hidden meanings, to deconstruct texts and behaviors in order to determine their true significance.[71] The technique has been glorified as the quintessential feminist intellectual technique in which the hidden meanings relate to the oppression of women.[72]

---

CAL. L. REV. 1763 (1990); Frank Michelman, *Law's Republic,* 97 YALE L.J. 1493, 1526 (1988); Frances Olsen, *Feminist Theory in Grand Style,* 89 COLUM. L. REV. 1147, 1168 (1989); Jeanne Schroeder, Abduction from the Seraglio: *Feminist Methodologies and the Logic of Imagination,* 70 TEX. L. REV. 109, 193–94, 206–07 (1991) ("Schroeder, *Abduction*"); Jeanne Schroeder, *The Taming of the Shrew: The Liberal Attempt to Mainstream Radical Feminist Theory,* 5 YALE J.L. & FEM. 123, 158–60 (1992); Carol Weisbrod, *Practical Polyphony: Theories of the State and Feminist Jurisprudence,* 24 GA. L. REV. 985, 990–91 (1990); Joan Williams, *Gender Wars: Selfless Women in the Republic of Choice,* 66 NYU L. REV. 1559, 1561, 1564–72, 1612–15 (1991).

70. *See* ANTONIO GRAMSCI, SELECTIONS FROM THE PRISON NOTEBOOKS 323–43 (Quintin Hoare & Geoffrey Smith trans. & eds. 1971). *See generally* STEPHEN WHITE, POLITICAL THEORY AND POSTMODERNISM 27–31 (1991); Richard Delgado, *Rodrigo's Sixth Chronicle: Intersections, Essences, and the Dilemma of Social Reform,* 68 NYU L. REV. 639, 653 (1993); Douglas Litowwitz, *Gramsci, Hegemony, and the Law,* 2000 BYU L. REV. 515. Marx himself seems not to have used the phrase "false consciousness," but it permeates his thinking about the alienation of workers from society through the appropriation of the fruits of their labor. *See* MICHELE BARRETT, THE POLITICS OF TRUTH FROM MARX TO FOUCAULT 4–17 (1991).

71. *See, e.g.* JONATHAN CULLER, ON DECONSTRUCTION: THEORY AND CRITICISM AFTER STRUCTURALISM (1982); JACQUE DERRIDA, ON GRAMMATOLOGY (Gayatri Chakravorty Spivak trans. 1976); PETER DEWS, LOGICS OF DISENTEGRATION: POST-STRUCTURALIST THOUGHT AND THE CLAIMS OF CRITICAL THEORY (1987); MICHEL FOUCAULT, ARCHEOLOGY OF KNOWLEDGE AND THE DISCOURSE ON LANGUAGE (A.M. Sheridan Smith trans. 1972); DAVID HARVEY, THE CONDITION OF POSTMODERNITY (1989); JEAN-FRANÇOIS LYOTARD, THE POSTMODERN CONDITION: A REPORT ON KNOWLEDGE (Geoff Bennington & Brian Massumi trans. 1984); ROGER KIMBALL, TENURED RADICALS: HOW POLITICS HAS CORRUPTED HIGHER EDUCATION (1990); CHRISTOPHER LASCH, THE TRUE AND ONLY HEAVEN: PROGRESS AND ITS CRITICS (1991); ADRIENNE RICH, ON LIES, SECRETS, AND SILENCE (1979); PAULINE MARIE ROSENAU, POST MODERNISM AND THE SOCIAL SCIENCES: INSIGHTS, INROADS, AND INTRUSIONS (1992); WHITE, *supra* note 70.

72. *See* PAOLO BONO & SANDRA KEMP, ITALIAN FEMINIST THOUGHT 40–59 (1991); DRUCILLA CORNELL, BEYOND ACCOMMODATION: ETHICAL FEMINISM, DECONSTRUCTION, AND THE LAW 200–01 (1991); SARA EVANS, BORN FOR LIBERTY: A HISTORY OF WOMEN IN AMERICA 263, 289–90 (1989); GORDON, *supra* note 25, at 409; CATHERINE HOSKINS, INTEGRATING GENDER: WOMEN, LAW, AND POLITICS IN THE EUROPEAN UNION 36–38 (1996); CATHARINE MACKINNON, TOWARD A FEMINIST THEORY OF THE STATE 8, 83–105, 120 215–34 (1989); ANITA SHREVE, WOMEN TOGETHER, WOMEN ALONE 10 (1989); Katherine Bartlett, *Feminist Legal Methods,* 103 HARV. L. REV. 829, 863–64 (1990); Leslie Bender, *A Lawyer's Primer on Feminist Theory and Tort,* 38 J. LEGAL EDUC. 3, 9 (1988); Cain, *Feminist Legal Scholarship, supra* note 69, at 24–25; Petra deVries, *Feminism in the Netherlands,* 4 WOMEN'S STUD. INT'L F. 389 (1981); Martha Minow, *Foreword: Justice Engendered,* 101 HARV. L. REV. 10, 64 (1987); Elizabeth Schneider, *The Dialectic of Rights and Politics: Perspectives from the Women's Movement,* 61 NYU L. REV. 589, 610–12, 648–52 (1986). *See generally* MARY FIELD BELENKY et al., WOMEN'S WAYS OF KNOWING: THE DEVELOPMENT OF SELF, VOICE, AND MIND (1986); SCYLA BENHABIH, SITUATING THE SELF: GENDER, COMMUNITY AND POSTMODERNISM IN CONTEMPORARY ETHICS (1992); ROSI BRAIDOTTI, PATTERNS OF DISCOURSE: A STUDY OF WOMEN IN CONTEMPORARY PHILOSOPHY (1991); DRUCILLA CORNELL, BEYOND FEMINISM: ETHICAL FEMINISM, DECONSTRUCTION, AND THE LAW (1991) MARY JOE FRUG, POSTMODERN LEGAL FEMINISM (1992); CAROL GILLIGAN, IN A DIFFERENT VOICE: PSYCHOLOGICAL THEORY AND WOMEN'S DEVELOPMENT (1982); SANDRA HARDING, THE SCIENCE QUESTION IN FEMINISM (1986); NANCY HIRSCHMANN, RETHINKING OBLIGATION: A FEMINIST METHOD FOR POLITICAL THEORY (1992); BELL HOOKS, TALKING BACK: THINKING FEMINIST, THINKING BLACK (1989); MARTHA MINOW, MAKING ALL THE DIFFERENCE: INCLUSION, EXCLUSION, AND AMERICAN LAW (1990) ("MINOW, DIFFERENCE"); NEL NODDINGS, CARING: A FEMININE APPROACH TO ETHICS AND MORAL EDUCATION (1984); SUSAN MILLER OKIN, JUSTICE, GENDER, AND THE FAMILY (1989); SARA RUDDING, MATERNAL THINKING: TOWARDS A POLITICS OF PEACE (1989); SUSAN SHERWIN, NO LONGER PATIENT: FEMINIST ETHICS AND HEALTH CARE (1992); SMART, *supra* note 44; ELIZABETH SPELLMAN, INESSENTIAL WOMAN: PROBLEMS OF EXCLUSION IN FEMINIST THOUGHT (1988); DEBORAH TANNEN, YOU JUST DON'T UNDERSTAND (1990); JANET TODD, GENDER AND LITERARY VOICE

The technique can, of course, be used by anyone and for almost any purpose.[73]

Some feminists, however, have now come to see consciousness raising as a dead end, leading only to more consciousness raising and rarely to action.[74] Law professor Jeanne Schroeder presents the criticism more subtly. Proponents of consciousness raising, she argues, confound its use for three separate functions (hypothesis formation, data collection, and hypothesis verification), and largely neglect hypothesis verification as if that were insignificant.[75] In any event, how those who deny the possibility of identifying any "truth"[76] can discern a "false" consciousness is not disclosed.[77] Only legal historian Morton Horwitz seems to have discussed, even briefly, the need to "revise" the concept of "false consciousness" in light of changing notions of "truth value."[78]

There is an even more basic problem when throwing around charges of "false consciousness" in legal debate. Law is designed to resolve disputes, not to seek ultimate truths, or even to ex-

---

(1980); WOMEN, KNOWLEDGE AND REALITY: EXPLORATIONS IN FEMINIST PHILOSOPHY (Ann Garry & Marylin Pearsall eds. 1989).

73. *See, e.g.,* Duncan Kennedy, *Sexual Abuse, Sexy Dressing and the Eroticization of Domination,* 26 N. ENG. L. REV. 1309, 1337–38 (1992); Michael Shapiro, *Fragmenting and Reassembling the World: Of Flying Squirrels, Augmented Persons, and Other Monsters,* 51 OHIO ST. L.J. 331, 390–91 (1990).

74. *See* ALICE ECHOLS, DARING TO BE BAD: RADICAL FEMINISM IN AMERICA, 1967–1975, at 148 (1989). *See also* Bartlett, *supra* note 72, at 864–67. *See generally* COLKER, *supra* note 69, at 22–38; ZILLAH EISENSTEIN, THE FEMALE BODY AND THE LAW 171–73 (1988); PAULINE JOHNSON, FEMINISM AS RADICAL HUMANISM (1994); REBECCA KLATCH, WOMEN OF THE NEW RIGHT 139 (1987); MACKINNON, *supra* note 69, at 115–16; SMART, *supra* note 44, at 77–80; Kathryn Abrams, *Feminist Lawyering and Legal Method,* 16 LAW & SOC. INQUIRY 373, 383–87, 391–93, 397–400 (1991); Katherine Bartlett, *MacKinnon's Feminism: Power on Whose Terms?* (book rev.), 75 CAL. L. REV. 1559, 1564 (1987); Alexandra Dobrowsky & Richard Devlin, *The Big Mac Attack: A Critical Affirmation of MacKinnon's Unmodified Theory of Patriarchal Power,* 36 MCGILL L.J. 576, 602–05 (1991); Lucinda Finley, *The Nature of Domination and the Nature of Women: Reflections on Feminism Unmodified* (book rev.), 82 NW. U.L. REV. 352, 380 (1988); Christine Littleton, *Women's Experience and the Problem of Transition: Perspectives on Male Battering of Women,* 1989 U. CHI. LEGAL F. 23, 26; Matsuda, *supra* note 69; Julie Mertus, *Beyond the Solitary Self: Voice, Community, and Reproductive Freedom,* 3 COLUM. J. GENDER & L. 247, 266 (1992); Katherine O'Donovan, *Engendering Justice: Women's Perspectives and the Rule of Law,* 39 U. TOR. L.J. 127, 139 n.61 (1989); Olsen, *supra* note 69, at 1175–77; Deborah Rhode, *Feminist Critical Theories,* 42 STAN. L. REV. 617, 623 (1990); Schroeder, *supra* note 54, at 37–38, 110–11; Robin West, *The Difference in Women's Hedonic Lives: A Phenomenological Critique of Feminist Legal Theory,* 3 WIS. WOMEN'S L.J. 81, 115–16 (1987).

75. Schroeder, *supra* note 54, at 151–61, 181–83.

76. *See, e.g.,* HARRY COLLINS & TREVOR PINCH, THE GOLEM: WHAT EVERYONE SHOULD KNOW ABOUT SCIENCE (1993); DECONSTRUCTION AND THE POSSIBILITY OF JUSTICE (Drucilla Cornell, Michel Rosenfeld, & David Gray Carlson eds. 1992); DEWS, *supra* note 71; FRUG, *supra* note 72; KENT GREENAWALT, LAW AND OBJECTIVITY (1992); SANFORD LEVINSON, CONSTITUTIONAL FAITH 170–77 (1988); MINOW, DIFFERENCE, *supra* note 72, at 173–214; CHRISTOPHER NORRIS, THE CONTEST OF FACULTIES: PHILOSOPHY AND THEORY AFTER DECONSTRUCTION (1985); ROSENAU, *supra* note 72; Arthur Austin, *Deconstruction Voice Scholarship,* 30 HOUS. L. REV. 1071 (1993); J.M. Balkin, *Understanding Legal Understanding: The Legal Subject and the Problem of Legal Coherence,* 103 YALE L.J. 105 (1993); Jules Coleman & Brian Leiter, *Determinacy, Objectivity, and Authority,* 142 U. PA. L. REV. 549 (1993); Anthony Cook, *Reflections on Postmodernism,* 26 N. ENG. L. REV. 751 (1992); Peter Goodrich, *Sleeping with the Enemy: An Essay on the Politics of Critical Legal Studies in America,* 68 NYU L. REV. 389 (1993); Allan Hunt, *The Big Fear: Law Confronts Postmodernism,* 35 MCGILL L.J. 507 (1990); Kenneth Kress, *A Preface to Epistemological Indeterminacy,* 85 NW. U. L. REV. 134, 134–38 (1990); Dragan Milovanovic, *The Postmodernist Turn: Lacan, Psychoanalytic Semiotics, and the Construction of Subjectivity in Law,* 8 EMORY INT'L L. REV. 67 (1994); Dennis Paterson, *The Poverty of Interpretive Universalism: Toward the Reconstruction of Legal Theory,* 72 TEX. L. REV. 1 (1993); Peter Schanck, *Understanding Postmodern Thought and Its Implications for Statutory Interpretation,* 65 S. CAL. L. REV. 2505 (1992); Symposium, *Postmodernism and Law,* 62 U. COLO. L. REV. 439 (1991).

77. *See* RICH, *supra* note 71, at 185; Judith Lichtenberg, *Objectivity and Its Enemies,* 2 THE RESPONSIVE COMMUNITY 59 (1991); Banu Ramachandran, Note, *Re-Reading Difference: Feminist Critiques of the Law School Classroom and the Problem of Speaking from Experience,* 98 COLUM. L. REV. 1757, at 1780–83 (1998).

78. Morton Horwitz, *Reconstructing Historical Theory from the Debris of the Cold War,* 102 YALE L.J. 1287, 1291–92 (1993).

plore various dimensions of human existence. To apply deconstruction theory, originally a form of literary theory, to legal problems demonstrates a fundamental misunderstanding of the functions of law in general and courts in particular.[79] While no shared value can withstand deconstruction, objective truth is not a precondition for a shared value to have legitimate social force.[80] Few feminist scholars seem even to note the problem, an example of the pervasive problem of category confusion (the inability to classify things correctly) that even some feminist scholars have noted as regrettably characteristic of much feminist thinking.[81]

The common consciousness in the past regarding abortion—namely, that it was a social and personal evil that should be repressed by law—illustrates the difficulties in a deconstructionist approach to the past that dismisses evidence of such a consensus as representing a "false consciousness." After all, the militant feminists of the nineteenth century uniformly condemned abortion as a crime against nature and against womanhood.[82] How do we know that the consciousness of those feminists was "false," and that the consciousness of most self-avowed feminists today is not? At the least, those who would dismiss the former consciousness as false must demonstrate, not merely assert, the truth of their claim. While neither value claim might be objectively true (or false), each in its time could serve as the basis of effective law so long as the value claim was widely shared in society. The question for historians is how did one form of consciousness give way to another, and how can the struggle between proponents of those different forms of consciousness be resolved. The obligation of jurists, and perhaps also of people generally, is to learn from our history and our traditions, as they were and not as we would have had them be, to adapt the values expressed in our history and traditions to the social and materials conditions of our lives.[83]

The Court in *Harmelin v. Michigan*[84] demonstrates the demands this process makes on our capacity to exercise judgment. The court resorted to history not simply to mimic the murmured echoes of the past. In the lead opinion in *Harmelin*, Justice Antonin Scalia appealed with limited success to the history of the "cruel and unusual punishment" language of the Eighth Amendment in an attempt to overturn 70 years of evolving jurisprudence requiring judicial review of the proportionality between the crime and the punishment.[85] Three Justices, in an opinion by Justice Byron White, disputed Scalia's history not only regarding medieval sources, but also by insisting that the 70 year-old recent tradition itself counted heavily in reading the relevant history.[86] In a third opinion, the *Casey* troika presaged their decision in *Casey* by declining to join the historical debate and resting the holding of the case purely on *stare decisis*.[87]

79. *See* Charles Collier, *The Use and Abuse of Humanistic Theory in Law: Reexamining the Assumptions of Interdisciplinary Legal Scholarship*, 41 Duke L.J. 191 (1991).

80. Celeste Michelle Condit, *Within the Confines of the Law: Abortion and a Substantive Rhetoric of Liberty* (book rev.), 38 Buff. L. Rev. 903, 913 (1990).

81. *See* Sandra Lee Bartky, *Toward a Phenomenology of Feminist Consciousness*, in Feminism and Philosophy 22, 29 (Mary Vetterling-Braggin, Frederick Elliston, & Jane English eds. 1981); Cheshire Calhoun, *Responsibility and Reproach*, 99 Ethics 389 (1989).

82. *See* Chapter 8.

83. John Hart Ely, *The Wages of Crying Wolf*, 82 Yale L.J. 920, 929 n.69 (1973) (the Court's duty is "to seek out the sorts of evils the Framers meant to combat and to move against their twentieth century counterparts.").

84. 501 U.S. 957 (1991).

85. *Id.* at 958–95 (Scalia, J., in a separate part of the opinion for the Court joined only by Rehnquist, C.J.).

86. *Id.* at 1008–27 (White, J., dissenting, joined by Blackmun, & Stevens, JJ.). *See also* Stephen Meltzer, Comment, Harmelin v. Michigan: *Contemporary Morality and Constitutional Objectivity*, 27 N. Eng. L. Rev. 749, 752–71 (1993).

87. *Harmelin*, 501 U.S. at 996–1009 (Kennedy, J., concurring, joined by O'Connor & Souter, JJ.).

What is perhaps most striking about the three opinions in *Harmelin* is how each Justice sought to avoid truly engaging with the history they sought to exploit to sustain their view of the case before them. In each opinion, the author sought to show how the result advocated was required by history rather than to use history to illuminate where we have come from and a little of where we are headed, let alone why these changes came about. Merely to pose these questions suggests how difficult meaningful reliance on history really is, and why the Court usually shies away from doing so—just as it did in *Casey*.[88]

# The Emerging Technomorality
# of the Life Sciences

*No one here gets out alive.*

—Jim Morrison[89]

Nearly 2,000 years of history presents us with a tradition that abortion is a grievous wrong, primarily to the unborn child but also to the mother. Why then did a dramatic change occur in the twentieth century, largely within the last 40 years? The repeal or reform of abortion laws that occurred in so many places so rapidly around the world suggests that something more was at work than a mere coincidence of changing opinion.[90] This pattern also suggests that something more than the working out of the meaning of the American Bill of Rights was involved.[91] Rather, we are at a crossroads created by the intersection of changing social roles for women with changing medical technologies that have fundamentally transformed both the experience of abortion and our interactions with prenatal life.

No one claims that the changing role expectations felt by many women result solely from changes in abortion technology, yet that technology (as well as wholly unrelated technologies) played a major role in shaping changed role expectations. This was noted, in a backhanded way, by the troika in *Casey*: "The ability of women to participate equally in the economic and social life of the Nation has been facilitated by their ability to control their reproductive lives."[92] Sexual mores, with attendant effects on the entire range of women's roles, historically were largely governed by a "prudential ethic" based upon the triple threat of infection, detection, and conception.[93] All three threats were eliminated by changing technology: antibiotics, the car, and the pill, respectively. As a complete explanation of the changes in social attitudes towards sexuality, this is, of course, an oversimplification. There have been other periods of sexual licentiousness (or liberation) in the past in particular cultures without any of these modern technologies. And the elimination of the three fears is no longer entirely true with the advent of AIDS. Still, the attribution of changes in attitude towards sexuality to such technological mechanisms is only somewhat of an oversimplification as becomes apparent in considering the specifics of each variable.

---

88. *See* Chapter 17, at notes 129–55.

89. Jim Morrison, *Five to One* (1968).

90. *See* Chapter 15, at notes 141–356.

91. Frank Easterbrook, *Bills of Rights and Regression to the Mean*, 15 HARV. J. L. & PUB. POL'Y 71, 79–80 (1992).

92. *Casey,* 505 U.S. at 856 (Kennedy, O'Connor, & Souter, JJ., joint plurality op.). On the backhandedness of this apparently straightforward statement, see Chapter 17, at notes 258–74.

93. Myron Bloy, *The Christian Norm*, in TECHNOLOGY AND HUMAN VALUES 18–21 (Chris Wilkinson ed. 1967).

Consider, for example, the problem of detection. Commentators have long seen the automobile as the root of all recent changes in our sexual mores.[94] The auto made it possible (as early as the 1920s—when the modern sexual revolution apparently made its first major inroads into Victorian sexuality in North America and Europe) for the unmarried young to isolate themselves from their families even when while continuing to live at home. It served as a mobile platform that could function as a crude bedroom.

Even if one insists that there were other, complementing factors, these factors often were also technological. Consider the demise, in the West, of the two-parent, woman-in-the-kitchen pattern. While millions of families around the world and even in western societies never conformed to that model at any given moment in history, this clearly was the dominant form of family life the United States at least from the middle of the nineteenth century to the middle of the twentieth century.[95] The same pattern was frequently dominant in Europe (including England) at least back to the Middle Ages despite considerable variation regionally and temporally.[96] The newly developed technologies for the mechanization of household chores made homemaking as a full-time occupation a thing of the past in a society organized around nuclear rather than extended families. Imagine, in contrast, doing laundry by beating clothes on rocks near a running stream, or doing all cooking, cleaning, and dish washing by entirely hand daily, as women still do in some parts of the world. These mechanical developments as much as any rendered the once dominant pattern of family life socially obsolete.[97]

The technological challenges to traditional modes of family life and to traditional social mores have continued unabated for more than a century, perhaps even at an accelerated pace in recent decades. Often, however, these technological changes cut in different directions relative to traditional social mores. Thus, the development of relatively safe and effective "morning-after" pills and related pharmacological techniques for inducing an abortion can only further the tendency to undermine the traditional family, particularly devaluing a conceptus at least early in pregnancy.[98] At the same time, the continuing developments in embryology (as well as fetology) tend to reinforce the valuing of that very same conceptus. [99]

---

94. *See, e.g.,* MICHAEL HARRINGTON, THE ACCIDENTAL CENTURY 18–19 (1965); ALVIN TOFFLER, FUTURE SHOCK 437 (1970).

95. *See generally* DEGLER, *supra* note 47, at 66–85; MICHAEL GROSSBERG, GOVERNING THE HEARTH: LAW AND THE FAMILY IN NINETEENTH-CENTURY AMERICA (1985); SMITH-ROSENBERG, *supra* note 46, at 26–29, 58, 68; BERNARD WISHY, THE CHILD AND THE REPUBLIC: THE DAWN OF EARLY AMERICAN CHILDREN AND YOUTH IN AMERICA (1968); BERTRAM WYATT-BROWN, SOUTHERN HONOR, ETHICS AND BEHAVIOR IN THE OLD SOUTH (1982); Gerda Lerner, *The Lady and the Mill Girl: Changes in the Status of Women in the Age of Jackson,* 10 AM. STUD. J. 5 (1969); Siegel, *supra* note 25, at 291–97; Lise Vogel, *The Contested Domain: A Note on the Family in the Transition to Capitalism,* 1 MARXIST PERSPECTIVES 50 (1978); Ronald Walters, *The Family and Antebellum Reform: An Interpretation,* 3 SOCIETAS 224 (1973).

96. 1 BONNIE ANDERSON & JUDITH ZINSSER, A HISTORY OF THEIR OWN: WOMEN IN EUROPE FROM PREHISTORY TO THE PRESENT 133–34 (1988); RALPH HOULBROOKE, THE ENGLISH FAMILY, 1450–1700 (1984); PETER LASLETT, THE WORLD WE HAVE LOST 91 (1966); MARTINE SEGALEN, LOVE AND POWER IN THE PEASANT FAMILY: RURAL FRANCE IN THE NINETEENTH CENTURY 57–59 (Sarah Matthews trans. 1983); E.A. WRIGLEY, POPULATION AND HISTORY 19 (1969). The evidence is summarized in Ralph Houlbrooke, *The Preindustrial Family,* 36 HIS. TODAY 49 (1986).

97. TOFFLER, *supra* note 94, at 238–59. *See generally* NANETTE DAVIS, FROM CRIME TO CHOICE 7–14 (1985); BETTY FRIEDAN, THE FEMININE MYSTIQUE (1963).

98. *See, e.g.,* A. Glasier *et al., Mifeprestone (RU 486) Compared with High-Dose Estrogen and Progestogen for Emergency Postcoital Contraception,* 327 N. ENG. J. MED. 1041 (1992); D.A. Grimes & R.J. Cook, *Mifeprestone (RU 486)—An Abortifacient to Prevent Abortion?,* 327 N. ENG. J. MED. 1088 (1992); Warren Hogue, *British Store Gives Women Emergency Pill, Igniting Debate,* N.Y. TIMES, Mar. 18, 2002, at A9.

99. *See* Chapter 15, at notes 357–500.

One could go on in ever widening circles about the interplay between changing technologies, social practices, and the values that both grow from and influence those social practices. For example, Lewis Mumford long ago pointed out how the invention of clear glass in thirteenth-century Italy created windows that framed a view of the world, not only introducing perspective into western painting, but, eventually, changing our entire relation to the world.[100] Mumford also noted how the invention of mechanical clocks in medieval monasteries shortly thereafter (to assure timely prayers) led to the reconceptualization of time and ultimately to modern science and mass production.[101] And Marshall McLuhan pointed out nearly 30 years ago that the invention of electronic media in the twentieth century already portends similar far-reaching changes in our society generally even down to the level of how we think and how we process information.[102] Others have predicted McLuhanesque consequences for our legal systems in particular.[103]

We can jump to what is undoubtedly the most profound of these changes, the emergence of a "quality of life" ethic to compete with the traditional "sanctity of life" ethic.[104] The need for such a new ethic as a justification for abortion was recognized even before *Roe*.[105] This new attitude

---

100. Lewis Mumford, Technics and Civilization 124–31 (1934).

101. *Id.* at 12–17. *See also* Kevin Casey, *The Barbed Wire Invention: An External Factor Affecting American Legal Development*, 72 J. Pat. & Trademark Office Soc'y 417 (1990).

102. Marshall McLuhan, Understanding Media (1964). *See generally* Elizabeth Eisenstein, The Printing Revolution in Early Modern Europe (1983); Jack Goody, The Interface between the Written and the Oral 75–76 (1987); Harold Innes, Empire and Communication (1972); Robert Logan, The Alphabet Effect: The Impact of the Phonetic Alphabet on the Development of Western Civilization (1986); Marshall McLuhan, The Gutenberg Galaxy: The Making of Typographic Man (1962); Walter Ong, Interfaces of the Word: Studies in the Evolution of Consciousness and Culture (1977); Walter Ong, Orality and Literacy: The Technologizing of the Word (1982); Walter Ong, Rhetoric, Romance, and Technology: Studies in the Interaction of Expression and Culture (1971); Brian Stock, The Implications of Written Language and Models of Interpretation in the Eleventh and Twelfth Century (1983); Berthold Ullman, Ancient Writing and Its Influence (1980).

103. M. Ethan Katsh, The Electronic Media and the Transformation of Law 33–35, 85–86, 215–18 (1989); Ronald Collins & David Skover, *Paratexts,* 44 Stan. L. Rev. 509 (1992); Joseph Dellapenna, *Law in a Shrinking World: The Interaction of Science and Technology with International Law,* 88 Ky. L.J. 809 (2000).

104. *See, e.g.* Minow, Difference, *supra* note 72, at 312–49; Helga Kuhse & Peter Singer, Should the Baby Live? The Problem of Handicapped Infants 118–39 (1985); Quality of Life: The New Medical Dilemma (James Walter & Thomas Shannon eds. 1990); Peter Singer, Rethinking Life and Death (1995); Who Speaks for the Child: The Problems of Proxy Consent (Willard Gaylin & Ruth Macklin eds. 1982); Glanville Williams, The Sanctity of Life and the Criminal Law 163–66 (1957, reprinted 1972); Hadley Arkes, *"Autonomy" and the "Quality of Life": The Dismantling of Moral Terms,* 2 Issues in L. & Med. 421 (1987); Peter Berkowitz, *Other People's Mothers: The Utilitarian Horrors of Peter Singer,* New Rep., Jan. 10, 2000, at 27; John Finnis, Bland: *Crossing the Rubicon?,* 109 Law Q. Rev. 329 (1993); John Keown, *The Legal Revolution: From "Sanctity of Life" to "Quality of Life" and "Autonomy,"* 14 J. Contemp. Health L. & Pol'y 253 (1998); Gina Kolata, *Ethicists Struggle to Judge the "Value" of Life: If Money Is Limited, Is It Better to Finance Hip Replacements or Kidney Replacements?,* N.Y. Times, Nov. 24, 1992, at C3; Gilbert Meilander, *Terra es animata: On Having a Life,* 23 Hastings Ctr. Rep. no. 4, at 25 (July–Aug. 1993); Margaret Somerville, *The Song of Death: The Lyrics of Euthanasia,* 9 J. Contemp. Health L. & Pol'y 1, 27–31 (1993); Symposium, *The Legal and Ethical Implications of Innovative Medical Technology,* 57 Albany L. Rev. 551 (1994).

105. *See A New Ethic for Medicine and Society,* 113 Cal. Med. 68 (Sept. 1970) (an editorial). *See also* Judith Boss, The Birth Lottery: Prenatal Diagnosis and Selective Abortion 231–50 (1993); Kristin Luker, Abortion and the Politics of Motherhood 189–90 (1984); Mohr, *supra* note 25, at 252–53; Dellapenna, *supra* note 10, at 422–27; Joseph Imber, *Abortion Policy and Medical Practice,* Society, July–Aug. 1990, at 27, 30–31, 34; Kenneth Ryan, *Humane Abortion Laws and the Health Needs of Society,* in Abortion and the Law 29, 68 (David Smith ed. 1967); Solinger, *supra* note 25, at 262–63.

sweeps within a single abstraction a broad pattern of changes of which abortion is only a part. The new ethic portends the possibility of even more sweeping changes in the future as we transform "the enduring problem of human happiness and well-being into one more medical problem to be dealt with by scientific means."[106] Yet what is an appropriate "quality of life" remains an entirely subjective value judgment, providing little guidance to a court or a physician.[107] The quality of life ethic, however, cannot be limited to the abortion debate. This leads to a certain irony when one finds those who favor the quality of life ethic also supporting "speech codes" that, in a variety of settings, would ban speech that "injures" other persons. Such advocates seem unconcerned that speaking about the quality of life ethic injures the feelings of those they themselves are careful to call "challenged" rather than "handicapped."[108]

Undoubtedly the most contentious aspect of the substitution of a quality of life ethic for a sanctity of life ethic is the struggle over when a quality of life is so low that the life itself should be terminated. Suicide traditionally was considered one of the most serious sins[109] and was a felony at common law.[110] In older times, this meant that one's property was forfeit to the Crown rather than passed to one's heirs; today, it would make an attempted suicide a felony. Also, assisting a suicide was a form of murder at common law.[111] Today, many societies are poised to accept "rational suicide" when the person in question faces what many would consider an intolerably low level of quality of life.[112] Furthermore, growing segments of the population of many coun-

---

106. DANIEL CALLAHAN, WHAT KIND OF LIFE: THE LIMITS OF MEDICAL PROGRESS 34 (1990). *See also* LARRY PALMER, LAW, MEDICINE, AND SOCIAL JUSTICE (1989).

107. *See* LINDA BECK FENWICK, PRIVATE CHOICES, PUBLIC CONSEQUENCES: REPRODUCTIVE TECHNOLOGY AND THE NEW ETHICS OF CONCEPTION, PREGNANCY, AND FAMILY 73–79 (1998); Thomas Gill & Alvan Feinstein, *A Critical Appraisal of Quality-of-Life Measurements,* 272 JAMA 619 (1994); Gordon Guyatt & Deborah Cook, *Health Status, Quality of Life, and the Individual,* 272 JAMA 630 (1994); Philip Prygoski, *Abortion and the Right to Die: Judicial Imposition of a Theory of Life,* 23 SETON HALL L. REV. 67 (1992).

108. Kristi Kirschner, Carol Gill, & Christine Cassel, *Physician-Assisted Death in the Context of Disability,* in PHYSICIAN-ASSISTED SUICIDE: ETHICS, MEDICAL PRACTICE, AND PUBLIC POLICY 155 (Robert Weir ed. 1997); Teresa Harvey Paredes, *The Killing Words? How the New Quality-of-Life Ethic Affects People with Severe Disabilities,* 46 SMU L. REV. 805 (1992); Wolf Wolfensberger, *The Growing Threat to the Lives of Handicapped People in the Context of Modernistic Values,* 9 DISABILITY & SOCIETY 395 (1994).

109. Darrel Amundsen, *The Significance of Inaccurate History in Legal Consideration of Physician-Assisted Suicide,* in PHYSICIAN-ASSISTED SUICIDE, *supra* note 108, at 3; Eltjo Schrage, *Suicide in Canon Law,* 21 J. LEGAL HIST. 57 (2000).

110. Life Ass'n of Am. v. Waller, 57 Ga. 533 (1876); Commonwealth v. Hicks, 82 S.W. 265 (Ky. Ct. App. 1904); State v. Willis, 121 S.E.2d 854 (N.C. 1961); Connecticut Mut. Life Ins. Co. v. Groom, 5 Pa. 92 (1878) (*dictum*); Phadenhauer v. Germania Life Ins. Co., 54 Tenn. (7 Heisk.) 567 (1872) (*dictum*); Plunkett v. Supreme Conclave, 55 S.E. 9 (Va. 1906) (*dictum*). *See generally* ALEXANDER MURRAY, SUICIDE IN THE MIDDLE AGES (1998); Roger Groot, *When Suicide Became Felony,* 21 J. LEGAL HIST. 1 (2000); Thomas Marzen *et al., Suicide: A Constitutional Right?,* 24 DUQ. L. REV. 1, 56–100 (1985); Gwen & Alice Seabourne, *The Law on Suicide in Medieval England,* 21 J. LEGAL HIST. 21 (2000); Schrage, *supra* note 109; Henry Summerson, *Suicide and the Fear of the Gallows,* 21 J. LEGAL HIST. 49 (2000).

111. Commonwealth v. Mink, 123 Mass. 422 (1877); People v. Roberts, 178 N.W. 690 (Mich. 1920); State v. Hembd, 232 N.W.2d 872 (Minn. 1975); Blackburn v. State, 23 Ohio St. 146 (1872); *In re* Marline B., 540 A.2d 1028 (R.I. 1988).

112. *See* Vacco v. Quill, 521 U.S. 793 (1997); Washington v. Glucksberg, 521 U.S. 702 (1997); Cooley v. Granholm, 291 F.3d 880 (6th Cir. 2002); Lee v. Oregon, 107 F.3d 1382 (9th Cir.), *cert. denied sub nom.* Lee v. Harcleroad, 522 U.S. 927 (1997); Sampson v. State, 31 P.3d 88 (Alaska 2001); Thor v. Superior Ct., 21 Cal. Rptr. 2d 357 (Ct. App. 1993); Krischer v. McIver, 697 So. 2d 97 (Fla. 1997); State v. McAfee, 385 S.E.2d 651 (Ga. 1989); *In re* E.G., a Minor, 549 N.E.2d 322 (Ill. 1989); Gentry v. State, 625 N.E.2d 1268 (Ind. Ct. App. 1993), *transfer denied;* Wright v. Johns Hopkins Health Systems Corp., 728 A.2d 166 (Md. 1999); *In re* Martin, 538 N.W.2d 399 (Mich. 1995); People v. Kevorkian, 527 N.W.2d 714 (Mich. 1994), *cert. denied,* 514 U.S. 1083 (1995); McKay v. Bergstedt, 801 P.2d 617 (Nev. 1990); *In re* Farrell, 529 A.2d 404 (N.J. 1987); *In re* Long Island Jewish Med. Ctr., 557 N.Y.S.2d 239 (Sup. Ct. 1990); Department of Pub. Welfare v. Kallinger, 580 A.2d 887 (Pa. Commw. Ct. 1990), *appeal dismissed,* 615 A.2d 730 (Pa. 1990); Laurie v. Senecal, 666 A.2d 806 (R.I.

tries appear ready to accept the termination of someone's life if the quality seems too low even if the person is no longer capable of making a choice in any but a fictitious sense.[113]

1995); Sanders v. State, 3 P.3d 891 (Wyo.), *cert. denied,* 531 U.S. 1024 (2000); Rodriguez v. British Columbia, 107 D.L.R.4th 342 (Can. 1993); Wake v. N. Terr., 124 F.L.R. 298 (N. Terr. 1996) (appeal pending when the Northern Territories euthanasia statute was overridden by the Australian Parliament). *See also In re* Joseph G., 667 P.2d 1176 (Cal. 1983) (minor who survived driving a car off a cliff as part of a suicide pact was guilty of aiding a suicide, rather than of murder); State v. Couser, 567 N.W.2d 657 (Iowa 1997) (adult survivor of a suicide pact is guilty of manslaughter).

*See generally* ASSISTED SUICIDE: FINDING COMMON GROUND (Lois Snyder & Arthur Caplan eds. 2002); ROBERT BARRY, BREAKING THE THREAD OF LIFE (1994); MARGARET PABST BATTIN, THE LEAST WORST DEATH: ESSAYS IN BIOETHICS ON THE END OF LIFE (1994); HAZEL BIGGS, EUTHANASIA, DEATH WITH DIGNITY, AND THE LAW (2001); DAN BROCK, LIFE AND DEATH: PHILOSOPHICAL ESSAYS IN BIOMEDICAL ETHICS (1993); GEORGE BURNELL, FINAL CHOICES: TO LIVE OR TO DIE IN AN AGE OF MEDICAL TECHNOLOGY (1993); DONALD COX, HEMLOCK'S CUP: THE STRUGGLE FOR DEATH WITH DIGNITY (1993); DEATH, DYING AND THE LAW (Sheila McLean ed. 1996); GERALD DWORKIN, R.G. FREY, & SISSELA BOK, EUTHANASIA AND ASSISTED SUICIDE (1998); RONALD DWORKIN, LIFE'S DOMINION: AN ARGUMENT ABOUT ABORTION, EUTHANASIA, AND INDIVIDUAL FREEDOM 179–86, 190–92, 199–208, 213–17, 222–29, 237–41 (1993); ETHICAL ISSUES IN DEATH AND DYING (Tom Beauchamp & Robert Veach eds. 1996); EUTHANASIA AND ASSISTED SUICIDE: THE CURRENT DEBATE (Ian Gentles ed. 1995); EUTHANASIA, CLINICAL PRACTICE, AND THE LAW (Luke Gormally ed. 1994); EUTHANASIA EXAMINED: ETHICAL, CLINICAL AND LEGAL PERSPECTIVES (John Keown ed. 1995); EUTHANASIA: OPPOSING VIEWPOINTS (Carol Wekesser ed. 1995); PETER FILENE, IN THE ARMS OF OTHERS: A CULTURAL HISTORY OF THE RIGHT-TO-DIE IN AMERICA (1998); GERE FULTON & EILEEN METRESS, PERSPECTIVES ON DEATH AND DYING (1995); HERBERT HENDIN, SEDUCED BY DEATH: DOCTORS, PATIENTS, AND THE DUTCH CURE (1996); DANIEL HILLYARD & JOHN DOMBRINK, DYING RIGHT: THE DEATH WITH DIGNITY MOVEMENT (2001); JAMES HOEFLER, DEATHRIGHT (1994); HOW SHALL WE DIE? HELPING CHRISTIANS DEBATE ASSISTED SUICIDE (Sally Geis & Donald Messers eds. 1997); DEREK HUMPHREY & MARY CLEMENT, FREEDOM TO DIE: PEOPLE, POLITICS AND THE RIGHT-TO-DIE MOVEMENT (1998); BRIAN JOHNSTON, DEATH AS A SALESMAN: WHAT'S WRONG WITH ASSISTED SUICIDE (1994); FRANCES KAMM, MORALITY, MORTALITY: DEATH, AND WHOM TO SAVE FROM IT (1993); NANCY KING, MAKING SENSE OF ADVANCE DIRECTIVES (1996); EDWARD LARSON & DARREL AMUNDSEN, A DIFFERENT DEATH: EUTHANASIA IN THE CHRISTIAN TRADITION (1998); WILLIAM MAY, ACTIVE EUTHANASIA AND HEALTH CARE REFORM(1996); CHARLES McKHANN, A TIME TO DIE: THE PLACE FOR PHYSICIAN ASSISTANCE (1998); ALAN MEISEL, THE RIGHT TO DIE (2nd ed. 1995); MERCY OR MURDER: EUTHANASIA, MORALITY AND PUBLIC POLICY (Kenneth Overberg ed. 1993); G. STEVEN NEELEY, THE CONSTITUTIONAL RIGHT TO SUICIDE: A LEGAL AND PHILOSOPHICAL EXAMINATION (1996); N.Y. STATE TASK FORCE, WHEN DEATH IS SOUGHT: ASSISTED SUICIDE AND EUTHANASIA IN THE MEDICAL CONTEXT (1994); SHERWIN NULAND, HOW WE DIE (1993); MARGARET OTLOWSKI, VOLUNTARY EUTHANASIA AND THE COMMON LAW (1997); LARRY PALMER, ENDINGS AND BEGINNINGS: LAW, MEDICINE, AND SOCIETY IN ASSISTED LIFE AND DEATH (2000); PHYSICIAN ASSISTED DEATH (James Humber *et al.* eds. 1993); PHYSICIAN-ASSISTED SUICIDE, *supra* note 108; PHYSICIAN-ASSISTED SUICIDE: EXPANDING THE DEBATE (REFLECTIVE BIOETHICS) (Margaret Battin, Rosamond Rhodes, & Anita Silvers eds. 1998); WESLEY SMITH, FORCED EXIT: THE SLIPPERY SLOPE FROM ASSISTED SUICIDE TO LEGALIZED MURDER (1997); BONNIE STEINBECK & ALASTAIR NORCROSS, KILLING AND LETTING DIE (2nd ed. 1994); GARY P. STEWART *et al.,* SUICIDE AND EUTHANASIA: ARE THEY EVER RIGHT? (1998); SUICIDE: A CHRISTIAN RESPONSE: CRUCIAL CONSIDERATIONS FOR CHOOSING LIFE (Timothy Denny & Gary Stewart eds. 1998); PATRICIA TALONE, FEEDING THE DYING: RELIGION AND END-OF-LIFE DECISIONS (1996); MARILYN WEBB, THE GOOD DEATH (1997); DICK WESTELY, WHEN ITS RIGHT TO DIE: CONFLICTING VOICES, DIFFICULT CHOICES (1995).

113. *See, e.g.,* Cruzan v. Director, Mo. Dep't Health, 497 U.S. 261 (1990); Knight v. Beverly Health Care Bay Manor Health Care Ctr., 820 So. 2d 92 (Ala. 2001); Rasmussen v. Fleming, 741 P.2d 674 (Ariz. 1987); *In re* Conservatorship of Wendland, 28 P.3d 151 (Cal. 2001); McConnell v. Beverly Enterprises-Conn., Inc., 553 A.2d 596 (Conn. 1989); *In re* Tavel, 661 A.2d 1061 (Del. 1995); *In re* K.I., 735 A.2d 448 (D.C. 1999); *In re* Guardianship of Browning, 568 So. 2d 4 (Fla. 1990); Bush v. Schiavo, 861 So. 2d 506 (Fla. Ct. App. 2003), *appeal pending*; *In re* Estate of Greenspan, 558 N.E.2d 1194 (Ill. 1990); *In re* Lawrence, 579 N.E.2d 32 (Ind. 1991); DeGrella v. Elston, 858 S.W.2d 698 (Ky. 1993); *In re* P.V.W., 424 So. 2d 1015 (La. 1982); Causey v. St. Francis Med. Ctr., 719 So. 2d 1072 (La. Ct. App. 1998); *In re* Swan, 569 A.2d 1202 (Me. 1990); Mack v. Mack, 618 A.2d 744 (Md. 1993); *In re* Guardianship of Doe, 583 N.E.2d 1263 (Mass.), *cert. denied sub nom.* Doe v. Gross, 503 U.S. 950 (1992); Martin v. Martin, 538 N.W.2d 399 (Mich. 1995); *In re* Jobes, 529 A.2d 434 (N.J. 1987); *In re* Quinlan, 355 A.2d 647 (N.J.), *cert. denied sub nom.* Garger v. New Jersey, 429 U.S. 922 (1976); *In*

As with so many other debates in medical ethics, the modern practice of euthanasia (and the fears of excess) can be traced back to the Nazis.[114] Yet the modern acceptance of euthanasia results not from the spread of Nazi ideals, but from the conundrums posed by modern medical technology.[115] That technology today gives physicians the ability to keep a human body "alive" long after any meaningful possibility that body's functioning as a human person has ended. As law professor Wolfgang Friedman pointed out more than two decades ago, changes such as these in medical technologies provide the means of preserving "lives" that formerly were beyond help and thus create unprecedented financial and emotional drains on individuals, families, and society—even at lesser extremes than a persistent vegetative state.[116] This has led to a widely shared reconceptualization of when death occurs as being when the brain becomes incapable of functioning rather than when the heart stops beating.[117]

---

re Westchester Cty. Med. Ctr., 531 N.E.2d 607 (N.Y. 1988); *In re* Guardianship of Myers, 610 N.E.2d 663 (Ohio C.P. 1993); *In re* Fiori, 673 A.2d 905 (Pa. 1996); San Juan-Torregosa v. Garcia, 80 S.W.3d 539 (Tenn. Ct. App. 2002); *In re* Guardianship of Grant, 747 P.2d 445 (Wash. 1987); *In re* Edna M.F., 563 N.W.2d 485 (Wis.), *cert. denied sub nom.* Spahn v. Wittman, 522 U.S. 951 (1997); Airedale NHS Trust v. Bland, [1993] 1 All E.R. 821 (H.L.).

See generally BROCK, *supra* note 112, at 356–85; DWORKIN, *supra* note 112, at 186–90, 192–98, 208–13, 218–22, 229–37; STEPHEN JAMISON, FINAL ACTS OF LOVE: FAMILIES, FRIENDS, AND ASSISTED SUICIDE (1995); KUHSE & SINGER, *supra* note 104; WILLIAM MAY, ACTIVE EUTHANASIA AND HEALTH CARE REFORM (1996); MINOW, DIFFERENCE, *supra* note 72, at 312–49; WESLEY SMITH, CULTURE OF DEATH: THE ASSAULT ON MEDICAL ETHICS IN AMERICA (2001); PATRICIA TALONE, FEEDING THE DYING: RELIGION AND END-OF-LIFE DECISIONS (1996); WHO SPEAKS FOR THE CHILD, *supra* note 104; Jonathan Black-Branch, *Being over Nothingness: The Right to Life under the Human Rights Act*, 26 EUR. L. REV., at H.R./22 (2001); Richard Fenigsen, *Dutch Euthanasia Revisited*, 13 ISSUES IN L. & MED. 301 (1997); Henk Jochemsen, *Dutch Court Decisions on Nonvoluntary Euthanasia Critically Reviewed*, 13 ISSUES IN L. & MED. 447 (1998); Roger Magnusson, *The Sanctity of Life and the Right to Die: Social and Jurisprudential Aspects of the Euthanasia Debate in Australia and the United States*, 6 PAC. RIM L. & POL'Y REV. 1, 52–58 (1997); Thomas Marzen & Daniel Avila, *Will the Real Michael Martin Please Speak Up? Medical Decisionmaking for Questionably Competent Persons*, 72 U. DET. L. REV. 833 (1995); Scott Obernberger, *When Love and Abuse Are Not Mutually Exclusive: The Need for Government Intervention*, 12 ISSUES IN LAW & MED. 355 (1997); Zev Schostak, *Jewish Ethical Guidelines for Resuscitation and Artificial Nutrition and Hydration of the Dying Elderly*, 20 J. MED. ETHICS 93 (1994); Britt van den Akker, Rien Janssens, & Henk ten Have, *Euthanasia and International Human Rights Law: Prolegomena for an International Debate*, 37 MED. SCI. L. 289 (1997); Martin Van Der Weyden, *Deaths, Dying and the Euthanasia Debate in Australia*, 166 MED. J. AUSTRAL. 173 (1997).

114. ALBERT JONSEN, THE BIRTH OF BIOETHICS (1998); WHEN MEDICINE WENT MAD: BIOETHICS AND THE HOLOCAUST (Arthur Caplan ed, 1992). *See also* Leo Alexander, *Medical Science under Dictatorship*, 241 N. ENG. J. MED. 39 (1949); Robert Burt, *The Suppressed Legacy of Nuremberg*, 26 HASTINGS CTR. REP. no. 5, at 30 (1996); Patrick Derr, *Hadamar, Hypocrites, and the Future of Medicine: Reflections on Euthanasia and the History of German Medicine*, 4 ISSUES IN L. & MED. 487 (1989); Wolf Wolfensberger, *A Reflection on Alfred Hoche, the Ideological Godfather of the German "Euthanasia" Program*, 8 DISABILITY, HANDICAP & SOC'Y 311 (1993).

115. *See* Stephen Goldberg, *The Changing Face of Death: Computers, Consciousness, and Nancy Cruzan*, 43 STAN. L. REV. 659 (1991).

116. Wolfgang Friedman, *Interference with Human Life: Some Jurisprudential Reflections*, 70 COLUM. L. REV. 1058, 1058–59 (1970). *See also* Daniel Callahan, *Transforming Mortality: Technology and the Allocation of Resources*, 65 S. CAL. L. REV. 205 (1991); Norman Daniels, *Technology and Resource Allocation: Old Problems in New Clothes*, 65 S. CAL. L. REV. 225 (1991); Margaret Lock, *Death in Technological Time: Locating the End of Meaningful Life*, 10 MED. ANTRHO. Q. 575 (1996).

117. *See* UNIFORM DETERMINATION OF DEATH ACT, 12 U.L.A. 443 (Supp. 1995); PRESIDENTIAL COMM'N FOR THE STUDY OF ETHICAL PROBLEMS IN MEDICINE & BIOMEDICAL & BEHAVIORAL RESEARCH, DEFINING DEATH (1981); P.D.G. Skegg, *Irreversibly Comatose Individuals: "Alive" or "Dead"?*, 33 CAMBRIDGE L.J. 130 (1974). *See also* Bassie v. Obstetrics & Gynecology Assocs., 828 So. 2d 280 (Ala. 2002); UNUM Life Ins. Co. v. Craig, 26 P.3d 510 (Ariz. 2001); Terrell v. State, 27 S.W.3d 423 (Ark. 2000); People v. Kelly, 822 P.2d 385 (Cal.), *cert. denied*, 506 U.S. 881 (1992); People v. Mann, 646 P.2d 352 (Colo. 1982); State v. Guess, 715 A.2d 64 (Conn. 1998); *In re* J.N., 406 A.2d 1275 (D.C. 1979); *In re* T.A.C.P., 609 So. 2d 588 (Fla. 1992); State v. Williams, 275 S.E.2d 62 (Ga. 1981); State v. Wakisaka, 78 P.3d 317 (Haw. 2003); People v. O'Quinn, 791 N.E.2d 1066 (Ill. App. Ct. 2003), *appeal denied*, 803 N.E.2d 494 (Ill. 2003); Lewis v. State, 740 N.E.2d 550

The reconceptualization of when death occurs in turn allowed considerably greater possibilities for the development and implementation of organ transplantation technologies—which itself created even further possibilities for extending human lives in ways that before had been imagined only in science fiction.[118] Yet the practical application of the "brain death" standard poses its own problems. How do physicians decide that the possibility of further brain function has ceased.[119] Debate over when death occurs, as well as over whether to terminate the lives of those no longer able to choose whether to go on living, expresses the view that to continue to prolong life when medical treatment becomes futile merely prolongs suffering without good rea-

---

(Ind. 2000); Wolbers v. Finley Hosp., 673 N.W.2d 728 (Iowa 2003); State v. Gholston, 35 P.3d 868 (Kan. 2001), *cert. denied*, 536 U.S. 963 (2002); Russell v. Commonwealth, 992 S.W.2d 871 (Ky. 1999); Carey v. Rao, 828 So. 2d 53 (La. Ct. App.), *writ denied*, 831 So. 2d 986 (La. 2002); Purty v. Kennebec Valley Med. Ctr., 551 A.2d 558 (Me. 1988); Sloan v. State, 522 A.2d 1364 (Md. Ct. Spec. App.), *cert. denied*, 528 A.2d 1287 (Md. 1987); *In re* Care of Beth, 587 N.E.2d 1377 (Mass. 1992); People v. Vanderford, 258 N.W.2d 502 (Mich. Ct. App. 1977); State v. Bock, 490 N.W.2d 116 (Minn. 1992); Jones v. State, 442 So. 2d 919 (Miss. 1983); State v. Ponder, 950 S.W.2d 900 (Mo. Ct. App. 1997); State v. Hartmann, 476 N.W.2d 209 (Neb. 1991); Harte v. State, 13 P.3d 420 (Nev. 2000); State v. Timmendequas, 737 A.2d 55 (N.J. 1999), *cert. denied*, 534 U.S. 858 (2001); State v. Mascareñas, 4 P.3d 1221 (N.M. 2000); People v. Eulo, 472 N.E.2d 286 (N.Y. 1984); State v. Walls, 463 S.E.2d 738 (N.C. 1995), *cert. denied*, 517 U.S. 797 (1996); Wilburn v. Cleveland Elec. Illum. Co., 599 N.E.2d 301 (Ohio Ct. App. 1991); Commonwealth v. Lambert, 765 A.2d 306 (Pa. Super. Ct. 2000); State v. Burton, 397 S.E.2d 90 (S.C. 1990); Bearden v. Memphis Dinettes, Inc., 690 S.W.2d 863 (Tenn. 1984); Duren v. State, 87 S.W.3d 719 (Tex. Ct. App. 2002); State v. Velarde, 734 P.2d 449 (Utah 1986); Emmett v. Commonwealth, 569 S.E.2d 39 (Va. 2002), *cert. denied*, 538 U.S. 929 (2003); Hay v. Medical Ctr. of Vt., 496 A.2d 939 (Vt. 1985); *In re* Guardianship of Hamlin, 689 P.2d 1372 (Was. 1984); Cranmore v. State, 271 N.W.2d 402 (Wis. Ct. App. 1978); Warren v. State, 835 P.2d 304 (Wyo. 1992).

*See generally* KAREN GERVAIS, REDEFINING DEATH (1986); ROBERT VEATCH, DEATH, DYING, AND THE BIOLOGICAL REVOLUTION (1989); A. EARL WALKER, CEREBRAL DEATH (2nd ed. 1981); Christopher De Giorgio & Mark Lew, *Consciousness, Coma, and the Vegetative State: Physical Basis and Definitional Character*, 6 ISSUES IN LAW & MED. 361 (1991); Amir Halevy & Baruch Brody, *Brain Death: Reconciling Definitions, Criteria, and Tests*, 119 ANN. INTERNAL MED. 519 (1993); A.A. Howsepian, *The 1994 Multi-Society Task Force Consensus Statement on the Persistent Vegetative State: A Critical Analysis*, 12 ISSUES IN L. & MED. 3 (1996); Magnusson, *supra* note 113, at 40–45; J.K. Mason & G.T. Laurie, *The Management of the Persistent Vegetative State in the British Isles*, 4 JURIDICAL REV. 263 (1996); Ann MacLean Massie, *Withdrawal of Treatment for Minors in a Persistent Vegetative State: Parents Should Decide*, 35 ARIZ. L. REV. 173 (1993); Multi-Society Task Force on PVS, *Medical Aspects of the Persistent Vegetative State*, 330 NEW ENG. J. MED. 1499 (1994); Kirk Payne et al., *Physicians' Attitudes about the Care of Patients in the Persistent Vegetative State: A National Survey*, 125 ANNALS INTERNAL MED. 104 (1996); David Powner et al., *Medical Diagnosis of Death in Adults: Historical Contribution to Current Controversies*, 348 LANCET 1219 (1996); D. Alan Shewmon, *Recovery from "Brain Death": A Neurologist's Apologia*, LINACRE Q., Feb. 1997, at 30; Symposium, *Beyond the Persistent Vegetative State*, 15 J. CONTEMP. HEALTH L. & POL'Y 425 (1999); Samantha Weyrauch, *Acceptance of Whole-Brain Death Criteria for Determination of Death: A Comparative Analysis of the United States and Japan*, 17 PAC. BASIN L.J. 91 (1999).

118. ORGAN SUBSTITUTION TECHNOLOGY: ETHICAL, LEGAL, AND PUBLIC POLICY ISSUES 69 (Deborah Mathieu ed. 1988); Derek Jones, *Retrospective on the Future: Brain Death and Evolving Legal Regimes for Tissue Replacement Technology*, 38 McGILL L. REV. 394 (1993). *But see* Jiro Nudeshima, *Obstacles to Brain Death and Organ Transplantation in Japan*, 338 LANCET 1063 (1991).

119. Marcia Angell, *After Quinlan: The Dilemma of the Persistent Vegetative State*, 330 NEW ENG. J. MED. 1524 (1994); James Bernat, *How Much of the Brain Must Die in Brain Death?*, 3 J. CLINICAL ETHICS 21 (1992); Christian Borthwick, *The Permanent Vegetative State: Ethical Crux, Medical Fiction?*, 12 ISSUES IN LAW & MED. 167 (1996); Paul Byrne & Richard Nilges, *The Brain Stem in Brain Death: A Critical Review*, 9 ISSUES IN L. & MED. 3 (1993); Nancy Childs & Walt Mercer, *Late Improvement in Consciousness after Post-Traumatic Vegetative State*, 334 N. ENG. J. MED. 24 (1996); Halevy & Brody, *supra* note 117; Alan Sherman, *"Brainstem Death," "Brain Death" and Death: A Critical Reevaluation of the Purported Equivalence*, 14 ISSUES IN L. & MED. 125 (1998); Nicholas Tonti-Filippini, *Revising Brain Death: Cultural Imperialism?*, LINACRE Q., May 1998, at 51; Robert Truog, *Is It Time to Abandon Brain Death?*, 27 HASTINGS CTR. REP. no. 1, at 29 (Jan.–Feb. 1997); Robert Veatch, *The Impending Collapse of the Whole-Brain Definition of Death*, 23 HASTINGS CTR. REP. no. 4, at 18 (July–Aug. 1993); Daniel Wilker, *Brain Death: A Durable Consensus?*, 7 BIOETHICS 239 (1993); Stuart Youngner, *Defining Death: A Superficial and Fragile Consensus*, 49 ARCH. NEUROLOGY 570 (1992).

son.[120] The question of when further medical treatment would be futile is as fraught with ambiguities as the notion of death itself has become.[121] With some physicians began opting for rather expansive concepts of brain death in order to free up organs for transplantation, there arises the even more troubling question of whether the declaration of death served the interests of the dying patient or of the prospective recipient of the organ.[122]

After society became accustomed to the idea of doctors' "pulling the plug" on apparently living patients who had been declared brain dead, it was perhaps inevitable that some physician would come forward to assert that doctors should more actively assist competent persons to terminate their own lives—at least if that decision appeared to be "rational."[123] Most likely, any number of physicians reached and implemented this conclusion quietly. A few, upon being dis-

---

120. Magnusson, *supra* note 113, at 52–54; Stuart Youngner & Edward Bartlett, *Human Death and High Technology: The Failure of the Whole-Brain Death Formulations,* 99 Ann. Internal Med. 252 (1983). *See generally* Callahan, *supra* note 106.

121. Medical Futility and the Evaluation of Life-Sustaining Interventions (1997); Allen Bennett, *When Is Medical Treatment "Futile"?,* 9 Issues in L. & Med. 35 (1993); Marni Bonnin *et al., Distinct Criteria for Termination of Resuscitation in the Out-of-Hospital Setting,* 270 JAMA 1457 (1993); Chris Bothwick, *The Proof of the Vegetable: A Commentary on Medical Futility,* 21 J. Med. Ethics 205 (1995); Miriam Cotler & Dorothy Gregory, *Futility: Is Definition the Problem?,* 2 Cambridge Q. Healthcare Ethics 219 (1993); J. Randall Curtis *et al., Use of the Medical Futility Rationale in Do-Not-Resuscitate Orders,* 273 JAMA 124 (1995); Paul Helft, Mark Siegler, & John Lantos, *Sounding Board: The Rise and Fall of the Futility Movement,* 343 N. Eng. J. Med. 293 (2000); Nancy Jecker & Lawrence Schneiderman, *Medical Futility: The Duty not to Treat,* 2 Cambridge Q. Healthcare Ethics 151 (1993); Marshall Kapp, *Futile Medical Treatment: A Review of the Ethical Arguments,* 9 J. Gen. Internal Med. 170 (1994); Steven Miles, *Futility and Medical Professionalism,* 25 Seton Hall L. Rev. 873 (1995); James Reitman, *The Dilemma of "Medical Futility"—A "Wisdom Model" for Decisionmaking,* 12 Issues in L. & Med. 231 (1996); Lawrence Schneiderman & Nancy Jecker, *Futility in Practice,* 153 Arch. Internal Med. 437 (1993); George Smith, II, *Utility and the Principle of Medical Futility: Safeguarding Autonomy and the Prohibition against Cruel and Unusual Punishment,* 12 J. Contemp. Health L. & Pol'y 1 (1995); Mildred Solomon, *How Physicians Talk about Futility: Making Words Mean too Many Things,* 21 J. Health L., Med. & Ethics 231 (1993); Marc Stern, *"And You Shall Choose Life"—Futility and the Religious Duty to Preserve Life,* 25 Seton Hall L. Rev. 997 (1995); Robert Taylor & John Lantos, *The Politics of Medical Futility,* 11 Issues in L. & Med. 3 (1995); Jane Teno *et al., Prognosis-Based Futility Guidelines: Does Anyone Win?,* 42 J. Am. Geriatrics Soc'y 1202 (1994); C. Weijer & C. Elliott, *Pulling the Plug on Futility,* 310 Brit. Med. J. 683 (1995); Stuart Youngner, *Medical Futility and the Social Contract (Who Are the Real Doctors on Howard Brody's Island?),* 25 Seton Hall L. Rev. 1015 (1995).

122. H.D.C. Roscam Abbing, *Transplantation of Organs: A European Perspective,* 21 J. Law, Med. & Ethics 54 (1993); Robert Arnold *et al., The Dead Donor Rule: Should We Stretch It, Bend It, or Abandon It[?],* 3 J. Kennedy Inst. Ethics J. 263 (1993); Bruce Braun & Dane Drobny, *Life, Death, and Organ Donation,* 24 Litigation no. 4, at 3 (1998); Alexandra Glazier, *"The Brain Dead Patient Was Kept Alive" and Other Disturbing Misconceptions: A Call for Amendments to the Uniform Anatomical Gift Act,* 9 Kan. J. Law & Pub. Pol'y 640 (2000); D.J. Hill, R. Munglani, & D. Sapsford, *Haemodynamic Responses to Surgery in Brain-Dead Organ Donors,* 49 Anaesthesia 835 (1994); S.H. Pennefather, J.H. Dark, & R.E. Bullock, *Haemodynamic Responses to Surgery in Brain-Dead Organ Donors,* 48 Anaesthesia 1034 (1993); John Robertson, *Relaxing the Death Standard for Organ Donation in Pediatric Situations,* in Organ Substitution Technology, *supra* note 118, at 69; Truog, *supra* note 119, at 34–36; Stuart Youngner & Robert Arnold, *Ethical, Psychological, and Public Policy Implications of Procuring Organs from Non-Heart-Beating Cadaver Donors,* 269 JAMA 2769 (1993).

123. Hendin, *supra* note 112; Catherine Bjorck, *Physician-Assisted Suicide: Whose Life Is It Anyway?,* 47 SMU L. Rev. 371 (1994); Howard Brody, *Assisting in Patient Suicides Is an Acceptable Practice for Physicians,* in Physician-Assisted Suicide, *supra* note 108, at 136; Daniel Callahan, *Self-Extinction: The Morality of the Helping Hand,* in Physician-Assisted Suicide, *supra,* at 69; Daniel Callahan & Margot White, *The Legalization of Physician-Assisted Suicide: Creating a Regulatory Potemkin Village,* 30 U. Rich. L. Rev. 1 (1996); Edward Grant & Paul Benjamin Linton, *Relief or Reproach?: Euthanasia Rights in the Wake of Measure 16,* 74 Ore. L. Rev. 449 (1995); Herbert Hendin, *Seduced by Death: Doctors, Patients, and the Dutch Cure,* 10 Issues in L. & Med. 123 (1994); Peter Rasmussen *et al., Physician-Assisted Suicide and Euthanasia,* 343 N. Eng. J. Med. 140 (2000); David Schanker, *Of Suicide Machines, Euthanasia Legislation, and the Health Care Crisis,* 68 Ind. L.J. 977 (1993).

covered, were charged with serious crimes.[124] In the United Kingdom, Dr. Nigel Cox was convicted in 1992 of attempted murder rather than murder because the 70-year old woman he had killed had been cremated, making it impossible to prove the cause of death.[125]

Dr. Timothy Quill (in New York) eventually went public. In an article in the *New England Journal of Medicine,* he described killing of a terminally ill woman who chose suicide over a slow, painful death.[126] Despite his public confession and the eventual identification of the deceased woman's body, a local grand jury declined to indict him.[127] Quill, however, was comparatively conservative about assisting suicide for he strongly opposes "active euthanasia"—the killing of the incompetent without their consent.[128] Quill also disapproved of physicians assisting in the suicide of patients with whom the physician had no relationship other than the killing.[129] Another physician, Dr. Jack Kevorkian, undertook to challenge all opposition to assisted suicide in a highly publicized program of activities in Michigan beginning in 1990 without any of the safeguards that Quill advocated.[130]

Kevorkian, a former pathologist who specialized in autopsies, seemed morbidly obsessed with death—his own and others. He undertook to assist people with terminal illnesses to kill themselves while threatening to kill himself by a hunger strike if he were ever sent to prison. Eventually he became involved in about 130 deaths.[131] Kevorkian's program prompted Michigan's legislature to enact a statute prohibiting assisted suicide.[132] Courts upheld the statute as constitutional.[133] Kevorkian was tried four times for violating the assisted suicide statute, obtain-

---

124. Magnusson, *supra* note 113, at 11–12.

125. Diana Brahams, *Euthanasia Doctor Convicted of Attempted Murder,* 340 THE LANCET 782 (1992); Magnusson, *supra* note 113, at 12–13; Harry Ognall, *A Right to Die? Some Medico-Legal Reflections,* 62 MEDICO-LEGAL J. 165 (1994).

126. Timothy Quill, *Death with Dignity: A Case of Individualized Decision Making,* 324 N. ENG. J. MED. 691 (1991). *See also* Magnusson, *supra* note 113, at 13–16; Peter Ubel, *Assisted Suicide and the Case of Dr. Quill and Diane,* 8 ISSUES IN L. & MED. 487 (1993); Patricia Wesley, *Dying Safely,* 8 ISSUES IN L. & MED. 467 (1993).

127. Lawrence Altman, *Jury Declines to Indict a Doctor Who Said He Aided in Suicide,* N.Y. TIMES, July 27, 1991, at A1.

128. Timothy Quill *et al., Core of the Hopelessly Ill: Proposed Clinical Criteria for Physician-Assisted Suicide,* 327 NEW ENG. J. MED. 1380, 1381 (1992). *See also* Timothy Quill, *Risk Taking by Physicians in Legally Gray Areas,* 57 ALBANY L. REV. 693 (1994).

129. Quill *et al., supra* note 128, at 1381–82.

130. *See* Jack Kevorkian, *A Letter from Dr. Kevorkian,* N.Y. REV. BOOKS, July 5, 2001, at 17 (with comments and editing by Mike Wallace). *See also* MICHAEL BETZOLD, APPOINTMENT WITH DOCTOR DEATH (1993); NINA CLARK, THE POLITICS OF PHYSICIAN-ASSISTED SUICIDE (1997); JACK KEVORKIAN, PRESCRIPTION: MEDICIDE—THE GOODNESS OF PLANNED DEATH (1991); Lisa Belkin, *Doctor Tells of First Death Using His Suicide Device,* N.Y. TIMES, June 6, 1990, at A1; Eric Chevlin, *Euthanasia Promises Marcus Welby, but Gives Us Jack Kevorkian: Physician Assisted Suicide,* 72 MED. ECON. 25 (1995); Steve Calandrillo, *Corralling Kevorkian: Regulating Physician-Assisted Suicide in America,* 7 VA. J. SOC. POL'Y & L. 41 (1999); Geoffrey Fieger, *Commentary: The Persecution and Prosecution of Doctor Death and His Mercy Machine,* 20 OHIO N.U. L. REV. 659 (1994); Magnusson, *supra* note 113, at 15–20; Marvin Zalman *et al., Michigan's Assisted Suicide Three Ring Circus—An Intersection of Law and Politics,* 23 OHIO N.U. L. REV. 863 (1997).

131. Dirk Johnson, *Kevorkian Sentenced to 10 to 25 Years in Prison,* N.Y. TIMES, Apr. 14, 1999, at A1. *See also* Zalman *et al., supra* note 130, at 948–65 (a detailed timeline of Dr. Kevorkian's activities, with brief description of each death he was involved with between June 1990 and November 1993).

132. MICH. COMP. LAWS ANN. § 750.1027 (West 1993).

133. People v. Kevorkian, 527 N.W.2d 714 (Mich. 1994), *cert. denied,* 514 U.S. 1083 (1995). A Michigan court also issued an injunction against Kevorkian, but he defied it. People v. Kevorkian, 534 N.W.2d 172 (Mich. Ct. App. 1995), *appeal denied,* 549 N.W.2d 566 (Mich.), *cert. denied,* 519 U.S. 928 (1996). *See also* Kevorkian v. Thompson, 947 F. Supp. 1152 (E.D. Mich. 1997); Kevorkian v. American Med. Ass'n, 602 N.W.2d 233 (Mich. Ct. App. 1999), *appeal denied,* 613 N.W.2d 720 (Mich. 2000); *See generally* Robert Sedler, *Constitutional Challenges to Bans on "Assisted Suicide": The View from Without and Within,* 21 HASTINGS CONST. L.Q. 777 (1994); Zalman *et al., supra* note 130, at 869–907.

ing three acquittals and a hung jury.[134] He defiantly continued to assist suicides openly, and Kevorkian himself injected the lethal dose for a patient (Thomas Youk) whose disease was too far advanced for suicide. Kevorkian, as if seeking martyrdom, videotaped the Youk episode and arranged for the tape to be shown on television.[135]

The prosecutor for Oakland County, Michigan, who had gone after Kevorkian in the earlier trials had been defeated for reelection by a candidate who had pledged not to expend further public resources in prosecuting assisted suicide cases.[136] Even for the new prosecutor, however, Kevorkian's brazen disregard of the law was too much. He prosecuted Kevorkian for murder, with Kevorkian acting as his own defense attorney. Kevorkian hardly presented a defense, arguing that he was only a doctor seeking to alleviate the pain of a patient—although Kevorkian had surrendered his license to practice medicine eight years earlier.[137] On March 26, 1999, a jury returned a verdict of guilty of second-degree murder.[138]

Judge Jessica Cooper, who presided at the trial, sentenced the 70 year-old Kevorkian to 10 to 25 years in prison[139]—tantamount to a life sentence for a man of his age even if he did not carry out his threat to commit suicide in prison. Cooper's sentencing order was notably caustic.[140] She stated that the issue at the trial was not assisted suicide, but a man who was determined to defy the law and the medical profession, to place himself above the law, and to refuse to abide by the results of democratic elections that had addressed the question of assisted suicide. She concluded thusly:

> You were on bond to another judge when you committed this offense, you were not licensed to practice medicine when you committed this offense and you hadn't been licensed for eight years. And you had the audacity to go on national television, show the world what you did and dare the legal system to stop you. Well, sir, consider yourself stopped.[141]

In a referendum in Michigan a few months before the last Kevorkian trial, the electorate had repudiated assisted suicide by about 70 percent to 30 percent.[142] Many other states enacted

---

134. *Doctor Faces Murder Trial for Suicide Aid,* N.Y. TIMES, Feb. 29, 1992, § 1, at 10; Johnson, *supra* note 131, at A23; Magnusson, *supra* note 112, at 16–19. *See also* Jack Lessenberry, *Prosecutor Goes against the Tide, Going after Kevorkian,* N.Y. TIMES, Nov. 25, 1996, at A12; Jack Lessenberry, *Kevorkian Aids in Suicide as Michigan Ban Expires,* N.Y. TIMES, Nov. 27, 1994, at A12; Ron Rosenbaum, *Angel of Death: The Trial of the Suicide Doctor,* VANITY FAIR, May 1991, at 147; Isabel Wilkerson, *Doctor Is Charged with Murder in Suicide by Device He Invited,* N.Y. TIMES, Dec. 4, 1990, at A1.

135. Bill Dedman, *Death "Appeared a Homicide," State Says,* N.Y. TIMES, Nov. 24, 1998, at A16; Dirk Johnson, *Kevorkian Faces a Murder Charge in Death of Man: Fallout from Broadcast: Both Sides Praise Decision by Prosecutor to Take Debate on Euthanasia to Court,* N.Y. TIMES, Nov. 26, 1998, at A1. At least one commentator has suggested that Kevorkian's apparently self-defeating actions arose from a craving for publicity because Kevorkian's killings had become so frequent that they no longer made the front pages of newspapers. *See* John Leo, *Taking a Right Turn,* U.S. NEWS & WORLD REP., Feb. 23, 1998, at 13.

136. Zalman *et al., supra* note 130, at 922–25.

137. Johnson, *supra* note 131, at A23.

138. Pam Belluck, *Dr. Kevorkian is a Murderer, The Jury Finds,* N.Y. TIMES, March 27, 1999, at A1.

139. Johnson, *supra* note 130, at A1.

140. *Statement from Judge to Kevorkian,* N.Y. TIMES, Apr. 14, 1999, at A23.

141. *Id.* Kevorkian's conviction and sentencing were upheld on appeal. People v. Kevorkian, 639 N.W.2d 391 (Mich. Ct. App. 2001), *appeal denied,* 642 N.W.2d 681 (Mich.), *cert. denied,* 537 U.S. 881 (2002). Kevorkian might have been stopped, but other doctors were ready to step in his place. *See New Suicide Machine Being Made, Euthanasia Group Told,* L.A. TIMES, Jan. 13, 2003, at B5.

142. DEREK HUMPHRY, A TWENTIETH CENTURY CHRONOLOGY OF VOLUNTARY EUTHANASIA AND PHYSICIAN-ASSISTED SUICIDE, 1906–2003 (Euthanasia Research & Guidance Org. 2003). *See generally* Jerald Bachman *et al., Attitudes of Michigan Physicians and the Public toward Legalizing Physician-Assisted Suicide and Voluntary Euthanasia,* 334 NEW ENG. J. MED. 303 (1996). Kevorkian's first attempt to get the issue on the ballot failed when he was unable to collect enough signatures to qualify. *Kevorkian's Ballot Drive on Suicide Stumbles,* N.Y. TIMES, July 6, 1996, at A14.

statutes to prohibit assisted suicide.[143] Oregon, however, legalized assisted suicide through a referendum.[144] Even in Oregon, Kevorkian's actions presumably would have been illegal. In Canada, the national Parliament enacted a prohibition of assisted suicide. Canada's Supreme Court recently declared that there is no constitutional right to assistance in suicide in upholding that country's ban against a claim that it violates the Canadian Charter of Rights and Freedoms.[145]

When physicians undertook to assist suicides, some commentators were troubled by the reality that the great majority of those assisted were women, suggesting yet another instance of (perhaps unintended) male dominance over women's lives.[146] Some African-Americans also tend to

---

143. ARIZ. REV. STAT. ANN. § 13-1103(A)(3) (West 2001); CAL. PENAL CODE § 401 (West 1999); COLO. REV. STAT. ANN. § 18-3-104 (West 2003); FLA. STAT. ANN. § 782.08 (West 2000); GA. CODE ANN. § 16-5-5 (2003); 720 ILL. COMP. STAT. ANN. 5/12-31 (West. Supp. 2002); IND. CODE ANN. § 35-42-1-2.5 (West 1997); IOWA CODE ANN. § 707A.2 (West 2003); KAN. STAT. ANN. § 21-3406 (Cumm. Supp. 2003); KY. REV. STAT. ANN. § 216.302 (Michie 1999); LA. REV. STAT. ANN. § 32.12 (West 2002); MINN. STAT. § 609.215 (West 2003); MISS. CODE ANN. § 97-3-49 (1999); MO. REV. STAT. § 565 .023 (West 1999); NEB. REV. STAT. § 28-307 (1995); N.H. REV. STAT. ANN. § 630:4 (1996); N.M. STAT. ANN. § 30-2-4 (Michie 1994); N.Y. PENAL LAW § 120.30 (McKinney 1997); OKLA. STAT. tit. 21, § 813 (West 2002); S.D. CODIFIED LAWS § 22-16-37 (LexisNexis 1998); TENN. CODE ANN. § 39-13-216 (2003); TEX. PENAL CODE § 22.08 (West 2003); WASH. REV. CODE ANN. § 9A.36.060 (West 2000). *See* Gentry v. State, 625 N.E.2d 1268 (Ind. Ct. App. 1993), *transfer denied;* State v. Bauer, 471 N.W.2d 363 (Minn. Ct. App. 1991). For one of the more publicized controversies such policies generate, see Abby Goodenough, *Governor of Florida Orders Woman Fed in Right-to-Die Case,* N.Y. TIMES, Oct. 22, 2003, at A1; David Sanger, *Bush Backs His Brother's Decision in Feeding Tube Case,* N.Y. TIMES, Oct. 29, 2003, at A23; Rob Stein, *Woman's Sustaining Care Resumed, But Experts Say No Hope for Her Recovery,* WASH. POST, Oct. 23, 2003, at A3.

144. *See The Oregon Death with Dignity Act,* OR. REV. STAT. §§ 127.800 to 127.897 (2003); Lee v. Oregon, 107 F.3d 1382 (9th Cir.), *cert. denied sub nom.* Lee v. Harcleroad, 522 U.S. 927 (1997); Oregon v. Ashcroft, 192 F. Supp. 2d 1077 (D. Or. 2002), *appeal pending;* Hamilton v. Myers, 943 P.2d 214 (Or. 1997). *See also* THE OREGON DEATH WITH DIGNITY ACT: A GUIDEBOOK FOR HEALTHCARE PROVIDERS (Donnie Reagan *et al.* ed. 1998); Ann Alpers & Bernard Lo, *Physician-Assisted Suicide in Oregon: A Bold Experiment,* 274 JAMA 483 (1995); George Annas, *Death by Prescription: The Oregon Initiative,* 331 N. ENG. J. MED. 1240 (1994); A.L. Back *et al., Physician-Assisted Suicide and Euthanasia in Washington State: Patient Requests and Physician Responses,* 275 JAMA 919 (1996); Stephen Bushong & Thomas Balmer, *Breathing Life into the Right to Die: Oregon's Death with Dignity Act,* 11 ISSUES IN L. & MED. 269 (1995); Calandrillo, *supra* note 130, at 88–100; Jonathan Cohen *et al., Attitudes toward Assisted Suicide and Euthanasia among Physicians in Washington State,* 331 N. ENG. J. MED. 89 (1994); Scott Gast, *Who Defines "Legitimate Medical Practice?" Lessons Learned from the Controlled Substances Act, Physician-Assisted Suicide, &* Oregon v. Ashcroft, 10 VA. J. SOC. POL'Y & L. 261 (2002); Kathy Graham, *Last Rights: Oregon's New Death with Dignity Act,* 31 WILLAM. L. REV. 601 (1995); Grant & Linton, *supra* note 123, at 481–501; Herbert Hendin, Kathleen Foley, & Margot White, *Physician-Assisted Suicide: Reflections on Oregon's First Case,* 14 ISSUES IN L. & MED. 243 (1998); Melinda Lee *et al., Legalizing Assisted Suicide—Views of Physicians in Oregon,* 334 N. ENG. J. MED. 310 (1996); Steven Miles, Demetra Pappas, & Robert Koepp, *Considerations of Safeguards Proposed in Laws and Guidelines to Legalize Assisted Suicide,* in PHYSICIAN-ASSISTED SUICIDE, *supra* note 108, at 205; Christine Neylon O'Brien, Gerald Madek, & Gerald Ferrera, *Oregon's Guidelines for Physician-Assisted Suicide: A Legal and Ethical Analysis,* 61 U. PITT. L. REV. 329 (2000); Mark Siegel, *Lethal Pity: The Oregon Death with Dignity Act, its Implications for the Disabled, and the Struggle for Equality in an Able-Bodied World,* 16 LAW & INEQ. J. 259 (1998); Sam Howe Verhovek, *Oregon Reporting 15 Deaths in 1998 under Suicide Law: Officials See No Abuses, but Findings Reignite Debate over Doctors' Prescribing Lethal Doses of Drugs,* N.Y. TIMES, Feb. 18, 1999, at A1; William Winslade, *Physician-Assisted Suicide: Evolving Public Policies,* in PHYSICIAN-ASSISTED SUICIDE, *supra,* at 224.

145. Rodriguez v. British Columbia, 107 D.L.R.4th 342 (Can. 1993); Neil Milton, *Lessons from* Rodriguez v. British Columbia, 11 ISSUES IN L. & MED. 123 (1995). *See also* Anthony DePalma, *Light Sentence in Mercy Death Is Overturned in West Ontario,* N.Y. TIMES, Nov. 24, 1998, at A8. *And see* Pretty v. United Kingdom, Application no. 2346/02 (Eur. Ct. H. Rts. Apr. 25, 2002), *available at* http://www.echr.coe.int/Eng/ Judgments/htm (holding there is no right to assisted suicide under the European Convention on human rights); *Dutch Doctor Loses Euthanasia Appeal,* N.Y. TIMES, Dec. 25, 2002, at A4 (the doctor was convicted of assisting a suicide and was not performing euthanasia which is legal in the Netherlands).

146. *See, e.g.,* Stephanie Guttmann, *Death and the Maiden: Dr. Kevorkian's Woman Problem,* NEW REP., June 24, 1996, at 20; Lynne Marie Kohm & Britney Brigner, *Women and Assisted Suicide: Exposing the Gender*

view the legalization of physician-assisted suicide as a special threat to their group rather than as a means for empowering patients.[147] Rather less attention was given to the ample evidence that the overwhelming majority of the elderly—even those in great pain and in the terminal stages of disease—want to live as long as possible rather than sacrifice some part of their remaining life for an enhanced, but shortened, quality of life.[148] Persons who become quadriplegic after serious spinal injuries not only nearly always choose life, but sometimes go so far as to describe their lives as "enriched" by the event.[149] And when persons born with serious defects requiring multiple operations throughout their life are asked whether they would have preferred to have been allowed to die as a newborn, their answers are a clear and nearly unanimous "no."[150]

The reality that the "handicapped" choose life is in sharp contrast to the perceptions of their caregivers and loved ones. The potential for conflict between the dying or irremediably disabled and those intimately involved with them in dying poses daunting challenges to determining competence to consent.[151] Indeed, one study concluded that it was loss of a sense of community,

---

*Vulnerability to Acquiescent Death,* 4 Cardozo Women's L.J. 241 (1998); Nancy Osgood & Susan Eisenhandler, *Gender and Assisted and Acquiescent Suicide: A Suicidologist's Perspective,* 9 Issues in L. & Med. 361 (1994); Susan Wolf, *Physician-Assisted Suicide, Abortion, and Treatment Refusal: Using Gender to Analyze the Difference,* in Physician-Assisted Suicide, *supra* note 158, at 167.

147. Patricia King & Leslie Wolf, *Empowering and Protecting Patients: Lessons for Physician-Assisted Suicide from the African-American Experience,* 82 Minn. L. Rev. 1015 (1998); Larry Pittman, *Physician-Assisted Suicide in the Dark Ward: The Intersection of the Thirteenth Amendment and Health Care Treatments Having Disproportionate Impacts on Disfavored Groups,* 28 Seton Hall L. Rev. 774 (1998). *See also* Timothy Coté et al., *Risk of Suicide among Persons with AIDS,* 268 JAMA 2066 (1992) (only 13% of AIDS patients who commit suicide are non-white); Jennifer Haas et al., *Discussions of Preferences for Life-Sustaining Care by Persons with AIDS,* 153 Arch. Internal Med. 1241 (1993) (finding non-whites to be less likely to discuss death as an option). For arguments that many persons suffering from AIDS "quietly" commit suicide, see Russel Ogden, Euthanasia, Assisted Suicide, and AIDS (1994); Peter Marzuk et al., *Increased Risk of Suicide in Persons with AIDS,* 259 JAMA 1333 (1988); Jeremy Sitcoff, Note, *Death with Dignity: AIDS and a Call for Legislation Securing the Right to Assisted Suicide,* 29 John Marshall L. Rev. 677 (1996); Lee Slome et al., *Physician-Assisted Suicide and Patients with Human Immunodeficiency Virus Disease,* 336 New Eng. J. Med. 417 (1997).

148. Susan Gilbert, *Elderly Seek Longer Life, Regardless,* N.Y. Times, Feb. 10, 1996, at F7; Larry Seidlitz et al., *Attitudes of Older People toward Suicide and Assisted Suicide: An Analysis of Gallup Poll Findings,* 43 J. Am. Geriatrics Soc'y 993 (1995); Joel Tsevat et al., *Health Values of Hospitalized Patients 80 Years or Older,* 279 JAMA 371. *See also* James Brown et al., *Is It Normal for Terminally Ill Patients to Desire Death?,* 143 Am. J. Psychiatry 208 (1986); Mark Chopko & Michael Moses, *Assisted Suicide: Still a Wonderful Life?,* 70 Notre Dame L. Rev. 519 (1995); Harvey Max Chochinov et al., *Desire for Death in the Terminally Ill,* 152 Am. J. Psych. 1185 (1995); Ezekiel Emmanuel et al., *Euthanasia and Physician-Assisted Suicide: Attitudes and Experiences of Oncology Patients, Oncologists, and the Public,* 347 Lancet 1805 (1996) (finding different levels of support for euthanasia among the three groups); Herbert Hendin & Gerald Klerman, *Physician-Assisted Suicide and the Dangers of Legalization,* 150 Am J. Psych. 143 (1993); Gregory Hinrichson, *Recovery and Relapse from Major Depressive Disorder in the Elderly,* 149 Am. J. Psych. 1575 (1992); Harold Koenig et al., *Attitudes of Elderly Patients and Their Families toward Physician-Assisted Suicide,* 156 Arch. Internal Med. 2240 (1996); Nancy Osgood, *Assisted Suicide and Older People—A Deadly Combination: Ethical Problems in Permitting Assisted Suicide,* 10 Issues in L. & Med. 415 (1995).

149. Fenwick, *supra* note 107, at 90–91; Oliver Sacks, *Foreward,* in Temple Grandin, Thinking in Pictures and Other Reports from My Life with Autism 11, 16 (1995). *See also* Joni Eareckson Tada, When Is It Right to Die? (1992); National Council on Disability, *Assisted Suicide: A Disability Perspective,* 14 Issues in L. & Med. 273 (1998); Siegel, *supra* note 144.

150. *See* C. Everett Koop, *Ethical and Surgical Considerations in the Care of the Newborn with Congenital Abnormalities,* in Infanticide and the Handicapped Newborn 89, 94–96 (Dennis Horan & Melinda Delahoyde eds. 1982); Stephen Mikochik, *When Life Becomes Optional: A Comment on Kevin O'Rourke's Approach to Forgoing Life Support,* 10 Issues in L. & Med. 343 (1994). *See also* Murray Campbell, *The Latimer Decision: Disabled Relieved by Court's Decision,* Globe & Mail (Toronto), Jan. 19, 2001 (leaders of organizations of handicapped individuals approve of sentencing a father to prison for killing his handicapped daughter).

151. *See* Becky Cox White, Competence to Consent (1994); Jeffrey Blustein, *The Family in Medical Decisionmaking,* 23 Hastings Ctr. Rep. no. 3, at 6 (May–June 1993); Ardath Hamann, *Family Surrogate*

as much as physical deterioration, that leads people to abandon their desire to live.[152] And how freely can consent be given when, as in Oregon, the state declines to fund pain management but does fund assisted suicide.[153]

All of this suggests that the question of deciding to terminate the life of incompetent patients is far more problematic than litigation or television drama might lead one to think.[154] The differences between an actual person's judgment and the "substituted judgment" by others should be self-evident, but apparently are not. And if society accepts allowing substituted judgments for those unable to express their own preferences, it is only a small step to denying medical care to persons who would benefit from it on the grounds that the benefit is not worth the cost. That line has already been reached, and many think it has been crossed, with the advent of "managed care" and in Oregon's refusal to fund pain management while funding assisted suicide.[155]

Given that most individuals no longer pay for their medical care, it is perhaps inevitable that decisions about medical care will gravitate to the institutions that bear the expense. These questions transcend issues about the quality of a life when the denied treatment results in a serious shortening of a patient's life. The actual decisions thus far seem mostly to have remained in the hands of the doctors rather than the insurance companies. Doctors are most willing to help someone to die who is likely to die quickly, relatively painlessly, and with dignity—at least in the eyes of the doctor.[156]

---

*Laws: A Necessary Supplement to Living Wills and Durable Powers of Attorney,* 38 VILLA. L. REV. 103 (1993); John Hardwig, *Is There a Duty to Die?,* 27 HASTINGS CTR. REP. no. 2, at 34 (Mar.–Apr. 1997); Mark Kuczewski, *Reconceiving the Family: The Process of Consent in Medical Decisionmaking,* 26 HASTINGS CTR. REP. no. 2, at 30 (Mar.–Apr. 1996); Thomas Mappes & Jane Zembaty, *Patient Choices, Family Interests, and Physician Obligations,* 4 KENNEDY INST. FOR ETHICS J. 27 (1994); Adam Milani, *Better off Dead than Disabled?: Should Courts Recognize a "Wrongful Living" Cause of Action when Doctors Fail to Honor Patients' Advance Directive?,* 54 WASH. L. REV. 149 (1997); Carson Strong, *Patients Should Not Always Come First in Treatment Decisions,* 4 J. CLINICAL ETHICS 63 (1993); Mark Sullivan, *Should Psychiatrists Serve as Gatekeepers for Physician-Assisted Suicide,* 28 HASTINGS CNTR. REP. no. 4, at 24 (July–Aug. 1998). *But see* Stephen Mikochik, *Assisted Suicide and Disabled People,* 46 DePAUL L. REV. 987 (1997); Paul Steven Miller, *The Impact of Assisted Suicide on People with Disabilities—Is It a Right without a Freedom?,* 9 ISSUE IN LAW & MED. 47 (1993).

152. *Euthanasia: Physical Disintegration, Loss of Community Identified as Primary Factors Prompting Request,* AIDS WEEKLY, Aug. 20, 2001, at 15.

153. Physicians for Compassionate Care, *Oregon Cuts Funds for Pain Care—Pays for Assisted Suicide,* 14 ISSUES IN L. & MED. 339 (1998). *See also* Ezekiel Emanuel & Margaret Battin, *What Are the Potential Cost Savings from Legalizing Physician-Assisted Suicide?,* 339 N. ENG. J. MED. 167 (1998); Ezekiel & Linda Emanuel, *The Economics of Dying: The Illusion of Cost Savings at the End of Life,* 330 N. ENG. J. MED. 540 (1994); Julie Madorsky, *Is the Slippery Slope Steeper for People with Disabilities?,* 166 W. J. MED. 410 (1997); Mark Mosley, *How Can We Best Care for Persons Who Are Medically Indigent in a World of Limited Resources?,* 6 ISSUES IN L. & MED. 175 (1990); Robert Risley, *Voluntary Active Euthanasia; The Next Frontier: Impact on the Indigent,* 8 ISSUES IN L. & MED. 361 (1992). On pain management and other forms of care for the dying that could serve as an alternative to suicide, see APPROACHING DEATH: IMPROVING CARE AT THE END OF LIFE (Marilyn Field & Christine Cassel eds. 1997).

154. *See, e.g.,* Ellen Fox & Carol Stocking, *Ethics Consultants' Recommendations for Life-Prolonging Treatment of Patients in a Persistent Vegetative State,* 270 JAMA 2578 (1993); Benjamin Freedman, *Respectful Service and Reverent Obedience: A Jewish View on Making Decisions for Incompetent Parents,* 26 HASTINGS CTR. REP. no. 4, at 31 (July–Aug. 1996); Lawrence Markson et al., *Physician Assessment of Patient Competence,* 47 J. AM. GERIATRICS SOC'Y 1074 (1994); Kevin McIntyre, *Loosening Criteria for Withholding Prehospital Cardiopulmonary Resuscitation,* 153 ARCHIVES INTERNAL MED. 2189 (1993); Edmund Pellegrino, *Compassion Needs Reason Too,* 270 JAMA 874 (1993).

155. *See, e.g.,* E. HAAVI MERREIM, BALANCING ACT: THE NEW MEDICAL ETHICS OF MEDICINE'S NEW ECONOMICS (1995). *See also* TOM BEAUCHAMP & JAMES CHILDRESS, PRINCIPLES OF BIOMEDICAL ETHICS 228–34 (3rd ed. 1989). On Oregon's funding priorities, see the authorities collected *supra* in note 153.

156. Nicholas Christakis & David Asch, *Biases in How Physicians Choose to Withdraw Life Support,* 342 THE LANCET 642 (1993). *See also* David Asch, *The Role of Critical Care Nurses in Euthanasia and Assisted Suicide,* 334 NEW ENG. J. MED. 1374 (1996); Russell Portenoy et al., *Determinants of the Willingness to Endorse Assisted Suicide: A Survey of Physicians, Nurses, and Social Workers,* 38 PSYCHOSOMATICS 277 (1997).

Some choose to deny the existence of a "slippery slope" leading from the right to refuse treatment to assisted suicide to "substituted judgment" to the denial of medical to those deemed not worth the expense.[157] Empirical evidence of the so-called foot-in-the-door effect,[158] however, validates the impression of the downward progression we seem to observe in the sequence of developments at the end of life. After all, moral perceptions have "the same earthy dependence on reinforcement schedules as all other kinds of human behavior."[159] If those in authority seem to validate the progression, the ability of many to resist the downward trend often will be reduced.[160] There is direct evidence of this last premise for assisted suicide—one survey found that most doctors refused to grant patients' requests to assist them to die, but many more would do so were it legal.[161]

How is one to approach such questions in light of the teaching of *Roe* or *Casey?* Is the right to die (or to kill an elderly or infirm relative) encompassed in *Roe's* right of privacy?[162] Does *Casey's* right to "define one's own concept of existence" or to make "personal decisions relating to... family relationships... [or] the private realm of family life"[163] create a right in "any competent person—physically ill or not—to enlist the aid of another in committing suicide"?[164] There is no gainsaying that the ethos that gave us abortion on demand (but without real consideration of

---

157. Magnusson, *supra* note 113, at 81–82.

158. Jonathan Freedman & Scott Fraser, *Compliance without Pressure: The Foot-in-the-Door Technique*, 4 J. PERSONALITY & SOC. PSYCH. 195 (1966). *See also* DAVID LAMB, DOWN THE SLIPPERY SLOPE (1988); DOUGLAS WALTON, SLIPPERY SLOPE ARGUMENTS (1992); Trudy Govier, *What's Wrong with Slippery Slope Arguments?*, 12 CAN. J. PHILOS. 303 (1982); Eric Lode, *Slippery Slope Arguments and Legal Reasoning*, 87 CAL. L. REV. 1469 (1999); David Mayo, *The Role of Slippery Slope Arguments in Public Policy Debates*, 21 PHILOS. EXCHANGE 81 (1990); Wibren van der Burg, *The Slippery Slope Argument*, 102 ETHICS 42 (1991); Jeffrey Whitman, *The Many Guises of the Slippery Slope Argument*, 20 SOC. THEORY & PRAC. 85 (1994); Bernard Williams, *Which Slopes Are Slippery?*, in MORAL DILEMMAS IN MODERN MEDICINE 126 (Michael Lockwood ed. 1985).

159. Thomas Wren, *Social Learning Theory, Self-Regulation, and Morality*, 92 ETHICS 409, 411 (1982). *See also* J. Phillipe-Rushton, *Altruism and Society: A Social Learning Perspective*, 92 ETHICS 425, 435 (1982) ("From a social learning perspective, the overwhelming majority of human social behavior is learned from observing others.").

160. STANLEY MILGRAM, OBEDIENCE TO AUTHORITY (1974); Alan Elms & Stanley Milgram, *Personality Characteristics Associated with Obedience and Defiance toward Authoritative Command*, 2 J. EXPERIMENTAL RESEARCH IN PERSONALITY 282 (1966); Stanley Milgram, *Behavioral Study of Obedience*, 67 J. ABNORMAL & SOC. PSYCH. 371 (1963).

161. Sheryl Gay Stolberg, *Assisted Suicides Are Rare, Survey of Doctors Finds; Patient Requests Denied*, N.Y. TIMES, Apr. 23, 1998, at A1.

162. *Roe*, 410 U.S. at 152–61. *See generally* Susan Frelich Appleton, *Assisted Suicide and Reproductive Freedom: Exploring Some Connections*, 76 WASH. U. L.Q. 15 (1998); James Bopp, jr. & Richard Coleson, Roe v. Wade *and the Euthanasia Debate*, 12 ISSUES IN LAW & MED. 343 (1997); Martha Field, *Killing "the Handicapped"— Before and after Birth*, 16 HARV. WOMEN'S L.J. 79 (1993); Grant & Linton, *supra* note 123, at 509–15; Seth Kreimer, *Does Pro-Choice Mean Pro-Kevorkian? An Essay on* Roe, Casey, *and the Right to Die*, 44 AM. U. L. REV. 803 (1995); Michael McConnell, *The Right to Die and the Jurisprudence of Tradition*, 1997 UTAH L. REV. 665; Pittman, *supra* note 147, at 780–86; Lois Shepherd, *Dignity and Autonomy after* Washington v. Glucksberg: *An Essay about Abortion, Death, and Crime*, 7 CORNELL J. LAW & PUB. POL'Y 431 (1998); Marc Spindelman, *Are the Similarities between a Woman's Right to Choose an Abortion and the Alleged Right to Assisted Suicide Really Compelling?*, 29 U. MICH. J.L. REFORM 775 (1996); Sandra Lynne Tholen & Lisa Baird, Note, *Con Law Is as Con Law Does: A Survey of* Planned Parenthood v. Casey *in State and Federal Courts*, 28 LOY. L.A. L. REV. 971, 1030–35 (1995).

163. *Casey*, 505 U.S. at 851. *See* Compassion in Dying v. Washington, 49 F.3d 586, 595 (9th Cir. 1995) (Wright, J., dissenting), *cev'd sub nom.* Washington v. Glucksberg, 521 U.S. 782 (1997).

164. The argument was made without success in: Washington v. Glucksberg, 521 U.S. 702 (1997); Lee v. Oregon, 107 F.3d 1382 (9th Cir.), *cert. denied sub nom.* Lee v. Harcleroad, 522 U.S. 927 (1997); Quill v. Koppell, 870 F. Supp. 78 (S.D.N.Y. 1994), *rev'd sub nom.* Quill v. Vacco, 80 F.3d 716 (2nd Cir. 1996), *rev'd*, 521 U.S. 973 (1997).

the interests of the fetus) also sustains the claimed right to death on demand—or even over an unworthy person's objection. Note, however, the different answers one arrives at if one sees these cases as turning on sexual equality rather than on personal equality given the disproportionate impact of the assisted suicide option on women.[165]

Similarly, nearly half of the states now recognize a cause of action for "wrongful birth" based on the premise that parents, at least, are entitled to a healthy and sound child and should be compensated for the "emotional trauma" of giving birth to a seriously deformed child.[166] This notion finds its application in the widely held view that "problem pregnancies"—situations where the fetus is significantly deformed or will face a serious disability in life—should be aborted.[167] Those who purport to counsel parents facing "problem pregnancies" tend to paint only the worst case scenarios, while the prospective parents are seldom invited to meet parents of children with such problems—parents who might present a more positive picture of going through with the birth[168] Ironically, pressures to abort "deformed" fetuses come at a time when the opportunities for social acceptance and fulfilling lives for children born with many severe problems are better than ever before in history.[169] No wonder persons who have lived with many of these deformities or disabilities all of their lives tend to oppose abortion both as a denial by the parents of the rights of the fetus and as a denial by society of the adult's dignity and self-worth.[170]

---

165. *See* Wolf, *supra* note 146.

166. *See* Phillips v. United States, 508 F. Supp. 544 (D.S.C. 1981); Keel v. Banach, 624 So. 2d 1022 (Ala. 1993); Walker v. Mart, 790 P.2d 735 (Ariz. 1990); Ramos v. Valley Vista Hosp., 234 Cal. Rptr. 608 (Ct. App. 1987); Lininger v. Eisenbaum, 764 P.2d 1202 (Colo. 1988); Garrison v. Medical Ctr. of Del., Inc., 581 A.2d 288 (Del. 1989); Kush v. Lloyd, 616 So. 2d 415 (Fla. 1992); Atlanta Obstet. & Gyn. Group v. Abelson, 398 S.E.2d 557 (Ga. 1990); Blake v. Cruz, 698 P.2d 315 (Idaho 1984); Bader v. Johnson, 732 N.E.2d 1212 (Ind. 2000); Arche v. United States, 798 P.2d 477 (Kan. 1990); Reed v. Campagnolo, 630 A.2d 1145 (Md. 1993); Viccaro v. Milunsky, 551 N.E.2d 8 (Mass. 1990); Girdley v. Coats, 825 S.W.2d 295 (Mo. 1992); Smith v. Cote, 513 A.2d 341 (N.H. 1986); Bani-Esrali v. Lerman, 505 N.E.2d 947 (N.Y. 1987); Jackson v. Bumgardner, 347 S.E.2d 743 (N.C. 1986); Jacobs v. Theimer, 519 S.W.2d 846 (Tex. 1975); Naccash v. Burger, 290 S.E.2d 825 (Va. 1982); Harbeson v. Parke-Davis, Inc., 656 P.2d 483 (Was. 1983); James G. v. Caserta, 332 S.E.2d 872 (W. Va. 1985); Dumer v. St. Michael's Hosp., 233 N.W.2d 372 (Wis. 1975); Beardsley v. Wierdsma, 650 P.2d 288 (Wyo. 1982). *Contra:* Cauman v. George Was. U., 630 A.2d 1104 (D.C. 1993); Williams v. University of Chi. Hosps., 688 N.E.2d 130 (Ill. 1997); Grubbs v. Barbourville Fam. Health Ctr., PSC, 120 S.W.3d 682 (Ky. 2003); Taylor v. Kurapati, 600 N.W.2d 670 (Mich. Ct. App. 1999); Simmerer v. Dabbas, 733 N.E.2d 1169 (Ohio 2000). For analyses of this development, see W. PAGE KEETON *et al.*, PROSSER AND KEETON ON TORTS §§ 54, 55 (5th ed. 1984); Shelly Ryan, *Wrongful Birth: False Representations of Women's Reproductive Lives,* 78 MINN. L. REV. 857 (1994).

167. *See* WILLIAM RAY ARNEY, POWER AND THE PROFESSION OF OBSTETRICS 183 (1982); EMBRYOS, ETHICS, AND WOMEN'S RIGHTS (Elaine Hoffman Baruch, Amadeo D'Adamo, & Joni Seager eds. 1988); HADLEY, *supra* note 24, at 130–37; RUDY, *supra* note 45, at 3–21; BARBARA KATZ ROTHMAN, THE TENTATIVE PREGNANCY: PRENATAL DIAGNOSIS AND THE FUTURE OF MOTHERHOOD (1987); TEST-TUBE WOMEN: WHAT FUTURE FOR MOTHERHOOD? (Rita Arditti, Renate Klein, & Shelley Minden eds. 1984); THE CUSTOM-MADE CHILD: WOMEN-CENTERED PERSPECTIVES (Helen Holmes, Betty Hoskins, & Michael Gross eds. 1981); Eva Alberman *et al.*, *Down's Syndrome: Births and Pregnancy Terminations in 1989 and 1993: Preliminary Findings,* 102 BRIT. J. OSTET. & GYNECOLOGY 445 (1995); Wendy Farrant, *Who's for Amniocentesis? The Politics of Prenatal Screening,* in THE SEXUAL POLITICS OF REPRODUCTION (Hilary Homans ed. 1985); Marsha Sexton, *Disability Rights and Selective Abortion,* in ABORTION WARS, *supra* note 23, at 374, 380–83.

168. FENWICK, *supra* note 107, at 1145–54; Bruce & Diane Rodgers, *Abortion: The Seduction of Medicine,* 2 LIBERTY LIFE & FAM. 285, 295 (1995).

169. *See, e.g.,* Michael Bérubé, *Life as We Know It,* HARPER'S, Dec. 1994, at 41.

170. *See* RUTH HUBBARD, THE POLITICS OF WOMEN'S BIOLOGY 197 (1990); Brock Eide, *"The Least A Parent Can Do": Prenatal Genetic Testing and the Welcome of Our Children,* 13 ETHICS & MED. no. 3, at 59 (1997); Sexton, *supra* note 167, at 374.

Such difficult choices, whether relating to the end or the beginning of life, actually are only somewhat troubling in terms of our society's traditional values when one decides for oneself.[171] Choices directed at the lives of others are far more difficult to justify in terms of our traditional values. Rather, imposing such choices on unwilling others recalls too strongly from the attitudes of the notorious Nazi physicians who similarly espoused a quality of life ethic.[172] Still, we find people ready to argue that the aged, the infirm, and the defective (at least at birth) should be killed without their consent. The argument, cast in terms of the interests of the person to be killed, erupted into print shortly after *Roe* was decided.[173] Abortion "reform" strikes some as an easy first step in reordering our societies values along those lines—as the enthusiastic embrace of the quality of life ethic by abortion rights advocates demonstrates.[174]

Unreflectively seeking after the convenient answer rather than the right answer threatens to lead us, through a succession of well-intentioned but thoughtless acts—not because of any conspiratorial design—to abandon any sense of reverence for life, to become inured to seeing ourselves simply as means and not as ends.[175] As Lewis Mumford pointed out, before machines can replace people, people must be reduced to the level of the machine.[176] Mumford cut to the heart of the problem when, more than 60 years ago, he asked:

> What is the use of conquering nature if we fall prey to nature in the form of unbridled men? What is the use of equipping mankind with the mighty powers to move and build and communicate, if the final result of this secure food supply and this excellent organization is to enthrone the morbid impulses of a thwarted humanity?[177]

Technologies related to abortion, however, have fueled not only the drive to lessen or remove restrictions on access to abortion, but also the struggle to preserve restrictions as protections for unborn lives. Nor are these countervailing effects limited to either gender. The need to fit concerns of and about physicians into one's analysis further complicate any attempt to explain the failure of the apparent majority to enact its will into law. The question to be confronted then is how should society respond to and manage the emerging technology of the life sciences and the consequent technomorality—a morality generated by our technological capacities rather than by social or cultural tradition (or for those who take such claims seriously, by divine revelation)?

---

171. Cruzan v. Director, Mo. Dep't Health, 497 U.S. 261 (1990); Charles Sabatino, *Death in the Legislature: Inventing Legal Tools for Autonomy,* 19 NYU REV. L. & SOC. CHANGE 309 (1991).

172. GERMAIN GRISEZ, ABORTION: THE MYTHS, THE REALITIES, AND THE ARGUMENTS 202–03 (1970). *See also* HELMUT SCHOECK, SCIENTISM AND VALUES (1960); Symposium, *Biomedical Ethics and the Shadow of Nazism,* 6 HASTINGS CENTER REP. no. 6, at S1 (Aug. 1976).

173. BIOETHICS (Thomas Shannon ed. 1976); ETHICS OF NEWBORN INTENSIVE CARE (Albert Jonsen & Michael Garland eds. 1976); LEONARD WEBER, WHO SHALL LIVE? (1976); A.G.M. Campbell & Raymond Duff, *Moral and Ethical Dilemmas in the Special-Care Nursery,* 289 N. ENG. J. MED. 890 (1973); John Robertson, *Involuntary Euthanasia of Defective Newborns: A Legal Analysis,* 27 STAN. L. REV. 213 (1975); Anthony Shaw, *Dilemmas of "Informed Consent" in Children,* 289 N. ENG. J. MED. 885 (1973).

174. *See, e.g.,* DANIEL CALLAHAN, ABORTION: LAW, CHOICE, AND MORALITY 307–46 (1970); MOHR, *supra* note 25, at 251–52, 255–59.

175. For arguments that we have already done so, see JACQUES ELLUL, THE TECHNOLOGICAL SOCIETY 141–46, 208–27, 319–40 (John Wilkinson trans. 1964); ALVIN GOULDNER, THE COMING CRISIS OF WESTERN SOCIOLOGY 276–82 (1970); MUMFORD, *supra* note 100, at 3–6, 24–31, 41–54; Morton Kaplan, *Means/Ends Rationality,* 87 ETHICS 61 (1976); Kai Nielson, *Distrusting Reason,* 87 ETHICS 49 (1976).

176. MUMFORD, *supra* note 100, at 31.

177. *Id.* at 366.

# The Past—and the Future

*There always will be critique, but critique is not all that there is.*

—Christopher Wolfe[178]

History and tradition do not often supply simple, direct answers in political and legal debates. Justice Robert Jackson explained the problem in these words:

> A judge...may be surprised at the poverty of really useful and unambiguous authority applicable to concrete problems....Just what our forefathers did envision, or would have envisioned had they foreseen modern conditions, must be divined from materials almost as enigmatic as the dreams Joseph was called upon to interpret for Pharaoh.[179]

Thus, even the relatively straightforward question of whether the Fourteenth Amendment "incorporates" the Bill of Rights, making those rights applicable against the states, is highly uncertain—at least once the question was politicized and legalized.[180] While history and tradition might not provide easy answers, history and tradition are necessary for an informed answer.

Only by paying careful and honest attention to the past can we learn how the community has defined its values in relation to the facts as then understood. As our values evolve or our understanding of the facts change, it may become necessary to revise laws (including constitutional interpretations) based on those values or understandings.[181] The clearest example are the related practices of slavery and segregation that were once an accepted tradition in this country yet are clearly (and correctly) unconstitutional today—the latter development coming without the necessity of a formal constitutional amendment. Yet if we are to be true to our selves as individuals in a social community, we must honestly confront our past and not simply pretend that the past was different than it was. As Judge Learned Hand pointed out, "wisdom is to be gained only as we stand upon the shoulders of those who have gone before."[182]

In *Roe* and since, the Court has never actually considered the values and perceived facts underlying the prohibition of abortion. All we have in *Roe* is a falsified argument that abortion was "contested" throughout history, a matter of taste rather than an expression of mores basic to

---

178. Christopher Wolfe, *Give Me That Old-Time Historiography: Mark Tushnet on Constitutional Law*, 15 Law & Soc. Inquiry 831, 876 (1990).

179. Youngstown Sheet & Tube Co. v. Sawyer, 343 U.S. 579, 634 (1952) (Jackson, J., concurring).

180. *See* Raoul Berger, The Fourteenth Amendment and the Bill of Rights (1989); Raoul Berger, Government by Judiciary 134–56 (1978); Michael Curtis, No State Shall Abridge (1986); Alfred Avins, *The Crosskey-Fairman Debates Revisited*, 6 Harv. J. Legis. 1 (1968); Richard Aynes, *On Misreading John Bingham and the Fourteenth Amendment*, 103 Yale L.J. 57 (1993); Alexander Bickel, *The Original Understanding of the Segregation Decisions*, 69 Harv. L. Rev. 1 (1955); William Crosskey, *Charles Fairman, "Legislative History" and the Constitutional Limitations on State Authority*, 32 U. Chi. L. Rev. 1 (1953); Michael Curtis, *The Bill of Rights as a Limitation on State Authority: A Reply to Professor Burger*, 16 Wake Forest L. Rev. 45 (1980); Charles Fairman, *Does the Fourteenth Amendment Incorporate the Bill of Rights?*, 2 Stan. L. Rev. 5 (1949); William Nelson, *History and Neutrality in Constitutional Adjudication*, 72 Va. L. Rev. 1237 (1986).

181. *See* Joseph Dellapenna, *Nor Piety Nor Wit: The Supreme Court on Abortion*, 6 Colum. H. Rts. L. Rev. 379, 400–01 (1974).

182. Learned Hand, *A Plea for the Open Mind and Free Discussion*, in The Spirit of Liberty: Papers and Addresses of Learned Hand 274, 283 (Irving Dilliard ed., 3rd ed. 1977).

our culture.[183] It is time that the Court took seriously its own premise that the constitutional status of a claimed right to abort is to be tested against the history and traditions of this nation.[184] The accumulated wisdom relating to abortion teaches us that the prohibition of abortion was always viewed as the protection of emerging, yet real, human life—a concern only been made more certain by the continual growth of medical knowledge of gestation during the last two centuries.

Neither a Supreme Court decision to return responsibility for abortion laws to the legislatures nor the Court's decisions to involve itself in the controversy were responsible for politicizing the issue. The issue was politicized already. I suggest that not only would moving the controversy from the courts to the legislatures be consistent with our nation's history and traditions, but it would also carry positive benefits in its own right. If I am right about this, returning the abortion issue to the political branches will move us closer to closure on the problem.

For anyone who does not accept fetal personhood, prohibition of abortions that are increasingly safe for mothers can only seem a serious intrusion into the liberty of women because of a "moral prejudice."[185] Thus a majority of the Supreme Court repeatedly stressed, as early as *Doe v. Bolton*[186] (the companion case to *Roe v. Wade*), the lack of "any reason" for treating abortion differently than other minor surgery. Sociologist Kristin Luker went so far as to call the physicians' crusade against abortion an "ideological sleight of hand."[187] Political scientist Beverly Harrison prefers to describe the physicians' purported moral outrage against abortion as a mere "rhetorical flourish."[188] And many supporters of "abortion rights" simply refuse to accept that opponents of abortion can be sincere in their opposition instead of being dedicated to the continued oppression of the women.[189] Those who think like this proposed a *"Freedom of Choice Act"* in Con-

---

183. See *Casey Historians' Brief, supra* note 25; *Webster Historians' Brief, supra* note 25; Sylvia Law, *Conversations between Historians and the Constitution*, 12 THE PUBL. HISTORIAN 11, 14 (1990). *See generally* Chapter 1, at notes 59–140; Chapter 14, at notes 390–95, 436–50; Chapter 17, at notes 39–69.

184. *Casey,* 505 U.S. at 901 (Kennedy, O'Connor, & Souter, JJ., joint plurality op.), 912 (Stevens, J., partially concurring), 926–27 (Blackmun, J., partially concurring), 952–53 (Rehnquist, C.J., partially dissenting, joined by Scalia, Thomas, & White, JJ.), 980 n.1, 984, 995–96 (Scalia, J., partially dissenting, joined by Rehnquist, C.J, & Thomas & White, JJ.).

185. *See, e.g.,* BARBARA HINKINSON CRAIG & DAVID O'BRIEN, ABORTION AND AMERICAN POLITICS 40 (1993); DEGLER, *supra* note 47, at 242–43; GORDON, *supra* note 25, at 59–60, 154; LUKER, *supra* note 105, at 214; MOHR, *supra* note 25, at 35–36, 128, 140, 143–44, 147–54, 164–70, 175–76, 182–99, 219–21, 238, 261–63, 307 n.69; PETCHESKY, *supra* note 46, at 74–80; Rachael Pine & Sylvia Law, *Envisioning a Future for Reproductive Liberty: Strategies for Making the Rights Real,* 27 HARV. C.R.-C.L. L. REV. 407, 423–25 (1992).

186. 410 U.S. at 93–194, 197–198, 199.

187. LUKER, *supra* note 105, at 39.

188. HARRISON, *supra* note 34, at 128–29.

189. JOHN ARTHUR, THE UNFINISHED CONSTITUTION: PHILOSOPHY AND CONSTITUTIONAL PRACTICE 259–60 (1989); DALLAS BLANCHARD, THE ANTI-ABORTION MOVEMENT AND THE RISE OF THE RELIGIOUS RIGHT: FROM POLITE TO FIERY PROTEST 1–9 (1994); DALLAS BLANCHARD & TERRY PREWITT, RELIGIOUS VIOLENCE AND ABORTION: THE GIDEON PROJECT xii, 227–28, 231, 241 (1993); JAMES MACGREGOR BURNS & STEWART BURNS, A PEOPLE'S CHARTER: THE PURSUIT OF RIGHTS IN AMERICA 356–58 (1991); CONDIT, *supra* note 6, at 30, 61–63, 74 n.9, 127–28; CRAIG & O'BRIEN, *supra* note 185, at 46–47; MARILYN FRALIK, IDEOLOGY AND ABORTION POLITICS (1983); GARROW, *supra* note 23, at 633 ELIZABETH FOX GENOVESE, FEMINISM WITHOUT ILLUSIONS 2, 81–83 (1991); FAYE GINSBURG, CONTESTED LIVES: THE ABORTION DEBATE IN AN AMERICAN COMMUNITY 1, 6–19, 140–45, 172–97, 212–21 (1989); HARRISON, *supra* note 34, at 2–4, 32–49, 59–62, 67, 181–82, 189–90; JUDGES, *supra* note 25, at 12–15; KENNETH KARST, LAW'S PROMISE, LAW'S EXPRESSION: VISIONS OF POWER IN THE POLITICS OF RACE, GENDER, AND RELIGION 52–57 (1993); LUKER, *supra* note 105, at 137–38, 159–75, 195, 224, 241; CONNIE PAIGE, THE RIGHT TO LIFERS: WHO THEY ARE; HOW THEY OPERATE; WHERE THEY GET THEIR MONEY (1983); PETCHESKY, *supra* note 46, at xiii, xvi–xviii, xx–xxi, 5, 82–84; DEBORAH RHODE, JUSTICE AND GENDER 214–15 (1989); JOHN ROBERTSON, CHILDREN OF CHOICE: FREEDOM AND THE NEW REPRODUCTIVE TECHNOLOGIES 66–68 (1994); ROGER ROSENBLATT, LIFE ITSELF: ABORTION IN THE AMERICAN MIND 37–38, 109, 121–31 (1992); PATRICK SHEEHAN, WOMEN, SOCIETY, THE STATE, AND ABOR-

gress to create a federal statutory right to choose abortion that goes beyond the strictures of *Roe* as construed by the Supreme Court.[190] In my view, Congress has the power to do so under section 5 of the Fourteenth Amendment, although others have questioned this.[191] The proposed statute, however, ignores the unbroken common law tradition of protecting unwanted children as far as possible from aggression by their parents and also ignores the reality that reproductive technology is one of the most rapidly advancing areas of medicine.

Although attention in the abortion controversy has come to focus ever more exclusively on the interests of women, the Supreme Court initially seemed almost as concerned to protect physician autonomy as to promote maternal autonomy. Thus, although the Supreme Court majority denied standing to a specific doctor in *Roe v. Wade* itself,[192] they repeatedly referred to medical opinions[193] and they finally gave the physician decision-making power equal to the mother.[194] In the companion case of *Doe v. Bolton,* the majority accorded doctors standing as a class[195] and repeatedly adverted to the doctors' privacy interest.[196] Indeed, many supporters of

---

TION 125–28 (1987); SUSAN SHERWIN, NO LONGER PATIENT: FEMINIST ETHICS AND HEALTH CARE 111–14 (1992); SMITH-ROSENBERG, *supra* note 46, at 217–18; RICKIE SOLINGER, THE ABORTIONIST: A WOMAN AGAINST THE LAW 237–38 (paperback ed. 1996); LAURENCE TRIBE, ABORTION: THE CLASH OF ABSOLUTES 52–53, 76, 115, 132, 213, 232–34, 237–38, 242 (1992); JAMES BOYD WHITE, ACTS OF HOPE: CREATING AUTHORITY IN LITERATURE, LAW, AND POLITICS 166–67 (1994); Jean Braucher, *Tribal Conflict over Abortion* (book rev.), 25 GA. L. REV. 595, 597–606, 619–24 (1991); Rhonda Copelon, *From Privacy to Autonomy: The Conditions for Sexual and Reproductive Freedom,* in FROM ABORTION TO REPRODUCTIVE FREEDOM: TRANSFORMING A MOVEMENT 27, 27–29 (Marlene Gerber Fried ed. 1990); Nancy (Ann) Davis, *The Abortion Debate: The Search for Common Ground, Part I,* 103 ETHICS 516, 526–39 (1993); Amy Fried, *Abortion Politics as Symbolic Politics: An Investigation into Belief Systems,* 69 SOC. SCI. Q. 137 (1988); Linda Gordon & Allen Hunter, *Sex, Family, & the New Right,* 11/12 RADICAL AM. 9 (Dec. 1977, Feb. 1978); Donald Granberg, *Pro-Life or Reflections of Conservative Ideology?—An Analysis of Opposition to Legalized Abortion,* 62 SOCIOLOGY & SOC. RES. 414 (1978); Christopher Hitchens, *Minority Report,* 248 THE NATION 546 (1989); Molly Ivins, *Sex Bullies: What Do the Anti-Abortion, Anti-Gay, Anti-Porn Groups Want? Nothing Less than Sex Control,* PLAYBOY, June 1990, at 88; Sylvia Law, *Abortion and Compromise—Inevitable and Impossible,* 1992 U. ILL. L. REV. 921, 933–37; Krisztina Morvai, *What Is Missing from the Rhetoric of Choice? A Feminist Analysis of the Abortion Dilemma in the Context of Sexuality* (book rev.), 5 UCLA WOMEN'S L.J. 445, 446–49 (1995); Mary Jo Neitz, *Family, State, and God: Ideologies of the Right to Life Movement,* 42 SOCIOLOGICAL ANALYSIS 265 (1981); Pine & Law, *supra* note 185, at 423–25; Stephen Schnably, *Beyond* Griswold: *Foucauldian and Republican Approaches to Privacy,* 23 CONN. L. REV. 861, 910–21 (1991); Jeanne Schroeder, *History's Challenge to Feminism,* 88 MICH. L. REV. 1889, 1897 (1990); Suzanne Staggenborg, *Life-Style Preferences and Social Movement Recruitment: Illustrations from the Abortion Conflict,* 68 SOCIAL SCI. Q. 779 (1987); Ellen Willis, *Putting Women Back into the Abortion Debate,* in FROM ABORTION TO REPRODUCTIVE FREEDOM, *supra,* at 131–38.

190. H.R. 25, 102d Cong., 1st. Sess (1991); S. 25, 102d Cong., 2nd Sess. (1992). *See generally* JUDGES, *supra* note 25, at 259–64, 281–95; 1 FEDERAL ABORTION POLITICS: A DOCUMENTARY HISTORY 519–655 (Neal Devins & Wendy Watson eds. 1995); Ira Lupu, *Statutes Revolving in Constitutional Law Orbits,* 79 VA. L. REV. 1, 37–38 (1993). Law professor Ira Lupu warned, however, that the actual text lends itself to more restrictive interpretations than envisioned by its authors. Lupu, *supra,* at 46–52, 72–76.

191. Dellapenna, *supra* note 181, at 409–13. For a more detailed (and skeptical) analysis of the constitutional basis of the statute, see Lupu, *supra* note 190, at 38–46, 76–83. *See generally* City of Boerne v. Flores, 521 U.S. 507 (1997).

192. 410 U.S. at 125–127.

193. *Id.* at 130–32, 141–46, 149–50, 159, 163.

194. *Id.* at 153, 162–66.

195. 410 U.S. at 188–89.

196. *Id.* at 192–93, 196–201. *See also* Webster v. Reproductive Health Services, Inc., 492 U.S. 490, 513–18 (plurality op. per Rehnquist, C.J., joined by Kennedy & White, JJ.), 525–27 (O'Connor, J., concurring) (1989); Thornburgh v. American College of Obstetricians, 476 U.S. 747, 759–65 (1986); Colautti v. Franklin, 439 U.S. 379, 387–89, 397–401 (1979); Planned Parenthood of Cent. Mo. v. Danforth, 428 U.S. 52, 61–65 (1976). *See generally* George Annas *et al., The Right of Privacy Protects the Doctor-Patient Relationship,* 263 JAMA 858, 861 (1990); Robert Destro, *Abortion and the Constitution: The Need for a Life-Protective Amendment,* 63 CAL. L. REV. 1250, 1306–10 (1975); Julie George, *Political Effects of Court Decisions on Abortion: A Comparison be-*

abortion rights charge that the entire edifice of *Roe v. Wade* was designed to enhance the professional power of (male) doctors over women rather than to serve women's needs.[197]

The scope of the proper deference to the professional judgments of physicians is, of course, an issue broader than the abortion controversy. Intense debates have over the exercise by physicians of excessive control over widely varying decisions affecting people's health.[198] Integrating an ethic of patient autonomy with the ethic of physician responsibility has become a serious

---

*tween the United States and the German Federal Republic,* 3 INT'L J.L. & FAM. 106, 114 (1989); Siegel, *supra* note 25, at 273–74.

197. *See, e.g.,* NINIA BAEHR, ABORTION WITHOUT APOLOGY: A RADICAL HISTORY FOR THE 1990s, at 4 (1990); G.J. BARKER-BENFIELD, THE HORRORS OF THE HALF-KNOWN LIFE: MALE ATTITUDES TOWARD WOMEN AND SEXUALITY IN NINETEENTH CENTURY AMERICA 61 (1976); ROBERT BLANK & JANNA MERRICK, HUMAN REPRODUCTION, EMERGING TECHNOLOGIES, AND CONFLICTING RIGHTS 32–33, 38 (1995); COLKER, *supra* note 67, at 104–06; CONDIT, *supra* note 6, at 102; DAVIS, *supra* note 97, at 10–12, 17–20, 179–206, 226–32; GARROW, *supra* note 23, at 408, 613–14; GINSBURG, *supra* note 189, at 41–42, 55–56; GORDON, *supra* note 25, at 344, 358; VICTORIA GREENWOOD & JACK YOUNG, ABORTION ON DEMAND 99 (1976); HARRISON, *supra* note 34, at 9–10; FREDERICK JAFFE, BARBARA LINDHEIM, & PHILIP LEE, ABORTION POLITICS 9–10 (1981); MARY KENNY, ABORTION: THE WHOLE STORY 260–67 (1986); MACKINNON, *supra* note 69, at 98, 100–01; MACKINNON, *supra* note 72, at 189, 192; BARBARA MILBAUER & BERT OBRENTZ, THE LAW GIVETH: LEGAL ASPECTS OF THE ABORTION CONTROVERSY 122–24 (1983); PETCHESKY, *supra* note 46, at 90–93, 123–25, 130–32, 192–97, 289–94; KERRY PETERSEN, ABORTION REGIMES 15–17, 76–78, 101–02, 154–55 (1993); RHODE, *supra* note 189, at 204–05; SMART, *supra* note 44, at 90–113; WHITE, *supra* note 189, at 165; Susan Frelich Appleton, *Doctors, Patients and the Constitution: A Theoretical Analysis of the Physician's Role in "Private" Reproductive Decisions,* 63 WASH. U. L.Q. 183 (1985); Andrea Asaro, *The Judicial Portrayal of the Physician in Abortion and Sterilization Decisions: The Use and Abuse of Medical Discretion,* 6 HARV. WOMEN'S L.J. 51 (1983); Marie Ashe, *Zig-Zag Stitching and the Seamless Web: Thoughts on "Reproduction" and the Law,* 13 NOVA L. REV. 355 (1989); Diane Curtis, *Doctored Rights: Menstrual Extraction, Self-Help Gynecological Care, and the Law,* 20 REV. L. & SOC. CHANGE 427, 428–29 (1994); Erin Daly, *Reconsidering Abortion Law: Liberty, Equality, and the New Rhetoric of Planned Parenthood v. Casey,* 45 AM. U. L. REV. 77, 79, 83–102, 108–09, 126–28 (1995); Janet Gallagher, *Fetus as Patient,* in REPRODUCTIVE LAWS FOR THE 1990s, at 190, 192, 205–10 (Sherill Cohen & Nadine Taub eds. 1989); Ruth Bader Ginsburg, *Some Thoughts on Autonomy and Equality in Relation to Roe v. Wade,* 63 N.C. L. REV. 375, 382–83 (1985); Karen Booth Glen, *Abortion in the Courts: A Lay Woman's Historical Guide to the New Disaster Area,* 4 FEMINIST STUD. 1 (1978); Patricia Karlan & Daniel Ortiz, *In a Different Voice: Relational Feminism, Abortion Rights, and the Feminist Legal Agenda,* 87 NW. U. L. REV. 858, 877 (1993); Sylvia Law, *Rethinking Sex and the Constitution,* 132 U. PA. L. REV. 955, 1020 (1984); Martha Minow, *Breaking the Law: Lawyers and Clients in Struggles for Social Change,* 52 U. PITT. L. REV. 723, 728–29 (1991); Laura Punnett, *The Politics of Menstrual Extraction,* in FROM ABORTION TO REPRODUCTIVE FREEDOM, *supra,* at 101; Sally Sheldon, *"Who Is the Mother to Make the Judgment?": The Constructions of Woman in English Abortion Law,* 1 FEMINIST LEG. STUD. 3, 13–14 (1993); Siegel, *supra* note 77, at 287–88, 314–15. *See also* JOHN NOONAN, JR., A PRIVATE CHOICE: ABORTION IN AMERICA IN THE SEVENTIES 38–40 (1979); Robert Araujo, *Abortion, Ethics, and the Common Good: Who Are We? What Do We Want? How Do We Get There?,* 76 MARQ. L. REV. 701, 707–10, 729–30 (1993); David Smolin, *The Jurisprudence of Privacy in a Splintered Supreme Court,* 75 MARQ. L. REV. 975, 1016–25 (1992).

Similar objections have been made to the English abortion legislation that permits an abortion only if performed by a doctor and only after it is approved by two doctors. Royal College of Nursing v. Department of Health, [1980] Crim. L.R. 714 (Q.B.), [1981] A.C. 800 (C.A. & H.L.); Paton v. British Pregnancy Advisory Service, [1979] 1 Q.B. 276, 281–82; C. v. S., [1988] 1 Q.B. 135. *See, e.g.,* SUSAN ATKINS & BRENDA HOGGETT, WOMEN AND THE LAW 86–90 (1984); GREENWOOD & YOUNG, *supra,* at 132–33; ELIZABETH KINGDOM, WHAT'S WRONG WITH RIGHTS?: PROBLEMS FOR FEMINIST POLITICS AND JURISPRUDENCE 52–53 (1991); J.K. MASON, MEDICO-LEGAL ASPECTS OF REPRODUCTION AND PARENTHOOD 116–19 (1990); DAVID MEYERS, THE HUMAN BODY AND THE LAW 28 (2nd ed. 1990). *See also* EVA RUBIN, ABORTION, POLITICS, AND THE COURTS 75–77 (rev. ed. 1987). The same charge has been leveled at the clergy who undertook abortion counseling, at some personal risk, when abortion was still illegal. DAVIS, *supra,* at 135, 157.

198. *See, e.g.,* Clark Havighurst, *The Professional Paradigm of Medical Care: Obstacle to Decentralization,* 30 JURIMETRICS J. 415 (1990); Eliot Freidson, *The Centrality of Professionalism to Health Care,* 30 JURIMETRICS J. 431 (1990).

problem.[199] Solicitousness for the medical profession, as is found in the Supreme Court's abortion decisions, perhaps expresses a judicial hope not to impede the remarkable progress in reproductive and other medical technologies that we have witnessed in recent decades. Law, however, cannot be fashioned solely to protect the autonomy of the technicians. Issues relating to abortion transcend mere technical competence,[200] just as questions relating to products liability cannot be left entirely to the engineers or issues relating to state involvement in religious practice cannot be left entirely to theologians. Indeed, the feminist critiques of *Roe* often have objected to its remarkable deference to the interests of physicians rather than concern for the interests of women.[201]

Deference to the technicians should be all the more suspect as the technicians responsible for abortion have an economic interest in deciding against life.[202] Usually, profit in abortions comes from the rather hefty fees the abortionist can command—fees that could be higher still if public funds were to foot the bill. If 1,500,0000 abortions are performed annually at an average cost of $500 each (a modest price), abortion is a $750,000,000/year industry in the United States. No wonder it is so easy to find experts willing to testify in favor of abortion or that any attempt to overturn abortion rights will meet a vocal, well organized, and well funded opposition.[203]

In England, at least, some doctors also profited from selling fetal tissue until that became such a public scandal that the government acted to stop it.[204] In the United States, concern to prevent the doing of abortions for the purpose of obtaining fetal tissue—whether to be sold or to be used for non-profit purposes—led to a long-term but temporary ban on the federal funding of research on fetal tissue.[205] This in turn led to abortionists simply discarding fetal remains in trash containers,[206] and subsequent laws to require "respectful" disposal.[207]

---

199. *See* Mary Briody Mahowald, Women and Children in Health Care: An Unequal Majority (1993).

200. *See* Alexander Morgan Capron & Vicki Michel, *Law and Bioethics,* 27 Loy.-L.A. L. Rev. 25, 36 (1993); Siegel, *supra* note 25, at 272–77; Smolin, *supra* note 197, at 1020–25; Richard Wilkins, Richard Sherlock, & Stephen Clark, *Mediating the Polar Extremes: A Guide to Post-*Webster *Abortion Policy,* in Abortion and the States: Political Change and Future Regulation 139, 148–50 (Jane Wishner ed. 1993). On the troubled (and troubling) relationship between law (and politics) and modern science, see Schuck, *supra* note 54.

201. *See, e.g.,* Atkins & Hoggett, *supra* note 197, at 86–90; Baehr, *supra* note 197, at 4; Colker, *supra* note 69, at 104–06; Condit, *supra* note 6, at 102; Davis, *supra* note 97, at 10–12, 17–20, 179–206, 226–32; Ginsburg, *supra* note 189, at 41–42, 55–56; Gordon, *supra* note 25, at 344, 358; Hadley, *supra* note 23, at 179–82, 198–201; Harrison, *supra* note 34, at 9–10; Kenny, *supra* note 197, at 260–67; Kingdom, *supra* note 197, at 52–53; MacKinnon, *supra* note 69, at 98, 100–01; MacKinnon, *supra* note 72, at 189, 192; Petchesky, *supra* note 46, at 90–93, 123–25, 130–32, 192–97, 289–94; Petersen, *supra* note 197, at 15–17, 76–78, 101–02, 154–55; Rhode, *supra* note 189, at 204–05; Smart, *supra* note 71, at 90–113; Appleton, *supra* note 197; Asaro, *supra* note 197; Ashe, *supra* note 197; Curtis, *supra* note 197, at 428–29; Daly, *supra* note 197, at 79, 83–102, 108–09, 126–28; Gallagher, *supra* note 197, at 190, 192, 205–10; Ginsburg, *supra* note 197, at 41–42; Glen, *supra* note 197; Law, *supra* note 197, at 1020; Minow, *supra* note 197, at 728–29; Punnett, *supra* note 197, at 101; Sheldon, *supra* note 197, at 13–14; Siegel, *supra* note 25, at 287–88, 314–15.

202. Brian Clowes, *The Role of Maternal Deaths in the Abortion Debate,* 13 St. L.U. Pub. L. Rev. 327, 345–49 (1993); Rodgers & Rodgers, *supra* note 168, at 306–08.

203. Denis Cavanagh, *Legal Abortion in America: Factors in the Dynamics of Change,* 2 Life Liberty & Fam. 309, 313 (1995).

204. Noonan, *supra* note 197, at 120.

205. *Id.* at 120–27; Jane Friedman, *The Federal Fetal Experimentation Regulations: An Establishment Clause Analysis,* 61 Minn. L. Rev. 961 (1977); Dennis Horan, *Fetal Experimentation and Federal Regulation,* 22 Villa. L. Rev. 325 (1977); Robert Levine, *The Impact on Fetal Research on the Report of the National Commission for the Protection of Human Subjects of Biomedical and Behavioral Research,* 22 Villa. L. Rev. 367 (1977); David Nathan, *Fetal Research: An Investigator's View,* 22 Villa. L. Rev. 384 (1977). *See also* Chapter 18, at notes 131–39.

206. Marvin Olasky, The Press and Abortion, 1838–1988, at 138–39, 147 (1988).

207. Ark. Code Ann. § 20-17-802 (LexisNexis 2000); Cal Health & Safety Code § 123445 (West 1996); Fla. Stat. Ann. §§ 390.0111(7), 390.012 (West 2002); Ga. Code Ann. § 16-12-141.1 (2003); La. Stat. Ann.

Candid appraisal of abortion in the United States today reveals a practice permeated by the profit motive. Consider the description proffered by Bruce and Diane Rodgers (a doctor and a registered nurse):

> Most pregnancy terminations in the United States take place in free-standing, profit motivated abortion clinics. Generally, the mother has little if any personal contact with the physician abortionist, and postabortion followup (*sic*) usually is not provided. Patients usually report to local hospital emergency rooms for complications. The proceedings are expensive, and in many cases, the bill is paid in cash by individuals with scant resources. Ironically, abortion in such settings bears little resemblance to the compassionate act it is purported to be.[208]

Occasionally, evidence of abortionists' commercial motivation creeps into the press, as when the *Philadelphia Inquirer* reported on an FBI investigation of the largest chain of abortion clinics in Massachusetts because it's physicians consistently diagnosed pregnancies as about three weeks further along that they actually were.[209] This pattern enabled the clinic to perform a larger percentage of the more profitable later term abortions. Another exposé found abortionists who routinely aborted women who were not even pregnant, without bothering to wear sterile gloves, and one whose nurse's dog lapped up blood off the operating room floor.[210] A number of cases have produced malpractice judgments for botched abortions.[211]

---

§ 40.1299.35.14 (West 2001); Minn. Stat. § 145.1621 (West 1998); Mont. Code Ann. § 50-20-105 (2003); Neb. Rev. Stat. § 71-20,121 (Supp. 2003); N.D. Cent. Code § 14-02.1-09 (Michie 1997); S.D. Codified Laws Ann. §§ 34-25-32.3 to 34-25-32.7 (LexisNexis Supp. 2003); Wyo. Stat. Ann. § 35-6-109 (LexisNexis 2003). *See also* Catholic Lg.v. Feminist Women's Health Center, Inc., 469 U.S. 1303 (1984).

208. Rodgers & Rodgers, *supra* note 168, at 291. *See also* Carol Everett, The Scarlet Lady: Confessions of a Successful Abortionist 121 (1991); Garrow, *supra* note 23, at 715–17. In at least one state, there is even a precedent for the proposition that husbands are not liable to pay for a wife's legal abortion on the grounds that an abortion is not a "necessary." Sharon Clinic v. Nelson R., 394 N.Y.S.2d 118 (Sup. Ct. 1977).

209. *Mass. Abortion Clinics Probed for Rigged Tests*, Phila. Inquirer, Dec. 10, 1995, at A28.

210. Olasky, *supra* note 206, at 133–35, 140–41 (1988).

211. Gaydar v. Sociedad Instituto Gineco-Quirurigico, 345 F.3d 15 (1st Cir. 2003); Arnold v. Board of Educ. of Escambia Cnty., 880 F.2d 305 (11th Cir. 1989); Baker v. Edman, 719 F.2d 122 (5th Cir. 1983); Fowler v. Bickham, 550 F. Supp. 71 (N.D. Ill. 1982); Boykin v. Magnolia Bay, Inc., 570 So. 2d 639 (Ala. 1990); Williams v. Robinson, 512 So. 2d 58 (Ala. 1987); Perguson v. Tamis, 937 P.2d 347 (Ariz. Ct. App. 1996); Vuitch v. Furr, 482 A.2d 811 (D.C. 1984); Sponaugle v. Pre-Term, Inc., 411 A.2d 366 (D.C. 1980); Atlanta Obstetrics v. Coleman, 398 S.E.2d 16 (Ga. 1990); Adams v. Family Planning Assoc. Med. Group, 733 N.E.2d 766 (Ill. App. Ct. 2000), *appeal denied*, 744 N.E.2d 283 (Ill. 2001); Shirk v. Kelsey, 617 N.E.2d 152 (Ill. App. Ct. 1993.), *appeal denied*, 622 N.E.2d 1228 (Ill. 1993); Kirby v. Jarrett, 545 N.E.2d 965 (Ill. App. Ct. 1989); Collins v. Thakkar, 552 N.E.2d 507 (Ind. Ct. App. 1990); Reynier v. Delta Women's Clinic, Inc., 359 So. 2d 733 (La. Ct. App. 1978); Hitch v. Hall, 399 A.2d 953 (Md. Ct. Spec. App.), *cert. denied*, 285 Md. 730 (1979); Blair v. Hutzel Hosp., 552 N.W.2d 507 (Mich. Ct. App. 1996), *rev'd mem.*, 569 N.W.2d 167 (Mich. 1997); Kiddy v. Lipscomb, 628 So. 2d 1355 (Miss. 1993); Eidson v. Reproductive Health Services, 863 S.W.2d 621 (Mo. Ct. App. 1993), *transfer denied*; Blackburn v. Blue Mt. Women's Clinic, 951 P.2d 1 (Mont. 1997), *cert. denied*, 524 U.S. 905 (1998); Ferrara v. Bernstein, 613 N.E.2d 542 (N.Y. 1993); Jessamy v. Parkmed Assocs., 761 N.Y.S.2d 639 (App. Div. 2003); Negron v. State, 638 N.Y.S.2d 977 (App. Div.), *appeal denied*, 670 N.E.2d 226 (N.Y. 1996); Ganapolskaya v. VIP Med. Assocs., 644 N.Y.S.2d 735 (App. Div. 1996); Nehorayoff v. Fernandez, 594 N.Y.S.2d 863 (App. Div. 1993); Martinez v. Long Island Jewish-Hillside Med. Ctr., 519 N.Y.S.2d 53 (App. Div. 1987); Kusterman v. Glick, 484 N.Y.S.2d 31 (App. Div. 1985); Jean-Charles v. Planned Parenthood, 471 N.Y.S.2d 622 (App. Div. 1984); Delaney v. Krafte, 470 N.Y.S.2d 936 (App. Div. 1984); Mears v. Alhadeff, 451 N.Y.S.2d 133 (App. Div. 1982); Phillips v. Triangle Women's Health Clinic, 573 S.E.2d 600 (N.C. Ct. App. 2002); Sorina v. Armstrong, 589 N.E.2d 1359 (Ohio Ct. App. 1990), *jurisdictional motion overruled*, 569 N.E.2d 512 (Ohio 1991); Davis v. Fieker, 952 P.2d 505 (Okla. 1997); Hunte v. Hinkley, 731 S.W.2d 570 (Tex. Ct. App. 1987), *writ refused, n.r.e.*; Lake v. Northern Va. Women's Med. Ctr., 483 S.E.2d 220 (Va. 1997); Ott v. Baker, 53 Va. Cir. 113 (2000); Senesac v. Associates in Obstet. & Gynecology, 449 A.2d 900 (Vt. 1982); S.R. v. City of

Supporters of abortion rights, however, generally succeed in silencing reports of abortionists' profit motives, purveying instead an image of abortionists as selfless friends of women.[212]

---

Fairmont, 280 S.E.2d 712 (W. Va. 1981). *See also* Sherman v. Ambassador Ins. Co., 670 F.2d 251 (D.C. Cir. 1981) (physician's suit against malpractice insurer); Broemmer v. Abortion Services of Phoenix, Ltd., 840 P.2d 1013 (Ariz. 1992) (a woman cannot be bound to arbitrate abortion-malpractice claim); Blanton v. Womancare, Inc., 696 P.2d 645 (Cal. 1985) (same); Lewis v. Family Plan. Mngt., Inc., 715 N.E.2d 743 (Ill. App. Ct. 1999) (upholding discovery orders in abortion-malpractice action); Bickham v. Selcke, 576 N.E.2d 975 (Ill. App. Ct. 1991) (upholding professional sanctions against a physician because of the negligent performance of an abortion); Rockefeller v. Chul Hwang, 484 N.Y.S.2d 206 (App. Div. 1985) (upholding discovery orders in abortion-malpractice action); Sanchez v. Sirmons, 467 N.Y.S.2d 757 (N.Y. Sup. Ct. 1983) (a woman cannot be bound to arbitrate abortion-malpractice claim).

*See generally* Thomas Eller, *Informed Consent Civil Actions for Post-Abortion Psychological Trauma,* 71 Notre Dame L. Rev. 639 (1996); Ray Kerrison, *Horror Tale of Abortion,* N.Y. Post, Jan. 7, 1991, at 2; Ray Kerrison, *Abort Patients Naivete Leads to Another Death,* N.Y. Post, Aug. 5, 1991, at 2; Tamar Lewin, *Malpractice Lawyers' New Target,* Med. Econ., July 1995, at 21; Rodgers & Rodgers, *supra* note 168 at 307–08 (1995); Thomas Strahan, *Negligent Physical or Emotional Injury Related to Induced Abortion,* 9 Regent U. L. Rev. 149 (1997). *See generally* Paige Comstock Cunningham & Clarke Forsythe, *Is Abortion the "First Right" for Women?: Some Consequences of Legal Abortion,* in Abortion, Medicine and the Law 100, 130–37 (J. Douglas Butler & David Walbert eds., 4th ed. 1992); Gary Roberts, *Medical Malpractice in Abortion Cases,* 3 Am. J. Trial Adv. 259 (1979).

For decisions denying recovery (none of which deny the legal possibility of bringing such a claim), see: Okpalobi v. Foster, 244 F.3d 405 (5th Cir. 2001) (the Governor and Attorney General of Louisiana are immune from suit challenging a statute providing for malpractice suits against abortion providers); Inland Empire Health Plan v. Superior Ct., 133 Cal. Rptr. 2d 735 (Ct. App. 2003) (the HMO is not liable for negligent credentialing after one of their accredited doctors committed malpractice during an abortion); Adams v. Family Plan. Assocs. Med. Group, Inc., 733 N.E.2d 766 (Ill. App. Ct. 2000) (failure to prove malpractice); Brown v. Moawad, 570 N.E.2d 490 (Ill. App. Ct.) (same), *appeal dismissed,* 575 N.E.2d 112 (Ill. 1991); Miller v. Vitner, 546 S.E.2d 917 (Ga. Ct. App. 2001) (suit barred by the statute of limitations), *state cert. denied*; Bryant v. Crider, 434 S.E.2d 161 (Ga. Ct. App. 1993) (same); Joplin v. University of Mich. Bd. of Regents, 433 N.W.2d 830 (Mich. Ct. App. 1988) (state-owned hospital immune from suit), *remanded on other grounds,* 450 N.W.2d 263 (Mich.), *dismissed on other grounds,* 459 N.W.2d 70 (Mich. Ct. App. 1990); Dunmore v. Babaoff, 386 N.W.2d 154 (Mich. Ct. App. 1986) (failure to prove malpractice); Baker v. Gordon, 759 S.W.2d 87 (Mo. Ct. App. 1988) (same); Koehler v. Schwartz, 399 N.E.2d 1140 (N.Y. 1979) (no liability for an attempted abortion that did not "terminate the pregnancy"); Perez v. Park Madison Professional Labs., Inc., 630 N.Y.S.2d 30 (App. Div. 1995) (action barred by informed consent given after appropriate warnings of risks), *appeal dismissed,* 663 N.E.2d 922 (N.Y. 1995); Symone T. v. Lieber, 613 N.Y.S.2d 404 (App. Div. 1994) (action barred when the plaintiff knowingly underwent an illegal abortion); Greene v. Legacy Emanuel Hosp., 60 P.3d 535 (Or. 2002) (malpractice action dismissed on statute of limitations grounds); Grandelli v. Methodist Hosp., 777 A.2d 1138 (Pa. Super. Ct. 2003) (failure to prove malpractice); Roddy v. Volunteer Med. Clinic, Inc., 926 S.W.2d 572 (Tenn. Ct. App. 1996) (same); Powers v. Floyd, 904 S.W.2d 713 (Tex. Ct. App. 1995) (a woman who underwent an abortion as a minor with the informed consent of her mother cannot sue the non-negligent physician upon becoming an adult), *cert. denied,* 516 U.S. 1126 (1996); Senesac v. Associates in Obstetrics & Gynecology, 449 A.2d 900 (Vt. 1982) (failure to prove malpractice).

212. Garrow, *supra* note 23, at 715; Olasky, *supra* note 206, at 135–37, 140–41; Solinger, *supra* note 189, at 4, 6, 8–9, 22, 27–28, 31, 37–38, 42–46, 54, 56, 162, 219–20, 228. *See, e.g.,* Warren Hern, *Life on the Front Lines,* in Abortion Wars, *supra* note 23, at 307; Jane Hodgson, *The Twentieth-Century Gender Battle: Difficulties in Perception,* in Abortion Wars, *supra,* at 290; Carol Joffe, Patricia Anderson, & Jody Steinauer, *The Crisis of Abortion Provision and Pro-Choice Medical Activism in the 1990s,* in Abortion Wars, *supra,* at 320; Karlin, *supra* note 23. *But see* Timothy Vinceguerra, *Notes of a Footsoldier,* 62 Alb. L. Rev. 1167, 1174 (1999). Consider also their defense of Bruce Steir who pleaded guilty to involuntary manslaughter after killing a patient in doing an abortion. *See* Chapter 15, at notes 110–23. Similarly, these "heroic" abortion providers are occasionally convicted of tax evasion for failure to report their income from their abortion clinics; in one case, two partners were convicted of tax evasion for failure to report hundreds of thousands of dollars of income, yet the government arranged for them to serve their sentences at different times to assure that their clinic remained open. James Risen & Judy Thomas, Wrath of Angels: The American Abortion War 145, 193 (1998),

They even succeeded in having a three-judge panel of a federal Court of Appeals declare unconstitutional (as unduly burdening the right to an abortion) a Louisiana statute declaring that abortion providers are liable for any injuries caused by the abortion to the "mother," although that decision was reversed in a rehearing *en banc*.[213] Nor are they willing to give an open hearing to research that raises the possibility of long-term health risks from abortion.[214] As a NARAL activist pointed out, "other groups [were] formed to keep abortion safe, and we decided to exclude that word from our mission statement. That's not part of our mission to keep it safe."[215]

In balancing the interests and values created or reinforced by changing medical technologies then, states need the same broad authority to regulate the conduct of physicians performing abortions as states have for other medical procedures.[216] A good case can be made, how-

---

213. Okpalobi v. Foster, 190 F.3d 337 (5th Cir. 1999), 244 F.3d 405 (5th Cir. 2001).

214. Hans-Olev Adami *et al.*, *Parity, Age at First Childbirth, and Risk of Ovarian Cancer*, 344 THE LANCET 1250 (1994); Grethe Albrektsen *et al.*, *Is the Risk of Cancer of the* Corpus Uteri *Reduced by a Recent Pregnancy? A Prospective Study of 765,756 Norwegian Women*, 61 INT'L J. CANCER 485 (1995); N. Andreau *et al.*, *Familial Risk, Abortion and Their Interactive Effect on the Risk of Breast Cancer—A Combined Analysis of Six Case-Control Studies*, 72 BRIT. J. CANCER 744 (1995); Valerie Beral *et al.*, *Does Pregnancy Protect against Ovarian Cancer?*, 8073 THE LANCET 1083 (1978); Joel Brind *et al.*, *Induced Abortion as an Independent Risk Factor for Breast Cancer: A Comprehensive Review and Meta-Analysis*, 50 J. EPIDEMIOLOGY & COMMUNITY HEALTH 481 (1996); Louise Brinton *et al.*, *Reproductive, Menstrual, and Medical Risk Factors for Endometrial Cancer: Results from a Case-Control Study*, 167 AM. J. OBSTET. & GYNECOLOGY 1317 (1992); Willard Cates, jr., *The Risks Associated with Teenage Abortion*, 309 N. ENG. J. MED. 621 (1983); Mei-Tzu Chen *et al.*, *Incomplete Pregnancies and Risk of Ovarian Cancer*, 7 CANCER CAUSES & CONTROL 415 (1996); Clowes, *supra* note 202; Janet Daling *et al.*, *Risk of Breast Cancer among White Women Following Induced Abortion*, 144 J. EPIDEMIOLOGY 373 (1996); M. Ewertz & S.W. Duffy, *Risk of Breast Cancer in Relation to Reproductive Factors in Denmark*, 58 BRIT. J. CANCER 99 (1988); Kathleen Franco *et al.*, *Dysphoric Reactions in Women after Abortion*, 44 J. AM. MED. WOMEN'S ASS'N 113 (1989); Bernard Harlow *et al.*, *Case-Control Study of Borderline Ovarian Tumors: Reproductive History and Exposure to Exogenous Female Tumors*, 48 CANCER RES. 5849 (1988); Patricia Hartge, *Editorial: Abortion, Breast Cancer, and Epidemiology*, 336 N. ENG. J. MED. 127 (1997); Aravanadinos Kalandidi *et al.*, *A Case-Control Study of Endometrial Cancer in Relation to Reproductive, Somatometric, and Life-Style Variables*, 53 ONCOLOGY 354 (1996); Nancy Kreiger, *Exposure, Susceptibility, and Breast Cancer Risk: A Hypothesis Regarding Exogenous Carcinogens, Breast Tissue Development, and Social Gradients, Including Black/White Differences in Breast Cancer Incidence*, 13 BREAST CANCER RES. & TREATMENT 205 (1989); Loren Lipworth *et al.*, *Abortion and the Risk of Breast Cancer: A Case-Control Study in Greece*, 61 BRIT. J. CANCER 181 (1995); Mads Melbye *et al.*, *Induced Abortion and the Risk of Breast Cancer*, 336 NEW ENG. J. MED. 81 (1997); Eva Negri *et al.*, *Incomplete Pregnancies and Ovarian Cancer Risk*, 47 GYENCOLOGIC ONCOLOGY 234 (1992); Polly Newcomb *eg al. Pregnancy Termination in Relation to Risk of Breast Cancer*, 275 JAMA 283 (1996); José & Irma Russo, *Susceptibility of the Mammary Gland to Carcinogenesis II: Pregnancy Interruption as a Risk Factor in Tumor Incidence*, 100 AM. J. PATHOLOGY 497 (1980); Kenneth Schulz, David Grimes, & Willard Cates, jr., *Measures to Prevent Cervical Injury during Suction Curretage Abortion*, 2 THE LANCET 1182 (May 28, 1983); Alice Whittemore, *Epithelial Ovarian Cancer and the Ability to Conceive*, 49 CANCER RES. 4047 (1989). *See also* Jennifer Kelsey *et al.*, *A Case-Control Study of Cancer of the Endometrium*, 116 AM. J. EPIDEMIOLOGY 333 (1982); Jennifer Kelsey *et al.*, *Exogenous Estrogens and Other Factors in the Epidemiology of Breast Cancer*, 67 J. NAT. CANCER INST. 327 (1981); Polly Newcomb *et al.*, *Lactation and a Reduced Risk of Premenopausal Breast Cancer*, 330 NEW ENG. J. MED. 81 (1994); Thomas Sellers, *Effect of Family History, Body-Fat Distribution, and Reproductive Risk Factors on the Risk of Postmenopausal Breast Cancer*, 326 NEW ENG. J. MED. 1323 (1992); Alice Whittemore, *Characteristics Relating to Ovarian Cancer Risk: Collaborative Analysis of 12 US Case-Control Studies II: Invasive Epithelial Ovarian Cancers in White Women*, 136 AM. J. EPIDEMIOLOGY 1184 (1992).

215. SUZANNE STAGGENBORG, THE PRO-CHOICE MOVEMENT: ORGANIZATION AND ACTIVISM IN THE ABORTION CONFLICT 107 (1991). *See generally* Lynne Marie Kohm, *Sex Selection Abortion and the Boomerang Effect of a Woman's Right to Choose: A Paradox of the Skeptics*, 4 WM. & MARY J. WOMEN & L. 91, 121–24 (1997); Lynne Marie Kohm & Colleen Holmes, *The Rise and Fall of Women's Rights: Have Sexuality and Reproductive Freedom Forfeited Victory?*, 6 WM. & MARY J. WOMEN & L. 381, 403–06 (2000).

216. Paul Bridenhagen, *Abortion: From Roe to Akron, Changing Standards of Analysis*, 33 CATH. U.L. REV. 393, 419–27 (Winter 1984); Roslyn Bazzelle, Mazurek v. Armstrong: *Should States Be Allowed to Restrict the*

ever, that the state's power to regulate abortion should not be vested in the courts. Justice Oliver Wendell Holmes, jr., summed up what ultimately is wrong with the Supreme Court's attempt to impose its view of the abortion on a badly divided society: "The first requirement of a sound body of law is, that it should correspond to with the actual feelings and demands of the community, whether right or wrong."[217] As the continuing struggle over abortion demonstrates, *Roe* has failed this elementary test of sound law. If I am right about the historical roots of the abortion crisis, it is clear not only that the old solutions cannot remain unquestioned, but also that an outcome that expresses only one set of the contending interests will remain divisive rather than serving as a judicial call on "the contending sides of a national controversy to end their national division by accepting a common mandate rooted in the Constitution."[218] Despite insistence of the troika in their joint plurality opinion in *Casey* that they are striking just such a balance,[219] they still attempt to stifle political debate while awarding victory to one side or the other rather than leaving the political branches to struggle with the problem.

Judge Frank Easterbrook adds a more general criticism of the Supreme Court's claim to strike balances to which all must pledge allegiance: "The 'balancing' so much in vogue amounts to the denial of law and the assumption by judges of the power to say what is reasonable."[220] To begin to resolve the controversy, we must escape the language of rights and the atomistic vision of society it entails.[221] We must get past simplistic constitutional claims and begin to face the complexities

---

*Performance of Abortions to Licensed Physicians Only?*, 24 T. Marshall L. Rev. 149, 166 (Fall 1998). *See generally* Cunningham & Forsythe, *supra* note 211, at 149–53.

217. Oliver Wendell Holmes, jr., The Common Law 36 (Mark Howe ed. 1963).

218. *Casey,* 505 U.S. at 867 (Kennedy, O'Connor, & Souter, JJ., joint plurality op.).

219. *Id.* at 846 (asserting the troika's simultaneous adherence to the three principles of protecting the right of the woman to choose, the power of the State to restrict abortions after fetal viability, and the State's legitimate interest in protecting the health of the woman and the life of the nonviable fetus).

220. Easterbrook, *supra* note 91, at 79. *See also* T. Alexander Aleinikoff, *Constitutional Law in the Age of Balancing*, 96 Yale L.J. 943, 972–78, 986–92 (1987).

221. Guido Calabresi, Ideals, Beliefs, Attitudes, and the Law: Private Law Perspectives on a Public Law Problem 109 (1985); Colker, *supra* note 69, at 133–38; Jean Bethke Elshtain, Power Trips and Other Journeys: Essays in Feminism as Civic Discourse 89–91 (1990); Mary Ann Glendon, A Nation under Lawyers: How the Crisis in the Legal Profession Is Transforming American Society 14, 24, 38–40, 131 (1994) ("Glendon, A Nation under Lawyers"); Hirschmann, *supra* note 72, at 148–51; Elizabeth Mensch & Alan Freeman, The Politics of Virtue: Is Abortion Debatable? 126–52 (1993); F.L. Morton, Pro-Choice vs. Pro-Life and the Courts in Canada 294–314 (1993); Michael Perry, Love and Power: The Role of Religion and Morality in American Politics (1991); Araujo, *supra* note 197, at 727–54; Annette Baier, *Trust and Antitrust*, 96 Ethics 275 (1986); Emily Jackson, *Catharine MacKinnon and Feminist Jurisprudence: A Critical Appraisal*, 19 J.L. & Soc'y 195, 196 (1992); Teresa Godwin Phelps, *The Sound of Silence Breaking: Catholic Women, Abortion, and the Law*, 59 U. Tenn. L. Rev. 547, 565–66 (1992); Wilkins, Sherlock, & Clark, *supra* note 200, at 165; David Smolin, *Regulating Religious and Cultural Conflict in a Postmodern America: A Response to Professor Perry*, 76 Iowa L. Rev. 1067 (1991). *See also* Daniel Bell, Communitarianism and Its Critics (1993); Law and the Community: The End of Individualism? (Allan Hutchinson & Leslie Green eds. 1989); Lawrence Friedman, The Republic of Choice: Law, Authority, and Culture (1990); Minow, *supra* note 72, at 146–72, 267–69, 277–83, 289–311; Helen Holmes & Susan Peterson, *Rights over One's Own Body: A Woman-Affirming Health Care Policy*, 3 Hum. Rts. Q. 71, 73–74 (1981); Andrew Siropoulos, *Natural Right and the Constitution: Principle as Purpose and Limit*, 13 St. L.U. L. Rev. 285 (1993). *See generally* William Galston, Liberal Purposes: Goods, Virtues, and Diversity in the Liberal State (1991); Mary Ann Glendon, Rights Talk: The Impoverishment of Political Discourse (1991); Symposium, *Roads Not Taken: Undercurrents of Republican Thinking in Modern Constitutional Theory*, 84 Nw. U. L. Rev. 1 (1989); Symposium, *1787: The Constitution in Perspective*, 29 Wm. & Mary L. Rev. 1 (1987); Symposium, *The Republican Civic Tradition*, 97 Yale L.J. 1493 (1988). Note that radical scholars tend to posit an ideal "critical community" of their own invention as an alternative to an actual (or, as the radicals term them, "traditional") communities, all in the name of fostering personal freedom even for those who prefer the existing community. *See, e.g.,* Marilyn Friedman, *Feminism and Modern Friendships:*

of self-government in the contexts of troubled lives.[222] We must balance concern for the dignity of women and the needs of poor and working mothers with the welfare of unborn children in a context continually reshaped by changing medical technologies.[223] No one should be content with a situation that Mary Ann Glendon so aptly described:

> [P]oor, pregnant women…have their constitutional right to privacy and little else. Meager social support for maternity and child-raising, and the absence of public funding for abortions in many jurisdictions, do in fact leave such women largely isolated in their privacy…. [T]echnically proper legal negations of responsibility can easily miseducate the public about what it means to be a citizen. Careless judicial pronouncements can harden the lines on a cultural grid which already seems to have decreasing room for a sense of public obligation.[224]

Theologian Karl Barth criticized sterile, rights-based approaches some 40 years ago even while he condemned abortion under most circumstances.[225] Even some feminists have begun to speak in communitarian terms.[226] In general, how ever, we have seen the "acceleration of claims" to rights, meaning the proliferation of newly discovered rights and a demand for immediate implementation of these suddenly essential demands.[227] This acceleration is most troubling when accomplished through judicial fiat rather than because a substantial majority of the population as a whole has been persuaded to support, or at least tolerate, the proposed new right, for the judiciary tends to carry matters to logical extremes.

This is not to suggest that legislative bodies cannot be pressured into hasty or ill-considered actions, but simply that they are more responsive to countervailing political pressures to a degree that judges, deliberately insulated from such pressures, are not. Consider, for example, the attempt to ram an anti-pornography ordinance through the Minneapolis City Council in 1983 and 1984.[228] The effort, orchestrated by Andrea Dworkin and Catharine MacKinnon, used deliberately confrontational tactics to silence opponents. MacKinnon in particular has been aptly

---

*Dislocating the Community*, 99 ETHICS 275 (1989). *See also* Timothy Terrell, *When Duty Calls*, 41 EMORY L.J. 1111 (1992).

222. Robert Nagel, *Political Pressure and Judging in Constitutional Cases*, 61 U. COLO. L. REV. 685, 685–90 (1990). *See generally* JEROME AUERBACH, JUSTICE WITHOUT LAW? (1983); COLKER, *supra* note 69, at 114–19; CAROL GREENHOUSE, PRAYING FOR JUSTICE: FAITH, ORDER, AND COMMUNITY IN AN AMERICAN TOWN (1986); PETCHESKY, *supra* note 46, at 7–8; John Brigham, *Rights, Rage, and Remedy: The Constitution of Legal Discourse*, 2 STUD. AM. POL. DEV. 303 (1987); Neil Milner, *The Denigration of Rights and the Persistence of Rights Talk: A Cultural Portrait*, 14 LAW & SOC. INQUIRY 631 (1989); Neil Milner, *The Intrigues of Rights, Resistance, and Accommodation*, 17 LAW & SOC. INQUIRY 313 (1992).

223. Note the factual changes between the trial and its review by the Court in *Planned Parenthood of Cent. Mo. v. Danforth*, 428 U.S. 52, 75–79, 95–99 (White, J., dissenting, with Burger, C.J., & Rehnquist, J.), 101–2 (Stevens, J., concurring) (1976). *See generally* Catherine Pap Mangel, *Legal Abortion: The Impending Obsolescence of the Trimester Framework*, 14 AM. J.L. & MED. 69 (1988).

224. GLENDON, A NATION UNDER LAWYERS, *supra* note 221, at 65, 104. *See also* Daniel Callahan, *Communitarian Bioethics: A Pious Hope?*, 6 RESPONSIVE COMMUNITY no. 4, at 26 (Fall 1996).

225. KARL BARTH, 3 CHURCH DOGMATICS pt. IV, at 415–23 (1960). *See also* DIETRICH BONHOEFFER, ETHICS 131 (1955); JAMES GUSTAFSON, PROTESTANT AND ROMAN CATHOLIC ETHICS 30–31 (1978); MENSCH & FREEMAN, *supra* note 221, at 63–65.

226. *See, e.g.,* ELIZABETH FOX GENOVESE, FEMINISM IS NOT THE STORY OF MY LIFE: HOW TODAY'S FEMINIST ELITE HAS LOST TOUCH WITH THE REAL CONCERNS OF WOMEN (1995); GENOVESE, *supra* note 189; Mertus, *supra* note 74.

227. Andrew Jacobs, *Rhetoric and the Creation of Rights: MacKinnon and the Civil Right to Freedom from Pornography*, 42 KAN. L. REV. 785, 785 (1994).

228. IN HARM'S WAY: THE PORNOGRAPHY CIVIL RIGHTS HEARINGS (Catharine MacKinnon & Andrea Dworkin eds. 1997).

termed an "authoritarian in the guise of a progressive."[229] She consistently refuses to debate many of her points even with other feminists, apparently in the smug confidence that there cannot be any other view than hers.[230] As one critic noted, "[t]he world for MacKinnon may be an ugly and violent place, but it is not complex—it remains undisturbed by competing visions of truth, moral worth, and struggles for the good life."[231]

Although the effort in Minneapolis narrowly passed the City Council on two occasions, it was successfully vetoed both times and never enacted.[232] Of course, such stories are never so simple as we would like. Courts had to rescue Indianapolis by declaring their anti-pornography ordinance, which was enacted by the city council there, unconstitutional for violating the First Amendment.[233] Courts, however, will not always support freedom of expression rather than laws

---

229. Carlin Romano, *Between the Motion and the Act*, THE NATION, Nov. 15, 1993, at 563, 570. *See also* Donna Haraway, *A Cyborg Manifesto: Science, Technology, and Socialist-Feminism in the Late Twentieth Century*, in SIMIANS, CYBORGS, AND WOMEN: THE REINVENTION OF NATURE 149, 159 (Donna Haraway ed. 1991) ("MacKinnon's radical theory of experience is totalizing in the extreme; it does not so much marginalize as obliterate the authority of any other woman's political speech and action."); Angela Harris, *Race and Essentialism in Feminist Legal Theory*, 12 HARV. L. REV. 581, 585 (1990) ("The result of gender essentialism...is not only that some voices are silenced in order to privilege others..., but that the voices that are silenced turn out to be the same voices silenced by the mainstream legal voice of 'We the People'—among them, the voices of black women."); Shelley Wright, *Patriarchal Feminism and the Law of the Father*, 1 FEMINIST LEG. STUD. 115, 120 (1993) (stating of MacKinnon that "there is no more masculinist writer and speaker.").

230. *See, e.g.*, David Margolick, *A: the Bar: Catering to an Academic Superstar, Judges Find Themselves in a Free-Speech Debate*, N.Y. TIMES, Nov. 13, 1993, at B11. *See also* Bartlett, *supra* note 74, at 1564; Lynn Chancer, *Pornography Debates Reconsidered*, 2 NEW POL. 72 (1988); Finley, *supra* note 74, at 380; Suzanne Gibson, *The Discourse of Sex/War: Thoughts on Catharine MacKinnon's 1993 Oxford* Amnesty Lecture, 1 FEMINIST LEGAL STUD. 179 (1993); Schroeder, Abduction, *supra* note 69, at 157–58.

231. Lawrence Douglas, *The Force of Words: Fish, Matsuda, MacKinnon, and the Theory of Discursive Violence*, 29 LAW & SOC'Y REV. 169, 188 (1995). For an elaborate attempt to develop MacKinnon's thinking to place her ideas on a more intellectually defensible (and less authoritarian) position, see Jeffrey Brand-Ballard, *Reconstructing MacKinnon: Essentialism, Humanism, Feminism*, 6 REV. L. & WOMEN'S STUD. 89 (1996).

232. *See* DONALD DOWNS, THE NEW POLITICS OF PORNOGRAPHY 51–94 (1989); Martha Allen, *Council Passes Pornography Law, Fraser Deciding Whether to Veto It*, MINNEAPOLIS STAR & TRIB., Dec. 31, 1983, at 1A; Paul Brest & Ann Vandenberg, *Politics, Feminism, and the Constitution: The Anti-Pornography Movement in Minneapolis*, 39 STAN. L. REV. 607 (1987); Jacobs, *supra* note 227. *See generally* MACKINNON, *supra* note 69, at 175–95; Andrea Dworkin, *Against the Male Flood: Censorship, Pornography, and Equality*, 8 HARV. WOMEN'S L.J. 1 (1985).

233. American Booksellers' Ass'n, Inc. v. Hudnut, 771 F.2d 323 (7th Cir. 1985), *aff'd*, 475 U.S. 1001 (1986). *See generally* LYNN CHANCER, RECONCILING DIFFERENCES: CONFRONTING BEAUTY, PORNOGRAPHY AND THE FUTURE OF FEMINISM (1998); DRUCILLA CORNELL, THE IMAGINARY DOMAIN: ABORTION, PORNOGRAPHY, AND SEXUAL HARASSMENT 95–166 (1995); RONALD DWORKIN, A MATTER OF PRINCIPLE 335–72 (1985); SUSAN EASTON, THE PROBLEM OF PORNOGRAPHY (1994); CATHARINE MACKINNON, ONLY WORDS (1993); GILLIAN RODGERSON & ELIZABETH WILSON, PORNOGRAPHY AND FEMINISM (1991); THE PRICE WE PAY: THE CASE AGAINST RACIST SPEECH, HATE PROPAGANDA, AND PORNOGRAPHY (Laura Lederer & Richard Delgado eds. 1995); WOMEN AGAINST CENSORSHIP (Varda Burstyn ed. 1985); Amy Adler, *What's Left?: Hate Speech, Pornography, and the Problem for Artistic Expression*, 84 CAL. L. REV. 1499 (1996); C. Edwin Baker, *Of Course, More than Words* (book rev.), 61 U. CHI. L. REV. 1181 (1994); Patricia Barnes, *A Pragmatic Compromise in the Pornography Debate*, 1 TEMP. POL. & CIV. RTS. L. REV. 117 (1992); Mary Kay Blakely, *Is One Woman's Sexuality Another Woman's Pornography?*, Ms., April 1, 1985, at 37; Joanna Calne, *In Defense of Desire*, 23 RUTGERS L.J. 305 (1992); Lynn Chancer, *From Pornography to Sadomasochism: Reconciling Feminist Differences*, 571 ANNALS AM. ACADEMY POL. & SOC. SCI. 77, 81–83 (2000) ("Chancer, *Pornography*"); Richard Delgado & Jean Stefanic, *Pornography and Harm to Women: "No Empirical Evidence?,"* 53 OHIO ST. L.J. 1037 (1992); Thomas Emerson, *Pornography and the First Amendment: A Reply to Professor MacKinnon*, 3 YALE L. & POL'Y REV. 130 (1984); Dan Greenberg & Thomas Tobiason, *The New Legal Puritanism of Catharine MacKinnon*, 54 OH. ST. L.J. 1375 (1993); Thomas Grey, *How to Write a Speech Code without Really Trying: Reflections on the Stanford Experience*, 29 U.C. DAVIS L. REV. 891 (1996); Peter Hamill, *Women on the Verge of a Legal Breakdown*, PLAYBOY, Jan. 1993, at 186; Alon Harel, *Bigotry, Pornography, and the First Amendment: A Theory*

prohibiting pornography. The Supreme Court of Canada upheld a similar statute against a challenge based upon the guarantee of free expression in the Canadian Charter of Rights on the grounds that the statue was necessary to achieve equality for women.[234]

We in the United States should consider the approach of most other western democracies: Leave abortion to legislative action in a search for an accommodation of the competing interests in a statute that can command sufficiently broad support to quiet the controversy.[235] The Canadian Supreme Court adopted such an approach in overturning Canada's national abortion statute.[236] Noted constitutional scholar Alexander Bickel made the same point shortly in his comment on *Roe's* trimester scheme:

> The Court...refused the discipline to which its function is properly subject. It simply asserted the result it reached. If medical considerations only were involved, a satisfactory rational answer might be arrived at. But, as the Court acknowledged, they are not. Should not the question then have been left to the political process, which in state after state can achieve not one but many accommodations, adjusting them from time to time as attitudes change?[237]

Legislatures, after all, are better for establishing policies for the future, leaving to the courts the fashioning remedies for past wrongs.[238] The advantage may only be relative, but it is real nonetheless.[239] A legislature can fund programs to reduce the need for abortion and can accu-

---

*of Unprotected Speech,* 65 S. Cal. L. Rev. 1887 (1992); Nan Hunter & Sylvia Law, *Brief of* Amici Curiae *of the Feminist Anti-Censorship Taskforce et al. in* American Booksellers Association, Inc. v. Hudnut, 21 U. Mich. J.L. Ref. 69 (1987); Caryn Jacobs, *Patterns of Violence: A Feminist Perspective on the Regulation of Pornography,* 8 Harv. Women's L.J. 1 (1985); Susan Etta Keller, *Viewing and Doing: Complicating Pornography's Meaning* (book rev.), 81 Geo. L.J. 2195 (1993); Elena Kagan, *When a Speech Code Is a Speech Code: The Stanford Policy and the Theory of Incidental Restraints,* 29 U.C. Davis L. Rev. 957 (1996); Rae Langton, *Whose Right? Ronald Dworkin, Women, and Pornographers,* 19 Phil. & Pub. Aff. 311 (1990); Arnold Loewy, *Obscenity, Pornography, and First Amendment Theory,* 2 Wm. & Mary L. Rev. 471 (1993); Catharine MacKinnon, *Pornography as Defamation and Discrimination,* 71 B.U. L. Rev. 793 (1991); Catharine MacKinnon, *Not a Moral Issue,* 2 Yale L. & Pol'y Rev. 321 (1984); Carlin Meyer, *Sex, Sin, and Women's Liberation: Against Porn-Suppression,* 72 Tex. L. Rev. 1097 (1994); Jeffrey Sherman, *Love Speech: The Social Utility of Pornography,* 47 Stan. L. Rev. 661 (1995); Nadine Strossen, *A Feminist Critique of "the" Feminist Critique of Pornography,* 79 Va. L. Rev. 1099 (1993); Cass Sunstein, *Pornography and the First Amendment,* 1986 Duke L.J. 589; Nadine Taub, *A New View of Pornography, Speech, and Equality or Only Words?* (book rev.), 46 Rutgers L. Rev. 595 (1993); West, *supra* note 74; Susan Williams, *Feminist Jurisprudence and Free Speech Theory* (book rev.), 68 Tulane L. Rev. 1563 (1994).

234. Butler v. Regina, [1992] 1 S.C.R. 452 (Can.). *See generally* Kevin Saunders, *The United States and Canadian Responses to the Feminist Attack on Pornography: A Perspective from the History of Obscenity,* 9 Ind. Int'l & Comp. L. Rev. 1 (1998). Ironically, Canadian authorities thereafter seized copies of a book by Andrea Dworkin—with Catharine MacKinnon, the principal architect of these laws—for its "pornographic" content because of its vivid descriptions of male sexual oppression of women. Chancer, *Pornography, supra* note 233, at 81.

235. *See generally* Mary Ann Glendon, Abortion and Divorce in Western Law 58–62 (1987); Mary Ann Glendon, *U.S. Abortion Law: Still the Most Permissive on Earth,* Wall St. J., July 1, 1992, at A15; Larry Letich, *Bad Choices,* 4 Tikkun, July/Aug. 1989, at 22; Richard Posner, *Legal Reasoning from the Top down and from the Bottom up: The Question of Unenumerated Constitutional Rights,* 59 U. Chi. L. Rev. 433, 443 (1992).

236. Morgantheler v. Regina, [1988] 1 S.C.R. 30 (Can.). *See generally* Daniel Conkle, *Canada's Roe: The Canadian Abortion Decision and Its Implications for American Constitutional Law and Theory,* 6 Const'l Commentary 299, 308–18 (1989).

237. Alexander Bickel, The Morality of Consent 28 (1975). *See also Roe,* 410 U.S. at 219–23 (Rehnquist & White, JJ., dissenting); Arnold Loewy, *Why* Roe v. Wade *Should Be Overruled,* 67 N. Car. L. Rev. 939, 942–43 (1989).

238. City of Richmond v. J.A. Croson Co., 469 U.S. 469, 513–14 (1989) (Stevens, J., concurring).

239. Mark Tushnet, *The Constitution Outside the Courts: A Preliminary Inquiry,* 26 Val. L. Rev. 437, 443, 453 (1992).

rately reflect the prevailing sentiments of the community on this divisive issue. Courts can only issue injunctions, an approach fraught with difficulty when attempting to resolve complex social problems.[240] Courts are simply not suited to serve as a board of review for issues of medical technology[241] — as the court in *Roe* recognized when it was unable to decide when an individual human life (a "person") begins.[242] Legislatures are simply better placed than courts to devise regulatory responses if any are appropriate to rapidly changing human reproductive technologies.[243] Legislatures are better able to assemble the information necessary to assess the import of the changing technologies and to balance the interests created or reinforced by the technologies.[244] And, as law professor Michael McConnell noted regarding a decision upholding the application of criminal sodomy statutes to private homosexual conduct between consenting adults,

> the discussion of gay rights in and around the Chicago City Council had more substance than the opinions in *Bowers v. Hardwick*....In contrast to the months, even years, that are devoted to major legislative deliberation, the Justices devote one hour to oral argument and somewhat less than that to discussion at conference.[245]

McConnell's comment underestimates the time Justices devote to consideration a hotly debated question, particularly one, like abortion, that returns to the Court year after year. His comment does catch the point, however, that judges are more circumscribed in their ability to marshal information and to hear all relevant arguments.[246] Yet the effect of *Roe* was to foreclose serious legislative deliberation, substituting for any serious discussion on the merits a simple declaration that any proposal to restrict access to abortion would be unconstitutional.[247] Nor should we overlook that women are not an "insular minority" in this or most nations; they are

---

240. *See* Linda Schwartzstein, *Bureaucracy Unbounded: The Lack of Effective Constraints in the Judicial Process,* 35 St. L.U. L.J. 597 (1991). Ms. Schwartzstein's analysis does not factor in the formality, cost, and delays entailed in litigation, which Judge Miles Lord says "have led to a deterioration in the quality of justice" since he began to practice law more than 40 years ago. Miles Lord, *The Practice of Law and the Quality of Justice,* 35 St. L.U. L.J. 525 (1991).

241. City of Akron v. Akron Center for Reproductive Health, Inc., 462 U.S. 416, 454–59 (1983) (O'Connor, J., dissenting). *See also* Margaret Farrell, *Revisiting Roe v. Wade: Substance and Due Process in the Abortion Debate,* 68 Ind. L.J. 269, 317–53 (1993). For the full range of medical issues the Court has considered regarding abortion, see Kathryn Ann Farr, *Shaping Policy through Litigation: Abortion Law in the United States,* 39 Crime & Delinquency 167, 174–75 (1993). *See also* Rhode, *supra* note 189, at 210. At least one commentator has noted that this was the error the Court fell into regarding sterilization statutes. Harry Kalvin, *A Special Corner of Civil Liberties: A Legal View I,* 31 NYU L. Rev. 1223, 1234 (1956).

242. *Roe,* 410 U.S. at 160.

243. On the problem of whether a state's regulations regarding abortion could be applied extraterritorially to a woman who travels outside the state to obtain an abortion lawful at her destination, see C. Steven Bradford, *What Happens If Roe Is Overruled? Extraterritorial Regulation of Abortion by the States,* 35 Ariz. L. Rev. 87 (1993); Lea Brilmeyer, *Interstate Preemption: The Right to Travel, the Right to Life, and the Right to Die,* 91 Mich. L. Rev. 873 (1993); Seth Kreimer, *"But Whoever Treasures Freedom...": The Right to Travel and Extraterritorial Abortions,* 91 Mich. L. Rev. 907 (1993); Seth Kreimer, *The Law of Choice and Choice of Law: Abortion, the Right to Travel, and Extraterritorial Regulation in American Federalism,* 67 NYU L. Rev. 451 (1992); Gerald Neuman, *Conflict of Constitutions? No Thanks: A Response to Professors Brilmeyer and Kreimer,* 91 Mich. L. Rev. 939 (1993).

244. *See generally* John Hart Ely, Democracy and Distrust 105–34 (1980).

245. Michael McConnell, *The Role of Democratic Politics in Transforming Moral Convictions into Law* (book rev.), 98 Yale L.J. 1501, 1536–37 (1989).

246. This point is lost on jurisprude Ronald Dworkin who has argued that the quality of public debate is higher, more focused, and more extensive when the decision is to be rendered by a court rather than by a legislature. Ronald Dworkin, *Mr. Liberty,* N.Y. Rev. Books, Aug. 11, 1994, at 17, 21–22 (a review of a biography of Judge Learned Hand). *See also* Neil Devins, *Through the Looking Glass: What Abortion Teaches Us about American Politics,* 94 Colum. L. Rev. 293, 315–28 (1994).

247. Earl Maltz, Rethinking Constitutional Law: Originalism, Interventionism, and the Politics of Judicial Review 98–100 (1994).

both the majority and an increasingly vocal and politically effective majority in the United States. They can be expected to look out after their own interests in legislative battles.[248] Finally, as Justice Louis Brandeis argued in justly famous dissent to *New State Ice Co. v. Liebman*,[249] for such morally and socially unsettled problems, the states should serve as laboratories for social experiment.[250]

Both sides of this troubling debate could benefit from returning the question to the political processes. A sustained political campaign by proponents of abortion rights could raise the consciousness of the nation about women's rights generally,[251] and perhaps lead us to alter the social structures that so often drive a woman "to desperate violence in taking life in their wombs."[252] Or perhaps, while frankly acknowledging that abortion kills a living being, we could develop a theory of a "just abortion" just as our society seems to have embraced a theory of a "just war."[253] We could, for example, couple a ban on abortion after, say, eight weeks of gestation,[254] with a program of publicly provided contraceptives and prenatal and postnatal medical care, as well as tax-funded nutritional subsidies to mother and child, while promoting sexual and contraceptive education and providing a national adoption service.[255] A sustained political campaign by opponents of abortion could recall us to our traditional values (including especially respect for life) on which this nation was founded, and for which untold numbers sacrificed their lives and labors in similar struggles to protect the rights of hitherto invisible people.[256] The process will probably result in laws that do not satisfy the most extreme on either side,[257] but the laws might

---

248. Ginsberg, *supra* note 27, at 1207 (noting that women are not only a majority, but that, unlike racial minorities, women live in intimate relation to men as mothers, sisters, wives, and daughters, whose interests are therefore not so easy to ignore in the political processes); Penny Miller, *Staking Their Claim: The Impact of Kentucky Women in the Political Process,* 84 KY. L.J. 1163 (1996) (detailing the impact of women on Kentucky politics where women have long formed a majority of registered voters but have remained underrepresented in public office). *See also* James McCristal Culp, jr., *Toward a Black Legal Scholarship: Race and Original Understandings,* 1991 DUKE L.J. 39, 62–67 (arguing that political processes have been central to achieving feminist goals, while judicial processes have been central to achieving African-American goals).

249. 285 U.S. 262, 309–11 (1932). *See also* Addington v. Texas, 441 U.S. 418, 431 (1979).

250. *See* Clarke Forsythe, *First Steps: A New Strategy for Pro-Lifers,* 51 NAT'L REV. 42 (Dec. 20, 1999). For a survey of the legislative struggles that ensued after the Webster decision, *see* CRAIG & O'BRIEN, *supra* note 185, at 279–303.

251. HADLEY, *supra* note 23, at 146–52, 191–208; Rosalind Pollack Petchesky, *Change Strategies, Change Vision,* 18 NEW DIMENSIONS FOR WOMEN 1 (Sept./Oct. 1989); Pine & Law, *supra* note 185, at 452–63; Williams, *supra* note 69, at 1588–94.

252. James Douglas, *Patriarchy and the Pentagon Make Abortion Inevitable,* 9 SOJOURNERS 14, 15 (Nov. 1980); Julia Hanigsberg, *Homologizing Pregnancy and Motherhood: A Consideration of Abortion,* 94 MICH. L. REV. 371 (1995).

253. KATHRYN ALLEN RABUZZI, MOTHER WITH CHILD: TRANSFORMATION THROUGH CHILDBIRTH 52–53 (1994).

254. For why I suggest eight weeks, see the *Personal Aside* at the opening of this book.

255. *See* Hitchens, *supra* note 189. *See also* ROSALIND BAXANDALL, WOMEN AND ABORTION: THE BODY AS BATTLEGROUND 10 (1992); PETCHESKY, *supra* note 46, at 25; RUDY, *supra* note 45, at 87–149; STAGGENBORG, *supra* note 215, at 110; Ruth Colker, *Feminist Consciousness and the State: A Basis for Cautious Optimism,* 90 COLUM. L. REV. 1146, 1165–70 (1990); Daniel Degnan, *When (If) "Roe" Falls,* COMMONWEAL, May 5, 1989, at 267; Marlene Gerber Fried, *Transforming the Reproductive Rights Movement,* in FROM ABORTION TO REPRODUCTIVE FREEDOM, *supra* note 189, at 1.

256. *See generally* ABORTION AND PUBLIC POLICY: AN INTERDISCIPLINARY INVESTIGATION WITHIN THE CATHOLIC TRADITION (R. Randall Rainey & Gerard Magill eds. 1996); MENSCH & FREEMAN, *supra* note 221, at 126–52; RICHARD MCMCORMICK, HEALTH AND MEDICINE IN THE CATHOLIC TRADITION: TRADITION IN TRANSITION 137–38 (1985); ROSENBLATT, *supra* note 189; KELLEY, *supra* note 33; Jeffrey Parness, *Your Bodies, Ourselves: Legal Protection of Potential Human Life,* 30 CATH. LAW. 370 (1986).

257. *See, e.g.,* CONDIT, *supra* note 6, at 151–66; DWORKIN, *supra* note 112, at 84–100; JUDGES, supra note 25, at 280–95; PETERSEN, *supra* note 197, at 109–70; LLOYD STEFFEN, LIFE/CHOICE: THE THEORY OF JUST ABORTION (2000); TRIBE, *supra* note 189, at 193–208; Annette Clark, *Abortion and the Pied Piper of Compro-*

prove more lasting than a judicial declaration that the position of one side or the other is utterly illegitimate.[258] In contrast, a judicial "conversation" about abortion tends simply to send one side or the other to prison.[259] In the end the political struggle just might make us better people for having confronted the struggle within our own consciences that abortion presents to us all.[260]

Finally, there is the question of why should we care about history in these debates. There are two reasons. First, of course, is because at present getting the history right is significant, some would say central, to getting the constitution right. Second is a strong belief on my part that history has something to tell us as we struggle within our consciences. Historian Garry Wills has expressed the second reason more eloquently that I ever could. Wills wrote:

> The lack of any historical memory (even a false one) is like an attack of amnesia at the personal level. It deprives us of an identity. Though we do not learn to predict the future from the past, the greater our understanding of long stretches of time, the better become our chances of judging the past that we all share in a convincing way.... History does not dictate that we must approve or disapprove of current trends like multiculturalism, the loosening of family ties, or the autonomy of youth culture. But the run of events affecting demography, urbanism, and technological education does help us put discussion of such matters in a wider setting. That kind of knowledge can teach us, at the least, the limits of our room for maneuver. We are all caught in a rushing flood of time that is hard to measure in meaningful ways. But the ride is more enjoyable if we can get just high enough in the waves to see the broad expanse of sea that carries us along.[261]

---

*mise,* 68 NYU L. Rev. 265, 296–316 (1993); Council on Ethical & Judicial Affairs, *Mandatory Parental Consent to Abortion,* 269 JAMA 82 (1993); B.J. George, jr., *State Legislatures versus the Supreme Court: Abortion Legislation into the 1990s,* in Abortion, Medicine, and the Law 3 (J. Douglas Butler & David Walbert eds., 3rd ed. 1986); Law, *supra* note 189, at 937–41; Gary Leedes, *Liberalism, Republicanism and the Abortion Controversy,* 35 Villa. L. Rev. 571, 603–08 (1990); Susan Oliver Renfer, Randal Shaheen, & Michael Hegarty, *The Woman's Right to Know: A Model Approach to the Informed Consent of Abortion,* 22 Loy. U. Chi. L.J. 409 (1991); J. Allison Strickland, *Rape Exceptions in Post-*Webster *Antiabortion Legislation: A Practical Analysis,* 26 Colum. J.L. & Soc. Prob. 163 (1992); Nadine Strossen & Ronald Collins, *The Future of an Illusion: Reconstructing* Planned Parenthood v. Casey, 16 Const'l Commentary 587, 592–93 (1999); Wilkins, Sherlock, & Clark, *supra* note 200, at 164–87; Jane Wishner, *The Changing Politics of Abortion,* in Abortion and the States, *supra* note 200, at 319–45. This is hardly a novel insight, nor is it confined to the abortion context. *See, e.g.,* J.B. Ruhl, *Working Both (Positivist) Ends toward a New (Pragmatist) Middle in Environmental Law,* 68 Geo. Wash. L. Rev. 522 (2000).

258. Nancy (Ann) Davis, *The Abortion Debate: The Search for Common Ground (Part 2),* 103 Ethics 731, 769–74 (1993).

259. *See* Richard John Neuhaus, *After* Roe, 41 Nat. Rev. 38 (1989). The concept of litigation as a "judicial conversation" is a favorite of law professor James Boyd White. *See* James Boyd White, Justice as Translation: An Essay in Cultural and Legal Criticism (1990). *But see* Mark Tushnet, *"Shut up He Explained,"* 95 Nw. U. L. Rev. 907 (2001).

260. For a skeptical view of the power of dialogue to resolve fundamental disagreements over moral issues, see Richard Delgado, *Zero-Based Politics and an Infinity-Based Response: Will Endless Talking Cure America's Racial Ills?,* 80 Geo. L.J. 1879 (1992). For a brief description of one small attempt to open such a dialogue, see Samuel Calhoun, *Impartiality in the Classroom: A Personal Account of a Struggle to Be Evenhanded in Teaching about Abortion,* 45 J. Legal Educ. 99 (1995).

261. Garry Wills, *A Reader's Guide to the Century,* N.Y. Rev. Books, July 15, 1999, at 24, 28.

# Table of Cases

(References in italics are to the text; all other references are found in footnotes.)

# Index